THE INTERNATIONAL DICTIONARY OF
FILMS AND FILMMAKERS: VOLUME II

DIRECTORS/ FILMMAKERS

THE INTERNATIONAL DICTIONARY
OF FILMS AND FILMMAKERS

Volume I
FILMS

Volume II
DIRECTORS/FILMMAKERS

Volume III
ACTORS AND ACTRESSES

Volume IV
WRITERS AND PRODUCTION ARTISTS

THE INTERNATIONAL DICTIONARY OF FILMS AND FILMMAKERS: VOLUME II

DIRECTORS/ FILMMAKERS

Editor:
Christopher Lyon

Assistant Editor:
Susan Doll

St J

Printed in The United States of America

ISBN
Films: 0-912289-04-X
Directors: 0-912289-05-8

First published in the U.K. and U.S.A. in 1984

Library of Congress Cataloging in Publication Data
Main entry under title:

Films and filmmakers.

    Includes bibliographies.
    Contents: v. 1. Films — v. 2, Directors/filmmakers.
    1. Moving-pictures—Plots, themes, etc. 2. Moving-picture producers and directors — Biography. I. Lyon, Christopher, 1949–   . II. Doll, Susan, 1954–
PN1997.8.F555   1984   791.43'09   83-24616
ISBN 0-912289-04-X (v. 1)
ISBN 0-912289-05-8 (v. 2)

Printed in the U.S.A.

CONTENTS

INTRODUCTION

This volume is the second of four in the series *International Dictionary of Films and Filmmakers*, and the first of three devoted to the principal creative figures in the history of film. Volume III, *Actors and Actresses*, and Volume IV, *Writers and Production Artists*, completes the series.

The subjects of *Directors/Filmmakers* are persons considered to have had the principal creative responsibility for a substantial body of work, whether or not they pursued filmmaking within an established film industry. We have tended to exclude those best known for achievement in arts other than cinema and certain figures whose principal contributions to film appears to be in areas other than directing.

Since directors have long been the subject of critical and scholarly attention, it was not thought necessary to propose criteria for their selection. Among our advisers, there seemed little disagreement over the final choice of directors active in the American, British, and major European industries. Outside those areas, we sought the advice of advisers and contributors with specialized interests.

We gratefully acknowledge their assistance, and wish particularly to thank Maria Racheva in Munich and Vladimír Opěla and his colleagues at the Czechoslovak Film Archives for their considerable help with Eastern European filmmakers; John Mraz in Mexico for his work on Cuban and Mexican cinema; and Ib Monty, Director of the Danish Film Museum, for his help with Scandinavian film. We are indebted to Dudley Andrew at the University of Iowa for his advice and assistance on French film; to Anthony Slide and Liam O'Leary who provided information on early filmmakers; Jack C. Ellis, chairman of Radio-TV-Film at Northwestern University, for his work on the British documentarists; Robin Wood and Roger Manvell who have been extremely generous with their time; P. Adams Sitney and Fred Camper for their help on avant-garde and experimental film; and the many film scholars in the Chicago area who have given their time to this project.

Research for this volume was carried out principally at the University of Chicago where we received the assistance of Professor Gerald Mast. A project of this scope could not have been undertaken without the support of the Computation Center at the University of Chicago and particularly James Lichtenstein, who designed the computerized editing system we have used and provided indispensable advice. We also wish to thank the Film Center of the School of the Art Institute of Chicago and its director Richard Peña; the Film Study Center of the Museum of Modern Art, New York, and especially Ron Magliozzi; Ephraim Katz, author of *The Film Encyclopedia*, for his advice and his hospitality in New York; Frances Thorpe of the British Film Institute who provided assistance at each stage of the project; and Patricia Coward who so efficiently carried out the research for this book done at the BFI.

We consider that a volume such as this is in need of constant revision, correction, and updating. We hope that interested readers will bring errors and omissions to our attention, and we also welcome additions to the bibliographies. Please address any correspondence on such matters to the editors, care of St. James Press, Chicago or London.

Christopher Lyon, Editor

Susan Doll, Assistant Editor

✦✦✦   *A NOTE ON THE ENTRIES*

Non-English language film titles are ordinarily given in the original language or a transliteration of it. Alternate release titles in the original language(s) are found within parentheses, in italic, and are followed by release titles in English (American then British if there is a difference). Titles have been placed within brackets if we know them to be literal translations not used as release titles.

The entry subject's principal function(s) on any given film will ordinarily be found, within parentheses, preceding the film on which the subject assumed those functions, as in this example from Hal Ashby's filmography:

FILMS (as editor): 1965 — *The Loved One* (Richardson) (co-ed)... (as director): 1970 — *The Landlord*;

Information within parentheses following each film modifies, if necessary, then adds to the subject's principal function(s):

1979 — *Being There* (+ ed);

The commonest abbreviations used are: "pr" — producer; "d" — director; "sc" — scenarist or scriptwriter; "ph" — cinematographer or director of photography; "ed" — editor; and "ro" — role taken, followed by name or description of character played, if known. "co-" preceding a function indicates collaboration with one or more persons. A name in parentheses following a film title is that of the director.

ADVISERS AND CONTRIBUTORS

Advisers

Andrew, Dudley
Bardarsky, Dimitar
Barnouw, Erik
Bodeen, DeWitt
Brito, Rui Santana
Burgoyne, Robert
Ciment, Michel
Cook, David

Ellis, Jack C.
Everson, William K.
Gomery, Douglas
Kaplan, E. Ann
Katz, Ephraim
Kehr, Dave
Khanna, Satti
MacCann, Richard Dyer

Mast, Gerald
Monty, Ib
O'Leary, Liam
Peña, Richard
Rabinovitz, Lauren
Sitney, P. Adams
Slide, Anthony
Thorpe, Frances

Contributors

Affron, Charles
Affron, Mirella Jona
Allegro, Anthony
Andrew, Dudley
Armes, Roy
Barnouw, Erik
Basinger, Jeanine
Baxter, John
Bock, Audie
Bodeen, DeWitt
Bordwell, David
Bowers, Ronald
Bowles, Stephen E.
Broeske, Pat H.
Burgoyne, Robert
Burton, Julianne
Camper, Fred
Ciment, Michel
Conley, Tom
D'Arpino, Tony
Derry, Charles
Doll, Susan
Dunagan, Clyde Kelly
Dunbar, Robert
Edelman, Rob
Edmonds, Robert
Ellis, Jack D.

Elsner-Sommer, Gretchen
Erens, Patricia
Estrin, Mark
Faller, Greg
Farnsworth, Rodney
Feinstein, Howard
FitzGerald, Theresa
Fonseca, M.S.
Foreman, Alexa
Gomery, Douglas
Gomez, Joseph
Habá, Věroslav
Hanson, Patricia King
Hanson, Steve
Harris, Ann
Heck-Rabi, Louise
Hirano, Kyoko
Holdstein, Deborah H.
Kaminsky, Stuart M.
Kanoff, Joel
Kehr, Dave
Kemp, Philip
Khanna, Satti
Kovács, Katherine Singer
Limbacher, James L.
Lockhart, Kimball
Lorenz, Janet E.

Lowry, Ed
Mancini, Elaine
Manvell, Roger
Marchetti, Gina
Mast, Gerald
Merhaut, G.
Merritt, Russell
Michaels, Lloyd
Monty, Ib
Mraz, John
Murphy, William T.
Narducy, Ray
Nastav, Dennis
Nichols, Bill
O'Kane, John
O'Leary, Liam
Obalil, Linda J.
Opěla, Vladimir
Peña, Richard
Phillips, Gene D.
Pick, Zuzana Mirjam
Polan, Dana B.
Porton, Richard
Rabinovitz, Lauren
Racheva, Maria
Reynolds, Herbert
Robson, Arthur G.

x

Rubinstein, E.
Saeli, Marie
Schade, W. Curtis
Schiff, Lillian
Schuth, H. Wayne
Selig, Michael
Silet, Charles L.P.
Simmon, Scott
Sitney, P. Adams
Skvorecký, Josef

Slide, Anthony
Small, Edward S.
Smoodin, Eric
Snyder, Thomas
Stam, Robert
Tabery, Karel
Telotte, J.P.
Thorpe, Frances
Tomlinson, Doug
Tudor, Anthony

Urgošíkova, B.
Verdaasdonk, Dorothee
Weinberg, Herbert
Welsh, James
West, Dennis
White, M.B.
Williams, Colin
Wine, William David
Woolf, Jessica
Wood, Robin

Translators

Robert Streit —
  Czechoslovakian

Zita Laus —
  Portuguese

Lillian Chorvat —
  Czechoslovakian

Stanley F. Smelhaus —
  Czechoslovakian

THE INTERNATIONAL DICTIONARY OF
FILMS AND FILMMAKERS: VOLUME II

DIRECTORS/ FILMMAKERS

Akerman, Chantal
Aldrich, Robert
Alexeieff, Alexander and Parker, Claire
Allégret, Marc
Allégret, Yves
Allen, Woody
Allio, René
Altman, Robert
Alvarez, Santiago
Anderson, Lindsay
Angelopoulos, Theodoros
Anger, Kenneth
Antonioni, Michelangelo
Arzner, Dorothy
Ashby, Hal
Asquith, Anthony
Astruc, Alexandre
Autant-Lara, Claude
Avery, Tex

Bacon, Lloyd
Baillie, Bruce
Bakshi, Ralph
Bardem, Juan Antonio
Becker, Jacques
Bellocchio, Marco
Benegal, Shyam
Benoit-Lévy, Jean
Beresford, Bruce
Bergman, Ingmar
Berkeley, Busby
Bertolucci, Bernardo
Birri, Fernando
Blackton, J. Stuart
Blasetti, Alessandro
Blier, Bertrand
Blom, August
Boetticher, Budd
Bogdanovich, Peter
Bolognini, Mauro
Boorman, John
Borau, José Luis
Borzage, Frank
Boulting, Roy and John
Brakhage, Stan
Breer, Robert
Brenon, Herbert
Bresson, Robert
Broca, Philippe de
Brocka, Lino
Brooks, Mel
Brooks, Richard
Broughton, James
Brown, Clarence
Browning, Tod
Buñuel, Luis

Capra, Frank
Carlsen, Henning
Carné, Marcel
Carpenter, John
Cassavetes, John
Castellani, Renato
Cavalcanti, Alberto
Cayatte, Andre
Chabrol, Claude

Chahine, Youssef
Chaplin, Charlie
Christensen, Benjamin
Christian-Jacque
Chytilová, Véra
Cimino, Michael
Clair, René
Clarke, Shirley
Clayton, Jack
Clément, René
Clouzot, Henri-Georges
Cocteau, Jean
Cohl, Emile
Comencini, Luigi
Conner, Bruce
Coppola, Francis Ford
Costa-Gavras, Constantin
Crichton, Charles
Cromwell, John
Crosland, Alan
Cruze, James
Cukor, George
Curtiz, Michael
Czinner, Paul

D'Arrast, Harry d'Abbadie
Dassin, Jules
Daves, Delmer
De Antonio, Emile
Dearden, Basil
De Fuentes, Fernando
Delannoy, Jean
Delluc, Louis
De Mille, Cecil B.
Demme, Jonathan
Demy, Jacques
De Palma, Brian
Deren, Maya
De Santis, Giuseppe
De Sica, Vittorio
De Toth, Andre
Dickinson, Thorold
Diegues, Carlos
Dieterle, William
Disney, Walt
Dmytryk, Edward
Donen, Stanley
Donner, Jörn
Donskoi, Mark
Dovzhenko, Alexander
Dreyer, Carl Theodor
Dudow, Slatan
Dulac, Germaine
Dupont, E.A.
Duras, Marguerite
Duvivier, Julien
Dwan, Allan

Edwards, Blake
Eggeling, Viking
Eisenstein, Sergei
Emshwiller, Ed
Epstein, Jean
Ermler, Friedrich

Fábri, Zoltán

Fassbinder, Rainer Werner
Fejös, Pál
Fellini, Federico
Fernández, Emilio
Ferreri, Marco
Feuillade, Louis
Feyder, Jacques
Fischinger, Oskar
Fisher, Terence
Flaherty, Robert
Fleischer, Max and Dave
Fleischer, Richard
Fleming, Victor
Florey, Robert
Ford, Aleksander
Ford, John
Forman, Milos
Fosse, Bob
Frampton, Hollis
Franju, Georges
Frankenheimer, John
Franklin, Sidney
Frič, Martin
Friedkin, William
Fuller, Samuel

Gaál, István
Gad, Urban
Gallone, Carmine
Gance, Abel
Garciá Berlanga, Luis
Garnett, Tay
Gehr, Ernie
Gerasimov, Sergie
Germi, Pietro
Godard, Jean-Luc
Gómez, Manuel Octavio
Gomez, Sara
Goretta, Claude
Gosho, Heinosuke
Goulding, Edmund
Grémillon, Jean
Grierson, John
Griffith, D.W.
Guerra, Ruy
Guitry, Sacha
Güney, Yilmaz
Gutiérrez Alea, Tomás
Guy, Alice
Guzmán, Patricio

Haanstra, Bert
Halas, John and Batchelor, Joy
Hamer, Robert
Hammid, Alexander
Hani, Susumu
Hathaway, Henry
Hauff, Reinhard
Hawks, Howard
Henning-Jensen, Astrid and Bjarne
Hepworth, Cecil
Herzog, Werner
Hill, George Roy
Hill, Walter
Hiller, Arthur
Hitchcock, Alfred

Holger-Madsen
Howard, William K.
Huston, John

Ichikawa, Kon
Imai, Tadashi
Imamura, Shohei
Ingram, Rex
Ioseliani, Otar
Ivens, Joris
Ivory, James

Jancsó, Miklós
Jennings, Humphrey
Jewison, Norman
Jireš, Jaromil
Jones, Chuck
Jutra, Claude

Kachyna, Karel
Kadár, Ján
Kapoor, Raj
Kawalerowicz, Jerzy
Kazan, Elia
Keaton, Buster
Kershner, Irvin
King, Henry
King Hu
Kinoshita, Keisuke
Kinugasa, Teinosuke
Kline, Herbert
Kluge, Alexander
Kobayashi, Setsuo
Korda, Alexander
Kovács, András
Kozintsev, Grigori
Kramer, Robert
Kramer, Stanley
Kubelka, Peter
Kubrick, Stanley
Kuleshov, Lev
Kurosawa, Akira

La Cava, Gregory
Landow, George
Lang, Fritz
Lattuada, Alberto
Leacock, Richard
Lean, David
Leduc, Paul
Leenhardt, Roger
Lefebvre, Jean-Pierre
Le Grice, Malcolm
Leisen, Mitchell
Lelouch, Claude
Leni, Paul
Lenica, Jan
Leone, Sergio
LeRoy, Mervyn
Lester, Richard
Lewis, Jerry
L'Herbier, Marcel
Littin, Miguel
Litvak, Anatole
Loach, Ken
Logan, Joshua

Lorentz, Pare
Losey, Joseph
Lubitsch, Ernst
Lucas, George
Lumet, Sidney
Lumière, Louis
Lye, Len

Mackendrick, Alexander
Makavejev, Dušan
Malick, Terence
Malle, Louis
Mamoulian, Rouben
Mankiewicz, Joseph
Mann, Anthony
Marker, Chris
Markopoulos, Gregory
Mauro, Humberto
Maysles, Albert and David
Mazursky, Paul
McCarey, Leo
McCay, Winsor
McLaren, Norman
McLeod, Norman
Mekas, Jonas
Méliès, Georges
Melville, Jean-Pierre
Menzel, Jiří
Mészáros, Márta
Micheaux, Oscar
Mikhalkov-Konchalovsky, Andrei
Milestone, Lewis
Milius, John
Miller, George
Minnelli, Vincente
Mizoguchi, Kenji
Molander, Gustaf
Monicelli, Mario
Mulligan, Robert
Munk, Andrzej
Murnau, F.W.

Naruse, Mikio
Negulesco, Jean
Neilan, Marshall
Němec, Jan
Niblo, Fred
Nichols, Mike

Olcott, Sidney
Oliveira, Manoel de
Olmi, Ermanno
Ophuls, Marcel
Ophüls, Max
Oshima, Nagisa
Oswald, Richard
Ozu, Yasujiro

Pabst, G.W.
Pagnol, Marcel
Pakula, Alan J.
Pal, George
Panfilov, Gleb
Paradzhanov, Sergei
Pasolini, Pier Paolo
Passer, Ivan

Pastrone, Giovanni
Pearson, George
Peckinpah, Sam
Penn, Arthur
Pereira dos Santos, Nélson
Peries, Lester James
Perrault, Pierre
Peterson, Sidney
Petri, Elio
Pick, Lupu
Polanski, Roman
Pollack, Sydney
Polonsky, Abraham
Pontecorvo, Gillo
Porter, Edwin S.
Powell, Michael and Pressburger, Emeric
Preminger, Otto
Protazanov, Yakov
Ptushko, Alexander
Pudovkin, Vsevolod

Rademakers, Fons
Rafelson, Bob
Rainer, Yvonne
Ray, Nicholas
Ray, Satyajit
Reed, Carol
Reichenbach, Francois
Reiniger, Lotte
Reisz, Karel
Renoir, Jean
Resnais, Alain
Richardson, Tony
Richter, Hans
Riefenstahl, Leni
Risi, Dino
Ritchie, Michael
Ritt, Martin
Rivette, Jacques
Robison, Arthur
Robson, Mark
Rocha, Gláuber
Roeg, Nicolas
Rohmer, George
Romm, Mikhail
Roos, Jorgen
Rosi, Francesco
Rossellini, Roberto
Rossen, Robert
Rouch, Jean
Roy, Bimal
Ruggles, Wesley
Ruiz, Raúl
Russell, Ken
Ruttmann, Walter

Sandrich, Mark
Saura, Carlos
Sautet, Claude
Saville, Victor
Schaffner, Franklin
Schatzberg, Jerry
Schlesinger, John
Schlöndorff, Volker
Schoedsack, Ernest
Schorm, Evald

Schrader, Paul
Scola, Ettore
Scorsese, Martin
Seaton, George
Sembene, Ousmane
Sen, Mrinal
Sennett, Mack
Shindo, Kaneto
Shinoda, Masahiro
Shub, Esther
Sidney, George
Siegel, Don
Siodmak, Robert
Sirk, Douglas
Sjöberg, Alf
Sjöman, Vilgot
Sjöström, Victor
Skolimowski, Jerzy
Smith, Harry
Snow, Michael
Solanas, Fernando and Getino, Octavio
Solás, Humberto
Spielberg, Steven
Stahl, John
Staudte, Wolfgang
Stevens, George
Stiller, Mauritz
Storck, Henri
Straub, Jean-Marie and Huillet, Danièle
Strick, Joseph
Sturges, John
Sturges, Preston
Sucksdorff, Arne
Sutherland, Edward
Syberberg, Hans-Jürgen
Szabó, István

Tanner, Alain
Tarkovsky, Andrei
Tashlin, Frank
Tati, Jacques
Taurog, Norman
Tavernier, Bertrand
Taviani, Paolo and Vittorio
Teshigahara, Hiroshi
Torre-Nilsson, Leopoldo
Tourneur, Jacques
Tourneur, Maurice
Trnka, Jiři
Troell, Jan
Truffaut, Francois

Ulmer, Edgar

Vadim, Roger
Vanderbeek, Stan
Van Dyke, Willard
Van Dyke, W.S.
Van Peebles, Melvin
Varda, Agnès
Vasiliev, Sergei and Georgi
Verneuil, Henri
Vertov, Dziga
Vidor, Charles
Vidor, King
Vigo, Jean

Visconti, Luchino
von Sternberg, Josef
von Stroheim, Erich
von Trotta, Margarethe

Wajda, Andrzej
Walsh, Raoul
Walters, Charles
Warhol, Andy and Morrissey, Paul
Watkins, Peter
Watt, Harry
Weber, Lois
Weir, Peter
Weiss, Jiři
Welles, Orson
Wellman, William
Wenders, Wim
Wertmuller, Lina
Whale, James
Wicki, Bernhard
Widerberg, Bo
Wieland, Joyce
Wiene, Robert
Wilcox, Herbert
Wilder, Billy
Wise, Robert
Wiseman, Frederick
Wolf, Konrad
Wood, Sam
Wright, Basil
Wyler, William

Yates, Peter
Yoshimura, Kozabura
Yutkevich, Sergei

Zampa, Luigi
Zanussi, Krzysztof
Zecca, Ferdinand
Zeffirelli, Franco
Zeman, Karel
Zetterling, Mai
Zinnemann, Fred
Zurlini, Valerio

AKERMAN, CHANTAL. Belgian. Born in Brussels, June 1950. Educated at INSAS film school, Brussels, 1967-68; studied one year at Université Internationale du Théâtre, Paris. Career: 1971—receives 1st attention when *Saute ma ville* entered in Oberhausen festival; 1972—lives in New York for most of year, returns in 1973 to finish *Hanging Out—Yonkers*; 1979—*Les Rendez-vous d'Anna*, produced by Gaumont, a financial failure; moves to Los Angeles, fails in attempt to fund project to film I.B. Singer's *The Manor and the Estate*; returns to Belgium.

Films (as director): 1968—*Saute ma ville*; 1971—*L'Enfant aimé*; 1972—*Hotel Monterey*; *La Chambre*; 1973—*Le 15/18* (co-d); *Hanging Out—Yonkers (Yonkers, Hanging Out)*; 1974—*Je, tu, il, elles*; 1975—*Jeanne Dielman, 23 Quai du Commerce, 1080 Bruxelles*; 1976—*News from Home*; 1978—*Les Rendez-vous d'Anna*; 1982—*Toute une nuit*; 1983—*Les Années 80 (The Golden Eighties)* (co-sc).

Publications:

By AKERMAN:

Articles—interview by C. Alemann and H. Hurst in *Frauen und Film* (Berlin), March 1976; interview by D. Dubroux and others in *Cahiers du cinéma* (Paris), July 1977; "Chantal Akerman", with interview, by B. Villien and P. Carcassonne in *Cinématographe* (Paris), June 1977; interview by P. Carcassonne and L. Cugny in *Cinématographe* (Paris), November 1978; interview by C. Champetier in *Cahiers du cinéma* (Paris), May 1978; interview by I. Aranda and A. Pagaolatos in *Contracampo* (Madrid), March 1981.

On AKERMAN:

Articles—"Women Working" by C. Creveling in *Camera Obscura* (Berkeley), fall 1976; "Chantal Akerman: il cinema puro" by G. Bertolina in *Filmcritica* (Rome), March 1976; "Jeanne Dielman, 23 Quai du Commerce, 1080 Bruxelles", with interview, by J. Bergstrom in *Camera Obscura* (Berkeley), fall 1977; "La qualifica di laboratorio alla prova dei film presentati. II: Akerman: una scoperta" by E. Comuzio in *Cineforum* (Bergamo), September 1977; "Apropos des films de C. Akerman: un temps atmosphere" by E. Mairesse in *Cahiers du cinéma* (Paris), October 1977; "Les Rendez-vous de Chantal" by M. Levieux and M. Martin in *Ecran* (Paris), December 1978; "Wahrnehmungsformen von Zeit und Raum am Beispiel der Filme von Marguerite Duras und Chantal Akerman" by N. Seni in *Frauen und Film* (Berlin), September 1979; "Notas sobre un nuevo cine: El de Chantal Akerman" by M. Orellana in *Cine* (Mexico), January/-February 1980.

*   *   *

At 15 Chantal Akerman saw Godard's *Pierrot le fou* and realized that filmmaking could be experimental and personal. She dropped in and out of film school and has since created short and feature films for viewers who appreciate the chance to think about sounds and images. Her films are often shot in real time, and in space that is part of the characters' identity.

During a self-administered apprenticeship in New York (1972-74) shooting short films on very low budgets, Akerman learned much, she said, from the work of innovators Michael Snow and Stan Brakhage. She was encouraged to explore organic techniques for her personal subject matter. In her deliberately paced films there are long takes, scenes shot with stationary camera, and a play of light in relation to subjects and their space. (In *Jeanne Dielman, 23 Quai du Commerce, 1080 Bruxelles*, as Jeanne rides up or down in the elevator, diagonals of light from each floor cut across her face in a regular rhythm.) There are vistas down long corridors, acting with characters' backs to the camera, and scenes concluded with several seconds of darkness. In Akerman films there are hotels and journeys, little conversation. Windows are opened and sounds let in, doors opened and closed; we hear a doorbell, a radio, voices on the telephone answering machine, footsteps, city noises. Each frame is carefully composed, each gesture the precise result of Akerman's direction. A frequent collaborator is her sensitive cameraperson Babette Mangolte who has worked with Akerman on *Jeanne Dielman 23 Quai du Commerce, 1080 Bruxelles*, *News from Home* and *Toute une nuit*. Mangolte has also worked with avant gardists Yvonne Rainer, Marcel Hanoun and Michael Snow.

In Akerman films plot is minimal, or non-existent. Old welfare clients come and go amid the impressive architecture of a once splendid hotel on New York's Upper West Side in *Hotel Monterey*. New York City plays its busy, noisy self for the camera as Akerman's voice on the sound track reads concerned letters from her mother in Belgium in *News from Home*. A young filmmaker travels to Germany to appear at a screening of her latest film, meets people who distress her, and her mother who delights her, and returns home in *Les Rendez-vous d'Anna*. Jeanne Dielman, super-efficient housewife, earns money as a prostitute to support herself and her son. Her routine breaks down by chance, and she murders one of her customers.

The films (some semi-autobiographical) are not dramatic in the conventional sense, nor are they glamorized or eroticized; the excitement is inside the characters. In a film Akerman calls a love letter to her mother, Jeanne Dielman is seen facing the steady camera as members of a cooking class might see her, and she prepares a meatloaf—in real time. Later she gives herself a thorough scrubbing in the bathtub; only her head and the motion of her arms are visible. Her straightening and arranging and smoothing are seen as a child would see and remember them.

In *Toute une nuit* Akerman continues her precision and control as she stages the separate, audience-involving adventures of a huge cast of all ages that wanders out into Brussels byways one hot, stormy night. In this film, reminiscent of Wim Wenders and his wanderers and Marguerite Duras with her inventive sound tracks, choreography and sense of place, Akerman continues to explore her medium using no conventional plot, few spoken words, many sounds, people leaving the frame to a lingering camera, and appealing images. A little girl asks a man to dance with her, and he does. The filmmaker's feeling for the child, and the child's independence can't be mistaken.

—Lillian Schiff

ALDRICH, ROBERT. American. Born in Cranston, Rhode Island, 9 August 1918. Educated at Moses Brown School, Providence, Rhode Island; University of Virginia (studied law and economics), degree 1941. Married Harriet Foster in 1941 (divorced 1965); children: Adell, William, Alida and Kelly; married fashion model Sibylle Siegfried in 1966. Career: 1941—becomes production clerk at RKO studios; soon made 3rd assistant director; 1942-44—works on RKO films for Edward Dmytryk,

Irving Reis and others; 1944—leaves RKO to freelance, begins work on *The Southerner* with Jean Renoir; 1945-48—under contract to Enterprise Studios, serves in production capacities and as assistant screenwriter; works as 1st assistant director on United Artists productions; 1952—begins to direct for television; TV work includes episodes of *4 Star Playhouse*, pilots for series *Adventurer in Paradise* and *The Sundance Kid*; 1955—"Associates and Aldrich Company" formed following success of *Kiss Me Deadly*, produces 12 features through 1972; 1956—contract with Columbia Pictures, fired after refusing to "soften" script of *The Garment Jungle*; 1957-62—directs films abroad; 1962—returns to Hollywood; 1967—success of *The Dirty Dozen* makes possible establishment of Aldrich Studios; 1973—forced to sell studio; 1975—elected President of Directors Guild; 1976—"Aldrich Company" reorganized. Died in Los Angeles of kidney failure, 5 December 1983. Recipient: Silver Prize, Venice Festival, for *The Big Knife*, 1955; Silver Bear Award for Best Direction, Berlin Festival, for *Autumn Leaves*, 1956; Italian Critics Award, Venice Festival, for *Attack!*, 1956.

Films (as 1st assistant director): 1945—*The Southerner* (Renoir); 1946—*The Story of G.I. Joe* (Wellman); *Pardon My Past* (Fenton); *The Strange Love of Martha Ivers* (Milestone); 1947—*The Private Affairs of Bel Ami* (Lewin); *Body and Soul* (Rossen); 1948—*Arch of Triumph* (Milestone); *So This is New York* (Fleischer); *No Minor Vices* (Milestone); 1949—*Force of Evil* (Polonsky); *The Red Pony* (Milestone); *A Kiss for Corliss* (Wallace); 1950—*The White Tower* (Tetzlaff); *Teresa* (Zinnemann) (pre-prod. work only); 1951—*The Prowler* (Losey); *M* (Losey); *Of Men and Music* (Reis); *New Mexico* (Reis); 1952—*Abbott and Costello Meet Captain Kidd* (Lamont); *Limelight* (Chaplin); *The Trio: Rubinstein, Heifetz and Piatigorsky (Million Dollar Trio)* (Dassin); *The Steel Trap* (Stone) (pr supervision only); (as director): 1953—*The Big Leaguer*; 1954—*World for Ransom* (+co-pr); *Apache*; *Vera Cruz*; 1955—*Kiss Me Deadly* (+pr); *The Big Knife* (+pr); 1956—*Autumn Leaves*; *Attack!* (+pr); 1957—*The Garment Jungle* (un-credited); *The Ride Back* (pr only); 1959—*The Angry Hills*; *10 Seconds to Hell* (+co-sc); 1961—*The Last Sunset*; 1962—*Whatever Happened to Baby Jane?* (pr); *Sodoma e Gomorra (Sodom and Gomorrah)* (co-d); 1963—*4 for Texas* (+co-pr, co-sc); 1964—*Hush...Hush, Sweet Charlotte* (+pr); 1966—*Flight of the Phoenix* (+pr); 1967—*The Dirty Dozen*; 1968—*The Legend of Lylah Clare* (+pr); *The Killing of Sister George* (+pr); 1969—*Too Late the Hero* (+pr, co-sc); *What Ever Happened to Aunt Alice?* (pr only); 1971—*The Grissom Gang* (+pr); 1972—*Ulzana's Raid*; 1973—*Emperor of the North (The Emperor of the North Pole)*; 1974—*The Longest Yard (The Mean Machine)*; 1975—*Hustle* (+co-pr); 1977—*Twilight's Last Gleaming*; *The Choirboys*; 1979—*The Frisco Kid*; 1981—*All the Marbles*.

Publications:

By ALDRICH:

Articles—interview by George Fenin in *Film Culture* (New York), July/August 1956; interview by François Truffaut in *Cahiers du cinéma* (Paris), November 1956; "High Price of Independence" in *Films and Filming* (London), June 1958; interview by François Truffaut in *Cahiers du cinéma* (Paris), April 1958; "Mes Deboires en Europe" in *Cahiers du cinéma* (Paris), May 1960; "Learning from My Mistakes" in *Films and Filming* (London), June 1960; "The Care and Feeding of Baby Jane" in the *New York Times*, 4 November 1962; "Hollywood.-

..Still an Empty Tomb" in *Cinema* (Beverly Hills), May/June 1963; "What Ever Happened to American Movies?" in *Sight and Sound* (London), winter 1963/64; "American Report" in *Cahiers du cinéma* (Paris), December/January 1964/65; "Director's Formula for a Happy Cast" in the *Los Angeles Times*, 7 February 1966; "Filmmaking in an Era of New Liberality" in the *Los Angeles Times*, 15 December 1968; interview by Joel Greenburg in *Sight and Sound* (London), winter 1968/69; "Why I Bought My Own Studio" in *Action* (Los Angeles), January/February 1969; "Impressions of Russia" in *Action* (Los Angeles), July/-August 1971; "Dialogue" with Bernardo Bertolucci in *Action* (Los Angeles), March/April 1974; "Robert Aldrich Discusses the Horror of Personality Directors" by C. Derry in *Cinefantastique* (Oak Park, Illinois), no.3, 1974; "Up to Date with Robert Aldrich", interview by Harry Ringel in *Sight and Sound* (London), summer 1974; "Aldrich Interview" by Pierre Sauvage in *Movie* (London), winter 1976/77; "I can't get Jimmy Carter to see my movie!", interview by Stuart Byron, in *Film Comment* (New York), March/April 1977; "Dialogue on Film: Robert Aldrich" in *American Film* (Washington, D.C.), November 1978.

On ALDRICH:

Books—*Robert Aldrich* by Rene Micha, Brussels 1957; *The Celluloid Muse: Hollywood Directors Speak* by Charles Higham, London 1969; *Robert Aldrich: A Guide to References and Resources* by Alain Silver and Elizabeth Ward, Boston 1979; articles—"On Revolution" by Jacques Rivette in *Cahiers du cinéma* (Paris), no.54, 1955; "La Photo du mois" by François Truffaut in *Cahiers du cinéma* (Paris), December 1955; "Hysteria and Authoritarianism in the Films of Robert Aldrich" by Ian Jarvie in *Film Culture* (New York), summer 1961; "Interview and Filmography" by Ian Cameron and Mark Shivas in *Movie* (London), April 1963; "La Fonction de Producer" by Charles Bitsch and B. Tavernier in *Cahiers du cinéma* (Paris), December/January 1964/65; "Directed By:" by Claude Chabrol in *Cahiers du cinéma* (Paris), December/January 1964/65; "Aldrich Weighs Hollywood's Future" by Charles Champlin in the *Los Angeles Times*, 24 August 1969; "Robert Aldrich", edited by James Silke in *Dialogue on Film* (Washington, D.C.), no.2, 1972; "Mr. Film Noir Stays at the Table" by Alain Silver in *Film Comment* (New York), spring 1972; "Aldrich Philosophizes on Biz Where You're 'Only as Good as Your Last Pic'" by Lee Beaupre in *Variety* (New York), 21 June 1973; "Bob Aldrich: Candid Maverick" by Lee Beaupre in *Variety* (New York), 27 June 1973; "Aldrich's Safari in Mogul Country" by Charles Champlin in the *Los Angeles Times*, 25 August 1974; "Robert Aldrich: The Director as Phoenix" by Harry Ringel in *Take One* (Montreal), September 1974; "*Kiss Me Deadly*: Evidence of a Style" by Alain Silver in *Film Comment* (New York), March/April 1975; "Worlds Apart: Aldrich Since *The Dirty Dozen*" by Richard Combs in *Sight and Sound* (London), spring 1976; "Aldrich le rebelle" by B. Duval in *Image et Son* (Paris), May 1976; "Robert Aldrich et l'incompletude du nihilism" by Gerard Legrand in *Positif* (Paris), June 1976; "L'Homme d'Aldrich" by R. Gazano and M. Cusso in *Cinéma* (Paris), June 1980.

*　　*　　*

Despite a commercially respectable career both within the studio system and as an independent producer-director, Robert Aldrich remains an ill-appreciated, if not entirely bothersome presence for most American critics. Andrew Sarris did praise Aldrich in 1968 as "one of the most strikingly personal directors of the past two decades"; yet, for the most part, it has remained to the French and the English to attempt to unravel the defiant quirkiness of Aldrich's career. Only the otherworldly *Kiss Me Deadly*, which Paul Schrader unequivocally dubbed "the masterpiece of film noir," has received anything like the attention it deserves on this side of the Atlantic; yet the film is quite indicative of the bitter ironies, bizarre stylistics and scathing nihilism characteristic of most of Aldrich's work.

In bringing Mickey Spillane's neo-fascist hero Mike Hammer to the screen, *Kiss Me Deadly* plays havoc with the conventions of the hardboiled detective, turning the existential avenger into a narcissistic materialist who exploits those around him for the benefit of his plush lifestyle. In an outrageous alteration of the novel's plot, Hammer becomes a modern neanderthal whose individualism is revealed as insanity when it causes him to botch a case involving a box of pure nuclear energy and thus the fate of the world. The result is a final shot of a mushroom cloud rising from a California beachhouse, consuming both Hammer and the bad guys. Only at this extreme and this distance in time has Aldrich's acute sense of irony impressed itself upon a liberal critical establishment whose repugnance to the surfaces of his films has usually served as an excuse for ignoring their savage, multi-layered critiques of Hollywood genres and American ideology.

The extremity of Aldrich's re-interpretations of the Western in *Ulzana's Raid*, of the war movie in *Attack!*, of the cop film in *The Choirboys*, and of the women's melodrama in *Autumn Leaves* betrays a cynicism so bitter that it could only arise from a liberal sensibility utterly disillusioned by an age in which morality has become a cruel joke. In fact, the shattering of illusions is central to Aldrich's work, and it is a powerfully self-destructive process, given the sweetness of the illusions and the anger of his iconoclasm. In *Whatever Happened to Baby Jane?*, a gothic horror film whose terms are explicitly the hideous realities hidden beneath the sugar-coating of the entertainment industry, Aldrich virtually defines the genre of camp, offering derisive laughter as the only alternative to an unbearably absurd cosmos. This sense of black comedy (which Aldrich shares with, and developed at the same time as Hollywood contemporary Stanley Kubrick) has frequently been responsible for the volatile relationship his films have had with popular audiences. Given the context of a life-and-death prison football game in *The Longest Yard*, Aldrich was able to enlist the audience in the hero's bitter laughter in the face of a triumphant totalitarian authority. But when he adopted the same black humor toward the scandalous chicanery of the marginally psychotic cops in *The Choirboys*, he angered almost everybody, not the least of whom was the novel's author Joseph Wambaugh.

Turned in an introspective direction, Aldrich's acid sensibility has resulted in an intensely discomforting, stylistically alienated version of Clifford Odets's Hollywood-hating *The Big Knife* and the madly ambitious *The Legend of Lylah Clare*, an 8½ cum *Vertigo* far too complex by any Hollywood standard. When turned outward toward the world at large, that same sensibility is responsible for a downbeat, disheartening masterpiece like the much-maligned *Hustle*, a film which succeeds better than almost any other in summing up the moral displacement and emotional anguish of the whole decade of the 1970s.

At his most skillful, Aldrich can juggle ideologically volatile issues so well that his most popular film *The Dirty Dozen*, made during the politically turbulent period of the Vietnam war, played equally well to hawks and doves. Its story of death row prisoners exploited by the military bureaucracy into participation in a suicide raid, where they are to attack a chateau, slaughtering both German officers and civilians, seemed explicitly antiwar in its equation of heroism and criminality and its critique of the body-count mentality of a morally corrupt system. Yet, *The Dirty Dozen* still managed to emerge as a gung-ho war movie in the best Hollywood tradition. The multiple contradictions of the film's stance are nowhere clearer than in its climactic scene, where Aldrich has black athlete Jim Brown re-create one of his famous touchdown runs in order to set off an underground holocaust explicitly parallelled to Auschwitz.

In a far less popular film, the revisionist western *Ulzana's Raid*, Aldrich does confront the horrors of Vietnam with a nearly intolerable accuracy via the properly bloody metaphor of a cavalry company using West Point tactics to fight a band of Apache guerilla warriors. The film relentlessly refuses to diminish the brutality of the red man; even as it demonstrates the poverty of the white man's Christian idealism. The result is perhaps the first western ever to cast America's doctrine of Manifest Destiny in explicitly colonial terms.

More than any other mainstream director, Aldrich has insisted on presenting the radical contradictions of American ideology. If we adopt a stance not nearly as cynical as his own in most of his films, we might observe that his capacity to do so has frequently resulted in sizable profits. Yet it is also important to remember that, while Stanley Kubrick (whose fifties films bear striking stylistic and thematic similarities to those of Aldrich) found it necessary to retreat to England, reducing his output to two or three films a decade, Aldrich chose to fight it out in Hollywood, where his capacity for money-making has allowed him the space to vent his own personal anger at the compromises we all must make.

—Ed Lowry

ALEXEIEFF and PARKER. Russian/American. Alexander Alexeieff (also spelled as 'Alexandre Alexieff') born in Kazan, Russia, 5 August 1901. Claire Parker born in Boston, 1907. Married in 1941; Alexeieff previously married to actress Alexandra Grinevsky, 1923 (divorced). Career: 1921—Alexeieff moves to Paris to study linguistics; becomes scenic designer for Diaghilev's Ballets Russes; 1920s—active as artist, book illustrator, and stage designer; 1931—Claire Parker, then his student, collaborates with Alexeieff and wife Alexandra Grinevsky on first pinboard ("l'écran d'épingles") animation; 1933—*Night on Bald Mountain* a commercial failure, Alexeieff turns to advertising films for theatrical exhibition; 1935-39—with collaborators Georges Violet and others, Alexeieff and Parker produce 25 films, mostly for sponsors or advertisers; some of these feature original scores by major composers such as Poulenc, Auric, and Milhaud; 1940—emigrate to U.S. and marry following year, continue work as illustrators; 1947—return to Paris; 1952-64—produce 21 advertising films using "totalization" technique; 1957—designed logo used on films of distribution company Cocinor; 1962—produce animated prologue to Orson Welles's *The Trial*; through 1970—illustrated books (some using serial photos made on pinboard) total more than 40. Alexeieff died in 1979, Parker in 1980.

Films (as directors and animators): 1933—*Une Nuit sur le Mont Chauve (Night on Bald Mountain)* (+pr); 1935—*La Belle au bois dormant* (puppet film); 1943—*En passant*; 1962—prologue to *Le Procès (The Trial)* (Welles); 1963—*Le Nez (The Nose)*; 1966—*L'Eau*; 1972—*Tableaux d'une exposition (Pictures at an Exhibition)*; 1980—*Trois Themes (3 Themes)*.

Advertising and Sponsored Films: 1936—*Lingner Werke*; *Opta empfangt*; 1937—*Le Trône de France*; *Grands Feux*; *Parade des chapeaux*; *Franck Aroma*; *La Crème Simon*; 1938—*Les Vêtements Sigrand*; *Huilor*; *L'Eau d'Evian*; *Les Fonderies Martin*; *Balatum*; *Les Oranges de Jaffa*; *Les Cigarettes Bastos*; 1939—*Gulf Stream*; *Les Gaines Roussel*; *Cenpa*; *Le Gaz* (unfinished); 1951—*Fumées*; 1952—*Masques*; 1954—*Nocturne*; *Pure Beauté*; *Esso*; *Rimes*; 1955—*La Sève de la terre*; *Le Buisson ardent*; 1956—*Quatre Temps*; *Bain d'X (Bendix)*; 1957—*Constance*; *Anonyme*; *Osram* (4 films); *Cent pour cent*; 1959—*Automation*; 1960—*La Dauphine Java*; 1962—*Divertissement*; *A propos de Jivago*.

Publications:

By ALEXEIEFF and PARKER:

Books—*Alexandre Alexeieff*, exhibition catalogue, National Library of Scotland, Edinburgh 1967; *Alexandre Alexeieff*, exhibition catalogue, by G. Rondolino, Cinema Incontri Abano Terme, Este 1971; *Alexandre Alexeieff*, exhibition catalogue, edited by G. Bendazzi, Ente provinciale per il turismo di Milano, Milan 1973; *A. Alexeieff, C. Parker: Films et eaux-fortes, 1925-75*, exhibition catalogue, Chateau d'Annecy, 1975; "Entretien avec A. Alexeieff et C. Parker" by N. Salomon, Annecy 1980; *Pages d'Alexeieff* edited by G. Bendazzi, Milan 1983; *A. Alexeieff ou la gravure animée*, exhibition catalogue, Chateau d'Annecy, 1983; articles—"Circuit fermé!" in *Cinéma 57* (Paris), no.14, 1957; "L'Écran d'épingles" in *Technicien du film* (Paris), no.27, 1957; "Reflections on Motion Picture Animation" in *Film Culture* (New York), no.32, 1964; interview in *Script*, no.10-12, 1964; "Synthèse cinématographique des mouvements artificiels" in *IDHEC* (Paris), 1966; interview in *Image et son* (Paris), no.207, 1967; "The Synthesis of Artificial Movements in Motion Picture Projection" in *Film Culture* (New York), no.48-49, 1970; "Chère Marthe" in *Bulletin d'information ASIFA*, no.1, 1972; "Le Chant d'ombres et de lumières de 1 250 000 épingles", edited by H. Arnault, in *Cinéma pratique* (Paris), no.123, 1973; "Alféoni par Alexeieff" edited by L. Olteanu, in *Nous mêmes*, ASIFA, Bucharest 1973; "Cinema d'animazione: strategia e tattica" in *Filmcritica* (Rome), no.31, 1980.

On ALEXEIEFF and PARKER:

Books—*Discovering the Movies* by Cecile Starr, New York 1972; *Experimental Animation* by R. Russett and C. Starr, New York 1976; articles—"Une Nuit sur le Mont Chauve, film en gravure animée par A. Alexeieff et C. Parker" by L. Cheronnet in *Art et décoration* (Paris), no.63, 1934; "Alexandre Alexeieff et les cinémas possibles" by A. Martin in *Cinéma 63* (Paris), no.81, 1963; "Alexeieff nez à nez" by P. Philippe in *Cinéma 63* (Paris), no.81, 1963; "Notes on The Nose" by Cecile Starr in *Film Society Review* (New York), November 1965; "The Road Less Travelled" by R.R. Rains in *The Lens & Speaker* (Univ. of Illinois Visual Aids Service), 15.1, 1977; "A. Alexeieff" by J.P. Jouvanceau and C. Gaudillière in *Banc-Titre*, no.25, 1982; "Alexeieff's The Nose" by A.G. Robson in *Purdue University Film Studies* (Lafayette, Indiana), no.6, 1982; films—*Alexeieff at the Pinboard* produced by Cinema Nouveau, Paris 1960 (English version produced by Cecile Starr, 1972); *Pinscreen* produced by the National Film Board of Canada, 1972; *Annecy Impromptu* produced by S.F.P. Films, Paris 1976 (English version distributed by Cecile Starr).

* * *

Even a brief scrutiny of Alexeieff's cinema must acknowledge his preliminary activities in other spheres, initially the severe challenge of designing and painting sets for the theatrical production companies of Paris. An autodidact in each of his areas of skill and artistry, he soon took up engraving, woodcuts, etching, and lithographs for book illustration, all of which profited from the assistance and critiques of his first wife, actress Alexandra Grinevsky, whose painting skills complemented his own.

Although Alexeieff and Claire Parker, who arrived in 1931, were participants in the avant-garde movements of Paris, as artists they remained largely separate from these spheres; their art is mainly a synthesis of their own experiences and conceptions. The key to the pinboard that he and Parker created lies in Alexeieff's engravings, especially his masterwork to this point, a 3-volume edition of Dostoevsky's *Brothers Karamazov* for which he created 100 lithographs. Until his edition of Pasternak's *Dr. Zhivago* in 1959 with 200 pinboard illustrations, the Dostoevsky work remained the most powerful example of "static film," i.e. a series of images joined together serially to create an implicit sense of movement, providing a visually powerful interpretation of the verbal narrative.

From this impetus Parker and Alexeieff conceived a desire to animate his engravings, to employ chiaroscuro with even more refinement than was possible with engravings. The blurred contours and indistinct forms of their poetic and anti-narrative films reflect the Freudian preoccupation with dreams of avant-garde cinema in the twenties, to which they add a sense of theater and spectacle that invest the engravings with vivid drama.

At the same time as Alexeieff planned the pinboard with Parker, his student from Boston, Berthold Bartosch created *L'Idée*, described in its premiere announcement as "animated engravings." Less an influence than an inspiration, *L'Idée* became for Alexeieff and Parker an example of poetic animation, great art, arduous craftsmanship, and imaginative techniques.

All the pinboard films build their visual poetry upon the stimulus of a musical track devoid of dialogue. The only apparent anomaly in their use of the pinboard as a medium of visual poetry is *The Nose*, based on Gogol's short story. It is, however, more an homage to Gogol than a duplication of his narrative. Reducing his narrative to a slight strand, they build a finely detailed illustration of 19th century Russia centered on a breathtaking realization of Kazan Cathedral. The story of an overreaching czarist clerk serves as the occasion for exploring spatial definitions in a new way.

Their final two pinboard films are derived from a single Mussorgsky composition. In the spirit of their first Mussorgsky-inspired film, four decades earlier, they continued to explore animated orchestrations of movement and time with their minds attuned to basic issues of mathematics and physics. In their final creative decade, Alexeieff and Parker focussed more sharply on the ability of their medium to represent the free play of time and space, the intuitive interaction of visual and musical modes in a continual metamorphosis of contrapuntal relationships. *Pictures at an Exhibition* lacks the nightmarish quality of their initial film, but possesses quite different strengths. One pinboard in front of another establishes a visual dialogue, juxtaposing past and present in a sinuous and melancholy poetry that captures, through interlaced allusions, the paradoxical relationships between youth and maturity.

In no pinboard film, least of all in their final one *Three Themes*, do Alexeieff and Parker try to simulate what they would call photographic prose. Their texture is suggestive rather than explicit, a 3-part complementing and contrasting sonata; their goal is a heuristic creation of reality's depths where the mind and heart correspond freely. *Three Themes* is a fiftyfold slowdown of the normal scherzo pace of animation, a meditative elegy.

—Arthur G. Robson

ALLÉGRET, MARC. French. Born in Basel, Switzerland, 22 December 1900. Educated in law and political science. Career: 1925—directs cabaret acts; 1925-26—makes documentary on Belgian Congo accompanying uncle André Gide on West African tour; 1927-30—assistant to Robert Florey and Augusto Genina; 1930s—gives first major roles to a number of French film stars including Raimu, Simone Simon and Michèle Morgan. Died in Paris, 3 November 1973.

Films (as director): 1927—*Voyage au Congo* (co-d); 1930—*Papoul*; *La meilleure Bobonne*; *J'ai quelque chose à vous dire*; *L'Amour chante* (Genina) (art d only); 1931—*Le Blanc et le noir* (co-d); *Les Amants de minuit* (co-d); *Mam'zelle Nitouche*; *Attaque nocturne*; *L'Amour à l'américain* (Heymann and Fejos) (sc only); 1932—*Fanny*; 1934—*Lac-aux-Dames* (+co-sc); *L'Hôtel du libre échange*; *Sans famille*; *Zouzou*; 1935—*Les beaux Jours*; 1936—*Sous les yeux d'Occident (Razumov)*; *Les Amants terribles*; *Aventure à Paris*; 1937—*Orage*; *La Dame de Malacca*; *Gribouille (Heart of Paris)*; 1938—*Entrée des artistes (The Curtain Rises)* (+co-sc); 1939—*Le Corsaire* (uncompleted); 1940—*Jeune Filles de France* (short; co-d); 1941—*Parade en sept nuits*; 1942—*L'Arlésienne*; *Félicie Nanteuil (Histoire comique)*; *La Belle Aventure (Twilight)*; 1943—*Les Petites du Quai aux Fleurs*; 1945—*Lunegarde*; 1946—*Pétrus* (+co-sc); 1947—*Blanche Fury*; 1950—*The Naked Heart (Maria Chapdelaine)* (+sc); 1951—*La Demoiselle et son revenant*; 1952—*Avec André Gide* (+co-sc; 2 versions, feature and medium-length); *Blackmailed*; 1953—*Jean Coton* (+sc; short); *Le Film de Jean*; *Julietta*; *L'Amante di Paride (The Face That Launched a 1000 Ships, Loves of 3 Queens)* (+co-sc); *Eterna femmina* (co-d); 1954—*Futures vedettes* (+co-pr, co-sc); 1955—*L'Amant de Lady Chatterley (Lady Chatterley's Lover)* (+co-adapt); 1956—*En effeuillant la Marguerite (Please Mr. Balzac)* (+co-adapt); 1957—*Ma Femme, mon gosse et moi (L'Amour est un jeu)*; 1958—*Sois belle et tais-toi (Be Beautiful But Shut Up)* (+co-sc); 1959—*Un Drôle de dimanche*; *Les Affreux*; 1961—*Les Démons de minuit* (co-d, +co-sc); "Sophie (The Tale of Sophie)" episode of *Les Parisiennes (Tales of Paris)*; 1963—*L'Abominable Homme des douanes* (+co-sc); 1967—*Exposition 1900* (+sc; short); *Lumière* (+sc; short); 1968—*Début de siècle* (+sc; medium length); *La Grande-Bretagne et les Etats-Unis de 1896 à 1900* (+sc; short); 1969—*Europe continentale avant 1900* (+sc; short); *Europe méridionale au temps des rois* (+sc; short); 1970—*Le Bal du Comte d'Orgell* (+sc). Role: 1960—*...Et mourir de plaisir* (Vadim).

Publications:

On ALLÉGRET:

Article—"Marc Allegret le dilettante" by Claude Beylie in *Ecran* (Paris), December 1973.

*   *   *

From the beginning an air of importance surrounded the name Marc Allégret. Born into a privileged family he was virtually adopted by a most famous uncle, André Gide, and actually got his start in cinema through the travel documentary he made accompanying Gide on his Congo voyage in 1925. The full-length film, which was really an ethnographic study, received some exhibition in Paris, but Allégret then had no serious intentions of devoting his life to this art. It was a hobby to him, and he organized evenings of experimental films (his own among them) for his friends.

When the introduction of sound made Paris a world center of film production, anyone with any experience was wanted. Allégret worked as assistant to Robert Florey, finishing their second project himself when Florey returned to Hollywood. He then began to work with Raimu whom he directed in three films, the last of which was Pagnol's *Fanny*. Unquestionably the 1930's are the best years of a career that produced more than 30 films. Marc Allégret has always had an instinct for cultural fads and moods. In the 1930s he engaged topics and actors that put him near the top of the profession.

Lac-aux-Dames is a quintessential Allégret film. It introduced Simone Simon and Jean-Pierre Aumont to the screen; both of them took the country by storm. The subject comes from Vicki Baum's best-selling novel. Allégret, again relying on the influence of Gide who visited the set, enticed Colette to write the dialogue. The film is scintillating in its depiction of the social pressures and private dreams of adolescents. The depiction of the island on the lake with its little inlets is among the most romantic of the period.

Allégret went on to discover other brilliant actors: Michelle Morgan, Bernard Blier, Odette Joyeux, Gérard Philipe, and of course in 1953 Brigitte Bardot. And he did so in roles designed to reveal the freshness and vitality they would bring to the French cinema over their long careers. In *Gribouille* Michelle Morgan is a delinquent taken in by Raimu who as a juror at her trial was unable to disbelieve her clear eyes. Nor would millions of spectators disbelieve them over the next twenty years. In *Futures vedettes* (1953) it was Brigitte Bardot's turn to shock high culture sensibilities (the film takes place in a ballet school) with her irrepressible sexuality. The film otherwise is a rather pathetic attempt by Allégret to recapture his successes of the 1930s, using another Vicki Baum story and one similar to his much acclaimed 1937 film *Entrée des artistes*.

Most critics even in the fifties felt that, despite a stunning beginning, Allégret hadn't enough depth to continue to develop. He has been called a dilettante, rubbing shoulders with Parisian intelligentsia, trying to shock them with the youth culture he has always espoused. His final major film *Lady Chatterley's Lover* reflects both these impulses. Andre Bazin pointed out the impossibility of the project, a tasteful and intelligent adaptation of a novel that despises taste and insults the intelligentsia. Here, as usual, Marc Allégret had his finger on issues crucial to the culture, but he was unable to contribute to it a convincing or serious cinematic meditation.

—Dudley Andrew

ALLÉGRET, YVES. French. Born in Paris, 13 October 1907. Married actress Simone Signoret, 1944 (divorced 1949); child: Cathérine. Career: 1929—introduced to film industry by brother Marc Allégret; 1930—hired by producer Pierre Braunberger to install sound at Billancourt studios; 1931—kept on as assistant to Jean Renoir on *La Chienne*; also assists Augusto Genina and Marc Allégret; early 1930s—makes advertising shorts; post-war—makes series of films noir starring wife Simone Signoret; 1981—reported preparing English-language film *Let Juan Montario Live* to be shot in Spain.

Films (as director): 1932—*Ténériffe* (short); 1933—*Ciboulette* (Autant-Lara) (co-costume des only); 1934—*Prix et profits* (short); 1935—*Le Gagnant* (short); 1936—*Vous n'avez rien à déclarer?* (co-d); 1937—*Forfaiture* (L'Herbier) (tech advisor only); 1939—*L'Émigrante* (co-d, +co-sc); 1941—*La Roue tourne* (unfinished); *Tobie est un ange* (unreleased, destroyed); 1942—*Les Deaux Timides (Jeunes Timides)* (under pseudonym Yves Champlain, +sc); 1943—*La Boîte aux rêves* (begun by Jean Choux) (+co-sc); 1945—*Les Démons de l'aube*; 1947—*Dédée d'Anvers (Dedee)* (+co-sc); 1948—*Une si jolie petite plage (Riptide)*; 1949—*Manèges (The Cheat)*; 1950—*Les Miracles n'ont lieu qu'une fois*; 1951—*Nez de cuir* (+adapt); "La Luxure (Lust)" episode of *Les Sept Péchés capitaux (The 7 Deadly Sins)*; 1952—*La Jeune Folle (Desperate Decision)*; 1953—*Mam'zelle Nitouche* (+co-sc); *Les Orgueilleux (The Proud and the Beautiful)* (+co-sc); 1954—*Oasis*; 1955—*La Meilleure Part* (+co-sc); 1957—*Quand la femme s'en mêle*; *Méfiez-vous fillettes (Young Girls Beware)*; 1958—*La Fille de Hambourg (Port of Desire)* (+co-sc); 1959—*L'Ambitieuse*; 1961—*La Chien de pique* (+co-sc); 1962—*Germinal*; *Terreur sur la savane (Konga-Yo)* (+co-sc—documentary); 1966—*Johnny Banco* (+co-sc); 1970—*L'Invasion*; 1975—*Orzowei*; 1976—*Mords pas—on t'aime* (+co-sc).

Publications:

By ALLÉGRET:

Article—"Why I Choose the Unusual" in *Films and Filming* (London), October 1955.

*   *   *

Yves Allégret followed his older brother Marc into the cinema in 1929. A friend from the outset of Cavalcanti, Renoir, and the producer Diamant-Berger, he was destined to find a place in the burgeoning Paris film industry at the birth of the sound era.

Displaying a sharp technical aptitude, he was hired by Pierre Braunberger to oversee the installation of sound in his suburban Billancourt studios. One of Braunberger's first productions was to be Renoir's *La Chienne* and Allégret was kept on to serve as assistant.

His apprenticeship was exemplary for he moved both in cinematic and theatrical circles (assisting his brother on the wonderful *Lac-aux-Dames* and Autant-Lara on *Ciboulette*) while helping the October Group put on their guerrilla theater sketches around Paris. He became a trusted resource and was even asked by Renoir to finish *A Day in the Country* when the master was forced to leave that little film to supervise *La Marseillaise*.

But *A Day in the Country* was shelved by Braunberger, initiating an excruciating series of unfinished and censored projects that dogged Allégret's career right through to the Liberation. It was not until 1948, nearly twenty years after he had entered the field, that Allégret made a notable film. The success of *Dédée d'Anvers* has been attributed by many to its scriptwriter Jacques Sigurd. In truth Sigurd and Allégret, working together for the first time here, discovered a theme and a style that would carry

them through several other successes. This approach, termed "psychological realism," was a product of script, direction, and acting alike.

All this sounds like a return to "poetic realism," and undoubtedly Allégret was hoping to repeat the Carné-Prévert pre-war successes. But the times had changed and his style was much more analytic just as Sigurd's scripts were far more bitter.

Dédée d'Anvers is the story of smalltime gangsters. Simone Signoret, Marcel Dalio, and Bernard Blier live lives of jealousy and distrust in the bistros and along the docks of Anvers. As their petty crimes move toward murder a film noir style is invoked, only the component of suspense is deliberately downplayed in favor of atmosphere and acting.

Both this film and its successor *Une si jolie petite place*, undoubtedly Allégret's greatest work, expend all their effort in depicting an atmosphere of despair that drives the hero of the latter, Gérard Philipe, to a Gabin-like suicide at the end. But Allégret doesn't share his hero's dreams the way Carné seemed to. Instead he observes, almost sadistically, the debilitating effect of small town life on a character whose past haunts him. The incessant rain, the grotesque visitors in the hotel, and the back-alley sex give him no reprieve from his past and drive him to his death.

In *Manèges* Sigurd and Allégret go further in taking apart the hypocritical lives of their characters. This time Simone Signoret is an undisguised cynic as she seduces a wealthy bourgeois and then robs him blind while consorting with lovers from her own lower class. The filmmakers' cynicism is as great as that of their heroine. While still wielding a powerfully evocative style in painting this atmosphere of upper-class hypocrisy and lower-class sex, Allégret's utter misanthropy begins to turn the film toward satire. With no respect for his characters and with a Darwinian view of private and social behavior, a patronizing tone results.

Of his many later films, only *Les Orgueilleux* compares in stature to the 1948-50 trilogy. Adapted from a novel by Sartre, Allégret's penchant for nasty details and intolerable living conditions comes out in this existentialist (non)morality play. The excessive wearing down of the characters that is part of his psychological realism this time was in tune with the film's philosophic theme.

Yves Allégret is not a likable director. His long career produced only four powerful films, all of which dwell excessively on human meanness. Yet his genius for making us feel this meanness and his audacious effort to make everything including plot serve the unveiling of human motivation make him perhaps the key filmmaker of the immediate postwar period.

—Dudley Andrew

ALLEN, WOODY. American. Born Allen (Alan in some sources) Stewart Konigsberg in Brooklyn, 1 December 1935. Educated at Midwood High School, Brooklyn; briefly at New York University and City College of New York (expelled from both). Married Harlene Rosen, 1954 (divorced); Louise Lasser, 1966 (divorced). Career: 1950—begins writing quips and sending them to Earl Wilson and other newspaper columnists under name Woody Allen; mention by Wilson leads to job with press agent writing one-liners for show business clients; 1952—following graduation from high school, joins staff of Sid Caesar TV show; 1961—quits job as writer for "Garry Moore Show" to become stand-up performer; 1964—producer Charles Feldman sees nightclub act, hires Allen to write *What's New, Pussycat?*;

1966—successful opening of 1st Broadway play, *Don't Drink the Water*; 1969-70—performs in successful Broadway run of his play *Play It Again, Sam*; 1976—begins collaboration with scriptwriter Marshall Brickman on *Annie Hall*. Recipient: Academy Award, Best Direction, Best Screenplay (co-recipient), for *Annie Hall*, 1977. Address: c/o Rollins & Joffe, 130 W. 57th Street, New York NY 10019.

Films (as scriptwriter): 1965—*What's New, Pussycat?* (+ro); 1966—*What's Up, Tiger Lily?* (co-sc, +assoc. pr, ro as host/narrator); *Don't Drink the Water* (play basis only); (as director, scriptwriter and actor): 1969—*Take the Money and Run*; 1971—*Bananas* (co-sc); 1972—*Play It Again, Sam* (Ross) (sc and ro only); *Everything You Always Wanted to Know About Sex but Were Afraid to Ask*; 1973—*Sleeper*; 1975—*Love and Death*; 1977—*Annie Hall* (co-sc); 1978—*Interiors* (d and sc only); 1979—*Manhattan* (co-sc); 1980—*Stardust Memories*; 1982—*A Midsummer Night's Sex Comedy*; 1983—*Zelig* (ro: *Leonard Zelig*).

Roles: (in films not directed): 1967—*Casino Royale* (Huston and others); 1976—*The Front* (Ritt).

Publications:

By ALLEN:

Books—*Getting Even*, New York 1971; *Without Feathers*, New York 1976; *The Floating Lightbulb*, New York 1982; articles—"Interview: Woody Allen" in *Playboy* (Chicago), May 1967; "How Bogart Made Me the Superb Lover I Am" in *Life* (New York), 21 March 1969; "Woody Allen Interview" by Robert Mundy and Stephen Mamber in *Cinema* (Beverly Hills), winter 1972/73; "Everything You've Always Wanted to Know About Sex You'll Find in My New Movie" in *Playboy* (Chicago), September 1972; "The Art of Comedy: Woody Allen and *Sleeper*", interview by J. Trotsky in *Filmmakers Newsletter* (Ward Hill, Mass.), summer 1974; "I have no yen to play Hamlet", interview by Guy Flatley, in *The New York Times*, 3 October 1976; "A Conversation with the Real Woody Allen (or Someone Just Like Him)" by K. Kelley in *Rolling Stone* (New York), 1 July 1976; "The Night Woody Allen Turned Me On", interview by J. Viorst, in *Redbook* (New York), October 1976; "Woody Allen is Feeling Better", interview by B. Drew, in *American Film* (Washington, D.C.), May 1977; "Comedy Directors: Interviews with Woody Allen" by M. Karman in *Millimeter* (New York), October 1977; interview in *Esquire* (New York), May 1977; "Scenes from a Mind", interview by I. Halberstadt in *Take One* (Montreal), November 1978; "I share my characters' views on men—and stuff like that", interview by Janet Maslin, in *The New York Times*, 20 May 1979; "Rencontre avec Woody Allen" by J. Raynal in *Cahiers du cinéma* (Paris), March 1978; "Woody Allen: Seit 50 Jahren hält der amerikanische Film den Mythos am Leben, dass gleich um die Ecke das Glück auf dich wartet", interview by J. Kritz, in *Filmfaust* (Frankfurt), October 1979; "Dos encuentros con Woody Allen" by J. Ruiz in *Casablanca* (Madrid), February 1981.

On ALLEN:

Books—*On Being Funny: Woody Allen and Comedy* by Eric Lax, New York 1975; *...But We Need the Eggs: The Magic of Woody Allen* by Diane Jacobs, New York 1982; articles—

"Pushing Back" in *Newsweek* (New York), 20 August 1962; "His Own Boswell" in *Time* (New York), 15 February 1963; "Woody, Woody Everywhere" in *Time* (New York), 14 April 1967; special issue of *Cinema* (Beverly Hills), winter 1972/73; "The Wooden Acting of Woody Allen" by B. Weiner in *Take One* (Montreal), December 1972; "Woody Allen: Stumbling Through the Looking Glass" by Harry Wasserman in *Velvet Light Trap* (Madison), winter 1972/73; "Provaci ancora, Woody" by E. Comuzio in *Cineforum* (Rome), April/May 1973; "Take Woody Allen—Please!" by Leonard Maltin in *Film Comment* (New York), March/April 1974; article in the *New Yorker*, 4 February 1974; "Les Nouveau Burlesques: Woody Allen, Mel Brooks" by D. Offroy in *Cinematographe* (Paris), August/September 1975; "Woody Allen—Together Again for the First Time" by G. Way in *Movietone News* (Seattle), 29 August 1976; "Annie Hall" by A. Remond in *Avant-Scène du cinéma* (Paris), 15 December 1977; "Woody Allen" in *Ecran* (Paris), June 1978; "Film View: Notes on Woody Allen and American Comedy" by Vincent Canby in *The New York Times*, 13 May 1979; "Forms of Coherence in the Woody Allen Comedies" by M. Yacowar in *Wide Angle* (Athens, Ohio), no.2, 1979; "The Autobiography of Woody Allen" by M. Dempsey in *Film Comment* (New York), May/June 1979; "Woody Allen's Jewish American Gothic" by D.M. Friend in *Midstream* (New York), June/July 1979; "The Maturing of Woody Allen" by N. Gitelson in *The New York Times*, 22 April 1979; "Woody Allen: Narr oder Poet?" by J. Gebski in *Film und Fernsehen* (Berlin), March 1980; "El cine de Woody Allen" by R. Median de la Serna in *Cine* (Mexico), March 1980; "Producing Woody: an Interview with Charles H. Joffe" by D. Teitelbaum in *Cinema Papers* (Melbourne), April/May 1980; "Avatar del buhonero" by M. Fuster in *Contracampo* (Madrid), February 1981; film—*Woody Allen: An American Comedy* directed by Harold Mantell, 1978.

* * *

Woody Allen fashioned a comic persona that came to embody the hip urban neurotic American of the 1970s, just as Harold Lloyd embodied the American go-getter of the 1920s and Jerry Lewis the American loudmouth of the 1950s. Allen's incarnation of the self-educated American popular artist-intellectual followed the path of Charles Chaplin and George Gershwin, to both of whom Allen films consciously allude.

His first film, *Take the Money and Run*, was an outright parody of gangster films in its study of a comically inept bank-robber who even has difficulty spelling the words in notes demanding money from bank tellers. Allen's taste for parody would continue in subsequent films, *Bananas*, *Sleeper*, and *Love and Death*, along with an evolving exploration of the comic schlepp character that Allen embodied.

Allen's work took a major leap forward, both visually and psychologically, with *Annie Hall*. The character Allen played, Alvie Singer, was as close to Allen himself as a fictional creation could be. A Jewish intellectual nightclub comedian, like Allen, Alvie examined his relationship to a beautiful Gentile performer-artist, played by Diane Keaton, Allen's own offscreen romance at the time. In this almost psychoanalytic comic film, the writer-director-actor began to explore the ways that his comic art tries to make sense of and communicate his personal feelings and beliefs in life. Allen used a variety of cinematic devices to achieve comedic and psychological effects—subtitles to reveal the subtext beneath superficial dialogue, a superimposed Annie who disinterestedly watches herself and Alvie making love, a split screen to compare the difference between dinner-table scenes at the Jewish Singer and Gentile Hall families. In addition to exploring the coming together and breaking apart of Annie and Alvie, the film also makes comic cultural comparisons between East Coast and West Coast "hip" life styles, Gentile and Jewish family life, intellectually self-conscious and emotionally spontaneous types of human personalities. The film's visual images and textures revealed a significant deepening and maturing of Allen's work, largely due to the beginning of Allen's collaboration with cinematographer Gordon Willis, who has shot all of Allen's films since.

Woody Allen has spent the years since *Annie Hall* experimenting with different ways of turning his personal concerns into popular forms with varying degrees of commercial and critical success. *Interiors*, like Chaplin's *A Woman of Paris*, is a serious study of human emotion in which the comedian himself does not appear. Modeled largely on *Cries and Whispers* by Ingmar Bergman, always one of Allen's favorite film figures for both affectionate parody and artistic emulation, *Interiors* continued Allen's psychoanalytic exploration of family life, of the attempt to escape the influence of a dominating mother, and of the contrast between neurotic, self-conscious, self-torturing human behavior and exuberant, spontaneous, unreflecting vitality. *Manhattan* was a return to Allen's comic form and persona, the study of another New York Jewish-intellectual comedian, who this time cannot make up his sexual-romantic mind between a sensitive, mature woman (Diane Keaton again) and an innocent adolescent (Mariel Hemingway). The film is most memorable for its striking visual choices—a CinemaScope film in black-and-white—and its musical score, an homage to George Gershwin. Both the use of the Gershwin music and of black-and-white film were nostalgic choices, summoning the spirit of the past when life and love seemed simpler and purer than they do now.

Stardust Memories, another black-and-white film, was popular with neither Allen fans nor critics primarily because it specifically attacked both his fans and his critics. Allen, playing another popular entertainer with both a past and present similar to his own, models his film consciously on Fellini's *8½*, wondering why his critics and fans won't let him explore his own dreams, images, and longings, rather than the ones they have decided he ought to develop. The film reveals a popular artist confronting the trap of his own popularity. He has been straitjacketed by the persona and the kind of comedy he previously defined, and prohibited by his public from expanding and exploring other avenues in the future. While *A Midsummer Night's Sex Comedy* left much of the bitterness behind, it also left much of its audience behind. It was too light, too frivolous for Allen's critics. A combination of Shakespeare's *A Midsummer Night's Dream* and Ingmar Bergman's *Smiles of a Summer Night*, Allen's *Midsummer Night* explores the relationship of love and magic in the twentieth century. These are synthesized by a magical-mechanical invention, a "spirit ball," which is an explicit Allen metaphor for the cinema itself.

Woody Allen has maintained an insistent schedule of making one film every year like those film comedians of the past such as Lloyd and Keaton who turned out films on regular schedules. As a result, Allen is building a canon of works which will probably look much richer as a whole, some time in the future, than some of the films may look now, subjected to the cavils of contemporary critics.

—Gerald Mast

ALLIO, RENÉ. French. Born in Marseilles, 1924. Educated in literature. Career: early 1950s—active as set and costume designer in Parisian avant-garde theater; 1957—begins theatrical collaboration with Planchon; beginning late 1950s—active as stage designer for Comédie Française, Paris Opéra, and in London and Milan; 1960s—participates in design and renovation of theaters including Théâtre d'Aubervilliers, Maison de la Culture in Lyon, and Théâtre de la Ville, Paris; early 1960s—first involvement with cinema designing animation film for Planchon production of Gogol's *Dead Souls*; 1963 to present—continues theatrical activity along with filmmaking; 1976—participates in creation of production organization Unité de production cinématographique at Vitrolles, near Marseilles; announces intention of making films set in his native region.

Films (as director and scriptwriter): 1963—*La Meule (The Haystack)*; 1965—*La Vieille Dame indigne (The Shameless Old Lady)*; 1967—*L'Une et l'autre*; 1968—*Pierre et Paul*; 1970—*Les Camisards*; 1973—*Rude Journée pour la reine* (co-sc); 1976—*Moi, Pierre Rivière, ayant égorgé ma mère, ma soeur et mon frère*; 1980—*Retour à Marseille*.

Publications:

By ALLIO:

Articles—interview by André Zavriew in *Film* (London), spring 1969; "Entretien avec René Allio" by B. Cohn and C. Gauteur in *Positif* (Paris), May 1972; "Entretien avec René Allio" by G. Gauthier in *Image et son* (Paris), March 1972; "René Allio et les Camisards", interview by A.J. Gili and M. Martin in *Ecran* (Paris), February 1972; "A propos de *Rude journée pour la reine*" in *Cahiers du cinéma* (Paris), February/March 1974; interview in special issue on *Rude journée...* of *Avant-Scène du cinéma* (Paris), January/February 1974; "Le Retour de Pierre Rivière", interview by G. Gauthier, in *Image et son* (Paris), December 1976; interview by M. Amiel in *Cinéma 76* (Paris), November 1976; interview by J.-C. Bonnet in *Cinématographe* (Paris), December 1976; "Le retour de Pierre Rivière: entretiens avec René Allio et Michel Foucault" by G. Gauthier in *Image et son* (Paris), December 1976; interview by S. Le Peron and others in *Cahiers du cinéma* (Paris), November 1976; "...denn rückwarts werde ich mich niemals wenden", interview by J.-P. Brossard in *Film und Fernsehen* (Berlin), July 1977; "L'Histoire au cinéma", discussion with Marc Ferro and others, in *Positif* (Paris), January 1977; interview by Guy Hennebelle and R. Koussim in *Ecran* (Paris), July 1977; interview by J.-P. Gatlato in *Cinéma* (Paris), May 1977; "La Place de l'artiste dans le cinéma politique", interview by B. Nave in *Jeune cinéma* (Paris), December/January 1979/80; "3 cinéastes en quête de l'histoire", interview by J.-P. Bertin-Maghit, in *Image et son* (Paris), July/August 1980.

On ALLIO:

Articles—"Pasolini—Varda—Allio—Sarris—Michelson" in *Film Culture* (New York), fall 1966; "2 Arts in One: René Allio and Antoine Bourseiller" by Jean-Luc Godard and Michel Delahaye in *Cahiers du Cinema in English* (New York), December 1966; "Le réalisateur: René Allio" in *Avant-Scène du cinéma* (Paris), February 1972; "Les rudes sentiers de la création" by G. Gauthier in *Image et son* (Paris), November 1973; "Le retour à Marseille de René Allio" by G. Delavaud in *Cahiers du cinéma* (Paris), February 1980.

*   *   *

René Allio was in his early forties and had already established his name and reputation as a stage director when he began his feature filmmaking career with two remarkable studies of characters who deliberately change their identity—to the consternation of those closest to them. *La Vieille Dame indigne* was adapted from a Brecht story and relocated in Allio's native Marseilles. It offered the veteran actress Sylvie one of her finest roles as an old woman who, on the verge of death, suddenly decides to spend the little money she has on herself rather than leave it to her heirs. *L'Une et l'autre*, which followed two years later, has an explicitly theatrical setting but shows the same mastery in the capturing of everyday detail and the tiny gestures by which people relate. The heroine is an actress who, realising that her life has become meaningless, takes on the identity of her sister as a prelude to finding the ability to express to the man she lives with her need to live an independent life.

The same blend of realism and theatricality together with an intense sympathy for ordinary people, capturing the banality of their existence and also their dreams, characterises his subsequent three films, despite their striking differences in subject matter. Pierre, the hero of *Pierre et Paul*, has an ordered existence on which he depends far more than he realises. When his father's death destroys his peace of mind and plunges him into debt, he cannot cope and is driven to a mad outburst of violence. In contrast, *Les Camisards* is a historical study made without stars or even star roles, which traces the failed revolt of the Protestants of the Ceyennes against the oppression of Louis XIV at the beginning of the 18th century. Just as the careful naturalistic detail of *Pierre et Paul* does not exclude comment on wider aspects of the consumer society, so here the historical costumes and period reconstruction do not prevent the issues of freedom and struggle, which have a quite contemporary relevance, from coming to the fore. *Rude Journée pour la reine* in 1973 is another new departure, which traces with precision and an involving rhythm the interaction of dream and reality in the head of an ordinary, aging housewife, played with characteristic forcefulness by Simone Signoret.

Allio was unable subsequently to maintain this rhythm of a film every two years or so, and only two films follow in the next ten years. *Moi, Pierre Rivière, ayant égorgé ma mère, ma soeur et mon frère* is a remarkable work. Based on a 50 page confessional text discovered and published by Michel Foucault, the film combines so exemplary naturalism of detail (the actual locations of the crime, real peasants, precise period reconstruction) with a refusal to dramatise events. These are simply presented for our attention, to engage our emotions but at the same time to give rise to thought about the shaping impact of social conditions. *Retour à Marseille*, a fictional account of a man's return to Marseilles which is also the filmmaker's own return to his native city did not have the same impact. But Allio's career over fifteen years is a striking and important one. To a French cinema which is still essentially Parisian, he gives an authentic provincial voice; in a cinema which tends to avoid social comment, he locates his characters precisely in period and class. His sense of realist detail is sure, but is balanced by a theatrical awareness of staging and creating dramatic involvement. As a result the figures Allio puts before us engage our sympathies and provoke our thought in a way which is both personal and original.

—Roy Armes

ALTMAN, ROBERT. American. Born in Kansas City, Missouri, 20 February 1925. Attended University of Missouri. Married (3rd time) Kathryn Reed; children: Robert and Matthew; children by first 2 marriages: Catherine, and Michael and Stephen. Career: 1943-47—military service; 1947—works as director of industrial films for Calvin Company in Kansas City; early 1950s—unsuccessfully attempts to break into Hollywood film industry; 1955-57—writes, produces, and directs 1st feature film, *The Delinquents*; 1957—collaborates with George W. George on compilation-documentary, *The Story of James Dean*; 1957-63—works as director in television on such programs as *Alfred Hitchcock Presents, Bonanza, Kraft Mystery Theater,* and *Combat;* 1963—forms partnership with Ray Wagner to produce television programs and films; 1966-67—returns to directing feature films with *Countdown;* 1970—directs *M*A*S*H,* 1st critical and financial success; establishes Lion's Gate production company; "Lion's Gate" is also name of Altman's 8-track sound system; mid-70s—forms Westwood Editorial Services for post-production and rentals of Lion's Gate Sound; 1976—financial failure of *Buffalo Bill and the Indians* leads to cancellation of projects including direction of E.L. Doctorow's *Ragtime* and Kurt Vonnegut's *Breakfast of Champions;* 1979-80—directs *Health* which fails to get distribution; directs adaptations of serious contemporary dramas. Address: 1861 S. Bundy Drive, Los Angeles, California 90025.

Films (as director): 1954—*The Builders* (medium length publicity film); 1955—*The Delinquents* (+pr, sc); 1957—*The James Dean Story* (co-d, +co-pr, co-ed); 1964—*The Party** (short); 1965—*Pot au Feu** (short); *The Katherine Reed Story** (short); 1967—*Countdown* (moon-landing sequence d uncred by William Conrad); 1969—*That Cold Day in the Park;* 1970—*M*A*S*H; Brewster McCloud* (+pr); 1971—*McCabe and Mrs. Miller* (+co-sc); 1972—*Images* (+pr, sc); 1973—*The Long Goodbye;* 1974—*Thieves Like Us* (+co-sc); *California Split* (+co-pr); 1975—*Nashville* (+co-pr, co-songwriter: "The Day I Looked Jesus in the Eye"); 1976—*Buffalo Bill and the Indians, or Sitting Bull's History Lesson* (+pr, co-sc); *Welcome to L.A.* (pr only); 1977—*The Late Show* (pr only); 1978—*A Wedding* (+pr, co-sc); *Remember My Name* (pr only); 1979—*Quintet* (+pr, co-sc); *A Perfect Couple* (+pr, co-sc); *Rich Kids* (pr only); 1979—*Health* (+pr, sc); 1980—*Popeye;* 1982—*Come Back to the Five and Dime, Jimmy Dean, Jimmy Dean;* 1983—*Streamers; The Diviners.*
* films of 1964-65 are 16 mm "home movies".

Publications:

By ALTMAN:

Book—*Buffalo Bill and the Indians, or Sitting Bull's History Lesson,* with Alan Rudolf, New York 1976; articles—interview by Aljean Harmetz in *The New York Times,* 20 June 1971; "Entretien avec Robert Altman" by M. Grisolia in *Cinéma* (Paris), July/August 1972; interview by S. Rosenthal in *Focus on Film* (London), spring 1972; interview by Russell Auwerter in *Directors in Action,* edited by Bob Thomas, New York 1973; "Entretien avec Robert Altman" in *Positif* (Paris), February 1973; "Images", interview by G. Braucourt in *Ecran* (Paris), April 1973; interview by Michel Ciment and Bertrand Tavernier in *Positif* (Paris), February 1973; "Robert Altman Speaking", interview by J. Dawson, in *Film Comment* (New York), March/-April 1974; "An Altman Sampler", interview by B.J. Demby in *Filmmakers Newsletter* (Ward Hill, Mass.), October 1974;

"Robert Altman et *Thieves Like Us*", interview by A. Lacombe in *Ecran* (Paris), July 1974; "Entretien avec Robert Altman" by Michel Ciment and M. Henry in *Positif* (Paris), February 1975; Robert Altman seminar in *Dialogue on Film* (Beverly Hills), February 1975; "The Artist and the Multitude Are Natural Enemies", interview by F.A. Macklin, in *Film Heritage* (Dayton, Ohio), winter 1976/77; "Playboy Interview: Robert Altman" by Bruce Williamson in *Playboy* (Chicago), August 1976; "Entretien avec Robert Altman" in *Positif* (Paris), September 1977; "Entretien avec Robert Altman" by Michel Ciment and M. Henry in *Positif* (Paris), September 1977; interview by Jean-André Fieschi in *Cinématographe* (Paris), June 1977; interview by R.T. Johnson and K. Murphy in *Movietone News* (Seattle), 16 September 1977; interview by Charles Michener in *Film Comment* (New York), September-October 1978; "Jumping Off the Cliff" in *Monthly Film Bulletin* (London), December 1978; "Robert Altman sur *A Wedding*", interview and article by C. Clouzot, in *Ecran* (Paris), November 1978; interview and article by J.-P. Le Pavec and others in *Cinéma* (Paris), November 1978; "Erratum", interview by K. Murphy, in *Movietone News* (Seattle), November 1977; "An Altman", interview by J. Rosenbaum and C. Michener, in *Film Comment* (New York), September/-October 1978; "Entretiens avec Robert Altman" by Michel Ciment and M. Henry in *Positif* (Paris), March 1979; "Robert Altman: Backgammon and Spinach", interview by Tom Milne and R. Combs in *Sight and Sound* (London), summer 1981; "Peripheral Vision", interview by A. Stuart, in *Films* (London), July 1981.

On ALTMAN:

Books—*On Making a Movie: Brewster McCloud*, edited by Nancy Hardin, New York 1971; *Persistence of Vision: The Films of Robert Altman* by Neil Feineman, New York 1976; *Robert Altman: American Innovator* by Judith M. Kass, New York 1978; *The Films of Robert Altman* by Alan Karp, Metuchen, New Jersey 1981; articles—"D.W. Griffith se porte bien, moi aussi, merci!" by Bertrand Tavernier in *Positif* (Paris), October 1970; "*MASH, McCloud*, and *McCabe*" by John Cutts in *Films and Filming* (London), November 1971; "*McCabe and Mrs. Miller*: Robert Altman's Anti-Western" by Gary Engle in *Journal of Popular Film* (Bowling Green, Ohio), fall 1972; "Le Chaos fertile de Bob Altman" by Robert Benayoun in *Positif* (Paris), January 1972; "Altman's Images" by J. Dawson in *Sight and Sound* (London), spring 1972; "Knight without Meaning?: Marlowe on the Screen" in *Sight and Sound* (London), summer 1973; "The Theme of Structure in the Films of Robert Altman" by C.A. Baker in *Journal of Popular Film* (Bowling Green), summer 1973; "From *The Big Sleep* to the *The Long Goodbye* and More or Less How We Got There" by Leigh Brackett in *Take One* (Montreal), January 1974; "Outlaws, Auteurs, and Actors" by Richard Corliss in *Film Comment* (New York), May/June 1974; "The Return of the Outlaw Couple" by Marsha Kinder in *Film Quarterly* (Berkeley), summer 1974; "Let Us Now Praise—Not Overpraise—Robert Altman" by Stephen Farber in *The New York Times*, 29 September 1974; "Altman, U.S.A." by Robert Benayoun in *Positif* (Paris), December 1975; "Jouer avec Altman (rencontres avec Ronee Blakeley et Keith Carradine)" in *Positif* (Paris), December 1975; "Entretien avec Joan Tewkesbury" by Michael Henry in *Positif* (Paris), December 1975; "*The Delinquents*" by Todd McCarthy in *King of the B's* edited by Todd McCarthy and Charles Flynn, New York 1975; "*Nashville*: America's Voices" in *Film Heritage* (Dayton, Ohio), fall 1975; "*The Long Goodbye* and *Chinatown*: Debunking the Private Eye Tradition" by Bill Oliver in *Literature/Film Quarterly* (Salisbury, Maryland), summer 1975; "Improvisations and Interactions in Altmanville" by Jonathan Rosenbaum in *Sight and Sound* (London), spring 1975; "*The Long Goodbye* from *Chinatown*" by Garrett Stewart in *Film Quarterly* (Berkeley), winter 1974-75; "Smart-ass and Cutie-pie: Notes Toward an Evaluation of Altman" by Robin Wood in *Movie*, autumn 1975; special issue of *Film Heritage* (Dayton, Ohio), fall 1975; "Altmanscope (sur le plateau de *Nashville*), A Journal of On-Set Observation" in *Positif* (Paris), January 1976; "Tracking Altman's Movies" by Bruce Pittman in *Take One* (Montreal), August 1976; "Invention and Death: The Commodities of Media in Robert Altman's *Nashville*" by Robert Self in *Journal of Popular Film* (Bowling Green, Ohio), no.5, 1976; "*Nashville* (An Interview Documentary) by Connie Byrne and William O. Lopez in *Film Quarterly* (Berkeley), winter 1975-76; "Robert Altman ou la mise en question" by A.-M. Bidaud in *Cinéma 76* (Paris), June 1976; "Robert Altman de *MASH* a *Nashville*" by P. Pitiot and H. Talvat in *Jeune Cinéma* (Paris), September/October 1976; "Robert Altman" in *Hollywood Renaissance* by Diane Jacobs, New York 1977; "The Art of Dreaming in *3 Women* and *Providence*: Structures of the Self" in *Film Quarterly* (Berkeley), fall 1977; "Notes sur les films TV de Robert Altman" by Jack Nolan in *Positif* (Paris), September 1977; "Robert Altman: repères biofilmographiques" by M. Henry in *Positif* (Paris), September 1977; "R. Altman & Co." by R. Levine in *Film Comment* (New York), January/February 1977; "Bob and Pauline: A Fickle Affair" by B. Cook in *American Film* (Washington, D.C.), December/January 1978/79; "Playing the Game, or Robert Altman and the Indians" in *Sight and Sound* (London), summer 1979; "Dialogue on Film" by Joan Tewkesbury in *American Film* (Washington, D.C.), March 1979; "Film View: Altman—A Daring Filmmaker Falters" by Vincent Canby in *The New York Times*, 18 February 1979; "Portrait de groupe avec hargne" by C. Clouzot in *Avant-Scène du cinéma* (Paris), March 1979; "Actors as Conventions in the Films of Robert Altman" by M. Yacowar in *Cinema Journal* (Evanston), fall 1980; "Dossier: Robert Altman" by J.-C. Bonnet and others in *Cinématographe* (Paris), January 1980; "Against Altman" by S. Eyman in *Focus on Film* (London), October 1980; "Building Sand Castles" by D. Altman in *Cinema Papers* (Melbourne), July/August 1981.

*   *   *

The American seventies may have been dominated by a "New Wave" of younger, auteurist-inspired filmmakers including George Lucas, Peter Bogdanovich, Steven Spielberg, Martin Scorsese, and Francis Ford Coppola, all contemporaries as well as sometime colleagues. It is, however, an outsider to this group, the older Robert Altman, perhaps the decade's most consistent chronicler of human behavior, who could be characterized as the artistic rebel most committed to an unswerving personal vision. If the generation of whiz kids tends to admire the American cinema as well as its structures of production, Altman tends to regard the American cinema critically and to view the production establishment more as an adversary to be cunningly exploited.

Although Altman has worked consistently within American genres, his work can instructively be seen as anti-genre: *McCabe and Mrs. Miller* is a kind of anti-western, exposing the myth of the heroic westerner (as described by Robert Warshow and executed by John Wayne and John Ford) and replacing it with an almost Marxist view of the Westerner as financier, spreading capitalism and corruption, with opportunism and good cheer. *The Long Goodbye* sets itself in opposition to certain aspects of the hard-boiled detective genre, as Elliott Gould's Philip Marlowe reflects a moral stance decidedly more ambiguous than that of Raymond Chandler's conventional lonely moralist. Similarly, *Countdown* can be seen in relationship to the science-fiction film; *Thieves Like Us* (based on *They Live by Night*) in relationship to the bandit-gangster film; *That Cold Day in the Park* in relationship to the psychological horror film inaugurated by Alfred Hitchcock's *Psycho*; and *California Split* in relationship to that generic phenomenon so common to the seventies, the "buddy film." Even *Nashville*, Altman's complex bicentennial musical released in 1975, can be seen in relationship to a generic tradition with roots in *Grand Hotel*.

Aside from his generic preoccupations, Altman seems especially interested in people. His films characteristically contain perceptive observations, telling exchanges, moments of crystal clear revelation of human folly, perhaps most persuasively in relationship to a grand social organization: that of the upper classes and *nouveau riche* in *A Wedding*; health faddists and, by metaphor, the American political process, in *Health*, and so forth. Certainly Altman's films offer a continuous critique of American society: people are constantly using and exploiting others, though often with the tacit permission of those being exploited. One thinks of the country-western singers' exploitation by the politician's p.r. man in *Nashville*, for instance; or the spinster in *That Cold Day in the Park*. Violence is often the climax of an Altman film—almost as if the tensions among the characters must ultimately explode, notable examples include the fiery deaths and subsequent "surprise ending" in *A Wedding*, or the climactic assassination in *Nashville*

Another recurring interest for Altman is his preoccupation with the psychopathology of women: one thinks of the subtly encroaching madness of Sandy Dennis's sexually repressed spinister in *That Cold Day in the Park*, an underrated, early Altman film; the disturbing instability of Ronee Blakley in *Nashville*; the relationships among the unbalanced subjects of *Three Women*, based on one of Altman's own dreams; and the real/surreal visions of Susannah York in the virtual horror film, *Images*. Because almost all of Altman's characters tend to be hypocritical, psychotic, weak, or morally flawed in some way, with very few coming to a good or happy end, Altman has often been attacked for a kind of trendy cynicism, yet this cynicism seems not a mannerism of the director as much as his genuine attempt to avoid the conventional myth-making of the American cinema by imbuing as many of his characters as possible with that sloppy imperfection associated with human beings as they are.

Performers enjoy working with Altman in part because of the freedom he allows them to develop their characters and often alter the script through improvisation and collaboration. Like Bergman, Altman has worked often with a stock company of performers who appear in one role after another, among them Elliott Gould, Sally Kellerman, Rene Auberjonois, Keith Carradine, Shelley Duvall, Michael Murphy, Bert Remsen, and Henry Gibson.

Altman's distinctive style transforms whatever subject he approaches. He often takes advantage of widescreen compositions in which the frame is filled with a number of subjects and details competing for the spectator's attention. Working with cinematographer Vilmos Zsigmond, he has achieved films that are visually distinguished and tend toward the atmospheric; especially notable are the use of the zoom lens in the smokey cinematography of *McCabe and Mrs. Miller*; the reds, whites, and blues of *Nashville*; the constantly mobile camera, specially mounted, of *The Long Goodbye*, which so effortlessly reflects the hazy moral center of the world the film presents; and the pastel prettiness of *A Wedding*, particularly the first appearance of that icon of the American cinema, Lillian Gish. Altman's use of multi-track sound is also incredibly complex:

sounds are layered upon one another, often emanating from different speakers in such a way that the audience member must also decide what to listen for. Indeed, watching and listening to an Altman film inevitably requires an active participant: events unroll with a Bazinian ambiguity. Altman's Korean War comedy *M*A*S*H* was the director's first public success with this kind of soundtrack. One of his more extreme uses of this technique can be found in *McCabe and Mrs. Miller*, generally thought to be among the director's two or three finest achievements.

Nashville, Altman's most universally acclaimed work, is a panoramic view of the American experience and society, following the interrelated experiences of 24 characters in the country-western capital. In its almost three-hour length, *Nashville* accumulates a power of the whole even greater than the vivid individual parts which themselves resonate in the memory: the incredibly controlled debut performance of Lily Tomlin and the sensitive performances of at least a dozen others; the lesson on sexual politics Altman delivers when he photographs several women listening to a song by Keith Carradine; the vulnerability of Ronee Blakley who suffers a painful breakdown in front of her surprisingly fickle fans; the expressions on the faces of the men who watch Gwen Welles's painfully humiliating striptease; the final cathartic song of Barbara Harris, as Altman suddenly reveals the conventional "Star is Born" myth in his apparent anti-musical like a magician stunning us with an unexpected trick.

Overall, Altman's career itself has been rather weird. His output since the 1971 *M*A*S*H* has been prodigious indeed, especially in light of the fact that a great number of his films have been financial and/or critical failures. In fact, several of his films, among them *A Perfect Couple* and *Quintet* (with Paul Newman) barely got a national release; and *Health* (which starred Glenda Jackson, Carol Burnett, James Garner, and Lauren Bacall) languished on the shelf for years before achieving even a limited release in New York City. The most amazing thing about Altman's *Popeye*, which was relatively successful with critics and public, was that Altman managed to secure the assignment at all, not that the film emerged as one of the most cynical and ultimately disturbing children's films, in line with Altman's consistent vision of human beings and social organization. The directions Altman's theater-inspired films-*Come Back to the Five and Dime, Jimmy Dean, Jimmy Dean, Streamers*, and *The Diviners*—will lead his increasingly curious and unique career remains to be seen.

—Charles Derry

ALVAREZ, SANTIAGO. Cuban. Born in Havana, 1919. Educated in philosophy and letters, University of Havana; studied psychology and history, Columbia University, New York. Career: 1950's—co-founds *Nuestro Tiempo* film society in Havana; late 1950's-1959—serves as member of underground struggle against Batista; 1959—Instituto Cubano del Arte e Industria Cinematograficos (ICAIC) is established by revolutionary government; serves as Vice-President of ICAIC, and in other capacities including artistic director of Animated Film Department at ICAIC; 1960—becomes Director of the Latin American ICAIC newsreel; 1960-1970's—directs many award-winning documentaries, predominantly in black and white; late 1960s-early 1970s—begins to make documentaries in color.

Films (as director) 1961—*Escambray*; *Muerte al invasor* (co-d);

1962—*Forjadores de la paz* [Forgers of Peace]; *Cumplimos* [We Accomplished]; *Crisis en el Caribe*; 1963—*Ciclon* [Cyclone]; *El Barbaro del ritmo* [The Rhythm Barbarian]; 1964—*Via libre a la zafra del '64* [Green Light for the 1964 Sugar Crop]; 1965—*Solidaridad Cuba y Vietnam* [Solidarity Cuba and Vietnam]; *Cuba Dos de Enero* [Cuba, January 2]; *Pedales sobre Cuba* [Pedals over Cuba]; *Now*; *Segunda Declaracion de la Habana*; *La Escalada del chantaje*; 1966—*Abril de Giron*; *Cerro Pelado*; *Año Siete*; 1967—*La Guerra olvidada (Laos, the Forgotten War)*; *Hasta la victoria siempre* [Till victory Always]; *Golpeando en la selva*; *Hanoi, Martes 13* [Hanoi, Tuesday 13th]; 1968—*La Hora de los Hornos* [The Hour of the Furnaces] (co-d); *Amarrando el cordon* [Tying Up the Cord]; *L.B.J.*; 1969—*Despegue a las 18:00*; *79 Primaveras (79 Springtimes of Ho Chi Minh)*; 1970—*Once por cero*; *Piedra sobre piedra*; *El Sueño del Pongo*; *Yanapanacuna*; 1971—*Quemando tradiciones*; *Como por que y para que asesina a un general?*; *La Estampida*; *El Pajaro del faro*; 1972—*De America soy hijo...y a ella me debo*; 1973—*Y el cielo fue tomado por asalto*; *El Tigre salto y mato...pero morira...morira (The Tiger Leaped and Killed, But He Will Die, He Will Die)*; 1974—*60 Minutos con el primer mundial de boxeo amateur*; *Rescate*; *Los Cuatro Puentes*; 1975—*Abril de Vietnam en el año del gato*; *(Realizador)*; 1976—*El Tiempo es el viento*; *El sol no se puede tapar con un dedo*; *Luanda ya no es de San Pablo*; *Morir por la patria es vivir*; *Maputo: Meridiano novo*; *Los Dragones de Ha-Long*; 1977—*Ma Hermano Fidel*; *El Octubre de todos*; 1978—*Sobre el problema fronterizo*; *Entre Kampuchea y Vietnam*; 1979—*El Gran Salto al vacio*; *Tengo fe en ti*; *La Cumbre que nos une*; *El Desafio*.

Publications:

By ALVAREZ:

Articles—"La noticia a traves del cine" in *Cine Cubano* (Havana), no.23-5; interview by Enrique Colina in *Cine Cubano* (Havana), no.58-9; "Santiago Alvarez habla de su cine" in *Hablemos de Cine* (Lima), July/August 1970; "Sinopsis de un film sobre Cuba 1971" in *Cine Cubano* (Havana), no.78-80, 1973; interview by V. Casaus in *Cine Cubano* (Havana), no.78-80, 1973; "5 Frames Are 5 Frames, Not 6, but 5", interview in *Cineaste* (New York), v.6, no.4, 1975; "Entrevista con Santiago Alvarez" in *Areito* (Verano), v.2, no.1, 1975; "Kinematograf, rozhdennyt Oktiabrem" in *Iskusstvo Kino* (Moscow), no.5, 1976; "Angaben zur Person", interview by H. Herlinghaus in *Film und Fernsehen* (Berlin), June, August and October 1978; "Revolutionäre Sensibilität und der filmische Gedanke", interview by R. Michel in *Film und Fernsehen* (Berlin), August 1979; "El Periodismo cinematografico" in *Cine Cubano* (Havana), no.94, 1979; interview by D. Toala in *Young/Jeune Cinema & Theatre* (Prague), winter 1980.

On ALVAREZ:

Books—*Cuba: The Measure of a Revolution* by L. Nelson, Minneapolis 1972; *Memories of Underdevelopment: The Revolutionary Films of Cuba* by Michael Myerson, New York 1973; *BFI Dossier Number 2: Santiago Alvarez* edited by Michael Chanán, London 1982; articles—"Cinema of Revolution—90 Miles From Home" by Elizabeth Sutherland in *Film Quarterly* (Berkeley), Winter 1961-62; "The Cuban Cinema" by M.E. Douglas in *Take One* (Montreal), July/August 1968; "Propaganda Fills Cuban Newsreels" by R. Adler in the *New York*

Times, 12 February 1969; "Cubans are Molding Movie Industry into a Pervasive Force" by R. Adler in the *New York Times*, 11 February 1969; "Cultural Life in Cuba Thriving Despite Rein" by R. Adler in the *New York Times*, 10 February 1969; "Solidarity and Violence" by A. Engel in *Sight and Sound* (London), Autumn 1969; article on *79 Springtimes of Ho Chi Minh* by Lenny Rubenstein in *Cinéaste* (New York), winter 1970-71; "The Spring 1972 Cuban Film Festival Bust" by Gary Crowdus in *Film Society Review* (New York), March/May 1972; "Cine Cubano" by P. Sauvage in *Film Comment* (New York), Spring 1972; "Retrospectiva del documental cubano" by A. Marrosu in *Cine al dia* (Caracas), February 1976; "Introduction to Revolutionary Cuban Cinema" by Julianne Burton in *Jump Cut* (Chicago), December 1978; "El internacionalismo en la obra de Santiago Alvarez" by R. Chávez in *Cine Cubano* (Havana), March 1978.

*   *   *

Predominantly associated with the educational or the exotic in the United States, the documentary film occupies a very different place in the cinema of revolutionary Cuba. 90-95% of the films produced under the revolution have been documentaries, and the man most responsible for the international stature of Cuban documentary cinema is Santiago Alvarez.

As the director of the weekly "Latin American Newsreel" produced by the Cuban Film Institute (ICAIC), Alvarez has directed an enormous number of newsreels as well as many other short and feature-length documentaries. Never having formally studied cinema, he became a filmmaker by "handling millions of feet of film." Alvarez feels himself to be a journalist, but believes that cinematic journalism should have a permanence beyond simple reportage. To achieve such transcendency, Alvarez's newsreels are typically monothematic and integrated, with the result that they appear more like individual documentary films than the sort of generalized news reporting normally associated with newsreels.

The dominant characteristic of Alvarez's style is the extraordinarily rhythmic blend of visual and audio forms. Alvarez utilizes everything at hand to convey his message: live and historical documentary footage, still photos, bits from TV programs and fiction films, animation, and an incredible range of audio accompaniment. Believing that "50% of the value of a film is in the soundtrack," Alvarez mixes rock, classical, and tropical music, sound effects, participant narration—even silence—to the furious pace of his visual images. For Alvarez, cinema has its own language, different from that of television or of radio, and the essence of this language is montage.

Alvarez's documentaries focus on both national and international themes. For example, *Ciclon* is an early newsreel on the effects of hurricane Flora in Cuba. Although it lacks the elaborate visual montage for which Alvarez later became famous, the film shows great skill in the use of sound. There is no verbal narration, and the track is limited to the source sound of trucks and helicopters, and the organ music which eerily punctuates the scenes of caring for the wounded and burying the dead.

Now, a short dealing with racism in the U.S. and edited to the rhythm of Lena Horne's song, shows the master at his best in working with still photographs. Paricularly effective is a sequence in which Alvarez cuts between the chained hands of arrested blacks and the linked hands of protestors to suggest a dynamic of collective struggle in which people are seen not only as products of their circumstances, but as historical actors capable of changing their circumstances. Here, Alvarez fuses ideology and art by making graphic the third of Marx's "Theses on Feuerbach." Alvarez's tribute to Che Guevara, *Hasta la victoria siempre*, deals with much the same concept. He begins with a series of beautifully shot stills of poverty in the Altiplano. Then, following footage of Che speaking in the Sierra Maestra of Cuba, he dissolves a still of Che into a still of a Gulf Oil Co. camp in Bolivia. Through this technique he links the earlier struggle in Cuba with the later guerrilla war in the Andes.

One of the finest examples of Alvarez's work is *79 Springtimes*, a beautifully controlled montage on Ho Chi Minh's life and death. He opens the short by ironically mixing elapsed-time photography of flowers opening with slow-motion footage of bombs falling from U.S. planes. He goes on to cut between scenes of U.S. atrocities in Viet Nam and protest marches in the U.S., visually depicting the position that the real enemy is not the people of the U.S., but the ruling class and its mercenaries. In the final sequence, Alvarez uses what seems to be every available visual effect—torn and burned strips of film, film frames, bits of paper—to create an incredible animated montage. The sound track underscores the visual dynamic with music and poems by Ho Chi Minh and Jose Martí.

Alvarez continues to be thought of as one of the foremost documentary filmmakers in Latin America, although some consider his earlier short films to be superior to the later and longer works. This may result from the fact that in the earlier films the line between heroes (Che, Ho Chi Minh) and villains (U.S. imperialism and racism) was more clearly drawn, while the later works reflect the international compromises with the Soviet Union and reformist Latin American governments that have been required of the Cuban revolution. Nonetheless, Alvarez persists in his indefatigable quest for an "audacious and constantly renewed optic."

—John Mraz

ANDERSON, LINDSAY. British. Born 17 April 1923 in Bangalore, South India. Educated at St. Ronan's School, Worthing, and at Cheltenham College. Career: during WWII—in Army Intelligence Corps; 1947—begins to edit *Sequence* magazine at Oxford; 1948—makes industrial documentary film, *Sequence* moved to London; 1950s—contributes to *Isis, Sight & Sound* and *New Statesman*; 1955—organizes retrospective of John Ford films for National Film Theatre; begins directing television series *Robin Hood* (5 episodes); 1956—helps organize first Free Cinema program, National Film Theatre; 1959-60—Artistic Director, Royal Court Theatre; 1959-present—active as stage director; 1969-70—Member of British Film Institute Board of Directors, resigns, with Karel Reisz, for political reasons in 1970; 1972—directs *Home* (play by David Storey) for TV; also has directed TV commercials. Recipient: Academy Award, Best Short Subject, for *Thursday's Children*, 1955; Golden Palm, Cannes Festival, for *If...*, 1969.

Films (as director): 1948—*Meet the Pioneers* (+sc, co-ed, narration); 1949—*Idlers That Work* (+sc, narration); 1952—*3 Installations* (+sc, narration); *Trunk Conveyor* (+sc, narration); *Wakefield Express* (+sc); 1953—*Thursday's Children* (co-d, +sc); *O Dreamland* (+sc); 1955—*Green and Pleasant Land* (+sc); *Henry* (+sc, ro); *The Children Upstairs* (+sc); *A Hundred Thousand Children* (+sc); *£20 a Ton* (+sc); *Energy First* (+sc); *Foot and Mouth* (+sc, narration); 1956—*Together* (Mazzetti) (supervising ed only); 1957—*Every Day Except Christmas* (+sc); 1958—*March to Aldermaston* (supervising ed only); 1960—*Let My People Go* (Krish) (sponsor only); 1963—*This Sporting Life*;

1967—*The White Bus*; *Raz, dwa, trzy (The Singing Lesson)* (+sc); 1969—*If...* (+pr); 1972—*O Lucky Man!* (+co-pr); 1974—*In Celebration*; 1982—*Brittania Hospital*. Roles: 1949—narrator, *Out of Season* (Brendon); 1952—*The Pleasure Garden* (Broughton) (+pr); 1962—narrator, *The Story of Private Pooley* (Alsen—English language version of *Der Schwur des Soldaten Pooley*); 1965—narrator, *The Threatening Sky* (Ivens—*English language version of Le Ciel, la terre*); 1966—*Mucednici lásky (Martyrs of Love)* (Němec); 1967—himself in *About 'The White Bus'* (Fletcher); 1968—narrator, *Abel Gance—The Charm of Dynamite* (Brownlow) (for TV); *Inadmissable Evidence* (Page); 1969—*The Parachute* (Page) (for TV); 1970—narrator, *Hetty King—Performer* (Robinson); 1971—narrator, *A Mirror from India* (Sarabhai); 1981—schoolmaster in *Chariots of Fire* (Hudson).

Publications:

By ANDERSON:

Books—*Making a Film: The Story of "Secret People"*, London 1952; *If...: A Film by Lindsay Anderson* by David Sherwin and Lindsay Anderson, New York 1969; *O Lucky Man!*, with David Sherwin, with songs by Alan Price, New York 1973; articles—"Angles of Approach" in *Sequence* (London), winter 1947; "The Manvell Approach" in *Sequence* (London), winter 1947; review of *Paisa* in *Sequence* (London), winter 1947; "Creative Elements" in *Sequence* (London), autumn 1948; "The Need for Competence" in *Sequence* (London), spring 1948; "A Possible Solution" in *Sequence* (London), spring 1948; review of *Sciuscia* in *Sequence* (London), summer 1948; review of *Strange Voyage* in *Sequence* (London), autumn 1948; "What Goes On" in *Sequence* (London), summer 1948; "British Cinema: The Descending Spiral" in *Sequence* (London), spring 1949; "The Film Front" in *Sequence* (London), summer 1949; "Film Review: *Louisiana Story*" in *Sequence* (London), winter 1949; "Films of Alfred Hitchcock" in *Sequence* (London), autumn 1949; review of *The History of Mr. Polly* in *Sequence* (London), spring 1949; "The Studio that Begs to Differ" in *Film and Theatre Today: The European Scene*, London 1949; "The Director's Cinema?" in *Sequence* (London), autumn 1950; "Notes at Cannes" in *Sequence* (London), New Year issue 1950; "Retrospective Review: *Wagonmaster* and *2 Flags West*" in *Sight and Sound* (London), December 1950; "*They Were Expendable* and John Ford" in *Sequence* (London), summer 1950; "Goldwyn at Claridges" in *Sequence* (London), New Year issue 1951; "John Ford" in *Films in Review* (New York), February 1951; "As the Critics Like It: Some Personal Choices" in *Sight and Sound* (London), October/December 1952; "Casque d'Or" in *Sight and Sound* (London), October/December 1952; "Minnelli, Kelly and *An American in Paris*" in *Sequence* (London), New Year issue 1952; "The Quiet Man" in *Sequence* (London), New Year issue 1952; "Cannes 1953" in *Sight and Sound* (London), July/September 1953; "Encounter with Prévert" in *Sight and Sound* (London), July/September 1953; "Only Connect: Some Aspects of the Work of Humphrey Jennings" in *Sight and Sound* (London), April/June 1953; review of *Birth of a Nation* in *Sight and Sound* (London), January/March 1953; review of *The Sun Shines Bright* in *Sight and Sound* (London), October/December 1953; review of *What Price Glory?* in *Sight and Sound* (London), January/March 1953; "French Critical Writing" in *Sight and Sound* (London), October/December 1954; "Perspectives at Cannes" in *Sight and Sound* (London), July/September 1954; "Cannes 1955" in *Sight and Sound* (London), summer 1955;

"The Last Sequence of *On the Waterfront*" in *Sight and Sound* (London), January/March 1955; review of *Positif* and *Cahiers du Cinéma* in *Sight and Sound* (London), January/March 1955; "Film Reviews: *The Searchers*" in *Sight and Sound* (London), autumn 1956; "Notes from Sherwood" in *Sight and Sound* (London), winter 1956; "Panorama at Cannes" in *Sight and Sound* (London), summer 1956; "Stand Up! Stand Up!" in *Sight and Sound* (London), autumn 1956; "10 Feet Tall" in *Sight and Sound* (London), summer 1957; "2 Inches Off the Ground" in *Sight and Sound* (London), winter 1957; "The Critical Issue: A Discussion Between Paul Rotha, Basil Wright, Lindsay Anderson, Penelope Houston" in *Sight and Sound* (London), autumn 1957; "Get Out and Push!" in *Declaration*, edited by Tom Maschler, New York 1958; review of *The Last Hurrah* in *Sight and Sound* (London), spring 1958; "3 to Cheer For" in *International Film Annual No. 2*, New York 1958; "The Filmmaker and the Audience: Replies to a Questionnaire" in *Film Book 1: The Audience and the Filmmaker*, edited by Robert Hughes, New York 1959; "Pre-Renaissance" in *International Theatre Annual*, London 1961; "Sport, Life and Art" in *Films and Filming* (London), February 1963; "An Interview with Lindsay Anderson" by Peter Cowie in *Film Quarterly* (Berkeley, California), summer 1964; "Class Theatre, Class Film: An Interview with Lindsay Anderson", edited by Kelly Morris, in *Tulane Drama Review*, (Alabama), fall 1966; interview with Lindsay Anderson in *Cinema International* (Montier, Switzerland), no.16, 1967; "The Film Maker and the Audience" in *Film Makers on Film Making*, edited by Harry Geduld, Bloomington, Indiana 1967; interview in *Directors in Action*, edited by Bob Thomas, New York 1968; "The Method of John Ford" in *The Emergence of Film Art*, edited by Lewis Jacobs, New York 1969; interview in *Documentary Explorations: 15 Interviews with Film-makers* by G. Roy Levin, New York 1971; "Financial Support for Film Makers from Mr. Lindsay Anderson and Others" in the *Times* (London), 15 August 1971; "John Ford" in *Cinéma* (Paris), spring 1971; "The 7th Seal" in *Focus on the 7th Seal*, edited by Birgitta Steene, Englewood Cliffs, New Jersey 1972; "Anderson: 'We have to make our own acts of courage'," interview by Guy Flatley in the *New York Times*, 1 July 1973; "The Anderson Tape", interview by Klas Freund and Lars-Olaf Löthwall in *Chaplin* (Stockholm), no.124, 1973; "Crisis in Film Industry: From Mr. Lindsay Anderson and Others" in the *Times* (London), 12 December 1973; "Stripping the Veils Away", interview with David Robinson in the *Times* (London), 21 April 1973; "O Lucky Man!", interview by J. Delson in *Take One* (Montreal), September 1973; interview by A. Head in *Image et son* (Paris), May 1973; "Some Aspects of the Work of Humphrey Jennings" in *The Documentary Tradition*, selected by Lewis Jacobs, New York 1974; "From Theater to Film...Lindsay Anderson", interview by M. Carducci in *Millimeter* (New York), January 1975.

On ANDERSON:

Books—*The Contemporary Cinema* by Penelope Houston, Baltimore 1963; *New Cinema in Britain* by Roger Manvell, New York 1969; *Lindsay Anderson* by Elizabeth Sussex, New York 1969; *Nonfiction Film* by Richard Barsam, New York 1973; *Lindsay Anderson* by Allison Graham, Boston 1981; articles—"Look at Britain!" by John Berger in *Sight and Sound* (London), summer 1957; "Looking for Documentary, Part 2: The Ones that Got Away" by David Robinson in *Sight and Sound* (London), autumn 1957; "*This Sporting Life*" by Tom Milne in *Sight and Sound* (London), summer 1962; "Anderson Shooting *If...*" by David Robinson in *Sight and Sound* (London), summer 1968; "Editing Anderson's *If...*" by David Gladwell in *Screen* (London), January/February 1969; "Lindsay Anderson" in *The Film*

Director as Superstar by Joseph Gelmis, Garden City, New Jersey 1970; "Biofilmographie—Lindsay Anderson" in *Avant-Scene du Cinéma* (Paris), November 1971; "O Lucky Man!" by James Delson in *Take One* (Montreal), May/June 1972; "Free Cinema" by Alan Lovell and Jim Hillier in *Studies in Documentary*, New York 1972; "The Unknown Cinema of Britain" by Alan Lovell in *Cinema Journal* (Evanston), spring 1972; "O Lucky Man!" by D. Wilson in *Sight and Sound* (London), summer 1973; "Lindsay Anderson" by Rafal Marszalek in *Kino* (Warsaw), October 1974; "Brecht in Britain—Lindsay Anderson" by Alan Lovell in *Screen* (London), winter 1975; "Lindsay Anderson" by John Taylor in *Directors and Directions*, London 1975; "Brittania Waives the Rules" by Raymond Durgnat in *Film Comment* (New York), July/August 1976.

*   *   *

In a 1958 essay entitled "Get Out and Push," Lindsay Anderson expressed his approach to working in the cinema and at the same time the world view which permeates his feature films: "I have learned that it is impossible to work in the cinema, or usefully discuss it, without reference to the system within which films are produced; and once that reference is made, it is impossible not to consider the basis of the system, the way it has grown, the motives which sustain it and the interests that it serves."

This examination of the cinema parallels the position Anderson puts forth in his films concerning an individual's relationship to his environment. If the system is not serving the interests of the creative growth of the individual, it is the responsibility of the individual to actively seek a new self-definition beyond the confines of the established system. This individualistic approach is especially well developed in *This Sporting Life, If...*, and *O Lucky Man!*

In *This Sporting Life*, Anderson approaches the repression of a traditionally structured society through the personal, subjective story of Frank Machin and Margaret Hammond. The social system is evident in the film, but the focus is on the emotional conflicts of the two main characters. The setting of *This Sporting Life*, an industrial northern city, is an environment divided into economic classes. The division of classes serves to emphasize the central problem of the film—the division within Frank Machin. Machin finds himself limited to the realm of the physical, and constantly attempts to connect with others on an emotional level. Despite his attempts, he is only seen in terms of his physical qualities; he is referred to as a "big cat" and a "great ape" and is valued only when he is participating in the physical act of playing rugby.

In contrast to Machin is his landlady, Margaret Hammond, a deeply emotional person; however, her emotions are hidden and suppressed. Although Mrs. Hammond has no desire to make connections outside herself, Machin sees her as his complement, as the key to his personal happiness and completeness. Machin, though, not knowing how to reach people on an emotional level, is often clumsy and coarse, and Mrs. Hammond, not wishing to be reached, does not attempt to aid or encourage him. Instead of sharing with each other and complementing each other, the two are in constant conflict.

Frank Machin is aware of his limitations but does not know how to change; he lacks direction. At one point in the film Mrs. Hammond states that "Some people have their lives made for them," and Machin quickly replies, "Some people make their own lives." But Machin tries to make others responsible for his happiness: Margaret Hammond, the rugby team, and even the elites of society who populate the world of Mr. and Mrs. Weaver, owners of the rugby team. Instead of acting upon his environment, Machin constantly attempts to break into the established system, seemingly unaware that it is this same system which controls and restrains him. Margaret's death leaves Machin alone, still trapped within himself and within the society which makes it so difficult for him to connect with others.

Mick Travis, the protagonist of Anderson's second feature film *If...*, also struggles to make connections outside himself; however, unlike Frank Machin, Mick struggles to break out of the established system. Mick takes on the responsibility of action, and although his revolution is not complete, he does not remain trapped like Frank Machin.

As in *This Sporting Life*, the principal purpose of the environment of *If...* is not solely to present authentic physical surroundings, but to contribute to the understanding of the central problem of the film. The English public school system is not the focus of the film, but a metaphor for, as Elizabeth Sussex states, the "separation of intellect from imagination." The environment of College House does not allow for the creative development of the individual; it encourages separation and fragmentation of the self. The students of College House are told to, "Work—play, but don't mix the two."

Film technique in *If...* also serves to reveal the narrative theme of the division of the self. The chapter headings physically divide the film into rigidly ordered sections, reflecting the separation of intellect and imagination encouraged by the nature of the tradition of College House. These chapter headings, along with the alternation between black and white and color film, function as distancing devices, making the viewer aware of the medium.

A narrative technique which Anderson uses to illustrate the process that leads to Mick's eventual break from the system is the establishment of verbal language as an essential part of the structure of College House. When Mick first expresses his disdain for College House through words, they are simply absorbed by the system. Even when Mick turns from insulting the Whips to making revolutionary statements his words remain empty and meaningless for lack of a concrete conviction. There is no change in Mick's situation until he initiates action by bayoneting the college chaplin. After this point in the film Mick no longer recites revolutionary rhetoric; in fact, he rarely speaks. He is no longer existing within the structure of College House. Totally free of the system, Mick launches into his final action of the destruction of the established order. Mick is no longer acted upon but is the creator of action; in this respect, he triumphs where Frank Machin fails. It is in Anderson's next feature, *O Lucky Man!*, that the character Mick Travis will go beyond the revolution in *If...* to achieve a new self-definition.

In *O Lucky Man!*, the thematic sequel to *If...*, the medium of film itself becomes one of the narrative themes, and self-reflexive film techniques serve to reveal not only the narrative theme of self-definition, but also the process of filmmaking. The titles used in *O Lucky Man!* announce different sections of the film but do not impose order; in fact, because of their abrupt appearance and their brevity these titles tend to interrupt the order of the narrative. It is as if the medium of film itself occasionally breaks through to remind the viewer of its existence.

The recording sessions with Alan Price provide the major interruptions of the narrative structure of the film. The reality of the process of filmmaking constantly breaks into the fantasy of the story. Again, as with the film *If...*, Anderson is using the Brechtian principle of distancing so the audience may view the film objectively. In this film, however, Anderson is not just making the viewer aware of the existence of the medium to clarify other narrative themes. The medium, specifically the energy the medium generates, is one of the themes of *O Lucky Man!*. The process of creation in the medium far exceeds anything Mick accomplishes in the narrative until the two meet in the final sequence.

Mick Travis, the character, confronts Lindsay Anderson, the director, at an audition for the film *O Lucky Man!*. Mick obediently projects the different emotions Anderson demands of him until he is asked to smile. It is at this point in the film that Mick finally takes action and rejects a direct order: "What is there to smile about?" he asks. Mick is looking outside himself for motivation, as he has done throughout the film, before he will take action. Anderson, exasperated, strikes Mick with a script. After receiving the blow, Mick is able to smile. He soon finds that he is one of the actors in the film; he too is capable of creating action.

Anderson's first two features, *This Sporting Life* and *If...* were well received. Critics were impressed with Anderson's individual style of poetic realism. Each film was praised for transcending the popular genre of its time. The release of *O Lucky Man!* once again brought praise for an individual style; critics applauded the film as Anderson's best and approved highly of his Brechtian techniques. Some reviewers, however, had reservations about the technique and were disturbed by the film's ending. The film was either admired or criticized, depending upon the reviewer, for its reflexive qualities, its lack of identification with the hero, and its tendency to move the viewer to think rather than feel.

All three of these films are audience pleasers, and overall Anderson is admired for his humor, his eye for detail, and his unique style. Anderson's subsequent films, *In Celebration* (1975) and *Brittania Hospital* (1982), have continued to explore the same themes as his previous work.

—Marie Saeli

ANGELOPOULOS, THEODOROS. (Surname also spelled "Anghelopoulos".) Greek. Born in Athens, 27 April 1935. Educated in law, Athens, 1953-59; Sorbonne, Paris, 1961-64; studies at IDHEC, Paris, 1962-63. Career: before 1969—works as lawyer, writes poetry, essays and short stories; 1959-60—military service; 1964-67—film critic for *Dimoktatiki Allaghi*, left-wing journal suppressed after 1967 coup; 1965—feature film *Forminx* begun then abandoned because of dispute with producer; 1966-68—actor and director of production for several films; 1970—on *Reconstruction* begins association with cinematographer George Arvanitis; 1970s—teaches at Stavrakou Film School. Recipient: British Film Institute Award for Best Film: *The Travelling Players*, 1976. Lives in Athens.

Films (as director and scriptwriter): 1968—*Ekpombi (The Broadcast, L'Emission)*; 1970—*Anaparastassi (Reconstruction, Reconstitution)* (+ro); 1972—*Mères tou 36 (Days of '36, Jours de 36)*; 1975—*O Thassios (The Travelling Players, Le Voyage des comédiens)*; 1977—*I Kynighi (The Hunters)*(+co-pr); 1980—*O Megalexandros* (+pr). Roles: 1968—in *Kieron* (Theos).

Publications:

By ANGELOPOULOS:

Articles—"Le Voyage des comédiens", interview by J.-P. Brossard and others in *Image et son* (Paris), November 1975; "Mes films sont des appels à la discussion...", interview by N. Ghali in *Cinéma* (Paris), September/October 1975; "Entretien avec Anghelopoulos" by P. Mereghetti and others in *Jeune cinéma*

(Paris), July/August 1975; "Les Chasseurs", interview by O. Barrot and M. Demopoulos in *Ecran* (Paris), November 1977; interview by P. Carcassonne in *Cinématographe* (Paris), June 1977; interview by Michel Ciment in *Positif* (Paris), June 1977; interview by D. Rabourdin in *Cinéma* (Paris), August/September 1977; "Animating Dead Space and Dead Time", interview and article by T. Mitchell, in *Sight and Sound* (London), winter 1980/81.

On ANGELOPOULOS:

Book—*The Contemporary Greek Cinema* by Mel Schuster, Metuchen, New Jersey 1979; articles—in *Avant-Scène du cinéma* (Paris), December 1975; article in *Ecran* (Paris), November 1975; articles in *Image et son* (Paris), September/October and November 1975; article in *Positif* (Paris), October 1975; article in *Cineforum* (Bergamo), September 1975; "La qualifica di laboratorio alla prova dei film presentati. III: Anghelopoulos: mito e metafora come instrumento e lezione di storia" by V. Giacci in *Cineforum* (Bergamo), September 1976; "Anghelopoulos et le non-dit" by P. Pitiot in *Cinéma* (Paris), August/September 1978; "Anghelopoulos and the New Greek Cinema" by A. Horton in *Film Criticism* (Edinboro, Pa.), fall 1981.

*　　*　　*

Angelopoulos's considerable achievement in the 1970's has made him not only the most important Greek filmmaker to date, but one of the truly creative and original artists of his time. In 1970 he convinced a young producer, George Papalios, to finance his first film, *Anaparastassi*. The story follows the pattern of a crime tale à la James Cain. A Greek peasant is killed by his wife and her lover on his return from Germany where he had gone to find work. A judge tries to reconstruct the circumstances of the murder but finds himself unable to communicate with the accused who belong to a totally different culture. To shoot this Pirandellian story of misunderstanding, Angelopoulos adopted an austere style with long camera movements that show a bleak and desolate Greek landscape, far from the tourist leaflets. Very much like Visconti's *Ossessione*, this is a film noir that opens the way to more daring aesthetic ventures.

His trilogy, *Days of 36*, *The Travelling Players* and *The Hunters* can be seen as an exploration of contemporary Greek history. If his style shows some influences—particularly Jancsó's with his use of the one reel-one take and Antonioni's for its slow, meditative mood—Angelopoulos has nevertheless created an authentic epic cinema akin to Brecht's theatre where aesthetic emotion is counterbalanced by a reflexive approach that questions the surfaces of reality. The audience is neither allowed to identify with a central character, nor to follow a dramatic development, or given a reassuring morality. The director boldly goes from the present to the past within the same shot and in *The Hunters* broadens his investigation by including the fantasies of his characters. The sweep of a movie like *Travelling Players*, which includes songs and dances, is breathtaking and its length (four hours) transforms it into the earth odyssey of an actors group circulating through Greece from 1939 to 1952 performing a pastoral play. Angelopoulos's masterpiece had been preceded by the haunting *Days of 36*, a political thriller about a murder in a prison which was a prelude to events of national importance. It is the director's most radical use of off-screen space and off-screen sound, of the dialectic between the seen and the unseen. With its closed doors, whispering voices in corridors, and silhouettes running to and fro, it evokes the mystery that surrounds the exercise of power.

Angelopoulos's fifth film, *Alexander the Great* breaks new ground: it deals with myth and develops the exploration of the popular unconscious already present in *Travelling Players* and *The Hunters*. At the turn of the 20th century, a bandit is seen as the reincarnation of the Macedonian king. He kidnaps some English residents in Greece, leads them to the mountains, tries to blackmail the British government and ends by killing his hostages. Angelopoulos opposes several groups: the foreigners, the outlaws, some Italian anarchists who have taken refuge in Greece, and village people who try to establish a utopian community. The director's indictment of hero-worshipping and his portrayal of diverse forms of political failure reveal a growing pessimism in his works. But his style is as masterly as ever, reaching a kind of austere grandeur reminiscent of Byzantine mosaics. Few have blended so satisfyingly a political investigation with a search for new forms of expression.

—Michel Ciment

———————

ANGER, KENNETH. American. Born in Santa Monica, California, 1930. Career: 1934—plays role of a changeling in Max Reinhardt's film *A Midsummer Night's Dream*; 1935—studies tap-dancing in class that includes Shirley Temple, Maurice Kossloff Dancing School, Hollywood; 1941—completes first film; early 1950s—moves to Europe; 1959—original version of *Hollywood Babylon* published in France; subsequently appears in U.S. in unauthorized version; 1962—returns to U.S. to make film celebrating arrival of Age of Aquarius; 1967—destruction of only print of *Lucifer Rising* by Bobby Beausoleil, Manson gang member who appeared in film; Anger places ad in *Village Voice* "In Memoriam Kenneth Anger 1947-1967" announcing end of filmmaking career; 1967-73—in Europe; 1974—completes 2nd version of *Lucifer Rising* (released 1980). Recipient: Ford Foundation Fellow, 1964. Address: c/o American Federation of Arts Film Program, 41 E. 65th St., New York, NY 10021.

Films (conception, direction, photography and editing): 1941—*Who Has Been Rocking My Dream Boat*; 1941-42—*Tinsel Tree*; 1942—*Prisoner of Mars*; 1943—*The Nest*; 1944—*Escape Episode*; 1945—*Drastic Demise*; 1946—*Escape Episode* (sound version); 1947—*Fireworks** (+ro as *The Dreamer*); 1948—*Puce Women* (unfinished); 1949—*Puce Moment**; *The Love That Whirls* (unfinished); 1950—*La Lune des Lapins (Rabbit's Moon)** (conception, d and ed only, +prod. design); 1951-52—*Maldoror* (unfinished); 1953—*Eaux d'artifice** (+costume design); *Le Jeune Homme et la mort*; 1954—*Inauguration of the Pleasure Dome** (+ro as *Hecate*); 1955—*Thelema Abbey* (conception, d and ed only); 1962-63—*Scorpio Rising**; 1965—*Kustom Kar Kommandos**; 1969—*Invocation of My Demon Brother**; 1971—*Rabbit's Moon*; 1974—*Lucifer Rising**; 1980—*Lucifer Rising** (second version). Note: * indicates films contained and distributed in Anger's definitive portfolio "The Magick Lantern Cycle".

Publications:

By ANGER:

Books—*Hollywood Babylon*, Phoenix, Arizona 1965; *Magick Lantern Cycle: A Special Presentation in Celebration of the Equinox Spring 1966*, New York 1966; *Hollywood Babylon*, San Francisco 1975; articles—interview in *Spider Magazine*, v.1, no.13, 1965; interview in *Film Culture* (New York), spring 1966;

"An Interview with Kenneth Anger" in *Film Culture* (New York), spring 1966; interview by Bruce Martin and Joe Medjuck in *Take One* (Montreal), August 1967; "Interview with Kenneth Anger" by Lenny Lipton in *Filmmakers Newsletter* (Ward Hill, Mass.), November 1967; article in *Film Makers on Filmmaking* edited by Harry Geduld, Bloomington, Indiana 1967.

On ANGER:

Books—*The New American Cinema* edited by Gregory Battcock, New York 1967; *Expanded Cinema* by Gene Youngblood, New York 1970; *Visionary Film* by P. Adams Sitney, New York 1974; *A History of the American Avant-Garde Cinema*, exhibition catalogue, by John Hanhardt and others, The American Federation of Arts, New York 1976; articles—"Thanatos in Chrome" by Kenneth Kelman in *Film Culture* (New York), winter 1963/64; "Imagism in 4 Avant-Garde Films" by P. Adams Sitney in *Film Culture* (New York), winter 1963/64; "Filmography of Kenneth Anger" in *Film Culture* (New York), no.31, 1963/64; "Appendix to Thanatos in Chrome" by Kenneth Kelman in *Film Culture* (New York), spring 1964; "Thanatos in Chrome" by Ken Kelman in *Film Culture* (New York), no.31, 1964; "Anger at the 3rd Los Angeles Filmmakers Festival" by Art Knuden in *Canyon Cinema News* (San Francisco), November 1964; "Le Nouveau Cinéma" by René Micha in *Les Temps modernes* (Paris), no.214, 1964; "San Francisco's Hipster Cinema" by Thomas Alexander in *Film Culture* (New York), no.44, 1967; "On Kenneth Anger" by Regina Cornwall in *December* (New York), no.1, 1968; "Lucifer: A Kenneth Anger Kompendium" by Tony Rayns in *Cinema* (Cambridge), October 1969; "3 Notes on *Invocation of My Demon Brother*" by Jonas Mekas, Richard Whitehall and P. Adams Sitney in *Film Culture* (New York), winter/spring 1970; "The Avant-Garde: Kenneth Anger and George Landow" by P. Adams Sitney in *Afterimage* (Rochester, New York), no.2, 1970; "Collectif jeune cinéma: 3e nuit blanche" by J. Magny in *Cinéma* (Paris), April 1972; "Anger at Work" in *Cinema Rising*, April 1972; "Illuminating Lucifer" by C. Rowe in *Film Quarterly* (Berkeley), summer 1974; "Kenneth Anger: Holding a Magick Lantern Up to the Future" by James Saslow in *Advocate*, 23 July 1981; "Kenneth Anger: Master in Hell" by Robin Hardy and "Kenneth Anger: Personal Traditions and Satanic Pride" by Michael Wade in *Body Politic*, April 1982.

*   *   *

One of the key figures of the postwar American avant-garde, Kenneth Anger represents a fiercely original talent, relatively free of the independent circles and movements which his own work managed to anticipate in almost every case. Creator of an oeuvre and a persona defined by their dialectical relationship to dominant representational, ideological, industrial, sexual and aesthetic practices, Anger embodies the "radical otherness" of the avant-garde filmmaker, casting himself not only outside the mainstream, but as its negative image. While other experimentalists were exploring "ways of seeing" through cinematic abstraction, Anger remained committed to a search for meanings, even as his films pursued a variety of aesthetic paths. Anger's meanings emerge from his subversive reworkings of sources already charged with significance: the iconography of American popular culture (movie stars, comic strips, car clubs), the conventional rhetoric of narrative forms (from the commedia dell'arte to the lyrics of rock songs), the imagery of classic cinema (Cocteau, Eisenstein, DeMille), and the symbolism of various mythologies (Egyptian, Greek, astrological, alchemical, centered by the cosmology of master "magickian" Aleister Crowley.

Anger gained international prominence and notoriety at the age of 17 with his film *Fireworks*, in which he appeared as the protagonist of a homoerotic fantasy in the oneiric tradition of Cocteau and Maya Deren, shot through with the romantic sadism of the American film noir. Three years later, he made *Rabbit's Moon*, a delicately humorous, Méliès-like fantasy involving a Pierrot character and a magic lantern, shot in Cocteau's own studio in Paris. Another three years found Anger in Italy, where he choreographed an elaborately baroque game of hide-and-seek through Tivoli's water gardens in *Eaux d'artifice*. Focusing at intervals on the visual patterns of water flowing from the fountains, this film experiments with the textures of an abstract filmic image a full two years before Brakhage's *Wonder Ring*. Yet, characteristically, the multiple superimpositions of Anger's colorful mass/masquerade *Inauguration of the Pleasure Dome* have less to do with abstraction than with an effort to achieve a magical condensation of mythological imagery. *Scorpio Rising*, however, remains Anger's most influential and original work. A tour-de-force collage of pop imagery, it is a paean to the American motorcyclist, a revelation of the violent, homoerotic undercurrent of American culture, and a celebration of the forces of chaos in the universe.

Anger spent most of the mid- to late-1960s on two abortive projects. His *Kustom Kar Kommandos* was cut short by the death of the young man playing its protagonist, although one sensual sequence, involving the dusting of a custom hot rod with a powder puff, has survived. Far more ambitious, however, was a master opus entitled *Lucifer Rising*, a project cut tragically short when, at a 1967 San Francisco screening of the work-in-progress, the single print of the film was stolen by one of the film's actors, Manson cultist Bobby Beausoleil, and was supposedly buried somewhere in Death Valley, never to be recovered. This event was followed by Anger's self-imposed retirement, interrupted in 1969 by the appearance of an 11-minute structural black mass constructed largely of *Lucifer's* outtakes, backed by a maddeningly monotonous soundtrack by Mick Jagger, and entitled *Invocation of my Demon Brother*.

By 1974, however, Anger had completed another version of *Lucifer Rising*, a dense meditative work shot mostly in Egypt, imbued with Crowleian mysticism and most memorable for the thoroughly uncanny image of a pinkish flying saucer hovering above the pyramids. The far more complete version finally released by Anger in 1980 marks a quantum leap in terms of *Lucifer Rising*'s complexity, and remains at this time the *chef-d'oeuvre* of Anger's career.

—Ed Lowry

ANTONIONI, MICHELANGELO. Italian. Born in Ferrara, Italy, 29 September 1912. Educated Faculty of Economics and Commerce, University of Bologna, degree 1935; attended Centro Sperimentale di Cinematografia, Rome, 1940-41. Career: 1935—writes for newspaper *Il Corriere Padano* in Ferrara, and attempts documentary on mental hospitals; 1935-39—works in bank; 1939—moves to Rome; 1940-49—writes criticism for film magazines, including *Cinema* (Rome); 1942—serves as assistant director on *I due Foscari* (Fulchignoni); in France assists Marcel Carné as Italian representative of French-Italian co-production *Les Visiteurs du soir*; 1942-52—serves as scriptwriter or co-scriptwriter on films including Rossellini's *Una pilota ritorna* (1946) and Fellini's *Lo sceicco bianco*; 1943-47—directs 1st film *Gente del Po*, a short documentary; 1957—directs 2 plays *Scan-*

dali segreti and *I Am a Camera*; 1960—gains international attention with *L'avventura*; 1966—directs 1st film in English, *Blow-Up*; 1970s—begins to experiment with video processes. **Recipient:** Special Jury Prize, Cannes Festival, for *L'avventura*, 1960; Special Jury Prize, Cannes Festival, for *L'eclisse*, 1962; Best Director, National Society of Film Critics, for *Blow-Up*, 1966. **Address:** Via Vincenzo Tiberio 18, Rome, Italy.

Films (as director and scriptwriter of short films): 1947—*Gente del Po*; 1948—*N.U. (Nettezza urbana)*; *Roma—Montevideo*; *Oltre l'oblio*; 1949—*L'amorosa menzogna*; *Bomarzo*; *Superstizione*; *Ragazze in bianco*; 1950—*Sette canne e un vestito*; *La villa dei mostri*; *La funivia del Faloria*; *Uomini in piú*; (as feature director and scriptwriter): 1950—*Cronaca di un amore (Story of a Love Affair)* (co-sc); 1952—*I Vinti (I nostri figli, The Vanquished)* (co-sc); 1953—*La signora senza camelie (Camille Without Camelias)* (co-sc); "Tentato suicidio" episode of *L'Amore in città*; 1955—*Le amiche (The Girlfriends)* (co-sc); 1957—*Il grido (The Outcry)* (co-sc); 1959—*L'avventura* (co-sc); 1960—*La notte (The Night)* (co-sc); 1962—*L'eclisse (The Eclipse)* (co-sc); 1964—*Deserto rosso (Red Desert)* (co-sc); 1965—"Prefizione" episode of *Tre Volti*; 1966—*Blow-Up* (co-sc); 1970—*Zabriskie Point* (co-sc); 1972—*Chung Kuo (La cina)*; 1975—*Professione: Reporter (The Passenger)* (co-sc); 1979—*Il mistero di Oberwald (The Oberwald Mystery)*; 1982—*Identificazione di una donna*.

Publications:

By ANTONIONI:

Books—*La Nuit: La Notte* with Tonino Guerra and E. Flaiano, translated by Michèle Causse, Paris 1961; *L'eclisse* with Tonino Guerra (collaboration by E. Bartolini), Capelli 1962; *Screenplays by Michelangelo Antonioni*, New York 1963; *Michelangelo Antonioni*, Rome 1964; *Blow-Up* with Tonino Guerra, Turin 1968; *L'Avventura*, with E. Bartolini, New York 1969; *Blow-Up* with Tonino Guerra, New York 1971; *Il Primo Antonioni* (screenplays or working scripts for early Antonioni documentaries and films) edited by Carlo di Carlo, Bologna 1973; *Il mistero di Oberwald*, Turin 1980/81; articles—"Marcel Carné parigino" in *Bianco e Nero* (Rome), December 1948; "Brevario del cinema" in *Cinema* (Rome), no.11, 16, 20, 37, 41, 1949; "Stanotte hanno sparato" in *Cinema nuovo* (Turin), 15 April 1953; "Le allegre ragazze del '24" in *Cinema nuovo* (Turin), 1956; "Fare un film è per me vivere" in *Cinema nuovo* (Turin), March-April 1959; "There Must Be a Reason for Every Film" in *Films and Filming* (London), April 1959; "Faire un film, c'est pour moi vivre" in *Premier Plan* (Paris), no.15, 1960; "La malattia dei sentimenti" in *Bianco e Nero* (Rome), February-March 1961; "Antonioni: Interview" by M. Manceaux and R. Roud in *Sight and Sound* (London), winter 1960-61; "Reflections on a Film Career" in *Film Culture* (New York), no. 22-23, 1961; "Eroticism—The Disease of Our Age" in *Films and Filming* (London), January 1961; "Interview with Antonioni" by André Labarthe in *New York Film Bulletin*, no. 8, 1961; "Making a Film is My Way of Life" in *Film Culture* (New York), spring 1962; "A Talk with Antonioni on His Work" in *Film Culture* (New York), spring 1962; "Talk with Antonioni" by H. Alpert in the *Saturday Review* (New York), 27 October 1962; "Makaroni" in *Cinema nuovo* (Turin), May/June 1963; "The Hollywood Myth Has Fallen" in *Popular Photography* (Boulder, Colorado), July 1963; "Prefizione" in *Sei Film*, Turin 1964; "The Event and the Image" in *Sight and Sound* (London), winter 1963-64; "Jean-Luc Godard Interviews Michelangelo Antonioni" in *Movie* (London), Spring 1965; "Antonioni Talks About His Work" in *Life* (New York), 27 January 1967; interview in *Playboy* (Chicago), November 1967; "Michelangelo Antonioni" in *Do You Sleep in the Nude* by Rex Reed, New York 1968; "What Directors are Saying" in *Action* (Los Angeles), September/October 1969; interview by C.T. Samuels in *Vogue* (New York), 15 March 1970; interview by C.T. Samuels in *Film Heritage* (Dayton, Ohio), Spring 1970; interview by L. Spagnoli in *Ecran* (Paris), December 1973; "Antonioni after China: Art versus Science", interview by G. Bachmann in *Film Quarterly* (Berkeley), summer 1975; "Conversazione con Michelangelo Antonioni" in *Filmcritica* (Rome), March 1975; interview by B.J. Demby and L. Sturhahn in *Fimmakers Newsletter* (Ward Hill, Mass.), July 1975; "Antonioni Speaks...and Listens", interview by R. Epstein in *Film Comment* (New York), July/August 1975; "Antonioni: nous en savons trop sur le soleil", interview by A. Ongaro in *Ecran* (Paris), May 1975; "Entretien avec Michelangelo Antonioni" by A. Tassone in *Image et son* (Paris), September 1975; "Quattro uomini in mare" in *Cinema nuovo* (Turin), November/December 1976; ; "'Quel bowling sul Tevere' e inoltre 'Il deserto dei soldi'" in *Cinema nuovo* (Turin), March/April 1976; "Antonioni and the 2-Headed Monster", interview by J.F. Lane, in *Sight and Sound* (London), winter 1979/80; interview by F. Cuel and B. Villien in *Cinematographe* (Paris), November 1981.

On ANTONIONI:

Books—*Michelangelo Antonioni* by Fabio Carpi, Parma 1958; *Michelangelo Antonioni*, Centro Universitario Cinematografico, Milan 1960; *Michelangelo Antonioni: An Introduction* by Pierre Leprohon, New York 1963; *Antonioni, Bergman, Resnais* by Peter Cowie, New York 1963; *Cinema Eye, Cinema Ear* by John Russell Taylor, New York 1964; *Antonioni* by Philip Strick, London 1965; *Interviews with Film Directors* by Andrew Sarris, New York 1967; *Man and the Movies* edited by W.R. Robinson, Baton Rouge, Louisiana 1967; *The Film* edited by Andrew Sarris, Indianapolis, Indiana 1968; *Antonioni* by Ian Cameron and Robin Wood, New York 1969; *Focus on 'Blow-Up'* edited by Roy Huss, Englewood Cliffs, New Jersey 1971; *Encountering Directors* by Charles Thomas Samuels, New York 1972; articles—"Il festival dell'Arlecchino" by Guido Aristarco in *Cinema* (Rome), 15 May 1949; "Il documentario: Michelangelo Antonioni" by Marcello Bollero and "Il cinema italiano del dopoguerra" by Guido Aristarco in *Sequenze* (Italy), December 1949; "Il documentario" in *Il neorealismo italiano* by Ermanno Contini, Venice 1951; "Antichi gesti: del documentario italiano" by Renzo Renzi in *Cinema* (Rome), 15 June 1952; "New Names" in *Sight and Sound* (London), winter 1955-56; "Michelangelo Antonioni, simbolo di una generazione" by Giambattista Cavallaro in *Bianco e nero* (Rome), September 1957; "Cronache dell'angoscia in Michelangeo Antonioni" by Renzo Renzi in *Cinema nuovo* (Turin), May/June 1959; "Antonioni" in *Positif* (Paris), July 1959; "Arrival of an Artist" by Stanley Kauffmann in the *New Republic* (New York), 10 April 1961; "Rebirth in Italy: 3 Great Movie Directors" by C.F. Pepper in *Newsweek* (New York), 10 July 1961; "Exploring the World Inside" by J.F. Lane in *Films and Filming* (London), January 1961; "Michelangelo Antonioni: 5 Films" by R. Roud in *Sight and Sound* (London), winter 1960-61; "Antonioni: Complete Filmography" by André Labarthe in *New York Film Bulletin*, no. 9, 1961; "A Diary" by J. F. Lane in *Films and Filming* (London), March 1962; "Letter" by R.W. Parkin in *Cinema Journal* (Australia), April 1962; special issue of *Film Quarterly* (Berkeley), fall 1962; "*La Dolce Vita* and *L'Avventura* as Controversy: *L'Avventura* and *Breathless* as Phenomenalist Film" by Marc Schleifer in *Film Culture* (New York), fall 1962; "Memento mori" in *Time*

(New York), 11 January 1963; "The Face of '63—Italy" by J.F. Lane in *Films and Filming* (London), April 1963; "Antonioni" by L. N. Gerard in *Films in Review* (New York), April 1963; "The Antonioni Trilogy" by Terence McNally, "The Music of Sound" by Gary Carey, and "To Be, Not to Understand" by Sibyl March in *7th Art* (New York), spring 1963; "L'lapse" by Donald Barthelme in the *New Yorker*, 2 March 1963; "2 On the Aisle" by P.V. Beckley in the *Saturday Review* (New York), 8 February 1964; "Most Controversial Director" by M.S. Davis in the *New York Times Magazine*, 15 November 1964; "Shape Around a Black Point: The Event and the Image" by Geoffrey Nowell-Smith in *Sight and Sound* (London), winter 1963-64; "Keeping up with the Antonionis" by Penelope Houston in *Sight and Sound* (London), autumn 1964; "Michelangelo Antonioni: l'homme et l'objet" in *Etudes cinématographiques* (Paris), no.36-37, 1964; "Watching Antonioni" by R. Garis in *Commentary* (New York), April 1967; "Antonioni in Transit" by M. Kinder in *Sight and Sound* (London), summer 1967; "Reply with Rejoinder to Garis" by P. Warshow in *Commentary* (New York), August 1967; "Antonioni Says New York is Too Vertical for Filmmaking" by E. Shaw in *Making Films* (New York), October 1967; "On the Scene: Michelangelo Antonioni" in *Playboy* (Chicago), June 1967; "Memories of Resnais" by Richard Roud in *Sight and Sound* (London), summer 1969; "Antonioni's America" by J. Hamilton in *Look* (New York), 18 November 1969; "Antonioni: What's the Point" by J. Simon, J. Gelmis, M. Last, H. Starr, and A. Lees in *Film Heritage* (Dayton, Ohio), spring 1970; "Antonioni Men" by Gordon Gow in *Films and Filming* (London), June 1970; "The Road to Death Valley" by A. Tudor in *Cinema* (London), August 1970; "Michelangelo Antonioni and the Imagery of Disintegration" by T. Hernacki in *Film Heritage* (Dayton, Ohio), autumn 1970; "Thalberg Didn't Look Happy" by B. Gindoff in *Film Quarterly* (Berkeley), Fall 1970; "Antonioni Report" by P. Strick in *Sight and Sound* (London), winter 1973/74; "Antonioni Discovers China" by J.F. Lane in *Sight and Sound* (London), spring 1973; "Un crollo di valori documentato dall'interno" by A. Frezzato in *Cineforum* (Rome), August/September 1974; "Altman: the Empty Staircase and the Chinese Princess" by M. Dempsey in *Film Comment* (New York), September/October 1974; "Antonioni nelle vesti del drago bianco" by R. Renzi in *Cinema nuovo* (Turin), May/June 1974; special issue on *Le Voyage des comédiens* with bio-filmography in *Avant-Scène du cinéma* (Paris), December 1975; "Antonioni Down Under" by G. Bachmann in *Sight and Sound* (London), no.4, 1976; "Antonioni: en souvenir de Conrad" by M. Martin in *Ecran* (Paris), October 1976; "The Natural Enmity of Words and Moving Images: Language, *La Notte*, and the Death of the Light" by F. Burke in *Literature/Film Quarterly* (Salisbury, Maryland), no.1, 1979; "Film Styles and Film Meanings" by T.A. Nelson in *Film Criticism* (Edinboro, Pa.), no.3, 1979; "Lettre à Antonioni" by Roland Barthes in *Cahiers du cinéma* (Paris), May 1980; "Antonioni: Moving On" by Clarke Taylor in the *Los Angeles Times Calender*, 17 October 1982; special issue of *Camera/Stylo* (Paris), November 1982.

*   *   *

Antonioni's cinema is one of non-identification and displacement. In almost all of his film shots can be found striking emphasis on visual structure works in opposition to the spectator's desire to identify, as in classical Hollywood cinema, with either a protagonist's existential situation or with anything like a seamless narrative continuity—the "impression of reality" so often evoked in conjunction with the effect of fiction films on the spectator.

Since his first feature, *Cronaca di un amore*, Antonioni's

introduction of utterly autonomous, graphically stunning shots into the film's narrative flow has gradually expanded to the point where, in his most recent films *Professione: Reporter*, but even more emphatically in *Il mistero di Oberwald* and *Identificazione di una donna*, the unsettling effect of these discrete moments in the narrative continuity of the earlier work has taken over entirely. If these graphically autonomous shots of Antonioni's films of the fifties and sixties functioned as striking "figures" which unsettled the "ground" of narrative continuity, his latest films undo altogether this opposition between form and content, technique and substance, in order to spread the strangeness of the previously isolated figure across the entirety of the film which will thus emphatically establish itself as a "text."

That which might at first seems to mark a simple inversion of this opposition—where narrative substance would take a back seat to formal technique—instead works to question, in a broad manner, the ways in which films establish themselves as fictions. Antonioni's cinema strains the traditional conventions defining fiction films to the breaking point where, beginning at least as early as *Professione: Reporter*, those aspects always presumed to define what is "given" or "specific" or "proper" to film (and which is commonly grouped together under the general heading of "technique") find themselves explicitly incorporated into the overall fabric of the film's narration; technique finds itself drawn into that which it supposedly presents neutrally, namely, the film's fictional universe. One might name this strategy the fictionalization of technique.

Such a strategy, however, is anything but self-reflexive, nor does it bear upon the thematics of Antonioni's films. In even those films where the protagonist has something to do with producing images, narratives, or other works of art (the filmmaker of *La signora senza camelie*, the architect of *L'avventura*, the novelist of *La notte*, the photographer of *Blow-up*, the television reporter of *Professione: Reporter*, the poet of *Il mistero di Oberwald*, and the film director of *Identificazione di una donna*), their professions remain important only on the level of the film's drama, never in terms of its technique. It is as though the image of the artist were trapped in a world where self-reflection is impossible. Indeed, one common strand linking the thematics of all of Antonioni's films—the impossibility for men to communicate with women—might be seen to illustrate, on the level of drama, the kind of communicational impasse to be found on the level of "technique" in his cinema. Though his films are far from "experimental" in the sense of the work of Hollis Frampton, Michael Snow or Andy Warhol, Antonioni's fictional narratives always feel flattened or, to borrow a term from Roland Barthes, they seem curiously *mat*, as if the spectator's ability to gain immediate access to the fiction were being impeded by something.

Antonioni's films, then, are not simply "about" the cinema, but rather, in attempting to make films which always side-step the commonplace or the conventional (modes responsible for spectatorial identification and the "impression of reality"), they call into question what is taken to be a "language" of cinema by constructing a kind of textual idiolect which defys comparison to any other film, even to Antonioni's other films. This may at least in part account for the formidable strangeness and difficulty of Antonioni's work, not just for general audiences but for mainstream critics as well. One constantly has the impression that the complexity of his films requires years in the cellar of critical speculation before they are ready to be understood; what was initially described as sour and flat ends up ten years later, as in the case of *L'avventura*, being proclaimed "one of the ten best films of all time" ("International Critics Poll," *Sight and Sound*). To judge from the reception in the United States of his most recent work, it appears that we are still at least ten years behind Antonioni.

As Antonioni has himself stressed repeatedly, the dramatic or the narrative aspect of his films—telling a story in the manner of literary narrative—comes to be of less and less importance; frequently, this is manifested by an absurd and complete absence of dramatic plausibility (*Zabriskie Point, Professione: Reporter, Il mistero di Oberwald*). The non-verbal logic of what remain narrative films depends, Antonioni says, upon neither a conceptual, nor emotional organization: "Some people believe I make films with my head; a few others think they come from the heart; for my part, I feel as though I make them with my stomach."

—Kimball Lockhart

ARZNER, DOROTHY. American. Born in San Francisco, 3 January 1900. Educated in medicine at the University of Southern California. Career: 1917—volunteers as ambulance driver in WWI; 1919-22—begins as typist at Famous Players-Lasky (Paramount) for William DeMille, becomes script supervisor then editor; 1922—becomes sole editor at "Realart", a subsidiary of Paramount; 1922-25—edits several major films, including *Blood and Sand* (Niblo) and *The Covered Wagon* (Cruze); 1925—serves as writer and editor for Cruze's *Old Ironsides*; 1929—directs Paramount's 1st sound film, *Wild Party*; 1943—retires from directing; 1943-45—produces WAC training films for Armed Services; after 1945—teaches film periodically at UCLA and makes commercials for Pepsi-Cola; 1972—is honored at 1st International Festival of Women's Films, New York; 1975—Director's Guild of America holds "A Tribute to Dorothy Arzner". Died 1 October 1979.

Films (as editor include): 1922—*Blood and Sand*; 1923—*The Covered Wagon*; 1924—*Inez from Hollywood* (+sc); *The Bread of the Border* (sc only); *The No-Gun Man* (sc only); 1925—*Red Kimono* (sc only); *When Husbands Flirt* (sc only); 1926—*Old Ironsides* (+sc); (as director) 1927—*Fashions for Women*; *Get Your Man*; *10 Modern Commandments*; 1928—*Manhattan Cocktail*; 1929—*The Wild Party*; 1930—*Sarah and Son*; "The Gallows Song—Nichavo" sequence in *Paramount on Parade*; *Anybody's Woman*; *Behind the Makeup* (co-d); *Charming Sinners* (co-d, uncredited); 1931—*Honor Among Lovers*; *Working Girls*; 1932—*Merrily We Go to Hell*; 1933—*Christopher Strong*; 1934—*Nana (Lady of the Boulevard)*; 1936—*Craig's Wife*; 1937—*The Bride Wore Red*; *The Last of Mrs. Cheyney* (co-d, uncredited); 1940—*Dance, Girl, Dance*; 1943—*First Comes Courage*.

Publications:

By ARZNER:

Interview by G. Peary in *Cinema* (Beverly Hills), no.34, 1974.

On ARZNER:

Books—*The Parade's Gone By* by Kevin Brownlow, New York 1968; *Notes on Women's Cinema* by Claire Johnston, London 1973; *Spellbound in Darkness: A History of Silent Film* by George Pratt, Greenwich, Connecticut 1973; *Popcorn Venus: Women, Movies, and the American Dream* by Marjorie Rosen, New York 1973; *From Reverence to Rape: The Treatment of*

Women in the Movies by Molly Haskell, New York 1974; *Women Who Make Movies* by Sharon Smith, New York 1975; *The Work of Dorothy Arzner: Towards a Feminist Cinema*, edited by Claire Johnston, London 1975; *Early Women Directors* by Anthony Slide, South Brunswick, New Jersy 1977; articles—"Sketch" by Adela Rogers St. John in *Photoplay* (New York), March 1927; "Hollywood Notes" in *Close-Up* (London), April 1928; "Sketch" by H. Cruikshank in *Motion Picture Classic* (Brooklyn), September 1929; "The Woman as Film Director" by H. A. Potamkin in *American Cinematographer* (Los Angeles), January 1932; "Get Me Dorothy Arzner" by Adela Rogers St. John in *Silver Screen* (New York), December 1933; "They Stand Out from the Crowd" in *Literary Digest* (New York), 3 November 1934; "Sketch" in *Movie Classic* (Brooklyn), December 1936; "Women Directors" by J. and H. Feldman in *Films in Review* (New York), November 1950; "Notes on Women Directors" by J. Pyros in *Take One* (Montreal, Canada), November/December 1970; "Women Directors" by Richard Henshaw in *Film Comment* (New York), November 1972; "Approaching the Art of Arzner" by F. Parker in *Action* (Los Angeles), July/August 1973; "Forgotten Early Woman Directors" by Anthony Slide in *Films in Review*, March 1974; "Dorothy Arzner" by G. Peary in *Cinema* (Beverly Hills), no.34, 1974; "Tribute to Dorothy Arzner" by W. Castle in *Action* (Los Angeles), March/-April 1975; "Aspects of British Feminist Film Theory" by E. Ann Kaplan in *Jump Cut* (Berkeley), no.12-13, 1976; article by Claire Johnston in *Jump Cut* (Berkeley), 30 December 1976; obituary in the *New York Times*, 12 October 1979; "Rereading the work of Claire Johnston" by J. Bergstrom in *Camera Obscura* (Berkeley), summer 1979.

*   *   *

Dorothy Arzner is an outstanding exception to the unwritten rule that has virtually excluded women from major directing careers in American commercial movies. Starting at Famous Players-Lasky (Later Paramount) as a script typist, Arzner soon realized that the director was "the whole works," and decided to become one. It took eight years before she achieved that goal, during which time she prepared herself by working as a script-girl, then a cutter and editor at Realart, a subsidiary of Paramount where she cut an estimated 52 pictures on a one-a-week treadmill schedule.

Recalled to Paramount, Arzner edited Fred Niblo's *Blood and Sand*, her first "big picture," starring movie idol Rudolph Valentino; later she said she had directed "some shots for the bull-fights." After editing James Cruze's *Covered Wagon* and several other films, she wrote scripts for other companies, then returned to Paramount to write Cruze's *Old Ironsides*, keep script for the production and edit the finished film.

After *Old Ironsides* (Cruze had told people she was his "right arm"), Arzner felt she was ready to direct. She was about to accept a low-budget offer from Columbia Pictures when Paramount's Benjamin Schulberg agreed to let her direct *Fashions for Women*, starring Esther Ralston. She directed two other films that same year (1927), gaining a reputation for finishing her films on time, at budget or under, and without displays of temperament. Recognition came in the late 1920s when the London International Festival of Women's Films awarded her first prize for directing *Fashions for Women*, and *Close-Up* magazine wrote that "in her so far brief career as a director, she has already won an established reputation and a following of discriminating admirers." Later she was named one of Hollywood's Top Ten directors.

Arzner's films were generally "women's pictures"—not the sob story variety, but films about strong women in unstereotyped oles. They starred or featured actresses of wide-ranging styles and personalities including Clara Bow, Katharine Hepburn, Rosalind Russell, Joan Crawford, Sylvia Sidney and Lucille Ball. She launched the screen careers of Ruth Chatterton, Anna Sten and Fredric March (the latter starred in four of her films).

"Men actors never showed any prejudice against working with me," Arzner told Adela Rogers St. John in a 1933 interview. Arzner also praised the technicians she worked with—cameramen, assistants, property men. "Everybody helped me," she said. She had also been helped by women like Nan Hernon, who started her in film editing, and writers like Zoe Akins and Tess Slesinger who wrote a number of the scripts she directed.

Arzner retired from filmmaking after a serious bout of pneumonia when she was in her mid-forties, at an age when many comparable male directors were just getting a second wind. She made a series of shorts for the WACs early in World War II, and later inagurated a filmmaking course at the Pasadena Playhouse. In the 1960s Arzner taught for four years at U.C.L.A. and directed a series of Pepsi-Cola commercials, thanks to her friend Joan Crawford.

Neither great art nor high camp, Arzner's films have been virtually ignored by male film critics and historians over the years. Lewis Jacobs in *The Rise of the American Film* (1939) mentioned her only among "the better cutters"; Arthur Knight in *The Liveliest Art* (1957) didn't mention her at all; Basil Wright, a good friend of Arzner, added a footnote to *The Long View* (1974), calling her "a top director". Andrew Sarris in an article entitled "The Ladies Auxiliary, 1976," credited Arzner for "the spectacular spinelessness of her male characters," and concluded that she had risen "from a mere footnote" to "a chapter heading all her own."

While every other run-of-the-mill film genre has several generations of devoted fans, "women's pictures" have generally been scorned and mocked. Feminist film critics have recently praised the way heroines in "the Arzner oeuvre" interrupt and reverse female stereotypes within the "dominant patriarchal ideology," but they assess work that is four decades old in terms of feminist ideals for the 1970s and '80s. Until "women's pictures" are recognized as a legitimate part of film history-along with horror films, westerns, cartoons and the like—the few women who pioneered in American film directing are not likely to be properly represented or fairly evaluated.

—Cecile Starr

ASHBY, HAL. American. Born in Ogden, Utah, 1932. Attended Utah State University. Career: 1950-51—hitchhikes to Los Angeles and eventually obtains job mimeographing screenplays in script department at Universal; early 1950s—a job at Republic Studios running multilith press indirectly leads to becoming apprentice to editor Robert Swink; thru 1963—works as assistant editor; 1963—becomes full editor, eventually for director Norman Jewison; 1970—directs 1st film *The Landlord*; 1978-82— directs 3 productions for Lorimar Films. Recipient: Best Film Editing Academy Award for *In the Heat of the Night*, 1967. Address: c/o Director's Guild of America, 7950 Sunset Blvd., Hollywood, California 90046.

Films (as assistant editor): 1958—*The Big Country* (Wyler); *The Diary of Anne Frank* (Stevens); 1961—*The Young Doctors* (Karlson); 1962—*The Children's Hour (The Loudest Whisper)* (Wyler); 1964—*The Best Man* (Schaffner); 1965—*The Greatest Story Ever Told* (Stevens); (as editor): 1965—*The Loved One*

(co-ed); *The Cincinnati Kid* (Jewison); *The Russians Are Coming, the Russians Are Coming* (Jewison); 1967—*In the Heat of the Night* (Jewison); (as associate producer): 1968—*The Thomas Crown Affair* (Jewison) (+supervising ed); 1969—*Gaily, Gaily* (Jewison); (as director) 1970—*The Landlord*; 1971—*Harold and Maude*; 1973—*The Last Detail*; 1975—*Shampoo*; 1976—*Bound for Glory*; 1978—*Coming Home*; 1979—*Being There* (+ed); 1980-81—*Second Hand Hearts* (+ed); 1982—*Lookin' to Get Out* (+ co-ed); 1983—*Time is On Our Side* (+ed).

Publications:

By ASHBY:

Articles—"Breaking Out of the Cutting Room" in *Action* (Los Angeles), September/October 1970; interview by L. Salvato and D. Schaefer in *Millimeter* (New York), October 1976; "Positive Thinking: Hal Ashby", interview by R. Appelbaum in *Films and Filming* (London), July 1978; "Dialogue on Film: Hal Ashby" in *American Film* (Washington, D.C.), May 1980.

On ASHBY:

Articles—"Hal Ashby—en auteur?" by U. Jørgensen in *Kosmorama* (Copenhagen), September 1974; "Gambling on a Film About the Great Depression" by A. Harmetz in *The New York Times*, 5 December 1976; "Hal Ashby" in *Hollywood Renaissance* by Diane Jacobs, New York 1977; "David Carradine and Hal Ashby on Bound for Glory", interview by C. Amata, in *Focus on Film* (London), no.27, 1977; "Neurotische zonen, kapotte huwelijken en oorlogsinvaliden" by H. Hosman in *Skoop* (Amsterdam), October 1978; "El cine norteamericano al día" by L. García Tsao in *Imagenes* (Mexico), April 1980; "Whatever Happened to Hal Ashby?" by Dale Pollock in the *Los Angeles Times Calendar*, 17 October 1982.

*   *   *

Hal Ashby has a reputation for showing a light touch as a director, stating that he prefers to let the actors develop their characters. During the filming of *Coming Home*, for example, he threw out a script when Jon Voight saw one of the major characters differently than the screenwriter. The people in his films generally face choices in situations that reflect major social concerns. In *The Landlord* characters have to make decisions involving the issue of race; in *Shampoo* they must decide which side they are on in a complex political and sexual skirmish set in the turbulent summer of 1968; and in *Coming Home*, the effects of the Viet Nam War force both characters involved directly with the war as well as those at home to deal with unexpected changes in their lives. The solutions to these decisions when faced by the characters are never facile. In *Harold and Maude*, Harold gains some degree of maturity but loses the love of his life, Maude; the military police of *The Last Detail* have given the prisoner a way to face life, but have also delivered him to prison; while George, in *Shampoo*, realizes how empty his life is and appears to want to change it, but at the same time has lost what chances he had for happiness.

Ashby's experience as an editor is evident as he will employ a wide variety of editing effects in his films. His use of both dissolves and rapid cutting to show the passage of time in *The Last Detail* serves as an example. His predilection for varying editing techniques could explain in part, what Ashby himself has admitted, that he has not shown a distinctive style as yet, but rather attempts to adapt his style to the type and subject of each film.

Though he has been called a "maverick director," Ashby's career has garnered him a good deal of respect from the critics, and his films have done well at the box office. *Shampoo, Coming Home,* and *Being There* represent his major financial successes, while the reputation of *Harold and Maude* was made in a slightly different manner. After an initial panning and a short general release, the film caught on in the Midwest, running in several theaters for over a year. The film has since become a cult favorite and has received positive critical response.

—Ray Narducy

ASQUITH, ANTHONY. British. Born in London, 9 November 1902; commonly known by childhood name 'Puffin'. Educated at Summer Fields, Oxford, Winchester, and Balliol College, Oxford, until 1925. Career: 1925—as founder-member of Film Society in London, invited to study American filmmaking as guest of Mary Pickford and Douglas Fairbanks; 1926—visits Hollywood,; 1928—returns to London and joins British Instructional Film Co. works in various capacities on *Boadicea* (Hill); 1937—invited to become 1st president of Association of Cinematographic Technicians; 1939—association with writer Terence Rattigan begins; 1953—produces *Carmen* for Covent Garden; mid-1950s—directs several ballets for television with Margot Fonteyn and Rudolf Nureyev. Died in London, 21 February 1968. Recipient: Fellow, British Film Academy; Commander of the Order of Al Merito della Repubblica, Italy.

Films (as assistant director and scriptwriter): 1927—*Shooting Stars* (Bramble) (d uncred, co-sc); 1928—*Boadicea* (Hill); (as director and scriptwriter): 1928—*Underground*; *The Runaway Princess*; 1929—*A Cottage on Dartmoor (Escape From Dartmoor)*; 1931—*Tell England (Battle of Gallipoli)* (co-d, co-sc); *Dance Pretty Lady* (+adapt); 1932—*Marry Me* (Thiele) (sc only); (as director): 1933—*The Lucky Number*; *Letting in the Sunshine* (Lane) (sc only); 1934—*Unfinished Symphony* (co-d for English version only); 1935—*Moscow Nights (I Stand Condemned)* (+co-sc); 1938—*Pygmalion* (co-d, +co-sc); 1939—*French Without Tears*; 1940—*Freedom Radio (The Voice in the Night)*; *Quiet Wedding*; *Channel Incident* (+pr); 1941—*Rush Hour*; *Cottage to Let (Bombsight Stolen)*; 1942—*Uncensored*; 1943—*We Dive at Dawn*; *The Demi-Paradise (Adventure for Two)*; *Welcome to Britain* (co-d); 1944—*Fanny by Gaslight (Man of Evil)*; *2 Fathers* (+sc); 1945—*The Way to the Stars (Johnny in the Clouds)*; 1947—*While the Sun Shines*; 1948—*The Winslow Boy*; 1950—*The Woman in Question (5 Angles on Murder)*; *The Browning Version*; 1951—*The Importance of Being Earnest* (+sc); 1952—*The Net (Project M7)*; *The Final Test*; 1954—*The Young Lovers (Chance Meeting)*; 1955—*On Such a Night*; 1956—*Carrington VC (Court Martial)*; 1958—*Orders to Kill*; *The Doctor's Dilemma*; 1959—*Libel!*; 1960—*The Millionairess*; *Zero*; 1961—*Two Living, One Dead*; 1962—*Guns of Darkness*; 1963—*The VIPs*; *An Evening with the Royal Ballet* (co-d); 1964—*The Yellow Rolls-Royce*.

Publications:

By ASQUITH:

articles—"Wanted—a Genius" in *Sight and Sound* (London), spring 1938; "Note on Americanization" in *Film* (London), September/October 1955; "The Play's the Thing" in *Films and Filming* (London), February 1959.

On ASQUITH:

books—*Anthony Asquith* by Peter Noble, London 1951; '*Puffin' Asquith* by R.J. Minney, London 1973; articles—"What Asquith Did for Me" by Paul Massie in *Films and Filming* (London), February 1958; "This England" by Peter Cowie in *Films and Filming* (London), October 1963; "The Champagne Set" by Anatole de Grunwald in *Films and Filming* (London), February 1965; "Anthony Asquith" by Michael Balcon in *Sight and Sound* (London), spring 1968.

*   *   *

"Tasteful" and "restrained" are the two adjectives critics use most when describing Anthony Asquith, the British director second only to Alfred Hitchcock as the most important British filmmaker of the 1930s and forties. Known as "Puffin" since childhood, young Anthony went to Hollywood in 1926 to study American filmmaking methods; in 1928, he returned to England to assist Sinclair Hall on the film *Boadicea*. Asquith also made his first feature in 1928, *Shooting Stars*, known for its experimental visual techniques and use of sound.

In 1930 he began to develop the first of his two favorite types of film, the near-documentary portrayal of English life and manners, with *A Cottage on Dartmoor*. In 1938, Asquith became internationally known for his direction of Shaw's *Pygmalion*, with Leslie Howard and Wendy Hiller, a good example of the second type of Asquith film, the theatrical adaptation. Other films of note in these categories include *The Browning Version*, with Michael Redgrave, and *The Importance of Being Earnest*.

Critics generally recognize Asquith's *The Way to the Stars* as his masterpiece. Seen as a "gentle, satisfying film," it focused on the RAF during World War II and featured a decidedly distinguished cast: Michael Redgrave, John Mills, Rosamund John, Stanley Holloway, and Douglass Montgomery. The action centers around the characters' existence in a small hotel near the airfield, with hardly any planes at all in view. The young man in the story must choose between love and his devotion to the military service. Critics noted the fine script (by Terence Rattigan) and meticulous production values.

After World War II, developments in film production and audience taste stranded Asquith in the two genres that had appealed to him. He had worked to present a quintessentially English type of theater on film, and assiduously avoided what he termed the "International style" of such directors as Alexander Korda. But in spite of his attempt to move beyond the two genres in which he had specialized, Asquith succeeded only in creating more tasteful, civilized, and "entertaining" films.

—Deborah H. Holdstein

ASTRUC, ALEXANDRE. French. Born in Paris, 13 July 1923. Educated at collège de Saint-Germain-en-Laye; Polytechnique, degrees in letters and law. Career: mid-1940s—literary and film critic (continues to write on film throughout career); 1945—publishes novel *Les Vacances*; 1946-47—assistant to Marcel Achard and Marc Allégret (on *Blanche Fury*); 1948-49—makes two short films; 1955—series of 6 feature length films begins with *Mauvaises rencontres*; 1960s—collaborates on several television productions, in particular on program of series "Cinéastes de notre temps" on Murnau.

Films (as director and scriptwriter): 1948—*Aller et retour (Aller-retour)*; *Jean de la Lune* (Achard) (co-sc only); 1949—*Ulysse ou Les Mauvaises rencontres*; *La P...respecteuse* (Pagliero) (co-sc only); 1950—*L'Affaire Manet* (Aurel) (commentary only); 1953—*Le Rideau cramoisi (The Crimson Curtain)*; 1954—*Le Vicomte de Bragelonne* (Cerchio) (co-sc only); 1955—*Les Mauvaises rencontres* (co-sc); 1958—*Une Vie (End of Desire)* (co-sc); 1960—*La Proie pour l'ombre* (co-sc); 1962—*L'Education sentimentale*; 1963—*Le Puits et le pendule (The Pit and the Pendulum)* (for TV); 1964—*Bassae* (Pollet) (sc only); 1965—*Evariste Galois*; 1966—*La Longue Marche* (co-sc); 1968—*Flammes sur l'Adriatique* (co-sc); 1976—*Sartre par lui-même* (co-d). Role: 1949—*La Valse de Paris* (Achard).

Publications:

On ASTRUC:

Articles—"Venice Film Festival" by Lotte Eisner in *Film Culture* (New York), v.2, no.1, 1956; "An Escapist Realism" by Eugene Weber in *Film Quarterly* (Berkeley), winter 1959; "Sur une émission de télévision" in *Cahiers du cinéma* (Paris), February/-March 1974; "4 de la forfanterie" by Claude Beylie in *Ecran* (Paris), October 1975.

* * *

Alexandre Astruc was the embodiment of the revolutionary hopes of a renewed cinema after the war. True, Clément, Bresson, and Melville were already making films in a new way, but making them in the age old industry. Astruc represented a new, arrogant sensibility. He had grown up on the ideas of Sartre and was one of the youthful literati surrounding the philosopher in the St. Germain-des-Prés cafes. There he talked of a new French culture being born, one that demanded new representations in fiction and film.

His personal aspirations were great and grew even greater when his novel *Les Vacances* was published by the prestigious N.R.F., almost winning an important prize. While writing essays on art and culture for *Combat* and *L'Ecran français* he became convinced that the cinema must replace the novel.

But first the cinema must become more like the novel. In his crucial essay "Le Caméra stylo," written the same year as Sartre's "Situation of the Writer in 1948," he called for an end to institutional cinema and for a new style that would be both personal and malleable. He wanted cinema to be able to treat diverse ideas and a range of expressions. He, like Sartre, wanted to become ethical.

This was the first loud clarion cry of the New Wave and it provoked attention in its own day. Astruc found himself linked with Bazin, Cocteau, Marker, and Tacchella against the Stalinists at *L'Ecran français* led by Louis Daquin. Banding together to form "Objectif 48," these men created a new atmosphere for cinema, attracting the young Truffaut and Godard to their screenings.

Everyone looked to Astruc to begin turning out short films, but his 16mm efforts ran aground. Soon he began writing scripts for acceptable standard directors like Marc Allégret. Finally in 1952 he was able to make *Le Rideau cramoisi* in his own way. It was a remarkable way: this 19th century mystery tale was reduced to a set of unforgettable images and a soundtrack that contained no dialogue whatsoever. Pushing the voice-over discoveries of Bresson and Melville to the limit, Astruc's narrational device places the film somewhere between dream and memory. This coincides perfectly with the haunting night photography and Anouk Aimée's inscrutably romantic performance.

There followed more adaptations, not because Astruc had joined the industry's penchant for such quality material, but because he always believed in the overriding import of style, seeing plots as pretexts only. The color photography in *Une Vie*, for example, explores the painterly concerns of the impressionists. But since the plot comes from a Maupassant tale written in the same era, the result is unpretentious.

In his older age Astruc has renounced this obsession with style. The themes that possess him now, crises in marriage and love, can actually be seen in all his earlier work as well. Now he can explore these issues in television, the medium that seems perfectly suited to his early ideas. Only now his ideas have changed and so has his following. Alexandre Astruc must always be mentioned in any chronicle of modern French cinema, but his career can only be thought of as disappointing.

—Dudley Andrew

AUTANT-LARA, CLAUDE. French. Born in Luzarches (Seine-et-Oise), 5 August 1903. Educated at Lycée Janson-de-Sailly, Paris; Ecole nationale supérieure des arts décoratifs; Ecole des Beaux Arts; Mill Hill School, London. Married Ghislaine Auboin. Career: 1919—begins film career as art director on L'Herbier's *Le Carnaval de verité*; 1923-25—makes several avant-garde films; assistant to René Clair on *Paris qui dort* and *Le Voyage imaginaire*; 1926—designs costumes for Renoir's *Nana*; uses early wide-screen process called "l'hypergonar" in *Construire un feu*; briefly visits U.S. because of some interest in process but fails to sell it; 1930-32—works in Hollywood making French versions of American films; 1933—returns to France; directs first feature film; 1937-39—co-directs 3 films with Maurice Lehmann; 1946—*Le Diable au corps* establishes international reputation; 1948-55—President of Syndicat des techniciens du cinéma; 1957-63—President of Fédération nationale du spectacle. Recipient: Grand prix de la critique internationale, 1947; Grand prix du Cinéma français, 1954; Prix Femina Belge du cinéma, 1965; Prix Europa for entire body of work, Rome 1974; Chevalier de la Légion d'honneur; Commandeur des Arts et des Lettres. Address: 66 rue Lepic, 75018 Paris, France.

Films (as art director and costume designer): 1919—*Le Carnaval des vérités* (L'Herbier); *L'Ex-voto* (L'Herbier); 1920—*L'Homme du large* (L'Herbier); 1921—*Villa Destin* (L'Herbier); *Eldorado* (L'Herbier) (co-); 1922—*Don Juan et Faust* (L'Herbier); 1923—*L'Inhumaine* (L'Herbier) (co-); *Le Marchand de plaisir* (Catelain) (co-); (as director): 1923—*Faits divers*; 1926—*Construire un feu*; *Vittel*; *Nana* (Renoir) (co-art d, co-costume des only); 1927—*Le Diable au coeur* (L'Herbier) (art d, cost des only); (as director of French versions of American films): 1930—*Buster se* marie (Sedgwick: *Parlor, Bedroom and Bath*); 1931—*Le Plomb-ier amoureux* (Sedgwick: *The Passionate Plumber*); *Le Fils du Rajah* (Feyder: *Son of India*); *La Pente*; *Pur Sang*; 1932—*L'Athlète incomplet*; (as director after return to France): 1932—*Le Gendarme est sans pitié*; *Un Client sérieux*; *Monsieur le Duc*; *La Peur des coups*; *Invite Monsieur à dîner*; 1933—*Ciboulette* (+co-sc, co-costume des); 1936—*My Partner Mr. Davis (The Mysterious Mr. Davis)* (+co-sc); 1937—*L'Affaire du courrier de Lyon (The Courier of Lyon)* (co-d); 1938—*Le Ruisseau* (co-d); 1939—*Fric-Frac* (co-d); 1942—*Le Mariage de Chiffon*; *Lettres d'amour*; 1943—*Douce (Love Story)*; 1944—*Sylvie et le fantôme (Sylvie and the Phantom)*; 1947—*Le Diable au corps (Devil in the Flesh)*; 1949—*Occupe-toi d'Amélie (Oh Amelia!)*; 1951—*L'Auberge rouge (The Red Inn)* (+co-sc); 1952—"*L'Orgueil*" [Pride] episode of *Les 7 Péchés capitaux (The 7 Deadly Sins)* (+co-sc); 1953—*Le Bon Dieu sans confession* (+co-sc); *Le Blé en herbe (The Game of Love)* (+co-sc); 1954—*Le Rouge et le noir*; 1956—*Marguerite de la nuit*; *La Traversée de Paris (4 Bags Full)*; 1958—*En Cas de malheur (Love Is My Profession)*; *Le Joueur*; 1959—*La Jument verte (The Green Mare)* (+pr); 1960—*Les Régates de San Francisco*; *Le Bois des amants*; 1961—*Tu ne tueras point (Non uccidere, Thou Shalt Not Kill)* (+co-pr); *Le Comte de Monte Cristo (The Story of the Count of Monte Cristo)*; 1962—*Vive Henri IV... Vive l'amour!*; 1963—*Le Meurtrier (Enough Rope)*; 1964—*Le Magot de Joséfa* (+co-sc); "La Fourmi" episode of *Humour noir*; 1965—*Le Journal d'une femme en blanc (A Woman in White)*; 1966—*Le Nouveau Journal d'une femme en blanc (Une Femme en blanc se révolte)*; 1967—"Aujourd' hui" [Paris Today] episode of *Le Plus Vieux Métier du monde (The Oldest Profession)*; *Le Franciscain de Bourges*; 1969—*Les Patates* (+co-sc); 1971—*Le Rouge et le blanc*; 1973—*Lucien Leuwen* (for TV); 1977—*Gloria* (+co-sc).

Publications:

By AUTANT-LARA:

Articles—"Styles du cinéma français" in *La Livre d'or du cinéma français 1947-48* edited by René Jeanne and Charles Ford, Paris 1948; numerous polemical articles on state of French cinema, studios, and attacking government policies appeared during early to mid-1950s in *La Technicien du film* (Paris), *Les Lettres françaises* (Paris), and other French periodicals; "La Traversée de Paris est un film insolite", interview by Martine Monod in *Les Lettres françaises* (Paris), 4 October 1956; "La Comédie du milliard" in *Les Lettres françaises* (Paris), 19 January 1956; "Les Etrennes du cinéma françaises" in *Les Lettres françaises* (Paris), 3 January 1957; "Attention, notre métier n'est pas un métier d'hurluberlus" in *La Technicien du film* (Paris), May 1958; "Comment j'ai pu réaliser *Le Diable au corps*" in *Ikon* (Milan), January/March 1972; "La Parole est à Claude Autant-Lara", interview by M. Oms, in *Cahiers de la Cinémathèque* (Paris), summer 1973; interview by J.-C. Bonnet and others in *Cinématographe* (Paris), April 1978; "Lausanne (Autant-Lara)" in *Positif* (Paris), December 1981.

On AUTANT-LARA:

Articles—"The Fighter" by Catherine de la Roche in *Films and Filming* (London), January 1955; "The Rebel with Kid Gloves" in 2 parts by Raymond Durgnat in *Films and Filming* (London), October and November 1960; special issue of *Cahiers de la Cinémathèque* (Paris), spring 1973; biofilmography in *Film Dope* (London), no.2, 1973.

*   *   *

Claude Autant-Lara is best known for his post-World War II films in the French "tradition of quality." His earliest work in the industry was more closely related to the avant-garde movements of the 1920s than to the mainstream commercial cinema with which he was later identified. He began as a set designer in the 1920s, serving as art director for several of Marcel L'Herbier's films, including *L'Inhumaine* and for Jean Renoir's *Nana*; and assisted René Clair on a number of his early shorts. After directing several films, he worked on an early wide-screen experiment, *Construire un feu* using the Hypergonar system designed by Henri Chretien. On the basis of his work in this format, he was brought to Hollywod and ended up directing French language versions of American films for several years. He returned to France, and directed his first feature of note, *Ciboulette*, in 1933.

During the war Autant-Lara exercised greater control in his choice of projects, and started working with scenarists Jean Aurenche and Pierre Bost who would continue to be among his most consistent collaborators. He also started assembling a basic crew that worked with him through the 1960s: composer René Cloerec, designer Max Douy, editor Madeleine Gug, and cameraman Jacques Natteau. Autant-Lara rapidly established his reputation as a studio director in the tradition of quality. For many, the names Aurenche, Bost, and Autant-Lara are synonymous with this movement. Their films are characterized by an emphasis on scripting and dialogue, a high proportion of literary adaptations, a solemn "academic" visual style, and general theatricality (due largely to the emphasis on dialogue and its careful delivery to create cinematic world determined by psychological realism. They frequently attack or ridicule social groups and institutions.

Autant-Lara's first major post-war film, *Le Diable au corps*, was adapted from a novel by Raymond Radiguet. Set during World War I, it tells the story of an adolescent's affair with a young married woman whose husband is away at war. While the film was considered scandalous by many for its valorization of adultery and tacit condemnation of war, it was also seen to express the cynical mood of post-war youth. Autant-Lara's films seem to revel in irreverent depictions of established authority and institutions. *L'Auberge rouge* is a black comedy involving murderous innkeepers, a group of insipid travellers (representing a cross-section of classes), and a monk trapped by the vows of confession.

Throughout the 1950s Autant-Lara was extremely active. His successes of the period include *Le Rouge et le noir*, adapted from Stendhal; *La Traversée de Paris*, a comedy about black market trading in occupied France; and *En cas de malheur*, a melodrama involving a middle-aged lawyer, his young client, and her student lover. At the same time Autant-Lara was an active spokesman for the French film industry. As head of several film trade unions and other groups promoting French film, he criticized (often harshly) the CNC (Centre National du cinéma française) for its inadequate support of the industry; the American film industry for its stultifying presence in the French market; and government censorship policies for limiting freedom of expression.

Autant-Lara's prominence was effectively eclipsed with the emergence of the French New Wave, although he continued directing films. In the 1950s he, along with Aurenche and Bost, had been subject to frequent critical attacks, most notably by François Truffaut. In the wake of the success of the new generation of directors, Autant-Lara's work is often seen as no more than the "stale" French cinema of the 1950s which was successfully displaced by the more vital films of the New Wave. Yet in spite of, indeed owing to, their "armchair" criticism of authority, bleak representation of human nature, and slow-paced academic style, they possess a peculiarly appealing, insolent sensibility.

—M.B. White

AVERY, TEX. American. Born Frederick Bean Avery in Taylor, Texas, 26 February 1907. Educated at North Dallas High School, graduated 1927. Career: 1930-35—animator with Universal-Walter Lantz Cartoons; 1936-41—works at Warners (4 films in Bugs Bunny series: *A Wild Hare, Tortoise Beats Hare, The Heckling Hare* and *All This and Rabbit Stew*); before 1941 credited as Fred Avery; 1942—brief period at Paramount, does 3 films in *Speaking of Animals* series then moves to MGM beginning with *The Blitz Wolf*; 1954-55—directs for Walter Lantz; 1955—quits MGM; 1956-78—makes commercials for Cascade Productions; 1979-80—with Hanna-Barbera Cartoons. Died 26 August 1980. Recipient: First Prize, Venice Publicity Festival, for *Calo-Tiger*, 1958; Television Commercials Council Award, 1960; Annie Award, ASIFA, 1974.

Films (as co-animator with Walter Lantz): *Elmer, the Great Dane; Town Hall Follies;* (as director, often credited as supervisor): 1936—*Golddiggers of '49; The Blow-Out; Plane Dippy; I'd Love to Take Orders from You; Miss Glory; I Love to Singa; Porky the Rain Maker; The Village Smithy; Milk and Money; Don't Look Now; Porky the Wrestler;* 1937—*Picador Porky; I Only Have Eyes for You; Porky's Duck Hunt; Uncle Tom's Bungalow; Ain't We Got Fun; Daffy Duck and Egghead; Egghead Rides Again; A Sunbonnet Blue; Porky's Garden; I Wanna Be a Sailor; The Sneezing Weasel; Little Red Walking Hood;* 1938—*The Penguin Parade; The Isle of Pingo Pongo; A Feud There Was; Johnny Smith and Poker-Huntas; Daffy Duck in Hollywood; Cinderella Meets Fella; Hamateur Night; The Mice Will Play; Daffy's Romance;* 1939—*A Day at the Zoo; Thugs with Dirty Mugs; Believe It or Else; Dangerous Dan McFoo; Detouring America; Land of the Midnight Fun; Fresh Fish; Screwball Football; The Early Worm Gets the Bird;* 1940—*Cross Country Detours; The Bear's Tale; A Gander at Mother Goose; Circus Today; A Wild Hare; Ceiling Hero; Wacky Wild Life; Of Fox and Hounds* (+voice of Willoughby the dog); *Holiday Highlights;* 1941—*The Crackpot Quail; Haunted Mouse; Tortoise Beats Hare; Hollywood Steps Out; Porky's Preview; The Heckling Hare* (+voice of Willoughby the dog); *Aviation Vacation; All This and Rabbit Stew; The Bug Parade; Aloha Hooey; The Cagey Canary* (completed by Bob Clampett); *Crazy Cruise;* 1942—*Speaking of Animals Down on the Farm; Speaking of Animals in a Pet Shop; Speaking of Animals in the Zoo; The Blitz Wolf; The Early Bird Dood It; Dumb-Hounded;* 1943—*Red Hot Riding Hood; Who Killed Who?; One Ham's Family; What's Buzzin', Buzzard?;* 1944—*Screwy Squirrel; Baty Baseball; Happy-Go-Nutty; Big Heel-watha;* 1945—*The Screwy Truant; The Shooting of Dan McGoo; Jerky Turkey; Swing Shift Cinderella; Wild and Woolfy;* 1946—*Lonesome Lenny; The Hick Chick; Northwest Hounded Police; Henpecked Hoboes* (+voice of Junior); 1947—*Hound Hunters* (+voice of Junior); *Red Hot Rangers* (+voice of Junior); *Uncle Tom's Cabana; Slap Happy Lion; King-Size Canary; Little Tinker;* 1948—*What Price Fleadom; Half-Pint Pygmy* (+voice of Junior); *Lucky Ducky; The Cat That Hated People;* 1949—*Bad Luck Blackie; Senor Droopy; The House of Tomorrow; Doggone Tired; Wags to Riches; Little Rural Riding Hood; Outfoxed; Counterfeit Cat;*

1950—*Ventriloquist Cat; The Cuckoo Clock; Garden Gopher; The Chump Champ; The Peachy Cobbler;* 1951—*Cock-a-Doodle Dog; Dare-Devil Droopy; Droopy's Good Deed; Symphony in Slang; The Car of Tomorrow; Droopy's Double Trouble; The Magical Maestro;* 1952—*One Cab's Family; Rock-a-Bye Bear;* 1953—*Little Johnny Jet; TV of Tomorrow; The 3 Little Pups; Drag-a-long Droopy;* 1954—*Billy Boy; Homesteader Droopy; Farm of Tomorrow; The Flea Circus; Dixieland Droopy; Crazy Mixed-Up Pup;* 1955—*Field and Scream; The 1st Bad Man; Deputy Droopy* (co-d); *Cellbound* (co-d); *I'm cold (Some Like It Not); Chilly Willy in the Legend of Rockabye Point (The Rockabye Legend); SH-H-H-H-H;* (remakes, respectively, of *Wags to Riches* and *Ventriloquist Cat*): 1956—*Millionaire Droopy; Cat's Meow;* 1958—*Polar Pests.*

Publications:

By AVERY:

Interview by Joseph Adamson in *Take One* (Montreal), January/February 1970.

On AVERY:

Books—*Le Surréalisme au cinéma* by Ado Kyrou, Paris 1952; *Le Dessin animé après Walt Disney* by Robert Benayoun, Paris 1961; *Tex Avery, King of Cartoons* by Joseph Adamson, New York 1975; articles—"Un Savoureaux Western animé" by Jacques Doniol-Valcroze in *Revue du cinéma* (Paris), February 1947; "Le Dossier Tex Avery" in *Positif* (Paris), July/August 1963; "The Hollywood Cartoon" by J. Canemakers in *Filmmakers Newsletter* (Ward Hill, Mass.), April 1974; "Tex Avery ou le délire lucide" by P. Kral in *Positif* (Paris), June 1974; "Cartoonographies" by J. Adamson in *Film Comment* (New York), January/February 1975; "Looney Tunes and Merrie Melodies" by M.S. Cohen in *Velvet Light Trap* (Madison), autumn 1975; "Dream Masters II: Tex Avery" by J. Rosenbaum in *Film Comment* (New York), January/February 1975; "Le Festival d'Annecy..." by A. Cornand in *Image et son* (Paris), January 1977; "Confessions of a Cell Washer" by Chuck Jones in *Take One* (Montreal), September 1978; "Additions and Corrections: Tex Avery" in *Film Dope* (London), February 1979; "The Showgirl and the Wolf" by J. Gaines in *Cinema Journal* (Evanston), fall 1980; "Tex Avery: L'accléré à 24 images seconde!" by G. Dagneau in *Cinéma* (Paris), October 1980; "Dos óbitos del ochenta" by A. Beltrán in *Contracampo* (Madrid), January 1981; "Look at me, folks, I'm just Tex Avery" by G. Colpart in *Image et son* (Paris), January 1981.

*   *   *

The cartoons of Tex Avery represent a style of animation that is the absolute antithesis to the Disney school of filmmaking. Whereas Disney strove for realism in animation (with such technical devices as sound, Technicolor, and the multiplane camera), Avery strove for the absurd and the surreal. Avery's "logic" had no bounds and his cartoons exhibited an anything goes policy. The characters in Avery's cartoons not only behaved in a crazy way, but actually seemed insane. Among the cartoon characters that he created were Daffy Duck, Screwball Squirrel, Droopy, and his most famous character, Bugs Bunny. Avery gave Bugs his familiar phrase "What's up, Doc?," which was an expression in Avery's home town in Texas.

The most striking feature of Avery's animation style is the

breakneck pace of gags. Avery believed in having as many gags as possible. While at Warner Brothers, Avery did a number of cartoons loosely structured as travelogues or newsreels. This simple framework gave Avery the opportunity to string together as many "black out" (short, self-contained) gags as could fit into seven minutes. Cartoons like *Believe It or Else* and *Wacky Wild Life* were short on plot, but bursting with Avery's sight gags.

Another trademark of Avery's cartoons is the elasticity of his characters. It would be fair to say that Avery puts his characters through a wider range of physical distortions than any other cartoon director. For example, in *King Size Canary*, the dog, cat, bird and mouse grow to absurd proportions. In *Screwball Football* a character literally yells his head off. Naturally, none of these physical distortions ever proves to be fatal.

Another source of Avery's humor is the medium of animation itself. Many times the characters in Avery's cartoons refer to the cartoon world in which they live. For example, in *Porky's Preview*, Porky Pig draws his own cartoon starring himself. In *Screwball Squirrel*, Screwy accidentally runs clear off the side of the frame of the film. In *The Magical Maestro* a hair keeps bobbing up and down in the projection gate until one of the characters finally reaches over and pulls it out. Avery rarely lets the audience forget that they are watching animation.

Another feature often associated with Tex Avery's cartoons are his jokes based on sexual innuendos. For example, Avery's character of the Wolf (who appeared in *Red Hot Riding Hood* and *Wild and Woolfy* among others) represents the most elementary of sexual beings. In these cartoons the Wolf cannot control his desire for Red: the Wolf's eyes pop out of his head, his jaw drops open, his tongue rolls out on the floor, and he literally falls to pieces. His lust is in no way subtle, and in fact, *Red Hot Riding Hood* had some trouble getting by the Hays Office because of the suggestion of bestiality. Nothing in Avery's cartoons ever went beyond suggestion, but Avery subsequently adopted the habit of padding his scripts with extra and outlandish "no-no's," which could then be dropped, in order that a few innuendos could slip by the censors.

During the latter part of his career, Tex Avery achieved an unusual degree of recognition in television even though his work was uncredited. He created a number of award-winning animated commercials with such characters as the Raid bugs and the Frito Bandito. The short 30 or 60 second format of commercial advertising was an ideal outlet for Avery's fast-paced gags. His work has certainly influenced a number of younger animators, although no one has yet been able to completely match Avery's achievement: the totally crazy cartoon.

—Linda Obalil

BACON, LLOYD. American. Born in San Jose, California, 16 January 1890. Educated in California public schools and at Santa Clara College. Married Margaret Balach. Career: 1911—member, David Belasco's Los Angeles stock company; 1913—stage actor in Lloyd Hamilton comedies; 1916—works in Chaplin comedies; 1917—serves during WW I in Photo Dept., U.S. Navy; 1918—actor at Mutual; 1919—actor at Triangle; 1921—begins as director for Lloyd Hamilton and Mack Sennett; 1926—moves to Warners and directs 1st feature, *Broken Hearts of Hollywood*; 1928—directs most popular early talkie, *The Singing Fool*; 1944 moves to 20th Century-Fox; 1953—finishes career with 2 films at Universal and 2 at RKO. Died in Burbank, California, 15 November 1955.

Films (as director): 1926—*Broken Hearts of Hollywood*; *Private Izzy Murphy*; 1927—*Finger Prints*; *White Flannels*; *The Heart of Maryland*; *A Sailor's Sweetheart*; *Brass Knuckles*; 1928—*Pay as You Enter*; *The Lion and the Mouse*; *Women They Talk About*; *The Singing Fool*; 1929—*Stark Mad*; *No Defense*; *Honky Tonk*; *Say It with Songs*; *So Long Letty*; 1930—*The Other Tomorrow*; *She Couldn't Say No*; *A Notorious Affair*; *Moby Dick*; *The Office Wife*; 1931—*Sit Tight*; *Kept Husbands*; *50 Million Frenchmen*; *Gold Dust Gertie*; *Honor of the Family*; 1932—*Manhattan Parade*; *Fireman Save My Child*; *Alias the Doctor*; *The Famous Ferguson Case*; *Miss Pinkerton*; *Crooner*; *You Said a Mouthful*; 1933—*42nd Street*; *Picture Snatcher*; *Mary Stevens M.D.*; *Footlight Parade*; *Son of a Sailor*; 1934—*Wonder Bar*; *A Very Honorable Guy*; *He Was Her Man*; *Here Comes the Navy*; *6-Day Bike Rider*; 1935—*Devil Dogs of the Air*; *In Caliente*; *Broadway Gondolier*; *The Irish in Us*; *Frisco Kid*; 1936—*Sons o' Guns*; *Cain and Mabel*; *Gold Diggers of 1937*; 1937—*Marked Woman*; *Ever Since Eve*; *San Quentin*; *Submarine D-1*; 1938—*A Slight Case of Murder*; *Cowboy from Brooklyn*; *Rocket Busters*; *Boy Meets Girl*; 1939—*Wings of the Navy*; *The Oklahoma Kid*; *Indianapolis Speedway*; *Espionage Agent*; 1940—*A Child Is Born*; *Invisible Stripes*; *3 Cheers for the Irish*; *Brother Orchid*; *Knute Rockne—All American*; 1941—*Honeymoon for 3*; *Footsteps in the Dark*; *Affectionately Yours*; *Navy Blues*; 1942—*Larceny, Inc.*; *Wings for the Eagle*; *Silver Queen*; 1943—*Action in the North Atlantic*; 1944—*Sunday Dinner for a Soldier*; 1945—*Captain Eddie*; 1946—*Home Sweet Homicide*; *Wake Up and Dream*; 1947—*I Wonder Who's Kissing Her Now*; 1948—*You Were Meant For Me*; *Give My Regards to Broadway*; *Don't Trust Your Husband (An Innocent Affair)*; 1949—*Mother Is a Freshman*; *It Happens Every Spring*; *Miss Grant Takes Richmond*; 1950—*Kill the Umpire*; *The Good Humor Man*; *The Fuller Brush Girl*; 1951—*Call Me Mister*; *The Frogmen*; *Golden Girl*; 1953—*The I Don't Care Girl*; *The Great Sioux Uprising*; *Walking My Baby Back Home*; 1954—*The French Line*; *She Couldn't Say No*. Roles: (in Chaplin comedies): 1915—*The Champion*; *In the Park*; *The Jitney Elopement*; *The Bank*; *The Tramp*; 1916—*The Floorwalker*; *The Vagabond*; *Behind the Screen*; *The Rink*; *The Fireman*; 1919-20—roles for Mutual and Triangle.

Publications:

On BACON:

Book—*Warner Brothers Directors* by William Meyer, New York 1978; *42nd Street* by Rocco Fuments, Madison, Wisconsin 1980; articles—"Lloyd Bacon...Warner Brothers' Ace" in *Cue* (New York), 6 April 1935; "Cosmopolitan's Citation for the Best Direction of the Month" by Louella Parsons in *Cosmopolitan* (New York), May 1949.

*   *   *

Lloyd Bacon is probably best known for his director's credit on such classic Warner Bros. films as *42nd Street*, *Footlight Parade*, *Knute Rockne—All American*, and *Action in the North Atlantic*. But others are more remembered for these films: choreographer Busby Berkeley for the musicals, and actors Pat O'Brien, Ronald Reagan, and Humphrey Bogart in the 1940s films. Today Bacon is lost in the literature about Warner Bros. and is not even ranked by Andrew Sarris in his *American Directors* book.

In his day Lloyd Bacon was recognized as a consummate

Hollywood professional. One cannot help standing in some awe of Bacon's directorial output in the era from the coming of sound to the Second World War. During these 14 years he directed an average of five films per annum for Warner Bros. (Seven were released in 1932 alone.) Bacon's *42nd Street* and *Wonder Bar* were among the industry's top-grossing films of the decade. For a time he was considered Warners' top musicals specialist. The corporation paid him accordingly, some $200,000 per year, making him one of its highest paid contract directors of the 1930s.

Bacon's status declined during the 1940s. His craftmanship remained solid for he knew the classical Hollywood system of production as well as anyone on the Warners lot. But Bacon never seemed to find his special niche, skipping from one genre to another. He seemed to evolve into Warners' handyman director. His greatest success came with war films. For example, *Wings of the Navy* had a million dollar budget, and helped kick off Warners' string of successful World War II films. Probably Bacon's best-remembered film of the 1940s is *Action in the North Atlantic*, a tribute to the U.S. Merchant Marine. (This also was Bacon's last film at Warners.)

In 1944 Bacon moved to Twentieth Century-Fox to work for his former boss, Darryl F. Zanuck. There he re-established himself in musicals as well as films of comedy and family romance, but still seemed unable to locate a long-term specialty. He finished at Fox with an early 1950s series of Lucille Ball comedies, and ended his directorial career in somewhat ignominious fashion, helping Howard Hughes create a 3-D Jane Russell spectacle, *The French Line*.

Bacon's most significant contribution to film history probably came during his early days at Warners as that studio pioneered new sound technology in the late 1920s. Bacon presided over several significant transitional films, none more important than *The Singing Fool*. Although *The Jazz Singer* usually gets credit as the first (and most important) transitional talkie, *The Singing Fool* should receive far more credit because for more than a decade, this film stood as the highest grossing feature in Hollywood annals. As its director, Bacon was honored by the trade publication *Film Daily* as one of the top ten directors of the 1928-29 season. As a consequence of this and other films, Bacon established his reputation as a director who helped thrust Hollywood into an era of movies with sound.

—Douglas Gomery

BAILLIE, BRUCE. American. Born in Aberdeen, South Dakota, 24 September 1931. Educated at University of Minnesota, B.A. 1955; graduate studies in education, University of California at Berkeley, 1956-58; London School of Film Technique, 1959. Career: serves in Korean War; 1958 and 1960—travels in Europe; 1960—volunteer apprentice at Marvin Becker Films, San Francisco, under Will Hindle; begins first personal film, *On Sundays*; 1961—starts Canyon Cinema, organization to exhibit and support independent film in San Francisco area; 1964-65—travels around U.S. filming *Quixote*; 1965-67—lives and works at Morning Star Commune, near Santa Rosa, California; 1967—travels to Mexico, contracts hepatitis; long recuperation period results in making of *Quick Billy*; 1970—teaches film at Rice University, Houston; 1971—begins work on multi-part film-in-progress *Roslyn Romance*; 1974—begins teaching at Bard College; 1981—begins teaching at Evergreen College; begins work on feature-length *The Cardinal's Visit*, a part of *Roslyn Romance*. Recipient: Creative Arts Award for Filmmaking, Brandeis

University, 1970. Agent: American Federation of Arts, 41 E. 65 St., New York, NY 10021. Address: 669 W. 1050 South, Camano Island, WA 98292.

Films: 1960-61—*On Sundays*; 1961—*David Lynn's Sculpture*; *Mr. Hayashi*; *The Gymnasts*; 1962—*Friend Fleeing* (unfinished); *Everyman*; *News No.3*; *Have You Thought of Talking to the Director?*; *Here I Am*; 1962-63—*A Hurrah for Soldiers*; 1963—*To Parsifal*; 1964—*Mass for the Dakota Sioux*; *The Brookfield Recreation Center*; 1964-65—*Quixote* (revised 1967); 1965—*Yellow Horse*; 1966—*Tung*; *Castro Street*; *All My Life*; *Still Life*; *Termination*; *Port Chicago*; *Show Leader*; 1967—*Valentin De Las Sierras*; 1970—*Quick Billy*; 1971-present—*Roslyn Romance* (multi-part film-in-progress); 1981-present—*The Cardinal's Visit* (final section of *Roslyn Romance*).

Publications:

By BAILLIE:

Articles—poems by and letters from Baillie have appeared frequently in *Canyon Cinema News* (San Francisco); "Letters: San Francisco Film Scene" in *Film Culture* (New York), summer 1963; interview by Richard Whitehall in *Film Culture* (New York), summer 1969; "Bruce Baillie—An Interview" in *Film Culture* (New York), spring 1971; "Bruce Baillie" in *Film Comment* (New York), spring 1971; "Dr. Bish" in *Downtown Review*, fall/winter 1979/80, spring 1980, fall 1980.

On BAILLIE:

Books—*A History of the American Avant-Garde Cinema*, exhibition catalogue, by John Hanhardt and others, The American Federation of Arts, New York 1976; *Bruce Baillie* by Ernest Callenbach, St. Paul, Minnesota 1979; articles—"The Films of Bruce Baillie" by Harriet Polt in *Film Comment* (New York), fall 1964; "Bruce Baillie" by Ernest Callenbach in *Film Quarterly* (Berkeley), fall 1964; special Baillie issue of *Harbinger* (Houston), July 1967; special section of *Film Culture* (New York), no.67-69, 1979.

*   *   *

The career of Bruce Baillie has two central aspects, which are also features of the whole American avant-garde film movement. First, his films are generally intensely poetic, lyrical evocations of persons and places in which the subject matter is transformed by the subjective methods used to photograph it. Second, many of his films display a strong social awareness, describing attitudes critical towards, and alienated from, mainstream American society. In many cases, Baillie fuses these concerns within single films.

Stylistically, Baillie's films are characterized by images of haunting, evanescent beauty. An object will appear with spectacular clarity, only to dissolve away an instant later. Light itself often becomes a subject, shining across the frame or reflected from objects, suggesting a level of poetry in the subject matter that lies beyond easy interpretation. Baillie combines images with other images, and images with sound, in dense, collage-like structures. Thus, many of his films cut frequently between scenes, or superimpose objects on each other. One is constantly aware of a restlessness, an instability, which seems to result from his images' appearance and flow. It is significant, too, that many of Baillie's films contain, or are structured as, journeys.

The effect of Baillie's films is to make the viewer feel that any moment of the viewing, any single image he is looking at is a mere illusion that will soon vanish. The sensuousness of the light and colors only heighten one's awareness of their unreality. It is as if there is a void, a nothingness, that lies behind all things. It is not irrelevant in this regard that Baillie has evidenced strong interest, over the years, in Eastern religious thought.

Some degree of social comment is present in most of Baillie's films, but in widely varying degrees. *Mr. Hayashi* places the poetic and the social in a very precise balance. The imagery consists of evocative, sun-drenched images forming a short, haiku-like portrait of a man. On the soundtrack, we hear the man speak of his life, and his difficulty in finding work. *Mass* and *Quixote* indict American society as overly aggressive, toward its citizens, toward Native Americans, and toward nature; as impersonal and dehumanizing; as lacking physical or moral roots. For *Quixote*, Baillie uses an extremely dense, collage-like form, in which images and fragments of images are intercut with and superimposed on others, with a similarly complex soundtrack. At times, the film's multiple themes seem to blur into each other, as if the filmmaker is acknowledging that he is as "lost" as the society he is depicting.

Castro Street, *Tung*, and *Valentin de las Sierras* are, by contrast, apparently simpler portraits of people and places. By keeping his camera very close to things, Baillie renders their details ever more stunning, while his collage editing and soundtrack again create an instability leading to "nothingness". *Castro Street*, which depicts an industrialized area, is extraordinary for its combination of diverse photographic representations—black and white, color, positive and negative—in editing and superimposition. *Quick Billy* contains thematic and stylistic elements of most of Baillie's previous films; its motifs include autobiography, "portrait"-like representation of people and events, and an underlying theme, made explicit in the film's final section, of Western man's aggressiveness toward his surroundings. Since the early seventies, Baillie has been working on a long, inclusive, multireel film, *Roslyn Romance*.

—Fred Camper

BAKSHI, RALPH. American. Born in Haifa, Palestine, 26 October 1938. Educated at Thomas Jefferson High School, Brooklyn, and High School of Industrial Arts , New York. Divorced from first wife; one son; married Elizabeth Bakshi; son and daughter. Career: 1956—following high school graduation, hired as cell painter for CBS Terrytoons unit, New Rochelle, New York; becomes animator after short period; 1964—becomes director; 1965—creative director for Terrytoons and in 1966 becomes director of Paramount cartoon dept. in New York; 1967—Paramount shuts down cartoon dept.; 1969—work begins on *Fritz the Cat*; 1969-73—association with producer Steve Krantz; 1974—preview of *Coonskin* at Museum of Modern Art picketed by Congress of Racial Equality; Bakshi roughed up in ensuing disturbance; Paramount drops plans to distribute film; 1975—completes *Hey Good Lookin'* (released 1982); 1978—begins filming live-action *If I Catch Her, I'll Kill Her* for Warner Bros. Address: Bakshi Productions, Inc., 8132 Sunland Blvd., Sun Valley, CA 91352.

Films (as director and scriptwriter): 1972—*Fritz the Cat*; 1973—*Heavy Traffic*; 1975—*Coonskin*; 1977—*Wizards* (+pr); 1978—*Lord of the Rings*; 1981—*American Pop* (+co-pr, R&B efx, animation supervisor); 1982—*Hey Good Lookin'* (largely completed in 1975); 1983—*Fire and Ice* (+pr).

Publications:

By BAKSHI:

Articles—"Rencontre avec Ralph Bakshi" by G. Hynek in *Image et son* (Paris), March 1974; "MOMA Will Never Be the Same", interview by G. Beke, in *Millimeter* (New York), April 1975; "The Young Turk", interview by S. Eyman, in *Take One* (Montreal), November 1978.

On BAKSHI:

Articles—"Animator Bakshi Shuns 'Racist' Caricature, Turns to Fantasy" by J. McBride in *Variety* (Los Angeles), 22 December 1976; "Animation Kit: Rings 'n Things" by H. Beckerman in *Filmmakers Monthly* (Ward Hill, Mass.), January 1979; "Rotoscoping, or Whatever Happened to Animation?" by H. Beckerman in *Filmmakers Monthly* (Ward Hill, Mass.), April 1981; "Lexique des réalisateurs de films fantastiques américains" by J.-P. Piton in *Image et son* (Paris), April 1981.

* * *

Totally animated feature films are a rather rare commodity in the film market. There are a couple of important reasons for this lack of product. One is cost. Animated films are very expensive to produce, mainly because of the volume of work involved and the man-hours required to draw and paint the approximately 108,000 frames needed for a 75 minute film. The other obstacle facing animated films is the attitude of movie audiences: it is generally assumed that cartoons are for kids. In most cases this has been true. Companies like Hanna-Barbera and Filmation have released a few feature-length cartoons, but they never have found a very wide audience. For many years Disney was the only studio that was regularly producing animated feature films—until Ralph Bakshi came on the scene. Bakshi devised his own formula to create a series of animated feature films, a formula that placed his films at the opposite end of the spectrum from Disney's.

Bakshi began his career in the mid-fifties as an animator at Terrytoons and eventually became the head of the studio at age 26. He later put in some time as head of the cartoon department at Paramount before venturing into the feature cartoon market in 1972. Beginning with *Fritz the Cat*, Bakshi found ways around the many obstacles that usually block the path of feature-length animated film production.

The first obstacle which Bakshi wanted to overcome was to produce a cartoon for adults. *Fritz the Cat*, based on the underground comics by Robert Crumb, makes this point quite clear with an "X" rating due to its language and subject matter. It was the first animated feature to receive an "X" rating and because of it the film gathered a lot of publicity. Bakshi's second feature, *Heavy Traffic*, also received an "X". Here were cartoons that were definitely *not* for kids.

The publicity (and controversy) which surrounded Bakshi's films continued to grow with *Coonskin*. The film's title alone brought down the wrath of an organization called CORE (Congress of Racial Equality). The group picketed and nearly rioted at a preview screening of the film at New York's Museum of Modern Art. As a result, Paramount Studios, which had been planning to distribute the film, dropped the picture and the film never received a proper release. Bakshi's next film, *Hey Good Lookin'!*, was also shelved because of possible racist connotations. (*Hey Good Lookin!* was eventually released in 1982.) At this point Bakshi moved away from his "social relevancy" period and into fantasy.

In order to produce his films within a reasonable budget, Bakshi has had to take some short cuts in technique. *Fritz the Cat* was produced for $700,000 which left no money in the budget for pencil tests or animation checkers. *Wizards* and *Lord of the Rings* had slightly higher budgets, but Bakshi still had to skimp in some areas, and these two films especially show the negative effects of rising costs on animation. Many of the scenes are rotoscoped (a process invented by the Fleischer brothers in the early thirties whereby live-action film is traced onto animation cels to copy the action) in order to save some animation time. Other scenes were not even rotoscoped, but left as live-action (often color tinted on hi-con film). This mixing and matching of styles is often jarring in the films, but it allows Bakshi to bring in his picture at a lower cost and in less time than other animated feature film directors.

Although some of Bakshi's films have been shelved because of their controversial nature, others have been very profitable. His formula for producing feature-length cartoons has made Bakshi one of the few successful animation directors in the marketplace today.

—Linda J. Obalil

BARDEM, JUAN ANTONIO. Spanish. Born Juan Antonio Bardem-Muñoz in Madrid, 2 July 1922. Educated in agriculture; Instituto de Investigaciones Cinematograficas, beginning 1947. Career: mid-1940s—works for Spanish Ministry of Agriculture, assigned to cinema section 1946; 1947—while studying filmmaking, writes for film periodicals and collaborates on scripts with Luis Berlanga; 1951—*Welcome, Mr. Marshall!* gains international recognition for Spanish film industry; 1953—begins film magazine *Objetivo* (banned by government 1955); 1956—arrested for political reasons during filming of *Calle Mayor*, released after 10 days; 1958-61—produces through Uninci company; 1972—begins shooting international co-production *The Mysterious Island* with Henri Colpi as 2nd unit director; film closed down March 1972; 1973—production resumed with Colpi as director (see filmography below for credits on different versions of film); 1970s—head of Spanish directors' guild. 1981—directs Bulgarian/U.S.S.R./East German co-production *The Warning*.

Films (as director and scriptwriter): 1949—*Paseo sobre una guerra antigua* (co-d, co-sc; silent short incorporated into feature *La honradez de la cerradura* by Luis Escobar); 1950—*Barajas, aeropuerto internacional* (short); 1951—*Esa pareja feliz (That Happy Pair)* (co-d, co-sc); 1952—*Bienvenido, Mr. Marshall! (Welcome, Mr. Marshall!)* (Berlanga) (co-sc only); 1953—*Novio a la vista* (Berlanga) (co-sc only); 1954—*Cómicos (Comedians)*; *El torero* (Wheeler: Spanish version of *Châteaux en Espagne*) (co-dialogue only); *Felices Pascuas* (co-sc); 1955—*Muerte de un ciclista (Death of a Cyclist, Age of Infidelity)*; *Playa prohibida (El esconocido)* (Soler) (sc only); 1956—*Calle Mayor (Grand Rue, The Lovemaker)*; *El amór de Don Juan (Don Juan)* (Berry) (co-sc only); *Carte a Sara* (Manzanos and Bercovici) (sc only); 1957—*La muerte de Pio Baroja* (unreleased); *La venganza (The Vengeance)*; (as producer, director and scriptwriter): 1958—*L'uomo dai calzoni corti (Tal vez mañana)* (Pellegrini) (pr only);

1959—*Sonatas*; 1960—*A las cinco de la tarde* (co-sc); 1961—*Viridiana* (Buñuel) (pr only); (as director and scriptwriter): 1962—*Los inocentes* (co-sc); 1963—*Nunca pasa nada* (co-sc); 1965—*Los pianos mécanicos (Les Pianos méchaniques, The Uninhibited)*; 1969—*El ultimo dia de la guerra (The Last Day of the War)* (co-sc); 1971—*Varietes*; (as director): 1973—4 versions of *The Mysterious Island* (see 1973 career entry above for production details): 1. *La isla misteriosa* (for Spanish and Latin American distribution, Bardem credited with direction); 2. *L'isola misteriosa e il Capitano Nemo* (for Italian distribution, Bardem credited with direction, but incorporates material directed by Henri Colpi); 3. *l'île mystérieuse* and *The Mysterious Island* (French, English and international version, credited as co-directed by Bardem and Colpi); 4. 6 hour TV version for international distribution; *La corrupción de Chris Miller (The Corruption of Chris Miller)* (+ro); *Behind the Shutters*; 1976—*El podor del deseo*; *Foul Play*; 1977—*The Dog*; *El puente*; 1979—*7 Dias de enero (7 Days in January)* (+sc); 1982—*The Warning*.

Publications:

By BARDEM:

Articles—"Spanish Highway" in *Films and Filming* (London), June 1957; statement in *Film Makers on Filmmaking* edited by Harry Geduld, Bloomington, Indiana 1967; "Cara a cara... Bardem-Berlanga" in *Cinema 2002* (Madrid), July/August 1980; "Interview mit Juan Antonio Bardem" by R. Heckmann in *Film und Fernsehen* (Berlin), April 1981.

On BARDEM:

Books—*J.A. Bardem* by Marcel Oms, *Premier Plan* no.21, Paris; articles—"The Arrest" in *Sight and Sound* (London), spring 1956; "Bardem: Une Méthode de travail" by J.F. Aranda in *Cinéma 59* (Paris), no.33, 1959; "Juan Antonio Bardem, homme d'Espagne" by Philippe Durand in *Image et son* (Paris), October 1959; "Despues de 27 años, Bardem se revitaliza" by M. Martinex Carril in *Cinemateca Revista* (Andes), July 1980.

*   *   *

A pioneer figure in Spanish film, Juan Antonio Bardem is also one of Spain's most consistently political filmmakers. In his early movies co-directed with Luis Garcia Berlanga, *Esa pareja feliz* and *Bienvenido Mr. Marshall*, he broke with prevailing Francoist film traditions which emphasized militarism, folklore, literary adaptations and costume dramas. Bardem and Berlanga chose instead to present scenes of contemporary Spanish life and used humor to describe and criticize aspects of Spanish society. With *Bienvenido Mr. Marshall* the two directors were recognized as leading filmmakers and along with others of their generation, they set about to revitalize the Spanish film industry and to rescue Spanish films from mediocrity. At a meeting held in Salamanca in 1955, they drafted a statement of principles in which Bardem wrote: "After 60 years, Spanish cinema is politically futile, socially false, intellectually worthless, esthetically valueless and industrially paralytic." Bardem went on to note that Spanish cinema "had turned its back on reality... (and was) totally removed from Spanish realistic traditions [as found] in paintings and novels."

Bardem and other filmmakers who attended the meeting at Salamanca also deplored the lack of general film culture in Spain, noting that it was not possible to see 95% of movies made abroad. Bardem felt the it was important for Spaniards to keep abreast of worldwide trends in filmmaking and especially to become familiar with Italian neo-realism. This was the single most important influence in the development of his own cinematic style. Both in his movies and in his writings he remained faithful to the tenets of Italian neo-realism. In order to foster a film culture in Spain, Bardem founded *Objetivo*, a cinema journal that was eventually banned by the government. During its brief existence, it nevertheless became a rallying point for Spanish cineastes, raised the level of film criticism in Spain and informed readers about prohibited films. Several years later in yet another effort to ensure the autonomy and integrity of Spanish film, Bardem joined with Berlanga, Carlos Saura, and other directors and founded a production company, UNINCI, which operated until 1962, when it was closed down for coproducing Luis Buñuel's *Viridiana*.

Because of these endeavors as well as his political outspokenness, Bardem was arrested seven times during the Franco years. He nevertheless persisted in his efforts to make political films in Spain. In spite of his lack of favor at home, he won many prizes at film festivals around the world and directed co-productions in Italy, France, Argentina, and Bulgaria.

The movies with which he is most closely associated are those that chronicle the negative effects of Francoism on the psyche of Spaniards of different classes, regions and social milieus. In several films he dramatizes the alienation fostered by Francoism by focusing upon a single individual who often bears his own name of Juan. This Spanish everyman feels frustrated and stifled in a closed society. He attempts to find outlets through hobbies, intrigues, even through radio contests but all means prove to be unsatisfactory. In the course of his efforts, Juan is led to reevaluate himself and the world around him in order to find new options. The spectator judges the choices that each Juan makes, becoming increasingly critical of individuals who act selfishly, cowardly, or who refuse to take a stand. These general themes continue in the movies he has made since the death of Franco.

—Katherine Singer Kovács

BECKER, JACQUES. French. Born in Paris, 15 September 1906. Educated at Lycée Condorcet, then Schola Cantorum, Paris. Married actress Françoise Fabian; son Jean and daughter. Career: before 1930—urged toward career as engineer by father, works in battery factory; other jobs include baggage supervisor on CGT line between New York and Le Havre; early 1930s—meets King Vidor, who offers him job in U.S. as assistant and actor, decides to remain in France; 1932—becomes assistant to Jean Renoir through 1939; 1935—makes first short film *Le Commissaire est bon enfant, le gendarme est sans pitie*, co-directed with Pierre Prévert; 1938—makes untitled documentary on congress of Communist Party at Arles; 1941-42—spends year in German prisoner-of-war camp; 1960—son and assistant Jean Becker finishes *Le Trou* following death. Died 1960.

Films (as assistant to Jean Renoir): 1932—*Boudu sauvé des eaux* (+ro); *La Nuit du carrefour*; 1933—*Chotard & Compagnie*; 1934—*Madame Bovary* (uncredited); 1935—*Le Commissaire est bon enfant, le gendarme est sans pitie* (co-d, co-sc with Pierre Prévert); *Tête de turc (Une Tête qui rapporte)* (d, +co-sc); *Le Crime de Monsieur Lange*; *Toni*; 1936—*Les Bas-Fonds* (+ro); *Une Partie de campagne* (+ro); *La Vie est à nous* (+ro); 1938—short documentary on Communist Party Congress at Arles (d);

La Grande Illusion (+ro); *La Marseillaise*; *La Bête humaine*; 1939—*La Règle du jeu*; *L'Héritier des Montdésir* (d: Valentin); (as director): 1939—*L'Or du Cristobal* (co-d, uncredited); 1942—*Le Dernier Atout* (+co-pr, co-sc); 1943—*Goupi Mains rouges (It Happened at the Inn)* (+co-sc); 1945—*Falbalas (Paris Frills)* (+co-sc); 1947—*Antoine et Antoinette* (+co-sc); 1949—*Rendez-vous de Juillet* (+co-sc); 1951—*Édouard et Caroline* (+co-sc); 1952—*Casque d'Or* (+co-sc); 1953—*Rue de l'Estrapade*; 1954—*Touchez pas au Grisbi (Grisbi)* (+co-sc); *Ali Baba et les quarante voleurs (Ali Baba)* (+co-sc); 1956—*Les Aventures d'Arsène Lupin (The Adventures of Arsène Lupin)* (+co-sc); 1957—*Montparnasse 19 (Modigliani of Montparnasse)* (+co-sc); 1960—*Le Trou (The Night Watch, The Hole)* (co-d, +co-sc). Roles: 1929—*Le Bled* (Renoir); appearance in *Le Rendez-vous de Cannes* (Petrossian—documentary).

Publications:

On BECKER:

Book—*French Cinema Since 1946: Vol.I—The Great Tradition* by Roy Armes, New York 1970; articles—"The Stylist" by Catherine de la Roche in *Films and Filming* (London), March 1955; "Microscope Director" by Joseph Lisbona in *Films and Filming* (London), December 1956; "Jacques Becker and *Montparnasse 19*" by Brian Baxter in *Film* (London), September/October 1958; "Becker" in *Sight and Sound* (London), spring 1960; "Becker—Sjöström" in *Sight and Sound* (London), spring 1960; "Jacques Becker: 2 Films" by Gilberto Perez Guillermo in *Sight and Sound* (London), summer 1969; "Un Couple sans histoire" by J.-L. Lederlé in *Cinématographe* (Paris), May 1977; film—*Portraits filmés...Jacques Becker* by Pierre Viallet and Marcel L'Herbier, 1954.

* * *

Next to Jean Grémillon, Jacques Becker is surely the most neglected of France's great directors. Known in France for *Goupi Mains rouges* and *Antoine et Antoinette*, his only film to reach an international critical audience was *Casque d'Or*. But from 1942 to 1959 Becker fashioned 13 films, none of which could be called a failure and each of which merits respect and attention.

Tied to Jean Renoir through a youthful friendship (their families were both close to the Cézannes), Becker began assisting Renoir in 1932. For eight years he helped put together some of the greatest films ever made, allowing the generous genius of Renoir to roam unconcerned over the details he had already prearranged. Becker gave Renoir the kind of grounding and order which kept his films from flying into thin air. His fastidiousness and precision made him the perfect assistant and many of his friends doubted that such a sensibility could ever command the energy needed to finish a film.

Nevertheless nearly from the first this was his ambition. It was he who developed the idea for *Le Crime de M. Lang* and when the producer insisted that Renoir take over, it cost them their friendship for a time. Soon Becker was directing a cheap anarchist subject *Le Commissaire est bon enfant* with the Octobre groupe company of actors. He wasn't to be held back.

Like so many others he was given his chance with the Occupation. The producer who had financed the 1936 short let him try a detective comedy *Le Dernier Atout* which he brought in under budget and to a good box office response. This opened his career, permitting him to film the unforgettable *Goupi*. Georges Sadoul claims that after the war an American firm bought up the film and had it destroyed so that it wouldn't compete with American products as *Open City* had done. Whether this is true or not, the film remains today impressive in the clarity of its partly cynical, partly mysterious tone; and it shows Becker to be a brilliant director of actors.

The sureness of touch in each of his films derives from a precision some link to craftsmanship; but Becker was striving for far more than competence, veneer, or "quality." He was first and always interested in rhythm. A musician, he was obsessed with jazz and ragtime. No other standard director spent so much time collaborating with his editor (who was Marguerite Renoir).

Goupi is only the first of a host of films whose subjects are difficult to define. Becker seems to have gone out of his way to set himself problems. Many of his films are about groups of characters, most notably his final work *Le Trou*. Others are about milieux: *Antoine et Antoinette* captures the working class quarters of Paris; *Rendez-vous de Juillet* must be the first film anywhere to explicitly bring out the youth culture of postwar Europe; *Falbalas* evokes the world of high fashion as only someone raised in such as world could know it; and of course, *Casque d'Or* makes the turn-of-the-century Parisian underworld come to life with a kind of grim romanticism.

Becker stated that his fastidious attention to milieu was the only way he could approach his characters. Bazin goes further, claiming that only through the exactitude of social particularity could the universality of his characters and their situations come to life. For Bazin, *Edouard et Caroline* is, if not his greatest film, at least his most revealing one. This brilliant farce in the style of Marivaux is virtually plotless. Becker was able, via the minuteness of his *découpage* and the sympathy he had for his actors to build a serious moral comedy from literally nothing. *Edouard et Caroline*, along with *Le Trou*, shows him working at his best, working without plots and without the luxury of breadth. Both films take place in prison cells, *Le Trou* in an actual prison, *Edouard et Caroline* in the dingy apartment they share and the more menacing jail of her uncle's mansion.

Becker has been called "the mechanic" of cinema, for he took a delight in its workings and he went about his own job with such order and method. This separates him further from such "quality" directors as Autant-Lara, Cayatte, and Delannoy, whose themes may seem grander. Becker was interested in what the cinema could do just as he was interested in what men and women do. Never searching for the extraordinary, he would go to endless lengths to bring out not some abstract rhythm in the lives of people (as René Clair did) but the true style and rhythm of their sensibilities.

In 1956 Max Ophuls bequeathed to Becker his project on the life of Modigliani. While the resultant film *Montparnasse 19* is one of his least successful, its style is illustrative. Within weeks after taking over the project, both the scriptwriter (Henri Jeanson) and the set designer (Annenkov) left in outrage, for Becker refused to let them show off with words and drapery. His was always a reduced idea of cinema even when, as in *Falbalas*, his subject was fashion. Nor did he ever choose name actors, except perhaps Gérard Philipe as Modigliani. He had a sureness of taste, backed up by scrupulous reflection. Filmmaking for him was an endless series of choices each of which could founder the project.

Yet his "divide and conquer" attitude toward filmmaking somehow did not remove him from the true source of his sensibility, the generous observation of human beings he shares with his teacher Renoir. *Antoine et Antoinette* was broken into nearly 1300 shots while *Grand Illusion* has fewer than 400; nevertheless they have in common a respect for their subject matter, for the actors and for the ambience which is their stage. Both are

observers, sympathetic and curious onlookers who never succomb to weeping for the tragedies they relate and never fully laugh at their comedies. Life is always bigger than the drama at hand as any steady storyteller knows. Becker was one of these.

Truffaut once claimed that Becker had his own pace of living; he would linger over meals, but race his car. He would spend hours of film over minor incidents in the lives of his characters, while whipping through the core of the intrigue which brought those characters together. Perhaps this is why *Le Trou* is a fitting finale to his career. For here the intrigue is given in advance and in a sense is without interest: five men struggling to escape from jail. For two and a half hours we observe the minutiae of their efforts and the silent camaraderie that develops among them. This is for Becker the state of life on earth: despite the ingenuity we bring to our struggle for freedom, we are doomed to failure; but in the effort we come upon another value, greater even than liberty, an awareness that our struggle is shared and the friendship and respect that confers. If *Casque d'Or* is destined to remain his most popular and most acclaimed film (it was his personal favorite), it will not betray these sentiments, for Manda gives up not only liberty, but life with Marie-Casque d'Or in order to be true to his friend. The stunning scene at the guillotine which ends that film evokes a set of emotions as contradictory as life itself. Jacques Becker was uniquely able to express such contradictions.

—Dudley Andrew

BELLOCCHIO, MARCO. Italian. Born in Piacenza, 9 November 1939. Educated in letters and philosophy, Milan; Centro Sperimentale di Cinematografia, Rome; studied on scholarship at School of Fine Arts, London, 1959-63. Career: 1968-70—renounces fictional for militant cinema, joins cooperative film group; collaborates on *Paola*, film about occupation of a town hall in Calabria, and propaganda documentary *Viva il primo maggio rosso*; 1973—accepts invitation of health authority for Parma and region of Emilia-Romagna to make film about conditions in mental hospitals and reintegration of patients into normal life; film *Nessuno o tutti— Matti da slegare* results; 1977-78—co-directs 5-part "inquest" on world of cinema for TV, *La macchina cinema.*

Films (as student at Centro Sperimentale): *La colpa e la pena, Abbasso lo zio,* and *Ginepro fatto uomo* (diploma film); (as director and scriptwriter): 1965—*I pugni in tasca (Fist in His Pocket)*; 1967—*La Cina è vicina (China is Near)* (co-sc); 1969—"Discutiamo discutiamo" episode of *Amore e rabbia (Vangelo 70)* (co-sc, +ro); 1971—*Nel nome del padre (In the Name of the Father)*; 1972—*Sbatti il mostro in prima pagina (Strike the Monster on Page One)* (co-d uncredited, co-sc); 1974—*Nessuno o tutti—Matti da slegare* (co-d, co-sc); 1976—*Marcia trionfale* (co-sc); 1977—*Il gabbiano* (co-sc); 1979—*Salto nel vuoto*; 1980—*Leap into the Void*; 1983—*Les Yeux, la bouche.*

Publications:

By BELLOCCHIO:

Articles—"Marco Bellocchio: an Interview" in *Film Society Review* (New York), January 1972; "La Place de la politique", interview by G. Fofi, in *Positif* (Paris), April 1972; "Entretien avec Bellocchio" by J. Delmas and A. Tournès in *Jeune cinéma* (Paris), March 1973; "Entretien avec Marco Bellocchio" by J.A. Gili in *Ecran* (Paris), February and March 1973; "Entretien avec Marco Bellocchio" by G. Sibilla in *Jeune cinéma* (Paris), February 1973; "Mon film est en prise directe avec l'Histoire", interview by N. Simsolo in *Cinéma* (Paris), March 1973; "Entretien avec Marco Bellocchio" by N. Zalaffi in *Image et son* (Paris), April 1973; "Interview with Marco Bellocchio" by N. Zalaffi in *Sight and Sound* (London), autumn 1973; "Marco Bellocchio on Victory March", interview by R. Schar, in *Cinema Papers* (N. Melbourne, Australia), September/October 1976; "Marco Bellocchio—l'alibi du grand public n'est qu'une justification hypocrite", interview by D. Rabourdin, in *Cinéma* (Paris), March 1977.

On BELLOCCHIO:

Articles—"Au nom du père et de la politique" by Max Tessier in *Ecran* (Paris), February 1973; "Marco Bellocchio apunta hacia paternalistas y dominantes" by Martínez Carril in *Cinemateca Revista* (Andes), March 1979; "Marco Bellocchio au miroir de Tchekhov" by E. Comuzio in *Jeune cinéma* (Paris), April/May 1979; "Perissinotto: Danse sur le film du rasoir", interview by P. Kral, in *Positif* (Paris), June 1980.

*   *   *

One of the healthiest aspects of the ever-more impressive cinematic output of the sixties was the greater respect accorded to different, even opposing, approaches to political filmmaking. Thus, a Godard or a Straub could comfortably accept being called a political filmmaker while their work analyzed the process of creating meaning in cinema. One of Italy's most gifted directors to have emerged since the war, Marco Bellocchio chose to delve into his own roots, and scrutinize those primary agents of socialization—the classroom, the church, and most crucially for him, the family. Besides serving to reproduce selected values and ideas about the world, these structures are depicted by Bellocchio to be perfect, if miniature, reflections of society at large.

Bellocchio's films are black comedies centered around the threat of impending chaos. Typically, Bellocchio's protagonists are outsiders who, after learning the rules by which societal structures remain intact, set about circumventing or ignoring them. Through their actions, they expose the fragility of the social order by exposing the fragility of all presumed truths. The judge, in *Leap into the Void*, for example, devises a bizzare plot to have his sister killed, in order not to suffer the embarrassment of sending her to a mental institution.

The nuclear family, as an incarnation of the social order, represents a system of clearly understood, if unexpressed, power relationships within a fixed hierarchy. These power relationships are expressed in familial terms: Bellocchio's women, for example, are usually defined as mothers or sisters. Even the radical political beliefs which some of his characters profess must be judged with regard to their application in the family sphere: shocked to discover that his sister is no longer a virgin, Vittorio in *China Is Near* admits "You can be a Marxist-Leninist but still insist that your sister doesn't screw around."

Along with his countryman Bernardo Bertolucci, Bellocchio is a primary example of the first European generation of film-school-educated directors .Often, these directors—under the influence of *la politique des auteurs* perhaps—tended to exhibit an extreme self-conciousness in their films. While watching a Bellocchio film, one is struck at how little or nothing is left open to interpretation—everything seems achingly precise and intentional. Yet what saves his films from seeming airless or hopelessly "arty" is that they're often outrageously funny. The havoc which his characters wreak on all those around them is ironically counterpointed to the controlled precision of the direction. There is a kind of mordant delight in discovering just how far Bellocchio's characters will go in carrying out their eerie intrigues. The sense of shrewd critical intelligence orchestrating comic pandemonium into lucid political analyses is one of the most pleasurable aspects of his cinema.

—Richrd Peña

BENEGAL, SHYAM. Indian. Born in in Alwal, near Hyderabad, 14 December 1934. Educated Osmania University, M.A. in economics. Married Nira Mukerji; daughter: Pia. Career: 1950s—moves to Bombay with promise of job in advertising firm; early 1960s—works as copywriter, Lintas Agency; begins scripting commercials, then directs them; 1960-66—makes over 620 advertising shorts; 1969—receives Bhabha Fellowship, works briefly in U.S. as associate TV producer; 1970—after return to India becomes independent producer of advertising shorts and documentaries; early 1980s—Director of the National Film Development Corporation.

Films (as director of documentary shorts): 1967—*A Child of the Streets*; 1968—*Close to Nature*; *Indian Youth—An Exploration*; *Sinhasta or The Path to Immortality*; 1969—*Poovanam (The Flower Path)*; 1970—*Horoscope for a Child*; 1971—*Pulsating Giant*; *Steel: A Whole New Way of Life*; *Raga and the Emotions*; 1972—*Tala and Rhythm*; *The Shruti and Graces of Indian Music*; *The Raag Yaman Kalyan*; *Notes on a Green Revolution*; *Power to the People*; *Foundations of Progress*; (as feature director of films in Hindi): 1974—*Ankur (The Seedling)* (+sc); 1974-75—*Learning Modules for Rural Children* (doc); 1975—*Nishant (Night's End)*; *Charandas Chor (Charandas the Thief)*; 1975—*A Quiet Revolution* (doc); 1976—*Manthan (The Churning)*; *Tomorrow Begins Today: Industrial Research* (short); *Epilepsy* (short); 1977—*Bhumika (The Role)* (+co-sc); *Kondura/Anugrahan* [Telugu version] (The Boon) (+co-sc); *New Horizons in Steel* (doc); 1978—*Junoon (The Obsession)*; 1980—*Hari Hondal Bargadar (Share Cropper)* (+sc); 1981—*Kalyug (The Machine Age)*; 1982—*Arohan (Ascending Scale)*; *Satyajit Ray—Film Maker* (doc); *Jawaharlal Nehru* (doc).

Publications:

By BENEGAL:

Article—interview by B. Gandhy in *Framework* (Norwich, England), no.12, 1980.

On BENEGAL:

Book—*Film India: The New Generation 1960-1980*, edited by Uma da Cunha, New Delhi 1981; articles—"Shyam Benegal", article and interview, in *Cinéma* (Paris), September/October 1975; "Shyam Benegal" by Anil Dharker in *International Film Guide 1979*, London 1978; "Film in India: interview—

achtergronden—Shyam Benegal" by P. Posthumus and T. Custers in *Skrien* (Amsterdam), winter 1980/81.

*   *   *

The career of Shyam Benegal, which began with a first feature in 1974 has some similarity in terms of both approach and tenacity to that of Satyajit Ray 20 years earlier. Among shared aspects one may note: a background in the film society movement, a strong western influence, commercial work in an advertising agency, and direction of work for children (in Benegal's case the feature length *Charandas the Thief*, made in 1975 for the Children's Film Society). But Benegal was 40 by the time he made his first feature and had already directed a large number of sponsored documentaries and commercials. Moreover, virtually all his filmmaking has been in Hindi, the language of the commercial "all-India" movie, not in a regional dialect.

Benegal's personal style is already apparent and fully formed in the loose trilogy of studies of rural oppression made between 1974 and 1976: *The Seedling*, *Night's End* and *The Churning*, the latter financed collectively—at two rupees apiece—by the farmers of Gujarat state. In each case the interaction of the rural populace and often well-meaning outsiders ends disastrously, but the note of revolt is very muted. Though Benegal's social commitment is unquestionable he does not offer any clear way out for his characters. In *The Seedling* the seduction and abandoning of the servant girl is followed by the savage beating of her deaf-mute husband, but the only answer is the stone thrown at the landlord's house by a small boy in the film's final sequence. This is the "seedling," but Benegal offers no indication as to how it can be nurtured. In *Night's End* a schoolmaster's efforts lead to violence when his wife is kidnapped by the landlord's family who are accustomed to exploiting and brutalizing the peasants at will. But the final peasant revolt stirred up by the middle class hero gets totally and blindly out of hand, and one knows that it will be put down—no doubt savagely—by the authorities and passivity will resume. *The Churning* is more optimistic, but even here the advocates of change are eventually defeated, though their efforts may some day bear fruit. Typical of Benegal's approach is the way in which women—so often a personification of new values in third world films—are depicted as passive suffering figures in these films. Always Benegal's style is solidly realistic, with stress on a carefully worked out narrative line and well-drawn characters. The pace is generally slow and measured, but enlivened by excellent observation and fine choice of significant detail.

In the late 1970s Benegal retained this somewhat austere style with a total professionalism but without ever slipping into the extravagance or melodrama of the conventional Hindi film. *The Role*, one of his richest films, tells of a more dynamic woman, a film star who tries desperately to live her own life, but is cruelly exploited by men from childhood onwards. The film, essentially a problem picture of a kind familiar in the West, has a muted, open ending and is enlivened by vigorously recreated extracts from the films in which the actress is purported to star. Subsequently Benegal continued the widening of his chosen area of subject matter with *The Boon*, a film shot in two language versions and known as *Kondura* in Hindi and *Anugrahan* in Telegu. A study of the tragic effect of a young man's belief that he has been granted supernatural powers, it was followed by *The Obsession*, a tale of inter-racial love set at the time of the Indian Mutiny, and *The Machine Age*, a story of bitter rivalry between industrialists which is also an archetypal tale of conflict based on an ancient Hindi epic. But *Ascending Scale*, which depicts a peasant family destroyed as it is pitted against the reactionary forces of rural India, shows Benegal's fidelity to the themes with which he had begun his career. Working aside from the dominant Hindi traditions, the director offers a striking example of integrity and commitment to an unrelenting vision.

—Roy Armes

BENOIT-LÉVY, JEAN. French. Born in Paris, 25 April 1888. Educated at University of Paris. Career: 1910—completes military service; works briefly for Pathé and Gaumont, joins uncle's educational film company; 1921-27—produces 4 features while continuing to make documentaries; 1922—artistic director, Jean Epstein's *Pasteur*; 1926-35—co-directs feature documentaries with Marie Epstein, sister of filmmaker Jean Epstein; 1930s—produces educational films through company Les Films Benoit-Lévy; late 1930s—president of Coopérative des Artisans d'Art du Cinéma (technicians' union); teaches at Ecole Nationale de Cinématographie, Paris; 1939—makes last feature, *Feu de paille*; 1940—takes refuge in U.S.; 1941-46—professor at New School for Social Research, New York; 1946—appointed Director of Films and Visual Information Division, United Nations; produces documentaries for UN; 1949—returns to France, named delegate general of UNESCO International Council of Cinema and Television; 1952—begins series of 25 ballet films for *March of Time* and French TV. Died in Paris, 2 August 1959. Recipient: Grand Prix du Cinéma, Paris International Exhibition, for *Ballerina*, 1938; French Legion of Honor, 1951.

Films (as producer and director made over 400 educational and instructional films—features only listed here): 1922—*Pasteur* (Epstein) (pr only, +art d); (as producer and co-director with Marie Epstein): 1925—*Peau-de-pêche*; 1926—*Le Nid (The Nest)* (sole d); *Le Voile sacré (The Holy Veil)* (sole d); 1927—*Maternité (Maternity)*; 1928—*Ames d'enfants (The Souls of Children)*; 1930—*Jimmy bruiteur (Le Petit Jimmy)*; 1931—*Le Coeur de Paris*; 1933—*La Maternelle*; 1934—*Itto*; (as producer and director): 1936—*Hélène*; 1937—*La Mort du cygne (Ballerina)*; 1938—*Altitude 3.002 (Youth in Revolt)*; 1939—*Feu de paille (Fire in the Straw)*.

Publications:

By BENOIT-LÉVY:

Books—*Le Cinéma d'enseignement et l'education*, 1929; *L'Instruction visuelle aux Etats-Unis*, 1936; *Les Grandes Missions du cinéma*, Paris 1945, translated as *The Art of the Motion Picture*, New York 1946.

On BENOIT-LÉVY:

Obituary in *Sight and Sound* (London), summer/autumn 1959.

*   *   *

When Jean Benoit-Lévy died in 1959, the film world mourned one of its most respected and versatile members. Producer, director, scholar, and diplomat, he devoted his life to expanding the horizons of the medium. One of France's pioneer entrepreneurs in cinema, Edmond Benoit-Lévy, was his uncle, a man who personally directed young Jean's career. Even before World War I Benoit-Lévy had begun making instructional films. After the war his uncle saw to it that he gained experience in every aspect of the medium.

Benoit-Lévy, whose family had always been involved in academics, would make the educational film his true passion. But he recognized early on that to make this a viable genre certain concessions would have to be made to art and entertainment. In the early twenties such a blend of genres was entirely feasible, and this young scholar soon found himself friends with many of the impressionist filmmakers. In 1922 he produced *Pasteur*, a feature length biography directed by Jean Epstein. During the production he became friends with Marie Epstein, initiating a productive collaboration that only the Second World War would break up.

Their first project, like all their later successes, was in the mode of the semi-documentary. *Peau de pêche* followed the exploits of a delightful slumchild in the 20th arrondissement of Paris. Shot largely on location, and with an engaging non-actor, this film found favor with the critics.

With the coming of sound, Benoit-Lévy helped launch the career of a music hall star with several light comedies. But he and Marie Epstein were eager to use the new technology to bring to the screen the immediacy of the world around them. They latched onto a recent bestseller and Goncourt Prize winner, *La Maternelle*, convinced an American producer to bring it to the screen. Naturally there were compromises to be made. Although the loose plot concerning the life of an upper class teacher in a slum school was kept intact, star actors were given the major roles. Foremost among these was Madeleine Renaud. The children, however, were of the district treated in the film and the performances teased out of them by Marie Epstein are incredibly fresh even today.

The remarkable success of this unlikely little picture permitted the team to make several more semi-documentaries during the thirties, the most notable of which are *Itto* and *La Mort du cygne*, known as *Ballerina* in its American distribution. Using the students of the ballet conservatory of Paris, this film records several exciting dance numbers, but ultimately the heavy melodrama of its plot tilts the film toward standard fictional fare. Still it was an international success except in Germany where it was banned because Benoit-Lévy's name was taken to be Jewish.

After one more feature in 1939, Benoit-Lévy fled to the United States as did so many of his French colleagues. Here his educational background made him more successful than most expatriates, for he had already written a book in 1936 on the instructional film in the United States. He taught at the New School for Social Research were he prepared his second book, *The Art of the Motion Picture*.

After the war he was appointed Director of several United Nations councils on film and visual information. His last years were spent with UNESCO in Paris where he returned to making short films, particularly on ballet.

—Dudley Andrew

BERESFORD, BRUCE. Australian. Born in 1940. Educated at Sydney University. Married, 3 children. Career: late 1950s—following graduation, works briefly in advertising and for ABC TV; 1961—moves to London, works at odd jobs, teaches at girls' school, Willesden; 1964-66—film editor with East Nigerian Film Unit; 1966—returns to London, hired as secretary to British Film Institute Production Board, becomes head of production; 1966-70—produces some 86 films including 3 features; becomes known as short film documentarian, especially for work on pop crazes and on artists (*Lichtenstein in London* and *The False Mirror* on Magritte); 1971—returns to Australia following government decision to help finance film industry; begins association with producer Philip Adams; 1981—shoots *Tender Mercies* in U.S. Recipient: Best Director, Australian Film Awards, for *Don's Party*, 1976; Best Director, American Film Institute Awards, for *Don's Party*, 1977; Best Director, Australian Film Awards, for *Breaker Morant*, 1980.

Films (as feature director): 1972—*The Adventures of Barrie MacKenzie* (+sc); 1974—*Barrie MacKenzie Holds His Own* (+co-sc); 1975—*Don's Party*; 1977—*The Getting of Wisdom*; 1978—*Money Movers* (+sc); 1980—*Breaker Morant* (+co-sc); *The Club*; 1981—*Puberty Blues*; 1982—*Tender Mercies*.

Publications:

On BERESFORD:

Articles—"Bruce Beresford's New Australian Cinema" by David Robinson in *The Times* (London), 23 October 1980; "The Films of Bruce Beresford" by K. Connolly in *Cinema Papers* (Melbourne), August/September 1980; "At the Movies" by Chris Chase in *The New York Times*, 18 June 1982.

*   *   *

Thought-provoking in their scrutiny of characters and relationships, the films of Bruce Beresford also pay painstaking attention to the environment in which those relationships take place. Whether that landscape is the Australian Outback or the American southwest, he ably fuses people and places with a straightforward, often near-documentary approach. Soft white lighting, effective use of close-ups (especially of faces) and melancholy panoramic studies of breathtaking vistas are also Beresford signatures.

It was the filmmaker's *Breaker Morant* that brought international attention and acclaim to the once-dormant Australian film industry. That Beresford was at the vanguard of this renaissance (along with countrymen Fred Schepisi and Peter Weir) is especially fitting; Beresford himself underwent a renaissance of outlook pertaining to the filmic passion, and talent, of his heritage. A cinema buff during his boyhood, he nonetheless thought his countrymen were incapable of creating lasting works. Australian cinema had virtually disappeared during the forties and fifties; between the years 1941 and 1945, for instance, only five Australian features were made. A turning point occurred for him during his teenage years, when he attended a tribute to Raymond Longford, actor and director of the silent era, whose 1919 work *The Sentimental Bloke* is hailed as Australia's *Birth of a Nation*. As Beresford was later to admit, "It was the first time I realized you could make great films in Australia. If Longford could do it, so could I."

If the majority of his works are Australian in setting, they have managed to be universal in attitude. Both *The Getting of Wisdom* and *Puberty Blues* deal with youth and coming-of-age; *The Club*, ostensibly about a soccer club, delves into the politics inherent in that club. Though the popular *Breaker Morant* concerns a historical figure who occupies a sturdy niche in Australian folklore, it purposely suggests a parallel between Victorian imperialism and the United States involvement in Vietnam. As a study of wartime hypocrisy and violence, the film speaks a language that knows no national boundaries.

Beresford's sense of accuracy that manages to be both startlingly realistic and lyrically poetic. His American-made *Tender Mercies*, a look at three intensely likable people coming to terms with changes in their lives, displays those trademarks. It features mesmerizing performances (including the much-applauded work of Robert Duvall as country singer Mac Sledge). But just as important is a stirring sense of honesty that came about after Beresford toured tiny towns throughout Texas, in an effort to discover if the film's Horton Foote screenplay was "true." Only after his tour was completed did Beresford agree to tackle the project. That he did so on a modest budget (less than $4 million but still a hefty sum compared to his Australian projects, which were all made for considerably less than $1 million), and with a modicum of production difficulties, can be attributed to his astute pre-production detail (including complete storyboarding), as well as his background of making low-budget, experimental films for the British Film Institute.

Beresford's cinematic pragmatism, combined with a somewhat laconic though acute sensibility, has resulted in a body of work of considerable appeal. The biblical saga of King David is next on Beresford's agenda; the filmmaker has announced that accuracy in locations and sets, as well as an "everyday" approach by the film's actors will distinguish the work.

—Pat H. Broeske

BERGMAN, INGMAR. Swedish. Born Ernst Ingmar Bergman in Uppsala, Sweden, 14 July 1918. Educated at Palmgren's School, Stockholm; Stockholm High School (the University of Stockholm). Married dancer Else Fisher, 1943; child: Lena; married Ellen Lundström, 1945 (divorced 1950); children: Eva, Jan, Anna and Mats; married Gun Grut, 1950; child: Ingmar; married pianist Käbi Laretei, 1959 (separated 1965); child: Daniel; married Ingrid von Rosen, 1971. Career: 1938-40—begins directing career at Mäster-Olofsgården, a Christian settlement for young people, Stockholm; 1942—favorable notices for production of first play, *The Death of Punch*, leads to offer to join Svensk Filmindustri (SF) as assistant scriptwriter; 1943—signs as scriptwriter; 1944—Victor Sjöstrom, then artistic director of SF, suggests Bergman's *Torment* script to director Alf Sjöberg; appointed director of Helsingborg City Theater; 1945—begins shooting *Crisis*, using players from stage productions; 1946—begins association with independent producer Lorens Marmstedt; begins long association with Gothenburg Civic Theater; 1948—begins working with cinematographer Gunnar Fischer; early 1950s—makes some cinema commercials; 1952—meets and falls in love with Harriet Andersson; appointed director, Municipal Theater in Malmö (through 1958); during fifties works 7 months of each year in theater; 1955—begins working and personal relationship with Bibi Andersson, and begins working with Max von Sydow; 1957—directs 1st TV production *Mr. Sleeman Is Coming*; 1959—joins Royal Dramatic Theater, Stockholm; affair with Bibi Andersson ends; begins working with cinematographer Sven Nykvist; 1961—becomes artistic advisor at SF; 1963-66—head of Royal Dramatic Theater, Stockholm; 1965—during long recuperation from illness writes *Persona* script; 1965-70—lives with Liv Ullmann (daughter Linn born 1966); 1966—settles on island of Fårö, setting of several subsequent films; 1968—establishes Cinematograph production company; 1972—directs *Scenes from a Marriage* for TV; 1976—arrested for allegedly avoiding payment of personal income tax,

hospitalized for resulting breakdown; goes into self-imposed exile, settling in Munich; 1977—forms production company Personafilm in Munich, begins directing stage plays at Munich Residenzteater (through 1982); 1978—returns to Sweden; 1979—tax matter settled with small additional payment; 1982—after completing *Fanny and Alexander* announces retirement from filmmaking. Recipient: Golden Bear, Berlin Festival, for *Wild Strawberries*, 1958; Gold Plaque, Swedish Film Academy, 1958; Academy Award, Best Foreign Language Picture, for *The Virgin Spring*, 1961; Academy Award, Best Foreign Language Film, for *Through a Glass Darkly*, 1962; Erasmus Prize (shared with Charles Chaplin), Netherlands, 1965; honorary doctorate of philosophy, Stockholm University, 1975.

Films (as scriptwriter): 1944—*Hets (Torment, Frenzy)* (Sjöberg); (as director and scriptwriter): 1946—*Kris (Crisis)*; *Det regnar på vår kärlek (It Rains on Our Love, The Man with an Umbrella)* (co-sc); 1947—*Skepp till Indialand (A Ship Bound for India, The Land of Desire)*; *Kvinna utan ansikte (Woman Without a Face)* (Molander) (sc only); 1948—*Musik i mörker (Music in Darkness, Night Is My Future)* (d only); *Hamnstad (Port of Call)* (co-sc); *Eva* (Molander) (co-sc only); 1949—*Fängelse (Prison, The Devil's Wanton)*; *Törst (Thirst, 3 Strange Loves)* (d only); 1950—*Till glädje (To Joy)*; *Sånt händer inte här (High Tension, This Doesn't Happen Here)* (d only); *Medan staden sover (While the City Sleeps)* (Kjellgren) (synopsis only); 1951—*Sommarlek (Summer Interlude, Illicit Interlude)* (co-sc); *Frånskild (Divorced)* (Molander) (sc only); 1952—*Kvinnors väntan (Secrets of Women, Waiting Women)*; 1953—*Sommaren med Monika (Monika, Summer with Monika)* (co-sc); *Gycklarnas afton (The Naked Night, Sawdust and Tinsel)*; 1954—*En lektion i kärlek (A Lesson in Love)*; 1955—*Kvinnodröm (Dreams, Journey into Autumn)*; *Sommarnattens leende (Smiles of a Summer Night)*; 1956—*Sista paret ut (Last Couple Out)* (Sjöberg) (sc only); 1957—*Det sjunde inseglet (The Seventh Seal)*; *Smultronstället (Wild Strawberries)*; 1958—*Nära livet (Brink of Life, So Close to Life)* (co-sc); *Ansiktet (The Magician, The Face)*; 1960—*Jungfrukällen (The Virgin Spring)* (d only); *Djävulens öga (The Devil's Eye)*; 1961—*Såsom i en spegel (Through a Glass Darkly)*; *Lustgården (The Pleasure Garden)* (Kjellin) (co-sc only under pseudonym "Buntel Eriksson"); 1963—*Nattvardsgästerna (Winter Light)*; *Tystnaden (The Silence)*; 1964—*För att inte tala om alla dessa kvinnor (All These Women, Now About These Women)* (co-sc under pseudonym "Buntel Eriksson"); 1966—*Persona*; 1967—"Daniel" episode of *Stimulantia* (+ph); 1968—*Vargtimmen (Hour of the Wolf)*; *Skammen (Shame, The Shame)*; 1969—*Riten (The Ritual, The Rite)*; *En passion (The Passion of Anna, A Passion)*; *Fårö-dokument (The Fårö Document)*; 1971—*The Touch (Beröringen)*; 1973—*Viskningar och rop (Cries and Whispers)*; *Scener ur ett äktenskap (Scenes from a Marriage)* (+narration, voice of the photographer) in 6 episodes: "Oskuld och panik (Innocence and Panic)"; "Kunsten att sopa unter mattan (The Art of Papering Over Cracks)"; "Paula"; "Tåredalen (The Vale of Tears)"; "Analfabeterna (The Illiterates)"; "Mitt i natten i ett mörkt hus någonstans i världen (In the Middle of the Night in a Dark House Somewhere in the World)" (shown theatrically in shortened version of 168 minutes); 1974—*Kallelsen (The Vocation)* (Nykvist) (pr only); 1975—*Trollflöjten (The Magic Flute)* (for TV); 1976—*Ansikte mot ansikte (Face to Face)* (+co-pr) (for TV—originally broadcast in serial format); *Paradistorg (Summer Paradise)* (Lindblom) (pr only); 1977—*Das Schlangenei (The Serpent's Egg, Örmens ägg)*; 1978—*Herbstsonate (Autumn Sonata, Höstsonaten)*; 1979—*Fårö-dokument 1979 (Fårö 1979)* (+narration); 1980—*Aus dem Leben der Marionetten (From the Life of the*

Marionettes); 1982—Fanny och Alexander (Fanny and Alexander). Role: 1977—interviewee in A Look at Liv (Kaplan).

Publications:

By BERGMAN:

Books—4 Screenplays of Ingmar Bergman translated by Lars Malmström and David Kushner, New York 1960; The Virgin Spring translated by Lars Malmström and David Kushner, New York 1960; Oeuvres translated by G.C. Bjurström and Maurice Fons, Paris 1962; A Film Trilogy (Through a Glass Darkly, Winter Light, and The Silence), translated by Paul Austin, New York 1967; Persona and Shame translated by Keith Bradfield, New York 1972; Bergman on Bergman edited by Stig Björkman and others, translated by Paul Austin, New York 1973; Scenes from a Marriage translated by Alan Blair, New York 1974; Face to Face, translated by Alan Blair, New York 1976; 4 Stories by Ingmar Bergman translated by Alan Blair, New York 1977; The Serpent's Egg translated by Alan Blair, New York 1978; Autumn Sonata translated by Alan Blair, New York 1979; Ur Marionetternas Liv, Stockholm 1980; From the Life of the Marionettes translated by Alan Blair, New York 1980; articles—"Dreams and Shadows" in Films and Filming (London), October 1956; "Self-Analysis of a Film-Maker" in Films and Filming (London), September 1956; interview by Jean Béranger in Cahiers du cinéma (Paris), October 1958; "Chacun de mes films est le dernier" in Cahiers du cinéma (Paris), no.100, 1959; "Each Film is My Last" in Films and Filming (London), July 1959; "Bergman on Victor Sjöström" in Sight and Sound (London), spring 1960; "A Page from My Diary" in Cinéma 60 (Paris), November/December 1960; "Wood Painting: A Morality Play" in Tulane Drama Review (Louisiana), 1961; "Interview" in Playboy (Chicago), June 1964; "The Snakeskin" in Sight and Sound (London), August 1965; "Ingmar Bergman: The Serpent's Skin" in Cahiers du Cinéma in English (New York), September 1967; transcription of Shame press conference in Continental Film Review (London), December 1967; "Schizophrenic Interview with a Nervous Film Director" by 'Ernest Riffe' (pseudonym for Bergman) in Film in Sweden (Stockholm), no.3, 1968, and in Take One (Montreal), January/February 1969; "Moment of Agony", interview by Lars-Olof Löthwall in Films and Filming (London), February 1969; "Conversations avec Ingmar Bergman" by Jan Aghed in Positif (Paris), November 1970; interview by Cynthia Grenier in Oui (New York), no.3, 1974; interview by William Wolf in New York, 27 October 1980.

On BERGMAN:

Books—Flashback 1: Ingmar Bergman by Alberto Tabbia and Edgardo Cozarinsky, Buenos Aires 1958; Ingmar Bergman et ses films by Jean Béranger, Paris 1959; Ingmar Bergman: teatermannen och filmskaparen by Fritiof Billquist, Stockholm 1960; Thèmes d'inspiration d'Ingmar Bergman by Jos. Burvenich, Brussels 1960; Ingmar Bergman by Jacques Siclier, Paris 1960; Ingmar Bergman by Marianne Höök, Stockholm 1962; Ingmar Bergman by Tommaso Chiaretti, Rome 1964; The Personal Vision of Ingmar Bergman by Jörn Donner, Bloomington, Indiana 1964; Ingmar Bergman by Jean Béranger and François Guyon, Lyon 1964; Ingmar Bergman: The Search for God by David Nelson, Boston 1964; La Crisi spirituali dell'uomo moderno nei film di Ingmar Bergman by Massimo Maisetti, Varese 1964; La Solitudine di Ingmar Bergman by Guido Oldrini, Parma 1965; Ingmar Bergman på teatern by Henrik Sjögren, Stockholm 1968; Ingmar Bergman by Birgitta Steene, New York 1968; The Silence of God: Creative Response to the Films of Ingmar Bergman by Arthur Gibson, New York 1969; Ingmar Bergman by Robin Wood, New York 1969; Regi: Ingmar Bergman by Henrik Sjögren, Stockholm 1970; Cinema Borealis: Ingmar Bergman and the Swedish Ethos by Vernon Young, New York 1971; Ingmar Bergman Directs by John Simon, New York 1972; Focus on The Seventh Seal by Birgitta Steene, Englewood Cliffs, New Jersey 1972; Encountering Directors by Charles Samuels, New York 1972; Bergman och Strindberg by Egil Törnqvist, Stockholm 1973; Ingmar Bergman by Tino Ranieri, Florence 1974; Ingmar Bergman: Essays in Criticism edited by Stuart Kaminsky, New York 1975; Changing by Liv Ullmann, New York 1976; Ingmar Bergman and Society by Maria Bergom-Larsson, San Diego 1978; L. 136. Diary with Ingmar Bergman by Vilgot Sjöman, translated by Alan Blair, Ann Arbor, Michigan 1978; Mindscreen: Bergman, Godard and the First-Person Film by Bruce Kawin, Princeton 1978; Der frühe Ingmar Bergman by Hauke Lange-Fuchs, Lübeck 1978; Ingmar Bergman by Denis Marion, Paris 1979; Ingmar Bergman: An Appreciation by Roger Manvell, New York 1980; My Story by Ingrid Bergman with Alan Burgess, New York 1980; Ingmar Bergman: The Cinema as Mistress by Philip Mosley, Boston 1981; Film and Dreams: An Approach to Bergman edited by Vlada Petrić, South Salem, New York 1981; Ingmar Bergman: A Critical Biography by Peter Cowie, New York 1982; Ingmar Bergman: 4 Decades in the Theatre by Lise-Lone and Frederick Marker, Cambridge, England 1982; A Reference Guide to Ingmar Bergman by Birgitta Steene, Boston 1982; articles—"Ingmar Bergman" by Claude Gauteur in Cinéma 58 (Paris), July/August 1958; "Bergmanorama" by Jean-Luc Godard in Cahiers du cinéma (Paris), July 1958; "Ingmar Bergman and the Devil" by Erik Ulrichsen in Sight and Sound (London), summer 1958; "The Rack of Life" by Eugene Archer in Film Quarterly (Berkeley), summer 1959; "Ingmar Bergman, Magician of Swedish Cinema" by Paul Austin in Anglo-Swedish Review (London), April 1959; "Bergman as Writer" by Hollis Alpert in Saturday Review (New York), 27 August 1960; "Style Is the Director" by Hollis Alpert in Saturday Review (New York), 23 December 1961; "Les Visages de la passion dans l'univers de Bergman" by Pierre Renaud in La Passion du Christ comme thème cinématographique edited by Michel Estève, Paris 1961; "Photographing the Films of Ingmar Bergman" by Sven Nykvist in American Cinematographer (Los Angeles), October 1962; "Ingmar Bergman: The Listener" by Oscar Hedlund in Saturday Review (New York), 29 February 1964; "L'Univers d'Ingmar Bergman" by Alain Hervé in Réalités (Paris), February 1964; "Bergmans trilogi" by Göran Persson in Chaplin (Stockholm), no.40, 1964; "Ants in a Snakeskin" by Frederic Fleisher in Sight and Sound (London), autumn 1965; "Der Spiegel ist verschlagen" by Frieda Grafe in Filmkritik (Frankfurt), November 1968; "Triebhaus der Neurosen: der frühe Bergman" by Herbert Holba in Action (Vienna), October 1968; Ingmar Bergman by Raymond Lefèvre in Image et son (Paris), March 1969; "A Visit with Ingmar Bergman" by A. Alvarez in New York Times Magazine, 7 December 1975; "Learning 'A Few Words in the Foreign Language': Ingmar Bergman's 'Secret Message' in the Imagery of Hand and Face" by Fritz Sammern-Frankenegg in Scandinavian Studies, summer 1977; "Ingmar Bergman: I Confect Dreams and Anguish" by Edith Sorel in The New York Times, 22 January 1978; "Ingmar Bergman: 'The Struggle with the Beyond'" by Peter Cowie in The New York Times, 26 October 1980; "From the Life of the Marionettes to The Devil's Wanton" by Marsha Kinder in Film Quarterly (Berkeley), spring 1981; films—appearance in The Directors produced by Nat Greenblatt, 1963; Tre scener med

Ingmar Bergman (3 Scenes with Ingmar Bergman) directed for Finnish TV by Jörn Donner, 1975; The Bergman File directed by Jörn Donner, 1978.

*   *   *

Bergman's unique international status as filmmaker would seem assured on many grounds: his prolific output of largely notable work (40 features 1946-82); the profoundly personal nature of his best films since the 1950s; the innovative nature of his technique combined with its essential simplicity even when employing surrealistic and dream-like treatments (as, for example, in Wild Strawberries and Persona); his creative sensitivity in relation to his players; and his extraordinary capacity to evoke distinguished acting from his regular interpreters, notably Gunnar Björnstrand, Max von Sydow, Bibi Andersson, Ingrid Thulin and Liv Ullmann.

After an initial period of derivative, melodramatic filmmaking largely concerned with bitter man-woman relationships ("I just grabbed helplessly at any form that might save me, because I hadn't any of my own," he owns in Bergman on Bergman), Bergman reached an initial maturity of style in Summer Interlude and Summer with Monika, romantic studies of adolescent love and subsequent disillusionment. In The Naked Night he used a derelict travelling circus—its proprietor with a faithless young mistress and its clown with a faithless middle-aged wife—as a symbol of human suffering through misplaced love and the ultimate loneliness of the human condition, a theme common to much of his work. Not that Bergman's films are all gloom and disillusionment. He has a recurrent, if veiled, sense of humour. His comedies, A Lesson in Love and Smiles of a Summer Night are ironically effective ("You're a gynocologist who knows nothing about women," says the man's mistress in A Lesson in Love), and even in Wild Strawberries the aged professor's relations with his housekeeper offer comic relief. Bergman's later comedies, the Shavian The Devil's Eye and Now About All These Women are both sharp and fantastic.

"To me, religious problems are continuously alive...not...on the emotional level, but on an intellectual one," wrote Bergman at the time of Wild Strawberries, The Seventh Seal, The Virgin Spring, Through a Glass Darkly, Winter Light, and The Silence lead progressively through to the rejection of religious belief, leaving only the conviction that human life is haunted by "a virulent, active evil." The crusading knight of The Seventh Seal who cannot face death once his faith is lost survives only to witness the cruelty of religious persecution. Faith belongs to the simple-minded and innocent. The Virgin Spring exposes the violence of vengeance in a period of primitive Christianity. Bergman no longer likes these films, considering them "bogus"; nevertheless, they are excellently made in his highly professional style. Disillusionment with Lutheran denial of love is deep in Winter Light, and the mad girl in Through a Glass Darkly perceives God as a spider. "In Winter Light I swept my house clean," Bergman has said, and the ailing sister in The Silence faces death with the loneliness that passes all understanding as a result of the frigid silence of God in the face of her sufferings. However, in The Face Bergman takes sardonic delight in letting the rationalistic miracle-man in the end suspect that his bogus miracles are in fact genuine.

With Wild Strawberries Bergman turned increasingly to psychological dilemmas and ethical issues in human and social relations once religion had proved a failure. Above all else love, understanding and common humanity seem lacking. The aged medical professor in Wild Strawberries comes through a succession of dreams to realize the truth about his cold and loveless nature. In Persona, the most psychologically puzzling, contro-

versial, yet significant of all Bergman's films, with its Brechtian alienation of technique and surreal treatment of dual personality, the self-imposed silence of the actress stems from her failure in love for husband and son, though she responds with horror to the self-destructive violence in the world around her. This latter theme is carried still further in The Shame in which an egocentric musician attempts non-involvement in his country's war only to collapse into irrational acts of violence himself through sheer panic. The Shame and Hour of the Wolf are concerned with artists who are too self-centered to care about the larger issues of the society in which they live.

"It wasn't until A Passion that I really got to grips with the man-woman relationship," says Bergman; this film deals with "the dark, destructive forces" in human nature which sexual urges can inspire. Bergman's later films reflect, he claims, his "ceaseless fascination with the whole race of women," adding that "the film...should communicate psychic states." The love and understanding needed by women is too often denied them, witness the case of the various women about to give birth in Brink of Life and the fearful, haunted, loveless family relationships in Cries and Whispers the latter, with The Shame and The Serpent's Egg is surely among the most terrifying of Bergman's films, though photographed in exquisite color by Bergman's principal cinematographer, Sven Nykvist.

Man-woman relationships are successively and uncompromisingly examined in The Touch, showing a married woman driven out of her emotional depth in an extra-marital affair; in Face to Face, one of Bergman's most moving films, concerning the nervous breakdown of a cold-natured woman analyst and the hallucinations she suffers; and in his film made in series for television, but reissued more effectively in a shortened, reedited form for the cinema, Scenes from A Marriage, about the troubled, long-term love of a professional couple who are divorced but unable to endure separation. Supreme performances were given by Bibi Andersson in Persona and The Touch, and by Liv Ullmann in Cries and Whispers, Scenes from a Marriage and Face to Face.

Bergman's latest films, made in Sweden or during his period of self-imposed exile, are more miscellaneous. The Magic Flute is one of the best, most delightful of opera-films, The Serpent's Egg a savage study in the sadistic origins of Nazism, and Autumn Sonata the case of a mother who cannot love. Bergman has declared his filmmaking at an end with his brilliant, German-made misanthropic study of a fatal marriage, From the Life of the Marionettes, and the semi-autobiographical television series Fanny and Alexander, Swedish produced, and with a reedited version for the cinema.

—Roger Manvell

BERKELEY, BUSBY. American. Born Busby Berkeley William Enos in Los Angeles, 29 November 1895. Educated Mohegan Military Academy, Peekskill, New York, 1907-1914. Married 1st wife, late 1920's (divorced 1930); Merna Kennedy, 1934 (divorced mid 1930's); Claire James, mid 1930s (annulled same year); Myra Steffin, 1944 (annulled 1944); Marge Pemberton, mid 1940s (divorced mid 1950's); Etta Dunn Judd, 1958. Career: 1900—makes 1st appearance on stage in New York City; 1914-17—works in shoe store in Athol, Massachusetts where he directs a dance band in his spare time; 1917—joins U.S. Army, is selected to attend Saumer Artillery School in France; 1917-19—while in the military, duties include choreographing and rehearsing marching drills for both the U.S. and French armies; after war organizes stage shows to tour army camps; 1919—begins acting in road companies and summer stock; 1923-27—works at various jobs in the theater such as stage manager, dance director, and actor; choreographs *A Connecticut Yankee* on Broadway; 1928—directs 1st show on Broadway, *A Night in Venice*; 1930—hired by Samuel Goldwyn to direct dance numbers in musical films beginning with *Whoopee*; 1935—arrested for manslaughter after hitting 3 people with his auto, acquitted after several trials; 1939—hired by MGM as a director and dance advisor; 1943—returns to Warners; 1944—released from Warners contract, returns to Broadway to direct and stage *Glad to See You*; mid 1940s—suffers nervous breakdown; 1948—returns to film supervising musical numbers in Warner Bros. *Romance on the High Seas*; 1949—directs last film *Take Me Out to the Ballgame*; 1950-54—directs musical numbers for various films; 1962—choreographs circus numbers in MGM's *Jumbo*; 1971—supervises production of Broadway revival of *No, No, Nanette* starring Ruby Keeler. Died 14 March 1976.

Films (as choreographer): 1930—*Whoopee*; 1931—*Palmy Days*; *Flying High*; 1932—*Night World*; *Bird of Paradise*; *The Kid from Spain*; 1933—*42nd Street*; *Gold Diggers of 1933*; *Footlight Parade*; *Roman Scandals*; *She Had to Say Yes* (+co-d); 1934—*Wonder Bar*; *Fashions of 1934*; *Dames*; 1935—*Go Into Your Dance*; *In Caliente*; *Stars Over Broadway*; (as director and choreographer): 1935—*Gold Diggers of 1935*; *Bright Lights*; *I Live for Love*; 1936—*Stage Struck*; 1937—*Gold Diggers of 1937* (ch only); *The Go-Getter*; *Hollywood Hotel*; *The Singing Marine* (ch only); *Varsity Show* (ch only); 1938—*Men Are Such Fools*; *Garden of the Moon*; *Comet over Broadway*; *Gold Diggers in Paris* (ch only); 1939—*They Made Me a Criminal*; *Babes in Arms*; *Fast and Furious*; *Broadway Serenade* (ch only); 1940—*Strike Up the Band*; *40 Little Mothers*; 1941—*Blonde Inspiration*; *Babes on Broadway*; *Ziegfeld Girl* (ch only); *Lady Be Good* (ch only); *Born to Sing* (ch only); 1942—*For Me and My Gal*; 1943—*The Gang's All Here*; *Girl Crazy* (ch only); 1946—*Cinderella Jones*; 1949—*Take Me Out to the Ballgame*; (as choreographer): 1950—*2 Weeks with Love*; 1951—*Call Me Mister*; *2 Tickets to Broadway*; 1952—*Million Dollar Mermaid*; 1953—*Small Town Girl*; *Easy to Love*; 1954—*Rose Marie*; 1962—*Jumbo*. Role: 1970—cameo appearance in *The Phynx*.

Publications:

By BERKELEY:

Book—*The Busby Berkeley Book*, with Tony Thomas and Jim Terry, New York 1973; articles—interview by John Gruen in *Close-Up*, New York 1968; "Entrevista con Busby Berkeley" by P. Brion and R. Gilson in *Contracampo* (Madrid), September 1981.

On BERKELEY:

Books—*The Making of 'No, No Nanette'* by Don Dunn, New York 1972; *The Genius of Busby Berkeley* by Bob Pike and Dave Martin, Reseda, California 1973; *The Warner Bros. Story* by Clive Hirschhorn, New York 1979; articles—"Berkeley and Santell: letter" by R. F. Cort in *Films in Review* (New York), June-July 1957; "Conversation with Roger Edens" by A. Johnson in *Sight and Sound* (London), spring 1958; "Likable but Elusive" by Andrew Sarris in *Film Culture* (New York), spring 1963; "Current Cinema" by B. Gill in *New Yorker*, 4 December

1965; "100 Lighted Violins" in *Newsweek* (New York), 13 December 1965; "The Great Busby" by P. Jenkinson in *Film* (London), spring 1966; "Dancing Images" by J.-L. Comolli and "A Style of Spectacle" by P. Brion and R. Gilson in *Cahiers du Cinéma in English* (New York), no.2, 1966; "A Berkeley Evening" by D.L. Bevis in *Films in Review* (New York), June/July 1967; "The Machineries of Joy" by John Thomas in *Film Society Review* (New York), February 1967; "Busby Berkeley" by R.C. Roman in *Dance* (New York), February 1968; "Where Are They Now" in *Newsweek* (New York), 8 April 1968; "The 3 Ages of the Musical" by George Sidney in *Films and Filming* (London), June 1968; "Return of Busby Berkeley" by W. Murray in the *New York Times Magazine*, 2 March 1969; "Busby Berkeley and his Gorgeous Girls" in *Vogue* (New York), May 1970; "What Directors are Saying" in *Action* (Los Angeles), May/June 1970; "Busby and Ruby" by D. Gorton in *Newsweek* (New York), 3 August 1970; "Busby Berkeley's Girls Glitter Again" by H. Winge in *Life* (New York), 19 February 1971; "Hollywood Dance Directors Were More Than Busby Berkeley" by G. Fernett in *Classic Film Collector* (Indiana, Pennsylvania), summer 1972; "Busby Berkeley" by Arthur Knight in *Action* (Los Angeles), May/June 1974; obituary by H. Béhar in *Image et son* (Paris), May 1976; "Some Warners Musicals and the Spirit of the New Deal" by M. Roth in *Velvet Light Trap* (Madison), winter 1977; "Busby Berkeley 1895-1976" by Max Tessier in *Avant-Scène du cinéma* (Paris), 15 April 1978; "Busby Berkeley: an American Surrealist" by J. Delameter in *Wide Angle* (Athens, Ohio), v.1, no.1, 1979; "Los mágicos delirios de Busby Berkeley" by T. Pérez Turrent in *Cine* (Mexico), December 1979.

*   *   *

No American film director explored the possibilities of the mobile camera more fully or ingeniously than Busby Berkeley. He was the Méliès of the musical, the corollary of Vertov in the exploration of the possibilities of cinematic movement. His influence has since been felt from movie musicals to television commercials.

Certain aspects of Berkeley's personal history are obvious in their importance to a discussion of his cinematic work, most specifically his World War I service and his work in the theatre. Born to a theatrical family, Berkeley learned early of the demands of the theatrical profession: when his father died, his mother refused to take the night off, instilling in Busby the work ethic of "the show must go on." Throughout most of his career, Gertrude Berkeley and her ethic reigned, no wife successfully displacing her as spiritual guide and confidante until after her death in 1948, while Berkeley drove himself at the expense of his many marriages.

Berkeley's World War I service was significant for the images he created in his musical sequences. He designed parade drills for both the French and U.S. armies and his later service as an aerial observer with the Air Corps formed the basis of an aesthetic which incorporated images of order and symmetry often seen from the peculiar vantage of an overhead position. In addition, that training developed his approach to economical direction which included storyboarding to effect his editing-in-the-camera approach, and the blackboard instruction of chorines by which he illustrated the formations they were to achieve.

Returning from war, Berkeley found work as a stage actor, his first role directed by John Cromwell with Gertrude serving as his dramatic coach. He soon graduated to direction and choreography, in 1929 becoming the first man on Broadway to direct a musical for which he also staged the dance numbers, setting a precedent for such talents as Jerome Robbins, Gower Champion, Bob Fosse and Tommy Tune. When Samuel Goldwyn invited him to Hollywood in 1930 as a dance director, that Broadway division of labor was in effect and Berkeley had to wait until *Golddiggers of 1935* before being allowed to do both jobs on the same film.

From 1933 through 1939 Berkeley worked for Warner Bros. where he created a series of dance numbers which individually and collectively represent much of the best Hollywood product of the period. An examination of his work in this period in relation to the Production Code and the developing conventions of the musical genre illustrates his unique contribution to cinema.

Boy/girl romance and the success story were standard narrative ingredients of thirties musicals and Berkeley's work contributed significantly to the formulation of these conventions. Where he was unique was in his visualization of the on-stage as opposed to the back stage segments of these dramas. Relying on his war service, he began to fashion on-stage spectacles which had been impossible on the Broadway stage. In his films he was able to explode any notion of the limitations of a proscenium stage and the relationship of the theater spectator to it: the fixed perspective of that audience was abandoned for one which lacked defined spatial or temporal coordinates. His camera was regularly mounted on a crane (or on the monorail he invented) and swooped over and around or toward and away from performers in a style of choreography for camera which was more elaborate than that mapped out for the dancers. Amusingly, in his direction of non-musical scenes, he generally reversed this procedure, making the back stage dramas appear confined within a stage-space and bound to the traditions of theatrical staging and dialogue.

As he created the illusion of theatre in his musical numbers, so too he created the illusion of dance. Having never studied dance, he rarely relied on trained dancers, preferring to create movement through cinematic rather than choreographic means. Occasionally when he would include sophisticated dance routines, such as in the Lullaby of Broadway number from *Golddiggers of 1935*, he would highlight the dancers' virtuosity in a series of shots which preserved the integrity of their movement without infringing on the stylistics of his camerawork.

The virtuosity of his camera movement remains important not only for a discussion of aesthetics, but also for the meaning Berkeley brought to the depiction of sexual fantasy and spectacle in a period of Hollywood history when the Production Code Administration was keeping close watch over screen morality. Throughout the thirties, Berkeley's camera caressed as if involved in foreplay, penetrated space as if seeking sexual gratification, and soared in an approximation of sexual ecstasy. Whether tracking through the legs of a line of chorus girls in *42nd Street*, swooping over an undulating vagina-shaped construction of pianos in *Golddiggers of 1935*, or caressing gigantic bananas manipulated by scantily clad chorines in *The Gang's All Here*, his sexual innuendos were titillating in both their obviousness and seeming naiveté. Berkeley's ability to inject such visual excitement meant that he was often called upon to rescue a troubled picture by adding one or more extravagantly staged musical numbers.

After leaving Warner Bros. in 1939, he returned to MGM where, although generally less innovative, his work set precedents for the genre: he directed the first Judy Garland/Mickey Rooney musical, the first Garland/Gene Kelly film, and with his last effort as a director, introduced the team of Gene Kelly and Stanley Donen. Undoubtedly the master director of American musicals in the first decade of sound film and a huge influence on many of the musical talents of succeeding decades, Berkeley worked only occasionally through the fifties, staging musical

numbers for various studios, his last being in the 1962 MGM film, *Jumbo*.

With the nostalgia craze of the late sixties, Berkeley's aesthetic was resurrected and in 1971 he triumphantly returned to the Broadway stage where he directed a revival of the twenties hit *No, No, Nanette*, starring his leading lady of the thirties, Ruby Keeler, herself in retirement for 30 years. That moment was surely the fulfillment of all the success stories he had directed over his long career.

—Doug Tomlinson

BERTOLUCCI, BERNARDO; Italian. Born in Parma, Italy, 16 March 1940. Attended University of Rome, about 1960-61. Career: 1952—writes poetry which is published in several periodicals; 1955—obtains 16mm movie camera and begins making amateur films; early 1950s—family moves to Rome; 1961—meets father's friend Pier Paolo Pasolini, becomes assistant director on Pasolini's *Accatone*; 1962—at suggestion of producer Antonio Cervi, directs *La commare secca*, adapted from story by Pasolini; publishes book of poetry *In cerca del mistero*;1965-66—directs and writes 3-part TV documentary, *La vie del Petrolio*, for Italian oil company in Iran; 1966-67—collaborates on scripts of *Ballata de un milliardo* (Puccini) and *Once Upon a Time in the West* (Leone); 1967—works with Julian Beck and Living Theater on episode in *Amore e rabbia*; late 1960s—joins Italian Communist Party (PCI); 1971-72—directs 2 films for PCI, *La salute è malata* on health reforms and unfinished short on work at home; 1972—leaves for Paris to make *Last Tango in Paris*. Address: Via del Balbuino 51, Rome, Italy.

Films (as director and scriptwriter): 1962—*La commare secca (The Grim Reaper)*; 1964—*Prima della rivoluzione (Before the Revolution)* (co-sc); 1965-66—*La vie del Petrolio*; *Il canale*; 1966-67—*Ballata de un milliardo (co-sc only)*; 1967—*"Il fico infruttuoso" episode of Amore e rabbia (Vangelo 70), Love and Anger)*; *C'era una volta il West (Once Upon a Time in the West)* (Leone) (co-sc only); 1968—*Partner* (co-sc); 1969—*La strategia del ragno (The Spider's Strategem)* (co-sc); 1970—*Il conformista (The Conformist)*; 1971—*La saluta e malato o I poveri muorioro prima (La Sante est malade ou Les Pauvres meurent les premiers)*; *L'inchiesa (co-sc only)*; 1972—*Ultimo tango a Parigi (Le Dernier Tango à Paris, Last Tango in Paris)* (co-sc); 1976—*1900 (Novecento)* (presented in 2 parts in Italy: Novecento atto I and Novecento atto II) (co-sc); 1979—*La luna* (co-sc); 1981—*La tragedia di un uomo ridicolo (La Tragedie d'un homme ridicule)*.

Publications:

By BERTOLUCCI:

Books—*In cerca del mistero*, Milan 1962; articles—interview by

Jacques Bontemps and Louis Marcorelles in *Cahiers du cinéma* (Paris), March 1965; "A Conversation with Bernardo Bertolucci" by John Bragin in *Film Quarterly* (Berkeley), fall 1966; "Versus Godard" in *Cahiers du cinéma* (Paris), January 1967; **"Versus Godard" in *Cahiers du Cinema in English* (New York), May 1967;** "Le Monde entier dans une chambre" in *Cahiers du cinéma* (Paris), no.194, 1967; "Prima della rivoluzione" in *Avant-Scène du cinéma* (Paris), June 1968; "Bernardo Bertolucci: An Interview" by Amos Vogel in *Film Comment* (New York), fall 1971; "Bertolucci on *The Conformist*" by Marilyn Goldin in *Sight and Sound* (London), spring 1971; "Conversazione con Bertolucci" by G. Bachmann in *Filmcritica* (Rome), September 1972; "Every Sexual Relationship is Condemned: Interview" by Gideon Bachmann in *Film Quarterly* (Berkeley), spring 1973; "Au cinéma le temps se glisse entre les choses et les gens...", interview by M. Amiel in *Cinéma* (Paris), January 1973; interview by M. Ciment and G. Legrand in *Positif* (Paris), March 1973; interview by M. Martin in *Ecran* (Paris), February 1973; "A Conversation with Bernardo Bertolucci" by Joan Mellen in *Cinéaste* (New York), v.5, no.4, 1973; interview by A. Tassone in *Image et son* (Paris), February 1973; "Dialogue on Film" in *American Film* (Washington, D.C.), April 1974; "Dialogue: Bertolucci and Aldrich" in *Action* (Los Angeles), March/April 1974; "Bertolucci: un demi-siècle d'histoire en Emilie", interview by G. Braucourt, in *Ecran* (Paris), December 1974; "Films Are Animal Events", interview by G. Bachmann in *Film Quarterly* (Berkeley), autumn 1975; interview and review of *1900* by D. Buckley and others in *Cineaste* (New York), winter 1976/77; interview by G. Bachmann in *Cinéma 76* (Paris), January 1976; "Propos de Bernardo Bertolucci", interview by G. Braucourt in *Ecran* (Paris), October 1976; "Klassenkampf mit harter Währung: im September kommt Bertoluccis *1900* in deutschen Kinos", interview by E. Kocian in *Film und Ton* (Munich), July 1976; "Bertolucci dans la polemique sur *1900*", interview by A. Tournes, in *Jeune cinéma* (Paris), September/October 1976; "History Lessons", interview by D. Young, in *Film Comment* (New York), November/December 1977; interview by D. O'Grady in *Cinema Papers* (Melbourne), July 1977; "*1900* rosa rote Dollars—gefälschte Bauern?" by B. Steinborn in *Filmfaust* (Frankfurt), April/May 1977; interview by Gordon Gow in *Films and Filming* (London), June 1978; "Vom Monolog zum Epos", interview by A. Karaganov, in *Film und Fernsehen* (Berlin), April 1978; "Förslag till alternativ verklighet", interview by S. Larsson and A. Sandgren, in *Chaplin* (Stockholm), v.20, no.6, 1978; "Luna and the Critics", interview by G. Crowdus and D. Georgakas in *Cineaste* (New York), winter 1979/80; "Bertolucci parle de *La Luna*" in *Jeune cinéma* (Paris), October 1979; interview by Michel Ciment and G. Legrand in *Positif* (Paris), November 1979; "Luna: the Last Taboo", interview by Jonathan Cott in *Rolling Stone* (New York), 15 November 1979; interview by G. Gosetti in *Ecran* (Paris), 20 October 1979; "Bertolucci on *La Luna*", interview by Richard Roud, in *Sight and Sound* (London), no.4, 1979; "Bernardo Bertolucci on *Luna*", interview by M. Sclauzero, in *Interview* (New York), October 1979; "Don't stop till you've had enough: San Sebastian '79", interview by A. Stuart, in *Films and Filming* (London), November 1979; "Dialogue on Film: Bernardo Bertolucci" in *American Film* (Washington, D.C.), January/February 1980; "J'ai toujours en moi un film que vous n'avez pas encore vu" in *Cinéma* (Paris), October 1981.

On BERTOLUCCI:

Books—*Le Cinéma italien* by Pierre Leprohon, Paris 1966; *The Film Director as Superstar* by Joseph Gelmis, Garden City, New York 1970; *Women and Sexuality in the New Film* by Joan Mellen, New York 1973; *Bertolucci* by F. Casetti, Florence 1975; articles—"Le Nouveau Cinéma italien" by Raymond Borde and André Bovisy in *Premier Plan* (Lyon), no.30, 1963; "Starburst by a Gifted 22-Year Old" by Pauline Kael in *Life* (New York), 13 August 1965; "Tourner avec Bertolucci" by Julian Beck in *Cahiers du cinéma* (Paris), October 1967; "Current Cinema" by Pauline Kael in the *New Yorker*, 13 January 1968; "Les Vacances rouges" by Roger Tailleur in *Positif* (Paris), May 1968; "Fathers and Sons" by Richard Roud in *Sight and Sound* (London), spring 1971; "Bernardo Bertolucci, an Italian young master" by R. Kreitzman in *Film* (London), spring 1971; "Bernardo Bertolucci" by N. Purdon in *Cinema* (London), no.8, 1971; special issue, including interview, of *Cinema* (Zurich), December 1972; "Last Tango in Paris" by Richard Roud in *Sight and Sound* (London), summer 1972; article in *Newsweek* (New York), 12 February 1973; article in *The New York Times*, 2 and 11 February 1973; "Bertolucci and the Dance of Danger" by Marsha Kinder and B. Houston in *Sight and Sound* (London), autumn 1973; "Le Dernier Tango à Paris" in *Avant-Scène du cinéma* (Paris), February 1973; article on filming of *1900* in *Sight and Sound* (London), winter 1974/75; "The Father Figure in The Conformist and in Last Tango in Paris" by D. Lopez in *Film Heritage* (New York), summer 1976; "*1900*—die Emilia Romagna, Verdi, Bertolucci" by F. Hanck in *Film und Ton* (Munich), November 1976; "Bertolucci's Gay Images" by W. Aitken in *Jump Cut* (Berkeley), November 1977; "Notes on some European directors" by A. Greenberg in *American Film* (Washington, D.C.), October 1977; "Bertolucci: 3 miradas sobre el Fascismo" by A. Volpone in *Cine* (Mexico), May 1979; "Bertolucci: He's Not Afraid to Be Shocking" by M. Kakutani in *The New York Times*, 4 October 1979; "Embarrass me more!" by P. Schwartzman in *Film Comment* (New York), November/December 1979; "La Luna" special issue of *Avant-Scène du cinéma* (Paris), 15 November 1980; "History as Myth and Myth as History in Bertolucci's *1900*" by A. Horton in *Film and History* (Newark, N.J.), February 1980; "Bernardo Bertolucci" by J.G. Requena and others in *Contracampo* (Madrid), March/April 1980; "Bernardo Bertolucci réévalué" by Pierre Verbraeken, Gilbert Cabasso, and Leila Weiss in *Cinéma* (Paris), October 1981; "Biofilmographie commentée de Bernardo Bertolucci" by Joël Magny in *Cinéma* (Paris), October 1981; "Form as Fatherscape: Bolognini and Bertolucci" by R.T. Witcombe in *The New Italian Cinema: Studies in Dance and Despair*, 1983.

*   *   *

At the age of 21, Bernardo Bertolucci established himself as a major artist in two distinct art forms, winning a prestigious award in poetry and receiving high critical acclaim for his initial film, *La commare secca*. This combination of talents is evident in all of his films, which have a lyric but exceptionally concrete style. As a poet, Bertolucci obtained the Italian Premiro Viareggio prize in 1962 for the collection entitled *In cerca del mistero*; he has been publishing poetry since childhood, benefiting from an early immersion in a literary milieu. His father, Attilio Bertolucci, was famous in his own right as a critic, professor, and poet, and in 1961 introduced Bernardo to Pier Paolo Pasolini, an esteemed literary figure. This friendship led both writers, ironically, away from poetry and into the cinema. Serving as the assistant director on Pasolini's inaugural film, *Accatone*, Bertolucci was very quickly entrusted with the full direction of Pasolini's next project, *La commara secca*, based on a story by the writer. Considering the youth and inexperience of the young artist, the decision by the producer, Antonio Cervi, to place Bertolucci in charge was a bold and prescient move.

La commare secca is an auspicious debut; as both screenwriter and director, Bertolucci found at once the high visual style and narrative complexity which distinguish his later films. The sex murder of a prostitute is its central narrative event; as the probable witnesses and suspects are brought in for questioning, a series of lives are unraveled, with each sad story winding toward the city park where the murder occurred. Formally, the film is an ambitious amalgam of a film noir atmosphere and narrative style with a neorealist concentration on behavioral detail and realistic settings.

In *Before The Revolution*, which won a prize at the Cannes Film Festival of 1964, Bertolucci first presents the theme which will become foremost in his work: the conflict between freedom and conformity. Fabrizio, the leading character, is obliged to decide between radical political commitment and an alluring marriage into the bourgeoisie. Drifting into an incestuous affair with his aunt, he in effect stacks the deck against an authentic life, giving himself no alternative but to reform—and to live in a conventional manner. To this reworking of Stendhal's *The Charterhouse of Parma*, Bertolucci expressly delineates the connection between politics and sexuality. The film also establishes the Freudian theme of the totemic father, which will recur throughout Bertolucci's work, here emblematized in the figure of Fabrizio's communist mentor, whom Fabrizio must renounce as a precondition to his entry into moneyed society.

Bertolucci diverged from the style of his first two critically successful films with *The Partner*, a complex, experimental work based on Doestoevski's *The Double*. Heavily influenced by the films of Godard and the events of May '68, it eschews narrative exposition, developing instead a critique of literary consumerism, academic pacifism, and the student left, through a series of polemical debates between a bookish student and his radical double. The film marks Bertolucci's first use of color in a theatrical film, heralding what will soon become a major stylistic feature. For the most part, however, *The Partner* is an anomalous film, which conveys very little of the heightened lyricism of his major works.

With *The Spider's Strategem*, originally made for television in 1969, and *The Conformist*, Bertolucci combines an experimental narrative technique with lavish visual design, achieving in *The Conformist* an unprecedented commercial and critical triumph. Sexuality is here explicitly posited as the motor of political allegiance, as Marcello, the lead character in *The Conformist*, becomes a Fascist in order to suppress his growing recognition of of his homosexuality. The character performs an outlandishly deviant act—killing his former professor, now a member of the Resistance, in order to declare his own conventionality and membership in the Fascist order. Conformity and rebellion are thus folded together, not only in the psyche of Marcello, but in the culture as a whole, as Bertolucci examines the interpenetrating structures, the twin pathologies, of family and politics. Bertolucci here unveils the full range of stylistic features—the elaborate tracking shots, the opulent color photography (realized by the virtuoso cinematographer Vittorio Storara), the odd, surrealistic visual incongruities—that give his work such a distinctive surface. It is here, also, that Bertolucci connects most directly with the general evolution of the post war Italian cinema. Beginning with Visconte, and continuing with Antonioni and Bellochio, an increasing emphasis is placed on the psychology of transgression, a motif which links politics and the libido. The inner life of the alienated protagonist becomes the lens displaying the spectrum of social forces, as the politics of the state are viewed in the mimetic behavior of disturbed individuals.

In *Last Tango in Paris* a similar study is carried out, and rendered in a classical style that conforms to Aristotle's definition of the three dramatic unities. The film depicts the last week in the life of Paul, played by Marlon Brando, as a man who is both geographically and spiritually in exile. His orbit crosses that of "the girl," played by Maria Schneider. The raw sexual encounters which ensue serve as a kind of purgation for the Brando character, who retaliates against the hypocrisy of cultural institutions such as family, church and state through the medium of Jeanne's body. Sex is used as a weapon and symbolic cure, as the libidinal rage of the character is focused on the entire apparatus of social constraints. Bertolucci writes: "At the base of modern sex you will find sadomasochism, that means, automatically, that you will find a dialectic of violence and aggression in *all* human relationships." The outsized human passion Bertolucci depicts, chiefly through the threatening figure of Marlon Brando, seems to literalize the filmmaker's comment that "films are animal events." *Last Tango* combines the talents of several artists noted for the emotional temperature of their work. In addition to the players, the music by Gatto Barbieri and the cinematography of Vittorio Storaro contribute to the febrile intensity of the work.

The world acclaim brought by *Last Tango* assured Bertolucci of the financial resources to complete the long-planned Marxian epic, *1900*. Setting the film in the rural areas of Parma, a few miles from his childhood home, Bertolucci set out to compose a paean to a way of life that was passing—the "culture of the land" of the peasant farmers, seen as a native and pure form of communism. The film depicts the cruel historical awakening of the farmers of the region, part of an entire class that has been regularly brutalized, first by aristocratic landowners, and then by the Fascist regime. Bertolucci localizes this conflict in the twin destinies of two characters born on the same day in *1900*—Olmo, who becomes a peasant leader, and Alfredo, the scion of the feudal estate. The whole of the film takes place in the environs of the estate, and such elements of landscape as the road, the railroad tracks, and the courtyard become poeticized internal frames enclosing the movement of History.

The controversial work was released in a six-hour form in Europe, and shortened to three hours for American release. Bertolucci had complete control of the cutting of the film, and considers the shorter version a more finished work. The epic sweep remains, as do the contradictions—for the film amalgamates the most divergent elements: a marxian epic, it is furnished with an international star cast; a portrait of the indiginous peasantry, its principle language is English. Intentionally fashioned for wide commercial appeal, it nonetheless broaches untried subject matter. The film keeps these elments in suspension, never dissolving these differences into an ideological portrait of life "after the revolution." The film's ending seems instead to return to the customary balance and tension between historical forces and class interests.

In *Luna*, Bertolucci turns to a much more intimate subject: the relation between mother and son. The work has a diminutive scale but a passionate focus, a quality crystallized in the opera scenes in which the mother, Caterina, performs. The reconciliation of mother, son and father occurs during a rehearsal in which the mother reveals, through song, the identity of father and son. This cathartic and bravura scene plays in high relief the characteristic patterns of Bertolucci's cinema, in which the family drama is played against the backdrop of a ritualized art form, opera in this case, dance in *Last Tango*, and theater (the *Macbeth* scene in *Before the Revolution*).

With *Tragedy of a Ridiculous Man*, Bertolucci continues his inquiry into the relations between politics and family life, here framing the ambivalent bond between father and son with the correlative conflict between capitalism and political terror. As of this writing, Bertolucci is seeking financing for a film based on the Dashiell Hammett story *Red Harvest*, which essays a similar family conflict. In general, Bertolucci's oeuvre must be considered the most original and accomplished cinema of the period, for it combines an extremely vivid and distinctive visual style with unique and challenging subject matter.

—Robert Burgoyne

BIRRI, FERNANDO. Argentine. Born 13 March 1925. Educated at Universidad Nacional del Litoral, Santa Fe, Argentina (UNL); Centro Sperimentale de Cinematografia, Rome, 1950-52. Career: early 1940s—member of Espadalirio, group of Santa Fe poets; 1942—director of itinerant puppet theater based at Universidad Nacional del Litoral; 1947—director of 1st theater group at UNL; 1954—assistant to Vittorio De Sica on *Il tetto*; 1956—returns to Argentina, organizes filmmaking seminar for Sociology Institute of UNL; helps found Instituto de Cinematografia, later La Escuela Documental de Santa Fe, 1st documentary film school in Latin America; 1958—1st exhibition of "foto-documentales" by students of Escuela Documentale, seen in Argentina and in Montevideo, Uruguay, where praised by visiting documentarist John Grierson; 1963—with wife and 3 colleagues leaves Argentina for political reasons; 1964—investigates filmmaking possibilities in Brazil, Mexico and Cuba before returning to Italy; 1979—returns to Latin America to attend 1st International Festival of the New Latin American Cinema, Havana; 1980—teaches at Universidad Nacional Autonoma de Mexico and at Film School of Universidad de Los Andes, Merida, Venezuela (through 1983). Recipient: Grand Prize, SODRE Festival Montevideo, for *Tire Die* (33 min. version), 1960; Golden Lion "Premio Opera Primo", Venice Festival, for *Los Inundados*, 1962.

Films (as director): 1951—*Selinunte* (short); *Alfabeto notturno* (short); 1952—*Immagini Populari Siciliane Sacre*; *Immagini Populari Siciliane Profane*; 1954—*Tire die (Toss Me a Dime)* (59 min. version—co-d, co-sc, co-ph with students of Instituto de Cinematografia, Santa Fe, Argentina); 1959—*La primera fundación de Buenos Aires* (medium-length animation); 1960—*Buenos dias, Buenos Aires* (short); 1961—*Los inundados (Flooded Out)*; 1962—*Che, Buenos Aires* (feature documentary comprising previous 2 films); *La pampa gringa* (compilation documentary); 1966—*Castagnino, diario romano* (short); 1979—*Org* (co-d). Roles: 1955—*Gli sbanditi* (Maselli).

Publications:

By BIRRI:

Book—*La Escuela Documental de Santa Fe*, Instituto de Cinematografia, Universidad Nacional del Litoral, Santa Fe, Argentina 1964; articles—"Cine y subdesarrollo" in *Cine Cubano* (Havana), May/July 1967; "Revolucion en la revolucion del nuevo cine latinoamericano" in *Cine Cubano* (Havana), August/-December 1968; "Apuntes sobre la 'guerra de guerrillas' del Nuevo Cine Latinoamericano" in *El rostro de America Latina* vol.7, Caracas 1970; interview by Julianne Burton in *Fernando Birri e la Escuela Documental de Santa Fe* edited by Lino Micciche, Pesaro, Italy 1981.

On BIRRI:

Books—*Breve historia del cine argentino* by Jose Agustin

Mahieu, Buenos Aires 1966; *Fernando Birri e la Escuela Documental de Santa Fe* edited by Lino Micciche, Pesaro, Italy 1981; *Breve historia del cine nacional* by Jose Agustin Mahieu, Buenos Aires; articles—"Breve historia del documental en la Argentina" by Dolly Pussi in *Cine Cubano* (Havana), October 1973; "The Camera as 'Gun': 2 Decades of Film Culture and Resistance in Latin America" by Julianne Burton in *Latin American Perspectives*, winter 1978; "Carta a Fernando Birri" by Manuel Pereira and "Pequena critica agradecida a *Tire die*" by Rigoberto Lopez in *Cine cubano* (Havana), no.100, 1981.

*   *   *

Because he was more interested in creating filmmakers than in creating films; because he attempted to offer a sustained and systematic counter-example to existing industrial modes of filmmaking and to the ideological assumptions which limited both the process and the product; because he developed a concrete theoretical-practical approach and founded the first school of documentary filmmaking in Latin America in order to teach that methodology; and finally because his students fanned out across the continent putting his ideas into practice, Fernando Birri is a key figure in the history of the New Latin American Cinema.

Born in the provincial capital of Santa Fe, Birri was a poet and puppeteer before turning to the cinema in search of a broad popular audience. Unable to break into the tightly controlled national film industry, Birri travelled to Italy to study at Rome's Centro Sperimentale de Cinematografia during the early fifties, when the neo-realist movement was still at its height. Profoundly influenced by the ideology, aesthetics and methodology of this first anti-industrial, anti-Hollywood model for a national cinema, Birri returned to Argentina in 1956 hoping to found a national film school. Rejecting the closed commercialism of the Buenos Aires-based film industry, one of the three largest in Latin America at the time, Birri returned to Santa Fe.

Birri recalls, "Fresh from Europe, what I had in mind was a film school modeled on the Centro Sperimentale, a fictional film school which would train actors, directors, cinematographers, set designers, etc. But when I confronted the actual conditions in Argentina and in Santa Fe, I realized that my plan was premature. What was needed was something else: a school which would not only provide apprenticeship in filmmaking, but also in sociology, and even in Argentine history, geography and politics, because the most essential quest is the quest for national identity, in order to recover and rediscover what had been alienated, distorted and destroyed by centuries of cultural penetration. This search for a national identity is what led me to pose the problem in strictly *documentary* terms, because I believe that the first step for any national cinema is to document its own reality."

La Escuela Documental de Santa Fe grew out of the *Instituto de Cinematografia*, which was in turn an outgrowth of a 4-day seminar on filmmaking led by Birri. Birri's goal was to lay the foundations for a regional film industry whose films would be "national, realist, and popular": national in that they would address the most pressing problems of national life; realist (documentary) in approach in contrast to the highly artificial style and milieux of the "official" film industry; popular in their focus on and appeal to the less privileged classes. Birri emphasized process over product, viewing each film project as the opportunity for practical apprenticeship on the part of the largest possible number of students, in keeping with his determination to integrate theory and practice. He was the first of the Latin American filmmakers to posit technical imperfection as a positive attribute, preferring *un sentido imperfecto a una perfeccion sin sentido* (an imperfect/sincere meaning to a meaningless perfection).

Birri's best-known films are the 33-minute documentary *Tire die (Toss Me a Dime)* and *Los inundados (Flooded Out)*, a picaresque feature in the neorealist style about the adventures of a squatter family displaced by seasonal floods. Both played to huge and enthusiastic audiences at their local premieres but could not achieve broad national exhibition even after winning important prizes in international festivals.

An inhospitable political climate compelled Birri to leave Argentina in 1963. Subsequent months in São Paulo catalyzed an important documentary movement there, but Birri himself returned to Italy and, until recently, relative obscurity. His presence at the First International Festival of the New Latin American Cinema in Havana in 1979 signaled renewed activity and recognition. Since then, Birri has taught at Mexico's national university and at the University of Los Andes in Venezuela. The Benalmadena and Pesaro Festivals (Spain, 1979 and Italy, 1981) organized special programs honoring his work.

—Julianne Burton

BLACKTON, J. STUART. American. Born James Stuart Blackton in Sheffield, England, 5 January 1875. Educated briefly at City College, New York. Married Isabelle Mabel MacArthur, early 1890s (divorced 1906); married Paula (Dean) Hilburn, 1906 (died 1930); married physician Helen Stahle, 1931 (died 1933); married Evangeline Russell, 1936. Career: 1885—family moves to U.S. 1894—works briefly as painter before becoming sketch artist for newspapers; 1895—as journalist-illustrator for *New York World*, interviews Edison; impressed by drawings, Edison suggests filming them with Kinetograph camera, resulting in film *Blackton, the Evening World Cartoonist*; 1896—buys a Kinetoscope from Edison; with friend Albert E. Smith forms partnership to make and exhibit films; 1897—3rd partner William T. Rock added and Vitagraph Company established; begin film production in open-air studio on roof of Morse Building, 140 Nassau St., New York, with *The Burglar on the Roof*; 1900-15—president, Vitaphone Company (mfr. of record players); 1905—Vitagraph forms stock company of actors; 1905-06—build 1st glass-enclosed studios in Flatbush, Brooklyn; over next decade Vitagraph actors include Maurice Costello, Mabel Normand, Anita Stewart, John Bunny and Norma Talmadge; 1906-10—makes series of animated cartoons, pioneering single-frame animation technique; 1915—organizes and becomes president of Motion Picture Board of Trade (later Association of Motion Picture Producers and Distributors of America); also publisher and editor, *Motion Picture Magazine*; 1917—begins independent producing; early 1920s—directs in England, makes several experiments with color film; 1925—Vitagraph sold to Warner Bros., reportedly for $1,000,000; retires from filmmaking; 1929—loses heavily in stock market crash; 1931—goes into bankruptcy; 1935—goes on relief, appointed director of a Federal work relief movie project; late 1930s—hired as director of production for Anglo-American Film Company. Died in Hollywood of injuries suffered in auto accident, 13 August 1941.

Films (as director—partial listing as no director's credit was given on Vitagraph's early films): 1898—*Burglar on the Roof* (+ro); 1899—*A Visit to the Spiritualist*; 1900—"Happy Hooligan" series (+ro); *The Enchanted Drawing*; 1905—*Monsieur Beaucaire* (+ro); *The Automobile Thieves* (+ro); *Raffles, the Amateur Cracksman*; 1906—*Humorous Phases of Funny Faces*; *100 to 1 Shot*; 1907—*The Haunted Hotel*; 1909-10—*The Life of Moses*; 1909—*The Magic Fountain Pen*; *Princess Nicotine*; (as scriptwriter): 1914—*Goodness Gracious*; *The Honeymooners*; *The Win(k)some Widow*; *The New Stenographer*; *The Park Honeymooners*; *Love, Luck and Gasoline*; (as producer and scriptwriter): 1915—*The Battle Cry of Peace*; 1916—*Whom the Gods Destroy* (co-sc); (films complete from 1917 on): 1917—*Womanhood, or The Glory of a Nation* (co-sc); (as director): 1917—*The Message of the Mouse*; "Country Life" series; (as producer and director): 1917—*The Judgment House* (+sc); 1918—*World for Sale*; *Missing* (+co-sc); *The Common Cause*; *Safe for Democracy*; 1919—*The Moonshine Trail* (+co-sc); *My Husband's Other Wife*; *A House Divided*; *Dawn*; 1920—*Respectable By Proxy*; *The Blood Barrier*; *Passers-By*; *The House of the Tolling Bell*; *Forbidden Valley*; 1922—*The Glorious Adventure*; *The Gypsy Cavalier*; 1923—*The Virgin Queen*; *On the Banks of the Wabash*; 1924—*Let Not Man Put Asunder*; *Between Friends*; *Behold This Woman*; *The Clean Heart*; *The Beloved Brute*; 1925—*The Redeeming Sin*; *Tides of Passion*; *The Happy Warrior*; 1926—*Bride of the Storm*; *The Gilded Highway*; *Hell-Bent for Heaven*; *The Passionate Quest*; 1933—*The Film Parade (March of the Movies, Cavalcade of the Movies)* (compilation film with some footage 'recreated' by Blackton).

Publications:

By BLACKTON:

Book—*Marine Studies*, undated; articles—"An Interview with J. Stuart Blackton" in *The Moving Picture World*, 19 December 1908; introduction to *The Photodrama* by Henry Phillips, 1914; "Awake America!" in *The Theatre* (New York), September 1915; "The Battle Cry of Peace" in *Motion Picture* (New York), September 1915/January 1916; "Yesterdays of Vitagraph" in *Photoplay* (New York), July 1919; "The Movies Are Growing Up" in *Motion Picture* (New York), February 1925.

On BLACKTON:

Books—*The Pioneer of the Photoplay*, pamphlet by Felix Orman, n.d. (*ca.* 1921); *The Big V: A History of the Vitagraph Company* by Anthony Slide, 1976; *J. Stuart Blackton* by Marian Blackton Trimble, Metuchen, N.J. 1984; articles—by H. Haskins in *Motion Picture Classic* (Brooklyn), September 1918; sketch in *Current Biography*, New York 1941; obituary in the *New York Times*, 14 August 1941; "Films on 8 & 16" by Anthony Slide in *Films in Review* (New York), February 1978.

*   *   *

J. Stuart Blackton was both a pioneering producer/director and a pioneering animator. The American film industry may well be said to have its origins in the founding by Blackton and Albert E. Smith of the Vitagraph Company, and most historians agree that animation originates with Blackton's 1907 production of *The Haunted Hotel*.

The Haunted Hotel combined animation, live action and special effects and had its origins in the fantasies of Georges Méliès. In France the film certainly influenced the work of Emile Cohl. Of course, Blackton had experimented with a form of animation long before *The Haunted Hotel*, notably with the undated *Cohen and Coon*, in which Blackton writes those two words on a blackboard and proceeds to translate each word into the appropriate stereotype, and with *Humorous Phases of Funny Faces*, which again had Blackton creating comic faces on blackboards.

As a pioneering producer, J. Stuart Blackton was required to serve as producer and director, as well as occasional cameraman and actor on the films released by Vitagraph through 1909. With his recreation of *The Battle of Manila Bay*, Blackton introduced a form of special effects to the cinema. The same film demonstrated the patriotic and propaganda value of the motion picture, which Blackton was later to exploit to its fullest with *The Battle Cry of Peace*, which he co-directed and conceived of in partnership with Theodore Roosevelt as a message for preparedness in the United States at a time when many were advocating U.S. noninvolvement in the First World War.

Albert E. Smith was the business head of Vitagraph, as well as the company's first cameraman, while J. Stuart Blackton took responsibility for the production end of the company, which with an artistic genius such as Blackton meant an influx of considerable creativity and ingenuity. Thanks to Blackton, the films of the Vitagraph Company through the mid-teens were and are considered some of the best produced in the United States.

However, Blackton failed to keep abreast of changes in the industry, as indicated by the poor quality and equally poor reception of the independent features he directed after leaving Vitagraph in 1917. Yet he remained an innovator, as evidenced by *The Glorious Adventure*, shot in Prizma Color in England, an impressive if dull attempt at historical spectacle. Blackton continued to direct through 1926, but his films received little attention, and those that have survived appear unimpressive.

A social climber who amassed and lost great sums of money during his career, Blackton was also a fun-loving filmmaker, and nowhere is this more evident than in his last fling, a highly personal history of the cinema, *The Film Parade* (also known as *The March of the Movies*), which Blackton made in association with his former director William P.S. Earle in the early thirties. Blackton blithely recreated his own early films and even donned blackface to impersonate Al Jolson in *The Jazz Singer*. *The Film Parade* is no masterpiece, but it is a fitting tribute to a major, and much underrated, figure in American film history.

—Anthony Slide

BLASETTI, ALESSANDRO. Italian. Born in Rome, 3 July 1900. Doctor of law. Career: 1924—gives up law practice; 1926—founds *Il Mondo dello Schermo* (Screen World); 1928—joins Alessandrini, Barbaro and others in filmmaking cooperative Augustus; founds *Cinematografo* and *Lo spettacolo d'Italia*; 1929—produces and directs 1st film *Sole*; 1932-34—directs 1st Italian film school at music academy S. Cecile, Rome.

Films (as director, co-scriptwriter and co-editor): 1929—*Sole* (ed, +pr); 1930—*Nerone*; 1931—*Resurrectio*; *Terra madre*; 1932—*Palio*; *La tavola dei poveri*; 1933—*Il caso Haller*; 1934—*1860 (Gesuzza la sposa Garibaldina)*; *L'impiegata di papà*; *Vecchia guardia*; 1935—*Aldebaran* (d and co-sc only, +ro); 1937—*La contessa di Parma*; 1938—*Ettore Fieramosca*; *Caccia alla volpe*; 1939—*Retroscena*; 1940—*Un'avventura di Salvator Rosa*; *Napoli e le terre d'oltremare* (unfinished); (as director and co-scriptwriter): 1941—*La corona di ferro (The Iron Crown)*; *La cena delle beffe*; 1942—*Quattro passi fra le nuvole (4 Steps in the Clouds)* (+ro); 1943—*Nessuno torna indietro*; 1946—*Un giorno nella vita*; *La gemma orientale di Papi*; *Il Duomo di Milano*; *Castel Sant'Angelo*; 1948—*Fabiola*; 1950—*Prima comunione (Father's Dilemma)*; *Ippodromi all'Alba*; 1952—*Altri tempi (Times Gone By)*; *La fiammata*; 1953—*Tempi nostri (Anatomy*

of Love); 1954—*Peccato che sia una canaglia (Too Bad She's Bad)*; 1955—*La fortuna di essere donna (Lucky to Be a Woman)*; 1957—*Amore e chiacchiere*; 1959—*Europa di notte (European Nights)* (d only); 1961—*Io amo, tu ami (I Love—You Love)*; 1963—"La lepre e la tartaruga" episode of *Le quattro verità*; 1964—*Liolà* (d only); 1966—*Io, io, io...e gli altri*; 1967—*La ragazza del bersagliere*; 1969—*Simon Bolivar*; 1982—*Venezia, una Mostra per il cinema* (documentary).

Publications:

By BLASETTI:

Books—*Come nasce un film*, Rome 1932; *Scritti sul cinema*, Marsilio Editori, 1982; *Il cinema che ho vissuto*, Dedalo Edizioni, 1982; articles—"Alessandro Blasetti/ogni volta da capo", interview in *Bianco e nero* (Rome), September/December 1975; "Alessandro Blasetti", interview and article by F. Cuel and B. Villien in *Cinématographe* (Paris), November 1981; "Sur le seuil de ma vie" in *Positif* (Paris), March 1981.

On BLASETTI:

Articles—"The Big Screens" in *Sight and Sound* (London), spring 1955; "Ni chemises noires, ni telephones blancs: cinema italien 1923-1943 (Pesaro)" by J.-P. Jeancolas in *Positif* (Paris), October 1976; "Blasetti, le fascisme et la virilite..." by P. Mereghetti in *Positif* (Paris), October 1976.

BLIER, BERTRAND. French. Born in Paris, 11 March 1939. Career: 1960-63—assistant director on films of John Berry, Georges Lautner, Christian-Jaque, Jean Delannoy, Denys de La Patellière and others; directs a number of short documentaries before first feature. Recipient: Academy Award, Best Foreign Film, for *Get Out Your Handkerchiefs*, 1978.

Films (as director and scriptwriter): 1963—*Hitler? Connais pas!*; 1966—*La Grimace*; 1967—*Si j'etais un espion (Breakdown, If I Were a Spy)* (co-sc); 1970—*Laisse aller, c'est une valse* (Lautner) (sc only); 1973—*Les Valseuses (Going Places)*; 1975—*Calmos (Femmes Fatales)* (co-sc); 1977—*Preparez vos mouchoirs (Get Out Your Handkerchiefs)*; 1979—*Buffet froid*; 1981—*Beau-père*.

Publications:

By BLIER:

Books—*Les Valseuses*, Paris 1972; *Beau-père*, Paris 1980; articles—"Les Valseuses de B. Blier: le nuvite du cinéma français", interview by R. Gay, in *Cinéma Québec* (Montreal), v.3, no.8, 1974; "Entretien avec Bertrand Blier" by B. Villien and P. Carcassonne in *Cinématographe* (Paris), January 1980; "Beau-père. Entretien avec Bertrand Blier" by C. de Béchade and H. Desrues, in *Image et son* (Paris), September 1981.

On BLIER:

Articles—"At the Movies: The Truth About Making a Movie in

"Singapore" by T. Buckley in *The New York Times*, 2 February 1979; "Buffet froid" (special Blier issue) by Y. Alion in *Avant-Scène du cinéma* (Paris), 15 March 1980; "El humor, el absurdo, la agresión y el mundo (desagradable) de Blier" by L. Elbert in *Cinemateca Revista* (Andes), June 1981; "Revoir l'oeuvre de Bertrand Blier" by G. Haustrate in *Cinéma* (Paris), July/August 1981.

*   *   *

Bertrand Blier directs erotic buddy movies featuring men who are exasperated by the opposite sex, who perceive of themselves as macho but are incapable of satisfying the women in their lives. Really, his heros are terrified of feminism, of the "new woman" who demands her right to experience and enjoy orgasm. But Blier's females are in no way villainesses. They are just elusive—and so alienated that they can only find fulfillment from oddballs, or young boys.

Going Places (*Les Valseuses*, which in French is slang for testicles), based on Blier's best-selling novel, was a box office smash in France. Gérard Depardieu and Patrick Dewaere both achieved stardom as a couple of outsiders, adult juvenile delinquents; chronicled are their sexual and sadistic adventures as they travel across France. They are both unable to bring to orgasm a young beautician (played by Miou-Miou) they pick up and take on as a sexual partner. They then attempt to please an older woman (Jeanne Moreau), who has just spent ten years in prison. After a night together, she commits suicide by shooting herself in the vagina. Eventually, Miou-Miou is satisfied by a crazy, physically unattractive ex-convict.

In *Femmes Fatales*, middle-aged Jean-Pierre Marielle and Jean Rochefort, one a gynecologist and the other a pimp, decide to abandon wives and mistresses for the countryside, but end up pursued by an army of women intent on enslaving them as studs. Again, men cannot escape women's sexual demands: here, the latter come after the former with tanks and guns. And, in *Get Out Your Handkerchiefs*, driving instructor Depardieu is so anxious to please bored, depressed wife Carol Laure that he finds her a lover, a total stranger, playground instructor Dewaere. Both men feel that she will be happy if she can only have a child. She in her own way does this, finding a substitute for them in a precocious young boy barely into his teens. *Handkerchiefs* is a prelude of sorts to *Beau Père*, which features only one male lead, a struggling pianist played by Dewaere. Here, he is seduced by the refreshingly self-confident 14-year-old daughter of his recently deceased lover. The teen-ager's feelings are deep and pure, while the "adult" is immature, too self-conscious and self-absorbed to accept her.

In Blier's films, men do not understand women. "Maybe one day I'll do *Camille*," the filmmaker says. "But I won't do *An Unmarried Woman*, because I don't feel I have the right to do it. I don't know what goes on in a woman's head. I believe I know what certain men think, but not women." As a result, in Blier's movies, the sexual barriers between the sexes seem irrevocable. His men are more at ease talking among themselves about women than with actually being with wives or lovers; their relationships with each other are for them more meaningful than their contacts with the opposite sex. There are alternatives to women: become homosexual (the characters in *Going Places* sleep with each other when they are lonely or celibate which, in *Femmes Fatales*, they are denied).

Another Blier film, *Buffet Froid*, is also about male bonding: Depardieu, as a psychopathic killer, becomes involved with a mass murderer (Jean Carmet) and a homicidal cop (the director's father, the distinguished character actor Bernard Blier). However, *Buffet Froid* is mostly a study of alienation in urban society,

and the acceptance of random, irrational violence. It is thematically more closely related to, for example, Jules Feiffer's *Little Murders* than *Going Places* or *Get Out Your Handkerchiefs*.

Bertrand Blier best explains what he attempts to communicate in his films: "The relations between men and women are constantly evolving and it's interesting to show people leading the lifestyle of tomorrow."

—Rob Edelman

BLOM, AUGUST. Danish. Born 26 December 1869. Married Agnete von Prangen, 1908; 2nd marriage to Johanne Fritz-Petersen. Career: 1893—acting debut in provinces; actor at Folketeatret, Copenhagen; 1908—begins acting in small roles at Nordisk Films Kompagni; 1910-25—directs for Nordisk; 1934 until death—manager of Copenhagen cinema. Died 10 January 1947; buried in Frederiksberg Kirkegård, Copenhagen.

Films (as director): 1910—*Livets Storme* (*Storms of Life*); *Robinson Crusoe*; *Den hvide Slavehandel I* (*The White Slave*); *Spionen fra Tokio* (*The Red Light*); *Den skaebnesvangre Opfindelse* (*Dr. Jekyll and Mr. Hyde*); *Jagten paa Gentlemanrøveren*; *Singaree*; *Hamlet*; *Spøgelset i Gravkaelderen* (*The Ghost of the Variety*); *Den Dødes Halsbaand* (*The Necklace of the Dead*); 1911—*Den hvide Slavehandel II* (*In the Hands of Impostors*); *Den farlige Alder* (*The Price of Beauty*); *Ved Faengslets Port* (*Temptations of a Great City*); *Vildledt Elskov* (*The Bank Book*); *Potifars Hustru* (*The Victim of a Character*); *Politimesteren* (*Convicts No.10 and No.13*); *Den blaa Natviol* (*The Daughter of the Fortune Teller*); *Damernes Blad* (*The Ladies' Journal*); *Balletdanserinden* (*The Ballet Dancer*); *Jernbanens Datter* (*The Daughter of the Railway*); *Den naadige Frøken* (*Lady Mary's Love*); *En Lektion* (*Aviatikeren og Journalistens Hustru*, *The Aviator and the Journalist's Wife*); *Ekspeditricen* (*Ungdom og Letsind*, *In the Prime of Life*); *Desdemona*; *En Opfinders Skaebne* (*The Aeroplane Inventor*); *Fader og Søn* (*Onkel og Nevø*, *A Poisonous Love*); *Dødsdrømmen* (*A Dream of Death*); *Min første Monocle* (*Herr Storms første Monocle*, *His First Monocle*); *Fru Potifar* (*Den skaebnesvangre Løgn*, *A Fatal Lie*); *Kaerlighedens Styrke* (*The Power of Love*); *Mormonens Offer* (*The Victims of the Mormon*); *Haevnet* (*Det bødes der for*, *Vengeance*); *Det mørke Punkt* (*Mamie Rose*, *Annie Bell*); *Eventyr paa Fodrejsen* (*Den udbrudte Slave*, *The 2 Convicts*); *Ungdommens Ret* (*The Right of Youth*); *Tropisk Kaerlighed* (*Love in the Tropics*); *Vampyrdanserinden* (*The Vampire Dancer*); *Det gamle Købmandshus* (*Midsommer*, *Midsummer-Time*); *Dødens Brud* (*A Bride of Death*); 1912—*Brillantstjernen* (*For Her Sister's Sake*); *Guvernørens Datter* (*The Governor's Daughter*); *Kaerlighed gør blind* (*Love is Blind*); *Dyrekøbt Venskab* (*Dearly Purchased Friendship*); *Den sorte Kansler* (*The Black Chancellor*); *Hjertets Guld* (*Et Hjerte af Guld*, *Faithful Unto Death*); *Direktørens Datter* (*Caught in His Own Trap*); *Det første Honorar* (*Hans første Honorar*, *His Firts Patient*); *Elskovs Magt* (*Gøgleren*, *Man's Great Adversary*); *Historien om en Moder* (*En Moders Kaerlighed*, *The Life of a Mother*); *De tre Kammerater* (*The 3 Comrades*); *Operabranden* (*Bedstemoders Vuggevise*, *The Song Which Grandmother Sang*); *Den første Kaerlighed* (*Her First Love Affair*); *Hjerternes Kamp* (*A High Stake*); *Hans vanskeligste Rolle* (*His Most Difficult Part*); *Den tredie Magt* (*The Secret Treaty*); *Fødselsdagsgaven* (*Gaven*, *The Birthday Gift*); *En Hofintrige* (*A Court Intrigue*); *Den sande Kaerlighed* (*Flugten gennem Skyerne*, *The Fugitives*); *Hvem var Forbryderen?* (*Samvittighedsnag*, *At the 11th Hour*); *Alt paa ét Kort* (*Guldmønten*, *Gold from the Gutter*); 1913—*Pressens*

Magt (Et Bankrun, A Harvest of Tears); Troløs (Gøglerblod, Artists); Højt Spil (Et forfejlet Spring, A Dash for Liberty); Naar Fruen gaar paa Eventyr (Pompadourtasken, The Lost Bag); Bristet Lykke (A Paradise Lost); Fem Kopier (5 Copies); Atlantis; En farlig Forbryder (Knivstikkeren, A Modern Jack the Ripper); Af Elskovs Naade (Acquitted); Elskovsleg (Love's Devotee); Vasens Hemmelighed (Den kinesiske Vase, The Chinese Vase); 1914—Sønnen (Her Son); Den store Middag (The Guestless Dinner Party); Tugthusfange No.97 (En Gaest fra en anden Verden, The Outcast's Return); Faedrenes Synd (Nemesis); Aegteskab og Pigesjov (Mr. King paa Eventyr, A Surprise Packet); Aeventyrersken (Exiled); En ensom Kvinde (Hvem er han?, The Doctor's Legacy); Revolutionsbryllup (A Revolution Marriage); Et Laereaar (The Reformation); Den lille Chauffør (The Little Chauffeur); Den største Kaerlighed (En Moders Kaerlighed, "Escaped the Law, But..."); Pro Patria; Kaerligheds-Vaeddemaalet (The Wager); 1915—Du skal elske din Naeste (For de Andre, The Samaritan); Giftpilen (The Poisonous Arrow); Hjertestorme; Kaerligheds Laengsel (Den Pukkelryggede, The Cripple Girl); Lotteriseddel No.22152 (Den blinde Skaebne, Blind Fate); Rovedderkoppen (Den røde Enke); Syndens Datter (Den, der sejrer, Nobody's Daughter); Syndig Kaerlighed (Eremitten, The Hermit); Truet Lykke (Et Skud i Mørket, The Evil Genius); Verdens Undergang (Flammesvaerdet, The Flaming Sword); For sit Lands Aere (Hendes Aere, For His Country's Honor); 1916—Den mystiske Selskabsdame (The Mysterious Companion); Gillekop; 1918—Grevindens Aere (Kniplinger, Lace); Maharadjaens Yndlingshustru II (The Favorite Wife of the Maharaja II, A Daughter of Brahma); Via Crucis; 1919—Prometheus I-II (Bonds of Hate); 1920—Hans gode Genius (Mod Stjernerne, His Guardian Angel); Praesten i Vejlby (The Vicar of Vejlby, The Land of Fate); 1924—Det store Hjerte (Lights from Circus Life, Side Lights of the Sawdust Ring); Den store Magt; 1925—Hendes Naade; Dragonen. Roles: 1909—Droske 519 (Cab No.519); En Kvinde af Folket (A Woman of the People); Dr. Nicola I (Den skjulte Skat); Dr. Nicola (Hvorledes Dr. Nicola erhvervede den kinesiske Stok, How Dr. Nicola Procured the Chinese Cane); Barnet (A Child's Love); Madame Sans Gène; Faderen (A Father's Grief); Museumsmysteriet (The Mystery of the Museum); Dr. Nicola III (Dr. Nicola in Tibet); Et Budskab til Napoleon paa Elba (A Message to Napoleon); Revolutionsbryllup (A Wedding During the French Revolution); 1910—Sølvdaasen med Juvelerne (The Jewel Case); Tyven (A Society Sinner); To Tjenestepiger (The Rival Servants); Kean; Medbejlerens Haevn (Caught in His Own Net); Forraederen (A Traitor to His Country).

* * *

When August Blom came to Nordisk Films Kompagni in 1909 it was the major film production company in Denmark, having been founded in 1906 by Ole Olsen. Nordisk dominated so-called "belle époque" (from 1910 to 1914) in Danish filmmaking, and August Blom was the leading force in this period. From 1911 Blom was head of production, besides being a director. He was in charge of scripts and actors, and he launched the career of Valdemar Psilander, who showed a natural talent for understated and realistic film acting and became an immensely popular star in Denmark and Europe until his premature death in 1917. In 1911 Blom directed 16 of Psilander's 17 films.

In 1910 Blom made Ved Faengslets Port (released 1911) which, with Urban Gad's Afgrunden, introduced the erotic melodrama, a genre refined by Blom in the following years. Ved Faengslets Port is typical of the kind of films which made Nordisk famous all over the world. The story is about a young aristocrat who is in the grip of a moneylender and at the same time loves the moneylender's daughter. Although Blom tried to introduce contemporary themes in his films, the stories were always the weak part of his and most other Danish films in this period. The compensation for the banal magazine stories was found in the way Blom told these stories. His films are often about contrasts, social and sexual. The films are passionate and reveal the many faces of love with great imagination. As a former actor Blom put great weight on the acting and he had a fine feeling for the direcion of actresses. His portraits of women are quite often subtle and daring.

Blom put immense care into the making of his films. The sets were used in a dramatic way, playing an important role in the story as a means of characterizing the people. His narrative technique made use of cross-cutting and, assisted by his favourite cameraman Johan Ankerstjerne, he was an innovator in lighting. One of his stylistic devices, used to great and suprising effect, was mirrors as a means of expanding the dramatic content of a scene.

Blom must be considered as one of the important pioneers in the early silent film. It was quite natural that Blom was commissioned to direct the greatest and most ambitious film of the period, a film which introduced a literary era in the Danish film. This was Atlantis, based on Gerhart Hauptmann's novel of 1912 It was an attempt to transpose a modern novel with a complicated plot and interesting characters to film. Blom's direction is astonishingly mature, confident and imaginative, and in many ways Atlantis is ahead of its time. Johan Ankerstjerne's camera work points forward to the expressionist-inspired German films. Another fine film by Blom was Verdens Undergang.

Blom made 78 of his approximately 100 films in the years 1910-14, but he was a company man, and he stayed with Nordisk in the years of decline. He left filming in 1924. During the golden age of the Danish cinema Blom was the great stylist, a gifted and civilized director.

—Ib Monty

BOETTICHER, BUDD. American. Born Oscar Boetticher, Jr., in Chicago, 29 July 1916. Educated at Ohio State University. Career: early 1930s—football star at Ohio State; while recuperating from football injury in Mexico, becomes interested in bullfighting; studies with Lorenzo Garza and becomes professional matador; 1940—engaged as technical advisor on Mamoulian's Blood and Sand (1941); 1941-43—messenger boy at Hal Roach Studios; 1943-44—assistant to William Seiter on Destroyer (1943), to George Stevens on The More the Merrier and to Charles Vidor (The Desperadoes and Cover Girl); 1946-47—military service, makes several propaganda films; 1956-60—makes cycle of Westerns written with Burt Kennedy, produced by Harry Joe Brown and starring Randolph Scott; 1960—leaves Hollywood to make documentary on matador Carlos Arruza; early 1960s—in Mexico encounters numerous setbacks with project, is divorced, jailed briefly, suffers physical and mental illness; 1967—returns to Hollywood, begins association with producer Audie Murphy (killed in plane crash, 1971).

Films (directed as Oscar Boetticher): 1944—One Mysterious Night; The Missing Juror; Youth on Trial; 1945—A Guy, a Gal and a Pal; Escape on the Fog; 1946—The Fleet That Came to Stay (and other propaganda films); 1948—Assigned to Danger; Behind Locked Doors; 1949—Black Midnight; Wolf Hunters; 1950—Killer Shark; (directed as Budd Boetticher): 1951—The Bullfighter and the Lady (+co-story); The Sword of D'Artagnan;

'he Cimarron Kid; 1952—Bronco Buster; Red Ball Express; Jorizons West; 1953—City Beneath the Sea; Seminole; The Man from the Alamo; Wings of the Hawk; East of Sumatra; 955—The Magnificent Matador (+story); The Killer is Loose; 956—7 Men from Now; 1957—The Tall T; Decision at Sundown; 1958—Buchanan Rides Alone; 1959—Ride Lonesome (+pr); Westbound; 1960—Comanche Station; The Rise and Fall f Legs Diamond; 1970—2 Mules for Sister Sara (Siegel) (sc nly); 1971—Arruza (+pr, co-sc: production completed 1968); A Time for Dying (+sc: production completed 1969).

Publications:

By BOETTICHER:

Book—When in Disgrace; articles—interview in The Director's Event by Eric Sherman and Martin Rubin, New York 1970; interview by Bertrand Tavernier in Cahiers du cinéma (Paris), July 1964; interviews by Michel Ciment and others in Positif (Paris), November 1969.

On BOETTICHER:

Books—Horizons West by Jim Kitses, Bloomington, Indiana 1969; Budd Boetticher: The Western edited by Jim Kitses, London 1969; articles—"The Director and the Public: a Symposium" in Film Culture (New York), March/April 1955; "Un Western exemplaire" in Qu'est-ce que le cinéma by André Bazin, Paris 1961; "Esoterica" by Andrew Sarris in Film Culture (New York), spring 1963; "B.B. wie Budd Boetticher" by Eckhart Schmidt in Film (Germany), October/November 1964; "Budd Boetticher" by Lee Russell in New Left Review, July/August 1965; "Boetticher Returns" by P. Coonradt in Cinema (Beverly Hills), December 1968; "Budd Boetticher" by Christopher Wicking in Screen (London), July/October 1969; "2 Westerns d'Oscar 'Budd' Boetticher" by Louis Seguin in Positif (Paris), November 1969; "Budd Boetticher: A Case Study in Criticism" by Paul Schrader in Cinema (Los Angeles), fall 1970.

*   *   *

Budd Boetticher will be remembered as a director of Westerns, although his bullfight films have their fervent admirers, as does his Scarface-variant, The Rise and Fall of Legs Diamond, notwithstanding its chilly and distanced title performance. Since Boetticher's Westerns are so variable in quality, it's tempting to overcredit Burt Kennedy, the scriptwriter for all of the finest. But Kennedy's own efforts as director (Return of the Seven, Hannie Caulder, The War Wagon, etc.) are tediously paced dramas or failed comedies. Clearly the Boetticher/Kennedy team clicked to make Westerns significantly superior to what either could create on their own. Indeed, The Tall T, Seven Men from Now, and (on a slightly lower level) Ride Lonesome look now like the finest work in the genre during the fifties, less pretentious and more tightly controlled than even that of Anthony Mann or John Ford.

Jim Kitses's still-essential Horizons West rightly locates Boetticher's significant Westerns in the "Ranown" cycle (a production company name taken from producer Harry Joe Brown and his partner Randolph Scott). But the non-Kennedy entries in the cycle have, despite Scott's key presence, only passing interest. One might have attributed the black comedy in the series to Kennedy without the burlesque Buchanan Rides Alone, which wanders into an episodic narrative opposite to the taut, unified

action of the others; Decision at Sundown is notable only for its remarkably bitter finale and a morally pointless showdown, as if it were a cynic's answer to High Noon.

The Tall T's narrative is typical of the best Boetticher/ Kennedy: it moves from a humanizing comedy so rare in the genre into a harsh and convincing savagery. Boetticher's villains are relentlessly cruel, yet morally shaded. In The Tall T, he toys with the redeemable qualities of Richard Boone, while deftly characterizing the other two (Henry Silva asks, "I've never shot me a woman, have I Frank?") Equally memorable are Lee Marvin (in Seven Men from Now) and Lee Van Cleef (Ride Lonesome).

Randolph Scott is the third essential collaborator in the cycle. He's generally presented by Boetticher as a loner not by principle or habit but by an obscure terror in his past (often a wife murdered). Thus he's not the asexual cowpoke so much as one who, temporarily at least, is beyond fears and yearnings. There's a Pinteresque sexual confrontation in Seven Men from Now among Scott, a pioneer couple, and an insinuating Lee Marvin when the four are confined in a wagon. And indeed the typical Boetticher landscape—smooth, rounded, and yet impassible boulders—match Scott's deceptively complex character as much as the majestic Monument Valley towers match Wayne in Ford's Westerns, or the harsh cliffs match James Stewart's in Mann's.

Clearly the Westerns of the sixties and seventies owe more to Boetticher than Ford. Even such very minor works as Horizons West, The Wings of the Hawk, and The Man from the Alamo have the tensions of Spaghetti Westerns (without the iciness), as well as the Peckinpah fantasy of American expertise combining with Mexican peasant vitality. If Peckinpah and Leone are the masters of the post-"classic" Western, then it's worth noting how The Wings of the Hawk anticipates The Wild Bunch, and how Once Upon a Time in the West opens like Seven Men from Now and closes like Ride Lonesome. Boetticher's films are the final great achievement of the traditional Western, before the explosion of the genre.

—Scott Simmon

BOGDANOVICH, PETER. American. Born in Kingston, New York, 30 July 1939. Educated at Collegiate School, New York; studied acting at Stella Adler's Theatre Studio. Married Polly Platt (separated 1971); children: Antonia and Alexandra. Career: 1955—stage debut as director at Cherry County Playhouse, Michigan; late 1950s—acts with American and New York Shakespeare Festivals; 1958—proposes to Clifford Odets off-Broadway production of The Big Knife, favorably reviewed; early 1960s—begins writing on film for numerous periodicals including Esquire, The New York Times and Cahiers du cinéma; 1964—following failure of production of Once in a Lifetime, moves to Hollywood; 1966—given job as 2nd unit director on Corman's The Wild Angels; 1967—directs The Great Professional—Howard Hawks for BBC TV; 1968—Corman backs first film Targets; 1968-71—intermittently works on documentary Directed by John Ford; 1973—Paramount forms and finances The Directors Company, independent unit partnership of Bogdanovich, Francis Ford Coppola and William Friedkin which produced Paper Moon and Daisy Miller; 1975—forms Copa de Oro production company. Address: 212 Copa de Oro Road, Los Angeles, CA 90077.

Films (as co-scriptwriter, 2nd unit director, co-editor, all uncredited): 1966—The Wild Angels (+bit role, voice); (supervising editor, narrator, directed add'l scenes under pseudonym Derek Thomas and/or Peter Stewart): *Voyage to the Planet of the Prehistoric Women (Gill-Women of Venus)* (from Russian science fiction film by Pavel Klushantsev *Planeta Burg (Cosmonauts on Venus, Storm Clouds of Venus)*, dubbed and reedited for American Int'l Pictures); (as director and scriptwriter): 1967—*Targets* (co-sc, +pr, ed, ro as *Sammy Michaels*); 1971—*Directed by John Ford*; *The Last Picture Show* (co-sc); (as producer, director and scriptwriter): 1972—*What's Up, Doc?* (co-sc); 1973—*Paper Moon* (pr and d only); 1974—*Daisy Miller* (pr and d only); 1975—*At Long Last Love* (+co-songwriter: "Poor Young Millionaire"); *The Gentleman Tramp* (Patterson) ("special thanks" credit for supervising scenes shot at Charles Chaplin's home in Switzerland); (as director and scriptwriter): 1976—*Nickelodeon* (co-sc); 1979—*Saint Jack* (co-sc, +ro as *Eddie Schuman*); 1983—*They All Laughed*. Roles: (in films not directed): 1966—small role in *The Wild Angels* (Corman); 1967—small role in *The Trip* (Corman); 1969—guest star in *Lion's Love* (Varda); 1970—*Higgan* in *The Other Side of the Wind* (Welles: unreleased); 1973—voice-over in *F for Fake* (Welles); 1975—appearance in reel 3 of *Diaries, Notes & Sketches—Volume 1, reels 1-6: Lost Lost Lost* (Jonas Mekas); 1978—guest star in *Opening Night* (Cassavetes).

Publications:

By BOGDANOVICH:

Books—*The Cinema of Orson Welles*, New York 1961; *The Cinema of Howard Hawks*, New York 1962; *The Cinema of Alfred Hitchcock*, New York 1963; *Fritz Lang in America*, New York 1967; *John Ford*, Berkeley, California 1968; *Alan Dwan: The Last Pioneer*, New York 1971 (rev. ed. 1981); *Pieces of Time*, New York 1973; *John Ford*, rev. ed., Berkeley, California 1978; *Fritz Lang in America*, New York 1981; articles—"Bogie in Excelsis" in *Esquire* (New York), September 1964; "Go-Go and Hurry: It's Later Than You Think" in *Esquire* (New York), February 1965; "Th' Respawnsibility of Bein' J...Jimmy Stewart. Gosh!" in *Esquire* (New York), July 1966; "Godard in Hollywood" in *Take One* (Montreal), June 1968; "Targets" in *Sight and Sound* (London), winter 1969/70; "Without a Dinosaur", interview by Gordon Gow in *Films and Filming* (London), June 1972; "Inter/View with Peter Bogdanovich" by G. O'Brien and R. Feiden in *Inter/View* (New York), March 1972; "Peter Bogdanovich on Paper Moon", interview by D. Lyons and others in *Interview* (New York), July 1973; "Cybill and Peter", interview by Andy Warhol and others in *Interview* (New York), June 1974; interview by B.J. Demby in *Filmmakers Newsletter* (Ward Hill, Mass.), June 1975; "Bogdanovich: 'Nessun omaggio al cinema'", interview edited by V. Giacci, in *Filmcritica* (Rome), May 1976; "Polly Platt: Sets the Style", interview by M. McAndrew, in *Cinema* (Beverly Hills), no.35, 1976; "Originaliteit als criterium voor kunst is belackelijk", interview by A. de Jong in *Skoop* (Amsterdam), April 1977; "Dialogue on Film: Peter Bogdanovich" in *American Film* (Washington, D.C.), December/January 1978/79; "American Journal" (interview with John Wayne) in the *New York Times*, 25 June 1979; "Peter Bogdanovich et Saint-Jack", interview by J. Meurice in *Amis du film et de la television* (Brussels), November 1979; "Bogdanovich ou le malentendu", interview and article by A. Garel and G. Grassard in *Image et son* (Paris), January 1980.

On BOGDANOVICH:

Books—*The Director's Event* by Eric Sherman and Martin

Rubin, New York 1970; *Bogdanovich* by V. Giacci, Florence 1975; articles—"Hitchcockery" by Penelope Houston in *Sight and Sound* (London), autumn 1968; "Directed by John Ford Producing a Compilation Documentary" by R. Patterson in *American Cinematographer* (Los Angeles), November 1971; "Bogged Down: a Twitch in the Auteur Niche" by P. Rainer in *Film Critic* (New York), September/October 1972; "The Continental Divide" by J. Dawson in *Sight and Sound* (London), winter 1973/74; "Peter Bogdanovich" by W.E. Bühler in *Filmkritik* (Munich), January 1973; "Noch einmal: Peter Bogdanovichs historische Kommerzfilme" by J. Ebert in *Filmkritik* (Munich), February 1973; "Peter Bogdanovich" by Martin Kasindorf in *Action* (Los Angeles), July/August 1973; "Peter Bogdanovich Remembered and Assessed" by C. Starr in *Filmmakers Newsletter* (Ward Hill, Mass.), September 1973; "Une Nouvelle Vague américaine. 2 Peter Bogdanovich" by M. Elia in *Sequences* (Montreal), July 1977; "At the Movies: How Bogdanovich Learned to Think Small Again" by T. Buckley in the *New York Times*, 20 April 1979; "At the Movies: The Truth About Making a Movie in Singapore" by T. Buckley in the *New York Times*, 2 February 1979; "Dossier: Hollywood 79: Peter Bogdanovich" by J. Fieschi in *Cinématographe* (Paris), March 1979.

* * *

Of all trades ancillary to the cinema, few offer worse preparation for a directing career than criticism. Bogdanovich's background as Hollywood historian and profiler of its legendary figures inevitably invited comparisons between his films and those of directors like Ford, Hawks and Dwan whom he had deified. That he should have occasionally created films which deserve such comparison argues for his skill and resilience.

He first attracted attention with *Targets*, a flashy exercise with an ailing Karloff playing straight man to Bogdanovich's film-buff director and a psychotic sniper menacing the audience at a drive-in cinema. The documentary *Directed by John Ford* likewise exploited Hollywood history, but with uncertain scholarship and even less certain taste. Yet in his first major fiction feature, based on Larry McMurtry's rural nocturne *The Last Picture Show*, Bogdanovich created a precise and moving chronicle of small-town values eroded by selfishness and disloyalty. He also showed a flair for casting in his choice of underrated veterans and fresh newcomers. Ben Johnson, Cloris Leachman and Ellen Burstyn earned new respect, while Timothy Bottoms, Jeff Bridges and Cybill Shepherd received boosts to nascent careers—though Shepherd, via her relationship with the director, was to prove a troublesome protegé.

What's Up Doc? and *Paper Moon* are among the shapeliest comedies of the seventies, trading on nostalgia but undercutting it with sly character/playing and deadpan wit. Ryan and Tatum O'Neal achieve a stylish ensemble performance in the latter as thirties con-man and unwanted orphan auxillary; in the former, O'Neal makes a creditable attempt at playing Cary Grant to Barbra Streisand's Hepburn, backed up by a typically rich character cast, notably Austin Pendleton, Kenneth Mars and the ululating Madeline Kahn.

Daisy Miller, a period vehicle for Shepherd more redolent of Henry King than Henry James, inaugurated Bogdanovich's decline. An attempt at a thirties Cole Porter musical, *At Long Last Love* likewise flopped, as did *Nickelodeon*, an unexpectedly leaden tribute to pioneer moviemaking. He returned to form with a low-budget adaptation of Paul Theroux's *Saint Jack*, dignified by Ben Gazzara's performance as the ironic man of honor coping with Occidental venality and Asian corruption. And the Manhattan comedy *They All Laughed*, though widely disliked, showed a truer synthesis of screwball humour and sentimentality than other equivalent films, and marked a return by Bogdanovich to the spirit of the classical directors he admires. In 1982 he announced his relocation to Texas, a state, he feels, with fewer restrictions on the making of film, and the one which inspired his first success. One hopes it will put him back in touch with the tradition of thirties program cinema he so clearly enjoys.

—John Baxter

BOLOGNINI, MAURO. Italian. Born in Pistoia, 28 June 1922. Educated in architecture, University of Florence; studied production and film directing at Centro Sperimentale di Cinematografia. Career: 1948-52—assistant to Luigi Zampa, Jean Delannoy and Yves Allégret; after 1964—active as opera and stage director; 1971—collaborated in *12 dicembre*, collective work produced by "Lotta continua" political group. Recipient: Best Script, Cannes Festival, for *Newlyweds*, 1958.

Films (as director and co-scriptwriter): 1953—*Ci troviamo in galleria*; *Canzone appasionata* (Simonelli) (sc only); 1954—*I cavalieri della regina*; *1955—La vena d'oro*; (as director): 1955—*Gli innamorati (Wild Love)*; 1956—*Guardia, guardia scelta, brigadiere e maresciallo*; 1957—*Marisa la civetta* (+co-sc); *Giovani mariti (Newlyweds, Young Husbands)* (+co-sc); 1959—*Arrangiatevi!*; *La notte brava (On Any Street, Bad Girls Don't Cry)*; 1960—*Il bell'Antonio* (+co-sc); *La giornata balorda (From a Roman Balcony, A Crazy Day, Pickup in Rome)*; *La viaccia (The Love Makers)*; 1961—*Senilità* (+co-sc); 1962—*Agostino* (+co-sc); 1963—*La corruzione*; 1964—"Gli amanti celebri" episode of *I tre volti*; "Monsignor Cupido" episode of *Le bambole*; "I miei cari" episode of *La mia signora*; "La balena bianca" and "Una donna dolce dolce" episodes of *La donna è una cosa meravigliosa*; 1965—*Madamigella di Maupin*; 1966—"Fata Elena" episode of *Le Fate*; 1967—"Nuits romaines (Notti romane)" episode of *Le Plus Vieux Métier du monde (The Oldest Profession)*; "Senso civico" episode of *Le streghe*; *Arabella*; 1968—"Perché?" and "La gelosa" episodes of *Capriccio all'italiana*; *Un bellissimo novembre*; 1969—*L'assoluto naturale* (+co-sc); *Metello* (+co-sc); 1970—*Bubú* (+co-sc); 1971—*Imputazione di omicidio per uno studente*; 1974—*Fatti di gente per bene (La Grande Bourgeoise)* (+co-sc); *Libera, amore mio!* (+co-sc); 1976—*Per le antiche scale (Down the Ancient Stairs)*; *L'eredità Ferramonti*; 1977—*La Signora degli Orrori (Black Journal)*; *Gran bollito*; 1978—"Sarò tutta per te" episode of *Dove vai in vacanza?*; 1981—*La vera storia della Signora delle Camelie (The True Story of Camille)* (+co-pr).

Publications:

On BOLOGNINI:

Book—*Bolognini* by Jean Gili and others, Rome 1977; articles—"Italy: The Moral Cinema" by Vernon Young in *Film Quarterly* (Berkeley), fall 1961; "The Italian Film: Antonioni, Fellini, Bolognini" by Anne Paolucci in *Massachusetts Review* (Amherst), summer 1966; "Sur 3 films de Mauro Bolognini" by R. Bassan and others in *Ecran* (Paris), April 1977; "Actualité de Bolognini" by B. Duval and A. Tassone in *Image et son* (Paris), May 1977.

*   *   *

Of the Italian directors who began their careers in the early fifties, Mauro Bolognini was among those who embrace the sociological themes of post-war neorealism but moved away from its aesthetic imperatives. Having worked in France as an assistant to Jean Dellanoy and Yves Allégret, Bolognini had been trained in a production style which involved the use of professional performers and studio settings, production aspects eschewed by neorealists. In his films Bolognini continued to place emphasis on these codes.

While many of his films were adaptations of literary works by writers such as Italo Svevo (*Senilità*), Alberto Moravia (*Agostino*) and Vasco Pratolini (*Metello*), the writer Bolognini claims to have affected his career most was Pier Paolo Pasolini. Bolognini had wanted to use Pasolini on his second feature, *Gli innamorati*, but was forbidden from doing so by producers who claimed Pasolini was not yet a 'known' writer. In spite of this, Bolognini claims the film to be very much in the spirit of Pasolini. In 1957 the two were finally allowed to collaborate (on *Marisa la civetta*) and before Pasolini turned to directing films in 1961, the two worked on three additional films, two of which were based on Pasolini stories (*La Notte brava* and *La giornata balorda*). The third collaboration, *Il bell'Antonio*, is among Bolognini's best films and among the best performances in the career of its star, Marcello Mastroianni. While many critics have persuasively argued that Bolognini's career flagged without Pasolini's contributions, such is far too easy an assessment, *Fatti di gente per bene* being an obvious exception to such an indictment.

Unlike other prominent Italian filmmakers, Bolognini has not considered himself a political filmmaker, openly admitting to a sentimentalized aspect of his treatment of the human condition. In many of his later films, his protagonists are defeated characters who fight only when pushed to the limit by a society which has not allowed for their individuality. In his direction Bolognini has characteristically built sympathy for the character rather than hatred against the state or institution.

Having come to cinema from architecture, Bolognini has consistently used settings and cinematography to most fully communicate a character's condition. In *Senilità* for example, the hopeless squalor of Emilio's (Anthony Franciosa) life as a public official involved in a masochistic love affair with the prostitute Angiolina (Claudia Cardinale) is best conveyed by the atmospheric cinematography of Arando Nannuzzi and the claustrophobic settings of Luigi Scaccianoce.

In line with this interest in performance values and his background in set design, Bolognini has regularly directed both opera and theatre.

—Doug Tomlinson

BOORMAN, JOHN. British. Born at Shepperton, Middlesex, England, 18 January 1933. Career: 1949-50—film critic for revues and on radio; 1953-54—military service; 1955—becomes assistant director for television; 1957—begins directing documentaries for Southern Television; 1962—becomes head of BBC documentary section; makes *Citizen 63*, *The Newcomers* and *The Quarry* for TV; 1965—1st feature, *Catch Us If You Can*; 1966—for BBC makes *The Great Director* on D.W. Griffith; while researching Griffith film in Los Angeles, meets producers Robert Chartoff and Irwin Winkler who propose adaptation of Richard Stark novel *The Hunter* (*Pointblank*); 1967—moves to U.S. to direct *Point Blank*. Business Manager: Edgar F. Gross, International Business Management, Los Angeles, California.

Films (as director): 1965—*Catch Us If You Can*; 1967—*Point Blank*; 1968—*Hell in the Pacific*; 1970—*Leo the Last*; 1972—*Deliverance*; 1973—*Zardoz*; 1977—*The Exorcist II: The Heretic*; 1980—*Merlin and the Knights of King Arthur*; 1981—*Excalibur* (+pr, co-sc).

Publications:

By BOORMAN:

Articles—"Déliverance", interview by G. Allombert, in *Image et son* (Paris), November 1972; "Brève rencontre avec John Boorman" by G. Braucourt in *Ecran* (Paris), November 1972; "Playboy in a Monastery", interview by Gordon Gow, in *Films and Filming* (London), February 1972; "L'Amerique s'est dissociée de la nature, par un sort de névrose commune...", interview by M. Grisolia, in *Cinéma* (Paris), November 1972; "Conversation with John Boorman" by L. Strawn in *Action* (Los Angeles), November/December 1972; "2 Entretiens avec John Boorman" by Michel Ciment in *Positif* (Paris), March 1974; "Zardoz", interview by P. Strick, in *Sight and Sound* (London), spring 1974; "Zardoz: Entretien avec John Boorman" by Max Tessier in *Ecran* (Paris), March 1974; "Director John Boorman Talks About His Work" in *American Cinematographer* (Los Angeles), March 1975; "Visual Metaphors for Violence", interview, in *Variety* (New York), 20 October 1976; "Rencontre expresse avec John Boorman" by H. Béhar in *Image et son* (Paris), March 1978; "Entretien avec John Boorman" by Michel Ciment in *Positif* (Paris), February 1978; interview by J.-P. Le Pavec and D. Rabourdin in *Cinéma* (Paris), March 1978; "The Technology of Style", interview by J. Verniere in *Filmmakers Monthly* (Ward Hill, Mass.), June 1981; "The Sorcerer: John Boorman Interviewed" by D. Yakir in *Film Comment* (New York), May/-June 1981.

On BOORMAN:

Articles—"The Writer in American Films" by Stephen Farber in *Film Quarterly* (Berkeley), summer 1968; "Islands of the Mind" by John Brown in *Sight and Sound* (London), winter 1969/70; "John Boorman" by D. McGillivray in *Focus on Film* (London), autumn 1972; "Deliverance/Boorman: Dickey in the Woods" by M. Dempsy in *Cinema* (Beverly Hills), spring 1973; article in *Avant-Scène du cinéma* (Paris), April 1974; "Hommage à Boorman" by G. Legrand in *Positif* (Paris), March 1974; "En travaillant avec Boorman" by Bill Stair in *Positif* (Paris), March 1974; "The Exorcism of *The Heretic*" by T. McCarthy in *Film Comment* (New York), September/October 1977; special issue on *Exorcist II* of *Avant-Scène du cinéma* (Paris), 1 February 1978; "L'inconscient chez John Boorman" by M. Mathieu in *Positif* (Paris), February 1978; biofilmography by J.-P. Piton in *Image et son* (Paris), April 1981; "Un Héraut de notre temps" by M. Sineux in *Positif* (Paris), October 1981.

*   *   *

John Boorman's career as a director has certainly had its ups and downs. He has made some films that were extremely popular with the public, such as *Deliverance*, and others that were so disliked that audiences reportedly threw popcorn at the screen (*Exorcist II: The Heretic*). Although his films have prompted such diverse reactions, they still maintain a consistent style that distinguishes Boorman as a very unique and individual film director.

One of the ties that links Boorman's films together is the idea of the quest. Boorman acknowledges that one of the greatest influences on his career has been the Arthurian legends. The most obvious example of this interest is his most recent film, *Excalibur*, which deals directly with the characters of King Arthur and Merlin. But many of Boorman's earlier characters also had to face a quest. For example, in *Deliverance* four men canoe down a river as a test of their manhood. Father Lamont in *Exorcist II* must go to Africa to find the secret of the ancient demon Pazuzu. All of these characters must make a journey of discovery in order to learn more about themselves.

Boorman's films also show a fascination with magic and nature. *Deliverance* is a story of men who have lost touch with nature; *Zardoz* deals with the breakdown of science and the "perfect" Utopian society in favor of nature and a "less perfect" but more real world. *Exorcist II* (unlike the first *Exorcist*) is a glorification of the positive side of psychic power.

Boorman's films, even those that are more "realistic," have a dream-like or fantasy element. He doesn't tell a story in a linear way, but floats in and out of scenes. There are many examples of this kind of editing in *Exorcist II* as Father Lamont makes his search for Pazuzu. Without the conventional signals of a dissolve or ripple glass, it becomes difficult to distinguish between reality and unreality (or perhaps they are one and the same). Fantasy is also brought out in Boorman's films through his use of lighting. In *Excalibur* Boorman lit his exteriors with colored lights (for example, green lights on the bushes and trees) to give the film a saturated and surreal quality. The opposite effect was created for *Deliverance*. In this case the colors were desaturated in the lab (leaving mostly browns, greys, and greens) to make the forest seem more terrifying. In all of these examples Boorman uses the elements of film to create a subtly fantastic effect.

In terms of success and popularity, Boorman's films have occupied both ends of the spectrum. *Deliverance* was one of the most popular films of 1972 and made Boorman one of the more sought after directors in Hollywood. *Exorcist II* nearly destroyed that reputation. The film received such a bad reception that it was re-cut within 24 hours after opening. Boorman himself takes most of the blame for the failure, saying that he was a "victim of audience expectations" and failed to give audiences what they wanted (in this case, more pea soup).

Eventually Boorman overcame this failure with *Excalibur*. He worked on the film at no salary (he did contract for a percentage of the profits) and produced it for $11.5 million, a bargain compared with the *Star Wars* and *Superman* sagas. *Excalibur* was both a critical and financial success which helped to put Boorman back on the track.

—Linda J. Obalil

BORAU, JOSÉ LUIS. Spanish. Born in Saragossa, 1929. Educated at University of Madrid, degree in law; diploma, Escuela Oficial de Cinematografía (Film School), Madrid. Career: 1953—film critic for Saragossan newspaper *El Heraldo de Aragon*; 1965-70—professor of screenwriting, Escuela Oficial de Cinematografía, Madrid; 1966-present—produces many documentaries and TV programs; 1967—establishes El Imán (The Magnet) production company; 1969—produces *Un dos tres...al escondite inglés (Hide and Seek, Popland)*, considered best Spanish film musical; 1970s-present—directs documentaries, publicity films, and for Spanish TV series including *Dichoso*

Mundo, Conozca, Ud. España, and *Fiesta.*

Films (as director): 1961—*En el rio (In the River)* (diploma film); 1963—*Brandy, el sheriff de Losatumba (Brandy, the Sheriff of Losatumba)*; 1964—*Crimen de doble filo (Double-edged Murder)*; (as producer and scriptwriter): 1969—*Uno dos tres...al escondite inglés (Popland)* (Zulueta); 1972—*Mi Querida señor- ita (My Dearest Señorita)* (de Armiñan) (art d, +ro as doctor); (as producer, director and scriptwriter): 1974—*Hay que matar a B (B Must Die)* (co-sc); 1975—*Furtivos (Poachers)* (+ro); 1977— *Camada Negra* (Guttiérez Aragon) (pr, sc only); *Adios Alicia* (San Miguel and Pérez) (pr only); *In Memoriam* (Brasó) (co-pr only); 1978—*El Monosabio* (pr, sc only); 1979—*La Sabina*; 1983—*Rio Abajo*; Roles: *El Juego de la Oca* (Summers); *La Adultera* (Bodegas); *Sonambulos* (Guttierez Aragon).

Publications:

By BORAU:

Articles—"Borau sobre *Furtivos*" by Jaime Millás in *Revista de occidente* (Madrid), February 1976; "Without Weapons" in *The Quarterly Review of Film Studies* (Pleasantville, New York), spring 1983; interview by José Maria Carreño in *Casablanca* (Madrid), June 1983.

On BORAU:

Articles—"José Luis Borau: El Francotirador responsable" by Marías Miguel in *Dirigido por* (Barcelona), September 1975; "Borau: Un realizador desaprovechado" by Jesus and Javier Martínez de Leon in *Possible* (Madrid), 19 June 1975; "Furtivos" by Roger Mortimore in *Sight and Sound* (London), winter 1975/76; "José Luis Borau, realizador furtivo" by César Santos-Fontenla in *Informaciones* (Madrid), 19 September 1975; "Fur- tivos" by Carolyn Lewis in *Monthly Film Bulletin* (London), April 1976; "Los Furtivos" by Gilles Dagneau in *Image et son* (Paris), September 1977; "A New Cinematic Age" by Reavis Ward in *Upstart Magazine* (New York), spring 1978; "José Luis Borau: La belleza y la racionalidad de un clásico" by Carlos Heredero in *Argumentos* (Madrid), February 1980; "Nuevo cine español: José Luis Borau", in 2 parts, by Katherine Kovács in *Suplemento cultural de la Opinion* (Los Angeles), 30 March and 13 April 1980.

*   *   *

José Luis Borau is one of the most versatile of Spain's film- makers. He has directed, written, produced, and even acted in a number of movies. A former professor of screenwriting at the official film school of Madrid, he taught some of Spain's most talented young writers and directors. Several of them subse- quently made their debut working with Borau in his own produc- tion company, El Iman, which he established in 1968.

With El Iman, Borau embarked upon a series of movies in which he sought artistic as well as financial independence. He produced and co-wrote some of them including *Uno, dos, tres ... al escondite inglés*, an offbeat musical, *Mi querida señorita*, the story of a middleaged woman who discovers that she is a man, nominated for an Oscar in 1973 and *Camada Negra*, a controver- sial political thriller about a band of right wing terrorists.

The movies written and directed by Borau display a compar-

able range in subject and style. *Hay que matar a B* takes place in an imaginary South American country where a foreigner unwit- tingly becomes involved in a ploy to assassinate the President, a plot in which he himself becomes trapped. *Furtivos* is also about individuals who become caught in traps that prove to be as deadly as those that the poacher in the title sets for his animals. *Furtivos* is set in rural Spain among people who live marginal "furtive" lives. Its setting recalls Franco's famous statement that Spain was a peaceful forest. And in the forest that Borau uses to represent Spain we see what is hidden in a stark and dramatic tale of violence, betrayal and incest. But in spite of its sensationalistic elements, the story unfolds with simplicity and even austerity as Borau omits the crucial scenes of violence, leaving it up to the spectators to reconstruct what has happened. *Furtivos* is a rich and complex film that operates on many levels. It is therefore all the more remarkable that it achieved not only critical acclaim but also great popular success. When it was released it immediately became the top-grossing Spanish film of all time. It later went on to win international awards, bringing Borau national and inter- national recognition.

In *La Sabina* Borau moves away from complex fables and tells a more straightforward story of superstition and love among people of different nationalities, cultural conditions and social classes who meet in a town in Andalusia. The movie, a Spanish- Swedish co-production with cast and crew from four different countries, is a meditation on the nature of myths and on the power of elemental forces to draw characters from different countries and backgrounds together. Although very different in style from *Furtivos*, in both movies Borau presents unusual female characters who are both victims and victimizers in a rigid social structure. Here as in all of his movies Borau is interested in character and story rather than in symbols, unusual camera angles, or striking cinematic effects. The meticulous elegance with which he tells his stories is in the best tradition of the filmmakers whom he most admires: Fritz Lang, Jean Renoir, and other "classical" directors whose styles are unobtrusive and unpretentious but perfectly suited to the stories that they tell. Like them, Borau is an independent, original talent and a world class filmmaker.

—Katherine Singer Kovács

BORZAGE, FRANK. American. Born in Salt Lake City, Utah, 23 April 1893. Married Rena Rogers (divorced 1945); married Edna Marie Stillwell, 1945 (divorced 1949); married Juanita Borzage, who survived him. Career: 1906—joins theatrical tour- ing company as prop boy; 1912—arrives in California, begins acting in bit parts; 1913-15—plays leading roles in many Ince Westerns and Mutual comedies; 1916—begins directing for Uni- versal; 1935-42—signs with MGM; 1945—joins Republic Pic- tures as producer-director; Died of cancer in Los Angeles, 19 June 1962. Recipient: Best Director Academy Award for *Sev- enth Heaven*, 1927/28; Best Director Academy Award for *Bad Girl*, 1931/32.

Films (as director): 1916—*That Gal of Burke's* (+ro); *Mammy's Rose* (co-d, +ro); *Life's Harmony* (co-d, +ro); *The Silken Spider* (+ro); *The Code of Honor* (+ro); *Nell Dale's Men Folks* (+ro); *The Forgotten Prayer* (+ro); *The Courtin' of Calliope Clew* (+ro); *Nugget Jim's Pardner* (+ro); *The Demon of Fear* (+ro); *Land o' Lizards (Silent Shelby)* (+ro); *Immediate Lee (Hair Trigger Casey)* (+ro); *Enchantment* (+sc, ro); *The Pride and the Man* (+sc, ro); *Dollars of Dross* (+sc); 1917—*Wee Lady Betty* (co-d, +ro); *Flying Colors*; *Until They Get Me*; 1918—*The Atom* (+ro); *The Gun Woman* (+ro); *Shoes That Danced*; *Innocent's Progress*; *An Honest Man*; *Society for Sale*; *Who Is to Blame?*; *The Ghost Flower*; *The Curse of Iku* (+ro); 1919—*Toton*; *Prudence of Broadway*; *Whom the Gods Destroy*; *Ashes of Desire*; 1920—*Humoresque*; 1921—*The Duke of Chimney Butte*; *Get-Rich-Quick Wallingford*; 1922—*Back Pay*; *Billy Jim*; *The Good Provider*; *Hair Trigger Casey* (re-edited version); *Silent Shelby* (reissue of *Land o' Lizzards*); *The Valley of Silent Men*; *The Pride of Palomar*; 1923—*The Nth Commandment*; *Children of the Dust*; *Age of Desire*; 1924—*Secrets*; 1925—*The Lady*; *Daddy's Gone A-Hunting*; *Lazybones*; *Wages for Wives*; *The Circle*; 1926—*The First Year*; *The Dixie Merchant*; *Early to Wed*; *Marriage License?*; 1927—*Seventh Heaven*; 1928—*Street Angel*; 1929—*The River*; *Lucky Star*; *They Had to See Paris*; 1930—*Song o' My Heart*; *Liliom*; 1931—*Doctors' Wives*; *Young as You Feel*; *Bad Girl*; 1932—*After Tomorrow*; *Young America*; *A Farewell to Arms*; 1933—*Secrets* (remake of 1924 film); *Man's Castle*; 1934—*No Greater Glory*; *Little Man What Now?* (+pr); *Flirtation Walk* (+pr); 1935—*Living on Velvet*; *Stranded*; *Shipmates Forever*; 1936—*Desire*; *Hearts Divided*; 1937—*Green Light*; *History Is Made at Night*; *Big City*; 1938—*Mannequin*; *3 Comrades*; *The Shining Hour*; 1939—*Disputed Passage* (+co-pr); 1940—*Strange Cargo*; *The Mortal Storm* (+co-pr); 1941—*Flight Command*; *Smilin' Through*; 1942—*The Vanishing Virginian*; *7 Sweethearts*; 1943—*Stage Door Canteen*; *His Butler's Sister* (+co-pr); 1944—*Till We Meet Again* (+pr); 1945—*The Spanish Main*; 1946—*I've Always Loved You* (+pr); *Magnificent Doll*; 1947—*That's My Man* (+pr); 1949—*Moonrise*; 1958—*China Doll* (+pr); 1959—*The Big Fisherman*.

Publications:

By BORZAGE:

Articles—in *Motion Picture Directing: The Facts and Theories of the Newest Art* by Peter Milne, New York 1922; interview by V. Tully in *Vanity Fair* (New York), February 1927; "What's Wrong with the Movies?" in *Motion Picture* (New York), September 1933.

On BORZAGE:

Books—*Amour, éroticisme et cinéma* by Ado Kyrou, Paris 1957; *The Hollywood Professionals* vol.3 by John Belton, New York 1974; articles—"Frank Borzage" by Henri Agel in *New York Film Bulletin*, no.12-14, 1961; obituary in the *New York Times*, 20 June 1962; "Second Line" by Andrew Sarris in *Film Culture* (New York), spring 1963; "Souls Made Great By Love and Adversity: Frank Borzage" by J. Belton in *Monogram* (London), no.4, 1972; "Sur 5 films de Frank Borzage" by Claude Beylie in *Ecran* (Paris), September 1976; "Disputed Passage" by Fred Camper in *Cinema* (London), v.9, no.10.

*   *   *

Frank Borzage had a rare gift of taking characters, even those who were children of violence, and fashioning a treatment of them abundant with lyrical romanticism and tenderness, even a spirituality that reformed them and their story.

He arrived in Hollywood in 1913, and Thomas H. Ince gave him his first small roles as a film actor, gradually promoted him to leads, and also to directing. He usually played the romantic lead in Westerns and romantic melodrama with such Triangle players as Sessue Hayakawa (*The Typhoon* and *Wrath of the Gods*, both 1914) and Olive Thomas (*Toton*, 1919). The first really important feature he directed was *Humoresque*, written by Frances Marion from a Fannie Hurst story. It had all the elements which were later to stamp a picture as a Borzage film—hope, love, and faith in himself and others in a world that was poverty-stricken and could be cruel. It won *Photoplay Magazine*'s award as Best Picture of the year.

He insisted that "Real art is simple, but simplicity requires the greatest art." He went on to say that "Naturalness is the primary requisite of good acting. I like my players to perform as though there were no camera on the set."

He did exceedingly well at Paramount's Cosmopolitan and at First National, where he directed two Norma Talmadge favorites, *Secrets* and *The Lady*. Then he moved over to Fox and in 1927 with *Seventh Heaven* he established himself as one of the best in the business. He directed two others with Janet Gaynor and Charles Farrell, *Street Angel* and *Lucky Star*. His *The River* of 1928, starring Farrell, is a virtual cinematic poem. In 1929 he directed his first all-talking feature, *They Had to See Paris*, starring Will Rogers, Fox's number one box-office star.

The year 1933 was probably his finest as a director, for he made three films which still rate as superb examples of the romantic cinema: *A Farewell to Arms*, from the Hemingway novel, with Gary Cooper and Helen Hayes; Mary Pickford's final and her very best, a re-make of *Secrets* in which Norma Talmadge had starred in the silent era; and *Man's Castle* with Spencer Tracy and Loretta Young, a very moving romance. Miss Pickford was desperate over *Secrets*. She had almost completely finished a version with Marshall Neilan directing, but had to halt production because it was obvious to her that Neilan was no longer able to direct because of his alcoholism. She junked that version, hired Frances Marion to write a complete new screenplay, and re-cast entirely. She started over this time with Borzage directing, an obvious choice because he had already directed Talmadge in the silent version, and had proved conclusively that he had mastered the talking picture. There was a lasting tenderness about Borzage's treatment of a love story, and during the days of the Depression and the rise of Fascism, his pictures were ennobling melodramas about the power of love to create a heaven on earth. He made four with Margaret Sullavan that clearly indicated that she was the quintessential heroine for Borzage films: *Little Man, What Now?*, a study of love in the midst of deprivation and the growing terror in Germany; *Three Comrades*, in which Sullavan played an ill-fated tubercular wife; *The Shining Hour* featuring her role as a self-sacrificing woman for which she was nominated by the Academy as Best Actress in 1938; and *The Mortal Storm*, a very moving film of the imminent battle with the Nazi forces. No director since Griffith had made love seem so timeless and eternal.

Also, he had directed three others during this time of stress that were extraordinary departures for him: *Desire*, a sleek romance in the Lubitsch tradition, starring Marlene Dietrich and Gary Cooper; *Mannequin*, co-starring Joan Crawford with Spencer Tracy, one of their best; and a drama that combined romance with effective disaster, *History Is Made at Night*, with Jean Arthur and Charles Boyer as lovers trapped in a Titanic-like explosion of violence. It is true that in the case of *Desire* Ernst Lubitsch was producer, but the picture has touches that are just as indicative of Borzage as they are of Lubitsch, for both were masters of cinematic subtlety.

In the post-war period, it began to be clear that Borzage's career was on the wane. His best picture was *Moonrise*. Penelope Gilliatt has remarked that "He had a tenderness rare in melodrama and absolute pitch about period. He understood adversity." Outside of Griffith, there has never been another director in the business who could so effectively triumph over sentimentality, using true sentiment with an honest touch.

—DeWitt Bodeen

BOULTING, ROY AND JOHN. British. Born as twins in Bray, Buckinghamshire, England, 21 November 1913. Educated at McGill University, Toronto. Roy married actress Hayley Mills, 1971 (divorced). Career: mid-1930s—John enters film industry as office boy, works as salesman, publicity writer and editor; introduced by brother, Roy begins working as assistant director; 1937—they found Charter Films; 1939—with capital from parents make short comedy (unreleased); 1940-45—John serves in film unit of Royal Air Force, Roy in British Army film unit; 1942—obtain leave at same time to make *Thunder Rock*; 1954—successful series of comedies begins with *Seagulls Over Sorrento*; 1958—both join board of British Lion Film Corp.

Films (Roy as director and John as producer, though functions overlap): 1938—*The Landlady*; *Ripe Earth*; *Seeing Stars*; *Consider Your Verdict*; 1939—*Trunk Crime*; 1940—*Inquest*; *Pastor Hall*; 1941—*Dawn Guard*; 1942—*Thunder Rock*; *They Serve Abroad*; 1943—*Desert Victory*; 1944—*Tunisian Victory* (co-d); 1945—*Burma Victory*; *Journey Together* (John d and Roy pr); 1947—*Fame Is the Spur*; *Brighton Rock (Young Scarface)* (John d and Roy pr); 1948—*The Guinea Pig (The Outsider)* (+co-sc); 1950—*7 Days to Noon* (John d and Roy pr); 1951—*Singlehanded (Sailor of the King)*; *High Treason* (+co-sc); *The Magic Box* (John d and Roy pr); 1954—*Seagulls Over Sorrento (Crest of the Wave)* (Roy and John co-d and co-pr, +sc); 1955—*Josephine and Men*; 1956—*Run for the Sun* (+co-sc); *Private's Progress* (John d and Roy pr, +co-sc); 1957—*Brothers in Law* (+co-sc); *Happy Is the Bride* (+co-sc); *Lucky Jim* (John d and Roy pr); 1959—*Carlton-Browne of the F.O. (Man in a Cocked Hat)* (co-d, +co-sc); *I'm All Right Jack* (John d and Roy pr, +co-sc); 1960—*A French Mistress* (+co-sc); *Suspect (The Risk)* (Roy and John co-d and co-pr); 1963—*Heavens Above!* (John d and Roy pr, +co-sc); 1965—*Rotten to the Core* (John d and Roy pr); 1966—*The Family Way* (+co-adaptation); 1968—*Twisted Nerve* (+co-sc); 1970—*There's a Girl in My Soup*; 1974—*Soft Beds and Hard Battles (Undercovers Hero)* (+co-sc); 1979—*The Number*.

Publications:

By BOULTING:

Articles—"What Makes the British Laugh?", interview with John Boulting by D. Conrad, in *Films and Filming* (London), February 1959; "Getting it Together" by Roy Boulting in *Films and Filming* (London), February 1974.

On BOULTING:

Articles—"The Boulting Twins" by S. Watts in *Films in Review* (New York), February 1960; "Pitfalls of Pratfalls: Boulting Brothers Comedies" by W. Sheed in *Commonweal* (New York), 5 July 1963.

BRAKHAGE, STAN. American. Born in Kansas City, Missouri, 14 January 1933. Educated at Dartmouth College, 1951; attended Institute of Fine Arts, San Francisco, 1953. Married Jane Collum, 1958; 5 children. Career: 1937-46—training as singer and pianist, performs as boy soprano on live radio and for recordings; 1952—drops out of college, begins making films in Colorado; runs small theater in Central City, Colorado; stages Wedekind and Strindberg; travels to San Francisco, meets poets including Kenneth Rexroth, Kenneth Patchen, Michael McClure, Louis Zukofsky; 1954—goes to New York, meets John Cage, studies informally with Edgard Varèse; becomes acquainted with avant-garde filmmakers including Maya Deren, Marie Menken, Willard Maas, Jonas Mekas; 1955—meets and shoots film for Joseph Cornell; 1956—works for Raymond Rohauer in Los Angeles, does first public lecturing on film in Rohauer's theater; 1956-64—does many commercial film projects including TV commercials and industrial films; 1957—moves to Denver, marries; subject matter of films shifts toward domestic family life; 1958—at Brussels film festival sees work of Peter Kubelka, Robert Breer; about 1960—begins presenting own films in public lecturing on his own and others' work; 1964-69—concentrates on 8mm filmmaking, in part due to 1964 theft of equipment; 1964—completes major works *The Art of Vision* and *Dog Star Man*; 1969—lectures in film history and aesthetics at Colorado University; 1970—begins teaching at the School of the Art Institute, Chicago; 1974—completes major "abstract" film *The Text of Light*; 1976—begins working in super-8mm; 1981—begins teaching at Colorado University. Recipient: James Ryan Morris Award, 1979; Telluride Film Festival Medallion, 1981. Agent: Film-Makers' Cooperative, 175 Lexington Ave., New York, NY 10016. Address: P.O. Box 170, Rollinsville, Colorado 80474.

Films: 1952—*Interim*; 1953—*Unglassed Windows Cast a Terrible Reflection*; *The Boy and the Sea*; 1954—*Desistfilm*; *The Extraordinary Child*; *The Way to Shadow Garden*; 1955—*In Between*; *Reflections on Black*; *The Wonder Ring* (with Joseph Cornell); "Tower House" (photographed for Joseph Cornell under working titles "Bolts of Melody" and "Portrait of Julie"; finally became Cornell's *Centuries of June*); *Untitled Film of Geoffery Holder's Wedding* (collaboration with Larry Jordan); 1956—*Zone Moment*; *Flesh of Morning*; *Nightcats*; 1957—*Daybreak and Whiteye*; *Loving*; 1958—*Anticipation of the Night*; 1959—*Wedlock House: An Intercourse*; *Window Water Baby Moving*; *Cat's Cradle*; *Sirius Remembered*; 1960—*The Dead*; 1961—*Thigh Line Lyre Triangular*; *Films By Stan Brakhage: An Avant-Garde Home Movie*; 1962—*Blue Moses*; *Silent Sound Sense Stars Subotnick and Sender*; 1963—*Oh Life—A Woe Story—The A Test News*; "Meat Jewel" (incorporated into *Dog Star Man: Part II*); *Mothlight*; 1964—*Dog Star Man* (in prelude and 4 parts dated as follows: *Prelude*, 1962; *Part I*, 1963; *Part II*, 1964; *Part III*, 1964; *Part IV*, 1964); 1965—*The Art of Vision* (derived from *Dog Star Man*); *3 Films* (includes *Blue White*, *Blood's Tone*, *Vein*); *Fire of Waters*; *Pasht*; *Two: Creeley/McClure* (also incorporated in *15 Song Traits*); *Black Vision*; 1968—*Lovemaking*; *The Horseman, The Woman and The Moth*; 1969—*Songs* (dated as follows: *Song 1*, 1964; *Songs 2 and 3*, 1964; *Song 4*, 1964; *Song 5*, 1964; *Songs 6 and 7*, 1964; *Song 8*, 1964; *Songs 9 and 10*, 1965; *Song 11*, 1965; *Song 12*, 1965; *Song 13*, 1965; *Song 14*, 1965; *15 Song Traits*, 1965; *Song 16*, 1965; *Songs 17 and 18*, 1965; *Songs 19 and 20*, 1965; *Songs 21 and 22*, 1965; *23rd Psalm Branch: Part I*, 1966 and *Part II and Coda*, 1967; *Songs 24 and 25*, 1967; *Song 26*, 1968; *My Mountain Song 27*, 1968; *Song 27 (Part II) Rivers*, 1969; *Song 28*, 1969; *Song 29*, 1969; *American 30's Song*, 1969; *Window Suite of Children's Songs*, 1969); 1970—*Scenes from Under Child-*

hood (dated as follows: *Section No.1*, 1967; *Section No.2*, 1969; *Section No.3*, 1969; *Section No.4*, 1970); *The Weir-Falcon Saga*; *The Machine of Eden*; *The Animals of Eden and After*; 1971—*"The Pittsburgh Documents": (Eyes; Deus Ex; The Act of Seeing with One's Own Eyes)*; *Foxfire Childwatch*; *Angels' Door*; *Western History*; *The Trip to Door*; *The Peaceable Kingdom*; 1972—*Eye Myth* (begun in 1968 as sketch for *The Horseman, The Woman and The Moth*) (16mm version); *Sexual Meditations* (titled and dated as follows: *Sexual Meditation No.1: Motel*, 1970; *Sexual Meditation: Room with View*, 1971; *Sexual Meditation: Faun's Room Yale*, 1972; *Sexual Meditation: Office Suite*, 1972; *Sexual Meditation: Open Field*, 1972; *Sexual Meditation: Hotel*, 1972); *The Process*; *The Riddle of Lumen*; *The Shores of Phos: A Fable*; *The Presence*; *The Wold Shadow*; 1973—*Gift*; *Sincerity*; *The Women*; 1974—*Skein*; *Aquarien*; *Hymn to Her*; *Star Garden*; *Flight*; *Dominion*; *he was born, he suffered, he died*; *Clancy*; *The Text of Light*; *The Stars Are Beautiful*; *Sol*; 1975—*Sincerity II*; *Short Films: 1975* (divided into Parts I-X); 1976—*Gadflies*; *Sketches*; *Airs*; *Window*; *Trio*; *Desert*; *Rembrandt, Etc. and Jane*; *Short Films: 1976*; *Tragoedia*; *Highs*; *The Dream, NYC, The Return, The Flower*; *Absence*; 1977—*Soldiers and Other Cosmic Objects*; *The Governor*; *The Domain of the Moment*; 1978—*Sincerity III*; *Nightmare Series*; *Duplicity*; *Duplicity II*; *Purity and After*; *Centre*; *Bird*; *Thot Fal'n*; *Burial Path*; *Sluice*; 1979—*Creation*; @; 1980—*Sincerity IV*; *Sincerity V*; *Duplicity III*; *Salome*; *Other*; *Made Manifest*; *Aftermath*; *Murder Psalm*; 1981—*Eye Myth* (original 35mm version); *Roman Numeral Series* (dated and titled as follows: 1979—*I, II*; 1980—*III, IV, V, VI, VII*; 1981—*VIII, IX*); *Nodes*; *RR*; *The Garden of Earthly Delights*; 1982—*Arabics* (dated and titled as follows: 1980—*1, 2, 3*; 1981—*4, 5, 6, 7, 8, 9, 0+10, 11, 12, 13, 14, 15, 16, 17, 18, 19*). Note: beginning 1978, many films first issued in 8mm or Super-8mm reissued in 16mm.

Commercial Work: 1957—*Martin Missil Quarterly Reports*; 1958—"Opening" for *G.E. Television Theatre*; 1959—*Untitled Film on Pittsburgh*; 1961—*The Colorado Legend and the Ballad of the Colorado Ute*; 1962—*Mr. Tomkins Inside Himself*; 1963-65—film on Mt. Rushmore, photographed for Charles Nauman's Part II film on Korczak Ziolkowski; film on Chief Sitting Bull.

Publications:

By BRAKHAGE:

Books—*Metaphors on Vision*, New York 1963; *A Motion Picture Giving and Taking Book*, West Newbury, Mass. 1971; *The Brakhage Lectures*, Chicago 1972; *Stan Brakhage, Ed Emshwiller* edited by Rochelle Reed, Washington, D.C. 1973; *Film Biographies*, Berkeley, California 1977; *Brakhage Scrapbook: Collected Writings 1964-1980*, New Paltz, New York 1982; articles—"The Silent Sound Sense" in *Film Culture* (New York), summer 1960; "Province-and-Providential Letters" in *Film Culture* (New York), spring 1962; "Excerpts from Letters" in *Film Culture* (New York), summer 1962; "Metaphors on Vision" in *Film Culture* (New York), no.30, 1963; "Letter to Gregory Markopoulos" in *Film Culture* (New York), winter 1963/64; "Interview with Stan Brakhage" by P. Adams Sitney in *Film Culture* (New York), fall 1963; "Sound and Cinema" (exchange of letters with James Tenney and Gregory Markopoulos) in *Film Culture* (New York), no.29, 1963; "Letter from Brakhage: On Splicing" in *Film Culture* (New York), winter 1964/65; "Letter to Yves Kovacs" in *Yale Literary Magazine* (New Haven), March 1965;

"Stan Brakhage Letters" in *Film Culture* (New York), spring 1966; "A Moving Picture Giving and Taking Book" in *Film Culture* (New York), summer 1966; "Letter to Jonas Mekas, September 1967" in *Filmmakers Newsletter* (Ward Hill, Mass.), December 1967; "On Dance and Film" in *Dance Perspectives*, summer 1967; "Transcription of Some Remarks..." in *Take One* (Montreal), September/October 1970; "In Defense of the Amateur Filmmaker" in *Filmmaklers Newsletter* (Ward Hill, Mass.), summer 1971; "Stan and Jane Brakhage Talking" by Hollis Frampton in *Artforum* (New York), January 1973; various writings in *Film Culture* (New York), no.67-69, 1979.

On BRAKHAGE:

Books—*Brakhage* by Dan Clark, New York 1966; *Stan Brakhage—A Retrospective* by Donald Richie, New York 1970; *Movie Journal, The Rise of a New American Cinema, 1959-1971* bu Jonas Mekas, New York 1972; *A History of the American Avant-Garde Cinema*, exhibition catalogue, by John Hanhardt and others, The American Federation of Arts, New York 1976; *Stan Brakhage*, exhibition catalogue for Filmex '76, by Fred Camper, Los Angeles 1976; *Stan Brakhage* by Marie Nesthus, Minneapolis/St. Paul 1979; *Visionary Film* by P. Adams Sitney, New York 1979; *Stan Brakhage*, catalogue introduction by Simon Field, Arts Council of Great Britain, 1980 or 1981; *By Brakhage: 3 Decades of Personal Cinema*, catalogue, by Fred Camper, New York 1981; articles—"Stan Brakhage" by Parker Tyler in *Film Culture* (New York), no.18, 1958; "Films of Stan Brakhage" by Ernest Callenbach in *Film Quarterly* (Berkeley), spring 1961; "Pioneer of the Abstract Expressionist Film" by Charles Boultenhouse in *Filmwise*, no.1, 1961; "Stan Brakhage's Critics" by Arthur Gordon in *Filmwise*, no.1, 1961; "A Love Affair: I Talk to Myself about Stan Brakhage" by Willard Maas in *Filmwise*, no.1, 1961; "A Note on Stan Brakhage" by Donald Sutherland in *Film Culture* (New York), no.24, 1962; "*Anticipation of the Night* and *Prelude*" by P. Adams Sitney in *Film Culture* (New York), no.26, 1962; "The Birth Film" by Jane Brakhage in *Film Culture* (New York), winter 1963/64; "Brakhage and Rilke" by Jerome Hill in *Film Culture* (New York), no.37, 1965; "Robert Kelly on *The Art of Vision*" in *Film Culture* (New York), summer 1965; "2 Essays on Brakhage and His Songs" by Jerome Hill and Guy Davenport in *Film Culture* (New York), spring 1966; "*The Art of Vision*, a Film by Stan Brakhage" by Fred Camper in *Film Culture* (New York), autumn 1967; "23rd Psalm Branch (Song XXIII) A Film by Stan Brakhage" by Fred Camper in *Film Culture* (New York), autumn 1967; "Up from the Underground" by K. Kroll in *Newsweek* (New York), 13 February 1967; "My Mtn. Song 27" by Fred Camper in *Film Culture* (New York), summer 1969; "Mehr Licht..." by Robert Creeley in *Film Culture* (New York), summer 1969; "Stan Brakhage: the Courage of Perception" by A. Sainer in *Vogue* (New York), 1 September 1970; "Avant Garde Film" by P. Adams Sitney in *Afterimage* (Rochester), autumn 1970; "Brakhage's Eyes" by Jerome Hill in *Film Culture* (New York), spring 1971; "Stan Brakhage: Transforming Personal Vision..." by Katherine Smith and "Discovering Stan Brakhage" by Douglas Lee in *Film Library Quarterly* (New York), summer 1971; "*Sexual Meditation No.1: Motel*, a Film by Stan Brakhage" by Fred Camper in *Film Culture* (New York), spring 1972; "Brakhage: A Learned Language" by P. Johnson in *Village Voice* (New York), 20 January 1972; article by Jonas Mekas in *Village Voice* (New York), 30 March 1972; "New Forms in Film" by Bill Simon in *Artforum* (New York), October 1972; "The Idea of Morphology" by P. Adams Sitney in *Film Culture* (New York), spring 1972; "Stan Brakhage: 4 Films" by P. Arthur in *Artforum* (New York), January 1973;

"Camera Lucida/Camera Obscura" by Annette Michelson, and "*Western History* and *The Riddle of Lumen*" by Fred Camper in *Artforum* (New York), January 1973; "*Scenes from Under Childhood*" by Phoebe Cohen in *Artforum* (New York), January 1973; "A Varied Burst of Brakhage" by Clinton Delancey in *Village Voice* (New York), 21 June 1973; "Brakhage's *The Act of Seeing with One's Own Eyes*" by Daniel Levoff in *Film Culture* (New York), spring 1973; "Movie Journal" by Jonas Mekas in *Village Voice* (New York), 14 November 1974; "Perspective Reperceived: Brakhage's *Anticipation of the Night*" in *The Essential Cinema* edited by P. Adams Sitney, New York 1975; "Brakhage: Artistic Development in 2 Childbirth Films" by William Barr in *Film Quarterly* (Berkeley), spring 1976; "The Super-8 Stan Brakhage" by Fred Camper in *Soho Weekly News* (New York), 23 December 1976; "Filmmaker Stan Brakhage: 'Movies Weaken Your Mind'" by William Gallo in *Denver* (Colorado), January 1976; "The Influence of Olivier Messiaen on the Visual Art of Stan Brakhage in *Scenes from under Childhood*" part 1 by M. Mesthus in *Film Culture* (New York), no.63-64, 1977; "Autobiography in Avant-Garde Film" by P. Adams Sitney in *Millenium* (New York), winter 1977/78; "Hyperkinetic Stan/dards" by Henry Hills in *Cinemanews* (San Francisco), November/December 1977; "Animal Cinema" by Ken Kelman in *Film Culture* (New York), no.63-64, 1977; "Brakhage and the Structuralists" by Jonas Mekas in *Soho Weekly News* (New York), 24 November 1977 (also see Brakhage reply in letters column 8 December 1977); "The Influence of Olivier Messiaen on the Visual Art of Stan Brakhage in *Scenes from Under Childhood*, Part 1" by Marie Nesthus in *Film Culture* (New York), no.63-64, 1977; articles in *Film Culture* (New York), no.67-69, 1979; "The Other Cinema" by Noel Carroll in *Soho Weekly News* (New York), 22 February 1979; "Brakhage's *Sincerity III*" by Phoebe Cohen in *Millenium Film Journal* (New York), no.4-5, 1979; "Stan Brakhage: Life Behind the Camera" by Jennifer Dunbar in *Boulder Monthly* (Colorado), September 1979; "*Text of Light*" by Bruce Jenkins and Noel Carroll in *Film Culture* (New York), no.67-69, 1979; "Brakhage's Dreamscape" by Christopher Sharrett in *Millennium Film Journal* (New York), spring 1980; "Brakhage's *I, II, III*" by Phoebe Cohen in *Millenium Film Journal* (New York), no.7-8-9, 1980/81; "Duplicitously Ours: Brakhage in New York" by J. Hoberman in *Village Voice* (New York), 8 April 1981; "Packaging Brakhage" by Amy Taubin in *Soho Weekly News* (New York), 15 April 1981.

*   *   *

Brakhage has been the most prolific and consistent of avant-garde filmmakers. Perhaps Andy Warhol made more films, or more hours of film, between 1963 and 1968, and James Broughton, Harry Smith, and Kenneth Anger have been making films for more years than Brakhage, but the outpouring of films he has created since he began in 1952 constitutes one of the most astounding achievements of any filmmaker. It is difficult to number Brakhage's films because so many of them are short and gathered into series under a collective title, e.g., thirty different *Songs* (some of which have subdivisions) or ten different *Short Films: 1975*. A conservative tally would list over a 100 titles. Only ten of them have soundtracks; and of those seven were made in his first five years, before his mature style emerged.

In his often obscure and poetic theoretical texts, Brakhage has at times held the position that sound has been an aesthetic error for the cinema. Yet generally he invokes the Emersonian argument of "necessity" to define his own production as not needing sound (in the sense of requiring it for clarity or effect) and of

himself not needing to make sound films (in the sense of hieratic inspiration, beyond his personal and rational decisions). The heart of Brakhage's theory (as forcefully represented in *Metaphors on Vision* and *Brakhage Scrapbook: Collected Writings* is the notion of cinema as the imitation of the act of seeing, which includes simultaneously the perpetually scanning eyes, the visual imagination and memory, and the phosphenes which are most distinct when the eyes are closed. For him, the act of making a film intensifies and makes conscious this perpetual process of vision. Any dramatic representation whatsoever is anathematized by him.

As a consequence of this thinking, the films of his maturity (since 1958) describe his daily life. The birth of his five children, his travels as a lecturer, visits to a hospital, morgue, grammar school, cemetery, a few days with the governor of Colorado, etc., are examples of the more thematically unified and conventionally intense experiences he has translated onto film. Yet more often the montage of glimpses from his daily life constructs a fabric of memory, fantasy, or dream, in which visual association plays a dominant role. No filmmaker, not even the great Soviet masters, can challenge the skill and diversity of Brakhage's editing. No major filmmaker has been as fanatical about performing all the operations of filmmaking himself.

Brakhage began to make films in 1952, in his native Colorado after dropping out of Dartmouth College as a freshman. He quickly met and fell under the influence of the chief figures of the avant-garde of the forties: Maya Deren, Willard Maas, Kenneth Anger, and Sidney Peterson. But it was the encounter with the very personal, and less expressionistic films of Marie Menken that seems to have had the most lasting influence, along with a passionate and prolonged reading of Gertrude Stein. There are hints of his turn from the acted psychodramas of his first period in the film Joseph Cornell commissioned about the soon-to-be-destroyed Third Avenue El, *Wonder Ring*, in his study of cats, *Nightcats*, and his portrait of friends necking, *Loving*. However, with his 42-minute long *Anticipation of the Night*, a melancholy meditation on suicide and the loss of innocent vision, he succeeded for the first time in making a film which described the act of seeing as well as the hopes and disappointments which attended his quest for a visionary experience.

In extreme poverty during the first years of his marriage, Brakhage had to conserve film materials penuriously, yet he managed to make a dozen films between 1959 and 1964 which established his reputation as the leading American avant-garde filmmaker. In this period of great intensity and invention, which includes his four part cosmological "epic" *Dog Star Man*, he wrote most of *Metaphors on Vision*. It was at that time that he actually sandwiched bits of flowers and mothwings between layers of mylar splicing tape to create the remarkable *Mothlight* because he could not afford film, but could not stop working. The complex achievements of this early period continue to define Brakhage's cinematic project: the representation of a lyrical self through camera movements, shifting light values, hand-painting over film, and above all associative editing, in response to the imagistic material presented on the screen.

The ineluctable need to keep making films led Brakhage to concentrate on 8mm filmmaking between 1964 and 1969. His complex series *Songs* began as an alternative to the painstaking editing of his 16mm films (and as an economic necessity when his equipment was stolen in 1964), but eventually they became even more painstaking and expensive as when he made the *23rd Psalm Branch*, his intricate, seven-part response to the Vietnam War.

The late sixties and seventies were dominated by a vast autobiographical film, still in progress, which contains the series *Scenes from Under Childhood* in four parts, *The Weir-Falcon Saga* in three, *Sincerity* in five, and *Duplicity* in three. In the same period he completed six *Sexual Meditations*, three "Pittsburgh Documents" consisting of *Eyes*, shot in a police car, *Deus Ex* in a surgery room, and the grisly *The Act of Seeing with One's Own Eyes* at an autopsy. In 1975 he began a series of films shot in Super-8mm and blown up to 16mm to enhance their grainy texture, and since 1979, after a plethora of short films, he has completed two series of purely abstract works, *Roman Numeral Series I-X* and *Arabics 1-0+10*.

—P. Adams Sitney

BREER, ROBERT. American. Born in Detroit, Michigan, 30 September 1926. Educated at Stanford University, BA 1949. Career: 1944—begins painting; 1949—moves to Paris, painting in mode of neo-plasticism; subsequently exhibits at Denise René Gallery and elsewhere; 1952—makes 1st film; 1955—following 1st one-person painting show, interest shifts to filmmaking; 1958—ceases painting; begins making mutoscopes; shows films at 1958 Brussels Avant-Garde Film Festival; sees films by Anger, Brakhage, Kubelka, Menken for 1st time; 1959—returns to U.S., settles in New York; 1965—exhibits kinetic and 'self-propelled' sculpture; 1971—film style shifts from abstract to more eclectic mode including use of rotoscoping and photographed images; 1973—begins teaching filmmaking at Cooper Union; 1981—paints large mural outside Film Forum, New York City. Agent: Film-Makers' Cooperative, 175 Lexington Ave., New York, NY 10016. Address: Cooper Union, Cooper Square, New York, NY 10013.

Films: 1952—*Form Phases I*; 1953—*Form Phases II and III*; 1954—*Form Phases IV*; *Image by Images I* (endless loop); *Un Miracle*; 1955—*Image by Images II and III*; 1956—*Image by Images IV*; *Motion Pictures*; *Cats*; 1956-57—*Recreation I*; *Recreation II*; 1957—*Jamestown Baloos*; 1958—*A Man and His Dog Out for Air*; *Par Avion*; 1958-59—*Cassis Colank*; *Chutes de pierres, danger du mort* (animation sequnce in film by Michel Fano); 1959—*Eyewash*; *Trailer*; 1960—*Homage to Jean Tinguely's "Homage to N.Y.";* *Inner and Outer Space*; 1961—*Blazes*; *Kinetic Art Show—Stockholm*; 1962—*Pat's Birthday*; *Horse Over Tea Kettle*; 1963—*Breathing*; 1964—*Fist Fight*; 1966—66; 1968—69; *PBL 2* and *PBL 3* (for PBL TV); 1970—70; 1971—*Elevator* (for CTW TV); *What?* (for CTW TV); 1972—*Gulls and Buoys*; 1974—*Fuji*; 1975—*Etc.*; *Rubber Cement*; 1977—77; 1978—*LMNO*; 1979—*TZ*; 1981—*Swiss Army Knife with Rats and Pigeons*; 1982—*Trial Balloons*.

Publications:

By BREER:

Articles—"On 2 Films" in *Film Culture* (New York), summer 1961; "Interview with Robert Breer" by Guy Cote in *Film Culture* (New York), winter 1962/63; "Robert Breer on His Work" in *Film Culture* (New York), fall 1966; "Tape Recorded Interview with Robert Breer" by Paul Cummings in *Archives of American Art* (New York), 10 July 1973; interview by Jonas Mekas and P. Adams Sitney in *Film Culture* (New York), spring 1973; interview in *The American Film Institute Report* (Washington, D.C.), summer 1974; "Independent Film: Talking with Robert Breer" by L. Fischer in *University Film Study Newsletter*

(Cambridge, Mass.), no.1, 1976; article in *Paris-New York*, exhibition catalogue, Centre Pompidou, Paris 1977.

On BREER:

Books—*The Machine as Seen at the End of the Mechanical Age*, exhibition catalogue, by K.G. Hulten, New York 1969; *A History of the American Avant-Garde Cinema*, exhibition catalogue, by John Hanhardt and others, The American Federation of Arts, New York 1976; *Experimental Animation* by Robert Russett and Cecile Starr, New York 1976; *Film as Film* by Birgit Hein, Arts Council of Great Britain, 1979; *Robert Breer* by Sandy Moore, St. Paul, Minnesota 1980; *Robert Breer: A Study of His Work in the Context of the Modernist Tradition* by Lois Mendelson, Metuchen, New Jersey 1982; articles—"*Images by Images, Cats, Jamestown Balloes, A Man and His Dog Out for Air* (films by Robert Breer)" by Noël Burch in *Film Quarterly* (Berkeley), spring 1959; "4 Artists as Filmmakers" by A. Mancia and W. Van Dyke in *Art in America* (New York), January 1967; "Motionless Motion" by H. Rosenstein in *Art News* (New York), November 1967; "Movie Journal" by Jonas Mekas in *The Village Voice* (New York), 24 April 1969; "Onward and Upward with the Arts" by Calvin Tomkins in the *New Yorker*, 3 October 1970; "Intellectual Cinema: A Reconsideration" by Annette Michelson in *Yale University Art Gallery Catalogue* (New Haven), April/May 1973; "*Gulls and Buoys*, an Introduction to the Remarkable Range of Pleasures Available from the Films of Robert Breer" by Scott Hammen in *Afterimage* (Rochester, New York), December 1974; "Avant Garde Film (Homage to Robert Breer)" by Lucy Fischer in *The Soho Weekly News* (New York), 3 April 1975; "Animated Dissection" by Fred Camper in *The Soho Weekly News* (New York), 20 May 1976; "At Long Last Breer" by Amy Taubin in *The Soho Weekly News* (New York), 14 April 1977; "Robert Breer: l'avant-garde revient aux sources" by A. Tournes in *Jeune cinéma* (Paris), March 1979; "The Other Cinema" by Noel Carroll in *The Soho Weekly News* (New York), 25 January 1979; "A Mixed Bag of Tricks" by J. Hoberman in *The Village Voice* (New York), 22 January 1979; "Robert Breer's Animated World" by J. Hoberman in *American Film* (Washington, D.C.), September 1980; "Robert Breer: Fuji, 77, LMNO and T.Z." by Fred Camper in *10 Years of Living Cinema*, New York 1982.

*   *   *

Robert Breer's work as a filmmaker has been primarily in animation. He has made two live-action films (*Pa's Birthday* and *Homage to Jean Tinguely's Homage to New York*), and many of his other films contain photographed images, but his films generally are made one or a few frames at a time, which is what distinguishes them from live-action cinema. However Breer is not simply one of many film animators: he is perhaps the most extraordinary maker of animated films the cinema has given us since Méliès.

Just as many avant-garde live-action filmmakers have defined their work in terms radically opposed to the "illusionistic" mainstream of commercial film, so Breer has defined his work in direct opposition to mainstream commercial animation. The Hollywood cartoon, and many of its offshoots, make use of the continuous movement of characters through connected spaces. Breer's films are full of disjunctive breaks, multiple and discontinuous spaces and rhythms, and acknowledgements, often humorous, of the animation process itself and the animator's presence.

The tremendous richness of Breer's cinema comes not from a simple exclusion of continuities, but rather from the attempt to *include* as much as possible. Thus he situates his films at a number of "thresholds." A burst of continuous movement will suddenly arrest itself in a freeze frame. Extremely jerky and irregular rhythms will unexpectedly become continuous ones. A drawn object will appear to rotate in three dimensions, creating the illusion of depth; a moment later we find ourself watching a flat surface once again. The soundtrack will oscillate between apparently synchronous effects that match the action, a more abstract accompaniment, and sounds that are intentionally, often humorously, at odds with the images. The viewer thus finds himself presented with a virtual panoply of styles and techniques. The effect is that the viewer is held literally at the edge of his perception by a continual process of surprise. Each time a brief section ("brief" being generally only a few seconds) establishes some form of continuity, the film leaps outside of the pattern just established into some new realm. While it should be clear from the foregoing that Breer's attitude toward his medium and its materials locates him clearly within the modernist tradition, the effect of his work is unique. Time and space are profoundly fragmented, and the film and its viewer are placed firmly in the infinitely uncertain realm of the instant.

While Breer's work as a whole is too various to be divided into periods, some categories can be mentioned. His earliest film, such as the *Form Phases* series, are abstract, and grew out of his work as an abstract painter. There are some hand-drawn animated films, such as *A Man and His Dog Out for Air* and *PBL 2*, in which tension is created between line as representation of figures and line as an abstraction. There are some highly eclectic works, such as *Eyewash* and *Fist Fight*, in which cut-outs, various kinds of animation, and live-action photography are intermixed. There are "abstract" animations such as *66*, *69*, and *70*, which are amazing for their fusion of purity and complexity. And there are Breer's films of the last decade, which form perhaps his most extraordinary sequence of works. In these films, hand-drawn abstract shapes are combined with images derived from photography or related media—created through rotoscoping, color photocopying, Polaroid still photography, or other similar means. Different kinds of image material interact in multiple ways, with the result being a new, and profoundly energized form of seeing, in which traces of recognizable objects perpetually oscillate between their existence as identifiable places and things and the multitudinous abstract shapes and colors that they contain, or suggest.

—Fred Camper

BRENON, HERBERT. American. Born in in Dublin, 13 January 1880; became citizen of of United States in 1918. Educated at St. Paul's School; studied medicine in King's College, London. Married Helen Oberg, 1904; son: Cyril Herbert Brenon. Career: 1896—emigrates to U.S., settles in New York; works as office boy for theatrical agent Joseph Vion; hired as extra in play *Sporting Life*; becomes call boy for producer Augustin Daly until Daly's death in 1899; 1900—becomes assistant stage manager to Shakespearean actor Walker Whiteside; 1903—engaged to direct Dick Ferris stock company, Minneapolis; 1908-10—joins and soon heads stock company in Johnstown, Pennsylvania, begins showing motion pictures as well; 1911—hired as scenario editor for Carl Laemmle's IMP Co.; 1912—directs 1st one-reeler; 1914-15—forms independent production company Tiffany Film Corp.; 1915—begins directing for William Fox with *The Kreutzer Sonata*; 1916—in budget dispute Fox removes

Brenon's name from credits of *A Daughter of the Gods*; sues Fox to no avail, severs association; forms production company in Hudson Heights, New Jersey, joins Lewis J. Selznick Alliance; 1st Selznick production is *War Brides*; 1918—dissolves production company; 1918—invited by British government to make propaganda film in England; 1918-20—directs for Select Film Company, London, then Unione Cinematografica Italiana, Rome; 1920—returns to U.S., directs 3 productions for Joseph Schenck; also directs 3 William Farnum films for Fox; 1923-27—under contract to Famous Players-Lasky (Paramount); 1930—makes 1st talkie *Lummox*; 1932—signs with independent producer I.E. Chadwick, releasing through Monogram; 1935-40—directs in Britain. Died 1958.

Films (as director—listing incomplete before 1921): 1912—*All for Her* (+sc, ro); *The Clown's Triumph*; *Leah the Forsaken* (+sc); 1913—*Ivanhoe* (+sc, ro as *Isaac of York*); *Time Is Money* (+ro); *Kathleen Mavourneen* (+sc); *The Angel of Death*; *The Anarchist*; 1914—*Absinthe*; *Neptune's Daughter* (co-d, +ro); *The Secret of the Air*; *Time Is Money*; *Across the Atlantic* (+ro as Japanese spy) (completed 1913); 1915—*The Heart of Maryland* (+pr); *The Kreutzer Sonata* (+sc); *The 2 Orphans* (+sc, ro as Pierre, the scissors-grinder); *The Clemenceau Case* (+sc); *Sin* (+sc); *The Soul of Broadway* (+sc); 1916—*A Daughter of the Gods* (d uncredited, +sc); *War Brides*; *Whom the Gods Destroy*; *Marble Heart* (+sc); *The Ruling Passion*; 1917—*The Eternal Sin*; *The Lone Wolf*; *The Fall of the Romanoffs*; *Empty Pockets*; *Kismet*; 1918—*The Passing of the Third Floor Back*; *Victory and Peace*; 1919—*Twelve: Ten* (+pr); *Princess Impudence*; *A Sinless Sinner*; 1920—*Sister Against Sister* (U.S. release 1922); *Chains of Evidence*; 1921—*The Passion Flower* (+co-sc); *The Sign on the Door* (+co-sc); *The Wonderful Thing* (+co-sc); 1922—*Any Wife*; *A Stage Romance*; *Shackles of Gold*; *Moonshine Valley* (+co-sc); *A Kiss for Cinderella*; 1923—*The Custard Cup*; *The Rustle of Silk*; *The Woman with 4 Faces*; *The Spanish Dancer* (+pr); 1924—*Shadows of Paris*; *The Side Show of Life* (+pr); *The Alaskan*; *Peter Pan*; *The Breaking Point*; 1925—*The Little French Girl*; *The Street of Forgotten Men*; 1926—*Dancing Mothers*; *Beau Geste*; *The Great Gatsby*; *God Gave Me 20 Cents*; *The Song and Dance Man*; 1927—*Sorrell and Son* (+sc); *The Telephone Girl* (+pr); 1928—*Laugh Clown Laugh*; 1929—*The Rescue*; 1930—*Lummox*; *The Case of Sergeant Grischa*; 1931—*Beau Ideal*; 1932—*Transgression*; *Girl of the Rio*; 1933—*Oliver Twist* (production supervisor only); *Wine, Women and Song*; 1934—*Sorrell and Son* (pr only—remake of 1927 film); 1935—*Royal Cavalcade (Regal Cavalcade)*; *Honours Easy*; 1936—*Living Dangerously*; *Someone at the Door*; 1937—*The Dominant Sex*; *Spring Handicap*; *The Live Wire*; 1938—*The Housemaster*; *Yellow Sands*; 1939—*Black Eyes*; 1940—*The Flying Squadron (The Flying Squad)*.

*   *   *

Dublin-born Herbert Brenon brought to the cinema an Irish temperament and a versatility which made him equally at ease with historical drama, fantasy and melodrama. After a year of learning his craft with Carl Laemmle's IMP Company, Brenon came to prominence as the director of *Ivanhoe*, a curtailed if respectable film version of Sir Walter Scott's novel, shot on location in England and starring the IMP Company's best-known leading man, King Baggot. *Ivanhoe* typified many of Brenon's productions; it was well-received critically and publicly, it offered spectacle and yet it was a somewhat static creation, lacking in zest.

In the mid-teens, Brenon directed Australian swimming star Annette Kellermann (who had become a vaudeville sensation thanks to her one-piece swimming costume) in *Neptune's Daughter* and *A Daughter of the Gods*. Both films were highly regarded, thanks in no small part to their star's "nude" sequences. Brenon's credit was removed from the latter film because its producer, William Fox, felt the director had spent an inordinate amount of time—nine months—on the production. The director sued Fox unsuccessfully, but his action did lead to Brenon's colleagues insisting on contracts granting them screen credit. Melodramas with Theda Bara (*The Kreutzer Sonata*) and about the Russian Revolution (*The Fall of the Romanoffs*) followed, and Brenon was even able to get a passable performance out of stage actor Sir Johnston Forbes-Robertson in *The Passing of the Third Floor Back*, but it was not until 1923 and the signing of a long-term contract with Famous Players-Lasky that Brenon again achieved the prominence he had held in the teens.

Brenon's Irish background should never be overlooked for assuredly it helped him bring just the right amount of whimsy to *Peter Pan* and *A Kiss for Cinderella*, which made a star of Betty Bronson. Its fantastical charm has seldom been equalled in the cinema. Whatever Brenon turned his directorial hand to, it seemed he could do no wrong in the twenties, be it the flapper revolution in *Dancing Mothers*, a foreign legion melodrama such as *Beau Geste*, or the first screen version of F. Scott Fitzgerald's *The Great Gatsby*. He seemed ill at ease with his first talkie, a stagey, depressing Fannie Hurst melodrama, *Lummox*. Brenon ended his career directing from 1935 through 1940 in England, where he was responsible for one minor masterpiece, *The Housemaster*, adapted from the Ian Hay play and a far more satisfactory study of public school life than, say, *Goodbye Mr. Chips*.

Herbert Brenon was not apparently an easy man to work with. He was a fierce taskmaster who was prone to fits of anger who failed to measure up to his demands. Nevertheless, he was a reliable technician who could rise to spectacular heights, as with *A Daughter of the Gods* and *Peter Pan*, and handle romantic melodrama, such as *Sorrell and Son*, without descending to the maudlin.

—Anthony Slide

BRESSON, ROBERT. French. Born in Bromont-Lamothe (Puy-de-Dôme), France, 25 September 1907. Educated Lycée Lakanal à Sceaux, Paris, Bachelor of Arts degree. Married Leidia van der Zee, 21 December 1926. Career: 1920s-1933—attempts career as painter; 1933-37—writes or co-writes film scripts for several directors; 1934—directs 1st film *Les Affaires publiques*; 1939—serves as assistant director to René Clair on the unfinished *Air pur*; 1940-41—prisoner of war in Germany; 1942-43—directs 1st major film *Les Anges du péché*; 1945—directs *Les Dames du Bois de Boulogne* co-written by Jean Cocteau; 1950—directs *Journal d'un curé de campagne (Diary of a Country Priest)*; using non-actors only; 1968—elected "Président d'honneur de la Société des réalisateurs de films"; 1969—directs 1st film in color, *Une Femme douce*; 1975—publishes book on filmmaking, *Notes sur le cinématographe*. Recipient: Venice Film Festival, International Prize for *Le Journal d'un curé de campagne*, 1951; Cannes Film Festival, Best Direction for *Un Condamné a mort s'est échappé*, 1957; Cannes Film Festival, Special Jury Prize for *Le Procès de Jeanne d'Arc*, 1962; Grand Prix national des Arts et des Lettres (Cinéma), France, 1978; Officier de la Légion d'honneur. Address: 49 Quai de Bourbon, 75004 Paris, France.

Films (dialogue): 1933—*C'était un musicien* (Zelnick and Gleize); (as director and scriptwriter): 1934—*Les Affaires publiques* (no known copies exist); 1936—*Les Jumeaux de Brighton* (Heymann) (co-sc only); *Courrier Sud* (Billon) (co-adaptation only); 1943—*Les Anges du péché (Angels of the Streets)* (co-sc); 1945—*Les Dames du Bois de Boulogne (The Ladies of the Bois de Boulogne)* (co-sc); 1950—*Journal d'un curé de campagne (Diary of a Country Priest)*; 1956—*Un Condamné a mort s'est échappé (Le Vent souffle où il veut, A Condemned Man Escapes)*; 1959—*Pickpocket*; 1962—*Le Procès de Jeanne d'Arc (The Trial of Joan of Arc)*; 1966—*Au hasard Balthazar (Balthazar)*; 1967—*Mouchette*; 1969—*Une Femme douce*; 1971—*Quatre Nuits d'un rêveur (4 Nights of a Dreamer)*; 1974—*Lancelot du Luc (Le Graal, Lancelot of the Lake)*; 1977—*Le Diable probablement*; 1983—*L'Argent*.

By BRESSON:

Books—*Notes sur le cinématographe*, Paris 1975; English edition *Notes on the Cinema*, New York 1977; *Notas sobra el cinematografo*, Mexico City 1980; articles—"Bresson on Location: Interview" by Jean Douchet in *Sequence* (London), no. 13, 1951; letter to Bosley Crowther in the *New York Times*, 2 May 1954; "An Interview with Robert Bresson" by Ian Cameron in *Movie* (London), February 1963; interview by Jean-Luc Godard and M. Delahaye in *Cahiers du Cinema in English* (New York), February 1967; "4 Nights of a Dreamer", interview by Carlos Clarens, in *Sight and Sound* (London), winter 1971/72; interview in *Sight and Sound* (London), winter 1971/72; "2 Nuits d'un rêveur", interview by Claude Beylie, in *Ecran* (Paris), April 1972; "Bresson's Isolation", interview by M. Knudsen and C. Braad Thomsen in *Kosmorama* (Copenhagen), February 1972; "Au hasard Balthazar" fiche by M. Mettey in *Image et son* (Paris), no.269, 1973; "Lancelot du Lac" in *Avant-Scène du cinéma* (Paris), February 1975; interview by Paul Schrader in *Film Comment* (New York), September/October 1977; interview in *Sight and Sound* (London), winter 1976-77; interview by J. Fieschi in *Cinématographe* (Paris), July/August 1977; "Robert Bresson, Possibly", interview by Paul Schrader in *Film Comment* (New York), September/October 1977.

On BRESSON:

Books—*The Film* edited by Andrew Sarris, Indianapolis, Indiana 1968; *The Films of Robert Bresson* by 5 reviewers, New York 1969; *French Cinema Since 1946, Vol.1* by Roy Armes, New York 1970; *The Films of Robert Bresson* by Ian Cameron, London 1970; *Transcendental Style on Film: Ozu, Bresson, Dreyer* by Paul Schrader, Los Angeles 1972; *Robert Bresson o cinematografo e o sinal* by C. de Pontes Leca, Lisbon 1978; articles—"Notes on Robert Bresson" by Gavin Lambert in *Sight and Sound* (London), summer 1953; "Working with Bresson" by Roland Monod in *Sight and Sound* (London), summer 1957; "The Quest for Realism" by Gordon Gow in *Films and Filming* (London), December 1957; "Robert Bresson" by Brian Baxter in *Film* (London), September/October 1958; "The Early Work of Robert Bresson" by Richard Roud in *Film Culture* (New York), no. 20, 1959; "Robert Bresson" by Charles Ford, translated by Anne and Thornton Brown in *Films in Review* (New York), February 1959; "Robert Bresson" by Marjorie Green in *Film Quarterly* (Berkeley, California), spring 1960; "French Outsider with the Inside Look" by Richard Roud in *Films and Filming*

(London), April 1960; "The French Film—A Discussion" in *Film* (London), November/December 1960; "The Face of 63—France" by Peter Cowie in *Films and Filming* (London), May 1963; "Conventional-Unconventional" by Colin Young in *Film Quarterly* (Berkeley, California), fall 1963; "Spiritual Style in the Films of Robert Bresson" by Susan Sontag in *Seventh Art* (New York), summer 1964; "Robert Bresson" in *Interviews with Film Directors* by Andrew Sarris, New York 1967; "Etc. in a Christian Framework" by Annette Michelson in *Commonweal* (New York), 29 November 1968; "Praxis as a Cinematic Principle in the Films of Robert Bresson" by Donald S. Skoller in *Cinema Journal* (Evanston, Illinois), fall 1969; "Ars Theologica: Man and God at the N.Y. Film Festival" by Calvin Green in *Cinéaste* (New York), fall 1969; "The Art of Robert Bresson" by Roy Armes in *London Magazine*, October 1970; "Dostoevsky and Bresson" by Eric Rhode in *Sight and Sound* (London), spring 1970; "The Suicide of Robert Bresson" by Marvin Zeman in *Cinema* (Los Angeles), Spring 1971; "Robert Bresson" in *Current Biography Yearbook*, New York 1971; "Bresson's Stylistics Revisited" by M. Prokosch in *Film Quarterly* (Berkeley), v.15, no.1, 1972; "Robert Bresson" in *Encountering Directors* by Charles Samuels, New York 1972; "Bresson's Stylistics Revisited" by M. Prokosch in *Film Quarterly* (Berkeley), winter 1971-72; "L'Idéologie moderniste dans quelques films récents" by J.-P. Oudart in *Cahiers du cinéma* (Paris), March/April 1972; filmography and article on *Au hasard Balthazar* in *Image et son* (Paris), no. 269, 1973; "Matter and Spirit in the Films of Robert Bresson" by H.M. Polhemus in *Film Heritage* (Dayton, Ohio), spring 1974; "Lancelot du Lac: Robert Bresson et ses armures" by J. Delmas in *Jeune cinéma* (Paris), November 1974; "Bresson's Lancelot du Lac" by J. Rosenbaum in *Sight and Sound* (London), summer 1974; "Léonce H. Burel", interview by R. Prédal, in *Cinéma* (Paris), July/August 1974; "4 de la forfanterie" by Claude Beylie in *Ecran* (Paris), October 1975; "Quand le film noir met ouvert" by R. Duval in *Ecran* (Paris), February 1975; "Burel and Bresson" by R. Nogueira in *Sight and Sound* (London), winter 1976/77; "Rencontre, a propos de l'évolution esthetique de l'image, avec Philippe Agostini" by M. Martin in *Cinéma pratique* (Paris), August/September 1976; "Robert Bresson's Austere Vision" by Colin Westerbeck, Jr., in *Artforum* (New York), November 1976; article on *Les Dames du Bois de Boulogne* and partial filmography in *L'Avant-Scène du cinéma* (Paris), 15 November 1977; "Bresson et l'argent" by M. Latil Le Dantec in *Cinématographe* (Paris), May 1977; "Das 'Tagebuch eines Landpfarrers' und die Stilistik von Robert Bresson" by André Bazin, translated by A. Spingler, in *Filmkritik* (Munich), May 1979; films—*Robert Bresson* by François Weyergans, 1965; *Zum Beispiel Bresson* by Theodor Kotulla, 1967.

*　　*　　*

Robert Bresson began and quickly gave up a career as a painter, turning to cinema in 1934. The short film he made that year, *Les Affaires publiques*, is never shown. His next work, *Les Anges du péché* was his first feature film, followed by *Les Dames du Bois du Boulogne* and *Le Journal d'un curé de campagne* which firmly established his reputation as one of the world's most rigorous and demanding filmmakers. In the next 15 years he made only four films: *Un Condamné à mort s'est échappé, Pickpocket, Le Procès de Jeanne d'Arc* and *Au hasard Balthazar*, each a work of masterful originality and unlike the others. Since then he has made films with more frequency and somewhat less intensity. In 1975 Gallimard published his gnomic *Notes sur le cinématographe*.

As a whole Bresson's oeuvre constitutes a crucial investigation of the nature of cinematic narration. All three films of the 1950s are variations on the notion of a written diary transposed to a voice-over commentary on the visualized action. More indirectly, *Le Procès de Jeanne d'Arc* proposes yet another variant through the medium of the written transcript of the trial; *Une Femme douce* is told through the voice of the husband as he keeps a vigil for his suicidal wife; and in *Quatre nuits d'un rêveur* both of the principle characters narrate their previous histories to each other. In all of these instances Bresson allows the tension between the continuity of written and spoken language and the fragmentation of shots in a film to become an important thematic concern. His narrators tell themselves (and us) stories in order to find meaning in what has happened to them. The elusiveness of that meaning is reflected in the elliptical style of Bresson's editing.

For the most part, Bresson employs only amateur actors. He avoids histrionics and seldom permits his "models" (as he calls them, drawing a metaphor from painting) to give a traditional performance. The emotional tensions of the films derive from the elaborate interchange of glances, subtle camera movements, offscreen sounds, carefully placed bits of baroque and classical music, and rhythmical editing.

The Bressonian hero is often defined by what he or she sees. We come to understand the sexual tensions of Ambricourt from a few shots seen from the country priest's perspective; the fierce desire to escape helps the condemned man to see the most ordinary objects as tools for his purpose; the risk the pickpocket initially takes to prove his moral superiority to himself leads him to see thefts where we might only notice people jostling one another: the film initiates its viewers into his privileged perspective. Only at the end does he realize that this obsessive mode of seeing has blinded him to a love which he ecstatically embraces. Conversely, Mouchette kills herself suddenly when she sees the death of a hare (with which she identified herself); the heroine of *Une Femme douce* kills herself because she can see no value in things, while her pawnbroker husband sees nothing but the monetary worth of everything he handles. The most elaborate form this concentration on seeing takes in Bresson's cinema is the structure of *Au hasard Balthazar*, where the range of human vices is seen through the eyes of a donkey as he passes through a series of owners.

The intricate shot-countershot of Bresson's films reinforces his emphasis on seeing, as does his careful use of camera movement. Often he reframes within a shot to bring together two different objects of attention. The cumulative effect of this meticulous and often obsessive concentration on details is the sense of a transcendent and fateful presence guiding the actions of characters who come to see only at the end, if at all, the pattern and goal of their lives.

Only in *Un Condamné, Pickpocket*, and *Quatre Nuits* does the protagonist survive the end of the film. A dominant theme of his cinema is dying with grace. In *Mouchette, Une Femme douce*, and *Le Diable probablement* the protagonists commit suicide. In *Les Anges* and *L'Argent* they give themselves up as murderers. Clearly Bresson, who is the most prominent of Catholic filmmakers, does not reflect the Church's condemnation of suicide. Death, as he represents it, comes as the acceptance of one's fate. The three suicides emphasize the enigma of human will; they seem insufficiently motivated, but are pure acts of accepting death.

—P. Adams Sitney

BROCA, PHILIPPE DE. French. Born in Paris, 15 March 1933. Educated at Ecole Technique de Photographie et du Cinéma, Paris. Career: 1950s—cameraman on documentary in Africa, then military service as cameraman in North Africa; 1958-59—assistant director to Claude Chabrol on *Le Beau Serge* and *Les Cousins* and on Truffaut's *The 400 Blows*; 1959—with profits from *Les Cousins*, Chabrol produces his 1st feature; 1965—forms Fildebroc production company.

Films (as director of documentary shorts): 1954—*Salon nautique* (+ph); 1955—*Opération Gas-oil* (+ph); *Sous un autre soleil* (+ph); (as assistant director): 1957—*Tous peuvent me tuer* (Decoin) (credit as 'stagiaire'); *Charmants garçons* (Decoin) (2nd asst d); *La Cargaison blanche* (Lacombe) (2nd asst d); 1958—*Ramuntcho* (Schoendoerffer); *Les Quatre Cents Coups (The 400 Blows)* (Truffaut); *Le Beau Serge* (Chabrol) (+ro); 1959—*Les Cousins* (Chabrol); *A Double Tour* (Chabrol); (as feature director and co-scriptwriter): 1960—*Les Jeux de l'amour (The Love Game)*; 1961—*Le Farceur (The Joker)*; *L'Amant de cinq jours (The 5 Day Lovers)*; 1962—"La Gourmandise (Gluttony)" episode of *Les Sept Péchés capitaux (The 7 Deadly Sins)* (d only); *Cartouche* (+bit ro); "La Vedette" episode of *Les Veinards*; 1963—*L'Homme de Rio (That Man from Rio)*; 1964—*Un Monsieur de compagnie (Male Companion)* (co-adapt); 1965—*Les Tribulations d'un chinois en Chine (Up to His Ears)*; 1966—*Le Roi de coeur (King of Hearts)* (d only, +pr); 1967—"Mademoiselle Mimi" episode of *Le Plus Vieux Métier du monde (The Oldest Profession)* (d only); *Ne jouez pas avec les Martiens* (Lanoë) (co-sc only, +pr); *O salto (Le Voyage du silence, Le Saut* (de Chalonge) (pr only); 1968—*Le Diable par la queue (The Devil by the Tail)*; 1969—*Les Caprices de Marie (Give Her the Moon)*; 1971—*La Poudre d'escampette (Touch and Go)*; 1972—*Chère Louise*; 1973—*Le Magnifique (Comment détruire la reputation du plus célèbre agent secret du monde, How to Destroy the Reputation of the Greatest Secret Agent)* (d only, +ro); 1975—*L'Incorrigible*; 1977—*Julie Pot de Colle* (d only); *Tendre Poulet (Dear Inspector, Dear Detective)*; 1978—*Le Cavaleur (Practice Makes Perfect)*; 1980—*On a vole la cuisse de Jupiter (Somebody's Stolen the Thigh of Jupiter)* (sc); 1983—*L'Africain (The African)*. Roles: 1959—bit in *A bout de souffle (Breathless)* (Godard); 1964—*Les Pieds-Nickelés* (Chambon); 1970—*Le Cinéma de papa* (Berri).

Publications:

By BROCA:

"What Directors Are Saying" in *Action* (Los Angeles), March/-April 1975.

On BROCA:

"Philippe de Broca" by T. Curran in *Films in Review* (New York), November 1980.

*   *   *

The most successful films of Philippe de Broca are honest, sincere comedies which stress illusion over reality. His characters are nonconformists who celebrate life and the joy of personal liberation. Structurally, de Broca's works are highly visual, more concerned with expression, with communication by images, than any specifics in the scenario. And these images are generally picturesque. The filmmaker acknowledges his desire to give plea-

sure to the esthetic sense and, as such, he is a popular artist. His films may not be as rich as those of Truffaut (with whom he worked as assistant director on *The 400 Blows* or as cinematic as those of Chabrol (he was this filmmaker's assistant on *Beau Serge* and *Les Cousins*, but he is still a solid stylist with his share of worthy credits.

De Broca's films are nontragic, with humorous treatments of characters and their situations. One of his favorite themes is the relationship between the sexes, explored in his earliest films *Les Jeux de l'Amour*, *Le Farceur* and *L'Amant de Cinq Jours*, all featuring Jean-Pierre Cassel as lighthearted lovers; this character ages 20 years in *Le Cavaleur*, with Jean Rochefort as a bored, self-centered womanizer. But his most popular features include *Cartouche*, a flavorful comedy-swashbuckler chronicling the exploits of kind-hearted criminals in 18th century Paris; *That Man from Rio*, a charming James Bond spoof about a soldier (Jean-Paul Belmondo, also toplined in *Cartouche*) on leave who is led to a stunningly photographed Brazil on a chase for treasure; and *King of Hearts*, featuring a town during World War I that has been abandoned by all except for the residents of its insane asylum. The last, de Broca's most renowned effort, is a staple on the cult film circuit. It ran for six-and-a-half years alone at a Cambridge, Massachusetts, moviehouse.

King of Hearts is de Broca's idea of an anti-war film. Typically, he does not focus on the calamity of a youthful hero who is robbed of his life (as in *All Quiet on the Western Front*), or soldiers needlessly and maddeningly put to death by a military bureaucracy (*Paths of Glory, Breaker Morant*), or the bloody slaughter of his protagonists (any of a score of films). Instead, he gently, satirically celebrates individual freedom: his inmates are more sane than the society which has labelled them mad while intent on blowing itself to smithereens. Deaths and tragedies in a de Broca feature are usually obscured by humorous situations.

De Broca is more concerned with good than evil. He began his career as a newsreel cameraman in Algeria, but switched to narrative filmmaking because he "decided the real world was just too ugly." The work in his first decade as filmmaker is generally more satisfying than his more recent efforts. But, at his best, de Broca deals with possibilities—for peace, beauty, hope, love.

While Philippe de Broca's scenarios may be a screenwriter's fantasy, their essence is emotionally genuine.

—Rob Edelman

BROCKA, LINO. Filipino. Born Lino Ortiz Brocka in San Jose, Nuevo Ecija, Philippines, 1940. Educated at University of the Philippines. Career: early 1960s—after university studies, converts to Mormon religion, sent as missionary to Hawaii; assigned to leper colony at Molocai following conflict with church authorities; visits U.S., then returns to Manila; acts and directs for theater, works with others on TV adaptation of *A Streetcar Named Desire*; 1965—begins work in film as script supervisor on *Flight to Fury* (Hellman and Romero); late 1960s—works for Philippine Educational Theater Association (P.E.T.A.), becomes head when former leader Cecile Guidole exiled; 1974—co-founds Cine Manila production company; 1978—presentation of *Insiang* at 1978 Cannes Festival leads to European recognition. Recipient: Best Direction, Filipino Academy of Movie Arts and Sciences, for *Tubog Sa Ginto*, 1971; Best Direction, Filipino Academy of Movie Arts and Sciences, for *Tinimbang Ka't Ngu nit Kulang*, 1975; Best Direction, Filipino Academy of Movie Arts and Sciences, for *Maynila sa Kuko nig Liwanag*, 1976.

Films (as director): 1970—*Wanted: Perfect Mother*; *Santiago*; 1971-73—*Tubog Sa Ginto*; *Now*; *Lumuha Pati Mga Anghel*; *Cadena de Amor*; *Cherry Blossoms*; *Villa Miranda*; *Stardoom*; 1974—*Tinimbang ka Nguni't Kulang (You Are Weighed in the Balance But Are Found Lacking)*; *Talto, Dalawa, Isa*; 1975—*Maynila sa Kuko nig Liwanag (Manila in the Claws of Light)*; 1976—*Lunes, Martes, Myerkoles...*; *Insiang*; 1977—*Tahan Na Empy, Tahan*; *Inay*; 1979—*Jaguar*; 1980—*Bona*; 1981—*Dung-Aw (Lamentations)* (+sc, for TV); 1982—*Cain at Abel*; *P.X.*.

Publications:

By BROCKA:

Articles—"Salut aux Philippines", interview and article by A. Garsault and A. Sotto, in *Positif* (Paris), June 1978; "Entretien avec Lino Brocka" by Michel Ciment in *Positif* (Paris), June 1980; "Philippine Cinema: Hollywood of the Pacific", includes interview, by I. Stocks in *Cinema Papers* (Melbourne), October/-November 1980.

*   *   *

Lino Ortiz Brocka is undoubtedly the most important Filipino filmmaker to date. Unknown outside of his own country until he was discovered by the French critics and revealed at the 1978 Cannes Film Festival with the presentation of *Insiang*, he has since become a focus of attention and the flagbearer of a new wave of filmmakers which includes Mike De Leon who had produced and photographed one of Brocka's films, *Manila in the Claws of Light*. There were forerunners, of course, like Lamberto Avellana and Gerardo De Leon, but it was Brocka who showed for the first time a consistent attempt at creating a body of work distinct from the crassly commercial and superficial entertainment produced by a national industry releasing some 200 films a year. In little more than a decade he has shot over 40 films and many of these are not distinguishable from the run-of-the-mill. They were made to pay his debts, to fund his other artistic activities or just to survive till the censor would accept one of his projects.

The son of a fisherman and a schoolteacher, he has always shown a concern for the poor and the lower middle class. He shoots films, he says, "to make people angry." His first film, *Wanted: Perfect Mother* uses the Filipino comic strips as a source of inspiration and reaches the audience by a clever use of popular culture. In his second venture *Santiago*, a war drama, he made use of actors he had worked with in theater. But it is with *You Are Weighed In The Balance But Are Found Lacking* that he makes his real breakthrough, mocking the shortcomings, the inhumanity, and the hypocrisy of a society in a brilliant ironical tale.

The ruthless social films of Brocka, often set in the slums or the poor districts of Manila, borrow from several sources: Italian neorealism, the Spanish melodrama and the American film noir of Kazan and Dassin. *Manila in the Claws of Light* shows the slow degradation of youths arriving from the country to face urban corruption and vice. In his trilogy, *Insiang, Jaguar* and *Bona*, he shows characters who are totally subservient, accepting the weight of societal pressures till they revolt in a final act, suddenly conscious of their alienation. In Brocka's films the social and human relationships are closely intertwined and the realistic approach is enhanced by a larger-than-life theatricality. Brutality is accompanied by sudden outbursts of lyricism (*Jaguar* is reminiscent of *You Only Live Once* or *They Live By Night*), the tragic and the comic alternating in a style that is at once feverish and precise.

—Michel Ciment

———————

BROOKS, MEL. American. Born Melvyn Kaminsky in Williamsburg section of Brooklyn, about 1926. Educated for a year at Brooklyn College. Married Florence Baum; children: Stefanie, Nicky and Edward; married actress Anne Bancroft, 1964; child: Maximilian. Career: 1943-45—military service as combat engineer; after war—plays drums in nightclubs in Catskills, changes name to avoid confusion with trumpeter Max Kaminsky; begins doing stand-up comedy in late 1940s; also social director for Grossinger's resort; 1949—asked by Sid Caesar to write for NBC TV series *Broadway Revue*; 1950—begins as writer and occasional performer on *Your Show of Shows*; 1950-58—writes for Sid Caesar shows; 1960—makes 1st recording as "The 2000-Year Old Man" with Carl Reiner; 1963—conceives, writes and narrates cartoon short *The Critic*; 1965—with Buck Henry creates *Get Smart* TV series. Recipient: Academy Award (Short Subjects) for *The Critic*, 1963; Best Story and Screenplay Academy Award for *The Producers*, 1968; Best Written Screenplay, Writers Guild, for *The Producers*, 1968. Address: Brooksfilms Ltd., 20th Century-Fox, 10201 West Pico Blvd., Los Angeles, CA 90064.

Films (as director and scriptwriter): 1963—*The Critic* (cartoon); 1968—*The Producers*; 1970—*The Twelve Chairs* (+ro); 1974—*Blazing Saddles* (co-sc, +ro); *Young Frankenstein* (co-sc); 1976—*Silent Movie* (co-sc, +ro); (as producer, director and scriptwriter): 1977—*High Anxiety* (co-sc, +ro); 1981—*The History of the World, Part I* (co-sc, +ro); 1983—*To Be or Not to Be* (co-sc).

Publications:

By BROOKS:

Articles—interview in *Playboy* (Chicago), October 1966; "Confessions of an Auteur" in *Action* (Los Angeles), November/December 1971; "Mel Brooks Interview" by James Atlas in *Film Comment* (New York), March/April 1975; "Fond Salutes and Naked Hate", interview by Gordon Gow in *Films and Filming* (London), July 1975; "Entretien avec Mel Brooks" by A. Remond in *Ecran* (Paris), November 1976; "And Now, in the Great Tradition of Mel Brooks, Mel Brooks on *High Anxiety*", interview and article by R. Rivlin, in *Millimeter* (New York), December 1977; "Comedy Directors: Interview with Mel Brooks" by R. Rivlin in *Millimeter* (New York), October 1977.

On BROOKS:

Book—*Mel Brooks: l'ultima follia di Hollywood* by G. Bendazzi, Milan 1977; articles—"2,000 Year Old Man" in *Newsweek* (New York), 4 October 1965; "What Makes Mel Brooks Run?" by Fred Robbins in *Show*, 17 September 1970; "Les Nouveau Burlesques: Woody Allen, Mel Brooks" by D. Offroy in *Cinématographe* (Paris), August/September 1975; "Mel Brooks" by D. Diehl in *Action* (Los Angeles), January/February 1975; "The

Mel Brooks Memos" by G. Lees in *American Film* (Washington, D.C.), October 1977; "Dossier: Hollywood 79: Mel Brooks" by P. Carcassonne in *Cinématographe* (Paris), March 1979; "The Splice is Right" by R. Rosenblum and R. Karen in *Penthouse* (New York), September 1979; "Woody Allen y Mel Brooks" by L. García Tsao in *Imagenes* (Mexico), July 1980.

*   *   *

Brooks's central concern (with *High Anxiety* and *To Be or Not to Be* as possible exceptions) is the pragmatic, absurd union of two males, starting with the more experienced member trying to take advantage of the other, and ending in a strong friendship and paternal relationship. The dominant member of the duo, confident but ill-fated, is Zero Mostel in *The Producers*, Frank Langella in *The 12 Chairs*, and Gene Wilder in *Blazing Saddles* and *Young Frankenstein*.

The second member of the duo, usually physically weak and openly neurotic, represents the victim who wins, who learns from his experience and finds friendship to sustain him. These "Jewish weakling" characters include Wilder in *The Producers*, Ron Moody, and Cleavon Little. Though this character, as in the case of Little, need not literally be Jewish, he displays the typical characteristics.

Women in Brooks's films are grotesque figures, sex objects ridiculed and rejected. They are either very old or sexually gross and simple. The love of a friend is obviously worth more than such an object. The secondary male characters, befitting the intentional infantilism of the films, are men-babies given to crying easily. The are set up as examples of what the weak protagonist might become without the paternal care of his reluctant friend. In particular, Brooks sees people who hide behind costumes—cowboy suits, Nazi uniforms, clerical garb, homosexual affectations—as silly children to be made fun of.

The plots of Brooks's films deal with the experienced and inexperienced man searching for a way to triumph in society. They seek a generic solution or are pushed into one. Yet there is no escape into generic fantasy in the Brooks films, since the films take place totally within the fantasy. There is no regard, as in Woody Allen's films, for the pathetic nature of the protagonist in reality. In fact, the Brooks films reverse the Allen films' endings as the protagonists move into a comic fantasy of friendship. (A further contrast with Allen is in the nature of the jokes and gags. Allen's humor is basically adult embarrassment; Brooks's is infantile taboo-breaking.)

In *The Producers* the partners try to manipulate show business and wind up in jail, planning another scheme because they enjoy it. In *The 12 Chairs* they try to cheat the government; at the end Langella and Moody continue working together though they no longer have the quest for the chairs in common. In *Blazing Saddles* Little and Wilder try to take a town; it ends with the actors supposedly playing themselves, getting into a studio car and going off together as pals into the sunset. In these films it is two men alone against a corrupt and childish society. Though their schemes fall apart—or are literally exploded as in *The Producers* and *The 12 Chairs*—they still have each other.

Young Frankenstein departs from the pattern with each of the partners, monster and doctor, sexually committed to women, and while the basic pattern of male buddies continued when Brooks began to act in his own films, he also winds up with the woman when he is the hero star (*High Anxiety, Silent Movie, The History of the World, To Be or Not to Be*). It is interesting that Brooks always tries to distance himself from the homosexual implications of his central theme by including scenes in which overtly homosexual characters are ridiculed. It is particularly striking that these characters are, in *The Producers*, *Blazing Saddles*, and *The 12 Chairs*, stage or film directors.

—Stuart M. Kaminsky

BROOKS, RICHARD. American. Born in Philadelphia, 8 May 1912. Educated at Temple University, Philadelphia. Married Jean Simmons, 1961. Career: 1932-34—reporter for *Philadelphia Record*; 1934-36—sports reporter for *Atlantic City Press Union*, then *World Telegram*; 1936—begins working for radio station WNEW, then for NBC; 1940—directs Mild Pond Theatre and mounts several plays in New York; 1941—does daily radio program from Hollywood, writing a story a day; collaborates on radio script with Orson Welles; begins to collaborate on film scripts; 1943-45—service in Marine Corps, writes novel *The Brick Foxhole* (source of Dmytryk's *Crossfire*); 1946—signs with MGM after having worked with producer Mark Hellinger; makes most of fifties and early sixties films for MGM; 1965—becomes independent producer. Recipient: Best Screenplay (Based on Material from Another Medium) Academy Award for *Elmer Gantry*, 1960; Best-Written American Drama, Writers Guild, for *Elmer Gantry*, 1960; Laurel Award for Achievement, Writers Guild, 1966. Attorney: Gerald Lipsky, Beverly Hills, CA.

Films (as co-scriptwriter): 1942—*Sin Town* (Enright); *Men of Texas*; 1943—*The White Savage* (Lubin); *Cobra Woman* (Siodmak); *My Best Gal* (Anthony Mann); *Don Winslow of the Coast Guard*; 1946—*Swell Guy* (Tuttle); *The Killers* (Siodmak); 1947—*Brute Force* (Dassin); 1948—*To the Victor* (Daves); *Key Largo* (Huston); *The Naked City* (Dassin); 1949—*Storm Warning* (Heisler); *Any Number Can Play* (John Sturges); 1950—*Mystery Street* (John Sturges); (as director and scriptwriter): 1950—*Crisis*; 1951—*The Light Touch*; 1952—*Deadline USA*; 1953—*Battle Circus*; *Take the High Ground* (d only); 1954—*The Flame and the Flesh* (d only); *The Last Time I Saw Paris* (co-sc); 1955—*The Blackboard Jungle*; 1956—*The Last Hunt*; *The Catered Affair* (d only); 1957—*Something of Value*; 1958—*The Brothers Karamazov* (co-sc); *Cat on a Hot Tin Roof* (co-sc); 1960—*Elmer Gantry*; 1961—*Sweet Bird of Youth*; 1965—*Lord Jim*; 1966—*The Professionals*; 1967—*In Cold Blood*; 1969—*The Happy Ending*; 1971—*Dollars* (co-sc); 1975—*Bite the Bullet*; 1977—*Looking for Mr. Goodbar*; 1982—*Wrong Is Right* (+pr).

Publications:

By BROOKS:

Books—*The Brick Foxhole*, New York 1946; *The Boiling Point*, New York 1948; *The Producer*, New York 1951; articles—"2 Story Conferences", with King Vidor, in *Sight and Sound* (London), October/December 1952; "A Novel Isn't a Movie" in *Films in Review* (New York), February 1952; extract from *The Producer* in *Cahiers du cinéma* (Paris), July 1956; "On Filming Karamazov" in *Films in Review* (New York), February 1958; "Dostoievsky, Love and American Cinema" in *Films in Review* (New York), April 1958; interview by Charles Bitsch in *Cahiers du cinéma* (Paris), February 1959; interview in *Positif* (Paris), January 1964; interview by Ian Cameron and others in *Movie* (London), spring 1965; "Lord Jim Interview" in *Cinema* (Beverly

Hills), March/April 1965; "In Cold Blood" interview in *Cahiers du Cinema in English* (New York), no.5, 1966; interview in *Positif* (Paris), May 1968; interview in *Cahiers du cinéma* (Paris), May/June 1965; "Richard Brooks" seminar in *American Film* (Washington, D.C.), October 1977; "Richard Brooks Directs *Looking for Mr. Goodbar*", interview by J. Mariani in *Millimeter* (New York), July/August 1977; "Richard Brooks: Le precheur du monde occidental", interview by C. Clouzot, in *Ecran* (Paris), June 1978.

On BROOKS:

Articles—"Personality of the Month" in *Films in Review* (New York), May 1956; various writings on Brooks in *Positif* (Paris), July 1956; "Richard Brooks ou la sincerité" by Louis Seguin in *Positif* (Paris), June/July 1956; "Richard Brooks" by A. Johnson in *Sight and Sound* (London), autumn 1960; "Brooks en marche" by Roger Tailleur in *Positif* (Paris), March 1963; "Note sur Richard Brooks" by Jean-Luc Godard in *Cahiers du cinéma* (Paris), December 1963; "Richard Brooks and *Lord Jim*", interview by Paul Joyce in *Film* (London), winter 1964; special section of *Movie* (London), spring 1965; special Brooks section of *Image et son* (Paris), May 1972; "The Secret Scripts of Richard Brooks" by B. Thomas in *Action* (Los Angeles), September/October 1975; "La lenta evolución de Richard Brooks" by J. Traverso in *Cinemateca Revista* (Andes), March 1979; "Dossier auteur Richard Brooks" by J.-P. Le Pavec and others in *Cinéma* (Paris), December 1980.

*   *   *

Richard Brooks had his literary education in the hard school of radio and the program picture, where "licking the story" and "getting out the pages" marked progress to an acceptable screenplay. In the tradition of such writers, he won critical acceptance with his bottom-drawer novel, *The Brick Foxhole*, later filmed (and traduced) as *Crossfire*. Projects of an increasing sophistication followed, until he reached his goal of writing and directing serious, "significant" films, only to find the cinema moving away from such material towards a self-regarding personal style he was ill-fitted to pursue. Today, he occupies almost the position of Hollywood's premier adapter of literary works, selling his wares to a market markedly less interested with each year.

What won Brooks his commmercial success, and will continue to sustain him where films like *The Brothers Karamazov, Lord Jim, In Cold Blood* and *Looking For Mr. Goodbar* may not, are his films of action, for which he displayed a notable skill in his program days, and on which he capitalized in a series of polished and thoughtful westerns. *The Last Hunt, Bite the Bullet* and particularly *The Professionals* all deal effectively with arresting by-ways of the frontier experience. Brooks is interested in the interface between old and new ways, old and new men; the buffalo hunters of *The Last Hunt* represent the conflicting forces of ruthless slaughter and environmental protection, and the long-distance horse racers of *Bite the Bullet* a set of rival motives in which an attitude to horses arises frequently as a symbol. The least overtly significant of them all, *The Professionals* is also the most entertaining, a stylish and character-rich variation on *The Magnificent Seven* which repays frequent re-viewing.

Brooks's literary adaptations are sustained by their bravura performances and little more. He coaxed high passion from Elizabeth Taylor in *Cat on a Hot Tin Roof*, and banked down the same fires in Burt Lancaster to make *Elmer Gantry* one of his best works. But in "licking" essentially unfilmable books like *Lord Jim, The Brothers Karamazov* and *In Cold Blood* he turned first-rate literature into second-rate film. It may be that

one of his most tawdry creations, the earliest of the teen exploitation films, *The Blackboard Jungle*, will be the production for which he is best remembered.

—John Baxter

———————

BROUGHTON, JAMES. American. Born in San Francisco, 1912. Educated at Stanford University, B.A. New School, New York, 1943-45. Career: before 1946—active as poet and in theater; 1946—Sidney Peterson proposes collaboration on experimental film; 1946-51—Associate of Art in Cinema, San Francisco Museum of Art; 1948—completes first solo film; 1951—invited by director of British Film Institute to make film in London (*The Pleasure Garden*); 1953-63—prevented by lack of funds, debt incurred on *The Pleasure Garden*, from completing any projects; 1953-55—works in Paris on *Paris Review* and with American Theater; 1954—resident filmmaker, Danish Film Institute, Copenhagen; 1955—editorial assistant, *Botteghe oscure*, Rome; 1958-64—resident playwright, Playhouse Repertory Theatre, San Francisco; after 1962—concert tours as poet; 1967—persuaded to make *The Bed* by director of Belgian Royal Cinematheque, Jacques Ledoux; resumes active filmmaking; 1969—Playwright Fellow, Eugene O'Neill Theater Foundation; 1976—begins filmmaking collaboration with Joel Singer on *Together*; on faculty of San Francisco Art Institute. Recipient: Guggenheim Fellowship, 1971; Guggenheim Fellowship, 1973; 12th Independent Film Award, *Film Culture*, 1975; individual grant, National Endowment for the Arts, 1976.

Films: 1946—*The Potted Psalm* (with Sidney Peterson); 1948—*Mother's Day*; 1950—*Adventures of Jimmy*; 1951—*4 in the Afternoon; Loony Tom, the Happy Lover*; 1953—*The Pleasure Garden*; 1968—*The Bed*; 1969—*Nuptiae*; 1970—*The Golden Positions*; 1971—*This Is It*; 1972—*Dreamwood*; 1973—*High Kukus*; 1974—*Testament*; 1975—*The Water Circle*; 1976—*Erogeny; Together*; 1977—*Windowmobile; Song of the Godbody*; 1979—*Hermes Bird*; 1981—*The Gardener of Eden; Shaman Psalm*.

Publications:

By BROUGHTON:

Books—*The Playground*, San Francisco 1949; *The Ballad of Mad Jenny*, San Francisco 1949; *Musical Chairs*, San Francisco 1950; *An Almanac for Amorists*, Paris 1955; *True and False Unicorn*, New York 1957; *The Right Playmate*, San Francisco 1964; *Tidings*, San Francisco 1965; *The Water Circle*, San Francisco 1965; *Look In Look Out*, Oregon 1968; *High Kukus*, North Carolina 1969; *A Long Undressing (Collected Poems 1949-1969)*, New York 1971; *Going Through Customs*, San Francisco 1976; *Erogeny*, San Francisco 1976; *Seeing the Light*, San Francisco 1977; *Odes for Odd Occasions*, San Francisco 1977; *The Androgyne Journal*, Oakland 1977; *Song of the Godbody*, San Francisco 1978; *Hymns to Hermes*, San Francisco 1979; articles—"Playground: Dance Drama of Our Precarious Times" in *Theatre Arts* (New York), August 1946; "Odd Birds in the Aviary: Some Notes on Poetry and Film" in *Sight and Sound* (London), January/March 1952; "The Gardener's Son" in *Sequence* (London), no.14, 1952; "Film as a Way of Seeing" in *Film Culture* (New York), summer 1963; "Knokke-le-Zoute" in *Film*

Quarterly (Berkeley), vol.17, no.3, 1964; "The Bed" in *Filmagazine*, vol.1, no.1, 1968; "A Manifesto: Concurrent Theater" in *Los Angeles Free Press*, 15 March 1968; "Excerpts from Script Writing Seminar at the San Francisco Art Institute" in *Canyon Cinemanews* (Sausalito, California), no.5, 1974; various writings and interviews in special Broughton issue of *Film Culture* (New York), no.61, 1975/76; "Broughton's Guide to Moviegoing" in *Canyon Cinemanews* (Sausalito, California), September/October 1976; "Cinema and the Tao" in *Canyon Cinemanews* (Sausalito, California), November/December 1976; recordings—*San Francisco Poets*, Evergreen Records, New York 1958; *Erotic Poetry*, Random House, 1963; *The Bard & the Harper*, MEA Records, Sausalito, California 1965.

On BROUGHTON:

Books—*The Essential Cinema* edited by P. Adams Sitney, New York 1975; *A History of the American Avant-Garde Cinema*, exhibition catalogue, by John Hanhardt and others, The American Federation of Arts, New York 1976; articles—"Quandary and Statement" by F. Gelffing in *Poetry* (Chicago), March 1951; "3 Créatures: Préambule à un cinéma poétique" by Michel Mayoux in *Cahiers du cinéma* (Paris), no.10, 1952; "San Francisco Letter" by H. Aigner in *Take One* (Montreal), July 1972; special Broughton issue of *Film Culture* (New York), no.61, 1975/76; "Autobiography in Avant-Garde Film" by P. Adams Sitney in *Millenium* (New York), winter 1977/78.

*   *   *

James Broughton began his career as a poet and playwright. He was an important literary figure of the so-called San Francisco Renaissance, after the Second World War. In 1946 he started to collaborate on a play with the sculptor and writer Sidney Peterson, but instead they made their first film, *The Potted Psalm*. After that they both continued film-making separately.

Mother's Day, Broughton's first solo film, incorporates a persistent strategy of his poetry: adults are seen as children and childhood is recreated from the perspective of adults. The filmmaker's fierce vision of the mother's solipsistic isolation from her husband and children is masked by his cheerful repetition, on the intertitles, of the platitudes the mother taught her children. In its wild concatenation of characters, its use of symbolical objects, and, above all, in its translation of moral isolation into the spatial arrangement of characters, *Mother's Day* was not only one of Broughton's greatest achievements, but one of the formative films of the American avant-garde.

He followed this major work with three somewhat more conventional film poems: the autobiographical *Adventures of Jimmy*, *Four in the Afternoon*, directly inspired by his volume of poems *Musical Chairs*, and *Loony Tom, the Happy Lover*. All three films describe erotic disasters as child's play, and they all benefit from poetic texts recited by the filmmaker or his intermediaries. After the economic disappointment of his 35mm, medium length, *The Pleasure Garden*, made in England as an homage to British eccentricity, Broughton gave up making films, but continued to write poetry and plays.

In 1967, Jaques Ledoux, director of the Cinemathéque Royale de Belgique, persuaded Broughton to make a film for his International Film Competition. *The Bed* was such a success that Broughton began to make films again with renewed vigor. His subject remained essentially the power of eros. *The Bed* depicts tableaux of erotic, domestic, and ritual life spontaneously occurring on a bed that has wandered into the woods. *Nuptiae* represents Broughton's wedding, which had occurred some seven years earlier. *This is it!* is a cosmological irony: the images show Broughton's young son, Orion, playing with a red plastic ball, but the poet's voice-over transforms the innocent images into a Zen genesis.

Since 1976 Broughton has made a number of films with Joel Singer. *Together, Windowmobile, Song of the Godbody, The Gardener of Eden,* and *Shaman Psalm* often incorporate minimalist concentration on a limited range of images—an influence form Singer's independent work—and they celebrate homoerotic themes which had never been explicit in Broughton's earlier cinema.

—P. Adams Sitney

BROWN, CLARENCE. American. Born in Clinton, Massachusetts, 10 May 1890. Educated at University of Tennessee, degree in mechanical and electrical engineering, 1910. Married actress Mona Maris; actress Alice Joyce; former secretary Marian Ruth Spies. Career: 1911-12—works for Moline Automobile Co. and Stevens Duryea Co.; founds Brown Motor Car Company, Birmingham, Alabama; 1913-14—meets and becomes assistant to Maurice Tourneur; becomes editor, then co-director; 1918—serves as aviator in World War I; 1925—joins MGM; 1971—helps found Clarence Brown Theatre for the Performing Arts, University of Tennessee, Knoxville. Business Manager: Parker, Miliken, Clark & O'Hara, Los Angeles, CA.

Films (as co-director with Maurice Tourneur): 1920—*The Great Redeemer; The Last of the Mohicans*; 1921—*The Foolish Matrons*; (as director): 1922—*The Light in the Dark*; 1923—*Don't Marry for Money; The Acquittal*; 1924—*The Signal Tower; Butterfly; Smouldering Fires*; 1925—*The Goose Woman; The Eagle*; 1926—*Kiki*; 1927—*The Flesh and the Devil*; 1928—*A Woman of Affairs*; 1929—*The Trail of '98; Wonder of Women; Navy Blues*; 1930—*Anna Christie; Romance*; 1931—*Inspiration; A Free Soul; Possessed*; 1932—*Emma; Letty Lynton; The Son-Daughter*; 1933—*Looking Forward; Night Flight*; 1934—*Sadie McKee; Chained*; 1935—*Anna Karenina; Ah Wilderness*; 1936—*Wife Versus Secretary; The Gorgeous Hussy*; 1937—*Conquest*; 1938—*Of Human Hearts*; 1939—*Idiot's Delight; The Rains Came*; 1940—*Edison the Man*; 1941—*Come Live with Me; They Met in Bombay*; 1943—*The Human Comedy*; 1944—*The White Cliffs of Dover; National Velvet*; 1946—*The Yearling*; (as producer and director): 1947—*Song of Love*; 1949—*Intruder in the Dust; The Secret Garden* (Ardrey) (pr only); 1950—*To Please a Lady*; 1951—*Angels in the Outfield*; episode of *It's a Big Country*; 1952—*When in Rome; Plymouth Adventure*; 1953—*Never Let Me Go* (Daves) (pr only).

Publications:

By BROWN:

Articles—"Bringing Saroyan to the Screen" in *Lion's Roar* (Hollywood), April 1943; "The Producer Must Be Boss" in *Films in Review* (New York), February 1951.

On BROWN:

Book—*The Parade's Gone By* by Kevin Brownlow, London

1968; articles—sketch by D. Manners in *Motion Picture Classic* (Brooklyn), April 1928; "Estimate" by J. Tully in *Vanity Fair* (New York), April 1928; "Redecouvrir Clarence Brown" by G. Cebe and others in *Ecran* (Paris), 15 June 1979; "Clarence Brown: un grand cinéaste intimiste" by P. Brion in *Cinéma* (Paris), February 1979; "Inspiration et romance chez Clarence Brown" by C. Viviani in *Positif* (Paris), March 1980.

*   *   *

It was in 1915 that Clarence Brown saw a movie being filmed at Fort Lee, New Jersey, and he was so fascinated that he sold his business as head of the Brown Motor Company, and apprenticed himself to Maurice Tourneur, who was about to direct Clara Kimball Young in a film version of *Trilby*. He was then 25 years old, and spent the next five years as assistant to Tourneur, whom he freely acknowledged as his god.

"I owe it all to him," he once said. "Before he got into filmmaking, he was a painter. He used the screen like a canvas. Everything I know about lighting and composition and arrangement I learned from him."

During the making of *The Last of the Mohicans*, Tourneur was injured, and Clarence Brown finished the picture for him; they share the directorial credit. Tourneur and Brown collaborated once again on directing another feature, *The Foolish Matrons*, and Tourneur then told him that he was ready to direct a feature on his own. Brown signed with Universal, then under the management of Carl Laemmle, where he found that he was happiest working with female stars like Pauline Frederick and Laura La Plante in *Smouldering Fires* and Louise Dresser in *The Goose Woman*. Joseph Schenck admired his work, and signed him to direct two for him at United Artists—*The Eagle*, one of the few really good pictures that Rudolph Valentino made, and *Kiki*, which starred Schenck's wife, Norma Talmadge.

Brown signed then with MGM, where he remained the rest of his career until 1952, save for only one loan-out to 20th Century-Fox for *The Rains Came*, a picture he wanted to make. Louis B. Mayer always held him in high regard; in fact, he is the only director at MGM with whom Mayer did not at some time or another quarrel.

The important thing was that MGM had a veritable galaxy of female stars, and it was the woman star with whom Brown felt most compatible. His range as a director at MGM was enviable; he was never typed. He moved from his first picture there, *Flesh and the Devil*, which made Garbo an important star, to an American epic like his last, *Plymouth Adventure*. In between he directed, among others, seven films for Garbo, five for Crawford, two for Shearer, and in spite of that record, will probably be known best for his cinematic adventures in Americana like *Ah, Wilderness, Of Human Hearts, The Human Comedy, The Yearling,* and *Intruder in the Dust*. Although he greatly admired Garbo, he sincerely believed that Mickey Rooney was the most talented actor in the business.

—DeWitt Bodeen

BROWNING, TOD. American. Born Charles Albert Browning in Louisville, Kentucky, 12 July 1880. Attended school in Churchill Downs. Married Alice Houghton (acted as Alice Wilson), 1918. Career: 1898—runs away from home to join a carnival; 1898-1913—works carnival circuit, then later joins various vaudeville and burlesque shows, including "The World of Mirth" and "Lizard and Coon"; 1913-14—joins Biograph film studio as comedic actor; later moves to Majestic-Reliance Pictures as actor; 1914-17—serves as assistant director and scriptwriter in Hollywood; 1915—directs 1st film, *The Lucky Transfer*; 1916—appears in Griffith's *Intolerance* as well as serving as assistant director; 1919—joins Universal Studios, and directs various film series; begins long term association with Lon Chaney, directing him in their 1st film together, *The Wicked Darling*; 1925—signed by MGM; 1939—directs last film, *Miracles for Sale*; 1944—his death is mistakenly reported. Died 6 October 1962. Recipient: Honorary Life Membership, Directors Guild of America.

Films (as director): 1915—*The Lucky Transfer*; *The Slave Girl*; *The Highbinders*; *The Living Death*; *The Burned Hand*; *The Woman from Warren's*; *Little Marie*; *The Story of a Story*; *The Spell of the Poppy*; *The Electric Alarm*; *The Queen of the Band* (Myers) (story only); 1916—*Puppets*; *Everybody's Doing It*; *The Deadly Glass of Beer (The Fatal Glass of Beer)*; *Sunshine Dad* (Dillon) (co-story only); *The Mystery of the Leaping Fish* (Emerson) (story only); *Atta Boy's Last Race* (Seligmann) (sc only); 1917—*Jim Bludso* (co-d, +co-sc); *Peggy, The Will o' th' Wisp*; *The Jury of Fate*; *A Love Sublime* (co-d); *Hands Up!* (co-d); 1918—*The Eyes of Mystery*; *The Legion of Death*; *Revenge*; *Which Woman*; *The Deciding Kiss*; *The Brazen Beauty*; *Set Free* (+sc); 1919—*The Wicked Darling*; *The Exquisite Thief*; *The Unpainted Woman*; *A Petal on the Current*; *Bonnie, Bonnie Lassie* (+sc); *The Pointing Finger* (Kull) (supervisor only); 1920—*The Virgin of Stamboul* (+sc); 1921—*Outside the Law* (+co-sc); *No Woman Knows* (+co-sc); *Society Secrets* (McCarey) (supervisor only); 1922—*The Wise Kid*; *Under 2 Flags* (+co-sc); *Man Under Cover* (+co-sc); 1923—*Drifting* (+co-sc); *White Tiger* (+co-sc); *Day of Faith*; 1924—*The Dangerous Flirt*; *Silk Stocking Girl (Silk Stocking Sal)*; 1925—*The Unholy 3* (+co-sc); *The Mystic* (+co-sc); *Dollar Down*; 1926—*The Black Bird* (+co-sc); *The Road to Mandalay* (+co-sc); 1927—*London After Midnight* (+co-sc); *The Show*; *The Unknown* (+co-sc); 1928—*The Big City* (+co-sc); *West of Zanzibar*; *Old Age Handicap* (Mattison) (story only under pseudonym Tod Underwood); 1929—*Where East is East* (+co-sc); *The 13th Chair*; 1930—*Outside the Law* (+co-sc); 1931—*Dracula* (+co-sc); *The Iron Man*; 1932—*Freaks*; 1933—*Fast Workers*; 1935—*Mark of the Vampire* (+sc); 1936—*The Devil-Doll* (+co-sc); 1939—*Miracles for Sale*; 1946—*Inside Job* (Yarborough) (story only).

Roles:

(for Biograph): 1913—*Scenting a Terrible Crime*; *A Fallen Hero*; (for Komic): 1914-15—*Mr. Hadley* in "Bill" series through no.17, *Ethel Gets Consent*; (other roles for Komic): 1914—*A Race for a Bride*; *The Man in the Couch*; *An Exciting Courtship*; *The Last Drink of Whiskey*; *Hubby to the Rescue*; *The Deceivers*; *The White Slave Catchers*; *Wrong All Around*; *Leave It to Smiley*; *The Wild Girl*; *Ethel's Teacher* ("Bill" series?); *A Physical Culture Romance*; *The Mascot*; *Foiled Again*; *The Million Dollar Bride*; *Dizzy Joe's Career*; *Casey's Vendetta*; *Out Again—In Again*; *A Corner in Hats*; *The Housebreakers*; *The Record Breakers*; 1915—*Cupid and the Pest*; *Music Hath Its Charms*; *A Costly Exchange*; 1916—*Intolerance* (Griffith) (+ass't d for crowd scenes).

Publications:

By TOD BROWNING:

Article—"A Maker of Mystery", interview by Joan Dickey in *Motion Picture Classic* (Brooklyn), March 1928.

On TOD BROWNING:

Articles—by Joan Dickey in *Motion Picture Classic* (Brooklyn), March 1928; "Tod Browning" by George Geltzer in *Films in Review* (New York), October 1953; obituary in *The New York Times*, 10 October 1962; "Tod Browning" by Jean-Claude Romer in *Bizarre* (Paris), no.3, 1962; "The Browning Version" by Rory Guy in *Cinema* (Beverly Hills), June/July 1963; "Tod Browning" by Eli Savada in *Photon* (New York), no.23, 1973; "Tod Browning" by Stuart Rosenthal in *The Hollywood Professionals* vol.4, London 1975; "Freaks", introduction by J.-M. Léger, in *Avant-Scène du cinéma* (Paris), July/September 1975; "Tod Browning: à la recherche de la réalité" by A. Garsault in *Positif* (Paris), July/August 1978; "Tod Browning's Side Show" by James Hoberman in the *Village Voice* (New York), 17 September 1979.

*   *   *

It was not through any comparision of his films to the poetry of his namesake Robert Browning that Tod Browning became recognized as a major Hollywood cult director, but rather to the works of Edgar Allen Poe. However, unlike Poe, Tod Browning was, by all accounts, a quiet and gentle man who could rise to sarcasm and sardonics when necessary to bring out the best from his players or to ward off interference from the front office.

Browning came to Hollywood as an actor, after working circus and vaudeville, a background obviously supplying elements in many of his films, notably *The Unholy Three*, *The Show* and *Freaks*. He worked initially in the film industry as an actor until D.W. Griffith (for whom Browning had worked on *Intolerance* as both a performer and assistant director) gave him the chance to direct at the Fine Arts Company. Browning directed a few films for Metro, but came to fame at Universal with a series of features starring Priscilla Dean. It was *The Virgin of Stamboul* which critics particularly admired, but it was his next film, *Outside the Law*, which has more historical significance, marking the first time that Browning was to direct Lon Chaney. (Browning remade the feature as a talkie.)

These Universal productions were little more than pretentious romantic melodramas, but they paved the way for a series of classic M-G-M horror films starring Lon Chaney, from *The Unholy Three* in 1925 through *Where East Is East* in 1929. They were notable for the range of Chaney's performances—a little old lady, a cripple, an armless circus performer, a gangster, and so on—and for Browning's penchant for the macabre. All were stylish productions, well directed, but all left the viewer with a sense of disappointment, of unfulfilled climaxes. Aside from directing, Tod Browning also wrote most of his films, and once explained that the plots were secondary to the characterizations, which perhaps explains the dismal, unexciting endings to many of his features.

Tod Browning made an easy transition to sound films, although surprisingly he did not direct the 1930 remake of *The Unholy Three*. Instead he directed the atmospheric *Dracula*, which made a legend of Bela Lugosi and skillfully blended elements of both comedy and horror. A year later, Browning directed another classic horror talkie, *Freaks*, a realistic and at times offensive melodrama about the physically deformed members of a circus troupe, one of whom, midget Harry Earles marries a trapeze artiste (Olga Baclanova).

Browning ended his career with *The Mark of the Vampire*, a remake of the Chaney feature *London After Midnight*; *The Devil Doll*, in which Lionel Barrymore appears as an old lady, a similar disguise to that adopted by Chaney in *The Unholy Three*; and *Miracles for Sale*, a mystery drama involving professional magicians. Tod Browning will, of course, be best remembered for his horror films, but it should also be recalled that during the first half of his directorial career he stuck almost exclusively to romantic melodrama.

—Anthony Slide

———

BUÑUEL, LUIS. Spanish. Born in Calanda, province of Teruel, Spain, 22 February 1900. Educated at Jesuit schools in Zaragoza, 1906-15; Residencia de Estudiantes, Madrid, 1917-20; University of Madrid, degree in 1924. Married Jeanne Rucar, 1933; sons: Juan-Luis and Rafael. Career: 1922—begins contributing to literary journals; 1925—goes to Paris; invited by Jean Epstein to be assistant on his films; 1929—enters Surrealist group in Paris, makes *Un Chien andalou*; 1930—offered contract by **MGM** after *L'Age d'or*, visits Hollywood; 1931—returns to Paris; 1933—works for Paramount in Paris; 1935—Filmófono Executive Producer, Madrid, supervising musicals and comedies; 1936-39—serves Republican government during Spanish Civil War, returns to Hollywood to supervise documentaries on war (unrealized); 1939-42 works at Museum of Modern Art, New York, reediting, dubbing and directing documentaries for Latin American distribution; 1942—dismissed because of suspicion of communist background; 1944—returns to Hollywood, producing Spanish versions of Warners films; 1946—moves to Mexico; 1947-60—directs films in Mexico; 1961—invited by Spanish government to return and makes *Viridiana*; film suppressed in Spain; 1960s-'70s—works mainly in France and Italy, lives in Mexico. Died in Mexico City, 29 July 1983. Recipient: Best Direction and International Critics Prize, Cannes Festival, for *Los olvidados*, 1951; Best Avant-Garde Film, Cannes Festival, for *Subida al cielo*, 1952; Gold Medal, Cannes Festival, for *Nazarín*, 1959; Gold Medal (co-recipient), Cannes Festival, for *Viridiana*, 1961; Silver Lion, Venice Festival, for *Simón del desierto*, 1965; Golden Lion, Venice Festival, for *Belle de jour*, 1967.

Films (as assistant director): 1926—*Mauprat* (Epstein) (+ro as monk); 1927—*La Sirène des tropiques* (Etiévant and Nalpas); 1928—*La Chute de la maison Usher* (Epstein); (as director): 1929—*Un Chien andalou* (+pr, co-sc, ed, ro as *Man with razor*); 1930—*L'Age d'or* (+co-sc, ed, mu); 1932—*Las Hurdes—Tierra sin pan (Land Without Bread)* (+sc, ed); 1935—*Don Quintín el amargao* (Marquina) (co-d uncredited, +pr, co-sc); *La hija de Juan Simón* (Sáenz de Heredia) (co-d uncredited, +pr, co-sc); 1936—*Quién me quiere a mi?* (Sáenz de Heredia) (pr, co-sc, ed only); *Centinela alerta!* (Grémillon) (co-d uncredited, +pr, co-sc); 1937—*Espagne 1937/España leal en armas!* (compilation only, +ed?); 1940—*Triumph of Will* (supervising editor, commentary only—edited compilation of Riefenstahl's *Triumph des Willens* and Hans Bertram's *Feuertaufe*); *El Vaticano de Pio XII (The History of the Vatican)* (short, special issue of *March of Time* series); 1947—*Gran Casino (Tampico)*; 1949—*El gran calavera*; 1950—*Los olvidados (The Forgotten, The Young and the Damned)* (+co-sc); 1950—*Susana (Demonio y carne)* (+co-sc); *Si usted no puede, yo sí* (Soler) (co-story only); 1951—*La hija del engaño (Don Quintín el amargao)*; *Cuando los hijos nos juzgan (Una mujer sin amor)*; *Subida al cielo* (+sc); 1952—*El Bruto* (+co-sc); *Las aventuras de Robinson Crusoe (Adventures of Robinson Crusoe)* (+co-sc); *El* (+co-sc); 1953—*Abismos de* pasión (Cumbres borrascoses) (+co-sc); La ilusión viaja en tranvía (+co-sc); 1954—El rio y la muerte (+co-sc); 1955—Ensayo de un crimen (La Vida Criminal de Archibaldo de La Cruz, The Criminal Life of Archibaldo de la Cruz) (+co-sc); Cela s'appelle l'Aurore (+co-sc); 1956—La Mort en ce jardin (La muerte en este jardin) (+co-sc); 1958—Nazarín (+co-sc); 1959—La Fièvre monte à El Pao (Los Ambiciosos) (+co-sc); 1960—The Young One (La Joven, La Jeune Fille) (+co-sc); 1961—Viridiana (+co-sc, story); 1962—El ángel exterminador (The Exterminating Angel) (+co-sc, story); 1963—Le Journal d'une femme de chambre (+co-sc); 1965—Simón del desierto (+co-sc); 1966—Belle de jour (+co-sc); 1969—La Voie lactée (The Milky Way, La via lattea) (+co-sc, mu); 1970—Tristana (+co-sc); 1972—Le Charme discret de la bourgeoisie (The Discreet Charm of the Bourgeoisie) (+co-sc); Le Moine (Kyrou) (co-sc only); 1974—Le Fantôme de la liberté (The Phantom of Liberty) (+sc, sound effects); 1977—Cet obscur objet du désir (That Obscure Object of Desire) (+co-sc). Roles: 1964—the Executioner in Llanto por un bandido (Lament for a Bandit) (Saura) (+tech advisor on arms and munitions); En este pueblo no hay ladrones (Isaac); 1973—La Chute d'un corps (Polac).

Publications:

By BUÑUEL:

Books—Viridiana, Paris 1962; Viridiana, Mexico City 1963; El ángel exterminador, Barcelona 1964; L'Age d'or and Une Chien andalou, translated from French by Marianne Alexander, London 1968; 3 Screenplays: Viridiana, The Exterminating Angel, Simon of the Desert, New York 1969; Belle de Jour, English translation and description of action by Robert Atkinson, London 1971; Tristana, London 1971; The Exterminating Angel/-Nazarín/Los Olvidados, London 1972; Los olvidados, Mexico City 1980; Quell'oscuro oggetto del desiderio, translated and edited by A.M. and F.Tato, Turin 1981; My Last Breath, New York 1983; articles—"Entretien avec Luis Buñuel" by Jacques Doniol-Valcroze and André Bazin in Cahiers du Cinéma (Paris), June 1954; "Luis Buñuel," interview by Daniel Aubry and Jean Lacor in Film Quarterly (Berkeley), winter 1958; "Poésie et cinéma" in Cinema 59 (Paris), June 1959; "Luis Buñuel—A Statement" in Film Culture (New York), summer 1960; "Sur Nazarín" in Cinéma 61 (Paris), January 1961; "The Cinema: An Instrument of Poetry" in New York Film Bulletin, February 1961; "Interview with Luis Buñuel" by Kenji Kanesaka in Film Culture (New York), spring 1962; "Illisible, fils de flûte: synopsis d'un scénario non réalisé" with Jean Larrea in Positif (Paris), March 1963; "Luis Buñuel: voix off", interview by Manuel Michel in Cinéma 65 (Paris), March 1965; "Luis Buñuel", interview by Ulrich Gregor in Wie Sie Filmen, Gütersloh, West Germany 1966; "Buñuel contre son mythe", interview by Manuel Michel in Cinéma 66 (Paris), April 1966; "Luis Buñuel" in Interviews with Film Directors, edited by Andrew Sarris, New York 1967; "Entretien avec Luis Buñuel" by J. Cobos and G.S. de Erice in Cahiers du Cinéma (Paris), June 1967; "Autobiographie", in 2 parts, in Positif (Paris), January and February 1973; "El Cine instrumento de poesía" and interview in Cine Cubano (Havana), no.78-80, 1973; "Entretien avec Luis Buñuel" by R. Saint-Jean, in Positif (Paris), October 1974; "Buñuel Scenes", interview by Carlos Fuentes, in Movietone News (Seattle), February 1975; "I am not a producer", interview with Serge Silberman by R. Conrad in Film Quarterly (Berkeley), fall 1979; "Poesie und Film" in Film und Fernsehen (Berlin), February 1980; "Aragón, Madrid, Paris...Entrevista con Luis Buñuel" by J. de la Colina and T. Pérez in Contracampo

(Madrid), October/November 1980; "Entretien avec Luis Buñuel" by J. de la Colina and T. Perez-Turrent in Positif (Paris), January 1981; film—Luis Buñuel by André Labarthe, with interview by Georges Sadoul, Paris 1967.

On BUÑUEL:

Books—Luis Buñuel, edited by Michel Estève, Paris 1962/63; Luis Buñuel by Ado Kyrou, Paris 1962; Luis Buñuel: odisea del demoledor by Eduardo Lizalde, Mexico 1962; Luis Buñuel by Frédéric Grange and Charles Rebolledo, Paris 1964; Luis Buñuel: eine Dokumentation by Alice Goetz and Helmut Banz, Verband der Deutschen Filmclubs 1965; Luis Buñuel by Raymond Durgnat, Berkeley, California 1968; Luis Buñuel: Biografia Critica, Madrid 1969; Luis Buñuel by Freddy Buache, Lausanne 1970; Surrealism and Film by J.H. Matthews, Ann Arbor, Michigan 1971; The Cinema of Luis Buñuel by Freddy Buache, translated by Peter Graham, London 1973; Buñuel (Cine e ideología) by Manuel Alcalá, Madrid 1973; Luis Buñuel: A Critical Biography by José Francisco Aranda, translated by David Robinson, New York 1975; El ojo de Buñuel by Fernando Cesarman, Barcelona 1976; Luis Buñuel, architecte du rêve by M. Drouzy, Paris 1978; Luis Buñuel by Raymond Durgnat, Berkeley, California 1978; The World of Luis Buñuel edited by Joan Mellen, New York 1978; Luis Buñuel by Virginia Higginbotham, Boston 1979; Luis Buñuel by Ian Cameron, Berkeley, California 1979; Luis Buñuel, Ediciones C: Directores de Cine, No.7, Madrid 1981; articles—"Une fonction de constat: notes sur l'oeuvre de Buñuel" by Pierre Kast in Cahiers du Cinéma (Paris), December 1951; "Quatrième période" by Jacques Brunius in En marge du cinéma français, Paris 1954; "Luis Buñuel" by Claude Mauriac in L'amour du cinéma, Paris 1954; "Luis Buñuel: poète de la cruaute" by Jacques Demeure in Positif (Paris), no.10, 1954; "The Films of Luis Buñuel" by Tony Richardson in Sight and Sound (London), January/March 1954; special Buñuel issue, Cinemages (New York), no.1, 1955; "A Mexico avec Luis Buñuel" by Emmanuel Robles in Cahiers du Cinéma (Paris), October 1956; "En travaillant avec Luis Buñuel" by Gabriel Arout in Cahiers du Cinéma (Paris), November 1957; "Buñuel espagnol" by José Francisco Aranda in Cinema 57 (Paris), Christmas 1957; "The Eternal Rebellion of Luis Buñuel" by Emilio Riera in Film Culture (New York), summer 1960; "Breve encuentro con Luis Buñuel" by Jean Baroncelli in Film Quarterly (Berkeley), April 1960; "Los Olvidados" in Qu'est ce que le cinéma vol.3 by André Bazin, Paris 1961; "Nazarín et Le Journal d'un curé de campagne: La Passion refusée et acceptée" in La Passion du Christ comme thème cinématographique by Michel Estève, Paris 1961; "Surrealist and Spanish Giant" by José Francisco Aranda in Films and Filming (London), October 1961; "Back from the Wilderness" by José Francisco Aranda in Films and Filming (London), November 1961; special issue on Buñuel, Positif (Paris), November 1961; issue on Buñuel, Image et son (Paris), December 1962; "The Old Surrealist" by David Robinson in London Magazine, November 1962; issue on Buñuel, La Methode (Paris), January 1962; "Interviewing Buñuel" by Derek Prouse in Sight and Sound (London), summer 1962; "Luis Buñuel" in Le Surréalisme au cinéma by Ado Kyrou, Paris 1963; "Luis Buñuel: Cinéaste hispanique" by Nestor Almendros in Objectif (Paris), July 1963; "Luis Buñuel" by Alan Lovell in Anarchist Cinema, London 1964; "Luis Buñuel" in Cinema Eye, Cinema Ear by John Taylor, New York 1964; "Los Olvidados" by R.C. Dale and "Viridiana" by Frederick Hoffman in Classics of the Film, Madison, Wisconsin 1965; "Luis Alcoriza and the Films of Luis Buñuel" by Robert Hammond in Film Heritage (Dayton, Ohio), autumn 1965; "The Mexican Buñuel" by Tom Milne in Sight and Sound (London), winter 1965/66; "Rebirth of Buñuel" by Luis Garcia-Abrines in Yale French Studies (New Haven, Connecticut), no.17, 1965; "L'Ange et la bête" by Jean-André Fieschi in Cahiers du cinéma (Paris), March 1966; "A Visit to Luis Buñuel" by Kenji Kanesaka in Film Culture (New York), summer 1966; "Film inédits de Buñuel" by Raymond Lefèvre in Image et son (Paris), April 1966; "Buñuel le mexicain" by Jean Delmas in Jeune Cinéma (Paris), February 1966; "Buñuel et le nouveau cinéma mexicain" by Charles Chabouel in Positif (Paris), March 1966; "Luis Buñuel: Spaniard and Surrealist" by Peter Harcourt in Film Quarterly (Berkeley), spring 1967; "Luis Buñuel/Glauber Rocha: échos d'une conversation" by Augusto Torres in Cinéma 68 (Paris), February 1968; series of articles and interviews in Jeune Cinéma (Paris), April 1969; "The Devil and the Nun: Viridiana" by Andrew Sarris in Renaissance of the Film, edited by Julius Bellone, London 1970; issue on Buñuel, with interviews, Image et son (Paris), May 1971; "Buñuel" by William Pechter in 24 Times a Second, New York 1971; "Max Aub et Luis Buñuel: le roman d'une génération" by M.P. Coterillo in Ecran (Paris), September/October 1972; "Buñuel se escribe con Ñ y tiene setenta años" by J.L. Egea in Cine Cubano (Havana), no.71-72, 1972; "Luis Buñuel anticapitalista romantico" by Fiesole in Cinema nuovo (Turin), September/October 1972; "Spain, Catholicism, Surrealism and Anarchism: The Discreet Charm of Luis Buñuel" by Carlos Fuentes in the New York Times Magazine, 11 March 1973; "Bunuels Oscar" by José Francisco Aranda in Kosmorama (Copenhagen), August 1973; articles discussing dream imagery in Buñuel films in Filmcritica (Rome), April 1973; special Buñuel issue of Cine Cubano, no.78-80, 1973; "L'exil de Buñuel à New York" by R. Gubern in Positif (Paris), January 1973; "Luis Buñuel: The Process of Dissociation in 3 Films" by E.H. Lyon in Cinema Journal (Evanston, Illinois), fall 1973; "Luis Buñuel: Spaniard and Surrealist" by Peter Harcourt in 6 European Directors, London 1974; "Saggi e studi su Luis Buñuel", special issue of Cinema nuovo (Turin), January/February 1974; "Le Fantôme de la liberté", special issue of Avant-Scène du cinéma (Paris), October 1974; "The Discreet Charm of Luis Buñuel" by G.L. George in Action (Los Angeles), November/December 1974; "Phantom of Liberty" by A. Madsen in Sight and Sound (London), summer 1974; "Erotic Moments in the Films of Luis Buñuel" by S. Murray in Cinema Papers (Melbourne), July 1974; "Un Chien andalou, L'Age d'or, Las Hurdes, Los Olvidados" by R.C. Dale in Movietone News (Seattle), February 1975; "Buñuel, Sáenz de Heredia and Filmófono" by R. Mortimore in Sight and Sound (London), summer 1975; "Procedimenti narrativi del film: il ribaltamento della favola come ribaltamento della fiction (1)" by G. Tiso in Filmcritica (Rome), January/February 1975; "The Minister of the Interior is on the Telephone: The Early Films of Luis Buñuel" by Randall Conrad in Cineaste (New York), no.7, 1976; "A Magnificent and Dangerous Weapon: The Politics of Luis Buñuel's Later Films" by Randall Conrad in Cineaste (New York), no.8, 1976; "The 'Commercial' Life of Luis Buñuel" by P. Hogue in Movietone News (Seattle), 29 August 1976; "Buñuel cinéaste hispanique" by Nestor Almendros in Cinématographe (Paris), September 1977; "Tristana" by A. Cornand in Image et son (Paris), no.319bis, 1977; "Buñuel in Mexico" by E. Rubinstein in Review 77 (New York), spring 1977; "Getting What You Need" by J. Ahrens in Movietone News (Seattle), 14 August 1978; "Le Marteau de Buñuel" by J. Chevallier in Image et son (Paris), September 1978; "La Critica perdurable" by P. Moctezuma de la Villa in Cine (Mexico), October 1979; "El cuchillo espectral" by J. de la Colina in Contracampo (Madrid), October/November 1980; "Ein Realist—streng und mitleidlos" by S. Yutkevich in Film und Fernsehen (Berlin), February 1980; special Buñuel issue of Contracampo (Madrid), October/November 1980; article by Michael Wood in American Film (Washington, D.C.), September 1982; film—Cinéastes de notre temps by Jeanine Bazin and André Labarthe, for TV, 1967.

*   *   *

For all the critical attention (and furious critical controversy) his work occasioned over half a century, Luis Buñuel resisted our best taxonomical efforts. To begin with, while no artist of this century strikes one as more quintessentially Spanish than Buñuel, how can one apply the term "Spanish filmmaker" to a man whose oeuvre is far more nearly identified with France and Mexico than with the land of his birth? By the same token, can one speak of any film as "typical" of the man who made both L'Âge d'or and Nazarín, both Los olvidados and Belle de jour, both Land Without Bread and Le Charme discret de la bourgeoisie? Nonetheless, from Un Chien andalou to Cet obscur objet du désir, a Buñuel film is always (albeit, as in many of the Mexican pieces of the 1940s and 1950s, only sporadically), a Buñuel film.

Perhaps the easiest way to deal with Buñuel's career is to suggest that certain avatars of Luis Buñuel may be identified at different (if sometimes slightly overlapping) historical periods. The first Luis Buñuel is the Surrealist: the man who slit eyeballs (Un Chien andalou), the man to whom blasphemy was less a matter of specific utterances and gestures than a controlling style out of which might emerge new modes of feeling and of expression (L'Âge d'or), the man who documentarized the unimaginable (Land Without Bread) and finally, the man who demonstrated more clearly than any other that surrealist perspectives demanded cinematographic realism. The second Luis Buñuel (and the saddest, and much the least identifiable, now as then) is the all-but-anonymous journeyman film professional: the collaborator, often unbilled and almost always unremarked, on Spanish films which to this day remain unknown to any but the most dogged researchers; the archivist and adapter and functionary in New York and Hollywood; the long-term absentee from the world's attention. The third is the Mexican director, the man who achieved a few works that at the time attracted varying degrees of notice outside the sphere of Latin American commercial distribution (Los olvidados, Él, Archibaldo de la Cruz, Robinson Crusoe) but also of others that at the time attracted no notice at all. The fourth is the Luis Buñuel who gradually made his way back to Europe by way of a few French films made in alternation with films in Mexico; and who then, with Viridiana, returned to appall, and so to reclaim, his native land; and who thenceforth, and no matter where or under what conditions he operated, persuasively reasserted himself as a figure of unmistakable moment in world cinema. The last Luis Buñuel, following his emergence in the mid-1960s, was the past master, at once awesome and beloved, as serene in his command of his medium as he was cheerfully intrepid in his pursuit of whatever of value might be mined from the depths of the previously unexplored.

Each of the Buñuels of the preceding catalogue, except for the obscure and essentially uncreative second one, is manifest, or at least implicit, in the others. Even in his Mexican work, including some otherwise less than exalted assignments (and Buñuel himself, unlike certain of his more indiscriminate adulators, was perfectly willing to acknowledge that much of his Mexican work was shoddy or aborted or simply dull), the scion of surrealism showed his hand. There are several astonishing dream sequences, of course: the vision of slabs of raw meat hanging from the racks of a Mexico City streetcar (La ilusión viaja en tranvía), the incongruous verticality of the skeletal skyscrapers rising from the Mexico City slums (Los olvidados), and the necrophiliac ragings at the end of the Buñuel version of Wuthering Heights (Abismos de pasión). At the same time, it was in his Mexican studio movies, with their often absurdly brief shooting schedules, that Buñuel developed the unobtrusive but sovereign sway over narrative continuity and visual construction that so exhilarates admirers of such later works as *Le Journal d'une femme de chambre* or *Cet obscur objet du désir*. (According to Francisco Aranda, Alfred Hitchcock in 1972 called Buñuel "the best director in the world.")

Similarly, one may recognize in *Tristana* that same merciless anatomy of a specific social milieu, and in *The Exterminating Angel* that same theme of inexplicable entrapment, that one first encountered in *Land Without Bread*. And when, in *El rio y la muerte*, we watch a man, all of him save his head imprisoned in an iron lung, submitting to a round of face-slapping, and when we recognize in the image (and in the gasp of laughter it provokes) something of the merciless attack on our pieties of Buñuel's early Surrealist works and something of the more offhand wicked humor of, say, *Le Charme discret*, then we know that the variety of styles and accents in which Buñuel addressed us over the years is almost irrelevant. The political and social (or anti-social) canons of early surrealism could not contain him, nor could the foolish melodramatic conventions of some of his Mexican films stifle his humor, nor could the elegant actors and luxurious color cinematography of some of the later French films finally seduce him. Against all odds, his vision sufficed to transcend any and all stylistic diversions.

"Vision," perhaps the most exhausted word in the critical vocabulary, struggles back to life when applied to Buñuel and his camera. In the consistent clarity of its perception, in its refusal to distinguish between something called "reality" and something called "hallucination," Buñuel's camera always acts in the service of a fundamental surrealist principle, one of the few principles of any kind that Buñuel was never tempted to call into question. Whether focused on the tragic earthly destiny of an inept would-be saint (*Nazarín*) or on the bizarre obsessions of an inept would-be sinner (the uncle in *Viridiana*, among a good many others), Buñuel's camera is the instrument of the most rigorous denotation, invoking nothing beyond that which it so plainly and patiently registers. The uncertainties and ambivalences we may feel as we watch a Buñuel film arise not from the camera's capacity to mediate but from the camera's capacity to record: our responses are inherent in the subjects Buñuel selects, in those extremes of human experiences that we recognize as his special domain.

—E. Rubinstein

CAPRA, FRANK. American. Born in Bisaquino, Sicily, 18 May 1897; emigrated with family to Los Angeles, 1903. Educated at Manual Arts High School, Los Angeles; studied chemical engineering at California Institute of Technology, Pasadena, graduated 1918. Married Helen Howell in 1924 (divorced 1938); married Lucille Reyburn in 1932; children: Frank, Jr., John (died 1938), Lulu and Thomas. Career: 1918—enlists in Army, teaches ballistics; 1919—released from Army, does odd jobs; 1922-23—lab assistant for Walter Bell; 1923-25—works as prop man, editor for Bob Eddy, writer for Hal Roach and Mack Sennett; 1927—fired by Harry Langdon; 1928—hired by Columbia Pictures; 1931—begins to work with Robert Riskin; 1935—elected president of Academy; mysterious illness leads to decision to make "committed" films; 1938—elected president of Screen Directors' Guild; 1939—forms Frank Capra Productions with writer Robert Riskin; 1942-45—commissioned as Major in Signal Corps, produces *Why We Fight* films; 1945—forms Liberty Films with Sam Briskin, William Wyler and George Stevens; 1948—Liberty Films sold to Paramount; 1952—U.S. Delegate to International Film Festival, Bombay; 1952-57—produces,writes and directs 4 science documentaries for Bell Telephone; 1961—during filming of *A Pocketful of Miracles* begins to suffer cluster headaches; 1962-64—works on series of abortive projects; 1963—visits Soviet Union as State Department representative; 1971-present—active as speaker and participant at film festivals; 1977—80th birthday celebration organized by Italian filmmakers. Recipient: Best Director Academy Award for *It Happened One Night*, 1934; Best Director Academy Award for *Mr. Deeds Goes to Town*, 1936; Best Director Academy Award for *You Can't Take It With You*, 1938; Distinguished Service Medal, U.S. Armed Forces, 1945; D.W. Griffith Award, Directors Guild of America, 1958; Society of Motion Picture and Television Engineers Award, 1973. Address: P.O. Box 98, La Quinta, CA 92253.

Films (as director): 1922—*Fultah Fisher's Boarding House*; (as co-scenarist with Arthur Ripley on films featuring Harry Langdon): 1924—*Picking Peaches*; *Smile Please*; *Shanghaied Lovers*; *Flickering Youth*; *The Cat's Meow*; *His New Mama*; *The 1st 100 Years*; *The Luck o' the Foolish*; *The Hansom Cabman*; *All Night Long*; *Feet of Mud*; 1925—*The Sea Squawk*; *Boobs in the Woods*; *His Marriage Wow*; *Plain Clothes*; *Remember When?*; *Horace Greeley, Jr.*; *The White Wing's Bride*; *Lucky Stars*; *There He Goes*; *Saturday Afternoon*; 1926—*Fiddlesticks*; *The Soldier Man*; *Tramp, Tramp, Tramp*; (as director): *The Strong Man* (+co-sc); 1927—*Long Pants*; *For the Love of Mike*; 1928—*That Certain Thing*; *So This is Love*; *The Matinee Idol*; *The Way of the Strong*; *Say It With Sables* (+co-story); *Submarine*; *The Power of the Press*; *The Swim Princess*; *The Burglar (Smith's Burglar)*; 1929—*The Younger Generation*; *The Donovan Affair*; *Flight* (+dialogue); 1930—*Ladies of Leisure*; *Rain or Shine*; 1931—*Dirigible*; *The Miracle Woman*; *Platinum Blonde*; 1932—*Forbidden* (+sc); *American Madness*; (as director and producer): 1933—*The Bitter Tea of General Yen*; *Lady for a Day* (d only); 1934—*It Happened One Night* (d only); *Broadway Bill* (d only); 1936—*Mr. Deeds Goes to Town*; 1937—*Lost Horizon*; 1938—*You Can't Take It With You*; 1939—*Mr. Smith Goes to Washington*; 1941—*Meet John Doe*; 1942—*Why We Fight (Part 1): Prelude to War*; 1943—*Why We Fight (Part 2): The Nazis Strike* (co-d); *Why We Fight (Part 3): Divide and Conquer* (co-d); *Why We Fight (Part 4): The Battle of Britain* (pr only); 1944—*The Negro Soldier* (pr only); *Why We Fight (Part 5): The Battle of Russia* (pr only); *Why We Fight (Part 6): The Battle of China* (co-d); *Tunisian Victory* (co-d); *Know Your Ally: Britain* (pr only); *Arsenic and Old Lace* (filmed 1942); 1945—*Why We Fight (Part 7): War Comes to America* (pr only); *Know Your Enemy: Germany* (pr only); *Know Your Enemy: Japan* (co-d); *2 Down, 1 to Go*; 1946—*It's a Wonderful Life* (+co-sc); 1948—*State of the Union*; 1950—*Westward the Women* (story only); *Riding High*; 1951—*Here Comes the Groom*; 1956—(Bell System Science Series Numbers 1 to 4): *Our Mr. Sun* (+sc); 1957—*Hemo the Magnificent* (+sc); *The Strange Case of the Cosmic Rays* (+co-sc); 1958—*The Unchained Goddess* (+co-sc); 1959—*A Hole in the Head*; 1961—*Pocketful of Miracles*.

Publications:

By CAPRA:

Book—*The Name Above the Title*, New York 1971; articles—"The Gag Man" in *Breaking Into Movies*, edited by Charles Jones, New York 1927; "The Cinematographer's Place in the

Motion Picture Industry" in *Cinematographic Annual 2*, Los Angeles 1932; "Sacred Cows to the Slaughter" in *Stage* (New York), 13 July 1936; "Ce sont les films qui font les stars" in *Anthologie du Cinéma*, edited by Marcel Lapierre, Paris 1946; "Breaking Hollywood's Pattern of Sameness" in the *New York Times Magazine*, 5 May 1946; "We Should All Be Actors" in *Silver Screen* (New York), September 1946; "Do I Make You Laugh?" in *Films and Filming* (London), September 1962; "Capra Today" with James Childs in *Film Comment* (New York), vol.8, no.4, 1972; "Mr. Capra Goes to College" with Arthur Bressan and Michael Moran in *Interview* (New York), June 1972; "Introduction" in *The Man Who Invented Hollywood: The Autobiography of D.W. Griffith*, Louisville, Kentucky 1972; "Introduction" in *Light Your Torches and Pull Up Your Socks* by Tay Garnett, New Rochelle, New York 1973; "Introduction" in *Directors in Action*, edited by Bob Thomas, Indianapolis 1973; "Introduction for William Wellman" in *Action* (Los Angeles), March/April 1973; "Frank Capra Interviewed at the 2nd Tehran International Film Festival" in *American Cinematographer* (Los Angeles), February 1974; interviews in *The Men Who Made the Movies* by Richard Schickel, New York 1975; "'Trends Change Because Trends Stink'—An Outspoken Talk with Legendary Producer/Director Frank Capra" by Nancy Anderson in *Photoplay* (New York), November 1975; "Why We (Should Not) Fight," interview by G. Bailey, in *Take One* (Montreal), September 1975; "What Directors Are Saying" in *Action* (Los Angeles), March/April 1975; interview by J. Mariani in *Focus on Film* (London), no.27, 1977; "Dialogue on Film" in *American Film* (Washington, D.C.), October 1978; "Frank Capra: a Lighthouse in a Foggy World," interview by W.A. Drew, in *American Classic Screen* (Shawnee Mission, Kansas), July/August 1979.

On CAPRA:

Books—*Frank Capra* by Richard Griffith, London 1951; *The Film Till Now* by Richard Griffith and Paul Rotha, Middlesex 1967; *King Cohn: The Life and Times of Harry Cohn* by Bob Thomas, New York 1967; *Frank Capra: One Man—One Film* by James Silke, Washington, D.C. 1971; *We're in the Money: Depression America and Its Films* by Andrew Bergman, New York 1972; *The Moviemakers: A History of American Movies Through the Lives of 10 Great Directors* by Alice Fleming, New York 1973; *The Films of Frank Capra* by Donald Willis, Metuchen, New Jersey 1974; *Frank Capra: The Man and His Films*, edited by Richard Glatzer and John Raeburn, Ann Arbor 1975; *The Cinema of Frank Capra: An Approach to Film Comedy* by Leland Poague, South Brunswick, New Jersey 1975; *Directing the Film: Film Directors on Their Art* by Eric Sherman, Boston 1976; *Hollywood Story*, Paris 1976; *An Historical and Descriptive Analysis of the 'Why We Fight' Series* by Thomas Bohn, New York 1977; *American Visions: The Films of Chaplin, Ford, Capra and Welles, 1936-1941* by Charles Maland, New York 1977; *The Films of Frank Capra* by Victor Scherle and William Levy, Secaucus, New Jersey 1977; *Close Up: The Hollywood Director*, edited by Jon Tuska, Metuchen, New Jersey 1978; *Frank Capra Study Guide*, edited by Dennis Bohnenkamp and Sam Grogg, Washington, D.C. 1979; *Frank Capra* by Charles Maland, Boston 1980; articles—"Hollywood's New Miracle Man" by Kirtley Baskette in *Photoplay* (Los Angeles), December 1934; "Hollywood" by James Hilton in *Cosmopolitan* (New York), vol.101, no.5, 1936; "Columbia's Gem" in *Time* (New York), 8 August 1938; "How Frank Capra Makes a Hit Picture" in *Life* (New York), 19 September 1938; "Capra Shoots as He Pleases" by A. Johnson in *Saturday Evening Post* (Philadelphia), 14 May 1938; "Mr. Capra Goes Someplace" by Otis

Ferguson in *The New Republic* (New York), 1 November 1939; "Democracy at the Box Office" by Otis Ferguson in *The New Republic* (New York), 24 March 1941; "Thinker in Hollywood" by Geoffrey Hellman in the *New Yorker*, 5 February 1940; "Frank Capra's Characters" by Herbert Biberman in *New Masses* (New York), 8 July 1941; "Frank Capra's Secret" by P. Benedict in *Silver Screen* (Los Angeles), January 1942; "Mild or Bitter?" by Winifred Holmes in *Sight and Sound* (London), January 1944; "Mr. Capra's Short Cuts to Utopia" by Harold Salemson in *Penguin Film Review* no.7, London 1948; "Comedy's Greatest Era" by James Agee in *Life* (New York), 4 September 1949; "Non-Heroic Heroes" by Barbara Deming in *Films in Review* (New York), April 1951; "Capra and the American Dream" by James Price in *The London Magazine*, vol.3, no.10, 1964; "The Telephone Company, the Nation, and Perhaps the World" by Mark Bergman in *Velvet Light Trap* (Madison, Wisconsin), winter 1971/72; "Capra, 74, Looks Back at Film Career" by Howard Thompson in the *New York Times*, 24 June 1971; issue devoted to Capra, *Positif* (Paris), December 1971; "Capra and Riskin" by Richard Corliss in *Film Comment* (New York), vol.8, no.4, 1972; "A Decade of Good Deeds and Wonderful Lives: Under Capracorn" by Stephen Handzo in *Film Comment* (New York), vol.8, no.4, 1972; "Capra & Langdon" by Richard Leary in *Film Comment* (New York), vol.8, no.4, 1972; "Frank Capra and the Cinema of Populism" by Jeffrey Richards in *Film Society Review* (New York), vol.7, no.6 and no.7-9, 1972; "Capra Counts His Oscars" by Elliott Stein in *Sight and Sound* (London), vol.41, no.3, 1972; "L'athlète incomplet" by N. Simsolo in *Image et son* (Paris), no.269, 1973; "Frank Capra" by D.J. Badder in *Film Dope* (London), November 1974; "Mr. Smith Goes to Washington: Capra, Populism and Comic-Strip Art" by J. Nelson in *Journal of Popular Film* (Bowling Green, Ohio), summer 1974; "Additions and Corrections: Frank Capra" in *Film Dope* (London), October 1975; "Why We (Should Not) Fight" by G. Bailey in *Take One* (Montreal), September 1975; "Lost and Found: The Films of Frank Capra" in *Film* (London), June 1975; "Capra Conks Creepy Pic Heroes" by Joseph McBride in *Variety* (New York), 23 April 1975; "The Making of Cultural Myths: Walt Disney and Frank Capra" in *Movie-Made America* by Robert Sklar, New York 1975; "Frank Capra and the Popular Front" by Leonard Quart in *Cineaste* (New York), summer 1977; "It's a Wonderful Life: The Stand of the Capra Hero" by B. Rose in *Journal of Popular Film* (Bowling Green, Ohio), v.6, no.2, 1977; "McCarey vs. Capra: A Guide to American Film Comedy of the '30s" by Wes Gehring in *The Journal of Popular Film and Television* (Bowling Green, Ohio), vol.7, no.1, 1978; "The 'Populist' Films of Frank Capra" by G.A. Phelps in *Journal of American Studies* (London), no.3, 1979; "It's a Wonderful Life, But..." by M. Dickstein in *American Film* (Washington, D.C.), May 1980; special Capra issue of *Film Criticism* (Edinboro, Pennsylvania), winter 1981; "Stanwyck and Capra" by R.T. Jameson in *Film Comment* (New York), March/April 1981.

*   *   *

The critical stock of Frank Capra has fluctuated perhaps more wildly than that of any other major director. During his peak years, the 1930s, he was adored by the press, by the industry and, of course, by audiences. In 1934 *It Happened One Night* won nearly all the Oscars in sight, and through the rest of the decade a film of Frank Capra was either the winner or the strong contender for that honor. Long before the formulation of the *auteur* theory, the Capra signature on a film was recognized. But after World War II his career went into serious decline. His first post-war film, *It's a Wonderful Life*, was not received with the enthusiasm he thought it deserved (it has gone on to become one of his most-revived films). Of his last five films, two are remakes of material he treated in the thirties. Many contemporary critics are repelled by what they deem indigestible Capracorn and have even less tolerance for an ideology characterized as dangerously simplistic in its populism, its patriotism, its celebration of all-American values.

Indeed, many of Capra's most famous films can be read as excessively sentimental and politically naive. These readings, however, tend to neglect the bases for Capra's success—his skill as a director of actors, the complexity of his staging configurations, his narrative economy and energy, and most of all, his understanding of the importance of the spoken word in sound film. Capra captured the American voice in cinematic space. The words often serve the cause of apple pie, mom, the little man and other greeting card clichés (indeed, the hero of *Mr. Deeds Goes to Town* writes verse for greeting cards). But often, in the sound of the voice we hear uncertainties about those very clichés.

Capra's career began in the pre-talkie era, when he directed silent comic Harry Langdon in two successful films. His action films of the early thirties are not characteristic of his later work. Yet already, in the flms he made with Barbara Stanwyck, his individual gift can be discerned. The narrative pretext of *The Miracle Woman* is the urgency of Stanwyck's voice, its ability to move an audience, to persuade listeners of its sincerity. Capra exploited the raw energy of Stanwyck in this and other roles, where her qualities of fervor and near-hysterical conviction are just as essential to her persona as her hard-as-nails implacability will be in the forties. Stanwyck's voice is theatricalized, spatialized in her revivalist circus-tent in *The Miracle Woman* and on the hero's suicide tower in *Meet John Doe*, where her feverish pleadings are the only possible tenor for the film's unresolved ambiguities about society and the individual.

John Doe is portrayed by Gary Cooper, who possesses another American voice with particular resonance in the films of Capra. A star who seems to have invented the "strong, silent" type, Cooper first plays Mr. Deeds, whose platitudinous doggerel comes from a simple, do-gooder heart, but who enacts a crisis of communication in his long silence at the film's climax, a sanity hearing. When Mr. Deeds finally speaks it is a sign that the community (if not sanity) is restored—the usual resolution of a Capra film. As John Doe, Cooper is given words to voice by reporter Stanwyck, and he delivers them with such conviction that the whole nation listens. The vocal/dramatic center of the film is located in a rain-drenched ball park filled with John Doe's "people." The hero's effort to speak the truth, to reveal his own imposture and expose the fascistic intentions of his sponsor, is stymied when the lines of communication are literally cut between microphone and loudspeaker. The Capra narrative so often hinges on the protagonist's ability to speak and be heard, on the drama of sound and audition.

The bank run in *American Madness* is initiated by a montage of telephone voices and images, of mouths spreading a rumor. The panic is quelled by the speech of the bank president (Walter Huston), a situation repeated in more modest physical surroundings in *It's a Wonderful Life*. The most extended speech in the films of Capra occurs in *Mr. Smith Goes to Washington*. The whole film is a test of the hero's voice, and it culminates in a filibuster, a speech that, by definition, cannot be interrupted. The climax of *State of the Union* involves a different kind of audience and audition. There, the hero confesses his political dishonesty and his love for his wife on television.

The visual contexts, both simple and complex, never detract from the sound of Capra's films. They enhance it. The director's most elaborately designed film, *The Bitter Tea of General Yen* (recalling the style of Josef von Sternberg in its chiaroscuro lighting and its exoticism) expresses the opposition of cultural values in its visual elements, to be sure, but also in the voices of Stanwyck and Nils Asther, a Swedish actor who impersonates a Chinese war lord. Less unusual but not less significant harmonies are sounded in *It Happened One Night*, where a society girl (Claudette Colbert) learns "real" American speech from a fast-talking reporter (Clark Gable). The love scenes in *Mr. Deeds* are for Gary Cooper and Jean Arthur, another quintessential Capra heroine, whose vocal personality is at least as memorable as her physical one. In James Stewart Capra finds his most disquieting voice, ranging in *Mr. Smith* from ingenuousness to hysterical desperation, and in *It's a Wonderful Life*, to an even higher pitch of hysteria when the hero loses his identity.

The sounds and sights of Capra's films bear the authority of a director whose autobiography is called *The Name above the Title*. With that authority comes an unsettling belief in authorial power, the power dramatized in his major films, the persuasiveness exercised in political and social contexts. That persuasion reflects back on the director's own power to engage the viewer in his fiction, to call upon a degree of belief in the fiction—even when we reject the meaning of the fable.

—Charles Affron

CARLSEN, HENNING. Danish. Born in Aalborg, Denmark, 4 June 1927. Married Else Heidary, 1975. Career: 1948-53—assistant director on documentary films at Minerva Film; 1953-57—works for Nordisk Films Junior; after 1957—free-lance director, and producer after 1960; 1962—first feature film, *Dilemma*; 1968-81—manager of Copenhagen cinema "Dagmar"; works as stage and television director, teaches at The Danish Film School. Address: Puggårdsgade 15, DK-1573 Copenhagen V, Denmark.

Films (as director): 1949—*I formerlaere*; 1950—*Dukkestuen*; *Civilforsvaret*; 1951—*Post mortem Technique*; 1952—*Haakon VII* (co-d); 1953—*El-gjort er velgjort*; *Danish Motorboat Story*; *På vej mod et job*; 1954—*Havets husmaend*; *Velkommen til Vendsyssel*; *Maelkehygiejne*; *Knive*; *Køleskabe*; *Penge og økonomi*; 1955—*Jeg et hus mig bygge vil*; *Gulvbehandling*; 1956—*A Kingdom of Islands*; *Copenhagen*; *Lifeguards*; *Tivoli*; *Circus-farm*; 1957—*Cyklisten*; 1958—*Ligeud ad luftvejen*; 1959—*Danfoss—jorden rundt døgnet rundt*; *Et knudeproblem*; 1960—*Souvenirs from Sweden*; 1961—*Limfjorden*; *De gamle*; 1962—*Ren besked om snavs*; *Dilemma*; 1963—*Hvad med os?*; 1964—*Familiebilleder*; *Kattorna*; 1966—*Sult*; 1967—*Mennesker mødes og sød musik opstår i hjertet*; 1968—*Hvor er magten blevet af?*; 1969—*Klabautermanden*; 1971—*Er I bange?*; 1972—*Man sku' vaere noget ved musikken*; 1975—*Un Divorce heureux*; *Da Svante forsvandt*; 1978—*Hør, var der ikke én, som lo*; 1982—*Pengene eller livet*.

Publications:

By CARLSEN:

Articles—"Copenhague. H.C.7," interview by P. Legrand, in *Cinéma* (Paris), January 1972; "Comment faire partie de l'orchestre," interview by G. Allombert, in *Image et son* (Paris), April 1974; "Le Cinéma danois + entretien avec Henning

Carlsen" by E. Decaux in *Cinématographe* (Paris), January 1980.

On CARLSEN:

Articles—"Bedroom Philosophers" by Denis Duperley in *Films and Filming* (London), May 1968; "Deux moments du cinéma danois" by F. Devaux in *Cinéma* (Paris), January 1980.

* * *

Henning Carlsen learned the hard way, working on documentaries, sponsored films and commercials. During the fifties he worked on Disney travelogues and Danish versions of foreign films. He won international acclaim at short film festivals for his *Cyklisten* in 1957. Carlsen had developed into an all-round craftsman, by 1960 when he was strongly inspired by the *cinéma vérité* and living cinema approach to filmmaking.

This was reflected in his finest documentary, *De gamle*. Through an interview technique he presented revealing but sensitive portraits of pensioners. The way he handled a social problem with curiosity and openmindedness brought about a change in documentary filmmaking in Denmark. Carlsen was immensely fascinated by the films of Jean Rouch, especially *Chronique d'un été* and he applied Rouch's searching interview technique to his own short films. *De gamle* and Carlsen's two subsequent films form a trilogy about family life in contemporary Denmark in which Carlsen refined his way of observing people.

His first long film, *Dilemma*, based on Nadine Gordimer's novel *A World of Strangers* and shot illegally in South Africa, was partly documentary and partly fiction. Its weaknesses were obvious, especially in the description of the characters, but still the film was a major effort. For the first time a Danish director manifested an interest in the political world outside Denmark. Carlsen took sides, and despite the modern film clichés of *Dilemma*, viewers found a precise and sensitive realism.

Carlsen's next feature was not successful, but in his third, *Kattorna*, produced in Sweden and based on a Finnish play, he succeeded in blending his observing documentary approach with an authoritative grasp of the acting. The film's mobile and dramatic visual style was efficient. In 1966 came *Sult*, which is still the most fascinating of Carlsen's films, and in which he showed himself in complete control of all the elements.

In the following years Carlsen, who is constantly trying to extend his range, made some highly ambitious, but not entirely successful films, based on novels. In 1971 he returned to the documentary form in *Er I bange?* about a fashionable Copenhagen commune. His most popular success was *Man sku' vaere noget ved musikken* in 1972, a serio-comedy about ordinary, anonymous people who meet at a cafe. The film's sympathetic everyday realism seemed somewhat marred, however, by the fundamental traditionalism of the characters.

In 1975 Carlsen made *Un Divorce heureux* in France, a film heavily influenced by Chabrol, about erotic complications among the *haute bourgeoisie*. The same year he made what is perhaps his happiest and most relaxed film, *Da Svante forsvandt*, a charming and imaginative burlesque about a fictional poet. His last two films, about unemployment problems in the thirties, and about an overworked architect in midlife crisis in the eighties, are not very significant. But still Carlsen is an honest, committed and careful *metteur-en-scène*, who by energy and will power has come a long way.

—Ib Monty

CARNÉ, MARCEL. French. Born in Paris, 18 August 1909. Career: mid-1920s—works as insurance clerk, studies filmmaking; 1928—Françoise Rosay secures introduction to her husband Jacques Feyder; becomes assistant to chief cameraman Georges Périnal on *Les Nouveaux Messieurs*; 1929—works briefly as film critic; makes short film *Nogent, Eldorado du dimanche*; 1930—René Clair, impressed by *Nogent*, takes on Carné as assistant on *Sous les toits de Paris*; makes first publicity films, from scenarios by Jean Aurenche; early 1930s—becomes editor-in-chief on *Hebdo-Films* journal; later collaborates on *Cinémagazine* and *Cinémonde*; meets future collaborator Jacques Prévert in connection with activities of group "October"; 1933-35—assistant to Feyder on *Le Grand Jeu, Pension Mimosa* and *La Kermesse héroïque*; 1935—enabled to direct first film by Feyder's recommendation; 1943-45—production of *Children of Paradise*; 1947—split with Prévert following cancellation in mid-production of *La Fleur de l'âge*. Recipient: Special Mention, Venice Festival, for direction of *Quai des brumes*, 1938.

Films (as director): 1929—*Nogent, Eldorado du dimanche*; 1936—*Jenny*; 1937—*Drôle de drame (Bizarre Bizarre)*; 1938—*Quai des brumes (Port of Shadows)*; *Hôtel du Nord*; 1939—*Le Jour se lève (Daybreak)*; *École communale* (abandoned due to war); 1942—*Les Visiteurs du soir (The Devil's Envoys)*; 1945—*Les Enfants du paradis (Children of Paradise)*; 1946—*Les Portes de la nuit (Gates of the Night)*; 1947—*La Fleur de l'âge* (not completed); 1949—*La Marie du port* (+co-sc); 1951—*Juliette ou la Clé des songes* (+co-sc); 1953—*Thérèse Raquin (The Adulteress)* (+co-sc); 1954—*L'Air de Paris* (+co-sc); 1956—*Le Pays d'où je viens* (+co-sc); 1958—*Les Tricheurs (The Cheaters)*; 1960—*Terrain vague* (+co-sc); 1962—*Du mouron pour les petits oiseaux* (+co-sc); 1965—*Trois Chambres à Manhattan* (+co-sc); 1967—*Les Jeunes Loups (The Young Wolves)*; 1971—*Les Assassins de l'ordre* (+co-sc); 1974—*La Merveilleuse Visite* (+co-sc); 1976—*La Bible* (feature documentary for TV and theatrical release).

Publications:

By CARNÉ:

Articles—interview by F. Cuel and others in *Cinématographe* (Paris), May 1978; "Comment est ne 'Le Quai des brumes'" in *Avant-Scène du cinéma* (Paris), 15 October 1979; "Marcel Carné sous la coupole" in *Avant-Scène du cinéma* (Paris), 1 July 1980.

On CARNÉ:

Books—*Marcel Carne* by Jean-Louis Béranger, Paris 1945; *Marcel Carne* by Robert Chazal, Paris n.d.; *Marcel Carné* by Jean Quéval, Paris 1952; *Marcel Carné, sa vie, ses films* by Bernard Landry, Paris n.d.; *Marcel Carné* by Jacques Meillant, Paris n.d.; *Children of Paradise* by Jacques Prévert, with interview of Carné, New York 1968; *Le Jour se leve* by Jacques Prévert, New York 1970; *La Vie a belles dents: souvenirs*, Paris 1975; articles—"Marcel Carné" by Roger Manvell in *Sight and Sound* (London), spring 1946; "The Cinema of Marcel Carné" by J.F. Lodge in *Sequence* (London), December 1946; "Marcel Carné" by Gavin Lambert in *Sequence* (London), spring 1948; "Les 20 Ans de cinéma de Marcel Carné" by Louis Daquin in *Les Lettres françaises* (Paris), 1 March 1956; "Carné ou la Clé des songes" by J. Michel in *Cinéma 56* (Paris), no.12, 1956; "Les Films de Marcel Carné, expression de notre époque" by Georges

Sadoul in *Les Lettres françaises* (Paris), 1 March 1956; "The Carné Bubble" by Alan Stanbrook in *Film* (London), November/December 1959; special issue of *Cahiers de la Cinémathèque* (Paris), winter 1972; "4 de la forfanterie" by Claude Beylie in *Ecran* (Paris), October 1975; "Le Quai des brumes," special issue of *Avant-Scène du cinéma* (Paris), 15 October 1979; "The Birth of Children of Paradise" by E.B. Turk in *American Film* (Washington, D.C.), July/August 1979; "Temoignages" by P. Tchernia and others in *Avant-Scène du cinéma* (Paris), 15 November 1979.

*   *   *

At a time when film schools were non-existent and training in filmmaking was acquired through assistantship, no one could have been better prepared for a brilliant career than Marcel Carné. He worked as assistant to Clair on the first important French sound film, *Sous les toits de Paris*, and to Feyder on the latter's three great films of 1934-35. Though he had also made a successful personal documentary, *Nogent, Eldorado du dimanche*, and a number of publicity shorts, it was only thanks to the support of Feyder and his wife, the actress Françoise Rosay, that Carné was able to make his debut as a feature filmmaker with *Jenny* in 1936. If this was a routine melodrama, Carné was able in the next three years to establish himself as one of Europe's leading film directors.

During the period up to the outbreak of war in 1939 Carné established what was to be a ten-year collaboration with the poet and screenwriter Jacques Prévert, and gradually built up a team of collaborators—including the designer Alexandre Trauner and composer Maurice Jaubert—which was unsurpassed at this period. In quick succession Carné made the comedy *Drôle de drame*, which owes more to Prévert's taste for systematic absurdity and surreal gags than to the director's professionalism, and a trio of fatalistic romantic melodramas, *Quai des brumes*, *Hôtel du nord* and *Le Jour se lève*.

These are perfect examples of the mode of French filmmaking which had been established by Jacques Feyder: a concern with visual style and a studio-created realism, a reliance on detailed scripts with structure and dialogue separately elaborated, and a foregrounding of star performers to whom all elements of decor and photography are subordinate. Though the forces shaping a character's destiny may be outside his or her control, the story focuses on social behavior and the script offers set-piece scenes and confrontations and witty or trenchant dialogue which enables the stars to display their particular talents to the full.

The various advocates of either Prévert or Carné have sought to make exclusive claims as to which brought the poetry to the nebulous and ill-defined "poetic realism" which these films are said to exemplify. In retrospect, however, these arguments seem over-personalized, since the pair seem remarkably well-matched. The actual differences seem less in artistic approach than in attitude to production. From the first, Carné, heir to a particular mode of quality filmmaking, was concerned with an industry, a technique, a career. Prévert, by contrast, though he is a perfect example of the archetypal 1930s screenwriter, able to create striking star roles and write dazzling and memorable dialogue, is not limited to this role and has a quite separate identity as surrealist, humorist and poet.

The pair share a certain fantastic conception of realism, with film seen as a studio construct in which fidelity to life is balanced by attention to a certain poetic atmosphere. Carné's coldly formal command of technique is matched by Prévert's sense of the logic of a tightly woven narrative. If it is Prévert's imagination that allows him to conceive both the *amour fou* which unites the lovers and the grotesque villains who threaten it, it is Carné's

masterly direction of actors which turns Jean Gabin and Michèle Morgan into the 1930s ideal couple and draws such memorable performances from Michel Simon, Jules Berry and Arletty.

The collaboration of Prévert and Carné was sustained during the very different circumstances of the German Occupation, when they together made two films which rank among the most significant of the period. Since all the films of the 1930s poetic realism were now banned, it is hardly surprising that they should have found the need to adopt a radically new style. Remaining within the concept of the studio-made film, but leaving behind the contemporary urban gloom of *Le Jour se lève*, they opted for a style of elaborate and theatrical period spectacle. The medieval fable of *Les Visiteurs du soir* was an enormous contemporary success but it has not worn well. Working with very limited resources the filmmakers—assisted clandestinely by Trauner and the composer Joseph Kosma—succeeded in making an obvious prestige film, a work in which Frenchmen could take pride at a dark moment of history. But despite the presence of such players as Arletty and Jules Berry, the overall effect is ponderous and stilted.

Prévert and Carné's masterpiece is *Les Enfants du paradis*, shot during the war years but released only after the Liberation. Running for over three hours and comprising two parts, each of which is of full feature length, *Les Enfants du paradis* is one of the most ambitious films ever undertaken in France. Set in the twin worlds of theatre and crime in nineteenth century Paris, this all-star film is both a theatrical spectacle in its own right and a reflection on the nature of spectacle. The script is one of Prévert's richest, abounding in wit and aphorism, and Carné's handling of both stars and crowd scenes is masterly. The sustained vitality and dynamism of the work as it moves seemingly effortlessly from farce to tragedy, from delicate love scenes to outrageous buffoonery is exemplary and its impact is undimmed by the years.

Marcel Carné was still only 36 and at the height of his fame when the war ended. Younger than most of those who now came to the fore, he had already made masterly films in two quite different contexts and it seemed inevitable that he would continue to be a dominant force in French cinema despite the changed circumstances of the postwar era. But in fact the first postwar Carné-Prévert film, *Les Portes de la nuit*, was an expensive flop and when a subsequent film, *La Fleur de l'âge*, was abandoned shortly after production had begun, one of the most fruitful partnerships in French cinema came to an end. Carné directed a dozen more films from *La Marie du port* in 1950 to *La Merveilleuse Visite* in 1973, but he was no longer a major force in French filmmaking.

Marcel Carné was an unfashionable figure long before his directing career came to an end. Scorned by a new generation of filmmakers—few if any of whom were to have a comparably rich set of credits by the age of 35—Carné grew more and more out of touch with contemporary developments, despite an eagerness to explore new subjects and use young performers. His failure is a measure of the gulf which separates 1950s and 1960s conceptions of cinema from the studio era of the war and immediate prewar years. He was, however, the epitome of this French studio style, its unquestioned master even if—unlike Renoir—he was unable to transcend its limitations. While future critics are unlikely to find much to salvage from the latter part of his career, films like *Drôle de drame* and *Quai des brumes*, *Le Jour se lève* and *Les Enfants du paradis* remain rich and complex monuments to a decade of filmmaking which will reward fresh and unbiased critical attention.

—Roy Armes

CARPENTER, JOHN. American. Born in Bowling Green, Kentucky, 1948. Educated at Western Kentucky University; studied filmmaking at University of Southern California, degree 1972. Married actress Adrienne Barbeau, 1979. Career: 1962—begins making short films; 1965—publishes film buff review *Fantastic Films Illustrated*; mid-1970s—with editor Tommy Wallace forms band "The Coupe de Villes"; 1978—begins scriptwriting collaboration with Debra Hill; *Halloween* is unexpected success, soon becomes top-grossing independent film ever made in U.S. Recipient: Academy Award for Best Short Subject (Live Action) for *The Resurrection of Bronco Billy*, 1970. Agent: David Gersh, The Gersh Agency, Inc., 222 North Canon Dr., Beverly Hills, CA. Address: P.O. Box 1334, North Hollywood, CA 91604.

Films (as maker of short films): 1962 and after—*Revenge of the Colossal Beasts*; *Gorgo versus Godzilla*; *Terror from Space*; *Sorcerer from Outer Space*; *Warrior and the Demon*; *Gorgon, the Space Monster*; 1970—*The Resurrection of Bronco Billy*; (as feature director): 1974—*Dark Star* (+pr, co-sc); 1977—*Assault on Precinct 13* (+sc); 1978—*Halloween* (+co-sc); *Eyes of Laura Mars* (Kershner) (sc only); 1979—*Elvis* (made for TV); 1980—*The Fog* (+sc); *Escape from New York* (+co-sc); 1982—*The Thing*.

Publications:

By CARPENTER:

Articles—"The Man in the Cryogenic Freezer", interview by Tom Milne and R. Combs in *Sight and Sound* (London), spring 1978; "Working with Numbers", interview by R. Appelbaum, in *Films and Filming* (London), September 1979; "Trick and Treat", interview by T. McCarthy, in *Film Comment* (New York), January/February 1980; "An Interview with Director John Carpenter: The Fog" by A. Oddie, in *Filmmakers Monthly* (Ward Hill, Mass.), March 1980; "New Fright Master: John Carpenter", interview by J. Wells in *Films in Review* (New York), April 1980.

On CARPENTER:

Articles—"Introducing John Carpenter" by G. Cebe in *Ecran* (Paris), September 1978; "From Cult Homage to Creative Control" by R. Appelbaum in *Films and Filming* (London), June 1979; "*The Fog*: a Spook Ride on Film" by P. Scanlon in *Rolling Stone* (New York), 28 June 1979; "Profiles: People Start Running" by James Stevenson in *The New Yorker*, 28 January 1980; "Lexique des réalisateurs de films fantastiques américains" by J.-P. Piton in *Image et son* (Paris), May 1981; "Las Máscaras del tiempo" by S. Zunzunegui in *Contracampo* (Madrid), October 1981.

*   *   *

It seems to be generally agreed that, after a promising start, John Carpenter's career has been, to date, singularly disappointing: those who hailed *Halloween* as at once fulfilling the promise of *Dark Star* and *Assault on Precinct 13* and definitively establishing Carpenter in the front rank of contemporary American filmmakers cannot but be dismayed and embarrassed by *The Fog*, *Escape from New York*, and *The Thing*. In retrospect, however, the early films seem scarcely more satisfying than their

successors, with the reasons for the failure significantly to develop visible from the outset.

The prime attraction of Carpenter's early work lay in its awareness of being rooted in a mainstream Hollywood tradition, its sophisticated play with genres, conventions, references, its delight in skills (learnt primarily from Hitchcock) of suspense and manipulation. Both the awareness and the sophistication, however, now look decidedly superficial: a matter of acquiring the skills without acquiring much understanding of what (in Hitchcock's or Hawks's best work) the skills were *for*.

The technical attainment is accompanied by a curious abeyance of thought. Thus, in *Assault on Precinct 13*, Carpenter combines *Rio Bravo* and *Night of the Living Dead* without any apparent awareness of the ideological consequences of converting Hawks's fascists and Romero's ghouls into an army of revolutionaries: the film's display of scepticism about established society and celebration of the individualistic outsider is oddly and confusingly juxtaposed with a strikingly reactionary political position. A parallel confusion vitiates *Halloween*: the arresting opening (derived from the Halloween sequence of *Meet Me in St. Louis* as much as from *Psycho*) offers us (in line with the major American horror films of the seventies) the monster as the direct product of the psychopathology of the nuclear family. He is subsequently diagnosed (by his own psychiatrist!) as Evil Incarnate, a horror that cannot be analysed, only repressed.

Each of Carpenter's films has an interesting premise, but the premise is never satisfactorily followed through, the interest progressively dissipated. *The Fog* offers a re-reading of the small town (microcosm of America) as founded, not in the purity of democratic idealism, but in corruption and repression, with "the repressed" returning to exact its revenge; but the realization is curiously half-hearted, the skills of *Halloween* largely absent. Carpenter's re-working of Hawks's *The Thing* (the original was "quoted" on a television set in *Halloween*) suggests that he has reached a (temporary?) bankruptcy: lacking a single sympathetic (or even interesting) character with whom to identify, the spectator merely waits for the next eruption (admittedly spectacular) of special effects.

Halloween has an undeniable, if scarcely positive, importance in the evolution of the horror film: with Tobe Hooper's greatly superior *The Texas Chainsaw Massacre*, it is the source of the twin cycles that have dominated the genre since the late seventies, the "violence against women" and "slaughter of promiscuous teenagers" movies. It is particularly saddening that Carpenter allowed his name (as producer) to be attached to one of the grossest and most inept of these, *Halloween II*.

—Robin Wood

CASSAVETES, JOHN. American. Born in New York City, 9 December 1929. Educated at Mohawk College; Colgate University; New York Academy of Dramatic Arts, degree 1950. Married Gena Rowlands; children: Nicholas, Alexander, and Xan. Career: 1950-52—acts in stock companies in Rhode Island; 1952—appears in bit role in 1st film *Taxi*; 1953—appears in television show *Omnibus*; 1956—conducts "method" workshop for unemployed actors; 1959-60—returns to television as title character in series *Johnny Staccato*; 1961—hired by Paramount to direct; contract terminated after critical and financial failure of *Too Late Blues*; hired by Stanley Kramer to direct *A Child is Waiting*; 1964—shoots and edits next independent film *Faces*;

1974—finances own film *Woman Under the Influence* (with film's star Peter Falk), using mainly family members as cast and crew; with Falk and Gena Rowlands promotes and distributes *Woman Under the Influence*. Recipient: Best Screenplay, National Society of Film Critics, for *Faces*, 1968. Address: c/o Esme Chandee, 9056 Santa Monica Blvd., 201 Los Angeles, California 90069.

Films (as director and scriptwriter): 1960—*Shadows*; 1961—*Too Late Blues* (+pr); 1962—*A Child is Waiting* (d only); 1968—*Faces*; 1970—*Husbands* (+ro as *Gus*); 1971—*Minnie and Moskowitz* (+ro as *Husband*); 1974—*A Woman Under the Influence*; 1976—*The Killing of a Chinese Bookie*; 1977-78—*Opening Night*; 1980—*Gloria* (d only).

Roles: 1951—extra in *14 Hours* (Hathaway); 1953—*Taxi* (Ratoff); 1955—*The Night Holds Terror* (Stone); 1956—*Crime in the Streets* (Siegel); 1957—*Edge of the City* (Ritt); 1958—*Saddle the Wind* (Parrish); *Virgin Island* (P. Jackson); 1962—*The Webster Boy* (Chaffey); 1964—*Johnny North* in *The Killers* (Siegel); 1967—*Victor Franko* in *The Dirty Dozen* (Aldrich); *Devil's Angels* (Haller); 1968—*Rosemary's Husband* in *Rosemary's Baby* (Polansky); *Gli Intoccabili (Machine Gun McCain)* (Montaldo); 1969—*Roma coma Chicago (Bandits in Rome)* (De Martino); cameo in *If It's Tuesday, This Must Be Belgium* (M. Stuart); 1976—*2-Minute Warning* (Peerce); 1978—*The Fury* (De Palma); 1982—*The Tempest* (Mazursky).

Publications:

By CASSAVETES:

Books—*Faces*, New York 1970; *John Cassavetes, Peter Falk* edited by Bruce Henstell, Washington, D.C. 1972; articles—"What's Wrong with Hollywood" in *Film Culture* (New York), April 1959; article in *Film Quarterly* (Berkeley), spring 1961; "...and the Pursuit of Happiness" in *Films and Filming* (London), February 1961; "Incoming Tide: Interview" in *Cinema* (Beverly Hills), no.1, 1962; "Masks and Faces: Interview" by David Austen in *Films and Filming* (London), September 1968; "*Faces*: Interview" in *Cinema* (Beverly Hills), Spring 1968; "The Faces of the Husbands" in the *New Yorker*, 15 March 1969; interview by Jonas Mekas in the *Village Voice* (New York), 23 December 1971; "Interview: John Cassavetes" in *Playboy* (Chicago), July 1971; interview by L. Gross in *Millimeter* (New York), April 1975; "A Woman Under the Influence", interview by L. McNally in *Filmmakers Newsletter* (Ward Hill, Mass.), January 1975; "Entretien avec John Cassavetes" by J. Farren in *Cinéma* (Paris), February 1977; "Cassavetes on Cassavetes" in *Monthly Film Bulletin* (London), June 1978; "John Cassavetes à Los Angeles", interview by L. Gavron, in *Positif* (Paris), April 1978; "Le Bal des vauriens. Entretien avec John Cassavetes" by Y. Lardeau and L. Marcorelles in *Cahiers du cinéma* (Paris), June 1978; "Crucial Culture", interview by R. Appelbaum, in *Films* (London), January 1981.

On CASSAVETES:

Books—*The Film Director: A Practical Guide to Motion Picture and Television Techniques* by Richard L. Bare, New York 1971; articles—"Broadway Love Story" in *Look* (New York), 11 June 1957; "No Torn Shirts for Him" in *TV Guide* (New York), 5 October 1957; "The Chip's Off His Shoulder" in *TV Guide* (New York), 28 November 1959; "Cassavetes in London" by John Russell Taylor in *Sight and Sound* (London), autumn 1960; "$40,000 Method" in *Time* (New York), 24 March 1961; "People on the Way Up" in the *Saturday Evening Post* (Philadelphia), 7 April 1962; "Cassavetes, the Improvisation" by Jonas Mekas in *Film Culture* (New York), spring 1962; "An Interview with Hugh Hurd" by Clara Hoover in *Film Comment* (New York), no.4, 1963; "The Face of 63—United States" by G. Fenin in *Films and Filming* (London), March 1963; "Oddities and One-Shots" by Andrew Sarris in *Film Culture* (New York), spring 1963; "After *Faces*, a Film to Keep the Man-Child Alive" by A. Guerin in *Life* (New York), 9 May 1969; "On the Scene: John Cassavetes" in *Playboy* (Chicago), April 1970; "New Hollywood is Old Hollywood" in *Time* (New York), 7 December 1970; article by Aljean Harmetz in *The New York Times*, 13 February 1962; "Robert Aldrich on John Cassavetes" in *Dialogue on Film* (Washington, D.C.), no.2, 1972; "Ainsi va l'amour" by G. Braucourt in *Ecran* (Paris), February 1973; "Films on TV" by J.E. Nolan in *Films in Review* (New York), December 1974; article by E. Comuzio in *Cineforum* (Bergamo), September 1976; "Femmes et maris dans l'oeuvre de Cassavetes" by C. Benoit and A. Tournes in *Jeune cinéma* (Paris), September/October 1976; "Shadow" by R. Lefèbvre in *Avant-Scène du cinéma* (Paris), 1 December 1977; "John Cassavetes" in *Hollywood Renaissance* by Diane Jacob, New York 1977; "John Cassavetes. Une caméra sur le qui-vivre" by R. Lefèvre in *Cinéma* (Paris), February 1977; "John Cassavetes" in *Ecran* (Paris), April 1978; "Notes sur le cinéma de John Cassavetes" by Noel Simsolo in *Cahiers du cinéma* (Paris), May 1978; "Das Leben an der Arbeit" by P. Lachat in *Cinéma* (Zurich), September 1979; "John Cassavetes" by G. Courant and J. Farren in *Cinéma* (Paris), October 1979; "'La sera della prima': la maniera del doppio" by G. Turroni in *Filmcritica* (Rome), March 1979; "The Cinema of John Cassavetes" by M. Landy and S. Shostack in *Ciné-Tracts* (Montreal), winter 1980; "John Cassavetes: Film's Bad Boy" by J. Stevenson in *American Film* (Washington, D.C.), January/February 1980.

*   *   *

As perhaps the most influential of the independently produced feature films of its era (1958-1967), *Shadows* came to be seen as a virtual breakthrough for American alternative cinema. The film and its fledgling writer-director had put a group of young, independent filmmakers on the movie map, together with their more intellectual, less technically polished, decidedly less commercial, low-budget alternatives to Hollywood features.

Beginning as an improvisational exercise in the method-acting workshop actor Cassavetes was teaching, and partly financed by his earnings from the *Johnny Staccato* television series, *Shadows* was a loosely plotted, heavily improvised work of cinema verité immediacy which explored human relationships and racial identity against the background of the beat atmosphere of the late fifties, given coherence by the jazz score of Charles Mingus.

The origins and style of *Shadows* were to characterize John Cassavetes's work throughout his directorial career, once he got the studio-financed production bug out of his system—and his system out of theirs.

The five prizes garnered by *Shadows*, including the prestigious Critics Award at the 1960 Venice Film Festival, led to Cassavetes's unhappy and resentful experience directing two studio-molded productions (*Too Late Blues*, *A Child is Waiting*), both of which failed critically and commercially. Thereafter, he returned to independent filmmaking, acting in mainstream movies such as *The Dirty Dozen*, *Rosemary's Baby*, and *Two Minute Warning*, in between directing feature films in his characteristic, controversial style.

That style, on display in the seven subsequent Cassavetes-directed films (all but *Gloria* also scripted by him), centers around a freedom afforded his actors to share in the creative process. Cassavete's scripts serve as sketchy blueprints for the performers' introspective explorations and emotional embellishments. Consequently, camera movements, at the command of the actors' intuitive behavior, are of necessity spontaneous.

The amalgam of improvisational acting, hand-held camera work, grainy stock, loose editing, and thread-bare plot give his films a texture of recreated rather than heightened reality, often imbuing them with a feeling of astonishing psychodramatic intensity as characters confront each other and lay bare their souls.

However, detractors see director Cassavetes as too dedicated to the performers' art, too trusting of the actor's self-discipline. The result: a mild form of aesthetic anarchy.

At the worst Cassavetes's films are admittedly formless and self-indulgent. Scenes are stretched excruciatingly far beyond their climactic moments, lines are delivered falteringly, dialogue is repetitious. But, paradoxically, these same blemishes seem to make possible the several lucid, provocative, and moving moments of transcendent human revelation that a Cassavetes film almost inevitably delivers.

As his career has progressed, Cassavetes has changed his thematic concerns, upgraded his technical production values, and, not surprisingly, attracted a wider audience—but without overhauling his actor-as-auteur approach.

Faces represented Cassavetes's return to his favored semi-documentary style, complete with the seemingly obligatory excesses and gaffes, but also containing moments of truth and exemplary acting. Not only did this highly charged drama about the disintegration of a middle-class marriage in affluent Southern California find favor with the critical and filmmaking communities, it broke through as one of the first independent films to find a sizable audience among the general moviegoing public.

In *Husbands*, Cassavetes continued his exploration of marital manners, morals and sexual identity by focusing on a trio of middle-class husbands—played by Cassavetes, Ben Gazzara, and Peter Falk—who confront their own mortality when a friend dies. Director Cassavetes's doubled-edged trademark—brilliant moments of intense acting amid the banal debris of overindulgence—had never been in bolder relief.

Minnie and Moskowitz was Cassavetes's demonstration of a lighter touch, an amusing and touching interlude prior to his most ambitious and commercially successful film. Starring Gena Rowlands (Cassavetes's wife) and Seymour Cassel as a pair of dissimilar but similarly lonely people ensnared in a manic romance, it was Cassavetes again examining miscommunication but in a much more playful vein.

By far his most polished, accessible, gripping, and technically proficient film was *A Woman Under the Influence*, for which Cassavetes departed from his accustomed style of working by writing a fully detailed script during pre-production. Starring Gena Rowlands in a magnificent performance as a lower-middle class housewife coming apart at the seams, and the reliable Peter Falk as the hardhat husband who is ill-equipped to deal with his wife's mental breakdown, *Woman* offered a more palatable balance of Cassavetes's strengths and weaknesses. The over-long scenes and overindulgent acting jags are there, but in lesser doses, while the privileged moments and bursts of virtuoso screen acting seem more abundant than usual.

Financed by Falk and Cassavetes, its crew and cast (including many family members) working on deferred salaries; promoted via a tour undertaken by the nucleus of the virtual repertory company (Cassavetes, Rowland, Falk); and booked without a major distributor, *Woman* collected generally ecstatic reviews,

Academy Award nominations for Cassavetes and Rowlands, and impressive box office returns.

Both of Cassavetes's next two films (*The Killing of a Chinese Bookie, Opening Night*) feature a return to his earlier structure (or lack thereof)—inaccessible, interminable, and insufferable for all but diehard buffs. However, *Gloria*, showcasing Rowlands as a former gangster's moll, while uneven in tone and erratic in pace, represented a concession by Cassavetes to filmgoers seeking heightened cinematic energy and narrative momentum.

"People who are making films today are too concerned with mechanics—technical things instead of feeling," Cassavetes told an interviewer in 1980. "Execution is about eight percent to me. The technical quality of a film doesn't have much to do with whether it's a good film."

—Bill Wine

CASTELLANI, RENATO. Italian. Born in Finale Ligure (Savona), 4 September 1913. Educated in Argentina until 1925, then in Geneva; studied architecture in Milan. Career: mid-1930s—begins film career as journalist, then scriptwriter for Mario Camerini, Augusto Genina, Mario Soldati and Alessandro Blasetti; 1940—assistant director to Blasetti on *Un'avventura di Salvator Rosa* and *La corona di ferro*; 1948—joins neorealist movement with *Sotto il sole di Roma*; 1971—writes and directs 5 programs on Leonardo da Vinci for Italian TV. Recipient: Best Italian Film, Venice Festival, for *Sotto il sole di Roma*, 1948; Best Film, Cannes Festival (*ex aequo*), for *2 Cents Worth of Hope*, 1952; Golden Lion, Venice Festival, for *Romeo and Juliet*, 1954.

Films (as co-scriptwriter): 1938—*L'orologio a Cucu* (Mastrocinque); *Batticuore* (Camerini); *Castelli in aria* (Camerini); 1939—*Grandi magazzini* (Camerini) (+asst d); *Il documento* (Camerini); *Un'avventura di Salvator Rosa* (Blasetti) (+asst d); *Due milioni per un sorriso* (Borghesio and Soldati); 1940—*Centomila dollari* (Camerini) (asst d only); *Una romantica avventura* (Camerini); *La corona di ferro* (Blasetti) (+asst d); 1941—*La cena della beffe* (Blasetti); (as director and co-scriptwriter): 1941—*Un Colpo di pistola*; 1942—*Zaza* (sc); *Malombra* (Soldati) (co-sc only); 1943—*La Donna del Montagna* (sc); 1944—*Quartieri alti* (Soldati) (co-sc only); 1945—*Malia* (Amato) (co-sc only); *Notte di tempesta* (Franciolini) (sc only); 1946—Mio Figlio Professore (Professor My Son); 1948—*Sotto il sole di Roma (Under the Sun of Rome)* (sc); 1949—*E'primavera (It's Forever Springtime)*; 1952—*Due Soldi di speranza (2 Cents Worth of Hope)* (sc); 1954—*Giulietta e Romeo (Romeo and Juliet)* (sc); 1957—*I sogni nel cassetto* (sc); 1958—*Resurrezione (Auferstehung)* (Hansen) (co-sc only); 1959—*Nella città l'inferno (And the Wild, Wild Women)*; 1961—*Il Brigante* (sc); 1962—*Mare Matto*; *Venere imperiale* (Delannoy) (idea only—begun by Castellani in 1958, discontinued due to dispute with producers and star Gina Lollobrigida); 1964—"La Vedova" episode of *Tre notti di amore (Three Nights of Love)*; "Una Donna d'Afari" episode of *Controsesso*; *Matrimonio all'italiana* (de Sica) (co-sc only); 1967—*Questi fantasmi (Ghosts Italian Style)*; 1969—*Una breve stagione*; 1972—*Leonardo da Vinci* (condensed from 5-part TV series).

Publications:

By CASTELLANI:

Article—"Putting Gloss on Prison" in *Films and Filming* (London), April 1959.

On CASTELLANI:

Books—*Giulietta e Romeo di Renato Castellani* edited by Stelio Martini, Cappelli; *Atti del Convegno della X mostra internazionale del nuovo cinema*, Venice 1975; *Cinema neo-realista da Rossellini a Pasolini* by Mario Verdone, Palermo 1977.

*   *   *

Poggioli, Lattuada, Chiarini, Soldati—the "calligraphers": with these directors, novelists, and critics Castellani is associated at the beginning of his film career (1940-1948). The "calligraphers" are interested in form above all, strongly attached to the narrative tradition of the nineteenth century, committed to an essentially bourgeois cinema, refined, cultivated, intellectual. Their aesthetic is articulated in theory and in practice, and resistent, even antithetical, to the demands of the new realism voiced by De Santis and others in *Cinema*, and by Visconti in *Ossessione*. *Un colpo di pistola*, *Zaza* (a comedy in the French manner set during the "belle époque"), and *La donna della montagna* are films of escape. Through them Castellani managed his own flight: from the reality of the present, to be sure, but also from fascist propaganda and fascist censorship.

The opposition between "calligraphy" and neorealism must be treated cautiously, as Roy Armes points out in *Patterns of Realism*. Not only did the two tendencies share a number of temptations (to historicism, for example), but individual artists, Castellani among them, passed with apparent ease from one to the other. "Calligrapher" as late as 1946, Castellani joined the neorealists with *Sotto il sole di Roma*, announcing his new allegiance in the very first frame with this intertitle: "This film was inspired by events that actually took place. It was performed by non-professional actors, and shot entirely in Rome, in the neighborhoods depicted in the film." While the presence of Alberto Sordi undermines the claim of a non-professional cast, his performance as a shoe salesman (recalling, in comic mode, the shoes of *Paisa* and *Shoe Shine*), the music of Nino Rota, the theme of black marketeering, the Roman locales and dialect, the events of early summer 1943 to the end of summer of 1944 (from the invasion of Sicily to the liberation of Rome), cast the film firmly in the honored mold of Rossellini and De Sica. The chronology of *Sotto il sole di Roma* is that of *Paisà*; it is the story of the coming of age of a group of adolescent boys, matured by destruction and death. At its conclusion, unlike the children of *Open City*, *Bicycle Thief*, and *Shoe Shine*, they face the future with confidence—in themselves and in the society of which they are a part.

Two films follow in the wake of *Sotto il sole di Roma* to shape a trilogy on youth and young love: *E primavera* and *Two Cents Worth of Hope*. To their scripts are linked the names of Suso Cecchi d'Amico, Cesare Zavattini, and Titina de Filippo, names in turn allied with Visconti, De Sica, and the master family of Italian comedy. Shot on location from one end of the peninsula to the other, the burning questions of the day—the *mezzogiorno*, unemployment, Communist vs. Christian Democrat—are cloaked in humor, more importantly in an optimism that, as Leprohon notes in *The Italian Cinema*, official Italy found reassuring. Threatened by the bleak view of Italy exported by the post-war Italian cinema, the government reacted by passing the Andreotti Law (1948) in the same year Castellani launched what came to be known as "rosy neorealism."

The trilogy was followed by *Giulietta e Romeo*. This story of young love thwarted by parents and convention had already found expression in the contemporary working class settings of the three previous films, and was drawn from two Renaissance versions: Shakespeare's and Luigi Da Porto's. Laurence Harvey, Flora Robson, highly professional, and non-professional actors including a Juliet chosen from an avalanche of responses to a talent search conducted in the neorealist style, combined to create a tension of text and performance that elicited considerable critical controversy—for the last time in Castellani's career. The ostensibly neorealist treatment of this ancient tale found its most original conception in the decor: real locations juxtaposed to reconstruct a renaissance city untouched by time. An ideal Verona was created through editing from extant streets, corners, interiors and exteriors in Venice, Siena, Verona, and elsewhere.

Once again, Castellani had adapted neorealism to his own uses. This time it was a literary neorealism, redefined to suit his inspiration, and dependent as always on the rejection of mimicry and doctrine.

—Mirella Jona Affron

CAVALCANTI, ALBERTO; Brazilian. Born Alberto de Almeida Cavalcanti in Rio de Janeiro, 6 February 1897. Attended law school, Brazil; Geneva Fine Art School, Switzerland. Career: after World War I—works in architect's atelier in Paris; late teens, early 1920s—turns to interior decoration to support himself, eventually becomes art director for avant-garde films; 1922—art director on Marcel L'Herbier's unfinished *Resurrection*; 1926—directs 1st film, *Rien que les heures*, documentary about Paris; 1929-30—directs French language versions of American films at Paramount Studios, Joinville; 1934—invited by John Grierson to join General Post Office (GPO) film unit in England; 1937—takes over as head of Unit following Grierson's departure (later in conjunction with J.B. Holmes); 1940—joins Michael Balcon's Ealing Studios as feature director; 1949-50—returns to Brazil, joins Vera Cruz group as head of production; helps found Brazilian Film Institute; 1952—fired from Vera Cruz production company on suspicion of communist activities; later that year, directs *Herr Puntila und sein Knecht Matti* in Austria with author Bertolt Brecht; 1955—settles in Europe; 1950s-68—works for British and French television, as well as directing other features; 1963-65—teaches course in film at UCLA; 1971-74—presents films and lectures in U.S. and Canada. Recipient: American States Medal for Superior Artistic Achievement, 1972.

Films (as art director): 1923—*L'Inhumaine* (L'Herbier) (co-art d); 1924—*L'Inondation* (Delluc); *La Galerie des monstres* (Catelain) (+asst d); *Feu Mathias Pascal* (L'Herbier); (as director, scriptwriter and editor): 1925—*Le Train sans yeux*; *Rien que les heures* (+pr); 1926—*The Little People* (Pearson) (art d only); 1927—*Yvette*; *En rade (Sea Fever)* (co-sc); *La P'tite Lilie* (ed supervisor); 1928—*La Jalousie du barbouillé* (+art d); *Le Capitaine Fracasse* (co-sc); 1929—*Le Petit Chaperon rouge* (+art d); *Vous verrez la semaine prochaine*; (as director): 1929—*A mi-chemin du ciel* (d only—French language version of George Abbott's *Half-Way to Heaven*); 1930—*Toute sa vie* (French language version of Dorothy Arzner's *Sarah and Son*); *A canção do berço* (Portuguese version of Arzner's *Sarah and Son*); *Les Vacances du diable* (French language version of Edmund Goulding's *The Devil's Holiday*); *Dans une île perdue* (French language version of William Wellman's *Dangerous Paradise*); 1931—*Au* *pays du scalp* (de Wavrin) (ed only); 1932—*En lisant le journal*; *Le Jour du frotteur* (+sc, ed); *Revue Montmartroise* (+sc); *Nous ne ferons jamais de cinéma*; *Le Truc du brésilien*; *Le Mari garçon (Le Garçon divorcé)*; 1933—*Plaisirs défendus*; *Tour de chant* (+sc); *Coralie et Cie.* (+sc); 1934—*Pett and Pott* (+sound supervisor, bit ro); *New Rates*; (as sound supervisor only): 1934—*Windmill in Barbados* (Wright); *Granton Trawler* (Anstey); *Song of Ceylon* (Wright); (as director): 1935—*Coalface* (+sound supervisor); 1936—*Message from Geneva*; (as producer and director): 1937—*We Live in 2 Worlds*; *The Line to Tschierva Hut*; *Who Writes to Switzerland*; 1938—*4 Barriers*; *The Chiltern Country*; 1939—*Alice in Switzerland*; *Midsummer Day's Work* (+sc); 1940—*La Cause commune* (made in Britain for showing in France); *Factory Front* (British version of preceding film); *Yellow Caesar (The Heel of Italy)*; 1941—*Young Veteran*; *Mastery of the Sea*; (as director): 1942—*Went the Day Well? (48 Hours)*; 1943—*Watertight (Ship Safety)*; 1944—*Champagne Charlie*; *Trois Chansons de la résistance (Trois Chants pour la France)*; 1945—"The Ventriloquist's Dummy (The Christmas Party)" episode of *Dead of Night*; 1947—*The Life and Adventures of Nicholas Nickleby*; *They Made Me a Fugitive (I Became a Criminal)*; 1948—*The 1st Gentleman (Affairs of a Rogue)*; 1949—*For Them That Trespass*; 1952—*Simão o caolho (Simon the One-Eyed)* (+pr); 1953—*O canto do mar (The Song of the Sea)* (+pr, co-sc—remake of *En rade*); 1954—*Mulher de verdade (A Real Woman)* (+pr); 1955—*Herr Puntila und sein Knecht Matti* (+co-sc); 1956—*Die Windrose* (d prologue only, collective film co-supervised with Joris Ivens); 1958—*La Prima notte (Les Noces vénitiennes)*; 1960—*The Monster of Highgate Ponds*; 1967—*Thus Spake Theodor Herzl (The Story of Israel)* (+sc). Role: 1969—*Lettres de Stalingrad* (Katz).

Films as producer: 1935—*Book Bargain* (McLaren); *Big Money* (Watt); 1936—*Rainbow Dance* (Lye); *Night Mail* (Wright and Watt) (+sound supervisor); *Calendar of the Year* (Spice); 1937—*The Saving of Bill Blewitt* (Watt); *Roadways* (Coldstream and Legg); 1938—*N. or N.W.* (Lye); *North Sea* (Watt) (+sound supervisor); *Distress Call* (Watt) (shortened silent version of preceding title); *Mony a Pickle* (McLaren); *Happy in the Morning* (Jackson); 1939—*The City* (Elton); *Men in Danger* (Jackson); *Spare Time* (Jennings); *Health of a Nation (Health for the Nation, 40 Million People)* (Monck); *Speaking from America* (Jennings); *Spring Offensive (An Unrecorded Victory)* (Jennings); *The First Days* (Watt, Jennings, and Jackson); 1940—*Men of the Lightship* (Macdonald); *Squadron 992* (Watt); *Sea Fort* (Dalrymple); *Salvage with a Smile* (Brunel); 1941—*Guests of Honour* (Pitt); *The Big Blockade* (Frend) (assoc pr); *Merchant Seamen (Merchant Convoy)* (Holmes); *The Foreman Went to France (Somewhere in France)* (Frend) (assoc pr); *Find, Fix and Strike* (Bennett); 1942—*Greek Testament (The Shrine of Victory)* (Hasse); 1944—*The Halfway House* (Dearden) (assoc pr); 1950—*Caicara (Loafer)* (Celi) (+supervisor); 1951—*Terra sempere terra (Land Is Forever Land)* (Payne); *Painel (Panel)* (Barreto); *Santuario (Sanctuary)* (Barreto); 1952—*Volta redonda (Round Trip)* (Waterhouse); *Film and Reality* (selection and compilation only).

Publications:

By CAVALCANTI:

Books—*Film and Reality*, London 1942; *Film e realidade*, Rio de Janeiro 1952; articles—"Sound in Films" in *Film* (London), November 1939; "Cavalcanti in Brazil" in *Sight and Sound*

(London), April/June 1953; interview by J. Hillier and others in *Screen* (London), summer 1972.

On CAVALCANTI:

Books—*Cavalcanti* by Wolfgang Klaue and others, Berlin 1952; *Grierson on Documentary* edited by H. Forsyth Hardy, revised edition, London 1966; *Studies in Documentary* by Alan Lovell and Jim Hillier, New York, 1972; *Documentary Diary* by Paul Rotha, London 1973; *The Non-Fiction Film* by Richard Barsam, New York 1973; *The Rise and Fall of British Documentary: The Story of the Film Movement Founded by John Grierson* by Elizabeth Sussex, Berkeley 1975; articles—"Alberto Cavalcanti" by Emir Rodriguez Monegal and "Cavalcanti: His Film Works" in *Quarterly of Film, Radio, and Television* (Berkeley), summer 1955; "Cavalcanti in Brazil" by Catherine De La Roche in *Sight and Sound* (London), January/March 1955; "The Big Screens" in *Sight and Sound* (London), spring 1955; "Cavalcanti in Paris" by Geoffrey Minish in *Sight and Sound* (London), summer 1970; "Surrealist Admen" by J.R. Taylor in *Sight and Sound* (London), autumn 1971; "Alberto Cavalcanti" by Claude Beylie and others in *Ecran* (Paris), November 1974; "Cavalcanti in England" by E. Sussex in *Sight and Sound* (London), autumn 1975.

CAYATTE, ANDRE. French. Born in Carcassonne, 3 February 1909. Educated in literature and law. Career: 1930s—lawyer and journalist; 1932—interest in case mishandled by French legal system, "l'affaire Seznec", leads to decision to become filmmaker; mid-1930s—abandons law practice to become writer and filmmaker; 1938—becomes scenarist in collaboration with Henri Jeanson and then Charles Spaak; Spaak subsequently is principal scriptwriter. Recipient: Lion of St. Mark, Venice Festival, for *Justice Is Done*, 1950; Special Jury Prize, Cannes Festival, for *Nous sommes tous des assassins*, 1952; Lion of St. Mark, Venice Festival, for *Le Passage du Rhin*, 1960.

Films (as scriptwriter): 1938—*Entrée des artistes* (Allegret) (co-sc); 1939—*Tempête sur Paris* (Bernard-Deschamps); 1941—*Remorques* (Grémillon) (co-sc); *Le Club des soupirants* (Gleize) (co-sc); *Montmartre sur Seine* (Lacombe) (co-sc); *Caprices* (Joannon) (co-sc); 1942—*Le Camion blanc* (Joannon) (co-sc); (as director and scriptwriter or co-scriptwriter): 1942—*La Fausse Maîtresse*; 1943—*Au bonheur des dames (Shop-Girls of Paris)*; *Pierre et Jean*; 1945—*Farandole* (Zwoboda) (co-sc only); 1946—*Le Dernier Sou* (completed 1944); *Sérénade aux nuages*; *Roger-la-Honte*; *La Revanche de Roger-la-Honte*; *La Couple idéal* (Roland) (synopsis only); 1947—*Le Chanteur inconnu*; 1948—*Le Dessous des cartes*; 1949—*Les Amants de Vérone (The Lovers of Verona)*; "Tante Emma" episode of *Retour à la vie*; 1950—*Justice est faite (Justice Is Done)*; 1952—*Nous sommes tous des assassins (We Are All Murderers)*; 1954—*Avant le déluge*; 1955—*Le Dossier noir*; 1957—*Œil pour œil (An Eye for an Eye)*; 1958—*Le Miroir à deux faces (The Mirror Has 2 Faces)*; 1960—*Le Passage du Rhin (Tomorrow Is My Turn)*; 1963—*Le Glaive et la balance (2 Are Guilty)*; 1964—*La Vie conjugale (Anatomy of a Marriage)* (composed of 2 films: *Françoise (My Nights with Francoise)* and *Jean-Marc (My Days with Jean Marc)*; 1965—*Piège pour Cendrillon (A Trap for Cinderella)*; 1967—*Les Risques du métier*; 1969—*Les Chemins de Katmandou*; 1970—*Mourir d'aimer (To Die of Love)*; 1973—*Il n'y a pas de fumée sans feu (Where There's Smoke)*; 1975—*Le Testament (The Verdict)*; 1977—*A chacun son enfer*; 1978—*La Raison d'état*; *Justices*; *L'Amour en question*.

Publications:

By CAYATTE:

Books—*Mesures pour rien* (poems), Paris 1927; *La Peau des autres* (novel), Paris 1936; *Le Traquenard*, Paris 1939; articles—interview in *Unifrance* (Paris), December/January 1954/55; "My Friend Bourvil" in *Unifrance* (Paris), October 1958; "La Cybernétique d'André Cayatte" in *Qu'est-ce que le cinéma?* by André Bazin, Paris 1961; "André Cayatte accuse les critiques", interview by André Parinaud in *Arts* (Paris), 20 February 1963.

On CAYATTE:

Book—*André Cayatte* by Guy Braucourt, Paris 1969; articles—by Jacques Audiberti in *Comœdia* (Paris), 22 August 1941 and 31 July 1943; "A French Winner at Venice" in *Films in Review* (New York), October 1950; article by Michel Ciment in *Positif* (Paris), April 1971; film—*Portraits filmées...André Cayatte*, for TV, by Pierre Viallet and Marcel L'Herbier, 1953.

*   *   *

Andre Cayatte is surely one of the most satisfied directors in history. He has known continual success and has made the kinds of films he felt it was his destiny to make. Moreover, these films in his eyes, and in the eyes of a great many others, are of the highest social value. The fact that they have scored well at the box office is a final indication of a long and happy career.

Cayatte chose the cinema because it was in his view the most powerful and efficient communications medium in the modern world. He was not drawn to its glamour, nor to its artistic potential. Rather it seemed to him the logical tool for anyone interested in formulating and conveying important ideas. As a young lawyer schooled in the humanities, Cayatte was full of ideas. At first he published stories and novels, winning an important prize in 1934. But the slowness of writing discouraged him, as did its oblique relation to a tangible public and to the themes he was devoted to.

The cinema, on the other hand, put one in contact with an audience. Its materials were not airy words but hard technology directed at actual social situations. Even if these situations were generally fabricated on sound stages, the confrontation of ideas, actors, settings, and points of view appeared authentic. Besides, he was certain he could dramatize situations on screen quickly. Cayatte has never been interested in refined subtlety.

With his usual self-confidence, Cayatte set out to enter this field through writing. His first script, *Entrée des artistes*, was a smash hit directed by Marc Allégret. After several more scripts, Cayatte had little trouble finding a directorial assignment, particularly in view of the paucity of directors after the Nazi takeover.

To learn the art, and to avoid wasting his time on trivial genre films, Cayatte became a specialist in literary adaptation. Balzac, Zola, and Maupassant served him in his first three ventures. As thin as these films seem today, they exhibit a clarity of purpose and rhetoric that would serve him later on. *Au bonheur des dames* from Zola is a genuinely interesting socio-economic melodrama concerned with the birth of the first department store in Paris and the demise of the small shops. Virtually the same theme guides *The Magnificent Ambersons* made the same year. But where Welles's *mise en scene* is deep, Cayatte's is two-dimensional, as if he were fascinated by the glittery surface of his tale, not its consequences.

In 1949 Cayatte made the film that gave him carte blanche in the industry, *The Lovers of Verona*. The script by Jacques Prévert flattered Cayatte's intellectual pretensions, while justifying his thin studio style, for this was a retelling of the Romeo and Juliet story, or rather a double retelling, as the actors playing the tragic roles find themselves condemned to live out those roles in real life.

From 1950 on Cayatte and his writer Charles Spaak have turned out over a dozen problem films dealing with such issues as euthanasia (*Justice est faite*), capital punishment (*Nous sommes tous des assassins*), delinquency (*Avant Le déluge*) and marriage. Even his more recent *To Die of Love* achieved international success in exposing prejudice against the sexual independence of an admirable schoolteacher (Annie Girardot).

But Cayatte's more standard films like *Passage du Rhin* display the shallowness of characterization that Bazin early on claimed was the ruin of his fabricated *"films à thèse."* There is little ambiguity in his point of view. This directness is both his best and most damaging trait.

—Dudley Andrew

CHABROL, CLAUDE. French. Born in Paris, 24 June 1930. Educated at University of Paris in law and pharmacy. Married Agnès Goute in 1952 (divorced); children: Jean-Yves, Matthieu; married Stéphane Audran in 1964; child: Thomas. Career: 1947—meets François Truffaut at a screening of *Rope*; early 1950s—writes film criticism for *Arts* (Paris); 1953-57—regular contributor to *Cahiers du cinéma* (under own name and also as 'Charles Eitel' and 'Jean-Yves Goute'); 1955—Paris publicity director for 20th Century-Fox; 1956-61—heads production company AJYM, produces films of Jacques Rivette, Philippe de Broca and others; 1957—book on Hitchcock, written with Eric Rohmer, published; 1959—technical director on *Breathless*; 1964—directed *Macbeth* at the Théâtre Recamier, Paris; 1967—with *La Route de Corinthe* begins association with producer André Génovès; 1974—directs following episodes for TV series *Histoires insolites*: "Monsieur Bébé"; "Nul n'est parfait"; "Une invitation à la chasse"; "Les Gens de l'été"; also directs several episodes of *Henry James* TV series: "De Grey" and "Le Banc de la désolation"; 1978—directs several episodes of *Madame le juge* TV series. Recipient: Golden Bear, Berlin Festival, for *Les Cousins*, 1959. Address: 20 rue Soyer, 92200 Neuilly-sur-Seine, France.

Films (as director): 1958—*Le Beau Serge (Bitter Reunion)* (+pr, sc, bit ro); 1959—*Les Cousins (The Cousins)* (+pr, sc); *A double tour (Web of Passion, Leda)* (+bit ro); *A bout de souffle* (Godard) (tech adv only); 1960—*Les Bonnes Femmes* (+adapt, bit ro); 1961—*Les Godelureaux* (+co-adapt, bit ro); "L'Avarice" episode of *Les Sept Péchés capitaux (The 7 Deadly Sins)* (+bit ro); *Ples v dezju (Dance in the Rain)* (Hladnik) (supervisor only); 1962—*L'Œil du malin (The Third Lover)* (+sc); *Ophélia* (+co-sc); 1963—*Landru (Bluebeard)* (+co-sc); 1964—"L'Homme qui vendit la tour Eiffel" episode of *Les Plus Belles Escroqueries du monde (The Beautiful Swindlers)*; *Le Tigre aime la chair fraîche (The Tiger Likes Fresh Blood)*; *La Chance et l'amour* (Tavernier, Schlumberger, Bitsch and Berry) (d linking sequences only); 1965—"La Muette" episode of *Paris vu par... (6 in Paris)* (+sc, ro); *Marie-Chantal contre le Docteur Kha* (+co-sc, bit ro); *Le*

Tigre se parfume à la dynamite (An Orchid for the Tiger) (+bit ro); 1966—*La Ligne de démarcation* (+co-sc); *Happening*(Bokanowski) (tech adv only); 1967—*Le Scandale (The Champagne Murders)*; *La Route de Corinthe (Who's Got the Black Box?, The Road to Corinth)* (+ro); 1968—*Les Biches (The Does, The Girlfriends)* (+co-sc, ro); 1969—*La Femme infidèle (Unfaithful Wife)* (+co-sc); *Que la bête meure (This Man Must Die, Killer!)*; 1970—*Le Boucher* (+sc); *La Rupture (Le Jour des parques, The Breakup)* (+sc, bit ro); 1971—*Juste avant la nuit (Just Before Nightfall)* (+sc); *Eglantine* (Brialy) (tech adv only); 1972—*La Décade prodigieuse (10 Days' Wonder)*(+co-sc); *Docteur Popaul* (+co-song); *Piège à pucelles* (Leroi) (tech adv only); 1973—*Les Noces rouges (Wedding in Blood)* (+sc); 1974—*Nada (The NADA Gang)*; *Histoires insolites* (series of 4 TV films); 1975—*Une Partie de plaisir (A Piece of Pleasure, Pleasure Party)*; *Les Innocents aux mains sales (Dirty Hands, Innocents with Dirty Hands))*(+sc); *Les Magiciens (Initiation à la mort, Profezia di un delitto)*; 1976—*Folies bourgeoises (The Twist)* (+co-sc); 1977—*Alice ou La dernière fugue (Alice or the Last Escapade)* (+sc); 1978—*Blood Relatives (Les Liens de sang)* (+co-sc); *Violette Nozière (Violette)*; 1982—*Les Fantômes du chapelier (The Hatmaker)*. Roles (in films other than his own—mainly small roles and bit parts): 1956—*Le Coup de berger* (Rivette) (+co-sc, uncred co-mu); 1959—*Les Jeux de l'amour* (de Broca); 1960—*Paris nous appartient* (Rivette); *Saint-Tropez blues* (Moussy); *Les Distractions* (Dupont); 1961—*Les Menteurs* (Gréville); 1964—*Les Durs à cuire* (Pinoteau); 1965—*Brigitte et Brigitte* (Moullet); 1966—*Zoé bonne* (Deval); 1968—*La Femme écarlate* (Valère); 1969—*Et crac!* (Douchet); *Version latine* (Détré); *Le Travail* (Détré); 1970—*Sortie de secours* (Kahane); 1971—*Aussi loin que l'amour* (Rossif); 1972—*Un Meurtre est un meurtre* (Périer); 1973—interviewee in *Le Flipping* (Volatron).

Publications:

By CHABROL:

Books—*Hitchcock*, with Eric Rohmer, Paris 1957; *Les Noces rouges*, Paris 1973; *Et pourtant, je tourne...*, Paris 1976; articles —contributed more or less regularly to *Cahiers du cinéma* (Paris) from 1953 to 1957; in *Cahiers* issues of 1956 and 1957 Chabrol's writings appear under the pseudonyms 'Charles Eitel' and 'Jean-Yves Goute'; continued to contribute occasionally to *Cahiers du cinéma* through the late 1960s; "Rencontre avec Hitchcock", with François Truffaut, in *Arts* (Paris), 9 February 1955; "Tout ce qu'il faut savoir pour mettre en scène s'apprend en 4 heures", interview by François Truffaut in *Arts* (Paris), 19 February 1958; "Vers un néo-romanticisme au cinéma" in *Les Lettres françaises* (Paris), March 1959; "Clés pour C. Chabrol", interview by Michel Mardore, in *Cinéma 62* (Paris), March 1962; "Big Subjects, Little Subjects" in *Movie* (London), June 1962; interview by Gilles Jacob in *Cinéma 66* (Paris), September/October 1966; in *Interviews with Film Directors* edited by Andrew Sarris, New York 1967; articles anthologized in *The New Wave* edited by Peter Graham, New York 1968; *La Femme Infidèle* and *La Muette* in *L'Avant-scène du cinéma* (Paris), no.42, 1969; interview by Noël Simsolo in *Image et son* (Paris), May 1969; "Non à la censure paternaliste" in *L'Actualité* (Paris), 19 October 1970; interview by Michel Ciment and others in *Positif* (Paris), April 1970; interview by Rui Nogueira in *Sight and Sound* (London), winter 1970/71; interview by Noah James in *Take One* (Montreal), September/October 1970; "Incontro con Chabrol" by E. Zocaro in *Filmcritica* (Rome), May 1974; "Entretien avec Claude Chabrol" by G. Braucourt in *Ecran*

(Paris), May 1975; "Entretien avec Claude Chabrol" by M. Rosier and D. Serceau in *Cinéma* (Paris), September/October 1973; "Alice ou la dernière fugue", interview by G. Braucourt, in *Ecran* (Paris), February 1977; interview by D. Maillet in *Cinématographe* (Paris), February 1977; "Chabrol's Game of Mirrors", interview by D. Overbey, in *Sight and Sound* (London), spring 1977; interview by J.-C. Bonnet and others on *Violette Nozière* in *Cinématographe* (Paris), June 1978; "I Fell in Love with Violette Nozière" in *Monthly Film Bulletin* (London), April 1979; "The Magical Mystery World of Claude Chabrol" by D. Yakir in *Film Quarterly* (Berkeley), no.3, 1979.

On CHABROL:

Books—*Essai sur le jeune cinéma français* by A.-S. Labarthe, Paris 1960; *French Cinema Since 1946: Vol.2—The Personal Style* by Roy Armes, New York 1966; *Claude Chabrol* by Robin Wood and Michael Walker, London 1970; *Claude Chabrol* by Guy Brancourt, Paris 1971; *Directors and Directions* by John Taylor, New York 1975; *Reihe Film 5: Claude Chabrol*, [Carl Hanser] 1975; *The New Wave* by James Monaco, New York 1976; articles—"Le Réalisme fantasmagorique de Claude Chabrol" by Luc Moullet in *Présence du cinéma* (Paris), no.1, 1959; "New Wave" issue of *Cinéma 60* (Paris), February 1960; special issue of *Movie* (London), June 1963; "The Films of Claude Chabrol" by Gordon Gow in *Films and Filming* (London), March 1967; special Chabrol issue of *L'Avant-scène du cinéma* (Paris), May 1969; "Chabrol and Truffaut" by Robin Wood in *Movie* (London), winter 1969/70; "Claude Chabrol" by Brian Baxter in *Film* (London), spring 1969; "Chabrol Rides the Waves" by Langdon Dewet in *Film* (London), summer 1969; "The Films of Chabrol—A Priest among Clowns" by Molly Haskell in the *Village Voice* (New York), 12 November 1970; "Chabrol's Schizophrenic Spider" by Tom Milne in *Sight and Sound* (London), spring 1970; "Claude Chabrol" by Don Allen in *Screen* (London), February 1970; "Songs of Innocence" by Tom Milne in *Sight and Sound* (London), winter 1970/71; "Welles and Chabrol" by F. Bucher and Peter Cowie in *Sight and Sound* (London), autumn 1971; "Chabrol's Iliad" by R. Giard in *Film Heritage* (New York), spring 1971; articles in *Movie Reader* edited by Ian Cameron, New York 1972; articles by M. Mancini and others in *Filmcritica* (Rome), April/May 1972; "Appetit auf Chabrol" by J. Ebert in *Filmkritik* (Munich), July 1972; "Chabrol, Truffaut, après quinze ans" by J.P. Jeancolas in *Jeune cinéma* (Paris), January 1972; "The Continental Divide" by J. Dawson in *Sight and Sound* (London), winter 1973/74; "Negazione e finzione nell'ultimo Chabrol" by G. Frezza in *Filmcritica* (Rome), August 1973; "The Eyehole of Knowledge" by A. Appel, Jr. in *Film Comment* (New York), May/June 1973; "Les Noces rouges, Chabrol et la censure" by A. Cornand in *Image et son* (Paris), April 1973; special issue of *Image et son* (Paris), December 1973; "The Cinema of Irony: Chabrol, Truffaut in the 1970s" by M. Le Fanu in *Monogram* (London), no.5, 1974; "Le 'cas' Chabrol" by T. Renaud in *Cinéma* (Paris), July/August 1974; "Télé-Chabrol" by G. Braucourt in *Ecran* (Paris), June/July 1975; "Histoires insolites" by M. Ricci in *Positif* (Paris), January 1975; "Claude Chabrol into the 70s" by M. Walker in *Movie* (London), spring 1975; "Chabrol ultima..." by E. Ghezzi in *Filmcritica* (Rome), April 1976; "Claude Chabrol: l'écorce et le noyau" by J. Magny in *Téléciné* (Paris), June 1976; "Insects in a Glass Case: Random Thoughts on Claude Chabrol" by Rainer Fassbinder in *Sight and Sound* (London), no.4, 1976; "Middle Chabrol" by P. Harcourt in *Film Comment* (New York), November/December 1976; "Additions and Corrections: Claude Chabrol" in *Film Dope* (London),

February 1979; "The Great God Orson: Chabrol's '10 Days' Wonder'" by L. Poague in *Film Criticism* (Edinboro, Pa.), no.3, 1979; film—*Getting Away with Murder or The Childhood of Claude Chabrol*, for TV, by Alan Yentob, Great Britain 1978.

*   *   *

Claude Chabrol provokes overwhelming loyalty from his coterie of admirers, who might claim for him a special honored position within the New Wave Pantheon: if Jean-Luc Godard appeals to critics because of his extreme interest in politics and film theory, if François Truffaut appeals to the popular audience because of his humanism and sentimentality, it is Chabrol—film critic, filmmaker, philosopher—whose work consistently offers the opportunity for the most balanced appeal. His partisans find especially notable the subtle tone of Chabrol's cinema: his films are apparently cold and objective portraits of profoundly psychological situations; and yet that coldness never approaches the kind of fashionable cynicism, say, of a Stanley Kubrick, but suggests, rather, something closer to the viewpoint of a god who, with compassion but without sentiment, observes the follies of his creations.

Chabrol's work can perhaps best be seen as a cross between the unassuming and popular genre film and the pretentious and elitist art film: Chabrol's films tend to be thrillers with an incredibly self-conscious, self-assured style—that is, pretentious melodrama, aware of its importance. For some, however, the hybrid character of Chabrol's work is itself a problem: indeed, just as elitist critics sometimes find Chabrol's subject matter beneath them, so too do popular audiences sometimes find Chabrol's style and incredibly slow pace alienating.

Chabrol's films are filled with allusions and references to myth (as in *La Rupture*, which begins with an epigraph from Racine's *Phaedra*: "What an utter darkness suddenly surrounds me!"). The narratives of his films are developed through a sensuousness of decor, a gradual accumulation of psychological insight, an absolute mastery of camera movement, and the inclusion of objects and images—beautiful and evocative, like the river in *Le Boucher* or the lighthouse in *Dirty Hands*—which are imbued with symbolic intensity. Like Balzac whom he admires, Chabrol attempts, within a popular form, to present a portrait of his society in microcosm.

Chabrol began his career as a critic for *Cahiers du cinéma*. With Eric Rohmer, he wrote a book-length study of Alfred Hitchcock, one of the first to take Hitchcock seriously and to recognize the director's formal and thematic elements, especially the concepts of guilt and sin which underlie Hitchcock's Roman Catholic *Weltanschauung*. Writing and thinking about film, Chabrol and his friends (Truffaut, Godard, Rohmer, Jacques Rivette, and others) were attempting to turn topsy-turvy the entire cinematic value system. That their theories of authorship remain today a basic (albeit modified and continuously examined) premise certainly indicates the success of their endeavor. Before long, Chabrol found himself functioning as financial consultant and producer for a variety of films inaugurating the directorial careers of his fellow critics who, like himself, were no longer content merely to theorize.

Chabrol's career can perhaps be divided into four semi-discreet periods: 1) the early personal films, beginning with *Le Beau Serge* in 1958 and continuing through *Landru* in 1962; 2) the commercial assignments, beginning with *The Tiger Likes Fresh Blood* in 1964 and continuing through *The Road to Corinth* in 1967; 3) the mature cycle of masterpieces, beginning

with *Les Biches* in 1968 and continuing through *Wedding in Blood* in 1973; and 4) the search for the new subject or perspective, beginning with *Nada* in 1974 and continuing to the present.

If Hitchcock's *Shadow of a Doubt*, as analyzed by Chabrol and Rohmer, is contructed upon exchange of guilt, Chabrol's first film, *Le Beau Serge*, modeled after it, is contructed upon an exchange of redemptions. Chabrol followed *Le Beau Serge*, in which a city-dweller visits a country friend, with *Les Cousins*, in which a country-dweller visits a city friend. Most notably, *Les Cousins* offers Chabrol's first "Charles" and "Paul," the names Chabrol would continue to use throughout his career, Charles to represent the more serious bourgeois man, Paul the more hedonistic id-figure. *A double tour*, Chabrol's first color film, is especially notable for its striking cinematography, its complex narrative structure, and exhuberance of its flamboyant style; it represents Chabrol's first studied attempt to examine and criticize the moral values of the bourgeoisie as well as to dissect the sociopsychological causes of the violence which inevitably erupts as the social and family structures prove inadequate. Perhaps the most wholly successful film of this period is the infrequently screened *L'Œil du malin*, which presents the most typical Chabrol situation: a triangle consisting of a bourgeois married couple—Hélène and her stolid husband—and the outsider whose involvement with the couple ultimately leads to violence and tragedy. Here can be found Chabrol's first "Hélène," the recurring beautiful and slightly aloof woman, generally played by Chabrol's wife, Stéphane Audran.

When these and other personal films failed to ignite the box-office, despite often positive critical responses, Chabrol embarked on a series of primarily commercial assignments, during which his career went into a considerable critical eclipse. Today, however, even these fairly inconsequential films seem to reflect a fetching style and some typically quirky Chabrolian concerns.

Chabrol's breakthrough occurred in 1968 with the release of *Les Biches*, an elegant thriller in which an outsider, Paul, disrupts the lesbian relationship between two women. All of Chabrol's films in this period were slow psychological thrillers which tended basically to represent variations upon the same theme: an outsider affecting a central relationship until violence results. In *La Femme infidèle*, one of Chabrol's most self-assured films, the marriage of Hélène and Charles is disrupted when Charles kills Hélène's lover. In the Jansenist *Que la bête meure*, Charles tracks down the unremittingly evil hit-and-run killer of his young son, and while doing so disrupts the relationship between the killer, Paul, and his sister-in-law Hélène. In *Le Boucher* the butcher Popaul, who is perhaps a homicidal killer, attempts a relationship with a cool and frigid schoolteacher, Hélène, who has displaced her sexual energies onto her teaching of her young pupils, particularly onto one who is conspicuously given the name Charles.

In the extravagantly expressive *La Rupture*, the outsider Paul attempts a plot against Hélène in order to secure a better divorce settlement desired by the rich parents of her husband Charles, who has turned to drug addiction to escape his repressive bourgeois existence. In *Juste avant la nuit* it is Charles who has taken a lover, and Charles's wife Hélène who must ultimately resort to an act of calculated violence in order to keep the bourgeois surface intact. In the detective variation *Ten Days' Wonder*, the relationship between Charles and Hélène is disrupted by the intervention of a character named Théo (*Theos*, representing God), whose false image must be unmasked by the outsider Paul. And in *Wedding in Blood*, based on factual material, it is the wife and her lover who team together to plot against her husband.

Jean Renoir said that all great directors make the same film over and over; perhaps no one has taken this dictum as seriously as Chabrol; indeed, all these films represent a kind of formal geometry as Charles, Hélène, and Paul play out their fated roles in a universe strongly influenced by Fritz Lang, the structures of their bourgeois existence unable to contain their previously repressed passions. Noteworthy too is the consistency of collaboration on these films: usually with Stéphane Audran, Michel Bouquet, and Jean Yanne as performers; Jean Rabier as cinematographer; Paul Gégauff as co-scriptwriter; André Génovès as producer; Guy Littaye as art director; Pierre Jansen as composer; Jacques Gaillard as editor; Guy Chichignoud on sound.

Chabrol's *Nada* in 1973 seemed to inaugurate a new period in Chabrol's career which is difficult as yet to assess. Preliminary indications suggest a search for a new subject or inspiration which may not yet be entirely fruitful. Increasingly interested in exploring different financing arrangements, Chabrol has made television films as well as several international co-productions and seems not to have given up on his hope to execute someday a English-language film. In any case, the director has announced the end of the cycle of psychological thrillers starring his wife, although his most recent critical and commerical success, *Violette Noziére*, with Audran subsidiary to Isabelle Huppert and the marital relationship subsidiary to the filial relationship, seems to have developed from his own established tradition.

—Charles Derry

CHAHINE, YOUSSEF. (also spelled "Shahin"). Egyptian. Born in Alexandria, 25 January 1926. Educated at Victoria College; year at Alexandria University; studied acting 2 years at Pasadena Playhouse, California. Career: 1948—returns to Egypt after studying at Pasadena Playhouse; works with Italian documentarist Gianni Vernuccio and continues to study acting; introduced to film production by Alvisi Orfanelli, "pioneer of Egyptian cinema"; 1953—discovers actor Omar Sharif, who debuts in *Struggle in the Valley*; 1963—makes 1st Egyptian epic *Saladin* as sign of admiration for Egyptian President Nasser; 1965-67—voluntary exile in Libya because of conflict with government cinema authorities; becomes acquainted with writer Abderrahmane Sherkawi whose novel *La Terre* he later films; 1972—directs 1st Egyptian-Algerian co-production, *Le Moineau*; subsequent films also coproductions with Algeria; mid-1970s—suffers heart attack leading to reevaluation of career, begins work on autobiographical *Alexandria... Why?*. Recipient: Special Jury Prize, Berlin Festival, for *Alexandria... Why?*, 1979.

Films (as director): 1950—*Baba Amine (Father Amine)*; 1951—*Ibn el Nil (The Nile's Son)*; *El Muharraj el Kabir (The Great Clown)*; 1952—*Sayidet el Kitar (The Lady in the Train)*; *Nessa bala Rejal (Women without Men)*; 1953—*Sera'a fil Wadi (Struggle in the Valley)*; 1954—*Shaitan el Sahara (Devil of the Desert)*; 1955—*Sera'a fil Mina (Struggle on the Pier)*; 1956—*Inta Habibi (You Are My Love)*; 1957—*Wadaat Hobak (Farewell to Your Love)*; 1958—*Bab el Haded (Iron Gate, Cairo Station, Gare centrale)* (+ro as *Kennawi*); *Gamila Bohraid (Djamila)*; 1959—*Hub illal Abad (Forever Yours)*; 1960—*Bayn Ideak (Between Your Hands)*; 1961—*Nedaa el Ochak (Lover's Call)*; *Rajolfi Hayati (A Man in My Life)*; 1963—*El Naser Salah el Dine (Saladin)*; 1964—*Fajr Yum Jadid (Dawn of a New Day)*; 1965—*Baya el Khawatim (The Ring Seller)*; 1966—*Rimal min Zahab (Sand of Gold)*; 1968—*El Nas wal Nil (People and the Nile)*; 1969—*El Ard (The Land)*; 1970—*Al Ekhtiar (The Choice)*; 1973—*Al Asfour (The Sparrow)*; 1976—*Awdat al Ibn al Dal (Return of the Prodigal Son)*; 1978—*Iskindria... Leh? (Alexandria... Why?)* (+sc); 1982—*Hadota Misreya (An Egyptian Story, La Memoire)* (+sc).

Publications:

By CHAHINE:

Articles—"Entretien avec Youssef Chahine" by C.M. Cluny in *Cinéma* (Paris), September/October 1973; "Youssef Chahine: Aller aussi loin qu'un peut", interview by N. Ghali in *Jeune Cinéma* (Paris), December 1974/January 1975; "Entretien avec Youssef Chahine (Le moineau)" by G. Gauthier in *Image et son* (Paris), December 1974; interview by Guy Hennebelle in *Ecran* (Paris), December 1974; "Entretien avec Youssef Chahine" by C. Ruelle and B. Duval in *Cinéma* (Paris), April 1980.

On CHAHINE:

Book—*Realistischer Film in Agypten* by Erika Richter, Berlin 1974; articles—"Youssef Chahine" by C. Arnaud in *Image et son* (Paris), January 1978; "Le Retour du fils prodigue" by M. Wassef and Guy Hennebelle in *Ecran* (Paris), April 1978; "Le Cinéma de l'immigration: la masse et le manque" by B. Duval in *Image et son* (Paris), December 1979; "Chahine, le nationalisme demystifie: 'Alexandrie pourquoi?'" by A. Tournes in *Jeune cinéma* (Paris), no.3, 1979; "Youssef Chahine and Egyptian Cinema" by Roy Armes in *Framework* (Norwich, England), spring 1981.

*   *   *

Youssef Chahine is one of the most forceful and complex of Egyptian filmmakers, whose progress over the 30 years or so since his debut at the age of 24 offers remarkable insight into the evolution of Egyptian society. A series of sharply critical social studies—of which *The Sparrow* in 1975 is undoubtedly the most successful—was interrupted by a heart attack while the director was still in his early fifties. This led him to question his own personal stance and development in a manner unique in Arab cinema and the result was the splendidly fluent autobiography, *Alexandria... Why?* in 1978, which was followed four years later by a second installment entitled *An Egyptian Story*, which was shot in a style best characterized as an amalgam of Fellini and Bob Fosse's *All That Jazz*.

As such references indicate, Chahine is an eclectic filmmaker, whose cosmopolitan attitudes can be traced back to his origins. He was born in Alexandria in 1926 of middle-class parents. His father, a supporter of the nationalist Wafd party, was a scrupulous but financially unsuccessful lawyer, and Chahine was brought up as a Christian, educated first at religious school and then at the prestigious Victoria College, where the language of tuition was English. After a year at Alexandria University he persuaded his parents to allow him to study drama for two years at Pasadena Playhouse, near Los Angeles, and on his return to Egypt plunged into the film industry, then enjoying a period of boom in the last years of King Farouk's reign.

Alexandria... Why? presents a vividly drawn picture of this vanished world: Alexandria in 1942, awaiting the arrival of Rommel's troops who, it is hoped, will finally drive out the British. The film is peopled with English soldiers and Egyptian patriots, aristocrats and struggling bourgeoises, the enthusiastic young and their disillusioned or corrupt elders. Chahine mocks the excesses of the nationalists (his terrorist patriots are mostly caricatures), leaves condemnation of Zionism to Jew, and tells love stories that cross the neatly drawn barriers separating Muslim and Jew, Egyptian aristocrat and English Tommy. The revelation of Chahine's own background and a few of his personal obsessions (as with the crucified Christ) seems to have released fresh creative powers in the director. His technique of intercutting the action with scenes from Hollywood musicals and newsreel footage from the Imperial War Museum in London as it is audacious, and the transitions of mood are brilliantly handled.

Youssef Chahine is a key figure in Third World Cinema. Unlike some of the other major filmmakers who also emerged in the 1950s—such as Satyajit Ray or Lester James Peries—he has not turned his back on commercial cinema. He has always shown a keen desire to reach a wide audience and *Alexandria...Why?*, though personal, is by no means an inaccessible or difficult work. Chahine's strength as a filmmaker lies indeed in his ability to combine mainstream production techniques with a very individual style and approach. Though intensely patriotic, he has shown a readiness to criticize government policies with which he does not agree, such as those of President Sadat. It is ironic therefore that the appearance of *Alexandria...Why?* should have coincided with the Camp David agreements between Egypt and Israel. As a result, Chahine's very personal statement of his belief in a tolerant society came to be widely criticized in the Arab world as an opportunistic political statement and a justification of Sadat's policies.

—Roy Armes

CHAPLIN, CHARLIE. Sir Charles Spencer Chaplin. British. Born in London, 16 April 1889. Married actress Mildred Harris in 1918 (divorced 1920); married Lita Grey in 1924 (divorced 1927); children: Charles Spencer and Sidney Earle; married Paulette Goddard in 1936 (divorced 1941); married Oona O'Neill in 1943; 8 children. Career: 1898—music hall performer; 1901—acts in provincial theatres with half-brother Sidney; 1907—engaged by Fred Karno troupe; 1910—Karno troupe tours U.S. and Canada; 1912—during 2nd Karno U.S. tour, noticed by Mack Sennett; 1913—signs with Keystone; moves to Hollywood; 1914—after acting in 11 Keystone comedies, begins directing (35 films for Keystone); 1915—signs with Essanay (14 films); 1916—signs with Mutual (11 films); 1917—signs with First National (9 films); 1919—with Griffith, Pickford and Fairbanks founds United Artists; 1927—divorce proceedings widely publicized; 1940—Hearst papers mount campaign against *The Great Dictator*; 1943—paternity suit brought by actress Joan Barry, judgment against Chaplin; 1947—attacked by politicians and press as communist sympathizer; 1952—leaves country to visit London, en route receives cable from Attorney General rescinding reentry permit; is told he'd face "charges of a political nature and of moral turpitude"; 1953—purchases estate near Vevey on Lake Geneva, Switzerland. Died in the night of 24/25 December 1977. Recipient: Best Actor, New York Film Critics, for *The Great Dictator* (award refused); Honorary Academy Award "for the incalculable effect he has had in making motion pictures the art form of this country," 1971; Medallion Award, Writers Guild of America, 1971; Best Original Dramatic Score Academy Award, with Raymond Rasch and Larry Russell, for *Limelight*, 1972.

Films (as director, scriptwriter and actor in role of 'Charlie'): 1914—*Caught in a Cabaret (Jazz Waiter, Faking with Society)* (co-d, co-sc); *Caught in the Rain (Who Got Stung?, At It Again)*; *A Busy Day (Lady Charlie, Militant Suffragette)*; *The Fatal Mallet (The Pile Driver, The Rival Suitors, Hit Him Again)* (co-d, co-sc); *Her Friend the Bandit (Mabel's Flirtation, A Thief Catcher)* (co-d, co-sc); *Mabel's Busy Day (Charlie and the Sausages, Love and Lunch, Hot Dogs)* (co-d, co-sc); *Mabel's Married Life (When You're Married, The Squarehead)* (co-d, co-sc); *Laughing Gas (Tuning His Ivories, The Dentist)*; *The Property Man (Getting His Goat, The Roustabout, Vamping Venus)*; *The Face on the Bar-Room Floor (The Ham Artist)*; *Recreation (Spring Fever)*; *The Masquerader (Putting One Over, The Female Impersonator)*; *His New Profession (The Good-for-Nothing, Helping Himself)*; *The Rounders (2 of a Kind, Oh, What a Night!, The Love Thief)*; *The New Janitor (The Porter, The Blundering Boob)*; *Those Love Pangs (The Rival Mashers, Busted Hearts)*; *Dough and Dynamite (The Doughnut Designer, The Cook)*; *Gentlemen of Nerve (Some Nerve, Charlie at the Races)*; *His Musical Career (The Piano Movers, Musical Tramps)*; *His Trysting Place (Family Home)*; *Getting Acquainted (A Fair Exchange, Hullo Everybody)*; *His Prehistoric Past (A Dream, King Charlie, The Caveman)*; (for Essanay): 1915—*His New Job*; *A Night Out (Champagne Charlie)*; *The Champion (Battling Charlie)*; *In the Park (Charlie on the Spree)*; *A Jitney Elopement (Married in Haste)*; *The Tramp (Charlie the Hobo)*; *By the Sea (Charlie's Day Out)*; *Work (The Paper Hanger, The Plumber)*; *A Woman (The Perfect Lady)*; *The Bank*; *Shanghaied (Charlie the Sailor, Charlie on the Ocean)*; *A Night in the Show*; 1916—*Carmen (Charlie Chaplin's Burlesque on Carmen)*; *Police! (Charlie the Burglar)*; (for Mutual): *The Floorwalker (The Store)*; *The Fireman*; *The Vagabond*; *One A.M.*; *The Count*; *The Pawnshop*; *Behind the Screen*; *The Rink*; 1917—*Easy Street*; *The Cure*; *The Immigrant*; *The Adventurer*; (for First National): 1918—*A Dog's Life*; (for Liberty Loan Committee): *The Bond*; *Triple Trouble* (compiled from 1915 footage plus additional non-Chaplin film by Essanay after he left); (for First National): *Shoulder Arms*; 1919—*Sunnyside*; *A Day's Pleasure*; (as producer, director, scriptwriter and actor): 1921—*The Kid*; *The Idle Class*; 1922—*Pay Day*; *Nice and Friendly* (made privately and unreleased); 1923—*The Pilgrim*; 1923—*A Woman of Paris*; 1925—*The Gold Rush* (+narration, mu for sound reissue); 1926—*A Woman of the Sea (The Sea Gull)* (von Sternberg—unreleased) (pr, d add'l scenes only); 1927—*The Circus* (+mu, song for sound reissue); (as producer, director, scriptwriter, actor, and composer of musical accompaniment): 1931—*City Lights*; 1936—*Modern Times*; 1940—*The Great Dictator*; 1947—*Monsieur Verdoux*; *Limelight* (+co-choreographer); 1957—*A King in New York*; 1959—*The Chaplin Revue* (comprising *A Dog's Life, Shoulder Arms*, and *The Pilgrim*, with commentary and music); 1967—*A Countess from Hong Kong* (d, sc, mu, guest ro only).

Roles (in films not directed): 1914—as reporter in *Making a Living (A Busted Johnny, Troubles, Doing His Best)* (Lehrman); (as 'Charlie'): *Kid Auto Races at Venice (The Kid Auto Race)* (Lehrman); *Mabel's Strange Predicament (Hotel Mixup)* (Lehrman and Sennett); *Between Showers (The Flirts, Charlie and the Umbrella, In Wrong)* (Lehrman); *A Film Johnnie (Movie Nut, Million Dollar Job, Charlie at the Studio)* (Sennett); *Tango Tangles (Charlie's Recreation, Music Hall)* (Sennett); *His Favorite Pastime (The Bonehead, His Reckless Fling)* (Nichols); *Cruel, Cruel Love* (Sennett); *The Star Boarder (The Hash-House Hero)* (Sennett); *Mabel at the Wheel (His Daredevil Queen, Hot Finish)* (Normand and Sennett); *20 Minutes of Love (He Loved Her So, Cops and Watches)* (Sennett) (+sc?); *The Knock Out*

(Counted Out, The Pugilist) (Arbuckle); *Tillie's Punctured Romance (Tillie's Nightmare, For the Love of Tillie, Marie's Millions)* (Sennett); guest appearance in *His Regeneration* (Anderson); 1921—guest appearance in *The Nut* (Reed); 1923—guest appearance in *Souls for Sale* (Hughes); 1928—guest appearance in *Show People* (King Vidor).

Publications:

By CHAPLIN:

Books—*Charlie Chaplin's Own Story*, Indianapolis 1916; *My Trip Abroad*, New York 1922; *My Autobiography*, London 1964; *My Life in Pictures*, London 1974; articles—"Interview with Chaplin" by Margaret Hinxman in *Sight and Sound* (London), autumn 1957; "Interview of Chaplin" by Richard Merryman in *Life* (New York), 10 March 1967; "Charles Chaplin parle", interviews excerpted by C. Gauteur, in *Image et son* (Paris), November 1972; "Textes" in *Positif* (Paris), July/August 1973; "Charles Chaplin (en) français" in *Image et son* (Paris), January 1977; "Chaplin est mort, vive Charlot!", interview by Philippe Soupault, text by Chaplin from 1921, and round-table discussion in *Ecran* (Paris), March 1978; "Chaplin: textos" in *Contracampo* (Madrid), June 1980.

On CHAPLIN:

Books—*Charlot* by Louis Delluc, Paris 1921; *Une Mélodie silencieuse* by René Schwob, Paris 1928; *Charlot* by Philippe Soupault, Paris 1931; *Chaplin, Last of the Clowns* by Parker Tyler, New York 1947; *La figura e l'arte di Ch. Chaplin* by Kosintsev, Eisenstein and others, Turin 1949; *The Little Fellow* by Peter Cotes and Thelma Niklaus, London 1951; *Charlie Chaplin* by Theodore Huff, New York 1951; *The Great God Pan: A Biography of the Tramp Played by Charlie Chaplin* by Robert Payne, New York 1952; *Vie de Charlot* by Georges Sadoul, Paris 1952; *Monsieur Chaplin ou le rire dans la nuit* by Maurice Bessy and Robert Florey, Paris 1952; *Chaplin, the Immortal Tramp* by Rubeigh Minney, London 1954; *Charlot et la "fabulation" chaplinesque* by Jean Mitry, Paris 1957; *My Father Charlie Chaplin* by Charles Chaplin Jr., New York 1960; *Charles Chaplin* by Barthelemy Amengual, Paris 1963; *The Films of Charlie Chaplin* by Gerald McDonald and others, Secaucus, New Jersey 1965; *My Life With Chaplin* by Lita Grey Chaplin, New York 1966; *Charlie Chaplin* by Marcel Martin, Paris 1966; *The Parade's Gone By* by Kevin Brownlow, London 1968; *4 Great Comedians: Chaplin, Lloyd, Keaton, Langdon* by Donald McCaffrey, London 1968; *Charlie Chaplin: Early Comedies* by Isabel Quigly, London 1968; *Charles Chaplin* by Pierre Leprohon, Paris 1970; *Focus on Chaplin* edited by Donald McCaffrey, Englewood Cliffs, New Jersey 1971; *Chaplin's Films* by Uno Asplund, Newton Abbot, Devon 1971; *Tout Chaplin: Tous les films, par le texte, par le gag et par l'image* by Jean Mitry, Paris 1972; *Spellbound in Darkness* by George Pratt, Greenwich, Connecticut 1973; *The Comic Mind* by Gerald Mast, New York 1973; *Chaplin* by Roger Manvell, Boston 1974; *Etude de sémiologie stylistique portant sur l'oeuvre cinématographique de Charles Chaplin* by Adolphe Nysenholc, Brussels 1975; *Charlie Chaplin* by Robert Moss, New York 1975; *Chaplin, Genesis of a Clown* by Raoul Sobel and David Francis, London 1977; *Charlie Chaplin* by P. Baldelli, Florence 1977; *Chaplin, todo sobre un mito* by H.A. Thevenet, Barcelona 1977; *Charles Chaplin—a Guide to References and Resources* compiled by T.J. Lyons, Boston 1977; *Über Chaplin* edited by

Wilfried Wiegand, Zurich 1978; *Charlie Chaplin Story ou Charlot l'immortel* by P. Lemoine and F. Pedron, Bologna 1978; *Charlie Chaplin* by J. McCabe, Garden City, New York 1978; *Vie de Charlot: Charles Spencer Chaplin, ses films et son temps* by Georges Sadoul, Paris 1978; *L'Age d'or du comique: sémiologie de Charlot* by Adolphe Nysenholc, Brussels 1979; *Charlot: ou, Sir Charles Chaplin* by J. Lorcey, Paris 1978; articles — reprinted from *Ciné-Magazine* in *Avant-Scène du cinéma* (Paris), 15 May and 15 June 1981; "Everybody's Language" by Winston Churchill in *Collier's* (New York), 26 October 1935; "Charlie Chaplin" by Alistair Cooke in *Atlantic Monthly* (Greenwich, Connecticut), August 1939; *Charlie The Kid* by Sergei Eisenstein in *Sight and Sound* (London), spring 1946; "Charlie the Grown Up" by Sergei Eisenstein in *Sight and Sound* (London), summer 1946; "Chaplin Among the Immortals" by Jean Renoir in *Screen Writer* (London), July 1947; "Comedy's Greatest Era" by James Agee in *Life* (New York), 5 September 1949; "Chaplin as Composer" by Theodore Huff in *Films in Review* (New York), September 1950; "2 Lectures" by Vsevolod Meyerhold in *TDR* (New York), fall 1966; "Accusations Against Charles Chaplin for Political and Moral Offenses" by Terry Hickey in *Film Comment* (New York), winter 1969; "Faces and Facets", 12 essays, in *Film Comment* (New York), September/October 1972; "Le Retour de Charlot" by F. Chevassu in *Image et son* (Paris), January 1972; "Roland H. Totheroh Interviewed: Chaplin Films" edited by T.J. Lyons, in *Film Culture* (New York), spring 1972; "The Second Coming" by C. Silver in *Film Comment* (New York), September/October 1972; articles by Robert Benayoun, P. Kral and G. Legrand in *Positif* (Paris), July/August 1973; articles by E. Hvidt and I. Lindberg, P. Malmkjaer, and P. Schepelern in *Kosmorama* (Copenhagen), August 1973; "The Limits of Silent Film Comedy" by J. Cott in *Literature/Film Quarterly* (Salisbury, Md.), spring 1975; "Chaplin, Adorno e la maschera di Charlot" by S. Coggiola in *Cinema nuovo* (Turin), September/October 1976; "Charlot à la une" by Y. Wild and G. Perron in *Lumière du cinéma* (Paris), March 1977; "Charlot et la dictature" by G. Blanco in *Ecran* (Paris), December 1977; "Charlot juif" by H. Blanco in *Ecran* (Paris), June 1977; "L'Enfance de l'art" by A. Nysenholc in *Revue Belge du cinéma* (Brussels), October 1977; special issue of *Film und Fernsehen* (Berlin), March 1978; "Chaplin" by Richard Corliss in *Film Comment* (New York), March/April 1978; "Chaplin ou le poids d'un mythe" by M. Latil le Dantec in *Cinématographe* (Paris), February 1978; "Hommages Charlie Chaplin" by R. Lefèvre and J. Magny in *Cinéma* (Paris), February 1978; "Pour saluer Charlot" in *Avant-Scène du cinéma* (Paris), 1 May 1978; special Chaplin issue of *University Film Association Journal* (Houston), no.1, 1979; "Le Gloire de Charlot" in *Avant-Scène du cinéma* (Paris), 1 January 1979; "The Comedy of Ozu and Chaplin—a Study in Contrast" by Tadao Sato in *Wide Angle* (Athens, Ohio), no.2, 1979; "Chaplin's Austerity" by A. Spiegel in *Salmagundi* (Saratoga Springs, New York), winter 1979; "Dossier: Charles Chaplin et l'opinion publique", special section of *Cinématographe* (Paris), January 1981; "Rediscovery: 'New' Chaplin Films" by William K. Everson in *Films in Review* (New York), November 1981; "Geraldine Chaplin: el recuerdo de su padre", interview by M. Pereira, in *Cine Cubano* (Havana), no.99, 1981; "The Weinberg Touch", photos, by H. Weinberg in *Films in Review* (New York), January 1981; films—*Introducing Charlie Chaplin* by Wallace Carlson, 1915; *The Funniest Man in the World* by Vernon Becker, 1967; *Chaplinesque, My Life and Hard Times (The Eternal Tramp)*, for TV, by Harry Hurwitz, 1967; "Upptäckten (Discovery)" episode of *Stimulantia* by Hans Abramson, Sweden 1967.

*   *   *

Charles Chaplin was the first and the greatest international star of the American silent comic cinema. He was also the twentieth century's first media "superstar," the first artistic creator and popularized creature of our global culture, whose face, onscreen antics, and offscreen scandals were disseminated around the globe by new media which knew no geographical or linguistic boundaries. But more than this, Chaplin was the first acknowledged artistic genius of the cinema, recognized as such by a young generation of writers and artists whose number included George Bernard Shaw, H.G. Wells, Bertolt Brecht, Pablo Picasso, James Joyce, Samuel Beckett, and the surrealist painters and poets of both Paris and Berlin. Chaplin may be the one cinema artist who might truly be called a seminal figure of the century—if only because of his influence on virtually every other recognized seminal figure of the century.

Born in London into a theatrical family, his mother and father alternated between periods of separation and union, activities onstage and difficulties offstage (his father's alcoholism, his mother's insanity). The young Chaplin spent his life on the London streets and in a London workhouse, until he started earning his living on the stage at the age of eight. Like Buster Keaton and Stan Laurel, Chaplin's career indicates that physical comedians develop their bodies as children (like concert pianists and ballet dancers) or never really develop them at all. By the time he was 20 Chaplin had become the star attraction of the Fred Karno Pantomime Troupe, an internationally acclaimed English music-hall act, and it was on his second tour of America that a representative of the Keystone comedy film company (either Mack Sennett himself, Mabel Normand, the Sennett comedienne, or Charles Bauman, co-owner of the company) saw Chaplin and in 1913 he was offered a job at Keystone. Chaplin went to work at the Keystone lot in Burbank, California, in January of 1914.

To some extent, the story of Chaplin's popular success and artistic evolution can be told with a series of numbers. In 1914 at Keystone, Chaplin appeared in 35 one- and two-reel films (with the exception of the six-reeler, *Tillie's Punctured Romance*), about half of which he directed himself, for the yearly salary of $7,800. In 1915, Chaplin made 14 one- and two-reel films for the Essanay Film Company—all of which he wrote and directed himself—for a salary of $67,000. In 1916-17, Chaplin wrote, directed and starred in 11 two-reel films for the Mutual Film Corporation for an even million dollars—to write, direct, produce, and star in 12 more two-reel films. The contract allowed him to build his own studio, which he alone used until 1952 (it is now the studio for A&M Records), but his developing artistic consciousness kept him from completing the contract until 1923 with nine films of lengths ranging from two to six reels. Finally, in 1919, Chaplin became one of the founders of his own film company, United Artists (along with Mary Pickford, Douglas Fairbanks, and D.W. Griffith), through which Chaplin released eight feature films, made between 1923 and 1952, after which he sold his interest in the company.

In his early one- and two-reel films Chaplin evolved the comic tools and means that would lead to his future success. His character of the Tramp, the "little fellow," with derby, cane, floppy shoes, baggy pants, and tight jacket debuted in his second Keystone film, *Kid Auto Races at Venice*. Because the tramp was a little guy, he made an easy target for the obviously larger and tougher, but his quick thinking, agile body, and surprising ingenuity in converting ordinary objects into extraordinary physical allies, helped him more than hold his own in a big, mean world. Although he was capable of lechery (*The Masquerader*, *Dough and Dynamite*) he could also selflessly aid the innocent woman under attack (*The New Janitor*, *The Tramp*, *The Bank*). Although he deserved her affection as a reward, he was fre-

quently rejected for his social or sexual inadequacies (*The Tramp*, *The Bank*, *The Vagabond*, *The Adventurer*). Many of his early films combined his dexterous games with physical objects with deliberate attempts at emotional pathos (*The Tramp*, *The Vagabond*, *The Pawnshop*) or with social commentary on the corruption of the police, the brutality of the slums, or the selfishness of the rich (*Police*, *Easy Street*, *The Adventurer*). Before Chaplin, no one had demonstrated that physical comedy could be simultaneously hilariously funny, emotionally passionate, and pointedly intellectual. While his cinema technique tended to be invisible—emphasizing the actor and his actions—he gradually evolved a principle of cinema based on framing: finding the exact way to frame a shot to reveal its motion and meaning completely without the necessity of making a disturbing cut.

Chaplin's later films evolved more complicated or ironic situations in which to explore the Tramp's character and the moral paradoxes of his existence. His friend and ally is a mongrel dog in *A Dog's Life*; he becomes a doughboy in *Shoulder Arms*; acquires a child in *The Kid*; becomes a preacher in *The Pilgrim*; and explores the decadent Parisian high life in *A Woman of Paris*, a comedy-melodrama of subtle visual techniques in which the Tramp does not appear. Chaplin's four feature films between 1925 and 1936 might be called his "marriage group," in which he explores the circumstances by which the tramp might acquire a sexual-romantic mate. In *The Gold Rush* the Tramp succeeds in winning the dance-hall gal who previously rejected him, because she now appreciates his kindness and he is loaded with new-found wealth. The happy ending is as improbable as the Tramp's sudden riches—perhaps a comment that kindness helps but money gets the girl. But in *The Circus* Charlie turns his beloved over to the romantic high-wire daredevil, Rex, since the girl rejects him not because of Charlie's kindness or poverty but because he cannot fulfill the woman's image of male sexual attractiveness. *City Lights* builds upon this problem as it rises to a final question it leaves deliberately and poignantly unanswered: can the blind flower seller, whose vision has been restored by Charlie's kindness, love him for his kindness alone since her vision now reveals him to look so painfully different from the rich and handsome man she imagined and expected? And in *Modern Times* Charlie successfully finds a mate, a social outcast and child of nature like himself; unfortunately, their marriage can find no sanctification or existence within contemporary industrial society. So the two of them take to the road together, walking away from society toward who knows where—the Tramp's final departure from the Chaplin world.

Although both *City Lights* and *Modern Times* used orchestral music and cleverly comic sound effects (especially *Modern Times*), Chaplin's final three American films were talking films—*The Great Dictator*, in which Chaplin burlesques Hitler and Nazism, *Monsieur Verdoux*, in which Chaplin portrays a dapper mass murderer, and *Limelight*, Chaplin's nostalgic farewell to the silent art of pantomime which nurtured him. In this film, in which Buster Keaton also plays a major role, Chaplin bids farewell not only to a dead movie tradition—silent comedy—but to a 200 year tradition of physical comedy on both stage and screen, the tradition out of which both Keaton and Chaplin came, which would produce no clowns of the future.

Chaplin's later years were scarred by personal and political difficulties produced by his many marriages and divorces, his supposed sexual philanderings, his difficulties with the Internal Revenue Service, his outspoken defence of liberal political causes, and his refusal to become an American citizen. Although never called to testify before the House Un-American Activities Committee, Chaplin's films were picketed and boycotted by right-wing activist groups. When Chaplin left for a trip abroad in

1952, the State Department summarily revoked his automatic re-entry permit. Chaplin sent his young wife, Oona O'Neill, daughter of the playwright, Eugene O'Neill, back to America to settle their business affairs. He established his family in Switzerland and conveyed his outrage against his former country by not returning to America for 20 years, by refusing to let any of his films circulate in America for two decades, and by making in 1957 a very uneven, often embarrassing satire of American democracy, *A King in New York*. This film, like *A Countess from Hong Kong*, made ten years later, was a commercial and artistic disappointment, perhaps partially because Chaplin was cut off from the familiar studio, the experienced production team, and the painstakingly slow production methods he had been using for over three decades.

—Gerald Mast

CHRISTENSEN, BENJAMIN. Danish. Born in Viborg, Denmark, 28 September 1879. Educated in medicine; entered dramatic school of the Royal Theatre, Copenhagen, 1901. Married Ellen Arctander about 1904; Sigrid Ståhl, 1922; Kamma Winther about 1927. Career: 1902—debut as singer in *Don Giovanni*; subsequently lost singing voice; spends 3 years as actor in Aarhus Theater (Jutland), then Folketeatret, Copenhagen; 1907—leaves stage, becomes agent for French champagne firm Lanson Père et Fils; 1912—begins acting in films; 1921—seeking opportunity to work on larger scale, makes *Häxan* in Sweden; 1923—goes to Germany, works for Erich Pommer; 1926-34—works in U.S.; 1934—returns to Denmark; after 1944—manager of a small suburban cinema. Died 2 April 1959; buried in Søndermark Kirkegård, Copenhagen.

Films (as director): 1913—*Det hemmelighedsfulde X (The Mysterious X)* (+ro); 1915—*Haevnens Nat (Blind Justice)* (+ro); 1922—*Häxan (Witchcraft Through the Ages)* (+sc, ro as Devil and doctor); 1923—*Seine Frau, die Unbekannte (His Mysterious Adventure)*; 1924—*Die Frau mit dem schlechten Ruf (The Woman Who Did)* (not completed); 1926—*The Devil's Circus*; 1927—*Mockery*; 1928—*Hawk's Nest*; *The Haunted House*; *House of Horror*; 1929—*7 Footprints to Satan*; 1939—*Skilsmissens Børn*; 1940—*Barnet*; 1941—*Gaa med mig hjem*; 1942—*Damen med de lyse handsker*.

Roles: 1912—*Skaebnebaeltet*; 1913—*Gidslet*; *Scenens Børn*; *Store Klaus og Lille Klaus*; *Rumaensk Blod or Søstrene Corrodi*; *Vingeskudt*; 1924—*Michael*.

Publications:

By CHRISTENSEN:

Book—*Hollywood Skaebner* (short stories), 1945.

On CHRISTENSEN:

Book—*Benjamin Christensen* by John Ernst, Copenhagen 1967; articles—"The Mysterious X" by John Gillett in *Sight and Sound* (London), spring 1966; "Christensen Continued" by Cha-

rles Higham in *Sight and Sound* (London), autumn 1966; *La Sorcellerie à travers les âges* by Max Tessier in *Cinéma 68* (Paris), no.130, 1968; "Buried Directors" by W.D. Routt in *Focus on Film* (London), spring 1972.

*   *   *

Benjamin Christensen's first film was one of the most amazing directorial debuts in the history of the film. *Det hemmelighedsfulde X* is a spy melodrama about a lieutenant accused of betraying his country who is saved at the last minute. If the story is conventional, the handling of it shows a natural instinct for the film that is way ahead of its time. It is completely free from literary clichés in its narrative style, being told in often very imaginatively composed pictures, and Christensen demonstrates an ability to transform the psychology of his characters into physical action. The camerawork (by Emil Dinesen) is full of significant contrasts, the cutting is dynamic and gives the film a marvelous drive. The film was received with admiration; everybody was stunned by its remarkable visual style, and Christensen was immediately recognized as the individualist and the experimenter of the Danish film of his day. His next film, *Haevnens Nat*, was a social melodrama, burdened by a pathetic story, but also distinguished by an inventive camera style. Christensen played lead roles in both these films.

Benjamin Christensen provoked his contemporaries and set himself in opposition to the filmmaking practices of his time. He had a strong belief in himself and worked consciously with film as a new art form. He considered the director as the author of the film and stated that "like any other artist he should reveal his own individuality in his own work." Thus Christensen can be regarded as one of the first auteurs of the cinema. Carl Th. Dreyer has characterized Christensen as "a man who knew exactly what he wanted and who pursued his goal with uncompromising stubbornness."

Christensen's main work is *Häxan*, an ambitious and unique film and a pioneer achievement in both the documentary and the fiction film. In this film Christensen combined his rationalistic ideas with his passionate temperament.

Christensen was always an isolated director in the Danish film, and after *Häxan* he left Denmark. He made an insignificant film in Germany and was seen in Dreyer's *Michael* as the master. He got an offer from Hollywood and made six films there. He used his talent for the strange and the peculiar in *Seven Footprints to Satan*, a witty horror comedy.

Christensen returned to Denmark in the thirties and in 1939 he was hired by Nordisk Films Kompagni. Again Christensen showed himself a controversial filmmaker. He wanted to break the trivial pattern of Danish cinema at that time, and he made three films which dealt with topical problems, arising from conflicts between generations. One is about children from divorce-ridden homes, another about abortion. Christensen's last film was a spy thriller in international settings. It was a total failure, and Christensen left film production. For the rest of his life he lived in splendid isolation as manager of a small and insignificant cinema in the suburbs of Copenhagen.

—Ib Monty

CHRISTIAN-JAQUE. French. Born Christian Maudet in Paris, 4 September 1904. Educated in architecture, art and music at Ecole des beaux-arts, and Ecole des arts décoratifs, Paris.

Married 5 times, including actresses Simone Renant, 1938; Renée Faure, 1945; Martine Carol, 1952. Career: 1926—film poster designer; 1927-30—film critic for *CINEGRAF*; set decorator, assistant director to Julien Duvivier, Henri Roussel, and André Hugon; from late 1960s—works mainly in television. Recipient: Best Director, Cannes Festival, for *Fanfan la Tulipe*, 1952.

Films (as art director): 1927—*Une Java* (Roussel); 1928—*La Marche nuptiale* (Hugon); *La Vie miraculeuse de Thérèse Martin* (Duvivier); 1929—*Au Bonheur des Dames* (Duvivier) (co-art d); *Maman Colibri* (Duvivier); *La Grande Passion* (Hugon); *Les Trois Masques* (Hugon); 1930—*La Femme et le rossignol* (Hugon); *Lévy et Cie* (Hugon); 1931—*La Tendresse* (Hugon); *Le Marchande de sable* (Hugon); *La Croix du Sud* (Hugon); *Les Galeries Lévy et Cie* (Hugon); (as director): 1931—*Bidon d'or*; 1932—*Le Tendron d'Achile*; *Adhémar Lampiot*; 1933—*Ça colle*; *Le Boeuf sur la langue*; *La Montre*; 1934—*Atroce menace*; *Vilaine histoire*; *Le Père Lampion*; *Compartiment pour dames seules*; 1935—*La Sonnette d'alarme*; *Voyage d'agrément*; *La Famille Pont-Biquet*; *Sacré Léonce*; *Sous la griffe*; 1936—*On ne roule pas Antoinette*; *L'École des journalistes*; *Un de la Légion*; *Rigolboche*; *Monsieur Personne*; *Josette*; *La Maison d'en face*; 1937—*Les Dégourdis de la onzième*; *Les Perles de la couronne (The Pearls of the Crown)* (co-d); *A Venise, une nuit*; *Les Pirates du rail*; *François Ier (Francis the First)*; 1938—*Les Disparus de St. Agil (Boys School)*; *Ernest le Rebelle (C'était moi)*; *Raphaël le Tatoué*; 1939—*Le Grand Élan*; *L'Enfer des anges*; *Tourelle III* (unfinished); 1941—*L'Assassinat du Père Noël (Who Killed Santa Claus?)*; *Premier Bal*; *La Symphonie fantastique*; 1943—*Carmen*; *Voyage sans espoir*; (as director and co-author of adaptation or script): 1944—*Sortilèges (The Bellman)*; 1945—*Boule de Suif (Angel and Sinner)*; 1946—*Un Revenant (A Lover's Return)*; 1947—*La Chartreuse de Parma (La certosa di Parma)*; 1948—*D'homme à hommes (Man to Men)*; 1949—*Singoalla (The Wind Is My Lover, The Mask and the Sword)*; *Barrières* (short); 1950—*Souvenirs perdus*; 1951—*Barbe-Bleue (Blaubart, Bluebeard)* (adapt); *Fanfan la Tulipe (Fanfan the Tulip)*; 1952—*Adorables Créatures (Adorable Creatures)*; *Lucrèce Borgia (Lucrezia Borgia, Sins of the Borgias)*; *"Lysistrata"* episode of *Destinées (Daughters of Destiny)*; *Koenigsmark (Térac)* (supervisor only); 1954—*Madame Du Barry*; *Nana*; 1955—*Si tous les gars du monde (If All the Guys in the World)*; 1957—*Nathalie (The Foxiest Girl in Paris)* (+pr); 1958—*La Loi...c'est la loi (The Law Is the Law)*; 1959—*Babette s'en va-t-en guerre (Babette Goes to War)* (d only); 1960—*"Divorce"* episode of *La Française et l'amour (Love and the Frenchwoman)*; 1961—*Madame Sans-Gêne (Madame)*; 1962—*Marco Polo (L'Échiquier de Dieu)* (unfinished); 1963—*Les Bonnes Causes (Don't Tempt the Devil)*; *La Tulipe noire (The Black Tulip)*; 1964—*Le Gentleman de Cocody (Man from Cocody)*; *Le Repas des fauves*; 1965—*La Guerre secrète (The Dirty Game, La guerra segreta, Spione unter sich)* (co-d); 1966—*La Seconde Vérité*; *Le Saint prend l'affût*; 1967—*Deux Billets pour Mexico (Dead Run)*; 1968—*Lady Hamilton (Les Amours de Lady Hamilton, Emma Hamilton, The Making of a Lady)*; 1970—*Don Camillo et les contestataires* (unfinished due to Fernandel's death); 1971—*Les Pétroleuses (The Legend of Frenchy King)* (d only); 1975—*Dr. Justice*.

Publications:

By CHRISTIAN-JAQUE:

Article—"Making It International" in *Films and Filming* (London), October 1960.

On CHRISTIAN-JAQUE:

Article—biofilmography in *Film Dope* (London), April 1975; film—*Portraits filmées...Christian-Jacque* by Pierre Viallet and Marcel L'Herbier, France 1954.

*   *   *

Of all France's important filmmakers, Christian-Jaque has unquestionably been the most prolific. Director of more than 50 films in virtually all genres, his facility has been a mark against him in the eyes of most critics. Nevertheless, no one denies the lusty dynamism of his action scenes nor the technical ingenuity he loves to display in even his most run-of-the-mill efforts. For a time between 1937 and 1950 he had to be reckoned as one of the leading men in French cinema, not only as regards box-office where he has always had success, but in terms of the possibilities of the art of the cinema.

Born Christian Maudet, he took on the name with which he and a collaborator signed the film ads they designed in the twenties, "Christian-Jaque." When the coming of sound made Paris the center of European film production, his peripheral relation to the movies and his training as an architect helped him secure a job with Paramount in Joinville. Always eager to please, and a favorite director for actors to work with, he found his first efforts well received. The steady production of cheap vehicles for Fernandel wore down his spirits but did give him immense technical training and the film industry's confidence.

At last he made use of that confidence, selling an idea for a film about a boy's school to an independent producer. *Les Disparus de St. Agil* was an enormous success. Its delicate romanticism, stemming largely from Pierre Very's novel as put into dialogue by Jacques Prévert, was set off against the truly disturbing role played by Erich von Stroheim. This film put Christian-Jaque in a position of power during the Occupation and no one made more films than he in this era.

He specialized in two genres, both very popular during the war, the romantic mystery tale and the transcription on film of past cultural monuments. Representative of the former are *Sortilèges* and *L'Assassinat du Père Noël*. Both films are rich in evocative images such as a wild horse galloping through town at midnight, its mane blowing behind it. Both feature clever intrigues about mysterious personalities and occurrances. Both are delightfully satisfying, if overly cute. The other genre contains films of music and musicians on the one side and literary adaptations on the other. His life of Berlioz, *La Symphonie fantastique*, goes beyond all limits in insisting on the grandeur of musical genius. Jean-Louis Barrault throws himself at women, converses in cafes with Balzac and Delacroix, and pounds out the composition after which the film is titled in a fever compounded by wild lighting and compositions. The later *Carmen* is equally unrestrained, as though the fame of the original gave license to the filmmaker to go beyond all realistic bounds. As for literary adaptations, his *Boule de suif* from Maupassant and *La Chartreuse de Parme* from Sterdhal are vehicles for France's most ostentatious actors to dress up as their favorite characters. The latter film has genuine moments of visual excitement and some of the brash tone of the original, but both films remain at best on the surface.

Concerned with decoration, Christian-Jaque is finally a frothy director. When dealing with a star (and he married three of his leading ladies, Martine Carol being the most famous) or with a light action picture such as *Fanfan la Tulipe* he is delightful, but aside from the short period surrounding World War II, little of his work merits a second look. That period, though, culminating with *Un Revenant* captures the dreamy romanticism to which much of the culture escaped in its most difficult moment.

—Dudley Andrew

CHYTILOVÁ, VĚRA. Czech. Born in Ostrava, 2 February 1929. Briefly studied architecture at Charles University ; Film Academy (FAMU), Prague, 1957-62. Married cinematographer Jaroslav Kučera. Career: early 1950s—works as draughtsman and fashion model; 1950s—script girl at Barrandov Studios; 1956—assistant director on *3 Men Missing* (Ztracenci), enrolls at Film Academy (FAMU); 1966—begins collaboration with Ester Krumbachová; 1969-mid-70s—forbidden to direct or work for foreign producers; since 1976—resumes directing, both in Prague and abroad. Address: c/o Barrandov Studios, Prague, Czechoslovakia.

Films (as director and scriptwriter): 1962—*Strop (The Ceiling)*; *Pytel blech (A Bag of Fleas)*; 1963—*O něčem jiném (Something Different, Something Else, Another Way of Life)*; 1965— *Automat Svět (The World Cafe)* segment of *Perličky na dně (Pearls of the Deep)* (co-sc); 1966—*Sedmikrásky (Daisies)* (co-sc); 1969—*Ovoce stromů rajských jíme (The Fruit of Paradise, The Fruit of the Trees of Paradise)* (co-sc); 1977—*(The Apple Game)*; 1981—*Panelstory (The Panel Story)* (co-sc); 1982— *Kalamita (Calamity)* (co-sc). Role: 1958—girl in bikini in *Konec jasnovidce (End of a Clairvoyant)*.

Publications:

By CHYTILOVÁ:

Articles—"Neznám opravdový čin, který by nebyl riskantní" [I Don't Know Any Action that Would Not Be Risky], interview by Galina Kopaněvová in *Film a doba* (Prague), no.1, 1963; "Režijní explikace k filmu *O něčem jiném*" [The Director's Comments on *Something Different*] in *Film a doba* (Prague), no.1, 1964; facsimile of page from Chytilová script in *Film a doba* (Prague), no.8, 1965; "*Sedmikrásky*: režijní explikace" [*Daisies*: the Directress Comments] in *Film a doba* (Prague), no.4, 1966; "Interview mit Vera Chytilova" by H. Heberle and others in *Frauen & Film* (Berlin), December 1978; "A Film Should Be a Little Flashlight", interview by H. Polt, in *Take One* (Montreal), November 1978; interview in *The New York Times*, 12 March 1978.

On CHYTILOVÁ:

Books—*Modern Czechoslovak Film 1945-1965* by Jaroslav Boček, Prague 1965; *3 Í* by Jiří Janoušek, Prague 1965; *All the Bright Young Men and Women* by Josef Skvorecký, Toronto 1971; *Outline of Czechoslovakian Cinema* by Langdon Dewey, London 1971; *Closely Watched Films* by Antonín Liehm, White Plains, New York 1974; articles—"Podobenství Věry Chytilové" [The Parable of Věra Chytilová] by Jaroslav Boček in *Film a*

doba (Prague), no.11, 1966; sketch in *Film* (London), spring 1968; "The Return of Vera Chytilova" by P. Hames in *Sight and Sound* (London), no.3, 1979; "En otoño, Věra Chytilová mantiene una primaveral polémica femenina" by G. Zapiola in *Cinemateca revista* (Andes), June 1981; "Filmový svět Věry Chytilové" [The Film World of Věra Chytilová] by Karel Martínek in *Film a doba* (Prague), no.3, 1982; also articles by Miroslav Zůna and Vladimir Solecký in *Film a doba* (Prague), no.5, 1982.

*   *   *

So far the only important woman director of the Czech cinema is Věra Chytilová, its most innovative and probably most controversial personality. She is the only contemporary Czech filmmaker to work in the Eisensteinian tradition. She combines didacticism with often daring experimentation, based in essence on montage. Disregarding chronology and illustrative realism, she stresses the symbolic nature of images as well as visual and conceptual shock. Influenced to some extent also by cinema verité, particularly by its female representatives, and militantly feminist in her attitudes, she nevertheless made excellent use of the art of her husband, the cameraman Jaroslav Kučera in her boldest venture to date, *Daisies*. This film, Chytilová's best known, is a dazzling display of montage, tinting, visual deformation, film trickery, color processing etc.; a multifaceted tour de force which, among other things, is also a tribute to the classics of the cinema, from the Lumière Brothers to Chaplin and Abel Gance. It contains shots, scenes and sequences that utilize the most characteristic techniques and motives of the masters. *Daisies* is Chytilová at her most formalist. In her later films, there is a noticeable shift towards realism. However, all the principles mentioned above still dominate the more narrative approach, and a combination of unusual camera angles, shots, etc., together with a bitterly sarcastic vision, lead to hardly less provocative shock effects.

The didactical content of these highly sophisticated and subtly formalist works of filmic art, as in Eisenstein, is naive and crude: young women should prefer "useful" vocations to "useless" ones (*The Ceiling*); extremes of being active and being inactive both result in frustration (*Something Different*); irresponsibility and recklessness lead to a bad end (*Daisies*); a sexual relationship is something serious, not just irresponsible amusement (*The Apple Game*); people should help each other (*Panel Story, The Calamity*). Given the fact that Chytilová has worked mostly under the conditions of an enforced and harshly repressive establishment, a natural explanation of this seeming incongruity offers itself: the "moral messages" of her films are simply libations that enable her, and her friends among the critics, to defend the unashamedly formalist films and the harshly satirical presentation of social reality they contain. This is corroborated by Chytilová's many clashes with the political authorities in Czechoslovakia: from an interpellation in the Parliament calling for a ban of *Daisies* because so much food—"the fruit of the work of our toiling farmers"—is destroyed in the film, to her being fired from the Barrandov studios after the Soviet invasion in 1968, to her open letter to President Husák printed in Western newspapers. In each instance she won her case by a combination of publicly stated kosher ideological arguments, stressing the alleged "messages" of her works, and of backstage manipulation, not excluding the use of her considerable feminine charm. Consequently, she is the only one from among the new wave of directors from the sixties who has been able to continue making films in Czechoslovakia without compromising her aesthetic creed and her vision of society, as so many others had to do in order to remain in business (e.g. Jaromil Jireš, Hynek Bočan, Jaroslav Papoušek, and to some extent Jiří Menzel).

Her latest films, *Panel Story* and *Calamity*, earned her hateful attacks from establishment critics, and intrigues by her second-rate colleagues who are thriving on the absence of competition from such exiled or banned directors as Miloš Forman, Ivan Passer, Jan Němec, Evald Schorm, and Vojtěch Jasný. The two films were practically withdrawn from circulation and can be occasionally seen only in suburban theatres. The only critical film periodical *Film a doba* published, in 1982, a series of three articles which, in veiled terms and using what playwright Václav Havel calls "dialectical metaphysics" ("on the one hand it is bad, but on the other hand it is also good"), defended the director and her right to remain herself. In her integrity, artistic boldness and originality, and in her ability to survive the most destructive social and political catastrophes, Chytilová is a unique phenomenon in post-invasion Czech cinema.

—Josef Skvorecký

CIMINO, MICHAEL. American. Born 1940 (or 1943), grew up in New York City and Old Westbury, Long Island. Educated at Yale University, M.F.A. 1963. Career: 1963—moves to New York, studies acting and ballet; works for company producing industrial and documentary films; late 1960s—director of TV commercials in New York; 1971—moves to Hollywood, begins screenwriting. Recipient: Best Director Academy Award for *The Deer Hunter*, 1978; Best Director, Directors Guild, for *The Deer Hunter*, 1978. Agent: William Morris Agency, 151 El Camino Dr., Beverly Hills, CA 90212.

Films (as scriptwriter): 1971—*Silent Running* (Trumbull) (co-sc); 1973—*Magnum Force* (Post) (co-sc only); (as director): 1974—*Thunderbolt and Lightfoot* (+sc); 1978—*The Deer Hunter* (+co-sc); 1980—*Heaven's Gate* (+sc).

Publications:

By CIMINO:

Articles—"Stalking the Deer Hunter: an Interview with Michael Cimino" by M. Carducci in *Millimeter* (New York), March 1978; *Entretien avec Michael Cimino* by Robert Benayoun and others in *Positif* (Paris), April 1979; "The Film that Took On a Life of Its Own", interview by Herb Lightman, in *American Cinematographer* (Los Angeles), November 1980.

On CIMINO:

Articles—"A Successful Filmmaker Appraises His Craft" by E. Shaw in *Making Films* (New York), February 1969; "Cimino to Direct 'Epic' for Warners" in *Variety* (New York), 21 February 1979; "Oscar-Winning *Deer Hunter* Is Under Attack as Racist Film" by A. Harmetz in the *New York Times*, 26 April 1979; "Michael Cimino's Battle to Make a Great Movie" by J. Valley in *Esquire* (New York), 2 January 1979.

*   *   *

It would be rhetorically convenient if *Heaven's Gate* were either the "unqualified disaster" that Vincent Canby found it, or

the masterpiece that James Ivory took it for. Instead, it remains Cimino's *Intolerance* in more than one sense: a film which answers critics who charged his previous epic with racism, but which remains in essence a monument to ambition.

The Deer Hunter is Cimino's single success (unless one counts his first directorial assignment, *Thunderbolt and Lightfoot*, easily the most involving of Clint Eastwood's post-Italian westerns. No other film since those of John Ford so fully captured through ceremonies the sense of American community. Critical complaints that the wedding sequence lingered too long missed that the film was "about" Vietnam in the sense that the war made dramatic existing tensions between the Hemingwayesque self-reliance of Mike (Robert De Niro) and a communal male bonding. Cimino was allowed the time in the opening third of the film to play with tense glances and eruptions of finely unexplained violence. Certainly *The Deer Hunter* owes much to Coppola—but if its ceremonies make it evidently a post-*Godfather* film, its surreal politics anticipate *Apocalypse Now*. Cimino's vicious Vietcong *are* uncomfortably close to a *Shanghai Express* Orient "where time and life have no value," or to General Westmoreland's woodland-glade explanation of how death means less to Vietnamese in *Hearts and Minds*. But Russian roulette was an evident metaphor (albeit disguised by the blood-and-guts filming), much of whose point became the lack of moral difference from the capitalist South where the death game was played out passionlessly for dollars.

Not that *The Deer Hunter* hasn't its revealing flaws: the music is unconvincingly "lyrical" and its second half is so disjointed that only De Niro's intensity holds it together. (Although that may be its point—his intensity holds together the community as well.) In *Heaven's Gate* such disastrous choices came to the fore. Cimino is evidently a better *metteur-en-scene* than scriptwriter, and he needs actors of De Niro's caliber, not Kris Kristofferson's, to make his discursive epics cohere. In its defense, *Heaven's Gate* was unquestionably more compelling in its original 220-minute version than in its general release version of 145 minutes, which cut key motivations (such as John Hurt's Harvard speech) and added self-evident titles and embarrassing voice-over narration ("In that lovely place, on that lovely day, I dreamed I could do anything...."), while retaining all the pageantry of the Harvard Square dance and the "Heaven's Gate" roller-skating. The history of the Johnson County Wars was revised to correspond with Cimino's continuing exploration of the immigrant experience in America—although in the western it's represented by an undifferentiated mob of Eastern Europeans, not the quirky Russian-American of *The Deer Hunter*.

For those who admire *Heaven's Gate*, its mutilation and the subsequent pariah-status of Cimino in "Post-*Heaven's Gate* Hollywood" put him in von Stroheim's company. Both are visual realists, with an obsession with detail that's fussy or brilliant (depending perhaps on whether one is paying for it). But the other way of placing Cimino is within that other Germanic tradition of Leni Riefenstahl and Luis Trenker: to judge from the landscapes and lone struggles in all three of his features, Cimino would have been quite at home making "Mountain Films." Clearly the rounded hills of Pennsylvania needed something grander for *The Deer Hunter*—Cimino couldn't resist substituting heroic Sierra cliffs and glaciers, complete with German opera music, for De Niro's deerhunt. The critical jury is still out on Cimino, even if the commercial one seems to have shown him the door.

—Scott Simmon

CLAIR, RENÉ. French. Born René Chomette in Paris, 11 November 1898. Educated at the Lycée Montaigne, Paris; Lycée Louis-le-Grand, Paris, 1913-17. Married Bronya Perlmutter, 1926; child: Jean-François. Career: 1917—serves in ambulance corps at the front, invalided out after several months; 1918—goes through religious crisis, retires to Dominican monastery; after Armistice begins career as journalist; 1919—reporter for *L'Intransigéant*, Paris newspaper; begins to write poetry and fiction; 1920—begins acting at Gaumont studios; 1921—adopts pseudonym René Clair; 1922—becomes film editor of *Le Théâtre et comœdia illustré*, rediscovers films of Méliès and Zecca; 1924—associates with artistic avant-garde; 1929—film reviewer in London; initially opposes introduction of sound in film; 1935—following Paris failure of *Le Dernier Milliardaire*, accepts Alexander Korda's invitation to direct in Britain; 1938—returns to France; 1939—after 5 weeks of filming, *Air pur* abandoned due to German invasion; 1940—Robert Sherwood secures visa for Clair and family to emigrate to U.S.; signs contract with Universal; 1943-44—plans to organize Service Cinématographique de l'Armée in Algeria, money withdrawn before his departure; 1946—returns to Paris; 1951—directs 1st radio production; 1959—directs 1st stage work; 1967-81—works on writing projects; 1973—produces Gluck's *Orphée et Eurydice* at the Paris Opera. Died in Neuilly, France, 15 March 1981. Recipient: honorary doctorate, Cambridge University, 1956; elected to Académie Française, 1960; Doctor *Honoris Causa*, Royal College of Arts, London 1967; Commander of the Legion of Honor; Commander of Arts and Letters; Commander of the Italian Order of Merit.

Films (as director and scenarist): 1923—*Paris qui dort* (+ed); 1924—*Entr'acte* (d only); *Le Fantôme du Moulin Rouge*; 1925—*Le Voyage imaginaire*; 1926—*La Proie du vent*; 1927—*Un Chapeau de paille d'Italie*; 1928—*La Tour*; *Les Deux Timides*; (as director and scriptwriter): 1930—*Sous les toits de Paris*; *Prix de beauté (Miss Europe)* (Genina) (sc contribution only); 1931—*Le Million*; *A Nous la liberté*; 1932—*Quatorze Juillet*; 1934—*Le Dernier Milliardaire*; 1935—*The Ghost Goes West* (co-sc); 1937—*Break the News* (co-sc); 1939—*Un Village dans Paris* (co-pr only); *Air pur* (not completed); 1940—*The Flame of New Orleans* (co-sc); 1942—sketch featuring Ida Lupino in *Forever and a Day* (Lloyd); *I Married a Witch* (co-sc, +pr); 1943—*It Happened Tomorrow* (co-sc); (as producer, director, and scriptwriter): 1945—*And Then There Were None* (co-sc); 1947—*Le Silence est d'or*; 1949—*La Beauté du diable* (co-sc); 1952—*Les Belles-de-nuit*; 1955—*Les Grandes Manoeuvres* (co-sc); 1957—*Porte des Lilas* (co-sc); 1960—"Le Mariage" episode of *La Française et l'amour* (d, sc only); 1961—*Tout l'or du monde* (co-sc); 1962—"Les Deux Pigeons" episode of *Les Quatres vérités* (d, sc only); 1965—*Les Fêtes galantes*. Roles: 1920—*Le Lys de la Vie* (Fuller); *Les Deux Gamines* (Feuillade—serial); 1921—*Le Sens de la mort* (Protozanoff); *L'Orpheline* (Feuillade); *Parisette* (Feuillade—serial); 1922—*Parisette* (Feuillade); 1959—narrator of *La Grande Époque* (French version of Robert Youngson's *The Golden Age of Comedy*).

Publications:

By CLAIR:

Books—*La Princesse de Chine* and *De fil en aiguille*, Paris 1951; *Réflexion faite*, Paris 1951; *Reflections on the Cinema*, London 1953; *Comédies et commentaires*, Paris 1959; *Tout l'or du monde*, Paris 1962; *À nous la liberté and Entr'acte*, New York

1970; *4 Screenplays*, New York 1970; *Cinema Yesterday and Today*, New York 1972; *Jeux d'hasard*, Paris 1976; *Star Turn*, translation of *Adams*, by John Marks, London n.d.; articles—"A Conversation with René Clair" by Bernard Causton in *Sight and Sound* (London), winter 1933; "The Ghost Goes West" in *Successful Film Writing* by Seton Margrave, London 1936; "It Happened Tomorrow", with Dudley Nichols, in *Theatre Arts* (New York), June 1944; "Television and Cinema" in *Sight and Sound* (London), January 1951; "René Clair in Moscow", interview, in *Sight and Sound* (London), winter 1955/56; "*Porte de lilas*" in *L'Avant-Scène du cinéma* (Paris), no.159, 1957; "Nothing is More Artificial than Neo-realism" in *Films and Filming* (London), June 1957; "Picabia, Satie et la première d'*Entr'acte*" in *L'Avant-Scène du cinéma* (Paris), November 1968; interview in *Gotta Sing Gotta Dance* by John Kobal, London 1970; "René Clair in Hollywood", interview by R.C. Dale in *Film Quarterly* (Berkeley), winter 1970/71; "René Clair in Hollywood", interview by R.C. Dale in *Film Quarterly* (Berkeley), winter 1970/71; interview in *Encountering Directors* by Charles Samuels, New York 1972; "A Conversation with René Clair" by J. Baxter and J. Gillett in *Focus on Film* (London), winter 1972; "René Clair", interview by Patrick McGilligan and Debra Weiner, in *Take One* (Montreal), January/February 1973; interview by P. McGilligan and D. Weiner in *Take One* (Montreal), May 1974; "Adelsbrief an die Filmkunst" in *Film und Fernsehen* (Berlin), July 1981.

On CLAIR:

Books—*René Clair* by G. Viazzi, Milan 1946; *René Clair* by J. Bourgeois, Geneva 1949; *La Beauté du Diable racontée et le problème de Faust* by J. Marcenac, Paris 1950; *Un Maître du cinéma: René Clair* by Georges Charensol and Roger Régent, Paris 1952; *René Clair et Les Belles de nuit* by Georges Charensol, Paris 1953; *Tre maestri del cinema* by A. Solmi, Milan 1956; *René Clair, an Index* by Catherine De La Roche, London 1958; *René Clair* by Jean Mitry, Paris 1960; *René Clair* by Barthélemy Amengual, Paris 1969; articles—"René Clair and Film Humor" by Harry Potamkin in *Hound and Horn* (New York), October/December 1932; "René Clair: Transition" by William Troy in *Nation* (New York), 1 November 1933; "The Films of René Clair" by Louis Jacobs in *New Theatre* (New York), February 1936; "Omaggio a Clair" by M. A. Antonioni in *Film rivista*, 13 September 1946; "De Méliès à Clair" by Lo Duca in *Revue du cinéma* (Paris), no.6, 1947; "René Clair et la notion d'objet" by Georges Sallet in *Revue internationale de filmologie* (Paris), no.2, 1947; "The Films of René Clair" by G. Lambert in *Sequence* (London), no.6, 1949; issue devoted to Clair, *Bianco e nero* (Rome), August/September 1951; "René Clair" by A. Philipe in *Les Lettres françaises* (Paris), 18-24 October 1961; "Chaplin e Clair ieri e oggi" by A. Ferrero in *Cinema nuovo* (Turin), January/Februray 1963; "René Clair, hélas...!" by Claude Gauteur in *Image et son* (Paris), June 1963; "L'arte del comico in René Clair" by V. Berti in *Bianco e nero* (Rome), March/April 1968; "Entr'acte, le film sans maître" by Claude Beylie in *Cinema 69* (Paris), February 1969; "It Happened Tomorrow" by Helene Fraenkel in *Films in Review* (New York), August/September 1974; "Rene Clair and James Mason at the 2nd Teheran International Film Festival" by T. Graham in *American Cinematographer* (Los Angeles), February 1974; "Entr'acte, Paris and Dada" by Noel Carroll in *Millenium Film Journal* (New York), winter 1977/78; "René Clair, *Le Million*, and the Coming of Sound" by Lucy Fischer in *Cinema Journal* (Evanston, Illinois), spring 1977; "Dr. Crase and Mr. Clair" by A. Michelson in *October* (Cambridge, Mass.), winter 1979; "Utopia Ltd., the Cinema of René Clair" by G. Adair in *Sight and Sound* (London), summer 1981; "René Clair: était-il un grand cinéaste?"by G. Haustrate in *Cinéma* (Paris), April 1981; "...und man findet einen Menschen" by G. Netzeband in *Film und Fernsehen* (Berlin), July 1981; obituary in *Image et son* (Paris), May 1981; film—*Le Rouge est mis*, documentary on making of *Les Belles de nuit*, by Hubert Knapp and Igor Barrère, 1952.

* * *

During the 1930s, when the French cinema reigned intellectually pre-eminent, René Clair ranked with Renoir and Carné as one of its greatest directors—perhaps the most archetypally French of them all. His reputation has since fallen (as has Carné's), and comparison with Renoir may suggest why. Clair's work, though witty, stylish, charming and technically accomplished, seems beside Renoir's to lack a dimension; there is a certain over-simplification, a fastidious turning away from the messier, more complex aspects of life. (Throughout nearly the whole of his career, Clair rejected location shooting, preferring the controllable artifice of the studio.) Critics have alleged superficiality, and emotional detachment. Yet, at their best, Clair's films have much of the quality of champagne—given so much sparkle and exhilaration, it would seem churlish to demand nourishment as well.

At the outset of his career, Clair directed one of the classic documents of surrealist cinema, *Entr'acte*, and this grounding in surrealism underlies much of his comedy. The Surrealists' love of sight gags (Magritte's cloud-baguettes, Duchamp's urinal) and mocking contempt for bourgeois respectability can be detected in the satiric farce of *Un Chapeau de paille d'Italie*, Clair's masterpiece of the silent era. Dream imagery, another surrealist preoccupation, recurs constantly throughout his career, from *Le Voyage imaginaire* to *Les Belles-de-nuit*, often transmuted into fantasy—touchingly poetic at its best, though in weaker moments declining into fey whimsicality.

The key films in Clair's early career, and those which made him internationally famous, were his first four sound pictures: *Sous les toits de Paris*, *Le Million*, *A Nous la liberté* and *Quatorze Juillet*. Initially sceptical of the value of sound—"an unnatural creation"—he rapidly changed his opinion on realizing the creative, non-realistic possibilities which the soundtrack offered. Sound effects, music, even dialogue could be used imaginatively, to counterpoint and comment on the image, or to suggest a new perspective on the action. Words and pictures, Clair showed, need not, and in fact should not, be tied together clumsily duplicating information. Dialogue need not always be audible; and even in a sound picture, silence could claim a validity of its own.

In these four films, Clair created a wholly individual cinematic world, a distinctive blend of fantasy, romance, social satire and operetta. Song and dance are introduced into the action with no pretence at literal realism, characters are drawn largely from stock, and the elaborate sets are explored with an effortless fluidity of camera movement which would be impossible in real locations. These qualities, together with the pioneering use of sound, and Clair's knack for effective pacing and brilliant visual gags, resulted in films of exceptional appeal, full of charm, gaiety and an ironic wit which at times—notably in the satire on mechanised greed in *A Nous la liberté*—darkened towards an underlying pessimism.

As always, Clair wrote his own scripts, working closely on all four films with the designer Lazare Meerson and cinematographer Georges Périnal. Of the four, *Le Million* most effectively integrated its various elements, and is generally rated Clair's finest film. But all were successful, especially outside France, and highly influential: both Chaplin (*Modern Times*) and the Marx Brothers (*A Night at the Opera*) borrowed from them. In some quarters, though, Clair was criticized for lack of social relevance. Ill-advisedly, he attempted to respond to such criticisms; *Le Dernier Milliardaire* proved a resounding flop, and led to Clair's long exile. For 13 years he made no films in France, apart from the abortive *Air pur*, and his six English-language pictures—two in Britain, four in America—have an uneasy feel about them, the fantasy strained and unconvincing. By the time Clair finally returned to France in 1946, both he and the world had changed.

The films that Clair made after the war rarely recapture the lighthearted gaiety of his early work. In its place, the best of them display a new-found maturity and emotional depth, while preserving the characteristic elegance and wit. The prevailing mood is an autumnal melancholy that at times, as in the elegiac close of *Les Grandes Manoeuvres*, comes near to tragedy. Characters are no longer the stock puppets of the pre-war satires, but rounded individuals, capable of feeling and suffering. More serious subjects are confronted, their edges only slightly softened by their context: *Porte des Lilas* ends with a murder, *La Beauté du diable* with a vision of the atomic holocaust. Nearest in mood to the earlier films is the erotic fantasy of *Les Belles-de-nuit*, but even this is darkly underscored with intimations of suicide.

In the late 1950s Clair came under attack from the writers of *Cahiers du cinéma*, François Truffaut in particular, who regarded him as the embodiment of the 'Old Guard', the ossified *cinéma du papa* against which they were in revolt. To what he saw as Clair's emotionless, studio-bound artifice, Truffaut opposed an alternative, more 'truly French' cinematic tradition, the lyrical freedom of Renoir and Jean Vigo. Clair's reputation never fully recovered from these onslaughts, nor from the lukewarm reception which met his last two films, *Tout l'or du monde* and *Les Fetes galantes*.

But although Clair no longer commands a place among the very first rank of directors, he remains undoubtedly one of the most original and distinctive stylists of the cinema. His explorations of sound, movement and narrative technique, liberating at the time, still appear fresh and inventive. For all his limitations, which he readily acknowledged—"a director's intelligence," he once wrote, "can be judged partly by his renunciations"—Clair succeeded in creating a uniquely personal vision of the world, which in his best films still retains the power to exhilarate and delight.

—Philip Kemp

CLARKE, SHIRLEY. American. Born Shirley Brimberg in New York City, 1925. Educated at Stephens College, Johns Hopkins University, Bennington College, and University of North Carolina; studied with Martha Graham Dancers. Married lithographer Burt Clarke; daughter: Wendy. Career: 1940s-early 1950s—dancer with Martha Graham, Doris Humphrey companies, and as soloist; 1946—becomes chairwoman of National Dance Association; 1953—stops dancing to make films; 1962—co-founds Filmmakers Cooperative with Jonas Mekas; late 1960s—works with Public Broadcast Lab (fired 1969); 1969—acquires portable video cameras, begins working exclusively with videotape; 1971—Museum of Modern Art retrospective; 1973-75—tours East and Midwest with troupe giving video workshops; 1975—moves to Los Angeles; 1975-present—professor of film and video at UCLA; 1981—collaborates with Joseph Chaikin and Sam Shepard on *Savage/Love* videotape;

1981-82—works on other video adaptations of theater pieces.

Films (as producer, director, photographer, editor and co-choreographer): 1954—*A Dance in the Sun*; *In Paris Parks*; 1955—*Bullfight* (co-ph); 1957—*A Moment in Love* (co-ph); 1958—*The Skyscraper* (pr, co-d only); (as director): 1958—*Brussels "Loops"* (12 film loops made for Brussels Exposition, destroyed) (+pr, co-ph, ed); 1959—*Bridges-Go-Round* (+pr, co-ph, ed); *Opening in Moscow* (Pennebaker) (co-ed only); 1960—*A Scary Time* (+co-sc, ph); 1961—*The Connection* (+co-pr, ed); 1963—*The Cool World* (+co-sc, ed); *Robert Frost: A Lover's Quarrel with the World* (co-d); 1967—*Portrait of Jason* (+pr, ed, voice); *Man in Polar Regions* (11-screen film for Expo '67); 1981—*Savage/Love* (videotape). Roles: 1969—as herself in *Lion's Love* (Varda).

Publications:

By CLARKE:

Articles—"*Bridges-Go-Round*," "*Bullfight*," "*A Moment in Love*," catalogue entries for 1958 International Experimental Film Competition, Brussels 1958; "The Expensive Art" in *Film Quarterly* (Berkeley), summer 1960; "The Cool World" in *Films and Filming* (London), December 1963; "Shirley Clarke at Venice", interview by Harriet Polt, in *Film Comment* (New York), no.2, 1964; "Rencontre avec Shirley Clarke" by Axel Madsen in *Cahiers du cinéma* (Paris), March 1964; interview by James Blue in *Objectif* (Paris), February/March 1965; "Interview with Shirley Clarke" by Gretchen Berg in *Film Culture* (New York), spring 1967; "A Conversation—Shirley Clarke and Storm DeHirsch" in *Film Culture* (New York), autumn 1967 and October 1968; "A Statement on Dance and Film" in *Dance Perspectives*, summer 1967; "Entretiens—Le Départ pour Mars" by Michael Delahaye in *Cahiers du cinéma* (Paris), October 1968; "Shirley Clarke: Image and Ideas", interview by S. Rice in *Take One* (Montreal), February 1972; "What Directors Are Saying" in *Action* (Los Angeles), March/April 1975.

On CLARKE:

Books—*A History of the American Avant-Garde Cinema*, exhibition catalogue, by John Hanhardt and others, The American Federation of Arts, New York 1976; articles—"Films of Shirley Clarke" by Henry Breitrose in *Film Quarterly* (Berkeley), summer 1960; "Woman Director Makes the Scene" by Eugene Archer in the *New York Times Magazine*, 26 August 1962; "Notes on Women Directors" by J. Pyros in *Take One* (Montreal), November/December 1970; article by Jonas Mekas in the *Village Voice* (New York), 20 May 1971; "Shirley Clarke" by K. Cooper in *Filmmakers Newsletter* (Ward Hill, Mass.), June 1972; "The Cool Medium of Shirley Clarke" by Bruce Bebb in the *Reader* (Los Angeles), 26 February 1982.

*   *   *

Shirley Clarke was a leader and major filmmaker in the New York film community in the 1950s and 1960s. Her films, which exemplify the artistic directions of the independent movement, are classic examples of the best work of American independent filmmaking. Clarke began her professional career as a dancer, and participated in the late 1940s in the avant-garde dance community centered around New York City's Young Men's-Young Women's Hebrew Association's (YM-YWHA) perfor-mance stage and Hanya Holm's classes for young choreographers. In 1953, Clarke adapted dancer-choreographer Daniel Nagrin's *Dance in the Sun* to film. In her first dance film, Clarke relied on editing concepts to choreograph a new cinematic space and rhythm. She then applied her cinematic choreography to a non-dance subject in *In Paris Parks*, and further explored the cinematic possibilities for formal choreography in her dance films, *Bullfight* and *A Moment in Love*.

Clarke, during this time period, studied filmmaking with Hans Richter at City College of New York and participated in informal filmmaking classes with director and cinematographer Peter Glushanok. In 1955, she became an active member of Independent Filmmakers of America (IFA), a short-lived New York organization that tried to improve promotion and distribution for independent films. Through the IFA, Clarke became part of the Greenwich Village artistic circle that included avant-garde filmmakers Maya Deren, Stan Brakhage, and Jonas Mekas. It also introduced her to the importance of an economic structure for the growth of avant-garde film, a cause she championed throughout the 1960s.

Clarke worked with filmmakers Willard Van Dyke, Donn Alan Pennebaker, Ricky Leacock, and Wheaton Galentine on a series of film loops on American life for the United States Pavilion at the 1958 World's Fair in Brussels. With the leftover footage of New York City bridges, she then made her experimental film masterpiece, *Bridges-Go-Round* utilizing editing strategies, camera choreography, and color tints to turn naturalistic objects into a poem of dancing abstract elements. It is one of the best and most widely seen examples of a cinematic Abstract Expressionism in the 1950s.

Clarke made the documentary film *Skyscraper* in 1958 with Van Dyke, Pennebaker, Leacock, and Galentine, followed by *A Scary Time* (1960), a film commissioned by the United Nations International Children's Emergency Fund (UNICEF). Clarke also began work on a public television film on Robert Frost, *A Lover's Quarrel With the World*, but due to artistic disagreements and other commitments, she left the project before the film's completion still retaining a credit as co-director.

Influenced by the developing cinema-verité style in documentary films by Leacock and Pennebaker, Clarke adapted cinema verité to two feature-length dramatic films, *The Connection* and *The Cool World*. *The Connection* was a landmark for the emergence of a New York independent feature film movement. It heralded a new style that employed a greater cinematic realism and addressed relevant social issues in black-and-white low budget films. It was also important because Clarke made the film the first test case in the courts in a successful fight to abolish New York State's censorship rules. Her next feature film, *The Cool World*, was the first movie to dramatize a story on black street gangs without relying upon Hollywood-style moralizing, and it was the first commercial film to be shot on location in Harlem. In 1967, Clarke directed a 90-minute cinema verité interview with a black homosexual. *Portrait of Jason* is an insightful exploration of one person's character while it simultaneously addresses the range and limitations of cinema verité style. Although Clarke's features had only moderate commercial runs and nominal success in the United States, they have won film festival awards and critical praise in Europe making Clarke one of the most highly regarded American independent filmmakers among European film audiences.

In the 1960s, Clarke also worked for the advancement of the New York independent film movement. She was one of the 24 filmmakers and producers who wrote and signed the 1961 manifesto, "Statement for a New American Cinema" which called for an economic, artistic, and political alternative to Hollywood moviemaking. With Jonas Mekas in 1962, she co-founded Film-

Makers Cooperative, a non-profit distribution company for independent films. Later, Clarke, Mekas and filmmaker Louis Brigante co-founded Film-Makers Distribution Center, a company for distributing independent features to commercial movie theatres. Throughout the 1960s, Clarke lectured on independent film in universities and museums in the United States and Europe, and in 1969 she turned to video as her major medium in which to work.

—Lauren Rabinovitz

CLAYTON, JACK. British. Born in Brighton, Sussex, 1921. Career: before 1935—trains as racing ice skater; 1935—begins working at London Films as 3rd ass't director; 1936-40—promoted to ass't director, then editor; 1940—volunteers for RAF, serves in RAF Film Unit as cameraman, editor, director, and finally Officer Commanding; 1944—present at liberation of Naples, writes and shoots most of *Naples Is a Battlefield*, released by Ministry of Information; 1946—demobilized, begins working as production manager, then associate producer; early 1950s—associate producer with James Woolf's Romulus Films; 1958—directs 1st feature; mid-1960s—develops several adaptations of John Le Carré's *The Looking Glass War*, backs out of project in dispute with producers; 1974—critical and box-office failure of *The Great Gatsby* is followed by decade of inactivity.

Films (as director): 1944—*Naples Is a Battlefield* (+sc, co-ph—uncredited); 1948—*Bond Street* (Parry) (2nd unit d); *An Ideal Husband* (A. Korda) (pr mgr only); (as associate producer): 1948—*The Queen of Spades* (Dickinson); 1951—*Flesh and Blood* (Kimmins); 1952—*Moulin Rouge* (Huston); 1953—*Beat the Devil* (Huston); 1954—*The Good Die Young* (Gilbert); 1955—*I Am a Camera* (Cornelius); (as producer): 1955—*The Bespoke Overcoat* (+d); 1956—*Sailor Beware! (Panic in the Parlor)* (Parry); *Dry Rot* (Elvey); *3 Men in a Boat* (Annakin); 1957—*The Story of Esther Costello* (Miller) (assoc pr, +2nd unit d); 1958—*The Whole Truth* (Guillermin); (as director): 1958—*Room at the Top*; 1961—*The Innocents* (+pr); 1964—*The Pumpkin Eater*; 1967—*Our Mother's House*; 1974—*The Great Gatsby*; 1983—*Something Wicked This Way Comes*.

Publications:

By CLAYTON:

Articles—"Challenge from Short Story Films" in *Films and Filming* (London), February 1956; "The Way Things Are", interview by Gordon Gow, in *Films and Filming* (London), April 1974; "I'm proud of that film", interview by M. Rosen, in *Film Comment* (New York), July/August 1974.

On CLAYTON:

Articles—"Clayton's Progress" by Peter Cowie in *Motion* (London), spring 1962; "The House that Jack Built" by Douglas McVay in *Films and Filming* (London), October 1967; "There'll Always Be Room at the Top for Nothing But the Best" by C.T. Gregory in *Journal of Popular Film* (Bowling Green, Ohio), winter 1973; "West Egg at Pinewood" by Penelope Houston in *Sight and Sound* (London), autumn 1973; "Gatsby" by Penelope Houston in *Sight and Sound* (London), spring 1974; "Gatsby le magnifique" in *Avant-Scène du cinéma* (Paris), January 1975.

* * *

With his first feature, *Room at the Top*, Jack Clayton's reputation as a daring, innovative, and thoroughly professional filmmaker was firmly established. The film, which in Clayton's words depicted "what happened to England when everybody came back from the war", was widely hailed and subsequently accepted as a seminal breakthrough for British cinema. Enormously successful, both critically and financially, despite its X certificate believed by distributors at that time to limit a film's potential, *Room at the Top* opened the way for filmmakers to deal in a realistic, adult fashion with contemporary issues and concerns previously held taboo. On the evidence of his later films, however, the "realist" label has proved inappropriate for Clayton; with hindsight, his interest in John Braine's novel may have lain elsewhere than its subject matter—"realism" being perhaps more a question of style than of point of view.

Clayton's themes are remarkably consistent throughout his six feature films to date. Most notably, he is preoccupied with the loss of innocence, often, though not invariably, in children. His films seem to form a series of repeated pairs: a work of nominal "realism" (*Room at the Top*, *The Pumpkin Eater*, *The Great Gatsby*) in which the main protagonists are adults, followed by one in which children and the specifically supernatural predominate (*The Innocents*, *Our Mother's House*, *Something Wicked This Way Comes*). Repeatedly, in his films, two worlds clash, and the more idealistic suffers defeat at the hands of sophistication and experience, though the victory often proves double-edged. For children, the forces which defeat their innocence are external while his adults are betrayed by their own fantasies and self-deceptions—the "innocence" which leaves them vulnerable to those who can manipulate the power of class, sex, or the venality of others.

This clash is reflected in Clayton's shooting style. A fluid, lyrical camera movement is often interrupted with harsh cuts which bring a character into brutal close-up; a simple, unobtrusive shot is balanced by a series of complicated dissolves. However, such techniques are usually employed to further the mood, to comment, or to reveal complexities rather than simply to show off the director's adeptness. But for many there is a coldness and distance in the handling of the films' material which undermines the strongly-charged performances which Clayton elicits from his actors, both adult and child.

Clayton's fascination with romantic, obsessed characters appears to have its counterpart in his own personality, in that he works obsessively on each film, taking it through every stage of development himself. "When I am working on a film I do not exist other than on the film; I have no private life. So that when the film is finished, it is really like a kind of life finishing." This might account both for the intermittent nature of Clayton's career—only six features in 25 years, with increasing gaps between them—and for the impression that the films are a little too calculated, too obsessively detailed to match the extraordinary power and spontaneity of the performances. Clayton may perhaps furnish a rare example of a director who has been hampered, above all, by the very skill and sensitivity which distinguish his work.

—Theresa FitzGerald

CLÉMENT, RENÉ. French. Born at Bordeaux, 18 March 1913. Educated in architecture at Ecole de Beaux-Arts. Career: early 1930s—while a student, makes animated film *César chez les Gaulois*; 1934—meets Jacques Tati, who stars in *Soigne ton gauche* (1936); 1936—begins making short documentaries in Arabia and North Africa; 1940—demobilized in south of France, begins working with cameraman Henri Alekan; 1945—with cooperation of group 'Résistance-Fer' begins shooting material for *La Bataille du rail*; 1946—technical consultant on Cocteau's *Beauty and the Beast*. Recipient: Best Director, Cannes Festival, for *La Bataille du rail*, 1946; Best Director, Cannes Festival, for *Au-delà des grilles*, 1949.

Films (as director of short films): 1936—*Soigne ton gauche*; 1937—*L'Arabie interdite*; 1938—*La Grande Chartreuse*; 1939—*La Bièvre, fille perdue*; 1940—*Le Triage*; 1942—*Ceux du rail*; 1943—*La Grande Pastorale*; 1944—*Chefs de demain*; (as feature director): 1945—*La Bataille du rail (Battle of the Rails)* (+sc); 1946—*Le Père tranquille (Mr. Orchid)*; 1947—*Les Maudits (The Damned)* (+co-adapt); 1948—*Au-delà des grilles (Le Mura di Malapaga, The Walls of Malapaga)*; 1950—*Le Chateau de verre* (+co-sc); 1951—*Jeux interdits (Forbidden Games)* (+co-sc); 1954—*Monsieur Ripois (Knave of Hearts; Lovers, Happy Lovers)* (+co-sc); 1956—*Gervais*; 1958—*Barrage contre le Pacifique (La Diga sul Pacifico; This Angry Age; The Sea Wall)* (+co-sc); 1959—*Plein soleil (Purple Noon; Lust for Evil)* (+co-sc); 1961—*Che gioia vivere (Quelle joie de vivre)* (+co-sc); 1962—*Le Jour et l'heure (The Day and the Hour)* (+co-sc); 1964—*Les Félins (Joy House; The Love Cage)* (+co-sc); 1966—*Paris brûle-t-il? (Is Paris Burning?)*; 1969—*Le Passager de la pluie (Rider on the Rain)*; 1971—*La Maison sous les arbres (The Deadly Trap)*; 1972—*La Course du lièvre à travers les champs (And Hope To Die)*; 1975—*La Baby-Sitter*.

Publications:

By CLÉMENT:

Articles—"Interview with Clément" by Francis Koval in *Sight and Sound* (London), June 1950; "On Being a Creator" in *Films and Filming* (London), October 1960.

On CLÉMENT:

Books—*René Clément* by Jacques Siclier, Brussels 1956; *René Clément* by André Farwagi, Paris 1967; *French Cinema Since 1946: Vol.1—The Great Tradition* by Roy Armes, New York 1970; articles—by Jean Queval in *L'Écran français* (Paris), 16 October 1946; article by Roger Régent in *L'Écran français* (Paris), 14 October 1947; "Style of René Clément" by Lotte Eisner in *Film Culture* (New York), no.12 and no.13, 1957; article by Madeleine Riffaud in *Les Lettres françaises* (Paris), 14 November 1957; article by René Gilson in *Cinéma 60* (Paris), no.44, 1960; article by Michel Mardore in *Cinéma 62* (Paris), no.62, 1962; article by Raymond Bellour in *Les Lettres françaises* (Paris), 11 June 1964; "The Darker Side of Life" by Douglas McVay in *Films and Filming* (London), December 1966; "Plein soleil", special issue devoted to Clément of *Avant-Scène du cinéma* (Paris), 1 February 1981; "Situation de René Clement" by Étienne Chaumeton in *Positif* (Paris), no.18; "Pour René Clément" by Claude Gauteur in *Image et son* (Paris), no.186; article by Marc Kravetz in *Image et son* (Paris), no.149.

* * *

René Clément was the most promising filmmaker to emerge in France at the end of World War II. He became the most technically adroit and interesting of the makers of "quality" films during the 1950s only to see his career begin to disappoint the critics. In the years of the New Wave it was Clément, above all, who tied the older generation to the younger, especially through a film like *Purple Noon*. In his most recent phase he was associated with grand-scale dramas (*Is Paris Burning?*) and with small, personal, lyric films (*Rider on the Rain*).

Clément began his career auspiciously, helping Cocteau with *Beauty and the Beast*, and directing France's only great resistance film, *La Bataille du rail*. These films showed the world his wide range. The first is a classic of fantasy while the second exhibits what can only be termed a "neorealist" style. Because *La Bataille du rail* was shot on location with non-actors, and because its episodic story was drawn from the chronicle of everyday life, Clément, at the end of the war, was championed as France's answer to the powerful Italian school of the liberation.

For a time Clément seemed anxious to live up to this reputation. He associated himself with the progressive journal *L'Ecran francais*, and sought other realist topics for his films. In *Les Maudits* he observed the plight of a group of Germans and refugees aboard a submarine. Evidently more concerned with the technical problems of filming in small spaces than with the moral dimensions of his plot, this film was not a great success. But with *The Walls of Malapaga* Clément recovered his audience. This film, which won the Academy Award for best foreign film, was in fact a Franco-Italian co-production and brought together on the screen the most popular star of each country: Jean Gabin and Isa Miranda. The plot and style returned Clément to the poetic-realist films of pre-war France and continued to exhibit that tension of realism and abstraction that characterized all his work.

Unquestionably he was, along with Claude Autant-Lara, the most important figure in the French film industry during the 1950s. His *Forbidden Games* remains a classic today and is notable both for the ingenuous performances of his child actors against a natural location and for the moral incisiveness of its witty plot and dialogue, scripted by the team Aurenche and Bost. Doubtless because he had begun working with these writers, Truffaut condemned Clément in his notorious 1954 essay, "A Certain Tendency in French Cinema," but Bazin, commenting on this essay, found Truffaut to have been too harsh in Clément's case. Indeed Bazin lobbied to have the Cannes Film Festival award its Golden Palm to Clément's next feature, *Monsieur Ripois*. Starring Gérard Philipe, this film makes extensive use of subjective camera and voice over. Shot on location in London, it is clearly an experimental project.

But Clément's experiments are always limited. Technical problems continue to interest him, but he will never relinquish his belief that a film must be well-crafted in the traditional sense of that term. This is what must always distinguish him from the New Wave filmmakers with whom he otherwise has something in common. His all-knowing pessimism, and his literary good taste, finally put him in the camp of the "quality" directors. It must be said, however, that his adaptation of Zola's *L'Assomoir*, titled *Gervaise*, must make one re-evaluate this tradition. It is an effective, well-balanced film, far above the average output of French cinema during its decade.

Clément, then, must be thought of as consummately French. His technical mastery sits well with his advanced political and moral ideas. He is cultured and trained. He makes excellent films both on a grand scale and on a smaller more personal one. But finally there is something impersonal about even these small films, for, before representing himself, René Clément represents the institution of filmmaking in France. He is a good representative, perhaps the best it had after the war right up through the New Wave.

—Dudley Andrew

CLOUZOT, HENRI-GEORGES. French. Born at Niort, 20 November 1907. Educated at École navale, Brest; studied law and political science. Married Véra Amado Gibson, 1950 (died 1960). Career: late 1920s—secretary to Louis Marin, Deputy, and to René Dorin, songwriter; reporter for *Paris-Midi*; 1930—offered job in film industry while interviewing producer Adolphe Osso; early 1930s—works as assistant to Carmine Gallone and Anatole Litvak among others; 1933—collaborates on French-language versions of German films; 1934-38—stricken with pleurisy and spends time in hospitals and sanatoriums studying literature; 1938—reenters film industry as writer; 1943—*Le Corbeau* attacked as pro-German propaganda; 1944-46—Clouzot inactive, regarded as collaborator; 1950—travels to Brazil, abortive film project; 1965-66—makes 5 TV films about music: *Le Requiem de Verdi, La Symphonie du Nouveau Monde de Dvorak, La Quatrième Symphonie de Schumann, La Cinquième Symphonie de Beethoven* and *Le Concerto en la majeur de Mozart.* Died 12 January 1977. Recipient: Best Direction, Venice Festival, for *Quai des Orfèvres,* 1947; Grand Prix, Cannes Festival, for *Le Salaire de la peur,* 1953; Prix Louis Delluc for *Les Diaboliques,* 1955; Jury Prize, Cannes Festival, for *Le Mystère Picasso,* 1955; Academy Award, Best Foreign Film, for *La Verite,* 1960.

Films (as scriptwriter): 1931—*Ma Cousine de Varsovie* (Gallone) (co-sc); *Un Soir de Rafle* (Gallone) (adaptation only); *Je serai seule après minuit* (de Baroncelli) (co-sc); *Le Chanteur inconnu* (Tourjansky) (co-adapt only); *La Terreur des Batignolles* (d: short); 1932—*Le Roi des palaces* (Gallone) (co-sc); *Le Dernier Choc* (de Baroncelli) (co-sc); *La Chanson d'une nuit* (French language version of Anatole Litvak's *Das Lied einer Nacht*) (co-adaptation and dialogue); *Faut-il les marier?* (French version, co-d by Pierre Billon, of Carl Lamac's *Die grausame Freundin*) (adaptation and dialogue); 1933—*Caprice de princesse* (French version of Karl Hartl's *Ihre Durchlacht, die Verkäuferin*) (adaptation, +assoc d, ed); *Chateau de rêve* (French version of Geza von Bolvary's *Das Schloss im Süden*) (adaptation, +assoc d, ed); *Tout pour l'amour* (French version of Joe May's *Ein Lied für dich*) (adaptation, co-dialogue, lyrics, +assoc d)(lyrics and dialogue); 1934—*Itto d'Afrique* (Benoit-Lévy) (lyrics); 1938—*Le Révolté* (Mathot) (co-sc); 1939—*Le Duel* (Fresnay) (co-sc); *Le Monde tremblera (La Révolté des vivants)* (Pottier) (co-sc); 1941—*Le Dernier des 6* (Lacombe); *Les Inconnus dans la maison* (Decoin) (co-adapt); (as director and co-scriptwriter): 1942—*L'Assassin habite au 21*; 1943—*Le Corbeau*; 1947—*Quai des Orfèvres*; 1948—*Manon*; 1949—"Le Retour de Jean" in *Retour à la vie*; *Miquette et sa mère*; 1952—*Le Salaire de la peur* (sc); 1954—*Les Diaboliques*; 1955—*Les Espions*; *Si tous les gars du monde...* (Christian-Jaque) (co-adapt only); 1960—*La Verite* (sc); 1968—*La Prisonnière* (sc).

Publications:

By CLOUZOT:

Books—*Le Corbeau*, with Louis Chavance, Paris 1948; *Retour à la vie*, with others, Paris 1949; *Le Cheval des dieux*, Paris 1951;

articles—"Le Salaire de la peur" in *Avant-Scène du cinéma* (Paris), no.17, 1962; *Quai des Orfèvres* in *Avant-Scène du cinéma* (Paris), no.29, 1963; "Voix off: Clouzot", interview by Claire Clouzot in *Cinéma 65* (Paris), May 1965; "An Interview with Henri-Georges Clouzot" by Paul Schrader in *Cinema* (Beverly Hills), no.4, 1969.

On CLOUZOT:

Books—*H.G. Clouzot* by François Chalais, Paris 1950; *H.G. Clouzot* by Pietro Bianchi, Parma 1951; *Le Premier Spectateur* by Michel Cournot, Paris 1957; *Le Proces Clouzot* by Francis Lacassin and others, Paris 1964; *H.G. Clouzot* by Philippe Pilard, Paris 1969; *French Cinema Since 1946: Vol.1—The Great Tradition* by Roy Armes, New York 1970; articles—"Clouzot vu par Jouvet" by Roger Régent in *L'Ecran française* (Paris), no.197, 1949; "The Necrophilist" by Stanley Goulder in *Films and Filming* (London), December 1958; "Frenchman's Horror" in *Newsweek* (New York), 28 November 1955; "Clouzot est-il vraiment diable?" by Claude Brulé in *Ciné-revue* (Paris), 1955; "Henri-Georges Clouzot" by Sylvia Tennant in *Film* (London), March/April 1956; "Henri-Georges Clouzot" by Pietro Bianchi in *Yale French Studies* (New Haven, Conn.), summer 1956; "Dangers et vertus de l'orfèverie" by Jacques Marilen in *Positif* (Paris), November 1956; "Clouzot: He Plans Everything from Script to Screen" by Gerard Sety in *Films and Filming* (London), December 1958; "Clouzot as Delilah" by John Berger in *Sight and Sound* (London), spring 1958; "Clouzot sort de sa légende" by A. Fontaine in *Les Lettres françaises* (Paris), July 1960; obituary by Blaude Beylie in *Ecran* (Paris), February 1977; "Henri-Georges Clouzot, 1907-1977" by R. Lacourbe in *Avant-Scène du cinéma* (Paris), 15 April 1977; "Hommage à Henri-Georges Clouzot" by J.-M. Lardinois in *Revue Belge du cinéma* (Brussels), April 1977; "La Prisonnière" by P. Pilard and others in *Image et son* (Paris), no.331bis, 1978; "Clouzot: the Wages of Film" by D. Yakir in *Film Comment* (New York), November/December 1981; "Esquisse d'un portrait de H.G. Clouzot" by Jacques Chevallier in *Image et son* (Paris), no.64.

*   *   *

In a country like France where good taste is so admired, Henri-Georges Clouzot has been a shocking director. A film critic during the age of surrealism, Clouzot was always eager to assault his audience with his style and concerns.

Like so many others, he found his chance to move from scriptwriting to directing during the Occupation when there was a paucity of directors in France. His first effort *L'Assassin habite au 21* was a safe film since its script followed two similar films he had written which had been well-received by audiences. These witty police dramas are exercises in style and cleverness, befitting the epoch. *Le Corbeau*, made the next year, was in contrast a shattering film, unquestionably hitting hard at the society of the war years. Retaining all the conventions of the thriller, Clouzot systematically exposed the physical and psychological grotesqueries of every character in the film. A grim picture of small-town mores, *Le Corbeau* was condemned by the Nazis and French patriots alike.

When the war ended Clouzot found himself barred from the industry for two years by the "purification committee", an industry-appointed watchdog group that self-righteously judged complicity with the Germans. Clouzot's crime was to have made films for a German-financed company, though he was officially arraigned on charges of having maligned the French character and having demoralized the country during its dark hours. But even at this time many critics claimed that *Le Corbeau* was the only authentically engaged film made during the entire Occupation.

When he did resume his career, Clouzot's grim view of life had not improved. Both *Quai des Orfèvres* and his 1948 adaptation of *Manon* emulate American film noir with their lowlife settings. Both are extremely well acted, but ultimately small works.

Clouzot's fame in the United States came in the mid-1950s when *The Wages of Fear* and *Diabolique* gave him a reputation as a French Hitchcock, interested in the mechanics of suspense. But in France these films, especially *Diabolique*, were seen as only well-made studio products. His 1960 *La Vérité*, starring Brigitte Bardot, was designed to win him favor in the youth culture obsessed by New Wave Life and movies. While the film outgrossed its New Wave competition, a cloyingly paternalistic style shows how far Clouzot is from the spontaneity of the New Wave. The cafe scenes are insincere and the inevitable indictment of society rings false.

All of Clouzot's films even up to the 1968 *La Prisonnière* were financial successes, but in the end he ceased being the instrumental force in the film industry he had been 20 years earlier.

—Dudley Andrew

COCTEAU, JEAN. French. Born at Maisons-Lafitte, near Paris, 5 July 1889. Educated at Lycee Condorcet and Fénelon, Paris. Career: 1906—poems read at Théâtre Fémina, Paris, by Edouard de Max; 1912—meets Igor Stravinsky and Serge de Diaghileff; before 1914—actor in Paris; 1917—collaborates with Picasso on play *Parade*, scandalized audience threatens authors; 1920s—active as poet (*L'Ange Heurtebise*), playwright (*Orphée*), librettist (Stravinsky's opera *Oedipus Rex*), and novelist (*Les Enfants terribles*); these and other literary activities continue throughout career; 1930—the Vicomte Charles de Noailles finances *Le Sang d'un poète*; 1937—becomes manager of boxer Al Brown, helps him regain championship; 1940—remains in Paris during the Occupation, play *Les Parents terribles* forbidden by authorities; 1947—acquires house at Milly-la-Forêt (Seine et Oise); 1950—most important period as graphic artist begins with decorations for Villa Santo Sospir in Saint-Jean-Cap-Ferrat. Died at Milly-la-Forêt, France, 11 October 1963. Recipient: Chevalier de la Légion d'Honneur, 1949; member, Académie Royale de Belgique, 1955; member, Académie Française, 1955; honorary doctorate, Oxford University, 1956.

Films (as director and scriptwriter): 1925—*Jean Cocteau fait du cinéma* (negative lost?); 1930—*Le Sang d'un poète* (originally *La Vie d'un poète*) (+ed, voice-over); 1940—*La Comedie du bonheur* (L'Herbier) (co-sc only); 1942—*Le Baron fantôme* (de Poligny) (sc only, +ro as *Le Baron*); 1943—*L'Eternel Retour* (Delannoy) (sc only); 1945—*Les Dames du Bois de Boulogne* (Bresson) (co-sc only); 1946—*La Belle et la bête*; 1947—*Ruy Blas* (Billon) (sc only); *L'Aigle à deux têtes*; 1948—*La Voix humaine* (Rossellini) (from Cocteau's play); *Les Noces de sable* (Zvoboda) (sc only, +voice-over); *Les Parents terribles* (+voice-over); 1950—a 1914 "dramatic scene" by Cocteau included in *Ce siècle a cinquante ans* (Tual); *Les Enfants terribles* (Melville) (sc only); *Orphée*; *Coriolan* (+ro); 1952—*La Villa Santo-Sospir*; 1952—*La Couronne noire* (Saslavski) (co-sc only); 1957—*Le Bel indifferent* (Demy) (from Cocteau's play); 1959—*Charlotte et son Jules* (Godard) (from same play as Demy film above); 1960—*Le Testament d'Orphée (Ne me demandez pas pourquoi)*

(+ro as *le poète*); 1961—*La Princesse de Cleves* (Delannoy) (co-sc only); 1963—*Anna la bonne* (Jutra) (from song by Cocteau); 1965—*Thomas l'imposteur* (Franju) (co-sc only); 1970—*La Voix humaine* (Delouche) (from Poulenc and Cocteau opera). Roles and narration: 1943—*Alfred de Musset* in *La Malibran* (Guitry); 1946—*L'Amitie noire* (Villiers and Krull); 1948—*La Légende de Sainte Ursule* (Emmer); 1949—*Tennis* (Martin); 1950—*Colette* (Bellon); *Venise et ses amants* (Emmer and Gras); 1951—*Desordre* (Baratier); 1952—*8 x 8* (Richter); 1953—*Le Rouge est mis* (Barrère and Knapp); 1956—*A l'aube d'un monde* (Lucot); *Pantomimes* (Lucot); 1958—*Django Reinhardt* (Paviot); *Le Musée Grevin* (Demy and Masson).

Publications:

By COCTEAU:

Books—*L'Aigle à deux têtes*, Paris 1946; *The Blood of a Poet*, translated by Lily Pons, New York 1949; *Diary of a Film* [*La Belle et la bête*], New York 1950; *Cocteau on the Film*, New York 1954; *Jean Cocteau par lui-même*, edited by André Fraigneau, Paris 1957; *Le Sang d'un poète*, with drawings, Monaco 1957; *Orphée* (filmscript), Paris 1961; *Le Testament d'Orphée* (filmscript), Paris 1961; *The Eagle with 2 Heads*, translated by Carl Wildman, London 1962; *The Journals of Jean Cocteau* edited and translated by Wallace Fowlie, Bloomington, Indiana 1964; *The Difficulty of Being* translated by Elizabeth Sprigge, London 1966; *2 Screenplays* [*The Blood of a Poet* and *The Testament of Orpheus*], New York 1968; *Beauty and the Beast*, script edited by Robert Hammond, New York 1970; *Professional Secrets: An Autobiography of Jean Cocteau* edited by Robert Phelps and translated by Richard Howard, New York 1970; *Cocteau on the Film*, New York 1972; *Jean Cocteau: 3 Screenplays* [*The Eternal Return, Beauty and the Beast and Orpheus*], New York 1972; articles—"Interview with Cocteau" by Francis Koval in *Sight and Sound* (London), August 1950; "Conversation" in *Sight and Sound* (London), July/September 1952; "Cocteau" in *Film* (London), March 1955; interview in *Film Makers on Filmmaking* edited by Harry Geduld, Bloomington, Indiana 1967; "Aphorismes cinématographiques" and "Cocteau face a La Belle et la bête" in *Avant-Scène du cinéma* (Paris), July/September 1973; "4 Letters by Jean Cocteau to Leni Riefenstahl" in *Film Culture* (New York), spring 1973.

On COCTEAU:

Books—*Jean Cocteau* by Margaret Crosland, London 1955; *Jean Cocteau chez les Sirènes* by Jean Dauven, Paris 1956; *Cocteau* by Jean-Jacques Kihm, Paris 1960; *Jean Cocteau tourne son dernier film* by Roger Pillaudin, Paris 1960; *Cocteau* by André Fraigneau, New York 1961; *Jean Cocteau: The History of a Poet's Age* by Wallace Fowlie, Bloomington, Indiana 1968; *Jean Cocteau: The Man and the Mirror* by Elizabeth Sprigge and Jean-Jacques Kihm, New York 1968; *An Impersonation of Angels* by Frederick Brown, New York 1968; *Jean Cocteau* by Roger Lannes, Paris 1968; *Cocteau* by René Gilson, translated by Ciba Vaughn, New York 1969; *French Cinema Since 1946: Vol.1—The Great Tradition* by Roy Armes, New York 1970; *Cocteau* by Francis Steegmuller, Boston 1970; *Jean Cocteau and His Films of Orphic Identity* by Arthur Evans, Philadelphia 1977; articles—"The Blood of a Poet" by C.G. Wallis in *Kenyon Review* (Ohio), winter 1944; "Cocteau and Orpheus" by Gavin Lambert in *Sequence* (London), autumn 1950; "On Cocteau" by Neal Oxenhandler in *Film Quarterly* (Berkeley), fall 1964; "Images of the Mind—Part 13: Time and

Timelessness" by Raymond Durgnat in *Films and Filming* (London), July 1969; "The Testament of Jean Cocteau" by G. Amberg in *Film Comment* (New York), winter 1971/72; "Jean Cocteau et le cinéma", special issue by C. Gauteur, of *Image et son* (Paris), June/July 1972; "Rétrospective. Jean Cocteau. Un cinéaste? Peut-être. Un auteur? Certainement." by T. Renaud in *Cinéma* (Paris), December 1973; special issue of *Avant-Scène du cinéma* (Paris), July/September 1973; "Il y a dix ans Jean Cocteau" in *Image et son* (Paris), September 1973; "Astonishments: Magic Film from Jean Cocteau" by Gordon Gow in *Films and Filming* (London), January 1978; "The Mirrors of Life" by Gordon Gow in *Films and Filming* (London), February 1978; films—*Une Melodie, quatre peintres*, documentary by Herbert Seggelke, Koenig-Films (Germany), 1954; *Saint-Blaise-des-Simples*, film by Philippe Joulia and Jacques Kihm set in Chapelle de la Maladrerie at Milly-la-Forêt decorated by Cocteau, Films du Septentrion (France), 1959.

*   *   *

Jean Cocteau's contribution to cinema is as eclectic as one would expect from a man who fulfilled on occasion the roles of poet and novelist, dramatist and graphic artist, and dabbled in such diverse media as ballet and sculpture. As well as directing his own films, Cocteau has also written scripts and dialogue, made acting appearances and realized amateur films. His work in other media has inspired adaptations by a number of filmmakers ranging from Rossellini to Franju and Demy, and he himself has published several collections of eclectic and stimulating thoughts on the film medium. Though he took his first real steps as a filmmaker at the very beginning of the sound era, his period of greatest involvement was in the 1940s, when he contributed to the scripts of a half-dozen films, at times dominating his director, as in *L'Eternel Retour*, at others submitting to the discipline of contributing to another's vision as in his dialogue for Bresson's *Les Dames du Bois de Boulogne*. In addition he directed his own adaptations of such diverse works as the fairy tale *La Belle et la bête*, his own period melodrama *L'Aigle à deux têtes* and his intense domestic drama, *Les Parents terribles*.

But Cocteau's essential work in cinema is contained in just three wholly original films in which he explores his personal myth of the poet as Orpheus: *Le Sang d'un poète, Orphée* and *Le Testament d'Orphée*. Though made over a period of 30 years, these three works have a remarkable unity of inspiration. They are works of fascination in a double sense. They convey Cocteau's fascination with poetry and his own creative processes, and at the same time his openness to all the ways of fascinating an audience by the use of stars and trickery, found material and sheer fantasy. The tone is characterized by a unique mixture of reality and dream and his definition of *Le Sang d'un pòete* as "a realistic documentary of unreal events" can stand for all his finest work. Crucial to the lasting quality of Cocteau's work, which at times seems so light and fragile, is the combination of artistic seriousness and persistent, but unemphatic, self-mockery. For this reason his enclosed universe with its curiously idyllic pre-occupation with death is never oppressive or constricting, allowing the spectator a freedom rare in mainstream cinema of the 1930s and 1940s. In technical terms there is a similar ability to cope with the contributions of totally professional collaborators, while still retaining a disarming air of ingenuousness, which has sometimes been wrongly characterized as amateurism.

Reviled by the Surrealists as a literary poseur in the 1920s and 1930s and distrusted as an amateur in the 1940s, Cocteau has nonetheless produced films of lasting quality. In retrospect he is to be admired for the freedom with which he expressed a wholly personal vision and for his indifference to the given rules of a

certain period of French "quality" filmmaking. He was one of the few French filmmakers of the past to whom the directors of the New Wave could turn for inspiration, and it is totally fitting that Cocteau's farewell to cinema, *Le Testament d'Orphée*, should have been produced by one of the most talented of these newcomers, François Truffaut.

—Roy Armes

COHL, EMILE. French; Born Emile Eugène Jean Louis Courtet in Paris, 4 January 1857. Educated at the Ecole Professionnelle, Pantin, beginning 1864; Ecole Turgot, Paris, ca. 1870. Married Marie Servat, 1879 (separated 1889); child: Andrée; married Suzanne Delpy in 1896; child: André. Career: 1872—apprenticed to jeweler; 1874—jeweler purchases the "Cercle Fantastique" magic theater, Cohl becomes assistant, venture fails; 1875-76—military service; 1877—father finances journal *Ba-ta-clan*, which appears for several issues; 1878—meets and studies with André Gill; 1879—begins career as caricaturist and illustrator for journals; 1881—begins designing for theater and writing comedies; 1884—founds portraiture company "Photographie d'Art"; 1907—begins work at Gaumont on animating his drawings; 1910—leaves Gaumont for Pathé; 1911—makes films combining live action and animation; quarrels with Pathé; 1912—joins Société Française des Films-Eclair, leaves for U.S. begins working at Eclair Film Co. studio, Fort Lee, N.J.; 1913—meets George McManus, author of comic-strip "The Newlyweds and Their Baby" (Baby Snookums); begins *Newlywed* series of cartoons; 1914—returns to France after Eclair American subsidiary sold; 1919-23—makes animated commercials. Died in Paris, 20 January 1938.

Films (as director, scriptwriter and animator): 1908—*Le Mouton enragé* (animator, sc only); *Le Violoniste (l'Agent et le violoniste, Violon et agent)*; *FANTASMAGORIE (Metamorphosis, Black and White)*; *Le Prince azur*; *Le Miracle des roses* (animator, sc only); *La Monnaie de 1.000 F.*; *Blanche comme neige*; *La Vengeance de Riri*; *La Séquestrée*; *La Force de l'enfant*; *Le Veau*; *Le Coffre-fort*; *Et si nous buvions un coup*; *Le Journal animé (Mon Journal)*; *L'Hôtel du silence*; *Le Cauchemar du Fantoche (The Puppet's Nightmare, Living Blackboard)*; *L'Automate*; *Un Drame chez les fantoches (A Love Affair in Toyland, Mystical Love-Making)*; *Les Allumettes animées (Animated Matches)*; *Le Cerceau magique (Magic Hoop)*; *Le Petit Soldat qui devient Dieu*; *Les Freres Boutdebois (Acrobatic Toys, Brothers Wood)*; *N.I. ni-c'est fini*; 1909—*Les Transfigurations*; *Soyons doncs sportifs (A Sportive Puppet)*; *La Valise diplomatique (La Bourse, The Ambassador's Despatch)*; *L'Omelette fantastique (Magic Eggs)*; *Les Beaux-Arts de Jocko (The Automatic Monkey, Jacko the Artist)*; *La Lampe qui file (The Smoking Lamp)*; *Japon de fantaisie (Japanese Magic, A Japanese Fantasy)*; *L'Agent de poche (Pocket Policeman)*; *Les Joyeaux Microbes (The Merry Microbes)*; *Moderne Ecole* (co-d); *Les Gricheux*; *Le Docteur Carnaval*; *L'Eventail animé (Historical Fan, Magic Fan)*; *Clair de lune espagnol (The Man in the Moon, The Moon-Struck Matador)*; *Les Locataires d'à côte (Next Door Neighbors)*; *Les Couronnes (Laurels)*; *Le Linge turbulent* (co-d); *La Bataille d'Austerlitz (The Battle of Austerlitz)*; *Monsieur Clown chez les Lilliputiens*; *Porcelaines tendres (Sevres Porcelain)*; *Les Chapeaux des belles dames*; *L'Armée d'Agenor (L'Ecole du soldat)*; *Génération spontanée (Les Génénerations comiqués, Magic Cartoons)*; *Les Chaus-*

sures matrimoniales; La Lune dans son tablier (Moon for Your Love); Don Quichotte (Don Quixote); Un Coup de Jarnac (Jarnac's Treacherous Blow); Un Chirurgien distrait; Les Lunettes féeriques (X-Ray Glasses); Affaires de coeur (Affairs of Hearts); 1910—*Cadres fleuris (Floral Studies); Le Binettoscope (The Comedy-Graph); Rêves enfantins; En route; Les Chaines; Singeries humaines (The Jolly Whirl); Le Songe d'un garçon de cafe (Le Rêve du garçon de café, The Hasher's Delirium, Cafe Waiter's Dream); Le Champion du jeu à la mode (Solving the Puzzle); Le Mobilier fidèle; Le Petit Chantecler; Les 12 Travaux d'Hercule (Hercules and the Big Stick); Le Tout Petit Faust (The Beautiful Margaret); Le Peintre neo-impressioniste; Les 4 Petits Tailleurs (The 4 Little Tailors); L'Enfance de l'art; Les Beaux Arts mysterieux; Monsieur Stop; Le Placier est tenace; Toto devient anarchiste; Histoire de chapeaux (Headdresses of Different Periods); La Telecouture sans fil; Rien n'est impossible à l'homme; 10 Siècles d'elegance; Monsieur de Crac (Le Baron de Crac, The Wonderful Adventures of Herr Munchhausen); Le Grand Machin et le petit chose; Bonsoirs Russes; Bonsoirs (in 8 languages); Les Chefs d'oeuvres de Bébé; La Musicomanie (last film for Gaumont);* 1911—*Le Retapeur de Cervelles (Brains Repaired); Les Aventures d'un bout de papier; Le Musée des grotesques; Les Bestioles Artistes; Les Fantaisies d'Agenor maltrace; Jobard est demande en mariage; Jobard ne peut pas rire; Jobard a tue sa belle-mere; Jobard change de bonne; Jobard garçon de recettes; Jobard amoureux timide; Jobard portefaix par amour; Jobard ne peut pas voir les femmes travailler; Jobard fiance par interim (Jobard chauffeur); La Vengeance des esprits; La Boite diabolique;* 1912—*Les Exploits de feu-follet; Les Jouets animés (Les Joujoux savants); Les Allumettes fantaisies (Les Allumettes magiques); Les Extraordinaires Exercices de la famille Coeur-de-Bois; Campbell Soups; Les Metamorphoses comiques; Dans la Vallée d'Ossau; Quelle drôle de blanchisserie; Une Poule mouillée qui se sèche; Poulot n'est pas sage; Ramoneur malgré lui; Le Marie a mal aux dents; Le Premier Jour de Vacances de Poulot; Jeunes Gens a marier; Le Prince de galles et fallières; La Marseillaise; Fruits et légumes vivants; Moulai Hafid et Alphonse XIII;* 1912-14 (for Eclair, New York)— Newlywed Series: *When He Wants a Dog He Wants a Dog; Business Must Not Interfere; He Wants What He Wants When He Wants It; Poor Little Chap He Was Only Dreaming; He Loves to Watch the Flight of Time; He Ruins His Family Reputation; He Slept Well; He Was Not Ill, Only Unhappy; It Is Hard To Please Him, But It Is Worth It; He Poses For His Portrait; He Loves To Be Amused; He Likes Things Upside-Down; He Doesn't Care to Be Photographed;* Animated Weekly (The Moving World) series—22 films, 15 to 25 meters long, based on news events of the day; *Bewitched Matches; Clara and Her Mysterious Toys; A Vegetarian's Dream; Unforeseen Metamorphosis; (Exposition de Caricatures);* other titles possibly belonging to Newlywed Series: *(Pick-Me-Up est un sportman); (La Baignoire); (Il aime le bruit); (Carte américaine); (Il joue avec Dodo)* (last U.S. film); 1914—*Le Ouistiti de Toto;* 1915—*Le Voisin trop gourmand;* Eclair Journal Series: 4 films, 10-12 meters long; *La Trompette anti-neurasthenique; Ses Ancêtres; Fantaisies truquées; La Blanchisserie américaine; Fruits et légumes animés; Les Braves Petits Soldats de plomb; Le Terrible Bout de papier; Un Drame sur la planche a chaussures;* 1916—Eclair Journal Series: 32 films, most between 10 and 30 meters and on subjects related to the war; *La Main mystérieuse; Les Exploits de Farfadet; Les Tableaux futuristes et incohérents; Pulcherie et ses meubles; Les Evasions de Bob Walter; Mariage par suggestion; Les Victuailles de Gretchen se revoltent; Figures de cire et têtes de bois; Croquemitaine et Rosalie; Jeux de cartes; La Journée de Flambeau (Flambeau, chien perdu)* (co-an, co-d only); *Flambeau au pays des surprises (Flambeau aux lignes)* (co-an, co-d only); *Les Aventures des Pieds-Nickles* series, numbers 1 through 5; *Les Fiançailles de Flambeau* (an, co-d only); *Les Aventures de Clementine* (an, co-d only); *La Maison du Fantoche (Fantoche cherche un logement); La Campagne de France 1814-(?); Pages d'histoire* numbers 1 and 2; numerous publicity and educational films; 1917—*L'Enlevement de Dejanire Goldebois* (made in 1914); *L'Avenir devoile par les lignes des pieds* (made in 1914); 1922-23—numerous publicity films for Publi-Ciné.

Publications:

On COHL:

Books—*Le Dessin animé—histoire, esthétique, technique* by Lo Duca, Paris 1948; *Emile Cohl and the Origins of the Animated Film,* unpublished doctoral dissertation, by Donald Crafton, Yale University 1977; articles—"Les Premiers dessins animés cinématographiques: Emile Cohl" by Jean Auriol in *La Revue du cinéma* (Paris), January 1930; "En visite chez M. Emile Cohl" by L.R. Dauven in *Pour Vous* (Paris), August 1933; "Emile Cohl (Emile Courtet), créateur du dessin animé sur pellicule cinématographique" by Henry d'Allemagne in *Bulletin de la Société d'Encouragement pour l'Industrie Nationale* (Paris), March/April 1937; "3 Hommes ont inventé le dessin animé—Reynaud, Cohl et Disney" by Marcel Lapierre in *Paris-Soir,* 28 April 1937; "Le Dessin animé revient à ses origines" by André Martin in *Arts* (Paris), 20 August 1958; "Les Beaux-arts mystérieuses—portrait d'Emile Cohl" by Pierre Courtet-Cohl in *Catalogue des 8e Journées Internationales du Cinéma d'Animation,* Annecy 1971; "Les Pionniers français de l'animation" by Raymond Maillet in *Ecran* (Paris), January 1973; "Emile Cohl 1857-1938" by R. Maillet in *Avant-Scène du cinéma* (Paris), 15 June 1978; "Emile Cohl 1857-1938" by Raymond Maillet in *Anthologie du cinéma* vol.10, Paris 1979.

*   *   *

The invention of animated cartoons goes back to the invention of film itself, making it difficult to trace its exact origins. However, one of the first (if not the first) to discover this art form was Emile Cohl. Before he began his career as a film animator (at age 50), Cohl had achieved some fame in France as a newspaper caricaturist and political satirist. With his background as a cartoonist it seemed only natural that he should add movement to his drawings.

Before Cohl's work, both drawn and object animation was used only as a novelty in "trick" films, such as those done by George Méliès and J. Stuart Blackton. Cohl expanded the form so that an entire story could be told using animation. One of Cohl's first films, *Fantasmagorie,* ran only two minutes, but was composed of 700 drawings narrating the adventures of a little clown.

Cohl's animation style is rather surreal and also makes good use of the medium. The cartoons are not formally structured, but the images flow easily from one to another as objects melt into other shapes. For example, an elephant turns into a house or a window changes into a man. These films have had an obvious influence on more modern animated films, such as George Dunning's *Yellow Submarine,* or the pink elephant sequence in Walt Disney's *Dumbo.*

Emile Cohl's films also contain many technical innovations used in later cartoons. For example, *Clair de lune espagnol* uses matte photography to combine animation with live-action. Although it is a "simple" split-screen technique, it is amazing that Cohl registered any synchronization at all between the live and animated halves since these scenes must have been composed in-the-camera.

Emile Cohl was the first animator to have to deal with the pressures of studio production schedules. While at the Gaumont Studios in France he was required to complete a film every two weeks. This time pressure forced him to take several shortcuts. In some cases his animated films were lengthened with live-action footage; at other times he was forced to use cut-out animation. (Cut-out animation uses a single figure with movable limbs in order to save time by not having to re-draw the figure every frame.) Cohl naturally disliked the look of the cut-out animation because of its obviously limited motion. His situation at Gaumont Studios can be compared to television animation today where time and money limits the potential of the animators in favor of more product.

In 1912 Cohl moved to the United States and New Jersey to work for the Eclaire Studios. In America Cohl worked on a number of cartoons known as "The Newlyweds," marking the first time that a continuing set of characters appeared in a cartoon series. Of course, many competitors, such as Krazy Kat and Mickey Mouse, soon followed.

Though Emile Cohl's films were extremely well-received in America (his French films were distributed here by Gaumont), he was, unfortunately, given no credit. The production companies received all the praise and the true artist went unknown. However, the influence which Emile Cohl has had on the shape of the animated cartoon is invaluable as it is the basis for the art form as it exists today.

—Linda Obalil

COMENCINI, LUIGI. Italian. Born in Saló, Brescia, 8 June 1916. Educated in architecture at Politecnico, Milan, 1934-39. Career: mid-1930s—meets Alberto Lattuada; with him and Mario Ferrari, begins private cinema club to view old films; 1937—makes short *La Novelletta*; early 1940s—correspondent for periodical *Tempo* and film critic of *Corrente*; ass't director on several films; after war—becomes editor of *Avanti!*; 1946—documentary *Bambini in città* shown at Venice and Cannes; 1948—invited by Carlo Ponti to Rome to direct; makes 1st feature; 1949—co-founds, with Alberto Lattuada, the Cineteca Italiana film archives, Milan; 1970s—begins directing for TV.

Films (as director of short films): 1937—*La Novelletta*; 1946—*Bambini in città*; 1948—*Il museo dei sogni*; *L'ospedale del delitto*; (as feature director): 1948—*Proibito rubare (Guaglio)* (+co-sc); 1949—*L'imperatore di Capri* (+co-sc); 1951—*Persiane chiuse (Behind Closed Shutters)*; 1952—*La tratta della bianche (Girls Marked Danger)* (+co-sc); *Heidi*; 1953—*Pane, amore e fantasia (Bread, Love and Dreams)* (+co-sc); *La valigia dei sogni* (+co-sc); 1954—*Pane, amore e gelosia (Frisky)* (+co-sc); 1955—*La bella di Roma* (+co-sc); 1956—*La finestra sul Luna Park* (+co-sc); 1957—*Mariti in città* (+co-sc); 1958—*Mogli pericolose* (+co-sc); 1959—*Und das am Montagmorgen* (+co-sc); *La sorprese dell'amore* (+co-sc); 1960—*Tutti a casa (Everybody Go Home!)* (+co-sc); 1961—*A cavallo della tigre* (+co-sc); 1962—*Il commissario*; 1963—*La ragazza di Bube (Bebo's Girl)* (+co-sc); 1964—"Fatebenefratelli" episode of *Tre notti d'amore (3 Nights of Love)* (+co-sc); "Eritrea" episode of *La mia signora* (+co-sc); "Il trattato di eugenetica" [Treatise in Eugenics] episode of *Le bambole (The Dolls)*; *Il compagno Don Camillo*; 1965—*La*

bugiarda (6 Days a Week) (+co-adaptation); 1967—*Incompreso (Vita col figlio)* (+co-sc); 1968—*Italian Secret Service* (+co-sc); 1969—*Senza sapere niente di lei* (+co-sc); *Infanzia, vocazione e prime esperienze di Giacomo Casanova veneziano* (+co-sc); 1970—*I bambini e noi* (for TV); 1971—*Le avventure di Pinocchio* (+co-sc); 1972—*Lo scopone scientifico*; 1974—*Delitto d'amore* (+co-sc); *Mio Dio, come sono caduta in basso!* (+co-sc); *Educazione civica* (short); 1975—*La donna della domenica (The Sunday Woman)*; 1976—2 episodes of *Signore e signori, buonanotte* (co-d); "L'equivoco" episode of *Basta che non si sappia in giro*; "L'ascensore" episode of *Quelle strane occasioni*; 1977—*Il gatto*; 1978—*L'amore in Italia* (for TV); 1979—*L'ingorgo, una storia impossibile* (+co-sc); 1980—*Voltati Eugenio* (+sc); 1982—*Cercasi Gesù*; *Il matrimonio di Caterina* (for TV).

Publications:

By COMENCINI:

Articles—"Entretien avec Luigi Comencini" by N. Zalaffi in *Image et son* (Paris), February 1973; "Entretien avec Luigi Comencini" by A. Cervoni in *Image et son* (Paris), September 1974; "Entretien avec Luigi Comencini" by L. Codelli in *Positif* (Paris), February 1974; "En guise d'autoportrait" in *Positif* (Paris), February 1974; "Luigi Comencini/li captiva", interview, in *Bianco e nero* (Rome), September/December 1975; "Un vrai crime d'amour", interview by J.-A. Gili, in *Ecran* (Paris), January 1975; "L'Idée de la mort" in *Positif* (Paris), December/January 1977/78; interview by E. Decaux and B. Villien in *Cinématographe* (Paris), December 1978; "Les Paradoxes de Luigi Comencini", interview by D. Rabourdin and J. Roy in *Cinéma* (Paris), May and June 1978; "Conversation avec Luigi Comencini" by L. Codelli and "Notes sur l'enquête *L'Amore in Italia*" in *Positif* (Paris), May 1979; "5 cinéastes pour Cannes: entretien avec Luigi Comencini" by J.A. Gili in *Ecran* (Paris), 15 May 1979; "Entrevista con Luigi Comencini" by A. Garcia del Vall and A. Gómez Olea in *Cinema 2002* (Madrid), May 1980; "8 questions à Luigi Comencini" by L. Codelli in *Positif* (Paris), January 1981; "En revoyant les notes de travail d'Eugenio" in *Positif* (Paris), January 1981.

On COMENCINI:

Articles—"Luigi Comencini" by L. Codelli and others in *Positif* (Paris), March 1974; "Comencini et la comédie italienne" by B. Duval in *Téléciné* (Paris), September/October 1974; "Comencini: le rire et les larmes" by A. Tournès in *Jeune cinéma* (Paris), September/October 1974; "Les Aventures de Pinocchio" by S. Champenier in *Image et son* (Paris), no.319bis, 1977; "L'incompris", special Comencini issue, by G. Braucourt and D. Dubois-Jallais in *Avant-Scène du cinéma* (Paris), 1 May 1978; "L'incompris" by B. Duval and others in *Image et son* (Paris), April 1978; "Minorités impudiques" by P. Kane in *Cahiers du cinéma* (Paris), May 1978; "Comencini pontissalien" by R. Lefevre in *Image et son* (Paris), October 1979.

*   *   *

With more than 30 feature films, several TV documentaries and a few shorts, Luigi Comencini's work is considerable, but has only attracted critical attention in the 1970s though he has always enjoyed popular success in his own country. It is this very popularity which has probably worked against his artistic status. Working within traditional genres (comedy, thrillers, melodramas), dependent on his scripts and the whims of producers, Comencini has been accused, together with his contemporaries Mario Monicelli and Dino Risi, of having betrayed the heritage of neorealism by using it as a background adjunct to conventional story-telling.

Squeezed between the great authors (Rossellini, Fellini, Antonioni, Visconti, De Sica, Zavattini) with their obvious stylistic preoccupations and the directors of the Italian renaissance of the early 1960s (Rosi, Olmi, Pasolini, the Tavianis), Comencini has been neglected much like some of his Hollywood colleagues. Starting as a documentary filmmaker, a photographer, a movie critic for the socialist paper *Avanti* and the co-founder of the Italian Film Archives, Comencini has had a checkered career but has finally been recognized particularly in France, as an important artist. His work owes much to the neorealist movement, being firmly grounded in a social context, showing humanitarian preoccupations, and displaying interest in all strata of society. Indeed the director has often found a stimulus for his fiction films by doing special documentary programs for Italian TV, exploring such topics as children or love (*I bambini e noi, L'amore in Italia*).

The enormous success in his early career of a picturesque and charming comedy about a *carabiniere* and a beautiful country girl, *Pane, amore e fantasia* and its sequel *Pane, amore e gelosia*, starring Vittorio De Sica and Gina Lollobrigida, have given a false image of Comencini as a specialist in folksy escapism. Much more revealing is his first film *Proibito rubare* about the relationship between a priest and street kids in post-war Naples. The sentimentality is accompanied by a firm stand on social iniquities. The theme of children proves itself a fruitful one for Comencini, allowing him to oppose innocence and experience and to show the dryness and hypocrisy of the adult world. Some of the best and most personal of his films thus deal with children: *La finestra sul Luna Park*; *Incompreso*, remade in 1983 by Jerry Schatzberg under the same title; *Infanzia, vocazione e prime esperienze di Giacomo Casanova Veneziano* using the first five chapters of Casanova's memoirs to evoke the life of Venice in the 18th century seen through the eyes of a child who later becomes a rake; *Pinocchio*, a masterful adaptation of Collodi's book; and *Voltati Eugenio* in which a young boy severely judges his parents who had themselves been rebellious youths in the 1960s.

Like many Italians, Comencini has turned to World War II as a key experience in his country's history. *Tutti a casa* is one of the best films on this period, an epic comedy about a soldier, Schweik (Alberto Sordi), slowly becoming a resistance fighter. *La ragazze di Bube*, which tells about the love of a country girl (Claudia Cardinale) for a communist partisan who killed a fascist after the war, is also a sensitive portrait of the Mussolini period's aftermath.

Comencini displays a clarity of vision, a satiric sense and a taste for fables and allegories as in *A cavallo della tigre*, *La scopone scientifico*, *L'ingorgo, una storia impossibile* and *Cercasi Gesù*. Comencini thus reveals himself as rational and reformist, but ultimately a sceptic with a philosophy close to that of the Enlightenment. However his ironical tone does not exclude at times an emotional inspiration which leads him to melodramatic subjects set for example in the world of prostitution (*Pagine chiuse*) or factory work (*Delitto d'amore*). Rich in human details, varied in inspiration, and served by some of the best Italian actors, his work deserves the re-evaluation which is underway.

—Michel Ciment

CONNER, BRUCE. American. Born in McPherson, Kansas, 1933. Studied at University of Wichita; University of Nebraska, B.F.A.; further study at Brooklyn Museum Art School, University of Colorado. Career: 1950s to present—active as artist, making assemblage works, sculpture, painting, and drawings; 1957—moves to San Francisco; with Larry Jordan organizes Camera Obscura film society; 1958—first film *A Movie* made to be shown in exhibit of Conner sculpture; through next decade makes about a dozen films in both 8 and 16mm; 1974-75—assembles *Crossroads* from declassified footage of atomic bomb tests. Recipient: Ford Foundation Fellowship Grant, 1964; Copley Foundation Award, 1965; Gold Medal, Sesta Biennale d'Arte Republica Di San Marino, 1967; National Endowment for the Arts Fellowship Grant, 1973; American Film Institute Grant, 1974; Guggenheim Fellowship, 1975; Citation in Film, Brandeis University Creative Awards, 1979.

Films (in 16mm): 1958—*A Movie*; 1960-62—*Cosmic Ray*; 1961-67—*Looking for Mushrooms*; 1963-67—*Report*; 1964—*Leader*; 1964-65—*Vivian*; 1965—*10 Second Film*; 1966—*Breakaway*; 1967—*The White Rose*; *Liberty Crown*; 1969—*Permian Strata*; 1969-73—*Marilyn Times Five*; 1976—*Crossroads*; *Take the 5:10 to Dreamland*; 1977—*Valse Triste*; 1978—*Mongoloid*; 1981—*America Is Waiting*.

Publications:

By CONNER:

Articles—"Interview with Bruce Conner" by Robert Brown in *Film Culture* (New York), no.33, 1964; "Bruce Conner Makes a Sandwich" in *Artforum* (New York), September 1967; "Bruce Conner", discussion with participants of 1968 Flaherty Seminar, in *Film Comment* (New York), winter 1969; "'I Was Obsessed...'" in *Film Library Quarterly* (New York), summer 1969; "Excerpts from an Interview with Bruce Conner Conducted in July of 1971" by R. Haller in *Film Culture* (New York), no.67-69, 1979; "Amos Vogel and Bruce Conner: 2 Views of the Money Crunch" in *Film Comment* (New York), September/October 1981.

On CONNER:

Books—*Experimental Cinema: A 50 Year Evaluation* by David Curtis, New York 1971; *Film: Space Time Light & Sound* by Lincoln Johnson, New York 1974; *Visionary Film* by P. Adams Sitney, New York 1974; *A History of the American Avant-Garde Cinema*, exhibition catalogue, by John Hanhardt and others, The American Federation of Arts, New York 1976; articles—"Report" by David Mosen in *Film Quarterly* (Berkeley), spring 1966; "3 Films by Bruce Conner" by Carl Belz in *Film Culture* (New York), spring 1967; "Bruce Conner and His Films" by Brian O'Doherty in *The New American Cinema* edited by Gregory Battcock, New York 1967; "Bruce Conner" in *Film Comment* (New York), winter 1969; "The Anti-Information Film (Conner's *Report*)" by Ken Kelman in *The Essential Cinema: Essays on the Films in the Collection of Anthology Film Archives* vol.1, New York 1975; "Countdown: Some Thoughts on Bruce Conner" by L. Fischer in *University Film Study Center Newsletter* (Cambridge, Mass.), no.2, 1976; "Bruce Conner's New Films" by Anthony Reveaux in *Artweek* (Oakland), 3 April 1976; "Fallout: Some Notes on the Films of Bruce Conner" by W. Moritz and B. O'Neill in *Film Quarterly* (Berkeley), summer 1978; "Valse Triste and Mongoloid" by Scott Cook in *Millenium Film Journal* (New York), fall/winter, 1980/81;

"Avant-garde Film in the Bay Area: A Romantic Tradition" by Anthony Reveaux in *Pacific Magazine* (San Francisco), March 1981.

*   *   *

After graduating from the University of Nebraska, Bruce Conner moved to San Francisco to begin an exceptionally successful and still very productive career as an experimental filmmaker. Conner's production over the past quarter century manifests certain salient characteristics typical in the works of this genre. His films tend to be brief (the shortest being his 1965 *Ten Second Film*; the longest, his 1975 *Crossroads*, running 36 minutes). Beyond grant subsidy, his production is financially independent, allowing him total freedom in creativity and distribution. And his works are essentially a-collaborative, being in essence solely under Conner's control from conception through all phases of construction. However, since Conner is particularly known for the techno-structural resource of "compilation" (i.e., the use of extant or "found" footage shot by other filmmakers for various purposes), this a-collaborative characteristic deserves special qualification.

While not all of Conner's films manifest compilation (e.g. each of the brief shots that form the hectic, three-minute montage of *Looking for Mushrooms* was the result of Conner's cinematography), compilation is clearly his hallmark and the intrinsic reflexivity of compilation probably accounts for the continued success of Conner's early and later films today. "Reflexivity" is indeed that contemporary preoccupation—both inside and outside the experimental film genre—with grasping and expressing the special materiality that distinguishes film from other forms such as written literature, theatre, music, etc. Since montage or editing has classically been regarded as essential to "film as film," Conner's work can best be experienced as an ongoing exploration of montage's quintessential qualities.

Early works like Conner's *A Movie* or *Cosmic Ray* easily exemplify this thesis. Constructed from bits and pieces of such things as old newsreels, animated cartoons, Hollywood features, war documentaries, academy ("count-down") leader, home movies, and fifties pornography, the actual cinematography is at once very varied and very anonymous. Indeed, such disparate footage is largely cut together with no attempt to disguise or mitigate abrupt changes in tonality, grain, cinematographic style, or subject matter. Conner's clear exhibition of the "joints" of his montage is in contradistinction to more commercial use of library or file footage in fictive features or television news, where such visibility would prove a liability. Instead, Conner always reminds his audience that they are watching "a movie," an artifact whose very essence is bound to the extraordinary power and sometimes subtle imitations of montage.

Conner's earlier works like *Report*, a 1967 review of sounds and images from the day of John F. Kennedy's shocking assassination, tend—stylistically—more to abrupt junctures enhanced by frenzied editing rates. Also the earlier films are marked more by humor and biting ironies. Later compilation pieces such as *Crossroads* (built totally from declassified film records of early atomic bomb tests) manifest much slower pacing and more wistful moods. Comparably, *Take the 5:10 to Dreamland* employs sepia print stock to homogenize tonality, and its bittersweet representation of the past constitutes a distinct, more mature sensibilty than Conner's earlier works. Still, all his production remains remarkably fresh, and remarkably appealing even to popular audiences who might otherwise find experimental production arcane or bizarre. He is doubtless one of the finest American experimental filmmakers working today.

—Edward Small

COPPOLA, FRANCIS FORD. American. Born in Detroit, Michigan, 7 April 1939. Educated at Hofstra College, 1957-60, B.A. 1960; University of California at Los Angeles, 1960-62, Master of Cinema 1968. Married Eleanor Neil in 1963; children: Gian-Carlo, Roman and Sophia. Career: 1962—hired by Roger Corman, works in various capacities including dubbing, sound recording and editing; 1964—hired by Seven Arts as scriptwriter; 1969—founds American Zoetrope production organization in San Francisco; 1971—begins producing activities with *THX 1138* (Lucas); 1972—directs *Private Lives* for American Conservatory Theater, San Francisco, and *The Visit of the Old Lady* for San Francisco Opera Company; forms the Directors Company with Peter Bogdanovich and William Friedkin; 1975—begins work on *Apocalypse Now*; 1980—opens Zoetrope Studio in Hollywood (sold 1982). Recipient: Academy Award, Best Story and Screenplay, with Edmund H. North, for *Patton* (Schaffner), 1970; Academy Award, Best Screenplay, with Mario Puzo, for *The Godfather*, 1972; Director Award, Directors Guild of America, for *The Godfather*, 1972; Academy Award, Best Director, for *The Godfather, Part II*, 1974; Academy Award, Best Screenplay, with Mario Puzo, for *The Godfather, Part II*, 1974. Address: office—American Zoetrope, Sentinal Building, 916 Kearny Street, San Francisco, California 94133.

Films (as director of short sex films): about 1961—*The Peeper*; *The Wide Open Spaces* (*The Peeper* combined with someone else's 'nudie' western); *The Belt Girls and the Playboy* (5 sketches cut into existing West German feature); *Come on Out*; (in capacities as indicated): 1962—*The Magic Voyage of Sinbad* (adaptation of reedited and dubbed version of Alexander Ptushko's *Sadko*, 1952); *Battle Beyond the Sun* (adaptation of reedited and dubbed version of Alexander Kozyr and Mikhail Karyukov's 1960 *Nebo zovet (The Heavens Call)*); *The Premature Burial* (Corman) (ass't to d); *Tower of London* (Corman) (dialogue d); 1963—*Dementia 13* (d, sc); *The Young Racers* (Corman) (sound, 2nd unit ph—uncredited); *The Terror* (Corman) (assoc pr, 2nd unit ph—uncredited); 1966—*This Property is Condemned* (Pollack) (co-sc); *Is Paris Burning? (Paris brûle-t-il?)* (Clément) (co-sc); 1967—*You're a Big Boy Now* (d, sc); *Reflections in a Golden Eye* (sc); 1968—*Finian's Rainbow* (d); 1969—*The Rain People* (d, sc); 1970—*Patton* (Schaffner) (co-sc); 1971—*THX 1138* (Lucas) (exec. pr); 1972—*The Godfather* (d, co-sc); 1973—*American Graffiti* (Lucas) (exec. pr); 1974—*The Conversation* (pr, d, sc); *The Godfather, Part II* (co-pr, d, co-sc); *The Great Gatsby* (Clayton) (sc); 1979—*Apocalypse Now* (pr, d, co-sc); *The Black Stallion* (exec. pr); 1981—*One From the Heart* (pr, d, sc); 1982 *Hammett* (Wenders) (exec. pr); 1983—*The Outsiders* (pr, d, sc); *Rumble Fish* (pr, d, sc).

Publications:

By COPPOLA:

Articles—"The Youth of Francis Ford Coppola", interview by R. Koszarski in *Films in Review* (New York), November 1968; "The Dangerous Age", interview by John Cutts in *Films and Filming* (London), May 1969; "Francis Ford Coppola", interview in *The Film Director as Superstar* by Joseph Gelmis, Garden City, New York 1970; "Francis Ford Coppola on the Director" in *Movie People* edited by Fred Baker, New York 1973; interview by Marjorie Rosen in *Film Comment* (New

York), August 1974; "Conversation avec Francis Ford Coppola" by G. Belloni and L. Codelli in *Positif* (Paris), September 1974; "The Making of *The Conversation*", interview by Brian De Palma in *Filmmakers Newsletter* (Ward Hill, Mass.), May 1974; interview by Max Tessier and J.-A. Gili in *Ecran* (Paris), July 1974; "Playboy Interview: Francis Ford Coppola" by William Murray in *Playboy* (Chicago), July 1975; "Entretien avec Francis Ford Coppola" in *Cahiers du cinéma* (Paris), July/August 1979; "Testimonianze: la storia di *Apocalypse Now*" in *Filmcritica* (Rome), May 1979; "Journey Up the River", interview by G. Marcus, in *Rolling Stone* (New York), 1 November 1979; "Francis Ford Coppola habla de *Apocalypse Now*", interview, in *Cine* (Mexico), March 1980.

On COPPOLA:

Books—*The Godfather Journal* by Ira Zuckerman, New York 1972; *Francis Ford Coppola* by Robert Johnson, Boston 1977; *Notes* by Eleanor Coppola, New York 1979; articles—"A National Anthem" by Joseph Morgenstern in *Newsweek* (New York), 20 February 1967; "Francis Ford Coppola" by J.R. Taylor in *Sight and Sound* (London), winter 1968/69; "Coppola and *The Godfather*" by Stephen Farber in *Sight and Sound* (London), Autumn 1972; "San Francisco's Own American Zoetrope" by Christopher Pearce in *American Cinematographer* (Los Angeles), October 1972; "Francis Ford Coppola" by D. McGillivray in *Focus on Film* (London), autumn 1972; "The Making of the Godfather" in *The Godfather Papers* by Mario Puzo, Greenwich, Connecticut 1973; "Director's Guild Winner: Francis Ford Coppola" by Charles Higham in *Action* (Los Angeles), May/June 1973; "Coppola's Conversation" by A. Madsen in *Sight and Sound* (London), autumn 1973; "The Final Act of a Family Epic" in *Time* (New York), 16 December 1974; "Godfather of the Movies" by Maureen Orth in *Newsweek* (New York), 14 November 1974; "Coppola's Progress" by William Pechter in *Commentary* (New York), July 1974; "Outs" by Jay Cocks in *Take One* (Montreal), December 1974; "Conversation secrète" in *Avant-Scène du cinéma* (Paris), November 1974; "Francis Ford Coppola: A Profile" by Susan Braudy in *Atlantic Monthly* (New York), August 1976; "Zoetrope and Apocalypse Now" by A. Bock in *American Film* (Washington, D.C.), September 1979; "Dossier: Hollywood 79: Francis Ford Coppola" by P. Carcassonne in *Cinématographe* (Paris), March 1979; "Francis Coppola Discusses *Apocalypse Now*" by G.R. Levin in *Millimeter* (New York), October 1979; "Meet Me in Las Vegas" by Mike Bygrave and Joan Goodman in *American Film* (Washington, D.C.), October 1981; "Coppola on the Beat" by P. McGilligan in *Films and Filming* (London), December 1981.

*   *   *

Just as Francis Ford Coppola's *Godfather* films are textbook examples of grand-scale Hollywood productions, equal in scope and majesty to *Gone With the Wind*, so the director is the godfather of all film school-trained moviemakers. He was the first of his generation to work professionally (for Roger Corman), and the first to become financially successful from his art.

Coppola's films may be commercially exploitable sages of epic proportion that garner high box office returns and Oscar nominations while maintaining artistic integrity: *The Godfather, The Godfather, Part II, Acopalypse Now*, or, they may be far more modest productions, with small casts and budgets, that are barely noticed by the public: *The Rain People, The Conversation*. But they are always personal. Although far from accurate as a document of the reality of Vietnam, *Apocalypse Now* is a private version of hell via Joseph Conrad's *Heart of Darkness*.

The Godfather (Coppola's commercial breakthrough, shot while allegedly under constant threat of dismissal by Paramount) and its more cerebral, less violent sequel pay as much attention to characterization and period detail as to the far more exploitable blazing machine guns and glossy production values. *The Rain People*, a strongly directed tale of a pregnant housewife who abandons her husband and picks up a simple-minded football player-hitchhiker, is refreshingly innovative in its attempt at a feminist statement. *The Conversation*, paralleling Watergate though conceived before the event, is the story of an obsessive wiretapper. A disturbing, perceptive essay on privacy, the film is arguably Coppola's masterpiece.

While the director earned his credentials within the industry, winning several Academy Awards, he is still clearly a maverick. In 1969, after Warners' bungled his *Finian's Rainbow* (after the film's completion, the studio decided to blow the film up to 70mm, but ignored the change-in-aspect ratio; as a result, Fred Astaire's feet were eliminated from the final print), he established his own production organization, American Zoetrope. Coppola envisioned the talent making the decisions as well as the movies. However, for the next decade the company was forever in the red, with the filmmaker constantly throwing in his own funds to keep it afloat. He was also involved with the formation of the Directors Company in 1972, to support the creative visions of unknown moviemakers unable to crash the gates of the major studios. Unfortunately, the organization folded after just a trio of production, *The Conversation* and Peter Bogdanovich's *Paper Moon* and *Daisy Miller*.

Unlike many Hollywood filmmakers, Coppola is willing to take risks not only by developing younger or lesser-known directors, but also in the exploration and presentation of his own work. He has, for example, produced the films of others—George Lucas's *American Graffiti* and *THX 1138*, Carroll Ballard's *The Black Stallion*, Wim Wenders's *Hammett*; he has distributed Hans-Jurgen Syberberg's *Our Hitler* in the United States; and he has presented with live orchestral accompaniment the reconstructed version of Abel Gance's *Napoléon*. He has screened his own *Apocalypse Now* at Cannes as a "work-in-progress," and has rented Radio City Music Hall to premiere *One from the Heart* before the public. He will shoot, reshoot, and reshoot again until he gets it right without regard for the budget.

If Coppola's filmography consisted only of the *Godfather* films or *The Conversation*, he would be guaranteed a prominent reference in any dictionary of great filmmakers. Yet, perhaps even more significantly, he is considered an innovator and the leader of an entire generation of filmmakers.

—Rob Edelman

COSTA-GAVRAS, CONSTANTIN. Greek. Born Konstantinos Gavras in Athens, 1933; became citizen of France in 1956. Educated at Sorbonne in comparative literature; studied filmmaking at I.D.H.E.C.. Married Michele Ray, 1968; children: Alexandre and Hélène. Career: about 1950—a leading ballet dancer in Greece; father politically suspect, so denied educational opportunity; 1952—denied visa to emigrate to U.S., settles in Paris; late 1950s—after studies at I.D.H.E.C., becomes assistant to Yves Allégret on *L'Ambitieuse*; also assistant to René Clair, René Clément and Jacques Demy; 1959-64—2nd and then 1st assistant director to René Clair, Henri Verneuil, René Clément, Jacques Demy and others; 1973-74—makes advertisements for Télé-Hachette. Recipient: Best Director,

New York Film Critics, for Z, 1969; Best Director, Cannes Festival, for *Special Section*, 1975.

Films (as director and scriptwriter): 1964—*Compartiment tueurs (The Sleeping Car Murders)*; 1967—*Un Homme de trop (Shock Troops)*; 1969—*Z* (co-sc); 1970—*L'Aveu (The Confession)*; 1972—*Etat de siège (State of Siege)* (co-sc); 1975—*Section speciale (Special Section)* (co-sc); 1979—*Clair de femme*; 1982—*Missing*. Roles: 1977—in *La Vie devant soi (Madame Rosa)*.

Publications:

By COSTA-GAVRAS:

Articles—"Costa-Gavras Talks" by Dan Georgakas and Gary Crowdus in *Take One* (Montreal), July/August 1969; "Costa-Gavras Talks About 'Z'" in *Cinéaste* (New York), winter 1969/70; "Pointing Out the Problems", interview by David Austen in *Films and Filming* (London), June 1970; "On the Scene: Costa-Gavras" in *Playboy* (Chicago), November 1970; "An Interview with Costa-Gavras and Jorge Semprun" in *Film Society Review* (New York), January 1971; "A Conversation with Costa-Gavras" by B. Berman in *Take One* (Montreal), November 1973; "Entretien avec Costa-Gavras et Franco Solinas (Etat de siège)" by R. Grelier in *Image et son* (Paris), April 1973; "A Film Is Like a Match, You Can Make a Big Fire or Nothing at All", interview by H. Kalishman and G. Crowdus in *Cinéaste* (New York), v.6, no.1, 1973; "State of Siege", interview by P. Solinas, in *Cinema* (Beverly Hills), no.34, 1974; "Costa-Gavras: Dossier d'une crise" in *Image et son* (Paris), February 1978; "Constantin Costa-Gavras", interview by F. Guérif and S. Levy-Klein in *Cahiers de la Cinémathèque* (Paris), spring/summer 1978.

On COSTA-GAVRAS:

Book—*State of Siege* by Franco Solinas, with articles and interview of Costa-Gavras, New York 1973; articles—"Agent Provocateur of Films" by M.S. Davis in *The New York Times*, 21 March 1971; "A propos de Costa-Gavras" by D. Sauvaget and others in *Image et son* (Paris), December 1977; "Costa-Gavras Explores the Politics of the Heart" by A. Insdorf in *The New York Times*, 27 May 1979.

*   *   *

The films of Costa-Gavras are exciting, enthralling, superior examples of dramatic moviemaking, but the filmmaker is far from being solely concerned with keeping the viewer in suspense. A Greek exile when he made *Z*, set in the country of his birth, Costa-Gavras is most interested in the motivations and misuses of power: politically, he may be best described as an anti-fascist, a humanist. As such, his films are as overtly political as any above-ground, internationally popular and respected filmmaker in history.

Costa-Gavras' scenarios are based on actual events in which citizens are deprived of human rights, and which expose the hypocrisies of governments to both the left and right of center. In *Z*, Greek pacifist leader Yves Montand is killed by a speeding truck, a death ruled accidental by the police. Journalist Jean-Louis Trintignant's investigation leads to a right-wing reign of terror against witnesses and friends of the deceased, and to revelations of a government scandel. *The Confession* is the story of a Communist bureaucrat (Montand) who is unjustifiably

tortured and coerced into giving false testimony against other guiltless comrades. *State of Siege* is based on the political kidnapping of a United States official in Latin America (Montand); the revolutionaries slowly discover the discreetly hidden function of this "special advisor"—to train native police in the intricacies of torture. In *Special Section*, a quartet of young Frenchmen are tried and condemned by an opportunistic Vichy government for the killing of a German naval officer in occupied Paris. In *Missing*, an idealistic young American writer (John Shea) is arrested, tortured, and killed in a fascist takeover of a Latin American country. His father, salt-of-the-earth businessman Jack Lemmon, first feels it's all a simple misunderstanding. After he realizes that he has been manipulated and lied to by the American embassy, he applies enough pressure and embarrasses enough people so that he can finally bring home the body of his son.

Despite these sobering, decidedly non-commercial storylines, Costa-Gavras has received popular as well as critical success, particularly with *Z* and *Missing*, because the filmmaker does not bore his audience by structuring his films in a manner that will appeal only to intellectuals. Instead, he casts actors who are popular—international stars with box office appeal. Apart from collective message, that fascism and corruption may occur in any society anywhere in the world, Costa-Gavras' films also work as mysteries and thrillers. He has realized that he must first entertain in order to bring his point of view to a wider, more diversified audience, as well as exist and even thrive within the boundaries of motion picture economics in the Western world. As Pauline Kael so aptly noted, *Z* is "something very unusual in European films—a political film with a purpose and, at the same time, a thoroughly commercial film." Costa-Gavras', however, is not without controversy: *State of Siege* caused a furor when it was cancelled for political reasons from the opening program of the American Film Institute theater in Washington.

Not all of Costa-Gavras' features are "political": *The Sleeping Car Murders* is a well-made, atmospheric murder mystery, while *Clair de Femme* is the dreary tale of a widower and a woman scarred by the death of her young daughter. Both, again, star Yves Montand. The filmmaker's most characteristic works, however, do indeed condemn governments that control other governments, or suppress the human rights of the masses.

—Rob Edelman

CRICHTON, CHARLES. British. Born in Wallasey, England, 6 August 1910. Educated at Oundle School; Oxford University. Career: 1931—begins as cutter for London Film Productions; 1935-40—editor on major Korda productions; 1962—begins directing *Birdman of Alcatraz*, quits in dispute over Burt Lancaster's role as de facto producer; mid-1960s—begins directing for British TV; TV series work includes episodes of *The Avengers* and *Danger Man* (1965), *Man in a Suitcase* (1967), *Strange Report* (1969), *Shirley's World* (1971), *The Adventures of Black Beauty* (1972 and 1973), *The Protectors* (1973), and *Space 1999* (1975).

Films (as assistant editor): 1932—*Men of Tomorrow* (Sagan); 1933—*Cash (For Love or Money)* (Z. Korda); *The Private Life of Henry VIII* (A. Korda); *The Girl from Maxim's* (A. Korda); (as editor): 1935—*Sanders of the River* (Z. Korda); *Things to Come* (Menzies) (co-assoc ed); 1937—*Elephant Boy* (Flaherty and Z. Korda); *21 Days (The First and the Last, 21 Days Together)* (Dean); 1938—*Prison without Bars* (Hurst); 1940—*Old Bill and Son* (Dalrymple); *The Thief of Bagdad* (Berger, Powell, Whelan); *Yellow Caesar (The Heel of Italy)* (Cavalcanti); 1941—*The Big Blockade* (Frend) (co-ed); *Guests of Honour* (Pitt); *Young Veteran* (Cavalcanti); *Find, Fix and Strike* (Bennett) (+assoc pr); 1942—*9 Men* (Watt) (+assoc pr); *Greek Testament (The Shrine of Victory)* (Hasse) (assoc pr only); (as director): 1944—*For Those in Peril*; 1945—*Painted Boats (The Girl on the Canal)*; "The Golfing Story" episode of *Dead of Night*; 1946—*Hue and Cry*; 1948—*Against the Wind*; *Another Shore*; 1949—"The Orchestra Conductor" episode of *Train of Events*; 1950—*Dance Hall*; 1951—*The Lavender Hill Mob*; *Hunted (The Stranger in Between)*; 1952—*The Titfield Thunderbolt*; 1953—*The Love Lottery*; 1954—*The Divided Heart*; 1956—*The Man in the Sky (Decision Against Time)*; 1958—*Law and Disorder*; *Floods of Fear* (+sc); 1959—*The Battle of the Sexes*; 1960—*The Boy Who Stole a Million* (+co-sc); 1964—*The Third Secret*; 1965—*He Who Rides a Tiger*; 1968—*Tomorrow's Island* (+sc); 1970—*London—Through My Eyes* (for TV).

Publications:

By CRICHTON:

Article—interview in *Directing Motion Pictures* edited by Terence Marner, New York 1972.

On CRICHTON:

Article—"British Feature Directors" in *Sight and Sound* (London), autumn 1958.

CROMWELL, JOHN; American. Born Elwood Dager in Toledo, Ohio, 23 December 1887. Educated Howe High School, Howe, Indiana, 1901-1905. Married Alice Indahl; Marie Goff; Kay Johnson; Ruth Nelson; son: James. Career: 1906—acting debut in *Dorothy Vernon of Haddon Hall*; 1910—Broadway debut in producer William Brady's *Baby Mine*; 1912—changes name to John Cromwell; 1913—begins directing for Brady with *The Painted Woman*; 1915-19—serves as actor and stage director for the New York Repertory Company; 1917-18—military service; after WWI—works as actor and/or producer on Broadway and for various regional theaters across America; 1928—tours with Edward G. Robinson in gangster play *The Racket*, appears in Los Angeles, is hired by Paramount as dialogue director; 1929—directs 1st film, *Close Harmony*, in collaboration with Edward Sutherland; continues to direct for Paramount until 1933, and begins association with producer David O. Selznick; 1933—after walking off lot of Paramount over directorial dispute, he is hired by RKO as director; 1936—after leaving RKO, he is re-united with O. Selznick, now with his own independent production company, on *Little Lord Fauntleroy*; 1944-45—President of Screen Actors' Guild; 1951—unable to get work in Hollywood, returns to Broadway in role of Henry Fonda's father in *Point of No Return*; 1961—makes last film, independent production in Sweden; early 1960s—with wife joins Tyrone Guthrie Theater, Minneapolis, performing repertory; 1977—resumes film acting career, appearing in Robert Altman's *3 Women* and *A Wedding* (1978); Died in Santa Barbara, California, 26 September 1979.

Films (as director): 1929—*Close Harmony* (co-d); *The Dance of Life* (co-d); *The Mighty*; 1930—*The Street of Chance*; *The*

Texan; *7 Days Leave (Medals)*; *For the Defense*; *Tom Sawyer*; 1931—*Scandal Sheet*; *Unfaithful*; *Vice Squad*; *Rich Man's Folly*; 1932—*The World and the Flesh*; 1933—*Sweepings*; *The Silver Cord*; 1934—*Of Human Bondage*; *The Fountain*; *Jalna*; *I Dream Too Much*; 1936—*Little Lord Fauntleroy; To Mary with Love*; *Banjo on My Knee*; 1937—*The Prisoner of Zenda*; 1938—*Algiers*; 1939—*Made for Each Other*; *In Name Only*; 1940—*Abe Lincoln in Illinois (Spirit of the People)*; *Victory*; 1941—*So Ends Our Night*; 1942—*Son of Fury*; 1944—*Since You Went Away*; 1945—*The Enchanted Cottage*; 1946—*Anna and the King of Siam*; 1947—*Dead Reckoning*; *Night Song*; 1950—*Caged*; 1951—*The Company She Keeps*; *The Racket*; 1958—*The Goddess*; 1959—*The Scavengers*; 1960—*De Sista Stegen (A Matter of Morals)*; Roles: 1929—*Walter Babbing* in *The Dummy* (R. Milton); *Doorkeeper* in *The Dance of Life* (Sutherland-Cromwell); *Mr. Jamieson* in *The Mighty* (Cromwell); 1930—*Imbrie* in *Street of Chance* (Cromwell); 1940—*John Brown* in *Abe Lincoln in Illinois (Spirit of the People)* (Cromwell); 1957—*General Grimshaw* in *Top Secret Affair (Their Secret Affair)* (H.C. Potter); 1977—in *3 Women* (Altman); 1978—as cardinal in *A Wedding* (Altman).

Publications:

By CROMWELL:

Articles—interview by D. Lyons in *Interview* (New York), February 1972; interview by Leonard Maltin in *Action* (Los Angeles), May-June 1973; "Entretien avec John Cromwell" by J.-L. Borget in *Positif* (Paris), March 1979.

On CROMWELL:

Articles—"Some Actors" by E. Reed in *Theatre Arts* (New York), June 1936; article on *The Goddess* by G.D. in *Films in Review* (New York), May 1958; article on *The Goddess* by Derek Prouse in *Sight and Sound* (London), autumn 1958; article on *The Goddess* by Paul Rotha in *Films and Filming* (London), August 1958; "The New Hollywood: Myth and Anti-Myth" by Robert Brustein in *Film Quarterly* (Berkeley), spring 1959; "Likable But Elusive" by Andrew Sarris in *Film Culture* (New York), spring 1963; "The Finest Zenda of Them All" by John Cutts in *Cinema* (Beverly Hills), spring 1968; article by John Cutts in *Films and Filming* (London), March 1971; "John Cromwell" by R. Frey in *Sight and Sound* (London), autumn 1972; "John Cromwell" by Leonard Maltin in *Action* (Los Angeles), May/June 1973; "John Cromwell: Memories of Love, Elegance, and Style" by Kingsley Canham in *The Hollywood Professionals, Vol. 5*, London 1976; "Cromwell, 88, Actor" in *Variety* (New York), 13 October 1976; "John Cromwell ou la mélodie du mélodrame" by J.-P. Bleys in *Cahiers de la Cinémathèque* (Paris), no.28, 1979; obituary in *Image et son* (Paris), 11 October 1979; "Le Cavalier Cromwell" by J. Segond in *Positif* (Paris), March 1979; "Reperes biofilmographiques" by Olivier Eyquem in *Positif* (Paris), March 1979; obituary in *The New York Times*, 28 September 1979; obituary in *Cinéma* (Paris), March 1980.

*   *   *

John Cromwell was a very fine New York actor, and had a distinguished list of credits when he was hired by Paramount in 1928. Talking films were a new medium then, and Cromwell was eminently qualified to direct dialogue. He started in collaboration with Edward Sutherland on *Close Harmony* and *The Dance of Life* (from the play, *Broadway*), and then Paramount promoted him to solo status, on such films as *The Street of Chance* with William Powell, and *The Texan* and *Seven Days Leave*, both with Gary Cooper.

Once established as an ace director, he went over to the new RKO studios where in 1933 he directed such movies as *The Silver Cord* (from Sidney Howard's play), starring Irene Dunne with Joel McCrea; and the adaptation of Maugham's novel *Of Human Bondage* with Leslie Howard and Bette Davis. He met David O. Selznick at this time, and subsequently directed such Selznick films as *Little Lord Fauntleroy*; *The Prisoner of Zenda*; *Made for Each Other*; and *Since You Went Away*.

Meanwhile, he continued as director for such RKO successes as *In Name Only*, with Cary Grant, Carole Lombard, and Kay Francis; and Robert Sherwood's *Abe Lincoln in Illinois* starring Raymond Massey. He also directed Hedy Lamarr's American film debut with Charles Boyer in *Algiers*; *Victory*, from the Joseph Conrad novel; and *So Ends Our Night*, a remarkably tense melodrama of World War, with Fredric March, Margaret Sullavan, Glenn Ford, Frances Dee, and Erich von Stroheim.

In 1944 Harriet Parsons at RKO signed him as director for *The Enchanted Cottage*, a sensitive drama of a plain girl (Dorothy McGuire) and a scarred, crippled war veteran (Robert Young) who begin to see one another as straight and beautiful through the power of love. By this time, Cromwell was a thorough craftsman. He believed in full rehearsals with camera before any shooting took place. "For every day of full rehearsal you give me," he was fond of saying, "I'll knock off a day on the shooting schedule." At RKO they gave him three days for rehearsal, and he obligingly came in three days early. *The Enchanted Cottage* was a tricky assignment; the love story was so sensitive that it could easily slip into sentimentality, but it never did. He treated it realistically, and as he said, "It's the only way to treat a fantasy. It always works."

Cromwell directed Irene Dunne and Rex Harrison in *Anna and the King of Siam*, a film of great pictorial beauty. His best subsequently was a woman's prison story, *Caged* and *The Goddess*, a realistic story about a film star.

Howard Hughes falsely accused Cromwell of being a Communist during the McCarthy era. He said, "I was never anything that suggested a Red, and there never was the slightest evidence with which to accuse me of being one." He was black-listed, however, and the assignments ceased coming his way. He simply returned to the theatre as an actor, and was brilliant as Henry Fonda's father in the stage play of John Marquand's, *Point of No Return*.

—DeWitt Bodeen

CROSLAND, ALAN. American. Born in New York City, 10 August 1894. Married actress Elaine Hammerstein; son: director Alan Crosland, Jr. Career: 1909—begins working as actor and stage manager, and in journalism; 1912—hired by Edison Studios publicity department; 1914-17—directs numerous shorts; 1917—first feature; 1919—serves in U.S. Signal Corps Photographic Section; 1925—joins Warner Bros. directs *Don Juan*, 1st feature with synchronized music; 1927—directs *The Jazz Singer*, 1st talkie. Died in car crash, 1936.

Films (as feature director): 1917—*Kidnapped*; *Chris and the Wonderful Lamp*; *Light in Darkness* (+adapt); *Knights of the Square Table, or The Grail*; *The Little Chevalier*; *Friends, Romans, and Leo* (short); *The Apple-Tree Girl*; *The Story That the Keg Told Me*; 1918—*The Unbeliever*; *The Whirlpool*; 1919—*The Country Cousin*; 1920—*Greater Than Fame*; *Youthful Folly*; *The Flapper*; *Broadway and Home*; *The Point of View*; 1921—*Worlds Apart*; *Is Life Worth Living?*; *Room and Board*; 1922—*Why Announce Your Marriage?* (+co-sc); *Shadows of the Sea*; *The Prophet's Paradise*; *The Face in the Fog*; *Slim Shoulders*; *The Snitching Hour*; 1923—*Enemies of Women*; *Under the Red Robe*; 1924—*3 Weeks (The Romance of a Queen)*; *Miami* (+pr); *Unguarded Women*; *Sinners in Heaven*; 1925—*Contraband*; *Compromise*; *Bobbed Hair*; 1926—*Don Juan*; 1927—*When a Man Loves (His Lady)*; *The Beloved Rogue*; *Old San Francisco*; *The Jazz Singer*; 1928—*Glorious Betsy*; *The Scarlet Lady (The Scarlet Woman)*; 1929—*On with the Show*; *General Crack*; 1930—*The Furies*; *Song of the Flame*; *Viennese Nights*; *Big Boy*; *Captain Thunder*; 1931—*Children of Dreams*; 1932—*The Silver Lining (30 Days)*; *Week Ends Only*; 1933—*Hello Sister*; 1934—*Massacre*; *The Personality Kid*; *Midnight Alibi*; *The Case of the Howling Dog*; 1935—*The White Cockatoo*; *It Happened in New York*; *Mister Dynamite*; *Lady Tubbs (The Gay Lady)*; *King Solomon of Broadway*; *The Great Impersonation*.

Publications:

On CROSLAND:

Articles—sketch by D. Calhoun in *Motion Picture Classic* (Brooklyn), June 1928; "Flicker Veteran" in *Cue* (New York), 20 July 1935.

*   *   *

Alan Crosland's career is almost completely undistinguished. He would deservedly merit no more than a paragraph or two in the most thorough of film encyclopedias if not for his credit as director of the first two sound films, *Don Juan* and *The Jazz Singer*.

Don Juan, with John Barrymore in the title role, is not actually a talking film: there is no dialogue, just synchronized symphonic music paralleling the story. *The Jazz Singer* is mostly silent: Al Jolson sings "Mammy" and recites a few lines ("You ain't heard nothing yet," "Hey, Ma, listen to this") that probably were improvised. This film's smashing success, however, indicated public acceptance of sound in films.

Crosland, who abandoned a budding career as a journalist to become an actor and director, did not instigate either production. Warner Brothers, with Bell Telephone and Western Electric, developed the technology for sound-on-film, called Vitaphone, and the studio assigned this contract director to both. Previously, Crosland had made only a couple of long-forgotten features (*Bobbed Hair*, *Compromise*) for Warners. His selection as director for *Don Juan* and *The Jazz Singer* remains an enigma.

Don Juan is not as outdated as many other swashbucklers and historical spectacles of its day. The film's best-recalled sequence is the climactic duel between Barrymore and villain Montagu Love, which ultimately cannot compare to Errol Flynn and Basil Rathbone's swinging swords in *The Adventures of Robin Hood*. *The Jazz Singer* is not so much a film as a curio, a permanent record of a great entertainer. *Don Juan* is more Barrymore's film than Crosland's; *The Jazz Singer*, of course, belongs only to Jolson. The director's participation in them seems an afterthought, a judgment in no way overly harsh.

Alan Crosland made one more film with Jolson, *Big Boy*, and several with Barrymore including *The Beloved Rogue*, *When a Man Loves*, and *General Crack*. He did direct many of the era's top stars, from Alice Brady to Warren William, and is also credited with *On With the Show*, a clunky musical described in a period press release as "the first all natural color, talking, singing, and dancing picture." Technically, *On With the Show* was hopelessly dated just a couple of years after its release, but it does predate *Forty-Second Street* as the first backstage musical featuring a young, inexperienced girl replacing a star in a Broadway musical comedy.

By the mid-1930s, Crosland was reduced to churning out such programmers as *The Case of the Howling Dog* and *King Solomon of Broadway*.

—Rob Edelman

CRUZE, JAMES. American. Born Jens Cruz Bosen in Five Points, near Ogden, Utah, 27 March 1884. Married actress Marguerite Snow, 1913 (divorced 1924); married actress Betty Compson, 1924 (divorced 1930). Career: 1900—runs away from home to San Francisco; 1900-03—works as fisherman in Alaska to pay for drama school; studies in "Colonel" F. Cooke Caldwell dramatic school; joins Billy Banks Travelling Stock Co. as barker selling snake-bite cure between acts; 1903—organizes own troupe which includes Luke Cosgrove and George Melford; 1906—becomes member of Belasco company, New York; 1906-11—acts in vaudeville and legit theater, New York; 1911—joins Thanhouser Film Company as featured player; 1916—moves to Lasky company; 1918—begins directing; 1921-22—several Fatty Arbuckle films unreleased due to Arbuckle scandal; 1927—begins production company James Cruze Inc., followed by James Cruze Productions Inc. in 1929. Died 3 August 1942.

Films (as director): 1918—*Too Many Millions*; *The Dub*; 1919—*Alias Mike Moran*; *The Roaring Road*; *You're Fired*; *The Love Burglar*; *The Valley of the Giants*; *The Lottery Man*; *An Adventure in Hearts*; *Hawthorne of the U.S.A.*; 1920—*Terror Island*; *Mrs. Temple's Telegram*; *The Sins of St. Anthony*; *What Happened to Jones*; *A Full House*; *Food for Scandal*; *Always Audacious*; *The Charm School*; 1921—*The Dollar-a-Year Man*; *Crazy to Marry*; *Gasoline Gus*; *The Fast Freight (Freight Prepaid, Via Fast Freight)* (unreleased); 1922—*Leap Year (Skirt Shy)* (unreleased); *One Glorious Day*; *Is Matrimony a Failure?*; *The Dictator*; *The Old Homestead*; *30 Days*; 1923—*The Covered Wagon*; *Hollywood*; *Ruggles of Red Gap*; *To the Ladies*; 1924—*The Fighting Coward*; *The Enemy Sex*; *Merton of the Movies*; *The City That Never Sleeps*; *The Garden of Weeds*; 1925—*Waking Up the Town* (+co-story); *The Goose Hangs High*; *Welcome Home*; *Marry Me*; *Beggar on Horseback*; *The Pony Express*; 1926—*Mannequin*; *Old Ironsides (Sons of the Sea)*; *The Waiter from the Ritz* (unreleased?); 1927—*We're All Gamblers*; *The City Gone Wild*; *On to Reno*; 1928—*The Mating Call*; *The Red Mark*; *Excess Baggage* (+pr); 1929—*A Man's Man* (+pr); *The Duke Steps Out* (+pr); *The Great Gabbo*; 1930—*Once a Gentleman*; *She Got What She Wanted*; 1931—*Salvation Nell*; 1932—*Racetrack*; *Washington Merry-Go-Round (Invisible Power)*; "The Condemned Man" episode (or, according to other sources, "The Streetwalker" and "The Old Ladies' Home" episodes) of *If I Had a Million*; 1933—*Sailor Be Good*; *I Cover the Waterfront*; *Mr. Skitch*; 1934—*David Harum*; *Their Big Moment (Afterwards)*; *Helldorado*; 1935—*2 Fisted*; 1936—*Sutter's Gold*; 1937—*The Wrong Road*;

1938—*Prison Nurse*; *Gangs of New York*; *Come On Leathernecks*. Roles: (mostly in short films) 1911—*A Boy of the Revolution*; *The Higher Law* (Nicholls); *She* (Nicholls); 1912—*Dr. Jekyll and Mr. Hyde* (Henderson); *The Arab's Bride* (Nicholls); *On Probation*; *Flying to Fortune*; *For Sale—A Life*; *Into the Desert* (Nicholls); *Rejuvenation*; *Miss Arabella Snaith*; *Love's Miracle*; *Jess* (Nicholls); *The Ring of a Spanish Grandee*; *East Lynne* (Nicholls); *Called Back* (Nicholls); *Whom God Hath Joined* (Nicholls); *Lucile*; *Undine*; *But the Greatest of These Is Charity*; *Put Yourself in His Place*; *Miss Robinson Crusoe*; *When Mercy Tempers Justice*; *The Thunderbolt*; *Cross Your Heart*; *The Other Half*; *A Militant Suffragette*; *The Cry of the Children*; *The Star of Bethlehem*; 1913—*The Dove in the Eagle's Nest* (Marston); *A Poor Relation*; *The Tiniest of Stars*; *When the Studio Burned* (Marston); *Good Morning, Judge*; *Napoleon's Lucky Stone*; *The Idol of the Hour*; *Her Gallant Knights*; *For Her Boy's Sake*; *Cymbeline*; *The Woman Who Did Not Care*; *The Marble Heart*; *Her Sister's Secret*; *The Snare of Fate*; *The Lost Combination*; *Tannhauser*; *Rosie's Revenge*; *The Ward of the King*; *The Message to Headquarters*; *Plot Against the Governor* (Heffron); *A Girl Worth While*; 1914—*Joseph in the Land of Egypt* (Moore); *Frou Frou*; *The Legend of Provence*; *Why Reginald Reformed*; *The Woman Pays*; *Cardinal Richelieu's Ward*; *A Leak in the Foreign Office*; *The Desert Tribesman*; *The Cat's Paw*; *The Million Dollar Mystery* (Hansel) (serial); *A Debut in the Secret Service*; *A Mohammedan Conspiracy*; *From Wash to Washington*; *Zudora (The Zudora Mystery)* (Sullivan) (serial); 1915—*The 20 Million Dollar Mystery* (Hansel) (serial); *The Heart of Princess Mitsari*; *The Patriot and the Spy*; *His Guardian Auto*; *Armstrong's Wife*; 1916—*The Snowbird* (Carewe); 1917—*What Money Can't Buy* (Tellegen); *The Call of the East* (Melford); *Nan of Music Mountain* (Melford); 1918—*Hidden Pearls* (Melford); *Wild Youth* (Melford); *Believe Me Xantippe* (Crisp); *The Source* (Melford); *Under the Top* (Crisp); 1919—*Johnny Get Your Gun* (Crisp).

Publications:

By CRUZE:

Articles—"'Jimmie' Cruze", interview by M. Condon in *Photoplay* (New York), September 1914; interview in *Motion Picture Classic* (Brooklyn), November 1918.

On CRUZE:

Articles—"Cruze, Trail-Breaker" by D. Donnell in *Motion Picture Classic* (Brooklyn), September 1925; "Cruze, Director" by Frank Condon in *Collier's* (New York), 28 March 1936; obituary in the *New York Times*, 5 August 1942; obituary in *Time* (New York), 17 August 1942; "James Cruze" by George Geltzer in *Films in Review* (New York), June/July 1954; "Cruze's Last Efforts", letter from J. Cohen, in *Films in Review* (New York), August/September 1954.

*   *   *

James Cruze was selected in the "Film Daily" annual nationwide poll as one of the top-ten Hollywood directors in 1926 and 1928. During the year in between, he was the highest salaried one, earning an impressive $7,000 a week. Yet, today, Cruze is no more than a footnote in film history, long deceased and long forgotten. His career did survive the advent of sound but, unlike Ford and Lubitsch and others, he did not really thrive. Cruze was far from a great director: even at his peak, his films were awkwardly constructed, unimaginative and even monotonous. But they were extremely popular, and his career is not unworthy of reappraisal.

Cruze began working in Hollywood in front of the camera, playing leads at Pathé and Thanhouser; in the second decade of the century, he was Thanhouser's most popular male star. He first directed Wallace Reid in *Too Many Millions*, then guided the actor through romantic farces and melodramas. He also made Fatty Arbuckle comedies.

Cruze's great contribution to cinema history came in 1923, with *The Covered Wagon*. The film is stagily directed, and plays quite badly today, but it is the first of its kind: a large-scale, larger-than-life western drama of epic proportion, centering on the travails of a wagon train on its way west. Previously, westerns focused mostly on character interaction and drama; while these ingredients are noticably lacking in *The Covered Wagon*, Cruze in this film was the first to open up and explore the possibility of setting them in the wide open spaces of the Southwest. Additionally, the film was responsible for renewing audience interest in westerns, which despite the popularity of Tom Mix and a few others, had been in decline. Cruze later unsuccessfully tried to repeat *The Covered Wagon's* popularity with *The Pony Express*, *Old Ironsides* and, during the 1930s, *Sutter's Gold*, the latter almost bankrupting Universal Pictures.

Cruze also directed two of the early satires detailing the frustrations of hopeful youngsters who trek from small towns to Hollywood in the hope of motion picture stardom: *Hollywood* and *Merton of the Movies*. In 1927, he organized his own independent production-distribution organization, and then made *The Great Gabbo*, one of the earliest talkies. Erich von Stroheim starred in *Gabbo*, the bizarre drama of an egomaniacal, intolerant ventriloquist whose love for a dancer is communicated via the mouth of his dummy. There have subsequently been numerous variations on this theme, most memorably in the Cavalcanti classic, *Dead of Night*, and the atmospheric, underrated 1960s mystery, *Devil Doll*.

Cruze's sound films are not all potboilers. He made *Washington Merry Go Round*, a political drama, the May Robson sequence in *If I Had a Million*, Will Rogers' *David Harum* and a solid drama, *I Cover the Waterfront*. But his star rapidly dimmed and, like so many other silent era personalites, his decline was striking. His last credits before retiring in 1938 were such Republic "B" films as *Prison Nurse*, *Gangs of New York* and *Come On, Leathernecks*.

As the Associated Press reported, on his death in 1942, "James Cruze, former motion picture director and producer, once had a hilltop mansion and a million dollars, but when he died, Aug. 3, his estate was valued at only $1,000."

—Rob Edelman

CUKOR, GEORGE. American. Born George Dewey Cukor in New York, 7 July 1899. Educated at DeWitt Clinton High School, New York. Career: 1918—begins in theater as ass't stage manager for Chicago production of *The Better 'ole*; 1919—stage manager on Broadway for Selwyn, then Shubert Brothers' organizations; 1924-26—manages stock company in Rochester, New York during summers and directs in New York City during theater season; 1926-29—directs in New York for theatrical manager Gilbert Miller; 1929—goes to Hollywood under contract to Paramount; 1930—as co-director assists in adapting stage plays to film; 1932—moves to RKO after legal dispute following removal from *One Hour with You*; directs *A Bill of Divorcement*, 1st of 10 films with Katherine Hepburn; 1939—removed from direction of *Gone with the Wind*; 1943—serves in U.S. Armed forces, makes training film for Signal Corps titled *Resistance and Ohm's Law*; 1947—period of collaboration with writers Ruth Gordon and Garson Kanin; 1955—only return to theatre: directs *The Chalk Garden* up to Boston opening; 1959—takes over direction of *Song Without End* following death of Charles Vidor, asks that Vidor be given sole credit; 1962—begins shooting *Something's Got to Give*, abandoned following Marilyn Monroe's failure to appear on set shortly before her death; 1969—replaces Joseph Strick as director on *Justine*; 1974—associate producer for CBS TV's 2-part broadcast *The Movies*; 1976—directs *The Blue Bird*, 1st Russian-American co-production; Died 24 January 1983. Buried at at Forest Lawn, Glendale, California. Recipient: Best Director Academy Award for *My Fair Lady*, 1964; Directors Guild of America Award for *My Fair Lady*, 1964; honorary Doctor of Fine Arts, University of Southern California, 1968; Best Director Emmy Award for *Love Among the Ruins*, 1975; honorary Doctor of Humane Letters, Loyola University, Chicago, 1976; D.W. Griffith Award, Directors Guild of America, 1981; Golden Lion, Venice Festival, 1982.

Films (as dialogue director): 1929—*River of Romance* (Wallace); (as director): 1930—*Grumpy* (co-d); *The Virtuous Sin* (co-d); *The Royal Family of Broadway* (co-d); *All Quiet on the Western Front* (Milestone) (dialogue director only); 1931—*Tarnished Lady*; *Girls About Town*; 1932—*What Price Hollywood?*; *A Bill of Divorcement*; *Rockabye*; *One Hour With You* (Lubitsch) (co-d, uncredited +dialogue director); *The Animal Kingdom* (co-d, uncredited); 1933—*Our Betters*; *Dinner at 8*; *Little Women*; *David Copperfield (The Personal History, Adventures, Experience, and Observations of David Copperfield, the Younger)*; *No More Ladies* (co-d, uncredited); 1936—*Sylvia Scarlett*; *Romeo and Juliet*; 1937—*Camille*; 1938—*Holiday*; 1939—*Zaza*; *The Women*; *Gone With the Wind* (co-d, uncredited); 1940—*Susan and God*; *The Philadelphia Story*; 1941—*A Woman's Face*; *2-Faced Woman*; 1942—*Her Cardboard Lover*; 1943—*Keeper of the Flame*; 1944—*Gaslight*; *Winged Victory*; 1945—*I'll Be Seeing You* (co-d, uncredited); 1947—*A Double Life*; *Desire Me* (co-d, uncredited); 1949—*Edward My Son*; *Adam's Rib*; 1950—*A Life of Her Own*; *Born Yesterday*; 1951—*The Model and the Marriage Broker*; 1952—*The Marrying Kind*; *Pat and Mike*; 1953—*The Actress*; 1954—*It Should Happen to You*; *A Star is Born*; 1956—*Bhowani Junction*; 1957—*Les Girls*; *Wild is the Wind*; 1958—*Hot Spell* (co-d, uncredited); 1960—*Heller in Pink Tights*; *Let's Make Love*; *Song Without End* (co-d, uncredited); 1962—*The Chapman Report*; 1964—*My Fair Lady*; 1969—*Justine*; 1972—*Travels With My Aunt*; 1975—*Love Among the Ruins* (for TV); 1976—*The Bluebird*; 1979—*The Corn is Green* (for TV); 1981—*Rich and Famous*.

Publications:

By CUKOR:

Articles—"Entretien avec George Cukor" by Eric Rohmer and Jean Domarchi in *Cahiers du Cinéma* (Paris), January 1961; "George Cukor: de Garbo à Marilyn il a instauré le Star-System", interview by Gilbert Guez, in *Cinémonde* (Paris), 1 January 1963; "Conversation with George Cukor" by John Gillett and David Robinson in *Sight and Sound* (London), autumn 1964; "Interview with George Cukor" by Richard Overstreet in

Film Culture (New York), fall 1964/65; interview by Richard Overstreet in *Interviews with Film Directors* edited by Andrew Sarris, New York 1969; interview in *The Celluloid Muse* by Charles Higham and Joel Greenberg, New York 1972; interview by Gene Phillips in *Film Comment* (New York), spring 1972; "Cukor and Cukor" by J. Calendo in *Interview* (New York), December 1973; interview in *The Men Who Made the Movies* by Richard Schickel, New York 1975; "The Director" in *Hollywood Directors: 1914-40* edited by Richard Koszarski, New York 1976; "Surviving", interview by John Taylor in *Sight and Sound* (London), summer 1977; "Dialogue on Film: George Cukor" edited by James Powers in *American Film* (Washington, D.C.), February 1978; "A Conversation with George Cukor" by Beverly Gray in *Performing Arts* (Los Angeles), August 1980; "Carry On, Cukor" by J. McBride and T. McCarthy in *Film Comment* (New York), September/October 1981.

On CUKOR:

Books—*Hommage à George Cukor* by Henri Langlois and others, Paris 1963; *George Cukor* by Jean Domarchi, Paris 1965; *Cukor and Company: The Films of George Cukor and His Collaborators* by Gary Carey, New York 1971; *On Cukor* by Gavin Lambert, New York 1972; *George Cukor* by Carlos Clarens, London 1976; *The Hollywood Professionals*, Cukor entry by Allen Estrin, New York 1980; *George Cukor* by Gene Phillips, Boston 1982; articles—"Cukor and the Kanins" by Penelope Houston in *Sight and Sound* (London), spring 1955; "George Cukor: His Success Directing Women Has Obscured His Other Directorial Virtues" by Romano Tozzi in *Films in Review* (New York), February 1958; "Petit panégyrique d'un grand directeur" by Jean Domarchi in *Cahiers du Cinéma* (Paris), November 1960; "So He Became a Lady's Man" by John Reid in *Films and Filming* (London), August 1960; "Connaissance de George Cukor" by Alain Jomy in *Cinéma 63* (Paris), June 1963; "Retrospective Cukor" issue of *Cahiers du Cinéma* (Paris), February 1964; "On Cukor" by E. Buscombe in *Screen* (London), autumn 1973; "3 cinéastes de la femme" by G. Braucourt and others in *Ecran* (Paris), August/September 1974; "George Cukor ou comment le désir vient aux femmes" by M. Grisolia in *Cinéma* (Paris), February 1974; "George Cukor: The Blue Bird" by J. McBride in *Action* (Los Angeles), November/-December 1975; "George Cukor filmographie commentee" by Claude Beylie and others in *Ecran* (Paris), November 1976; "George Cukor: A Tribute" by A. Friedman in *Cinema* (Beverly Hills), no.35, 1976; "Cukor" by Andrew Sarris in *Film Comment* (New York), March/April 1978; "After Making 9 Films Together, Hepburn Can Practically Direct Cukor" by B. Nightingale in *The New York Times*, 28 January 1979; "Cukor and Hepburn" by Gene Phillips in *American Classic Screen* (Shawnee Mission, Kansas), fall 1979; "George Cukor" by DeWitt Bodeen in *Films in Review* (New York), November 1981; "George Cukor's Loving Marriage to the Movies" by Garson Kanin in *The New York Times*, 30 January 1983; obituary by Peter Flint in *The New York Times*, 26 January 1983.

* * *

George Cukor's films range from classics like Greta Garbo's *Camille*, through his films with Spencer Tracy and Katharine Hepburn such as *Adam's Rib*, to the Judy Garland musical *A Star is Born*. He won an Academy Award as best director (after five nominations) for *My Fair Lady* and an Emmy for directing his first television film, *Love Among the Ruins*, and also received the prestigious D.W. Griffith Award from the Directors' Guild in 1981.

Throughout the years he managed to "weather the changes in public taste and the pressures of the Hollywood studio system without compromising his style, his taste, or his ethical standards," as his honorary degree from Loyola University of Chicago is inscribed. Indeed, Cukor informed each of the stories which he brought to the screen with his affectionately critical view of humanity. In film after film he sought to prod the mass audience to reconsider their cherished illusions in order to gain fresh insights into the problems that confront everyone. Film critics have pointed to his films both entertaining and thought-provoking. "When a director has provided tasteful entertainment of a high order consistently" over a period of half a century, "it is clear that he is much more than a mere entertainer," Andrew Sarris has written; "he is a genuine artist."

Although most of Cukor's films are adaptations of pre-existing novels and plays, the sum total of his motion pictures nevertheless reflects the personal vision of the man who directed them because he has always chosen material that has been consistent with his view of reality. Most often he has explored the conflict between illusion and reality in peoples' lives. The chief characters in his films are frequently actors and actresses; for they, more than anyone, run the risk of allowing the world of illusion with which they are constantly involved to become their reality. This theme is obvious in many of Cukor's best films and appears in some of his earliest work including *The Royal Family of Broadway*, which he co-directed. In it he portrays a family of troupers, based on the Barrymores, who are wedded to their world of fantasy in a way that makes a shambles of their private lives.

The attempt of individuals to reconcile their cherished dreams with the sober realities of life continues in films as superficially different as *Dinner at Eight*, *The Philadelphia Story*, and *A Double Life*. Ronald Colman earned an Academy Award in the latter as an actor who becomes so identified with the parts he plays that, while enacting Othello, he develops a murderous streak of jealousy which eventually destroys him.

While it is true that Cukor was often drawn to stories about show people, his films also suggest that everyone leads a double life that moves between illusion and reality, and everyone must seek to sort out fantasy from fact if they are to cope realistically with their problems—something Cukor's characters frequently fail to do. *Les Girls* is the most explicit of all Cukor's films in treating this theme. Here the same events are told from four different points of view at a libel trial, each version differing markedly from the others. Because Cukor allows each narrator "equal time," he is sympathetic to the way each of them has subconsciously revised their common experiences in a manner that enables him or her to live with the past in the present. As Sarris remarks, Cukor does not imply that people necessarily are liars, but rather that they tell the truth in their own fashion.

Though Cukor must have harbored some degree of affection and sympathy for the world of romantic illusion, for there is always a hint of regret in his films when actuality inevitably asserts itself in the life of one of his dreamers, his movies nonetheless remain firmly rooted in, and committed to, the workaday world of reality.

Although his personal view of life permeates his pictures, Cukor sought to be faithful to the film's original source. "I think you have to follow the original work closely," he commented; "otherwise why make a movie of it in the first place? You can tone down the sentimental parts of the original text, for example; but you really can't change it in any major fashion. When my film of *David Copperfield* came out in 1935, some critics said that the second half wasn't as good as the first half. I replied that the second volume of the novel isn't as good as the first volume, so what can you do? Dickens couldn't straighten the story out either. On the whole, though, *David Copperfield* holds up very well indeed."

Directing his last film, *Rich and Famous*, merited Cukor the distinction of being perhaps the oldest filmmaker ever to direct a major motion picture, and likewise marked him as enjoying the longest continuous career of any director in film or television. Some of the satisfaction which he derived from his long career was grounded in the fact that few directors have commanded such a large portion of the mass audience. "His movies," Richard Schickel has noted, "can be appreciated—no, liked—at one level or another by just about everyone."

For his part, Cukor once reflected that "I look upon every picture that I make as the first one I've ever done—and the last. I love each film I have directed, and I try to make each one as good as I possibly can. Mind you, making movies is no bed of roses. Every day isn't Christmas. It's been a hard life, but also a joyous one."

—Gene D. Phillips

CURTIZ, MICHAEL. Hungarian. Born Mihály Kertész in Budapest, Hungary, 24 December 1888. (Also known as Michael Courtice.). Educated at Markoszy University and Royal Academy of Theater and Art, Budapest. Married actress Lucy Dorraine in 1915 (divorced 1923); Bess Meredyth. Career: 1906-1912—works as stage actor; 1912—enters Hungarian film industry in its infancy, and is credited with directing 1st Hungarian feature film; 1912-14—spends time at Nordisk Studios in Denmark, learning filmmaking techniques; 1914-15—serves in Hungarian infantry in WWI; 1915—is returned to civilian life to serve as newsreel cameraman, but soon returns to directing features; 1917—managing director of Hungarian Phönix Studios; 1918—flees Hungary when Béla Kun's Communist regime nationalizes the film industry; 1918-19—is credited with working in Swedish, then French, then German film industries during this time; 1919-26—directs films for Sascha Films of Austria; 1926—is contracted by Jack Warner to direct films in Hollywood; directs 1st American film, *The 3rd Degree*; 1933—directs industry's 1st all-color horror film, *The Mystery of the Wax Museum*; 1935-early '40s—association with Errol Flynn begins with *Captain Blood*; ends following production dispute. Died 11 April 1962. Recipient: Academy Award, Best Direction for *Casablanca*, 1943.

Films (as Kertész Mihály, director): 1912—*Az utolsó bohém (The Last Bohemian)*; *Ma es holnap (Today and Tomorrow)* (+ro); 1913—*Rablélek (Captive Soul)*; *Hazasodik az uram (My Husband Lies)*; *Atlantis (Blom)* (ass't d only, +ro); 1914—*A hercegnö Pongyolában (Princess Pongyola)*; *Az éjszaka rabjai (Slaves of the Night)* (+ro); *A kölcsönkért csecsemök (Borrowed Babies)*; *Bánk bán*; *A tolonc (The Vagrant)*; *Aranyáso (The Golden Shovel)*; 1915—*Akit ketten szeretnek (Loved By 2)* (+ro); 1916—*Az ezust kecske (The Silver Goat)* (+co-sc); *A medikus (The Apothecary)*; *Doktor ur (The Doctor)*; *Farkas (The Wolf)*; *A fekete szivarvany (The Black Rainbow)*; *Makkhetes (7 of Clubs)*; *Karthauzi (The Carthusian)*; *A Magyarföld ereje (The Strength of the Hungarian Soil)*; 1917—*Arendás zsidó (John, the Tenant)*; *Az ezredes (The Colonel)*; *A föld embere (The Man of the Soil)*; *Halálcsengö (The Death Bell)*; *A kuruzslo (The Charlatan)*; *A Szentjóbi erdö titka (The Secret of St. Job Forest)*; *A senki fia (Nobody's Son)*; *Tavasz a télben (Spring in Wintertime)*; *Zoárd Mester (Master Zoard)*; *Tatárjárás (Invasion)*; *A béke utja (The Road to Peace)*; *A vörös Sámson (The Red Samson)*; *Az utolsó hajnal (The Last Dawn)*; *Egy krajcár története (The Story of a Penny)*; 1918—*Kilencvenkilenc (99)*; *Judás*; *Lulu*; *Az ördög (The Devil)*; *A napraforgós hölgy (The Lady with Sunflowers)*; *Alraune* (co-d); *Vig özvegy (The Merry Widow)* (+sc); *Varázskeringö (Magic Waltz)*; *Lu, a kokott (Lu, the Cocotte)*; *A Wellingtoni rejtély (The Wellington Mystery)*; *Szamárbör (The Donkey Skin)*; *A csunya fiu (The Ugly Boy)*; *A skorpió (The Scorpion)*; 1919—*Jön az öcsem (John the Younger Brother)*; *Liliom* (unfinished); (in Austria, as Michael Kertesz): 1919—*Die Dame mit dem schwarzen Handschuh (The Lady with the Black Glove)*; 1920—*Der Stern von Damaskus*; *Die Dame mit den Sonnenblum* (+sc); *Herzogin Satanella*; *Boccaccio* (+pr); *Die Gottesgeisel*; 1921—*Cherchez la femme*; *Dorothys Bekenntnis (Frau Dorothys Bekenntnis)*; *Wege des Schreckens (Labyrinth des Grauens)*; *Miss Tutti Frutti*; 1922—*Sodom und Gomorrah (Die Legende von Sünde und Strafe): Part I. Die Sünde* (+co-sc); 1923—*Sodom und Gomorrah (Die Legende von Sünde und Strafe): Part II. Die Strafe* (+co-sc); *Samson und Dalila* (co-d); *Der Lawine (Avalanche)*; *Der junge Medardus*; *Namenlos (Der Scharlatan, Der falsche Arzt)*; 1924—*Ein Spiel ums Leben*; *Harun al Raschid*; *Die Slavenkönigin (Moon of Israel)*; 1925—*Celimene, Poupee de Montmartre (Das Spielzeug von Paris, Red Heels)*; 1926—*Der goldene Schmetterling (The Road to Happiness)*; *Fiaker Nr.13 (Einspänner Nr.13)*; (in U.S., as Michael Curtiz): 1926—*The 3rd Degree*; 1927—*A Million Bid*; *Good Time Charley*; *A Desired Woman*; 1928—*Tenderloin*; 1929—*Noah's Ark*; *The Glad Rag Doll*; *Madonna of Avenue A*; *Hearts in Exile*; *The Gamblers*; 1930—*Mammy*; *Under a Texas Moon*; *The Matrimonial Bed (A Matrimonial Problem)*; *Bright Lights*; *A Soldier's Plaything (A Soldier's Pay)*; *River's End*; 1931—*Dämon des Meeres* (German language version of Lloyd Bacon's *Moby Dick*); *God's Gift to Women (Too Many Women)*; *The Mad Genius*; 1932—*The Woman from Monte Carlo*; *Alias the Doctor*; *The Strange Love of Molly Louvain*; *Doctor X*; *Cabin in the Cotton*; 1933—*20,000 Years in Sing Sing*; *The Mystery of the Wax Museum*; *The Keyhole*; *Private Detective 62*; *Goodbye Again*; *The Kennel Murder Case*; *Female*; 1934—*Mandalay*; *British Agent*; *Jimmy the Gent*; *The Key*; 1935—*Black Fury*; *The Case of the Curious Bride*; *Front Page Woman*; *Little Big Shot*; *Captain Blood*; 1936—*The Walking Dead*; *Stolen Holiday*; *Charge of the Light Brigade*; 1937—*Kid Galahad*; *Mountain Justice*; *The Perfect Specimen*; 1938—*Gold is Where You Find It*; *The Adventures of Robin Hood* (co-d); *4 Daughters*; *4's a Crowd*; *Angels with Dirty Faces*; 1939—*Dodge City*; *Sons of Liberty*; *The Private Lives of Elizabeth and Essex*; *4 Wives*; *Daughters Courageous*; 1940—*Virginia City*; *The Sea Hawk*; *Santa Fe Trail*; 1941—*The Sea Wolf*; *Dive Bomber*; 1942—*Captains of the Clouds*; *Yankee Doodle Dandy*; *Casablanca*; 1943—*Mission to Moscow*; *This is the Army*; 1944—*Passage to Marseille*; *Janie*; 1945—*Roughly Speaking*; *Mildred Pierce*; 1946—*Night and Day*; 1947—*Life with Father*; *The Unsuspected*; 1948—*Romance on the High Seas (It's Magic)*; 1949—*My Dream is Yours* (+pr); *Flamingo Road* (+exec pr); *The Lady Takes a Sailor*; 1950—*Young Man with a Horn (Young Man of Music)*; *Bright Leaf*; *Breaking Point*; 1951—*Jim Thorpe—All American (Man of Bronze)*; *Force of Arms*; 1952—*I'll See You in My Dreams*; *The Story of Will Rogers*; 1953 *The Jazz Singer*; *Trouble Along the Way*; 1954—*The Boy from Oklahoma*; *The Egyptian*; *White Christmas*; 1955—*We're No Angels*; 1956—*The Scarlet Hour* (+pr); *The Vagabond King*; *The Best Things in Life Are Free*; 1957—*The Helen Morgan Story (Both Ends of the Candle)*; 1958—*The Proud Rebel*; *King Creole*; 1959—*The Hangman*; *The Man in the Net*; 1960—*The Adventures of Huckleberry Finn*; *A Breath of Scandal (Olympia)*; 1961—*Francis of Assisi*; 1962—*The Comancheros*.

Publications:

By CURTIZ:

Article—"Talent Shortage is Causing 2-Year Production Delay" in *Films and Filming* (London), June 1956.

On CURTIZ:

Book—*Hollywood Without Makeup* by Pete Martin, New York 1948; articles—"Biographical Sketch" in *Time* (New York), 19 August 1940; "Hollywood's Champion Language Assassin" by Pete Martin in the *Saturday Evening Post* (New York), 2 August 1947; "Director Hollywood's Leading Man" by G. Samuels in the *New York Times Magazine*, 26 October 1952; "Likable but Elusive" by Andrew Sarris in *Film Culture* (New York), Spring 1963; "Hitch Your Genre to a Star" by Harris Dienstfrey in *Film Culture* (New York), Fall 1964; "Michael Curtiz" by Jack Edmund Nolan in *Films in Review* (New York), No. 9 1970; "Comparative Anatomy of Folk-Myth Films: *Robin Hood* and *Antonio das Mortes*" by Ernest Callenbach in *Film Quarterly* (Berkeley), Winter 1969-70; "The Way to Make a Future: A Conversation with Glauber Rocha" by Gordon Hitchens and Elliot Stein in *Film Quarterly* (Berkeley), Fall 1970; "Captain Blood" by John Davis in *Velvet Light Trap* (Madison, Wisconsin), June 1971; "Letters" by R. Behlmer and A. Pinto in *Films in Review* (New York), February 1971; "The Tragedy of Mildred Pierce" by John Davis in *Velvet Light Trap* (Madison, Wisconsin), Fall 1972; "*The Unsuspected*" by John Davis in *Velvet Light Trap* (Madison, Wisconsin), Summer 1972; "Michael Curtiz" by Kingsley Canham in *The Hollywood Professionals, Vol. 1*, London 1973; "Michael Curtiz' 20,000 Years in Sing Sing" by J. Shadoian in *Journal of Popular Film* (Bowling Green, Ohio), spring 1973; "When Will They Ever Learn?" by J. Davis in *Velvet Light Trap* (Madison), autumn 1975; "Det stulna paradiset" by T. Manns in *Chaplin* (Stockholm), no.4, 1976.

*   *   *

The films of Michael Curtiz have come to symbolize Warner Brothers Studios of the 1930s and 1940s. Many favorites from that era were directed by this one man: *Captain Blood, The Charge of the Light Brigade, The Sea Hawk, Yankee Doodle Dandy, 20,000 Years in Sing Sing*, and *Mildred Pierce*. He helped guide Bette Davis as her popularity rose in the 1930s, and helped establish Erroll Flynn as the symbol of the swashbuckling hero. James Cagney (*Yankee Doodle Dandy*) and Joan Crawford (*Mildred Pierce*) both won Oscars under Curtiz's direction. His long career and directorial strengths benefited from the constant work available in the studios of the 1930s and 1940s. Most observers note a precipitous decline in the quality of Curtiz's films after World War II.

Surely Curtiz's most famous creation for today's audience is his only Oscar-winning film for Best Director, *Casablanca*. This cult favorite now has achieved a life of its own, making Bogart and Bergman into modern folk heroes. Director Curtiz has been lost in the shuffle. The anti-auteurist argument seems to be that this particular film represents a happy "accident" of the studio system, and its popularity should not be credited to its director. What is lost in this analysis is the fact that *Casablanca* was a major hit of 1943 (finishing among the top grossing films of the year), won three Academy Awards (Best Picture, Director and Screenplay), and earned Curtiz several awards as the year's best director. Critics of the day recognized Curtiz's input. Certainly today we should give proper credit to the director of a film which was popular upon release, continues to be popular today, and

has influenced countless other works.

Curtiz has been difficult for film historians to deal with because of the length and breadth of his career. Usually overlooked is the time he spent in Europe; Curtiz did not begin with Warners until he came to the United States at age 38. His career began in Hungary where he participated in the beginning of the Hungarian film industry, usually receiving credit for directing that country's first feature film. Curtiz remained active until the outbreak of the first World War. After the war, he moved to Vienna where he directed several important films, including the epic *Sodom and Gomorrha*. But this is about all scholars know about this part of this important director's career. Accounts of other activities lead only to contradictions; no reliable list of credits even exists. Sadly, historians have written off the first two decades of Curtiz's career. We know a great deal of the work of other emigrés, such as Fritz Lang and F.W. Murnau, but virtually nothing of Curtiz.

Not unexpectedly there exist several versions of why and how Warner Brothers' contacted Curtiz, and brought him to the United States. Regardless, from 1926 on Curtiz became intertwined with all the innovations of the Warner Brothers' studio. In the mid-1920s he was thrust into Warners' attempts to innovate sound. His *Tenderloin* and *Noah's Ark* were two-part talkies which achieved considerable popularity and millions in box-office revenues. In a key transitional year, 1930, Curtiz directed no less than six Warners' talkies. In that same year Warner Brothers tried to introduce color, but with none of the success associated with the studio's efforts with sound. Curtiz's *Mammy*, one of Jolson's follow-ups to *The Jazz Singer* and *The Singing Fool*, had color sequences. In 1933 he directed the well-regarded all-color horror film, *The Mystery of the Wax Museum*.

Curtiz's record during the transition to sound elevated him to the top echelon of contract directors at Warners. Unlike others, Curtiz seemed not to utilize this success to push for greater freedom and independence, but rather seemed content to take what was assigned, and execute it in a classic style. He produced crisp flowing narratives, seeking efficiency of method. He was a conservative director, adapting, borrowing and ultimately utilizing all the dominant codes of the Hollywood system. Stylistic innovations were left to others. Today critics praise the film noir look of *Mildred Pierce*, but in its day, this film was never thought of as one of the forerunners of that style. Curtiz could do film noir, and then move on to his next two projects, *Night and Day*, the fictionalized life of Cole Porter with Cary Grant, and *Life With Father*, a nostalgic, light family romance starring William Powell and Irene Dunne. Both of these latter features took in a great deal of money, and earned considerable critical praise, once again demonstrating how well Curtiz could operate when called upon by his employer.

If there is a way to get a handle on the enormous output of Curtiz's career, it is through genre analysis. In the early 1930s Curtiz stuck to formula melodramas. His limited participation in the Warners' social realism cycles came with films like *Black Fury* which looked at strikebreaking. Curtiz seemed to hit his stride with the Warners' Errol Flynn pirate cycle of the late 1930s. *Captain Blood* and *The Sea Hawk* stand as symbols to Hollywood's ability to capture the sweep of romantic adventure. Warners also sent director Curtiz and star Flynn to the Old West in *Dodge City*, and *Virginia City*.

In the early 1940s the Warners studio returned to the musical, establishing its niche with the biographical film. Curtiz participated, directing *Yankee Doodle Dandy* (George M. Cohan's life), *This Is the Army* (Irving Berlin), and the aforementioned *Night and Day* (Cole Porter). *Yankee Doodle Dandy* demonstrated how well this European emigré had taken to the United States. Curtiz would continue to deal with Americana in his

1940s films. For example, he touched deep American ideological strains with *Casablanca*, while *Mildred Pierce* examined the dark side of the American family. Feminist critics have noted how this portrait of a strong woman mirrors the freedom women achieved during World War II—a freedom withdrawn after the war when the men, feeling threatened, returned home. The family in *Mildred Pierce* is constructed in an odd, bitter way, contrasting with Curtiz's affectionate portrait in *Life with Father*.

Genre analysis is helpful but in the end still tells us too little of what we want to know about this important director. As critics and historians continue to go through the films, and utilize the records now available at the University of Wisconsin, University of Southern California, and Princeton, more will come to light about Curtiz's participation in the Hollywood studio system. And always, Curtiz's films will live on for the fans with continual re-screenings of *Casablanca*, *Mildred Pierce*, and *The Adventures of Robin Hood*.

—Douglas Gomery

CZINNER, PAUL. Hungarian. Born in Budapest, 1890; became citizen of Great Britain, 1933. Educated in philosophy and literature, Vienna. Married actress Elizabeth Bergner. Career: mid-'teens—works as journalist, writes play and produces several plays; 1919—directs first film in Vienna; 1924—*Nju*, starring Elizabeth Bergner, establishes reputation; 1930—begins directing in England; 1933—emigrates to England following Nazi rise to power; 1940—moves to U.S., produces and directs on Broadway; 1950s—in England develops multi-camera techniques to record opera and ballet performances. Died in 1972.

Films (as director): 1919—*Homo immanis (Der Unmensch)*; 1920—*Inferno*; 1924—*Nju (Husbands or Lovers)* (+sc); 1926—*Der Geiger von Florenz (Impetuous Youth, The Violinist of Florence)* (+sc); *Liebe* (+sc); *Eifersucht* (Grune) (sc only); 1927—*Dona Juana* (+co-sc); 1929—*Fräulein Else* (+sc); 1930—*The Woman He Scorned (The Way of Lost Souls)*; 1931—*Ariane* (+co-sc); *The Loves of Ariane* (+co-sc: English-language version of *Ariane*); 1932—*Der träumende Mund (Dreaming Lips)* (+co-sc); 1934—*Catherine the Great*; 1935—*Escape Me Never*; 1936—*As You Like It*; 1937—*Dreaming Lips* (re-make); 1939—*Stolen Life*; *Der träumende Mund* (von Baky) (sc only); 1955—*Don Giovanni*; 1956—*Kings and Queens* (short); *Salzburg Pilgrimage* (short); 1957—*The Bolshoi Ballet*; 1959—*The Royal Ballet*; 1962—*Der Rosenkavalier*; 1966—*Romeo and Juliet*.

* * *

When one thinks of Paul Czinner, one also must recall Elizabeth Bergner, his actress-wife and constant star. Czinner and Bergner were a creative team for almost a decade before they married and became British citizens in 1933; all of Bergner's films, from *Nju* in 1924 through *Stolen Life* 15 years later, were guided by her husband.

Great and enduring off-screen romances—Tracy and Hepburn most readily come to mind—have produced many a memorable on-screen comedy, drama or, most appropriately, love story. Ironically, such was not the case with Czinner and Bergner. Even the best of their collaborations, though tasteful and conceived to be aesthetically satisfying, remain seriously flawed. *Catherine the Great* is most typical, an extravagant but ponderously slow-moving account of the Russian tsarina whose life was ruined by a planned marriage. *As You Like It*, with Bergner as Rosalind and a wondrously young Laurence Olivier as Orlando, is lesser Shakespeare. *Stolen Life* features Bergner as twins, one of whom replaces the other in the life of the man they both love. The project was handled more successfully by Curtis Bernhardt seven years later in an American version with Bette Davis, though the film does not rank anywhere near the zenith of the Davis filmography. Such is a commentary on the quality of the Czinner-Bergner features.

Czinner was not a hack filmmaker, but a cultured, creative artist. A child prodigy as a violinist, he later wrote plays and produced them, then directed films in Europe and, after the advent of World War II, directed plays in the United States. His skills and artistic vision as a film director, however, were often overwhelmed by opulence, by luxurious settings that could not compensate for a lack of cinematic craftsmanship. Czinner's earlier silent films were said to be effectively moody, his reputation derives from his more familiar talkies.

For almost 20 years, Czinner did not direct a film. Then, for the final decade of his career, he specialized in shooting reproductions of ballets and operas from *Don Giovanni* and *Romeo and Juliet* to *The Bolshoi Ballet*, the last a chronicle of that group's Covent Garden season. All are at best serviceable historical records, in no way cinematic in any sense of the meaning. Though Paul Czinner was a serious filmmaker, effort, unfortunately, does not always result in quality.

—Rob Edelman

D'ARRAST, HARRY D'ABBADIE. American. Born in Argentina, 1897. Educated at Lycée Janson-de-Sailly, Paris; Bradford University, England. Married Eleanor Boardman (former wife of King Vidor), around 1937. Career: WWI—serves in French army, wounded and decorated; after war meets Irish director George Fitzmaurice in Paris, is urged to go to Hollywood; 1922—d'Arrast arrives in Hollywood; Chaplin offers position as technical advisor on *A Woman of Paris*; 1925—assistant on *The Gold Rush*; meets William Randolph Hearst, directs first picture for Hearst's Cosmopolitan Productions, released through MGM; 1927—signs 4-picture contract with Paramount; 1928—quits Paramount for Fox; 1929—makes first sound film *Laughter* for Monta Bell at Paramount (Long Island studio); 1930—assigned to direct *Hallelujah I'm a Bum*, fired by producer Joseph Schenck; 1933—fired by Samuel Goldwyn from *Raffles*; 1934—goes to Spain, makes *It Happened in Spain* on release contract for United Artists; 1935—returns to Hollywood, briefly engaged by Pickford-Lasky Productions; 1937—returns to France; 1940-46—idle in Hollywood; 1946—returns to France. Died 16 March 1968.

Films (as director): 1927—*Service for Ladies*; *A Gentleman of Paris*; *Serenade*; 1928—*The Magnificent Flirt* (+co-sc); *Dry Martini*; 1930—*Raffles* (co-d, uncredited); *Rive gauche* (co-story only: French-language version of Alexander Korda's *Laughter*); *Die Männer um Lucie* (co-story only: German-language version of Korda's *Laughter*); *Lo mejor es reir* (co-story only: Spanish-language version of Korda's *Laughter* directed by Emerich Emo); 1933—*Topaze*; 1934—*It Happened in Spain (The 3-Cornered Hat)* (co-d); *La traviesa molinera (El sombrero de tres picos)* (co-d: Spanish-language version of *It Happened in Spain*); *La Meunière débauchée (Le Tricorne)* (French-language version of *It Happened in Spain*); Note:

according to Herman Weinberg, *Laughter* and *Topaze* are the only existing d'Arrast films.

Publications:

On D'ARRAST:

Book—*Saint Cinema: Selected Writings (1929-1970)* by Herman Weinberg, New York 1970; article—"In Memoriam: H. D'Abbadie D'Arrast, 1897-1968" by Herman Weinberg in *Film Comment* (New York), fall 1969.

* * *

It is almost as if Harry d'Abbadie d'Arrast had never existed. Certainly he occupies no niche at all in the cinema pantheon, where he belongs. Of course, d'Arrast had a short career, hardly spanning seven years, from 1927 to 1934, during which he managed to make eight films. In a quantitative sense, this was, perhaps, not much, though by movie standards it was rather more than is usually the case with stubborn artists up against equally stubborn financial backers.

Qualitatively, however, they were very much indeed, these eight by Harry d'Arrast (as he was popularly known at the time of his florescence)—eight quiet, witty comedies, sometimes edged with satire but always with elegance, made by a civilized gentleman who thought that it was something to dedicate oneself to laughter as Chaplin and Lubitsch did, as René Clair did.

Nor did d'Arrast eschew the niceties of film technique. He cloaked his urbanity in a silken sheen, his photography being so incandescent that it was said he could not photograph even a telephone in close-up without making it a thing of beauty. This is especially true of d'Arrast's quintet of silent films, where the physical aspect of the scenes (as the choice of words in a story by, say, Katherine Mansfield) was a part of what the films were about. A master (I would say, an instinctive one) of pace and cutting, with never a frame too much, he made the slightest gesture count and the human face—most important of all—reflect the joy of living.

His films were comedies of manners done in high comic style—as if the cinema were not a mass medium but a patrician one, an aristocratic and cerebral one. His films were like a string quartet, in which the subtlest effects are obtained in the least ostentatious manner, for an audience that brings to the work its own worldly wisdom, its own capacity for appreciation for what is being done, its own delight in meaningful nuances.

D'Arrast celebrated that most evanescent of virtues—charm. He was a disciple of both Chaplin and Lubitsch, and he was one of that short-lived glittering galaxy that had learned their Lubitsch lesson well and had set forth on their own to emulate the "Sultan of Satire," notably Malcolm St. Clair with whom d'Arrast had much in common.

D'Arrast's first picture, which starred Adolphe Menjou, was *Service for Ladies*, and few directorial debuts have been more auspicious. From a delectable truffle by Ernest Vajda and Benjamin Glazer, d'Arrast had spun a completely winning tale of a *maître d'hôtel*, so expert as a concocter of sauces that he was the confidant of kings and princes, who falls in love with a visiting American debutante and follows her, incognito, to the Swiss Alps.

The second film was *A Gentleman of Paris*, a sort of denatured *Affairs of Anatol* with a harsh touch of *Daybreak*—indeed, if Schnitzler could ever have compromised with Hollywood and lent his talents as a writer to the film capital, the result might have been something like *A Gentleman of Paris*, for though this, too, was a gay and scintillating comedy of a charming roué, eternally "on the make", it also had sombre glints when the "gentleman of Paris" is framed by his valet to appear as a card cheat and is faced with the only honorable way out—a gun. But the Hollywood of 1927 was not the pre-World War I of Vienna, and so an ironic twist at the end preserves the happy ending.

Again Menjou was the star, and again he showed how beautifully he could respond to intelligent direction; while Nicholas Soussanin as the faithful valet—faithful, that is, until he learns that one of his master's light o'loves is his own wife—showed that the director could elicit sterling performances even from his secondary players, as he had elicited the much talked about performance by Lawrence Grant as the Balkan monarch in *Service for Ladies*. His third picture, *Serenade*, was again derived from a gossamer fluff by Ernest Vajda and again starred Menjou, this time as an operetta composer in Vienna.

How often have you seen in the movies someone hailing a taxicab? It is always going in the direction the person wishes it to go. In *The Magnificent Flirt*, the cab is going in the opposite direction and has to make a turn to pick up its passenger. This is such a little detail as to be almost not worth mentioning, save for the fact that even in these minute details, d'Arrast was fresh and original in his approach. This last of his incomparable quartet of silent comedies for Paramount was a dream to watch.

Could d'Arrast keep it up with the advent of the sound film? D'Arrast's old friend, Monta Bell, was in 1929 a producer at Paramount's Long Island Studio. He sent for d'Arrast and asked him to make his first sound film. The result was *Laughter*, a wry comedy about an ex-chorus girl (Nancy Carroll) who marries a millionaire (Frank Morgan) only to find that she prefers one of her erstwhile "bohemian" friends, a struggling composer (Fredric March). Out of the smallest things d'Arrast made a delight; when Nancy Carroll puts out her hands to receive several diamond bracelets from her maid, she places her wrists together with a tired smile as if she were to be handcuffed, for that's what her jeweled bracelets are, handcuffs that keep her tied to her dull millionaire.

In 1933 an opportunity came at RKO to direct John Barrymore in *Topaze*, from the satirical comedy by Marcel Pagnol, in an adaptation by Ben Hecht. In 1934 d'Arrast went to Spain, and with a release contract with United Artists he made *The Three Cornered Hat*, based on the 19th century tale by Pedro de Alarcón that had already served Manuel de Falla so well for the heady and irrepressible ballet he composed in 1919. D'Arrast accomplished hardly a whit less. The film was made in three versions—English, French and Spanish, and it was released as *It Happened in Spain*. It did not do well at the box office.

The New York Times and *Variety* on March 17, 1968 briefly noted d'Arrast's death in Monte Carlo, where he had been living in seclusion for many years. Richard Watts Jr.—he alone of all the critics in America, and one of d'Arrast's early appreciators during the years when Watts was film reviewer of the *New York Herald Tribune*—paid him a tribute in the *New York Post*: "The late Harry d'Arrast was one of the distinguished directors from the great days of the silent cinema."

—Herman Weinberg

DASSIN, JULES. American. Born in Middletown, Connecticut, 12 December 1911. Educated at Morris High School, the Bronx, New York. Married Beatrice Launer, 1933 (divorced

1962); children: Joseph, Richelle and Julie; married Melina Mercouri, 1966. Career: 1936—studies acting in Europe briefly, returns to U.S. and joins Artef Players (Jewish socialist theater collective); late 1930s—joins Communist Party (reportedly left it in 1939); 1939—directs 1st Broadway production, *Medicine Show* (Living Newspaper-type show); 1940—writing for Kate Smith radio show and other radio productions; leaves for Hollywood with RKO contract; "observer" during shooting of Kanin's *They Knew What They Wanted* and Hitchcock's *Mr. and Mrs. Smith*; moves to MGM after 8 months; 1946—leaves MGM, collaborates with producer Mark Hellinger on several films; late 1940s, early 1950s—continues to direct on Broadway: *Joy to the World* and *Magdalena* (1948), and *Two's Company* (1952); 1951—named by Edward Dmytryk and Frank Tuttle in HUAC testimony as member of Hollywood "Communist faction"; 1952—subpoenaed by HUAC, obtains several postponements; 1953—finds self unemployable, leaves for Europe; supports family by writing; 1956—meets Melina Mercouri; with help of her father, Greek member of Parliament, makes *He Who Must Die* in Crete; 1962—directs *Isle of Children* on Broadway; 1967—directs *Illya Darling* (adapted from *Never on Sunday*) on Broadway; 1967—with novelist Irwin Shaw, films documentary *Survival* on 1967 Arab-Israeli war. Recipient: Best Director (co-recipient), Cannes Festival, for *Rififi*, 1955. Agent: Sue Mengers, ICM, Hollywood. Address: 25 Anagnostopoulou St., Athens, Greece.

Films (as director): 1941—*The Tell-Tale Heart* (short); 1942—*Nazi Agent*; *The Affairs of Martha (Once Upon a Thursday)*; *Reunion (Reunion in France, Mademoiselle France)*; 1943—*Young Ideas*; 1944—*The Canterville Ghost*; 1946—*A Letter for Evie*; *2 Smart People*; 1947—*Brute Force*; 1948—*The Naked City*; 1949—*Thieves' Highway*; 1950—*Night and the City*; 1955—*Du Rififi chez les hommes (Rififi)* (+co-sc, ro as jewel thief under pseudonym Perlo Vita); 1958—*Celui qui doit mourir (He Who Must Die)* (+co-sc); 1959—*La legge (La Loi)* (released in U.S. 1960 as *Where the Hot Winds Blow*) (+sc); 1960—*Pote tin kyriaki (Never on Sunday)* (+pr, sc, ro); 1962—*Phaedra* (+pr, co-sc); 1964—*Topkapi* (+pr); 1966—*10:30 P.M. Summer* (+co-pr, sc, bit ro); 1967—*Survival 67* (+co-pr, appearance: documentary); 1968—*Uptight!* (+pr, co-sc); 1971—*La Promesse de l'aube (Promise at Dawn)* (+pr, sc, ro as Ivan Mozhukhin under pseudonym Perlo Vita); 1974—*The Rehearsal* (+sc); 1978—*A Dream of Passion* (+pr, sc); 1979—*Circle of Two*.

Publications:

By DASSIN:

Articles—interview by Claude Chabrol and François Truffaut in *Cahiers du cinéma* (Paris), April and May 1955; interview by Cynthia Grenier in *Sight and Sound* (London), winter 1957/58; interview by George Bluestone in *Film Culture* (New York), February 1958; "I See Dassin Make *The Law*", interview by John Lane in *Films and Filming* (London), September 1958; "Talk with a Movie Maker" in *Newsweek* (New York), 24 October 1960; "Style and Instinct", interview by Gordon Gow in *Films and Filming* (London), February and March 1970; "'A Dream of Passion': An Interview with Jules Dassin" by D. Georgakas and P. Anastasopoulos in *Cinéaste* (New York), fall 1978.

On DASSIN:

Books—*Jules Dassin* by Adelio Ferrero, Parma 1961; *Under-*

world USA by Colin McArthur, London 1972; *The Contemporary Greek Cinema* by Mel Schuster, Metuchen, New Jersey 1979; articles—"Greek Passion" by Hollis Alpert in *Saturday Review* (New York), 20 December 1958; "A Director's Return" by F. Hammel in *Cue* (New York), 10 March 1962; "Jules Dassin: Filmography" by J. Nolan in *Films in Review* (New York), November 1962; biographical note and filmography in *Film Dope* (London), April 1976; "Los vaivenes de Jules Dassin" by M. Martínez Carril in *Cinemateca revista* (Andes), July 1981.

*   *   *

Between the mid-1940s and the late 1950s, Jules Dassin directed some of the better realistic, hard-bitten, fast-paced crime dramas produced in America, before his blacklisting, and Europe. However, while he has made some very impressive films, his career as a whole is lacking in artistic cohesion.

Dassin's films are occasionally innovative: *The Naked City* is one of the first police dramas shot on location, on the streets of New York; *Rififi* is a forerunner of detailed jewelry heist dramas, highlighted by a 35-minute sequence chronicling the break-in, shot without a word of dialogue or note of music; *Never on Sunday*, starring his wife Melina Mercouri as a happy hooker, made the actress an international star, won her an Academy Award nomination and popularized in America the Mediterranean *bouzouki* music. *The Naked City* and *Rififi* are particularly exciting, as well as trend-setting, while *Brute Force* remains a striking, naturalistic prison drama, with Burt Lancaster in one of his most memorable early performances and Hume Cronyn wonderfully despicable as a Hitlerish guard captain. *Thieves' Highway*, also shot on location is a vivid drama of truck driver Richard Conte taking on racketeer Lee J. Cobb. *Topkapi* is a *Rififi* remake, with a delightful touch of comedy.

Many of Dassin's later films, such as *Brute Force* and *Thieves' Highway*, attempt to observe human nature: they focus on the individual fighting his own demons while trying to survive within a chaotic society. For example, in *A Dream of Passion*, an up-dating of Sophocles' *Medea*, an American woman is jailed in Greece for the murder of her three children; *Up Tight*, the filmmaker's first American-made release after the McCarthy hysteria, is a remake of *The Informer* set in a black ghetto. Unfortunately, they are all generally flawed: with the exception of *Never on Sunday* and *Topkapi*, his collaborations with Melina Mercouri (from *He Who Must Die* to *A Dream of Passion*) are disappointing, while *Up Tight* pales beside the original. *Circle of Two*, with teen-ager Tatum O'Neal baring her breasts for aging Richard Burton, had a limited release. Dassin's early triumphs have been obscured by his more recent fiascos, and as a result his critical reputation is now irrevocably tarnished.

The villain in his career is the blacklist, which tragically clipped his wings just as he was starting to fly. Indeed, he could not find work in Europe for five years, as producers felt American distributors would automatically ban any film with his signature. When *Rififi* opened, critics wrote about Dassin as if he were European. The *New York Herald Tribune* reported in 1961, "At one ceremony, when the award to *Rififi* was announced, (Dassin) was called to the dais, and a French flag was raised above him. "It should have been a moment of triumph but I feel awful. They were honoring my work and I'm an American. It should have been the American flag raised in honor." The blacklist thus denied Jules Dassin his roots. In 1958, it was announced that he was planning to adapt James T. Farrell's *Studs Lonigan*, a project that was eventually shelved. It is one more tragedy of the blacklist that Dassin was not allowed to follow up *Brute Force*,

The Naked City and *Thieves' Highway* with *Studs Lonigan.*

—Rob Edelman

DAVES, DELMER. American. Born in San Francisco, 24 July 1904. Educated in civil engineering; law degree, Stanford University. Married actress Mary Lou Lender. Career: 1923—works as prop boy on Cruze's *The Covered Wagon*; 1925—lives for several months in Arizona desert among Hopi and Navajo, renounces law career; with friend Lloyd Nolan joins Pasadena Playhouse; 1927—joins James Cruze production company as property boy; 1929—scriptwriter at Warner Bros., also acts in several films; 1950s—makes series of Westerns beginning with *Broken Arrow*; forms Diamond-D Productions; late 1960s—following retirement lectures frequently on filmmaking. Died 1977.

Films (as scriptwriter): 1929—*So This Is College* (Wood) (co-sc, +ro); 1931—*Shipmates* (Pollard) (co-adapt, co-dialogue, +ro); 1932—*Divorce in the Family* (Riesner) (+ro); 1933—*Clear All Wires* (Hill) (continuity only); 1934—*No More Women* (Rogell) (co-story, co-sc); *Dames* (Enright); *Flirtation Walk* (Borzage); 1935—*Stranded* (Borzage) (co-sc); *Page Miss Glory* (LeRoy) (co-sc); *Shipmates Forever* (Borzage); 1936—*The Petrified Forest* (Mayo) (co-sc); 1937—*The Go Getter* (Berkeley); *Slim* (Enright) (co-sc, uncredited); *The Singing Marine* (Enright); *She Married an Artist* (Gering) (co-sc); 1938—*Professor Beware* (Nugent); 1939—*Love Affair* (McCarey) (co-sc); *$1,000 a Touchdown* (Hogan); 1940—*The Farmer's Daughter* (Hogan) (story); *Safari* (Edward Griffith); *Young America Flies* (Eason) (short); 1941—*The Night of January 16th* (Clemens) (co-sc); *Unexpected Uncle* (Godfrey) (co-sc); 1942—*You Were Never Lovelier* (Seiter) (co-sc); 1943—*Stage Door Canteen* (Borzage); (as director and scriptwriter or co-scriptwriter): 1944—*Destination Tokyo*; *The Very Thought of You*; *Hollywood Canteen*; 1945—*Pride of the Marines* (*Forever in Love, Body and Soul*); 1947—*The Red House*; *Dark Passage*; 1948—*To the Victor* (d only); 1949—*A Kiss in the Dark* (d only); *Task Force*; 1950—*Broken Arrow* (d only); 1951—*Bird of Paradise* (+pr); 1952—*Return of the Texan* (d only); 1953—*Treasure of the Golden Condor*; *Never Let Me Go* (d only); 1954—*Demetrius and the Gladiators* (d only); *Drum Beat* (+pr); 1955—*White Feather* (Webb) (co-sc only); 1956—*Jubal*; *The Last Wagon*; 1957—*3:10 to Yuma* (d only); *An Affair to Remember* (McCarey) (co-sc only: re-make of *Love Affair*, 1939); 1958—*Cowboy* (d only); *Kings Go Forth* (d only); *The Badlanders* (d only); 1959—*The Hanging Tree* (d only); (as producer, director and scriptwriter): 1959—*A Summer Place*; 1961—*Parrish*; *Susan Slade*; 1962—*Rome Adventure* (*Lovers Must Learn*); 1963—*Spencer's Mountain*; 1964—*Youngblood Hawke*; 1965—*The Battle of the Villa Fiorita*. Roles: (as bit player): 1915—*Christmas Memories* (Leonard); 1925—*Zander the Great* (Hill); 1928—*The Night Flyer* (Lang) (+prop man); *3 Sinners* (Lee); *The Red Mark* (Cruze) (+prop man); *Excess Baggage* (Cruze) (+prop man); 1929—*A Man's Man* (Cruze) (+prop man); (as actor): 1929—*The Duke Steps Out* (Cruze) (+tech adv); 1930—*The Bishop Murder Case* (Grinde and Burton); *Good News* (Grinde and McGregor); 1972—appearance in *75 Years of Cinema Museum* (Hershon and Guerra).

Publications:

By DAVES:

Articles—interview by Christopher Wicking in *Screen* (London), July/October 1969.

On DAVES:

Book—*Delmer Daves* by M. Pigenet, IDHEC, Paris 1960; articles—"On the 3:10 to Yuma—Delmer Daves" by Richard Whitehall In *Films and Filming* (London), April and May 1963; "Auteur and Genre: The Westerns of Delmer Daves" by Mike Wallington in *Cinema* (Cambridge), October 1969; "Screenwriters Symposium" in *Film Comment* (New York), winter 1970/71; special Daves issue of *Filmkritik* (Munich), January 1975; obituary by G. Cebe in *Ecran* (Paris), October 1977; obituary by J.-L. Passek in *Cinéma* (Paris), November 1977; "Delmer Daves ou le secreat perdu" by D. Rabourdin in *Cinéma* (Paris), October 1977; "Delmer Daves ou 'la raison du cœur'" by Christian Ledieu in *Etudes cinématographiques* (Paris), no.12-13; film—*The Critic and "3:10 to Yuma"* directed by Hazel Wilkinson, Great Britain 1961.

*   *   *

Delmer Daves is perhaps best remembered for the highly successful youth-oriented movies which he made for Warner Brothers in the late 1950s and early 1960s. *A Summer Place*, the definitive teenage love film, was the most financially successful of these. Yet it is unfair to relegate Daves to the realm of glossy soap opera directors. When analyzed as a whole, the body of his work reveals some fine moments. *Pride of the Marines, Broken Arrow*, and *3:10 to Yuma* are all very different films, yet each is regarded by film historians as a classic.

After an early career in films as an actor, Daves turned to screenwriting in the early 1930s and worked, often in collaboration with others, on a variety of films, the most prominent of which were *The Petrified Forest* and *Love Affair*. When he began directing he continued to write the screenplays for his own films. His directorial debut was *Destination Tokyo*, not a great film but at least a cut above the glut of wartime propaganda movies being made at the time. It was also noteworthy as the only film which Cary Grant ever made with no romance, or even any women in the plot.

Another war film, *Pride of the Marines*, was one of Hollywood's first attempts to dramatize the plight of the returning G.I.'s. On a par with such other celebrated movies as *Bright Victory* and *The Men*, *Pride of the Marines* simply and without over-dramatizing, showed the anxieties and frustrations of war veterans who were wounded both physically and psychologically by their experiences. It also dealt, albeit briefly, with the sociological issue of minority soldiers who would return home to a nation perhaps unaware of the value of their contributions to their country.

Some of Daves's most significant movies were westerns which were both sympathetic to Indians and unglamorizing in their approach to traditional western themes. *Broken Arrow* is often cited as the first film to portray Indians without stereotyping them, even if most of the actors were white. *3:10 to Yuma* was one of the earliest "anti-hero" westerns and is regarded as a classic both in the United States and Europe. *Cowboy* was another atypical western. Although ostensibly a comic western, *Cowboy* was a film which had an underlying anti-macho theme ahead of its time. In the beginning of the film the main characters, played by Glenn Ford and Jack Lemmon, are opposites: Ford a traditional "he-man" cowboy, and Lemmon a tender foot. By the end of the film both characters become aware of the opposite sides of their own natures. At least a decade before the theme became popular, *Cowboy* showed that men's hard and soft sides could co-exist and could make entertaining subject matter for a motion picture.

Daves' final film, *The Battle of Villa Fiorita*, is regarded by most critics as a run-of-the-mill soap opera, yet even that shows his ability to build a film around an important social theme before it became popular. In its story, which like *Cowboy* begins like a comedy and gradually becomes a drama, Daves's characters are part of the currently popular social issue of divorce, re-marriage (or in this case co-habitation), and the rearing of step children. In this film, like *A Summer Place* and his other well known "soap operas" Daves's writing and direction make the work much better than its subject matter would suggest. Like his contemporary Douglas Sirk, who has had criticisms of his own films similar to those directed at Daves, his films are actually more meaningful than general critical opinion would seem to indicate.

—Patricia King Hanson

DE ANTONIO, EMILE. American. Born in Scranton, Pennsylvania, 1920. Educated at Harvard; graduate work at Columbia University. Career: military service in WW II; after war—teaches philosophy at College of William and Mary, City University of New York; works as longshoreman, editor; late 1950s—produces concerts of Merce Cunningham and John Cage; befriends major figures in New York art world including Rauschenberg, Stella; 1958—forms G-String Productions to distribute *Pull My Daisy* (Robert Frank and Alfred Leslie); 1961—begins making compilation documentaries with *Point of Order* on Army-McCarthy hearings; 1976—co-directs, with Haskell Wexler, *Underground* on fugitive Weather Underground members; FBI tries to subpoena film and crew.

Films: 1961—*Sunday* (Drasin) (pr only); (as director and producer): 1963—*Point of Order* (co-pr); 1965—*That's Where the Action Is* (for TV); 1966—*Rush to Judgment* (co-pr); 1968—*In the Year of the Pig*; 1969—*America Is Hard to See* (co-pr); 1971—*Millhouse: A White House Comedy (Millhouse: A White Comedy)*; 1972—*Painters Painting*; 1976—*Underground* (co-d); 1982—*In the King of Prussia*; Role: 1965—*Drunk* (Warhol).

Publications:

By DE ANTONIO:

Articles—interview by Jonas Mekas in the *Village Voice* (New York), 13 November 1969; "Radical Scavenging: An Interview with Emile de Antonio" by Bernard Weiner in *Film Quarterly* (Berkeley), fall 1971; "Brève rencontre avec Emile de Antonio" by M. Martin in *Ecran* (Paris), April 1972; interview by G. O'Brien in *Inter/View* (New York), February 1972; interview by P. Séry in *Cinéma* (Paris), April 1972; "Herausforderung durch ein Festival", interview by H. Schröder and H. Schmidt in *Film und Fernsehen* (Berlin), February 1974; "Rencontre avec Emile de Antonio" by L. Marcorelles in *Cahiers du cinéma* (Paris), December 1976; "Débat à Lincoln après la projection de 'Under-

ground'" in *Positif* (Paris), December/January 1977/78; "Filmer de que ne montre pas l'histoire 'officielle'", interview by M. Euvrard, in *Cinéma Quebec* (Montreal), v.5, no.19, 1977; interview by A. Rosenthal in *Film Quarterly* (Berkeley), fall 1978.

On DE ANTONIO:

Articles—"Background of Point of Order" by David Bazelon in *Film Comment* (New York), winter 1964; "Some Out-Takes from Radical Film Making: Emile de Antonio" by Colin Westerbeck Jr. in *Sight and Sound* (London), summer 1970; "Definizione de spazio" by M. Bacigalupo in *Filmcritica* (Rome), January 1972; "Political Filmmaking: Feds Harrass Film Crew" by J. Hess in *Jump Cut* (Berkeley), September 1975; interview in *Cineaste* (New York), v.12, no.2, 1982; "De Antonio's Day in Court" by Susan Linfield in *Village Voice* (New York), 8 February 1983.

DEARDEN, BASIL. British. Born Basil Dear in Westcliffe-on-Sea, 1 January 1911. Married actress Melissa Stribling, 1947; 2 sons. Career: late 1920s—acts in repertory, tours U.S. with Ben Greet Company; 1931-36—general stage manager for Basil Dean, sometimes working on Dean's films; changes name to avoid confusion with that of Dean; 1936-40—production manager, associate producer and scriptwriter at Ealing studios; 1941-43—co-directs several Will Hay comedies with Hay; 1943—begins collaboration with designer Michael Relph on first solo directing effort *The Bells Go Down*; 1949-71—works with Michael Relph as producer and designer beginning with *The Blue Lamp*; mid-1960s—television directing including episodes of *The Persuaders*. Died in auto accident, 23 March 1971. Recipient: British Film Academy Award, with Michael Relph, for *The Blue Lamp*, 1950; British Film Academy Award, with Michael Relph, for *Sapphire*, 1960.

Films (as assistant director): 1938—*It's in the Air* (Kimmins); *Penny Paradise* (Reed); *This Man Is News* (MacDonald) (co-sc only); 1939—*Come On, George!* (Kimmins); 1940—*Let George Do It* (Varnel) (co-sc only); *Spare a Copper* (Carstairs) (assoc pr only); 1941—*Young Veteran* (Cavalcanti); (as director): 1941—*The Black Sheep of Whitehall* (co-d); *Turned Out Nice Again* (Varnel) (assoc pr only); 1942—*The Goose Steps Out* (co-d); 1943—*The Bells Go Down*; *My Learned Friend* (co-d); 1944—*The Halfway House*; *They Came to a City*; 1945—"The Hearse Driver" episode and linking story of *Dead of Night*; 1946—*The Captive Heart*; 1947—*Frieda*; 1948—*Saraband for Dead Lovers (Saraband)*; 1949—"The Actor" and "The Prisoner of War" episodes of *Train of Events* (+co-sc—Michael Relph producer); *The Blue Lamp*; 1950—*Cage of Gold*; *Pool of London*; (as co-producer and co-director with Michael Relph): 1951—*I Believe in You* (+co-sc); 1952—*The Gentle Gunman*; 1953—*The Square Ring*; 1954—*The Rainbow Jacket*; *Out of the Clouds*; 1955—*The Ship That Died of Shame (P.T. Raiders)* (+co-sc); *Who Done It?*; 1956—*The Green Man* (Day) (supervisor only, uncredited); (as director): 1957—*The Smallest Show on Earth*; *Davy* (Relph) (pr only); 1958—*Violent Playground*; *Rockets Galore (Mad Little Island)* (Relph) (pr only); 1959—*Sapphire*; *The League of Gentlemen*; *Desert Mice* (Relph) (pr only); 1960—*Man in the Moon*; *The Secret Partner*; 1961—*Victim*; *All Night Long* (co-d, +co-pr with Relph); 1962—*Life for Ruth (Walk in the Shadow)*; 1963—*The Mind Benders*; *A Place to Go*; 1964—*Woman of Straw*; *Masquerade*; 1966—*Khartoum*; 1968—

Only When I Larf; The Assassination Bureau; 1970—*The Man Who Haunted Himself* (+co-sc).

Publication:

On DEARDEN:

Article—"Dearden and Relph: 2 on a Tandem" in *Films and Filming* (London), July 1966.

*   *   *

Basil Dearden is, par excellence, the journeyman-director of British cinema, standing in much the same relation to Ealing (the studio for which he directed the greater part of his output) as, say, Michael Curtiz did to Warner Brothers. More than any other director, Dearden personified the spirit of Ealing films: concerned, conscientious, socially aware, but hampered by a certain innately British caution. Dearden was the complete professional, unfailingly competent and meticulous; his films were never less than thoroughly well-constructed, and he enjoyed a reputation in the industry for total reliability, invariably bringing in assignments on schedule and under budget.

Such careful craftsmanship, though, should not be equated with dullness. Dearden's films may often have been safe, but they were rarely dull (despite the allegations of some critics). His work shows a natural flair for pace and effective action: narrative lines are clear and uncluttered, and although in many ways they have dated, his films remain eminently watchable and entertaining. In the moral climate of the time, too, his choice of subjects showed considerable boldness. Dearden tackled such edgy topics as race (*Sapphire*), homosexuality (*Victim*), sectarian bigotry (*Life for Ruth*), and post-war anti-German prejudice (*Frieda*), always arguing for tolerance and understanding. It was perhaps inevitable, given his background and the ethos of the studio, that these "social problem" movies tended towards overly reasonable solutions. "Dearden's films," Charles Barr has pointed out in his definitive study *Ealing Studios*, "insistently *generalize* their moral lessons."

For most of his directing career Dearden worked closely with Michael Relph, who produced nearly all his films, collaborated with him on the scripts, and occasionally co-directed; after the demise of Ealing, the two men formed their own production company. Their joint output covered a wide variety of genre, including costume drama (*Saraband for Dead Lovers*) and comedy (*The Smallest Show on Earth*), as well as large scale epic (*Khartoum*). Dearden's flair for action was effectively exploited in the classic "heist" movie, *The League of Gentlemen*, and in *The Blue Lamp*, a seminal police drama and one of the first Ealing films shot almost entirely on location. Early in his career, Dearden also evinced a weakness for slightly stagey allegories such as *Halfway House*, and *They Came To A City*, in which groups of disparate individuals are brought to a change of heart through supernatural intervention.

There can also be detected in Dearden's films, perhaps slightly unexpectedly, a muted but poetic vision of an idealized community—seen most clearly in his first film with Relph, *The Captive Heart*, a sympathetic study of prisoners-of-war. "The community" Charles Barr has noted "is presented as part of a wider society involving all of us—and encompassing England." In his strengths and in his weaknesses—the restraint verging on inhibition, the competent versatility tending towards lack of directorial character—Dearden was in many ways an archetypally "British" director. Anyone wishing to understand the suc-

cess and limitations of post-war British cinema, and indeed of post-war British society, could do far worse than study the films of Basil Dearden.

—Theresa FitzGerald

———

DE FUENTES, FERNANDO. Mexican. Born in Veracruz, 1894. Career: 1920s—works in theater and as manager of cinema (Olympia); serves for several years as film editor and assistant director; 1932—becomes 1st Mexican offered opportunity to direct by Compañia Nacional Productora de Películas; 1942—creation of Grovas production company for which De Fuentes will produce and direct; 1945—forms Diana Films with other Mexican directors and producers; 1954—ceases film activity. Died 1958.

Films (as director): 1932—*El anónimo;* 1933—*El prisionero trece; La calandria; El tigre de Yautepec; El compadre Mendoza;* 1934—*El fantasma del convento; Cruz diablo;* 1935—*Vámonos con Pancho Villa; La familia Dressel;* 1936—*Las mujeres mandan; Allá en el rancho grande;* 1937—*Bajo el cielo de México; La Zandunga;* 1938—*La casa del ogro;* 1939—*Papacito lindo;* 1940—*Allá en el trópico; El jefe máximo; Creo en Dios;* 1941—*La gallina clueca;* 1942—*Así se quiere en Jalisco;* 1943—*Doña Barbara; La mujer sin alma;* 1944—*El rey se divierte;* 1945—*Hasta que perdió Jalisco; La selva de fuego;* 1946—*La devoradora;* 1948—*Allá en el Rancho Grande; Jalisco canta en Sevilla;* 1949—*Hipólito el de Santa;* 1950—*Por la puerta falsa; Crimen y castigo;* 1952—*Los hijos de María Morales; Canción de cuna;* 1953—*Tres citas con el destino.*

Publications:

On DE FUENTES:

Books—*Historia documental del cine mexicano,* vol.1-6, by Emilio García Riera, Mexico City 1969/74; *La aventura del cine mexicano* by Jorge Ayala Blanco, Mexico City 1979; *Mexican Cinema: Reflections of a Society, 1896-1980* by Carl Mora, Berkeley 1982.

*   *   *

The first Mexican cineaste of note, Fernando De Fuentes is still considered the director whose interpretations of the revolution and whose contributions to typical Mexican genres have not been surpassed. Early sound film production in Mexico was dominated by foreigners: Russians who accompanied Eisenstein in the making of *Que Viva México,* Spaniards who passed through Hollywood, Cubans and U.S. citizens who somehow ended up there. De Fuentes was one of the first Mexicans to be given a chance to direct sound films in his country.

After several false starts with "grey and theatrical melodramas," De Fuentes indicated first in *Prisionero trece* that his métier was the "revolutionary tragedy." During 1910-17, Mexico passed through a cataclysmic social revolution whose cultural expression resounded principally in the extraordinary murals of Diego Rivera, David Siqueiros, and José Orozco. Fiction films did not examine this watershed event seriously until 1933 when

De Fuentes made *El compadre Mendoza*. Far from the epic monumentality of revolutionary transformation painted on the walls by Rivera or Siquieros, *El compadre Mendoza* recreates the revolution from a perspective similar to Orozco's vision of individual tragedies and private pain.

Rosalio Mendoza is the owner of a large hacienda which is constantly threatened by the conflict's warring factions. In order to appease them, Mendoza pretends to support whichever group is currently visiting him—something he accomplishes by wining and dining his guests in a room conspicuously decorated with a portrait of the appropriate leader. Eventually, Mendoza and General Nieto (a follower of Emiliano Zapata's agrarian revolt) become close friends. Mendoza names his son after Nieto and asks him to be the *compadre* (godfather). But after Mendoza is ruined economically, he betrays Nieto in order to flee to Mexico City. The emphasis on fraternal bloodletting, the corruption of ideals, and the disillusion in the aftermath of the revolution is powerfully conveyed in both *El compadre Mendoza* and *Vámonos con Pancho Villa*. They remain even today the best cinematic treatments of the Mexican revolution.

De Fuentes's work in traditional Mexican genres is also important. *Allá en el Rancho Grande* is the progenitor of the *charro* genre, the Mexican singing cowboy having received his widespread cinematic introduction to Mexico and the rest of Latin America in this immensely popular film. The attraction of such nostalgia for a never-existent Arcadia can be seen in the fact that the year following the release of *Rancho Grande* more than half of the Mexican films produced were similar pastoral fantasies, and these have continued to be a staple of Mexican cinema. The *charro* genre's domination of Mexican cinema is almost matched by films about the Mexican mother. De Fuentes directed perhaps the most palatable of such works, *La gallina clueca* starring Sara García, the character actress who is the national paradigm of the sainted, long-suffering, self-sacrificing mother. In De Fuentes's hands the overworked Oedipal melodrama is denied its usual histrionics and becomes an interesting work as well as the definitive film of this sub-genre.

His better films demonstrate De Fuentes's strong narrative style, noted for its consistency and humor. They do not seem particularly dated, and De Fuentes utilizes visual techniques such as the rack focus or the dissolve particularly effectively and unobtrusively. He also makes telling use of overlay montages, à la Eisenstein or Vertov, to convey moods or concepts. In regard to singing—one of the banes of Mexican cinema—De Fuentes has been uneven. For example, in the 2 films on the revolution, restraint is shown and songs function well in relation to the story line. Unfortunately, *Allá en el Rancho Grande* and its various sequels are characteristically glutted with songs.

De Fuentes's career as a director went from the sublime to the ridiculous. In one year he plummeted from the heights of *Vámonos con Pancho Villa* to the depths of *Allá en el Rancho Grande*, whose enormous commercial success throughout Latin America sealed De Fuentes's fate. It was popular because De Fuentes is a talented director; but the commercial rewards for those talents came at a high price. After *Vámonos con Pancho Villa*, De Fuentes settled into the repetition of mediocre and conventional formula films.

—John Mraz

DELANNOY, JEAN. French. Born in in Noisy-le-Sec, 8 August 1908. Educated at Lille University; studied literature at Paris University. Career: late 1920s—begins acting in film while studying at Paris University (sister is silent film actress Henriette Delannoy); 1930-32—in Service Cinématographique des Armées; then becomes chief editor, Paramount Studios, Joinville; 1935—begins as feature director; co-writes or co-adapts most of his films and edits about 15 of the early ones; 1975—becomes President of French film school, Institut des Hautes Etudes Cinématographiques (IDHEC). Recipient: Best Film, Cannes Festival, for *La Symphonie pastorale*, 1946; International Prize, Venice Festival, for *Dieu a besoin des hommes*, 1950.

Films (as editor, partial list): 1932—*La Belle Marinière* (Lachman); *Une Étoile disparaît* (Villers); *Le Fils improvisé* (Guissart); 1933—*Le Père prématuré* (Guissart); *Les Aventures du roi Pausole* (Granowsky); (as director of short films): 1933—*Franches lippées*; 1934—*Une Vocation irrésistible*; *L'École des detectives*; *Le Roi des Champs-Elysées* (Nosseck) (ed only); (as feature director plus co-scriptwriter or co-adaptor on films including those not so credited): 1935—*Paris-Deauville*; *Michel Strogoff* (de Baroncelli and Eichberg) (ed only); *Tovaritch* (Deval) (co-ed only); 1936—*La Moule* (medium-length); *Club de femmes* (Deval) (tech adv only, +co-ed); *Nitchevo* (de Baroncelli) (ed only); 1937—*Ne tuez pas Dolly!* (medium-length); *Tamara la complaisante* (Gandera) (tech adv only, +co-sc uncredited); *Feu!* (de Baroncelli) (ed only); 1938—*La Vénus de l'or* (co-sc); *Le Paradis de Satan* (Gandera) (tech adv only); 1939—*Macao, l'enfer du jeu*; *Le Diamant noir*; 1941—*Fièvres*; 1942—*L'Assassin a peur la nuit*; *Pontcarral, Colonel d'Empire*; 1943—*Macao, l'enfer du jeu* (partially re-shot version with Pierre Renoir in role played by Erich von Stroheim who was forbidden by German authorities; original version of *Macao* re-released after war); *L'Éternel Retour (The Eternal Return)*; 1944—*Le Bossu*; 1945—*La Part de l'ombre (Blind Desire)* (co-sc); 1946—*La Symphonie pastorale* (co-adapt); 1947—*Les Jeux sont faits (The Chips Are Down)* (co-adapt); 1948—*Aux yeux du souvenir (Souvenir)* (co-adapt); 1949—*Le Secret de Mayerling* (co-adapt); 1950—*Dieu a besoin des hommes (God Needs Men)*; 1951—*Le Garçon sauvage (Savage Triangle)* (co-adapt); 1952—*La Minute de vérité (L'ora della verità, The Moment of Truth)* (co-sc); "Jeanne (Joan of Arc)" episode of *Destinées (Daughters of Destiny)*; 1953—*La Route Napoléon* (co-sc); "Le Lit de la Pompadour" episode of *Secrets d'alcôve* (co-adapt); 1954—*Obsession* (co-adapt); 1955—*Chiens perdus sans collier* (co-sc); *Marie-Antoinette* (co-sc); 1956—*Notre-Dame de Paris (The Hunchback of Notre Dame)*; 1957—*Maigret tend un piège (Inspector Maigret)* (co-adapt); 1958—*Guinguette* (co-adapt); *Maigret et l'affaire Saint-Fiacre* (co-adapt); 1959—*Le Baron de l'Ecluse* (co-adapt); 1960—"L'Adolescence" episode of *La Française et l'amour (Love and the Frenchwoman)*; *La Princesse de Clèves*; 1962—*Le Rendez-vous* (co-adapt); *Venere imperiale (Vénus impériale)* (co-sc); 1964—*Les Amitiés particulières (This Special Friendship)* (co-sc); *Le Majordôme* (co-sc); 1965—"Le Berceau" and "La Répétition" episodes of *Le Lit à deux places (The Double Bed)*; *Les Sultans* (co-adapt); 1967—*Le Soleil des voyous (Action Man)* (co-adapt); 1969—*La Peau de Torpédo* (co-adapt); 1972—*Pas folle la guêpe* (co-sc).

Roles: (partial list): 1926—*Miss Helyett* (Monca and Keroul); 1927—*Casanova* (Volkoff); 1929—*La Grande Passion* (Hugon).

Publications:

By DELANNOY:

Article—"Le Réalisateur" in *Le Cinéma par ceux qui le font*,

Paris 1949.

On DELANNOY:

Article—biofilmography in *Film Dope* (London), September 1976; film—*Echos de plateau* on making of *La Minute de vérité*, by Hubert Knapp and Igor Barrère, 1952.

* * *

Critics have not been kind to Jean Delannoy although the public certainly has, for nearly all his films were solid box-office hits. But Dellanoy, both by personal pretention and by the subject matter of his major films, demanded more serious attention. Just as André Cayatte is France's director of social problem films, so Delannoy may be considered its moral philosopher. *La Symphonie pastorale* and *God Needs Man*, made just after the war, brought him this reputation and remain his best known work along with *Les Jeux sont faits* made in collaboration with Sartre. But more than a score of films surround this core, few of which measure up to the ambition and values for which they stand.

Delannoy flirted with the cinema in the 1920s while working at a bank. Godard would later recall these beginnings in his caricature of Delannoy "going into the Billancourt studios briefcase in hand; you would have sworn he was going into an insurance office." His initial training as an editor provided him with a sense of dramatic economy that may be at the origin of his popular success and critical failure. A Protestant, his calculated distance, even coolness, alienated many critics, most notably the passionate New Wave cinephiles at *Cahiers*.

No one would have paid Delannoy any attention had he not turned away from the competent studio dramas he first directed to stronger material. *Fontcarral* was his first remarkable effort, bringing him fame as a man of conviction when this Napoleonic adventure tale was interpreted as a direct call to resistance against the Nazi occupation forces.

He was then chosen to help Jean Cocteau bring to the screen *L'Eternel Retour*. Whether, as some suspect, Cocteau pushed him far beyond his usually cautious methods, or because the legendary tragedy of this Tristan and Isolde update was perfect material for the frigidity of his style, the film was a striking success, haunting in its bizarre imagery and in the mysterious implications of its plot and dialogue.

Just after the war came the films already mentioned as central to Delannoy as an auteur. Evidently Gide, Sartre, and Queffelec inspired him to render great moral and philosophical issues in a dramatically rigorous way. Today these films seem overly cautious and pretty, even prettified. But in their day they garnered worldwide respect, the first winning the Grand Prize at Cannes in 1946 and the last the Grand Prize at Venice in 1950. The cinematic ingenuity they display, particularly in the use of geography as a moral arena (a snowy alpine village, a destitute seacoast village), and in the taut editing, gives some, though not sufficient, justification for the staginess of the weighty dialogue.

Delannoy became perhaps the director most maligned by *Cahiers du cinéma* because of the battle he fought with Bresson over rights to *Diary of a Country Priest* (which Bresson won) and *La Princesse de Clèves* (which Delannoy won). Their accusations of his inauthenticity were borne out in the many hack productions he directed in the 1950s, including a super-production of *Notre Dame de Paris*. While none of these films is without some merit, the 1960 *Princesse de Clèves* being full of tasteful production values, his style more and more represented the most deprecated face of the "cinema of quality."

—Dudley Andrew

DELLUC, LOUIS. French. Born Louis-Jean-René Delluc at Cadouin, Dordogne, 14 October 1890. Educated at Lycée Henri IV, Paris, until 1909. Married actress Eve Francis, 1919. Career: 1909—abandons schooling to pursue journalism and writing; 1910—publishes 1st dramatic criticism; 1917—1st critical article on cinema published in *Film*; named editor-in-chief of *Film*; 1918—begins writing regular column for *Paris-Midi*; 1920—participates in creation of *Journal du ciné-club*; 1921—helps start *Cinéa* magazine, inaugurates "Matinées de *Cinéa*", forerunner of cine-clubs; 1923-24—writes for *Bonsoir*; 1923—after finishing *L'Inondation* succombs to tuberculosis; 1926—novel *Le Train sans yeux* filmed by Alberto Cavalcanti; beginning 1937 Prix Louis Delluc awarded annually (except during war years) to an outstanding French feature film. Died of tuberculosis in Paris, 22 March 1924.

Films (as scriptwriter): 1919—*La Fête espagnole* (Dulac); (as director and scriptwriter): 1920—*Fumée noire* (co-d); *Le Silence*; 1921—*Fièvre*; *Le Chemin d'Ernoa (L'Américain)*; *Le Tonnerre (Évangeline et la tonnerre)*; 1922—*La Femme de nulle part*; 1923—*L'Inondation*. Roles: 1921—*Prométhée banquier* (L'Herbier).

Publications:

By DELLUC:

Books—*Cinéma et Cie*, Paris 1919; *Photogénie*, Paris 1920; *Charlot*, Paris 1921; *La Jungle du cinéma*, Paris 1921; *Charlie Chaplin*, translated by H. Miles, London 1922; *Drames de cinéma* (including *La Fête espagnole*, *Le Silence*, *Fièvre* and *La Femme de nulle part*), Paris 1923.

On DELLUC:

Books—*Cinéma! Cinéma!* by Philippe Amiguet, Lausanne 1923; *Prisme* by Abel Gance, Paris 1930; *Temps héroïques* by Eve Francis, Paris 1949; *Louis Delluc* by Marcel Tariol, Paris 1965; articles—special issue of *Ciné-club* (Paris), March 1949; articles by Eve Francis and others in *Les Lettres françaises* (Paris), 19 March 1964; "Louis Delluc, Film Theorist, Critic and Prophet" by E.C. McCreary in *Cinema Journal* (Evanston), fall 1976; "'Le Delluc': un prix de copains" by R. Régent in *Avant-Scène du cinéma* (Paris), 15 April 1981.

* * *

Louis Delluc was one of the key figures in the renewal of French cinema after the collapse of the industry's world dominance in the years before World War I. Though in no sense the leader of a unified movement or faction, Delluc has considerable importance as both critic and filmmaker. His impact was crucial during the years after 1919, though he died in 1924 before the full flowering of the French film renaissance to which he had made such a contribution.

Like so many of his contemporaries, Delluc initially had literary ambitions. Abandoning his studies for a career in journalism, he wrote poetry, plays, novels and dramatic criticism. He continued to write even after he had turned to filmmaking and published—despite his early death—over a dozen literary works of various kinds, in addition to three collections of film criticism.

He was also one of the few filmmakers of the early 1920s to publish a collection of his screenplays, under the title *Drames de cinéma*, in 1923. The work which opened Delluc's eyes to the potential of film as an artistic medium was Cecil B. DeMille's *The Cheat*, distributed in France under the title *Forfaiture*. Though Delluc's writings show his clear awareness of the specific limitations of this particular work, which became a cult film for the cinematically-inclined French intellectuals of the period, he was very responsive to the form of cinema which it represented. This was the narrative continuity cinema which had developed during the previous five years or so in the United States and from which French filmmakers had been shielded by the economic power of the French commercial giants, Pathé and Gaumont.

Like André Bazin some thirty years later, Delluc developed his ideas in relation to specific films—attacking the Feuillade of *La Nouvelle Mission de Judex*, while offering a keen appreciation of American and Swedish cinema and the films of French contemporaries such as Antoine, L'Herbier and Gance. Delluc does not offer a worked-out theory of cinema, but a number of key ideas recur: the importance of cinema as a popular art, the crucial significance of rhythm and pacing in a form now based on sequences of shots instead of the long-held *plan séquences*, the importance of expressive, poetic imagery and the choice of concrete realistic detail, together with the need for restraint in acting. He sought a cinema which would be truly the expression of its author and put stress on the inner life of its characters.

Between 1919 and 1923 Delluc scripted one film, *La Fête espagnol*, and directed eight others, from *Fumée noire* in 1920 to *L'Inondation* in 1923. With one exception, all of these were from original scripts, conceived directly for the screen. Though Delluc drew inspiration from American movies and advocated a popular cinema, he placed little emphasis on physical action. These films concentrate on the ramifications of a single incident and depict the intense interaction of a handful of characters. For none of this work did Delluc enjoy adequate resources and he was denied the popular success which would have given him bigger budgets. Moreover, unlike Gance and L'Herbier, he did not have an instinctive flair for images, and the interest of his films lies more in their construction than their realization. Almost all contain some noteworthy stylistic exploration: the atmosphere of a single set in *Fièvres*, the use of landscape in *Le Chemin d'Ernoa*, or the interaction of past and present in *Le Silence* and his generally recognised masterpiece, *La Femme de nulle part*. The fact that he died at the age of 34, while his contemporaries Gance and L'Herbier survived into their nineties, makes Delluc something of a figure apart, but his place among the formative influences on French cinema is assured.

—Roy Armes

DEMILLE, CECIL B. American. Born Cecil Blount DeMille in Ashfield, Massachusetts, 12 August 1881. Educated at Pennsylvania Military Academy, Chester, 1896-98; American Academy of Dramatic Arts, New York, 1898-1900. Married Constance Adams, 16 August 1902; children: Cecilia, Katherine (adopted), John and Richard. Career: 1900—acting debut; before 1913—playwright, stage producer; organized Standard Opera Company; associate with mother in the DeMille Play Co. (a theatrical agency); 1913—with Samuel Goldfish (Goldwyn), Arthur S. Friend and Jesse Lasky founds Jesse L. Lasky Feature Play Co., and is made Director-General; 1918—merger creates Paramount Pictures Corp.; 1919—founds Mercury Aviation Co.; 1924—establishes DeMille Pictures Corp.; 1928—joins Metro-

Goldwyn-Mayer as producer-director; 1931—helps found Screen Directors Guild; 1932—returns to Paramount as independent producer; 1936-45—producer, Lux Radio Theatre of the Air; 1938—declines nomination as U.S. Senator; 1945—opposes closed shop policy of American Federation of Radio Artists, ends radio work. Died 21 January 1959. Recipient: Outstanding Service Award, War Agencies of the Government of the U.S. Special Academy Award "for 37 years of brilliant showmanship", 1949; Irving Thalberg Award, Academy, 1952; Milestone Award, Screen Producers' Guild, 1956; George Eastman House Award for contributions to motion pictures, 1915-1925; Chevalier of the Legion of Honor, France; Honorary Doctor of Fine Arts, University of Southern California.

Films (as director and scriptwriter): 1914—*The Squaw Man (The White Man)* (co-d, +bit ro); *The Call of the North* (+introductory appearance); *The Virginian* (+co-ed); *What's His Name* (+ed); *The Man from Home* (+ed); *Rose of the Rancho* (+ed); *Brewster's Millions* (co-d, uncredited); *The Master Mind* (co-d, uncredited); *The Man on the Box* (co-d, uncredited); *The Only Son* (co-d, uncredited); *The Ghost Breaker* (co-d, uncredited, co-sc); *Ready Money* (Apfel) (co-sc only); *The Circus Man* (Apfel) (co-sc only); *Cameo Kirby* (Apfel) (co-sc only); 1915—*The Girl of the Golden West* (+ed); *The Warrens of Virginia* (+ed); *The Unafraid* (+ed); *The Captive* (co-sc, +ed); *The Wild Goose Chase* (co-sc, +ed); *The Arab* (co-sc, +ed); *Chimmie Fadden* (co-sc, +ed); *Kindling* (+ed); *Carmen* (+ed); *Chimmie Fadden Out West* (co-sc, +ed); *The Cheat* (+ed); *The Golden Chance* (co-sc, +ed); *The Goose Girl* (Thompson) (co-d, uncredited, co-sc); *The Country Boy* (Thompson) (co-sc only); *A Gentleman of Leisure* (Melford) (sc only); *The Governor's Lady* (Melford) (co-sc only); *Snobs* (Apfel) (co-sc only); (as director): 1916—*Temptation* (+co-story, ed); *The Trail of the Lonesome Pine* (+sc, ed); *The Heart of Nora Flynn* (+ed); *Maria Rosa* (+ed); *The Dream Girl* (+ed); *The Love Mask* (Reicher) (co-sc only); 1917—*Joan the Woman* (+ed); *A Romance of the Redwoods* (+co-sc, ed); *The Little American* (co-sc, +ed); *The Woman God Forgot* (+ed); *The Devil Stone* (+ed); *Nan of Music Mountain* (Melford) (co-d, uncredited); *Lost and Won*; *Betty to the Rescue* (Reicher) (co-sc only, +supervisor); 1918—*The Whispering Chorus* (+ed); *Old Wives for New* (+ed); *We Can't Have Everything* (+co-ed); *Till I Come Back to You*; *The Squaw Man*; 1919—*Don't Change Your Husband*; *For Better, For Worse*; *Male and Female (The Admirable Crichton)*; 1920—*Why Change Your Wife?*; *Something to Think About*; 1921—*Forbidden Fruit* (+pr); *The Affairs of Anatol (A Prodigal Knight)*; *Fool's Paradise*; 1922—*Saturday Night*; *Manslaughter*; *Don't Tell Everything* (Wood) (co-d, uncredited—incorporates 2 reel unused *The Affairs of Anatol* footage); 1923—*Adam's Rib*; *The 10 Commandments*; 1924—*Triumph* (+pr); *Feet of Clay*; 1925—*The Golden Bed*; *The Road to Yesterday*; 1926—*The Volga Boatman*; 1927—*The King of Kings*; 1929—*The Godless Girl*; (as director and producer): 1929—*Dynamite*; 1930—*Madame Satan*; 1931—*The Squaw Man*; 1932—*The Sign of the Cross* (re-released 1944 with add'l footage); 1933—*This Day and Age*; 1934—*4 Frightened People*; *Cleopatra*; 1935—*The Crusades*; 1937—*The Plainsman*; 1938—*The Buccaneer*; 1939—*Union Pacific*; 1940—*North West Mounted Police* (+prologue narration); 1942—*Reap the Wild Wind* (+prologue narration); 1944—*The Story of Dr. Wassell*; 1947—*Unconquered*; 1949—*Samson and Delilah* (+prologue narration); 1952—*The Greatest Show on Earth* (+narration, introductory appearance); 1956—*The 10 Commandments* (+prologue narration); 1958—*The Buccaneer* (pr only, +supervisor, introductory appearance). Roles: 1923—guest appearance in *Hollywood* (Cruze); 1930—guest appearance in *Free and Easy* (Sedgwick); 1935—seen directing *Cleopatra* in *The Hollywood*

You Never See (short); seen directing *The Crusades* in *Hollywood Extra Girl* (Moulton); 1942—guest appearance in *Star Spangled Rhythm* (Marshall); 1947—guest appearance in *Variety Girl* (Marshall); guest appearance in *Jens Månsson i Amerika (Jens Månsson in America)* (Janzon); appearance in *Aid to the Nation* (short); 1950—as himself in *Sunset Boulevard* (Wilder); 1952—guest appearance in *Son of Paleface* (Tashlin); 1956—guest appearance in *The Buster Keaton Story* (Sheldon); 1957—narrator, *The Heart of Show Business* (Staub).

Publications:

By DEMILLE:

Book—*The Autobiography of Cecil B. DeMille*, Englewood Cliffs, New Jersey 1959; articles—"Building a Photo-Play" in *The Story of the Films* by J.P. Kennedy, New York 1927; "After 70 Pictures" in *Films in Review* (New York), March 1956; "DeMille Answers His Critics" in *Films and Filming* (London), March 1958; plays—*The Royal Mounted* (1899); *The Return of Peter Grimm*, with David Belasco.

On DEMILLE:

Books—*Cinéma & Cie* by Louis Delluc, Paris 1919; *Photogénie* by Louis Delluc, Paris 1920; *Such Sweet Compulsion* by Geraldine Farrar, New York 1938; *Hollywood Saga* by William DeMille, New York 1939; *Dance to the Piper* by Agnes de Mille, New York 1951; *Le Cinéma au service de la Foi* by Charles Ford, Paris 1953; *Merely Colossal* by Arthur Mayer, New York 1953; *Sunshine and Shadow* by Mary Pickford, New York 1955; *The Lion's Share* by Bosley Crowther, New York 1957; *Homenaje a Cecil B. DeMille* by Carlos Cuenca, Madrid 1959; *Yes, Mr. DeMille* by Phil Koury, New York 1959; *The Movies in the Age of Innocence* by Edward Wagenknecht, Oklahoma 1962; *Sur un art ignoré* by Michel Mourlet, Paris 1965; *Cecil B. DeMille* by Michel Mourlet, Paris 1968; *The Films of Cecil B. DeMille* by Gene Ringgold and DeWitt Bodeen, New York 1969; *DeMille: The Man and His Pictures* by Gabe Essoe and Raymond Lee, New York 1970; *Cecil B. DeMille* by Charles Higham, New York 1973; articles—"Filmland" by Robert Florey in *Cinémagazine* (Paris), 1923; "60 Reels of DeMille" by Frank Nugent in the *New York Times Magazine*, 10 August 1941; "The Sign of the Boss" by Ring Lardner, Jr. in *Screen Writer* , November 1945; "Cecil B. DeMille's Virtues" by Joseph and Harry Feldman in *Films in Review* (New York), December 1950; "The Siegfried of Sex" by Simon Harcourt-Smith in *Sight and Sound* (London), February 1951; "Revisione di DeMille" by Roberto Chiti and Mario Quargnolo in *Bianco e Nero* (Rome), August 1955; "The 10th Muse in San Francisco" by Albert Johnson in *Sight and Sound* (London), January/March 1955; "Showman for the Millions" by Peter Baker in *Films and Filming* (London), October 1956; "Forget the Spectacle—It's the Story That Counts" by Clayton Cole in *Films and Filming* (London), October 1956; "The Greatest Showman on Earth" by James Card in *Image* (Rochester, New York), November 1956; "Goodnight, C.B." by Agnes DeMille in *Esquire* (New York), January 1964; special issue on DeMille in *Présence du cinéma* (Paris), autumn 1967; "C.B. DeMille's Human Side" by Art Arthur in *Films in Review* (New York), April 1967; "Cecil B. de Mille" by Charles Ford in *Anthologie de Cinéma* vol.3, Paris 1968; "Claudette Colbert Still Tells DeMille Stories" by M. Kakutani in the *New York Times*, 16 November 1979; "Cecil B. DeMille" by Dewitt Bodeen in *Films in Review* (New York), August/September 1981.

*   *   *

For much of his 40-year career, the public and the critics associated Cecil B. DeMille with a single kind of film, the epic. And, certainly, he made a great many of them: *The Sign of the Cross*, *The Crusades*, *King of Kings*, two versions of *The Ten Commandments*, and others. As a result, DeMille became a symbol of Hollywood during its "Golden Age." He represented that which was larger than life, often too elaborate, but always entertaining. By having such a strong public personality, however, DeMille came to be neglected as a director, even though many of this films, and not just the epics, stand out as extraordinary.

Although he made films until 1956, DeMille's masterpiece may well have come in 1915 with *The Cheat*. Even this early in his career, we can locate some of the motifs that turn up again and again in DeMille's work: a faltering upper-class marriage, the allure and exoticism of the Far East, and sexual attraction equated with hypnotic control. He also made a major aesthetic advancement in the use of editing in *The Cheat* that soon became a part of the repertoire of most filmmakers.

For the cinema's first 20 years, editing was based primarily on following action. During a chase, when actors exited screen right, the next shot had them entering screen left; or, a director might cut from a person being chased to those characters doing the chasing. In either case, the logic of the action controls the editing, which in turn gives us a sense of the physical space of a scene. But in *The Cheat*, through his editing, DeMille created a sense of psychological space. Richard Hardy, a wealthy businessman, confronts his wife with her extravagant bills, but Mrs. Hardy can think only of her lover, Haka, who is equally obsessed with her. DeMille provides a shot/counter-shot here, but the scene does not cut from Mr. Hardy to his wife, even though the logic of the action and the dialogue seems to indicate that it should. Instead, the shots alternate between Mrs. Hardy and Haka, even though the two lovers are miles apart. The alternation of shots from widely separated spaces indicate that Mrs. Hardy and Haka think more about someone who is absent than about anyone present in their homes with them. This sort of editing, which follows thoughts rather than actions, may seem routine today, but in 1915 it was a major development in the method of constructing a sequence.

As a visual stylist, however, De Mille became known more for his wit than for his editing innovations. At the beginning of *The Affairs of Anatol*, for instance, our first view of the title character, Anatol DeWitt Spencer, is of his feet. He taps them nervously while he waits for his wife to make breakfast. Our first view of Mrs. Spencer is also of her feet—a maid gives them a pedicure. In just seconds, and with only two shots, DeMille lets us know that this couple is in trouble. Mrs. Spencer's toenails must dry before Anatol can eat. Also from these opening shots, the viewers realize that they have been placed firmly within the realm of romantic comedy. These closeups of feet have no place within a melodrama.

One normally does not think of DeMille in terms of pairs of shots. Instead, one thinks on a large scale, and remembers the crowd scenes (the lions versus Christians extravaganza in *The Sign of the Cross*), the huge upper-crust social functions (the charity gala in *The Cheat*), the orgiastic parties (one of which takes place in a dirigible in *Dynamite*), and the bathrooms that DeMille turns into colossal marble shrines.

DeMille began directing in the grand style quite early in his career. In 1915, with opera star Geraldine Farrar in the lead role, he made one of the best film versions of *Carmen*, and two years later, again with Farrar, he directed *Joan the Woman*. Even at the beginning of his career, DeMille not only made use of history (Joan of Arc's martyrdom) to bring a certain respectability to his films, but also made use of high art for the same purpose (Bizet's opera acting as the source for the silent *Carmen*). Again and again, DeMille would refer to history as a foundation for the believability of his stories, as if his most obvious excesses could be justified if they were at least remotely based on real-life incidents. Just a quick look at his filmography shows many films base on historical events (often so far back in the past that accuracy hardly becomes an issue): *The Sign of the Cross*, *The Crusades*, *Union Pacific*, *Northwest Mounted Police*, and others. When history was inconvenient, DeMille made use of a literary text to give his films a high gloss of acceptability and veracity. In the opening credits of *The Affairs of Anatol*, for instance, DeMille stresses that the story derives from the play by Schnitzler. This acknowledgement of a famous literary source works to strengthen the credibility of the story presented in the film. No matter how little the movie may resemble the play, the mere mention of a playwright known for his keen observations of social mores might have made the film more believable for the audiences of *Anatol*.

In both his silent and sound films, DeMille mixes Victorian morality with sizable doses of sex and violence. The intertitles of *Why Change Your Wife?*, for example, rail against divorce as strongly as any nineteenth century marital tract, but the rest of the film deals openly with sexual obsession, and shows two women in actual physical combat over one man. Similarly, all of the religious epics extol the Christian virtues while at the same time revelling in scenes depicting all of the deadly sins. Though it is tension between extremes that makes DeMille's films so intriguing, critics have often made this aspect of his work seem laughable. Even today DeMille has barely received the serious recognition and study that he deserves.

—Eric Smoodin

DEMME, JONATHAN. American. Born in Rockville Center, New York, 1944. Educated at University of Florida (film critic for student newspaper, *The Florida Alligator*). Married producer Evelyn Purcell. Career: 1960—father, p.r. director for Miami's Fontainebleu Hotel, introduces him to producer Joseph E. Levine; Levine, pleased by review of *Zulu* hires him to write releases; moves to New York; early 1960s—does publicity for United Artists, Avco Embassy, and Pathe Contemporary Films; 1966-68—writes for trade publication *Film Daily*; 1969—moves to London as sales rep. and producer for small company, writes some reviews; 1970—works as musical coordinator on Irwin Allen production *Sudden Terror* (original title *Eyewitness*); taken on as unit publicist for Roger Corman film, invited to write for Corman. Recipient: Best Director, New York Film Critics, for *Melvin and Howard*, 1980. Agent: Arnold Stiefel, William Morris Agency, Beverly Hills, CA. Business Manager: Lee Winkler, Global Business Management, 9000 Sunset Blvd. Suite 1115, Beverly Hills, CA 90069.

Films (as producer and co-writer with director Joe Viola): 1972—*Angels Hard as They Come*; *The Hot Box*; (as director): 1974—*Caged Heat*; 1975—*Crazy Mama*; 1976—*Fighting Mad*; 1976—*Fighting Mad*; 1977—*Handle with Care* (original title: *Citizens Band*); 1978—*Murder in Aspic* (*Columbo* series TV movie); 1979—*The Last Embrace*; 1980—*Melvin and Howard*; 1982—"Who Am I This Time?" segment of PBS series *American Playhouse*; 1983—*Swing Shift*.

Publications:

By DEMME:

Article—"Demme Monde", interview by Carlos Clarens, in *Film Comment* (New York), September/October 1980.

On DEMME:

Articles—"Velvet Vampires and Hot Mamas: Why Exploitation Films Get to Us" by Michael Goodwin in *Village Voice* (New York), 7 July 1975; "From Vixen to Vindication: Erica Gavin Interviewed" by Dennis Peary in *Velvet Light Trap* (Madison), fall 1976; "4 Auteurs in Search of an Audience" by Dave Kehr in *Film Comment* (New York), September/October 1977; "*Caged Heat*" by Louis Black and "*Caged Heat*: 2nd Thoughts" by Marjorie Baumgarten in *CinemaTexas Program Notes* (Austin), spring 1978; "Demme's Newest Film Sets a Record of Sorts" by Janet Maslin in the *New York Times*, 13 May 1979; "*Crazy Mama*" by Louis Black in *CinemaTexas Program Notes* (Austin), fall 1981.

*   *   *

Renowned for the critically acclaimed *Melvin and Howard*, Jonathan Demme is the most personally inventive and creatively stylish director to emerge from the talent groomed at Roger Corman's exploitation mill, New World Pictures. The integrity of Demme's work, which combines a nearly delirious appreciation of everyday kitsch with a brand of humanism almost forgotten in the cynical seventies, is evident from his first film, *Caged Heat*. The last of New World's women's prison cycle, this flamboyant film demonstrates amazing stylistic flair as well as political intelligence in a depiction of women's solidarity too strong for mainstream Hollywood. Its Buñuelian audacity in mounting three dream sequences in its first quarter-hour, its John Cale soundtrack, and its self-consciously campy sense of humor are ample testimony to the freedom available to the creative filmmaker within the parameters of the Corman formula.

In Demme's second film, *Crazy Mama*, four generations of women (and a fifth unborn) blythely blaze a trail of crime from California to Arkansas in pursuit of the American dream. An outrageously visual celebration of fifties' decadence, the film presents characters quirky enough, and relationships off-beat enough, to recall the heyday of screwball comedy. Demme's capacity to maintain the free-wheeling energy and odd-ball daring of this early work, even as he began to shed its exploitive excesses, was a key factor in his critical breakthrough with *Handle with Care*. Originally titled *Citizens Band*, this rambling, *Nashville*-style narrative exploring the populist premises of the CB-radio craze has already been compared to the wry tales of Eric Rohmer, although it bears even greater resemblances to Jean Renoir's comedies of manners, since everyone (including a bigamist truckdriver, and his two wives who rally to one another's support) has their reasons.

After a largely failed attempt at a bigger-budget, DePalma-type thriller *The Last Embrace*, Demme finally found a property ideally suited to his sense of character, style and humor in the true story of Melvin Dummar, the Utah gas-station owner who claimed to have been left a substantial portion of Howard

Hughes' fortune after giving the old man a lift in his pickup. *Melvin and Howard*, which won Demme international acclaim and a Best Director award from the New York Film Critics, is a clever, compassionate comedy which asserts the insanities of success myths and consumer culture without patronizing the character of Melvin, the peculiarly American dreamer and loser at its center. Despite critical accolades and Academy Award nominations, *Melvin and Howard* (like *Handle with Care*) never gained the audience it deserved—less the fault of the film than of a distribution system virtually incapable of handling films which cannot be easily pigeonholed.

Demme's career since leaving Corman's employ illustrates the difficulties currently faced by independent commercial filmmakers who choose to pursue projects they find personally rewarding. But whether or not a major hit eventually launches him into the first ranks of New Hollywood, Demme remains one of the brightest lights in the current American cinema, and his track record warrants the hope that his best work is still to come.

—Ed Lowry

DEMY, JACQUES. French. Born at Pontchâteau (Loire-Atlantique), 5 June 1931. Educated at technical college, Nantes; Ecole des Beaux-Arts, Nantes; Ecole Technique de Photographie et de Cinématographie, Paris. Married director Agnès Varda, 1962. Career: 1952—becomes assistant to animator Paul Grimault; 1954—assistant to Georges Rouquier; 1955—with Rouquier's support, makes short *Le Sabotier du Val de Loire*; begins association with editor Anne-Marie Cotret; 1969—makes *The Model Shop* in U.S. early 1970s—directs stage productions in Salzburg and Paris.

Films (as assistant director): 1954—*Lourdes et ses miracles* (Rouquier); 1955—*Arthur Honegger* (Rouquier); 1956—*S.O.S. Noronha* (Rouquier); (as director and scriptwriter of short and medium length films): 1956—*Le Sabotier du Val de Loire*; 1957—*Le Bel Indifférent*; 1958—*Le Musée Grévin*; 1959—*La Mère et l'infant* (co-d); *Ars*; (as feature director and scriptwriter): 1961—*Lola*; 1962—"La Luxure (Lust)" episode of *Les Sept Péchés capitaux (7 Deadly Sins)*; 1963—*La Baie des Anges (Bay of the Angels)*; 1964—*Les Parapluies de Cherbourg (The Umbrellas of Cherbourg)*; 1967—*Les Demoiselles de Rochefort (The Young Girls of Rochefort)*; 1969—*The Model Shop* (+pr); 1971—*Peau d'ane (Donkey Skin)*; 1972—*The Pied Piper of Hamelin (The Pied Piper)*; 1973—*L'Évènement le plus important depuis que l'homme a marché sur la lune (A Slightly Pregnant Man)*; 1978—*Lady Oscar*; 1982—*Une Chambre en ville (A Room in Town)* (+sc). Roles: 1959—policeman in *Les Quatre Cents Coups* (Truffaut); 1960—guest at party in *Paris nous appartient* (Rivette).

Publications:

By DEMY:

Articles—"I Prefer the Sun to the Rain" in *Film Comment* (New York), spring 1965; interview by Marsha Kinder in *Film Heritage* (Dayton, Ohio), spring 1967; "Frenchman in Hollywood", interview by Philip Scheuer in *Action* (Los Angeles), November/December 1968; "Lola in Los Angeles" in *Films and Film-ing* (London), April 1970; "Cinéastes et musiciens", round table including Demy, in *Ecran* (Paris), September 1975; interview by M. Amiel in *Cinéma 76* (Paris), January 1976; interview and biofilmography in *Film Dope* (London), September 1976; interview by G. Haustrate in *Cinéma* (Paris), July/August 1981.

On DEMY:

Articles—"Rondo Galant" by Richard Roud in *Sight and Sound* (London), summer 1964; "Jacques Demy and His Other World" by Ginette Billard in *Film Quarterly* (Berkeley), fall 1964; "Jacques Demy" by G. Petrie in *Film Comment* (New York), winter 1971/72; "Demy Calls the Tune" by P. Strick in *Sight and Sound* (London), autumn 1971; "Journals: Gilbert Adair from Paris" in *Film Comment* (New York), March/April 1979; special Demy issue of *Cinéma* (Paris), July/August 1981; film—*Derrière l'écran* by André Delvaux, 1966.

*   *   *

Demy's first film, *Lola*, is among the early distinguished products of the New Wave and is dedicated to Max Ophuls: two facts that in conjunction define its particular character. It proved to be the first in a series of loosely interlinked films (the intertextuality is rather more than a charming gimmick, relating as it does to certain thematic preoccupations already established in *Lola* itself); arguably, it remains the richest and most satisfying work so far in Demy's erratic, frustrating, but also somewhat underrated career.

The name and character of Lola (Anouk Aimée) herself relate to two previous celebrated female protagonists: the Lola Montès of Max Ophuls's film of that name, and the Lola-Lola (Marlene Dietrich) of von Sternberg's *The Blue Angel*, to which Demy pays homage in a number performed by Aimée in a top hat. The explicit philosophy of Lola Montès ("For me, life is movement") is enacted in Demy's film by the constant comings and goings, arrivals and departures, and intricate intercrossings of the characters. Ophuls's work has often been linked to concepts of fate; at the same time the auteurs of the early New Wave were preoccupied with establishing Freedom—as a metaphysical principle, to be enacted in their professional methodology. The tension between fate and freedom is there throughout Demy's work. *Lola's* credit sequence alternates the improvisatory freedom of jazz with the slow movement of Beethoven's 7th Symphony which is explicitly associated with destiny in the form of the huge white American car that brings back Michel, Lola's lover and father of her child, who, like his predecessors in innumerable folk songs, has left her for seven years to make his fortune. No film is more intricately and obsessively patterned, with all the characters interlinked: the middle-aged woman used to be Lola (or someone like her), her teenage daughter may become Lola (or someone like her). Yet neither resembles Lola as she is in the film: everyone is different, yet everyone is interchangeable.

Two subsequent Demy films relate closely to *Lola*: in the all-sung *Les Parapluies de Cherbourg* Roland, Lola's rejected lover, recounts his brief liaison with Lola, to the visual accompaniment of a flashback to the arcade that was one of their meeting-places; and Lola herself re-appears in *The Model Shop*. Two other films are bound in to the series, *Les Demoiselles de Rochefort* by means of a certain cheating—Lola has been found murdered and dismembered in a laundry basket, but it's a different Lola. Especially poignant, as the series continues, is the treatment of the abrupt, unpredictable, seemingly fortuitous happy ending. At the end of *Lola*, Lola drives off with Michel and their child (as Roland of *Parapluies*, discarded and embittered, departs on his diamond-smuggling trip to South Africa);

at the end of *Le Baie des Anges*—a film that, at the time, revealed no connection with *Lola*—Jackie (Jeanne Moreau), a compulsive gambler, manages to leave the casino to follow her lover *before* she knows the result of her bet: two happy endings which are exhilarating precisely because they are so arbitrary. Then, several films later, in *Model Shop*, Lola recounts how her great love Michel abandoned her to run off with a compulsive gambler called Jackie: both happy endings reversed in a single blow. Yet it is not so much that Demy doesn't believe in happy endings: he simply doesn't believe in *permanent* ones (as "life is movement"). The ambivalent, bittersweet "feel" of Demy is perhaps best summed up in the end of *Les Parapluies de Cherbourg*, where the lovers, now both married to others, accidentally meet, implicitly acknowledge their love, and return with acceptance to the relationships to which they are committed.

Outside the *Lola* series, Demy's touch has been uncertain. His two fairy-tale films, *Peau d'ane* and *The Pied Piper*, unfortunately tend to confirm the common judgment that he is more a decorator than a creator. But he should not be discounted. His latest film, *A Room in Town*, a return to the *Lola* mode if not to the *Lola* characters, has been favorably received.

—Robin Wood

DE PALMA, BRIAN. American. Born in Newark, New Jersey, 11 September 1940. Educated at Columbia University, New York. Sarah Lawrence College. Career: 1960—begins making amateur films while undergraduate at Columbia University; 1962-63—short *Wotan's Wake* wins Rosenthal Foundation Award and others, goes to Sarah Lawrence College on writing fellowship; 1965-66—collaborates with Cynthia Munroe and Wilford Leach on *The Wedding Party*; 1966—success of *The Responsive Eye* on Op Art exhibition at Museum of Modern Art leads to feature directing. Personal Business: Fetch Productions, New York, NY 10003. Business Manager: Richard Roemer, 605 3rd Avenue, New York, NY 10158.

Films (as maker of short films): 1960—*Icarus*; 1961—*660214, the Story of an IBM Card*; 1962—*Wotan's Wake*; 1964—*Jennifer*; *Mod*; 1965—*Bridge that Gap*; 1966—*Show Me a Strong Town and I'll Show You a Strong Bank*; *The Responsive Eye*; (as feature director): 1967—*Murder à la Mod* (+sc, ed); 1968—*Greetings* (+co-sc, ed); 1969—*The Wedding Party* (co-d, +co-pr, co-sc, co-ed: release delayed from 1966); 1970—*Dionysus in '69* (co-d, +co-ph, co-ed: completed 1968); *Hi, Mom!* (+co-sc); 1972—*Get to Know Your Rabbit*; 1973—*Sisters* (+co-sc); 1974—*Phantom of the Paradise* (+sc); 1976—*Obsession* (+co-sc); *Carrie*; 1978—*The Fury*; 1979—*Home Movie*; 1980—*Dressed to Kill*; 1981—*Blow-Out*; 1983—*Scarface*.

Publications:

By DE PALMA:

Articles—interview in *The Film Director as Superstar* by Joseph Gelmis, Garden City, New York 1970; interview by E. Margulies in *Action* (Los Angeles), September/October 1974; "The Making of *Phantom of the Paradise*", interview by J. Coates, in *Filmmakers Newsletter* (Ward Hill, Mass.), February 1975; "Phantoms and Fantasies", interview by A. Stuart, in *Films and*

Filming (London), December 1976; "interview by M. Henry in *Positif* (Paris), May 1977; "Brian de Palma discusses *The Fury*", interview by P. Madell in *Filmmakers Newsletter* (Ward Hill, Mass.), May 1978; "Things That Go Bump in the Night", interview by S. Swires, in *Films in Review* (New York), August/September 1978.

On DE PALMA:

Articles—"The Making of Sisters" by R. Rubinstein in *Filmmakers Newsletter* (Ward Hill, Mass.), September 1973; "Considering de Palma" by R.S. Brown in *American Film* (Washington, D.C.), July/August 1977; "Une Nouvelle Vague américain 1—Brian de Palma" by M. Elia in *Séquences* (Montreal), April 1977; "Brian de Palma" by A. Garel in *Image et son* (Paris), December 1977; "Le Fantôme de la cinémathèque" by F. Guérif in *Image et son* (Paris), December 1977; "L'Oeil du malin (à propos de Brian de Palma)" by M. Henry in *Positif* (Paris), May 1977; "Note sur le cinéma de Brian de Palma" by P. Kané in *Cahiers du cinéma* (Paris), June 1977; "Corruption and Catastrophe: De Palma's *Carrie*" by P. Matusa in *Film Quarterly* (Berkeley), fall 1977; "An Exciting Contest: Next DePalma Script" by A. Harmetz in the *New York Times*, 31 January 1979; "Brian de Palma True to 'Menace'" in *Variety* (New York), 29 August 1979; "At the Movies: Brian de Palma Makes a Thriller Near the Docks" by T. Buckley in the *New York Times*, 30 November 1979; "Rules of the Game" by Stuart Byron in the *Village Voice* (New York), 5 November 1979; "Dossier: Hollywood 79: Brian de Palma" by G. Gourdon in *Cinématographe* (Paris), March 1979; "Style vs. 'Style'" by R.T. Jameson in *Film Comment* (New York), March/April 1980; "Donaggio Domani" by L. O'Toole in *Film Comment* (New York), September/October 1981; "Lexique des réalisateurs de films fantastiques américains" by J.-P. Piton in *Image et son* (Paris), June 1981; "Las Máscaras del tiempo" by S. Zunzunegui in *Contracampo* (Madrid), October 1981; "The Art of Film Editing", interview with Paul Hirsch by J. Verniere in *Filmmakers Monthly* (Ward Hill, Mass.), September 1981.

* * *

Unlike his contemporaries, Brian De Palma has failed to garner the enthusiastic critical acclaim of Martin Scorsese or Francis Coppola or the financial success of George Lucas or Steven Spielberg. De Palma is the black sheep in this group of youthful filmmakers, whose impact on Hollywood in the last decade rivals that of the German filmmakers in the 1930s and 1940s.

De Palma has concentrated on two kinds of films: satirical, offbeat comedies influenced by New York underground films of the 1960s and his own work in documentary, and stylized horror films or thrillers influenced by, and highly derivative of, Alfred Hitchcock's films. Despite the differences between these two kinds of films, there still exist a great many similarities. For example, references to Hitchcock appear in De Palma's comedy/satires, and his interest in foregrounding the process of film and other media, especially video, appears in most, if not all, of his films. *Phantom of the Paradise* is particularly noteworthy because it can be viewed as both a horror film and a comedy/satire.

Obsession, sexuality and death are key themes in De Palma's work. There are no simple resolutions to his narratives—obsessions do not die and open sexuality often leads to death. Although a specific political doctrine is unimportant in his films, politics is sometimes linked with violence, particularly in *Greetings*, *Hi Mom!*, *The Fury* and *Blow Out*.

Some critics have accused De Palma of imitating Hitchcock to the point of outright theft, but De Palma is not simply copying Hitchcock, he is creating new works of horror and mystery that use Hitchcock as a popular mythic background. In psychological terms, Hitchcock's films are focused more on repression, while De Palma is more concerned with the guilt and response of the victim.

Above all De Palma's films are noted for their bold visual style. Reputed for his elaborate camera movements, De Palma not only reminds us of the process of film but also of the process of dream. In every De Palma dream sequence, we have to ask ourselves where the dream begins and where the film takes over. Ultimately, De Palma's films are a discourse on the medium itself. Seeing replaces doing in his films, and fantasy is inseparable from reality.

—Tom Snyder

DEREN, MAYA. Russian/American. Born in Kiev, 1917; became citizen of United States. Educated at League of Nations School, Geneva, Switzerland; studied journalism at University of Syracuse, New York; New York University, B.A.; Smith College, M.A. Married (2nd time) Alexander Hackenschmied (Hammid), 1942 (divorced); married Teiji Ito. Career: 1922—parents emigrate to America; father, a psychiatrist, works for and eventually directs State Institute for the Feeble-Minded, Syracuse, New York; 1940-41—travels with dancer Katherine Dunham on tour working on book on modern dance (unrealized); introduced by Dunham to filmmaker Alexander Hammid in Los Angeles; 1942—marries Hammid, collaborates with him on *Meshes of the Afternoon*; 1946—receives first Guggenheim Fellowship for work in creative film, travels to Haiti to film rituals and dances; begins writing study of Haitian mythology, *Divine Horsemen*; 1960—works as secretary for Creative Film Foundation; 1977—Haitian film footage and wire recordings edited into film by widower Teiji Ito and his wife. Died of cerebral hemorrhage in St. Alban's Naval Hospital, Queens, New York, 13 October 1961.

Films: 1943—*Meshes of the Afternoon* (with Alexander Hammid) (+ro); *The Witches' Cradle* (unfinished); 1944—*At Land* (+ro); 1945—*A Study in Choreography for Camera*; *The Private Life of a Cat* (home movie, with Hammid); 1946—*Ritual in Transfigured Time* (+ro); 1948—*Meditation on Violence*; 1959—*The Very Eye of Night*.

Publications:

By DEREN:

Books—*An Anagram of Ideas on Art, Form and the Film*, New York 1946; *The Divine Horseman: The Living Gods of Haiti*, New York 1953; *Divine Horsemen: Voodoo Gods of Haiti*, New York 1970; articles—"Choreography of Camera" in *Dance* (New York), October 1943; reply to Manny Farber in *New Republic* (New York), 11 November 1946; "Creative Cutting. Parts I and II" in Movie Makers, May/June 1947; "Meditation on Violence" in *Dance Magazine* (New York), December 1948; "Movie Journal" in the *Village Voice* (New York), 25 August 1960; "Cinema as an Art Form" in *Introduction to the Art of the Movies* edited by Lewis Jacobs, New York 1960; "Adventures in Creative Film-making" in *Home Movie Making*, 1960; "Cinematography: The Creative Use of Reality" in *Daedalus: The Visual Arts Today*, 1960; "A Statement of Principles" in *Film Culture* (New York), summer 1961; "Movie Journal" in the *Village Voice* (New York), 1 June 1961; "Chamber Films" in *Filmwise*, no.2, 1962; "A Lecture..." in *Film Culture* (New York), summer 1963; "The Very Eye of Night" in *Film Culture* (New York), summer 1963; "Film in Progress..." in *Film Culture* (New York), winter 1965; "Notes, Essays, Letters" in *Film Culture* (New York), winter 1965; "A Statement on Dance and Film" in *Dance Perspectives*, no.30, 1967; "Tempo and Tension" in *The Movies as Medium* edited by Lewis Jacobs, New York 1970.

On DEREN:

Books—*A History of the American Avant-Garde Cinema*, exhibition catalogue, by John Hanhardt and others, The American Federation of Arts, New York 1976; *The Legend of Maya Deren* by VeVe Amasasa Clark and others, New York 1978; *Visionary Film*, second edition, by P. Adams Sitney, New York 1979; articles—"Maya Deren's Films" by Manny Farber in the *New Republic* (New York), 28 October 1946; "For Maya Deren" by Jerry Tallmer in the *Village Voice* (New York), 19 October 1961; obituary in the *New York Times*, 14 October 1961; special issue of *Filmwise*, no.2, 1961; "To Maya Deren" by Rudolf Arnheim in *Film Culture* (New York), no.24, 1962; "Notes on Women Directors" by J. Pyros in *Take One* (Montreal), November/December 1970; "Maya Deren and Germaine Dulac: Activists of the Avant-Garde" by Regina Cornwell in *Film Library Quarterly* (New York), winter 1971/72; "The Idea of Morphology" by P. Adams Sitney in *Film Culture* (New York), No. 53, 54, and 55, 1971; "Maya Deren, il tempo trasfigurante" by R. Milani in *Filmcritica* (Rome), September 1975; "Zu Maya Derens Filmarbeit" by M. Bronstein and S. Grossmann in *Frauen und Film* (Berlin), December 1976; excerpts from interview with Camera Obscura Collective on 'The Legend of Maya Deren Project' in *Camera Obscura* (Berkeley), summer 1979; "The Legend of Maya Deren: Champion of American Independent Film" by T. Mayer in *Film News* (New York), September/October 1979.

*   *   *

Maya Deren was the best-known independent, experimental filmmaker in the United States during and after World War II. She developed two types of short, subjective films: the psychodrama and the ciné-dance film. She initiated a national nontheatrical network to show her six independently-made works, which have been referred to as visual lyric poems, or dream-like trance films. She also lectured and wrote extensively on film as an art form. Her films remain as provocative as ever; her contributions to cinematic art indisputable.

Intending to write a book on dance, Deren toured with Katherine Dunham's dance group as a secretary. Dunham introduced Deren to Alexander Hammid, and the following year the couple made *Meshes of the Afternoon*. Considered a milestone in the chronology of independent film in the United States, it is famous for its four-stride sequence (from beach to grass to mud to pavement to rug). Deren acted the role of a girl driven to suicide. Continuous action is maintained while time-space unities are severed, establishing a trance-like mood by the use of slow motion, swish-pan camera movements, and well executed point-of-view shots.

In her next film, *At Land*, a woman (Deren) runs along a beach and becomes involved in a chess game. P. Adams Sitney refers to this work às a "pure American trance film." The telescoping of time occurs as each scene blends with the next in unbroken sequence, a result of pre-planned editing. *At Land* is also studded with camera shots of astounding virtuosity.

Other films include her first ciné-dance film, the three-minute *A Study in Choreography for Camera*. Filmed in slow motion, a male ballet dancer, partnered by the camera, moves through a variety of locales. Continuity of camera movement is maintained as the dancer's foot changes location, and space is compressed, time expanded. According to Sitney, the film's importance resides in two fresh observations: space and time in film are *created* space and time, and the camera's optimal use is as a dancer itself. *Ritual in Transfigured Time*, another dance-on-film, portrays psycho-dramatic ritual by use of freeze frames, repeated shots, shifting character identities, body movements, and locales. *Meditation on Violence* explores Woo (or Wu) Tang boxing with the camera as sparring partner, panning and zooming to simulate human response. *The Very Eye of Night* employed Metropolitan Ballet School members to create a celestial ciné-ballet of night. Shown in its negative state, Deren's handheld camera captured white figures on a total black background. Deren evolved, in her four dance-films, a viable form of ciné-choreography which was adapted and adjusted to commercial feature films later, meritoriously exampled in *West Side Story*.

Deren traced the evolution of her six films in "A letter to James Card", dated April 19, 1955. *Meshes* was her "point of departure" and "almost expressionist"; *At Land* depicted dormant energies in mutable nature, and *Choreography* distilled the essence of this natural changing. In *Ritual* she defined the processes of changing while *Meditation* extends the study of metamorphosis. In *The Very Eye* she express her love of life and its living. "Each film was built as a chamber and became a corridor, like a chain reaction."

In 1946, Deren published *An Anagram of Ideas on Art, Form, and the Film*, a monograph declaring two major statements: the rejection of symbolism in film, and a strong support for independent film after an analysis of industrial and independent filmmaking activities in the United States.

Although *Meshes* remains the most widely-seen film of its type, with several of its affects unsurpassed by filmmakers, Deren had been forgotten until recently. Her reputation now enjoys a renaissance well-deserved by the filmmaker that Rudolf Arnheim eulogized as one of the film's "most delicate magicians".

—Louise Heck-Rabi

DE SANTIS, GIUSEPPE. Italian. Born in Fondi, Latina, 11 February 1917. Educated in letters and philosophy, University of Rome; Centro Sperimentale di Cinematografia, Rome. Married Giovanna Valeri, 1943. Career: 1935—influenced by writer Giovanni Verga, writes series in realistic ("verista") style; late 1930s—studies at Centro Sperimentale di Cinematografia, Rome; begins collaborating on periodical *Cinema*, advocating approach later known as neorealism; 1942—collaborates on script of Visconti's *Ossessione*; 1943—assists Roberto Rossellini on *Scala Merci* (completed by Marcello Pagliero as *Desiderio*); Address: Piazza Faleri, I, Fiano Romano, Italy.

Films (as scriptwriter): 1940—*Don Pasquale*; (as co-scriptwriter and assistant director): 1942—*Ossessione* (Visconti); 1943—*Desiderio* (Rossellini and Pagliero—ass't to Rossellini only); 1945—*Il sole sorge ancora* (+ro uncredited); (as director and co-scriptwriter): 1945—episode of *Giorni di gloria*; 1946—*Ultimo amore* (co-sc only); 1947—*Caccia tragica (Tragic Hunt)*; 1948—*Riso amaro (Bitter Rice)*; 1949—*Non c'è pace tra gli ulivi (Under the Olive Tree)*; 1952—*Roma ore undici (Rome 11 O'Clock)*; 1953—*Un marito per Anna Zaccheo (A Husband for Anna)*; *Donne proibite* (sc only); 1954—*Giorni d'amore (Days of Love)*; 1956—*Uomini e lupi (Men and Wolves)*; 1957—*L'Uomo senza domenica*; 1958—*Cesta duga godinu dana (La strada lunga un anno)*; 1960—*La Garçonnière*; 1964—*Italiani, brava gente*; *La visita* (co-sc only); 1972—*Un Apprezzato professionista di sicuro avvenire*.

Publications:

By DE SANTIS:

Books—*Riso amaro: un film diretto da Giuseppe de Santis* by C. Lizzani, Rome 1978; *Giuseppe De Santis verso il neorealismo* edited by Callisto Cosulich, Bologna 1982; articles—interview by Claude Souef in *Les Lettres françaises* (Paris), November 1952; article in *Rivista del cinema italiano*, January/February 1953; "Una lettera di De Santis" in *Cinema nuovo* (Turin), 15 February 1957.

On DE SANTIS:

Books—*Giuseppe De Santis* by Alberto Farnassino, Milan 1978; *Giuseppe De Santis* by Stefano Masi, Florence 1981; articles—"De Santis and Italian Neo-Realism" by John Lane in *Sight and Sound* (London), August 1950; "Giuseppe De Santis est à Paris" by Jacques Krier in *L'Écran français* (Paris), 29 May 1950; "L'Évolution de De Santis" by Eduardo Bruno and "Température du néo-realisme de De Santis et Castellani" by Guy Jacob and "Giuseppe De Santis" by Marcel Oms in *Positif* (Paris), no.5, n.d. article by Marcel Oms in *Positif* (Paris), no.23, 1957; interview by Michel Delahaye and Jean Wagner in *Cinéma 59* (Paris), April 1959; "De Santis" by Andrea Martini and Marco Melani in *Il neorealismo cinematografico italiano*, Venice 1975; "America, cinema e mass media nel neorealismo italiano" by Roberto Campari in *Cinema e cinema* (Venice), January/March 1977; entire issue of *Cinema e cinema* (Venice), January/March 1982.

*   *   *

For a brief five years, Giuseppe De Santis's film career was the most often discussed, the most highly applauded and the most commercially successful of the Italian neorealist directors. His writings in the magazine *Cinema* from 1941 until 1943 took an active, prescriptive, and radical stance previously unknown to film criticism.

Like the later generation of French critics-turned-directors, such as Jean-Luc Godard or François Truffaut, De Santis's first films showed new approaches while displaying a mastery of the medium, but also succeeded in capturing popular imagination. "Popular" is the key to appreciating De Santis's work. Despite a college education (albeit never diplomaed), rigorous theorizing, and a profound dedication to Marxist principles, De Santis's films never appeared aloof or difficult to understand to a mass audience. He proved that the popular world was no longer something to be considered as different, but was actually the norm. While his first features are concerned with Italy, they are most significant as studies of changes in cultures, and as commentaries upon filmmaking and other mass media as the modern international culture. De Santis was the first Italian director to truly appreciate the effects of the mass media which appear in their various forms—newspapers, radio, television, cinema, posters, pop music, magazines, photo novels, pin-ups, advertisements, dancing, etc.—throughout all of his films. Like many of his colleagues, he displayed an admiration of American literature and American cinema, but he perceived more clearly why those were popular—not merely in a commercial sense but because they were creating a new culture that international audiences found meaningful in their daily lives and habits.

Mass media, and cinema in particular, formed the modern means of education, cultural formation, and inspiration in addition to providing role models. Two aspects of this phenomenon were the star system and eroticism, joined together in Silvana Mangano's most famous performance—in *Bitter Rice*, a film nominated for an Academy Award in 1949. In this, her film debut, De Santis transformed Mangano into an instant star. The eroticism in the film liberated the human body from something to be leered at to something that could be celebrated and enjoyed, thus starting a trend in the Italian cinema which made stars of such women as Mangano, Gina Lollabrigida and Sophia Loren.

Ironically, the very director who freed Italian cinema from provincialism found it increasingly difficult to get his projects accepted and funded in his own country. His best works of the second half of his career were made only partially with Italian capital, and often outside the country. *La Strada lunga un anno*, about the building of a road, was filmed in and financed by Yugoslavia, and indicated the possibility of a socialist cinema by joyfully depicting the solidarity of unpaid workers. Much applauded in the United States, it received the Golden Globe from the Hollywood critics as well as an Academy Award nomination. *Italiani brava gente* was the first Italian-Soviet coproduction, with some American financing. Successfully and convincingly, De Santis creates a gallery of characters at the Russian front during the war: a Roman, a Sicilian, a Pugliese, and Emilian played by a Soviet actor, a Milanese commandant played by Arthur Kennedy, and a Neopolitan of the medical corps played by Peter Falk! The circumstances of this production permitted De Santis to express one of this strongest beliefs: differences between people are no longer based on nationalities but on class and occupation.

—Elaine Mancini

DE SICA, VITTORIO. Italian. Born in Sora (near Rome), 7 July 1902; became citizen of France, 1968. Attended Institut Supérieur de Commerce, Rome, 1917-18; also graduated from University of Rome with accounting degree. Married Giuditta Rissone (div. 1968); married Maria Mercader, 1968; children: Manuel and Christian. Career: 1918—appears in small role in 1st film *Il processo Clémenceau* (Bencivenga); 1923—joins Tatiana Pavlova's stage company; mid 1920s—serves in Italian military; late 1920s—forms own stage company to produce plays starring himself and actress-wife Giuditta Rissone; 1931—appears in film *La Vecchia Signora*, establishing himself as matinee idol; 1935—while acting in *Darò un milione* meets future scriptwriting collaborator Cesare Zavattini; 1968—becomes citizen of France in order to obtain divorce from 1st wife and marry Maria Mercader. Died 13 November 1974 in Paris.

Films (as director): 1940—*Rose scarlette* (co-d, +ro as *The Engineer*); 1941—*Maddelena zero in condotta* (+dialogue, ro as Carlo Hartman); *Teresa Venerdí* (+co-sc, ro); 1942—*Un garibaldino al convento* (+co-sc, ro as Nino Bixio); 1943—*I bambini ci guardano* (+co-sc); 1946—*La porta del cielo* (+co-sc—completed 1944); *Sciuscia (Shoeshine)* (+co-sc); *Roma città libera* (co-sc only); *Il marito povero* (Amata) (co-sc only); 1948—*Ladri di biciclette (The Bicycle Thief)* (+pr, co-sc); 1950—*Miracolo a Milano (Miracle in Milan)* (+co-sc); 1952—*Umberto D* (+pr +co-sc); 1953—*Stazione Termini (Indiscretion of an American Wife, Indiscretion)* (+co-pr); 1954—*L'oro di Napoli (Gold of Naples)* (+co-sc, ro); 1956—*Il tetto (The Roof)* (+pr); 1960—*La ciociara (2 Women)*; 1961—*Il giudizio universale* (+ro); 1962—"La Riffa (The Raffle)" episode of *Boccaccio '70*; *I sequestrati di Altona (The Condemned of Altona)*; 1963—*Il boom*; *Ieri, oggi, domani (Yesterday, Today, and Tomorrow)*; 1964—*Matrimonio all'italiana (Marriage, Italian Style)*; 1965—*Un Monde nouveau (Un Monde jeune, Un mondo nuovo, A Young World)*; 1966—*Caccia alla volpe (After the Fox)* (+guest ro); "Un sera come le altre (A Night Like Any Other)" episode of *Le streghe (The Witches)*; 1967—*Woman Times 7 (Sept fois femmes)*; 1968—*Amanti (A Place for Lovers)* (+co-sc); 1970—*I girasoli (Sunflower)*; *Il giardino dei Finzi Contini (The Garden of the Finzi-Continis)*; "Il leone" episode of *Le coppie (Les Couples)*; 1971—"Il 2 giugno (Dal referendum alla Costituzione)" episode of *Nascita della Repubblica* (for TV); 1972—*Lo chiameremo Andrea*; 1973—*Una breve vacanza (A Brief Vacation)*; 1974—*Il viaggio (The Journey, The Voyage)*.

Roles (in films not directed): 1918—*Il processo Clémenceau (L'Affaire Clemenceau* (Bencivenga); 1926—*La bellezza del mondo* (Almirante); 1928—*La compagnia dei matti (La compagnie des fous)* (Almirante); 1932—*La vecchia signora* (Palermi); *La segretaria per tutti* (Palermi); *Due cuori felici* (Negroni); *Gli uomini...che mascalzoni* (Camerini); 1933—*Un cattivo soggetto* (Bragaglia); *Il signore desidera?* (Righelli); *The Secretary* in *La canzone del sole* (German version: *Das Lied der Sonne* (Neufeld); *Lisetta* (Boese); 1934—*Tempo massimo* (Mattòli); 1935—*The Millionaire* in *Darò un millione* (Camerini); *Amo te sola* (Mattòli); 1936—*Lohengrin* (Malasomma); *Ma non è una cosa seria!* (Camerini); *Non ti conosco più* (Malasomma); *L'uomo che sorride* (Mattòli); 1937—*Hanno rapito un uomo* (Righelli); *Il signor Max* (Camerini); *Questi ragazzi* (Mattòli); 1938—*Napoli d'altri tempi* (Palermi); *L'orologio a cucù* (Mastrocinque); *Partire* (Palermi); *La mazurka di papà* (Biancoli); *Le due madri* (Palermi); *Ai vostri ordini, signora!* (Mattòli); *Castelli in aria* (German version: *Ins blaue Leben*, 1939) (Genina); 1939—*Grandi magazzini* (Camerini); *Finisce sempre così* (Susini); *Napoli che non muore* (Palermi); 1940—*La peccatrice* (Palermi); *Pazza di gioia* (Bragaglia); *Manon Lescaut* (Gallone); 1941—*L'avventuriera del piano di sopra* (Matarazzo); 1942—*Se io fossi onesto!* (Bragaglia) (+co-sc); *La guardia del corpo* (Bragaglia) (+co-sc); 1943—*I nostri sogni* (Cottafavi) (+co-sc); *Non sono superstizioso, ma...!* (Bragaglia) (+co-sc); *L'ippocampo* (Rosmino) (+co-sc); *Diece minuti di vita* (Longanesi) (unfinished—another version made in 1944 with different cast); *Nessuno torna indietro* (Blasetti); 1945—*Lo sbaglio di essere vivo* (Bragaglia); *Il mondo vuole così* (Bianchi); 1946—*Abbasso la ricchezza!* (Righelli) (+co-sc); 1947—*Nanzio* in *Sperduti nel buio* (Mastrocinque) (+co-sc); *The noble Neopolitan* in *Natale al campo 119* (Francisci) (+supervisor); 1948—*The Proprietor* in *Lo sconosciuto di San Marino* (Waszinsky); *The Landlord* in *Cuore* (Coletti) (+co-sc); 1950—*Professor Landi* in *Domani è troppo tardi* (Moguy); 1951—*The Actor* in *Cameriera bella presenza offresi* (Pastina); *The Barrister* in "Il processo di Frine" episode of *Altri tempi* (Blasetti); *Gli uomini non guardano il cielo* (Scarpelli); 1952—*Garetti* in *Buongiorno elefante! (Sabú principe ladro)* (Franciolini) (+co-sc); *Count* in "Scena all'aperto" and *Don Corradino* in "Don Corradino" episodes of *Tempi nostri* (Blasetti); 1953—*Fabrizio Donati* in *Madame De...* (Ophuls); *Marshal Carotenuto* in *Pane, amore e fantasia* (Comencini); "Pendolin" episode of *Cento anni d'amore* (De Felice); "Incidente a Villa Borghese" episode of *Villa Borghese* (Franciolini); *Il matrimonio* (Petrucci); "Il fine dicitore" episode of *Gran varietà* (Paolella); "Le Divorce (Il divorzio)" episode of *Secrets d'alcôve (Il letto)* (Franciolini); 1954—*The Banker* in *Vergine moderna* (Pagliero); *The General* in *L'Allegro Squadrone* (Moffa); *Pane, amore e gelosia* (Comencini); *Mr. Stroppiani* in *Peccato che sia una canaglia* (Blasetti); 1955—*Alessio Spano, the Poet* in *Il segno di Venere* (Risi); *Carlo* in *Gli ultimi cinque minuti (The Last 5 Minutes)* (Amato); *The Governor* in *La bella mugnaia* (Camerini); *Carotenuto* in *Pane, amore e...* (Risi); *Racconti romani* (Franciolini); *The Barrister* in *Il bigamo* (Emmer); 1956—*Sénèquel* in *Mio figlio Nerone (Nero's Weekend)* (Steno); *The Celebrity* in *Tempo di villegiatura* (Racioppi); *Count Dino Giocondo Della Fiaba* in *The Monte Carlo Story (Montecarlo)* (Taylor); *The Banker* in *I giorni più belli (I nostri anni più belli, Gli anni più belli)* (Mattòli); *Celimontani* in *Noi siamo le colonne* (D'Amico); 1957—*The tailor Corallo* in *Padri e figli* (Monicelli); *The barrister Vasari* in *I colpevoli* (Vasile); *The Count* in *Souvenir d'Italie (It Happened in Rome)* (Pietrangeli); 1957—*Bordigin* in *La donna che venne dal mare* (De Robertis); *Occhipinti* in *Vacanze a Ischia* (Camerini); *Count Max Orsini Baraldo* in *Il conte Max* (Bianchi); *Bonelli* in *Amore e chiacchiere* (Blasetti); *Locoratolo* in *Il medico e lo stregone* (Monicelli); *The sick nobleman* in *Totò, Vittorio e la dottoressa* (Mastrocinque); *Alexandre Gordy* in *Casino de Paris* (Hunebelle); 1958—*Count Alessandro Rinaldi* in *A Farewell to Arms* (Vidor); *Mr. Guastaldi* in *Domenica è sempre domenica* (Mastrocinque); *The Policeman, the taxi driver, and the costume porter* in *Ballerina e buon Dio* (Leonviola); *Count Ernesto De Rossi* in *Kanonenserenade (Pezzo, capopezzo e capitano)* (Staudte); *Don Luigino* in *Anna di Brooklyn* (Denham and Lastricati) (+supervisor, co-music); *Armando Conforti* in *La ragazza di Piazza S. Pietro* (Costa); *Professor Landi* in *Gli zitelloni* (Bianchi); *Carotenuto* in *Pane, amore e Andulasia* (Setò); *Alfredo* in *La prima notte* (Cavalcanti); 1959—*Spartaco* in *Nel blu dipinto di blu (Volare)* (Tellini); *The Husband* in *Il nemico di mia moglie* (Puccini); *Manrizie* in *Vacanze d'inverno* (Mastrocinque); *The President* in *Il moralista* (Bianchi); *Giovanni Bertone* in *Il Generale Della Rovere* (Rossellini); *Pietro Giordani* in *Il mondo dei miracoli* (Capuano); *Marquis Nicolas Peccoli* in *Uomini e nobiluomini* (Bianchi); *Ceccano* in *Ferdinando I, re di Napoli* (Franciolini); *The Prince* in *Gastone* (Bonnard); *Colonel Belalcazar* in *Les trois etc ... du colonel (Le tre eccetera del colonnello)* (Boissol); 1960—*The Trustee* in *Il vigile* (Zampa); *Colonel Pietro Cuocolo* in *Le pillole di Ercole* (Salce); *Pope Pius VII* in *Austerlitz* (Gance); *General Clave* in *The Angel Wore Red (La sposa bella)* (Johnson); *Joe* in *The Millionairess* (Asquith); *Mario Vitale* in *It Started in Naples* (Shavelson); *Comic actor* in *Gli incensurati* (Giaculli); *Un amore a Roma* (Risi); 1961—*Colonel Bitossi* in *Gli attendenti* (Bianchi); *Antonio Cotone* in *I due marescialli* (Corbucci); *The Genie* in *Le meraviglie di Aladino (The Wonders of Aladdin)* (Bava and Levin); *The Chef* in *L'onorata società* (Pazzaglia); *Bancroft* in *La Fayette (La Fayette, una spada per due bandiere)* (Dréville); 1962—*don Pedro* in *Vive Henry IV, vive l'amour* (Autant-Lara); 1965—*The Count* in *The Amorous Adventures of Moll Flanders* (T. Young); 1966—*Count Trepossi* in *Io, io, io...e gli altri* (Blasetti); 1967—*Man on Pension* in *Gli altri, gli altri e noi* (Arena); *Giuseppe's Father* in *Un italiano in America* (Sordi); *Cesare Celli* in *The Biggest Bundle of Them All* (Annakin); *Count de Bièvres* in *Caroline Cherie* (de la Patellière); 1968—*Cardinal Rinaldi* in *The Shoes of the Fisherman (Les Souliers de Saint-Pierre)* (M. Anderson); 1969—*The Shoemaker* in *If It's Tuesday, This Must Be Belgium* (M. Stuart); *Di Seta* in *Una su tredici (12 + 1)* (Gessner and Lucignani); 1970—*The Lawyer* in *Cose di Cosa Nostra* (Steno); *Milord* in *L'Odeur des fauves* (Balducci); 1971—*Enrico Formichi* in *Trastevere* (Tozzi); *Count at the Casino* in *Io non vedo, tu non parli, lui non sente* (Camerini); 1972—*The Judge* in *Pinocchio* (Comencini) (for TV); *Dolphi* in *Snow Job (The Ski Raiders)* (Englund); *Giove* in *Ettore lo fusto* (Castellari); *Siamo tutti in libertà provvisoria* (Scarpelli); 1973—*The Marshal* in *Storia de fratelli e de cortelli* (Amendola); *Mauro del Giudice* in *Il delitto Matteotti* (Vancini); 1974—*Marquis di Fiori* in *Andy Warhol's Dracula (Dracula cerca sangue di vergine e . . . morì di sete!!, Blood for Dracula)* (Morrissey); *himself* in *C'eravamo tanto amati* (Scola); *Vittorio De Sica, il Regista, l'attore, l'uomo* (Gragadze).

Publications:

By DE SICA:

Books—*Umberto D.*, with Cesare Zavattini, Rome 1954; *The Bicycle Thief*, with C. Zavattini, New York 1968; *Miracle in Milan* (plus filmography and 2 articles by De Sica), with C. Zavattini and others, New York 1968; articles—"*Le voleur de bicyclette*", with C. Zavattini and others in *Ciné-Club* (Paris), January 1950; interview in *L'Ecran français* (Paris), Christmas 1950; interview by F. Koval in *Sight and Sound* (London), April 1950; "*Miracle a Milan*" (extract), with C. Zavattini and others in *Cinémonde* (Paris), 1953; "The Most Wonderful Years of My Life" in *Films and Filming* (London), December 1955; "On ne peut pas être heureux sans toit" in *Lettres françaises* (Paris), May 1956; "Illiberal Censorship" in *Film* (London), January-February 1956; "Money, the Public, and *Umberto D*" in *Films and Filming* (London), January 1956; "Hollywood Shocked Me" in *Films and Filming* (London), February 1956; "I Must Act to Pay My Debts" in *Films and Filming* (London), March 1956; "British Humor? It's the Same in Italy" in *Films and Filming* (London), April 1959; "De Sica on Sophia Loren" in *Vogue* (New York), 1 November 1962; "What's Right With Hollywood" in *Films and Filming* (London), November 1963; "*Le voleur de bicyclette*", with C. Zavattini and others in *L'Avant-Scène du cinéma* (Paris), December 1967; "*Le voleur de bicyclette*" (extracts), with C. Zavattini and others in *Cinémathèque belge* (Brussels), 1958; "Le Jardin des Finzi-Contini", interview by G. Braucourt in *Ecran* (Paris), February 1972; entire issue of articles by De Sica in *Bianco e Nero* (Rome), fall 1975; "El humanista De Sica", interview by A. García Rayo in *Cinema 2002* (Madrid), July/August 1980.

On DE SICA:

Books—*Il cinema italiano* by Carlo Lizzani, Florence 1954; *Il cinema neorealistico italiano* by G.C. Castello, Turin 1956; *Il neorealismo italiano* by Brunello Rondi, Parma 1956; *Il nuovo cinema italiano* by Giuseppe Ferrara, Florence 1957; *Le Néo-Réalism italien et ses créateurs* by Patrice G. Hovald, Paris 1959; *Le Néo-Réalism italien* by Borde-Bouissy, Lausanne, France 1960; *Vittorio De Sica* by Henri Agel, 2nd ed., Paris 1964; *Vittorio De Sica* by Pierre Leprohon, Paris 1966; *Encountering Directors* by Charles Thomas Samuels, New York 1972; *Qu'est-ce que le cinéma* by André Bazin, 2nd ed., Paris 1975; *Neorealismo e vita nazionale: Antologia di cinema nuovo* edited by Mario Guaraldi-Rimini, Florence 1975; *La mia vita con Vittorio De Sica* by Maria Mercader, Milan, Italy 1978; *Anthologie du cinéma* vol.10, Paris 1979; articles—"De Sica's Bicycle Thieves and Italian Humanism" by H.L. Jacobson in *Hollywood Quarterly*, fall 1949; "De Sica Dissected" by R.F. Hawkins in *Films in Review* (New York), May 1951; "The Case of De Sica" by Gavin Lambert in *Sight and Sound* (London), June 1951; "Miracle Man" in the *New Yorker*, 5 April 1952; "De Sica in Chicago" by M. Picker in *Films in Review* (New York), May 1952; "Bread, Love, and Neo-Realism" by W. Sargeant in the *New Yorker*, 29 June 1957 and 6 July 1957; "Why Neo-Realism Failed" by Eric Rhode in *Sight and Sound* (London), winter 1960/61; "Italy: the Moral Cinema: Notes on Some Recent Films by Vernon Young in *Film Quarterly* (Berkeley, California), fall 1961; "The Face of '63—Italy" by John Francis Lane in *Films and Filming* (London), April 1963; "How They Live and Die in Naples" in *Horizon* (Los Angeles), September 1963; "A Case of Artistic Inflation" by J.F. Lane in *Sight and Sound* (London), summer 1963; "Poet of Poverty" by D. McVay in *Films and Filming* (London), November 1964; interview in *Travel and Camera* (New York), April 1970; interview by D. Lyons in *Interview* (New York), February 1972; "What Directors are Saying" in *Action* (Los Angeles), May/June 1972; issue devoted to De Sica edited by O. Caldiron, *Bianco e nero* (Rome), September/December 1975; "Vittorio de Sica: Always a True Window" by Gideon Bachmann in *Sight and Sound* (London), spring 1975; "De Sica o della doppia costante: il sorriso e il tarlo segreto" by E. Comuzio in *Cineforum* (Bergamo), January 1975; "Le Cinéma du néo-realisme italien est en berne: Vittorio de Sica" by J.-L. Passek in *Cinéma* (Paris), January 1975; "Le Tombeau de Sica" by T. Ranieri in *Positif* (Paris), January 1975; biofilmography in *Film Dope* (London), January 1977; "Vittorio de Sica 1902-1974" by Henri Agel, special issue of *Avant-Scène du cinéma* (Paris), 15 October 1978; "Vittorio de Sica" by J. Passalacqua in *Films in Review* (New York), April 1978; "Dossier: le neo-realisme: De Sica 'le menteur'" by P. Carcassonne in *Cinématographe* (Paris), January 1979; films—*Meet De Sica* by Bika De Reisner; *Vittorio De Sica: Il regista, l'attore, l'uomo*, for TV, by Peter Dragadze, 1974.

*   *   *

The films of Vittorio De Sica are among the most enduring of the Italian post-war period. His career suggest an openness to form and a versatility uncommon among Italian directors. De Sica began acting on stage as a teenager and played his first film role in 1918. In the twenties, his handsome features and talent made him something of a matinee idol, and from the mid-thirties he appeared in a number of films by Mario Camerini including *Gliuomini, che mascalzoni, Daro un milione...* and *Grandi magazzine*. During his lifetime, he made over 100 films in Italy and abroad as actor, using this means to finance his own films. He specialized in breezy comic heroes, men of great self assurance or confidence men (as in Rossellini's *Generale della Rovere*). The influence of his tenure as actor cannot be overestimated in his directorial efforts, where the expressivity of the actor in carefully written roles was one of his foremost technical implements. In this vein De Sica has continually mentioned the influence on his work of Charlie Chaplin. The tensive continuity between tragic and comic, the deployment of a detailed yet poetic gestural language, and a humanist philosophy without recourse to the politically radical are all paralleled in the silent star's films.

De Sica's directorial debuts, *Rose scarlatte* and *Maddalena, zero in condotta*, are both attempts to bring theater pieces to the screen with suitable roles for himself. With his fourth film, *I bambini ci guardano*, De Sica teamed with Cesare Zavattini, who was to become his major collaborator for the next three decades, and together they began to demonstrate elements of the

post-war realist aesthetic which, more than any other director except Visconti and Rossellini, De Sica helped shape and determine. Despite the overt melodrama of the misogynistic story (a young mother destroys her family by deserting them), the filmmaker has refused to narrow the perspective through an overwrought Hollywoodian mise-en-scene, preferring instead a refreshing simplicity of composition and a subdued editing style. Much of the film's original flavor can be traced to the clear, subjective mediation of a child as promised in the title.

De Sica's intense feeling for children's sensibilities led him to imagine how children viewed the failing adult reconstruction of society after the war. *Sciuscia*, a realistic look at the street and prison life of poor, abandoned children, was the result. It is the story of how the lasting friendship of two homeless boys, who make their living shining shoes for the American G.I.'s, is betrayed by their contact with adults. At the end one inadvertently causes the other's death. Although Zavattini insists that his creative role was minimal in this instance, the presence of his poetic imagination is evident in the beautiful white horse which cements the boys' mutual bond and their hope for a future. Though a miserable failure in Italy, *Sciuscia* marked De Sica's entry into international prominence. It won a special Oscar in 1947.

For the balance of the neorealist period it was an uphill fight to finance his films through friends and acting salaries. *Ladri di biciclette* anchors searching social documentation in metaphor and a non-traditional but highly structured marrative. The workman Ricci's desperate search for his bicycle is an odyssey that enables us to witness a varied collection of characters and situations among the poor and working class of Rome. Each episode propels the narrative toward a sublimely Chaplinesque but insufficiently socially critical ending in which Ricci is defeated in his search and therefore in his attempts to provide for his family. Reduced to being a thief himself, he takes his son's hand and disappears into the crowd. Like De Sica's other neorealist films, *Ladri di biciclette* gives the impression of technical nonchalance only to the indiscriminate eye for De Sica planned his work with attention to minute details of characterization, mise-en-scene, and camera technique. During this period he preferred the non-professional actor for his or her ability to accept direction without the mediation of learned acting technique.

The story of Toto the Good in *Miracolo a Milano* remains one of the outstanding stylistic contradictions of the neorealist period (there are many) yet one which sheds an enormous amount of light on the intentions and future of the De Sica-Zavattini team. The cinematography and setting, markedly neorealist in this fable about the struggle to found a shanty town for the homeless, is undercut at every moment with unabashed clowning both in performance and in cinematic technique. Moreover, the film moves toward a problematic fairy tale ending in which the poor, no longer able to defend their happy, makeshift village now beleaguered by the voracious appetite of capitalist entrepreneurs, take to the skies on magic broomsticks. (The film has more special effects than anyone would ever associate with neorealism; could De Sica have left his mark on Steven Spielberg?) Still, Zavattini, who had wanted to make the film for a number of years, and De Sica defend it as the natural burlesque transformation of themes evident in their earlier work together.

By this time De Sica's films were the subject of a good deal of controversy in Italy, and generally the lines were drawn between Catholic and Communist critics. The latter had an especially acute fear (one which surfaced again with Fellini's *La Strada*) that the hard-won traits of neorealism had begun to backslide into those of the so-called "calligraphic" films of the Fascist era. These were based on an ahistorical, formal concern for aesthetic, compositional qualities and the nuances of clever storytelling. However their next film *Umberto D*, comes closest to Zavattini's ideas on the absolute responsibility of the camera eye to observe life as it is lived without the traditional compromises of entertaining narratives. The sequence of the maid waking up and making the morning coffee has been praised many times for its day-in-the-life directness and simplicity. *Il Tetto*, about a curious attempt to erect a small house on municipal property, is generally recognized as the last neorealist film of this original period.

Continually wooed by Hollywood, De Sica finally acquiesced to make *Stazione termini* in 1953, produced by Selznick and filmed in Rome with Jennifer Jones and Montgomery Clift. Unfortunately, neorealist representation formed only an insignificant background to this typically American star vehicle. A similar style is employed in *La ciociara* from a Moravia story about the relationship of a mother and daughter uprooted by the war. De Sica attempted in it to reconstruct reality in the studio making use of a somewhat unsuccessful stylized lighting technique but, as usual, he obtains excellent performances in an engaging dramatic vehicle. (Sophia Loren won an Oscar.)

The filmmakers returned to comedic vehicles in 1954 in *L'oro di Napoli*. Human comedy emerges from the rich diversity and liveliness of Neapolitan life. Three episodes featuring Totò as the little man set upon by a bullying thug, Loren as the amorous wife of a baker, and Silvana Mangano as a dignified prostitute trapped into marriage, complete the comic gallery though still within the confines of realism, the film foreshadows the director's entrance into the popular Italian market for sexual satire and farce. The exactitude with which he sculpts his characters and his reluctance to reduce the scenario to a mere bunch of gags demonstrates his intention to fuse comedy and drama, putting De Sica at the top of his class in this respect—among Risi, Comencini, and Monicelli. Often with Zavattini but also with Eduardo De Filippo, Tonino Guerra, and even Neil Simon (*After the Fox*), De Sica turned out about eight such films for the lucrative international market between 1961 and 1968, the best of which are: *Il giudizio universale* with an all-star cast of international comedians; *Ieri, oggi, domani* and *Matrimonio all'Italiana* both with Loren and Mastroianni; and *Sette volte donna*. Many of these films deserve more critical attention than they have received.

Il giardino dei Finzi Contini from a Bassani novel about the incarceration of Italian Jews during the war shows a strong Viscontian influence in its lavish setting and thematics, dealing with the dissolution of the bourgeois family. *Una breve vacanza*, an examination of a woman who has managed to break out of the confines of a oppressive marriage during a sanitorium stay, reinstitutes the tensive relationship between comedy and tragedy of the earlier films. De Sica's last film, *Il viaggio*, is from a Pirandello novel.

—Joel Kanoff

DE TOTH, ANDRÉ. Hungarian. Born Sásvrái Farkasfawi Tóthfalusi Tóth Endre Antai Mihaly in Mako, Hungary, 1910. Educated at the University of Budapest, degree in law 1926. Married Veronica Lake, 1944 (divorced 1952). Career: 1926—joins theatrical troupe; 1929—visits Vienna and makes publicity film for department store; continues to work in Vienna for Bavarisch Pictura Productions; 1930s—works on Hungarian films as scriptwriter, editor, 2nd-unit director and occasional actor; 1939—with outbreak of war, sent as correspondent to German-Polish front; obtains visa, emigrates to England, engaged

by Alexander Korda; early 1940s—works on London Film productions including *The Thief of Bagdad, Sahara, 4 Feathers* and *Jungle Book*; 1943—moves to Hollywood; 1953—directs 3-D feature *House of Wax*; 1960s—directs 16 episodes of U.S. TV series including *77 Sunset Strip, Bronco, Maverick*, and *The Westerner*; 1964—serious skiing accident temporarily halts career. Agent: Marvin Moss, Marvin Moss Inc., Los Angeles, CA 90069. Address: 3690 Barham Blvd., Los Angeles, CA 90068.

Films (as scriptwriter): 1937—*Falu rossza (Evil Village)* (Pásztor) (story only); *The Life of Emile Zola* (Dieterle) (co-sc uncredited); (directed in Hungary as Tóth Endre): 1939—*Öt óra 40 (At 5:40)*; *Két lány az utcán (2 Girls of the Street)*; *Semmelweiss*; *Hat hét boldogság (6 Weeks of Happiness)*; *Balalaika*; *Toprini nász (Wedding in Toprin)* (+co-sc); 1941—*Lydia* (Duvivier) (pr ass't, +co-sc both uncredited); (directed in U.S. as André de Toth): 1943—*Passport to Suez* (+story, uncredited); 1944—*None Shall Escape*; *Dark Waters*; *Guest in the House* (Brahm) (d several scenes, +co-sc, both uncredited); 1946—*Young Widow* (Marin) (co-sc only, uncredited); 1947—*Ramrod*; *The Other Love*; *Dishonored Lady* (Stevenson) (co-sc only, uncredited); 1948—*Pitfall*; 1949—*Slattery's Hurricane*; 1950—*The Gunfighter* (King) (co-story only); 1951—*Man in the Saddle (The Outcast)*; 1952—*Carson City*; *Springfield Rifle*; *Last of the Comanches (The Sabre and the Arrow)*; *Riding Shotgun*; 1953—*House of Wax*; *Thunder Over the Plains*; *The Stranger Wore a Gun*; 1954—*The Bounty Hunter*; *Tanganyika*; *Crime Wave (The City Is Dark)*; *Riding Shotgun*; 1955—*The Indian Fighter*; 1956—*Westward Ho the Wagons!* (Beaudine) (co-sc only uncredited); 1957—*Monkey on My Back*; *Hidden Fear* (+co-sc); 1959—*The 2-Headed Spy*; *Day of the Outlaw*; 1960—*Man on a String (Confessions of a Counterspy)*; 1961—*Morgan il pirata (Morgan the Pirate)* (co-d, +co-sc); *I Mongoli (The Mongols)* (co-d); 1962—*Oro per i Cesari (Gold for the Caesars)* (co-d); 1967—*Billion Dollar Brain* (Russell) (exec pr only); 1968—*Play Dirty* (+exec pr); 1970—*El Condor* (Guillermin) (pr only).

Publications:

On DE TOTH:

Articles—"Problem Child with Good Intentions" by B. Bangs in *Silver Screen* (New York), March 1945; "The Amazing de Toths" by M. Howard in *Silver Screen* (New York), July 1947; biofilmography in *Film Dope* (London), January 1977.

*   *   *

André De Toth is a superb visual stylist of remarkable control and intensity whose work is virtually unknown today except to a few scholars who see him as a true artist. His excellent body of work contains a unifying set of thematic and visual characteristics which add up to a strong personal cinema.

The films of André De Toth seem to begin in the middle of events which are already under way. Both the main characters and the viewers find themselves in an already determined chain of events in which one's position is not fully understood. The films use space, geography, location and setting to represent the inner psychology of the characters. In *Dark Waters*, the leading lady (Merle Oberon) has been psychologically damaged by a wartime experience in which the boat carrying her and her parents was torpedoed. The "dark waters" of her emotions, her confused memories of the resulting deaths of her parents, and her deep fears for her own safety are represented on screen by the swamp that surrounds the southern mansion she visits. Ultimately, she must save herself from the villains by entering the swamp and plunging into the dark waters to hide, confronting her fear.

The universe in which the characters in a De Toth film live is a treacherous one. It is a world in which safety falls away, and danger is objectively demonstratd through "deep waters," quicksands, and hostile terrain. In such circumstances, a hero frequently has to behave villainously in order to survive. In *Pitfall*, Dick Powell is supposedly safe inside his typical suburban home of the 1950s, but a killer stalks him there. Powell is forced to move outside and begin to stalk the killer. Thus the hero and the villain exchange places, a change which De Toth demonstrates skillfully through camera movement, point of view, and composition.

Whether working in the film noir tradition in such films as *Dark Waters* and *Pitfall* or in westerns such as *Ramrod, Day of the Outlaw*, and *Indian Fighter*, De Toth's films reflect common themes. Ordinary people are trapped in situations beyond their control and are forced to struggle for mastery. They are subject to betrayals by those they considered friends, and characters reverse themselves as to behavior patterns. A desire for escape or adventure can lead a character into a nightmare situation. Above all, the films reflect a cynical attitude toward human nature. Deception and treachery are everyday occurrences, and the ambiguous endings of the films seem to be happy, but upon reflection may not be. De Toth uses a moving camera to create tension, employing reverse pans against tracks to demonstrate the treacherous nature of events upon the screen. His camera explores the space of the frame, guiding the viewer through the uncertain events of the narrative much as the characters are guided through their story. The frequent reversals of character are ably demonstrated formally on the screen, as De Toth matches his manipulation of the tools of film technique to story events with great skill. In the opening sequence of *Play Dirty*, a German soldier is seen driving a jeep across the North African desert during World War II. The radio loudly plays "Lili Marlene." At a certain point, the soldier checks his map, calmly removes his German cap and jacket, and dons a British uniform, switching the radio to an English broadcast. This is the perfect statement of De Toth's world and his characters. The world is tricky and can change swiftly, because human beings are tricky and capable of being the opposite of what they seem. Furthermore, such behavior is necessary for survival.

André De Toth was never a popular director with critics, most of whom ignored his low-budget films. If he was known at all, it was as a former husband of the glamorous actress Veronica Lake, or perhaps as the one-eyed man who directed a 3-D smash hit of the fifties, *House of Wax*, even though he could not perceive true depth. His cruel themes and deliberately visual form of story-telling did not create beloved, well-remembered films which pleased either audiences or critics, In the great re-evaluation of film directors inspired by the first waves of American auteurism in the 1960s, he was more or less overlooked. His work, with its visual and thematic rewards, is yet to be fully discovered and analyzed.

—Jeanine Basinger

DICKINSON, THOROLD. British. Born in Bristol, 16 November 1903. Educated at Clifton College, Keble College, Oxford.

Married Joanna Macfadyen (architect), 1929. Career: 1925—entered film industry as interpreter for George Pearson working in France; subsequently film editor, director and scriptwriter; 1929-39—in charge of program presentation for The Film Society, London, and member of the Council (1932-39); 1936-53—Vice-President, Assn. of Cine-Technicians; visits Soviet Union 1937 as representative of that group; 1942-43—organizes Army Kinematograph Service Production Group, produces 17 military training films; 1946—spends 4 months in India on unrealized film project for Viceroy of India, Lord Wavell; 1950-53—Chairman of the British Film Academy; 1953-54—film advisor in Israel; 1956-60—Chief of the Film Service, Office of Public Information, United Nations; 1958-66—President of the International Federation of Film Societies; 1959-present—jury chairman for numerous international film festivals; 1960—introduces Film Studies in Higher Education in the Slade School of Fine Art, University College, London; 1967—appointment at London University makes him first Professor of Film at a British university. Recipient: Commander of the British Empire, 1973. Address: Wing Cottage, Sheepdrove, Lambourn, Berkshire.

Films (as assistant director): 1926—*The Little People* (Pearson) (+co-sc); 1927—*Huntingtower* (Pearson); (as editor): 1928—*Love's Option* (Pearson) (co-ed, +ass't d); 1929—*Auld Lang Syne* (Pearson) (co-ed, +synchronization of song sequences); 1930—*The School for Scandal* (Elvey); 1931—*The Sport of Kings* (Saville); *Contraband Love* (Morgan); *Other People's Sins* (Hill); *The Great Gay Road* (Hill); *Lloyd of the CID (Detective Lloyd)* (12 episode serial) (MacRae); (ed 8 episodes); 1932—*The First Mrs. Fraser* (Hill); *Karma* (Rai and Freer-Hunt); *Perfect Understanding* (Gardner); 1933—*Going Gay (Kiss Me Goodbye)* (Gallone—completed 1931); *For Love of You* (Gallone—completed 1931); *Loyalties* (Dean); 1934—*Java Head* (Ruben) (+completion of film after director fell ill); *Sing as We Go!* (Dean); 1935—*The Silent Passenger* (Denham); *Midshipman Easy (Men of the Sea)* (Reed) (+supervisor); 1936—*Whom the Gods Love (Mozart)* (Dean); *Calling the Tune* (Denham) (co-ed); *The House of the Spaniard* (Denham); (as director): 1937—*The High Command*; 1938—*Spanish ABC* (short) (co-d, +co-ed); *Behind the Spanish Lines* (short) (co-d, +co-ed); 1939—*The Arsenal Stadium Mystery* (+co-adapt); 1939—*The Mikado* (Schertzinger) (2nd unit d only); 1940—*Gaslight (Angel Street)*; (short films for Ministry of Information): *Westward Ho! 1940* (+pr, co-ed); *Yesterday Is Over Your Shoulder* (+pr, co-ed); *The Horseshoe Nail* (abandoned because of objections of Ministry of Aircraft Production); 1941—*The Prime Minister*; 1942—*The Next of Kin* (+co-sc); (as producer/-supervisor of films for Army Kinematograph Service—partial list): 1942—*The New Lot* (Reed); *Tank Tactics* series (F.A. Young and others) (6 2-reelers); (plus 10 other titles); (as director): 1946—*Men of 2 Worlds (Kisenga, Man of Africa)* (+co-sc); 1948—*The Queen of Spades*; 1951—*Secret People* (+story, co-sc); 1954—*Hakarka ha a dom (The Red Ground)* (short) (+co-sc, ed, bit ro as man playing cards); 1955—*Hill 24 Doesn't Answer* (+co-pr, co-sc, co-ed); (as producer/supervisor of short films for United Nations): 1957—*Question in Togoland* (Porter); *Out* (Rogosin); *Blue Vanguard* (feature) (McNeill); *3 of Our Children* (Reed and Estelle); 1958—*Overture* (Polidoro and Singh); *Exposure* (Hughes and Singh); *Pablo Casals Breaks His Journey* (Sarma); *Big Day in Bogo* (N. Reed); *Power Among Men* (feature) (Hammid, Polidoro and Sarma) (+co-sc, ed); 1959—*In Our Hands* (Sarma); *A Scary Time* (Clarke); *Workshop for Peace* (Hammid—revised version of a 1955 film); 1960—*The Farmers of Fermathe* (Polidoro) (footage from *Power Among Men*, 1958).

Publications:

By DICKINSON:

Books—*Soviet Cinema*, with Catherine de la Roche, London 1948 (reissued New York, 1972); screenplay of *Secret People* in *Making a Film* by Lindsay Anderson, London 1952; *The Technique of Film Editing* by Karel Reisz, introduction and guidance by Thorold Dickinson, London 1952; *A Discovery of Cinema*, London 1971; *A Discovery of the Cinema*, New York 1971; articles—"Shooting in the Tropics Is No Fun" in *Picturegoer* (London), November 1944; "Search for Music" and "Indian Spring" in *Penguin Film Review*, London 1948; "The Filmwright and the Audience" in *Sight and Sound* (London), March 1950; "The Third Eye" in *Diversion* (London), 1950; "A Film Is Made" in *Pelican Film Annual*, London 1951; "Griffith and the Development of the Silent Film" in *Sight and Sound* (London), October 1951; "A Day in the Life of a Film" in *Sight and Sound* (London), August 1951; "The Work of Sir Michael Balcon" in *The Year's Work in Film*, London 1951; "Secret People" in *Cinema* (London), 1952; "Heaven Preserve Us from the Passive Audience!" in *Film* (London), September/October 1955; "The Sponsoring of Films" in *Film* (London), March/April 1956; "Conference in Paris" in *Sight and Sound* (London), summer 1956; "This Documentary Business" in *Film Culture* (New York), October 1957; "The Personal Style" in *Film* (London), March/April 1957; "Films to Unite the Nations" in *Film Book 2* (London), 1962; interview and biofilmography in *Film Dope* (London, January 1977.

On DICKINSON:

Article—"Closeups" by Frank Sainsbury in *Cine-Technician* (London), August 1940; film—*A Film Is Made*, BBC with Roger Manvell, 1948.

*   *   *

Though his work has received far less attention and acclaim than that of his contemporary Michael Powell, Thorold Dickinson has stong claims to be considered as one of British cinema's major artists. Like Powell, he belongs to the studio era of the 1940s and 1950s but marked out a highly individual path, rejecting both the literary adaptation style of Reed and Lean and the cosy conformities of Balcon's Ealing studios. Dickinson is the most English of feature directors. He learned his craft from the veteran George Pearson while still an undergraduate at Oxford and later as an editor in the mainstream of British commercial film production of the 1930s. His breakthrough to feature filmmaking came with *The High Command* in 1937 and his work soon began to show his interest in the psychological motivation of his characters and his concern to analyse British liberal values.

The 1940 *Gaslight*, his third feature film, is his first major work. A stylish period thriller, it is a version of the play later adapted in Hollywood by George Cukor. Though overshadowed by Cukor's version, this is a fine professional piece, which shows a characteristic Dickinson concern with the psychological state of the characters and their reactions under the intense pressure. In a very different vein, *The Next of Kin* began as a project for a military training film before being transformed by Dickinson and his producer Balcon into a feature-length fiction which achieved considerable commercial success. Though imbued with the patriotic spirit typical of its period, *The Next of Kin* avoids the rhetoric and self-glorification so common in the 1940s. Indeed its unsparing portrayal of a country ill-prepared for the war in which it is engaged caused it some initial problems with the film censors.

The early postwar years saw three further remarkably diverse features, all of enormous interest and power. *Men of Two Worlds* is one of the few British studies of the impact of colonialism on the educated African elite which remains viable in its analysis. In contrast to its highly constructed realism (it was researched in Tanganyika but shot in the studio), Dickinson's adaptation of Pushkin's *The Queen of Spades* has an elegant period style which shows the influence of Jean Cocteau and the German expressionists in its creation of atmosphere. Again the director's interest in the madness which stems from the failure to control passion is evident. *Secret People*, again produced by Balcon, but in no way an "Ealing film," probed another sensitive area for the liberal conscience: the use of violence for political ends, with the focus again on questions of identity and motivation. It proved to be Dickinson's last major film as a director, though he subsequently made a fictional feature in Isreal, *Hill 24 Doesn't Answer*, worked as a producer for the United Nations, and became British's first professor of film at the Slade School of Fine Art, University College London.

Dickinson's work in the feature film has a restraint and subtlety akin to that displayed by Jennings in the documentary. It is exemplary in its use of the imaginative potential of the film studio and for the director's acute moral sense. The handful of films which Dickinson directed in the course of just a dozen or so years are among the most rewarding—as well as most neglected British films of their period.

—Roy Armes

DIEGUES, CARLOS. Brazilian. Born in Maceio, state of Alagoas, 19 May 1940. Educated in law, Catholic University of Rio de Janeiro. Married entertainer Nara Leao. Career: about 1960—organizer and member of Metropolitan Union of Students, and film critic for its publication *O Metropolitano*; early 1960s—active as poet and film critic; 1964—first feature film; established as a principal figure of "Cinema Novo" movement; late 1960s—emigrates to France following Brazilian military takeover, 1968; attempts several European projects without success; mid-1970s—returns to Brazil.

Films (as director of short films): 1960—*Fuga* (co-d); 1961—*Domingo*; 1962—"Escola de samba, alegria de viver" episode of *Cinco vêzes Favela*; (as feature film director): 1964—*Ganga Zumba* (+co-adapt); 1965—*A 8a. Bienal de São Paulo* (short); *O Circo* (Jabor) (ed only); 1966—*A grande cidade (The Big City)* (+co-sc); 1967—*Oito Universitários* (short); *Terra em transe (Land in Trance)* (Rocha) (assoc pr only); 1968—*Capitu* (Saraceni) (assoc pr only); 1969—*Os herdeiros (The Inheritors)*; 1970—*Séjour* (medium-length, for French TV); 1972—*Quando o Carnaval chegar (When Carnival Comes)*; 1973—*Joana a Francesa (Jeanne la française)* (+sc); 1976—*Xica da Silva (Xica)*; 1977—*Chuvas de verao (Summer Showers, A Summer Rain)* (+sc); 1978—*Os filhos do medo (Les Enfants de la peur)* (TV documentary); 1980—*Bye Bye Brasil* (+sc); *Prova de Fogo* (Altberg) (assoc pr only).

Publications:

By DIEGUES:

Articles—"Géographie et cinéma d'un pays américain" in *Positif* (Paris), no.92; "Brésil: 39 (degrees) ou le cinéma novo sera toujours nouveau" in *Positif* (Paris), no.116; "Diegues fala de Moreau e 'Joana'", interview, in *Filme cultura* (Rio de Janeiro), January/February 1973; "Carlos Diegues: 'cette chose trés simple, aimer le peuple'", interview by J. Delmas, in *Jeune Cinéma* (Paris), July/August 1978; "Le Cinéma nuovo dix ans aprés", interview by G. Haustrate and D. Rabourdin in *Cinéma* (Paris), November 1980; "Exploration d'un continent", interview by A. Tournès in *Jeune Cinéma* (Paris), September/October 1980; "The Mind of Cinema Novo", interview by D. Yakir in *Film Comment* (New York), September/October 1980; "Adieu, cinema novo", interview by P.A. Paranagua in *Positif* (Paris), May 1981.

On DIEGUES:

Article—"Bio-filmographie: Carlos Diegues" by R. Prédal in *Etudes cinématographiques* (Paris), no.93-96, 1972.

DIETERLE, WILLIAM. German. Born Wilhelm Dieterle in Ludwigshafen, 15 July 1893; became citizen of United States, late 1930s. Studied acting with Paul Tietsch, Mannheim. Married comedienne and writer Charlotte Hagenbruch, 1921 (died about 1965); married Elisabeth Dieterle. Career: 1911—engaged by Westphälisches Städtebundtheater, Arnsberg; 1912—debuts at Stadttheater, Heilbronn; 1914-17—works under director Ludwig Berger at Mainz; 1917—called up for military service, quickly accepts engagement at Stadttheater, Zurich, acts opposite Elisabeth Bergner and meets Max Reinhardt; 1918—engaged by Berger for Neue Freie Volksbühne, Berlin; 1920-23—member of Reinhardt company, Berlin; 1921—first major film role, under E.A. Dupont, in *Die Geier-Wally*; 1923—directs first film, *Der Mensch am Wege*; 1924—begins avant-garde theater in Berlin, Dramatisches Theater, with Georg Kaiser and others; 1927—ceases theater work, founds film company Charha-Film, produces *Ich Habe im Mai von der Liebe geträumt*; 1929—success of Dieterle's pictures attracts attention of Carl Laemmle, Dieterle signed by Deutsch Universal for 5 films; 1930—with wife leaves for U.S. at invitation of Warner Bros.-First National, leaving serious debts unpaid; works on American-German co-productions; 1931—signs 7-year contract with Warners; changes name to William; 1935—convinces Warners to allow Reinhardt to make *A Midsummer Night's Dream*, and co-directs; 1936—success of *The Story of Louis Pasteur* begins series of Dieterle-Paul Muni biopics for Warners; 1941—quits Warners for R.K.O. where becomes own producer; with Fritz Lang, finances emigration of Brecht, Helene Weigel and Kurt Weill to U.S.; financial failure of *All That Monet Can Buy* ends "Dieterle Productions," goes to MGM in 1942; early 1940s—plans several abortive projects with Brecht; 1942—signs long-term contract with Hal Wallis, producing for Paramount; 1945—takes over direction of *Duel in the Sun* from King Vidor; 1945—planned film *Das Lied vom Weib des Nazisoldaten*, written by Brecht, intended for German war prisoners in U.S., stopped by U.S. government; 1947—McCarthyist attacks on Dieterle films; 1951—passport confiscated (again in 1953); 1958—returns to Germany; after unsatisfying attempt to make films in Germany, begins working in theater once again; 1961—becomes director of Bad Hersfeld Theater Festival; Died at Ottobrunn, 9 December 1972.

Films (as director): 1923—*Der Mensch am Wege* (+sc, ro as the angel); 1927—*Das Geheimnis des Abbé X (Der Mann, der nicht lieben darf)* (+pr, sc, ro); 1928—*Die Heilige und ihr Narr (La Sainte et le fou)* (+pr, ro as *Harro, Count of Torstein*); *Geschlecht in Fesseln—Die Sexualnot der Gefangenen (Chaînes, Les Sexes enchaînés)* (+ro as *Franz Sommer*); 1929—*Ich liebe für dich (Le Triomphe de la vie)* (+ro as *Bergson*); *Frühlingsrauschen (Tränen die ich dir geweint, Rêves de printemps, Nostalgie)* (+ro as *Friedrich*); *Das Schweigen im Walde (Le Silence dans la forêt, La Nuit de la Saint-Jean)* (+ro as *Ettingen*); 1930—*Ludwig der Zweite, König von Bayern* (+co-sc, ro as *Ludwig II of Bavaria*); *Eine Stunde glück* (+co-sc, ro as *Eddy*); (films made in U.S.): 1930—*Der Tanz geht weiter* (German version of William Beaudine's *Those Who Dance*) (+ro as *Fred Hogan*); *Die Maske fällt* (German version of Frank Lloyd's *The Way of All Men*); *Kismet* (German version of Dillon film); *Dämon des Meeres* (co-d: German version of Curtiz's *Moby Dick*); 1931—*Die Heilige Flamme* (co-d: German version of Archie Mayo's *The Sacred Flame*); *The Last Flight*; *Her Majesty, Love*; 1932—*Man Wanted*; *Jewel Robbery*; *6 Hours to Live!*; *The Crash*; *Scarlet Dawn*; 1933—*Lawyer Man*; *Grand Slam*; *Adorable*; *The Devil's in Love*; *Female* (co-d); *From Headquarters*; 1934—*Fashions of 1934* (co-d); *Madame du Barry*; *Fog Over Frisco*; *Doctor Monica* (co-d); *The Firebird*; *The Secret Bride*; 1935—*A Midsummer Night's Dream* (co-d); *Dr. Socrates*; 1936—*The Story of Louis Pasteur*; *The White Angel*; *Satan Met a Lady*; 1937—*The Great O'Malley*; *Another Dawn*; *The Life of Emile Zola*; 1938—*Blockade*; 1939—*Juarez*; *The Hunchback of Notre Dame*; 1940—*Dr. Ehrlich's Magic Bullet (The Story of Dr. Ehrlich's Magic Bullet, The Magic Bullet)*; *A Dispatch from Reuter's (This Man Reuter)*; *All That Money Can Buy (The Devil and Daniel Webster)* (+pr, co-sc); 1942—*Syncopation* (+pr, co-sc); *Tennessee Johnson (The Man on America's Conscience)*; 1943—*Kismet*; 1944—*I'll Be Seeing You* (co-d); 1945—*This Love of Ours*; *Love Letters*; 1946—*Duel in the Sun* (co-d); *The Searching Wind*; 1948—*Paid in Full*; *The Accused*; 1949—*Portrait of Jennie (Tidal Wave)* (production begun 1947); *Rope of Sand*; *Vulcano*; 1950—*September Affair*; *Dark City*; 1952—*Red Mountain* (co-d, produced in 1950); *Boots Malone*; *The Turning Point*; 1953—*Salome*; 1954—*Elephant Walk*; 1956—*Magic Fire* (co-pr, shot in 1954); *One Against Many* (+co-sc, made for TV); 1957—*Peking Express* (produced in 1951); *The Loves of Omar Khayyam*; (after return to Germany): 1959—*Il Vendicatore (Dubrowsky, L'Aigle noir, Révolte sur la Volga)*; 1960—*Herrin der Welt (Apocalisse sull fiume giallo, Les Mystères d'Angkor)* in 2 parts: "Herrin der Welt" and "Angkor-Vat" (co-d); *Die Fastnachtsbeichte*; 1961—*Die grosse Reise* (for TV); *Das Vergnügen, Anständig zu sein* (for TV); 1962—*Spiel um Job, Antigone, Das grosse Vorbild* (for TV); *Gabriel Schillings Flucht* (for TV); 1965—*The Confession (Quick, Let's Get Married, 7 Different Ways)*; *Samba* (for TV).

Roles (in films not directed by Dieterle): 1913—*Fiesko*; 1915—*Der Erbföster* (Oberländer); 1921—*Die Geier-Wally* (Dupont); *Die Hintertreppe* (Jessner and Leni); *Fräulein Julie* (Basch); *Die Silbermöwe* (Sauer); 1922—*Frauenopfer* (Grüne); *Es leuchtet meine Liebe* (Stein); *Der Graf von Charolais* (Grüne); *Lukrezia Borgia* (Oswald); *Marie-Antoinette—Das Leben einer Königin* (Meinert); 1923—*Boheme—Künstlerliebe* (Righelli); *Der zweite Schuss* (Krol); *Die Pagode* (Fekete); *Die grüne Manuela* (Dupont) (+co-d); *Die Austreibung—Die Macht der zweiten Frau* (Murnau); 1924—*Carlos und Elisabeth—Eine Herrschertragödie* (Oswald); *Das Wachsfigurenkabinett* (Leni) (+co-d); *Moderne Ehen* (Otto); *Mutter und Kind* (Froehlich); 1925—*Wetterleuchten* (Walther-Fein); *Lena Warnstetten* (Eriksen); *Die Blumenfrau vom Potsdamer Platz* (Speyer); *Sumpf und Moral* (Walther-Fein); *Die vom Niederrhein* (Walther-Fein); *Der Hahn im Korb* (Jacoby); *Der Rosa Diamant* (Gliese); *Die Dame aus Berlin* (von Kabdebo); *Die Gesunkenen* (Walther-

Fein); *Gerechtigkeit*; *Der Traumkönig*; 1926 —*Die Mühle von Sanssouci* (Philippini); *Die Försterchristel* (Zelnik); *Qualen der Nacht* (Bernhardt); *Familie Schimeck (Wiener Herzen)* (Halm); *Die Flucht in den Zirkus (Verurteilt nach Sibirien—Moskau 1912)* (Bonnard and Schamberg); *Zopf und Schwert (Eine tolle Prinzessin)* (Janson); *Faust—Eine Deutsche Volkssage* (Murnau); *Hölle der Liebe—Erlebnisse aus einem Tanzpalais* (Rahn); *Wie bliebe ich jung und schön (Ehegeheimnisse)* (Rahn); *Der Jäger von Fall* (Seitz); *Der Pfarrer von Kirchfeld* (Fleck); 1927 —*Unter Ausschluss der Öffentlichkeit* (Wiene); *Der Zigeunerbaron (Sandor, Prince Vagabond)* (Zelnik); *Violantha* (Froehlich); *Die vom Schicksal verfolgten* (Kleinmann); *Am Rande der Welt* (Grüne); *Die Weber* (Zelnik); *Ich habe im Mai von der Liebe geträumt* (Seits) (+pr); *Liebesreigen* (Walther-Fein); *Petronella* (Schwartz); *Heimweh* (Righelli); *Das Geheimnis des Abbe (Der Mann der nicht lieben darf, Behind the Altar)* (+pr, sc); 1928 —*Frau Sorge* (Land); *Apachenliebe (Die Apachen von Paris)* (Malikoff); *Diebe* (Heuberger); *Ritter der Nacht (Le Gentilhomme des bas-fonds, Les Chevaliers de la nuit)* (Reichmann).

Publications:

By DIETERLE:

Book—*The Good Tidings*, New York 1950; articles—in *Wir über uns selbst: Filmkünstler-Autobiographien*, Berlin 1928; "Ein Schicksalstag: 9. November 1918" in *Film-Kurier* (Berlin), 9 November 1928; "Gesinnung im Film" in *Reichsfilmblatt* (Berlin), 26 January 1929; "Warum ich Ganghofer verfilmte" in *Film-Kurier* (Berlin), 29 November 1929; "Brief aus Hollywood" in *Reichsfilmblatt* (Berlin), 21 February 1931; "Views on Historical Movies" in *New York World Telegram*, 18 October 1937; "The Great God Box-Office" in *Cinema Progress* (Los Angeles), February/March 1938; "Intervista con me stesso" in *Cinema* (Rome), no.50, 1938; "Do Films Have a Pedagogical Mission for the Masses?" in *Decision* (New York), March 1941; "Hollywood and the European Crisis" in *Studies in Philosophy and Social Science* (New York), v.9, 1941; interview by Marcel Idzkowski in *Cinémonde* (Paris), 17 January 1949; "Interview with Dieterle" by Francis Koval in *Sight and Sound* (London), May 1950; "Europeans in Hollywood" in *Sight and Sound* (London), July/-September 1952; "Directors in a Rut" in *The Cine-Technician* (London), April 1954; "Busby Berkeley, Bette Davis, William Powell" in *Retrospektive 1971*, Berlin 1971; "Max Reinhardt in Hollywood" in *A Centennial Festschrift*, New York 1973; "Erlebtes Theater" in *Retrospektive 1973*, Berlin 1973; "William Dieterle: the Plutarch of Hollywood," interview by T. Flinn in *Velvet Light Trap* (Madison), autumn 1975.

On DIETERLE:

Book—*Von Deutschland nach Hollywood: W. Dieterle*, Berlin 1973; articles—"Osterspaziergang mit Dieterle" by Rulo in *Der Film* (Berlin), no.6, 1928; "Dieterle daheim" by S. Berndt in *Filmwoche* (Berlin), 6 November 1929; "William Dieterle und der Filmschnitt" by Waldemar Lydo in *Reichsfilmblatt* (Berlin), 5 October 1929; "W. Dieterle, pionnier du film biographique" by Arthur Göpfert in *Ciné-Suisse* (Zurich), 13 November 1943; "William Dieterle" by Herbert Luft in *Films in Review* (New York), April 1957; also see Dieterle's response in *Films in Review* of May 1957, and Luft's response in June/July issue; "The Films of William Dieterle" by Alfonso Pinto and Francisco Rialp in *Films in Review* (New York), October 1968; "William

Dieterle l'hétéroclite" by Claude Beylie in *Ecran* (Paris), February 1973; "L'Homme aux gants blancs" by Hervé Dumont in *Travelling* (Lausanne), September/October 1973; "William Dieterle 1893-1972" by Hervé Dumont in *Avant-Scène du cinéma* (Paris), 15 November 1977; biofilmography in *Film Dope* (London), January 1977.

* * *

Dieterle came from that cradle of film talent, the theatre of Max Reinhardt. Although he appeared in a the film *Fiesko* in 1913 it was in Dupont's *Die Geierwally* with Henny Porten that he established himself as a screen actor. He became much sought after and appeared with Asta Nielsen in *Fraulein Julie*, in Jessner's *Hintertreppe*, Oswald's *Lukretia Borgia* and *Carlos and Elizabeth*, Leni's *Waxworks*, Dupont's *Die grüne Manuela* and Murnau's *Die Austreibung* and *Faust*.

He ran his own theatre in Berlin in 1924 and had married the actress Charlotte Hagenbruch who was to be his close collaborator in both Europe and America. Already in 1915 he had directed *Der Erbförster*. In 1923 he directed Marlene Dietrich in a small part. By 1928 and 1929 he was directing many films two of which, *Die Heilige und ihr Narr* and *Geschlecht in Fesseln*, were outstanding. The latter, dealing with the sexual problems of prisoners, ran into censor trouble and was banned at one stage. He played in his own productions including *Ludwig der Zweite* with a script by his wife and design by Ernst Stern. In 1927 he appeared in Karl Grüne's unusual anti-war film *Am Rande der Welt* and Friedrich Zelnik's version of Hauptmann's *Die Weber*.

In 1930 he went to Hollywood to direct German versions of American films. Soon he was directing in English and was one of the most popular and successful of immigrant filmmakers. He directed Janet Gaynor in *Adorable* with story by Billy Wilder. In 1934 he made two Bette Davis films, *Fashions of 1934* and *Fog Over Frisco*. He collaborated with his old master Reinhardt on *A Midsummer Night's Dream*. Then followed *The Story of Louis Pasteur* for which Paul Muni won an Academy Award as best actor, and the brilliant *Juarez*, with Muni, Davis, and Brian Aherne. Another biographical film, *Dr. Ehrlich's Magic Bullet*, starred Edward G. Robinson. *Blockade* proved controversial as it touched on the Spanish Civil War. Perhaps the best film he made in America was *All That Money Can Buy* based on Steven Vincent Benet's *The Devil and Daniel Webster*. This was a transposition of the Faust legend to a rural New England setting. The film was remarkable for its atmosphere and the fact that in it the supernatural really worked. It was visually very beautiful with impeccable acting from a distinguished cast including Edward Arnold as Webster and Walter Huston as Mr. Scratch, the homely and rogueish Mephistopheles of the story. He directed Charles Laughton in *The Hunchback of Notre Dame* in 1939 and made two distinguished films with Jennifer Jones, *Love Letters* and *Portrait of Jenny*. His version of *Salome* with Rita Hayworth, appearing in 1953, added nothing to his reputation and a decline set in. He returned to Germany in 1955, directing a film on Richard Wagner, *Magic Fire*, and the Pushkin story *Dubrovsky*, which he made in Yugoslavia.

He had begun life as a carpenter in Ludwigshaven. He was a man of large stature and dynamic energy coupled with a cultured elegance which made his Hollywood home a salon where artists and writers met. In the studios he appeared with large hat and white gloves marking him out as *the director*. His skilled artistry enabled him to cover a wide range of subject matter and all his films carried an air of refinement of thought and feeling.

—Liam O'Leary

DISNEY, WALT. American. Born Walter Elias Disney in Chicago, 5 December 1901. Educated at McKinley High School, Chicago; attended Kansas City Art Institute, 1915. Married Lillian Bounds, 1925; children: Diane, Sharon; Career: 1918—in France with Red Cross Ambulance Corps, arriving just after Armistice; 1919—returns to Kansas, becomes commercial art studio apprentice, meets Ub Iwerks; with Iwerks briefly in business, doing illustrations and ads; 1920—joins Kansas City Film Ad Co., making cartoon commercials for local businesses; 1922—incorporates Laugh-o-Gram Films, 1st studio, goes bankrupt; 1923—to Hollywood, contract with M.J. Winkler, begins *Alice in Cartoonland* series; soon joined by Iwerks; 1927—ends *Alice* series, begins *Oswald the Lucky Rabbit* series; salary dispute with Winkler; forms Walt Disney Productions; 1928—*Steamboat Willie* released, 1st synchronized sound cartoon, featuring Mickey Mouse; makes deal with Pat Powers for independent distribution; 1930—begins distributing through Columbia; 1932—*Flowers and Trees*, 1st cartoon in Technicolor and 1st to win an Academy Award; releasing through United Artists; 1937—*Snow White*, 1st feature length cartoon, marks innovative use of multi-plane camera, developed by Disney Studios; begins releasing through RKO; 1941—strike by Disney staff belonging to Cartoonists Guild; Art Babbitt fired, later rehired; changes introduced include credit titles on cartoon shorts; 1944—"Mickey Mouse" is password on D-Day invasion of Europe; 1945—"True Life Adventure" series begins, Disney's 1st live action films; 1951-60—Disney develops several television programs; 1954—forms Buena Vista Distributing Co. for release of Disney and occasionally other films; begins hosting *Disneyland* TV series (later *Walt Disney Presents, Walt Disney's Wonderful World of Color, The Wonderful World of Disney*); 1955—Disneyland opens, Anaheim, California; *The Mickey Mouse Club* premieres on TV; 1960—*Walt Disney's Wonderful World of Color* premieres on television; 1971—Walt Disney World opens in Orlando, Florida; Died in California, 1966. Recipient:Special Academy Award, 1932; French Legion of Honor, 1936; Honorary M.S., University of Southern California, 1938; Honorary M.A., Yale University, 1938; Honorary M.A., Harvard University, 1938; Special Academy Award for contributions to sound, with William Garity and John N.A. Hawkins, 1941; Irving G. Thalberg Award, Academy of Motion Picture Arts and Sciences, 1941; Best Director for his work as a whole, Cannes Film Festival, 1953.

Films (as producer, director and animator): 1920—*Newman Laugh-O-Grams* series; 1922—*Cinderella; The 4 Musicians of Bremen; Goldie Locks and the 3 Bears; Jack and the Beanstalk; Little Red Riding Hood; Puss in Boots*; 1923—*Alice's Wonderland; Tommy Tucker's Tooth; Martha;* ("Alice" series): 1924—*Alice and the Dog Catcher; Alice and the 3 Bears; Alice Cans the Cannibals; Alice Gets in Dutch; Alice Hunting in Africa; Alice's Day at Sea; Alice's Fishy Story; Alice's Spooky Adventure; Alice's Wild West Show; Alice the Peacemaker; Alice the Piper; Alice the Toreador;* 1925—*Alice Chops the Suey; Alice Gets Stung; Alice in the Jungle; Alice Loses Out; Alice on the Farm; Alice Picks the Champ; Alice Plays Cupid; Alice Rattled by Rats; Alice's Balloon Race; Alice's Egg Plant; Alice's Little Parade; Alice's Mysterious Mystery; Alice Solves the Puzzle; Alice's Ornery Orphan; Alice Stage Struck; Alice's Tin Pony; Alice the Jail Bird; Alice Wins the Derby;* 1926—*Alice Charms the Fish; Alice's Monkey Business; Alice in the Wooly West; Alice the Fire Fighter; Alice Cuts the Ice; Alice Helps the Romance; Alice's Spanish Guitar; Alice's Brown Derby; Clara Cleans Her Teeth;* 1927—*Alice the Golf Bug; Alice Foils the Pirates; Alice at the Carnival; Alice's Rodeo (Alice at the Rodeo); Alice the Collegiate; Alice in the Alps; Alice's Auto Race; Alice's*

Circus Daze; Alice's Knaughty Knight; Alice's 3 Bad Eggs; Alice's Picnic; Alice's Channel Swim; Alice in the Klondike; Alice's Medicine Show; Alice the Whaler; Alice the Beach Nut; Alice in the Big League; ("Oswald the Lucky Rabbit" series): 1927—*Trolley Troubles; Oh, Teacher; The Ocean Hop; All Wet; The Mechanical Cow; The Banker's Daughter; Great Guns; Rickety Gin; Empty Socks; Harem Scarem; Neck 'n Neck;* 1928—*The Ol' Swimmin' 'ole; Africa Before Dark; Rival Romeos; Bright Lights; Sagebrush Sadie; Ozzie of the Mounted; Ride 'em Plow Boy!; Hungry Hoboes; Oh, What a Knight; Sky Scrappers; Poor Papa; The Fox Chase; Tall Timber; Sleigh Bells; Hot Dog;* (as head of Walt Disney Productions and co-director with Ub Iwerks) (featuring Mickey Mouse): 1928—*Steamboat Willie;* 1929—*Plane Crazy* (made as silent 1928 but released with synch sound); *The Gallopin' Gaucho* (made as silent 1928 but released with synch sound); *The Barn Dance; The Opry House; When the Cat's Away; The Barnyard Battle; The Plow Boy; The Karnival Kid; Mickey's Choo Choo; The Jazz Fool; Jungle Rhythm; The Haunted House;* (Silly Symphonies): *The Skeleton Dance; El Terrible Toreador; The Merry Dwarfs* (d alone); (as head of Walt Disney Productions and director) (featuring Mickey Mouse): 1930—*The Barnyard Concert; Just Mickey (Fiddling Around); The Cactus Kid;* (Silly Symphonies): *Night;* 1935—*The Golden Touch;* (cartoon features as head of Walt Disney Productions): 1937—*Snow White and the 7 Dwarfs* (supervising d Hand); 1940—*Pinocchio* (supervising d Sharpsteen); *Fantasia* (pr supervisor Sharpsteen); 1941—*The Reluctant Dragon* (cartoon d's Luske, Handley, Beebe, Verity, Blystone; live-action d Werker) (+appearance); *Dumbo* (supervising d Sharpsteen); 1942—*Bambi* (supervising d Hand); *Saludos Amigos* (pr supervisor Ferguson) (+appearance); 1943—*Victory through Air Power* (supervising d Hand, live-action d Potter); 1944—*The 3 Caballeros* (supervising d Ferguson); 1946—*Make Mine Music* (pr supervisor Grant); *Song of the South* (cartoon d Jackson, live-action d Foster); 1947—*Fun and Fancy Free* (pr supervisor Sharpsteen); 1948—*Melody Time* (pr supervisor Sharpsteen); *So Dear to my Heart* (cartoon d Luske, live-action d Schuster); 1949—*Ichabod and Mr. Toad (The Adventures of Ichabod and Mr. Toad)* (pr supervisor Sharpsteen); 1950—*Cinderella* (pr supervisor Sharpsteen); (cartoon ['ct'] and live-action features for theatrical distribution as head of Walt Disney Productions): 1950—*Treasure Island* (Haskin); 1951—*Alice in Wonderland* (ct) (pr supervisor Sharpsteen); 1952—*The Story of Robin Hood and His Merrie Men* (Annakin); 1953—*Peter Pan* (ct) (Luske, Geronimi, and Jackson); *The Sword and the Rose* (Annakin); *Rob Roy, the Highland Rogue* (French); 1954—*20,000 Leagues Under the Sea* (Fleischer); *The Littlest Outlaw (El pequino proscrito)* (Gavaldon); 1955—*Lady and the Tramp* (ct) (Luske, Geronimi, Jackson); *Davy Crockett and the River Pirates,;* 1956—*The Great Locomotive Chase* (Lyon); *Westward Ho the Wagons!* (Beaudine); 1957—*Johnny Tremain* (Stevenson); *Old Yeller* (Stevenson); 1958—*The Light in the Forest* (Daugherty); *Sleeping Beauty* (pr supervisor Geronimi); *Tonka* (L. Foster); 1959—*The Shaggy Dog* (Barton); *Darby O'Gill and the Little People* (Stevenson); *Third Man on the Mountain* (Annakin); *Toby Tyler, or 10 Weeks with a Circus* (Barton); 1960—*Kidnapped* (Stevenson); *Pollyanna* (Swift); *10 Who Dared* (Beaudine); *Swiss Family Robinson* (Annakin); *One Hundred and One Dalmatians* (ct) (Reitherman, Luske, Geronimi); *The Absent-Minded Professor* (Stevenson); 1961—*Moon Pilot* (Neilson); *In Search of the Castaways* (Stevenson); *Nikki, Wild Dog of the North* (Couffer and Haldane); *The Parent Trap* (Swift); *Greyfriars Bobby* (Chaffey); *Babes in Toyland* (Donohue); 1962—*Son of Flubber* (Stevenson); *The Miracle of the White Stallions (Flight of the White Stallions)* (Hiller); *Big Red* (Tokar); *Bon Voyage* (Neilson); *Almost Angels (Born* to Sing) (Previn); *The Legend of Lobo* (Algar and Couffer); 1963—*Savage Sam* (Tokar); *Summer Magic* (Neilson); *The Incredible Journey* (Markle); *The Sword in the Stone* (ct) (Reitherman); *The Misadventures of Merlin Jones* (Stevenson); *The 3 Lives of Thomasina* (Chaffey); 1964—*A Tiger Walks* (Tokar); *The Moon-Spinners* (Neilson); *Mary Poppins* (Stevenson); *Emil and the Detectives* (Tewksbury); *Those Calloways* (Tokar); *The Monkey's Uncle* (Stevenson); 1965—*That Darn Cat* (Stevenson); 1966—*The Ugly Dachsund* (Tokar); *Lt. Robin Crusoe, U.S.N.* (Paul) (+story under pseudonym Retlaw Yensid); *The Fighting Prince of Donegal* (O'Herlihy); *Follow Me, Boys!* (Tokar); *Monkeys, Go Home!* (McLaglen); *The Adventures of Bullwhip Griffin* (Neilson); *The Gnome-Mobile* (Stevenson); 1967—*The Jungle Book* (ct) (Reitherman).

Publications:

By DISNEY:

Articles—"What I've Learned From Animals" by Walt Disney in *American Magazine*, February 1953; "The Lurking Camera" by Walt Disney in *Atlantic Monthly* (New York), August 1954; "Too Long at the Sugar Bowls: Frances C. Sayers Raps with Disney" in *Library Journal* (New York), 15 October 1965.

On DISNEY:

Books—*Celluloid, the Film Today* by Paul Rotha, New York 1931; *Histoire du Cinéma* by Maurice Bardeche and Robert Brasillach, Paris 1935; *The Art of Walt Disney* by Robert D. Field, New York 1942; *Film Sense* by Sergei Eisenstein, translated and edited by Jay Leyda, New York, 1947; *Reflections on the Cinema* by René Clair, translated by Vera Traill, London 1953; *The Technique of Film Music* by Roger Manvell and J. Huntley, New York 1957; *The Story of Walt Disney* by Diane Disney Miller, edited by Pete Martin, New York 1957; *Behind the Screen: the History and Techniques of Motion Pictures* by Kenneth McGowan, New York 1965; *Animation in the Cinema* by Ralph Stephenson, New York 1967; *The Disney Version: The Life, Times, Art and Commerce of Walt Disney* by Richard Schickel, New York 1968; *Walt Disney* by Maurice Bessy, Paris 1970; *Grierson on Documentary* by John Grierson, edited by Forsyth Hardy, New York 1971; *Walt Disney: the Master of Animation* by Gerald Kurland, edited by Steve D. Rahmas, Charlottesville, N.Y. 1971; *The Art of Walt Disney, from Mickey Mouse to the Magic Kingdoms* by Christopher Finch, New York 1973; *The Disney Films* by Leonard Maltin, New York 1973; "Disney and Animation" in *Film and Reality* by Roy Armes, Baltimore 1974; "The Making of Cultural Myths: Walt Disney and Frank Capra" in *Movie Made Ameica: a Social History of American Movies* by Robert Sklar, New York 1975; *Walt Disney: An American Original* by Bob Thomas, New York 1976; *Full Length Animated Features* by Bruno Edera, edited by John Halas, New York 1977; *Disney Animation: The Illusion of Life* by Frank Thomas and Ollie Johnston, New York 1982; articles—"The Mechanized Mouse" in *The Saturday Review of Literature* (New York), 11 November 1933; "Straws in the Wind" by Claude Bragdon in *Scribner's Magazine* (New York), July 1934; article by Arthur Mann in *Harper* (New York), May 1934; "A Famous Fairytale is Brought to the Screen as the Pioneer Feature Length Cartoon in Color" by Andrew R. Boone in *Popular Science Monthly* (New York) 1938; "Comment naquirent les dessins animés" by René Jeanne in *Revue des deux Mondes* (Paris), 15 March 1938; "Remarks on the Poplarity of Mickey Mouse" by F. Moellenhoff in *American Imago*, no. 3 1940; "Mickey Mouse Goes Classical" by Andrew R. Boone in

Popular Science Monthly (New York), January 1941; "Disney Techniques in Educational Film" by Frances Norene Ahl in *The Social Studies*, December 1941; "Mickey Mouse and Donald Duck Work for Victory" in *Popular Science Monthly* (New York), September 1942; "Walt Disney: Great Teacher" in *Fortune* (New York), August 1942; "Film Review" by D. Mosdell in *Canadian Forum*, November 1946; "Mickey Mouse and How He Grew" by Irving Wallace in *Colliers* (New York), 9 April 1949; "A Silver Anniversary for Walt and Mickey: Disney's Magic Wand Has Enriched the World with Birds, Beasts and Fairy Princesses" in *Life* (New York), 2 November 1953; "Cinema: Father Goose—Walst Disney: To Enchanted Worlds on Electronic Wings" in *Time* (New York), 27 December 1954; "Disney Comes to Television" in *Newsweek* (New York), 12 April 1954; "Aesop in Hollywood: The Man and the Mouse" by Marshall Fishwick in *Saturday Review* (New York), 10 July 1954; "A Wonderful World: Growing Impact of the Disney Art" in *Newsweek* (New York), 18 April 1955; "McEvoy in Disneyland: A Visit with the Wonderful Wizard of Filmdom" by J.P. McEvoy in *Reader's Digest* (Pleasantville, New York), February 1955; "Hayley Mills on the Pickford Path" by Dilys Powell in *The New York Times*, 13 August 1961; "Sur le 'huitiéme art'" by Georges Sadoul in *Cahiers du cinéma* (Paris), June 1962; "The Wide World of Walt Disney" in *Newsweek* (New York), 31 December 1963; "Animation: Mickey Mouse Explains the Art to Mr. G.O. Graphic" in *National Geographic* (Washington, D.C.), August 1963; "The Magic Worlds of Walt Disney" by Robert De Roose in *National Geographic* (Washington, D.C.), August 1963; "Genius of Laughter and Learning: Walt Disney" by Melville Bell Grosvenor in *National Geographic* (Washington, D.C.), August 1963; "A Day with Disney" by Frederic Whitaker in *American Artist* (New York), September 1965; "Walt Disney, Cross Breeder of Movies and TV Dies at 65" in *Broadcasting*, 19 December 1966; "Le vrai Walt Disney est mort il y a des annes mais ne soyons pas injustes..." by Michel Aubriant in *Paris Presse*, 21 December 1966; "Disney Without Walt...Is Like a Fine Car Without an Engine. Will the Great Entertainment Company Find a New Creative Boss? Or Will it Slowly Lose Momentum?" in *Forbes* (New York), 1 July 1967; "Le Cinéma à l'expo de Montréal" by Jean-Louis Comolii and Michel Delahaye in *Cahiers du Cinéma* (Paris), April 1967; "Who's Afraid of Walt Disney" by N. Tucker in *New Society*, no.11, 1968; "Letters to the Editor: Class in Fantasia" by Robert Gessner in *The Nation* (New York), 30 November 1970; "The 10 Greatest Men of American Business—As You Picked Them" in *Nation's Business*, March 1971; special Disney issue of *Kosmorama* (Copenhagen), November 1973; "Lest We Forget" by J.C. Murray in *Lumiere* (Melbourne), November 1973; "Decay of an American Dream" by A. Stuart in *Films and Filming* (London), November 1973; "Walt Disney, una pedagogía reaccionaria" by F. Pérez in *Cine Cubano* (Havana), no.81-83, 1973; "A Visit to the Walt Disney Studio" by J. Canemaker in *Filmmakers Newsletter* (Ward Hill, Mass.), January 1974; "Animation Kit: Movies, Myth and Us" by H. Beckerman in *Filmmakers Newsletter* (Ward Hill, Mass.), September 1975; "Dream Masters" by Jonathan Rosenbaum in *Film Comment* (New York), January/-February 1975; "Ben Sharpsteen...33 Years with Disney" by D.R. Smith in *Millimeter* (New York), April 1975; "The Wonderful World of Disney: Its Psychological Appeal" by M. Brody in *American Imago* (Detroit), no.4, 1976; "Disney Night at the A.S.C." in *American Cinematographer* (Los Angeles), February 1977; "Art, Music, Nature and Walt Disney" by W. Paul in *Movie* (London), spring 1977; biofilmography in *Film Dope* (London), June 1977; "Disney Animation: History and Technique" by J. Canemaker in *Film News* (New York), January/-February 1979; "Disney Design: 1928-1979" by J. Canemaker in

Millimeter (New York), February 1979; "'Building a Better Mouse': 50 Years of Disney Animation" by M. Barrier in *Funnyworld* (New York), summer 1979; "A Star is Drawn" by S. Hulett in *Film Comment* (New York), January/February 1979; "Disney Before Burbank: the Kingswell and Hyperion Studios" by D.R. Smith in *Funnyworld* (New York), summer 1979; "The Remarkable Visions of Peter Ellenshaw" by J. Culhane in *American Film* (Washington, D.C.), September 1979; "Mickey a 50 ans" by P. Schupp in *Sequences* (Montreal), January 1979; "Disney Out-Foxed: the Tale of Reynard at the Disney Studio" by J. Cawley, Jr., in *American Classic Screen* (Shawnee Mission, Kansas), July/August 1979; "Journals: Tom Allen from New York" in *Film Comment* (New York), September/October 1981; recording—"The Magical Music of Walt Disney: 50 Years of Original Motion-Picture Soundtracks", 1979.

*   *   *

Before Walt Disney, there was Emile Cohl (the "first animator," who made over 250 films in the early years of the century), Winsor McCay (whose Gertie the Dinosaur, created in 1914, was the original animated personality), John Randolph Bray (the Henry Ford of animation, whose technological and organizational contributions revolutionized the art form), and Otto Messmer, inventor of Felix the Cat, the Charlie Chaplin of animated characters, the most popular cartoon creation of the 1920s, entertaining audiences before Mickey Mouse ever uttered a squeak.

So why is Walt Disney synonymous with animation? How can *Fantasia*, *Snow White and the Seven Dwarfs* and *Bambi* be re-released every few years, to delight generation after generation of children? Simply because no other animator ever duplicated the Disney studio's appealingly lifelike cartoon characters and wonderful flair for storytelling.

First, Disney was an innovator, a perfectionist who was forever attempting to improve his product and explore the medium to its fullest potential. He was the first to utilize sound in animation, in *Steamboat Willie*, which was the third Mickey Mouse cartoon. The soundtrack here is more than just a gimmick: for example, in an animal concert, a cow's udder is played like a bagpipe and its teeth are transformed into a xylophone. The musical accompaniment thus emerges from the background, becoming an integral element in the film's structure.

In *Flowers and Trees*, Disney was the first to utilize three-strip Technicolor in animation, a process devised by Joseph Arthur Ball: three different negatives, each recording a primary color, replaced the single camera film previously used. *Snow White and the Seven Dwarfs* was the first full-length cartoon feature: during the production, Disney staffers developed the multiplane camera, and animation rostrum which realistically created the illusion of perspective and depth. The camera, operated by several technicians, filled an entire room. A sequence was drawn and painted on several panes of glass, with each one carefully placed and rigidly held down. Cels, of the animated characters, were placed on the various planes, which would then be moved past the camera at varying speeds: those close to the camera would go by rapidly; those in the rear would be moved more slowly.

Just as significantly, however, Disney was a master organizer and administrator. As a result, from the 1930s on the Disney Studio practically monopolized the animation industry. He established an industrialized assembly line, employing hundreds of animators and technicians who regularly churned out high-quality, Academy Award-caliber product. In the early 1930s, he opened distribution offices in London and Paris. He instigated large merchandising campaigns to reap additional profits via tee shirts, toys and watches. Today, Disneyland and Disneyworld are living monuments to his memory. And it is not surprising that

Disney eventually stretched his talents beyond pure animation, first combining cartoons with actors and, finally, producing live-action features, wildlife documentaries and television series.

Yet Walt Disney's ultimate legacy remains his animated stories, and the narrative elements which lifted them above his competition. His characters are not just caricatures who insult each other, bash each other with baseball bats, or push each other off cliffs. They are lifelike, three-dimensional creatures with personalities all their own: they are simple, but never simplistic, and rarely if ever fail to thoroughly involve the viewer.

It is virtually impossible to rank the best of Disney's animated features in order of quality or popularity. *Snow White*, with its enchanting storyline and sweet humor, remains a joy for audiences over 45 years after its release. It is the perfect romantic fairy tale, with Snow White and her Prince Charming in a happy-ever-after ending, the comic relief of the lovable dwarfs and the villainy of the evil Queen. The film's financial history is typical of most Disney features: originally budgeted at $250,000, it eventually cost $1,700,000 to produce. It earned $4.2 million in the United States and Canada alone when first released; to date, it has grossed over $30 million.

Jiminy Cricket singing "When You Wish Upon a Star" is the highlight of *Pinocchio*. *Bambi* is easily the most delicate of all Disney features. And there is *Fantasia*, a series of animated sequences set to musical classics conducted by Leopold Stokowski and performed by the Philadelphia Orchestra: Tchaikovsky's *The Nutcracker Suite*, Dukas's *The Sorcerer's Apprentice*, Stravinsky's *The Rite of Spring*, and Beethoven's *Symphony No.6 in F Major*, among others, *Fantasia* is ambitious, innovative, and controversial—how dare anyone attempt to visually interpret music?—and, ultimately, timeless.

An essay on Walt Disney would be incomplete without a note on Mickey Mouse, the most famous of all Disney creations and one of the world's most identifiable and best-loved characters. Appropriately, Disney himself was the voice of Mickey, who was originally named Mortimer. The filmmaker himself best explained the popularity of his mouse: "...Mickey is so simple and uncomplicated, so easy to understand, that you can't help liking him."

With pen, pencil, ink and paint, Walt Disney created a unique, special world. Max and Dave Fleischer, Walter Lantz, Chuck Jones and many others may all be great animators, but Disney is unarguably the most identifiable name in the art form.

—Rob Edelman

DMYTRYK, EDWARD. American. Born in Grand Forks, British Columbia, Canada, 4 September 1908; became citizen of of United States, 1939. Studied 1 year at California Institute of Technology, 1926-27. Married first wife 1932 (divorced 1948); married actress Jean Porter, 1948; son: Michael. Career: 1923—hired as messenger and handy boy at Famous Players-Lasky; soon becomes projectionist; 1926-27—spends year at California Institute of Technology, returns to Paramount; 1929—becomes cutter; 1931—fired in studio shake-up, hired back as ass't cutter; 1934—full editor; 1935—directs 1st film independently; 1939—offered directing contract by Paramount making B pictures; 1940-42—directs series of films for Columbia; 1942-47—with RKO; 1944 or early 1945—joins Communist Party; 1947—subpoenaed to appear before House Un-American Activities Committee; becomes 1 of "Hollywood Ten"; 1948-50—lives in England; 1950—forced back to U.S. to renew passport; fined and serves 6 months prison term for contempt of Congress; 1951—appears as friendly witness before HUAC; hired by producer Stanley Kramer; 1971—moves to England; 1978—begins teaching at University of Texas at Austin; 1981—professor of filmmaking, University of Southern California. Agent: Kurt Frings, Beverly Hills, California.

Films (as editor): 1930—*Only Saps Work* (Gardner and Knopf); *The Royal Family of Broadway* (Cukor and Gardner); 1932—*Million Dollar Legs* (Cline); 1934—*Belle of the '90s* (McCarey) (co-ed, uncredited); *College Rhythm* (Taurog) (co-ed); (as director): 1935—*The Hawk*; (as editor): 1935—*Ruggles of Red Gap* (McCarey); 1936—*Too Many Parents* (McGowan); *3 Cheers for Love* (Ray McCarey); *3 Married Men* (Buzzell); *Easy to Take* (Tryon); 1937—*Murder Goes to College* (Riesner); *Turn Off the Moon* (Seiler); *Double or Nothing* (Reed); *Hold 'em Navy (That Navy Spirit)* (Neumann); 1938—*Bulldog Drummond's Peril* (Hogan); *Prison Farm* (Louis King); 1939—*Zaza* (Cukor); *Love Affair* (McCarey) (co-ed); *Some Like It Hot* (Archainbaud); (as director): 1939—*Television Spy*; *Emergency Squad*; *Million Dollar Legs* (Grinde) (co-d, uncredited); 1940—*Golden Gloves*; *Mystery Sea Raider*; *Her First Romance*; 1941—*The Devil Commands*; *Under Age*; *Sweetheart of the Campus (Broadway Ahead)*; *The Blonde from Singapore (Hot Pearls)*; *Secrets of the Lone Wolf (Secrets)*; *Confessions of Boston Blackie (Confessions)*; 1942—*Counter-Espionage*; *7 Miles from Alcatraz*; 1943—*Hitler's Children*; *The Falcon Strikes Back*; *Captive Wild Woman*; *Behind the Rising Sun*; *Tender Comrade*; 1944—*Farewell, My Lovely (Murder My Sweet)*; 1945—*Back to Bataan*; *Cornered*; 1946—*Till the End of Time*; 1947—*Crossfire*; *So Well Remembered*; 1949—*Obsession (The Hidden Room)*; *Give Us This Day (Salt to the Devil)*; 1950—*The Hollywood Ten* (Berry) (co-sc, appearance only); 1952—*Mutiny*; *The Sniper*; *8 Iron Men*; 1953—*The Juggler*; *3 Lives* (short); 1954—*The Caine Mutiny*; *Broken Lance*; *The End of the Affair*; 1955—*Soldier of Fortune*; *The Left Hand of God*; *Bing Presents Oreste* (short); 1956—*The Mountain* (+pr); 1957—*Raintree County*; 1958—*The Young Lions*; 1959—*Warlock* (+pr); *The Blue Angel*; 1962—*The Reluctant Saint* (+pr); *Walk on the Wild Side*; 1963—*The Carpetbaggers*; 1964—*Where Love Has Gone*; *Mirage*; 1966—*Alvarez Kelly*; 1968—*Lo sbarco di Anzio (Anzio, The Battle for Anzio)*; *Shalako*; *Hamlet* (Wirth) (dubbing d only); 1972—*Barbe-Bleue (Bluebeard)* (+co-sc); 1975—*The "Human" Factor*; 1976—*He Is My Brother*. Roles: 1976—interviewee in *Hollywood on Trial* (Helpern).

Publications:

By DMYTRYK:

Book—*It's a Hell of a Life But Not a Bad Living*, New York 1978; articles—"Reply to R. English" in *Nation* (New York), 26 May 1951; "The Director-Cameraman Relationship", interview by Herb Lightman in *American Cinematographer* (Los Angeles), May 1968; "The Director and the Editor" in *Action* (Los Angeles), March/April 1969; "Whose is the Right of the 1st Cut?" in *Making Films* (New York), June 1969; "Verden er den beste filmskole", interview by A. Dreesen in *Filmavisa* (Norway), v.4, no.3-4, 1980.

On DMYTRYK:

Articles—"What Makes a Hollywood Communist?" by R. English in the *Saturday Evening Post* (Philadelphia), 19 May 1951; "Edward Dmytryk" by Romano Tozzi in *Films in Review* (New York), February 1962; "The Cinema of Edward Dmytryk" in *Films Illustrated* (London), October 1971; biofilmography in *Film Dope* (London), June 1977; "Films: Major Transforma-

tions" in *USA Today* (New York), April 1979; "Edward Dmytryk: the Director as Professor" by L. McClure in *Filmmakers Monthly* (Ward Hill, Mass.), January 1979.

*   *   *

Edward Dmytryk rose through the Hollywood ranks, beginning as a projectionist in the twenties, working as an editor through most of the 1930s and directing low-budget films during the first half of the 1940s before making his first A-budget film, *Tender Comrade*, in 1943. He continued to make notable films like *Crossfire* and *Murder My Sweet* before being subpoenaed to testify before HUAC. Dmytryk subsequently became one of the Hollywood Ten and, after completing his jail sentence, the only member of the Ten to become a friendly witness and name names. After doing one film for the King brothers, *Mutiny*, in 1952, Stanley Kramer hired him to direct four features that culminated with *The Caine Mutiny*. He continued to direct films regularly through the 1950s and sixties and now teaches at U.S.C. in Los Angeles.

In many of his films Dmytryk displays much the same sensibility informing the work of Frank Capra: a faith in ordinary people, a belief in the virtues of working together, a deep reverence for traditional American ideals and heros, and a strongly utopian bent that tends to see evil as a localized aberration capable of correction. Characters often "see the light" (*Hitler's Children*, or *Salt to the Devil*,) find themselves transformed by the example or expectations of others (*The Left Hand of God* or *The Juggler*), or reveal a tender, committed side that is not immediately apparent (*Soldier of Fortune* and *Broken Lance*). Utopianism, then, instead of becoming a positive affirmation of values, becomes more an implicit trust in goodness that sometimes defuses dramatic conflict by rendering evil ineffectively or by side-stepping intense confrontations or issues. (*Walk on the Wild Side*, for example, presents a more pollyannaish view of down-and-out Depression life in New Orleans, affirming the nobility of true love despite adversity, than the Nelson Algren novel it is based on.)

Dmytryk directs with an essentially serious tone that minimizes comedy and seldom romanticizes the agrarian or nonurban ethos so dear to Capra. He also tends to work with more interiorized states of personal feeling that run counter to Capra's tendency to play conflicts out in public among a diverse, somewhat stereotyped range of characters. But, like Capra, Dmytryk dwells upon the issue of faith—the need for it and the tests it is subjected to. *Salt to the Devil*, *Tender Comrade*, *Soldier of Fortune*, *Raintree County*, *The Juggler*, *Broken Lance*, *The Left Hand of God*, *The Caine Mutiny*, *Hitler's Children*, these and other films involve tests of faith and commitment for their central characters. Characters strive to find and affirm a sense of personal dignity, whatever the odds, and usually do so within a private setting that uses the broader social context as a dramatic backdrop, even in *Hitler's Children* or *The Young Lions*, two films dealing with Nazism. Some have argued that Dmytryk's work simply deteriorated after his testimony before HUAC; it may also be that recurring themes bridge this period and offer intriguing parallels between the political climate, Dmytryk's personal view of life, and his overall film accomplishments.

—Bill Nichols

DONEN, STANLEY. American. Born in Columbia, South Carolina, 13 April 1924. Studied dance at Town Theatre, Columbia, S. Carolina; enrolled at University of South Carolina until 1940. Married actress Yvette Mimieux, 1972. Career: 1940—Broadway debut as chorus boy in *Pal Joey* starring Gene Kelly; 1941—assists Kelly in choreography for *Best Foot Forward*; also stars in George Abbott's *Beat the Band*; 1943—moves to Hollywood to act in film version of *Best Foot Forward*, becomes assistant choreographer; 1943-49—choreographs numerous MGM musicals; 1949—co-scripts, co-choreographs and directs sequence of *Take Me Out to the Ball Game*; co-directs with Kelly *On the Town*; 1952—co-directs with Kelly *Singin' in the Rain* (also *It's Always Fair Weather*, 1955). Agent: Stan Kamen, William Morris Agency, 151 El Camino, Beverly Hills, CA 90210. Business Manager: Edward Traubner, Traubner & Flynn, 2049 Century Park East No.2500, Los Angeles, CA 90067.

Films (as choreographer or co-choreographer): 1943—*Best Foot Forward* (Buzzell); 1944—*Hey Rookie* (Barton); *Jam Session* (Barton); *Kansas City Kitty* (Lord); *Cover Girl* (Vidor); 1945—*Anchors Aweigh* (Sidney); 1946—*Holiday in Mexico* (Sidney); *No Leave, No Love* (Martin); 1947—*This Time for Keeps* (Thorpe); *Living in a Big Way* (La Cava); *Killer McCoy* (Rowland); 1948—*A Date with Judy* (Thorpe); *The Big City* (Taurog); *The Kissing Bandit* (Benedek); 1949—*Take Me Out to the Ball Game* (Berkeley; +co-sc); (as director): 1949—*On the Town* (co-d, +co-chor); 1951—*Royal Wedding (Wedding Bells)*; 1952—*Singin' in the Rain* (co-d, +co-chor); *Love Is Better Than Ever (The Light Fantastic)*; *Fearless Fagan*; 1953—*Give a Girl a Break* (+co-chor); 1954—*7 Brides for 7 Brothers*; *Deep in My Heart* (+co-chor); 1955—*It's Always Fair Weather* (co-d, +co-chor); 1957—*Funny Face*; *The Pajama Game* (co-d, +co-pr); *Kiss Them For Me*; 1958—*Indiscreet* (+pr); *Damn Yankees (What Lola Wants)* (co-d, +co-pr); (as producer and director): 1960—*Once More with Feeling*; *Surprise Package*; *The Grass Is Greener*; 1963—*Charade*; 1966—*Arabesque*; 1967—*2 For the Road*; *Bedazzled*; 1969—*Staircase*; 1974—*The Little Prince*; 1975—*Lucky Lady*; 1978—*Movie Movie*; 1979—*Saturn 3* (pr only).

Publications:

By DONEN:

Articles—"Giving Life an Up-Beat" in *Films and Filming* (London), July 1958; "What to Do with Star Quality" in *Films and Filming* (London), August 1960; interview by Bertrand Tavernier and Gilbert Palas in *Cahiers du cinéma* (Paris), May 1963; "Stanley Donen," interview by Gilbert Guez in *Cinémonde* (Paris), 23 July 1963; "Bavardons sous la pluie", interview by Monique Vernhes in *Cinéma 66* (Paris), July/August 1966; "Talking in the Sun", interview by Colo and Bertrand Tavernier in *Positif* (Paris), December 1969; interview by S. Harvey in *Film Comment* (New York), July/August 1973; interview by J. Hillier in *Movie* (London), spring 1977.

On DONEN:

Book—*Singin' in the Rain*, script, by Betty Comden and Adolph Green, New York 1972; articles—"From Dance to Film Director" by Arthur Knight in *Dance* (New York), August 1954; "The 10th Muse in San Francisco" by Albert Johnson in *Sight and Sound* (London), summer 1956; "Dance in the Movies" by Arthur Knight in *Dance* (New York), October 1958; special issue on musical comedy, *Cinéma 59* (Paris), August/September 1959; "Moanin' for Donen" by Douglas McVay in *New York Film Bulletin*, no.9, 1961; "Donen at Work" by Herbert Luft in

Films in Review (New York), February 1961; biofilmography in *Film Dope* (London), June 1977; "Saturn 3" by G. Colpart in *Image et son* (Paris), June 1980.

*   *   *

Stanley Donen is most frequently remembered for his work as a musical director/choreographer at MGM under the "Arthur Freed Unit," a production team that Donen claims existed only in Arthur Freed's head (*Movie* interview, spring 1977). With Gene Kelly, he co-directed three of the musical genre's best films: *On the Town*, *Singin' in the Rain*, and *It's Always Fair Weather*. Kelly was, in a sense, responsible for giving Donen his start in Hollywood; their first collaboration being the "doppelganger" dance in *Cover Girl*. Donen followed a path typical of that time, from Broadway dancer to Hollywood dancer and choreographer to director. Directing solo, he won recognition for *Royal Wedding* (his first effort), *Seven Brides for Seven Brothers*, *Funny Face*, *The Pajama Game*, and *Damn Yankees*.

Andrew Sarris believes that Donen always seems to function best as a "hyphenated director" or a "genial catalyst;" that any personal style he may possess is usually submerged under that of the performer's (Kelly, Astaire, Fosse) or choreographer's (Michael Kidd, Eugene Loring, Bob Fosse) and hence is difficult to assess. This view may simply reflect that period of studio production (mid 1940s to late 1950s), when there was a constant melding of creative personnel. As Jerome Delamater explains: "Performers, choreographers, and directors worked together and in many instances one cannot discern the auteur, as it were, or—more accurately—there seem to be several auteurs." Donen credits Astaire for his inspiration and it comes as no surprise that he feels his musical work is an extension of the Astaire/Rogers format (which itself is derived from the films of Clair and Lubitsch). This format is not logically grounded in reality, but functions more or less in the realm of pure emotion. Such a world of spontaneous singing and dancing can most accurately be presented in visual terms through forms of surrealism.

Donen's oeuvre demonstrates a reaction against the presentation of musical numbers on the stage, choreographing them instead on the streets of everyday life. It is this combination of a visual "reality" and a performing "unreality" (a performing "reality" is some type of stage that is clearly delineated from normal, day to day activity), that creates the tension inherent in surrealism. What Donen did with the integrated musical was geared towards the unreal; our functional perception of the real world does not include singing and dancing as a means of normal interpersonal communication. As he said in an interview with Jim Hillier, "A musical...is anything but real." It possesses its own peculiar internal reality, not directly connected to everyday life. Leo Braudy points out that Donen's musical films explore communities and the reaction/interaction of the people that dwell within. Even though Donen left the musical genre after *Damn Yankees* (returning to it in 1973), he continued to explore the situation of the individual in a social community, and the absurd, occasionally surrealistic experiences that we all face, in such deft "comedies" as *Bedazzled*, *Two for the Road*, and *Charade* (the last an hommage to Hitchcock).

—Greg Faller

DONNER, JÖRN. Finnish. Born Jörn Johan Donner in Helsinki, Finland, 5 February 1933. Educated in political science and Swedish literature at Helsinki University, beginning 1951.

Career: 1951—publishes collection of stories, begins to be interested in cinema; early 1950s—founds literary-political magazine *Arena*; film critic for *Ny Tid* and then *Vapaa Sana*; 1953—meets principal Italian neorealist directors; late 1950s, early 1960s—publishes widely on European affairs and culture; books include *Report from Berlin, Report from the Danube*; 1959-61—as conscientious objector, serves 18 months as hospital orderly in Pori; 1961—offered post as film critic for *Dagens Nyheter*, then largest Swedish morning paper, moves to Stockholm; 1962—begins living with Harriet Andersson, star of 1st few films; 1967—*Rooftree* a failure in Sweden, returns to Finland; begins to promote Finnish directors, acquires majority interest in FJ-Filmi, merging it with Jörn Donner Productions; 1972-75—Curator, Swedish Film Institute; 1975-77—executive producer with Institute; 1978—named president of Swedish Film Institute.

Films (as director, scriptwriter and editor of short films): 1954—*Aamua Kaupungissa (Morning in the City)*; 1955—*Näinä Päivinä (In These Days)*; 1956—*Porkala*; 1957—*Vettä (Water)*; 1962—*Vittnesbörd om Henne (Testimonies)*; (as feature director and scriptwriter): 1963—*En Söndag i September (A Sunday in September)*; 1964—*Att Älska (To Love)*; 1965—*Här Börjar Äventyret (Adventure Starts Here)*; 1967—sequence in *Teenage Rebellion (Mondo Teeno)* (Herman); episode no.3, "Han-Hon (He-She)" in *Stimulantia*; *Tvärbalk (Rooftree, Crossbeam)* (+ed); (as executive or co-executive producer, director and scriptwriter): 1968—*Mustaa Valkoisella (Black on White)* (+ed, ro as *Juha Holm*); 1969—*Sixtynine* (+ro as *Timo*); 1970—*Naisenkuvia (Portraits of Women)* (+ed, ro as *Pertti*); *Anna* (co-sc); 1971—*Perkele! Kuvia Suomesta (Fuck Off! Images of Finland)* (documentary); 1972—*Hellyys (Tenderness)*; *Marja pieni! (Poor Marja!)* (Bergholm) (pr only); 1973—*Baksmälla (Hangover, Sexier Than Sex)* (rev. version of *Tenderness* for int'l distribution); *Laukaus Tehtaalla (Shot in the Factory)* (Kivikoski) (pr only); *Mommilan Veriteot 1917 (The Mommila Murders)* (Pennanen) (pr only, +ed); 1975—*The World of Ingmar Bergman*; 1976—*Drömmen om Amerika (The American Dream)* (Abrahamsen) (exec. pr only); *Långt Borta och Nära (Near and Far Away)* (Ahrne) (pr only); 1977—*Hemåt i Natten (Harri! Harri!, Homeward in the Night, Home and Refuge)* (Lindström) (pr only); *Tabu (Taboo)* (Sjöman) (pr only); *Elvis! Elvis!* (Pollak) (pr only); 1978—*Bluff Stop* (exec. pr only); *Manrape (Man Cannot Be Raped)*; 1982—*Yhdeksan Tapaa Lahestya Helsinkia (9 Ways to Approach Helsinki)* (+co-ed, narration, for TV). Role: 1968—*Asfalttilampaat (The Asphalt Lambs)* (Niskanen).

Publications:

By DONNER:

Books—*Filmipulmamme* [Our Film Problem], pamphlet with Martti Savo, Helsinki 1953; *The Personal Vision of Ingmar Bergman*, Bloomington, Indiana 1966; *The Films of Ingmar Bergman*, New York 1972; articles—"After 3 Films" in *Sight and Sound* (London), autumn 1966; "After 6 Films" in *Sight and Sound* (London), spring 1970; "Den svenska filmens uselhet år 1973" in *Chaplin* (Stockholm), v.15, no.8, 1973; "Efter tolv filmer" in *Chaplin* (Stockholm), v.20, no.3, 1978; "Filminstitutet som idébank", interview by B. Heurling and L. Åhlander in *Chaplin* (Stockholm), v.20, no.4, 1978.

On DONNER:

Articles—"Jörn Donner: An Outsider at Home" in *Films and Filming* (London), December 1968; "Jörn Donner" in *Films and Filming* (London), December 1968; "Jörn Donner" by L. Reyner in *Film* (London), spring 1969; "Director of the Year" in *International Film Guide*, London 1972; biofilmography in *Film Dope* (London), June 1977; "Donner Steers Swedish Film Biz to Int'l B.O. Via Co-Prod. Deals" in *Varity* (New York), 9 May 1979; "Jorn Donner from Stockholm credits Yank 'storytelling' lure: Europeans are Too Artsy-Craftsy" by F. Segers in *Variety* (New York), 11 April 1979; "Donner on Swedish Cinema" in *Variety* (New York), 19 September 1979; "Donner Fears Swedes Too 'Local'" by G. Moskowitz in *Variety* (New York), 14 November 1979.

DONSKOI, MARK. Soviet. Born Mark Semyonovich Donskoi in Odessa, 6 March 1901. Educated in medicine and music; studied law at University of Simferopol, graduated 1925. Married scriptwriter Irina Sprink, 1936; 2 sons. Career: 1919-21—serves in Red Army during civil war, prisoner for a year; early 1920s—works on Ukrainian police force as detective and attorney; 1925—publishes *The Prisoners*, stories based on period when imprisoned by White Guards in Crimea; 1926—attends State Film School, studies under Eisenstein; 1927—joins Belgoskino studios, Leningrad; 1934—first sound film for Vostokkino; 1935—meets Maxim Gorky, makes trilogy based on Gorky's autobiographical novels 1938-40; 1940—begins working at Soyuzdietfilm, Moscow (Children's Film Studios); 1942-45—works at Kiev Studios, evacuated to Ashkhabad, capital of Turkmen Soviet Socialist Republic; 1945—joins Communist Party; 1946—returns to Soyuzdietfilm, Moscow (renamed Maxim Gorky Studios); 1948—displeases Stalin with *Alitet Leaves for the Hills*; 1217 meters celebrating Lenin cut from film; 1949—assigned to Kiev Studios through late 1950s; late 1950s—returns to Gorky Studios, Moscow. Died 24 March 1981. Recipient: Stalin Prize, 1941, 1946, 1948; Merited Artist, Turkmen Soviet Socialist Republic, 1943; Order of Lenin, 1944, 1971; Silver Seal, Locarno Film Festival, 1960; People's Artist of the Soviet Union, 1966; Hero of Socialist Labor, 1971.

Films (as director): 1927—*Zhizn (Life)* (co-d, +co-sc); *V bolshom gorode (In the Big City)* (co-d, +co-sc); *Yevo prevosoditelstvo (His Excellency)* (Roshal) (ed only); 1928—*Tsena cheloveka (The Price of Man, Man's Value, The Lesson)* (co-d); 1929—*Pizhon (The Fop)*; 1930—*Chuzoi bereg (The Other Shore)*; *Ogon (Fire)*; 1934—*Pesnya o shchastye (Song about Happiness)* (co-d); 1935—*Nevidimi chelovek (The Invisible Man)* (Whale) (supervisor of dubbing and reediting); 1938—*Detstvo Gorkovo (Childhood of Gorky, The Childhood of Maxim Gorki)* (+co-sc); 1939—*V lyudyakh (Among People, My Apprenticeship)* [In the World] (+co-sc); 1940—*Moi universiteti (My Universities)* (+co-sc); *Brat geroya (Brother of a Hero)* (Vasilchikov) (art d only); 1941—*Romantiki (Children of the Soviet Arctic)* (+co-sc); 1942—*Kak zakalyalas stal (How the Steel Was Tempered, Heroes Are Made)* (+sc); "*Mayak (Beacon, The Signal Tower)*" segment and supervisor of "*Kvartal (Block 14)*" and "*Sinie skali (Blue Crags)*" segments of *Boevi kinosbornik (Fighting Film Album)* No.9; 1944—*Raduga (The Rainbow)* (+co-sc); 1945—*Nepokorenniye (Semya tarassa, Unvanquished, Unconquered)* (+co-sc); 1947—*Selskaya uchitelnitsa (Varvara, An Emotional Education, Rural Institute, A Village Schoolteacher)*; 1949—*Alitet ukhodit v gory (Zakoni Bolshoi zemli, Alitet Leaves for the Hills)* (+co-sc—film banned, partially destroyed); 1950—*Sportivnaya slava (Nachi chempiony, Sporting Fame, Our Champions)* (short); 1956—*Mat (Mother)* (+co-sc);

1957—*Dorogoi tsenoi (At Great Cost, The Horse That Cried)*; 1959—*Foma Gordeyev* (+co-sc); 1962—*Zdravstvuitye deti (Hello Children)* (+co-sc); 1966—*Serdtse materi (A Mother's Heart, Heart of a Mother)*; 1967—*Vernost materi (A Mother's Loyalty, A Mother's Devotion)*; 1972—*Chaliapin*; 1973—*Nadezhda*. Role: 1926—passerby in *Prostitutka (The Prostitute)* (Frelikh).

Publications:

By DONSKOI:

Articles—"Ceux qui savent parler aux dieux..." in *Cinéma 59* (Paris), November 1959; "Travaillons pour tous les coeurs humains!" in *L'Humanité* (Paris), 14 December 1963; "Mon Idéal c'est un humanisme combattant" in *Les Lettres françaises* (Paris), 19 December 1963; "Essai de portrait de Mark Donskoï", interview by Albert Cervoni in *France nouvelle* (Paris), 18 December 1963; interview by Yves Kovacs in *Télérama* (Paris), 15 March 1964; "Voix off", text and interview by Marcel Martin in *Cinéma 64* (Paris), April 1964; text in *La Table ronde* (Paris), May 1966; interview by Robert Grelier in *Cinéma 67* (Paris), December 1967; "My—propagandisty partii" in *Iskusstvo Kino* (Moscow), November 1972; "Tret'e izmerenie" in *Iskusstvo Kino* (Moscow), December 1974; "Vernost' teme: k 75-letiiu Very Pavlovny Stroevoi" in *Iskusstvo Kino* (Moscow), no.11, 1978.

On DONSKOI:

Books—*Kino: A History of the Russian and Soviet Film* by Jay Leyda, London 1960; *Marc Donskoi* by Albert Cervoni, Paris 1966; *The Most Important Art: Eastern European Film After 1945* by Mira and Antonín Liehm, Berkeley, California 1977; articles—"Mark Donskoi" by Catherine de la Roche in *Sequence* (London), autumn 1948; "Umanesimo di Donskoi" by Paolo Mondello in *Bianco e nero* (Rome), March 1950; "Marc Donskoï" by André Desvallées in *Positif* (Lyon), no.5, 1953; "The Gorky Trilogy" by John Minchinton in *Films and Filming* (London), January 1955; "The Gorki Trilogy—The Poetry of Cinema" by Charles Fox in *Film* (London), February 1955; article by Marcel Martin in *Cinéma 58* (Paris), September/October 1958; article by Louis Marcorelles in *Cahiers du cinéma* (Paris), no.93, 1959; "Au prix de sa vie" by Claude Beylie in *Cinéma 61* (Paris), November/December 1961; "Les Roseaux pensants" by Michel Mardore in *Cahiers du cinéma* (Paris), November 1961; "Donskoï" by Albert Cervoni in *Contre-Champ* (Marseilles), October 1962; "Mark Donskoï" by Philippe Haudiquet in *Image et son* (Paris), November 1964; "Mark Donskoï, un idéaliste à la tête dure dans un monde matérialiste" by Jean d'Yvoire in *Télérama* (Paris), 15 August 1965; "Mark Donskoi: Filmography" by J. Gillett in *Focus on Film* (London), March/April 1970; "Mark Donskoy" by J. Gillett in *Focus on Film* (London), March/April 1970; "Director of the Year" in *International Film Guide*, London 1971; "Mark Donskoj a Gorkij" by G. Kopaněvová in *Film a Doba* (Prague), November 1977; biofilmography in *Film Dope* (London), June 1977; "Biofilmographie de Marc Donskoi" in *Avant-Scène du cinéma* (Paris), 15 February 1979; "Mark Donskoy: Irrepressible Youth" by Y. Fadeeva in *Soviet Film* (Moscow), no.3, 1979; ; "Hommage: Marc Donskoï" by C.M. Cluny in *Cinéma* (Paris), May 1981; "Die plastischen Bilder des Mark Donskoi" by H.-J. Schlegel in *Film und Fernsehen* (Berlin), August 1981; "V kontekste istorii" by M. Zak and others in *Iskusstvo Kino* (Moscow), March 1981.

* * *

Mark Donskoi may not be as familiar to western audiences as Eisenstein, Pudovkin or Dovzhenko; his films are in no way as readily recalled as *Battleship Potemkin*, *Mother* or *Earth*. Like other Soviet filmmakers, he does propagandize about the glories of the Bolshevik Revolution and highlight the life of Lenin. But Donskoi's great and unique contribution to Russian cinema is his adaption to the screen of Maxim Gorki's autobiographical trilogy: *The Childhood of Gorki, My Apprenticeship* and *My Universities,* all based on the early life of the famed writer and shot during the late 1930s. (Years later, Donskoi adapted two other Gorki works, *Mother*—the same story filmed by Pudovkin in 1926—and *Foma Gordeyev.*)

In the trilogy, Donskoi chronicles the life of a child who grew up to become Gorki, and the experiences which alter his view of the world. At their best, they are original and pleasing in a high degree: the first especially presents a comprehensive richly detailed view of rural life in Russia during the 1870s. While delineating the dream of 19th century Russian youth, Donskoi lovingly recreates the era. The characters are presented in terms of their conventional ambitions and relationships within the family structure. They are not revolutionaries, but farmers and other provincials with plump bodies and commonplace faces. The result is a very special sense of familiarity, of fidelity to a time and place. Of course, villains in Gorki's childhood are not innately evil, but products of the repressive czarist society. They are thus compassionate: within them, there is both good and bad. Donskoi shoots the Russian countryside with imagination, and sometimes even with grandeur. In this regard, the Gorki trilogy is an original: arguably no other filmmaker has ever depicted Russia in this manner.

Donskoi's later noteworthy works include *How the Steel Was Tempered*, one of the first Russian films to deal with World War II. While based on the civil war story, the filmmaker includes only the sequences pertaining to Ukrainian resistance to German invaders in 1918, paralleling them to the then-current situation in his country. The story also mirrors the Gorki trilogy in that it presents a boy who is changed by the encounters of his life.

The Rainbow, an appropriately angry drama shot at the height of World War II, details the travails of life in a German-occupied village. The message: even small boys may be shot by the Nazis, but the spirit of the Soviet people will endure. This film is particulary inspirational; its aesthetics may have even influenced Italian neorealism. *The Unvanquished*, about occupied Kiev, is sort of a sequel to *The Rainbow.* Most significantly and graphically, Jews are crowded into Babi Yar, and then slaughtered.

The careers of a few Russian filmmakers have outlasted that of Mark Donskoi, who in his youth had fought in the Civil War and been imprisoned by the White Russians; his films span 50 years, but his Gorki trilogy alone assures him of his niche in cinema history.

—Rob Edelman

DOS SANTOS, NELSON PEREIRA
see **PEREIRA DOS SANTOS, NELSON**

DOVZHENKO, ALEXANDER. Ukrainian. Born in Sosnytsia, Chernigov province of Ukraine, 12 September 1894. Educated at

Alexandrovsk Parish School, Sosnytsia, 1902-06; secondary school in Sosnytsia, 1907-11; Hlukhiv Teachers' Institute, 1911-14; Kiev University Dept. of Science and Kiev Commercial Institute School of Economics, 1917-18; Academy of Fine Arts, Kiev, 1919. Married Barbara Krylova, 1920 (divorced about 1926); married actress Julia Solntseva, 1927. Career: 1914—teacher at 2nd Zhitomir High School; 1917—teacher at 7th High School, Kiev; organizes student demonstrations against conservative regime; 1919-20—military service; 1920—becomes member, Communist Party of Ukraine, works in underground during Polish occupation; serves as Commissar of Shevchenko Theater, organizes village governments; 1921—chargé d'affaires, Embassy of Ukrainian SSR in Warsaw; 1922—attached to Ukrainian Embassy in Berlin, studies painting with Erich Heckel; 1923—returns to Ukraine, expelled from Communist Party, becomes cartoonist in Kharkiv; 1925—co-founder of VAPLITE (Free Academy of Proletarian Literature); 1926—goes to Odessa Film Studio; 1927—meets Eisenstein and Pudovkin; 1928—moves to Kiev Film Studio; 1929—Julia Solntseva begins to work as Dovzhenko's assistant; 1930—premiere of Earth, travels through Europe showing film and giving press conferences; 1932—first lectures at State Cinema Institute (VGIK), Moscow; 1933—dismissed from Ukrainfilm, assigned to Mosfilm by Stalin; 1935—begins writing Shchors after Stalin suggests making a "Ukrainian Chapayev"; 1940—Artistic Supervisor, Kiev Studio; 1941—evacuated with Kiev Studio to Central Asia following German invasion; 1942-43—correspondent at front lines for Red Army and for Izvestia in the Ukraine; 1943—Stalin bans script for Ukraine in Flames; 1944—denounced as "bourgeois nationalist", transferred to Mosfilm; 1945-47—works on theater projects; 1952—settles in Kakhiva; 1952-56—works on writings, submits treatments for films (unrealized); 1958—Dovzhenko's widow Julia Solntseva completes Poem of an Inland Sea, the 1st of 5 of Dovzhenko's unfinished projects she will complete. Died in Moscow, 26 November 1956. Recipient: Lenin Prize, 1935; Honored Art Worker of the Ukrainian SSR, 1939; 1st Degree Stalin Prize for Shchors, 1941; Order of the Red Flag, 1943; 2nd Degree Stalin Prize for Michurin, 1949; People's Artist of the RSFSR, 1950; Order of the Red Labor Flag, 1955.

Films (as director and scenarist): 1926—Vasya-reformator (Vasya the Reformer) (co-d); Yahidka kokhannya (Love's Berry, Russ.: Yagodki lyubvi); 1927—Teka dypkuryera (The Diplomatic Pouch, Russ.: Sumka dipkuryera) (revised sc, +ro); 1928—Zvenyhora (Russ.: Zvenigora) (revised sc); 1929—Arsenal (Arsenal: The January Uprising in Kiev in 1918); 1930—Zemlya (Earth); 1932—Ivan; 1935—Aerograd (Air City, Frontier); 1939—Shchors (co-d, co-sc); 1940—Osvobozhdenie (Liberation) (co-d, +ed); (as artistic supervisor): Bukovyna-Zemlya Ukrayinska (Bucovina-Ukrainian Land) (Solntseva); 1941—Bohdan Khmelnytsky (Savchenko); 1942—Alexander Parkhomenko (Lukov); 1943—Bytva za nashu Radyansku Ukrayinu (The Battle for Our Soviet Ukraine) (Solntseva and Avdiyenko) (+narration); (as director): 1945—Pobeda na pravoberezhnoi Ukraine i izgnanie Nemetskikh zakhvatchikov za predeli Ukrainskikh Sovetskikh zemel (Victory in Right-Bank Ukraine and the Expulsion of the Germans from the Boundaries of the Ukrainian Soviet Earth) (co-d, +commentary); 1946—Strana rodnaya (Native Land, Our Country) (co-ed uncredited, narration only); 1948—Michurin (co-d, +pr, sc).

Films directed by Julia Solntseva and prepared or written by Dovzhenko or based on his writings: 1958—Poema o more (Poem of an Inland Sea); 1961—Povest plamennykh let (Story of the Turbulent Years, The Flaming Years, Chronicle of Flaming Years); 1965—Zacharovannaya Desna (The Enchanted Desna);

1968—Nezabivaemoe (The Unforgettable, Ukraine in Flames); 1969—Zolotye vorota (The Golden Gates).

Role: 1927—The Diplomatic Pouch.

Publications:

By DOVZHENKO:

Books—Izbrannoie, Moscow 1957; Tvori v triokh tomakh, Kiev 1960; Sobranie sotchinenyi (4 toma), izdatelstvo, Moscow 1969; "Polum'iane zhyttia: spogadi pro Oleksandr a Dovzhenka" compiled by I. Solntseva, Kiev 1973; articles—"Interview de A. Dovjenko" by Georges Sadoul in Les Lettres françaises (Paris), 1956; "Avtobiographia" in Iskusstvo Kino (Moscow), no.5, 1958; "Iz zapisnykh knijek" in Iskusstvo Kino (Moscow), no.1, 2, 4, 5, 1963; "Carnets de notes, fragments" in 20 Ans de cinéma sovietique, Paris 1963.

On DOVZHENKO:

Books—Alexander Dovzhenko by R. Yourenev, Moscow 1958 (name transliterated as R. Jurenew in German translation, 1964); Poetika Dovzhenko by Igor Rachuk, Moscow 1964; Dovjenko by Luda and Jean Schnitzer, Paris 1966; Alexandre Dovjenko by Marcel Oms, Lyon 1968; Dovjenko by Alexandr Mariamov, Moscow 1968; Alexandre Dovjenko by Barthélemy Amengual, Paris 1970; Alexander Dovzhenko: The Poet as Filmmaker, edited by Marco Carynnyk, Cambridge, Massachusetts 1973; articles—"Dovzhenko at 60" in Sight and Sound (London), autumn 1955; obituary in The New York Times, 27 November 1956; special issue of Film (Venice), August 1957; "Dovzhenko—Poet of Life Eternal" by Ivor Montagu in Sight and Sound (London), summer 1957; "The Films of Alexander Dovzhenko" by Charles Shibuk in New York Film Bulletin, no.11-14, 1961; "Dovzhenko" by D. Robinson in The Silent Picture (London), autumn 1970; "The Dovzhenko Papers" by Marco Carynnyk in Film Comment (New York), fall 1971; "Celovek, proživšij tysjaču žiznej" by L. Arnstam in Iskusstvo Kino (Moscow), May 1972; special issue of Iskusstvo Kino (Moscow), September 1974; "Fin unserer Epoch" and "Ein Poet des Films" by S. Frejlih in Film und Fernsehen (Berlin), August and September 1974; "Verteidiger der Poesie" by G. Netzeband in Film und Fernsehen (Berlin), March 1975; "Dal linguaggio metaforico al linguaggio denotativo" by G. Cremonini in Cinema nuovo (Turin), March/April 1976; "Zu Problemen des stilistischen Einflusses der bildenden Kunst auf die Stummfilme Alexander Dowshenko" by A. Krautz in Information (Berlin), no.2, 1977; "Die wichtigste der Künste" by A. Karaganov in Film und Fernsehen (Berlin), April 1977; biofilmography in Film Dope (London), January 1978; "Iabloni" by V. Sytin and "Tvorchestvo A.P. Dovzhenko i narodnaia kul'tura" by S. Trimbach in Iskusstvo Kino (Moscow), no.10, 1979; film—Alexander Dovzhenko by Yevheniya Hryhorovych (Evgeni Grigorovich), 1964.

*　　*　　*

Unlike many other Soviet filmmakers, whose works are boldly and aggressively didactic, Alexander Dovzhenko's cinema is personal, fervently private. His films are clearly political, yet at the same time he is the first Russian director whose art is so emotional, so vividly his own. His best films, Arsenal, Earth and Ivan, are all no less than poetry on celluloid. Their emotional and poetic expression, almost melancholy simplicity, and celebration of life ultimately obliterate any external event in their scenarios. His images—most specifically, farmers, animals, and crops drenched in sunlight—are penetratingly, delicately real. With Eisenstein and Pudovkin, Dovzhenko is one of the great inventors and masters of the Russian cinema.

As evidenced by his very early credits, Dovzhenko might have become a journeyman director and scenarist, an adequate technician at best: *Vasya the Reformer*, his first script, is a forgettable comedy about an overly-curious boy; *The Diplomatic Pouch* is a silly tale of secret agents and murder. But in *Zvenigora*, his fourth film, he includes scenes of life in rural Russia for the first time. This film is complex and confusing, but it is the forerunner of *Arsenal*, *Earth*, and *Ivan*, a trio of classics released within four years of each other, all of which honor the lives and struggles of peasants.

In *Arsenal*, set in the Ukraine in a period between the final year of World War I and the repression of a workers' rebellion in Kiev, Dovzhenko does not bombard the viewer with harsh, unrealistically visionary images. Despite the subject matter, the film is as lyrical as it is piercing and pointed; the filmmaker manages to transcend the time and place of his story. While he was not the first Soviet director to unite pieces of film with unrelated content to communicate a feeling, his *Arsenal* is the first feature in which the totality of its content rises to the height of pure poetry. In fact, according to John Howard Lawson, "No film artist has ever surpassed Dovzhenko in establishing an intimate human connection between images that have no plot relationship."

The storyline of *Earth*, Dovzhenko's next—and greatest—film, is deceptively simple: a peasant leader is killed by a landowner after the farmers in a small Ukrainian village band together and obtain a tractor. But these events serve as the framework for what is a tremendously moving panorama of rustic life and the almost tranquil admission of life's greatest inevitability: death. Without doubt, *Earth* is one of the cinema's few authentic masterpieces.

Finally, *Ivan* is an abundantly eloquent examination of man's connection to nature. Also set in the Ukraine, the film chronicles the story of an illiterate peasant boy whose political consciousness is raised during the building of the Dnieper River dam. This is Dovzhenko's initial sound film: he effectively utilizes his soundtrack to help convey a fascinating combination of contrasting states of mind.

None of Dovzhenko's subsequent films approach the greatness of *Arsenal*, *Earth* and *Ivan*. Stalin suggested that he direct *Shchors*, which he shot with his wife, Yulia Solntseva. Filmed over a three-year period, and under the ever-watchful eye of Stalin and his deputies, the scenario details the revolutionary activity of a Ukrainian intellectual, Nikolia Shchors. The result, while unmistakably a Dovzhenko film, still suffers from rhetorical excess when compared to his earlier work.

Eventually, Dovzhenko headed the film studio at Kiev, wrote stories and made documentaries. His final credit, *Michurin*, about the life of a famed horticulturist, was based on the play he wrote during World War II. After *Muchurin*, the filmmaker spent several years putting together a trilogy set in the Ukraine, chronicling the development of a village from 1930 on. He was sent to commence shooting when he died, and Solntseva completed the projects.

It is unfortunate that Dovzhenko never got to direct these last features. He was back on familiar ground: perhaps he might have been able to recapture the beauty and poetry of his earlier work. Still, *Arsenal*, *Ivan* and especially *Earth* are more than ample accomplishments for any filmmaker's lifetime.

—Rob Edelman

DREYER, CARL THEODOR. Danish. Born in Copenhagen, 3 February 1889. Married Ebba Larsen, November 1911; children: daughter Gunni (born 1913) and Erik (born 1923). Career: before 1909—office job in a telegraph company; 1909-12—reporter for *Berlingske Tidende* and *Riget*, Copenhagen newspapers; 1912—feature writer for daily *Ekstrabladet*; series of celebrity profiles leads to contact with film industry; 1912-13—writes 3 scripts for Skandinavisk-Russiske Handelshus; 1913—joins Nordisk Films Kompagni part-time (full-time in 1915); 1918—given opportunity to direct *The President*; 1920—shoots *The Parson's Widow* for Svensk Filmindustri in Sweden; 1921—moves to Primusfilm in Berlin, works with actors associated with Stanislavsky and Reinhardt; 1922—returns to Denmark to film *Once Upon a Time*; 1924—joins Ufa in Berlin but leaves after less than a year; 1925—returns to Copenhagen; *Thou Shalt Honor Thy Wife* secures European reputation; 1926—hired by Société Generale de Films, begins work on *Jeanne d'Arc*; 1930—contract with Dreyer broken; 1932—after *Vampyr* begins work on *Mudundu* (unrealized) in Africa; quits film and returns to practicing journalism in Denmark; 1942—after documentary project *Good Mothers*, begins work on *Day of Wrath*; 1946-56—works on documentary projects; 1948—comes to America seeking support for film on life of Jesus; 1952—awarded managership of film theater, as a form of pension, by Danish government; 1964—*Gertrud* receives Paris premiere, attacked by critics; 1964-68—works on *Jesus* project, visits Israel, learns Hebrew; receives promises of support from Danish government and RAI, Italy. Died in Copenhagen, 20 March 1968; buried at Frederiksberg Kirkegård, Copenhagen. Recipient: Golden Lion Award for *Ordet*, Venice Film Festival, 1955.

Films (as scriptwriter): 1912—*Bryggerens Datter (The Brewer's Daughter)* (Ottesen) (co-sc); 1913—*Balloneksplosionen (The Balloon Explosion)*; *Krigskorrespondenten (The War Correspondent)* (Glückstadt); *Hans og Grethe (Hans and Grethe)*; *Elskovs Opfindsomhed (Inventive Love)* (Wolder); *Chatollets Hemmelighed, eller Det gamle chatol (The Secret of the Writing Desk, or, The Old Writing Desk)* (Davidsen); 1914—*Ned Med Vabnene (Lay Down Your Arms)* (Holger-Madsen); 1915—*Juvelerernes Skræk, eller Skelethaanden, eller Skelethaandens sidste bedrift (The Jeweller's Terror, or, The Skeleton's Hand, or, The Last Adventure of the Skeleton's Hand)* (Christian); 1916—*Penge (Money)* (Mantzius); *Den Hvide Djævel, eller Djævelens Protege (The White Devil, or, The Devil's Protegé)* (Holger-Madsen); *Den Skonne Evelyn (Evelyn the Beautiful)* (Sandberg); *Rovedderkoppen, eller Den røde Enke (The Robber Spider, or, The White Widow)* (Blom); *En Forbryders Liv og Levned, eller En Forbryders Memoirer (The Life and Times of a Criminal, or, The Memoirs of a Criminal)* (Christian); *Guldets Gift, eller Lerhjertet (The Poison of Gold, or, The Clay Heart)* (Holger-Madsen); *Pavillonens Hemmelighed (The Secret of the Pavilion)* (Mantzius); 1917—*Den Mystiske Selskabsdame, eller Legationens Gidsel (The Mysterious Lady's Companion, or, The Hostage of the Embassy)* (Blom); *Hans Rigtige Kone (His Real Wife)* (Holger-Madsen); *Fange Nr. 113 (Prisoner No. 113)* (Holger-Madsen); *Hotel Paradis (Hotel Paradiso)* (Dinesen); 1918—*Lydia* (Holger-Madsen); *Glaedens Dag, eller Miskendt (Day of Joy, or, Neglected)* (Christian); 1919—*Gillekop* (Blom); *Grevindens Aere (The Countess's Honor)* (Blom); (as director and scriptwriter): *Praesidenten (The President)* (+co-art director); 1920—*Prästänkan (The Parson's Widow, The Witch Woman, The 4th Marriage of Dame Margaret)*; 1921—*Blade af Satans Bog (Leaves from Satan's Book)* (co-sc+co-art direction, shot in 1919); 1922—*Die Gezeichneten (The Stigmatized One, Love One Another)*; *Der Var Engang (Once Upon a Time)* (co-sc +ed); 1924—*Michael* (co-sc); 1925—*Du Skal Aere Din Hustru (Thou Shalt Honor Thy Wife, The Master of the House)* (co-sc +art direction); 1926—*Glomdalsbruden (The Bride of Glomdal)* (+art direction); 1928—*La Passion de Jeanne d'Arc* (co-sc); 1932—*Vampyr (The Dream of Allan Gray)* (co-sc +pr); 1942—*Mødrehjaelpen (Good Mothers)* (d only); 1943—*Vredens Dag (Day of Wrath)* (co-sc); 1945—*Två Manniskor (2 People)* (co-sc +ed); 1946—*Vandet Pa Låndet (Water from the Land)* (never finished); 1947—*De Gamle (The 7th Age)* (sc only); *Landsbykirken (The Danish Village Church)* (co-sc); *Kampen Mod Kraeften (The Struggle Against Cancer)* (co-sc); 1948—*De Naaede Faergen (They Caught the Ferry)*; 1949—*Thorvaldsen* (co-sc); *Radioens Barndom* (ed only); 1950—*Storstrømsbroen (The Bridge of Storstrøm)*; *Shakespeare og Kronborg (Shakespeare and Kronborg)* (sc only); 1954—*Rønnes og Nexøs Genopbygning (The Rebuilding of Rome and Nexos)* (sc only); *Et Slot I Et Slot (Castle within a Castle)*; 1955—*Ordet (The Word)*; 1964—*Gertrud*.

Publications:

By DREYER:

Books—*La Passione di Giovanna d'Arco*, edited by Guido Guerrasio, Milan 1945; *Vampyr. L'Etrange Aventure de David Gray*, edited by A. Buzzi and B. Lattuada, Milan 1948; *La Parola* [Ordet], edited by Guido Cincotti, Rome 1956; *Om filmen*, articles and interviews, Copenhagen 1959; *Om filmen*, Copenhagen 1964; *Fire Film af Carl Th. Dreyer*, edited by Ole Storm, Copenhagen 1964; *Cinque Film*, Turin 1967; *Jesus fra Nazaret. Et filmmanuskript*, Copenhagen 1968; *Gesú. Racconto di un film*, Turin 1969; *4 Screenplays*, New York 1970; *4 Screenplays* translated by Oliver Stallybrass, London 1970; *Jesus*, original manuscript, New York 1972; *Dreyer in Double Reflection*, edited by Donald Skoller, New York 1973; articles—"Realisierte Mystik" in *Film-Photos wie noch nie*, 1929; "Lunch with Carl Dreyer" by Ragna Jackson in *Penguin Film Review* (London), August 1947; interview by Judith Podselver in *Revue du cinéma* (Paris), no.8, 1947; "Interview with Dreyer" by John Winge in *Sight and Sound* (London), January 1950; "Visit with Carl Th. Dreyer" by James Card in *Image* (Rochester, New York), December 1953; "Rencontre avec Carl Dreyer" by Lotte Eisner in *Cahiers du cinéma* (Paris), June 1955; "Thoughts on My Craft" in *Sight and Sound* (London), no.3, 1955/56; "Metaphysic of Ordet", letter in *Film Culture* (New York), no.1, 1956; "The Filmmaker and the Audience" in *Film: Book One*, edited by Robert Hughes, New York 1959; interview by Herbert Luft in *Films and Filming* (London), no.9, 1961; preface to *The Story of Danish Film* by Ebbe Neergaard, Copenhagen 1962; "Dreyer Mosaik", edited by John Ernst and others in *Kosmorama* (Copenhagen), December 1963; "Carl Dreyer, l'un des hommes les plus mystérieux du cinéma, est à Paris", interview by Guy Allombert in *Arts* (Paris), 16 December 1964; "The Passion of Carl Dreyer", interview by Peter Lennon in the *Guardian* (London), 21 December 1964; "Carl Dreyer nous dit: 'Le principal intérêt d'un homme: les autres hommes.'", interview by Georges Sadoul in *Les Lettres Françaises* (Paris), 24 December 1964; interview by Guy Allombert in *Arts* (Paris), no.985, 1964; interview by Bjørn Rasmussen in *Cineforum* (Bergamo), no.35, 1964; interview by Georges Sadoul in *Les Lettres françaises* (Paris), 24 December 1964; interview by Michel Delahaye in *Cahiers du cinéma* (Paris), no.170, 1965; "Liminaire" in *Dictionnaire du Cinéma*, edited by Raymond Bellour and Jean-Jacques Broch-

ier, Paris 1966; "My Way of Working is in Relation to the Future: A Conversation with Carl Dreyer" by Carl Lerner in *Film Comment* (New York), fall 1966; "Interview with Carl Dreyer" by Børge Trolle in *Film Culture* (New York), summer 1966; "Carl Dreyer om film" in *Louisiana Revy* (Denmark), no.4, 1967; "Parmi les acteurs émigrés à Berlin" in *Cahiers du Cinéma* (Paris), December 1968; "Filmographie commentée" in *Cahiers du Cinéma* (Paris), December 1968; "Carl Dreyer: Utter Bore or Total Genius?" by Denis Duperley in *Films and Filming* (London), February 1968; "Carl Dreyer", interview by Michel Delahaye in *Interviews with Film Directors*, edited by Andrew Sarris, New York 1969; "Metaphysic of *Ordet*" in *The Film Culture Reader*, edited by P. Adams Sitney, New York 1970; "Dies Irae" in *Avant-Scène du cinéma* (Paris), no.100; "Vampyr" in *Avant-Scène du cinéma* (Paris), no.228.

On DREYER:

Books—*Carl Theodor Dreyer: A Film Director's Work* by Ebbe Neergaard, London 1950; *The Art of Carl Dreyer: An Analysis* by Børge Trolle, Copenhagen 1955; *Tre maestri del cinema* by Angelo Solmi, Milan 1956; *Dreyer* by Jean Sémolué, Paris 1962; *The Films of Carl Dreyer* by Eileen Bowser, New York 1964; *Carl Theodor Dreyer* by Carlos Cuenca, Madrid 1964; *Portrait of Carl Th. Dreyer* by Ib Monty, Copenhagen 1965; *Carl Th. Dreyer, Danish Film Director*, edited by Soren Dyssegaard, Copenhagen 1968; *Le Cinéma et sa vérité* by Amédée Ayfre, Paris 1969; *Carl Th. Dreyer* by Claude Perrin, Paris 1969; *Carl Theodor Dreyer*, Amsterdam 1970; *Carl Th. Dreyer* by Jean Sémolué, Paris 1970; *The Cinema of Carl Dreyer* by Tom Milne, New York 1971; *Dreyer: Carl Th. Dreyer—en dansk filmskaber* by Helge Ernst, Copenhagen 1972; *Transcendental Style in Film: Ozu, Bresson, Dreyer* by Paul Schrader, Los Angeles 1972; *Dreyer* by David Bordwell, London 1973; *Dreyer in Double Reflection* edited by Donald Skoller, New York 1973; *Dreyer*, edited by Mark Nash, London 1977; *Carl Theodor Dreyer* by Pier Giorgio Tone, Florence 1978; *The Films of Carl-Theodor Dreyer* by David Bordwell, Berkeley, California 1981; *Carl Th. Dreyer tøat Nilsson* I and II by M. Drouzy, Copenhagen 1982 (French edition: *Carl Th. Dreyer, né Nilsson*, Paris 1982); articles—special issue of *Ecran français* (Paris), 11 November 1947; "Carl Dreyer: The Director as Artist" by Dilys Powell in *Screen and Audience*, edited by Cross and Rattenburry, London 1947; "Carl Théo Dreyer et sa situation en 1947" by Judith Podselver in *La Revue du cinéma* (Paris), no.8, 1947/48; "Parabola creativa di Carl Th. Dreyer" by Giulio Castello in *Bianco e nero* (Rome), no.7, 1948; "Carl Theodor Dreyer e la sua opera" by Carl Vincent in *Bianco e nero* (Rome), no.10, 1949; "The Rise, the Fall, and the Rise of Danish Film" by Ebbe Neergaard in *Hollywood Quarterly*, no.3, 1949/50; "Carl Dreyer's World" by Richard Rowland in *Hollywood Quarterly*, no.1, 1950; "The Tyrannical Dane" by Paul Moor in *Theatre Arts* (New York), no.4, 1951; "Trilogie mystique de Dreyer" by Lo Duca in *Cahiers du Cinéma* (Paris), February 1952; "Carl Theodor Dreyer et le cinéma danois" by Frédéric Laurent in *Image et son* (Paris), no.65, 1953; "Carl Dreyer, poète tragique du cinéma" by Ernst Rehben in *Positif* (Paris), no.8, 1953; "Bresson et Dreyer" by B. Amengual in *Image et son* (Paris), no.69, 1954; "The World of Carl Dreyer" by Børge Trolle in *Sight and Sound* (London), winter 1955/56; "Réalisme et irréel chez Dreyer" by Lotte Eisner in *Cahiers du cinéma* (Paris), December 1956; "Carl Dreyer—A Master of His Craft" by Herbert Luft in *The Quarterly of Film, Radio and Television* (Berkeley), no.2, 1956; "Dreyer" by Herbert Luft in *Films and Filming* (London), June 1961; "'Douleur, Noblesse Unique' ou la passion chez Carl Dreyer" by Jean Sémolué in *Etudes cinématographiques* (Paris), fall 1961; "Dreyer at 75" by Peter Cowie in *Films and Filming* (London), no.6, 1964; "Dreyer" by Ken Kelman in *Film Culture* (New York), no.35, 1964/65; "The World of Carl Dreyer" by Kirk Bond in *Film Quarterly* (Berkeley), fall 1965; "Una Giornata con Dreyer" by Giacomo Gambetti in *Bianco e nero* (Rome), no.10-11, 1965; "Darkness and Light" by Tom Milne in *Sight and Sound* (London), no.4, 1965; "L'Archaisme nordique de Dreyer" by André Téchiné in *Cahiers du cinéma* (Paris), no.170, 1965; "Dreyer: cadres et mouvements" by Philippe Parrain in *Etudes cinématographiques* (Paris), no.53-56, 1967; "Dreyer in memoriam..." by Alexandre Astruc in *Kosmorama* (Copenhagen), June 1968; special issue on Dreyer, *Cahiers du cinéma* (Paris), December 1968; special issue od *Kosmorama* (Copenhagen), June 1968; "Great Dane" by Ib Monty in *Sight and Sound* (London), spring 1968; "Féroce" by Jean-Marie Straub in *Cahiers du cinéma* (Paris), December 1968; "Dreyer" by Ken Kelman in *The Film Culture Reader* edited by P. Adams Sitney, New York 1970; "Carl Th. Dreyer" by Jean Sémolué in *Avant-Scène du cinéma* (Paris), 1970; "Carl Th. Dreyer" by Jacques-Pierre Amette in *Dossiers du cinéma: Cinéastes I*, Paris 1971; "Passion, Death and Testament: Carl Dreyer's Jesus Film" by David Bordwell in *Film Comment* (New York), summer 1972; "Carl Dreyer and the Theme of Choice" by Dai Vaughan in *Sight and Sound* (London), summer 1974; "Carl Dreyer" by Robin Wood in *Film Comment* (New York), March/April 1974; "Dreyer's Concept of Abstraction" by Vlada Petric in *Sight and Sound* (London), spring 1975; "Döden forener", script and article by G. Werner in *Chaplin* (Stockholm), no.4, 1975; "Deux moments du cinéma danois" by F. Devaux in *Cinéma* (Paris), January 1980.

* * *

Carl Th. Dreyer is the greatest filmmaker in the Danish cinema, in which he was always a solitary personality. But he is also among the few international directors who turned films into an art and made them a new means of expression for the artistic genius. Of Dreyer's feature films, seven were produced in Denmark, three in Germany, two in France, two in Sweden and one in Norway.

If one tries to understand the special nature of Dreyer's art, one can delve into his early life to find the roots of his never failing contempt for pretentions and his hatred of bourgeois respectability, of his preoccupation with suffering and martyrdom. In the first biography of Dreyer, which was published in 1982, M. Drouzy has revealed the fate of Dreyer's biological mother, who died in the most cruel way following an attempted abortion. Dreyer, who was adopted by a Copenhagen family, learned about this when he was 18, and Drouzy's psychoanalytical study finds the victimized woman in all of Dreyer's films. But of what value is the biographical approach to the understanding of a great artist? The work of an artist need not be the illumination of his private life. This may afford some explanation when we are inquiring into the fundamental point of departure for an artist, but Dreyer's personality is expressed very clearly and graphically in his films. Therefore we can well admire the consistency which has always characterized his outlook on life.

Like many great artists, Dreyer is characterized by the relatively few themes that he constantly played upon. One of the keynotes in Dreyer's work is suffering, and his world is filled with martyrs. Yet suffering and martyrdom are surely not the fundamentals. They are merely manifestations, the results of something else. Suffering and martyrdom are the consequences of wickedness, and it is malice and its influence upon people that his films are concerned about. Already in his second film, *Leaves From Satan's Book*, Dreyer tackled this theme which he was

never to let go: the power of evil over the human mind.

If the popular verdict is that Dreyer's films are heavy and gloomy, naturally the idea is suggested by the subjects which he handled. Dreyer never tried to make us believe that life is a bed of roses. There is much suffering, wickedness, death and torment in his films, but they often conclude in an optimistic conviction in the victory of spirit over matter. With death comes deliverance. It is beyond the reach of malice.

In his delineation of suffering man, devoid of any hope before the arrival of death, Dreyer was never philosophically abstract. Though his films were often enacted on a supersensible plane, were concerned with religious problems, his method as an artist was one of psychological realism, and his object was always the individual. Dreyer's masterly depiction of milieu has always been greatly admired; his keen perception of the characteristic detail is simply dazzling. But this authenticity in settings has never been a means towards a meticulous naturalism. He always sought to transcend naturalism so as to reach a kind of purified, or classically simplified realism.

Though Dreyer occupied himself with the processes of the soul, he always preserved an impartiality when portraying them. One might say that he maintained a high degree of objectivity in his description of the subjective. It can be sensed in his films as a kind of presentation rather than forceful advocacy. Dreyer himself, when describing his method in *La Passion de Jeanne d'Arc*, once employed the expression "realized mysticism." It indicates quite precisely his endeavours to render understandable things that are difficult to comprehend, to make the irrational appear intelligible. The meaning behind life lies in just this recognition of the necessity to suffer in order to arrive at deliverance. The characters nearly always suffered defeat in the outward world because Dreyer considered defeat or victory in the human world to be of no significance. For him the triumph of the soul over life was what was most important.

There are those who wish to demonstrate a line of development in Dreyer's production, but there is no development in the customary sense. Quite early Dreyer's world seemed established, and his films merely changed in their way of viewing the world. There was a complete congruity between his ideas and his style, and it was typical of him to have said: "The soul is revealed in the style, which is the artist's expression of the way he regards his material. For Dreyer the image was always the important thing, so important that there is some justification when described as being first and foremost the great artist of the silent film. On the other hand, his last great films were concerned with the effort to create a harmony between image and sound, and to that end he was constantly experimenting.

Dreyer's pictorial style has been characterized by his extensive and careful employment of the close-up. His films are filled with faces. In this way he was able to let his characters unfold themselves, because he was chiefly interested in the expression which is the result of spiritual conflicts. Emphasis has often been given to the slow lingering rhythm in Dreyer's films. It is obvious that this dilatoriness springs from the wish to endow the action with a stamp of monumentality, though it could lead dangerously close to empty solemnity, to the formalistic.

Dreyer quickly realized the inadequacy of the montage technique, which had been regarded as the foundation of film for so many years. His films became more and more based on long uncut sequences and at the end of his career his calm, elaborating style was quite in conformity with the newer trends in the cinema.

—Ib Monty

DUDOW, SLATAN. Bulgarian. Born in Zaribrod, Bulgaria, 30 January 1903. Educated in architecture and theatre, Berlin; Institute of Theatrical Studies, University of Berlin, 1925-29. Career: 1917—begins involvement with Bulgarian revolutionary organizations; 1920—participates in street fighting resulting from general strike in Sofia; 1922—leaves for Berlin to study architecture; begins taking classes in theatre; 1923—enrolls in dramatic school of Emanuel Reicher; 1929—travels to Moscow to study Soviet theatre following University of Berlin studies, meets Eisenstein; upon return from Moscow, meets Bertolt Brecht; becomes editor and assistant to Victor Blum on documentaries *Hunderttausende unter roten Fahnen* (1929), and *Rotsport marschiert* and *Sprengt die Ketten* (1930); 1930—plans series of short documentaries *Wie lebt die Berliner Arbeiter* (How Does the Berlin Worker Live?); first film in series is forbidden by censor; 1932—*Kuhle Wampe* is severely cut by censors before being shown; 1933—prevented from working for German film companies by Goebbels edict demanding the purification of the cinema of foreign elements; works for Davis-Film, Berlin, as editing specialist; 1934—moves to Paris; abandons filmmaking and returns to theatre, directing several Paris productions of Brecht plays; 1939-45—spends war years in Switzerland; 1946—returns to East Berlin, begins working in film again; 1963—filming of *Christine* interrupted by Dudow's death. Died in car crash, 1963.

Films (as cameraman and editor in collective productions): 1929—*Hunderttausende unter Roten Fahnen* (Hundreds of Thousands under Red Flags); 1930—*Rotsport Marschiert* (Red Sport on the March); *Springt die Ketten* (Break the Chains); (as director and scriptwriter): 1930—*Wie der Berliner Arbeiter wohnt* [How the Berlin Worker Lives] (+ph, ed); *Kuhle Wampe oder Wem Gehört die Welt?* [Kuhle Wampe or Who Owns the World?] (co-sc); 1934—*Bulles de Savon (Seifenblasen)* (co-sc); 1949—*Unser täglich Brot* [Our Daily Bread] (co-sc); 1950—*Familie Benthin* [The Benthin Family] (co-d, co-sc); 1952—*Frauenschicksale* [Women's Destiny] (co-sc); 1954—*Stärker als die Nacht* [Stronger than the Night] (d only); 1956—*Die Hauptmann von Köln* [The Captain of Cologne] (co-sc); 1959—*Verwirrung der Liebe* [Craziness of Love].

Publications:

By DUDOW:

Articles—"La Responsabilité sociale du cinéaste" in *Cinéma d'aujourd'hui*, Paris 1945; "Kuhle Wampe und der Rotstift" in *Junge Welt* (Berlin), 1 March 1958; article in *Neues Deutschland* (Berlin), 31 May 1958; "Aus einem Drehbuch: Christine" in *Film* (Velber bei Hannover), no.3, 1963; "Komedijata i nejnoto obštestveno značenie" in *Kinoizkustvo* (Sofia), April 1978; "Die Komödie und ihre gesellschaftliche Bedeutung" in *Film und Fernsehen* (Berlin), January 1978.

On DUDOW:

Books—*From Caligari to Hitler* by Siegfried Kracauer, Princeton 1947; *Slatan Dudow* by Hermann Herlinghaus, Leipzig 1965; *Le Cinéma réaliste allemand* by R. Borde, Freddy Buache and F. Courtade, Paris 1965; *The Haunted Screen* by Lotte Eisner, Berkeley 1968; articles—"Der Filmregisseur Slatan Dudow" by K. Wischnewski in *Deutsche Filmkunst*, no.7, 1958; "No. spécial consacré à Bertolt Brecht" of *Cahiers du cinéma* (Paris), December 1960; "Stil- und Sujetlinien in den DEFA-Filmen" by Hans Lohmann in *Film* (Velber bei Hannover), no.3,

1962; "Un Cinéma didactique" by Robert Grelier in *Positif* (Paris), December 1962; "Zum Tode Slatan Dudows" in *Film* (Velber bei Hannover), no.2, 1963; "Slatan Dudow" by Yves Aubry in *Anthologie du cinéma*, Paris 1971; "Alltag und Geschichte" by E. Richter in *Filmwissenschaftliche Beitrage* (Berlin), v.14, 1973; "Wer kein woher hat, hat kein wohin" by K. Wischnewski in *Film und Fernsehen* (Berlin), September 1973; "Vietato il suicidio nella Repubblica di Weimar" by Bertolt Brecht in *Cinema nuovo* (Turin), May/June 1974; "A qui est le monde?—Leçons d'histoire" by D. Sauvaget in *Image et son* (Paris), December 1975; "Slatan Dudow" in *Information* (Berlin), no.3-6, 1976; biofilmography in *Film Dope* (London), January 1978.

DULAC, GERMAINE. French. Born Charlotte-Elisabeth-Germaine Saisset-Schneider at Amiens, 17 November 1882. Married Marie-Louis Albert-Dulac, 1905 (divorced 1920). Career: 1909-13—writer and editor for feminist journal *La Française*, then drama critic; 1914—actress friend Stacia de Napierkowska offers Dulac position as camerawoman on *Caligula*; 1915—with husband as administrative director and in association with scenarist Irène Hillel-Erlanger, forms production firm D.H.; 1918—begins collaboration with Louis Delluc on *La Fête espagnole*; 1921—travels to U.S., observes production techniques, meets D.W. Griffith; 1922—made general secretary of Ciné-Club de France, continues promotion of advanced filmmaking through career; 1923—*La Souriante Madame Beudet* establishes reputation; 1925—term "cinéma integrale" used to describe intentions in avant-garde filmmaking; 1928—collaboration with Antonin Artaud on *La Coquille et la clergyman* results, according to some sources, in violent disagreement over her "surrealistic" realisation of film; 1928-29—works from musical sources; 1930s—directs newsreels for Gaumont. Died in Paris, end of July 1942.

Films (as director): 1915—*Les Soeurs ennemies*; 1916—*Geo le mystérieux*; *Venus Victrix*; *Dans l'ouragan de la vie*; 1917—*Ames de fous* (+sc); 1918—*Le Bonheur des autres*; 1919—*La Fête espagnole*; *La Cigarette* (+co-sc); 1920—*Malencontre*; *La Belle Dame sans merci*; 1921—*La Mort du soleil*; 1922—*Werther* (incomplete); 1923—*La Souriante Madame Beudet (The Smiling Madame Beudet)*; *Gossette*; 1924—*Le Diable dans la ville*; 1925—*Ame d'artiste* (+co-sc); *La Folie des vaillants*; 1926—*Antoinette Sabrier*; 1927—*La Coquille et le clergyman (The Seashell and the Clergyman)*; *L'Invitation au voyage*; *Le Cinéma au service de l'histoire*; 1928—*La Princesse Mandane*; *Mon Paris* (Guyot) (supervision only); *Disque 927*; *Thèmes et variations*; *Germination d'un haricot*; 1929—*Etude cinégraphique sur une arabesque*; 1932—*Le Picador* (Jacquelux) (supervision only).

Publications:

By DULAC:

Articles—"Un Article? Mais que faut-il prouver?" in *Le Film* (Paris), 16 October 1919; "Aux amis du cinéma" address in *Cinémagazine* (Paris), 19 December 1924; "L'Art des nuances spirituelles" in *Cinéa-Ciné pour tous* (Paris), January 1925; "Du sentiment à la ligne" in *Schémas* no.1, 1927; "Les Esthètiques, les entraves, la cinégraphie intégrale" in *L'Art cinématographique*,

Paris 1927; "Sur le cinéma visuel" in *Le Rouge et le noir* (Paris), July 1928; "Jouer avec les bruits" in *Cinéa-Ciné pour tous* (Paris), 15 August 1929.

On DULAC:

Articles—biography by Charles Ford in *Anthologie du cinéma* (Paris), no.31, January 1968; "Maya Deren and Germaine Dulac: Activists of the Avant-Garde" by Regina Cornwell in *Film Library Quarterly* (New York), winter 1971/72; "Germaine Dulac: 1st Feminist Filmmaker" by W. Van Wert in *Women and Film* (Santa Monica, Calif.), v.1, no.5-6, 1974; "Dulac Versus Artaud" by W. Dozoretz in *Wide Angle* (Athens, Ohio), no.1, 1979.

*   *   *

Before becoming a film director, Germaine Dulac had studied music, was interested in photography and had written for two feminist journals—all of which played a role in her development as a filmmaker. There were three phases to her filmmaking career: in commercial production, in the avant-garde, and in newsreels. In addition, filmmaking was only one phase of her film career; she also was prominent as a theorist and promoter of the avant-garde film, and as an organizer of the French film unions and the ciné-club movement. The French historian Charles Ford, in *Femmes Cinéastes*, writes that Dulac was the "heart" of the avant-garde in France, that without her there would have been no avant-garde. Her role in French film history has been compared to that of Maya Deren in the U.S., three decades later.

Dulac learned the rudiments of filmmaking by assisting a friend who was making a film in 1914. The following year she made her first film, *Les Soeurs ennemies*, which was distributed by Pathé. It was the ideal time for a woman to enter commercial production, since many men had been called into the army. After directing several other conventional story films, Dulac became more and more drawn to the avant-garde cinema, which she defined in 1927 as—"Lines, surfaces, volumes, evolving directly without contrivance, in the logic of their forms, stripped of representational meaning, the better to aspire to abstraction and give more space to feelings and dreams—INTEGRAL CINEMA."

It is generally reported that Dulac became involved in the French film avant-garde movement through her friendship with Louis Delluc; but Ester Carla de Miro, who is writing Dulac's biography, says that it was in fact through her that he became involved in film. Dulac wrote that her first film was worth "more than a dozen of each of her colleagues...But the cinema is full of people...who cannot forgive her for being an educated woman...or for being a woman at all".

Dulac's best-known and most impressive film (of the few that have been seen outside France) is *The Smiling Madame Beudet*, based on a play by Andre Obey. It depicts the life and dreams of a housewife in a small town married to a coarse, if not repulsive, businessman and created a sensation in its day. Iris Barry, in The Museum of Modern Art's program notes, found Dulac's direction "sensitive and bold"; the use of slow-motion photography and trick-work, however, was "somewhat excessive," but Barry added that Dulac succeeded with what was, at the time, "signal originality" in expressing by pictorial means the atmosphere and implications of this study of domestic conflicts. In later years critics (male) have called the film "clichéd" and "oversimplified."

Currently, showings of *The Seashell and the Clergyman*, based on an original screenplay by Antonin Artaud, have generally been accompanied by program notes indicating Artaud's outrage at Dulac's "feminized" direction. Yet, as P. Adams Sitney points

out in his introduction to *The Avant-Garde Film*, Artaud in an essay entitled "Cinema et l'abstraction" praised the actors and thanked Dulac for her interest in his script. (Wendy Dozoretz, in a doctoral dissertation on Dulac, indicates in her article "Dulac versus Artaud" that the protest aimed against Dulac at the film's Paris opening in 1928 was based on a misunderstanding; at least one protester, Georges Sadoul, later said he had thought he was protesting against Artaud.)

At the other end of the cinema spectrum, Dulac almost revered the use of time-lapse cinematography to reveal the magical effects of tiny plants emerging from the soil with leaf after leaf unfolding and stretching to the sun. "Here comes Germaine Dulac and her lima bean," became a popular joke among film-club devotees, a joke that did not exclude admiration.

The last decade of Dulac's life was spent directing newsreels for Gaumont. She died in 1942, during the German occupation. Charles Ford, who has collected her articles, indicates that she expressed ideas in "clear and accessible language," which others often set forth "in hermetic formulas." One American writer, Stuart Liebman, sums up the opposing view: "Despite their undeniable importance for the film culture of the 1920s, the backward-looking character of Dulac's film theory, constituted by her nostalgia for the aesthetic discourse of the past, both defines and delimits our interest in her theoretical contributions today." The final assessment of Germaine Dulac's life and work as filmmaker and theorist still awaits the availability of a well-documented biography, of all her writings (five short pieces are now available in English translations), and all her existing films.

—Cecile Starr

DUPONT, E.A. German. Born Ewald André Dupont in Seitz, Saxony, 25 December 1891. Educated at University of Berlin. Career: 1911—film critic for *BZ am Mittag* (Berlin); 1916—sells scenario of *Horse Race Fever* to Richard Oswald who takes him on as story editor; collaborates on Oswald's *Let There Be Light*; 1917—directs 1st feature, *The Secret of the America Docks*; 1924—spends season in Mannheim directing vaudeville; invited by Erich Pommer to direct *Variety* for UFA; 1925—put under contract by Universal; 1926—directs in Hollywood; 1928—leaves Hollywood for England, signs long-term contract with British-International; next 3 co-productions under Carr-Gloria-Dupont organization; 1929—makes 1st European all-talkie *Atlantic*; 1931—returns to Berlin; 1933—in U.S. finishing *The Marathon Runner*, remains when Hitler seizes power, begins working for Universal; 1936-37—4 films for Paramount; 1938-39—works for Warner's; 1939—dismissed from *Hell's Kitchen* after reportedly slapping one of the Dead End Kids; begins editing *Hollywood Tribune*; 1941—forms talent agency; late 1940s—with Bachman agency; 1951—attempts comeback with *The Scarf*, does some TV work; 1953-55—makes series of quickies. Died of cancer in Los Angeles, 12 December 1956.

Films (as scriptwriter): 1917—*Rennfieber (Horse Race Fever)* (Oswald); *Der Onyxkopf* (May); *Sturmflut* (Zeyn); *Die sterbende Perlen* (Meinert); *Die Faust des Riesen* parts 1 and 2 (Biebrach); (as director and scriptwriter): 1917—*Das Geheimnis des Amerika-Docks (The Secret of the America Dock)*; 1918—*Es Werde Licht (Let There Be Light)* part 2 (co-d, co-sc); *Europa-Postlagernd (Post Office Europe)*; *Mitternacht*; *Der Schatten (Der lebender Schatten)*; *Der Teufel*; *Die Japanerin*; *Ferdinand Lassalle* (Meinert) (sc only); *Der Saratoga-Koffer* (Meinert) (sc only); *Die Buchhalterin* (von Woringen) (co-sc only); *Nur um tausend Dollars* (Meinert) (sc only); 1919—*Grand Hotel Babylon*; *Die Apachen (Paris Underworld)*; *Das Derby*; *Die Würger der Welt*; *Die Maske*; *Die Spione*; 1920—*Der Mord ohne Täter (Murder Without Cause)* (co-sc); *Die weisse Pfau (The White Peacock)* (co-sc); *Herztrumpt*; *Whitechapel*; 1921—*Der Geier-Wally (Ein Roman aus den Bergen, Geierwally, The Woman Who Killed a Vulture)*; 1922—*Kinder der Finsternis (Children of Darkness)* part 1—*Der Mann aus Neapel (The Man from Naples)* (co-sc); *Kinder der Finsternis* part 2—*Kämpfende Welten (Worlds in Struggle)* (co-sc); *Sie und die Drei (She and the 3)*; 1923—*Die grüne Manuela (The Green Manuela)* (d only); *Das alte Gesetz (Baruch, The Ancient Law)* (d only); 1925—*Der Demütige und die Sängerin (The Humble Man and the Singer, La Meurtrière)* (co-sc); *Variété (Variety, Vaudeville, Varietes)* (co-sc); 1927—*Love Me and the World Is Mine (Implacable Destiny)* (co-sc); *Madame Pompadour* (Wilcox) (sc only); (as director and producer): 1928—*Moulin-Rouge* (+sc); *Piccadilly* (sound version released 1929); 1929—*Atlantic*; *Atlantik* (German version) (co-sc); 1930—*Atlantis* (co-d—French version); *Cape Forlorn (The Love Storm)* (+co-sc); *Menschen im Käfig* (German version); *Le Cap perdu* (French version); *2 Worlds* (+co-story); *Zwei Welten* (German version); *Les Deux Mondes* (French version); (as director): 1931—*Salto Mortale (The Circus of Sin)*; 1932—*Peter Voss, der Millionendieb (Peter Voss, Who Stole Millions)* (+co-sc); 1933—*Der Läufer von Marathon (The Marathon Runner)*; (in U.S.): *Ladies Must Love*; 1935—*The Bishop Misbehaves (The Bishop's Misadventures)*; 1936—*A Son Comes Home*; *Forgotten Faces*; 1937—*A Night of Mystery (The Greene Murder Case)*; *On Such a Night*; *Love on Toast*; 1939—*Hell's Kitchen* (Seiler) (co-d, uncredited); 1951—*The Scarf (The Dungeon)* (+sc); 1953—*Problem Girls*; *The Neanderthal Man*; *The Steel Lady (Secret of the Sahara, The Treasure of Kalifa)*; 1954—*Return to Treasure Island (Bandit Island of Karabei)*; *Miss Robin Crusoe* (co-d, uncredited); 1956—*Magic Fire* (Dieterle) (sc only).

Publications:

By DUPONT:

Books—*Wie ein Film geschrieben wird und wie man ihn verwertet*, with Podehl Fritz, Berlin 1925; *Varieté*, with Leo Birinski, in *Antologia di Bianco e nero*, Rome 1943. article—interview by Ezra Goodman in *Daily News* (Los Angeles), 10 April 1950.

On DUPONT:

Books—*From Caligari to Hitler* by Siegfried Kracauer, Princeton 1947; *The Haunted Screen* by Lotte Eisner, Berkeley 1968; *E.A. Dupont* by Herbert Luft, Anthologie du Cinéma, Paris; articles—"Reflections on the Current Scene" by Herman Weinberg in *Take One* (Montreal), January/February 1970; "E.A. Dupont 1891-1956" by Herbert Luft in *Films in Review* (New York), June/July 1977; letter from A. Pinto in *Films in Review* (New York), October 1977; biofilmography in *Film Dope* (London), January 1978.

*   *   *

Some directors are able to maintain a steady flow of talent in all their work. Others, like E.A. Dupont are remembered for one outstanding moment in their career. *Variété*, or *Vaudeville* as it is also known, was one of the most exciting films to come from Germany in the twenties and Dupont must receive full credit for its creation although it was a film brimming with other talents. He made many other good films but his career as a whole is a rather tragic one. This was partly due to personal deficiencies and partly due to circumstances over which he had no control. He is an example of a director who withers when removed from the soil in which his art was nourished. Some European directors flourished in Hollywood; Dupont was not one of them.

He had been a film critic and also wrote film scripts, before becoming Richard Oswald's story editor and contributing to the latter's sensational sex films *Es werde Licht*. In 1917 he began to direct thrillers like *Das Geheimnis des America Docks* and *Europa Postlagernd*. Recognition came with *Die Geierwally* in 1921. This Henny Porten film was distinguished by settings of Paul Leni, and camera work by Karl Freund. It also popularized Wilhelm Dieterle. Dupont had previously launched the careers of Paul Richter and Bernhardt Goetzke, later featured in the films of Fritz Lang. Freund photographed his next film, *Kinder der Finsternis*, which was in two parts with striking sets by Leni. 1923 was a bumper year for Dupont. his *Die grueme Manuela*, about a young dancer who falls in love with a smuggler whose brother gives his life to ensure their happiness, won international appreciation as did *Das alte Gesetz*, a story of a young Jew's flight from his orthodox home to seek fame in the Austrian theater. In the depiction of Jewish rituals and the life of the Austrian court and theatre, the film had a rich authenticity.

Dupont worked outside the then-current German expressionist style, being more human and realistic in his approach to filmmaking. This was evident in his tour de force *Variété*, a tale of jealousy and death amongst trapeze artists. Its powerful realism, its visual fluidity and daring techniques, coupled with the superb performances of Jannings, Lya de Putti and Warwick Ward, made it stand out in a year rich with achievement. The virtuoso camerawork of Karl Freund contributed not merely to the spatial and temporal aspects of the film but in the revelation of motive and thought. The uninhibited sensuality depicted by the film led to censorship problems in many countries. Inevitably Dupont went to Hollywood where he directed a not entirely successful *Love Me and the World Is Mine* for Universal. In 1928 he made two stylish films in England: *Moulin Rouge*, exploiting the sensual charms of Olga Tschechowa, and *Piccadilly* with Gilda Gray and Anna May Wong and with Charles Laughton making his film debut in a small role.

With the coming of sound, *Atlantic*, made in German and English proved a considerable version of the Titanic story but the two British sound films that followed suffered from weak acting that belied the striking sets. With *Salto Mortale*, made in Germany in 1931 with Anna Sten and Adolph Wohlbruch, Dupont returned to the scene of his earlier *Variété*. Two more films were made in Germany before he found himself a Jewish refugee in Hollywood. Here his career was uneven. B pictures, factory produced, gave him no scope for his talents.

Being dismissed for slapping a Dead End Kid who was mocking his foreign accent was a humiliating experience which played havoc with his morose and withdrawn personality. He became a film publicist, a talent agent, wrote some scripts and returned in 1951 to direct *The Scarf*, a film of some merit for United Artists. He dabbled in television. He wrote the script for a film on Richard Wagner, directed by his former protege Wilhelm Dieterle in 1956. In December of the same year he died of cancer in Los Angeles. A sad case. Sad too to see the name of his great photographer Karl Freund on the credits of "I Love Lucy."

—Liam O'Leary

DURAS, MARGUERITE. French. Born Marguerite Donnadieu in Giadinh, French Indo-China, 1914. Educated in mathematics, law and political science at the Sorbonne. Career: late 1930s—works for Paris publishing houses, and in Colonial Ministry; 1943—publishes first novel *Les Impudents*; 1945—joins French Communist Party (expelled 1955); 1950s-present—active as novelist, journalist, playwright in addition to filmmaking activities; 1955—first play produced; 1957—Clement's *Barrage contre le Pacifique (This Angry Age, The Sea Wall)* made from Duras novel; 1959—writes original screenplay for Resnais's *Hiroshima mon amour*, nominated for Academy Award; 1966—begins film directing; 1967—Tony Richardson's *The Sailor from Gibralter* adapted from her novel *Le Marin de Gibralter*.

Films (as scriptwriter): 1959—*Hiroshima mon amour* (Resnais); 1960—*Moderato cantabile* (Brook) (co-adapt from her novel); 1961—*Une Aussi Longue Absence (The Long Absence)* (Colpi) (co-sc from her novel); 1964—*Nuit noire, Calcutta* (Karmitz) (short); 1965—"Les Rideaux blancs" (Franju) episode of *Der Augenblick des Friedens (Un Instant de la paix)* (for W. German TV); 1966—*10:30 P.M. Summer* (Dassin) (co-sc uncredited from her novel *Dix Heures et demie du soir en été*); *La Voleuse* (Chapot) (dialogue); (as director and scriptwriter): 1966—*La Musica* (co-d); 1969—*Détruire, dit-elle (Destroy She Said)*; 1971—*Jaune de soleil* (+pr, co-ed—from her novel *Abahn, Sabana, David*); 1972—*Nathalie Granger* (+music); 1974—*La Femme du Ganges*; *Ce que savait Morgan* (Béraud) (dialogue only—for TV); 1975—*India Song* (+voice); 1976—*Des journées entières dans les arbres (Days in the Trees)*; *Son Nom de Venise dans Calcutta desert*; 1977—*Baxter, Vera Baxter*; *Le Camion* (+ro); 1978—*Le Navire Night*; 1978-79—*Aurelia Steiner* (4-film series): *Cesarée* (1978); *Les Mains negatives* (1978); *Aurelia Steiner—Melbourne* (1979); *Aurelia Steiner—Vancouver* (1979); 1981—*Agatha et les lectures illimitées (Agatha)*.

Publications:

By DURAS:

Books—*Les Impudents*, Paris 1943; *La Vie tranquille*, Paris 1944; *Un Barrage contre le Pacifique*, Paris 1950; translated as *A Sea of Troubles*, Harmondsworth, 1969; *Le Marin de Gibralter*, Paris 1952; translated as *The Sailor from Gibralter*, New York 1967; *Les Petits Chevaux de Tarquinia*, Paris 1953; *Des Journées entières dans les arbres*, and other plays, Paris 1954; *Le Square*, Paris 1955; *Moderato cantabile*, Paris 1958; *Hiroshima mon amour*, screenplay, Paris 1959; translated as *Hiroshima Mon Amour*, New York 1961; *Dix Heures et demie du soir en été*, Paris 1960; *Les Viaducs de la Seine-et-Oise*, play, Paris 1960; *Une Aussi Longue Absence*, scenario and dialogues, with Gerard Jarlot, Paris 1961; *L'Apres-midi de Monsieur Andesmas*, Paris 1962; *Le Ravissement de Lol V. Stein*, Paris 1964; translated as *The Ravishing of Lol V. Stein*, New York, 1966; *Le Vice-Consul*, Paris 1964; translated as *The Vice-Consul*, London 1968; *4 Novels (The Square, Moderato Cantabile, 10:30 on a Summer Night, The Afternoon of Mr. Andesmas)*, New York 1965; *Theatre I: Les Eaux et forêts, Le Square, La Musica*, plays, Paris 1965; *3 Plays: The Square, Days in the Trees, The Viaducts of Seine-et-Oise*, London 1967; *L'Amante anglaise*, play, Paris 1968; *Theatre II: Suzanna Andler, Des Journées entières dans les arbres, Yes, peut-être, Le Shaga, Un Homme est venu me voir*, plays, Paris 1968; *Détruire, dit-elle*, Paris 1969; translated as *Destroy, She Said*, New York 1970; *Abahn, Sabana, David*,

Paris 1970; *L'Amour*, Paris 1970; *Nathalie Granger, suivi de La Femme du Gange*, screenplays, Paris 1973; *India Song—texte—theatre—film*, Paris 1973; translated as *India Song*, New York 1976; *Marguerite Duras*, Paris 1975; *Suzanna Andler, La Musica, L'Amante Anglaise*, plays, London 1975; *L'Eden Cinema*, play, Paris 1977; *Le Camion* and *Entretien avec Michelle Porte*, screenplays, Paris 1977; *L'Amante anglaise*, Paris 1978; *Le Navire Night, Cesaree, Les Mains negatives, Aurelia Steiner, Aurelia Steiner*, screenplays, Paris 1979; *L'Homme assis dans le couloir*, Paris 1980; *Vera Baxter ou les plages de l'Atlantique*, screenplay, Paris 1980; *L'Été 80*, Paris 1981; *Agatha*, Paris 1981; articles—"Conversation with Marguerite Duras" by Richard Roud in *Sight and Sound* (London), winter 1959/60; "Un Barrage contre le Pacifique", screenplay, in *L'Avant-Scène du cinéma* (Paris), January 1960; "Hiroshima mon amour", decoupage and dialogue, in *L'Avant-Scène du cinéma* (Paris), no.61-62, 1966; "Marguerite Duras en toute liberté", interview by F. Dufour, in *Cinéma* (Paris), April 1972; "Autour d'un film: India Song", interviews by N.L. Bernheim in *Image et son* (Paris), December 1974; "Du livre au film" in *Image et son* (Paris), April 1974; "India Song and Marguerite Duras", interview by Carlos Clarens in *Sight and Sound* (London), winter 1975/76; "India Song, a Chant of Love and Death", interview by F. Dawson in *Film Comment* (New York), November/December 1975; "Entretien avec Marguerite Duras" by J. Grant in *Cinéma* (Paris), July/August 1975; "Son nom de Venise dans Calcutta Desert", interview by C. Clouzot in *Ecran* (Paris), July 1976; interview by J.-C. Bonnet and J. Fieschi in *Cinématographe* (Paris), November 1977; "Entretien avec Marguerite Duras" by J. Grant and J. Fresnais in *Cinéma* (Paris), July 1977; "Le Camion", interview by René Predal in *Jeune Cinéma* (Paris), July/August 1977; "Das Unbezahlbare hat seinem Preis" by R. Halter in *Frauen und Film* (Berlin), October 1980; "Les Yeux verts", special issue written and edited by Duras of *Cahiers du cinéma* (Paris), June 1980; "Aus einem Gespräch zwischen Marguerite Duras und Elia Kazan" in *Filmkritik* (Munich), March 1981; "Cinéma, dit-elle...", interview by J.-P. Wauters, in *Film en Televisie* (Brussels), September 1981.

On DURAS:

Books—*Marguerite Duras tourne un film* by N.-L. Bernheim, Paris 1976; *La Texte divisé* by Marie-Claire Ropars-Wuilleumier, Paris 1981; articles—"French Writers Turned Film Makers" by Judith Gollub in *Film Heritage* (New York), winter 1968/69; "Cinema/Psicanalisi/Politica" by F. Ferrini and A. Rossi in *Bianco e nero* (Rome), July/August 1972; "Digne" by P. Queyrel in *Cinéma* (Paris), July/August 1973; "Reflections in a Broken Glass" in *Film Comment* (New York), November/December 1975; "Marguerite Duras: un exploratrice de l'indicible" by M. Martin in *Cinéma pratique* (Paris), October/November 1976; "Marguerite Duras in 1977" by M.J. Lakeland in *Camera Obscura* (Berkeley), fall 1977; "3 cinéastes du texte" by J.-C. Bonnet in *Cinématographe* (Paris), October 1977; biofilmography in *Film Dope* (London), January 1978; "Wahrnehmungsformen von Zeit und Raum am Beispiel der Filme von Marguerite Duras and Chantal Akerman" by N. Seni in *Frauen und Film* (Berlin), September 1979; "The Cinema of Marguerite Duras: Sound and Voice in a Closed Room" by W.F. Van Wert in *Film Quarterly* (Berkeley), fall 1979; "Biblio-filmographie de Marguerite Duras" in *Avant-Scène du cinéma* (Paris), 1 April 1979; "Marguerite Duras à l'action" in *Positif* (Paris), July/August 1980; bibliography and filmography by Elizabeth Lyon in *Camera Obscura* (Berkeley), fall 1980.

*　　　*　　　*

As a writer, Duras's work is identified, along with that of such authors as Alain Robbe-Grillet and Jean Cayrol, with the tradition of the New Novel. Duras began working in film as a screenwriter, with an original script for Alain Resnais's first feature, *Hiroshima mon amour*. She subsequently wrote a number of film adaptations from her novels, and directed her first film, *La Musica*, in 1966. If *Hiroshima mon amour* remains her best known work in cinema, her later films have won widespread praise for the profound challenge they offer to conventional dramatic narrative.

The nature of narrative and the potential contained in a single text are major concerns of Duras's films. Many of her works have appeared in several forms, as novels, plays, and films. This not only involves adaptations of a particular work, but also extends to cross-referential networks that run through her texts. The film *Woman of the Ganges* combines elements from three novels—*The Ravishing of Lol V. Stein*, *The Vice-Consul*, and *L'Amour*. *India Song* was initially written as a play, taking characters from *The Vice-Consul* and elaborating on the structure of external voices developed in *Woman of the Ganges*. *India Song* was made as a film in 1975, and its verbal track was used to generate a second film, *Son Nom de Venises dans Calcutta Desert*.

This process of transformation suggests that all works are "in progress," inherently subject to being otherwise constructed. In part this is because Duras's works are more concerned with the quality or intensity of experience than with events *per se*. The films evoke narrative, rather than presenting a linear, unambiguous sequence of events. In *Le Camion* two characters, played by Gerard Depardieu and Duras, sit in a room as the woman describes a movie about a woman who hitches a ride with a truck driver and talks with him for an hour and twenty minutes. This conversation is intercut with scenes of a truck driving around Paris, picking up a female hitchhiker (with Depardieu as the driver, and Duras as the hitchhiker). Thus the verbal description of a potential film is juxtaposed its images of what that film might be.

An emphasis on the soundtrack is also a crucial aspect of Duras's films; her verbal texts are lyrical and are as important as the images. In *India Song*, sound and image function contrapuntally, and the audience must actively assess the relation between them, reading across the body of the film, noting continuities and disjunctions. The verbal text often refers in past tense to events and characters on screen, as the viewer is challenged to figure out the chronology of events described and depicted—which name on the soundtrack corresponds to which actor, whether the voices belong to on or off screen characters, and so forth. In this way the audience participates in the search for a story, constructing possible narratives.

As minimal as they are, Duras's narratives are partially derived from melodrama, focusing on relations between men and women, the nature or structure of desire, and colonialism and imperialism in both literal and metaphoric senses. In pursuing these issues through non-conventional narrative forms, and shifting the burden of discovering meaning to the audience, Duras's films provide an alternative to conventional ways of watching movies. Her work is seen as exemplifying a feminine writing practice that challenges the patriarchal domination of classical narrative cinema. In an interview Duras said, "I think the future belongs to women. Men have been completely dethroned. Their rhetoric is stale, used up. We must move on to the rhetoric of women, one that is anchored in the organism, in the body." It is this new rhetoric, a new way of communicating, that Duras strives for in her films.

—M. B. White

DUVIVIER, JULIEN. French. Born in Lille, 8 October 1896. Educated at Lille University; studied acting in Paris; Career: 1916—enters acting company of Odéon, Paris; works in Théâtre Libre of André Antoine who introduces him to cinema; assistant to several directors including Feuillade, Antoine on *Les Travailleurs de la mer* and to Marcel L'Herbier; 1919—directing debut; 1920—negative of 2nd film destroyed by fire before release, temporarily returns to assistant directing; 1925—joins "Film d'Art" of Marcel Vandal and Charles Delac; 1937—success of *Pepe-le-Moko* leads to MGM offer of 1-picture contract; 1938—after directing *The Great Waltz* for MGM, returns to France; 1938—episodic structure of *Un Carnet de Bal* sets pattern for many subsequent films; 1940—moves to U.S. 1941-45—makes films in U.S. 1945—returns to France. Died in auto accident, 26 October 1967.

Films (as assistant director): 1918—*Les Travailleurs de la mer* (Antoine); (as director and scriptwriter): 1919—*Haceldama ou Le Prix du Sang*; 1920—*La Réincarnation de Serge Renaudier* (negative destroyed by fire before film shown); *L'Agonie des aigles* (Bernard-Deschamps) (adaptation only); *La Terre* (Antoine) (asst d only); 1921—*Crépuscule d'épouvante* (Etiévant) (sc only); 1922—*Les Roquevillard*; *L'Ouragan sur la montagne*; *Der unheimliche Gast (Le Logis de l'horreur)*; *L'Arlésienne* (Antoine) (asst d only); 1923—*Le Reflet de Claude Mercoeur*; 1924—*Credo ou La Tragédie de Lourdes*; *Coeurs farouches*; *La Machine à refaire la vie* (co-d—re-released with sound 1933); *L'Oeuvre immortelle*; *La Nuit de la revanche* (Etiévant) (story only); 1925—*L'Abbé Constantin*; *Poil de carotte* (co-sc); 1926—*L'Agonie de Jerusalem*; *L'Homme à l'Hispano* (d only); 1927—*Le Mariage de Mademoiselle Beulemans*; *Le Mystère de la Tour Eiffel*; 1928—*Le Tourbillon de Paris* (d only); 1929—*La Divine croisière*; *Maman Colibri* (co-sc); *La Vie miraculeuse de Thérèse Martin*; *Au bonheur des dames* (co-sc); (sound films): 1930—*David Golder*; 1931—*Les Cinq Gentlemen maudits*; *Allo Berlin? Ici Paris! (Hallo! Hallo! Hier spricht Berlin)*; *Die funf verfluchten Gentlemen* (German version); 1932—*Poil de carotte* (remake); *La Tête d'un homme* (co-sc); 1933—*Le Petit Roi*; *Le Paquebot 'Tenacity'* (co-sc); 1934—*Maria Chapdelaine*; 1935—*Golgotha* (adapt); *La Bandera* (co-sc); 1936—*L'Homme du jour* (co-sc); *Golem (Le Golem)* (co-sc); *La Belle Équipe* (co-sc); 1937—*Pépé-le-Moko* (co-sc); *Un Carnet de bal*; 1938—*The Great Waltz (Toute la ville danse)*; *La Fin du jour* (co-sc); *Marie Antoinette* (Van Dyke) (d uncredited); 1939—*La Charrette fantôme*; 1940—*Untel père et fils* (co-sc); 1941—*Lydia* (co-story); 1942—*Tales of Manhattan* (co-sc); 1943—*Flesh and Fantasy* (d only, +co-pr); 1944—*The Imposter*; 1946—*Panique* (co-sc); *Collège swing (Amours, délices et orgues)* (Berthomieu) (co-sc only); 1948—*Anna Karenina (Anna Karénine)* (co-sc); 1949—*Au royaume des cieux* (+pr); 1950—*Black Jack* (co-sc, +pr); *Sous le ciel de Paris* (co-sc); 1951—*Le Petit Monde de Don Camillo (Il piccolo mondo di Don Camillo)* (co-sc); 1952—*La Fête à Henriette* (co-sc); 1953—*Le Retour de Don Camillo (Il ritorno di Don Camillo)* (co-sc); 1954—*L'Affaire Maurizius*; 1955—*Marianne de ma jeunesse*; 1956—*Voice le temps des assassins* (co-sc); 1957—*L'Homme à l'imperméable* (co-sc); *Pot Bouille* (co-sc); 1958—*La Femme et le pantin* (co-adapt); 1959—*Marie Octobre* (co-sc); 1960—*Das kunstseidene Mädchen (La Grande Vie)* (co-sc); *Boulevard* (co-sc); 1962—*La Chambre ardente* (co-sc); *Le Diable et les dix commandements* (co-sc); 1963—*Chair de poule* (co-sc); 1967—*Diaboliquement vôtre* (co-adapt).

Publications:

By DUVIVIER:

Articles—"Les Confidences de M. Julien Duvivier" by Nino Frank in *Pour vous* (Paris), 12 February 1931; interview by Pierre Leprohon in *Cinémonde* (Paris), 9 February 1933; "Un Réalisateur compare 2 méthodes", interview by Pierre Leprohon in *Cinémonde* (Paris), 6 May 1946; "Julien Duvivier fête ses 30 ans de cinéma", interview by M. Idszkowski in *Cinémonde* (Paris), 29 October 1946; "De la création à la mise en scène" in *Cinémonde* (Paris), Christmas 1946; "Julien Duvivier nous parle" in *Unifrance-Film Informations* (Paris), January/February 1952; "Julien Duvivier: 'Pourquoi j'ai trahi Zola'", interview by Yvonne Baby in *Les Lettres françaises* (Paris), 31 October 1957; reminiscences of Harry Baur in *Avant-Scène du cinéma* (Paris), 1 February 1977.

On DUVIVIER:

Books—*Julien Duvivier* by Raymond Chirat, Lyon 1968; "Julien Duvivier" by Pierre Leprohon in *Anthologie du cinéma* vol.4, Paris 1969; articles—"Julien Duvivier" by Pierre Leprohon in *Cinémonde* (Paris), 13 February 1930; "Voyage autour de Julien Duvivier" by Robert Vernay in *Cinégraph* (Paris), July 1930; "Quand je revois ma vie" by Jean Gabin in *Pour vous* (Paris), 3/10 October 1935; "Julien Duvivier" by Michel Aubriant in *Cinémonde* (Paris), 28 November 1952; "Débat sur Duvivier" in *Arts* (Paris), 18 April 1956; "Parabola di Duvivier" by Roberto Chiti and Mario Quargnolo in *Bianco e nero* (Rome), January 1956; "Comment ils travaillent? Julien Duvivier" by Marie Epstein in *Technique cinématographique* (Paris), December 1958; "Les Français à Hollywood" by P. Marcabru in *Arts* (Paris), 8 February 1961; obituary in *The New York Times*, 30 October 1967; obituary in *Time* (New York), 10 November 1967; "Duvivier, le professionel" by Jean Renoir in *Le Figaro littéraire* (Paris), 6 November 1967; "Défense de Duvivier" by Bernard Amengual in *Cahiers de la Cinémathèque* (Paris), spring 1975; "Pépé le Moko" by Claude Beylie and M. Marie, special issue, in *Avant-Scène du cinéma* (Paris), 1 June 1981; "A propos de Julien Duvivier" by Noel Simsolo in *Image et son* (Paris), November 1981; film—*Portraits filmées...Julien Duvivier* by Pierre Viallaet and Marcel l'Herbier, for TV, 1953.

*   *   *

No one speaks of Julien Duvivier without apologizing. So many of his 50-odd films are embarrassing to watch that it is hard to believe he was ever in charge of his career in the way we like to imagine Renoir or Clair were in charge of theirs. There is justice in this response. Duvivier had neither the luxury nor the contacts to direct his career. He hadn't the schooling that an aristocratic upbringing gives even to the sons of the avant-garde. Duvivier began and remained a yeoman in the industry. A director at the Théâtre Antoine in the teens, he began his film career in 1922 and made over a score of silent films, mainly melodramas. From the first he separated himself from the experiments in narration and visual style that characterized much of that period.

His reputation as a reputable, efficient director jumped in the sound era when he made a string of small but successful films (*David Golder*, *Les Cinq Gentilhommes maudits*, *Allo Berlin? Ici Paris!*, *Poil de carotte*, *La Tête d'un homme*). Evidently his flair for the melodramatic and his ability to control powerful actors put him far ahead of the average French director trying to cope with the problems of sound. But in this era as always, Duvivier discriminated little among the subjects he filmed. This couldn't

be more evident than in 1935. First came *Golgotha*, a religious epic starring Gabin, Le Vigan, Edwige Feuillère, and other celebrities of French cinema. A throwback to the religious films he made in the silent era, *Golgotha* is completely outmoded in 1935. Duvivier struggles to energize the static tableaux the film settles into. He moves his camera wildly, but seldom reaches for a key closeup or for an authentic exchange among his actors. It is all picture postcards, or rather holy cards, set off to Jacques Ibert's operatic score.

This solemn, even bombastic, film which rises and falls on technologically induced miracles, could not be farther from the swiftness and authentic feeling of the romantic Foreign Legion film *La Bandera* made the same year. Where *Golgotha* is an official presentation of French cinema, *La Bandera* seems more intimate, more in the spirit of the times. Its success was only the first of a set of astounding films that include *La Belle Équipe*, *Pépé-le-Moko*, *Un Carnet de bal*, and *Le Fin du jour*.

It is tempting to surmise that cultural history and Julien Duvivier came for once into perfect coincidence in this age of poetic realism. Like Michael Curtiz and *Casablanca*, Duvivier's style and the actors who played out the roles of his dramas spoke to a whole generation. In France it was a better generation, vaguely hopeful with the popular front, but expecting the end of day.

Duvivier's contribution to these films lies in more than the direction of actors. Every film contains at least one scene of remarkable expressiveness, like the death of Regis in *Pépé-Le-Moko*, gunned down by his own victim with the jukebox blaring. Duvivier's sureness of pace in this era brought him a Hollywood contract even before the Nazi invasion forced him to leave France. Without the strong personality of Renoir or Clair, and with far more experience in genre pictures, Duvivier fit in rather well with the American methods. He deplored the lack of personal control or even personal contribution in the industry, but he acquitted himself well until the Liberation.

Hoping to return to the glory years of poetic realism, his first postwar project in France, *Panique*, replicated the essence of its style: sparse sets, atmosphere dominating a reduced but significant murder drama, the evocative play of Michel Simon and Vivian Romance in an offbeat policier from Simenon. But the country had changed. The film failed, and Duvivier began what would become a lifelong search for the missing formula. With varying degrees of box office success and with the winking eyes of critics he turned out contemporary and historical comedies and melodramas; the only one which put him in the spotlight was *Don Camillo* with Fernandel.

Believing far more in experience, planning, and hard work than in spontaneity and genius, he never relaxed. Every film taught him something and, by rights, he shold have ended a better director than ever. But he will be remembered for those five years in the late 1930s when his every choice of script and direction was in tune with the romantically pessimistic sensibility of the country.

—Dudley Andrew

DWAN, ALLAN. American. Born Joseph Aloysius Dwan in Toronto, Canada, 3 April 1885; family moved to Detroit and then Chicago about 1893. Educated at the Alcott School and North Division High School, Chicago; Notre Dame University, South Bend, Indiana, degree in electrical engineering 1907. Married Pauline Bush in 1915 (divorced about 1920); married Marie Shelton in early 1920s (died in 1954). Career: 1907—teaches mathematics and physics and coaches football at Notre Dame; 1908—joins Peter Cooper Hewitt Company in Chicago as illuminating engineer; 1909—work on mercury vapor arc light leads to association with Essanay film company; begins writing stories while supervising lighting; 1910—American Film Company ('Flying A') formed by Essanay staff, Dwan joins as chief scenario editor; replaces Beal as director on location at San Juan Capistrano, California; 1913—signs on with Universal Pictures, takes Flying A production units with him; supervises Wallace Reid and Marshall Neilan in addition to directing; 1914—signs with Famous Players Company in New York; 1915—introduces sustained travelling shot, in *David Harum*; leaves Famous Players to join Triangle Company under Griffith's supervision; 1916—designs elevator device on tracks for crane shot over Babylon set on *Intolerance* (Griffith); 1916-22—does 11 pictures with Douglas Fairbanks culminating with *Robin Hood*; 1932-34—works in England; 1943—organizes and trains camera units for U.S. Armed Services photographic division; 1945-54—works under exclusive contract with Republic Pictures; 1955-56—directs "It's Always Sunday" and "High Air" for TV *Screen Directors' Playhouse*; 1961—retires following *The Most Dangerous Man Alive*; 1967—prepares *Marine!* for Warner Bros., abandoned when studio is sold. Died in Woodland Hills, California, 21 December 1981.

Films (as producer, director and scenarist): Note—Dwan estimated that he had directed 1,850 films, so following list is very incomplete: 1911—*Branding a Bad Man* and *A Western Dreamer* (split reel); *A Daughter of Liberty* and *A Trouper's Heart* (split reel); *Rattlesnakes and Gunpowder* and *The Ranch Tenor* (split reel); *The Sheepman's Daughter*; *The Sagebrush Phrenologist* and *The Elopements on Double L Ranch* (split reel); *$5000 Reward—Dead or Alive*; *The Witch of the Range*; *The Cowboy's Ruse* and *Law and Order on Bar L Ranch* (split reel); *The Yiddisher Cowboy* and *The Broncho Buster's Bride* (split reel); *The Hermit's Gold*; *The Actress and the Cowboys* and *The Sky Pilot's Intemperance* (split reel); *A Western Waif*; *The Call of the Open Range*; *The School Ma'am of Snake* and *The Ranch Chicken* (split reel); *Cupid in Chaps*; *The Outlaw's Trail*; *The Ranchman's Nerve*; *When East Comes West*; *The Cowboy's Deliverance*; *The Cattle Thief's Brand*; *The Parting Trails*; *The Cattle Rustler's End*; *Cattle, Gold and Oil*; *The Ranch Girl*; *The Poisoned Flume*; *The Brand of Fear*; *The Blotted Brand*; *Auntie and the Cowboys*; *The Western Doctor's Peril*; *The Smuggler and the Girl*; *The Cowboy and the Artist*; *3 Million Dollars*; *The Stage Robbers of San Juan*; *The Mother of the Ranch*; *The Gunman*; *The Claim Jumpers*; *The Circular Fence*; *The Rustler Sheriff*; *The Love of the West*; *The Trained Nurse at Bar Z*; *The Miner's Wife*; *The Land Thieves*; *The Cowboy and the Outlaw*; *3 Daughters of the West* and *Caves of La Jolla* (split reel); *The Lonely Range*; *The Horse Thief's Bigamy*; *The Trail of the Eucalyptus*; *The Stronger Man*; *The Water War*; *The 3 Shell Game*; *The Mexican*; *The Eastern Cowboy*; *The Way of the West*; *The Test*; *The Master of the Vineyard*; *Sloppy Bill of the Rollicking R*; *The Sheriff's Sisters*; *The Angel of Paradise Ranch*; *The Smoke of the 45*; *The Man Hunt*; *Santa Catalina, Magic Isle of the Pacific*; *The Last Notch*; *The Gold Lust*; *The Duel of the Candles*; *Bonita of El Cajon*; *The Lawful Holdup*; *Battleships*; *Dams and Waterways*; 1912—*A Midwinter Trip to Los Angeles*; *The Misadventures of a Claim Agent* and *Broncho Busting for Flying A Pictures* (split reel); *The Winning of La Mesa*; *The Locket*; *The Relentless Outlaw*; *Justice of the Sage*; *Objections Overruled*; *The Mormon*; *Love and Lemons*; *The Best Policy*; *The Real Estate Fraud*; *The Grubstake Mortgage*; *Where Broadway Meets the Mountains*; *An Innocent Grafter*; *Society and Chaps*; *The Leap Year Cowboy*; *The Land Baron of San Tee*; *An Assisted Elopement*; *From the 400 to the Herd*; *The Broken Ties*; *After School*; *A Bad Investment*; *The Full Value*; *The Tramp's Gratitude*; *Fidelity*; *Winter Sports and Pastimes of

Coronado Beach; *The Maid and the Man*; *The Cowboy Socialist*; *Checkmate* and *The Ranchman's Marathon* (split reel); *The Coward*; *The Distant Relative*; *The Ranch Detective*; *Driftwood*; *The Eastern Girl*; *The Pensioners*; *The End of the Feud*; *The Wedding Dress*; *Mystical Maid of Jamasha Pass*; *The Other Wise Man*; *The Haters*; *The Thread of Life*; *The Wandering Gypsy*; *The Reward of Valor*; *The Brand*; *The Green Eyed Monster*; *Cupid Through Padlocks*; *For the Good of Her Men*; *The Simple Love*; *The Weaker Brother* and *50 Mile Auto Contest* (split reel); *The Wordless Message*; *The Evil Inheritance*; *The Marauders*; *The Girl Back Home*; *Under False Pretences*; *Where There's a Heart*; *The Vanishing Race*; *The Fatal Mirror* and *Point Loma, Old Town* (split reel); *The Tell Tale Shells*; *Indian Jealousy* and *San Diego* (split reel); *The Canyon Dweller*; *It Pays to Wait*; *A Life for a Kiss*; *The Meddlers*; *The Girl and the Gun*; *The Battleground*; *The Bad Man and the Ranger*; *The Outlaw Colony*; *The Land of Death*; *The Bandit of Point Loma*; *The Jealous Rage*; *The Will of James Waldron*; *The House that Jack Built*; *Curtiss's School of Aviation*; *The Stepmother*; *The Odd Job Man*; *The Liar*; *The Greaser and the Weakling*; *The Stranger at Coyote*; *The Dawn of Passion*; *The Vengeance that Failed*; *The Fear*; *The Foreclosure*; *White Treachery*; *Their Hero Son*; *Calamity Anne's Ward*; *Father's Favorite*; *Jack of Diamonds*; *The Reformation of Sierra Smith*; *The Promise*; *The New Cowpuncher*; *The Best Man Wins*; *The Wooers of Mountain Kate*; *1,2,3*; *The Wanderer*; *Maiden and Men*; *God's Unfortunate*; *Man's Calling*; *The Intrusion at Lompoc*; *The Thief's Wife*; *The Would-Be Heir*; *Jack's Word*; *Her Own Country*; *Pals*; *The Animal Within*; *The Law of God*; *Nell of the Pampas*; *The Daughters of Senor Lopez*; *The Power of Love*; *The Recognition*; *Blackened Hills*; *The Loneliness of Neglect*; *Paid in Full*; *Ranch Life on the Range*; *The Man from the East*; *The Horse Thief*; *The Good Love and the Bad*; 1913—*The Fraud that Failed*; *Another Man's Wife*; *Calamity Anne's Inheritance*; *Their Masterpiece*; *His Old-Fashioned Mother*; *Where Destiny Guides*; *The Silver-Plated Gun*; *A Rose of Old Mexico*; *Building the Great Los Angeles Aqueduct*; *Women Left Alone*; *Andrew Jackson*; *Calamity Anne's Vanity*; *The Fugitive*; *The Romance*; *The Finer Things*; *Love is Blind*; *When the Light Fades*; *High and Low*; *The Greater Love*; *The Jocular Winds*; *The Transgression of Manuel*; *Calamity Anne, Detective*; *The Orphan's Mine*; *When a Woman Won't*; *An Eastern Flower*; *Cupid Never Ages*; *Calamity Anne's Beauty*; *The Renegade's Heart*; *Matches*; *The Mute Witness*; *Cupid Throws a Brick*; *Woman's Honor*; *Suspended Sentence*; *In Another's Nest*; *the Ways of Fate*; *Boobs and Bricks*; *Calamity Anne's Trust*; *Oil on Troubled Waters*; *The Road to Ruin*; *The Brothers*; *Human Kindness*; *Youth and Jealousy*; *Angel of the Canyons*; *The Great Harmony*; *Her Innocent Marriage*; *Calamity Anne Parcel Post*; *The Ashes of 3*; *On the Border*; *Her Big Story*; *When Luck Changes*; *The Wishing Seat*; *Hearts and Horses*; *The Reward of Courage*; *The Soul of a Thief*; *The Marine Law*; *The Road to Success*; (as director): *The Spirit of the Flag*; *The Call to Arms* (+sc); *Women and War*; *The Powder Flash of Death* (+sc); *The Picket Guard*; *Mental Suicide*; *Man's Duty*; *The Animal* (+sc); *The Wall of Money*; *The Echo of a Song*; *Criminals*; *The Restless Spirit* (+sc); *Jewels of a Sacrifice*; *Back to Life*; *Red Margaret, Moonshiner*; *Bloodhounds of the North*; *He Called Her In* (+sc); *The Menace* (+sc); *The Chase*; *The Battle of Wills*; 1914—*The Lie*; *The Honor of the Mounted*; *Remember Mary Magdalene* (+sc); *Discord and Harmony*; *The Menace to Carlotta*; *The Embezzler* (+sc); *The Lamb, the Woman, the Wolf* (+sc); *The End of the Feud*; *Tragedy of Whispering Creek*; *The Unlawful Trade*; *The Forbidden Room*; *The Hopes of Blind Alley*; *The Great Universal Mystery*; *Richelieu* (+sc); *Wildflower*; *The Country Chairman* (+sc); *The Small Town Girl*; *The Straight Road*; *The Conspi-*

racy; *The Unwelcome Mrs. Hatch*; *The Man on the Case*; 1915—
The Dancing Girl; *David Harum*; *The Love Route*; *The Commanding Officer, May Blossom*; *The Pretty Sister of Jose*; *A Girl of Yesterday*; *The Foundling*; *Jordan is a Hard Road* (+sc);
1916—*Betty of Greystone*; *The Habit of Happiness (Laugh and the World Laughs)* (+sc); *The Good Bad Man (Passing Through)*; *An Innocent Magdalene*; *The Half-Breed*; *Manhattan Madness*;
50-50 (+sc); 1917—*Panthea* (+sc); *The Fighting Odds*; *A Modern Musketeer* (+sc); 1918—*Mr. Fix-It* (+sc); *Bound in Morocco* (+sc); *He Comes Up Smiling*; 1919—*Cheating Cheaters*; *Getting Mary Married*; *The Dark Star*; *Soldiers of Fortune*; 1920—*The Luck of the Irish*; (as producer and director): *The Forbidden Thing* (+co-sc); 1921—*A Perfect Crime* (+sc); *A Broken Doll* (+sc); *The Scoffer*; *The Sin of Martha Queed* (+sc); *In the Heart of a Fool*; 1922—*The Hidden Woman*; *Superstition*; *Robin Hood* (d only); 1923—*The Glimpses of the Moon*; *Lawful Larceny*; *Zaza*; *Big Brother*; 1924—*A Society Scandal*; *Manhandled*; *Her Love Story*; *Wages of Virtue* (d only); *Argentine Love*; 1925—*Night Life in New York*; *Coast of Folly*; *Stage Struck*; 1926—*Sea Horses*; *Padlocked*; *Tin Gods*; *Summer Bachelors*; 1927—*The Music Master*; *West Point*; *The Joy Girl*; *East Side, West Side* (d only, +sc); *French Dressing*; 1928—*The Big Noise*; (as director): 1929—*The Iron Mask*; *Tide of Empire*; *The Far Call*; *Frozen Justice*; *South Sea Rose*; 1930—*What a Widow!* (+pr); *Man to Man*; 1931—*Chances*; *Wicked*; 1932—*While Paris Sleeps*; 1933—*Her First Affaire*; *Counsel's Opinion*; 1934—*The Morning After (I Spy)*; *Hollywood Party* (uncredited); 1935—*Black Sheep* (+sc); *Navy Wife*; 1936—*Song and Dance Man*; *Human Cargo*; *High Tension*; *15 Maiden Lane*; 1937—*Woman-Wise*; *That I May Live*; *One Mile from Heaven*; *Heidi*; 1938—*Rebecca of Sunnybrook Farm*; *Josette*; *Suez*; 1939 *The 3 Musketeers*; *The Gorilla*; *Frontier Marshal*; 1940— *Sailor's Lady*; *Young People*; *Trail of the Vigilantes*; 1941— *Look Who's Laughing* (+pr); *Rise and Shine*; 1942—*Friendly Enemies*; *Here We Go Again* (+pr); 1943—*Around the World* (+pr); 1944—*Up in Mabel's Room*; *Abroad with 2 Yanks*; 1945—*Brewster's Millions*; *Getting Gertie's Garter*; 1946— *Rendezvous with Annie* (+co-pr); 1947—*Calendar Girl* (+co-pr); *Northwest Outpost* (+co-pr); *Driftwood*; 1948—*The Inside Story* (+pr); *Angel in Exile*; 1949—*Sands of Iwo Jima*; 1950— *Surrender* (+co-pr); 1951—*Belle le Grand*; *The Wild Blue Yonder*; 1952—*I Dream of Jeannie (With the Light Brown Hair)*; *Montana Belle*; 1953—*Woman They Almost Lynched*; *Sweethearts on Parade* (+co-pr); 1954—*Flight Nurse*; *Silver Lode*; *Passion*; *Cattle Queen of Montana*; 1955—*It's Always Sunday* (for *Screen Director's Playhouse* television series); *Escape to Burma*; *Pearl of the South Pacific*; *Tennessee's Partner*; 1956—*Slightly Scarlet*; *Hold Back the Night*; *High Air* (episode for *Screen Director's Playhouse* television series); 1957—*The River's Edge*; *The Restless Breed*; 1958—*Enchanted Island*; 1961—*Most Dangerous Man Alive*.

Publications:

By DWAN:

Articles—interview by A.R. St. Johns in *Photoplay* (New York), August 1920; interview by F.T. Pope in *Photoplay* (New York), September 1923; "Must actors have temperament?" in *Motion Picture* (New York), February 1926; "As It Was" in *Making Films* (New York), June 1971; "What Directors Are Saying" in *Action* (Los Angeles), August 1971; "Angel in Exile: Alan Dwan", interview by G. Morris and H. Mandelbaum in *Bright Lights* (Los Angeles), no.4, 1979.

On DWAN:

Books—*The Parade's Gone By* by Kevin Brownlow, New York 1968; *Allan Dwan, the Last Pioneer* by Peter Bogdanovich, New York 1971; Articles—"Esoterica" by Andrew Sarris in *Film Culture* (New York), spring 1963; "Allan Dwan" by J.M. Smith in *Brighton Film Review*, February 1970; "Good Days, Good Years" by Richard Schickel in *Harper's* (New York), October 1970; "6 Pioneers" in *Action* (Los Angeles), November/December 1972; "Allan Dwan: Master of the American Folk Art of Filmmaking" by J.H. Dorr in *Take One* (Montreal), September 1973; "The Griffith Tradition" by J. Dorr in *Film Comment* (New York), March/April 1974.

*　　*　　*

Alan Dwan was a pioneer among pioneers, men like D.W. Griffith and Cecil B. DeMille, whose careers spanned the birth and the growth of the American motion picture industry. Active in the industry for over 50 years, he participated in creating at least 800 films—his own estimate was 1,850. Most of these were one-to four-reel silents of which some two-thirds are lost and for that reason his career remains one which has never been properly assessed. The artistic disparity of his 70-odd sound films fail to adequately represent this technically innovative, unpretentious, avid storyteller and his is surely a career which will undergo considerable re-evaluation as the study of film history progresses.

It was the scientific aspect of motion picures which attracted Dwan to the medium and in 1909 he joined Essanay as a lighting man. He then joined the American Flying A Company as a writer but soon found himself directing short films, mostly Westerns. He moved next to Universal, then to Famous Players where in 1915 he invented the dolly shot for *David Harum*, and directed Mary Pickford in *The Foundling*.

The same year he joined Fine Arts-Triangle where his films were supervised by D.W. Griffith. He directed many of Griffith's top stars including Dorothy Gish in *Betty of Greystone* and her sister Lillian in *An Innocent Magdalene* and he once stated how impressed he was with the "economy of gesture" of Griffith's players. He credits Griffith with developing his clean, spare visual style and Griffith frequently sought out Dwan for his technical knowledge. One such request resulted in Dwan's improvising an elevator on a moving track to film the massive sets of *Intolerance*. Also at Fine Arts-Triangle, Dwan established his association with Douglas Fairbanks, a professional relationship which resulted in 11 films including *The Half-Breed*, *A Modern Musketeer*, *Bound in Morocco* and the celebrated *Robin Hood*, which Robert Sherwood called "the high-water mark of film production in the farthest step that the silent drama has ever taken along the high road to art."

In 1923, Dwan directed his favorite film *Big Brother*, about under-privileged boys and then embarked on the first of eight buoyant comedies starring Gloria Swanson, the best of which were *Zaza* and *Manhandled*. With the arrival of sound, Dwan signed a long-term contract with Fox (1930-41) where he was unfortunately relegated to their B unit except for occasional reprieves—Shirley Temple's *Heidi* and *Rebecca of Sunnybrook Farm*, and *Suez*, much admired for its typhoon sequence. He then signed with producer Edward Small for whom he directed a delightful quartet of farces—*Up in Mabel's Room*, *Getting Gertie's Garter*, *Abroad with Two Yanks*, and *Brewster's Millions*. He then unwisely signed an exclusive deal with Republic Pictures where, except for *Sands of Iwo Jima*, his creativity was constricted by studio head Herbert Yates. Moving to RKO, he persevered despite the many obstacles of 1950s filmmaking, churning out entertaining actioners.

Dwan loved movie making and has been called the "last of the journeyman filmmakers" by Richard Roud. Of his self-imposed retirement in 1958, Dwan explained: "It was no longer a question of 'Let's get a bunch of people together and make a picture.' It's just a business that I stood as long as I could and I got out of it when I couldn't stand it any more."

—Ronald Bowers

EDWARDS, BLAKE. American. Born William Blake McEdwards in Tulsa, Oklahoma, 26 July 1922. Educated at Beverly Hills High School. Married Patricia Walker, 1953 (divorced 1967); children: Jennifer and Geoffrey; married actress Julie Andrews, 1969; adopted children: Amy and Joanna. Career: 1942—small role in *10 Gentlemen from West Point*; 1944-45—serves in Coast Guard; 1947—co-scripts with John Champion *Panhandle*; 1948—begins association with director Richard Quine on *Leather Gloves*; 1949—creates NBC radio series *Richard Diamond, Private Detective* for Dick Powell; also writes for *Yours Truly, Johnny Dollar*, and *The Line-up*; 1955—assigned as writer/director to Columbia B-picture unit, directs 2 Frankie Laine vehicles; 1957—directs first A picture *Mister Cory* for Universal; 1958—creates *Peter Gunn* TV series, followed by *Mr. Lucky* in 1959; 1960—creates *Dante's Inferno* TV series; 1962—writes and directs *The Boston Terrier*, for TV *Dick Powell Theater*; 1964—begins *Pink Panther* series with Peter Sellers as Inspector Clouseau; 1970—*Darling Lili* a financial disaster; 1972—reacting to increasing studio interference, quits *The Carey Treatment* when principal photography completed; unsuccessfully tries to have name removed from credits; 1972-78—lives and works mainly in Europe; 1974-78—reestablishes commercial viability with *Pink Panther* sequels; 1978—signs contract guaranteeing creative control with Orion Pictures for 3 films to be released through Warners; agreement terminated after *10*. Agent: Marty Baum, Creative Artists, Los Angeles, CA. Business Manager: Mary Prappas, Trellis Enterprises, Inc., Los Angeles, CA. Address: lives in Gstaad, Switzerland.

Films (as scriptwriter): 1947—*Panhandle* (co-sc, +co-pr, ro); 1948—*Leather Gloves (Loser Take All)* (Quine and Asher) (+ro); 1949—*Stampede* (Selander) (co-sc, +pr); 1952—*Sound Off* (Quine); *Rainbow Round My Shoulder* (Quine); 1953—*All Ashore* (Quine); *Cruisin' Down the River* (Quine); 1954—*Drive a Crooked Road* (Quine); *The Atomic Kid* (Martinson) (story); 1955—*My Sister Eileen* (Quine); (as director and scriptwriter): 1955—*Bring Your Smile Along*; 1956—*He Laughed Last*; *Operation Mad Ball* (Quine) (co-sc only); 1958—*This Happy Feeling*; 1959—*The Perfect Furlough*; *Operation Petticoat*; 1960—*High Time*; 1961—*Breakfast at Tiffany's* (d only); *The Couch* (Crump) (co-story only); 1962—*Experiment in Terror (The Grip of Fear)* (+pr); *The Notorious Landlady* (Quine) (co-sc only); *Days of Wine and Roses* (d only); *Walk on the Wild Side* (Dmytryk) (d add'l scenes, uncred); 1963—*Soldier in the Rain* (Nelson) (co-sc only, +pr); 1964—*The Pink Panther* (co-sc); *A Shot in the Dark*; 1965—*The Great Race* (co-story, +bit ro as troublemaker); *What Did You Do in the War, Daddy?* (co-story, +pr); 1967—*Gunn* (co-sc); 1968—*The Party* (co-sc, +pr); *Inspector Clouseau* (Yorkin) (sc only); 1970—*Darling Lili* (co-sc, +co-pr); 1971—*The Wild Rovers* (+co-pr); 1972—*The Carey Treatment (Emergency Ward)* (d only); 1974—*The Tamarind Seed*; (as producer, director, and scriptwriter): 1974—*The Return of the Pink Panther* (co-sc); 1976—*The Pink Panther Strikes Again* (co-sc); 1978—*Revenge of the Pink Panther* (co-

sc); 1979—*10*; 1981—*S.O.B.*; 1982—*Victor/Victoria*.

Roles: (in minor or bit parts): 1942—*10 Gentlemen from West Point* (Hathaway); *Lucky Legs* (Barton); 1943—*A Guy Named Joe* (Fleming); 1944—*In the Meantime, Darling* (Preminger); *Marshal of Reno* (Grissell); *See Here, Private Hargrove* (Ruggles); *Ladies Courageous* (Rawlins); *The Eve of St. Mark* (Stahl); *Marine Raiders* (Schuster); *Wing and a Prayer* (Hathaway); *My Buddy* (Sekely); *The Unwritten Code* (Rotsten); *30 Seconds over Tokyo* (LeRoy); *She's a Sweetheart* (Lord); 1945—*This Man's Navy* (Wellman); *A Guy, a Gal, and a Pal* (Boetticher); *Gangs of the Waterfront* (Blair); *What Next, Corporal Hargrove?* (Thorpe); *They Were Expendable* (Ford); *Tokyo Rose* (Landers); *Strangler of the Swamp* (Wisbar) (major role); 1946—*The Strange Love of Martha Ivers* (Milestone); *Till the End of Time* (Dmytryk); *The Best Years of Our Lives* (Wyler); 1947—*The Beginning or the End* (Taurog).

Publications:

By EDWARDS:

Articles—interview in *Présence du cinéma* (Paris), September/-October 1962; "Un Humour sérieux" in *Cahiers du cinéma* (Paris), May/June 1965; interview in *Cinéma 65* (Paris), March 1965; "Sophisticated Naturalism", interview by Jean-François Hauduroy in *Cahiers du Cinema in English* (New York), no.3, 1966; interview in *Cahiers du cinéma* (Paris), February 1966; "Confessions of a Cult Figure", interview by Stuart Byron in *Village Voice* (New York), 5 August 1971; "Dans la tradition classique", interview by C. Viviani in *Positif* (Paris), June 1973; interview by P. Stamelman in *Millimeter* (New York), January 1977; "Riding Herd on a Chinese Fire Drill", interview, in *American Cinematographer* (Los Angeles), July 1978; "Too much to do, not enough time to do it", interview by P. Lehman and W. Luhr in *Wide Angle* (Athens, Ohio), v.3, no.3, 1980.

On EDWARDS:

Articles—in *Présence du cinéma* (Paris), September/October 1962; round table and filmography in *Filmcritica* (Rome), May 1964; "'Peter Gunn': The Private Eye of Blake Edwards" by Robert Haller in *Film Heritage* (New York), summer 1968; "Un Assez Beau Doublé" by Gérard Legrand in *Positif* (Paris), February 1968; "Wild Rovers, Case History of a Film" by Herb Lightman in *American Cinematographer* (Los Angeles), July 1971; "Blake Edwards ou la sophistication de l'innocence" by Robert Benayoun in *Positif* (Paris), June 1973; "Il vuoto dell'assurdo" by G. Turroni in *Filmcritica* (Rome), January/February 1976; "You'll Never Work in Hollywood Again" by W. Luhr and P. Lehman in *Wide Angle* (Athens, Ohio), v.1, no.4, 1977; biofilmography in *Film Dope* (London), March 1978; "The Case of the Missing Lead Pipe Cinch" by W. Luhr and P. Lehman in *Wide Angle* (Athens, Ohio), v.1, no.1, 1979; "Crime in the Bedroom" by P. Lehman and W. Luhr in *Wide Angle* (Athens, Ohio), no.2, 1979; "Blake Edwards Takes *10*" by G. Morris in *Film Comment* (New York), November/December 1979; films—*Experiment on "Experiment"*, for TV, by Will Hindle, 1962; *Gift of Laughter* by Edward Anderson, Great Britain 1975.

*   *   *

Blake Edwards is one of the few filmmakers formed in the late classical period of American movies (the late forties and fifties) to survive and prosper in the eighties. If anything, Edwards's work has deepened with the passing decades, though it no longer bears much resemblance to the norms and styles of contemporary Hollywood. Edwards is an isolated figure, but a vital one.

His critical and box office reputation first peaked in the early sixties with such films as *Operation Petticoat, Breakfast at Tiffany's, Days of Wine and Roses*, and *The Pink Panther*. But as the new, post-studio Hollywood moved away from his brand of classicism, Edwards had a string of commercial disappointments—*What Did You Do in the War, Daddy?, Gunn, The Party*—leading up to the total failure of the multi-million dollar musical *Darling Lili*. In the early seventies, Edwards was barely visible, issuing occasional programmers—*The Wild Rovers, The Carey Treatment, The Tamarind Seed*—until his decision to revive the Inspector Clouseau character for *The Return of the Pink Panther*. The mordant slapstick of the panther films was back in style, and Edwards rode the success of *Return* through three more sequels, with the promise (despite the death of Clouseau's interpreter, Peter Sellers) of more to come. The success of the Panther films allowed Edwards to capitalize more personal projects, one of which—the 1979 *10*—became a sleeper hit. Now in his sixties, he has again become a brand name, with his own production company, Blake Edwards Entertainment, and a measure of security.

For all his artistic independence, Edwards has always chosen to work within well-defined, traditional genres—the musical, the melodrama, the slapstick farce, the thriller. There is little continuity in tone between a film like *The Tamarind Seed* (a transcendant love story) and *S.O.B.* (a frenzied black farce), yet there are the more important continuities of personality. Edwards has no particular commitment to any single genre (though his greatest successes have been comedies); he varies his choices as a painter varies the colors of his palette, to alter the tonal mix. The single stylistic constant has been Edwards's use of Panavision; with very few exceptions, his films have used the widescreen format as the basic unit of organization and expression.

At their most elemental level, Edwards's films are about space—crossing it, filling it, transcending it. In the comedies, the widescreen space becomes a vortex fraught with perils—hidden traps, aggressive objects, spaces that abruptly open onto other, unexpected spaces. Edwards extends the principles of silent comedy into modern technology and modern absurdism; his comic heroes are isolated in the hostile widescreen space, unable to conquer it as Chaplin and Keaton could conquer the more manageable dimensions of the silent frame. (Though the Panther films employ this principle, Edwards's masterpiece in this vein is the relatively unknown 1968 film, *The Party*.)

Visually, Edwards's thrillers appear to be more dense, more furnished, more confining than his comedies (and two of the best of them, *Gunn* and *Experiment in Terror*, were photographed in the standard screen ratio); the threat comes not from empty space, but from the crowding of objects, colors, surfaces—the hard, cold *thingness* of things: a deathly solidity that gives way, when the surfaces dissolve, to a more deathly chaos. In the romances, that operative space is the space between the characters; it must be collapsed, transformed, overcome. In *Darling Lili*, a room full of red roses is an emblem of love; it is not the trite symbolism of the flowers that gives the image its power, but the complete filling in of the widescreen space, its emotional conquest. In *The Tamarind Seed*, the lovers' conquest of space entails, as it does in the sublime thirties romances of Frank Borzage, a conquest of death.

With *10* and *Victor/Victoria*, Edwards has managed to blend the styles and assumptions of his comedies and romances; the strict genre divisions that once ruled his work have broken down, and with their dissolution a new humanism, has appeared. *10*

uses its long lenses trained on Bo Derek's face (as perfect a blank, deathly surface as any in Edwards's films) to create looming, overlarge images of romantic fantasy; balances wide-screen compositions—two lovers occupying the same, stable space—are the images of romantic reality and responsibility. *Victor/Victoria*, with its theatrical metaphors, builds small proscenium spaces for each of its role-playing characters; as the constricting roles are cast off, these isolating spaces give way to an overall openness and warmth. The widescreen space is no longer inherently hostile, but contains the promise of closeness and comfort. It is a new direction for Edwards, and perhaps the beginning of a brilliant late period.

—Dave Kehr

EGGELING, VIKING. Swedish. Born in Lund, Sweden, 21 October 1880. Educated in business at Flensburg; art studies at Brera Academy, Milan. Married Nora Fiernkranz, 1903; Marion Klein, 1914 or 1915. Career: 1897—emigrates to Germany and begins business studies at Flensburg; about 1900—bookkeeper in a clock factory at Le Locle, Switzerland; 1901-07—bookkeeper in Milan, evening courses at Brera Academy; about 1907—bookkeeper and art teacher at Lyceum Alpinum, Zuoz, Switzerland; 1910—short visit to Berlin; 1911—begins working as artist in Paris, comes to know Modigliani, Arp, and others; 1915-17—lives in Switzerland, makes first sketches for his scrolls *Horizontal/Vertical Orchestra* and *Diagonal Symphony*; 1918—lives in Zurich, renews contact with Hans Arp, meets other members of Dada group; comes to know Hans Richter through Tristan Tzara; 1918—participant in radical "Novembergruppe" of artists and architects; 1919—returns to Germany with Richter; at Klein-Kölzig, near Berlin, both begin to work on experiments with form; 1920—with Richter begins film experiments; 1921—ends collaboration with Richter, lives in Berlin; 1922—through Russian exhibition at Galerie van Diemen, comes in contact with Constructivist artists; 1923—meets Erna Niemeyer, begins collaboration with her on *Diagonal Symphony*; 1924—short visit to Paris, meets Fernand Léger; *Diagonal Symphony* shown privately in Berlin on 5 November; 1925—first public showing of *Diagonal Symphony*. Died in Berlin, 19 May 1925.

Films 1923—*Horizontal-Vertikal Orchester (Horizontal-Vertical Orchestra)* (unfinished); 1925—*Diagonal Sinfonie (Diagonal Symphony)*.

Publications:

By EGGELING:

Articles—"Theoretische Präsentationen der Kunst der Bewegung" in *MA* (Vienna), 1 August 1921; "Elvi fejtegetések a mozgómüvészetről" in *MA* (Vienna), v.6, no.8, 1921; "Zweite präsentistische Deklaration. Gerichtet an die internationalen Konstruktivisten", with Raoul Haussmann, in *MA* (Vienna), v.8, no.5/6, 1923; "Aus dem Nachlass Viking Eggelings" edited by Hans Richter in *G. Zeitschrift für elementare Gestaltung* (Berlin), no.4, 1926; "Anteckningar" in *Konstrevy* (Stockholm), v.43, no.4, 1967 (also see corrections in no.5/6, 1967).

On EGGELING:

Books—*Viking Eggeling*, exhibition catalogue, Nationalmuseum, Stockholm 1950; *Apropå Eggeling* edited by Karl Hultén, Stockholm 1958; *Viking Eggeling, 1880-1925, Artist and Filmmaker* by Louise O'Konor, Stockholm 1971; *The Cubist Cinema* by Standish Lawder, New York 1975; *Experimental Animation* by Robert Russett and Cecile Starr, New York 1976; articles—"Horizontal-Vertikal Orchester" by Theo van Doesburg in *De Stijl* (Amsterdam), 10 May 1921; "Bewegungskunst" by Ludwig Hilbersheimer in *MA* (Vienna), v.8, no.5/6, 1923; articles reprinted in special issue "Zehn Jahre Novembergruppe" of *Kunst der Zeit* (Berlin), v.3, no.1/3, 1928; "The Film Experiments of Viking Eggeling" by Louise O'Konor in *Cinema Studies* (England), June 1966; "Step by Step. An Account of the Transition from Painting to the First Abstract Films, 1919-1921" by Hans Richter in *Studies in the 20th Century* (Troy, N.Y.), fall 1968.

*   *   *

Eggeling's fame and influence as an experimental film artist is remarkable in that it is largely based upon a single work, *Diagonal Symphony*. Indeed, his death in Berlin, in 1925, followed the film's first public screening by only two weeks. Certainly any appreciation of Eggeling's place in film history rests upon the extraordinary influence *Diagonal Symphony* was to have, first on the European avant-garde of the 1920s, and then upon that movement's heritage: the international experimental film, a genre of major proportion which continues to flourish throughout the industrialized world.

Eggeling's personal theory of art was based upon the synaesthetic notion of *Augenmusik* ("optical music"). His early paintings were devoted to restructuring natural forms along geometric patterns in a fashion similar to Cubist strategies. He then began developing a personal dictionary of abstract forms which he hoped would function as contrapuntal hieroglyphs. His delicate drawings of these were done on long paper scrolls such as "Horizontal Vertical Mass" (1919).

As Standish Lawder details in his book *The Cubist Cinema*, it was about this time that Eggeling began to collaborate with the German painter Hans Richter. Together they formulated the theoretical monograph *Universelle Sprache* to detail a proposed "elemental pictorial language of abstract form and its articulation through counterpoint of contrast and analogy." Through this writing they gained precious access to the UFA film studio's animation facilities.

Diagonal Symphony is a delicately beautiful work, difficult to describe with its essential abstraction and unique shapes and forms. Unlike popular cartoons, but very much like countless experimental films which would follow it, its stucture operates independent of narrative. Instead, its white-on-black figures, which at times seem to be harps or wings, metamorphose with a subtle luminosity curiously similar to neon advertising lights, which became popular during the 1920s.

This single work, crafted in perfect independence over a half century ago continues to attract the attention of film historians, theoreticians, and experimental artists. With a running time of only about five minutes, its fleeting abstractions remain remarkably popular with contemporary audiences. Such appreciation helps explain Eggeling's fame and influence, despite such a meager cinematic legacy.

—Edward S. Small

EISENSTEIN, SERGEI. Russian. Born Sergei Mikhailovich Eisenstein in Riga, Latvia, 23 January 1898. Educated in St. Petersburg and at gymnasium in Riga; Institute of Civil Engineering, St. Petersburg, 1914-17 (studied architecture); briefly studied Japanese at General Staff Academy, Moscow, 1920. Married Pera Attasheva. Career: 1917—joins student recruits for defense of Petrograd; mobilized and is sent for officers' training; 1920—serves as poster artist on front at Minsk, demobilized; joins Proletkult Theater, Moscow, as scenic artist; becomes a co-director; 1921—studies in Vsevolod Meyerhold's "director's workshop"; 1922—joins Meyerhold as designer, meets Grigori Alexandrov; 1923-24—directs Tretiakov's *Listen, Moscow!* and his *Gas Masks*, the latter in a Moscow gas works; 1924—begins work on *Strike!*; 1925—commissioned to make film celebrating 1905 revulution; during filming in Odessa, *1905* becomes *Battleship Potemkin*; 1926—travels to Berlin for *Potemkin* premiere; begins work on *Old and New*, sets project aside to work on commission for film to celebrate 10th anniversary of 1917 Revolution; made professor at State Institute for Cinema; 1929-30—with collaborators Alexandrov and cinematographer Eduard Tisse leaves U.S.S.R. and travels first through Europe then the U.S., arriving finally in Hollywood; 1930—contract signed with Paramount, works on scripts for *The Glass House*, *Sutter's Gold* and *An American Tragedy*; Paramount breaks contract, State Department refuses to issue work permits; travels to Mexico to begin work on *Que Viva Mexico!* financed by Sinclair Lewis; 1932—Sinclair orders shooting halted and remains in possession of uncut film; refused visa to reenter U.S., then allowed only to cross to New York without stopping in Hollywood; returns to U.S.S.R. 1933—begins to teach at Moscow Film Institute; 1936—influenza stops shooting on *Bezhin Meadow*, works on script with Isaac Babel; 1937—*Bezhin Meadow* denounced, production halted; 1939—goes to Central Asia to plan *Ferghana Canal* project, abandoned as World War II begins; 1940—works on Pushkin film project, named Artistic Director of Mosfilm Studios; 1946—finishes shooting *Ivan the Terrible*, suffers heart attack; *Ivan* condemned by Central Committee on Cinema and Theater; 1947—prepares a 3rd part to *Ivan*, to have been made in color. Died in Moscow, 11 February 1948. Recipient: Gold Medal for *Strike*, Exposition Internationale des Arts Décoratifs, Paris, 1925; Order of Lenin, 1939; Stalin Prize, 1st Class, for *Ivan the Terrible, Part I*, 1946.

Films (as director and scriptwriter): 1923—*Kinodnevik Glumova (Glurumov's Film Diary)* (short film inserted in production of Ostrovsky's *Enough Folly in a Wise Man*, Proletkult Theater, Moscow); 1924—*Doktor Mabuze—Igrok* (co-ed only)(Russian version of Lang's *Dr. Mabuse der Spieler*); 1925—*Stachka (Strike)* (co-sc, +ed); *Bronenosets Potemkin (Battleship Potemkin)* (+ed); 1928—*Oktiabr (October, 10 Days That Shook the World)* (co-d, co-sc); 1929—*Staroie i novoie (Old and New)* (film produced as *Generalnaia linnia (The General Line)*, title changed before release) (co-d, co-sc); 1930—*Romance sentimentale* (co-d); 1933—*Thunder Over Mexico* (unauthorized, produced by Sol Lesser from *Que Viva Mexico!* footage, seen by Eisenstein in 1947 and disowned); *Death Day* and *Eisenstein in Mexico* (also unauthorized productions by Sol Lesser from *Que Viva Mexico!* footage; 1938—*Alexandr Nevskii (Alexander Nevsky)* (co-sc, +set des, costume des, ed); 1939—*Time in the Sun* (produced by Marie Seton from *Que Viva Mexico!* footage); *The Ferghana Canal* (short documentary out of footage from abandoned feature project on same subject); 1941—shorts edited by William Kruse for Bell and Howell from *Que Viva Mexico!* footage: *Mexico Marches*; *Conquering Cross*; *Idol of Hope*; *Land and Freedom*; *Spaniard and Indian*; *Mexican Symphony* (feature combining previous 5 titles); *Zapotecan Village*;

1944—*Ivan Grozny (Ivan the Terrible, Part I)* (+set des, costume des, ed); 1958—*Ivan Grozny II: Boyarskii Zagovor (Ivan the Terrible, Part II: The Boyars' Plot)* (completed 1946); *Eisenstein's Mexican Project* (unedited sequences of *Que Viva Mexico!* assembled by Jay Leyda); 1966—*Bezhin Lug (Bezhin Meadow)* (25 minute montage of stills from original film assembled by Nahum Kleimann, with music by Prokoviev). Role: as London policeman in *Everyday* (Hans Richter), shot in London, 1929.

Publications:

By EISENSTEIN:

Books—*The Soviet Screen*, Moscow 1939; *The Film Sense*, edited and translated by Jay Leyda, New York 1942; *Notes of a Film Director*, Moscow 1948; *Film Form*, edited and translated by Jay Leyda, New York 1949; *Que Viva Mexico*, London 1951; *Drawings*, Moscow 1961; *Charlie Chaplin*, Zurich 1961; *Ivan the Terrible: A Screenplay*, translated by Montagu and Marshall, New York 1962; *Erinnerungen*, Zurich 1963; *Potemkin*, translated by Gillon Aiten, New York 1968; *The Battleship Potemkin*, text by Andrew Sinclair, London 1968; *Film Essays with a Lecture*, edited by Jay Leyda, London 1968; *Notes of a Film Director*, New York 1970; *Collected Works of Sergei Eisenstein*, edited and translated by Herbert Marshall, Cambridge, Massachusetts 1971; *The Complete Works of Sergei M. Eisenstein*, edited by Marcel Martin, Guy Lecouvette and Abraham Segal, New York 1971; *The Complete Films of Eisenstein*, translated by John Hetherington, New York 1974; *Eisenstein: 3 Films* edited by Jay Leyda, New York 1974; *La Non-Differente nature*, Paris 1975; *Über Mich und meine Filme*, edited by L. Kaufmann, Berlin 1976; *S.M. Eisenstein: esquisses et dessins*, Paris 1978; articles—"Mass Movies" in *The Nation* (New York), 9 November 1927; letter to the editor in *The New Republic* (New York), 9 December 1931; "Mexican Film and Marxian Theory" in *New Republic* (New York), 9 December 1931; "The Cinematographic Principle and Japanese Culture" in *Experimental Cinema*, no.3, 1932; "Film Forms: New Problems" in *New Theatre*, April, May, June 1936; "Through Theatre to Cinema" in *Theatre Arts* (New York), September 1936; "The Mistakes of *Bezhin Lug*" in *International Literature* (Moscow), no.1, 1937; "My Subject is Patriotism" in *International Literature* (Moscow), no.2, 1939; "Charlie the Kid" in *Sight and Sound* (London), spring 1946; "Charlie the Grownup" in *Sight and Sound* (London), summer 1946; "The Birth of a Film" in *Hudson Review* (Nutley, New Jersey), no.2, 1951; "Sketches for Life" in *Films and Filming* (London), April 1958; "Mein Weg zum Film" in *Der russische Revolutionsfilm* by Boris Lawrenjew, Zurich 1960; "One Path to Colour: An Autobiographical Fragment" in *Sight and Sound* (London), spring 1961; "Betrachtung über No und das japanische Theater" in *No—vom Genius Japans* by Ezra Pound and Ernest Fenellosa, Zurich 1963; interview in *Interviews with Film Directors* edited by Andrew Sarris, New York 1967; "Iz neosuščestvlĕnnyh zamyslov: Kapital" in *Iskusstvo Kino* (Moscow), January 1973; "Filmer 'Le Capital'" in *Ecran* (Paris), December 1974; "Lehrprogramm für Theorie und Praxis der Regie" in *Filmkritik* (Munich), December 1974; "Die marxistisch-leninistische Methode im Film" in *Filmkritik* (Munich), November 1974; "La Quatrième Dimension du cinéma" in *Cahiers du cinéma* (Paris), September/October 1976; special section of Eisenstein's writings in *Film und Fernsehen* (Berlin), January 1978; "Briefe aus Mexico" in *Film und Fernsehen* (Berlin), August 1979; "Prometheus (expérience)" in *Cahiers du cinéma* (Paris), January 1980; "MMM (Scenariusz)", with S. Yutkevich and M. Andronikova, in *Kino* (Warsaw), April 1980.

On EISENSTEIN:

Books—*Film Problems of Soviet Russia* by Winifred Bryher, London 1929; *Eisenstein, 1898-1948* by Paul Rotha, Ivor Montagu and John Grierson, London 1948; *Film as Art* by Rudolph Arnheim, Berkeley 1957; *Kino* by Jay Leyda, London 1960; *Sergei Eisenstein—Künstler der Revolution*, Berlin 1960; *S.M. Eisenstein* by Jean Mitry, Paris 1961; *Sergej Michailowitsch Eisenstein*, edited by Konlecher and Kubelka, Vienna 1964; *Montaz w Tworezosci Eisenstein* by Regina Dreyer-Sfard, Warsaw 1964; *With Eisenstein in Hollywood* by Ivor Montagu, New York 1969; *Lessons with Eisenstein* by Vladimir Nizhny, translated by Montagu and Leyda, New York 1969; *Sergei Eisenstein* by Léon Moussinac, translated by Sandy Petrey, New York 1970; *Sergei Eisenstein and Upton Sinclair: The Making and Unmaking of Que Viva Mexico!* by Harry Geduld and Ronald Gottesman, Bloomington, Indiana 1970; *The Brakhage Lectures* by Stan Brakhage, Chicago 1972; *Eisenstein* by Yon Barna, Bloomington, Indiana 1973; *6 European Directors—Essays on the Meaning of Film Style* by Peter Harcourt, Baltimore 1974; *Eisenstein* by Yon Barna, Bloomington, Indiana 1974; *Eisenstein* by Dominique Fernandez, Paris 1975; *Eisenstein* by D. Fernandez, Paris 1975; *Sergei M. Eisenstein: Materialien zu Leben und Werk* by W. Sudendorf and others, Munich 1975; *Sergei M. Eisenstein in Selbstzeugrissen und Bilddokumenten*, edited by E. Weise, Reinbek bei Hamburg 1975; *Eisenstein: a Documentary Portrait* by N. Swallow, London 1976; *Octobre. Ecriture et idéologie* by Marie-Claire Ropars-Wuilleumier and others, Paris 1976; *Eisenstein: A Documentary Portrait* by Norman Swallow, New York 1977; *Image/Music/Text* by Roland Barthes, New York 1977; *Sergei M. Eisenstein* by Marie Seton, London 1978; *S.M. Eisenstein* by Jean Mitry, Paris 1978; *La Révolution figurée* by Marie-Claire Ropars-Wuilleumier and others, Paris 1979; *Montage Eisenstein* by Jacques Aumont, Paris 1979; *Eisenstein's Ivan the Terrible, a Neoformalist Analysis* by Kristin Thompson, Princeton 1981; *Eisenstein at Work* by Jay Leyda and Zina Voynow, New York 1982; articles—"Sergei Michailovitch Eisenstein" by Alfred Barr, Jr. in *The Arts* (New York), December 1928; "Paris Hears Eisenstein" by Samuel Brody in *Close Up* (London), no.4, 1930; "Eisenstein in Hollywood" by Edmund Wilson in *New Republic* (New York), 4 November 1931; "2 Masters: Ernst Lubitsch and Sergei M. Eisenstein" by H. Wollenberg in *Sight and Sound* (London), spring 1948; "Sergei Eisenstein" by Ivor Montagu in *Penguin Film Review* (London), September 1948; "The End of Sergei Eisenstein" by Waclaw Solski in *Commentary* (New York), March 1949; "Unfair to Eisenstein?" in *Sight and Sound* (London), June 1951; "Eisenstein's Images and Mexican Art" by Marie Seton in *Sight and Sound* (London), September 1953; "Aesthetics of the Film: The Pudovkin-Arnheim-Eisenstein Theory" by D. Harrah in *Journal of Aesthetics and Art Criticism*, December 1954; "Eisenstein and the Mass Epic" by Arthur Knight in *The Liveliest Art*, New York 1957; "Entretiens sur Eisenstein" by Georges Sadoul in *Cinéma 60* (Paris), 1960; chapter in *The Director's Counterpoint* by S. Yutkevich, Moscow 1960; "The Stage Antecedents of the Film Theory of S.M. Eisenstein" by John Kuiper in *Educational Theatre Journal*, December 1961; "Care of the Past" by Jay Leyda in *Sight and Sound* (London), winter 1961/62; "Cinematic Expression: A Look at Eisenstein's Silent Montage" by John Kuiper in *Art Journal*, fall 1962; "Cinema Scope: Before and After" by Charles Barr in *Film Quarterly* (Berkeley), summer 1963; "Missing Reel" by Jay

Leyda in *Sight and Sound* (London), spring 1965; "Eisenstein" by Rostislav Yourenev in *Anthologie du Cinéma*, Paris 1966; "Masquage, an Extrapolation of Eisenstein's Theory of Montage-as-Conflict to the Multi-image Film" by R. Siegler in *Film Quarterly* (Berkeley), spring 1968; "Eisenstein: Cinema and the Avant-Garde" by Peter Wollen in *Art International* (Lugano), November 1968; "Eisenstein, Pudovkin and Others" by Dwight Macdonald in *The Emergence of Film Art*, edited by Lewis Jacobs, New York 1969; chapter in *In Close-up* by Esther Shub, Moscow 1969; "The Influence of the Kabuki Theater on the Films of Eisenstein" by Norma Levine in *Modern Drama* (Toronto), May 1969; "2 Types of Film Theory" by Brian Henderson in *Film Quarterly* (Berkeley), spring 1971; "Kuleshov, Eisenstein, and the Others" by Lev Kuleshov in *Film Journal* (New York), fall/winter 1972; "The 'Left' Front of Art: Eisenstein and the Old 'Young' Hegelians" by M. Pleynet in *Screen* (London), spring 1972; "Eisenstein's Aesthetics: A Dissenting View" by P. Seydor in *Sight and Sound* (London), winter 1973/74; "Eisenstein et les hiéroglyphes" by Bernard Amengual in *Ecran* (Paris), June 1973; "Un Disciple inattendu d'Eisenstein: Antonin Artaud" by Bernard Amengual in *Ecran* (Paris), September/October 1973; "Ivan, una tragedia atea dello storico S.M. Eisenstein" by G. Aristarco in *Cinema nuovo* (Turin), May/June and July/August 1973; "Dialettica del vecchio e nuovo nella poetica di Ejzenštejn" by M. Del Ministro in *Cinema nuovo* (Turin), January/February 1973; "Il sistema Eisenstein" by A. Grasso in *Bianco e nero* (Rome), January/February 1973; "The Eisenstein-Prokoviev Correspondence" by R. Levaco in *Cinema Journal* (Evanston), fall 1973; "*Filmcritica*, Eisenstein, Brecht" by Jean-Marie Straub in *Filmkritik* (Berlin), July 1973; "Eisenstein's Epistemological Shift" by David Bordwell in *Screen* (London), winter 1974/75 (also see Bordwell letter in *Screen*, spring 1975); "Propos sur et autour de S.M. Eisenstein" by Bernard Amengual in *Cinéma* (Paris), March 1974; "Diderot, Brecht, Eisenstein" by Roland Barthes in *Screen* (London), summer 1974; "Eisensteins Weg zum *Streik*" by V. Shklovsky in *Filmwissenschaftliche Beitrage* (Berlin), v.15, 1974; Eisenstein issue of *Cine Cubano* (Havana), no.89-90, 1974; "Comment Eisenstein pensait filmer Le Capital" by Bernard Amengual in *Cinéma* (Paris), February 1975; "La Conception de la tragédie et de l'histoire chez Eisenstein" by G. Aristarco in *Cahiers de la Cinémathèque* (Paris), Christmas 1975; "Le Gai Savoir: Godard and Eisenstein: Notions of Intellectual Cinema" by R. Perlmutter in *Jump Cut* (Berkeley), May/July 1975; "Eisenstein et le sacre" by Bernard Amengual in *Cinéma* (Paris), October 1976; "Eisenstein par les autres et par lui-meme" by J. Aumont in *Cahiers du cinéma* (Paris), February 1976; 3 articles in *Cinema Journal* (Evanston), fall 1977; "Die Tendenz, den Kopf zu heben" by H.-J. Rother in *Filmwissenschaftliche Beitrage* (Berlin), v.18, no.2, 1977; "Fonctions du gros plan chez Eisenstein" by J.-C. Bonnet in *Cinématographe* (Paris), February 1977; "Die wichtigste der Künste" by A. Karaganov in *Film und Fernsehen* (Berlin), April 1977; "Eizennshtein i Stanislavskii" by V. Tereshkovich in *Iskusstvo Kino* (Moscow), no.12, 1978; "Eisenstein et la question graphique" by F. Albera in *Cahiers du cinéma* (Paris), December 1978; "S.M. Eisenstein and W. Reich, correspondences" by F. Albera in *Cahiers du cinéma* (Paris), June 1978; "Les Dessins mexicains d'Eisenstein" by A.-M. Blanchard in *Image et son* (Paris), March 1978; "The Prokoviev-Eisenstein Collaboration" by D.W. Gallez in *Cinema Journal* (Evanston), spring 1978; "Eisenstein: Ideology and Intellectual Cinema" by J. Goodwin and "A Note on Eisenstein's Shot Montage..." by H. Marshall in *Quarterly Review of Film Studies* (Pleasantville, N.Y.), spring 1978; "Unter fremden Himmel", in 2 parts, by R. Yurenev in *Film und Fernsehen* (Berlin), January and February 1978; "Die Kraft der Dialektik" by H.-J. Schlegel in *Film und Fernsehen* (Berlin), August 1979; "Na tom my stoim" by E. Tisse in *Iskusstvo Kino* (Moscow), no.2, 1979; "Film's Institutional Mode of Representation and the Soviet Response" by Noel Burch in *October* (Cambridge, Mass.), winter 1979; "Alienation and De-Alienation in Eisenstein and Brecht" by T. Gutiérrez Alea in *Cinema Papers* (Melbourne), July/August 1981; "Print the Legend" by P. Viota in *Contracampo* (Madrid), March 1980; films—*Eisenstein in Nederland (Eisenstein in Holland)* by Henk Aslem, Holland 1930; *In Memory of Eisenstein* directed and scripted by Pera Attasheva, U.S.S.R.; *Eisenstein Survey* by Marie Seton and John Minchinton, Great Britain 1952; *S.M. Eisenstein (Sergei Eisenstein Film Biography)* by V. Katanyan, U.S.S.R. 1958; *Eisenstein Directs Ivan* (derived from previous film), Great Britain 1969; *Eisenstein in Mexico* by Philip Hudsmith, Canada 1977.

* * *

Eisenstein is widely regarded as one of the most important figures in the history of the cinema. He was both a master filmmaker whose *Battleship Potemkin* ranks among the finest examples of film art, and a brilliant theorist whose ideas about montage have had enormous effect on film communication theory. He formed his eclectic theory of montage—a fusion of ideas drawn from such diverse sources as Japanese language and culture, Freud, Vsevolod Meyerhold, Pavlov, and Marx—while working within the atmosphere of revolution that characterized Soviet life of the 1920s.

Two pioneers of the Soviet cinema—Dziga Vertov, who founded the Kino Eye documentary group and experimented with an expressive use of editing in his documentaries, and Lev Kuleshov, who conducted numerous editing and acting experiments—heavily influenced Eisenstein, V.I. Pudovkin, and other young Soviet filmmakers. Furthermore, D.W. Griffith's *Intolerance* had a strong impact on all of the Soviet filmmakers because of its complexly intercut stories, one of which (the Modern story) was anti-capitalist and pro-labor.

Eisenstein entered filmmaking by way of the Proletkult Theater, from which he learned to distrust the traditional character-based theater and to seek instead a proletarian theater in which masses become a collective hero and social problems are explored. He rebelled against the idea that dialogue is the dominant element and all other elements—set design, lighting, costumes—merely support it. Instead, he considered that all elements, which he called "attractions," should function on equal terms and that the director ought to compose these attractions according to his formal designs.

Eisenstein's "montage of attractions"—the combination of attractions in order to create meaning—is derived from the Japanese language and from Marxist dialectic.

Eisenstein applied his theory of montage to film by taking the individual shot to be film's basic unit of construction and then creating meaning through the juxtaposition of shots. Unlike Pudovkin, whose idea of montage involved the linkage of shots for narrative purposes, Eisenstein favored the collision of contradictory shots, to shock and agitate the audience. Eisenstein identified five kinds of montage: metric, rhythmic, tonal, overtonal, and intellectual, which deal with conflict generated by, respectively, shot length, the rhythm of movement within the shot, visual tones and overtones in the shot, and the juxtaposition of two terms of a visual metaphor.

Eisenstein gave his early films a documentary look by casting according to the notion of typage—the selection of a non-actor to play a role because he/she is the correct physical type for the part—and by shooting on location, thereby placing non-actors against realistic backgrounds. He eschewed the individual hero, as he had done in the Proletkult Theater, in favor of a collective hero—e.g. the undifferentiated mass of striking workers in *Strike*. Moreover, the combination of Edward Tisse's carefully composed shots (Tisse was Eisenstein's cameraman on nearly all of his films) and Eisenstein's dynamic montage editing—as in the famous Odessa Steps sequence in *Battleship Potemkin*—encouraged audience identification with the collective hero and added dramatic impact.

In his last silent film, *Old and New*, which traces the growth of a poor Russian village into a prosperous collective farm, Eisenstein used for the first time an individual hero, a peasant woman who struggles for the establishment of the collective. He also experimented with an expressive use of color and composition in depth—a dozen years before the much-acclaimed deep-focus cinematography of *Citizen Kane*. Furthermore, while editing *Old and New*, Eisenstein discovered the "filmic fourth dimension", overtonal montage, a synthesis of metric, rhythmic, and tonal montage that does not appear at the level of the individual frame, but only at the level of the projected film.

Although Eisenstein's political enemies within the Communist Party denounced his silent films and charged him with "formalism"—a preference for aesthetic form over ideological content—Soviet and foreign audiences and critics loved the films, particulary *Battleship Potemkin*. Once it was clear that Eisenstein's films had brought the Soviet cinema and Eisenstein himself to the attention of the world, the Stalin government grudgingly lent Eisenstein its support; Eisenstein was compelled, however, to cut *October* and *Old and New* according to Stalin's wishes.

After he completed *Old and New* in 1929, Eisenstein embarked on a tour of Western Europe and America, to exchange ideas with other prominent intellectuals and to learn the new sound technology. In Hollywood, he worked on several projects for Paramount Pictures, but ideological differences between Eisenstein and the studio heads prevented the completion of the projects; the studio wanted, for example, *An American Tragedy* to be a simple love triangle-murder story, while Eisenstein saw the film as a criticism of the relations in American society that led to the murder. From Hollywood he went to Mexico, where he worked on *Que viva Mexico!*, a film about Mexican culture and the revolutionary spirit. When that project was cancelled in 1932 because Eisenstein had gone over budget, he returned to the Soviet Union.

In spite of his disappointing experiences in Hollywood and Mexico, Eisenstein was eager to apply his ideas on montage to the new medium of the sound film. The Stalin government, however, which had always disapproved of Eisenstein's formalist tendencies, now felt that Eisenstein had grown too independent during his tour of the West. In order to discredit him, the government launched a series of attacks on Eisenstein in the press, and prevented him from completing any films for the next six years.

Finally, Eisenstein was allowed to work on *Alexander Nevsky*, a historical epic about a 13th Century Russian hero. Unlike Eisenstein's early films, *Nevsky* focused on a central character played by a professional actor, and emphasized the plastic qualities of the image through composition in depth. He worked with composer Sergei Prokofiev to create a score that operated in counterpoint to the film's visual rhythms; such a contrapuntal use of sound was, of course, a logical extension of Eisenstein's montage aesthetics. *Alexander Nevsky* became a worldwide popular and critical success, and Eisenstien temporarily regained his position of importance in the Soviet cinema.

His last two films were the first parts of an intended trilogy about the 16th century Czar Ivan. In *Ivan the Terrible* parts I and II Eisenstein used actors to play his main characters, he made contrapuntal use of scores composed by Prokofiev, he replaced the montage editing of his silent films with ornate pictorial compositions, and he made expressive use of color in a dance sequence in *Ivan* part II. *Ivan* part I was a success inside the Soviet Union and abroad, but *Ivan* part II was banned in the Soviet Union because Stalin didn't like the film's negative portrayal of Ivan's secret police. Eisenstein never made *Ivan* part III: he suffered a heart attack in 1946 and, after a long illness, died in 1948.

Although Eisenstein is best known for the dynamic editing in his early films, we should keep in mind that he did not limit his montage approach to the juxtaposition of shots in the black-and-white silent film. He favored the use of montage techniques in literature, theater, and the other arts, montage within the frame by means of composition in depth, and the use of sound, color, and even 3-D in counterpoint to the graphics of the visual image.

—Clyde Kelly Dunagan

———

EMSHWILLER, ED. American. Born in East Lansing, Michigan, 1925. Educated at University of Michigan, Bachelor of Design, 1949; studied graphics, Ecole des Beaux-Arts, Paris, 1949-50; studied at Art Students League, New York, 1951. Career: 1951-64—active as painter, and illustrator of books and magazines (as "EMSH"); 1963-73—period of collaboration on dance films with choreographer Alwin Nikolais; 1965-present—produces or collaborates on many mixed-media shows; 1969-75—Member of Board of Trustees, American Film Institute; 1971-present—included in numerous exhibitions of video art in addition to one-man shows; 1972-79—Artist in Residence, WNET-TV/Channel 13 TV Lab, New York; Member of Board of Directors, Association of Independent Video and Filmmakers; 1975—Ford Foundation research fellow at Center for Music Research, University of California at San Diego; 1979-present—Provost and Dean of the School of Film and Video, California Institute of the Arts, Valencia. 1980—visual consultant, PBS production *The Lathe of Heaven*. Recipient: filmmaking grant, Ford Foundation, 1964; Special Award, Oberhausen Festival, for *Relativity*, 1967; Von Stroheim Prize for most original feature, Mannheim Festival, for *Image, Flesh and Voice*, 1970; video grant, National Endowment for the Arts, 1972 (and 1973, 1975, and 1979); CAPS Grant, New York State Council on the Arts, 1973; filmmaking grant, Guggenheim Foundation, 1973; awards for best drama and most innovative program, Corporation for Public Broadcasting, for *Pilobolus and Joan*, 1975; video grant, Rockefeller Foundation, 1976; video grant, Corporation for Public Broadcasting, 1976; INDY Award, Association of Independent Video and Filmmakers, 1976; video grant, Guggenheim Foundation, 1978. Film Distributor: Filmmakers Cooperative, 175 Lexington Ave., New York, NY 10016. Videotape Distributor: Electronic Arts Intermix, 84 Fifth Ave., New York, NY 10011. Address: lives in Valencia, California.

Films: 1955-58—*Paintings by Ed Emshwiller*; 1959—*Dance Chromatic*; *Transformation*; 1960—*Lifelines*; 1960-61—*Variable Studies*; 1961—*Time of the Heathen* (collaboration with Peter Kass); 1962—*Thanatopsis*; 1963—*Totem* (collaboration with Alwin Nikolais); *Scrambles*; 1964—*George Dumpson's Place*; 1965—*Dlugoszewski Concert*; *Faces of America*; 1966—*Relativity*; *Art Scene USA*; 1967—*Fusion* (collaboration with Alwin Nikolais); 1968—*Project Apollo*; 1969—*Image, Flesh and Voice*; 1970—*Carol*; *Film with 3 Dancers*; *Branches*; 1971—*Choice*

Chance Woman Dance; 1971—*Images* (video); 1972—*Computer Graphics No.1* (video); *Thermogenesis* (video—short version of *Computer Graphics No.1*; *Woe Oh Ho No*; *The Chalk Line*; *Inside the Gelatin Factory*; *Scape-Mates* (video); 1973—*Chrysalis* (collaboration with Alwin Nikolais); *Positive Negative Electronic Faces* (video—collaboration with Tony Bannon); *Identities*; 1974—*Pilobolus and Joan* (video); *Interrupted Solitude*; *Crossings and Meetings* (video); (videotapes): 1975—*Inside Edges*; *Family Focus*; 1976—*New England Visions Past and Future* (collaboration with William Thompson); *Short and Very Short Films* (compilation of films from 1952-76); *Collisions*; *Self Trio*; 1977—*Slivers* (multi-monitor installation with partly masked screens); *Sur Faces*; *Face Off*; 1978—*Dubs*; 1979—*Sunstone* (computer animation); 1982—*Passes* [4-monitor installation comprised of following videotapes: *Space Passes* (1981); *Vascular Passes* (1982); *Cut Passes* (1981); *Pan Passes* (1982); *Echo Passes* (1979-82)].

Films photographed (partial listing): 1961—*The American Way*; 1963—*Hallelujah the Hills* (Mekas); *Film Magazine No.1*; *The Streets of Greenwood*; *The Quiet Takeover*; 1964—*The Opinion Makers*; *The Existentialist*; 1965—*Oysters*; 1967—*Norman Jacobson*; 1972—*Painters Painting*.

Publications:

By EMSHWILLER:

Book—*Stan Brakhage, Ed Emshwiller*, edited by Rochelle Reed, Washington, D.C. 1973; articles—"A Statement" in *Film Culture* (New York), summer 1963; interview by James Mullins in *Film Culture* (New York), fall 1966; "Cine-dance" in *Dance Perspectives* (New York), summer 1967; "Movies" in *New Worlds*, no.178, 1968; "Images from the Underground" in *Dialogue*, vol.4, no.1, 1971; "AFI Seminar" in *Dialogue on Film* (Washington, D.C.), January 1973; interview by Scott Hammon in *Afterimage* (Rochester, New York), September 1974; article in *Directing the Film, Film Directors on Their Art* by Eric Sherman, Washington, D.C. 1976; "An Interview with Ed Emshwiller" by G. Jamison in *Filmmakers Newsletter* (Ward Hill, Mass.), November 1977; "Image Maker Meets Video, or, Psyche to Physics and Back" in *The New Television* edited by Douglas Davis and Allison Simmons, Cambridge, Mass. 1977.

On EMSHWILLER:

Books—*Experimental Cinema* by David Curtis, New York 1971; *Movie Journal: The Rise of the New American Cinema, 1959-1971* by Jonas Mekas, New York 1972; articles—"The Films of Ed Emshwiller" by Richard Whitehall in *Film Quarterly* (Berkeley), spring 1967; "Relativity Re-Affirms Emshwiller's Stature" by Richard Whitehall in *Filmmakers Newsletter* (Ward Hill, Mass.), November 1967; "4 Artists as Filmmakers" by Adrienne Mancia and Willard Van Dyke in *Art in America* (New York), January/February 1967; article by Jonas Mekas in the *Village Voice* (New York), 25 June 1970; "Ed Emshwiller: Beginnings" by Letty Lou Eisenhauer in *Art and Artists* (London), March 1974.

*   *   *

Ed Emshwiller's first major film was *Dance Chromatic* which, like *Transformations* and *Life Lines*, was an admixture of animated and live action images. By the early 1970s he had completed over 20 works, many of them very famous and—for the experimental film genre—very successful. His film *Relativity*, made under a Ford Grant, displays the fine craftsmanship and technical precision that helped assure an international appeal and repeated awards for his various productions. His concerns during this early period were diverse, ranging from animated graphics through dance films to live action experimental constructions—all characterized by compositional and cinematographic virtuosity that made them mainstays of the American underground film. During the same period he was active as cinematographer on other artist's shorts, features, and documentaries. Further, Emshwiller himself produced or collaborated on many mixed-media productions (e.g. *Split 5th*, with the Denver Symphony) which were quite innovative for the time.

Since the early 1970s, Emshwiller has extended his skill in cinematographic construction to electronic image making. His *Images 1971* Whitney Museum video exhibition was followed by over a dozen experimental video projects that augment his continuing experimental film production. Such fluency with diverse technological resources has always marked Emshwiller's career. But because changes in technology are invariably structurally consequential his recent vidio productions—often predicated upon computer generated or synthesized graphics—have resulted in essential differences from his earlier film work. The silent three minute *Sunstone* of 1980 an eight month endeavor employing a digital computer, is a case in point. With its poststructuralist attention to cathode-ray tube dimensionality and to movement and radiated color, *Sunstone* is so distinct from the limbo-lighting and cinematic superimpositions of *Dance Chromatic* that audiences might find difficulty in assigning both constructions to the same author.

Thus Emshwiller's personal evolution from painter's graphics, through film and mixed media, into vidio provides scholars a fine microcosmic example of progressions making the larger technostructural transformation of experimental film as a historical genre.

—Edward S. Small

EPSTEIN, JEAN. French. Born in Warsaw, 25 March 1897. Educated at collège français, Villa Saint-Jean, Fribourg; Ecole Centrale, Lyons, degree in medicine 1916. Career: 1916—meets Auguste Lumière while doing medical residency at Hôtel-Dieu, Lyon; 1920—meets Blaise Cendrars, then collaborating on script of Gance's *La Roue*; founds revue *Le Promenoir*; 1921—*La Poésie d'aujourd'hui* favorably received, becomes assistant to Louis Delluc on *Le Tonnerre*; hired as editor by Editions de la Sirène, continues to write; 1922—Jean Benoit-Lévy offers direction of film on Pasteur; 1923—put under contract by Pathé; sponsors 2 conferences on cinematic issues; 1924—at suggestion of sister, scenarist Marie Epstein, joins Alexandre Kamenka's Films Albatros; 1926-28—producing organization is Les Films Jean Epstein; early 1940s—with sister arrested by Gestapo, saved from deportation through intervention of friends and Red Cross; after war—teaches at I.D.H.E.C., writes on cinema, makes several films. Died of cerebral hemmhorage in Paris, 3 April 1953.

Films (as assistant director): 1921—*Le Tonnerre* (Delluc); (as director): 1922—*Pasteur*; *Les Vendanges*; 1923—*L'Auberge rouge* (+sc); *Coeur fidèle* (+sc); *La Montagne infidèle*; *La Belle Nivernaise* (+sc); 1924—*Le Lion des Mogols* (+adaptation); *L'Affiche*; *La Goutte de sang* (Mariaud) (uncredited d); 1925—*Le Double Amour*; *Les Aventures de Robert Macaire*; (as producer and director): 1926—*Mauprat*; *Au pays de George Sand*; 1927—*Six et demi onze*; *La Glace a trois faces*; 1928—*La Chute* de la maison Usher; 1929—Finis terrae (+sc); Sa Tête (+sc); 1930—Le Pas de la mule; 1931—Mor-Vran (La Mer des corbeaux); Notre-Dame de Paris; La Chanson des peupliers; Le Cor; 1932—L'Or des mers (+sc); Les Berceaux; La Villanelle des Rubans; Le Vieux Chaland; 1933—L'Homme a l'Hispano (+sc); La Chatelaine du Liban (+sc); 1934—Chanson d'armor (+adaptation); La Vie d'un grand journal; 1936—Coeur de Gueux (+adaptation); La Bretagne; La Bourgogne; 1937—Vive la vie; La Femme du bout de monde (+sc); 1938—Les Batisseurs; Eau vive (+sc); 1939—Arteres de France; La Charrette fantôme (Duvivier) (d superimpositions and special photographic effects only); 1947—Le Tempestaire (+sc); 1948—Les Feux de la mer; La Bataille de l'eau lourde (Kampen om tungtvannet) (Marin and Vibe-Müller) (d prologue only).

Publications:

By EPSTEIN:

Books—La Poésie d'aujourd'hui—Un nouvel état d'intelligence, Paris 1921; Bonjour cinéma, Paris 1921; La Lyrosophie, Paris 1922; Le Cinématographe vu de l'Etna, Paris 1926; L'Or des mers, Valois 1932; Les Recteurs et la sirène, Paris 1934; Photogénie de l'impondérable, Paris 1935; L'Intelligence d'une machine, Paris 1946; Le Cinéma du diable, Paris 1947; Esprit de cinéma, Paris 1955; articles—"Jean Epstein nous parle de ses projets et du film parlant", interview by Pierre Leprohon in Pour vous (Paris), 17 October 1929; article in Cahiers du cinéma (Paris), June 1953.

On EPSTEIN:

Books—Jan Epstein by Zbigniew Gawrak, Warsaw 1962; Jean Epstein by Pierre Leprohon, Paris 1964; articles—"Un Poète de l'image" by Pierre Leprohon in Cinémonde (Paris), 28 February 1929; "Jean Epstein" by Catherine Wunscher in Sight and Sound (London), October/December 1953; issue devoted to Epstein, edited by Gideon Bachmann, of Cinemages (New York), v.2, 1955; "Souvenirs en l'honneur de Jean Epstein" by R. Toussenot in L'Age nouveau (Paris), October 1956; "Epstein" by Philippe Haudiquet in Anthologie du cinéma vol.2, Paris 1967; biofilmography in Film Dope (London), March 1978; "Jean Epstein" in Travelling (Lausanne), summer 1979; "Cinema Rising: Epstein in the 20s", special section, in Afterimage (Rochester), no.10, 1981

*   *   *

Jean Epstein belongs to the generation of 1920s French filmmakers who were drawn to the cinema from early interest in literature by the impact of the Hollywood productions of Griffith, Chaplin, and Ince. Gifted with a precocious intelligence, Epstein had already published books on literature, philosophy, and the cinema when he made his debut as a filmmaker with a documentary on Pasteur in 1922 at the age of only 25. Three fictional features in the following year, including Coeur fidèle which contains virtuoso passages to rank with the work of Gance and L'Herbier, put him in the forefront of French avant-garde filmmaking.

The four films he made during 1925-26 for the Albatros company run by the Russian emigré Alexandre Kamenka include two, L'Affiche and Le Double Amour, from scripts by Jean's sister Marie Epstein. The spectacular Le Lion des Mogols from a preposterous script by its star, the great actor Ivan Mosjoukine,

was followed by Les Aventures de Robert Macaire, an adaptation of the play parodied by Frédéric Lemaître in Carné's Les Enfants du paradis. None of these are generally considered to be among Epstein's work but they established him as a director after the controversies which had surrounded the showings of Coeur fidèle, and enabled him to set up his own production company in 1926.

The films which he both produced and directed are very varied. He began with two films in which his own artistic aspirations were balanced by demands of commercial popularity: an adaption of George Sand's novel, Mauprat, which had formed part of his childhood reading, and Six et demi onze, again from a script by his sister. But the last two films of Les Productions Jean Epstein were resolutely independent works. The short feature La Glace à trois faces is remakable for its formal pattern which looks foward to experiments in narrative structure of a kind which were still striking to audiences 30 years later when Alain Resnais made Hiroshima mon amour. Even more accomplished in terms of acting and setting, and as intriguing in terms of narrative, is Epstein's atmospheric evocation of the dark world of Edgar Allan Poe, La Chute de la maison Usher. This tale of love, art, and madness is told in a marvellously controlled style which makes extensive use of slow motion and multiple superimposition. Just as the hero refuses to accept the division of life and death and through the effort of will, summons back the woman he has killed through devotion to his art, so too Epstein's film creates a universe where castle and forest, interior and exterior interpenetrate.

After this masterly evocation of a world of Northern imagination, which can rank with Dreyer's Vampyr and is a reminder of Epstein's part-Polish ancestry, the director largely withdrew from the world of Parisian film production. With only occasional forays into commercial filmmaking, Epstein devoted much of his efforts over the 18 years that spread from the silent Finis terrae in 1929 to the short Le Tempestaire in 1947 to a masterly series of semi-documentary evocations of the Breton countryside and seascape.

Epstein is a complex and uncompromising figure whose filmmaking was accompanied by a constant theoretical concern with his chosen medium. If the central concept of his 1930s writing—La photogénie—remains not merely undefined but undefinable, and he makes recourse to notions of a magical or mystical essence of cinema unfortunately typical of the period, his theoretical work remains of great interest. The republication of his complete works, Ecrits sur le Cinéma, in 1974-75, demonstrated the modernity and continuing interest of his explorations of key aspects of the relationship between the spectator and the screen.

—Roy Armes

ERMLER, FRIEDRICH. Soviet. Born Friedrich (or Fridrich) Markovich Ermler in Rechitsa (Rezekne), Latvia, 13 May 1898. Educated in Leningrad Institute of Screen Arts, enrolled 1923. Career: 1908—pharmacist's apprentice; 1916—mobilized for war; 1917—deserts army; participates in October Revolution, St. Petersburg; 1919—joins Red Army and becomes member of Communist Party; is captured on Northern Front and tortured by Whites; 1923—while in school organizes the Cinema Experimental Workshop (KEM); 1924—persuades authorities to support film on public health (Skarlatina); 1927—collaborates with Eduard Ioganson on first feature Children of the Storm; early 1930s—suffers crisis of confidence with coming of sound, asked by Sergei Yutkevich to collaborate on Counterplan; 1935—

travels to Hollywood with delegation led by Boris Shumyatski to promote Soviet films; group given cool reception; 1939-43—artistic director of Lenfilm Studio, supervises evacuation of studio to interior of Soviet Union during war; early 1960s—works in Soviet television. Died in 1967. Recipient: Stalin Prize for *She Defends Her Country*.

Films (as assistant director): 1924—*Krasnye partizany (Red Partisans)* (Viskovsky) (+ro); (as director): 1924—*Skarlatina (Scarlet Fever)*; 1926—*Deti buri (Children of the Storm)* (co-d, +co-sc); *Katka bumazhnyi ramet (Katka's Reinette Apples)* (co-d); 1928—*Parizhsky sapozhnik (Parisian Cobbler)*; *Dom v sugribakh (The House in the Snow-Drifts)* (+sc); 1929—*Oblomok imperii (Fragment of an Empire)* (+co-sc); 1932—*Vstrechnyi (Counterplan)* (co-d, +co-sc); 1935—*Krestyaniye (Peasants)* (+co-sc); 1938—*Velikii grazhdanin (A Great Citizen)*: Part I (+co-sc); 1939—*Velikii grazhdanin (A Great Citizen)*: Part II (+co-sc); 1940—*Osen (Autumn)* (short—co-d); 1941—*Anton Ivanovic serditsya (Anton Ivanovich Gets Mad)* (Ivanovski) (supervisor only); 1943—*Ona zashchishchayet rodinu (She Defends Her Country)*; 1946—*Velikii perelom (The Great Turning-Point)*; 1950—*Velikaya sila (Great Power, Great Strength)* (+sc); 1954—*Kortik (Dagger)* (Vengerov and Schveitzer) (supervisor only); 1955—*Neokonchennaya povest (Unfinished Story)*; 1958—*Den pervyi (The First Day)*; 1962—*Zvanyi uzhin* (short); *Starozhil (Old Inhabitant)* (Khamraev) (supervisor only); 1967—*Pered sudom istorii (Before the Judgment of History)*. Role: 1924—*Chai (Maybe)* (Viskovsky) (banned).

Publications:

By ERMLER:

Article—"Programma iz pjati punktov" in *Iskusstvo Kino* (Moscow), September 1973.

On ERMLER:

Books—*Kino: A History of the Russian and Soviet Film* by Jay Leyda, London 1960; *The Most Important Art: Eastern European Film After 1945* by Mira and Antonín Liehm, Berkeley, California 1977; articles—"A Fragment of Ermler" by Leonid Trauberg in *Films and Filming* (London), March 1968; special isssue of *Iskusstvo Kino* (Moscow), September 1973; biofilmography in *Film Dope* (London), March 1978.

FÁBRI, ZOLTÁN. Hungarian. Born in Budapest, 1917. Educated at Academy of Fine Arts and Academy of Dramatic and Film Art, Budapest, diploma 1941. Career: 1941-45—stage designer, actor and director, interned as prisoner of war; 1945-49—at Artists Theater, Budapest; 1949—appointed artistic director of Hunnia Studios; 1952—makes first feature; 1956—*Hannibál tanár úr*, indirectly attacking Stalinist period, banned; 1964—begins ongoing collaboration with cameraman György Illés on *Húsz óra*; 1968—directs Hungarian-American coproduction *The Boys of Paul Street*, nominated for Oscar in 1968; currently President of Union of Hungarian Cinema and Television Artists; Professor at Academy of Dramatic and Cinema Arts, Budapest. Recipient: Special Jury Prize, Moscow Festival, for *141 perc a Befejezetlen mondatból*, 1975; Grand Prize, Moscow Festival, for *Az ötödik pecsét*, 1977.

Films (as director): 1951—*Gyarmat a föld alatt* [Colony Beneath the Earth] (co-d); 1952—*Vihar (Storm)*; 1954—*Életjel (Vierzehn Menschenleben)* [Life Signs]; 1955—*Körhinta (Merry-Go-Round, Karussell)* (+co-sc, art d); 1956—*Hannibál tanár úr (Professor Hannibal)* (+co-sc); 1957—*Bolond április (Summer Clouds)* [Crazy April]; *Édes Anna (Anna, Schuldig?)* (+co-sc); 1959—*Dúvad (The Brute, Das Scheusal)* (+sc); 1961—*Két félidö a pokolban (The Last Goal)* (+art d); 1963—*Nappali sötétség (Darkness in Daytime, Dunkel bei Tageslicht)* (+sc, art d); 1964—*Húsz óra (20 Hours)*; 1965—*Vizivárosi nyár (A Hard Summer)* (for TV); 1967—*Utószezon (Late Season)*; 1968—*A Pál utcai fiúk (The Boys of Paul Street)* (+co-sc); 1969—*Isten hozta, örnagy úr! (The Toth Family)* (+co-sc); 1971—*Hangyaboly* (+co-sc); 1973—*Plusz mínusz egy nap (One Day More, One Day Less)*; 1974—*141 perc a Befejezetlen mondatból (141 Minutes from the Unfinished Sentence)* (+co-sc); 1976—*Az ötödik pecsét (The Fifth Seal)* (+sc); 1977—*Magyarok (The Hungarians)* (+sc); 1979—*Fábián Bálint találkozása Istennel (Balint Fabian Meets God)* (+sc); 1981—*Reqiem*.

Publications:

By FÁBRI:

Articles—"A morális készületlenség tragikuma", interview, in *Filmkultura* (Budapest), March/April 1973; "Mit és mennyit tehet sorsáert és sorsa ellen az ember?", interview by M. Ember in *Filmkultura* (Budapest), April 1975; "Az emberi méltóság védelme foglalkoztat" in *Filmkultura* (Budapest), September/October 1977; "Bálint Fábián's Encounter with God" in *Hungarofilm Bulletin* (Budapest), no.4, 1979.

On FÁBRI:

Articles—biographical note in *International Film Guide*, London 1965; "Zoltán Fábri" by Michael Hanisch in *Regiestühle*, Berlin 1972; bio-filmography in *Film und Fernsehen* (Berlin), no.3, 1976; "Egy életmü—a társadalom fejlödésében" by K. Nemes in *Filmkultura* (Budapest), September/October 1977; film—*Fábri portré* directed by László Nádassy, 1980.

*   *   *

Having been a theater director and designer, Zoltán Fábri began to work in films in 1950 and quickly discovered his true vocation. In 1952 he made his first film, *Vihar*, a drama about the collectivization of a village. *Körhinta*, presented at Cannes in 1956, was astonishing for the beauty of its images and feelings, and for the appearance of a young actress, Mari Törocsik, whom he picked again two years later for his film *Édes Anna*.

Also in 1956 he made *Hannibál tanár úr*, the tragedy of a man broken by the pressure of his conformist milieu, with the outstanding Ernö Szabó in the main role. This film, honored at the Karlovy Vary Festival in 1957, raised the problem of the heritage of a fascist past and indirectly attacked the oppressive atmosphere of the Stalinist period. Following the political events which supervened in 1956, it was excluded from Hungarian screens.

In all of his work, nourished by Hungarian literature, Fábri deals with moral problems bound up with the history of his country, making use of a vigorous realism. Besides the meticulous composition of his narratives, and precise evocation of atmosphere and the milieu where they unfold, it's necessary to underline the importance given to his work with actors and his own participation in the creation of some set designs.

Following a drama showing the present-day problems of life in the countryside, *Dúvad*, Fábri continued with *Két félidö a pokolban*, set in a concentration camp. The moral behavior of men in times of crisis, the confrontation of ideas and of characters, of cowardice and heroism, totally absorb him and are at the heart of all his films. In *Húsz óra*, made in 1964, he uses an investigation undertaken by a journalist as the starting point for a brilliant reflection on the impact in Hungary of political events in the recent past, confirming anew his abilities as an analyst and director. For this film he was able to engage again György Illés as cameraman, and they have continued a constant collaboration since.

Having given the Hungarian cinema an international audience, Fábri in 1968 directed a Hungarian-American coproduction, *The Boys of Paul Street*, faithfully adapted from the popular novel by Ferenc Molnár. This touching story of childhood heroism was nominated for an Oscar in 1968. After *Hangyaboly*, a drama that unfolds behind the walls of a convent, with Mari Töröcsik, he made *141 perc a Befejezetlen mondatból*, which brought him the Special Jury Prize at Moscow in 1975. He returned then to a moral analysis of the wartime period with *Az ötödik pecsét*, a work of deep psychological insight, which received the Grand Prize at the Moscow Festival in 1977 and remains one of the director's best films. With *Magyarok*, nominated for an Oscar in 1978, and its sequel *Fábián Bálint találkozása Istennel*, he traces in epic style and more conventional form the fate of the peasants in the period between the wars.

Having received the Kossuth Prize three times, today President of the Union of Hungarian Cinema and Television Artists, and professor at Budapest's Academy of Dramatic and Cinema Arts, Fábri is now considered a classic of the Hungarian cinema. In his last film, *Reqiem*, he sets against the drama of a young girl the tragic consequences of the postwar political dislocations. In attempting thus to renew his method, he succeeds once again in powerfully expressing the message of a great moralist.

—Karel Tabery

FASSBINDER, RAINER WERNER. German. Born in Bad Wörishofen, Bavaria, 31 May 1946. Educated at the Rudolf Steiner School and secondary schools in Augsburg and Munich until 1964; studied acting at Fridl-Leonhard Studio, Munich. Married Ingrid Caven in 1970 (divorced). Career: 1964-66—after leaving school, does office work, decorating, and works in archives of *Süddeutsche Zeitung*, Munich; 1965—applies to West Berlin Film and Television Academy, fails entrance examination; 1967—joins *action-theater*, Munich, with Hanna Schygulla whom he met in acting school; 1968—1st original play produced (*Katzelmacher*); *action-theater* closed by police in May; co-founds *anti-teater*; 1969—begins making films with members of *anti-teater*; 1969-82—works in theater throughout Germany, produces a number of radio plays and acts in own films and in others'; 1971—founds Tango Film, independent company; 1974—with Kurt Raab and Roland Petri takes over Theater am Turm (TAT), Frankfurt; 1975—founds Albatros Produktion, mainly for co-productions; TAT project fails, he returns to Munich and concentrates more exclusively on films; 1978—begins directing photography of his films. Died, probably

of overdose of sleeping pills and cocaine, in Munich, 10 June 1982. Recipient: Golden Bear, Berlin Festival, for *Die Sehnsucht der Veronika Voss*, 1982.

Films (as director, scriptwriter, editor under pseudonym 'Franz Walsch', and uncredited producer): 1965—*Der Stadtstreicher (The City Tramp)* (+ro); 1966—*Das kleine Chaos (The Little Chaos)* (+ro); 1969—*Liebe ist kälter als der Tod (Love is Colder than Death)* (+ro as *Franz*); *Katzelmacher* (+art direction, ro as *Jorgos*); *Götter der Pest (Gods of the Plague)* (+ro as *Porno Buyer*); *Warum läuft Herr R amok? (Why Does Herr R Run Amok?)* (co-d, co-sc, co-ed); *Fernes Jamaica (Distant Jamaica)* (Moland) (sc only); 1970—*Rio das Mortes* (d and sc only, +ro as *Discotheque-goer*); *Whity* (co-ed, +ro as *Guest in Saloon*); *Die Niklashauser Fahrt (The Niklashausen Journey)* (co-d, co-sc, co-ed, +ro as *Black Monk*); *Der amerikanische Soldat (The American Soldier)* (d and sc only, + song and ro as *Franz*); *Warnung vor einer heiligen Nutte (Beware of a Holy Whore)* (co-ed, +ro as *Sascha*); (as director, scriptwriter and uncredited producer): 1971—*Pioniere in Ingolstadt (Pioneers in Ingolstadt)*; *Das Kaffeehaus (The Coffee House)* (for TV); *Der Händler der vier Jahreszeiten (The Merchant of the Four Seasons)* (+ro as *Zucker*); 1972—*Die bitteren Tränen der Petra von Kant (The Bitter Tears of Petra von Kant)* (+des); *Wildwechsel (Wild Game)*; *Acht Stunden sind kein Tag (8 Hours Don't Make a Day)* (shown on German television in 5 monthly segments, each between 88 and 101 minutes long); *Bremer Freiheit ("Bremen Freedom")* (for TV); 1973—*Welt am Draht (World on a Wire)* (in 2 parts) (co-sc); *Angst essen Seele auf (Fear Eats the Soul)* (+des); *Martha*; *Nora Helmer* (for TV); 1974—*Fontane Effi Briest (Effi Briest)* (+ro as narrator); *Faustrecht der Freiheit (Fox)* (co-sc, +ro as *Franz Biberkopf—'Fox')*; *Wie ein Vogel auf dem Draht ("Like a Bird on a Wire")* (for TV); 1975—*Mutter Küsters Fahrt zum Himmel (Mother Küster's Trip to Heaven)* (co-sc); *Angst vor der Angst (Fear of Fear)*; 1976—*Ich will doch nur, dass Ihr mich liebt (I Only Want You to Love Me)*; *Satansbraten (Satan's Brew)*; *Chinesisches Roulette (Chinese Roulette)* (co-pr); *Schatten der Engel (Shadow of Angels)* (Schmid) (sc only); 1977—*Bolwieser*; *Frauen in New York (Women in New York)* (d only); *Eine Reise ins Licht (Despair)(Despair)* (d only); 1978—episode of *Deutschland im Herbst (Germany in Autumn)* (+ro); *Die Ehe der Maria Braun (The Marriage of Maria Braun)* (d only, +story); (as director, scriptwriter, cinematographer and uncredited producer): *In einem Jahr mit 13 Monden (In a Year with 13 Moons)*; 1979—*Die dritte Generation (The 3rd Generation)*; 1980—*Berlin Alexanderplatz* (for TV, in 13 episodes with epilogue) (+ro as himself in dream sequence); *Lili Marleen*; 1981—*Lola*; *Theater in Trance* (documentary for TV) (d only, +commentary); 1982—*Die Sehnsucht der Veronika Voss (Veronika Voss)*; *Querelle*.

Roles (in films other than his own): 1967—*Mallard* in *Tony Freunde* (Vasil); 1968—*The Pimp* in *Der Bräutigam, die Komödiantin und der Zuhalter (The Bridegroom, the Comedienne and the Pimp)* (Straub); 1969—*the man in uniform* in *Alarm* (Lemmel); *Heini* in *Al Capone im deutschen Wald* (Wirth); *Baal* in *Baal* (Schlöndorff); *the mechanic* in *Frei bis zum nächsten Mal* (Köberle); 1970—*Flecklbauer* in *Matthias Kneissl* (Hauff); a peasant in *Der plötzliche Reichtum der armen Leute von Kombach* (Schlöndorff); the man who looks through window in *Supergirl* (Thome); 1973—*Wittkowski* in *Zärtlichkeit der Wölfe* (Lommel); 1974—as himself in *1 Berlin-Harlem* (Lambert); 1976—*Raoul, the pimp* in *Schatten der Engel* (Schmid); 1978—in *Bourbon Street Blues* (Sirk, Schonherr, and Tilman); 1980—*Lili Marleen* (Weisenborn).

Publications:

By FASSBINDER:

Books and scripts—*Liebe ist kälter als der Tod* in *Film* (London), no.8, 1969; *Antiteater*, Frankfurt a. M. 1973; *Antiteater 2*, Frankfurt a. M. 1974; *Stücke 3*, Munich 1978; articles—interview in *Filmkritik* (Munich), August 1969; "Imitation of Life: Über die Filme von Douglas Sirk" in *Film und Fernsehen* (Berlin), no.2, 1971; "Imitation of Life: On the Films of Douglas Sirk" in *Douglas Sirk*, edited by Mulvey and Halliday, Edinburgh 1972; also in *New Left Review*, May/June 1975; interview in *Ecran* (Paris), December 1974; interview in *Cinéma 74* (Paris), December 1974; interview in *Sight and Sound* (London), winter 1974/75; interview in *Film Comment* (New York), November/December 1975; "Insects in a Glass Case" in *Sight and Sound* (London), autumn 1976; interview in *Cineaste* (New York), autumn 1977; interview in *Cinema* (Paris), no.2, 1978; interview in *Image et son* (Paris), November 1978; record—*Antiteater's Greatest Hits* (Kuckuck label), 1973.

On FASSBINDER:

Books—*Fassbinder* by Wolfgang Limmer, Munich 1973; *I Fassbinders Spejl* by Christian Thomsen, Copenhagen 1975; *Das bisschen Realität, das ich brauche* by Hans Pflaum, Munich 1976; *Reihe Film 2: Rainer Werner Fassbinder*, edited by Peter Jansen and Wolfram Schütte, Munich 1979; articles—"Anti-Cinema, Rainer Werner Fassbinder" by David Wilson in *Sight and Sound* (London), no.2, 1972; special section on Fassbinder and Douglas Sirk in *Film Comment* (New York), November/December 1975; featured in issue on melodrama, *Positif* (Paris), July/August 1976; article by Paul Thomas in *Film Quarterly* (Berkeley), winter 1976/77; article by Serge Daney in *Cahiers du Cinéma* (Paris), April 1977; 'Gay Men and Film' section, *Jump Cut* (Berkeley), no.16, 1977; biofilmography in *Film Dope* (London), September 1978; "Explorations" by J. Hoberman in *American Film* (Washington, D.C.), September 1982; films—*Ende einer Kommune* by Joachim von Mengershausen, West Germany 1970; *Fassbinder produziert: Film Nr.8* by Michael Ballhaus and Dietmar Buchmann, West Germany 1971; *Rainer Werner Fassbinder* by Christian Braad Thomsen, Denmark 1972; *Glashaus-TV Intern* by Martin Wiebel and Ludwig Metzger, West Germany 1973.

*   *   *

Rainer Werner Fassbinder was the leading member of a group of second-generation, alternative filmmakers in West Germany, the first consisting of Alexander Kluge and others who in 1962 drafted the Oberhausen manifesto, initiating what has come to be called the "New German Cinema." Fassbinder's most distinguishing trait within the tradition of "counter-cinema" aside from his reputation for rendering filmically fragments of the new left ideology of the sixties, was his modification of the conventions of political cinema initiated in the twenties, and subsequently tailored to modern conditions of Hollywood cinema to a greater degree than Godard, who is credited with using these principles as content for filmic essays on narrative.

In an interview in 1971 Fassbinder asserted what has come to represent his most convincing justification for his innovative attachment to story: "The American cinema is the only one I can take really seriously, because it's the only one that has really reached an audience. German cinema used to do so, before 1933, and of course there are individual directors in other countries who are in touch with their audiences. But American cinema has generally had the happiest relationship with its audience, and that is because it doesn't try to be 'art.' Its narrative style is not so complicated or artificial. Well, of course it's artificial, but not 'artistic.' "

This concern with narrative and popular expression (some of his productions recall the good story telling habits of Renoir) was evident early in the theatrical beginnings of his career, when he forged an aesthetic that could safely be labeled a creative synthesis of Brecht and Artaud oriented toward the persuasion of larger audiences. This began with a turn to the stage in 1967, having finished his secondary school training in 1964 in Augsburg and Munich. He joined the Action-Theater in Munich, with Hanna Schygulla whom he had meet in acting school. After producing his first original play in 1968, the Action-Theater was closed by the police in May of that year, whereupon he founded the "anti-teater," a venture loosely organized around the tenets of Brechtian theater translated into terms alluring for contemporary audiences. Though the 1969 *Liebe ist kälter als der Tod* marks the effective beginning of his feature film career (*Der Stadtsreicher* and *Das kleine Chaos* constituting minor efforts), he was to maintain an intermittent foothold in the theater all the way until his premature death, working in various productions throughout Germany as well as producing a number of radio plays in the early seventies. The stint with "anti-teater" was followed by the assuming of directorial control, with Kurt Raab and Roland Petri, over the Theater am Turm (TAT) of Frankfurt in 1974, and the founding of Albatross Productions for coproductions in 1975.

When TAT failed, Fassbinder became less involved in the theater, but a trace of his interest always remained in the form of his frequent appearances in his own films. In fact, out of the more than forty feature films produced during his lifetime there have only been a handful or so where Fassbinder has not appeared in one way or another, and he has had a major role in at least ten of them.

Fassbinder's mixing together of Hollywood and avantgarde forms took a variety of turns throughout his brief career. In the films made during the time of the peak of sixties activism in Germany—specifically *Katzelmacher*, *Liebe ist kälter als der Tod*, *Götter der Pest*, and *Warum läuft Herr R. Amok?*—theatrical conventions, principally those derived from his Brechtian training, join forces with a "minimalist" aesthetic and the indigenous energies of the *Heimatfilm* to portray such sensitive issues as the foreign worker problem, contradictions within supposedly revolutionary youth culture, and concerns of national identity. These early "filmed theater" pieces, inevitably conforming to a static, long-take style because of a dearth of funding, tended to resemble parables or fables in their brevity and moral, didactic structuring. As funding from the Government increased proportionate to his success, the popular forms associated with Hollywood became his models. His output from 1970 through the apocalyptic events of October 1977 (the culmination of a series of terrorists actions in Hans-Martin Schleyer's death, etc.) is an exploration of the forms of melodrama and the family romance as a way to place social issues within the frame of sexual politics. *Whity*, *Der Händler der vier Jahreszeiten*, *Die bitteren Tränen der Petra von Kant*, *Martha*, *Faustrecht der Freiheit*, and *Frauen in New York* are perhaps the most prominent examples. A self-reflexive pastiche of the gangster film is evident as well in *Der amerikanische Soldat*. This attention to the mediation of other forms ultimately began to assume the direction of a critique of the "art film": *Warnung vor einer heiligen Nutte*, an update of *8½*; *Satansbraten*, a comment on aesthetics and politics around the figure of Stephen George; and *Chinesisches*

Roulette, a parody concerning an inbred aristocracy.

The concern with the continuation of fascism into the present day receives some attention in this period (specifically in *Wildweschsel*, *Despair* and *Bolwieser*), but it becomes the dominant structuring motivation in the final period, 1977-82. Here there is a kind of epic recombination of all earlier innovations in service to the understanding of fascism and its implications for the immediate postwar generation. Fassbinder's segment in *Deutschland im Herbst* (a collective endeavor of many German intellectuals and filmmakers) inaugurates this period. It and *Die Ehe der Maria Braun*, *Lili Marleen*, *Lola*, and *Die Sehnsucht der Veronika Voss* may been seen as a portrayal of the consolidation of German society to conform to the "American Model" of social and economic development. *In einem Jahr mit 13 Monden*, *Berlin Alexanderplatz*, and *Querelle* are depictions of the crisis in sexual identity, and the criminal and counter-cultural worlds associated with that process in relation to "capitalism in crisis." *Die dritte Generation* is a kind of cynical summation of the German new left in the wake of a decade of terrorist activities. This final phase, perhaps Fassbinder's most brilliant cinematically, will be the one given the most critical attention in future years. It is the one which evinces the greatest awareness of the intellectual spaces traversed in Germany since the years of fascism (and especially since the mid-sixties), and the one as well which reveals the most effective assimilation of the heritage of forms associated with art and political cinema.

—John O'Kane

FEJÖS, PÁL. Hungarian. Born Pal Fejös in Budapest, 24 January 1897; became citizen of the United States in 1930. Educated at school at Veszprem, and at Kecskemet; studied medicine. Career: 1914-18—serves on Italian front, organizes plays for soldiers; after Armistice begins to design sets for opera, then Orient-Film studios; 1919 (1920 according to some sources)—begins to direct for Studio Mobil; 1920-22—directs series of light films; economic situation of Hungarian film industry worsens; 1922—stages Passion play at village in northeast Hungary; early 1923—travels across Austria and France, said to have worked briefly with Reinhardt and Fritz Lang; 1923—leaves for U.S. in October; 1924—works in piano factory, is hired as medical research assistant at Rockefeller Institute; 1926—resigns, buys Buick for 45 dollars and sets out for Hollywood; meets young producer Edward Spitz who finances 1st U.S. film; 1928—Chaplin's interest in *The Last Moment* leads to contract with Universal; 1929—with cameraman Hal Mohr, designs crane allowing great camera mobility; 1930—while directing *Captain of the Guard*, suffers fall and is hospitalized (film completed and credited to John Stuart Robinson); quits Universal, signs with MGM; directs French and German versions of *Big House* (Hill); 1931—invited to Paris by Pierre Braunberger, quits Hollywood; 1932—returns to Hungary to direct for Films Osso; MGM demands return to Hollywood, Fejos refuses, violating contract; 1933—in Vienna makes *Sonnenstrahl*; 1934-35—in Denmark makes 3 films; under contract to Nordisk Films which proposes journey to Madagascar (1935-36); 1937—for Svensk Filmindustri travels to Indonesia and New Guinea; 1937-38—in East Indies and Thailand makes several films and collects artifacts for Danish and Swedish museums; 1938—is relieved of responsibility for *A Handful of Rice* after production problems; returning from Thailand, meets industrialist Wenner-Gren who finances Peru documentary; 1941—returns to New York, becomes director of Viking Fund and later of Wenner-Gren Foundation for Anthropological Research; ceases filmmaking activity. Died in New York, 23 April 1963.

Films (as director in Hungary): 1920—*Pan*; *Lidércnyomás (Nightmare, Hallucination, Lord Arthur Saville's Crime)* (+co-sc); *Ujraélök (Reincarnation)*; *Jóslat (Prophecy)*; 1921—*Fekete Kapitany (The Black Captain)*; *Arsén Lupin utolsó kalandja (The Last Adventure of Arsène Lupin)*; 1922—*Szenzáció (Sensation)*; 1923—*Egri csillagok (The Stars of Eger)* (+sc—incomplete); *Land of the Lawless* (Buckingham) (adapt only); (in U.S.): 1928—*The Last Moment (Le Dernier Moment)* (+sc, ed); *Lonesome (Solitude)*; 1929—*Broadway*; *The Last Performance (Last Performance)* (working title: "Erik the Great"); 1930—*Captain of the Guard (Marseillaise)* (co-d, uncredited); *Menschen hinter Gittern* and *Big House* (German and French versions of George Hill's *The Big House*); (in France): 1931—*L'Amour a l'américaine* (supervision only); *Fantômas* (+co-sc); (in Hungary): 1932—*Tavaszi zápor (Marie, legende hongroise, Une Histoire d'amour)* (+co-sc); *Ítél a Balaton (Storm at Balaton)*; (in Austria): 1933—*Sonnenstrahl (Gardez le sourire)* (+co-pr, co-sc); *Frühlingsstimmen (Les Voix du printemps)*; (in Denmark): 1934—*Flugten fra millionerne (Flight from the Millions, Les Millions en fuite)* (+sc); 1935—*Fange nr.1 (Prisoner No.1)* (+co-sc); *Det gyldne Smil (The Golden Smile, Le Sourire d'or)* (+sc); (in Madagascar): 1935-36—*Svarta Horisonter (Horizons noirs)* series: 1. Danstävlingen i Esira (Dance Contest in Esira); 2. Skönhetsvård i djungeln (Beauty Care in the Jungle); 3. Världens mest Användbara Träd (The Most Useful Tree in the World); 4. Djungeldansen (Jungle Dance); 5. Havets Djävul (The Sea Devil); 6. Våra Faders Gravar (Tombs of Our Ancestors); (in Indonesia and New Guinea): 1937-38—*Stammen Lever an (The Tribe Lives On)*; *Bambuåldern på Mentawei (The Age of Bamboo at Mentawei)*; *Hövdingens Son är död (The Chief's Son Is Dead)*; *Draken på Komodo (The Dragon of Komodo)*; *Byn vid den Trivsamma Brunnen (The Village Near the Pleasant Fountain)*; *Tambora*; *Att Segla är Nödvändigt (To Sail Is Necessary)* (completed by Åke Leijonhufvud); (in Thailand): 1938—*En Handfull Ris (A Handful of Rice, Une Poignee de riz)* or *Man och Kvinna (Homme et femme)* (co-d); (in Peru): 1940-41—*Yagua* ("directed" by Yagua tribe shaman with Fejos controlling camera).

Publications:

On FEJÖS:

Book—*The Several Lives of Paul Fejos* by John Dodds, New York 1973; articles—"La Carrière de Paul Fejos by Jean-Vincent Bréchignac in *Pour vous* (Paris), 31 January 1929; "Paris—Pourquoi Paul Fejos vient travailler en France" by Jean-Vincent Bréchignac in *Pour vous* (Paris), 10 September 1931; "Fantômas reparait" by Claude Doré in *Ciné-Miroir* (Paris), 22 January 1932; "Paul Fejos" by Catherine Wunscher in *Films in Review* (New York), March 1954; "Fejos's Broadway", letter, by R. Kraft in *Films in Review* (New York), April 1954; "Paul Fejos—Had He Directed *All Quiet on the Western Front*, He Might Still Be Making Films" by Catherine Wundscher in *Films in Review* (New York), March 1954; "Fejös Pal es a Tavaszi Zapor" by Istvan Molnar in *Filmkultura* (Budapest), October 1960; "Paul Fejos (1897-1963)" by David Bidney in *The American Anthropologist* (New York), February 1964; "Fejös Pal—A Tavolbalato" by Lajos Balint in *Filmvilag* (Budapest), 15 July 1966; "Paul Fejos 1897-1963" by Philippe Haudiquet in *Anthologie du cinéma* vol.4, Paris 1968; "A film vilagtörténetéböl: 10 arckép—10 élet regénye: Akit elfelejtettek: Fejös Pal" by Robert Ban in *Film, Szinhaz, Muzsika* (Budapest), 17 August 1968; "A filmstudiotol az egyetemi katedraig—Fejös Pal élet-müve a Pécsi filmszemien" by Istvan Molnar in *Film, Szinhaz, Muszika* (Budapest), no.42, n.d.; "Fejos" by G. Petrie in *Sight and Sound* (London), summer 1978; biofilmography in *Film Dope* (London), September 1978; "Paul Fejos in America" by G. Petrie in *Film Quarterly* (Berkeley), no.2, 1979; issue devoted to Fejos of *Filmkritik* (Munich), August 1979; "Fejos—den fremmede fugl" by P. Schepelern in *Kosmorama* (Copenhagen), May 1980.

*   *   *

Few directors can have had such a curious and diverse career as that of Paul Fejos, who was equally at home behind a camera directing entertainment features and documentaries or on anthropoligical expeditions to South America and the Far East.

After an early career in his native Hungary which embraced medicine, painting and play production, Paul Fejos became a film director in the late teens. A trip to Paris persuaded him that he wanted to direct in the West, specifically the United States. In 1921 he arrived in the New World and started to work at the Rockefeller Institute. Eventually Fejos came to Hollywood—penniless—and made his first American film, *The Last Moment*, for $5,000, borrowed from Edward Spitz. An experimental drama in which a drowning man (Otto Matiesen) relives his life, *The Last Moment* was hailed by the Hollywood intelligentsia and landed Fejos a contract at Universal. The film also indicated that Fejos was to be no ordinary Hollywood-style producer. He was going to use every technical trick the cinema offered to put over his films be they melodramas about magicians (*The Last Performance*) or screen adaptations of popular Broadway productions (*Broadway*).

Paul Fejos's one genuine screen masterpiece (and the only one of his films which is readily available for appraisal today) is *Lonesome*, which uses cinéma vérité to provide a study of two lonely New Yorkers who spend a Saturday afternoon and evening at Coney Island. Not only are the visuals in *Lonesome* stunningly exciting, but the director manages to obtain realistic performances from his two stars, Barbara Kent and Glenn Tryon, neither of whom had previously shown much sign of histrionic greatness.

The director's Hollywood career ended as suddenly as it had begun. There were arguments over the direction of *All Quiet on the Western Front* (a project which he cherished) being assigned to Lewis Milestone, and Fejos returned to Hungary, where he directed *Marie*, generally considered the best pre-war production from that country. He also directed films in Austria and Denmark, and then embarked on a documentary filmmaking trip to the Far East, China and Japan, where he made *Black Horizons* and *A Handful of Rice*, among others. In 1941, he joined the Wenner-Gren Foundation in New York and spent the rest of his life directing anthropological research.

—Anthony Slide

FELLINI, FEDERICO; Italian. Born in Rimini, Italy, 20 January 1920. Educated at primary level by nuns of San Vicenzo, Rimini, and at boarding school run by Carissimi Fathers at Fano; secondary school at Rimini until 1938. Married Giulietta

Masina in Rome, 30 October 1943; child: "Federichino" (died when 3 weeks old). Career: 1938—takes job in Florence with *420,* a humor magazine, and *Avventuroso,* a comic strip magazine; 1939—moves to Rome, works as caricature artist, submits cartoons and stories to *Marc'Aurelio,* satirical magazine; meets comic and actor Aldo Fabrizi who assists him in getting screenwriting jobs, 1941-43; 1939-40—writes sketches for radio and gags for movies; 1943—meets actress Giulietta Masina; 1944—meets Roberto Rossellini, becomes involved in film project *Rome, Open City*; 1946-52—screenwriter or assistant director for Rossellini, Alberto Lattuada and Pietro Germi; 1950—with Alberto Lattuada forms production company Capitolium for *Variety Lights*; 1961—with Angelo Rizzoli forms Federiz production company; goes bankrupt without producing any films, taken over by Clemente Fracazzi and subsequently involved in production of several Fellini films; 1967—backing withdrawn for project *Il viaggio di G. Mastorna* (*A Director's Notebook* subsequently shot among the abandoned sets for *Mastorna*); 1967—hospitalized with serious illness, reorganizes production team following recovery. Address: lives at Fregene, near Rome.

Films (as gagman for Mario Mattòli): 1939—*Lo vedi come soi...lo vedi come sei?!* (Mattòli); 1940—*Non me lo dire!* (Mattòli); *Il pirata sono io!* (Mattòli); (as author of or collaborator on screenplay): 1941—*Documento Z3* (Guarini) (uncredited); 1942—*Avanti, c'è posto* (Bonnard) (uncredited); *Chi l'ha vistro?* (Alessandrini); *Quarta pagina* (Manzari and Gambino); 1943—*Apparizione* (de Limur) (uncredited); *Campo dei fiori* (Bonnard); *Tutta la città canta* (Freda); *L'ultima carrozzella* (Mattòli); (as assistant director and screenwriter): 1945—*Roma, città aperta* (Rossellini) (co-sc); 1946—*Paisà* (Rossellini) (co-sc); 1947—*Il delitto di Giovanni Episcopo* (Lattuada) (co-sc only); *Il passatore* (Coletti) (co-sc only); *La fumeria d'oppio (Ritorna Za-la-mort)* (Matarazzo) (co-sc only); *L'ebreo errante* (Alessandrini) (co-sc only); 1948—"Il miracolo" episode of *L'amore* (Rossellini) (co-sc, +role as stranger mistaken for St. Joseph); *Il mulino del Po* (Lattuada) (co-sc only); *In nome della legge* (Germi) (co-sc only); *Senza pietà* (Lattuada) (co-sc only); *La città dolente* (Bonnard) (co-sc only); 1949—*Francesco, giullare di Dio* (Rossellini) (co-sc); 1950—*Il cammino della speranza* (Germi) (co-sc only); (as director and collaborator on or author of screenplay): *Luci del varietà* (co-d, +co-pr); *Persiane chiuse* (Comencini) (co-sc only); 1951—*La città si difende* (Germi) (co-sc only); *Cameriera bella presenza offresi* (Pastina) (co-sc only); *Lo Sceicco Bianco*; 1952—*Il brigante di Tacca del Lupo* (Germi) (co-sc only); *Europa '51* (Rossellini) (co-sc only, uncredited); 1953—*I Vitelloni*; "Un'agenzia matrimoniale" in *Amore in città* (Zavattini); 1954—*La strada*; 1955—*Il bidone*; 1956—*Le notti di Cabiria (Nights of Cabiria)*; 1958—*Fortunella* (De Filippo) (co-sc only); 1960—*La dolce vita*; 1962—"Le tentazioni del dottor Antonio" in *Boccaccio '70* (Zavattini); 1963—*Otto e mezzo (8 1/2)*; 1965—*Giulietta degli spiriti (Juliet of the Spirits)*; 1968—"Toby Dammit (Il ne faut jamais parier sa tête contre le diable" in *Histoires extraordinaires / Tre passi nel delirio* (anthology film); 1969—*Block-notes di un regista (Fellini: A Director's Notebook)* (for TV) (+narration, appearance); *Satyricon (Fellini Satyricon)*; 1970—*I clowns (The Clowns)*; 1972—*Roma (Fellini Roma)* (+ro); 1974—*Amarcord*; 1976—*Casanova (Il Casanova di Federico Fellini)*; 1978—*Prova d'orchestra (Orchestra Rehearsal)* (for TV); 1980—*La città delle donne (City of Women)*; 1983—*E la nave va (And the Ship Sailed On)*.

Roles: 1970—as himself in *Alex in Wonderland* (Mazursky); 1974—guest appearance in *C'eravamo tanto amati* (Scola).

Publications:

By FELLINI:

Books and filmscripts—*Moraldo in città*, with Ennio Flaiano and Tullio Pinelli, in *Cinema* (Rome), August through December 1954; *La strada* in *Bianco e nero* (Rome), September/October 1954; *Il Bidone*, with Ennio Flaiano and Tullio Pinelli, Paris 1956; *Le notti di Cabiria di Federico Fellini*, edited by Lino del Fra, Rocca San Casciano, Italy 1957; *La Dolce Vita*, edited by Giuseppe Lo Duca, Paris 1960; *La dolce vita di Federico Fellini*, edited by Tullio Kezich, Bologna 1960; *La Douceur de vivre*, edited by Giuseppe Lo Duca, Paris 1960; *La Dolce Vita*, translated by Oscar DeLiso and Bernard Shir-Cliff, New York 1961; *Entretiens avec Federico Fellini*, edited by Jacques Delcorde, Belgium 1962; *Boccaccio '70 di De Sica, Fellini, Monicelli, Visconti*, edited by Carlo di Carlo and Gaio Fratini, Rocca San Casciano, Italy 1962; *8 1/2 de Fellini*, Paris 1963; *8 1/2 di Federico Fellini*, edited by Camilla Cederna, Rocca San Casciano, Italy 1963; *Juliet of the Spirits*, edited by Tullio Kezich, New York 1965; *Giulietta degli spiriti*, edited by Tullio Kezich, Rocca San Casciano, Italy 1965; *La mia Rimini*, Bologna 1967; *Tre passi nel delirio*, with Louis Malle and Roger Vadim, Bologna 1968; *Fellini Satyricon di Federico Fellini*, edited by Dario Zanelli, Bologna 1969; *Il primo Fellini: Lo sceicco blanco, I vitelloni, La strada, Il bidone*, edited by Renzo Renzi, Bologna 1969; *Federico Fellini. Discussion* no.1, Beverly Hills 1970; *I clowns*, edited by Renzo Renzi, Bologna 1970; *Fellini's Satyricon*, edited by Dario Zanelli, New York 1970; *3 Screenplays*, translated by Judith Green, New York 1970; *Early Screenplays: Variety Lights, The White Sheik*, translated by Judith Green, New York 1971; *Roma* in *Avant-Scène du cinéma* (Paris), October 1972; *Roma*, Paris 1972; *Roma di Federico Fellini*, Rocca San Casciano, Italy 1972; *Amarcord*, with T. Guerra, Milan 1973; *Federcord: disegni per Amarcord di Federico Fellini*, edited by L. Betti and O. Del Buono, Milan 1974; *Il film Amarcord di Federico Fellini*, Bologna 1974; *4 film: I vitelloni, La dolce vita, 8 1/2, Giulietta degli spiriti*, Turin 1974; *Il Casanova di Fellini: sceneggiatura originale*, with Bernardino Zapponi, Turin 1974; *Amarcord: Portrait of a Town*, with Tonino Guerra, London 1974; *Fellini on Fellini*, edited by Christian Strich, New York 1976; *Fellinis Zeichnungen*, edited by Christian Strich, Zurich 1976; *Il Casanova di Federico Fellini*, with Bernardino Zapponi, Bologna 1977; *Fare un film*, Turin 1980; *Casanova. Federico Fellini's Film- und Frauenheld...*, edited by A.A. De Saint-Gall, Zurich 1981; *Bottega Fellini. La città delle donne*, with text by Raffaele Monti, Rome 1981; articles—"I vitelloni", with Ennio Flaiano and Tullio Pinelli in *Cinema* (Rome), December 1952; "Strada sabarrata: via libera ai vitelloni" in *Cinema nuovo* (Turin), 1 January 1953; "In tre si chiacchiera" in *Cinema nuovo* (Turin), 15 July 1954; "Ogni margine è bruciato" in *Cinema* (Rome), 10 August 1954; "Enquête sur Hollywood" in *Cahiers du cinéma* (Paris), Christmas 1955; "An Interview with Federico Fellini" by George Bluestone in *Film Culture* (New York), October 1957; "A Personal Statement" in *Film* (London), January/February 1957; "Prefazione" in *Cinemà e realtà* by Brunello Rondi, Rome 1957; "Les Femmes libres de Magliano" in *Cahiers du cinéma* (Paris), February 1957; "*Les Nuits de Cabiria:* extraits du dernier film de Fellini" in *Cahiers du cinéma* (Paris), February 1957; "Fellini parla del suo mestiere di regista" in *Bianco e nero* (Rome), May 1958; "Mon métier" in *Cahiers du cinéma* (Paris), June 1958; "Crisi e neorealismo" in *Bianco e nero* (Rome), July 1958; "My Experiences as a Director" in *International Film Annual*, New York 1959; "Federico Fellini: An Interview" by Gideon Bachmann in *Film: Book I*, edited by Robert Hughes, New York 1959; "My Sweet Life" in *Films and Filming* (London), April 1959; "Témoignage à André Bazin" in *Cahiers du cinéma* (Paris), January 1959; "Su *La dolce vita* la parola a Fellini" in *Bianco e nero* (Rome), January/February 1960; "The Bitter Life—of Money" in *Films and Filming* (London), January 1961; "Federico Fellini: An Interview" by Enzo Peri in *Film Quarterly* (Berkeley), fall 1961; "Federico Fellini: A Self-Portrait" in *Esquire* (New York), February 1962; "The Screen Answers Back" in *Films and Filming* (London), May 1962; "End of the Sweet Parade" in *Esquire* (New York), January 1963; "Confessione in pubblico: colloquio con Federico Fellini" in *Bianco e nero* (Rome), April 1963; "Interview with Federico Fellini" by Gideon Bachmann in *Sight and Sound* (London), spring 1964; "Federico Fellini vous parle" in *Cinéma 65* (Paris), September/October 1965; "Fellini et les fumetti", interview by Michael Caen and Francis Lacassin in *Cahiers du cinéma* (Paris), November 1965; "The Long Interview" by Tullio Kezich in *Juliet of the Spirits*, New York 1965; "Playboy Interview: Federico Fellini" in *Playboy* (Chicago), February 1966; "'I Was Born for the Cinema': A Conversation with Federico Fellini" by Irving Levine in *Film Comment* (New York), fall 1966; interview in *Interviews with Film Directors*, edited by Andrew Sarris, Indianapolis 1967; "Anouk Aimée: A Face of the Hour" in *Vogue* (New York), 1 October 1967; "Interview with Fellini" by Pierre Kast in *Interviews with Film Directors*, Indianapolis 1967; "Federico Fellini: Famous Italian Film Director", interview by Oriana Fallaci in *The Egotists: 16 Surprising Interviews*, Chicago 1968; "An Interview with Fellini" in *Cinema* (Beverly Hills), fall 1969; "Fellini che va, Fellini che viene", interview by Renzo Renzi in *Il primo Fellini*, Bologna 1969; "L'Autre Nuit au Colisée" in *Cinema 70* (Paris), January 1970; "Fellini's Formula" in *Esquire* (New York, August 1970); "*Satyricon*: Pictorial Essay" in *Playboy* (Chicago), May 1970; "Un viaggio nell'ombra" in *I clowns*, edited by Renzo Rienzi, Bologna 1970; "Preface" in *Fellini's Satyricon*, edited by Dario Zanelli, New York 1970; "Now! In the Center Ring!! Fellini!!!", interview by Alfred Friendly, Jr., in *The New York Times*, 19 July 1970; "Fellini on Satyricon: Agony, Indulgence, Enigma, Dream—A Talk with Moravia" by Alberto Moravia in *Vogue* (New York), 1 March 1970; "Entretien avec Federico Fellini" by Roger Borderie and others in *Cahiers du cinéma* (Paris), May/June 1971; "Come non detto" in *Fellini TV. Block-notes di un regista. I clowns*, Bologna 1972; "*Fellini Roma*: texte écrit par Federico Fellini durant la préparation du film" in *Cinéma 72* (Paris), July 1972; interview in *Encountering Directors* by Charles Samuels, New York 1972; "As Fellini Sees Rome: A City of Desolation, Fossilized Ruins, and Children" in *The New York Times*, 3 June 1973; "My *Dolce Vita*", with José Luis de Vilallonga in *Oui* (New York), March 1973; "Federico Fellini: Chacun de mes films se rapporte a une saison de ma vie" in *Écran 73* (Paris), September/October 1973; "Fellini", interview by Alberto Arbasino in *Vogue* (New York), October 1974; "Entretien avec Federico Fellini" by Valerio Riva in *Positif* (Paris), 1 April 1974; "Il fascismo dentro di noi", interview by Valerio Riva in *Il film Amarcord di Federico Fellini*, Bologna 1974; "Entretien avec Federico Fellini" by Aldo Tassone in *Positif* (Paris), May 1976; "Conversation with Federico Fellini" by Melton Davis in *Oui* (New York), January 1977; "Fellini dixit" by A. Tassone in *Cinéma* (Paris), February 1977; "8 Entretiens autour du Casanova de Fellini" by O. Volta in *Positif* (Paris), March 1977; "Lettre à Alberto Grimaldi sur un projet de film et dessins" in *Positif* (Paris), December/January 1977/78; "C'était comme si on m'avait dit que je serais devenu amiral", interview by J.A. Gili in *Positif* (Paris), July/August 1981.

On FELLINI:

Books—*La Strada*, edited by François-Régis Bastide, Juliette

Caputo and Chris Marker, Paris 1955; *Les Chemins de Fellini, suivi du Journal d'un bidoniste par Dominique Delouche* by Geneviève Agel, Paris 1956; *Il cinema neorealistico italiano* by Giulio Castello, Milan 1956; *Federico Fellini* by Renzo Renzi, Parma 1956; *Federico Fellini* by Renzo Renzi, Lyons 1960; *Storia di Federico Fellini* by Angelo Solmi, Milan 1962; *Federico Fellini* by Gilbert Salachas, Paris 1963; *Il cinema di Fellini* by Brunello Rondi, Rome 1965; *Fellini* by Suzanne Budgen, London 1966; *Fellini* by Angelo Solmi, New York 1967; *Federico Fellini: An Investigation into his Films and Philosophy* by Gilbert Salachas, New York 1969; *Fellini TV: I clowns*, edited by Mario Novi, Rome 1970; *On the Set of Fellini Satyricon: A Behind-the-Scenes Diary* by Eileen Hughes, New York 1971; *The Italian Cinema* by Pierre Leprohon, New York 1972; *Roma di Federico Fellini* edited by Bernardino Zapponi, Rocca San Casciano, Italy 1972; *Il film Amarcord di Federico Fellini*, Bologna 1974; *Federico Fellini* by Franco Pecori, Florence 1974; *Casanova, rendezvous con Federico Fellini* by Liliana Betti and Gianfranco Angelucci, Milan 1975; *Fellini* by Liliana Betti, Zurich 1976; *Federico Fellini: The Search for a New Mythology* by Charles Ketcham, New York 1976; *Fellini the Artist* by Edward Murray, New York 1976; *The Cinema of Federico Fellini* by Stuart Rosenthal, London 1976; *Fellini's Filme*, edited by Christian Strich, Zurich 1976; articles—"Una diversità complementare" by Tullio Pinelli in *Cinema* (Rome), 10 August 1954; "Le Cas Fellini" by Cecilia Mangini in *Cinéma 55* (Paris), January 1955; "I problemi dell' indecisione" by Renzo Renzi and "La mia posizione di fronte a Fellini" by Georges Sadoul in *Cinema nuovo* (Turin), 25 November 1955; "Fellini e la critica", edited by Leonardo Autera in *Bianco e nero* (Rome), June 1957; "A proposito di Fellini" by Lino del Fra in *Bianco e nero* (Rome), June 1957; "Regards sur l'oeuvre de Federico Fellini" by Raymond Lefèvre in *Image et son* (Paris), February 1958; "Federico Fellini: l'arracheur de masques" in *Le Nèo-Réalisme italien* by Patrice Hovald, Paris 1959; "Itinéraire de Fellini: du spectacle au spectaculaire" by Barthélemy Amengual in *Etudes cinématographiques* (Paris), winter 1963; "Gli antenati di Federico Fellini" by Renzo Renzi in *Cinema nuovo* (Turin), May/June 1964; "Federico Fellini" in *Cinema Eye, Cinema Ear* by John Taylor, New York 1964; "Profiles: 10 1/2" by Lillian Ross in the *New Yorker*, 30 October 1965; "Federico Fellini: Wizard of Film" by Eugene Walter in *Atlantic* (Greenwich, Connecticut), December 1965; "Masina contre Fellini" by Claude Gauteur in *Image et son* (Paris), April 1966; "The Secret Life of Federico Fellini" by Peter Harcourt in *Film Quarterly* (Berkeley), spring 1966; "Federico Fellini" in *Tower of Babel* by Eric Rhode, Philadelphia 1966; "The Wizardry of Fellini" by Eugene Walter in *Films and Filming* (London), June 1966; "Fellini's Back and Mae West's Got Him" by Mark Shivas in *The New York Times*, 13 October 1968; "Fellini at Work" by Hollis Alpert in the *Saturday Review* (New York), 12 July 1969; "Notes on Double Structure and the Films of Fellini" by Patrick Eason in *Cinema* (London), March 1969; "Federico Fellini" by David Herman in *American Imago*, fall 1969; "Fellini Finds 'An Unknown Planet for Me to Populate'" by Tom Burke in *The New York Times*, 8 February 1970; "The Purpose of the Grotesque in Fellini's Films" by Harvey Cox, Jr. in *Celluloid and Symbols*, edited by Cooper and Skrade, Philadelphia 1970; "Federico Fellini" by Eugene Walter in *Behind the Scenes: Theater and Film Interviews from the Transatlantic Review*, New York 1971; "Dilatazione visionaria del documento e nostalgia della madre chiesa in Fellini" in *Cinema dell'ambiguità: Rossellini, De Sica e Zavattini, Fellini* by Pio Baldelli, Rome 1971; issue devoted to Fellini of *L'Arc* (Aix-en-Provence, France), no.45, 1971; "Federico Fellini" in *Dibattiti de film* by Antonio Covi, Padua 1971; "Psychanalyse de Fellini" by

Jacques Julia in *Cinéma 71* (Paris), May 1971; "Un Artiste sous le chapiteau: perplexe" by Marcel Martin in *Cinéma 71* (Paris), May 1971; "La (Tres) Pudique Agonie de Federico Fellini" by Mireille Amiel in *Cinéma 74* (Paris), September/October 1974; "Autobiografia di uno spettatore" by Italo Calvino in *Quattro film* (by Federico Fellini), Turin 1974; "Vita (presunta, provvisoria, precaria) con Federico Fellini" by Oreste del Buono in *Federcord: disegni per Amarcord di Federico Fellini*, Milan 1974; "The Secret Life of Federico Fellini" and "Conclusion" in *6 European Directors* by Peter Harcourt, Harmondsworth, England 1974; "Autobiographie d'un spectateur" by Italo Calvino in *Positif* (Paris), May 1976; "Fellini's *Casanova*: The Final Nights" by Antonio Chemasi in *American Film* (Washington, D.C.), September 1976; "More Films About Filmmakers" by J.M. Welsh in *Literature/Film Quarterly* (Salisbury, Md.), fall 1976; "Le Voyageur immobile" by L. Audibert in *Cinématographe* (Paris), April 1977; biofilmography in *Film Dope* (London), September 1978; "Meeting Fellini" by M. Sarne in *Films and Filming* (London), April 1978; "Reason and Unreason in Federico Fellini's 'I vitelloni'" by F.M. Burke in *Literature/Film Quarterly* (Salisbury, Md.), v.8, no.2, 1980; "Federico Fellini, écrivain au *Marc' Aurelio*" by F. Pieri in *Positif* (Paris), July/August 1981; "Ein unermüdlicher Sucher" by M. Winter in *Filmfaust* (Frankfurt), February/March 1981; films—*Fellini*, for TV, by Peter Goldbarb, Canada 1968; *Ciao, Federico!* by Gideon Bachmann, U.S. 1970.

* * *

Federico Fellini is, perhaps, one of the most controversial figures in the recent history of Italian cinema. Though his successes have been spectacular as in the cases of *La strada*, *La dolce vita* and *Otto e mezzo*, his failures have been equally flamboyant. This has caused considerable doubt in some quarters as to the validity of his ranking as a major force in contemporary cinema and has made it somewhat difficult for him to acheive sufficient financial backing in recent years to support his highly personalized film efforts. Certainly, few directors in any country can equal Fellini in his interest in the history of the cinema or share his moral certainly as to the appropriate place within its progression of films for the body of his work. Consequently, he has molded each of his film projects in such a way that any discussion of their individual merits is inseparable from the autobiographical details of his personal legend.

His first film, *La sceicco bianco* gave a clear indication of autobiographical nature of the works to follow by drawing upon his experience as a journalist and merging it with many of the conceits he had developed in his early motion picture career as a gag writer and script writer. However, he also had been an instrumental part of the development of the neorealistic film in the 1940s, writing parts of the screenplays of Roberto Rossellini's *Roma città aperta* and *Paisà*, and his reshaping of that tradition toward an autobiographical mode of expression in his first film troubled a number of his former collaborators. But, on his part, Fellini was seemingly just as critical of the brand of neorealism practiced by Rossellini with its penchant for overt melodrama.

In a succeeding film, *La strada*, he took his autobiographical parallels a step farther, even casting his wife, Giulietta Masina in the major female role. This highly symbolic work was variously interpreted as a manifesto on human rights or, at least, a treatise on women's liberation. In these contexts, however, it roused the ire of strict neorealists who regarded it as containing too much justification for political oppression. Yet, as a highly metaphorical personal parable about the relationship between a man and a woman it was a critical success and a confirmation of the validity of Fellini's autobiographical instincts. This gave him the confidence to indulge in a subtle criticism of the neorealistic style in his next film. *Il bidone* which became, in effect, a tongue-in-cheek criticism of the form's sentimental aspects.

In the films of his middle period, beginning in 1959 with *La dolce vita*, Fellini became increasingly preoccupied with his role as an international "auteur" and as a result, the autobiographical manifestations in his films became more introspective and extended to less tangible areas of his psyche than anything that he had previously brought to the screen. While *La dolce vita* is a relatively straightfoward psychological extension of what might have become of Moraldo, the director's earlier biographical persona (*I vitelloni*) after forsaking his village for the decadence of Rome, its successors increasingly explored the areas of its creator's fears, nightmares and fantasies.

After establishing actor Marcello Mastroianni as his alter ego in *La dolce donne*, Fellini again employed him in his masterpiece, *Otto e mezzo (8½)* as a vehicle for his analysis of the complex nature of artistic inspiration. Then, in a sequel of sorts, he examined the other side of the coin. In *Giulietta degli spiriti (Juliet of the Spirits)*, he casts his wife as the intaglio of the Guido figure in *8½*. Both films, therefore, explored the same problems from different sexual perspectives while, on the deeper, ever-present, autobiographical plane, the two characters became corresponding sides of Fellini's mythic ego.

Subsequent films have continued the rich, flamboyant imagery that has become a Fellini trademark, but with the exception of the imaginative fantasy *Fellini Satyricon*, they have, for the most part, returned to the vantage point of direct experience that characterized his earlier works. Finally, in 1980, with *La città delle donne*, again featuring Mastroianni, he returned to the larger than life examination of his psyche. In fact, a number of critics regarded it as the ultimate statement in an ideological trilogy, begun with *8½* and continued in *Juliet of the Spirits*, in which he finally attempts a rapprochement with his inner sexual and creative conflicts. Unfortunately, however, *City of Women* is too highly derivative of the earlier work and, consequently, does not resolve the issues raised in the earlier two films.

Perhaps, then, it is his future films that will ultimately establish the director's place in the pantheon of filmmakers. Certainly, several of his films are masterpieces by anyone's standards and yet in no other director's body of films does each work identifiably relate a specific image of himself that its creator wishes to present to the world and to posterity. Whether any of the films are truly autobiographical in any traditional sense is open to debate. They definitely do not interlock to provide a history of a man and yet each is a deliberately crafted building block in the construction of a larger than life Fellini legend which may eventually come to be regarded as the "journey of a psyche."

—Stephen L. Hanson

FERNÁNDEZ, EMILIO (nicknamed "El Indio"). Mexican. Born in Del Hondo, Coahuila, 1904. Married actress Columba Dominguez. Career: 1923—takes part in Mexican Revolution on side of Adolfo de la Huerta; attains rank of lieutenant colonel; captured, sentenced to 20 years imprisonment; escapes to U.S. 1923-33—in California, does manual labor, plays bit and supporting roles in Hollywood films; 1934—returns to Mexico following 1933 declaration of amnesty; begins acting in Mexican films, given lead in *Janitzio*; 1941—begins directing; 1958—returns to acting, directs intermittently; 1976—kills farm laborer, allegedly in self-defense, while scouting location in northern

Mexico; serves 6 months of 4½ year manslaughter sentence. Recipient: Best Film, Cannes Festival, for *María Candelaria*, 1946.

Films (as director and co-scriptwriter): 1941—*La isla de la pasión (Passion Island)*; 1942—*Soy puro mexicano*; 1943—*Flor silvestre* (+ro); *María Candelaria*; 1944—*Las abandonadas*; *Bugambilia*; 1945—*Pepita Jiménez*; *La perla (The Pearl)*; 1946—*Enamorada*; 1947—*Río Escondido (Hidden River)*; 1948—*Maclovia*; *Salón México*; *Pueblerina*; 1949—*La malquerida*; *Duelo en las montañas*; *Del odio nació el amor (The Torch, Beloved)*; 1950—*Un dia de vida*; *Víctimas del pecado*; *Islas Marías*; *Siempre tuya*; 1951—*La bien amada*; *Acapulco*; *El mar y tú*; 1952—*Cuando levanta la niebla*; 1953—*La red (The Net)*; *Reportaje*; *El rapto*; *La rosa blanca*; 1954—*La rebelión de los colgados*; *Nostros dos*; 1955—*La Tierra de Fuego se apaga*; 1956—*Una cita de amor*; *La pasionaria*; 1961—*Pueblito*; 1963—*Paloma herida*; 1964—*The Night of the Iguana* (Huston) (assoc. d only); 1967—*Un dorado de Pancho Villa (A Loyal Soldier of Pancho Villa)*; 1968—*El crepúscolo de un Dios*; 1973—*La Choca*; 1975—*Zona roja*.

Roles: (partial list): 1934—*Corazón bandolero* (Chacal); *Toparca*, bandolero, in *Cruz diablo*; *Tribu*; *Zirahuén* in *Janitzio*; 1935—*María Elena*; 1936—*El Indio* in *Mariguana, El monstruo verde*; *bailarín* in *Allá en el rancho grande*; 1937—*Nicanor* in *Adíos Nicanor*; *Las cuatro milpas*; 1939—*Con los dorados de Villa*; 1943—*Rogelio Torres* in *Flor silvestre*; 1958—*La cucaracha*; 1964—*La recta final*; 1965—*The Reward* (Bourguignon); 1966—*The Appaloosa* (Furie); *Return of the Seve ī* (Kennedy); 1967—*A Covenant with Death* (Johnson); *The War Wagon* (Kennedy); 1969—*The Wild Bunch* (Peckinpah); 1972—*Detras de esa puerta*; 1973—*Pat Garrett and Billy the Kid* (Peckinpah); 1974—*Bring Me the Head of Alfredo Garcia* (Peckinpah); 1975—*Lucky Lady* (Donen).

Publications:

By FERNÁNDEZ:

Articles—"After the Revolution" in *Films and Filming* (London), June 1963; interview in *The Mexican Cinema: Interviews with 13 Directors* by Beatriz Reyes Navares, Albuquerque, New Mexico 1976.

On FERNÁNDEZ:

Books—*Historia documental del cine mexicano*, vol.1-9, by Emilio García Riera, Mexico City 1969—; *La busqueda del cine mexicano* by Jorge Ayala Blanco, Mexico City 1974; *La aventura del cine mexicano* by Jorge Ayala Blanco, Mexico City 1979; *Mitología de un cine en crisis* by Alberto Ruy Sanchez, Mexico City 1981; *Mexican Cinema: Reflections of a Society, 1896-1980* by Carl Mora, Berkeley 1982; articles—"El Indio" in *Time* (New York), 11 November 1946; "The 2 Kinds of Mexican Movies" by Natalia Askenazy in *Films in Review* (New York), May 1951; "Vet Actor-Helmer Back in Pix: Mexico's Emilio Fernandez, Released from Jail on Manslaughter Rap, Cast in *Luna*" in *Variety* (New York), 22 December 1976.

*   *   *

If he did not already exist, it would be necessary to invent Emilio "El Indio" Fernández. His manneristic visual style, his folkloric themes and characters, and his distinctively Indian physiognomy make him an integral element of Mexico's culture of nationalism, as well as the nation's best-known director. Fleeing Mexico with the defeat of his faction in the revolution of 1910-17, Fernández ended up digging ditches in Hollywood. As has been the case with so many Latin American artists and intellectuals, Fernández discovered his fatherland by leaving it: "I understood that it was possible to create a Mexican cinema, with our own actors and our own stories....From then on the cinema became a passion with me, and I began to dream of Mexican films." Making Mexican cinema became Fernández's obsession and, as is so often true of cultural nationalism, a short-term gain was to turn into a long-term dead end.

Perhaps that which most distinguishes Fernández's films is their strikingly beautiful visual style. Fernández and Gabriel Figueroa, the cinematographer, created the classical visual form of Mexican cinema. Ironically, their expressive cinematic patriotism was significantly inspired by foreign models—the most important of which was that of Sergei Eisenstein and his cameraman Eduard Tisse. Fernández evidently saw *Qué Viva Mexico!* in Hollywood, and he later played the lead in *Janitzio*, a film influenced by Eisenstein and the documentaries of Robert Flaherty and Willard Van Dyke and which he went on to "re-make" twice as *María Candelaria* and *Maclovia*. Another important antecedent was Paul Strand's photography in *Los Redes*, which must itself have reflected Eisenstein's examples as well as Strand's experiences in the Film and Photo League.

Foreign models were prominent at a formal level, but nationalism was presumably communicated in the content of the visual images. Fernández's and Figueroa's films are a celebration of Mexico's natural beauty: stony Indian faces set off by dark rebozos and white shirts, *charros* and their stallions riding through majestic cactus formations, fishermen and their nets reflected in the swirling ocean tides, flower vendors in Xochimilco's canals moving past long lines of tall poplar trees; and over it all, the monumentally statuesque masses of rolling clouds made impossibly luminous by photographic filters.

In the earlier films, the incredible beauty of the visual structures functioned as a protagonist, contexting the story and resonating with the characters' emotions. However, Fernández and Figueroa apparently became victims of their own myths, for their later films manifest a coldness and immobility which indicate an emphasis on visual form at the expense of other cinematic concerns. The dangers inherent in their "tourist's" images of Mexico were ever-present, of course; but they became increasingly obvious with the petrification of the style.

Fernández's stories have been summed up by Carlos Monsiváis, a leading Mexican critic, as "monothematic tragedies: the couple is destroyed by the fate of social incomprehension, Nature is the essence of the Motherland, beauty survives crime, those who sacrifice themselves for others understand the world." One is tempted to add: the Indian is a cretin, the *charro* a blustering *macho*, women are long-suffering and self-denying saints—and the revolution a confused tangle of meaningless atrocities.

Fernández's picturesque myths still retain vigor in the statist nationalism which dominates ideological discourse in Mexico. And, judging from the international attention that Fernández received for his early works, they were evidently also what the world expected from Mexican cinema. The pity is that Emilio "El Indio" Fernández did not demand a little more from himself.

—John Mraz

FERRERI, MARCO. Italian. Born in Milan, 11 May 1928. Educated in veterinary medicine. Married Jacqueline (Ferreri). Career: late 1940s—drops out of university, works with little success as liquor salesman and advertising agent; 1950-51—produces 2 issues of filmic "magazine" *Documento mensile* including shorts by Antonioni, De Sica, Visconti, and others; 1952-53—participates as actor and writer in various film projects; 1954—temporarily abandons cinema, sells optical instruments in Spain; meets Castilian writer Rafael Fernandez Azcona, collaborates on adaptation of Azcona short story which becomes first feature, *El Pisito*. Recipient: International Film Critics Award, Venice Festival, for *The Wheelchair*, 1960; International Critics Award, Cannes Festival, for *La Grande Bouffe*, 1973.

Films (as production manager): 1951—*Documento mensile* (2 "issues" or 3 according to other sources); *Il cappotto* (Lattuada); 1953—*Amore in città* (anthology film); *La spiaggia* (Lattuada) (+ro); 1954—*Donne e soldati* (Malerba and Marchi) (+co-sc, ro); 1956—*Fiesta brava (Toro bravo)* (Cottafavi—unauthorized release); (as director and scriptwriter): 1958—*El Pisito* (co-sc); 1959—*Los chicos* (co-sc); 1960—*El cochecito (The Wheelchair, The Motorcart)* (co-sc); *Le Secret des hommes bleus (Caravan pour Zagora, El secreto de los hombres azules)* (d only begun by Ferreri, completed by Edmon Agabra); 1961—"Gli adulteri (L'infidelità coniugale)" episode of *Le italiane e l'amore*; 1962—*Mafioso* (Lattuada) (co-sc only); 1963—*Una storia moderna: l'ape regina (The Conjugal Bed)* (co-sc); 1964—*La donna scimmia (The Ape Woman)* (co-sc); "Il professore" episode of *Controsesso* (co-sc); 1965—"L'uomo dei cinque palloncini (The Man with the Balloons)" episode of *Oggi, domani, dopodomani* (co-sc); 1966—*Marcia nuziale* (co-sc); 1967—*L'harem* (co-sc); 1968—*Dillinger è morto (Dillinger Is Dead)* (co-sc); *Break-Up* (revised version of episode from 1964 film *Oggi, domani, dopodomani*); 1969—*Il seme dell'uomo (The Seed of Man)* (co-sc); 1970—*Perché pagare per essere felici!* (documentary, for TV); 1971—*L'udienza* (co-sc); 1972—*Liza (La cagna)* (co-sc); 1973—*La grande abbuffata (La Grande Bouffe, Blow-Out)*; *Non toccate la donna bianca (Touche pas la femme blanche)* (co-sc, +ro); 1976—*L'ultima donna (La Dernière Femme, The Last Woman)* (co-sc); 1978—*Bye Bye Monkey (Ciao maschio)* (co-sc); 1979—*Chiedo asilo (My Asylum)*; 1981—*Tales of Ordinary Madness (Storie di ordinaria follia)* (+co-sc); 1983—*Storia di Piera (Piera's Story)* (co-sc).

Roles: (mainly in bit parts): 1950—*Il principe ribelle* (Mercanti); 1964—*Casanova '70* (Monicelli); 1967—*Il fischio al naso* (Tognazzi); 1969—*Porcile* (Pasolini); *Le vent d'est* (Godard); 1970—*Ciao Gulliver* (Tuzii); *Sortilegio* (Bonomi); 1971—*Lui per lei* (Rispoli).

Publications:

By FERRERI:

Articles—"Entretien" by M. Amiel in *Cinéma* (Paris), June 1972; "Entretien" by G. Fofi in *Positif* (Paris), April 1972; "Entretien" by R. Gardies in *Image et son* (Paris), June/July 1972; "Entretien" by J.-A. Gili in *Ecran* (Paris), July/August 1973; "L'Audience", interview by M. Martin, in *Ecran* (Paris), February 1973; "Je fais du cinéma commercial parce que je ne suis pas un héros", interview by Noel Simsolo, in *Cinéma* (Paris), January 1973; "Touche pas la femme blanche", interview by J.A. Gili and G. Braucourt, in *Ecran* (Paris), March

1974; "Perché ho fatto un film fisiologico", interview edited by P. Mereghetti, in *Cineforum* (Bergamo), May 1974; "Entretien avec Marco Ferreri" by O. Volta in *Positif* (Paris), February 1974; "Marco Ferreri on l'ultima donna" by R. Schar in *Cinema Papers* (Melbourne), September/October 1976; interview by P. Bonitzer and others in *Cahiers du cinéma* (Paris), July/August 1976; interview by D. Rabourdin in *Cinéma* (Paris), July/August 1976; "Why? Why Not?", interview by P.-L. Thirard in *Positif* (Paris), June 1978; "Les Premiers Cris de l'homme nouveau", interview by E. Matacena, in *Cahiers du cinéma* (Paris), February 1980; "interview by G. Buscaglia and others in *Framework* (Norwich, England), no.12, 1980; "Retour sur Ferreri", interview by J. Magny and others in *Cinéma* (Paris), April 1980.

On FERRERI:

Articles—"The Face of '63—Italy" by J.F. Lane in *Films and Filming* (London), April 1963; "L'Audience" in *Avant-Scène du cinéma* (Paris), March 1973; "Il Recupero del fantastico nell'opera di Marco Ferreri" by G. Peruzzi in *Cinema nuovo* (Turin), July/August 1973; "Ferreri: un cinéma de moeurs-fiction" by C. Depuyper in *Cinéma* (Paris), September/October 1974; "La Grand Bouffe" in *Avant-Scène du cinéma* (Paris), January/February 1974; "Dillinger est mort" by G. Vialle in *Image et son* (Paris), June/July 1975; biofilmography in *Film Dope* (London), September 1978; "La Libertad, un camino elegido por Marco Ferreri" by J.R. Solares in *Cinemateca Revista* (Andes), January 1979.

*   *   *

Marco Ferreri's films are daringly excessive, outrageous, to some even obscene. But the filmmaker does not wish to shock or startle or offend the viewer solely for effect. Rather, he wants to jar his audience into pondering his themes: the break-up of the nuclear family, the redefinition of sex roles, the alienation inherent in modern city living. He is a social critic who captures in his images a contemporary world on the edge of social chaos. Ferreri is if anything a humanist—and a pessimist—so frustrated by his perceptions of society that his art can only border on the absurd.

Ferreri's early films center around the crumbling institution of marriage. In *The Conjugal Bed* (*L'Ape Regina*, the translation of which is *The Queen Bee*), a pleasant, fortyish bachelor (Ugo Tognazzi) cannot keep up with youthful wife Marina Vlady's sexual demands, becoming an invalid and dying before the final credits. The heavy, though, is not always the wife. *The Ape Woman*, played by Annie Girardot, has her body and face covered with hair. She is exploited by a two-bit showman (Tognazzi, again), who eventually must marry her to keep her from leaving his freak show. In the film's Italian-released print, the title character dies in childbirth and her husband has her stuffed, putting her on exhibit. *Dillinger Is Dead*, arguably Ferreri's masterpiece, sums up the first phase of his career. It is the surreal, ambiguous tale of an industrial designer (Michel Piccoli), disenchanted with his wife, job and home, who polishes and fixes an old revolver, kills his mate, and escapes to Tahiti. But, perhaps, all this might have occurred in his imagination, as he is driving home from work.

The filmmaker's scenarios during the 1970s expand beyond familial relationships. In *La Grande Bouffe*, a quartet of bored middle-aged men (a chef, airline pilot, judge, and television producer) eat themselves to death in an orgy of gluttony. In *Bye Bye Monkey*, Ferreri's first English language feature, Gerard Depardieu is gang-raped by several women and a rat colony that

has overrun New York City devours a baby chimp. Ben Gazzara stars in *Tales of Ordinary Madness* as a rumpled, booze-loving beat poet who rambles through a maze of hookers, nymphomaniacs, neurotics and weirdos. *The Last Woman* is the story of a male chauvinist factory engineer (Depardieu), who appears throughout almost entirely in the nude. He has his consciousness raised by nursery school teacher Ornella Muti and, at the finale, slices off his sex organ with an electric carving knife. In this last film, Ferreri's characters exist in an ambience of stark, impersonal, dehumanizing factories, high-rises, shopping centers, and superhighways.

Marco Ferreri's films range from the superb (*Dillinger Is Dead*) to the dreadful (*Tales of Ordinary Madness*). But they are unified in their despair for modern society. He offers no positive solutions: his characters gorge themselves to death, or deny themselves of the sexuality that is the essence of their lives. The filmmaker explains it best: "...society is finished. The values that once existed no longer exist. The family, the bourgeoisie—I'm talking about values, morals, economic relationships—they no longer serve a purpose. My films are reactions translated into images. The Roman Empire is over. We are entering the new Middle Ages. What interests me are moments when the world is dissolving and exploding."

—Rob Edelman

———————————

FEUILLADE, LOUIS. French. Born in Lunel, France, 19 February 1873. Educated at the Institut de Brignac; secondary school at the Petit Séminaire, Carcassonne. Married Jeanne-Léontine Janjou in 1895. Career: 1891-95—serves with Army at Chambéry; 1898—moves to Paris, works in publishing; 1903—founds satirical journal *La Tomate*; 1904—begins writing for monarchist periodical *Soleil* and for *Revue Mondiale*; 1905—takes scenarios to Gaumont Studios, is hired by Alice Guy; 1907—Alice Guy leaves Paris, recommends him as her replacement; 1915—serves 4 months in French army, invalided out; 1916—begins series of "ciné-romans" (serials) with *Judex*; 1916-24—serials adapted into novels in "ciné-roman" series; credited as author in collaboration; 1917-18—1st President of the Société des Auteurs de Films; 1918—moves to Nice where Gaumont studio built in 1916. Died in Nice, 26 February 1925.

Films—Feuillade wrote and directed an estimated 800 films; this partial listing includes all of the series titles and the known titles of those films which are not part of the various series: (as director and scenarist): 1905—*Le coup de vent (Le chapeau)* (sc only); 1906—*Le billet de banque*; *C'est Papa qui prend la purge*; *La course au potiron* (sc only); *Les deux Gosses*; *La Porteuse de pain*; *Mireille* (co-d); *N'te promène donc pas toute nue*; 1907—*Un accident d'auto*; *La course des belles-mères*; *Un facteur trop ferré*; *L'homme aimanté*; *La légende de la fileuse*; *Un paquet embarrassant*; *La sirène*; *Le thé chez la concierge*; *Vive le sabotage*; 1908—*Les agents tels qu'on nous les présente*; *Une dame vraiment bien*; *La grève des apaches*; *Nettoyage par le vide*; *Une nuit agitée*; *Prométhé*; *Le récit du colonel*; *Le roman de Sœur Louise*; *Un tic*; 1909—*L'aveugle de Jérusalem*; *La chatte métamorphosée en femme*; *La cigale et la fourmi*; *Le collier de la reine*; *Les filles du cantonnier*; *Les heures*; *Histoire de puce*; *Le huguenot*; *Judith et Holopherne*; *Fra Vincenti*; *La légende des phares*; *La mère du moine*; *La mort de Mozart*; *La mort*; *La possession de l'enfant*; *Le savetier et le financier*; *Le printemps*; *Vainqueur de la course pédestre*; 1910—*Benvenuto Cellini*; *Le*

Christ en croix; Esther; L'Exode; Le festin de Balthazar; La fille de Jephté; Mil huit cent quatorze; Mater dolorosa; Maudite soit la guerre; Le pater; Le roi de Thulé; 1910-11—"Le Film Esthétique" series [(alphabetically by year): 1910: Les sept péchés capitaux, La nativité; 1911: La vierge d'Argos]; 1910-13—"Bébé" series (74 films: length varies from 88 to 321 meters); the series begins with Bébé fume (1910); the final title is Bébé en vacances (1913); 1911—L'aventurière, dame de compagnie; Aux lions les chrétiens; Dans la vie; Les doigts qui voient; Fidélité romaine; Le fils de la sunamite; Le fils de Locuste; Les petites apprenties; Quand les feuilles tombent; Sans le joug; Le trafiquant; 1911-13—"La vie telle qu'elle est" series: 1911 [Les vipères, Le mariage de l'aînée, Le roi Lear au village, En grève, Le bas de laine (Le Trésor), La tare, Le poison, La souris blanche, Le trust (Les batailles de l'argent), Le chef-lieu de Canton, Le destin des mères, Tant que vous serez heureux; 1912: L'accident, Les braves gens, Le nain, Le pont sur l'Abime; 1913: S'affranchir]; 1912—Amour d'automne; Androclès; L'anneau fatal; L'attrait du bouge; Au pays des lions; L'Aventurière; La cassette de l'émigrée; Le chateau de la peur; Les cloches de Paques; Le cœur et l'argent; La course aux millions; Dans la brousse; La demoiselle du notaire; La fille du margrave; La hantise; Haut les mains!; L'homme de proie; La maison des lions; Le maléfice; Le mort vivant; Les noces siciliennes; Le Noël de Francesca; Préméditation; La prison sur le gouffre; Le témoin; Le tourment; Tyrtée; La vertu de Lucette; La vie ou la mort; Les yeux qui meurent; 1912-16—"Bout-de-Zan" series (53 films: length varies from 79 to 425 meters; the series begins with Bout-de-Zan revient du cirque (1912); the final title is Bout-de-Zan et la torpille (1916); 1912-13—"Le Detective Dervieux" series [1912: Le Proscrit, L'oubliette; 1913: Le guet-apens, L'écrin du rajah]; 1913—L'agonie de Byzance; L'angoisse; Les audaces du cœur; Bonne année; Le bon propriétaire; Le browning; Les chasseurs de lions; La conversion d'Irma; Un drame au pays basque; L'effroi; Erreur tragique; La gardienne du feu; Au gré des flots; L'intruse; La marche des rois; Le mariage de miss Nelly; Le ménestrel de la reine Anne; La mort de Lucrèce; La petite danseuse; Le revenant; La rose blanche; Un scandale au village; Le secret du forçat; La vengeance du sergent de ville; Les yeux ouverts; 1913-14—"Fantômas" series: 1913: Fantômas, Juve contre Fantômas, La mort qui tue; 1914: Fantômas contre Fantômas, Le faux magistrat; 1913-16—"La vie drôle" series (35 films of which 26 are preserved); series begins with Les millions de la bonne (1913) and includes L'Illustre Machefer (1914), Le colonel Bontemps (1915) and Lagourdette, gentleman cambrioleur (1916); 1914—Le calvaire; Le coffret de Tolède; Le diamant du Sénéchal; L'enfant de la roulotte; L'épreuve; Les fiancés de 1914; Les fiancés de Séville; Le gendarme est sans culotte; La gitanella; L'hôtel de la gare; Les lettres; Manon de Montmartre; La neuvaine; Paques rouges; La petite Andalouse; La rencontre; Severo Torelli; 1915—L'angoisse au foyer; La barrière; Le blason; Celui qui reste; Le collier de perles; Le coup du fakir; La course a l'abîme; Deux Françaises; L'escapade de Filoche; L'expiation; Le fer a cheval; Fifi tambour; Le furoncle; Les noces d'argent; Le Noël du poilu; Le sosie; Union sacrée; 1915-16—"Les vampires" series [1915: 1. and 2. La tête coupée and La bague qui tue; 3. Le cryptogramme rouge; 1916: 4. Le spectre; 5. L'évasion du mort; 6. Les yeux qui fascinent; 7. Satanas; 8. Le maître de la foudre; 9. L'homme des poisons; 10. Les noces sanglantes]; 1916—L'aventure des millions; C'est le printemps; Le double jeu; Les fiançailles d'Agénor; Les fourberies de Pingouin; Le malheur qui passe; Un mariage de raison; Les mariés d'un jour; Notre pauvre cœur; Le poète et sa folle amante; La peine du talion; Le retour de Manivel; Si vous ne m'aimez pas; Judex (serial in a prologue and 12 episodes); 1917—L'autre; Le bandeau sur les yeux; Débrouille-toi; Déserteuse; La femme fatale; La fugue de Lily; Herr Doktor; Mon oncle; La nouvelle mission de Judex (serial in 12 episodes); Le passé de Monique; 1918—Aide-toi; Les petites marionnettes; Tih Minh (serial in 12 episodes); Vendémiaire; 1919—Barrabas (serial in 12 episodes); L'engrenage; L'énigme (Le mot de l'); L'homme sans visage; Le nocturne; 1920—Les deux Gamines (serial in 12 episodes); 1921—L'Orpheline (serial in 12 episodes); Parisette (serial in 12 episodes); 1921-22—"Belle humeur" series [1921: Gustave est médium, Marjolin ou la fille manquée, Saturnin ou le bon allumeur, Séraphin ou les jambes nues, Zidore ou les métamorphoses; 1922: Gaétan ou le commis audacieux, Lahire ou le valet de cœur]; 1922—Le fils du flibustier (serial in 12 episodes); 1923—Le gamin de Paris; La gosseline; L'orphelin de Paris (serial in 6 episodes); Vindicta (film released in 5 parts); 1924—La fille bien gardée; Lucette; Pierrot Pierrette; Le stigmate (serial in 6 episodes).

Publications:

By FEUILLADE:

Books—Le Clos (play), with Etienne Arnaud, Paris 1905; Les Vampires, with Georges Meirs, Paris 1916; Judex, with Arthur Bernède, Paris 1917 (and 1934); La nouvelle Mission de Judex, with Arthur Bernède, Paris 1919; Tih Minh, with Georges Le Faure, Paris 1919; Barrabas, with Maurice Level, Paris 1920; Les Deux Gamines adapted by Paul Cartoux, Paris 1921; L'Orpheline adapted by Frédéric Boutet, Paris 1922; Parisette adapted by Paul Cartoux, Paris 1922; Le Fils du Flibustier adapted by Paul Cartoux, Paris 1923; Vindicta adapted by Paul Cartoux, Paris 1924; L'Orphelin de Paris adapted by Paul Cartoux in Le Petit Journal (Paris), 28 March through 2 May 1924; Le Stigmate adapted by Paul Cartoux, Paris 1925; articles—"Naundor, la genèse d'un crime historique" by 'P. Valergues' (pseudonym) in Revue mondiale (Paris), 10 November 1904 through 25 October 1905; interview by André Lang in Déplacements et villégiatures littéraires, Paris 1923; interview by Gaston Phelip in Le Courrier Cinématographique (Paris), 16 August 1924; manifestos on the series "Le film esthétique" and "La vie telle qu'elle est" in L'Anthologie du Cinéma edited by Marcel Lapierre, Paris 1946.

On FEUILLADE:

Books—Cinéma et Compagnie by Louis Delluc, Paris 1919; Images du cinéma français by Nicole Védrès, Paris 1945; La Foi et les montagnes by Henri Fescourt, Paris 1959; Louis Feuillade by Francis Lacassin, Paris 1964; Le Cinéma muet à Nice by René Prédal, Aix-en-Provence 1964; La Lanterne magique by Robert Florey, Lausanne 1966; articles—"Le souvenir de Louis Feuillade" by Arthur Bernède in Courrier cinématographique (Paris), 26 August 1933; "Louis Feuillade" by Pierre Leprohon in Radio-Cinéma-Télévision (Paris), 27 July 1958; "Louis Feuillade" by Claude Beylie in Ecrans de France (Paris), 15 May 1959; "En effeuillant la Marguerite" by F. Lacassin and R. Bellour in Cinema 61 (Paris), March through June 1961; "Une Saison dans la cage à mouches avec Feuillade" by Robert Florey in Cinéma 62 (Paris), June 1962; "Feuillade (l'homme aimanté)" by Jean-André Fieschi in Cahiers du cinéma (Paris), November 1964; "Louis Feuillade" by Francis Lacassin in Sight and Sound (London), winter 1964/65; "Les lettres de Léon Gaumont à Louis Feuillade" by Francis Lacassin in Cinéma 65 (Paris), no.95, 1965; "Feuillade" in Anthologie du cinéma vol.2, Paris 1967; "Memories of Resnais" by Richard Roud in Sight and

Sound (London), summer 1969; "Maker of Melodrama" by Richard Roud in *Film Comment* (New York), November/December 1976; biofilmography in *Film Dope* (London), September 1978; "Quand Louis Feuillade cinématographiait à la cité de Carcassonne" by C. Cartier and M. Oms in *Cahiers de la Cinémathèque* (Paris), winter 1979; "Un Beau Revolver" by P. Le Guay in *Cinématographe* (Paris), December 1980; "Louis Feuillade, poète de la réalité" by J. Champreux in *Avent-Scène du cinéma* (Paris), 1 July 1981; special Fantômas issue of *Avant-Scène du cinéma* (Paris), 1 July 1981.

*   *   *

Louis Feuillade was one of the most solid and dependable talents in French cinema during the teens. He succeeded Alice Guy as head of production at Gaumont in 1906 and worked virtually without a break—aside from a period of war service—until his death in 1925, producing some 800 films of every conceivable kind: comedies and contemporary melodramas, biblical epics and historical dramas, sketches and series with numerous episodes adding up to many hours of running time. Though most of these films were made from his own scripts, Feuillade was not an innovator. The years of his apprenticeship in the craft of filmmaking were those in which French producers reigned supreme and he worked uncomplainingly in a context in which commercial criteria were paramount. For Feuillade—as for so many of his successors in the heyday of Hollywood—aesthetic strategies not rooted in sound commercial practices were inconceivable, and a filmmaker's only viable ambition was to reach the widest possible audience.

Most of Feuillade's output forms part of a series of some kind and he clearly saw films in generic terms rather than as individually sculpted works. Though not an originator in terms of the forms or styles he adopted, he made films which are among the finest examples of the various popular genres he successively explored. Before 1914 his work is enormously diverse: thirty comic films in the series of *La Vie drôle*, a group of seriously intended dramas in which a concern with the quality of the pictorial image is apparent, marketed under the banner of the *Film esthétique*, and a number of contemporary dramas, *La Vie telle qu'elle est*, with somewhat ambiguous claims to realism. In addition he made some 76 films with a four-year-old child star, Bébé, and a further 50 or so with the urchin Bout-de-Zan.

But the richest vein of Feuillade's work is the series of crime melodramas from *Fantômas* in 1913-14 to *Barrabas* in 1920. Starting with his celebration of Fantômas, master criminal and master of disguise, who triumphs effortlessly over the dogged ordinariness of his opponent Inspector Juve, Feuillade went on to make his wildest success with *Les Vampires*. Made to rival the imported American serials, this series reflects the chaotic wartime state of French production in its improvised stories refusing all logic, its bewildering changes of casting (necessary as actors were summoned to the war effort), its economical use of real locations and dazzling moments of total incongruity. *Les Vampires* reach a level Feuillade was never subsequently to achieve. *Judex* and especially *La Nouvelle Mission de Judex* are marked by a new tone of moralising, with the emphasis now on the caped avenger rather than the feckless criminals. If the later serials, *Tih Minh* and *Barrabas*, contain sequences able to rank with the director's best, Feuillade's subsequent work in the 1920s lacks the earlier forcefulness.

It was the supreme lack of logic, the disregard of hallowed bourgeois values—so appropriate at a time when the old social order of Europe was crumbling under the impact of World War I—which led the surrealists such as André Breton and Louis Aragon to hail *Fantômas* and *Les Vampires*, and most of Feuillade's subsequent advocates have similarly celebrated the films' anarchistic poetry. But this should not lead us to see Feuillade as any sort of frustrated artist or poet of cinema, suffocating in a world dominated by business decisions. On the contrary, the director was an archetypal middle class family man, who prided himself on the commercial success of his work and conducted his personal life in accord with strictly ordered bourgeois principles.

—Roy Armes

FEYDER, JACQUES. Belgian. Born Jacques Frédérix in Ixelles, Belgium, 21 July 1885; became citizen of France in 1928. Educated at the Ecole régimentaire, Nivelles, 1905. Married Françoise Rosay in 1917; children: Marc Frédérix, Paul Feyder, Bernard Farrel. Career: 1906-07—works in family's cannon foundry; 1907—announces intention to become actor, father forbids use of family name, 'Feyder' chosen as pseudonym; 1911—moves to Paris; 1911-13—performs supporting roles in theatre; 1912—first film role in Georges Méliès fantasy; subsequently acts in films of Charles Burguet, Victorien Jasset, Feuillade, and Gaston Ravel; 1913-14—engaged by theatre in Lyon, meets Françoise Rosay; 1914—assistant to director Gaston Ravel; 1916—begins directing for Gaumont on Ravel's recommendation; 1917-19—serves with Belgian army, member of acting troupe directed by Victor Francen; 1919—returns to France; 1928—*Les Nouveaux Messieurs* banned in France for insulting "the dignity of Parliament and its ministers"; accepts MGM offer and moves to Hollywood; 1933—contract with MGM terminated; 1940—*La Kermesse héroïque* banned by Goebbels after German invasion, takes refuge in southern France; 1942—moves to Switzerland for duration of war; 1945—returns to Paris, begins producing. Died in Prangins, Switzerland, 25 May 1948. Recipient: Best Foreign Film for *La Kermesse héroïque*, New York Film Critics, 1935; Best Direction for *La Kermesse héroïque*, Venice Festival, 1935.

Films (as director and scriptwriter): 1915—*Monsieur Pinson, policier* (co-d only); 1916—*Têtes de femmes, femmes de tête* (d only); *L'Homme au foulard à pois*; *Le Bluff*; *Un conseil d'ami*; *L'Homme de compagnie* (d only); *Tiens, vous êtes à Poitiers?*; *L'Instinct est maître* (d only); *Le Frère de lait*; *Le Billard cassé*; *Abrégeons les formalités*; *La Trouvaille de Buchu*; 1917—*Le Pardessus de demi-saison*; *Les Vieilles Femmes de l'Hospice* (d only); 1919—*La Faute d'orthographe*; 1921—*L'Atlantide*; 1922—*Crainquebille* (+art direction); 1925—*Visages d'enfants* (+art direction); *L'Image* (+ro); *Gribiche*; *Poil de Carotte* (Duvivier) (sc only); 1926—*Carmen*; 1927—*Au pays du Roi Lépreux*; 1928—*Thérèse Raquin (Du sollst nicht Ehe brechen)* (co-sc); *Les Nouveaux Messieurs* (co-sc); *Gardiens de Phare* (Grémillon) (sc only); 1929—*The Kiss* (co-sc); *Anna Christie* (German version of Clarence Brown film); 1930—*Le Spectre vert* (French version of Lionel Barrymore's *The Unholy Night*); *Si l'Empereur savait ça* (French version of *His Glorious Night*); *Olympia* (French version); 1931—*Day Break* (d only); *Son of India* (d only); 1934—*Le Grand Jeu* (co-sc); 1935—*Pension Mimosas* (co-sc); *La Kermesse héroïque* (co-sc); 1936—*Die klugen Frauen* (German version of *La Kermesse héroïque*); 1937—*Knight without Armour* (d only); 1938—*Les Gens du voyage* (co-sc); *Fahrendes Volk* (German version of *Les Gens du voyage*); *La Loi du nord* (made 1939: during Occupation titled *La Piste du nord*) (co-sc); *Une Femme disparaît* (co-sc); *Maturareise (Jeunes filles d'aujourd'hui)* (Steiner) (technical and artistic supervision only); 1946—

Macadam (Blistène) (art direction only).

Roles: 1913—1st episode of series *Protéa* (Jasset); 1914—*Quand minuit sonna*; 1915—*Autour d'une bague* (Ravel); bit role in *Les Vampires* (serial) (Feuillade).

Publications:

By FEYDER:

Books and scripts—*Le Cinéma, notre métier*, with Françoise Rosay, Geneva 1946; *La Kermesse héroïque* in *L'Avant-scène du cinéma* (Paris), no.26, 1965; articles—preface to *Histoire de l'art cinématographique* by Carl Vincent, Brussels 1939; "Transposition visuelle" in *Intelligence du cinématographe* edited by Marcel l'Herbier, Paris 1946; "Impressions de Hollywood, L'Ordre" in *Anthologie du cinéma* edited by Marcel Lapierre, Paris 1946; "Je crois au film parlant, Pour vous" in *L'Art du cinéma* edited by Pierre Lherminier, Paris 1960; "Der internationale Film" in *Film Kunst* (Vienna), no.74, 1976.

On FEYDER:

Books—*Jacques Feyder ou le Cinéma concret* (anthology), Brussels 1949; *Jacques Feyder* by Victor Bachy, Paris 1966; *Jacques Feyder, artisan du cinéma* by Victor Bachy, Louvain 1968; *Jacques Feyder* by Charles Ford, Paris 1973; articles—"Souvenirs sur Jacques Feyder" by Georges Chaperot in *La Revue du cinéma* (Paris), 1 July 1930; special issue of *L'Ecran français* (Paris), 8 June 1948; special issue of *Ciné-Club* (Paris), 2 November 1948; obituary in *The New York Times*, 26 May 1948; "Hommage à Jacques Feyder" by Jean Lambotte in *Films et Documents* (Paris), February/March 1959; biofilmography in *Film Dope* (London), September 1978; film—*Jacques Feyder et son chef d'oeuvre* by Raymond Antoine and Charles Van Der Hagen, Belgium 1974.

*   *   *

Underneath everything Jacques Feyder did was a great love and mastery of his medium, giving integrity and style to his work. As a young man he rejected the bourgeois background of his Belgian home and became an actor. He fell in love with the talented Françoise Rosay who became his life's partner. He acted in the cinema of Victorin Jasset, Feuillade, and Léon Gaumont, then became a scriptwriter, and finally began directing.

His individual approach to *La Faute d'orthographe* did not commend itself to Gaumont and Feyder raised the money to make the popular novel of Pierre Benois, *L'Atlantide*. This, in spite of an ill-chosen Napierkowska in the lead, was an international success. Its scenes shot in the Sahara under difficult conditions balanced the picturesque and exotic interiors, depicting an underground city.

Dining out in Montmartre he and Françoise discovered a boy playing in the street. This was little Jean Forest whom Feyder directed with consummate skill in three films, *Crainquebille*, *Visages d'enfants* and *Gribiche*. The first, based on the Anatole France story, added to Feyder's reputation while the second, shot with simplicity and sensitivity in the Haut Valais, Switzerland, showed a remarkable skill in directing child actors. *Gribiche* was his first film for the Russian-inspired Albatros Com-

pany, and introduced the designer Lazare Meerson, working in the Art Deco style. It also featured Françoise Rosay in her first major role. Following a pictorially beautiful *Carmen*, with a recalcitrant Raquel Meller in the title role, came Feyder's masterpiece *Thérèse Raquin*, shot in a German studio with Gina Manes in her greatest part. Zola's somber bourgeois tragedy was brought vividly to life. The details of the Raquin home, the human tensions, the unspoken words and the looming shadows created an unforgettable effect. At the end the old dumb and paralysed woman watches through those shadows the dead bodies of the murderous lovers lying on the floor. One of the great moments of cinema.

After an irreverent satire on French politics, *Les Nouveaux Messieurs* which succeeded in getting itself banned, Feyder set out for Hollywood where he directed Garbo in *The Kiss*, her last silent film and one of her most intelligent. Feyder now tackled the sound film with European versions of *Anna Christie*, *Le Spectre vert* and *Olympia*. In 1931 he directed Ramon Novarro in *Son of India* and *Day Break* before returning to France. Teaming up with his fellow countryman Charles Spaak he made in quick succession *Le Grand Jeu*, one of the best films of the Foreign Legion, *Pension Mimosas* with Rosay in a great tragic role, and the delightful, decorative and witty *La Kermesse héroïque*, a costume film that defies the ravages of time. The latter outraged the sensibilities of his fellow Belgians even as it delighted the rest of the world.

He directed *Knight without Armour* for Alexander Korda in London, Dietrich playing opposite Robert Donat. This story of the revolution in Russia saw an elegant Marlene moving through picturesque landscapes and great buildings designed by Lazare Meerson in one of his last assignments. Feyder then went to Germany to make *Les Gens du voyage* in two versions. After this story of circus life he returned to France and made his last important film *La Loi du nord* with Michele Morgan. The story of a Mounted Police search for a murderer in the Far North still showed the Feyder quality. It just managed to be completed by the time France was invaded. Feyder chose to live in Switzerland during the war, turning out a star vehicle for Françoise Rosay, *Une Femme disparait* in 1941. He died in Switzerland in 1948, a year which saw the passing of Eisenstein and Griffith. Feyder was in the company of his peers. But in 1970 René Clair could still say "Jacques Feyder does not occupy today the place his work and his example should have earned him."

—Liam O'Leary

FISCHINGER, OSKAR. German. Born Wilhelm Oskar Fischinger in Gelnhausen, Germany, 22 June 1900. Educated in Gelnhausen, finishing course of technical studies 1914. Married Elfriede (Fischinger) in 1932; 5 children. Career: 1914-15—apprentice to organ builder; 1915—architectural draftsman, city of Gelnhausen; 1916-22—draftsman, tool designer and then engineer, Pokorny and Wittekind Turbine factory, Frankfurt; 1920—1st experiments with animated film; 1921—meets Walther Ruttman, invents wax slicing machine for animation, later used by Ruttman; 1923—manager for film producer Louis Seel Co.; 1926—moves to Berlin; 1928—works on special effects for *Frau im Mond* (Lang); begins independent commercial production; 1931-32—collaborates with brother Hans; 1933—produces 1st color-on-film movie in Europe, *Kreise*, for advertising firm; 1935—*Composition in Blue* leads to Paramount offer; 1936—moves to Hollywood; contract terminated; 1936-67—active as oil painter, exhibits widely; 1937-38—under contract to MGM;

1939—on visit to New York where paintings being shown, meets Baroness Hilla Rebay von Ehrenwiesen; she becomes source of small-scale funding for film projects, but seeks to gain control over his work; works at Disney Studios, suggests idea for *Fantasia*, disowns work on film when designs altered; 1940-45—with Rebay's assistance receives funding from Guggenheim Foundation; 1940-44—in house on Hammond Street and at studio on Sunset Strip at Sawtelle Blvd., group of young film artists gathers, including the Whitney brothers, Maya Deren, and Kenneth Anger, and musicians John Cage and Edgard Varèse; 1942— works with Orson Welles on *Life of Louis Armstrong* (unrealized); 1950—invents Lumigraph, instrument for "playing" light (patent granted 1955); 1950-57—produces television commercials. Died in Los Angeles, 31 January 1967; buried at at Holy Cross Cemetery, Los Angeles. Recipient: special award, Venice Festival, for *Composition in Blue*, 1935; Grand Prix, Brussels International Film Festival, for *Motion Painting No.1*, 1949.

Films (as director and animator) by years of production: 1921-26—*Wax Experiments*; 1923-27—*Orgelstäbe (Staffs)*; 1924—*Pierrette No.1*; 1924-26—*Münchener Bilderbogen*; about 1927—*R-1*; *Staffs (colored)*; *Seelische Konstruktionen* [Spiritual Constructions]; special effects sequences in *Sintflut*; 1927—*München-Berlin Wanderung*; 1928—*Dein Schicksal* [Your Destiny]; 1929—special effects for *Frau im Mond* (Lang); about 1929—*Study No.1*; about 1930—*Study No.2*; 1930—*Das Hohelied der Kraft* [The Hymn of Energy]; *Study No.3*; *Study No.4*; *Study No.5*; *Study No.6*; 1930-31—*Study No.7*; 1931—*Study No.8*; *Study No.9*; *Liebesspiel* [Love-games]; 1932—*Study No.10*; *Study No.11*; *Study No.12*; *Koloraturen* [Coloratura]; *Synthetic Sound Experiments*; 1933—*Eine Viertelstunde Grossstadtstatistik* [A Quarter Hour of City Statistics] (d only); *Study No.14*; 1933-34—*Study No.13* (unfinished); *Kreise* [Circles]; 1934—*Ein Spiel in Farben* [A Play in Colors]; *Quadrate* [Squares]; *Muratti greift ein* [Muratti Marches On]; *Cigarette Tests*; *Swiss Trip (Rivers and Landscapes)*; 1935—*Muratti Privat*; *Komposition in Blau (Composition in Blue)*; *Lichtkonzert No.2*; 1936—*Allegretto*; 1937—*An Optical Poem*; 1939—"Toccata and Fugue" section of *Fantasia* (adapted from Fischinger's designs); 1941—*American March*; 1942—*Radio Dynamics*; *Color Rhythm* (unedited version of *Radio Dynamics*); ca. 1945—*Organic Fragment*; 1947—*Motion Painting No.1*.

Publications:

By FISCHINGER:

Articles—"Was ich mal sagen möchte..." in *Deutsche allgemeine Zeitung*, 23 July 1932; "Klingende Ornamente" in *Deutsche allgemeine Zeitung, Kraft und Stoff* (Sunday supplement), 28 July 1932; "Een gesprek met Oskar Fischinger" by Lou Lichtveld in *Nieuwe Rotterdamsche Courant*, 27 July 1932; "Der absolute Tonfilm: Neue Möglichkeiten für den bildenden Künstler" in *Dortmunder Zeitung* (Dortmund), 1 January 1933 (also appeared in *Schwäbischer Merkur* and other newspapers); "Zum Internationalen Filmcongress...", interview with Fischinger and Lotte Reiniger by Fritz Böhme in *Deutsche allgemeine Zeitung*, 27 April 1935; "My Statements Are in My Work" in *Art in Cinema* edited by Frank Stauffacher, San Francisco 1947; "Veritable création" in *Le Cinéma à Knokke-le-Zoute*, 1950; "Paintings—and Painters Today", brochure, Pasadena Art Museum, California, 1956.

On FISCHINGER:

Books—*Bildmusik: Art of Oskar Fischinger*, Long Beach (California) Museum of Art, 1970; *Experimental Animation* by Robert Russett and Cecile Starr, New York 1976; *Retrospective Oskar Fischinger, the Working Process*, with articles by William Moritz and Andre Martin, International Animated Film Festival, Ottawa 1976; *Film als Film, 1910 bis Heute* edited by Birgit Hein and Wulf Herzogenrath, Cologne 1978; articles—"Die Filme des lebenden Lichts" by Franz Böhme in *Deutsche allgemeine Zeitung*, 11 July 1931; "Die Filme Oskar Fischingers" by Paul Hatschek in *Filmntechnik*, 7 March 1931; "Abstrakte Filmstudie Nr.5 von Oskar Fischinger (Synästhetischer Film)" by Walther Behn in *Farbe-Ton-Forschungen* edited by Georg Anschütz, vol.III, Hamburg 1931; "A New Break in Movies: The Fischinger Films" by Caroline Lejeune in *The Observer* (London), 20 December 1931; "Über Fischingerfilme: das ästhetische Wunder" by Bernhard Diebold in *Lichtbildbühne*, 1 June 1932; "Lichtertanz" by Lotte Eisner in *Film-Kurier* (Berlin), 1 June 1932; "Tönende Ornamente: Aus Oskar Fischingers neuer Arbeit" by Fritz Böhme in *Film-Kurier* (Berlin), 30 July 1932; "Elektrische Musik" by Dr. M. Epstein in *Berliner Tageblatt*, 24 August 1932; "Ornamente musizieren" by Dr. Albert Neuberger in *Deutsche Musiker Zeitung*, 15 October 1932; "Fischinger" by Schu. in *Film-Kurier* (Berlin), 1 October 1934; "Der absolute Film: Oskar Fischingers Arbeiten" by Alman in *Filmwelt* (Sunday supplement of *Film-Kurier*) (Berlin), 16 June 1935; "Film als Ausdrucksform" by Leonhard Fürst in *Film-Kurier* (Berlin), 11 November 1935; "The Last of the Mohicans" by L.J. Jordaan in *Filmliga*, 15 November 1935; "Master of Motion" by Lou Jacobs, Jr., in *International Photographer*, October 1949; "Pioneer of Abstract Films at Perls Gallery, Los Angeles" in *Art News* (New York), September 1951; "Oskar Fischinger: Abstract Movie Master" by Ty Cotta in *Modern Photography* (Cincinnatti), July 1952; "Concrete films of Oskar Fischinger" by M. Weaver in *Art and Artists* (London), May 1969; review by Peter Plagens in *Artforum* (New York), October 1970; "Oskar Fischinger et la crème de l'animation" by Max Tessier in *Ecran* (Paris), January 1973; "The Films of Oskar Fischinger" by William Moritz in *Film Culture* (New York), no.58-60, 1974; "Fischinger at Disney: or, Oskar in the Mousetrap" by W. Moritz in *Millimeter* (New York), February 1977; "Oskar Fischinger" by Georges Daumelas in *Filmer*, summer 1978; "Elfriede! On the Road with Mrs. Oskar Fischinger" by John Canemaker in *Funnyworld* (New York), summer 1978; "Oskar Fischinger" in *Travelling* (Lausanne), summer 1979; "Oskar Fischinger Remembered" by H. Weinberg in *Films in Review* (New York), June/July 1980; "You Can't Get Then from Now" by William Moritz in *Journal* (Los Angeles Institute of Contemporary Art), summer 1981; film—*The Art of Oskar Fischinger* with John Canemaker, William Moritz, and Elfriede Fischinger, for CBS Camera Three, May 1977.

* * *

Oskar Fischinger's contributions to the art of the motion picture were both artistic and scientific.

Moving to Frankfurt, he apprenticed as an engineer, and he began experimenting with film animation around age 20. In 1921, Fischinger met filmmaker Walter Ruttmann who purchased a wax slicing machine Fischinger had invented for animating special effects.

In 1923, Fischinger moved to Munich where he began animating theatrical cartoons during the day for film producer Louis Seel, while privately pursuing his own film experiments which included the surrealist silhouette film *Spiritual Constructions*, and several three-, five-, and seven-projector "light shows." During the summer of 1927, Fischinger walked from Munich to Berlin, making a single-frame diary film of the trip. By 1928, he was working on special effects for director Fritz Lang's *Woman in the Moon*. He also began making highly successful commercials which were shown in German movie theaters.

Fischinger worked on a series of 16 experimental film *Studies* over a five-year period. In 1933 he helped perfect a color film process invented by Dr. Bela Gaspar, Gasparcolor, which allowed Fischinger to create the first color abstract films, *Circles* and *Composition in Blue*, which was awarded a major prize at the Venice Biennale in 1935.

For Metro-Goldwyn-Mayer in 1937, Fischinger made a masterpiece of film animation, *An Optical Poem*, an abstract short synchronized to Liszt's Second Hungarian Rhapsody. In 1939, Walt Disney hired him to design the Bach "Toccata and Fugue" sequence for *Fantasia*. Fischinger's designs, however, were altered by the studio and he disowned his contribution to the comleted film.

In 1941, Orson Welles hired him to work at Mercury Productions on *It's All True* for RKO Radio Pictures. After a year, however, the entire film was abandoned before completion. Because he was an enemy alien, Fischinger could not work at regular jobs during World War II, but fortunately the Solomon Guggenheim Foundation extended several grants so that he could buy the rights to *Allegretto*, and complete three more films, *American March*, *Radio Dynamics* and *Motion Painting No. 1*, which won the Grand Prize at the Brussels International Film Festival in 1949.

In the 1950s Fischinger produced and designed television commercials and invented the Lumigraph, a color-organ instrument for home performance. Although he continually attempted to raise money to finance another abstract film, he never again received a grant or other backing. His wife Elfriede continues his work at the Fischinger Studio in Hollywood.

—James L. Limbacher

FISHER, TERENCE. British. Born in London, 23 February 1904; Educated at Christ Hospital, Horsham, Sussex. Career: mid-1920s—becomes sailor; 1926-28—apprenticeship aboard training ship H.M.S. Conway; 1929—signs as junior officer in English Merchant Marine, serves with P & O Lines; 1930—becomes window-dresser for London department store; 1931—begins frequenting cinemas; 1933—begins working as assistant film editor at Shepherd's Bush Studios, after working as clapper boy and runner; [Note: other sources date this initial film work as 1930]; 1936—becomes full editor on Robert Stevenson's *Tudor Rose*; 1948—given first directing opportunity by Rank Organisation; 1952—joins Hammer company, becomes identified with Hammer's low-budget, quick schedule horror films; 1952-56—directs episodes of *Robin Hood* for British TV; other TV work includes *Dial 999* and episodes for *Three's Company*. Died 18 June 1980.

Films (as assistant editor): 1935—*Brown on Resolution (Forever England, Born for Glory)* (Asquith); (as editor): 1936—*Tudor Rose (9 Days a Queen)* (Stevenson); *Jack of All Trades (The 2 of Us)* (Stevenson and Hulbert); *Where There's a Will* (Beaudine); *Everybody Dance* (Reisner) (co-ed); *Windbag the Sailor* (Beaudine); 1938—*Mr. Satan* (Woods); 1939—*On the Night of the Fire (The Fugitive)* (Hurst); 1940—*George and Margaret* (King); 1941—*Atlantic Ferry (Sons of the Sea)* (Forde); *The 7th Survi-*

vor (Hiscott); 1942—*Flying Fortress* (Forde); *The Peterville Diamond* (Forde); *Tomorrow We Live (At Dawn We Die)* (King) (supervising ed); *The Night Invader* (Mason) (supervising ed); 1943—*The Dark Tower* (Harlow); *The 100 Pound Window* (Hurst) (supervising ed); *Candlelight in Algeria* (King) (supervising ed); 1944—*One Exciting Night (You Can't Do Without Love)* (Forde); *Flight from Folly* (Mason) (supervising ed); 1945—*The Wicked Lady* (Arliss); 1947—*The Master of Bankdam* (Forde) (supervising ed); (as director): 1948—*A Song for Tomorrow*; *Colonel Bogey*; *To the Public Danger*; *Portrait from Life (The Girl in the Painting)*; 1949—*Marry Me*; *The Astonished Heart* (co-d); 1950—*So Long at the Fair* (co-d); 1951—*Home to Danger*; 1952—*The Last Page (Manbait)*; *Stolen Face*; *Wings of Danger (Dead on Course)*; *Distant Trumpet*; 1953—*Mantrap (Man in Hiding)* (+co-sc); *4 Sided Triangle* (+co-sc); *Spaceways*; *Blood Orange*; 1954—*Face the Music (The Black Glove)*; *The Stranger Came Home (The Unholy 4)*; *Final Appointment*; *Mask of Dust (Race for Life)*; *Children Galore*; 1955—*Murder by Proxy (Blackout)*; *Stolen Assignment*; *The Flaw*; 1956—*The Gelignite Gang*; *The Last Man to Hang?*; 1957—*Kill Me Tomorrow*; *The Curse of Frankenstein*; 1958—*Dracula (Horror of Dracula)*; *The Revenge of Frankenstein*; 1959—*The Hound of the Baskervilles*; *The Man Who Could Cheat Death*; *The Mummy*; *The Stranglers of Bombay*; 1960—*The Brides of Dracula*; *The 2 Faces of Dr. Jekyll (House of Fright)*; *Sword of Sherwood Forest*; 1961—*The Curse of the Werewolf*; 1962—*The Phantom of the Opera*; *Sherlock Holmes und der Halsband des Todes*; *Sherlock Holmes and the Deadly Necklace* (English language version of preceding); 1964—*The Horror of It All*; *The Earth Dies Screaming*; *The Gorgon*; 1965—*Dracula—Prince of Darkness*; 1966—*Island of Terror*; *Frankenstein Created Woman*; 1967—*Night of the Big Heat (Island of the Burning Damned)*; 1968—*The Devil Rides Out (The Devil's Bride)*; 1969—*Frankenstein Must Be Destroyed*; 1973—*Frankenstein and the Monster from Hell*.

Publications:

By FISHER:

Articles—"Horror Is My Business", interview by Raymond Durgnat and John Cutts in *Films and Filming* (London), July 1964; "Entretien" by S. Levy-Klein and G. Parfitt in *Ecran* (Paris), July/August 1973; "Entretien avec Terence Fisher" by P. Bachmann in *Positif* (Paris), January 1975.

On FISHER:

articles—"The Horrible Hammer Films of Terence Fisher" by H. Ringel in *Take One* (Montreal), May 1973; "Le Cauchemar de Dracula" in *Avant-Scène du cinéma* (Paris), July/September 1975; "Sang et encens" by É. Caron-Lowins in *Positif* (Paris), January 1975; "Prométhée délivré (sur les 'Frankenstein' de Terence Fisher)" by E. Carrère in *Positif* (Paris), July/August 1977; "Terence Fisher" by M. Salmi in *Film Dope* (London), February 1979; "Fantastique Angleterre Terence Fisher vingt ans aprés" by F. Guérif in *Image et son* (Paris), May 1980; "Ga er niet alleen heen! Bij de dood van Terence Fisher (1904-1980)" by T. Ockersen in *Skoop* (Amsterdam), August 1980; "Terence Fisher, le prince des ténèbres" by P. Ross in *Image et son* (Paris), September 1980.

*　　　*　　　*

Although he directed more than two dozen movies before his first horror film in 1957 (*The Curse of Frankenstein*), Terence Fisher is best remembered for his gruesome interpretations of the supernatural and the macabre. Fisher made most of these films in England for Hammer, a small production company that specialized in "B" pictures. When Hammer began producing a series of sensational horror films in the late fifties, it became world famous. Much of the credit for its success can be attributed to the directing talents of Fisher.

The Curse of Frankenstein, made in 1957, began a revitalization of the horror genre. Although the Hammer films were often based on the same characters and stories as the Universal horror films of the thirties and forties, Hammer presented its versions with an added exploitive twist—sex and violence. While the sex and violence of the Hammer films is certainly mild by today's standards (compared, for example, to *Dawn of the Dead* and *Friday the 13th*), it was very explicit for its time. For example, Fisher's *Horror of Dracula* showed very graphically the women vampires being impaled through the heart with a stake. Hammer produced the first Gothic horror films to be done in color, so the flowing of deep red blood gained its maximum effect. The critics often lambasted Hammer for the violence of its films, but it did get them noticed.

Part of Fisher's formula (and an element often missing in the horror films of today) is the importance of character. His monsters aren't typical in the evil and destructive sense of the word; they are often victims and are played very sympathetically. Christopher Lee as *The Mummy* is being punished through eternity for loving a woman he can never have. Oliver Reed in *Curse of the Werewolf* is also a victim of love. The "monster" in *Revenge of Frankenstein* wants only to be like normal people. All of these characters are victims of forces they cannot control.

The Curse of Frankenstein, Hammer's first horror film, was a huge financial success. So was *The Horror of Dracula*. Fisher seemed to find his niche at Hammer, and the partnership was long and mutually beneficial. Contemporary reviews did not go out of their way to praise Fisher's horror films—perhaps they were too trend-setting. But his influence on today's films is unmistakable, and Terence Fisher has risen to the status of a cult director, having created a new kind of horror film, with style.

—Linda J. Obalil

FLAHERTY, ROBERT. American. Born Robert Joseph Flaherty in Iron Mountain, Michigan, 16 February 1884. Educated Upper Canada College, Toronto; Michigan College of Mines. Married Frances Hubbard, 12 November 1914. Career: early 1900s—serves as explorer, surveyor, and prospector for Canadian Grand Trunk Railway and Canadian mining syndicates; 1910-16—works for industrial entrepreneur William MacKenzie searching for iron ore deposits along the Hudson Bay, is introduced to Eskimo culture during these journeys; 1913-14—takes motion picture camera on expedition for 1st time; 1915—rough cut of Eskimo footage destroyed when cigarette dropped on editing room floor results in fire; from surviving footage constructs travelogue-type film which proves unsuccessful when screened privately; publishes book *The Drawings of Ennoosweetok of the Sikosilingmiut Tribe of the Eskimo*; 1920-22—returns to Hudson Bay area to film Eskimo way of life, resulting in 1st feature *Nanook of the North*; 1923-25—in Samoa makes *Moana* with backing of Paramount (then Famous Players-Lasky), wife Francis Flaherty collaborates on production; 1928—invited by

Irving Thalberg of MGM to co-direct *White Shadows in the South Seas* with W.S. Van Dyke; discouraged by Hollywood system and quits; forms company with F.W. Murnau to produce *Tabu*; when Murnau forced to finance film himself, personal difficulties between them result in Flaherty's resignation; 1929—*Acoma the Sky City* production shut down following disagreements with Fox; 1931—hired by John Grierson of Empire Marketing Board to make film about England; *Industrial Britain* shot mainly by Flaherty but edited by Grierson; 1932-34—moves to Aran Islands and makes *Man of Aran*; 1939-41—for American government makes *The Land* which he also narrates; 1942—hired by Frank Capra to work in his Army orientation film unit, but Flaherty project proves unsuccessful; 1944-45—supervises 3 films directed by his brother David for U.S. Office of Price Administration; 1946-48—sponsored by Standard Oil to do *Louisiana Story*, last successful venture; 1948-51—embarks on number of projects never completed and also lends name to brother David's projects; 1953—Robert Flaherty Foundation established (later renamed International Film Seminars, Inc.). Died 23 July 1951; ashes scattered across Black Mountain, Vermont. Recipient: Venice Film Festival, International Prize for *Louisiana Story* for it's "lyrical beauty", 1948.

Films (as director, photographer, and scenarist): 1922—*Nanook of the North* (+ed); 1925—*The Potterymaker (Story of a Potter)* (short); 1926—*Moana (Moana: A Romance of the Golden Age, Moana: The Love Life of a South Sea Siren)* (co-sc, co-ph, co-ed); 1927—*The 24-Dollar Island* (short); 1931—*Tabu* (co-d, co-sc, uncredited co-ph); 1933—*Industrial Britain* (co-d and co-ph only); *The English Potter* (short) (d and ph only—edited by Marion Grierson from footage shot for *Industrial Britain*); *The Glassmakers of England* (short) (d and ph only—edited from *Industrial Britain* footage); *Art of the English Craftsman* (short) (d and ph only—from *Industrial Britain* footage); 1934—*Man of Aran* (co-ph); 1937—*Elephant Boy* (co-d only); 1942—*The Land* (co-ph, +narration); 1945—*What's Happened to Sugar* (David Flaherty) (pr only); 1948—*Louisiana Story* (co-sc, co-ph, +pr); 1949—*The Titan: The Story of Michelangelo* (co-pr only); 1950—*Green Mountain Land* (short) (David Flaherty) (pr only); 1951—*St. Matthew's Passion* (ed, narration only—reedited version of Ernst Marischka's 1949 *Matthäus-Passion*); 1967—*Studies for Louisiana Story* (15 hours of outtakes from *Louisiana Story* edited by Nick Cominos).

Publications:

By FLAHERTY:

Books—*Anerca: Drawings by Enooesweetof*, revised ed., Toronto 1959; *Eskimo* by Edmund Carpenter with Frederick Varley and Robert Flaherty, Toronto 1959; "How I Filmed *Nanook of the North*" in *Film Makers on Filmmaking* edited by Harry M. Geduld, Bloomington, Indiana 1971; articles—"Producer of *Nanook* joins Metro-Goldwyn" by Donald H. Clarke in *The New York Times*, 26 June 1927; interview by S.M. Weller in *Motion Picture Classic* (New York), October 1927; article on *North Sea*, a film by Harry Watt, in *Sight and Sound* (London), summer 1938; "The Giant Shinnies Down the Beanstalk: Interview" by Theodore Strauss in the *New York Times*, 12 October 1941.

On FLAHERTY:

Books—*The Film Till Now* by Paul Rotha, London 1930; *Ele-*

phant Dance by Frances Flaherty, New York 1937; Sabu: The Elephant Boy by Frances Flaherty, New York 1937; Footnotes to the Film edited by Charles Davy, London 1938; 2 Pioneers: Robert Flaherty, Hans Richter by Herman Weinberg, supplement to Sight and Sound, index series, London 1946; 20 Years of British Film by Michael Balcon, London 1947; Robert Flaherty: Nota biografica, filmografica e bibliografica... by Mario Gromo, Parma, Italy 1952; Documentary Film by Paul Rotha, New York 1952; The Odyssey of a Film-Maker: Robert Flaherty's Story by Frances Flaherty, Urbana, Illinois 1960; Robert Flaherty et le Documentaire Poetique: Etudes Cinématographique No. 5 by Fuad Quintar, Paris 1960; Robert Flaherty by Jose Clemente, Madrid 1963; Robert Flaherty by Carlos Fernandez Cuenca, Madrid 1963; Robert Flaherty compiled by Wolfgang Klaue, Berlin 1964; Robert J. Flaherty by Henri Agel, Paris 1965; Pare Lorentz and the Documentary Film by Robert L. Snyder, Norman, Oklahoma 1968; The World of Robert Flaherty by Richard Griffith, New York 1970; The Innocent Eye: The Life of Robert Flaherty by Arthur Calder-Marshall, London 1970; Grierson on Documentary edited by Forsyth Hardy, revised ed., New York 1971; Documentary Explorations: 15 Interviews with Film-makers by G. Roy Levin, Garden City, New York 1971; Nonfiction Film: A Critical History by Richard Barsam, New York 1973; Film and Reality: An Historical Survey by Roy Armes, Baltimore 1974; Documentary: A History of the Non-Fiction Film by Erik Barnouw, New York 1974; Robert J. Flaherty by Antonio Napolitano, Florence 1975; Robert Flaherty: A Guide to References and Resources by William T. Murphy, Boston 1978; articles—"Nanook of the North" by Frances Taylor Patterson in the New Republic (New York), 9 August 1922; "Robert Flaherty's Nanook of the North" in The Best Moving Pictures of 1922-23 by Robert E. Sherwood, Boston 1923; "Flaherty, Great Adventurer" by Terry Ramsaye in Photoplay (New York), May 1928; "1st Principles of Documentary" by John Grierson in Cinema Quarterly (London), winter 1932; "Sentimentality and the Screen" by Miriam R. Flaherty in Commonweal (New York), 5 October 1934; "Flaherty" by John Grierson in Cinema Quarterly (London), autumn 1934; "Documentary Daddy" in Time (New York), 3 February 1941; "Flaherty and the Future" by Richard Griffith in New Movies (New York), January 1943; "Un Poete de l'exoticisme: Robert J. Flaherty" in L'Exoticisme et le cinéma by Pierre Leprohon, Paris 1945; "Post-War Patterns" by John Grierson in Hollywood Quarterly, January 1946; "They Make Documentaries: No. 1—Robert Flaherty" by Arthur Rosenheimer (Arthur Knight) in Film News (New York), April 1946; "The Flahertys: Pioneer Documentary Filmmakers" by John M. Brinnin in Harper's Bazaar (New York), December 1947; "Un Maitre du documentaire: Robert Flaherty" by Arthur Rosenheimer (Arthur Knight) in Revue du cinéma (Paris), January 1947; "My Friend Flaherty" in Morning Became Mrs. Spendlove by Oliver St. John Gogarty, New York 1948; "Partners and Pioneers" by Inez Foster in Christian Science Monitor (Boston), 15 January 1949; "Profile of Flaherty" by Robert Lewis Taylor in the New Yorker, 11, 18 and 25 June 1949; "Robert Flaherty and the Naturalist Documentary" by Hugh Gray in Hollywood Quarterly, fall 1950; "Flaherty—Education for Wanderlust" in The Running Pianist by Robert Lewis Taylor, New York 1950; "Flaherty in Review" in Sight and Sound (London), November/December 1951; "E'morto un poeta" by Giulio Castello in Bianco e Nero (Rome), July 1951; "Significato di Flaherty" by Luigi Chiarini in Cinema (Rome), 15 August 1951; "The Flaherty Way" by Frances Flaherty in Saturday Review (New York), 13 September 1951; "Flaherty as Innovator" by John Grierson in Sight and Sound (London), October/November 1951; "Robert Flaherty: An Appreciation" by John Grierson in The New York Times, 29

July 1951; "A Flaherty Festival" by Arthur Knight in Saturday Review (New York), 6 January 1951; "Hommage a Robert Flaherty" by Georges Sadoul in Les Lettres françaises (Paris), 13 September 1951; "Regarding Flaherty" by John Huston in Sequence (London), no.14, 1952; "Robert Flaherty und seine Film" by Fritz Kempe in Film Bild Ton (Munich), December 1952; "The World of Robert Flaherty" by George L. George in Film News (New York), no.4, 1953; "Ideas on Film: Film Seminar in Vermont" by Cecile Starr in Saturday Review (New York), 13 October 1956; "Robert Flaherty, Geographer" by Roger Manvell in The Geographical Magazine (New York), February 1957; "Robert Flaherty" by J. Eckardt in Film, Bild, Funk (Stuttgart), no.2, 1959; "Bob" by Gideon Bachmann in Film (London), September/October 1959; "The Understood Antagonist and Other Observations" by Ernest Callenbach in Film Quarterly (Berkeley), summer 1959; "A Few Reminiscences" by David Flaherty in Film Culture (New York), no.2, 1959; "Flaherty's Quest for Life" by Frances Flaherty in Films and Filming (London), January 1959; "Explorations" by Frances Flaherty and "Robert Flaherty—The Man and the Filmmaker" by Charles Siepmann in Film Book I: The Audience and the Filmmaker edited by Robert Hughes, New York 1959; The Cinema and Social Science: A Survey of Ethnographic and Sociological Films by Luc De Heusch, Paris 1962; "Robert Flaherty" by Marcel Martin in L'Avant-Scène du cinéma (Paris), vol.1, 1965; "Robert J. Flaherty, 1884-1951" by Helen Van Dongen in Film Quarterly (Berkeley), summer 1965; "Bob Flaherty Remembered" by Harvey Fondiller in Popular Photography (Boulder, Colorado), March 1970; "A Farewell to Flaherty" in Saint Cinema: Selected Writings by Herman Weinberg, New York 1970; "Robert Flaherty (Barnouw's File)" by Erik Barnouw in Film Culture (New York), spring 1972; "Remembering Frances Flaherty" by Ricky Leacock in Film Comment (New York), November/December 1972; "Robert Flaherty's Brief Career as a Radio Announcer" by Charles Siepmann in Film Culture (New York), spring 1972; "Robert Flaherty: The Man in the Iron Myth" by Richard Corliss in Film Comment (New York), November/December 1973; "Robert Flaherty albo rytual odkrywania formy" by A. Helman in Kino (Warsaw), March 1973; "Helen Van Dongen: An Interview" by Ben Achtenberg in Film Quarterly (Berkeley), winter 1976; "Looking Back...at the Pirogue Maker, Louisiana Story and the Flaherty Way" by Arnold Eagle in Film Library Quarterly (New York), no.1, 1976; "Remembering Robert Flaherty" by Fred Zinnemann in Action (Los Angeles), May/June 1976; biofilmography in Film Dope (London), February 1979; radio program—"Portrait of Flaherty" produced by W.R. Rodgers for BBC-Radio, broadcast 2 September 1952; films—Odyssey: The World of Robert Flaherty produced by Charles Romine for CBS-TV in cooperation with the Museum of Modern Art, broadcast 17 February 1957; How the Myth Was Made: A Study of Robert Flaherty's Man of Aran (for TV) by George Stoney, 1978.

*   *   *

Robert Flaherty was already 36 years old when he set out to make a film, Nanook of the North, as his primary purpose. Before that he had established himself as a prospector, surveyor, and explorer, having made several expeditions to the sub-Artic regions of the Hudson Bay. He had shot motion picture footage on two of these occasions, but before Nanook, filmmaking was only a sideline.

Yet these years in the wilderness were to have a profound effect on his development as a filmmaker. First, the expeditions brought Flaherty into intimate contact with the Eskimo culture. Second, they enhanced his knowledge about the human condition in a natural setting. Third, the numerous evenings that he spent in isolation encouraged him to contemplate the day's events by writing in his diaries, from which he developed highly skilled powers of observation which sharpened his sense of photographic imagery and detail. Also a violinist and an accomplished storyteller, Flaherty had clearly cultivated an artistic sensibility before becoming a filmmaker. Filmmaking became a compelling mechanism for expressing this sensibility.

Flaherty turned to filmmaking not only as a means of creation but also to communicate to the outside world his rare, close look at Eskimo culture. He held a profound admiration for these people who lived close to nature and whose daily existence was an unrelenting struggle to survive. The struggle ennobled this proud race. Flaherty sought to portray their existence in manner that would illustrate the purity and nobility of their lives, a purpose underlying each of his films.

Flaherty develped a method of working that was fairly consistent from film to film. The films about the people of Hudson Bay, Samoa, the Aran Islands, and the Louisiana Bayou demonstrate a more or less constant concern with people who live in natural settings. These geographical locations are incidental; others would have done just as well. Eskimo culture was the only one in which he was deeply versed. Nevertheless, the locations were chosen because they represented societies on the verge of change. Indeed, Flaherty has often been criticized for presenting his subjects as they existed years ago, not as he found them. But for Flaherty this meant the last opportunity to capture a way of life on film.

Another consistent feature of his technique was the selection of a "cast." Although he pioneered the use of real people to reenact their own everyday lives before the camera lens, he deliberately chose ideal types on the basis of physical appearance and even created artificial families to act before the camera.

Flaherty worked without a plot or script, allowing for a maximum of improvisation. The Flaherty method entailed total immersion in these cultures in order to discover the basic patterns of life. *Nanook* represented the least difficulty because of his thorough familiarity with Eskimo culture. However, *Moana* and *Man of Aran* represented unfamiliar territory. Flaherty had to become steeped in strange cultures. His search for struggle and conflict in Savaii misled him and he later abandoned it. Struggle was more readily apparent in the Aran Islands, in terms of conflict between man and the sea; the hunt for the basking shark which he portrayed, abandoned in practice some years earlier, helps us to visualize this conflict.

Flaherty's technical facility also served him well. Generally he carried projectors and film printers and developing equipment to these far off places so that he could view his rushes on a daily basis. Flaherty, a perfectionist, shot enormous quantities of footage for his films; the lack of a script or scenario contributed to this. He went to great lengths to achieve photographic excellence, often shooting when shadows were longest. In *Moana* he used the new panchromatic film stock which was much more sensitive to color than orthochromatic film. He pioneered the use of long lenses for closeup work allowing an intimacy with his subjects that was novel for its time.

Flaherty's films were generally well received in the popular press and magazines as well as in the more serious critical literature. *Nanook* was praised for its authenticity and its documentary value as well as its pictorial qualities. John Grierson first used the term documentary as applying to a film in his review of *Moana*. Subsequently Grierson, through his filmmaking activities and writings, began to formulate a documentary aesthetic dealing with social problems and public policy, subjects that Flaherty (except for *The Land*) tried to avoid. Nevertheless, Grierson's writings, which were to influence the development of

the modern sponsored film, had their foundations in Flaherty's work. Their purposes were ultimately quite different, but Grierson gave due credit to Flaherty for working with real people, shaping the story from the material, and bringing a sense of drama to the documentary film.

Man of Aran aroused the most critical responses to Flaherty's work. It was released at a time when the world was beset with enormous political, social, and economic problems, and many enthusiasts of documentary film believed it was irresponsible and archaic of Flaherty to produce a documentary making no reference to these problems or concealing them from public view. *Louisiana Story*, on the other hand, was greeted as the culminating work of a master filmmaker, and recognized for its skillful interveaving of sound and image, an audiovisual symphony as one critic described it. However, in today's world of pollution and oil spills it is much more difficult to accept the benign presence of the oil industry in the bayou.

Although Flaherty made a relatively small number of films in his long career, one would be hard pressed to find a more influential body of work. He always operated outside the mainstream of the documentary movement. Both he and Grierson, despite their contradictory purposes, can be credited with the development of a new genre and a documentary sensibility; Flaherty by his films, Grierson by his writing. Watching today's 16mm distribution prints and video cassettes it is often difficult to appreciate the photographic excellence of Flaherty's work. Nevertheless, the clean lines are there as well as an internal rhythm created by the deft editing touch of Helen Van Dongen. Although his films were improvised, the final product was never haphazard. It showed a point of view which he wished to share.

—William T. Murphy

FLEISCHER, MAX AND DAVE. American. Max: born in Vienna, 17 July 1883 (or 1885); Dave: born in New York City, 14 July 1894. Max studied at New York Art Students League, Cooper Union, and Mechanics and Tradesmen's School; Married; children (Max): Ruth and Richard. Career: 1887—Fleischer family moves to New York City; before 1912—Dave works as theater usher and in engraving company art dept.; 1912—Dave is cutter for Pathe Films; before 1914—Max works as errand boy for Brooklyn *Daily Eagle* and for Boston photoengraver; 1914—Max is commercial artist for Crouse-Hinds, and *Popular Science Monthly* art editor; 1915—Max invents Rotoscope, device for tracing live action film for conversion to animation; 1916—begins working for John Randolph Bray at Paramount, producing animation sequences for *Bray Pictograph* series; joined by Dave who works as assistant and Rotoscope model; 1917—Dave joins Army; edits live action training films; 1917-18—Max makes Army instructional films; 1919—brothers form Out of the Inkwell, Inc. production company; 1925—distribution company Red Seal Pictures acquired; 1929—Fleischer Studios, Inc. formed, distributing through Paramount; 1936—produce medium-length *Popeye the Sailor Meets Sinbad the Sailor*; 1937—studio artists strike for more pay; 1939—studio moved from New York to Miami; 1939—first full-length feature *Gulliver's Travels*; 1941—second feature *Mr. Bug Goes to Town* a financial failure; Paramount forecloses on loans, shutting down studio; 1942—Dave becomes head of Columbia cartoon dept. Max produces instructional films for Jam-Handy company; 1944—Dave moves to Universal, holds various positions until 1967 retirement; 1962—Max forms a new Out of the Inkwell,

Inc., produces cartoons for TV; 1963—Max retires; Max Fleischer died in 1972; Dave Fleischer died in 1979.

Films (by Max Fleischer as director): 1915—*Out of the Inkwell* (+pr, sc, anim, +Dave as ass't d, Rotoscope model); 1918—*How to Read an Army Map; How to Fire a Lewis Gun; How to Fire a Stokes Mortar;* (Max as producer and Dave as director of cartoon shorts, and both collaborating—often uncredited—on scripts): "Out of the Inkwell" series: 1919—*The Clown's Pup; The Tantalizing Fly; Slides;* 1920—*The Boxing Kangaroo; The Chinaman; The Circus; The Clown's Little Brother; The Ouija Board; Perpetual Motion; Poker (The Card Game); The Restaurant;* 1921—*The Automobile Ride; Cartoonland; The First Man to the Moon; Fishing; Invisible Ink; November; The Sparring Partner;* 1922—*Birthday; Bubbles; The Challenge; The Dresden Doll; The Fish* (possibly alternate title for *Fishing,* 1921); *The Hypnotist; Jumping Beans; Mosquito; Pay Day; Reunion; The Show;* 1923—*Balloons; The Battle; Bedtime; The Contest; False Alarm; Flies; The Fortune Teller; Fun from the Press* (series of 3 inserts); *Laundry; Modeling; The Puzzle; Shadows; Surprise; Trapped; The Einstein Theory of Relativity* (d Max only—live action, in 2-reel version, and 4-reel with some cartoon sequences); *Adventures in the Far North (Captain Kleinschmidt's Adventures in the Far North)* (Kleinschmidt) (co-pr and ed Max only—live action); 1924—*The Cure; Ko-Ko in 1999; Ko-Ko the Hot Shot; League of Nations; The Masquerade; The Runaway; Vacation; Vaudeville;* "Song Car-Tune" series: *Come Take a Trip in My Airship; Mother, Mother, Mother, Pin a Rose on Me; Oh, Mabel!; Old Folks at Home;* "Fleischer Novograph": *Echo and Narcissus;* for Pathe Review: *The Proxy Lover: A Fable of the Future;* 1925—"Out of the Inkwell" series: *Big Chief Ko-Ko; The Cartoon Factory; Ko-Ko Celebrates the 4th; Ko-Ko Eats; Ko-Ko in Toyland; Ko-Ko Nuts; Ko-Ko on the Run; Ko-Ko Packs 'em; Ko-Ko Sees Spooks; Ko-Ko's Thanksgiving; Ko-Ko the Barber; Ko-Ko Trains Animals; Mother Goose Land; The Storm;* "Song Car-Tune" series: *Daisy Bell; Dixie; Good-bye My Lady Love; I Love a Lassie; My Bonnie; Suwanee River; Evolution* (d Max only—part-live action feature); 1926—"Out of the Inkwell" series: *The Fadeaway; It's the Cat's; Ko-Ko at the Circus; Ko-Ko Baffles the Bulls; Ko-Ko Gets Egg-cited; Ko-Ko Hot After It; Ko-Ko Kidnapped; Ko-Ko's Paradise; Ko-Ko Steps Out; Ko-Ko the Convict; Toot! Toot!;* "Song Car-Tune" series: *By the Light of the Silvery Moon; Comin' Through the Rye; Darling Dolly Gray; Has Anybody Here Seen Kelly?; In the Good Old Summertime; My Old Kentucky Home; Oh You Beautiful Doll; Old Black Joe; Pack Up Your Troubles; Sailing, Sailing Over the Bounding Main; Sweet Adeline; Take a Trip; Ta? Ra-Ra-Boom-Der-A; Trail of the Lonesome Pine; Tramp, the Boys Are Marching;* "Carrie of the Chorus" live action series: *Morning Judge; Berth Mark; Another Bottle, Doctor* (not released); 1927—"Out of the Inkwell" series: *Inklings* (series of 18); *East Side, West Side* ("Song Car-Tune"?); *Ko-Ko Back Tracks; Ko-Ko Makes 'em Laugh; Koko Plays Pool; Ko-Ko's Kane; Koko the Knight; Koko Hops Off; Koko the Kop; Koko Explores; Koko Chops Suey; Ko-Ko's Klock; Koko Kicks; Koko's Quest; Ko-Ko the Kid; Ko-Ko Needles the Boss;* advertising cartoon: *That Little Big Fellow* (d Dave only—for American Telephone and Telegraph Co.); 1928—"Out of the Inkwell" series: *Koko's Kink; Koko's Kozy Korner; Koko's Germ Jam; Ko-Ko's Bawth; Ko-Ko Smokes; Ko-Ko's Tattoo; Ko-Ko's Earth Control; Ko-Ko's Hot Dog; Ko-Ko's Haunted House; Ko-Ko Lamps Aladdin; Koko Squeals; Ko-Ko's Field Daze; Koko Goes Over; Ko-Ko's Catch; Ko-Ko's War Dogs; Ko-Ko's Chase; Ko-Ko Heaves-Ho; Ko-Ko's Big Pull; Ko-Ko Cleans Up; Ko-Ko's Parade; Ko-Ko's Dog-Gone; Telefilm; Ko-Ko in the Rough; Ko-Ko's Magic; Ko-Ko on the Track; Ko-Ko's*

Act; Ko-Ko's Courtship; 1929—*No Eyes Today; Noise Annoys Ko-Ko; Ko-Ko Beats Time; Ko-Ko's Reward; Ko-Ko's Hot Ink; Ko-Ko's Crib; Ko-Ko's Saxophonies; Ko-Ko's Knock-down; Ko-Ko's Signals; Ko-Ko's Focus; Ko-Ko's Conquest; Ko-Ko's Harem-Scarem; Ko-Ko's Big Sale; Ko-Ko's Hypnotism; Chemical Ko-Ko; Noah's Lark* (sound); advertising cartoon: *Finding His Voice* (co-d Max only—for Western Electric Co.); "Screen Songs" series: *The Sidewalks of New York; Yankee Doodle Boy; Old Black Joe* (remake of 1926 title); *Ye Olde Melodies; Daisy Bell* (remake of 1925 title); *Mother Pin a Rose on Me* (remake of 1924 title); *Chinatown My Chinatown; Dixie* (remake of 1925 title); *Good-bye My Lady Love* (remake of 1925 title); *My Pony Boy; Smiles; Oh You Beautiful Doll* (remake of 1926 title); *After the Ball; Put on Your Old Gray Bonnet; I've Got Rings on My Fingers;* 1930—*Bedelia; In the Shade of the Old Apple Tree; I'm Afraid to Come Home in the Dark; La Paloma; Prisoner's Song; I'm Forever Blowing Bubbles; Yes! We Have No Bananas; Come Take a Trip in My Airship* (remake of 1924 title); *In the Good Old Summer Time* (remake of 1926 title); *A Hot Time in the Old Town Tonight; The Glow Worm; The Stein Song; Strike Up the Band; My Gal Sal; Mariutch; On a Sunday Afternoon; Row, Row, Row;* "Betty Boop" series: *Dizzy Dishes; Barnacle Bill; Swing, You Sinner; Accordion Joe; Mysterious Mose;* other cartoons: *Marriage Wows; Radio Riot; Hot Dog; Fire Bugs; Wise Flies; The Grand Uproar; Sky Scraping; Up to Mars;* 1931—"Screen Songs" series: *Please Go 'way and Let Me Sleep; By the Beautiful Sea; I Wonder Who's Kissing Her Now; I'd Climb the Highest Mountain; Somebody Stole My Gal; Any Little Girl That's a Nice Little Girl; Alexander's Ragtime Band; And the Green Grass Grew All Around; My Wife's Gone to the Country; That Old Gang of Mine; Mr. Gallagher and Mr. Shean; You're Driving Me Crazy; Little Annie Rooney; Kitty from Kansas City* (also "Betty Boop" series); *By the Light of the Silvery Moon* (remake of 1926 title); *My Baby Just Cares for Me; Russian Lullaby;* "Betty Boop" series: *The Bum Bandit; Silly Scandals; Bimbo's Initiation; Bimbo's Express; Minding the Baby; In the Shade of the Old Apple Sauce; Mask-a-Raid; Jack and the Beanstalk; Dizzy Red Riding Hood; Betty Co-ed;* advertising cartoons: *Graduation Day in Bugland* (for Listerine Co.); *Suited to a T.* (for India Tea Co.); *Hurry Doctor* (for Texaco); *In My Merry Oldsmobile* (for Oldsmobile Co.); *Texas in 1999* (for Texaco); *A Jolt for General Germ* (for Listerine Co.?); other cartoons: *Ace of Spades; Teacher's Pest; Tree Saps; The Cow's Husband; The Male Man; 20 Legs Under the Sea; Step on It; The Herring Murder Case;* 1932—"Betty Boop" series: *Any Rags; Boop-Oop-a-Doop; The Robot; Minnie the Moocher; Swim or Sink; Crazy Town; The Dancing Fool; A Hunting We Will Go; Chess-nuts; Let Me Call You Sweetheart* (also "Screen Song"); *Hide and Seek; Admission Free; The Betty Boop Limited; Stopping the Show; Betty Boop's Bizzy Bee; Betty Boop M.D.; Betty Boop's Bamboo Isle; Betty Boop's Ups and Downs; Romantic Melodies* (also "Screen Song"); *Betty Boop for President; I'll Be Glad When You're Dead, You Rascal* (also "Screen Song"); *Betty Boop's Museum;* "Screen Songs" series: *Sweet Jenny Lee; Show Me the Way to Go Home; When the Red Red Robin Comes Bob Bob Bobbin' Along; Wait Till the Sun Shines, Nellie; Just One More Chance; Oh! How I Hate to Get Up in the Morning; Shine On Harvest Moon; I Ain's Got Nobody; You Try Somebody Else; Rudy Vallee Melodies; Down Among the Sugar Cane; Just a Gigolo; School Days; Sleepy Time Down South; Sing a Song; Time on My Hands;* 1931—*Dinah; Ain't She Sweet; Reaching for the Moon; Aloha Oe; Popular Melodies; The Peanut Vendor; Song Shopping; Boilesk; Sing, Sisters, Sing!; Down by the Old Mill Stream; Stoopnocracy; When Yuba Plays the Rumba on the Tuba; Boo, Boo, Theme Song; I Like Mountain Music; Sing, Babies, Sing;*

"Betty Boop" series: *Betty Boop's Ker-choo; Betty Boop's Crazy Inventions; Is My Palm Read; Betty Boop's Penthouse; Snow White; Betty Boop's Birthday Party; Betty Boop's May Party; Betty Boop's Big Boss; Mother Goose Land; The Old Man of the Mountain; I Heard; Morning, Noon, and Night; Betty Boop's Hallowe'en Party; Parade of the Wooden Soldiers;* "Popeye" series: *Popeye the Sailor* (also "Betty Boop" series); *I Yam What I Yam; Blow Me Down; I Eats My Spinach; Season's Greetinks; Wild Elephinks;* 1934—"Betty Boop" series: *She Wronged Him Right; Red Hot Mama; Ha! Ha! Ha!; Betty in Blunderland;* **Betty Boop's Rise to Fame** (compilation of sequences from *Stopping the Show, Betty Boop's Bamboo Isle,* and *The Old Man of the Mountain,* + new material); *Betty Boop's Life Guard; There's Something About a Soldier; Betty Boop's Little Pal; Betty Boop's Prize Show; Keep in Style; When My Ship Comes in;* "Screen Songs" series: *Keeps Rainin' All the Time; Let's All Sing Like the Birdies Sing; Tune Up and Sing; Lazybones; This Little Piggie Went to Market; She Reminds Me of You; Love Thy Neighbor;* "Popeye" series: *Sock a Bye Baby; Let's You and Him Fight; Can You Take It?; The Man on the Flying Trapeze; Shoein' Hosses; Strong to the Finich; Shiver Me Timbers!; Axe Me Another; A Dream Walking; The Two-Alarm Fire; The Dance Contest; We Aim to Please;* other cartoons: *Poor Cinderella; Little Dutch Mill;* 1935—*An Elephant Never Forgets; The Song of the Birds; The Kids in the Shoe; Dancing on the Moon; Time for Love; Musical Memories;* "Betty Boop" series: *Baby Be Good; Taking the Blame; Stop That Noise; Swat the Fly; No! No! A Thousand Times No!; A Little Soap and Water; A Language All My Own; Betty Boop and Grampy; Judge for a Day; Making Stars; Betty Boop with Henry the Funniest Living American; Little Nobody;* "Popeye" series: *Be Kind to Aminals; Pleased to Meet Cha; The Hyp-nut-tist; Choose Your Weppins; Beware of Barnacle Bill; For Better or Worser; Dizzy Divers; You Gotta Be a Football Hero; King of the Mardi Gras* (also "Betty Boop" series); *Adventures of Popeye* (compilation with sequences from *I Eats My Spinach, Popeye the Sailor,* and *Axe Me Another); The Spinach Overture;* "Screen Songs" series: *I Wished on the Moon; It's Easy to Remember;* 1936—*No Other One; I Feel Like a Feather in the Breeze; I Don't Want to Make History; The Hills of Old Wyomin'; I Can't Escape from You; Talking Through My Heart;* "Popeye" series: *Vim, Vigor and Vitaliky; A Clean Shaven Man; Brotherly Love; I-ski Love-ski You-ski; Bridge Ahoy!; What No Spinach?; I Wanna Be a Life Guard; Let's Get Movin'; Never Kick a Woman; Little Swee' Pea; Hold the Wire; Popeye the Sailor Meets Sinbad the Sailor* (2-reeler); *The Spinach Roadster; I'm in the Army Now* (compilation); "Betty Boop" series: *Betty Boop and the Little King; Not Now; Betty Boop and Little Jimmy; We Did It; A Song a Day; More Pep; You're Not Built That Way; Happy You and Merry Me; Training Pigeons; Grampy's Indoor Outing; Be Human; Making Friends;* other cartoons: *Somewhere in Dream Land; The Little Stranger; The Cobweb Hotel; Greedy Humpty Dumpty; Hawaiian Birds; Play Safe; Christmas Comes But Once a Year;* 1937—*Bunny-mooning; Chicken a la King; A Car-Tune Portrait; Peeping Penguins; Educated Fish; Little Lamby;* "Betty Boop" series: *House Cleaning Blues; Whoops! I'm a Cowboy; The Hot Air Salesman; Pudgy Takes a Bow-wow; Pudgy Picks a Fight; The Impractical Joker; Ding Dong Doggie; The Candid Candidate; Service with a Smile; The New Deal Show; The Foxy Hunter; Zula Hula;* "Popeye" series: *The Paneless Window Washer; Organ Grinder's Swing; My Artistical Temperature; Hospitaliky; The Twisker Pitcher; Morning, Noon, and Night Club; Lost and Foundry; I Never Changes My Altitude; I Like Babies and Infinks; The Football Toucher Downer; Protek the Weakerist; Popeye the Sailor Meets Ali Baba's 40 Thieves* (2-reeler); *Fowl Play;* "Screen Songs" series:

Never Should Have Told You; Twilight on the Trail; Please Keep Me in Your Dreams; You Came to My Rescue; Whispers in the Dark; Magic on Broadway; 1938—*You Took the Words Right Out of My Heart; Thanks for the Memory; You Leave Me Breathless; Beside a Moonlit Stream;* "Popeye" series: *Let's Celebrake; Learn Polikeness; The House Builder-Upper; Big Chief Ugh-Amugh-Ugh; I Yam Love Sick; Plumbing Is a Pipe; The Jeep; Bulldozing the Bull; Mutiny Ain't Nice; Goonland; A Date to Skate; Cops Is Always Right;* "Betty Boop" series: *Riding the Rails; Be Up to Date; Honest Love and True; Out of the Inkwell; Swing School; Pudgy and the Lost Kitten; Buzzy Boop; Pudgy and the Watchman; Buzzy Boop at the Concert; Sally Swing; On with the New; Thrills and Chills;* other cartoons: *The Tears of an Onion; Hold It; Hunky and Spunky; All's Fair at the Fair; The Playful Polar Bears;* 1939—*Always Kickin'; Aladdin and His Wonderful Lamp* (2-reeler); *Small Fry; Barnyard Brat; The Fresh Vegetable Mystery* (in 3-D); "Betty Boop" series: *My Friend the Monkey; So Does an Automobile; Musical Mountaineers; The Scared Crows; Rhythm on the Reservation; Yip, Yip, Yippy;* "Popeye" series: *Leave Well Enough Alone; Customers Wanted; Wotta Nitemare; Ghosks in the Bunk; Hello, How Am I?; It's the Natural Thing to Do; Never Sock a Baby;* 1940—*Shakespearian Spinach; Females Is Fickle; Stealin' Ain't Honest; My Feelin's Is Hurt; Onion Pacific; Wimmin Is a Myskery; Nurse Mates; Fightin' Pals; Doing Imposikible Stunts; Wimmin Hadn't Oughta Drive; Puttin' on the Act; Popeye Meets William Tell; My Pop, My Pop; Poopdeck Pappy; Eugene, the Jeep;* "Stone Age Cartoons" series: *Way Back When a Triangle Had Its Points; Way Back When a Nag Was Only a Horse; Way Back When a Night Club Was a Stick; Granite Hotel; The Foul Ball Player; The Ugly Dino; Wedding Belts; Way Back When a Razzberry Was a Fruit; The Fulla Bluff Man; Springtime in the Rockage; Pedagogical Institution (College to You); Way Back When Women Had Their Weigh;* other cartoons: *Little Lambkin; Ants in the Plants; Kick in Time; Snubbed by a Snob; You Can't Shoe a Horsefly; The Dandy Lion; King for a Day; Sneak, Snoop and Snitch; The Constable; Mommy Loves Puppy; Bring Himself Back Alive;* 1941—*All's Well; Pop and Mom in Wild Oysters; 2 For the Zoo; Zero, the Hound; Twinkletoes Gets the Bird; Raggedy Ann and Andy* (2-reeler); *Swing Cleaning; Sneak, Snoop and Snitch in Triple Trouble; Fire Cheese; Twinkletoes—Where He Goes Nobody Knows; Copy Cat; Gabby Goes Fishing; The Wizard of Arts; It's a Hap-hap-happy Day; Vitamin Hay; Twinkletoes in Hat Stuff; Superman; Superman in The Mechanical Monsters;* "Popeye" series: *Problem Pappy; Quiet! Pleeze; Olive's Sweepstake Ticket; Flies Ain't Human; Popeye Meets Rip Van Winkle; Olive's Boithday Presink; Child Psykolojiky; Pest Pilot; I'll Never Crow Again; The Mighty Navy; Nix on Hypnotricks;* 1942—*Kickin' the Conga 'round; Blunder Below; Fleets of Stren'th; Pip-eye, Pup-eye, Poop-eye and Peep-eye; Many Tanks; Olive Oyl and Water Don't Mix; Baby Wants a Bottleship;* other cartoons: *Superman in Billion Dollar Limited; Superman in The Arctic Giant; Superman in The Bulleteers; The Raven* (2-reeler); *Superman in The Magnetic Telescope; Superman in Electric Earthquake; Superman in Volcano; Superman in Terror on the Midway;* (Dave as producer for Columbia Screen Gems series): 1942—*Song of Victory* (Wickersham); *The Gullible Canary* (Geiss); *The Dumbconscious Mind* (Sommer and Hubley); *Tito's Guitar* (Wickersham); *Malice in Slumberland* (Geiss); *Toll Bridge Troubles* (Wickersham); *King Midas, Junior* (Sommer and Hubley); *Cholly Polly* (Geiss); 1943—*Slay It with Flowers* (Wickersham); *The Vitamin G-Man* (Sommer and Hubley); *There's Something About a Soldier* (Geiss); *Kindly Scram* (Geiss); *Prof. Small and Mr. Tall* (Sommer and Hubley); *Willoughby's Magic Hat* (Wickersham); *Plenty Below*

Zero (Wickersham); *Duty and the Beast* (Geiss); *Mass Mouse Meeting* (Geiss); *Tree for 2* (Wickersham); *He Can't Make It Stick* (Sommer and Hubley); *The Fly in the Ointment* (Sommer); *Dizzy Newsreel* (Geiss); *A Hunting We Won't Go* (Wickersham); *The Rocky Road to Ruin* (Sommer); *Room and Bored* (Wickersham); *Nursery Crimes* (Geiss); *The Cocky Bantam* (Sommer); *Imagination* (Wickersham); *Way Down Yonder in the Corn* (Wickersham); *The Playful Pest* (Sommer); *Polly Wants a Doctor* (Swift); 1944—*Sadie Hawkins Day* (Wickersham); *The Herring Murder Mystery* (Roman); *Magic Strength* (Wickersham); *Lionel Lion* (Sommer); *Amoozin' But Confoozin'* (Marcus); *Giddy-yapping* ((Swift); *The Dream Kids* (Wickersham); *The Disillusioned Bluebird* (Swift); *Tangled Travels* (Geiss); *Trocadero* (Nigh) (live action—d animated sequences only, +ro); (Dave as animation supervisor on Universal's "Sing and Be Happy" series, live action with cartoon inserts): 1946—*Merrily We Sing* (Moore); *A Bit of Blarney* (Moore); *The Singing Barbers* (Moore); 1947—*Let's Sing a College Song* (Moore); *Let's Sing a Western Song* (Moore); *Kernels of Corn* (Moore); *Let's Go Latin* (Moore); *Manhattan Memories* (Moore); 1948—*Lamp Post Favorites* (Moore); *Singin' the Blues* (Parker); *Spotlight Serenade* (Parker); *Choo Choo Swing* (Cowan); *River Melodies* (Parker); *Clap Your Hands* (Cowan); *Hits of the Nineties* (Parker); *Let's Sing a Love Song* (Parker); *Sing While You Work* (Parker); *Songs of the Seasons* (Parker); *The Year Around* (Cowan); *Rudolph, the Red-nosed Reindeer* (Max d); 1949—*Minstrel Mania* (Cowan); *Songs of Romance* (Cowan); *Sailing with a Song* (Cowan); *Singing Along* (Cowan); *Francis* (Lubin) (live action—storyboard only); ("Cartoon Melody" series, live action with cartoon inserts): 1950—*Brother John* (Cowan); *Lower the Boom* (Cowan); *Peggy, Peg and Polly* (Cowan); 1951—*Bedtime for Bonzo* (de Cordova) (live action—d animation sequences for trailer only); *Bubbles of Song* (Cowan); *Readin' 'ritin' and 'rithmetic* (Cowan); *Down the River* (Cowan); *Hilly Billy* (Cowan); *MacDonald's Farm* (Cowan); *Reuben, Reuben* (Cowan); *Uncle Sam's Songs* (Cowan); 1952—*Memory Song Book* (Cowan); *Songs that Live* (Cowan); *Toast of Song* (Cowan).

Publications:

By FLEISCHER:

Book—*Betty Boop* by Max Fleischer, New York 1975.

On FLEISCHER:

Book—*The Fleischer Story* by L. Cabarga, New York 1976; articles—"Les Épinards par la racine" (obituary for Max) by Claude Beylie in *Ecran* (Paris), November 1972; "Max Fleischer, de koning van de voorfilm" by K. de Bree in *Skoop* (Amsterdam), v.8, no.5, 1972; "Max and Dave Fleischer" by M. Langer in *Film Comment* (New York), January/February 1975; "Even Popeye Couldn't Hold Fleischer's Studio Together" by G. Fernett in *Classic Film Collector* (Muscatine, Iowa), winter 1978; "Max & Dave Fleischer": by B. Baker in *Film Dope* (London), February 1979; "In Memoriam Dave Fleischer" by K. de Bree in *Skoop* (Amsterdam), August 1979; obituary for Dave by H. Moret in *Ecran* (Paris), 20 October 1979; obituary in *Variety* (New York), 4 July 1979.

* * *

Max and Dave Fleischer were important stylistic and technical innovators in American animation in the 1920s and 1930s. Their cartoon series, which included *Out of the Inkwell*, *Betty Boop*, *Popeye*, and *Superman*, relied on a flair for ingenuity and comic imagination that made their work stylistically distinctive. The best of the Fleischer brothers' work features an un-self-conscious surrealism and fluid imagery unparalleled in pre-World War Two animation.

Max Fleischer emigrated with his family in 1887 from Vienna to New York City, where his brother Dave was born seven years later. Max studied art at the Art Students League and Cooper Union in New York City. After his schooling, he became a staff artist on the *Brooklyn Daily Eagle*. There he met cartoonist John R. Bray, whose subsequent move into animation later furthered Fleischer's own career. By 1915, Max was an art editor at *Popular Science Monthly*. His job heightened his interest in mechanics and inspired him to invent a machine that would enable an animator to trace over live-action film frame-by-frame. Fleischer was assisted by his brothers Joe and Dave in his new invention, the rotoscope.

The Fleischers put the rotoscope to use in a series of cartoons that were produced by Bray and were called *Out of the Inkwell*. The series featured the "out-of-the-inkwell" appearances and adventures of a cartoon clown (later named Koko) in live action settings. Max and Dave collaborated on the *Out of the Inkwell* series for Bray until 1921, when they established their own company. Max took over responsibility for managing the business and distributing the films. Dave, meanwhile, assumed creative directorship over all the company's cartoons. The Fleischers released their cartoons from 1921 to 1927 through their own distribution company, Red Seal Pictures. After Red Seal collapsed in 1927, they distributed through Paramount Pictures until they were forced out of business in 1942.

The brothers' success increased in the late 1920s with *Talkartoons*, a series of sound cartoons. One of the *Talkartoons'* characters became so popular that she got her own series. Betty Boop, modelled after the flapper actress Helen Kane and individualized by Mae Questel's vocals, was the first sexualized cartoon character. Frequently likened to actress Mae West for her suggestive body language and natural insouciance, Betty Boop appealed to adults as well as to children. The best of the series capitalized on good-natured sexual innuendo, constantly metamorphosizing images, and thinly veiled Freudian symbolism. But in 1934, Hollywood's new Production Code called for so much revision that a sanitized and desexed Betty Boop destroyed the series' imaginative flair even though it continued until 1939.

When Betty's popularity waned, another Fleischer cartoon character became the studio's main attraction. The *Popeye* series based on the Elzie Segar comic strip character, featured new songs, comic twists, and a more ambitious graphic style that used perspective and a range of values. The peak of the series came in the late 1930s in three two-reel Popeyes (*Popeye the Sailor Meets Sinbad the Sailor*, *Popeye the Sailor Meets Ali Baba's 40 Thieves*, and *Aladdin and His Wonderful Lamp*). The three films featured Technicolor, and the first two used Max Fleischer's Turntable Camera, a device for photographing animation cels in front of revolving miniature sets that created three-dimensional effects.

Soon after, the Fleischers attempted to compete with Walt Disney's successful animated feature, *Snow White and the Seven Dwarfs*. They made two feature-length cartoons, *Gulliver's Travels* and *Mr. Bug Goes to Town*. The financial failure of the latter prompted Paramount Pictures to foreclose on the Fleischers' company. Paramount took over the management, renamed the studio (Famous Studio), and fired the Fleischers. The two brothers, who had not been speaking to each other for some time, went their separate ways. Dave worked at Columbia Pictures cartoon studio and Universal studios. He retired in 1969. Max worked on a series of industrial and educational projects, mechanical inventions, and television animation. But he never achieved his former success. He died in 1972 at the Motion Picture Country Home, where he had been a resident for almost ten years.

—Lauren Rabinovitz

FLEISCHER, RICHARD. American. Born in Brooklyn, New York, 8 December 1916. Educated in medicine, Brown University, B.A.; studied drama at Yale University, M.F.A. Married Mary Dickson, 1943. Career: 1937—organized theatrical group Arena Players; 1942—begins editing Pathe newsreels at RKO; 1943—begins directing shorts in RKO series *This Is America*; also producer-director of "Flicker Flashbacks" series compiled from silent films; 1952—*The Narrow Margin*, last film for RKO, is first considerable success; 1955—founds Nautilus Productions. Agent: Phil Gersh, Phil Gersh Agency, Beverly Hills, California.

Films (as co-scriptwriter): 1943—*Air Crew* (short) (O'Reilly); (as director—also credited as Richard O. Fleischer): 1944—*Memo for Joe* (short); 1946—*Child of Divorce*; 1947—*Banjo*; *Design for Death* (no d credit—co-pr from newsreel material); 1948—*So This Is New York*; 1949—*The Clay Pigeon*; *Follow Me Quietly*; *Make Mine Laughs* (co-d—mainly compilation); *Trapped*; 1950—*Armored Car Robbery*; 1952—*The Narrow Margin*; *The Happy Time*; 1953—*Arena*; 1954—*20,000 Leagues Under the Sea*; 1955—*Violent Saturday*; *The Girl in the Red Velvet Swing*; 1956—*Bandido*; *Between Heaven and Hell*; 1958—*The Vikings*; *These Thousand Hills*; 1959—*Compulsion*; 1960—*Crack in the Mirror*; *The Big Gamble*; *North to Alaska* (Hathaway) (pre-production only); 1961—*Barabba (Barabbas)*; 1966—*Fantastic Voyage*; 1967—*Doctor Dolittle*; 1968—*The Boston Strangler*; 1969—*Che!*; 1970—*Tora! Tora! Tora!* (co-d); *10 Rillington Place*; 1971—*Blind Terror (See No Evil)*; *The Last Run*; 1972—*The New Centurions (Precinct 45 Los Angeles Police)*; 1973—*Soylent Green*; *The Don Is Dead*; 1974—*Mr. Majestyk*; *The Spikes Gang*; 1975—*Mandingo*; 1976—*The Incredible Sarah*; 1977—*The Prince and the Pauper (Crossed Swords)*; 1979—*Ashanti*; 1980—*The Jazz Singer*; 1982—*Tough Enough*.

Publications:

By FLEISCHER:

Articles—"Underwater Filming" in *Films in Review* (New York), August/September 1954; interview by Bertrand Tavernier in *Cahiers du cinéma* (Paris), January 1967; "Multi-Image Technique for the Boston Strangler", interview with others, in *American Cinematographer* (Los Angeles), February 1969; "Don't Throw Them Away", interview by Gordon Gow, in *Films and Filming* (London), December 1970; "The Professional Director Speaks" in *Making Films* (New York), August 1971; "Entretien" by D. Rabourdin and P. Collin in *Cinéma* (Paris), May 1979.

On FLEISCHER:

Book—*Barabbas: The Story of a Motion Picture*, edited by Lon

Jones, Bologna 1962; articles—"Un Américain à Cannes: Richard Fleischer" by Michel Delahaye in *Cinéma 59* (Paris), May 1959; articles and interview in *Films ideal* (Madrid), 1 March 1964; biofilmography in *Film Dope* (London), February 1979.

* * *

Fleischer is neither muddled nor mindless as Andrew Sarris has more than implied. He is a rapid, efficient director with some distinct concerns and interests which dominate any film he directs. Since 1968, especially, Fleischer's films have dealt with middle-aged professionals forced to review their life and accomplishments when faced with the threat of a younger rival or a situation beyond their power to control.

The Fleischer hero has usually committed himself to a way of life in which others respect his detached professionalism—Henry Fonda in *The Boston Strangler*, George C. Scott in *The Last Run* and *The New Centurions*, Charlton Heston in *Soylent Green*, Anthony Quinn in *The Don Is Dead*, Lee Marvin in *The Spikes Gang*, and Warren Oates in *Tough Enough*.

Confronted with a new challenge, however, the weary, aging protagonist finds it too much for him, his past methods no longer viable (*Mr. Majestyk* is an atypical Fleischer film in that Charles Bronson's past proves to be that which saves him; his violence and guerrilla tactics result in his triumph, which is generally the case with Bronson's screen persona). In *10 Rillington Place*, this confrontation is most bizarre with Richard Attenborough's Christie as a horrible distortion of the Fleischer hero. In a particularly gruesome conclusion, Christie, the murderer of women, is caught, but his younger, pathetic rival is executed for a murder Christie committed.

These aging heroes are inevitably overwhelmed by a challenge too great for their diminished abilities. The war is too much for Martin Balsam in *Tora! Tora! Tora!*, Scott is destroyed by the vision of his wasted life in both *The New Centurions* and *The Last Run*, Marvin in *The Spikes Gang* both destroys and is destroyed by the three young men he has taught to rob banks, and Heston at the end of *Soylent Green* has not saved the world from starvation, but deprived it of a source of food. The conclusion of *Soylent Green* indicates clearly the dilemma which drives the Fleischer protagonist to despair and neurosis: the moral decision may turn out to be destructive, painful and deadly, yet the protagonist cannot escape the decision. He stays with it even if it destroys him and society.

Fleischer, the son of film animator Max Fleischer who created Betty Boop, Koko the Clown and the Popeye cartoons, is particularly adept at working with and coaxing out subdued performances from his often larger-than-life stars. Charlton Heston's reaction to the death of Edward G. Robinson in *Soylent Green* is one of the most poignant moments in Heston's career. Conversely, Fleischer has recognized the emotional possibilities of young actors and has given them the opportunity for initial serious recognition. Notable examples of this are John Hurt in *10 Rillington Place*, Tony Curtis in *The Boston Strangler* and Bradford Dillman in *Compulsion*.

—Stuart M. Kaminsky

FLEMING, VICTOR. American. Born in Pasadena, California, 23 February 1883. Career: before 1910—car-racing driver and chauffeur; 1910—hired as assistant cameraman at American

Film Company; 1911—begins working on Allan Dwan films; 1915—begins as cameraman at Triangle, works under D.W. Griffith; 1917—joins photographic section of U.S. Army Signal Corps; 1919—cameraman for Walter Wanger at Versailles Peace Conference; returns to Hollywood, begins directing with 2 Douglas Fairbanks, Sr., films; from 1932—contract director for MGM; 1939—receives directing credit, and Academy Award, for *Gone With the Wind*. Died in 1949. Recipient: Best Director Academy Award for *Gone With the Wind*, 1939.

Films (as photographer—incomplete listing): 1916—*His Picture in the Papers* (Emerson); *The Habit of Happiness (Laugh and the World Laughs)* (Dwan); *The Good Bad Man (Passing Through)* (Dwan); *Betty of Greystone* (Dwan); *Macbeth* (Emerson); *Little Meena's Romance* (Powell); *The Mystery of the Leaping Fish* (Emerson—short); *The Half-breed* (Dwan); *An Innocent Magdalene* (Dwan); *A Social Secretary* (Emerson); *Manhattan Madness* (Dwan); *50-50* (Dwan); *American Aristocracy* (Ingraham); *The Matrimaniac* (Powell); *The Americano* (Emerson); 1917—*Down to Earth* (Emerson); *The Man from Painted Post* (Henabery); *Reaching for the Moon* (Emerson) (co-); *A Modern Musketeer* (Dwan); 1919—*His Majesty, the American (One of the Blood)* (Henabery); (as director): 1919—*When the Clouds Roll By* (co-d); private film, featuring Douglas Fairbanks, Sr., made for the Duke of Sutherland; 1920—*The Mollycoddle*; 1921—*Mamma's Affair*; *Woman's Place*; 1922—*The Lane That Had No Turning*; *Red Hot Romance*; *Anna Ascends*; 1923—*Dark Secrets*; *The Law of the Lawless*; *To the Last Man*; *The Call of the Canyon*; 1924—*Code of the Sea*; *Empty Hands*; 1925—*The Devil's Cargo*; *Adventure*; *A Son of His Father*; *Lord Jim*; 1926—*The Blind Goddess*; *Mantrap*; 1927—*The Rough Riders (The Trumpet Call)*; *The Way of All Flesh*; *Hula*; 1928—*The Awakening*; 1929—*Abie's Irish Rose*; *Wolf Song*; *The Virginian*; 1930—*Common Clay*; *Renegades*; 1931—*Around the World With Douglas Fairbanks (Around the World in 80 Minutes With Douglas Fairbanks)* (+ro); 1932—*The Wet Parade*; *Red Dust*; 1933—*The White Sister*; *Bombshell (Blonde Bombshell)*; 1934—*Treasure Island*; 1935—*Reckless*; *The Farmer Takes a Wife*; 1937—*Captains Courageous*; *The Good Earth* (Franklin) (co-d, uncredited); *A Star Is Born* (Wellman) (d add'l material); 1938—*Test Pilot*; *The Crowd Roars* (Thorpe) (d add'l scenes); *The Great Waltz* (Duvivier) (co-d, uncredited); 1939—*The Wizard of Oz*; *Gone With the Wind*; 1941—*Dr. Jekyll and Mr. Hyde* (+pr); 1942—*Tortilla Flat*; 1943—*A Guy Named Joe*; 1945—*Adventure*; 1948—*Joan of Arc*.

Publications:

On FLEMING:

Articles—obituary in *The New York Times*, 7 January 1949; "The Man Who Made *Gone With the Wind*" and "Fleming: The Apprentice Years" by John Reid in *Films and Filming* (London), December 1967 and January 1968; "Checklist 109—Victor Fleming" in *Monthly Film Bulletin* (London), October 1977; "Victor Fleming" by Kevin Brownlow in *Film Dope* (London), February 1979; "Victor Fleming" in *Contracampo* (Madrid), October/November 1980.

*　　*　　*

In his day, Victor Fleming was a successful, respected director of some of Metro-Goldwyn-Mayer's biggest and most celebrated films (*Red Dust, Captains Courageous, Test Pilot*) as well as two undisputed Hollywood classics by the standards of popular taste, *The Wizard of Oz* and *Gone with the Wind*. Ironically, it is probably the enormous continuing popularity of the latter two titles that has eclipsed Fleming's personal reputation. Correctly perceived as producer-dominated, studio-influenced cinema, both *Oz* and *Gone with the Wind*, are talked and written about extensively, but never as Victor Fleming films. They are classic examples of the complicated collaborations which took place under the old studio system. Although Fleming received directorial credit (and 1939's Oscar as Best Director) for *Gone with the Wind*, others made significant contributions to the final film, among them George Cukor.

Fleming served his film apprenticeship as a cinematographer, working with such pioneers as Allan Dwan at the Flying A company and D.W. Griffith at Triangle. He photographed several Douglas Fairbanks films, among them *The Americano*, *Wild and Woolly*, and *Down to Earth*. He developed a skillful sense of storytelling through the camera, as well as a good eye for lighting and composition during those years. After he became a director, his critical reputation became tied to the studio at which he made the majority of his films, Metro-Goldwyn-Mayer. Known unofficially as a "producer's studio," MGM concentrated on showcasing its well-known stable of stars in suitable vehicles.

At Metro, Fleming was frequently thought of as a counterpart to George Cukor; Cukor was labelled a "woman's director," Fleming a "man's director." Besides being a close personal friend and favorite director of Clark Gable, Fleming was responsible for directing the Oscar-winning performance of Spencer Tracy in *Captains Courageous*. His flair for getting along with male stars enabled him to create an impressive group of popular films that were loved by audiences, who saw them as "Gable films" or "Tracy films." Both Henry Fonda (whose screen debut was in Fleming's *The Farmer Takes a Wife*) and Gary Cooper (whose first big screen success was in *The Virginian*) owed much of their early recognitions to Fleming's talent for directing actors. One of Fleming's chief characteristics was that of spotting potential stars and understanding the phenomenon of the star persona. In addition to his work with male actors, he also played a key role in the career development of Jean Harlow. Under Fleming's direction, she was encouraged to mix comedy with her sex appeal.

The Virginian, Fleming's first sound film, is an under-rated movie which demonstrates a remarkable ability to overcome the problems of the early sound era, shooting both outdoors and indoors with equal fluidity and success. Fleming's use of naturalistic sound in this film did much to influence other early films. However, Fleming's work is not unified by a particular cinematic style, although it is coherent in thematic terms. His world is one of male camaraderie, joyous action, pride in professionalism, and lusty love for women who are not too ladylike to return the same sort of feelings. In this regard, his work is not unlike that of Howard Hawks, but Fleming lacks of Hawks's ability to refine style and content into a unified vision.

Fleming's name is not well-known today. Although he received directorial credit for what is possibly the most famous movie ever made in Hollywood (*Gone with the Wind*), he is not remembered as its director. His work stands as an example of the best done by those directors who worked within the studio system, allowing the studio stamp to become the style of the film rather than creating a personal vision of their own.

—Jeanine Basinger

FLOREY, ROBERT. French. Born in Paris, 14 September 1900. Educated in private schools, Switzerland. Career: 1918-19—acts in and collaborates on script of several films in Switzerland; 1920—returns to Paris, makes contact with filmmaking community, contributes to revues *Cinémagazine* and *La Cinématographie française*; sent to write on Feuillade's studios at Nice, is taken on as actor and assistant director on *L'Orpheline* serial; 1921—returning to Paris, persuades Jean Pascal to send him as special envoy for *Cinémagazine* to Hollywood; hired as historical advisor on *Monte Cristo* (Flynn); gagman for "Fox Sunshine Comedies"; 1921-23—director of foreign publicity for Douglas Fairbanks and Mary Pickford; 1923—handles publicity for Valentino's tour of U.S. and Europe; on return to Hollywood directs first film, 2-reel comedy *50-50*; 1924-26—assistant director to von Sternberg, King Vidor, John Stahl, and others at M.G.M.; 1926—quits M.G.M. to direct *One Hour of Love* for Tiffany; 1927-28—directs 4 experimental shorts; 1928—at Paramount Long Island studios directs 24 shorts featuring New York theater stars; directs Paramount's first feature talkie *Night Club*; 1929—invited by producer Pierre Braunberger to make first French talking film *La Route est belle* (shot in Britain and France); also makes 2 films at UFA studios, Neubabelsberg; becomes familiar with German expressionistic techniques, invited by Carl Laemmle to adapt *Frankenstein*; 1930—*Frankenstein* assignment given to James Whale, receives Poe's *The Murders in the Rue Morgue* as compensation; 1948—publishes *Hollywood d'hier et d'aujourd'hui*, first of a series of outstanding histories of Hollywood's development; 1950—abandons filmmaking for TV, beginning with "Four Star TV" series; makes hundreds of TV dramas and series episodes. Died at Santa Monica, California, 16 May 1979. Recipient: French Légion d'Honneur, 1950.

Films (as director and scriptwriter): 1919—*Heureuse Intervention*; *Isidore sur le lac*; *Isidore a la deveine*; (as assistant director): 1921—*L'Orpheline* (serial in 12 episodes) (Feuillade) (+ro as *un apache*); *Saturnin (Le Bon Allumeur)* (Feuillade) (+ro as *un gazier*); (as historical advisor): *Monte Cristo* (Flynn); (French sub-titles): 1922—*Robin Hood* (Dwan); (as director and scriptwriter): 1923—*Valentino en Angleterre*; *50-50*; (as assistant director): 1923—*Wine* (Gasnier); 1924—*Parisian Nights* (Santell) (+tech advisor); *The Exquisite Sinner* (von Sternberg); *Time the Comedian* (Leonard); 1925—*The Masked Bride* (von Sternberg); *La Boheme* (King Vidor); *Escape* (Rosen); *Paris (Shadows of Paris)* (Goulding) (+tech advisor); *Dance Madness* (Leonard); *Toto* (Stahl); 1926—*Monte Carlo (Dreams of Monte Carlo)* (Cabanne); *Bardelys the Magnificent* (King Vidor); (as director): 1926—*One Hour of Love*; *That Model from Paris* (Gasnier) (co-d, uncredited, +sc); *The Magic Flame* (King) (ass't d only); 1927—*The Romantic Age*; *The Cohens and the Kellys* (Beaudine) (2nd unit d only); *Face Value*; *The Woman Disputed* (King) (ass't d only); *Life and Death of a Hollywood Extra (The Life and Death of 9413—A Hollywood Extra)* (+sc); *Johann the Coffin Maker* (+sc); *The Loves of Zero* (+sc); 1928—series of 24 shorts for Paramount featuring New York stage stars; *Night Club*; *Skyscraper Symphony* (+sc, ph); *The Pusher-in-the-Face*; *Bonjour, New York!* (+sc); *The Hole in the Wall*; 1929—*The Cocoanuts* (co-d); *The Battle of Paris (The Gay Lady)*; *Eddie Cantor* (+sc); *La Route est belle*; 1930—*L'Amour chante* (also directed German version: *Komm' zu mir zum Rendezvous*, and Spanish: *Professor de mi Señora (El professor de mi mujer)*); *Anna Christie* (Brown) (d New York exteriors only, uncredited); 1932—*Le Blanc et le noir* (co-d); *Frankenstein* (Whale) (sc only); *The Murders in the Rue Morgue* (+co-sc); 1932—*The Man Called Back*; *Those We Love*; *A Study in Scarlet* (+sc); *The Blue Moon Murder Case*; *Girl Missing*; *Ex-Lady*; 1933—*The House on 56th Street*; *Bedside*; *Registered Nurse*; *Smarty (Hit Me Again)*; 1934—*Oil for the Lamps of China* (LeRoy) (d exteriors only); *Shanghai Orchid* (d exteriors only); *I Sell Anything*; *I Am a Thief*; *The Woman in Red*; 1935—*Go into Your Dance* (Mayo) (co-d, uncredited); *The Florentine Dagger*; *Going Highbrow*; *Don't Bet on Blonds*; *The Payoff*; *Ship Cafe*; *The Rose of the Rancho* (Gering) (d add'l scenes, uncredited); *The Preview Murder Mystery*; 1936—*Till We Meet Again*; *Hollywood Boulevard* (+co-sc); *Outcast*; 1937—*The King of the Gamblers*; *This Way Please*; *Mountain Music*; *Daughter of Shanghai (Daughter of the Orient)*; *Disbarred*; *King of Alcatraz*; 1938—*Dangerous to Know*; *Hotel Imperial*; 1939—*The Magnificent Fraud*; *Parole Fixer*; *Death of a Champion*; *Women without Names*; 1940—*Meet Boston Blackie*; *The Face Behind the Mask*; 1941—*2 in a Taxi*; *Dangerously They Live*; *Lady Gangster*; 1942—*The Desert Song* (+co-sc); 1943—*Bomber's Moon* (Fuhr) (co-d, uncredited); *Roger Touhy, Gangster (The Last Gangster)*; *The Man from Frisco*; 1944—*Escape in the Desert* (Blatt) (co-d, uncredited); *God Is My Co-Pilot*; 1945—*Danger Signal*; *The Beast with 5 Fingers*; 1947—*Monsieur Verdoux* (Chaplin) (co-associate d only); *Tarzan and the Mermaids*; 1948—*Adventures of Don Juan* (Sherman) (sc only under pseudonym "Florian Roberts"); *Rogue Regiment* (+sc); *Outpost in Morocco*; 1949—*The Crooked Way*; *Johnny One-Eye*; 1950—*The Vicious Years (The Gangster We Made)*. Role: 1918—*le détective* in *Le Cirque de la mort* (Lindt).

Publications:

By FLOREY:

Books—*Filmland*, Paris 1923; *Deux Ans dans les studios américains*, Paris 1924; *Douglas Fairbanks, sa vie, ses films, ses aventures*, Paris 1926; *Pola Negri*, Paris 1926; *Charlie Chaplin*, preface by Lucien Wahl, Paris 1927; *Ivan Mosjoukine*, with Jean Arnoy, preface by René Jeanne, Paris 1927; *Adolphe Menjou*, with André Tinchant, Paris 1927; *Hollywood d'hier et d'aujourd'hui*, preface by René Clair, Paris 1948; *Monsieur Chaplin, or Le Rire dans la nuit*, with Maurice Bessy, Paris 1952; *La Lanterne magique*, preface by Maurice Bessy, Lausanne 1966; *Hollywood années zéro. La Prehistoire l'invention, les pionniers, naissance des mythes*, Paris 1972; articles—Note: from 1921 to 1926, Florey wrote several hundred articles for *Cinémagazine* (Paris); he also wrote numerous articles for Parisian publications including *Pour vous*, *Saint Cinéma des Prés*, *Ciné-Club*, *Le Technicien du film*, *La Cinématographie française*, and *Cinéma*.

On FLOREY:

Articles—"Robert Florey" by Jack Spears in *Films in Review* (New York), April 1960 (collected in his *Hollywood: The Golden Era*, New York 1971); "Visitors to Sydney" by Charles Higham in *Sight and Sound* (London), summer 1962; "Directors on TV: Robert Florey" by Leonard Maltin in *Film Fan Monthly*, December 1971; "En attendant Verdoux" by G. Braucourt in *Ecran* (Paris), July/August 1972; "Robert Florey" by M. Salmi in *Film Dope* (London), February 1979; obituary by Claude Beylie in *Ecran* (Paris), 15 July 1979; "Robert Florey", letter from Herbert Luft in *Films in Review* (New York), August/September 1979.

*   *   *

It is not easy to define Robert Florey's status in the history of the American film. As a list of his films quite clearly attests, he was not a major director, but he was certainly an interesting and intriguing one who seemed able to keep abreast with trends and changes in the methodology of filmmaking.

After working on a number of minor silent program features, Florey reached the peak of his artistic filmmaking career in the late twenties with the production of four experimental shorts—*The Life and Death of 9413—A Hollywood Extra, The Loves of Zero, Johann the Coffin Maker*, and *Skyscraper Symphony*—which showed a skillful understanding of editing and the influence of German expressionist cinema. The best known of these shorts is *A Hollywood Extra*, which no longer appears to survive in its entirety, but which nonetheless illustrates Florey's grasp of montage and satire. Florey never again returned to this form of filmmaking, but thanks to these shorts he was invited to direct a number of early talkies at Paramount. Aside from *Cocoanuts*, which is more Marx Brothers than Florey, these Paramount features—notably *The Battle of Paris*—again demonstrate that the director was not only totally cognizant of developments in the sound film but also was able to bring ingenuity and fluidity to the medium.

A crucial point in Florey's career came in 1931 when he was asked to script and direct *Frankenstein*. Although some elements of the Florey screenplay are utilized, his script was basically scrapped and he was replaced as director by James Whale. Had Florey been allowed to keep the assignment, he would doubtless have become a major Hollywood director. Instead he was assigned *Murders in the Rue Morgue*, which certainly contains some nice atmospheric lighting effects as well as moments of surprising brutality, but has never achieved the cult popularity of *Frankenstein*. For the next 20 years Robert Florey toiled away as a reliable contract director, whose films were never more than pleasant and diverting entertainments. Even when he worked as co-director with Chaplin on *Monsieur Verdoux*, Florey saw his more daring directing ideas rejected by the comedian in favor of a static filmmaking style which Chaplin favored. Florey moved exclusively into television direction in 1950, and seemed very much at ease working on programs such as *The Loretta Young Show*, whose star and content suited his own conservative temperament.

Aside from his work as a director, Robert Florey deserves recognition as a commentator on and witness to the Hollywood scene. He *loved* cinema from his first involvement in his native France as an assistant to Louis Feuillade. That love led to his coming to Hollywood in the early twenties as a correspondent for a French film magazine and to the writing of eight books, all in French, on the history of the cinema, all of which are exemplary works of scholarship.

—Anthony Slide

FORD, ALEKSANDER. Polish. Born in Lodz, Poland, 24 November 1908; emigrated to Israel 1969. Educated in History of Arts, Warsaw University. Career: 1929-30—makes 2 documentaries about native city, Lodz; early 1930s—belongs to S.T.A.R.T. ("Society of Friends of Artistic Films") with Wanda Jakubowska, Stanislaw Wohl and others, organization to promote a socially useful cinema; 1934—in Palestine makes *Sabra*, story of a Jewish and an Arab village; film forbidden by Zionists; 1935—joins Polish Communist party; 1939—emigrates to USSR, begins making instructional and documentary films for Red Army; 1943—with founding of Armia Polska, becomes head of film group of 1st Polish Division; 1944—after area around Lub-

lin liberated, returns to Poland; makes documentary *Majdanek—Cemetery of Europe*, one of first documentaries about concentration camps; made head of Polish Army film studios; 1945—Polish film industry nationalized; 1945-47—1st director of Film Polski; 1946-47—makes *Border Street* in former Warsaw Jewish ghetto; 1948—helps found Lodz film school, and serves as its head for several years; begins again to make feature films; mid-1950s to 1968—head of film production group "Studio"; 1960s—begins to encounter difficulties in realizing projects; supports directors such as Skolimowski and Nasfeter accused of "anti-Polish tendencies"; 1969—though denied visa to U.S., is allowed to emigrate to Israel; 1973—directs first Israeli-German co-production, *The Martyr*; 1973—in West Germany makes *Sie sind frei, Dr. Korszak*. Died in Los Angeles, 29 April 1980. Recipient: award for direction, Cannes Festival, for *5 Boys of Barska Street*, 1954.

Films (as director): 1928—*Nad ranem*; *Tetno Polskiego Manchesteru*; 1930—*Mascotte (A Mascot)*; 1931—*Narodziny gazety*; 1932—*Legion ulicy (The Street Legion)*; 1934—*Przebudzenie (The Awakening)*; *Sabra*; 1935—*Na start!*; 1936—*Droga mlodych (The Road for Youth)*; *Spolem*; 1937—*Ludzie wisly (The Vistula People)* (co-d); 1943—*Przysiegam u Ziemi Polskiej* (co-d); *Bitwa pod Lenino*; 1944—*Majdanek—Cmentarzysko Europy*; 1949—*Ulica graniczna (Border Street)* (+co-sc); 1952—*Mlodosc Chopina (The Youth of Chopin)* (+sc); 1954—*Piatka z ulicy Barskiej (5 Boys of Barska Street)* (+co-sc); 1957—*Osmy dzien tygodnia (The 8th Day of the Week)* (+sc); 1960—*Krzyzacy (The Knights of the Teutonic Order)* (+co-sc); 1964—*Pierszwy dzien wolnosci (The First Day of Freedom)* (+sc); 1966—*Angeklagt nach N.218*; 1973—*The Martyr*; 1973—*Sie sind frei, Dr. Korczak*; 1974—*The First Circle*.

Publications:

By FORD:

Articles—"Questions à Aleksander Ford" by Jacques Chevallier in *Image et son* (Paris), no.136-7, 1960; "L'Itinéraire d'Aleksander Ford", interview by Antonin Liehm in *Cinéma* (Paris), April 1974.

On FORD:

Articles—"The Uneasy East: Aleksander Ford" by Gene Moskowitz in *Sight and Sound* (London), winter 1957/58; obituary by M. Martin in *Image et son* (Paris), September 1980.

FORD, JOHN. American. Born Sean Aloysius O'Feeney (or John Augustine Feeney) in Cape Elizabeth, Maine, 1 February 1895. Educated at Portland High School, Maine; University of Maine, 1913 or 1914 (for 3 weeks). Married Mary McBryde Smith in 1920; children: Patrick and Barbara. Career: 1914—joins his brother Francis (director for Universal) in Hollywood; 1914-17—works for Universal as actor, does stunts and special effects; 1916—assumes name "Jack Ford"; assistant director to brother; credited as Jack Ford on films through *Cameo Kirby* (1923); 1917-21—contract director for Universal; 1921—leaves Universal for Fox Film Corp. (through 1931); 1930—begins collaboration with screenwriter Dudley Nichols on *Men without*

Women; 1940—assembles film crew that becomes Field Photographic Branch of U.S. Office of Strategic Services; pioneers documentary film techniques for use in intelligence gathering; 1942-45—serves as Lieutenant-Commander, U.S. Marine Corps, wounded at Battle of Midway; 1945—begins supervising 8-hour documentary on Nuremberg trials, project abandoned; after WWII—becomes officer in U.S. Naval Reserve, eventually being given rank of Admiral by President Nixon. Died in Palm Desert, California, 31 August 1973. Recipient: Academy Award, Best Director, for *The Informer*, 1935; Best Direction, New York Film Critics, for *The Informer*, 1935; Best Direction, New York Film Critics, for *Stagecoach*, 1939; Academy Award, Best Director, for *The Grapes of Wrath*, 1940; Academy Award, Best Director, for *How Green Was My Valley*, 1941; Best Direction, New York Film Critics, for *How Green Was My Valley*, 1941; Academy Award, Best Documentary, for *Battle of Midway*, 1942; Legion of Merit and Purple Heart; Annual Award, Directors Guild of America, 1952; Grand Lion of Venice Award, Venice Film Festival, 1971; Lifetime Achievement Award, American Film Institute, 1973.

Films (as director): 1917—*The Tornado* (+sc, ro); *The Trail of Hate* (may have been directed by Francis Ford); *The Scrapper* (+sc, ro); *The Soul Herder*; *Cheyenne's Pal* (+story); *Straight Shooting*; *The Secret Man*; *A Marked Man*; *Bucking Broadway*; 1918—*The Phantom Riders*; *Wild Women*; *Thieves' Gold*; *The Scarlet Drop* (+story); *Hell Bent* (+co-sc); *A Woman's Fool*; *3 Mounted Men*; 1919—*Roped*; *The Fighting Brothers*; *A Fight for Love*; *By Indian Post*; *The Rustlers*; *Bare Fists*; *Gun Law*; *The Gun Packer (The Gun Pusher)*; *Riders of Vengeance* (+co-sc); *The Last Outlaw*; *The Outcasts of Poker Flat*; *The Ace of the Saddle*; *The Rider of the Law*; *A Gun Fightin' Gentleman* (+co-story); *Marked Men*; 1920—*The Prince of Avenue A*; *The Girl in Number 29*; *Hitchin' Posts*; *Just Pals*; *The Big Punch* (+co-sc); 1921—*The Freeze Out*; *Desperate Trails*; *Action*; *Sure Fire*; *Jackie*; 1922—*The Wallop*; *Little Miss Smiles*; *The Village Blacksmith*; *Silver Wings* (Carewe) (d prologue only); 1923—*The Face on the Barroom Floor*; *3 Jumps Ahead* (+sc); *Cameo Kirby*; *North of Hudson Bay*; *Hoodman Blind*; 1924—*The Iron Horse*; *Hearts of Oak*; 1925—*Lightnin'*; *Kentucky Pride*; *The Fighting Heart*; *Thank You*; 1926—*The Shamrock Handicap*; *3 Bad Men*; *The Blue Eagle*; 1927—*Upstream*; 1928—*Mother Machree*; *4 Sons*; *Hangman's House*; *Napoleon's Barber*; *Riley the Cop*; 1929—*Strong Boy*; *Salute*; *The Black Watch*; 1930—*Men Without Women* (+co-story); *Born Reckless*; *Up the River* (+co-sc, uncredited); 1931—*Seas Beneath*; *The Brat*; *Arrowsmith*; *Flesh*; 1933—*Pilgrimage*; *Dr. Bull*; 1934—*The Lost Patrol*; *The World Moves On*; *Judge Priest*; 1935—*The Whole Town's Talking*; *The Informer*; *Steamboat Round the Bend*; 1936—*The Prisoner of Shark Island*; *Mary of Scotland*; *The Plough and the Stars*; 1937—*Wee Willie Winkie*; *The Hurricane*; 1938—*4 Men and a Prayer*; *Submarine Patrol*; 1939—*Stagecoach*; *Drums Along the Mohawk*; *Young Mr. Lincoln*; 1940—*The Grapes of Wrath*; *The Long Voyage Home*; 1941—*Tobacco Road*; *Sex Hygiene*; *How Green Was My Valley*; 1942—*The Battle of Midway* (+co-ph); *Torpedo Squadron*; 1943—*December 7th* (co-d); *We Sail at Midnight*; 1945—*They Were Expendable*; 1946—*My Darling Clementine*; 1947—*The Fugitive* (+co-pr); 1948—*Fort Apache* (+co-pr); *3 Godfathers* (+co-pr); 1949—*She Wore a Yellow Ribbon* (+co-pr); 1950—*When Willie Comes Marching Home*; *Wagonmaster* (+co-pr); *Rio Grande* (+co-pr); 1951—*This is Korea!*; 1952—*What Price Glory*; *The Quiet Man* (+co-pr); 1953—*The Sun Shines Bright*; *Mogambo*; 1955—The Long Gray Line; *Mister Roberts* (co-d); *Rookie of the Year* (episode for *Screen Directors Playhouse* television series); *The Bamboo Cross* (episode for *Fireside*

Theater television series); 1956—*The Searchers*; 1957—*The Wings of Eagles*; *The Rising of the Moon*; 1958—*So Alone*; *The Last Hurrah*; 1959—*Gideon of Scotland Yard (Gideon's Day)*; *Korea*; *The Horse Soldiers*; 1960—*The Colter Craven Story* (episode for *Wagon Train* television series); *Sergeant Rutledge*; 1961—*2 Rode Together*; 1962—*The Man Who Shot Liberty Valance*; *Flashing Spikes* (episode for *Alcoa Premiere* television series); *How the West Was Won* (directed *The Civil War* segment); 1963—*Donovan's Reef* (+pr); 1964—*Cheyenne Autumn*; 1965—*Young Cassidy* (co-d); 1966—*7 Women*; 1970—*Chesty: A Tribute to a Legend*; 1971 *Vietnam! Vietnam!* (Beck—for U.S.I.A.) (executive pr only).

Roles: 1914—*Lucille Love, the Girl of Mystery* (15 episode serial) (Francis Ford); *The Mysterious Rose* (Francis Ford); 1915—*The Birth of a Nation* (Griffith); *3 Bad Men and a Girl* (Francis Ford); *The Hidden City* (Francis Ford); *The Doorway of Destruction* (Francis Ford) (+ass't d); *The Broken Coin* (22 episode serial) (Francis Ford); 1916—*The Lumber Yard Gang* (Francis Ford); *Peg o' the Ring* (15 episode serial) (Francis Ford and Jacques Jaccard); *Chicken-Hearted Jim* (Francis Ford); *The Bandit's Wager* (Francis Ford); 1929—as himself in *Big Time* (Kenneth Hawks).

Publications:

By FORD:

Book—*John Ford's Stagecoach* edited by Richard Anobile, New York 1975; articles—"John Ford Wants It Real", interview in *Christian Science Monitor Magazine* (Boston), 21 June 1941; interview by Lindsay Anderson in *Sequence* (London), New Year issue 1952; "Rencontre avec John Ford" in *Cahiers du cinéma* (Paris), March 1955; "Poet in an Iron Mask", interview by Michael Barkun in *Films and Filming* (London), February 1958; "Rencontre avec John Ford" by Jean-Louis Rieupeyrout in *Cinéma 61* (Paris), February 1961; "Ford on Ford" in *Cinema* (Beverly Hills), July 1964; "Rencontre avec John Ford" by Axel Madsen in *Cahiers du cinéma* (Paris), July 1965; interview by Jean Mitry in *Interviews with Film Directors*, edited by Andrew Sarris, New York 1967; "Our Way West", interview by Burt Kennedy in *Films and Filming* (London), October 1969.

On FORD:

Books—*John Ford* by Jean Mitry, Paris 1954; *John Ford* by Philippe Haudiquet, Paris 1966; *The Cinema of John Ford* by John Baxter, New York 1971; *Filmguide to The Grapes of Wrath* by Warren French, Bloomington, Indiana 1973; *John Ford* by Joseph McBride and Michael Wilmington, London 1975; *The John Ford Movie Mystery* by Andrew Sarris, London 1976; *John Ford* by Claude Beylie in *Anthologie du cinéma*, Paris 1976; *John Ford* by Peter Bogdanovich, Berkeley, California 1978; *John Ford* by Andrew Sinclair, New York 1979; *Pappy: The Life of John Ford* by Dan Ford, Englewood Cliffs, New Jersey 1979; articles—"Days of a Pioneer" by Peter Baker in *Films and Filming* (London), November 1955; "The 5 Worlds of John Ford" by Douglas McVay in *Films and Filming* (London), November 1955; "Working with John Ford" by Michael Killanin in *Films and Filming* (London), 1958; "Notes on the Art of John Ford" by Michael Barkun in *Film Culture* (New York), summer 1962; "Ford on Ford" by George Mitchell in *Films in Review* (New York), March 1963; article in *Films in Review* (New York), June/July 1964; "Autumn of John Ford" by Peter

Bogdanovich in *Esquire* (New York), April 1964; John Ford issue, *Présence du cinéma* (Paris), March 1965; "Special John Ford" in *Cahiers du cinéma* (Paris), October 1966; "John Ford, un homme très peu tranquille" by Anne Capelle in *Arts* (Paris), 20 July 1966; "John Ford à Paris" by Bertrand Tavernier in *Positif* (Paris), March 1967; "La quatrième dimension de la vieillesse" by Claudine Tavernier in *Cinéma 69* (Paris), June 1969; "Decline of a Master" by Bruce Beresford in *Film* (London), autumn 1969; "A Persistence of Vision" by William Pechter in *24 Times a Second: Films and Film-makers*, New York 1971; "Special Issue Devoted to John Ford and His Towering Achievement, *Stagecoach*", *Action* (Los Angeles), September/-October 1971; "John Ford" by Lindsay Anderson in *Cinema* (Beverly Hills), spring 1971; articles on Ford's late films in *Film Comment* (New York), autumn 1971; issue devoted to Ford, *Focus on Film* (London), spring 1971; John Ford issue, *Velvet Light Trap* (Madison, Wisconsin), August 1971; issue on "Ford's Stock Company" in *Filmkritik* (Munich), January 1972; "John Ford's Young Mr. Lincoln" by the Editors of *Cahiers du cinéma* in *Screen* (London), autumn 1972; "Drums Along the Mekong: I Love America, I Am Apolitical" by J. McBride in *Sight and Sound* (London), autumn 1972; "Après la mort de John Ford" by J. Magny in *Téléciné* (Paris), November 1973; "About John Ford" in *Action* (Los Angeles), November/December 1973; "L'Ouest en deuil. John Ford—1895-1973" by R.-C. Bérubé in *Séquences* (Paris), October 1973; "Fordissimo" by Claude Beylie and Marcel Martin in *Ecran* (Paris), November 1973; "Wer ist Don Quichotte? Die Ideen und die Quadratfüsse" by W.-E. Bühler in *Filmkritik* (Munich), February 1974; "John Ford: l'uomo del passato, da progressista a reazionario" by A. Frezzato in *Cineforum* (Bergamo), September 1973; "Bringing in the Sheaves" by J. McBride in *Sight and Sound* (London), winter 1973/74; "Ford and Mr. Rogers" by M. Rubin in *Film Comment* (New York), January/February 1974; "Ceremonies of Innocence: 2 Films by John Ford" by E.R. Belton in *Velvet Light Trap* (Madison), winter 1975; "John Ford (1895-1973)" special issue of *Anthologie du cinéma* (Paris), March 1975; "John Ford: A Reassessment" by M. Dempsey in *Film Quarterly* (Berkeley), summer 1975; "John Ford: Midway. The War Documentaries" by T. Gallagher in *Film Comment* (New York), September/October 1975; "A Home in the Wilderness: Visual Imagery in John Ford's Westerns" by M. Budd in *Cinema Journal* (Evanston), fall 1976; "Vietnam! Vietnam!" by F. Kaplan in *Cineaste* (New York), fall 1976; "John Ford's Literary Sources: From Realism to Romance" by H.P. Stowell in *Literature/Film Quarterly* (Salisbury, Md.), spring 1977; "Gelbe Streifen strenges blau Passage durch Filme von John Ford" by H. Bitomsky and M. Müller in *Filmkritik* (Munich), June 1978; "John Ford: Tribut an eine Legende" by W.-E. Bühler in *Filmkritik* (Munich), August 1978; "Approche du rite, de la discipline et de la transgression chez John Ford" by J. Funck in *Positif* (Paris), April 1978; "Print the Fact: For and Against the Films of John Ford" by P. Greenfield in *Take One* (Montreal), November 1977; "John Ford and Monument Valley" by T. McCarthy in *American Film* (Washington, D.C.), May 1978; "Where Have You Gone, My Darling Clementine?" by W. Roth in *Film Culture* (New York), no.63-64, 1977; special issue by W.C. Siska and others of *Wide Angle* (Athens, Ohio), v.2, no.4, 1978; "Passage durch Filme von John Ford gelbe Streifen, strenges Blau" by H. Bitomsky in *Filmkritik* (Munich), August 1980; "Shadow and Substance" by R. Combs in *Monthly Film Bulletin* (London), June 1980; "Ford, Ozu, et nous" by W.K. Guérin in *Cinéma* (Paris), February 1981; films—*John Ford: Memorial Day 1970* by Mark Haggard, U.S. 1970; *Directed by John Ford* by Peter Bogdanovich, U.S. 1971; *The American West of John Ford* by Denis Sanders, U.K. 1971.

*   *   *

John Ford has no peers in the annals of cinema. This is not to place him above criticism, merely above comparison. His faults were unique, as was his art, which he pursued with a single-minded and single-hearted stubbornness for 60 years and 112 films. He grew up with the American cinema. That he should have begun his career as an extra in the Ku Klux Klan sequences of *The Birth of a Nation* and ended it supervising the documentary *Vietnam! Vietnam!* conveys the remarkable breadth of his contribution to film, and the narrowness of its concerns.

Ford's subject was his life and times. Immigrant, Catholic, Republican, he speaks for the generations that created the modern United States between the Civil and Great Wars. Like Walt Whitman, Ford chronicles the society of that half century, expansionist by design, mystical and religious by conviction, hierarchical by agreement; an association of equals within a structure of command, practical, patriotic and devout: the society Whitman celebrated as "something in the doings of man that corresponds with the broadcast doings of night and day."

Mythologizing the armed services and the church as paradigms of structural integrity, Ford adapted their rules to his private world. All may speak in Ford's films, but when divine order is invoked, the faithful fall silent, to fight and die as decreed by a general, a president or some other member of a God-anointed elite.

In Ford's hierarchy, Indians and blacks share the lowest rung, women the next. Businessmen, uniformly corrupt in his world, hover below the honest and unimaginative citizenry of the United States. Above them begins Ford's elite, within which members of the armed forces occupy a privileged position. In authority over them is an officer class of career military men and priests, culminating in a few near-saintly figures of which Abraham Lincoln is the most notable, while over all rules a retributory, partial and jealous God.

The consistency of Ford's work lies in his fidelity to the morality implicit in this structure. *Mary of Scotland*'s Mary Queen of Scots, the retiring Nathan Brittles in *She Wore a Yellow Ribbon* and outgoing mayor Frank Skeffington in *The Last Hurrah* can thus all be seen to face the decline in their powers with a moral strength drawn from a belief in the essential order of their lives. Mary goes triumphant to the scaffold, affirming Catholicism and the divine right of kings. Duty to his companions of the 7th Cavalry transcending all, Brittles returns to rejoin them in danger. Skeffington prefers to lose rather than succumb to modern vote-getters like TV.

"I make westerns," Ford announced on one well-publicized occasion. Like most of his generalizations, it was untrue. Only a third of his films are westerns, and of those a number are rural comedies with perfunctory frontier settings: *Doctor Bull, Judge Priest, Steamboat Round the Bend, The Sun Shines Bright*. Many of his family films, like *Four Men and a Prayer* and *Pilgrimage*, belong with the stories of military life, of which he made a score. A disciple of the US Navy, from which he retired with the emeritus rank of Rear Admiral, Ford found in its command structure a morality much like that of his films. In *They Were Expendable*, he chose to falsify every fact of the Pacific war to celebrate the moral superiority of men trained in its rigid disciplines—men who obey, affirm, keep faith.

Acts, not words, convey the truth of mens' lives; public affirmations of this dictum dominate Ford's films. Dances and fights convey in their vigor a powerful sense of community; singing and eating and getting drunk together are the great acts of Fordian union. A film like *The Searchers*, perhaps his masterpiece, makes clear its care for family life and tradition in a series of significant actions that need no words. Ward Bond turns away from the revelation of a woman's love for her brother-in-law exposed in her reverent handling of his cloak—the instinctive act of a natural gentleman. Barred from the family life his anger and independence make alien to his character, John Wayne clutches his arm in a gesture borrowed from Ford's first star, Harry Carey, and, in a memorable final image, the door closes on him, rejecting the eternal clan-less wanderer.

Ford spent his filmmaking years in a cloud of critical misunderstanding, each new film compared unfavorably with earlier works. *The Iron Horse* established him as an epic westerner in the mold of Raoul Walsh, *The Informer* as a Langian master of expressionism, the cavalry pictures as Honest John Ford, a New England primitive whose work, in Lindsay Anderson's words, was "unsophisticated and direct." When, in his last decades of work, he returned to reexamine earlier films in a series of revealing remakes, the sceptical saw not a moving reiteration of values but a decline into self-plagiarism. Yet it is *The Man Who Shot Liberty Valance*, in which he deals with the issues raised in *Stagecoach*, showing his beloved populist west destroyed by law and literacy, that stands today among his most important films.

Belligerent, grandiose, deceitful and arrogant in real life, Ford seldom let these traits spill over into his films. They express at their best a guarded serenity, a sceptical satisfaction in the beauty of the American landscape, muted always by an understanding of the dangers implicit in the land, and a sense of the responsibility of all men to protect the common heritage. In every Ford film there is a gun behind the door, a conviction behind the joke, a challenge in every toast. Ford belongs in the tradition of American narrative art where telling a story and drawing a moral are twin aspects of public utterance. He saw that he lived in history, and that history embodies lessons we must learn. When Fordian man speaks, the audience is meant to listen—and listen all the harder for the restraint and circumspection of the man who speaks. One hears the authentic Fordian voice nowhere more powerfully than in Ward Bond's preamble to the celebrating enlisted men in *They Were Expendable* as they toast the retirement of a comrade. "I'm not going to make a speech," he states. "I've just got something to say."

—John Baxter

FORMAN, MILOS. Czech. Born in Cáslav, 18 February 1932; became citizen of of the United States in 1975. Educated at Academy of Music and Dramatic Art, Prague; at Film Academy (FAMU), Prague, 1951-56. Married Jana Brejchová (divorced); married Věra Křesadlová (divorced). Career: 1955—collaborates on screenplay for Frič's *Leave It to Me*; 1956—for Alfred Radok directs first few productions of Prague's Laterna Magika; 1962—returns to film work as assistant to Pavel Blumenfeld on *Beyond the Wood*; collaborated with Josef Skvorecký on *The Band Has Won*, banned 1962; 1968—in Paris at time of Russian invasion of Czechoslovakia, remains an expatriate, moves to New York 1969; 1975—becomes co-director of Columbia University Film Division. Recipient: Czechoslovak Film Critics' Prize for *Peter and Pavla*, 1963; Czechoslovak State Prize, 1967; Best Director Academy Award for *One Flew Over the Cuckoo's Nest*, 1975; Director Award, Directors Guild of America, for *One Flew Over the Cuckoo's Nest*, 1975; Best Direction British Academy Award for *One Flew Over the Cuckoo's Nest*, 1976. Agent: Robert Lantz, The Lantz Office, 888 Seventh Ave., New York, NY 10106. Address: Hampshire House, 150 Central Park South, apt.3204, New York, NY 10019.

Films (as scriptwriter): 1955—*Nechte to na mně (Leave It to Me)* (Frič) (co-sc); *Dědeček automobil (Old Man Motorcar)* (Radok) (ass't d, ro only); 1957—*Stěnata (The Puppies)* (co-sc); (as assistant director): 1962—*Tam za lesem (Beyond the Forest, Beyond the Wood)* (Blumenfeld) (+ro as the physician); (as director and co-scriptwriter): 1963—*Cerný Petr (Black Peter, Peter and Pavla)*; *Konkurs (Talent Competition)*; 1965—*Lásky jedné plavovlásky (Loves of a Blonde)*; *Dobře placená procházka (A Well Paid Stroll)*; 1967—*Hoří, má panenko (The Fireman's Ball)*; 1968—*La Pince à ongles* (Carrière) (co-sc only); 1970—*Taking Off*; 1972—"Decathlon" segment of *Visions of 8*; (as director only): 1975—*One Flew Over the Cuckoo's Nest*; 1975—*Le Mâle du siècle* (Berri) (story only); 1979—*Hair*; 1981—*Ragtime*; 1983—*Amadeus*.

Publications:

By FORMAN:

Books—*Taking Off*, with John Guare and others, New York 1971; *Milos Forman*, with others, London 1972; articles—"Více duvěry mládeži" ["More Confidence in the Youth"], interview by Galina Kopaněvová, in *Film a doba* (Prague), no.8, 1963; "Closer to Things" in *Cahiers du Cinema in English* (New York), January 1967; "Interview with Milos Forman" by James Blue and Gianfranco de Bosio in *Cahiers du Cinema in English* (New York), February 1967; commentary on *Firemen's Ball* in *Film a doba* (Prague), no.10, 1967; "Dvě hodiny s Milošem Formanem" ["2 Hours with Miloš Forman"], interview by Galina Kopaněvová, in *Film a doba* (Prague), no.8, 1968; interview in *The Film Director as Superstar* edited by Joseph Gelmis, Garden City, New York 1970; "Getting the Great 10%", interview by Harriet Polt, in *Film Comment* (New York), fall 1970; "How I Came to America to Make a Film and Wound Up Owing Paramount $140,000" in *Show*, February 1970; "A Czech in New York", interview by Gordon Gow, in *Films and Filming* (London), September 1971; interview in *Dialogue on Film* (Washington, D.C.), vol.3, no.1, 1972; "Milos Forman at the Olympic Games", interview, in *American Cinematographer* (Los Angeles), November 1972; interview by D. Maillet in *Cinématographe* (Paris), April/May 1976; "One Flew Over the Cuckoo's Nest", interview by L. Sturhahn in *Filmmakers Newsletter* (Ward Hill, Mass.), December 1975; "Milos Forman Lets His Hair Down", interview by T. McCarthy, in *Film Comment* (New York), March/April 1979; "Entretien" in *Ecran* (Paris), 15 July 1979; "Auf einen Sprung nach Hause", interview by J. Kliment in *Film und Fernsehen* (Berlin), February 1980.

On FORMAN:

Books—*Modern Czechoslovak Film 1945-1965* by Jaroslav Boček, Prague 1965; *All the Bright Young Men and Women* by Josef Skvorecký, Toronto 1971; *Milos Forman, Ingrid Thulin* edited by Bruce Henstell, Washington, D.C. 1972; *Closely Watched Films* by Antonín Liehm, White Plains, New York 1974; *The Milos Forman Stories* by Antonín Liehm, White Plains, New York 1975; articles—"Star-Crossed in Prague" by Peter Dyer in *Sight and Sound* (London), winter 1965/66; "Red Youth" by Gordon Gow in *Films and Filming* (London), February 1966; "Watch Out for the Hook, My Friend" by Alan Levy in *Life* (New York), 20 January 1967; "Formanovský film a některé předsudky" ["The Formanesque Film and Some Prejudices"] by Vladimír Bor in *Film a doba* (Prague), no.1, 1967; "Obraz člověka v českém film" ["The Portrayal of Man in the Czech

Cinema"] by Vratislav Effenberger in *Film a doba* (Prague), no.7, 1968; "Director of the Year" in *International Film Guide*, London 1969; "Milos Forman's America Is Like Kafka's—Basically Comic" by J. Conaway in *The New York Times*, 11 July 1971; "Vol au-dessus d'un nid de coucou" in *Avant-Scène du cinéma* (Paris), May 1976; "Sentimental Jorney" by Richard Combs in *Sight and Sound* (London), summer 1977; "Milos Forman" by B. Baker in *Film Dope* (London), April 1979; "A Day in the Life: Milos Forman: Moment to Moment with the Director of *Hair*" by H. Stein in *Esquire* (New York), 8 May 1979; "Milos Forman and *Hair*: Styling the Age of Aquarius" by J. Cameron in *Rolling Stone* (New York), 19 April 1979; "On Screen: Milos Forman in America" by L. Quart and A. Auster in *USA Today* (New York), July 1979; "Ragtime ve Formanově virtuozním rytmu" ["Ragtime in Forman's Virtuoso Rhythm"] in *Západ* (Ottawa), no.1, 1982; film—*Meeting Milos Forman* by Mira Weingarten, U.S. 1971.

*   *   *

In the context of Czechoslovak cinema in the early sixties, Milos Forman's first films (*Black Peter* and *Competition*) amounted to a revolution. Influenced by Czech novelists who revolted against the establishment's aesthetic dogmas in the late fifties rather than by Western cinema (though the mark of late neorealism, in particular Ermanno Olmi, is visible), Forman, in these early films, introduced to the cinema after 1948 (the year of the Communist coup) portrayals of working-class life untainted by the formulae of socialist realism.

Though initially he was fiercely attacked by Stalinist reviewers, the more liberal faction of the Communist party, then in the ascendancy, appropriated Forman's movies as expressions of the new concept of "socialist" art. Together with great box office success and an excellent reputation gained at international festivals, these circumstances made Forman into the undisputed star of the Czech New Wave. His style was characterized by a sensitive use of non-actors (usually coupled with professionals); by refreshing, natural-sounding, semi-improvised dialogue which reflected Forman's intimate knowledge of the milieu he was capturing on the screen; and by an unerring ear for the nuances of Czech folk-rock and for music in general.

All these characteristic features of the two early films are even more prominent in *Loves of a Blonde*, and especially in *Firemen's Ball* which works equally well on the level of a realistic humorous story, and on the allegorical level that points to the aftermath of the party's decision to reveal some of the political crimes committed in the fifties (the Slánský trial). In all these films—developed, except for *Black Peter*, from Forman's original ideas—he closely collaborated with his scriptwriters Ivan Passer and Jaroslav Papousek, who later became directors in their own right.

Shortly after the Soviet invasion of 1968, *Firemen's Ball* was banned and Forman decided to remain in the West, where he was during the events of August 1968. He was working on the script for what was to become his only American film in which he would apply the principles of his aesthetic method and vision to indigenous American material. It is also his only American movie developed from his original idea; the rest are adaptations. Traces of the pre-American Forman are easily recognizable in his most successful U.S. film to day, *One Flew Over the Cuckoo's Nest*, which radically changed Ken Kesey's story and—just as in the case of Papousek's novel *Black Peter*—brought it close to the director's own objective and comical vision. The work received an Oscar in 1975. In that year Forman became an American citizen. Unfortunately, the Forman touch is much less evident in his reworking of the musical *Hair*, and almost—though not entirely—absent from his version of Doctorow's novel *Ragtime*. Of marginal importance are the two remaining parts of Forman's oeuvre, *The Well-Paid Stroll*, a jazz opera adapted from the stage for Prague TV, and *Decathlon*, his contribution to the 1972 Olympic documentary *Visions of Eight*.

Forman is a merciless observer of the *comedie humaine* and, both in Czechoslovakia and in the West, has often been accused of cynicism. To such criticisms he answers with Chekhov, pointing out that what is cruel in the first place is life itself. But apart for such arguments, the rich texture of acutely observed life and the sensitive portrayal of and apparent sympathy for people as victims—often ridiculous—of circumstances over which they yield no power, render such critical statements null and void. Forman's vision is deeply rooted in the anti-ideological, realistic and humanist tradition of such "cynics" of Czech literature as Jaroslav Hasek (*The Good Soldier Svejk*), Bohumil Hrabal (*Closely Watched Trains*) or Josef Skvorecky (whose novel *The Cowards* Forman was prevented from filming by the invasion of 1968). Though the influence of his method may be felt even in some North American films, his lasting importance will, very probably, rest with his three Czech movies to which *Taking Off* should be added, a valiant attempt to show America to Americans through the eyes of a sensitive, if caustic foreign observer. After the mixed acceptance of this film, Forman took off in the direction of adaptations of best sellers and stage hits. He remains an outstanding craftsman and a first-class actors' director; however, in the context of American cinema he does not represent the innovative force he was in Prague.

—Josef Skvorecký

FOSSE, BOB. American. Born Robert Louis Fosse in Chicago, 23 June 1927. Educated at Amundsen High School, Chicago, graduated 1945; studied acting at American Theatre Wing, New York, 1947. Married dancer Mary Ann Niles (divorced); married musical comedy actress Joan McCracken (divorced); married dancer Gwen Verdon, 1960 (divorced). Career: 1940—with Charles Grass forms dance team "The Riff Brothers," appearing in vaudeville and burlesque; 1942—master of ceremonies in small night club; 1945—enlists in U.S. Navy, assigned to entertainment units in Pacific; 1948-50—chorus dancer in touring companies; 1950—Broadway debut in revue *Dance Me a Song*; 1951-52—dances on TV shows including *Show of Shows*, *Toni Review*, and *Hit Parade*; appears in New York nightclubs; 1953—signs with MGM and goes to Hollywood; 1954—returns to Broadway; Broadway debut as choreographer with *The Pajama Game*; later 1950s—works both on Broadway and in Hollywood as choreographer; 1959—debut as Broadway director/choreographer with *Redhead*; 1968—film directing debut with screen version of his Broadway hit *Sweet Charity*. Recipient: 7 Antoinette Perry ("Tony") Awards for stage work; Best Director Academy Award for *Cabaret*, 1972; Best Direction British Academy Award for *Cabaret*, 1972.

Films (as choreographer): 1955—*My Sister Eileen* (Quine) (+ro); 1957—*The Pajama Game* (Donen and Abbott); 1958—*Damn Yankees (What Lola Wants)* (Donen and Abbott) (+dancer in "Who's Got the Pain" number); (as director): 1968—*Sweet Charity* (+chor); 1972—*Cabaret* (+chor); 1974—*Lenny*; 1974—*The Little Prince* (Donen) (chor "Snake in the Grass" number only, +ro); 1979—*All That Jazz* (+chor); 1983—*Star 80*.

Roles: 1953—*The Affairs of Dobie Gillis* (Weis); *Kiss Me Kate* (Sidney); *Give a Girl a Break* (Donen); 1976—*Thieves* (Berry).

Publications:

By FOSSE:

Articles—"Inter/View with Bob Fosse" by L. Picard in *Inter/-View* (New York), March 1972; "The Making of *Lenny*", interview by S. Hornstein in *Filmmakers Newsletter* (Ward Hill, Mass.), February 1975.

On FOSSE:

Articles—"Bob Fosse" by T. Vallance in *Focus on Film* (London), summer 1972; "Bob Fosse" by P. Gardner in *Action* (Los Angeles), May/June 1974; "Life as a Long Rehearsal" by B. Drew in *American Film* (Washington, D.C.), November 1979; "Bob Fosse" by D.J. Badder in *Film Dope* (London), April 1979; "Film: When Bob Fosse's Art Imitates Life, It's Just *All That Jazz*" by M. Hodgson in *The New York Times*, 30 December 1979; "Bob Fosse, ejemplo demovimiento continuo" by J. Abbondanza in *Cinemateca revista* (Andes), August 1980; "In Camera: The Perfectionist" by E. Braun in *Films and Filming* (London), January 1980.

* * *

Rex Reed once said of Bob Fosse (in a review of his performance as The Snake in *The Little Prince*), "The man can do anything!" Somewhat effusive, Reed's comment nonetheless has more than a kernel of truth: Fosse has won 8 Tonys, 1 Oscar, and 1 Emmy. In fact, he garnered four of the awards (the Oscar for *Cabaret*, the Emmy for *Liza with a Z*, and two Tonys for *Pippin*) in one year.

Fosse started his career as a dancer and choreographer on Broadway and still divides his time almost equally between directing for the stage and for films. All of Fosse's films have been musicals (with the exception of *Lenny*) and it is within this genre that he has made significant contributions. The directorial choices employed by Fosse stem, not surprisingly, from his style of dancing and choreography: a type of eccentric jazz that isolates and exaggerates human motion, breaking it up into small components. It has been noted that there appears to be little difference between the dance material for Fosse's stage and film choreography. But the presentation of the dance is radically different. On the stage, only the performers can create the fragmentation of Fosse's choreography. In film, the use of multiple camera set-ups and editing allows an amplification of this fragmentation, essentially obliterating the dance material and the mise-en-scène.

This style can be seen as the complete opposite of Astaire's presentation which strives to preserve spatial and temporal integrity. "I love the camera," Fosse has said, "I love camera movement and camera angles. As a choreographer you see everything with a frame." Camera angle and camera image become more important choreographically than the dancing. The routine itself is non-essential, subordinated to a more complex system of integration and commentary, as Jerome Delameter has noted.

Fosse's notions of integration and commentary drastically altered the structure of the American musical film. Reacting against 30-odd years of the Arthur Freed musical, Fosse broke new ground in 1972 with *Cabaret*. No longer were the musical numbers "integrated" into the narrative with people singing to each other. All performance was logically grounded, occurring where it might be expected—on a stage for example (and never leaving that stage as Berkeley did)—and was distinctly separated from the narrative. The "integration" took place in the sense that each performance was a comment on the narrative action. In an interview with Glenn Loney for *After Dark*, Fosse sheds some light on his approach. "I don't think there is any such thing as a realistic musical. As soon as people start to sing to each other, you've already gone beyond realism in the usual sense...I have generally tried to make the musical more believable." (Not more realistic, just more plausible or more logical.) Fosse expounded on his concepts of "believability," "integrated commentary," and visual fragmentation of performance via camera angle and editing with *All That Jazz*, a film in which musical numbers are literal hallucinations, obviously separated from the narrative but still logically grounded within it.

—Greg Faller

FRAMPTON, HOLLIS. American. Born in Wooster, Ohio, 11 March 1936. Educated at Western Reserve University, 1954-58. Career: 1957-58—visits with Ezra Pound; 1958—moves to New York City, begins to work in photography; 1960-68—works as technician in film laboratories, specializes in dye-imbibition processes; 1962-66—makes a number of unreleased films; 1966—finishes *Manual of Arms*, first released film; 1967—teaches film at Free University of New York; 1969—teaches film and photography at Hunter College; 1971—publishes first of many theoretical texts on film and photography; 1972-present—works on large, multi-part film *Magellan*; 1973—begins teaching at State University of New York at Buffalo; 1977—works with computer graphics in connection with *Magellan*. Agent: Film-Makers' Cooperative, 175 Lexington Ave., New York, NY 10016. Address: State University of New York at Buffalo, Media Study, 207 Wende Hall, Buffalo, NY 14214.

Films: 1966—*Manual of Arms*; *Information*; *Process Red*; 1967—*States* (revised 1970); *Heterodyne*; 1968—*Snowblind*; *Maxwell's Demon*; *Surface Tension*; 1969—*Palindrome*; *Carrots & Peas*; *Lemon (for Robert Huot)*; *Prince Ruperts Drops*; *Works and Days*; *Artificial Light*; 1970—*Zorn's Lemma*; 1971-72—*Hapax Legomena* series, dated as follows: *Hapax Legomena I: (nostalgia)*, 1971; *Hapax Legomena II Poetic Justice*, 1972; *Hapax Legomena III: Critical Mass*, 1971; *Hapax Legomena IV: Travelling Matte*, 1971; *Hapax Legomena V: Ordinary Matter*, 1972; *Hapax Legomena VI: Remote Control*, 1972; *Hapax Legomena VII: Special Effects*, 1972; 1972-present—*Magellan*, film-in-progress, in many parts, some of which have already been released separately.

Publications:

By FRAMPTON:

Books—"Poetic Justice", Rochester, New York: The Visual Studies Workshop, 1973; *Fictcryptokrimsographs*, Buffalo, NY 1975; *Circles of Confusion*, Rochester, NY 1983; articles—"Filmmakers vs. The Museum of Modern Art", with Ken Jacobs and Michael Snow, in *Filmmakers' Newsletter* (Ward Hill, Mass.), May 1969; interview by Michael Snow in *Film Culture* (New York), winter/spring 1970; "For a Meta-History of Film:

Commonplace Notes and Hypotheses" in *Artforum* (New York), September 1971; "Voice-Over Narration for a Film of That Name: 1-8-71" in *Film Culture* (New York), spring 1972; "Digressions on the Photographic Agony" in *Artforum* (New York),November 1972; interview by Simon Field in *Afterimage* (Rochester, New York), fall 1972; "Meditations Around Paul Strand" in *Artforum* (New York),February 1972; "A Pentagram for Conjuring the Narrative" in *Form and Structure in Recent Film* edited by Dennis Wheeler, Vancouver 1972; "Notes on Nostalgia" in *Film Culture* (New York), no.53-55, spring 1972; "Eadweard Muybridge: Fragments of a Tesseract" in *Artforum* (New York),March 1973; "Stan and Jane Brakhage Talking" in *Artforum* (New York),January 1973; "A Stipulation of Terms from Maternal Hopi" in *Options and Alternatives*, exhibition catalogue, Yale University Art Gallery, New Haven 1973; interview by Jonas Mekas in *Village Voice* (New York), 11 January 1973; "Incisions in History/Segments of Eternity" in *Artforum* (New York),October 1974; "The Withering Away of the State of Art" in *Artforum* (New York),December 1974; "To the Editor" in *Artforum* (New York),March 1975; interview by Peter Gidal and "Letter from Hollis Frampton..." in *Structural Film Anthology* edited by Peter Gidal, London 1976; "Notes on Composing in Film" in *October* (Cambridge, Mass.), spring 1976; "3 Dialogues on Photography", with Carl Andre, in *Interfunktionen* (Cologne), spring 1976; "Frampton at the Gates", interview by M. Tuchman in *Film Comment* (New York), September/October 1977; articles from 1977 to present in *October* (Cambridge, Mass.); interview by S. MacDonald in *Film Culture* (New York), no.67-69, 1979; interview by S. MacDonald in *Quarterly Review of Film Studies* (Pleasantville, N.Y.), no.1, 1979.

On FRAMPTON:

Book—*The Films of Hollis Frampton*, Minneapolis: Walker Art Center, 1972; articles—"Structural Film" by P. Adams Sitney in *Film Culture Reader*, New York 1970; "Hollis Frampton's Zorn's Lemma" by Mark Segal in *Film Culture* (New York), spring 1971; "Zorn's Lemma" by Wanda Bershen in *Artforum* (New York), September 1971; "Hollis Frampton" by P. Adams Sitney in *The American Independent Film*, Boston: Boston Museum of Fine Arts, 1971; "New Forms in Film" by Bill Simon in *Artforum* (New York), October 1972; "Some Formalist Tendencies in the Current American Avant-Garde Film" by Regina Cornwell in *Kansas Quarterly*, spring 1972; "Stan Brakhage on Hollis Frampton" in *Form and Structure in Recent Film*, exhibition catalogue, Vancouver 1972; "Alphabet as Ideogram" by Simon Field in *Art and Artists* (London), August 1972; "Seeing...Decoding" by Pierre Francastel in *Afterimage* (Rochester, New York), spring 1974; "Hollis Frampton" by Douglas Resnick in *Options and Alternatives: Some Directions in Recent Art*, exhibition catalogue, Yale University Art Gallery, New Haven 1974; "Lines Describing an Impasse: Experimental 5" by Tony Rayns in *Sight and Sound* (London), spring 1975; "The Participatory Film" by Tom Gunning in *American Film* (Washington, D.C.), October 1975; "Narrative Space" by S. Heath in *Screen* (London), no.3, 1976; "Animated Dissection" by Fred Camper in *The Soho Weekly News* (New York), 20 May 1976; "Hollis Frampton—Film as Symbol" by Dave Weinstein in *Artweek* (Oakland), 8 May 1976; "Frampton and the Magellan Metaphor" by L. Fischer in *American Film* (Washington, D.C.), May 1979.

*　　　*　　　*

Hollis Frampton worked in poetry, painting, and photo-

graphy before coming to filmmaking. In addition, he has studied widely in a variety of disciplines outside of as well as within the arts. Much of the richness and complexity of his films results from influences culled from many diverse fields and fused within single works.

Many of Frampton's films exhibit complex, spectacularly strict structures. *Zorn's Lemma*, his best-known work, has a long central section in which alphabetized signs are gradually replaced with wordless images. This and similar devices involve the audience in an overtly participatory way. In *(nostalgia)*, we hear still photographs described before seeing them, and are thus involved with constructing a mental image from the description, which generally is quite different from the actual photograph we then see. Many of Frampton's pre-*Magellan* films involve game-like activities of counting, reading, guessing. While carefully controlled structures and audience participation were common to other avant-garde films and other arts in the late sixties, Frampton's films in this mode are characterized by a unique rigor. He seeks to bring to cinema some of the precision of the sciences, of mathematics.

True to the modernist tradition of which he is a part, Frampton has devoted much of his cinema's energy to the act of investigating the medium itself. In a great number of early films made before *Zorn's Lemma*, he has explored a vast range of cinematic possibilites, from the simplest use of black and white portrait imager (*Manual of Arms*) to abstract shapes (*Palindrome*) to various modifications of photo imagery (*Artificial Light*). He has said that film itself "is what all films are about," and much of his work can be taken as the proffering of possible alternative definitions of the medium. But by defining Frampton does not mean to delimit, so not only do different films offer different definitions: each film tries to be the most perfect example of its possibility that it can. These works are characterized by their frequently spectacular photographic qualities, and their absolute formal precision.

In seeking to investigate the properties of his medium, rather than placing primary emphasis on the idiosyncratic qualities of his own inner vision, Frampton has set different goals for himself than those of Brakhage or Baillie. But an autobiographical element is often also present in Frampton's work, most strongly in his serial film *Hapax Legomena*, of which *(nostalgia)* is the first of seven parts. The sections that make up this work simultaneously display a range of possible interactions between film and other media (still photography, writing, video, spoken language), and tell an implied story of the birth of a filmmaker via an evolution through film-related media (photography, a film script) to cinema itself. The sequence's seventh and final section, *Special Effects*, completes this movement by presenting a moving white-outlined rectangle at the edge of a black frame, and is a meditation on one of cinema's essences, the frame itself. The evolution within *Hapax Legomena* can also be seen to lead to Frampton's current, massive, multi-part film-in-progress, *Magellan*.

Of Frampton's other areas of involvement, still photography seems to have had the strongest influence on his filmmaking. He has seen in photographers like Weston the possibility that a photo image, in the sensuality of its tiniest modulations, can constitute an ineluctable mystery which is finally outside of language. The subject matter and photographic and editing styles of *Magellan*'s completed sections are many and various, but again and again the editing functions to return the viewer to a contemplation of the graphic qualities of the screen imagery, as if cinematically recreating the process of looking at a still photograph. The filmmaker's exhibition scheme for the completed film defies anything yet attempted in the medium; for instance, there is to be at least one different film for each day of the year.

Magellan's encyclopedic goal is perhaps best expressed by Frampton himself, as being an attempt to record, and render comprehensible, the sights and sounds of the visible world.

—Fred Camper

FRANJU, GEORGES. French. Born in Fougères, Brittany, 12 April 1912. Educated at religious school at Fougères. Career: 1927—works briefly for insurance company; 1928-32—military service in Algeria; 1932-33—studies theatre decor, builds sets for Folies Bergère and the Casino de Paris; 1934—with Henri Langlois begins Cercle du Cinéma programs, and directs *Le Metro*; 1937—with Langlois founds Cinémathèque Française and *CINEMAtographe* magazine; 1938—becomes Executive Secretary of La Fédération Internationale des Archives du Film (FIAF); 1945-54—Secretary-General of the Institut de Cinématographie Scientifique; 1946—founds L'Académie du Cinéma; 1958—makes first feature-length film *La Tête contre les murs*; 1965-76—directs *Chroniques de France* series for TV; 1966-68—directs *Pour le plaisir* series for TV; 1970—directs for TV *La Service des affaires classées* series; 1974—adapts *L'Homme sans visage* as series for TV. Recipient: Chevalier de la Légion d'honneur; Officier de l'ordre national du Mérite et des Arts et des Lettres. Address: 13 quai des Grandes-Augustins, 75006 Paris.

Films (as director and scriptwriter of short films): 1934—*Le Metro* (co-d); 1949—*Le Sang des bêtes*; 1950—*En passant par la Lorraine*; 1951—*Hôtel des Invalides*; 1952—*Le Grand Méliès*; 1953—*Monsieur et Madame Curie*; 1954—*Les Poussières*; *Navigation marchande (Marine marchande)* (disowned by Franju); 1955—*A propos d'une rivière (Le Saumon Atlantique)*; *Mon chien*; 1956—*Le Théâtre National Populaire (Le T.N.P.)*; *Sur le Pont d'Avignon*; *Décembre, mois des enfants* (Storck) (co-sc only); 1957—*Notre Dame, cathédrale de Paris*; 1958—*La Première nuit*; (as director of feature-length films): *La Tête contre les murs*; 1959—*Les Yeux sans visage* (+co-adaptation); 1960—*Pleins feux sur l'assassin*; 1962—*Thérèse Desqueyroux* (+co-sc); 1963—*Judex*; 1964—*Thomas l'imposteur (Thomas the Imposter)* (+co-sc); 1965—*Les Rideaux blancs* (episode for television feature *L'Instant de la paix*); 1970—*La Faute de l'Abbé Mouret (The Demise of Father Mouret)* (+co-sc); 1971—*La Ligne d'ombre* (for TV) (+co-sc); 1974—*Nuits rouges (L'Homme sans visage, Shadowman)* (+co-music).

Publications:

By FRANJU:

Books—*Le Sang des bêtes*, with Jean Painleve, in *L'Avant-Scène du cinéma* (Paris), no.41, 1964; *Hôtel des Invalides* in *L'Avant-Scène du cinéma* (Paris), no.38, 1964; *De Marey à Renoir, trésors de la Cinémathèque française 1882-1939*, Paris 1981; articles—"Entretien avec Georges Franju" by Freddy Buache in *Positif* (Paris), September 1957; "Le Style de Fritz Lang" in *Cahiers du cinéma* (Paris), November 1959; "Entretien avec Georges Franju..." by Jean-Marc Lebouits and Francis Tranchant in *Cinéma 59* (Paris), March 1959; "Entretien avec Georges Franju" by François Truffaut in *Cahiers du cinéma* (Paris), November 1959; "Franjudex: Entretien avec Georges Franju et Marcel Champreux" by Bernard Cohn in *Positif*

(Paris), November 1963; "Nouvel entretien avec Georges Franju" by Jean-Louis Fieschi and André Labarthe in *Cahiers du cinéma* (Paris), November 1963; "Réalisme et Surréalisme" in *Etudes cinématographiques*, edited by Yves Kovacs, no.41-42, 1965; "Entretien avec Georges Franju" by Michel Ciment and others in *Image et son* (Paris), March 1966; "Les Nuits rouges", interview by Claude Beylie in *Ecran* (Paris), January 1975; "Georges Franju: The Haunted Void", interview by Tom Milne, in *Sight and Sound* (London), spring 1975; "A propos du 'Grand Méliès'" in *Positif* (Paris), December/January 1977/78; interview by F. Guérif and S. Levy-Klein in *Cahiers de la cinémathèque* (Paris), spring/summer 1978.

On FRANJU:

Book—*Miroirs de l'insolite dans le cinéma francais* by Henri Agel, Paris 1957; articles—"Le Plus grand cinéaste français" by Jacques Demeure and Ado Kyrou in *Positif* (Paris), May 1956; "Franju" by Cynthia Grenier in *Sight and Sound* (London), spring 1957; "Georges Franju" by Jean-Luc Godard in *Cahiers du cinéma* (Paris), December 1958; "Pour un portrait" by Roger Tailleur in *Présence du cinéma* (Paris), June 1960; "Les Paradoxes de la fidélité" by Claude Beylie in *Cahiers du cinéma* (Paris), January 1963; "Georges Franju ou la terreur comme un des beaux-arts" by Pierre Ajame in *Les Nouvelles littéraires* (Paris), 30 January 1964; "Feuillade et son double" by Jean-André Fieschi in *Cahiers du cinéma* (Paris), April 1964; "Undertones" by James Price in *London Magazine*, April 1965; special issue of *Image et son* (Paris), March 1966; "Franju et la critique" by Claude Gauteur in *Image et son* (Paris), March 1966; "A propos de Georges Franju" by Gabriel Vialle in *Image et son* (Paris), March 1966; "Songs of Innocence" by T. Milne in *Sight and Sound* (London), winter 1970/71; "Franju" by G. Gow in *Films and Filming* (London), August 1971; "The Films of Luis Buñuel and Georges Franju" by A. MacLochlainn in *Film Journal* (New York), summer 1971; "Terrible Buildings: The World of Georges Franju" by Robin Wood in *Film Comment* (New York), November/December 1973; "Nuits rouges" in *Avant-Scène du cinéma* (Paris), January 1975; "Les Yeux sans visage", special issue of *Avant-Scène du cinéma* (Paris), 1 June 1977; "Georges Franju" by D.J. Badder in *Film Dope* (London), April 1979.

*   *   *

Franju's career falls clearly into two parts, marked by the format of the films: the early period of documentary shorts, and a subsequent period of fictional features. The parts are connected by many links of theme, imagery, attitude, and iconography. Critical attention has focused primarily on the short's and there is some justice in this. While it is difficult to accept Noel Burch's assertion that "the magic that is so much a part of his nonfiction work no longer survives in his fiction features," it is true that nothing in the later work surpasses *Le Sang des bêtes* and *Hôtel des Invalides*, and the intensity and poetic concentration of those early masterpieces are recaptured only in intermittent moments. It is necessary to define the *kind* of documentary Franju made (it is highly idiosyncratic, and I can think of no close parallels; though Resnais' documentaries are often linked with his, the differences seem more important than the similarities). The traditional documentary has three main modes: the factual, the lyrical, and the politically tendentious. It is the peculiar distinction of Franju's documentaries that they correspond to none of these modes. The kind of organization that structures them is essentially poetic, built upon imagery, juxtaposition, rather than on overt statement or clear-cut symbolism. *Hôtel des Invalides* might well have been expected, from its genesis, to correspond to either the second or third type of documentary (or an amalgamation of the two, a quite common phenomenon): it was commissioned by an organization called *Forces et Voix de France*, and the intention was to celebrate a national monument-institution: the Musée de L'Armée, home of Napoleon's tomb, an edifice dedicated to the glory of France and of war. Franju seized upon and made central to his film the fact that the building also houses the *victims* of war and "Glory": the veterans' hospital of the film's title, peopled with the shell-shocked, the crippled, the mutilated, who continue to carry military banners, wear their medals, attend the religious ceremonies that constitute an aspect of their oppression. Beyond the skillful use of purely cinematic codes (lighting, camera movement, editing, etc.) and Maurice Jarre's music, Franju adds nothing extraneous to his raw maaterial: the introductory commentary (spoken by Michel Simon), locating the museum in place and history, is rigorously factual and unemotional; once inside, we have only the "authentic" commentary of the museum guides. Yet the application of cinematic codes to this material transforms its meaning totally, producing a continuous irony that modulates back and forth between the violent and the subtle: the emblems of military glory and national pride become sinister, monstrous, terrifying.

A politically tendentious documentary after all, then? Certainly not in any simple or clear-cut way. Ultimately, *Hôtel des Invalides* is no more an anti-war movie than *Le Sang des bêtes* is an appeal for vegetarianism—though those meanings can and will be read by many viewers. The film's elements of rage and protest are finally subordinated to an overriding sense of irredeemable insanity, an intimation of a world and a species so fundamentally crazy that protest is almost superfluous. The supreme irony Franju produces out of his material involves the museum's very status as a national monument: here, at the heart of civilization, regarded with pride, admiration and wonderment, stands what amounts to a monument to pain, cruelty, ugliness, death—and no one notices.

The basic problem with Franju's feature films is that he does not seem greatly interested in narrative. He has usually relied on the support of a preexistent literary work, whose structure, characters, and movement he recreates with a generally scrupulous fidelity, delicacy, and discretion, the changes being mainly of emphasis and omission. The curious feat of *Thérèse Desqueyroux* has often been noted: a faithful, almost literal translation of a novel by a famous Catholic writer (Mauriac) that never violates the integrity of Franju's atheism. Cocteau singled out Franju as the director to whom he would most confidently entrust his work, and Franju justified that confidence fully with his version of *Thomas l'imposteur*. Nonetheless, these films are discernibly Franju's: the directorial reticence should not be mistaken for abdication. The clearest way to demonstrate the continuity is to show how the Franjuesque iconography that is already fully developed in the documentaries recurs in the features, to produce those moments of poetic density and resonance that are the films' chief distinction.

If *Les Yeux sans visage* remains the finest of Franju's feature films, it is because it is the one that permits the greatest concentration of poetry created out of the association of these elements.

—Robin Wood

*Note: See Robin Wood's essay on *Le Sang des bêtes* in *Films*, vol. 1 of this series.

FRANKENHEIMER, JOHN. American. Born in Malba, New York, 19 February 1930. Educated at LaSalle Military Academy, graduated 1947; Williams College, B.A. in English 1951. Married actress Evans Evans, 1963. Career: 1951-53—serves in U.S. Air Force, assigned at his request to newly formed Film Squadron; 1953—following discharge, joins CBS-TV in New York as assistant director; works on *The Garry Moore Show, Lamp Unto My Feet,* and *Person to Person*; 1954—promoted to director of *You Are There* program following departure of Sidney Lumet; 1955—moves to Hollywood; directs altogether over 125 TV plays, including for *Playhouse 90* series; 1956—first feature film *The Young Stranger* remake of play directed for *Climax* TV series; 1963—forms John Frankenheimer Productions. Agent: Jeff Berg, ICM, Los Angeles, California. Business: John Frankenheimer Productions, 2800 Olympic Blvd., Suite 201, Santa Monica, CA 90404.

Films (as director): 1957—*The Young Stranger*; 1961—*The Young Savages*; 1962—*The Manchurian Candidate* (+co-pr); *All Fall Down*; *Birdman of Alcatraz*; 1963—*7 Days in May*; 1964—*The Train*; 1966—*Grand Prix*; *Seconds*; 1968—*The Extraordinary Seaman*; *The Fixer*; 1969—*The Gypsy Moths*; 1970—*I Walk the Line*; *The Horsemen*; 1973—*L'Impossible Objet (Impossible Object)*; *The Iceman Cometh*; 1974—*99 44/100% Dead* (retitled *Call Harry Crown* for general release in U.K.); 1975—*French Connection II*; 1976—*Black Sunday* (+bit ro as TV controller); 1979—*Prophecy*; 1982—*The Challenge*.

Publications:

By FRANKENHEIMER:

Book—*The Cinema of John Frankenheimer* by Gerald Pratley, New York 1969; articles—"7 Ways with *7 Days in May*" in *Films and Filming* (London), June 1964; "Criticism as Creation" in *Saturday Review* (New York), 26 December 1964; interview in *The Celluloid Muse* edited by Charles Higham and Joel Greenberg, London 1969; interview by Russell Au Werter in *Action* (Los Angeles), May/June 1970; interview by J. O'Brien in *Interview* (New York), August 1971; interview by N. Zalaffi in *Image et son* (Paris), January 1973; "Filming *The Iceman Cometh*" in *Action* (Los Angeles), January/February 1974; interview by L. Gross and R. Avrech in *Millimeter* (New York), July/August 1975; interviews by R. Appelbaum in *Films and Filming* (London), October and November 1979; interview by David Castell in *Films Illustrated* (London), September 1979.

On FRANKENHEIMER:

Articles—"John Frankenheimer" by Paul Mayersberg in *Movie* (London), December 1962; "Black King Takes 2" by J.H. Fenwick in *Sight and Sound* (London), summer 1964; "John Frankenheimer, the Smile on the Face of the Tiger" by John Thomas in *Film Quarterly* (Berkeley), winter 1965/66; "Realism and Beyond: The Films of John Frankenheimer" by Alan Casty in *Film Heritage* (New York), winter 1966/67; "Frankenheimer" by Charles Higham in *Sight and Sound* (London), spring 1968; "3 Frankenheimer Films: A Sociological Approach" by Paul Filmer in *Screen* (London), July/October 1969; "99 and 44/100% Dead" by A. Madsen in *Sight and Sound* (London), winter 1973/74; "Frankenheimer is First Par Exclusive in 2 Decades" in *Variety* (New York), 8 December 1976; "John Frankenheimer: His Fall and Rise" by B. Drew in *American Film* (Washington, D.C.), March 1977; "The War Between the Writers and the

Directors: Part II: The Directors" by B. Cook in *American Film* (Washington, D.C.), June 1979; "John Frankenheimer" by M. Salmi in *Film Dope* (London), April 1979; "A Matter of Conviction" by Richard Combs in *Sight and Sound* (London), no.4, 1979.

*   *   *

The seven features John Frankenheimer directed between 1961 and 1964 stand as a career foundation unique in American cinema. In a single talent, film had found a perfect bridge between television and Hollywood drama, between the old and new visual technologies, between the cinema of personality and that of the corporation and the computer.

Frankenheimer's delight in monochrome photography, his instinct for new light cameras, fast stocks and lens systems like Panavision informed *The Manchurian Candidate*, *Seven Days in May* and *Seconds* with a flashing technological intelligence. No less skillful with the interior drama he's mastered as a director of live TV, he turned *All Fall Down* and *The Young Savages* into striking personal explorations of familial disquiet and social violence. He seemed unerring. Even *Birdman of Alcatraz* and *The Train*, troubled projects taken over at the last minute from Charles Crichton and Arthur Penn respectively, emerged with the stamp of his forceful technique.

His career began to sour with *Seconds*, arguably too selfconscious with its fish-eye sequences and rampant paranoia. *Grand Prix*, an impressive technical feat in Super Panavision, showed less virtuosity in the performances. His choices thereafter were erratic; heavy handed comedy, rural melodrama, a further unsuccessful attempt at spectacle in the Afghanistan-shot *The Horsemen*. Frankenheimer relocated in Europe, no doubt mortified that Penn, Lumet and Delbert Mann, lesser lights of live TV drama, had succeeded where he failed.

Despite a revival with the 1975 *French Connection II*, a sequel which equalled its model in force and skill, he has not since hit his stride. The choices remain variable in intelligence, though by staying within the area of violent melodrama he has at least ceased to dissipate his talent in the pursuit of production values. *Black Sunday* is a superior terrorist thriller, *Prophecy* a failed but worthy horror film with environmental overtones, and *The Challenge* a stylish Japanese romp in the style of *The Yakuza*. Unfortunately, new directors who grew up with the Frankenheimer work as benchmarks do such work better; he appears to have suffered the fate of bridges everywhere, and been passed over.

—John Baxter

FRANKLIN, SIDNEY. American. Born Sidney Arnold Franklin in San Francisco, 21 March 1893. Married; son: Sidney Franklin, Jr. Career: before 1913—works as traveling salesman, factory worker, and oil-field laborer; 1913—enters films as extra in Colin Campbell film; 1914—works as assistant cameraman, then assistant director for Hobart Bosworth company; begins collaborating on comedy shorts with brother Chester M. Franklin; 1918—Chester drafted, end of directing collaboration; early 1920s—directs for First National and Warner Bros.; 1926-57— works for MGM first as director, then mainly as producer after finishing *The Good Earth* in 1937; 1938—production of *Goodbye, Mr. Chips* reassigned to Sam Wood just before Fleming was to begin shooting; 1956—attempted remake of *The Barretts of Wimpole Street* fails; 1957—retired. Died in 1972. Recipient: Irving G. Thalberg Memorial Academy Award, 1942.

Films (as assistant director): 1914—*An Odyssey of the North* (Bosworth); *Burning Daylight* (Bosworth); (as co-director of shorts with Chester Franklin): 1914—*The Sheriff* (+co-ed, ro); 1915—*The Baby*; *The Rivals*; *Little Dick's First Case*; *The Ash Can or Little Dick's First Adventure*; *Her Filmland Hero*; *Dirty Face Dan*; *Pirates Bold*; *The Kid Magicians*; *A 10 Cent Adventure*; *The Runaways*; *The Straw Man*; *The Little Cupids*; *The Doll-house Mystery* (+bit ro); *Smoke Bellew* (Bosworth) (ass't d only); 1916—*Let Katie Do It*; *Martha's Vindication*; *The Children in the House*; *Little Schoolma'am*; *Gretchen the Greenhorn*; *A Sister of Six*; 1917—*Going Straight*; *Jack and the Beanstalk* (+co-sc); *Aladdin and the Wonderful Lamp*; *Treasure Island*; *The Babes in the Woods* (d alone, though credited and copyrighted to both); 1918—*6 Shooter Andy* (d alone, though credited and copyrighted to both); *Fan Fan*; *Ali Baba and the 40 Thieves*; (as director): 1918—*The Bride of Fear* (+sc); *Confession* (+sc); *The Safety Curtain* (+co-sc); *Her Only Way* (+co-story); *The Forbidden City*; *The Heart of Wetona*; 1919—*The Probation Wife*; *The Hoodlum (The Ragamuffin)*; *Heart o'the Hills*; 1920—*2 Weeks*; *Unseen Forces*; 1921—*Not Guilty*; *Courage*; 1922—*Smilin' Through* (+co-sc); *The Primitive Lover*; *East Is West*; 1923— *Brass*; *Dulcy*; *Tiger Rose*; 1924—*Her Night of Romance*; 1925— *Learning to Love*; *Her Sister from Paris*; 1926—*Beverly of Graustark*; *The Duchess of Buffalo*; 1927—*Quality Street*; 1928—*The Actress (Trelawney of the Wells)*; 1929—*Wild Orchids*; *The Last of Mrs. Cheyney*; *Devil May Care*; 1930—*The Lady of Scandal (The High Road)*; *A Lady's Morals (The Soul Kiss, Jenny Lind)*; 1931—*The Guardsman*; *Private Lives*; 1932— *Smilin' Through* (remake of 1922 film); 1933—*Reunion in Vienna*; 1934—*The Barretts of Wimpole Street*; 1935—*The Dark Angel*; 1937—*The Good Earth*; 1938—*Marie Antoinette* (Van Dyke) (planning and pre-prod only); (as producer): 1939— *On Borrowed Time* (Bucquet); *The Women* (Cukor) (+co-sc, uncredited); 1940—*Waterloo Bridge* (LeRoy); 1942—*Mrs. Miniver* (Wyler); *Random Harvest* (LeRoy); *Bambi* (supervising d Hand) (credited with "inspiring collaboration", worked on script); 1943—*Madame Curie* (LeRoy); 1944—*The White Cliffs of Dover* (Brown); 1946—*The Yearling* (Brown); 1947—*Homecoming* (LeRoy); 1948—*Command Decision* (Wood); 1950— *The Miniver Story* (Potter); 1953—*The Story of 3 Loves* (Reinhardt and Minnelli); *Young Bess* (Sidney); 1956—*The Barretts of Wimpole Street* (d only—remake of 1934 film); 1957—*The 7th Sin* (Neame) (co-pr, uncredited). Role: 1913—*The Hoyden's Awakening* (Parker).

Publications:

On FRANKLIN:

Articles—"The Franklin Kid Pictures" by Kevin Brownlow in *Films in Review* (New York), August/September 1972; "The Modest Pioneer: Sidney Franklin" by Kevin Brownlow in *Focus on Film* (London), summer 1972; obituary in *The New York Times*, 20 May 1972; "Sidney Franklin" by Kevin Brownlow in *Film Dope* (London), April 1979.

*   *   *

Sidney Franklin began in films in the teens, and like many early directors, moved from acting to direction. By the 1920s he began to direct features starring some of the biggest female stars of the silent era, Mary Pickford, Constance and Norma Talmadge, and Greta Garbo. His last silent film, *Wild Orchids* starring Garbo, is an excellent example of Franklin's ability to bring out the best in his female stars despite the limitations of a weak, melodramatic script.

Franklin was one of several directors prominent at Metro-Goldwyn-Mayer during the early 1930s whose own style seemed to be submerged beneath the "high gloss" look of most of that studio's output. Under the guidance of Irving G. Thalberg who was his sponsor at M-G-M, Franklin made a number of popular dramatic vehicles, several of which starred Thalberg's wife, Norma Shearer. Among his most successful films of the period were *The Last of Mrs. Cheyney* and *The Barretts of Wimpole Street*, both starring Shearer, and *The Guardsman*, the only film made by the legendary Broadway acting team of Alfred Lunt and Lynn Fontanne.

His last directorial assignment before a hiatus of 20 years was *The Good Earth* in 1937, an adaptation of Pearl Buck's Nobel Prize-winning novel about China. The film involved a very long pre-production and shooting schedule which began in 1934, but was not completed until several months after Thalberg's premature death. There were other directors who worked on the project, among them Sam Wood, George Hill, and Fred Niblo, but Franklin was the only one to receive director's credit on the screen. The film won two Oscars, including Best Actress for Luise Rainer and Best Cinematography for Karl Freund, but it was been highly criticized for its lack of oriental actors. Although to modern moviegoers seeing mostly Caucasions in oriental make-up seems ludicrous, it must be remembered that this was a common practice of the time, and not the exclusive fault of one or two filmmakers.

After completion of *The Good Earth*, Franklin turned to producing for M-G-M. His most prominent motion pictures as a producer were again "women's pictures" like *Waterloo Bridge*, *Mrs. Miniver*, which won an Oscar for the Best Picture, *Random Harvest*, and *Young Bess*. Most of his films as a producer are dismissed today by critics as saccharine weepies, but they still have their audience and are frequently revived on television.

Following his years as a producer, Franklin decided to direct one more film in 1957, a remake of *The Barrettes of Wimpole Street* starring Jennifer Jones. The film was not a success—perhaps it was too reminiscent of the type of movies produced in a bygone era. After the failure of the film, Franklin retired from all aspects of the picture business.

There is hardly a film of Franklin's either as producer or director which are highly regarded by contemporary critics, but many are still enjoyed for the quality of individual performances and their overall entertainment value.

—Patricia King Hanson

FRIC, MARTIN. Czech. Born in Prague, 29 March 1902. Married Czech film star Suzanne Marwille, 1932. Career: 1918—actor in Prague and Bratislava; 1919-21—lab man, cameraman, designer; 1922—begins film acting, scriptwriting; 1924—collaboration with Karel Lamač begins; 1931—begins editing own films; early 1940s—billed as Mac Fric on films made during Occupation; 1961—begins directing for TV; after 1965—chairman of Union of Czechoslovakian Film and Television Artists; 1965—1st chairman, Union of Czechoslovakian Film and Television Artists. Died 22 August 1968. Recipient: National Artist; Order of the Republic; laureate, State Prize.

Films (partial listing of 85 as director): 1928—*Páter Vojtěch (Father Vojtech)* (+sc, ro); 1929—*Varhaník v sv. Víta (The Organist at St. Vitus)* (+co-sc); *Chudá holka (Poor Girl)* (+sc); 1930—*Vše pro lásku (All for Love)* (+co-sc); 1931—*Der Zinker (The Informer)* (co-d); *On a jeho sestra (He and His Sister)* (co-d); (as director and editor): 1931—*Dobrý voják Svejk (The Good Soldier Schweik)*; 1932—*Kantor Ideál (Master Ideál)* (d only); *Sestra Angelika (Sister Angelica)*; 1933—*Revisor (The Inspector)*; *U snědeného krámu (The Emptied-out Grocer's Shop)*; *Pobočník Jeho Výsosti (Adjutant to His Highness, Der Adjutant seiner Hoheit)*; *Zivot je pes (A Dog's Life* (d only, +co-sc); *Dvanáct křesel (The 12 Chairs* (co-d only); *S vyloučením veřejnosti (Closed Doors)* (d only); 1934—*Hej rup! (Heave-ho!)* (+co-sc); *Poslední muž (The Last Man)* (d only); *Mazlíček (Darling)* (+co-sc); 1935—*Hrdina jedné noci (Hero for a Night)*; *Jánošík* (+co-sc); *Jedenácté přikázání (The 11th Commandment)*; *Ať žije nebožtík (Long Live the Deceased)* (+co-sc); (as director): 1936—*Páter Vojtěch (Father Vojtech)* (re-make); *Svadlenka (The Seamstress)*; *Ulička v ráji (Paradise Road)*; 1937—*Svět patří nám (The World Is Ours)* (+co-sc, ro); *Hordubalové (The Hordubals)*; *Lidé na kře (People on a Glacier)*; 1938—*Krok do tmy (Madman in the Dark)*; *Skola, základ života (School, the Basis of Life)*; 1939—*Eva tropí hlouposti (The Escapades of Eva)*; *Kristián (Christian)* (+co-sc); *Muž z neznáma (The Reluctant Millionaire)*; 1940—*Muzikantská Liduška (Liduška of the Stage, Musicians' Girl)*; *Baron Prášil (Baron Munchhausen)*; *Katakomby (Catacombs)*; *Druhá směna (Second Tour)*; 1941—*Těžký život dobrodruha (Hard is the Life of an Adventurer)*; *Hotel Modrá hvězda (The Hotel Blue Star)* (+co-sc); 1942—*Barbora Hlavsová*; 1943—*Experiment*; *Der zweite Schuss (The Second Shot)* (+co-sc); 1944—*Počestné paní pardubické (The Virtuous Dames of Pardubice)*; *Prstýnek (The Ring, The Wedding Ring)*; 1945—*13. revír (Beat 13)*; 1947—*Varuj! (Warning!, Reiterate the Warning)* (+co-sc); *Capkovy povídky (Tales from Capek)* (+co-sc); 1948—*Návrat domu (Lost in Prague)*; *Polibek ze stadionu (A Kiss from Stadium)* (+co-sc); 1949—*Pětistovka (Motorcycles)*; *Pytlákova schovanka (The Kind Millionaire)*; 1950—*Past (The Trap)*; *Zocelení (Tempered Steel, Steel Town)*; 1951—*Císařuv pekař a Pekařuv pekař (The Emperor's Baker and the Baker's Emperor)* (+co-sc); *Akce B (Action B)* (+co-sc); 1953—*Tajemství krve (The Secret of Blood, The Mystery of Blood)* (+co-sc); 1954—*Psohlavci (Dog-Heads)* (+co-sc); 1955—*Nechte to na mně (Leave It to Me)* (+co-sc); 1956—*Zaostřit, prosím (Watch the Birdie!)* (+co-sc); 1958—*Povodeň (The Flood)*; *Dnes naposled (Today for the Last Time)*; 1959—*Princezna se zlatou hvězdou (The Princess with the Golden Star)* (+co-sc); 1960—*Dařbuján a Pandrhola (A Compact with Death)*; *Bílá spona (The White Slide)*; 1961—*Medvěd (The Bear)* (+sc, for TV); *Slzy, které svět nevidí (Tears the World Can't See)* (for TV); *Námluvy (Courting)* (for TV); 1963—*Krák Králu (King of Kings)*; *Tři zlaté vlasy děda Vševěda (The 3 Golden Hairs of Old Man Know-All)*; 1964—*Hvězda zvaná Pelyněk (A Star Named Wormwood)*; 1966—*Lidé z maringotek (People on Wheels)* (+co-sc); 1967—*Přísně tajné premiéry (Recipe for a Crime, Strictly Secret Previews)*; 1968—*Nejlepší ženská mého života (The Best Woman of My Life)* (+co-sc).

Publications:

By FRIC:

Article—interview in *Closely Watched Films* by Antonín Liehm, White Plains, New York 1974.

On FRIC:

Book—*Modern Czechoslovak Film*, Prague 1965; articles—"Martin Frič: Lidový vyprávěč" (in 4 parts) by J. Hrbas in *Film a Doba* (Prague), January through April 1972; "Czechoslovakia: Silence into Sound" by L. Dewey in *Film* (London), no.60, n.d.

*   *   *

Scion of a notable middle-class Prague family, Martin Fric left the road marked out by family tradition at the age of 16 to follow the uncertain path of a cabaret performer, actor, and filmmaker. In 1919 he designed a poster for Jan Stanislav Kolár's film *Dáma s malou nozkou (Lady With a Little Foot)*, and thus began his years of apprenticeship. He was by turns an actor, a scenarist, a film laboratory worker, a cameraman. Of crucial importance to the young Fric was his collaboration and friendship with the most influential director in Czech film, Karel Lamac, who taught him the film trade and enabled him to become familiar with the film studios of Berlin and Paris.

In 1928 he made his debut with the film *Páter Vojtech (Father Vojtech)* and followed it immediately with his most important film of the silent era, *Varhaník u sv. Vita (The Organist at St. Vitus)*, which dealt with the tragedy of a man suspected of murder. In the sound era Fric quickly gained a position of prominence, chiefly through his ability to work fast (making up to six films a year) and, no matter what, with surprising ease and dexterity. Comedy became his domain. His comedies, often produced in two language versions (German or French), featured popular comedians but also actors and actresses whose comic talent he recognized and helped to develop. First and foremost was Vlasta Burián in the situation comedies *On a jeho sestra (He and His Sister)* with Anny Ondráková, *Pobocník jeho Výsosti (Adjutant to His Highness)*, *Dvanáct kresel (The 12 Chairs)*, *Katakomby (Catacombs)*, and also in the film adaptation of Gogol's *Revisor (The Inspector)*. Fric had much to do with shaping the film acting of Hugo Haas in such films as *Zivot je pes (A Dog's Life*—the first Czech screwball comedy with Adina Mandlová). *Ať žije nebožtík (Long Live the Deceased)*, *Jedenácté přikázání (The Eleventh Commandment)*, and *Ulička v ráji (Paradise Road)*. Together with Voskovec and Werich he made the social comedy *Hej rup! (Heave-ho)* and he modern political satire *Svět patří nám (The World Is Ours)*. Then came *Kristián (Christian)*, a social comedy with Oldrich Nový that is undoubtedly Fric's best work.

But Fric also demonstrated his directorial abilities in infrequent excursions into other genres. His *Jánosik (Jánosik)*, a poetic epic about a legendary highwayman, is one of the pinnacles of Czechoslovak cinematography. Fric showed sensitivity and an understanding of the atmosphere of the time in his film rendition of *U snedeného Krámu (The Emptied-Out Grocer's Shop)*, a story by the 19th-century Czech writer Ignát Hermann. He also made felicitous film versions of the dramas *Hordubalové (The Hordubals)*, based on the novel by Karel Capek, *Lidé na kře (People on a Glacier)*, and *Barbora Hlavsová*.

Following the nationalization of Czechoslovak filmmaking, Fric aided in the development of filmmaking in Slovakia with his film *Varúj...! (Warning!)*. In 1949, in collaboration with Oldrich Nový, he fashioned his next masterpiece, *Pytláková schovanka (The Kind Millionaire)*, a parody of film kitsch. Following the successful costume comedy *Cisaruv pekar a pekaruv cisar (The Emperor's Baker and the Baker's Emperor)* with Jan Werich, and an excursion into the biographical genre with the film *Tajemstvi krve (The Secret of Blood)*, Fric made a few films that were—for the first time, actually—neither a popular nor a criti-

cal success.

Fric's last creative surge came at the beginning of the 1960s. He made fine adaptations for Czechoslovak telelvision and directed Chekhov's tales *Medved (The Bear)*, *Slzy, které svě nevidí (Tears the World Can't See)*, and *Námluvy (Courting)*, and once more returned to the studios. The tragicomedy *Hvězda zvaná Pelyněk (A Star Named Wormwood)* and the comedy *Nejlepši ženská mého života (The Best Woman of My Life)*, the premieres of which he did not live to see, close out his final period of creativity.

Fric's creation is the work of a solid and honest artist who demonstrated his talent in diverse genres from psychological drama to madcap comedy. He produced two masterful comedies, *Kristián* and *Pytlákova schovanka*, which can be numbered among the world's best comedies of the period. The best proof of the quality and vitality of his creative work is the fact that almost a third of the films he made are still shown in the theaters of Czechoslovakia, where they bring pleasure and joy to new generations of viewers.

—Vladimír Opela

FRIEDKIN, WILLIAM. American. Born in Chicago, 29 August 1939. Married Jeanne Moreau, 1977 (divorced). Career: 1955—begins working in Chicago TV station in mail room; soon becomes studio floor manager; 1956—becomes TV director; 1957-67—directs numerous TV shows, including many documentaries; 1973—partner, with Francis Ford Coppola and Peter Bogdanovich, in The Directors Company, financed by Paramount; 1974—withdraws from Directors Company because of other commitments. Recipient: Best Director Academy Award for *The French Connection*, 1971.

Films (as director): 1967—*Good Times*; 1968—*The Night They Raided Minsky's*; *The Birthday Party*; 1970—*The Boys in the Band*; 1971—*The French Connection*; 1973—*The Exorcist*; 1977—*Sorcerer (Wages of Fear)* (+pr); 1978—*The Brink's Job*; 1980—*Cruising* (+sc); 1983—*Deal of the Century*.

Publications:

By FRIEDKIN:

Articles—"Anatomy of a Chase" in *Take One* (Montreal), July/August 1971; "French Connection", interview by G. Braucourt, in *Ecran* (Paris), March 1972; "Police Oscar", interview by M. Shedlin in *Film Quarterly* (Berkeley), summer 1972; "Photographing *The French Connection*" by Herb Lightman in *American Cinematographer* (Los Angeles), February 1972; interview by D. Brandes in *Cinema Papers* (Melbourne), July 1974; "Mervyn LeRoy Talks with William Friedkin" in *Action* (Los Angeles), November/December 1974; interview by Max Tessier and A. Lacombe in *Ecran* (Paris), November 1974; "William Friedkin" in *Dialogue on Film* (Washington, D.C.), February/March 1974; "L'Exorciste", interview by J. Zimmer and Guy Allombert in *Image et son* (Paris), November 1974; "Tense Situations", interview by R. Appelbaum, in *Films and Filming* (London), March 1979.

On FRIEDKIN:

Articles—"Everyone's Reading It: Billy's Filming It" by C. Chase in *The New York Times*, 27 August 1972; "Friedkin

Defends His *Cruising*" by Janet Maslin in *The New York Times*, 18 September 1979; "William Friedkin" by M. Salmi in *Film Dope* (London), September 1979.

* * *

William Friedkin's career is generally noted for the two extremely popular films he directed in the seventies, *The French Connection* and *The Exorcist*.

Based on the real life exploits of New York City policeman Eddie Egan, *The French Connection* is the story of a drug investigation with international complexities. The film came out at a time when the American public was deeply concerned about crime in the streets and had begun to lose its faith in nearly all forms of government. Watergate would soon be a household word. Friedkin's film certainly reflects these attitudes. Crime is not shown as being contained in a small section of New York. Corruption is evident everywhere. No one is clean and no one appears able to stop or control crime.

Friedkin's hero, Popeye Doyle, is no traditional clean-cut individual. Differing little in appearance from the criminals he collars, he wears ill-fitting clothes and often is unshaven. Popeye's dedication to his job borders on the fanatical. He shows no sympathy for minorities or any one else. He is brutal in his handling of suspects. His language is coarse, full of obscenities and ethnic slurs.

One way Friedkin makes Doyle a sympathetic character is by showing the contrast between Doyle and the very successful and sophisticated French drug dealer and mobster that Doyle is chasing. Controlled, cultured, well dressed, the mobster is everything Doyle is not. This underdog status allows the audience to side with Doyle even when he accidentally kills a Federal agent.

What makes the famous car chase so effective is this sympathy, heightened by Gene Hackman's portrayal, the realistic settings, and frantic editing pace. As Doyle destroys cars, commandeers replacements, and wreaks havoc in the streets below the targeted train, the audience is with him on a thrilling urban "amusement ride."

Friedkin has said "I know how to do it; how to, for one hour and a half, just throw everything I have at an audience and give them a real thrill. That's what they want. They don't go to a theater and treat it like a book." Full of shocks generated by special effects, *The Exorcist* seems to be proof that Friedkin can do exactly what he said.

But the key to the audience involvement in the battle for a little girl's soul is in Friedkin's development of character. In particular he portrays Father Karras as a once deeply committed priest whose faith is wavering. Karras's battle is not only with the demon but with himself. Thus his sacrifice is both the winning move in the struggle for the child and the solution to his own problems.

Friedkin's other films have not been greeted with much positive response from either critics or audiences. It has been suggested that Friedkin's success in the seventies was the product of doing the right film at the right time but both films still find audiences in revival houses and on television. It has also been suggested that Friedkin's success has become a burden: too much is expected from the director of *The French Connection* and *The Exorcist*. With time perhaps his other films can find a more positive response.

—Ray Narducy

FULLER, SAMUEL. American. Born Samuel Michael Fuller in Worcester, Massachusetts, 12 August 1911. Married actress Christa Lang in 1965. Career: 1924—copy-boy on *New York Journal*, assists journalist Arthur Brisbane; also works for *San Diego Sun*; 1928—becomes crime reporter; 1931—begins publishing fiction; 1936—moves to Hollywood, begins writing screenplays; 1942-45—serves in 16th regiment of Army 1st Division ("The Big Red One"), receives Bronze Star, Silver Star, and Purple Heart; 1946-48—screenwriter at Warner Bros. 1948—convinces producer Robert Lippert to let him direct his script of *I Shot Jesse James*; 1951-57—works for 20th Century-Fox; subsequently produces own films; 1962—directs "It Tolls for Thee" episode of *The Virginian* and "330 Independance S.W." episode of *The Dick Powell Reynolds Aluminum Show*, both for TV; 1966—suggests concept for and directs 5 episodes of *Iron Horse* TV series; 1974-78—negotiation process to make *The Big Red One*. Recipient: Best-Written American Low-Budget Film by Writers Guild of America, for *The Steel Helmet*, 1951.

Films (as screenwriter): 1936—*Hats Off* (Petroff); 1937—*It Happened in Hollywood* (Lachman); 1938—*Gangs of New York* (Cruze), remade in 1945 as *Gangs of the Waterfront* (Blair); *Adventure in Sahara* (Lederman); *Federal Man-Hunt* (Grinde); 1940—*Bowery Boy* (Morgan); 1941—*Confirm or Deny* (Lang, Mayo); 1943—*Power of the Press* (Landers); 1948—*Shockproof* (Sirk); (as director and scriptwriter): 1948—*I Shot Jesse James*; 1950—*The Baron of Arizona*; *The Steel Helmet* (+co-pr); 1951—*Fixed Bayonets*; *The Tanks Are Coming* (Seiler) (sc only); 1952—*Park Row* (+co-pr); *Scandal Sheet* (Karlson) (sc only); 1953—*Pick Up on South Street*, remade in 1968 as *Cape Town Affair* (Webb); *The Command* (Butler) (sc only); 1954—*Hell and High Water* (co-sc); 1955—*The House of Bamboo* (co-sc, +ro as Japanese policeman); (as producer, director and scriptwriter): 1957—*Run of the Arrow*; *China Gate*; *40 Guns*; 1958—*Verboten*; 1959—*The Crimson Kimono*; 1960—*Underworld USA*; 1962—*Merrill's Marauders* (co-sc and d only); 1963—*Shock Corridor*; *The Naked Kiss* (co-pr); (as director and scriptwriter): 1967—*Caine*; 1973—*Dead Pigeon on Beethoven Street* (+ro as United States Senator); 1974—*The Klansman* (Young) (sc only); 1980—*The Big Red One*.

Roles: 1965—as himself in *Pierrot le fou* (Godard); 1966—as himself in *Brigitte et Brigitte* (Moullet); 1971—as himself in *The Last Movie* (Hopper); 1976—*The American Friend* (Wenders); 1979—small role in *1941* (Spielberg).

Publications:

By FULLER:

Books—*Burn, Baby, Burn*, New York 1935; *Test Tube Baby*, New York 1936; *Make Up and Kiss*, New York 1938; *The Dark Page*, New York 1944 (published as *Murder Makes a Deadline*, New York 1952); *The Naked Kiss*, screenplay novelization, New York 1964; *Crown of India*, New York 1966; *144 Picadilly*, New York 1971; *Dead Pigeon on Beethoven Street*, screenplay novelization, New York 1973; articles—"What is Film?" in *Cinema* (Beverly Hills), July 1964; "Samuel Fuller: 2 Interviews" by Stig Björkman and Mark Shivas in *Movie* (London), winter 1969/70; interview in *The Director's Event* by Eric Sherman and Martin Rubin, New York 1970; interview by Ian Christie and others in *Cinema* (Cambridge, Mass.), February 1970; "Dead Pigeon on Beethoven Street", interview by H. Weigel, in *Filmkritik* (Munich), January 1973; interview by D. Rabourdin and T.

Renaud in *Cinéma* (Paris), December 1974; "Sam Fuller Returns", interview by Claude Beylie and J. Lourcelles in *Ecran* (Paris), January 1975; "War That's Fit to Shoot" in *American Film* (Washington, D.C.), November 1976; "3 x Sam: The Flavor of Ketchup", interview by R. Thompson in *Film Comment* (New York), January/February 1977; "'A Privilege to Work in Films': Sam Peckinpah Among Friends" in *Movietone News* (Seattle), February 1979; "Entretien" by A. Masson and others in *Positif* (Paris), July/August 1981.

On FULLER:

Books—*Samuel Fuller* edited by David Will and Peter Wollen, Edinburgh 1969; *Samuel Fuller* by Phil Hardy, New York 1970; "Samuel Fuller by Nicholas Garnham, New York 1971; *Underworld U.S.A.* by Colin MacArthur, London 1972; articles—"Samuel Fuller" by Russell Lee in *New Left Review*, January/February 1964; "Low-Budget Movies with Pow" by Ezra Goodman in *The New York Times Magazine*, 28 February 1965; "Notes Toward a Structural Analysis of the Films of Samuel Fuller" by Peter Wollen in *Cinema* (Cambridge, Mass.), December 1968; "The World of Samuel Fuller" by Kingsley Canham in *Film* (London), November/December 1969; "Samuel Fuller's Action Films" by Kingsley Canham and "Samuel Fuller's Gangster Films" by Colin McArthur in *Screen* (London), November/December 1969; "Are You Waving the Flag At Me: Samuel Fuller and Politics" by John Belton in *Velvet Light Trap* (Madison, Wisconsin), spring 1972; "Pickup on South Street and the Metamorphosis of the Thriller" by F. McConnell in *Film Heritage* (New York), spring 1973; "Sam Fuller Lands with the Big One" by B. Cook in *American Film* (Washington, D.C.), June 1979; "Samuel Fuller" by B. Baker in *Film Dope* (London), September 1979; "Samuel Fuller—Survivor", interview by T. Ryan in *Cinema Papers* (Melbourne), December/January 1980/81; "Sam Fuller's War" by Tom Milne in *Sight and Sound* (London), Autumn 1980; "Love, Action, Death, Violence: Cinema Is Emotion (sur quelques films de Samuel Fuller)" by J. Valot in *Image et son* (Paris), July/August 1980; "La Violence de Fuller" by O.-R. Veillon in *Cinématographe* (Paris), September 1980; "Notes sur Samuel Fuller: anarchiste, moraliste et américain" by Noël Simsolo in *Image et son* (Paris), April 1981; special section on Fuller in *Image et son* (Paris), April 1981; "The Big Red One", special issue of *Avant-Scène du cinéma* (Paris), 1 November 1981.

*   *   *

Sam Fuller's narratives investigate the ways that belonging to a social group simultaneously functions to sustain and nurture individual identity and, conversely, to pose all sorts of emotional and ideological threats to that identity. Fuller's characters are caught between a solitude that is both liberating and debilitating, and a communality that is both supportive and oppressive. Unlike, say, Howard Hawks, whose films suggest the triumph of the group over egoism, Fuller is more cynical and shows that neither isolation nor group membership is without its hardships and tensions.

Many of the films touch upon a broad kind of belonging: membership in a nation specifically the United States (although *China Gate* comments on several other nationalities) as a driving idea and ideal, national identity becoming a reflection of personal identity. For example, in Fuller films about the building of the West, such as *Forty Guns*, *The Baron of Arizona*, or *Run of the Arrow*, the central characters initially understand their own quests as necessarily divergent from the quest of America for its own place in the world. Even though the course of the films suggests the moral and emotional losses that such divergence leads to, the films also imply that there is something inadequate in the American quest itself, in the ways such a quest undercuts its own purity by finding strength in a malevolent violence (the readiness of "ordinary" people in *The Baron of Arizona* to lynch at a moment's notice), in mistrust and prejudice (unbridled racism in *Run of the Arrow*), or in political corruption.

Similarly, in several films, such as *House of Bamboo*, *Underworld USA*, and *Pickup on South Street*, about criminal organizations infiltrated by revenging outsiders, the narrative trajectory will begin by suggesting the moral separation of good guys and bad guys, but will then continue to demonstrate their parallelism, their interweaving, even their blurring. For example, in *Underworld USA*, the criminals and crimefighters resemble each other in their methods, in their cold calculation and determination, and in their bureaucratic organization. Tolly, the film's central character, may agree to map his own desire for revenge onto the crimefighters' desire to eliminate a criminal element, but the film resolutely refuses to unambiguously propagandize the public good over personal motives.

At a narrower level of group concern, Fuller's films examine the family as a force that can be nurturing, but is often stifling and riddled with contradictions. Not accidentally, many of Fuller's films concentrate on childless or parentless figures: the family here is not a given but something that one loses or that one has to grope towards. Often, the families that do exist are, for Fuller, like the nation-state initially presenting an aura of innocent respectability but ultimately revealing a corruption and rotted perversity. Indeed, *The Naked Kiss* connects questions of political value to family value in its story of a woman discovering that her fiance, a town's benefactor, its model citizen, is actually a child molester. Similarly, *Verboten!* maps the story of postwar America's self-image as benefactor to the world onto an anti-love love story composed of a German woman initially marrying a G.I. for financial support and then finding she really does love him, only to discover that he no longer loves her.

Love, to be sure, is a redemptive promise in Fuller's films but it is run through by doubt, anger, mistrust, deception. Any reciprocity or sharing that Fuller's characters achieve comes at a great price ranging from mental and physical pain to death. For example, in *Underworld USA*, Tolly is able to drop his obsessional quest and give himself emotionally to the ex-gangster moll, Cuddles, only when he is at a point of no return that will lead him to his death. Against the possibility of love (which, if it ever comes, comes so miraculously as to call its own efficacy into doubt), Fuller's films emphasize a world where everyone is potentially an outsider and therefore a mystery and even a menace. No scene in Fuller's cinema encapsulates this better than the opening of *Pickup on South Street* where a filled subway car becomes the site of intrigued and intriguing glances as a group of strangers warily survey each other as potential victims and victimizers. Echoing the double-entendre of the title (the pickup is political—the passing on of a secret microfilm—as well as sexual), the opening scene shows a blending of sexual desire and aggression as a sexual come-on reveals itself to be a cover for theft, and passive passengers reveal themselves to be government agents.

In a world of distrust, where love can easily betray, the Fuller character survives either by fighting for the last vestiges of an honest, uncorrupted love (in the most optimistic of the films) or, in the more cynical cases, by displacing emotional attachment from people to ideas; to myths of masculine power in *Forty Guns*; to obsessions (for example, Johnny Barratt's desire in *Shock Corridor* to win the Pulitzer Prize even if that desire leads him to madness); to mercenary self-interest; to political or social ideals;

and ultimately, to a professionalism that finally means doing nothing other than doing your job right without thinking about it. This is especially the case in Fuller's war films which show characters driven to survive for survival's sake, existence being defined in *Merrill's Marauders* as "put(ting) one foot in front of the other."

Fuller's style, too, is one based on tensions: a conflict of techniques that one can read as an enactment for the spectator of Fuller themes. Fuller is both a director of rapid, abrupt, shocking montage, as in the alternating close-ups of robber and victim in *I Shot Jesse James*, and a director who uses extremely long takes incorporating a complex mix of camera movement and character action. Fuller's style is the opposite of graceful; his style seems to suggest that in a world where grace provides little redemption, its utilization would be a kind of lie. Thus, a stereotypically beautiful shot like the balanced image of Mount Fujiyama in *House of Bamboo* might seem a textbook example of the well-composed nature shot but for the fact that the mountain is framed through the outstretched legs of a murdered soldier.

As with other American genre and action directors, Fuller has only gradually become a subject for critical investigation, except in France. Anglo-American criticism of Fuller tends to be in journals such as Seattle's *Movie-Tone News* which devoted a special issue to him. However, there are two excellent book-length British analyses of the interweavings of style and theme in Fuller's films and their relations to national and personal quests for identity: Phil Hardy's *Samuel Fuller* (1970) and Nicholas Garnham's *Samuel Fuller* (1971).

—Dana B. Polan

GAÁL, ISTVÁN. Hungarian. Born in Salgótarján, 25 August 1933. Educated at Academy of Theatre and Film Art, Budapest, graduated 1959; studied at Centro Sperimentale, Rome, 1959-61. Career: 1961—works briefly as director and cameraman for Hungarian Newsreel Dept.; 1961-64—makes several shorts before first feature; 1977—for Hungarian TV directs 2 adaptations from Maxim Gorky novels, *2 Trains a Day* and *Customs Frontier*.

Films (as director, scriptwriter, and editor): 1957—*Pálya-munkások (Surfacemen)* [Railroaders] (short); 1961—*Etude* (short); 1962—*Tisza—öszi vázlatok (Tisza—Autumn Sketches)* (short); *Oda—vissza (To and Fro)* (short); *Cigányok (Gypsies)* (Sára—short) (ed, ph only); 1964—*Sodrásban (The Stream, Current)*; *Férfiarckép (Portrait of a Man)* (Gyöngyössy—short) (co-ph only); 1965—*Zöldár (Green Flood, The Green Years)* (co-sc); 1967—*Krónika (The Chronicle)* (short) (+ph); *Keresztelö (Baptism, Christening Party)*; *Vizkereszet (Twelfth Night)* (Sára—short) (co-sc only); 1969—*Tiz éves Kuba (Cuba's 10 Years, 10 Years of Cuba)* (short) (+ph); 1970—*Bartók Béla: az éjszaka zenéje (Béla Bartók: The Music of the Night, The Night Music)* (short); *Magasiskola (The Falcons)*; 1971—*Holt vidék (The Dead Country, Dead Landscape)* (co-sc); 1977—*Legato (Ties)* (co-sc); *Naponta két vonat (2 Trains a Day)* (for TV); *Vámhatár (Customs Frontier)* (for TV) (d, ed only); 1981—*Cserepek (Buffer Zone, Shards)*.

Publications:

By GAAL:

Articles—"Un Réalisateur hongrois", interview by J. Camerlain in *Séquences* (Paris), January 1973; interview by Kiss/Koller and A. Ibrányi-Kiss in *Cinema Canada* (Montreal), April/May 1973; "Interviewing Istváa Gaál" in *Hungarofilm Bulletin* (Budapest), no.4, 1977.

On GAAL:

Book—*History Must Answer to Man* by Graham Petrie, London 1978; articles—"István Gaál, de *Remous* à *Paysage mort*: itinéraire d'un témoin" by M. Martin and Y. Biro in *Ecran* (Paris), March 1974; "István Gaál and *The Falcons*" by G. Petrie in *Film Quarterly* (Berkeley), spring 1974; "Istvan Gaal" by M. Salmi in *Film Dope* (London), September 1979; "Istvan Gaal: les remous de la quarantaine" by René Predal in *Jeune cinéma* (Paris), October 1981; "Filmröl zenéröl" by György Czigány in *Filmvilág* (Budapest), no.1, 1981; "István Gaál" in *Filmowy serwis Prasowy* (Warsaw), no.5, 1982.

*   *   *

The artistic personality of the film editor, cameraman, scriptwriter, and director István Gaál was formed by his study at the Higher School of Theatrical and Film Art in Budapest, where he arrived as a young electrical engineer determined to devote himself to the art of film. Here he shaped and precisely defined his artistic viewpoint in a classroom that is already legandary today as the meeting place of later notable personalities in Hungarian cinematography—Judit Elek, Pál Gábor, Imre Gyöngössy, Zoltán Huszárik, Ferenc Kardos, Zsolt Kérdi-Kovács, János Rózsa, István Szabó, Sándor Sára, Ferenc Kósa, and others. He took his first, already conspicuous step in a creative workshop, the experimental studio of Béla Balázs. The artistic path he chose was a difficult one, because it was specific, individual form of documentary. In the course of his creative career he returns constantly to this basic source, but at the same time he applies its elements in his not very extensive but masterfully suggestive artistic film work.

He is one of the founders of the Hungarian new wave of the mid-1960s, which he inaugurated with his deeply emotive debut *Sodrásban*. Not only did this work reflect the positive social events of the time, but the author also applied genuine elements of a subjectively motivated poetics. With every important subsequent film—and these are for the most part adaptions of his own literary work—Gaál reveals the strange world of the Hungarian countryside, a world of desolation and unromantically flat landscapes with scattered lonely settings where solitary tree trunks, well-beams, and the whitewashed walls of old buildings loom from time to time. In this microcosm he uncovers human community, relationships, and problems of morality. In intimate episodes he manages to take up and treat delicate problems of the past and generalize them in the form of a profound philosophical drama that reveals the roots of violence and evil and the dangerous elements of apathy and indifference, despair and loneliness. At the same time, his films, with their limited dialogue and almost totally graphic conception, are poetic pictures that have dramatic tension. However, István Gaál is not the romantic poet of the countryside he may appear to be. In a brief moment and in simple fashion he suggests the atmosphere and the relationships among characters, and he is equally adept at capturing the essence of a hunting lodge in the wilderness, a depopulated village, or the smell of a provincial town. For him the environment is merely a symbolic medium, because each of his works offers a kind of parallel between the world of nature and human society, a metaphor with deep ideological and moral significance.

There is a close union of all artistic components in films under his direction—a carefully constructed script, a poetic form of screen photography, simple non-illustrative music, and dramatically motivated editing, along with prodigious acting by the noted performers whom the director gets to "shed their theatrical skin," enabling them to achieve quite remarkable degree of expression before the camera.

In the intervals between making his fictional film works, István Gaál constantly returns to the pure documentary, which is for him a starting point and perhaps also an experimental station. But he shapes his documentaries with the same fire and originality. Here again, there is an altertion between people and nature, and a struggle between the two.

In his most recent films, István Gaál turns more to the inner world of his contemporaries. His works delineate masterful psychological portraits in which there is more and more reflection of history on a general plane. His films are personal, poetically veiled confessions about present-day people, their problems and relations.

—G. Merhaut

GAD, URBAN. Danish. Born in Korsør, 12 February 1879. Educated in Copenhagen until 1897; attended art school in Paris. Married Asta Nielsen, 1912 (divorced 1918); married Esther Burgert Westenhagen, 1922. Career: before 1910—artistic advisor for 2 Copenhagen theaters; also wrote several plays; 1910—directs first film; discovers actress Asta Nielsen; 1911-22—works in German film industry; 1922-47—becomes manager of "Grand," prominent Copenhagen film theater; 1926—makes last film. Died 26 December 1947; buried at Humlebaek Kirkegaard.

Films (as director): 1910—*Afgrunden (The Abyss)*; 1911—*Den sorte Drøm*; *Hulda Rasmussen or Dyrekøbt Glimmer (When Passion Blinds Honesty)*; *Aedel Daad or Den store Flyver (Generosity)*; *Gennem Kamp til Sejr (Through Trials to Victory)*; *Der fremde Vogel*; *Die Verräterin*; *Heisses Blut*; *In dem grossen Augenblick*; *Nachtfalter*; *Zigeunerblut (Gypsy Blood)*; 1912—*Den hvide Slavehandel III or Det berygtede Hus (Nina, In the Hands of the Impostors)*; *Das Mädchen ohne Vaterland*; *Der Totentanz*; *Die arme Jenny*; *Die Kinder des Generals*; *Die Macht des Goldes*; *Jugend und Tollheit*; *Komödianten*; *Wenn die Maske fällt*; *Zum Tode gehetz*; 1913—*Der Tod in Sevilla*; *Die Filmprimadonna*; *Die Sünden der Vater*; *Die Suffragette*; *Engelein*; *S.I.*; 1914—*Aschenbrödel*; *Das Feuer*; *Das Kind ruft*; *Die ewige Nacht*; *Die Tochter der Landstrasse*; *Engeleins Hochzeit*; *Vordertreppe und Hintertreppe*; *Weisse Rosen*; *Zapatas Bande*; 1916—*Der rote Streifen*; 1917—*Der breite Weg*; *Die Gespensterstunde*; *Die Vergangenheit rächt sich*; *Die verschlossene Tür*; *Klosterfriede*; 1918—*Das sterbende Modell*; *Das verhängnisvolle Andenken*; *Der Schmuck des Rajah*; *Die Kleptomanin*; *Die neue Dalila*; *Vera Panina*; 1919—*Das Spiel von Liebe und Tod*; *Mein Mann—der Nachtredakteur*; 1920—*Der Abgrund der Seelen*; *Der Liebes-Korridor*; *So ein Mädel*; *Weltbrand*; 1921—*Christian Wahnschaffe*; *Der vergiftete Brunnen*; *Die Insel der Verschollenen*; 1922—*Hanneles Himmelfahrt*; 1926—*Lykkehjulet (The Gay Huskies)*.

Publications:

By GAD:

Book—*Filmen: Dens Midler og Maal*, Copenhagen 1919 (translated as *Der Film: seine Mittel—seine Ziele*, 1921).

On GAD:

Article—obituary by H.H. Wollenberg in *Penguin Film Review* (London), September 1948.

*   *   *

"The part he played in the early history of European film art can be compared with that of D.W. Griffith in America," wrote H.H. Wollenberg in his obituary of Urban Gad (in *Penguin Film Review*, September 1948). These kind words are—to put it mildly—an exaggeration of Urban Gad's importance in the history and development of the film. Considering his total output, Urban Gad might better be characterized as a cultivated craftsman, who was mainly occupied with the handling of actors. With his background, coming from a high-society milieu with a cultural leaning, and having worked as a dramatic consultant for Copenhagen theaters, this is quite natural. He was an intellectual with a great affection for and belief in the film as an artistic means of expression. His book *The Film: Its Means and Ends*, published in 1919 and two years later translated into German, was a very intelligent, open-minded and stimulating theoretical work, which was remarkable at a time when few intellectuals had any respect for film.

Gad's position in early film history is secured by one work, and this was his first, *Afgrunden*, which he wrote and directed, assisted by the experienced cameraman Alfred Lind. The story was about a young bourgeois girl, who is infatuated with a circus artist. She abandons her quiet and safe life, follows the performer, and in the end she murders him in a rage of jealousy. *Afgrunden* introduced the erotic melodrama, with a background of social contrast, which became in the next few years a Danish speciality, influencing the international film. Gad had written the role of the girl for Asta Nielsen. She made her screen debut in the film and was an instant sensation. Her sensuality and frankness shocked the audience and one scene, in which Nielsen performs a gaucho dance with Poul Reumert, the leading man, was a hitherto unseen demonstration of sexual provocation. Urban Gad had created the first European film star.

Gad was known for his meticulous care when filming and he had a reputation for being a very demanding director. In the next two films, made for Nordisk before he went to Germany, he used more sets than was customary. Gad left Denmark with Asta Nielsen and he wrote and directed 34 of her films until 1914, when they separated. Asta Nielsen rose to stardom; but Gad never played an important part in German film. After a couple of films in Denmark in the twenties he left film production in 1926. For the rest of his life he was held in great esteem as the manager of one of Copenhagen's prestige cinemas.

—Ib Monty

GALLONE, CARMINE. Italian. Born in Taggia, 18 September

1886. Married Soava (Gallone), 1912. Career: early 1900s—writes plays and poetry; 1911—wins national prize for poetry collection; 1911—begins working at Teatro Argentina, Rome; 1913—begins screenwriting at Cines studio; late 1920s, early 1930s—works outside Italy; 1936—invited by Fascist government to direct spectacle and propaganda film *Scipione l'Africano*; after war makes opera films and historical spectacles. Died in April 1973.

Films (as director): 1913—*Il bacio di Cirano*; *La donna nuda*; 1914—*Turbine d'odio*; 1915—*Avatar*; *Redenzione*; *Fior di male*; *Marzia nuziale*; 1916—*La falena*; *Malombra*; *Fede*; *Tra i gorghi*; *La storia dei tredici*; 1917—*Lo chiamavano Cosetta*; *Madonna Grazia*; 1918—*Storia di un peccato*; 1919—*Maman Popee*; *La figlie del mare*; *Il destino e il timoniere*; *Il mare di Napoli*; 1920—*La Vie d'une femme*; *Il bacio di Cirano*; *Marcella*; *La Fanciulla, il poeta e la laguna*; *La figlia del tempesta* (+sc); *Il Colonello Chabert*; *Sterimator Vesevo* (sc only); *La grande tormenta*; *Amleto e il suo clown*; *Nemesis*; *L'ombra di un trono*; 1922—*La madre folle* (+pr); *Le braccia aperte*; *Il Reggimento Royal Cravate*; *Il segreto della grotta azzurra*; *La vedova scaltra*; 1923—*Amore* (+pr); *Tormenta (Nella tormenta)*; *I volti dell'amore*; 1924—*Il corsaro* (co-d); *La signorina madre di familglia*; *Jerry*; *La fiammata*; 1926—*Gli ultimi giorni di Pompeii (The Last Days of Pompeii)*; 1927—*La cavalcata ardente*; *Celle qui domine* (co-d); *Die Stadt der tausend Freuden*; *Liebeshölle (L'inferno dell'amore, Pawns of Passion)*; *Marter der Liebe*; *S.O.S.*; 1929—*Das Land ohne Frauen (Terra senza donne, Bride 68)*; 1930—*Die singende Stadt*; 1931—*Un Soir de rafle*; *The City of Song (Farewell to Love)*; 1932—*Le Chant du marin*; *Un Fils d'Amerique*; *Ma Cousine de Varsovie*; *Le Roi des palaces*; 1933—*King of the Ritz* (American version of *Le Roi des palaces*); *Eine Nacht in Venedig*; 1934—*2 Hearts in Waltz Time*; *Going Gay*; *For Love of You*; 1935—*Wenn die Musik nicht wär*; *Im Sonnenschein (Opernring, Thank You Madame)*; *Mein Herz ruft nach Dir (E lucean le stelle, My Heart Is Calling, Mon Coeur t'appelle)*; *Casta Diva (The Divine Spark)*; *Al sole*; 1937—*Scipione l'Africano (Scipio Africanus)*; 1938—*Solo per te*; *Manège (Un dramma al circo)*; *Marionette (Dir gehört mein Herz)*; *Giuseppe Verdi*; 1939—*Das Abenteuer geht weiter*; *Il sogno di Butterfly*; *Manon Lescaut*; 1940—*Oltre d'amore*; *Melodie eterne (Eternal Melodies)*; *Marcella*; *Amami, Alfredo!*; 1941—*L'amante segreta*; *Primo amore*; *La Regina di Navarra*; 1942—*Le due orfanelle (The 2 Orphans)*; *Odessa in fiamme*; *Harlem*; 1943—*Tristi amori*; 1945—*Il canto della vita*; 1946—*Biraghin*; *Devanti a lui tremava tutta Roma (Before Him All Rome Trembled, Tosca)*; 1947—*Rigoletto*; 1948—*La signora delle camelie (La traviata, The Lost One)*; 1949—*La leggenda di Faust (Faust and the Devil)*; *Il trovatore*; 1950-*La forza del destino*; *Taxi di notte (Singing Taxi Driver)* (+pr); 1951—*Addio Mimi (Her Wonderful Lie)* (completed 1947); *Messalina (The Affairs of Messalina)* (+co-sc); 1953—*Puccini* (+co-sc); *Cavalleria rusticana (Fatal Desire)* (+co-sc); *Senza veli* (+co-sc); 1954—*Casa Ricordi (House of Ricordi)*; 1955—*Madama Butterfly* (+co-sc); *Don Camillo e l'onorevole Peppone*; *Casta Diva*; *La figlia di Mata Hari* (supervisor only); 1956—*Tosca*; *Michele Strogoff*; 1958—*Polijuschka*; 1959—*Cartagine in fiamme*; 1961—*Don Camillo Monsignore ma non troppo*; 1962—*La Monaca di Monza*; *Carmen di Trastavere*.

Publications:

By GALLONE:

Articles—partial script of *Marcella* in *Bianco e nero* (Rome), March 1940; "L'arte di inscenare" in *Bianco e nero* (Rome),

July/August 1952.

On GALLONE:

Articles—issue devoted to *Scipione l'Africano* of *Bianco e nero* (Rome), no.7-8, 1937; article by Roberto Paolella in *Bianco e nero* (Rome), no.7-8, 1952; "Carmine Gallone le grandiloquent" by Claude Beylie in *Ecran* (Paris), May 1973.

*   *   *

Gallone started his career in 1911 at the Teatro Argentina in Rome but was quickly attracted to the cinema, entering the Cines studio as scriptwriter in 1913. His directorial talent being immediately recognized, Cines gave him the project of adapting a version of *Cyrano de Bergerac*. From then on, most notably working with Lucio D'Ambra, Gallone became a leading director during the golden age of Italian silent cinema that lasted until the end of the First World War. He was largely responsible for the growth of an elaborate star system, wherein the films were tailored specifically to the stars' talents and personae. Such films dominated Italian production. Gallone's favorite players were Soava Gallone, a polish actress, who married him in 1912 and starred in a dozen of his films, Lyda Borelli, Emilio Ghione, and Amleto Novelli. Even though Gallone could film in a realist style, for example in *Storia di un peccato*, he seemed more adept at torrid love stories, historical epics, and adaptations of famous literature. In a period governed by the artistic style and philosophy of Gabriele D'Annunzio, Gallone was perhaps the best at portraying the prevailing sensibility on a grand scale. Gallone placed great emphasis on composition, the pictorial elements of the image, and set decoration. He believed in visual orchestration whereby concepts are realized through the mise-en-scène itself. He insisted that actors work very closely with the set designer so that the design and performances would be consonant with each other. His films were enormously successful both in his native country and abroad, so much so that their popularity demanded remakes by Gallone, as in the cases of *Il Bacio di Cirano*, *La grande tormenta*, and *Casta Diva*.

During the years of extreme crisis in the Italian cinema in the late 1920s, Gallone, like many of his contemporaries, made films in other countries, and multiple-language versions of sound films for national markets. For a decade, he directed in Germany, Austria, France, and worked for the continental studios of British Gaumont. He had no difficulty making the transition to sound and, in fact, one of his first sound films, the French *Un soir de rafle*, starring Annabella and Albert Prejean (who made three films with Gallone) proved to be a huge success. Outside of Italy as well he worked with popular stars: Conrad Veidt, Martha Eggerth, Brigitte Helm. He was called back to Italy in 1936 for the colossal project in praise of the Roman empire, *Scipione l'Africano*, famous because it is one of the few outright pieces of propaganda produced by the film industry under Fascism, and for its immense scope: 20 principal actors, 32,848 extras, 50 elephants, 1,000 horses, and a shooting schedule of 232 days lasting from August 1936 until March 1937.

During the sound period, before and after the war, Gallone was best known as a director of musicals, lavishly produced, and filmed operas. Most of the films starring the tenor Beniamino Gigli just before the war were directed by Gallone. His 1946 Resistance film, which he co-scripted, was, in fact, an operatic depiction of Fascism starring Anna Magnani and Tito Gobbi.

—Elaine Mancini

GANCE, ABEL. French. Born in Paris, 25 October 1889. Educated at Collège de Chantilly; Collège Chaptal, Paris, baccalaureate 1906. Married actress Odette Vérité in 1933; child: Clarisse (Mme Jacques Raynaud). Career: 1906—becomes clerk in law office; 1907—begins acting career in Brussels; 1908-09—acts at Théâtre du Parc, Brussels; 1909—first leading screen role in *Molière* (Perret), begins selling screenplays to Gaumont; 1911—forms production company Le Film Français; 1917—appointed artistic director of Le Film d'Art; mobilized for war, gassed at a poison gas factory; serves several months with Service Cinématographique et Photographique et la Armée; 1921—following death of first wife, suspends work on *La Roue*, travels to U.S., meets D.W. Griffith; 1922—returns to France; 1925—begins shooting *Napoléon*; 1926—patents widescreen "Polyvision" process; 1929—patents "Perspective Sonore"—stereophonic sound process; 1931—*La Fin du monde* (his first talking film) a financial failure; 1939—begins work on *Christophe Colomb* (unrealized); 1954—*La Tour de Nesle* a commercial success, leads to renewed activity; 1965—adapts and directs *Marie Tudor* for TV; 1970s—lives in Nice and in home for aged actors, continues to work on screenplay for *Christophe Colomb*; 1981—*Napoleon*, reassembled, is premiered in New York. Died in Paris, 10 November 1981. Recipient: Gold Medal, Union Française des Inventeurs, 1952; Cinérama Gold Medal, Société des Auteurs, 1952; Théâtre de l'Empire, Paris, named for Gance, 1961; Silver Medal of the city of Paris, 1971; Grand prix national de Cinéma, 1974; César award, 1980; Commandeur de la Légion d'honneur; Grand Officier de l'ordre national du Mérite, et des Arts et des Lettres.

Films (as scriptwriter): 1909—*Le Portrait de Mireille* (Perret); *Le Glas du Père Césaire*; *La Legende de l'arc-en-ciel*; 1910—*Paganini*; *La Fin de Paganini*; *Le Crime de Grand-père* (Perret); *Le Roi des parfums*; *L'Aluminité*; *L'Auberge rouge*; *Le Tragique Amour de Mona Lisa* (Capellani); 1911—*Cyrano et D'Assoucy* (Capellani); *Un Clair de lune sous Richelieu* (Capellani); *L'Électrocuté* (Morlhon); (as director and scriptwriter): 1911—*La Digue, ou Pour sauver la Hollande*; 1912—*Le Nègre blanc* (+ro); *Il y a des pieds au plafond*; *Le Masque d'horreur*; *Une Vengeance d'Edgar Poe* (Capellani) (sc only); *La Mort du Duc d'Enghien* (Capellani) (sc only); *La Conspiration des drapeaux* (sc only); *La Pierre philosophe* (sc only); 1914—*L'Infirmière* (Pouctal) (sc only); 1915—*Un drame au Château d'Acre (Les Morts reviennent-ils?)*; 1915—*Ecce Homo* (unfinished); 1916—*La Folie du Docteur Tube*; *L'Enigme de dix heures*; *Le Fleur des ruines*; *L'Héroïsme de Paddy*; *Le Fou de la falaise*; *Ce que les flots racontent*; *Le Périscope*; *Barberousse*; *Les Gaz mortels (Le Brouillard sur la ville)*; *Strass et compagnie*; 1917—*Le Droit à la vie*; *La Zone de la mort*; *Mater Dolorosa*; 1918—*La Dixième Symphonie*; 1918—*Le Soleil noir* (unfinished); 1919—*J'Accuse*; 1920—*L'Atre* (Boudrioz) (pr only); 1923—*La Roue*; *Au secours!*; 1927—*Napoléon vu par Abel Gance*; 1928—*Marines* and *Cristeaux* (experimental footage for "Polyvision"); 1929—*Napoléon auf St. Helena (Napoléon à Saint-Hélène)* (Pick) (sc only); 1931—*La Fin du monde*; 1932—*Mater Dolorosa*; 1933—*Le Maître de forges* (Rivers) (sc only, +supervisor); 1934—*Poliche*; *La Dame aux Camélias*; *Napoléon Bonaparte* (sound version, with additional footage); *La Dame aux camélies* (Rivers) (sc only, +supervisor); 1935—*Le Roman d'un jeune homme pauvre*; *Lucrèce Borgia* (d only); 1936—*Un Grande Amour de Beethoven (The Life and Loves of Beethoven)*; *Jérome Perreau, héros des barricades (The Queen and the Cardinal)* (d only); *Le Voleur de femmes*; 1937—*J'accuse (That They May Live)*; 1939—*Louise* (co-sc); *Le Paradis perdu (4 Flights to Love)* (co-sc); 1941—*La Vénus aveugle*;

1942—*Le Capitaine Fracasse* (co-sc); 1944—*Manolete* (unfinished); 1953—*Lumière et la invention du cinématographe (Louis Lumière)* (Paviot) (commentary only, +narr); 1954—*Quatorze Juillet*; *La Tour de Nesle*; *La Reine Margot* (Dréville) (sc only); 1956—*Magirama* (co-pr: demonstration of Polyvision in color); 1960—*Austerlitz* (co-d, co-sc); 1964—*Cyrano et d'Artagnan* (co-sc); 1971—*Bonaparte et la révolution* (co-pr).

Roles: 1909—*Molière* (Perret); 1909-10—appears in some Max Linder short comedies as Max's brother.

Publications:

By GANCE:

Books and scripts—*J'Accuse* in *La Cinématographie Française* (Paris), April 1919; *J'Accuse*, Paris 1922; *Napoléon vu par Abel Gance*, Paris 1927; *Prisme*, Paris 1930; *La Roue, scénario original arrangé par Jean Arroy*, Paris 1930; *La Fin du Monde, scénario arrangé par Joachim Renez*, Paris 1931; *Mater Dolorosa, scénario original arrangé par Joachim Renez*, Paris 1932; articles—"La Beauté à travers le cinéma" in *Bulletin, Institut Général Psychologique* (Paris), no.1-3, 1926; "Qu'est-ce que le cinématographe? Un sixième art" in *Intelligence du cinématographe* by Marcel L'Herbier, Paris 1946; "Les nouveaux chapitres de notre syntaxe" in *Cahiers du cinéma* (Paris), October 1953; "Départ vers la polyvision" in *Cahiers du cinéma* (Paris), December 1954; "Entretien avec Jacques Rivette et François Truffaut" in *Cahiers du cinéma* (Paris), January 1955; "The Kingdom of the Earth (*Le Royaume de la Terre*)" in *Film Culture* (New York), December 1957; "La Digue" in *L'Ecran* (Paris), April/May 1958; "Film as Incantation: An Interview with Abel Gance" in *Film Comment* (New York), March/April 1974.

On GANCE:

Books—*En tournant "Napoléon" avec Abel Gance* by Jean Arroy, Paris 1927; *Abel Gance, hier et demain* by Sophie Daria, Paris 1959; *Abel Gance* by Roger Icart, Toulouse 1960; *Le Sunlight d'Austerlitz* by Nelly Kaplan, Paris 1960; *The Parade's Gone By* by Kevin Brownlow, New York 1969; *Abel Gance* by Steven Kramer and James Welsh, Boston 1978; articles—"Mon ami Gance" by Jean Epstein in *Cahiers du cinéma* (Paris), August/September 1955; "Filmographie d'Abel Gance" by Philippe Esnault in *Cahiers du cinéma* (Paris), January 1955; special Gance issue, *L'Ecran* (Paris), April/May 1958; "*Napoleon* and *La Roue*" by Arthur Lenning in *The Persistence of Vision*, edited by Joseph McBride, Madison, Wisconsin 1968; "*Bonaparte et la révolution*" by Kevin Brownlow in *Sight and Sound* (London), winter 1971/72; "Abel Gance's *Bonaparte and the Revolution*" by Vincent Canby in *Film 71/72*, edited by David Denby, New York 1972; "The Contribution of the French Literary Avant-Garde to Film Theory and Criticism (1907-1924)" by Richard Abel in *Cinema Journal* (Evanston), spring 1975; "Abel Gance's Accusation Against War" by J.M. Welsh and S.P. Kramer in *Cinema Journal* (Evanston), spring 1975; "The Current Cinema: Work of a Master" by Penelope Gilliatt in the *New Yorker*, 6 September 1976; "'Napoleon'—A Personal Involvement" by Kevin Brownlow in *Classic Film Collector* (Muscatine, Iowa), 23 August 1977; "Abel Gance: Prometheus Bound" by W.M. Drew in *Take One* (Montreal), July 1978; "Un Grand Amour de Bee-thoven" by C. Nerguy and Y. Alion in *Avant-Scène du cinéma* (Paris), 1 October 1978; "Abel Gance" by Kevin Brownlow, with biofilmography, in *Film Dope* (London), September 1979; obit-uary in the *New York Times*, 11 November 1981; "Abel Gance: trop grand pour le cinéma?" by C.M. Cluny in *Cinéma* (Paris), December 1981. films—*Les Éloquents* by Charles Ford and Jacques Guillon, France 1956; *Abel Gance, hier et demain (Abel Gance, Yesterday and Tomorrow)* by Nelly Kaplan, Paris 1964; *Abel Gance—the Charm of Dynamite* by Kevin Brownlow, Great Britain 1968.

*   *   *

Abel Gance's career as a director was long and flamboyant. He wrote his first scripts in 1909, turning to directing a couple of years later, and made his last feature, *Cyrano et d'Artagnan*, in 1964. As late as 1971 he reedited a four hour version of his Napoleon footage to make *Bonaparte et la révolution*, and he lived long enough to see his work again reach wide audiences.

Gance's original aspirations were as a playwright and throughout his life he treasured the manuscript of his verse tragedy *La Victoire de Samothrace*, written for Sarah Bernhardt and on the brink of production when the war broke out in 1914. If Gance's beginnings in the film industry he then despised were unremarkable, he was already showing a characteristic audacity and urge for experiment with the unreleased *La Folie du Docteur Tube*, which made great use of distorting lenses, in 1916. Learn-ing his craft in a dozen or more films during 1916-17, best remembered of which are *Les Gaz mortels*, *Barberousse*, and *Mater dolorosa*, he reached fresh heights with a somewhat pre-tentious and melodramatic study of a great and suffering com-poser, *La Dixième Symphonie*, and especially his ambitious and eloquent antiwar drama, *J'Accuse*, released in 1919. These films estalished him as the leading French director of his generation and gave him a preeminence he was not to lose until the coming of sound.

The 1920s saw the release of just three Gance films. If *Au secours!*, a comedy starring his friend Max Linder, is something of a lighthearted interlude, the other two are towering landmarks of silent cinema. *La Roue* began as a simple melodramatic tale but in the course of six months scripting and a year's location shooting, the project took on quite a new dimension. In the central figure of Sisif, Gance seems to have struggled to create an amalgam of Oedipus, Sisyphus, and Lear, while the cut portions of the film also apparently developed a social satire of such ferocity that the railway unions demanded its excision. This was the most expensive film as yet made in France and its production was again delayed when the death of Gance's wife caused him to abandon work and take a five month trip to the U.S. Like his previous work, *La Roue* had been conceived and shot in the pre-1914 style of French cinema, which was based on a concep-tion of film as a series of long takes, each containing a significant section of the action, rather than as a succession of scenes made up of intercut shots of different lengths, taken from varying distances. But in Hollywood, where he met D.W. Griffith, Gance came into contact with the new American style of editing and on his return to France spent a whole year reediting his film. On its release in 1923 *La Roue* proved to be one of the stunning films of the decade, even in its shortened version comprising a prologue and four parts, with a combined running time of nearly eight hours.

Gance's imagination and energy at this period seemed limitless and almost immediately he plunged into an even vaster project, whose title clearly reflects his personal approach, *Napoléon vu par Abel Gance*. If *La Roue* was particularly remarkable for its editing, with certain sequences becoming classic moments of French 1920s avant-garde experiment, *Napoléon* attracted immediate attention for its incredibly mobile camerawork created by a team under the direction of Jules Kruger. *Napoléon* thus emerges as a key masterpiece of French cinema at a time when visual experimentation took precedence over narrative and the disorganization of production offered filmmakers the chance to produce extravagant and ambitious personal works within the heart of the commercial industry. Gance's conception of himself as visionary filmmaker and of Napoleon as a master of his destiny points to the roots of Gance's style in the 19th century and a very romantic view of the artist as hero. The scope of Gance's film, bursting into triple screen effects at the moment of Napoleon's climactic entry into Italy, remains staggering even today.

The 1920s in France were a period of considerable creative freedom and a widespread urge to experiment with the full potential of the medium. If the freedom came from the lack of a tightly controlled studio system, the desire to explore new forms of filmic expression can be traced to a reaction against the situation imposed by Pathé and Gaumont before 1914, when film was seen as a purely commercial product, underfinanced and devoid of artistic or personal expression. This had been the cinema in which Gance had made his debut, and he was one of those striving most forcefully in the 1920s both to increase the possibilities for personal expressiveness and to widen the techni-cal scope of cinema. He pioneered new styles of cutting and camerawork, and also widescreen and multiscreen techniques. It's ironic, then, that the advent of the greatest technical innova-tion of the period should have left him stranded. The explanation for this lies less in the irrelevance of sound to his personal vision of the medium—he was pioneering a new stereophonic system with *La Fin du monde* as early as 1929—than in the new forms of tighter production control which came as a result of the greater costs involved in sound filmmaking.

The 1930s emerge as a sad era for a man accustomed to being in the forefront of the French film industry. Gance, whose mind had always teemed with new and original projects, was now reduced to remaking his old successes: sound versions of *Mater dolorosa* in 1932, *Napoléon Bonaparte* in 1934 and *J'accuse* in 1937. Otherwise the projects he was allowed to make were largely adaptations of fashionable stage dramas or popular novels: *Le Maître de forges*, *Poliche*, *La Dame aux camélias*, *Le Roman d'un jeune homme pauvre*. In the late 1930s he was able to treat subjects in which his taste for grandly heroic figures is again apparent: Savonarola in *Lucrèce Borgia*, or the great composer —played by Harry Faur—in *Un Grand Amour de Beethoven*, but by 1942, when he made *Le Capitaine Fracasse*, Gance's career seemed to have come to an end. Though a dozen years were to pass before he directed another feature film, he main-tained his incredible level of energy and refusal to be beaten, continuing his experiments with "polyvision" which were to culminate in his *Magirama* spectacle, and eventually making three further features, all historical dramas in which his zest, if not the old towering imagination, is still apparent: *La Tour de Nesle*, *Austerlitz* and *Cyrano et d'Artagnan*.

The French 1920s cinema of which Gance is the major figure has consistently been undervalued by film historians, largely because its rich experimentation with visual style and expres-siveness was not accompanied by an similar concern with the development of film narrative. Gance's roots are in the 19th century romantic tradition and despite his literary background, he, like his contemporaries, was willing to accept virtually any melodramatic story which would allow him to pursue his visual interests. For this reason French 1920s work has been marginalized in accounts of film history which see the growth of storytelling techniques as the central unifying factor. The rediscovery of Gance's *Napoléon* in the 1980s—thanks largely to 20 years of effort by Kevin Brownlow—has made clear to the most sceptical the force and mastery achieved in the years preceding the advent of sound, and restored Gance's reputation as a master of world cinema.

—Roy Armes

GARCÍA BERLANGA, LUIS. Spanish. Born Luis García-Berlanga Martí in Valencia, 12 July 1921. Jesuit education in Switzerland, then at private school in Valencia, studying architecture, law and letters; studied philosophy and humanities at Valencia University; studied at IIEC (School of Cinema), Madrid. Career: early 1940s—serves in División Azul (Blue Division) of Spanish volunteers with German forces on Russian front; 1942-47—paints and writes poetry; seeing Pabst's *Don Quichotte* leads to decision to become filmmaker; 1947—moves to Madrid, enrolls in School of Cinema (IIEC); 1951—with Antonio Bardem directs first film (Bardem in charge of actors, Berlanga photography and *mise en scène*; mid-1950s—several projects banned by censor prior to *Calabuch*; 1961—on *Plácido* begins continuing collaboration with novelist and scriptwriter Rafael Azcona; after 1967—acts occasionally in others' films; 1970s—professor at IIEC; currently President of Filmoteca Nacional.

Films (as student at IIEC): 1948-49—*Paseo sobre una guerra antigua*; *Tres cantos*; *El circo (sc, +ed)*; (as director and co-scriptwriter): 1951—*Esa pareja feliz (That Happy Couple)* (co-d, +ph); 1952—*¡Bienvenido, Mr. Marshall! (Welcome, Mr. Marshall)*; 1953—*Novio a la vista (Fiancé in sight)*; *Sangre y luces* (Muñoz) (sc only—Spanish language version of Georges Rouquier's *Sang et lumières*); 1955—*Familia provisional* (Rovira Beleta) (co-sc only); 1956—*Calabuch*; 1957—*Los jueves, milagro (Thursdays, Miracle)*; 1961—*Plácido*; 1962—"La muerte y el leñador (Death and the Woodcutter)" episode of *Las cuatro verdades*; 1963—*El verdugo (The Executioner, Not On Your Life)*; 1967—*Las pirañas*; 1969—*Vivan los novios (Long Live the Bride and Groom)*; 1973—*Tamaño natural (Life Size, Grandeur náture)*; 1978—*La escopeta nacional (The National Rifle, The Spanish Shotgun)*; 1980—*Patrimonio nacional*. Roles: 1967—*No somos de piedra (We Are Not Made Out of Stone)* (Summers); 1968—*Sharon vestida de rojo* (Lorente); 1971—*Apunte sobre Ana (Memorandum on Ana)* (Galán); 1979—*Cuentos eróticos (Erotic Tales)* (collectively directed).

Publications:

By GARCÍA BERLANGA:

Articles—"The Day I Refused to Work" in *Films and Filming* (London), December 1961; "Reflexiones sobre el cine" in *Cine* (Mexico), December 1978; "Cara a cara...Bardem-Berlanga" in *Cinema 2002* (Madrid), July/August 1980; "Berlanga Life Size", interview by Katherine Kovacs in *The Quarterly Review of Film Studies* (Pleasantville, New York), spring 1983.

On GARCÍA BERLANGA:

Books—*Carta abierta a Berlanga* by Diego Galan, Huelva 1978;

Luis G. Berlanga by Ernesto Santolaya, Victoria 1979; *Sobre Luis G. Berlanga* by Julio Pérez Perucha, Valencia 1980, 1981; articles —"Spanish Fighter" by Juan Cobos in *Films and Filming* (London), February 1958; "Luis G. Berlanga, createur Grandeur nature" by G. Braucourt in *Ecran* (Paris), October 1974; "Grandeur nature" in *Avant-Scène du cinéma* (Paris), November 1974; "Luis Berlanga aujourd'hui et hier" by J. Hernandez Les in *Jeune cinéma* (Paris), April/May 1979; "Berlanga—B. Wilder: Buscando un punto común" by J.L. Acosta in *Cinema 2002* (Madrid), April 1980; "Cuando Berlanga toma puntería y dispara contra (malas) costumbres" by J.R. Solares in *Cinemateca Revista* (Montevideo, Uruguay), August 1981; "Luis G. Berlanga" by José Luis Guarner in *International Film Guide 1981*, London 1982; "El Patrimonio de Berlanga" by Miguel Marías in *Casablanca* (Madrid), April 1981.

*   *   *

For many years in Spain strict censorship guidelines inhibited the development of a vital and creative film industry. The first original *auteur* of the post-Civil War period was Luis García Berlanga. When he began to make movies in the early 1950's, Berlanga and fellow filmmaker Juan Antonio Bardem were referred to as the two palm trees in the desert of Spanish film. Since then, and in spite of the fact that he could make relatively few films under Franco, Berlanga has remained one of Spain's foremost talents.

In the early years, the most important influence on Berlanga's filmmaking was Italian neo-realism. At the Conversations of Salamanca (1955) Berlanga and other young directors enthusiastically supported it as an antidote to Francoist cinema, a way of making authentic films that dealt with the everyday problems of ordinary people. From his first movie, *Esa pareja feliz*, which he co-directed with Bardem in 1951, to his most recent "trilogy" on the Spanish aristocracy, Berlanga has remained true to the spirit of Salamanca.

In many movies he has exposed the pitfalls of Spanish society and satirized those institutions or individuals who take themselves too seriously, often using black humor to deflate their pretentions. Berlanga's sympathies are with the underdogs of whatever social class, those who are victims of fate, institutions, or other forces which they cannot control. In a number of his films, we follow the efforts of an individual who wants to achieve something or attain some goal, struggles to do so, and in the end is defeated, ending up in the same or in a worse situation than before. This unfortunate outcome reflects Berlanga's pessimism about a society in which the individual is powerless and in danger of being devoured. There are no winners in Berlanga's movies; all of the victories are Pyrrhic ones. But never one to deliver messages or lessons, Berlanga expresses his pessimistic viewpoint with such verve, vitality and humor that audiences leave the theatre elated with the spontaneity and inventiveness of his films.

Berlanga prefers working with groups of characters rather than concentrating on the fate of a single protagonist. Rarely does one individual dominate the action. Usually we move from one person to the next so that our point of view on the action is constantly shifting. This approach is supported by Berlanga's distinctive camera style. He tends to use very long takes in which the camera surreptitiously follows the movement of the characters, the shot lasting as long as the sequence. (In *Patrimonio nacional* there are some takes that last six or seven minutes.) These sequences are not, however, the carefully arranged and choreographed efforts of a Jancsó. As Berlanga explains it, until he begins shooting he has no specific setup in mind: "What I do is organize the actors' movements and then tell the cameraman how to follow them. When we bump into some obstacle, we stop shooting." In shooting the often feverish activities of his characters in this way, Berlanga gives a fluid, spontaneous feeling to his films. His predilection for these shots expresses what Berlanga calls his "god complex"—his desire to be everywhere at once and to express the totality of any scene.

In his scrutiny of contemporary Spanish life, Berlanga is also attached to much older Spanish literary and cultural traditions, most notably to that of the picaresque novel, in which a *pícaro* or rogue is thrust out into the world and forced to fend for himself. At the bottom of the social heap, the *pícaro* is afforded "a worm's eye view" of society and learns to be tricky in order to survive. The *pícaro* keeps hoping and waiting for a miracle, a sudden change in fate that will change his or her fortune in one stroke. Berlanga's *pícaros*, whether they be naive like Placido (*Placido*) or noble like the Marquis of Leguineche (*Patrimonio nacional*) share the same hopes and tenacious desire to survive. These characters, like Berlanga himself, are deeply attached to Spanish cultural traditions. In fact, one might even consider Berlanga to be a sort of picaresque hero who managed to survive the vagaries of the Franco regime and its system of censorship. A popular director since *Welcome Mr. Marshall*, Berlanga has gone on to even greater success since Franco's death with *La escopeta nacional*, a satiric look at a hunting party of Spain's notables during the Franco regime. In this irreverent and amusing comedy and in its two sequels, Berlanga introduced himself and his vision of his country to a new generation of Spaniards.

—Katherine Singer Kovács

GARNETT, TAY. American. Born in Los Angeles, 13 June 1894. Educated at Los Angeles High School. Married actress Patsy Ruth Miller (divorced); married actress and writer Helga Moray (divorced); married actress Mari Aldon (divorced). Career: before WW I—contributes stories and cartoons to *Photoplayer's Weekly*, and sells stories to adventure magazines; 1917—joins Naval Air Service, studies at Massachusetts Institute of Technology, and in Navy schools before becoming instructor at San Diego Air Station; writes shows for servicemen's entertainment; 1920—goes to Hollywood, begins trying to sell stories; early 1920s—gag man and title writer for Hal Roach and Mack Sennett; briefly works as stuntman; 1927—joins DeMille unit at Pathé as scriptwriter; 1928—begins directing; 1935—sails around world on his yacht "The Athene"; 1940—produces and directs 26 segments of *3 Sheets to the Wind* radio series with John Wayne; 1949—with Bert Friedlob forms Thor Productions; late 1950s—begins directing mainly for television; series include *4 Star Playhouse*, *Loretta Young Show*, *Wagon Train*, *Laramie*, *Rawhide*, *Bonanza*, and *The Untouchables*. Died in 1977.

Films (as scriptwriter): 1922—*Broken Chains* (Holubar) (co-sc, uncredited); *The Hottentot* (Horne) (co-sc); 1924—*Don't Park There!* (Wagner) (co-sc); *Off His Trolley* (Cline) (co-story); *Honeymoon Hardships* (Cedar) (co-story); 1925—*Somewhere in Wrong* (Pembroke) (titles); *The Snow Hawk* (Pembroke) (titles); *Half a Man* (Sweet) (titles); *Who's Your Friend* (Sheldon) (continuity); 1926—*That's My Baby* (Beaudine) (co-sc, uncredited); *Up in Mabel's Room* (Hopper) (co-sc); *The Strong Man* (Capra) (co-sc, uncredited); *There You Are!* (Sedgwick) (co-sc); *The Cruise of the Jasper B.* (Horne) (co-adapt); 1927—*Rubber Tires (10,000 Reward)* (Hale) (co-sc); *Getting Gertie's*

Garter (Hopper) (co-sc, uncredited); *White Gold* (Howard) (co-sc); *Long Pants* (Capra) (co-sc, uncredited); *No Control* (Sidney) (co-sc); *The Wise Wife* (Hopper) (co-sc); *Turkish Delight* (Sloane); 1928—*Skyscraper* (Higgin) (co-sc); *The Cop* (Crisp); *Power* (Higgin); (as director): 1928—*Celebrity* (+co-sc); *The Spieler (The Spellbinder)* (+co-adapt); 1929—*The Flying Fool* (+co-sc); *Oh, Yeah! (No Brakes)* (co-d, +adapt, co-lyrics); 1930—*Officer O'Brien*; *Her Man* (+co-story); 1931—*Bad Company* (+co-sc); *One Way Passage*; 1932—*Prestige* (+co-adapt); *Okay America (The Penalty of Fame)*; 1933—*Destination Unknown*; *S.O.S. Iceberg* (English language version of Fanck's *S.O.S. Eisberg*—location footage shot by Fanck); 1935—*Professional Soldier*; *China Seas*; *She Couldn't Take It (Woman Tamer)*; 1937—*Love Is News*; *Slave Ship*; *Stand-in*; 1938—*Joy of Living*; *Trade Winds* (+story); 1939—*Eternally Yours* (+bit ro as pilot); 1940—*Slightly Honorable*; *7 Sinners*; 1941—*Cheers for Miss Bishop*; *Unexpected Uncle* (Godfrey) (pr only); *Weekend for 3* (Reis) (pr only); 1942—*My Favorite Spy*; 1943—*Bataan*; *The Cross of Lorraine*; 1944—*Mrs. Parkington*; *See Here, Private Hargrove* (Ruggles) (co-d, uncredited); 1945—*The Valley of Decision*; 1946—*The Postman Always Rings Twice*; 1947—*Wild Harvest*; 1948—*A Connecticut Yankee (A Connecticut Yankee in King Arthur's Court, A Yankee in King Arthur's Court)*; 1950—*The Fireball* (+co-sc); *Cause for Alarm!*; 1951—*Soldiers 3*; 1952—*One Minute to Zero*; 1953—*Main Street to Broadway*; 1954—*The Black Knight*; 1955—*7 Wonders of the World* (d Indian sequence only); 1960—*A Terrible Beauty (The Night Fighters)*; 1963—*Cattle King (Guns of Wyoming)*; 1970—*The Delta Factor* (+pr, sc); 1975—*Challenge to Be Free* (co-d, +ro—completed 1972); *Timber Tramps* (completed 1972).

Publications:

By GARNETT:

Books—*A Man Laughs Back*, 1935; *Light Up Your Torches and Pull Up Your Tights*, New Rochelle, New York 1973; articles—"The Director's Problems" in *Photoplay* (New York), September 1939; "Les 44 films de Tay Garnett" by Claude Beylie in *Ecran* (Paris), April and May 1977; "Tay Garnett" by J.-L. Passek in *Cinéma* (Paris), December 1977; "Tay Garnett Speaking", interview by R. Fernandez in *Velvet Light Trap* (Madison, Wisconsin), spring 1978.

On GARNETT:

Articles—"Likable but Elusive" by Andrew Sarris in *Film Culture* (New York), spring 1963; "Tay Garnett: A Man for All Films" by B. Thomas in *Action* (Los Angeles), September/October 1972; "Hommage à Tay Garnett" by T. Navacelle in *Cinéma* (Paris), January 1978; "Tay Garnett" by M. Salmi in *Film Dope* (London), September 1979; "Tay Garnett (1898-1977)" by C. Viviani in *Avant-Scène du cinéma* (Paris), 1 April 1980; "Tay Garnett" by J. Gallagher in *Films in Review* (New York), December 1981.

*   *   *

Tay Garnett's career can best be described as chaotic. He has directed comedies and dramas, war films and women's pictures, a couple of classics, more than a couple of solid entertainments, and one too many turkeys.

Garnett's career did not develop in a cohesive manner, one that can be successfully charted. Most of his best films were made during the early part of his career. *Her Man*, a Frankie and Johnny story set in Cuba, is exceptional for its period ambience and smooth camerawork. *One Way Passage*, a sophisticated drama about a romance between terminally ill Kay Francis and con man William Powell, remains a woman's picture of the highest caliber. *China Seas*, a melodrama with Clark Gable, Jean Harlow and a stellar cast aboard a Hong Kong-bound ship, is corny but exciting. *Stand-in* is a funny, underrated satire of Hollywood.

Garnett's one outstanding post-1940 feature is *The Postman Always Rings Twice* a sizzling drama of adultery and murder, from the James M. Cain story, that is far superior to Bob Rafelson's recent remake. In fact, of all Garnett's credits, only *One Way Passage* and *The Postman Always Rings Twice* approach the level of greatness. The rest are all good examples of their respective types, but are in no way linked by any artistic vision. However, Garnett's films are generally evenly paced. Even in his less auspicious productions the narrative flows smoothly, and there is an effective union of background and storyline. Garnett was aware that a film was sometimes unevenly paced because it was too slow, rather than fast. He would often reshoot scenes, attempting to trim them down by an all-important eight or ten seconds.

Garnett was also a keen observer of actors. When necessary, he could be stern as with Wallace Beery, a difficult star with a large ego. Yet he was particularly patient with a performer (for instance, Jean Harlow) who was not naturally gifted but still was willing to work and learn. As a result, he would accentuate the strengths of his actors. He insisted on casting Humphrey Bogart, then known solely for gangster roles, as a leading man in *Stand-in*.

Andrew Sarris wrote, in 1968, "Inconsistency is the hobgoblin of Tay Garnett's career, and inconsistency can never be defined satisfactorily....For the moment, Garnett's ultimate reputation is still unusually elusive." From the late 1940s on, Garnett's films do become increasingly mediocre. At their best, however, they're likable as well as competently made, and Garnett deserves to be called an entertainer—not an uncomplimentary appellation.

—Rob Edelman

GEHR, ERNIE. American. Born in Milwaukee, Wisconsin, 20 July 1943. Career: 1966—moves to New York City; sees first independent films, begins working in 8mm; 1967—makes first publicly released films in 16mm: *Morning* and *Wait*; 1970— teaches film at State University of New York at Binghamton; 1972-73—teaches film at Bard College; 1974-75—returns to SUNY Binghamton; 1977—resumes showing films publicly after hiatus of several years; 1980—begins releasing films made during 1970s; 1980—teaches at SUNY Buffalo; 1983—teaches at the School of the Art Institute of Chicago. Agent: Film-Makers' Cooperative, 175 Lexington Ave., New York, NY 10016.

Films: 1968—*Morning*; *Wait*; 1969—*Reverberation*; *Transparency*; 1969-71—*Still*; 1970—*History*; *Serene Velocity*; *Field*; 1972-74—*Shift*; 1974—*Eureka*; 1976—*Table*; 1977—*Untitled (77)*; 1981—*Mirage*; *Untitled*.

Publications:

By GEHR:

Article—"Program Notes by Ernie Gehr..." and interview by Jonas Mekas in *Film Culture* (New York), spring 1972.

On GEHR:

Book—*Ernie Gehr* by P. Adams Sitney, Minneapolis 1980; Articles—"New Forms in Film" by Bill Simon in *Artforum* (New York), October 1972; "Some Formalist Tendencies in the Current American Avant-Garde Film" by Regina Cornwell in *Kansas Quarterly*, spring 1972; "Letter from New York" by Bob Cowan in *Take One* (Montreal), September/October 1972; "Ernie Gehr" by David Cuthell in *Options and Alternatives: Some Directions in Recent Art*, exhibition catalogue, Yale University Art Gallery, New Haven 1974; "New Film Forms" by Simon Field in *Art and Artists* (London), November 1974; "Works of Ernie Gehr from 1968 to 1972" by Regina Cornwell in *Film Culture* (New York), no.63-64, 1977; "Ernie Gehr's Recent Work" by John Pruitt in *10 Years of Living Cinema*, New York 1982; "The Critique of Seeing with One's Own Eyes: Ernie Gehr's Untitled (1975)" in *Millenium Film Journal* (New York), no.12, 1983.

*   *   *

An Ernie Gehr film appears, at first glance, to be very sparse. His films most frequently depict a single location, which is shown through several cinematic techniques that are applied consistently throughout. The adjectives "formal," "minimal," and "structural" have been applied to Gehr's films, though the filmmaker himself disclaims them. While there may be some relation between Gehr's filmmaking and the "minimal" art that emerged contemporaneously, his films are unique, in themselves and in the redefinition they offer for cinema.

Gehr's most acclaimed film is *Serene Velocity*. A single corridor is filmed in images four frames (about ¼ second) long; Gehr cuts between images with different focal length lens settings so that the corridor appears to advance or recede, and to alter in its spatial aspect, quite rapidly. The perceptual effects that result are complex and diverse; Gehr's choice of frame-length places his film at a kind of threshold: the images are barely perceptive as separate stills; they also begin to fuse into movement. In *Transparency*, Gehr films passing cars, from very close; their colors fill the frame with beautiful, moving flat surfaces, making an apparent metaphor for the film surface itself. in *Table*, he cuts between two adjacent views of a table, with different color filters over the lens; the mind's eye is violently divided between different representations of the same view.

Gehr avoids using subject matter or techniques that will appeal to the viewer's emotions, or encourage symbolic readings. He tries to use cinematic techniques that will dominate the material filmed so strongly as to make the two inseparable. Thus he denies that cinema can be about any "subject matter" other than film itself, and the effects that film can have. The result is that a Gehr film addresses the viewer's *perception* directly, rather than his emotions, sense of human empathy, intellect, or aesthetic sense, as most other films do. While some other independent filmmakers have appealed to their viewers' perception, Gehr's application of this form of address has been the most radical, consistent, and rigorous.

The result is that his films work on two levels. First, the

viewer experiences complex, and often new, perceptual phenomena. By constructing some of his films at such a rapid pace that movement almost fuses into stillness, Gehr allows both to be experienced at once. His films hover, for the viewer, around paradoxes of depth/flatness, recognizable shape/abstract color, and stillness/movement. The films acknowledge cinema as illusion, through their devices, while at the same time trying to unmask the illusion to form a more direct relationship between viewer and work. The viewer of *Serene Velocity* or *Table* experiences optical phenomena he has not seen before, but those phenomena lead him to reconsider the nature not only of film viewing but of his own perception.

The result can be, at its best, an opening up of film's possibilities. Instead of the viewer sensing he is *receiving* messages, emotions, ideas or visions from the screen, the viewer is placed in a new position of equality with the filmic image. Indeed, the power of Gehr's technique is such that the viewer is almost forced to continually *interact* with what is on the screen. Since a Gehr film activates so much of one's perceptual/mental system, including aspects of it that may have been long dormant, the viewer comes away from the screening with a vastly deepened awareness. In an interview with Jonas Mekas, Gehr himself articulates this as a goal: "...[my] desire [is] less to express myself and more of making something out of the film material itself relevant to film for spiritual purposes...What I mean by 'spiritual' is sensitizing the mind to its own consciousness.."

—Fred Camper

GERASIMOV, SERGEI. Soviet. Born Sergei Apollinarievich Gerasimov in Zlatoust, Ural region, 21 May 1906. Educated at Leningrad Art School in painting; studied scenic design at State Institute of Dramatic Art, Leningrad (1920-25). Career: 1920—leaves school, moves to Leningrad; early 1920s—while in college, joins FEKS group founded by fellow teen-agers Grigori Kozintsev and Leonid Trauberg; 1925-30—becomes actor in their films, specializing in villains; 1929-30—also works as 1st assistant director on their films; 1930—directs 1st film; 1930-41—works at Lenfilm Studios and is Head of Acting and Directing Master Class there; 1931-41; 1941—moves to Moscow, takes charge of *Fighting Film Album No. 1* and directs its opening short; co-directs feature with Mikhail Kalatozov; 1942-44—continues war work, makes feature and takes charge of official films of Yalta and Berlin Conferences; 1944—joins Communist Party, becomes head of Central Newsreel and Documentary Studios, Moscow; 1944—1970s—Professor and Head of Acting and Directing Workshop at Moscow Film School (VGIK); 1949—attends "Cultural and Scientific Conference for World Peace" in New York, makes anti-American speech; 1955—works at Gorki Film Studios as Artistic Supervisor; 1970s—serves as Deputy to the Supreme Soviet of the RSFSR, Secretary of Soviet Union of Cinematographers, and on editorial board of *Iskusstvo Kino*. Recipient: Red Banner of Labor, 1940 and 1950; State Prize for *Uchitel*, 1941; Red Star, 1944; Peoples' Artist of USSR, 1948; State Prize for *The Young Guard*, 1949; State Prize for *Liberated China*, 1951.

Films (as assistant director): 1929—*Novyi Vavilon (The New Babylon)* (Kozintsev and Trauberg) (as director): 1930—*22 Misfortunes (22 Mishaps)* (co-d); 1931—*The Forest (The Woods)* (+sc); *Odna (Alone)* (Kozintsev and Trauberg) (ass't d only); 1932—*Solomon's Heart* (co-d, +sc); 1934—*Do I Love You? (If I Love You?)* (+sc); 1936—*Semero smelykh (The Bold 7)*; 1938—*Komsomolsk* (+co-sc); 1939—*Uchitel (Teacher)* (+sc); 1941—*Masquerade* (+sc, ro as *the Stranger*); *Meeting with Maxim* segment of *Fighting Film Album No.1*; *Chapayev is with Us* (co-sc only); *The Old Guard*; 1943—*The Invincible (The Unconquerable)* (co-d, +co-sc); *Film-Concert Dedicated to the 25th Anniversary of the Red Army (Cine-Concert...)* (co-d, +co-sc); 1944—*Great Land (The Mainland)* (+sc); *The Yalta Conference* (pr supervisor only); 1945—*The Berlin Conference* (pr supervisor only); 1947—*Molodaya gvardiya (Young Guard)* (+sc); 1950—*Liberated China* (+sc); 1951—*Selskiy vrach (Country Doctor)*; 1954—*Nadezhda* (+sc); 1955—*Damy* (Oganisyan and Kulidzhanov) (artistic supervisor only); 1956—*The Road of Truth* (Frid) (sc only); 1957-58—*Tikhy Don (And Quiet Flows the Don)* (+sc); 1958—*Memory of the Heart* (Lioznova) (sc only); 1959—*Sputnik Speaking (The Sputnik Speaks)* (co-d, +co-sc); 1961—*Dimy Gorina (Career of Dima)* and Mirski) (artistic supervisor only); 1962—*Men and Beasts* (+sc); *U Krutovo Yara (On the Steep Cliff)* (K. and A. Morakov) (artistic supervisor only); 1963—*Venski Les (Vienna Woods)* (Grigoriev) (artistic supervisor only); 1964—*Sostyazanie (Controversy)* (Mansurev) (artistic supervisor only); 1967—*Zhurnalist (The Journalist)* (+sc); 1969—*U ozera (By the Lake, At the Lake)* (+sc); 1972—*Lyubit cheloveka (To Love a Man, For the Love of Man)* (+sc); 1974—*Materi i docheri (Mothers and Daughters)*; 1976—*(Le Rouge et le noir)* (+sc: 5-part series for Soviet tv).

Roles: (in Kozintsev and Trauberg films unless title followed by other name): 1925—the spy in *Michki protiv Youdenitsa (Mishka Against Yudenitch)*; 1926—the conjuror in *Chyortovo koleso (The Devil's Wheel)*; the card-sharp in *Shinel (The Cloak)*; the driver in *Bratichka (Little Brother)*; 1927—Medoks in *S.V.D. (The Club of the Big Deed)*; Skalkovsky in *Someone Else's Jacket* (Boris Shpis); 1929—The journalist Lutreau in *Novyi Vavilon (The New Babylon)* (+ass't d); *the Menshevik* in *Oblomok imperii (Fragment of an Empire)* (Ermler); 1931—the chairman of the village soviet in *Odna (Alone)*; 1932—*Commander of the Iron Regiment* in *3 Soldiers* (Ivanov); 1933—*the bonze in Dezertir (Deserter)* (Pudovkin); *Razbudite Lenochky (Wake Up Lenochka)* (Kudryavtseva); 1935—*Yakov the Tailor* in *(The Frontier)* (Dubson); 1939—*The Socialist-Revolutionary* in *Vyborgskaya storona (New Horizons, The Vyborg Side)*.

Publications:

By GERASIMOV:

Book—*Vospitanie kinorezhisseva*, Moscow 1978; articles—"Socialist Realism and the Soviet Cinema" in *Films and Filming* (London), December 1958; "All Is Not Welles" in *Films and Filming* (London), September 1959; "A Clash of Conscience" in *Films and Filming* (London), March 1961; "Sergei Gerasimov", interview by Roger Hudson, in *Film* (London), spring 1969; "Auf der Suche nach der Heimat: ein Entwurf, der nie verwirklicht wird" in *Film und Fernsehen* (Berlin), no.8, 1976; "V dobryi chas!" in *Iskusstvo Kino* (Moscow), no.10, 1976; "Byt dostoinymi narodnogo priznaniia", with G. Aleksandrov, in *Iskusstvo Kino* (Moscow), no.8, 1979; "Arbenin v kino", with N. Mordvinov, in *Iskusstvo Kino* (Moscow), no.10, 1979; "Narodnyi khudozhnik", with others, in *Iskusstvo Kino* (Moscow), no.7, 1979; "Soviet Cinema: Films, Personalities, Problems", with others, in *Soviet Film* (Moscow), no.271, 1979; "Akyual'nost' istorii", interview by G. Maslovskij in *Iskusstvo Kino* (Moscow), September 1980.

On GERASIMOV:

Articles—"Recent Russian Cinema" by J. Vronskaya in *Film* (London), summer 1971; "Sergei Gerasimov" in *Soviet Film* (Moscow), no.261, 1979.

* * *

The brilliant, original, almost iconoclastic young Sergei Gerasimov became a successful survivor, whose very survival has tended to obscure the importance of his earlier contributions to cinema. The somewhat stern image of a grim conservative headmaster he seemed to project to students at the Moscow Film School (VGIK) in the early seventies was a tragic antithesis of his prewar self.

His own career started in Leningrad when, after graduating as a theatrical designer he joined the "Factory of Eccentric Actors" (FEKS) and became one of the strongest and most original actors in Soviet silent cinema, much attracted to complex roles, which he always tried to motivate, managing to convey a character's whole biography even when playing "cameo" villains. Instead of relying on mystification to enhance the mysterious people he liked to portray, he preferred to analyse the social and psychological pressures that caused his villains to behave as such, and he played them with a cold realism very much more chilling than the antics of the usual silent film "heavy." Together with what he learned from Kozintsev and Trauberg, who directed most of the productions in which he appeared, this deep study of acting was an important part of Gerasimov's apprenticeship as a filmmaker.

After doubling up as assistant director as well as actor on a couple of Kozintsev and Trauberg films he cut his directorial teeth on three silent productions in the early thirties; but it was not until 1936, with his first sound film *Semero Smelykh* (*The Bold 7*) that Gerasimov came into his own as a major talent. In this and his next film (*Komsomolsk*) he broke new ground in his choice of subject and in his sincere and unusually successful attempt to portray ordinary young people as varied, breathing, living human beings rather than animated heroic sculptures. His sympathetic direction of his young cast; together with his romantic but naturalistic scripts (pitting teams of young people against the elements) achieved something approaching that elusive ideal of socialist realism which so many sought and failed to find. Another measure of his skill and discernment is that many of his young actors later became well-known film stars.

Uchitel (*Teacher*) in 1939 completed his trio of lyrical but down-to-earth and unpretentious evocations of the new Soviet generation in the Russian countryside, by far the most successful films of their genre during the thirties. Scripted (as usual) by the enthusiastic but modest young director, this tale of a young man who leaves the bright lights of the city to return to his native village as a schoolmaster, begins, perhaps, to show some signs of the stress imposed by the increasing rigidity of official dogma, not quite achieving throughout the total freshness of the previous two films. Yet, sadly, some seven years later Gerasimov castigated himself for not having adhered more strictly to the party line. "I loved the film," he wrote, "and I still love it, despite the fact that it is far too polished...and not a little too obsequious in its attitude to Art." By this time the war had intervened and Gerasimov (in 1944) had become a member of the Communist Party; the faintest suspicion of art for art's sake (though hardly justified in this case) had become less acceptable than ever.

Besides his rural trilogy, his only other prewar feature, *Masquerade*, was a lavish version of Lermontov's verse tragedy which, although successful at the time, was also criticized by the director himself, a stern exponent of "socialist self-criticism". Admitting that the film had helped him "refine his art," he considered it "haphazard and unplanned" and lacking sufficient appreciation of Lermontov's particular genius. He had certainly set himself an uphill task in trying to combine his FEKS style with the tradition of stage drama and dialogue in verse, although his own performance as "The Stranger" was an echo of his old FEKS philosophy and the Leningrad setting was spectacular.

During the war, after being involved with various propaganda features and documentaries (like most filmmakers around the world at the time) Gerasimov was put in charge of the documentary film studios, where he brought together the talents of feature directors and documentartists and once more proved his flair for encouraging good work from others, which perhaps led to his appointment in 1944 as head of the directing and acting workshops of the Moscow Film School (VGIK). Occupying this seminal position through the following 30 years, he has had an enormous influence on the whole present generation of Soviet filmmakers; and even if some students belittled him in later years he must have given them a thorough grounding in the basic techniques.

After the war his own work seems drastically to have swung from his self-effacing, sympathetic form of filmmaking to the opposite, the grandiose style fashionable during Stalin's final phase. Fadeev's patriotic, lyrical novel *The Young Guard* would seem to have been ideal source material for a typical Gerasimov film, yet it turned out to be bombastic, pompous, and overblown. To be fair, it was made at the height of that maelstrom of newthink and massive interference caused by the artistic purge of the late forties. Unfortunately, his other huge epic—*And Quiet Flows the Don*—in three full-length parts suffered from similar grandiosity: it was said by one wit to be much more representative of the older Mikhail Sholokhov than of his youthful novel; sad, perhaps, that the young Gerasimov had not filmed it in the thirties. Apart from this foray into gigantism, and a documentary on China, much of Gerasimov's post-Stalin output saw a return to his themes of the thirties. Though always a highly competent director, however, he never quite recaptured his freshness of approach and lightness of touch.

His careeer exemplifies the survivor who swims with the tide and, by sacrificing a fair measure of his personal integrity, can continue to deal with contemporary themes—in contrast to those (like Paradjanov) who are submerged by the tide or (like Gerasimov's original mentor, Kozintsev) preserve their individuality by turning to historical subjects. Such dilemmas in various forms face filmmakers everywhere. Whatever our assessment of his massive contribution to Russian cinema, and whether or not we think him misguided, a man of Gerasimov's stature and stamina doubtless feels he made the best choice for himself, his industry, and his country.

—Robert Dunbar

GERMI, PIETRO. Italian. Born in Genoa, 14 September 1914. Educated at Instituto Nautico; studied acting and directing at Centro Sperimentale di Cinematografia, Rome. Career: 1939—co-scriptwriter and assistant director to Alessandro Blasetti on *Retroscena*; 1974—retires from *Amici miei* project because of ill health, film completed by Mario Monicelli. Died in Rome, 5 December 1974. Recipient: Best Story and Screenplay Academy Award, with Ennio de Concini and Alfredo Giannetti, for *Divorce Italian Style*, 1962; Best Film (co-recipient), Cannes

Festival, for *Signore e signori*, 1966.

Films (as assistant director): 1939—*Retroscena* (Blasetti) (+co-sc); 1943—*Nessuno torna indietro* (Blasetti); 1945—*I dieci comandamenti* (Chili) (co-sc only); (as director and co-script-writer): 1946—*Il testimone*; 1947—*Gioventù perduta (Lost Youth)*; 1949—*In nome della legge (Mafia)*; 1950—*Il cammino della speranza (The Path of Hope)* (co-story, co-adapt); 1951—*La città si difende (4 Ways Out)*; 1952—*La presidentessa (Mademoiselle Gobette)*; *Il brigante di Tacca del Lupo*; 1953—*Gelosia*; 1954—"*Guerra 1915-1918*" episode of *Amori di mezzo secolo* (d only); 1956—*Il ferroviere (The Railroad Man, Man of Iron)* (+ro); 1957—*L'uomo di paglia* (+ro); 1962—*Divorzio all'i-taliana (Divorce Italian Style)*; 1964—*Sedotta e abbandonata (Seduced and Abandoned)*; 1965—*Signore e signori (The Birds, the Bees and the Italians)* (+co-pr); 1967—*L'immorale (The Climax, Too Much for One Man)*; 1968—*Serafino* (+pr); 1970—*Le castagne sono buone (Till Divorce Do You Part)* (+pr); 1972—*Alfredo, Alfredo* (+pr); 1975—*Amici miei* (Monicelli) (co-sc only, +credit "A Film by Pietro Germi").

Roles: 1946—*Monte Cassino* (Gemmiti); 1948—*Fuga in Francia* (Soldati); 1959—*Jovanka e le altre (5 Branded Women)* (Ritt); 1960—*Il rossetto* (Damiani); 1961—*La viaccia* (Bolognini); *Il sicario* (Damiani); 1963—appearance in *The Directors* (pr: Greenblatt).

Publications:

By GERMI:

Articles—"Man Is Not Large Enough for Man" in *Films and Filming* (London), September 1966; "Govorjat laureaty festivalja" in *Iskusstvo Kino* (Moscow), July 1973.

On GERMI:

Articles—"Notes on 5 Italian Films" by Lauro Venturi in *Hollywood Quarterly*, summer 1951; "Pietro Germi" by J.A. Gili in *Ecran* (Paris), February 1975; "Pietro Germi" by J.-L. Passek in *Cinéma* (Paris), February 1975; "Pietro Germi, mon amour" by M. Monicelli in *Ecran* (Paris), September 1976; "Pietro Germi" by B. Pattison in *Film* (London), October 1976; biofilmography in *Film Dope* (London), December 1979.

*   *   *

Pietro Germi, though often regarded by scholars as fundamentally a neorealist director who made a transition in mid-career to social comedy, never actually considered himself to be an adherent to the style popularized by Roberto Rossellini. Like several other Italian directors achieving prominence in the late 1940s, notably Alberto Lattuada, Alberto De Santis and, of course, Vittorio DeSica, he produced films notable for breaking with prevailing themes that dealt with the immediate aftermath of World War II. His early works addressed themselves instead to the fundamental, even timeless, social issues affecting postwar Italy and in particular, those exemplified in the poverty of the island of Sicily.

His early films, notable *In nome della legge* and *Il cammino della speranza*, owe as much, if not more, to the influence of American director John Ford as they do to a strictly neorealist

filmmaker like Luchino Visconti. Sicily easily replaces Ford's Monument Valley and the island's traditional knife duels supplant the American director's classic showdowns. In all other respects, however, the fundamental issues in Germi's first few films differ little from a typical John Ford production like *Stagecoach*. Indeed the themes of the aforementioned Germi films consisting, in the first instance, of the clash between a young judge and the local Mafia over his attempts to enforce the law and, in the second, of the problem of illegal immigration, deal with problems not too far removed from those of the actual post-Civil War American west.

Interestingly, the fact that Germi dared to propose solutions to the problems that he examined in these and in succeeding films effectively removed him from the realm of pure neorealism which, as construed by Rossellini and his immediate followers, must limit itself merely to the exposition of a particular social condition. It cannot suggest solutions. Unfortunately, in a number of cases (*Il cammino della speranza* in particular), the director's solutions were overly romanticized, pat and simplistic.

During the latter part of the 1950s, Germi began to compress the scope of his social concerns to those affecting the individual and his relationship to the family unit albeit as components of the larger society. In *Il ferroviere* and *L'uomo di Paglia*, however, he continued to be plagued by his penchant for simplistic and overly contrived solutions as well as a tendency to let the films run on too long. They are redeemed to some extent by their realistic portrayals of working class characters which, though considered melodramatic by many reviewers at the time of their release, have come to be more highly regarded.

He corrected his problems in the 1960s by changing his narrative style to one dominated by satirical devices. Yet he did not compromise his family-centered social vision. *Divorzio all'italiana*, for which he won an Academy Award for best screeenplay, *Sedotta e abbandonata*, and *Signori e signore*, the winner of the Palm d'or at Cannes, all magnify social questions all out of proportion to reality and thus, through the chaos that results, reduce the issues to absurdity.

Divorzio all'italiana, in particular, is a craftsmanlike portrayal of the internal upheavals within a family, set in the oppressive atmosphere of a small Sicilian village. It features the deft use of a moving camera that passes swiftly, almost intimately, through endless groups of gawking townspeople. Also, his use of actors, including Marcello Mastroianni and Daniella Rocca, as well as his own latent sense of humor, make the social commentary in this film quite possibly more penetrating than in his early neorealist films.

Though he shifted over the length of his career from social dramas to socio-moral satires, his social concerns and his favorite setting for them—Sicily—remained constant. As is not normally the case with many artists of his stature, his most polished and commercially successful efforts also turned out to be the critical equals of his earlier and more solemn ones.

—Stephen L. Hanson

GODARD, JEAN-LUC. French. Born in Paris, 3 December 1930; became citizen of Switzerland. Educated (elementary and secondary education) at Nyon, Switzerland; Lycée Buffon, Paris; Sorbonne, 1947-49, certificate in ethnology 1950. Married Anna Karina, 1960 (divorced); Anne Wiamzensky, 1967 (divorced). Career: 1949-56—moves repeatedly between Switzerland and Paris, working as a delivery boy, cameraman, assistant editor for Zurich television, construction worker, and gossip columnist for *Les Temps de Paris*; 1950—meets André Bazin, François Truffaut, Jacques Rivette, Eric Rohmer, and Claude Chabrol while attending films at the Cinémathèque and Left Bank cine clubs; finances and appears in an experimental film, *Quadrille*, by Rivette; 1950-51—founds short-lived *Gazette du cinéma*, writing criticism under the pseudonym "Hans Lucas"; 1952—begins to write criticism for *Cahiers du cinéma*; 1954—directs first film, *Opération Béton*, a 20 minute short on the construction of a dam; 1956—works professionally as a film editor; 1957—works in publicity department of 20th Century Fox, Paris; Here he meets producer and friend Georges de Beauregard; directs 3 shorts for de Beauregard; 1959—begins working for de Beauregard; directs first feature film, *A bout de souffle*; 1964—founds Anouchka films with wife and star of his films, Anna Karina; 1965—begins to become politically involved with leftist groups as he criticizes the ideological and financial aspects of the film industry; 1968—leads protests over firing of Henri Langlois, director of Cinémathèque; instigates (along with Truffaut, Claude Lelouche, and Claude Barrie) shut down of 1968 Cannes Festival; 1968-72—becomes affiliated with various Marxist-Leninist and Maoist groups; "reclaims" his work from 1969-72 as that of the Dziga Vertov Group; 1969—begins close collabortion with Jean-Pierre Gorin, editor of *Cahiers marxistes-léninistes*; 1971—injured seriously in motorcycle accident; 1972—*Tout va bien*, 1st feature film addressed to popular audience since 1967, released; 1973—Gorin and Godard terminate partnership; 1974-75—establishes Sonimage film and video studio in Grenoble with Anne-Marie Miéville. Recipient: Berlin Film Festival, Best Direction for *Breathless*, 1960. Address: 15 rue du Nord, 1180 Roulle, Switzerland.

Films (as director and screenwriter) 1954—*Opération Béton* (+pr) (released 1958); 1955—*Une Femme coquette* (d as "Hans Lucas" +pr, ph, bit ro as man visiting prostitute); 1956—*Kreutzer Sonata* (Rohmer) (pr only); 1957—*Charlotte et Véronique ou Tous les garçons s'appellent Patrick*; 1958—*Une Histoire d'eau* (co-d—actual shooting by Truffaut, co-sc) (released 1961); *Charlotte et son Jules* (+ dubbed voice of Jean-Paul Belmondo) (released 1961); 1960—*A bout de souffle* (+ro as passerby who points out Belmondo to police); 1961—*Une Femme est une femme*; 1962—"La Paresse" episode of *Les Sept Péchés capitaux*; *Vivre sa vie* (+dubbed voice of Peter Kassowitz); "Il nuovo mondo (Le Nouveau Monde)" in *RoGoPaG (Laviamoci il cervello)* (+bit ro); 1963—*Le Petit Soldat* (+bit ro as man at railway station) (completed 1960); *Les Carabiniers*; *Le Mépris* (+ro); 1964—"Le Grand Escroc" in *Les Plus Belles Escroqueries du monde* (+narration, bit ro as man wearing Moroccan chéchia); *Bande à part*; *La Femme mariée (Une Femme mariée)*; *Reportage sur Orly* (short); 1965—"Montparnasse—Levallois" in *Paris vu par...*; *Alphaville: Une Étrange aventure de Lemmy Caution*; *Pierrot le fou*; 1966—*Masculin-féminin (Masculin féminin: 15 faits précis)*; *Made in U.S.A.* (+voice on tape recorder); 1967—*Deux ou trois choses que je sais d'elle*; "Anticipation" episode of *Le Plus Vieux Métier du monde*; *La Chinoise ou Plutôt à la chinoise*; "Caméra-oeil" in *Loin du Viêt-Nam* (+appearance); *Week-end*; 1968—*Le Gai Savoir*; 1968—*Cinétracts* (series of untitled, creditless newsreels); *Un Film comme les autres* (+voice); *One Plus One (Sympathy for the Devil)* (+voice); *One A.M. (One American Movie)* (unfinished); 1969—*British Sounds (See You at Mao)* (co-d, co-sc); *Pravda* (collective credit to Groupe Dziga-Vertov); *Lotte in Italia (Luttes en Italie)* (collective credit to Groupe Dziga-Vertov); "L'amore" episode of *Amore e rabbia* (completed 1967: festival showings as "Andante e ritorno dei figli prodigi" episode of *Vangelo 70*); 1970—*Vent d'est* (co-d, co-sc); *Jusqu'à la victoire (Till Victory)* (co-d) (unfinished); *One P.M. (One Parallel Movie)* (Pennebaker) (includes footage from abandoned *One A.M.* and documentary footage of its making); 1971—*Vladimir et Rosa* (collective credit to Groupe Dziga Vertov, +ro as U.S. policeman, appearance, narration); *Tout va bien* (co-d, co-sc, +pr); *A Letter to Jane or Investigation About a Still (Lettre à Jane)* (co-d, co-sc, +co-pr, narration); 1975—*Numéro deux* (co-sc, +co-pr, appearance); 1976—*Ici et ailleurs* (co-d, co-sc) (includes footage from *Jusqu'à la victoire*); *Comment ça va* (co-d, co-sc); 1977—*6 x 2: sur et sous la communication* (for TV) (co-d, co-sc); 1980—*Sauve qui peut (La Vie)* (co-sc, +co-ed); 1982—*Passion*.

Roles: 1950—*Quadrille* (Rivette) (+pr); 1951—*Présentation ou Charlotte et son steack* (Rohmer); 1956—*Le Coup du berger* (Rivette); 1958—Godard's silhouette in *Paris nous appartient* (Rivette); 1959—*Le Signe du lion* (Rohmer); 1961—with Anna Karina in comic sequence in *Cléo de 5 à 7* (Varda); *Le Soleil dans l'oeil* (Bourdon); 1963—*Schehérézade* (Gaspard-Huit); appearance in *The Directors* (pr: Greenblatt); appearance in *Paparazzi* (Rozier); appearance in *Begegnung mit Fritz Lang* (Fleischmann); appearance in *Petit Jour* (Pierre); 1966—*L'Espion (The Defector)* (Levy).

Publications:

By GODARD:

Books—*Jean-Luc Godard par Jean-Luc Godard: articles, essais, entretiens* edited by Jean Narboni, Paris 1968; *Interviews with Film Directors* by Andrew Sarris, New York, reissued 1969; *Wind from the East* and *Weekend*, New York 1972; *A bout de souffle*, Paris 1974; *Introduction à une véritable histoire du cinema*, Paris 1980; articles—"Chronique du 16 mm" in *La Gazette du cinéma* (Paris), November 1950; "Ditte Menneskebarn" in *La Gazette du cinéma* (Paris), November 1950; "La Femme à écharpe pailletee" in *La Gazette du cinéma* (Paris), November 1950; articles on *Gaslight* and *The Great McGinty* in *La Gazette du cinéma* (Paris), November 1950; "Joseph Mankiewicz" in *La Gazette du cinéma* (Paris), November 1950; articles on *Panique dans les rues*, *Que viva Mexico!*, and *La Ronde* in *La Gazette du cinéma* (Paris), October 1950; "Pour un cinéma politique" in *La Gazette du cinéma* (Paris), September 1950; "Le Trésor ..." in *La Gazette du cinéma* (Paris), November 1950; "Works of Calder et L'Histoire d'Agnès" in *La Gazette du cinéma* (Paris), October 1950; articles on Alfred Hitchcock and Rudolph Mate in *Cahiers du cinéma* (Paris), March 1952; "Défense et illustration du découpage classique" in *Cahiers du cinéma* (Paris), September 1952; "Le Chemin des écoliers: *The Man Who Knew Too Much*" in *Cahiers du cinéma* (Paris), November 1956; "Mirliflores et bécassines: *The Lieutenant Wore Skirts*" in *Cahiers du cinéma* (Paris), August/September 1956; "Montage, mon beau souci" in *Cahiers du cinéma* (Paris), December 1956; "Les Acteurs françaises: de bons produits sans mode d'emploi" in *Arts* (Paris), no.619 1957; "Biofilmographie de Jean Renoir" in *Cahiers du cinéma* (Paris), December 1957; "Le Cinéaste bien-aimé: *The True Story of Jesse James*" in *Cahiers du cinéma* (Paris), August/September 1957; "Le Cinéma et son double: *The Wrong Man*" in *Cahiers du cinéma* (Paris), June 1957; articles on Roger Vadim and *Hollywood or Bust* in *Cahiers du cinéma* (Paris), July 1957; "Les 10 Meilleurs Films de 1956" in *Cahiers du cinéma* (Paris), January 1957; articles on *L'Ardente Gitane* and Abel Gance in *Cahiers du cinéma* (Paris), February 1957; "Au petit Trot: *Courte-tête*" in *Cahiers du cinéma* (Paris), April 1957; articles on *Logare* and *40 Guns* in

Cahiers du cinéma (Paris), November 1957; "60 Metteurs en scène français" in *Cahiers du cinéma* (Paris), May 1957; "Tournage: *Will Success Spoil Rock Hunter*" in *Cahiers du cinéma* (Paris), August/September 1957; articles on *Une Vie* and *Les Cousins* in *Cahiers du cinéma* (Paris), November 1958; "Un Athlète complet: *Un Américaine bien tranquille*" in *Arts* (Paris), 22 July 1958; articles on *Bitter Victory* and "10 Meilleurs Films de 1957" in *Cahiers du cinéma* (Paris), January 1958; "B.B. Rhènne: *Liane, l'esclave blanche*" in *Arts* (Paris), 10 December 1958; articles on *L'Eau vive, The Long Hot Summer, The Pajama Game*, and Ingmar Bergman in *Cahiers du cinéma* (Paris), July 1958; "Un Bon Devoir: *The Killing* in *Cahiers du cinéma* (Paris), February 1958; articles on *The Wayward Bus* and Max Ophuls in *Cahiers du cinéma* (Paris), March 1958; "*La Chatte*" in *Arts* (Paris), no.668, 1958; "Désespérant: *La Femme en robe de chambre*" in *Arts* (Paris), 30 July 1958; "17 jeune metteurs en scène donnent leur mot de passe" in *Arts* (Paris), 27 May 1958; "Un Drôle de dimanche" in *Arts* (Paris), 26 November 1958; articles on *Les Temps des oeufs durs* and *Raffles sur la ville* in *Cahiers du cinéma* (Paris), April 1958; "Georges Franju" in *Cahiers du cinéma* (Paris), December 1958; "Ignorès du jury: Demy, Resnais, Rozier et Varda dominent le festival de Tours 1958" in *Arts* (Paris), 10 December 1958; "Jean-Luc Godard fait parler Astruc..." in *Arts* (Paris), 20 August 1958; "Jean-Luc Godard fait parler François Reichenbach" in *Arts* (Paris), 27 August 1958; "Jean Rouch remporte le prix Delluc" in *Arts* (Paris), 17 December 1958; articles on *Montparnasse 19*, "Malraux mauvais français", and "Petit journal du cinéma in *Cahiers du cinéma* (Paris), May 1958; "Mizoguchi fut le plus grand cinéaste japonais: la Cinémathèque lui rend hommage après sa mort" in *Arts* (Paris), 5 February 1958; "Monika" in *Arts* (Paris), 30 July 1958; "La Ronde de l'aube" in *Arts* (Paris), no.682, 1958; "Les Seigneurs de la fôret" in *Arts* (Paris), 24 December 1958; "Si le roi savait ça" in *Arts* (Paris), no.680, 1958; "Télégramme de Berlin" in *Cahiers du cinéma* (Paris), August 1958; articles on *A Time to Love and a Time to Die, Boris Barnett*, and "Petit journal du cinéma" in *Cahiers du cinéma* (Paris), April 1959; articles on *Auberge du sixième bonheur*, "Cigarettes, whiskey, et p'tites pépées", and *Esclave des son dèsir* in *Arts* (Paris), 4 March 1959; "Une Bête humaine: *Un Simple Histoire*" in *Arts* (Paris), 8 April 1959; articles on *Babosse, Moana*, and Roberto Rosselini plus an interview with Rosselini in *Arts* (Paris), 1 April 1959; articles on *Orfeu negro* and *Hiroshima Mon Amour* in *Cahiers du cinéma* (Paris), July 1959; articles on *Tarawa Beachhead* and the Cannes Festival of 1959 in *Cahiers du cinéma* (Paris), June 1959; articles on *Man of the West, 400 Coups*, "10 Meilleurs Films de 1958", and "Chacun son Tours" in *Cahiers du cinéma* (Paris), February 1959; articles on *Les Rendez-vous du diable, La Loi*, and *La Ligne de mire* in *Cahiers du cinéma* (Paris), March 1959; articles on *Asphalte, Le Petit Prof..., Ramuntcho*, and *Le Bel Age* in *Arts* (Paris), 25 February 1959; articles on *Les Dragueurs* and "Les Tripes au soleil" in *Arts* (Paris), 13 May 1959; articles on *Le Grand Chef, Les Motards*, and *La Tête contre les murs* in *Arts* (Paris), 25 March 1959; "Entretien avec J.P. Mocky" in *Arts* (Paris), no.709, 1959; articles on *Moi, un noir* and *Les Cousins* and an interview with René Clément in *Arts* (Paris), 11 March 1959; articles on *Les 400 Coups, Vacances à Paris*, and "Le Jeune Cinéma à gagné" in *Arts* (Paris), 22 April 1959; "Fade et grotesque: *Le Vent se lève* in *Arts* (Paris), 4 February 1959; "Faiblard: *Faibles femmes*" in *Arts* (Paris), 18 February 1959; "*Les Fauve est lâche*" in *Arts* (Paris), no.707, 1959; articles on *Houla-Houla* and *Les Jeux dangereux* in *Arts* (Paris), no.706, 1959; "Jean Renoir: La Télévision m'a révélé un nouveau cinéma" in *Arts* (Paris), 22 April 1959; articles on *La Tête contre les murs* and *The Perfect Furlough* in *Cahiers du cinéma* (Paris), May

1959; "Sainte simplicité: *Goha* in *Arts* (Paris), 20 May 1959; "Les Vignes du seigneur: Pourvu ou'on ait l'ivresse" in *Arts* (Paris), 21 January; "Scenario" (*Une Femme est une Femme*) in *Cahiers du cinéma* (Paris), August 1959; "Les 10 Meilleurs Films de 1959" and "Entretien avec Robert Bresson" in *Cahiers du cinéma* (Paris), February 1960; "Frère Jacques" in *Cahiers du cinéma* (Paris), April 1960; "Tournage: *Le Petit Soldat*" in *Cahiers du cinéma* (Paris), July 1980; "Jean-Luc Godard: 'Je ne suis pas à bout de souffle'" in *Arts* (Paris), 23 March 1960; "Un Entretien avec J.-L. Godard, le réalisateur du *Petit Soldat*" by Yvonne Baby in *Le Monde* (Paris), 13 September 1960; "Mon Film est documentaire sur Jean Seberg et J.-P. Belmondo" interview by Yvonne Baby in *Le Monde* (Paris), 18 March 1960; "But 'Wave' Adds Brightness" in *Films and Filming* (London), September 1961; "Les 10 Meilleurs Films de 1960" in *Cahiers du cinéma* (Paris), February 1961; "*Le Petit Soldat*" in *Cinéma 61* (Paris), January 1961; *Charlotte et son Jules* in *L'Avant-Scène du cinéma* (Paris), June 1961; *Une Histoire d'eau* in *L'Avant-Scène du cinéma* (Paris), September 1961; "Entretien avec le petit soldat: Michel Subor" and "Le Soldat de Godard: questions à l'auteur" in *Cinéma 61* (Paris), January 1961; "Les 10 Meilleurs Films de 1961" in *Cahiers du cinéma* (Paris), February 1962; "Du Stylo à la caméra" in *Études cinématographiques: Théâtre et cinéma (2)—l'acteur* (Paris), no.14-15, 1962; "*Vivre sa vie*" in *Vivre sa vie: L'Avant-Scène du cinéma* (Paris), October 1962; "*Vivre sa vie*" in *L'Avant-Scène du cinéma* (Paris), October 1962; "Scenario" (*Vivre sa vie*), translated by Louis Brigante, in *Film Culture* (New York), winter 1962; "Entretien avec Jean-Luc Godard" by Jean Collet and others in *Cahiers du cinéma* (Paris), December 1962; "Jean-Luc Godard and *Vivre sa vie*" by Tom Milne in *Sight and Sound* (London), winter 1962; "Questions and Answers on Peace and War" in *Film: Book 2: Films of Peace and War* edited by Robert Hughes, New York 1962; "Un Conte de faits" in *Cinéma 63* (Paris), March 1963; "L'Odysée selon Jean-Luc" in *Cinéma 63* (Paris), June 1963; "Les 10 Meilleurs Films de 1962" in *Cahiers du cinéma* (Paris), February 1963; articles on *Les Carabiniers* and *Le Mépris* in *Cahiers du cinéma* (Paris), August 1963; "Godard on Pure Film" in *Cinema* (Beverly Hills), March/April 1963; "Note per *Il disprezzo*" in *Filmcritica* (Rome), October 1963; interview on *Le Mépris* by Yvonne Baby in *Le Monde* (Paris), 20 December 1963; "Jean-Luc Godard a repeint dans *Le Mépris* le sourire des statues grecques" by Michel Mardore in *Les Lettres françaises* (Paris), 26 December 1963/1 January 1964; articles on American directors, "10 Meilleurs Films américains du parlent", and "Sept hommes à debattre" in *Cahiers du cinéma* (Paris), December/-January 1964; "Les 10 Meilleurs Films de 1963" and "*Orphée*" in *Cahiers du cinéma* (Paris), February 1964; "Entretien avec Antonioni" in *Cahiers du cinéma* (Paris), December 1964; "*La Femme mariée*" in *Cahiers du cinéma* (Paris), October 1964; "Entretien avec Jean-Luc Godard à propos d'*Une Femme mariée*: 'L'Idée de la femme dans un société primitive de 1964" by Yvonne Baby in *Le Monde* (Paris), 5 December 1964; "Jean-Luc Godard s'explique" by Raymond Bellour in *Les Lettres françaises* (Paris), 14 May 1964; "Entretien avec Jean-Luc Godard" by Michael Caen, et al. in *Cinématographie française* (Paris), June/July 1964; "An Interview with Jean-Luc Godard" by Herbert Feinstein in *Film Quarterly* (Berkeley), spring 1964; "Entretien avec J.-L. Godard" by Gérard Guégan in *Les Lettres françaises* (Paris), 19 November 1964; "*Les Carabiniers*" in *L'Avant-Scène du cinéma* (Paris), March 1965; "*La Femme Mariée* in *L'Avant-Scène du cinéma* (Paris), March 1965; "Apprenez le François" in *L'Avant-Scène du cinéma* (Paris), May 1965; "Chacun ses dix" and Response to "Qui? Pourquoi? Comment?: Questionnaire" in *Cahiers du cinéma* (Paris), January 1965; "Les 10 Meilleurs Films de 1964" in *Cahiers du cinéma*

(Paris), February 1965; "Le Dossier du mois" in *Cinéma 65* (Paris) March 1965; "Jean-Luc Godard: Lemmy Caution..." in *Les Lettres françaises* (Paris), 22-28 April 1965; "Mon film, un apologue" in *Une Femme mariée: L'Avant-Scène du cinéma* (Paris), March 1965; articles on *Montparnasse-Levallois* and "Pierrot mon ami" in *Cahiers du cinéma* (Paris), October 1965; interview with Godard in *Les Lettres françaises* (Paris), 9 September 1965; "Entretien avec Jean-Luc Godard: 'Dresser des embuscades dans la planification'" by Yvonne Baby in *Le Monde* (Paris), 6 May 1965; "Les Cravates rouges: convérsation avec Jean-Luc Godard" by Jacques Benismon and others in *Objectif* (Montreal), August/September 1965; "Parlons de *Pierrot*: nouvel entretien avec Jean-Luc Godard" by Jean-Louis Comolli in *Cahiers du cinéma* (Paris), October 1965; "Deux arts en un: René Allio..." in *Cahiers du cinéma* (Paris), April 1966; "Les 10 Meilleurs Films de 1965" in *Cahiers du cinéma* (Paris), January 1966; article on and interview with Bresson in *Cahiers du cinéma* (Paris), May 1966; "Trois milles heures de cinéma" in *Cahiers du cinéma* (Paris), November 1966; "Jean-Luc Godard: 'Ce que j'ai à dire'" by Pierre Daix in *Les Lettres françaises* (Paris), 21-27 April 1966; "*Deux ou trois choses que je sais d'elle*" in *L'Avant-Scène du cinéma* (Paris), May 1967; "Impressions anciennes" in *Cahiers du cinéma* (Paris), February 1967; "Dans ma journeé d'artiste" by Yvonne Baby in *Le Monde* (Paris), 27 January 1967; "Der Mensch ist Gott..." by Gideon Bachmann, translated by Christa Maeker, in *Film* (Hanover, Germany), November 1967; "Lutter sur deux fronts" by Jacques Bontemps and others in *Cahiers du cinéma* (Paris), October 1967; "Godard par Godard" by Guy Gauthier in *Image et son: Revue du cinéma* (Paris), December 1967; "Entretien avec Jean-Luc Godard" by Phillipe Pilard in *Image et son: Revue du cinéma* (Paris), December 1967; "*A Bout de souffle*" in *L'Avant-Scène du cinéma* (Paris), March 1968; "Conférence de presse: l'affaire Langlois" in *Cahiers du cinéma* (Paris), March 1968; "Struggle on 2 Fronts: A Conversation with Jean-Luc Godard" by Jacques Bontemps in *Film Quarterly* (Berkeley), winter 1968; "Jean-Luc Godard: montage à partir d'un entretien avev Jean-Luc Godard" by Abraham Segal in *Image et son: Revue du cinéma* (Paris), March 1968; "Cinema-provcazione" in *Filmcritica* (Rome), January 1969; "Lettera ai miei amici" in *Cineforum* (Bergamo), February 1969; "Premiers 'Sons Anglais'" in *Cinéthique* (Paris), September/October 1969; "Un Cinéaste comme les autres" by Gérard Leblanc in *Cinéthique* (Paris), January 1969; "Splicing Together Jean-Luc Godard" by Walter Ross in *Esquire* (New York), July 1969; "Notes on *Pravda*" in *Afterimage* (New York), April 1970; "What Is to Be Done?", translated by Mo Tietelbaum, in *Afterimage* (New York), April 1970; "Godard Says Bye-Bye to Bardot and All That" by Guy Flatley in *The New York Times*, 17 May 1970; "Le Groupe 'Dziga Vertov': Jean-Luc Godard parle au nom de ses camarades du groupe:..." by Marcel Martin in *Cinéma 70* (Paris), December 1970; "*La Chinoise*" in *L'Avant-Scène du cinéma* (Paris), May 1971; "Dziga Vertov Notebook" in *Take One* (Montreal), June 1971; "Che faire?" in *Bianco e nero* (Rome), July/August 1972; "Juin 1973: Jean-Luc Godard fait le point" by Philippe Durand in *Cinéma pratique* (Paris), July/August 1973; "Let's See Where We Are" by Ken Mate and others in *Velvet Light Trap* (Madison, Wisconsin), summer 1973; "L'Adolescent et l'homme" in *L'Avant-Scène du cinéma* (Paris), March 1974; "Jean-Luc Godard paroles..." in *Téléciné* (Paris), September/October 1975; "Warum ich hier spreche..." in *Filmkritik* (Munich), September 1975; interview in *Téléciné* (Paris), September/October 1975; "Un Entretien avec Jean-Luc Godard: faire les films possibles là où on est" by Yvonne Baby in *Le Monde* (Paris), 25 September 1975; "*Pierrot le fou*" in *L'Avant-Scène du cinéma* (Paris), July/September 1976; interview by W. Reichart in

Filmkritik (Munich), February 1977; interview by A. Grivas and A. Head in *Cine* (Mexico), October/November 1980; "La invención del cinema", interview by I. Bosch and M. Vidal Estevez in *Contracampo* (Madrid), January 1981; interview by P. Carcassonne and J. Fieschi in *Cinématographe* (Paris), March/April 1981; "Zum zweiten Mal habe ich das Gefühl, dass ich mein gesamtes Leben vor mir habe mein zwetes Leben im Kino", interview by C. David in *Filmfaust* (Frankfurt), February/March 1981; "Es ist absolut unmöglich in der Stadt Ideen zu haben" in *Filmfaust* (Frankfurt), April/May 1981; "Rette sich wer kann (das Leben)" in *Filmfaust* (Frankfurt), February/March 1981; "Jean-Luc Godard...for Himself" in *Framework* (Norwich, England), autumn 1980; "Kain-Arriflex was hast du mit deinem Bruder Abelsony gemacht?" in *Filmfaust* (Frankfurt), April/May 1981.

On GODARD:

Books—*Nouvelle Vague* by Jacques Siclier, Collection 7e Art, Paris 1961; *Jean-Luc Godard* by Jean Collet, Paris 1963; *Cinema Eye, Cinema Ear: Some Key Filmmakers of the 60's* by John Russell Taylor, New York 1964; *Jean-Luc Godard* by Richard Roud, New York 1967; *Movie Man* by David Thomson, New York 1967; *Jean-Luc Godard: A Critical Anthology* edited by Tony Mussman, New York 1968; *Elements of Film* by Lee R. Bobker, New York 1969; *The Films of Jean-Luc Godard* edited by Ian Cameron, London 1969; *Godard polémico* by Roman Gubern, Barcelona, Spain 1969; *Godard* by Michele Mancini, Rome 1969; *Signs and Meaning in the Cinema* by Peter Wollen, Bloomington, Indiana 1969; *French Cinema since 1946: Vol. 2: The Personal Style* by Roy Armes, rev. ed. London 1970; *Jean-Luc Godard* edited by Jean Collet, translated by Ciba Vaughan, New York 1970; *De la littérature au cinéma: genèse d'une écriture* by Marie-Claire Ropars-Wuilleumier, Paris 1970; *Il cinema è il cinema* edited and translated by Adriano Aprà, Rome 1971; *Cinéma et société moderne: le cinéma de 1968 à 1968: Godard, Antonioni, Resnais, Robbe-Grillet* by Annie Goldman, Paris 1971; *Cinema e pubblicita nell'opera di Jean-Luc Godard* by Gianni Rondolino, Turin 1971; *Focus on Godard* edited by Royal Brown, Englewood Cliffs, New Jersey 1972; *Le Cinéma française depuis la nouvelle vague* by Claire Clouzot, Paris 1972; *Guerre et cinéma: grandes illusions et petits soldats, 1895-1971* by Joseph Daniel, Paris 1972; *Double Feature: Movies and Politics* by Greil Marcus and Michael Goodwin, New York 1972; *Godard on Godard* edited and translated by Tom Milne, London 1972; *On Film: Unpopular Essays on a Popular Art* by Vernon Young, Chicago 1972; *Jean-Luc Godard* by Alberto Farassino, Florence 1974; *6 European Directors: Essays on the Meaning of Film Style* by Peter harcourt, Baltimore 1974; *Film and Revolution* by James MacBean, Bloomington, Indiana 1975; *Jean-Luc Godard: 3 Films—'A Woman is a Woman', 'A Married Woman', '2 or 3 Things I Know about Her'*, New York 1975; *The New Wave* by James Monaco, New York 1976; articles—"Charlotte et Véronique" by François Truffaut in *Cahiers du cinéma* (Paris), May 1958; "Un Cinéma des gens de lettres" by Jean Douchet in *Arts* (Paris), no.730, 1959; "Censure: *Le Petit Soldat*" in *Image et son* (Paris), no.134, 1960; "*Le Petit Soldat* de J.-L. Godard est interdit" in *Le Monde* (Paris), 14 September 1960; "Films nouveaux: *A bout de souffle*" by J. Chevallier in *Image et son: Revue du cinéma* (Paris), April 1960; "*A bout de souffle*": naissance du cinéma vaudois" by René Cortade in *Arts* (Paris), 23 March 1960; "Views of the New Wave" by Louis Marcorelles in *Sight and Sound* (London), spring 1960; "Jean-Luc Godard" by Luc Moullet in *Cahiers du cinéma* (Paris), April 1960; "L'Important est de se poser des questions" by Georges Sadoul in *Les Lettres françaises* (Paris),

3-9 November 1960; "Quoi de neuf (suite): *A bout de souffle*" by Louis Seguin in *Positif* (Paris), no.33, 1960; "Cubist Crime" in *Time* (New York), 17 February 1961; "Movies Abroad: Larcenous Talent" in *Time* (New York), 17 March 1961; "Nonconformist on the Crest of the New Wave" by Eugene Archer in *The New York Times*, 5 February 1961; "*Breathless*" by Arlene Croce in *Film Quarterly* (Berkeley), spring 1961; "Films: The New Cinema, the Old Nonsense" in *Esquire* (New York), July 1961; "Cinema of Appearance" by Eric Rhode and Gabriel Pearson in *Sight and Sound* (London), autumn 1961; "Le Brave Petit Soldat" in *Positif* (Paris), June 1962; "Un Palmarès sans surprise au festival de Venise" by Jean de Baroncelli in *Le Monde* (Paris), 11 September 1962; "Le Roi est nu" by Robert Benayoun in *Positif* (Paris), June 1962; "Jean-Luc Godard, *Le Petit Soldat ou la résistance à la tyrannie*" by Michel Capdenac in *Les Lettres françaises* (Paris), 18-24 January 1962; "Sérénade à trois" by Michel Delahaye in *Cahiers du cinéma* (Paris), no.132, 1962; "La Difficulté d'être de Jean-Luc Godard" by Jean-André Fieschi in *Cahiers du cinéma* (Paris), November 1962; "How Art is True" by Tom Milne in *Sight and Sound* (London), autumn 1962; "The Sound Track" by T.M.F. Steen in *Films in Review* (New York), February 1962; "Que chacun vive sa vie" by François Truffaut in *L'Avant-Scène du cinéma* (Paris), 15 October 1962; "Checklist 5—Jean-Luc Godard" in *Monthly Film Bulletin* (London), August 1963; "Anna et les paradoxes" in *Cinéma 63* (Paris), July/August 1963; "Godard: Cut-Sequence: *Vivre sa vie*" by Jean-André Fieschi, translated by Gary Broughton, in *Movie* (London), January 1963; "La Censure et *Le Soldat*" by Marcel Martin in *Cinéma 63* (Paris), March 1963; "En écoutant Jean-Luc Godard" by Marcel Martin in *Les Lettres françaises* (Paris), 31 January—6 February 1963; "Le Cinémois de Jean-Pierre Melville" by Jean-Pierre Melville in *Cinéma 63* (Paris), April 1963; "Conventional-Unconventional" by Colin Young in *Film Quarterly* (Berkeley), fall 1963; "A Fad Is Not a Revolution: Gadget-Laden France Alters" in *Variety* (New York), 29 April 1964; "France's Far-Out Filmmaker" by Eugene Archer in *The New York Times*, 27 September 1964; "French New Wave" by Eugene Archer in *The New York Times*, 4 November 1964; "Godard or Not Godard" by Raymond Bellour in *Les Lettres françaises* (Paris), 14 May 1964; "A Movie is a Movie is a Movie" by Andrew Sarris in *New York Film Bulletin*, summer 1964; "Waiting for Godard" by Andrew Sarris and Andrew Blasi in *Film Culture* (New York), summer 1964; "Une Rencontre nommée Godard" in *Cinéma 65* (Paris), January 1965; "*Tous les garçons s'appellent Patrick*" in *Movie* (London), spring 1965; "Qu'est que l'art, Jean-Luc Godard" by Louis Aragon in *Les Lettres françaises* (Paris), 9-15 September 1965; "*Cahiers*—And in a Word that Means Far Out" by Eugene Archer in *The New York Times*, 23 May 1965; "I debiti della 'nouvelle vague'" by Leobardi Autera in *Bianco e nero* (Rome), January 1965; "Le Miroir critique" by Raymond Bellour in *La Nouvelle Revue française* (Paris), August 1965; "Lecture et réflexion faites" by Pierre Billard in *Cinéma 65* (Paris), March 1965; "Light of Day" by Raoul Coutard in *Sight and Sound* (London), winter 1965; "Jean-Luc Godard, cinéaste masqué" by Jacques Doniol-Valcroze in *L'Avant-Scène du cinéma* (Paris), March 1965; "Godard Est Godard" by Pauline Kael in *New Yorker*, 9 October 1965; "A Film is a Film: Some Notes on Jean-Luc Godard" by James Price in *Evergreen Review* (New York), November 1965; "La Langage des signes" by Gilles Sainte-Marie in *Objectif* (Montreal), August/September 1965; "Encyclopédie permanent du cinématographe: Carre (dernier)" in *Positif* (Paris), no.74, 1966; "Masters and Mavericks" in *Newsweek* (New York), 14 February 1966; article on Godard in *Filmcritica* (Rome), March 1966; "*Pierrot le fou*: la machine à décerveler" by Robert Benayoun in *Positif* (Paris), February

1966; "Les Jeunes devant de jeune cinéma:..." by Jean-Louis Bory in *Arts* (Paris), 27 April—3 May 1966; "Jean-Luc Godard et l'enfance de l'art" by Michel Delahaye in *Cahiers du cinéma* (Paris), June 1966; "Rigore e coerenza di Jean-Luc Godard" by Giacomo Gambetti in *Bianco e nero* (Rome), July/August 1966; "Godard—Cult or Culture?" by Judith Goldman in *Films and Filming* (London), June 1966; "...Unissez-vous!" by Michel Hautecouverture in *Positif* (Paris), May 1966; "Movie Brutalists" by Pauline Kael in *New Republic* (New York), 24 September 1966; "Godard: Instinkt und Reflexion" by Herbert Linder in *Filmkritik* (Munich), March 1966; "Le Cinéma moderne et la narrative" by Christian Metz in *Cahiers du cinéma* (Paris), December 1966; "Film and the Radical Aspiration" by Annette Michaelson in *Film Culture* (New York), fall 1966; "Les Facettes d'un miroir brisé" by Georges Sadoul in *Les Lettres françaises* (Paris), 29 December—4 January 1966; "Godard ne passera pas" by Georges Sadoul in *Les Lettres françaises* (Paris), May 1966; "The Verge and After: Film by 1966" by Vernon Young in *Hudson Review* (Nutley, New Jersey), spring 1966; "Jean-Luc Godard—au delà du récit" in *Etudes cinématographiques* (Paris), no.57-61, 1967; "Box Office de Jean-Luc Godard" and "Jean-Luc Godard et la Centrale Catholique du Cinéma" in *Image et son: Revue du cinéma* (Paris), December 1967; "An Alpha for Godard" by John Ardagh in *Manchester Guardian*, 12 March 1967; "Versus Godard" by Bernardo Bertolucci in *Cahiers du cinéma* (Paris), January 1967; "Interview with Geoges de Beauregard" by Ginette Billard in *Film Quarterly* (Berkeley), spring 1967; "Jean-Luc Godard, ou, l'urgence de l'art" by Michel Delahaye in *Cahiers du cinéma* (Paris), February 1967; "Topografia dell'oggetto" by Francesco Dorigo in *Bianco e nero* (Rome), February 1967; "Interview de Jean-Luc Godard à Alger" by Guy Hennebelle in *Cinéma intérnational* (Montier, Switzerland), September/October 1967; "Shooting at Wars: 3 Views" by Max Kozloff and William Johnson in *Film Quarterly* (Berkeley), winter 1967; "Without and Within..." by Michael Kustow in *Sight and Sound* (London), summer 1967; "Godard sans sous-titres" by Raymond Lefèvre in *Image et son: Revue de cinéma* (Paris), December 1967; "Peter Lennon Watches Godard at Work" by Peter Lennon in *Manchester Guardian*, 27 September 1967; "Godard: la dissoluzionne del personaggio" by Angelo Mascariello in *Filmcritica* (Rome), September 1967; "2nd Opinion: Jean-Luc Godard" by Paul Mayersburg in *Sunday Times* (London), 9 April 1967; "Godard as Godard" by Tony Mussman in *Medium* (Frankfurt), winter 1967; "Jean-Luc Godard's Non-Endings" by Tony Mussman in *Arts* (New York), November 1967; "Jean-Luc Godard: thèmes et variations" by Phillipe Pilard in *Image et son: Revue du cinéma* (Paris), December 1967; "La Logique de Godard" by Pierre-Felix de Ravel d'Esclapon in *Take One* (Montreal), April 1967; "Modern Life" by Sylvain Regard, translated by Jean Billard, in *Take One* (Montreal), February 1967; "Godard" by Richard Roud in *Making Films* (New York), October 1967; "Godard: essai collage" by Abraham Segal in *Image et son: Revue du cinéma* (Paris), December 1967; "Godard and the Godardians: A Study in the New Sensibility" in *Private Screenings* by John Simon, New York 1967; "Adler Loves Godard—Sort Of" by Renata Adler in *The New York Times*, 27 October 1968; articles on the events of May 1968 in Paris by Renata Adler in *The New York Times*, 19 May, 25 May, 26 May, and 2 June 1968; "The Beautiful Swindlers" in *Film-Facts* (New York), January 1968; "Cannes Officials Close Festival" in *The New York Times*, 19 May 1967; "Directors: Infuriating Magician" in *Time* (New York), 16 February 1967; "What Makes Us Hate, or Love, Godard?" by Eugene Archer in *The New York Times*, 28 January 1968; "Godard and the U.S." by Claire Clouzot in *Sight and Sound* (London), summer 1968;

"Fin d'un festival: Cannes" by Michel Delahaye in *Cahiers du cinéma* (Paris), August 1968; "The Films of Jean-Luc Godard" by Manny Farber in *Artforum* (New York), October 1968; "Jean-Luc Godard and Americanism" by Raymond Federman in *Film Heritage* (Dayton, Ohio), spring 1968; "L'Affaire Godard" by Joel Finler in *International Times* (London), December 1968; "Godard et ses critiques" by Claude Gauteur in *Image et son: Revue du cinéma* (Paris), February 1968; "A Minority Movie" by Pauline Kael in *New Yorker*, 6 April 1968; "Cannes '68" by Richard Roud in *Sight and Sound* (London), summer 1968; "Jean-Luc vs. Saint Jean" by Andrew Sarris in *Film Heritage* (Dayton, Ohio), spring 1968; "The Trying Genius of M. Godard" by Richard Schickel in *Life* (New York), 12 April 1968; "Between Art and Life: The Films of Jean-Luc Godard" by Joel E. Siegel in *Film Heritage* (Dayton, Ohio), spring 1968; "The Truth 24 Times a Second" by Raymond Solokov in *Newsweek* (New York), 12 February 1968; "Going to the Movies" by Susan Sontag in *Partisan Review* (New Brunswick, New Jersey), spring 1968; "How the Revolution Came to Cannes" by Harvey Swados in *The New York Times*, 9 June 1968; "Interview: John Whitley Watches Godard..." by John Whitley in *Sunday Times* (London), 23 June 1968; series of interviews with Godard by Gene Youngblood in *Los Angeles Free Press*, 8 March, 15 March, 22 March, and 29 March 1968; "Personal Cinema in the 60's: Jean-Luc Godard" in *The Technique of Film Editing* by Gavin Millar and Karel Reisz, 2nd ed. London 1968; "Die Kunst ist eine Idee der Kapitalisten" in *Film* (Hanover), April 1969; "Fritz Lang on Godard and *Contempt*" by Gretchen Berg in *Take One* (Montreal), 22 June 1969; "Interview with Godard" by Jonathan Cott in *Rolling Stone* (New York), June 1969; "Politics, Poetry, and the Language of Signs in Godard's *Made in U.S.A.*" by James MacBean in *Film Quarterly* (Berkeley), spring 1969; "Godard the Wrecker is at It Again..." by Gene Moskowitz in *Variety* (New York), 26 March 1969; "Cinema provocazione" by Paola Rispoli in *Filmcritica* (Rome), January 1969; "How Good is Godard?" by Andrew Sarris in *The Village Voice* (New York), 23 January 1969; "La rivola degli studenti" by Giuseppe Turroni in *Bianco e nero* (Rome), March/April 1969; "Cinema as a Gun: An Interview with Fernando Solanas" by Gianni Volpi in *Cineaste* (New York), fall 1969; "Godard to Direct *Little Murderers* Film" by A.H. Weiler in *The New York Times*, 29 May 1969; "Cinéma et citation" by Jean-Louis Alexandre in *Cinéma* (Paris), October/November 1970; "Movies? They Are No Joke, Mes Amis" by Vincent Canby in *The New York Times*, 31 May 1970; "Film and Revolution: An Interview with Jean-Luc Godard" by Kent Carroll in *Evergreen Review* (New York), October 1970; "Le Cinéma dans la politique: debat" in *Positif* (Paris), February 1970; "Une Reapparition de Jean-Luc Godard" by Guy Gauthier in *Image et son: Revue du cinéma* (Paris), December 1970; "Toward a Non-Bourgeois Cinema Style" by Brian Henderson in *Film Quarterly* (Berkeley), winter 1970; "Jean-Luc Godard" by Peter Sainsbury in *Afterimage* (New York), April 1970; "Godard and the Revolution" by Andrew Sarris in *The Village Voice* (New York), 30 April 1970; "Godard and Revolution" by Norman Silverstein in *Films and Filming* (London), June 1970; "Dziga Vertov Notebook" by Robert Altman in *Take One* (Montreal), May/June 1971; articles on Godard's motorcycle accident in *Times* (London), 10 June, 11 June, and 30 June 1971; "Godard's Truths" by David Cast in *Film Heritage* (Dayton, Ohio), summer 1971; "The Dziga Vertov Group in America" by Michael Goodwin and others in *Take One* (Montreal), March/April 1971; "Notes on Solanas and Godard" by Joel Haycock in *Film Society Review* (New York), November and December 1971; "Godard Burns Italian Film Org..." by Judith Moore in *Variety* (New York), 31 March 1971; "Struggles in Italy" by Bill Nichols in *Film Quar-*

terly (Berkeley), fall 1971; "Jean-Luc Godard: 'Le Cinéma est un moment de la révolution'" by Patrick Sery in *Le Monde* (Paris), 1 April 1971; "A Terrible Duty is Born" by Colin Westerbeck, Jr. in *Sight and Sound* (London), summer 1971; "Politics and Production:..." by Christopher Williams in *Screen* (London), winter 1971; "Jean-Luc Godard selon deux points de vue" by Jean-Louis Bory in *Dosier du cinéma, cinéastes, I* edited by Jean-Louis Bory and Claude Cluny, Paris 1971; "Jean-Luc Godard and the Sensibility of the 60's" by Haywood Gould in *The Imagemaker* edited by Ron Henderson, Richmond, Virginia 1971; "Godard Back to Commercial Pix with *All is Well*" in *Variety* (New York), 26 April 1972; "Marx, le cinéma, et la critique de film" by Guido Aristarco, translated by Barthélemy Amengual, in *Etudes cinématographiques* (Paris), no.88-92, 1972; "Jean-Luc Godard: 'Pour mieux écouter les autres'" by Yvonne Baby in *Le Monde* (Paris), 27 April 1972; "Politica/-cinema/actilop" by F. Carlini in *Bianco e nero* (Rome), July/August 1972; "Oltre l'inscrizione, la scrittura" by F. Casetti in *Bianco e nero* (Rome), July/August 1972; "Jean-Luc Godard Wants to Live for the Revolution, Not Die for It" by James Conway in *The New York Times*, 24 December 1972; "Le Groupe Dziga Vertov" by Lou Sin Groupe d'intervention idéologique in *Cahiers du cinéma* (Paris), May/June 1972; "Godard and the Dziga Vertov Group: Film and Dialectic" by James MacBean in *Film Quarterly* (Berkeley), fall 1972; "Black Panthers in the New Wave" by Martha Merrill in *Film Culture* (New York), spring 1972; "I Didn't Always Understand Him" by Anna Karina in *Film* (London), May 1973; "Angle and Reality: Godard and Gorin in America" by R.P. Kolkein in *Sight and Sound* (London), summer 1973; "Film and Style: The Fictional Documentary" by Joan Mellen in *Antioch Review* (Yellow Springs, Ohio), no.3, 1973; "Tout ne va pas bien" by Colin Westerbeck, Jr. in *Commonweal* (New York), 5 January 1973; "Programming Works by a Single Filmmaker: Jean-Luc Godard" by Ron Green in *Film Library Quarterly* (New York), no.3-4, 1974; "*Godard on Godard*: Notes for a Reading" by Brian Henderson in *Film Quarterly* (Berkeley), summer 1974; "Realism and the Cinema: Notes on Some Brechtian Theses" by Colin McCabe in *Screen* (London), Summer 1974; "The Godard Film Forum" by Tony Rayns in *Film* (London), January 1974; "Breathless Again" by Martin Evan in *Manchester Guardian Weekly*, 9 June 1975; "Le Remake de *A bout de souffle*: recontre avec Godard sur un îlot de socialisme" by Martin Evan in *Le Monde* (Paris), 8 May 1975; "Humanism Breaks Camp" by Penelope Gilliat in *New Yorker*, 14 August 1975; "Bertolt Brecht et le cinéma: des rapports difficiles et inaboutis" by J. Petrat in *Cinéma 75* (Paris), November 1975; "Godard Image" by Richard Roud in *Manchester Guardian Weekly*, 16 August 1975; "J-M.S. et J.-L. G." by Pascal Bonitzer in *Cahiers du cinéma* (Paris), February 1976; "Profiles: The Urgent Whisper" by Penelope Gilliatt in *New Yorker*, 25 October 1976; "Visual Distancing in Godard" by Julia Lesage in *Wide Angle* (Athens, Ohio), no.3, 1976; "Godard et le groupe Dziga Vertov" by Abraham Segal in *L'Avant-Scène du cinéma* (Paris), July/September 1976; "Le Hasard arbitraire" by Serge Toubiana in *Cahiers du cinéma* (Paris), January 1976; "Godard and Me" by Martin Walsh in *Take One* (Montreal), February 1976; "Looking for Mr. Godard: Grenoble Savage—How It Goes with Godard" by Terry Curtis Fox in *The Village Voice* (New York), 31 October 1977; "Atlantic City: John Hughes on Godard's Made in U.S.A." in *Film Comment* (New York), March/April 1977; "La Lettre et le cinématographe: L'Écrit dans les films de Godard" by R. Lefèvre in *Image et son* (Paris), May 1977; "La Troisième 'Époque' de Jean-Luc Godard" by René Predal in *Jeune Cinéma* (Paris), March 1977; "Veränderung, was ist das?" by Gilles Deleuze in *Filmkritik* (Munich), February 1977; "Le Petit Théatre de Jean-Luc Godard" by J.-C. Bonnet in *Cinématographe* (Paris), November 1978; "Godard de la nuit" by G. Gauthier in *Image et son* (Paris), January 1978; "Jean-Luc Godard Sauve qui peut (La Vie): Une Journée de tournage 1" by A. Bergala and L. Carax in *Cahiers du cinéma* (Paris), December 1979; "Godard's 'Week-end': Totem, Taboo, and the 5th Republic" by D. Nicholls in *Sight and Sound* (London), winter 1979/80; "Jean-Luc Godard: 2 into 3" by J. Forbes in *Sight and Sound* (London), winter 1980/81; "Gilbert Adair from London" in *Film Comment* (New York), May/June 1981; "Jean-Luc Godard", with biofilmography, by Sheila Whitaker in *Film Dope* (London), April 1980. films--*Jean-Luc Godard, ou le cinéma de défi*, for TV, directed by Janine Bazin, André-S. Labarthe, and Hubert Knapp, filmed 6-8 November 1964; *Pour le plaisir*, for TV, directed by Jacques Doniol-Valcroze, 1965; *Godard in America*, directed by Ralph Thanhauser on Godard's tour of the U.S., 1970; *La Longue Marche de Jean-Luc Godard* directed by Jean-Pierre Berckmans, Belgium 1972; *Der kleine Godard* directed by Hellmuth Costard, West Germany 1978.

*   *   *

If influence on the development of world cinema be the criterion, Godard is certainly the most important filmmaker of the past 30 years; he is also one of the most problematic.

His career so far falls roughly into three periods: the early works from *A bout de souffle* to *Weekend* (1959-1968), a period whose end is marked decisively by the latter film's final caption, "Fin de Cinéma"; the period of intense politiciztion, during which Godard collaborated (mainly though not exclusively) with Jean-Pierre Gorin and the Dziga Vertov group (1968-1972); and the recent work, divided between attempts to renew communication with a wider, more "mainstream" cinema audience and explorations in the potentialities of video (in collaboration with Anne-Marie Miéville). (One might separate off the films from *Masculin-Féminin* to *Weekend* inclusive as representing a transitional phase from the first to the Dziga Vertov period; though in a sense all Godard's work is transitional.) What marks the middle period off from its neighbours is above all the difference in intended audience: the Dziga Vertov films were never meant to reach a general public, being aimed at already committed Marxist or leftist groups, campus student groups, and so on, to stimulate discussion of revolutionary politics and aesthetics and, crucially, the relationship between the two.

Godard's importance lies in his development of an authentic modernist cinema in opposition to (though, during the early period, at the same time *within*) mainstream cinema; it is with his work that film becomes central to our century's major aesthetic debate, the controversy developed through such figures as Lukács, Brecht, Benjamin, and Adorno as to whether realism or modernism is the more progressive form. As ex-*Cahiers du cinéma* critic and New Wave filmmaker, Godard was initially linked with Truffaut and Chabrol in a kind of revolutionary triumvirate; it is easy, in retrospect, to see that Godard was from the start the truly radical figure, the "revolution" of his colleagues operating purely on the aesthetic level and easily assimilable into the mainstream. A simple way of demonstrating the essential thrust of Godard's work is to juxtapose his first feature, *Breathless*, with the excellent American remake. Jim McBride's film follows the original fairly closely, with the fundamental difference that in it all other elements are subordinated to the narrative and the characters. In Godard's film, on the contrary, this traditional relationship between signifier and signified shows a continuous tendency to come adrift, so that the *process of*

narration (which mainstream cinema strives everywhere to conceal) becomes foregrounded; *A bout de souffle* is "about" a story and characters, certainly, but it is also about the cinema, about film techniques, about Jean Seberg, etc.

This foregrounding of the process—and the means—of narration is developed much further in subsequent films, in which Godard systematically breaks down the traditional barrier between fiction/documentary, actor/character, narrative film/experimental film to create freer, "open" forms. Persons appear as themselves in works of fiction, actors address the camera/audience in monologues or as if being interviewed, materiality of film is made explicit (the switches from positive to negative in *Une Femme mariée*, the turning on and off of the soundtrack in *Deux ou trois choses que je sais d'elle*, the showing of the clapper-board in *La Chinoise*). The initial motivation for this seems to have been the assertion of personal freedom: the filmmaker shatters the bonds of traditional realism in order to be able to say and do whatever he wants, creating films spontaneously. (*Pierrot le fou*—significantly, one of Godard's most popular films—is the most extreme expression of this impulse.) Gradually, however, a political motivation (connected especially with the influence of Brecht) takes over. There is a marked sociological interest in the early films (especially *Vivre sa vie* and *Une Femme mariée*), but the turning-point is *Masculin, féminin* with its two male protagonists, one seeking fulfilment through personal relations, the other a political activist. The former's suicide at the end of the film can be read as marking a decisive choice: from here on, Godard increasingly listens to the voice of revolutionary politics and eventually (in the Dziga Vertov films) adopts it as his own voice.

The films of the Dziga Vertov group (named after the great Russian documentarist who anticipated their work in making films that foreground the means of production and are continuously self-reflexive) were the direct consequence of the events of May, 1968. More than ever before the films are directly concerned with their own process, so that the ostensible subjects—the political scene in Czechoslovakia (*Pravda*) or Italy (*Lotte in Italia*), the trial of the Chicago Eight (*Vladimir and Rosa*)—become secondary to the urgent, actual subject: how does one make a revolutionary film? It was at this time that Godard distinguished between making political films (i.e. films on political subjects: Costa-Gavras's *Z* is a typical example) and making films politically, the basic assumption being that one cannot put radical content into traditional form without seriously compromising, perhaps negating, it. Hence the attack on Realism initiated at the outset of Godard's career manifests its full political significance: realism is a bourgeois art form, the means whereby the bourgeoisie endlessly reassures itself, validating its own ideology as "true," "natural," "real"; its power must be destroyed. Of the films from this period, *Vent d'est* (the occasion for Peter Wollen's seminal essay on "Counter-Cinema" in *After Image*) most fully realized this aesthetic: the original pretext (the pastiche of a Western) recedes into the background, and the film becomes a discussion about itself—about the relationship between sound and image, the materiality of film, the destruction of bourgeois forms, the necessity for continuous self-criticism and self-awareness.

The assumption behind the Dziga Vertov films is clearly that the revolutionary impetus of May '68 would be sustained, and it has not been easy for Godard to adjust to its collapse. That difficulty is the subject of one of his finest works, *Tout va bien* (again in collaboration with Gorin), an attempt to return to commercial fimmaking without abandoning the principles (both aesthetic and political) of the preceding years. Beginning by foregrounding Godard's own problem (how does a radical make a film within the capitalist production system?), the film is strongest in its complex use of Yves Montand and Jane Fonda (simultaneously fictional characters/personalities/star images) and its exploration of the issues to which they are central: the relationship of intellectuals to the class struggle; the relationship between professional work, personal commitment, and political position; the problem of sustaining a radical impulse in a non-revolutionary age. *Tout va bien* is Godard's most authentically Brechtian film, achieving radical force and analytical clarity without sacrificing pleasure and a degree of emotional involvement.

Godard's relationship to Brecht has not always been so clear-cut. While the justification for Brecht's distanciation principles was always the communication of clarity, Godard's films often leave the spectator in a state of confusion and frustration. He continues to seem by temperament more anarchist than Marxist. One is troubled by the continuity (pointed out by Peter Harcourt in *Six European Directors*) between the criminal drop-outs of the earlier films and the political activists of the later. The insistent intellectualism of the films is often offset by a wilful abeyance of systematic thinking, the abeyance, precisely, of that self-awareness and self-criticism the political works advocate. Even in *Tout va bien*, what emerges from the political analysis as the film's own position is an irresponsible and ultimately desperate belief in spontaneity. Desperation, indeed, is never far from the Godardian surface, and seems closely related to the treatment of heterosexual relations: even through the apparent feminist awareness of the recent work runs a strain of unwitting misogyny (most evident, perhaps, in *Sauve qui peut*). The central task of Godard criticism, in fact, is to sort out the remarkable and salutary nature of the positive achievement from the temperamental limitations that flaw it.

—Robin Wood

GÓMEZ, MANUEL OCTAVIO. Cuban. Born in Havana, 14 November 1934. Married Idalia Anreus. Career: 1950s—works as newspaper and television writer as well as film critic; 1950s—member of Vision, a cine-club in Havana; 1959—immediately after revolution, becomes part of National Board of Culture organized by Julio García Espinosa; Instituto Cubano del Arte e Industria Cinematograficos (ICAIC) established by the revolutionary government; 1959-61—assistant director on documentary shorts by Tomás Gutiérrez Alea and Espinosa, and later assists Gutiérrez Alea on his 1st feature *Historias de la Revolucion*; 1965—directs 1st feature *El encuentro: La salacion*; 1965-82—continues to direct films.

Films (as director): 1960—*Cooperativas agricolas: El Agua*; 1962—*Historia de una batalla (History of a Battle)*; 1963—*Cuentos del alhamnara: Guancanayabo*; 1965—*El encuentro: la salacion*; 1967—*Tulipa*; 1968—*Nuevitas*; 1969—*La primera carga al machete (First Charge of the Machete)*; 1972—*Days of Water*; 1974—*Ustedes tienen la palabara (Now It's Up to You)*; 1977—*La tierra y el cielo*; 1978—*Una mujer, un hombre, una ciudad (A Woman, A Man, A City)*.

Publications:

By GÓMEZ:

Articles—"Manuel Octavio Gómez Interviewed: Popular Cul-

ture, Perpetual Quest" by Julianne Burton in *Jump Cut* (Chicago), May 1979; "Emotion—Dramaturgie—Improvisation", interview by W. Becker and R. Schenk in *Film und Fernsehen* (Berlin), June 1980.

On GÓMEZ:

Books—*Cuba: The Measure of a Revolution* by L. Nelson, Minneapolis 1972; *Memories of Underdevelopment: The Revolutionary Films of Cuba* by Michael Myerson, New York 1973; articles—"The Cuban Cinema" by M.E. Douglas in *Take One* (Montreal), July/August 1968; "Propaganda Fills Cuban Newsreels" by R. Adler in *The New York Times*, 12 February 1969; "Cubans are Molding Movie Industry into a Pervasive Force" by R. Adler in *The New York Times*, 11 February 1969; "Cultural Life in Cuba Thriving Despite Rein" by R. Adler in *The New York Times*, 10 February 1969; "Solidarity and Violence" by A. Engel in *Sight and Sound* (London), autumn 1969; "The Spring 1972 Cuban Film Festival Bust" by G. Crowdus in *Film Society Review* (New York), March/May 1972; "Cine Cubano" by P. Sauvage in *Film Comment* (New York), spring 1972; "Introduction to Revolutionary Cuban Cinema" by Julianne Burton in *Jump Cut* (Chicago), December 1978; "*Now It's Up to You* and *A Woman, A Man, A City*: The Personal is Political in Cuba" by John Hess in *Jump Cut* (Chicago), May 1979.

*   *   *

Perhaps best known for his capacity to rework traditional and popular film forms into exciting, innovative, and revolutionary cinema, Manuel Octavio Gómez is a member of the first generation of filmmakers trained in Cuba since the triumph of the revolution in January of 1959. Prior to that date, he worked as a film critic while informally studying film direction—even though "being a filmmaker seemed like an impossible dream in pre-revolutionary Cuba."

Gómez entered the Cuban Film Institute (ICAIC) upon its founding, and "learned to make films by making them." He began with documentaries, a characteristic path for ICAIC's directors, as it requires that they first immerse themselves in the material reality and national culture of Cuba. Among his better documentaries is *History of a Battle*, a fine encapsulation of the first years of the revolution, which juxtaposes the victory at the Bay of Pigs with the successes achieved in the Literacy Campaign. Gómez feels that this background in documentary film has been an essential formative experience for Cuban cineastes, and argues that "The documentary medium constitutes one of the most efficient ways to understand and portray a problem—and to put the idea into practice that art shouldn't just reflect reality, but should be one of the conscious factors that assists in its transformation."

The first of the traditional genres receiving Gómez's attention was historical cinema, which he considers "unbearable." Although he views the distinction of "historical" and "contemporary" cinema as a mystification, he does feel that there exists "a national necessity—rather, one for the whole Third World—a necessity to rescue, to revise, to de-alienate our true history—a thousand times falsified, twisted, and hidden...in order to feel ourselves more deeply rooted in our nationality and with a greater consciousness of our present." To accomplish this, films must make history "more alive, more urgent."

To make contemporary the "100 years of anti-imperialist struggles that give Cuba a historical continuity," Gómez directed *First Charge of the Machete*. This film links past and present through several devices: the formal contrast of modern and archaic film styles; the centrality of the machete, tool of war and weapon in the economic struggles of 1968; and the implied relationship of Maximo Gómez (Dominican rebel leader in the 1868 uprising) to Che Guevara, both foreigners who joined Cubans in their liberation movements.

Manuel Octavio Gómez reinterpreted other traditional genres in his following films. *Days of Water* contains a sequence critical of the pre-revolutionary cabaret aesthetic, one example of the ways in which authentic forms of popular culture were distorted and commercialized. *Now It's Up to You* and *A Woman, a Man, a City* both penetrating analyses of contemporary problems in Cuba, rework the courtroom drama and detective genres, respectively, by inverting the traditional narrative structure we associate with these forms. Although they begin with the sort of individualist focus usual in bourgeois cinema, they open up into historical and political analyses rather than remain at the level of personal melodrama.

In his "perpetual quest," Gómez has been guided through his early "confused and erroneous notions about personal expression and 'being or not being' an artist" by the concrete reality of Cuba's revolutionary transformation. He stated, "On top of this small, 'painful,' and individual conflict, a revolution was generating changes, inverting values, and engendering new social, ideological, and cultural duties." Among the duties of Gómez has been the production of vigorous and critical films, worthy of his revolutionary commitment.

—John Mraz

GOMEZ, SARA. Cuban. Born in Havana, 1943. Educated Conservatory of Music, Havana. Career: 1960s—works as journalist on youth publication *Mella* and on the Sunday supplement *Hoy Domingo*; 1961—begins working at Instituto Cubano del Arte e Industria Cinematograficos (ICAIC) as assistant director under Tomás Gutiérrez Alea, Jorge Fraga, and Agnes Varda; 1964—directs 1st film, *Ire a Santiago*, a documentary; 1964-74—continues to direct documentaries; 1974—shoots and edits 1st feature film *De cierta manera (One Way or Another)*; original negative for *De cierta manera* is damaged in processing; 1974-76—footage for *De cierta manera* is restored in various labs in Sweden, and Gutiérrez Alea and Rigoberto Lopez oversee postproduction stages in preparation of its release. Died 2 June 1974.

Films (as director): 1964—*Ire a Santiago*; 1965—*Excursion a Vueltabajo*; 1967—*Y tenemos sabor*; 1968—*En la otra isla*; 1969—*Isla del tesoro*; 1970—*Poder local, poder popular*; 1971—*Un documental a proposito del transito*; 1972—*Atencion prenatal*; *Ano uno*; 1973—*Sobre horas extras y trabajo voluntario*; 1977—*De cierta manera (One Way or Another)*.

Publications:

On GOMEZ:

Articles—"Individual Fulfillment and Collective Achievement: An Interview with Tomás Gutiérrez Alea" by Julianne Burton in *Cinéaste* (New York), January 1977; "*One Way or Another*: The Revolution in Action" by Carlos Galiano in *Jump Cut* (Chicago), December 1978; "Introduction to the Revolutionary Cuban Cinema" by Julianne Burton in *Jump Cut* (Chicago), December 1978; "*One Way or Another*" by Julia Lesage in *Jump Cut* (Chicago), May 1979.

*   *   *

We shall never know all that Sara Gomez might have given to us. We have her one feature film, the marvelous *De cierta manera*, and a few short documentaries to indicate what might have been had she lived beyond the age of 31. But we will never really know all that this prodigiously talented black woman was capable of.

Sara Gomez could be seen as prototypical of the new Cuban directors. Entering the Cuban Film Institute (ICAIC) at a early age, she worked as assistant director for various cineastes, including Tomás Gutiérrez Alea, whose influence marked her work as it has so many of the young directors. During a ten-year period (1964-74) she fulfilled the usual apprenticeship among Cuban cineastes by directing documentary films. Documentaries are seen as an important training ground for Cuban directors because they force them to focus on the material reality of Cuba and thus emphasize the use of cinema as an expression of national culture. As Gutiérrez Alea noted, "The kind of cinema which adapts itself to our interests, fortunately, is a kind of light, agile cinema, one that is very directly founded upon our own reality." This is precisely the kind of cinema Sara Gomez went on to produce, beginning work on *De cierta manera* in 1974 and finishing the editing of the film shortly before her death of acute asthma.

Her early training in documentaries and the influence of Gutiérrez Alea is evident in *De cierta manera*. The film combines the documentary and fiction forms so inextricably that they are impossible to disentagle. Through this technique, she emphasized the material reality that is at the base of all creative endeavor and the necessity to bring a critical perspective to all forms of film.

In choosing this style, which I call "dialectical resonance," Gómez appeared to follow Gutiérrez Alea's example in the superb *Memories of Underdevelopment*. But, there is a crucial difference between the two films—a difference that might be said to distinguish the generation of directors who came of age before the triumph of the revolution (e.g., Gutiérrez Alea) from those who have grown up within the revolution. In spite of its ultimate commitment to the revolutionary process, *Memories* remains in some ways the perspective of an "outsider" and might be characterized as "critical bourgeois realism." However, *De cierta manera* is a vision wholly from within the revolution, despite the fact that every position in the film is subjected to criticism—including that of the institutionalized revolution, which is presented in the form of an annoyingly pompous omniscient narration. Thus, the perspective of Gomez might be contrasted to that of *Memories* by calling it "critical socialist realism." The emphasis on dialectical criticism, struggle, and commitment, is equally great in both films, but the experience of having grown up within the revolution created a somewhat different perspective.

Despite its deceptively simple appearance—a result of being shot in 16mm on a very low budget—*De cierta manera* is the work of an extremely sophisticated filmmaker. Merely one example among many of Gómez's sophistication is the way in which she combined a broad range of modern distanciation techniques with the uniquely Cuban tropical beat to produce a film that is simultaneously rigorously analytic and powerfully sensuous—as well as perhaps the finest instance to date of a truly dialectical film. Although we are all a little richer for the existence of this work, we remain poorer for the fact that she will make no more films.

—John Mraz

GORETTA, CLAUDE. Swiss. Born in Geneva, 23 June 1929. Educated in law at Université de Genève; studied at British Film Institute. Career: early 1950s—while at University of Geneva founds cine club with Alain Tanner; 1955—joins Tanner in London, briefly works at department store; 1956-57—works at British Film Institute, makes documentary *Nice Time* with Alain Tanner; 1958—returns to Switzerland, begins TV directing; 1958-61—makes 3 TV documentaries; 1961-66—makes 25 "reportages" for monthly series "Continents sans visa"; 1961-present—directs numerous plays adapted for TV; 1968—forms production company "Groupe de 5": Goretta, Tanner, Jean-Louis Roy, Claude Soutter, and Yves Yersin; 1970—makes first feature *Le Fou*. Recipient: Ecumenical Prize, Cannes Festival, for *The Lacemaker*, 1977.

Films (as director and scriptwriter): 1957—*Nice Time* (co-d, co-sc); 1961—*Le Retour* (short—for TV); 1963—*Un Dimanche de mai* (co-sc—for TV); *La Miss à Raoul* (short—for TV); 1965—*Tchékhov ou Le Miroir des vies perdues* (for TV); *Jean-Luc persecuté* (co-sc—for TV); 1968—*Vivre ici* (for TV); 1970—*Le Fou (The Madman)* (+co-pr); *Le Jour des noces (The Wedding Day)* (co-sc—for TV); 1971—*Le Temps d'un portrait* (co-sc—for TV); 1973—*L'Invitation (The Invitation)* (co-sc); 1975—*Pas si méchant que ça (Not as Wicked as That, The Wonderful Crook)* (co-sc); 1975—*Passion et mort de Michel Servet* (d only—for TV); 1977—*La Dentellière (The Lacemaker)* (co-sc); *Jean Piaget (The Epistemology of Jean Piaget)*; 1978—*Les Chemins de l'exil ou Les Dernières Années de Jean-Jacques Rousseau* (co-sc—for TV); 1980—*La Provinciale*; 1983—*The Death of Mario Ricci*.

Publications:

By GORETTA:

Book—*Goretta, Claude: La Dentellière*, Paris 1981; articles—"Goretta au travail", interview in *Jeune cinéma* (Paris), September/October 1973; "L'Invitation", interview by G. Braucourt in *Ecran* (Paris), May 1973; interview by G. Langlois in *Cinéma* (Paris), April 1973; interview by D. Gain in *Image et son* (Paris), January 1974; "Claude Goretta Opus 3", interview by M. Boujut in *Cinema* (Zurich), vol.21, no.1, 1975; interview by D. Maillet in *Cinématographe* (Paris), June 1977; "Trotz allem hoffe ich", interview by J.-P. Brossard in *Film und Fernsehen* (Berlin), October 1978; "Claude Goretta and Isabelle Huppert", interview by Judith Kass in *Movietone News* (Seattle), 14 August 1978.

On GORETTA:

Articles—"Tanner, Goretta, la Suisse et nous" by J. Delmas in *Jeune cinéma* (Paris), September/October 1973; "Claude Goretta" in *Cinema* (Zurich), v.20, no.1, 1974; "Vier Temperamente" by M. Schaub in *Cinema* (Zurich), v.20, no.1, 1974; "Goretta's *Roads of Exile*" by Tom Milne in *Sight and Sound* (London), no.2, 1979; "Claude Goretta", with biofilmography, by Tom Milne in *Film Dope* (London), April 1980; "La Dentellière", special issue of *Avant-Scène du cinéma* (Paris), 15 April 1981.

* * *

Claude Goretta's gentle comedies and sensitive depictions of provincial naifs have been among the most successful Swiss films of recent years. Although Goretta shares his countryman Alain Tanner's preoccupation with Renoiresque evocations of landscape and lovable eccentrics, there is a sharp disparity between these two idiosyncratic Swiss directors. As Goretta himself has observed, "Tanner's film's always have a discourse, while mine do everything they can to avoid one."

Goretta's first film, an experimental short called *Nice Time*, was in fact made with the collaboration of Alain Tanner when both men were affiliated with the British Film Institute. This impressionistic view of Piccadilly Circus, one of the sleazier venues in central London, prefigures both directors' subsequent interest in whimsical vignettes with serious, and occasionally acerbic, sociological underpinnings. Like many contemporary directors of note, Goretta served his apprenticeship in television. Many of his early television films were literary adaptations. His adaptation of four Chekhov stories, *Chekov ou le miroir des vies perdues*, is reportedly one of the most intriguing of these projects.

Goretta's first feature film, *Le Fou*, featured one of his favorite actors, the distinguished character player, François Simon. Despite a mixed critical reception, *Le Fou* was awarded a prize as the best Swiss film of 1970 by the Swiss Critics' Association. *L'Invitation* was the first of Goretta's films to receive widespread international recognition. This unpretentious comedy about the loss of inhibitions experienced by a group of office workers during a mildly uproarious party was ecstatically reviewed by British and American critics who casually invoked the names of both Buñuel and Renoir for the sake of comparison. *Pas si mechant que ça* fared less well with both the critics and public, although Gerard Depardieu's charming portrayal of a whimsical thief was widely praised.

Le Dentelliére, an incisive character study of a guileless young beautician played flawlessly by Isabelle Huppert (in her first major role), received an even more rhapsodic critical reception than *L'Invitation*. Jean Boffety's pristine cinematography and Goretta's restrained direction were singled out for praise, although several feminist critics cogently observed that Goretta's reverence for the Huppert character's enigmatic passivity was a singularly insidious example of male condescension.

Les Chemins de l'exil marked Goretta's return to his roots in documentary filmmaking. This leisurely biographical portrait of Jean Jacques Rousseau stars François Simon as the famed *philosophe* who remains one of the most celebrated figures in Swiss cultural history. *La Provincale* was a somewhat muddled attempt to reiterate many of the themes first explored in *La Dentelliére*, although Nathalie Baye's performance was suffused with integrity. *The Death of Mario Ricci*, Goretta's most recent film, was favorably received at the 1983 Cannes film festival.

—Richard Porton

GOSHO, HEINOSUKE. Japanese. Born in Tokyo, 1 February

1902. Educated at Keio Commerce School, graduated 1921. Married actress Emiko Kasuga, 1927 (separated; she died in 1931); teacher in Nagauta, 1934 (divorced 1943); daughter of clothing store owner, 1944. Career: 1923—enters Shochiku-Kamata studio, sponsored by Yasujiro Shimazu; works as assistant to Shimazu; fired by studio director, rehired 1924; 1925—directs first film; this and next 4 films poorly received, last one not released; 1926—*She* is first film to attract positive attention; 1928—after *The Village Bride* career goes into slump until making Japan's first talking picture *Next Door Madame and My Wife*, 1931; 1941—leaves Shochiku-Ofuna for Daiei studio; 1945—returns to Shochiku-Ofuna; then to Toho until 1948; 1951—establishes "Studio 8 Productions," affiliated with Shin-Toho; from 1954—works for Shin-Toho, Nikkatsu, Kabuki-za Film, Shochiku-Kyoto, Shochiku-Ofuna, and other studios; also writes for TV; 1964-75—President of the Japanese Association of Film Directors; also Director of the Japanese Haiku Art Association. Died 1 May 1981. Recipient: 11 films placed among Kinema Jumpo Best Films of the Year between 1927 and 1968; Shiju Ho sho Order of the Japanese Government, 1941; Mainichi Film Prize, Japan, for *One More Time*, 1947; Kun Yon-to Asahi Shoju sho Order of the Japanese Government, 1947; International Peace Prize, Berlin Festival, for *Where Chimneys Are Seen*, 1953.

Films (as director): 1925—*Nanto no haru (Spring of Southern Island, Spring in Southern Islands)* (+sc); *Sora wa haretari (The Sky Shines, No Clouds in the Sky, The Sky Is Clear)*; *Otoko-gokoro (Man's Heart)* (+sc); *Seishun (Youth)* (+sc); *Tosei tamatebako (Contemporary Jewelry Box, A Casket for Living)*; 1926—*Machi no hitobito (People in the Town, Town People)*; *Hatsukoi (First Love)* (+sc); *Hahayo koishi (Mother, I Miss You, Mother's Love)*; *Honryu (A Torrent, A Rapid Stream)*; *Musume (A Daughter)* (+sc); *Kaeranu sasabue (Bamboo Leaf Flute of No Return, No Return)*; *Itoshi no wagako (My Loving Child, My Beloved Child)* (+sc); *Kanojo (She, Girl Friend)* (+sc); 1927—*Sabishiki ranbomono (Lonely Hoodlum, The Lonely Roughneck)*; *Hazukashii yume (Shameful Dream, Intimate Dream)*; *Karakuri musume (Fake Girl, Tricky Girl)* (+sc); *Shojo no shi (Death of a Virgin, Death of a Maiden)* (+co-sc); *Okame (A Plain Woman, Moon-faced)* (+sc); *Tokyo koshinkyoko (Tokyo March)*; 1928—*Sukinareba koso (Because I Love, If You Like It)* (+co-sc); *Mura no hanayome (The Village Bride)*; *Doraku shinan (Guidance to the Indulgent, Debauchery Is Wrong)* (+co-sc); *Kami e no michi (The Way to the God, Road to God)*; *Hito no yo no sugata (The Situation of the Human World, Man's Worldly Appearance)*; *Kaido no kishi (Knight of the Street)*; *Haha yo, kimi no na o kegasu nakare (Mother, Do Not Shame Your Name)*; 1929—*Yoru no mesuneko (Cat of the Night)*; *Shin josei kagami (New Woman's Guidance, A New Kind of Woman)*; *Oyaji to sono ko (Father and His Child, Father and His Son)*; *Ukiyo-buro (Bath of the Transitory World, The Bath Harem)* (+sc); *Netsujo no ichiya (A Night of Passion, One Night of Passion)* (+co-sc); 1930—*Dokushinsha goyojin (Bachelors Beware)* (+co-sc); *Dai-Tokyo bi ikkaku (A Corner of Great Tokyo)* (+add'l dialogue); *Hohoemu jinsei (A Smiling Life)*; *Onna yo, kini no na o kegasu nakare (Women, Do Not Shame Your Names, Woman, Don't Make Your Name Dirty)*; *Shojo nyuyo (We Need Virgins, Virgin Wanted)*; *Kinuyo monogatari (The Kinuyo Story, Story of Kinuyo)*; *Aiyoku no ki (Record of Love and Desire, Desire of Night)*; 1931—*Jokyu aishi (Sad Story of a Barmaid)*; *Yoru hiraku (Blooming at Night, Open at Night)*; *Madamu to nyobo (Next Door Madame and My Wife, The Neighbor's Wife and Mine, Madame and Wife)*; *Shima to ratai jiken (Naked Murder Case of the Island, Island of Naked Scandal)* (+add'l dialogue); *Gutei kenkei (Stupid Young Brother and Wise Old Brother, Silly Younger Brother and Clever Elder Brother)* (+add'l dialogue); *Wakaki hi no kangeki (Excitement of a Young Day, Memories of Young Days)*; 1932—*Niisan no baka (You Are Stupid, My Brother, My Stupid Brother)*; *Ginza no yanagi (Willows of Ginza, A Willow Tree in the Ginza)*; *Tengoku ni musubu koi (Heaven Linked with Love)*; *Satsueijo romansu: Renai annai (Romance at the Studio: Guidance to Love, A Studio Romance)*; *Hototogisu (A Cuckoo)*; *Koi no Tokyo (Love in Tokyo)*; 1933—*Hanayome no negoto (Sleeping Words of the Bride, The Bride Talks in Her Sleep)*; *Izu no odoriko (Dancer of Izu, Dancing Girls of Izu)*; *Jukyu-sai no haru (Spring of a 19-year-old, The 19th Spring)*; *Shojo yo sayonara (Virgin, Goodbye, Goodbye My Girl)*; *Lamuru (L'Amour)*; 1934—*Onna to umaretakaranya (Now That I Was Born a Woman)*; *Sakura Ondo (Sakura Dance, Cherry Blossom Chorus)*; *Ikitoshi Ikerumono (The Living, Everything That Lives)*; 1935—*Hanamuko no negoto (Sleeping Words of the Bridegroom, The Bridegroom Talks in His Sleep)*; *Hidari uchiwa (Good Financial Situation, Left-handed Fan, A Life of Luxury)*; *Fukeyo koikaze (Blow, Love Wind, Breezes of Love)*; *Akogare (Longing, Yearning)*; *Jinsei no onimotsu (Burden of Life)*; 1936—*Oboroyo no onna (A Woman of a Misty Moonlight, Woman of Pale Night)*; *Shindo (New Way)* parts I and II; *Okusama shakuyosho (A Married Lady Borrows Money)*; 1937—*Hanakago no uta (Song of the Flower Basket)* (+adapt); 1940—*Mokuseki (Wood and Stone, Wooden Head)*; 1942—*Shinsetsu (New Snow)*; 1944—*Goju-no to (The Pagoda, The 5-storied Pagoda)*; 1945—*Izu no musume-tachi (Girls of Izu)*; 1947—*Ima hitotabi no (One More Time, Once More)*; 1948—*Omokage (A Vestige, Image)*; 1951—*Wa-kare-gumo (Spreading Cloud, Dispersing Clouds, Drifting Clouds)* (+co-sc); 1952—*Asa no hamon (Trouble in the Morning, Morning Conflicts)*; 1953—*Entotsu no mieru basho (4 Chimneys, Where Chimneys Are Seen)*; 1954—*Osaka no yado (Inn of Osaka, An Inn at Osaka, Hotel at Osaka)* (+co-sc); *Niwatori wa futatabi naku (A Hen Will Squawk Again, The Cock Crows Twice)*; *Ai to shi no tanima (The Valley Between Love and Death)*; 1955—*Takekurabe (Comparison of Heights, Growing Up, Daughters of Yoshiwara)*; 1956—*Aruyo futatabi (Again One Night, Twice on a Certain Night)* (+co-sc); 1957—*Kiiroi karasu (Yellow Crow, Behold Thy Son)*; *Banka (An Elegy, Elegy of the North)*; 1958—*Hotaru-bi (Firefly's Light, Firefly Light)*; *Yoku (Desire, Avarice)*; *Ari no Machi no Maria (Maria of the Street of Ants, Maria of the Ant Village)*; 1959—*Karatachi nikki (The Trifoliate Orange Diary, Journal of the Orange Flower)*; 1960—*Waga ai (My Love, When a Woman Loves)*; *Shiroi kiba (White Fang, White Fangs)*; 1961—*Ryoju (Hunting Rifle)*; *Kumo ga chigireru toki (As the Clouds Scatter)* (+co-pr); *Aijo no keifu (Record of Love, Love's Family Tree)* (+co-pr); 1962—*Kachan kekkon shiroyo (Mother, Get Married, Get Married Mother)* (+co-sc); 1963—*Hyakumanin no musumetachi (A Million Girls)* (+co-sc); 1964—*Osore-zan no onna (A Woman of the Osore Mountains, An Innocent Witch)*; 1966—*Kachan to Juichi-nin no Kodomo (Mother and 11 Children, Our Wonderful Years)*; 1967—*Utage (Feast, Rebellion in Japan)*; 1968—*Onna no misoshiru (Women and Miso Soup, Woman and Bean Soup)*; *Meiji haruaki (Seasons of Meiji, A Girl of the Meiji Period)*.

Publications:

On GOSHO:

Books—*The Japanese Film* by Joseph Anderson and Donald Richie, New York 1961; *The Waves at Genji's Door* by Joan

Mellen, New York 1976; articles—"The Films of Heinosuke Gosho" by J.L. Anderson and Donald Richie in *Sight and Sound* (London), autumn 1956; "Coca-Cola and the Golden Pavilion" by John Gillett in *Sight and Sound* (London), summer 1970; "Heinosuke Gosho", with biofilmography, by John Gillett in *Film Dope* (London), April 1980; "Heinosuke Gosho" by Max Tessier in *Image et son* (Paris), June 1981.

*   *   *

At the beginning of his career in 1925 as a disciple of Yasujiro Shimazu at Shochiku Studio, Gosho proved his skill at the genre of "shomin-geki," stories of the life of ordinary people, characteristic of his mentor's work at that studio. Gosho's early films were criticized as "unsound" because they often involved characters physically or mentally handicapped (e.g. *The Village Bride* and *Faked Daughter*. Gosho's intention, however, was to illustrate a kind of warm and sincere relationship born in pathos. Today, these films are estimated highly for their critique of feudalistic village life. Gosho was affected by this early criticism, however, and made his next films about other subjects. This led him into a long creative slump, although he continued to make five to seven films annually.

His first film to attract attention was *Lonely Hoodlum* of 1927, his 14th film, which is a depiction of the bittersweet life of common people, Gosho's characteristic subject. In 1931, Shochiku gave him the challenge of making the first Japanese "talkie" (because many established directors had refused). The film, *Next Door Madame and My Wife*, was welcomed passionately by both audiences and critics. It is a light and clever comedy, using ambient sounds such as a baby's cries, an alarm clock, a street vendor's voice, and jazz music from next door. Because every sound had to be sychronized, Gosho explored many technical devices, and also used multiple cameras, different lenses, and frequent cuts to produce a truly "filmic" result.

Gosho preferred many cuts and close-up shots and he related it to his studying Lubitsch carefully in his youth. Gosho's technique of creating a poetic atmosphere with editing is most successful in *Dancer of Izu*, in which he intentionally chose the silent film form after making several successful talkies.

Even after the success of these films, Gosho had to accept many projects which he did not want to do. He later reflected that only those films that he really wanted to do were well-made. For example, he found the subject of *The Living* most appealing—its protagonist tries to protest against social unjustice but is unable to continue his struggle to the end.

Gosho is believed to be best at depicting the human side of the life in his native Tokyo (e.g. *Woman of Pale Night*, *Song of the Flower Basket*, *Where Chimneys Are Seen*, and *Comparison of Heights*). However, the director also worked in many other genres, including romantic melodrama, family drama, light comedy, and social drama. He further extended his range in such films *An Elegy*, a contemporary love story, and *A Woman of Osore-zan*, which is unusual for its unfamiliar dark tones and its eccentricity. His experimental spirit is illustrated by his story of the treatment of a disturbed child with color-oriented visual therapy in *Yellow Crow*.

Throughout his career, Gosho expressed his basic belief in humanistic values. The warm, subtle, and sentimental depiction of likable people is characteristic both of Gosho's major studio productions and his own independent films.

—Kyoko Hirano

GOULDING, EDMUND. British. Born in London, 20 March 1891. Career: 1903—stage debut in London; 1903-14—performs, writes, and directs stage plays in London; 1915—New York stage debut; 1915-18—serves with British Army in France; 1919—returns to U.S., begins screenwriting; also writes novel *Fury* (wrote film adaptation 1923), and successful play *Dancing Mothers* (1924); 1925—hired by MGM as director-scriptwriter; 1945—writes, directs and produces stage play *The Ryan Girl*. Died in Los Angeles, 24 December 1959.

Films (as scriptwriter): 1916—*Quest of Life* (co-play basis); 1917—*The Silent Partner* (Neilan) (story); 1918—*The Ordeal of Rosetta* (Chautard) (story); 1919—*The Perfect Love* (Ralph Ince); *The Glorious Lady* (Irving) (story); *A Regular Girl* (Young) (co-story); *Sealed Hearts* (Ralph Ince) (co-story); *The Imp* (Ellis) (co-story); 1920—*A Daughter of 2 Worlds* (Young); *The Sin That Was His* (Henley); *The Dangerous Paradise* (Earle) (story); *The Devil* (Young); 1921—*Dangerous Toys (Don't Leave Your Husband)* (Bradley) (story); *The Man of Stone* (Archainbaud) (co-story); *Tol'able David* (King) (co-sc); *Peacock Alley* (Leonard); 1922—*The 7th Day* (King); *Fascination* (Leonard); *Broadway Rose* (Leonard); *Till We Meet Again* (Cabanne); *Heroes of the Street* (Beaudine) (co-sc); *Fury* (King) (d erroneously attributed to Goulding in Library of Congress Copyright Catalogue); 1923—*Dark Secrets* (Fleming); *Jazzmania* (Leonard); *The Bright Shawl* (Robertson); *Bright Lights of Broadway (Bright Lights and Shadows)* (Campbell); *Tiger Rose* (Franklin) (co-sc); 1924—*Dante's Inferno* (Otto); *The Man Who Came Back* (Flynn); *Gerald Cranston's Lady* (Flynn); 1925—*The Dancers* (Flynn); *The Scarlet Honeymoon* (Hale) (story—some sources credit story to Fannie Davis); *The Fool* (Millarde); *Havoc* (Lee); *The Beautiful City* (Webb) (story); (as director and scenarist): 1925—*Sun-up*; *Sally, Irene and Mary*; 1926—*Paris (Shadows of Paris)*; *Dancing Mothers* (Brenon) (co-play basis only); 1927—*Women Love Diamonds* (story); *Love (Anna Karenina)* (adapt, uncredited, +pr); 1928—*Happiness Ahead* (Seiter) (story only); *A Lady of Chance* (Leonard) (adapt only); 1929—*The Broadway Melody* (Beaumont) (story only); 1930—"Dream Girl" episode of *Paramount on Parade* (d only, +ro); *The Devil's Holiday* (+music, song) (foreign language versions: *Les Vacances du diable* (Cavalcanti); *La vacanza del diavolo* (Salvatori); *La fiesta del diablo* (Millar); *Sonntag des Lebens* (Mittler); *En kvinnas morgondag* (Bergman)); *The Grand Parade* (Newmeyer) (sc only, +pr, songs); 1931—*Reaching for the Moon*; *The Night Angel* (+song melodies); (as director): 1932—*Grand Hotel*; *Blondie of the Follies* (+co-lyrics, bit ro as Follies director); *Flesh* (Ford) (story only); *No Man of Her Own* (Ruggles) (co-story only); 1934—*Riptide*; *Hollywood Party* (co-d, uncredited); 1935—*The Flame Within* (+sc); 1937—*That Certain Woman* (+sc); 1938—*White Banners*; *The Dawn Patrol*; 1939—*Dark Victory* (+song); *The Old Maid*; *We Are Not Alone*; 1940—*'Til We Meet Again*; *2 Girls on Broadway (Choose Your Partner)* (Simon) (remake of *The Broadway Melody*, 1929); 1941—*The Great Lie*; 1943—one episode of *Forever and a Day*; *The Constant Nymph*; *Claudia*; 1944—*Flight from Folly* (Mason) (story basis only); 1946—*Of Human Bondage*; *The Razor's Edge*; *The Shocking Miss Pilgrim* (Seaton) (d several scenes while Seaton ill); 1947—*Nightmare Alley*; 1949—*Everybody Does It*; 1950—*Mr. 880*; 1952—*Down Among the Sheltering Palms*; *We're Not Married*; 1956—*Teenage Rebel* (+music for song *Dodie*); 1958—*Mardi Gras*.

Roles: 1911—*Henry VIII* (Parker); 1914—*The Life of a London Shopgirl* (Raymond); 1922—*3 Little Ghosts* (Fitzmaurice).

Publications:

By GOULDING:

Book—*Fury*, 1922; article—"*The Razor's Edge*" in *Life* (New York), 12 August 1946.

On GOULDING:

Articles—in *Movies and People*, no.2, 1940; article in *Time* (New York), 19 May 1947; obituary in *The New York Times*, 25 December 1959; "Likable But Elusive" by Andrew Sarris in *Film Culture* (New York), spring 1963; "Why I Will Never Write My Memoirs" by Louise Brooks in *Film Culture* (New York), no.67-69, 1979; "Edmund Goulding", with biofilmography, by Michael Walker in *Film Dope* (London), April 1980.

*   *   *

Our sense of Edmund Goulding is, of course, skewed by his frequently revived *Grand Hotel* and *Dark Victory*. These films are viewed today not as examples of the director's art, but rather as star acting vehicles, the second also being seen as a prototypical "woman's film." It is generally assumed that such films were primarily authored by the studio and the stars. Yet, without suggesting that Goulding had a visual signature as distinctive as von Sternberg's or a thematic/ideological one as coherent as Capra's, we must recognize the director's personality in the care of the stagings and in the vitality of the performances complemented by those stagings.

Grand Hotel seems, at first, a product of MGM's collective enterprise rather than Goulding's particular imagination. The sleekness of the writing, photography and art direction are exemplary of the studio that defined cinematic luxury. The assembly of stars—Garbo, Crawford, Beery, John and Lionel Barrymore—in a "hotel" as grand as the studio itself would seem sufficient *direction* of the film. Yet we must give Goulding credit for the exceptionally involved choreography of faces, voices, and bodies in *Grand Hotel* when we look at the same stars in other movies of the period. The film's numerous two-shots are organized with a nuance that makes us as attentive to the shifting relationships between those starry faces as we are to the faces themselves. And we need only see Garbo as directed by Clarence Brown or George Fitzmaurice to appreciate the contribution of Edmund Goulding. He is exceptionally sensitive to the time it takes the actress to register thought through her mere act of presence.

That sensitivity is not diminished when Goulding directs Bette Davis, whose rhythm is totally dissimilar to Garbo's. In *Dark Victory* and *The Old Maid* the director presides over shots that permit us to perceive star and character simultaneously, a requisite of successful screen star performance. Goulding's strength is in characterization, in creating the kind of atmosphere in which actors explore the richest areas within themselves, and in creating the visual/aural contexts that put such exploration in relief for the viewer. This is certainly the case in *The Constant Nymph*. Its precious narrative conceit—a soulful adolescent girl (Joan Fontaine) inspires an excessively cerebral composer (Charles Boyer) to write music with emotion—both reflects the emotional qualities of Goulding's films and displays the actors at their most courageous.

For Goulding, the mature Joan Fontaine is able to sustain her impersonation of an impulsive, loving girl for the whole length of a film. And in *Nighmare Alley*, Tyrone Power is pushed to expose his own persona in the most unflattering light—the "handsome leading man" as charlatan. But that exposure, one of many in the films of Goulding, is also evidence of his affinity for the dilemma of performing artist, vulnerable in the magnifying exposures of the cinematic medium and dependent on the director's empathy if that vulnerability is to become a meaningful cinematic sign.

—Charles Affron

GRÉMILLON, JEAN. French. Born in Bayeux, Normandy, 3 October 1901. Educated at l'école communale de Saint-Lô, Lycée de Brest, and Ecole des Cordeliers, Dinan; Schola Cantorum, Paris (studied with Vincent d'Indy), 1920. Married Christiane (Grémillon). Career: 1920-22—military service; 1923—works as film titler, becomes interested in editing; 1923-25—makes short films; 1935-38—works in Spain and Germany; 1939—mobilized for war as cinematographer; 1944—elected president of Cinématheque Française; 1946-50—President of C.G.T. film technicians union; 1947—works on *Le Printemps de la liberté* (unrealized), subsequently adapted for radio; 1948—replaces Jean Anouilh on *Pattes blanches*; 1953—makes *L'Amour d'une femme*, last feature-length film. Died 25 November 1959.

Films (as director and editor): 1923—*Chartres (Le Cathédrale de Chartres)*; *Le Revêtement des routes*; 1924—*La Fabrication du fil*; *Du fil à l'aiguille*; *La Fabrication du ciment artificiel*; *La Bière*; *Le Roulement à billes*; *Les Parfums*; *L'Étirage des ampoules électriques*; *La Photogenie mécanique*; 1925—*L'Éducation professionelle des conducteurs de tramway* (6 short films); *L'Électrification de la ligne Paris-Vierzon*; *L'Auvergne*; *La Naissance des cigognes*; *Les Aciéries de la marine et d'Homécourt*; 1926—*La Vie des travailleurs italiens en France*; *La Croisière de L'Atalante*; *Un Tour au large* (+sc, music—recorded on piano rolls); 1927—*Maldone* (+co-music); *Gratuités*; 1928—*Bobs*; 1929—*Gardiens de phare*; 1930—*La Petite Lise*; 1931—*Dainah la métisse* (disowned due to unauthorized reediting); *Pour un sou d'amour* (no d credit on film); 1932—*Le Petit Babouin* (+mu); (as director): 1933—*Gonzague ou L'Accordeur* (+sc); 1934—*La Dolorosa*; 1935—*La Valse royale* (French version of Herbert Maisch's *Königswalzer*); 1936—*Centinella alerta!* (not completed by Grémillon); *Pattes de mouches* (+co-sc); 1937—*Gueule d'amour*; 1938—*L'Étrange Monsieur Victor*; 1941—*Remorques*; 1943—*Lumière d'été*; 1944—*Le Ciel est à vous*; 1945—*Le Six Juin à l'aube (Sixth of June at Dawn)* (+sc, mu); 1949—*Pattes blanches* (+co-dialogue); *Les Charmes de l'existence* (co-d, +co-sc, co-commentary, mu advisor); 1951—*L'Étrange Madame X*; *Desastres de la guerre* (Kast) (commentary and co-mu only); 1952—*Astrologie ou Le Miroir de la vie* (+sc, co-mu); "Alchimie" épisode de *L'Encyclopédie filmée—Alchimie, Azur, Absence* (+sc); 1954—*L'Amour d'une femme* (+sc, dubbed actor Paolo Stoppa); *Au cœur de l'Ile de France* (+sc, co-mu); 1955—*La Maison aux images* (+sc, mu); 1956—*Haute Lisse* (+sc, mu adapt); 1958—*André Masson et les quatre éléments* (+sc, mu).

Publications:

By GRÉMILLON:

Books—*Hommage à Jacques Feyder*, Paris 1948; *Le Printemps de la Liberté*, with introduction and notes by Pierre Kast, Paris

1948; articles—"Propositions" in *Comoedia* (Paris), 27 November 1925; "Le Cinquantenaire du Cinéma" in *Plaquette du cinquantenaire*, Paris 1946; "Le Cinema? Plus qu'un art..." in *L'Ecran français* (Paris), August 1947; "Jacques Feyder, ce combattant" in *L'Ecran français* (Paris), 8 June 1948; "Remarques sur l'Exercice de la Création du Cinéma" in *Combat* (Paris), February 1949; article in *La Réalité des faits*, Brussels 1949; "La Malédiction du style" in *Le Film maudit*, Biarritz 1949; "Cinéma et documents" in *Ciné-Club* (Paris), January/February 1951; "*Le Massacre des Innocents*", script excerpt, in *Ciné-Club* (Paris), January/February 1951; "Aller au cœur des choses" in *L'Ecran français* (Paris), 9 May 1951; "Grémillon? Il est unique", interview by José Zendel, in *Ciné-Club* (Paris), January/February 1951; "Conférences sur Flaherty" in *Cinéma 56* (Paris), no.9-10, 1956; "Ma rencontre avec André Masson" in *Les Lettres françaises* (Paris), 24 November 1960; "Comprendre et Faire voir" in *Labyrinthe* (Paris), no.12, n.d.

On GRÉMILLON:

Books—*Jean Grémillon*, *Premier Plan* no.5, Paris 1960; *Jean Grémillon* by Henri Agel in *Cinéma d'aujourd'hui* no.58, Paris 1969; articles—"Jean Grémillon" by Hazel Hackett in *Sight and Sound* (London), summer 1947; "Exercice d'un tragique quotidien..." by Pierre Kast in *Revue du cinéma* (Paris), August 1948; "Grémillon ou le tragique moderne" by Henri Agel in *Ciné-Club* (Paris), January/February 1951; "Jean Grémillon travaille au scalpel" by A.G. Brunelin in *Ciné-Club* (Paris), January/February 1951; "Le nez de Cléopatre est dans le champ" by Pierre Kast in *Ciné-Club* (Paris), January/February 1951; "Jean Grémillon face à la réalité" by Jacques Krier in *l'Ecran français* (Paris), 9 May 1951; "Sur Jean Grémillon" by F. Laurent in *Image et Son* (Paris), February 1955; "C'est auprès de lui que j'ai appris le cinéma" by Louis Daquin in *L'Humanité* (Paris), 27 November 1959; "Jean Grémillon et les images témoins" by Michèle Firk in *Les Lettres françaises* (Paris), 11 June 1959; "Jean Grémillon, grand réalisateur français" by Samuel Lachize in *L'Humanité* (Paris), 27 November 1959; "Jean Grémillon, les chefs-d'œuvre perdus" by Henri Langlois in *Le Lettres françaises* (Paris), 3 December 1959; "Jean Grémillon...ou la rigueur" by Georges Sadoul in *Les Lettres françaises* (Paris), 3 December 1959; "Jean..." by Charles Spaak in *Les Lettres françaises* (Paris), 3 Decmeber 1959; "Jean Grémillon" by Henri Agel in *Les Grands Créateurs du cinéma* no.18, Paris 1960; "Jean Grémillon, cinéaste tendre et discret" by Guy Allombert in *Image et son* (Paris), January 1960; "Jean Grémillon fut un cinéaste maudit" by Claude Beylie in *Radio-Cinéma-Television* (Paris), 10 July 1960; "Jean Grémillon" by Pierre Billard in *Cinéma 60* (Paris), January 1960; "Textes choisis de Jean Grémillon" by A.G. Brunelin in *Cinéma 60* (Paris), March 1960; "Dossier Jean Grémillon" by François Chevassu in *Image et son* (Paris), January 1960; "Jean Grémillon devant l'avenir" by René Clair in *Les Lettres françaises* (Paris), 24 November 1960; "Jean Grémillon devant l'avenir" by Maurice Druon in *Les Lettres fraçaises* (Paris), 24 November 1960; "Jean Grémillon" by Philippe Esnault in *Cinéma 60* (Paris), March 1960; "Jean Grémillon ou l'amour du risque" by Pierre Kast in *Cinéma 60* (Paris), March 1960; "Jean Grémillon cinéaste de la réalité" by Michel Mayoux in *Cahiers du cinéma* (Paris), February 1960; "Mémoire Idhec sur Jean Grémillon: l'Homme et la nature ou jalons sur la progression lyrique de Jean Grémillon" by Alain Jomy in *Etudes cinématographiques* (Paris), no.8-9, 1961; "Hommage à Jean Grémillon" by J.-P. Vivet in *Avant-scène du cinéma* (Paris), 15 September 1962; "Jean Grémillon" by Pierre Billard in *Anthologie du cinéma* vol.2, Paris 1967; "Portrait: Jean Grémillon" by Jacques Siclier in *Radio-Télé-Cinéma* (Paris), 24 November 1969; "Notes sur une rétrospective" by Philippe Haudiquet in *Image et son* (Paris), January 1970; "La nostalgie d'un très lointain pays" by Gabriel Vialle in *Image et son* (Paris), January 1970; article on Grémillon in *French Cinema Since 1946: Vol.1—The Great Tradition* by Roy Armes, New York 1970; "Jean Grémillon" in *Dossier du cinéma*, Paris 1971; "Jean Grémillon: le réalisme et le tragique" and "Le Cinéma de Jean Grémillon" by M. Latil Le Dantec in *Cinématographe* (Paris), no.40 and no.41, 1978; "David Overbey from Paris" in *Film Comment* (New York), September/October 1978; biofilmography in *Film Dope* (London), October 1980; "Hommage à Jean Grémillon", special section of *Cinéma* (Paris), November 1981; "Le Ciel est à vous", special issue of *Avant-Scène du cinéma* (Paris), 15 November 1981; "Retour sur Jean Grémillon" by J.-C. Guiguet and P. Vecchiali in *Cinéma* (Paris), December 1981.

* * *

Jean Grémillon is finally beginning to enjoy the reputation most French film scholars always bestowed upon him. Although Americans have until recently been able to see only one or two of his dozen important works, he has generally been placed only slightly below Renoir, Clair, and Carné in the hierarchy of French classical cinema.

Evidently no one was more versatile than Grémillon. A musician, he composed many of his own scores and supervised all aspects of his productions scrupulously. Along with the search for a romantic unity of feeling and consistency of rhythm, his films also display an attention to details and locations that derives from his earliest documentaries. No one was more prepared than Grémillon for the poetic realist sensibility that dominated French cinema in the 1930s. Even in the silent period his *Maldone* and *Gardiens de phare* reveal a heightening of strange objects as they take on fatal proportions in these tense and dark melodramas. *La Petite Lise* displayed these same qualities with an incredibly imaginative and rigorous use of sound. It should be called the first poetic realist film, anticipating Carné's work in particular. After a few years of obscurity, Grémillon reemerged with *Gueule d'amour*, a Foreign Legion love story with Jean Gabin. Then came a series of truly wonderful films: *L'Étrange M. Victor*, *Remorques*, *Le Ciel est à vous*, and *Lumière d'été*. Spanning the period of French subjugation by the Nazis, these films capture the sensibility of the times with their wistful romanticism, the fatality of their conclusions, and their attention to social classes.

Le Ciel est à vous must be singled out as a key film of the Occupation. Enormously popular, this tale of a small town couple obsessed with aviation has been variously interpreted as promoting Vichy morality (family, small-town virtues, hard work) and as representing the indomitable French spirit ready to soar beyond the temporary political restraints of the Occupation. Charles Vanel and Madeleine Renaud give unforgettable performances.

Grémillon often sought mythic locations (mysterious villages in the Alps or Normandy, the evocative southern cities of Orange and Toulon) where his quiet heroes and heroines played out their destinies of passion and crime. Unique is the prominent place women hold in his dramas. From the wealthy femme fatale murdered by Gabin in *Gueule d'amour* to the independent professional woman refusing to give up her medical career even for love (*L'Amour d'une femme*) women are shown to be far more prepossessed than the passionate but childish men who pursue them.

It is perhaps the greatest tragedy of French cinema that Gremillon's career after World War II was derailed by the conditions of the industry. His *Sixth of June at Dawn* shows how even a documentary project could in his hands take on poetic proportions and become a personal project. Yet the final years before his death in 1959 (when he was only 57) were spent in teaching and preparing unfinanced scripts. This is a sad end for the man some people claim to have been the most versatile cinematic genius ever to work in France.

—Dudley Andrew

GRIERSON, JOHN. Scottish. Born in Deanstown, Scotland, 18 April 1898. Educated Glasgow University, Scotland, degree in philosophy 1923. Married Margaret Taylor, 1930. Career: *ca.*1914-18—service in Navy; 1924—granted Rockefeller Research Fellowship in social science; 1924-27—travels to U.S. to study press, cinema, and other aspects of mass media; associated with University of Chicago during this time; 1927—joins Empire Marketing Board (EMB) Film Unit under Stephen Tallents, for research into government use of mass media; 1928-29—produces and directs *Drifters* for EMB; 1933—becomes head of General Post Office (GPO) Film Unit when EMB dissolved and former EMB film unit transferred to GPO; 1933-37—serves as producer for films made by GPO unit; 1937—resigns from GPO to form Film Centre with Arthur Elton, Stuart Legg, and J.P.R. Golightly; 1937-40—Film Advisor to Imperial Relations Trust, and to Canadian, Australian, and New Zealand Governments; 1939-45—Film Commissioner of Canada, guides legislation leading to establishment of National Film Board of Canada; produces series of films with Stuart Legg, *The World in Action*; 1947—Co-ordinator of Mass Media at UNESCO; 1948-50—Controller, Films Division of Central Office of Information, England; 1951-54—Joint Executive Producer of Group 3, an experimental group established by National Finance Company to produce feature films; 1954—becomes member of Films Of Scotland Committee; 1955—produces and presents television series for Scottish TV, *This Wonderful World*, which ran for 10 years. Died 19 February 1972. Recipient: Honorary Doctorate of Laws, 1948; Commander of the British Empire, 1961; Edinburgh Film Festival, Golden Thistle Award, 1968.

Films (as producer): 1929—*Drifters* (+d, sc); 1930—*Conquest* (+co-ed); 1931—*The Country Comes to Town*; *Shadow on the Mountain*; *Upstream*; 1931-32—*Industrial Britain* (+co-ed); 1932—*King Log*; *The New Generation*; *The New Operator*; *O'er Hill and Dale*; *The Voice of the World*; 1933—*Aero-Engine*; *Cargo from Jamaica*; *The Coming of the Dial*; *Eskimo Village*; *Line Cruising South*; *So This Is London*; *Telephone Workers*; *Uncharted Waters*; *Windmill in Barbados*; 1934—*BBC: Droit-wich*; *Granton Trawler* (+ph); *Pett and Pott*; *Post Haste*; *6:30 Collection*; *Song of Ceylon* (+co-sc); *Spring Comes to England* (co-pr); *Spring on the Farm*; *Weather Forecast*; 1935—*BBC: The Voice of Britain* (co-pr); *Coalface*; *Introducing the Dial*; 1936—*Night Mail* (+co-sc); *The Saving of Bill Blewett*; *Trade Tattoo*; 1937—*Calender of the Year*; *Children at School* (co-pr); *4 Barriers*; *Job in a Million*; *Line to Tschierva Hut*; *The Smoke Menace* (co-pr); *We Live in 2 Worlds*; 1938—*The Face of Scotland*; 1939—*The Londoners* (co-pr); (as executive producer): 1951—*Judgment Deferred*; *Brandy for the Parson*; 1952—*The Brave Don't Cry*; *Laxdale Hall*; *The Oracle*; *Time Gentlemen Please*; *You're Only Young Twice*; 1953—*Man of Africa*; *Orders are Orders*; (treatments by Grierson): 1959—*Seawards the Great Ships*; 1961-62—*Heart of Scotland*.

Publications:

By GRIERSON:

Book—*Grierson on Documentary* edited by Forsyth Hardy, revised edition London 1966; articles—in *Cinema Quarterly* (London), Winter 1932; "Future for British Film" in *Specatator* (London), 14 May 1932; "The Symphonic Film I" in *Cinema Quarterly* (London), spring 1933; article on the EMB Film Unit in *Cinema Quarterly* (London), summer 1933; "The Symphonic Film II" in *Cinema Quarterly* (London), spring 1934; article in *Sight and Sound* (London), autumn 1934; "100% Cinema" in *Spectator* (London), 23 August 1935; "Dramatising Housing Needs and City Planning" in *Films* (London), November 1939; article in *Theatre Arts* (New York), December 1946; "Post-War Patterns" in *Hollywood Quarterly*, January 1946; "Notes on the Tasks of an International Film Institute" in *Hollywood Quarterly*, January 1947; "Prospect for Documentary" in *Sight and Sound* (London), summer 1948; "Flaherty as Innovator" in *Sight and Sound* (London), October/December 1951; "The Front Page" in *Sight and Sound* (London), April/June 1952; "Making of *Man of Africa*" in *Films and Filming* (London), October 1954; "The BBC and All That" in *Quarterly of Film, Radio, Television* (Berkeley), fall 1954; "The Prospect for Cultural Cinema" in *Film* (London), January/February 1956; "I Derive My Authority from Moses" in *Take One* (Montreal), January/February 1970; "Grierson on Documentary: Last Interview" by Elizabeth Sussex in *Film Quarterly* (Berkeley), fall 1972; "The Golden Years of Grierson", interview by Elizabeth Sussex in *Sight and Sound* (London), summer 1972; "The Last Word" in *Films and Filming* (London), December 1973.

On GRIERSON:

Books—*Rotha on Film* by Paul Rotha, London 1958; *Documentary Film* by Paul Rotha, 4th edition London 1964; *Studies in Documentary* by Alan Lovell and Jim Hillier, New York 1972; *The Rise and Fall of British Documentary: The Story of the Film Movement Founded by John Grierson* by Elizabeth Sussez, Berkeley, California 1975; *John Grierson—Film Master* compiled by J.A. Beveridge, New York 1978; *John Grierson: A Documentary Biography* by Forsyth Hardy, London 1979; articles—"Mickey's Rival" by Hay Chowl in *Close-Up* (London), no.6, 1930; "Story of Grierson" in *Time* (New York), 16 December 1946; "Who Wants True?" by Gavin Lambert in *Sight and Sound* (London), April/June 1952; "The Young Grierson in America" by Jack C. Ellis in *Cinema Journal* (Evanston, Illinois), fall 1968; "John Grierson's 1st Years at the National Film Board" by Jack C. Ellis in *Cinema Journal* (Evanston, Illinois), fall 1970; "The Golden Years of Grierson" by Elizabeth Sussex in *Sight and Sound* (London), summer 1972; "John Grierson" by Elizabeth Sussex in *Sight and Sound* (London), spring 1972; obituary in *The New York Times Biography Edition*, 21 February 1972; "Grierson's Hammer" in *Films and Filming* (London), July 1972; "Le Rêve de Grierson" by R. James in *Cinéma Québec* (Montreal), May 1972; "The Unknown Cinema of Britain" by A. Lovell in *Cinema Journal* (Evanston), spring 1972; "Grierson at University" by Jack Ellis in *Cinema Journal* (Evanston), spring 1973; "There's More to the Film Board Than Meets the Eyes" by R. Blumer in *Cinema Canada* (Montreal), August/September 1974; "The Rise and Fall of the British Documentary" by T. Dickinson in *Film Comment* (New York), January/February 1977; "The Canadian Wartime Documentary" by W. Goetz in *Cinema Journal* (Evanston), spring 1977; "Subsidy for the Screen: Grierson and Group 3/1951-55" by R.D. MacCann in *Sight and Sound* (London), summer 1977; "The Canadian Connection: John Grierson" by D. Herrick in *Cinema Canada* (Montreal), September/October 1978; "The Grierson Files" by K. Cox and "The Politics of Propaganda" by G. Evans in *Cinema Canada* (Montreal), June/July 1979; exhaustive biofilmography, with appendices on principal collaborators, in *Film Dope* (London), October 1980.

* * *

More than any one other person, Grierson was responsible for the documentary film as it has developed in the English-speaking countries. He was the first to use the word *documentary* in relation to film, applying it to Robert Flaherty's *Moana* while Grierson was in the United States in the 1920s.

He took the term and his evolving conception of a new kind and use of film back to Britain with him in 1927. There he was hired by Stephen Tallents, Secretary of the Empire Marketing Board, a unique government public relations agency intended to promote the marketing of the products of the British Empire.

The first practical application of Grierson's ideas at the EMB was *Drifters* in 1929, a short feature about herring fishing in the North Sea. Following its success, Grierson established, with the full support of Tallents, the Empire Marketing Board Film Unit instead of pursuing a career as an individual filmmaker. He staffed the Film Unit with young people, mostly middle class and well educated (many from Cambridge University). Basil Wright, Arthur Elton, Edgar Anstey, and Paul Rotha were among the early recruits; Stuart Legg and Harry Watt came later, as did Humphrey Jennings. Alberto Cavalcanti joined the group, shortly after it had moved to the General Post Office as a sort of co-producer and co-teacher with Grierson.

The training at the EMB Film Unit and subsequently the General Post Office Film Unit was ideological as well as technical and aesthetic. The young filmmakers exposed to it came to share Grierson's broad social purposes, and developed an extraordinary loyalty to him and to his goals. It was in this way that the British documentary movement was given shape and impetus.

What Grierson wanted documentary to do was to inform the public about their nation and involve them emotionally with the workings of their government. His assumptions were as follows: if people at work in one part of the Empire are shown to people in the other parts, and if a government service is presented to the population at large, an understanding and appreciation of the interrelatedness of the modern world, and of our dependency on each other, will develop and everyone will want to contribute his or her share to the better functioning of the whole. On these assumptions were based the first phase in Grierson's lifelong activity on behalf of citizenship education. Phase one included some of the most innovative, lovely, and lasting of the British documentaries: *Drifters*, *Industrial Britain*, *Granton Trawler*, *Song of Ceylon*, *Coal Face*, and *Night Mail*.

Phase two, which began in the mid-thirties, consisted of calling public attention to pressing problems faced by the nation, of insistence that these problems needed to be solved, of suggestions about their causes and possible solutions. Since these matters may have involved differing political positions and in any case did not relate directly to the concerns of the sponsoring General Post Office, Grierson stepped outside the GPO to enlist sponsorship from private industry. Big oil and gas concerns were especially responsive to his persuasion. The subjects dealt with in this new kind of documentary included unemployment (*Workers and Jobs*), slums (*Housing Problems*), malnutrition among the poor (*Enough to Eat?*), smog (*The Smoke Menace*), and education (*Children at School*). Unlike the earlier British documentaries, these films were journalistic rather than poetic, and seemed quite unartistic. Yet they incorporated formal and technical experiments. Most notable among these was the direct interview, with slum dwellers in *Housing Problems*, for example, presaging the much later cinéma vérité method, and a standard technique of television documentary today.

The use of institutional sponsorship, public and private, to pay for his kind of filmmaking, rather than dependence on returns from the box office, was a key Grierson innovation in the development of documentary. A second innovation, complementing the first, was nontheatrical distribution and exhibition: going outside the movie theaters to reach audiences in schools and factories, union halls and church basements.

During the ten years between *Drifters* and Grierson's departure for Canada, in 1939, the 60 or so filmmakers who comprise the British documentary movement made over 300 films. These films and the system they came out of became models for other countries. Paul Rotha, one of Grierson's principal lieutenants, went on a six month missionary expedition to the United States in 1937, and film people from America and other countries visited the documentary units in Britain. Grierson carried his ideas himself not only to Canada, where he drafted legislation for the National Film Board and became its first head, but to New Zealand, Australia, and later South Africa, all of which established national film boards.

The National Film Board of Canada stands as the largest and most impressive monument to Grierson's concepts and actions relating to the use of film by governments in communicating with their citizens. During his Canadian years he moved beyond national concerns to global ones. The Film Board's *The World in Action*, a monthly series for the theaters along *March of Times* lines, expressed some of these concerns. His ideas regarding the education of citizens required in a world at war, and a new world to follow, were expressed in major essays that have inspired many who have read them. "The Challenge of Peace," reprinted in *Grierson on Documentary*, pp. 317-28, is one of them.

It is for his many-faceted, innovative leadership in film and in education that Grierson is most to be valued. As a theoretician he articulated the basis of the documentary film, its form and function, its aesthetic and its ethic. As a teacher he trained and, through his writing and speaking, influenced many documentary filmmakers, not only in Britain and Canada but throughout the world. As a producer he was responsible to one extent or another for thousands of films and played a decisive creative role in some of the most important of them. And almost all of his life he was an adroit political figure and dedicated civil servant. Whether being paid by a government or not, his central concern was always with communicating to the people of a nation and of the world the information and attitudes that he thought would help them to lead more useful and productive, more satisfying and rewarding lives.

—Jack C. Ellis

GRIFFITH, D.W. American. Born David Wark Griffith on Oldham County farm near Centerfield, Kentucky, 23 January 1875. Educated at district schools in Oldham County, Shelby County, and Louisville, Kentucky. Married Linda Arvidson in 1906 (separated 1911, divorced 1936); married Evelyn Baldwin in 1936 (separated 1946, divorced 1947). Career: 1895-99—performs small roles with local and regional stock companies stock companies as "Lawrence Griffith," "Alfred Lawrence,"

"Lawrence Brayington," and "Thomas Griffith"; 1897-99—reporter for Louisville *Courier Journal*; 1899-1906—performs supporting roles in New York and tours country with various companies; 1901—vaudeville playlet *In Washington's Time* produced; 1906—plays lead in *The Clansman* in New York; play *A Fool and a Girl* produced; 1907—hired by J. Searle Dawley to act for Edison Company, plays lead in *Rescued from the Eagle's Nest*; sells several scenarios to American Mutoscope and Biograph Company and acts in Biograph pictures; 1908—hired by Biograph as scriptwriter and director; 1908-13—makes approximately 485 one- and two-reelers for Biograph; 1909—begins association with cinematographer G.W. (Billy) Bitzer; first films with Mary Pickford, then billed as "Dorothy Nicholson"; 1910—supervises Mack Sennett's first films; 1912—does *An Unseen Enemy*, first film with Lillian and Dorothy Gish; 1913—leaves Biograph and joins Reliance Majestic (affiliated with Mutual); 1914—begins shooting *The Birth of a Nation* in May; begins to prepare *The Mother and the Law*, transformed into the modern segment of *Intolerance*; 1915—becomes partner in Triangle Pictures; 1915-17—in addition to directing, supervises 77 films by directors under contract to Triangle; 1916—releases *Intolerance*; 1917—travels to Britain to aid war effort; 1918—engaged by Paramount; 1919—joins First National; 1920—forms United Artists with Pickford, Fairbanks and Chaplin; builds own studio at Mamaroneck, New York; 1924—leaves United Artists; 1925-26—works for Paramount; 1927—signs with United Artists (through 1930); 1930—makes his 1st talking picture, *Abraham Lincoln*; 1939—returns to Hollywood and works on *One Million B.C.*. Died in Los Angeles, 23 July 1948; buried at Mount Tabor Cemetery, Centerfield, Kentucky. Recipient: Director of the Year, Academy of Motion Picture Arts and Sciences, 1931; Special Award, Academy of Motion Picture Arts and Sciences, 1936; Honorary Doctorate, University of Louisville, 1945.

Films (as director and scriptwriter at Biograph, in order and by year of production): 1908—*The Adventures of Dolly*; *The Redman and the Child*; *The Tavern Keeper's Daughter*; *The Bandit's Waterloo*; *A Calamitous Elopement*; *The Greaser's Gauntlet*; *The Man and the Woman*; *For Love of Gold*; *The Fatal Hour*; *For a Wife's Honor*; *Balked at the Altar*; *The Girl and the Outlaw*; *The Red Girl*; *Betrayed by a Hand Print*; *Monday Morning in a Coney Island Police Court*; *Behind the Scenes*; *The Heart of Oyama*; *Where the Breakers Roar*; *The Stolen Jewels*; *A Smoked Husband*; *The Zulu's Heart*; *The Vaquaro's Vow*; *Father Gets in the Game*; *The Barbarian, Ingomar*; *The Planter's Wife*; *The Devil*; *Romance of a Jewess*; *The Call of the Wild*; *After Many Years*; *Mr. Jones at the Ball*; *Concealing a Burglar*; *Taming of the Shrew*; *The Ingrate*; *A Woman's Way*; *The Pirate's Gold*; *The Guerrilla*; *The Curtain Pole*; *The Song of the Shirt*; *The Clubman and the Tramp*; *Money Mad*; *Mrs. Jones Entertains*; *The Feud and the Turkey*; *The Test of Friendship*; *The Reckoning*; *One Touch of Nature*; *An Awful Moment*; *The Helping Hand*; *The Maniac Cook*; *The Christmas Burglars*; *A Wreath in Time*; *The Honor of Thieves*; *The Criminal Hypnotist*; *The Sacrifice*; *The Welcome Burglar*; *A Rural Elopement*; *Mr. Jones Has a Card Party*; *The Hindoo Dagger*; *The Salvation Army Lass*; *Love Finds a Way*; *Tragic Love*; *The Girls and a Daddy*; 1909—*Those Boys*; *The Cord of Life*; *Trying to Get Arrested*; *The Fascinating Mrs. Frances*; *Those Awful Hats*; *Jones and the Lady Book Agent*; *The Drive for Life*; *The Brahma Diamond*; *Politician's Love Story*; *The Jones Have Amateur Theatricals*; *Edgar Allen Poe*; *The Roue's Heart*; *His Wife's Mother*; *The Golden Louis*; *His Ward's Love*; *At the Altar*; *The Prussian Spy*; *The Medicine Bottle*; *The Deception*; *The Lure of the Gown*; *Lady Helen's Escapade*; *A Fool's*

Revenge; *The Wooden Leg*; *I Did It, Mama*; *The Voice of the Violin*; *And a Little Child Shall Lead Them*; *The French Duel*; *Jones and His New Neighbors*; *A Drunkard's Reformation*; *The Winning Coat*; *A Rude Hostess*; *The Road to the Heart*; *The Eavesdropper*; *Schneider's Anti-Noise Crusade*; *Twin Brothers*; *Confidence*; *The Note in the Shoe*; *Lucky Jim*; *A Sound Sleeper*; *A Troublesome Satchel*; *Tis an Ill Wind That Blows No Good*; *The Suicide Club*; *Resurrection*; *One Busy Hour*; *A Baby's Shoe*; *Eloping with Auntie*; *The Cricket on the Hearth*; *The Jilt*; *Eradicating Auntie*; *What Drink Did*; *Her First Biscuits*; *The Violin Maker of Cremona*; *2 Memories*; *The Lonely Villa*; *The Peach Basket Hat*; *The Son's Return*; *His Duty*; *A New Trick*; *The Necklace*; *The Way of Man*; *The Faded Lilies*; *The Message*; *The Friend of the Family*; *Was Justice Served?*; *Mrs. Jones' Lover* or "*I Want My Hat!*"; *The Mexican Sweethearts*; *The Country Doctor*; *Jealousy and the Man*; *The Renunciation*; *The Cardinal's Conspiracy*; *The 7th Day*; *Tender Hearts*; *A Convict's Sacrifice*; *A Strange Meeting*; *Sweet and Twenty*; *The Slave*; *They Would Elope*; *Mrs. Jones' Burglar*; *The Mended Lute*; *The Indian Runner's Romance*; *With Her Card*; *The Better Way*; *His Wife's Visitor*; *The Mills of the Gods*; *Franks*; *Oh, Uncle*; *The Sealed Room*; *1776* or *The Hessian Renegades*; *The Little Darling*; *In Old Kentucky*; *The Children's Friend*; *Comata, the Sioux*; *Getting Even*; *The Broken Locket*; *A Fair Exchange*; *The Awakening*; *Pippa Passes*; *Leather Stockings*; *Fools of Fate*; *Wanted, a Child*; *The Little Teacher*; *A Change of Heart*; *His Lost Love*; *Lines of White on the Sullen Sea*; *The Gibson Goddess*; *In the Watches of the Night*; *The Expiation*; *What's Your Hurry*; *The Restoration*; *Nursing a Viper*; *2 Women and a Man*; *The Light that Came*; *A Midnight Adventure*; *The Open Gate*; *Sweet Revenge*; *The Mountaineer's Honor*; *In the Window Recess*; *The Trick That Failed*; *The Death Disc*; *Through the Breakers*; *In a Hempen Bag*; *A Corner in Wheat*; *The Redman's View*; *The Test*; *A Trap for Santa Claus*; *In Little Italy*; *To Save Her Soul*; *Choosing a Husband*; *The Rocky Road*; *The Dancing Girl of Butte*; *Her Terrible Ordeal*; *The Call*; *The Honor of His Family*; *On the Reef*; *The Last Deal*; *One Night, and Then—*; *The Cloister's Touch*; *The Woman from Mellon's*; *The Duke's Plan*; *The Englishman and the Girl*; 1910—*The Final Settlement*; *His Last Burglary*; *Taming a Husband*; *The Newlyweds*; *The Thread of Destiny*; *In Old California*; *The Man*; *The Converts*; *Faithful*; *The Twisted Trail*; *Gold is Not All*; *As It Is in Life*; *A Rich Revenge*; *A Romance of the Western Hills*; *Thou Shalt Not*; *The Way of the World*; *The Unchanging Sea*; *The Gold Seekers*; *Love Among the Roses*; *The 2 Brothers*; *Unexpected Help*; *An Affair of Hearts*; *Ramona*; *Over Silent Paths*; *The Implement*; *In the Season of Buds*; *A Child of the Ghetto*; *In the Border States*; *A Victim of Jealousy*; *The Face at the Window*; *A Child's Impulse*; *The Marked Time-table*; *Muggsy's First Sweetheart*; *The Purgation*; *A Midnight Cupid*; *What the Daisy Said*; *A Child's Faith*; *The Call to Arms*; *Serious 16*; *A Flash of Light*; *As the Bells Rang Out*; *An Arcadian Maid*; *The House with the Closed Shutters*; *Her Father's Pride*; *A Salutary Lesson*; *The Usurer*; *The Sorrows of the Unfaithful*; *In Life's Cycle*; *Wilful Peggy*; *A Summer Idyll*; *The Modern Prodigal*; *Rose o'Salem Town*; *Little Angels of Luck*; *A Mohawk's Way*; *The Oath and the Man*; *The Iconoclast*; *Examination Day at School*; *That Chink at Golden Gulch*; *The Broken Doll*; *The Banker's Daughters*; *The Message of the Violin*; *2 Little Waifs*; *Waiter No.5*; *The Fugitive*; *Simple Charity*; *The Song of the Wildwood Flute*; *A Child's Stratagem*; *Sunshine Sue*; *A Plain Song*; *His Sister-in-law*; *The Golden Supper*; *The Lesson*; *When a Man Loves*; *Winning Back His Love*; *His Trust*; *His Trust Fulfilled*; *A Wreath of Orange Blossoms*; *The Italian Barber*; *The 2 Paths*; *Conscience*; *3 Sisters*; *A Decree of Destiny*; *Fate's Turning*; *What Shall We Do with Our Old?*; *The Diamond Star*;

The Lily of the Tenements; Heart Beats of Long Ago; 1911—*Fisher Folks; His Daughter; The Lonedale Operator; Was He a Coward?; Teaching Dad to Like Her; The Spanish Gypsy; The Broken Cross; The Chief's Daughter; A Knight of the Road; Madame Rex; His Mother's Scarf; How She Triumphed; In the Days of '49; The 2 Sides; The New Dress; Enoch Arden, Part I; Enoch Arden, Part II; The White Rose of the Wilds; The Crooked Road; A Romany Tragedy; A Smile of a Child; The Primal Call; The Jealous Husband; The Indian Brothers; The Thief and the Girl; Her Sacrifice; The Blind Princess and the Poet; Fighting Blood; The Last Drop of Water; Robby the Coward; A Country Cupid; The Ruling Passion; The Rose of Kentucky; The Sorrowful Example; Swords and Hearts; The Stuff Heroes Are Made Of; The Old Confectioner's Mistake; The Unveiling; The Eternal Mother; Dan the Dandy; The Revue Man and the Girl; The Squaw's Love; Italian Blood; The Making of a Man; Her Awakening; The Adventures of Billy; The Long Road; The Battle; Love in the Hills; The Trail of the Books; Through Darkened Vales; Saved from Himself; A Woman Scorned; The Miser's Heart; The Failure; Sunshine Through the Dark; As in a Looking Glass; A Terrible Discovery; A Tale of the Wilderness; The Voice of the Child; The Baby and the Stork; The Old Bookkeeper; A Sister's Love; For His Son; The Transformation of Mike; A Blot on the 'Scutcheon; Billy's Strategem; The Sunbeam; A String of Pearls; The Root of Evil;* 1912—*The Mender of the Nets; Under Burning Skies; A Siren of Impulse; Iola's Promise; The Goddess of Sagebrush Gulch; The Girl and Her Trust; The Punishment; Fate's Interception; The Female of the Species; Just Like a Woman; One is Business, the Other Crime; The Lesser Evil; The Old Actor; A Lodging for the Night; His Lesson; When Kings Were the Law; A Beast at Bay; An Outcast Among Outcasts; Home Folks; A Temporary Truce; The Spirit Awakened; Lena and the Geese; An Indian Summer; The Schoolteacher and the Waif; Man's Lust for Gold; Man's Genesis; Heaven Avenges; A Pueblo Legend; The Sands of Dee; Black Sheep; The Narrow Road; A Child's Remorse; The Inner Circle; A Change of Spirit; An Unseen Enemy; 2 Daughters of Eve; Friends; So Near, Yet So Far; A Feud in the Kentucky Hills; In the Aisles of the Wild; The One She Loved; The Painted Lady; The Musketeers of Pig Alley; Heredity; Gold and Glitter; My Baby; The Informer; The Unwelcome Guest; Pirate Gold; Brutality; The New York Hat; The Massacre; My Hero; Oil and Water; The Burglar's Dilemma; A Cry for Help; The God Within; 3 Friends; The Telephone Girl and the Lady; Fate; An Adventure in the Autumn Woods; A Chance Deception; The Tender Hearted Boy; A Misappropriated Turkey; Brothers; Drink's Lure; Love in an Apartment Hotel;* 1913—*Broken Ways; A Girl's Strategem; Near to Earth; A Welcome Intruder; The Sheriff's Baby; The Hero of Little Italy; The Perfidy of Mary; A Misunderstood Boy; The Little Tease; The Lady and the Mouse; The Wanderer; The House of Darkness; Olaf—An Atom; Just Gold; His Mother's Son; The Yaqui Cur; The Ranchero's Revenge; A Timely Interception; Death's Marathon; The Sorrowful Shore; The Mistake; The Mothering Heart; Her Mother's Oath; During the Round-up; The Coming of Angelo; An Indian's Loyalty; 2 Men of the Desert; The Reformers or The Lost Art of Minding One's Business; The Battle at Elderbush Gulch* (released 1914); *In Prehistoric Days* (original title: *Wars of the Primal Tribes* and released as *Brute Force*); *Judith of Bethulia* (released 1914); (as director after quitting Biograph, by year of release): 1914—*The Battle of the Sexes; The Escape; Home, Sweet Home; The Avenging Conscience;* 1915—*The Birth of a Nation* (+co-sc, co-music); 1916—*Intolerance* (+co-music); 1918—*Hearts of the World* (+sc under pseudonyms, co-music arranger); *The Great Love* (+co-sc); *The Greatest Thing in Life* (+co-sc); 1919—*A Romance of Happy Valley* (+sc);

The Girl Who Stayed at Home; True-Heart Susie; Scarlet Days; Broken Blossoms (+sc, co-music arranger); *The Greatest Question;* 1920—*The Idol Dancer; The Love Flower; Way Down East;* 1921—*Dream Street* (+sc); *Orphans of the Storm;* 1922—*One Exciting Night* (+sc); 1923—*The White Rose* (+sc); 1924—*America; Isn't Life Wonderful* (+sc); 1925—*Sally of the Sawdust;* 1926—*That Royle Girl; The Sorrows of Satan;* 1928—*Drums of Love; The Battle of the Sexes;* 1929—*Lady of the Pavements;* 1930—*Abraham Lincoln;* 1931—*The Struggle* (+pr, co-music arranger).

Publications:

By GRIFFITH:

Books—*The Rise and Fall of Free Speech in America*, Hollywood 1967 (originally published in Los Angeles, 1916); *The Man Who Invented Hollywood: The Autobiography of D.W. Griffith*, edited by James Hart, Louisville, Kentucky 1972; articles—"Defense of *The Birth of a Nation* and Attack on the Sullivan Bill" by D.W. Griffith in *Boston Journal*, 26 April 1915; "Reply to the New York Globe" by D.W. Griffith in the *New York Globe*, 10 April 1915; "D.W. Griffith Recalls the Making of *The Birth of a Nation*" by Henry Stephen Gordon in *The Photoplay Magazine* (Hollywood), October 1916; "The Rise and Fall of Free Speech in America" by D.W. Griffith, a pamphlet written in answer to the reaction against *The Birth of a Nation*, 1916; "Pictures Versus One Night Stands" in *The Independent*, 11 December 1916; "What I Demand of Movie Stars" in *Motion Picture Magazine* (Los Angeles), February 1917; "How a Leading Screen Director Picks His Leading Women" in *Current Opinion*, January 1919; "The Miracle of Modern Photography" in *The Mentor*, July 1921; "Are Motion Pictures Destructive of Good Taste" in *Arts and Decoration*, September 1923; "The Real Truth about Breaking into the Movies" in *Women's Home Companion* (New York), February 1924; "How Do You Like the Show" in *Collier's* (New York), 24 April 1926; "The Motion Picture Today—and Tomorrow" in *Theatre Magazine* (New York), October 1929; "An Old Timer Advises Hollywood" in *Liberty* (New York), 17 June 1939.

On GRIFFITH:

Books—*A Biography of David Wark Griffith* by Charles Hastings and Herman Holland, New York 1920; *David Griffith* by Leonid Trauberg and Georg Ronen, Moscow 1926; *David Wark Griffith, A Brief Sketch of His Career* by Robert Long, New York 1946; *An Index to the Creative Work of D.W. Griffith* by Seymour Stern, supplement to *Sight and Sound*, index series, London 1946-47; *Le Cinéma devient un art, 1909-1920*, in 2 volumes, by Georges Sadoul, Paris 1952; *The Birth of a Nation Story* by Roy Aitken, Middleburg, Virginia 1956; *Star-Maker* by Homer Croy, New York 1959; *A Shot Analysis of D.W. Griffith's 'Birth of a Nation'* by Theodore Huff, New York 1961; *The Movies in the Age of Innocence* by Edward Wagenknecht, Norman, Oklahoma 1962; *The Birth of a Nation Story* by Roy Aitken as told to Al P. Nelson, Middleburg, Virginia, 1965; *D.W. Griffith: American Film Master* by Iris Barry and Eileen Bowser, New York 1965; *Griffith* by Jean Mitry in *Anthologie du cinéma*, Paris 1966; *Spellbound in Darkness* by George C. Pratt, Rochester, New York 1966; *The Parade's Gone By* by Kevin Brownlow, New York 1968; *When the Movies Were Young* by Linda Arvidson Griffith, New York reprinted 1969; *Lillian Gish: The Movies, Mr. Griffith, and Me* by Lillian Gish with Ann Pinchot, Englewood Cliffs, New Jersey 1969; *Griffith and the Rise of Hollywood* by Paul O'Dell, New York 1970; *D.W. Griffith: The Years at Biograph* by Robert Henderson, New York 1970; *Focus on Birth of a Nation* edited by Fred Silva, New York 1971; *Focus on D.W. Griffith*, edited by Harry Geduld, Englewood Cliffs, New Jersey 1971; *Dreams for Sale: The Rise and Fall of the Triangle Film Corporation* by Kalton Lahue, New York 1971; *The Man Who Invented Hollywood: The Autobiography of D.W. Griffith* edited by James Hart, Louisville, Kentucky 1972; *D.W. Griffith: His Life and Work* by Robert Henderson, New York 1972; *The Brakhage Lectures* by Stan Brakhage, Chicago 1972; *Billy Bitzer: His Story* by G.W. Bitzer, New York 1973; *Adventures with D.W. Griffith* by Karl Brown, New York 1973; *The Griffith Actresses* by Anthony Slide, New York 1973; *Billy Bitzer: His Story* by G.W. Bitzer, New York 1973; *D.W. Griffith: His Biograph Films in Perspective* by Kemp Niver, Los Angeles 1974; *Nascita del racconto cinematografico Griffith 1908-1912* by Gian Piero Brunetta, Padua 1974; *The Films of D.W. Griffith* by Edward Wagenknecht and Antony Slide, New York 1975; *Ragioni di una proposta ovvero The Adventures of Dollie* by Angelo Humouda and Alessandro Cozzani, Turin 1975; *Griffith: 1st Artist of the Movies* by Martin Williams, New York 1980; articles—"D.W. Griffith—Film Wizard" in *Motion Picture Magazine* (Los Angeles), 1920; "Le Maitre et le prophète" by Louis Delluc in *Photogénie* (Paris), n.d.; "D.W. Griffith" by James Tully in *Vanity Fair* (New York), November 1926; "D.W. Griffith: *The Birth of a Nation*" in *The Rise of the American Film* by Lewis Jacobs, New York 1939; "D.W. Griffith, Creator of Film Form" by Barnet Braverman in *Theatre Arts* (New York), 1945; "Panorama de l'oeuvre de Griffith" by Jacques Manuel in *Revue du Cinéma* (Paris), November 1946; "Griffith Not Anti-Negro" by Seymour Stern in *Sight and Sound* (London), spring 1947; "Griffith, Pioneer of Film Art" by Seymour Stern in *The New York Times*, 10 November 1948; "The Griffith Controversy" by Seymour Stern in *Sight and Sound* (London), v.7, 1948; article by J.C. Trewin in *Sight and Sound* (London), spring 1949; "Dickens, Griffith and the Film Today" by Sergei Eisenstein in *Sight and Sound* (London), June, July and November 1950; "The D.W. Griffith Influence" by Joseph and Harry Feldman in *Films in Review* (New York), July/August 1950; "Griffith and Poe" by Seymour Stern in *Films in Review* (New York), November 1951; "11 East 14th Street" by Seymour Stern in *Films in Review* (New York), v.3, 1952; "The Cold War Against D.W. Griffith" by Seymour Stern in *Films in Review* (New York), February 1956; "The Decline of a Mandarin" by Peter Dyer in *Sight and Sound* (London), v.28, 1958/59; "Biographical Hogwash" by Seymour Stern in *Films in Review* (New York), May and June/July 1959; "In the Nick of Time, D.W. Griffith and the Last-Minute Rescue" by George Pratt in *Image* (Rochester, New York), 2 May 1959; "The Soviet Director's Debt to D.W. Griffith" by Seymour Stern in *Films in Review* (New York), v.10, 1959; "Editing in *The Birth of a Nation*" in *Motion Pictures: The Development of an Art from Silent Pictures to the Age of Television* by A.R. Fulton, Norman, Oklahoma 1960; "Flashback" by Ezra Goodman in *The 50 Year Decline and Fall of Hollywood*, New York 1962; special Griffith issue, *Film Culture* (New York), spring/summer 1965; "D.W. Griffith: American Film Master" in *Film Comment* (New York), summer 1965; "David Wark Griffith: In Retrospect" by G. Charles Niemeyer in *Film Heritage* (Dayton, Ohio), fall 1965; issue devoted to *Birth of a Nation*, *Film Culture* (New York), summer 1965; "D.W. Griffith and Anarchy in American Films" by Norman Silverstein in *Salmagundi* (New York), winter 1966; "The Films of David Wark Griffith: The Development of Themes and Techniques in 42 of His Films" by Richard Meyer in *Film Comment* (New York), fall/winter 1967; "D.W. Griffith" by Arthur Lennig in *The Silent Voice: A Text*, New York 1969; "Griffith in Hollywood" by John Dorr in *Take One* (Montreal), September/October 1971; "The Movies, Mr. Griffith, and Carol Dempster" by John Dorr in *Cinema* (Beverly Hills), fall 1971; special Griffith issue of *Les Cahiers de la Cinémathèque* (Lyon), spring 1972; "The Films of D.W. Griffith: A Style for the Times" by Alan Casty in *Journal of Popular Film* (Bowling Green), spring 1972; special Griffith issue of *Ecran* (Paris), February 1973; "D.W. Griffith and the Moral Landscape" by Stephen Zito in *A.F.I. Report* (Washington, D.C.), winter 1973; "Theme, Felt Life, and the Last Minute Rescue in Griffith after *Intolerance*" by William Cadbury in *Film Quarterly* (Berkeley), fall 1974; special issue of *Films in Review* (New York), October 1975; special issue of *Filmcritica* (Rome), May/June 1975; special issue of Kosmorama (Copenhagen), summer 1975; special issue of *Les Cahiers de la Cinémathèque* (Lyon), Christmas 1975; "Spazio della fiction e macchina fissa" by Michele Mancini in *Filmcritica* (Rome), August 1975; special issue of *Filmkritik* (Berlin), April 1975; "'Lo! The Entertainers': D.W. Griffith and Dance" by Elizabeth Kendall in *Ballet Review* (New York), 1975-76; special issue of *Griffithiana* (Genoa), March/July 1980; "David Wark Griffith" by Vlada Petric in *Cinema: A Critical Dictionary* vol.1, edited by Richard Roud, New York 1980; biofilmography and appendices on principal collaborators in *Film Dope* (London), October 1980; "Rescued from a Perilous Nest: D.W. Griffith's Escape from Theatre into Film" by Russell Merritt in *Cinema Journal* (Evanston), fall 1981; "D.W. Griffith Directs the Great War: The Making of *Hearts of the World*" by Russell Merritt in *Quarterly Review of Film Studies* (Salisbury, Md.), winter 1981; special issue of *Griffithiana* (Genoa), January 1982.

*   *   *

Perhaps no other director has generated such a broad range of critical reaction as D.W. Griffith. For students of the motion picture, Griffith's is the most familiar name in film history. Generally acknowledged as America's most influential director (and certainly one of the most prolific), he is also perceived as being among the most limited. Praise for his mastery of film technique is matched by repeated indictments of his moral, artistic, and intellectual inadequacies. At one extreme, Kevin Brownlow has characterized him as "the only director in America creative enough to be called a genius." At the other, Paul Rotha calls his contribution to the advance of film "negligible" and Susan Sontag complains of his "supreme vulgarity and even inanity"; his work "reeks of a fervid moralizing about sexuality and violence" and his energy comes "from suppressed voluptuousness."

Griffith started his directing career in 1908, and in the following five years made some 485 films, almost all of which have been preserved. These films, one or two reels in length, have customarily been regarded as apprentice works, films in which, to quote Stephen Zito, "Griffith borrowed, invented, and perfected the forms and techniques that he later used to such memorable effect in *The Birth of a Nation*, *Intolerance*, *Broken Blossoms*, and *Way Down East*." These early "Biographs" (named after the studio at which Griffith worked) have usually been studied for their stylistic features, notably parallel editing, camera placement, and treatment of light and shadow. Their most famous structuring devices are the last-minute rescue and the cross-cut.

In recent years, however, the Biographs have assumed higher status in film history. Many historians and critics rank them with the most accomplished work in Griffith's career. Vlada Petric, for instance, calls them "masterpieces of early cinema, fascinating lyrical films which can still affect audiences today, conveying the content in a cinematic manner often more powerful than that of Griffith's later feature films."

Scholars have begun studying them for their characters, images, narrative patterns, themes, and ideological values, finding in them a distinctive signature based on Griffith's deep-seated faith in the values of the woman-centered home. Certain notable Biographs—*The Musketeers of Pig Alley, The Painted Lady, A Corner in Wheat, The Girl and Her Trust, The Battle of Elderbush Gulch, The Unseen Emeny,* and *A Feud in the Kentucky Hills*—have been singled out for individual study.

Griffith reached the peak of his popularity and influence in the five years between 1915 and 1920, when he released *The Birth of a Nation, Intolerance, Hearts of the World, Broken Blossoms,* and *Way Down East.* Of these, only *Hearts of the World,* a First World War propaganda epic, is ignored today; but in 1918 it was the most popular war film of its time, and rivalled *The Birth of a Nation* as the most profitable of all Griffith's features. Today, it is usually studied as an example of World War I hysteria or as a pioneering effort at government-sponsored mass entertainment which incorporates newsreel and faked documentary footage into an epic fictional narrative.

Although Griffith's epics are generally grouped together, Paul Goodman points out that his films are neither so ideologically uniform nor so consistent as recent writers have generally assumed. With equal fervor Griffith could argue white supremacy and make pleas for toleration, play the liberal crusader and the reactionary conservative, appear tradition-bound yet remain open to experimentation, saturate his work in Victorian codes while struggling against a Victorian morality. Frustrated by his inability to find consistent ideological threads in Griffith's work, Norman Silverstein has called Griffith the father of anarchy in American films because his luminous movements in these epics never appear to sustain a unified whole.

Yet, the epics do share broad formal characteristics, using history as a chaotic background for a fictional drama that stresses separation and reunification. Whether set in the French Revolution (*Orphans of the Storm*), the American Revolution (*America*), the Civil War (*Birth of a Nation*), or in the various epochs of *Intolerance,* the Griffith epic is an action-centered spectacle that manipulates viewer curiosity with powerfully propulsive, intrinsically developmental scenes culminating in a sensational denouement.

But Griffith made a much different sort of feature during these years which only recently has received serious critical attention—the pastoral romance. In these films stripped of spectacle and historical surroundings, the cast of principal characters does not exceed two or three, the action is confined in time and space, and the story is intimate. Here, in films like *Romance of Happy Valley, True-heart Susie,* and *The Greatest Question,* Griffith experiments with alternative narrative possibilities, whereby he extends the techniques of exposition to the length of a feature film. Strictly narrative scenes in these films are suspended or submerged to convey the illusion of near-plotlessness. The main figures, Griffith implied (usually played by Lillian Gish and Bobby Harron), would emerge independent of fable; atmosphere would dominate over story line.

From the start, critics and reviewers found the near absence of action sequences and overt physical struggle noteworthy in the Griffith pastorals, but differed widely in their evaluation of it. Most of the original commentators assumed they had found a critical shortcoming, and complained about the thinness of plot, padded exposition, and frequent repetition of shots. Even Kenneth MacGowan, who alone among his contemporaries preferred Griffith's pastorals to his epics, scored the empty storyline

of *The Romance of Happy Valley* for its "loose ends and dangling characters." More recent critics, on the other hand—notably Jean Mitry, John Belton, and Rene Kerdyk—have found transcendental virtues in the forswearing of event-centered plots. Ascribing to Griffith's technique a liberating moral purpose, Mitry called *True-heart Susie* "a narrative which follows characters without entrapping them, allowing them complete freedom of action and event." For John Belton, *True-heart Susie* is one of Griffith's "purest and most immediate films" because, "lacking a 'great story' there is nothing between us and the characters." Equating absence of action sequences with the elimination of formal structure, Belton concludes that "it is through the characters not plot that Griffith expresses and defines the nature of the characters' separation."

If these judgments appear critically naive (plainly these films have plots and structures even if these are less complex than in *Intolerance* and *Birth*), they raise important questions Griffith scholars continue to debate: how does Griffith create the impression that characters exist independent of action, and, in a temporal medium, how does Griffith create the impression of narrative immobility?

By and large, Griffith's films of the mid-and late-1920s have not fared well critically, although they have their defenders. The customary view—that Griffith's work became dull and undistinguished when he lost his personal studio at Mamaroneck in 1924—continues to prevail, despite calls from John Dorr, Arthur Lennig, and Richard Roud for re-evaluation. The seven films he made as a contract director for Paramount and United Artists are usually studied (if at all) as examples of late twenties studio style. What critics find startling about them—particularly the United Artists features—is not the lack of quality, but the absence of any identifiable Griffith traits. Only *Abraham Lincoln* and *The Struggle* (Griffith's two sound films) are recognizable as his work, and they are usually treated as early 1930s oddities.

—Russell Merritt

GUERRA, RUY. Mozambiquan. Born in Lourenço Marques, Mozambique, 22 August 1931. Educated in Mozambique and Portugal; attended I.D.H.E.C., Paris, 1952-54; Théâtre National Populaire, 1955. Career: 1955—assistant director to Jean Delannoy on *Chiens perdus sans collier;* 1957—works with Georges Rouquier on *S.O.S. Noronha;* 1958—invited by producer to Brazil to direct *Joana* (unrealized), remains in Brazil; early 1960s—leader of Brazilian "cinema novo" movement; 1960s—writes lyrics for pop songs; 1966—translator and musical advisor to Pierre Kast on *Carnets brésiliens;* 1967—artistic advisor on *Valmy* (Gance); returns to France, makes *Chanson pour traverser la rivière,* intended as part of *Loin du Vietnam;* late 1970s—following independence of Mozambique, returns to help plan film industry; 1982—goes to Mexico to adapt Gabriel Garcia Marquez's *Erendira.*

Films (as director and scriptwriter): 1954—*Les Hommes et les autres* (short—IDHEC diploma work); (as assistant director): 1955—*Souvenir de Paris* (Théocary); *Chiens perdus, sans colllier* (Delannoy); 1957—*S.O.S. Noronha* (Rouquier) (+ro); 1958—*Le Tout pour le tout* (Dally); (as director and scriptwriter): 1960—*Oros* (short—unfinished); 1961—*O cavalo de Oxumaire (The Horse of Oxumaire)* (co-d, co-sc—unfinished); 1962—*Os cafajestes (The Unscrupulous Ones, La Plage du désir)* (co-sc);

1964—*Os fuzis* (*The Guns, Les Fusils*) (co-sc, +co-ed); 1967—
"Vocabulaire" episode of *Loin du Viêt-nam* (not included in
released version); 1969—*Sweet Hunters* (co-sc); 1970—*Os deuses
e os mortos* (*The Gods and the Dead, Les Dieux et les morts*)
(co-sc, +co-ed); 1978—*A queda* (*The Fall, La Chute*) (co-d,
+co-sc, co-mu, co-ed); 1979—*Mueda, memória e massacre*
(*Mueda, Memory and Massacre*) (d only, +co-ph, ed);
1983—*Erendira*.

Roles: 1963—*Os mendigos*; 1969—*Benito Cereno* (Roullet);
1970—*Le Maître du temps* (Pollet); *Le Mur* (Roullet); 1971—
Les Soleils de l'Ile de Pâques (Kast); *O homem das estrelas (Man
and the Stars)* (Barreto); 1972—*Aguirre, der Zorn Göttes (Aguirre, the Wrath of God)* (Herzog).

Publications:

By GUERRA:

Articles—interview by F. Leduc on *Os fuzis* in *Jeune Cinéma*
(Paris), April 1967; interview by J.A. Fieschi and J. Narboni in
Cahiers du cinéma (Paris), April 1967; interview by G. Langlois
in *Cinéma* (Paris), June 1967; interview by P. Pelegri in *Positif*
(Paris), July 1967; interview by A. Berman in *Image et son*
(Paris), May 1969; interview by Michel Ciment in *Positif* (Paris),
May 1970; interview by R. Nogueira in *Cinéma* (Paris), December
1970; on *Sweet Hunters* in *L'Avant-Scène du cinéma* (Paris),
March 1971; "Entretien avec Ruy Guerra" by Jean Gili in *Études
cinématographiques* (Paris), no.93-96, 1972; "Entretien avec
Ruy Guerra" by Rui Nogueira in *Image et son* (Paris), December
1974; "Interview" by T. Elsaesser in *Monogram* (London), no.5,
1974; "Les Dieux et les morts", interview by M. Martin and J.-L.
Douin in *Ecran* (Paris), January 1975; "Entretien avec Rui
Guerra" by Jeanine Meerapfel in *Positif* (Paris), June 1978;
"Entretien" by J. Meerapfel in *Positif* (Paris), June 1978.

On GUERRA:

Articles—"Diaphragme à 4" by Michel Mardore in *Cahiers du
cinéma* (Paris), November 1964; "La Plage du désir" by Paul
Thirard in *Cinéma 64* (Paris), November 1964; "Le Dieu, le
diable et les fusils" by Michel Ciment in *Positif* (Paris), May
1967; "Os Fuzis" by Van Zele in *Image et son* (Paris), November
1969; "Ruy Guerra" by Michel Ciment in *Second Wave*, New
York 1970; "Pour un réalisme magique" by Jacques Demeure in
Positif (Paris), January 1971; "Le 'cinema nôvo' brésilien" issue
of *Études cinématographiques* (Paris), no.93-96, 1972; "Filmen
in Mozambique", interview by F. Sartor, in *Film en Televisie*
(Brussels), May/June 1981; biofilmography in *Film Dope* (London), March 1981.

*   *   *

A truly cosmopolitan artist, Ruy Guerra was born in Mozambique of Portuguese settlers, got a higher education in Lisbon,
and studied cinema at the the Paris I.D.H.E.C. He was one of the
leaders of the Brazilian *cinema novo* with two films that broke
new ground both ethical and aesthetic, *Os cafajestes* and *Os
fuzis*. He shot *Sweet Hunters*, in French and in English, and went
back to Mozambique after it became independent to organize the
newly born cinema industry and to shoot a documentary,
Mueda, memória e massacre before going to Mexico to adapt
Gabriel Garcia Marquez's *Erendira* in 1983. Besides writing his

own scripts, Guerra is the author of lyrics for Latin American
pop songs (sung in particular by Baden Powell), and an actor in
his own right (he plays in Herzog's *Aguirre* and in Serge Roullet's
adaptation of *Benito Cereno*).

The product of a cultural melting pot, Guerra's style is hard to
define. Very classical in form (except in the extraordinary *Os
deuses e os mortes*, the epitome of Brazilian tropicalist aesthetics
with virtuoso camera movements and sequence shots), it shows
none of the *external* signs of modernity such as non-chronological
sequences, manipulation of the sound track, or elaborate framing. On the other hand, it displays a very unusual use of rhythm,
and makes use of great variety of tempos akin to that found in
some Japanese films such as those of Kurosawa.

Guerra is preoccupied, even obsessed with the theme of frustration and disappointed expectations. Guerra's interest in social
issues is already evident in his first film, *Os cafajestes*, about
penniless young loafers in Rio who blackmail a girl after having
taken photos of her in the nude. *Os fuzis*, set in the northeast of
Brazil, opposes a sergeant and four soldiers guarding a harvest
destined for town (to profit the landowner mayor) and the cove-
tous desires of hungry peasants. 13 years later Guerra shot a
sequel, *A queda* (*The Fall*), with the same actors to show what
happened to the characters after a decade spent in the big city.

Os deuses e os mortes presents in grand operatic manner a feud
between two families of farmers. This film reveals another aspect
of Guerra's personality: a taste for magic and dream, an interest
in myths and surrealism. The economic and the psychic are
bound together in this difficult and fascinating work. *Sweet
Hunters*, Guerra's most poetic film (with Sterling Hayden, Susan
Strasberg, and Stuart Whitman), is set on an island where the
three characters act out their obsessions and frustrated desires.
Allan, a keen ornithologist, is waiting for the migration of birds,
his wife Clea for the arrival of a man who has escaped from a
nearby prison, and his sister for her departure. Very logically,
Guerra was picked to adapt Garcia Marquez's novella *Erendira*
set in an imaginary country where a mythical and monstrous
grandmother (Irene Pappas) sells her granddaughter as a prostitute. A picaresque tale of economic exploitation, with ironical
characters and nightmarish situations, it offers a good synthesis
of Guerra's style even if the faithfulness of his adaptation does
not allow him to give full vent to his ordinarily richer and more
personal inspiration.

—Michel Ciment

GUITRY, SACHA. French. Born Alexandre-Georges Pierre
Guitry in St. Petersburg, Russia, 21 February 1885. Educated at
lycée Jeanson-de-Sailly, St. Petersburg, 1894; attended 12 different schools through 1902. Married Charlotte Lysès in 1907
(divorced 1918); married Yvonne Printemps in 1919 (divorced
1935); married Jacqueline Delubac in 1935 (divorced 1938); married Geneviève de Séréville in 1942 (divorced 1949); married
Lana Marconi in 1949. Career: 1903—publishes 1st book of
caricatures, meets Alfred Jarry; 1904—makes acting debut in
company of father, Lucien Guitry; pursues enormously successful theatrical career as playwright and actor through 1930s;
1931—supervises film based on his play *White and Black*; 1942—
on list of collaborators to be executed after war; 1944—arrested
for collaborating with Nazis, released after 2 months; 1947—
officially cleared of charges, ban on works lifted; 1953—last
stage appearance; writes and narrates radio series "Et Versailles
vous est conté". Died in Paris, 24 July 1957. Recipient: Chevalier
de la Légion d'Honneur, 1923; Commander of the Légion

d'Honneur, 1936; elected to the Goncourt Academy, 1939; Grande Médaille d'Or de la Société des Auteurs, 1955.

Films (as director and scriptwriter): 1915—*Ceux de chez nous* (+ph); 1931—*Le Blanc et le noir* (sc only); 1935—*Pasteur* (co-d, +ro as *Pasteur*); *Bonne chance* (+ro as *Claude*); *Les Deux coverts* (sc only); 1936—*Le Nouveau Testament* (+ro as *Jean Marcelin*); *Le Roman d'un tricheur (The Story of a Cheat)* (+ro as the cheat); *Mon Père avait raison* (+ro as *Charles Bellanger*); *Faisons un rêve* (+ro as *He*); 1937—*Le Mot de Cambronne* (+ro as *Cambronne*); *Les Perles de la couronne (Pearls of the Crown)* (+ro as *François I, Barras, Napoleon III, Jean Martin*); *Désiré* (+ro as *Désiré Tronchais*); 1938—*Quadrille* (+ro as *Philippe de Moranes*); *Remontons les Champs-Elysées* (+ro as the teacher, *Louis XV, Ludovic at 54 years of age, Jean-Louis at 54, Napoleon III*); *L'Accroche-coeur* (sc only); 1939—*Ils étaient neuf célibataires* (+ro as *Jean Lécuyer*); 1942—*Le Destin fabuleux de Desirée Clary* (+ro as *Napoleon I*); 1943—*Donne-moi tes yeux* (+ro as *François Bressoles*); 1944—*La Malibran* (+ro as *M. Malibran*); 1948—*Le Comédien* (+ro as *Lucien Guitry* at 40); 1949—*Le Diable boiteux* (+ro as *Talleyrand*); *Aux deux colombes* (+ro as *Jean-Pierre Walter*); *Toâ* (+ro as *Michel Desnoyers*); 1950—*Le Trésor de Cantenac* (+ ro as *Baron de Cantenac*); *Tu m'as sauvé la vie* (+ ro as *Baron de Saint-Rambert*); 1951—*Deburau* (+ro as *Jean-Gaspard Deburau*); *La Poison*; *Adhemar* or *Le Jouet de la fatalité* (sc only); 1952—*Je l'ai été trois fois* (+ro as *Jean Renneval*); 1953—*La Vie d'un honnête homme*; 1954—*Si Versailles m'etait conté* (+ro as *Louis XIV*); 1955—*Napoleon* (+ro as *Talleyrand*); 1956—*Si Paris nous était conté*; 1957—*Assassins et voleurs*; *Les Trois font la paire*; 1958—*La Vie a deux* (sc only).

Roles: 1918—*Un Roman d'amour...et d'aventures* (Hervil and Mercanton); 1938—guest appearance as man leaving hotel with girl on arm in *Bluebeard's 8th Wife* (Lubitsch).

Publications:

By GUITRY:

Books—*Si j'ai bonne mémoire*, Paris 1934; *Mémoires d'un tricheur*, Paris 1935; *De Jeanne d'Arc à Philippe Pétain*, Paris 1944; *Toutes réflexions faites*, Paris 1947; *Le Comédien*, Paris 1948; *Et Versailles vous est conté*, Paris 1954; *Théâtre, je t'adore!*, Paris 1958; *Théâtre*, Volumes I-XIV, Paris 1959-62; *Les Femmes et l'amour*, Paris 1959; *Le Cinéma et moi*, Paris 1977; *Le Petite Carnet rouge et autres souvenirs inedits*, Paris 1979; *A bâtons rompus*, Paris 1981; article—"Entretien" by J. Meerapfel in *Positif* (Paris), June 1978.

On GUITRY:

Books—*Sacha* by Alex Madis, Paris 1950; *Sacha Guitry hors sa légende* by Stéphane Prince, Paris 1959; *Sacha Guitry et les femmes* by Hervé Lauwick, Paris 1965; *Sacha Guitry* by Jacques Sicilier in *Anthologie du Cinéma* II, Paris 1967; *Sacha Guitry: The Last Boulevardier* by James Harding, New York 1968; *Sacha Guitry par les témoins de sa vie* by Jacques Lorcey, Paris 1976; *Sacha Guitry monstre sacré de l'époque rétro* by Vincent Badaire, Montivilliers 1977; *Sacha Guitry* by Bettina Knapp, Boston 1981; articles—"Ordeal of Sacha Guitry" in *Time* (New York), 7 June 1948; "Sacha Guitry" by Louis Marcorelles in *Sight and Sound* (London), autumn 1957; obituary in the *New York Times*, 24 July 1957; "Sacha Guitry" issue, *Cahiers du cinéma* (Paris), no.173, 1965; issue devoted to Guitry, *Revue du cinéma* (Paris), v.3, 1971; "La Mise en pièce du film" by J. Fieschi in *Cinématographe* (Paris), no.40, 1978; "Sacha, an Introduction to Guitry" by G. Adair in *Sight and Sound* (London), winter 1980/81; biofilmography in *Film Dope* (London), March 1981; films—*Le Musée de Sacha Guitry* (Prince) (short); *Cinéastes de notre temps: Sach Guitry*, for TV, by Claude de Givray, France 1965.

*   *   *

Values change and time plays tricks on one's memory of how it really was. Back in the early thirties, when talking pictures were gaining a foothold in this country and all foreign nations were exhibiting their product in America, it seemed as if there were nobody in films as charming, witty, and multi-talented as Sacha Guitry. His films made in France appeared at all the best art houses; he was a delightful actor, a director with a Lubitsch-like wit, and a writer of amusing sophisticated comedy. Seeing his films today in revival, they don't seem that funny; they are old-fashioned and often dull; and his preoccupation with sex is too often mere lechery. Only two films are still diamond-bright: one that he co-directed with Christian-Jaque, *Les Perles de la couronne*, and *Le Roman d'un tricheur*.

The first has a narrative device that enables Guitry to skip back and forth from one century to another and from one country to another, and still keep the story clear and funny; the second is a razor-sharp treatise on the rewards of dishonesty. It involves a hero who as a young boy is punished by being sent to bed without dinner because of a lie he has told. Because he does not eat the meal that has been prepared, he lives while all other members of his family perish, having consumed a dish prepared from toadstools rather than fresh mushrooms. In *Les Perles de la couronne* Guitry plays tricks with actual events and people. The comedy has a nice bite, and Guitry pulls off a narrative resolution that is masterly in its irony.

Sacha Guitry was once the toast of Paris, where one season he had as many as three plays running simultaneously. When he turned his talents to talking pictures, the medium seemed to have been invented expressly for his convenience. His father, Lucien Guitry, was France's greatest actor, and in time his talented son wrote two plays that his father turned into pure gold—*Pasteur* and *Mon Père avait raison*. In all, Sacha Guitry wrote more than a hundred plays; his films were often adaptations of these. Most were boudoir farces, remarkable in that they always seemed to work thanks to skilfull construction, though they were also generally feather light and too often highly forgettable.

He married five actresses who all rose to prominence in whatever he wrote before he divorced them. The one who became a star in her own right was Yvonne Printemps, the second actress he married; she divorced him finally to marry her leading man, handsome Pierre Fresnay, while Guitry that same year married a new leading lady, the beautiful Jacqueline Delubac.

In World War Two Guitry was trapped in Paris, and he was not permitted by the Nazis to act on the Parisian stage. After four years, when the Germans were forced to quit Paris, Guitry was arrested by a ridiculous quirk of fate for having collaborated with the enemy; he was released after two months, exonerated, and freed to go on with his career.

—DeWitt Bodeen

GÜNEY, YILMAZ. Turkish. Born in village near Adana in southern Turkey, 1937. Educated in law in Ankara; studied economics at Istanbul. Career: 1952—works for film distribution company; 1958—publishes first short stories; begins working with director Atif Yilmaz as scriptwriter, assistant director, and actor; 1961—arrested, sentenced to 18 month prison term and 6 months exile for publishing "communist" novel *Equations with 3 Strangers*; 1963—begins career in commercial cinema, writing and starring in heroic melodramas; becomes matinee idol, nicknamed "Cirkin kral" (The Ugly King); 1968—founds production company Güney-Filmcilik (Güney Film) for own productions, continues to write and star in films by others; 1972—during production of *The Poor Ones* arrested on charge of sheltering anarchist students wanted by authorities; imprisoned for 26 months without trial; 1974—released under general amnesty; in August of 1974 allegedly shoots judge in restaurant after being insulted; sentenced to 24 years' hard labor for homicide (commuted later to 18 years); 1974-80—while in prison is allowed privileges because of popularity, continues to script films and oversee production of them; success of *The Herd* and *The Enemy* brings international attention; 1980—films banned following military takeover; 1981—moved to another prison, decides he is safer outside of country, escapes to France; stripped of citizenship by Turkish government after refusing to return to Turkey. Recipient: Best Film (co-recipient), Cannes Festival, for *Yol*, 1982.

Films (as scriptwriter and actor): 1958—*Alageyik (The Hind)* (Yilmaz) (co-sc); *Bu vatanin cocuklari (The Children of This Country)* (Yilmaz) (co-sc); 1959—*Karacaoğlanin kara sevdasi (Karacaoğlan's Mad Love)* (Yilmaz) (co-sc only); (as assistant director to Atif Yilmaz): 1960—*Clum perdesi (The Screen of Death)*; 1961—*Dolandiricilar (The King of Thieves)*; *Kizil vazo (The Red Vase)*; *Seni kaybederesen (If I Lose You)*; (as scriptwriter and actor): 1961—*Yaban gülü (The Desert Laughs)* (Utku) (co-sc only); 1963—*Ölüme yalniz gidilar (The Dead Only Perish)* (Yalinkilic) (sc only); *Ikisi de cesurdu (2 Brave Men)* (co-sc); 1964—*Hergün ölmektense* (Ceylan); *Kamali zeybek (Hero with a Knife)* (Akinci); *Dağlarin kurdu Kocero (Kocero, Mountain Wolf)* (Utku); 1965—*Kasimpasali* (Akinci); *Kasimpasali recep* (Akinci); *Konyakci (The Drunkard)* (Basaran); *Kirallar kirali (King of Kings)* (Olgac); (as director, scriptwriter, and actor): 1966—*At avrat silah (The Horse, the Woman, and the Gun)*; *Burcak tarlasi* (Utku) (sc only); *Aslanlarin dönüsü (Return of the Heroes)* (Atadeniz) (sc, ro only); *Esrefpasali* (Tokatli) (sc, ro only); *Hudutlarin kanunu (The Law of Smuggling)* (Akad) (sc, ro only); *Yedi dağin aslani (7 Wild Lions, The Mountain King)* (Atadeniz) (sc, ro only); *Tilki Selim (Crafty Selim)* (Hancer) (sc, ro only); 1967—*Bana kursun islemez (Bullets Cannot Pierce Me)*; *Benim adim Kerim (My Name Is Kerim)*; *At hirsizi banus* (Jöntürk) (sc, ro only); *Seytanin oğlu* (Aslan) (sc, ro only); 1968—*Pire Nuri (Nuri the Flea)* (co-d); *Seyyit Han "Topragin Gelini" (Seyyit Khan, Bride of the Earth)* (ro as *Seyyit Han*); *Azrail benim (The Executioner)* (sc, ro only); *Kargaci Halil (Halil, the Crow-Man)* (Yalinkilic) (sc, ro only); 1969—*Ac kurtlar (The Hungry Wolves)*; *Bir cirkin adam (An Ugly Man)*; *Belanin yedi türlüsü (7 Kinds of Trouble)* (Ergün) (sc, ro only); 1970—*Umut (Hope)* (co-sc, ro as *Cabar*); *Piyade Osman (Osman the Wanderer)* (co-d); *Yedi belalilar (The 7 No-goods)* (co-d); *Imzam kanla yazilir (I Sign in Blood)* (Aslan) (sc, ro only); *Sevgili muhafizin (My Dear Bodyguard)* (Jöntürk) (sc, ro only); *Seytan kayaliklari (Devil Crag)* (Filmer) (sc, ro only); 1971—*Kacaklar (The Fugitives)*; *Vurguncular (The Wrongdoers)*; *Ibret (The Example)* (co-d); *Yarin son gündür (Tomorrow Is the Final Day)*; *Umutsuzlar (The Hopeless Ones)*; *Aci (Pain)*; *Ağit (Elegy)* (ro as *Copanoğlu*); *Baba (The Father)* (ro as Cemal, the Boat-

man); 1974—*Arkadas (The Friend)* (ro as *The Friend*); *Endise (Anxiety)* (co-d, sc only); 1975—*Zavallilar (The Poor Ones)* (co-d, co-sc, ro as *Abu*) (begun 1972); *Izin (Leave)* (Gürsu) (sc only); *Bir gün mutlaka (One Day Certainly)* (Olgac) (sc only); 1978—*Sürü (The Herd)* (Ökten) (sc only, +pr supervision); 1979—*Düsman (The Enemy)* (Ökten) (sc only, +pr supervision); 1981—*Yol (The Way)* (sc only, +pr supervision, ed); 1982—*Le Mur (The Wall)*.

Roles: (in films not scripted or directed): 1959—*Tütün zamani* (Arlburnu); 1961—*Dolandiricilar sahi* (Yilmaz); *Tatli-Bela* (Yilmaz); 1964—*Halimeden mektup var* (Doğan); *Kocaoğlan* (Demirel); *Kara sahin* (Akinci); *Mor defter* (Ergün); *10 Korkusuz adam* (Basaran); *Prangasiz mahkumlar* (Ariburnu); *Zimba gibi delikanli* (Jöntürk); 1965—*Ben öldükce yasarim* (Sağiroğlu); *Beyaz atli adam* (Jöntürk); *Dağlarin oğlu* (Atadeniz); *Davudo* (Kazankaya); *Gönül kusu* (Gülnar); *Sayili kabadayilar* (Kazankaya); *Kan Gövdeyi götürdü* (Atadeniz); *Kahreden kursun* (Atadeniz); *Haracima dokunma* (Kazankaya); *Kanli buğday* (Ceylan); *Korkuszlar* (Evin); *Silaha yeminliydim* (Inci); *Sokakta kan vardi* (Türkali); *Tehlikeli adam* (Kazankaya); *Torpido Yilmaz* (Okcugil); *Ücünüzü de mihlarim* (Olgac); *Yarali kartal* (Dursun); 1966—*Aanasi yiğit doğurmas* (Kurthan); *Cirkin kiral* (Atadeniz); *Kovboy Ali* (Atadeniz); *Silahlarin kanunu* (Atadeniz); ...*Veda silahlara veda...* (Jöntürk); *Yiğit yarali olur* (Görec); 1967—*Balatli arif* (Yilmaz); *Bomba Kemal* (Kurthan); *Büyük cellatlar* (Duru); *Cirkin kiral affetmez* (Atadeniz); *Eskiya celladi* (Jöntürk); *Ince cumali* (Duru); *Kizilirmak-Karakoyun* (Akad); *Kozanoğlu* (Yilmaz); *Kuduz recep* (Sağirğlu); *Kurbanlik katil* (Akad); 1968—*Aslan bey* (Yalinkilic); *Beyoğlu canavari* (Görec); *Canpazari* (Görec); *Marmara hasan* (Aslan); *Öldürmek hakkimdir* (Ergün); 1969—*Bin defa ölürüm* (Aslan); *Cifte tabancali kabadayi* (Aslan); *Güney ölüm saciyor* (Aslan); *Kan su gibi akacak* (Atadeniz); *Kursunlarin kanunu* (Ergün); 1970—*Cifte yürekli* (Evin); *Kanimin son damlasina kadar* (Figenli); *Onu Allah affetsin* (Elmas); *Son kizgin adam* (Davutoğlu); *Zeyno* (Yilmaz); 1971—*Cirkin ve cesur* (Ozer); *Namus ve silah* (Görec); 1972—*Sabte yar* (Görec).

Publications:

By GÜNEY:

Articles—"Entretien avec Yilmaz Güney (1977)" in *Positif* (Paris), April 1980; interview in *Framework* (Norwich, England), summer 1981.

On GÜNEY:

Articles—"Repères pour une chronologie du cinéma turc" by G. Bosseno in *Image et son* (Paris), June/July 1975; "Yilmaz Güney miroir du peuple turc" by N. Gürsel in *Jeune cinéma* (Paris), September/October 1975; "Istanbul Journal" by G. Weales in *Film Comment* (New York), January/February 1975; "Cinéastes en danger" by M. Martin in *Ecran* (Paris), September 1976; "A propos d'un artiste qui m'est inconnu mais que j'admire" by Elia Kazan in *Positif* (Paris), April 1977; "The View from a Turkish Prison" by Elia Kazan in *The New York Times Magazine*, 4 February 1979; special issue of *Positif* (Paris), April 1980; "Yilmaz Guney: The Limits of Individual Action" by Roy Armes in *Framework* (Norwich, England), summer 1981; "Sürü: le troupeau de Yilmaz Guney, cinéaste en prison" by A. Nysenholc in *Revue Belge du cinéma* (Brussels), October/November 1981; "Guney (Dernières nouvelles)" by Y. Tobin in *Positif* (Paris),

June 1981; "L'Oeuvre de Yilmaz Güney à Berlin" by A. Tournès in *Jeune cinéma* (Paris), April/May 1981; "Yilmaz Güney" by Derek Elley in *International Film Guide 1983*, London 1982; film—*Besuch auf Imrali (Portrait of Yilmaz Güney)* by Hans Stempel and Martin Ripken, 1979.

*　　*　　*

Yilmaz Güney's life has been fully as dramatic as any of his films. The son of a rural worker, he supported himself through studies at university in Ankara and Istanbul. Though his career was interrupted by a series of arrests for political activities, he established himself as a scriptwriter and actor in the 1960s and developed a wide popular following. More than a film star in the conventional sense, he became something of a popular myth, a figure in whose sufferings and ruthless quest for vengeance the poor and oppressed could see their lives and aspirations reflected. When he turned to directing in the late 1960s, his first films were in the same commercial tradition as his early hits. But the early 1970s saw a fresh burst of creativity, brought to an end by a new prison sentence of two years. On his release he completed one of his most interesting films, *Arkadas*, (*The Friend*) in 1974, before finding himself back in prison, this time on a murder charge for which he received a sentence of 24 years imprisonment. But even this could not put a stop to his career. He maintained contact with the outside world and continued scripting films, some of which, like *Sürü (The Herd)*, achieved international success. When he finally made his escape from Turkey in 1981 he was able to work on yet another film he had scripted, *Yol (The Way)*, which won the Cannes Grand Prix in 1982. While there can be no doubts about Güney's talent and commitment as a filmmaker, only time will tell whether his career will continue to develop successfully in exile, since all his work has been profoundly rooted in the Turkish national situation.

Perhaps Güney's major achievement as an actor-director in the early 1970s was to make the transition from the heroic superman figure of the early films such as *Ac Kurtlar (The Hungry Wolves)*, to the vulnerable individual of his later work. In the series of masterly films beginning with the ironically titled *Umut (Hope)* in 1970, the failure of the isolated individual acting alone becomes the uniting thread of Güney's work. Already in *The Hungry Wolves* the picture of Turkish society is most remarkable for what is lacking: no concerned government to maintain the law, no self-help for the terrorized peasants, no acceptable role for women, no vision beyond instinctive revolt on the part of the bandits. These factors continue to form the background for the series of defeated individuals in both rural settings (the new bandit film, *Ağit (Elegy)* and the urban environment as in *Baba (The Father)* and *Zavallilar (The Poor Ones)*. The one film which posits a set of positive values is his last completed work as a director before his arrest in 1974, *The Friend*. But even here the vision is a dark one, for the intellectual hero (played by Güney) confronts an erstwhile friend with his empty life and thereby drives him to suicide.

The next film he began, *Endise (Anxiety)*, was completed by his friend and former assistant Serif Gören following Güney's arrest. He was to spend eight years in prison, but he continued to write film scripts indefatigably. Among his best films of this period are those which offer a vivid picture of the life of peasants in the still feudal world of his native district, Adana: *Anxiety* and *The Herd*, the latter directed by Zeki Ökten. Güney's final Turkish work, *Yol*, which he edited himself in exile, is even wider in its scope, offering an image of the whole breadth of Turkey through its intercut stories of five detainees released from prison for a week and travelling home to their families. Despite Güney's strong political commitment, his films are social studies rather than overtly political tracts. He himself never fails to make the distinction between his political activity, which is directed towards revolutionary change in society, and his filmmaking. For Güney, the fictional feature film remains first and foremost a popular form, a way of communicating with a mass audience, and, as *Yol* shows, he uses in an exemplary way the possibilities it offers for stating and examining the contradictions that underlie contemporary Turkish society.

—Roy Armes

GUTIÉRREZ ALEA, TOMÁS. Cuban. Born in Havana, 11 December 1928. Educated at University of Havana, law degree 1950; Centro Sperimentale, Rome, 1951-53. Career: 1954-55—works on 1st film *El megano* in collaboration with Julio Garcia Espinosa and others who will later play major roles in ICAIC, the Cuban film institute; late 1950s—works with Cine-Revista, a guerrilla-like newsreel organization; 1959—Instituto Cubano del Arte e Industria Cinematograficos (ICAIC) is established by revolutionary government; Gutiérrez Alea begins making documentaries about social realities of Cuba; 1960-61—directs 1st feature films, *Historias de la revolucion*, 3 short dramatic features on urban underground struggle against Batista; 1960s—collaborates on numerous films by less experienced filmmakers, in keeping with ICAIC's policy of assisting younger filmmakers in their development; 1967-68—directs *Memorias del subdesarrollo (Memories of Underdevelopment)* gaining him international attention.

Films (as director): 1955—*El megano* (co-d); 1959—*Esta tierra nuestra*; 1960—*Asemblea General*; 1961—*Muerte al invasor* (co-d); *Historias de la revolucion*; 1962—*Las doce sillas (The 12 Chairs)*; 1964—*Cumbite*; 1966—*La muerte de un burócrata (The Death of a Bureaucrat)*; 1968—*Memorias del subdesarrollo (Memories of Underdevelopment)*; 1971—*Una pelea cubana contra los demonios (A Cuban Struggle Against the Demons)*; 1974—*El arte del tobaco*; 1976—*La última cena (The Last Supper)*; 1979—*Los sobrevivientes (Survivors)* (+co-sc).

Publications:

By GUTIÉRREZ ALEA:

Articles—"Individual Fulfillment and Collective Achievement: An Interview with Tomás Gutiérrez Alea" by Julianne Burton in *Cineaste* (New York), January 1977; "Das letzte Abendmahl", interview by G. Chijona in *Film und Fernsehen* (Berlin), no.7, 1979; "Towards a Renewal of Cuban Revolutionary Cinema", group interview by Z.M. Pick in *Cine-Tracts* (Montreal), no.3/4, 1978; interview by G. Chijona in *Framework* (Norwich, England), spring 1979; "Cuban Cinema", with interview by M. Ansara in *Cinema Papers* (Melbourne), May/June 1981.

On GUTIÉRREZ ALEA:

Books—*Cuba: The Measure of a Revolution* by L. Nelson, Minneapolis 1972; *Memories of Underdevelopment: The Revolutionary Films of Cuba* by Michael Myerson, New York 1973; articles—"Cinema of Revolution—90 Miles From Home" by Elizabeth Sutherland in *Film Quarterly* (Berkeley), winter 1961-

62; "The Cuban Cinema" by M.E. Douglas in *Take One* (Montreal), July/August 1968; "Propaganda Fills Cuban Newsreels" by R. Adler in *The New York Times*, 12 February 1969; "Cubans are Molding Movie Industry into a Pervasive Force" by R. Adler in *The New York Times*, 11 February 1969; "Cultural Life in Cuba Thriving Despite Rein" by R. Adler in *The New York Times*, 10 February 1969; "Solidarity and Violence" by A. Engel in *Sight and Sound* (London), autumn 1969; "2 Third World Films" by William Murphy in *Take One* (Montreal), January/-February 1971; "The Spring 1972 Cuban Film Festival Bust" by G. Crowdus in *Film Society Review* (New York), March/May 1972; "Cine Cubano" by P. Sauvage in *Film Comment* (New York), spring 1972; "Images of Underdevelopment" by Julia Lesage in *Jump Cut* (Chicago), May/June 1974; "Introduction to Revolutionary Cuban Cinema" by Julianne Burton in *Jump Cut* (Chicago), December 1978; "Cuba 1: Introduction: Cuban Images" by M. Chanan in *Framework* (Norwich, England), spring 1979; "Slavery and Cinema in Cuba: The Case of Gutiérrez Alea's *The Last Supper*" by Dennis West in *The Western Journal of Black Studies*, summer 1979.

*   *   *

The narrative and structural approaches and the style of Gutiérrez Alea's films have varied widely, but his best works show a significant thematic unity stemming from the director's position as a committed revolutionary filmmaker working within a film industry controlled by a socialist state. The director's greatest films all explore aspects of revolution. This central theme of revolution is announced in the neorealist-influenced *Historias de la revolución*, the first feature made by Gutiérrez Alea after the triumph of the Cuban revolution.

Gutiérrez Alea believes that bureaucracy is a part of revolutionary Cuba's bourgeois heritage. His *La muerte de un burócrata* is a polemical yet humorous feature on bureaucratization in a revolutionary socialist society. This masterful satire is outstanding for its dimension of playful inventiveness: credits which are typed in "bureaucratese," the humorous use of animated cartoons, and the many well-integrated parodies of renowned sequences from world cinema. *La muerte de un burócrata* demonstrates that socialist cinema need not resort to heavy-handed methods to express important themes.

Gutiérrez Alea's masterpiece, *Memorias del subdesarrollo*, is a critique of the colonized bourgeois mentality. The protagonist is a man without a future: a middle-aged bourgeois intellectual who refuses to flee to Miami but who is unable to integrate himself into the Cuban revolutionary process. Gutiérrez Alea successfully draws on historical motifs (speeches by Kennedy and Castro) and elements of other film genres (documentary and newsreel) in order to show this individual's place in the march of history.

A primary goal of Cuba's revolutionary filmmakers has been to decolonize the taste of the Cuban film-going public, which for decades had been subjected to standard Hollywood fare. In *Memorias del subdesarrollo*, Gutiérrez Alea contributes overtly to this effort by including a sequence in which clips from a pornographic film are shown in order to critique that genre. *Memorias del subdesarrollo* also features more subtle efforts at decolonization; the director subverts and questions conventional film techniques and strategies through self-conscious and self-reflective devices. Two of these devices: the director appears as himself in the Instituto Cubano del Arte e Industria Cinematográficos (ICAIC) commenting on this very film; and the author of the novel *Memorias del subdesarrollo* participates in a round table on literature and underdevelopment.

In *La última cena*, Gutiérriz Alea abandons self-conscious and self-reflective techniques in favor of a realist style and a conventional chronological treatment of the story line. He uses traditional Christian motifs associated with the Last Supper and the Resurrection in order to reveal the religious ideology of the white planter class—a dead-letter Christianity which reinforced the socioeconomic status quo and reconciled black slaves to a life of bondage. One of the goals of ICAIC has been to contribute to the forging of an authentic national identity through the reassessment of Cuban history. *La última cena*, based on an actual incident, reexamines the historical role of blacks by depicting a slave revolt. Gutiérrez Alea and others at ICAIC supported this film project because Cuba's tradition of black resistance (to slavery and to Spanish colonial powers) was seen as a major contribution to today's socialist Cuba, whose proclaimed objectives include an end to the oppressive legacy of colonialism and to all forms of domination.

The films of Gutiérrez Alea have been well received by Cuban audiences and by critics of many nations. Gutiérrez Alea is one of the greatest Latin American filmmakers because of his ability to mold widely different structural and stylistic approaches to a variety of significant revolutionary themes. This achievement is particularly impressive for having been accomplished in a developing country with modest financial and technical resources.

—Dennis West

GUY, ALICE; also known as Alice Guy-Blaché and Alice Blaché. French. Born in Saint-Mandé, 1 July 1873. Educated at convent du Sacré-Coeur, Viry, France, 1879-85; religious school at Ferney, and brief term in Paris; studied stenography. Married Herbert Blaché-Bolton in 1907 (divorced 1922); children: Simone and Reginald. Career: 1895—hired as secretary by Léon Gaumont, manufacturer of photographic equipment; 1896—films *La Fée aux choux*, thought to be 1st narrative film (but date of film is disputed on basis that the title appears in Gaumont catalogue for 1900); 1897-1907—director of Gaumont film production; 1900—using Gaumont "chronophone", makes 1st sound films; 1905—hires Louis Feuillade as scenarist and assistant; 1907—moves with husband to U.S. where he is to supervise Gaumont subsidiary; Solax becomes Blache Features 1913-14, U.S. Amusement Corporation, 1914-16, and Popular Plays and Players from 1916 to about 1918; 1917—ceases independent production; lectures on filmmaking at Columbia University; 1919-20—assistant director to Herbert Blaché; 1922—returns to France, fails to find work as director; 1964—moves to U.S. and lives with daughter in New Jersey. Died in Mahwah, New Jersey, 24 March 1968. Recipient: Legion of Honor, 1955.

Films (as director and author of script or adaptation): 1896—*La Fée aux choux (The Cabbage Fairy)*; 1897—*Le Pêcheur dans le torrent; Leçon de danse; Baignade dans le torrent; Une nuit agitée; Coucher d'Yvette; Danse fleur de lotus; Ballet Libella; Le Planton du colonel; Idylle; L'Aveugle; 1897-98—L'Arroseur arrosé; Au réfectoire; En classe; Les Cambrioleurs; Le Cocher de fiacre endormi; Idylle interrompue; Chez le magnétiseur; Les Farces de Jocko; Scène d'escamotage; Déménagement à la cloche de bois; Je vous y prrrrends!; 1898-99—Leçons de boxe; La Vie du Christ (11 tableaux); 1899-1900—Le Tondeur de chiens; Le Déjeuner des enfants; Au cabaret; La Mauvaise Soupe; Un Lunch; Erreur judiciaire; L'Aveugle; La Bonne Absinthe; Danse serpentine par Mme Bob Walter; Mésaventure* *d'un charbonnier; Monnaie de lapin; Les Dangers de l'acoolisme; Le Tonnelier; Transformations; Le Chiffonier; Retour des champs; Chez le Maréchal-Ferrant; Marché à la volaille; Courte échelle; L'Angélus; Bataille d'oreillers; Bataille de boules de neige; Le marchand de coco;* 1900—*Avenue de l'Opera; La petite magicienne; Leçon de danse; Chez le photographe; SIDNEY'S JOUJOUX* series (9 titles); *Dans les coulisses; AU BAL DE FLORE* series (3 titles); *BALLET JAPONAIS* series (3 titles); *Danse serpentine; Danse du pas des foulards par des almées; Danse de l'ivresse; Coucher d'une Parisienne; LES FREDAINES DE PIERRETTE* series (4 titles); *VÉNUS ET ADONIS* series (5 titles); *La Tarantelle; DANSE DES SAISONS* series (4 titles); *La Source; Danse du papillon; La Concierge; DANSES* series (3 titles); *Chirurgie fin de siècle; Une Rage de dents; Saut humidifié de M. Plick;* 1900-01—*La Danse du ventre; Lavatory moderne; Lecture quotidienne;* 1900-07—(Gaumont "Phonoscènes", i.e. films with synchronized sound recorded on a wax cylinder): *Carmen* (12 scenes); *Mireille* (5 scenes); *Les Dragons de Villars* (9 scenes); *Mignon* (7 scenes); *Faust* (22 scenes); *POLIN* series (13 titles); *MAYOL* series (13 titles); *DRANEM* series of comic songs (12 titles); Series recorded in Spain (11 titles); *La Prière* by Gounod; 1901—*FOLIES MASQUÉES* series (3 titles); *Frivolité; Les Vagues; Danse basque; Hussards et grisettes; Charmant FrouFrou; Tel est pris qui croyait prendre;* 1902—*La fiole enchantée; L'Equilibriste; En faction; La Première Gamelle; La Dent récalcitrante; Le Marchand de ballons; Les Chiens savants; MISS LINA ESBRARD DANSEUSE COSMOPOLITE ET SERPENTINE* series (4 titles); *Les Clowns; Sage-femme de première classe; Quadrille réaliste; Une Scène en cabinet particulier vue à travers le trou de la serrure; Farces de cuisinière; Danse mauresque; Le Lion savant; Le Pommier; La Cour des miracles; La Gavotte; Trompé mais content; Fruits de saison; Pour secourir la salade;* 1903—*Potage indigeste; Illusioniste renversant; Le Fiancé ensorcelé; Les Apaches pas veinards; Les Aventures d'un voyageur trop pressé; Ne bougeons plus; Comment monsieur prend son bain; La Main du professeur Hamilton ou Le Roi des dollars; Service précipité; La Poule fantaisiste; Modelage express; Faust et Méphistophélès; Lutteurs américains; La Valise enchantée; Compagnons de voyage encombrants; Cake-Walk de la pendule; Répétition dans un cirque; Jocko musicien; Les Braconniers; La Liqueur du couvent; Le Voleur sacrilège; Enlèvement en automobile et mariage précipité;* 1903-04—*Secours aux naufragés; La Mouche; La Chasse au cambrioleur; Nos Bons Étudiants; Les Surprises de l'affichage; Comme on fait son lit on se couche; Le Pompon malencontreux1; Les Enfants du miracle; Pierrot assassin; Les Deux Rivaux;* 1904—*L'Assassinat du Courrier de Lyon; VIEILLES ESTAMPES* series (4 titles); *Mauvais cœur puni; Magie noire; Rafle de chiens; Cambrioleur et agent; SCÈNES DIRECTOIRE* series (3 titles); *Duel tragique; L'Attaque d'un diligence; Culture intensive ou Le Vieux Mari; Cible humaine; Transformations; Le Jour du terme; Robert Macaire et Bertrand; Electrocutée; La Rêve du chasseur; Le Monolutteur; Les Petits Coupeurs de bois vert; Clown en sac; Triste Fin d'un vieux savant; Le Testament de Pierrot; Les Secrets de la prestidigitation dévoilés; La Faim...L'occasion...L'herbe tendre; Militaire et nourrice; La Première Cigarette; Départ pour les vacances; Tentative d'assassinat en chemin de fer; Paris la nuit ou Exploits d'apaches à Montmartre; Concours de bébés; Erreur de poivrot; Volée par les bohémiens (Rapt d'enfant par les romanichels); Les Bienfaits du cinématographe; Pâtissier et ramoneur; Gage d'amour; L'Assassinat de la rue du Temple (Le Crime de la rue du Temple); Le Réveil du jardinier; Les Cambrioleurs de Paris;* 1905—*Réhabilitation; Douaniers et contrebandiers (La Guérité); Le Bébé embarrassant; Comment on dort à Paris!; Le Lorgnon accusateur; La Charité du prestidi-*

gitateur; Une Noce au lac Saint-Fargeau; Le Képi; Le Pantalon coupé; Le Plateau; Roméo pris au piège; Chien jouant à la balle; La Fantassin Guignard; La Statue; Villa dévalisée; Mort de Robert Macaire et Bertrand; Le Pavé; Les Maçons; La Esmeralda; Peintre et ivrogne; On est poivrot, mais on a du cœur; Au Poulailler!; 1906—*La Fée au printemps; La Vie du marin; La Chaussette; La Messe de minuit; Pauvre pompier; Le Régiment moderne; Les Druides; VOYAGE EN ESPAGNE* series (15 titles); *LA VIE DE CHRIST* (25 tableaux); *Conscience de prêtre; L'Honneur du Corse; J'ai un hanneton dans mon pantalon; Le Fils du garde-chasse; Course de taureaux à Nîmes; La Pègre de Paris; Lèvres closes (Sealed Lips); La Crinoline; La Voiture cellulaire; La Marâtre; Le Matelas alcoolique; A la recherche d'un appartement;* 1907—*La vérité sur l'homme-singe (Ballet de Singe); Déménagement à la cloche de bois; Les Gendarmes; Sur la barricade (L'enfant de la barricade);* 1910—*A Child's Sacrifice (The Doll);* 1911—*Rose of the Circus; Across the Mexican Line; Eclipse; A Daughter of the Navajos; The Silent Signal; The Girl and the Bronco Buster; The Mascot of Troop 'C'; An Enlisted Man's Honor; The Stampede; The Hold-Up; The Altered Message; His Sister's Sweetheart; His Better Self; A Revolutionary Romance; The Violin Maker of Nuremberg;* 1912—*Mignon or The Child of Fate; A Terrible Lesson; His Lordship's White Feather; Falling Leaves; The Sewer; In the Year 2000; A Terrible Night; Mickey's Pal; Fra Diavolo; Hotel Honeymoon; The Equine Spy; 2 Little Rangers; The Bloodstain; At the Phone; Flesh and Blood; The Paralytic; The Face at the Window;* 1913—*The Beasts of the Jungle; Dick Whittington and His Cat; Kelly From the Emerald Isle; The Pit and the Pendulum; Western Love; Rogues of Paris; Blood and Water; Ben Bolt; The Shadows of the Moulin Rouge; The Eyes that Could Not Close; The Star of India; The Fortune Hunters;* 1914—*Beneath the Czar; The Monster and the Girl; The Million Dollar Robbery; The Prisoner of the Harem; The Dream Woman; Hook and Hand; The Woman of Mystery; The Yellow Traffic; The Lure; Michael Strogoff or The Courrier to the Czar; The Tigress; The Cricket on the Hearth;* 1915—*The Heart of a Painted Woman; Greater Love Hath No Man; The Vampire; My Madonna; Barbara Frietchie* (co-d); 1916—*What Will People Say?; The Girl with the Green Eyes; The Ocean Waif; House of Cards;* 1917—*The Empress; The Adventurer; A Man and the Woman; When You and I Were Young; Behind the Mask;* 1918—*The Great Adventure;* 1919—*The Divorcee* (ass't d); *The Brat* (ass't d); 1920—*Stronger than Death* (ass't d); *Tarnished Reputation.*

Publications:

By GUY:

Book—*Autobiographie d'une pionnière du cinéma 1873-1968,* Paris 1976; articles—"Woman's Place in Photoplay Production" by Alice Blaché in *The Moving Picture World,* 11 July 1914; letter in *Films in Review* (New York), May 1964; "La Naissance du cinéma" in *Image et Son* (Paris), April 1974; "Tornez, mesdames..." in *Ecran* (Paris), August/September 1974.

On GUY:

Book—*Early Women Directors* by Anthony Slide, New York 1977; articles—"Madame Alice Blaché" by H.Z. Levine in *Photoplay* (New York), March 1912; "The First Female Producer" by Charles Ford in *Films in Review* (New York), March 1964;

"Alice Guy Blache" by F.L. Smith in *Films in Review* (New York), April 1964; "Out of Oblivion: Alice Guy Blaché" by Francis Lacassin in *Sight and Sound* (London, summer 1971; "Czarina of the Silent Screen" by G. Peary in *Velvet Light Trap* (Madison, Wisconsin), fall 1972; "Sur Alice Guy: polemique" by J. Deslandes in *Ecran* (Paris), September 1976; "A propos d'Alice Guy" by Jean Mitry in *Ecran* (Paris), July 1976; "Czarina of the Silent Screen" by G. Peary in *Velvet Light Trap* (Madison), winter 1977.

* * *

Alice Guy was the first person, or among the first, to make a fictional film. The story-film was quite possibly "invented" by her in 1896 when she made *La Fée aux choux (The Cabbage Fairy)*. Certain historians claim that films of Louis Lumière and Georges Méliès preceded Guy's first film. The question remains debatable; Guy claimed precedence, devoting much effort in her lifetime to correcting recorded errors attributing her films to her male colleagues, and trying to secure her earned niche in film history. There is no debate regarding Guy's position as the world's first woman filmmaker.

Between 1896 and 1901 she made films averaging just 75 feet in length; from 1902 to 1907 she made numerous films of all types and lengths using acrobats, clowns, and opera singers as well as large casts in ambitious productions based on fairy and folk tales, Biblical themes, paintings, and myths. The "tricks" she used—running film in reverse and the use of double exposure—were learned through trial-and-error. In this period she also produced "talking pictures," in which Gaumont's Chronophone synchronized a projector with sound recorded on a wax cylinder.

One of these sound films, *Mireille*, was made by Guy in 1906. Herbert Blaché-Bolton joined the film crew of *Mireille* to learn directing. Alice Guy and Herbert were married in early 1907, and moved to the U.S. where they eventually set up a studio in Flushing, N.Y. The Blachés then established the Solax Company, with a Manhattan office. In its four years of existence, Solax released 325 films including westerns, military movies, thrillers, and historical romances. Mme. Blaché's first picture in the U.S. was *A Child's Sacrifice* (in 1910) centering on a girl's attempts to earn money for her family. In her *Hotel Honeymoon* of 1912, the moon comes alive to smile at human lovers, while in *The Violin Maker of Nuremberg* two apprentices contend for the affections of their instructor's daughter.

The Blachés built their own studio at Fort Lee, N.J., with a daily printing capacity of 16,000 feet of positive film. For its inauguration, in February 1912, Mme. Blaché presented an evening of Solax films at Weber's Theatre on Broadway. In that year she filmed two movies based on operas: *Fra Diavolo* and *Mignon*, each 3-reelers, with orchestral accompaniment. Her boldest enterprises were films using animals and autos.

Cataclysmic changes in the film industry finally forced the Blachés out of business. They rented, and later sold, their studio, then directed films for others. In 1922, the Blachés divorced. Herbert directed films until 1930, but Alice could not find film work and never made another film. She returned to France but without prints of her films, she had no evidence of her accomplishments. She could not find work in the French film industry either. She returned to the U.S. in 1927 to search the Library of Congress and other film depositories for her films, but in vain: only a half-dozen of her one-reelers survive. In 1953, she returned to Paris, where, at 78, she was honored as the first woman filmmaker in the world. Her films, characterized by innovation and novelty, explored all genres, and successfully appealed to both French and American audiences. Today she is finally being recognized as a unique pioneer of the film industry.

—Louise Heck-Rabi

GUZMÁN, PATRICIO. Chilean. Born in Santiago de Chile, 11 August 1941. Educated at EOC—Escuela oficial de cinematografía (Official Film School), Madrid, degree 1969. Career: 1958—publication of 1st short stories; 1964—2 novels published in Santiago; 1965—joins Filmic Institute, Catholic University in Santiago; 1967—leaves for Spain; 1970—returns to Chile, joins Chile-Films (national film production company), heading Documentary Film Workshops; 1973—constitutes Group of the Third Year to produce *The Battle of Chile*; imprisoned shortly after coup d'etat of Sept. 11; 1974—leaves Chile for Cuba; 1974-77—completes *The Battle of Chile* in Cuba; 1980—goes to Spain, begins to prepare *La rosa de los vientos*.

Films (as director): 1965—*Viva la libertad (Hail to Freedom)**; 1966—*Artesania popular (Popular Crafts)**; *Electroshow**; 1967—*Cien Metros con Charlot (100 Meters with Chaplin)*; *Escuela de sordomudos (School for Deafmutes)*; 1968—*La tortura (Torture)*; *Imposibrante*; 1969—*Opus seis (Opus 6)*; *El Paraiso ortopedico (Orthopedic Paradise)*; 1970—*Elecciones municipales (Municipal Elections)*; *El primer año (The 1st Year)*; 1972—*La respuesta de Octubre (The Response in October)*; *Comandos comunales (Communal Organization)*; *Manuel Rodriguez* (unfinished); 1974—*La batalla de Chile: La lucha de un pueblo sin armas(The Battle of Chili: The Struggle of an Unarmed People)* Part 1: *La insurreccion de la burguesia (Insurrection of the Bourgeoisie)*; 1976—Part 2: *El golpe de estado (Coup d'état)*; 1979—Part 3: *El poder popular (The Popular Power)*; 1981—*La rosa de los vientos (Rose of the Winds)*; note: * denotes short feature.

Publications:

By GUZMÁN:

Books—*La insurrección de la burgesia*, edited by Racinante, Caracas 1975; *La batalla de Chile: La lucha de un pueblo sin armas*, Madrid 1977; *El cine contra el fascismo*, with P. Sempere, edited by Fernando Torres, Valencia 1977; articles—"Más vale una sólida formación política que la destreza artesanal", interview by S. Salinas and H. Soto in *Primer Plano* (Valparaiso), vol.2, no.5, 1973; "Chili: le cinéma de l'unité populaire", interview by H. Ehrmann and others in *Ecran* (Paris), February 1974; "Le Cinéma dans la politique de l'Unité Populaire" in *Jeune cinéma* (Paris), November 1974; "Stadion Chile" in *Film und Fernsehen* (Berlin), February 1974; "Il cinema cileno nel periodo del governo popolare" in *Quaderno informativo* (Pesaro), September 1974; "La Bataille du Chili II", interview by Marcel Martin in *Ecran* (Paris), January 1977; "Politics and the Documentary in People's Chile", interview by Julianne Burton in *Socialist Review*, October 1977; reprinted by Angry Arts Film Series, Cambridge, Mass., 1978; "*La batalla de Chile*", interview by Carlos Galiano in *Cine Cubano* (Havana), no.91-92, 1978; "Chile: 3: Guzmán" and "Chile" in *Framework* (Norwich, England), spring and autumn 1979; "Wirklichkeit und Dokument", interview by C. Galiano in *Film und Fernsehen* (Berlin), November 1980; "Interview with Patricio Guzmán" by Z.M. Pick in *Ciné-Tracts* (Montreal), winter 1980.

On GUZMÁN:

Articles—"Chili: la première année" by Guy Gauthier in *Image et son* (Paris), March 1973; "*La Bataille du Chili*" by Ginette Delmas in *Jeune Cinéma* (Paris), July/August 1975; "*La Bataille du Chili*, première partie: *L'Insurrection de la bourgeoisie*" by Guy Gauthier in *Image et son* (Paris), January 1976; "*La Batalla du Chili: el golpe de estado*" by Hubert Niogret in *Positif* (Paris), July/August 1976; "Patricio Guzman—ein Filmschöpfer der Unidad Popular" by J. Hönig in *Information* (Berlin), no.1, 1977; "*La Batalla du Chile*, deuxième partie: *Le Coup d'état*" by Jean Delmas in *Jeune Cinéma* (Paris), February 1977; "De l'histoire déjà" by Paul-Louis Thirard in *Positif* (Paris), February 1977; "La Batalla de Chile", special section of *Cine Cubano* (Havana), March 1978; "The Battle of Chile" by Dennis West in *Cineaste* (New York), v.11, no.2; "Documenting the End of the Chilean Road to Socialism: *La Batalla de Chile*" by Dennis West in *The American Hispanist*, February 1978; "*Battle of Chile*: Struggle of People without Arms" by V. Wallis in *Jump Cut* (Chicago), November 1979; "*Battle of Chile* in Context" by Angry Arts group in *Jump Cut* (Chicago), November 1979.

* * *

Chilean director Patricio Guzmán studied fiction filmmaking in Spain in the 1960s, but he eventually dropped plans to make fiction features when he returned to Chile during the presidency of the Marxist-socialist Salvador Allende (1970-73). Guzmán is above all a political filmmaker, and the intense everyday political activities in Allende's Chile stimulated Guzmán to take to the streets and factories in order to make documentary records of those fast-paced events. In all three of his documentaries on Allende's Chile—*El primer año*, *La repuesta de octubre*, and *La batalla de Chile*—the director rejected archival footage and the compilation approach in favor of immersing himself in significant political events in order to obtain actuality footage.

Guzmán's success in obtaining meaningful and abundant actuality footage is owing in large part to his (and his colleagues') marked ability to understand and foresee the flow of political events. Political savvy coupled with rigorous and disciplined production techniques allowed Guzmán and his production groups to overcome formidable obstacles, including financial and technical difficulties. To film the three feature-length parts of the masterwork *La batalla de Chile*, the director and his collective had access to one 16mm Eclair camera and one Nagra tape recorder; film stock, unavailable in Chile, had been sent from abroad by a European colleague.

During his stay in Allende's Chile, Guzmán successfully combined his personal political militancy with his concept of the role of the filmmaker. Guzmán, a committed Marxist, wished to make films that would help Allende's leftist Popular Unity coalition take power. Marx and Engels (*Manifesto of the Communist Party*) viewed classes as the protagonists of history, and conflict as an inherent dimension of class societies; Guzmán follows this Marxist conception in that classes are the protagonists of his films and events are framed in terms of class conflict. In accordance with the Marxist-Leninist revolutionary view that there can be no peaceful transition to socialism before the repressive machinery of the bourgeois state is broken up and replaced, the first two parts of *La batalla de Chile* follow the military's drift to the right as well as the anti-Allende activities of the opposition-dominated legislature. Both *La respuesta de octubre* and part three of *La batalla de Chile* center on workers organizing as a class in order to achieve self-emancipation and transform the world the bourgeoisie created.

The style of the journalistic *El primer año* is unexceptional, and it was only with *La batalla de Chile* that Guzmán found a distinctive documentary style. This style is characterized by the frequent use of the sequence shot, which the director prefers because it is a synthetic device allowing spectators to see events unfolding in front of their eyes without breaks in the flow of the images.

El primer año and *La respuesta de octubre* have not circulated widely outside of Allende's Chile. Inside Allende's Chile, these documentaries were well received by working-class audiences. *La respuesta de octubre* was particularly popular with workers who, heartened to see their efforts to create worker-controlled industrial zones documented on film, facilitated the documentary's distribution in the factories. Guzmán's international reputation as a documentary filmmaker has been secured by *La batalla de Chile*, hailed by both Marxist and non-Marxist critics in many countries as a landmark in the history of the political documentary.

—Dennis West

HAANSTRA, BERT. Dutch. Born in Holten, Holland, 31 May 1916. Educated at Academy of Arts, Amsterdam. Career: late 1930s—works as painter and press photographer; 1952—begins association with Royal Dutch Shell Film Unit; 1956—producer and manager of Shell Film Unit, Venezuela; 1960—sets up Bert Haanstra Filmproductie as production company; Recipient: Grand Prix (documentary), Cannes Festival, for *Mirror of Holland*, 1951.

Films (as director, scriptwriter, photographer, and editor): 1948—*De Muiderkring herleeft (The Muyder Circle Lives Again)*; 1949—*Myrte en de demonen (Myrte and the Demons)* (Schreiber) (ph only); *Boer Pietersen schiet in de roos (Bull's Eye for Farmer Pietersen)* (Brusse) (ph only); 1950—*Spiegel van Holland (Mirror of Holland)*; 1951—*Nederlandse beeldhouwkunst tijdens de late Middeleeuwen (Dutch Sculpture)* (d, co-ed only); *Panta Rhei (All Things Flow)*; (as director and scriptwriter): 1952—*Dijkbouw (Dike Builders)* (+ed); 1954—*Ontstaan en vergaan (The Changing Earth)*; *De opsporing van aardolie (The Search for Oil)*; *De verkenningsboring (The Wildcat)*; *Het olieveld (The Oilfield)*; 1955—*The Rival World (Strijd zonder einde)* (+ed); (as producer, director, scriptwriter, and editor): 1955—*God Shiva*; *En de zee was niet meer (And There Was No More Sea)*; *Belgian Grand Prix* (Hughes) (co-ph only); 1957—*Rembrandt, schilder van de mens (Rembrandt, Painter of Man)*; *De gouden Ilsy (The Golden Ilsy)* (van der Linden) (ph only); *Olie op reis (Pattern of Supply)* (Pendry) (pr only); 1958—*Over glas gesproken (Speaking of Glass)*; *Glas (Glass)* (co-ed); *Fanfare* (d, co-sc, co-ed only); 1959—*Paleontologie (Schakel met het verleden, Story in the Rocks)* (van Gelder) (pr, tech advisor only); 1960—*De zaak M.P. (The M.P. Case)* (co-sc, co-ed); *Lage landen (Hold Back the Sea)* (Sluizer) (tech advisor only); 1962—*Zoo*; *Delta Phase I*; *De overval (The Silent Raid)* (Rotha) (co-sc only, uncredited); 1963—*Alleman (The Human Dutch)* (co-sc, +narration for English and German versions); 1966—*De stem van het water (The Voice of the Water)* (co-sc); 1967—*Retour Madrid (Return Ticket to Madrid)* (co-pr, d only, +co-ph); 1968—*Pas assez (Not Enough, Niet genoeg)* (van der Velde) (ed only); 1970—*Trafic* (Tati) (collaborator only); *Summer in the Fields* (van der Linden) (ed only); 1972—*Bij de beesten af (Ape and Super Ape)* (+co-commentary, co-add'l ph, narration); 1975—*Dokter Pulder zaait papavers (Dr. Pulder Sows Poppies, When the Poppies Bloom Again)* (pr, d only); 1978—*Nationale Parken...noodzaak (National Parks...a Necessity, National Parks* *in the Netherlands)*; 1979—*Een pak slaag (Mr. Slotter's Jubilee)* (pr, d only); *Juliana in zeventig bewogen jaren (Juliana in 70 Turbulent Years)* (Kohlhaas) (advisor only); 1983—*Vroeger kon je lachen (One Could Laugh in Former Days, Formerly, You Had a Big Time)* (pr, d, sc only); *Nederland (The Netherlands)*; Role: 1972—interviewee in *Grierson* (Blais).

Publications:

By HAANSTRA:

Articles—"Gesprek met Bert Haanstra en prof. dr. G.P. Behrends" by R. du Mée and others in *Skoop* (Amsterdam), v.8, no.6, 1972; "Geen klachten over hoeveelheid aandacht voor Nederlandse film" in *Skoop* (Amsterdam), February 1976.

On HAANSTRA:

Articles—"Director of the Year" in *International Film Guide*, London 1966; "Bert Haanstra" by Peter Cowie in *Focus on Film* (London), spring 1972; biofilmography in *Film Dope* (London), March 1981.

*   *   *

Bert Haanstra is one of Holland's most renowned filmmakers. The 28 films he has made from 1948 until the present day belong to various genres. His first films were documentaries. Typical of these, and a hallmark of Haanstra's personal style, is the frequent use of "rhyming images" and of images blending into each other. Critics responded warmly to the lyrical and pictorial qualities of Haanstra's early work. In his films about oil drilling, commissioned by Shell, Haanstra showed that instructional films can be of artistic as well as informative value.

Haanstra tutored numerous younger Dutch filmmakers, among them George Sluizer, Kees Hin, Wim van der Velde, and Rolf Orthel, who have worked as his assistants. A more permanent cooperation was established with Anton van Munster (camera) and Simon Carmiggelt and Anton Koolhaas, two important Dutch authors who scripted and narrated a number of Haanstra's films.

Haanstra's first feature film, *Fanfare*, was a comedy and a big hit at the box-office. The film, however, was also praised for its artistic importance and considered by many as a turning point in the situation of the Dutch film: "This film should set the tone for the future production of Dutch feature-films," wrote a critic. His second feature film, *De zaak M.P.*, was very coolly received, however, and Haanstra turned again to making documentaries.

Discussions in the sixties about the establishment of a tradition of Dutch feature films—a tradition which was lacking at that time—were heavily influenced by the views on film expressed by the French *nouvelle vague* cineasts. Haanstra's long documentaries, *Alleman*, *De stem van het water*, and *Bij de beesten af*, show that the filmmaker is perfectly able to catch the peculiarities of human behaviour, especially those of the Dutch. These three films still enjoy a firm reputation in Holland and also in other countries. *Alleman* and *Bij de beesten af* were nominated for Academy awards. Although the number of movie-goers in Holland has sharply decreased, Haanstra's public has remained large and loyal.

In 1975 Haanstra made his first novel-based film. *Dokter Pulder zaait papavers* gives a subtle and detailed analysis of a number of fundamental human problems: loss of love, social failure, aging, addiction to drugs and liquor. The film is psycho-logically convincing and full of tension. *Een pak slaag*, again based on a novel by Anton Koolhaas, failed to interest the public. In 1983 Haanstra brought out another feature film with Simon Carmiggelt as the main character listening to the tragicomical monologues of all kinds of ordinary people. Carmiggelt's art, as an author, in rendering this type of monologue had won a wide audience for his daily columns which have appeared since 1945 in a Dutch newspaper. The film, *Vroeger kon je lachen*, was well received.

By virtue of the diversity of genres to which his films belong, and of the great reputation they have won him with critics and the public, Haanstra has made an invaluable contribution to the establishment of a Dutch film tradition. He is a very important representative of the Dutch documentary shcool which grew to fame in the sixties and won countless awards at international film festivals. Haanstra's own films have won over 70 prizes; he received an Oscar for *Glas*, a short documentary film. As a director of feature films he has convinced a large audience that Dutch films can (and should) be judged according to the same standards by which important foreign films are judged.

His films, and also his cooperation with Simon Carmiggelt and Anton Koolhaas, show that Haanstra's work is firmly rooted in Dutch culture which, however, he transcends by taking it as an example of more general aspects of human behavior. This is beautifully exemplified in *Bij de beesten af*. Although his films do not contain explicit political statements, Haanstra is anything but a "neutral observer". By the art of montage he gives his films a deeper meaning which not infrequently embodies a critical view of human society. His eye for humorous, often tragicomical, situations yields poignant scenes in which general values mark individual lives and make them seem typical.

—Dorothee Verdaasdonk

HALAS, JOHN, and BATCHELOR, JOY. British. Janos Halasz born in Budapest, 16 April 1912; Joy Batchelor in Watford, England, 12 May 1914. Married. Career: 1928-31—Halas apprentice to George Pal; early 1930s—spends 18 months in Paris, returns to Budapest and teaches at Atelier, graphic design school; 1934—Halas opens 1st animation studio, Halas, Macskasi and Kassowitz; 1935—Batchelor begins working in films as artist; 1936—Halas moves to England; 1937—Joy Batchelor hired as designer and animator to work on *Music Man*; 1940—Halas & Batchelor Cartoon Films formed; 1940-45—make numerous information and propaganda films for British government; 1952-54—produce only feature-length British cartoon, *Animal Farm*, based on George Orwell novel; 1967—computerized animation used on series of films about mathematics; 1968—Halas & Batchelor bought by Trident Television; Batchelor and Halas concentrate on individual projects working through their other company, Educational Film Centre; from 1968 to 1972 not responsible for films produced by Halas & Batchelor production company; 1970—Halas elected President of International Council of Graphic Design Associations (ICOGRADA); 1973—Joy Batchelor retires but continues to act as advisor to animation students at International Film School, London; 1974—Halas & Batchelor sold back to Halas after losing money for corporation; 1975—Halas made President of International Animated Film Association (ASIFA); also Chairman of the Federation of Film Societies; and Contributing Editor and Film/TV correspondent to *Novum* (Munich).

Animated Films (as co-animators): 1938—*The Music Man*

(+Halas d). Principal productions of Halas & Batchelor production companies (John Halas and Joy Batchelor as co-producers and co-directors unless otherwise indicated, and in other capacities following '+' sign): 1940—*Train Trouble* (+anim); 1940—*Carnival in the Clothes Cupboard* (+co-des, co-anim); 1941—*Filling the Gap* (+co-sc, co-anim); *Dustbin Parade* (+co-sc, co-des, co-anim); 1942—*Digging for Victory* (+co-sc, co-anim, des: Batchelor); 1943—*Jungle Warfare* (+co-des, co-anim); 1944/45—*Handling Ships* (feature) (Halas only pr, co-d, des, anim); 1946—*Modern Guide to Health* (+co-des, sc: Batchelor); *Old Wives' Tales* (+co-des, sc: Batchelor); 1946/47—"Charley" series [*Charley in the New Towns*; *Charley in the New Schools*; *Charley in "Your Very Good Health"*; *Charley in the New Mines*; *Charley Junior's Schooldays*; *Charley's March of Time*] (+co-sc, co-des); *Robinson Charley* (+co-des); 1947—*First Line of Defence* (+co-sc); *This Is the Air Force* (+co-sc); *What's Cooking?* (+co-des, sc: Batchelor); *Dolly Put the Kettle On* (+co-des, sc: Batchelor); 1948—*Oxo Parade* (+co-des, sc: Batchelor); *Magic Canvas* (co-pr only, +Halas d, sc, co-des); *Water for Fire Fighting* (feature) (Halas only co-d); *Heave Away My Johnny* (+co-sc); 1949—*The Shoemaker and the Hatter* (+co-sc, co-des); *Submarine Control* (pr: Crick, co-d: Privett and Crick); *Fly About the House* (+co-des, sc: Batchelor); (John Halas as producer and director): 1950—*As Old as the Hills* (co-pr only); *Earth in Labour* (co-pr, +co-sc); 1951—*Moving Spirit* (co-pr, co-d, +co-sc: Batchelor); "Poet and Painter" series [Programme 1: *Twa Corbies, Spring and Winter*; Programme 2: *Winter Garden, Sailor's Consolation, Check to Song*; Programme 3: *In Time of Pestilence, The Pythoness*; Programme 4: *John Gilpin*]; (Halas & Batchelor productions with John Halas and Joy Batchelor serving in capacities as indicated): 1952—*We've Come a Long Way* (H: co-pr, B: co-sc); *The Owl and the Pussycat* (stereoscopic) (H: pr, co-d, co-sc); *Linear Accelerator*; 1953—*Power to Fly* (H: co-pr, B: co-sc)); 1954—*Animal Farm* (feature—begun 1951) (H & B: co-pr, co-d, co-sc, co-des); *Down a Long Way* (H: co-pr, B: co-sc); *The Sea* (H: pr, sc); 1955—*Animal Vegetable Mineral* (H: co-pr, B: co-sc); "Popeye" series [*The Billionaire*; *Dog Gone Dog Catcher*; *Matinee Idol*; *Model Muddle*; *Weight for Me*; *Potent Lotion*; *Which Is Witch?*] (H: pr, co-d); 1956—*The World of Little Ig* (H & B: co-pr, H: d, B: sc); *The Candlemaker* (H & B: co-d, H: pr, B: co-sc); *To Your Health* (H: pr, B: co-sc); 1957—*History of the Cinema* (H: pr, d, co-sc, co-des); *Midsummer Nightmare* (H & B: co-pr, co-sc, H: d, co-des); 1958—*The First 99* (H & B: co-pr, B: d, co-sc); *The Christmas Visitor* (H & B: co-pr, co-sc, H: d); *Dam the Delta* (H & B: d, B: sc); *Speed the Plough* (H: co-pr, B: co-sc); *Early Days of Communication* (H: co-pr, d); 1959—*How to Be a Hostess* (live action) (H: pr, B: sc); *Man in Silence* (H: co-d); *All Lit Up* (H & B: co-pr, co-d, B: sc); *Piping Hot* (H & B: co-pr, co-d, B: sc); *Energy Picture* (H & B: co-pr, B: sc); *For Better for Worse* (H & B: co-pr, co-d, B: sc); 1960—"Foo-Foo" series [*The Gardener*; *The Birthday Treat*; *A Denture Adventure*; *A Misguided Tour*; *The Caddies*; *Burglar Catcher*; *The Art Lovers*; *The 3 Mountaineers*; *Foo Foo's New Hat*; *The Big Race*; *The Treasure Hunt*; *The Magician*; *The Spy Train*; *Insured for Life*; *Automation Blues*; *The Beggar's Uproar*; *Sleeping Beauty*; *The Reward*; *The Dinner Date*; *Beauty Treatment*; *The Ski Resort*; *Lucky Street*; *The Stowaway*; *A Hunting We Will Go*; *The Pearl Divers*; *Foo Foo's Sleepless Night*; *The Salesman*; *Art for Art's Sake*; *The Dog Pound*; *The Hypnotist*; *Low Finance*; *The Scapegoat*] (H: pr); "Habatales" series [*The Lion Tamer*; *Hairy Hercules*; *The Cultured Ape*; *The Insolent Matador*; *The Widow and the Pig*; *I Wanna Mink*] (H: pr, co-d); "Snip and Snap" series [*Bagpipes*; *Treasure of Ice Cake Island*; *Spring Song*; *Snap's Rocket*; *Snakes and Ladders*; *In the Jungle*; *Lone World Sail*; *Thin Ice*; *Magic Book*; *Circus Star*; *Moonstruck*; *Snap and the Beanstalk*; *Goodwill to All Dogs*; *In the Cellar*; *The Grand Concert*; *The Beggar's Uproar*; *The Birthday Cake*; *Snap Goes East*; *The Hungry Dog*; *Top Dogs*] (H: pr, co-d, co-sc); *History of Inventions* (H: co-pr, co-sc); *Wonder of Wool* (H: pr, d); *Guns of Navarone* (Foreman) (H: des of excerpts); 1961—*The Monster of Highgate Pond* (live action) (H: pr, B: sc); *Hamilton the Musical Elephant* (H: pr, d, co-sc); *Hamilton in the Music Festival* (H: pr, d, co-sc); 1961/69—"Concept Films" series [200 titles in areas of "Biology," "Science," and "Maths"] (H: pr); 1962—*Barnaby—Father Dear Father* (H & B: co-pr, H: d, co-des); *Barnaby—Overdue Dues Blues* (H & B: co-pr, H: d, co-des); *The Showing Up of Larry the Lamb* (H: pr); 1963—*Automania 2000* (H & B: co-pr, co-sc, H: d); *The Axe and the Lamp* (H: pr, d); 1964—*The Tale of the Magician* (H: pr); *Ruddigore* (feature) (H & B: co-pr, B: d, sc); *Paying Bay* (H & B: co-pr, B: co-sc); *Follow That Car* (H & B: co-pr, B: co-sc); (Halas as producer and co-scriptwriter): "The Tales of Hoffnung" series [*The Symphony Orchestra*; *The Palm Court Orchestra* (+d); *The Music Academy* (+co-d); *The Vacuum Cleaner*; *Professor Ya-Ya's Memoirs* (+co-d); *The Maestro* (+co-d); *Birds Bees and Storks* (+d)]; "The Carters of Greenwood" English language teaching series (12 films) (H: pr, d); "Martian in Moscow" Russian language teaching series (12 films) (H: pr, d); "Evolution of Life" series (8 films) (H: pr); "Do Do" series (72 episodes) (H: pr, d); "Les Aventures de la famile Carre" French language teaching series (12 films) (H: pr, co-d); 1966—*ICOGRADA Congress* (live action) (H: pr, d); "Classic Fairy Tales" series (6 films) (H & B: co-pr, B: d, sc); *Matrices* (H: pr); *Dying for a Smoke* (H: pr, d, B:co-sc); *Deadlock* (H: pr); *Flow Diagram* (H: pr); *Linear Programming* (H: pr); 1966/67—"Lone Ranger" series (37 episodes) (H: co-pr, co-d); 1967—*The Question* (H: pr, d); *What Is a Computer?* (H: co-pr); *Girls Growing Up* (H: pr); *Mothers and Fathers* (H: pr); *Colombo Plan* (H & B: co-pr, B: d, sc); *The Commonwealth* (H & B: co-pr, B: d, sc); 1968—*Bolly* (H & B: co-pr, B: d, sc); *Functions and Relations* (H: pr); 1969—*Measure of Man* (H: pr); *To Our Children's Children* (H: pr, d, des); 1970—*Short Tall Story* (H & B: co-pr, H: d); *The Five* (H & B: co-pr, B: d, sc); *Wot Dot* (H & B: co-pr, B: d, sc); *Flurina* (H & B: co-pr, H: d); "Tomfoolery" series (17 episodes) (H: pr, d); *This Love Thing*; 1971—*Children and Cars* (H & B: co-pr, co-sc, H: d); *Football Freaks*; "The Condition of Man" series [*Condition of Man*; *Quartet*; *Up*; *Let It Bleed*; *It Furthers One to Have Somewhere to Go*; *Xeroscopy*] (H: pr); 1972—"The Addams Family" series (17 episodes); "The Jackson 5" series (17 episodes); 1973—"The Osmonds" series (17 episodes); *Children Making Cartoons* (live action) (H: pr); "Britain Now" series (live action) [*Animals*; *Sports*; *Roads*] (H: pr); *Contact* (H & B: co-d, B: co-sc); *Making Music Together*; *The Glorious Musketeers* (feature) (H: d); *The 12 Tasks of Asterix* (Watrin and Gruel) (animation in last reel only); 1974—*Kitchen Think*; *The Ass and the Stick* (H & B: co-sc, B: d); *Christmas Feast* (H & B: co-sc, H: d); *Carry On Milkmaids* (B: d, sc); *Butterfly Ball*; 1975—*How Not to Succeed in Business* (H: pr, d); *Life Insurance Training Film* (excerpts) (H: pr); 1976—*Skyrider* H: pr, d, co-sc); 1977—*Making It Move* (live action) (H: pr, d, co-sc); *Noah's Ark* (H: pr); 1978—*Max and Moritz* (feature) (H: co-pr, d); "Wilhelm Busch Album" series (13 films) (H: co-pr); 1979—*Bravo for Billy* (H: co-pr); *10 for Survival* (H: co-pr, d, B: sc); *Autobahn* (H: pr, d, co-sc); *Dream Doll* (H: co-pr); 1980—*Bible Stories.*

Publications:

By HALAS:

Books—*Archibald the Great*, illustrations by Halas, London

1937; *How to Cartoon for Amateur Films*, London 1951; *Technique of Film Animation*, with Roger Manvell, London 1959; *Design in Motion*, with Roger Manvell, London 1962; *Film and Television Graphics*, with Walter Herdeg, London 1967; *Art in Movement*, with Roger Manvell, London 1970; *Visual Scripting* edited by Halas, London 1976; *Film Animation*, Paris 1976; *Computer Animation*, London 1976; *Timing for Animation*, London 1981; articles—"The Film Cartoonist" in *Working for the Films*, London 1947; "The Animated Film" in *Art and Industry* (London), July 1947; "From Script to Screen" in *Art and Industry* (London), August 1947; "Cartoon Films in Commerce" in *Art and Industry* (London), November 1947; "The Approach to Cartoon Film Scriptwriting" in *This Film Business*, London 1948; "Introducing Hamilton...And Some of the People Who Gave Him Birth" in *Films and Filming* (London), June 1962; introduction to *The Great Movie Cartoon Parade* compiled by D. Rider, New York 1976; "Talking with Halas and Batchelor" in *1000 Eyes* (New York), February 1976; "The Way Forward" in *Film* (London), March 1979.

On HALAS and BATCHELOR:

Book—*Art and Animation* by Roger Manvell, London 1980; articles—"Halas and Batchelor: Profile of a Partnership" in *Film* (London), March 1955; "Halas and Batchelor" in *International Film Guide*, London 1965; "Halas and Batchelor" in *Film* (London), spring 1966.

*   *   *

Halas and Batchelor, the distinguished animation studio, and film research and production center, was established in London in 1940. It was the result of the partnership (and subsequent marriage) of two artists, John Halas and Joy Batchelor. John Halas was educated in Budapest and Paris, and had originally worked as an assistant to George Pal before establishing himself as an independent animator in 1934. In 1936 he had come to England; while working on a cartoon film, *Music Man*, he had met Joy Batchelor, who entered films in 1935 as a commerial artist.

Their unit made its name during the Second World War for its imaginative and excellently designed government-sponsored cartoon propaganda and informational films, some 70 of which were produced between 1941-45. They injected into such forbidding subjects as saving scrap metal both wit and distinction of design, turning them into a ballet of movement with the constant collaboration of two celebrated composers, Francis Chagrin and Matyas Seiber. Highly technical instructional films, for example *Handling Ships* and the post-war *Water for Firefighting* and *Submarine Central*, extended range and proved their capacity to match clarity of exposition with design in technological subjects. This was especially notable in the extensive series of informational films sponsored by British Petroleum on oil exploration and technology, such as *Moving Spirit*.

In the 1950's, Halas and Batchelor were able to expand their work yet further, producing films on purely artistic subjects such as their *Poet and Painter* series (working with such artists as Henry Moore, Ronald Searle, and Mervyn Peake). The climax of this came with the feature cartoon version of George Orwell's *Animal Farm*, Britain's first full-length animated entertainment film. By now their London-based studio had become one of the largest in Western Europe, and the unit was capable of attracting international talent from Europe and America to supplement the work of such long-term resident animators as Harold Whitaker, Bob Privett, Digby Turpin, Vic Bevis, Tony Guy, and Brian

Borthwick. The Canadian, Gerry Potterton, and the American, Philip Stapp, for example, directed their brilliant film on alcoholism, *To Your Health*, sponsored by the World Health Organization. Jack King supervised editing and sound, and supplemented the composition of innumerable original music scores by Chagrin, Seiber and others with his own witty and tuneful compositions. The unit had from its start been distinguished for its sponsorship of fine scores; apart from Chagrin and Seiber (between them responsible for some 250 original compositions), contributing composers have included Benjamin Fraenkel, Tristram Cary, and Johnny Dankworth.

Animal Farm, still perhaps the best-known internationally of Halas and Batchelor films, was sponsored in 1952 by the American producer, Louis de Rochemont; Orwell's fatalistic fable had been published in 1945. In a period when almost all cartoon films featuring animal characters were cutely comic, Orwell's novel demanded a basically serious approach to animal characterization. The 1,800 background drawings involved represented in somewhat stylized form a realistic farm setting, while the animals themselves were strongly developed as serious dramatic characters. Seiber wrote a powerful score, orchestrated for 36 instruments, and all the animals were voiced by a single, highly versatile actor, Maurice Denham. A controversial point was the provision of a somewhat uplifting end, in which it seemed the oppressed animals might be led to revolt against the police state established by the pigs, in place of Orwell's wholly negative view of a society irrevocably lost to any hope of democratic revival.

The economics of animation have always been precarious, and Halas and Batchelor primarily supported their unit by the mass production of commercials for television, the production of sponsored public relations films, films made in association with other production companies, and by sponsored entertainment series undertaken for television, such as the *Foo-Foo* cartoon series and the *Snip and Snap* series, the latter introduced paper sculpture animals and both series, made in association with ABC-TV, enjoyed world-wide distribution.

Experimental work as early as the 1950's included stereoscopy (work with Norman McLaren for the 1951 Festival of Britain, and *The Owl and the Pussycat*); and advanced form of film puppetry, with Alan Crock, in *The Figurehead*; work in New York (1953-54) for the original three-projection form of Cinerama; cooperation with the Czech stage presentation, *Living Screen*, combining the multi-projection of film in close synchronization with the live player on the stage; and the production from 1960 of some 200 8mm cassettes to illustrate through brief animation loops points in scientific and technological instruction linked directly to the textbook. Other subjects the studio pioneered were the first animated film version of a Gilbert and Sullivan opera, *Ruddigore*, *The Tales of Hoffnung*, a series co-sponsored with BBC-TV, and two animated series of language teaching films in Russian and French.

In association with Roger Manvell (who worked for three years with the unit on research and scriptwriting) John Halas has written over a span of some 20 years several books on the art and technology of animation, *The Technique of Film Animation*, *Design in Motion* and *Art in Movement*, while Roger Manvell recorded the 40-year history of the unit (very fully illustrated by John Halas) in *Art and Animation*, which contains an extensive filmography. Other books edited by John Halas include *Computer Animation* and, with Walter Herdeg, *Film and TV Graphics*.

John Halas's interest in the most advanced form of technolgy in animation took him into computer animation in the early period of its development in the 1960s. The computer, once mastered as an ally, can cut costs as well as increase limitlessly the artistic propensities of the filmmaker. Halas's first production using the computer was a series of films on mathematics made in

1967; he originated his own computer language: HALAB. His later interests have included the investigation of hologram and laser techniques.

Looking back over its forty years' existence and its wide variety of prize-winning productions exemplifying many styles, from hand-drawn animation to computerized graphics, certain titles among others must stand out as examples of their kind in the period of their production. For education, propaganda, and public relations: *Dustbin Parade, Fly about the House, As Old as the Hills, Down a Long Way, To Your Health, Wonder of Wool,* and *The Colombo Plan*; and as artistic works for entertainment: *Magic Canvas,* the *Poet and Painter* series, *The Owl and the Pussycat, The Figurehead, Animal Farm, History of the Cinema,* the *Snip and Snap* series, *Automania 2000* (the unit's record prize-winner), *The Tales of Hoffnung, Ruddigore, The Question, Butterfly Ball, Autobahn,* and *Dream Doll*. In the second half of the twentieth century, the names of John Halas and Joy Batchelor will inevitably be linked with the history of the fuller development of international animation.

—Roger Manvell

HAMER, ROBERT. British. Born in Kidderminster, 31 March 1911. Educated at Rossall; Corpus Cristi College, Cambridge. Career: 1934—begins working in films as clapper boy; 1935—becomes cutter at London Films; 1938—begins as editor on Erich Pommer's *Vessel of Wrath*; 1943—becomes associate producer; 1945—makes directing debut; 1963—at time of death planning adaptation of *Lady Windermere's Fan.* Died 1963.

Films (as editor): 1938—*Vessel of Wrath (The Beachcomber)* (Pommer); *St. Martin's Lane W.C.2 (Sidewalks of London)* (Whelan) (co-ed); 1939—*Jamaica Inn* (Hitchcock); 1940—*La Cause commune (Factory Front)* (Cavalcanti—short); *French Communique* (Cavalcanti—short); 1941—*Mastery of the Sea* (Cavalcanti—short); *Turned Out Nice Again* (Varnel) (uncredited); *Ships with Wings* (Nolbandov); *The Foreman Went to France (Somewhere in France)* (Frend); (as associate producer): 1943—*My Learned Friend* (Dearden and Hay) (uncredited); *San Demetrio London* (Frend) (+co-sc); 1944—*Fiddlers 3* (Watt) (+d add'l scenes, co-lyrics); (as director): 1945—"The Haunted Mirror" episode of *Dead of Night*; 1947—*It Always Rains on Sunday* (+co-sc); *The Loves of Joanna Godden* (Frend) (d some scenes while director ill); 1949—*Kind Hearts and Coronets* (+co-sc); *The Spider and the Fly*; 1951—*His Excellency* (+sc); 1952—*The Long Memory* (+co-sc); 1954—*Father Brown (The Detective)* (+co-sc); *To Paris with Love*; 1955—*Rowlandson's England* (Hawkesworth—short) (co-sc only); *Molière* (Tildian and de Chessin—short) (commentary for English-language version only); 1958—*The Scapegoat* (+sc); 1959—*School for Scoundrels or How to Win without Actually Cheating*; 1962—*55 Days at Peking* (Ray) (add'l dialogue only); 1963—*A Jolly Bad Fellow (They All Died Laughing)* (Chaffey) (co-sc only).

Publications:

By HAMER:

Articles—interview by Freda Lockart in *Sight and Sound* (London), October/December 1951; "A Free Hand" in *Sight and Sound* (London), spring 1959.

On HAMER:

Articles—"Hamer's Potted Lifemanship" by J. Vincent in *Films and Filming* (London), July 1959; "'Projecting Britain and the British Character: Ealing Studios" by C. Barr in *Screen* (London), summer 1974; biofilmography in *Film Dope* (London), March 1981.

*   *   *

Rarely can a director's career have risen and declined quite so abruptly as that of Robert Hamer. (Only Preston Sturges, perhaps, furnishes a comparable example.) Within the space of 15 years, Hamer directed an episode of one film and two further films evincing increasing mastery and promise; he achieved one outstanding masterpiece, then went into virtually instantaneous decline, and produced half a dozen disappointing pictures culminating with a dismal flop. Three years later he was dead, at the age of 52: in David Thomson's words, "the most serious miscarriage of talent in the post-war British cinema."

Something of the forces that contributed to Hamer's sadly blighted career can be inferred from his films—especially the later ones, which often center around lonely, unattached individuals, victims of emotional atrophy. (Four of his pictures starred Alec Guinness, whose remote, withdrawn quality as an actor clearly matched Hamer's requirements.) The protagonists of *The Scapegoat, The Long Memory,* and *The Spider and the Fly* are all isolated, at odds with society; and a similarly bleak despair pervades the Chestertonian humor of *Father Brown,* preventing laughter. Only once, in *Kind Hearts and Coronets,* did Hamer strike the ideal balance between comedy and the blackness of his vision.

From the first, Hamer's films evoked a dark, dangerous world lurking below the calm surface of everyday life. (This, in itself, is enough to set them apart from the commonsense mainstream of Ealing Studios, for whom all Hamer's early films were made.) In his *Haunted Mirror* episode from *Dead of Night,* a bland young man is drawn into a past filled with sexual jealousy and madness. The son in *Pink String and Sealing Wax* escapes from his stiflingly respectable Victorian family into a glittering night-world of drink, lust and, ultimately, murder. The exciting, threatening past, in the person of her convict ex-lover, returns to confront the heroine of *It Always Rains on Sunday.* In all these films, Hamer displays an exceptional flair for the vivid recreation of atmosphere and milieu, as sure with the lush Victoriana of *Pink String* as with the contemporary East End realism of *It Always Rains on Sunday.* The latter offers a rare example of the pre-war fatalism of Carné effectively transposed to a British context.

All these elements—the black humour, the concern with suppressed passion, the sense of atmosphere, as well as Hamer's savagely ambiguous view of family life—come together in his one masterpiece, *Kind Hearts and Coronets.* Undoubtedly the finest black comedy ever produced by the British cinema, *Kind Hearts* blends wit, elegance, and unfailingly apt visual effects into a stylish and consistently satisfying film. The humor, both verbal and visual, is wickedly subversive, and complemented by superb performances—especially from Dennis Price, Joan Greenwood, and Alec Guinness in his famous eight-fold role.

From there on, it was all down hill. Neither *The Spider and the Fly* nor *Father Brown* could be dismissed as failures, but they never approach the sustained mastery of *Kind Hearts,* and the vitality of the early films is also lacking. Michael Balcon, the head of Ealing, felt that Hamer was "engaged on a process of self-destruction." In the light of the artistic deterioration of the later films, paralleled by the director's gradual descent into alcoholism, Balcon's verdict would, sadly, appear to be justified.

—Philip Kemp

HAMMID, ALEXANDER. Czech and American. Born Alexander Hackenschmied of Czech parents in Linz, Austria, 17 December 1907; became citizen of United States in 1947. Educated first in architecture, then in photography and cinema at Polytechnic, Prague. Married Maya Deren, 1942 (divorced 1947). Career: 1929—while student, taken on as scenic designer by Czech director Gustav Machaty; works on *Erotikon* (1929) and *From Saturday to Sunday* (1931); 1930—borrows camera and shoots 1st experimental film; reviews films for Prague daily *Národní osvobození* (until 1933) and weekly *Pestrý týden* (until 1931); 1934—engaged by producer Ladislav Kolda to make series of short films on Czech spa towns; 1935-38—works at Baťa studios at Zlín making commercials and promotional films; 1937—travels to India and Ceylon for Baťa Enterprises, filming whatever interested him; 1938—meets American filmmaker Herbert Kline and begins collaborating on *Crisis*, first of 3 feature documentaries with him; 1939—leaves Czechoslovakia following Nazi takeover; 1940—works on *Lights Out in Europe* with Kline in London; moves to U.S., works on *The Forgotten Village* in Mexico; 1942—meets Maya Deren in Los Angeles, begins to do experimental work again; 1943-45—directs for the Overseas Branch of the U.S. Office of War Information; 1945-50—works with Affiliated Film Producers, New York; 1947—changes last name to "Hammid"; 1950s—freelances for U.S. Information Agency, National Broadcasting Company, and others; 1952—goes to work at United Nations under temporary contract and joins staff 1954; 1962-present—collaboration with filmmaker Francis Thompson; 1964—they make 3-screen *To Be Alive!* for Johnson Wax Pavilion at New York World's Fair; as Francis Thompson Inc., specialize in multi-screen and very large-screen films for exhibitions. Recipient: New York Critics Special Citation for the Creative Use of the Motion Picture for *To Be Alive!*, 1965; Best Documentary Short Subject Academy Award for *To Be Alive!*, 1965.

Films (as production assistant): 1929—*Erotikon* (Machaty); (as maker of short experimental films): 1930—*Bezúčelná procházka (Aimless Walk)*; 1931—*Ze soboty na neděli (From Saturday to Sunday)* (Machaty) ("Artistic collaborator" only); 1932—*Na Pražském hradě (Prague Castle)*; (as director, or in capacities as indicated): 1933—*Zem spieva (The Earth Sings)* (Plicka) (ed); 1934—*Jaro v Praze (Prague Spring)* (Plicka—from footage originally shot for *The Earth Sings*) (ed, credited for ph); *Listopad (November)* (Vávra) (ph); *Město živé vody (City of Live Water)*; *Karlovy Vary*; *Jáchymov*; 1937—*Poslední léto (The Last Summer)* (co-ph, co-ed); *Silnice spívá (The Highway Sings)* (Bata studio) (co-ph); 1938—*Crisis: A Film of "The Nazi Way" (Kline)* (ph, tech d, ed); *Historie fíkového listu (History of the Fig Leaf)* (co-ph); *Pojďte námi (Come with Us)* (co-ph); 1939—*Lights Out in Europe* (Kline) (ph, ed); *Chudí lidé (Poor People)* (Klos) (ph); 1939-40—*Vzpomínka na ráj (Souvenir of Paradise)* (Klos) (ph); *Reka života a smrti (The River of Life and Death)* (Klos) (ph); *Přístav v srdci Europy (Harbor in the Heart of Europe)* (co-ph); *Dvakrát kauček (Rubber Twice)* (co-ph); 1940—*The Forgotten Village* (Kline) (ph, tech d, ed); 1943—*Meshes of the Afternoon* (collaboration with Deren—tech d, ph, ed); 1944—*Valley of the Tennessee* (+ed); *Toscanini: Hymn of the Nations*; *At Land* (Deren) (co-ph, co-ed only); 1945—*A Better Tomorrow* (+ed); *Library of Congress* (+ed); *A Study in*

Choreography for Camera (Deren) (co-ph, co-ed only); *The Private Life of a Cat* (in silent and sound versions); 1945-46—*Ritual in Transfigured Time* (Deren) (co-ph, co-ed, tech advisor, uncredited); 1947—*Georgia O'Keeffe* (Rodakiewicz) (ed); 1948—*Princeton* (ed); *The Photographer* (Jacoby and Van Dyke) (ed); 1949—*Marriage for Moderns*; 1950—*Angry Boy*; 1950—last of 4 segments of *Of Men and Music* (pr: Polk and Luber); 1951—*The Medium* (film of Menotti opera); *Gentlemen in Room 8*; 1953—*Shrimp Fisherman*; 1954—*Workshop for Peace*; *Conversation with Arnold Toynbee*; 1955—*Operation Hourglass*; 1956—*Kid Brother*; 1957—*Israel, an Adventure* (co-d, ph); 1958—2 of 4 segments in *Power Among Men* (pr: Dickinson); 1960—*Night Journey* (+ed); *Pablo Casals Master Class*; 1961—*Family Centered Maternity Care*; *Collage*; *River Music*; 1962—*Jascha Heifetz Master Class*; (in collaboration with Francis Thompson): 1962—*To Be Alive!* (co-d, ph); 1964—*To the Fair!* (co-d); 1967—*We Are Young* (for Expo '67, Montreal (co-d, ph); 1968—*US* (for Hemisfair '68, San Antonio (co-d, ph); 1973—*City Out of Wilderness* (ph, co-ed); 1976—*American Years* (collaborating ed); *To Fly* (supervising ed); 1978—*The Living Earth* (supervising ed).

Publications:

By HAMMID:

Book—*To Be Alive!*, with Francis Thompson and others, New York 1966; articles—"Film and Music", translated by Karel Santar, in *Cinema Quarterly* (Edinburgh), spring 1933; "New Fields—New Techniques" in *The Screen Writer*, May 1946; interview in *Documentary Explorations: 15 Interviews with Filmmakers* edited by G. Ray Levin, New York 1971; writings in *Film Culture* (New York), no.67-69, 1979.

On HAMMID:

Books—*Alexander Hackenschmied* by Jaroslav Brož, Prague 1973; *Nonfiction Film: A Critical History* by Richard Barsam, New York 1973; *The People's Films* by Richard Dyer MacCann, New York 1973; *Visionary Film: The American Avant-Garde* by P. Adams Sitney, New York 1974; articles—"The Interpretive Camera in Documentary Films" by Willard Van Dyke in *Hollywood Quarterly*, July 1946; "*The Private Life of a Cat*" by Maya Deren in *Mademoiselle* (New York), July 1947; "Comment fut realisé *The Forgotten Village*" in *Positif* (Paris), no.10, 1954; "Films at the Fair" by Edward Conner in *Films in Review* (New York), November 1964; "Movie Man" in *The New Yorker*, 10 October 1964; "Notes, Essays, Letters" by Maya Deren in *Film Culture* (New York), winter 1965; "*To Be Alive!* and the Multi-Screen Film" by Maxine Haleff in *Film Culture* (New York), winter 1966; "The Greatest Film Show on Earth" by Herb Lightman in *American Cinematographer* (Los Angeles), August 1967; "Expo 67: Audio-Visual Revolution" by Arthur Rosien and "Multi-screen, Multi-media Trend" in *Industrial Photography*, June 1967; "*We Are Young*" in *American Cinematographer* (Los Angeles), August 1967; "Confluence, U.S.A. and a Film Called *US*" in *American Cinematographer* (Los Angeles). August 1968; "Alexander Hammid: A Survey of His Filmmaking Career" by T.E. Valasek in *Film Culture* (New York), no.67-69, 1979.

HANI, SUSUMU. Japanese. Born in Tokyo, 10 October 1926. Graduated from Jiyu Gakuen, Tokyo. Married actress Sachiko Hidari, 1960. Career: 1945—begins working for Kyoto News Agency; 1950—joins Iwanami Eiga production company; works first as still photographer, then director of commercials and sponsored documentaries; 1959—produces TV series *Nenrin no himitsu (Tricks of Their Trades)*, directing 5 of the 52 episodes; 1964—writes and directs TV play *Futatabi gotatsu (Once in May)*; mid-'60s—forms Hani Productions; 1970s—makes wildlife documentaries. Recipient: First Prize (educational short), Venice Festival, for *Children Who Draw*, 1955; First Prize (short film), Cannes Festival, for *Children Who Draw*, 1955; Special Jury Prize for Best Direction, Moscow Festival, for *Children Hand in Hand*, 1965.

Films (as director and scriptwriter of short and medium-length films): 1952—*Seikatsu to mizu (Water in Our Life)*(co-d, co-sc); *Yuki matsuri (Snow Festival)*; 1953—*Machi to gesui (The Town and Its Drains)*; 1954—*Anata no biru (Your Beer)*; *Kyoshitsu no kodomotachi (Children in the Classroom)*; 1955—*Eo kaku kodomotachi (Children Who Draw)*; 1956—*Group no shido (Group Instruction)*; *Soseiji gakkyu (Twin Sisters)*; *Dobutsuen nikki (Zoo Story)*(feature length); 1958—*Shiga Naoya*; *Horyu-ji (Horyu Temple)*; *Umi wa ikiteiru (The Living Sea)* (feature length); *Nihon no buyo (Dances in Japan)*; *Tokyo 1958* (co-d, co-sc, +co-ed); (as director of feature films): 1960—*Furyo shonen (Bad Boys)*; 1962—*Mitasareta seikatsu (A Full Life)*(+co-sc); *Te o tsunagu kora (Children Hand in Hand)*; 1963—*Kanojo to kare (She and He)* (+co-sc); 1965—*Bwana Toshi no uta (The Song of Bwana Toshi, Bwana Toshi)* (+co-sc); 1966—*Andesu no hanayome (Bride of the Andes)*(+sc); 1968—*Hatsuoki jigokuhen (Inferno of First Love, Nanami: Inferno of First Love)* (+co-sc); 1969—*Aido (Aido, Slave of Love)*; 1970—*Mio* (+sc, co-ed); 1972—*Gozenchu no jikanwari (Timetable, Morning Schedule)* (+co-sc); 1981—*Afurika monogatari (A Tale of Africa)* (co-d).

Publications:

By HANI:

Books—*Engishinai shuyakutachi* [The Leading Players Who Do Not Act, The Non-professional Actor], 1958; *Camera to maiku no ronri* [Aesthetics of Camera and Microphone], 1960; *Afurika konnan ryoko* [My Travels in Africa, Report About Film Making in Africa], 1965; *Andes ryoko* [Travels in the Andes, Report About Film Making in the Andes], 1966; articles—interview by James Blue in *Film Comment* (New York), spring 1969; "En préparant *Mio*" in *Ecran* (Paris), July/August 1972; "Susumu Hani: a decouvrir avec *Bwana Toshi*", interview by A. Tournes in *Jeune cinéma* (Paris), April/May 1979.

On HANI:

Article—biofilmography in *Film Dope* (London), September 1981.

*   *   *

Hani was born in Tokyo in 1928, the son of a famous liberal family. After schooling, he worked for a while as a journalist at Kyodo Press and entered filmmaking as a documentarist in 1950 when he joined Iwanami Productions. Most of his later dramatic features reflect his early documentary training, relying on authentic locations, amateur actors, hand-held camera techniques, and emphasis upon contemporary social issues.

His film career comprises three areas: documentary films; narratives relating to social problems, especially among the young; and dramas focusing on the emerging woman.

Of the eighteen documentaries made between 1952 and 1960, the best known are *Children in the Classroom* and *Children Who Draw Pictures*. The latter won the 1957 Robert Flaherty Award.

Hani's first dramatic feature, *Bad Boys*, emanated from many of his previous concerns. The film, a loose series of situations about reform school, was reenacted by former inmates who improvised dialogue. For Hani, truth emerges from the juxtaposition of fiction and fact. He also believes that all people have an innate capacity for acting.

Subsequent films which deal with the effect of post-war urban realities on the lives of the young include: *Children Hand in Hand* and *Inferno of First Love*. The former depicts young children in a provincial town and especially one backward child who becomes the butt of the other children's malicious teasing and pranks; the latter is a story of two adolescents in modern Tokyo, each of whom has been exploited, who find with each other a short-lived refuge.

Like his earlier documentaries, these films explore the themes of broken homes, the alienation of modern society, the traumatic effects of childhood, the oppressiveness of a feudal value system, and the difficulty of escaping, even in an alternative social structure. To all these films Hani brings a deep psychological understanding of the workings of the human psyche. Finally, each of these films focuses on individual growth and self-awakening, although Hani is clear to indicate that the problems cannot be solved on a personal level. Both topics—growing self-awareness and a critique of the existing social order—connect these works with Hani's second major theme, the emergence of women.

Hani's first film on this subject was *A Full Life*, which deals with the efforts of a young wife, married to a self-involved older man, to forge a life of her own in the competitive world of modern Tokyo. After demeaning work and involvement in the student demonstrations of the early 1960s, the wife returns home, a changed woman.

Hani's other films on this theme are *She and He*, the depiction of a middle-class marriage in which the wife gains independence by her kindness to a local ragpicker, and *Bride of the Andes*, the story of a mail-order Japanese bride in Peru, who finds personal growth through her relationship with the South American Indians. As in *A Full Life*, none of these women are able to make a full break with their husbands. However, through personal growth (usually affected by contact with a group or person marginal to society), they are able to challenge the patriarchal values of Japanese society as represented by their husbands and to return to the relationship with new understanding and dignity. Both films starred Sachiko Hidari, who was then his wife.

Contact with non-Japanese society, a challenge to deep-seated Japanese xenophobia, is also the theme of Hani's *The Song of Bwana Toshi*, which was filmed in Kenya and deals with Toshi, an ordinary Japanese man living in Central Africa. Here he cooperates with the natives and thus rises above his isolation to establish brotherhood with foreigners.

Hani's subsequent work *Timetable* combines his interest in contemporary youth with his continued interest in modern women. The story deals with two high school girls who decide to take a trip together. The fiction feature, which is narrated, was filmed in 8mm and each of the major actors was allowed to shoot part of the film. Further, the audience is informed of who is shooting, thereby acknowledging the filmmaker within the context of the work. The use of 8mm is not new for Hani. More than half of his fourth film was originally shot in 8mm. Likewise, the use of a narrator dates back to *A Full Life*.

Throughout his career Hani has concerned himself with people who have difficulty in communicating with one another and he remains one of the foremost psychologists of the Japanese cinema.

—Patricia Erens

HATHAWAY, HENRY; American. Born Marquis Henri Leopold de Frennes in Sacramento, 13 March 1898. Left school at age 14. Career: 1850—his grandfather, Marquis Henri Leopold, is commissioned by the King of the Belgians to acquire the Sandwich Islands (Hawaii), but failing to do so, settles in San Francisco; 1908—through contacts of actress mother and theatrical manager father, enters film industry as child actor and protégée of Allan Dwan; 1912—works as prop boy for Universal studios; 1912-17—plays juvenile roles in films; 1918-19—military service; 1919-32—serves as assistant director for Sam Goldwyn's studio and later Paramount, under such directors as Paul Bern, Victor Fleming, and Josef von Sternberg; 1921—briefly works as prop man for producer-director Frank Lloyd; 1932—directs 1st film *Heritage of the Desert* for Paramount; 1935—directs 1st critical and financial success, *The Lives of a Bengal Lancer*; 1945—directs *The House on 92nd Street*, a semi-documentary which uses documentary footage of real events in dramatized fashion, and initiates a cycle of films in this style; 1974—directs last film *Hangup*.

Films (as assistant director): 1923—*The Spoilers* (Hillyer); *To the Last Man* (Fleming); 1924—*The Heritage of the Desert* (Willat); *The Border Legion* (Howard); 1925—*The Thundering Herd* (Howard); *Wild Horse Mesa* (Seitz); 1926—*Bachelor Brides (Bachelor's Brides)* (Howard); *Mantrap* (Fleming); *Man of the Forest* (Waters); 1927—*Hula* (Fleming); *The Rough Riders (The Trumpet Call)* (Fleming); *Underworld (Paying the Penalty)* (von Sternberg); 1928—*The Last Command* (von Sternberg); *Under the Tonto Rim* (Raymaker); *The Shopworn Angel* (Wallace); 1929—*Sunset Pass* (Brower); *Wolf Song* (Fleming); *Thunderbolt* (von Sternberg); *The Virginian* (Fleming); *Redskin* (Schertzinger); 1930—*7 Days Leave (Medals)* (Wallace); *The Texan* (Cromwell); *Morocco* (von Sternberg); *The Spoilers* (Carewe); 1931—*Dishonored* (von Sternberg); 1932—*The Shanghai Express* (von Sternberg); (as director): 1932—*Heritage of the Desert*; *Wild Horse Mesa*; 1933—*Under the Tonto Rim*; *Sunset Pass*; *Man of the Forest*; *To the Last Man*; *The Thundering Herd*; 1934—*The Last Round-Up*; *Come on Marines!*; *The Witching Hour*; *Now and Forever*; 1935—*The Lives of a Bengal Lancer*, *Peter Ibbetson*; 1936—*Trail of the Lonesome Pine*; *Go West, Young Man*; *I Loved a Soldier* (unfinished); 1937—*Souls at Sea*; *Lest We Forget*; 1938—*Spawn of the North*; 1939—*The Real Glory*; 1940—*Johnny Apollo*; *Brigham Young (Brigham Young—Frontiersman)*; *Sundown*; 1941—*The Shepherd of the Hills*; 1942—*10 Gentlemen from West Point*; *China Girl*; 1944—*Home in Indiana*; *Wing and a Prayer*; 1945—*Nob Hill*; *The House on 92nd Street*; 1946—*The Dark Corner*; *13 Rue Madeleine*; 1947—*Kiss of Death*; 1948—*Call Northside 777*; 1949—*Down to the Sea in Ships*; 1950—*The Black Rose*; *Rawhide*; 1951—*You're in the Navy Now (U.S.S. Tea Kettle)*; *14 Hours*; *The Desert Fox (Rommel—Desert Fox, The Story of Rommel)*; 1952—*Diplomatic Courier*; "The Clarion Call" episode of *O. Henry's Full House (Full House)* (+d linking scenes, uncredited); *Red Skies of Montana* (Newman) (co-d uncredited); 1953—*Niagara*; *White Witch Doctor*; *The Coronation Parade*; 1954—*Prince Valiant*; *Garden of Evil*; 1955—*The Racers (Such Men Are Dangerous)*; 1956—*The Bottom of the Bottle (Beyond the River)*; *23 Paces to Baker Street*; 1957—*Legend of the Lost* (+co-pr); 1958—*From Hell to Texas (Manhunt)*; 1959—*Woman Obsessed*; 1960—*North to Alaska* (+pr); *7 Thieves*; 1962—"The Rivers," "The Plains," and "The Outlaws" episodes of *How the West Was Won*; 1963—*Rampage* (Karlson) (d begun by Hathaway); 1964—*Circus World (The Magnificent Showman)*; *Of Human Bondage* (Hughes) (began film and d add'l scenes); 1965—*The Sons of Katie Elder*; 1966—*Nevada Smith* (+pr); 1967—*The Last Safari* (+pr); 1968—*5 Card Stud*; 1969—*True Grit*; 1970—*Airport* (some direction when George Seaton became ill); 1971—*Raid on Rommel*; *Shootout*; 1974—*Hangup*.

Roles: 1917—*The Storm Boy* (Baldwin); 1972—appearance in *75 Years of Cinema Museum* (Hershon and Guerra).

Publications:

By HATHAWAY:

Articles—interview by Michel Ciment and Bertrand Tavernier in *Positif* (Paris), March 1972; Interview by Rui Nogueira in *Focus on Film* (Washington, D.C.), v.7.

On HATHAWAY:

Articles—"Lives of a Hollywood Director" by K. Crichton in *Collier's* (New York), 5 September 1936; "The Best 2nd Fiddle" by John Howard Reid in *Films and Filming* (London), November 1962; "Likable but Elusive" by Andrew Sarris in *Film Culture* (New York), spring 1963; "The Directors Choose the Best Films" in *Cinema* (Beverly Hills), August/September 1963; "No Pro Like an Old Pro" by Arthur Knight in *Saturday Review* (New York), 21 June 1969; "Henry Hathaway: Filmography" by A. Eyles in *Focus on Film* (Washington, D.C.), January/February 1970; article by Michael Kerbel in *Village Voice* (New York), 18 November 1971; "Sur Henry Leopold de Fienne, dit Hathaway" by Bertrand Tavernier in *Positif* (Paris), February 1972; "An Appreciation of Henry Hathaway" by Kingsley Canham in *The Hollywood Professionals, Vol. 1*, London 1973; article and "Hathaway's Films" by Kingsley Canham in *Focus on Film* (Washington, D.C.), v.7; "Legend of the Lost" by Stuart Kaminsky in *Velvet Light Trap* (Madison), winter 1975; biofilmography in *Film Dope* (London), September 1981.

* * *

Henry Hathaway had a reputation for being difficult on actors, but efficient with film. Aside from strictly biographical information, very little is generally said or known about Hathaway, and to a large extent this neglect is due to film critics.

Hathaway's career can be seen in terms of four distinct periods, each period representing a change in his assignments, control and interests. His western period (1932-34) comprises nine films including *Wild Horse Mesa, To the Last Man*, and *Under the Tonto Rim*. "Commercial versatility" characterizes films from 1934-45 including such contract projects as *Lives of a Bengal Lancer, Peter Ibbetson, Souls at Sea, Johnny Apollo*, and *Sundown*. The noir and semi-documentary films of 1945-52 include *The House on 92nd Street, The Dark Corner, 14 Hours, 13 Rue Madeleine, Kiss of Death*, and *Call Northside 777*. It is the films of Hathaway's mature period, beginning with *Niagara*, in 1952, that have been most neglected by critics.

Hathaway is clearly interested in foreign or exotic locales. This has been true throughout his career, but most strikingly in his mature period when only four of his films have had a contemporary or American setting. He has tended to see all of his exotic settings—Africa, the Old West, Mexico—as primitive, mysterious, grotesque, and even comic, dominated by a visual unreality. It has generally been accepted that Hathaway's one major excursion into surrealism was *Peter Ibbetson*. The evidence of the film shows, however, that depiction of unreality, the conversion of supposedly "real" settings into personal, unreal visions, is a growing interest with Hathaway. Unreality frequently intrudes on Hathaway's films, most strikingly in his use of painted backdrops and optical effects.

Hathaway's heroes are always remarkably humble and humanly weak. They drink, wench, cheat, but always respect and believe in the unknown. They are, like John Wayne in *Legend of the Lost*, mystics in a strange landscape, god-fearing men who have either been through a terrible crisis which taught them humility, or are undergoing that crisis in the course of the film.

The films in the mature period are about specific, dangerous quests undertaken by small groups in hostile, barren lands (with this in mind, *Prince Valiant* is not an act of commercial pandering, but a quintessential Hathaway film). The quest, for the hero, is an act of communion with nature or he learns that it should be. If the protagonist-hero is a younger man, he transgresses intentionally or by accident and is shown the way back to righteousness by an older, paternal figure. Invariably, the young protagonist or the woman must face the crisis of a father or husband who proves to have been less than he should have been. The woman, young man, or even villain must have the strength to accept this Jobian lesson or be destroyed by it and by their own hatred.

As should be obvious by now, Hathaway's films are filled with striking mixtures of Christianity and paganism. Mystical omens and forebodings abound, and Hathaway characters frequently quote from the Old Testament to gain strength or understanding.

—Stuart M. Kaminsky

HAUFF, REINHARD. German. Born in in Marburg, 23 May 1939. Educated in German studies, sociology, and theater in Vienna and Munich. Married film director Christel Buschmann. Career: 1963—becomes script and directing assistant for TV shows and teleplays; 1970—directs 1st feature *Mathias Kneissl*; this and subsequent films co-produced with WDR (Cologne) television; 1973—with Volker Schlöndorff and B. von Junkersdorf forms Bioskop production company. Recipient: Deutscher Filmpreis: Filmband in Silber for *Messer im Kopf*, 1979.

Films (as director): 1969—*Untermann—Obermann* (+co-sc—documentary); *Die Revolte* (+co-sc); *Ausweg los* (+co-sc—documentary); 1970—*Offener Hass gegen Unbekannt* (+co-sc); 1971—*Mathias Kneissl* (+co-sc); 1972—*Haus am Meer* (+co-sc); 1973—*Desaster*; 1974—*Die Verrohung des Franz Blums*; *Zündschnüre*; 1975—*Paule Pauländer*; 1977—*Der Hauptdarsteller (The Main Actor)* (+co-sc); 1978—*Messer im Kopf*; 1980—*Endstation Freiheit*; 1982—*Der Mann auf der Mauer*.

Publications:

By HAUFF:

Articles—interview in *Die Filmemacher. Der neue deutsche*

Film nach Oberhausen by Barbara Bronnen and Corinne Brocher, Munich 1973; commentary on *Desaster* in *Fernsehspiele Westdeutscher Rundfunk*, July-December 1973; interview in *Jeune Cinéma* (Paris), June 1978; "Versuche mit der Wirklichkeit. Gespräche mit den Filmregisseuren Reinhard Hauff und Christian Ziewer" in *Frankfurter Rundschau* (Frankfort), 16 January 1979; "Reinhard Hauff—Ein Protestant in der Unterwelt", interview by Thomas Timm and Christoph Meier-Siem in *Kino* (Hamburg), no.4, 1980.

On HAUFF:

Articles—"La Blessure symbolique" by Jean-Luc Pouillaude in *Positif* (Paris), June 1979; "Unterhaltung muss weder Cola noch Discothek bedeuten" by Maria Ratschewa in *Westermanns Monatshefte* (Munich), no.1, 1979; "The Man in the Crowd" by Wendy Lesser in *The Threepenny Review* (San Francisco), summer 1981; "Il coltello in testa di Reinhard Hauff" in *Cineforum* (Bergamo), no.221, 1983.

*   *   *

Reinhard Hauff's first feature was *Mathias Kneissl*, the story of a legendary Bavarian highwayman. He then made the television films *Haus am Meer* and *Desaster*. Finally he achieved his impressive film *Die Verrohung des Franz Blum*, about the drastic situation in the prisons, and *Zündschnüre*, from the Resistance novel of Franz Josef Degenhardt. In 1976 he made *Paule Pauländer*, the story of a bright young woman in a village, whose desire for culture and a spiritual life is crushed by the brutal upbringing given her by her primitive father.

This theme is expanded upon in Hauff's next film, *Der Hauptdarsteller*. The sensitive youth Pepe, who has appeared in a film, encounters the big city. This experience leaves deep scars—he cannot come to terms with his new surroundings but he can also no longer live in a small town. Hauff has said "I like directors who work realistically, and whose method is not derived from other films but from life. There are so many dramas in life, but not every filmmaker has the ability to give them form. It has become difficult today to portray a convincing rage or love or obsession."

In his next film, *Messer im Kopf*, which received various awards, Hauff achieved a contemporary political film on the highest artistic level. It concerns a biogeneticist, Hoffmann (Bruno Ganz), who, in a police raid, is accidentally shot, loses his memory, and must learn everything anew. He is branded a terrorist and dismissed from his position. By the other side he is acclaimed as a resistance fighter. For him there is nothing left but to uncover his identity and discover the truth—what actually happened to him and why.

Paralleling *The Lost Honor of Katharina Blum* by Volker Schlöndorff, and Margarethe von Trotta's *Die bleierne Zeit*, *Messer im Kopf* remains one of the most courageous analytical works in the history of West German film, a witness to the harshest conflicts of the seventies in its treatment of terrorism.

Of his influences Hauff has said "Rossellini impressed me deeply, because he understood the making of films not as a photographic act, but as a way of communicating a vision of humanistic morality. For me that means one attempts, from a certain position, to define one's time, not with a pretended objectivity, but from a given point of view."

In *Endstation Freiheit* scriptwriter Burkhard Driest and the director portray the vain efforts of an ex-convict to return to society, and to gain a foothold in everyday life.

Hauff's 1982 *Der Mann auf der Mauer* provoked intense controversy. The hero flees from East Germany and settles in West Berlin in order not to let the wall which separates the two Germanys out of his sight. The wall becomes a waking nightmare, a kind of personal challenge, and he soon tries to go over it again, this time in the opposite direction. In the end he becomes psychotic, and runs once more at the wall. In this film realism serves a socially critical parable about the spiritual condition of the nation.

—Maria Racheva

HAWKS, HOWARD. American. Born Howard Winchester Hawks in Goshen, Indiana, 30 May 1896. Educated at Pasadena High School, California, 1908-13; attended Phillips Exeter Academy, New Hampshire, 1914-16; Cornell University, New York, 1916-17, graduating with a degree in mechanical engineering. Married Athole (Hawks), 1924 (divorced 1941); writer Nancy Roe Gross (divorced); Mary (Dee) Hartford (divorced); children: David, Greg, Barbara McCampbell, and Kitty Tanen. Career: 1916-17—works in the property department at Famous Players-Lasky in Hollywood during vacations from Cornell; 1917-19—serves in U.S. Army Air Corps; after demobilization, designer in airplane factory; 1922—becomes involved with independent film productions in Hollywood with Allan Dwan, Marshall Neilan, and Allen Holubar, working as an editor and assistant director; writes, directs, and finances 2 short comedies; 1924-25—in charge of story dept. at Paramount; 1925—employed by William Fox to write original story and script *The Road to Glory*, which Fox agrees to let him direct; 1925-29—under contract to Fox; afterwards not under contract to a studio; 1944—with Borden Chase forms Motion Picture Alliance for the Preservation of American Ideals; 1962—Museum of Modern Art retrospective; 1970—makes last film, *Rio Lobo*; 1975—wins honorary Academy Award for career's work; 1977—planning western film at time of death. Died in Palm Springs, California, 26 December 1977. Recipient: Quarterly Award, Directors Guild of America, for *Red River*, 1948/49; Honorary Academy Award, 1974.

Films (as prop boy): 1917—*A Little Princess* (Neilan) (+d some scenes, uncredited); (as scriptwriter): 1923—*Quicksands* (Conway) (story, +pr); 1924—*Tiger Love* (Melford); 1925—*The Dressmaker from Paris* (Bern) (co-story); 1926—*Honesty—the Best Policy* (Bennett and Neill) (story); (as director): 1926—*The Road to Glory* (+story); *Fig Leaves* (+story); *Underworld (Paying the Penalty)* (von Sternberg) (co-sc, uncredited); 1927—*The Cradle Snatchers*; *Paid to Love*; *Fazil*; 1928—*A Girl in Every Port* (+co-sc); *The Air Circus* (co-d); 1929—*Trent's Last Case*; 1930—*The Dawn Patrol*; 1931—*The Criminal Code*; 1932—*Red Dust* (Fleming) (co-sc only, uncredited); *The Crowd Roars* (+story); *Tiger Shark*; *Scarface: The Shame of a Nation* (+pr, bit ro as man on bed); 1933—*The Prizefighter and the Lady (Everywoman's Man)* (Van Dyke) (d parts of film—claim disputed); *Today We Live*; 1934—*Viva Villa!* (Conway) (d begun by Hawks); *20th Century*; 1935—*Barbary Coast*; *Ceiling Zero*; 1936—*The Road to Glory*; *Come and Get It* (co-d); *Sutter's Gold* (Cruze) (co-sc, uncredited); 1937—*Captain Courageous* (Fleming) (co-sc, uncredited); 1938—*Test Pilot* (Fleming) (co-sc, uncredited); *Bringing Up Baby*; 1939—*Gone with the Wind* (Fleming) (add'l dialogue, uncredited); *Gunga Din* (Stevers) (co-sc, uncredited); *Only Angels Have Wings*; 1940—*His Girl Friday*; 1941—*The Outlaw* (Hughes) (d begun by Hawks); *Sergeant York*; *Ball of Fire*; 1943—*Air Force*; *Corvette K-225 (The Nelson Touch)* (Rosson) (pr only); 1944—*To Have and Have Not*; 1946—*The Big Sleep*; 1947—*A Song Is Born* (remake of *Ball of Fire*); (as director and producer): 1947—*Red River*; 1949—*I Was a Male War Bride (You Can't Sleep Here)* (d only); 1951—*The Thing (The Thing from Another World)* (Nyby) (pr only); 1952—*The Big Sky*; "The Ransom of Red Chief" episode of *O. Henry's Full House* (episode cut from some copies); *Monkey Business* (d only); 1953—*Gentlemen Prefer Blondes* (d only); 1955—*Land of the Pharaohs*; 1959—*Rio Bravo*; 1962—*Hatari!*; 1963—*Man's Favorite Sport*; 1965—*Red Line 7000* (+story); 1966—*El Dorado*; 1970—*Rio Lobo*.

Publications:

By HAWKS:

Articles—"Entretien avec Howard Hawks" by Jacques Becker, Jacques Rivette, and François Truffaut in *Cahiers du cinéma* (Paris), February 1956; "Interview with Howard Hawks" in *Movie* (London), 5 November 1962; article in *Movie* (London), 5 December 1962; "Man's Favorite Director, Howard Hawks", interview, in *Cinema* (Beverly Hills), November/December 1963; "Entretien avec Howard Hawks" by James R. Silke, Serge Daney, and Jean-Louis Noames in *Cahiers du cinéma* (Paris), November 1964; "Brève rencontre avec Hawks" by Axel Madsen in *Cahiers du cinéma* (Paris), November 1965; "Entretien avec Howard Hawks" by Jean-Louis Comolli, Jean Narboni, and Bertrand Tavernier in *Cahiers du cinéma* (Paris), July/August 1967; "Howard Hawks poète et businessman aux yeux clairs" by Patrick Bureau in *Les Lettres françaises* (Paris), 5 July 1967; "Howard Hawks: Il n'y a qu'une façon de pleurer, il y en a mille de rire" by Claude-Jean Philippe in *Télérama* (Paris), 9 July 1967; interview in *Interviews with Film Directors* by Andrew Sarris, New York 1967; "Gunplay and Horses" by David Austen in *Films and Filming* (London), October 1968; "Do I Get to Play the Drunk this Time", interview, in *Sight and Sound* (London), spring 1971; "An Interview with Howard Hawks" by Naomi Wise and Michael Goodwin in *Take One* (Montreal), November/December 1971; "Entretien avec Howard Hawks" by Claude Beylie in *Cinéma 71* (Paris), April 1971; "Howard Winchester Hawks ou le cinéma (américain) par excellence" by Rui Nogueira in *Les Lettres françaises* (Paris), 10 March 1971; "Howard Hawks: un divertissement immuable in *Le Monde* (Paris), 11 March 1971; interview in *Filmkritik* (Munich), April 1973; interview by M. Goodwin and N. Wise in *Take One* (Montreal), March 1973; "Hawks Talks", interview by J. McBride in *Film Comment* (New York), May/June 1974; "Hawks on Film, Politics, and Childrearing", interview by C. Penley and others in *Jump Cut* (Berkeley), January/February 1975; "You're goddam right I remember", interview by K. Murphy and R.T. Jameson in *Movietone News* (Seattle), June 1977.

On HAWKS:

Books—*The Cinema of Howard Hawks* by Peter Bogdanovich, New York 1962; *La Grande Aventure du Western* by Jean-Louis Rieupeyrout, Paris 1964; *Howard Hawks* by Jean-Claude Missiaen, Paris 1966; *Howard Hawks* by Robin Wood, London 1968, revised 1977; *Howard Hawks* by J.-A. Gili, Paris 1971; *The Films of Howard Hawks* by D.C. Willis, Metuchen, New Jersey 1975; *Howard Hawks, Storyteller* by Gerald Mast, New

York 1982; articles—"Today's Hero: A Review" by John Houseman in *Hollywood Quarterly*, January 1947; "Génie de Howard Hawks" by Jacques Rivette in *Cahiers du cinéma* (Paris), May 1953; "Quelques réalisateurs trop admirés" by Louis Seguin in *Positif* (Paris), September/October 1954; "Howard Hawks" by Jacques Rivette and François Truffaut in *Films in Review* (New York), November 1956; "Howard Hawks et le western" by Michel Perez in *Présence du cinéma* (Paris), July/September 1959; "Filmography" in *Movie* (London), 5 December 1961; "Depuis 40 ans Howard Hawks glorifie dans ses films l'amité, l'action et l'amour de la vie" by Claude-Jean Philippe in *Télérama* (Paris), 30 December 1962; "Sling the Lamps Low" by John Peter Dyer in *Sight and Sound (London), summer 1962; article by V.F. Perkins in Movie* (London), 5 December 1962; "The World of Howard Hawks" by Andrew Sarris in *Films and Filming* (London), July and August 1962; "Rivette on Hawks" in *Movie* (London), 5 December 1962; "Tout sur Howard Hawks" in *Bio-filmographie commentée" by Yves Boisset and others in Cinéma 63* (Paris), January and February 1963; "Hawks homme moderne" by Henri Langlois in *Cahiers du cinéma* (Paris), January 1963; special issue of *Cahiers du cinéma* (Paris), January 1963; "Howard Hawks ou l'ironique" by Jean-Louis Comolli in *Cahiers du cinéma* (Paris), November 1964; "Die Welt von Howard Hawks" in *Film* (Hanover), no.8, 1966; "Une conscience toute neuve" by Roger Tailleur in *Positif* (Paris), November 1967; "Reflections on the Tradition of the Movie Western" by Douglas Brode in *Cineaste* (New York), fall 1968; "A Comment on the Hawksian Woman" by Leigh Brackett in *Take One* (Montreal), July/August 1971; "The Hawksian Woman" by Naomi Wise in *Take One* (Montreal), April 1972; special issue edited by W.-E. Bühler of *Filmkritik* (Munich), May/June 1973; "Howard Hawks" by W.-E. Bühler and others in *Filmkritik* (Munich), April 1973; "L' Oeuvre de Howard Hawks" by Olivier Eyquem in *Avant-Scène du cinéma* (Paris), January 1973; "La Captive aux yeux clairs" by G. Gauthier in *Image et son* (Paris), no.269, 1973; "To Have (Written) and Have Not (Directed)" by Robin Wood in *Film Comment* (New York), May/June 1973; "Howard Hawks e le possibilità del cinema" by G. Frezza in *Filmcritica* (Rome), May 1974; "Howard Hawks: Masculine Feminine" by Molly Haskell in *Film Comment* (New York), March/April 1974; "Hawks in the 30s" by M. Cohen in *Take One* (Montreal), December 1975; "How It Is" by P. Hogue in *Movietone News* (Seattle), April 1975; "The Silent Films of Howard Hawks" by J. Richards in *Focus on Film* (London), summer/autumn 1976; "Hawks Isn't Good Enough" by Raymond Durgnat in *Film Comment* (New York), July/August 1977; special section by Olivier Eyquem and others in *Positif* (Paris), July/August 1977; "Sur 2 films d' Howard Hawks" by P. Mérigeau in *Image et son* (Paris), April 1977; "Dossier: le cinéma de Howard Hawks" by M. Devillers and others in *Cinématographe* (Paris), March 1978; "Last Round in the Great Hawks Debate" by Raymond Durgnat in *Film Comment* (New York), March/April 1978; "La Dernière Sequence (à propos de la femme chez Hawks)" by J. Fresnais in *Cinéma* (Paris), May 1978; "Hommage à Hawks" by Eric Rohmer and others in *Cinéma* (Paris), March 1978; "Hawks" by J. McBride in *Film Comment* (New York), March/April 1978; "Howard Hawks: cinéaste américain" by J. Magny in *Cinéma* (Paris), February 1978; "Hawks vs. Durgnat" by W. Paul in *Film Comment* (New York), January/February 1978; "Hommage to Howard Hawks: François Truffaut's Day for Night" by W.J. Douglass in *Literature/Film Quarterly* (Salisbury, Maryland), v.8, no.2, 1980; "Howard Hawks", with biofilmography, by Michael Walker in *Film Dope* (London), September 1981; films—*The Great Professional—Howard Hawks*, for TV, by Peter Bogdanovich, Great Britain 1967; *Interview with Howard Hawks*, for TV, by Richard Guinea, Great Britain 1968; *The Men Who Made the Movies: Howard Hawks*, for TV, by Richard Schickel, U.S. 1973; *Ein verdammt gutes Leben (A Hell of a Good Life)* by Hans Blumenberg, West Germany 1978.

* * *

Howard Hawks was perhaps the greatest director of American genre films. Hawks made films in almost every American genre, and each of these films could well serve as one of the very best examples and artistic embodiments of the type: gangster (*Scarface*), private eye (*The Big Sleep*), western (*Red River, Rio Bravo*), screwball comedy (*Bringing Up Baby*), newspaper reporter (*His Girl Friday*), prison picture (*The Criminal Code*), science fiction (*The Thing*), musical (*Gentlemen Prefer Blondes*), race-car drivers (*The Crowd Roars, Red Line 7000*), air pilots (*Only Angels Have Wings*). But into each of these narratives of generic expectations Hawks infused his particular themes, motifs, and techniques. Born in the midwest at almost the same time that the movies themselves were born in America, Hawks migrated with his family to southern California when the movies did; he spent his formative years working on films, learning to fly, and studying engineering at Cornell University. His initial work in silent films as a writer and producer would serve him well in his later years as a director, when he would produce and, if not write, then control the writing of his films as well. Although Hawks's work has been consistently discussed as exemplary of the Hollywood studio style, Hawks himself did not work for a single studio on a long-term contract but was an independent producer who sold his projects to every Hollywood studio.

Whatever the genre of a Hawks film, it bore traits that made it unmistakably a Hawks film. The narrative was always elegantly, symmetrically structured and patterned, a sign of both Hawks's sharp sense of storytelling and his good sense to work closely with very talented writers: Ben Hecht, William Faulkner, and Jules Furthman being the most notable among them. Hawks's films were devoted to characters who were professionals with fervent vocational commitments, men who were good at what they did, whether flying the mail, driving race cars, driving cattle, or reporting the news. These vocational commitments were usually fulfilled by the union of two apparently opposite physical types who were spiritually one: either the union of the harder, tougher, older male and a softer, younger, prettier male (John Wayne and Montgomery Clift in *Red River*, Wayne and Ricky Nelson in *Rio Bravo*), or by a sharp, tough male and an equally sharp, tough female (Cary Grant and Rosalind Russell in *His Girl Friday*, Bogart and Bacall in *To Have and Have Not* and *The Big Sleep*, John Barrymore and Carole Lombard in *Twentieth Century*). This spiritual alliance of physical opposites revealed Hawks's unwillingness to accept the cultural stereotype that those who are able to accomplish difficult tasks are those who appear able to accomplish them.

This tension between appearance and ability, surface and essence in Hawks's films led to several other themes and techniques. Characters talk very tersely in Hawks films, refusing to put their thoughts and feelings into explicit speeches which would either sentimentalize or vulgarize those internal abstractions. Instead, Hawks's characters reveal their feelings in action, not in talk, showing what they mean by what they do, not what they say. Hawks deflects his portrayal of the inner life from explicit speeches to symbolic physical objects—concrete visual images of things that convey the intentions of the person who handles, uses, or controls the piece of physical matter. One of those things, the coin which George Raft nervously flips in *Scarface*, has become a mythic icon of American culture itself—symbolic in itself of American gangsters and American gangster movies (and used as such in both *Singin' in the Rain* and *Some Like It Hot*). Another of Hawks's favorite things, the lighting of cigarettes, became his subtextual way of showing who cares about whom without recourse to dialogue.

Consistent with his narratives, Hawks's visual style was one of dead-pan understatement, never proclaiming its trickiness or brilliance but effortlessly communicating the values of the stories and the characters. Hawks was a master of point-of-view, knowing precisely which camera perspective would convey the necessary psychological and moral information. That point of view could either confine us to the perceptions of a single character (Marlowe in *The Big Sleep*), ally us with the more vital of two competing life styles (with the vitality of Oscar Jaffe in *Twentieth Century*, Susan Vance in *Bringing Up Baby*, Walter Burns in *His Girl Friday*), or withdraw to a scientific detachment that allows the viewer to weigh the paradoxes and ironies of a love battle between two equals (between the two army partners in *I Was a Male War Bride*, the husband and wife in *Monkey Business*, or the older and younger cowboy in *Red River*). Hawks's films are also masterful in their atmospheric lighting, and the hanging electric or kerosene lamp that dangles into the top of a Hawks frame became almost as much his signature as the lighting of cigarettes.

Hawks's view of character in film narrative was that in movies actor and character were inseparable. As a result his films were very improvisatory, allowing actors to add, interpret, or alter lines as they wished, rather than forcing them to stick to the script. This trait not only led to the energetic spontaneity of many Hawks films but also to their helping to create or shape the human archetype that the star came to represent in our culture. John Barrymore, John Wayne, Humphrey Bogart, and Cary Grant all refined or established their essential personae under Hawks's direction, while many who would become stars were either discovered by Hawks or given their first chance to play a major role in one of his films. Among Hawks's most important discoveries were Paul Muni, George Raft, Carole Lombard, Angie Dickinson, Montgomery Clift, and his Galatea, Lauren Bacall.

Although Hawks continued to make films until he was almost 75, there is disagreement about the artistic energy and cinematic value of the films he made after 1950. For some, Hawks's artistic decline in the 1950s and 1960s was both a symptom and an effect of the overall decline of the movie industry and the studio system itself. For others, Hawks's later films—slower, longer, less energetically brilliant than his studio-era films—were more probing and personal explorations of the themes and genres he had charted for the three previous decades.

—Gerald Mast

HENNING-JENSEN, ASTRID AND BJARNE. Danish. Born in Frederiksberg, Denmark; Astrid: *née* Astrid Smahl, 10 December 1914, Bjarne: 6 October 1908. Married 10 August 1938. Career: 1931-38—Bjarne actor at various theaters, Astrid actress at "Riddersalen", Copenhagen; 1940-50—Bjarne directs at Nordisk Films Kompagni; 1941-43—Astrid assistant director at Nordisk, becomes director 1943; since 1950—Bjarne freelance scriptwriter and director, works for radio and television; has also written stage play; 1950-52—Astrid at Norsk Film A/S, Oslo; since 1953—Astrid freelances, writes and directs for United Nations, Omnibus Television, Ford Foundation; also works as stage director, writes and directs for radio and television. Recipient: Astrid: Catholic Film Office Award, Cannes Festival, for *Paw*, 1960; Astrid: Best Director, Berlin Festival, for *Winter Children*, 1979. Address: Astrid: Frederiksberg Allé 76, DK-1820 Copenhagen V, Denmark; Bjarne: Fasangården, Svennerup, DK-4683 Rønnede, Denmark.

Films (Bjarne as director): 1940—*Cykledrengene i Tørvegraven*; 1941—*Hesten paa Kongens Nytorv*; *Brunkul*; *Arbejdet kalder*; *Chr. IV som Bygherre (Christian IV: Master Builder)*; 1942—*Sukker (Sugar)*; 1943—*Korn (Corn)*; *Hesten (Horses)*; *Føllet*; *Papir (Paper)*; *Naar man kun er ung (To Be Young)*; (Astrid and Bjarne as co-directors): 1943—*S.O.S. Kindtand (S.O.S. Molars)*; 1944—*De danske Sydhavsøer (Danish Island)* (Bjarne d only); 1945—*Flyktingar finner en hamn (Fugitives Find Shelter)*; *Dansk politi i Sverige* (Astrid d only); *Folketingsvalg 1945*; *Brigaden i Sverige (Danish Brigade in Sweden)* (Bjarne d only); *Frihedsfonden (Freedom Committee)* (Bjarne d only); 1946—*Ditte Menneskebarn (Ditte: Child of Man)* (Bjarne d only); 1947—*Stemning i April*; *De pokkers unger (Those Blasted Kids)*; *Denmark Grows Up* (Astrid co-d only); 1948—*Kristinus Bergman*; 1949—*Palle alene i Verden (Palle Alone in the World)* (Astrid d only); 1950—*Vesterhavsdrenge (Boys from the West Coast)*; 1951—*Kranes Konditori (Krane's Bakery Shop)* (Astrid d only); 1952—*Ukjent mann (Unknown Man)* (Astrid d only); 1953—*Solstik*; 1954—*Tivoligarden spiller (Tivoli Garden Games)*; (Astrid as director except where noted): 1954—*Ballettens børn (Ballet Girl)*; 1955—*Kaerlighed på kredit (Love on Credit)*; *En saelfangst i Nordgrønland* (Bjarne); *Hvor bjergene sejler (Where Mountains Float)* (Bjarne); 1959—*Hest på sommerferie*; *Paw (Boy of 2 Worlds, The Lure of the Jungle)*; 1961—*Een blandt mange*; 1962—*Kort är sommaren (Short Is the Summer)* (Bjarne); 1965—*De blå undulater*; 1966—*Utro (Unfaithful)*; 1967—*Min bedstefar er en stok*; 1968—*Nille*; 1969—*Mig og dig (Me and You)*; 1974—*Skipper & Co.* (Bjarne); 1978—*Vinterbørn (Winter Children)* (+sc, ed); 1980—*Øjeblikket (The Moment)*.

Roles: Astrid: 1937—*Cocktail*; Bjarne: 1938—*Kongen bød*; 1939—*Genboerne*; 1940—*Jens Langkniv*; 1942—*Damen med de lyse Handsker*.

* * *

Astrid and Bjarne Henning-Jensen started as stage actors, but shortly after they married in 1938 they began working in films. Bjarne Henning-Jensen directed several government documentaries beginning in 1940 and he was joined by Astrid in 1943. At that time the Danish documentary film, strongly influenced by the British documentary of the thirties, was blooming, and Bjarne Henning-Jensen played an importnat part in this. In 1943 he made his first feature film, Astrid serving as assistant director. *Naar man kun er ung* was a light, everyday comedy, striving for a relaxed and charming style, but it was too cute, and it was politely received. Their next film, *Ditte Menneskebarn*, was their breakthrough, and the couple was instantly considered as the most promising directors in the post-war Danish cinema. The film was an adaptation of a neoclassical novel by Martin Andersen-Nexø. It was a realistic story of a young country girl and her tragic destiny as a victim of social conditions. The novel, published between 1917 and 1921, was in five volumes, but the Henning-Jensens used only parts of the novel. The sentimentality of the book was, happily, subdued in the film, and it is a sensitive study of a young girl in her milieu. The film was the first example of a more realistic and serious Danish film and it paralleled similar trends in contemporary European cinema, even if one would refrain from calling the film neorealistic. It was a tremendous success in Denmark and it also won a certain international recognition.

Astrid and Bjarne Henning-Jensen's film was a sincere attempt to introduce reality and authentic people to the Danish film. They continued this effort in their subsequent films, but a certain facile approach, a weakness for cute effects, and a sensibility on the verge of sentimentality, made their films less and less interesting. In the fifties Bjarne Henning-Jensen returned to documentaries. In 1955 he made the pictorially beautiful *Hvor bjergene sejler*, about Greenland. He attempted a comeback to features in 1962 with a rather pedestrian adaptation of Knut Hamsun's novel *Pan called Kort är sommaren*. His last film, in 1974, was a failure. Astrid Henning-Jensen continued making films on her own. She made two carefully directed and attractive films in Norway, and in the sixties she tried to keep up with the changing times in a couple of films. But it was not until the last few years that she regained her old position. In *Vinterbørn*, about women and their problems in a maternity ward, and in *Øjeblikket*, treating the problems of a young couple when it is discovered that the woman is dying of cancer, she worked competently within an old established genre in Danish films, the problem-oriented popular drama.

—Ib Monty

HEPWORTH, CECIL. British. Born in Lambeth, London, 19 March 1874. Career: 1895—patents hand-feed lamp for optical lantern; 1896—becomes assistant projectionist to Birt Acres; 1898—writes 1st book on cinematography, *Animated Photography*; 1898—becomes cameraman for Charles Urban; subsequently forms Hepwix Films at Walton-on-Thames, acting in and directing films; patents film developing system; 1904—forms Hepworth Manufacturing Company, April 1904; 1905-13—concentrates on running studio, business, and producing; 1910—patents Vivaphone, primitive "Talking film" device; first chairman, Kinematograph Manufacturers' Association; 1911—founds British Board of Film Censors; 1919—forms Hepworth Picture Plays, April 1919; 1923—company goes bankrupt; 1936—joins National Screen Service as technical advisor and producer, works on trailers and nature shorts; also later serves as chairman of the History Research Committee of the British Film Institute. Died at Greenford, Middlesex, 9 February 1953.

Films (as director of short films): 1898—*Oxford and Cambridge Boat Race*; *The Interrupted Picnic*; *Exchange Is No Robbery*; *The Immature Punter*; *The Quarrelsome Anglers*; *2 Fools in a Canoe*; 1899—*Express Train in a Railway Cutting*; 1900—*Wiping Something Off the Slate*; *The Conjurer and the Boer*; *The Punter's Mishap*; *The Gunpowder Plot*; *Explosion of a Motor Car*; *The Egg-Laying Man*; *Clown and Policeman*; *Leapfrog as Seen by the Frog*; *How It Feels to be Run Over*; *The Eccentric Dancer*; *The Bathers*; *The Sluggard's Surprise*; *The Electricity Cure*; *The Beggar's Deceit*; *The Burning Stable*; *Topsy Turvy Villa*; *The Kiss*; 1901—*How the Burglar Tricked the Bobby*; *The Indian Chief and the Seidlitz Powder*; *Comic Grimacer*; *Interior of a Railway Carriage*; *Funeral of Queen Victoria*; *Coronation of King Edward VII*; *The Glutton's Nightmare*; 1902—*The Call to Arms*; *How to Stop a Motor Car*; 1903—*The Absent-Minded Bootblack*; *Alice in Wonderland*; *Firemen to the Rescue*; *Saturday's Shopping*; 1904—*The Jonah*

Man; 1905—*Rescued by Rover*; *Falsely Accused*; *The Alien's Invasion*; *A Den of Thieves*; 1907—*A Seaside Girl*; 1908—*John Gilpin's Ride*; 1909—*Tilly the Tomboy*; 1911—*Rachel's Sin*; 1914—*Blind Fate*; *Unfit or The Strength of the Weak*; *The Hills Are Calling*; *The Basilisk* (feature); *His Country's Bidding*; *The Quarry Mystery*; *Time the Great Healer* (feature); *Morphia the Death Drug*; *Oh My Aunt*; (as director of features): 1915—*The Canker of Jealousy*; *A Moment of Darkness* (short); *Court-Martialled*; *The Passing of a Soul* (short); *The Bottle*; *The Baby on the Barge*; *The Man Who Stayed at Home*; *Sweet Lavender*; *The Golden Pavement*; *The Outrage*; *Iris*; 1916—*Trelawney of the Wells*; *A Fallen Star*; *Sowing the Wind*; *Annie Laurie*; *Comin' Thro' the Rye*; *The Marriage of William Ashe*; *Molly Bawn*; *The Cobweb*; 1917—*The American Heiress*; *Nearer My God to Thee*; 1918—*The Refugee*; *Tares*; *Broken in the Wars*; *The Blindness of Fortune*; *The Touch of a Child*; *Boundary House*; 1919—*The Nature of the Beast*; *Sunken Rocks*; *Sheba*; *The Forest on the Hill*; 1920—*Anna the Adventuress*; *Alf's Button*; *Helen of Four Gates*; *Mrs. Erricker's Reputation*; 1921—*Tinted Venus*; *Narrow Valley*; *Wild Heather*; *Tansy*; 1922—*The Pipes of Pan*; *Mist in the Valley*; *Strangling Threads*; *Comin' Thro' the Rye* (2nd version); 1927—*The House of Marney*; 1929—*Royal Remembrances*.

Publications:

By HEPWORTH:

Books—*Animated Photography*, London 1898; *Came the Dawn: Memories of a Film Pioneer*, New York 1951; articles—"My Film Experiences" in *Pearson's Magazine* (London), 1920; "Those Were the Days" in *Penguin Film Review* (London), no.6, 1948.

On HEPWORTH:

Articles—"Cecil Hepworth Comes Through" in *Era* (London), 3 May 1935; "Hepworth: His Studios and Techniques" in *British Journal of Photography* (London), 15 and 22 January 1971.

*   *   *

The son of a famous magic lanternist and photographer named T.C. Hepworth (who authored an important early volume titled *The Book of the Lantern*), Cecil Hepworth was—along with Robert W. Paul—the best known and most important of early British film pioneers. In the first 20 years of British cinema, Hepworth's place is easy to determine. He was a major figure, who wrote the first British book on cinematography, *Animated Photography, the A.B.C. of the Cinematograph* (published in 1897) and who produced *Rescued by Rover*, which is to British cinema what D.W. Griffith's *The Adventures of Dollie* is to the American film industry. But as the industry grew, Cecil Hepworth failed to grow along with it, and as the English critic and historian Ernest Betts has written, "Although a craftsman and a man of warm sympathies, an examination of his career shows an extremely limited outlook compared with Americans or his contemporaries."

A cameraman before turning to production in the late 1890s, "Heppy," as he was known to his friends and colleagues, founded the first major British studio at Walton-on-Thames (which was later to become Nettlefold Studios). He experimented with sound films before 1910 and was also one of the few British pioneers to build up his own stable of stars, not borrowed from the stage, but brought to fame through the cinema. Alma Taylor, Chrissie White, Stewart Rome, and Violet Hopson were his best known "discoveries." So omnipotent was Hepworth in British cinema prior to the First World War that major American film-makers such as Larry Trimble and Florence Turner were eager to associate with him when they came over from the United States to produce films.

Hepworth's problem and the cause of his downfall was symp-tomatic of that effecting many other pioneers. He did not move with the times. His films were always exquisitely photographed, beautiful to look at, but totally devoid of drama. The editing techniques which he had displayed in *Rescued by Rover* were forgotten by the teens. His productions were all too often like the magic lantern presentations of his father, lifeless creations, with slow dissolves from one sequence or even one bit of action to the next, when it was obvious to anyone that quick cuts were needed. Hepworth appeared to despise anything that would bring movement to his films, preferring that the camera linger on the pictorial beauty of the scene. Nowhere is this more apparent than in Hepworth's best-known feature, *Comin' thro' the Rye* (which he filmed twice, in 1916 and 1922). As Iris Barry was forced to admit, when writing of the latter version, it is "a most awful film."

Bankruptcy and a closed mind drove Cecil Hepworth from the industry which he had helped to create. He returned late in life to supervise the production of trailers for National Screen Service, and also served as Chairman of the History Research Committee of the British Film Institute, at which time he also wrote his autobiography, *Came the Dawn.*

—Anthony Slide

HERZOG, WERNER. German. Born Werner Stipetič in Sach-rang, 5 September 1942. Educated at classical Gymnasium, Munich, degree 1961; University of Munich and Duquesne Uni-versity, Pittsburgh, early 1960s. Married to journalist Martje Grohmann; child: Rudolph Amos Ahmed. Career: 1957—writes 1st film script; 1961—works at night in steel factory to make money for films; 1966—works for U.S. National Aeronautics and Space Administration; 1974—walks on foot from Munich to Paris to visit film historian Lotte Eisner, writes *Vom Gehen im Eis*. Recipient: Carl-Meyer-Preis, Club of Munich Film Journal-ists, for script of *Feuerzeichen (Signs of Life)*, 1964; Bundesfilm-preis for *Signs of Life*, 1968; Silver Bear, Berlinale, for best first film *Signs of Life*, 1968; Bundesfilmpreis for *Every Man for Himself and God Against All*, 1975; Special Jury Prize, Cannes Festival, for *Every Man for Himself and God Against All*, 1975; German Film Critics Prize for *Stroszek*, 1977 (money shared with Bruno S.); Rauriser Literaturpreis for *Vom Gehen im Eis*, 1978; Best Director, Cannes Festival, for *Fitzcarraldo*, 1982. Address: Neureutherstr. 20, D-8000 München 13, West Germany.

Films (as producer, director and scriptwriter—beginning 1966 films are produced or co-produced by Werner Herzog Filmpro-duktion): 1962—*Herakles*; 1964—*Spiel im Sand* [Playing in the Sand] (incomplete); 1966—*Die beispiellose Verteidigung der Festung Deutschkreuz* [The Unparalleled Defense of the For-tress of Deutschkreuz] ; 1968—*Lebenszeichen (Signs of Life)*; *Letzte Worte* [Last Words]; 1969—*Massnahmen gegen Fana-tiker* [Measures Against Fanatics]; 1970—*Die fliegenden Ärzte von Ostafrika (The Flying Doctors of East Africa)*; *Auch Zwerge haben klein angefangen (Even Dwarfs Started Small)* (+mu arrangements); *Behinderte Zukunft (Frustrated Future)*; *Fata Morgana*; 1971—*Land des Schweigens und der Dunkelheit (Land of Silence and Darkness)*; 1972—*Aguirre, der Zorn Göttes (Aguirre, the Wrath of God)*; 1974—*Die große Ekstase des Bildschnitzers Steiner (The Great Ecstasy of the Sculptor Steiner)*; *Jeder für sich und Gott gegen alle (Every Man for Himself and God Against All, The Mystery of Kaspar Hauser)*; 1976—*How Much Wood Would a Woodchuck Chuck*; *Mit mir will keiner spielen* [No One Will Play with Me]; *Herz aus Glas (Heart of Glass)* (co-sc, +bit ro as glass carrier); 1977—*La Sou-frière* (+narration, appearance); *Stroszek*; 1979—*Nosferatu— Phantom der Nacht (Nosferatu the Vampire)* (+bit ro as monk); *Woyzeck*; 1982—*Fitzcarraldo*.

Publications:

By HERZOG:

Books and scripts—*L'énigme de Kaspar Hauser*, cutting conti-nuity and dialogue, in *Avant-Scène du cinéma* (Paris), June 1976; *Werner Herzog: Drehbücher I*, Munich 1977; *Werner Her-zog: Drehbücher II*, Munich 1977; *Vom Gehen im Eis*, Vienna 1978; *Aguirre, la colère de Dieu*, cutting continuity and dialogue, in *Avant-Scène du cinéma* (Paris), 15 June 1978; *Werner Herzog: Stroszek, Nosferatu: 2 Filmerzählungen*, Munich 1979; *Sur le chemin des glaces: Munich-Paris du 23.11 au 14.12.1974*, Paris 1979; articles—"Rebellen in Amerika" in *Filmstudio* (Frank-furt), May 1964; "9 Tage eines Jahres" in *Filmstudio* (Frankfurt), September 1964; "Mit den Wölfen heulen" in *Filmkritik* (Munich), July 1968; interview in *Die Filmemacher* by Barbara Bronnen and Corinna Brocher, Munich 1973; "Warum ist über-haupt Seiendes und nicht vielmehr Nichts?" in *Kino* (West Ber-lin), March/April 1974; "Comme un rêve puissant...", interview by Noureddine Ghali in *Jeune Cinéma* (Paris), September/Oc-tober 1974; interview by S. Murray in *Cinema Papers* (Mel-bourne), December 1974; "Entretien avec Werner Herzog" by Michel Ciment in *Positif* (Paris), May 1975; "Die große Ekstase des Werner Herzog", interview by Thomas Brandlmeier in *Film und Ton Magazin* (Munich), January 1975; "Every Man for Himself", interview by D.L. Overbey in *Sight and Sound* (Lon-don), spring 1975; interview by C. Clouzot in *Ecran* (Paris), November 1975; interview by J. Delmas in *Jeune cinéma* (Paris), July/August 1975; interview by Noel Simsolo in *Ecran* (paris), April 1975; interview by J. Zimmer in *Image et son* (Paris), March 1975; "Signs of Life: Werner Herzog", interview by Jona-than Cott in *Rolling Stone* (New York), 18 November 1976; "Playboy Interview: Werner Herzog by Raimund le Viseur and Werner Schmidmaier in *Playboy* (Chicago), January 1977; "10 Gedichte" in *Akzente*, June 1978; "Herzog", interview and article by J. Cott in *Filmkritik* (Munich), September 1978; interview by S. Mizrahi in *Ecran* (Paris), 15 February 1979; interview by V. Bachy in *Image et son* (Paris), September 1979; interview by J.B. Christensen in *Cinéma* (Paris), October 1979; "I Feel That I'm Close to the Center of Things", interview by L. O'Toole in *Film Comment* (New York), November/December 1979.

On HERZOG:

Books—*Herzog/Kluge/Straub* by Wolfram Schütte and others, Vienna 1976; *Heart of Glass* by Alan Greenberg, Munich 1976; articles—"Werner Herzog and Jean-Marie Straub" by Brian Baxter in *Film* (London), spring 1969; special issue of *Cinema* (Zurich), v.18, no.1, 1972; "Werner Herzog" by Kraft Wetzel in *Kino* (West Berlin), April/May 1973; "Zur Musik bei Werner Herzog" by Karsten Witte in *Kino* (West Berlin), 15 November 1974; "Werner Herzog: le réel saisi par le rêve" by Noreddine

Ghali in *Jeune Cinéma* (Paris), November 1974; "Dossier-Auteur établi par Noureddine Ghali" in *Cinéma* (Paris), May 1975; "Signs of Life" by Jonathan Cott in *Rolling Stone* (San Francisco), 18 November 1976; "Le Visionnaire Werner Herzog" by Ulrich Gregor in *Jeune Cinéma* (Paris), April 1976; "The Enigma of Werner Herzog" by John Dorr in *Millimeter* (New York), October 1977; "Notes on Some European Directors: Bertolucci, Schroeter, Herzog" by Alan Greenberg in *American Film* (Washington, D.C.), October 1977; "The Man on the Volcano" by Gideon Bachmann in *Film Quarterly* (Berkeley), autumn 1977; "Im Reich der Zwerge und des Wahns..." by Vinzenz Burg in *Film-Dienst*, November 1978; "Werner Herzog" by George Morris in *International Film Guide 1979*, London 1978; "L'État second du cinéma" by Jean-Claude Bonnet in *Cinématographe* (Paris), January 1978; "Dracula in Delft" by N. Andrews in *American Film* (Washington, D.C.), October 1978; "Werner Herzog's Nosferatu" by B. Walker in *Sight and Sound* (London), autumn 1978; "Le monde croule...je deviens lèger" by Jean-Philippe Domecq in *Positif* (Paris), April 1979; "Werner Herzog's Ecran Absurde" by J.-C. Horak in *Literature/Film Quarterly* (Salisbury, Maryland), v.7, no.3, 1979; "The Cinema of the Grotesque" by R. Perlmutter in *Georgia Review* (Athens, Georgia), no.1, 1979; "The Great Ecstasy of the Filmmaker Herzog" by L. O'Toole in *Film Comment* (New York), November/December 1979; "Dialectique du surhomme et du sous-homme dans quelques films de Werner Herzog" by M.-L. Portel-Dorget in *Image et son* (Paris), September 1979; "Hallowing the Ordinary, Embezzling the Everyday: Werner Herzog's Documentary Practice" by W.F. Van Wert in *Quarterly Review of Film Studies* (Pleasantville, New York), spring 1980; "3 Films by Werner Herzog" by E. Cleere in *Wide Angle* (Athens, Ohio), v.3, no.4, 1980; "Borne Out of Darkness: the Documentaries of Werner Herzog" by D. Davidson in *Film Criticism* (Edinboro, Penna.), fall 1980; "Les Lieux de Werner Herzog" by J.-C. Bonnet in *Cinématographe* (Paris), February 1981; "Werner Herzog (et l'affaire Fitzcarraldo)" by F. de Cardenas in *Positif* (Paris), March 1981; "Werner Herzog", with biofilmography, by Derek Owen in *Film Dope* (London), March 1982; films— *Was ich bin sind meine Filme* by Christian Weisenborn and Erwin Keusch, Munich 1978; *Werner Herzog Eats His Shoe* by Les Blank, U.S. 1980; *Burden of Dreams* by Les Blank, U.S. 1982.

*   *   *

The nature of Herzog's talents is hard to define because they are still evolving, and because his often contradictory qualities can only be encompassed within paradoxes. "Grotesque" presents itself as a useful term to define Herzog's work. His use of an actor like Klaus Kinski, whose singularly ugly face is sublimated by Herzog's camera, can best be described by such a term. Persons with physical defects like deafness, and blindness, and dwarfs are given a type of grandeur in Herzog's artistic vision. Herzog, as a contemporary German living in the shadow of remembered Nazi atrocities, demonstrates a penchant for probing the darker aspects of human behavior. His characters run the gamut from a harmlessly insane man (played by a mentally-ill actor) who is murdered for no apparent reason, to a Spanish conquistador lusting after gold, power, and blood. Herzog's vision renders the ugly and horrible sublime, while the beautiful is omitted or destroyed.

Closely related to the grotesque in Herzog's films is the influence of German expressionism on him. Two of Herzog's favorite actors, Klaus Kinski and Bruno S., have been compared to Conrad Veidt and Fritz Kortner, prototypical actors of German expressionistic dramas and films during the teens and twenties.

Herzog's actors make highly stylized, indeed often stock, gestures; in close-ups, their faces are set in exaggerated grimaces.

The characters of Herzog's films often seem deprived of free will, merely reacting to an absurd universe. Any exertion of free will in action leads ineluctably to destruction and death. He is a satirist who demonstrates what is wrong with the world but, as yet, seems unable or unwilling to articulate the ways to make it right; indeed, one is at a loss to find in his world view any hope, let alone prescription, for improvement.

Herzog's mode of presentation has been termed by some critics as romantic and by others as realistic. This seeming contradiction can be resolved by an approach that compares him with those romantic artists who first articulated elements of the later realistic approach. The scientific objectivity with which Géricault renders his series of portraits treating inmates of an insane asylum offers an art-historical parellel to the style and content of Herzog's films. A similar disinterestedness coupled with abnormal subject matter in the novels of Balzac offers itself for comparison with Herzog's approach. Critics have found in the quasi-photographic paintings of Caspar David Friedrich an analogue for Herzog's super-realism. As with these artists, there is an aura of unreality in Herzog's realism. Everything is seen through a camera that rarely goes out of intense, hard focus. Often it is as if his camera is deprived of the normal range of human vision, able only to perceive part of the whole through a telescope or a microscope.

In this strange blend of romanticism and realism lies the paradoxical quality of Herzog's talent: he, unlike Goddard, Resnais, or Altman, has not made great innovations in film language; if his style is to be defined at all it is as an eclectic one; and yet, his films do have a distinctive stylistic quality. He renders the surface reality of things with such an intensity that the viewer has an uncanny sense of seeing the essence beyond. *Aguirre*, for example, is unrelenting in its concentration on filth, disease, and brutality; and yet it is also an allegory which can be read on several levels: in terms of Germany under the Nazis, America in Vietnam, and more generally on the bestiality that lingers beneath the facade of civilized conventions. In one of Herzog's romantic tricks within his otherwise realistic vision, he shows a young Spanish noblewoman—accompanying and eventually becoming a prisoner of the bank of conquistadors—wearing an ever-pristine velvet dress amid mud and squalor; further, only she of all the rest is not shown dying through violence and is allowed to disappear almost mystically into the dense vegetation of the forest: clearly, she represents that transcendent quality in human nature that incorruptably endures. This figure is dropped like a hint to remind us to look beyond mere surface.

Some of the qualities of Herzog's vision may be due to the nature of the German film industry. Between the end of the Second World War and the sixties, American films dominated the German market. In 1967 the West Germany government passed a Film Subsidies Bill to support the production of artistically valid films. This induced what has been termed a "cultural ghetto" in which film directors made films not for the German public but for export to international film festivals and, above all, for themselves. Herzog's films, with their almost morbid sense of aesthetic closure, are examples. His films have developed their own uncanny structures, like forms of rare hothouse plants. As he says himself, his films will only come to be appreciated "in the next fifty years." For the most part, he avoids making films in Germany; indeed, he delights in going to strange locations, like the South American rain forests of *Aguirre*. This film however demonstrates an important recent development in German cinema: it was a TV-cinema coproduction. During the seventies, German TV set out to make New German Cinema available to Germans and, judging from his later films, Herzog seems to have profited by this change.

—Rodney Farnsworth

HILL, GEORGE ROY. American. Born in Minneapolis, Minnesota, 20 December 1922. Educated at Blake School, Hopkins, Minnesota; in music at Yale University, B.A. 1943; Trinity College, Dublin, B.Litt. 1949. Married Louisa Horton, 1951; 4 children. Career: 1943-45—serves as Marine Corps transport pilot; after war—works briefly for Texas newspaper; 1948—while studying in Dublin, makes stage debut in walk-on part in *The Devil's Disciple*, Gaiety Theatre; 1950—after returning to U.S., appears off-Broadway in Strindberg's *The Creditors*, tours with Margaret Webster's Shakespeare Repertory Company; early 1950s—acts in radio soap opera *John's Other Wife*, recalled for Marine service during Korean War; 1953—writes and performs in *My Brother's Keeper* for *Kraft Television Theater*; 1954-57—writes, produces, and directs teleplays including *A Night to Remember* (*Kraft Television Theater* 1954); *The Helen Morgan Story* (*Playhouse 90* 1954); and *Judgment at Nuremberg* (*Playhouse 90* 1957); 1957-62—directs on and off Broadway, beginning with adaptation of Thomas Wolfe's *Look Homeward, Angel*; 1962—goes to Hollywood to direct screen version of his production of *Period of Adjustment*; 1964-66—works on adaptation of Michener's *Hawaii* after replacing Fred Zinnemann as director; 1967—staging of *Henry, Sweet Henry*, musical version of *The World of Henry Orient*, fails on Broadway; 1975—signed to 5-year 15 project contract by Universal. Recipient: Emmy Awards for writing and direction for *A Night to Remember*, 1954; Best Direction, British Academy, for *Butch Cassidy and the Sundance Kid*, 1970; Jury Prize, Cannes Festival, for *Slaughterhouse-Five*, 1972; Best Director Academy Award for *The Sting*, 1973; Director Award, Directors Guild of America, for *The Sting*, 1973. Business address: Warner Bros. Studios, 4000 Warner Blvd., Burbank, CA 91522.

Films (as director): 1962—*Period of Adjustment*; 1963—*Toys in the Attic*; 1964—*The World of Henry Orient*; 1966—*Hawaii*; 1967—*Thoroughly Modern Millie*; 1969—*Butch Cassidy and the Sundance Kid*; 1972—*Slaughterhouse-Five*; 1973—*The Sting*; 1975—*The Great Waldo Pepper* (+story); 1977—*Slap Shot*; 1979—*A Little Romance*; 1982—*The World According to Garp* (+pr). Role: 1952—*Walk East on Beacon (Crime of the Century)* (Werker).

Publications:

By HILL:

Articles—interview by C. Flynn in *Focus* (London), spring 1970; "Abattoir 5", interview by G. Braucourt in *Ecran* (Paris), July/August 1972; interview by J.-A. Gili and others in *Ecran* (Paris), November 1972; "Flying High: George Roy Hill", interview by R. Appelbaum in *Films and Filming* (London), August 1979; interview by B.L. Zito in *Millimeter* (New York), October 1979; "Butch & Millie", interview in *Films* (London), March 1981.

On HILL:

Articles—"Stage to Film" in *Action* (Los Angeles), October 1968; "L'Arnaque" in *Avant-Scène du cinéma* (Paris), June 1974; "Award Winner" by B. Thomas in *Action* (Los Angeles), May/June 1974; article in *The New York Times Magazine*, 16 March 1975; "George Roy Hill" by Derek Owen in *Film Dope* (London), March 1982; film—*The Making of Butch Cassidy and the Sundance Kid* by Robert Crawford, U.S. 1970.

*   *   *

George Roy Hill has found his greatest popular success when he works with actors Paul Newman and Robert Redford. Before the emergence of George Lucas and Steven Spielberg, Hill's two collaborations with the duo earned him the distinction of being the only director to have made two among the ten most financially successful films.

Butch Cassidy and the Sundance Kid is an examination of the western hero, the myth and the reality. Butch and Sundance are nearly Robin Hood characters of the Old West but they are also shown to be trapped in their criminal profession and in their own myths. Their violent deaths are inevitable as there is no way for heros or criminals to get old. Helped considerably by the screen charm of Newman and Redford, Hill makes the pair into lovable, wisecracking rogues. The freeze frame death scene seems to be Hill's acknowledgment that the western myth must be recognized as a viable entity even though most of the action preceding their end seem to undercut the myth.

Hill's second film with Newman and Redford was *The Sting*. Illusions abound as experienced con men set up an elaborate scheme to avenge a friend's death. Redford's character's first big successful con is actually a mistake that leads to his mentor's death. Newman's character seems to be a down and out drunk but soon proves his merit as an extremely competent con man and schemer. Hill's ultimate illusion in the film is the con game the film plays on the audience.

Hill again directed Redford in *The Great Waldo Pepper*, focusing on the myth and reality of the barnstorming early years of aviation. Redford's character finally achieves his goal of showing how good a pilot he is when he turns an illusion (a filmed aerial battle) into a real aerial battle. Newman's character in *Slap Shot* is similar. In this, the most underrated film of Hill's career (mostly criticized for the profane but accurately observed locker room talk), Hill shows the development of a minor league hockey coach Reg Dunlop. Reg, late in his career, recognizes that sport in America is just an illusionary entertainment and that a sport can be manipulated to please a blood-thirsty audience. His team wins the championship when his star player breaks down and strips, thus joining "the team" Reg has created.

Hill has not yet found great acceptance with the popular film critics. Generally his films are regarded as superficial entertainment rather than serious works, in much the same way that Redford and Newman are regarded as "pretty faces" rather than actors. Critics do acknowledge Hill's ability to tell a narrative compellingly and completely. This ability coupled with charismatic stars certainly are at the base of the appeal of Hill's films. Audiences know that a Hill film will tell a story and allow the star to shine. Perhaps this might be labeled an old fashion approach, but Hill has shown that this can work time and time again.

—Ray Narducy

HILL, WALTER. American. Born in Long Beach, California; 10 January 1942. Educated at Michigan State University.

Career: mid-1960s—works in construction and oil drilling; 1967—begins in films as 2nd assistant director; 1977—creates *Dog and Cat* TV series; 1981—*Southern Comfort* produced by Phoenix Company, founded with David Giler and Joseph Gallagher. Agent: Jeff Berg, ICM, Los Angeles, California.

Films (as 2nd assistant director): 1968—*The Thomas Crown Affair* (Jewison); 1969—*Take the Money and Run* (Allen); (as scriptwriter): 1972—*Hickey and Boggs* (Culp); *The Getaway* (Peckinpah); 1973—*The Thief Who Came to Dinner* (Yorkin); *The Mackintosh Man* (Huston); 1975—*The Drowning Pool* (Rosenberg) (co-sc); (as director and scriptwriter): 1975—*Hard Times (The Streetfighter)* (co-sc); 1978—*The Driver*; 1979—*The Warriors* (co-sc); 1980—*The Long Riders* (d only); 1981—*Southern Comfort* (co-sc); 1982—*48 Hours*.

Publications:

By HILL:

Articles—"Scriptwriter and Director", interview by A.J. Silver and E. Ward in *Movie* (London), winter 1978/79; "Making *Alien*: Behind the Scenes: Walter Hill, Producer", interview by M.P. Carducci in *Cinefantastique* (Oak Park, Illinois), no.1, 1979; "Hard Riding", interview by M. Greco in *Film Comment* (New York), May/June 1980; interview by P. Broeske in *Films in Review* (New York), December 1981.

On HILL:

Article—"Walter Hill", with biofilmography, in *Film Dope* (London), March 1982.

*   *   *

Established in the early seventies as a writer of action movies, Hill went almost unnoticed for his first two directorial ventures. Not so with his third. *The Warriors* reportedly occasioned gang fights in the U.S., while one British newspaper dubbed it "the film they mustn't show here." Replete with highly stylized violence, *The Warriors* has been described by Hill as "a comic book rock 'n' roll version of the Xenophon story." It is a precise description: the movie takes the *Anabasis* and adapts it to an appropriately mythical setting among the street gangs of modern New York. The stranded Warriors fight their way home through the subways and streets of an extraordinary fantasy city. This world, as so often in Hill's movies, is evacuated of any sense of the everyday, and is rendered with the use of the strong reds, yellows, and blues of comic book design. In its subway scenes especially, colors leap from the screen much as, say, a Roy Lichtenstein picture leaps from the canvas, its direct assault on our vision as basic as that of a comic strip.

The pleasure of the movie lies in that style, transforming its much maligned violence into a sort of ritual. You could as well accuse Hill of celebrating gang warfare as you could accuse Lichtenstein of condoning aerial combat in his painting *Whaam!*. Hill's cinema evokes and elaborates upon mythical worlds, in this case grounded in ancient Greece and in comics, though in his

other movies more often based in the cinema itself. Thus *Driver* eliminates orthodox characterization in favor of thriller archetypes: the Driver, the Detective, and the Girl, as the credits list them. They revolve around each other in a world of formally defined roles, roles made archetypal by movies themselves. *The Long Riders*, in presenting a version of the Jesse James story, traps its characters in their own movie mythology so that they even seem to be aware that they are playing out a sort of destiny. *Southern Comfort* manipulates and undermines the war-movie ideology of the small military group, while Hill's most recent film, *48 Hours*, pursues its unstoppable action in precisely the fashion of the Don Siegel cop-movie—*Madigan*, say, or *Dirty Harry*.

As he tours the popular genres Hill is emerging as the major action director of the eighties. He is highly skilled in the narrative use of chase and confrontation, adept at the montage techniques so central to the genre's tension, while offering us not a "reality" but a distillation of the rules of the genre game. In his films we witness the *enmything* of characters, if that neologism is not too pompous for so pleasurable an experience, a self-conscious evocation of genre but without the knowing wink which often attends such exercises. Hill manages to take the genre seriously *and* to reflect upon it.

Inevitably such immersion in popular genre conventions, however skilled, risks critical opprobrium. *The Warriors*, *Southern Comfort*, and *48 Hours* have all been dismissed as shallow and morally suspect, lacking in the "seriousness" considered necessary to redeem their almost exclusive focus on action. This, however, is to miss the pleasures of Hill's cinema, its visual power, its narrative force, and its absorbing concern with myth-making and myth-breaking. These, too, are qualities to which the label "serious" properly may be applied.

—Andrew Tudor

———————

HILLER, ARTHUR. Canadian. Born in Edmonton, Alberta, 22 November 1923. University of Toronto, B.A.; studied law for year at University of British Columbia; University of Alberta, M.A. in psychology, 1950. Married Gwen Pechet, 1948; children: Henryk and Erika. Career: WW II—flys as navigator with Royal Canadian Air Force Bomber Group in England; 1950—begins working for Canadian Broadcasting Company, directing public affairs broadcasts; 1954—joins CBC Television; mid-1950s—brought to Hollywood by Albert McCleery of NBC to direct *Matinee Theater* shows; 1956-62—works mainly in TV, directing for *Playhouse 90* ("Massacre at Sand Creek" nominated for Emmy), *Naked City*, *Climax!*, *Perry Mason*, *Alfred Hitchcock Presents*, *Wagon Train*, *Gunsmoke*, *Route 66*, and many others. Agent: Phil Gersh Agency, Beverly Hills, California.

Films (as director): 1957—*The Careless Years*; 1962—*This Rugged Land* (for TV); *Miracle of the White Stallions (Flight of the White Stallions)*; 1963—*The Wheeler Dealers (Separate Beds)*; 1964—*The Americanization of Emily*; 1965—*Promise Her Anything*; 1966—*Penelope*; *Tobruk*; *Eye of the Devil* (Thompson) (d uncredited); 1967—*The Tiger Makes Out*; 1969—*Popi*; *The Out of Towners*; 1970—*Love Story*; *Confrontation* (short); *Plaza Suite*; 1971—*The Hospital*; 1972—*Man of La Mancha*; 1974—*The Crazy World of Julius Vrooder* (+co-pr); *The Man in the Glass Booth*; 1976—*W.C. Fields and Me*; *Silver Streak*; 1979—*Nightwing*; *The In-Laws* (+co-pr); 1981—*Making Love*; 1983—*The Terry Fox Story*.

Publications:

By HILLER:

Articles—"Dialogue on Film" in *American Film* (Washington, D.C.), October 1979; interview by D. Teitelbaum in *Cinema Papers* (Melbourne), December/January 1979/80.

On HILLER:

Articles—"Instinct" by Gordon Gow in *Films and Filming* (London), August 1974; "Arthur Hiller", with biofilmography, by T.S. Rutherford in *Film Dope* (London), March 1982.

*   *   *

Arthur Hiller is strictly a commercial Hollywood filmmaker, a competent technician whose films are at best inspired: on occasion, he chides the powers that be, or compassionately chronicles the exploits of underdogs attempting to cope with a crazy, uncaring world. But, too often, the style or structural approach of his work may be traced not to Hiller but to a screenwriter or star. Unlike a Martin Scorsese or Woody Allen or Paul Mazursky, his projects do not seem carefully selected and nurtured. His films are slick and trendy: Hiller reflects contemporary Hollywood in that he is a director of deals, packages.

The filmmaker's best works are light and entertaining escapist fare: the joyously frantic *In-Laws*; and *Silver Streak*, a diverting example of Hollywood fun. They might be satirical: he spoofs Texas millionaires in *The Wheeler Dealers*; knocks the military mentality in *The Americanization of Emily*; caricatures the medical establishment's bureaucracy and incompetency in *The Hospital*. Or, they may focus on society's victims: he sympathetically examines the plight of a Puerto Rican widower concerned with the future of his offspring in *Popi*; and chronicles the antics of a Vietnam veteran relating to the insanity of his environment in *The Crazy World of Julius Vrooder*.

Yet most of Hiller's films are ultimately signed not by the director but by another creative participant. *The Americanization of Emily* and *The Hospital* are more the products of their screenwriter, Paddy Chayefsky (and in the latter case star George C. Scott). *The Out of Towners* and *Plaza Suite* bear more of a stamp of Neil Simon. *Silver Streak* is one-quarter Gene Wilder, three-quarters Richard Pryor. *Popi* is Alan Arkin's film, while *The In-laws* is Arkin, Peter Falk and Richard Libertini's.

Occasionally, Hiller's films do break creative ground, or initiate trends. *Making Love* may be, with *Personal Best* and a handful of other 1982 releases, Hollywood's long-overdue attempt to depict homosexuals as three-dimensional characters rather than limp-wristed stereotypes; nevertheless, the film is in and of itself a bland soap opera, and Hiller is in no way a mover or shaker on this theme. In *Love Story*, a commercial blockbuster and Hiller's best-known feature, the title tells almost all: an idyllic romance between a boy and girl climaxes when she becomes terminally ill. The story of *Love Story*—death tragically intruding on the life of a vibrant, happy young woman—may not be original: *Dark Victory*, released in 1939 and starring Bette Davis, remains the definitive film featuring this theme. The box office success of *Love Story* did, however, revive its popularity: this film was the first in a series of theatrical releases with similar scenarios, none of which were as financially successful as the original. Yet *Love Story* is still pap disguised as profundity ("Love means you never have to say you're sorry"); *Brian's Song*,

a 1970 made-for-television movie focusing on the demise of football player Brian Piccolo and *The Terry Fox Story*, a 1983 Home Box Office made-for-pay film about a cancer-striken young man's "Marathon of Hope" across Canada, are both infinitely superior. And, even in *Love Story*, the names of Ali MacGraw, Ryan O'Neal and Erich Segal are more closely associated with the film than Hiller.

Arthur Hiller is certainly no hack. But his artistic style or narrative approach remains linked to his collaborators, or to the simple fact that he has been hired to direct a given project. In a modern-era Hollywood devoid of the old studio system, Hiller is the current equivalent of a contract director.

—Rob Edelman

HITCHCOCK, ALFRED. British. Born Alfred Joseph Hitchcock in Leytonstone, London, 13 August 1899; became citizen of United States, 1955. Educated briefly at Faithful Companions of Jesus convent school; attended briefly a secular primary school in South London; attended Salesian College, Battersea, England, 1908; St. Ignatius College, Stamford Hill, England, 1908-13; entered School of Engineering and Navigation, 1914; attended drawing and design classes at London University, under E.J. Sullivan, 1917. Married Alma Reville, 2 December 1926; child: Patricia, born 1928. Career: 1914-19—technical clerk, W.T. Henley Telegraph Co.; 1919—employed as a designer of title cards for Famous Players-Lasky British studio at Islington; 1922—directs 1st film, *No: 13* or *Mrs. Peabody*, 2-reeler not completed; Balcan-Saville-Freeman takes over studios, hired as scriptwriter and assistant director; 1925—directs 2 films for Michael Balcon in Germany, visiting the various German studios while there; 1926—*The Lodger* brings acclaim, also marks 1st Hitchcock cameo appearance; 1927—signs with British International Pictures as director; 1929—directs *Blackmail*, 1st British film to use synchronized sound; 1933—signs with Gaumont-British Studios, working for independent producer Tom Arnold; 1939—moves to U.S. to direct *Rebecca* for Selznick International Studios and decides to remain; 1944—on visit to Britain directs *Bon Voyage* and *Aventure Malgache* for British Ministry of Information; 1948—directs his 1st color film *Rope*, notable for experimental shooting technique, using long takes interrupted only to re-load film; 1954-60—films released through Paramount, except for *The Wrong Man* and *North by Northwest*; 1955-62—produces and hosts television anthology mystery series *Alfred Hitchcock Presents*; 1962-65—becomes *The Alfred Hitchcock Hour*; 1977—directs last film *Family Plot*; 1980—knighted. Died in Los Angeles, 29 April 1980. Recipient: Irving Thalberg Academy Award, 1968; Chevalier de la Légion d'Honneur, 1971; Commander of the Order of Arts and Letters, France, 1976; Life Achievement Award, American Film Institute, 1979; Honorary Ph.D., University of Southern California; Knight of the Legion of Honour of the Cinémathèque Français.

Films (as inter-titles designer): 1920—*The Great Day* (Ford); *The Call of Youth* (Ford); 1921—*The Princess of New York* (Crisp); *Appearances* (Crisp); *Dangerous Lies* (Powell); *The Mystery Road* (Powell); *Beside the Bonnie Brier Bush (The Bonnie Brier Bush)* (Crisp); 1922—*3 Live Ghosts* (Fitzmaurice); *Perpetua (Love's Boomerang)* (Robertson and Geraghty); *The Man from Home* (Fitzmaurice); *Spanish Jade* (Robertson and Geraghty); *Tell Your Children* (Crisp); (as director) 1922—

Number 13 (or Mrs. Peabody) (uncompleted); 1923—Always Tell Your Wife (Croise) (completed d only); (as scriptwriter): 1923—Woman to Woman (Cutts) (co-sc, +ass't d, art d, ed); 1923—The White Shadow (White Shadows) (Cutts) (art d, ed only); 1924—The Passionate Adventure (Cutts) (co-sc, +ass't d, art d); The Prude's Fall (Cutts) (+ass't d, art d); 1925—The Blackguard (Die Prinzessin und der Geiger) (Cutts) (+ass't d, art d); (as director): 1926—The Pleasure Garden (Irrgarten der Leidenschaft); The Mountain Eagle (Der Bergadler, Fear o' God); The Lodger: A Story of the London Fog (The Case of Jonathan Drew) (+co-sc, bit ro as man in newsroom, and onlooker during Novello's arrest); 1927—Downhill (When Boys Leave Home); Easy Virtue; The Ring (+sc); 1928—The Farmer's Wife (+sc); Champagne (+adapt); The Manxman; 1929—Blackmail (+adapt, bit ro as passenger on "tube") (silent version also made); Juno and the Paycock (The Shame of Mary Boyle) (+co-sc); 1930—Elstree Calling (Brunel) (d after Brunel dismissed, credit for "sketches and other interpolated items"); Murder (+co-adapt, bit ro as passer-by) (1931 German version Mary (Sir John greift ein!)); An Elastic Affair (short); 1931—The Skin Game (+co-sc); 1932—Rich and Strange (East of Shanghai) (+co-sc); Number 17 (+co-sc); Lord Camber's Ladies (Levy) (pr only); 1933—Waltzes from Vienna (Strauss's Great Waltz, The Great Waltz); 1934—The Man Who Knew Too Much; 1935—The 39 Steps (+bit ro as passerby); 1936—Secret Agent; Sabotage (The Woman Alone); 1937—Young and Innocent (The Girl Was Young) (+bit as photographer outside courthouse); 1938—The Lady Vanishes (+bit ro as man at railway station); 1939—Jamaica Inn; 1940—Rebecca (+bit ro as man outside phone booth); Foreign Correspondent (+bit as man reading newspaper); The House Across the Bay (Mayo) (d add'l scenes only); Men of the Lightship (MacDonald—short) (reediting, dubbing of U.S. version only); 1941—Mr. and Mrs. Smith (+bit ro as passerby); Suspicion; Target for Tonight (Watt) (supervised reediting of U.S. version only); 1942—Saboteur (+bit ro as man by newsstand); 1943—Shadow of a Doubt (+bit ro as man playing cards on train); 1944—Life Boat (+bit ro as man in "Reduco" advertisement); Bon Voyage (short); Aventure Malgache (The Malgache Adventure) (short); 1945—Spellbound (+bit ro as man in elevator); 1946—Notorious (+story, bit ro as man drinking champagne); 1947—The Paradine Case (+bit ro as man with cello); 1948—Rope (+bit ro as man crossing street); 1949—Under Capricorn; Stage Fright (+bit ro as passerby); 1951—Strangers on a Train (+bit ro as man boarding train with cello); 1953—I Confess (+bit ro as man crossing top of flight of steps); 1954—Dial M for Murder (+bit ro as man in school reunion dinner photo); Rear Window (+bit ro as man winding clock); To Catch a Thief (+bit ro as man at back of bus); The Trouble with Harry (+bit ro as man walking past exhibition); 1955—The Man Who Knew Too Much (+bit ro as man watching acrobats); 1956—The Wrong Man (+intro appearance); 1957—Vertigo (+bit ro as passerby); 1959—North by Northwest (+bit ro as man who misses bus); 1960—Psycho (+bit ro as man outside realtor's office); 1963—The Birds (+bit ro as man with 2 terriers); 1964—Marnie (+bit ro as man in hotel corridor); 1966—Torn Curtain (+bit ro as man in hotel lounge with infant); 1969—Topaz (+bit ro as man getting out of wheelchair); 1972—Frenzy (+bit ro as man in crowd listening to speech); 1976—Family Plot (+bit ro as silhouette on office window).

Television productions: (directed for Alfred Hitchcock Presents unless otherwise noted): 1955—Revenge; Breakdown; The Case of Mr. Pelham; 1956—Back for Christmas; Wet Saturday; Mr. Blanchard's Secret; 1957—One More Mile to Go; The Perfect Crime; Four o'Clock (for Suspicion series); 1958—Lamb to the Slaughter; Deep in the Pool; Poison; 1959—Banquo's Chair;

Arthur; The Crystal Trench; 1960—Mrs. Bixby and the Colonel's Coat; Incident at a Corner (for Ford Star Time series); 1961—The Horseplayer; Bang! You're Dead; (for The Alfred Hitchcock Hour): 1962—I Saw the Whole Thing.

Roles: 1960—voice on telephone telling Glenn Ford how to dispose of corpse in The Gazebo (Marshall); 1963—appearance in The Directors (pr: Greenblatt); 1970—documentary appearance from early 1930s in Makin' It (Hartog); 1977—interviewee in Once Upon a Time...Is Now (Billington—for TV).

Publications:

By HITCHCOCK:

Articles—"My Own Methods" in Sight and Sound (London), summer 1937; "On Suspense and Other Matters" in Films in Review (New York), April 1950; "Rencontre avec Hitchcock" by Claude Chabrol and François Truffaut in Arts (Paris), 9 February 1955; "Entretien" by Claude Chabrol in Cahiers du cinéma (Paris), February 1955; "Hitchcock anglais in Cahiers du cinéma (Paris), September 1956; "Rencontre avec Alfred Hitchcock" by François Truffaut in Cahiers du cinéma (Paris), September 1956; "Conversation with Hitchcock" by Catherine de la Roche in Sight and Sound (London), winter 1955/56; "Hitchcock, les médecins, les oeufs et les espions" in Cahiers du cinéma (Paris), May 1958; "Alfred Hitchcock Talking" in Films and Filming (London), July 1959; "Pourquoi j'ai peur la nuit" in Arts (Paris), June 1960; "Je suis une légende" by Nancy Kaplan in Les Lettres françaises (Paris), 27 October 1960; "Hitchcock" by Ian Cameron and V.F. Perkins in Movie (London), 6 January 1963; "Hitchcock on Style" in Cinema (Beverly Hills), August/September 1963; "Hitch" in Take One (Montreal), September/October 1966; "Rear Window" in Take One (Montreal), November/December 1968; "Frenzy. Hitchcock s'explique" in Cinéma Québec (Montreal), October 1972; "Hitch, Hitch, Hitch, Hourra!", interview by Ruy Nogueira and N. Zalaffi in Ecran (Paris), July/August 1972; "Alfred Hitchcock: The German Years", interview by B. Thomas in Action (Los Angeles), January/February 1973; "Conversazione con Alfred Hitchcock" by G. Turroni in Filmcritica (Rome), October 1972; "Hitchcock", transcript of address to Film Society of Lincoln Center, 29 April 1974, in Film Comment (New York), July/August 1974; "Hitchcock", interview by Andy Warhol in Interview (New York), September 1974; "Surviving", interview by John Taylor in Sight and Sound (London), summer 1977.

On HITCHCOCK:

Books—An Index to the Creative Work of Alfred Hitchcock by Peter Noble, supplement to Sight and Sound, index series, London 1949; Hitchcock by Eric Rohmer and Claude Chabrol, Paris 1957; Alfred Hitchcock by Barthélémy Amengual and Raymond Borde, Paris 1957; The Cinema of Alfred Hitchcock by Peter Bogdanovich, New York 1962; Alfred Hitchcock by Hans Peter Manz, Zürich 1962; Hitchcock's Films by Robin Wood, London 1965; The Films of Alfred Hitchcock by George Perry, London 1965; Le Cinéma selon Hitchcock by François Truffaut, Paris 1966; Alfred Hitchcock by Jean Douchet, Paris 1967; Alfred Hitchcock by Noel Simsolo, Paris 1969; Hitch by John Russell Taylor, New York 1978; L'Analyse du film by Raymond Bellour, Paris 1979; Hitchcock. La dimensione nacosta, Venice 1980; Hitchcock by J.-A. Fieschi and others, Paris 1981; Hitchcock—The Murderous Gaze by William Rothman, Cambridge, Massachusetts, 1982; *The Dark Side of Genius: The Life of Alfred Hitchcock* by Donald Spoto, New York, 1982; articles—"Alfred Hitchcock's Working Credo" by Gerald Pratley in *Films in Review* (New York), December 1952; special issue of *Cahiers du cinéma* (Paris), October 1953; "Maître de l'humour plus que de l'angoisse, Alfred Hitchcock" by André Bazin in *Radio, cinéma, télévision* (Paris), 18 July 1954; "Figurant et grand metteur en scène..." by Pierre Feuga in *Arts* (Paris), May 1954; article by Derwent May in *Sight and Sound* (London), October/December 1954; "Alfred Hitchcock" by André Bazin in *Radio, cinéma, télévision* (Paris), 23 January 1955; "Hitchcock aime l'invraisemblance" by Claude Chabrol in *Arts* (Paris), December 1955; "Hitchcock presque parfait" by Etienne Chaummetton in *Cinéma 55* (Paris), 28 March 1955; "Petit bilan pour Alfred Hitchcock" by Louis Seguin in *Positif* (Paris), November 1955; "The Trouble with Hitchcock" by Andrew Sarris in *Film Culture* (New York), winter 1955; "Festival Alfred Hitchcock" by Claude Chabrol in *Arts* (Paris), June 1956; special issue of *Cahiers du cinéma* (Paris), August/September 1956; "Réalisateur de 45 films en 34 ans..." by François Truffaut in *Arts* (Paris), 4 December 1957; "British Feature Directors" in *Sight and Sound* (London), autumn 1958; "Alfred Hitchcock: Je suis prisonnier des compromis commerciaux: je veux revenir à la comédie" by Charles Bitsch in *Arts* (Paris), January 1959; "La troisième clé d'Hitchcock" by Jean Doucher in *Cahiers du cinéma* (Paris), September and December 1959; "La nouvelle vague, c'est moi" by Luc Moullet in *Arts* (Paris), October 1959; "Murderers Among Us" by Peter Dyer in *Films and Filming* (London), December 1958; "A Master of Suspense" by John Pett in *Films and Filming* (London), November and December 1959; "Alfred Hitchcock" by Guillaume Allombert in *Image et son* (Paris), November 1960; "Un Gros monsieur souriant appelé Hitchcock" by Raymond Barkan in *Ciné-Amateur* (Paris), January 1960; "Hitchcock et son public" by Jean Douchet in *Cahiers du cinéma* (Paris), November 1960; "Versuch über Hitchcock" by Helmut Faber in *Filmkritik* (Munich), August 1960; "Un certain Alfred Hitchcock" by Pierre Marcabru in *Arts* (Paris), February 1961; "Si j'étais amateur" by Guillaume Allombert in *Cinéma pratique* (Paris), February 1962; "Hitchcock and the Mechanics of Suspense" by Ian Cameron in *Movie* (London), October 1962; "Hitchcock's World" by Charles Higham in *Film Quarterly* (Berkeley), December/January 1962/63; "The Figure in the Carpet" by Penelope Houston in *Sight and Sound* (London), autumn 1963; "Skeleton Keys" by François Truffaut in *Film Culture* (New York), spring 1964; "Hitchcock économe ou le procès de Lucullus" by Jean Douchet in *Cahiers du cinéma* (Paris), February 1965; "The Universal Hitchcock" by Ian Cameron and Richard Jeffrey in *Movie* (London), spring 1965; article by Kirk Bond in *Film Culture* (New York), summer 1966; "An Alfred Hitchcock Index" in *Films in Review* (New York), April 1966; "Alfred Hitchcock: Master of Morality" by Warren Sonbert in *Film Culture* (New York), summer 1966; "Cinéma selon Hitchcock par Truffaut: Ce que savait Hitchcock" by Raymond Bellour in *Cahiers du cinéma* (Paris), May 1967; "Hitchcock talk about Light, Camera, Action" by Lightman in *American Cinematographer* (Hollywood), May 1967; "Hitchcock, Truffaut, and the Irresponsible Audience" by Leo Braudy in *Film Quarterly* (Berkeley), summer 1968; "Hitchcockery" by Penelope Houston in *Sight and Sound* (London), autumn 1968; "Hitchcock versus Truffaut" by Gavin Millar in *Sight and Sound* (London), spring 1969; "The Strange Case of Alfred Hitchcock" by Raymond Durgnat in *Films and Filming* (London), February 1970 through November 1970; "The Television Films of Alfred Hitchcock" by Steve Mamber in *Cinema* (Beverly Hills), fall 1971; "Alfred Hitchcock's Frenzy" by W.-E. Bühler and others in *Filmkritik*

(Munich), December 1972; "Lost in the Wood" by G. Kaplan in *Film Comment* (New York), November/December 1972; "Hitchcock avec frénésie" by J.-L. Mercier in *Ecran* (Paris), January 1972; "Conservative Individualism: A Selection of English Hitchcock" by J.M. Smith in *Screen* (London), autumn 1972; "The Eyehole of Knowledge..." by Alfred Appel, Jr. in *Film Comment* (New York), May/June 1973; "Hitch and Unhitch" by S. Lawson in *Lumiere* (Melbourne), April 1973; "The Detective in Hitchcock's Frenzy: His Ancestors and Significance" by Lee Poague in *Journal of Popular Film* (Bowling Green, Ohio), winter 1973; "Lest We Forget" by T. Ryan in *Lumiere* (Melbourne), October 1973; "The Discreet Qualms of the Bourgeoisie: Hitchcock's 'Frenzy'" by J. Sgammato in *Sight and Sound* (London), summer 1973; "Blackmail: The Opening of Hitchcock's Surrealist Eye" by H. Ringel in *Film Heritage* (Dayton, Ohio), winter 1973/74; "Alfred Hitchcock, Prankster of Paradox" by Andrew Sarris in *Film Comment* (New York), March/April 1974; "De quelques problèmes de mise en scène" by J.-F. Tarnowski in *Positif* (Paris), April 1974; "The Hitchcock Camera 'I'" by R. Fisher in *Filmmakers Newsletter* (Ward Hill, Mass.), December 1975; "Hitchcock and the Well-Wrought Effect" by D. Simer in *Literature/Film Quarterly* (Salisbury, Md.), summer 1975; "Alfred Hitchcock zu einer Retrospektive" by W.-E. Bühler in *Filmkritik* (Munich), June 1977; "Fragments of a Mirror: Uses of Landscape in Hitchcock" by A.J. Silver in *Wide Angle* (Athens, Ohio), v.1, no.3, 1976; "Cet anglais méconnu, Alfred Hitchcock. 1925-1939: entre frisson et sourire" by Guy Allombert in *Image et son* (Paris), March 1978; "Hitchcock, the Enunciator" by R. Bellour in *Camera Obscura* (Berkeley), fall 1977; "He Who Gets Hitched" by E. Lehman in *American Film* (Washington, D.C.), May 1978; "The Sound of One Wing Flapping" by E. Wise in *Film Comment* (New York), September/October 1978; "Dexterity in a Void" by J. Belton in *Cineaste* (New York), summer 1980; "Les Bonheurs d'Alfred Hitchcock" by the editors of *Séquence* (Paris), July 1980; special issue of *Cinématographe* (Paris), July/August 1980; "Perché Hitchcock?" by R. Combs in *Sight and Sound* (London), summer 1980; "Alfred Hitchcock zum 80. Geburtstag—'Suspense—eine subversive Kraft'" by R. Fischer in *Filmfaust* (Frankfurt), October 1979; "La Mise en scène & Petit diptyque pour 'Sir Alfred'", with text by Hitchcock, by G. Legrand in *Positif* (Paris), September 1980; "Alfred Hitchcock (1899-1980)" by J. Magny in *Cinéma* (Paris), June 1980; "Hitch" by E. Lehman in *American Film* (Washington, D.C.), August 1980; "Working with Hitchcock" by I. Montagu in *Sight and Sound* (London), summer 1980; "Hitch n'a plus la mort aux trousses" by D. Sauvaget in *Image et son* (Paris), no.351, 1980; "It's Only a Film/ou La face du néant" by P. Bonitzer in *Framework* (Norwich, England), spring 1981; "Les 39 Marches", special issue of *Avant-Scène du cinéma* (Paris), 1 June 1980; "Hybrid Plots in Psycho" by P. Wollen in *Framework* (Norwich, England), autumn 1980; "special issue of *Camera/Stylo* (Paris), November 1981; "Alfred Hitchcock", with biofilmography, by Michael Walker in *Film Dope* (London), March 1982; films—*Interview with Alfred Hitchcock*, for TV, by Philip Casson, Great Britain 1966; *Im Hitchcock bi Yerushalayin (With Hitchcock in Jerusalem)*, sort, by M. Ya'acovolitz and S. Melul, Israel 1967; *The Men Who Made the Movies: Alfred Hitchcock*, for TV, by Richard Schickel, U.S. 1973.

* * *

In a career spanning just over 50 years (1925-1976), Hitchcock completed 53 feature films, 23 in the British period, 30 in the

American. Through the early British films we can trace the evolution of his professional/artistic image, the development of both the Hitchcock style and the Hitchcock thematic. His third film (and first big commercial success), *The Lodger*, was crucial in establishing him as a maker of thrillers, but it was not until the mid-1930s that his name became consistently identified with that genre. Meanwhile, he had assimilated the two aesthetic influences that were major determinants in the formation of his mature style: German Expressionism and Soviet montage theory. The former, with its aim of expressing emotional states through a deformation of external reality, is discernible in his work from the beginning (not surprisingly, as he has acknowledged Lang's *Die müde Tod* as his first important cinematic experience, and as some of his earliest films were shot in German studios). Out of his later contact with the Soviet films of the 1920s evolved his elaborate editing techniques: he particularly acknowledged the significance for him of the Kuleshov experiment, from which he derived his fondness for the point-of-view shot and for building sequences by cross-cutting between person seeing/thing seen.

The extreme peculiarity of Hitchcock's art (if his films do not seem very odd it is only because they are so familiar) can be partly accounted for by the way in which these aesthetic influences from high art and revolutionary socialism were pressed into the service of British middle-class popular entertainment. Combined with Hitchcock's all-pervasive scepticism ("Everything's perverted in a different way, isn't it?"), this process resulted in an art that at once endorsed (superficially) and undermined (profoundly) the value system of the culture within which it was produced, be that culture British or American.

During the British period the characteristic plot structures that recur throughout Hitchcock's work are also established. I want here to single out three, not because they account for *all* of the films, but because they link the British to the American period, because their recurrence is particularly obstinate, and because they seem, taken in conjunction, central to the thematic complex of Hitchcock's total *oeuvre*.

1. The story about *the falsely accused man*.

This is already established in *The Lodger* (in which the male protagonist is suspected of being Jack the Ripper); it often takes the form of the "double chase," in which the hero is pursued by the police and in turn pursues (or seeks to unmask) the actual villains. Examples in the British period are *The 39 Steps* and *Young and Innocent*. In the American period it becomes the commonest of all Hitchcock plot structures: *Saboteur*, *Spellbound*, *Strangers on a Train*, *I Confess*, *To Catch a Thief*, *The Wrong Man*, *North by Northwest* and *Frenzy* are all based on it.

2. The story about *the guilty woman*.

Although there are guilty women in earlier films, the structure is definitively established in *Blackmail*, Hitchcock's (and Britain's) first sound film. To it, in the British period, we may add *Sabotage*, but it is in the American period that examples proliferate: *Rebecca* (Hitchcock's first Hollywood film), *Notorious*, *Under Capricon*, *The Paradine Case*, *Vertigo*, *Psycho* (the first third), *The Birds* and *Marnie* are all variations on the original structure.

Before proceeding, it is necessary to add some notes on these two plot-structures and their relationship to each other. First, it is striking that the opposition of the two is almost complete; there are very few Hitchcock films in which the accused man turns out to be guilty after all (*Shadow of a Doubt* and *Stage Fright* are the obvious exceptions; *Suspicion* would have been a third if Hitchcock had been permitted to carry out his original intentions), and really none in which the accused woman turns out to be innocent (*Dial M for Murder* comes closest, but even there, although the heroine is innocent of murder, she is guilty of adultery). Second, it should be noticed that while the falsely accused man is usually

(not quite always) the central consciousness of type 1, it is less habitually the case that the guilty woman is the central consciousness of type 2: frequently, she is the object of the male protagonist's investigation. Third, the outcome of the guilty woman films (and this may be dictated as much by the Motion Picture Production Code as by Hitchcock's personal morality) is dependent upon the *degree* of guilt: the woman can sometimes be "saved" by the male protagonist (*Blackmail*, *Notorious*, *Marnie*), but not if she is guilty of murder or an accomplice to it (*The Paradine Case*, *Vertigo*). Fourth, one should note the function of the opposite sex in the two types. The heroine of the falsely accused man films is, typically, hostile to the hero at first, believing him guilty; she subsequently learns to trust him, and takes his side in establishing his innocence. The function of the male protagonist of the guilty woman films is either to save the heroine or to be destroyed (at least morally and spiritually) by her. Fifth, it is important to recognize that the true nature of the guilt is always sexual, and that the falsely accused man is usually seen to be contaminated by this (though innocent of the specific crime, typically murder, of which he is accused). Richard Hannay in *The 39 Steps* can stand as the prototype of this: when he allows himself to be picked up by the woman in the music hall, it is in expectation of a sexual encounter, the notion of sexual disorder being displaced on to "espionage," and the film moves from this systematically towards the construction of the "good" (i.e. socially approved) couple. The very title of *Young and Innocent*, with its play on the connotations of the last word, exemplifies the same point, and it is noteworthy that in that film the hero's *sexual* innocence remains in doubt (we only have his own word for it that he was not the murdered woman's gigolo). Finally, the essential Hitchcockian dialectic can be read from the alternation, throughout his career, of these two series. On the whole, it is the guilty woman films that are the more disturbing, that leave the ·most jarring dissonances: here, the potentially threatening and subversive female sexuality, precariously contained within social norms in the falsely accused man films, erupts to demand recognition, is answered by an appalling violence (both emotional and physical), the cost of its destruction or containment leaving that "nasty taste" often noted as the dominant characteristic of Hitchcock's work.

3. It is within this context that the third plot structure takes on its full significance: the story about the *psychopath*.

Frequently, this structure occurs in combination with the falsely accused man plot (see, for example, *Young and Innocent*, *Strangers on a Train*, *Frenzy*,) with a parallel established between the hero and his perverse and sinister adversary, who becomes a kind of shadowy alter ego. Only two Hitchcock films have the psychopath as their indisputably central figure, but they (*Shadow of a Doubt*, *Psycho*) are among his most famous and disturbing. The Hitchcock villain has a number of characteristics which are not necessarily common to all but unite in various combinations: a) Sexual "perversity" or ambiguity: a number are more or less explicitly coded as gay (the transvestite killer in *Murder!*, Philip in *Rope*, Bruno Anthony in *Strangers on a Train*); others have marked mother-fixations (Uncle Charlie in *Shadow of a Doubt*, Anthony Perkins in *Psycho*, Bob Rusk in *Frenzy*), seen as a source of their psychic disorder. (b) Fascist connotations: this becomes politically explicit in the U-boat commander of *Lifeboat*, but is plain enough in, for example, *Shadow of a Doubt* and *Rope*. (c) The subtle associations of the villain with the devil: Uncle Charlie and Smoke in *Shadow of a Doubt*, Bruno Anthony in the paddle-boat named Pluto in *Strangers on a Train*, Norman Bates remarking to Marion Crane that "No one ever comes here unless they've gotten off the main highway" in *Psycho*. (d) Closely connected with these characteristics is a striking and ambiguous fusion of power and impotence.

operating on both the sexual and non-sexual levels. What is crucially significant here is that this feature is by no means restricted to the villains. It is shared, strikingly, by the male protagonists of what are perhaps Hitchcock's two supreme masterpieces, *Rear Window* and *Vertigo*. It also relates closely to the obsession with control and fear of losing it that characterized Hitchcock's own methods of filmmaking: his preoccupation with a totally finalized and story-boarded shooting-script, his domination of actors and shooting conditions. (e) Finally, it's notable that the psychopath/villain is invariably the most fascinating and seductive character of the film, its chief source of energy, his inevitable destruction leaving behind an essentially empty world.

If one adds together all these factors, one readily sees why Hitchcock is so much more than the skilful entertainer and master-craftsman he was once taken for. His films overall represent an incomparable exposure of the sexual tensions and anxieties (especially *male* anxieties) that characterize a culture built upon repression, sexual inequality, and the drive to domination.

—Robin Wood

HOLGER-MADSEN. Danish. Born Holger Madsen, 11 April 1878; in 1911 began spelling name with hyphen between first name and surname. Career: 1896-1904—acts in Danish provinces; beginning 1904—performs in Copenhagen theaters; 1907—begins acting in films; 1912—directs 1st film; 1913-20—directs for Nordisk Films Kompagni; 1920-30—works in Germany; 1930—returns to Denmark, makes several sound films; also appears in small stage and film roles; 1938-43—manager of small Copenhagen cinema. Died 30 November 1943; buried at Assistens kirkegård, Copenhagen.

Films (as director): 1912—*Kun en Tigger* (+ro); 1913—*Under Savklingens Taender (The Usurer's Son)* (+ro); *Under Mindernes Trae or Den gamle Baenk (Left Alone)*; *Skaebnes Veje or Under Kaerlighedens Aag (In the Bonds of Passion)*; *Det mørke Punkt or Staalkongens Vilje (The Steel King's Last Wish)*; *Mens Pesten raserr or Laegens Hustru or Under Pesten (During the Plague)*; *Ballettens Datter or Danserinden (Unjustly Accused)*; *Elskovsleg (Love's Devotee)*; *Prinsesse Elena (The Princess's Dilemma)*; *Den hvide Dame (The White Ghost)*; *Fra Fyrste til Knejpevaert (The Gambler's Wife)*; *Millionaerdrengen (The Adventures of a Millionaire's Son)*; *Guldet og vort Hjerte or Et vanskeligt Valg (The Heart's Voice)*; 1914—*Tempeldanserindens Elskov or Bajaderens Haevn (The Bayadere's Revenge)*; *Børnevennerne (A Marriage of Convenience)*; *En Opstandelse or Genopstandelsen (A Resurrection)*; *Husassistenten or Naar Fruen skifter Pige (The New Cook)*; *Søvngaengersken (The Somnambulist)*; *Opiumsdrømmen (The Opium Smoker's Dream)*; *Den mystike Fremmede (A Deal with the Devil)*; *Endelig Alene (Alone at Last)*; *Min Ven Levy (My Friend Levy)*; *Ned med Vaabnene (Lay Down Your Arms)*; *Trold kan taemmes (The Taming of the Shrew)*; *De Forviste or Uden Faedreland (Without a Country)*; *Et Huskors or Lysten styret (Enough of It)*; *Barnets Magt or Barnet (The Child)*; *Et Haremseventyr (An Adventure in a Harem)*; *Evangeliemandens Liv (The Candle and the Moth)*; *Kaerlighedens Triumf or Testamentet (The Romance of a Will)*; *Kys og Kaerlighed (Love and War)*; *Spiritisten (A Voice from the Past)*; *Det stjaalne Ansigt or Ansigtet (The Missing Admiralty Plans)*; *En Aeresoprejsning (Misunderstood)*; 1915—*Cigaretpigen (The Cigarette Maker)*; *Hvem er Gentle-*

mantyven (Strakoff the Adventurer); *En Ildprøve (A Terrible Ordeal)*; *Danserindens Haevn (Circus Arrives, The Dancer's Revenge)*; *Danserindens Kaerlighedsdrøm or Den Dødsdømte (A Dancer's Strange Dream, The Condemned)*; *Den frelsende Film (The Woman Tempted Me)*; *Grevinde Hjerteløs (The Beggar Princess)*; *Guldets Gift (The Tempting of Mrs. Chestney)*; *Den hvide Djaevel (Caught in the Toils, The Devil's Protegé)*; *Hvo som elsker sin Fader or Faklen (Who So Loveth His Father's Honor)*; *I Livets Braending (The Crossroads of Life)*; *Manden uden Fremtid (The Man without a Future)*; *Den omstridte Jord or Jordens Haevn (The Earth's Revenge)*; *Sjaeletyven or Sjaelens Ven (The Unwilling Sinner, His Innocent Dupe)*; *Det unge Blod (The Buried Secret)*; *Et Aeresoprejsning (Misunderstood)*; *Krigens Fjende or Acostates føste Offer (The Munition Conspiracy)*; *En Kunstners Gennembrud or Den Dødes Sjael (The Sound of the Violin)*; 1916—*For sin Faders Skyld (The Veiled Lady, False Evidence)*; *Maaneprinsessen or Kamaeleonen (The Mysterious Lady, The May-Fly)*; *Børnenes Synd (The Sins of the Children)*; *Fange no.113 (Convict No.113)*; *Hans rigtige Kone (Which Is Which)*; *Hendes Moders Løfte or Dødens Kontrakt (A Super Shylock)*; *Hittebarnet (The Foundling of Fate)*; *Hvor Sorgerne glemmes or Søster Ceciles Offer (Sister Cecilia)*; *Livets Gøglespil (An Impossible Marriage)*; *Manden uden Smil*; *Nattens Mysterium or Klubvennen (Who Killed Barno O'Neal)*; *Nattevandreren or Edison Maes Dagbog (Out of the Underworld)*; *Pax Aeterna*; *Lydia (The Music Hall Star)*; *Lykken (The Road to Happiness, Guiding Conscience)*; *Praestens Datter*; *Testamentets Hemmelighed or Den Dødes Røst (The Voice of the Dead, Nancy Keith)*; *Den Aereløse (The Infamous, The Prison Taint)*; *Smil or Far's Sorg (Father Sorrow, The Beggar Man of Paris)*; 1917—*Himmelskibet (A Trip to Mars)*; *Retten sejrer (Justice Victorious)*; *Hendes Helt or Vogt dig for dine Venner*; 1918—*Folkets Ven (A Friend of the People)*; *Mod Lyset (Towards the Light)*; *Manden, der sejrede (The Man Who Tamed the Victors, Fighting Instinct)*; 1919—*Gudernes Yndling or Digterkongen (Trials of Celebrity, The Penalty of Fame)*; *Har jeg Ret til at tage mit eget Liv or Flugten fra Livet (The Flight from Life, Beyond the Barricade, Can We Escape)*; *Det Største i Verden or Janes gode Ven (The Greatest in the World, The Love That Lives)*; 1921—*Am Webstuhl der Zeit*; *Tobias Buntschuh* (+ro); 1922—*Pömperly's Kampf mit dem Schneeschuh* (co-d); 1923—*Das Evangelium*; *Zaida, die Tragödie eines Modells*; 1924—*Der Mann um Mitternacht*; 1925—*Ein Lehenskünstler*; 1926—*Die seltsame Nacht*; *Die Sporck'schen Jäger*; *Spitzen*; 1927—*Die heilige Lüge*; 1928—*Freiwild*; *Die seltsame Nacht der Helga Wansen*; *Was ist los mit Nanette*; 1934—*København, Kalundborg og—?* (co-d); 1936—*Sol over Danmark*.

Roles: 1907—*Den sorte Hertung*; 1908—*Magdalene*; *En grov Spøg (A Practical Joke and a Sad End)*; *Verdens Herkules (Hercules the Athlete)*; *Karneval (The Bank Director, Carnival)*; *Svend Dyrings Hus (The Stepmother)*; *De smaa Landstrygere (Sold to Thieves)*; *Smaeklaasen (The Spring Lock)*; *Naten før Kristians Fødelsdag (The Night Before Christian's Birthday)*; *Rulleskøjterne (On Roller Skates)*; *Sherlock Holmes I*; *Sherlock Holmes III*; 1909—*Den graa Dame (The Gray Dame)*; 1911—*Det store Fald or Malstrømmen*; *Dødssejleren or Dynamitattentatet paa Fyrtaarnet*; 1912—*Paa Livets Skyggeside*; *Praesten i Vejlby*; 1933—*Lynet*; *7-9-13*; 1935—*Kidnapped*; 1943—*Krudt med Knald*.

* * *

The two leading directors at Nordisk Films Kompagni in the

Golden Age of the Danish cinema from 1910 to 1914 were August Blom and Holger-Madsen. They were similar in many respects. They both started as actors, but unlike Blom, Holger-Madsen began as a director with companies other than Nordisk. When he came to Nordisk he worked in almost all of the genres of the period—sensational films, comedies, farces, dramas, and tragedies. But little by little Holger-Madsen developed his own personality, both in content and style.

Holger-Madsen specialized in films with spiritual topics. His main film in this genre was *Evangeliemandens Liv*, in which Valdemar Psilander plays the leading part of a dissolute young man of good family who suddenly realizes how empty and pointless his life is. He becomes a Christian and starts working as a preacher among the poor and the social outcasts of the big city. He succeeds in rescuing a young man from the path of sin. There are several of the cliches of the period in this tale, but the characterization of the hero is largely free of sentimentality, and Holger-Madsen has coached Psilander into playing the role with a mature, calm and genuine strength of feeling. Formally the film is exquisite. The sets, the camerawork, and the lighting are executed with great care, and the film is rich in striking pictorial compositions, which was the forte of Holger-Madsen. He had a predilection for extraordinary, often bizarre images and picturesque surroundings. With his cameraman, Marius Clausen, he emphasized the visual look of his films. His use of side light, inventive camera angles and close-ups, combined with unusual sets, made him an original stylist. He was not very effective in his cutting technique, but he could establish marvelously choreographed scenes, in which people are moving in elegant patterns within the frame.

Holger-Madsen's reputation as an idealistic director lead him to direct the big prestige films with pacifist themes which Ole Olsen, the head of Nordisk Films Kompagni, wanted to make in the naive hope that he could influence the fighting powers in the First World War. The films were often absurdly simple, but Holger-Madsen brought his artistic sense to the visual design of these sentimental stories. One of his most famous films is *Himmelskibet* from 1917 about a scientist who flies to Mars in a rocket ship. There he is confronted with a peaceful civilization. The film has obtained a position as one of the first science fiction films.

When the Danish cinema declined, Holger-Madsen went to Germany. Returning to Denmark after the twenties, he was offered the opportunity of directing during the early sound film period, but his productions were insignificant. He was a silent film director; the image was his domain, and he was one of the craftsmen who molded and refined the visual language of film.

—Ib Monty

HOWARD, WILLIAM K. American. Born in St. Mary's, Ohio, 16 June 1899. Educated in engineering and law, Ohio State University, degree in engineering. Career: 1916-17—works for Cincinnati film distributor; becomes exhibitor for brief period, then Vitagraph sales manager in Minnesota; 1917-18—serves with American Expeditionary Force in France; 1919—fails to find job in New York, goes to Hollywood; becomes sales advisor for Universal; 1920—becomes assistant director; 1921—begins directing for Fox; 1924—signed for series of films by Famous Players-Lasky; 1926—Cecil B. DeMille leaves Famous Players-Lasky, invites Howard to join him in newly-formed Producers Distributing Corp.; 1928-33—under contract to Fox after

DeMille company folds; 1938—after making *Fire Over England* abroad in 1937, reputation declines; 1946—Republic offers series of films but only *A Guy Could Change* is made. Died 21 February 1954.

Films (as assistant director): 1920—*The Skywayman* (Hogan); (as director): 1921—*Get Your Man* (co-d); *Play Square*; *What Love Will Do*; *The One-Man Trail* (Durning) (sc only); 1922—*Extra! Extra!*; *Lucky Dan*; *Deserted at the Altar* (co-d); *Captain Fly-by-Night*; *Trooper O'Neill* (Dunlap and Wallace) (sc only); *The Crusader* (Mitchell) (co-sc only); 1923—*The Fourth Musketeer*; *Danger Ahead*; *Let's Go*; 1924—*The Border Legion*; *East of Broadway*; 1925—*The Thundering Herd*; *Code of the West*; *The Light of Western Stars*; 1926—*Red Dice*; *Bachelor Brides (Bachelor's Brides)*; *Volcano*; *Gigolo*; 1927—*White Gold*; *The Main Event*; 1928—*A Ship Comes in (His Country)*; *The River Pirate*; 1929—*Christina*; *The Valiant*; *Love, Live and Laugh* (dialogue scenes d by Henry Kolker); *Sin Town* (co-sc only); 1930—*Good Intentions* (+co-sc, dialogue scenes d by Henry Kolker); *Scotland Yard (Detective Clive, Bart.)*; 1931—*Don't Bet on Women (More than a Kiss)*; *Transatlantic*; *Surrender*; 1932—*The Trial of Vivienne Ware*; *The First Year*; *Sherlock Holmes*; 1933—*The Power and the Glory (Power and Glory)*; *The Cat and the Fiddle*; 1934—*This Side of Heaven*; *Evelyn Prentice*; 1935—*Vanessa, Her Love Story*; *Rendezvous*; *Mary Burns, Fugitive*; 1936—*The Princess Comes Across*; *Fire over England*; 1937—*The Squeaker (Murder on Diamond Row)*; *Over the Moon* (Freeland) (d, uncredited); *The Green Cockatoo (4 Dark Hours, Race Gang)* (Menzies) ("A William K. Howard Production"); 1939—*Back Door to Heaven* (+pr, story); 1940—*Money and the Woman*; *Knute Rockne—All American (A Modern Hero)* (Bacon) (d begun by Howard); 1941—*Bullets for O'Hara*; 1942—*Klondike Fury*; 1943—*Johnny Come Lately (Johnny Vagabond)*; 1944—*When the Lights Go on Again*; 1946—*A Guy Could Change* (+associate pr).

Publications:

On HOWARD:

Articles—"William K. Howard" by William K. Everson in *Films in Review* (New York), May 1954; obituary in *The New York Times*, 22 February 1954; "William K. Howard", with biofilmography, by T.S. Rutherford in *Film Dope* (London), November 1982.

*   *   *

For more than 20 years, William K. Howard was a reliable Hollywood director, able to turn his attention with ease to most types of features. He was not a major director, the majority of his films being no better than those turned out by his contemporaries, but Howard does deserve more than passing recognition for his work on *White Gold*, *Sherlock Holmes*, *The Power and the Glory*, and *Fire Over England*.

Howard's silent features were always well-made commercial successes, with the best-known titles being a version of Zane Grey's *The Thundering Herd*, starring Jack Holt and Tim McCoy, and a spectacular melodrama featuring Bebe Daniels, *Volcano*. Most historians agree that Howard's best silent film work is *White Gold*, which owes much to German expressionist cinema and which one historian, William K. Everson, has compared favorably to *The Last Laugh*. Certainly the film's star,

Jetta Goudal, has never given a more impressive performance, one that is immediately reminiscent of Lillian Gish in *The Wind*. In the early forties, Howard actively considered a remake of *White Gold*.

Curiously, William K. Howard semed to establish far more of a visual style with his sound films than with his silent efforts. This is particularly apparent in *Sherlock Holmes* and, above all, in *The Power and the Glory*. The latter utilizes a series of flashbacks—rather like *Citizen Kane* some years later—to tell of a railroad executive's rise to power. Highly regarded at the time, the film's continuing appeal owes as much to Howard's direction as to its obviously brilliant script by Preston Sturges. For example, it is doubtful that a lesser team than Howard and Sturges could have created the sequence in which Spencer Tracy and Colleen Moore become engaged, told as the couple climb a steeper and steeper hill with no dialogue except for the commentary by Ralph Morgan.

From 1936 through 1938 Howard worked in England, notably on *Fire Over England*, based on the A.E.W. Mason historical romance set during the reign of Elizabeth I. Obviously Howard was aided by a cast which included Flora Robson (as Elizabeth), Laurence Olivier, Vivien Leigh, and Raymond Massey, not to mention the cinematography of James Wong Howe, but even so the director deserves credit for his capable handling of both sweeping historical spectacle and intimate drama.

With his return to the States, Howard settled down to directing routine melodramas. He did create something of a sensation in the film community in 1936 when he ordered his supervising producer off the set during the filming of *The Princess Comes Across*, the first time a director had enforced the policies of the fledgling Screen Directors Guild. Contemporaries of Howard have described him as both brilliant and cynical, and it is perhaps the latter trait which enabled the director to add a reasonable amount of artistry to films which might otherwise have been nothing more than mere box office successes.

—Anthony Slide

HUSTON, JOHN. Irish. Born John Marcellus Huston in Nevada, Missouri, 5 August 1906; became citizen of Ireland in 1964. Educated at boarding school in Los Angeles, 1918; Lincoln High School, Los Angeles, 1923-24. Married Dorothy Jeanne Harvey in 1926 (divorced 1933); Leslie Black in 1937 (divorced 1944); Evelyn Keyes in 1946 (divorced 1950); adopted Pablo Albarran, 1947; married Ricki Soma in 1950 (died 1969); children: Walter, Anjelica and Allegra; child (by Zoë Sallis): Daniel; married Celeste Shane in 1972 (divorced 1977). Career: 1916—doctors in St. Paul, Minnesota, diagnose enlarged heart and kidney disease, taken to California for cure; early 1920s—boxer in California; 1924—moves to New York, acts in *The Triumph of the Egg* at Provincetown Playhouse; 1927—competition horseman, Mexico; 1928—decides on career as writer; 1928-30—works as journalist in New York; 1930—goes to Hollywood where father Walter Huston appearing in 1st picture; works on script for *A House Divided* (Wyler); 1932—moves to London, works for Gaumont-British; 1933—moves to Paris, intending to study painting; 1934—returns to New York, edits *Midweek Pictorial*; resumes acting career in title role of *Abe Lincoln in Illinois*, Chicago Federal Theater production; 1935—returns to Hollywood, begins to write for Warner Bros. in 1936; 1939—directs father in *A Passage to Bali* on Broadway; 1942-45—serves in

Signal Corps, Army Pictorial Service; discharged as Major; 1943-45—makes war documentaries; 1945—*Let There Be Light* suppressed by Army; 1947—directs Sartre's *No Exit*, New York; with William Wyler and Phillip Dunne forms Committee for the 1st Amendment to counteract HUAC investigation; 1948—forms Horizon Pictures with Sam Spiegel; 1952—forms John Huston Productions for unrealized project *Matador*; 1955—buys home in Ireland; 1963—directs Richard Bennett's opera *The Mines of Sulphur*, Milan; mid-1960s to present—appears in and narrates for television; 1972—moves to Mexico; 1977—undergoes open-heart surgery, Los Angeles. Recipient: Legion of Merit, U.S. Armed Services, 1944; Best Direction Academy Award for *Treasure of the Sierra Madre*, 1947. Address: c/o Jess S. Morgan and Company, 6420 Wilshire Blvd., Los Angeles, CA 90048.

Films (as scriptwriter): 1931—*A House Divided* (Wyler) (dialogue); 1932—*Murders in the Rue Morgue* (Florey) (dialogue); 1935—*It Started in Paris* (Robert Wyler) (co-adapt); *Death Drives Through* (Cahn) (co-story); 1938—*Jezebel* (Wyler) (co-sc); *The Amazing Dr. Clitterhouse* (Litvak) (co-sc); 1939—*Juarez* (Dieterle) (co-sc); 1940—*The Story of Dr. Ehrlich's Magic Bullet (Dr. Ehrlich's Magic Bullet)* (Dieterle) (co-sc); 1941—*High Sierra* (Walsh) (co-sc); *Sergeant York* (Hawks) (co-sc); (as director): 1941—*The Maltese Falcon* (+sc); 1942—*In This Our Life* (+co-sc, uncredited); *Across the Pacific* (co-d); 1943—*Report from the Aleutians* (+sc); *Tunisian Victory* (Capra and Boulting) (d some replacement scenes when footage lost, +co-commentary); 1945—*San Pietro (The Battle of San Pietro)* (+sc, co-ph, narration); 1946—*Let There Be Light* (unrealeased) (+co-sc, co-ph); *The Killers* (Siodmak) (sc, uncredited); *The Stranger* (Welles) (co-sc, uncredited); *3 Strangers* (Negulesco) (co-sc); *A Miracle Can Happen (On Our Merry Way)* (King Vidor and Fenton) (d some Henry Fonda/James Stewart sequences, uncredited); 1948—*The Treasure of the Sierra Madre* (+sc, bit ro as man in white suit); *Key Largo* (+co-sc); 1949—*We Were Strangers* (+co-sc, bit ro as bank clerk); 1950—*The Asphalt Jungle* (+co-sc); 1951—*The Red Badge of Courage* (+sc); *Quo Vadis* (LeRoy) (pre-production work only); 1952—*The African Queen* (+co-sc); 1953—*Moulin Rouge* (+pr, co-sc); 1954—*Beat the Devil* (+co-pr, co-sc); 1956—*Moby Dick* (+pr, co-sc); 1957—*Heaven Knows, Mr. Allison* (+co-sc); *A Farewell to Arms* (Charles Vidor) (d begun by Huston); 1958—*The Barbarian and the Geisha*; *The Roots of Heaven*; 1960—*The Unforgiven*; 1961—*The Misfits*; 1963—*Freud (Freud: The Secret Passion)* (+narration); *The List of Adrian Messenger* (+bit ro as *Lord Ashton*); 1964—*The Night of the Iguana* (+co-pr, co-sc); 1965—*La bibbia (The Bible)* (+ro, narration); 1967—*Casino Royale* (co-d, +ro); *Reflections in a Golden Eye* (+voice heard at film's beginning); 1969—*Sinful Davey*; *A Walk with Love and Death* (+ro); 1970—*The Kremlin Letter* (+co-sc, ro); 1971—*The Last Run* (Fleischer) (d begun by Huston); 1972—*Fat City* (+co-pr); *The Life and Times of Judge Roy Bean* (+ro as *Grizzly Adams*); 1973—*The Mackintosh Man*; 1975—*The Man Who Would Be King* (+co-sc); 1976—*Independence* (short); 1979—*Wise Blood* (+ro); 1980—*Phobia*; 1981—*Victory (Escape to Victory)*; 1982—*Annie*.

Roles: 1929—small role in *The Shakedown* (Wyler); small role in *Hell's Heroes* (Wyler); 1930—small role in *The Storm* (Wyler); 1963—*Cardinal Glennon* in *The Cardinal* (Preminger); appearance in *The Directors* (pr: Greenblatt—short); 1968—*Dr. Dunlap* in *Candy* (Marquand); interviewee in *The Rocky Road to Dublin* (Lennon); 1969—*The Abbé* in *De Sade* (Enfield) (+d, uncredited); 1970—*Buck Loner* in *Myra Breckenridge* (Sarne); 1971—*Sleigh* in *The Bridge in the Jungle* (Kohner); *General*

Miles in *The Deserter* (Kennedy); *Captain Henry* in *Man in the Wilderness* (Sarafian); 1974—*Lawgiver* in *Battle for the Planet of the Apes* (Thompson); *Noah Cross* in *Chinatown* (Polanski); 1975—*Harris* in *Breakout* (Gries); *John Hay* in *The Wind and the Lion* (Milius); 1976—*Professor Moriarty* in *Sherlock Holmes in New York* (Sagal); 1977—*Ned Turner* in *Tentacles* (Hellman); *Il grande attacco (La battaglia di Mareth, The Biggest Battle)* (Lenzi); *El triangulo diabolico de la Bermudas (Il triangolo delle Bermude, Triangle: The Bermuda Mystery, The Mystery of the Bermuda Triangle)* (Cardona); *Angela* (Sagal); 1978—*Il visitatore (The Visitor)* (Paradise, i.e. Paradisi); 1979—*Jaguar Lives* (Pintoff); *Winter Kills* (Richert); 1980—*Head On* (Grant); interviewee in *Agee* (Spears); 1981—narrator of *To the Western World* (Kinmonth); 1982—narrator of *Cannery Row* (Ward); 1983—psychiatrist in *Lovesick* (Brickman).

Publications:

By HUSTON:

Books and scripts—*Frankie and Johnny*, New York 1930; *In Time to Come* in *The Best Plays of 1941-1942* edited by Burns Mantle, New York 1942; *Juarez* in *20 Best Film Plays* edited by Gassner and Nichols, New York 1943; *Let There Be Light* in *Film: Book 2* by Robert Hughes, New York 1962; *An Open Book*, New York 1980; articles—"Fool" in *American Mercury*, March 1929; "Figures of Fighting Men" in *American Mercury*, May 1931; "The African Queen" in *Theatre Arts* (New York), February 1952; "Interview with Huston" by Karel Reisz in *Sight and Sound* (London), January/March 1952; "Humphrey Bogart est mort lundi matin" in *Positif* (Paris), no.21, 1957; "Home is Where the Heart is—and So Are Films" in *Screen Producers Guild Journal* (Los Angeles), March 1963; "How I Make Films", interview by Gideon Bachmann, in *Film Quarterly* (Berkeley), fall 1965; "Monkeys I Have Known" in *Pageant*, August 1965; "Interview with John Huston" by Curtice Taylor and Glenn O'Brien in *Interview* (New York), September 1972; "The Innocent Bystander", interview by D. Robinson in *Sight and Sound* (London), winter 1972/73; "2 soirées avec John Huston" by J. Aghed and Michel Ciment in *Positif* (Paris), September 1972; "A Talk with John Huston" by D. Ford in *Action* (Los Angeles), September/October 1972; "Huston!", interview by C. Taylor and G. O'Brien in *Inter/View* (New York), September 1972; "Talking with John Huston" by Gene Phillips in *Film Comment* (New York), May/June 1973; interview by D. Brandes in *Filmmakers Newsletter* (Ward Hill, Mass.), July 1977; "John Huston: souvenirs d'Hollywood", interview by E. Decaux and B. Villien in *Cinématographe* (Paris), November 1979; interview by P.S. Greenberg in *Rolling Stone* (New York), June/July 1981.

On HUSTON:

Books—*Picture* by Lillian Ross, New York 1952; *John Huston* by Paul Davay, Paris 1957; *John Huston* by Jean-Claude Allais, Paris 1960; *Agee on Film* by James Agee, Boston 1964; *John Huston, King Rebel* by William Nolan, Los Angeles 1965; *Agee on Film: 5 Film Scripts* by James Agee, foreword by John Huston, Boston 1965; *John Huston* by Robert Benayoun, Paris 1966; *John Huston* by Riccardo Cecchini, 1969; *John Huston, A Picture Treasury of his Films* by Romano Tozzi, New York 1971; *John Huston* by Axel Madsen, New York 1978; *John Huston: Maker of Magic* by Stuart Kaminsky, London 1978; articles—"Wyler, Wellman and Huston" by Richard Griffith in *Films in Review* (New York), February 1950; "The Way John Huston

Works" by David Mage in *Films in Review* (New York), October 1952; special Huston issue of *Positif* (Paris), August 1952; "The Director on Horseback" by Peter Barnes in *Film Quarterly* (Berkeley), spring 1956; "An Encounter with John Huston" by Edouard Laurot in *Film Culture* (New York), no.8, 1956; special Huston issue of *Positif* (Paris), January 1957; special number of *Bianco e nero* (Rome), April 1957; "Huston at Fontainbleu" by Cynthia Grencer in *Sight and Sound* (London), autumn 1958; "John Huston—The Hemingway Tradition in American Film" by Eugene Archer in *Film Culture* (New York), no.19, 1959; "Huston avant le déluge" by Robert Benayoun in *Positif* (Paris), June 1965; "John Huston, *The Bible* and James Bond" in *Cahiers du Cinema in English* (New York), no.5, 1966; "John Huston: As He Was, Is and Probably Always Will Be" by Brian St. Pierre in *The New York Times*, 25 September 1966; "From Book to Film—via John Huston" by Hans Koningsberger in *Film Quarterly* (Berkeley), spring 1969; "John Huston and the Figure in the Carpet" by John Russell Taylor in *Sight and Sound* (London), spring 1969; "Talking with John Huston" by Gene Phillips in *Film Comment* (New York), May/June 1973; "Beating the Devil" by D. Jones in *Films and Filming* (London), January 1973; "Reflections on a Golden Boy" by H. Koch in *Film Comment* (New York), May/June 1973; "Ray Bradbury on Hitchcock, Huston and Other Magic of the Screen" by A.R. Kunert in *Take One* (Montreal), September 1973; "Huston Meets the Eye" by T. Reck in *Film Comment* (New York), May/June 1973; "John Huston" by Rosemary Lord in *Transatlantic Review*, autumn/winter 1974; "Details from the Master's Painting" by R. Riger in *Action* (Los Angeles), September/October 1975; "Watching Huston" by Gideon Bachmann in *Film Comment* (New York), January/February 1976; "John Huston as Survivor of the 2nd Hollywood Generation" by A. Spiegel in *Salmagundi* (Saratoga Springs, New York), fall 1976; "3 regards critiques" by L. Audibert and J.-C. Bonnet in *Cinématographe* (Paris), April 1977; "John Huston: At 74 No Formulas" by B. Drew in *American Film* (Washington, D.C.), September 1980; "At War with the Army" by S. Hammen in *Film Comment* (New York), March/April 1980; "John Huston" by R.T. Jameson in *Film Comment* (New York), May/June 1980; "Huston, la Warner y las ideas previas" by F. Llinás in *Contracampo* (Madrid), June/July 1981; "John Huston" by G. Millar in *Sight and Sound* (London), summer 1981; biofilmography in *Film Dope* (London), January 1983; films—*On Location: The Night of the Iguana*, for TV, by William Kronick, U.S. 1964; *On the Trail of the Iguana*, short, by Russ Lowell, U.S. 1965; *The Life and Times of John Huston, Esq.* by Roger Graef, Great Britain 1967; *Ride This Way Grey Horse* by Paul Joyce, Great Britain 1970.

*　　*　　*

Few directors have been as interested in the relationship of film to painting as has John Huston and, perhaps, none has been given as little credit for this interest. This lack of recognition is not completely surprising in a medium which, in spite of its visual nature, criticism has tended to be derived primarily from literature and not from painting or, as might be more reasonable, a combination of the traditions of literature, painting, theater, and the uniqueness of film itself.

In a 1931 profile in *The American Mercury* accompanying a short story by John Huston, the future director said that he wanted to write a book on the lives of French painters. The following year, unable to or dissatisfied with work as a film writer in London, Huston moved to Paris to become a painter. He studied for a year and a half making money by painting portraits on street corners and singing for pennies. Huston's interest in painting has continued throughout his life and he from time to time "retires" from filmmaking to concentrate on his painting.

Each of Huston's films has reflected this prime interest in the image, the moving portrait and the use of color, as well as the poetic possibilities of natural dialogue. Each film has been a moving canvas on which Huston explores his main subject: the effect of the individual ego on the group and the possibility of the individual's survival.

Huston began exploring his style of framing in his first film, *The Maltese Falcon*. Following his sketches, he set up shots like the canvases of paintings he had studied. Specifically, Huston showed an interest in characters appearing in the foreground of a shot, with their faces often covering half the screen. Frequently, too, the person whose face half fills the screen is not talking, but listening. The person reacting thus becomes more important than the one speaking or moving.

Huston's first film as a director presented situations he would return to again and again. Spade is the obsessed professional, a man who will adhere to pride and dedication, to principle unto death. Women are a threat, temptations that can only sway the hero from his professional commitment. They may be willfully trying to deceive, as with Brigid and Iva, or they may, as in later Huston films, be the unwitting cause of the protagonist's defeat or near-defeat. In *The Asphalt Jungle*, for example, the women in the film are not evil; it is the men's obsession with them that causes disaster.

Even with changes and cuts, a film like *The Red Badge of Courage* reflects Huston's thematic and visual interests. Again, there is a group with a quest that may result in death. These soldiers argue, support each other, pretend they are not frightened, brag, and some die.

In the course of the action, both the youth and the audience discover that the taking of an isolated field is not as important as the ability of the young men to face death without fear. Also, as in other Huston films, the two central figures in *The Red Badge of Courage*, the youth and Wilson, lie about their attitudes. Their friendship solidifies only when both confess that they have been afraid during the battle and have run.

Visually, Huston has continued to explore an important aspect of his style, the placement of characters in a frame so that their size and position reflect what they are saying and doing. He developed this technique with Bogart, Holt, and Walter Huston in *The Treasure of the Sierra Madre* and Audie Murphy and Bill Mauldin in *The Red Badge of Courage*.

Early in *The African Queen*, after Rosie's brother dies, there is a scene with Rosie seated on the front porch of the mission. Charlie, in the foreground, dominates the screen while Rosie, in the background, is small. As Charlie starts to take control of the situation and tell Rosie what must be done, he raises his hand to the rail and his arm covers our view of her. Charlie is in command.

Thematically, *Moulin Rouge* was a return to Huston's pessimism and exploration of futility. The director identified with Lautrec who, like Huston, was given to late hours, ironic views of himself, performing for others, sardonic wit, and a frequent bitterness toward women, Lautrec, like Huston, loved horses, and frequently painted pictures of them.

The narrative as developed by Huston and Ray Bradbury in *Moby Dick* is in keeping with the director's preoccupation with failed quests. Only one man, Ishmael, survives. All the other men of the Pequod go down in Ahab's futile attempt to destroy the whale. But Huston sees Ahab in his actions and his final gesture as a noble creature who has chosen to go down fighting.

The Roots of Heaven is yet another example of Huston's exploration of an apparently doomed quest by a group of vastly

different people led by a man obsessed. In spite of the odds, the group persists in its mission and some of its members die. As in many Huston films, the quest is not a total failure; there is the likelihood of continuation, if not success, but the price that must be paid in human lives is high.

In *The Misfits* there was again the group on a sad and fruitless quest. This time they are searching for horses. But they find far fewer than they had expected. The expedition becomes a bust and the trio of friends are at odds over a woman, Roslyn (Marilyn Monroe), who opposes the killing and capturing of the horses.

With the exception of Guido, the characters represent the least masked or disguised group in Huston's films. Perhaps it is this very element of never-penetrated disguise in Guido that upset Huston about the character and drove him to push for a motivation scene, an emotional unmasking.

As a Huston film, *Freud* has some particular interests: Huston serves as a narrator, displaying an omnipotence and almost Biblical detachment that establishes Freud as a kind of savior and messiah. The film opens with Huston's description of Freud as a kind of hero or God on a quest for mankind. "This is the story of Freud's descent into a region as black as hell, man's unconscious, and how he let in the light," Huston says in his narration. The bearded, thin look of Freud, who stands alone denounced before the tribunal of his own people, also suggests a parallel with Christ. Freud brings a message of salvation which is rejected, and he is reluctantly denounced by his chief defender, Breuer.

Of all Huston's films, *The List of Adrian Messenger* is the one that deals most literally with people in disguise. George, who describes himself as unexcused evil, hides behind a romantic or heroic mask that falls away when he is forced to face the detective, who functions very much like Freud. The detective penetrates the masks, revealing the evil, and the evil is destroyed.

Huston's touch was evident in *The Night of the Iguana* in a variety of ways. First, he again took a group of losers and put them together in an isolated location. The protagonist, Shannon, once a minister, has been reduced to guiding tourists in Mexico. At the furthest reaches of despair and far from civilization, the quest for meaning ends and the protagonist is forced to face himself. Religion is an important theme. The film opens with Richard Burton preaching a sermon to his congregation. It is a startling contrast to Father Mapple's sermon in *Moby Dick*. Shannon is lost, confused, his speech is gibberish, an almost nonsensical confession about being unable to control his appetites and emotions. The congregation turns away from him.

This choice between the practical and the fantastic is a constant theme in Huston's life and films. There is also a choice between illusion and reality, a choice Huston finds difficult to make. Religion is seen as part of the fantasy world, a dangerous fantasy that his characters must overcome if they are not to be destroyed or absorbed by it. This theme is present in *The Bible, Wise Blood*, and *Night of the Iguana*.

There are clearly constants in Huston's works—man's ability to find solace in animals, and nature, the need to challenge oneself—but his world is unpredictable, governed by a whimsical God or no God at all. Each of Huston's characters seeks a way of coming to terms with that unpredictability, establishing rules of behavior by which he can live.

The Huston character, like Cain or Adam, is often weak, and frequently his best intentions will not carry him through to success or even survival. The more a man thinks in a Huston film, the more dangerous it is for his survival, but carried away by emotion, or too much introspection, a man is doomed. Since the line between loss of control and rigidity is difficult to walk, many Huston protagonists do not survive. It takes a Sam Spade,

Sergeant Allison, or Abraham, very rare men indeed, to remain alive in this director's world.

Reflections in a Golden Eye raised many questions about the sexuality inherent in many of the themes that most attracted Huston: riding horses, hunting, boxing, and militarism. The honesty with which the director handles homosexuality is characteristic of his willingness to face what he finds antithetical to his own nature. In the film, the equation of Leonora and her horse is presented as definitely sexual, and at one point Penderton actually beats the horse in a fury because he himself is impotent. Huston also includes a boxing match in the film which is not in the novel. The immorally provocative Leonora watches the match, but Penderton watches another spectator, Williams. *Reflections* becomes an almost comic labyrinth of voyeurism, with characters spying on other characters.

Huston's negative religious attitude is strong in *A Walk with Love and Death*, in which there are three encounters with the clergy. In the first, Heron is almost killed by a group of ascetic monks who demand that he renounce the memory of Claudia and "repent his knowledge of women." The young man barely escapes with his life. These religious zealots counsel a move away from the pleasure of the world and human love, a world that Huston believes in.

Huston's protagonists often represent extremes. They are either ignorant, pathetic, and doomed by their lack of self-understanding (Tully and Ernie in *Fat City*, Dobbs in *The Treasure of the Sierra Madre*, Peachy and Danny in *The Man Who Would Be King*) or intelligent, arrogant, and equally doomed by their lack of self-understanding (Penderton in *Reflections in a Golden Eye* and Ahab in *Moby Dick*). Between these extremes is the cool, intelligent protagonist who will sacrifice everything for self-understanding and independence (Sam Spade in *The Maltese Falcon*, and Freud). Huston always finds the first group pathetic, the second tragic, and the third heroic. He reserves his greatest respect for the man who retains his dignity in spite of pain and disaster.

Many of Huston's films can de divided between those involving group quests that fail and those involving a pair of potential lovers who must face a hostile world generally, Huston's films about such lovers end in the union of the couple or, at least, their survival. In that sense, *A Walk with Love and Death*, starring his own daughter, proved to be the most pessimistic of his love stories, and *Annie*, his most commerical venture, proved to be his most optimistic.

—Stuart M. Kaminsky

ICHIKAWA, KON. Japanese. Born Uji Yamada in Ise, Mie Prefecture, 20 November 1915. Educated at Ichioka Commercial School, Osaka. Married scriptwriter Natto Wada, 1948. Career: 1933—goes to work in animation dept. of J.O. studios, Kyoto; later 1930s—becomes assistant director on feature-filmmaking staff; early 1940s—transferred to Tokyo when J.O. becomes part of Toho company; 1946—U.S. occupation authorities confiscate print of *A Girl at Dojo Temple* because of its "traditionalist and medieval spirit"; 1948-56—collaborates on scripts with wife Natto Wada; after 1957—uses pen name "Shitei Kuri" (after Japanese rendering of Agatha Christie's name, as homage to her) for his own scenarios; 1958-66—writes and directs extensively for television. Recipient: San Giorgio Prize, Venice Festival, for *Harp of Burma*, 1956.

Films (as director): 1946—*Musume Dojoji (A Girl at Dojo Temple)* (+co-sc); 1947—*Toho senichi-ya (1001 Nights with Toho)* (responsible for some footage only); 1948—*Hana hiraku (A Flower Blooms)*; *Sanbyaku rokujugo-ya (365 Nights)*; 1949—*Ningen moyo (Human Patterns, Design of a Human Being)*; *Hateshinaki jonetsu (Passion without End, The Endless Passion)*; 1950—*Ginza Sanshiro (Sanshiro of Ginza)*; *Netsudeichi (Heat and Mud, The Hot Marshland)* (+co-sc); *Akatsuki no tsuiseki (Pursuit at Dawn)*; 1951—*Ieraishan (Nightshade Flower)* (+co-sc); *Koibito (The Lover, The Sweetheart)* (+co-sc); *Mukokuseki-sha (The Man without a Nationality)*; *Nusumareta koi (Stolen Love)* (+co-sc); *Bungawan Solo (River Solo Flows)* (+co-sc); *Kekkon koshinkyoku (Wedding March)* (+co-sc); 1952—*Rakkii-san (Mr. Lucky)*; *Wakai hito (Young People, Young Generation)* (+co-sc); *Ashi ni sawatta onna (The Woman Who Touched Legs)* (+co-sc); *Ano te kono te (This Way, That Way)* (+co-sc); 1953—*Puu-san (Mr. Pu)* (+co-sc); *Aoiro kakumei (The Blue Revolution)*; *Seishun Zenigata Heiji (The Youth of Heiji Zenigata)* (+co-sc); *Ai-jin (The Lover)*; 1954—*Watashi no subete o (All of Myself)* (+co-sc); *Okuman choja (A Billionaire)* (+co-sc); *Josei ni kansuru juni-sho (12 Chapters on Women)*; 1955—*Seishun kaidan (Ghost Story of Youth)*; *Kokoro (The Heart)*; 1956—*Biruma no tategoto (The Burmese Harp, Harp of Burma)*; *Shokei no heya (Punishment Room)*; *Nihonbashi (Bridge of Japan)*; 1957—*Manin densha (The Crowded Streetcar)* (+co-sc); *Tohoku no zummu-tachi (The Men of Tohoku)* (+sc); *Ana (The Pit, The Hole)* (+sc); 1958—*Enjo (Conflagration)*; 1959—*Sayonara, konnichiwa (Goodbye, Hello)* (+co-sc); *Kagi (The Key, Odd Obsession)* (+co-sc); *Nobi (Fires on the Plain)*; *Jokyo II: Mono o takaku uritsukeru onna (A Woman's Testament, Part 2: Women Who Sell Things at High Prices)*; 1960—*Bonchi* (+co-sc); *Ototo (Her Brother)*; 1961—*Kuroi junin no onna (10 Dark Women)*; 1962—*Hakai (The Sin, The Outcast, The Broken Commandment)*; *Watashi wa nisai (I am Two, Being Two Isn't Easy)*; 1963—*Yukinojo henge (An Actor's Revenge, The Revenge of Yukinojo)*; *Taiheiyo hitoribotchi (My Enemy, the Sea, Alone on the Pacific)*; 1964—*Zeni no odori (The Money Dance, Money Talks)* (+sc); 1965—*Tokyo Orimpikku (Tokyo Olympiad)* (+co-sc); 1967—*Toppo Jijo no botan senso (Toppo Gigio and the Missile War)* (+co-sc); 1968—*Seishun (Youth, Tournament)* (for TV) (+sc); 1969—*Kyoto* (+sc); 1970—*Nihon to Nihonjin (Japan and the Japanese)* (+sc); *Dodes'ka-den* (Kurosawa) (pr only); 1972—*Ai futatabi (To Love Again, Pourquoi)*; 1973—*Matatabi (The Wanderers)* (+pr, co-sc); "The Fastest" episode of *Visions of 8*; 1975—*Wagahai wa neko de aru (I Am a Cat)*; 1976—*Tsuma to onna no aida (Between Women and Wives)* (co-d); *Inugami-ke no ichizoku (The Inugami Family)* (+co-sc); 1977—*Akuma no temari-uta (A Rhyme of Vengeance, The Devil's Bouncing Ball Song)* (+sc); *Gokumonto (The Devil's Island, Island of Horrors)* (+co-sc); 1978—*Jo-bachi (Queen Bee)* (+co-sc); 1980—*Koto (Ancient City)* (+co-sc); *Hi no tori (The Phoenix)* (+co-sc); 1982—*Kofuku (Lonely Hearts, Happiness)* (+co-sc).

Publications:

By ICHIKAWA:

Book—*Seijocho 271 Banchi*, with Natto Wada, Tokyo 1961; articles—in *Film Makers on Filmmaking* edited by Harry Geduld, Bloomington, Indiana 1967; "Kon Ichikawa at the Olympic Games", interview in *American Cinematographer* (Los Angeles), November 1972.

On ICHIKAWA:

Books—*The Japanese Film, Art and Industry* by Joseph Anderson and Donald Richie, new edition, New York 1971; *Japanese Film Directors* by Audie Bock, Tokyo 1978; articles—"Portrait de Kon Ichikawa" by Donald Richie in *Cinéma 60* (Paris), June 1960; "The Skull Beneath the Skin" by Tom Milne in *Sight and Sound* (London), autumn 1966; "The Several Sides of Kon Ichikawa" by Donald Richie in *Sight and Sound* (London), spring 1966; "Kon Ichikawa l'entomologiste" by Max Tessier in *Jeune Cinéma* (Paris), March 1967; "The Uniqueness of Kon Ichikawa" in *Cinema* (Beverly Hills), fall 1970; "Kon Ichikawa" by Langdon Dewey in *International Film Guide 1970*, London 1969; "Ichikawa and the Wanderers" by W. Johnson in *Film Comment* (New York), September/October 1975; "Kon Ichikawa", with biofilmography, by John Gillett in *Film Dope* (London), January 1983.

*   *   *

Kon Ichikawa is noted for a wry humor which often resembles black comedy, for his grim psychological studies, portrayals of misfits and outsiders, and for the visual beauty of his films. Noted as one of Japan's foremost cinematic stylists, he has commented, "I began as a painter and I think like one."

His early films show a perverse sense of humor as they reveal human foibles and present an objective view of corruption. In *Mr. Pu* a projector breaks down while showing scenes of an atomic explosion; in *A Billionaire*, a family dies from eating radioactive tuna, leaving only a lazy elder son and a sympathetic tax collector. In *The Key*, a group of rather selfish, despicable people are poisoned inadvertently by a senile old maid, who becomes the only survivor. The film is a study of an old man who becomes obsessed with sex to compensate for his fears of impotency. He becomes a voyeur and through the manipulation of the camera, we come to share in this activity. Slowly, however, he emerges as being sympathetic while the other characters are revealed in their true light.

Throughout his career Ichikawa has proven himself a consistent critic of Japanese society, treating such themes as the rebirth of militarism (*Mr. Pu*), the harshness and inhumanity of military feudalism (*Fires on the Plain*), the abuse of the individual within the family (*Bonchi* and/*Her Brother*), as well as familial claustrophobia and the tendency of repression to result in perversion and outbreaks of violence (*The Key*). His films usually refuse a happy ending and Ichikawa has been frequently criticized for an unabashed pessimism, bordering on nihilism.

Two of his most important films, *Harp of Burma* and *Fires on the Plain*, deal with the tragedies of war. The former concerns a soldier who adopts Buddhist robes and dedicates himself to burying the countless Japanese dead on Burma; the latter is about a group of demoralized soldiers who turn to cannibalism. A third work, *Tokyo Olympiad*, provided a new approach to sports films, giving as much attention to human emotions and spectator reactions as to athletic feats.

Ichikawa is a master of the wide screen and possesses a strong sense of composition, creating enormous depth with his use of diagonal and overhead shots. Often he utilizes black backgrounds, so as to isolate images within the frame, or a form of theatrical lighting, or he blocks out portions of the screen to alter the format and ratio.

Ichikawa remains fascinated with experimental techniques. His excellent use of the freeze frame in *Kagi* reflects his case study approach to characterization. He has also done much in the way of color experimentation. *Kagi* is bathed in blues which bleach skin tones to white, thus creating corpse-like subjects. *Her Brother* is so filtered that it resembles a black and white print with dull pinks and reds. On most of his films, Ichikawa has used cameramen Kazuo Miyagawa or Setsuo Kobayashi.

After *Tokyo Olympiad* Ichikawa encountered many studio difficulties. His projects since then include a 26-part serialization of *The Tale of Genji*, *The Wanderers*, a parody of gangster films with a nod to *Easy Rider*, plus a dozen documentaries and fiction features, among which *The Inugami Family*, a suspense thriller, proved to be the biggest box office success in Japanese film history.

—Patricia Erens

IMAI, TADASHI. Japanese. Born in Tokyo, 8 January 1912. Educated at Tokyo Imperial University, left in 1935. Married in 1934 and 1955. Career: 1935—enters J.O. Studio, Kyoto; works as assistant to directors Ishida, Namiki, and Nakagawa; 1937—J.O. Studio absorbed by Toho; appointed director; 1939—1st film *Numazu Military School* completed; during war—makes propaganda films; after war—begins to make "democratic" films; joins Communist party; 1950—due to persecution of leftists by American Occupation authorities, leaves Toho and helps initiate independent film production movement; during 1950s—5 Imai films place at top of *Kinema Jumpo* annual 10 Best Films list; 1953 through 1960s—"prestige director" for Toei, Daiei, and other studios; 1969—resumes independent production with *River without Bridges*. Recipient: Mainichi Film Competition Award for *The People's Enemy*, 1946. Address: 1-4-1 Yazaki-cho, Fuchu City, Tokyo, Japan.

Films (as director): 1939—*Numazu Hei-gakko (Numazu Military Academy)*; *Waga kyokan (Our Teacher, Our Instructor)*; 1940—*Tajiko mura (Tajiko Village, The Village of Tajiko)*; *Onna no machi (Women's Street, Women's Town)*; *Kakka (Your Highness)*; 1941—*Kekkon no seitai (Married Life, The Situation of Marriage)*; 1943—*Boro no kesshitai (The Suicide Troops of the Watch Tower, The Death Command of the Tower)*; 1944—*Ikari no umi (Angry Sea)*; 1945—*Ai to chikai (Love and Pledge)*; 1946—*Minshu no teki (An Enemy of the People, The People's Enemy)*; *Jinsei tonbo-gaeri (Somersault of Life, Life Is Like a Somersault)*; 1947—*Chikagai nijuyo-jikan (24 Hours of a Secret Life, 24 Hours of the Underground Street)*; 1949—*Aoi sanmyaku (Green Mountains)* parts I and II; *Onna no kao (A Woman's Face)*; 1950—*Mata au hi made (Until the Day We Meet Again, Until We Meet Again)*; 1951—*Dokkoi ikiteiru (Still We Live, And Yet We Live)*; 1952—*Yamabiko gakko (Echo School, School of Echoes)*; 1953—*Himeyuri no to (Himeyuri Lily Tower, The Tower of Lilies)*; *Nigori-e (Muddy Water)*; 1955—one episode of *Aisureba koso (Because I Love)*; *Koko ni izumi ari (Here Is a Fountain, Here Is a Spring)*; *Yukiko*; 1956—*Mahiru no ankoku (Darkness at Noon)*; 1957—*Kome (Rice)*; *Junai monogatari (The Story of Pure Love)*; 1958—*Yoru no tsuzumi (The Adulteress, Night Drum)*; *Kiku to Isamu (Kiku and Isamu)*; 1960—*Shiroi gake (The Cliff, White Cliff)*; 1961—*Are ga minato no hikari da (That Is the Port Light)*; 1962—

Nippon no obachan (Japanese Grandmothers, The Old Women of Japan); 1963—*Bushido zankoku monogatari (Bushido: Samurai Saga, Cruel Story of the Samurai's Way)*; 1964—*Echigo tsutsuishi oyashirazu (A Story for Echigo, Death in the Snow)*; *Adauchi (Revenge)*; 1967—*Sato-gashi ga kazureru toki (When the Cookie Crumbles, When Sugar-Cookies Are Broken)*; 1968—*Fushin no toki (The Time of Reckoning, Time of Losing Faith)*; 1969—*Hashi no nai kawa (River without Bridges, Bridge Across No River)*; 1970—*Hashi no nai kawa (River without Bridges, Bridge Across No River)* Part II; 1971—*En to iu onna (A Woman Named En)*; 1972—*Aa koe naki tomo (Ah! My Friends without Voice)*; *Kaigun tokubetsu shonen hei (Special Boy Soldiers of the Navy)*; 1974—*Kobayashi Takiji (Takiji Kobayashi, The Life of a Communist Writer)*; 1976—*Ani imoto (Mon and Ino, His Younger Sister, Older Brother and Younger Sister)*; *Yoba (The Old Woman Ghost)*; 1982—*Himeyuri no to (Himeyuri Lily Tower)* (remake).

Publications:

On IMAI:

Books—*The Japanese Film* by Joseph Anderson and Donald Richie, New York 1961; *Voices from the Japanese Cinema* by Joan Mellen, New York 1975; *The Waves at Genji's Door* by Joan Mellen, New York 1976; articles—"Imai: La Femme infidèle" by Pierre Philippe in *Cinéma* (Paris), February 1964; "Imai Tadashi" by Rikiya Tayama in *Image et son* (Paris), July 1964; "La Production indépendante" by Akira Iwasaki in *Cinéma* (Paris), September/October 1969.

*   *   *

Despite his early Marxist commitment, Imai was forced to give up politics under the wartime military regime. Because of the regime's ideological restriction, Imai's first works were so-called "war-collaboration" films. Some of them are nonetheless valued for a Western-style action sequence technique (e.g. *The Death Command of the Tower*) and for the successful depiction of the personality of an army officer (*Our Teacher*).

Imai's postwar return to Marxism surprised his audience. As early as 1946, he made a film which severely attacked the corruption of the wartime rulers, and he preached on behalf of the postwar democracy in *The People's Ememy*. Imai's real fame came with his record-breaking commercial success, *Green Mountains I* and *II*, which became legendary for its reflection of the almost revolutionary excitement of the postwar period. The film depicts, in a light, humorous style, the struggle at a small town high school against established institutions and values.

Until We Meet Again became another legendary film for its romantic, lyrical treatment of tragic wartime love. In particular, the scene of the young lovers kissing through the window glass became famous. The Red Purge at the time of the Korean War drove Imai out of the organized film industry. He then became one of the most active filmmakers, initiating the postwar leftist independent film production movement.

His subsequent films fall into two main genres—films analyzing social injustice and oppression from the Communist point of view, and maticulously made literary adaptations. The films of the first category outnumber the second. Imai was much influenced by Italian neorealism in his themes and semi-documentary method based on location shooting. The hardship and tribulations of the proletariat are depicted in *Still We Live* (about day-laborers), *Rice* (concerning farmers), and *That Is the Port Light* (about fishermen and the Japan-Korea problems). Social problems are treated in *School of Echoes* (concerning the progressive education movement in a poor mountain village), *Kiku and Isamu*, which deals with Japanese-black mixed-blood children, *Japanese Grandmother* (on the aged), and *River without Bridges I* and *II*, about discrimination against the outcast class.

The mistaken verdict in a murder case is the subject of *Darkness at Noon* which condemns the police and the public prosecutor. *Himeyuri Lily Tower*, another commercial hit, depicts the tragic fighting on Okinawa toward the end of the war, showing the cruelty of both the Japanese and the American forces. *Night Drum*, *The Cruel Story of the Samurai's Way*, *Revenge*, and *A Woman Named En* focus on feudalism and its oppression from the viewpoint of its victims.

These films all embody an explict and rather crude leftist point-of-view. However, Imai's talent at entertaining the audience with deft story-telling and comfortable pacing attracted popular and critical support for his work. Imai is especially skillful in powerful appeals to the audience's sentimentalism. His distinctive lyrical and humanistic style is valued and helps us to differentiate Imai from other more dogmatic leftist directors.

Imai is also appreciated for his depiction of details. This trait helped make his literary adaptations (e.g. *Muddy Water*) so successful that every ambitious actress was said to want to appear in Imai's films to obtain prizes. The collaboration of the excellent scenario writer, Yoko Mizuki, is indispensable to Imai's success.

Imai's unchanged formula of the poor being oppressed by the authorities has been increasingly out-of-date through the 1960s and '70s. However, his lyricism still proved to be attractive in recent works such as *Older Brother and Younger Sister*.

—Kyoko Hirano

IMAMURA, SHOHEI. Japanese. Born in Tokyo, 1926. Educated in technical school, Tokyo, until 1945; studied occidental history, Waseda University, Tokyo, graduated 1951. Career: late 1940s—acts and writes stage plays at university; 1951—becomes assistant director at Shochiku's Ofuna studios; assists Ozu on his early '50s films; 1954—leaves Shochiku for reestablished Nikkatsu studios; 1955-58—assistant to director Yuzo Kawashima; 1965—forms Imamura Productions; 1969—collaborates on book about director Yuzo Kawashima, *Life Is Only Goodbye*; 1970-78—"retires" from feature filmmaking, works mainly in television; early 1970s—makes TV documentaries on former Japanese soldiers living in southeast Asia who didn't return home after WWII; 1975—founds and begins teaching at Yokohama Broadcast Film Institute. Recipient: Gold Palm, Cannes Festival, for *The Ballad of Narayama*, 1983.

Films (as assistant director): 1951—*Bakushu (Early Summer)* (Ozu); 1952—*Ochazuke no aji (The Flavor of Green Tea over Rice)* (Ozu); 1953—*Tokyo monogatari (Tokyo Story)* (Ozu); 1954—*Kuroi ushio (Black Tide)* (Yamamura); 1955—*Tsukiwa noborinu (The Moon Rises, Moonrise)* (Tanaka); (as scriptwriter): 1956—*Fusen (The Balloon)* (Kawashima) (co-sc); 1958—*Bakumatsu Taiyoden (Saheiji Finds a Way, Sun Legend of the Shogunate's Last Days)* (Kawashima) (co-sc); (as director): 1958—*Nusumareta yokujo (Stolen Desire); Nishi Ginza eki mae (Lights of Night, Nishi Ginza Station)* (+sc); *Hateshinaki yokubo (Endless Desire)* (+co-sc); 1959—*Nianchan (My Second Brother, The Diary of Sueko)* (+co-sc); *Jigoku no magarikago (Turning to Hell)* (Kurahara) (co-sc only); 1961—*Buta to gunkan (The Flesh Is Hot, Hogs and Warships, Pigs and Battleships)* (+co-sc); 1962—*Kyupora no aru machi (The Street with the Cupola, Cupola Where the Furnaces Glow)* (Urayama) (sc only); 1963—*Nippon konchuki (The Insect Woman)* (+co-sc); *Samurai no ko (Son of a Samurai, The Young Samurai)* (Wakasugi) (co-sc only); 1964—*Akai satsui (Unholy Desire, Intentions of Murder)* (+co-sc); *Keirin shonin gyojoki* (Nishimira) (co-sc only); (as producer and director): 1966—*Jinruigaku nyumon (The Pornographers: Introduction to Anthropology)* (+co-sc); 1967—*Ningen johatsu (A Man Vanishes)* (+sc, ro); *Neon taiheiki-keieigaku nyumon (Neon Jungle)* (Isomi) (co-sc only); 1968—*Kamigami no fukaki yokubo (The Profound Desire of the Gods, Kurage-jima: Tales from a Southern Island)* (co-pr, +co-sc); *Higashi Shinaki (East China Sea)* (Isomi) (story, co-sc only); 1970—*Nippon sengoshi: Madamu Omboro no seikatsu (History of Postwar Japan as Told by a Bar Hostess)* (co-pr, +planning, ro as interviewer); 1975—*Karayuki-san (Karayuki-san, the Making of a Prostitute)* (for TV) (co-pr, +planning); 1979—*Fukushu suruwa wareni ari (Vengeance Is Mine)* (d only); 1980—*Eijanaika (Why Not?)* (d only, +co-sc); 1983—*The Ballad of Narayama.*

Publications:

By IMAMURA:

Book—*Sayonara dake ga jinsei-da* [Life Is Only Goodby: biography of director Yuzo Kawashima], Tokyo 1969; articles—"Monomaniaque de l'homme..." in *Jeune Cinéma* (Paris), November 1972; interview by S. Hoass in *Cinema Papers* (Melbourne), September/October 1981.

On IMAMURA:

Books—*Imamura Shohei no eiga* [The Films of Shohei Imamura], Tokyo 1971; *Sekai no eiga sakka 8: Imamura Shohei* [Film Directors of the World 8: Shohei Imamura] by Heiichi Sugiyama, Tokyo 1975; articles—"Les Cochons et les dieux: Imamura Shohei" by Koichi Yamada in *Cahiers du cinéma* (Paris), May/June 1965; "Shohei Imamura" by John Gillett in *Film Dope* (London), January 1983.

*   *   *

Outrageous, insightful, sensuous, and great fun to watch, the films of Shohei Imamura are among the greatest glories of the postwar Japanese cinema. Yet, Imamura remains largely unknown outside of Japan. Part of the reason, to be sure, lies in the fact that Imamura has until recently worked for small studios such as Nikkatsu or on his own independently financed productions. But it may also be because Imamura's films fly so furiously in the face of what most westerners have come to expect Japanese films to be like.

After some amateur experience as a theater actor and director, Imamura joined Shochiku Studios in 1951 as an assistant director, where he worked under, among others, Yasujiro Ozu. His first important work, *My Second Brother*, an uncharacteristically gentle tale set among Korean orphans living in postwar Japan, earned him third place in the annual *Kinema Jumpo* "Best Japanese Film of the Year" poll, and from then on Imamura's place within the Japanese industry was more or less firmly established. Between 1970 and 1978, Imamura "retired" from feature filmmaking, concentrating his efforts instead on a series of remarkable television documentaries which explored little-known sides of postwar Japan. In 1978, Imamura returned to features with his greatest commercial and critical success, *Vengeance Is Mine*, a complex, absorbing study of a cold-blooded killer. In 1983, his film *The Ballad of Narayama* was awarded the Gold Palm at the Cannes Film Festival, symbolizing (hopefully) Imamura's belated discovery by the international film community.

Imamura has stated that he likes to make "messy films," and it is the explosive, at times anarchic quality of his work which makes him appear "uncharacteristically Japanese" when seen in the context of Ozu, Mizoguchi, or Kurosawa. Perhaps no other filmmaker anywhere has taken up Jean-Luc Godard's challenge to end the distinction between "documentary" and "fiction" films. In preparation for filming, Imamura will conduct exhaustive research on the people whose story he will tell, holding long interviews, not only to extract information, but also to become familiar with different regional vocabularies and accents (many of his films are set in remote regions of Japan). Insisting always on location shooting and direct sound, Imamura has been referred to as the "cultural anthropologist" of the Japanese cinema. Even the titles of some of his films—*The Pornographers: Introduction to Anthropology* and *The Insect Woman* (whose Japanese title literally translates to "Chronicle of a Japanese Insect")—seem to reinforce the "scientific" spirit of these works. Yet, if anything, Imamura's films argue against an overly-clinical approach to understanding Japan, as they often celebrate the irrational and instinctual aspects of Japanese culture.

Strong female protagonists are usually at the center of Imamura's films, yet it would be difficult to read these films as "women's films" in the way that critics describe works by Mizoguchi or Naruse. Rather, women in Imamura's films are always the ones more directly linked to "ur-Japan,"—a kind of primordial fantasy of Japan not only before "westernization" but before any contact with the outside world. In *The Profound Desire of the Gods*, a brother and sister on a small southern island fall in love and unconsciously attempt to recreate the myth of Izanagi and Izanami, sibling gods whose union founded the Japanese race. Incest, a subject which might usually be seen as shocking, is treated as a perfectly natural expression, becoming a crime only due to the influence of "westernized" Japanese who have come to civilize the island. Imamura's characters indulge freely and frequently in sexual activity, and sexual relations tend to act as a kind of barometer for larger, unseen social forces. The lurid, erotic spectacles in *Eijanaika*, for example, are the clearest indication of the growing frustration that finally bursts forth with the massive riots which conclude the film.

—Richard Peña

INGRAM, REX. American. Born Reginald Ingram Montgomery Hitchcock in Dublin, 15 Januray 1893. Educated at Saint Columba's College, Dublin; studied sculpture at Yale, 1911. Married actress Doris Pawn, 1917 (divorced 1920); Alice Terry, 1921. Career: 1911—offered job by friend of father on New

Haven Railroad, emigrates to U.S.; 1912—acts briefly in England, then returns to New York; 1913—meets Charles Edison, son of Thomas Edison, becomes interested in films and joins Edison Co. as assistant; 1913—writes several scenarios filmed by Stuart Blackton, works as screen actor; 1914—moves to Vitagraph; 1915—hired by Fox, changes name to Rex Ingram; 1916—begins directing at Universal; 1917—contracted by Paralta-W.W. Hodkinson Corp.; 1918—enlists in Canadian Air Force, wounded in action; 1920—joins Metro Pictures; 1921—success of *The 4 Horsemen of the Apocalypse* secures reputation; 1923—dissatisfied with Hollywood production system, moves to France; 1924—settles in Nice, modernizing Studios de la Victorine de Saint-Augustin; 1928—Ingram Hamilton Syndicated Ltd. production company established in London; early 1930s—engaged in law suit with Franco-Films; 1932—decides to devote himself to travelling and writing; 1934—leaves France for good, settles in Egypt; 1936—returns to U.S., settles in Hollywood, becoming more deeply innvolved with Islamic mysticism. Died 1950; buried at Forest Lawn, Glendale, California. Recipient: honorary degree, Yale University; Légion d'honneur française.

Films (as scriptwriter): 1913—*Hard Cash* (Reid) (+ro); *The Family's Honor* (Ridgely); 1915—*Should a Mother Tell?* (Edwards); *The Song of Hate* (Edwards) (+ro); *The Wonderful Adventure* (Thompson); *The Blindness of Devotion* (Edwards); *A Woman's Past* (Powell); *The Galley Slave* (Edwards) (co-sc, uncredited); 1916—*The Cup of Bitterness*; (as director and scriptwriter): 1916—*The Great Problem (Truth)*; *Broken Fetters (A Human Pawn)*; *Chalice of Sorrow (The Fatal Promise)*; *Black Orchids (The Fatal Orchids)*; 1917—*The Reward of the Faithless (The Ruling Passion)*; *The Pulse of Life*; *The Flower of Doom*; *Little Terror*; (as director): 1918—*His Robe of Honor*; *Humdrum Brown*; 1919—*The Day She Paid*; 1920—*Under Crimson Skies (The Beach Comber)*; *Shore Acres*; *Hearts Are Trumps*; 1921—*The 4 Horsemen of the Apocalypse* (+pr); *The Conquering Power (Eugenie Grandet)*; *Turn to the Right*; 1922—*The Prisoner of Zenda*; *Trifling Women* (+sc) (remake of *Black Orchids*); *Where the Pavement Ends* (+sc); 1923—*Scaramouche* (+pr); 1924—*The Arab (L'Arabe)* (+sc); 1925—*Mare Nostrum* (+co-pr); *Greed* (von Stroheim) (co-ed 2nd cut only); 1926—*The Magician* (+co-pr, sc); 1927—*The Garden of Allah*; 1929—*The Three Passions (Les Trois Passions)* (+sc); 1931—*Baroud (Love in Morocco, Passion in the Desert, Les Hommes bleus)* (+pr, co-sc).

Roles: 1913—*Beau Brummel* (Young); *The Artist's Great Madonna* (Young); *A Tudor Princess* (Dawley); 1914—*Witness to the Will* (Lessey); *The Necklace of Ramses* (Brabin); *The Price of the Necklace* (Brabin); *The Borrowed Finery*; *Her Great Scoop* (Costello and Gaillord); *The Spirit and the Clay* (Lambart); *The Southerners* (Ridgely and Collins); *Eve's Daughter* (North); *The Crime of Cain* (Marston); *The Circus and the Boy* (Johnson); *David Garrick* (Young); *The Upper Hand* (Humphrey); *Fine Feathers Make Fine Birds* (Humphrey); *His Wedded Wife* (Humphrey); *Goodbye, Summer* (Brooke); *The Moonshine Maid and the Man* (Gaskill); 1915—*The Evil Men Do* (Costello and Gaillord); *Snatched From a Burning Death* (Gaskill); 1923—guest in *Mary of the Movies* (McDermott).

Publications:

By INGRAM:

Articles—interview by L. Montanye in *Motion Picture Classic*

(Brooklyn), July 1921; interview with Ingram by J. Robinson in *Photoplay* (New York), August 1921; article on directing in *Motion Picture Directing* by Peter Milne, New York 1922.

On INGRAM:

Books—*The Spirit and the Clay* by Liam O'Leary, London 1970; *Rex Ingram* by Rene Predal, Paris 1970; *Rex Ingram, Master of the Silent Cinema* by Liam O'Leary, Dublin 1980; articles—"6 Men with Names" by C. Morz in *New Republic* (New York), 2 April 1924; "Fairbanks and Valentino: The Last Heroes" by Gavin Lambert in *Sequence* (London), summer 1949; obituary in *The New York Times*, 23 July 1950; "Hollywood's Handsomest Director" by George Geltzer in *Films in Review* (New York), May 1952; "Rex Ingram and the Nice Studios" by Liam O'Laoghaire in *Cinema Studies* (England), December 1961; "Rex Ingram and Alice Terry" in 2 parts by Dewitt Bodeen in *Films in Review* (New York), February and March 1975; "Rex Ingram", with biofilmography, by Liam O'Leary in *Film Dope* (London), July 1983.

*   *   *

Due to his retirement from films in the early thirties when sound had taken over, Ingram has tended to be overlooked and forgotten. He began his career in films in 1913, working as designer, script-writer and actor for Edison, Vitagraph and Fox, until in 1916 he directed his own story *The Great Problem* for Universal at the age of only 23. His educational background was that of an Irish country rectory and the Yale School of Fine Arts where he studied sculpture under Lee Lawrie, and developed an aesthetic sense which informed all his films.

The early films he made for Universal have disappeared. His version of *La Tosca* transferred to a Mexican setting as *Chalice of Sorrow*, and *Black Orchids* remade in 1922 as *Trifling Women*, earned critical attention for the quality of the acting and their visual beauty. Cleo Madison starred in both these films. The fragment that exists of *The Reward of the Faithless* shows a realism that is reminiscent of von Stroheim who was later to acknowledge his indebtedness by allowing Ingram to do the second cutting on *Greed*. It may be noted also that greed was the theme of *The Conquering Power*. A characteristic element of Ingram's work was the use of grotesque figures like dwarfs and hunchbacks to offset the glamour of his heroes. After a period of ups and downs, he made another film for Universal in 1920, *Under Crimson Skies*, which won critical acclaim.

With *The Four Horsemen of the Apocalypse* in 1921 he achieved top status in his profession. Ordinarily, Valentino dominates discussion of this film but Ingram's work is of the highest quality, and with his team of cameraman John Seitz, and editor Grant Whytock he went on to make a dazzlingly successful series of films for Metro. His financial and artistic success gave him carte blanche and his name won a box-office draw. *The Conquering Power*, *The Prisoner of Zenda* and *Scaramouche* featured his wife, the beautiful and talented Alice Terry, and the latter two films introduced the new star, Ramon Novarro, who also played with Alice Terry in the South Sea romance *Where the Pavement Ends*. Ingram made stars and knew how to get the best out of players. He was now considered the equal of Griffith, von Stroheim, and DeMille.

In 1924 the formation of Metro-Goldwyn-Mayer saw a tightening up of front office control over the creative director and Ingram sought fresh fields to conquer. He made *The Arab* with Terry and Novarro in North Africa with which he fell in love. He next moved to Nice where he founded the Rex Ingram Studios and released his masterpiece *Mare Nostrum* in 1926 for "Metro-Goldwyn" (He would never allow his arch-enemy Louis B. Mayer to have a credit.) In this Alice Terry gave her best performance as the Mata Hari-like heroine. This film as well as *The Four Horsemen* was later suppressed because of its anti-German feeling, both being authored by Blasco Ibañez.

The German-inspired *The Magician* featured Paul Wegener (the original *Golem*) and was based on a Somerset Maugham story. After *The Garden of Allah* Ingram broke with MGM in 1926. *The Three Passions*, with an industrial background, followed in 1929, and his last film *Baroud*, a sound film in which he himself played the lead, completed a distinguished career. He sold his studios in Nice where he had reigned as an uncrowned king; as the Victorine Studios they were to become an important element in Frendh Film production. Ingram retired to North Africa and later rejoined his wife Alice Terry in Hollywood. He indulged his hobbies of sculpture, writing and travel.

Ingram was the supreme pictorialist of the screen, a great director of actors, a perfectionist whose influence was felt not least in the films of David Lean and Michael Powell. The themes of his films ranged over many locations but his careful research gave them a realism and authenticity that balanced the essential romanticism of this work.

—Liam O'Leary

IOSELIANI, OTAR. Soviet Georgian. Born 2 February 1934. Educated in music, Tbilisi Conservatory; studied graphic art; degree in mathematics, Moscow University; studied under Alexander Dovzhenko, V.G.I.K., Moscow. Career: 1961—*April* fails to receive authorization for distribution; decides to abandon filmmaking, works for a time in factory and as sailor; 1966—makes 1st feature; 1983—shoots film in France. Recipient: FIPRESCI Prize, Berlin Festival, for *Pastorale*, 1982.

Films (as director of short films): 1958—*Watercolor* (for TV); 1959—*The Song About Flowers*; 1961—*April (Stories About Things)* (feature—not released) (+sc); 1964—*Cast-Iron* (+sc); (as feature director): 1966—*Listopad (When Leaves Fall, Falling Leaves)*; 1972—*Zil pevcij drozd (There Was a Singing Blackbird, There Lived a Thrush)* (+co-sc); 1976—*Pastoral (The Summer in the Country)* (+co-sc).

Publications:

By IOSELIANI:

Articles—interview by G. Kopaněvová in *Film a doba* (Prague), May 1974; "Pour saluer *Pastorale* et *Le Bonheur d'Assia*", interview by M. Ciment in *Positif* (Paris), May 1978; interview by Marcel Martin in *Ecran* (Paris), February 1978; interview by Serge Daney and S. Toubiana in *Cahiers du cinéma* (Paris), November 1979; "Syntetické umění neexistuje...", interview by A. Gerber in *Film a doba* (Prague), February 1981.

On IOSELIANI:

Articles—"Stat'ja iz gazety 'Zarja Vostoka'" by K. Cereteli in *Iskusstvo Kino* (Moscow), November 1973; "Il était une fois un merle chanteur de O. Iosseliani" in *APEC—Revue Belge du cinéma* (Brussels), v.13, no.1-2, 1975/76; "Le Cinéma soviétique

revient de loin" by M. Martin *Ecran* (Paris), February 1978; "L'Art 'Comme la vie' d'Otar Iosseliani" by M. Martin in *Image et son* (Paris), September 1980.

*   *   *

The Georgian cinema has a long history that goes back to the twenties and it has known a renaissance in the sixties with Otar Ioseliani as its most remarkable representative. Together with Tarkovsky (but in a very different way) he is the young Soviet director who has been the most uncompromising and the most consistent in his aesthetic approach. Born in 1934, he has studied music at the Tbilisi Conservatory, as well as graphic art, and graduated from Moscow University in mathematics. But finally he chose cinema as his favorite field and graduated from V.G.I.K. after attending Alexander Dovzhenko's class. His first film, *April*, of which little is known, was not released. His second, *When leaves Fall*, shows the characteristics of his style. Ioseliani, like many of his contemporaries, is hostile to the cinema of Eisenstein, to his intellectual montage, to the theoretical aspect of his work. In presenting Jean Vigo as his master, Ioseliani insists that he tries "to capture moments of passing life," and in doing so wants to reach the ultimate goal of art. In a way his films are close to the Czech new wave (Forman, Passer, Menzel) but the realism is counterbalanced by a more formal treatment, particularly in the use of sound and off-screen space.

His films also show a disregard for conventional ways of life. Ioseliani's nonconformity, his stubbornness, his frankness, have alienated the authorities. *When Leaves Fall* takes place in a wine factory and shows an innocent and honest young man trying to live in a bureaucratic universe. He does not wear a moustache, that Georgian symbol of bourgeois respectability.

There Was a Singing Blackbird, Ioseliani's third film, portrays the life of a musician in the Tbilisi orchestra who always arrives at the last minute to perform, being busy enjoying his life, drinking and courting girls. His behavior is an insult to an official morality based on work and duty. Ioseliani's fancifulness and sense of humor are shown at their best in this sprightly comedy that ends tragically with the hero's death. *Pastoral*, which had problems with the Moscow authorities (though the film was shown regularly in Georgia), is about a group of five musicians from the city who come to live with a peasant family. Ioseliani observes the opposition of city and country, and makes a young peasant girl the observer of his delightful conflict of manners and morals. Using many non-professionals—as in his earlier films—the director manages to show us poetically and with truthfulness the life of the Georgian people. Discarding any kind of plot, observing his characters with affection and irony, he is faithful to his anti-dogmatic stance: "Everyone is born to drink the glass of his life." Ioseliani's limited output is of a very high level indeed. Finding it difficult to work in the U.S.S.R., he shot a film in France in 1983, following the example of Tarkovsky who directed *Nostalghia* in Italy. In both cases: the refusal to compromise.

—Michel Ciment

IVENS, JORIS. Dutch. Born Georg Henri Anton Ivens in Nijmegen, Holland, 18 November 1898. Educated at Economische Hogeschool, Rotterdam, 1916-17 and 1920-21; studied chemistry and photography at Technische Hochschule, Charlottenburg, 1922-23. Married Marceline Loridan. Career: 1911—makes *Flaming Arrow* film about Indians using family members; 1917-18—military service as lieutenant in artillery; 1924-25—works for phtographic equipment manufacturers ICA and Ernemann, Dresden, and Zeiss, Jena; 1926—technical director for CAPI (father's firm selling photographic equipment) in Amsterdam; sees *The Mother* (Pudovkin); associated with Filmliga Amsterdam; 1929-30—success of *The Bridge* and *Rain* in Paris leads to invitation by Soviet filmmakers to visit U.S.S.R.; 1930—meets Pudovkin and Dovjenko; 1931—makes industrial documentaries in the Netherlands; begins association with cinematographer John Fernhout (John Ferno); 1932—invited to return to U.S.S.R.; 1933—in Belgium clandestinely films striking miners for *Borinage*; 1936—visits New York, befriends Robert Flaherty; with Hemingway, Dos Passos, Lillian Hellman, Fredric March and Luise Rainer, forms group to finance films on contemporary events; 1937—films *Spanish Earth* during Spanish Civil War; 1938—following Japanese attack on China, films *400 Million* in China; 1939-40—industrial documentary projects in U.S.; 1941—teaches at University of Southern California; 1942-43—invited by John Grierson to direct *Alarm!* for National Film Board of Canada; 1943-44—works on *Why We Fight* series in Hollywood; 1945—invited to become Commissioner for cinema in Dutch East Indies on condition that Dutch colonial interests promoted, refuses; 1945-46—in Sydney, Australia, makes *Indonesia Calls*, regarded as traitorous act by Dutch authorities; 1947—establishes residence in Prague; 1950-51—teaches in Lodz, Poland; 1957—moves to Paris; 1958—teaches filmmaking in Peking; 1959-60—filming in Italy and Africa; 1960-61—teaches young documentary filmmakers in Cuba; 1962-63—teaches in Chile; 1964—invited to Holland by Nederlands Filmmuseum for retrospective; 1965—makes 1st of Vietnam war documentaries; principal films in Vietnam and Laos done during 1967-69; 1971-75—in China with Marceline Loridan makes documentary in 12 parts (almost 12 hours) *Comment Yu-Kong déplaça les montagnes*; Ivens retrospective organized by Nederlands Filmmuseum, Amsterdam, tours Europe. Recipient: World Peace Prize, Helsinki, 1955; Palme d'Or for best documentary *La Seine a rencontré Paris*, Cannes Festival 1958; Diploma *Honoris Causa*, Royal College of Art, London, 1978.

Films (as director, cinematographer and editor): 1911—*De brandende straal* or *Wigwam* (*Flaming Arrow*); 1927—*Zeedijk-Filmstudie (Filmstudy—Zeedijk)*; 1928—*Etudes de mouvements*; *De Brug (The Bridge)* (+sc); 1929—*Branding (The Breakers)* (co-d); *Regen (Rain)* (sound version prepared 1932 by Helen van Dongen); *Ik-Film ("I" Film)* (co-d—unfinished); *Schaatsenrijden (Skating, The Skaters)* (unfinished); *Wij bouwen (We Are Building)* (+co-sc); [footage shot for but not used in *Wij bouwen* used for following films: *Heien (Pile Driving)* (+co-sc); *Nieuwe architectur (New Architecture)* (+co-sc); *Caissounbouw Rotterdam* (+co-sc); *Zuid Limburg (South Limburg)* (+co-sc)]; 1929-30—*N.V.V. Congres (Congres der Vakvereeinigingen)*; *Jeugddag (Days of Youth)* (co-ed only); *Arm Drenthe*; 1930—*De Tribune film: Breken en bouwen (The Tribune Film: Break and Build)*; *Timmerfabriek (Timber Industry)* (co-ph, co-ed); *Filmnotities uit de Sovjet-Unie (News from the Soviet Union)* (d, ed only); *Demostratie van proletarische solidariteit (Demonstration of Proletarian Solidarity)* (d, ed only); 1931—short film in *VVVC Journal* series (ed only); *Philips-Radio (Symphonie industrielle, Industrial Symphony)* (co-ph, co-ed); *Creosoot (Creosote)* (+sc); 1932—*Pesn o Gerojach (Komsomol, Youth Speaks, Song of Heroes)* (d, ed only); (as director): 1933—*Zuyderzee* (+sc, co-ph); 1934—*Misère au Borinage (Borinage)*

(co-d, +co-sc, co-ed, co-ph); *Nieuwe Gronden (New Earth)* (+sc, co-ph, co-ed, narration); 1937—*The Spanish Earth* (+sc, co-ph); 1939—*The 400 Million (China's 400 Million)* (co-d, +sc); 1940—*Power and the Land* (+co-sc); *New Frontiers* (unfinished); 1941—*Bip Goes to Town*; *Our Russian Front* (co-d); *Worst of Farm Disasters*; 1942—*Oil for Aladdin's Lamp*; 1943—*Alarme!* or *Branle-Bas de combat (Action Stations!)* (+sc, ed) (released in shorter version *Corvette Port Arthur*); 1946—*Indonesia Calling* (+sc, ed); 1949—*Pierwsze lata (The 1st Years)* (+co-ed, produced 1947); 1951—*Pokoj zwyciezy swiat (Peace Will Win)* (co-d); 1952—*Naprozod mlodziezy (Freundschaft siegt, Friendship Triumphs)* (co-d); *Wyscig pokoju Warszawa-Berlin-Praga (Friedensfahrt, Peace Tour)* (+sc); 1954—*Das Lied der Ströme (Song of the Rivers)* (+co-sc); 1956—*Mein Kind (My Child)* (Pozner and Machalz) (artistic supervisor only); 1957—*La Seine a rencontré Paris* (+co-sc); *Die Windrose (The Wind Rose)* (Bellon and others) (co-supervisor only); *Die Abenteuer des Till Ulenspiegel (The Adventures of Till Eulenspiegel)* (co-d); 1958—*Before Spring (Early Spring, Letters from China)* (+sc, ed); *600 Million People Are with You* (+ed); 1960—*L'Italia non e un paese povero (Italy is Not a Poor Country)* (+co-sc, co-ed); *Demain à Nanguila (Nanguila Tomorrow)*; 1961—*Carnet de viaje* (+sc); *Pueblos en armas (Pueblo armado, Cuba, pueblo armado, An Armed Nation)* (+sc); 1963—*..à Valparaiso* (+sc); *El circo mas pequeño (Le Petit Chapiteau)*; 1964—*El tren de la victoria (Le Train de la victoire)*; 1966—*Pour le mistral* (+co-sc); *Le Ciel, la terre (The Sky, the Earth)* (+narration, appearance); *Rotterdam-Europoort (Rotterdam—Europort, The Flying Dutchman)*; 1967—Hanoi footage in *Loin du Viêt-nam (Far from Vietnam)* (co-d); 1968—*Le Dix-septième parallèle (The 17th Parallel)* (co-d +co-sc); *Aggrippés à la terre* (co-d); 1969—*Rencontre avec le Président Ho Chi Minh* (co-d); (next 7 titles made as part of collective including Marceline Loridan, Jean-Pierre Sergent, Emmanuele Castro, Suzanne Fen, Antoine Bonfanti, Bernard Ortion, and Anne Rullier): *Le Peuple et ses fusils (The People and Their Guns)*; *L'Armée populaire arme le peuple*; *La Guerre populaire au Laos*; *Le Peuple peut tout*; *Qui commande aux fusils*; *Le Peuple est invincible*; *Le Peuple ne peut rien sans ses fusils*; 1976—*Comment Yukong déplaça les montagnes* (in 12 parts totaling 718 minutes) (co-d); 1977—*Les Kazaks—Minorité nationale—Sinkiang* (co-d); *Les Ouigours—Minorité nationale—Sinkiang* (co-d). Roles: 1972—interviewee in *Grierson* (Blais); 1981—interviewee in *Conversations with Willard Van Dyke* (Rothschild).

Publications:

By IVENS:

Books—*Lied der Ströme*, with Vladimir Pozner, Berlin 1957; *Joris Ivens*, edited by W. Klaue and others, Berlin 1963; *Autobiografie van een Filmer*, Amsterdam 1970; *The Camera and I*, Berlin 1974; *Entretiens avec Joris Ivens* by Claire Devarrieux, Paris 1979; articles—numerous articles in Filmliga (Amsterdam), 1928-32; "Notes on Hollywood" in *New Theatre* (New York), 28 October 1936; article on China in *The New York Times*, 28 August 1938; "Pacific Flight" in *Asia* (New York), September 1939; "Collaboration in Documentary" in *Film* (New York), 1940; "Apprentice to Film" in *Theatre Arts* (New York), March and April 1946; "...parce que le documentariste ne faurait être seulement un sémoin" in *L'Ecran français* (Paris), 13 March 1950; "Les Films de Joris Ivens, modèles de réalisme", interview by Pol Gaillard, in *Parallel* (Paris), 10 March 1950; "La Réalite est plus passionante que toutes les inventions de Hollywood" in

L'Humanité (Paris), 10 March 1953; "Der Mensch im Dokumentarfilm in *Deutsche Filmkunst* (Berlin), no.6, 1955; "Borinage—A Documentary Experience" in *Film Culture* (New York), no.1, 1956; "Meine Filmarbeit mit Hanns Eisler" in *Musik und Gesellschaft* (Berlin), no.5, 1956; "Till Ulenspiegel", with Gérard Phillipe, in *Aufbau* (Berlin), no.5, 1956; "Making Documentary Films in China" in *China Reconstructs* (Peking), no.1, 1959; "El papel del cine en el Frente" in *Verde Olivo* (Havana), 1962; "Vive le Cinéma-Vérité" in *Les Lettres françaises* (Paris), 21 March 1963; "Notes de Pekin en Notes de Paris" in *Artsept* (Paris), June 1963; "Ik-Film" in *Skoop* (Amsterdam), no.2, 1964; "Erinnerungen an Robert Flaherty" in *Robert Flaherty*, Berlin 1964; "Monolog auf Hanns Eisler" in *Sonderheft Sinn und Form*, Berlin 1964; "Joris Ivens Interviewed by Gordon Hitchens" (1968) in *Film Culture* (New York), spring 1972; "Chine: naissance du cinéma rouge", with Jay Leyda, in *Ecran* (Paris), January 1972; "Joris Ivens on the Search for Film Truth" and "My Future Post-Graduate Work in Film-Making" in *Film Culture* (New York), spring 1972; "Les 3 yeux du cinéaste militant" in *Cinéma d'aujourd'hui* (Paris), March/April 1976; "Interview mit Joris Ivens and Marceline Loridan" by B. Steinborn and A. Kluge in *Filmfaust* (Frankfurt), December 1976; interview by Serge Daney and others in *Cahiers du cinéma* (Paris), May 1976; "Entretien avec Joris Ivens and Marceline Loridan" by J. Grant and G. Frot-Coutaz in *Cinéma* (Paris), April 1976; "Joris Ivens Filming in China", interview by D. Bickley in *Filmmakers Newsletter* (Ward Hill, Mass.), February 1977; "Die Verantwortung der Kinos und der Filmemacher muss öffentlich werden", interview by A. Kluge and B. Steinborn in *Filmfaust* (Frankfurt), June/July 1977; interview by E. Naaijkems and others in *Skrien* (Amsterdam), October 1977; "Terre d'espagne", interview by H. Oms and R. Grelier in *Cahiers de la Cinémathèque* (Paris), January 1977; "Brève rencontre avec Joris Ivens" by Marcel Martin in *Ecran* (Paris), November 1978; "Johan van der Keuken: Wie kannst du Gehör finden, wenn du die Sprache der Macht ablehnst?", interview by B. Hervo in *Filmfaust* (Frankfurt), October 1979; interview by A. Segal in "Spécial Ivens" issue of *Avant-Scène du cinéma* (Paris), 1 January 1981.

On IVENS:

Books—*The Spanish Earth* by Ernest Hemingway, Cleveland 1938; *Joris Ivens* by Abraham Zalzman, Paris 1963; *Joris Ivens, Dokumentarist den Wahrheit* by Hans Wegner, Berlin 1965; *Joris Ivens* by Robert Grelier, Paris 1965; *17e Parallèle, la guerre du peuple* by Marceline Loridan, Paris 1968; *Joris Ivens, de weg naar Vietnam* by Han Meyer, Utrecht 1970; *Joris Ivens, ein Filmer an den Fronten der Weltrevolution* by Klaus Kremeier, Berlin 1976; *Il cinema di Joris Ivens* by Klaus Kremeier, Milan 1977; *Joris Ivens, 50 jaar wereldcineast*, Nederlands Filmmuseum, Amsterdam 1978; *Joris Ivens: 50 ans de cinéma* edited by Jean-Loup Passek, Paris 1979; articles—"Too Much Reality" by Friedrich Wolf in *New Theatre* (New York), March 1935; "Joris Ivens in America" by Helen van Dongen in *Filmart* (London), autumn 1936; "Guest Artist" by Otis Ferguson in the *New Republic* (New York), 15 April and 13 May 1936; "Joris Ivens: Social Realist vs. Lyric Poet" by Cynthia Grenier in *Sight and Sound* (London), spring 1958; "Retrato del artista revolucionario" by Jorge Fraga in *Cine Cubano* (Havana), no.3, 1960; "Cuba vu par Joris Ivens" by Anne Philipe in *Les Lettres Françaises* (Paris), 15 December 1960; issue devoted to Ivens, *Cine Cubano* (Havana), no.3, 1960; "Eine Reise nach China" in *Filmkritik* (Munich), November 1976; "*How Yukong Moved the Mountains*: Filming the Cultural Revolution" by T. Waugh in *Jump Cut* (Berkeley), 30 December 1976; "Joris Ivens en het VVVC-journaal" by B. Hogenkamp in *Skrien* (Amsterdam), April 1977; "Archive et mémoire" by R. Munoz-Suay in *Cahiers de la Cinémathèque* (Paris), January 1977; "Joris Ivens—The China Close-Up" by Roberta Sklar in *American Film* (Washington, D.C.), June 1978; "'Ik kwam Joris Ivens tegen': 'waarom ben je bij de film gegaan?'" by Helen van Dongen in *Skoop* (Amsterdam), November 1978; "Joris Ivens 50 jaar wereldcineast" by B. Hogenkamp in *Skrien* (Amsterdam), November 1978; "Het Parool en de eeuwige jacht op de Vliegende Hollander: deopdracht van Ivens" by W. Verstappen in *Skoop* (Amsterdam), March 1978; "Sotto i tre occhi di Joris Ivens..." by G. Bernagozzi in *Cineforum* (Bergamo), March 1979; "Joris Ivens and the Problems of the Documentary Film" by B. Hogenkamp in *Framework* (Norwich, England), autumn 1979; "L'Homme du peuple fait l'histoire: Joris Ivens" by G. Gervais in *Jeune cinéma* (Paris), June 1979; "The Chinese Connection: Filmmaking in the People's Republic" by N. Jervis in *Film Library Quarterly* (New York), no.1, 1979; "Joris Ivens Defended", letters from T. Waugh and P. Pappas in *Cineaste* (New York), fall 1980; "Know Your Enemy: Japan" by P. Pappas in *Cineaste* (New York), summer 1980; "Travel Notebook—A People in Arms: Joris Ivens' Work in Cuba" by T. Waugh in *Jump Cut* (Berkeley), May 1980; "Spécial Ivens" issue of *Avant-Scène du cinéma* (Paris), 1 January 1981; film—*A chacun son Borinage* by Wieslaw Hudon, Belgium 1978.

*   *   *

Since his debut with *The Bridge* in 1928, Joris Ivens has made over 50 documentary films. A great advocate for a socialist society, Ivens had attacked fascism and colonialism in all of his films made after 1930. His first two films, *The Bridge* and *Rain*, are rather abstract. Here Ivens's main concern is the elaboration of varied, often breath-taking, rhythm of pictures. In this, he appears to be indebted to the French and German avant-garde films, notably those by Ruttmann and Man Ray.

In 1930 Ivens visited the USSR at the invitation of Pudovkin. He became very familiar with Russian revolutionary films. The compelling expressiveness of Russian agit-prop films had a deep influence upon Ivens in shaping his unique and powerful style. According to Ivens, films should convey social and political insights by confronting the public directly with reality. This analytical and didactic viewpoint is already exemplified in *Komsomol*, the first film Ivens made in Russia. *Misère au Borinage* not only shows in ruthless and often violent images the miserable conditions under which the Belgian coalminers lived and worked; the film also indicates that the desperate situation of the workers follows necessary from a specific social order. To deepen his analysis and to strengthen the urgency of his message, Ivens has reconstructed a number of scenes, e.g. the May-Day celebration. This procedure also reflects Ivens's conviction that a documentary film is an emotional presentation of facts. Ivens has said that the maker of a documentary film should be in search of truth. To attain truth, one must have solidarity with the people whose situation is depicted. Mutual confidence and understanding are essential to a good documentary film.

Ivens's techniques bear the mark of such filmmakers as Eisenstein and Pudovkin. In addition to developing specific ways of shooting and styles of montage, Ivens has always attached great importance to spoken commentary. In *Spanish Earth*, a film about the Spanish civil war, Ernest Hemingway speaks the commentary; Jacques Prévert does so in *La Seine a rencontré Paris*. Commentary plays a secondary role in the films Ivens made during the seventies, notably in *How Yukong Moved the Mountains*. In this documentary epos about daily life in China after the cultural revolution, people tell about their own situation. Ivens's style here is descriptive, with many long sequences and with less dramatic montage.

Ivens's was one of the founders in 1977 of the Dutch Film League which united a number of intellectuals and Dutch filmmakers. Their efforts to promote quality films included the publication of a review, the organization of film screenings and inviting important foreign avant-garde filmmakers to give talks. Among these were René Clair and Man Ray. Ivens's contacts with Pudovkin and Eisenstein date to this period. Ivens's contribtions to Dutch film culture are immense. In spite of this, he has remained rather controversial to the Dutch authorities. His manifest sympathy for the struggle of the Indonesian people against colonialism (*Indonesia Calling*) has brought him into conflict with the Dutch government. Until 1956 Ivens was deprived of his Dutch passport.

Joris Ivens had consequently served important social and political issues. From 1938 till 1945 he lived in the U.S. *Power and the Land* is about the improvements in farming brought about by the use of electricity. With *Our Russian Front* Ivens intended to urge the Americans to enter World War II and to support the Russians. the films was financed by Ivens himself and some of his New York Russian friends. He hoped to make more films of this kind, but the project titled *Letters to the President* was cooly received. It led to only one film *A Sailor on Convoy Duty to England* which was financed by the National Film Board of Canada. In the fifties Ivens worked in Eastern Europe (Poland, the German Democratic Republic, and Czechoslovakia). The *First Years* shows the tranformation of a capitalist society into a socialist one; the film concentrates on episodes from postwar life in Bulgaria, Czechoslovakia, and Poland.

In 1956 the Dutch Government returned Ivens's passport; he then took up residence in Paris, where he still lives. From then he worked in Latin America (Cuba, Chile) and above all in Asia (Vietnam, Laos, and China). *Travel Notebook* is about daily life on Cuba; *An Armed People* shows how the militia of the people of Cuba captures a small group of counter-revolutionaries. *Le Train de la victoire* is a report on the election campaign of Salvador Allende, later President of Chile.

Ivens taught Vietnamese filmmakers. His engagement with the cause of the Vietnamese people manifests itself in films such as *The Threatening Sky* and *The 17th Parallel.*

Ivens always has had great influence in new technical developments in the domain of film equipment. He has hailed the professionalization of the 16mm camera as a big step foward: this development enabled the camera to take part in the action. It goes without saying that Ivens has excellent knowledge of all developments in the realm of documentary films. He has taught at numerous film schools and advised many colleagues. All this has contributed decisively to make the exemplary status which is attributed to Ivens's films. In the fifties he was an advisor to the Defa Studios (GDR) and collaborated on many films. Together with a number of leftist French filmmakers, Jean-Luc Godard, Alain Resnais, Agnès Varda and others, Ivens made the filmic pamplet of solidarity, *Loin du Vietnam.*

For Ivens the documentary film constitutes the only possiblity of surviving as an artist outside the field of commercial films. Despite the high esteem which Ivens's films enjoy, they never have been great successes at the box office. Ivens, however, had always succeeded in financing his projects on such terms that he has conserved maxium artistic freedom and full responsibility for the final product. This even holds for the two films which he made at an early stage in his career and which were commissioned by commercial firms (*Creosoot* and *Philips Radio*).

Within his lifetime Ivens has become a legend. His films comment on many events which shaped the modern world. His art,

his intelligence, his sophisticated political views, his great sincerity are constitutive of the unique position Joris Ivens holds among documentary film makers.

—Dorothee Vardaasdonk

IVORY, JAMES. American. Born in Berkeley, California, 7 June 1928. Educated in architecture and fine arts at the University of Oregon; in filmmaking at the University of Southern California, Los Angeles. Career: mid-1950s—2 years as NCO with U.S. Army Special Services, works on military entertainment shows in Germany; 1960—*The Sword and the Flute* leads to commission from Asia Society, New York, to make documentary on Delhi, India; meets Indian movie producer Ismail Merchant at 1st screening of film in New York; 1963—Merchant-Ivory Productions incorporated; begins association with scriptwriter Ruth Prawer Jhabvala on *The Householder.* Address: office—Merchant Ivory Productions, 655 Madison Ave., New York, NY 10021; home—400 E. 52nd Street, New York, NY 10022.

Films (as student at USC): 1953—*4 in the Morning*; 1957—*Venice: Theme and Variations* (MA thesis film, USC); (as director and scriptwriter): 1960—*The Sword and the Flute* (+pr, ph, ed); 1963—*The Householder*; 1964—*The Delhi Way* (+pr, ph, ed); 1965—*Shakespeare Wallah* (co-sc); 1968—*The Guru* (co-sc); 1970—*Bombay Talkie* (co-sc); 1972—*Adventures of a Brown Man in Search of Civilization* (for TV); *Savages* (story); *Helen, Queen of the Nautch Girls* (Korner) (sc only); (as director): 1974—*The Wild Party*; 1975—*Autobiography of a Princess*; 1977—*Roseland*; 1978—*Hullabaloo over Georgie and Bonnie's Pictures* (for British TV); 1979—*The Europeans* (+bit ro as connoisseur in warehouse); *The 5:48* (for U.S. TV— originally shown as part of NET series "3 Cheever Stories"); 1980—*Jane Austen in Manhattan*; 1981—*Quartet*; 1982—*Heat and Dust*; *The Courtesans of Bombay* (Merchant) (co-story—for TV).

Publications:

By IVORY:

Articles—"*Savages*" in *Sight and Sound* (London), autumn 1971; "James Ivory, un cinéaste entre 2 mondes", interview by Max Tessier in *Ecran* (Paris), April 1973; interview by Judith Trojan in *Take One* (Montreal), January/February 1974; "James Ivory and Ismail Merchant Tell D. Eisenberg About Their Wild Party with Raquel" in *Interview* (New York), January 1975; "The Merchant-Ivory Synthesizer" by J. Trojan in *Take One* (Montreal), May 1975; interview by S. Varble in *Interview* (New York), vol.2, no.2, n.d.

On IVORY:

Book—*The Wandering Company* by John Pym, London 1983; articles—"Merchant-Ivory" by John Gillett in *Sight and Sound* (London), spring 1973; "Le Choc des mondes et la crise de l'esprit" by G. Braucourt in *Ecran* (Paris), April 1973; "A Princess in London" by J. Gillett in *Sight and Sound* (London), summer 1974; "The Wild Party" by John Taylor in *Sight and*

Sound (London), autumn 1974; "The Making of *Roseland*" by D. Hillgartner in *Filmmakers Newsletter* (Ward Hill, Mass.), January 1978; "Quartet", special issue of *Avant-Scène du cinéma* (Paris), 1 October 1981; biofilmography in *Film Dope* (London), July 1983.

* * *

Perhaps one of the most cosmopolitan and independent directors in the history of the cinema, James Ivory has ranged over three continents for the setting and subject matter of his 18 films to date. Of these, many have been set in, or directly concerned with, India, a country which for Ivory exerts a perennial fascination, offering as it does an ideal ground for the meeting of cultures, a theme which provides the basis, in one form or another, for all Ivory's films.

The focal point of almost every Ivory film is the collision, in more or less mutual misapprehension, of representatives of different races, religions, cultural backgrounds or social assumptions. Those who attempt to bridge the gaps usually come to grief, suffering at best ridicule, and at worst (like Olivia in *Heat and Dust*) rejection and social exile. Ivory rarely judges or takes sides, preferring to observe with irony and quiet humor the quirks and vicissitudes of his characters, and taking particular delight in eccentricity and intrigue. Frequently the tone is elegiac, as in *Roseland* or *Shakespeare Wallah*, where Ivory finds poignancy in the representatives of a dying tradition which refuses to relinquish its feeble hold on existence. The same theme, handled with a robustness of humor which surprised some critics, underlies *The Wild Party*, in which a fading silent movie star attempts a disastrous comeback. Ivory's satirical side also emerged strongly in *Savages*, an engagingly absurdist parable on the rise and fall of civilization.

All of Ivory's films have been produced by Merchant Ivory Productions, a doggedly independent company which he set up in partnership with the Indian producer Ismail Merchant. A third close collaborator is the novelist Ruth Prawer Jhabvala, who has scripted the majority—and, some would claim, the best—of Ivory's work. To a large extent, as Ivory himself readily concedes, the characteristic tone and preoccupations of his films are the creation of this exceptional partnership.

Ivory's films are perhaps to be criticized—and indeed have been—for being too intellectual, too detached and tasteful, at the expense of dramatic involvement, a weakness which Ivory himself acknowledges. "Pace has often played second fiddle to atmosphere in my films and sometimes it should have been the other way round." This tendency, in conjunction with his characteristically elegant camera work and pictorial composition, can result (as in *The Europeans* or *Quartet*) in an impression of coldness, a beautiful surface lacking emotional depth. Ivory is probably at his best when, as in *Heat and Dust*, he allows the emotional values of a situation to speak for themselves, rather than retreating from them into protective irony.

Despite such weaknesses, though, Ivory's movies have consistently offered stylish and intelligent pleasures—not least being his rare eye for social idiosyncrasy. Over two decades, his films have appeared with encouraging regularity; and with the imminent completion of a long-nurtured project, Henry James's *The Bostonians*, the offbeat enterprise of Merchant-Ivory shows, happily, little sign of flagging.

—Theresa FitzGerald

JANCSÓ, MIKLÓS. Hungarian. Born in Vác, 27 September 1921. Educated in law at Kolozsvár University, Romania, doctorate 1944; Budapest Academy of Dramatic and Film Art, graduated 1950. Married director Márta Mészáros. Career: after war—active in Hungarian youth movement; early 1950s—makes newsreels; 1957—travels to China, shooting several documentaries; 1958—makes first feature-length film; 1960s—associated with "25th Theater", Budapest, stages versions of his films; 1966—presentation of *The Round-Up* at Cannes leads to international recognition; 1974—directs *Othello*, Venice. Recipient: Hungarian Critics' Prize for *Cantata*, 1963; Best Director, Cannes Festival, for *Red Psalm*, 1972; Special Prize for ensemble of his work, Cannes Festival, 1979.

Films (as director of short films and documentaries): 1950—*Kezunbe vettuk a béke ugyét (We Took Over the Cause of Peace)* (co-d); *A Maksimenko brigád (The Maximenko Brigade)* (Koza) (story only); 1951—*Szovjet mezögazdasági hüldöttsek tanításai (The Teachings of a Soviet Agricultural Deputation)* (co-d); 1952—*A 8. szabad Május 1 (Ezerkilencszázötvenkettö. 1952 Május 1, The 8th Free May Day)*; 1953—*Választás elótt (Before Election)*; *Arat az Orosházi Dözsa (Harvest in the Cooperative "Dosza")*; *Közös útan (Ordinary Ways, On a Common Path)* (co-d); 1954—*Galga mentén (Along the Galgu River, At the River Galga)*; *Ösz Badacsonyban (Autumn in Badacsony)*; *Éltetö Tisza-víz (The Health-Giving Waters of Tisza, Life-Bringing Water)*; *Emberek! Ne engedjétek! (Comrades! Don't Put Up with It, Don't Allow It!)* (+co-d, co-sc); *Egy kiállítás képei (Pictures at an Exhibition)*; 1955—*Angyalföldi fiatalok (Children of Angyalfold, The Youth of "The Land of Angels")*; *A Varsói vit (Varsoí Világifjusági Találkozó I-III, Warsaw World Youth Meeting I-III, World Youth Festival in Warsaw)*; *Egy délután Koppánymonostorban (One Afternoon in Koppanymonostor, An Afternoon in the Village)*; *Emlékezz, ifjúság (Young People, Remember)*; 1956—*Móricz Zsigmond (Zsigmond Moricz 1879-1942)*; 1957—*A város peremén (In the Outskirts of the City)*; *Dél-Kína tájain (In the South China Countryside, The Landscapes of Southern China)*; *Színfoltok Kínaböl (Colorful China, Colors of China)*; *Pekingi palotái (Palaces of Peking)*; *Kína vendégei voltunk (Our Visit to China, We Have Been the Guests of China)*; 1958—*Derkovitz Gyula 1894-1934*; *A harangok Römába mentek (The Bells Have Gone to Rome)* (feature); 1959—*Halhatatlanság (Immortality)* (+sc, ph); *Izotöpok a gyögyászatban (Isotopes in Medical Science)*; 1960—first episode of *Három csillag (Three Stars)*; *Az eladás müvészete (The Art of Revival, The Art of Salesmanship)* (co-d); *Szerkezettervezés (Construction Design)* (+sc); 1961—*Az idö kereke (The Wheels of Time)* (+sc); *Alkonyok és hajnalok (Dusks and Dawns, Twilight and Dawn)* (+sc); *Indiántörténet (Indian Story, Indian Adventure)* (+sc); 1963—*Oldás és kötés (Cantata)* (+co-sc); *Hej, te eleven Fa...(Living Tree..., An Old Folk Song)* (+sc); (as director of feature films): 1964—*Így jöttem (My Way Home)*; 1965—*Szegénylegények (The Round-Up)*; *Jelenlét (The Presence)* (+sc—short); *Közelrölia: a vér (Close-up: The Blood)* (short); 1967—*Csillagosok, katonák (The Red and the White)* (+co-sc); 1968—*Csend és kiáltás (Silence and Cry)* (+co-sc); *Vörös Május (Red May)* (short); 1969—*Fényes szelek (The Confrontation)*; *Sirokkó (Teli sirokkó lek, Sirocco d'hiver, Winter Wind)* (+co-sc); 1970—*Égi bárány (Agnus Dei)* (+co-sc); *La pacifista (The Pacifist)* (+co-sc); *Füst (Smoke)* (short); 1971—*La tècnica ed il rito (Il giovane Attila, The Technique and the Rite)* (+co-sc—for TV); 1972—*Még kér a nép (Red Psalm, Red Song, People Still Ask)*; 1974—*Roma rivuole Cesare (Rome Wants Another Caesar)* (+co-sc—for TV); 1975—*Szerelmem, Elektra (Elektreia)*; 1976—*Vizi privati, pubbliche virtù (Vices and Pleasures)*; 1978—*Eletünket és vérunket: Magyar rapszödia 1 (Hun-*

garian Rhapsody) (+co-sc); *Allegro barbaro: Magyar rapszödia 2 (Allegro barbaro)* (+co-sc); 1981—*A zsarnok szíve avagy Boccaccio Magyarországon (The Tyrant's Heart or Boccaccio in Hungary)* (+co-sc). Roles: 1968—*A Pál utcai fiúk (The Boys of Paul Street)* (Fabri); 1977—*Difficile morire* (Silva).

Publications:

By JANCSÓ:

Articles—interview in *Cinéma 67* (Paris), February 1967; interview in *The Image Maker* edited by Ron Henderson, Richmond, Virginia 1971; "Miklos Jancso: conversazione" by E. Chaluja and others in *Filmcritica* (Rome), March 1972; "L'Idéologie, la technique et le rite", interview by Claude Beylie in *Ecran* (Paris), December 1972; interview by G. Langlois in *Cinéma* (Paris), December 1972; "Une dialectique de l'oppression" by I. Zsugán in *Cinéma* (Paris), April 1972; interview by A. Cornand in *Image et son* (Paris), January 1973; "I Have Played Christ Long Enough: A Conversation with Miklos Jancso" by Gideon Bachmann in *Film Quarterly* (Berkeley), fall 1974; interview by Gideon Bachmann in *Cinéma* (Paris), April 1974; "Films of Change", interview by F. Zaagsma in *Lumiere* (Melbourne), January/February 1974; interview by P. Haudiquet in *Image et son* (Paris), November 1975; "L'Electre de Jancso notre contemporaine", interview by René Predal in *Jeune cinéma* (Paris), November 1975; "A forma es a tartalom egysegenek iskolapeldaja" in *Filmkultura* (Budapest), May/June 1976; "'Bizom benne, hogy a végcél nem utópia'", interview by L. Nádasy in *Filmkultura* (Budapest), October 1978; "Entretien...sur *Vitam et sanguinem*" by Michel Ciment and J.-P. Jeancolas in *Positif* (Paris), May 1979; "'A szabadsag kerdeseit probaljuk koruljarni': beszelgetes Hernadi Gyulaval", interview by L. Nadasy in *Filmkultura* (Budapest), May/June 1979; "5 cinéastes pour Cannes", interview by U. Rossi in *Ecran* (Paris), 15 May 1979; "A jelenlét", interview by I. Antal in *Filmkultura* (Budapest), November/December 1981.

On JANCSÓ:

Books—*Directors and Directions* by John Taylor, New York 1975; *History Must Answer to Man: The Contemporary Hungarian Cinema* by Graham Petrie, London 1978; articles—"Jeune Cinéma hongrois" in *Premier Plan* (Lyon), no.43, 1966; "Miklós Jancsó" in *International Film Guide 1969* edited by Peter Cowie, London 1968; "The Horizontal Man" by Penelope Houston in *Sight and Sound* (London), summer 1969; "Polarities: The Films opf Miklós Jancsó" by James Price in the *London Magazine*, August/September 1969; "Sur 3 films de Miklós Jancsó" by Frédéric Vitoux in *Positif* (Paris), May 1969; "Lectures de Jancsó: hier et aujourd'hui" by P. Kane and others in *Cahiers du cinéma* (Paris), March and May 1969, and April 1970; "3 East European Directors" by P. Crick in *Screen* (London), March/April 1970; "Quite Apart from Miklos Jancso" by D. Robinson in *Sight and Sound* (London), spring 1970; "Jancso Country: Miklos Jancso and the Hungarian New Cinema" by Lorant Czigany in *Film Quarterly* (Berkeley), fall 1972; "Jancsó Country" by L. Czigany in *Film Quarterly* (Berkeley), fall 1972; "Jancsó par ses collaborateurs" by Z. Farkas and others in *Cinéma* (Paris), April 1972; "Jancso est-il un cinéaste révolutionnaire?" by Guy Hennebelle in *Ecran* (Paris), December 1972; "Un 'Rouge' noir sur blanc" by Marcel Martin in *Ecran* (Paris), December 1972; "Rouges et blancs" by M.-C. Mercier in *Image et son* (Paris), no.269, 1973; "Jancso Plain" by Gideon Bachmann in *Sight and Sound* (London), autumn 1974; "Dalla dialettica marxista alla ritualitá metafisica" by G. Giuricin in *Cinema*

nuovo (Turin), September/December 1975; "Ripensando alla violenza dei 'rossi' e dei 'bianchi'" by R. Alemanno in *Cinema nuovo* (Turin), January/February 1975; "Letter from Hungary" by Gideon Bachmann in *Take One* (Montreal), June 1975; special issue by Michel Estève and others of *Etudes cinématographiques* (Paris), no.104-108, 1975; "Miklos Jancso: i riti della rivoluzione la morte, la resurrezione, il futuro" by R. Escobar and V. Giacci in *Cineforum* (Bergamo), November 1976; "Old Jancso Customs" by David Robinson in *Sight and Sound* (London), no.1, 1978/79; "Landscape During the Battle" by Y. Biro in *Millenium* (New York), summer/fall 1979; "Miklos Jancso" by C. Losada in *Cinema 2002* (Madrid), December 1979; "A forma elvének változásai Jancsó Miklós filmjeiben" by P. Milosevits in *Filmkultura* (Budapest), September/October 1980; "Jancsó Miklós a magyar kritikák tükrében" by E. Komár in *Filmkultura* (Budapest), November/December 1981; "Miklos Jancso", with biofilmography, by John Gillett in *Film Dope* (London), July 1983; films—*Kamerával Kosztromában (With a Camera in Kosztroma)*, short, by Zsolt Kovács, 1967; *Miklos Jancso*, for TV, by Jean-Louis Comolli, France 1969.

JENNINGS, HUMPHREY. English. Born in Walberswick, England, 1907. Educated Perse School and Pembroke College, England. Career: *c.* 1930-34—remains at Cambridge doing postgraduate research, painting and writing poetry; 1934—joins General Post Office (GPO) film unit as scenic designer and as editor of compilation films; 1936—begins working with Len Lye at Shell Films; 1938—returns to GPO film unit (became Crown Film Unit, 1940), directing documentaries for them throughout and after the war; paintings shown; late 1930's—becomes associated with Mass Observation, conducting a nationwide investigation of public opinion; 1949—begins directing for Wessex Films; directs *Family Portrait* an official film for Festival of Britain; 1950—fatally injured in fall from a cliff in Greece while scouting locations for film.

Films (as editor): 1934—*Post-Haste*; *Pett and Pott* (sets only); *The Story of the Wheel*; 1935—*Locomotives*; 1936—*The Birth of a Robot* (color direction and production only); (as director): 1938—*Penny Journey*; 1939—*Spare Time* (+sc); *Speaking from America*; *SS Ionian (Her Last Trip)*; *The 1st Days (A City Prepares)* (co-d); 1940—*London Can Take It* (co-d); *Spring Offensive (An Unrecorded Victory)*; *Welfare of the Workers* (co-d); 1941—*Heart of Britain (This is England)*; *Words for Battle* (+sc); 1942—*Listen to Britain* (co-d +co-sc, co-ed); 1943—*Fires Were Started (I Was a Fireman)* (+sc); *The Silent Village* (+pr, sc); 1944—*The 80 Days* (+pr); *The True Story of Lilli Marlene* (+sc); *VI* (+pr); 1944-45—*A Diary for Timothy* (+sc); 1946—*A Defeated People*; 1947—*The Cumberland Story* (+sc); 1949—*Dim Little Island* (+pr); 1950—*Family Portrait* (+sc). Roles: 1934—*telegraph boy* in *Glorious 6th of June* (Cavalcanti); *grocer* in *Pett and Pott* (Cavalcanti).

Publications:

By JENNINGS:

Articles—essay on the theater in *The Arts Today* edited by Geoffrey Grigson, London 1935; essay in *London Symphony, Portrait of an Orchestra, 1904-54* by Hubert Foss and Noël Goodwin, London 1954; "Work Sketches of an Orchestra" in *Film Quarterly* (Berkeley), winter 1961/62.

On JENNINGS:

Books—*Humphrey Jennings: A Tribute* by John Grierson, London 1951; *Grierson on Documentary* by Forsyth Hardy, revised edition London 1966; *Studies in Documentary* by Alan Lovell and Jim Hillier, New York 1972; *The Rise and Fall of British Documentary: The Story of the Film Movement Founded by John Grierson* by Elizabeth Sussex, Berkeley, California 1975; *Humphrey Jennings: More than a Maker of Films* by Anthony Hodgkinson and Rodney Sheratsky, Hanover, New Hampshire 1982; *Humphrey Jennings: Film-Maker/Painter/-Poet* edited by Mary-Lou Jennings, London 1982; articles— "Humphrey Jennings" by Basil Wright in *Sight and Sound* (London), December 1950; "Humphrey Jennings—A Memoir" by Nicole Védrès in *Sight and Sound* (London), May 1951; "Jennings' Britain" by Gavin Lambert in *Sight and Sound* (London), May 1951; "Only Connect: Some Aspects of the Work of Humphrey Jennings" by Lindsay Anderson in *Sight and Sound* (London), April/June 1954; "Index to the Creative Work of Humphrey Jennings" by Jonas Mekas in *Film Forum* (Mesdetten, Germany), 8 July 1954; "Britain's Screen Poet" by Charles Dand in *Films in Review* (New York), February 1955; "Great Films of the Century, 11, *Fires Were Started*" by Philip Strick in *Films and Filming* (London), May 1961; special issue of *Film Quarterly* (Berkeley), winter 1961-62; "Cinema of Appearance" by Eric Rhode and Gabriel Pearson in *Sight and Sound* (London), autumn 1961; "Rogosin and the Documentary" by Peter Davis in *Film Culture* (New York), no.24 1962; "*Fires Were Started*" by Daniel Millar in *Sight and Sound* (London), spring 1969; "Humphrey Jennings, 1907-1950" by Jacques Belmans in *Anthologie du cinéma, Vol. VI*, Paris 1971; "The Unknown Cinema of Britain" by A. Lovell in *Cinema Journal* (Evanston), spring 1972; "Über Humphrey Jennings und einige seiner Filme" by H. Bitomsky in *Filmkritik* (Munich), November 1975; "Humphrey Jennings: Artist of the British Documentary", special issue, by R.E. Sharatsky in *Film Library Quarterly* (New York), v.8, no.3-4, 1975; "Propaganda für das Alltägliche: Filme von Humphrey Jennings im WDF" by E. Netenjakob in *Medium* (Frankfurt), October 1976; "Humphrey Jennings" by O. Barrot in *Cinéma d'aujourd'hui* (Paris), February/March 1977; "Humphrey Jennings' Film *Family Portrait*: The Velocity of Imagistic Change" by T.A. Zaniello in *Literature/Film Quarterly* (Salisbury, Maryland), no.1, 1979.

*   *   *

Though Jennings was (from 1934 on) part of the Grierson documentary group, he was never fully part of it. Grierson regarded him as something of a dilettante; Jennings's taste and interests were subtler and gentler than Grierson's. It wasn't until Grierson had left England to become wartime head of the National Film Board of Canada that Jennings gained creative control over the films on which he worked.

The outbreak of World War II seemed to loose in Jennings a special poetic eloquence, and his finest work was done at the Crown Film Unit during the war years. *Listen to Britain*, *Fires Were Started*, and *A Diary for Timothy* are generally regarded as his masterpieces.

Jennings was part of the English intellectual aristocracy. Extremely well educated, he had done a good deal of research into English literature and cultural history. He was also a surrealist painter and poet. In his wartime films his deep-felt affection for English tradition mingles with impressionist observations of the English people under the stress of war. Rather than following the sociological line of the Griersonian documentaries of the 1930's, Jennings offered a set of cultural notations—sights and sounds, people and places—illuminated by his very special aesthetic sensibility and complete mastery of technique of the black and white sound film. His films present an idealized English tradition in which class tensions don't appear. They record and celebrate contemporary achievement in preserving the historical heritage, along with commonplace decenies and humor in the face of enemy threat. They also are experiments with form, of such breathtaking distinctiveness that they never really have been imitated. (Though Lindsay Anderson and other Free Cinema film makers would later acknowledge the importance of Jennings's work to them as inspiration, the Free Cinema films are radically different from Jennings's films in what they say about England, and are also much simpler in form.)

Listen to Britain, a short, is a unique impressionistic mosaic of images and sounds, including much music (as is usual in Jennings's work)—a sort of free-association portrait of a nation at a particular historical moment. The feature-length *Fires Were Started* carries the understated emotionality of the British wartime semi-documentary form to a kind of perfection: a very great deal about heroic effort and quiet courage is suggested through an austere yet deeply moving presentation of character and simple narrative. In *A Diary for Timothy*, which runs about forty minutes, Jennings attempted to fuse the impressionism of *Listen To Britain* with the narrativity of *Fires Were Started*. In its formal experimentation it is the most complex and intricate of all of Jennings's films.

With the Germans massed across the Channel, and bombs and then rockets being dropped on Britain, the British people needed a kind of emotional support different from the wartime psychological needs in other countries. In rising to this particular occasion Jennings became one of the few British filmmakers whose work might be called poetic. He is also one of a small international company of film artists whose propaganda for the state resulted in lasting works of art.

—Jack C. Ellis

JEWISON, NORMAN. American. Born in Toronto, Canada, 21 July 1926. Educated at Malvern Collegiate Institute, graduated 1944. Victoria College, University of Toronto, B.A. 1950. Married Margaret Ann Dixon, 1953; children: Kevin, Michael, and Jennifer. Career: 1944—joins Canadian Navy; 1950-52—lives in London, occasionally acting and selling some scripts for children's shows to BBC; 1952—accepts position in Canadian Broadcasting Company training program; mid-1950s—produces and directs top Canadian TV variety shows including Wayne and Shuster, The Big Review, and Showtime; 1958—on basis of Canadian work, signed by CBS in New York as director, successfully revives *Your Hit Parade*; 1959-61—stages TV specials, several nominated for Emmy awards; 1961—moves to Hollywood; 1963—success of *40 Pounds of Trouble* leads to 7-picture contract with Universal; executive producer for *The Judy Garland Show* on TV; 1965—gets out of Universal contract through technicality, takes over direction of *The Cincinnati Kid* from Sam Peckinpah for MGM; 1966—begins producing as well as directing for *The Russians Are Coming, The Russians Are Coming*. Recipient: Emmy award for best single variety program, for *The Fabulous Fifties*, 1960. Agent: William Morris, Beverly Hills, California; business manager: Capell, Flekman, Coyne & Co., Beverly Hills, California.

Films (as director): 1963—*40 Pounds of Trouble*; *The Thrill of It All*; 1964—*Send Me No Flowers*; 1965—*The Art of Love*; *The Cincinnati Kid*; (as producer and director): 1966—*The Russians Are Coming, the Russians Are Coming*; 1967—*In the Heat of the Night* (d only); 1968—*The Thomas Crown Affair*; 1969—*Gaily, Gaily*; 1970—*The Landlord* (Ashby) (pr only); 1971—*Fiddler on the Roof*; 1973—*Jesus Christ Superstar* (co-pr, +co-sc); *Billy Two-Hats* (Kotcheff) (pr only); 1975—*Rollerball*; 1978—*F.I.S.T.*; 1979—*And Justice for All* (co-pr); 1982—*Best Friends*.

Publications:

By JEWISON:

Articles—"Norman Jewison Discusses Thematic Action in The Cincinnati Kid", interview in *Cinema* (Beverly Hills), July/August 1965; "Turning On in Salzburg" in *Action* (Los Angeles), July/August 1969; interview in *Directors at Work* edited by Bernard Kantor and others, New York 1970; "Confrontations: Norman Jewison Interviewed" by Gordon Gow in *Films and Filming* (London), January 1971; "The Man Behind Fiddler on the Roof", interview by J. Williams in *Films Illustrated* (London), December 1971.

On JEWISON:

Articles—"Rollerball Superstar" by G. Braucourt in *Ecran* (Paris), November 1974; "Norman Jewison Directs *Rollerball*" by M. Carducci in *Millimeter* (New York), March 1975; "Film: Futures Past" by H.E. Phillips in the *National Review* (New York), 12 November 1976; "Norman Jewison Directs *And Justice for All*" by J. Mariani in *Millimeter* (New York), October 1979; entry in *Current Biography 1979*, New York 1980.

*   *   *

The very model of the modern up-market commercial director, Jewison is cut out to make the kind of prestige pictures once handled at MGM by Clarence Brown and Victor Fleming. No theme is so trashy or threadbare that he cannot elevate it by stylish technique and apt casting into a work of merit, even on occasion art.

Early work with an aging and cantankerous Judy Garland marked him as a man at ease with the cinema's sacred monsters; in the indifferent sex comedies of the early sixties, he acquired equal skill with the pastels of Hollywood color and the demands of widescreen. A recognizable Jewison style was first evident in *The Cincinnati Kid*. Its elements—rich crimsons; the sheen of faces, tanned or sweating, in shadowed rooms; an edgy passion in performance—reappeared in *In the Heat of the Night* and *The Thomas Crown Affair*, novelettes redeemed by their visual flair and a sensual relish, not for sex, but for the appurtenances of power.

Not at home in the domestic or the comic, Jewison brought little to Ben Hecht's film memoir *Gaily, Gaily*, the literary ellipsis of *The Landlord* or, more recently, to comedies like *Best Friends*. Two musicals, *Fiddler on the Roof* and *Jesus Christ, Superstar*, did, however, offer an invitation to location shooting and unconventional staging which Jewison confidently accepted. Though little liked on release, the latter shows a typical imagination and sensuality applied to the subject, which Jewison relocated in contemporary Israel to spectacular effect. *Rollerball*, his sole essay in science fiction, belongs with *Thomas Crown* in its

relish for high life. The strong points are not the eponymous gladiatorial game but the dark glamor of life among his future power elite.

A pattern of one step forward, two steps backward, dominates Jewison's career into the eighties. The Israel-shot western *Billy Two Hats* was a notable miscalculation, as was the Sylvester Stallone union melodrama *F.I.S.T.*, a program picture that needed to be an epic to survive. He was on surer ground in *And Justice for All*, a dark and sarcastic comedy/drama about the idiocy of the law, with a credible Al Pacino in command. It is a cause for concern that he could never put together his projected musical remake of *Grand Hotel*, whose elements seem precisely those with which he works most surely. A taint of the high-class advertising lay-out characterises Jewison's best work, just as the style and technique of that field rescues his often banal material. Within the ambit of the glossy magazine, with its rich colours and crepuscular compositions, he seems destined to spend his career.

—John Baxter

———————

JIRES, JAROMIL. Czech. Born in Bratislava, 10 December 1935. Educated at film technical school, Cmelice; the FAMU Film Faculty, Prague; graduated in 2 branches: photography, 1958, and direction, 1960. Married computer engineer Hana Jirešová. Career: 1960-62—experimental work with Polyecran and the Magic Lantern; 1963—begins directing feature films at Barrandov Film Studio; after 1965—director of documentary films at Short Film Prague; after 1974—also directs TV films. Address: Na ostrohu 16, 160 00 Praha 6, Ceskoslovensko.

Films (as director): 1958—*Horečka (Fever)* (+sc); 1959—*Strejda (Uncle)* (+sc); 1960—*Sál ztracených kroku (The Hall of Lost Steps)* (+sc, ph); *Stopy (Footprints)*; *Polyekrán pro BVV (Polyecran for the Brno Industrial Fair)* (co-d); 1961—*Polyekrán pro Mezinárodní výstavu práce Turin (Polyecran for International Exposition of Labor Turin)* (co-d); 1962—*Houslový koncert (The Violin Concert)* (co-d, Magic Lantern program); 1963—*Křik (The Cry)* (+co-sc); 1964—"Romance" episode of *Perličky na dně (Pearls in the Deep)* (+sc); 1965—*Srub (The Log Cabin)* (+sc); 1966—*Občan Karel Havlíček (Citizen Karel Havlíč ek)* (+co-sc); 1967—*Hra na krále (The King Game)* (+sc); 1968—*Zert (The Joke)* (+sc); *Don Juan 68* (+sc); *Dědáček (Granpa)* (+sc); 1969—*Cesta do Prahy Vincence Moštek a Simona Pešla z Vlčnova l.p. 1969 (The Journey of Vincenc Moštek and Simon Pešl of Vlčnov to Prague, 1969 A.D.)* (co-d, +co-sc); 1970—*Valerie a týden divu (Valerie and a Week of Wonders)* (+sc); 1972—*...a pozdravuji vlaštovky (My Love to the Swallows, Greetings to the Swallows)* (+sc); 1973—*Kasař (The Safe Cracker)* (+sc); 1974—*Lidé z metra (People from the Metro, People in the Subway)* (+co-sc); *Leoš Janáč ek* (+sc, for TV); 1975—*Il Divino Boemo* (+sc); 1976—*Ostrov stříbrných volavek (The Island of Silver Herons)*; 1977—*Taliře nad Velkým Malíkovem (Flying Saucers Coming!, Flying Saucers Over Our Town)* (+sc); 1978—*Mladý muž a bílá velryba (The Young Man and Moby Dick, The Young Man and the White Whale)* (+sc); 1979—*Causa králík (The Rabbit Case)* (+sc); *Zápisník zmizelého (The Diary of One Who Disappeared)* (+sc, for TV); 1980—*Svět Alfonso Muchy (The World of Alphonse Mucha)* (+sc); *Bohuslav Martinu* (+sc, for TV); *Útěky domu (Escapes Home)* (+co-sc); 1981—*Opera ve vinici (Opera in the Vineyard)*

(+sc); 1982—*Kouzelná Praha Rudolfa II (The Magic Prague of Rudolph II)*(+sc); *Neúplné zatmění (Partial Eclipse)*(+co-sc); *O labuti (On the Swan)* (+sc—for TV).

Publications:

By JIRES:

Articles—interview in *The Image Maker* edited by Ron Henderson, Richmond, Virginia 1971; "O lidech—hudbě a filmu", interview by A. Bechtoldová in *Film a doba* (Prague), January 1977; "Rozhovor s Jaromilem Jirešem o filmech a nejen vlastních", interview by E. Zaoralová in *Film a doba* (Prague), February 1981.

On JIRES:

Book—*3½ po druhé* by Jiří Janoušek, Prague 1969; article—"Movers" by Andrew Sarris in *Saturday Review* (New York), 23 December 1967.

*   *   *

Having finished his studies at the Prague Film School, Jireš entered filmmaking at the end of the 1950s with several short films, the most engaging of which was *Sál ztracených kroku (The Hall of Lost Steps)*. In 1963 he made his debut in feature-length films with the picture *Křik (The Cry)*, which earned him a place among the ranks of young directors striving for new content and a new film language. In his debut Jireš reacts to modern film currents, above all to the stylistics of the cinéma vérité, whose elements he utilizes, conscious, of course, of the danger that this can hold for the representation of reality and the expression of truth. The story of *The Cry* suppresses traditional dramatic structure. It consists of the fragmentary memories of the two main protagonists, a husband and wife, on the day their child is to be born. Arranging individual recollections, combining fictional segments with documentary shots, and using a hidden camera, Jireš seeks to convince the viewer of man's connection with the present, the past, and the future, and his close and immediate link with the whole world. (Jireš: "We live in a time when a person's most intimate experiences are connected with the major currents of world events.") *The Cry* was very well received and won several awards; it is the first pinnacle of Jireš's creative work.

The second pinnacle was achieved in two totally disparate pictures from the early 1970s. One film was *Valerie a týden divu (Valerie and a Week of Wonders)*, based on a novel by the eminent modern Czech poet Víítězslav Nezval. What interested Jireš about the novel was "the juncture of reality and dream and the playful struggle between horror and humor." The other film, *...a pozdravuji vlaštovky (My Love to the Swallows)*, is purely Jireš's own. The director was inspired by the life and death of the real-life character of Maruška Kudeříková, a young woman who fought against German fascism during the Second World War. Here, in a different connection, Jireš used the same method of alternating real-life elements and reminiscences, as in *The Cry*, but for a different purpose, namely, to demonstrate a person's inner strength, the source of her faith and hope.

The following years, in which Jireš made three pictures, were a period of stagnation. The fairy-tale film *Lidé z metra (The People from the Metro)* is about the same as *Ostrov stříbrných volavek (The Island of Silver Herons)*, in which he returns to the days of the First World War. Even less noteworthy is the fantastic tale *Talíře nad Velkým Malíkovem (Flying Saucers Over Velký Malík).*

Jireš's creative path took a new turn in 1978 with *Mladý muž a bílá velryba (The Young Man and the White Whale)*. The film is an adaptation of Vladimír Páral's novel of the same name and deals with modern man's uneasy oscillation between a mask of cynicism and pure human feeling. Next came *Causa králík (The Rabbit Case)*, an apparently humorous morality piece with a bitter finale on the struggle for justice against cunning and evil. The heroine of Jireš's next work, *Utěky domu (Escapes Home)*, is a young woman who must face a conflict between her desire for self-fulfillment in a challenging profession and her duties as a wife and the mother of a family. In his last film, *Neúplné zatmění (Partial Eclipse)*, about a little blind girl, he speculates on an emotional level about the meaning of life and the quest for human personality. All of these recent films have a common feature—they address problems of modern life in the area of the ethics of human relations.

Documentary films form an integral part of Jireš's creative work. Unlike his friends of the same generation, Jireš remained faithful to the documentary genre throughout his artistic career. This segment of his work shows great thematic breadth. However, we can nonetheless delineate two fundamental areas of interest for Jireš. In the 1960s his attention was drawn to the folklore of southern Moravia, where several of his short films have their setting. Jireš returns to this region and to this subject matter in a modified form in 1981 with the ballad story *Opera ve vinici (Opera in the Vineyard)*. In the 1970s his documentary films turn more and more to the world of art, to music, painting, and architecture. Examples include *Il divino Boemo, Leoš Janáček, Zápisník zmizelého (Notebook of Things Gone), Bohuslav Martinů, Svět Alfonse Muchy (The World of Alfonse Mucha)*, and *Kouzelná Praha Rudolfa II (The Enchanting Prague of Rudolph II)*.

—Vladimir Opela

[translated by Robert Streit]

JONES, CHUCK. American. Born in Spokane, Washington, 21 September 1912. Educated at Chouinard Art Institute, Los Angeles. Married Dorothy Webster (deceased). Career: early 1930s—works at various animation studios in variety of capacities, including for Charles Mintz at Screen Gems, Ub Iwerks at Flip the Frog Productions, and for Walter Lantz; about 1935—joins Warner Brothers as animator; works as animator under Ub Iwerks, Robert Clampett, and Tex Avery; 1938-62—cartoon director for Warners; 1955—works 4 months at Disney Studios, then returns to Warners; 1963-67—directs for MGM; 1970-present—directs and produces television specials. Recipient: Best Animated Cartoon Academy Award for *For Scent-Imental Reasons*, 1949; Best Short Subject Academy Award for *So Much for So Little*, 1950; Best Animated Cartoon Academy Award for *The Dot and the Line*, 1965; Peabody Award for *Horton Hears a Who*, 1971.

Cartoons (as director for Warner Brothers): 1938—*Night Watchman; Dog Gone Modern*; 1939—*Robin Hood Makes Good; Presto Change-O; Daffy Duck and the Dinosaur; Naughty But Mice; Old Glory; Snowman's Land; Little Brother Rat; Little Lion Hunter; The Good Egg; Sniffles and the Bookworm; Curious Puppy*; 1940—*Mighty Hunters; Elmer's Candid Camera*;

Sniffles Takes a Trip; Tom Thumb in Trouble; The Egg Collector; Ghost Wanted; Good Night Elmer; Bedtime for Sniffles; Sniffles Bells the Cat; 1941—*Toy Trouble; The Wacky Worm; Inki and the Lion; Snow Time for Comedy; Joe Glow the Firefly; Brave Little Bat; Saddle Silly; The Bird Came C.O.D.; Porky's Ant; Conrad the Sailor; Porky's Prize Pony; Dog Tired; The Draft Horse; Hold the Lion, Please; Porky's Midnight Matinee;* 1942—*The Squawkin' Hawk; Fox Pop; My Favorite Duck; To Duck or Not to Duck; The Dover Boys; Case of the Missing Hare; Porky's Cafe;* 1943—*Flop Goes the Weasel; Super Rabbit; The Unbearable Bear; The Aristo Cat; Wackiki Wabbit; Fin 'n Catty; Inki and the Mynah Bird;* 1944—*Tom Turk and Daffy; Angel Puss; From Hand to Mouse; The Odor-able Kitty; Bugs Bunny and the 3 Bears; The Weakly Reporter; Lost and Foundling;* 1945—*Trap Happy Porky; Hare Conditioned; Hare Tonic; Hush My Mouse; Fresh Airedale; Quentin Quail; Hair Raising Hare; The Eager Beaver;* 1946—*Roughly Squeaking; Scenti-Mental Over You; Fair and Worm-er; A Feather in His Hare;* 1947—*Little Orphan Airedale; What's Brewin' Bruin; House Hunting Mice; Haredevil Hare; Inki at the Circus; A Pest in the House; Rabbit Punch;* 1948—*You Were Never Duckier; Mississippi Hare; Mouse Wreckers; Scaredy Cat; My Bunny Lies Over the Sea; Awful Orphan; The Bee-Deviled Bruin; Daffy Dilly; Long-Haired Hare;* 1949—*Frigid Hare; Rabbit Hood; Often an Orphan; Fast and Furry-ous; For Scent-imental Reasons; Bear Feat; Homeless Hare;* 1950—*The Hypo-Chondri-Cat; Dog Gone South; The Scarlet Pumpernickel; 8-Ball Bunny; The Ducksters; Rabbit of Seville; Caveman Inki;* 1951—*Two's a Crowd; A Hound For Trouble; Rabbit Fire; Chow Hound; The Wearing of the Grin; A Bear for Punishment; Bunny Hugged; Scent-Imental Romeao; Cheese Chasers; Drip-Along Daffy;* 1952—*Operation Rabbit; Water, Water Every Hare; The Hasty Hare; Mousewarming; Don't Give Up the Sheep; Feed the Kitty; Little Beau Pepe; Beep Beep; Going! Going! Gosh!; Terrier Stricken; Rabbit Seasoning; Kiss Me Cat;* 1953—*Forward March Hare; Wild Over You; Bully for Bugs; Duck Amuck; Much Ado About Nutting; Duck Dodgers in the 24 1/2 Century; Zipping Along; Feline Frame-Up;* 1954—*Punch Trunk; From A to ZZZZ; Bewitched Bunny; Duck! Rabbit!; No Barking; Stop, Look, and Hasten!; Sheep Ahoy; My Little Duckaroo;* 1955—*The Cat's Bah; Claws for Alarm; Lumber Jack Rabbit* (in 3-D); *Ready, Set, Zoom!; Rabbit Rampage; Double or Mutton; Baby Buggy Bunny; Beanstalk Bunny; Past Performance; Jumpin' Jupiter; Guided Muscle; Knight-Mare Hare;* 1956—*Two Scents' Worth; One Froggy Evening; Bug's Bonnets; Rocket Sqaud; Heaven Scent; Rocket-Bye Baby; Gee Whizzzz; Barbary Coast Bunny;* 1957—*Deduce You Say; There They Go-Go-Go!; Scrambled Aches; Go Fly a Kit; Steal Wool; Zoom and Bored; To Hare Is Human; Ali Baba Bunny; Boyhood Daze; What's Opera, Doc?; Touché and Go;* (as director and scriptwriter): 1958—*Hare-Way to the Stars; Hook, Line, and Stinker; Robin Hood Daffy; Whoa, Begone!; To Itch His Own;* 1959—*Baton Bunny; Hot Rod and Reel; Cat Feud; Hip Hip—Hurry!; Really Scent;* 1960—*Fastest with the Mostest; Who Scent You?; Rabbit's Feat; Wild About Hurry;* 1961—*High Note; Hopalong Casualty; The Abominable Snow Rabbit; A Scent of the Matterhorn; Lickety Splat; Zip 'n Snort; The Mouse on 57th Street; Compressed Hare;* 1962—*Louvre Come Back to Me; Beep Prepared; A Sheep in the Deep; Nelly's Folly; Zoom at the Top; Gay Purr-ee* (feature—story only); 1963—*Martian Thru Georgia; Now Hear This; Hare-Breadth Hurry; I Was a Teenage Thumb; Woolen Under Where;* (as director at MGM—all Tom and Jerry cartoons unless asterisked): 1963—*Penthouse Mouse;* 1964—*The Cat Above and the Mouse Below; Is There a Doctor in the Mouse; Much Ado About Mousing; Snowbody Loves Me; Unshrinkable Jerry Mouse;* 1965—*The Dot and the Line*; Ah*

Sweet Mouse-Story of Life; Bad Day at Cat Rock; Brothers Carry Mouse Off; Haunted Mouse; I'm Just Wild About Jerry; Of Feline Bondage; Year of the Mouse; Cat's Me-Ouch; 1966—*Duel Personality; Jerry Jerry Quite Contrary; Love Me, Love My Mouse* (with Ben Washam); 1967—*The Bear That Wasn't*; Cat and Duplicat;* (television specials): 1970—*How the Grinch Stole Christmas;* 1971—*The Phantom Toll Booth* (feature film); *Horton Hears a Who; The Pogo Special Birthday Special; A Christmas Carol* (exec. pr only); *The Cricket in Times Square; A Very Merry Cricket;* 1974—*Yankee Doodle Cricket;* 1975-*Riki-Tiki-Tavy.*

Publications:

By JONES:

Articles—"The Road Runner and Other Characters", interview by R. Benayoun in *Cinema Journal* (Evanston), spring 1969; interview by M. Barrier in *Funnyworld* (New York), spring 1971; interview by J. Colombat in *Image et son* (Paris), January 1972; "Animation Is a Gift Word" in *AFI Report* (Washington, D.C.), summer 1974; interview by G. Ford and R. Thompson in *Film Comment* (New York), January/February 1975; "L'Animation, un art nu" in *Positif* (Paris), February 1975; "Cel Washer: 'Kidvid' Is a Dirty Word" in *Take One* (Montreal), no.4, 1976; "Frix Freleng and How I Grew" in *Millimeter* (New York), November 1976; interview by J. Rubin in *Classic Film Collector* (Muscatine, Iowa), summer 1976; "Chuck Jones Interviewed" by Joe Adamson in *The American Animated Cartoon* edited by Gerald and Danny Peary, New York 1980.

On JONES:

Book—*Of Mice and Magic* by Leonard Maltin, New York 1980; articles—"The Hollywood Cartoon", interview by J. Canemaker in *Filmmakers Newsletter* (Ward Hill, Mass.), April 1974; "Looney Tunes and Merrie Melodies" by M.S. Cohen in *Velvet Light Trap* (Madison), autumn 1975; "Duck Amuck" by R. Thompson in *Film Comment* (New York), January/February 1975; "Master Animator Chuck Jones: The Movement's the Thing" by A. Ward in *The New York Times*, 7 October 1979; "Meep Meep!" and "Pronoun Trouble by Richard Thompson in *The American Animated Cartoon* edited by Gerald and Danny Peary, New York 1980.

*   *   *

During a career of over 50 years (and still going strong) in cartoon animation, Chuck Jones has created over 250 animated films. His most famous work was done at the Warner Brothers' Studios where from 1938 to 1962 he directed such "stars" as Bugs Bunny, Daffy Duck, and Porky Pig. Although many different animators worked with these characters, Jones developed his own particular style of animation that set his cartoons apart from the others.

Part of Jones' animation style has to do with the development of his characters which have very strong personalities. For example, Pepe LePew is an ever confident Casinova. No matter how many times he is pushed off the road to romance, he remains undaunted in his attempts to pursue his heart's "true love." Daffy Duck on the other hand is a self-centered egotist. He is always looking out for Number One and he must, above all, maintain his dignity. By using such strong characters in his films, Jones creates humor not out of what is happening to the character, but rather how the character reacts to what is happening. For example, the Roadrunner series (one of Jones's own creations) relies on character reaction throughout the story. Whenever the Coyote finds that he is about to go over the edge of a cliff, he remains in mid-air, looks down, realizes his predicament, gulps, looks to the audience for sympathy, and *then* falls. The humor is not in the act of his falling, but in the way the Coyote reacts to his situation.

Another characteristic found in many of Jones's cartoons is his distinctive use of the medium. It is not uncommon to find references to the techniques of animation in his films. The most manifest example of Jones's self-reflexivity in a cartoon is *Duck Amuck*. In this film Daffy Duck is plagued by the animator who, in a series of gags, erases Daffy, gives him the wrong voice, rolls the picture, collapses the frame line, and finally blows up Daffy by drawing in a bomb. Another of Jones's cartoons that is filled with inside jokes is *What's Opera, Doc?* In this cartoon (which can be viewed as a parody of Disney's *Fantasia*) Bugs Bunny and Elmer Fudd continue to play their roles of the hunter and hunted, but as "actors" within the very formal structure of a Wagnerian opera. It is the only cartoon in which Bugs "dies", but as he says as the camera irises out, "What did you expect in an opera, a *happy* ending?"

Another distinctive trait that can be found in Chuck Jones's cartoons is his sense of comic timing. Whereas some cartoon directors pile gag upon gag at a frantic pace, Jones often uses pauses within his gags. For example, whenever the Coyote would fall off a cliff, the overhead point of view would show him getting smaller and smaller until he was invisible, and a few frames later a puff a smoke could be seen where he crashed. Jones knew exactly how many frames it would take to create the right amount of tension before the Coyote actually hit the ground. It was a piece of timing he had to teach all of his animators on the Roadrunner series.

With the closing of the studio cartoon departments, Jones moved his animation talents into television and feature-length production. His newer work (such as *How the Grinch Stole Christmas*) has proven to be very popular with audiences and his older work shows no sign of age. The stories and characters which Chuck Jones has created in his animated films have that special kind of universal appeal that will make them timeless for generations to come.

—Linda J. Obalil

JUTRA, CLAUDE. Canadian. Born in Montreal, 11 March 1930. Doctor of Medicine, University of Montreal, 1952. Career: 1947—makes first films in collaboration with Michel Brault; 1953—author of 1st original teleplay produced in Canada, *L'École de la peur*; 1954-66—works intermittently with National Film Board; 1957—collaborates with Norman McLaren on *A Chairy Tale*; early 1960s—works with Jean Rouch in Niger Republic; 1961—founds Films Cassiopée to produce *A tout prendre*. Recipient: First Prize for experimental film, Venice Festival, co-recipient with Norman McLaren, for *A Chairy Tale*, 1958; Best Film, Canadian Film Awards, for *A tout prendre*, 1964.

Films (as director): 1947—*Le Dément du Lac Jean Jeune* (co-d); 1949—*Mouvement perpétuel* (co-d, +sc); 1956—*Pierrot des bois* (+sc, ed, ro); *Les Jeunesses musicales* (+sc); 1957—*A Chairy Tale* (*Il était une chaise*) (co-d with Norman McLaren, +ro); 1958—

Les Mains nettes; 1959—*Anna la bonne*; *Félix Leclerc, troubadour*; *Fred Barry, comédien* (+sc); 1961—*Le Niger—jeune république* (+ed); *La Lutte (Wrestling)* (co-d, +co-ph, co-ed, co-sound); 1962—*Québec-USA (L'Invasion pacifique, Visit to a Foreign Country)* (co-d, +ed); 1963—*Les Enfants du silence* (co-d, +ed, commentary); *Petit Discours de la méthode* (co-d, +ed, commentary); *A tout prendre (Take It All)* (+sc, ed, ro); 1966—*Comment savoir (Knowing to Learn)*; *Rouli-Roulant (The Devil's Toy)* (+ph, ed, commentary); 1969—*Wow* (+sc, co-ed); *Au coeur de la ville*; 1970—*Marie-Christine*; 1971—*Mon Oncle Antoine* (+ro as Fernand); 1972—*Kamouraska*; 1975—*Pour le meilleur et pour le pire*; 1976—*Pennies for My Chocolate* (for TV); *Dream Speaker* (for TV); 1978—*Surfacing*; 1980—*By Design*. Role: 1978—*Two Solitudes*.

Publications:

By JUTRA:

Articles—"Michel Brault et Claude Jutra racontent Jean Rouch" in *Objectif* (Paris), December 1960; "En courant derrière Rouch", in 3 parts, in *Cahiers du cinéma* (Paris), November 1960, and January and February 1961; "Entretien avec 2 cinéastes" in *Ecran* (Paris), May 1961; interview in *Cahiers du cinéma* (Paris), April/May 1968; "Kamouraska: Claude Jutra", interview by K. Cox and Baltazar in *Cinema Canada* (Montreal), April/May 1973; "Claude Jutra: Une Exploration dans une morale pathologique", interview by G. Langlois in *Cinéma* (Paris), January 1973; "Un espèce de joie dans la création", interview by J.-P. Tadros in *Cinéma Québec* (Montreal), March/April 1973; "A pied? à joual?...ou en ski-doo?" in *Cinéma Québec* (Montreal), v.2, no.9, 1973; "Jutra in 2 Takes", interview by G.C. Koller and P. Wronski in *Cinema Canada* (Montreal), November 1975; "Jutra on the Tube", interview by P. Kelman in *Cinema Canada* (Montreal), March 1979.

On JUTRA:

Books—*Le Cinéma canadien* by Gilles Marsolais, Paris 1968; *Cinéastes du Québec 4: Claude Jutra* by Jean Chabot, Montreal 1970; *A Handbook of Canadian Film* by Eleanor Beattie, Toronto 1973; articles—"Petit éloge des grandeurs et des misères de la colonie française de l'office national du film" by Jean-Pierre Lefebvre in *Objectif* (Paris), August/September 1964; *Jeune Cinéma canadien* by René Predal in *Premier Plan* (Lyon), no.45, 1967; "Dr. Claude Jutra: Filmmaker" by Ronald Blumer in *McGill Medical Journal* (Montreal), December 1969.

KACHYNA, KAREL. Czechoslovakian. Born at Vyškov, 1 May 1924. Educated at Film Academy (FAMU), Prague. Career: 1949—begins association with co-director Vojtěch Jasný; 1955—last film with Jasný; later 1950s—begins association with writer Jan Procházka; 1970—last film with Procházka. Recipient: Czech Film Critics' Award for *Smugglers of Death*, 1959.

Films (as co-director and co-scriptwriter with Vojtěch Jasný): 1950—*Není stále zamrečeno (The Clouds Will Roll Away)* (+ph); *Věděli si rady (They Know What to Do)* (+ph); 1951—*Za život radostný (For a Joyful Life)*; 1952—*Neobyčejná léta (Extraordinary Years, Unusual Years)*; *Věda jde s lidem (Science Goes with People)* (ph only); 1953—*Lidé jednoho srdce (People of One Heart)* (co-d, +co-ph); 1954—*Stará čínská opera (Old Chinese Opera)* (+ph); *Z čínskěo zápisníku (From a Chinese*

Notebook) (+ph); 1955—*Dnes večer všechno skončí (Everything Ends Tonight)*; (as director and scriptwriter): 1956—*Ztracená stopa (The Lost Track, The Lost Trail)*; *Křivé zrcadlo (Crooked Mirror)*; 1957—*Mistrovství světa leteckých modelářu (World Championship of Air Models)*; *Pokušení (Temptation)* (+ph); 1958—*Tenkrát o vánocích (That Christmas)* (+co-sc); *Ctyřikrát o Bulharsku (4 Times About Bulgaria)*; *Městomä svou tvář (The City Has Your Face)*; 1959—*Král Sumavy (The King of the Sumava, Smugglers of Death)* (+co-sc); 1960—*Práče (The Slinger)* (co-sc); (as director and co-scriptwriter with Jan Procjázka): 1961—*Pouta (The Country Doctor, Fetters)*; *Trápení (Stress of Youth, The Proud Stallion, Piebald, Lenka and Prim)*; 1962—*Závrat (Vertigo)*; 1963—*Naděje (Hope)*; 1964—*Vysoká zed (The High Wall)*; 1965—*Ať žije republika (Long Live the Republic)*; 1966—*Kočár do Vídně (Carriage to Vienna)*; 1967—*Noc nevěsty (Night of the Bride)*; 1968—*Vánoce s Alžbětou (Christmas with Elizabeth)*; 1969—*Směšný pán (Funny Old Man)*; (as director): 1970—*Už zase skáču přes kaluže (Jumping the Puddles Again)* (+co-sc); *Lásky Alexandra Dumase St. (The Loves of Alexander Dumas Sr.)* (for TV); 1971—*Tajemství velkého vypravěče (Secret of the Big Narrator)* (+co-sc—for TV); 1972—*Vlak do stanice nebe (Train to Heaven)* (+co-sc); *Láska (Love)* (+co-sc); *Horká zima (Hot Winter)* (+co-sc); 1974—*Pavlínka*; *Robinsonka (Robinson Girl)*; 1975—*Skaredá dědina (The Ugly Village)*; *Smrt mouchy (The Death of the Fly)*; 1976—*Malá mořská víla (The Little Mermaid, The Little Sea Nymph)* (+co-sc); 1977—*Setkání v červenci (Meeting in July)*; 1978—*Cekání na déšť (Waiting for the Rain)*; 1979—*Láska mezi kapkami deště (Love Between the Raindrops)*; 1980—*Cukrová bouda (Sugar Cottage, The Little Sugar House)*; 1981—*Vizita (Doctor's Round)*; 1982—*Fandy ó Fandy*; 1983—*Sestřičky (Nursing Sisters)*.

Publications:

By KACHYNA:

Articles—"Zastavení se zasloužilým uměleem Karlem Kachyňou", interview, in *Kino*, 20 July 1974; "Malá mořská víla", interview by E. Hepnerová in *Film a doba* (Prague), February 1976.

On KACHYNA:

Books—*Modern Czechoslovak Film 1945-1965* by Jaroslav Boček, Prague 1965; *Filmové profily* by Sárka and Luboš Bartoškovi, Prague 1966; *Closely Watched Films* by Antonín Liehm, White Plains, New York 1974; *CSF—Czechosklovak Cinema*, Czechoslovak Film Institute, Prague 1982.

*   *   *

Karel Kachyňa is an artist with a broad range of ideas which constitute the starting point for his thinking in images. Despite their formal variety, his works bear an individual creative stamp characterized by a play of poetic images precisely tailored to the dramatic structure of the story. Like any original artist who continuously seeks new paths of self-expression, Kachyňa has brief periods which seem to be at odds with the rest of his work. These are the exceptions, the experiments, the preparations for great artistic work to come.

At first it seemed that Kachyňa's main calling would be making documentary films. He has gone beyond these; they served as a point of departure for his dramatic films. His first creative period is characterized in innovatively-conceived documentaries which not only captured the facts but also expressed the view of the filmmaker. His attempts to combine elements of fantasy, story, and style led him to the dramatic film, where he concentrated on films of wartime adventure and suspense. In so doing he did not forget what he had learned in making documentaries: to capture reality and transform it into a new artisitc image in a carefully conceived story. The culmination of this period is *Král Sumavy (The King of the Sumava)*.

Gradually other elements asserted themselves in his films: detailed psychological characterization and a precise portrayal of relationships against the backdrop of a given historical situation. Since he was never an independent writer of his own films, he was able to detach himself from the given material and consider it from a unique viewpoint. He was most interested in the contradiction-fraught relationships of people taking their first steps into adulthood, or the world of children on the verge of some kind of awakening, a discovery of life in the brief interval in which reality stimulates the world of thoughts, dreams, and memories and becomes itself only a framework for a profound catharsis of feelings: *Trápení (Worries), Závral (Vertigo), Užz zase skáču přs kaluže (I'm Jumping Puddles Again), Smrt mouchy (Death of a Fly)*, and others. His films are first and foremost images interspersed with brief dialogue, where small details, objects, and nature come to life. He directs his actors, be they amateurs or professionals, in a way that enables them to live the roles they play, to create the truth of life, to shape and work their own feelings and views in a made-up story. A tendency to create intimate dramas, however, leads to formal refinement in which an objective view of reality is often lost.

Karel Kachyňa is served by several literary works which may be sensitively adapted for the screen. But the foundation of his work remains the cinematic poem of feelings (for example, *Pavlínka, Robinsonka, Skaredá dědina (The Ugly Village)*, or the made-for-television film *Zlatiúhoři (The Golden Eels)*. "I like drawing-room stories set in an atmosphere of feelings, where the leading role is played by image, music, and often by what cannot even be expressed, that which is a part of our lives but is not concrete and cannot even be described. Apprehensions, hopes, dreams, someone's touch...I would always like to have these things in my films. I think they are an essential part of the truth of life. And this truth is what film is mainly about. A film will never be a work of art unless it mirrors that truth, however subtly it may strive in other ways to express the most sublime thought," said Karel Kachyňa in one conversation. And it is this credo that he strives strictly to uphold in his own films. After a lengthy period in which he focused on the world of children at the threshold of adulthood, he turns in his latest works to an adult milieu. His films show no lack of humor or the outlook that will enable the filmmaker to delve without hesitation into the depths of human nature.

—G. Merhaut

KADÁR, JÁN. Czech. Born in Budapest, 1 April 1918. Career: 1938—gives up law studies to study photography at Bratislava school; early 1940s—prisoner in Nazi labor camp; after war—producer and director, Bratislava Studio of Short Films; 1947—moves to Prague, begins as scriptwriter and assistant director at Barrandov Studio; meets Elmar Klos; 1952—begins directing and scriptwriting collaboration with Klos (born in Brno, 26 January 1910); 1968—with Klos begins work on Czech-American coproduction *Adrift*, shooting interrupted due to Soviet invasion of Czechoslovakia; 1969—moves to U.S.; 1970—directs 1st

U.S. film, *The Angel Levine.* Died in Los Angeles, 1 June 1979. Recipient: Best Foreign-Language Film Academy Award for *The Shop on Main Street,* 1965; National Artist of Czechoslovakia, 1969.

Films (as director): 1945—*Life is Rising from the Ruins*; 1947—*Nevité o bytě? (Looking for a Flat)* (sc only); 1950—*Katka (Kitty, Katya)* (+co-sc); (as co-director and co-scriptwriter with Elmar Klos): 1952—*Unos (Kidnap)*; 1954—*Hudba z Marsu (Music from Mars)*; 1957—*Tam na konečné (The House at the Terminus)* (co-d only); 1958—*Tři přání (3 Wishes)*; 1963—*Smrt si říká Engelchen (Death Is Called Engelchen)*; 1964—*Obžalovaný (The Accused, The Defendant)*; 1965—*Obchod na korze (The Shop on Main Street, Shop in the High Street)*; (as director): 1970—*The Angel Levine*; 1971—*Touha zvaná Anada (Adrift, Something Is Drifting on the Water)* (completed 1969, co-d with Klos); 1975—*Lies My Father Told Me*; 1978—*Freedom Road.*

Publications:

By KADÁR:

Articles—"Elmar Klos and Jan Kadar", interview by Jules Cohen, in *Film Culture* (New York), fall/winter 1967; "En för alla...", interview by Antonin Liehm in *Chaplin* (Stockholm), v.14, no.1, 1972; "Interview with Jan Kadar" by Robert Haller in *Film Heritage* (Dayton, Ohio), spring 1973; interview by L. Vigo in *Image et son* (Paris), June 1973.

On KADÁR:

Books—*Modern Czechoslovak Film 1945-1965* by Jaroslav Boček, Prague 1965; *Closely Watched Films* by Antonín Liehm, White Plains, New York 1974; articles—"Director" in the *New Yorker*, 12 February 1966; "Czechs in Exile" in *Newsweek* (New York), 27 July 1970; "The Czech Who Bounced Back" in *Films Illustrated* (London), April 1972; obituaries by G. Gervais in *Jeune cinéma* (Paris), July/August 1979, and by H. Moret in *Ecran* (Paris), 15 July 1979; obituary in *The New York Times*, 4 June 1979.

KAPOOR, RAJ. Indian. Born in Peshawar (now in Pakistan), 14 December 1924. Educated in Calcutta and Bombay. Married Krishna (Kapoor); 3 sons, 2 daughters. Career: late 1930s—enters film industry as clapper boy; early 1940s—assistant on Bombay Talkies; Production Manager, Art Director and actor for Prithvi Theatres; 1947—first leading role in *Neel Kamal*; 1948—produces 1st film as director, *Aag*. Recipient: Filmfare Award for Best Director, for *My Name Is Joker*, 1970. Address: R.K. Studios, Chembur, Bombay-400071, India.

Films (as producer and director): 1948—*Aag (Fire)* (+ro); 1949—*Barsaat* (d only, +ro); 1951—*Awara (The Vagabond)* (d only, +ro); 1953—*Aah* (pr only, +ro); 1954—*Boot Polish* (pr only); 1955—*Shri 420 (Mister 420)* (d only, +ro); 1956—*Jagte Raho* (pr only, +ro); 1957—*Ab Dilli Dur Nahin* (pr only); 1960—*Jis Desh Me Ganga Behti Hai (Where the Ganges Flows)* (pr only, +ro); 1964—*Sangam* (+ro); 1970—*Mera Naam Joker (My Name Is Joker)* (+ro); 1972—*Kal, Aaj Aur Kal* (pr only, +ro); 1974—*Bobby*; 1975—*Dhadram Karam* (pr only); 1978—*Satyam Shivam Sundaram*; 1981—*Biwi O Biwi* (pr only); 1982—*Prem Rog.*

Roles: 1935—*Inquilab*; 1943—*Hamari Baat*; *Gowri*; 1946—*Valmiki*; 1947—*Neel Kamal*; *Chithod Vijay*; *Jail Yaatra*; *Dil Ki Raani*; 1948—*Gopinath*; 1949—*Andaz*; *Parivartan*; *Sunehere Din*; 1950—*Banwara*; *Banware Nayan*; *Dastaan*; *Jaan Pehchan*; *Pyaar*; *Sargam*; 1952—*Ambar*; *Anhonee*; *Aashiyana*; *Bewafa*; 1953—*Dhoon*; *Paapi*; 1956—*Chori Chori*; 1958—*Sharada*; *Parvarish*; *Phir Subah Hogi*; 1959—*Anadi*; *Char Dil Char Rahen*; *Do Ustad*; *Kanhaiya*; *Main Nashe Me Hoon*; 1960—*Chaliya*; *Shriman Satyavadi*; 1961—*Nazraana*; 1962—*Aashik*; 1963—*Dil Hi To Hai*; *Ek Dil Sou Afsane*; 1964—*Dulha Dulhan*; 1966—*Teesri Kasam*; 1967—*Around the World*; *Diwana*; 1968—*Sapnon Ka Saudgar*; 1975—*Do Jasoos*; 1976—*Khaan Dost*; 1977—*Chandi Sona*; 1981—*Abdullah*; 1982—*Gopichand Jasoos.*

Publications:

By KAPOOR:

Article—"We Sell Them Dreams", interview by K. Singh in *The New York Times*, 31 October 1976.

*   *   *

Raj Kapoor is the best-known screen personality in India. He has acted major roles in over 50 films, produced more than a dozen films, and, during the course of a 35-year career directed six of the most popular films of the Hindi cinema. (*Awara, Shri 420, Sangam, Mera Nam Joker, Bobby,* and *Satyam Shivam Sundaram*). The popularity of Raj Kapoor's work derives from a paradoxical achievement: he intensifies in his films both the lavishness and the social consciousness of the Hindi cinema. His films are characterized by elaborate sets, evocative music, new stars, dramatic confrontations and narrow escapes from heartbreak. At the same time he introduces into his films the themes of poverty and injustice, and the plight of individuals insisting on their own way against the massive force of social conventions. Indian audiences respond enthusiastically to Raj Kapoor's mixture of entertainment and concern; it is clear that his films articulate at some level the longings of an entire people.

Raj Kapoor's first film *Aag* is restrained by smallness of scale; the set is modest and the fiery character of the emotional triangle in the story is rendered chiefly through high-contrast lighting. But his third and fourth films (*Awara* and *Shri 420*) disclose a fully operatic style. In *Awara*, the key court scene is played in a deep, amply lit hall; and in both *Awara* and *Shri 420*, the houses of the rich are magnificently spacious, fitted with winding stairs, high ceilings and tall, curtained windows. For music, Raj Kapoor employs the lyricist Shailendra and the composers Shankar-Jaikishen, who specialized in brightening up traditional melodies; a number of their songs for Raj Kapoor (*Awara Hun, Mera Joota Hai Japani*) are among the songs which run through the heads of most people in India. Raj Kapoor also delights in soaring camera movements, as over the courtroom in *Awara* and under the circus tent in *Mera Nam Joker*. The speed and freedom of the camera contributes to the audience's sense of dynamic onward progress in Raj Kapoor's films.

Raj Kapoor's films deal with important cultural experiences: *Shri 420* is concerned with the ruthlessness which confronts new migrants to the city; *Awara* with the malign influence of slum environments; *Sangam, Bobby* and *Satyam Shivam Sundaram* with tensions between spontaneous affection and the social protocols for intimacy; and *Mera Nam Joker* presents the loneliness of a circus clown as an archetype for people who have been uprooted. Both plot and music invite viewers to identify with the experience of unfortunate protagonists. Meanwhile the mise-en-scène directs the attention of viewers to the furnishings of rich houses (*Shri 420* and *Awara*), to the mountain spectacle of various Himalayan resorts (*Bobby*), to a spacious temple court-yard and a daringly costumed dancer (*Satyam Shivam Sunda-ram*) and to entire acts of the Soviet State Circus (*Mera Nam Joker*).

Since the time of Raj Kapoor's first films, filmmaking in India has moved towards greater generic variety and coherence. From the perspective of the new political films, Raj Kapoor's produc-tions seem complacent; from the perspective of the new realist films, his work seems gaudy. Nonetheless, his work is certain to be remembered for its spectacular vitality.

—Satti Khanna

KAWALEROWICZ, JERZY. Polish. Born in Gwózda (Gwozdziec), now part of Soviet Ukraine, 19 January 1922. Educated at Film Institute, Cracow. Married actress Lucyna Winnicka. Career: 1946-51—assistant director and scriptwriter; 1952—co-directs 1st feature with Kazimierz Sumerski; 1955—becomes head of Studia Kadr. Recipient: Premio Evrotecnica, Venice Festival, for *Night Train*, 1959; Silver Palm, Cannes Festival, for *Mother Joan of the Angels*, 1961; Silver Bear, Berlin Festival, for *The President's Death*, 1977.

Films (as assistant director): 1946—*Jutro premiera (Morning Premiere)*; 1947—*Zakazane piosenki (Forbidden Songs)*; *Ostatni etap (The Last Stage)*; 1948—*Stalowe serca (Steel Hearts)*; *Czarci źleb (The Devil's Pass)*; (as director): 1952—*Gromada (The Village Mill, Commune, Rural Community)* (co-d); 1954—*Celuloza (A Night of Remembrance, Cellulose)* (+co-sc); *Pod gwiazda frygijska (Under the Phrygian Star)* in 2 parts (+co-sc); 1956—*Cién (The Shadow)*; 1957—*Prawdziwy koniec wielkiej wojny (The Real End of the Great War)* (+co-sc); 1959—*Pociag (Night Train, Baltic Express)* (+co-sc); 1961—*Matka Joanna od Aniolów (Mother Joan of the Angels, Joan of the Angels?)* (+co-sc); 1965—*Faraon (The Pharaoh)* (+co-sc); 1968—*Gra (The Game)* (+sc); 1970—*Maddalena*; 1977—*Śmierć Prezydenta (The President's Death)* (+co-sc); 1979—*Spotkanie na Atlan-tyku (Chance Meeting on the Ocean, Meeting on the Atlantic)* (+co-sc); 1982—*Austeria* (+co-sc).

Publications:

By KAWALEROWICZ:

Articles—"Primer sovetskogo kino" in *Iskusstvo Kino* (Mos-cow), no.5, 1976; "Historia i forma", interview by K. Zórawski in *Kino* (Warsaw), September 1977; "'Spotkanie na Atlantyku' czyli o filmach nie zrealizowanych", interview by M. Dipont in *Kino* (Warsaw), October 1980; interview by K. Sčerbakov in *Iskusstvo Kino* (Moscow), August 1980; interview in *Filmowy serwis prasowy* (Warsaw), no.2, 1983.

On KAWALEROWICZ:

Books—*20 Years of Polish Cinema* by Stanislaw Grzelecki,

Warsaw 1969; *Film—sztuka w ewolucji* by Boleslaw Michalek, Warsaw 1975; *Contemporary Polish Film* by Stanislaw Kus-zewski, Warsaw 1978; articles—"Jerzy Kawalerowicz czyli miłść do geometrii" by M. Kornatowska in *Kino* (Warsaw), February 1978; "Ḱawalerowicz twórczość kapryśna" by Urszula Bielous in *Żicie Literackie* (Cracow), April 1982.

*   *   *

It is no simple matter to give a precise characterization of this filmmaker. His work is not uniform, but full of twists and turns, strange shifts, and new experiments. The films of Jerzy Kawale-rowicz are uneven; it is as though the filmmaker, after momen-tary triumphs and outstanding artistic achievemnet, would lapse into a crisis which prepared him for yet another masterpiece. His films are long in the making. Between individual works come the lengthy pauses in which the director carefully absorbs raw mate-rial from a wide range of disciplines, in order to personally work it into film form. Only in a very few directors' works do we find such range, from the realistic film to the profound psychological drama, from the historical epic to the political drama.

Jerzy Kawalerowicz has always gone his own way. And it has not been an easy path, especially when we realize that he has never turned back, never given a particular theme further devel-opment. Although he begun at the same time as Wajda and Munk, he never created a work that belonged to the "Polish school of film." After his first independent film, *Celuloza (Cellu-lose)*, which was both a realistic portrayal and a literary adapta-tion, he never came back to this subject or form. In his next creative period he quickly turned out several films which are unusual analytic studies of human relationships, probings into human psychology with a profound motif of loneliness. These are earnest pyschological portraits of lonely people marked by war (The Real End of the Great War), isolated en route on an overnight express *Night*, or within the walls of a cloister (*Mother Joanna of the Angels*). Kawalerowicz achieves creative mastery with these films. In fact, they initiated an entire trend in intimate dramas, which became fashionable only several years later. Thanks to the filmmaker's skill in directing, the last film in this series was a masterpiece which overcame elements of melodrama.

The historical epic *Faraon (Pharaoh)*, adapted from the cele-brated novel by Boleslaw Prus, is once again unusual in composi-tion. It is a film on a grand scale, a monumental fresco, but at the same time an unusual psychological film with political and philo-sophical elements. In this drama of a struggle for power in ancient Egypt, the director finds room for an account of human qualities, motives, and feelings.

Emotions are the leitmotif of Kawalerowicz'a work. After the grand epic *Faraon* the filmmaker attempts a return to the inti-mate psychologically-oriented film. A crisis sets in. His subse-quent work fails to attain the level of his earlier pieces. There is a kind of break, a respite which will bear fruit in the later purely political film and documentary drama *Death of a President*. For some time the method employed for this film, which Kawalero-wicz produced as a chronicle of an actual event—the assassina-tion of President Gabriel Natutowicz in the 1930s—served as the director's credo. "When we studied the documents and the tes-timony and compiled the chronology of events, we ascertained that the drama of history, the drama of real events is far more persuasive than what we ourselves could invent." Captivated by the facts, Kawakerowicz relates not only a real-life event but also an ordinary human story that is timeless. After this film the critics expected the director to continue in the same genre in which he had attained even greater mastery. But things turned out differently. Once more, Jerzy Kawalerowicz is experiment-ing with new genres and forms. But outstanding literary works and actual political or historical events, shaped into suggestive individual dramas, remain the foundation of his creative work.

—G. Merhaut

KAZAN, ELIA. American. Born in Constantinople (now Istanbul), Turkey, 7 September 1909. Educated at Mayfair School; New Rochelle High School, New York; Williams College, Massachusetts, B.A. *cum laude* 1930; studied at Yale drama school, 1930-32. Married Molly Day Thatcher, 1932 (died 1963); children: Judy, Nick, Katherine and Chris; married actress Barbara Loden, 1967. Career: 1913—father establishes carpet business in New York, brings over family from Turkey; 1933—Elia Kazan moves to New York, joins Group Theatre as apprentice; works as actor, property manager, then director; 1933-34—appears in *Men in White* and *Gold Eagle Guy*, directed by Lee Strasberg; 1934—co-writes and directs *Dimitroff* for League of Workers Theatres; 1935—appears in Odets's *Waiting for Lefty*; 1935-41—continues stage acting, productions include Odets's *Till the Day I Die* and *Paradise Lost* (1935), *Golden Boy* (1937), and *Night Music* (1940), Irwin Shaw's *The Gentle People* (1939), and Benno Schneider's production of *Liliom*; 1935 to mid-'60s—directs many now-famous premiere productions of plays such as Wilder's *The Skin of Our Teeth* (1942), Miller's *All My Sons* and Williams's *A Streetcar Named Desire* (both 1947), and Miller's *Death of a Salesman* (1949); continues to be principal director for premieres of work by Tennessee Williams and Arthur Miller through early 1960s; 1940-41—acts in 1st feature films, *City for Conquest* and *Blues in the Night*, both directed by Anatole Litvak; 1948—co-founds Actors' Studio with Cheryl Crawford; 1952—appears voluntarily before House Un-American Activities Committee (HUAC),; admits membership in Communist Party from 1934 to 1936 and gives names of former friends also active in the Party at that time, including Arthur Miller; 1954—production of *On the Waterfront*, seen by some as justification for cooperation with HUAC; 1962—quits Actors' Studio to direct newly-formed Lincoln Center Repertory Company (resigned 1964); begins successful career as novelist with *America, America*. Recipient: New York Drama Critics' Award for directing *The Skin of Our Teeth*, 1942; New York Drama Critics' Award for directing *All My Sons*, 1947; Donaldson Award for directing *All My Sons*, 1947; Antoinette Perry Award for directing *All My Sons*, 1947; Best Director Academy Award for *Gentleman's Agreement*, 1947; Best Direction, New York Film Critics, for *Gentleman's Agreement*, 1947; Antoinette Perry Award for directing *A Streetcar Named Desire*, 1949; New York Drama Critics' Award for directing *Death of a Salesman*, 1949; Donaldson Award for directing *Death of a Salesman*, 1949; Antoinette Perry Award for directing *Death of a Salesman*, 1949; International Prize, Venice Festival, for *Panic in the Streets*, 1950; Special Jury Prize, Venice Festival, for *A Streetcar Named Desire*, 1951; Donaldson Award for directing *Tea and Sympathy*, 1953; Best Director Academy Award for *On the Waterfront*, 1954; Most Outstanding Directorial Achievement, Directors Guild of America, for *On the Waterfront*, 1954; Donaldson Award for directing *Cat on a Hot Tin Roof*, 1955; honorary degree, University of Leyden, 1978; Honorary D.Litt., Wesleyan University; Honorary D.Litt., Carnegie Institute of Technology; Honorary D.Litt., Williams College. Address: 22 West 68th St., New York, NY 10023.

Films (as director): 1937—*The People of the Cumberlands* (+sc—short); 1941—*It's Up to You*; 1945—*A Tree Grows in Brooklyn*; 1947—*The Sea of Grass*; 1947—*Boomerang*; 1947—*Gentleman's Agreement*; 1949—*Pinky*; 1950—*Panic in the Streets*; 1952—*A Streetcar Named Desire*; *Viva Zapata!*; *Man on a Tightrope*; 1954—*On the Waterfront*; (as producer and director): 1955—*East of Eden*; 1956—*Baby Doll* (+co-sc); 1957—*A Face in the Crowd*; 1960—*Wild River*; 1961—*Splendor in the Grass*; 1964—*America, America* (+sc); 1969—*The Arrangement* (+sc); (as director): 1972—*The Visitors*; 1976—*The Last Tycoon*.

Roles: 1934—*Pie in the Sky* (Steiner) (short); 1940—*Googie*, a gangster, in *City for Conquest* (Litvak); 1941—a clarinetist in *Blues in the Night* (Litvak).

Publications:

By KAZAN:

Books—*America America*, New York 1961; *The Arrangement*, New York 1967; *The Assassins*, New York 1972; *The Understudy*, New York 1974; *Acts of Love*, New York 1978; *Anatolian*, New York 1982; articles—"A Quiz for Kazan", interview, in *Theatre Arts* (New York), November 1956; "The Writer and Motion Pictures" in *Sight and Sound* (London), summer 1957; interview by Jean Domarchi and André Labarthe in *Cahiers du cinéma* (Paris), April 1962; article in *Cahiers du cinéma* (Paris), December 1963/January 1964; "Préface à un entretien avec Elia Kazan" and "Un Phénomène de la nature", interview, by Michel Delahaye in *Cahiers du cinéma* (Paris), October and November 1966; translation in *Cahiers du Cinema in English* (New York), no.9, 1967; interview by Michel Ciment and Roger Tailleur in *Positif* (Paris), October 1966; "Kazan vieux comme le monde", interview by Claudine Tavernier, in *Cinéma 70* (Paris), February 1970; interview by S. Byron and M. Rubin in *Movie* (London), winter 1971/72; interview by Michel Ciment in *Positif* (Paris), May 1972; "Elia Kazan et les multiples visages de l'Amériqie", interview by A. Leroux in *Cinéma Québec* (Montreal), December/January 1972/73; interview by G. O'Brien in *Inter/View* (New York), March 1972; "Visiting Kazan", interview by C. Silver and J. Zukor in *Film Comment* (New York), summer 1972; "All You Need to Know, Kids" in *Action* (Los Angeles), January/February 1974; "The Movie We Made Is Realistic Hollywood", interview by A. Whitman in *The New York Times*, 14 November 1976; interview by Michel Ciment in *Positif* (Paris), April 1977; "A propos d'un artiste qui m'est inconnu mais que j'admire" in *Positif* (Paris), April 1977; "Notes sur Monroe Stahr" in *Positif* (Paris), April 1977; "Hollywood Under Water", interview by C. Silver and M. Corliss in *Film Comment* (New York), January/February 1977; "Visite à Yilmaz Güney ou vue d'une prison turque", with O. Adanir, in *Positif* (Paris), February 1980; "Elia Kazan à la croisée des chemins" by Michel Ciment in *Positif* (Paris), April 1981; special section of *Positif* (Paris), April 1981.

On KAZAN:

Books—*The Fervent Years: The Story of the Group Theatre and the Thirties* by Harold Clurman, New York 1946; *Elia Kazan*, revised edition, by Roger Tailleur, Paris 1971; *Kazan on Kazan* by Michel Ciment, London 1972; articles—"Elia Kazan: Actor and Director of Stage and Screen" by Virginia Stevens in *Theatre Arts* (New York), December 1947; article on Kazan and the Actors' Studio by Louis Marcorelles in *Cahiers du cinéma* (Paris), Christmas 1956; "Elia Kazan: The Genesis of a Style" by Eugene Archer in *Film Culture* (New York), v.2, no.2, 1956;

"Genesis of a Genius" by Eugene Archer in *Films and Filming* (London), December 1956; "The Theatre Goes to Hollywood" by Eugene Archer in *Films and Filming* (London), January 1957; "What Kazan Did for Me" by Patricia Neal in *Films and Filming* (London), October 1957; "Personality of the Month: Elia Kazan" and article by Warren Beatty in *Films and Filming* (London), April 1961; "Elia Kazan on 'The Young Agony'" by Robin Bean in *Films and Filming* (London), March 1962; "The Anatolian Smile" by Robin Bean and "The Life and Times of Elia Kazan" in *Films and Filming* (London), May 1964; "Les Incertitudes d'Elia Kazan" by Michel Ciment in *Positif* (Paris), no.64/5, 1964; "Elia Kazan's Great Expectations" by Thomas Morgan in *Self-Creation: 13 Impersonalities*, 1966; "Elia Kazan and the House Un-American Activities Committee" by Roger Tailleur in *Film Comment* (New York), fall 1966; "Elia Kazan: The Genesis of a Style" by Eugene Archer in *The Film*, edited by Andrew Sarris, New York 1968; "Elia Kazan" in *International Film Guide 1971*, London 1970; special Kazan issue of *Movie* (London), spring 1972; "Elia Kazan: a Structural Analysis" by Jim Kitses in *Cinema* (Beverly Hills), winter 1972/73; "Elia Kazan's America" by E. Changas in *Film Comment* (New York), summer 1972; "A l'est d'Eden", special issue of *Avant-Scène du cinéma* (Paris), November 1975; "The Politics of Power in *On the Waterfront*" by P. Biskind in *Film Quarterly* (Berkeley), autumn 1975; "3 Regards critiques" by L. Audibert and J.-C. Bonnet in *Cinématographe* (Paris), April 1977; "Pour en finir avec les mises en point (Elia Kazan et les folliculaires)" in *Positif* (Paris), April 1977; "Aus einem Gespräch zwischen Marguerite Duras und Elia Kazan" in *Filmkritik* (Munich), March 1981.

*   *   *

Elia Kazan's career has spanned more than three decades of enormous change in the American film industry. Often he has been a catalyst for these changes. He became a director in Hollywood at a time when, following World War Two, the studios were interested in producing the kind of serious mature, and socially conscious stories Kazan had been putting on the stage since his Group Theatre days. During the late forties and mid-fifties, under first the influence of Italian neorealism and then the pressure of American television, he was a leading force in developing the aesthetic possibilities of location shooting (*Boomerang, Panic in the Streets, On the Waterfront*) and CinemaScope (*East of Eden, Wild River*). At the height of his success, Kazan formed his own production unit and moved back east to become a pioneer in the new era of independent, "personal" filmmaking which emerged during the sixties and contributed to revolutionary upheavals within the old Hollywood system. As an archetypal *auteur*, he progressed from working on routine assignments to developing more personal themes, producing his own pictures, and ulimately directing his own scripts. At his peak during a decade and a half (1950-1965) of anxiety, gimmickery, and entropy in Hollywood, Kazan remained among the few American directors who continued to believe in the cinema as a medium for artistic expression and who brought forth films that consistently reflected his own creative vision.

Despite these achievements and his considerable influence on a younger generation of New York-based filmmakers including Sidney Lumet, John Cassavetes, Arthur Penn, Martin Scorsese, and even Woody Allen, Kazan's critical reputation in America currently rests at it lowest ebb. The turning point both for Kazan's own work and the critics' reception of it was almost certainly his decision to become a friendly witness before the House Un-American Activities Committee in 1952. While "naming names" cost Kazan the respect of many liberal friends and colleagues (Arthur Miller most prominent among them), it ironi-cally ushered in the decade of his most inspired filmmaking. If Abraham Polonsky, himself blacklisted during the fifties, is right in claiming that Kazan's post-HUAC movies have been "marked by bad conscience," perhaps he overlooks how that very quality of uncertainly may be what makes films like *On the Waterfront*, *East of Eden*, and *America America* so much more compelling than Kazan's previous studio work.

His apprenticeship in the Group Theater and his great success as a Broadway director had a natural influence on Kazan's films, particularly reflected in his respect for the written script, his careful blocking of scenes, and, pre-eminently, his depiction of Method acting to the screen. While with the Group, which he has described as "the best thing professionally that ever happened to me," Kazan acquired from its leaders, Harold Clurman and Lee Strasberg, a fundamentally artistic attitude toward his work, from Marx, a political view of art as an instrument of social change, and from Stanislavski, a method of acting which sought the play's "spine" and emphasized the characters' psychological motivation. Although he developed a lyrical quality which informs many later films, Kazan generally works out of the social realist mode he learned from the Group. Thus, he prefers location shooting over studio sets, relatively unfamiliar actors over stars, long shots and long takes over editing, and naturalistic forms over genre conventions. *On the Waterfront* and *Wild River*, though radically different in style, both reflect the Group's quest, in Kazan's words, "to get poetry out of the common things of life." And while one may debate the ultimate ideology of *Gentleman's Agreement*, *Pinky*, *Viva Zapata!* and *The Visitors*, one can hardly the deny the premise they all share, that art should illuminate society's problems and the possibility for their reform.

Above all else, however, it is Kazan's skill in directing actors that has secured his place in the history of American cinema. 21 of his performers have been nominated for Academy Awards; nine have won. He was instrumental in launching the film careers of Marlon Brando, Julie Harris, James Dean, Carroll Baker, Warren Beatty, and Lee Remick. Moreover, he elicted from such undervalued Hollywood players as Dorothy McGuire, James Dunn, Eva Marie Saint, and Natalie Wood perhaps the best performances of their careers. For all the long decline in critical appreciation, Kazan's reputation among actors has hardly wavered. The Method, which became so identified with Kazan's and Lee Strasberg's teaching at the Actors' Studio, was once simplisticity defined by Kazan himself as "turning psychology into behavior." An obvious example from *Boomerang* would be the suspect Waldron's gesture of covering his mouth whenever he lies to the authorities. But when Terry first chats with Edie in the park in *On the Waterfront*, unconsciously putting on one of the white gloves she has dropped as he sits in a swing, such behavior becomes not merely psychological but symbolic and poetic—and Method acting transcends Kazan's own mundane definition.

His films have been most consistently concerned with the theme of power, expressed as either the restless yearning of the alienated or the uneasy arrangements of the strong. The struggle for power is generally manifested through wealth, sexuality, or, most often, violence. Perhaps because every Kazan film except *A Tree Grows in Brooklyn* and *The Last Tycoon* (excluding a one-punch knockout of the drunken protagonist) contains at least one violent scene, some critics have complained about the director's "horrid vulgarity" (Lindsay Anderson) and "unremitting stridency" (Robin Wood), yet even his most "overheated" work contains striking examples of restrained yet resonant interludes: the rooftop scenes of Terry and his pigeons in *On the Waterfront*, the tentative reunion of Bud and Deanie at the end of *Splendor in the Grass*, the sequence in which Stavros tells his betrothed not to trust him in *America America*. Each of these scenes could be regarded not simply as a necessary lull in the dramatic structure but as a priviliged, lyrical moment in which the ambivalence underlying Kazan's attitude toward his most pervasive themes seem to crystallize. Only then can one fully realize how Terry is both confined by the *mise-en-scène* within the coop wire and free on the roof to be himself, how Bud and Deanie are simultaneously reconciled and estranged, how Stavros becomes honest only when he confesses to how deeply he has been compromised.

—Lloyd Michaels

KEATON, BUSTER. American. Born Joseph Francis Keaton in Piqua, Kansas, 4 October 1895. Married Natalie Talmadge in 1921 (divorced 1932); children: Joseph, renamed James, and Robert Talmadge; married Mae Scribbens in 1933 (divorced 1935); Eleanor Norris in 1940. Career: Reportedly named "Buster" after tumbling down a flight of stairs when 6 months old; Harry Houdini picked him up and was surprised to find him unhurt after such a 'buster' (i.e. pratfall); 1898—is incorporated into parents' vaudeville act which becomes The 3 Keatons; 1899—the act appears in New York; 1917—Keaton family act breaks up; meets Roscoe (Fatty) Arbuckle, begins acting for Comique Film Corp. supervised by Joseph Schenck; moves with film company to California; 1917-19—appears in 15 2-reelers for Comique; 1918—7 months' Army service in France; 1919—Schenck offers Keaton own production company within Metro Pictures Corp. 1920-23—produces 19 2-reelers; 1923-28—produces 10 features; 1928—dissolves production company, joins M-G-M; 1933—announces retirement from screen; 1934-39—stars in 16 comedies for Educational Pictures; 1937-50—works intermittently as gag writer for MGM; 1939-41—appears in 10 2-reelers for Columbia; 1949—begins appearing on television programs and in commercials; 1950—makes 2 series of *The Buster Keaton Show* for KTTV Los Angeles; 1962—Cinémathèque Française Keaton retrospective. Died in Woodland Hills, California, 1 February 1966.

Films (as co-director and co-scriptwriter with Eddie Cline, and principal actor): 1920—*One Week*; *Convict 13*; *The Scarecrow*; 1921—*Neighbors*; *The Haunted House*; *Hard Luck*; *The High Sign*; *The Goat* (d and sc with Mal St. Clair); *The Playhouse*; *The Boat*; 1922—*The Paleface*; *Cops*; *My Wife's Relations*; *The Blacksmith* (d and sc with Mal St. Clair); *The Frozen North*; *Day Dreams*; *The Electric House*; 1923—*The Balloonatic*; *The Love Nest*; (as director and principal actor): 1923—*The 3 Ages*; *Our Hospitality* (co-d); 1924—*Sherlock Jr.* (co-d); *The Navigator* (co-d); 1925—*7 Chances*; *Go West* (+story); 1926—*Battling Butler*; *The General* (co-d, +co-sc); 1927—*College* (no d credit); 1928—*Steamboat Bill, Jr.* (no d credit); *The Cameraman* (no d credit, +pr); 1929—*Spite Marriage* (no d credit); 1938—*Life in Sometown, U.S.A.*; *Hollywood Handicap*; *Streamlined Swing*; 1939—*The Jones Family in Hollywood* (co-sc only); *The Jones Family in Quick Millions* (co-sc only).

Roles: (in Fatty Arbuckle comedies): 1917—as a village pest in *The Butcher Boy*; as a rival in *A Reckless Romeo*; *The Rough House*; *His Wedding Night*; *Oh, Doctor!*; as a husband touring Coney Island with his wife in *Fatty at Coney Island (Coney Island)*; *A Country Hero*; 1918—as a dude gambler in *Out West*; as a village pest in *The Bell Boy*; as an assistant revenue agent in *Moonshine*; as the doctor and a visitor in *Good Night, Nurse!*; as the waiter and helper in *The Cook*; 1919—as a stagehand in *Back*

Stage; as a helper in *The Hayseed*; 1920—as a garage mechanic in *The Garage*; (subsequent roles): 1920—as an Indian in *The Round Up*; as Bertie "the Lamb" Van Alstyne in *The Saphead*; 1922—*Screen Snapshots, No.3*; 1929—as an oriental dancer in *The Hollywood Revue*; 1930—as Elmer Butts in *Free & Easy (Easy Go)*; as Elmer Stuyvesant (+pr) in *Doughboys*; 1931—as Reginald Irving (+pr) in *Parlor, Bedroom & Bath*; as Homer Van Tine Harmon (+pr) in *Sidewalks of New York*; 1932—as Elmer Tuttle (+pr) in *The Passionate Plumber*; as Prof. Timoleon Zanders Post in *Speak Easily*; 1933—as Elmer J. Butts in *What! No Beer!*; 1934—as Wally in *The Gold Ghost*; as Elmer in *Allez Oop*; as Buster Garnier and Jim le Balafre in *Le Roi des Champs Elysées*; 1935—as Leander Proudfoot in *The Invader (The Intruder, An Old Spanish Custom)*; as Jim in *Palookah from Paducah*; (as "Elmer" in the following, except as noted): 1935—*One Run Elmer*; *Hayseed Romance*; *Tars & Stripes*; *The E-Flat Man*; *The Timid Young Man*; 1936—*3 On a Limb*; *Grand Slam Opera*; as one of several stars in *La Fiesta de Santa Barbara*; *Blue Blazes*; *The Chemist*; *Mixed Magic*; 1937—*Jail Bait*; *Ditto*; *Love Nest on Wheels* (last appearance as "Elmer"); 1939—as a traveler in Mexico in *Pest from the West*; as a Civil War veteran in *Mooching through Georgia*; *Hollywood Cavalcade*; 1940—as a vacationer in *Nothing But Pleasure*; as a reporter in *Pardon My Berth Marks*; as an innocent accomplice in *The Taming of the Snood*; as a magician's housekeeper in *The Spook Speaks*; *The Villain Still Pursued Her*; as Lonesome Polecat in *Li'l Abner*; *His Ex Marks the Spot*; 1941—*So You Won't Squawk*; *She's Oil Mine*; *General Nuisance*; 1943—as a plumber in *Forever and a Day*; 1944—as a bus driver in *San Diego, I Love You*; 1945—as L.M. in *That's the Spirit*; *That Night with You*; 1946—*God's Country*; as a prisoner of Mexicans who is sent to moon in *El Moderno Barba azul*; 1949—as a suitor in *The Loveable Cheat*; as Hickey in *In the Good Old Summertime*; as a butler in *You're My Everything*; 1950—as a comic duellist in *Un Duel à mort*; as a bridge player in *Sunset Boulevard*; 1952—as the piano accompanist in a music-hall sketch in *Limelight*; in a brief sketch in *L'incantevole nemica*; *Paradise for Buster*; 1955—*The Misadventures of Buster Keaton*; 1956—as a train conductor in *Around the World in 80 Days*; 1960—in a clip from *Cops* in *When Comedy was King*; as a lion tamer in *The Adventures of Huckleberry Finn*; 1963—in clips in *30 Years of Fun*; as Lester in *The Triumph of Lester Snapwell*; as Jimmy the Crook in *It's a Mad, Mad, Mad, Mad World*; 1964—as an Indian chief in *Pajama Party*; 1965—as a would-be surfer in *Beach Blanket Bingo*; as Object/Eye in *Film*; as Bwana in *How to Stuff a Wild Bikini*; as Private Blinken in *Sergeant Deadhead*; *The Railrodder*; *Buster Keaton Rides Again*; 1966—*The Scribe*; as Erronius in *A Funny Thing Happened on the Way to the Forum*; 1967—as the German general in *Due Marines e un Generale (War, Italian Style)*; 1970—*The Great Stone Face*.

Publications:

By KEATON:

Book—*My Wonderful World of Slapstick*, with Charles Samuels, New York 1960; articles—"Why I Never Smile" in *The Ladies Home Journal* (New York), June 1926; "Buster Keaton: 'On ne peut pas faire ça à Charlie Chaplin'", interview by José Zendel in *Les Lettres françaises* (Paris), 2 October 1952; "Then and Now", interview by Milton Shulman in *The New York Times Magazine*, 9 May 1954; "An Interview with Buster Keaton" by Christopher Bishop in *Film Quarterly* (Berkeley), fall 1958; "Buster Keaton Hopes for a Revival", interview, in *London Times*, 17 August 1960; "Buster Keaton: An Interview" by Herbert Feinstein in *Massachusetts Review* (Amherst), winter 1963; "An Interview with Buster Keaton" by Penelope Gilliatt in the *London Observer Weekend Review*, 24 May 1964; "Buster Keaton", interview by Kevin Brownlow, in *Film* (London), no.42, 1965; "Keaton at Venice", interview by John Gillett and James Blue, in *Sight and Sound* (London), winter 1965; "Keaton: Still Making the Scene", interview by Rex Reed, in *The New York Times*, 17 October 1965; "Buster Keaton: An Interview" by Arthur Friedman in *Film Quarterly* (Berkeley), summer 1966; "Buster Keaton", interview by Christopher Bishop, in *Interviews with Film Directors* edited by Andrew Sarris, New York 1967; "'Anything Can Happen—And Generally Did': Buster Keaton on His Silent Film Career", interview by George Pratt in *Image* (Rochester), December 1974; 1920s articles reprinted in *Cahiers du cinéma* (Paris), January 1979.

On KEATON:

Books—*L'Originalissimo Buster Keaton* by José Pantieri, Milan 1963; *Buster Keaton* by Davide Turconi and Francesco Savio, Venice 1963; *Keaton et Compagnie: Les Burlesques américaines du "muet"* by Jean-Pierre Coursodon, Paris 1964; *Buster Keaton* by Marcel Oms, Premier Plan No.31, Lyon 1964; *Keaton* by Rudi Blesh, New York 1966; *Buster Keaton* by Jean-Pierre Lebel, New York 1967; *The Parade's Gone By* by Kevin Brownlow, New York 1968; *4 Great Comedians* by Donald McCaffrey, New York 1968; *Buster Keaton* by David Robinson, London 1968; "Buster Keaton" by Michel Denis in *Anthologie du cinéma* vol.7, Paris 1971; *Buster Keaton* by Jean-Pierre Coursodon, Paris 1973; *The Silent Clowns* by Walter Kerr, New York 1975; *The Best of Buster* edited by Richard Anobile, New York 1976; *Buster Keaton and the Dynamics of Visual Wit* by George Wead, New York 1976; *Keaton: The Silent Features Close Up* by Daniel Moews, Berkeley, California 1977; *The Film Career of Buster Keaton* by George Wead and George Ellis, Boston 1977; *Keaton: The Man Who Wouldn't Lie Down* by Tom Dardis, New York 1979; articles—"Poor Child" by Elizabeth Peltret in *Motion Picture Classic* (New York), March 1921; "They Told Buster to Stick to It" by Harry Brand in *Motion Picture Classic* (New York), June 1926; "Cinématographe" by Luis Buñuel in *Les Cahiers d'art* (Paris), no.10, 1927; "The Cyclone Baby" by Joe Keaton in *Photoplay* (New York), May 1927; "Comedy" by L. Saalschutz in *Close Up* (London), April 1930; "Strictly for Laughs" by Ashton Reid in *Collier's* (New York), 10 June 1944; "Portrait de Buster Keaton" by Henriette Nizan in *Magasin du spectacle* (Paris), August 1946; "Great Stone Face" by James Agee in *Life* (New York), 5 September 1949; "Gloomy Buster is Back Again" in *Life* (New York), 13 March 1950; "Circus in Paris" by Paul Gallico in *Esquire* (New York), August 1954; "Last Call for a Clown" in *Pieces at 8* by Walter Kerr, New York 1957; "Comedy's Greatest Era" in *Agee on Film* by James Agee, New York 1958; "Buster Keaton" by Brian Baxter in *Film* (London), November/December 1958; "The Great Stone Face" by Christopher Bishop in *Film Quarterly* (Berkeley), fall 1958; "Cops, Custard—and Keaton" by Peter Dyer in *Films and Filming* (London), August 1958; special Keaton issue of *Cahiers du cinéma* (Paris), August 1958; "Rediscovery: Buster" by David Robinson in *Sight and Sound* (London), winter 1959; "Buster Keaton" by Jean-Marc Leuwen in *Cinéma 60* (Paris), August/-September 1960; "Rétrospective Buster Keaton" by Claude Beylie and others in *Cahiers du cinéma* (Paris), April 1962; "Sportif par amour" by Luis Buñuel in *Luis Buñuel* edited by Ado Kyrou, Paris 1962; "Charlot et l'anti-Charlot" by Claude Gauteur in *Cinéma 62* (Paris), September/October 1962; "Le Plus Bel Animal du monde" by Michel Mardore in *Cahiers du cinéma* (Paris), April 1962; "Un dîner avec Keaton" by Georges Sadoul in *Les Lettres françaises* (Paris), 1 March 1962; "Le Mécano de la générale" by Georges Sadoul in *Les Lettres françaises* (Paris), 28 June 1962; "Happy Pro" in *The New Yorker*, 27 April 1963; "Battling Butler [College]" by Luis Buñuel in *Luis Buñuel: An Introduction* edited by Ado Kyrou, New York 1963; "Sur le film comique et singulièrement sur Buster Keaton" by Judith Erèbe in *Crapouillot* (Paris), January 1963; "Buster Keaton nel periodo muto" by Ernesto Laura in *Bianco e nero* (Rome), September/October 1963; "Beckett—Producer of 1st Screenplay" in the *New Yorker*, 8 August 1964; "Watch Out, Buster, You're Being Watched!" in *Life* (New York), 14 August 1964; "Buster Keaton Takes a Walk" by Federico García Lorca in *Sight and Sound* (London), winter 1965; "Buster Keaton, 'L'Aristocrate de la culbute'" by Claude-Jean Philippe in *Télérama* (Paris), 25 July 1965; "Le Colosse de silence" and "Le Regard de Buster Keaton" by Robert Benayoun in *Positif* (Paris), summer 1966; "Dignity in Deadpan" by Bosley Crowther in *The New York Times*, 2 February 1966; obituary and "Buster Agonistes" by Hugh Kenner in *National Review* (New York), 22 February and 9 August 1966; "Buster Keaton vu de dos" by André Martin in *Cinéma 66* (Paris), March 1966; "Razionalismo e 'conformismo' di Buster Keaton" by Claudio Rispoli and Adriano Aprà in *Filmcritica* (Rome), February 1966; "Le Génie de Buster Keaton" by Georges Sadoul in *Les Lettres françaises* (Paris), 10 February 1966; "The Mutual Approval of Keaton and Lloyd" by Donald McCaffrey in *Cinema Journal* (Evanston), no.6, 1967; "Buster Keaton" by Eric Rhode in *Encounter* (London), December 1967; "The Great Blank Page" by Penelope Houston in *Sight and Sound* (London), spring 1968; "On Directing *Film*" by Alan Schneider in *Film* by Samuel Beckett, New York 1969; "Current Cinema" by Penelope Gilliatt in the *New Yorker*, 26 September 1970; "Buster Keaton" by Anne Villelaur in *Dossiers du cinéma: Cinéastes* I, Paris 1971; "Buster Keaton" in *The Great Movie Shorts* by Leonard Maltin, New York 1972; "Un volto impassibile sull' American way of life" by F. Prono in *Cinema nuovo* (Turin), May/June 1972; "Buster Keaton vu par..." by Raymond Devos and others in *Écran 73* (Paris), January 1973; "Buster Keaton's Gags" by Sylvain de Pasquier in *Journal of Modern Literature* (Philadelphia), April 1973; "Buster Keaton" in *Unholy Fools* by Penelope Gilliatt, New York 1973; "Keaton" in *The Comic Mind* by Gerald Mast, New York 1973; "Buster Keaton" in *The Primal Screen* by Andrew Sarris, New York 1973; "The Limits of Silent Comedy" by Jeremy Cott in *Literature/Film Quarterly* (Salisbury, Maryland), spring 1975; "Keaton algebrique" by J.-J. Bernard in *Cinématographe* (Paris), August/September 1975; "The Limits of Silent Film Comedy" by J. Cott in *Literature/Film Quarterly* (Salisbury, Maryland), spring 1975; "Rediscovery" by William Everson in *Films in Review* (New York), March 1975; "Le Mécano de la *General*", special issue of *Avant-Scène du cinéma* (Paris), February 1975; "Observations on Keaton's Steamboat Bill Jr." by E. Rubinstein in *Sight and Sound* (London), autumn 1975; "Ganz und gar nicht Lustiges: Buster Keaton, der weisses Clown" by T. Brandlmeier in *Film und Ton* (Munich), April 1976; "Rediscovery: Le Roi des Champs Elysees" by William Everson in *Films in Review* (New York), December 1976; "The Great Locomotive Chase" by G. Wade in *American Film* (Washington, D.C.), July/August 1977; "Keaton Through the Looking Glass" by G. Stewart in *Georgia Review* (Athens, Georgia), no.2, 1979; "Les Avatars de Buster" in *Image et son* (Paris), September 1980; "Discours sur le cinéma dans quelques films de Buster Keaton: by J. Valot in *Image et son* (Paris), February 1980; "Reprises: Buster Keaton—et sa poetique de l'action" by A. Charbonnier in *Cinéma* (Paris), October 1981.

*   *   *

Buster Keaton is the only creator-star of American silent comedies who equals Chaplin as one of the artistic giants of the cinema. He is perhaps the only silent clown whose reputation is far higher in the 1980s than it was in the 1920s, when he made his greatest films. Like Chaplin, Keaton came from a theatrical family and served his apprenticeship on stage in the family's vaudeville act. Unlike Chaplin, however, Keaton's childhood and family life was less troubled, more serene, lacking the darkness of Chaplin's youth that would lead to the later darkness of his films. Keaton's films were more blithely athletic and optimistic, more committed to audacious physical stunts and cinema tricks, far less interested in exploring moral paradoxes and emotional resonances. Keaton's most famous comic trademark, his "great stone face," itself reflects the commitment to a comedy of the surface, but attached to that face was one of the most resiliently able and acrobatic bodies in the history of cinema, and Keaton's comedy was based on the conflict between that imperviously dead-pan face, his tiny but almost superhuman physical instrument, and the immensity of the physical universe that surrounded them.

After an apprenticeship in the late 1910s making two-reel comedies that starred his friend Fatty Arbuckle, and after service in France in 1918, Keaton starred in a series of his own two-reel comedies beginning in 1920. Those films displayed Keaton's comic and visual inventiveness: the delight is bizarrely complicated mechanical gadgets (*The Scarecrow*, *The Haunted House*), the realization that the cinema itself was an intriguing mechanical toy (his use of split-screen in *The Playhouse* of 1921 allows Buster to play all members of the orchestra and audience, as well as all nine members of a minstrel troupe), the games with framing and composition *The Balloonatic* is a comic disquisition on the surprises one can generate merely by entering, falling out of, or supressing information from the frame), the breathtaking physical stunts and chases (*Daydreams*, *Cops*), and the underlying fatalism when his exuberent efforts produce ultimately disastrous results (*Cops*, *One Week*, *The Boat*).

In 1923, Keaton's producer, Joseph M. Schenck, decided to launch the comic star in a series of feature films, to replace a previously slated series of features starring Schenck's other comic star, the now scandal-ruined Fatty Arbuckle. Between 1923 and 1929, Keaton made an even dozen feature films on a regular schedule of a two year—always leaving Keaton free in the early autumn to travel East for the World Series. This regular pattern of Keaton's work—as opposed to Chaplin's lengthy laboring and devoted concentration on each individual project— reveals the way Keaton saw his film work. He was not making artistic masterpieces but knocking out everyday entertainment, like the vaudevillian playing the two-a-day. Despite the casualness of this regualr routine (which would be echoed decades later by Woody Allen's regular one-a-year rhythm), many of those dozen silent features are comic masterpieces, ranking alongside the best of Chaplin's comic work.

Most of those films begin with a parodic premise—the desire to parody some serious and familiar form of stage or screen melodrama—the Civil War romance (*The General*), the mountain feud (*Our Hospitality*), the Sherlock Holmes detective story (*Sherlock, Jr.*), the Mississippi Riverboat race (*Steamboat Bill, Jr.*), or the western (*Go West*). Two of the features were built around athletics (boxing in *Battling Butler* and every sport but football in *College*, and one was built around the business of motion picture photography itself (*The Cameraman*). The narrative lines of these films were thin but fast-paced, usually based on the Keaton character's desire to satisfy the demands of his highly conventional lady love. The film's narrative primarily served to allow the film to build to its extended comic sequences, which, in Keaton's films, continue to amaze with their cinematic inge-

nuity, their dazzling physical stunts, and their hypnotic visual rhythms. Those sequences usually forced the tiny but dexterous Keaton into combat with immense and elemental antagonists—a rockslide in *Seven Chances*; an entire ocean liner in *The Navigator*; a herd of cattle in *Go West*; a waterfall in *Our Hospitality*. Perhaps the cleverest and most astonishing of his elemental foes appears in *Sherlock, Jr.* when the enemy becomes cinema itself— or, rather, cinema time and space. Buster, a dreaming movie projectionist, becomes imprisoned in the film he is projecting, subject to its inexplicable laws of monatage, of shifting spaces and times, as opposed to the expected continuity of space and time in the natural universe. Perhaps Keaton's most satisfyingly whole film is *The General*, virtually an extended chase from start to finish, as the Keaton character chases north, in pursuit of his stolen locomotive, then races back south with it, fleeing his Union pursuers. The film combines comic narrative, the rhythms of the chase, Keaton's physical stunts, and his fondness for mechanical gadgets into what may be the greatest comic of the cinema.

Unlike Chaplin, Keaton's stardom and comic brilliance did not survive Hollywood's conversion to synchronized sound. It was simply a case of a voice's failing to suit the demands of both physical comedy and the microphone. Keaton's personal life was in shreds, after a bitter divorce from Natalie Talmadge. Always a heavy social drinker, Keaton's drinking increased in direct proportion to his personal troubles. Neither a comic spirit nor an acrobatic physical instrument could survive so much alcholic abuse. In addition, Keaton's contract had been sold by Joseph Schenck to MGM (conveniently controlled by his brother, Nicholas Schenck, head of Loew's Inc., MGM's parent company). Between 1929 and 1933, MGM assigned Keaton to a series of dreary situation comedies—many of them Jimmy Durante's co-star and straight man. For the next two decades, Keaton survived on cheap two-reel sound comedies and occasional public appearances, until his major role in Chaplin's *Limelight* led to a comeback. Keaton remarried, went on the wagon, and made stage, television, and film appearances in featured roles. In 1965 he played the embodiment of existential consciousness in Samuel Beckett's only film work, *Film*, followed shortly by his final screen appearance in Richard Lester's *A Funny Thing Happened on the Way to the Forum*.

—Gerald Mast

KERSHNER, IRVIN. American. Born in Philadelphia, Pennsylvania, 29 April 1923. Educated at Tyler School of Fine Arts, Temple University, Philadelphia; Art Center School, University of California at Los Angeles in design; studied filmmaking at University of Southern California. Career: World War II— serves in U.S. Air Force as flight engineer on B-24 bombers; 1946-47—active as painter, studies with Hans Hoffmann, lives in Provincetown for a time; 1948—decides to study photography, moves to Los Angeles to attend UCLA; about 1950—studies filmmaking at USC while teaching courses in photography; 1950-52—works on documentaries for U.S. Information Service in Iran, Jordan, Greece, and Turkey; 1953-55—director and cameraman on West Coast TV documentary series *Confidential File*; mid-1950s—directs for series *The Rebel* and numerous pilots; 1958—directs and co-scripts 1st feature *Stakeout on Dope Street* for producer Roger Corman. Recipient: Catholic Film Office Award, Cannes Festival, for *The Hoodlum Priest*, 1961. Agent: Michael Marcus, CAA, 1888 Century Park East, Los

Angeles, CA 90067; business manager: Charles Silverberg, Silverberg, Rosen, Leon Behr, 2029 Century Park East #1900, Los Angeles, CA 90067; address: Box 232, Route 7 North, Kent, CT 06757.

Films (as director): 1958—*Stakeout on Dope Street* (+co-sc); 1959—*The Young Captives*; 1961—*The Hoodlum Priest*; 1963—*A Face in the Rain*; 1964—*The Luck of Ginger Coffey*; 1966—*A Fine Madness*; 1967—*The Flim-Flam Man*; 1970—*Loving*; 1972—*Up the Sandbox*; 1974—*S*P*Y*S*; 1976—*Return of a Man Called Horse*; *Raid to Entebbe* (for TV); 1978—*Eyes of Laura Mars*; 1980—*The Empire Strikes Back*; 1983—*Never Say Never Again*.

Publications:

By KERSHNER: articles—in *Film Quarterly* (Berkeley), spring 1961; interview by S. Mamber and R. Mundy in *Positif* (Paris), March 1973; interview by A. Leroux in *Séquences* (Paris), January 1975; "Director Irvin Kershner and The Eyes of Laura Mars", interview by D. Chase in *Millimeter* (New York), August 1978; "Visual Effects in Eyes of Laura Mars", interview by S. Mitchell in *Filmmakers Monthly* (Ward Hill, Mass.), November 1978; interview by Paul Most in *Cinegram*, summer 1978; "Dialogue on Film: Irvin Kershner" in *American Film* (Washington, D.C.), January/February 1981.

On KERSHNER:

Book—*Women and Sexuality in the New Film* by Joan Mellen, New York 1973; articles—"Director of the Month" by Andrew Sarris in *Show* (Hollywood), May 1970; special section of *Positif* (Paris), March 1973.

*   *   *

If anything characterizes Irwin Kershner's directorial career, it is his apparent willingness—or circumstantial need—to submerge his artistic ego and voice either in those of the more dominant artist, personality, or studio in command of a given project, or a set of audience expectations which determines the aesthetic parameters of a sequel.

Kershner's background as an academician and documentarian has contributed to his ability to undertake technically sophisticated, location-shot projects of moderate intellectual substance; his cinematic self-effacement has proven to be both strength and weakness, rendering him a journeyman craftsman rather than an artist of formidable vision.

Whether overshadowed (Rogar Corman on *Stakeout on Dope Street*, George Lucas on *The Empire Strikes Back*), shackled by the personas of the above-the-title performers (Barbara Streisand in *Up the Sandbox*, Donald Sutherland and Elliott Gould reteaming in *S*P*Y*S*, Faye Dunaway in *Eyes of Laura Mars*), pulled aloft by the umbrella covering of a series (the sequel *Return of a Man Called Horse*, *Star Wars* sequel *The Empire Strikes Back*, James Bond sequel *Never Say Never Again*), or reputedly re-edited by the supervising studio (*The Hoodlum Priest* and *A Fine Madness* were severely re-cut), Kershner has frequently disappeared into the murkiness or clarity of somebody else's vision.

Still his most substantial works, perhaps best exemplified by *Loving*, have demonstrated a sensitive feel for fully dimensional characters, a casual effectiveness with actors, a flexible and utilitarian visual sophistication, and a keen interest in themes related to humen weakness, social aliention, and survival in an impersonal universe.

His independently-concocted, idiosyncratically directed works have showcased interesting, memorable performances—George Segal as the frustrated, middle-class artist, husband, and breadwinner in *Loving*, George C. Scott as the ingratiating con artist in *The Flim-Flam Man*, Sean Connery as the rebellious New York City poet in *A Fine Madness*, Don Murray as the criminal-befriending title character in *The Hoodlum Priest*, Robert Shaw as the struggling Irish immigrant in *The Luck of Ginger Coffey*.

In each of the three stages of his career, Kershner has concentrated on a different genre. His early films (1958-1965) were suspense melodramas, seldom transcendant but consistently taut and tense. The string of quirky comedies which followed (1966-1974) varied widely in quality, but allowed Kershner's artistic sensibilities and philosphical viewpoints to come closer to the surface. Thereafter, however, he specialized (with the exception of *Eyes of Laura Mars*), in epic adventures with predetermined commercial appeal, thus gaining access to a much wider audience at the expense of his directorial signiture.

Loving, generally regarded as Kershner's best work, quietly established for him a reputation he has never quite lived up to again. A sensitive, sustained, maturalistic comedy about a dissatisfied middle-class illustrator, *Loving* seems to stand as Irwin Kershner's tender tribute to a failed artist—perhaps a prophetic self-portrait.

—Bill Wine

———————————

KING, HENRY. American. Born in Christianburg, Virginia, 24 January 1888. Married twice. Career: early 1900s—leaves school, joins Empire Stock Company, travelling repertory show; also works in circus, burlesque, vaudeville; 1912-16—acts, then writes for Lubin Co., working in Philadelphia; 1916—begins directing and acting for Balboa Films, Long Beach, California; 1918—moves to American Film Company; also makes one film for Thomas Ince (*23 1/2 Hours Leave*); 1923—shoots *The White Sister* in Italy, giving Ronald Colman first role and becoming one of first American directors to make film on location outside of U.S.; 1925—enters into partnership with Sam Goldwyn to make *Stella Dallas*; 1930s through 1961—works mainly at Fox; 1961—makes last film, *Tender Is the Night*. Died at home in San Fernando Valley, 29 June 1982.

Films (as director): 1915—*Who Pays?*; 1916—*Little Mary Sunshine*; *Joy and the Dragon*; *Pay Dirt*; *The Strained Pearl*; 1917—*The Mainspring*; *The Climber*; *Southern Pride*; *A Game of Wits*; *The Mate of the Sally Ann*; *Twin Kiddies*; *Told at Twilight*; *Sunshine and Gold*; 1918—*Beauty and the Rogue*; *Powers That Prey*; *Hearts or Diamonds*; *Up Romance Road*; *The Locked Heart*; *Hobbs in a Hurry*; *The Unafraid*; *Souls in Pawn*; *The Spectre of Suspicion*; *The Bride's Silence*; 1919—*When a Man Rides Alone*; *Where the West Begins*; *Brass Buttons*; *Some Liar*; *Sporting Chance*; *This Hero Stuff*; *Six Feet Four*; *A Fugitive from Matrimony*; *23 1/2 Hours Leave*; *Haunting Shadows*; 1920—*The White Dove*; *Uncharted Channels*; *One Hour Before Dawn*; *Help Wanted—Male*; *Dice of Destiny*; 1921—*When We Were 21*; *Mistress of Shenstone*; *Salvage*; *The Sting of the Lash*; *Tol'able David*; 1922—*The 7th Day*; *Sonny*; *The Bond Boy*; 1923—*Fury*; *The White Sister*; 1925—*Sackcloth and Scarlet*; *Any Woman*; *Romola*; 1926—*Stella Dallas*; *Partners Again*; *The Winning of Barbara Worth*; 1927—*The Magic Flame*;

1928—*The Woman Disputed*; 1929—*She Goes to War*; 1930—*Hell Harbor*; *Eyes of the World*; *Lightnin'*; 1931—*Merely Mary Ann*; *Over the Hill*; 1932—*The Woman in Room 13*; 1933—*State Fair*; *I Love You Wednesday*; 1934—*Carolina*; *Marie Galante*; 1935—*One More Spring*; *Way Down East*; 1936—*The Country Doctor*; *Ramona*; *Lloyd's of London*; 1937—*7th Heaven*; 1938—*In Old Chicago*; *Alexander's Ragtime Band*; 1939—*Jesse James*; *Stanley and Livingston*; 1940—*Little Old New York*; *Maryland*; *Chad Hanna*; 1941—*A Yank in the RAF*; *Remember the Day*; 1942—*The Black Swan*; 1943—*The Song of Bernadette*; 1944—*Wilson*; 1945—*A Bell for Adano*; 1946—*Margie*; 1947—*Captain from Castille*; 1948—*Deep Waters*; 1949—*The Prince of Foxes*; 1950—*12 O'Clock High*; *The Gunfighter*; 1951—*I'd Climb the Highest Mountain*; *David and Bathsheba*; 1952—*Wait 'til the Sun Shines, Nellie*; "The Gift of the Magi" episode of *O. Henry's Full House*; *The Snows of Kilimanjaro*; 1953—*King of the Khyber Rifles*; 1955—*Untamed*; *Love Is a Many-Splendored Thing*; 1956—*Carousel*; 1957—*The Sun Also Rises*; 1958—*The Bravados*; 1959—*This Earth Is Mine*; *Beloved Infidel*; 1961—*Tender Is the Night*.

Publications:

By KING:

Articles—interview by M. Cheatham in *Motion Picture Classic* (Brooklyn), March 1921; "Filmmakers as Goodwill Ambassadors" in *Films in Review* (New York), October 1958; "Henry King: The Flying Director", interview by Richard Cherry in *Action* (Los Angeles), July/August 1969; "6 Pioneers" in *Action* (Los Angeles), November/December 1972; "Il mito di fronte alla storia" by M. Buffa in *Filmcritica* (Rome), May/June 1973; "Pioneers '73" by C. Kirk in *Action* (Los Angeles), November/-December 1973; interview by S. Eyman in *Focus on Film* (London), winter 1976; interview by D. Badder in *Sight and Sound* (London), winter 1977/78; interviews and article by J. Lacourcelles and P. Guinle in *Ecran* (Paris), June and July 1978;

On KING:

Books—*The Parade's Gone By* by Kevin Brownlow, London 1968; *The Hollywood Professionals Vol.2: Henry King, Lewis Milestone, Sam Wood* by Clive Denton and others, New York 1974; articles—"Give Me a Volcano" by Pete Martin in the *Saturday Evening Post* (Philadelphia), 31 May 1947; "The Life and Films of Henry King" by Charles Shibuk and Christopher North in *Films in Review* (New York), October 1958; "Henry King" by G.J. Mitchell in *Films in Review* (New York), July 1964; "The Tough Race" by Roy Pickard in *Films and Filming* (London), September 1971; obituary in *The New York Times*, 1 July 1982.

*　　*　　*

Henry King has been called the "pastoral poet" of American motion pictures by a small coterie of film historians for the most part of his lengthy and prominent career as a director has been slighted by film historians partly because many of his silent films remain inaccessible and partly because his interpretation of life in rural America has been overshadowed by the works of such directors as King Vidor, John Ford, and D.W. Griffith.

At their best, King's films recreated a charming and honestly sentimental America, evoking a sincere nostalgia and naturalism, and expressing an optimistic and durable view of romantic love. He presented his stories in a simple, straightforward manner rather than attempting any "between-the-lines" analyses. He relied on plot and the competance of his actors to interpret his stories. Technically his films were spare and unnumbered by cinematic tricks. No technical virtuoso, he nevertheless possessed a remarkable facility for creating rustic tableaux which represented the verities of American country life.

King came to motion pictures via acting in theatre stock companies and, like his contemporaries John Ford and Raoul Walsh, acting in silent pictures. Acting led him to directing and his first film of note was *23½ Hours Leave*, produced by Thomas Ince. *Tol'able David*, his interpretation of life in his native rural Virginia, brought his first real acclaim, including from the Russian master Pudovkin. The Lillian Gish vehicle *The White Sister* was a beautifully-conceived religious tragedy and the first major U.S. production filmed abroad. His *Stella Dallas* remains the best and least maudlin version of that oft-filmed tear-jerker and contains a most remarkable performance by Belle Bennett.

With the arrival of sound, King signed a contract with Fox, where he would remain for the balance of his career, frequently working with the esteemed cinematographer Leon Shamroy. King proved a supreme studio craftsman and his first sound masterpiece was the memorable *State Fair*, starring the beloved Will Rogers. The best of his many films for Fox relied heavily on nostalgia and Americana, exhibited a steadfast earnestness, e.g. *In Old Chicago*, *Alexander's Ragtime Band*, *Jesse James* and *Stanley Livingston*. In *Song of Bernadette* he transcended the sentimentality of the novel. *Wilson*, for all its nobility, was really more Darryl F. Zanuck than King and today is a bit tedious.

Twelve O'Clock High ia a compelling depiction of a U.S. Air Force commander's breakdown and contains Gregory Peck's best performance, and *The Gunfighter* is a vivid, albeit off-beat western. *I'll Climb the Highest Mountain*, a greatly underrated film, is the synthesis of all of King's love of ordinary country life and romance, and *The Snows of Kilimanjaro* is better Hemingway than most critics admit and was the author's favorite film adaptation of his writing.

Love Is a Many-Splendored Thing is another example of how King could make audiences believe in pure, romantic love and *The Bravados*, an austere western, was his last good film. Certainly *Beloved Infidel* is an embarrassment and *Tender Is the Night*, which has its moments, was botched by David O. Selznick's meddling.

Before his death in 1982, King began to see a renewed interest in his work through numerous retrospectives. In 1969, the International Motion Picture Almanac listed what it deemed the "Greatest Hundred" films and six of King's works appeared on that list: *Tol'able David*, *The White Sister*, *Stella Dallas*, *Alexander's Ragtime Band*, *The Song of Bernadette*, and *Wilson*.

King's venerable career deserves more recognition than it has yet received; as Andrew Sarris has stated, King is a "Subject for Further Research."

—Ronald Bowers

KING HU [Pseudonym of Hu Chin-Ch'üan; as actor known as Chin Ch'üan; name in pinyin: Hu Jinquan.]. Chinese. Born in Peking, 29 April 1931. Educated at Hui-Wen Middle School, Peking; Peking National Art College. Married scriptwriter Chong Ling. Career: 1949—visiting Hong Kong at time of Communist take-over; remains, works at first as proof-reader and graphic draughtsman; 1950-54—in design department of

Yong Hua Film Company; actor (especially for radio), assistant director and scriptwriter; mid-1950s—works as set designer for Great Wall Film Company; 1954-58—producer of radio programs; works for The Voice of America; 1958-65—actor, scriptwriter, and director under contract to the Shaw Brothers; works closely with director Li Han-hsiang before being allowed to direct *The Story of Sue San* under strict supervision; later disowns this film; 1964—*Sons and Daughters of the Good Earth* severely cut by Shaw Brothers, censored in Singapore and Malaysia for depiction of Sino-Japanese conflict; 1965—quits Shaw Brothers; 1965-70—joins Union (Lianbang) Film Company as director and production manager; 1967—directs *Dragon Gate Inn* which breaks all box-office records in Taiwan, Korea, Hong Kong, and Southeast Asia; success of film allows undertaking 3-year production of *A Touch of Zen*; 1970—founds King Hu Film Productions. Recipient: Grand Prix de Technique Supérieur, Cannes Festival, for *A Touch of Zen*, 1975.

Films (as scriptwriter): 1958—*Hung Hu-tzu (Red Beard)* (P'an Lei); 1961—*Hua t'ien-t'so (Bridenapping)* (Yen Chun); (as director): 1962—*The Story of Sue San* (credit as "executive director"—disowned); 1963—*Liang Shan-po yü Chu Ying-t'ai (The Love Eterne, Eternal Love)* [Liang Shan-po and Chu Ying-t'ai] (co-d); 1964—*Ta-ti nü-erh (Sons of the Good Earth)* [Children of the Good Earth]; *Ting Yi-Shan* (+sc—not completed); 1965—*Ta tsui hsia (Come Drink with Me)* [Big Drunken Hero] (+co-sc, lyrics); 1966—*Lung men k'o-chan (Dragon Gate Inn, Dragon Inn)* (+sc); 1969—*Hsia nü (A Touch of Zen)* [The Gallant Girl] (+sc, ed]; 1970—"Nu (Anger)" episode of *Hsi nu ai le (4 Moods)* (+sc); (as producer and director): 1973—*Ying-ch'un ko chih feng-po (The Fate of Lee Khan)* [Trouble at Spring Inn] (+co-sc); 1975—*Chung lieh t'u (The Valiant Ones)* [Portrait of the Patriotic Heroes] (+sc); 1976—*Lung men feng-yün (Dragon Gate)* (Ou-yang Chün) (sc only); 1979—*K'ung shan ling yü (Raining in the Mountains)* (+sc); *Shan chung ch'uan-ch'i (Legend in the Mountain)*; 1981—*Chung-shen ta-shih (The Juvenizer)*.

Publications:

By KING HU:

Article—interview by Michel Ciment in *Positif* (Paris), May 1975.

On KING HU:

Articles—"Introduction à King Hu" by H. Niogret in *Positif* (Paris), May 1975; "Director: King Hu" by Tony Rayns in *Sight and Sound* (London), winter 1975/76; "King Hu" by Derek Elley in *International Film Guide 1978*, London 1977; "King Hu dans les montagnes" by Max Tessier in *Ecran* (Paris), July 1978; "King Hu's 4 from Hong Kong" by R.J. Landry in *Variety* (New York), 26 September 1979; "Jacobean Drama and the Martial Arts Films of King Hu: A Study in Power and Corruption" by V. Ooi in *Australian Journal of Screen Theory* (Kensington N.S.W.), no.7, 1980; "King Hu" by J.-M. Vos and others in *Film en televisie* (Brussels), January 1980.

KINOSHITA, KEISUKE. Japanese. Born in Hamamatsu City, Shizuoka Prefecture, 5 December 1912. Educated at Hamamatsu Engineering School; Oriental Photography School, Tokyo, 1932-33. Career: 1933—enters Shochiku's Kamata studios as laboratory assistant; 1934-36—camera assistant under chief cinematographer for Yasujiro Shimazu; 1936—enters Shimazu's production group as assistant director (through 1942); 1939—becomes chief assistant to director Kozaburo Yoshimura; 1940-41—military service; 1943—promoted to director; 1964—leaves Shochiku, begins to work for TV; enjoys considerable success with weekly series "Kinoshita Keisuke Gekijo" (1964-67); "The Kinoshita Keisuke Hour" (1967-74); "Kinoshita Keisuke: Ningen no Uta" (1970-80). Recipient: Films placed on *Kinema Jumpo* Ten Best Films of the Year lists 18 times; placed no.1 for *The Morning of the Osone Family*, 1946, *24 Eyes*, 1954, and *The Ballad of Narayama*, 1958. Address: Mamiana Mansion #910, 44 Maniana-cho, Minato-ku, Tokyo, Japan.

Films (as director): 1943—*Hanasaku minato (The Blossoming Port)*; *Ikite-iru Magoroku (The Living Magoroku)* (+sc); 1944—*Kanko no machi (Jubilation Street, Cheering Town)*; *Rikugun (The Army)*; 1946—*Osone-ke no asa (Morning for the Osone Family)*; *Waga koiseshi otome (The Girl I Loved, The Girl That I Love)* (+sc); 1947—*Kekkon (Marriage)* (+story); *Fujicho (Phoenix)* (+sc); 1948—*Onna (Woman)* (+sc); *Shozo (The Portrait)*; *Hakai (Apostasy)*; 1949—*Ojosan kanpai (A Toast to the Young Miss, Here's to the Girls)*; *Yotsuya kaidan, I-II (The Yotsuya Ghost Story, Parts I and II)*; *Yabure daiko (Broken Drum)* (+co-sc); 1950—*Konyaku yubiwa (Engeiji ringu, Engagement Ring)* (+sc); 1951—*Zemma (The Good Fairy)* (+co-sc); *Karumen kokyo ni kaeru (Carmen Comes Home)* (+sc); *Shonen ki (A Record of Youth)* (+co-sc); *Umi no hanabi (Fireworks over the Sea)* (+sc); (as director and scriptwriter): 1952—*Karumen junjo su (Carmen's Pure Love)*; 1953—*Nihon no higeki (A Japanese Tragedy)*; 1954—*Onna no sono (The Garden of Women)*; *Nijushi no hitomi (24 Eyes)*; 1955—*Toi kumo (Distant Clouds)* (co-sc); *Nogiku no gotoki kimi nariki (You Were Like a Wild Chrysanthemum)*; 1956—*Yuyake-gumo (Clouds at Twilight)* (d only); *Taiyo to bara (The Rose on His Arm)*; 1957—*Yorokobi mo kanashimi mo ikutoshitsuki (Times of Joy and Sorrow, The Lighthouse)*; *Fuzen no tomoshibi (A Candle in the Wind, Danger Stalks Near)*; 1958—*Narayamabushi-ko (The Ballad of the Narayama)*; *Kono ten no niji (The Eternal Rainbow, The Rainbow of This Sky)*; 1959—*Kazabana (Snow Flurry)*; *Sekishun-cho (The Bird of Springs Past, The Bird Missing Spring)*; *Kyo mo mata kakute arinan (Thus Another Day)*; 1960—*Haru no yume (Spring Dreams)*; *Fuefuki-gawa (The River Fuefuki)*; 1961—*Eien no hito (The Bitter Spirit, Immortal Love)*; 1962—*Kotoshi no koi (This Year's Love)*; *Futari de aruita iku-haru-aki (The Seasons We Walked Together)*; 1963—*Utae, wakodo-tachi (Sing, Young People!)* (d only); *Shito no densetsu (Legend of a Duel to the Death, A Legend, or Was It?)*; 1964—*Koge (The Scent of Incense)*; 1967—*Natsukashiki fue ya taiko (Lovely Flute and Drum)* (+pr); 1976—*Suri Lanka no ai to wakare (Love and Separation in Sri Lanka)*; 1979—*Shodo satsujin: Musukoyo (My Son)*; 1983—*Konoko o nokoshite (Leaving This Child)*.

Publications:

By KINOSHITA:

Article—"Jisaku o kataru" [Keisuke Kinoshita Talks About His Films] in *Kinema Jumpo* (Tokyo), no.115, 1955.

On KINOSHITA:

Books—*The Japanese Film* by Joseph Anderson and Donald Richie, New York 1961; *The Waves at Genji's Door* by Joan

Mellen, New York 1976; *Japanese Film Directors* by Audie Bock, Tokyo 1978; article—note in *International Film Guide*, London 1965.

*   *   *

Kinoshita's films are characteristic of the Shochiku Studio's work: healthy home drama and melodrama as conventionalized by the studio's two masters, Shimazu and Ozu. The latter two specialized in the genre of depicting everyday family life. Kinoshita gravitated towards sentimentalism and a belief in the eventual triumph of good will and sincere efforts. It was against this "planned unity" that the new generation of Shochiku directors (e.g. Oshima and his group) reacted.

Within this framework, Kinoshita is skilled in various genres. The light satiric comedies started with Kinoshita's first film, *The Blooming Port*. Although obtensibly it illustrated the patriotism of two con men in a small port town, this film demonstrated Kinoshita's extraordinary talent for witty mise-en-scène and briskly paced story-telling. His postwar comedies include *Broken Drum*, *Carmen Comes Home*, *Carmen's Pure Love* and *Light in Front of Wind*, which captured the liberated spirit of postwar democratization. *A Toast to the Young Miss* was a kind of situation comedy which became unusually successful due to its excellent cast.

The romantic melodrama became the favorite of women filmgoers. *Marriage* and *Phoenix* surprised the audience with their bold and sophisticated expression of love, which pioneered the new social morality. *You Were Like a Wild Chrysanthemum* is a romantic, sentimental love story. They were followed years later by *Distant Clouds*, *Immortal Love*, *The Scent of Incense* and *Love and Separation in Sri Lanka*.

The sentimental human drama became Kinoshita's most characteristic genre. It is typified by *24 Eyes*, which deftly appeals to the Japanese audience's sentimentality, depicting the life of a woman teacher on a small island. This was followed by films such as *Times of Joy and Sorrow*, *The Seasons We Walked Together* and *Lovely Flute and Drum*. The Shochika Studio was proud that these films could attract "women coming with handkerchiefs to wipe away their tears."

Films of rather straightfoward social criticism include *Morning for the Osone Family*, *Apostasy*, *A Japanese Tragedy*, *The Garden of Women*, *The Sun and the Rose*, *The Ballad of Narayama* and *Snow Flurry*. They vary from rather crude "postwar democratization" films to ones which deal with the world of folkloric convention, struggles against the feudalistic system, and current social problems.

Kinoshita is adventurous in his technical experimentation. *Carmen Comes Home* is the first Japanese color film, and is highly successful in its use of the new technology. In its sequel, *Carmen's Pure Love*, he employs tilting composition throughout the film, producing a wry comic atmosphere. In *A Japanese Tragedy*, newsreel footage is inserted to connect the historical background with the narrative. *You Were Like a Wild Chrysanthemum*, a film presented as an old man's memory of his youth, creates a nostalgic effect by vignetting with an oval shape and misting images. *Ballad of Narayama*, except for the last outdoor sequence, takes place on a set which accentuates artificiality and theatricality, with the added effects of a peculiar use of color. Kabuki-style acting, music, and story-telling create the fable-like ambience of this film. In *The River Fuefuki*, the film is entirely tinted with colors corresponding to the sentiment of each scene (e.g. red for fighting scenes, blue for funerals, and green for peaceful village life).

After the Japanese film industry sank into a depression in the 1960s, Kinoshita successfully continued his career in TV for a long period. His skill at entertaining and his sense of expeimentation have kept him popular with television audiences as well.

—Kyoko Hirano

KINUGASA, TEINOSUKE. Japanese. Born Teinosuke Kogame in Mie Prefecture, 1 January 1896. Educated at Sasayama Private School. Career: about 1913—runs away to Nagoya, begins theatrical apprenticeship; 1915—stage debut; 1918—enters Nikkatsu Mukojima studio as *oyama* actor (playing female roles); 1921—writes and directs 1st film; 1922—moves to Makino Kinema; mid-1920s—contract director for Shochiku Company; forms Kinugasa Motion Picture League, makes *A Page of Madness*; becomes involved with new actors' and technicians' unions; leads mass walkout over plan to replace *oyama* actors with female performers; 1928—releases *Crossroads*; travels to Russia, meets Eisenstein, then to Germany; 1929—UFA screens *Crossroads*, film is released in Paris; out of money, returns to Japan, resumes contract directing for Shochiku; 1935—begins collaboration with kabuki actor Hasegawa on *The Revenge of Yukinojo*, still one of most financially successful Japanese films; 1939—moves to Toho Company; 1949—moves to Daiei Company; 1958—appointed to board of directors, Daiei Company; 1967—directs last film, Japanese-Russian co-production *The Little Runaway*. Died in Kyoto, 27 February 1982. Recipient: Best Film, Cannes Festival, for *Gate of Hell*, 1954; Best Foreign Film Academy Award for *Gate of Hell*, 1954; Best Foreign Film, New York Film Critics, for *Gate of Hell*, 1954; Purple Ribbon Medal, Japan, for distinguished cultural service, 1958.

Films (as director and scriptwriter): 1921—*Imoto no shi (The Death of My Sister)* (+ro); 1922—*Niwa no kotori (2 Little Birds)*; *Hibana (Spark)*; 1923—*Hanasake jijii*; *Jinsei o Mitsumete*; *Onna-yo ayamaru nakare*; *Konjiki yasha (The Golden Demon)*; *Ma no ike (The Spirit of the Pond)*; 1924—*Choraku no kanata (Beyond Decay)*; *Kanojo to unmei (She Has Lived Her Destiny)* (in 2 parts); *Kire no ame (Fog and Rain)*; *Kishin yuri keiji*; *Kyoren no buto (Dance Training)*; *Mirsu (Love)*; *Shohin (Shuto)*; *Shohin (Shusoku)*; *Jashumon no onna (A Woman's Heresy)*; *Tsuma no himitsu (Secret of a Wife)* (d only); *Koi (Love)* (d only); *Sabishi mura (Lonely Village)* (d only); 1925—*Nichirin (The Sun)* (d only); *Koi to bushi (Love and a Warrior)*; *Shinju yoimachigusa* (d only); *Tsukigata hanpeita* (d only); *Wakaki hi no chuji* (d only); 1926—*Kurutta ippeiji (A Page of Madness, A Crazy Page)* (d only); *Kirinji* (d only); *Teru hi kumoru hi (Shining Sun Becomes Clouded)* (d only); *Hikuidori (Cassowary)* (d only); *Ojo Kichiza* (d only); *Oni azami* (d only); *Kinno jidai (Epoch of Loyalty)* (d only); *Meoto boshi (Star of Married Couples)* (d only); *Goyosen* (d only); *Dochu sugoruku bune* (d only); *Dochu sugoruku kago (The Palanquin)* (d only); *Akatsuki no yushi (A Brave Soldier at Dawn)* (d only); *Gekka no kyojin (Moonlight Madness)* (d only); 1928—*Jujiro (Crossroads, Crossways, Shadows over Yoshiwara)*; *Benten Kozo (Gay Masquerade)* (d only); *Keiraku hichu* (d only); *Kaikokuki (Tales from a Country by the Sea)* (d only); *Chokon yasha (Female Demon)* (d only); 1931—*Reimei izen (Before Dawn)*; *Tojin okichi* (d only); 1932—*Ikinokata Shinsengumi (The Surviving Shinsengumi)*; *Chushingura (The Loyal 47 Ronin, The Vengeance of the 47 Ronin)*; 1933—*Tenichibo to iganosuke*; *Futatsu doro (2 Stone Lanterns)*; *Toina no Ginpei (Ginpei from Koina)*; 1934—*Kutsukate tokijiro*; *Fuyaki shinju*; *Ippan gatana*

dohyoiri (A Sword and the Sumo Ring); Nagurareta kochiyama;
1935—*Yukinojo henge (The Revenge of Yukinojo, Yukinojo's
Revenge, Yukinojo's Disguise)* (co-sc—in 3 parts, part 3 released
1936); Kurayama no ushimatsu; 1937—*Hito hada Kannon (The
Sacred Protector)*; (in 5 parts); *Osaka natsu no jin (The Summer
Battle of Osaka)*; 1938—*Kuroda seichuroku*; 1940—*Hebi hime-
sama (The Snake Princess, Miss Snake Princess) (in 2 parts)*;
1941—*Kawanakajima kassen (The Battle of Kawanakajima)*;
1943—*Susume dokuritsuki (Forward Flag of Independence)* (d
only); 1946—*Aru yo no tonosama (Lord for a Night)* (d only);
1945—*Umi no bara (Rose of the Sea)* (d only); 1947—"Koi no
sakasu (The Love Circus)" section of *Yottsu no koi no monogatari (The Story of 4 Loves)* (d only); *Joyu (Actress)* (co-sc);
1949—*Kobanzame* (part 2); *Koga yashiki (Koga Mansion)*; *Sat-
sujinsha no kao (The Face of a Murderer* (d only); 1951—*Beni
komori*; *Tsuki no watari-dori (Migratory Birds Under the
Moon)*; *Meigatsu somato (Lantern Under a Full Moon)*; 1952—
*Daibutsu kaigen (Saga of the Great Buddha, The Dedication of
the Great Buddha)*; *Shurajo hibun* (in 2 parts); 1953—*Jigokumon
(Gate of Hell)*; 1954—*Yuki no yo ketto (Duel of a Snowy Night)*;
Hana no nagadosu (End of a Prolonged Journey); *Tekka bugyo*;
1955—*Yushima no shiraume (The Romance of Yushima, White
Sea of Yushima)*; *Kawa no aru shitamachi no hanashi (It Hap-
pened in Tokyo, The Story of a River Downtown)*; *Bara ikutabi
(A Girl Isn't Allowed to Love)*; 1956—*Yoshinaka o meguru
sannin no onna (3 Women Around Yoshinaka)*; *Hibana (Spark)*;
Tsukigata hanpeita (in 2 parts); 1957—*Shirasagi (White Heron,
The Snowy Heron)*; *Ukifune (Floating Vessel)*; *Naruto hicho (A
Fantastic Tale of Naruto)*; 1958—*Haru koro no hana no en (A
Spring Banquet)*; *Osaka no onna (A Woman of Osaka)*; 1959—
Joen (Tormented Flame); *Kagero ezu (Stop the Old Fox)*;
1960—*Uta andon (The Old Lantern)*; 1961—*Midare-gami (Dis-
hevelled Hair)*; *Okoto to Sasuke (Okoto and Sasuke)*; 1963—
Yoso (Priest and Empress, The Sorcerer); episode of *Uso (When
Women Lie, Lies)* (d only); 1967—*Chiisana tobosha (The Little
Runaway)* (co-d only).

Roles: (incomplete listing): 1918—*Nanairo yubi wa (The 7
Colored Ring)* (Oguchi) (film acting debut); 1920—*Ikeru shika-
bane (The Living Corpse)* (Tanaka).

Publications:

By KINUGASA:

Articles—interview by H. Niogret in *Positif* (Paris), May 1973;
"Une Page folle", interview by Max Tessier in *Ecran* (Paris),
April 1975; "'Dat ik de grote prijs in Cannes won, vond ik echt
belachelijk'", interview by I. Buruma in *Skoop* (Amsterdam),
August 1977.

On KINUGASA:

Article—"Yasujiro Ozu et le cinéma japonais à la fin du muet"
by Max Tessier in *Ecran* (Paris), December 1979.

KLINE, HERBERT. American. Born in Chicago, 13 March
1909. Married Rosa Harvan (divorced); Josine (Kline); children:
Ethan and Elissa. Career: 1930s—member of John Reed Club,
Chicago; sees 1st Soviet films, arranges for showings in home

town of Davenport, Iowa; editor of *New Theatre and Film*; early
1930s—joins New York Film and Photo League; 1936—visits
Moscow with Moscow Theatre Festival; 1936—goes to Spain
after outbreak of Civil War; 1946—in Palestine, makes semi-
documentary *My Father's House*; late '40s-early '50s—works in
Hollywood, mainly as scriptwriter; 1974—resumes documentary directing with *Walls of Fire*. Recipient: First Prize, Best
Feature Documentary, Brussels World Film Festival, for *The
Forgotten Village*, 1947.

Films (as director of short films): 1937—*Heart of Spain*; *Return
to Life*; 1938—*Crisis: A Film of "The Nazi Way"*; 1939—*Lights
Out in Europe* (+co-sc); (as director of feature-length films):
1940—*The Forgotten Village*; 1944—*Youth Runs Wild* (Robson) (co-sc only); 1947—*My Father's House*; 1949—*The Kid
from Cleveland*; 1952—*The Fighter* (+co-sc); 1953—*Prince of
Pirates* (Salkow) (sc only); 1974—*Walls of Fire* (+co-sc); 1976—
The Challenge: A Tribute to Modern Art; 1981—*Acting: Lee
Strasberg and the Actors Studio* (+pr, sc).

Publications:

By KLINE:

Articles—"Hollywood Fights Back" in *Nation* (New York), 13
May 1936; "Extract from a Letter" in *Sight and Sound* (Lon-
don), autumn 1940; "Forgotten Village" in *Theatre Arts* (New
York), May 1941; "Films Without Make-Believe" in *Magazine
of Art*, February 1942; "Filmmaking in Mexico City" in *Theatre
Arts* (New York), November 1943; "About the Shape of Films to
Come" in *Theatre Arts* (New York), January 1946.

KLUGE, ALEXANDER. German. Born in Halberstadt, 14
February 1932. Educated at Domgymnasium, Halberstadt;
Charlottenburger Gymnasium, Berlin, Abitur 1949; studied law
and history at Freiburg, Marburg, and Johann-Wolfgang-
Goethe Universität, Frankfurt (degree in law 1953). Career:
1950s—lawyer, published novelist, political writer; 1958—begins
working in films as assistant to Fritz Lang; 1960—makes 1st
film, with Peter Schamoni, *Brutality in Stone*, about Nazi architecture's ideological implications; 1962—leader and spokesman
of group of young German filmmakers who protest condition of
German filmmaking at Oberhausen Festival; publishes 1st book,
collection of stories *Lebensläufe*; 1962 to present—heads film
division of Hochschule für Gestaltung in Ulm (known as "Institut für Filmgestaltung"); 1963—founds Kairos-Film. Recipient:
Berliner Kunstpreis—Junge Generation for *Lebensläufe*, 1964;
Bayrischer Staatspreis für Literatur for *Porträt einer Bewärung*;
Bayrischer Staatspreis für Literatur for *Schlachtbeschreibung*;
Silver Lion, Venice Festival, for *Abschied von gestern*, 1966;
Golden Lion, Venice Festival, for *Die Artisten in der Zirkus-
kuppel: ratlos*, 1967; Honorary Professor, University of Frank-
furt am Main, 1973; International Critics Award, Cannes Festi-
val, for *Ferdinand the Strongman*, 1976; Fontane-Preis, 1979;
Grosser Bremer Literatur-preis, 1979.

Films (as director of short films): 1960—*Brutalität in Stein (Die
Ewigkeit von gestern)* [Brutality in Stone, Yesterday Goes On
for Ever] (co-d); 1961—*Rennen* [Racing] (co-d); 1963—*Lehrer
im Wandel* [Teachers in Transformation] (co-d); 1964—*Porträt*

einer Bewährung [Portrait of One Who Proved His Mettle]; 1965—*Unendliche Fahrt—aber begrenzt* (Reitz—feature) (text only); 1966—*Pokerspiel*; (as director of feature-length films): 1966—*Abschied von gestern (Yesterday Girl)*; 1967—*Frau Blackburn, geb. 5. Jan. 1872, wird gefilmt* [Frau Blackburn, Born 5 Jan. 1872, Is Filmed] (short); *Die Artisten in der Zirkuskuppel: ratlos (Artistes at the Top of the Big Top—Disoriented)*; 1968—*Feuerlöscher E.A. Winterstein* [Fireman E.A. Winterstein] (short); 1969—*Die unbezähmbare Leni Peickert* [The Indomitable Leni Peickert]; *Ein Arzt aus Halberstadt* [A Doctor from Halberstadt] (short); 1970—*Der grosse Verhau* [The Big Dust-up]; 1971—*Wir verbauen 3 X 27 Milliarden Dollar in einen Angriffsschlachter (Der Angriffsschlachter)* [We'll Blow 3 X 27 Billion Dollars on a Destroyer (The Destroyer)] (short); *Willi Tobler und der Untergang der 6. Flotte (Willi Tobler and the Wreck of the 6th Fleet)*; 1972—*Besitzbürgerin, Jahrgang 1908* [A Woman from the Property-owning Middle Class, Born 1908] (short); 1973—*Gelegenheitsarbeit einer Sklavin (Occasional Work of a Female Slave, Part-Time World of a Domestic Slave)*; *Die Reise nach Wien* (Reitz) (sc only); 1974—*In Gefahr und grösster Not bringt der Mittelweg den Tod (The Middle of the Road Is a Very Dead End)*; 1975—*Der starke Ferdinand (Strongman Ferdinand)*; *Augen aus einem anderen Land*; 1977—*Die Menschen, die die Staufer-Ausstellung vorbereiten (Die Menschen, die das Stauferjahr vorbereiten)* [The People Who Are Preparing the Year of the Hohenstaufens] (co-d—short); *'Zu böser Schlacht schleich'ich heut' Nacht so bang'* ["In Such Trepidation I Creep Off Tonight to the Evil Battle"] (revised version of *Willi Tobler and the Wreck of the 6th Fleet*); 1978—contribution to *Deutschland im Herbst (Germany in Autumn)*; 1979—*Die Patriotin* [The Patriotic Woman]; 1980—*Der Kandidat* (co-d); 1983—*Krieg und Frieden*.

Publications:

By KLUGE:

Books—*Die Universitäts-Selbstverwaltung*, dissertation, Frankfurt a.M., 1958; *Kulturpolitik und Ausgabenkontrolle*, Frankfurt a.M., 1961; *Lebensläufe*, Stuttgart 1962; *Schlachtbeschreibung*, Olten and Freiburg 1964; *Abschied von gestern*, filmscript transcribed by Enno Patalas, Reihe Cinemathek 17, Frankfurt a.M., n.d. *Die Artisten in der Zirkuskuppel: ratlos. Die Ungläubige. Projekt Z. Sprüche der Leni Peickert*, filmscripts, Munich 1968; *Der Untergang der 6. Armee—Schlachtbeschreibung*, Munich 1969; *Öffentlichkeit und Erfahrung. Zur Organisationsanalyse bürgerlicher und proletarischer öffentlichkeit*, with Oskar Negt, Frankfurt a.M. 1972; *Filmwirtschaft in der BRD und in Europa. Götterdämmerung in Raten*, with Florian Hopf and Michael Dost, Munich 1973; *Lernprozesse mit tödlichem Ausgang*, Frankfurt a.M. 1973; *Lebensläufe*, new edition, Frankfurt a.M. 1974; *Gelegenheitsarbeit einer Sklavin. Zur realistischen Methode*, filmscript and essay, Frankfurt a.M., 1975; *In Gefahr und grösster Not bringt der Mittelweg den Tod*, filmscript with Edgar Reitz, in *Kursbuch*, no.41, 1975; *Neue Erzählungen. Hefte 1-18 "Unheimlichkeit der Zeit"*, Frankfurt a.M. 1977; *Schlachtbeschreibung*, new and expanded edition, Munich 1978; *Die Patriotin*, filmscript, Frankfurt a.M., 1979; *Die Patriotin*, text, Frankfurt a.M. 1979; *Geschichte und Eigensinn*, with Oskar Negt, 1982; articles—"Was wollen die Oberhausener?" in *Kirche und Film*, no.11, 1962; "An einen Kritiker der 'Oberhausener'" in *Kirche und Film*, no.10, 1963; "Hauptfeldwebel Hans Peickert", story, in *Akzente*, no.2, 1963; "Totenkapelle für Bechtolds" in *Der Spiegel*, 30 September

1964; "Die Utopie Film" in *Merkur* (Cologne), Heft 201, 1964; "Wort und Film", with Edgar Reitz andf Wilfried Reinke, in *Sprache im technischen Zietalter*, no.13, 1965; "Ungeduld hilft nicht, aber Geduld auch nicht", in 2 parts, in *film*, no.3 and 4, 1967; "Traurig, traurig, sieht man hin, sieht man nicht hin, traurig, traurig!'" in *film*, no.7, 1967; "Schnulzen-Kartell versperrt die Zukunft" in *Die Welt*, 22 September 1967; "Die Artisten in der Zirkuskuppel: ratlos" in *film*, no.10, 1968; interview by F. Hopf in *Jeune Cinéma* (Paris), December/January 1972/73; interview by J. Dawson in *Film Comment* (New York), November/December 1974; "Gelegenheitsarbeit einer Sklavin: Gespräch mit Alexander Kluge" in *Filmkritik* (Munich), June 1974; "Medienproduktion" in *Perspektiven der kommunalen Kulturpolitik* edited by Hoffman and Hilmar, Frankfurt a.M. 1974; "Das ganze Maul voll Film'" (on Edgar Reitz) in *Frankfurter Rundschau*, 21 November 1974; "Pesaro '76", interview by A. Cappabianca and G. Graziani in *Filmcritica* (Rome), September 1976; "Irmi" and "Zur realistischen Methode" in *Filmkritik* (Munich), December 1976; interview by G. Graziani in *Filmcritica* (Rome), September 1976; "Die Rebellion des Stoffs gegen die Form und der Form gegen den Stoff", interview with Heiner Boehncke, in *Das B. Traven Buch*, edited by J. Beck and others, Reinbek 1976; "Zäh weiterarbeiten", interview by F. Hopf, in *Filmdienst*, 14 June 1976; "Wir müssen gewissermassen unterm Eis wegtauchen", interview by H.G. Pflaum in *Frankfurter Rundschau*, 22 December 1976; "Gespräche mit Alexander Kluge" in *Filmkritik* (Munich), no.12, 1976; "Film ist das natürliche Tauschverhältnis der Arbeit...", interview by B. Steinborn in *Filmfaust* (Frankfurt), December 1977; "Die Hexenjagd und eine Antwort", interview, in *Nicht heimlich und nicht kühl, Entgegnungen an Dienst- und andere Herren, Ästhetik und Kommunikation akut*, Berlin 1977; "Realismus ist anstrengend", interview by Christel Buschmann in *Konkret*, no.8, 1977; "Das Theater der spezialisten, Kraut und Rüben", interview by M. Schaub in *Cinema* (Zurich), May 1978; "Films d'auteurs ...Films de spectateurs...", interview by B. Steinborn in *Jeune Cinéma* (Paris), April/May 1978; "Gesprach mit Alexander Kluge: über *Die Patriotin*, Geschichte und Filmarbeit" by H. Bitomsky and others in *Filmkritik* (Munich), November 1979; "*Die Patriotin*: Entstehungsgeschichte—Inhalt" in *Filmkritik* (Munich), November 1979; "Ach ja, die Deutschen und die Lust" in *lui*, no.2, 1979; "Eine neue Tonart von Politik" in *Der Spiegel*, 30 April 1979; "Das Politische als Intensität der Gefühle" in *Freibeuter* (West Berlin), September 1979; "Ein lebhaftes Kontaktbedürfnis", "Alte schlafsüchtige Frau", and "Das Rennpferd" in *ZEITmagazin*, no.11, 9 March 1979; "Eine realistische Haltung müsste der Zuschauer haben, müsste ich jaben, müsste der Film Haben", with R. Frey, in *Filmfaust* (Frankfurt), November 1980.

On KLUGE:

Books—*In Gefahr und grösster Not bringt der Mittelweg den Tod. Zur Operativität bei Alexander Kluge* by M. Buselmeier, Heidelberg 1975; *Herzog, Kluge, Straub*, with commentary by Ulrich Gregor and others, Munich 1976; *Sinnlichkeit des Zusammenhangs, Zur Filmstrategie Alexander Kluges* by M. Kötz and P. Höhe, Frankfurt a.M. 1979; *The New German Cinema* by John Sandford, Totowa, New Jersey 1980; *Die Filme von Alexander Kluge* by Rainer Lewandowski, Hildesheim 1980; *Alexander Kluge* by Rainer Lewandowski, Munich 1980; articles—filmography in *Die Information* (Wiesbaden), no.12, 1973; "Alexander Kluge" by C. Brocher and B. Bronnen in *B.B., Die Filmemacher*, Munich, Gütersloh, Vienna 1973; "KINO-Gespräch mit Alexander Kluge", interview by A. Meyer, in *KINO* (Berlin), May 1974; "Alexander Kluges Filmtheorie" by

Wilfried Wiegand in *Frankfurter Allgemeine Zeitung*, 13 December 1975; special Kluge issue of *Filmkritik* (Munich), December 1976; "Heitere Thesen und Stossgebete—Mit Alexander Kluge in Pesaro" by Th. Petz in *Süddeutsche Zeitung* (Munich), 20 December 1976; "Il Cinema di Kluge: il realismo e l'utopia" by R. Escobar in *Cineforum* (Bergamo), February 1977; filmography in *Die Information* (Wiesbaden), July/September 1978; "Directed Change in the Young German Film: Alexander Kluge and Artists under the Big Top: Perplexed" by H.-B. Moeller and C. Springer in *Wide Angle* (Athens, Ohio), v.2, no.1, 1978.

*   *   *

Alexander Kluge, the chief ideologue of the new German cinema, is the author of various books in the areas of sociology, contemporary philosophy, and social theory. In 1962 he helped initiate, and was the spokesman for, the "Oberhausen Manifesto" in which "Das Opas Kino" ("grandpa's cinema") was declared dead.

At the same time Kluge published his first book, *Lebensläufe*: a collection of stories that presented a comprehensive cross-section of contemporary life along with its deeply-rooted historical causes. His method is grounded in a rich and representative mosaic of sources: fiction, public records and reports, essays, actual occurrences, news, quotations, observations, ideas, and free associations; the method is used by Kluge as a principle of construction in his best films such as *Abschied von gestern*, *Die Artisten...*, *In Gefahr...*, and in the series of collective films: *Deutschland im Herbst*, *Der Kandidat*, and *Krieg und Frieden*. The theme of war, in particular the Second World War, appears in all Kluge's works.

Kluge views filmmaking as another form of writing since it essentially continues the recording of his participation in the development of society and in everyday life. His unifying creative trait could be called verbal concentration, or image concentration. His filmic activity is a living extension of his comprehensive epistemological and sociological researches, which he has published, together with Oskar Negt (associated with the "Frankfurt School" of Adorno and Horkheimer), as *Öffentlichkeit und Erfahrung* (1972) and *Geschichte und Eigensinn* (1982).

Kluge's films probe reality—not by way of the fantastic fictions of Fassbinder, or film school pictures as with Wenders—but through establishing oppositions and connections between facts, artifacts, reflections, and bits of performance. The protagonists of his feature films are mostly women who seek to grasp and come to terms with their experiences. For the sake of continuity these women are played either by Alexandra Kluge, his sister, or by Hannelore Hoger. They move through the jungle of contemporary life, watching and witnessing, suffering and fighting. The director mirrors their experiences.

As a filmmaker, Kluge is unique, but not isolated. The three collective films, which together with Volker Schlöndorff, Fassbinder, Stephan Aust, and others, he has devoted to the most pressing contemporary events, are something new and original in the history of world cinema. Without Kluge these would be inconceivable, since it is he who pulls together and organizes, aesthetically and ideologically, the fragments filmed by the others. He creates film forms and image structures to transform the various narrative modes and artistic conceptions into a new, conscious, mobilized art of cinema, free of fantasy. This cinema is not only non-traditional, but conveys a socio-historical content.

It is doubtless that without Kluge a new German cinema is scarcely conceivable, since creative inspiration needs to be supported by a strong film-political foundation. It is thanks to him, above all, that film is officially promoted in the Federal Republic, and that film has been taken seriously in the last decade. An untiring fighter for the interests of his colleagues, Kluge gets involved whenever the fate of the new German cinema is at stake.

—Maria Racheva

KOBAYASHI, MASAKI. Japanese. Born in Hokkaido, 4 February 1916. Educated in Oriental art at Waseda University, Tokyo, 1933-41. Career: 1941—enters Shochiku's Ofuna studios as assistant to Kinoshita, works 8 months before being drafted; 1942-44—serves in Manchuria; refuses to be promoted above rank of private as expression of opposition to conduct of war; 1944—transferred to Ryukyu Islands until end of war, then interned in detention camp on Okinawa; 1946—returns to Shochiku; 1947-52—assistant director on staff of Keisuke Kinoshita; 1952—completes first film as director; 1957—begins work on trilogy *The Human Condition*. Recipient: Special Jury Prize, Cannes Festival, for *Seppuku*, 1963; Special Jury Prize, Cannes Festival, for *Kwaidan*, 1965.

Films (as director): 1952—*Musuko no seishun (My Sons' Youth)*; 1953—*Magokoro (Sincerity, Sincere Heart)*; 1954—*Mittsu no ai (3 Loves)* (+sc); *Kono hiroi sora no dokoka ni (Somewhere under the Broad Sky, Somewhere Beneath the Wide Sky)*; 1955—*Uruwashiki saigetsu (Beautiful Days)*; 1956—*Kabe atsuki heya (The Thick-Walled Room, Room with Thick Walls)* (completed 1953); *Izumi (The Spring, The Fountainhead)*; *Anata kaimasu (I'll Buy You)*; 1957—*Kuroi kawa (Black River)*; 1959—*Ningen no joken I (The Human Condition, Part I: No Greater Love)* (+co-sc); *Ningen no joken II (The Human Condition, Part II: Road to Eternity)* (+co-sc); 1961—*Ningen no joken III (The Human Condition, Part III: A Soldier's Prayer)* (+co-sc); 1962—*Karami-ai (The Entanglement, The Inheritance)*; *Seppuku (Harakiri)*; 1964—*Kaidan (Kwaidan)*; 1967—*Joiuchi (Rebellion, Samurai Rebellion)*; 1968—*Nihon no seishun (The Youth of Japan, Hymn to a Tired Man)*; 1971—*Inochi bo ni furo (Inn of Evil, At the Risk of My Life)*; 1975—*Kaseki (Fossils)* (originally made for TV as 8-part series); 1983—*Tokyo saiban (The Tokyo Trial, The Far East Martial Court)* (documentary).

Publications:

By KOBAYASHI:

Articles—"*Harakiri*, Kobayashi, Humanism", interview by James Silke in *Cinema* (Beverly Hills), June/July 1963; interview by Georges Sadoul in *Les Lettres françaises* (Paris), 23 May 1963; "5 japonais en quête de films: Masaki Kobayashi", interview by Max Tessier in *Ecran* (Paris), March 1972; interview in *Voices from the Japanese Cinema* by Joan Mellen, New York 1975; "Den Menschen die Augen öffnen", interview by S. Certoc in *Film und Fernsehen* (Berlin), June 1977.

On KOBAYASHI:

Book—*The Japanese Film: Art and Industry* by Joseph Anderson and Donald Richie, New York 1971; articles—"The Younger Talents" by Donald Richie in *Sight and Sound* (London), spring 1960; "Kobayashi's Trilogy" by M. Iwabuchi in *Film Culture* (New York), spring 1962; "Drame et noblesse d'un homme d'hier et de notre temps" by Mireille Boris in 'L'Humanité (Paris), 27 July 1963; "L'Astre japonais" by Philippe Esnault in *Image et son* (Paris), February 1969; "Kobayashi, l'homme et l'oeuvre" by C.R. Blouin and "Kobayashi, à l'uquam: anarchiste ou utopiste?" by G. Thérien in *Cinéma Québec* (Montreal), February/-March 1974; "Masaki Kobayashi" by Richard Tucker in *International Film Guide 1977*, London 1976.

*   *   *

The dilemma of the dissentient—the individual who finds himself irrevocably at odds with his society—is the overriding preoccupation of Kobayashi's films, and one which stems directly from his own experience. In 1942, only months after starting his career at Shochiku studios, Kobayashi was drafted into the Imperial Japanese Army and sent to Manchuria. A reluctant conscript, he refused promotion above the rank of private, and was later made a prisoner of war. Released in 1946, he returned to filmmaking, becoming assistant to Keisuke Kinoshita, whose flair for lyrical composition clearly influenced Kobayashi's own style—though he succeeded, fortunately, in shaking off the older director's penchant for excessive sentimentality.

Initially, Kobayashi's concern with social justice, and the clash between society and the individual, expressed itself in direct treatment of specific current issues: war criminals in *Kabe atsuki heya* (*The Thick-Walled Room*)—a subject so sensitive that the film's release was delayed three years; corruption in sport in *Anata kaimasu* (*I'll Buy You*); and in *Kuroi Kawa* (*Black River*) the organized crime and prostitution rampant around U.S. bases in Japan. This phase of Kobayashi's career culminated in his towering three-part, nine-hour epic, *Ningen no joken* (*The Human Condition*), a powerful and moving indictment of the systematized brutality inherent in a militaristic society.

The ordeal of the pacifist Kaji, hero of *Ningen no joken* (played by Tatsuya Nakadai, Kobayashi's favorite actor), closely parallels the director's own experiences during the war. Kaji is the archetypal Kobayashi hero, who protests, struggles, and is finally killed by an oppressive and inhumane system. His death changes nothing, and will not even be recorded; yet the mere fact of it stands as an assertion of indomitable humanity. Similarly, the heroes of Kobayashi's two finest films, *Seppuku (Harakiri)* and *Joiuchi (Rebellion)*, revolt, make their stand, and die—to no apparent avail. In these films Kobayashi turned the conventions of the *jidai-geki* (period movie) genre to his own ends, using historical settings to universalize his perennial theme of the dissident individual. The masterly blend of style and content, with the unbending ritual of samurai convention perfectly matched by cool, reticent camera movement and elegantly geometric composition, marks in these two films the peak of Kobayashi's art.

By Japanese standards, Kabayashi has made few films, working slowly and painstakingly with careful attention to detail. From *Seppuku* onwards, an increasing concern with formal beauty has characterized his work, most notably in *Kaidan (Kwaidan)*. This film, based on four of Lafcadio Hearn's ghost stories, carried for once no social message, but developed a strikingly original use of color and exquisitely stylized visual composition.

Since the crisis which hit Japanese cinema in the late 1960s, Kobayashi's activities have been yet further circumscribed. His umcompromising seriousness of purpose, and the slow, measured cadences of his style, have held little appeal to an industry resorting increasingly to sex, violence and disaster movies to lure back shrinking audiences. Nor, unlike his contemporary Kon

Ichikawa, does he take readily to working in television; he refused to watch the eight-part TV version of *Kaseki (Fossils)*, regarding it merely as rough footage from which to edit the cinematic version. Regrettably, few of Kobayashi's recent projects have come to fruition. His reputation still rests on *Ningen no joken* and on his *jidai-geki* films of the 1960s.

—Philip Kemp

KORDA, SIR ALEXANDER. Hungarian and British. Born Sándor László Kellner in Puszta Turpósztó, Hungary, 16 September 1893. Educated in secondary schools at Kisújszállás and Mezötúr, Hungary, 1902-06; secondary school in Budapest, 1906-09. Married Maria Farkas (subsequently acted as Maria Corda), 1919 (divorced 1930); child: Peter; married Merle Oberon, 1939 (divorced 1945); Alexandra Boycun, 1953. Career: about 1907—begins writing for Budapest periodicals, signing articles 'Sursum Corda' ("lift up your hearts") from which he takes surname Korda about 1910; 1909—works as reporter for newspaper *Független Magyarország*; 1911—goes to Paris, spends time at Pathé studios; 1912—returns to Budapest, takes secretarial job at Pictograph company and writes titles for imported films; begins film journal *Pesti mozi* (Budapest Cinema); 1914—makes 1st films with actor Gyula Zilahy; 1915—begins 2nd film journal *Mozihét*; 1916—Jenö Janovics hires Korda as director; 1917—forms own production company (Corvin) with Miklós Pásztory, builds studio near Budapest; 1919—arrested after Horthy regime takes power; flees to Vienna; 1920—adopts Alexander as first name; forms Corda Film Consortium (dissolved 1922); 1923—moves to Berlin, forms Korda-Film; 1926—with Maria Corda, offered contract by First National, goes to Hollywood 1927; 1930—returns to Berlin, then moves to Paris, hired by Paramount French subsidiary; 1931—offered contract by British Paramount, moves to London; 1932—founds London Films; 1933—with *Men of Tomorrow* begins to act exclusively as producer on most projects; 1935—made a partner in United Artists (sold interest in 1944); begins construction of Denham Studios; 1938—suffering financial reverses, loses control of Denham Studios; 1939—forms Alexander Korda Productions, retains positions as head of London Films; 1940-43—based in Hollywood; 1943—enters into partnership with MGM (dissolved 1946); 1946—revives and reorganizes London Films, purchases controlling interest in British Lion Film Corporation (distribution organization); 1947—founds British Film Academy (now Society of Film and Television Arts); 1949—British government loans British Lion £ 3,000,000; 1954—British Lion goes into receivership. Died in London, 23 January 1956. Knighted in 1942.

Films (as director): 1914—*A becsapott újságíró* [The Duped Journalist] (co-d); *Tutyu és Totyo* [Tutyu and Totyo] (co-d); 1915—*Lyon Lea* [Lea Lyon] (co-d); *A tiszti kardbojt* [The Officer's Swordknot] (+sc); 1916—*Fehér éjszakák* [White Nights] or *Fedora* (+sc); *A nagymama* [The Grandmother] (+sc); *Mesék az írógépröl* [Tales of the Typewriter] (+sc); *A kétszívü férfi* [The Man with 2 Hearts]; *Az egymillió fontos bankó* [The One Million Pound Note] (+sc); *Ciklámen* [Cyclamen]; *Vergödö szívek* [Struggling Hearts]; *A nevetö Szaszkia* [The Laughing Saskia]; *Mágnás Miska* [Miska the Magnate]; as producer and director): 1917—*Szent Péter esernyöje* [St. Peter's Umbrella]; *A* *gólyakalifa* [The Stork Caliph]; *Mágia* [Magic]; *Harrison és Barrison* [Harrison and Barrison]; 1918—*Faun*; *Az aranyember* [The Man with the Golden Touch]; *Mary Ann*; 1919—*Ave Caesar!*; *Fehér rózsa* [White Rose]; *Yamata*; *Se ki, se be* [Neither In Nor Out]; *A 111-es* [Number 111]; 1920—*Seine Majestät das Bettelkind (Prinz und Bettelknabe, The Prince and the Pauper)* (d only); 1922—*Heeren der Meere* [Masters of the Sea] (d only); *Eine Versunkene Welt (Die Tragödie eines Verschollenen Fürstensohnes)* [A Vanished World] (d only); *Samson und Delilah (Samson and Delilah)*; 1923—*Das unbekannte Morgen (The Unknown To-morrow)*; 1924—*Jedermanns Frau (Jedermanns Weib)* [Everybody's Woman]; *Tragödie im Hause Habsburg (Das Drama von Mayerling, Der Prinz der Legende)* [Tragedy in the House of Hapsburg]; (as director): 1925—*Der Tänzer meiner Frau (Dancing Mad)* (d only); 1926—*Madame wünscht keine Kinder (Madame Wants No Children)* (d only); 1927—*Eine Dubarry von heute (A Modern Dubarry)*; *The Stolen Bride*; *The Private Life of Helen of Troy*; 1928—*Yellow Lily*; *Night Watch*; 1929—*Love and the Devil*; *The Squall*; *Her Private Life*; 1930—*Lilies of the Field*; *Women Everywhere*; *The Princess and the Plumber*; (as producer and director): 1931—*Die Manner um Lucie*; *Rive Gauche* (French version of *Die Manner um Lucie*); *Marius* (d only); *Zum Goldenen Anker* (German version of *Marius*); 1932—*Service for Ladies (Reserved for Ladies)*; 1933—*Wedding Rehearsal*; *The Private Life of Henry VIII*; *The Girl from Maxim's* (co-p); 1934—*La Dame de Chez Maxim* (French version); *The Private Life of Don Juan*; 1936—*Rembrandt*; 1941—*That Hamilton Woman (Lady Hamilton)*; 1945—*Perfect Strangers (Vacation from Marriage)*; 1947—*An Ideal Husband*.

Publications:

By KORDA:

Articles—"50 Million Questions—and only one Answer" in *Daily Express Film Book* edited by Ernest Betts, London 1935; "Foreword" in *British Film Yearbook* edited by Peter Noble, London 1946; "The Future and the Film" in *Winchester's Screen Encyclopedia*, London 1948; "The 1st Talking Pictures" in *Radio Times* (London), 25 December 1953.

On KORDA:

Books—*20 Years of British Films, 1925-45* by Michael Balcon and others, London 1947; *Nice Work: The Story of 30 Years in British Film Production* by Adrian Brunel, London 1949; *Alexander Korda* by Paul Tabori, London 1959; *Korda* by Peter Cowie in *Anthologie du Cinéma* no.6, Paris 1965; *Word and Image: A History of the Hungarian Cinema* by István Nemeskürty, Budapest 1968; *Alexander Korda: The Man Who Could Work Miracles* by Karol Kulik, London 1975; *Charmed Lives: A Family Romance* by Michael Korda, New York 1979; articles—"Alexander Korda and the International Film" by Stephen Watts in *Cinema Quarterly*, autumn 1933; "Alexander Korda: A Sketch" by C.A. Lejeune in *Sight and Sound* (London), spring 1935; "Alexander Korda: Man of Destiny" by Lydia Sherwood in *Vogue* (New York), September 1936; "British Films: To-day and To-morrow" in *Footnotes to the Film* edited by Charles Davy, London 1937; "'Alex': A Study of Korda" by Jympson Harman in *British Film Yearbook 1949-50*, London 1949; "The Impresario Urge" by Peter Price in *Sight and Sound* (London), November 1950; "The Producer: Sir Alexander Korda" by Colin Campbell in *Sight and Sound* (London), summer 1951; "Alex"

by Ian Dalrymple in *Journal of the British Film Academy* (London), spring 1956; "Sir Alexander Korda" by Sidney Gilliat and others in *Sight and Sound* (London), spring 1956; "Korda's Empire: Politics and Films in *Sanders of the River*, *The Drum* and *The 4 Feathers*" by J. Richards in *Australian Journal of Screen Theory* (Kensington N.S.W.), no.5-6, 1980; film—*The Golden Years of Alexander Korda*, BBC television documentary by Robert Vas, 1968.

*   *   *

Alexander Korda may be Britian's most controversial film figure, but there is no doubt that his name stands everywhere for the most splendid vision of cinema as it could be, if one had money and power. Both of these Korda had, although several times he was close to bankruptcy, living on pure Hungarian charm and know-how. He at least had a dream that came near reality on several occasions.

He had two younger brothers, Zolten, who worked with him as a director, and Vincent, who was an art director; both were outstanding in their fields. He worked as a journalist and film magazine editor before he directed his first film in Hungary in 1914. He labored long in the cinematic fields of Vienna and Berlin when finally in 1926 his film production of *A Modern Dubarry* earned him a contract in Hollywood with First National, where his initial film was *The Private Life of Helen of Troy*, starring his wife Maria Corda as Helen. It brought him instant recognition. One extravagantly beautiful feature, and he was among the top as a director. He directed four specials starring Billie Dove (who should have played Helen of Troy for him)—*The Stolen Bride*, *The Night Watch*, and *The Yellow Lily*, and *Her Private Life*, a remake of Zoe Akins's play, which Corinne Griffith had filmed earlier under its play title, *Declassé*. Korda also directed a sound feature starring Miss Griffith, *Lilies of the Field*. Alexander Korda could soon write his own ticket. He did just that, leaving Hollywood to return to England where, in 1931, he set up his own production company, London Film Productions. There he was almost fully occupied with production details, and only directed eight of the many films which his company produced. It was an exciting era for an ambitious producer like Korda. His company's product was so lavish that he seemed in a fair way not only to rival Hollywood but to surpass it. His first big one was *The Private Life of Henry VIII*, starring Charles Laughton as Henry and with Merle Oberon making her debut as the unfortunate Anne Boleyn. As soon as he could, Korda was divorced from Maria, married Miss Oberon, and started to set the stage for her stardom.

Hers was not the only career he established, for he had much to do with the film careers of Laurence Olivier, Vivien Leigh, Robert Donat, and Leslie Howard, among others. He was the power behind it all who set up financial deals for pictures that starred these actors.

While the pictures he directed, like *Rembrandt*, *That Hamilton Woman*, and *Vacation from Marriage* were done in exquiste taste, production details involved him in such pictures as *Catherine the Great*, *The Scarlet Pimpernel*, *Elephant Boy*, *The Ghost Goes West*, *Drums*, *The Four Feathers*, *The Thief of Bagdad*, *The Fallen Idol*, and *The Third Man*.

Three times Korda built and rebuilt his company and the third time it was with national aid. Even after the Korda empire collapsed he was able to secure new financial alliances which allowed him to keep producing until his death in 1956. His name stood for glory and when, after 1947, his name ceased to appear as part of the film credits, the lustre surrounding a London Film Production vanished.

—DeWitt Bodeen

KOVÁCS, ANDRÁS. Hungarian. Born in Kide, 20 June 1925. Educated at Academy of Theatre and Film Art, Budapest, 1946-50. Career: 1951-57—works at Film Studios of Budapest as head of scenario department; 1960—directs 1st film; 1964—receives 1st international attention with *Difficult People*; currently President of the Union of Hungarian Filmmakers. Recipient: Hungarian Critics Prize for *Difficult People*, 1965; Silver Prize, Moscow Festival, for *Temporary Paradise*, 1981. Address: Magyar Jakobinusok tere 2-3, 1122 Budapest, Hungary.

Films (as director): 1960—*Zápor (A Summer Rain)*; 1961—*Pesti háztekök (On the Roofs of Budapest)*; 1962—*Isten öszi csillaga (Autumn Star)*; 1964—*Nehéz emberek (Difficult People)* (+sc); 1965—*Két arckép (2 Portraits)* (documentary); *Ma vagy holnap (Today or Tomorrow)* (documentary); 1966—*Hideg napok (Cold Days)* (+sc); 1968—*Falak (Walls)* (+sc); 1969—*Extázis 7-töl 10-ig (Ecstasy from 7 to 10)* (documentary—for TV); 1970—*Örökösök (Heirs)* (documentary); *Staféta (Relay Race)* (+sc); 1972—*A magyar ugaraon (Fallow Land)* (+sc); *Találkozás Lukács Györggyel (Meeting György Lukács)* (for TV—in 2 parts); 1973—*Együtt Károlyi Mihállyal—Beszélgetés Károlyi Mihálynéval (My Life with Mihály Károlyi)* (for TV); 1975—*Bekötött szemmel (Blindfold)* (+sc); *Kié a müvészet (People and Art)* (documentary); 1976—*Labirintus (Labyrinth)* (+sc); 1978—*Ménesgazda (The Chief of the Horse Farm, The Stud Farm)* (+sc); 1979—*Októberi vasárnap (A Sunday in October)* (+sc); 1980—*Ideiglenes paradicsom (Temporary Paradise)* (+sc—for TV); 1983—*Közelkép.*

Publications:

By KOVÁCS:

Books—*Falak*, Budapest 1968; *Egy fiěm forrásvidéke*, Budapest 1971; *Októberi vasárnap*, Budapest 1980; articles—"Aucune fin ne justifie les moyens...", interview by F. Dufour in *Cinéma* (Paris), June 1973; "A müvészet értelme a konfliktusok tudatositása és végigharcolása" in *Filmkultura* (Budapest), January/-February 1973; interview by I. Zsugán in *Filmkultura* (Budapest), September/October 1974; "Labirintus" (script) in *Filmkultura* (Budapest), March/April 1976; "Aby dobré bylo nahrazeno lepším", interview by K. Pošová in *Film a Doba* (Prague), July 1977; "A szovjet film demokratizmusarol" in *Filmkultura* (Budapest), July/August 1979.

On KOVÁCS:

Books—*András Kovács* by Trosin, Moscow 1979; *Kovács András* by J. Veres, Budapest 1980; *Kovács* by G. Giuricin, Florence 1981; article—"La dialettica marxista nel cinema di Andras Kovacs" by G. Giuricin in *Cinema nuovo* (Turin), September/October 1976.

*   *   *

András Kovács, together with Zoltán Fábri and Miklós Jancsó, was the filmmaker who provoked discussions about a new Hungarian cinema at the beginning of the sixties. After making many more or less conventional films in the 1950s, most of which show traces of Stalinistic aesthetics from the period of the cult of personality, these filmmakers, at the time in their thirties, tried to introduce another kind of cinema.

Thematically their films treated "difficult" subjects, controversial moments from the nation's history. They portrayed events in which heroes often turned out to be villians, and the usual interpretation of historical facts was put into question. A typical example of this trend is *Cold Days*, which dealt with the liquidation of hundreds of Bosnians by the Hungarian fascists during the Second World War.

In his subsequent films—*Walls, Relay Race*, and *Labyrinth*, Kovács treats contemporary problems of Hungarian society. These films are constructed as discussions during which a number of protagonists express in detail their arguments and points of view. Because of this approach, Kovács came to be called a "publicist with a camera," the communist conscience of the Hungarian cinema. Stylistically these works are uneven, rough, overloaded with dialogue. This is the reason why many Hungarian and foreign critics consider him as a social, but not artistic phenomenon, as opposed to Miklós Janscó.

In 1978 Kovács created the film *The Chief of the Horse-Farm*, which demonstrated a new aspect of his cinematic gift. The film presents the birth pains of the socialist system in Hungary in 1950, and analyzes why and how that birth took place in the midst of bloody tragedies.

This is the story of the ancient peasant Buso, who is given the task of ruling a farm where the former owners and supervisors have become the grooms. The resulting conflicts end in the death of Buso and the others, because none of them manages to understand and master the complicated situation of political fighting and intrigue. This is Kovács's best film, dealing profoundly with the first years of the new system in Hungary and illustrating processes which everyone who wishes to understand the Hungarian experience must grasp. Stylistically, it is a very beautiful, poetically narrated ballad, with masterfully lit and composed shots, and with strong acting.

With this film Kovács buried the prejudice that he is a chronicler, a polemicist, a quasi-documentary director. He proved that a beautiful, lyrical film need not lead to mythologizing, but can demythologize. Once more Kovács managed to create a masterpiece, overcoming the greatest resistance. He is what one calls an artist, engaged in the problems of reality.

—Maria Racheva

KOZINTSEV, GRIGORI. Russian. Born in Kiev, 22 March 1905. Educated at gymnasium, Kiev; studied art with Alexandra Exter, Kiev; Academy of Fine Arts, Petrograd, 1919. Career: 1918—scenic artist in Lenin Theater, Kiev; with Sergei Yutkevich stages several plays; 1919—sent to Petrograd by Union of Art Workers of Kiev to further training; 1921—with Leonid Trauberg founds The Factory of the Eccentric Actor (FEKS); collaboration with Trauberg continues through 1946; 1924—with Trauberg makes 1st film, *The Adventures of Oktyabrina*; 1939-40—Kozintsev and Trauberg prepare film on the life of Karl Marx (unrealized); 1945—*Simple People* attacked in resolution of Central Committee of Communist Party; film suppressed until 1956; 1947—debut as solo director; 1953—stages *Hamlet*. Died in Leningrad, 11 May 1973. Recipient: Stalin Prize for the Maxim Trilogy, 1941; Lenin Prize for *Hamlet*, 1965.

Films (as co-director with Leonid Trauberg): 1924—*Pok-hozdeniya Oktyabrini* [The Adventures of Octyabrina] (+co-sc); 1925—*Michki protiv Youdenitsa* [Mishka Against Yudenitch] (+co-sc); 1926—*Chyortovo Koleso* [The Devil's Wheel]; *Shinel* [The Cloak]; 1927—*Bratichka* [Little Brother] (+co-sc); *S.V.D. (Soyuz Velikogo Dela)* [The Club of the Big Deed]; 1929—*Novyi Vavilon (The New Babylon)*; 1931—*Odna (Alone)* (+co-sc); 1935—*Yunost Maksima (The Youth of Maxim)* (+co-sc); 1937—*Vozvrashcheniye Maksima (The Return of Maxim)* (+co-sc); 1939—*Vyborgskaya storona (New Horizons)* [The Vyborg Side] (+co-sc); 1945—*Prostiye Lyudi (Simple People, Plain People)* (released in reedited version 1956 which Kozintsev disowned) (+co-sc); (as director): 1947—*Pirogov*; 1953—*Belinski* (+co-sc); 1957—*Don Quixote*; 1963—*Hamlet* (+sc); 1971—*Karol Lear (King Lear)* (+sc).

Publications:

By KOZINTSEV:

Books—*Shakespeare: Time and Conscience*, New York 1966; *Glubokij ekran*, Moscow 1971; *King Lear: The Space of Tragedy*, Berkeley, California 1977; articles—"Deep Screen" in *Sight and Sound* (London), summer/autumn 1959; "Over the Parisiana" in *Sight and Sound* (London), winter 1962/63; "The Hamlet Within Me" in *Films and Filming* (London), September 1962; "Prostrantsvo tragedii" in *Iskusstvo Kino* (Moscow), January, April, June, August, and November 1972; "A Child of the Revolution" in *Cinema in Revolution* edited by Luda and Jean Schnitzer, New York 1973; "Er widmete sein Talent der Revolution", interviews in *Film und Fernsehen* (Berlin), September 1973; "Peterburgskie povesti" in *Iskusstvo Kino* (Moscow), October 1973; "Prostranstvo tragedii" in *Iskusstvo Kino* (Moscow), January 1973; "L'Espace de la tragédie" in *Ecran* (Paris), March 1974; "Gogoliada" in *Iskusstvo Kino* (Moscow), May, June and July 1974; "Tagebuch" in *Film und Fernsehen* (Berlin), January 1974; "Iz rabočih tetradej" in *Iskusstvo Kino* (Moscow), July 1977; "Propos" in *Positif* (Paris), June 1977.

On KOZINTSEV:

Books—*Kino* by Jay Leyda, London 1960; *La Feks* by Mario Verdone and Barthelemy Amengual, Paris 1970; *Focus on Shakespearean Films* edited by Charles Eckert, Englewood Cliffs, New Jersey 1972; *The Most Important Art* by Antonin and Mira Liehm, Berkeley, California 1977; *Grigori Kozintsev* by Barbara Leaming, Boston 1980; *La Nouvelle Babylone*, anthology of texts on FEKS by Bernard Eisenschiytz and others, Paris n.d.; *La Feks: Kozintsev e Trauberg* edited by Giusi Rapisarda, Rome n.d.; articles—"A Meeting with Grigori Kozintsev" in *Film* (London), autumn 1967; "One Day with *King Lear*" by Yevgeniya Barteneva in *Soviet Film* (Moscow), no.9, 1969; "La metaphore 'commune'" by Jacques Aumont and others in *Cahiers du cinéma* (Paris), July 1971; "*La Nouvelle Babylon*" by Jean Narboni and Jean-Pierre Oudart in *Cahiers du cinéma* (Paris), October 1971; "The Conscience of the King" by Sergei Yutkevitch in *Sight and Sound* (London), autumn 1971; Director of the Year entry in *International Film Guide 1972*, London 1971; "Grigori Kozintsev, 1905-1973" by David Robinson in *Sight and Sound* (London), summer 1973; obituaries in *Iskusstvo Kino* (Moscow), October 1973; "G.M. Kozincev, kakim my ego znali..." by I. Hejfic and others in *Iskusstvo Kino* (Moscow), November 1974; "Slovo v spore" by A. Lipkov in *Iskusstvo Kino* (Moscow), September 1977; "La Nouvelle Babylone", special section by M. Tsikounas and Leonid Trauberg in *Avant-Scène du cinéma* (Paris), 1 December 1978; "Iz rabočih tetradej: Pis'ma" by V.G. Kozintseva and "Iz myslej o G.M. Kozinceve" by V. Shklovsky and others in *Iskusstvo Kino* (Moscow), April 1980.

*   *   *

A man of enormous enthusiasms, bursting with theories which were always intended to be put into practice as soon as possible, Kozintsev started his career at the age of 15 by giving public performances of plays in his family's sitting room in Kiev. When he went to art school in Petrograd he met Sergei Yutkevich and the two boys joined with Leonid Trauberg—a mature fellow of 20—to found FEKS, the Factory of the Eccentric Actor. They produced a book on *Eccentrism*, "published in Eccentropolis (formerly Petrograd)" and they produced all sorts of street theater, an amalgam of music hall, jazz, circus, and posters, meanwhile exhibiting their paintings at avant-garde shows.

Kozintsev was barely 19 when he and Trauberg brought all this flashy modernism, their love of tricks and devices, their commitment to a new society, and their boundless energy together in their first film *The Adventures of Oktyabrina*. Through their next few productions the two young directors perfected their art, learned how to control the fireworks and developed a mature style which, however, never lost its distinctive FEKS flavor.

In *The New Babylon*, a story about the Paris Commune of 1870, largely set in a fantastic department store, they reached that standard of excellence only achieved by the greatest silent films: in complete control of the medium, using Enei's brilliant art direction to the full, but peopling a gripping story with human characters only the correct degree larger than life that the medium demanded. A young composer, Shostakovich, was commissioned to write the accompanying score.

Kozintsev and Trauberg were themselves a little disappointed with their first sound film, *Alone*, a contemporary subject, although it was by no means a failure and it at least brought Shostakovich to the notice of the world at large. For the *Maxim Trilogy* they returned to a "historical-revolutionary" subject with tremendous success, building on their own experience with *New Babylon*, but completely integrating sound and dialogue rather than merely adding them to the previous recipe.

Sadly, the trilogy was really the last work of this highly successful partnership; their *Plain People*, about the wartime evacuation of a Leningrad factory to Central Asia, ran into serious official trouble and, although completed in 1945, was not released until 1956 in a version that Kozintsev refused to acknowledge.

For the rest of his independent career he remained loyal to the Leningrad studios and, perhaps because of the troubles with *Plain People*, devoted himself exclusively to historical or literary themes. After two "biopics"—*Pirogov* and *Belinski*—he turned to *Don Quixote*, which was well received at home and abroad. His *Hamlet*, with its brooding Scandinavian background, superb photography and beautifully handled acting, won even wider international acclaim; and his even more brooding and original *King Lear* must surely appeal to thinking people all over the world. These films were not merely very accomplished interpretations of Shakespeare's plays: they were the result of Kozintsev's own "brooding," years of deep research and careful thought, electrified, however, by equally profound emotions—the final flowering, in fact, of that enthusiastic 15-year-old in Kiev.

He himself wrote to Yutkevich after *King Lear*, "I am certin that every one of us...in the course of his whole life, shoots a single film of *his own*...this *own film* is made...in your head, through other work, on paper...in conversation: but it lives, breathes, somehow prolongs into age something that began its existence in childhood!" (*Sight and Sound*, Autumn 1971.) And indeed *King Lear* still combines Kozintsev's original emotionalism with his commitment to a cause; it is no accident that, despite its humanistic values, the film can be analyzed in terms of dialectical materialism. His enthusiam never deserted him. Not long before his death, after a private London showing of *King Lear*, triggered by a question about which translation of the play he had used, Kozintsev, waving his arms in excitement, his eyes flashing, his voice rising several octaves launched himself into a passionate eulogy and defense of the officially discredited poet, Boris Pasternak. So Kozintsev was an "eccentric actor" to the last—but, as always, with a deep concern for humanity and truth, regardless of any personal consquences.

—Robert Dunbar

KRAMER, ROBERT. American. Born in New York, June 1939 (or 1940). Career: early 1960s—writes several novels (unpublished); 1965—works for Newark Community Union Project (N-CUP), black community organization; project is subject of film *The Troublemakers* by Norman Fruchter; becomes interested in filmmaking, meets Robert Machover, cameraman on 1st 2 films; begins to work with Peter Gessner and Mike Robinson in production organization Alpha 60; also becomes associated with New York-based documentary team Blue Van Films; 1968—co-founds radical filmmaking/distribution organization *Newsreel*; early 1970s—part of political collective in Putney, Vermont; 1979—begins working in France. Recipient: Prix Georges Sadoul for *The Edge*, 1967; Special Jury Mention, Venice Festival, for *Guns*, 1980.

Films (as director): 1965—*FALN*; 1966—*In the Country*; 1968—*The Edge*; 1969—*People's War* (co-d); 1970—*Ice* (+sc, ro); 1975—*Milestones* (co-d); 1977—*Scenes from the Portuguese Class Struggle* (co-d); 1980—*Guns*; 1981—*Naissance*; *A toute allure*.

Publications:

By KRAMER:

Articles—interview by Jonas Mekas in the *Village Voice* (New York), 14 March 1968; "Entretiens avec Robert Kramer" by Jean Narboni in *Cahiers du cinéma* (Paris), April/May 1968; "Entretien avec Douglas et Kramer" by G. Gervais and G. Lionet in *Jeune Cinéma* (Paris), September/October 1975; "Milestones", interview by M. Martin in *Ecran* (Paris), December 1975; "Milestones", interview in *Cahiers du cinéma* (Paris), July/August 1975; "Filming in the Fist of the Revolution", interview by T. Brom in *Jump Cut* (Berkeley), no.12/13, 1976; interview by S. Toubiana in *Cahiers du cinéma* (Paris), December 1978; interview by P. Carcassonne and C. McMullin and "Notes sur une breve rencontre avec Franco Piperno" in *Cinématographe* (Paris), no.50, 1979; "Naissance d'une contre-culture", interview by G. Gervais in *Jeune cinéma* (Paris), December/-

January 1980/81; "Guns", interview by A. Garel in *Image et son* (Paris), December 1980.

On KRAMER:

Articles—"The Newsreel, première déclaration" in *Positif* (Paris), sumer 1968; "Blue Van, Alpha 60: 3 films politiques américains" by Jean-Pierre Jeancolas in *Jeune Cinéma* (Paris), May 1969; "Débat" by Jacques Aumont and others in *Cahiers du cinéma* (Paris), November/December 1970; "Ice et les USA" by Bernard Eisenschitz in *Cahiers du cinéma* (Paris), November/December 1970; "Tribune: cinema, fragments d'un expérience" by J.-P. Oudart in *Cahiers du cinéma* (Paris), February 1979.

*   *   *

Robert Kramer first tried his hand at literature, writing two unpublished novels, poetry, and plays. In 1965 he got involved in the organization of "N-Cup" (Newark Community Union Project) and simultaneously in the New York-based documentary team Blue Van Films. He founded a free federation of directors and producers, Alpha 60, and frequently collaborated with Newsreel, founded in 1968. Kramer never studied at a film school. He was influenced by sixties cinéma-vérité in the U.S. and more recently by directors such as Boorman and Altman. He has applied the devices of cinéma-vérité to fiction. "Fiction interests me, but I want to give it the life of a documentary," says Kramer.

His films deal mainly with political subjects: *In the Country* (story of a draft dodger), *The Edge*, *Ice* (urban guerillas); and with relationship among people as in *Milestones* (life in a commune). Kramer likes to work with non-actors, usually his close friends, although he increasingly uses professionals. His scripts are often improvised. He experiments with editing, avoids aesthetic embellishments, uses few colors. His films often seem to be of poor technical quality and visually "uncouth."

Kramer rejects classic narrative, leaving out exposition, and has no central heroes. He strives for a balance between acts and words. Refraining from pathos and revolutionary romanticism, he shows the failures and confusion of his characters. His concentration on explanatory details sometimes tends to be didactic and tedious, as are the pauses intended for viewers' reflection.

As a leftist filmmaker, Kramer has been accused of negative propaganda on the one hand, and of an inconsistent Marxist-Leninist standpoint on the other (although he is a supporter of Marxism-Leninism). The brutal, disturbing style of his films has elicited some negative response from audiences, but he has been generally acclaimed by critics. *Milestones* was banned in South Africa and a castration scene was censored in Great Britian.

Kramer currently lives in France (Italy would have been his second choice), where he has made three films. He left the U.S. because of a feeling of isolation and for the challenges of working in another culture. However, he is ready to face the U.S. public and even willing to accept a high-budget project with an interesting subject. Before moving to France, Kramer lived in various communes with friends and his second child, condemning the capitalist ideology of the family.

Robert Kramer believes that to be a filmmaker is both a profession and a pleasure, but that one can not separate the profession of a filmmaker from the work of a political agitator.

—Veroslav Hába

KRAMER, STANLEY. American. Born Stanley Earl Kramer in New York, 29 September 1913. Educated at New York University, degree in business administration 1933. Married Anne Pearce, 1950; children: Larry and Casey (daughter); married Karen Sharpe, 1966; children: Katherine and Jennifer. Career: 1934—takes job at 20th Century-Fox, becomes apprentice writer; 1938—senior editor at Fox; 1939-40—staff writer for Columbia and Republic Pictures, writes for radio series; 1942—joins MGM; 1943-45—serves in Army Signal Corps making training films; 1947—with Herbert Baker and Carl Foreman forms Screen Plays Inc.; 1949—forms Stanley Kramer Productions (becomes Stanley Kramer Co. in 1950); 1951—Stanley Kramer Co. joins Columbia Pictures with arrangement guaranteeing producing freedom; 1954—forms Stanley Kramer Pictures Corp. after agreement with Columbia terminated; 1955—begins directing as well as producing. Recipient: One World Award, San Remo, Italy, 1950; Best Director, New York Film Critics, for *The Defiant Ones*, 1958; Irving G. Thalberg Award, Academy of Motion Picture Arts and Sciences, 1961; Gallatin Medal, New York University, 1968. Address: c/o Stanley Kramer Productions, PO Box 158, Bellevue, Washington 90889.

Films (as producer): 1948—*So This Is New York* (Fleischer); 1949—*Champion* (Robson); *Home of the Brave* (Robson); 1950—*The Men* (Zinnemann); *Cyrano de Bergerac* (Gordon); 1951—*Death of a Salesman* (Benedek); 1952—*My 6 Convicts* (Fregonese); *The Sniper* (Dmytryk); *High Noon* (Zinnemann); *The Happy Time* (Fleischer); *The Four Poster* (Reis); *8 Iron Men* (Dmytryk); *The Member of the Wedding* (Zinnemann); 1953—*The Juggler* (Dmytryk); *The 5,000 Fingers of Dr. T* (Rowland); 1954—*The Wild One* (Benedek); *The Caine Mutiny* (Dmytryk); (as producer and director): 1955—*Not as a Stranger*; 1957—*The Pride and the Passion*; 1958—*The Defiant Ones*; 1959—*On the Beach*; 1960—*Inherit the Wind*; 1961—*Judgement at Nuremberg*; 1962—*Pressure Point* (Cornfield) (pr only); 1963—*A Child is Waiting* (Cassavetes) (pr only); *Its a Mad Mad Mad Mad World*; 1964—*Invitation to a Gunfighter* (Wilson) (pr only); 1965—*Ship of Fools*; 1967—*Guess Who's Coming to Dinner?*; 1969—*The Secret of Santa Vittoria*; 1970—*RPM*; 1971—*Bless the Beasts and Children*; 1973—*Oklahoma Crude*; 1976—*The Domino Principle*; 1979—*The Runner Stumbles*.

Publications:

By KRAMER:

Articles—"The Independent Producer" in *Films in Review* (New York), March 1951; "Kramer on the Future" in *Films in Review* (New York), May 1953; "Politics, Social Comment, and My Emotions" in *Films and Filming* (London), June 1960; "Sending Myself the Message" in *Films and Filming* (London), February 1964; interview in *A Special Kind of Magic* by Roy Newquist, Chicago 1967; "9 Times Across the Generation Gap" in *Action* (Los Angeles), March/April 1968; interview in *Directors at Work* edited by Bernard Kantor and others, New York 1970; "Soznanie otvetstvennosti" in *Iskusstvo Kino* (Moscow), December 1973; "Stanley Kramer: The Man and His Film", interview in *American Cinematographer* (Los Angeles), November 1979.

On KRAMER:

Book—*Stanley Kramer: Film Maker* by Donald Spoto, New York 1978; articles—"A Movies on B Budgets" by Bosley Crowther in *The New York Times Magazine*, 12 November 1950; "New Horizon" in *Time* (New York), 13 November 1950; *Kramer and Company* by Penelope Houston in *Sight and Sound* (London), July/September 1952; "Half a Step Behind" in *Time* (New York), 14 December 1953; "Talk with the Director" in *Newsweek* (New York), 17 October 1960; "Dore Schary—Stanley Kramer Syndrome" by Peter Bogdanovich in *New York Film Bulletin*, no.12-14, 1960; "Haunting Question:Producer-Director at Work" by Hollis Alpert and Arthur Knight in *Saturday Review* (New York), 2 December 1961; "Hollywood's Producer of Controversy" by Bosley Crowther in *The New York Times Magazine*, 10 December 1961; "An Actor's Director" by Spencer Tracy and Montgomery Clift in *Films and Filming* (London), January 1962; "The Defiant One" by Peter Cowie in *Films and Filming* (London), March 1963; "The Different One" by Peter Cowie in *Films and Filming* (London), March 1963; "Movies and Messages" by Midge Decter in *Commentary* (New York), November 1965; "Guess Who Came to Lunch?" by Mary Omatsu in *Take One* (Montreal), v.1, no.9, 1968; "A Recipe for Greatness" in *Films and Filming* (London), March 1968; "Stanley Kramer" by D. McGillivray in *Focus on Film* (London), autumn 1973.

*   *   *

Kramer was among the first of the successful, postwar independent producers in Hollywood. His oeuvre offers testimony to the virtues of such a position in terms of control over subject-matter, while also confirming the power of the tacit constraints that limit social criticism in Hollywood. Films produced, or produced and directed by Stanley Kramer remain close to the typical styles of postwar Hollywood narrative: location realism in *The Sniper*, *The Juggler*, *On the Beach*, and *Judgment at Nuremberg*; a clean narrative trajectory, except for somewhat "preachy" scenes when characters discuss the overt issues confronting them (medical care for the psychopath in *The Sniper* and *Pressure Point*, the need to support those with legal authority in *High Noon* or *The Caine Mutiny*); and a stress on the dilemmas of particular individuals via the mechanisms of psychological realism, although Kramer's characters bear a greater than average burden of representing social types and prominent social attitudes or beliefs.

What gives Kramer's work its greatest distinction is its frequent attention to topical social issues (criminality vs. mental illness, G.I. rehabilitation, racism, campus unrest in the sixties, juvenile delinquency, the need for and limits to legitimate authority, the hazard of nuclear war, and so on), even though some of Kramer's work is only obliquely issue-related (*The Four Poster*, *Cyrano de Bergerac*, *It's a Mad Mad Mad Mad World*, and *The 5000 Fingers of Dr. T*). When, through most of the 1950s, fewer and fewer topical, social issue films were being produced, Kramer continued to bring such fare to the screen. His films are not radical or revolutionary by any means: they tend to plead for a respect for the existing institutions of law and authority although they do point to serious structural rather than individual flaws in need of redress. They lack the idiosyncratic, more stylistically expressive sensibility of filmmakers less overtly socially-conscious who nevertheless raise similar issues such as Samuel Fuller or John Cassavetes. Even so, Kramer's films continue a long-standing Hollywood tradition of marrying topical issues to dramatic forms, a tradition in which we find many of Hollywood's more openly progressive films. In many ways, Kramers's films address the kind of issues those who were blacklisted during the fifties hoped to address within the terms of popular culture as defined by Hollywood. (Kramer himself was not blacklisted though he was and is still regarded by many as a socially concerned liberal.)

In fact, Stanley Kramer's career is ripe for reinvestigation. Criticized or dismissed by the left for failing to support blacklisted individuals or for not taking a sufficiently critical view of existing institutions, Kramer has also been criticized and dismissed by auteurist critics for failing to evince a personal enough stylistic signature (or the kind of fascination evoked by the romantic individualism of a Fuller or Ray). Structuralists have also overlooked his work, and so it remains a scantily studied, poorly assessed body of very significant work—as revealing of the limits of critical approaches as it may be of Kramer's own artistic or political sensibilities.

—Bill Nichols

KUBELKA, PETER. Austrian. Born in Taufkirchen, 3 March 1934. Educated in filmmaking at Akademie für Musik und darstellende Kunst, Vienna; Centro Sperimentale de Cinematografia, Rome. Career: late 1940s—member of Vienna Boys' Choir; co-founder and curator, Austrian Film Museum, Vienna; 1957-60—makes 3 "metrical" films, establishing reputation as avant-garde filmmaker; *Adebar* and *Schwechater* originally made as commercials; 1958—commissioned by painter Arnulf Rainer to make film portrait of himself; since 1967—numerous lecture appearances at American universities; late 1960s to present—at work on project *Monument for the Old World*; active as lecturer on film theory and as teacher; continues as joint director (with Peter Konlechner) of Österreichisches Filmmuseum, Vienna.

Films: 1954-55—*Mosaik im Vertrauen (Mosaic in Confidence)* (16.5 minutes); 1957—*Adebar* (90 seconds); 1958—*Schwechater* (1 minute); 1958-60—*Arnulf Rainer* (6.5 minutes); 1961-66—*Unsere Afrikareise* (12.5 minutes); 1976—*Pause*; [*Monument for the Old World*] (in progress); [*Body Language*] (in progress).

Publications:

By KUBELKA:

Book—*Histoire du cinéma: exposition concue par Peter Kubelka, organisée par Alain Sayag...*, Paris 1976; articles—interview by Jonas Mekas in *Film Culture* (New York), spring 1967 (collected in *Film Culture Reader* edited by P. Adams Sitney, New York 1970); interview by Jonas Mekas in *The Village Voice* (New York), 11 November 1971; "The Invisible Cinema" in *Design Quarterly* (Minneapolis), no.93, 1974; "Restoring Enthusiasm", interview by L. Fischer in *Film Quarterly* (Berkeley), winter 1977/78.

On KUBELKA:

Articles—"Kubelka Concrete (Our Trip to Vienna)" by P. Adams Sitney in *Film Culture* (New York), fall 1964; "The Films of Peter Kubelka" by Earl Bodien in *Film Quarterly* (Berkeley), winter 1966/67; "Structural Film" by P. Adams Sitney in *Film Culture* (New York), summer 1969; (collected in *Film Culture*

Reader edited by P. Adams Sitney, New York 1970); "Avant-Garde Film in Austria: Current Activities" by Peter Weibel in *Studio International* (London), November/December 1975.

* * *

Kubelka, the son of a musician, was a member of the Vienna boys choir; he remains a serious student of Baroque flute music, occasionally giving concerts. He studied filmmaking at the Centro Sperimentale di Cinematografia in Rome, where, he claims, he was nearly expelled for making his first film, *Mosaik im Vertrauen*, even though he made it on vacation and not under the auspices or with the equipment of the school.

A perfectionist, his entire oeuvre runs less than one hour of screen time. Between 1957 and 1960 he had made three short "metrical" films which established his reputation as a major avant-garde filmmaker. *Adebar*, and *Schwechater* were commissioned to advertise a cafe and a beer, but the resulting 90-second films were such rigorous manifestations of pure cinema that the filmmaker's incipient career as a maker of commercials was aborted and, instead, the foundation was laid for his prestige as a wholly original artist. The painter Arnulf Rainer commissioned a portrait of himself, but once again Kubelk seized the opportunity to make an abstract film; his *Arnulf Rainer* is a six-and-one-half-minute montage of black and white leader, synchronized with blasts of white noise. All these films were edited according to different schemata preestablished by the filmmaker, with every frame accounted for. They constitute the highest achievement of the European avante-garde of the 1950s, and they remain unmatched in their intricacy and formal rigor.

In 1966 Kubelka completed *Unsere Afrikareise*, a portrait of a group of Austrians on a safari. Shifting his attention from the dynamics of the changes which occur between film frames to the more traditional montage of whole shots, the filmmaker succeeded in making a sound/picture montage of incomparable ingenuity. Although none of the sound was shot synchronously, he found what he calls a "synch event" to correspond to every image.

All of Kubelka's films, including his later *Pause*, a study of the body performances of Arnulf Rainer, share a denial of temporality as we experience it conventionally. In any case he constructs *ad hoc* continuities through editing. His films are all systematic and have had a considerable influence on American and European filmmakers since the tendency toward the elaboration of abstract systems began in the late 1960s.

For the first fifteen years Kubelka has been at work on his *Monument for the Old World* but he has devoted considerable energy to lecturing on film theory and to teaching. His theoretical position stresses the autonomy and uniqueness of cinema as an art divorced from our commonsense notion of reality; it polemically asserts the value of extreme condensation and the discovery of purely cinematic rhythms, as exemplified by his own work. In this respect, his position reflects the tradition of the 20th century Vienese music, and more immediately the poetics of the generation of advanced Austrian artists who are his contemporaries.

—P. Adams Sitney

KUBRICK, STANLEY. American. Born in New York, 26 July 1928. Educated in New York City public schools; attended evening classes at City College of the City University of New York, 1945. Married Toba Metz, 1947 (divorced 1952); married dancer Ruth Sobotka, 1952; child: Katherine; married actress Suzanne Christiane Harlan; 1958—children: Anya and Vivian. Career: 1946—apprentice photographer for *Look* magazine, New York; 1950—makes 1st film, quits job as photographer; 1955—meets James Harris, forms Harris-Kubrick Productions; 1957—*Paths of Glory* released, Kubrick seen as "marketable" director; 1958—works on *One-Eyed Jacks* with Marlon Brando, quits film after 6 months; 1959—takes over direction of *Spartacus*, later disowns film; 1962—partnership with Harris dissolved amicably; 1964—begins research for *2001*; 1969—plans to film *Napoleon* (unrealized); 1971—release of *A Clockwork Orange*, violent critical reaction; 1974 to present—continues to work in England. Recipient: Best Direction for *Dr. Strangelove*, New York Film Critics 1964; Best Written American Comedy (screenplay), with Peter George and Terry Southern, Writers Guild of America, for *Dr. Strangelove*, 1964; Academy Award for Special Visual Effects for *2001*, 1968; Best Direction for *A Clockwork Orange*, New York Film Critics 1971; Best Direction British Academy Award for *Barry Lyndon*, 1975. Address: Boreham Wood, Hertfordshire, England.

Films (as producer or co-producer and director): 1950—*Day of the Fight* (+sc, ph); 1951—*Flying Padre* (+sc, ph); 1953—*The Seafarers* (d only, +ph); *Fear and Desire* (+ph, ed, co-sc); 1955—*Killer's Kiss* (+ph, sc, ed); 1956—*The Killing* (+sc); 1957—*Paths of Glory* (+co-sc); 1959—*Spartacus* (d only); 1962—*Lolita* (d only); 1964—*Dr. Strangelove: Or How I Learned to Stop Worrying and Love the Bomb* (+co-sc); 1968—*2001: A Space Odyssey* (+co-sc, director and designer of special photographic effects); 1971—*A Clockwork Orange* (+sc); 1975—*Barry Lyndon* (+sc); 1980—*The Shining* (+co-sc).

Publications:

By KUBRICK: Book—*Stanley Kubrick's A Clockwork Orange*, New York 1972; articles—"Bonjour, Monsieur Kubrick", interview by Raymond Haine in *Cahiers du cinéma* (Paris), July 1957; interview in the *Observer* (London), 4 December 1960; "Interview with Kubrick" by Charles Reynolds in *Popular Photography* (Boulder, Colorado), December 1960; "Words and Movies" in *Sight and Sound* (London), winter 1961; "How I Learned to Stop Worrying and Love the Cinema" in *Films and Filming* (London), June 1963; "Quotesmanship" in *Action* (Los Angeles), May/June 1968; "Kubrick Reveals All" in *Cinéaste* (New York), summer 1968; "Interview with Stanley Kubrick" by Eric Norden in *Playboy* (Chicago), September 1968; "A Talk with Stanley Kubrick" by Maurice Rapf in *Action* (Los Angeles), January/February 1969; "Entretien avec Stanley Kubrick" by Renaud Walter in *Positif* (Paris), December/January 1969/70; "What Directors Are Saying" in *Action* (Los Angeles), January/-February and November/December 1971; "Entretien avec Stanley Kubrick" by Michel Ciment in *Positif* (Paris), June 1972; "Kubrick", interview by Gene Phillips in *Film Comment* (New York), winter 1971/72; "Interview with Stanley Kubrick" by Phillip Strick and Penelope Houston in *Sight and Sound* (London), spring 1972; "Something More", interview by Gordon Gow in *Films and Filming* (London), October 1975.

On KUBRICK: Books—*The Cinema of Stanley Kubrick* by David Austen, London 1969; *The Making of Kubrick's 2001* by Jerome Agel, New York 1970; *Stanley Kubrick Directs* by Alexander Walker, New York 1972; *The Cinema of Stanley Kubrick* by Norman Kagan, New York 1972; *The Films of Stanley*

Kubrick by Daniel Devries, Grand Rapids, Michigan 1973; *Elements of Film* by Lee Bobker, New York 1974; *Stanley Kubrick: A Film Odyssey* by Gene Phillips, New York 1977; *Voices of Film Experience* edited by Jay Leyda, New York 1977; *How to Read a Film* by James Monaco, New York 1977; *Kubrick* by Michel Ciment, Paris 1980; articles—"The Current Cinema: Amateur" by John McCarten in the *New Yorker*, 11 April 1953; review by Arlene Croce in *Film Culture* (New York), spring 1956; "29 and Running: The Director with Hollywood By the Horns" in *Newsweek* (New York), 2 December 1957; "Film Fan to Film Maker" in *The New York Times Magazine*, 12 October 1958; "No Art and No Boxoffice" by Dwight MacDonald in *Encounter* (London), July 1959; "The Hollywood War of Independence" by Colin Young in *Film Quarterly* (Berkeley), spring 1959; "Killers, Kisses, and *Lolita*" by Robin Noble in *Films and Filming* (London), December 1960; article in *The Dreams and the Dreamers* by Hollis Alpert, New York 1962; "10 Questions to 9 Directors" in *Sight and Sound* (London), spring 1964; "Stanley Kubrick" in *Cahiers du cinéma* (Paris), December/January 1964/65; "Out of This World" by Robert Brustein in *New York Review of Books*, 6 February 1964; "The Antimilitarism of Stanley Kubrick" by Jackson Burgess in *Film Quarterly* (Berkeley), fall 1964; "Stanley Kubrick's Divided World" by James Price in *London Magazine*, May 1964; "Beyond the Stars" by Jeremy Bernstein in the *New Yorker*, 24 April 1965; "Profiles: How About a Little Game?" by Jeremy Bernstein in the *New Yorker*, 12 November 1966; "L'Odyssee de Stanley Kubrick" by Michel Ciment in *Positif* (Paris), October 1968; "Mind's Eye" by Jack Hofsess in *Take One* (Montreal), May/June 1971; "Kubrick Country" by Penelope Houston in *Saturday Review* (New York), 25 December 1971; "Nice Boy From the Bronx?" by Craig McGregor in *The New York Times*, 30 January 1972; "Kubrick Tells What Makes *Clockwork Orange* Tick" by Bernard Weinraub in *The New York Times*, 4 January 1972; "Kubrick's Brilliant Vision" by Paul Zimmerman in *Newsweek* (New York), 3 January 1973; "The Films of Stanley Kubrick" by James Monaco in the *New School Bulletin* (New York), summer 1973; "Stanley Kubrick" in *The Movie Makers: Artists in Industry* by Gene Phillips, Chicago 1973; "The Eyehole of Knowledge: Voyeuristic Games in Film and Literature" by Alfred Appel, Jr. in *Film Comment* (New York), May/June 1973; "Kubrick and the Structures of Popular Culture" by Harriet and Irving Deer in *Journal of Popular Film* (Bowling Green, Ohio), summer 1974; "Barry Lyndon" by Penelope Houston in *Sight and Sound* (London), spring 1974; "In Search of Stanley K." by Mark Carducci in *Millimeter* (New York), December 1975; "Kubrick's Grandest Gamble" by Martha Duffy and Richard Schickel in *Time* (New York), 15 December 1975; "Stanley Kubrick" in *Directors and Directions: Cinema for the 70s* by John Taylor, New York 1975; "Kubrick and His Discontents" by Hans Feldmann in *Film Quarterly* (Berkeley), fall 1976; "Clockwork Violence" by Ken Moskowitz in *Sight and Sound* (London), winter 1976/77; "'Orange mécanique' de Stanley Kubrick" by D. Sotiaux in *Revue belge du cinéma* (Brussels), January 1977; "Kubrick Goes Gothic" by H. Kennedy in *American Film* (Washington, D.C.), June 1980; "Stanley Kubrick se ha puesto reflexivo y ahora terrorifico" by A. Migdal in *Cinemateca revista* (Montevideo, Uruguay), July 1981; "La Symphonie Kubrick" by M. Sineux in *Positif* (Paris), February 1981.

* * *

Few American directors have been able to work within the studio system of the American film industry with the independence which Stanley Kubrick has achieved. By steadily building a reputation as a filmmaker of international importance, he has gained full artistic control over his films, guiding the production of each of them from the earliest stages of planning and scripting through post-production. Kubrick has been able to capitalize on the wide artistic freedom that the major studios have accorded him because he learned the business of filmmaking from the ground up.

In the early fifties he turned out two documentary shorts for RKO; he was then able to secure financing for two low-budget features which he says today were "crucial in helping me to learn my craft," but which he would otherwise prefer to forget. He made both films almost singlehandedly, acting as his own cameraman, sound man, editor, as well as directing the films.

Then, in 1955, he met James Harris, an aspiring producer; together they made *The Killing*, about a group of small-time crooks who rob a race track. *The Killing* not only turned a modest profit but prompted the now legendary remark of *Time* magazine that Kubrick "has shown more imagination with dialogue and camera than Hollywood has seen since the obstreperous Orsen Welles went riding out of town."

Kubrick next acquired the rights to Humphrey Cobb's 1935 novel *The Paths of Glory*, and in 1957 turned it into one of the most uncompromising anti-war films ever made. One film historian has written that Kubrick uses his camera in the film "unflinchingly, like a weapon," as it sweeps across the slopes to record the wholesale slaughter of a division.

Spartacus, a spectacle about slavery in pre-Christian Rome, Kubrick recalls as "the only film over which I did not have absolute control," because the star, Kirk Douglas, was also the movie's producer. Although *Spartacus* turned out to be one of the better spear-and-sandal epics, Kubrick vowed never to make another film unless he was assured of total artistic freedom and he never has.

Lolita, about a middle-aged man's obsessive infatuation with his pre-teen step-daughter, was the director's first comedy."The surprising thing about *Lolita*," Pauline Kael wrote, "is how enjoyable it is. It's the first new American comedy since those great days in the forties when Preston Sturges re-created comedy with verbal slapstick. *Lolita* is black slapstick and at times it's so far out that you gasp as you laugh."

For those who appreciate the dark humor of *Lolita*, it is not hard to see that it was just a short step from that film to Kubrick's masterpiece in that genre, *Dr. Strangelove: Or How I Learned to Stop Worrying and Love the Bomb*, concerning a lunatic American general's decision to launch an attack inside Russia. The theme implicit in the film is man's final capitulation to his own machines of destruction. Kubrick further examined his dark vision of man in a mechanistic age in *2001: A Space Odyssey*.

Kubrick's view of life, as it is reflected in *2001*, seems to be somewhat more optimistic than it was in his previous pictures. *2001* holds out hope for the progress of mankind through man's creative encounters with the universe. In *A Clockwork Orange*, however, the future appears to be less promising than it did in *2001*: in the earlier film Kubrick showed (in the "person" of the talking computer Hal) the machine becoming human, whereas in *A Clockwork Orange* he shows man becoming a machine through brainwashing and thought control.

Ultimately, however, the latter film only reiterates in somewhat darker terms a repeated theme in all of Kubrick's previous work, i.e. that man must retain his humanity if he is to survive in a dehumanized, highly mechanized world. Moreover, *Clockwork Orange* echoes the warning of *Dr. Strangelove* and *2001* that man must strive to gain mastery over himself if he is to master the machines of his own invention.

After a trio of films set in the future, Kubrick reached beck into the past and adapted Thackeray's historical novel *Barry Lyndon* to the screen in 1975. Kubrick has portrayed Barry, an eighteenth century rogue, and his times in the same critical fashion as Thackeray did before him.

The film echoes a theme which appears in much of the director's best work, that through human error the best-laid plans often go awry; and hence man is often thwarted in his efforts to achieve his goals. The central character in *Lolita* fails to possess a nymphet exclusively; the "balance of terror" between nations designed to halt the nuclear arms race in *Dr. Strangelove* does not succeed in averting global destruction; and modern technology turns against its human instigators in *Dr. Strangelove, 2001*, and *A Clockwork Orange*. In this list of films about human failure the story of Barry Lyndon easily finds a place, for its hero's lifelong schemes to become a rich nobleman in the end come to nothing. And the same can be said for the frustrated writing aspirations of the emotionally disturbed hero of Kubrick's horror film, *The Shining*.

It is clear, therefore, that Kubrick can make any source material fit comfortably into the fabric of his work as a whole, whether it be a remote and almost forgotten Thackeray novel, or a provocative "thinking man's thriller" by a comtemporary novelist such as *The Shining*.

Furthermore, it is equally evident that Kubrick wants to continue to create films that will stimulate his audience to think about serious human problems, as his pictures have done from the beginning. Because of the success of his movies in the past, Kubrick can go on making films in the way he wants to, proving in the future as he has in the past, that he values the artistic freedom which he has worked so hard to win and he has used so well.

—Gene D. Phillips

KULESHOV, LEV. Soviet. Born Lev Vladimirovich Kuleshov in Tambov, Russia, 14 January 1899. Educated in painting at Fine Arts School, Moscow, enrolled 1914. Married Alexandra Khokhlova. Career: 1916—becomes set designer for filmmaker Yevgeni Bauer; late 'teens—begins editing experiments leading to formulation of "Kuleshov effect" by which varying emotions can be evoked through juxtaposing same shot of actor with different objects; 1918—publishes 1st theoretical article; 1919—participates in creation of First National Film School, begins teaching there 1920; 1919-21—makes short *agitki* and forms film workshop; late 1920s—increasing conflict with authorities; 1933—temporarily halts filmmaking activities, continues writing theoretical works on film; 1944—appointed director of State Institute of Cinematography, Moscow; 1960s—rediscovered in the West, becomes subject of retrospectives; 1966—on jury of Venice Film Festival. Died 29 March 1970. Recipient: Merited Artist of the RSFSR, 1935.

Films (as director): 1918—*Proyekt inzhenera Praita (Engineer Prite's Project)* (+art d); 1919—*The Unfinished Love Song* (co-d, +art d); 1920—*Na krasnom fronte (On the Red Front)* (+sc, ro); 1924—*Neobychainiye priklucheniya Mistera Vesta v stranye bolshevikov (Extraordinary Adventures of Mr West in the Land of the Bolsheviks)*; 1925—*Luch smerti (The Death Ray)* (+ro); 1926—*Po zakonu (Dura Lex, By the Law)* (+co-sc); *Locomotive No.1000b*; 1927—*Vasha znakomaya (Your Acquaintance, Journalist)* (+co-sc); 1929—*The Gay Canary*; *2-Buldi-2* (co-d); 1931—*40 Hearts*; 1932—*Horizon (Horizon—The Wandering*

Jew) (+co-sc); 1933—*Velikii uteshitel (The Great Consoler)* (+co-sc); 1940—*The Siberians*; 1941—*Incident in a Volcano* (co-d); 1942—*Timur's Oath*; 1944—*We Are From the Urals* (co-d).

Publications:

By KULESHOV:

Books—*Eisenstein: Potiemkine*, with Shklovsky and Tisse, Moscow 1926; *The Art of Cinema*, in Russian, Moscow 1929; *Fundamentals of Film Direction*, in Russian, Moscow 1941; *Traité de mise en scène. Les Premières Prises de vues*, Paris 1962; *Kuleshov on Film* translated and edited by Ronald Levaco, Berkeley 1974; articles—in *Vestnik Kinematografia* (Moscow), no.127, 1917; "From 'West' to 'Canary'", in Russian, in *Sovietski Ekran* (Moscow), 12 March 1929; "Our First Experiences", in Russian, in *Sovetskoye Kino* (Moscow), November/December 1934; "20 Years", in Russian, in *Iskusstvo Kino* (Moscow), March 1940; "Bonjour, Paris!" in *Les Lettres françaises* (Paris), 18 October 1962; "Souvenirs (1918-1920)" in *Cahiers du cinéma* (Paris), July 1970; interview by André Labarthe and Bertrand Tavernier in *Cahiers du cinéma* (Paris), May/June 1970; "Selections from Lev Kuleshov's Art of the Cinema" in *Screen* (London), winter 1971/72.

On KULESHOV:

Books—*Kino* by Jay Leyda, London 1960; *Le Cinéma soviétique par ceux qui l'ont fait*, edited by Luda and Jean Schnitzer, Paris 1966; articles—"Au début du cinéma soviétique était Lev Koulechov. Portrait d'un ami" by Georges Sadoul in *Les Lettres françaises* (Paris), 18 October 1962; "Lev Koulechov grand théoreticien du cinéma by Georges Sadoul in *Le Technicien du film* (Paris), January 1965; "Kuleshov—Prophet Without Honor?" by Steven Hill in *Film Culture* (New York), spring 1967; "Lev Kuleshov, 1899-1970" by Richard Taylor in *Silent Picture* (London), autumn 1970; "Lev Kuleshov: 1899-1970" in *Afterimage* (Rochester, New York), April 1970; "Lev Koulechov" by Neïa Zorkaia in *Cahiers du cinéma* (Paris), May/June 1970; "Kuleshov" by Ronald Levaco in *Sight and Sound* (London), spring 1971; "Lev Koulechov, inventeur et pédagogue (1899-1970)" by Jerzy Toeplitz in *Cinéma 71* (Paris), December 1971; "The Classic Period of Soviet Cinema" in *Film Journal* (New York), fall/winter 1972.

* * *

KUROSAWA, AKIRA. Japanese. Born in Tokyo, 23 March 1910. Educated at Kuroda Primary School, Edogawa; Keika High School; studied at Doshusha School of Western Painting, about 1927. Married Yoko Yaguchi in 1945; children: Hisao (son) and Kazuko (daughter). Career: late 1920s—attempts to make living as painter, does illustrations for popular magazines; joins Japan Proletariat Artists' Group; 1936—answers newspaper advertisement seeking applicants for assistant-directorships at P.C.L. Studios (Photo-Chemical Laboratory, later Toho Motion Picture Co.), and is selected; learns basic filmmaking in Kajiro Yamamoto's production group; late 1930s—writes scripts in addition to other duties; 1948—begins collaboration with actor Toshiro Mifune on *Drunken Angel*; with Yamamoto and others organizes production organization Motion Picture Artists Association (Eiga Geijutsuka Kyokai); 1959—forms Kurosawa Productions; 1966—signs contract with producer Joseph E. Levine to work in U.S., engaged in several abortive projects through 1968; 1971—forms Yonki no Kai production company with directors Keisuke Kinoshita, Kon Ichikawa and Masaki Kobayashi; despair over career and commercial failure of *Dodeskaden* leads to suicide attempt on December 22; 1972-75—works on *Dersu Uzala* following Russian invitation. Recipient: *Mainichi* newspaper best director award for *Regrets for Our Youth*, 1947; Lion of St. Mark, Venice Film Festival, for *Rashomon*, 1951; Academy Award for Best Foreign Language Film for *Rashomon*, 1951; Golden Bear (Best Direction), Berlin Festival, for *The Hidden Fortress*, 1959; International Critics' Prize, Berlin Festival, for *The Hidden Fortress*, 1959; Ramon Magsaysay Memorial Award, Philippines, 1965; Best Foreign-Language Film Academy Award for *Dersu Uzala*, 1975; made a 'Person of Cultural Merits' by Japanese government, 1976; Best Direction British Academy Award for *Kagemusha*, 1980.

Films (as scriptwriter): 1941—*Uma* [Horses] (Yamamoto) (co-sc); 1942—*Seishun no kiryu* [Currents of Youth] (Fushimizi); *Tsubasa no gaika* [A Triumph of Wings] (Yamamoto); (as director and scriptwriter): 1943—*Sugata Sanshiro (Sanshiro Sugata, Judo Saga)*, remade as same title by Shigeo Tanaka, 1955, and by Seiichiro Uchikawa, 1965 (and edited by Kurosawa); 1944—*Ichiban utsukushiku (The Most Beautiful, Most Beautifully)*; *Dohyo-matsuri* [Wrestling-Ring Festival] (Marune) (sc only); 1945—*Zoku Sugata Sanshiro (Sanshiro Sugata—Part 2, Judo Saga—II)*; *Appare Isshin Tasuke* [Bravo, Tasuke Isshin!] (Saeki) (sc only); *Tora no o o fumu otokotachi (Men Who Tread on the Tiger's Tail, They Who Step on the Tiger's Tail)*; 1946—*Asu o tsukuru hitobito (Those Who Make Tomorrow)* (co-d only); *Waga seishun ni kuinashi (No Regrets for Our Youth, No Regrets for My Youth)* (co-sc); 1947—*Subarashiki nichiyobi (One Wonderful Sunday, Wonderful Sunday)* (co-sc); *Ginrei no hate (To the End of the Silver Mountains)* (Taniguchi) (sc only); *Hatsukoi (1st Love)* segment of *Yottsu no koi no monogatari (4 Love Stories)* (Toyoda) (sc only); 1948—*Yoidore tenshi (Drunken Angel)* (co-sc); *Shozo (The Portrait)* (Kinoshita) (sc only); 1949—*Shizukanaru ketto (The Quiet Duel, A Silent Duel)* (co-sc); *Nora inu (Stray Dog)* (co-sc); *Yakoman to Tetsu (Yakoman and Tetsu)* (Taniguchi) (sc only); *Jigoku no kifujin (The Lady from Hell)* (Oda) (sc only); 1950—*Shubun (Scandal)* (co-sc); *Rashomon* (co-sc), remade as *The Outrage* by Martin Ritt, 1964; *Akatsuki no dasso (Escape at Dawn)* (Taniguchi) (sc only); *Jiruba no Tetsu (Tetsu 'Jilba')* (Kosugi) (sc only); *Tateshi danpei (Fencing Master)* (Makino) (sc only); 1951—*Hakuchi (The Idiot)* (co-sc); *Ai to nikushimi no kanata e (Beyond Love and Hate)* (Taniguchi) (sc only); *Kedamono no yado (The Den of Beasts)* (Osone) (sc only); *Ketto Kagiya no tsuji (The Duel at Kagiya Corner)* (Mori) (sc only); 1952—*Ikiru (Living, To Live)* (co-sc); 1954—*Shichinin no samurai (Seven Samurai)* (co-sc), remade as *The Magnificent Seven* by John Sturges, 1961; 1955—*Ikimono no kiroku (Record of a Living Being, I Live in Fear, What the Birds Knew)* (co-sc); 1957—*Kumonosu-jo (The Throne of Blood, The Castle of the Spider's Web, Cobweb Castle)* (co-sc, +co-pr); *Donzoko (The Lower Depths)* (co-sc, +co-pr); *Tekichu odan sanbyakuri (300 Miles through Enemy Lines)* (Mori) (sc only); 1958—*Kakushi toride no san-akunin (The Hidden Fortress, 3 Bad Men in a Hidden Fortress)* (co-sc, +co-pr); 1960—*Warui yatsu hodo yoku nemuru (The Bad Sleep Well, The Worse You Are the Better You Sleep, The Rose in the Mud)* (co-sc, +co-pr); *Sengoku guntoden (The Saga of the Vagabond)* (Sugie) (sc only); *Yojimbo (The Bodyguard)* (co-sc), remade as *Per un pungo di dollari (A Fistful of Dollars)* by Sergio Leone; 1962—*Sanjuro* (co-sc); 1963—*Tengoku to jigoku (High and Low, Heaven and Hell, The Ransom)* (co-sc); 1965—

Akahige (Red Beard) (co-sc); 1970—*Dodesukaden (Dodeskaden)* (co-sc, +co-pr); 1975—*Dersu Uzala* (co-sc); 1980—*Kagemusha (The Shadow Warrior)* (co-sc +co-pr).

Publications:

By KUROSAWA:

Books and scripts—*Ikiru*, with Shinobu Hashimoto and Hideo Oguni, edited by Donald Richie, New York 1968; *Rashomon*, with Shinobu Hashimoto, edited by Donald Richie, New York 1969; *The 7 Samurai* translated by Donald Richie, New York 1970; *Kurosawa Akira eiga taikei* [Complete Works of Akira Kurosawa] edited by Takamaro Shimaji, in 12 volumes, Tokyo 1970-72; articles—"Jokantoku jidai no omoide" [Recollections of My Time as an Assistant Director] in *Nihon eiga kaikoroku* [A Retrospective of Japanese Cinema], Tokyo 1963; "Waga eiga jinsei no ki" [Diary of My Movie Life] in *Kinema jumpo* (Tokyo), April 1963; "Notes à propos de mes films" in *Études cinématographiques* (Paris), spring 1964; "Why Mifune's Beard Won't Be Red" in *Cinema* (Los Angeles), July 1964; "Visite à l'empereur du Japon: un entretien avec Akira Kurosawa" by *Michel Mesnil in Cinema 66* (Paris), February 1966; "L'Empereur: entretien avec Kurosawa" by Yoshio Shirai and others in *Cahiers du cinéma* (Paris), September 1966; "Akira Kurosawa", interview by Donald Richie, in *Interviews with Film Directors* edited by Andrew Sarris, New York 1967; "Dits" in *Positif* (Paris), December 1971; "Kurosawa Akira kantoku to *Dersu Uzala* staff ni kiku" [Listening to Kurosawa and His Staff of *Dersu Uzala*], with others, in *Kinema jumpo* (Tokyo), October 1974; "Akira Kurosawa", interview, in *Voices from the Japanese Cinema* by Joan Mellen, New York 1975; "Moscow Film Festival", with interview, by B.J. Demby in *Filmmakers Newsletter* (Ward Hill, Mass.), October 1975; "Der Film ist mein Leben", interview with S. Certok in *Film und Fernsehen* (Berlin), January 1977; "Declaraciones", interview, in *Contracampo* (Madrid), April/May 1981; "Tokyo Stories: Kurosawa", interview by Tony Rayns in *Sight and Sound* (London), summer 1981.

On KUROSAWA:

Books—*Le Cinéma japonais, (1896-1955)* by Shinobu and Marcel Giuglaris, Paris 1956; *The Japanese Film: Art and Industry* by Joseph Anderson and Donald Richie, New York 1960; *Kurosawa Retrospektive* by Donald Richie and Werner Schwier, Munich 1961; *Kurosawa* by Sacha Ezratti, Classiques du cinéma no.15, Paris 1964; *Kurosawa* by Sacha Ezratty, Paris 1964; *Kurosawa Akira no sekai* [The World of Akira Kurosawa] by Tadao Sato, Tokyo 1968; *The Films of Akira Kurosawa* by Donald Richie, Berkeley, California 1970; *Sekai no eiga sakka—Kurosawa Akira* [Film Directors of the World—Akira Kurosawa] edited by Chieko Kofujita, Tokyo 1970; *Japanese Cinema: Film Style and National Character* by Donald Richie, New York 1971; *Focus on Rashomon* edited by Donald Richie, Englewood Cliffs, New Jersey 1972; *Kurosawa* by Michel Mesnil, Paris 1973; *The Waves at Genji's Door: Japan Through Its Cinema* by Joan Mellen, New York 1976; *Akira Kurosawa: A Guide to References and Resources* by Patricia Erens, Boston 1979; articles—"Introducing Japan's Top Director" by Ray Falk in *The New York Times*, 6 January 1952; "The Films of Kurosawa" by Jay Leyda in *Sight and Sound* (London), October/December 1954; "Humanism in Film" by A. Rosenthal in *Film* (London), October 1954; "2 Inches Off the Ground" by Lindsay Anderson in *Sight and Sound* (London), winter 1957; "Les deux visages d'Akira Kurosawa" by F. Gaffary in *Positif* (Paris), no.22, 1957; "Traditional Theater and the Film in Japan" by Joseph Anderson and Donald Richie in *Film Quarterly* (Berkeley), fall 1958; "Season in the Sun" by Arthur Knight in the *Saturday Review* (New York), 13 February 1960; "A Personal Record" by Donald Richie in *Film Quarterly* (Berkeley), fall 1960; "The Rebel in a Kimono" by Douglas McVay in *Films and Filming* (London), July 1961; "Samurai and Small Beer" by Douglas McVay in *Films and Filming* (London), August 1961; "Akira Kurosawa" in *Cinema* (Los Angeles), August/September 1963; articles translated from Japanese in *Cinema* (Los Angeles), August/September 1963; "Heaven and Hell" by Donald Richie in *Films and Filming* (London), January 1963; special Kurosawa issue of *Kinema jumpo* (Tokyo), April 1963; "Akira Kurosawa" issue of *Etudes cinématographiques* (Paris) no.30-31, spring 1964; special issue of *Kinema jumpo* (Tokyo), 5 September 1964; "Kurosawa's Humanism" by Charles Higham in *Kenyon Review* (Ohio), autumn 1965; "Au Japon: Akira Kurosawa et Georges Sadoul" in *Cinema 65* (Paris), January 1965; "Kurosawa and His Work" by Iwasaki Akira in *Japan Quarterly* (New York), January/March 1965; articles by Koichi Yamada in *Cahiers du cinéma* (Paris), September 1966; "Akira Kurosawa: Japan's Poet Laureate of Film" in *Film Makers on Film Making* edited by Harry Geduld, Bloomington, Indiana 1967; "Dostoevsky with a Japanese Camera" by Donald Richie in *The Emergence of Film Art* edited by Lewis Jacobs, New York 1969; "A Few Stones from a Glass House" by B. Chekhonin in *Atlas*, March 1970; "Akira Kurosawa's *Macbeth, The Castle of the Spider's Web*" by Roger Manvell in *Shakespeare and the Film*, London 1971; "Notes sur quelques films de Kurosawa" by Hubert Niogret in *Positif* (Paris), December 1971; "Kurosawa, Akira" by Arne Svenson in *Japan*, London 1971; "The Samurai Film and the Western" by Stuart Kaminsky in *The Journal of Popular Film* (Bowling Green, Ohio), fall 1972; "*Dodeskaden* Spectrum" by Yoichi Matsue and others in *Cinema* (Los Angeles), spring 1972; "The Epic Cinema of Kurosawa" by Joan Mellen in *Take One* (Montreal), June 1972; "Cinq japonais en quete de films: Akira Kurosawa" by Max Tessier in *Ecran* (Paris), March 1972; "Kurosawa and Ichikawa: feudalist and individualist" by Richard Tucker in *Japan: Film Image*, London 1973; special Kurosawa issue of *Kinema jumpo* (Tokyo), 7 May 1974; "On Akira Kurosawa" by Barbara Wolf in the *Yale Review* (New Haven), v.64, no.2, 1974; "Samurai" by Alain Silver in *Film Comment* (New York), September/October 1975; "Tovaritch Kurosawa" by Max Tessier in *Ecran* (Paris), February 1975; "Kurosawa: A Television Script" by Donald Richie in *1000 Eyes* (New York), May 1976; "Some Comments on Dersu Uzala" by J. Hrbas in *Young/Jeune Cinema & Theatre* (Prague), summer 1976; "Akira Kurosawa" in *The Samurai Film* by Alain Silver, Cranbury, New Jersey 1977; "Kurosawa: The Nature of Heroism" by Ruth McCormick in *1000 Eyes* (New York), April 1977; "Tokyo, Kyoto et Kurosawa" by Satyajit Ray in *Positif* (Paris), December 1979; "Kurosawa. Kagemusha", special section by Max Tessier of *Image et son* (Paris), October 1980; "Kurosawa redécouvert" by B. Nave in *Jeune Cinéma* (Paris), February 1981; "Tutto Kurosawa" by H. Niogret in *Positif* (Paris), December 1981; film—*Akira Kurosawa: Film Director* by Donald Richie, 1975.

* * *

Unquestionably Japan's best-known film director, Akira Kurosawa introduced his country's cinema to the world with his

1951 Venice Festival Grand Prize winner, *Rashomon*. His international reputation has broadened over the years with numerous citations, including an Academy Award for Best Foreign-Language Film for his 1975 Siberian epic *Dersu Uzala*. When 20th Century-Fox distributed his 1980 Cannes Grand Prize winner, *Kagemusha*, it was the first time a Japanese film achieved world-wide circulation through a Hollywood major.

At the time *Rashomon* took the world by surprise, Kurosawa was already a well-established director in his own country. He had received his six-year assistant director's training at the Toho Studios under the redoubtable Kajiro Yamamoto, director of both low-budget comedies and war epics such as *The War at Sea from Hawaii to Malaya*. Yamamoto described Kurosawa as more than fully prepared to direct when he first grasped the megaphone for his own screenplay *Sanshiro Sugata* in 1943. This film based on a best-selling novel about the founding of judo launched lead actor Susumu Fujita as a star and director Kurosawa as a powerful new force in the film world. Despite numerous battles with wartime censors, Kurosawa managed to get approval on three more of his scripts for production before the Pacific War ended in 1945. He was already fully established with his studio and his audience as a writer-director. His films were so successful commercially that he would, until late in his career, receive a free creative hand from his producers, ever-increasing budgets and extended schedules, and never would he be subjected to a project that was not of his own initiation and his own writing.

In the pro-documentary, female emancipation atmosphere that reigned briefly under the Allied Occupation of Japan, Kurosawa created his strongest woman protagonist and produced his most explicit pro-left message in *No Regrets for Our Youth*. But internal political struggles at Toho left bitterness and creative disarray in the wake of a series of strikes, and Kurosawa's 1947 *One Wonderful Sunday* is as a result perhaps his weakest film, an innocuous and sentimental story of a young couple who are too poor to get married.

The mature Kurosawa appears in the 1948 *Drunken Angel*. Here he displays not only a full command of black-and-white filmmaking technique with his characteristic variety of pacing, lighting, and camera angle for maximum editorial effect, but his first use of sound-image counterpoints in the "Cuckoo Waltz" scene where the lively music contrasts with the dying gangster's dark mood. Here too is the full-blown appearance of the typical Kurosawan master-disciple relationship first suggested in *Sanshiro Sugata*, and here is the over riding humanitarian message despite a tragic outcome to the story. The master-disciple roles assume great depth in the blustery alcoholic doctor played by Takashi Shimura opposite the vain, hotheaded young gangster played by Toshiro Mifune, through the tension generated by Shimura's questionable worthiness as a mentor and Mifune's violent unwillingness as a pupil. These two actors would recreate similar testy relationships in numerous Kurosawa films from the late 1940s through the mid-1950s, including the noir police drama *Stray Dog*, the doctor dilemma film *Quiet Duel*, and the all-time classic *Seven Samurai*. In the 1960s Yuzo Kayama would assume the disciple role to Mifune's master in the feudal comedy *Sanjuro* and the struggle for humanity in modernizing portrayed in *Red Beard*.

Part of Kurosawa's characteristic technique is the typical Japanese studio practice of using the same crew or "group" on each production. He consistently worked with cinematographer Asakazu Nakai and composer Fumio Hayasaka, for example. Kurosawa's group became a kind of family that extended to actors as well. Mifune and Shimura were the most prominent names of the virtual private repertory company that through lifetime studio contracts could survive protracted months of

production on a Kurosawa film and fill in with more normal four-to-eight-week shoots in between. Kurosawa was thus assured of getting the performance he wanted every time.

Kurosawa'a own studio contract and consistent box-office record enabled him to exercise creativity never permitted lesser talents in Japan. He was responsible for numerous technical innovations as a result. He pioneered the use of long lenses and multiple cameras in the famous final battle scenes in the driving rain and splashing mud of *Seven Samurai*. His was the first use of widescreen in Japan in the 1958 samurai entertainment classic *Hidden Fortress*. To the dismay of the leftist critics and the delight of audiences he invented realistic swordfighting and serious portrayals of violence in such extravagant confrontations as those of *Yojimbo*, which spawned the entire Clint Eastwood spaghetti western genre in Italy. Kurosawa further experimented with long lenses on the set in *Red Beard*, and accomplished breathtaking work with his first color film *Dodeskaden*, now no longer restorable. A firm believer in the importance of motion picture science, Kurosawa pioneered the use of Panavision and multi-track Dolby sound in Japan with *Kagemusha*. His only reactionary practice is his editing, which he does entirely himself on an antique Moviola, better and faster than anyone else in the world.

Western critics have most often chastised Kurosawa for using symphonic music in his films. His reply to this is to point out that he and his entire generation grew up on more Western music than native Japanese, which to a contemporary audience sounds artificially exotic. Nevertheless, he has succeeded in his films in adapting not only boleros and elements of Beethoven, but snatches of Japanese popular songs and musical instrumentation from Noh theater and folk song.

Perhaps most startling of Kurosawa'a achievements in a Japanese context, however, have been his innate grasp of a storytelling technique that is not culture bound, and his flair for adapting Western classical literature to the screen. No other Japanese director would have dared to set Dostoevski's *Idiot*, Gorki's *Lower Depths*, or Shakespeare's *Macbeth* (*Throne of Blood)* and the projected *King Lear (Ran)* in Japan. But he also adapted works from the Japanese Kabuki theater (*Men Who Tread on the Tiger's Tail*) and used Noh staging and music in both *Throne of Blood* and *Kagemusha*. Like his counterparts and most admired models, Jean Renoir, John Ford, and Kenji Mizoguchi, Kurosawa has taken his cinematic inspirations from the full store of world film, literature, and music. And yet the completely original screenplays of his two greatest films, *Ikiru*, the story of a bureaucrat dying of cancer who at last finds purpose in life, and *Seven Samurai*, the saga of seven hungry warriors who pit their wits and lives against marauding bandits in the defense of a poor farming village, reveal that his natural story-telling ability and humanistic convictions transcend all impediments of genre, period and nationality.

—Audie Bock

LA CAVA, GREGORY. American. Born in Towanda, Pennsylvania, 10 March 1892. Educated in Rochester, New York, high school; Art Institute of Chicago; Art Students League and National Academy of Design, New York. Married (2nd time) Grace Garland, 1941; son: Billy. Career: early teens—cartoonist for American Press Association, *Evening World* and *Sunday Herald*, New York; 1917—organizes and heads animated cartoon unit of Hearst Enterprises; works on *Mutt and Jeff* series;

1921—begins writing *Torchy* stories for Johnny Hines, starring in 2-reel comedies for Charles Burr; 1922—begins directing Johnny Hines pictures; 1924—hired as writer and director for Paramount, moves to Hollywood with company in 1927; 1929—accepts offer by First National to direct *Saturday's Children*; film's success leads him to pursue directing full time; 1930—directs for Pathe, then RKO-Radio when it absorbs Pathe; develops reputation as difficult director in series of feuds with studio managements; 1933—signs with 20th Century Pictures; 1934—refuses directing contract with MGM, begins freelancing under non-exclusive contract; 1942—failure of *Lady in a Jam* followed by 5 years' inactivity; 1948—hired by Mary Pickford company to direct *One Touch of Venus*, walks off set after 11 days in dispute over script; brings unsuccessful breach-of-contract suit against Pickford. Died in 1952. Recipient: New York Film Critics Circle Award for *Stage Door*, 1937.

Films (as director of animated shorts—partial list): 1917—*Der Kaptain Discovers the North Pole* ("Katzenjammer Kids" series) (co-d); 1919—*How Could William Tell?* ("Jerry on the Job" series); 1920—*Smokey Smokes (and) Lampoons* ("Judge Rummy Cartoons" series); *Judge Rummy in Bear Facts*; *Kats Is Kats* ("Krazy Kat Cartoon"); (as director of 2-reelers): 1922—*His Nibs* (5 reels); *Faint Heart*; *A Social Error*; 1923—*The 4 Orphans*; *The Life of Reilly*; *The Busybody*; *The Pill Pounder*; *So This Is Hamlet?*; *Helpful Hogan*; *Wild and Wicked*; *Beware of the Dog*; *The Fiddling Fool*; (as feature director): 1924—*The New School Teacher* (+co-sc); *Restless Wives*; 1925—*Womanhandled*; 1926—*Let's Get Married*; *So's Your Old Man*; *Say It Again*; 1927—*Paradise for Two* (+pr); *Running Wild*; *Tell It to Sweeney* (+pr); *The Gay Defender* (+pr); 1928—*Feel My Pulse* (+pr); *Half a Bride*; 1929—*Saturday's Children*; *Big News*; 1930—*His First Command* (+co-sc); 1931—*Laugh and Get Rich* (+sc, co-dialogue); *Smart Woman*; 1932—*Symphony of 6 Million*; *Age of Consent*; *The Half Naked Truth* (+co-sc); 1933—*Gabriel over the White House*; *Bed of Roses* (+co-dialogue); *Gallant Lady*; 1934—*Affairs of Cellini*; *What Every Woman Knows* (+pr); 1935—*Private Worlds* (+co-sc); *She Married Her Boss*; 1936—*My Man Godfrey* (+pr, co-sc); 1937—*Stage Door*; 1939—*Fifth Avenue Girl* (+pr); 1940—*Primrose Path* (+pr, co-sc); 1941—*Unfinished Business* (+pr); 1942—*Lady in a Jam* (+pr); 1947—*Living in a Big Way* (+story, co-sc).

Publications:

On LA CAVA:

Articles—sketch by D. Thorpe in *Motion Picture Classic* (Brooklyn), May 1926; article in *Collier's* (New York), 26 March 1938; article in *Life* (New York), 15 September 1941; article in *Time* (New York), 15 September 1941; obituary in *The New York Times*, 2 March 1952; "Esoterica" by Andrew Sarris in *Film Culture* (New York), spring 1963; "Enfin, La Cava vint..." by Claude Beylie in *Ecran* (Paris), May 1974; "Gregory La Cava" by R. McNiven in *Bright Lights* (Los Angeles), no.4, 1979.

*   *   *

Although many of his individual films are periodically reviewed and reassessed by film scholars, Gregory La Cava remains today a relatively under-appreciated director of some of the best "screwball comedies" of the 1930s. Perhaps his apparent inability to transcend the screwball form or his failure with a number of straight dramas contributed to this lack of critical recognition. Yet, at his best, he imposed a vitality and sparkle on his screen comedies that overcame their often weak scripts and some occasionally pedestrian performances from his actors

The great majority of his films reflect an instinctive comic sense undoubtedly gained during his early years as a newspaper cartoonist and as an animator with Walter Lantz on such fast and furious cartoons in "The Katzenjammer Kids" and "Mutt and Jeff" series. He subsequently became one of the few directors capable of transferring many of these techniques of animated comedy to films involving real actors. His ability to slam a visual gag home quickly sustained such comedies as W.C. Fields's *So's Your Old Man* and *Running Wild*. Yet his real forte emerged in the sound period when the swiftly-paced sight gags were replaced by equally quick verbal repartee.

La Cava's "screwball comedies" of the 1930s were characterized by improbable plots and brilliantly foolish dialogue but also by a dichotomous social view that seemed to delight in establishing satirical contrasts between the views of themselves held by the rich and by the poor. Although treated in varying degrees in *Fifth Avenue Girl*, *She Married Her Boss* and *Stage Door*, La Cava'a classic treatment of this subject remains 1936's *My Man Godfrey*. Made during the depths of the Depression, it juxtaposes the world of the rich and frivolous with the plight of the real victims of the economic disaster through the sharply satiric device of a scavenger hunt. When one of the hunt's objectives turns out to be "a forgotten man," in this case a hobo named Godfrey Parke (William Powell), it provides a platform for one of the Depression's victims to lash out at the upper class as being composed of frivolous "nitwits." However, the film seemingly pulls its punches at the end when, although one socialite, Irene Bullock (Carole Lombard) achieves some realization of the plight of the less fortunate, the hobo Godfrey turns out to be a formerly wealthy Harvard man who actually renews his fortune through his association with her, although he has been somewhat tempered by his experience with the hoboes.

La Cava, perhaps more than other directors working in the screwball genre, was able, by virtue of doing much of the writing on his scripts, to impose his philosophical imprint upon the majority of his films. While he was often required to keep a foot in both the conservative and the liberal camps, his films do not suffer. On the contrary, they maintain an objectivity that has allowed them to grow in stature with the passage of years. *My Man Godfrey*, *Stage Door* and *Gabriel Over the White House*, which is only now being recognized as a political fantasy of great merit, give overwhelming evidence that critical recognition of Gregory La Cava is considerably overdue.

—Stephen L. Hanson

LANDOW, GEORGE. [Also known as George Lando; changed name to Owen Land, 1980.]. American. Born 10 September 1944. Educated in painting at Pratt Institute and Art Students League, New York. Career: 1969—moves to San Francisco; 1970—becomes convert to Messianic Judaism; 1980—changes name to Owen Land; has taught at the School of the Art Institute of Chicago, Northwestern University, and the San Francisco Art Institute. Address: lives in San Francisco.

Films: 1961—*2 Pieces for the Precarious Life*; *Faulty Pronoun Reference, Comparison, and Punctuation of the Restrictive or Non-restrictive Element*; *A Stringent Prediction at the Early Hermaphroditic Stage*; 1963—*Fleming Faloon*; 1963-65—*Studies and Sketches*; 1965—*Film in Which There Appear Sprocket Holes, Edge Lettering, Dirt Particles, Etc.*; 1966—*Film in Which There Appear Sprocket Holes, Edge Lettering, Dirt Particles, Etc.* (wide screen); 1967—*Diploteratology or Bardo Folly*; 1968—*The Film That Rises to the Surface of Clarified Butter*; 1969—*Institutional Quality*; 1970—*Remedial Reading Comprehension*; 1971-72—*What's Wrong with This Picture?*; 1973—*Thank You Jesus for the Eternal Present: 1*; 1974—*Thank You Jesus for the Eternal Present: 2—A Film of Their 1973 Spring Tour Commissioned by Christian World Liberation Front of Berkeley, California*; 1975—*Wide Angle Saxon*; *"No Sir, Orison"*; *New Improved Institutional Quality: In the Environment of Liquids and Nasals a Parasitic Vowel Sometimes Develops*; 1979—*On the Marriage Broker Joke as Cited by Sigmund Freud in Wit and Its Relation to the Unconscious, or Can the Avant-Garde Artist Be Wholed*.

Publications:

By LANDOW:

Articles—interview by P. Adams Sitney in *Film Culture* (New York), summer 1969; "New Improved George Landow Interview" by P. Gregory Springer in *Film Culture* (New York), no.67-69, 1979.

On LANDOW:

Articles—by George Stoller in *The Village Voice* (New York), 6 June 1968; "*The Tibetan Film of the Dead*" by Ken Kelman in *Film Culture* (New York), no.47, 1969; "Avant-Garde Film" by P. Adams Sitney in *Afterimage* (Rochester, New York), autumn 1970; "The Calisthenics of Vision: Open Instructions on the Films of George Landow" by Paul Arthur in *Artforum* (New York), September 1971; "*Remedial Reading Comprehension*" by Fred Camper in *Film Culture* (New York), spring 1971; "Autobiography in Avant-Garde Film" by P. Adams Sitney in *Millenium* (New York), winter 1977/78.

*   *   *

George Landow attended art schools, contemplating a career as a painter or sculptor, but had already begun to make and show films in highschool, at which time he was one of the founding editors of the short-lived avant-garde film journal, *Filmwise*.

Some of his most important films reflect his flirtations with spiritual movements: *Bardo Follies* and *The Film that Rises to the Surface of Clarified Butter* with Tantrism; *Thank You, Jesus, for the Eternal Present* and, *Wide Angle Saxon* with Messianic Judaism. But Landow is always more of an ironist that a cultist. His witty manipulation of puns, palindromes, and paradoxes, and his use of found film footage, testify to the abiding influence of Marcel Duchamp on his films.

Landow's earliest films, from 1962-68, arose out of his fascination with the surface and texture of filmic materials. At the time he was the youngest and most original of generation of filmmakers absorbed with critiquing the illusion inherent in films. This dimension is never wholly absent from his later work as well. In 1969 he moved from New York to San Francisco where he completed *Institutional Quality* and *Remedial Reading Comprehension*, two quasi-autobiographical films which cultivate the paradoxes he finds at stake in all filmmaking. Like the two-part *What's Wrong with this Picture?* which he made in Chicago, where he had gone to teach at the School of the Art Institute, these short films are inspired by educational and industrial films. The rhetorical stance implied by such neglected genres became a basis for Landow's critical scrutiny.

In *Wide Angle Saxon*, *New Improved Institutional Quality: In the Environment of Liquids and Nasals a Parasitic Vowel Sometimes Develops*, and *On the Marriage Broker Joke as Cited by Sigmund Freud in Wit and Its Relation to the Unconscious* he satirizes the institutions of the avant-garde cinema. In his oblique criticism of Brakhage's preoccupation with pure seeing, Deren's fascination with dream life, and the apodictic cinema of many of his own generation, he does not spare his own work from hilarious spoofing.

The whole thrust of Landow's cinema is a quest for meaning, an insight into a transcendental order, even when he seems to admit that such a quest is preposterous or doomed to defeat. Those filmmakers who settle for anything less, or who propose a purely aesthetic substitute for revelation, become the objects of his witty attacks.

Landow changed his name to Owen Land in 1980. Since then he has finished no films, but has directed several performances and been involved in making videotapes.

—P. Adams Sitney

———————

LANG, FRITZ. German. Born in Vienna, 5 December 1890; became citizen of the United States, 1935. Educated in engineering at the Technische Hochschule, Vienna. Married (second time) writer Thea von Harbou, 1924 (separated 1933). Career: 1911-12—travels in Russia, Asia Minor, North Africa; 1913—lives in Paris, paints watercolors, designs fashions, and contributes cartoons to German newspapers; 1914—returns to Vienna, joins army; 1916—discharged as lieutenant, writes scripts while in army hospital; begins working as actor, sells scripts to Decla; 1918—moves to Berlin, joins Decla as reader and story editor; assistant director to Joe May on *Herrin der Welt*; 1919—scripts and directs 1st film *Halbblut*; 1920—works with Thea von Harbou for 1st time on *Die Vier um die Frau*; 1924—visits New York and Hollywood, studies film production methods; 1931—directs his 1st sound film, *M*; 1933—*Das Testament des Dr. Mabuse*, last film before leaving Germany, banned by Nazis; summoned to office of Joseph Goebbels, Nazi propaganda minister, informed apologetically of ban, offered post as supervisor of Nazi film productions; flees Germany, suspecting trap and afraid Nazis will discover his Jewish background; 1933-34—directs *Liliom* in Paris, signs contract with David Selznick in London; 1934—goes to Hollywood, works on several unrealized projects, travels extensively; 1935-36—directs *Fury*, 1st U.S. film; 1940—signs with Paramount, makes first color film, *The Return of Frank James*; 1942—works on *Hangmen Also Die!* with Bertolt Brecht; 1945—helps found Diana Productions, becomes president; produces and directs *Scarlet Street*; 1956—decides to quit Hollywood, citing continuing disputes with producers and others; revisits Germany on way to India to plan *Taj Mahal* (unrealized); 1958-59—directs *Der Tiger von Eschnapur* and *Das Indische Grabmal* in India from scripts originally written with von Harbou; 1960—last film, directed in Germany;

1963—appears as himself in Godard's *Contempt*. Died in Beverly Hills, 2 August 1976. Recipient: Officier d'Art et des Lettres, France.

Films (as scenarist): 1917—*Die Hochzeit im Ekzentrik Klub (The Wedding in the Eccentric Club)* (May); *Hilde Warren und der Tod (Hilde Warren and Death)* (May); *Joe Debbs* (series); 1918—*Die Rache ist mein (Revenge Is Mine)* (Neub); *Herrin der Welt (Men of the World)* (May) (ass't d only); *Bettler GmbH*; 1919—*Wolkenbau und Flimmerstern (Castles in the Sky and Rhinestones)* (d unknown, co-sc); *Totentanz (Dance of Death)* (Rippert); *Die Pest in Florenz (Plague in Florence)* (Rippert); *Die Frau mit den Orchiden (The Woman with the Orchid)* (Rippert); *Lilith und Ly*; (as director): 1919—*Halbblut (Half Caste)* (+sc); *Der Herr der Liebe (The Master of Love)* (+ro); *Hara-Kiri*; *Die Spinnen (The Spiders)* Part I: *Der Goldene See (The Golden Lake)* (+sc); 1920—*Die Spinnen (The Spiders)* Part II: *Das Brillantenschiff (The Diamond Ship)* (+sc); *Das Wandernde Bild (The Wandering Image)* (+co-sc); *Kämpfende Herzen (Die Vier um die Frau, 4 Around a Woman)* (+co-sc); 1921—*Der müde Tod: Ein Deutsches Volkslied in 6 Versen (The Weary Death, Between 2 Worlds, Beyond the Wall, Destiny)* (+co-sc); *Das Indische Grabmal* (in 2 parts: *Die Sendung des Yoghi* and *Der Tiger von Eschnapur)* (co-sc only); 1921-22—*Dr. Mabuse, der Spieler (Dr. Mabuse, the Gambler, The Fatal Passions)* in 2 parts: *Ein Bild der Zeit (Spieler aus Leidenschaft, A Picture of the Time)* and; *Inferno—Menschen der Zeit (Inferno des Verbrechens, Inferno—Men of the Time)* (+co-sc); 1924—*Die Nibelungen* in 2 parts: *Siegfrieds Tod (Death of Siegfried)* and *Kriemhilds Rache (Kriemhild's Revenge)* (+co-sc, uncredited); 1927—*Metropolis* (+co-sc, uncredited); 1928—*Spione (Spies)* (+pr, co-sc—uncredited); 1929—*Die Frau im Mond (By Rocket to the Moon, The Girl in the Moon, The Woman in the Moon)* (+pr, co-sc—uncredited); 1931—*M, Mörder unter Uns (M)* (+co-sc, uncredited); 1933—*Das Testament des Dr. Mabuse (The Testament of Dr. Mabuse, The Last Will of Dr. Mabuse)* (+co-sc, uncredited) (German and French versions); 1934—*Liliom* (+co-sc, uncredited); 1936—*Fury* (+co-sc); 1937—*You Only Live Once*; 1938—*You and Me* (+pr); 1940—*The Return of Frank James*; 1941—*Western Union*; *Man Hunt*; *Confirm or Deny* (co-d, uncredited); 1942—*Moontide* (co-d, uncredited); 1943—*Hangmen Also Die!* (+pr, co-sc); 1944—*Ministry of Fear*; *The Woman in the Window*; 1945—*Scarlet Street* (+pr); 1946—*Cloak and Dagger*; 1948—*Secret Beyond the Door* (+co-pr); 1950—*House by the River*; *An American Guerrilla in the Philippines*; 1952—*Rancho Notorious*; *Clash by Night*; 1953—*The Blue Gardenia*; *The Big Heat*; 1954—*Human Desire*; 1955—*Moonfleet*; 1956—*While the City Sleeps*; *Beyond a Reasonable Doubt*; 1959—*Der Tiger von Eschnapur (The Tiger of Bengal)* and *Das Indische Grabmal (The Hindu Tomb)* (+co-sc) (released in cut version as *Journey to the Lost City*); 1960—*Die Tausend Augen des Dr. Mabuse (The Thousand Eyes of Dr. Mabuse)* (+pr, co-sc).

Roles: 1917—four roles in *Hilde Warren und der Tod*; 1963—as himself in *Le Mépris (Contempt)* (Godard).

Publications:

By LANG:

Articles— "Äusserungen zum Thema Kontingents-Verfahren und Qualitätsfilme" in *Der Film* (Berlin), no.30, 1922; "Arbeitsgemeinschaft im Film" in *Der Kinematograph* (Düsseldorf and Berlin), 2 February 1924; "Kitsch—Sensation—Kultur und Film" in *Das Kulturfilmbuch*, edited by Beyfuss and Kossowsky, Berlin 1924, reprinted in part in *UFA und der frühe deutsche Film*, Zurich 1963; "Zwischen Bohrturmen und Palmen" in *Filmland* (Berlin), 3 January 1925; "Ausblick auf Morgen: Zum Pariser Kongress" in *Lichtbildbühne* (Berlin), 25 October 1926; "Moderne Filmregie" in *Die Filmbühne* (Berlin), April 1927; "Über sich selbst" in *Filmkünstler: Wir über uns selbst*, edited by Hermann Treuner, Berlin 1928; "Die mimische Kunst des Lichtspiele" in *Der Film* (Berlin), no.1, 1929; "Mein Film *M*: Ein Tatsachenbericht" in *Die Filmwoche* (Berlin), May 1931; "Mes Amis, les Ouvriers" (1934) reprinted in "A Propos de *Liliom*" in *Positif* (Paris), December 1976; "Director Presents His Case Against the Censorship of Films" in *Los Angeles Daily News*, 15 August 1946; "The Freedom of the Screen" (1947) reprinted in *Hollywood Directors 1941-1976* by Richard Koszarski, New York 1977; "Happily Ever After" (1948) collected in *Film Makers on Film Making*, edited by Harry Geduld, Bloomington, Indiana 1969; "Fritz Lang Today", interview by H. Hart in *Films in Review* (New York), June/July 1956; "The Impact of Television on Motion Pictures", interview by G. Bachmann in *Film Culture* (New York), December 1957; interview by Michel Delahaye and Jean Wagner in *Présence du Cinéma* (Paris), July/September 1959; "Entretien avec Fritz Lang" by Jean Domarchi and Jacques Rivette in *Cahiers du cinéma* (Paris), September 1959; "Fritz Lang: 43 ans de métier", interview in *L'Express* (Paris), 6 July 1961; "Rencontre avec Fritz Lang" by Yvonne Baby in *Le Monde* (Paris), 3 July 1961; "Mon film le plus important depuis *M*", interview by Yvonne Baby in *Le Monde* (Paris), 9 December 1961; "Fritz Lang dit: L'Amérique ne m'a pas devoré", interview by Michel Mardore in *Les Lettres Françaises* (Paris), 7 December 1961; "Fritz Lang S'Explique: 'Je ne recherche pas le crime pour lui-même.'", interview by Pierre Mazars in *Le Figaro Littéraire* (Paris), 9 December 1961; "Une Entretien avec Fritz Lang" by Claude-Jean Philippe in *Télérama* (Paris), 9 July 1961; "The Dark Struggle", interview by Nicholas Bartlett in *Film* (London), summer 1962; "On the Problems of Today" in *Films and Filming* (London), June 1962; "Fritz Lang vous parle" in *Cinéma 62* (Paris), no.70, 1962; "Fritz Lang Talks About Dr. Mabuse", interview by Mark Shivas in *Movie* (London), November 1962; "Fritz Lang über *M*: Ein Interview" by Gero Gandert in *M*, Hamburg 1963; "Was bin ich, was sind wir?" in *Filmkritik* (Munich), no.7, 1963; "Bilder der Zeit" in *Frankfurter Rundschau*, 25 July 1964; "Avec Fritz Lang", interview by Michèle Manceaux in *L'Express* (Paris), 7 May 1964; "Nouvel Entretien avec Fritz Lang", interview by Jean-Louis Noames in *Cahiers du cinéma* (Paris), June 1964; "La Nuit viennoise: Une Confession de Fritz Lang" (Part 1), edited by Gretchen Berg in *Cahiers du cinéma* (Paris), August 1965; "Zum Selbstverständnis des Films IV" in *Filmkritik* (Munich), no.12, 1965; "La Nuit viennoise: Une Confession de Fritz Lang", part 2, edited by Gretchen Berg in *Cahiers du cinéma* (Paris), June 1966; "Fritz Lang: An Interview" by Axel Madsen in *Sight and Sound* (London), summer 1967; "Fritz Lang", interview by Gretchen Berg in *Take One* (Montreal), November/December 1968; "Fritz Lang à Venise" by Michel Ciment and others in *Positif* (Paris), April 1968; "Autobiography" in *The Celluloid Muse: Hollywood Directors Speak* by Charles Higham and Joel Greenberg, London 1969; "What Directors are Saying" in *Action* (Los Angeles), November/December 1969; "Fritz Lang: Une main tendue vers la jeunesse", interview by Gérard Langlois in *Les Lettres françaises* (Paris), 16 April 1969; "Autobiography" in *The Real Tinsel* by Rosenberg, Bernard and Silverstein, London 1970; "Ein Brief von Fritz Lang (über Kracauer's 'Caligari' Interpretation)" in *Caligari und Caligarismus*, Berlin 1970; "Pioneer '73: 4 Evenings with Directors Fritz Lang, Henry King, Norman Taurog and

Robert Lee" by Cynthia Kirk in *Action* (Los Angeles), November/December 1973; "Interviews" in *Dialogue on Film* (Beverly Hills), April 1974; "Fritz Lang: An Interview" by Gene Phillips in *Focus on Film* (London), spring 1975; "Fritz Lang Gives His Last Interview" by Gene Phillips in the *Village Voice* (New York), 16 August 1976.

On LANG:

Books—*From Caligari to Hitler: A Psychological History of the German Film* by Siegfried Kracauer, Princeton, New Jersey 1947; *Fritz Lang* by Francis Courtade, Paris 1963; *Fritz Lang* by Luc Moullet, Paris 1963; *Fritz Lang*, edited by Alfred Eibel, Paris 1964; *The Sociology of Film Art* by George Huaco, New York 1965; *Tower of Babel* by Eric Rhode, London 1966; *The Haunted Screen: Expressionism in the German Cinema and the Influence of Max Reinhardt* by Lotte Eisner, translated by Robert Greaves, Berkeley and Los Angeles 1969; *Fritz Lang in America* by Peter Bogdanovich, New York 1969; *The Cinema of Fritz Lang* by Paul Jensen, New York 1969; *Fritz Lang* by Claire Johnston, London 1969; *Le Cinéma expressioniste allemand* by Michael Henry, Paris 1971; *Fritz Lang* by Frieda Grafe, Enno Patalas and Hans Prinzler, Munich 1976; *Fritz Lang* by Lotte Eisner, translated by Gertrud Mander, edited by David Robinson, New York 1977; *Fritz Lang* by Robert Armour, Boston 1978; *The Films of Fritz Lang* by Frederick Ott, Secaucus, New Jersey 1979; *Fritz Lang*, edited by Stephen Jenkins, London 1980; *Fritz Lang: The Image and the Look* edited by Stephen Jenkins, London 1980; *Fritz Lang: A Guide to References and Resources* by E. Ann Kaplan, Boston 1981; articles—"German Director Tells of Visit to Hollywood" in *The New York Times*, 30 November 1924; "The Story of Fritz Lang, Maker of *Siegfried*" by Heinrich Fraenkel in *Motion Picture Classic* (Brooklyn), 23 March 1926; "Bis eine Szene so weit ist..." by Thea von Harbou in *Ufa Magazine* (Berlin), 14-20 January 1927; "La Femme sur la Lune" by Jean Arroy in *Cinémagazine* (Paris), June 1930; "Fritz Lang Bows to Mammon" by D.W.C. in *The New York Times*, 14 June 1936; "Fritz Lang, Director of Fury, Discusses His Film 'You Only Live Once'" by Eileen Creelman in the *Sun* (New York), 28 January 1937; "Fritz Lang Likes Hollywood, America, and Social Themes" by Marguerite Tazelaar in the *Herald Tribune* (New York), 7 February 1937; "Fritz Lang, Master of Mood" by Ram Bagai in *Cinema Progress* (Los Angeles), May/June 1938; "Cinema and Stage" by W.L. Snyder in *Cinema Progress* (Los Angeles), June/July 1939; "Footnote on a Patriotic Occasion" by Theodore Strauss in *The New York Times*, 11 August 1940; "Fritz Lang Puts on Film the Nazi Mind He Fled From" in the *World Telegram* (New York), 11 June 1941; "Behind the Camera" by Otis Ferguson (1941) collected in *The Film Criticism of Otis Ferguson*, edited by Robert Wilson, Philadelphia 1971; "Watching Them Make Movies" by Sidney Skolsky in the *Post* (New York), 19 April 1941; "Lettre de Londres: Hollywood n'a pas standardisé Fritz Lang" by Jacques Borel in *L'Écran française* (Paris), 5 June 1946; "Notes sur le style de Fritz Lang" by Lotte Eisner in *La Revue du cinéma* (Paris), 1 February 1947; "The Genius of Fritz Lang" by Harry Wilson in *Film Quarterly* (Berkeley), summer 1947; "Fritz Lang: Suggestion und Stimmung" in *Gestalter der Filmkunst, von Asta Nielsen bis Walt Disney* by Ludwig Gesek, Vienna 1948; "Ich Spreche mit Fritz Lang (in Hollywood)" by Ernst Jaeger in *Film Review* (Baden-Baden), no.5-6, 1948; "Fritz Lang" in *Histoire générale du cinéma* vol.3, by Georges Sadoul, Paris 1953; "Il parabola di Fritz Lang" by Leonardo Autera in *Cinema* (Rome), 15 January 1954; "Un realisme méchant" by Eric Rohmer (Maurice Schérer) in *Cahiers du cinéma* (Paris), June 1954; "Aimer Fritz Lang" by François Truffaut in *Cahiers du cinéma* (Paris),

January 1954; "Fritz Lang's America" by Gavin Lambert in *Sight and Sound* (London), summer 1955; "Europa ist immer noch unbequem" (1956) collected in *Stimmt es Stimmt es Nicht?* by Karena Niehoff, Munich 1962; "La Cinquième Victime" by François Truffaut in *Arts* (Paris), 22-24 August 1956; "La Hautaine Dialectique de Fritz Lang" by Phillipe Demonsablon in *Cahiers du cinéma* (Paris), September 1959; "Le Style de Fritz Lang" by Georges Franju in *Cahiers du cinéma* (Paris), November 1959; "Trajectoire de Fritz Lang" by Michel Mourlet in *Cahiers du cinéma* (Paris) September 1959; "Lang" by Vernon Howard in *Cahiers du cinéma* (Paris), September 1960; "Fritz Lang Aujourd'hui" by Philippe Brunel in *L'Express* (Paris), 4 May 1961; "Fritz Lang, un vieux seigneur" by Jean Douchet in *Arts* (Paris), 21-28 June 1961; "L'Étrange Obsession" by Jean Douchet in *Cahiers du cinéma* (Paris), August 1961; "The 9 Lives of Dr. Mabuse" by John Taylor in *Sight and Sound* (London), winter 1961; "Cloak and Dagger: esempi dello stile di Fritz Lang" by Adriano Aprà in *Filmcritica* (Rome), October 1963; "Notes pour un éloge de Fritz Lang" by Gérard Legrand in *Positif* (Paris), March 1963; "Fritz Lang" by Andrew Sarris in *Film Culture* (New York), spring 1963; "Ornament und Ideologie: Zu einer Fritz Lang Retrospective" by Peter Schröder in *Film* (Munich), June/July 1964; "Zwischen Kunst und Kolportage" by Rudolf Freund in *Filmspiegel* (East Berlin), 1 December 1965; "Orientalischer Irrgarten und Grossberlin" by Peter Schröder in *Filmkritik* (Munich), no.12, 1965; "Sur Fritz Lang" (1966) in *Le Livre des autres* by Raymond Bellour, Paris 1971; "Fritz Lang (The German Period, 1919-1933)" in *Tower of Babel* by Eric Rhode, London 1966; "Fritz Lang" in *Les Grands Cinéastes que je propose* by Henri Agel, Paris 1967; "Caligari is Dead—Long Live Caligari" in *Films and Feelings* by Raymond Durgnat, London 1967; issue devoted to Lang, *Image et son* (Paris), April 1968; "Nouvelles Notes sur un éloge de Fritz Lang" by Gérard Legrand in *Positif* (Paris), April 1968; "Hollywood regisseur mit deutscher Filmvergangenheit" by Heiko Blum in *Filmreport* (West Berlin), 2 December 1970; "Aspects of Fritz Lang" by Paul Joannides in *Cinema* (London), August 1970; "Prophet im Ausland" by Enno Patalas in *Die Zeit* (Hamburg), 25 November 1970; "Der Regisseur von *M*" by Wilfried Wiegand in *Frankfurter Allgemeine Zeitung*, 5 December 1970; "Fritz Lang-Mythos—für wen?" by Rolf Hempel in *Prisma*, edited by Horst Knietzsch, East Berlin 1972; "De Mabuse à M: Le Travail de Fritz Lang" by Noel Burch in *Revue d'esthétique* (Paris), special issue 1973; "Film Noir: The Director. Fritz Lang's American Nightmare" by Alfred Appel, Jr. in *Film Comment* (New York), November/December 1974; "Propositions" by Noel Burch and Jorge Dana in *Afterimage* (Rochester, N.Y.), spring 1974; "*Hangmen Also Die!*: Fritz Lang und Bertolt Brecht" by Wolfgang Gersch und others in *Filmkritik* (Munich), July 1975; "Hommage à Fritz Lang: La Borgne visionnaire" by Marcel Doneux in *Revue belge du cinéma* (Brussels), November 1976; "Fritz Lang, Film Director Noted for 'M', Dead at 85" by Albin Krebs in *The New York Times*, 3 August 1976; "Homage à Fritz Lang: 1890-1976" by Gérard Legrand in *Positif* (Paris), December 1976; "Fritz Lang, 1890-1976" by David Overby in *Sight and Sound* (London), autumn 1976; "Fritz Lang (1890-1976) Was the Prophet of Our Paranoia" by Andrew Sarris in *The Village Voice* (New York), 16 August 1976; "Sein Tod ist keine Lösung" by Wim Wenders (1976) reprinted in *Jahrbuch Film 77/78*, Munich 1977; "Fritz Lang Remembered" by Scott Eyman in *Take One* (Montreal), March 1977; "Fritz Lang in America" in *The Films of My Life* by François Truffaut, New York 1978; "The Film-Work" by Thierry Kuntzel in *Enclitic* (Minneapolis), spring 1978; "Fritz Lang: Only Melodrama" by Don Willis in *Film Quarterly* (Berkeley, California), winter 1979/80; film—*Künstlerporträt: Fritz Lang*, for TV, by Friedrich Luft and

Guido Schütte, Germany 1959; *Begegnung mit Fritz Lang* by Peter Fleischmann, Germany 1963; *Das war die Ufa* by Erwin Leiser, Germany 1964; *Zum Beispiel Fritz Lang*, for TV, by Erwin Leiser, Germany 1968; *Die Schweren Träume des Fritz Lang*, for TV, by Werner Dütsch, Germany 1974.

*   *   *

Fritz Lang's career can be divided conveniently into three parts: the first German period, 1919-1933, from *Halbblut* to the second Mabuse film, *Das Testament des Dr. Mabuse*; the American period, 1936-1956, from *Fury* to *Beyond a Reasonable Doubt*; and the second German period, 1959-60, which includes the two films made in India and his last film, *Die tausend Augen des Dr. Mabuse*.

Lang's apprentice years as a scriptwriter and director were spent in the studios in Berlin where he adopted certain elements of expressionism, and was imbued with the artistic seriousness with which the Germans went about making their films. In Hollywood this seriousness would earn Lang a reputation for unnecessary perfectionism, a criticism also thrown at fellow émigrés von Stroheim and von Sternberg. Except for several films for Twentieth Century-Fox, Lang never worked long for a single studio in the United States, and he often preferred to work on underbudgeted projects which he could produce, and therefore control, himself. The rather radical dissimilarities between the two studio worlds within which Lang spent most of his creative years not surprisingly resulted in products which look quite different from one another, and it is the difference in look or image which has produced the critical confusion most often associated with an assessment of Lang's films.

One critical approach to Lang's work, most recently articulated by Gavin Lambert, argues that Lang produced very little of artistic interest after he left Germany; the *Cahiers du cinéma* auteurists argue the opposite, namely that Lang's films made in America are superior to his European films because the former were clogged with self-conscious artistry and romantic didacticism which the leanness of his American studio work eliminated. A third approach, suggested by Robin Wood and others, examines Lang's films as a whole, avoiding the German-American division by looking at characteristic thematic and visual motifs. Lang's films can be discussed as exhibiting certin distinguishing features: economy, functional precision, detachment, and as containing basic motifs such as the trap, a suppressed underworld, the revenge motive, and the abuse of power. Investigating the films from this perspective reveals a more consistent development of Lang as a creative artist and helps to minimize the superficial anomolies shaped by his career.

In spite of the narrowness of examining only half of a filmmaker's creative output, the sheer number of Lang's German movies which have received substantial critical attention as "classic" films has tended to submerge the critical attempt at breadth and comprehensiveness. Not only did these earlier films form an important intellectual center for the German film industry during the years between the wars, as Sigfried Kracauer later pointed out, but they had a wide international impact as well and were extensively reviewed in the Anglo-American press. Lang's reputation preceded him to America, and although it had little effect ultimately on his working relationship, such as it was, with the Hollywood moguls, it has affected Lang's subsequent treatment by film critics.

If Lang is a "flawed genius," as one critic has described him, it is less a wonder that he is "flawed" than his genius had a chance to develop at all. The working conditions Lang survived after his defection would have daunted a less dedicated director. Lang, however, not only survived but flourished, producing films of undisputed quality: the four war movies *Man Hunt*, *Hangman Also Die!*, *Ministry of Fear* and *Cloak and Dagger*; and the urban crime films of the fifties: *Clash by Night*, *The Blue Gardenia*, *The Big Heat*, *Human Desire*, and *While the City Sleeps*.

These American films reflect a more mature director, tighter mise-en-scène, and more control as a result of Lang's American experience. The films also reveal continuity. As Robin Wood has written, the formal symmetry of his individual films is mirrored in the symmetry of his career, beginning and ending in Germany. All through his life, Lang adjusted his talent to meet the changes in his environment, and in so doing produced a body of creative work of unquestionable importance in the development of the history of cinema.

—Charles L.P. Silet

LATTUADA, ALBERTO. Italian. Born in Milan, 13 November 1914. Educated in architecture. Married Carla Del Poggio, 1945 (divorced). Career: 1933—participates in founding of avant-garde journal *Camminare*; 1936—collaborates with Baffico on experimental short *La danza del lancette*; 1938—helps found review *Corrente*; 1940—with Mario Ferreri and Luigi Comencini founds Cineteca Italiana, Italian film archive; 1940-41—assistant to Mario Soldati and Poggiolo; 1949—directs opera *Didone e Enea*, Teatro dell'Opera, Rome; 1970—directs opera *La Vestale*, Maggio Musicale Fiorentino, Florence. Address: Via N. Paganini, 7, Rome.

Films (as assistant director): 1935—*Il museo dell'amore*; (as collaborator on experimental short): 1936—*La danza delle lancette*; (as assistant director): 1941—*Piccolo mondo antico*; 1942—*Si signora* (+co-sc); (as director and co-scriptwriter): 1942—*Giacomo l'idealista*; 1945—*La freccia nel fianco*; *La nostra guerra* (doc); 1946—*Il bandito*; 1947—*Il delitto di Giovanni Episcopo (Flesh Will Surrender)*; 1948—*Senza pietà (Without Pity)*; 1949—*Il mulino del Po (The Mill on the Po)*; 1950—*Luci del varietà (Variety Lights)* (co-d, +co-pr); 1952—*Anna* (d only); *Il cappotto (The Overcoat)*; 1953—*La lupa (The She-Wolf)*; "Gli italiani si voltano" episode of *Amore in città (Love in the City)*; 1954—*La spiaggia (The Beach)*; *Scuola elementare*; 1956—*Guendalina*; 1958—*La tempesta (Tempest)*; 1960—*I dolci inganni*; *Lettere di una novizia (Rita)*; 1961—*L'imprevisto* (d only); 1962—*Mafioso* (d only); *La steppa*; 1965—*La mandragola (The Love Root)*; 1966—*Matchless*; 1967—*Don Giovanni in Sicilia* (+co-pr); 1968—*Fräulein Doktor*; 1969—*L'amica*; 1970—*Venga a prendere il caffè...da noi (Come Have Coffee With Us)*; 1971—*Bianco, rosso e... (White Sister)*; 1973—*Sono stato io*; 1974—*Le farò da padre... (Bambina)*; 1976—*Cuore di cane*; *Bruciati da cocente passione (Oh Serafina!)*; 1978—*Così come sei*; 1980—*La cicala*; 1983—*Christopher Columbus* (for TV). Role: 1958—*Un eroe dei nostri tempi* (Monicelli).

Publications:

By LATTUADA:

Books—*Occhio quadrato*, album of photos, Milan 1941; *La tempesta*, script, Bologna 1958; *La steppa*, script, Bologna 1962;

Gli uccelli indomabili, Rome 1970; *Cuore di cane*, script, Bari 1975; *A proposito di Cosi come sei*, script, edited by Enrico Oldrini, Bologna 1978; *Diario di un grane amatore*, Milan 1980; *Feuillets au vent*, Paris 1981; *La massa*, Rome 1982; articles— "We Took the Actors into the Streets" in *Films and Filming* (London), April 1959; interview by J.-A. Gili and C. Viviani in *Ecran* (Paris), June 1972; "Alberto Lattuada: du néoréalisme au réalisme magique", interview by A. Tournès in *Jeune Cinéma* (Paris), December/January 1974/75; interview by N. Zalaffi in *Image et son* (Paris), December 1974; "'Moi et le diable' je ne puis vivre ni avec toi ni sans toi" in *Positif* (Paris), June 1978; "Pipi caca" (short story) in *Positif* (Paris), October 1978; interview by G. Volpi in *Positif* (Paris), September and October 1978; "Alberto Lattuada à Nice", interview by E. Ballerini and G. Bertolino in *Jeune Cinéma* (Paris), June 1981; "Alberto Lattuada: une foi dans la beauté", interview by C. Depuyper and A. Cervoni in *Cinéma* (Paris), April 1981; interview by Enzo Ungari in *Cult Movie* (Florence), April/May 1981.

On LATTUADA:

Books—*Alberto Lattuada* by Filippo Mario De Sanctis, Parma 1961; (translated by Barthelemy Amengual in *Premier Plan* (Lyon), no.37, 1965); *Alberto Lattuada* by Lino Peroni, Pavia: Inquadrature no.11, autumn 1963; *Lattuada o la proposta ambigua* by Edoardo Bruno, Rome 1968; *Alberto Lattuada* by J.J. Broher, Brussels 1971; *Alberto Lattuada* by Giuseppe Turroni, Milan 1977; *L'uomo (cattivo sorte): il cinema di Lattuada* by Angelo Zanellato, Padua 1978; *Italian Directors: Alberto Lattuada* by Edoardo Bruno, Rome 1981; *Alberto Lattuada* by Claudio Camerini, Florence 1982; articles—"Notes sur Alberto Lattuada" by G. Volpi in *Positif* (Paris), June 1978; biofilmography by G. Volpi in *Positif* (Paris), October 1978; "Lattuada: un précursor perpetuel" by Bernard Duval in *Image et son* (Paris), July 1979; "Film e figurazione: la riflessione metalinguistica" by G. Turroni in *Filmcritica* (Rome), January 1979.

*   *   *

One of the most consistently commercially-successful directors in Italy, Lattuada has continued to enjoy a freedom of subject matter and style despite ideological shifts and methodological changes. His main films during the neorealist period (which he claims never to have taken part in) succeeded in further establishing the Italian cinema in the international market and, unlike many of his colleagues' works, also proved popular in the domestic market. *Il bandito* and *Il mulino del Po*, for example, combined progressive ideology, realistic detail due to location shooting and attention to quotidian activities, and tight narrative structure due to an attention to editing. In fact, Lattuada's entire career has demonstrated an on-going interest in editing, which he considers more fundamental than the script, and which gives his films a strictly controlled rhythm with no wasted footage. He shoots brief scenes that, he claims, are more attractive to an audience and that can be easily manipulated at the editing stage.

Lattuada's background stressed the arts and his films display a sophisticated cultural appreciation. As a boy, he took an active interest in his father's work as musician in the orchestra of La Scala in Milan. As a young man, Lattuada worked as a film critic, wrote essays on contemporary painters, co-founded cultural magazines, and worked as an assistant director and scriptwriter. Lattuada co-scripts most of his films, as well as occasionally producing them. He also co-founded what became the Milan film archive, the Cineteca Italiana.

As a director, he has been most often called eclectic because of his openness to projects and his ability to handle a wide variety of subject matter. His major commercial successes have been *Bianco, rosso e...* which he wrote especially for Sophia Loren; *Matchless*, a parody of the spy genre; *Anna*, the first Italian film to gross over one billion lire in its national distribution; *La spiaggia*, a bitter satire of bourgeois realism; and *Mafioso*, starring Alberto Sordi and filmed in New York, Sicily, and Milan.

Lattuada has also filmed many adaptations of literary works, which remain faithful to the source but are never simply static re-enactments. These range from the comically grotesque *Venga a prendere...*, to a version of Brancati's satirical *Don Giovanni in Sicilia*, and include the horror film *Cuore di cane* taken from a Bulgakov novel; a version of a D'Annunzio novel in 1947 praised for its set design, interpretation of the text and the high quality of the acting; the spectacular big-budget *La tempesta* from two Pushkin stories; and Chekhov's metaphorical journey in *La steppa*. His 1952 version of *The Overcoat* is considered his masterpiece for its portrayal of psychological states and the excellence of Renato Rascel's performance. Lattuada is famous for his handling of actors, and has launched many an actress's career, among whom are Catherine Spaak, Giulietta Masina and Nastassia Kinski.

Notwithstanding the diversity of subject matter he has directed, Lattuada'a main interest has been pubescent sexuality, the passage of a girl into womanhood, and the sexual relationship of a couple as the primary attraction they have for each other. Thus, his films deal with eroticism as a central theme and he chooses actresses whose physical beauty and sensuousness are immediately apparent. This theme appeared in Lattuada's work as early as his second feature and has been his main preoccupation in his films since 1974.

His films have been critically well-received in Italy, although rarely given the attention enjoyed by some of his contemporaries. In France, however, his work is highly acclaimed; *Il bandito* and *Il cappotto* received much praise at the Cannes festivals when they were shown. With a few exceptions, his more recent work is little known in Britain and the United States, although when *Come Have Coffee with Us* was released commercially in the U.S. ten years after it was made, it enjoyed a fair success at the box office and highly favorable reviews.

—Elaine Mancini

LEACOCK, RICHARD. British. Born in the Canary Islands, 18 July 1921. Educated in secondary schools in England; Harvard University, degree in physics 1943. Career: 1935—begins making documentaries in Canary Islands; 1938—moves to US; during WW II—serves as combat photographer; 1948—associate producer and photographer for Robert Flaherty on *Louisiana Story*; 1950s—works on numerous documentaries with Louis de Rochemont, John Ferno, and Willard Van Dyke among others; 1960s—with Robert Drew of Time-Life, makes series of experimental TV documentaries which initiate style of cinema verite in America; eventually goes into partnership with Donn Alan Pennebaker; 1969—founds and becomes head of Department of Film at Massachusetts Institute of Technology.

Films (as director and cinematographer): 1935—*Canary Bananas*; 1938—*Galápagos Islands*; 1940—*To Hear My Banjo Play* (ph only); 1946—*Louisiana Story* (Flaherty) (ph only, +assoc. pr); 1944-49—*Geography Films Series* (ph only); *Pelileo Earth-*

quake; 1950—*New Frontier (Years of Change)* (ph only, +ed); 1951—*The Lonely Night* (ph only); 1952—*Head of the House* (ph only);; 195?—*New York* (ph only); *The Lonely Boat*; 1954—*Toby and the Tall Corn* (+ed); 1955—*How the F-100 Got Its Tail*; 1958—*Bullfight at Málaga* (ph only); *Bernstein in Israel*; 1959—*Balloon* (co-ph only); *Bernstein in Moscow* (d only); *Coulomb's Law*; *Crystals*; *Magnet Laboratory*; *Points of Reference*; 1960—*Primary* (co-d, co-ph, +ed); *On the Pole* (co-d, co-ph, +co-ed); *Yanqui No* (co-d, co-ph); 1961—*Petey and Johnny* (co-d, co-ph); *The Children Were Watching* (co-d, co-ph); 1962—*The Chair* (co-d, co-ph); *Kenya, South Africa* (co-d, co-ph); 1963—*Crisis* (co-d, co-ph); *Happy Mother's Day* (co-d, co-ph, +co-ed); 1964—*A Stravinsky Portrait* (+ed); *Portrait of Geza Anda* (+ed); *Portrait of Paul Burkhard* (+ed); *Republicans—The New Breed* (co-d, co-ph); 1965—*The Anatomy of Cindy Fink* (co-d, co-ph); *Ku Klux Klan—The Invisible Empire*; 1966—*Old Age—The Wasted Years*; *Portrait of Van Cliburn* (+ed); 1967—*Monterey Pop* (co-ph); *Lulu*; 1968—*Who's Afraid of the Avant-Garde* (co-d, co-ph, +co-ed); *Hickory Hill*; *Maidstone* (co-ph only); 1969—*Chiefs* (+ed); 1970—*Queen of Apollo* (+ed); 1971—*Sweet Toronto* (co-ph only); *One P.M.* (co-ph only); *Keep On Rockin'* (co-ph only).

Publications:

By LEACOCK:

Articles—"To Far Places with Camera and Sound-Track" in *Films in Review* (New York), March 1950; "Richard Leacock Tells How to Boost Available Light" by H. Bell in *Popular Photography* (Boulder, Colorado), February 1956; "For an Uncontrolled Cinema" in *Film Culture* (New York), summer 1961; "The Work of Ricky Leacock: Interview" in *Film Culture* (New York), no.22-23, 1961; interview in *Movie* (London), April 1963; "Ricky Leacock on *Stravinsky* Film" in *Film Culture* (New York), fall 1966; "On Filming the Dance" in *Filmmakers Newsletter* (Ward Hill, Mass.), November 1970; "Richard Leacock" in *Documentary Explorations* edited by G. Roy Levin, Garden City, New York 1971; "Remembering Frances Flaherty" in *Film Comment* (New York), November/December 1973; "Leacock at M.I.T.", interview by L. Marcorelles in *Sight and Sound* (London), spring 1974; "(Richard) Leacock on Super 8, Video Discs and Distribution", interview by M. Sturken in *Afterimage* (Rochester, New York), May 1979.

On LEACOCK:

Book—*Cinema Verite* by M. Ali Issari, East Lansing, Michigan 1971; articles—"Weddings and Babies" in *Harper* (New York), September 1958; "The Frontiers of Realist Cinema: The Work of Ricky Leacock" by Gideon Bachmann in *Film Culture* (New York), summer 1961; "Going Out to the Subject" by Ernest Callenbach in *Film Quarterly* (Berkeley), spring 1961; "Notes on the New American Cinema" by Jonas Mekas in *Film Culture* (New York), no.24 1962; "One Man's Truth" by James Blue in *Film Comment* (New York), spring 1965; "Richard Leacock Uses Super 8" by A Vanderwildt in *Lumiere* (Melbourne), September 1973.

*   *   *

Richard Leacock has been an important contributor to the development of the documentary film, as cinematographer, pro-

ducer, director, and editor, specifically in *cinéma vérité*, now often called *direct cinema*.

For direct cinema filming, the lightweight 16mm camera, handheld, synced to a quiet recorder, is essential for its mobility, and because it allows the filmmaker to intrude as little as possible into the lives of those being filmed. From the very beginning of his interest in this kind of filming, Leacock has been an active experimenter, and inventor of mobile 16mm equipment for filming events, lifestyles, ongoing problematic situations, and other varieties of live history. At Massachusetts Institute of Technology where he heads the department of film, he has developed super-8 sync-sound equipment and related technology. As a patient, courteous and informative lecturer to hundreds of teachers in many workshops, he has demonstrated this equipment and its use for TV, shown his films, and indirectly taught many youngsters who went on to work in film, TV, and related fields.

At 14, Leacock, already an active still photographer, impressed his schoolmates in England with a 16-minute film made on his home island. An indicator, perhaps, of his later concentration on non-subjective filming, his 1935 *Canary Bananas* is still a good, straightforward silent film about what workers do on a banana plantation. Leacock's later work on such diverse subjects as the life of a traveling tent show entertainer, communism and democracy in South America, excitement about quintuplets in South Dakota, a recent portrait of the mind and work of an artist, and his opera filming attest to the breadth of his interests.

Leacock treasures his experience as photographer with poetic filmmaker/explorer Robert Flaherty on *Louisiana Story*, commissioned by Standard Oil to show preliminary steps in searching and drilling for oil, but emerging as a film poem about a boy in the bayou. From Flaherty, Leacock learned, he says, to discover with a camera. Leacock having realized how difficult Flaherty's ponderous un-synced equipment had made direct shooting, Leacock later joined a group, led by Robert Drew of Time-Life in 1960, committed to making direct cinema films for TV.

An example of the Drew unit's work was *Primary* which Leacock worked on with Donn Alan Pennebaker, Robert Drew, and Terry Filgate, an account of the campaign of Democratic Senators John F. Kennedy and Hubert Humphrey in the Wisconsin presidential primary. Critics and other viewers called this film an excellent report on the inner workings of a political campaign as well as an appealing glimpse of the personal lives of candidates and their families. But Leacock was not satisfied because the camera people could never get in to film behind-the-scenes activity such as p.r. methods.

Leacock has frequently indicated his own and other documentarists concerns about obstacles to achieving direct cinema. It is often controversial, now more than ever-explorations of poverty, exploitation, disease, and war. Leacock, always critical of his own work, is concerned about distribution problems, thoughtful about the role of films in effecting social change. His attachment to creating less expensive, more manageable apparatus, to portraying art and artists, to experimenting, to letting situation and event tell their own story, and to teaching, continues as strongly as ever.

—Lillian Schiff

———

LEAN, DAVID. British. Born in Croydon, England, 25 March 1908. Educated at Leighton Park Quaker School, Reading.

Married Kay Walsh in 1940 (divorced 1949); Ann Todd in 1949 (divorced 1957); Leila Matkar in 1960 (divorced 1978). Career: 1926—clapboard boy at Lime Grove Studios under Maurice Elvoy; 1928—camera assistant, then cutting room assistant; 1930—becomes chief editor for Gaumont-British Sound News; cuts, writes, and speaks commentaries; 1931—editor for British Movietone News; 1934—editor on "quota quickies" for British Paramount; 1942—invitation by Noel Coward to co-direct *In Which We Serve* leads to association with Coward on next 3 films; 1943—with Ronald Neame and Anthony Havelock-Allan founds Cineguild (dissolved 1950); 1956—begins association with producer Sam Spiegel; 1977—begins project with producer Dino De Laurentiis to make 2 films based on story of the HMS Bounty. Recipient: British Film Academy Award for *The Sound Barrier*, 1952; Commander Order of the British Empire, 1953; Best Direction, New York Film Critics, for *Summertime*, 1955; Best Direction, New York Film Critics, for *The Bridge on the River Kwai*, 1957; Best Director Academy Award for *The Bridge on the River Kwai*, 1957; Officier de l'Ordre des Arts et des Lettres, France, 1968. Address: B.P. 2871, Papeete, Tahiti, French Polynesia.

Films (as editor): 1935—*Escape Me Never* (Czinner); 1936—*As You Like It* (Czinner); 1937—*Dreaming Lips* (Czinner); 1938—*Pygmalion* (Asquith and Howard); 1939—*French Without Tears* (Asquith); 1941—*Major Barbara* (Pascal); 1942—*The Invaders (49th Parallel)* (Powell); *One of Our Aircraft Is Missing* (Powell); (as director): 1942—*In Which We Serve* (co-d); 1944—*This Happy Breed* (+co-adapt); 1945—*Blithe Spirit* (+co-adapt); *Brief Encounter* (+co-sc); 1946—*Great Expectations* (+co-sc); 1948—*Oliver Twist* (+co-sc); 1949—*The Passionate Friends (One Woman's Story)* (+co-adapt); 1950—*Madeleine*; 1952—*The Sound Barrier (Breaking Through the Sound Barrier, Breaking the Sound Barrier)* (+p); 1954—*Hobson's Choice* (+p, co-sc); 1955—*Summer Madness (Summertime)* (+co-sc); 1957—*The Bridge on the River Kwai*; 1962—*Lawrence of Arabia*; 1965—*Doctor Zhivago*; 1970—*Ryan's Daughter*.

Publications:

By LEAN:

Articles—"Brief Encounter" in *The Penguin Film Review* (New York), no.4, 1947; "David Lean on What You Can Learn from Movies" in *Popular Photography* (Boulder, Colorado), March 1958; "Out of the Wilderness" in *Films and Filming* (London), January 1963; in *Interviews with Film Directors* edited by Andrew Sarris, New York 1967; interview by S. Ross in *Take One* (Montreal), November 1973.

On LEAN:

Books—*The Movie Makers* by Gene Phillips, Chicago 1973; *The Cinema of David Lean* by Gerald Pratley, New York 1974; *David Lean and His Films* by Alain Silver and James Ursini, London 1974; *David Lean: A Guide to References and Resources* by Louis Castelli and Caryn Lynn Cleeland, Boston 1980; articles—"The Up and Coming Team of Lean and Neame" by C.A. Lejeune in *The New York Times*, 15 June 1947; "Career Inventory From the Lean Viewpoint" by Howard Thompson in *The New York Times*, 9 November 1952; "A Study of David Lean" by J. Holden in *Film Journal* (New York), April 1956; "David Lean, Lover of Life" in *Films and Filming* (London), August 1959; "David Lean" by Stephen Watts in *Films in*

Review (New York), April 1959; "The David Lean Recipe: A Whack in the Guts" by Hollis Alpert in *The New York Times Magazine*, 23 May 1965; "Letter Home" by Helen Laurenson in *Esquire* (New York), December 1965; "*Doctor Zhivago*: The Making of a Movie" by R.S. Stewart in *Atlantic Monthly* (Greenwich, Conn.), August 1965; "David Lean" by Charles Higham in *London Magazine*, January 1965; "On Location with *Ryan's Daughter*" by Herb Lightman in *American Cinematographer* (Los Angeles), August 1968; "Bolt and Lean" by Pauline Kael in the *New Yorker*, 21 November 1970; "Lean Years" by Colin Westerbeck Jr. in *Commonweal* (New York), 18 December 1970; "Lean at SF" by Cathy Furniss in *Films in Review* (New York), April 1971; "In Defense of David Lean" by Steven Ross in *Take One* (Montreal), July/August 1972; "In Defence of David Lean" by S. Ross in *Take One* (Montreal), November 1973; "David Lean" by B. Thomas in *Action* (Los Angeles), November/December 1973; "David Lean: Supreme Craftsman" by Ron Pickard in *Films in Review* (New York), May 1974; "Unresolved 'Ifs' on De Laurentiis Pair" in *Variety* (New York), 14 December 1977; "De Laurentiis on Bora Bora" in *Variety* (New York), 30 August 1978; "A Cinematographic Adventure with David Lean" by George Andrews in *American Cinematographer* (Los Angeles), March 1979; film—*David Lean—A Self Portrait*, Thomas Craven Film Corp., Santa Monica, California 1970.

* * *

There is a trajectory that emerges from the shape of David Lean's career, and it is a misleading one. Lean first achieved fame as a director of seemingly intimate films, closely based on plays of Noel Coward. His first directorial credit was shared with Coward, for *In Which We serve*. In the 1960s he was responsible for extraordinarily ambitious projects, for an epic cinema of grandiose effects, difficult location shooting, and high cultural, even literary pretention. But, in fact, Lean's essential approach to the movies never changed. All of his films, no matter how small or large their dimensions, demonstrate an obsessive cultivation of craft, a fastidious concern with production detail that defines the "quality" post-war British cinema. That craft and concern are as hyperbolic in their devices as is the medium itself. Viewers surprised at the attention to detail and to composition in Lean's last film, *Ryan's Daughter*, a work whose scope would appear to call for a more modest approach, had really not paid attention to the truly enormous dimensions of *Brief Encounter*, a film that defines, for many, intimist cinema.

Lean learned the movies during long years of apprenticeship, with particularly important experience as an editor. It is clear, even in the first films he directed with and then for Coward, that his vision is not bound to the playwright's West End proscenium.- *This Happy Breed*, a lower class version of *Cavalcade*, makes full use of the modest attached house that is the film's prime locus. The nearly palpable patterns of the mise-en-scene are animated by the highly professional acting characteristic of Lean's early films. Watching the working out of those patterns created by the relationsdhip between camera, decor and actor is like watching choreography at the ballet, where the audience is made aware of the abstract forms of placement on the stage even as that placement is vitalized by the individual quality of the dancer. The grief of Celia Johnson and Robert Newton is first expressed by the empty room that they are about to enter, then by the way the camera's oblique backward movement respects their silence.

It is in *Brief Encounter* that the fullness of the director's talent becomes clear. This story of chance meeting, love and renunciation is as apparently mediocre, conventional and echoless as Flaubert's *Madame Bovary*. What could be more boringly middle-class than the romantic longing of a nineteenth century French provincial housewife or the oh-so-tasteful near adultery of two "decent" Britishers. In both cases, the authorial interventions are massive. Lean conveys the film's passion through a set of disproportions, through the juxtaposition of the trite situation against the expressionistic violence of passing express trains and the wrenching departure of locals, against the decadent romanticism of the Rachmaninoff score, and most emphatically against one of the most grandiose and hyperbolic exposures of an actress in the history of film. The size of Celia Johnson's eyes finally become the measure of *Brief Encounter*, eyes whose scope is no less expansive than Lawrence's desert or Zhivago's tundra.

Lean's next two successes are his adaptations (with Ronald Neame) of novels of Dickens, *Great Expectations* and *Oliver Twist*. And again, intimacy on the screen becomes the moment of gigantic display. The greatness of Pip's expectations are set by the magnitude of his frightful encounter with an escaped convict who, when he emerges into the frame, reminds us all what it is like to be a small child in a world of oversized, menacing adults. A variation of this scale is in Pip's meeting with mad Miss Havesham, in all her gothic splendor.

Lean's next few films seem to have more modest ambitions, but they continue to demonstrate the director's concern with expressive placement. Of his three films with his then wife Ann Todd, *Madeleine* most fully exploits her cool blond beauty. Then there occurs a significant change in the development of his career. Lean's reputation as a "location" director with a taste for the picturesque is made by *Summertime*, an adaptation of the play *The Time of the Cuckoo*, in which the city of Venice vies with Katharine Hepburn for the viewer's attention. It is from this point that Lean must be identified as an international rather than an English director. And the international packages that result are perhaps the reasons for the widespread (and unjust, I think) opinion that Lean is more of an executive than a creator with a personal vision.

The personality of Lean is in his compulsive drive to the perfectly composed shot, whatever the cost in time, energy and money. In this there is some affinity between the director and his heroes. The Colonel (Alex Guinness) in *The Bridge on the River Kwai* must drive his men to build a good bridge, even if it is for the enemy. Lawrence (Peter O'Toole) crosses desert after desert in his quest for a self purified through physical ordeal, and the viewers must wonder about the ordeals suffered by the filmmakers to photograph those deserts. The same wonder is elicited by the snowy trek of Dr. Zhivago (Omar Sharif) and the representation of life in early twentieth century Russia.

That perfectly composed shot is emblemized by the principal advertising image used for *Ryan's Daughter*—an umbrella floating in air, suspended over an oceanside cliff. This is a celebration of composition per se, composition that holds unlikely elements in likely array. Composition is an expressive tension, accessible to viewers as it simultanously captures the familiar and the unfamiliar. It is the combination that makes so many viewers sensitive to *Brief Encounter*, where middle-class lives (the lives of film-goers) are filled with overwhelming passion and overwhelming style. Laura and Alex fall in love when they go to the movies.

—Charles Affron

LEDUC, PAUL. Mexican. Born in in Mexico City, 11 March 1942. Educated in architecture and theater, Universidad Nacional

Autónoma de México; IDHEC, Paris. Career: early 1960s—leading organizer of cine clubs while student at university; writes film criticism for *Nuevo cine* and newspaper *El dia*; mid-1960s—obtains grant from French government and enters IDHEC (Institut des hautes etudes cinématographiques, Paris), then works for year in French television; 1967—returns to Mexico, makes 17 documentary shorts for Olympic committee; 1970-76—government active as film producer during terms of President Luis Echeverria; pays for amplification of *Reed: Insurgent Mexico* and co-produces *Mezquital* with Canadian Film Board; 1976-present—films funded independently, through collective efforts, and through universities and unions.

Films (as director): 1973—*Reed: México insurgente (Reed: Insurgent Mexico)*; 1978—*Etnocidio: notas sobre el Mezquital*; 1979—*Historias prohibidas de Pulgarcito*; 1981—*Complot petrolero: La cabeza de la hidra*.

Publications:

By LEDUC:

Article—"Entrevista con Paul Leduc" by Nelson Carro in *Imagenes* (Mexico City), October 1979.

On LEDUC:

Books—*La búsqueda del cine mexicano* by Jorge Ayala Blanco, Mexico City 1974; *Mitología de un cine en crisis* by Alberto Ruy Sánchez, Mexico City 1981; *Mexican Cinema: Reflections of a Society, 1896-1980* by Carl Mora, Berkeley 1982.

*   *   *

Generally acknowledged as the most talented and socially conscious of contemporary Mexican directors, Paul Leduc has been forced to make his films on the margins of commercial cinema. Leduc began his career in a university department of film studies, an initiation increasingly prevalent among the younger generation of Mexican filmmakers. His first films were documentaries, a typical beginning for directors of the "New Latin American Cinema." Then, Leduc was able to take some advantage of a novel situation: during the reign of President Luis Echeverria (1970-76) the Mexican government actively intervened as a producer of cinema, the only time since the 1930s (e.g., *Redes*) that it has attempted to create some sort of alternative to the wretched fare provided by the country's commercial film industry. The government paid for the amplification of *Reed: Insurgent Mexico* to 35mm and co-produced *Mezquital* with the Canadian National Film Board. Since that time, however Leduc has funded his films independently, through universities and unions, and with collective efforts.

Reed: Insurgent Mexico is perhaps Leduc's most accomplished fiction film, and was the first really distinctive work of the "New Cinema" movement in Mexico. Although the film was shot on a minuscule budget in 16mm, it has an exquisite sepia tone which reproduces the ambience of antique revolutionary photographs. Deliberately undramatic, *Reed* demystified the Mexican revolution (1910-17) in a way that had not been seen since Fernando De Fuentes's masterpieces of 1933-35. One Mexican critic, Jorge Ayala Blanco, described *Reed* as "raging against, incinerating, and annihilating the spider web that had been knitted over the once-living image of the revolution, while briefly illuminating the nocturnal ruins of our temporal and cultural distance from the men who participated in that upheaval." The film is a dramatization of John Reed's famous account of the revolution, *Insurgent Mexico*, with Reed as the main protagonist. Although the film is a beautiful and important work, it doesn't really rise above the level of a vignette (perhaps too greatly influenced by the book's form), nor does it achieve the heights of De Fuentes's films.

Leduc's other major works reflect his concern for actuality. *Etnocidio: notas sobre el Mezquital* is probably the best documentary on the extermination of the native peoples in Latin America, allowing the Otomi Indians of the Mezquital region in Mexico to relate their experiences with "civilization." The film is an interesting example of collaborative effort, for the "script" was written by Roger Bartra, Mexico's leading rural sociologist, who based it on his years of research in the area. *Historias prohibidas* is a flawed work that Leduc made in a collective; but it does contain a lively analysis of El Salvador's history. *Complot petrolero* is a made-for-TV thriller about an attempt by right-wing elements (including the CIA and anti-Castro Cubans) to take over the oil and uranium resources of Mexico. Actually a mini-series totaling 3 1/2 hours, it has never been shown on Mexican television, which is largely dominated by series and made-for-TV movies imported from the U.S.

Mexico has proven to be a difficult context for Leduc, who appropriately describes cinema there as "a perfect disaster, composed of *churros*—vulgar, cheap, and badly-made films." Dominated by the "fastbuck" mentality typical of dependent capitalism, Mexican commercial cinema has offered few opportunities for Leduc to direct the kind of films which interest him.

—John Mraz

LEENHARDT, ROGER. French. Born in Montpellier, 23 July 1903. Educated in literature and philosophy, the Sorbonne. Career: 1933—begins working in films as editor, notably on de Baroncelli's *Crainquebille*; and on documentary series "Eclair Journal"; 1934—founds production company Les Films du Compas; makes 1st short documentaries in collaboration with René Zuber; 1935-38—cinema critic for revue *Esprit*; also writes for *Fontaine, Les Lettres françaises, Les Temps modernes*; 1945—with Georges Sadoul and Alexandre Astruc, film critic for *L'Ecran français*; 1949—with Bresson and Cocteau founds *Objectif 49*, precursor of *Cahiers du cinéma*; 1970s—directs television documentaries. Recipient: Best Documentary Film, Brussels World Film Festival, for *Naissance du cinéma*, 1947.

Films (as director of short documentary films): 1934—*En Crête sans les Dieux* (co-d); *L'Orient qui vient* (co-d); *Rezzou* (co-d); 1935—*Le Tapis moquette*; 1937—*R N 37*; 1938—*Revêtements routiers*; *La Course au pétrole* (+pr); 1939—*Fêtes de France*; 1943—*Le Chant des ondes*; *A la poursuite du vent*; 1945—*Lettre de Paris*; *Le Chantier en ruines*; 1946—*Départs pour l'Allemagne*; *Naissance du cinéma*; *Le Barrage de l'Aigle*; 1948—*Côte d'Azur*; *Entrez dans la danse*; 1949—*Le Pain de Barbarie*; *Les Dernières Vacances* (+co-sc—feature); 1950—*L'Héritage du croissant*; *Les Hommes du Champagne* (+pr); *Le Métro*; *La Fugue de Mahmoud*; 1951—*Victor Hugo*; 1952—*Du charbon et des hommes* (+pr); *La France est un jardin*; 1954—*François Mauriac*; *Louis Capet*; 1955—*La Conquête de l'Angleterre*; 1956—*Bâtir à notre âge* (+pr); 1957—*Jean-Jacques Rousseau*

(co-d); *En plein Midi* (co-d); *Paris et le désert français*; 1958—*Daumier*; 1959—*Paul Valéry*; 1960—*Entre Seine et mer*; *Le Maître de Montpellier*; 1961—*La Traversée de la France* (co-d, +pr); 1962—*Le Coeur de la France*; *L'Homme à la pipe*; *Le Rendez-vous de minuit* (feature); 1963—*Des femmes et des fleurs*; *Monsieur de Voltaire*; 1964—*Demain Paris*; *Europe*; *Daguerre ou la naissance de la photographie*; *Une Fille dans la montagne* (+co-sc—feature, for TV); 1965—*Corot*; 1967—*Monsieur Ingres*; *Le Beatnik et le minet* (fiction film); 1970—*Douze mois en France* (co-d, +pr); 1972—*Abraham Bosse*; 1975—*Pissarro*; 1976—*La Languedocienne*; *Var-matin*; 1977—*Anjou*; 1978—*Du plaisir à la joie*; 1980—*Manet ou le novateur malgré lui*.

Roles: 1964—appearance as "l'intelligence" in *La Femme mariée* (Godard); 1977—silhouette in *L'Homme qui aimait les femmes* (Truffaut).

Publications:

By LEENHARDT:

Books—*Les Yeux ouverts: entretiens avec Jean Lacouture*, Paris 1979; *Les Dernières Vacances*, screenplay, Paris 1980; articles—interview in *Le Figaro littéraire* (Paris), 23 September 1961; "Entretien avec Roger Leenhardt" in *Cahiers du cinéma* (Paris), November 1962; "Interview with Roger Leenhardt and Jacques Rivette" by Louis Marcorelles in *Sight and Sound* (London), autumn 1963; "Entretien avec Roger Leenhardt" in *Les Lettres françaises* (Paris), 7 June 1972; "Les Dernières Vacances", special issue of *Avant-Scène du cinéma* (Paris), 1 November 1980.

On LEENHARDT:

Book—*French Cinema Since 1946: Vol.1* by Roy Armes, New York 1970; articles—"Le Style c'est l'homme même" by André Bazin in *Revue du cinéma* (Paris), June 1948; "Roger Leenhardt, l'homme des valeurs centrales" in *L'Avant-Scène du cinéma* (Paris), 1 November 1980; films—*Roger Leenhardt ou le dernier humaniste*, for TV, by André-S. Labarthe, 1965; *Roger Leenhardt, homme de parole*, directed for TV by Robert Réa, 1979; *Roger Leenhardt, homme du Midi*, directed for TV by Claude Fayard, 1979.

*   *   *

Roger Leenhardt has made only two feature films, yet his reputation as a sage of the cinema is fabled and his influence on the course of French film has been great.

Leenhardt is a rare man indeed, for in no way did he decide to give himself up to a profession as cineaste. To this Renaissance man the cinema has been only one interest among many animating his life. He leaped at the opportunity to make his two feature films, and he struggled to bring a few other personal projects to the screen, projects which were for one reason or another abandoned; but he has never been tempted to become a contract director or to work as assistant on major films.

Many feel that Leenhardt, an intellectual from Montpellier, initiated modern film criticism in France. In any case his writings in *Esprit* were virtually the only serious essays on the cinema to be published in the 1930s and they had a great effect. André

Bazin, for instance, was lured into studying the cinema by these essays, and contiued to consider Leenhardt his inspiration, dedicating *What is Cinema?* to him.

Men of letters intrigued by the cinema, such as Gide and Sartre, found in Leenhardt a sensibility they could rely on and an expertise they could respect. As early as 1940 Leenhardt had proven his intellectual worth (in serious philosophical and political essays published in *Esprit*) and had become a serviceable filmmaker, auteur of a half-dozen shorts.

At the close of World War II he stood in an enviable position, for he was respected and experienced at a time when it appeared that the film industry was opening up to new blood. In fact it was in 1948 that he made *Les Dernières Vacances*. A charming hymn to the end of adolescence, set in the society of the grande bourgeoisie, this film also puts into play a number of the principles of film theory Leenhardt had long advocated in print. Philippe Agostini's mobile camera and Léon Barsacq's decor give the film the appearance of a quality production. But the direction is so insistently personal that it became a harbinger of the New Wave movement. Bazin wrote about it lavishly in *Esprit*. Astruc, another close friend from the St. Germain cafe circle, considered it to be an example of "le caméra-stylo." The whole pre-*Cahiers* community (Cocteau, Bresson, Doniol-Valcroze, etc.) hailed it. And, predictably, Leenhardt became the father figure for the New Wave. Jean-Luc Godard underlined this in 1966 when he gave Leenhardt a role in *A Married Woman* flashing "l'intelligence" as an intertitle upon his appearance.

During the humdrum 1950s Leenhardt occupied himself with short films. His *Birth of the Cinema* is a classic, and his biographical portraits of Rousseau, Mauriac, Valéry, and others stand out for their technical excellence and ingenuity as well as for their depth of understanding of their subjects. Leenhardt claims that filmmaking has been a way for him to pursue his other interests (biography, geography, art history).

At the coming of the New Wave it was only natural for Leenhardt to be given another chance at a major film; in 1961 the aid laws made it profitable for producers to risk money on new directors. Leenhardt was both new and old, a safe bet. *Le Rendez-vous de minuit*, starring Lili Palmer, was a perfect New Wave idea, a film within a film. But either because it came too late in the movement (1962) or because Leenhardt's cool classicism didn't fit the passionate excesses for which that movement is known, the film found little success.

Leenhardt went back to documentaries with television an obvious market for his productions. His encyclopedic knowledge of French culture, his personal acquaintance with many of the most vibrant figures of the century (Dos Passos, Merleau-Ponty, etc.), and his technical and theoretical mastery of the medium have justified his reputation.

—Dudley Andrew

LEFEBVRE, JEAN-PIERRE. Canadian. Born in Montreal, 17 August 1942. Educated in French literature, University of Montreal. Career: 1960-67—staff writer for *Objectif* (Montreal); 1963-65—professor of French; 1969—forms own production company Cinak; 1969-71—initiates "Premières Oeuvres" section of Office National du Film; 1974—President of Association des Réalisateurs de Films du Québec.

Films (as producer, director, and scriptwriter): 1964— *L'Homoman* (short) (+ph); 1965—*Le Révolutionnaire*; 1966—

Patricia et Jean-Baptiste; *Mon Oeil (My Eye)* (unrealized); 1967—*Il ne faut pas mourir pour ça (Don't Let It Kill You)* (co-sc); (as director and scriptwriter): *Mon Amie Pierrette*; 1968—*Jusqu'au coeur*; 1969—*La Chambre blanche (House of Light)*; 1970—*Un Succès commercial (Q-bec My Love)*; 1971— *Les Maudits sauvages (Those Damned Savages)*; *Ultimatum*; 1973—*On n'engraisse pas les cochons à l'eau claire*; *Les Deniéres Fiançailles (The Last Betrothal)*; 1975—*Le Gars des vues*; *L'Amour blessé*; 1977—*Le Vieux Pays ou Rimbaud est mort*; 1978—*Avoir 16 ans*; 1981—*Les Fleurs sauvages (The Wild Flowers)*.

Publications:

By LEFEBVRE:

Book—*Parfois quand je vis*, poems, Editions HMH 1970; articles—"Complexes d'une technique" in *Objectif* (Montreal), March 1961; "L'Equipe française souffre-t-elle de Roucheole?", with Jean-Claude Pilon, in *Objectif* (Montreal), August 1962; "Petit Eloge des grandeurs et des misères de la colonie française de l'Office National du Film" in *Objectif* (Montreal), August/-September 1964; "Les Années folles de la critique ou petite histoire des revues de cinéma au Québec" in *Objectif* (Montreal), October/November 1964; "La Crise du language et le cinéma canadien" in *Objectif* (Montreal), April/May 1965; "La Méche et la bombe" in *Cahiers du cinéma* (Paris), March 1966; "Les Paradis perdus du cinéma canadien, chapitre 1: notes en guise d'introduction à une préface éventuelle" in *Objectif* (Montreal), November/December 1966; "Un Cinéma de l'ambiguïté" in *Culture Vivante*, no.1, 1966; "Le Coup de dès: entretien avec Jean-Pierre Lefebvre" by Michel Delahaye in *Cahiers du cinéma* (Paris), January 1967; interview by Michèle Favreau in *La Presse* (Montreal), 15 April 1967; "Les Paradis perdus du cinéma canadien, chapitre 2: illustration existentielle du chapitre 1 à partir de données oniriques" in *Objectif* (Montreal), May 1967; "A propos du cours d'initiation au cinéma au secondaire classique" in *Objectif* (Montreal), August/September 1967; "Les Paradis perdus du cinéma canadien, chapitre 3: Saint Gabias, priez pour nous" in *Objectif* (Montreal), August/September 1967; interview by Michèle Favreau in *La Presse* (Montreal), 16 March 1968; "Les Quatres Saisons" in *Cahiers du cinéma* (Paris), April/May 1968; "Jean-Pierre Lefebvre: transformer le cours des choses", interview by Gérard Langlois in *Les Lettres françaises* (Paris), 9 October 1968; "La Confession d'un cinéaste du Québec qui pourrait bien être un adieu définitif au cinéma" in *Revue du cinéma international*, February 1969; "Un Martien en exil", interview by Luc Perreault in *La Presse* (Montreal), 2 August 1969; interview by M. Amiel in *Cinéma* (Paris), December 1972; "Jean-Pierre Lefebvre fait le point", interview by J.-P. Tadros in *Cinéma Québec* (Montreal), December/January 1973/74; interview by J. Beaulieu in *Séquences* (Montreal), April 1974; interview by G. Haustrate in *Cinéma* (Paris), May 1974; "Les Dernières Vacances", interview by M. Martin and J.-A. Gili in *Ecran* (Paris), November 1974; "Une Nouvelle Époque pour Jean-Pierre Lefebvre", interview by B. Oheix in *Jeune Cinéma* (Paris), September/October 1974; "On n'engraisse pas les cochons à l'eau claire", interview by J.-A. Gili in *Ecran* (Paris), January 1975; "Commission d'enquête sur le cinéma organise" in *Cinéma Québec* (Montreal), no.5, 1976; "Des lois et des cadres: La Guerre des gangs" in *Cinéma Québec* (Montreal), no.4, 1976; interview by F. Gévaudan in *Cinéma* (Paris), August/September 1977; "'Ecouter l'image et regarder le son'", interview by J.-P. Tadros in *Cinéma Québec* (Montreal), v.5, no.6, 1977; "Le Vieux Pays où Rimbaud est mort, Jean-Pierre Lefebvre, Le Québec et la France", interview by René Predal in *Jeune Cinéma* (Paris), February 1978.

On LEFEBVRE:

Books—*Le Cinéma canadien* by Gilles Marsolais, Paris 1968; *Cinéastes du Québec 3: Jean-Pierre Lefebvre*, Ottawa 1970; *Jean-Pierre Lefebvre* edited by Renald Bérubé and Yvan Patry, Montreal 1971; articles—"The Gentle Revolutionary" by Graham Fraser in *Take One* (Montreal), October 1967; article in *Jeune Cinéma canadien* by René Prédal, Premier Plan no.45, Lyon, October 1967; "Le Sens de la contestation et Jean-Pierre Lefebvre" by André Larsen in *Le Cinéma Québecois: Tendances et prolongements*, Cahiers Ste-Marie, 1968; article by Jean Chabot in *Second Wave*, New York 1970; "Political Situation of Quebec Cinema" by Real La Rochelle and Gilbert Maggi in *Cineaste* (New York), summer 1972; "Il Cinemardi Lefebvre (Sorrento 74)" by E. Bruno in *Filmcritica* (Rome), August/September 1974; "Un Tour de France d'un cinéaste" by J. Courcier in *Cinéma Québec* (Montreal), v.3, no.8, 1974; "Sur 2 films de Jean-Pierre Lefebvre" by G. Gauthier in *Image et son* (Paris), January 1975.

LE GRICE, MALCOLM. British. Born in Plymouth, Devon, 15 May 1940. Educated in painting at Plymouth Art College, 1957-61; Slade School of Fine Art, 1961-64. Career: since 1966—activity consists mainly in film-performance and projection works; 1967—begins working with London Film-Makers Co-op, founds and builds workshop; 1968—first one-man painting and film show, Drury Lane Arts Lab; 1968-present—teaches film production and film studies, St. Martin's College, London; 1976—*Abstract Film and Beyond* published; contributor to *Undercut*, magazine of London Film-Makers Co-op; 1977—takes part in Documenta 6, Kassel.

Films 1966—*Castle 1; China Tea*; 1967—*Little Dog for Roger* (double projection version 1968); *Yes No Maybe Maybenot*; *Talla; Blind White Duration*; 1968—*Castle 2; Grass; Wharf*; 1970—*Spot the Microdot; Your Lips No.1; Lucky Pigs; Reign of the Vampire; Berlin Horse; Horror Film 1*; 1971—*Love Story 1; Love Story 2; 1919, A Russian Funeral; Your Lips 3*; 1972—*Love Story 3; Horror Film 2; Newport; Whitchurch Down (Duration); Threshold; Blue Field Duration; White Field Duration*; 1973—*Pre-Production; Four Wall Duration; Gross Fog; Matrix and Joseph's Coat; After Leonardo; Don't Say; Principles of Cinematography; After Leslie Wheeler; FRPS; MBKS*; 1974—*Screen—Entrance Exit; After Lumiere, L'Arroseur Arrose*; 1975—*After Manet, After Giorgione, Le Dejeuner sur l'herbe*; 1977—*Blackbird Descending (Tense Alignment); Art Works 1: Academic Still Life (Cézanne); Art Works 2: Time and Motion Study*; 1979—*Emily (Third Party Speculation)*; 1983—*Finnegan's Chin*.

Publications:

By LE GRICE:

Book—*Abstract Film and Beyond*, Cambridge, Mass. 1977; articles— "Film" in *Studio International* (Lugano), September/-

October 1976; "Towards Temporal Economy" in *Screen* (London), winter 1979/80.

On LE GRICE:

Article—"More British Sounds" by J. Dawson and C. Johnston in *Sight and Sound* (London), summer 1970.

*   *   *

Malcolm Le Grice is a British film artist, theoretician, and educator. He may be best known in the United States for his 1977 MIT Press publication *Abstract Film and Beyond*, a complex and very sophisticated theoretical/historical comparison of American and European contemporary experimental film. However, with over 40 experimental productions to his credit, he is foremost an experimental filmmaker of international reputation.

By his own account, Le Grice's artistic career has enjoyed "three interconnected phases." All are related to his theoretical writings and insightful regard for the evolution of experimental film as a historical quest to establish cinema's distinct elements—that is, those characteristics and artistic resources which distinguish film from alternate modes such as written literature, the theater, painting, music, etc. Of all the major genres of film, experimental film seems especially qualified for this very theoretical task. Its independence of financing and controls, its attraction for technical and structural innovation, and its acollaborative construction allowing expression of a single artist's vision *sans* the filtered metamorphosis of more typical crews and companies—all this allows experimental film to reflexively examine cinema's essence for the sake of either pure or applied research goals.

During the earliest phase of his career, from 1967 to 1970, Le Grice advanced such research through concentration upon the medium's "material aspects" (such as emulsion or sprocket holes) in works like *Little Dog for Roger, Yes, No, Maybe, Maybe Not*, and *Berlin Horse*. During the middle phase, Le Grice concentrated upon elements of screening and projection. Indeed, multi-projection formats or the employ of pure shadows mark works like *Horror Film Two* and the four-screen *Matrix and Joseph's Coat*. Some works from this period—such as his 1972 *Pre-production*—are classified more as media-events than distributional motion-picture products.

His more recent, third phase works, such as the 1974 *After Lumière*, at once return to distributional units and to cinema's classic history. Faithful to experimental film's characteristics, Le Grice's productions are brief (though exceptions to such brevity exist, such as his 1977 work, *Blackbird Descending*, which runs over two hours). *After Lumière* is a 16-minute, single screen work that is largely a cinematic allusion to Lumière's nineteenth-century classic, *L'Arroseur Arrose*. Le Grice's strategy was to add an observing female character to Lumière's original, simple, one-shot story of a boy's trick upon a gardener with his garden hose. This character practices piano throughout the many repetitions of the core event, providing the study with a musical track that helps distinguish it from its 1895 prototype. Indeed, Le Grice's employ of such elements as sound, loop-like repetitions, editing, and subjective camera only gain their aesthetic force through implicit contradistinction to the original French film—a classic well-known to film artists and scholars throughout the world.

In *Abstract Film and Beyond*, Le Grice contends that film has evolved "towards a form which is not dependent on other areas of art for the source of its conventions." Le Grice's own film work can well be regarded as related exploration, "genuinely cinematographic in concept," beyond the confines of theater, literature, painting, and music.

—Edward S. Small

LEISEN, MITCHELL. American. Born in Menominee, Michigan, 6 October 1898. Educated in art, Art Institute of Chicago; studied architecture, Washington University, St. Louis. Career: 1919—goes to Hollywood, works as costume designer for Cecil B. De Mille; 1920—becomes set dresser, then art director, working with De Mille among others until 1932; 1933—begins directing for Paramount with 2 films co-directed by Stuart Walker; 1950s—begins directing for TV, series include *G.E. Theatre, Markham, Thriller, Wagon Train, Twilight Zone*; also works as interior designer and is co-owner of Beverly Hills tailor shop. Died 1972.

Films (as director): 1933—*Tonight Is Ours* (co-d); *Eagle and the Hawk* (co-d); *Cradle Song*; 1934—*Death Takes a Holiday*; *Murder at the Vanities*; 1935—*Behold My Wife*; *Four Hours to Kill*; *Hands Across the Table*; 1936—*13 Hours by Air*; *The Big Broadcast of 1937*; 1937—*Swing High, Swing Low*; *Easy Living*; 1938—*The Big Broadcast of 1938*; *Artists and Models Abroad*; 1939—*Midnight*; 1940—*Remember the Night*; *Arise, My Love*; 1941—*I Wanted Wings*; *Hold Back the Dawn*; 1942—*The Lady Is Willing*; *Take a Letter, Darling*; 1943—*No Time for Love*; 1944—*Lady in the Dark*; *Frenchman's Creek*; *Practically Yours*; 1945—*Masquerade in Mexico*; *Kitty*; 1946—*To Each His Own*; 1947—*Suddenly It's Spring*; *Golden Earrings*; 1948—*Dream Girl*; 1949—*Bride of Vengeance*; *Song of Surrender*; 1950—*No Man of Her Own*; *Captain Carey, U.S.A.*; 1951—*The Mating Season*; *Darling, How Could You*; 1952—*Young Man with Ideas*; 1953—*Tonight We Sing*; 1955—*Bedevilled*; 1957—*The Girl Most Likely*; 1967—*Spree* (co-d) (filmed in 1963 as *Here's Las Vegas*).

Publications:

By LEISEN:

Articles—"You Women Won't Like This" in *Silver Screen* (New York), May 1946; "A Visit with Mitchell Leisen" by Leonard Maltin in *Action* (Los Angeles), November/December 1969; "FFM Interviews Mitchell Leisen" by Leonard Maltin in *Film Fan Monthly* (Teaneck, N.J.), 1970; interview by J.B. Kelley and J. Schultheiss in *Cinema* (Beverly Hills), spring 1973.

On LEISEN:

Book—*Hollywood Director* by David Chierichetti, New York 1973; articles—"Likable but Elusive" by Andrew Sarris in *Film Culture* (New York), spring 1963; "Mitchell Leisen" by J. Greenberg in *Films in Review* (New York), March 1966; obituary by Claude Beylie in *Ecran* (Paris), January 1973; "Hollywood Contract Director: Mitchell Leisen" by J.B. Kelley and J. Schultheiss in *Cinema* (Beverly Hills), spring 1973; "The Magic Mountain" by G. Adair in *Sight and Sound* (London), summer 1980.

* * *

Costume and set designers who turn to direction are sufficiently rare for the career of Mitchell Leisen to be worthy of comment. As a soldier in the De Mille entourage of the twenties, he responded meekly to the master's demands for decorative camera-fodder. But in his first directing job, as "associate" to Stuart Walker in *The Eagle and the Hawk*, Leisen contrived, even while displaying the lovely young Carole Lombard to striking advantage in an extravagant silver gown, to turn her scene with Fredric March into an encounter humming with passion. He was no less skillful with the languid melodrama of *Death Takes a Holiday*, where once again he worked with the talented March to create scenes that transcend the high-life setting.

Such legerdemain became a Leisen trademark. He directed much that was beneath his intelligence, but always with style, taste, and decorative flair. The musicals are lush exemplars of Paramount's up-market European approach, from the backstage peep-show of *Murder at the Vanities* through the drama-with-music of *Swing High Swing Low* to *Lady in the Dark*'s lavish Broadway pastels and psychoanalytic fantasy.

Leisen directed some of the best Billy Wilder/Charles Brackett screenplays, including the sublime comedy *Midnight*, and those curious romantic melodramas *Arise My Love* and *Hold Back the Dawn*, cultured and ironic reflections of a world of refugees, intrigue and casual passion. Also for Leisen, Preston Sturges wrote the sarcastic *Remember the Night* for MacMurray and Stanwyck, and in *Easy Living* created a superb wise-cracking parody of capitalistic excess. Both were handled by the director with flawless skill.

Perhaps in reaction against De Mille, Leisen avoided costume pictures. Those he did make are notable less for couture than performance. *Kitty* is a regency sex comedy for Paulette Goddard, and *Bride of Vengeance* a Renaissance romp for the same star, this time playing an improbably Lucrezia Borgia to John Lund's distracted Duke of Ferrara, who has invasion and intrigue to contend with in city and bedroom both.

The typus of the Hollywood gay director, Leisen seldom slipped below a self-imposed standard of visual elegance, nor rose above a stylish superficiality. As the leader of Paramount's directorial second string, he was often saddled with its less-accomplished leads. He extracted creditable work from MacMurray, Lund, Goddard, and even Betty Hutton, but was moved to greater heights by Fontaine, Milland, Boyer, and Lombard. That he is remembered by *Cahiers du cinéma* as little more than "a great couturier" and by other reference books more for the writers and performers he directed is a fate suffered by many artists of Hollywood's thirties cinema, stronger on wit and taste than self-advertisement.

—John Baxter

LELOUCH, CLAUDE. French. Born in Paris, 30 October 1937. Married Christine Cochet (divorced); child: Simon. Career: 1955—sells travelogue on New York to French television; just before presentation, switches reels so that viewers see indictment of working conditions in New York instead; 1956-58—makes numerous short films as "cinereporter"; 1958-60—serves in Service-Cinéma des Armées (S.C.A.), makes about 10 films including *La Guerre du silence* on war in Algeria; 1960—founds production company "Les Films 13"; 1960-62—makes some 250 "scopitones", 2 or 3-minute mini-musicals shown on a type of jukebox; makes first feature; 1963—release of *La Femme spectacle* blocked by censors; 1966—international reputation established by *A Man and a Woman*. Recipient: Best Story and Screenplay Academy Award for *A Man and a Woman*, 1966; Palme d'oro, Cannes Festival, for *A Man and a Woman*, 1966; Grand prix du Cinéma français for *Vivre pour vivre*, 1967; Prix Raoul Levy, 1970. Address: 15 avenue Hoche, 75008 Paris, France.

Films (as producer, director, scriptwriter and editor): 1953—*Le Mal du siècle; USA en vrac*; 1957—*Quand le rideau se lève*; 1959—*La Guerre du silence; Les Mécaniciens de l'armée de l'air; S.O.S. hélicoptère*; (as producer, director and scriptwriter): 1960—*Le Propre de l'homme (The Right of Man)* (+ro as Claude); *La Femme spectacle (Night Women)*; 1964—*Une Fille et des fusils (To Be a Crook)* (+ph); *24 heures d'amant*; 1965—*Les Grands Moments* (+ph); *Jean-Paul Belmondo; Pour un maillot jaune*; 1966—*Un Homme et une femme (A Man and a Woman)* (+co-ed, ph); 1967—*Vivre pour vivre (Live for Life)*; episode of *Loin du Vietnam (Far From Vietnam)* (d only); 1968—*13 jours en France (Grenoble)* (+co-ph); *La Vie, l'amour, la mort (Life Love Death)* (co-sc); 1969—*Un Homme qui me plaît (Love Is a Funny Thing)* (co-p, co-sc); 1970—*Le Voyou (The Crook)*; 1971—*Smic Smac Smoc* (+ph); 1972—*L'Aventure c'est l'aventure (Money Money Money)* (co-sc); *La Bonne année (Happy New Year)* (co-pr, co-sc, +ph); 1973—"The Losers" episode in *Visions of 8* (co-sc); 1974—*Toute une vie (And Now My Love)*; *Mariage (Marriage)* (co-sc); 1975—*Le Chat et la souris (Cat and Mouse)*; *Le Bon et les méchants (The Good and the Bad)*; 1976—*Rendez-vous; Si c'était à refaire (If I Had to Do It All Over Again)* (+ph); 1977—*Another Man, Another Chance* (co-pr); 1978—*Molière* (4-hour TV drama: pr only); *Robert et Robert*; 1979—*A nous deux (An Adventure for 2, Us Two)*; 1981—*Les uns et les autres*; 1982—*Edith et Marcel*.

Publications:

By LELOUCH:

Book—*A Man and a Woman*, with Pierre Uytterhoeven, New York, 1971; articles—"Un homme, une femme" screenplay in *L'Avant-scène du cinéma* (Paris), December 1966; "Claude Lelouch at the Olympic Games", interview in *American Cinematographer* (Los Angeles), November 1972; interview by J. Craven in *Filmmakers Newsletter* (Ward Hill, Mass.), March 1974; interview by P. Lev in *Take One* (Montreal), August 1977; interview by S. McMillin in *Filmmakers Newsletter* (Ward Hill, Mass.), February 1978.

On LELOUCH:

Books—*French Cinema Since 1946: Vol.2—The Personal Style* by Roy Armes, New York 1966; *Claude Lelouch* by Guylaine Guidez, Paris 1972; *Claude Lelouch* by Pierluigi Ronchetti, Città di Castello, Italy 1979; articles—"A 26 ans, Lelouch cinéaste méconnu mérite d'être découvert" by Christian Ledieu in *Arts* (Paris), 20 May 1964; "Lelouch: table ronde" in *Cinéma 65* (Paris), May 1965; "Claude Lelouch, ou la bonne conscience retrouvée" by Jean-Louis Comolli in *Cahiers du cinéma* (Paris), June 1966; "L'amore piccolo borghese" by Fernaldo Di Giammatteo in *Bianco e nero* (Rome), no.6, 1966; "Zoom sur Lelouch" in *Technique cinématographique* (Paris), May 1969; "Le Cas Lelouch" by Maurice Perisset in *Cinéma 69* (Paris), May 1969; "Lelouch, portrait d'un condamné à mort" in *Les Lettres françaises* (Paris), January 1969; "Claude Lelouch, une vocation de voyou" by Gérard Sire in *Nouveau Cinémonde* (Paris), Janu-

ary 1971; "And Now My Love" by A. Eyles in *Focus on Film* (London), summer 1975; "A propos de *Toute une vie* ou Lelouchiens si vous saviez" by A. Garel in *Image et son* (Paris), January 1975; "Vom poetischen Realismus zum 'nouveau naturel'" by J.-P. Brossard in *Film und Fernsehen* (Berlin), May 1977.

*   *   *

The films of Claude Lelouch may be classified under three diverse headings: romance, crime, and liberal politics. Occasionally, they focus on one specific area; more often, the categories will be combined.

A Man and a Woman is a love story simply and purely. Despire Lelouch's many commercial successes, he is most identified with this glossy, gimmicky, tremendously popular tale of script girl Anouk Aimee, a widow, and her widower counterpart, race car driver Jean-Louis Trintignant. *A Man and a Woman* became one of the most beloved romantic films of its time, a favorite of young couples. The scenario may be a soap opera, photographed on what some critics perceive as superficially postcard-pretty locations; still, it is emotionally touching and truthful. Most significantly, there is refreshingly flexible camera work. Lelouch, who also photographed (as well as co-editing the film and co-authoring the screenplay), uses his camera like a paintbrush, with total ease and freedom.

More typically, Lelouch mixes love and politics in *Live for Life*, the story of television journalist Yves Montand, whose work takes him to Vietnam and Africa; this character leaves devoted wife Annie Girardot for fashion model Candice Bergen. The filmmaker combines love and crime in *Happy New Year*, in which two robbers plan a caper and one falls for the proprietress of a nearby antique store. He blends crime and politics in *Money, Money, Money*, in which a gang of crooks realize that the changing times will allow them to gain greater profits by committing political crimes.

Lelouch has always had one eye on box office receipts, once too often selecting his subject matter with commercial potential being the sole consideration. Early in his career he directed *Night Woman*, a relatively erotic film about, as the filmmaker explains, "all the kinds of women one wouldn't like to marry," in the hope of earning a financial success. His first box office hit was *To Be a Crook*, the story of four men and a deaf-and-dumb girl who become kidnappers and murderers; highlighted are gunfights, and a striptease.

Lelouch does have political concerns: he participated (with Alain Resnais, Jean-Luc Godard, Joris Ivens, William Klein, and Agnes Varda) in the anti-war compilation film *Far From Vietnam*. And he has made quite a few delightfully clever entertainments: *Happy New Year; Money, Money, Money; Cat and Mouse*, a mystery-comedy about a police inspector's efforts to uncover a rich philanderer's killer; *The Crook* and *And Now My Love*, which utilizes comedy, music, and drama to unite lovers Marthe Keller and Andre Dussollier. Yet he will all too often repeat himself, with uninspired results. For example, *Live for Life*, the follow-up to *A Man and a Woman*, is just too frilly, a slickly photographed soap opera lacking the warmth of its predecessor. *Another Man, Another Chance* is a blatant rip-off of *A Man and a Woman*, with James Caan the widower and Genevieve Bujold the widow. Despite his many successes, Claude Lelouch ultimately cannot be ranked with the top filmmakers of his generation.

—Rob Edelman

LENI, PAUL. German. Born in Stuttgart, 8 July 1885. Career: 1900—moves to Berlin; early 1900s—as painter participates in avant-garde movement around publication *Der Sturm*; before 1914—active as stage designer for Max Reinhardt among others; 1914—begins career as production designer on Joe May's *Das Panzergewölbe*; 1916—begins directing with *Das Tagebuch des Dr. Hart*; before 1920—also active as scenarist (von Antalffy's *Das Rätzel von Bangalor* in 1917) and actor in Joe May's *Die Schuld der Lavinia Morland* (1920); 1926—designs 2 films for Michael Kertesz in Vienna; 1927—hired for Universal by Carl Laemmle; 1927-29—makes 4 films for Universal. Died of blood poisoning, 2 September 1929.

Films (as production designer): 1914—*Das Panzergewölbe* (May); 1915—*Der Katzensteg* (Mack); *Das achte Gebot* (Mack); (as director): 1916—*Das Tagebuch des Dr. Hart*; 1917—*Das Rätsel von Bangalor* (assoc. d, +co-sc); *Dornröschen* (+sc); 1919—*Platonische Ehe* (+co-prod des); *Prinz Kuckuk* (+co-prod des); (as production designer): 1920—*Der weisse Pfau* (Dupont) (co-prod des, +co-sc); *Die Schuld der Lavinia Morland* (May) (co-prod des, +ro); *Veritas Vincit* (May) (co-prod des); (as director and production designer): 1920—*Patience* (+sc); 1921—*Fiesco (Die Verschwöhrung zu Genua)* (co-prod des); *Das Gespensterschiff*; *Hintertreppe (Backstairs)* (co-d); *Komödie der Leidenschaften; (as production designer): 1921—Die Geier Wally* (Dupont); *Kinder der Finsternis* (Dupont); 1922—*Frauenopfer* (Grüne); 1923—*Tragödie der Liebe* (May); (as director and production designer): 1924—*Das Wachsfigurenkabinett (Waxworks, 3 Wax Works, 3 Wax Men)*; (as production designer): 1925—*Die Frau von vierzig Jahren* (Oswald); *Der Farmer aus Texas* (May); *Der Tänzer meiner Frau* (Korda); 1926—*Manon Lescaut* (Robison) (costumes only); *Fiaker Nr. 13* (Kertesz); *Wie einst im Mai* (Wolff); *Der goldene Schmetterling* (Kertesz); (as director in U.S.): 1927—*The Cat and the Canary*; *The Chinese Parrot*; 1928—*The Man Who Laughs*; 1929—*The Last Warning*.

Publications:

On LENI:

Books—*From Caligari to Hitler* by Siegfried Kracauer, Princeton 1947; *The Haunted Screen: Expressionism in the German Cinema and the Influence of Max Reinhardt* by Lotte Eisner, Berkeley 1969; article—"Paul Leni 1885-1929" by Freddy Buache in *Anthologie du cinéma* vol.4, Paris 1968.

*   *   *

Siegfried Kracauer, in *From Caligari to Hitler*, calls Leni "one of the outstanding film directors of the post-World War I era," and refers to the Jack-the-Ripper episode of *Waxworks* as being "among the greatest achievements of film art." Yet Leni's name is familiar only to film scholars today.

He predates Hitchcock as a maker of thrillers; the screen cliches of trembling hands intent on murdering unsuspecting innocents, and corpses falling from opened doors, were first presented in his *The Cat and the Canary*. Excluding the films of Lon Chaney, he was the foremost practitioner of utilizing make-up to create grotesque creatures, silent-screen monsters who terrified audiences by looks alone.

Leni's death from blood poisoning at 44 denied the cinema what might have developed into a major career. Leni commenced his work in the German cinema as a painter, set designer and art director, most notably collaborating with Max Reinhardt. These concerns carry through into his own films: his sets are strikingly stylized, dreamlike, expressionistic.

Leni's attempt to go beyond the limits of photographed reality utilizing set and costume design was never more successfully realized than in *Des Wachsfigurenkabinett* (*Waxworks*). The film, with its distorted sets and ingenious lighting, is as profound an example of surreal cinematic madness as *The Cabinet of Dr. Caligari*. Three of the best-known actors in the post-World War I German cinema starred as the wax-work villains: Emil Jannings, Conrad Veidt and Werner Krauss. Each appears in a separate episode as, respectively, Haroun-al-Raschid, Ivan the Terrible (who places hourglasses near each of his poison victims, so that they will know the exact moment of their deaths), and Jack the Ripper (a sequence that, in its dreaminess, is extremely Caligari-like). Veidt's Ivan allegedly influenced Sergei Eisenstein's conception of the character.

Like many foreign talents of the period, Leni ended up in Hollywood. As a result of his success with *Waxworks*, he was signed by Universal's Carl Laemmle. His first project was *The Cat and the Canary*, the original haunted house movie and quite unlike its successor: here, heiress Laura La Plante and her nervous cronies spend a night in an old dark house. To his credit, Leni did not sensationalize the material. The film's chills result from atmosphere, from stylized, expressionistic set design. The mansion, seen in the distance, is eerily gothic; inside are long, winding corridors and staircases. *The Cat and the Canary* is not just a chiller, in that Leni adds charming touches of humor to the scenario. Paul Leni made only four features in Hollywood. His final one, prophetically titled *The Last Warning*, was his only talkie.

—Rob Edelman

———————

LENICA, JAN. Polish. Born in Poznan, 4 January 1928; became citizen of France. Educated in architectural engineering, Polytechnic, Warsaw, until 1952. Married Merja Alanen, 1969; children: Anneli and Maia. Career: 1945—begins publishing humorous and satirical drawings; 1948—first one man show, Warsaw; 1950—begins designing posters; 1957—begins making films with Walerian Borowczyk; 1958—leaves Poland to work in France; 1960s—poster designs featured in numerous international exhibitions; 1963—leaves France for West Germany; 1966-69—works on feature-length animation *Adam II*; 1966-present—subject of many one-man shows for designs and drawings; 1974—Artist in Residence, Carpenter Center, Harvard University; currently Professor of animated film, University of Kassel, West Germany. Recipient: Polish Film Critics Prize for *Once Upon a Time*, 1957; Grand Prix for Experimental Film, Brussels World's Fair, for *Dom*, 1958; "Golden Dragon", Cracow, for *New Janko the Musician*, 1960; Polish Film Critics Prize for *New Janko the Musician*, 1960; Toulouse Lautrec Award for film posters, 1961; "Golden Dragon", Cracow, for *Labyrinth*, 1962; Grand Prix, Oberhausen Festival, for *A*, 1964; Golden Lion, Venice Festival, for *Woman the Flower*, 1965; Max-Ernst Award for animated film, 1966; First Prize, International Poster Biennale, Warsaw, 1966; Award of the City of Essen for graphic work, 1980. Address: 3, rue Saint Christophe, 75015 Paris, France.

Films (as director and animator, in collaboration with Walerian Borowczyk): 1957—*Był sobie raz (Once Upon a Time)*; *Nagrod-*

zone uczucie (Love Required); 1958—Dom (The House); 1959—Monsieur Tête (Mr. Head); (as director and animator): 1960—Nowy Janko muzykant (New Janko the Musician); 1962—Labirynt (Labyrinth); 1963—Die Nashörner (Rhinoceroses); 1964—A; 1965—La Femme-Fleur (Woman the Flower); 1969—Adam II (Adam 2) (feature-length); Stilleben (Still Life); 1970—Nature morte; 1972—Fantorro, le dernier justicier (Fantorro, the Last Just Man); 1974—Landscape; 1976—Ubu Roi (King Ubu); 1979—Ubu et la Grande Gidouille (Ubu and the Great Gidouille) (feature-length).

Films of less than 3 minutes: 1957—Strip-Tease (with Borowczyk); 1958—Sztandar młodych (Banner of Youth) (with Borowczyk); 1961—Italia 61 (Italy 61) (with W. Zamecznik) (film lost); 1964—trailer for Cul-de-sac (Polanski); 1966—Weg zum Nachbarn (for Oberhausen Festival); 1972—trailer for 4 Mouches de velours gris; trailer for César et Rosalie (Sautet); 1973—"générique" for Le Petit Poucet (Boisrond); Life Size; 1975—"générique" for Das kleine Fernsespiel (for West German TV).

Publications:

By LENICA:

Books—Plakat Tadeusza Trepkowskiego, Warsaw 1958; Population Explosion, with Alfred Sauvy, New York 1962; Monsieur Tête, text by Eugène Ionesco, Munich 1970; articles—[has written some 40 articles for Polish periodical Projekt and international design journals such as GRAPHIS].

On LENICA:

Books—Jan Lenica by Zygmunt Kałuzyński, Warsaw 1963; Jan Lenica edited by Heinz-Jürgen Kristahn, (Fröhlich & Kaufmann) 1981; Das polnische Plakat von 1892 bis heute edited by Heinz-Jührgen Kristahn, Berlin 1981; articles—"Jan Lenica" in Film (London), summer 1963; "Animation Quartet" in International Film Guide, London 1966; "Artist and Animator" in Film (London), spring 1972; "Jan Lenica" in Polish Film Polonaise (Warsaw), no.5, 1976; "Le Festival d'Annecy et les Rencontres internationales du cinéma d'animation" by A. Cornand in Image et son (Paris), January 1977; "L'Enfer tranquille de Jan Lenica" by R. Bassan in Image et son (Paris), July/August 1980.

LEONE, SERGIO. Italian. Born in Rome, 3 January 1929. Attended law school, Rome. Married: Carla Leone, 1960; children: Raffaella, Francesca and Andrea. Career: 1947—appears in small part in Vittorio De Sica's Ladri di biciclette (The Bicycle Thief); 1947-56—works as assistant for both Italian filmmakers and American directors working in Italy such as Mervyn LeRoy, Raoul Walsh, and William Wyler; also works as 2nd unit director for Italian and American productions; late 1950s—works as screenwriter on costume adventure films; 1959—relieves ailing Mario Bonnard as director on Last Days of Pompeii starring Steve Reeves, but refuses credit; 1961—directs 1st film Il colosso di Rodi (The Colossus of Rhodes); 1961-62—works as assistant to Robert Aldrich on Sodom and Gomorrah; 1964—directs A Fistful of Dollars, launching sub-genre of the "spaghetti Western"; 1970s—heads own production company, Rafran Cinema-

tografica; late 1970s—briefly lives in France; plans production of Once Upon a Time in America.

Films (as scriptwriter): 1958—Nel segno di Roma (Sign of the Gladiator) (co-sc); 1959—Gli ultimi giorni di Pompei (The Last Days of Pompeii) (Bonnard) (co-sc, +co-d, uncredited); (as director and co-scriptwriter): 1961—Il colosso di Rodi (The Colossus of Rhodes); Sodoma e Gommorra (Sodom and Gomorrah) (Aldrich) (2nd unit d only—co-d according to some sources); 1964—Per un pugno di dollari (A Fistful of Dollars); 1965—Per qualche dollaro in più (For a Few Dollars More); 1966—Il buono il brutto il cattivo (The Good, the Bad, and the Ugly); 1968—C'era una volta il West (Once Upon a Time in the West); 1972—Giù la testa (Duck You Sucker, Il était une fois la révolution); 1973—My Name is Nobody (story idea only); 1975—Un genio due compari e un pollo; 1978—Il gatto (pr only); 1984—Once Upon a Time in America.

Publications:

By LEONE:

Articles—interview in Take One (Montreal), January/February 1972; "Il était une fois la révolution", interview by G. Braucourt in Ecran (Paris), May 1972; interview by E. Verdi in Cinéma (Paris), May 1972; "Pastalong Cassidy Always Wears Black" by Cynthia Grenier in Oui (Chicago), April 1973.

On LEONE:

Books—Les Bons, les sales, les méchants et les propres de Sergio Leone by Gavin Lambert, Paris 1976; Spaghetti Westerns: Cowboys and Europeans: From Karl May to Sergio Leone by Christopher Frayling, London 1981; articles—"Hi-Ho Denaro!" in Time (New York), 4 August 1967; article by Andrew Sarris in The Village Voice (New York), 19 and 26 September 1968; "Meanwhile...Back at Cinecitta" by Peter Witonski in Film Society Review (New York), fall 1965; "Sergio Leone" by C. Frayling in Cinema (London), August 1970; article by Stuart Kaminsky in Take One (Montreal), January/February 1972; "Something To Do With Death" by Richard Jameson in Film Comment (New York), March/April 1973; "Por un puñado de mitos: El oeste de Sergio Leone" by L. García Tsao in Cine (Mexico), June 1979; "Il etait une fois...le western: de Sergio Leone" by A. Garel and F. Joyeux in Image et son (Paris), July 1979; "Encuentro con 2 cineastas italianos" by A. Garcia del Vall and A. Gomez Olea in Cinema 2002 (Madrid), February 1980; "Once Upon a Time in Italy" by D. Nicholls in Sight and Sound (London), winter 1980/81; article in Sight and Sound (London), winter 1980-81; "From Spaghetti Cowboys to the Jewish Gangsters of New York" by Lewis Beale in the Los Angeles Times Calender, 7 November 1982.

* * *

Not since Franz Kafka's America has a European artist turned himself with such intensity to the meaning of American culture and mythology, Sergio Leone's career is remarkable in its unrelenting attention to both America and American genre film. In France, Truffaut, Godard and Chabrol have used American film as a touchstone for their own vision, but Leone, an Italian, a Roman who began to learn English only after five films about the

United States, has devoted most of his creative life to this examination.

Leone's films are not realistic or naturalistic visions of the American nightmare or fairy tale, but comic nightmares about existence. The feeling of unreality is central to Leone's work. His is a world of magic and horror. Religion is meaningless, a sham which hides honest emotions; civilization is an extension of man's need to dominate and survive by exploiting others. The Leone world, while not womanless, is set up as one in which men face the horror of existence. In this, Leone is very like Howard Hawks: as in Hawks's films, death erases a man. A man who dies is a loser, and the measure of a man is his ability to survive, to laugh or sneer at death. This is not a bitter point in Leone films. There are few lingering deaths and very little blood. Even the death of Ramon (Gian Maria Volonte) in *Fistful of Dollars* takes place rather quickly and with far less blood than the comparable death in *Yojimbo*. A man's death is less important than how he faces it. The only thing worth preserving in Leone's world is the family—and his world of American violence is such a terrible place that few families survive. In *Fistful of Dollars*, Clint Eastwood's primary emotional reaction is to the attempt to destroy the family of the woman Ramon has taken. In the later films, *The Good, the Bad, and the Ugly* and *Once Upon a Time in the West*, *Duck, You Sucker* and *Once Upon a Time in America*, family life is minimal and destroyed by self-serving evil not out of hatred but by a cold, passionless commitment to self-interest. Leone's visual obsessions contribute to his thematic interests. Many directors could work with and develop the same themes and characters, but Leone's forte lies in the development of these themes and characters in a personal world. No director, with the possible exception of Sam Fuller, makes as extensive use of the close-up as does Leone, and Leone's close-ups often show only a portion of the face, usually the eyes of one of the main characters. It is the eyes of these men that reveal what they are feeling—if they are feeling anything.

Such characters almost never define their actions in words. Plot is of minimal interest to Leone. What is important is examination of the characters, watching how they react, what makes them tick. It appears almost as if everything is, indeed, happening randomly, as if we are watching with curiosity the responses of different types of people, trying to read meaning in the slightest flick of an eyelid. The visual impact of water dripping on Woody Strode's hat, or Jack Elam's annoyed reaction to a fly, is of greater interest to Leone than the gunfight in which the two appear in *Once Upon a Time in the West*.

The use of the pan in Leone films is also remarkable. The pan from the firing squad past the church and to the poster of the governor, behind which Rod Steiger watches in bewilderment through the eyes of the governor's image, is a prime example in *Duck, You Sucker*. the shot ties the execution to the indifferent church, to the non-seeing poster, and to Steiger's reaction in one movement.

The apparent joy and even comedy of destruction and battle in Leone films are often followed immediately by some intimate horror, some personal touch that underlines the real meaning of the horror which moments before had been amusing. The death of Dominick and his final words, "I slipped," in *Once Upon a Time in America* undercut the comedy and zest for battle. There is little dialogue; the vision of the youthful dead dominates as it does in the cave scene in *Duck, You Sucker* in which Juan's family lies massacred.

At the same time, Leone's fascination with spontaneous living, his zeal for existence in the midst of his morality films, can be seen in his handling of details. For example, food in his films is always colorful and appetizing and people eat it ravenously.

The obsession of Leone protagonists and villians, major and

minor, with the attainment of wealth can be seen as growing out of a dominant strain within American genres, particularly western and gangster films. The desire for wealth and power turns men into ruthless creatures who violate land and family.

Leone's films are explorations of the mythic America he has created. Unlike many directors, he does not simply repeat the same convention in a variety of ways. Each successive film takes the same characters and explores them in greater depth, and Leone's involvement with this exploration is intense.

—Stuart M. Kaminsky

LEROY, MERVYN. American. Born in San Francisco, 15 October 1900. Attended night school, 1919-1924. Married Doris Warner, 1933 (divorced); children: Warner Lewis and Linda Mervyn; married Kathryn Spiegel, 1946. Career: 1910—begins working as newsboy; 1912—actor Theodore Roberts hires him to portray newsboy in West coast film production of *Barbara Fritchie*; 1912-15—works as extra or in small parts in films; works in vaudeville as the "Singing Newsboy" and later the "Boy Tenor of This Generation"; 1917-19—teams with Clyde Cooper for act "Leroy and Cooper: 2 Kids and a Piano"; 1919—asks cousin Jesse Lasky (of Famous Players-Lasky) for work in film industry and given job folding costumes; 1919-24—appears in juvenile roles in films; 1924—becomes gag writer and comedy construction specialist for director Alfred E. Green; 1927—directs 1st film, *No Place to Go*, for 1st National; 1930—directs *Little Caesar*, 1st of a number of social dramas made for Warners and First National through Depression; 1938—hired by MGM as producer and director; 1944—starts own production company; 1945—produces 1st documentary, *The House I Live In*. Recipient: Special Academy Award for *The House I Live In*, 1945; Victoire du Cinéma Français for *Quo Vadis*, 1954; Irving Thalberg Academy Award, 1976. Business: Mervyn LeRoy Productions, 9200 Sunset Blvd., Suite 1229, Los Angeles, California 90069.

Films (as gag writer): 1924—*In Hollywood with Potash and Perlmutter (So This is Hollywood)*; 1925—*Sally*; *The Desert Flower*; *The Pace That Thrills*; *We Moderns*; 1926—*Irene*; *Ella Cinders*; *It Must Be Love*; *Twinkletoes*; 1927—*Orchids and Ermines*; (as director): 1927—*No Place to Go*; 1928—*Flying Romeos*; *Harold Teen*; *Oh, Kay!*; 1929—*Naughty Baby (Reckless Rosie)*; *Hot Stuff*; *Broadway Babies (Broadway Daddies)*; *Little Johnny Jones*; 1930—*Playing Around*; *Showgirl in Hollywood*; *Numbered Men*; *Top Speed*; *Little Caesar*; *Too Young to Marry*; *Broad-Minded*; *5 Star Final (1 Fatal Hour)*; *Tonight or Never*; 1932—*High Pressure*; *Heart of New York*; *2 Seconds*; *Big City Blues*; *3 on a Match*; *I Am a Fugitive from a Chain Gang*; *The Dark Horse* (Green) (uncredited help); 1933—*Hard to Handle*; *Tugboat Annie*; *Elmer the Great*; *Gold Diggers of 1933*; *The World Changes*; 1934—*Heat Lightning*; *Hi, Nellie!*; *Happiness Ahead*; 1935—*Oil for the Lamps of China*; *Page Miss Glory*; *I Found Stella Parish*; *Sweet Adeline*; 1936—*Anthony Adverse*; *3 Men on a Horse*; 1937—*The King and the Chorus Girl*; *They Won't Forget*; *The Great Garrick* (pr only); 1938—*Fools for Scandal*; *Stand Up and Fight* (pr only); *Dramatic School* (pr only); *At the Circus* (pr only); 1939—*The Wizard of Oz* (pr only); 1940—*Waterloo Bridge*; *Escape* (+pr); 1941—*Blossoms in the Dust* (+pr); *Unholy Partners*; *Johnny Eager*; 1942—*Random Harvest*; 1944—*Madame Curie*; 1945—*30 Seconds Over Tokyo*; *The House I Live In* (pr only); 1946—

Without Reservations; 1947—*Desire Me* (uncredited direction); 1948—*Homecoming*; 1949—*Little Women* (+pr); *Any Number Can Play*; *The Great Sinner* (Siodmak) (uncredited direction and editing); 1950—*East Side, West Side*; *Quo Vadis?*; 1952—*Lovely to Look At*; *Million Dollar Mermaid (The 1-Piece Bathing Suit)*; 1953—*Latin Lovers*; (as producer and director): 1954—*Rose Marie* (+pr); 1955—*Strange Lady in Town*; *Mister Roberts* (co-d only); 1956—*The Bad Seed*; *Toward the Unknown (Brink of Hell)*; 1958—*No Time for Sergeants*; *Home Before Dark*; 1959—*The FBI Story*; 1960—*Wake Me When It's Over*; 1961—*The Devil at 4 O'Clock*; *A Majority of One*; 1962—*Gypsy*; 1963—*Mary, Mary*; 1965—*Moment to Moment*; 1968—*The Green Berets* (Wayne and Kellogg) (assisted Wayne).

Roles (partial list): 1920—*Juvenile* in *Double Speed* (Wood); 1922—*A Ghost* in *The Ghost Breaker* (Green); 1923—*George Nelson* in *Little Johnny Jones* (Rosson and Hines); *Bellboy* in *Going Up* (Ingraham); *Jack Rawlins* in *The Call of the Canyon* (Fleming); 1924—*Carl Fisher* in *Broadway After Dark* (Bell); *Duke* in *The Chorus Lady* (Ralph Ince).

Publications:

By LEROY:

Books—*It Takes More Than Talent*, as told to Alyce Canfield, New York 1953; *Mervyn LeRoy: Take One*, New York 1974; articles—"The Making of Mervyn LeRoy" in *Films in Review* (New York), May 1953; "What Directors Are Saying" in *Action* (Los Angeles), May/June 1970; "Mervyn LeRoy Talks with William Friedkin" in *Action* (Los Angeles), November/December 1974.

On LEROY:

Articles—"Shooting Stars" by Q. Reynolds in *Colliers* (New York), 9 February 1935; "Straight-Shooter" in *Literary Digest* (New York), 13 February 1937; "Sock!" by A. Eveleve in *Silver Screen* (New York), December 1937; "How He Transforms Unknowns into Movie Stars" in *Cosopolitan* (New York), March 1943; "Best Direction of the Month" in *Cosmpolitan* (New York), May 1946; "The Filming of *Quo Vadis* in Italy" by Robert Surtees in *American Cinematographer* (Hollywood), October 1951; "Dance of the Reels" by L. Rosten in the *Saturday Review* (New York), 30 May 1953; "Likable, but Elusive" by Andrew Sarris in *Film Culture* (New York), spring 1963; "Should Directors Produce?" in *Action* (Los Angeles), July/August 1968; "*I Am a Fugitive From a Chain Gang*" by Russell Campbell in *Velvet Light Trap* (Madison, Wisconsin), June 1971; "*Little Caesar* and Its Role in the Gangster Film Genre" by Stuart Kaminsky in *Journal of Popular Film* (Bowling Green, Ohio), summer 1972; "Mervyn LeRoy: Star-making, Studio Systems and Style" by Kingsley Canham in *The Hollywood Professionals Vol. 5*, London 1976.

*　　　*　　　*

The career of Mervyn LeRoy, one of the most successful in the heyday of the studio system, is a reflection of that system. When at Warner Brothers, through most of the thirties, LeRoy was a master of the style dominant at that studio, demonstrated in the fast-paced toughness of films like his *Little Caesar* and *I Am a*

Fugitive from a Chain Gang. As producer-director at MGM, until the mid-fifties, he presided over lushly romantic vehicles for Greer Garson and Vivien Leigh. Prolific, versatile (at home in action films, women's films, musicals, historical spectacles), LeRoy's fluency marks him as the kind of director who validates collaborative creativity. Sensitive to the particular individuals with whom he works, and to the wide-ranging needs of the various materials he treats, LeRoy offers us an image of the Hollywood technique during the development of the classic Hollywood narrative.

This often makes it difficult to locate that which is LeRoy's specific contribution to films as dissimilar as the taut courtroom drama, *They Won't Forget* (that featured the memorable debut of Lana Turner, the "sweater girl" under personal contract to the director) and the colossal pageantry of *Quo Vadis?*, where decor completely submerges character. But if LeRoy lacks the recognizable visual and thematic coherence we notice in the works of "auteurs" (Welles, Ford, Griffith) it would be incorrect to characterize him as a director without a personal vision, or at least an affinity for specific subjects. Some of his best remembered films contain narrative configurations that display the protagonists in situations of pathetic isolation. It is as if the director's eye and the spectator's eye spied a character in a state of embarrassing vulnerability. At the end of *I Am a Fugitive*, a film about a man wrongly charged with a crime and perpetually hounded by the police, the hero confesses that he must now steal to live. Staged in a dark alley, the last words emerge from total blackness that ironically hides the speaker's face in this moment of painful revelation. (It has been said that the blackout was due to a power failure on the set. This in no way lessens the significance of the decision to leave the scene in, as shot.) In *Random Harvest*, one of the most popular films LeRoy made at MGM, the director repeatedly finds ways to underscore the pain of the wife who "plays" at being the secretary of her husband, an amnesia victim who has forgotten her identity. Here, as in *Waterloo Bridge* where the heroine represents one thing to the audience (a prostitute) and another to the hero (his long-lost fiancée), the staging exploits this ironic brand of double identity.

In a film made at Warners in 1958, *Home Before Dark*, the dual representation of character is extended into the figure of the schizophrenic (Jean Simmons) who, wishing to be like her sister, appears in a crowded nightclub wearing an oversized gown and garishly inappropriate makeup. This sort of embarrassing exposure reaches a theatrical peak in *Gypsy* where the mother of the striptease artists does her own "turn" on the bare stage of an empty theater, stripping down to her raw ambition and envy.

—Charles Affron

———————————

LESTER, RICHARD. American. Born in Philadelphia, 19 January 1932. Educated at the William Penn Charter School, Germantown, Pennsylvania; University of Pennsylvania, Philadelphia, B.S. in clinical psychology 1951. Married dancer and choreographer Deirdre Vivian Smith in 1956; 2 children. Career: 1951—performs with singing group on Philadelphia television; becomes TV director; quits position to travel in Europe, makes living as musician; 1955—writes and composes *Curtains for Harry*, 1st original musical comedy on British commercial television; 1956-57—directs various programs on British television including *Goon Show* episodes; 1957—works for Canadian Broadcasting Company; 1959-60—works in British television; 1960s to present—extensive work as director of television commercials. Recipient: Palme d'or, Cannes Festival, for *The Knack*, 1965; Ghandi Peace Prize, Berlin Festival, for *The Bed Sitting Room*, 1969.

Films (as director): 1959—*The Running, Jumping and Standing Still Film* (+ph, mu, co-ed); 1962—*It's Trad, Dad (Ring-a-Ding Rhythm)*; 1963—*The Mouse on the Moon*; 1964—*A Hard Day's Night*; 1965—*The Knack—and How to Get It*; *Help!*; 1966—*A Funny Thing Happened On the Way to the Forum*; 1967—*How I Won the War* (+p); 1968—*Petulia*; 1969—*The Bed Sitting Room* (+co-p); 1974—*The 3 Musketeers (The Queen's Diamonds)*; *Juggernaut*; 1975—*The 4 Musketeers (The Revenge of Milady)*; *Royal Flash*; 1976—*Robin and Marian* (+co-pr); *The Ritz*; 1979—*Butch and Sundance: The Early Days*; *Cuba*; 1981—*Superman II*.

Publications:

By LESTER:

Articles—"In Search of the Right Knack" in *Films and Filming* (London), July 1965; "Lunch with Lester" by George Bluestone in *Film Quarterly* (Berkeley), summer 1966; "Richard Lester and the Art of Comedy" in *Film* (London), spring 1967; "Interview with Richard Lester" by Ian Cameron and Mark Shivas in *Movie* (London), winter 1968/69; "Londres: Encuentro con Richard Lester", interview, in *Nuestro Cine*, March 1969; "What I Learned from Commercials" in *Action* (Los Angeles), January/February 1969; "Richard Lester", interview by William Hall, in *Directors in Action* edited by Bob Thomas, Indianapolis, Indiana 1973; "Running, Jumping and Standing Still: An Interview with Richard Lester" by Joseph McBride in *Sight and Sound* (London), spring 1973; "The Pleasure in the Terror of the Game", interview by Gordon Gow in *Films and Filming* (London), October 1974; "Deux Entretiens avec Richard Lester" by Michel Ciment in *Positif* (Paris), November 1975; "Richard Lester: Doing the Best He Can", interview by Gerald Pratley in *Film* (London), February 1975; interview by A. Tassone in *Image et son* (Paris), May 1975; interview by T. Ockersen in *Skoop* (Amsterdam), February/March 1977.

On LESTER:

Books—*Hollywood U.K.* by Alexander Walker, New York 1974; *Richard Lester: A Guide to References and Resources* by Diane Rosenfeldt, Boston 1978; articles—"The Knack of Being Richard Lester" by Anthony Carthew in *The New York Times Magazine*, 8 August 1965; "New Faces—III" by Hollis Alpert in the *Saturday Review* (New York), 24 December 1966; "Richard Lester" in the *New Yorker*, 28 October 1967; "Richard Lester" in *Directors at Work* edited by Bernard Kantor and others, New York 1970; "Richard Lester" in *The Film Director as Superstar* by Joseph Gelmis, Garden City, New York 1970; "War as Movie Theater—2 Films" by M. Dempsey in *Film Quarterly* (Berkeley), winter 1971/72; "The Return of Richard Lester" by Roy Armes in *London Magazine*, December/January 1974/75; "Richard Lester" by Joseph McBride in *International Film Guide 1975*, London 1974; "Some Late Clues to the Lester Direction" by James Monaco in *Film Comment* (New York), May 1974; "Biofilmographie de Richard Lester" by Olivier Eyquem in *Positif* (Paris), November 1975; "Something More", interview of Malcolm McDowell by Gordon Gow in *Films and Filming* (London), October 1975; "Richard Lester: Robin and Marian" by Bob Thomas in *Action* (Los Angeles), November/-

December 1975; "Richard Lester" by D. Maillet in *Cinématographe* (Paris), March 1977.

*   *   *

Richard Lester has said that his obituaries will proclaim "Beatles' Film Director Dies." This is probably accurate, but to overlook the rest of his career would be an injustice. Lester's films range widely in genre, from musicals and comedies to swashbucklers and social commentary dramas, and they show a consistency in theme and style.

Part of Lester's distinctive style comes from his work in commercials. His comedies are full of "small bits," fast and to the point. But he also presents the "world," whether it be the Old West or Robin Hood's England, in a documentary style. One could almost say he tries to sell the viewers his created world. D'Artagnan's walk through the marketplace in the *Three Musketeers* is a prime example. One sees a full-fledged market of that day and age. It is not forced upon the viewer; the background is incorporated into the main action naturally and without intrusion.

As shown by his films, Lester's view of the world is a comic one. He sees it as a tangled mess of contradictions and confusions. It is not a world that can't be handled and heroes of Lester's works face it with humor. They persistently try to find peace and are not usually looking for much to achieve it. The Beatles are only looking for laughs and a place to perform. The romantic heroes of *Three Musketeers* and *Robin and Marian* have only the goal of being allowed to do their duty to their monarch and achieving personal, romantic happiness. However, Lester's vision is not entirely bright. Robin and Marian die heroically and with dignity, but their wishes for a glorious victory and a return to their lost days of youth are denied.

If Lester is known as the Beatles' film director, then he has a title that really brings him no shame. For *A Hard Day's Night* Lester was faced with several problems. The center of the film was a charismatic group that had no film acting experience and that was heading very quickly into international superstardom. A tight schedule and a small budget also presented obstacles. The fact that he directed a film that captured the charisma of the Beatles at the height of their "mop top" form, redefined rock and roll films, and was critically and commercially successful was no small feat. He faced a different challenge the next year with *Help!*, a parody of spy films, was a commercially successful work that did little to detract from the reputation of the Beatles or Lester.

—Ray Narducy

LEWIS, JERRY. American. Born Joseph Levitch in Newark, New Jersey, 16 March 1926. Educated at Irvington High School, Irvington, N.J. through 10th grade. Married singer Patti Palmer, 1944; children: Gary, Ronnie (adopted), Scott, Christopher, and Joseph. Career: 1931—makes debut at hotel on "borscht circuit" where father working as master of ceremonies, sings "Brother, Can You Spare a Dime?"; early 1940s—develops comedy routine based on mouthing songs being played on records; 1942—comedian Irving Kaye sees record routine, becomes Lewis's manager; 1946—begins working with Dean Martin at Atlantic City club; 1948—team is signed for Paramount by producer Hal Wallis; 1949—first Lewis and Martin picture, *My Friend Irma*; founds private production company and directs series of pastiches of Hollywood films; 1950-55—stars with Martin on the "Colgate Comedy Hour"; 1952—becomes national chairman of the Muscular Dystrophy Associations of America; continues to raise funds through annual telethons; 1956—team breaks up, gives last night club performance; Lewis begins career as solo club comedian, taking over Las Vegas engagement when Judy Garland cancels; 1957—produces *The Delicate Delinquent*, first film without Martin; begins recording career; 1959—seven-year contract signed between Paramount-York and Jerry Lewis Productions; 1972—production problems on *The Day the Clown Cried* lead to abandonment of film; concentrates on television and nightclub work, and on charity activities through rest of seventies. Agent: William Morris Agency, Beverly Hills, California. Business: Jerry Lewis Films, Inc., 1888 Century Park East, Suite 830, Los Angeles, CA 90067.

Films (as director of short pastiches of popular Hollywood films—partial list): 1949—*Fairfax Avenue* (after *Sunset Boulevard*); *A Spot in the Shade* (after *A Place in the Sun*); *Watch on the Lime*; *Come Back, Little Shicksa*; *Son of Lifeboat*; *The Re-Inforcer*; *Son of Spellbound*; *Melvin's Revenge*; *I Should Have Stood in Bedlam* (after *From Here to Eternity*); *The Whistler*; (as director, scriptwriter, and principal actor): 1960—*The Bellboy* (ro as *Stanley*, +pr); 1961—*The Ladies' Man* (ro as *Herbert H. Heebert* and his mother *Mrs. Heebert*, +pr); *The Errand Boy* (ro as *Morty S. Tachman*); 1963—*The Nutty Professor* (ro as *Julius F. Kelp* and *Buddy Love*); 1964—*The Patsy* (ro as *Stanley Belt*); (as producer, director, scriptwriter, and principal actor): 1965—*The Family Jewels* (ro as *Willard Woodward, Uncle James Peyton, Uncle Eddie Peyton, Uncle Julius Peyton, Uncle Shylock Peyton, Uncle Bugs Peyton*); 1966—*Three on a Couch* (ro as *Christopher Prise, Warren, Ringo Raintree, Rutherford, Heather*, +pr, d only); 1967—*The Big Mouth* (ro as *Gerald Clamson, Sid Valentine*); 1970—*One More Time* (d only); *Which Way to the Front?* (ro as *Brendan Byers III, Kesselring*, +pr, d only); (as director and principal actor): 1972—*The Day the Clown Cried* (not completed); 1980—*Hardly Working* (+sc); 1982—*Smorgasbord* (+sc).

Roles: 1949—*Seymour* in *My Friend Irma* (Marshall); 1950—*Seymour* in *My Friend Irma Goes West* (Walker); 1951—*Soldier Korwin* in *At War with the Army* (Walker); *"Junior" Jackson* in *That's My Boy* (Walker); 1952—*Melvin Jones* in *Sailor Beware* (Walker); *Hap Smith* in *Jumping Jacks* (Taurog); 1953—*Ted Rogers* in *The Stooge* (Taurog); *Myron Myron Mertz* in *Scared Stiff* (Marshall); *Harvey Miller* in *The Caddy* (Taurog); 1954—*Virgil Yokum* in *Money from Home* (Marshall); *Homer Flagg* in *Living It Up* (Taurog); *Jerry Hotchkiss* in *3 Ring Circus* (Pevney); 1955—*Wilbur Hoolick* in *You're Never Too Young* (Taurog); *Eugene Fullstack* in *Artists and Models* (Tashlin); 1956—*Wade Kingsley Jr.* in *Pardners* (Taurog); *Malcolm Smith* in *Hollywood or Bust* (Tashlin); 1957—*Sidney Pythias* in *The Delicate Delinquent* (McGuire) (+pr); *Meredith T. Bixby* in *The Sad Sack* (Marshall); *Gilbert Wooley* in *The Geisha Boy* (Tashlin) (+pr); 1958—*Clayton Poole* in *Rock-a-Bye Baby* (Tashlin) (+pr); 1959—*John Paul Steckley VII* in *Don't Give Up the Ship* (Taurog); 1960—*Kreton* in *Visit to a Small Planet* (Taurog); *Fella* in *Cinderfella* (Tashlin) (+pr); brief appearance in *Li'l Abner* (Frank); 1962—*Lester March* in *It's Only Money* (Tashlin); 1963—the man who drives over Culpepper's hat in *It's a Mad, Mad, Mad, Mad World* (Kramer); *Raymond Phiffier* in *Who's Minding the Store?* (Tashlin); 1964—*Jerome Littlefield* in *The Disorderly Orderly* (Tashlin); 1965—*Robert Reed* in *Boeing Boeing* (Rich); 1966—*Peter Mat-*

amore in *Way Way Out* (Douglas); 1967—*George Lester* in *Don't Raise the Bridge, Lower the River* (Paris); 1969—*Peter Ingersoll alias Dobbs* in *Hook, Line and Sinker* (Marshall) (+pr); 1982—*Jerry Langford* in *The King of Comedy* (Scorsese); *Slapstick* (Paul).

Publications:

By LEWIS:

Book—*The Total Film-Maker*, New York 1971; articles—"I'm in Love with My Best Friend's Wife" in *Photoplay* (New York), August 1952; "Mr. Lewis is a Pussycat", interview by Peter Bogdanovich in *Esquire* (New York), November 1962; "America's Uncle: Interview with Jerry Lewis" by Axel Madsen in *Cahiers du Cinema in English* (New York), no.4, 1966; interview in *Directors at Work*, edited by Bernard Kantor and others, New York 1970; "5 Happy Moments" in *Esquire* (New York), December 1970; "Dialogue on Film: Jerry Lewis" in *American Film* (Washington, D.C.), September 1977; interview by D. Rabourdin in *Cinéma* (Paris), April 1980.

On LEWIS:

Books—*That Kid—The Story of Jerry Lewis* by Richard Gehman, New York 1964; *Movie Comedy Teams* by Leonard Maltin, New York 1970; *Everybody Loves Somebody Sometime (Especially Himself): The Story of Dean Martin and Jerry Lewis* by Arthur Marx, New York 1974; articles—"Funny Men: Dean Martin and Jerry Lewis" by Daniel Farson in *Sight and Sound* (London), July/September 1952; "Jerry Lewis Analyzed" by Robert Kass in *Films in Review* (New York), March 1953; "Martin and Lewis—Are Their Critics Wrong?" by Rod Hume in *Films and Filming* (London), March 1956; "Jerry Lewis" by John Taylor in *Sight and Sound* (London), spring 1965; "Editor's Eyrie" by Andrew Sarris in *Cahiers du Cinema in English* (New York), no.4, 1966; "Le Roi du Crazy" by Hollis Alpert in *The New York Times Magazine*, 27 February 1966; "Jerry Lewis Retrieves a Lost Ideal" by Richard Schickel in *Life* (New York), 15 July 1966; "Essays in Visual Style" by Fred Camper in *Cinema* (London), no.8, 1971; "Jerry Lewis" by G. Vialle in *Image et son* (Paris), no.274, 1973; "Jerry Lewis" by G. Vialle and others in *Image et son* (Paris), no.278, 1973; "Films for Fun" by R. Gansera in *Filmkritik* (Munich), April 1974; "Jerry Lewis's Films: No Laughing Matter?" by J.-P. Coursodon in *Film Comment* (New York), July/August 1975; "Which Way to Jerry Lewis?" by F. LeBour and R. DeLaroche in *Ecran* (Paris), July 1976; "Jerry Lewis Tries a Film Comeback" by N.B. Jackson in *The New York Times*, 29 April 1979; "Telethon" by H. Shearer in *Film Comment* (New York), May/June 1979; "Recycling Jerry Lewis" by P. McGilligan in *American Film* (Washington, D.C.), September 1979; "American Journal: All Night with Jerry: Pitch with Kitsch" by B. Sobol in *New York*, 17 September 1979.

*   *   *

In France, Jerry Lewis is called "Le Roi de Crazy" and adulated as a genius by filmmakers as respectable as Alain Resnais, Jean-Luc Godard, and Claude Chabrol. In America, Jerry Lewis is still an embarrassing and unexplained paradox, awaiting a persuasive critical champion. This incredible gulf can in part be explained by American access, on television talk shows and Lewis's annual muscular dystrophy telethon, to Lewis's contradictory public persons: egotistical yet insecure, insulting yet sentimental, juvenile yet adult, emotionally naked yet defensive. Were not the real Lewis apparently so hard to love, the celluloid Lewis might be loved all the more. And yet a Lewis cult thrives among American cinephiles; and certainly *The Bellboy*, *The Errand Boy*, *The Nutty Professor*, and *Which Way To The Front?* appear today to be among the most interesting and ambitious American films of the sixties.

Lewis's career can be divided into four periods: first, the partnership with singer Dean Martin which resulted in a successful nightclub act and popular series of comedies, including *My Friend Irma* and *At War with the Army*, as well as several highly-regarded films directed by former cartoonist and Lewis mentor, Frank Tashlin; second after professional and personal tensions fueled by Lewis's more extensive artistic ambitions irrevocably destroyed the partnership, an apprenticeship as a solo comedy star, beginning with *The Delicate Delinquent* and continuing through Tashlin's *Cinderfella*; third, the period as the self-professed "total filmmaker," inaugurated in 1960 with *The Bellboy* and followed by a decade of Lewis films directed by and starring Lewis which attracted the attention of auteurist critics in France and overwhelming boxoffice response in America, culminating with a string of well-publicized financial failures, including *Which Way to the Front?* and the unreleased, nearmythical *The Day the Clown Cried*, in which clown Lewis leads Jewish children to Nazi ovens; and fourth, the present period as valorized, if martyred auteur, exemplified by Lewis's work as an actor in Martin Scorsese's *The King of Comedy* and Lewis's attempts to re-establish his own directorial career.

Lewis's appeal is significantly rooted in the American silent film tradition of the individual comedian: like Chaplin, Lewis is interested in pathos and sentiment; like Keaton, Lewis is fascinated by the comic gag which could only exist on celluloid; like Harry Langdon, Lewis exhibits, within an adult persona, behavior of a childishness which is often disturbing and embarrassing; like Stan Laurel, whose first name Lewis adopts as an *hommage* in several of his films, Lewis is the lovable innocent often endowed with almost magical qualities. What Lewis brings uniquely to this tradition, however, is his obsession with the concept of the schizophrenic self; his typical cinema character has so many anxieties and tensions that it must take on other personalities in order to survive. Often, the schizophrenia becomes overtly autobiographical, with the innocent, gawky kid escaping his stigmatized existence by literally becoming "Jerry Lewis," beloved and successful comedian (as in *The Bellboy* and *The Errand Boy*) or romantic leading man, perhaps representing the now absent Dean Martin (as in *The Nutty Professor*). Jerry Lewis's physical presence on screen in his idiot persona emphasizes movement disorders in a way which relates provocatively to his highly publicized work for the Muscular Dystrophy Association. Schizophrenia is compounded in *The Family Jewels*: what Jean-Pierre Coursodon calls Lewis's "yearning for self-obliteration" is manifested in seven distinct personalities. Ultimately, Lewis escapes by turning himself into his cinema, as evidenced by the credits in his comeback film, which proudly announce: "Jerry Lewis is...*Hardly Working*." This element of cinematic escape and schizophrenia is especially valued by the French who politicize it as a manifestation of the human condition under American capitalism.

Much must also be said about the strong avant-garde qualities to Lewis's work: his interest in surrealism; his experimentalism and fascination with self-conscious stylistic devices; his movement away from conventional gags toward structures apparently purposely deformed; his interest in plotlessness and ellipsis; the reflexivity of his narrative; his studied use of extended silence and gibberish in a sound cinema; the ambiguous sexual subtext of his work; and finally, his use of film as personal revelation in a tradition which ultimately recalls Maya Deren and Stan Brakhage more than Chaplin and Keaton. Perhaps only Lewis's death will allow any definitive American evaluation of his substantial career.

—Charles Derry

L'HERBIER, MARCEL. French. Born in Paris, 23 April 1888. Educated at lycée Voltaire, Sainte-Marie de Monceau; Faculté des Lettres, Faculté de Droit, and Ecole des Hautes Etudes Sociales, University of Paris. Career: 1914-18—military service, first with Service Auxiliaire, and from 1917 with Section Cinématographique de l'Armée; 1917—writes 2 scenarios for "L'Eclipse" company; 1918—directs first film *Rose-France*; 1922—organizes Cinégraphic production company; 1929—secretary general of Association des Auteurs de Films; 1936—co-founds Cinematheque Française; 1937—co-founds and in 1938 becomes president of Syndicat des Techniciens; 1943—founds and becomes president of the I.D.H.E.C. (Institut des Hautes Etudes Cinématographiques), French film school; 1947—president of Comité de Défense du Cinéma français; 1952-62—producer for French, Swiss, and Luxembourg TV; notable TV productions directed include *Adrienne Mesurat* (1953), *Zamore* and *Le Jeu de l'amour et du hasard* (1954), and *Les Fausses Confidences* and *Le Ciel de lit* (1955); 1978—working on film *La Féérie des fantasmes*. Died 26 November 1979. Recipient: Commander of the Légion d'Honneur et des Arts et Lettres.

Films (as scriptwriter): 1917—*Le Torrent* (Hervil); *Bouclette (L'Ange de minuit)* (Mercanton and Hervil); (as director and scriptwriter): 1918—*Phantasmes* (incomplete); *Rose-France*; 1919—*Le Bercail*; *Le Carnaval des vérités*; 1920—*L'Homme du large*; *Villa Destin*; 1921—*El Dorado*; *Prométhée...banquier* (d only); 1922—*Don Juan et Faust*; 1923—*Résurrection* (incomplete); 1924—*L'Inhumaine (The New Enchantment)* (co-sc); 1925—*Feu Mathias Pascal (The Late Mathias Pascal, The Living Dead Man)*; 1926—*Le Vertige*; 1927—*Le Diable au coeur (L'Ex-Voto)*; 1928—*L'Argent*; *Nuits de Prince*; (sound films): 1929—*L'Enfant de l'amour*; 1930—*La Femme d'une nuit (La donna d'una notte)*; *La Mystère de la chambre jaune*; 1931—*Le Parfum de la dame en noir*; 1932—*Le Martyre de l'Obèse* (Chenal) (supervisor only); 1933—*L'Epervier (Les Amoureux, Bird of Prey)*; *La Bataille* (Farkas) (supervisor only); 1934—*Le Scandale* (d only); *L'Aventurier*; *Le Bonheur*; 1935—*La Route impériale*; *Veille d'armes (Sacrifice d'honneur)* (co-sc); 1936—*Les Hommes nouveaux*; *La Porte du large (The Great Temptation)*; *Nuits de feu (The Living Corpse)* (co-sc); 1937—*La Citadelle du silence (The Citadel of Silence)*; *Forfaiture*; 1938—*La Tragédie impériale (Rasputin)*; (as director): 1938—*Adrienne Lecouvreur*; *Terre de feu*; *Terra di fuoco* (Ferroni: Italian version of *Terre de feu*) (supervisor only); *La Brigade sauvage (Savage Brigade)* (completed by J. Dréville); 1939—*Entente cordiale*; *Children's Corner* (short); *La Mode rêvée* (+sc—short); 1940—*La Comédie du bonheur* (+sc); 1941—*Histoire de rire (Foolish Husbands)*; 1942—*La Nuit fantastique*; *L'Honorable Catherine*; 1943—*La Vie de Bohême*; *Le Loup des Malveneur* (Radot) (supervisor only); 1945—*Au petit bonheur*; 1946—*L'Affaire du collier de la Reine (The Queen's Necklace)*; 1947—*La Révoltée (Stolen Affections)* (+sc); *Une Grande Fille tout simple* (Manuel) (supervisor only); 1948—*Les Derniers Jours de Pompéi (Gli ultimi giorni di Pompei, The Last Days of Pompeii)* (+co-sc); 1953—*Le Père de mademoiselle* (co-d); 1963—

Hommage à Debussy (short); 1967—*Le Cinéma du diable* (anthology film).

Publications:

By L'HERBIER:

Books—*Au jardin des jeux secrets*, Paris 1914; *L'Enfantement du mort*, Paris 1917; *Intelligence du cinématographe* (anthology), Paris 1947 (revised 1977); *La Tête qui tourne*, Paris 1979; articles—interview in *Cahiers du cinéma* (Paris), no.202, 1968; interview by J. Fieschi and others in *Cinématographe* (Paris), no.40, 1978; "Mise en scène et mise en film" in *Cinématographe* (Paris), December 1978; "Un Cinéaste..." in *Avant-Scène du cinéma* (Paris), 1 January 1980; reprinted interview from *Ciné-magazine* in *Avant-Scène du cinéma* (Paris), 15 October 1981.

On L'HERBIER:

Books—*Jaque-Catelain présente Marcel L'Herbier*, Paris 1950; *Marcel L'Herbier* by Noël Burch, Paris 1973; *Hommage à Marcel L'Herbier en cinq films de l'art muet*, brochure for retrospective, Centre National de la Cinématographie, Paris 1975; *Marcel L'Herbier et son temps*, edited by Jean-Pierre Brossard, La Chaux-de-Fonds, Switzerland 1980; articles—"The Big Screens" in *Sight and Sound* (London), spring 1955; "Memories of Resnais" by Richard Roud in *Sight and Sound* (London), summer 1969; "The Camera as Snowball: France 1918-1927" by R.H. Blumer in *Cinema Journal* (Evanston), spring 1970; article on 5 films of L'Herbier in *Ecran 76* (Paris), no.43, 1976; "Marcel L'Herbier ou l'intelligence du cinématographe" by Claude Beylie and M. Marie in *Avant-Scène du cinéma* (Paris), 1 June 1978; special issue of *Avant-Scène du cinéma* (Paris), 1 June 1978; "Archeologie du cinéma" by S. Trosa in *Cinématographe* (Paris), December 1978; "Marcel L'Herbier" by J. Fieschi in *Cinématographe* (Paris), December 1979; obituary in *Image et son* (Paris), January 1980; obituary in *The New York Times*, 28 November 1979.

*   *   *

Marcel L'Herbier was one of the most prominent members of the French 1920s avant-garde. His direct involvement with film-making extended into the 1950s and he made important contributions to the organization of the industry, to the foundation of the film school, the IDHEC, and to early television drama.

Like so many of his generation he turned to cinema after an early enthusiasm for literature and the theatre and in his case it was Cecil B. De Mille's *The Cheat* with Sessue Hayakawa which opened his eyes to the unrealized potential of the new medium. He came to prominence in the years 1919-22 with a series of films made for Léon Gaumont's "Pax" series. Among the half-dozen films made for Gaumont, two at least stand out as artistic and commercial successes: *L'Homme du large* a melodrama shot partly on location on the Britanny coast where the director's interest in visual effects and symbolism is very apparent, and *El Dorado*, a Spanish drama in which L'Herbier's use of cinema to convey the mental and psychological states of characters finds perfect expression. *El Dorado* achieved a success to match that of Gance's *La Roue* the following year.

Difficulties with Gaumont over the production of the ambitious *Don Juan et Faust* led L'Herbier to set up his own company, Cinégraphic, in 1922. He was able to assist the debuts of young filmmakers such as Jaque Catelain and Claude Autant-Lara as well as produce the last film of Louis Delluc, *L'Inondation*. His own films were made largely in co-production and ranged widely in style and approach. The celebrated but controversial *L'Inhumaine*, partly financed by its star the singer Georgette Leblanc, aimed to offer a mosaic of the decorative modern art of 1925, with sets produced by four very individual designers, including Fernand Léger and Robert Mallet-Stevens. In total contrast, *Feu Matthias Pascal* was essentially an experiment with complex narrative structures, co-produced with the Albatros company which had been set up by Russian exiles and starring the great silent actor, Ivan Mosjoukine. L'Herbier's eclectic approach and love of juxtapositions are very apparent in these films, together with his immense visual refinement. After a couple of commercial works he made his silent masterpiece, an updating of Zola's *L'Argent* in 1929. Inspired by the scope of Gance's *Napoléon*, L'Herbier created a strikingly modern work marked by its opulent, oversized sets and a complex, multi-camera shooting style.

L'Herbier was in no way hostile to the coming of sound, but despite a pair of interesting adaptations of comic thrillers by Gaston Leroux, *Le Mystère de la chambre jaune* and *Le Parfum de la dame en noir*, L'Herbier was largely reduced to the role of efficient but uninspired adaptor of stage plays in the 1930s. During the occupation years L'Herbier again came to prominence with his delicately-handled dreamlike *La Nuit fantastique* but his subsequent work, which included a spectacular version of *Les Derniers Jours de Pompei* in 1948, attracted little critical favor. In more recent years, however, L'Herbier's reputation has utive Committee of Latin American Filmmakers. Recipient: Chilean Critics' Prize for *El chacal de Nahueltoro*, 1970. by the towering figure of Abel Gance, L'Herbier emerges as a figure of considerable interest. In particular the work of the critic and theorist Noël Burch has emphasized the modernity of the approach to shooting and to narrative construction displayed in his ambitious *L'Argent*. There seems little doubt that French 1920s cinema offers a rich and largely unexplored area of study for future film studies and L'Herbier's reputation can only benefit from fresh investigation of his varied 1920s oeuvre.

—Roy Armes

LITTIN, MIGUEL. Chilean. Born in Palmilla (Colchagua), Chile, 9 August 1942. Educated at Theater School of the University of Chile (Santiago). Married Eli Menz. Career: 1958—participates in election campaign of Salvador Allende; 1961—publishes 1st stageplay; 1963—works in television as director and producer; 1964-67—stage director and actor and assistant on several films; 1969—founding member, Committee of the Popular Unity Filmmakers; 1970—named director of Chile Films (national production company) by Allende; 1970-71—makes weekly newsreels for Chile Films; 1973—emigrates to Mexico following coup d'etat; 1974—becomes member of Executive Committee of Latin American Filmmakers. Recipient: Chilean Critics' Prize for *El Chacal de Nahueltoro*, 1970.

Films (as director and scriptwriter): *Por la tierra ajena (On Foreign Land)*; 1969—*El chacal de Nahueltoro (The Jackal of Nahueltoro)*; 1971—*Compañero Presidente*; 1972-73—*La tierra prometida (The Promised Land)*; 1975—*El recurso del método (Viva el Presidente, Reasons of State)* (co-sc); 1979—*La viuda de*

Montiel (Montiel's Widow) (co-sc); 1982—*Alsino y el condór (Alsino and the Condor).*

Roles: 1965—*Yo tenía un camarada (I Had a Comrade)* (Soto); 1966—*Mundo mágico (Magic World)* (Soto); *ABC do amor (The ABC of Love).*

Publications:

By LITTIN:

Books—*La tierra prometida*, Caracas 1974; *El chacal de Nahueltoro*, Mexico 1976; articles—"Film in Chile", interview in *Cineaste* (New York), spring 1971; "Nuevo vine, nuevos realizadores, nuevos filmes", interview in *Cine Cubano* (Havana), no.63-65, 1971; interview by F. Martinez and others in *Hablemos de cine* (Lima), January/March 1972; interview by M. Torres in *Cine Cubano* (Havana), no.76-77, 1972; "El cine: herramienta fundamental" in *Cine Cubano* (Havana), no.66-67, 1972; "Primero hay que aprovechar el dividendo ideológico del cine", interview in *Primer Plano* (Valparaiso), fall 1972; "Chili: le cinéma de l'unité populaire", interview by H. Ermann and others in *Ecran* (Paris), February 1974; "La Terre promise", interview by Guy Hennebelle and M. Martin in *Ecran* (Paris), November 1974; "Culture populaire et lutte impérialiste", interview by J.-R. Huleu and others in *Cahiers du cinéma* (Paris), July/August 1974; "Journal de tournage" in *Jeune Cinéma* (Paris), June 1974; interview by G. Braucourt in *Ecran* (Paris), September 1976; interview by M. Martin in *Ecran* (Paris), November 1977; "Miguel Littin: Cinéma révolutionnaire et cinéma en exil", interview by A. Pierquet and B. Morissette in s*Cinéma Québec* (Montreal), v.5, no.3, 1976; "Propos d'auteur: Miguel Littin", interview by L. de la Fuente in *Cinéma* (Paris), March 1979; "Cine Chileno en exilio", interview by Gastón Ancelovici in *Contracampo* (Madrid), December 1979; interview by A.M. Amado and G. Garcia Riera in *Imagenes* (Mexico), April 1980; interview by R. Grelier and J.-C. Avellar in *Image et son* (Paris), November 1980; "*El chacal de Nahueltoro*: Tiempo de re-encuentro con su destinatario", interview by Emilia Palma in *Cine Cubano* (Havana), no.100, 1981.

On LITTIN:

Books—*El cine de Allende* by Francesco Bolzoni, Valencia 1974; *Chilean Cinema* edited by Michael Chanan, London 1976; articles—"Aspects of Latin American Political Cinema" by David Wilson in *Sight and Sound* (London), summer 1972; "The Promised Land" by Julianne Burton in *Film Quarterly* (Berkeley), fall 1975; "Cinéma du Chili: en exil ou sur place" by Françoise Le Pennec in *Cinéma* (Paris), February 1983.

LITVAK, ANATOLE. Russian. Born Mikhail Anatol Litvak in Kiev, 21 May 1902; became citizen of the United States, 1940. Educated at University of St. Petersburg (then University of Leningrad), PhD. in philosophy 1921; State School of Theatre, 1922. Married Miriam Hopkins, 1937 (divorced 1939); Sophie Steur, 1949. Career: 1923—directs for theater and begins as assistant director, Nordkino film studios, Leningrad; 1923-25—reportedly assistant director on 3, and art director on 6 films; 1925—leaves for Paris, goes then to Berlin and begins working at

Ufa studios as editor for G.W. Pabst; 1926-30—assistant to emigré director Nicholas Alexander Volkoff; 1930—begins directing on multiple-language productions; 1933—after Hitler's rise to power, relocates in Paris; 1936—international success of *Mayerling* leads to Hollywood offer; 1937-41—contract director at Warners; 1942—joins Special Services Film Unit, U.S. Army; works with Frank Capra on *Why We Fight* series, co-producing and co-directing 4 of the films; 1949—returns to Paris; 1970—directs last film *Lady in a Car*. Died in Paris, 15 December 1974. Recipient: Croix de guerre; Légion d'honneur; International Prize, Venice Festival, for *The Snake Pit*, 1949; Quarterly Award, Directors Guild of America, for *The Snake Pit*, 1948/49.

Films (as director of short features): 1923—*Tatiana*; 1924—*Hearts and Dollars*; 1925—*Samii yunii pioner* [A Very Young Pioneer] (Derzhavin) (co-sc only); (as assistant director to Alexander Volkoff): 1927—*Casanova (The Loves of Casanova)*; 1929—*Sheherazade (Secrets of the Orient)*; 1930—*Der weisse Teufel (The White Devil)* (+d dialogue and musical sequences); (as feature director): 1930—*Dolly macht Karriere*; 1931—*Nie wieder Liebe* (+co-adapt); French version: *Calais-Douvres*; 1932—*Coeur de Lilas* (+sc); *Das Lied einer Nacht*; English version: *Be Mine Tonight*; French version: *La Chanson d'une nuit* (Clouzot and Colombier) (artistic supervisor only); 1933—*Cette vielle canaille* (+co-adapt); *Sleeping Car*; 1935—*L'Équipage* (+co-sc); 1936—*Mayerling*; 1937—*The Woman I Love*; *Tovarich*; 1938—*The Amazing Dr. Clitterhouse*; *The Sisters*; 1939—*Confessions of a Nazi Spy*; 1940—*Castle on the Hudson*; *City for Conquest*; *All This and Heaven Too*; 1941—*Out of the Fog*; *Blues in the Night*; 1942—*This Above All*; *Why We Fight* series—No.2: *The Nazis Strike* (co-d); 1943—No.3: *Divide and Conquer* (co-d); 1944—No.7: *The Battle of Russia* (d, +co-sc); No.8: *The Battle of China* (co-d); 1945—No.9: *War Comes to America* (d, +co-sc); 1947—*Meet Me at Dawn* (co-play basis only); *The Long Night*; 1948—*Sorry, Wrong Number* (+co-pr); *The Snake Pit* (+co-pr); 1951—*Decision Before Dawn* (+co-pr); 1954—*Act of Love* (+co-sc); 1955—*The Deep Blue Sea* (+co-pr); 1956—*Anastasia*; 1957—*Mayerling* (remake for TV); 1959—*The Journey* (retitled after release as *Some of Us May Die)*(+pr); 1961—*Aimez-vous Brahms? (Goodbye Again)* (+pr, appearance in nightclub scene); 1962—*Le Cocteau dans la plaie (5 Miles to Midnight)*; 1966—*10:30 P.M. Summer* (+pr); 1967—*The Night of the Generals*; 1970—*The Lady in a Car with Glasses and a Gun (La Dame dans l'auto avec des lunettes et un fusil)* (+co-pr).

Publications:

By LITVAK:

Article—"A Cutter at Heart", interview by Allen Eyles and Barrie Pattison in *Films and Filming* (London), February 1967.

On LITVAK:

Articles—article on production of *The Snake Pit* in *Time* (New York), 20 December 1948; "Anatole Litvak" by Jack Nolan in *Films in Review* (New York), November 1967; obituary in *Ecran* (Paris), February 1975.

*   *   *

Anatole Litvak was a minor, commercially successful director whose personal and professional life can be characterized in one word: disingenuous. He was a multi-lingual cosmopolitan who possessed an anti-establishment political consciousness. He understood the technique and potential of the film medium, e.g. he opted for location shooting and realistic documentary effects as early as the 1930s; he emphasized realistic sound effects over dialogue in sound films; and he capably used camera tracking shots and pans. Yet his films were eratic in quality and subject matter and he never seemed able to coalesce his intelligence and talents into a cinematic unity.

Litvak acted and directed at the State School of Theatre and probably was assistant director and/or set decorator for at least nine silent Russian films at Leningrad's Nordkino studios. He was evasive about his background and life in Russia. Little is known except that he fled to Berlin in 1925 where he was an editor on G.W. Pabst's *Die freudlose Gasse*, worked as general assistant to Russian imigré director Nicholas Alexander Bolkoff, claims to have been one of the many editors on Abel Gance's *Napoléon*, and made his directorial debut with Ufa's *Dolly macht Karriere* in 1929. Two years later he directed *Nie wieder Liebe*, which was filmed simultaneously in a French version entitled *Calais-Douvres*, and had Max Ophüls as Litvak's assistant. He went to Paris to direct *Coeur de lilas* in which he used natural street sounds which he found to be "another support for a film's images, heightening their pictoral values, underscoring their visual beauty."

Paris became his home after he fled Hitler's Germany, and a favorite locale for his films—13 of his 37 pictures were set in Paris. It was also the city where he directed *Mayerling*, the internationally popular film which brought him to Hollywood.

Upon arriving in Hollywood he directed *The Woman I Love* for RKO (a re-make of *L'Equipage* which he had directed in Paris with Annabella and Charles Vanel) and which starred Miriam Hopkins whom he later married. Litvak then signed a 4-year contract with Warner Brothers and while that studio was deeply entrenched in its politically-conscious period, an atmosphere which would have seemed very well suited to his temperment, he was apparently too independent, if not overtly iconoclastic, to fit into the studio mold. For the most part his films there were sophisticated women's fare—*Tovarich*, *The Sisters*, and *All This and Heaven Too*. One exception was the now-dated, anti-Nazi propaganda film, *Confessions of a Nazi Spy*. Here Edward G. Robinson played a FBI agent who breaks up a ring of Nazi spies in the U.S., and Litvak used newsreels of actual U.S. Nazi rallies for a docu-drama effect.

During World War II he directed or co-directed for the U.S. Army's Special Services Film Unit and was in charge of motion picture operations during the Normandy invasion. His war efforts brought him the *Légion d'honneur* and the *Croix de guerre*.

Following the war Litvak produced and directed his two best and most popular American films—*Sorry, Wrong Number* and *The Snake Pit*, a starkly realistic depiction of life in an insane asylum. Litvak then left the United States to live and work in Paris for the remainder of his career. There he produced and directed what is probably his best film—*Decision Before Dawn*, a compelling drama about German prisoners of war who returned to spy in their native Germany in an effort to defeat Nazism.

Thereafter, Litvak's films were star-studded trifles with the exception of the immensely dramatic and moving *Anastasia* which was Ingrid Bergman's return to mainstream films. The most notable of Litvak's late films was the sadistic and lurid *The Night of the Generals* starring Peter O'Toole. His last picture was a non-entity entitled *The Lady in the Car with Glasses and a Gun*.

—Ronald Bowers

LOACH, KEN. British. Born Kenneth Loach in Nuneaton, 17 June 1936. Read law at Oxford. Married Lesley (Loach); 3 children. Career: serves 2 years with Royal Air Force; performs with repertory company, Birmingham; 1963—joins BBC; directs episodes of *Z Cars*; 1965—begins collaborating with producer Tony Garnett; first film together is *Up the Junction*; 1968—begins ongoing collaboration with writer Barry Hines on *Kes*; Loach and Garnett set up Kestrel Films production company; late 1970s—begins working mainly for independent TV producers, and releasing TV films theatrically abroad. Recipient: TV Director of the Year Award, British TV Guild, 1965. Address: lives in London.

Films (as director and co-scriptwriter): 1967—*Poor Cow*; 1969—*Kes*; 1971—*The Save the Children Fund Film* (short); *After a Lifetime*; *Family Life*; 1979—*Black Jack*.

Television films: 1964—*Catherine*; *Profit By Their Example*; *The Whole Truth*; 1965—*Tap on the Shoulder*; *Wear a Very Big Hat*; *3 Clear Sundays*; *Up the Junction*; *The End of Arthur's Marriage*; *The Coming Out Party*; 1966—*Cathy Come Home*; 1967—*In 2 Minds*; 1968—*The Golden Vision*; 1969—*The Big Flame*; 1971—*The Rank and File*; 1973—*A Misfortune*; 1976—*Days of Hope* (in 4 parts); 1977—*The Price of Coal*; 1979—*The Gamekeeper*; 1980—*Auditions*; 1981—*A Question of Leadership*; *Looks and Smiles* (also theatrical release).

Publications:

By LOACH:

Articles—"Solidaires des courants de pensée qui dépassent le cinéma...", interview by M. Amiel in *Cinéma* (Paris), December 1972; "Spreading Wings at Kestrel", interview by P. Bream in *Films and Filming* (London), March 1972; "Ken Loach: Famille et névrose", interview by C. and R. Hardwick in *Jeune Cinéma* (Paris), November 1972; "Ken Loach—Days of Hope", interview by J. O'Hara in *Cinema Papers* (Melbourne), April 1977; interview in *Image et son* (Paris), May 1980; "A Fidelity to the Real", interview by L. Quart in *Cineaste* (New York), fall 1980; interview by Julian Petley in *Framework* (Norwich, England), no.18, 1982; "Continuing...the State of Things", interview by Robert Brown, in *Monthly Film Bulletin* (London), January 1983.

On LOACH:

Articles—"Case Histories of the Next Renascence" by D. Robinson in *Sight and Sound* (London), winter 1968; "The 'Kes' Dossier" by John Taylor in *Sight and Sound* (London), summer 1970; "Tony Garnett and Kenneth Loach" in *Documentary Explorations: 15 Interviews with Filmmakers* by G. Roy Levin, New York 1971; "La Télévision des autres" by D. Serceau in *Téléciné* (Paris), March 1973; "One More Time" by Iain McAsh in *Films Illustrated* (London), December 1978; "Ken Loach aux rencontres de Saint-Etienne" by B. Nave in *Jeune cinéma* (Paris), April/May 1981.

* * *

The career of Ken Loach illustrates the continuing resiliency of the "social problem" film as well as the limitations of a rigorous naturalism. The Oxford-educated Loach is the most intelligent British director to focus on the problems of the working class in recent years, and his work constitutes a logical extension of the less militant films of the so-called "British New Wave"— Richardson, Reisz, Anderson et al.

Loach first gained wide recognition with a series of television-films produced for the BBC series, "Wednesday Play." Loach's anger had been aroused by the popularity of right-wing films such as *The Angry Silence* and his ire was shared by Tony Garnett who soon became both his producer and sometime collaborator. *Up the Junction*, a compassionate study of three working class teenage girls, was the first noteworthy Loach-Garnett "Wednesday Play." They followed this minor *succès d'estime* with *Cathy Come Home* in one of the most celebrated programs in the history of British television. *Cathy Come Home's* fictionalized exposé of the housing industry inspired a parliamentary inquiry, and established the Loach-Garnett reputation for timely social documentary.

Poor Cow marked Loach's first foray into feature filmmaking, although the enterprise did not entirely fulfill its initial promise. Despite Carol White's excellent performance and a characteristic commitment to conveying the nuances of everyday life, *Poor Cow* remains an interesting failure and a film that Loach himself has disavowed. *Kes*, an adaption of Barry Hines's novel *A Kestrel for a Knave*, was a much more effective blend of pathos and political indignation. This simple tale of a Yorkshire boy's rapport with a kestrel combined an almost Dickensian talent for acerbic social observation with carefully modulated sentiment that never degenerated into bathos.

Family Life, anthough an overly schematic dramatization of R.D. Laing's unorthodox theories concerning the origins of schizophrenia, is nonetheless an impressive achievement. The film is a triumph of ensemble acting (the performance of Sandy Ratcliff in the central role of Janice is particularly impressive), and David Mercer's meticulous evocation of a claustrophobic working class milieu is a crucial component of the film's unsubtle, but nonetheless memorable, impact.

Days of Hope, a fictionalized chronicle of the General Strike of 1926 produced for the BBC, is Loach's most significant synthesis of documentary and committed pathos to date. Despite occasional melodramatic interludes and *longeurs*, *Days of Hope* is a militant (The screenwriter, Jim Allen, is a committed Trotskyite) reevaluation of antiquated historical assumptions that avoids the pitfalls of standard agit-prop.

Loach's recent films have been more modest in scope, but continue in the tradition of earnest social realism. *Black Jack* was a slight formal departure, since this children's fable avoided explicit political allusions. *The Gamekeeper* and *Looks and Smiles* were minor works that nonetheless demonstrated Loach's ongoing concern with the preoccupations of Britain's "have nots" in the age of Thatcherism.

—Richard Porton

LOGAN, JOSHUA. American. Born Joshua Lockwood Logan in Texarkana, Texas, 5 October 1908. Educated at Culver Military Academy, Culver, Indiana, graduated 1927; Princeton University, 1927-31. Married Barbara O'Neill (divorced); Nedda Harrigan; children: Thomas and Sue. Career: 1931—leaves Princeton during senior year to study in Moscow for 8 months with Stanislavsky at Moscow Art Theatre; 1931-35—director and actor with University Players, summer stock company at West Falmouth, Massachusetts; company members include Henry Fonda, James Stewart, Margaret Sullavan, and Mildred Natwick; 1932—Broadway acting debut in *Carry Nation*; stages 2 productions in London; 1935—begins directing and producing on Broadway; 1936—works briefly in Hollywood as dialogue director, and co-director of *I Met My Love Again*; 1938—first big Broadway success *On Borrowed Time*; 1942-45—serves in Air Force, discharged as captain; 1946—beginning with *Annie Get Your Gun*, directs acclaimed series of Broadway dramas and musicals including *Mister Roberts* and *South Pacific*; 1977—directs and performs in own nightclub act at Rainbow Grill, New York. Recipient: Pulitzer Prize, as co-author of musical *South Pacific*, 1950; Honorary M.A., Princeton University, 1953; Best-Written American Comedy, Writers Guild of America, for *Mr. Roberts*, 1955; Outstanding Directorial Achievement, Directors Guild of America, for *Picnic*, 1955; Outstanding Directorial Achievement, Directors Guild of America, for *Sayonara*, 1957;

Films (as dialogue director): 1936—*Garden of Allah* (Boleslawski); *History Is Made at Night* (Borzage); 1937—*I Met My Love Again* (co-d with Arthur Ripley); (as director): 1955—*Picnic*; *Mister Roberts* (Ford and LeRoy) (co-sc only); 1956—*Bus Stop*; 1957—*Sayonara*; *South Pacific*; 1959—*Tall Story* (+pr); 1961—*Fanny* (+pr); 1964—*Ensign Pulver* (+pr, co-sc); 1967—*Camelot*; 1969—*Paint Your Wagon*. Role: 1953—as himself in *Main Street to Broadway* (Garnett).

Publications:

By LOGAN:

Books—*My Up and Down, In and Out Life*, New York 1976; *Movie Stars, Real People, and Me*, New York 1978; articles— "Fear Is My Enemy", "My Greatest Crisis", and "Recovery from Fear", with Bill Davidson, in *Look* (New York), 22 July 1958, 5 August 1958, and 19 August 1958; "Gold Diggers of 1969", interview by Gordon Gow in *Films and Filming* (London), December 1969; "Fonda Memories" in *Show* (Los Angeles), April 1970; "A Memory of Marilyn Monroe the Actress" in *Show* (Los Angeles), September 1972; "Success is being in the right spot at the right time, says Josh Logan" in *Boxoffice* (Kansas City, Missouri), 19 February 1979.

On LOGAN:

Articles—"Joshua Logan" by Ely Kahn, Jr., in the *New Yorker*, 4 April and 11 April 1953; "Soft Psyche of Joshua Logan" by Gay Talese in *Esquire* (New York), April 1963.

* * *

Joshua Logan's fame rests mostly with his contributions to the Broadway stage as both producer and author: he was involved in the original staging of such classic plays and musicals as *Annie Get Your Gun*, *Charley's Aunt*, *Mister Roberts*, *South Pacific*, and *Fanny*. His filmography is short, and most of his credits here are adaptations of theatrical hits. While he has never signed his name to an all-out clinker, Logan's films generally suffer from a staginess and artificiality that betrays his non-cinematic background. His films are musicals, comedies and dramas, but they are rarely visual.

For example, in *Picnic*, Logan unnecessarily positions Betty

Field, who is imploring daughter Kim Novak not to run off with drifter William Holden, as he might had she been performing on stage for the last row of the balcony as well as the front row of the orchestra. Yet, in spite of Logan's ineptitude, the film remains a pleasing adaptation of the William Inge play because of the solid performances from Holden and a supporting case that includes Rosalind Russell, Arthur O'Connell, and Verna Felton.

Generally, Logan is bailed out by the talents of his players. *Bus Stop* (also based on Inge) is noteworthy as Marilyn Monroe's most fully realized work on film. *Fanny* features the charming presences of Charles Boyer and Maurice Chevalier, handsome cinematography, and a beautiful score. *Sayonara* (his major feature without theatrical origin) is highlighted by the award calibre acting of Marlon Brando, Red Buttons, and Miyoshi Umeki. But *Tall Story*, from a Howard Lindsay-Russell Crouse play, is noteworthy mainly as Jane Fonda's screen debut.

Then there are his musicals, all of which are lavish but disappointing nonetheless. In each case, Logan's direction is the major culprit. *Paint Your Wagon* is the best of the lot, an entertaining saga of the California gold rush. However, the performances—notably that of Harve Presnell, who outshines his non-singing co-stars—and various technical contributions easily overshadow Logan's staging. *South Pacific* (which, like *Sayonara*, is from the writings of James Michener) is adequate at best, but a major disappointment considering the material. Again, Mitzi Gaynor, Ray Walston, and Juanita Hall triumph over their direction. *Camelot* is easily Logan's least successful adaptation, with an overabundance of close-ups (an attempt at creativity that is ultimately an exercise in pretention) and inadequate musical performances. But the film is not as bad as some critics maintain; it is fairly well-acted (when the players are reciting their lines instead of singing the lyrics), and Vanessa Redgrave is actually quite radiant.

Joshua Logan's failing is his lack of a cinematic sensibility. Even the best of his films ultimately suffer because he was never able to transcend this limitation.

—Rob Edelman

LORENTZ, PARE. American. Born in Clarksburg, West Virginia, 11 December 1905. Educated at Wesleyan College; University of West Virginia. Married Eliza Meyer. Career: 1930—writes book *Censorship: The Private Lives of the Movies*; 1930s—film critic for *McCall's* and *Town and Country*; 1933—assembles book of photos entitled *The Roosevelt Year*; 1934-36—writes movie column for Ring Features; 1935-36—directs 1st film, *The Plow That Broke the Plains*, for the U.S. Resettlement Agency; 1936-37—directs *The River* for U.S. Farm Security Administration; 1938-40—is director of short-lived U.S. Film Service; during this time is responsible for bringing in Robert Flaherty and Joris Ivens to make films for U.S.F.S.; 1941—makes a number of shorts for RKO; 1941-45—makes 275 navagational films for U.S. Air Force; 1946-47—serves as chief of film section of War Department's Civil Affairs Division; 1948-52—attempts but fails to raise money to make documentary based on book *No Place to Hide* by a doctor who witnessed A-bomb testing at Bikini Islands; 1960s—opens consulting firm in New York; 1981—"saluted" by Academy of Motion Pictures Arts and Sciences. Recipient: Narration for *The River* nominated for Pulitzer Prize in poetry.

Films (as director-screenwriter) 1936—*The Plow That Broke the*

Plains; 1937—*The River*; 1939—*The City* (co-sc only); 1940—*The Fight for Life*; 1946—*Nuremburg Trials*.

Publications:

By LORENTZ:

Articles—"Moral Racketeering in the Movies" in *Scribner's* (New York), September 1930; "Young Man Goes to Work" in *Scribner's* (New York), February 1931; "Movie Platform" in the *Literary Digest* (New York), 7 August 1937; "The Narration of *The River*" by Pare Lorentz in *Film Comment* (New York), spring 1965.

On LORENTZ:

Books—*Pare Lorentz and the Documentary Film* by Robert L. Synder, Norman, Oklahoma 1968; *The People's Films* by Richard Dyer MacCann, New York 1973; *Non-Fiction Film* by Richard Barsam, New York 1973; *Documentary—A History of the Non-Fiction Film* by Erik Barnouw, New York 1974; articles—"The American Documentary" by Ezra Goodman in *Sight and Sound* (London), autumn 1938; "Award to Pare Lorentz" in the *Magazine of Art* (New York), July 1938; "Pare Lorentz" by W.L. White in *Scribner's* (New York), January 1939; "Young Man with a Camera" by W.L. White in the *Reader's Digest* (Pleasantville, New York), August 1940; "He Serves Up America: Pare Lorentz" by C.M. Black in *Collier's (New York), 3 August 1940; "Pare Lorentz"* in *Current Biography Yearbook*, New York 1940; "Fight for Survival" in *McCalls* (New York), January 1957; "A Rare Treat" in *Newsweek* (New York), 25 September 1961; "Letter from *The River*" by Willard Van Dyke in *Film Comment* (New York), spring 1965; "Conscience of the 30's" in *Newsweek* (New York), 5 August 1968; "Hollywood Hails Lorentz, Documentary Pioneer" by Aljean Harmetz in *The New York Times*, 22 October 1981; film—"Pare Lorentz on Film" in 4 installments produced by WGBH in Boston for NET network.

*   *   *

In this country it was Pare Lorentz who was in a position for leadership in relation to documentary film comparable to that of John Grierson in Britain and later in Canada. Lorentz was founding head and leader of the short-lived government program, which began in 1935, became the United States Film Service in 1938, and ended in 1940. He established American precedent for the government use of documentaries, which would be continued during World War II (by the Armed Forces and the Office of War Information) and afterwards (by the United States Information Agency, now International Communication Agency). From Lorentz's efforts five large and important films resulted, the first three of which he directed: *The Plow that Broke the Plains, The River, The Fight for Life, Power and the Land* (directed by Joris Ivens), and *The Land* (directed by Robert Flaherty).

In *The Plow that Broke the Plains* and *The River*, Lorentz developed an original, personal style of documentary that also became a national style (similiarities can be seen in the films of others, *The City* and *And So They Live*, for example). In his two mosaic patterns of sight (carefully composed images shot silent) and sound (symphonic music, spoken words, noises), no one element says much by itself. Together they offer a form and content that resemble epic poems. They seem close to the attitudes of American populism and are rooted in frontier tradition. The sweeping views of a big country, the free verse commentaries with their chanted litany of place names and allusions to historic events, make one think of Walt Whitman. The use of music is quite special, with composer Virgil Thomson sharing more fully than usual in the filmmaking process; a sort of operatic balance is achieved between the musical score and the other elements. (Thomson made his scores for these two films into concert suites which have become part of the standard orchestral repertoire.)

In *The Fight for Life*, Lorentz is much less sure in his control of its narrative form than he was of the poetic form of the two preceding films. He seems to have been much more comfortable with land and rivers than with people. *Fight for Life* is about the work of the Chicago Maternity Center in delivering babies among the impoverished. It is an interesting film, if curiously flawed by melodramatic excesses. It is important in its innovations and might be regarded as a prototype for the postwar Hollywood semi-domumentaries; e.g. *The House on 92nd Street, Boomerang, Call Northside 777.*

In contributing two lasting masterpieces to the history of documentary—*The Plow* and, especially, *The River*—Lorentz joins a very select company, that of the artists of documentary. (Flaherty and Jennings would be other members of that company.) Some would argue that *The River* is the finest American documentary to date—aesthetically and in terms of expressing aspects of the American spirit. Lorentz's major limitations appear most sharply in the light that Grierson would cast on them.

First, Lorentz relied on the impermanent partisan support of the party in power. Lorentz had the support of President Franklin Roosevelt and the films were associated with Democratic policies. When the balance in Congress shifted to Republican in 1940, the United States Film Service was not allowed to continue. Second, even within that New Deal context Lorentz opted for a few big films sponsored by agencies related to one department (four of the five films were on agricultural subjects), rather than many smaller films from various departments that would have broadened the base of sponsorship and made for a steady flow of film communication. Third, he was creating art at public expense—making personal films à la Flaherty—with no real commitment to public service. (Lorentz disliked the term documentary and much of Grierson's work in England as being too school-teacherish; instead Lorentz was trying to create, he said, "films of merit.") Finally, Lorentz remained aloof in Washington. He made no efforts to seek sponsorship for documentary film making outside the government; he had no real connection with the New York City documentarians responsible for the nongovernmental documentaries of the 1930s (though some of them had worked with him on the government films).

On the other hand, the situation was not the same here as in Britain or Canada. If Lorentz couldn't establish a film unit, he couldn't follow through on the other things Grierson called for. The government of the United States *is* highly partisan; we don't have the centuries-old tradition of public servants working outside party as in England. (Lorentz claimed that Grierson had stolen his plan: that the National Film Board accepted by the Canadian Parliament was essentially the same as the U.S. Film Service which Congress abolished.) It is not clear that Grierson could have done any better here than Lorentz did; Grierson's criticisms tend to ignore the central differences of government structure and tradition.

However one chooses to look at the matter, it would be generally agreed that documentary in the United States remained a non-movement of individual rivalries, competitiveness, and political differences. The closing down of the U.S. Film Service proved a great waste and inefficiency. Shortly after its demise the United States entered World War II and government film making on a vast scale had to be started from scratch. It was the Hollywood filmmakers, without documentary experience, who assumed leadership in the wartime government production. Lorentz spent the war making films as guides to navigation for the U.S. Air Corps. Subsequent to his film on the Nuremberg war-crimes trials he made no more films, working instead mainly as a "film consultant."

—Jack C. Ellis

LOSEY, JOSEPH. American. Born in La Crosse, Wisconsin, 14 January 1909. Educated at Dartmouth College, New Hampshire, B.A. 1929; Harvard University, M.A. in English Literature 1930. Career: 1930—writes theater and book reviews for New York publications; 1932-34—stage director in New York; 1935—in Moscow attends Eisenstein film classes, stages *Waiting for Lefty*; 1936-37—stages Living Newspaper productions and other plays for Federal Theater Project, New York; 1940-43—directs War Relief shows in major cities; 1943-44—writes 90 radio programs for NBC and CBS including "Worlds at War" and "Days of Reckoning" series; 1947—directs Brecht's *Galileo* in Los Angeles and New York; 1948—hired by Dore Schary for RKO; 1951—blacklisted, directs *Stranger on the Prowl* in Italy, settles in London; 1954-55—directs London stage productions; 1963—collaborations with writer Harold Pinter and actor Dirk Bogarde begin with *The Servant*; 1971-74—works with Pinter on adaptation of Proust's *Remembrance of Things Past* (unrealized); 1980—directs *Boris Godunov*, Paris Opera. Recipient: Chevalier de l'Ordre des Arts et des Lettres, 1957; special jury prize, Cannes Festival, for *Accident*, 1967; International Critics Award, Cannes Festival, for *Accident*, 1967; Palme d'or, Cannes Festival, for *The Go-Between*, 1971; Honorary Doctorate in Literature and Humanities, Dartmouth College, 1973. Address: c/o Cowan Bellew Associates, 45 Poland Street, London W1, England.

Films (as director of short films): 1939—*Pete Roleum and His Cousins* (+p, sc); 1941—*A Child Went Forth* (+co-p, sc); *Youth Gets a Break* (+sc); 1945—*A Gun in His Hand*; (as director of feature films): 1949—*The Boy with Green Hair*; 1950—*The Lawless*; 1951—*The Prowler*; *M*; *The Big Night* (+co-sc); 1952—*Stranger on the Prowl (Encounter)* (d as "Andrea Forzano"); 1954—*The Sleeping Tiger* (d as "Victor Hanbury"); 1955—*A Man on the Beach*; 1956—*The Intimate Stranger (Finger of Guilt)* (d as "Joseph Walton"); 1957—*Time Without Pity*; 1958—*The Gypsy and the Gentleman*; 1959—*Blind Date (Chance Meeting)*; 1960—*The Criminal (The Concrete Jungle)*; 1962—*Eve*; 1963—*The Damned (These Are the Damned)*; *The Servant* (+co-p); 1964—*King and Country* (+co-p); 1966—*Modesty Blaise*; 1967—*Accident* (+co-p); 1968—*Boom!*; *Secret Ceremony*; 1970—*Figures in a Landscape*; *The Go-Between*; 1972—*The Assassination of Trotsky* (+co-p); 1973—*A Doll's House*; 1975—*Galileo* (+co-sc); *The Romantic Englishwoman*; 1977—*Mr. Klein*; 1979—*Don Giovanni*; 1982—*The Trout.*

Publications:

By LOSEY:

Books—*Losey on Losey* edited by Tom Milne, New York 1968;

Le Livre de Losey: entretiens avec le cinéaste, Paris 1979; articles—"A Mirror to Life" in *Films and Filming* (London), June 1959; "Entretiens" in *Cahiers du cinéma* (Paris), September 1960; interview by Penelope Houston and John Gillett in *Sight and Sound* (London), autumn 1961; "The Monkey on My Back" in *Films and Filming* (London), October 1963; "Notes sur *The Servant*" in *Positif* (Paris), June 1964; "Entretiens" in *Positif* (Paris), no.104, 1969; "Speak, Think, Stand Up" in *Film Culture* (New York), fall/winter 1970; "Entretiens" in *Positif* (Paris), no.128, 1971; interview by S. Schadhauser in *Filmcritica* (Rome), February 1972; "L'Assassinat de Trotsky. Dialectique de la fatalité", interview by P. Sory in *Cinéma* (Paris), May 1972; interview by Gene Phillips in *Séquences* (Montreal), April 1973; "Losey and Trotsky", interview by Tony Rayns in *Take One* (Montreal), March 1973; "Something More", interview by Gordon Gow in *Films and Filming* (London), October 1975; interview by A. Girard in *Cinématographe* (Paris), August/September 1975; interview by Michel Ciment in *Positif* (Paris), October 1976; "Notes de travail (sur *Mr. Klein*)" in *Positif* (Paris), October 1976; "Notes sur les personnages" in *Avant-Scène du cinéma* (Paris), 1 November 1976; "Original, lyrique, imposant" in *Avant-Scène du cinéma* (Paris), June 1976; interview by P. Carcassonne and M. Devillers in *Cinématographe* (Paris), no.40, 1978; "Tra il vecchio e il nuovo una varieta di simboli morbosi", interview by U. Finetti in *Cinema nuovo* (Turin), August 1979; "The Reluctant Exile", interview by Richard Roud in *Sight and Sound* (London), no.3, 1979.

On LOSEY:

Books—*The Cinema of Joseph Losey* by James Leahy, New York 1967; *Joseph Losey* by Christian Ledieu, Paris 1970; *Joseph Losey* by Foster Hirsch, Boston 1980; articles—special Losey issue, *Cahiers du cinéma* (Paris), September 1960; "L'oeil du maitre" in *Cahiers du cinéma* (Paris), October 1961; "Puritan Maids" by Raymond Durgnat in *Films and Filming* (London), April and May 1966; "Joseph Losey, or The Camera Calls" by Gilles Jacob in *Sight and Sound* (London), spring 1966; "Notes on an Early Losey" by T.J. Ross in *Film Culture* (New York), spring 1966; "Secret Ceremony" by Roger Greenspun in *The New York Times*, 17 November 1968; "The Critical Camera of Joseph Losey" by Gene Phillips in *Cinema* (Beverly Hills), spring 1968; "The Mice in the Milk" by Philip Strick in *Sight and Sound* (London), spring 1969; "Weapons" by Gordon Gow in *Films and Filming* (London), October 1971; "Losey, Galileo, and the Romantic Englishwoman" by Richard Combs in *Sight and Sound* (London), summer 1975; "Pro-positions a propos de Losey" by G. Legrand in *Positif* (Paris), October 1976; "The Blacklisting Era: 3 Cases" by Gene Phillips in *America* (New York), 18 December 1976; "The Losey-Pinter Collaboration" by B. Houston and Marcia Kinder in *Film Quarterly* (Berkeley), fall 1978; "*Don Giovanni*: Opera into Film" by R. Gelatt in *American Film* (Washington, D.C.), April 1979; "Dialogue on Film: Joseph Losey" in *American Film* (Washington, D.C,), November 1980; "Le Tsar noir de Losey" by E. Decaux in *Cinématographe* (Paris), July/August 1980.

*   *   *

Joseph Losey's career has spanned five decades and has included work in both theater and film. Now an American expatriate living in Europe, the early years of his life as a director were spent in the very different milieus of New Deal political theater projects and the paranoia of the Hollywood studio system during the McCarthy era. He was blacklisted in 1951 and left America for England where he continued making films, at first under a variety of pseudonyms. His work is both controversial and critically acclaimed, and Losey has long been recognized as a director with a distinctive and highly personal cinematic style.

Although Losey rarely writes his own screenplays, preferring instead to work closely with other authors, there are nevertheless several distinct thematic concerns which recur throughout his work. It is his emphasis on human interaction and the complexity of interior thought and emotion that makes a Losey film an intellectual challenge, and his interest has always lain with detailed character studies rather than with so-called "action"pictures. Losey's domain is interior action and his depiction of the physical world centers on those events which are an outgrowth or reflection of his characters inner lives. From *The Boy with Green Hair* to *The Trout*, his films have focused on individuals and their relationships to themselves, to those around them, and to their society as a whole.

One of Losey's frequent subjects is the intruder who enters a preexisting situation and irrevocably alters its patterns. In his earlier films, this situation often takes the form of a community reacting with violence to an individual its members perceive as a threat. The "boy with green hair" is ostracized and finally forced to shave his head by the inhabitants of the town in which he lives; the young Mexican-American in *The Lawless* becomes the object of a vicious manhunt after a racially motivated fight; and the child-murderer in Losey's 1951 version of *M* inspires a lynch mob mentality in the community he has been terrorizing. In each of these cases, the social outsider who, for good or evil, does not confirm to the standards of the community, evokes a response of mass rage and suspicion. And as the members of the group forsake their individuality and rational behavior in favor of mob rule, they also forfeit any hope of future self-deception regarding their own capacity for unthinking brutality.

In Losey's later films, the scope of the "intruder" theme is often narrowed to explore the effect of a newcomer on the relationship of a husband and wife. *The Sleeping Tiger*, *Eve*, *Accident*, *The Romantic Englishwoman*, and *The Trout* all feature married couples whose lives are disrupted and whose relationships are shattered or redefined by the arrival of a third figure. In each of these films, either the husband or the wife is strongly attracted to the outsider. In *The Sleeping Tiger*, *Eve*, and *The Trout*, this attraction leads to tragedy and death for one of the partners, while the couples in *Accident* and *The Romantic Englishwoman* are forced to confront a serious rift in a seemingly untroubled relationship. A further level of conflict is added by the fact that the intruder in all of the films is either of a different social class (*The Sleeping Tiger*, *Eve*, *The Trout*) or a different nationality (*Accident*, *The Romantic Englishwoman*) than the couple, representing not only a sexual threat but a threat to the bourgeois status quo as well.

This underlying theme of class conflict is one which runs throughout Losey's work, emerging as an essential part of the framework of films as different as *The Lawless*, *The Servant*, and *The Go-Between*. Losey's consistent use of film as a means of social criticism has its roots in his theatrical work of the 1930s and his association with Bertolt Brecht. The two collaborated on the 1947 staging of Brecht's *Galileo Galilei*, starring Charles Laughton—a play which 27 years later Losey would bring to the screen—and Brecht's influence on Losey's own career is enormous. In addition to his interest in utilizing film as an expression of social and political opinions, Losey has adapted many of Brecht's theatrical devices to the medium as well. The sense of distance and reserve in Brechtian theatre is a keynote to Losey's filmic style, and Brecht's use of a heightened dramatic reality is also present in Losey's work. The characters in a Losey film are very much of the "real" world, but their depiction is never achieved through a documentary-style approach. We are always aware that it is a drama that is unfolding, as Losey makes use of carefully chosen music on the soundtrack or photography that borders on expressionism or deliberately evokes an atmosphere of memory to comment on the characters and their state of mind. It is this approach to the intellect rather than the emotions of the viewer that ties Losey's work so closely to Brecht.

Losey's films are also an examination of illusion and reality, with the true nature of people or events often bearing little resemblance to their outer appearances. The friendly community that gives way to mob violence, the "happy" marriage that unravels when one thread is plucked; these images of actual vs. surface reality abound in Losey's work. One aspect of this theme manifests itself in Losey's fascination with characters who discover themselves through a relationship which poses a potential threat to their position in society. Tyvian, in *Eve*, can only acknowledge through his affair with a high-class prostitute that his fame as a writer is actually the result of plagiarism, while Marian, in *The Go-Between*, finds her true sexual nature, which her class and breeding urge her to repress, in her affair with a local farmer.

Several of Losey's films carry this theme a step further, offering characters who find their own sense of self-identity becoming inextricably bound up in someone else. In *The Servant*, the complex, enigmatic relationship between Tony and his manservant, Barrett, becomes both a class struggle and a battle of wills as the idle young aristocrat slowly loses control of his life to the ambitious Barrett. This is an idea Losey pursues in both *Secret Ceremony* and *Mr. Klein*. In the former, a wealthy, unbalanced young girl draws a prostitute into a destructive fantasy in which the two are mother and daughter, and the prostitute finds her initial desire for money becoming a desperate need to believe the fantasy. Alain Delon in *Mr. Klein* portrays a man in occupied France who becomes obsessed with finding a hunted Jew who shares his name. At the film's conclusion, he boards a train bound for the death camps rather than abandon his search, in effect becoming the other *Mr. Klein*. Losey emphasizes his characters' identity confusion cinematically, frequently showing them reflected in mirrors, their images fragmented, prism-like, or only partially revealed.

Losey's choice of subject has led to his successful collaboration with playwright Harold Pinter on *The Servant*, *Accident*, and *The Go-Between*, and Losey once hoped to film Pinter's screenplay of Proust's *Remembrance of Things Past*. Their parallel dramatic interests have served both men well, and their work together is among the finest in their careers. Yet if Losey has found his most nearly perfect voice in Pinter's screenplays, his films with a wide variety of other writers have still resulted in a body of work remarkably consistent in theme and purpose. His absorbing, sometimes difficult films represent a unique and uncompromising approach to cinema, and guarantee Losey's place among the world's most intriguing directors.

—Janet E. Lorenz

LUBITSCH, ERNST; German-American. Born in Berlin, 28 January 1892; became citizen of the United States in 1936. Educated at the Sophien Gymnasium. Married Irni (Helene) Kraus in August 1922 (divorced 1930); married Sania Bezencenet (Vivian Gaye), 1935 (divorced 1943); child: Nicola. Career: 1911—taken into Max Reinhardt theater company; 1913—

begins to appear in short films; begins to write 1-reelers, directs 1st films; 1918—directs 1st dramatic feature, with Pola Negri; leaves Reinhardt company; 1921—Europäischen Film-Allianz (Efa) initiated by Adolph Zukor: includes Lubitsch; visits America 1st time; 1922—Mary Pickford invites him to direct her, finds him difficult; 1923—joins Warner Brothers; sees *A Woman of Paris*, claims it as influence; 1926—breaks contract with Warners; 1928—begins association with Paramount, sound film career begins; 1930—begins collaboration with writer Ernest Vajda; 1935—named head of production at Paramount; relieved of post after a year; 1938—leaves Paramount; signs 3-year contract with 20th Century—Fox; 1943—massive heart attack, long recuperation period. Died in Hollywood, 29 November 1947. Recipient: Special Academy Award (for accomplishments in the industry), 1947.

Films (as director): 1914—*Fräulein Seifenschaum* (+ro); *Blindkuh* (+ro); *Aufs Eis geführt* (+ro); 1915—*Zucker und Zimt* (+co-d, co-sc, ro); 1916—*Wo ist mein Schatz?* (+ro); *Schuhpalast Pinkus* (+ro as *Sally Pinkus*); *Der gemischte Frauenchor* (+ro); *Der G.m.b.H. Tenor* (+ro); *Der Kraftmeier* (+ro); *Leutnant auf Befehl* (+ro); *Das schönste Geschenk* (+ro); *Seine neue Nase* (+ro); 1917—*Wenn vier dasselbe Tun* (+co-sc, ro); *Der Blusenkönig* (+ro); *Ossis Tagebuch*; 1918—*Prinz Sami* (+ro); *Ein fideles Gefängnis*; *Der Fall Rosentopf* (+ro); *Der Rodelkavalier* (+co-sc); *Die Augen der Mumie Mâ*; *Das Mädel vom Ballett*; *Carmen*; 1919—*Meine Frau, die Filmschauspielerin*; *Meyer aus Berlin* (+ro as *Apprentice*); *Das Schwabemädle*; *Die Austernprinzessin*; *Rausch*; *Madame DuBarry*; *Der lustige Ehemann* (+sc); *Die Puppe* (+co-sc); 1920—*Ich möchte kein Mann sein!* (+co-sc); *Kohlhiesels Töchter* (+co-sc); *Romeo und Julia im Schnee* (+co-sc); *Sumurun* (+co-sc); *Anna Boleyn*; 1921—*Die Bergkatze* (+co-sc); 1922—*Das Weib des Pharao*; 1923—*Die Flamme*; *Rosita*; 1924—*The Marriage Circle*; *3 Women*; *Forbidden Paradise* (+co-sc); 1925—*Kiss Me Again* (+pr); *Lady Windermere's Fan* (+pr); 1926—*So This Is Paris* (+pr); 1927—*The Student Prince in Old Heidelberg* (+pr); 1928—*The Patriot* (+pr); 1929—*Eternal Love* (+pr); *The Love Parade* (+pr); 1930—*Paramount on Parade* (anthology film); *Monte Carlo* (+pr); 1931—*The Smiling Lieutenant* (+pr); 1932—*The Man I Killed (Broken Lullaby)* (+pr); *One Hour with You* (+pr); *Trouble in Paradise* (+pr); *If I Had a Million* (anthology film); 1933—*Design for Living* (+pr); 1934—*The Merry Widow* (+pr); 1936—*Desire* (co-d, + pr); 1937—*Angel* (+pr); 1938—*Bluebeard's 8th Wife* (+pr); 1939—*Ninotchka* (+pr); 1940—*The Shop Around the Corner* (+pr); 1941—*That Uncertain Feeling* (+co-pr); 1942—*To Be or Not to Be* (co-source, +co-pr); 1943—*Heaven Can Wait* (+pr); 1946—*Cluny Brown* (+pr); 1948—*That Lady in Ermine* (co-d).

Roles: 1913—*Meyer* in *Meyer auf der Alm*; 1914—*Moritz Abramowski* in *Dir Firma Heiratet* (Wilhelm); *Siegmund Lachmann* in *Der Stolz der Firma* (Wilhelm); *Fräulein Piccolo* (Hofer); *Arme Marie* (Mack); *Bedingung—Kein Anhang!* (Rye); *Die Ideale Gattin*; *Meyer* in *Meyer als Soldat*; 1915—in *Robert und Bertram* (Mack); *Wie Ich Ermordert Wurde* (Ralph); *Der Schwarze Moritz* (Taufstein and Berg); *Dr. Satansohn* in *Doktor Satansohn* (Edel); *Devil* in *Hans Trutz im Schlaraffenland* (Wegener).

Publications:

By LUBITSCH:

Articles—"American Cinematographers Superior Artists" in

American Cinematographer (Los Angeles), December 1923; "Concerning Cinematography...as Told to William Stull" in *American Cinematographer* (Los Angeles), November 1929; "A Chat with Mr. Lubitsch" in *The New York Times*, 28 February 1932; "Lubitsch's Analysis of Pictures Minimizes Director's Importance" in *Variety* (New York), 1 March 1932; "Hollywood Still Leads...Says Ernst Lubitsch", interview by Barney Hutchinson in *American Cinematographer* (Los Angeles), March 1933; "Film Directing" in *The World Film Encyclopedia*, London 1933; "A Word with Mr. Lubitsch", interview by Andre Sennwald in *The New York Times*, 14 October 1934; "Garbo, as Seen by Her Director" in *The New York Times*, 22 October 1939; "Mr. Lubitsch Takes the Floor for Rebuttal" in *The New York Times*, 29 March 1942; "Lubitsch Looks at His 'Oscar'", interview by Philip Scheuer in the *Los Angeles Times*, 6 April 1947; "A Tribute to Lubitsch, with a Letter in Which Lubitsch Appraises His Own Career" in *Films in Review* (New York), August/September 1951; letter to Herman Weinberg (July 10, 1947) in *Film Culture* (New York), summer 1962.

On LUBITSCH:

Books—*Let's Go to the Pictures* by Iris Barry, London 1926; *Hollywood: Legende und Wirklichkeit* by Ali Hubert, Leipzig 1930; *Das Gab's nur Einmal* by Kurt Riess, Hamburg 1957; *Ernst Lubitsch* by Mario Verdone, Lyon 1964; *The Movie Musical from Vitaphone to 42nd Street*, edited by Miles Kreuger, New York 1975; *The Hollywood Exiles* by John Baxter, New York 1976; *The Cinema of Ernst Lubitsch: The Hollywood Films* by Leland Poague, London 1977; *The Lubitsch Touch: A Critical Study* by Herman Weinberg, 3rd revised edition, New York 1977; *Ernst Lubitsch: A Guide to References and Resources* by R. Carringer and B. Sabath, Boston 1978; *The Cinema of Ernst Lubitsch* by Leland Poague, South Brunswick, New Jersey 1978; articles—"Ernst Lubitsch: German Director" in *Motion Picture Directing* by Peter Milne, New York 1922; "Lubitsch on Directing" in *The New York Times*, 16 December 1923; "Ernst Lubitsch Looks at Life and the Cinema" by Robert Grosvenor in *Cinema Art*, October 1927; "Movie Magician" by Grover Jones in *Collier's* (New York), 21 September 1935; "Camera Work Fails True Mission When It Sinks Realism for Beauty" by William Stull in *American Cinematographer* (Los Angeles), February 1938; "E. Lubitsch Dead: Film Producer, 55" in *The New York Times*, 1 December 1947; "25 Years of the 'Lubitsch Touch' in Hollywood" by Mollie Merrick in *American Cinematographer* (Los Angeles), July 1947; "Ernst Lubitsch: A Symposium" in *Screen Writer*, January 1948; "2 Masters: Ernst Lubitsch and Sergei M. Eisenstein" by H.H. Wollenberg in *Sight and Sound* (London), spring 1948; special Lubitsch section in *La Revue du cinéma* (Paris), September 1948; "Contributo alla storia della 'Sophisticated Comedy'" by Giulio Castello in *Bianco e nero* (Rome), September 1949; "Ernst Lubitsch, regista del tempo perduto" by Roberto Paolella in *Bianco e nero* (Rome), January 1958; "The Films of Ernst Lubitsch", special issue of *Film Journal* (Australia), June 1959; "4 x Lubitsch: Die Komödie als Zeitkritik" by Michael Prager in *Action* (Vienna), no.1, 1966; "A Tribute to Lubitsch (1892-1947)" by various filmmakers in *Action!* (Los Angeles), November/December 1967; special Lubitsch feature in *Cahiers du cinéma* (Paris), February 1968; "Lubitsch (1892-1947)" by Bernard Eisenschitz in *Anthologie du Cinéma* vol.3, Paris 1968; "Lubitsch and the Costume Film", chapter 4 in *The Haunted Screen* by Lotte Eisner, Berkeley 1969; "Ernst Lubitsch: A Parallel to George Feydeau" by Herman Weinberg in *Film Comment* (New York), spring 1970; "Lubitsch in the '30s" by Andrew Sarris in *Film Comment* (New York), winter 1971/72 and summer 1972; "Hol-

lywood" by Peter Bogdanovich in *Esquire* (New York), November 1972; "Lubitsch in the '30s" by Andrew Sarris in *Film Comment* (New York), winter 1971/72 and summer 1972; "Ernst Lubitsch, le maître" by F. Vitoux in *Positif* (Paris), April 1972; "The 'Lubitsch Touch' and the Lubitsch Brain" in *The Comic Mind: Comedy and the Movies* by Gerald Mast, Indianapolis, Indiana 1973; "Lubitsch: l'être et le paraître" by F. Dufour in *Cinéma* (Paris), June 1973; "The Importance of Being Ernst" by J. McBride in *Film Heritage* (New York), summer 1973; "The Pre-Hollywood Lubitsch" by Jan-Christopher Horak in *Image* (Rochester, New York), December 1975; "Lubitsch's Widow: The Meaning of a Waltz" by N. Schwartz in *Film Comment* (New York), March/April 1975; "The Continental Touch" by John Baxter in *American Film* (Washington, D.C.), September 1976; special feature in *Kosmorama* (Copenhagen), spring 1976; "Ernst Lubitsch" in *Passport to Hollywood: Film Immigrants: Anthology* by Don Whittemore and Philip Cecchettini, New York 1976; "Ernst Lubitsch" by Kirk Bond in *Film Culture* (New York), no.63-64, 1977; "Munich's Cleaned Pictures" by John Gillett in *Sight and Sound* (London), winter 1977/78; "Sur 3 moments du cinéma allemand" by P. Stefani in *Cinéma* (Paris), January 1978; "Lubitsch Was a Prince" by François Truffaut in *American Film* (Washington, D.C.), May 1978; "At Long Last Lubitsch!" by D. McVay in *Film* (London), April 1979; "Lubitsch: The American Silent Films" by D. McVay in *Focus on Film* (London), April 1979; "Les Années courtes" by J. Fieschi in *Cinématographe* (Paris), February 1981.

* * *

Ernst Lubitsch's varied career is often broken down into periods to emphasize the spectrum of his talents—from an actor in Max Reinhardt's Berlin Theater company to Head of Production at Paramount. Each of these periods could well provide enough material for a sizeable book. It is probably most covenient to divide Lubitsch's output into 3 phases: his German films between 1913 and 1922; his Hollywood films from 1923 to 1934; and his Hollywood productions from 1935 till his death in 1947.

During the first half of Lubitsch's filmmaking decade in Germany he completed about 19 shorts. They were predomiantly ethnic slapsticks in which he played a "dumkopf" character by the name of Meyer. Only three of these one-to five-reelers still exist. He directed 18 more films during his last five years in Germany, almost equally divided between comedies, some of which anticipate the concerns of his Hollywood works, and epic costume dramas. Pola Negri starred in most of these historical spectacles and the strength of her performances together with the quality of Lubitsch's productions brought them both international acclaim. Their *Madame Dubarry* (retitled *Passion* in the U.S.) was not only one of the films responsible for breaking the American blockade on imported German films after World War I, but it also began the "invasion" of Hollywood by German talent.

Lubitsch came to Hollywood at Mary Pickford's invitation. He had hoped to direct her in *Faust*, but they finally agreed upon *Rosita*, a costume romance very similar to those he had done in Germany. After joining Warner Brothers, he directed five films that firmly established his thematic interests. The films were small in scale, dealt openly with sexual and psychological relationships in and out of marriage, refrained from offering conventional moral judgements, and demystified women as Molly Haskell and Marjorie Rosen point out, Lubitsch created complex female characters who were aggressive, unsentimental, and able to express their sexual desires without suffering the usual pains of banishment or death. Even though Lubitsch provided a new and healthy perspective on sex and increased America's understanding of woman's role in society, he did so only in a superficial way. His women ultimately affirmed the status quo. The most frequently cited film from this initial burst of creativity, *The Marriage Circle*, also exhibits the basic narrative motif found in most of Lubitsch's work—the third person catalyst. An essentially solid relationship is temporarily threatened by a sexual rival. The possibility of infidelity serves as the occasion for the original partners to reassess their relationship. They acquire a new self-awareness and understand the responsibilities they have towards each other. The lovers are left more intimately bound than before. This premise was consistently reworked until *The Merry Widow* in 1934.

The late 1920s were years of turmoil as every studio tried to adapt to sound recording. Lubitsch, apparently, wasn't troubled at all; he considered the sound booths nothing more than an inconvenience, something readily overcome. Seven of his ten films from 1929 to 1934 were musicals, but not of the proscenium-bound "all-singing, all-dancing" variety. Musicals were produced with such prolific abandon during this time (what better way to exploit the new technology?) that the public began avoiding them. Film histories tend to view the period from 1930 to 1933 as a musical void, yet it was the precise time that Lubitsch was making significant contributions to the genre. As Arthur Knight notes, "He was the first to be concerned with the 'natural' introduction of songs into the development of a musical-comedy plot." Starting with *The Love Parade*, Lubitsch eliminated the staginess that was characteristic of most musicals by employing a moving camera, clever editing, and the judicial use of integrated musical performance. Lubitsch constructed a seminal film musical format that is predominantly used today.

In 1932 Lubitsch directed his first non-musical sound comedy, *Trouble in Paradise*. Most critics consider this film to be, if not his best, than at least the complete embodiment of everything that has been associated with Lubitsch: sparkling dialogue, interesting plots, witty and sophisticated characters, and an air or urbanity, all part of the well-known "Lubitsch Touch." What constitutes the "Lubitsch Touch" is open to continual debate, the majority of the definitions being couched in poetic terms of idolization. Andrew Sarris comments that the "Lubitsch Touch" is a counterpoint of poignant sadness during a film's gayest moments. Leland A. Poague sees Lubitsch's style as being gracefully charming and fluid, with an "...ingenious ability to suggest more than he showed...." Observations like this last one earned Lubitsch the unfortunate moniker of "director of doors," since a number of his jokes relied on what unseen activity was being implied behind a closed door.

Regardless of which romantic description one chooses, the "Lubitsch Touch" can be most concretely seen as deriving from a standard narrative device of the silent film: interrupting the dramatic interchange by focusing on objects or small details that make a witty comment on or surprising revelation about the main action. Whatever the explanation, Lubitsch's style was exceptionally popular with critics and audiences alike. Ten years after arriving in the United States he had directed 18 features, parts of two anthologies, and was recognized as one of Hollywood's top directors.

Lubitsch's final phase began when he was appointed head of production at Paramount in 1935, a position that lasted only one year. Accustomed to pouring all his energies into one project at a time, he was ineffective juggling numerous projects simultaneously. Accused of being out of step with the times, Lubitsch up-dated his themes in his first political satire, *Ninotchka*, today probably his most famous film. He continued using parody and

satire in his blackest comedy, *To Be or Not to Be*, a film well liked by his contemporaries, and today receiving much reinvestigation. If Lubitsch's greatest talent was his ability to make us laugh at the most serious events and anxieties, to use comedy to make us more aware of ourselves, then *To Be or Not to Be* might be considered the consummate work of his career.

Lubitsch, who Gerald Mast terms the greatest technician in American cinema after Griffith, completed only two more films. At his funeral in 1947, Mervyn LeRoy presented a fitting eulogy: "...he advanced the techniques of screen comedy as no one else has ever done. Suddenly the pratfall and the double-take were left behind and the sources of deep inner laughter were tapped."

—Greg S. Faller

LUCAS, GEORGE. American. Born in Modesto, California, 14 May 1944. Attended Modesto Junior College; University of Southern California film school, graduated 1966. Married Marcia Griffen, 1969; daughter: Amanda (adopted). Career: 1965—wins several awards for *THX-1138: 4EB*, a student film made at USC; six-month internship at Warner Bros.; 1967-68—assistant to Francis Coppola on *Finian's Rainbow*; shoots documentary on the making of *The Rain People* and on making of *Mackenna's Gold* by Carl Foreman and J. Lee Thompson; 1970—Coppola persuades Warners to sign contract with Lucas to direct feature version of *THX-1138*; 1973—directs and co-scripts *American Graffiti* bringing 1st financial and critical success; 1976—establishes special effects company Industrial Light and Magic at San Rafael, California, for *Star Wars*; 1977—writes and directs *Star Wars*, top moneymaking film to date; 1978—forms Lucasfilm, Ltd. production company; 1980-81—produces *Raiders of the Lost Ark* in collaboration with Steven Spielberg; 1980—begins research and development firm Sprocket Systems; 1983—subject of *Time* magazine cover story; announces 2-year sabbatical following release of *Return of the Jedi*; engaged in completing filmmaking center "Skywalker Ranch". Recipient: New York Film Critics Award, Best Screenwriting for *American Graffiti*, with Gloria Katz and Willard Huyck, 1973. Address: P.O. Box 2009, San Rafael, California 94912.

Films (as maker of short films): 1965 and after—*Look at Life Freiheit*; *1.42.08*; *Herbie Anyone Lived in a Pretty Hometown*; *6.18.67*; *The Emperor*; *THX 1138: 4 EB*; (as director and scriptwriter): 1971—*THX-1138*; 1973—*American Graffiti*; 1977—*Star Wars*; 1978—*Corvette Summer* (Robbins) (exec. pr only); 1979—*More American Graffiti* (Norton) (exec. pr only); (as producer and scriptwriter): 1980—*The Empire Strikes Back* (Kershner); 1981—*Raiders of the Lost Ark* (Spielberg); 1983—*Return of the Jedi* (Marquand) (co-sc, exec. pr); 1984—*Indiana Jones and the Temple of Doom* (Spielberg) (pr only).

Publications:

By LUCAS:

Articles—"*THX-1138*" in *American Cinematographer* (Hollywood), October 1971; "The Filming of American Graffiti", interview by L. Sturhahn in *Filmmakers Newsletter* (Ward Hill, Mass.), March 1974; interview by Robert Benayoun and Michel Ciment in *Positif* (Paris), September 1977; "Le Matin du magicien", interview by C. Clouzot in *Ecran* (Paris), September 1977;

"George Lucas Goes Far Out" by S. Zito in *American Film* (Washington, D.C.), April 1977; interview by A. Bock in *Take One* (Montreal), no.6, 1979; "I'm the Boss", interview by M. Tuchman and A. Thompson in *Film Comment* (New York), July/August 1981.

On LUCAS:

Book—*Star Wars: The Making of the Movie* by Larry Weinberg, New York 1980; articles—"California Dreamin'" by Axel Madsen in *Sight and Sound* (London), summer 1970; article in *Newsweek* (New York), 3 May 1971; "Amateurs on the Campus Make Professional Films" by T. Fensch in *Making Films* (New York), April 1971; article in *The New York Times*, 7 October 1973; article in the *Saturday Review* (New York), 23 February 1974; "George Lucas: The Stinky Kid Hits the Big Time" by Steven Farber in *Film Quarterly* (Berkeley), spring 1974; article in *The New York Times*, 12 September 1976; article in *Time* (New York), 30 May 1977; "Behind the Scenes of Star Wars" in *American Cinematographer* (Los Angeles), July 1977; article in *Time* (New York), 6 March 1978; "George Lucas" in *Current Biography Yearbook*, New York 1978; "Songs of Innocence and Experience" by B.H. Fairchild, Jr., in *Literature/Film Quarterly* (Salisbury, Maryland), no.2, 1979; "The Man Who Made Star Wars" by M. Pye and L. Miles in *Atlantic Monthly* (Greenwich, Conn.), March 1979; "Can the Maker of *Star Wars* Do It Again?" by D. Lewin in *The New York Times*, 2 December 1979; "The Empire Strikes Back: Monsters from the Id" by Andrew Gordon in *Science Fiction Studies* (Montreal), November 1980; "Lexique des réalisateurs de films fantastiques américains" by Jean-Pierre Piton in *Image et son* (Paris), July/August 1981; "'I've Got to Get My Life Back Again'" by Gerald Clarke in *Time* (New York), 23 May 1983.

*   *   *

The career of George Lucas has been motivated by two strong desires: to make films for the general audience, films that he himself would like to see, and to make enough money from them so that he can free himself totally from the Hollywood production system and make the kind of abstract, experimental films that he truly wants to make. Apparently his taste is shared by the general audience; Lucas's films are among the most popular ever made.

As a result of his phenomenal success, his second desire is well on its way to being realized. His \$20 million filmmaking center, Skywalker Ranch, is now under construction in northern California's Marin County. There Lucas's production company (Lucasfilm, Ltd.) plans to house a computerized video digital printing, editing, and sound-mixing system which Lucas says will free him from the Hollywood studios' printing and distribution system. Lucas also says that *Return of the Jedi* will be the last picture his company will shoot on film. Skywalker Ranch will also serve as a filmmaking facility for some of his friends.

More than any other filmmaker, Lucas is responsible for the recent explosion of big-budget science fiction/fantasy films that continue to flood the film market. The immense popularity of *Star Wars* proved to the industry that the science fiction/fantasy film could be a powerful attraction at the box office.

All of his major film productions have been developed from original story ideas by Lucas. Except perhaps for *THX-1138*, each of these films relies on a romantic blend of fantasy and nostalgia. Even the *Star Wars* films, despite their science fiction sets, take place "a long time ago in a galaxy far, far away."

Yet, alongside their ability to evoke a wistful yearning for ages long past, there exists in these films a strong sense of satire. In *American Graffiti*, for instance, we have the antics of Terry the Toad who, in his desperation to appear "cool," mocks the tough fifties greaser attitude of hot-rodder John Milner. The robots in *Star Wars* also have a satirical function.

Whether one thinks of Lucas's films as reliving the fantasies of our youth or as creating new fantasies for today's children, Lucas remains a filmmaker for all ages and a product of his generation, perhaps the only one who can honestly be called the Walt Disney of the eighties.

—Thomas Snyder

———

LUMET, SIDNEY. American. Born in Philadelphia, 25 June 1924. Educated at Professional Children's School, New York; Columbia University extension school. Married Rita Gam (divorced); Gloria Vanderbilt in 1956 (divorced 1963); Gail Jones in 1963 (divorced 1978); Mary Gimbel in 1980. children: Amy and Jenny. Career: 1928—acting debut in Yiddish Theatre production, New York; late 1920s, early 1930s—acts in radio series; 1935—Broadway acting debut in *Dead End*; 1939—begins acting in films; 1941-46—serves in Army Signal Corps; 1947—forms off-Broadway acting group, begins stage directing; 1950—offered assistant director position at CBS; 1951-53—directs 150 episodes of *Danger* series, 26 *You Are There* shows and other television programs; 1953-56—directs for *Playhouse 90*, *Kraft Television Theatre*, *Studio One* and other "anthology" programs; 1960—for television directs *The Sacco and Vanzetti Story*, O'Neill's *The Iceman Cometh* and 4 NBC *Play of the Week* productions. Recipient: Directors Guild award for *12 Angry Men*, 1957; Directors Guild award for *Long Day's Journey into Night*, 1962. Address: c/o LAH Film Corp., 156 W. 56th Street, 2nd floor, New York, NY 10019.

Films (as film director): 1957—*12 Angry Men*; 1958—*Stage Struck*; 1959—*That Kind of Woman*; 1960—*The Fugitive Kind*; 1961—*A View from the Bridge*; 1962—*Long Day's Journey into Night*; 1964—*Fail Safe*; 1965—*The Pawnbroker*; 1966—*The Group*; 1967—*The Hill*; *The Deadly Affair* (+pr); 1968—*Bye, Bye Braverman* (+pr); *The Sea Gull* (+pr); 1969—*The Appointment*; *King: A Filmed Record...Montgomery to Memphis* (co-d); 1970—*Last of the Mobile Hot-Shots* (+pr); 1971—*The Anderson Tapes*; 1972—*Child's Play*; 1973—*The Offence*; 1974—*Serpico*; *Lovin' Molly*; *Murder on the Orient Express*; 1975—*Dog Day Afternoon*; 1976—*Network*; 1977—*Equus*; 1978—*The Wiz*; 1979—*Just Tell Me What You Want*; 1981—*Prince of the City*; *Deathtrap*; 1983—*The Verdict*.

Roles: 1939—as Joey Rogers in *One Third of a Nation* (Murphy); 1940—as youthful Jesus in *Journey to Jerusalem*.

Publications:

By LUMET:

Articles—"Le Point de vue du metteur en scene" in *Cahiers du cinéma* (Paris), April 1959; "An Interview with Sidney Lumet" by Peter Bogdanovich in *Film Quarterly* (Berkeley), winter 1960; "On a Film 'Journey'" in *The New York Times*, 7 October

1962; "Sidney Lumet" in *Cahiers du cinéma* (Paris), December/-January 1963/64; "Keep Them on the Hook" in *Films and Filming* (London), October 1964; "The Insider: Sidney Lumet Talks to Robin Bean about His Work in Films" in *Films and Filming* (London), June 1965; "Why I Like It Here: A Statement by Sidney Lumet" in *Making Films in New York*, March 1969; "*Long Day's Journey into Night*: An Interview with Sidney Lumet" by Luciano Dale in *Film Quarterly* (Berkeley), fall 1971; "Sidney Lumet on the Director" in *Movie People: At Work in the Business of Film* edited by Fred Baker, New York 1972; "Sidney Lumet: *The Offence*. An Interview with Susan Merrill" in *Films in Review* (New York), November 1973; "What's Real? Real? What's True?", interview by Gordon Gow in *Films and Filming* (London), May 1975; interview by Richard Eder in *The New York Times*, 31 December 1976; "Colour and Concepts", interview by Gordon Gow in *Films and Filming* (London), May 1978; "Wiz Kid", interview by D. Yakir in *Film Comment* (New York), December 1978.

On LUMET:

Book—*Sidney Lumet: A Guide to References and Resources* by Stephen Bowles, Boston 1979; articles—"The Tight Close-Up" by Gene Moskowitz in *Sight and Sound* (London), summer/autumn 1959; "Why Am I Happy?" in *Newsweek* (New York), 12 June 1961; "The Films of Sidney Lumet: Adaptation as Art" by Graham Petrie in *Film Quarterly* (Berkeley), winter 1967/68; "The Making of *The Group*" in *Kiss Kiss Bang Bang* by Pauline Kael, New York 1968; "Lumet—the Kid Actor Who Became a Director" by Guy Flatley in *The New York Times*, 20 January 1974; "Across the Board" by Tony Rayns in *Sight and Sound* (London), summer 1974; "What's Real? What's True?" by Gordon Gow in *Films and Filming* (London), May 1975; "'La Sera della prima': la maniera del doppio" by G. Turroni in *Filmcritica* (Rome), March 1979; "Plädoyer für Sidney Lumet" by F. Gehler in *Film und Fernsehen* (Berlin), August 1981.

*   *   *

Sidney Lumet must certainly be regarded as one of the most durable of contemporary directors. His career has spanned almost three decades and nearly 30 films. Although Lumet has applied his talents to a variety of genres (drama, comedy, satire, caper, romance, and even a musical), he has proven himself most comfortable and effective as a director of serious psychodramas and was most vulnerable when attempting light entertainments. His Academy Award nominations, for example, have all been for character studies of men in crisis, from his first film, *Twelve Angry Men*, through his most recent, *The Verdict*.

Lumet was, literally, a child of the drama. At the age of four he was appearing in productions of the highly popular and acclaimed Yiddish theatre in New York. He continued to act for the next two decades but increasingly gravitated toward directing. At 26 he was offered a position as an assistant director with CBS television. Along with John Frankenheimer, Robert Mulligan, Martin Ritt, Delbert Mann, George Roy Hill, Franklin Schaffner, and others, Lumet quickly won recognition as a competent and reliable director in a medium where many faltered under the pressures of producing live programs. It was in this environment that Lumet learned many of the skills that would serve him so well in his subsequent career in films: working closely with performers, rapid preparation for production, and working within tight schedules and budgets.

Because the quality of many of the television dramas was so impressive, several of them were adapted as motion pictures. Reginald Rose's *Twelve Angry Men* brought Lumet to the cinema. Although Lumet did not direct the television production, his expertise made him the ideal director for this low budget film venture. *Twelve Angry Men* was an auspicious beginning for Lumet. It was a critical and commercial success, and Lumet received his first nomination for an Academy Award. The film also established Lumet as a director skilled at adapting theatrical properties to motion pictures. Fully half of Lumet's complement of films have originated in the theater. Another precedent set by *Twelve Angry Men* was Lumet's career-long disdain for Hollywood.

Lumet prefers to work in contemporary urban settings, especially New York. Within this context, Lumet is consistently attracted to situations in which crime provides the occasion for a group of characters to come together. Typically these characters are caught in a vortex of events that they can neither understand nor control but which they must work to resolve. *Twelve Angry Men* explores the interaction of a group of jurors debating the innocence or guilt of a man being tried for murder; *The Hill* concerns a rough group of military men who have been sentenced to prison; *The Deadly Affair* involves espionage in Britian; *The Anderson Tapes* revolves around the robbery of a luxury apartment building; *Child's Play*, about the murder at a boy's school, conveys an almost supernatural atmosphere of menace; *Murder on the Orient Express*, *Dog Day Afternoon*, and *The Verdict* all involve attempts to find the solution to a crime, while *Serpico* and *Prince of the City* are probing examinations of men who have rejected graft practices as police officers.

Lumet's protagonists tend to be isolated, unexceptional men who oppose a group or institution. Whether the protagnoist is a member of a jury or party to a bungled robbery, he follows his instincts and intuition in an effort to find solutions. Lumet's most important criterion is not whether the actions of these men are right or wrong but whether the actions are genuine. If these actions are justified by the individual's conscience, this gives his heroes uncommon strength and courage to endure the pressures, abuses, and injustices of others. Frank Serpico, for example, is the quintessential Lumet hero in his defiance of peer group authority and the assertion of his own code of moral values.

Nearly all the characters in Lumet's gallery are driven by obsessions or passions that range from the pursuit of justice, honesty, and truth to the clutches of jealousy, memory, or guilt. It is not so much the object of their fixations but the obsessive condition itself that intrigues Lumet. In films like *The Fugitive Kind*, *A View from the Bridge*, *Long Day's Journey into Night*, *The Pawnbroker*, *The Sea Gull*, *The Appointment*, *The Offense*, *Lovin' Molly*, *Network*, *Just Tell Me What You Want*, and many of the others, the protagonists, as a result of their complex fixations, are lonely, often disillusioned individuals. Consequently, most of Lumet's central characters are not likable or pleasant and sometimes, not admirable figures. And, typically, their fixations result in tragic or unhappy consequences.

Lumet's fortunes have been up and down at the box office. One explanation seems to be his own fixation for uncompromising studies of men in crisis. His most intense characters present a grim vision of idealists broken by realities. From Val in *A View from the Bridge* and Sol Nazerman in *The Pawnbroker* to Danny Ciello in *Prince of the City*, Lumet's introspective characters seek to penetrate the deepest of the psyche.

—Stephen E. Bowles

LUMIÈRE, LOUIS. French. Born in Besançon, 5 October 1864. Educated at l'école de la Martinière, Besançon, degree 1880; Conservatoire de Lyon, 1880/81. Career: Chemist and inventor, son of an industrialist specializing in photographic chemistry and the making of emulsions; 1894—sees Edison Kinetoscope demonstrated in Paris, develops with brother Auguste Lumière (1862-1954) the "Cinématographe Lumière", camera capable of projecting film and incorporating invention of claw driven by eccentric gear for advancing film; 1895—projects 1st film, showing workers leaving the Lumière factory; on 28 December projects 1st program for a paying audience at Grand Café, Boulevard des Capucines, Paris; 1896—"Société du Cinématographe Lumière" formed; 1900—shows films on 16 by 21 foot screen at Paris Exposition; 1905—company ceases film production; through 1930s—invents and manufactures photographic equipment; after 1921—works on stereo projection method; 1936—premiere of "cinéma en relief" in Paris. Died at Bandol, France, 6 June 1948.

Films (as director and producer): 1896-1900—directed about 60 films and produced some 2000, mostly of a documentary nature; films attributed to Louis Lumière as director: 1894 or 1895—*La Sortie des usines* (version no.1); 1895—*La Sortie des usines* (version no.2); *L'Arroseur arrosé (Le Jardinier)*; *Forgerons*; *Pompiers: Attaque du feu*; *Le Repas de Bébé (Le Déjeuner de Bébé, Le Gouter de Bébé)*; *Pêche aux poissons rouges*; *La Voltige*; *Débarquement (Arrivée des congressistes à Neuville-sur-Saône)*; *Discussion de M. Janssen et de M. Lagrange*; *Saut à la couverture (Brimade dans une caserne)*; *Lyon, place des Cordeliers*; *Lyon, place Bellecour*; *Récréation à la Martinière*; *Charcuterie mécanique*; *Le Maréchal-ferrant*; *Lancement d'un navire à La Ciotat*; *Baignade en mer*; *Ateliers de La Ciotat*; *Barque sortant du port (La Sortie du port)*; *Arrivée d'un train à La Ciotat*; *Partie d'écarté*; *Assiettes tournantes*; *Chapeaux à transformations (Trewey: Under the Hat)*; *Photographe*; *Démolition d'un mur (Le Mur)*; *Querelle enfantine*; *Aquarium*; *Bocal aux poissons-rouges*; *Partie de tric-trac*; *Le Dejeuner du chat*; *Départ en voiture*; *Enfants aux jouets*; *Course en sac*; *Discussion*; 1896-97—*Barque en mer*; *Baignade en mer*; *Arrivée d'un bateau à vapeur*; *Concours de boules*; *Premiers pas de Bébé*; *Embarquement pour le promenade*; *Retour d'une promenade en mer*; *Marché*; *Enfant et chien*; *Petit frèree et petite soeur*; *Douche après le bain*; *Ronde enfantine*; *Enfants au bord de la mer*; *Bains en mer*; *Touristes revenant d'une excursion*; *Scènes d'enfants*; *Laveuses*; *Repas en famille*; *Bal d'enfants*; *Leçon de bicyclette*; *Menuisiers*; *Radeau avec baigneurs*; *Le Goûter de Bébé*; 1900—*Inauguration de l'Exposition universelle*, *La Tour Eiffel*, *Le Pont d'Iéna*, *Danses espagnoles* and other films shown on large screen at Paris Exposition 1900; 1936—*Arrivée d'un train en gare de La Ciotat* and other films presented in "cinéma en relief" program.

Publications:

By LUMIÈRE:

Books—*Cinématographe Auguste et Louis Lumière: Catalogue des Vues*, first through seventh lists, Lyon, France 1897-98; *Catalogue des vues pour cinématographe*, Lyon 1907; articles—"Lumière—The Last Interview" by Georges Sadoul in *Sight and Sound* (London), summer 1948; "Bellecour—Monplaisir" by H. Bitomsky in *Filmkritik* (Munich), August 1978.

On LUMIÈRE:

Books—*Les Frères Lumière* by Henri Kubnick, Paris 1938; *Au seuil de paradis des images avec Louis Lumière* by Paul Leroy, Paris 1948; *Louis Lumière, inventeur* by Maurice Bessy and Lo Duca, Paris 1948; *Histoire générale du cinéma* vols. 1 and 2 by Georges Sadoul, Paris 1949; *A Paris, il y a soixante ans, naissait le cinéma* by Victor Pernot, Paris 1955; *Louis Lumière* by Georges Sadoul, Paris 1964; *Filmographie Universelle* vol.2 by Jean Mitry, Paris 1964; articles—"Artisan in Light" by Mallory Browne in the *Christian Science Monitor Magazine* (Boston), 7 August 1935; "Lumiere Jubilee" in *Time* (New York), 18 November 1935; "Structural Patterning in the Lumière Films" by M. Deutelbaum in *Wide Angle* (Athens, Ohio), no.1, 1979; "Lieux du cinéma: lettre du Chateau Lumière" by E. Decaux in *Cinématographe* (Paris), January 1979; "Let There Be Lumière" by D. Vaughan in *Sight and Sound* (London), spring 1981.

LYE, LEN. New Zealander. Born in Christchurch, 5 July 1901; became citizen of of United States, 1950. Educated at Wellington Technical College; Canterbury College of Fine Arts. Career: 1921—assistant for Australian film company; makes first hand-painted film; 1926—comes to England, works as stage hand, Lyric Theatre, London; 1927—begins work on first animated film with support of the London Film Society; 1931—property boy at Wembley Studio; 1933—resumes experiments with "direct film": drawing and painting on celluloid; 1935—begins sporadic association with G.P.O. Film Unit under John Grierson; 1940-44—works on wartime propaganda films; 1944—goes to U.S. to work on March of Time series; 1958—devotes attention to kinetic sculpture. Died in Warwick, Rhode Island, 15 May 1980.

Films 1921—untitled handmade films, Australia; (as director, scriptwriter, and animator of short films): 1929—*Tusalava* (begun 1927); 1933—*Experimental Animation: Peanut Vendor* (not completed); 1935—*A Color Box (Colour Box)* (handmade film); *Kaleidoscope*; 1936—*The Birth of a Robot* (puppet animation) (co-d); *Rainbow Dance*; 1937—*Trade Tattoo (In Time with Industry)*; 1938—*N or NW (N. or N.W., North or North West)* (live action); *Colour Flight*; 1939—*Swinging the Lambeth Walk*; 1940—*Musical Poster No.1*; (live action shorts): *Profile of Britain* ("March of Time" series); 1941—*When the Pie Was Opened*; *Newspaper Train*; 1942—*Work Party*; *Kill or Be Killed*; *German Calling*; 1943—*Planned Crops*; 1944—*Cameramen at War*; 1944-51—collaborated on 7 films of "March of Time" series; 1952—*Fox Chase*; (handmade films): 1953—*Color Cry*; *Rhythm*; 1957—*Free Radicals*; 1961-66—*Particles in Space*; 1980—*Tal Farlow*.

Publications:

By LYE:

Books—*No Trouble*, Majorca 1930; *Figures of Motion*, Auckland, New Zealand 1982; articles—"Colour and the Box Office" in *Life and Letters Today*, September 1935; "Experiment in Colour" in *World Film News*, December 1936; "Television: New Axes to Grind" in *Sight and Sound* (London), summer 1939; "The Man Who Was Colour Blind" in *Sight and Sound* (London), spring 1940; "On the End of Audiences" in *Film Culture* (New York), summer 1961; interview by Gretchen Weinberg in

Film Culture (New York), no.29, 1963; "Is Film Art?" in *Film Culture* (New York), no.29, 1963; "Len Lye Speaks at the Film Makers Cinematheque" in *Film Culture* (New York), spring 1967; "Len Lye—Composer of Motion", interview by J. Kennedy in *Millimeter* (New York), February 1977; interview by R. Del Tredici in *Cinemanews* (San Francisco), no.2/4, 1979; "Len Lye: Some Unpublished Writings" in *Film Library Quarterly* (New York), 1981.

On LYE:

Book—*Experimental Animation* by Robert Russett and Cecile Starr, New York 1976; articles—"Len Lye Visuals" by Oswell Blakeston in *Architectural Review* (London), July 1932; "Presenting Len Lye" by Alberto Cavalcanti in *Sight and Sound* (London), winter 1947/48; "My Best Films Will Never Be Made" by James Breslin in *The Village Voice* (New York), 28 May 1958; "Forms in Air: Tangibles" in *Time* (New York), 24 August 1959; "Visionary Art of Len Lye" by P. Dandignac in *Craft Horizons* (New York), May 1961; "Timehenge" in *Newsweek* (New York), 22 March 1965; "Artist as Filmmaker" by A. Mancis and W. Van Dyke in *Art in America* (New York), July 1966; "Len Lye's Figures of Motion" by R. Horrocks in *Cantrill's Filmnotes* (Melbourne), November 1979; "Len Lye, 1901-1980" in *Cantrill's Filmnotes* (Melbourne), August 1980; "Len Lye and *Tusalava*" by W. Curnow in *Cantrill's Filmnotes* (Melbourne), February 1979; "The Len Lye Lists" in *Bulletin of New Zealand Art History*, 1980.

*   *   *

Until fairly recent times, it was no exaggeration to state that Len Lye was all that New Zealand had contributed to international cinema. An artist—equally at home with painting or sculpture—Len Lye was the progenitor of experimental cinema, yet, at the same time, he was willing to work within a more mainstream cinema (unlike so many of his successors). Lye's closest present-day equivalent in the cinema would be Norman McLaren, who continues the technique of drawing directly on film which was created by Len Lye in the early thirties.

Len Lye came to London in the twenties and there he made his first attempt at experimental filmmaking with *Tusalava*, which tried to merge elements of European modern art with the primitive art which Lye had experienced in the South Sea Islands. It was not until 1935 that Lye was able to complete another film, and that was his revolutionary *Colour Box*, for which he painted directly on the film. John Grierson's G.P.O. Film Unit sponsored the production, and Grierson hired Lye to work for his organization. Here Lye experimented with the use of color—in this instance Gasparcolor—and with puppet animation, creating the highly praised *The Birth of a Robot*. What is perhaps most extraordinary about Len Lye's work at this time is that he took mundane subjects handed to him by the Unit, which was established to create short propaganda films for the British mail service, and transformed them into surrealistic exercises. Nowhere is this more apparent than in *N. or N.W.*, which warns its audience of the danger in incorrectly addressing envelopes through a series of bizarre close-ups and superimpositions.

During the Second World War, Len Lye's films were more realistic in content, as he worked for the British Ministry of Information. Most were live action, although in *When the Pie Was Opened* he combines live action and animation to present a wartime recipe for vegetable pie. All those films support Cavalcanti's claim that "Len Lye could be described in the history of British cinema by one word—Experiment."

Coming to the United States in 1944, Lye put his experimental filmmaking behind him and settled down to creating live action documentaries, initially for March of Time. He returned briefly to experimental filmmaking in the fifties with *Color Cry*, based on a method of "shadow casting" created by Man Ray, and *Free Radicals* and *Particles in Space*, in both of which the images were scratched on the film. Lye eventually seemed to lose interest in film, becoming more involved in movable and kinetic sculpture. In *The New York Times*, Grace Glueck described him thus, "Bald as an egg, with a pointed goatee, Len Lye was a sprightly man who, despite his fascination with technology, referred to himself as 'an old-brain guy who can't even drive a car.' "

The most important period in Len Lye's filmmaking career was when he worked in Britain for the G.P.O. and the Ministry of Information. As Dave Curtis has written in *Experimental Cinema*, "Len Lye is one of the few significant figures in British cinema between the wars. He is as important to personal (informal) animation as Griffith is to the traditional narrative film."

—Anthony Slide

———————

MACKENDRICK, ALEXANDER. Scottish. Born in Boston, 1912. Educated at School of Art, Glasgow. Career: early 1930s—commercial artist, animator of advertising films; works in Holland with George Pal; 1937—joins script department of Pinewood Studios, London; during WW II—makes short propaganda films for Ministry of Information; then made head of documentary and newsreel dept. of Psychological Warfare Branch, Rome; 1946—joins Ealing Studios as scriptwriter; 1949—first feature, *Whiskey Galore*; 1956—signs contract with Hecht-Lancaster (Harold Hecht, Burt Lancaster) company to make *Sweet Smell of Success* in U.S.; 1969—appointed Dean, Film Dept. of the California Institute of the Arts, Valencia; 1978—resigns deanship, continues to teach at CalArts.

Films (as feature director): 1949—*Whiskey Galore (Tight Little Island)* (+co-sc); 1951—*The Man in the White Suit* (+co-sc); 1952—*Mandy (The Story of Mandy, Crash of Silence)*; 1954—*The Maggie (High and Dry)* (+story); 1955—*The Ladykillers*; 1957—*The Sweet Smell of Success*; 1963—*Sammy Going South (A Boy Ten Feet Tall)*; 1965—*A High Wind in Jamaica*; 1967—*Oh Dad, Poor Dad, Mamma's Hung You in the Closet and I'm Feelin' So Sad* (Quine) (d add'l scenes only); *Don't Make Waves*.

Publications:

By MACKENDRICK:

Article—interview by Bernard Cohn in *Positif* (Paris), February 1968.

On MACKENDRICK:

Articles—"Mackendrick Finds the Sweet Smell of Success" by John Cutts in *Films and Filming* (London), June 1957; "Alexander Mackendrick" in *Films and Filming* (London), January 1963; "Oddities and One-Shots" by Andrew Sarris in *Film Culture* (New York), spring 1963; entire issue of *Dialogue on Film* (Washington, D.C.), no.2, 1972; "'Projecting Britain and the British Character': Ealing Studios" by C. Barr in *Screen* (London), summer 1974; "Focus on Education: The MacKendrick

Legacy" by P. Goldstone in *American Film* (Washington, D.C.), March 1979.

* * *

In 1955 Alexander Mackendrick made *The Ladykillers*, the last of his four Ealing comedies. Two years later, in Hollywood, came his brilliantly acid study of corruption and betrayal, *The Sweet Smell of Success*. At first glance, the gulf is prodigious. Yet on closer examination, it narrows considerably: the apparent contrast between the two films becomes little more than a matter of surface tone. For behind the comedies that Mackendrick made for Ealing can be detected a mordant humor, a pessimism, and even an instinct for cruelty which sets them apart from the gentle sentimentality of their stablemates (Hamer's *Kind Hearts and Coronets* always excepted). The mainstream of Ealing comedy, even including such classics as *Passport to Pimlico* and *The Lavender Hill Mob*, presents (as Charles Barr has pointed out) "a whimsical daydream of how things might be." There is little of that daydream about Mackendrick's films; at times—as in *The Ladykillers*—they edge closer to surrealist nightmare.

In *Whisky Galore* the English outsider, Captain Waggett, is subjected by the islanders to continual humiliation, unalleviated even in their triumph by the slightest friendly gesture. Similarly Marshall, the American tycoon in *The Maggie*, is abused, exploited, and physically assulted by the Scots he encounters. Both workers and bosses, in *The Man in the White Suit*, turn violently upon Sidney Stratton, the idealistic inventor; and *The Ladykillers* culminates in a whole string of brutal murders. Not that this blackness detracts in the least from the effectiveness of the comedy. Rather, it lends the films a biting edge which makes them all the funnier, and may well explain why they have dated far less than most other Ealing movies.

A constant theme of Mackendrick's films is the clash between innocence and experience. Innocence connotes integrity, but also blindness to the interests of others; experience brings shrewdness, but also corruption. Generally, innocence is defeated, but not always: in *The Ladykillers* it is serenely innocent Mrs. Wilberforce who survives—as does Susan Hunsecker in *The Sweet Smell of Success*, albeit at a price. Children feature prominently in Mackendrick's films—*Mandy*, *Sammy Going South*, *The Maggie*—and often embody the principle of innocence, though again not always. In *A High Wind in Jamaica*, against all audience expectations, it is the pirates, not the children they capture, who prove to be the innocents, and who suffer death for it. As so often with Mackendrick's characters, they are doomed by their lack of perception; trapped, like the deaf heroine of *Mandy*, in a private world, they see only what they expect to see.

Mackendrick established a reputation as an exacting and perfectionist director, bringing to his films a visual acuteness and a flair for complex fluid composition to support the tight dramatic structure. After *Sweet Smell of Success*, though the quality of his work is generally considered to have declined, and he has made no films since 1967. A planned project on *Mary Queen of Scots* (intriguingly outlined by Mackendrick as "a sophisticated French lady landed in Boot Hill") never materialised. From 1969 to 1978 he headed an outstanding film department at the California Institute of the Arts; but the withdrawal of such a subtle and individual director from active filmmaking is greatly to be regretted.

—Philip Kemp

MAKAVEJEV, DUSAN. Yugoslavian. Born in Belgrade, 13 October 1932. Educated in psychology at Belgrade University, degree 1955; studied direction at the Academy for Theater, Radio, Film and Television, Belgrade. Married Bojana Marijan in 1964. Career: 1953—makes 1st 16mm short; 1955-58—makes experimental films through Kino-Club; 1958—joins Zagreb Films; 1959-60—military service; 1961—works for Avala Film; 1962—play *New Man of the Flower Market*, written for Belgrade Students' Theater, suppressed; 1968—goes to U.S. on Ford Foundation grant; 1969—offered financing for Wilhelm Reich documentary to be shown on German TV; project develops into *WR*; 1971—*WR* withdrawn from circulation in Yugoslavia due to Soviet pressure.

Films (as director and scriptwriter of shorts and documentaries): 1953—*Jatagan Mala*; 1955—*Pečat (The Seal)*; 1957—*Antonijevo razbijeno ogledalo (Anthony's Broken Mirror)*; 1958—*Spomenicima ne treba verovati (Don't Believe in Monuments)*; *Slikovnica pčelara (Beekeeper's Scrapbook)*; *Prokleti praznik (Damned Holiday)*; *Boje sanjaju (Colors Are Dreaming)*; 1959—*Sto je radnički savjet? (What is a Workers' Council?)*; 1961—*Eci, pec, pec (One Potato, 2 Potato...)*; *Pedagoška bajka (Educational Fairy Tale)*; *Osmjeh 61 (Smile 61)*; 1962—*Parada (Parade)*; *Dole plotovi (Down with the Fences)*; *Ljepotica 62 (Miss Yugoslavia 62)*; *Film o knjizi A.B.C. (Film about the Book)*; 1964—*Nova igračka (New Toy)*; *Nova domaća zivotinja (New Domestic Animal)*; (as director and scriptwriter of feature films): 1966—*Covek nije tica (Man Is Not a Bird)*; 1967—*Ljubavni Slučaj, tragedija sluzbenice PTT (Love Affair, Switchboard Operator, An Affair of the Heart)*; 1968—*Nevinost bez zaštite (Innocence Unprotected)*; 1971—*W.R.: Misterije organizma (W.R.: Mysteries of the Organism)*; 1974—*Sweet Movie* (co-sc); 1981—*Montenegro (Or Pigs and Pearls)* (+sc).

Publications:

By MAKAVEJEV:

Books—*A Kiss for Komradess Slogan*, 1964; *Nevinost bez zaštite* [Innocence Unprotected], Zagreb 1968; *WR: Mysteries of the Organism*, New York 1972; articles—"Fight Power with Spontaneity and Humor: An Interview with Dusan Makavejev" by Robert Sutton and others in *Film Quarterly* (Berkeley), winter 1971/72; interview by R. Colacielo in *Interview* (New York), February 1972; interview by G. Braucourt in *Ecran* (Paris), September/October 1972; interview by A. Cervoni in *Cinéma* (Paris), September/October 1972; "2 cinéastes yougoslaves", interview by A. Tournès in *Jeune Cinéma* (Paris), September/October 1972; interview by Robert Benayoun and Michel Ciment in *Positif* (Paris), June 1974; "Let's Put the Life Back in Political Life", interview by C.B. Thompson in *Cinéaste* (New York), v.6, no.2, 1974; "Dusan Makavejev Interview" by Edgardo Cozarinsky and Carlos Clarens in *Film Comment* (New York), May/June 1975; "Film Censorship in Yugoslavia" in *Film Comment* (New York), July-August 1975; interview by J. Hernandez Les in *Cinema 2002* (Madrid), September 1979.

On MAKAVEJEV:

Book—*Directors and Directions* by John Taylor, New York 1975; articles—"Movers" by Andrew Sarris in *Saturday Review* (New York), 23 December 1967; "Dušan Makavejev" by Robin Wood in *Second Wave*, New York 1970; "3 East European Directors" by P. Crick in *Screen* (London), March/April 1970;

"Makavejev in Montreal" by O. Oppenheim in *Sight and Sound* (London), spring 1970; "Joie de Vivre at the Barricades: The Films of Dušan Makavejev" by David Robinson in *Sight and Sound* (London), autumn 1971; "Makavejev and the Mysteries of the Organism" in *Film* (London), autumn 1971; "Why Did He Do That to Wm. Reich?" by David Bienstock in *The New York Times*, 7 November 1971; "Sex and Politics" by J.R. MacBean in *Film Quarterly* (Berkeley), spring 1972; article in *Film Journal* (Australia), September 1972; article in *Film Quarterly* (Berkeley), spring 1972; article in *Cineaste* (New York), winter 1971-72; "Portrait a Dušan et Bojana" by A. Cervoni in *Cinéma* (Paris), September/October 1972; "Directors of the Year" in *Filmguide 73*, London 1972; "Makavejev: Toward the Edge of the Real ...and Over" by Amos Vogel in *Film Comment* (New York), November/December 1973; "Yugoslavia" edited by Maurice Speed in *Film Review* (New York), 1973-74; "Dušan Makavejev" in *50 Major Filmmakers* edited by Peter Cowie, South Brunswick, New Jersey 1974; "Sweet Movie" in *Avant-Scène du cinéma* (Paris), October 1974; article in *Positif* (Paris), December 1975; "Unbeschützte und verlorene Unschuld, Dusan Makavejevs Spekulationen" by M. Schaub in *Cinema* (Zurich), v.21, no.2, 1975; article in *Velvet Light Trap* (Madison, Wisconsin), fall 1976; "On Makavejev on Bergman" by Stanley Cavell in *Critical Inquiry* (Chicago), no.2, 1979; "The Cinema of the Grotesque" by R. Perlmutter in *Georgia Review* (Athens, Ohio), no.1, 1979.

*   *   *

Before making his first feature film, *Man Is Not a Bird*, Makavejev had developed his filmmaking skills and formulated his chief thematic and formal concerns by producing a number of 35mm experimental shorts and documentaries. His second feature, *Love Affair*, furthered Makavejev's reputation and situated him within a growing community of Eastern European filmmakers committed to exploring the potential of the film medium by opening it up to new subject matter and experimenting with non-conventional narrative forms. *Love Affair* deals with the romance between a Hungarian-born switchboard operator, Isabella, and Ahmed, an Arab sanitation engineer, the breakdown of the relationship, Isabella's death and Ahmed's arrest for her murder. However, this straightforward plot is only the skeleton which supports the rest of the film. Influenced by Eisenstein and Godard, Makavejev builds an elaborate, Brechtian amalgam of documentary-like examinations of rat extermination, interviews with a sexologist and criminologist, actual stock footage of the destruction of church spires during the October Revolution, as well as almost quaint digressions on how mattress stuffing is combed and how strudel is made. Makavejev questions the nature of sexual relationships in a changing, post-revolutionary, but still puritanical society by juxtaposing ostensibly unrelated images. For example, the razing of the church spires is intercut with and comments on Isabella's seduction of Ahmed and the destruction of his archaic sexual inhibitions.

Innocence Unprotected also manifests Makavejev's interest in the dialections of montage, the ability to create new ideas from the juxtaposition of incongruous or contradictory images. In this film, Makavejev rescues a little bit of "unprotected innocence" from oblivion by incorporating the original *Innocence Unprotected*, the first Serbian "all-talking" feature into a new cinematic context. This 1940s romance-adventure—filmed by a well known local strongman-daredevil during the Nazi Occupation, censored by the occupation government, and ironically later denounced as being Nazi-inspired—is intercut with interviews Makavejev con-

ducted with members of the original production crew as well as newsreel footage from the period of the occupation. Moreover, Makavejev hand-tints portions of the original film to contribute to the critical distance created by the archaic quality of the footage. Perhaps more than any of his other films, *Innocence Unprotected* shows Makavejev's loving interest in traditional Yugoslavian folk culture and humor.

WR—Mysteries of the Organism deals with the sexuality of politics and the politics of sexuality. A radical condemnation of both the sterility of Stalinism and the superficial commercialism of Western capitalism, *WR* is certainly a document of its time—of Yugoslavia attempting to follow its "other road" to socialism while America fights in Vietnam and Moscow invades Czechoslovakia. Makavejev looks to Wilhelm Reich (the 'WR' of the title) for enlightenment. Reich was, early in his career, one of the first to recognize the profound interconnections between socio-political structure and the individual psyche. His radical sexual ideas alienated the psychoanalytic profession and his unorthodox medical theories and practices eventually led to his imprisonment in the U.S.

Although elaborate cross-cutting blends the two sections of the film, roughly the first half of *WR* is devoted to a documentary study of Wilhelm Reich's life in the U.S. Interviews with Reich's therapists, Reich's relatives, even people who knew him casually including his barber, are intercut with an examination of American sexual mores circa 1970 via interviews with Jackie Curtis, Barbara Dobson, one of the editors of *Screw* magazine, etc. The second half of the film is primarily a fictional narrative set in Belgrade, which concerns the love affair between a young female admirer of Reich (Milena) and a rather priggish and prudish Soviet ice skater named Vladimir Ilyich. Freed of his inhibitions by Milena's persistence, Vladimir makes love to her and then, unable to deal with his sexuality, decapitates her with his ice skate. However, after death, Milena's severed head continues to speak. Vladimir sings a song with a lyric written by a Soviet citizen critical of his government. *WR* ends with a photo of the smiling Reich—a sign of hope, a contradictory indication of the possibilty for change and new beginnings.

WR was never released in Yugoslavia, and Makavejev made his two most recent films, *Sweet Movie* and *Montenegro* in the U.S. and Europe. Like *WR*, *Sweet Movie* has two parts. In the first a beauty contestant, Miss World, is wedded to and violated by Mr. Kapital and, after other humiliations, ends up in Otto Muehl's radical therapy commune. Miss World is taken in and nurtured by actual commune members who engage in various types of infantile regressions (including carrying their shit displayed on dinner plates) as therapy. The second part of the film is an allegorical commentary on the East. A ship, with a figurehead of Karl Marx, sails about under the command of Anna Planeta, who seduces and murders young men and boys, while providing for their rebirth out of a hold filled with white sugar and corpses.

Montenegro continues this development of allegory in favor of Makavejev's earlier documentary interests. Marilyn, an American-born Swedish housewife, is lured into a world peopled by earthy and sexually active Yugoslavian immigrants, who run a club called Zanzibar as an almost anarchistic communal venture. Like the heroes and heroines of Makajevev's earlier films, Marilyn cannot deal with her newly acquired sexual freedom, and she, like Ahmed, Vladimir Ilyich, and Anna Planeta, kills her lovers. *Montenegro*'s linear plot contrasts sharply with the convoluted narrative structure and elaborate montage techniques characteristic of Makavejev's earlier works.

While being accused of making needlessly ambiguous films with scenes of gratuitous violence and sexuality, Makavejev has consistently explored the interrelationship of sexual life and socioeconomic structure while experimenting with narrative forms that challenge traditional notions of Hollywood filmmaking.

—Gina Marchetti

MALICK, TERRENCE. American. Born in Waco, Texas, 1945. Educated at Harvard University; attended Oxford University on Rhodes Scholarship; Center for Advanced Film Studies, American Film Institute. Career: late 1960s—works for *Newsweek*, *Time*, and *New Yorker* magazines; lecturer in philosophy for a year, Massachusetts Institute of Technology; leaves to study at American Film Institute; directs graduation short *Lanton Mills*. Recipient: Best Director, National Society of Film Critics, for *Days of Heaven*, 1978; Best Director, New York Film Critics, for *Days of Heaven*, 1978; Best Director, Cannes Festival, for *Days of Heaven*, 1979. Agent: Evarts Ziegler, Hollywood, California.

Films (as scriptwriter): 1972—*Pocket Money* (Rosenberg); (as director and scriptwriter): 1973—*Badlands* (+pr); 1978—*Days of Heaven*.

Publications:

By MALICK:

Articles—"The Filming of *Badlands*", interview by G.R. Cook in *Filmmakers Newsletter* (Ward Hill, Mass.), June 1974; interview by Michel Ciment in *Positif* (Paris), June 1975; "Malick on Badlands", interview by B. Walker in *Sight and Sound* (London), spring 1975.

On MALICK:

Articles—"Badlands" by William Johnson in *Film Quarterly* (Berkeley), spring 1974; "Terrence Malick: Days of Heaven's Image Maker" by Chris Hodenfield in *Rolling Stone* (Boulder, Colorado), 16 November 1978; "Dossier: Hollywood 79: Terrence Malick" by P. Maraval in *Cinématographe* (Paris), March 1979; "Sweeping Cannes" in *Time* (New York), 4 June 1979; "Days of High Seriousness" by Arthur Schlesinger in *Saturday Review* (New York), 6 January 1979; "The Last Ray of Light" by Terry Curtis Fox and interview with Nestor Almendros in *Film Comment* (New York), September/October 1978; "The Eyes of Texas" by Richard Combs in *Sight and Sound* (London), spring 1979.

* * *

Though he has directed only two feature films in ten years, Terrence Malick has received the kind of critical attention normally reserved for more experienced and prolific filmmakers. His career reflects a commitment to quality instead of quantity—an unusual and not always profitable gamble in the film industry.

In 1972, Malick wrote the screenplay for *Pocket Money* which starred Paul Newman and Lee Marvin, a film memorable more for character study than story. The following year, Malick made

his first feature, *Badlands*. The film was an amazing debut. Based loosely on the sensational Starkweather-Furgate murder spree, *Badlands* concerns Kit Carruthers, a 25-year old James Dean look-alike, and Holly Sargis, his 15-year-old girlfriend. After murdering Holly's father, they begin a flight across the northeastern United States, killing five others along the way.

This disturbing and beautiful film is narrated by Holly (Sissy Spacek) who unemotionally describes the couple's actions and feelings. Her partner in crime, Kit (Martin Sheen), is a likable, unpredictable, and romantic killer who is so confident of his place in American history as a celebrity that he marks the spot where he is arrested, and gives away his possessions as souvenirs to police officers.

Days of Heaven, Malick's long-awaited second feature was released five years later. The film was critically acclaimed in the United States, and Malick was named best director at the Cannes Film Festival. *Days of Heaven* is a homage to silent films (the director even includes a glimpse of Chaplin's work) with stunning visual images, and little dialogue. Moving very slowly at first, the film's pace gradually accelerates as the tension heightens. Its plot and style elaborate on that of *Badlands*: the flight of two lovers following a murder, and the use of unemotional narration, and off-beat characterizations.

Malick now lives in Paris, and as critics wait for his next endeavor, some wonder how the director will remain profitable to any studio with his lapses between projects, his aversion to interviews, and his refusal to help in the marketing of his films. Paramount, however, is confident of Malick's value, and has been sending the director scripts plus a yearly stipend for the last five years.

—Alexa Foreman

MALLE, LOUIS. French. Born in Thumeries, Nord, France, 30 October 1932. Educated at Collège des Carmes, Avon; University of Paris; Institut des Hautes Études Cinématographiques (IDHEC). Married Anne-Marie Deschodt (divorced 1967); married Candice Bergen, 1980. Career: 1954-55—becomes assistant and cameraman to Jacques Cousteau, co-directs *Le Monde du silence* (1956); 1956—assistant to Robert Bresson on *Un Condamné à mort s'est échappé*; 1957—cameraman on Tati's *Mon Oncle*; 1962-64—reports from Algeria, Vietnam and Thailand for French television; 1968—sells home in Paris, divorces and moves to India, begins shooting *Phantom India*. Recipient: Prix Louis-Delluc for *Ascenseur pour l'échafaud*, 1958; special jury prize, Venice Festival, for *Les Amants*, 1958; special jury prize, Venice Festival, for *Le Feu follet*, 1963; Prix Raoul Lévy and Prix Méliès for *Lacombe, Lucien*, 1974. Business Manager: Gelfand, Rennert & Feldman, New York, 489 Fifth Avenue, New York, NY 10017. Address: c/o N.E.F., 92 av. des Champs-Elysées, 75008 Paris, France.

Films (as co-director and cinematographer): 1956—*Le Monde du silence (The Silent World)*; (as producer, director and scriptwriter): 1958—*Ascenseur pour l'échafaud (Elevator to the Gallows, Frantic)* (co-sc); *Les Amants (The Lovers)* (co-sc); 1960—*Zazie dans le Métro (Zazie)* (co-sc); 1962—*Vie privée (A Very Private Affair)* (co-sc); 1963—*Le Feu follet (The Fire Within, A Time to Live, a Time to Die)* ; 1965—*Viva Maria* (co-sc, co-pr); 1967—*Le Voleur (The Thief of Paris)* (co-sc); 1968—"William Wilson" episode of *Histoires extraordinaires (Spirits of the Dead)*; 1969—*Calcutta*; *L'Inde fantôme (Phan-*

tom India) (6 hour feature presentation of TV documentary);
1971—*Le Souffle au coeur (Murmur of the Heart)*; 1972—
Humain trop humain; 1973—*Lacombe, Lucien* (co-sc); 1975—
Black Moon (co-sc); 1978—*La Petite*; *Pretty Baby* (co-story);
1980—*Atlantic City*; 1981—*My Dinner with Andre*. Role:
1969—Portuguese worker in *La Fiancée du pirate* (Kaplan).

Publications:

By MALLE:

Books—*Lacombe, Lucien*, with Patrick Modiano, New York
1975; *Louis Malle par Louis Malle*, with S. Kant, Paris 1978;
articles—"Avec *Pickpocket*, Bresson a trouvé" in *Arts* (Paris), 3
January 1960; "Les Amants" (text) in *L'Avant-scène du cinéma*
(Paris), 15 March 1961; interview in *Cinéma 62* (Paris), Febru-
ary 1962; "Le Feu follet" (text) in *L'Avant-scène du cinéma*
(Paris), 15 October 1963; "Louis Malle", interview in *Film*
(London), spring 1964; "Dorénavant, je mettrai les points sur les
i" in *Combat* (Paris), 7 January 1964; "Louis Malle: Murmuring
From the Heart", by N. Pasquariello in *Inter/View* (New York),
July 1972; "Phantom India" by E.L. Rodrigues in *Film Heritage*
(New York), fall 1973; interview by G. Braucourt in *Ecran*
(Paris), May 1974; interview by G. Jacob in *Positif* (Paris),
March 1974; interview by D. Lyons in *Interview* (New York),
November 1974; "Louis Malle on Lacombe Lucien" in *Film
Comment* (New York), September/October 1974; "Like Acid",
interview by Gordon Gow in *Films and Filming* (London),
December 1975; interview by Guy Flatley in *The New York
Times*, 19 November 1976; interview by D. Brandes in *Cinema
Papers* (Melbourne), July 1977; "From The Lovers to Pretty
Baby", interview by D. Yakir in *Film Quarterly* (Berkeley),
summer 1978; "Louis Malle's Pretty Baby", interview by D.
Yakir in *Film Comment* (New York), May/June 1978; "Creat-
ing a Reality That Doesn't Exist", interview by A. Horton in
Literature/Film Quarterly (Salisbury, Maryland), no.2, 1979.

On MALLE:

Book—*Louis Malle* by Henri Chapier, Paris 1964; articles—
"Talk with the Director" in *Newsweek* (New York), 27 November
1961; "Louis Malle" by P. Strick in *Film* (London), spring 1963;
"Louis Malle détruit son passé à chaque nouveau film" by Chris-
tian Ledieu in *Arts* (Paris), 9 October 1963; "Louis Malle's
France" by Gordon Gow in *Films and Filming* (London),
August 1964; "Night and Solitude: The Cinema of Louis Malle"
by James Price in *London Magazine*, September 1964; "Louis
Malle" by Russell Lej in the *New Left Review* (New York),
March/April 1965; "Director of the Year" in *International Film
Guide*, London 1965; "Louis Malle, Murmuring of the Heart"
by N. Pasquariello in *Interview* (New York), July 1971; "There's
More to Malle than Sex, Sex, Sex" by C. Grenier in *The New
York Times*, 6 February 1972; "Louis Malle" by D. McVay in
Focus on Film (London), summer 1974; "Black Moon" in
Avant-Scène du cinéma (Paris), December 1975; "Louis Malle"
in *Current Biography 1976*, New York 1976; "Pretty Baby: Love
in Storyville" by A. Chemasi in *American Film* (Washington,
D.C.), November 1977; "The Documentary Films of Louis
Malle" by R.T. Rollet and others, special issue of *Film Library
Quarterly* (New York), v.9, no.4, 1977; article by P. Strick in
Film (London), November 1979; interview by P. Carcassonne
and J. Fieschi in *Cinématographe* (Paris), March/April 1981.

*   *   *

In the scramble for space and fame that became the *nouvelle
vague*, Louis Malle began with more hard experience than
Godard, Truffant, or Chabrol, and showed in *Ascenseur pur
l'échafaud* that his instincts for themes and collaborators were
faultless. Henri Decaë's low-light photography and Malle's use
of Jeanne Moreau established him as emblematic of the new
French cinema. But the *Cahiers* trio with their publicist background made artistic hay while Malle persisted in a more personal voyage of discovery with his lovely star. As the cresting
New Wave battered at the restrictions of conventional narrative
technique, Malle created a personal style, sexual and emotional,
which was to sustain him while flashier colleagues failed. Of the
New Wave survivors, he is the most old-fashioned, the most
erotic, and, arguably, the most widely successful.

Re-viewing reveals *Ascenseur* as clumsy and improbable, a
failure redeemed only by the Moreau and Maurice Ronet performances. A flair for coaxing the unexpected from his stars had
often saved Malle from the consequences of too-reverent respect
for production values, a penchant for burnished low-lit interiors
being his most galling stylistic weakness. But playing Bardot
against type in *Vie privée* as a parody of the harried star, with
Moreau, as one of a pair of comic Western trollops (in *Viva
Maria*) showed the irony that was to make his name.

Thereafter he became a gleeful chronicler of the polymor-
phously perverse. Moreau's hand falling eloquently open on the
sheet in *Les Amants* as she accepts the joy of cunnilingus is
precisely echoed in her genuflection to fellate a yoked George
Hamilton in *Viva Maria*. Incest in *Souffle au coeur*, child prostitution in *Pretty Baby*, and, in particular, the erotic and sado-
masochistic overtones of Nazism in *Lacombe, Lucien* found in
Malle a skillful, committed and sensual celebrant.

The Indian documentaries of 1969 belong more to the literature of the mid-life crisis than to film history. *Black Moon*
likewise explores an arid emotional *couloir*. Malle returned to
his richest sources with the US-based films in the late seventies
and after. *Pretty Baby*, *Atlantic City*, and *My Dinner With
Andre* delight in overturning the stones under which closed
communities seethe in moist darkness. The ostensible source
material of the first, Bellocq's New Orleans brothel photographs,
receives short shrift in favour of the lingering interest in the
pre-pubescent Brooke Shields. *Atlantic City* relishes the delights
of post-climacteric potency, giving Burt Lancaster one of his
richest roles as the fading ex-strong arm man, dubbed "Numb
Nuts" by his derisive colleagues, who seizes a last chance for
sexual passion and effective action as the friend and protector of
Susan Sarandon's ambitious night-club croupier.

My Dinner With Andre focuses with equal originality in the
social eroticism of urban intellectuals. A globe-trotting theatrical
voluptuary reviews his Thespain conquests to the grudging
admiration of his stay-at-home colleague. An account of theatrical high-jinks in a Polish wood with Jerzy Grotowski and friends
becomes in Andre Gregory's fruity re-telling, and with Malle's
lingering attention, something very like an orgy. Again, production values intrude on, even dominate the action; mirrors, table
settings, the intrusive old waiter and even the food itself provide a
rich, decorated background that adds considerably to the sense
of occasion. Malle sends his audiences out of the cinema conscious of having taken part in an event as filling as a five-course
meal.

Given this general richness, it may be by contrast that certain
of his quieter, less vivid works shine. *Zazie dans le Metro*, his
fevered version of Queneau's farce, marked his first break with
the stable pattern of the New Wave, and, compared with Godard's
Une Femme est une femme, shows Malle as the more skillful of
the two at remaking the genre film. The terse *Le Feu follet*, a
vehicle for Maurice Ronet, adapted from E. Scott Fitzgerald's

Babylon Revisited, showed Malle moving towards what had become by then the standard "new" French film, characterized by the work of the so-called "Left Bank" group of Resnais, Varda, Rivette, and Rohmer. But again Malle found in the character a plump, opulent self-regard that turned *Le Feu follet*, despite its black and white cinematography and solemn style, into a celebration of self-pity, Ronet at one point caressing the gun with which he proposes to put an end to his life. Like the relish with which Belmondo's gentleman thief in *Le Voleur* savours the objects he steals, Malle's love of physicality, of weight and color and texture, seems so deeply rooted as to be almost religious. (And Malle did, after all, work as assistant to Bresson on *Un Condamné à mort s'est échappé*.) Sensual and perverse, Malle is an unlikely artist to have sprung from the reconstructed film-buffs of the *nouvelle vague*. It is with his early mentors—Bresson, Cousteau, Tati—that he seems, artistically and spiritually, to belong, rather than with Melville, spiritual hero of the *Cahiers* group. If Traffaut has turned into the René Clair of the new French cinema, Malle may yet become its Max Ophüls.

—John Baxter

MAMOULIAN, ROUBEN. American. Born in Tiflis, Caucasus, Russia, 8 October 1897; became citizen of the United States in 1930. Educated at Lycée Montaigne, Paris; gymnasium in Tiflis; University of Moscow; Vakhtangov Studio Theater, Moscow. Married Azadia Newman in 1945. Career: 1920—travels to London to visit sister, remains in Britain and begins stage directing; 1923—invited to Rochester, New York, by George Eastman, becomes production director of Eastman Theater through 1926; 1927—Broadway directing career begins with production of *Porgy*; 1929—accepts offer to direct for Paramount; 1935—stages original production of *Porgy and Bess*; 1944—casts, prepares shooting script, and shoots some footage for *Laura* before resigning as director; through 1940s—continues active career as director of musicals, especially noted for original productions of *Oklahoma!* (1943) and *Carousel* (1945); 1958—fired by Goldwyn as director of *Porgy and Bess*; 1959-60—prepares and begins shooting *Cleopatra*, resigns; 1966—directs *Shakespeare's Hamlet, A New Version* adapted by himself, University of Kentucky. Recipient: Best Direction, New York Film Critics, for *The Gay Desperado*, 1936; Award of Excellence, Armenian American Bicentennial Celebration 1976. Address: 1112 Schuyler Road, Beverly Hills, California 90210.

Films (as director): 1929—*Applause*; 1931—*City Streets*; 1932—*Dr. Jekyll and Mr. Hyde* (+pr); *Love Me Tonight* (+pr); 1933—*Song of Songs* (+pr); *Queen Christina*; 1934—*We Live Again*; 1935—*Becky Sharp*; 1936—*The Gay Desperado*; 1937—*High, Wide and Handsome*; 1939—*Golden Boy*; 1940—*The Mark of Zorro*; 1941—*Blood and Sand*; 1942—*Rings on Her Fingers*; 1948—*Summer Holiday*; 1957—*Silk Stockings*.

Publications:

By MAMOULIAN:

Books—*Abigail*, New York 1964; *Hamlet Revised and Interpreted*, New York 1965; *Rouben Mamoulian: Style is the Man* edited by James Silke, Washington, D.C. 1971; articles—"Some Problems in the Direction of Color Pictures" in *International Photographer*, July 1935; "Bernhardt versus Duse" in *Theatre Arts* (New York), September 1957; "Painting the Leaves Black: Rouben Mamoulian Interviewed" by David Robinson in *Sight and Sound* (London), summer 1961; interview by Jean Douchet and Bertrand Tavernier in *Positif* (Paris), no.64-65, 1965; in *Interviews with Film Directors* by Andrew Sarris, Indianapolis 1967; interview in *The Celluloid Muse* edited by Charles Higham and Joel Greenberg, London 1969; "Dr. Jekyll and Mr. Hyde", interview by T.R. Atkins in *Film Journal* (New York), January/-March 1973; interview by Wayne Warga in *Action* (Los Angeles), September/October 1974; "Bulletin Board: Mamoulian on Griffith" in *Action* (Los Angeles), September/October 1975.

On MAMOULIAN:

Book—*Rouben Mamoulian* by Tom Milne, London 1969; article—"Rouben Mamoulian: The Start of a Career" by P. Horgan in *Films in Review* (New York), August/September 1973.

* * *

Rouben Mamoulian is certainly one of the finest directors in American film history. While not considered strictly an *auteur* with the unifying theme running through his films, the importance of his movies on an individual basis is significant. Mamoulian did not have a large output, having completed only 16 assignments in his 20-year career in motion pictures, principally because he was also very active in the theater. His most famous stage successes were the highly innovative productions of Richard Rodgers and Oscar Hammerstein II's musicals *Oklahoma!* and *Carousel* in the mid-1940s.

His first film, *Applause*, was a very poignant story of a third-rate vaudevillian played by the popular singer Helen Morgan. The first film to utilize two sound tracks instead of one to produce a better quality sound, *Applause* was also noteworthy for its innovative use of a moving camera.

Mamoulian's third film, *Dr. Jekyll and Mr. Hyde*, is still regarded by most historians as the definitive film version of the Robert Louis Stevenson novella, as well as being one of the best horror films of all time. Yet it would be doing the film a disservice to call it "just" a horror movie. The use of light and shadows, the depth of emotion expressed by the main character, and the evocation of the evil hidden in all men make it a classic. For the time it was a very sensual film. Miriam Hopkins as Ivy Pearson is not just a girl from the lower strata of society as the character was in other versions. In Mamoulian's film she is deliberately sensual. Fredric March, in a truly magnificent performance, is troubled by his desire for Ivy long before he turns into Hyde, which is especially evident in the erotic dream sequence. What Mamoulian was able to do in this film is show the similtaneous existence of good and evil in Jekyll before it erupted into the drug-induced schizophrenic manifestation of Mr. Hyde.

Becky Sharp, although not particularly noteworthy for its dramatic style, is today remembered as being the first film in the three strip Technicolor process. Unusual perhaps for a director more closely associated with the stage than film, Mamoulian tried to learn and perfect virtually all of the techniques of film-making, and he could be accomplished in almost any genre: horror, musical, swashbuckler, or historical drama. Perhaps the only genre at which he was not successful was light comedy. His only real comedy, *Rings on Her Fingers*, was entertaining, but did not live up to the standards which he set in his other films. The three previous films, *Golden Boy*, *The Mark of Zorro*, and *Blood and Sand*, were all very successful films which are still applauded by critics and audiences alike.

Mamoulian's last film, *Silk Stockings*, was a very popular adaption of the musical play derived from *Ninotchka*, with a lively score by Cole Porter. The combination of Cyd Charisse and Fred Astaire in the lead roles was naturally responsible for a great part of the movie's success, and Mamoulian's direction and staging allowed their talents to be shown to their best advantage. *Silk Stockings* has a variety of delightful "speciality" numbers which do not detract from the main action, notably "Stereophonic Sound," besides some charming character roles played by Peter Lorre, Jules Munshin, and George Tobias.

Rouben Mamoulian was one of the most talented, creative filmmakers of all time, and while his films are few, virtually every one is a tribute to his genius.

—Patricia King Hanson

MANKIEWICZ, JOSEPH L. American. Born Joseph Leo Mankiewicz in Wilkes-Barre, Pennsylvania, 11 February 1909. Educated at P.S. 64, New York City; Stuyvesant High School, New York; Columbia University, B.A. 1928. Married Elizabeth Young in 1934 (divorced 1937); child: Eric; married Rosa Stradner in 1939 (died 1958); children: Christopher and Thomas; married Rosemary Matthews in 1962; child: Alexandra. Career: 1928—reporter for *Chicago Tribune*, and stringer for *Variety* in Berlin; 1929—brother Herman Mankiewicz arranges job as junior writer at Paramount; 1933—signed as writer by MGM; 1935—begins producing at MGM; 1943—contract taken over by Twentieth Century-Fox; 1952—directs *La Bohème* for Metropolitan Opera, New York; 1953—forms Figaro Inc., independent production company; 1964—directs *Carol for Another Christmas* for TV. Recipient: Best Director and Best Screenplay Academy Awards for *A Letter to 3 Wives*, 1949; Best Director and Best Screenplay Academy Awards for *All About Eve*, 1950. Address: RFD 1, Box 121, Bedford, New York 10506.

Films (as screenwriter): 1929—*Fast Company* (dialogue); 1930—*Slightly Scarlet* (co-sc); *The Social Lion* (adaptation and dialogue); *Only Saps Work* (dialogue); 1931—*The Gang Buster* (dialogue); *Finn and Hattie* (dialogue); *June Moon* (co-sc); *Skippy* (co-sc); *Newly Rich (Forbidden Adventure)* (co-sc); *Sooky* (co-sc); 1932—*This Reckless Age*; *Sky Bride* (co-sc); *Million Dollar Legs* (co-sc); "Rollo and the Roadhogs" and "The 3 Marines" sketches of *If I Had a Million*; 1933—*Diplomaniacs* (co-sc); *Emergency Call* (co-sc); *Too Much Harmony* (co-sc); *Alice in Wonderland* (co-sc); 1934—*Manhattan Melodrama* (co-sc); *Our Daily Bread* (dialogue); *Forsaking All Others*; 1935—*I Live My Life*; (as producer): 1936—*3 Godfathers*; *Fury* (+co-story, uncredited); *The Gorgeous Hussy*; *Love on the Run*; 1937—*The Bride Wore Red*; *Double Wedding*; 1938—*Mannequin*; *3 Comrades*; *The Shopworn Angel*; *The Shining Hour*; *A Christmas Carol*; 1939—*The Adventures of Huckleberry Finn (Huckleberry Finn)*; 1940—*Strange Cargo*; *The Philadelphia Story*; 1941—*The Wild Man of Borneo*; *The Feminine Touch*; 1942—*Woman of the Year*; *Cairo*; *Reunion in France*; 1944—*The Keys of the Kingdom* (+co-sc); (as director): 1946—*Dragonwyck* (+sc); *Somewhere in the Night* (+co-sc);

1947—*The Late George Apley*; *The Ghost and Mrs. Muir*; 1948—*Escape*; 1949—*A Letter to 3 Wives* (+sc); *House of Strangers* (+co-sc, uncredited); 1950—*No Way Out* (+co-sc); *All About Eve* (+sc); 1951—*People Will Talk* (+sc); 1952—*5 Fingers* (+dialogue, uncredited); 1953—*Julius Caesar* (+sc); 1954—*The Barefoot Contessa* (+sc); 1955—*Guys and Dolls* (+sc); 1958—*The Quiet American* (+sc); 1959—*Suddenly, Last Summer*; 1963—*Cleopatra* (+co-sc); 1967—*The Honey Pot* (+co-p, sc); 1970—*There Was a Crooked Man...* (+pr); 1972—*Sleuth*.

Publications:

By MANKIEWICZ:

Book—*More About ALL ABOUT EVE*, with Gary Carey, New York 1972; articles—"Putting on the Style" in *Films and Filming* (London), January 1960; "Measure for Measure: Interview with Joseph L. Mankiewicz" by Jacques Bontemps and Richard Overstreet in *Cahiers du Cinema in English* (New York), February 1967; interview by Michel Ciment in *Positif* (Paris), September 1973; "Auteur de films! Auteur de films!" in *Positif* (Paris), September 1973; interview by A. Charbonnier and D. Rabourdin in *Cinéma* (Paris), June 1981; television—*Carol for Another Christmas*, 1964.

On MANKIEWICZ:

Books—*Joseph L. Mankiewicz: An Index to His Work* by John Taylor, London 1960; *The Cleopatra Papers: A Private Correspondence* by Jack Brodsky and Nathan Weiss, New York 1963; *Pictures Will Talk* by Kenneth Geist, New York 1978; articles—"All About Joe" by Frank Nugent in *Collier's* (New York), 24 March 1951; "Cleo's Joe" by John Reid in *Films and Filming* (London), August and September 1963; "Cocking a Snook" by Gordon Gow in *Films and Filming* (London), November 1970; "The Films of Joseph Mankiewicz" by John Springer in *Films in Review* (New York), March 1971; "Un Labyrinthe pour tout un royaume" by M. Henry in *Positif* (Paris), September 1973; "More About Joseph L. Mankiewicz" by J. Segond in *Positif* (Paris), September 1973; "Mankiewicz: The Thinking Man's Director" by K. Geist in *American Film* (Washington, D.C.), April 1978; "Dossier-auteur (II): Joseph L. Mankiewicz—le temps et la parole" by A. Charbonnier in *Cinéma* (Paris), July/August 1981.

*   *   *

Few of his contemporaries experimented so radically with narrative form. In *The Barefoot Contessa*, Mankiewicz (who wrote most of the films he directed) let a half-dozen voice-over narrators tell the Contessa's story, included flashbacks within flashbacks, and even showed one event twice (the slapping scene in the restaurant) from two different points of view. Multiple narrators tell the story in *All About Eve*, too, and in the non-narrated framing story for that film, Mankiewicz uses slow motion to make it seem as if the elapsed time between the beginning of the film and the end is only a few seconds. For much of the film, *The Quiet American* also has a narrator, and he seems almost totally omniscient. Apparently, he looks back at events with a firm understanding of their development and of the motivation of the people involved. But in the end, we find out that the narrator was wrong about practically everything, and so gave us an inaccurate account of things. *A Letter to Three Wives* is made up, primarily, of several lengthy flashbacks, and hallucinogenic flashback sequences provide the payoff to the story in Mankiewicz's adaption of the Tennessee Williams play, *Suddenly Last Summer*.

Mankiewicz's films, then, stand out in part because of the way they tell their stories. But there are also thematic motifs that turn up again and again, and one of the most important is the impact of the dead upon the living. Frequently, a dead character is more important in a Mankiewicz film than any living one. *The Late George Apley*, of course, concerns someone who has already died. Understanding a mother's dead son is the key for the psychiatrist in *Suddenly Last Summer*. In *The Ghost and Mrs. Muir*, it is the presence of the non-corporeal sea captain that makes the film so entertaining. *The Barefoot Contessa* opens with the Contessa's funeral, and then various mourners tell us what they know about the woman who has just been buried. And, of course, a famous funeral scene forms the centerpiece of another Mankiewicz film; Mark Antony's oration in *Julius Caesar*.

It is Antony's stirring performance as a eulogist that turns his countrymen against Brutus. Indeed, Mankiewicz's films deals constantly with the notion of effective and highly theatrical performance. *All About Eve*, for instance, is all about performing, since it concerns people who work on the Broadway stage. The barefoot contessa goes from cabaret dancer to Hollywood star. In *The Honey Pot*, an aging man pretends to be dying, to see how it affects his mistress. And in *Sleuth*, one marvels at the number of disguises worn by one man in his attempt to gain revenge on another.

Perhaps because he began as a screenwriter, Mankiewicz has often been thought of as a scenarist first and a director only second. But not only is he an eloquent scriptwriter, he is also an elegant visual stylist whose talents as a director far exceed his reputation. He is one of the few major American directors who was more appreciated during the early years of his career than during the later stages. He won consecutive Best Director Academy Awards in 1949 and 1950 (for *A Letter to Three Wives* and *All About Eve*), but after the 1963 diasaster *Cleopatra*, Mankiewicz's standing as a filmmaker declined rapidly.

—Eric Smoodin

MANN, ANTHONY. American. Born Anton or Emil Bundsmann in Point Loma or San Diego, California, about 1907. Educated in New York City public schools. Married Mildred Kenyon in 1931 (divorced 1956); children: Nina and Anthony; married Sarita Montiel in 1957 (marriage annulled 1963); married Anna (Mann) in 1964. child: Nicholas. Career: 1923—leaves school to work in theater following father's death; late 1920s, early 1930s—Production Manager for Theater Guild, New York; 1933—for Theater Guild directs *The Squall* and *Thunder on the Left*; 1936-38—directs for Federal Theater Project, New York; 1938 or 1939—hired as talent scout by David Selznick, goes to Hollywood, also works as casting director and conducts screen tests; 1939—works as assistant director at Paramount with Preston Sturges and others; 1943—goes to Republic Pictures; 1945—goes to RKO; 1949—signs with MGM; 1960—withdraws from *Spartacus* after quarrelling with Kirk Douglas; quits *Cimarron*, though film retains his name. Died in Germany during shooting of last film, 29 April 1967.

Films (as director): 1942—*Dr. Broadway*; *Moonlight in Havana*; 1943—*Nobody's Darling*; 1944—*My Best Gal*; *Strangers in the Night*; 1945—*The Great Flamarion*; *2 O'Clock Courage*; *Sing Your Way Home*; 1946—*Strange Impersonation*; *The Bamboo Blonde*; 1947—*Desperate*; *Railroaded*; 1948—*T-Men* (+co-sc, uncredited); *Raw Deal*; *He Walked by Night* (co-d, uncredited); 1949—*Reign of Terror (The Black Book)*; *Border Incident*; 1950—*Side Street*; *Devil's Doorway*; *The Furies*; *Winchester '73*; 1951—*The Tall Target*; 1952—*Bend of the River*; 1953—*The Naked Spur*; *Thunder Bay*; 1954—*The Glenn Miller Story*; 1955—*The Far Country*; *Strategic Air Command*; *The Man from Laramie*; *The Last Frontier*; 1956—*Serenade*; 1957—*Men in War*; *The Tin Star*; 1958—*God's Little Acre*; *Man of the West*; 1961—*Cimarron*; *El Cid*; 1964—*The Fall of the Roman Empire*; 1965—*The Heroes of Telemark*; 1968—*A Dandy in Aspic* (co-d).

Publications:

By MANN:

Articles—interview in *Cahiers du cinéma* (Paris), March 1957; "Now You See It: Landscape and Anthony Mann", interview by J.H. Fenwick and Jonathan Green-Armytage in *Sight and Sound* (London), autumn 1965; "A Lesson in Cinema", interview by Jean-Claude Missiaen in *Cahiers du Cinema in English* (New York), December 1967; interview in *Cahiers du cinéma* (Paris), May 1967; interview in *Positif* (Paris), April 1968; "Interview with Anthony Mann" by Christopher Wicking and Barrie Pattison in *Screen* (London), July/October 1969; "Empire Demolition" in *Hollywood Directors 1941-1976* edited by Richard Koszarski, New York 1977; interview by J.-C. Missiaen (from 1967) in *Framework* (Norwich, England), summer 1981.

On MANN:

Books—*Anthony Mann* by Jean-Claude Missiaen, Paris 1964; *Horizons West* by Jim Kitses, Bloomington, Indiana 1970; *Six-guns and Society* by Will Wright, Berkeley, California 1975; *Anthony Mann* by Jeanine Basinger, Boston 1979; articles—"Mann and His Environment" and "Tension at Twilight" by J.H. Reid in *Films and Filming* (London), January and February 1962; "Anthony Mann" by Jean Wagner in *Anthologie du cinéma* vol.4, Paris 1968; "Cote 465" by G. Allombert in *Image et son* (Paris), June/July 1975; "Through the Devil's Doorway: The Early Westerns of Anthony Mann" by Stephen Handzo in *Bright Lights* (Los Angeles), summer 1976; "Mann in the Dark" by Robert Smith in *Bright Lights* (Los Angeles), fall 1976; "Widescreen" by Michael Stern in *Bright Lights* (Los Angeles), fall 1976; "Eagle-Lion: The Violent Years" by Don Miller in *Focus on Film* (London), November 1978; special Mann double issue of *Movietone News* (Seattle), fall 1978; "Anthony Mann—Looking at the Male" by P. Willeman in *Framework* (Norwich, England), summer 1981.

*   *   *

Though he incidentally directed films in various genres (the musical, the war movie, the spy drama), Anthony Mann's career falls into three clearly marked phases: the early period of low-budget, B-feature films noir; the central, most celebrated period of westerns, mostly with James Stewart; and his involvement in the epic (with Samuel Bronston as producer). All three periods produced distinguished work (in particular, *El Cid* has strong claims to be considered the finest of all the 1950s-'60s wide screen historical epics, and the first half of *The Fall of the Roman Empire* matches it) but it is the body of work from the middle period in which Mann's achievement is most consistent and on which his reputation largely depends.

The first of the Stewart westerns, *Winchester 73*, contains most of the major components Mann was to develop in the series that followed. There is the characteristic use of landscape, never for the superficial beauty or mere pictorial effect that is a cliché of the genre, nor to ennoble the human figures through monumental grandeur and harmonious man-in-nature compositions, as in the classical westerns of Ford. In Mann, the function of landscape is primarily dramatic, and nature is felt as inhospitable, indifferent or hostile. If there is a mountain, it will have to be climbed, arduously and painfully; barren rocks provide a favourite location for a shoot-out, offering partial cover but also the continued danger of the ricochet. The preferred narrative structure of the films is the journey, and its stages are often marked by a symbolic progression in landscape, from fertile valley to bare rock or snow-covered peak, corresponding to a stripping-away of the trappings of civilization and civilized behavior: *Bend of the River* represents the most systematic treatment of this prior to *Man of the West*. *Winchester 73* also establishes the Mann hero ("protagonist" might be a better word): neurotic, obsessive, driven, usually motivated by a desire for revenge that reduces him emotionally and morally to a brutalized condition scarcely superior to that of the villian. Hero and villian, indeed, become mirror reflections of one another: in *Winchester 73* they are actually brothers (one has murdered the father, the other seeks revenge); in *Bend of the River*, both are ex-gunfighters, Stewart bearing the mark around his neck of the hangman's noose from which, at the beginning of the film, he saves Arthur Kennedy. Violence in Mann's westerns is never glorified: it is invariably represented as ugly, disturbing and painful (emotionally as much as physically), and this is true as much when it is inflicted by the heroes as by the villians.

Mann's supreme achievement is certainly *Man of the West*, the culmination of the Stewart series despite the fact that the Stewart role is taken over by Gary Cooper: one of the great American films and one of the great films *about* America. It carries to their fullest development all the components I have described, offering a magnificently complete realization of their significance. Cooper plays Link Jones (the "link" between the old West and the new), a reformed outlaw stranded in the wilderness while on a mission to hire a teacher for the first school in the new township of Good Hope, sucked back into involvement with his old gang of "brother," "cousins," and monstrous adoptive father Dock Tobiṇ (Lee J. Cobb), forced into more and more excessive violence, as he destroys his doubles in order finally to detach himself, drained and compromised, from his own roots.

—Robin Wood

MARKER, CHRIS. French. Born Christian François Bouche-Villeneuve in Neuilly sur Seine, 29 July 1921. Career: during war—resistance fighter, then joins American army; before 1950—novelist, poet, and journalist; 1949—writes play *Veillée de l'homme et de sa liberté*; 1967—forms SLON film cooperative (Société pour le Lancement des Ouevres Nouvelles); produces *Far From Vietnam* anthology film; 1973—supplies production

assistance to Patricio Guzmán for *The Battle of Chile*. Recipient: Golden Bear, Berlin Festival, for *Description d'un combat*, 1961; International Critics Prize, Cannes Festival, for *Le Jolie Mai*, 1963.

Films (as director and scriptwriter): 1952—*Olympia 52* (+co-ph); 1953—*Les Statues meurent aussi* (co-d, co-sc); 1956—*Dimanche à Pekin* (+ph); 1957—*Le Mystère de l'atelier* (commentary only, +collaborator on production); 1958—*Lettre de Sibérie (Letter from Siberia)*; 1960—*Description d'un combat*; *Les Astronautes* (co-d); 1961—*Cuba Si!* (+ph); 1963—*Le Jolie Mai*; 1964—*La Jetée* (completed 1962); 1965—*Le Mystère Koumiko (The Koumiko Mystery)*; 1966—*Si j'avais quatre dromadaires*; 1967—*Loin du Viêtnam (Far from Vietnam)* (pr only, +ed); 1968—*La Sixième Face du Pentagone* (collaboration with François Reichenbach); 1969—*A bientôt j'espère*; 1970—*L'Aveu (The Confession)* (Costa-Gavras) (asst ph only); *La Bataille des dix millions (Cuba: Battle of the 10,000,000)*; *Les Mots ont un sens*; 1973—*Le Train en marche*; *Kashima Paradise* (commentary only); 1975-76—*La batalla de Chile (The Battle of Chile)* (Guzmán) (co-pr only); 1976—*La Spirale* (contributor only); 1977—*Le Fond de l'air est rouge* (in 2 parts).

Publications:

By MARKER:

Books—*Le Coeur net*, Lausanne 1950; *Giraudoux par lui-même*, Paris 1952; *Coreennes*, photographs, Paris 1962; *Commentaires*, Paris 1962; articles—"Kashima Paradise", interview by G. Braucourt and Max Tessier in *Ecran* (Paris), November 1974.

On MARKER:

Articles—"'Cuba Si!' Censor No!" by Ian Cameron in *Movie* (London), October 1962; "I Am Writing to You from a Far Country..." by Ian Cameron in *Movie* (London), October 1962; "Cinéma Vérité in France" by Peter Graham in *Film Quarterly* (Berkeley), summer 1964; "Chris Marker and the Mutants" by Gilles Jacob in *Sight and Sound* (London), autumn 1966; "SLON" by Richard Roud in *Sight and Sound* (London), spring 1973; "Si j'avais 4 dromadaires. La Solitude du chanteur de fond" in *Avant-Scène du cinéma* (Paris), March 1975; "Un Programme Chris Marker" by P. Valade in *Jeune Cinéma* (Paris), February 1975; "Le Cinéma militant, en France, aujourd'hui 2" in *Cinéma d'aujourd'hui* (Paris), March/April 1976; "Le Fond de l'air est rouge" by Guy Hennebelle in *Ecran* (Paris), December 1977; "The Left Bank Revisited" by Richard Roud in *Sight and Sound* (London), summer 1977; "Marker and Resnais: Myth and Reality" by S. Gaggi in *Literature/Film Quarterly* (Salisbury, Maryland), no.1, 1979; "Chris Marker: the SLON Films" by W.F. Van Wert in *Film Quarterly* (Berkeley), no.3, 1979.

MARKOPOULOS, GREGORY. American. Born in Toledo, Ohio, 12 March 1928. Educated at University of Southern California. Career: 1948—completes first experimental films; 1954-55—in Greece, lectures on film at University of Athens; ; 1955-60—works on *Serenity*; continues to write extensively on experimental film.

Films: 1947—*Du sang de la volupté et de la mort* (trilogy comprising *Psyche*, *Lysis*, and *Charmides*); 1948—*The Dead Ones*; 1949—*Flowers of Asphalt*; 1950—*Swain*; 1951—*Arbres aux champignons*; 1953—*Eldora*; 1955-61—*Serenity*; 1963—*Twice a Man*; 1965—*The Death of Hemingway*; 1966—*Galaxie*; *Through a Lens Brightly: Mark Turbyfill*; *Ming Green*; 1967—*Himself as Herself*; *Eros, O Basileus*; *The Iliac Passion*; *Bliss*; *The Divine Damnation*; *Gammelion*; 1968—*Mysteries*; 1969—*Index Hans Richter*; 1970—*Genius*; 1971—*Doldertal 7*; *Hagiographia*; *35 Boulevard General Koenig*.

Publications:

By MARKOPOULOS:

Books—*Quest for Serenity*, New York 1965; *A Bibliography Containing the Marvelous Distortions of My Films as Reviewed in Books, Programs, Periodicals and Newspapers during 33 Years: 1945-1978*, St. Moritz 1978; articles—"On 'Serenity'" in *Film Culture* (New York), summer 1961; "Toward a New Narrative Form in Motion Pictures" in *Film Comment* (New York), fall 1963; interview by Robert Brown in *Film Culture* (New York), spring 1964; "Random Notes During a 2-Week Lecture Tour of the United States" in *Film Culture* (New York), fall 1964; "From 'Fanshawe' to 'Swain'" in *Film Culture* (New York), summer 1966; "The Driving Rhythm" in *Film Culture* (New York), spring 1966; "'Galaxie' (Production and Critical Notes)" in *Film Culture* (New York), fall 1966; interview by Jonas Mekas in *The Village Voice* (New York), 14 April 1966; "The Film-Maker as Physician of the Future" in *Film Culture* (New York), spring 1967; "Correspondences of Smells and Visuals" in *Film Culture* (New York), autumn 1967; "Gregory Markopoulos: Free Association—Rough Transcription for Paper on Levels of Creative Consciousness", interview by David Brooks in *Film Culture* (New York), summer 1967; interview by Jonas Mekas in *The Village Voice* (New York), 2 February 1967; "The Redeeming of the Contrary" in *Film Culture* (New York), spring 1971; "Index to the Work of Gregory Markopoulos, Years 1967-70" by Jonas Mekas in *Film Culture* (New York), spring 1971; letter in *Filmmakers Newsletter* (Ward Hill, Mass.), January 1972; "The Adamantine Bridge" in *Film Culture* (New York), spring 1972; "In altre parole è la sua lingua" in *Filmcritica* (Rome), February 1972; "The Theory Is the Work: 2 Gesprächen mit Gregory J. Markopoulos" by Thomas Brandelmeier in *Film und Ton* (Munich), February 1974; "L'usura dello spirito creativo e la conscienza individuale" in *Filmcritica* (Rome), July 1976.

On MARKOPOULOS:

Book—*Visionary Film: The American Avant-Garde 1943-1978* by P. Adams Sitney, New York 1979; articles—"Harrington, Markopoulos, and Boultenhouse: 2 Down and 1 to Go?" by Parker Tyler in *Film Culture* (New York), summer 1960; *Filmwise 3 & 4: Gregory Markopoulos*, spring 1963; "Markopoulos: cinema come oggettivazione del pensiero 'sublime'" by R. Milani in *Filmcritica* (Rome), January/February 1975; "Portrait of the Young Man as Artist: From the Notebook of Robert Beavers" by K. Kelman in *Film Culture* (New York), no.67/69, 1979.

Gregory J. Markopoulos made his first film (a version of *A Christmas Carol*) in 1940 with a borrowed 8mm silent movie camera. By the time he left the University of Southern California in 1947, he completed a trilogy titled *Du sang de la volupté et de la mort* (comprising *Psyche*, *Lysis*, and *Charmides*). His first 35mm film was *The Dead Ones* in 1948. With these beginnings, Markopoulos became one of the best-known avant-gardists of the post-World War II period, although his output in the 1950s was limited to four films—*Flowers of Asphalt*, *Arbres aux champignons*, *Eldora*, and *Serenity*.

Elements of homoeroticism pervade many of the Markopoulos experiments and they are as audacious and outrageous as the works of Adolfas and Jonas Mekas. In his trilogy, a battering ram becomes a phallic symbol. When the film was shown to a class at New York University in 1951, it caused Henry Hart, than the far-right editor of *Films in Review* magazine, to berate professor George Amberg for allowing it to be shown. Hart described some of the images included in the films—"a male nipple, a painted and coiffeured male head, a buttock...and quite a few suggestions that abnormal perceptions and moods are desirable." Markopoulos soon became a much talked-about and controversial filmmaker.

The first Markopoulos film of the sixties was *Serenity*, a dramatic film about the Greco-Turkish War of 1921-22, shot in Greece and released in 1962. This was followed by *Twice a Man*, a recreation of the Greek myths of Hippolytus, Phaedra and Ascleoius dealing openly for the first time (for Markopoulos) with male homosexuality.

Galaxie consisted of 30 three-minute 16mm silent clips of his friends (Parker Tyler, Jonas Mekas, W.H. Auden, Allen Ginsberg, Shirly Clarke, Maurice Sendak, Susan Sontag, and Gian Carlo Menotti, among others) with an electronic "clang" ending each segment as the only sound on the film. Markopoulos's subsequent films are in 16mm.

Single-frame editing and superimpositions were used in *Himself as Herself*, a strange film about a half man/half woman shot in and around Boston and released in 1967. In March of that year, *Eros, O Basileus* appeared, consisting of nine sequences involving a young man representing Eros. The *Markopoulos Passion*, a dramatic movie filmed over a three-year period, was finally released in 1968 as *The Iliac Passion*, a version of the Prometheus legend set in New York City.

Until 1981, he resided in St. Moritz, and there published a 1978 folio entitled *A Bibliography Containing the Marvelous Distortions of My Films as Reviewed in Books, Programs, Periodicals and Newspapers during Thirty-Three Years: 1945-1978*. He has been a leader in the avant-garde film movemnet for nearly 40 years.

—James L. Limbacher

MAURO, HUMBERTO. Brazilian. Born in Volta Grande, Minas Gerais, 30 April 1897. Educated in engineering. Career: 1925—begins filmmaking at Cataguases, small town near birthplace; participates in founding of production company Sul América Filme (later Brasil Filme S.A.); 1927—receives top prize of Rio de Janeiro film publication *Cineaste* for *Thesouro perdido*; 1930—*Cineaste* publisher Adhemar Gonzaga hires Mauro to direct company's first production in Rio, *Labios sem beijos*; 1937—begins making short fiction films and documentaries for Instituto Nacional de Cinema Educativo (INCE); 1960s—acclaimed by Cinema Novo figures as forefather of Brazilian national cinema.

*   *   *

Films (as director and scriptwriter of feature films): 1925—
Valadão, o cratera (Valadao the Disaster) (+ph); 1926—*Na primavera da vida (In the Springtime of Life)*; 1927—*Thesouro perdido (Tesouro perdido, Lost Treasure)*; 1928—*Brasa dormida (Sleeping Ember, Extinguished Cinders)*; 1929—*Sangue Mineiro (Minas Blood, Blood of Minas)*; 1930—*Labios sem beijos (Lips without Kisses)* (d only); 1932—*Ganga bruta (Rough Diamond)*; 1934—*Favela dos meus amores (Favela of My Loves)*; *Cidade mulher* (d only); 1937—*O descobrimento do Brasil*; 1940—*Argila (Clay)* (d only); 1944—*O segredo das Asas* (medium-length) (+pr); 1952—*O canto da saudade (The Song of Sadness)* (+pr).

Short films directed for Instituto Nacional de Cinema Educativo (partial list of 230) beginning 1937: 1939—*Um apólogo*; 1940—*Bandeirantes*; 1942—*O despertar da redentora*; 1945-56—"Brasilianas" series (includes *Manhã na Roça* and *Engenhos e usinas*); 1956—*Meus oito anos*; 1964—*A velha a Fiar*.

Publications:

On MAURO:

Articles—"Humberto Mauro" by Carlos Vieira in *Celuloide* (Rio Maior, Portugal), 1966; article in *Filme Cultura* (Rio de Janeiro), October/November 1967.

*   *   *

One of the greatest of all Latin American filmmakers, Humberto Mauro was a fascinating, deeply original talent whose best work exhibited a lyrical integration of characters and envionment reminiscent of Dovzhenko. Trained as an engineer, Mauro was living in the small city of Cataguazes—a city in the state of Minas Gerais, north of Rio, which produced an impressive number of important writers and artists in that era—when friends encouraged him to make a short documentary, *Valadão, O cratera*, in 1925. After another amateur experience, on the fiction feature *In the Springtime of Life*, Mauro attempted his first professional production with *Lost Treasure*, an exciting adventure story clearly influenced by the American westerns Mauro would continue to love all his life. *Lost Treasure* received some small circulation around Brazil, and in 1927 was awarded *Conearte* magazine's "Best Brazilian Film of the Year," the first such award ever given. His next film, *Sleeping Ember*, also made in Cataguazes, was one of his very finest; here Mauro demonstrated his extraordinary talent for eliciting sensitive, nuanced performances from non-professional actors, a feature of many of his best works.

Lost Treasure and *Sleeping Ember* brought Mauro to the attention of Adhemar Gonzaga and Carmen Santos, two film enthusiasts who had plans to found a professional film studio in Rio. In 1930, Mauro moved to Rio, where he became the principal director at Gonzaga's fledgling Cinedia Studios in the early thirties. Curiously, he continued to make silent films, even though the first Brazilian talkie, Luiz de Barro's *The End of the Hicks*, premiered in 1929. Mauro's final silent feature, *Rough Diamond*—released with a musical soundtrack—is unquestionably his masterpiece. After murdering his wife on their honeymoon night—he had discovered that she wasn't a virgin—a man attempts to piece together again his life and his relations with women. Some of the film's blatantly Freudian symbolism seems too contrived, and the plot's resolution isn't totally satisfying, but these shortcomings are more than made up for by the film's many exquisite passages.

After a few more studio films, notably the now-lost *Favela of My Loves*, Mauro began working as filmmaker-in-residence for the National Institute of Educational Cinema, a newly-founded branch of the Ministry of Education. For the next 30 years, Mauro would continue to work for this agency, producing well over 100 documentaries on a variety of subjects. During this period, he occasionally did return to work on features—*Clay*, with Carmen Santos, in 1940, and the tender pastoral romance, *The Song of Sadness*, in 1952.

Unlike other "naive geniuses" which with Brazilian cinema produced—Mario Peixoto—Mauro was happily able to cope with the seemingly insurmountable difficulties of working in a film industry as beleaguered as that of Brazil. Mauro's greatest strength lay in his sensitivity for the people and places of his native state of Minas Gerais; curiously, by concentrating on mostly regional ways of life and themes, Mauro created the single body of film work of any universal significance before the explosion of Cinema Novo in the early sixties. That generation of filmmakers—Glauber Rocha, Nelson Pereira dos Santos, Joaquim Pedro—lionized Mauro, and saw him as the spiritual grandfather of their movement to create a truely Brazilian cinema.

—Richard Peña

MAYSLES, ALBERT AND DAVID. American. Albert born in Brookline, Massachusetts, 26 November 1926; David born in Brookline, 10 January 1932. Albert educated Brookline High School; Syracuse University, New York, degree in psychology; Boston University, M.A. in psychology. David educated Brookline High School; Boston University, degree in psychology. Career: during WW II—Albert serves in Army Tank Corps; later David serves in the Army at Headquarters, Military Intelligence School, Oberammergau, Germany; after WW II—Albert teaches psychology at Boston University, travels in 1955 to Russia to make 1st film; 1956—David works as assistant to producer on *Bus Stop* and *The Prince and the Showgirl*; 1957—they make 1st film together, *Youth in Poland*, about the aftermath of Polish student revolution; late 50's-early 60's—David works as reporter on the *Adventures on the New Frontier* TV series; 1960—Albert serves as cameraman on Richard Leacock's *Primary* and *Yanqui No*; 1962—together form production company and release film *Showman* the following year; 1965—Albert works as cameraman on one section of 4-part film *Paris vu par (6 in Paris)* for Godard; the brothers receive Guggenheim Fellowship in experimental film; 1969—Albert serves as cameraman on Leacock's *Monterey Pop*; both team with Charlotte Zwerin to make *Salesman* which gains much critical attention, and on *Gimme Shelter*; 1970-82—the brothers continue to work together on full-length documentaries as well as on industrial and corporate promotional films.

Films: 1955—*Psychiatry in Russia* (Albert only); 1957—*Youth in Poland*; 1962—*Showman*; 1964—*What's Happening: The Beatles in the USA*; 1965—*Meet Marlon Brando*; 1966—*With Love From Truman*; 1969—*Salesman* (co-d); 1970—*Gimme Shelter* (co-d); 1972—*Christo's Valley Curtain* (co-d); 1975—*Grey Gardens* (co-d); 1977—*Running Fence*.

Publications:

By the MAYSLES:

Articles—interview in *Movie* (London), April 1963; "An Interview: Albert and David Maysles" by Bob Sitton in *Film Library Quarterly* (New York), summer 1969; interview by R.P. Kolker in *Sight and Sound* (London), autumn 1971; "*Gimme Shelter*: Production Notes" in *Filmmakers Newsletter* (Ward Hill, Mass.), December 1971; "Albert and David Maysles" in *Documentary Explorations* edited by G. Roy Levin, Garden City, New York 1971; "Financing the Independent Non-fiction Film", interview in *Millimeter* (New York), June 1978; "'Truthful Witness': An Interview with Albert Maysles" by H. Naficy in *Quarterly Review of Film Studies* (Pleasantville, N.Y.), spring 1981.

On the MAYSLES:

Book—*Cinema Verite* by M. Ali Issari, Ann Arbor, Michigan 1971; articles—"Focus on Al Maysles" by C. Reynolds in *Popular Photography* (Boulder, Colorado), May 1964; "The Maysles Brothers and Direct Cinema" by Maxine Heleff in *Film Comment* (New York), no.2, 1964; "Thoughts on Cinéma Vérité and a Discussion with the Maysles Brothers" by James Blue in *Film Comment* (New York), no.4, 1964; "Survey Among Unsuccessful Applicants for the Ford Foundation Film Grants" in *Film Comment* (New York), summer 1964; "Beatlemania and Cinema Verite" by Gary Carey in the *7th Art* (New York), summer 1964; "Maysles Brothers" in *Film Culture* (New York), fall 1966; "*Meet Marlon Brando*" by Robert Steele in *Film Heritage* (Dayton, Ohio), fall 1966; "The Amazing Maysles Exhibit *The Salesman*" in *Making Films* (New York), April 1969; "*Salesman*" in *The New Documentary in Action: A Casebook in Film Making* by Alan Rosenthal, Berkeley, California 1971; "*Gimme Shelter*: A Corkscrew or a Cathedral?" by David Sadkin in *Film News* (New York), December 1971; "Shooting Hidden Camera/-Real People Spots" by A.M. Safier in *Millimeter* (New York), April 1979.

*   *   *

Shooting unobtrusively in sync sound with no instructions to the subject, the Maysles brothers make films in what they prefer to call "direct cinema." Albert, gifted photographer and director of all their projects, carries the lightweight, silent camera that he perfected on his shoulder, its accessories built in and ready for adjustment. Mayles characters, who occasionally talk to the filmmakers on screen, seem astonishingly unaware that strangers and apparatus are in the room. They may not even know when the camera is on or off because Albert can operate it without apparent movement.

David, the soundman, carries a strong directional mike and a Nagra unattached to the camera. He is often involved in the editing and as producer has final say. During the shooting a story may become apparent to the director/cameraman, or a dominant character may surface. These elements may also become clear only as the editors examine and cut the vast amounts of footage to be structured that they receive in the dailies.

In 1962, after Albert's brief experience in documentary filmmaking and David's in Hollywood feature films, they formed a partnership committed to direct cinema. Commercials and industrial filmmaking have supported their preferred activity from time to time.

The company's production of two feature documentaries, dis-tributed by them commercially, *Salesman*, a study of four bible salesmen, and *Grey Gardens*, an essay on two eccentric women, fed the constantly boiling discussions between documentarists and critics about whether objectivity is at all possible in documentaries. Both films were charged with a dishonesty, exploitation, tastelessness, but from other quarters received praise for the Maysles' sensitivity, rapport with their subjects, and choice of situations that viewers could identify with.

The Maysles have answered the criticism and described their philosophy and working methods at screening of their films, in articles and in letters to editors. Their instinct takes them, they say, to situations related to closeness between human beings, an instinct arising sometimes from feelings that people they become interested in portraying remind them of their parents with whom they were very close, or of themes in their own lives. They have mentioned that they cannot do films about people they dislike. They look on their work as discovery of how people really are, first spending time with them to get acquainted, then filming their lives as lived. All their subjects agree to the project beforehand, and several have spoken of their satisfaction with the finished film and their good relationship with Albert and David whom they trust.

The Maysles do not deny that their choices affect their creation in some way; much footage, for example must be discarded. They emphasize that nothing is staged and that structure eventually emerges from the material. In their own work they see a relationship to Truman Capote's concepts and methods for his "nonfiction novel": no preconceptions about the subjects, concentration on learning about them and understanding their motivations and feelings. It is difficult to get spontaneous activity and words on film, but the Maysles keep working at it.

Albert and David Maysles have an important place in the history of the documentary for many reasons. They have produced a large, varied, evocative body of work in their chosen style, as very active members of their own small company. Despite some severe criticism of their work, they are admired, and probably envied for qualities that Americans value. They are devoted to family, tenacious in experimenting and researching, stubbornly committed to direct cinema; they show what's happening to recognizable people in America.

Directly influential or not on documentaries today, their work is certainly part of the flow of films that aim to show the truth about contemporary problems. While many other filmmakers' reports and studies embrace large communities, or even whole countries, Maysles productions are about individuals and their concerns which often illuminate larger aspects of society as well as its general attitudes toward non-traditional behavior.

—Lillian Schiff

MAZURSKY, PAUL. American. Born Irwin Mazursky in Brooklyn, New York, 25 April 1930. Educated Brooklyn College, degree 1951; studied acting with Paul Mann, Curt Conway, and Lee Strasberg. Married Betsy Purdy in 1953; children: Meg and Jill. Career: 1951—film acting debut in *Fear and Desire* (Kubrick); 1954-60—works as night club comedian; acts and directs off-Broadway; 1959—moves to Los Angeles to join, with Larry Tucker, the west coast extension of Second City; 1963-67—works as writer on *Danny Kaye Show* with Tucker; 1965—co-creates TV program *The Monkees*; 1968—co-scripts film *I Love You Alice B. Toklas*; 1969—co-scripts and directs 1st film *Bob & Carol & Ted & Alice*; 1971—writes 1st film alone *Blume* *in Love.* Agent: International Creative Management, 8899 Beverly Boulevard, Los Angeles, California 90048.

Films (as director and scriptwriter): 1969—*Bob & Carol & Ted & Alice* (co-sc); 1970—*Alex in Wonderland* (co-sc, +ro as *Hal Stern*); 1973—*Blume in Love* (+pr, ro as *Hellman*); 1974—*Harry and Tonto* (co-sc +pr); 1976—*Next Stop, Greenwich Village* (+co-pr); 1978—*An Unmarried Woman* (+co-pr, ro as *Hal*); 1980—*Willie and Phil*; 1982—*The Tempest.*

Roles: 1951—*Fear and Desire* (Kubrick); 1955—*Emmanuel Stoken* in *Blackboard Jungle* (Brooks); 1966—*A petty thief* in *Deathwatch* (Morrow); 1976—*John Norman's manager* in *A Star is Born* (Pierson).

Publications:

By MAZURSKY:

Articles—"What Directors Are Saying" in *Action* (Los Angeles), November/December 1970; "Paul Mazursky Seminar" in *Dialogue on Film* (Washington, D.C.), November 1974; "Paul Mazursky: The 4-year 'Overnight' Success of 'Harry and Tonto'", interview by N. Pasquariello in *Millimeter* (New York), v.3, no.5, 1975; interview by Guy Flatley in *The New York Times*, 1 October 1976; "Next Stop: Greenwich Village", interview by Max Tessier in *Ecran* (Paris), July 1976; "Paul Mazursky and Willie and Phil", interview and article by James Monaco in *American Film* (Washington, D.C.), July/August 1980.

On MAZURSKY:

Articles—"Paul Mazursky in Wonderland" by J. Greenfield in *Life* (New York), 4 September 1970; article on *Bob & Carol & Ted & Alice* by John Burgess in *Film Society Review* (New York), May 1970; article in *Life* (New York), 4 September 1970; article in *The New York Times*, 26 July 1970; "Portrait of the Artisan" by J. Cocks in *Time* (New York), 18 January 1971; "Paul Mazursky: The Horace with the Heart of Gold" by Richard Corliss in *Film Comment* (New York), March/April 1975; "Paul Mazursky" in *Hollywood Renaissance* by Diane Jacobs, New York 1977; "Experience and Expression", interview by R. Appelbaum in *Films and Filming* (London), August 1978; "A propos d'Une Femme libre", interview by H. Béhar in *Image et son* (Paris), June 1978; interview by Terry Fox in *Film Comment* (New York), March/April 1978; interview by Cecile Starr in *Filmmakers Newsletter* (Ward Hill, Mass.), April 1978; "Dossier: Hollywood 79: Paul Mazursky" by J. Fieschi in *Cinématographe* (Paris), March 1979; "Paul Mazursky" in *Current Biography Yearbook*, New York 1980; "Directors Series: Paul Mazursky" by P. Mascuch in *Films in Review* (New York), November 1980.

*   *   *

Paul Mazursky makes movies about people. Modern ones, complex ones, with modern problems. People who lose their partners (a constant Mazursky theme), or dream, or grow old. People who, as their institutions break down around them, are perplexed, courageous, victimized, and, finally, human. This comes to seem quite unusual in the era dominated by cinematic earthquakes, exorcists, star wars, star treks, and raiders of lost arks.

Mazursky's characters are undeniably, uniquely American. Bob and Carol and Ted and Alice are adults confronted by encounter group chic and the new sexuality—a first in major Hollywood feature. Pot smoking, wife swapping, extramartial affairs, and Esalen come to quite, conservative suburbia, as Bob and Carol experience "liberation" at a sensivity institute and preach their new consciousness to skeptical Ted and Alice.

Alex is a filmmaker in his own reality and wonderland who, like Mazursky, contemplates what his next project should be after his first hit. (Every truly American director should make at least one film about Hollywood.) Divorce lawyer Blume is hopelessly in love with his wife, who had left him because of an indiscretion with his secretary. Harry, an old man, journeys across the country with his cat, Tonto: *Harry and Tonto* is his transitional film, in that all his earlier efforts are set in California while his most recent ones are set in New York. Larry Lapinsky, like Mazursky a nice Jewish boy from Brooklyn, abandons that very special provincial borough and subways to his next but most assuredly not last stop, Greenwich Village. An unmarried woman adjusts to the sudden, awkward feeling of being unmarried. Willie and Phil, idealists both. love and lose the same woman like the characters in their favorite film, *Jules and Jim.* And Mazursky's *Tempest* is loosely updated from Shakespeare: a New York architect, in mid-life crisis, escapes America to a remote Greek isle.

Mazursky's characters may be young or elderly, male or female, New Yorkers or Californians. But they are, like the filmmaker, all white and middle-class. Mazursky may not be a great storyteller; he presents his characters, who cope with whatever befalls them until the final credits. However, he is a master craftsman, a wizard at making a point in a seemingly throwaway scene. In *Willie and Phil*, a quick sequence depicts the characters' affairs with pretty but mindless models: Mazursky establishes that his protagonists are seeking relationships that are not casual, that are deeper and more meaningful than instant orgasm. They already know what Bob, Carol, Ted and Alice learn.

Some of Mazursky's films – *An Unmarried Woman* is the best example – work better than others: *Alex in Wonderland* and *Tempest,* despite some wonderful sequences, are ultimately self-indulgent and even ridiculous. But, from *Bob & Carol & Ted & Alice* to *Tempest*, Mazursky has remained consistently moral. This is a very impressive achievement, in an era when so many filmmakers exploit both their characters and audience.

Paul Mazursky is the Preston Sturges of his generation. While attempting to comment on a rapidly changing society, he has perceptively documented on celluloid the manner in which Americans relate, feel, live.

—Rob Edelman

———————

MCCAREY, LEO. American. Born in Los Angeles, 3 October 1898. Educated at Los Angeles High School; University of Southern California Law School. Married Stella Martin in 1920; child: Mary. Career: 1916-17—pursues unsuccessful law career in San Francisco and Los Angeles; 1918—becomes 3rd assistant to Tod Browning at Universal; 1919—script supervisor, Universal; 1923-28—supervises and directs about 300 comedy shorts at Hal Roach studios; 1923-24—gagman for Our Gang series; 1927—teams Stan Laurel and Oliver Hardy; 1930—signs with Fox Studios; 1933—signs with Paramount; 1946—with Bing Crosby and others forms Rainbow Productions. Died 5 July 1969. Recipient: Best Direction Academy Award for *The*

Awful Truth, 1937; Best Direction and Best Original Story Academy Awards for *Going My Way*, 1944.

Films (as director and producer): *Society Secrets*; (as director and co-scriptwriter): 1924—*Publicity Pays*; *Young Oldfield*; *Stolen Goods*; *Jeffries Jr.*; *Why Husbands Go Mad*; *A 10 Minutes Egg*; *Seeing Nellie Home*; *Sweet Daddy*; *Why Men Work*; *Outdoor Pajamas*; *Sittin' Pretty*; *Too Many Mamas*; *Bungalow Boobs*; *Accidental Accidents*; *All Wet*; *The Poor Fish*; *The Royal Razz*; 1925—*Hello Baby*; *Fighting Fluid*; *The Family Entrance*; *Plain and Fancy Girls*; *Should Husbands Be Watched?*; *Hard Boiled*; *Is Marriage the Bunk?*; *Bad Boy*; *Big Red Riding Hood*; *Looking For Sally*; *What Price Goofy?*; *Isn't Life Terrible*; *Innocent Husbands*; *No Father to Guide Him*; *The Caretaker's Daughter*; *The Uneasy 3*; *His Wooden Wedding*; 1926—*Charley My Boy*; *Mama Behave*; *Dog Shy*; *Mum's the Word*; *Long Live the King*; *Mighty Like a Moose*; *Crazy Like a Fox*; *Bromo and Juliet*; *Tell 'em Nothing*; *Be Your Age*; 1927—*2nd Hundred Years* (story only); 1928—*We Faw Down (We Slip Up)* (d only); *Should Married Men Go Home?* (co-sc, +supervisor); *2 Tars* (story, +supervisor); *Should Women Drive?*; *A Pair of Tights*; *Blow By Blow*; *The Boy Friend*; *Came the Dawn*; *Do Gentlemen Snore?*; *Dumb Daddies*; *Going Ga-ga*; *Pass the Gravy*; *Tell It to the Judge*; *That Night*; 1929—*Liberty*; *Wrong Again*; *Dad's Day*; *Freed 'em and Weep*; *Hurdy Gurdy*; *Madame Q*; *Sky Boy*; *The Unkissed Man*; *When Money Comes*; *Why is Plumber*; (as feature director): 1929—*The Sophomore* (+co-sc); *Red Hot Rhythm* (+co-sc); 1930—*Wild Company*; *Part Time Wife* (+co-sc); 1931—*Indiscreet*; 1932—*The Kid from Spain*; 1933—*Duck Soup*; 1934—*6 of a Kind*; *Belle of the '90s (It Ain't No Sin)*; *Ruggles of Red Gap*; 1935—*The Milky Way*; 1937—*Make Way for Tomorrow (The Years Are So Long, When the Wind Blows)* (+pr); *The Awful Truth*; 1938—*The Cowboy and the Lady* (co-story only); *Love Affair*; 1940—*My Favorite Wife* (+co-sc); 1942—*Once Upon a Honeymoon* (+pr); 1944—*Going My Way* (+pr, story); 1945—*The Bells of Saint Mary's* (+pr, story); 1948—*Good Sam* (+pr, co-story); 1952—*My Son John* (+pr, story, co-sc); 1957—*An Affair to Remember* (+co-sc); 1958—*Rally 'round the Flag, Boys!* (+pr, co-sc); 1961—*Satan Never Sleeps (China Story)* (+pr, co-sc).

Publications:

By MCCAREY:

Articles—"What Makes a Box Office Hit?" in *Cinema* (Hollywood), June 1947; "Leo et les alias", interview by Serge Daney and Jean-Louis Noames in *Cahiers du Cinéma* (Paris), February 1965.

On MCCAREY:

Books—"Leo McCarey" by Jacques Lourcelles in *Anthologie du cinéma* vol.7, Paris 1973; *Leo McCarey and the Comic Anti-Hero in American Film* by Wes Gehring, New York 1980; articles—"Everything Happens to McCarey" by Sidney Carroll in *Esquire* (New York), May 1943; "Almost Everything Went His Way" by Alyce Canfield in *Liberty* (New York), 26 May 1946; "Going His Way" by Pete Martin in the *Saturday Evening Post* (Philadelphia), 30 November 1946; "L'Art et la manière de Leo McCarey" by Jean-Louis Noames in *Cahiers du cinéma* (Paris), February 1965; "Remembering Leo McCarey" by David Butler in *Action* (Los Angeles), September/October 1969; "Remembering Leo McCarey" by Bing Crosby in *Action* (Los

Angeles), September/October 1969; "A Session with McCarey" by H. Allen Smith in *Variety* (New York), January 1970; "Hollywood" by Peter Bogdanovich in *Esquire* (New York), February 1972; "Some Affairs to Remember: the Style of Leo McCarey" by P. Lloyd in *Monogram* (London), no.4, 1972; "Great Moments: Leo McCarey" by J. Richards in *Focus on Film* (London), spring 1973; "Journals: Paris" by Jonathan Rosenbaum in *Film Comment* (New York), November/December 1973; "Leo McCarey: From Marx to McCarthy" by C. Silver in *Film Comment* (New York), September/October 1973; "McCarey and McCarthy" by George Morris in *Film Comment* (New York), January/February 1976; "Leo McCarey: The Man Behind Laurel & Hardy" by W. Gehring in *Films in Review* (New York), November 1979; "McCarey/Laurel & Hardy", letters from William Everson and others, and "Laurel & Hardy", letter from W. Gehring, in *Films in Review* (New York), February and April 1980.

*   *   *

McCarey has always presented *auteur* criticism with one of its greatest challenges and one that has never been convincingly met. The failure to do so should be seen as casting doubt on the validity of *auteurism* (in its cruder and simplier forms) rather than on the value of the McCarey oeuvre. He worked consistently (and apparently quite uncomplainingly) within the dominant codes of shooting and editing that comprise the anonymous "classical Hollywood" style; the films that bear his name as director, ranging from *Duck Soup* to *The Bells of St. Marys*, from Laurel and Hardy shorts to *My Son John*, from *The Awful Truth* to *Make Way for Tomorrow* (made the same year!), resist reduction to a coherent thematic interpretation. Yet his name is on some of the best—the best-loved—Hollywood films (as well as on some that embarrass many of even his most fervent defenders).

In fact, it might be argued that McCarey's work validates a more sophisticated and circumspect *auteur* approach: not the author as divinely inspired individual creative genius, but the author as the animating presence in a project within which multiple determinants—collaborative, generic, ideological—complexly interact. The only adequate approach to a McCarey film would involve the systematic analysis of that interaction. A few notes can be offered, however, towards defining the "animating presence."

McCarey's formative years as an artist were spent working with the great clowns of the late silent/early sound period: Harold Lloyd, Mae West, W.C. Fields, the Marx Brothers and (especially) Laurel and Hardy, for whom he was "supervising manager" for many years, personally directing two of their greatest shorts (*Liberty* and *Wrong Again*). His subsequent career spans (with equal success) the entire range of American comedy from screwball (The Awful Truth) to romantic (*An Affair to Remember*). The director's congenial characteristic seems to have been a commitment to a spontaneous, individualist anarchy which McCarey never entirely abandoned, accompanied by a consistent scepticism about institutions and restrictive forms of social organization, a scepticism which produces friction and contradiction even within the most seemingly innocuous, conservative projects. *Going My Way* and *The Bells of St. Mary's* are usually rejected outright by the intelligentsia as merely pious and sentimental, but their presentation of Catholocism is neither simple, straightfoward, nor uncritical, and it is easy to mistake for sentimentality, in contexts where you expect to find it anyway (such as Hollywood movies about singing priests), qualities such as tenderness and generosity. The celebration of individualism is of course a mainspring of American ideology, yet, pushed far enough in certain directions, it can expose contradictions *within* that ideology: its oppressive response to many forms of individuality, for example.

Make Way for Tomorrow (which, understandably, remained McCarey's favorite among his own films) is exemplary in this respect. Taking as its starting point an apparently reformable social problem (with Lee Grant's *Tell Me a Riddle* it is one of the only important Hollywood films about the aged), and opening with an unassailably respectable Biblical text ("Honor thy father and thy mother"), it proceeds to elaborate what amounts to a systematic radical analysis of the constraints, oppression and divisiveness produced by capitalist culture, lending itself to a thoroughgoing Marxist reading that would certainly have surprised its director. Typically, the film (merely very good for its first three-quarters) suddenly takes off into greatness at the moment when Victor Moore asks the ultimate anarchic question "Why not?", and proceeds to repudiate his family in favour of rediscovering the original relationship with his wife before they become absorbed into the norms of democratic-capitalist domesticity. The process is only completed when, in one of the Hollywood cinema's most poignant and subversive moments, he "unmarries" them as they say their last farewell at the train station: "Its been a pleasure knowing you, Miss Breckenridge."

—Robin Wood

MCCAY, WINSOR. American. Born Winsor Zenis McCay in Spring Lake, Michigan, 26 September 1871. Educated at Ypsilanti Normal School, Michigan. Married Maud Defore, 1891; children: Robert and Marion. Career: before 1889—works for poster firm, Chicago; 1891—employed as scenic artist, Vine Street Dime Museum, Cincinnati, Ohio; 1898—reporter for Cincinnati *Commercial Tribune*, and later for *Enquirer*; 1903—drawings in strip form parodying Kipling's *Just So Stories* attract attention of James Gordon Bennett, Jr., of *New York Herald*; hired to draw for New York *Evening Telegram*; creates strip *Dreams of a Rarebit Fiend* using pseudonym "Silas"; begins comic strips for *Herald*; 1905—creates *Little Nemo in Slumberland*; 1906—begins giving chalk talks on vaudeville circuit; 1908—successful Broadway musical based on *Little Nemo*; 1909—introduced to cartoon animation by J. Stuart Blackton; begins work on *Little Nemo*, first cartoon; 1911—premieres *Little Nemo* in vaudeville act; 1914—uses *Gertie the Dinosaur* as part of vaudeville act; 1918—premiere of *The Sinking of the Lusitania*, probably first cartoon feature; 1967—at Expo 67, Montreal preservation of deteriorating film undertaken. Died in 1934.

Films (as director, writer, and animator of short cartoons): 1909—*Little Nemo*; 1911—*Winsor McCay* (*Little Nemo* with live-action sequence in which McCay explains how a cartoon is made); 1912—*How a Mosquito Operates* (*The Story of a Mosquito*); 1914—*Gertie the Dinosaur* (*Gertie the Trained Dinosaur*); 1916—*Winsor McCay and His Jersey Skeeters* (*How a Mosquito Operates* with live-action prologue featuring McCay and daughter); 1918—*The Sinking of the Lusitania* (feature); c. 1918-21—*The Centaurs*; *Flip's Circus*; *Gertie on Tour*; 1921—"Dreams of a Rarebit Fiend" series: *The Pet*; *Bug Vaudeville*; *Flying House* (co-d with son Robert McCay).

Publications:

On MCCAY:

Articles—"The Birth of Animation" by J. Canemaker in *Millimeter* (New York), April 1975; "Winsor McCay" by J. Canemaker in *Film Comment* (New York), January/February 1975; "Le Festival d'Annecy et les Rencontres internationales du cinéma d'animation" by A. Cornand in *Image et son* (Paris), January 1977.

*   *   *

Winsor McCay is generally regarded as the first American *auteur* animator. Although not the first to experiment with animated films, McCay achieved artistic and technical heights that established animation as a viable form and that set ground rules for a style of pictorial illusionism and closed figurative forms in American animated cartoons.

McCay studied art and worked as an illustrator and sign painter before settling down in 1889 as a newspaper cartoonist in Cincinatti. McCay's success as a cartoonist led him to move in 1903 to the New York *Evening Telegram*. There he worked as a staff illustrator and developed the comic strips that brought him international fame.

During the next several years, McCay created such comic strips as *Hungry Henrietta*, *Little Sammy Sneeze*, *Dream of the Rarebit Fiend*, *Pilgrim's Progress*, and his most famous work, *Little Nemo in Slumberland*. *Little Nemo*, which ran from 1905 to 1911, is the pinnacle of comic strip art in the first decade of the century. It displays an unparalleled application of art nouveau graphic style, translating sinewy, irregular forms and rhythms into a delightfully decorative comic strip design. The strips related the fantastic adventures which befell the child Little Nemo, who always woke up in the last panel of the comic strip.

Sometime about 1909, McCay set to work on making an animated film of *Little Nemo in Slumberland*. (He credits his son's interest in flip books as the source of inspiration for his cinematic experiment.) After drawing and hand-coloring more than 4,000 detailed images on rice paper, McCay employed his animated film in his vaudeville act while Vitagraph, the company that shot and produced the film, simultaneously announced its release of *Little Nemo*. The animation did not employ a story but rather showed the characters of the comic strip continuously moving, stretching, flipping, and metamorphosing. McCay used foreshortening and exact perspective to create depth and an illusionistic sense of space even without the aid of any background. The animation sequence is framed by a live-action story in which McCay's friends scoff at the idea that he can make moving pictures and then congratulate him when he succeeds.

The advertisements and the prologue for the film stressed the monumental amount of labor and time required to do the drawings. McCay promoted and flaunted not only his role as an artist but the animator's "trade secrets." Throughout his career, McCay emphasized the revelation of the mechanics and process of animation, a self-reflexive approach that grew naturally out of the way he self-consciously undermined conventions of comic strip art and constantly called attention to the form itself.

McCay made his second animated cartoon in 1911 and 1912. *How A Mosquito Operates* relies on a simplier, less intricately graphic style in order to tell the story of a large mosquito's encounter with a sleeping victim. Two years later, McCay completed the animated film for which he is most famous, *Gertie the Dinosaur*. Like his previous two films, McCay incorporated the cartoon into his vaudeville act and, like *Little Nemo*, Gertie's animation is framed by a live-action sequence. But in *Gertie*, McCay combined the lessons of his earlier two films in order to create a character who is animation's first cartoon personality.

After *Gertie the Dinosaur*, McCay continued doing other animated cartoons but began utilizing celluloid (instead of rice paper) and stationary backgrounds that did not have to be redrawn for every frame. He also devised a system of attaching pre-punched sheets to pegs so that he could eliminate the slight shifting that occurred from drawing to drawing. His discovery represents the first instance of peg registration, a technique commonly employed in modern animation.

Although McCay's later cartoons were popular and praised for their naturalness (*Centaurs* and *Sinking of the Lusitania*), McCay's elaborate full animation proved too time-consuming and costly to inspire others, more concerned with production, to adhere to McCay's high standards. Neither a full-time animator nor part of a movie studio, McCay was free to pursue his own ends, his success is due to his ability to translate graphic style to animation as well as to his gregarious showmanship.

McCay stopped making animated films in 1921, and by the time he died of cerebral hemorrhages in 1934, his contribution as an animator was almost forgotten. Only in the 1960s was McCay rediscovered as an American artist, and in 1966 New York's Metropolitan Museum sponsored an exhibit of his work.

—Lauren Rabinovitz

MCLAREN, NORMAN. Scottish. Born in Stirling, 11 April 1914. Educated at Stirling public schools; Glasgow School of Art. Career: 1934—while a student at Glasgow School of Art makes anti-war film with animated sequence which wins first prize, Scottish Film Festival; 1936—after graduation hired by John Grierson at General Post Office Film Unit; 1936-38—works on live-action documentaries; 1938—makes first professional animated film *Love on the Wing*; contains first example of his drawing-directly-on-film technique; 1939-41—works in New York independently, and for company producing publicity shorts and Museum of Non-Objective Art; 1941—hired by Grierson at Canada's National Film Board to set up animation department; begins by making animations to help war effort; 1949—begins long collaboration with Evelyn Lambert on *Begone Dull Care*; 1952—for anti-war film *Neighbors* develops process of animating film of live actors called "pixillation". Recipient: Best Documentary Short Subject Academy Award for *Neighbors*, 1952.

Films (made as student at Glasgow School of Art): 1934-35—*Hand Painted Abstraction*; *Seven Till Five*; *Camera Makes Woopee*; *Colour Cocktail*; (made independently): 1936-37—*Hell Unlimited*; *Defense of Madrid*; (made for G.P.O. Film Unit, London): 1937-39—*Book Bargain*; *News for the Navy*; *Mony a Pickle*; *Love on the Wing*; 1939—*The Obedient Flame* (for the Film Center, London); (made for the Museum of Non-Objective Art, New York): 1939-41—*Dots**; *Scherzo*; *Loops**; *Rumba* (lost); *Stars and Stripes**; *Boogie Doodle**; (made for the National Film Board of Canada): 1941—*Mail Early*; *V for Victory*; 1942—*Five for Four*; *Hen Hop**; 1943—*Dollar Dance*; 1944—*C'est l'aviron*; *Keep Your Mouth Shut*; 1945—*La Haut sur ces montagnes*; 1946—*A Little Phantasy*; *Hoppity Pop**; 1947—*Fiddle-de-dee**; *Poulette grise*; 1948-52—*A Phantasy*; 1949—*Begone Dull Care**; 1950-51—*Around Is Around*; *Now*

Is the Time; 1952—*Neighbors (Les Voisins)*** (+mu); *Two Bagatelles*** (+mu); 1954-55—*Blinkity Blank**; 1956—*Rythmetic* (+mu); 1957—*A Chairy Tale (Il était une chaise)***; 1958—*Le Merle*; 1959—*Serenal**; *Short and Suite**; *Mail Early for Christmas*; credit sequence for *The Wonderful World of Jack Paar* (for TV); 1960—*Lignes verticales (Lines Vertical)**; *Opening Speech (Discours de bienvenue de McLaren)***; 1961—*New York Lightboard*; 1962—*Lignes horizontales (Lines Horizontal)**; 1963—credit sequence and intertitles for *Caprice de Noël (Christmas Crackers)***; 1964—*Canon***; 1965—*Mosaic (Mosaïque)** (+mu); 1967—*Pas de deux* (live action); 1969—*Sphères (Spheres)*; 1971—*Synchromy*; 1972—*Ballet adagio*; 1973—*L'Écran d'épingles* (co-d with Alexeieff and Parker—documentary); 1976-78—*Le Mouvement image par image* (series of 5 animation instruction films); 1981-83—*Narcissus* (live action).

* films without camera (direct drawing, engraving, or painting on film)

** "pixillation"

Publications:

By MCLAREN:

Book—*The Drawings of Norman McLaren*, Montreal 1975; articles—"L'Animation stéréographique" in *Cahiers du cinéma* (Paris), July/August 1952; "Notes on Animated Sound" in *Quarterly of Film, Radio, and Television* (Berkeley), spring 1953; "Making Films on Small Budgets" in *Film* (London), December 1955; interview by Robin Joachin in *Cahiers du cinéma* (Paris), December 1955; "L'Écran et le pinceau" in *Séquences* (Montreal), December 1955; interview in *Séquences* (Montreal), October 1965; interview in *Film Library Quarterly* (New York), spring 1970; "The Synthesis of Artificial Movements in Motion Picture Projection", with Guy Glover, in *Film Culture* (New York), no.48-49, 1970; "Où va l'animation?" in *Ecran* (Paris), January 1973; "Rhythm 'n Truths", interview by D. Elley in *Films and Filming* (London), June 1974; "A Dictionary of Movement", interview by M. Magistros and G. Munro in *Wide Angle* (Athens, Ohio), v.3, no.4, 1980.

On MCLAREN:

Books—*Dots and Loops: The Story of a Scottish Film Cartoonist* by Hardy Forsyth, Edinburgh 1951; *Norman McLaren*, La Cinémathèque québécoise, Montreal 1965; *Norman McLaren* by Maynard Collins, Canadian Film Institute 1975; *Experimental Animation* by Robert Russett and Cecile Starr, New York 1976; articles—"Hen Tracks on Sound Tracks" in *Popular Mechanics*, April 1949; "Norman McLaren ou le cinéma du VVIe siècle" by Jean Queval in *Cahiers du cinéma* (Paris), October/November 1951; "Movies Without a Camera, Music Without Instruments" in *Theatre Arts* (New York), October 1952; "Norman McLaren: His Career and Techniques" by William Jordan in *Quarterly of Film, Radio and Television* (Berkeley), fall 1953; special animation issue, with interview, of *Cinéma 57* (Paris), January 1957; "Le Cinéma de deux mains" by André Martin, in 2 parts, in *Cahiers du cinéma* (Paris), January and February 1958; "Mystère d'un cinéma instrumental" by André Martin, in 3 parts, in *Cahiers du cinéma* (Paris), February, March, and April 1958; "Les Démons de McLaren" by Jean D'Yvoire in *Radio-Cinéma-Télévision* (Paris), 29 June 1958; "The Craft of Norman McLaren" in *Film Quarterly* (Berkeley), winter 1962/63; "The 2nd Story—Honoring the Only Canadian

Artist" by Adolfas Mekas in *Film Culture* (New York), summer 1962; "Mc et Moi" by Gretchen Weinberg in *Film Culture* (New York), summer 1962; "The Unique Genius of Norman McLaren" by May Cutler in *Canadian Art*, May/June 1965; "Klee, Steinberg, McLaren" by Max Egly in *Image et son* (Paris), March 1965; "Multi-McLaren" by Pierre Vinet in *Take One* (Montreal), September/October 1966; "Pixillation" by Dan Burns in *Film Quarterly* (Berkeley), fall 1968; "The Career of Norman McLaren" in *Cinema Canada* (Montreal), August/September 1973; "Rhythm 'n Truths" by D. Elley in *Films and Filming* (London), June 1974; "Norman McLaren au fil de ses films", special issue of *Séquences* (Montreal), October 1975; film—*The Eye Hears the Ear Sees*, produced by the BBC.

MCLEOD, NORMAN Z. American. Born Norman Zenos McLeod in Grayling, Michigan, 20 September 1898. Educated in Natural Science, University of Washington, B.S., M.S. Married Evelyn Ward. Career: World War I—service in Royal Canadian Air Force as combat pilot; 1919-27—gagman and writer for Al Christie Comedies; 1927—assistant director on Wellman's *Wings*; 1928—joins Fox Film Company as director; 1930-36—directs mainly for Paramount; 1931—first film with Marx Brothers released; 1937-46—directs for MGM, United Artists, and RKO; after 1947—directs mainly for RKO and Paramount; late fifties—directs for TV, episodes of *My Little Margie* and *Twilight Zone*; 1962—suffers stroke. Died 27 January 1964.

Films (as director): 1928—*Taking a Chance*; 1930—*Along Came Youth* (co-d); 1931—*Finn and Hattie* (co-d, +co-sc); *Monkey Business*; *Touchdown*; *Skippy* (Taurog) (co-sc only); *Sooky* (Taurog) (co-sc only); 1932—*The Miracle Man*; *Horse Feathers*; "The Forger" episode of *If I Had a Million*; 1933—*A Lady's Profession*; *Mama Loves Papa*; *Alice in Wonderland* (+co-sc); 1934—*A Melody in Spring*; *Many Happy Returns*; *It's a Gift*; 1935—*Redheads on Parade*; *Here Comes Cookie*; *Coronado*; 1936—*Early to Bed*; *Pennies from Heaven*; 1937—*Mind Your Own Business*; *Topper*; 1938—*Merrily We Live*; *There Goes My Heart*; 1939—*Topper Takes a Trip*; *Remember?* (+co-sc); 1940—*Little Men*; 1941—*The Trial of Mary Dugan*; *Lady Be Good*; 1942—*Jackass Mail*; *Panama Hattie*; 1943—*The Powers Girl (Hello Beautiful)*; *Swing Shift Maisie (The Girl in Overalls)*; 1946—*The Kid from Brooklyn*; 1947—*The Secret Life of Walter Mitty*; *Road to Rio*; 1948—*Isn't It Romantic?*; *The Paleface*; 1950—*Let's Dance*; 1951—*My Favorite Spy*; 1953—*Never Wave at a WAC (The Private Wore Skirts, The Newest Profession)*; 1954—*Casanova's Big Night*; 1957—*Public Pigeon No.1*; 1959—*Alias Jesse James*.

Publications:

On MCLEOD:

Articles—articles in *Lion's Roar* (Los Angeles), 1942 and 1943; "Gamble with Music" by K. Crichton in *Collier's* (New York), 23 March 1946; obituary in *The New York Times*, 28 January 1964.

* * *

The film career of Norman Z. McLeod is rather unique in the fact that he worked exclusively within the field of comedy. Several of his films have been recognized as classics of the genre, including *It's a Gift*, *Topper*, and *The Secret Life of Walter Mitty*. His films were generally box-office successes, which in turn led to his directing more comedies.

McLeod specialized in working with comic personalities, including the Marx Brothers, W.C. Fields, Red Skelton, Danny Kaye, and Bob Hope. His directing style was very unobtrusive (almost to the point of being non-existent), which allowed these comic personalities to shine through. He was known as a quiet director since, by his own admission, he could easily be out-talked by people like Bob Hope or Danny Kaye. Much of McLeod's instruction came in the form of sketches and little caricatures. He felt that it was easier to show the kinds of physical reactions he wanted by drawing comic postures for his actors.

Most of McLeod's films are shot on plot; they are mainly comprised of a series of gags and routines only loosely tied together. For example, underneath *The Secret Life of Walter Mitty* lies a spy story which exists only as a framework for Danny Kaye's daydreaming sequences. *The Paleface* is a western vehicle to support the comic antics of Bob Hope. The Marx Brothers tear their way through an ocean liner in *Monkey Business* to no particular end. The stories in McLeod's films are often unmemorable, being secondary to the comedians who dominate them.

Most of the comedians who worked in Norman McLeod's films came from a vaudeville or stage background, and McLeod photographed them as if they were still on the stage. The framing was often full or three-quarter figure and the camera rarely moved. Most of the scenes in McLeod's films were done as long continuous takes. This technique did little to establish any kind of an editing style, but it did allow the comedy of a scene to play out to its full extent.

Many of the gags in McLeod's films are based on the use of comic props. For example, in *Monkey Business* Harpo works in perfect harmony with the puppets from a Punch and Judy show (at no time is there any indication of a puppeteer). In *It's a Gift*, W.C. Fields's sleep on the back porch is interrupted by a coconut that insists on banging its way down every inch of three flights of stairs. In these (and other) examples, inanimate objects seem to take on a life of their own and exhibit comic characteristics.

On a few occasions the gags in McLeod's films are based on self-reflexive humor. For example, when in *Horse Feathers* Groucho is forced to sit through one of Chico's piano recitals, Groucho gets up and tells the audience, "I *have* to stay here, but there's no reason why you folks shouldn't go out in the lobby until this thing blows over." At the end of *Casanova's Big Night*, Bob Hope is about to be beheaded by the executioner's axe when the scene is interrupted by a freeze frame. What follows is Bob Hope's version of a happy ending where he triumphs and wins the girl. The audience is left to decide which ending they prefer.

—Linda J. Obalil

MEKAS, JONAS. Lithuanian. Born in Semeniskiai, 24 December 1922. Educated at Gymnasium, Birzai, Lithuania, graduated 1942; studied philosophy and literature, Johannes Gutenberg University, Mainz, and University of Tübingen. Married Hollis Melton, 1974; child: Oona. Career: 1944—during German occupation taken to forced labor camp near Hamburg with brother Adolfas; 1945—they escape and hide near Danish border; 1945-49—in Displaced Person camps;

while studying at German universities edits Lithuanian emigré literary magazine *Zvilgsniai* [Glimpses]; also writes and publishes collections of fairy tales and short stories, and first book of poetry "The Idylls of Semeniskiai"; 1950—comes to New York; through 1950s works in factories and shops as loader, machine operator, and in other capacities; 1955—founds *Film Culture* magazine, remains Editor-in-Chief; 1958—begins "Movie Journal" column for *The Village Voice*; 1960—shoots first film *Guns of the Trees*; helps organize New American Cinema Group; 1961—co-organizes The Film-Makers' Cooperative; 1964—organizes the Film-Makers' Cinematheque; arrested and charged with showing obscene film (Jack Smith's *Flaming Creatures*), given 6-month suspended sentence; 1970—with P. Adams Sitney founds Anthology Film Archives and serves as acting director; 1971—with filmmaker brother Adolfas visits Lithuania, makes *Reminiscences of a Journey to Lithuania*. Recipient: documentary award, Venice Festival, for *The Brig*, 1965.

Films: 1961—*Guns of the Trees*; 1963—*Film Magazine of the Arts*; 1964—*The Brig*; *Award Presentation to Andy Warhol*; 1966—*Report from Millbrook*; *Hare Krishna*; *Notes on the Circus*; *Cassis*; 1968—*Walden (Diaries, Notes, and Sketches)*; 1969—*Time & Fortune Vietnam Newsreel*; 1972—*Reminiscences of a Journey to Lithuania*; 1976—*Lost, Lost, Lost*; 1978—*In Between*; 1980—*Paradise Not Yet Lost, or Oona's Fifth Year*; 1981—*Notes for Jerome*.

Publications:

By MEKAS:

Articles—Mekas founded *Film Culture* magazine in 1955, contributes to it regularly, and remains Editor-in-Chief; "A Call for a New Generation of Film Makers" in *Film Culture* (New York), April 1959; Mekas's weekly column "Movie Journal" has appeared in *The Village Voice* (New York) since 1958; statement in *Film Comment* (New York), winter 1964; interview by B.L. Kevles in *Film Culture* (New York), fall 1965; interview by Gerald Barrett in *Literature/Film Quarterly* (Salisbury, Maryland), spring 1973; interview by Antonin Liehm in *Thousand Eyes* (New York), October 1976.

On MEKAS:

Articles—"Pornography is Undefined at Film-Critic Mekas' Trial" by Stephanie Harrington in *The Village Voice* (New York), 18 June 1964; "Voice of the Underground Cinema" by Alan Levy in *The New York Times Magazine*, 19 September 1965; "New Forms in Film" by Bill Simon in *Artforum* (New York), October 1972; "Profile: All Pockets Open" by Calvin Tompkins in the *New Yorker*, 6 January 1973; "Give It Away on 2nd Avenue" by R. Goldstein in *The Village Voice* (New York), 29 January 1979.

*   *   *

Born in Lithuania in 1922, Jonas Mekas was a poet and resistance worker against both the German and Soviet occupations during the Second World War. After some years in a German camp for displaced persons, he and his brother, Adolphas, also a filmmaker, emigrated to New York where they later founded the journal *Film Culture*. Initially hostile to the Ameri-

can avant-garde, Mekas became its champion and spokesman in the 1960s. Throughout that decade he exerted great influence through *Film Culture*, his "Movie Journal" column in the *Village Voice* and his founding of the Film-makers Cooperative (in 1962) to distribute independent films, and the Film-makers Cinematheque (founded in 1963) as a New York showcase.

His first film, *Guns of the Trees*, a 35mm feature, describes aspects of Beat culture in New York through the lives of four fictional characters. It reflects his hopes, at that time, for the establishment of a feature length narrative cinema on the model of the French and Polish "New Waves." By the time he made *The Brig* with his brother, directly filming Ken Brown's stage play in the Living Theatre Production as if it were a documentary, he had already shifted his energies to his on-going cinematic diary. The diary had actually begun in the mid-fifties when he reached the United States, but it took the liberating inspiration of Stan Brakhage and Marie Menken for Mekas to acknowledge that his artistic talent was focused outside of the feature film tradition he had been espousing.

The first installment of his *Diaries, Notes, and Sketches*, the nearly three-hour long *Walden*, records his life. With numerous portraits of his friends and colleagues in the mid-sixties. Its techniques are characteristic of the filmmaker's mature work: staccato, single-frame flashes, composed directly in the camera, are counterpointed to longer sketches of weddings, trips to the circus, meetings. Printed intertitles often occur. Long passages have musical accompaniment. The filmmaker repeatedly breaks in on the soundtrack to offer private reflections and aphorisms.

In 1976 he released *Lost, Lost, Lost*, another three hour section of the megadiary. This time, he went back to his initial experiments with the camera, in a more conventional and leisurely style, to document the aspirations and frustrations of his life as an exile dreaming of the reestablishment of an independent Lithuanian republic. Bits of this material had already appeared in his masterly and moving *Reminiscences of a Journey to Lithuania*, a three-part film made with the help of German television. The middle section of that film describes the emotional reunion of both brothers with their mother, then almost 90 years old, when they returned home for their first visit since the war. The film opens with a summary of Mekas's initial experiences in America and ends with a recognition of the impossibility of recovering the past, as he joins a group of his friends, mostly artists, in Vienna.

That elegiac tone is sustained and refined in *Notes for Jerome*, the record of his visits to the estate of Jerome Hill, in Cassis, France, in the late sixties, and edited after Hill's death in 1972. Mekas married Hollis Melton in 1974. Their first child Oona was born the next year. *Paradise Not Yet Lost: or Oona's Fifth Year* treats of his family life, but continues the theme of lost childhood which permeates Mekas's vision. It is filmed in the style of *Walden* as is *In Between* which records the years between *Lost, Lost, Lost* and *Walden*.

—P. Adams Sitney

MÉLIÈS, GEORGES. French. Born in Paris, 8 December 1861. Educated at the Lycée Imperial, Vanves, 1868-70; Lycée Louis-le-Grand, Paris, 1871-80. Married Eugénie Genin in 1885; children: Georgette and André; married Fanny Manieux (born Charlotte-Stéphanie Faës, stage name Jehanne D'Arcy) in 1925. Career: 1884—introduced to illusionism by English conjuror John Maskelyne; 1888—buys Théâtre Robert Houdin, Paris, begins to present performances of magic and illusionism; begins association with technician Eugène Calmels; 1895—attends premiere of Cinematographe Lumière; 1896—buys Animatographe projector in London after Antoine Lumière refuses to sell him the brothers' device; develops camera with Lucien Reulos, builds 1st studio at Montreuil; begins shooting first film *Une Partie des cartes (Playing Cards)*, "Star Film Company" begun; 1897—transforms theater into cinema; 1901-04—peak production period; 1903—brother Gaston Méliès opens Star Films branch in New York; 1905—2nd Montreuil studio built; 1909—studio closes temporarily due to American competition; 1910—returns to stage as magician (last performance 1920); 1929—Méliès retrospective, Paris, after "rediscovery" by Leon Druhot; 1932—given an apartment at Chateau d'Orly by the Mutuelle du Cinéma. Died in Paris, 21 January 1938. Recipient: Legion of Honor, 1933.

Films (as producer, director, scenarist, art director and frequent actor): 1896—78 films, 2 extant: *Une Nuit terrible (A Terrible Night)*; *Escamotage d'une dame chez Robert-Houdin (The Vanishing Lady)*; 1897—52 films, 4 extant: *Entre Calais et Douvres (Between Calais and Dover)*; *L'Auberge ensorcelée (The Bewitched Inn)*; *Aprés le bal (After the Ball)*; *Danse au sérail (Dancing in a Harem)*; 1898—30 films, 8 extant: *Visite sousmarine du Maine (Divers at Work on the Wreck of the Maine)*; *Panorama pris d'un train en marche (Panorama from Top of a Moving Train)*; *Le Magicien*; *Illusions fantasmagoriques (The Famous Box Trick)*; *La Lune à un mètre (The Astronomer's Dream)*; *Un Homme de tête (The 4 Troublesome Heads)*; *La Tentation de Saint-Antoine (The Temptation of Saint Anthony)*; *Salle à manger fantastique (A Dinner Under Difficulties)*; 1899—34 films, 4 extant: *Cléopâtre (Robbing Cleopatra's Tomb)*; *L'Impressioniste fin de siècle (An Up-To-Date Conjurer)*; *Le Portrait mystérieux (A Mysterious Portrait)*; *L'Affaire Dreyfus (The Dreyfus Affair)*; 1900—33 films, 7 extant: *Les Miracles de Brahmane (The Miracles of Brahmin)*; *L'Exposition de 1900 (Paris Exposition, 1900)*; *L'Homme orchestre (The One-Man Band)*; *Le Rêve de Noël (The Christmas Dream)*; *Gens qui pleurent et gens qui rient (Crying and Laughing)*; *Nouvelles Luttes extravagantes (The Wrestling Sextette)*; *Le Malade hydrophobe (The Man with Wheels in His Head)*; 1901—29 films, 4 extant: *Le Brahmane et le papillon (The Brahmin and the Butterfly)*; *Dislocations mystérieuses (Extraordinary Illusions)*; *Le Charlatan (Painless Dentistry)*; *Barbe-Bleue (Blue Beard)*; 1902—23 films, 5 extant: *L'Homme à la tête de caoutchouc (The Man with the Rubber Head)*; *Eruption volcanique à la Martinique (The Eruption of Mount Pelée)*; *Le Voyage dans la lune (A Trip to the Moon)*; *Le Sacré d'Édouard VII (The Coronation of Edward VII)*; *Les Trésors de Satan (The Treasures of Satan)*; 1903—29 films, 28 extant: *La Corbeille enchantée (The Enchanted Basket)*; *La Guirlande merveilleuse (The Marvellous Wreath)*; *Les Filles du Diable (Beelzebub's Daughters)*; *Un Malheur n'arrive jamais seul (Misfortune Never Comes Alone)*; *Le Cake-walk infernal (The Infernal Cake Walk)*; *La Boîte à malice (The Mysterious Box)*; *Le Puits fantastique (The Enchanted Well)*; *L'Auberge du bon repos (The Inn Where No Man Rests)*; *La Statue animée (The Drawing Lesson)*; *La Flamme merveilleuse (The Mystical Flame)*; *Le Sorcier (The Witch's Revenge)*; *L'Oracle de Delphes (The Oracle of Delphi)*; *Le Portrait spirite (A Spiritualist Photographer)*; *Le Mélomane (The Melomaniac)*; *Le Monstre (The Monster)*; *Le Royaume des Fées (The Kingdom of the Fairies)*; *Le Chaudron infernal (The Infernal Cauldron)*; *Le Revenant (The Apparition)*; *Le Tonnerre de Jupiter (Jupiter's Thunderbolts)*; *La Parapluie fantastique (10 Ladies in One Umbrella)*; *Tom Tight et Dum Dum (Jack Jaggs and Dum Dum)*; *Bob Kick, l'enfant terrible (Bob Kick the Mischievous Kid)*; *Illusions funambulesques (Extraordinary Illusions)*; *L'Enchanteur Alcofrisbas (Alcofrisbas, the Master Magician)*; *Jack et Jim*; *La Lanterne magique (The Magic Lantern)*; *La Rêve du maître de ballet (The Ballet Master's Dream)*; *Faust aux enfers (The Damnation of Faust)*; 1904—35 films, 19 extant: *Le Bourreau turc (The Terrible Turkish Executioner)*; *Au Clair de la lune ou Pierrot malheureux (A Moonlight Serenade, or The Miser Punished)*; *Un Bonne Farce avec ma tête (Tit for Tat)*; *Le Coffre enchanté (The Bewitched Trunk)*; *Les Apparitions fugitives (Fugitive Apparitions)*; *Le Roi du maquillage (Untamable Whiskers)*; *La Rêve d'horloger (The Clockmaker's Dream)*; *Les Transmutations imperceptibles (The Imperceptible Transformations)*; *Un Miracle sous l'inquisition (A Miracle Under the Inquisition)*; *Benvenuto Cellini ou une curieuse évasion (Benvenuto Cellini, or a Curious Evasion)*; *La Damnation du Docteur Faust (Faust and Marguerite)*; *Le Thaumaturge chinois (Tchin-Chao, the Chinese Conjurer)*; *Le Merveilleux éventail vivant (The Wonderful Living Fan)*; *Sorcellerie culinaire (The Cook in Trouble)*; *La Sirène (The Mermaid)*; *Le Rosier miraculeux (The Wonderful Rose Tree)*; *Le Voyage à travers l'impossible (The Impossible Voyage)*; *Le Juif errant (The Wandering Jew)*; *La Cascade de feu (The Firefall)*; 1905—22 films, 11 extant: *Les Cartes vivants (The Living Playing Cards)*; *Le Diable noir (The Black Imp)*; *Le Menuet lilliputien (The Lilliputian Minuet)*; *Le Bacquet de Mesmer (A Mesmerian Experiment)*; *Le Palais des mille et une nuits (The Palace of the Arabian Nights)*; *La Compositeur toqué (A Crazy Composer)*; *La Chaise à porteurs enchantée (The Enchanted Sedan Chair)*; *Le Raid Paris-Monte Carlo en deux heures (An Adventurous Automobile Trip)*; *Un Feu d'artifice improvisé (Unexpected Fireworks)*; *La Légende de Rip van Winkle (Rip's Dream)*; *Le Tripot clandestin (The Scheming Gambler's Paradise)*; 1906—18 films, 10 extant: *Une Chute de cinq étages (A Mix-up in the Galley)*; *La Cardeuse de Matelas (The Tramp and the Mattress-Makers)*; *Les Affiches en goguette (The Hilarious Posters)*; *Histoire d'un crime (A Desperate Crime)*; *L'Anarchie chez Guignol (Punch and Judy)*; *L'Hôtel des voyageurs de commerce (A Roadside Inn)*; *Les Bulles de savon animées (Soap Bubbles)*; *Les 400 Farces du Diable (The Merry Frolics of Satan)*; *L'Alchimiste Prarafaragamus ou la Cornue infernale (The Mysterious Retort)*; *La Fée caraboose ou le Poignard fatal (The Witch)*; 1907—19 films, 7 extant: *La Douche d'eau bouillanie (Rogue's Tricks)*; *Le Mariage de Victorine (How Bridget's Lover Escaped)*; *Le Tunnel sous la manche ou Le Cauchemar franco-anglais (Tunnelling the English Channel)*; *L'Eclipse du soleil en pleine lune (The Eclipse, or the Courtship of the Sun and the Moon)*; *Pauvre John ou Les Aventures d'un buveur de whiskey (Sight-Seeing Through Whiskey)*; *La Colle universelle (Good Glue Sticks)*; *Ali Barbouyou et Ali Bouf à l'huile (Delirium in a Studio)*; 1908—68 films, 21 extant: *Le Tambourin fantastiqyue (The Knight of the Black Art)*; *Il y a un dieu pour les ivrognes (The Good Luck of a Souse)*; *La Génie de feu (The Genii of Fire)*; *Why the Actor Was Late*; *Le Rêve d'un fumeur d'opium (The Dream of an Opium Fiend)*; *La Photographie électrique à distance (Long Distance Wireless Photography)*; *Salon de coiffure (In the Barber Shop)*; *Le Nouveau Seigneur du village (The New Lord of the Village)*; *Sideshow Wrestlers*; *Lulli ou le violon brisé (The Broken Violin)*; *The Woes of Roller Skates*; *Le Fakir de Singapoure (The Indian Sorcerer)*; *The Mischances of a Photographer*; *His First Job*; *French Cops Learning English*; *A Tricky Painter's Fate*; *Au patys des jouets (Grandmother's Story)*; *Buncoed Stage Johnnie*; *Not Guilty*; *Hallucinations pharmaceutiques (Pharmaceutical Hallucinations)*; *La Bonne Bergère et la méchante princesse (The Good Shepherdess and the Evil Princess)*; 1909—9 films, none extant: 1910—13 films, 3 extant: *Hydrothérapie fantastique (The Doc-*

tor's Secret); *Le Locataire diabolique (The Diabolic Tenant)*; *Les Illusions fantaisistes (Whimsical Illusions)*; 1911—2 films, 1 extant: *Les Hallucinations du Baron Münchausen (Baron Münchausen's Dream)*; 1912—4 films, 3 extant: *À la conquête du Pôle (The Conquest of the Pole)*; *Cendrillon ou la pantoufle mystérieuse (Cinderella or the Glass Slipper)*; *Le Chevalier des neiges (The Knight of the Snows)*.

Publications:

By MÉLIÈS:

Articles—"En marge de l'histoire du cinématographe" in *Ciné journal* (Paris), August 1926; "Les Phénomènes du spiritisme" in *Journal de l'Association Française des artistes prestidigitateurs* (Paris), July/August 1936; "The Silver Lining" in *Sight and Sound* (London), spring 1938.

On MÉLIÈS:

Books—*Warwick Film Catalogue*, London 1901; *Star Film Catalogue*, New York-Paris 1905; *Georges Méliès* by Charles Ford, Brussells 1959; *Georges Méliès, Mage* by Maurice Bessy and Lo Duca, Paris 1961; *Georges Méliès* by Georges Sadoul, Paris 1961; *Exposition commémorative du Centenaire de Georges Méliès*, exhibition catalogue, Paris 1961; *Le Boulevard du cinéma à l'époque de Georges Méliès* by Jacques Deslandes, Paris 1963; *De Méliès à l'expressionisme, le surréalisme au cinéma* by Ado Kyrou, Paris 1963; Georges Méliès, créateur du spectacle cinématographique, 1861-1938 by Madeleine Malthête-Méliès, Paris 1966; "Méliès" by Maurice Bessy in *Anthologie du cinéma* vól.2, Paris 1967; *The Brakhage Lectures* by Stan Brakhage, Chicago 1972; *Méliès, l'enchanteur* by Madeleine Malthête-Méliès, Paris 1973; *Marvellous Méliès* by Paul Hammond, New York 1975; *Film Biographies by Stan Brakhage*, Berkeley , California 1977; *Artificially Arranged Scenes*: *The Films of Georges Méliès* by John Frazer, Boston 1979; *Georges Méliès, Film Pioneer*, collected by Merritt Crawford and John Mulholland, New York n.d.; articles—"From Georges Méliès to S.M. Eisenstein" by Léon Moussinac in *Experimental Cinema*, June 1930; "Father of the Fantasy Film" by Alberto Cavalcanti in *The Listener* (London), 2 June 1938; "Georges Méliès, Magician and Film Pioneer" by Iris Barry in *Art in Our Time*, New York 1939; "An Index to the Creative Work of Georges Méliès" by Georges Sadoul in *Sight and Sound* (London), no.11, 1947; "L'Homme au cent mille images" by Paul Gilson and Nino Frank in *La Revue du cinéma* (Paris), March 1948; "Méliès père du cinéma, fils de Jules Verne" by Marcel Lapierre in *Cahiers du cinéma* (Paris), no.10, 1952; "Tribute to Mme Méliès" by Lotte Eisner in *Film* (London), January/February 1957; "Commemorating Méliès" by Ralph Stephenson in *Sight and Sound* (London), autumn 1961; "A Film a Day" by Ralph Stephenson in *Films and Filming* (London), December 1961; "Entre les mains de Méliès le Cinématographe devint une boîte magique" by Jacques Siclier in *Télérama* (Paris), September 1964; "An Interview with Madeleine Méliès" in *Film Culture* (New York), winter/spring 1970; "A Georges Méliès Scrapbook" by Paul Hammond in *Cinema* (Beverly Hills), summer 1971; "Le Classicisme de Méliès et Zecca" by Georges Franju in *Cinéma 71* (Paris), January 1971; "Georges Méliès and La Féerie" by Katherine Kovas in *Cinema Journal* (Evanston, Illinois), fall 1976; "A propos du 'Grand Méliès'" by Georges Franju in *Positif* (Paris), December/January 1977/78; "Le Cinéma retrouvé: Méphistoméliès" by E. Carrere in *Positif*

(Paris), June 1977; "The Magician and the Movies" by Eric Barnouw in *American Film* (Washington, D.C.), April 1978; "André Méliès Interviewed" by M. Haleff in *Film Culture* (New York), no.67-69, 1979; "Revoir Méliès: Méliès et la proliferation" and interview with Albert Levy by M.-C. Questerbert in *Cahiers du cinéma* (Paris), April 1979; "Les Burlesque de Méliès" by R. Bezombes in *Cinématographe* (Paris), April 1979; "Point d'histoire: Méliès: la fin d'un mythe?" by G. Courant in *Cinéma* (Paris), May 1979; "The American Méliès" by P. McInroy in *Sight and Sound* (London), no.4, 1979; "L'Idéologie de Méliès et son epoque" by M.A.M. Quevrain in *Cinéma* (Paris), September 1979; "Portrait de l'artiste en magicien" by O.-R. Veillon in *Cinématographe* (Paris), January 1981; "Film Body: An Implantation of Perversions" by L. Williams in *Ciné-Tracts* (Montreal), winter 1981; films—*Film and Reality* by Alberto Cavalcanti, 1943; *Le Grand Méliès* by Georges Franju, 1952; *Georges Méliès* by Madeleine Malthête-Méliès, 1969; *Georges Méliès: Cinema Magician* by Patrick Montgomery, 1977.

*　　*　　*

George Méliès, prestidigitator and master illusionist in the Parisian theater of the late 19th century, turned to the cinema and made some 500 films of every kind fashionable at the time between 1896 and 1912. Of these less than 90 survive, though working drawings (Méliès was a prolific and considerable graphic artist) remain to supplement his work.

Born in Paris in 1861, Méliès as a youth habitually attended the Theatre Robert-Houdin, a first-floor establishment with 200 seats and a stage carefully devised to present Jean-Eugene Robert-Houdin's technically advanced forms of conjuring and illusion. He was also influenced by visits to Maskelyne and Cooke's Egyptian Hall in London, where for a while his father, a wealthy bootmaker, sent him to work. Maskelyne presented spectacular dramatic shows involving illusion of the kind Méliès was himself to develop when, in 1888, selling his share in his late father's business to his brothers, he was able to buy the Theatre Robert-Houdin and take over as showman illusionist. In addition, he exhibited lantern-slide shows with an illusion of movement achieved by continuities of superimposition. After seeing celebrated Cinèmatographe in Paris in December 1895, Méliès could not rest until he had obtained equipment for himself. He acquired his first motion picture apparatus in 1896 from R.W. Paul in London, and presented his first film show at the Robert – Houdin on 4 April 1896, using Edison's kinetoscope loops; his own initial ventures into filmmaking – moving snapshots much like Lumière's – were exhibited in the fall.

In the first year Méliès made 78 films, all but one running about one minute; the exception *The Devil's Castle,* a vampire film playing three minutes. Within a year, by March 1897, he had constructed a glass studio in the garden of his house in Montreuil, near Paris, its equipment modelled on that for the stage in the Theatre-Robert-Houdin, which he seen turned over, in part at least, to screening programs made up exclusively of films. With his staff he built the sets, designed and made the costumes, photographed and processed the films, using cameras made mainly by Gaument, Lumière, and Pathé. He sold the prints outright to fairground and music-hall showmen, initially in France and England. He worked at a furious pace, being a tough employer of both artists and technicians. At first he used non-professional players, often performing himself.

Although he was to try his hand at every kind of film, his more lasting reputation was for burlesque, magical pantomine, and stage-derived illusion, but like other producers he made money out of the bogus, newsreel reconstruction, theatrical melodrama, adaptions from literary sources, historical costume drama, and even so-called "stag" films (mild strip-tease) and advertising films. Among his staged newreels were films that purported to be coverage of the Graeco-Turkish war (1897), and American involvement in Cuba and in the Philippines (1898). He even reconstructed *The Eruption of Mount Pelée* of Martinique in 1902, using models, and *The Coronation of Edward VII* before that event, which in any case was postponed.

It is well-known that Méliès was an exponent of trick photography, inspired, according to Georges Sadoul, the French film historian, by the publication in 1897 of Albert Allis Hopkins's *Magic, Stage Illusions and Scientific Diversions, Including Trick Photography*, though his most reliable biographer, Paul Hammond, claims Méliès would have been familiar with such devices long before. His standard technique included duplex photography (through which a single man could appear as himself and a double in a single frame) and spirit (ghost) photography using multiple image. These techniques enabled him to make films projecting stage illusions like *The Vanishing Lady* and *The Astronomer's Dream*—dream films are recurrent in his catalogue—and *The Four Troublesome Heads*, in which a magician repeatedly removes his head. Méliès was to specialize in comic dismemberment of heads and limbs.

By the turn of the century he was handling historical subjects-*Joan of Arc* and even a pro-Dreyfus film of 13 minutes, *The Dreyfus Affair*; literary adaptions, such as *The Damnation of Faust*; and coverage (backed by phonograph recordings) of the comedian-singer Paulus in a series of films, using for the first time electric arc-lights. He even made *Christ Walking on the Water* as well as simple travel or view films, including panoramas of Paris for the 1900 World Fair. He also reproduced in modern form the past glories of celebrated ghost and skelton exihibitions, such as *Pepper's Ghost* of London in 1862 and Robertson's *Fantasmagorie* of Paris in 1794. His mildly pornographic "stag" films included *After the Ball* and *The Bridegroom's Dilemma*, in which the actress Jehanne d'Arcy (Méliès's mistress, to become much later, in 1925, his second wife) appeared.

Most of Méliès's more celebrated films depended on illusion, comic burlesque, and pantomine, such a *The Man with the Rubber Head*—in which Méliès's own head is seen expanding to giant size and exploding—the delightfully absurd *A Trip to the Moon*—with acrobats playing the Selenites and hand-waving dancing girls sitting on stars—*The Melomaniac*, in which Méliès conjures with numerous images of his own head, creating out of them musical notes, the space-travelling burlesque, *The Impossible Voyage* (length 24 minutes), the pantominic *The Merry Frolies of Satan*, with its animated, skeletonic puppet horse, a 9 1/2 minute version of *Hamlet*, *The Conquest of the Pole*, with its man-eating Giant of the Snows, a vast marionette, and *Cinderella and the Glass Slipper*, produced in association with pathé and cut by his order from 54 to 33 minutes.

Until around 1909 Méliès remained a largely successful filmmaker. In 1900 he had been elected president of the International Convention of Cinematograph Editors (a position he held until 1912), and in 1904 he became president of the Chambre Syndicale de la Prestidigitation. There were agencies for his Star Film company in Berlin, Barcelona, London, and New York. Some of his films were available at double or treble cost in hand-tinted color prints. But the introduction of the practice of renting films, advocated by Pathé and other high-financed producers, was finally to defeat Méliès. He began to turn his attention back to theatrical presentation, producing pantomines in Paris. However, his brother Gaston, based now in America, began to produce live-action films for Star, including westerns in Texas and California, even for a while employing Francis Ford, John

Ford's older brother, and later in 1912 touring the South Seas and Far East to make travelogues. (Gaston was to die of food poisoning in Algeria in 1914.) Georges Méliès ceased filmmaking in 1912, his kind of work out-dated and unwanted, and by 1914, now a widower in his sixties, he was forced to rent his properties or see them taken over for war purposes, though one of his studios was converted into a vaudeville theater and run from 1917 to 1923 by his daughter, Georgette. Méliès gave his last show in the Théâtre Robert—Houdin in 1920, by which time he was deeply in debt. Many of his negatives and prints were destroyed for scrap.

As an artist of stage and screen, Méliès was at once illusionist and pantominist; in his films, human beings became comic creatures with fantastic costumes and make-up, liable to disintegrate or metamorphose into anything. Méliès's world was one of ceaseless change, a product partly of fairground magic and of costume tableaux vivants. Chaplin described him as an "alchemist of light." His sets, often beautifully painted in trompe-l'oeil with deceptive perspective, were essentially theatrical. His remarkable drawings, many happily preserved, show what a magnificent cartoon animator he could have become with his Protean imagination for the grotesque and the marvelous. As it was, adopting the cinema in the very year of its birth, he endowed it with the work of his highly individualist imagination, an imagination unlike that of any other filmmaker of his time. The best study of him in English is that by Paul Hammond, *Marvellous Méliès* (1974).

—Roger Manvell

MELVILLE, JEAN-PIERRE. French. Born Jean-Pierre Grumbach in Paris, 20 October 1917. Educated at the Lycées Condorcet, and Charlemagne, Paris, and Michelet, Vanves. Career: 1937—begins military service; evacuated to England after Dunkirk; serves with Free French forces in North Africa and Italy; 1945—founded O.G.C. (Organisation générale cinématographique) as production company; 1949—builds own studio, Paris; 1967—fire destroys studio. Died in Paris, 2 August 1973. Recipient: Prix René-Jeanne for *Le Cercle rouge*, 1970; Chevalier de la Légion d'honneur; Chevalier des Arts et des Lettres.

Films (as director and scriptwriter): 1946—*Vingt quatre heures de la vie d'un clown* (+pr); 1948—*Le Silence de la mer* ((+pr); 1950—*Les Enfants terribles* (co-sc, +pr, art direction); 1953—*Quand tu liras cette lettre*; 1956—*Bob le flambeur* (+pr, co-art direction); 1959—*Deux hommes dans Manhattan* (+pr, ro as *Moreau*); 1963—*Léon Morin, prêtre*; *Le Doulos*; *L'Aîné des Ferchaux*; 1966—*Le Deuxième Souffle*; 1967—*Le Samourai*; 1969—*L'Armée des ombres*; 1972—*Le Cercle rouge*; 1972—*Un Flic*.

Roles: 1948—*Les Dames du Bois de Boulogne* (Bresson); 1949—as hotel director in *Orphée* (Cocteau); 1957—as police commissioner in *Un Amour de poche*; 1960—as the writer Parvulesco in *A bout de souffle* (Godard); 1962—as Georges Mandel in *Landru* (Chabrol).

Publications:

By MELVILLE:

Articles—interview by Claude Beylie and Bertrand Tavernier in *Cahiers du cinéma* (Paris), October 1961; "Finding the Truth Without Faith" in *Films and Filming* (London), March 1962; interview by Jean Collet in *Télérama* (Paris), November 1962; "*Léon Morin, prêtre*: Découpage intégrale" in *Avant-Scène du cinéma* (Paris), no.10; "An Interview with Jean-Pierre Melville" by Eric Brietbart in *Film Culture* (New York), winter 1964/65; "*Le Doulos*: Découpage intégral" in *Avant-Scène du cinéma* (Paris), no.24; interview by Michel Dancourt in *Arts* (Paris), 25 April 1966; "A Samurai in Paris", interview by Rui Nogueira and François Truchaud in *Sight and Sound* (London), summer 1968; "Après Un Flic, Jean-Pierre Melville a-t-il besoin d'un deuxième souffle?", interview by R. Elbhar in *Séquences* (Paris), April 1973; interview by F. Guérif in *Cahiers de la Cinémathéque* (Paris), spring/summer 1978.

On MELVILLE:

Books—*Jean-Pierre Melville* by Jean Wagner, Paris 1964; *French Cinema Since 1946: Vol.2—The Personal Style* by Roy Armes, New York 1966; *Melville on Melville* by Rui Nogueira, London 1971; *Underworld U.S.A.* by Colin McArthur, London 1972; *Le Cinéma selon Melville* by Rui Nogueira, Paris 1973; articles—"Saluer Melville?" by Claude Chabrol in *Cahiers du cinéma* (Paris), October 1956; "Melville le flambeur" by Claude Beylie in *Cinéma 59* (Paris), no.40, 1959; "Plaisir à Melville" by Jean Domarchi in *Cahiers du cinéma* (Paris), December 1959; "Jean-Pierre Melville" by Christian Ledieu in *Études cinématographiques* (Paris), no.6 and 7, 1960; "Melville ou l'amour du cinéma" by François Porcile in *Cinéma-texte* (Paris), January 1963; "All Guns and Gangsters" by David Austen in *Films and Filming* (London), June 1970; "Quand tu liras cette lettre..." by Claude Beylie in *Ecran* (Paris), September/October 1973; "Il fut quand même Melville..." by T. Renaud in *Cinéma* (Paris), September/October 1973; "L'Armée des ombres" in *Image et son* (Paris), no.331bis, 1978; "A Parisian-American in Paris" by Volker Schlöndorff in *The Village Voice* (New York), 6 July 1982.

* * *

The career of Jean-Pierre Melville is one of the most independent in modern French cinema. The tone was set with his first feature film, *Le Silence de la mer*, made quite outside the confines of the French film industry. Without union recognition or even the rights to the novel by Vercors which he was adapting, Melville proceeded to make a film which, in its counterpointing of images and a spoken text, sets the pattern for a whole area of French literary filmmaking, extending from Bresson and Resnais down to Duras in the 1980s. *Les Enfants terribles*, made in close collaboration with Jean Cocteau, was an equally interesting amalgam of literature and film, but more influential was *Bob le flambeur*, a first variation on gangster film themes which emerged as a striking study of loyalty and betrayal. But by the time that the New Wave directors were drawing from *Bob le flambeur* a set of stylistic lessons which were to be crucial to their own breakthrough—economical location shooting, use of natural light, improvisatory approaches and use of character actors in place of stars—Melville himself had moved in quite a different direction. *Léon Morin, prêtre* marks Melville's decision to leave this directly personal world of low-budget filmmaking for a mature style of solidly commercial genre filmmaking, using

major stars and tightly wrought scripts to capture a wide audience.

This style is perfectly embodied in the trio of mid-1960s gangster films which constitute the core of Melville's achievement in cinema. Melville's concern with the film as a narrative spectacle is totally vindicated in these films, each of which is built around a star performance: Jean-Paul Belmondo in *Le Doulos*, Lino Ventura in *Le Deuxième Souffle* and Alain Delon in *Le Samourai*. Drawing on his 1930s viewing and his adolescent reading of American thrillers, Melville manipulates the whole mythology of the gangster film, casting aside all pretence of offering a social study. His criminals are idealized figures, their appearance stylized with emphasis on the belted raincoat, soft hat, and ever present handgun. Their behavior oddly blends violence and ritualized politeness, and lifts them out from their settings. Melville has no interest in the realistic portrayal of life as it is and disregards both psychological depth and accuracy of location and costume. He uses his stars to portray timeless, tragic figures caught up in ambiguous conflicts and patterns of deceit, relying on the actor's personality and certainty of gesture to fill the intentional void.

Le Samourai is a perfect distillation of the cinematic myth of the gangster, and remains Melville's masterpiece. Subsequent attempts to widen his range by transposing his characters into the world of Occupation and Resistance in *L'Armée des ombres*, or combining his particular gift for atmosphere with a *Rififi* style presentation of the mechanics of a robbery in *Le Cercle rouge* produced interesting but flawed works. Melville's frustration and dissatisfaction is reflected in his last work, *Un Flic*, which completes the passage towards abstration begun in the mid-1960s and offers a derisory world lacking even the human warmth of loyalty and friendship which the director had earlier celebrated. In retrospect, it seems likely that Melville's reputation will rest largely on this ability, almost unique in French cinema, to contain deeply-felt personal attitudes within the tight confines of commercial genre production. Certainly his thrillers are unequalled in European cinema.

—Roy Armes

MENZEL, JIRI. Czechoslovak. Born in Prague, 23 February 1938. Educated at Film Academy (FAMU), Prague, 1957-62. Career: 1963—assistant director on Věra Chytilová's *Something Different*; since 1965—director at Barrandov Studios; since 1967 has also directed plays at Drama Club, Prague (*Mandragola*, 1967), and at Semafor Theater, Prague (*The Last Stop*, 1968). Recipient: Best Foreign Film Academy Award for *Closely Watched Trains*, 1967; Grand Prize, Karlovy Vary Festival, for *Capricious Summer*, 1968. Address: Solidarita E/31, 100 00 Praha 10, Czechoslovakia.

Films (as director and co-scriptwriter): 1965—*Zločin v dívčí škole (Crime at a Girls' School)*; *Smrt pana Baltisbergra (The Death of Mr. Baltisberger)*; 1966—*Ostře sledované vlaky (Closely Watched Trains)* (+ro as the doctor); 1968—*Rozmarné léto (Capricious Summer)* (+ro as the magician *Arноštek*); *Zločin v šantánu (Crime in a Night Club)*; 1969—*Skřivánci na niti (Larks on a String)*; 1975—*Kdo hledá zlaté dno (Who Seeks the Gold Bottom)* (d only); 1977—*Na samotě u lesa (Seclusion Near a Forest)*; 1979—*Báječní muži s klikou (Magicians of the Silver Screen)* (+ro as the director); 1980—*Postřižiny (Short Cut, Cutting It Short)*. Roles: (in films not directed—incomplete list): 1964—guest in a pub in *Courage for Every Day*; soldier Schulze in *If One Thousand Clarinets*; secretary of the SCM in *A Place in* *a Crowd*; the young defense lawyer in *The Defendant*; 1965—*Dohnal* in *Wandering*; a bicyclist in *Nobody Shall Be Laughing*; 1967—the shy suitor in *Dita Saxová*; 1977—the doctor in *The Apple Game*.

Publications:

By MENZEL:

Books—*Closely Watched Trains*, script, with Bohumil Hrabal, New York 1977; articles—"Ostře sledované vlaky" in *Film a doba* (Prague), no.6, 1966; "O režii a herectví, o filmu a dicadle—Rozhovor s Jiřím Menzelem", interview by K. Pošová in *Film a Doba* (Prague), December 1977.

On MENZEL:

Books—*All the Bright Young Men and Women* by Josef Skvorecký, Toronto 1971; *Closely Watched Films* by Antonin Liehm, White Plains, New York 1974; *Cinema Beyond the Danube* by Michael Stoil, Metuchen, New Jersey 1974; *The Most Important Art* by Mira and Antonin Liehm, Berkeley 1977; *Jiří Menzel and the History of the Closely Watched Trains* by Josef Skvorecký, Boulder, Colorado 1982; articles—"Zádný strach o Jiřího Menzela" [Never Fear for Jiří Menzel] by A.J. Liehm in *Film a doba* (Prague), no.1, 1967; "The Man Who Made *Closely Watched Trains*" by Irving Kolodny in *Action* (Los Angeles), May/June 1968; "A Promised Land..." by Alan Levy in *The New York Times Magazine*, 9 February 1969; "Czech Jiri Menzel Directs a Movie" by Alan Levy in *The New York Times Magazine*, 9 February 1969; "3 East European Directors" by P. Crick in *Screen* (London), March/April 1970.

*   *   *

Menzel's chief claim to a firm place in the history of the Czech cinema to date is his masterpiece, *Closly Watched Trains*. He received an Oscar for it in 1967, and the film was the biggest box office success of all the works of the New Wave in Czechoslovakia. Banned from the industry after the Soviet invasion of 1968, Menzel eventually saved his career by recanting and publicly dissociating himself from his pre-invasion films, including *Closely Watched Trains*. However, even in his humiliation he scored one important point against the establishment: he refused to return his Oscar to Hollywood as the authorities had demanded (he was supposed to explain that he "did not accept awards from Zionists") and merely made a repentance movie, *Who Seeks the Gold Bottom*; a social realist formula story about the workers building a huge dam.

Like Milos Forman, Menzel was influenced by Czech novelists rather than by western filmmakers, and for a considerable time worked under the tutelage of his teacher from the Film Academy, Otakar Vávra, and one of his admired older colleagues, Věra Chytilová. Except for *Crime in a Night Club*, which was based on an original idea by novelist Josef Skvorecký, his pre-invasion films are adaptions of novels and short stories by Czech authors, either modern classics (*Capricious Summer* from a novella by Vladislav Vančura), or his contemporaries (Bohumil Hrabal's *Closely Watched Trains*, *The Death of Mr. Baltisberger* and *Larks on a String* and Skvorecký's *Crime at a Girls' School*). Except for *Capricous Summer*, all these films were banned, *Larks on a String* even before release. after three hesitant efforts

following his recantation, all developed from original ideas, Menzel found his old self in another adaption of Hrabal, *Short Cut*.

Except in his black comedies (*Crime at a Girls' School, Crime in the Night Club*), Menzel is essentially a realist whose method could, perhaps, be described by the theories of André Bazin: he reveals rather than describes reality. There is very little of the formalist elements of movie making, and if, occasionally, there are some (e.g. the opening montage in *Closely Watched Trains*), they are used mainly for comic effect. Menzel even dropped the achronological structure of the novella from which he made the *Closely Watched Trains*, and replaced it with linear narrative. However, there is inventive use of subtle symbolism (e.g. the clocks and their chiming in *Closely Watched Trains*), excellent work with actors, both professional and non-profesional, and superb editing. The trend towards subtle symbolism culminates in *Short Cut*, a Rabelaisian tribute to *elan vital*, which, however, hides a caustic, encoded comment on "goulash socialism," on the Marxist refutation of Freud (the commanding image of the pretty girl sitting on a high chimney), and on various smaller malpractices of "Realsozialismus" such as jamming foreign broadcasts. The nearly subliminal nature of such satirical stabs is a nut too hard for the censors to crack.

Unlike his mentor Chytilová's crude defensive moral statements, the messages of Menzel's pre-1968 works (and of *Short Cut*) are—in the light of establishment philosophy—extremely provocative. In a way, his entire *oeuvre* is one continuous eulogy of sex—a subject at best tolerated by Marxist aestheticians in Czechoslovakia. The shock value of *Closely Watched Trains* is the combination of commendable resistence heroism with an embarrassing sexual problem: an anathema in socialist realism. Similarly, the "crime" in *Crime at a Girls' School* turns out to be not murder but loss of virginity, and the "philosophical" ruminations of the three elderly Don Juans in *Capricious Summer* concentrate on a young artiste. The main theme of *Short Cut*—characterized by the phallic symbolism of the chimney which dominates the small central Bohemian Sodom—is simply the joy of sex. Considering that sex has always been the most dangerous enemy of puritancial revolutions, Menzel's message is clear. It is a much less acceptable one than the moralizing of Chytilová, whose eccentric form and merciless vision, on the other hand, stand against everything the government watchdogs would like to see. The two artists, taken together, represent the two basic headaches any repressive aesthetic necessarily faces—the objectionable form, and the objectionable content. The survival of Menzel and Chytilová in a national cinema so full of victims demonstrates that, with perseverance, intelligence, cunning, and good luck, art can occasionally triumph over censorship.

—Josef Skvorecký

MÉSZÁROS, MÁRTA. Hungarian. Born in Budapest, 19 September 1931. Educated at VGIK (Film School), Moscow. Divorced first husband 1959; married director Miklós Jancsó, mid-1960s. Career: 1936—family forced to leave Hungary for U.S.S.R.; 1946—returns briefly to Hungary; mid-1950s—lives in Romania for 2 years, makes 3 films for Alexandru Sahia Documentary Studio, Bucharest; 1959—following divorce from first husband, returns to Budapest; 1959-68—makes science popularization shorts and documentary shorts; mid-1960s—joins Mafilm Group 4, meets director Miklós Jancsó.

Films (as director of short films—in Hungary): 1954—*Ujra mosolyognak (Smiling Again)*; 1955—*Albertfalvai történet (A History of Albertfalva)*; *Tul a Kálvin-téren (Beyond the Square)*; *Mindennapi történetek (Everyday Stories)*; 1956—*Országutak vándora (Wandering on Highways)*; (in Romania): 1957—*Sa zimbeasca toti copiii*; 1958—*Femeile zilelor noastre*; *Popas in tabara de vara*; 1959—*Schimbul de miine*; (in Hungary): *Az élet megy tovább (Life Goes On)*; 1960—*Az eladás müvészete (Salesmanship)*; *Riport egy TSZ-elnökröl (Report on the Chairman of a Farmers' Co-Operative)*; *Rajtunk is mulik (It Depends on Us Too...)*; 1961—*Szivdobogás (Heartbeat)*; *Vásárhelyi szinek (Colors of Vásárhely)*; *Danulon gyártás (Danulon Production)*; *A szár és a gyökér fejlödése (The Development of the Stalk and the Root)*; 1962—*Tornyai János (János Tornyai)*; *Gyermekek, könyvek (Children, Books)*; *Kamaszváros (A Town in the Awkward Age)*; *Nagyüzemi tojástermelés (Mass Production of Eggs)*; *A labda varásza (The Spell of the Ball)*; 1963—*1963. julius 27. szombat (Saturday, July 27, 1963)*; *Munka vagy hivatás? (Work or Profession?)*; *Szeretet (Care and Affection)*; 1964—*Festök városa—Szentendre (Szentendre—Town of Painters)*; *Bóbita (Blow-Ball)*; *Kiáltó (Proclamation)*; 1965—*15 perc 15 évröl (15 Minutes on 15 Years)*; 1966—*Borsós Miklós (Miklós Borsós)*; *Harangok városa—Veszprém (Veszprém—Town of Bells)*; (as feature director): 1968—*Eltávozott nap (The Girl)* (+sc); *Mészáros László emlékére (In Memoriam László Mészáros)* (short); *A "holdudvar" (Binding Sentiments)* (+sc); 1970—*Szép lányok, ne sirjatok (Don't Cry, Pretty Girls)*; 1971—*A lörinci fonóban (At the Lörinc Spinnery, Women in the Spinnery)* (short); 1973—*Szabad lélegzet (Riddance, Free Breathing)* (+sc); 1975—*Örökbefogadás (Adoption)* (+co-sc); 1976—*Kilenc hónap (9 Months)*; 1977—*Ök ketten (The Two of Them, Two Women)*; 1978—*Olyan, mint otthon (Just Like at Home)*; 1979—*Utközben (En cours de route)*; 1980—*Örökség (The Heiresses, The Heritage)*; 1981—*Anya és leánya (Mother and Daughter)* (+co-sc); 1982—*Nema kiáltás (Silent Cry)* (+sc).

Publications:

By MÉSZÁROS:

Articles—"Látogatás rendezoi mühelyekben (II)", interview in *Filmkultura* (Budapest), November/December 1972; "Adopce", scenario extract, with others, in *Film a doba* (Prague), February 1976; "Nem vagyok, soha nem is voltam feminista", interview by A. Földes in *Filmkultura* (Budapest), March/April 1977; "Unter anderem zum Thema Frau", interview by R. Herlinghaus in *Film und Fernsehen* (Berlin), January 1977; "'Mary and Julie' and Márta Mészaros", interview in *Hungarofilm Bulletin* (Budapest), no.2, 1977; "9 mois", interview by F. Oukrate in *Ecran* (Paris), December 1977; interview by T. Giraud and D. Villain in *Cahiers du cinéma* (Paris), January 1978; "La Hongrie au coeur: Marta Meszaros", interview by C. Clouzot and others in *Ecran* (Paris), 15 January 1979; "Ganz wie zu Hause", photo essay in *Film und Fernsehen* (Berlin), no.2, 1979.

On MÉSZÁROS:

Articles—"Hiding It Under a Bushel: Breaking Free" by D. Elley in *Films and Filming* (London), February 1974; "Marta Meszaros: 'Senza legami' (Respiro libero)" by P. Rauzi in *Cineforum* (Bergamo), July/August 1976; "Az átlagok és a végletek" by K. Csala in *Filmkultura* (Budapest), July/August 1978; "Márta

Mészáros" by Derek Elley in *International Film Guide 1979*, London 1978.

* * *

Márta Mészáros is the sole contemporary woman filmmaker consistently making films both critically and commercially successful for an international audience. Her eight feature films made from 1968 to 1979 are concerned with the social oppression, economic constraints, and emotional challenges faced by Hungarian women. Mészáros explains: "I tell banal, commonplace stories, and then in them the leads are women—I portray things from a woman's angle."

Trained in filmmaking on a scholarship at Moscow's film school, she worked at the Newsreel Studios in Budapest, made four short films at the Bucharest Documentary Studios, married a Rumanian citizen in 1957, and was divorced in 1959. She returned to Budapest where she made more than 30 documentaries before attempting a feature. Mészáros's documentaries deal with subjects as diverse as science (*Mass Production of Eggs*), a Hungarian hero (*Saturday, July 27th 1963*), orphans (*Care and Affection*), and artists (*Szentendre—Town of Painters*, which she consideres her best documentary.)

In the mid-sixties Mészáros joined Mafilm Group 4 where she met Miklós Jancsó whom she later married. She wrote and directed her first feature, *The Girl*, in 1968. A hopeless mood pervades this story of the quest by an orphan girl for her biological parents who had abandoned her. The girl leaves her textile factory job to comfort her mother, who introduces her as her niece to her husband and relatives. The girl meets a man whom she believes is her father. The man neither confirms nor denies this. The girl returns home, attends a factory dance where she meets a young man interested in her. As with most Mészáros features the film is open-ended, lacking a conventional plot. Dialogue is sparse. Derek Elley asserts that *The Girl* is a model to which Mészáros adheres in her subsequent features; her visual compositions are "carefully composed, rarely showy," and "characterisation never remains static."

In *Binding Sentiments* the conflicts between an aging mother and her son's fiancé are delineated with understated solemnity and subtle humor. A semi-musical, *Don't Cry, Pretty Girls*, lightheartedy captures the romance between a rural girl and a city musician in a hostel and youth camp setting. Mészáros's short, *Woman in the Spinnery*, studies the working status and condictions of the factory worker that are also the subject of her feature *Riddance*. In this generation gap tale, a pair of lovers must deceive the young man's parents who object to his love for a girl who was raised in a children's home with no family. *Riddance* urges assertiveness and truth to oneself, and shows little sympathy for the older generation, as Derek Elley points out.

A fortyish woman wants a child from her unmarried lover in *Adoption*. She meets a teenager raised by the state who wants to marry her boyfriend. The relationship which develops between these two women and the man in their lives becomes the subject of Mészáros's most illuminating work.

A factory woman with one child has an affair with an engineer in *Nine Months*. The conflicts in their relationship are never resolved; they cannot agree on the terms and conditions of a life together; neither can surrender enough self to form a partnership. The woman leaves him to bear her second child alone. The actual birth of Lila Monari's child was photographed for the film.

The aptly titled *Two Women* depicts a friendship. Juli has a daughter and a husband attempting to find a cure for his alcoholism. Mari directs a hostel for working women, and tolerates a lackluster husband. Juli and Mari enjoy more rapport with each other than with the men in their lives. Situations depicting humiliation of and discriminating against women recur. The subject of Mészáros's next film, about a young man's attraction to a little girl, makes *Just Like at Home* a departure from her focus on women. Andras returns to Budapest after study in the U.S. and strikes up a friendship with a ten-year-old Zsuzsi whose parents agree that she live with Andras in Budapest and be educated there. Their chaste friendship resists the intrusion of Andras's lady friend. Andras learns more from Zsuzsi than she learns from him, to the bewilderment of their parents.

In *The Heiresses* Meszaros used a period setting for the first time. In the World War II era, a young, sterile woman marries a military officer. Because she needs an heir to inherit her father's money, she persuades a Jewish woman to bear a child sired by her husband. After the birth, the woman and her husband become deeply attached, and a second child is born. Then the wife "turns in" the Jewish woman (Jews were deported from Hungary in 1944), the husband is arrested, and the wife is given custody of the second child.

Meszaros's films deal with realities usually ignored in Eastern European cinema: the subordinaton of women, conflicts of urban and rural cultures, antagonism between the bureaucracy and its employees, alcoholism, the generation gap, dissolution of traditional family structures, and the plight of state-reared children. In her unpretentious works, she creates a composition picture of life in Hungary today.

In Derek Elley's words, she "has created a body of feature work which, for sheer thematic and stylistic homogeneity, ranks among the best in current world cinema." Her features examine emotional struggles "in the search for human warmth and companionship in a present-day, industrialised society."

—Heck-Rabi

MICHEAUX, OSCAR. American. Born in in Metropolis, Illinois, 1884. Married actress Alice Russell, 1929. Career: before 1909—works as Pullman porter and farmer; 1909—purchases homestead in South Dakota, expands holdings to 500 acres by 1914; 1914—publishes *The Homesteader*, based on ranching experiences; 1915—founds Western Book and Supply Company, Sioux City, Iowa; 1918—contacted by black-owned Lincoln Film Company, Nebraska, about producing film based on *The Homesteader*; insists on supervising production and deal falls through; founds Micheaux Film and Book Corporation, based in Sioux City and Chicago, to produce *The Homesteader* (later Micheaux Pictures Corporation); 1918-48—produces and distributes more than 30 films with black casts; 1920—unsuccessful attempts made in Chicago to block showing of *Within Our Gates*, containing scene of lynching; 1921—establishes office in New York City; 1928—company files for bankruptcy; reorganized 1929; 1931—first "all-talkie" *The Exile*. Died in Charlotte, North Carolina, 1951.

Films (as producer, director, scriptwriter, and editor—partial list of an estimated 30 or more films): 1919—*The Homesteader*; *Circumstantial Evidence*; 1920—*Within Our Gates*; 1921—*Deceit*; *The Gunsaulus Mystery*; 1922—*The Dungeon*; 1924—*Son of Satan*; *Birthright*; 1925—*Body and Soul*; mid-1920s—*The House Behind the Cedars*; 1928—*Easy Street*; 1930—*A Daughter of the Congo*; 1931—*The Exile*; 1932—*Ten Minutes*

to Live; *The Girl from Chicago*; 1936—*Swing*; *Underworld*; *Temptation*; 1937—*Miracle in Harlem*; 1938—*God's Stepchildren*; 1939—*Lying Lips*; *Birthright* (sound version); 1940—*The Notorious Elinor Lee*; 1948—*The Betrayal*.

Publications:

By MICHEAUX:

Article—in *Philadelphia Afro-American*, 24 January 1925.

On MICHEAUX:

Book—*Blacks in Black and White* by Henry Sampson, Metuchen, New Jersey 1977; article—"We Were Stars in Those Days" by Clinton Cox in the *New York Sunday News*, 9 March 1975.

*   *   *

Until the late 1940s, film roles for blacks in Hollywood were clichéd and demeaning: mammies, butlers, maids, Pullman porters, all decimating the English language while happily, mindlessly serving their white masters. As a result, independent filmmakers—a majority of whom were white—produced approximately 300 "race" films especially for ghetto audiences. Easily the most famous and prolific was a black, Oscar Micheaux, a one-man production and distribution company who shot over 30 features between 1918 and 1948.

Micheaux's origins—and even an accurate list of his films—cannot be clearly determined at least from existing volumes on the black cinema, but several facts are certain. Micheaux was a vigorous promoter who would tour the nation's black ghettos, establishing contact with community leaders and convincing theater owners to screen his films. Then he would dispatch his actors for personal appearances. Micheaux's budgets were practical infinitesimal, between $10,000 and $20,000 per feature, and he economized on sets, shooting schedules and behind-the-scenes personnel. He often filmed a complete feature on a single set, which may have been a private home or office. Scenes were rarely shot in more than one take; if an actor blew his lines, he just recovered his composure and completed his business. As a result, production values and performances were generally dreadful.

Some of Micheaux's films do attempt to address serious issues. *Within Our Gates* features a sequence in which a black is lynched. *Birthright* (the 1939 version) is the tale of a black Harvard graduate who experiences opposition from those of his own race as well as whites. *God's Stepchildren* centers on a light-skinned black who tries to pass for white. Because of this subject matter, Micheaux was occasionally threatened by local censors.

However, the filmmaker was concerned mostly with entertaining and earning profits, not with controversy. Actors' screen personas were modelled after those of contemporary Hollywood stars: Lorenzo Tucker was the "Black Valentino" and, after the advent of sound, the "colored William Powell"; Bee Freeman became the "sepia Mae West"; Slick Chester the "colored Cagney"; Ethel Moses the "negro Harlow." Plotlines also aped those of Hollywood products: *The Underworld* is a gangster film; *Temptation* a De Mille-like sex epic; *Daughter of the Congo* a melodrama set in Africa. Micheaux did direct the first all-talking black inde-pendent feature, *The Exile*, and 26-year-old Paul Robeson made his screen debut in a Micheaux melodrama, *Body and Soul*.

—Rob Edelman

MIKHALKOV-KONCHALOVSKI, ANDREI. (Also known by Christian name Andron.) Russian. Born in in Moscow, 1937. Educated as pianist, Moscow Conservatoire, 1947-57; State Film School (VGIK) under Mikhail Romm, diploma 1964. Married Natalya Arinbasarova; married second time 1969, divorced, 1 child. Career: 1960s—works as scriptwriter, especially with Andrei Tarkovsky; 1962—assistant to Andrei Tarkovsky on *Ivan's Childhood*; 1980—moves to United States at invitation of Jon Voight. Recipient: Special Jury Prize, Cannes Festival, for *Siberiade*, 1979. Lives in Malibu, California.

Films (as director of short film): 1961—*Malchik i golub (The Boy and the Pigeon)*; (as scriptwriter): *Katok i skripka (The Steamroller and the Violin)* (Tarkovsky); 1964—*Andrey Rubliov (Andrei Rublev)* (Tarkovsky); (as director and scriptwriter): 1965—*Pyervy uchityel (The First Teacher)* (co-sc—diploma film); 1966—*Istoriya Asi Klyachinoy, kotoraya lyubila, da nye vyshla zamuzh (The Story of Asya Klyachina, Who Loved But Did Not Marry, The Happiness of Asya, Happy Asya, Asya's Happiness)*; 1969—*Dvoryanskoye gnezdo (A Nest of Gentlefolk)* (+co-sc); *Tashkent—gorod khlyebny (Tashkent—City of Bread)* (sc only); *Pyesn o Manshuk (The Song of Manshuk)* (sc only); 1970—*Dyadya Vanya (Uncle Vanya)*; *The End of the Chieftain* (sc only); 1974—*Romans o uljublennyh (Lover's Romance, The Romance of Lovers)*; 1978—*Siberiade (The Siberiad)*; 1982—*Split Cherry Tree* (short—for U.S. cable TV).

Publications:

On MIKHALKOV-KONCHALOVSKI:

Articles—in *Films and Filming* (London), September 1967; "Andréi Kontchalovski ou les silences d'un jeune maître" by Michel Ciment in *Positif* (Paris), November 1969.

*   *   *

Probably the most gifted of the young Soviet directors who appeared in the sixties, Andrei Mikhalkov-Konchalovski did not manage to maintain his artistic level when cultural policy stiffened after the relatively liberal Khrushchev era. Andrei belongs to one of the most established families in Moscow. His grandfather was a famous pianist, his uncle a painter, his father (Sergei) a writer and the head of the writers' union, his brother (Nikita) an actor and a film director. Andrei studied music, but realizing he would not become a new Richter, he went to the V.G.I.K. (film school) in Moscow where he graduated after studying with Mikhail Romm. He wrote, together with Andrei Tarkovsky, the script of the short film *The Streamroller and the Violin* and *Andrei Rublev*, both directed by Tarkovsky.

His first film as director was the masterly *The First Teacher*, from a novel by Tenguiz Aitmatov, shot on the Central Asian steppes. Using mostly non-professionals except for the lead

characters, Konchalovski conveyed in lyrical terms the contradictions of his story: in the years following the Revolution, a young Russian soldier attempts to educate the people of a newly conquered land. The conflict of the old and the new and also the one between Asia and Europe, the beauty of tradition and the need for change, were expressed with a simplicity of style and a rare quality of emotion.

Konchalovski went even further in his attempt at freeing the Russian cinema from its academic straight jacket by shooting his next film, *Asya's Happiness*, in an actual peasant collective. With a script serving merely as a canvas, several cameras, and using improvisation techniques (which he compared in some respects to Altman's method in *Nashville*) he gave an astonishing force to his rural melodrama. Asya is pregnant by a man that she loves but who is indifferent to her, while she is courted by a man from the town whom she does not like. The realism of the film has probably so shocked the censors that the film was banned and has never been shown abroad or in the U.S.S.R. Konchalovski, following a well-known pattern, next directed literary adaptations from Turgenev (*A Nest of Gentlefolk*) and from Chekhov (*Uncle Vanya*). His love for Russia and for the past, and his great culture and sensitivity, give these films an elegance and a real emotional imapct, though they indulge, sometimes, particulary in the first film, in a certain mannerism. *The Romance of Lovers* is a mawkish story *à la* Lelouch which was heavily attacked—and deservedly so—by the ciritcs, but had a huge popular success. *Siberiade*, a kind of Soviet *Novecento* (the story of two families since the 1917 Revolution) show the director's ability to command a huge production. The early years of the colonization of Siberia allow him to express again his lyrical temperament, but the parts of the film concerned with more recent periods avoid controversial material (the camps, etc.), show dangerous signs of academicism, and make us regret an absence of the freedom, energy, and invention of his first films.

—Michel Ciment.

MILESTONE, LEWIS. American. Family name Milstein; born in Chisinau, near Odessa, Russia, 30 September 1895; became citizen of the United States in 1919, changing name to Milestone. Educated at Jewish schools in Kishinev, Russia; University of Ghent, Belgium; engineering college in Mitweide, Germany. Married Kendall Lee Glaezner in 1935 (died 1978). Career: 1913—emigrates to United States; 1915—photographer's assistant; 1917-19—serves in Army Signal Corps photography section; 1919—moves to Hollywood, becomes assistant to Henry King; 1920-21—works at Ince and Sennett studios; 1922—assistant editor at Fox; 1923—editor at Warner Brothers; 1927—signs contract with Howard Hughes's Caddo Company; 1932—production head for United Artists; 1938—out-of-court settlement of suit against Hal Roach finances adaptation of *Of Mice and Men*; 1942—with Joris Ivens compiles documentary *Our Russian Front*; 1946—appears as unfriendly witness before House Un-American Activities Committee; 1957-58—directs television series; 1962—replaces Carol Reed as director of *Mutiny on the Bounty*. Died in Los Angeles, 25 September 1980. Recipient: Best Comedy Direction Academy Award for *2 Arabian Knights*, 1927; Best Direction Academy Award for *All Quiet on the Western Front*, 1930.

Films (as director): 1925—*7 Sinners* (+co-sc); 1926—*The Caveman*; *The New Klondike*; 1927—*2 Arabian Knights*; 1928—*The Garden of Eden*; *The Racket*; 1929—*Betrayal*; *New York*

Nights; 1930—*All Quiet on the Western Front*; 1931—*The Front Page*; 1932—*Rain*; 1933—*Hallelujah, I'm a Bum*; 1934— *The Captain Hates the Sea*; 1935—*Paris in the Spring*; 1936— *Anything Goes*; *The General Died at Dawn*; 1939—*The Night of Nights*; 1940—*Of Mice and Men* (+pr); *Lucky Partners*; 1941— *My Life with Caroline*; 1942—*Our Russian Front* (co-d, +co-pr, ed); 1943—*Edge of Darkness*; *The North Star*; 1944—*The Purple Heart*; 1946—*A Walk in the Sun* (+pr); *The Strange Love of Martha Ivers*; 1948—*Arch of Triumph* (+co-sc); *No Minor Vices* (+pr); 1949—*The Red Pony* (+pr); 1951—*Halls of Montezuma*; 1952—*Kangaroo*; *Les Miserables*; 1953—*Melba*; *They Who Dare*; 1957—*La Vedova (The Widow)*; 1959—*Pork Chop Hill*; 1960—*Ocean's Eleven* (+pr); 1962—*Mutiny on the Bounty*.

Publications:

By MILESTONE:

Articles—"An Interview with Lewis Milestone" by Herbert Feinstein in *Film Culture* (New York), September 1964; "Lewis Milestone", interview, in *The Celluloid Muse: Hollywood Directors Speak* by Charles Higham and Joel Greenberg, Chicago 1969; "An Interview with Lewis Milestone" by Digby Diehl in *Action* (Los Angeles), July/August 1972; "The Reign of the Director" in *Hollywood Directors: 1914-1940* edited by Richard Koszarski, New York 1976; "First Aid for a Sick Giant" in *Hollywood Directors: 1941-1976* edited by Richard Koszarski, New York 1977.

On MILESTONE:

Books—*The Hollywood Professionals—Vol.2: Henry King, Lewis Milestone, Sam Wood* by Clive Denton and others, New York 1974; *Close Up: The Contract Director* by David Parker and Burton Shapiro, Metuchen, New Jersey 1976; *Lewis Milestone* by Joseph Millichap, Boston 1981; articles—"Directed by Lewis Milestone" by Ezra Goodman in *Theater Arts* (New York), February 1943; "Milestone and War" by Karel Reisz in *Sequence* (London), 1950; "Directors Go to Their Movies: Lewis Milestone" by Digby Diehl in *Action* (Los Angeles), July/August 1972; "Lewis Milestone 'Action!'" by Otis Ferguson in *Film Comment* (New York), March/April 1974; "Thoughts on a Great Adaptation" by William Everson in *The Modern American Novel and the Movies* edited by Gerald Peary and Roger Shatzkin, New York 1978; "Style vs. 'Style'" by R.T. Jameson in *Film Comment* (New York), March/April 1980.

*   *   *

Lewis Milestone is undoubtedly best remembered for his classic statement against the horrors of war, *All Quiet on the Western Front*, for which he won an Academy Award. The film, coming so early in his career, raised high hopes that subsequent efforts would expand upon the brilliant potential exhibited in his first effort. In the minds of many, his following work, with the exception of 1931's *The Front Page*, failed to live up to this early promise.

Through films like *Rain*, *Of Mice and Men*, *Pork Chop Hill*, and *Mutiny on the Bounty*, he achieved a lesser reputation, as a competent journeyman director and an excellent craftsman who, with good actors and a strong script, was capable of producing solid, entertaining films. The fundamental charge leveled against

him by most critics was that he maintained a lackadaisical attitude toward run-of-the-mill projects.

Such assessments, however, overlook the outstanding acheivement of at least one film, the much undervalued *A Walk in the Sun* in which the director's inspired use of sound, coupled with some shifts in perspective, turned a routine war drama into a small classic that compares favorably with his best work. Stylistically and thematically, it expands on the innovations of *All Quiet on the Western Front* and, at the same time, represents perhaps the most creative use of sound since it was introduced to films.

Milestone's experimentation with what the audience hears began with a unique approach to the film's narration which is accompanied by a brooding, recurring ballad. It functions much like a chorus in a Greek play by introducing and commenting on the action. The sentiments of the song are then fleshed out through the audible thoughts, and the dialogues and monologues of individual soldiers. The war is perceived through sound, allowing the audience to experience it as the fighting men do. Modern war is fought against an enemy that the average soldier rarely sees; bomb blasts, strafing from the air and mortar fire are heard as soldiers crouch in foxholes fearing to lift their eyes. *A Walk in the Sun*, by its very refusal to gratify the eye with images of battle and by its emphasis on the small talk of soldiers, creates a microcosm of war that effectively epitomizes the men who must fight all wars. Through Milestone's inspired use of previously-overlooked audio techniques, he achieves sensitivity of treatment in delineating his characters that many critics had found lacking in his work.

Milestone has yet to receive the critical reassessment that he undoubtedly deserves. Films as diverse as *A Walk in the Sun* and the *Strange Love of Martha Ivers* indicate that his later films contain moments of high achievement comparable to his two great early efforts, and that there is also a greater correlation between his technical innovations and his sensitivity-handled theme of men in groups than many scholars give him credit for.

—Stephen L. Hanson

MILIUS, JOHN. American. Born in St. Louis, 1944. Whitman School, Steamboat Springs, Colorado; studied English literature, Los Angeles City College; studied filmmaking at University of Southern California. Married (2nd time) actress Celia Kaye; 2 sons by previous marriage. Career: 1967—attempts to enlist in Marines, rejected because of chronic asthma; 1968-69— participates in founding of American Zoetrope production company; 1969—American International Pictures buys *The Devil's 8* co-written with Willard Huyck and James Gordon White; for Francis Coppola develops with George Lucas a screenplay about Vietnam (*Apocalypse Now*); 1970—does extensive writing, without screen credit, on *Dirty Harry* (Siegel); 1973—writes and directs *Dillinger*; 1975—forms A-Team production company at Warners (producer of Schrader's *Hard Core* and Spielberg's *1941*).

Films (as scriptwriter): 1969—*The Devil's 8* (Topper); 1971— *Evel Knievel* (Chomsky) (co-sc); *Dirty Harry* (Siegel) (co-sc, uncredited); 1972—*Jeremiah Johnson* (Pollack) (co-sc); *The Life and Times of Judge Roy Bean* (Huston); *Magnum Force* (Post) (co-sc); (as director and scriptwriter): 1973—*Dillinger*; 1974—*Melvin Purvis—G-Man* (Curtis—for TV) (sc only); 1975—*The Wind and the Lion*; 1978—*Big Wednesday* (co-sc);

1979—*Apocalypse Now* (Coppola) (co-sc only); 1982—*Conan the Barbarian* (+bit ro).

Publications:

By MILIUS:

Articles—"The Making of Dillinger", interview by A.C. Bobrow in *Filmmakers Newsletter* (Ward Hill, Mass.), November 1973; interview by L. Salvato and D. Schaefer in *Millimeter* (New York), September 1975; "Stoked", interview by R. Thompson in *Film Comment* (New York), July/August 1976; "John Milius 'Hangs 10' on Film", interview by G. MacGillivray in *Americam Cinematographer* (Los Angeles), June 1978; "Francis Ford Coppola: court histoire d'un scenario", interview by R. Thompson in *Ecran* (Paris), 15 September 1979; "John Milius, autor del argumento original, habla de 'Apocalypse Now'", interview in *Cine* (Mexico), March 1980; "Redneck Maverick, Zen Anarchist, or Both?", interview by Giovanni Dadomo in *Time Out* (London), 24-30 September 1982.

On MILIUS:

Articles—"Mr. Macho" by Burr Snider in *Esquire* (New York), June 1973; "'Heart' Transplant" by B. Riley in *Film Comment* (New York), September/October 1979; "Milius the Barbarian" by Kirk Honeycutt in *American Film* (Washington, D.C.), May 1982.

*   *   *

At the University of Southern California, Milius produced a short animated film entitled *Marcello, I'm So Bored*. It contains many of the themes and motifs which would later appear in his feature work, both as a writer and as director: will to power, violence, greed, and a world of almost total anarchy. All this is implied while a black man gently sings to himself as he sweeps a city street.

Neither heroism not villainy *per se* fascinate Milius but rather what he sees as a link between the two: ruthlessness in the pursuit of goals. He is not concerned with the methods used to achieve these ends for his heroes believe that the end justifies the means. A hero's justice can be swift, violent, and bloody. What distinguishes the Mulius hero from his villain is the particular goals. Thulsa Doom of *Conan* enslaves youths in an evil snake cult sending them forth to kill their parents with cult knives (a not-so-veiled comment on today's religious fringe). Conan's goal is to rescue the princess (at first for wealth but later for revenge) and decapitate Doom before his entire following, recalling the decapitation in *Apocalypse Now*. If Conan were a cop, he would be Harry of *Dirty Harry* or *Magnum Force*, and if Thulsa Doom were a colonel in View Nam he might be Kurtz. Whether his heroes are taken from comic book mythology, like Conan, contemporary sociology, like Harry, or American history in the case of Teddy Roosevelt (*The Wind and the Lion*), Milius praises the threat or use of violence in achieving a "moral" goal.

Milius co-authored *Apocalypse Now* with Francis Coppola and his influence in the story can easliy be identified in characters like Kurtz, and Kilgore whose very name suggests violence. The entire film poses the question of methods versus goals, One gets the sense that Milius and Coppola intend to show that to win a dirty war you can not fight a clean war. Kurtz was successful precisely because his methods were as barbaric as those of the enemy. What attracts Milius to Teddy Roosevelt is that if speaking softly did not work, he would use the big stick without hesitation. The Milius hero must not only threaten force, but it must use it without remorse or pity. The world of *Apocalypse Now* and *Wind* are diametrically opposed. Roosevelt and Raisuli are admired for their action while the generals who dispatch men like Willard to kill Kurtz (a man of action) are seen as weak and decadent. Their inaction results in a prolonged war and much needless death.

Milius as director characterizes his style as "ruthless." In a recent interview he said: "One of the things I've learned is to be ruthless. People don't throw star fits, and they don't complain about the food, and they don't wonder about their part because there's just no room for that on my set. They want the director to know what he wants and thats what I mean by 'ruthless.' You have to have a ruthless concept of your vision and nothing distracts you."

As a result of this directness and simplicity of motivation, Milius's characters have been criticized as shallow as have his plots. Psychological, philosophical, or literary complexity have little place in his work. Like the comic book hero, he wants characters which are immediately identified in the mind of his audience by a single trait. This frees him to create action scenes. His tampering with the facts of history (as in *Wind*) is more related to the exigencies of entertainment filmmaking than to any sort of historical revisionism. There is an underlying conservative philosophy in his work. While some feel it distorts history and misrepresents events, others might point to Costa-Gavras on the other end of the political spectrum, who does exactly the same thing. Milius, however, is far less overtly political.

Milius lauds the freedom and strength of individuals. He applauds commitment to a belief and acting on that belief, at any cost. We see this even in his villains. They are bad to the last with no remorse or regrets. Kurtz knows right away that Willard is there to kill him, just as Thulsa Doom knows that Conan is there to kill him. Both Conan and Willard kill their adversaries in the midst of their enemies and walk through them confidently. Those who use violence muct accept the possibility that it will be turned upon them, Milius also respects those who expose themselves to physical danger to prove their courage and worth. We see this in such films as *Big Wednesday*, a surfing movie with a "serious" plot, *Evil Knievel*, co-authored by Milius and two other writers, and *Jeremiah Johnson* which he also co-authored.

Big Wednesday and *Jeremiah Johnson* share the theme of man agianst the forces of nature, while *Evil Knievel* explores that of man and machine. Milius is also drawn to the late 19th and early 20th century in America. He admires the west still wild, unbridled by the laws and social graces of effete society (*The Life and Times of Judge Roy Bean*). Of all his films the least typical is *Big Wednesday*. It departs from his action formula and explores vague, internalized conflicts. It fails as a film. Surely it is filled with the nostalgia of Milius's youth in Cailfornia but it lacks the sort of "ruthlessness" and focus on his other screenplays and films.

—Anthony T. Allegro

MILLER, GEORGE. Australian. Born in Brisbane, 3 March 1945. Educated in medicine, University of New South Wales, M.D. Career: worked in St. Vincent's Hospital, Sydney; 1971—meets Byron Kennedy, collaborates with him on short *Violence* in the Cinema: Part I; 1975—begins working on Mad Max; 1983—president of jury, Avoriaz Festival du film fantastique; producer Byron Kennedy dies in crash of his helicopter.

Films (as director): 1971—Violence in the Cinema: Part I (+co-sc—short); 1973—Devil in Evening Dress (+sc—documentary); Frieze, an Underground Film (ed only—short); 1979—Mad Max (+co-sc); 1980—Chain Reaction (Barry) (assoc. pr only, +collaborator on waterfall scenes); 1981—Mad Max 2 (The Road Warrior) (+co-sc); 1982—The Dismissal (first episode only—for TV) (+exec. pr); 1983—"Nightmare at 2000 Feet" episode of Twilight Zone.

Publications:

By MILLER:

Articles—"Production Report" 'Mad Max': George Miller, Director", interview by P. Beilby and S. Murray in Cinema Papers (Melbourne), May/June 1979; interview by P. Westfield in Cinema Papers (Melbourne), September/October 1979; interview by Tony Crawley in Starburst (London), no.51, 1983.

*   *   *

At the time of his writing, George Miller's place in film history is linked to his nationality and the major cult character he has created in his two films. Along with his Australian contemporaries like Peter Weir and Gillian Armstrong, Miller has helped to bring Australian films to the forefront in international film. The world-wide success of his two "Mad Max" films has cut short Miller's first career as a physician.

Teamed with producer Byon Kennedy, Miller created on film a futuristic savage world of burnt-out men and women. He achieved this by his use of Australia's desolate highways as a setting and his ability to create larger-than-life villains and a distinctive yet familiar anti-hero. The highways seem to stretch for miles and lead nowhere; there is no shade, no comfort, and no shelter. Even the compound in Road Warrior is no more than a few tents and an oil refinery.

Dressed in a mixture of football uniforms, leather jackets and desert wear, the villains are hard and desperate, with a touch of insanity. They attack in groups like intelligent insects, and rape and murder with glee. To counter this evil, the hero Max is presented as a "burnt-out desolate man, a man haunted by the demons of his past," but who can to some extent civilize this wasteland by using his talent for driving. In interviews, Miller has openly admitted Max's resemblence to the Japanese samurai, a knight of the Round table, or the classic western hero, and cites that as one of the reasons for the success of the character and the film.

The pace of his films is very contolled. Action moves very quickly: motorcycles seem to fly, cars crashing flip over and over. Miller will end an action sequence with a fade to black and then begin a slow build up to the next action sequence. Both "Max" films could be plotted as hills and valleys of action.

—Ray Narducy

MINNELLI, VINCENTE. American. Born in Chicago, 28 February 1910. Educated at the Art Institute of Chicago, mid-1920s. Married Judy Garland in 1945 (divorced 1951); child: Liza; married Georgette Magnani (divorced); child: Christiana; married Denise Gigante in 1961 (divorced). Career: child actor with Minnelli Bros. Dramatic Tent Show; late 1920s—works as stage designer at Chicago Theatre for Balaban and Katz organization; 1931—moves to New York, working initially as costume designer; 1932—hired by Earl Carroll to design 1932 Vanities; 1933—chief costume designer, Radio City Music Hall; 1935—begins directing on Broadway with At Home Abroad; 1936—hired by Paramount as producer-director; buys out of contract after 8 months; 1940—joins MGM under producer Arthur Freed, serves in various production capacities before directing; 1942—directs certain sequences of Babes on Broadway (Berkeley) and Panama Hattie (McLeod); 1943—directs first film Cabin in the Sky; 1965—ends 26-year contract with MGM; 1967—directs Broadway-bound production Mata Hari, closes after 2-week Washington run. Recipient: Best Direction Academy Award for Gigi, 1958. Address: c/o Paul Kohner, Kohner-Levy Agency, 9169 Sunset Blvd., Hollywood CA 90069.

Films (as director): 1942—Cabin in the Sky; 1943—I Dood It (By Hook or By Crook); 1944—Meet Me in St. Louis; 1945—The Clock (Under the Clock); Yolanda and the Thief; 1946—Ziegfeld Follies (co-d); Undercurrent; 1947—Judy Garland sequences in Till the Clouds Roll By (Whorf); 1948—The Pirate; 1949—Madame Bovary; 1950—Father of the Bride; 1951—An American in Paris; Father's Little Dividend; 1952—fashion show sequence in Lovely to Look At (LeRoy); 1953—"Mademoiselle" episode of The Story of 3 Loves; The Bad and the Beautiful; The Band Wagon; 1954—The Long, Long Trailer; Brigadoon; 1955—The Cobweb; Kismet; 1956—Lust for Life; Tea and Sympathy; 1957—Designing Woman; The Seventh Sin (Neame) (replaced Neame as director, refused credit); 1958—Gigi; The Reluctant Debutante; 1959—Some Came Running; 1960—Home from the Hill; Bells Are Ringing; 1962—The 4 Horsemen of the Apocalypse; 2 Weeks in Another Town; 1963—The Courtship of Eddie's Father; 1964—Goodbye Charlie; 1965—The Sandpiper; 1970—On a Clear Day You Can See Forever; 1976—A Matter of Time.

Publications:

By MINNELLI:

Book—I Remember It Well, with Hector Arce, New York 1974; articles—"Entretien avec Vincente Minnelli" by Charles Bitsch and Jean Domarchi in Cahiers du cinéma (Paris), August/September 1957; "So We Changed It" in Films and Filming (London), November 1958; "Rencontre avec Vincente Minnelli" by Jean Domarchi and Jean Douchet in Cahiers du cinéma (Paris), February 1962; "The Rise and Fall of the Musical" in Films and Filming (London), January 1962; "On the Relationship of Style to Content in The Sandpiper" in Cinema (Los Angeles), July/August 1965; interview in The Celluloid Muse: Hollywood Directors Speak edited by Charles Higham and Joel Greenberg, London 1969; "Vincente Minnelli and Gigi", interview by Digby Diehl in Action (Los Angeles), September/October 1972; "The Nostalgia Express", interview by Gideon Bachmann in Film Comment (New York), November/December 1976; interview by D. Rabourdin in Cinéma (Paris), January 1978; "2 Weeks in Another Town", interview by P. Lehman and others in Wide Angle (Athens, Ohio), no.1, 1979.

On MINNELLI:

Books—*Vincente Minnelli* by François Truchaud, Paris 1966; *The Magic Factory: How M-G-M Made "An American in Paris"* by Donald Knox, New York 1973; articles—"Vincente Minnelli" by Simon Harcourt-Smith in *Sight and Sound* (London), January/March 1952; "L'Oeuvre de V.M." by Etienne Chaumeton in *Positif* (Paris), November/December 1954; "The Films of Vincente Minnelli" by Albert Johnson in *Film Quarterly* (Berkeley), winter 1958 and spring 1959; "The Magic of Minnelli" by Douglas McVay in *Films and Filming* (London), June 1959; "Minnelli's Method" by Mark Shivas in *Movie* (London), June 1962; "The Testament of V. Minnelli" by Paul Mayersberg in *Movie* (London), October 1962; Minnelli issue of *Movie* (London), June 1963; "V.M. ou Le Peintre de la vie rêvée" by Jean-Paul Torok and Jacques Quincey in *Positif* (Paris), March 1963; "V.M. is One of the Few Hollywood Directors Who Has an Art Sense" by Dennis Galling in *Films in Review* (New York), March 1964; "La Tentation du rêve" by Jean Douchet in *Objectif 64* (Paris), February/March 1964; "Lo spettacolo di Minnelli e il carro della Metro" by M. Del Ministro in *Cinema nuovo* (Turin), January/February 1975; "Minnelli and Melodrama" by G. Nowell-Smith in *Australian Journal of Screen Theory* (Kensington N.S.W.), no.3, 1977; "Mémoire musicale" by J. Fieschi in *Cinématographe* (Paris), January 1978; "Minnelli and 'The Pirate'" by D. McVay in *Velvet Light Trap* (Madison), spring 1978; "Vincente Minnelli" by George Morris in *International Film Guide 1978*, London 1977; "Sur quelques films de Minnelli" by Noel Simsolo in *Image et son* (Paris), October 1981.

* * *

Between 1942 and 1962, Vincente Minnelli directed 29 films and parts of several others at Metro-Goldwyn-Mayer, eventually becoming the studio's longest-tenured director. Brought to Hollywood following a tremendously successful career as a Broadway set designer and director of musicals, he was immediately placed at the helm of MGM's biggest musical productions, beginning with the all-black *Cabin in the Sky*. Over the next decade-and-a-half, he gained a reputation as the premiere director at work in the genre, based on a remarkable series of productions including *Meet Me in St. Louis*, *The Pirate*, *An American in Paris*, and *The Band Wagon*, and culminating with a Best Director's Oscar for *Gigi*. Yet Minnelli's career was by no means restricted to musicals. During the same period he also directed a series of successful comedies and melodramas with flair and stylistic elegance.

If anything, Minnelli's accomplishments as a stylist, which were recognized from the beginning of his Hollywood career, worked against his being taken seriously as a director-auteur. By the late fifties, he had been dubbed (by critic Albert Johnson) "the master of the decorative image," which seemed, at the time, the highest compliment which might be paid a director of musicals. Indeed, Minnelli's films are impeccably crafted—filled with lushly stylized sets, clever, graceful performances, a partiality for long tales, and a fluid mobile camera suited to the filming of dance, mounting and perserving performance spatially, even as the camera involves the audience in the choreographed movement. Yet it also informs the non-musical sequences of Minnelli's films with the same kind of liberal sensibilty associated with contemporaries like Otto Preminger and Nicholas Ray, one that allows both the characters and the eyes of the audience a certain freedom of movement within a nearly seamless time and space. An accompanying theatricality (resulting from a tendency to shoot scenes from a fourth-wall position) blends with Minnelli's specifically cinematic flourishes in a clever realization of the themes of art and artificiality themes which run throughout his films.

Stylization and artifice are necessarily addressed by musical films in general, and Minnelli's films do so with great verve— most thoroughly in the baroque outworldliness of *Yolanda and the Thief*; most brilliantly in the interplay of character and actor, stage and screen in *The Band Wagon*. But an equal concern with levels of unreality informs most of his films, most obviously perhaps in the Pirandellian meditation on Hoolywood, *The Bad and the Beautiful*, and it bizarre, Cinecitta-made quasi-sequel, *Two Weeks in Another Town*. This exploration surely reaches a kind of limit in Minnelli's last film, *A Matter of Time*, where the story of an aspiring actress, played by Liza Minnelli, becomes an examination his own daughter's talents and persona (haunted by the ghost of Judy Garland), making the film into the director's own *Vertigo*, a fitting conclusion to a career devoted to the interplay of various levels of fantasy.

Filmic fantsy is almost always present in Minnelli's films, even when they address the most mundane human problems in basically realistic settings. Virtually every Minnelli film contains a fantasy sequence, which is to say a moment in which the narrative recedes in order to allow a free play of symbols on an almost exclusively formal level. In the musicals, this is invariably an extended "ballet"—most memorably, the 20-minute number which concludes *An American in Paris*; but perhaps most powerfully, Judy Garland's erotic fantasy of Gene Kelly as "Mack the Black" in *The Pirate*. In *Meet Me in St. Louis*, the burst of pure style occurs in the non-musical, and surprisingly horrific Halloween sequence. In the comedy *Father of the Bride*, it is a tour-de-force dream sequence in which all of Spencer Tracy's fatherly anxieties are unleashed. The position is filled by a hallucinatory chase through a carnival in *Some Came Running*, by fantastic visions of the title figures in *The Four Horsemen of the Apocalypse*, and by mad car rides in both *The Bad and the Beautiful* and *Two Weeks in Another Town*. Such extra-narrative sequences serve to condense and resolve plot elements on a visual/emotional plane, providing the only escape routes from the exigencies of a world which Minnelli otherwise depicts as emotionally frustrating, overly complex, and terribly delicate.

Indeed, Andrew Sarris quite rightly noted that "Minnelli had an unusual, sombre outlook for musical comedy," a fact which seems responsible for lending most of his films an unexpected depth. Certainly one of the factors responsible for the continued interest in *Meet Me in St. Louis* is the overt morbidity of its nostalgic tone. Yet Minnelli's troubled perspective is probably most evident in the existential isolation of his characters, add in the humanistic, yet stoic attitude he adopts in treating equally of their petty jealousies and their moral fears. A genuinely pained sense of the virtual impossibility of meaningful human contact informs the machinations of such stylized melodramas as *Some Came Running*, *Home from the Hill*, and *The Four Horsemen*. And the tenuousness of love and power is nowhere more artfully rendered than in his generic masterpiece, *The Cobweb*, where an argument over drapes for the rec room of a mental hospital reveals a network of neuroses, amongst the staff and their families, as deep-seated as the disorders of the patients.

At worst, Minnelli has been cited as the epitome of Hollywood's "middlebrow" aspirations toward making art accessible to the mass audience. At best, he was championed by the British critics at *Movie* during the early sixties as one of Hollywood's consummate auteurs. For one such critic, V.F. Perkins, Minnelli's films provided some of the best examples of classical narrative style, which naturalized meaning through understated flourishes of mise-en-scène. It is certainly this capacity which enabled Minnelli to employ a 40-foot trailer as a effortless metaphor for the marriage of newlyweds Lucille Ball and Desi Arnaz (*The Long, Long Trailer*), to critique the manipulations of parental love by consumer culture in terms of an increasingly overblown wedding (*Father of the Bride*), and to displace a child's incapacity to deal with his mother's death onto his horror at the discovery of his dead goldfish (*The Courtship of Eddie's Father*).

We must certainly categorize Minnelli as something more than a decorative artist, for the stylistic devices of his films are informed with a remarkably resilient intelligence. And even if we are finally to conclude that, throughout his work, there is a dominance of style over theme, it ultimately serves only to confirm his contribution to the refinement of those techniques by which Hollywood translates meanings into style and presents both as entertainment.

—Ed Lowry

MIZOGUCHI, KENJI. Japanese. Born in Tokyo, 16 May 1898. Educated at Aohashi Western Painting Research Institute, Tokyo, enrolled 1914. Career: 1913—becomes apprentice to textile designer; about 1916—newspaper illustrator in Kobe; 1922—hired as assistant by director Osamu Wakayama; 1923—begins directing; late 1920s—makes several leftist "tendency films" severely cut by censors; 1933—begins association with art director Hiroshi Mizutani on *Gion Festival*; 1936—beginning with *Osaka Elegy*, collaborates with scriptwriter Yoshikata Yoda; 1940—becomes member of Cabinet Film Committee, publishes statements supporting nationalistic spirit in films; 1949—elected president of Japanese directors association; 1952—signs with Daiei company, and remains with it for rest of career. Died of leukemia in Kyoto, 24 August 1956. Recipient: International Prize, Venice Festival, for *The Life of Oharu*, 1952.

Films (as director): 1923—*Ai ni yomigaeru hi (The Resurrection of Love)*; *Furusato (Hometown)* (+sc); *Seishun no yumeji (The Dream Path of Youth)* (+sc); *Joen no chimata (City of Desire)* (+sc); *Haizan no uta wa kanashi (Failure's Song is Sad)* (+sc); *813 (813: The Adventures of Arsène Lupin)*; *Kiri no minato (Foggy Harbor)*; *Chi to rei (Blood and Soul)* (+sc); *Yoru (The Night)* (+sc); *Haikyo no naka (In the Ruins)*; 1924—*Toge no uta (The Song of the Mountain Pass)* (+sc); *Kanashiki hakuchi (The Sad Idiot)* (+story); *Gendai no joo (The Queen of Modern Times)*; *Josei wa tsuyoshi (Women Are Strong)*; *Jinkyo (This Dusty World)*; *Shichimencho no yukue (Turkeys in a Row)*; *Samidare zoshi (A Chronicle of May Rain)*; *Musen fusen (No Money, No Fight)*; *Kanraku no onna (A Woman of Pleasure)* (+story); *Akatsuki no shi (Death at Dawn)*; 1925—*Kyohubadan no joo (Queen of the Circus)*; *Gakuso o idete (Out of College)* (+sc); *Shirayuri wa nageku (The White Lily Laments)*; *Daichi wa hohoemu (The Earth Smiles)*; *Akai yuhi ni terasarete (Shining in the Red Sunset)*; *Furusato no uta (The Song of Home)*; *Ningen (The Human Being)*; *Gaijo no suketchi (Street Sketches)*; 1926—*Nogi Taisho to Kuma-san (General Nogi and Kuma-san)*; *Doka o (The Copper Coin King)* (+story); *Kaminingyo haru no sayaki (A Paper Doll's Whisper of Spring)*; *Shin ono ga tsumi (My Fault, New Version)*; *Kyoren no onna shisho (The Passion of a Woman Teacher)*; *Kaikoku danji (The Boy of the Sea)*; *Kane (Money)* (+story); 1927—*Ko-on (The Imperial Grace)*; *Jihi shincho (The Cuckoo)*; 1928—*Hito no issho (A Man's Life)*; 1929—*Nihombashi* (+sc); *Tokyo koshinkyoku (Tokyo March)*; *Asahi wa kagayaku (The Morning Sun Shines)*; *Tokai kokyogaku (Metropolitan Symphony)*; 1930—*Furusato (Home Town)*; *Tojin okichi (Mistress of a Foreigner)*; 1931—*Shikamo karera wa yuku (And Yet They Go)*; 1932—*Toki no ujigami (The Man of the Moment)*; *Mammo Kenkoku no Reimei (The Dawn of Manchukuo and Mongolia)*; 1933—*Taki no Shiraito (Taki no Shiraito, the Water Magician)*; *Gion matsuri (Gion Festival)* (+sc); *Jimpuren (The Jimpu Group)* (+sc); 1934—*Aizo toge (The Mountain Pass of Love and Hate)*; *Orizuru osen (The Downfall of Osen)*; 1935—*Maria no Oyuki (Oyuki the Madonna)*; *Gubijinso (Poppy)*; 1936—*Naniwa ereji (Osaka Elegy)* (+story); *Gion no shimai (Sisters of the Gion)* (+story); 1937—*Aienkyo (The Straits of Love and Hate)*; 1938—*Aa furusato (Ah, My Home Town)*; *Roei no uta (The Song of the Camp)*; 1939—*Zangiku monogatari (The Story of the Last Chrysanthemum)*; 1944—*Danjuro sandai (3 Generations of Danjuro)*; *Miyamoto Musashi (Musashi Miyamoto)*; 1945—*Meito Bijomaru (The Famous Sword Bijomaru)*; *Hisshoka (Victory Song)* (co-d); 1946—*Josei no shori (The Victory of Women)*; *Utamaro o meguru gonin no onna (Utamaro and His 5 Women)*; 1947—*Joyu Sumako no koi (The Love of Sumako the Actress)*; 1948—*Yoru no onnatachi (Women of the Night)*; 1949—*Waga koi wa moenu (My Love Burns)*; 1950—*Yuki Fujin ezu (A Picture of Madame Yuki)*; 1951—*Oyu-sama (Miss Oyu)*; *Musashino Fujin (Lady Musashino)*; 1952—*Saikaku ichidai onna (The Life of Oharu)*; 1953—*Ugetsu monogatari (Ugetsu)*; *Gion bayashi (Gion Festival Music)*; 1954—*Sansho dayu (Sansho the Bailiff)*; *Uwasa no onna (The Woman of the Rumor)*; *Chikamatsu monogatari (A Story from Chikamatsu, Crucified Lovers)*; 1955—*Yokihi (The Princess Yang Kwei-fei)*; *Shin Heike monogatari (New Tales of the Taira Clan)*; 1956—*Akasen chitai (Street of Shame)*.

Publications:

By MIZOGUCHI:

Articles—texts by Mizoguchi in *Cahiers du cinéma* (Paris), May 1959; "Kenji Mizoguchi" in *Positif* (Paris), November 1980; "Table ronde avec Kenji Mizoguchi (I)" in *Positif* (Paris), December 1980; interview by K. Matsuo translated in *Contracampo* (Madrid), February 1981; "Table ronde avec Kenji Mizoguchi (II)" in *Positif* (Paris), January 1981.

On MIZOGUCHI:

Books—*The Japanese Film: Art and Industry* by Joseph Anderson and Donald Richie, New York 1960; *Kenji Mizoguchi* by Ve-Ho, Paris 1963; *Mizoguchi Kenji* by Michel Mesnil, Paris 1965; "Mizoguchi" by Akira Iwazaki in *Anthologie du cinéma* vol.3, Paris 1968; *Mizoguchi Kenji no hito to geijutsu* [Kenji Mizoguchi: The Man and His Art] by Yoshikata Yoda, Tokyo 1970; *Kenji Mizoguchi* edited by Michel Mesnil, Paris 1971; *Voices from the Japanese Cinema* by Joan Mellen, New York 1975; *The Waves at Genji's Door: Japan Through Its Cinema* by Joan Mellen, New York 1976; *Japanese Film Directors* by Audie Bock, New York 1978; articles—special issue of *Cinéma 55* (Paris), no.6, 1955; *Kenji Mizoguchi* by Joseph Anderson and Donald Richie in *Sight and Sound* (London), autumn 1955; "Mizoguchi vu d'ici" by Jacques Rivette in *Cahiers du cinéma* (Paris), no.81, 1958; "L'Art de Kenji Mizoguchi" by Jean-Luc Godard in *Art* (Paris), no.656, 1958; special issue of *Cahiers du cinéma* (Paris), March 1958; special issue of *L'Ecran* (Paris), February/March 1958; articles by Philippe Demonsablon and Luc Moullet in *Cahiers du cinéma* (Paris), May 1959; "What is Mise-en-Scène?" by Alexandre Astruc in *Film Culture* (New

York), summer 1961; "Dossier Mizoguchi" in *Cahiers du cinéma* (Paris), August/September 1964; "Souvenirs sur Mizoguchi" by Yoshikata Yoda in *Cahiers du cinéma* (Paris), no.174, 1966; "Kenji Mizoguchi" by Akira Iwasaki in *Anthologie du cinéma* (Paris), November 1967; "The Density of Mizoguchi's Scripts", interview with Yoshikata Yoda, in *Cinema* (Los Angeles), spring 1971; "Memories of Mizoguchi" in *Cinema* (Los Angeles), spring 1971; "Mizoguchi: The Ghost Princess and the Seaweed Catcher" by Robin Wood in *Film Comment* (New York), March/April 1973; "3 cinéastes de la femme" by G. Braucourt and others in *Ecran* (Paris), August/September 1974; "Les Contes de la lune vague après la pluie", special issue of *Avant-Scène du cinéma* (Paris), 1 January 1977; "L'Espace de Mizoguchi" by H. Bokanowski in *Cinématographe* (Paris), November 1978; "Mizoguchi and Modernism" by R. Cohen in *Sight and Sound* (London), spring 1978; "Connaissance de Kenji Mizoguchi" by J. Douchet in *Cinéma* (Paris), August/September 1978; special section by G. Legrand and others in *Positif* (Paris), November 1978; "Notes sur Kenji Mizoguchi" by Noel Simsolo in *Image et son* (Paris), March 1979; "Il fantasma di Mizoguchi non e quello di Oshima" by M. Buffa in *Filmcritica* (Rome), January 1979; "Mizoguchi: un art sans artifice" by H. Niogret in *Positif* (Paris), December 1980; "On Kenji Mizoguchi" by Tadao Sato and Dudley Andrew in *Film Criticism* (Edinboro, Pennsylvania), spring 1980; "Tom Allen from New York" in *Film Comment* (New York), July/August 1981; "Kenji Mizoguchi: La Passion de la identification" by Dudley Andrew in *Positif* (Paris), January 1981; "Esa silla vacía, o el plano secuencia en Mizoguchi" by I. Bosch in *Contracampo* (Madrid), February 1981.

*   *   *

By any standard Kenji Mizoguchi must be considered among the world's greatest directors. Known in the West for the final half-dozen films which crowned his career, Mizoguchi considered himself a popular as well as a serious artist. Having made 85 films is evidence of that popularity and makes him, like John Ford, one of the few directorial geniuses to play a key role in a major film industry. In fact, Mizoguchi once headed the vast union governing all production personnel in Japan, and was awarded more than once the industry's most coveted citations. But it is as a meticulous, passionate artist that Mizoguchi will be remembered. His temperament drove him to astounding lengths of research, rehearsal, and execution. Decade after decade he refined his approach while energizing the industry with both his consistency and his innovations.

Mizoguchi's obsessive concern with ill-treated women, as well as his maniacal pursuit of a lofty notion of art, stems from his upbringing. His obstinate father, unsuccessful in business, refused to send his older son beyond primary school. With the help of his sister, a onetime geisha who had become the mistress of a wealthy nobleman, Mizoguchi managed to enroll in a western-style art school. For a short time he did layout work and wrote reviews for a newspaper, but his real education came through the countless books he read and the theater he attended almost daily. In 1920 he presented himself as an actor at Nikkatsu studio, where a number of his friends worked. He moved quickly into scriptwriting, then became an assistant director, and finally a director. Between 1922 and 1935, he made 55 films, mostly melodramas, detective stories, and adaptations. Only six of these are known to exist today.

Though these lost films might show the influences on his development of other Japanese films, of German expressionism, and of American dramatic filmmaking (not to mention Japanese theatrical style and western painting and fiction), Mizoguchi himself dismissed his early efforts, claiming that his first real achievement as an artist came in 1936. Working for the first time with scriptwriter Yoshikata Yoda, who would be his collaborator on nearly all his subsequent films, he produced *Osaka Elegy* and *Sisters of the Gion*, stories of exploited women in contemporary Japan. Funded by Daiichi, a tiny independent company he helped set up to by-pass big-studio strictures, these films were poorly distributed and had trouble with the censors on account of their dark realism and touchy subject. While effectively bankrupting Daiichi, these films caused a sensation among the critics and further secured Mizoguchi's reputation as a powerful, if renegade, force in the industry.

Acknowledged by the wartime culture as Japan's chief director, Mizoguchi busied himself during the war mainly with historical dramas which were ostensibly non-political, thus acceptable to the wartime government. Under the Allied occupation Mizoguchi was encouraged to make films about women, in both modern and historical settings, as part of America's effort to democratize Japanese society. With Yoda as scriptwriter and with actress Kinuyo Tanaka as star, the next years were busy but debilitating for Mizoguchi. He was beginning to be considered old-fashioned in technique even if his subjects were volatile. Ironically it was the West which resuscitated this most oriental director. With his critical and box-office reputation on the decline, Mizoguchi decided to invest everything in *The Life of Oharu*, a classic seventeenth-century Japanese picaresque story, and in 1951 he finally secured sufficient financing to produce it himself. Expensive, long, and complex, *Oharu* was not a particular success in Japan, but it gained an international reputation for Mizoguchi when it won the grand prize at Venice. Daiei Films, a young company aimed at the export market recently opened for Japanese films, then gave Mizoguchi virtual carte blanche, under which he was able to create his final string of masterpieces, beginning with his most famous film *Ugetsu*.

Mizoguchi's fanatic attention to detail, his insistence on multiple rewritings of Yoda's scripts, and his calculated tyranny over actors are legendary, as he sought perfection demanded by few other film artists. He saw his later films as the culmination of many years work, his style evolving from one in which a set of tableaux were photographed from an imperial distance and then cut together (one scene/one shot) to one in which the camera moves between two moments of balance, beginning with the movements of a character, then coming to rest at its own proper point.

It was this later style which hypnotized the French critics and through them the West in general. The most striking oppositions in his themes and dramas (innocence vs. guilt, good vs. bad) unroll like a seamless scroll until in the final camera flourish one feels the achievement of a majestic, stoic contemplation of life.

More recently Mizoguchi's early films have come under scrutiny, both for their radical stylistic innovations such as the shared flashbacks of the 1935 *Downfall of Osen*, and for the radical political position which they virtually shriek (the final close-ups of *Sisters of the Gion* and *Osaka Elegy*). When charges of mysticism are levelled at Mizoguchi, it is good to recall that his final film, *Street of Shame*, certainly helped bring about the ban on prostitution in Japan in 1957.

A profound influence on the New Wave directors, Mizoguchi continues to fascinate those in the forefront of the art (Godard, Straub, Rivette). Complete retrospectives of his 31 extant films in Venice, London, and New York resulted in voluminous publications about Mizoguchi in the 1980s. A passionate but contemplative artist, struggling with issues crucial to cinema and society, Mizoguchi will continue to reward anyone who looks closely at his films. His awesome talent, self-discipline, and productivity guarantee this.

—Dudley Andrew

MOLANDER, GUSTAF. Swedish. Born in Helsingfors (now Helsinki), Finland, 11 (or 18) November 1888. Educated at Royal Dramatic Theatre, Stockholm. Married to Karin Molander, 1910-18. Career: 1909-11—member of Swedish National Theatre company, Helsingfors, directed by father; 1913-26—stage actor in Stockholm; 1917—begins writing filmscripts for Mauritz Stiller; 1920—directs first film *The King of Boda*; 1923—joins Svensk Filmindustri as director; 1935—introduces Ingrid Bergman, one of series of Swedish stars who first played in Molander films. Died 21 June 1973.

Films (as scriptwriter): 1917—*Terje Vigen* (Sjöstrom) (co-sc); *Thomas Graals bästa film (Thomas Graal's Best Film)* (Stiller) (co-sc); 1918—*Thomas Graals bästa barn (Thomas Graal's First Child)* (Stiller); *Sängen om den eldröda blomman (Song of the Scarlet Flower)* (Stiller); 1919—*Herr Arnes pengar (Sir Arne's Treasure)* (Stiller); (as director and scriptwriter): 1920—*Bodakunden (King of Boda)*; 1922—*Thomas Graals myndling (Thomas Graal's Ward)*; 1923—*Pärlorna (The Amateur Film)*; 1923—*Mälarpirater (Pirates on Lake Mälar)* (sc only); 1924—*33.333*; *Polis Paulus påskasmäll (Constable Paulus's Easter Bomb)*; 1925—*Ingmarsarvet (The Ingmar Inheritance)* (co-sc); 1926—*Till Österland (To the Orient)* (co-sc); (as director): *Hon den enda (She's the Only One)*; *Hans engelska fru (His English Wife)*; 1927—*Förseglade löppar (Sealed Lips)*; 1928—*Parisiskor (Women of Paris)*; *Synd (Sin)*; 1929—*Hjärtats triumf (Triumph of the Heart)*; 1930—*Charlotte Löwenskjöld (Charlotte Löwensköld)*; 1930—*Fridas visor (Frida's Songs)*; 1931—*Från yttersta skären*; *En natt (One Night)*; 1932—*Svarta rosor (Black Roses)*; *Kärlek och kassabrist (Love and Deficit)* (+co-sc); *Vi som går köksvägen (We Go Through the Kitchen)* (+co-sc); 1933—*Kära släkten (Dear Relatives)* (+co-sc); 1934—*En stilla flirt (A Quiet Affair)* (+co-sc); *Fasters miljoner (My Aunt's Millions)*; *Ungkarlspappan (Bachelor Father)* (+co-sc); 1935—*Under falsk flagg (Under False Colors)* (+co-sc); *Swedenhielms* (+co-sc); *Bröllopsresan (The Honeymoon Trip)* (+co-sc); 1936—*På solsidan (On the Sunny Side)* (remade for TV 1966); *Intermezzo* (+co-sc); *Familjens hemlighet (The Family Secret)*; 1937—*Sara lär sig folkvett (Sara Learns Manners)*; *Dollar* (+co-sc); 1938—*En kvinnas ansikte (A Woman's Face)* (+co-sc); *En enda natt (One Single Night)* (+co-sc); *Ombyte förnöjer (Variety Is the Spice of Life)*; 1939—*Emilie Högqvist* (+co-sc); 1940—*En, men ett lejon (One But a Lion)*; *Den ljusnande framtid (Bright Prospects)* (+co-sc); 1941—*I natt eller aldrig (Tonight or Never)*; *Striden går vidare (The Fight Goes On)* (+co-sc); 1942—*Jacobs stege (Jacob's Ladder)*; *Rid i natt (Ride Tonight!)* (+sc); 1943—*Det brinner en eld (There Burned a Flame)*; *Älskling, jag ger mig (Darling I Surrender)*; *Ordet (The Word)*; 1944—*Den osynliga muren (The Invisible Wall)*; *Kejsaren av Portugallien (The Emperor of Portugal)* (+co-sc); 1945—*Galgamannen (Mandragora)* (+co-sc); 1946—*Det är min modell (It's My Model)*; 1947—*Kvinna utan ansikte (Woman without a Face)*; 1948—*Nu börjar livet (Life Begins Now)* (+co-sc); *Eva* (+co-sc); 1949—*Kärleken segrar (Love Will Conquer)*; 1950—*Kvartetten som sprängdes (The Quartet That Split Up)*; 1951—*Fästmö uthyres (Fiancée for Hire)*; *Fränskild (Divorced)*; 1952—*Trots (Defiance)* (+sc); *Kärlek (Love)* (+co-sc); 1953—*Glasberget (Unmarried)* (+co-sc); 1954—*Herr Arnes pengar (Sir Arne's Treasure)* (+co-sc—remake); 1955—*Enhörningen (The Unicorn)* (+co-sc); 1957—*Sången om den eldröda blommon (Song of the Scarlet Flower)* (remake); 1967—"*Smycket (The Necklace)*" episode of *Stimulantia* (shot 1965).

*   *   *

Gustav Molander was a screenwriter/director whose work remains largely unknown outside his native Sweden. Although his career spanned nearly 50 years and resulted in over 60 feature films, he is best remembered as the man who "discovered" Ingrid Bergman and who wrote and directed *Intermezzo*, the film which brought that remarkably beautiful and talented actress to the attention of producer David O. Selznick.

Molander was a cultivated man whose career was mostly devoted to making elegant comedies and romantic dramas. Along with Victor Seastrom and Mauritz Stiller, he was one of the noted directors of Sweden's "golden age of cinema"—1913-1924—and although not as artistically creative as those two masters, he was a respected journeyman director. Further unlike Seastrom and Stiller, he chose not to emigrate to Hollywood, refusing Selznick's invitation in 1937.

In 1917 he had written the screenplay for Seastrom's milestone, *Terje Vigen*, about the English blockade of Norway during the Napoleonic wars. He also wrote the scripts for three important films directed by Mauritz Stiller—*Thomas Graal's Best Film*; *Thomas Graal's Best Child*, and the sophisticated sex comedy, *Erotikon*. These three films starred Karin Molander, Molander's vivacious wife, who later married Lars Hanson. Molander began directing with *King of Boda*, very often writing his own screenplays. He was also the director of the Royal Dramatic Theatre and it was he who, in the spring of 1923, suggested the young Greta Gustaffsson—later Garbo—for Stiller's *Gösta Berlings Saga*.

Following the decline of Sweden's "golden age," much of Molander's creativity was directed toward launching the career of Ingrid Bergman. He directed her first screen test, encouraged her, directed her in seven films, most notably *Intermezzo*, which he wrote especially for her. Years later he would modestly state: "The truth is nobody discovered her. Nobody launched her. She discovered herself." His first film with the lovely young actress was the intelligent romantic comedy, *Swedenhielms*, about a wealthy girl who is engaged to the son of a brilliant but impoverished scientist, played by the great Gosta Ekman. *On the Sunny Side* was a charming, lightweight comedy co-starring Bergman and Lars Hanson. *Intermezzo*, again with Hanson, followed, after which Bergman went to Hollywood to film the U.S. version of that romantic classic about the love between a beautiful young pianist and a famous, married violinist. That film made an international star of Ingrid Bergman but she did return to her native Sweden to star in three more films directed by Molander. *Dollar* was a sophisticated farce with Bergman playing an actress; *A Woman's Face* the dramatic story of a facially-scarred criminal, was later re-made with Joan Crawford; and *En enda natt* was another elegant film which dealt with illegitimacy and extra-marital sex.

During World War II, Molander directed several anti-Nazi dramas, and the ambitious religious allegory, *The World*, remade by Carl Dreyer in 1955. Molander also helped launch the career of another young Swedish actress from the Royal Dramatic Theatre, Signe Hasso. Molander's post-World War II career consisted mostly of rather pedestrian filmic renderings of plays and novels which relied heavily on dialogue, such as the turgid remaking of *Sir Arne's Treasure*. Molander's version of that popular novel by Selma Lagerlof bore little comparison to Stiller's masterful 1919 production. Two exceptions to this stagnant period in Molander's career were *Eva* and *Divorce*, both derived from scripts by Ingmar Bergman.

After *Song of the Scarlet Flower*, Molander retired, but interrupted his retirement in 1964 to direct Ingrid Bergman one last time in *Stimulantia*, a four-episode film released in 1967. The Molander segment was entitled "The Necklace" and was based on Guy de Maupassant's short story. Upon completion of that film a reporter asked, "And what are your plans for the future?" Molander replied, "The graveyard." Molander died in 1973, and while little-known outside Sweden, his lengthy career spanned the history of Swedish cinema.

—Ronald Bowers

MONICELLI, MARIO. Italian. Born at Viareggio (Tuscany), 16 May 1915. Studied history and philosophy at Universities of Pisa and Milan. Career: 1932-33—contributes film articles to student revue *Camminare*; 1935—wins prize at Venice Festival for 16mm film *I ragazzi della via Paal*, a collaboration with Alberto Mondadori; success of film leads to position as assistant director, notably on Gustav Machaty's *Ballerine* (1936), and on films of Pietro Germi, Mario Camerini, Mario Bonnard, and others; 1940-43—army service; 1944—resumes working in film as scriptwriter; in all writes or collaborates on over 40 filmscripts; 1949—forms directing and scriptwriting team with Steno (Stefano Vanzina) through 1953; they collaborate on 8 films starring Totò; 1953—begins solo directing with *Proibito*. Recipient: Best Direction, Berlin Festival, for *Fathers and Sons*, 1957; Golden Lion, Venice Festival, for *The Great War*, 1959; Best Director, Berlin Festival, for *Caro Michele*, 1976; Silver Bear (Best Direction), Berlin Festival, for *Il Marchese del Grillo*, 1982. Address: Via del Babuino, 135, Rome, Italy.

Films (as director): 1935—*I ragazzi della via Paal*; *Il cuore rivelatore* (short); (as scriptwriter—partial list of about 40): 1946—*Aquila Nera (The Black Eagle)* (Freda); 1947—*I miserabili* (in 2 parts: *La caccia all'uomo* and *Tempesta su Parigi*) (Freda); *Gioventù perduta (Lost Youth)* (Germi) (+ass't d); 1948—*Il cavaliere misterioso* (Freda); 1949—*Il Conte Ugolino (Il cavaliere di ferro)* (Freda); *In nome della legge (Mafia)* (Germi); (as director with Steno, and scriptwriter in collaboration with Steno and others): 1949—*Al diavolo la celebrità*; 1950—*Totò cerca casa*; *Vita da cani*; *È arrivato il cavaliere*; 1951—*Guardie e ladri (Cops and Robbers)*; *Il tradimento* (Freda) (co-sc only); 1952—*Totò e i re di Roma*; 1953—*Totò e le donne*; *Le infedeli*; (as director and co-scriptwriter): 1954—*Proibito*; 1955—*Totò e Carolina* (shot in 1953); *Un eroe dei nostri tempi*; 1956—*Donatella*; 1957—*Padri e figli (Fathers and Sons)*; *Il medico e lo stregone*; 1958—*I soliti ignoti (Big Deal on Madonna Street)*; 1959—*La grande guerra (The Great War)*; 1960—*Risate di gioia (The Passionate Thief)*; 1961—*A cavallo della tigre* (Comencini) (co-sc); 1962—"Renzo e Luciana" episode of *Boccaccio '70*; 1963—*I compagni (The Organizer)*; 1964—"Gente moderne (Modern People)" episode of *Alta infidelità (High Infidelity)*; 1965—*Casanova '70*; *L'armata Brancaleone*; 1966—"Fata Armenia (Queen Armenia)" episode of *Le fate (The Queens)*; 1968—*La ragazza con la pistola (Girl with a Gun)*; "La bambinaia" episode of *Capriccio all'italiana*; 1969—*Tò, è morta la nonna!*; 1970—"Il frigorifero" episode of *Le coppie*; *Brancaleone alle Crociate (Brancaleone alla crusada)*;

1971—*La mortadella (Lady Liberty)*; 1973—*Vogliamo di colonnelli*; 1974—*Romanzo popolare*; 1975—*Amici miei (My Friends)* (co-d only, took over from Pietro Germi); 1976—*Caro Michele*; one episode of *Signore e signori, buonanotte*; one episode of *La Goduria*; 1977—*Un borghese piccolo piccolo*; *I nuovi mostri* (co-d); 1978—*Viaggio con Anita (Travels with Anita)*; 1979—*Temporale Rosy*; 1980—*Camera d'albergo*; 1982—*Amici miei atto II (My Friends Act II)*; *Il Marchese del Grillo*.

Publications:

By MONICELLI:

Books—*La grande guerra*, edited by Franco Calderoni, Bologna 1959; *Boccaccio '70* edited by Carlo di Carlo and Gaio Fratini, Bologna 1962; *I compagni*, edited by Pio Baldelli, Bologna 1963; *Romanzo popolare*, with Age and Scarpelli, novelization of script, Milan 1974; articles—interview by A. Tassone in *Image et son* (Paris), February 1974; "Pietro Germi, mon ami" in *Ecran* (Paris), September 1976; interview by L. Codelli in *Positif* (Paris), June 1977; interview by L. Dahan and B. Villien in *Cinématographe* (Paris), June 1977; "À la recherche de la comédie italienne", interview by L. de La Fuente and D. Rabourdin in *Cinéma* (Paris), February 1978; interview by J.-L. Comolli and F. Gere in *Cahiers du cinéma* (Paris), March 1979.

On MONICELLI:

Article—"Hay de todo en la viña de Monicelli" by J.R. Solares in *Cinemateca revista* (Andes), September 1981.

* * *

The cinema quickly attracted Monicelli who, at the age of 21, co-directed a short 16mm film with A. Mondadori, called *I ragazzi della Via Paal* which received a fair amount of attention in the non-professional category at the Venice Biennial. However, Monicelli underwent a long apprenticeship as assistant director and/or scriptwriter before he was able to debut as a director in 1949. Even then his first eight features were co-directed with Steno (Stefano Vanzina). They were modest comedies usually serving as vehicles for the talents of the famous comedian, Totò. Monicelli's first significant film came with *Un eroe dei nostri tempi* starring Alberto Sordi. Although its production values were quite modest, its ironic description of a common man, typical of his time and society, who refuses any responsibility, insists on never taking a stand, and lives in conformism and fear, was quite well-drawn and insightful. From then on, Monicelli has concentrated on using popular genres to investigate the social positions and internal dilemmas of common people, in his features and his frequent collaborations on episode films, a popular Italian form since 1954. Monicelli enjoys collaboration, having worked closely with the scriptwriters Age and Scarpelli. Also, he directed the two *Amici miei* in honor of his friend, fellow filmmaker Pietro Germi, who conceived the idea but was too ill to realize the project.

One of Monicelli's best-known films, in Italy and abroad (it is one of the few Italian films that has always been available from distributors in the U.S., at least in 16mm) is *Big Deal on Madonna Street*. It is a comedy about a group of totally inept thieves (including Renato Salvatori and Marcello Mastroianni), led by master thief Totò (in one of his most subtle performances) who bungle a robbery and return home empty-handed. It also remains Monicelli's personal favorite because it appeared on the screen exactly as he imagined it.

Despite the fact that Monicelli is regarded as a director of comedies, some of his finest works have used comic elements in highly dramatic situations. Two outstanding examples in this regard are *La grande guerra* and *I compagni*. The first won a Golden Lion at Venice although, in pre-production, it caused a controversy among government and military officials who considered it unpatriotic and harmful to the country's morale. It expresses the point-of-view of two common soldiers (Alberto Sordi and Vittorio Gassman) and the experiences through four years in the First World War. These soldiers, despite the enormous significance of the situations in which they find themselves, remain ignorant and naive, the source of the film's comedy. Despite having chosen Sordi and Gassman, Monicelli wanted to play down the impact of the star system and concentrate on collective protagonists, which he succeeded in doing.

I compagni tells the story of a strike in Turin at the turn of the century. Even though the strike fails, it is shown to be a necessary experience for the workers' maturation and understanding of the forces that control them. Again, although it has an all-star cast including Mastroianni, Salvatori, Annie Girardot, and Benard Blier, Monicelli wanted a collective protagonist and a portrait of a group of people.

On the other hand, *Un borghese piccolo piccolo* (which received a fair distribution in the United States) is predominantly a bitter portrait of the petit-bourgeois world in all its grotesque and melodramatic manifestations. However, it is also a comedy and not without sympathy for the protagonist, a living fossil who is overly protective of his son and suspicious and afraid of everything else. The main role offered Sordi a complex character to interpret which gave full range to his talents. In its ambiguity of tone, the film contains all the traits of Italian comedy, but has gone beyond the formula, approaching nearer to tragedy.

—Elaine Mancini

MULLIGAN, ROBERT. American. Born in the Bronx, New York, 23 August 1925. Educated in theological seminary; studied radio communications, Fordham University. Career: WW II—service as Marine radio operator; after war works in editorial dept. of *The New York Times*; begins working in television as messenger at CBS; mid-1950s—becomes recognized for TV dramas directed for *Suspense, TV Playhouse, Playhouse 90*, and other series; 1956—directs first feature film *Fear Strikes Out*; collaborates on this film with producer Alan Pakula; 1962—*To Kill a Mockingbird* first production of Pakula-Mulligan Productions (active through 1969). Agent: Stan Kamen, William Morris Agency, Beverly Hills, CA 90212.

Films (as director): 1957—*Fear Strikes Out*; 1960—*The Rat Race*; 1961—*The Great Imposter*; *Come September*; 1962—*The Spiral Road*; *To Kill a Mockingbird*; 1963—*Love with a Proper Stranger*; 1965—*Baby the Rain Must Fall*; 1966—*Inside Daisy Clover*; 1967—*Up the Down Staircase*; 1968—*The Stalking Moon*; 1971—*The Pursuit of Happiness*; *Summer of '42*; 1972—*The Other* (+pr); 1975—*The Nickel Ride* (+pr); 1978—*Blood Brothers*; 1979—*Same Time, Next Year* (+co-pr); 1982—*Kiss Me Goodbye* (+co-pr).

Publications:

By MULLIGAN:

Articles—"L'Autre", interview by G. Braucourt in *Ecran* (Paris), January 1973; interview by Michel Ciment in *Positif* (Paris), January 1973; "Robert Mulligan: Le Redoutable Credo de bonheur", interview by M. Grisolia in *Cinéma* (Paris), January 1973; "The Nickel Ride", interview by J.-A. Gili in *Ecran* (Paris), October 1974; "Time for Thought", interview by R. Appelbaum in *Films and Filming* (London), January 1975.

On MULLIGAN:

Articles—"Flawed Genius: The Work of Robert Mulligan" by Lionel Godfrey in *Films and Filming* (London), January 1967; "Inside Robert Mulligan" by John Taylor in *Sight and Sound* (London), autumn 1971; "A Loss of Innocence" by J. Mercer in *Film* (London), autumn 1971; "Mysterious Islands: Summer of '42" by M. Falonga in *Film Heritage* (New York), fall 1972; "Du silence et des ombres" by Michel Ciment in *Positif* (Paris), January 1973; "Biofilmographie" by Olivier Eyquem in *Positif* (Paris), January 1973.

*   *   *

In an era in which consistent visual style seems perhaps too uniformly held as the prerequisite of the valorized auteur, one can all too easily understand why Robert Mulligan's work has failed to evince any passionate critical interest. His films all look so different; for instance, *To Kill a Mockingbird*, with its black-and-white measured pictorialism; *Up the Down Staircase*, photographed on location with a documentary graininess; *The Other*, with its heightened Gothic expressionism rather conventional to the horror genre, if not to Mulligan's previous work; and *The Summer of '42*, with a pastel prettiness which suffuses each image with the nostalgia of memory. If some would claim this visual eclecticism reflects the lack of a strong personality, others could claim that Mulligan has too much respect for his material to impose arbitrarily upon it some monolithic consistency and instead brings his subjects the sensibilty of somewhat self-effacing Hollywood craftsman. Yet there are certainly some sequences in Mulligan's work which spring vividly to mind: The silent, final seduction in *The Summer of '42*; the almost surreal walk home by a child dressed as a ham in *To Kill a Mockingbird*; the high school dance in *Up the Down Staircase*; the climatic camera movement in *The Other*, from Niles to that empty space where Holland, were he not imaginary, would be sitting.

Even Mulligan's two biggest critical successes, *To Kill a Mockingbird* and *The Summer of '42*, both examples of the kind of respectable Hollywood filmmaking which garners Academy Award nominations, have not yet been greeted by any significant critical cult. And yet, if Mulligan's good taste has been steadfastly held against him, it must be noted that his films, albeit generally ignored, hold up remarkably well. Mulligan has a strong sense of narrative; and all his films are imbued with human values and a profound compassion which make for compelling audience identification with Mulligan's characteristic protagonists. Mulligan's tendency is to work in less-familiar movie genres (such as Hollywood exposé, the family drama, the teacher film, the cinematic *Bildungsroman*), but to avoid—though sincerity and human insight—that emphasis on the purely formal which sometimes makes genre works "go dead" for their audiences upon repeated viewings. Perhaps it is American mistrust of male emotional expression which contributes to Mulligan's facile dismissal by many; certainly it appears that those critics who attacked as sentimental *The Summer of '42*, Mulligan's tasteful and bittersweet paean to lost virginity, failed to assess negatively those same qualities in so many of the French New Wave films, especially, for instance, the Antoine Doinel cycle by François Truffaut, which were instead praised for their lyrical and compassionate exploration of human interaction. Is nostalgia somehow more acceptable when it is French?

An eventual reevaluation of Robert Mulligan as a significant, if minor artist, may eventually materialize, especially if the consistency of his thematic motifs is more extensively examined. Certainly Mulligan seems especially interested in the deviant, the outsider, the loner: the mentally unbalanced Jimmy Peirsall in *Fear Strikes Out*, the enlightened attorney whose values put him in conflict with a bigoted community in *To Kill a Mockingbird*, the ex-convict trying to accustom himself to life outside the penitentiary in *Baby the Rain Must Fall*, the character of Ferdinand Demara, based on real life, who, in *The Great Imposter*, succeeds by the sheer force of his skillful impersonations in insinuating himself into a variety of environments in which he would otherwise never be accepted; the students in *Up the Down Staircase* who, psychologically stunted and economically deprived, may—even with a committed teacher's help—never fit into mainstream society. Like Truffaut, Mulligan has an extraordinary insight into the world of the child or adolescent and the secret rituals of that world. Mulligan's children never display that innocence conventionally associated with children, instead participating in often traumatic ceremonies of passage. One thinks of the child through whose eyes the innate racism of small-town America is seen in *To Kill a Mockingbird*, the precocious child-star in *Inside Daisy Clover*; the lost and often already jaded students in *Up the Down Staircase*; the pubescent adolescents who learn about sex and morality in *The Summer of '42*; and the irrevocably evil child, Niles, and his twin, Holland, in *The Other*.

Some final note too must be made of the consistently fine performances elicited by Mulligan from his players: Anthony Perkins in *Fear Strikes Out*, Gregory Peck and Mary Badham in *To Kill a Mockingbird*, Sandy Dennis in *Up the Down Staircase*, Jennifer O'Neill in *The Summer of '42*, Richard Gere in *Blood Brothers*, and all the children and adolescents who populate Mulligan's world.

—Charles Derry

MUNK, ANDRZEJ. Polish. Born in Cracow, 16 October 1921. Educated in engineering and law; State Cinema School, Lodz, degree 1950. Married Joanna Prochnik. Career: war years—works as laborer in construction; active in resistance; 1946—after war, studies law and becomes general secretary of Z.N.M.S., organization of socialist students; late 1940s—abandons law studies, admitted to State Cinema School; 1950-55—works as director at documentary film studio, Warsaw; 1957-61—teaches in State Cinema School, Lodz; 1961—dies in auto accident while filming *The Passenger*; film assembled and presented as incomplete by Witold Lesiewicz. Died 20 September 1961.

Films (as director): 1949—*Kongres kombatantów* [Congress of Fighters] (co-d); 1950—*Sztuka młodych* [Art of Youth] (co-d, +sc); *Zaczeło sie w Hiszpanii* [It Began in Spain] (+ed); 1951—*Kierunek Nowa Huta* [Direction: Nowa Huta]; *Nauka bliżej życia* [Science Closer to Life] (+co-ph); 1952—*Bajka w Ursusie* [The Tale of Ursus] or *Poemat symfoniczny "Bajka" Stanislawa Moniuszki* [The Symphonic Poem "Fable" of Stanislas Moniuszko]; *Pamietniki chłopów* [Diaries of the Peasants] (+sc); 1953—*Kolejarskie słowo* [A Railwayman's Word] (+sc); 1954—*Gwiazdy musza płonać* [The Stars Must Shine] (co-d, +co-sc); 1955—*Niedzielny poranek (Sunday Morning, Un Dimanche Matin, Ein Sonntagmorgen in Warschau)* (+sc); *Błekitny krzyż (Men of the Blue Cross, Les Hommes de la croix bleue, Die Männer vom blauen Kreuz)* (+sc); 1956—*Człowiek na torze (Man on the Track, Un Homme sur la voie, Der Mann auf den Schienen)* (+co-sc); 1957—*Eroica (Eroica—Polen 44)*; 1958—*Spacerek staromiejski (A Walk in the Old City of Warsaw)* (+sc); 1959—*Kronika jubileuszowa* or *Polska kronika filmowa nr 52 A-B*; 1960—*Zezowate szcześćie (Bad Luck, De la veine a revendre, Das schielende Glück)* (+ro as bureaucrat); 1963—*Pasażerka (The Passenger, La Passagère, Die Passagierin)* (+co-sc).

Publications:

By MUNK:

Articles—"Rozmowa o", with Krzysztof Tœplitz, in *Nowa kultura* (Warsaw), no.45, 1955; "Expérience du cinéma polonais", interview by P.-L. Thirard in *Les Lettres françaises* (Paris), no.790, 1959; "Entretien avec Andrzej Munk" by J.-J. Camelin in *Image et son* (Paris), December/January 1960/61; "O filmie", interview by Stefania Beylin, in *Film* (Warsaw), no.41, 1961; "Entretiens polonais, Andrzej Munk" in *Cinéma 61* (Paris), no.60, 1961; "Naszych tworcow laczy jedna cecha—powazne podejscie do tematu i powazne traktowanie odbiorcy" [That which unites our filmmakers is a serious attitude toward the subject and the public]; in *Ekran* (Warsaw), no.22, 1961; "O filmie intelektualnym, szkole polskiej i snobizmie" [On intellectual cinema, the Polish school and snobism] in *Nowa kultura* (Warsaw), no.9, 1961; "National Character and the Individual" in *Films and Filming* (London), vol.8, no.2, 1961; interview by Maria Benesova in *Cinéma 62* (Paris), December 1962; "Le dernier entretien avec..." in *Cinéma 62* (Paris), no.71, 1962.

On MUNK:

Books—*Seans mitologiczny* by Krzysztof Tœplitz, Warsaw 1961; *Nouveaux cinéastes polonais* by Philippe Haudiquet, Premier Plan no.27, Lyon 1963; *Andrzej Munk*, collective work, Warsaw 1964; *Historia Filmu Polskiego IV*, Warsaw 1981; articles—"Candidek Langdonczyk" by René Gison in *Cinéma 60* (Paris), no.47, 1960; "Andrzej Munk" by Georges Sadoul in *Les Lettres françaises* (Paris), no.894, 1961; "Andrzej Munk: ricerca del vero" by Giacomo Gambetti in *Bianco e nero* (Rome), no.9-10, 1962; "La Responsabilité et la conscience" by Georges Sadoul in *Les Lettres françaises* (Paris), no.1053, 1963; "Andrzej Munk" by Philippe Haudiquet in *Image et son* (Paris), January 1964; "Andrzej Munk" issue of *Études cinématographiques* (Paris), no.45, 1964; "Le Regard de Munk" by Raymond Bellour in *Nouvelle Revue française* (Paris), 1 May 1965; "Munk et *La Passagère*" by Andrzej Brzozowski in *Cahiers du cinéma* (Paris), no.163, 1965; "Andrzej Munk" by Luc Moullet in *Cahiers du cinéma* (Paris), no.163, 1965; "Die Unruhe eines Moralisten" by Fred Gehler in *Film-Studio* (Frankfurt), no.49, 1966; "Andrzej Munk" by Jerzy Plazewsky in *Anthologie du cinéma* vol.3, Paris 1968; "Andrzej Munk" by Jacques-Pierre Amette in *Dossiers du cinéma*, Cinéastes I, Paris 1971; "Andrzej Munk" by Fred Gehler in *Regiestühle*, Berlin 1972; "Andrzej Munks Vermächtnis" by L. Bukowiecki in *Film und Fernsehen* (Berlin), August 1981; "Andrzej Munk (1921-1961)" by J. Cieslar in *Film a Doba* (Prague), October 1981.

* * *

Andrzej Munk is one of the creators of the so-called Polish school of filmmaking and one of the most important Polish film directors. He belongs to the skeptical generation of directors who spent their early youth in the difficult years of the Second World War and embarked on filmmaking in the 1950s with no rosy illusions but with a sense of responsibilty for themselves, their actions, and the time in which they lived, a time which shaped them but was also transformed by them. Their common trait is their critical view of the present and the recent events in their people's history (the defeat of Poland in September 1939, the Warsaw Uprising of 1944, the post-war disputes and struggles over the face of Poland, and the years marked by the cult of personality). In comparison with others in his generation and members of the "school," Munk stands out as a perceptive analyst and the rationist with a sober and searching view of people and events, a view which is only seldom presented metaphorically. Andrzej Munk adopted this sober and restrained view at the outset of his film career in the Documentary Film Studio, where he made several short pictures. Some of these were attributable to the prevailing schematic conception of socialist realism, but three of them (*Kolejarsie słowo*, *Gwiazdy muszą płonąć*, *Niedzielny poranek*) already show the rudiments of Munk's later inclination toward the dramatic film. Munk termed these films dramatic reportage, for they combine the authenticity of reality with certain dramatic elements. This step is further developed in Munk's first long film, *Błękitny krzyź*, about a successful action by the mountain service to rescue wounded partisans from territory still occupied by German units. The result, however, did not match the potential. Alongside successful sequences were others which shattered the unity of the work; dramatic sequences clashed with the paradocumentary parts.

Munk resolved this contradiction in his very next film, *Człowiek na torze*, which is the first manifestation of Munk's style based on rational reflection and analysis. Through a system of successive returns to the past, the director analyzes individual situations in the human face of a railway worker who faces a conflict between his own sense of responsibility and the demands of society; the director's purpose is then to combine these forces in a synthesis that reveals the truth that is sought. His next two films, *Eroica* and *Zezowate szczęście*—both films are keys words in the Polish film school—reveal another salient feature of Munk's artistic personality; added to his critical insight are irony, sarcasm, and, in the context of the Polish filmmaking of the time, a unique sense of comic exaggeration in exposing the function of certain national myths. In the tragic-grotesque stylization of *Eroica* he critizes the superficiality of the prevalent conception of heroism (Wajda does the same thing in a tragic key), while in the film *Zezowate szczęście* he engages in a polemic with the simplistic depiction of the hero in contemporary Polish films by making his hero a man who constantly adapts to various changes in the social situation.

Munk's last major work in *Pasażerka*, produced only after his death in a reworking by Witold Lesiewicz. It returns once again to the Second World War, to the horrible environment of a concentration camp, and confronts this period with post-war recollections. Despite the cogency of the Lesiewicz reconstruction, in which already completed film clips alternate with stills from the unfinished sequences, it is impossible to make a safe guess as to where Munk's future path would have taken him. He was unmistakably tending toward a certain change in his artistic methods. But his work is closed. It is not extensive—a few short pictures, five dramatic films, one of them unfinished. Nevertheless, right up to the present time, his work, by the strength of its artistic appeal, has exercised an influence on the following generation of young filmmakers and viewers. It continues to attract them with its individual, unifying style, whose components are a perfect composition of shots, meaningful camera movement, eloquent montage, sober action, laconic dialogue, and counterpoint of image and sound; it is a style that serves precisely what Munk wished to communicate to the viewer.

—B. Urgošíková

MURNAU, F.W. German. Born Friedrich Wilhelm Plumpe in Bielefeld, Germany, 28 December 1888. Educated at Universities of Berlin, in philology, and Heidelberg, in art history and literature. Career: about 1908—attends Max Reinhardt theater school, later joins company; 1914—called up for military service; after seeing action and being made lieutenant, is transferred to air force; 1917—interned in Switzerland after crash-landing in fog; 1919—with other Reinhardt school colleagues founds Murnau Veidt Filmgesellschaft; 1926—invited by William Fox to Hollywood; 1927—returns to Germany; 1929—sails to Tahiti with Robert Flaherty to prepare *Tabu*. Died in automobile accident, California, 11 March 1931; buried at Stahnsdorf cemetery in Plumpe family vault, Berlin.

Films (as director): 1919—*Der Knabe in Blau (Der Todessmaragd, The Boy in Blue)*; 1920—*Satanas*; *Sehnsucht (Bajazzo)*; *Der Bucklige und die Tänzerin* [The Hunchback and the Dancer]; *Der Januskopf (Schrecken, Janus-Faced)*[Janus Head]; *Abend...Nacht...Morgen* [Evening...Night...Morning]; 1921—*Der Gang in die Nacht* [Journey into the Night]; *Schloss Vogelöd (Haunted Castle)*; 1922—*Marizza, genannt die Schmuggler-Madonna* [Marizza, called the Smuggler's Madonna]; *Nosferatu—Eine Symphonie des Grauens (Nosferatu the Vampire)* [Nosferatu, a Symphony of Horror]; *Der Brennende Acker (Burning Soil)* [The Burning Earth]; *Phantom*; 1923—*Die Austreibung (Driven from Home)*[The Expulsion]; 1924—*Die Finanzen des Grossherzogs (The Grand Duke's Finances)*; *Der Letzte Mann (The Last Laugh)*[The Last Man]; 1926—*Tartüff* [Tartuffe]; *Faust*; 1927—*Sunrise (Sunrise: A Song of 2 Humans)*; 1928—*Four Devils*; 1930—*Die zwölfte Stunde—Eine Nacht des Grauens (Nosferatu the Vampire)*[The Twelfth Hour—A Night of Horror] (*Nosferatu* adapted for sound); *Our Daily Bread*; 1931—*Tabu* (+co-pr, co-sc).

Publications:

By MURNAU:

Book—*Sunrise (Sonnenaufgang), Ein Drehbuch von Carl Mayer mit handschriftlichen Bemerkungen von Friedrich Wilhelm Murnau*, German Institute for Film Studies, Wiesbaden 1971; articles—interview in *Cinéa-Ciné* (Paris), 1 April 1927; "The Ideal Picture Needs No Titles" in *Theatre Magazine* (New York), January 1928; "Étoile du Sud" in *La Revue du cinéma* (Paris), May 1931; "Turia, an Original Story" and "Tabu

(Tabou), a Story of the South Seas", with Robert Flaherty, in *Film Culture* (New York), no.20, 1959.

On MURNAU:

Books—"Murnau" by Jean Domarchi in *Anthologie du cinéma* vol.1, Paris 1966; *Murnau* by Charles Jameux, Paris 1965; *From Caligari to Hitler* by Siegfried Kracauer, New York 1966; *The Haunted Screen* by Lotte Eisner, Berkeley, California 1969; *Murnau* by Lotte Eisner, Berkeley, California 1973; *Hollywood Babylon* by Kenneth Anger, San Francisco 1975; articles— "F.W. Murnau—The German Genius of the Films" by Matthew Josephson in *Motion Picture Classic* (New York), October 1926; "Murnau—ses films" by Roger Blin in *La Revue du cinéma* (Paris), July 1931; "Vanité que la peinture" by Maurice Scherer in *Cahiers du cinéma* (Paris), no.3, 1951; "Le Feu et la glace" by Alexandre Astruc in *Cahiers du cinéma* (Paris), December 1952; "Un Cinéaste moderne—Frédéric Murnau" by Henri Agel in *Radio, cinéma, télévision* (Paris), 9 August 1959; "Murnau et les courants d'air glacés" by René Gilson in *Cinéma 63* (Paris), May 1963; "Fire and Ice" by Alexandre Astruc in *Cahiers du Cinema in English* (New York), January 1966; "Tabu" by Robin Wood in *Film Culture* (New York), summer 1971; "L'Envers du paradis" by M. Henry in *Positif* (Paris), February 1972; "I fantasmi impressionistici del giovane Murnau" by G. Oldrini in *Cinema nuovo* (Turin), January/February 1972; "L'Aurore", special issue of *Avant-Scène du cinéma* (Paris), June 1974; "The Griffith Tradition" by J. Dorr in *Film Comment* (New York), March/-April 1974; "Per una ri-lettura critica di F.W. Murnau", special issue of *Filmcritica* (Rome), July 1974; "Dossier: Le Pont traversé" by L. Audibert in *Cinématographe* (Paris), January 1977; "De Murnau à Rohmer: les pièges de la beauté" in 2 parts by M. Latil Le Dantec in *Cinématographe* (Paris), January and February 1977; "Special Murnau" issue of *Avant-Scène du cinéma* (Paris), July/September 1977; "Griffith, Murnau et les historiens" by Jean Mitry and others in *Avant-Scène du cinéma* (Paris), 15 March 1978; "Les Années courtes" by J. Fieschi in *Cinématographe* (Paris), February 1981; "F.W. Murnau, Hollywood und die Südsee" by F. Gehler in *Film und Fernsehen* (Berlin), May 1981.

*   *   *

Murnau was studying with Reinhardt when the First World War began. He was called up for military service, and after achieving his lieutenancy, he was transferred to the air service, where he served as a combat pilot; but his plane was forced down in Switzerland, where he was interned for the duration. Through the German Embassy, however, he managed to direct several independent stage productions, and he began his lifelong dedication to the motion picture, compiling propaganda film material and editing them, which made it possible for him to enter the reborn film industry after peace as a full-fledged director.

His first feature film as director was in 1919, *The Boy in Blue*, and he made 21 full-length features from that year until 1926, when Fox Studios brought him to Hollywood. Unfortunately, most of the pictures he made in his native country no longer exist except in fragmentary form. They are tempting to read about, especially items like *Janus-Faced*, a study of a Jekyll and Hyde personality, which he made in 1920 with Conrad Veidt and Bela Lugosi. Critics found it more artistic than the John Barrymore version of the story made at about the same time in Paramount's New York studios.

Extant today in a complete version is *Nosferatu*, which was subtitled "a symphony of horror." It was a more faithful version of Bram Stoker's *Dracula* than any made thereafter, and the film is still available, starring the incredibly gaunt and frightening figure of the actor, Max Schreck, as the vampire.

The next film of Murnau's that is still viewable is *The Last Laugh*, which starred Emil Jannings. At the time of its release, it was noted as being a picture without subtitles, told almost completely in pantomine. Its real innovation was the moving camera, which Murnau used brilliantly. The camera went everywhere; it was never static. Audiences watched spellbound as the camera moved upstairs and down, indoors and out, although it was in this case only the simple story of a proud commissionaire reduced by his old age to work menially as a lavatory attendant. The camera records, nevertheless, a very real world in an impressionistic way. In fact, Mirnau, because of his skill with the moving camera, was generally known at the Great Impressionist, for he gave a superb impression of actual reality.

That title fits him even more aptly in his next two features, both of which also starred Emil Jannings. They are *Tartuffe*, a screen adaption of Moliere's black comedy, in which Lil Dagover and Werner Krauss were also featured. It is topped by what must be the most definitive film version of Goethe's *Faust*, starring Jannings as Mephistofeles, with the handsome Swedish favorite, Gosta Ekman, in the title role; Camilla Horn as Marguerite; the great Parisian star, Yvette Guilbert, as Marthe; and a young William Dieterle as Valentine. Again, the camera not only moved, it soared, especially in the sequence where Faust is shown the world which will be his if he sells his soul to the devil. Murnau was a master of light and shadow, and his work is always brilliantly choreographed as it moves from lightness to the dark.

It came as no surprise when in 1926 Murnau was invited to Hollywood, where the red carpet at Fox was unrolled for him. He was allowed to bring his cameraman, writers, and other craftsmen to work with him, and his initial feature was to be called *Sunrise*, subtitled "a song of two human beings." The two stars were to be Janet Gaynor and George O'Brien playing a young farm couple who make their first trip to the big city, which was constructed on the Fox lot, so that Murnau and his camera could follow them everywhere indoors and out of doors and onto a moving streetcar. Again, the story was very simple, adapted from a Hermann Suderman novel, *A Trip to Tilsit*, and simply proved that real love will always be triumphant.

Sunrise was highly praised by all critics, and was one of three pictures which brought Janet Gaynor an Academy Award as Best Actress in the 1927-28 year. Quite naturally, awards also went to cinematographers Charles Rosher and Karl Struss, to interior decorator Harry Oliver, and *Sunrise* was given a special award for its Artistic Quality of Production, a category never again specified.

For all that, *Sunrise* was not a box-office success, and the studio moved in to supervise Murnau closely on his next two productions. *Four Devils* was a circus story of four young aerialists, which gave Murnau's camera a chance to fly with them from one performing trapeze to another. All prints of *Four Devils* are unfortunately lost, which is a fate common to most of the last great silent films. Murnau began shooting on his final film at Fox, called *Our Daily Bread*, with Charles Farrell and Mary Duncan, but he was not allowed to finish the picture. The overwhelming popularity of the talking screen was allowed to flaw it, for the only version of it now shown is called *City Girl*, and is only effective when it is recognizably silent and all Murnau. As a part-talkie, it is crude and not at all Murnau.

Murnau then allied himself with Robert Flaherty, and the two men journeyed to the South Seas to make *Tabu*. Flaherty, however, withdrew, and *Tabu* is pure Murnau; some praise it as his greatest film. Murnau returned to California and was on the eve of signing at Paramount, which treated directors like Mamoulian, Lubitsch, and von Sternberg very kindly in their talking debuts. Unfortunately, Murnau lost his life in a motor accident on the Pacific Coast highway. He was only 42, and after the success of *Tabu*, a new fame might have been his.

—DeWitt Bodeen

NARUSE, MIKIO. Japanese. Born in Tokyo, 1905. Educated in Tokyo technical school, 1918-20. Married actress Sachiko Chiba, 1937 (separated 1942); one child; later remarried. Career: 1920—enters Shochiku film company as prop man at Tokyo Kamata studios; 1921-28—assistant to director Yoshinobu Ikeda; writes comedy scripts under pen name "Chihan Miki"; 1929—joins staff of Heinosuke Gosho; 1930—given first opportunity to direct comedy *Mr. and Mrs. Swordplay* (lost); 1934—leaves Shochiku, joins P.C.L. studios (later Toho Company); after 1945—leaves Toho to freelance. Died 1969.

Films (as director): 1930—*Chambara fufu (Mr. and Mrs. Swordplay)*; *Junjo (Pure Love)*; *Fukeiki jidai (Hard Times)* (+story); *Ai wa chikara da (Love Is Strength)*; *Oshikiri shinkonki (A Record of Shameless Newlyweds)* (+story); 1931—*Nee kofun shicha iya yo (Now Don't Get Excited)*; *Nikai no himei (Screams from the Second Floor)* (+sc); *Koshiben gambare (Flunky, Work Hard!)* (+sc); *Uwaki wa kisha ni notte (Fickleness Gets on the Train)* (+sc); *Hige no chikara (The Strength of a Moustache)* (+sc); *Tonari no yane no shita (Under the Neighbors' Roof)*; 1932—*Onna wa tamoto o goyojin (Ladies, Be Careful of Your Sleeves)* (+sc); *Aozora ni naku (Crying to the Blue Sky)*; *Eraku nare (Be Great!)* (+sc); *Mushibameru haru (Motheaten Spring)*; *Chokoreito garu (Chocolate Girl)*; *Nasanu naka (Not Blood Relations)*; 1933—*Kimi to wakarete (Apart from You)* (+sc); *Yogoto no yume (Every Night Dreams)* (+story); *Boku no marumage (A Man with a Married Woman's Hairdo)*; *Sobo (2 Eyes)*; 1934—*Kagirinaki hodo (Street Without End)*; 1935—*Otome-gokoro sannin shimai (3 Sisters with Maiden Hearts)* (+sc); *Joyu to shijin (The Actress and the Poet)*; *Tsuma yo bara no yo ni (Kimiko, Wife! Be Like a Rose)* (+sc); *Sakasu gonin-gumi (5 Men in the Circus)*; *Uwasa no musume (The Girl in the Rumor)* (+sc); 1936—*Tochuken Kumoemon (Kumoemon Tochuken)* (+sc); *Kimi to iku michi (The Road I Travel with You)* (+sc); *Asa no namikimichi (Morning's Tree-lined Street)* (+sc); 1937—*Nyonin aishu (A Woman's Sorrows)* (+co-sc); *Nadare (Avalanche)* (+sc); *Kafuku I, II (Learn from Experience, Parts I, II)*; 1938—*Tsuruhachi tsurujiro (Tsuruhachi and Tsurujiro)* (+sc); 1939—*Hataraku ikka (The Whole Family Works)* (+sc); *Magokoro (Sincerity)* (+sc); 1940—*Tabi yakusha (Travelling Actors)* (+sc); 1941—*Natsukashi no kao (A Face from the Past)* (+sc); *Shanhai no tsuki (Shanghai Moon)*; *Hideko no shasho-san (Hideko the Bus Conductor)* (+sc); 1942—*Haha wa shinazu (Mother Never Dies)*; 1943—*Uta andon (The Song Lantern)*; 1944—*Tanoshiki kana jinsei (This Happy Life)* (+co-sc); *Shibaido (The Way of Drama)*; 1945—*Shori no hi made (Until Victory Day)*; *Sanjusangendo toshiya monogatari (A Tale of Archery at the Sanjusangendo)*; 1946—*Urashima Taro no koei (The Descendants of Taro Urashima)*; *Ore mo omae mo (Both You and I)* (+sc); 1947—*Yottsu no koi no monogatari, II: Wakare mo tanoshi (4 Love Stories, Part II: Even Parting Is Enjoyable)*; *Haru no mezame (Spring Awakens)* (+co-sc); 1949—*Furyo shojo (Delinquent Girl)* (+sc); *Ishinaka sensei gyojoki (Conduct Report on Professor Ishinaka)*; *Ikari no*

machi (The Angry Street) (+co-sc); *Shiroi yaju (White Beast)* (+co-sc); *Bara gassen (The Battle of Roses)*; 1951—*Ginza gesho (Ginza Cosmetics)*; *Maihime (Dancing Girl)*; *Meshi (Repast)*; 1952—*Okuni to Gohei (Okuni and Gohei)*; *Okasan (Mother)*; *Inazuma (Lightning)*; 1953—*Fufu (Husband and Wife)*; *Tsuma (Wife)*; *Ani imoto (Older Brother, Younger Sister)*; 1954—*Yama no oto (Sound of the Mountain)*; *Bangiku (Late Chrysanthemums)*; 1955—*Ukigumo (Floating Clouds)*; *Kuchizuke, III: Onna doshi (The Kiss, Part III: Women's Ways)*; 1956—*Shu-u (Sudden Rain)*; *Tsuma no kokoro (A Wife's Heart)*; *Nagareru (Flowing)*; 1957—*Arakure (Untamed)*; 1958—*Anzukko* (+co-sc); *Iwashigumo (Herringbone Clouds)*; 1959—*Kotan no kuchibue (Whistling in Kotan, A Whistle in My Heart)*; 1960—*Onna ga kaidan o agaru toki (When a Woman Ascends the Stairs)*; *Musume tsuma haha (Daughters, Wives and a Mother)*; *Yoru no nagare (Evening Stream)* (co-d); *Aki tachinu (The Approach of Autumn)*; 1961—*Tsuma toshite onna toshite (As a Wife, as a Woman, The Other Woman)*; 1962—*Onna no za (Woman's Status)*; *Horoki (A Wanderer's Notebook, Lonely Lane)*; 1963—*Onna no rekishi (A Woman's Story)*; 1964—*Midareru (Yearning)*; 1966—*Onna no naka ni iru tanin (The Stranger Within a Woman, The Thin Line)*; *Hikinige (Hit and Run, Moment of Terror)*; 1967—*Midaregumo (Scattered Clouds, 2 in the Shadow)*.

Publications:

On NARUSE:

Books—*Japanese Film Directors* by Audie Bock, Tokyo 1978; *To the Distant Observer* by Noel Burch, London 1979; *The Japanese Movie* by Donald Ritchie, revised edition, Tokyo 1982; *Currents in Japanese Cinema: Essays* by Tadao Sato, translated by Gregory Barrett, Tokyo 1982; articles—"Naruse Mikio" by Audie Bock in *FC*, no.55, 1979; "Mikio Naruse. Le Quatrième Grand" by Louella Interim in *Cahiers du cinéma* (Paris), February 1983.

NEGULESCO, JEAN. Romanian. Born in Craiova, 29 February 1900. Educated at Lyceul Carol; studied painting at Academie Julian, Paris. Married Ruth (Dusty) Anderson, 1946. Career: 1914-15—lives in Paris, attempting to study art; returns to Romania when war breaks out, serves as hospital orderly; early 1920s—studies art and exhibits in Paris; 1925-26—works in Art Theatre, Craiova, Romania; 1929—comes to United States to exhibit paintings (date according to Negulesco interview—other sources give 1927); 1932—assists in 2nd unit direction on Borzage's *A Farewell to Arms*; 1933—hired by producer Benjamin Glazer to do sketches for *The Story of Temple Drake*; becomes Glazer's assistant; continues through 1930s doing 2nd-unit work at Paramount and Universal; 1937—begins collaborating on stories and scripts; 1940s—directs for Warners; 1941—taken off direction of *Singapore Woman*, but nevertheless receives screen credit; 1948—signs with 20th Century-Fox; 1969—shoots *The Heroes* in Iran, returns to Iran in early seventies, helping with establishment of a film industry.

Films (as collaborator on script or story): 1937—*Expensive Husbands* (Connolly); *Fight for Your Lady* (Stoloff); 1938—*Beloved Brat* (Lubin) (story); *Swiss Miss* (Blystone); 1939—*Rio*

(Brahm) (story); (as director): 1940-44—approximately 50 1and 2-reel films released under Warner Bros. "Melody Masters" series; 1941—*Singapore Woman* (co-d, though received d credit); 1944—*The Mask of Dimitrios*; *The Conspirators*; 1946—*3 Strangers*; *Nobody Lives Forever*; *Humoresque*; 1947—*Deep Valley*; 1948—*Johnny Belinda*; *Road House*; 1949—*The Forbidden Street*; 1950—*Under My Skin*; *3 Came Home*; *The Mudlark*; 1951—*Take Care of My Little Girl*; 1952—*Phone Call from a Stranger*; *Lydia Bailey*; *Lure of the Wilderness*; "The Last Leaf" episode of *O. Henry's Full House*; 1953—*Titanic*; *Scandal at Scourie*; *How to Marry a Millionaire*; 1954—*3 Coins in the Fountain*; *A Woman's World*; 1955—*Daddy Long Legs*; *The Rains of Ranchipur*; 1957—*Boy on a Dolphin*; 1958—*The Gift of Love*; *A Certain Smile*; 1959—*Count Your Blessings*; *The Best of Everything*; 1962—*Jessica*; 1964—*The Pleasure Seekers*; 1970—*Hello-Goodbye*; *The Heroes (The Invincible 6)*.

Publications:

By NEGULESCO:

Article—interview in *The Celluloid Muse* edited by Charles Higham and Joel Greenberg, London 1969.

On NEGULESCO:

Articles—"Director-Artist" in *Life* (New York), 19 June 1944; "Jean Negulesco" by R. Campion in *Films in Review* (New York), April 1973 (also see addendum by R. Braff in August/-September 1973 issue).

*   *   *

Jean Negulesco is a good example of a director whose modest talents were dissipated by the studio system. He was a painter-turned-director who at Warner Brothers during the 1940s exhibited a painter's vision and an ability to handle actors and plot intricacies. Warner Brothers was an autocratic studio which held a tight rein on its directors, a disciplined atmosphere which Negulesco apparently needed. When he moved to the more lenient milieu of 20th Century-Fox in the 1950s, his career immediately descended into one of making sentimental divertissements enhanced only occasionally by exceptional imagery.

It was Negulesco's art work that brought him to Hollywood where he worked on the second unit of Frank Borzage's *A Farewell to Arms* and was hired as assistant to Benjamin Glazer, producer of *The Story of Temple Drake*, after Negulesco had created some sketches depicting Miriam Hopkin's rape scene which were deemed capable of passing the censors for that filmization of William Faulkner's controversial *Sanctuary*. He was then hired to direct short subjects at Warner Brothers—mostly ballet and musical shorts—and almost made his feature film debut as the director of *The Maltese Falcon*, but when that assignment was handed to its screenwriter John Huston, Negulesco went on to direct part of a B-picture called *Singapore*. More short subjects followed until he finally got his chance to direct with *The Mask of Dimitrios*, based on Eric Ambler's novel, *The Coffin of Dimitrios*.

That film was a clever and intricate story of a master criminal which teamed Sidney Greenstreet and Peter Lorre and in which, says Negulesco, "I established a sombre, low-key mood that I followed in a number of subsequent films. I learned that the public loves to share the actor's situation, to be a vicarious part of the action. It's curious that when you see the actors moving and talking in semi-darkness it's always more exciting than seeing them plainly, because you identify with them more."

Negulesco used Greenstreet and Lorre successfully again in *The Conspirators* and in *Three Strangers*, after which he used his exceptional painter's eye, with remarkable results, directing the popular *Humoresque*, a superior woman's picture. Joan Crawford was at her best as the wealthy, sophisticated patron of violinist John Garfield, and Ernest Haller's black and white photography complemented Negulesco's artistic vision.

Johnny Belinda is Negulesco's best film and here too his visual sensibilty was evident as he superbly captured the everyday life in a small Nova Scotia town. Jack Warner objected to *Johnny Belinda* as being too preachy and off-beat—it was the story of a deaf mute girl (Jane Wyman) who is raped then murders her rapist—and he shelved the picture and fired Negulesco. By the time it had received 12 Oscar nominations, including one for Best Director, Negulesco had been hired by 20th Century-Fox.

In comparing the two studios, Negulesco described Warners as "a very tough training ground, with schedules which you couldn't exceed by so much as a day"; but, he says, "Fox was much more relaxed."

Unfortunately, despite the apparently comfortable atmosphere, Negulesco's tenure at Fox was one of steady decline. He made the modestly respectable *Three Came Home*, *The Mudlark*, and *Phone Call From a Stranger*, and the above average *Titanic*. But increasingly Negulesco sank from making gripping melodramas to frothy, shallow entertainments which were little more than colorful travelogues in CinemaScope, e.g. *How to Marry a Millionaire*, which did have a few good Marilyn Monroe moments, and the sugary sudser *Three Coins in the Fountain*. *The Best of Everything* was patent soap opera, and after directing the miniscule *Hello-Goodbye*, Negulesco retired.

—Ronald Bowers

NEILAN, MARSHALL. (Known as "Mickey" Neilan.) American. Born in San Bernardino, California, 11 April 1891. Educated one year, Harvard Military Academy, Los Angeles. Married Gertrude Bambrick, 1913 (divorced 1921); child: Marshall, Jr.; married Blanche Sweet, 1922 (divorced 1929). Career: 1902—leaves school to become messenger boy for California Fruit Growers Assn.; also works for Santa Fe Railway, and as blacksmith's helper; plays boy's parts with Belasco Stock Company, Los Angeles; 1905—plays bit roles with Barney Bernard Stock Company, San Francisco; about 1908—salesman for Simplex Motor Car Company, Los Angeles; chauffeur for entrepreneur Oliver Morosco; 1909-10 and 1911—meets D.W. Griffith, and is driver for him briefly, on winter trips of Biograph company; urged by Griffith to try acting; 1911—begins acting at Kalem Studios, Santa Monica; 1912—invited by Allan Dwan to join his company, American (Flying A); plays 2nd leads and juvenile roles; 1913—hired by Griffith at Biograph; 1914—signed as director by Kalem; continues acting after Kalem contract expires, works for Dwan; 1915—writes for and acts opposite Mary Pickford; begins directing for Selig; 1916—directs first feature *The Cycle of Fate* at Selig Chicago studios; 1917—hired by Samuel Goldwyn as Blanche Sweet's director at Lasky Company; 1917-18—directs series of Mary Pickford vehicles; 1920—begins directing for First National; 1922—signs with Goldwyn

Company (through 1924); mid-1920s—last films as independent producer, including *The Skyrocket*; 1930s—does some writing and 2nd-unit directing, works briefly as agent; 1933—files for bankruptcy (and again in 1937); during WW II—on payroll of 20th Century-Fox as writer. Died in Hollywood, 27 October 1958.

Films (as feature director): 1916—*The Cycle of Fate*; *The Prince Chap*; *Country That God Forgot*; 1917—*Those without Sin*; *The Bottle Imp*; *Tides of Barnegat*; *The Girl at Home*; *Silent Partner*; *Freckles*; *The Jaguar's Claws*; *Rebecca of Sunnybrook Farm*; *The Little Princess*; 1918—*Stella Maris*; *Amarilly of Clothes-Line Alley*; *M'liss*; *Hit-the-Trail Holliday*; *Heart of the Wilds*; *Out of a Clear Sky*; 1919—*3 Men and a Girl*; *Daddy--Long-Legs*; *The Unpardonable Sin*; *In Old Kentucky*; 1920—*Her Kingdom of Dreams*; *The River's End*; *Don't Ever Marry* (co-d); *Go and Get It*; *Dinty* (co-d); 1921—*Bob Hampton of Placer*; *Bits of Life* (co-d); *The Lotus Eater*; 1922—*Penrod* (co-d); *Fools First*; *Minnie* (co-d); *Stranger's Banquet*; 1923—*Eternal Three* (co-d); *The Rendezvous*; 1924—*Dorothy Vernon of Haddon Hall*; *Tess of the D'Urbervilles*; 1925—*Sporting Venus*; *The Great Love*; 1926—*Mike*; *The Skyrocket*; *Wild Oats Lane*; *Diplomacy*; *Everybody's Acting*; 1927—*Venus of Venice*; *Her Wild Oat*; 1928—*3-Ring Marriage*; *Take Me Home*; *Taxi 13*; *His Last Haul*; 1929—*Black Waters*; *The Awful Truth*; *Tanned Legs*; *The Vagabond Lover*; 1930—*Sweethearts on Parade*; 1934—*Chloe*; *Social Register*; *The Lemon Drop Kid*; 1935—*This Is the Life*; 1937—*Sing While You're Able*; *Swing It, Professor*.

Roles: beginning 1911—numerous supporting and then leading roles through late teens; 1956—*Senator Fuller* in *A Face in the Crowd* (Kazan).

Publications:

By NEILAN:

Articles—interview by E. Peltret in *Motion Picture Classic* (Brooklyn), April.May 1920; interview by K. McGaffey in *Motion Picture Classic* (Brooklyn), December 1921.

On NEILAN:

Books—*Motion Picture Directing: The Facts and Theories of the Newest Art* by Peter Milne, New York 1922; *Hollywood: The Golden Era* by Jack Spears, New York 1971; articles—"Director 'Mickey'" by A.A. Cohn in *Photoplay* (New York), September 1917; sketch by Adela St. Johns in *Photoplay* (New York), March 1923; obituary in *The New York Times*, 28 October 1958; obituary in *Time* (New York), 10 November 1958; "Marshall Neilan" by J. Gribbel in *Films in Review* (New York), March 1960; "Marshall Neilan" by Jack Spears in *Films in Review* (New York), November 1962; "Blanche Sweet and Marshall Neilan" by K. Lewis in *Films in Review* (New York), June/July 1981.

*   *   *

In the late teens, Marshall Neilan was hailed as the "youngest director genius of the industry." Yet, by the coming of sound he was reduced to directing "B" features, and at the age of 46 he was

unemployable. His was an extraordinary career, begun out of a zest for the excitement which film directing offered and ended through a drinking problem and a failure to work within the studio system. During the height of his career, Marshall Neilan could afford to insult the studio bosses—he inscribed one photograph with the words, "May you never miss the love that Louis B. Mayer does"—but when his drinking and his volatile temper got the better of him, the industry was happy to forget Neilan's successes and assign him to the depths of ignominy which are reserved for those unable to come to terms with the studio system.

From leading man to the likes of Blanche Sweet (whom he was to marry), Marguerite Clark, Mary Pickford, and Ruth Roland—and Neilan was a handsome leading man—he became one of Hollywood's most talented directors, equally at home with the comedy of *Daddy-Long-Legs*, the pathos of *Stella Maris* and the miliatristic propaganda of *The Unpardonable Sin*. Neilan was particularly at ease directing Mary Pickford (whom he directed in seven features), who has said, "I can truthfully say that no director, not even the great D.W. Griffith or Cecil DeMille, could wring the performance from me that Mickey did." As Jack Spears has written, Marshall Neilan was "the boy wonder of Hollywood," a director who could do no wrong as far as the stars, the public or the critics were concerned. All of his films seemed destined to be automatic box-office successes, and all displayed Neilan's remarkable understanding of lighting and emotional audience involvement. Despite his quick temper and apparent private lack of decency (particularly after the ever more frequent bouts of drinking), Neilan was able to come to the set and produce a film of exquisite tenderness and charm.

Through the twenties Marshall Neilan was able to keep a hold on the medium, directing such major achievements as *Dorothy Vernon of Haddon Hall* and *Tess of the D'Urbervilles*, but the coming of sound found Neilan not only at a low personal ebb (following a divorce from Blanche Sweet), but also apprehensive about the future. He simply destroyed his own career (although *Social Register* illustrates that Neilan could produce a competent and pleasurable little picture), and nothing is more depressing than to see this once-great director reduced to playing a small role in Elia Kazan's 1956 *A Face in the Crowd*.

—Anthony Slide

NEMEC, JAN. Czech. Born in Prague, 12 July 1936. Educated at Film Faculty, Academy of Music and Arts (FAMU), Prague 1955-60. Married Ester Krumbachová (divorced); married Marta Kubisova. Career: while at film academy, assistant director to Vaclav Krska, whom Nemec cites as principal influence, and Martin Frič; 1964-66—co-scripts 2 features with then-wife Ester Krumbachovà; also directs 5 shorts and 5 mini-musicals for TV; 1966—after completing *Martyrs of Love*, blacklisted by Barrandov Studios for political reasons; 1968—screening of *The Party and the Guests* at New York Film Festival following 2 year struggle to release film in Czechoslovakia, brings international recognition; films entry of Soviet forces into Prague, footage broadcast around world, later used in both U.S. and Soviet propaganda films; 1969—blacklisted following Soviet occupation of Czechoslovakia; 1972—makes short documentary about intensive care unit in Prague, only film work in Czechoslovakia following Soviet invasion; 1974—able to leave Czechoslovakia on 2 year visa after not working for 6 years; joins with Veronika Schamoni to make several short films in Germany; subsequently moves to U.S., but unable so far to revive career. Address: 21607 Rambla Vista, Malibu, California 90265.

Films (as director): 1960—*Sousto (The Loaf, A Loaf of Bread, A Bite to Eat, The Morsel)*; 1963—*(The Memory of Our Day)*; (as director and co-scriptwriter): 1964—*Demanty noci (Diamonds of the Night)*; "Pdvodníci (The Liars, Impostors)" segment of *Perličky na dně (Pearls of the Deep)*; 1966—*O slavnosti a hostech (The Party and the Guests, Report on the Party and the Guests)*; 1967—*Mučednící lásky (Martyrs of Love)*; *Mother and Son* (short); 1968—*Oratorio for Prague (Oratorium for Prague)* (documentary); 1972—*Between 3 and 5 Minutes* (documentary short); 1975—*Le Décolleté dans le dos*; *Metamorphosis* (short); *The Czech Connection*.

Publications:

On NEMEC:

Books—*All the Bright Young Men and Women* by Josef Skvorecký, Toronto 1971; *Closely Watched Films* by Antonin Liehm, White Plains, New York 1974; *Cinema Beyond the Danube* by Michael Stoil, Metuchen, New Jersey 1974; *The Most Important Art* by Mira and Antonin Liehm, Berkeley 1977.

*   *   *

Nemec's Czech filmography includes three shorts, three features and a segment of a compilation work. All three features were co-scripted by his then wife, Ester Krumbachová. He reached international fame with the 1968 screening of *The Party and the Guests* at the New York Film Festival, which followed a two-year struggle to screen the film within Czechoslovakia. After completing *The Martyrs of Love* in 1966, Nemec was blacklisted by Barrandov Studios for political reasons and was unable to work in Czechoslovakia. He emigrated to the West in 1974, settling first in Paris, then in Germany, and finally in the United States, but he was unable to reestablish his film career despite the fact that he was one of the foremost talents of the Czech New Wave.

Thematically all of Nemec's films deal with obstacles to human freedom and the ways which men and women cope with these limitations. He has stated, "In *Diamonds of the Night* man is not free as a result of that most external of pressures called war. In *The Party and the Guests*, it is a lack of freedom that people bring on themselves by being willing to enter into any sort of collaborative relationship. In *Martyrs of Love*, it is a matter of a lack of freedom or opportunity to act out one's own folly, one's own madness, or dreams of love and human happiness." Within the context, Nemec is most concerned with the psychological effects of these restrictions.

Stylistically Nemec developed a highy metaphoric cinema utilizing several experimental techniques. He calls this style "dream realism." His works function as political and psychological parables. His first feature *Diamonds of the Night*, based on a novel by Holocaust survivor Arnost Lustig, follows two Jewish boys who jump from a Nazi transport on its way to the concentration camps. As the boys wander through the forest looking for food, time shifts back and forth. There are memories of war-torn Prague, distorted visions of elongated trams, and menacing looks of strangers. The boys hallucinate about falling trees and swarming ants. Eventually they are arrested by the Home Guard, composed of old men more concerned with drinking and singing than with the boys. The film ends ambiguously with the fate of the two still an open question. Jaroslav Kučera's hand-held camera creates tension as the boys scamper like animals or stare subjectively into the impassive faces of their captors.

The Party and the Guests begins with a summer picnic. Suddenly a group of men appear, forcing the picnickers to obey new rules. Next they are feted at an elaborate banquet. Only one man is unwilling to participate in the festivities. At the end, accompanied by a menacing dog, the group set out to capture the non-conformist. Here again are the themes of impersonal group control, conformity, man's indifferences, and the casual use of violence, and Nemec again creates a surreal world where the extraordinary takes on the look of everyday events.

Nemec's last major work, *Martyrs of Love*, is composed of three comic stories about young men in pursuit of romance. Their inability to achieve their goal ultimately turns comedy into sadness. In creating the dream-like world of the film, Nemec used only minimal dialogue. The images are accompanied by a jazzy score, reflecting the passion for American music among young Czechs during the sixties.

Nemec's short works deal with the same themes developed in his features. His graduation film *The Loaf of Bread*, portrays a group of prisoners who steal a loaf of bread from their Nazi captors. Here Nemec depicts human beings under stress. As he has commented, "I am concerned with man's reactions to the drastic situation in which, through no fault of his own, he may find himself." *Mother and Son*, made in Holland in 1967, deals with the death of a sadistic soldier, who has beaten and executed prisoners. When young boys try to desecrate his grave, his old mother staunchly protects it. The film ironically concludes with the title, "Love between one human being and another is the only important thing in life."

Nemec's contribution to *Pearls from the Deep* is an episode entitled "The Poseurs." Here two senile patients at a private clinic ramble on about their former achievements, despite their failing memories. Nemec's shots of the mortuary, the place where they will ultimately reside, provide a sad and chilling commentary on all human life. Nemec's remaining works are *Metamorphosis*, an adaptation of the Kafka story filmed in Germany in 1957, and *The Czech Connection*, made the same year.

—Patricia Erens

NIBLO, FRED. American. Born Federico Nobile in York, Nebraska, 6 January 1874. Married Josephine Cohan (died 1916); son: Fred, Jr.; married actress Enid Bennett; 1917; children: Peter, Lorie, and Judith. Career: before 1907—vaudeville performer, blackface monologist; 1907—shoots travelogues on round-the-world cruise, uses them in travel lectures on return; 1910—becomes company manager and actor for George M. Cohan and Sam Harris; toured with George M. Cohan's troupe, and appeared in Cohan's Broadway shows; 1912-15—takes American repertory company to Australia; 1915—for Australian theatrical company J.C. Williamson directs and stars in one film and takes lead in another; 1918—joins Ince company, Hollywood, directs films starring wife Enid Bennett; 1926—directs *Ben-Hur*, assisted by Bennett; 1928—co-founder of Academy of Motion Picture Arts and Sciences; 1930—unable to make transition to sound; attempts directing comeback in England; subsequently resumes acting. Died in New Orleans, 11 November 1948.

Films (as director): 1915—*Get-Rich-Quick Wallingford* (+ro); 1918—*Coals of Fire*; *The Marriage Ring*; *When Do We Eat?*; *A Desert Wooing*; *Fuss and Feathers*; 1919—*Happy Though Married*; *The Haunted Bedroom*; *Partners 3*; *The Virtuous Thief*; *Stepping Out*; *What Every Woman Learns*; 1920—*The Woman in the Suitcase*; *The False Road*; *Her Husband's Friend*; *Dangerous Hours*; *Sex*; *Hairpins*; *The Mark of Zorro*; 1921—*Silk Hosiery*; *Mother o' Mine*; *Greater than Love*; *The 3 Musketeers*; 1922—*The Woman He Married*; *Rose o' the Sea*; *Blood and Sand*; 1923—*The Famous Mrs. Fair*; *Strangers of the Night* (+co-pr); 1924—*Thy Name Is Woman*; *The Red Lily* (+story); 1926—*Ben-Hur*; *The Temptress*; 1927—*Camille* (+pr); *The Devil Dancer* (+pr); 1928—*The Enemy* (+pr); *2 Lovers* (+pr); *The Mysterious Lady*; *Dream of Love*; 1930—*Redemption* (+pr); *Way Out West*; 1931—*Donovan's Kid*; *The Big Gamble*; 1932—*2 White Arms*; *Diamond Cut Diamond* (co-d); *Blame the Woman*; 1944—*4 Jills in a Jeep* (Seiter) (co-sc only).

Roles: 1915—*Officer 666*; 1930—*Free and Easy* (Sedgwick); 1940—*Ellery Queen, Master Detective* (Bellamy); *I'm Still Alive*; 1941—*Life with Henry* (Reed).

Publications:

By NIBLO:

Articles—interview by M. Cheatham in *Motion Picture Classic* (Brooklyn), July 1920; "Sketch" by K. McGaffey in *Motion Picture Classic* (Brooklyn), October 1921; "The Filming of *Ben Hur*", interview by R. Wharton in *Classic Film/Video Images* (Indiana, Pennsylvania), winter 1978.

On NIBLO:

Book—*The Parade's Gone By* by Kevin Brownlow, New York 1968; articles—obituary in *The New York Times*, 12 November 1948; obituary in *Variety* (New York), 12 November 1948; "Buried Directors" by W.D. Route in *Focus* (Chicago), spring 1972.

*   *   *

Fred Niblo directed some of the most legendary stars of the 1920s, in some of that decade's biggest films: *Blood and Sand* (with Valentino); *The Mark of Zorro* and *The Three Musketeers* (Fairbanks); and *Ben Hur*. He guided Garbo through *The Temptress* (replacing her mentor, Mauritz Stiller) and *The Mysterious Lady*. He worked with Lillian Gish, Ronald Colman and Conrad Nagel, Lionel Barrymore, Vilma Banky and Norma Talmadge.

Valentino, Fairbanks, and Garbo first come to mind at the mention of their films with Niblo. The other actors' best work was done elsewhere, for other more rightfully distinguished filmmakers. Niblo's one distinction is his credit on *Ben Hur*, the cinema's first real super-spectacle. *Ben Hur* is the *Cleopatra* of its day, a boondoggle that ran way over budget and took two years to complete. It was begun by the Goldwyn Company, and passed along when Goldwyn, Loew's Metro, and Louis B. Mayer joined together to form Metro-Goldwyn-Mayer. *Ben Hur* was initially shot on location in Italy. The dissatisfied studio ordered a revised script. Ramon Novarro replaced George Walsh in the title role and Niblo, the choice of Mayer and Irving Thalberg, took over for Charles Brabin. The Coliseum was rebuilt several blocks from the MGM lot; inside the studio, Roman galleys floated inside a large tank. Eventually, the budget climbed to $3-million—perhaps even higher—with over one million feet of film shot.

Niblo not so much directed as coordinated *Ben Hur*, and the result was all effect and no drama. Sometimes the film is confusing, and even tiring, yet it is also at its best thrilling. The image of Navarro and Francis X. Bushman (as Messala) racing their chariots remains one of the best-recalled of the silent era. This sequence is supposed to have influenced the staging of the same one in William Wyler's far superior remake.

Ultimately, Niblo's career is more a case of luck than any inherent talent or aesthetic vision. In 1917, he married Enid Bennett, who worked for Thomas Ince; the following year, he began making films for Ince. Later, Niblo was hired by Mayer, who liked him and brought him along to MGM. Niblo's career as an A-film director did not last many years past *Ben Hur*. He made only a handful of films during the 1930s, even working in Britain before retiring in 1941. In his later years, he took small roles in films—he had commenced his career as an actor, in vaudeville, on tour and Broadway—and was employed as a radio commentator and master of ceremonies.

Before *Don Juan*, *The Jazz Singer*, and the demise of silent movies, Niblo made some intriguing prognostications. He foresaw the advent of sound, declaring that motion picture music would be synchronized by radio to replace the live piano; subtitles would be synchronized and broadcast in the same way, in the actual voices of the actors. He predicted the wide use of color cinematography, and three-dimensional screens to prevent distortion, and theaters specializing in children's films.

While Niblo may be at best called a decent technician, he was far more adept with a crystal ball than in a director's chair.

—Rob Edelman

NICHOLS, MIKE. American. Born Michael Igor Peschkowsky in Berlin, 6 November 1931; became citizen of the United States in 1944. Educated at the University of Chicago, 1950-53; studied acting with Lee Strasberg in 1954. Married Patricia Scott in 1957 (divorced); child: Daisy; married Margot Callas in 1974 (divorced); married to Annabel (Nichols); children: Max and Jenny. Career: 1955-57—member of Compass Players improvisational theater group, Chicago; 1957-61—partnership with Elaine May, culminating in Broadway run of *An Evening with Mike Nichols and Elaine May*; 1963—begins directing on Broadway with *Barefoot in the Park*; 1976—produces television series "Family". Recipient: Best Director Tony Award for *Barefoot in the Park*, 1963; Best Director Tony Award for *Luv*, 1964; Best Director Tony Award for *The Odd Couple*, 1965; Best Direction Academy Award for *The Graduate*, 1967; Best Director Tony Award for *Plaza Suite*, 1968; Best Director Tony Award for *The Prisoner of 2nd Avenue*, 1971. Agent: Sam Cohn, International Creative Management, 40 W. 57th Street, New York, NY 10019.

Films (as director): 1966—*Who's Afraid of Virginia Woolf?*; 1967—*The Graduate*; 1970—*Catch-22*; 1971—*Carnal Knowledge*; (+pr); 1973—*The Day of the Dolphin*; 1975—*The Fortune*; (+co-pr); 1980—*Gilda Live*; 1983—*Silkwood*.

Publications:

By NICHOLS:

Articles—"Playboy Interview: Mike Nichols" in *Playboy* (Chicago), June 1966; "And Now—An Evening with Nichols and Hellman", interview by Lillian Hellman, in the *New York Times*, 9 August 1970; interview in *The Film Director as Superstar* by Joseph Gelmis, New York 1971; recording—*Retrospect*, with Elaine May, Chicago 1971.

On NICHOLS:

Books—*Carnal Knowledge* by Jules Feiffer, New York 1971; *A "Catch-22" Casebook* edited by Frederick Kiley and Walter McDonald, New York 1973; *Mike Nichols* by H. Wayne Schuth, Boston 1978; articles—"A Tilted Insight" by Robert Rice in the *New Yorker*, 15 April 1961; "The Cold Loneliness of It All" by Vincent Canby in *The New York Times*, 23 January 1966; "Mike Nichols, Moviemaniac" by Peter Bart in *The New York Times*, 1 July 1967; "Some Are More Yossarian Than Others" in *Time* (New York), 15 June 1970; "On Location with *Carnal Knowledge*" by Herb Lightman in *American Cinematographer* (Los Angeles), January 1971; "Pictures of Innocence" by John Brown in *Sight and Sound* (London), spring 1972; "Mike Nichols Tries to Make a Talkie with Dolphins" by Peter Feibleman in *Atlantic* (New York), January 1974; "The Misfortune of Mike Nichols: Notes on the Making of a Bad Film" by Frank Rich in *New Times*, 11 July 1975; "Hollywood 79: Mike Nichols" by J. Fieschi in *Cinématographe* (Paris), March 1979.

*   *   *

The films of Mike Nichols are guided by an eye and ear of a satirist whose professional gifts emerge from a style of liberal, improvisational comedy that originated in a Chicago theater club and developed into a performing partnership with Elaine May in the late fifties and early sixties. In clubs and recordings, on radio, television and Broadway, Nichols and May routines gnawed hilariously close to the bone. Aimed at literate, self-aware audiences, their skits (anticipating key elements of Nichols's films) gleefully anatomized men and women dueling in post-Freudian combat, by turns straying from the marriage bond and clinging to it for dear life.

Before directing *Who's Afraid of Virginia Woolf?* for the screen in 1966, Nichols earned a reputation as a skillful Broadway director with particular flair for devising innovative stage business and eliciting unusually polished performances from his casts. That sure theatrical sense, honed by his subsequent direction of Broadway plays by writers as diverse as Neil Simon, Anton Chekhov, Lillian Hellman, David Rabe, and Tom Stoppard, combines in his best films with the sardonic attitude toward American life underlying even the gentlest of his collaborations with Elaine May.

Nichols's major films began as comedies and evolve into mordant, generically ambiguous dissections of the American psyche. Their central characters exist in isolation from the landscapes they inhabit, manufacturing illusions to shield themselves against reality (George and Martha in *Virginia Woolf*, Sandy and Jonathan in *Carnal Knowledge*) or fleeing with mounting desperation societies whose values they alone perceive as neurotic (Benjamin Braddock in *The Graduate*) or muderous (Yossarian in *Catch-22*).

Martha and George, Edward Albee's Strindbergian couple, flail at each other on their New England campus and reveal a tormented relationship that concludes with a glimmer of hope but seems nevertheless to imply the futility of monogamy, a view reenforced by *Carnal Knowledge* and *The Graduate*. Until he dates Elaine Robinson, Ben Braddock is segregated by script and

camera from the company of friends. In a packed airplane, on the Berkeley campus teeming with students, surrounded by his parents' partying guests: Ben is alone. His detachment, italicized by numerous shots within the film, permits him to function as the funnel for *The Graduate*'s social satire. In this respect he is Nichols's surrogate but the director complicates the viewer's empathetic response to Ben by scrutinizing him rather as an experimenting scientist scrutinizes a mouse darting about a maze, especially as he scampers in frantic pursuit of Elaine.

In Dustin Hoffman's memorable screen debut, Ben became the moralistic spokesman for a generation that mistrusted anyone over thirty and vowed never to go into plastics. But like other Nichols heroes Ben is himself more than a little crazy, the inevitable child of a Southern California lifestyle that leads him to anticipate instant gratification. Nichols, moreover, intentionally undermines the comic resolution toward which the film has been heading through ambivalent shots of Ben and Elaine on their departing bus, implicating them in mutual recognition of a colossal mistake. At film's end, Ben Braddock still has considerable cause to be "worried about [his] future."

For Yossarian, worrying about the future means literally staying alive. To survive a catch-22 universe he must behave like a lunatic but the more bizarrely he acts the more sanely is he regarded according to the military chop-logic that drives him toward madness. In *Catch-22* time is fractured (in Buck Henry's screenplay) to retain the basic storytelling method of Joseph Heller's novel. Flashbacks occur within flashbacks. Conversations are inaudible (as in the opening scene), incidents only partially revealed (as in the first Snowden sequences), to be played later in the film with deleted elements restored.

Fond of foreground shooting, long takes and distorting close-ups to intensify the sense of his characters' entrapment, Nichols also frequently employs overlapping sound and a spare, modernistic mise-en-scène (the latter at times reminiscent of Antonioni) to convey an aura of disorientation and sterility. In the underpraised and misunderstood *Carnal Knowledge*, Nichols uses whiteouts (also prominent in *Catch-22*) and Bergmanesque talking heads as structural and thematic devices to increase the viewer's alienation from the two central characters and to ridicule notions of male sexual fantasy at the core of the film. Visually and textually (in Jules Feiffer's original screenplay) Jonathan and Sandy are the most isolated and self-deluded of Nichols's characters.

Things are seldom what they initially seem in this director's work. Like Nick and Honey, misled by George and Martha's pretense of hospitality in *Who's Afraid of Virginia Woolf?*, the viewer is easily duped by a deceptively comic tone, enticing visual stylization, and innovative storytelling technique into misreading the bleak vision that the films usually harbor. Even *The Fortune*, a farce in the screwball tradition, hinges on the attempted murder by the film's two heroes of its heroine, whose fate hangs in the balance at the final fadeout.

Nichols directs literate, intelligent scripts that pull few punches in their delineations of sexual subjects (*Virginia Woolf*, *The Graduate*, *Carnal Knowledge*) and political ones (*Catch-22*, *Day of the Dolphin*, *Silkwood*). The same production designer (Richard Sylbert) and editor (Sam O'Steen) worked on the six films from *Virginia Woolf* to *The Fortune*, contributing substantially to a developing visual style and pace. While *The Graduate* continues to be regarded as an American classic, Nichols is sometimes undervalued for his film work because he prefers the New York theater and because his contributions to his pictures are periodically credited to their writers' screenplays (Buck Henry, Jules Feiffer) or their theatrical and literary sources (Edward Albee, Joseph Heller, Charles Webb). But Nichols is very much the auteur who works intimately with his collaborators on all aspects of his films, principally the writing. (See his interview with Josef Gelmis in *The Film Directors as Superstar*, 1970.)

The films uphold Nichols's original reputation as a gifted director of actors: Hoffman in *The Graduate*, Elizabeth Taylor and Richard Burton in *Who's Afraid of Virginia Woolf?*, Jack Nicholson, Ann-Margret, and Art Garfunkel in *Carnal Knowledge*, Alan Arkin in *Catch-22*, Meryl Streep in *Silkwood*. And they reveal, even in their intermittent self-indulgence, a director of prodigious versatility and insight.

—Mark W. Estrin

OLCOTT, SIDNEY. American. Born John Sidney Alcott in Toronto, 20 January 1874. Married actress Valentine Grant. Career: early 1890s—after experience in amateur theatricals in Toronto, moves to New York to pursue stage career; assumes surname "Olcott"; 1903—first important acting jobs secured by John Ince, father of Thomas H. Ince; appears in *When the Harvest Days Are Over*, *From Rags to Riches*, and *Billy the Kid* with Joseph Santley; 1904—appears in short films for American Mutoscope and Biograph companies; 1904-06—works intermittently at Biograph as actor and assistant; 1907—joins newly-formed Kalem company, directs its first picture *The Sleigh Bells*; works through 1908 at Kalem studio in Fort Lee, New Jersey; 1908—at end of year operations transferred to Jacksonville, Florida; 1910—takes film company to Ireland, first time American film made on location outside country; also shoots in England and Germany; 1911—shoots in North Africa; 1912—makes *From the Manger to the Cross* in Palestine; resigns from Kalem company; forms independent company in Jacksonville, G.G. Feature Players, with actress and scenarist Gene Gauntier; 1914—produces series of films in Ireland; 1915—signs with Famous Players; 1927—directs last film in U.S., goes to England to direct for British Lion; objects to story material, successfully sues; returns to U.S. Died in Hollywood, 16 December 1949; buried in Toronto.

Films (as director and scenarist—also edited early films and acted in many of them): 1907—*The Sleigh Bells*; *Ben Hur*; *The Scarlet Letter*; 1908—*Washington at Valley Forge*; *A Florida Feud (Florida Crackers)*; *Dr. Jekyll and Mr. Hyde*; *The Wooing of Miles Standish*; 1909—*The Escape from Andersonville*; *The Factory Girl*; *The Tomboy*; *The Queen of the Quarry*; *Out of Work*; *The Pay Car*; *Hiram's Bride*; *The Conspirators*; *The Winning Boat*; *The Mystery of the Sleeper Trunk*; *The Hand Organ Man*; *The Girl Scout*; *The Cattle Thieves*; *The Man and the Girl*; *A Brother's Wrong*; *Dora*; *The Governor's Daughter*; *The Rally Round the Flag*; *The Geisha Who Saved Japan*; *The Law of the Mountains*; *Her Indian Hero*; *The Cardboard Baby*; 1910—*The Lad from Old Ireland*; *The Feud*; *Further Adventures of the Girl Spy*; *The Priest of Wilderness*; *Hannah Dusten*; *The Sacred Turquoise of the Zuni*; *The Forager*; *The Bravest Girl in the South*; *The Love Romance of the Girl Spy*; *The Aigrette Hunter (The Egret Hunt)*; *The Stranger*; *The Seminole Halfbreed*; *Her Soldier Sweetheart*; *The Canadian Moonshiners*; *For a Woman's Honor*; *Up the Thames to Westminster* (documentary); *The Little Spreewald Maiden*; *The Indian Mother*; *Seth's Temptation*; *A Romance of Old Erin*; *The Girl Spy Before Vicksburg*; 1911—*Rory O'Moore*; *Arrah-na-Pogue*; *The Colleen Bawn*; *You Remember Ellen?*; *The Sister*; *Grandmother's War Story*; *The Irish Honeymoon*; *Her Chum's Brother*; *In Old Florida*; *The Carnival*; *Tangled Lives*; *To the*

Aid of Stonewall Jackson; *The Little Soldier of '64*; *The Seminole's Vengeance*; *Hunted Through the Everglades*; *When the Dead Return*; *The Fishermaid of Bally David*; *Sailor Jack's Reformation*; *Little Sister*; *The Fiddle's Requiem*; *In Blossom Time*; 1912—*From the Manger to the Cross*; *An Irish Girl's Love*; *Missionaries in Darkest Africa* (documentary); *Driving Home the Cows*; *The O'Kalems' Visit to Killarney* (documentary); *His Mother*; *The Vagabonds*; *The Kalemites Visit Gibralter* (documentary); *The Fighting Dervishes*; *Egypt* (documentary); *Captured by Bedouins*; *Tragedy of the Desert*; *Egypt the Mysterious* (documentary); *Making Photoplays in Egypt* (documentary); *An Arabian Tragedy*; *Winning a Widow*; *A Prisoner of the Harem*; *Egyptian Sports* (documentary); *Easter Celebration at Jerusalem* (documentary); *Palestine* (documentary); *From Jerusalem to the Dead Sea* (documentary); *Ancient Temples of Egypt* (documentary); *A Day in Jerusalem* (documentary); *Along the River Nile* (documentary); *The Kerry Gow*; *The Major from Ireland*; *Conway the Kerry Dancer*; *Ireland the Oppressed*; *The Shaughraun*; 1913—*The Wives of Jamestown*; *Lady Peggy's Escape*; *A Daughter of the Confederacy*; *The Mystery of Pine Tree Camp*; *In the Power of the Ku-Klux-Klan*; *The Little Rebel*; (as director): 1914—*When Men Would Kill*; *The Eye of the Government*; *Come Back to Erin*; *The Brute*; *A Mother of Men*; *Tricking the Government*; *The Moth and the Flame*; 1915—*The Melting Plot*; *The Irish in America*; *All for Old Ireland*; *Bold Emmett*; *Ireland's Martyr* (+sc); *Nan o' the Backwoods* (+sc); *The Ghost of the Twisted Oaks*; *The Taint*; *Madame Butterfly*; *7 Sisters*; 1916—*The Innocent Lie*; *Poor Little Peppina*; *The Daughter of MacGregor*; *The Innocent Lie*; *My Lady Incog*; *Jean o' the Heather*; 1918—*The Belgian*; 1919—*A Marriage for Convenience*; 1920—*Scratch My Back*; 1921—*The Right Way* (+pr); *Pardon My French*; *God's Country and the Law*; 1922—*Timothy's Quest*; 1923—*The Green Goddess*; *Little Old New York*; 1924—*Monsieur Beaucaire*; *The Humming Bird*; *The Only Woman*; 1925—*The Charmer*; *Not So Long Ago*; *Salome of the Tenements*; *The Best People*; 1926—*Ranson's Folly*; *The White Black Sheep*; *The Amateur Gentleman*; 1927—*The Claw*.

Publications:

By OLCOTT:

Article—"Blazing a Trail in the Movies", interview by P. Gaddis in *Photoplay* (New York), September 1914.

On OLCOTT:

Articles—obituary in *The New York Times*, 18 December 1949; obituary in *Time* (New York), 26 December 1949; "Ireland's First Films" by Proinsias Conluain in *Sight and Sound* (London), October/December 1953; "Sidney Olcott" by George Mitchell in *Films in Review* (New York), April 1954 (see also letter from G. Geltzer, May 1954, and Mitchell reply June/July 1954).

*   *   *

A pioneer in location shooting, Olcott was the first director of the Kalem Company and a filmmaker of taste and refinement whose work continued successfully into the twenties. From newspaper boy and touring actor he moved to the Biograph Company of New York, departing from this organization with

Frank Marion to direct for Kalem their first film *The Sleigh Bells*. His production of the first *Ben Hur* led to the first check on film piracy when the film was declared in breach of copyright and Kalem had to pay heavy indemnities. Olcott continued to direct many films in the New York and Florida Kalem studios often acting in his films and using the scripting and acting talents of Miss Gene Gauntier. With her and George Hollister, the cameraman, he visited the land of his fathers in 1910 making his first Irish film *The Lad From Old Ireland*. The plot was a stereotype. Irish peasant boy makes good in America and returns in time to save his boyhood sweetheart from eviction. But Olcott was observing the Irish at first hand and he returned to Beaufort, Killarney, to the home of Annie O'Sullivan which became his headquarters for four summers to come. He filmed patriotic dramas which led to conflict with the British authorities in Ireland and indeed he was denounced on another level from the local pulpit as the director of "these painted actors desecrating the homes of our ancestors". He filmed the popular dramas of Don Boucicault, *The Colleen Bawn, Arrah-na-Pogue*, and *The Shaughraun*. With his company of players he also travelled to Egypt and Palestine where his *From the Manger to the Cross* was filmed. The depiction of sacred figures of the New Testament led to violent controversy, one Irish newspaper denouncing it as "American simony at its worst." After he and Miss Gauntier left Kalem they returned again to Killarney in 1913, and in 1914 Olcott returned with his wife, Valentine Grant. The outbreak of war put an end to his plans for building a film studio in Killarney.

His *The Belgian* was much admired and touched directly on the war. Before this, however, he directed Mary Pickford in two films. *Madame Butterfly* did not run smoothly and star clashed with director on interpretation. Olcott demanded oriental restraint while Pickford wanted girlish high spirits. The presense of Marshall Neilan as Pinkerton did not make for harmony either. One recalls that Miss Pickford also clashed with Lubitsch in a similar matter. *Poor Little Peppina*, which followed, found a more docile Miss Pickford. Olcott's recognized talent as a director brought him the opportunity to direct many of Hollywood's leading players of the twenties, notably George Arliss (*The Green Goddess*), Marion Davis (*Little Old New York*), Valentino (*Monsieur Beaucaire*), Gloria Swanson, Pola Negri and Richard Barthelmess. Relying less on star appeal, he made some other films which revealed his own talents such as *Scratch My Back*, *Timothy's Quest*, and *The Right Way*. In 1927 he directed his last film *The Claw*. A plan to film in England came to nothing as Olcott refused to direct a subject he considered to glorify crime.

He lived on to 1949 and died at the home of his old-time friend, Robert Vignola, with whom he lived after the death of his wife Valentine Grant. He was a great-hearted man, demanding in his pursuit of perfection, hypnotic in his control of actors, and tasteful in his film presentations.

—Liam O'Leary

OLIVEIRA, MANOEL DE. Portuguese. Born Manoel Cândido Pinto de Oliveira in Oporto, 10 December 1908. Married Maria Isabel Carvalhais, 1940; 4 children. Career: 1920-27— athlete and racing car driver, winner of several awards; 1929— directs first film; also does some film acting in early 1930s, but fails to launch career in film and returns to sports activities and tending to family business; 1941—makes 1st feature *Aniki-Bóbó*; 1943-56—unable to make films, works in agriculture, introducing new farm production methods; 1956-71—continues

working in agriculture, resumes making shorts and documentaries; 1971—makes 2nd fiction feature with support of Portuguese Cinema Center, production cooperative created by filmmakers and supported by Gulbenkian Foundation; from 1972 concentrates entirely on filmmaking.

Films (as producer, director, scriptwriter, and editor): 1931— *Douro, faina fluvial (Hard Labor on the River Douro)* (short); 1939—*Miramar praia das rosas* (short); *Ja se fabricam automovels em Portugal* (short); 1940—*Famalicão* (short); 1942— *Aniki-Bóbó* (d, sc only); 1956—*O pintor e a cidade (The Painter and the Town)* (+ph) (short); (as director and scriptwriter): 1959—*O pão (Bread)* (+ed, ph); 1960—*O coração (The Heart)* (short); 1963—*Acto da primavera (The Passion of Jesus)* (+pr, ed, ph); *A caça (The Hunt)* (+ph, ed); (as director): 1965—*As pinturas de meu irmão Júlio (Pictures of My Brother Julio)* (+pr, ph, ed) (short); 1972—*O passado e o presente (Past and Present)* (+co-pr, ed); 1975—*Benilde ou a Virgem Mãe (Benilde: Virgin and Mother)* (+ed); 1978—*Amor de perdição (Ill-Fated Love)*; 1981—*Francisca*; 1982—*Memórias e confissões (Memories and Confessions)* (+sc, ed) (to be released only after Oliveira's death); 1983—*Lisboa Cultural (Cultural Lisbon)*; 1984—*À propos de Vigo*.

Role: 1933—*A Canção de Lisboa* (Telmo).

Publications:

By OLIVEIRA:

Book—*Aniki-Bóbó*, continuity and dialogue, Porto 1963; articles—"O cinema e o capital" in *Movimento* (Lisbon), October 1933; interview by Paulo Rocha in *Critica* (Lisbon), March 1972; interview by João Botelho and Cabral Martins in *M*, (Lisbon), August/September 1975; "Oliveira, Straub, Huillet, Robert Kramer e M. Hanoun", round table, in *Expresso* (Lisbon), October 1975; "Lettre de Manuel de Oliveira à Rui Nogueira" and "A propos de Benilde ou a Virgem-Mãe" in *Image et son* (Paris), February 1977; interview by J.C. Bonnet and E. Decaux in *Cinématographe* (Paris), November 1981; "Los Paisajes pintados", interview by F. Llináa and S. Zunzunegui in *Contracampo* (Madrid), January 1981; interview by C. Tesson and J.C. Biette in *Cahiers du cinéma* (Paris), October 1981.

On OLIVEIRA:

Books—*Manoel de Oliveira*, Ciné-Club of Estremoz, 1955; *Manoel de Oliveira*, with "Diálogo com Manoel de Oliveira", Cinemateca Portuguesa, Lisbon 1981; *Introdução à obra de Manoel de Oliveira* by J.A. França, L. Pina, and A. Costa, Lisbon 1982; articles—"Douro, faina fluvial" by José Régio in *Presença* (Coimbra), 1931; "Manoel de Oliveira" by Jacques Demeure in *Positif* (Paris), no.25-26, 1957; "Notes sur l'oeuvre de Manoel de Oliveira" by J.C. Biette in *Cahiers du cinéma* (Paris), February 1966; "Biennale cinéma '76: la realta portoghese vista attraverso il cinema di M. De Oliveira" by B. Fornara in *Cineforum* (Bergamo), November 1976; "Manuel de Oliveira" by A. Costa in *Image et son* (Paris), February 1977; "Notes sur les films de Manuel de Oliveira" by Serge Daney in *Cahiers du cinéma* (Paris), May 1977; "O voto de Simão e Teresa" by João Lopes in *Diário de Noticias* (Lisbon), November 1979; "Retrospective Manoel de Oliveira" by R. Bassan in *Image et son* (Paris), February 1980; "Dossier-auteur Manoel de Oliveira" by

J. Magny in *Cinéma* (Paris), March 1980; "Manuel de Oliveira: le passé et le présent" by F. Ramasse in *Positif* (Paris), March 1980; "Manuel de Oliveira: du regard au style" by H. Welsh in *Jeune Cinéma* (Paris), April/May 1980; "Manoel de Oliveira" by John Gillett in *Sight and Sound* (London), summer 1981; "Artificio, enunciacion, emocion: La Obra de Manoel de Oliveira" by S. Zunzunegui in *Contracampo* (Madrid), January 1981; "Francisca ou o cavalo na sala" by E. Prado Coelho in *Expresso* (Lisbon), September 1981; "Manoel de Oliveira, o cinema e a crueldade" by M.S. Fonseca in *Expresso* (Lisbon), October 1981; television—"Écran", with interview, by A.M. Seabra, RTP production, Portugal, September 1981.

*　　*　　*

Simultaneously rugged and tender, the tortured work of Manoel de Oliveira, in which a personal vision is transformed into a unique expression of Portuguese culture, finds its only counterpart in that of Carl Th. Dreyer. The radical aesthetic and ethical programs of both filmmakers met with imcomprehension; in both, one finds a tragic fusion of profane desire and an aspiration toward the sacred.

No man is a prophet in his own country; Oliveira, an artist of magnitude disproportionate to such a diminutive nation, confirms this aphorism. He found no favor under the Salazar regime, being condemned by its pettiness to silence and inactivity. Persecution did not cease with the death of the dictator. Oliveira continued to be charged with "not being natural" and was accused of the sin of "elitism." This is the reason there are so many films that Oliveira *did not* make. Only relatively late in his career did international acclaim force a measure of national recognition.

The first phase of Oliveira's work, what he calls "the stage of the people," is dominated by an intense dialogue between documentary and fiction. From the very beginning Oliveira had refused to subjugate himself to the "genres" and "schools." An unmistakable movement toward fiction, toward the autonomy of the cinema vis à vis *the real*, can be seen in his documentaries from *Douro* to *Pinturas*. In registering its images, Oliveira's camera approaches quotidien reality as a stage. Through montage, the world can be fixed, cut, and reproduced as a series of fragments.

The second phase begins in 1972 and is characterized by a more complete expression of the impulse towards fiction, There is a concomitant change of objectives: the "stage of the people" is replaced by the "stage of the bourgeoisie." This phase comprises four films, from *O passado e o presente* to *Francisca*, known as the "Tetralogy of Frustrated Loves." Alluringly romantic, possessed in particular by 19th century literature and its ethos of perdition, by the love of perdition as expressed in the Portuguese literature of the time, these films attain an esthetic refinement unsurpassed in European cinema.

In the 1930s Oliveira belonged to the cinematic vanguard. From 1940 to 1963 this cinematic craftsman anticipated many of the innovative esthetic experiments of later filmmakers—from Italian neorealism to the cinema of Straub—without reducing his work to mere formalism. With the *Tetralogy*, a risky and original project makes its appearance: the destruction of the narrative grammer, which relies on the shot/countershot, and the destruction of the psychological correspondences through the creation, in these films, of a *point of view belonging to no one*. Refusing to identify itself with either the characters or the spectator, the camera alters spatial relationships in an effort not exactly to neutralize itself, but to situate itself in a space without a subject in order to fix faces and voices. "Voices" because, being

films adapted from literary works, they resolutely assume the literary nature of the *text*, to which long and fixed planes or the repetition of such planes confers a temporality without parallel in the history of the cinema. The obsessive use of the studio is also underscored, re-enforcing a sense of enclosure and restriction. A similar emphasis is placed on the style or *representation* which situates actors and objects on the same level; their function is simply to be present.

Linking this formal experimentation with undeniably vigorous fiction, *Francisca* is Oliveira's masterpiece. In *Francisca*, a grandiose synthesis of literary, musical and pictorial materials, a telluric mark flourishes—and it is for this reason a possible similarity with Hans-Jurgen Syberberg disappears—which determines desire, fear, guilt, and perdition, i.e. the principle themes of Oliveira. After all, such a mark echoes an entire culture which, at its best, transcends a tormented pessimism and bitter irony, offering only the consolation of melancholy. This culture is Portuguese and Oliveira is its filmmaker.

—Manuel Dos Santos Fonseca

OLMI, ERMANNO. Italian. Born in Bergamo, Italy, 24 July 1931. Attended Accadémia d'Arte Drammatica, Milan. Married Loredana Detto; 3 children. Career: 1949—begins working for Italian electric company, Edisonvolta S.p.A. (Milan); 1952—becomes involved with directing the theatrical and cinematic activities sponsored by Edisonvolta; 1952-61—directs or supervises over 40 short 16mm and 35mm documentary films; 1959—directs 1st feature film, semi-documentary *Il Tempo si è fermato*, also sponsored by Edisonvolta; 1961—forms with Tullio Kezich and other friends production company "22 December S.p.A."; since 1964—directs regularly for television. Recipient: Catholic Film Office Award, Cannes Festival, for *The Fiancés*, 1963.

Films (as supervisor and director): 1953—*La digi sul ghiaccio*; 1954—*La pattuglia di passo San Giacomo*; 1955—*Società Ovesticino-Dinamo*; *Cantiere d'inverno*; *La mia valle*; *La tesatura meccanica della linea a 220.000 volt* (supervised only); *San Massenza (Cimego)* (supervised only); *L'onda*; *Buongiorno natura*; 1956—*Pantano d'avio* (supervised only); *Michelino la B*; *Construzione meccaniche riva*; *Peru—Istituto de Verano* (supervised only); *Fertilizzanti complessi* (supervised only); 1957—*Fibre e civilta* (supervised only); *Progresso in agricoltura* (supervised only); *Campi sperimentali* (supervised only); 1958—*Colonie Sicedison* (supervised only); *Bariri* (supervised only); *Tre fili fino a Milano*; *Giochi di Colonia*; *Il frumento* (supervised only); *Venezia città minore*; 1959—*Il tempo si è fermato (Time Has Stopped, Time Stood Still)* (feature) (+sc); *El frayle* (supervised only); *Fertiluzzanti produtti dalla Societá del Gruppo Edison* (supervised only); *Cavo olio fludio 220.000 volt* (supervised only); *Auto chiese* (supervised only); *Natura e chimica* (supervised only); 1960—*Il grande paese d'Acciaio*; 1961—*Il pomodoro* (supervised only); *Il sacco in Plypac* (supervised only); *Le grand barrage*; *Un metro lungo cinque*; *Po: forza 50.000* (pr only); (as feature director): 1961—*Il posto (The Sound of Trumpets, The Job)* (+sc); 1963—*I fidanzati (The Fiancés, The Engagement)* (+pr, sc); 1965—*...e venne un uomo (A Man Named John, A Man Called John, And There Came a Man)* (+co-sc); 1968—*Un certo giorno (One Fine Day)* (+sc, ed); 1969—*I recuperanti (The Scavengers)* (+co-sc, ph—for TV); *Un certo giorno (One Fine Day)* (+sc); 1971—*Durante l'estate (During the Summer, In the Summertime)* (+co-sc, ph, ed—for

TV); 1974—*La circostanza (The Circumstance)* (+pr, sc, ph, ed—for TV); 1978—*L'albero degli zoccoli (The Tree of the Wooden Clogs)*(+sc, ph, ed—for TV); 1983—*Camminacammina (Walking Walking)*. Role: 1962—*Una storia milanese* (E. Visconti).

Publications:

By OLMI:

Articles—interview by G. Bachmann in *Nation* (New York), 25 May 1964; interview in *Cahiers du cinéma* (Paris), July 1964; "Ermanno Olmi, A Conversation with John Francis Lane" in *Sight and Sound* (London), summer 1970; "Entretien avec Ermanno Olmi" by Lorenzo Codelli in *Positif* (Paris), September 1976; interview by A. Tassone in *Cinéma* (Paris), January 1976; interview by M. Devillers and others in *Cinématographe* (Paris), no.40, 1978.

On OLMI:

Book—*Encountering Directors* by Charles Thomas Samuels, New York 1972; articles—"The Triumph of Italy's Realism" by J.F. Lane in *Films and Filming* (London), December 1961; "Ermanno Olmi in London" by Penelope Houston in *Sight and Sound* (London), winter 1961-62; "Ermanno Olmi" by G.P. Solomos in *Film Culture* (New York), spring 1962; "3 Italian Films" by G.P. Solomos in *Film Comment* (New York), fall 1963; "A Fine Italian Hand" by Stanley Kauffman in the *New Republic* (New York), 15 February 1964; "The New Italian Films" by G. Bachmann in *Nation* (New York), 25 May 1964; "The Organisation Man" by Penelope Houston in *Sight and Sound* (London), spring 1964; "Filmography" in *Monogram* (London), summer 1971; "Ermanno Olmi" by M. Walsh in *Monogram* (London), summer 1971; article by Richard Corliss in *The Village Voice* (New York), 21 October 1971; "4 auteurs en quête d'un distributeur" by A. Tassone in *Image et son* (Paris), September 1975; "Bio-Filmographie d'Ermanno Olmi" by Lorenzo Codelli in *Positif* (Paris), September 1976; "Noblesse oblige ou l'art de l'héraldique" by Eithe Bourget in *Positif* (Paris), September 1976; "Du Côté de Brescia" by Jacques Segond in *Positif* (Paris), September 1976; "Ermanno Olmi: Humanism in the Cinema" by M. Gervais in *Sight and Sound* (London), autumn 1978; special section on *L'Albero degli zoccoli* by A. Masson and others in *Positif* (Paris), September 1978; "De cómo el amor y la caridad son la clave estética de Ermanno Olmi" by M. Martínez Carril in *Cinemateca revista* (Andes), June 1980; article in *Sight and Sound* (London), winter 1980-81; "Ermanno Olmi" by Derek Elley in *International Film Guide 1981*, London 1980.

*   *   *

Olmi, born in Bergamo in 1931, is the Italian filmmaker most committed to and identified with a regional heritage. His films are distinctly Lombardian; for the most part they describe life in Milan, the provincial capital (e.g. *Il posto*, *Un certo giorno*, *Durante l'estate* (1971), *La circonstanza*. He has also filmed in the Lombardian Alps (*Il tempo si è fermato*), and his native Bergamo (*L'albero degli zoccoli*), but even when he ventures to Sicily, it is to make a film of a Milanese worker temporarily assigned to the south who longs for home (*I fidanzati*), and when

he makes a semi-documentary biography (*...e venne un uomo*), it is of the Lombardian Pope, John XXIII.

Furthermore, his work bears affinities to the central literary figure of the Lombardian tradition, Alessandro Manzoni, whose great historical novel, *I promessi sposi*, is variously reflected in at least three of Olmi's films: most directly in *I findanzati*, whose very title recasts the 1827 novel, but also in the idealization of a great ecclesiastic (*L'albero degli zoccoli*, which portrays peasant life in the late 19th century rather than Manzoni's 17th). The most significant Manzonian characteristic of Olmi's cinema is its Catholicism; of all the major Italian filmmakers he has the least problematic relationship to the Church. He embodies the spirit of the "opening to the Left" which has characterized both religious and parliamentary politics in Italy since the early 1960s. For the most part, his films center upon an individual worker caught between employment and an individual quest to assert dignity through labor. Quite often this tension carries over from work to the conjugal or preconjugal love life of the protagonist.

Like Pasolini, Rosi, and Bertolucci, Olmi is a filmmaker nurtured by post-war neorealism. Like his great precursors, Rossellini, De Sica, and Visconti, he has worked extensively with amateur actors, chosen simplified naturalistic settings, eschewed elaborate artifices or lighting, and employed an ascetic camera style. What mobility his camera has comes largely from his extensive use of the zoom lens. In contrast, however, to the first generation of neorealists, he has a high tolerance for abstraction and ambiguity in his story telling. Dramatic and emotional moments are consistently understated. Instead of a mobile camera, he has relied heavily upon montage (especially in the intercutting of scenes between Milan and Sicily in *I fidanzati*) and even more on the overlapping of sounds, In fact, Olmi's meticulous attention to sound, his isolation and manipulation of auditory details, tends to transform his realistically photographed scenes into psychologically-inflected domains of space and time.

—P. Adams Sitney

OPHULS, MARCEL. French, American. Born in Frankfurt-am-Main, Germany, 1 November 1927; became citizen of France, 1938, and of the United States, 1950. Educated at Hollywood High School, graduated 1945; Occidental College; University of California at Berkeley; studied philosophy, the Sorbonne. Married Regina Ackermann, 1956; 3 daughters. Career: 1932—father, director Max Ophuls, takes family to France; 1941—family moves to U.S., settles in Hollywood; 1946—service with Occupation forces in Japan; performs with theater unit, Tokyo; 1951—begins working in French film industry as 3rd assistant director, using name "Marcel Wall"; 1956-59—radio and TV story editor (dramaturg) for Sudwestfunk, Baden-Baden, West Germany; radio and stage directing debuts; directs 4 productions for German TV; 1960-62—returns to Paris, begins directing and writing filmscripts and occasionally contributes to *Cahiers du cinéma* and *Arts*; 1966—begins working for French TV as journalist and director of *Zoom*, news magazine; 1966-68—works for ORTF (French TV monopoly) as reporter and director of news magazine features, learns interview technique; 1967—directs *Munich, or Peace in Our Time* for French TV, broadcast over 2 evenings, first major historical documentary; 1968—after unsuccessful television strike in wake of May protests, moves family to Hamburg; 1968-71—senior story editor at NDR (German TV, 1st channel); directs *The Sorrow and the*

Pity for German TV (banned by French television until 1981); 1973-74—Senior Visiting Fellow, Council of the Humanities, Princeton University; 1973-76—works on *The Memory of Justice* about Nuremberg trials and their aftermath; 1975-78—staff producer at CBS-News, then ABC News; 1979—returns to Europe; resumes making TV documentaries (*Kortnergeschichte* for German TV, 1980, and *Yorktown, le sens d'une bataille*, 1982); 1980-83—acts in films, contributes to various publications including *American Film*, *Newsday*, *The Nation*, *Positif*, and *Les Nouvelles Littéraires*; serves as Secretary General, French Filmmakers' Society, on Board of Directors, Société des gens de lettres. Recipient: Prix de Dinard for *The Sorrow and the Pity*; Prix Georges Sadoul for *The Sorrow and the Pity*; British Film and TV Academy Award for *The Sorrow and the Pity*; Special Award, National Society of Film Critics, for *The Sorrow and the Pity*, 1971; Special Citation for the year's best documentary, New York Film Critics, for *The Sorrow and the Pity, 1972*.

Films (as assistant director—partial list): 1953—*Moulin Rouge* (Huston); 1954—*Un Acte d'amour (Act of Love)* (Litvak); *Marianne de ma jeunesse* (Duvivier); 1955—*Lola Montès* (Ophüls); (as director and scriptwriter): 1960—*Matisse, or The Talent for Happiness*; 1961—German episode of *L'Amour à vingt ans (Love at 20)*; 1963—*Peau de banane (Banana Peel)* (co-sc); 1964—*Feu à volonté (Faites vos jeux, Mesdames, Fire at Will)* (co-sc); 1966—*Till Eulenspiegel* (co-sc, co-d—quit during filming—in 2 parts, for German TV); 1967—*Munich, ou La Paix pour cent ans (Munich, or Peace in Our Time)* (for French TV); 1969—*Le Chagrin et la pitié (The Sorrow and the Pity)* (for TV, in 2 parts—4.5 hours long); 1970—*Clavigo* (d only—for TV); *The Harvest of My Lai* (for TV); 1971—*America Revisited* (for TV, in 2 parts); *Zwei ganze tage (2 Whole Days)* (d only, for TV); 1972—*A Sense of Loss*; 1976—*The Memory of Justice*.

Publications:

By OPHULS:

Articles—"The Sorrow and the Pity, A Sense of Loss, a Discussion with Marcel Ophuls" by B.J. Demby in *Filmmakers Newsletter* (Ward Hill, Mass.), December 1972; "Politics and Autobiography", interview by D. Yergin in *Sight and Sound* (London), winter 1973/74; interview by L. Codelli in *Positif* (Paris), June 1973; "Why Should I Give You Political Solutions?", interview in *Film Critic* (New York), November/December 1973; "Marcel Ophuls Tells Us We Cannot Afford to Forget", interview by Terry Fox in the *Village Voice* (New York), 11 October 1976; "A Decent Man, an Indecent Subject", interview by M. Wood in *The New York Times*, 17 October 1976; interview by Timothy Crouse in *Rolling Stone* (New York), 13 January 1977; "Memory of Justice", interview by P. Lehman and others in *Wide Angle* (Athens, Ohio), v.2, no.2, 1978; "A War Over Justice", interview by F. Manchel in *Literature/Film Quarterly* (Salisbury, Maryland), winter 1978; "La Zivilcourage et les dîners en ville" in *Positif* (Paris), April 1980; article about Max Ophüls in *Positif* (Paris), July/August 1980; article on effect of Mitterand's election on French television in *American Film* (Washington, D.C.), November 1982.

On OPHULS:

Articles—"Jean-Pierre Melville Talks to Rui Nogueira About *Le Chagrin et la pitié*" in *Sight and Sound* (London), winter

1971/72; "La Chagrin et la pitié", special issue of *Avant-Scène du cinéma* (Paris), July/September 1972; "Marcel Ophuls and *The Sorrow and the Pity*" by Frederick Busi in *Massachusetts Review* (Amherst), winter 1973.

OPHÜLS, MAX. French. Born Max Oppenheimer in Saarbrucken, Germany, 6 May 1902; became citizen of of France in 1938. Married actress Hilde Wall in 1926; child: Marcel. Career: 1919—makes acting debut, changes name to Ophüls because of family objections to stage career; 1924—begins stage directing career, directs almost 200 plays by 1930; 1926—begins work at Burgtheater, Vienna; 1929—enters films at UFA as dialogue director to Anatole Litvak; 1930—directing debut; 1932—with family leaves Germany; 1933-40—directs in France, Italy and Holland; 1934—invited to Soviet Union, offered 2-year contract, declines after visiting country; 1940—goes to Switzerland after fall of France, directs at Zurich Schauspielhaus, works on film of Molière's *Ecole des femmes* (unrealized); 1941—moves to Hollywood; 1944—"rediscovered" by Preston Sturges, resumes directing (surname billed as "Opuls"); 1949—returns to France; mid-1950s—directs for German radio; 1957—stages Beaumarchais's *Mariage de Figaro* in Hamburg. Died in Hamburg, 26 March 1957; buried at in Père Lachaise cemetery, Paris.

Films (as director): 1930—*Dann schon lieber Lebertran* (+co-adaptation); 1932—*Die verliebte Firma*; *Die verkaufte Braut (The Bartered Bride)*; 1933—*Die lachende Erben* (produced 1931); *Liebelei*; *Une Histoire d'amour* (French version of *Liebelei*); 1934—*On a volé un homme*; *La Signora di tutti* (+co-sc); 1935—*Divine* (+co-sc); 1936—*Komedie om Geld* (+co-sc); *Ave Maria* (short); *La Valse brillante* (short); *La Tendre Ennemie (The Tender Enemy)* (+co-sc); 1937—*Yoshiwara* (+co-sc); 1938—*Werther (Le Roman de Werther)* (+co-adaptation); 1940—*Sans lendemain*; *De Mayerling à Sarajevo (Mayerling to Sarajevo)*; *L'Ecole des femmes* (unfinished); 1946—*Vendetta* (co-d, uncredited); 1947—*The Exile*; 1948—*Letter from an Unknown Woman*; 1949—*Caught*; *The Reckless Moment*; 1950—*La Ronde* (+co-sc); 1952—*Le Plaisir (House of Pleasure)* (+co-sc); 1953—*Madame de... (The Earrings of Madame De)* (+co-sc); 1955—*Lola Montès (Lola Montez, The Sins of Lola Montes)* (+co-sc).

Publications:

By OPHÜLS:

Books—*Novelle* by Goethe, radio adaptation, Frankfurt am Main 1956; *Max Ophüls par Max Ophüls*, Paris 1963; articles—"Hollywood, petite île..." in *Cahiers du cinéma* (Paris), December 1955; "Le Dernier Jour de tournage" in *Cahiers du cinéma* (Paris), May 1956; "Entretien avec Max Ophuls" by Jacques Rivette and François Truffaut in *Cahiers du cinéma* (Paris), June 1957; "*Lola Montès: séquence inédite*", with Jacques Natanson, edited by Claude Beylie, in *Education et cinéma* (Paris), no.14, 1958; "Mon experience" and "Les Infortunes d'un scenario" in *Cahiers du cinéma* (Paris), March 1958; "*La Ronde*: Scenario et adaptation", with Jacques Natanson, in *Avant-Scène du cinéma* (Paris), April 1963; "Memory and Max Ophüls" in *Interviews with Film Directors* edited by Andrew Sarris, New York 1967; "*Lola Montès*: Scenario et adaptation", with Jacques Natanson, in *Avant-Scène du cinéma* (Paris), January 1969; interview by Robert Aldrich in *The Celluloid Muse* edited by Charles Higham and Joel Greenberg, Chicago 1971; "Interview with Ophüls (1950)" by Francis Koval in *Masterworks of the French Cinema* edited by John Weightman, New York 1974.

On OPHÜLS:

Books—*Max Ophuls: An Index* by Richard Roud, London 1958; *Max Ophuls* by Georges Annenkov, Paris 1962; *Max Ophuls* by Claude Beylie, Paris 1963; *Ophuls* edited by Paul Willemen, London 1978; *Max Ophuls and the Cinema of Desire* by Alan Williams, New York 1980; articles—obituary in *The New York Times*, 12 November 1948; "Kosmopolit der Leinwand" by Ben Eichsfelder in *Filmforum* (Emsdetten, Germany), December 1953; "Une Certaine Tendence du cinéma français" by François Truffaut in *Cahiers du cinéma* (Paris), January 1954; "Max Ophüls" by Henri Agel in *Antares* (Baden-Baden), May 1955; "Ophuls and the Romantic Tradition" by Eugene Archer in *Yale French Studies* (New Haven), no.17, 1956; tributes to Ophuls in *Sight and Sound* (London), summer 1957; "Esquisse d'une théatrographie de Max Ophuls" by Claude Beylie in *Cahiers du cinéma* (Paris), March 1958; "Retrospective Ophuls" by Charles Bitsche and Jacques Rivette on *Cahiers du cinéma* (Paris), March 1958; Ophuls issue of *Cahiers du cinéma* (Paris), March 1958; "Max Ophüls" by Claude Beylie in *Anthologie du cinéma* (Paris), June 1965; "Max Ophüls" in *Retrospektive* [1] edited by Peter Schumann, Berlin 1966; "Alles bewegt sich..." by Elke Kummer in *Film* (Velber bei Hannover, Germany), January 1967; "Emigration in Babylon...Warum ging Max Ophüls nach Hollywood?" by Hans Blumenberg in *Film* (Velber bei Hannover), July 1969; "The Mastery of Movement" by Forrest Williams in *Film Comment* (New York), winter 1969; "Script to Screen with Max Ophuls" by Howard Koch in *Film Comment* (New York), winter 1970/71; special Ophuls issue of *Film Comment* (New York), summer 1971; "Max Ophuls" by Andrew Sarris in *Film Comment* (New York), summer 1971; "The Long Take" by Brian Henderson in *Film Comment* (New York), summer 1971; "Buried Directors" by W.D. Route in *Focus* (Chicago), spring 1972; "Distance and Style: The Visual Rhetoric of Max Ophüls" by Fred Camper in *Monogram* (London), no.5, 1974; "On Carl Dreyer" by Robin Wood in *Film Comment* (New York), March/April 1974; 2 issues devoted to Ophuls of *Filmkritik* (Munich), November and December 1977; special section by L. Audibert and others of *Cinématographe* (Paris), December 1977; "Theatre et cinéma: Schnitzler, Ophuls et Ronconi" by S. Tolnay in *Cinématographe* (Paris), February 1979; "Max Ophuls", special section of *Positif* (Paris), July/August 1980; "The Visual Rhetoric of Max Ophuls" by Fred Camper in *Monogram* (London), no.5, n.d.; television—"Der große Verzauberer", documentary by Ulrich Lauterbach, Baden-Baden: Südwestfunk, September 1977.

*   *   *

Ophüls's work falls neatly into three periods, marked by geographical locations and diverse production conditions, yet linked by common thematic concerns and stylistic/formal procedures: the pre-Second World War European period (during which he made films in four countries and four languages); the four Hollywood films of the late forties (to which one might add the remarkable Howard Hughes-produced *Vendetta*, on which he worked extensively in its early pre-production phases and which bears many identifiable Ophülsian traces, both thematic and stylistic); the four films made in France in the fifties, on which Ophüls's current reputation chiefly rests, and in which certain stylistic traits (notably the long take with elaborately mobile camera) are carried to their logical culmination.

Critical estimation of Ophüls has soared during the past 20 years; prior to that, the prevailing attitude was disparaging (or at best condescending), and the reasons for this now seem highly significant, reflecting far more on the limitations of the critics than of the films. The general consensus was that Ophüls's work had distinctive qualities (indeed, this would be difficult to deny), but was overly preoccupied with "style" regarded as a kind of spurious, slightly decadent ornamentation) and given over to trivial or frivolous subjects quite alien to the "social" concerns considered to characterize "serious" cinema. In those days, the oppression of women within the patriarchal order was not identified as a "social concern"—especially within the overwhelmingly male-dominated field of film criticism. Two developments have contributed to the revaluation of Ophüls: the growth of *auteur* criticism in the sixties and of feminist awareness, and I shall consider his work in relation to these phenomena.

1. *Ophüls and auteurism.* One of the first aims of auteur criticism was to dethrone the "subject" as the prime guarantee of a film's quality, in favor of style, mise-en-scène, the discernible presence of a defined directorial "voice": in Andrew Sarris's terms, the "how" was given supremacy over the "what." "Subject," in fact, was effectively redefined as what the auteur's mise-en-scène created. Ophüls was a perfect rallying-point for such a reformulation of critical theory. For a start, he offered one of the most highly developed and unmistakable styles in world cinema, consistent through all changes of time and place (though inevitably modified in the last two Hollywood melodramas, *Caught* and *The Reckless Moment*): elaborate tracking-and-craning camera movements, ornate décor, the glitter of glass and mirrors, objects intervening in the foreground of the image between characters and camera: a style that can be read as in itself implying a meaning, a metaphysic of entrapment in movement, time and destiny. Further, this style could be seen as developing, steadily gaining in assurance and definition, through the various changes in cultural background and circumstances of production—from, say, *Liebelei* through *Letter from an Unknown Woman* to *Madame de....* Ophüls could be claimed (with partial justice) as a major creative artist whose personal vision transcended the most extreme changes of time and place.

The stylistic consistency was underlined by an equally striking thematic consistency. For example, the same three films mentioned above, though adapted from works by fairly reputable literary figures (respectively, Arthur Schnitzler, Stefan Zweig, Louise de Vilmorin), all reveal strong affinities in narrative/thematic structure: all are centered on romantic love, which at once celebrated and regarded with a certain irony; all move towards a climactic duel in which the male lover is destroyed by an avenging patriarch, an offended husband; in all three, patriarchal authority is embodied in military figures. Finally, style and theme were perceived as bound together by a complicated set of visual motifs recurring from period to period. The eponymous protagonist of Ophüls's last film, *Lola Montès*, declares "For me, life is movement"; throughout his work, key scenes take place in vehicles of travel, places of transition: carriages, trains, staircases, and railway staions figure prominently in many of the films. Even a superficially atypical work like *The Reckless Moment* (set in modern California rather than the preferred "Vienna, 1900" or its equivalent) contains crucial scenes on the staircase, in moving cars, on a ferry, at a bus station. Above all, the dance was recognized as a central Ophülsian motif, acquiring complex significance from film to film: the romantic/ironic waltz scene of *Letter from an Unknown*

Woman, the fluid yet circumscribed dances of *Madame de...*, the hectic and claustrophobic *palais de danse* of *Le Plaisir*, the constricted modern dance floor of *Caught*, the moment in *De Mayerling à Sarajevo* where the lovers are *prevented* from attending the ball: reminders that "life is movement" is not the simple proposition it may at first appear.

There is no doubt that the development of auteur theory enormously encouraged and extended the appreciation of Ophüls's work. In its pure form (the celebration of the individual artist), however, auteurism tends towards a dangerous imbalance in the evaluation of specific films: a tendency, for example, to prefer the "typical" but slight *La Ronde* (perhaps the film that most nearly corresponds to the "primitive" account of Ophüls) to a masterpiece like *The Reckless Moment*, in which Ophüls's engagement with the structural and thematic marterials of the Hollywood melodrama results in an amazingly rich and radical investigation of ideological assumptions.

2.   *Ophüls and feminism.* Nearly all of Ophüls's films are centered on a female consciousness. Before the 1960s this tended merely to confirm the diagnosis of them as decorative, sentimental, and essentially frivolous: the social concerns with which "serious" cinema should be engaged were those which could be resolved within the patriarchal order, and more fundamental social concerns that threatened to undermine the order itself simply could not be recognized. The films belong, of course, to a period long before the eruption of what we now know as radical feminism; they do not (and could not be expected to) explicity engage with feminist politics, and they are certainly not free of a tendency to mythologize women. In retrospect, however, from the standpoint of the feminist theory and consciousness that evolved in the seventies, they assume a quite extraordinary significance: an incomparably comprehensive, sensitive and perspective analysis of the position of women (subject to oppression) within patriarchal society. The films repeatedly present and examine the options traditionally available to women within our culture—marriage, prostitution (in both the literal and the looser sense), romantic love—and the relationship between those options. *Letter from an Unknown Woman*, for example, dramatizes marriage (Lisa's to von Stauffer, her mother's to the "military tailor") and prostitution ("modelling") as opposite cultural poles, then goes on to show that they really amount to the same thing: in both cases, the women are selling themselves (this opposition/parallel is brilliantly developed through the three episodes of *Le Plaisir*). Essentially, *Letter from an Unknown Woman* is an enquiry into the validity of romanic love as the only possible means of transcending this illusory dichotomy. Clearly, Ophüls is emotionally committed to Lisa and her vision; the extraordinary complexity and intelligence of the film lies in its simultaneous acknowledgement that romantic love can only exist as narcissistic fantasy and is ultimately both destructive and self-destructive.

Far from being incompatible, the auteurist and feminist approaches to Ophüls demand to be synthesized. The identification with a female consciousness and the female predicament is the supreme characteristic of the Ophülsian thematic; at the same time, the Ophüls style—the commitment to grace, beauty, sensitivity—amounts to a celebration of what our culture defines as "femininity," combined with the force of authority, the drive, the organizational (directorial) abilities construed as masculine. In short, the supreme achievement of Ophüls's work is its concrete and convincing embodiment of the collapsibility of our culture's barriers of sexual difference.

—Robin Wood

OSHIMA, NAGISA. Japanese. Born in Kyoto, 31 March 1932. Educated in political history at Kyoto University, graduated 1954. Career: early 1950s—as student leader participates in left-wing activities; 1954—enters Shochiku Ofuna Studios as assistant director; 1956—begins writing film criticism; becomes editor-in-chief of film revue *Eiga hihyo*; 1959—promoted to director; 1961—leaves Shochiku after *Night and Fog in Japan* pulled from circulation; founds production company Sozosha (dissolved 1973); 1962—commercial failure of *The Rebel* leads to 3 years' work exclusively in TV; 1962-64—makes television documentaries in Korea and Vietnam; 1975—creates Oshima Productions; 1976—book of *Realm of the Senses* seized by police, Oshima and editor prosecuted for obscenity; acquitted on obscenity charge.

Films (as scriptwriter): 1956—*Shinkei gyogun* (unproduced but published); 1959—*Tsukimiso* (Iwaki); *Donto okoze* (Nomura) (co-sc); *Jusan nichi no kinyobi* (unproduced); (as director): 1959—*Ai to kibo no machi (A Town of Love and Hope)* (+sc); *Asu no taiyo* (short); 1960—*Seishun zankoku monogatari (Cruel Story of Youth, Naked Youth, a Story of Cruelty)* (+sc); *Taiyo no hakaba (The Sun's Burial)* (+co-sc); *Nihon no yoru to kiri (Night and Fog in Japan)* (+co-sc); 1961—*Shiiku (The Catch)*; 1962—*Amakusa shiro tokisada (Shiro Tokisada from Amakusa, The Rebel)* (+co-sc); 1964—*Chiisana boken ryoko (Small Adventure, A Child's First Adventure)* (+co-sc); *Watashi wa Bellet* (collective direction—advertising film); 1965—*Etsuraku (Pleasures of the Flesh)* (+sc); *Yunbogi no nikki (The Diary of Yunbogi)* (+pr, sc, ph—short); 1966—*Hakuchu no torima (Violence at Noon, Violence at High Noon)*; 1967—*Ninja bugeicho (Band of Ninja)* (+co-pr, co-sc); *Nihon shunka-ko (A Treatise on Japanese Bawdy Song, Sing a Song of Sex)* (+co-pr, co-sc); *Muri-shinju: Nihon no natsu (Japanese Summer: Double Suicide)* (+co-sc); 1968—*Koshikei (Death by Hanging)* (+co-pr, co-sc); *Kaettekita yopparai (3 Resurrected Drunkards, A Sinner in Paradise)* (+co-sc); 1969—*Shinjuku dorobo nikki (Diary of a Shinjuku Thief, Diary of a Shinjuku Burglar)* (+co-sc); *Shonen (Boy)*; *Yoiyami semareba* (Jissoji) (sc only); 1970—*Tokyo senso sengo hiwa (He Died After the War, The Man Who Left His Will on Film)* (+co-sc); 1971—*Gishiki (The Ceremony)* (+co-sc); 1972—*Natsu no imoto (Summer Sister, Dear Summer Sister)* (+co-sc); 1976—*Ai no corrida (In the Realm of the Senses, Empire of the Senses)* (+sc); 1978—*Ai no borei (Empire of Passion, The Phantom of Love)* (+co-pr, sc); 1983—*Merry Christmas Mr. Lawrence.*

Publications:

By OSHIMA:

Books—*Sengo eiga: Hakai to sozo* [Postwar Film: Destruction and Creation], Tokyo 1963; *Taikenteki sengo eizo ron* [A Theory of the Postwar Image Based on Personal Experience], Tokyo 1975; *Écrits (1956-1978): Dissolution et jaillissement*, translated by Jean-Paul Le Pape, Paris 1980; articles—"Conversazione con Oshima" (from 1960) by A. Gennari and others in *Filmcritica* (Rome), October 1972; interview by K. Nei on *Une Petite Soeur pour l'été* in *Positif* (Paris), October 1972; "Situation et sujet du cinéma japonais (1)" in *Positif* (Paris), October 1972; "Je suis constamment concerné par le temps où je vis...", interview by Noel Simsolo in *Cinéma* (Paris), November 1972; interview by Max Tessier in *Ecran* (Paris), July/August 1972; interview by R. McCormick in *Cineaste* (New York), v.6, no.2, 1974; "Une Petite Soeur pour l'été", interview by Max Tessier in *Ecran* (Paris), January 1974; interview by N.L. Bernheim in *Cinématographe* (Paris), June 1976; "Oshima Uncensored", interview by M. de la F. McKendry in *Interview* (New York), November 1976; "Oshima, Disappointed at the Barring of His Film, Says He Expected 'Some Reaction'", interview in *The New York Times*, 3 October 1976; interview by J.-C. Bonnet and others in *Cinématographe* (Paris), June 1978; interview by M. Henry in *Positif* (Paris), May 1978; "Ecrits" in *Positif* (Paris), May 1978; "L'Empire de la passion", interview by Max Tessier in *Ecran* (Paris), September 1978; "Currents in Japanese Cinema: Nagisa Oshima, Sachiko Hidari" by S. Hoass in *Cinema Papers* (Melbourne), September/October 1979; "Destruction et creation" and "Ecrits (II): la révolution" in *Positif* (Paris), November 1979; "Tokyo Stories: Oshima", interview by Tony Rayns in *Sight and Sound* (London), summer 1981.

On OSHIMA:

Books—*Oshima Nagisa no sekai* [The World of Nagisa Oshima] by Tadao Sato, Tokyo 1973; *Japanese Film Directors* by Audie Bock, New York 1978; articles—"Nagisa Oshima" by Ian Cameron in *Movie* (London), winter 1969/70; "Nagisa Oshima" by Ian Cameron in *Second Wave*, New York 1970; "Oshima" in *Film* (London), spring 1970; "Director of the Year" in *International Film Guide 1971*, London 1970; "Cinéma japonais d'après-guerre" by J. Delmas in *Jeune Cinéma* (Paris), November 1972; "La Cérémonie", special issue of *Avant-Scène du cinéma* (Paris), May 1973; "Ritual, the Family and the State: a Critique of Nagisa Oshima's The Ceremony" by R. McCormick in *Cineaste* (New York), v.6, no.2, 1974; "Nagisa Oshima: Forms and Feelings Under the Rising Sun" by J. Dawson in *Cinema Papers* (Melbourne), September/October 1976; "In the Realm if the Senses" by R. McCormick in *Cineaste* (New York), winter 1976/77; "Portrait de l'artiste en révolutionnaire: Nagisa Oshima" by M. Martin in *Ecran* (Paris), January 1977; "Oshima: A Vita Sexualis on Film" by P.B. High in *Wide Angle* (Athens, Ohio), v.2, no.4, 1978; "Oshima in Paris: Reaching for the Flame" by J. Hughes in *Take One* (Montreal), September 1978; "La Pendaison" dossier in *Image et son* (Paris), no.331bis, 1978; "Oshima: amour et fantôme" by Max Tessier in *Ecran* (Paris), February 1978; "Biofilmographie de Nagisa Oshima" by H. Niogret in *Positif* (Paris), November 1979; "Nagisa Oshima", special section by J.G. Requena and others in *Contracampo* (Madrid), July/August 1980; "Oshima documentariste" by A. Tournès in *Jeune Cinéma* (Paris), June 1981.

OSWALD, RICHARD. Austrian. Born in Vienna, 5 November 1880. Married Käte Waldeck about 1912. Career: 1900-13—actor on Austrian and German stages; 1910-12—acts at Düsseldorfer Schauspielhaus; 1911—acts in 1st film with other actors at Düsseldorf Theater; 1913—hired as dramaturge by Vitascope in Berlin; 1916—founds production organization "Richard-Oswald-Film", Berlin; 1919—Opens cinema "Richard Oswald Lichtspiele" with *Die sich verkaufen* under title "Prostitution Part 2"; 1934—leaves Germany for England, makes films in Austria and France through 1939; 1939—emigrates to U.S. Died in Düsseldorf, 11 September 1963.

Films (as scriptwriter): 1914—*Der Hund von Baskerville* Part 1 and 2; *Ein seltsamer Fall* [Dr. Jekyll and Mr. Hyde]; (as director and scriptwriter): 1914—*Iwan Koschula*; *Die Geschichte der stillen Mühle*; *Lache, Bajazzo* [Laugh, Bajazzo]; *Sie kann nicht Nein sagen* [You Can't Say No] (sc only); 1915—*Dämon und Mensch*; *Das eiserne Kreuz* [The Iron Cross]; *Und wandern sollst du ruhelos...(Die schöne Sünderin)* [And you will wander restless...(The Beautiful Sinner)]; *So rächt die Sonne* (sc only); *Schlemihl (Ein Lebensbild)* (co-sc); *Hampels Abenteuer* (co-sc); *Die verschleierte Dame*; *Das Laster*; *Der Fund im Neubau*; *Der Hund von Baskerville* Part 3; *Die Sage vom Hund von Baskerville*; *Die silberne Kugel* (d only); *Hoffmanns Erzählungen* (co-sc); (as producer, director and scriptwriter): 1916—*Das unheimliche Haus*; *Das unheimliche Haus* Part 2: "Freitag, der 13"; *Der chinesischen Götze (Das unheimliche Haus*, Part 3); *Seine letzte Maske*; *Zirkusblut*; 1917—*Das Bildnis des Dorian Gray*; *Der Schloßherr von Hohenstein*; *Die Rache der Toten*; *Die zweite Frau*; *Es werde Licht!* (co-sc); *Königliche Bettler* (d only); *Rennfieber*; *Schatten der Vergangenheit*; 1918—*Der Weg ins Freie*; *Es werde Licht!* Part 2 and 3; *Das Dreimäderlhaus*; *Das Tagebuch einer Verlorenen*; *Der lebende Leichnam*; *Die seltsame Geschichte des Barons Torelli*; *Henriette Jacoby*; *Jettchen Gebert*; *Peer Gynt* (co-d only); 1919—*Anders als die Andern* (co-sc); *Das Kainszeichen*; *Die Arche* (co-sc); *Die letzten Menschen (Die Arche* Part 2, co-sc); *Die Prostitution*; *Die Reise um die Erde in 80 Tagen (Die Reise um die Welt)*; *Die sich verkaufen* (co-sc); *Unheimliche Geschichten* (co-sc); 1920—*Das vierte Gebot*; *Der Reigen (Ein Werdegang)*; *Die Geheimnisse von London/Das siebente Gebot (Die Tragödie eines Kindes)*; *Kurfürstendamm (Ein Höllenspuk in 6 Akten)*; *Manolescus Memoiren/Fürst Lahory, der König der Diebe*; 1921—*Nachtgestalten (Eleagabl Kuperus)*; *Die Liebschaften des Hektor Dalmore*; *Lady Hamilton*; *Sündige Mütter*; *Das Haus in der Dragonergasse* (d only); 1922—*Lucrezia Borgia*; 1924—*Carlos und Elisabeth*; 1925—*Lumpen und Seide* (d only); *Die Frau von vierzig Jahren*; *Halbseide*; *Vorderhaus und Hinterhaus* (co-d, co-sc); 1926—*Als ich wiederkam* (d only); *Dürfen wir schweigen?*; *Im weißen Rössl* (d only); *Wir sind vom K. und K. Infanterie-Regiment*; (as producer and director): 1927—*Eine tolle Nacht* (+sc); *Dr. Bessels Verwandlung*; *Feme*; *Funkzauber*; *Gehetzte Frauen (Lebende Ware)*; *Lützows wilde werwegene Jagd*; 1928—*Die Rothausgasse*; *Villa Falconieri*; *Cagliostro*; 1929—*Ehe in Not (Ehen zu Dritt)*; *Frühlingserwachen*; *Die Herrin und ihr Knecht*; *Der Hund von Baskerville*; 1930—*Wien, du Stadt der Lieder*; *Die zärtlichen Verwandten*; *Alraune*; *Dreyfus*; 1931—*1914, die letzten Tage vor dem Weltbrand*; *Arm wie eine Kirchenmaus*; *Der Hauptmann von Köpenick*; 1932—*Unheimliche Geschichten*; *Gräfin Mariza*; 1933—*Ganovenehre*; *Die Blume von Hawaii*; *Ein Lied geht um die Welt*; 1935—*My Song Goes Round the World*; 1936—*Heute ist der schönste Tag in meinem Leben*; 1938—*Tempête sur l'Asie*; 1941—*The Captain of Koepenick (I Was a Criminal)*; 1942—*The Isle of Missing Men*; 1949—*The Lovable Cheat*.

Publications:

On OSWALD:

Book—*Richard Oswald* edited by Walter Kaul and Robert Scheuer, Berlin 1970; articles—"Richard Oswald" by Herbert Luft in *Films in Review* (New York), October 1958; letter from R. Tozzi in *Films in Review* (New York), June/July 1960; "Richard Oswald, een beroddelde Duitse filmpionier" by C. Boost in *Skoop* (Amsterdam), June/July 1980.

OZU, YASUJIRO. Japanese. Born in Tokyo, 12 December 1903. Educated at the Uji-Yamada (now Ise) Middle School, Matsuzaka, graduated 1921. Career: 1922-23—teacher in remote village; 1923—uncle introduces him to manager of Shochiku Motion Picture Co.; begins as assistant cameraman; 1924-25—called up for armed service, spends most of year feigning illness; 1926—asks to be assigned as assistant director; 1937-39—military service in China; 1943—sent to Singapore to make propaganda films; 1945—interned for 6 months as British POW. Died in Kamakura, 12 December 1963.

Films (as director): 1927—*Zange no yaiba* [The Sword of Penitence]; 1928—*Wakodo no yume* [The Dreams of Youth] (+sc); *Nyobo funshitsu* [Wife Lost]; *Kabocha* [Pumpkin]; *Hikkoshi fufu* [A Couple on the Move]; *Nikutai bi* [Body Beautiful] (+co-sc); 1929—*Takara no yama* [Treasure Mountain] (+story); *Wakaki hi* [Days of Youth] (+co-sc); *Wasei kenka tomodachi* [Fighting Friends, Japanese Style]; *Daigaku wa deta keredo* [I Graduated, But...]; *Kaisha-in seikatsu* [The Life of an Office Worker]; *Tokkan kozo* [A Straightforward Boy] (+co-story); 1930—*Kekkon-gaku nyumon* [An Introduction to Marriage]; *Hogaraka ni ayume* [Walk Cheerfully]; *Rakudai wa shita keredo* [I Flunked, But...] (+story); *Sono yo no tsuma* [That Night's Wife]; *Erogami no onryo* [The Revengeful Spirit of Eros]; *Ashi ni sawatta koun* [Lost Luck]; *Ojosan* [Young Miss]; 1931—*Shukujo to hige* [The Lady and the Beard]; *Bijin aishu* [Beauty's Sorrows]; *Tokyo no gassho* [Tokyo Chorus]; 1932—*Haru wa gofujin kara* [Spring Comes from the Ladies] (+story); *Umarete wa mita keredo* [I Was Born, But...] (+story); *Seishun no yume ima izuko* [Where Now Are the Dreams of Youth?]; *Mata au hi made* [Until the Day We Meet Again]; 1933—*Tokyo no onna* [A Tokyo Woman] (+story); *Hijosen no onna* [Dragnet Girl] (+story); *Dekigokoro* [Passing Fancy] (+story); 1934—*Haha o kowazu-ya* [A Mother Should Be Loved]; *Ukigusa monogatari* [A Story of Floating Weeds]; 1935—*Hakoiri musume* [An Innocent Maid]; *Tokyo no yado* [Tokyo Chorus]; 1936—*Daigaku yoi toko* [College Is a Nice Place] (+story); *Hitori musuko* [The Only Son] (+story); 1937—*Shukujo wa nani o wasuretaka* [What Did the Lady Forget?] (+co-story); 1941—*Toda-ke no kyodai* [The Brothers and Sisters of the Toda Family] (+co-sc); 1942—*Chichi ariki* [There Was a Father] (+co-sc); 1947—*Nagaya no shinshi roku* [The Record of a Tenement Gentleman] (+co-sc); 1948—*Kaze no naka no mendori* [A Hen in the Wind] (+co-sc); (as director and co-scriptwriter with Kogo Noda) 1949—*Banshun* [Late Spring]; 1950—*Munekata shimai* [The Munekata Sisters]; 1951—*Bakushu* [Early Summer]; 1952—*Ochazuke no aji* [The Flavor of Green Tea over Rice]; 1953—*Tokyo monogatari* [Tokyo Story]; 1956—*Soshun* [Early Spring]; 1957—*Tokyo boshoku* [Twilight in Tokyo]; 1958—*Higanbana* [Equinox Flower]; 1959—*Ohayo*; *Ukigusa* [Floating Weeds]; 1960—*Akibiyori* [Late Autumn]; 1961—*Kohayagawa-ke no aki* [The End of Summer]; 1962—*Samma no aji* [An Autumn Afternoon].

Publications:

On OZU:

Books—*The Japanese Film: Art and Industry* by Joseph Anderson and Donald Richie, New York 1960; *5 Pictures of Yasujiro Ozu* by Donald Richie, Tokyo 1962; *The Japanese Movie: An Illustrated History* by Donald Richie, Tokyo 1966; *Ozu Yasujiro no Geijutsu* [The Art of Yasujiro Ozu] by Tadao Sato, Tokyo 1971; *Japanese Cinema: Film Style & National Character* by Donald Richie, New York 1971; *Ozu Yasujiro—Hito to Shigoto*

[Yasujiro Ozu: The Man and His Work] edited by Jun Satomi and others, Tokyo 1972; *Transcendental Style in Film: Ozu, Bresson, Dreyer* by Paul Schrader, Berkeley, California 1972; *Theory of Film Practice* by Noël Burch, New York 1973; "Yasujiro Ozu" by Max Tessier in *Anthologie du cinéma* vol.7, Paris 1973; *Ozu* by Donald Richie, Berkeley, California 1974; *Masters of Japanese Film* edited by Leonard Schrader and Haruji Nakamura, Tokyo 1975; *Japanese Film Directors* by Audie Bock, New York 1978; *To the Distant Observer* by Noel Burch, Berkeley 1979; articles—"The Japanese Cinema" by Akira Iwasaki in *Film* (London), November/December 1956; special issue of *Kinema Jumpo* (Tokyo), June 1958; "Un trés grand réalisateur japonais est mort" by Georges Sadoul in *Les Lettres françaises* (Paris), 19 December 1963; "Yasujiro Ozu" by Chishu Ryu in *Sight and Sound* (London), spring 1964; special Ozu issue of *Kinema Jumpo* (Tokyo), February 1964; "Ozu" by Akira Iwasaki in *Film* (London), summer 1965; "Ozu Spectrum" in *Cinema* (Beverly Hills), summer 1970; "Ozu" by Manny Farber in *Art Forum* (New York), June 1970; "Yasujiro Ozu" by Jean-Claude Philippe in *Dossiers du cinéma: Cinéastes* no.1, Paris 1971; "Mizoguchi and Ozu—2 Masters from Japan" by Roger Greenspun in *The New York Times*, 9 July 1972; "Ozu" by Jonathan Rosenbaum in *Film Comment* (New York), summer 1972; "The Art of Ozu" by Jonathan Scott in *Rolling Stone* (New York), 13 April 1972; "The Zen Artistry of Yasujiro Ozu: The Serene Poet of Japanese Cinema" by Marvin Zeaman in *Film Journal* (New York), fall/winter 1972; "Space and Narrative in the Films of Ozu" by Kristin Thompson and David Bordwell in *Screen* (London), summer 1976; "The Space of *Equinox Flower*" by Edward Branigan in *Screen* (London), summer 1976; "Notes on the Spatial System of Ozu's Early Films" by Kristin Thompson in *Wide Angle* (Athens, Ohio), v.1, no.4, 1977; "L'Homme qui se lève" by Alain Bergala in *Cahiers du cinéma* (Paris), May 1980; "Le Cinéma toujours recommencé de Yasujiro Ozu", special section if *Cinéma* (Paris), January 1981; "La Netteté est l'ornement de la justesse" by A. Masson in *Positif* (Paris), February 1981; special Ozu section of *Cinéma* (Paris), February 1981; recordings—*Ozu Yasujiro no sekai* [The World of Yasujiro Ozu], Tokyo 1972; *Ozu Yasujiro meisaku eiga ongaku shu* [Yasujiro Ozu Memorial Album: Music from His Masterpieces], Tokyo 1972.

*   *   *

Throughout his career, Yasujiro Ozu worked in the mainstream film industry. Obedient to his role, loyal to his studio (the mighty Shochiku), he often compared himself to the tofu salesman, offering nourishing but supremely ordinary wares. For some critics, his greatness inheres in his resulting closeness to the everyday realities of Japanese life. Yet since his death another critical perspective has emerged. This modest conservative has come to be recognized as one of the most formally intriguing filmmakers in the world, extending the genre he worked within and developing a rich and unique cinematic style.

Ozu started his career within a well-established genre system, and he quickly proved himself versatile, handling college comedies, wistful tales of office workers, even gangster films. By 1936, however, he had started to specialize. The "home drama," a Shochiku speciality, focused on the trials and joys of middle-class or working-class life—raising children, finding a job, marrying off sons and daughters, settling marital disputes, making grandparents comfortable. It was this genre in which Ozu created his most famous films and to which he is said to have paid tribute on his deathbed: "After all, Mr. President, the home drama."

Ozu enriched this genre in several ways. He strengthened the pathos of family crisis by suggesting that many of them arose from causes beyond the control of the individual. In the 1930s works, this often leads to strong criticism of social forces like industrialization, bureaucratization, and Japanese "paternalistic" capitalism. In later films, causes of domestic strife tend to be assigned to a mystical super-nature. This "metaphysical" slant ennobles the characters' tribulations by placing even the most trivial action in a grand scheme. The melancholy resignation that is so pronounced in *Tokyo Story* and *An Autumn Afternoon* constitutes a recognition of a cycle of nature that society can never control.

To some extent, the grandiose implications of this process are qualified by a homely virtue: comedy. Few Ozu films wholly lack humor, and many involve outrageous sight gags. As a genre, the home drama invited a light touch, but Ozu proved able to extend it into fresh regions. There is often an unabashed vulgarity, running to joke about eating, bodily functions, and sex. Even the genrally sombre *Autumn Afternoon* can spare time for a gag about an elderly man run ragged by the sexual demands of a young wife. *Ohayu* is based upon equating talk, especilly polite vacuities, with farting. Ozu risks breathtaking shifts in tone: in *Passing Fancy*, after a tearful scene at a boy's sickbed, the father pettishly says that he wishes his son had died. The boy responds that the father was singly looking foward to a good meal at the funeral.

Ozu also developed many narrative tendencies of the home drama. He exploited the family-plus-friends-and-neighbors cast by creating strict parallels among characters. If family A has a son of a certain type, family B will have a daughter of that type, or a son of a different sort. The father may encounter a younger or older man, whom he sees as representing himself at another point in his life. The extended-family format allows Ozu to create dizzying permutations of comparisons. The sense is again of a vast cycle of life in which an individual occupies many positions at different times.

Ozu has one of the most distinctive visual styles in the cinema. Although critics have commonly attributed this to the influence of other directors or to traditions of Japanese art, these are insufficient to account for the rigor and precision of Ozu's technique. No other Japanese director exhibits Ozu's particular style, and the connections to Japanese aesthetics are general and often tenuous. (Ozu once remarked: "Whenever Westerners don't understand something, they simply think it's Zen.") There is, however, substantial evidence that Ozu built his unique style out of deliberate imitation of and action against Western cinema (especially the work of Chaplin and Lubitsch).

Ozu limited his use of certain technical variables, such as camera movement and variety of camera position. This can seem a wilful asceticism, but it is perhaps best considered a ground-clearing that let him concentrate on exploring minute stylistic possibilities. For instance, it is commonly claimed that every Ozu shot places the camera about three feet off the ground, but this is false. What Ozu keeps constant is the perceived *ratio* of camera height to the subject. This permits a narrow but nuanced range of camera positions, making every subject occupy the same sector of each shot. Similarly, most of Ozu films employ camera movements, but these are also systematized to a rare degree. Far from being an ascetic director, Ozu is quite virtuosic, but within self-imposed limits. His style reveals vast possibilities within a narrow compass.

Ozu's compositions rely on the fixed camera-subject relation, adopting angles that stand at multiples of 45 degrees. He employs sharp perspectival depth; the view down a corridor or street is common. Ozu enjoyed playing with the positions of objects within the frame, often rearranging props from shot to shot for the sake of minute shifts. In the color films, a shot will be enhanced by a fleck of bright and deep color, often red; this accent will migrate around the film, returning as an abstract motif in scene after scene.

Ozu's use of editing is no less idiosyncratic. In opposition to the 180-degree space of Hollywood cinema, Ozu employed a 360-degree approach to filming a scene. This "circular" shooting space yields a series of what Western cinema would consider incorrect matches of action and eyelines. While such devices crop up in the work of other Japanese filmmakers, only Ozu used them so rigorously—to undermine our understanding of the total space, to liken characters, and to create abstract graphic pattrns. Ozu's shots of objects or empty locales extend the concept of the Western "cutaway": he will use them not for narrative information but for symbolic purposes or for temporal prolongation. Since Ozu early abjured the use of fades and dissolves, cutaways often stand in for such punctuations. And because of the unusually precise compositions and cutting, Ozu is able to create a sheerly graphic play with the screen surface, "matching" contours and regions of one shot with those of the next.

Ozu's work remains significant not only for its extraordinary richness and emotional power but also because it suggests the extent to which a filmmaker working in popular mass-production filmmaking can cultivate a highly individual approach to film form and style.

—David Bordwell

PABST, G.W. Austrian. Born Georg Wilhelm Pabst in Raudnitz, Bohemia, 27 August 1885. Educated in engineering at technical school, Vienna; at Academy of Decorative Arts, Vienna, 1904-06. Married Gertrude (Pabst); child: Peter. Career: 1906—begins acting career, appears in Switzerland, Austria and Bohemia; 1910—travels to U.S. with German language troupe; 1914—returns to Europe to recruit new actors, interned in France as enemy alien; 1914-18—as prisoner-of-war in camp near Brest, organizes theater group; 1918-19—plays season in Prague; 1919—returns to Vienna; directs season of Expressionist theater in Prague; 1920—appointed artistic director, Neuen Wiener Bühne; joins Carl Froelich's film production company; 1922—scenarist and assistant on *Luise Millerin*; 1928—with Heinrich Mann, Erwin Piscator and Karl Freund forms leftist Volksverband für Filmkunst (Popular Association for Film Art); sees Louise Brooks in *A Girl in Every Port* and *Beggars of Life*, invites her to Berlin to make *Pandora's Box*; 1929—studies sound film techniques in London; 1933—decides to remain in France after Hitler becomes Chancellor; invited to Hollywood by Warners; 1935—returns to France; 1939—offered French citizenship, refuses, afraid son will be drafted into French army; decides to emigrate to U.S., returns to Austria to gather belongings, falls ill and remains in Austria after outbreak of war; 1941-44—makes historical films under Nazi aegis; 1949—forms Pabst-Kiba Filmproduktion in Vienna; 1950-53—works in Italy; Died in Vienna, 29 May 1967. Recipient: Légion d'honneur, 1931; Best Director, Venice Festival, for *Der Prozess*, 1948.

Films (as director): 1923—*Der Schatz (The Treasure)* (+co-sc); 1924—*Gräfin Donelli (Countess Donelli)*; 1925—*Die freudlose Gasse (The Joyless Street)*; *Geheimnesse einer Seele (Secrets of a Soul)*; 1926—*Man spielt nicht mit der Liebe (One Does Not Play with Love)*; 1927—*Die Liebe der Jeanne Ney (The Love of*

Jeanne Ney); 1928—*Abwege (Begierde)* [Crisis (Desire)]; *Die Büchse der Pandora (Pandora's Box)*; 1929—*Die weisse Hölle vom Pitz-Palu (The White Hell of Pitz-Palu)* (co-d); *Das Tagebuch einer Verlorenen (Diary of a Lost Girl)* (+pr); 1930—*Westfront 1918*; *Skandal um Eva (Scandalous Eva)*; 1931—*Die Dreigroschenoper (The Threepenny Opera)*; *Kameradschaft (Comradeship)*; 1932—*L'Atlantide (Die Herrin von Atlantis)*; 1933—*Don Quichotte*; *Du haut en bas (High and Low)*; 1934—*A Modern Hero*; 1936—*Mademoiselle Docteur (Salonique, nid d'espions)*; 1938—*Le Drame de Shanghai*; 1939—*Jeunes Filles en detress*; 1941—*Komödianten* (+co-sc); 1943—*Paracelsus* (+co-sc); 1944—*Der Fall Molander* (unfinished and believed destroyed); 1947—*Der Prozess (The Trial)*; 1949—*Geheimnisvolle Tiefen* (+pr); 1952—*La Voce del silenzio*; 1953—*Cose da pazzi*; 1954—*Das Bekenntnis der Ina Kahr*; 1955—*Der letzte Akt (The Last 10 Days, 10 Days to Die)*; *Es geschah am 20 Juli (Jackboot Mutiny)*; 1956—*Rosen für Bettina*; *Durch die Walder, durch die Auen*.

Role: 1921—*Im Banne der Kralle* (Fröhlich).

Publications:

By PABST:

Book—*Classic Film Scripts: Pandora's Box (Lulu)* translated by Christopher Holme, New York 1971; articles—"Un Déjeuner avec Pabst", interview by Alexandre Arnoux in *Pour vous* (Paris), 29 January 1931; "Servitude et grandeur de Hollywood" in *Le Rôle intellectuel du cinéma* Cahier 3, Paris 1937; "Censor the Censor!", interview by Beatrix Moore in *Sight and Sound* (London), winter 1938/39; "Le Réalisme est un passage" in *Revue du cinéma* (Paris), October 1948; "Il cinema domani" in *Cinema* (Rome), no.28, 1949; "Über zwei meiner Filme" in *Filmkunst* (Vienna), 1960; "The Threepenny Opera" edited by Roger Manvell in *Masterpieces of the German Cinema*, New York 1973.

On PABST:

Books—*From Caligari to Hitler* by Siegfried Kracauer, Princeton, New Jersey 1947; *Der Regisseur: G.W. Pabst* edited by Rudolph Joseph, Munich 1963; *Le Cinéma réaliste allemande* by Raymond Borde and others, Lyons 1965; *G.W. Pabst*, Premier Plan No.39, by Freddy Buache, Lyons 1965; *Georg Wilhelm Pabst* by Barthelemy Amengual, Paris 1966; "G.W. Pabst" by Yves Aubry and Jacques Pétat in *Anthologie du cinéma* vol.4, Paris 1968; *The Haunted Screen* by Lotte Eisner, Berkeley 1969; *Film in the Third Reich* by David Hull, Berkeley 1969; *G.W. Pabst* by Lee Atwell, Boston 1977; *Lulu in Hollywood* by Louise Brooks, New York 1981; articles—"G.W. Pabst: A Survey by Bryher in *Close Up* (London), December 1927; "Pabst, Dovjenko: A Comparison" by John Moore in *Close Up* (London), September 1932; "Pabst and the Social Film" by Harry Potamkin in *Hound & Horn* (New York), January-March 1933; "Pabst, Pudovkin and the Producers" by Paul Rotha in *Sight and Sound* (London), summer 1933; "6 Talks on G.W. Pabst" edited by Gideon Bachmann in *Cinemages* (New York), no.3, 1955; special issue of *Filmkunst* (Vienna), no.18, 1955; "Index to the Creative Work of Pabst" by H. Weinberg and L. Boehm in *Cinemages* (New York), no.3, 1955; "Mr. Pabst" by Louise Brooks in *Image* (Rochester, New York), September 1956; "Out of Pandora's Box" by James Card in *Image* (Rochester, New York), September 1956; "The Intense Isolation of Louise Brooks" by James Card in *Sight and Sound* (London), summer 1958; "Brecht et le cinéma" by Alan Stanbrook in *Cahiers du cinéma* (Paris), December 1960; "Die Dreigroschenoper" by Alan Stanbrook in *Films and Filming* (London), April 1961; essays on *Don Quichotte* and *The Threepenny Opera* in *Classics of the Foreign Film* by Parker Tyler, New York 1962; "Il Cinema tedesco e il passato nazista" by Aristarco Guido in *Cinestudio*, March 1963; "G.W. Pabst" by Herbert Luft in *Films in Review* (New York), February 1964; "Pabst and Lulu" by Louise Brooks in *Sight and Sound* (London), summer 1965; "G.W. Pabst" by Herbert Luft in *Films and Filming* (London), April 1967; "Meeting with Pabst" by Lotte Eisner in *Sight and Sound* (London), Autumn 1967; "Thoughts on Pabst" by Paul Rotha in *Films and Filming* (London), February 1967; "Working with Pabst" by John Stuart in *Silent Picture* (London), autumn 1970; "G.W. Pabst—Mensch seiner Zeit" by C. Broda in *Filmkunst* (Vienna), no.74, 1976; "Le Réalisme libertaire de G.W. Pabst" by R. Borde in *Avant-Scène du cinéma* (Paris), 1 December 1980; "Sur 4 films de Pabst" by Bernard Amengual in *Jeune Cinéma* (Paris), June 1981; "Les Perdants de l'histoire" by R. Bezombes in *Cinématographe* (Paris), February 1981; "Pabst, aujourd'hui?—une réévaluation nécessaire" by J. Petat in *Cinéma* (Paris), April 1981; "4 films de G.W. Pabst" by D. Sauvaget in *Image et son* (Paris), March 1981; "Actors and the Pabst Spirit" by Louise Brooks in *Focus on Film* (London), vol.8, n.d.

*　　*　　*

Bryher, writing in *Close Up* in 1927, noted that "it is the thought and feeling that line gesture that interest Mr. Pabst. And he has what few have, a consciousness of Europe. He sees psychologically and because of this, because in a flash he knows the sub-conscious impulse or hunger that prompted an apparently trivial action, his intense realism becomes, through its truth, poetry."

Pabst was enmeshed in the happenings of his time, which ultimately engulfed him. He is the chronicler of the churning maelstrom of social dreams and living neuroses, and it is this perception of his time which raises him above many of his contemporary filmmakers.

Like other German directors, he drifted to the cinema through acting and scripting. His first film, *Der Schatz*, dealt with a search for hidden treasure and the passions it aroused. Expressionist in feeling and design, it echoed the current trend in German films, but in *Die freudlose Gasse* he brought clinical observation to the tragedy of his hungry postwar Europe. For Pabst the cinema and life grew closer together. In directing the young Greta Garbo and the more experienced Asta Nielsen, Pabst was beginning his gallery of portraits of women to whom he would add Brigitte Helm, Louise Brooks and Henny Porten.

Geheimnisse einer Seele carried Pabst's interest in the subconscious further, dealing with a Freudian subject of the dream and using all the potential virtues of the camera to illuminate the problems of his central character, played by Werner Krauss. *Die Liebe der Jeanne Ney*, based on a melodramatic story by Ilya Ehrenburg, reflected the upheavals and revolutionary ideas of the day. It also incorporated a love story that ranged from the Crimea to Paris. Through his sensitive awareness of character and environment Pabst raised the film to great heights of cinema. His individual style of linking image to create a smoothly flowing pattern induced a rhythm which carried the spectator into the very heart of the matter.

Two films have a special significance. *Die Büchse der Pandora* and *Das Tagebuch einer Verlorenen* featured the American actress Louise Brooks, in whom Pabst found an ideal interpreter for his analysis of feminine sensuality.

Between the high spots of his career there were such films as *Grafin Donelli* which brought more credit to its star, Henny Porten, then to Pabst. *Man spielt nicht mit der Liebe* featured Krauss and Lily Damita in a youth and age romance. *Abwege*, a more congenial subject of a sexually frustrated woman, gave Pabst the opportunity to direct the beautiful and intelligent Brigitte Helm. His collaboration with Dr. Arnold Fanck on *Die weisse Hölle vom Pitz-Palu* resulted in the best of the mountain films, aided by the talented Leni Rienfenstahl and a team of virtuoso camaramen, Angst, Schneeberger and Allgeier.

The coming of sound was a challenge met by Pabst. Not only did he enlarge the scope of filmmaking techniques, but he extended the range of social committments in his choice of subject matter. Hans Casparius, his distinguished still cameraman and friend, has stressed the wonderful teamwork involved in a Pabst film. There were no divisions of labor all were totally involved. *Westfront 1918*, *Die Dreigroschenoper* and *Kameradschaft* were made in this manner when Pabst began to make sound films. Vajda the writer, Fritz Arno Wagner the cameraman (who had filmed *Jeanne Ney*) and Ernö Metzner, another old colleague, worked out the mise-en-scène with Pabst, assuring the smooth fluid process of cinema. With Pabst the cinema was still a wonder of movement and penetrating observation. The technical devices used to ensure this have been described by the designer Metzner.

Westfront 1918 was an uncompromising anti-war film which made *All Quiet on the Western Front* look contrived and artificial. Brecht's *Die Dreigroschenoper*, modified by Pabst, is still a stinging satire on the pretensions of capitalist society. *Kameradschaft*, a moving plea for international cooperation, shatters the boundries that tend to isolate people. All these films were studio-made and technically stupendous, but the heart and human warmth were given to them by G.W. Pabst.

Germany was now in the grip of growing Nazi domination. Pabst looked elsewhere to escape from that Germany which he had once been so much a part. *L'Atlantide* was based on the Pierre Benoit novel of adventure in the Sahara, the former success of Jacques Feyder and now featuring Brigitte Helm as the mysterious Antinea. *Don Quixote* with Chaliapin did not fulfil its promise. *A Modern Hero* made in Hollywood for Warner Brothers had little of Pabst in it. On his return to France he handled with some competence *Mademoiselle Docteur*, *Le Drame de Shanghai*, and *Jeunes Filles en aetresse*.

In 1941 circumstances compelled him to return to his estate in Austria. He was trapped, and if he was to make films, it had to be for the Nazi regime. *Komödianten* was a story of a troupe of players who succeed in establishing the first National Theatre at Weimar. Its leading player was Pabst's old friend Henny Porten, who gave an excellent performance. The film won an award at the then Fascist-controlled Venice Biennale. *Paracelsus*, again an historical film, showed Pabst had lost none of his power. For his somewhat reluctant collaboration with the Nazis, Pabst has been savagely attacked, but it is hard to believe that any sympathy could have ever existed from the man who made *Kameradschaft* for the narrow chauvinists who ruled his country.

After the war Pabst made *Der Prozess*, dealing with Jewish pogroms in 19th-century Hungary. It was a fine film. After some work in Italy he made *Der letze Akt* dealing with the last days of Hitler, and *Es geschah am 20 Juli* about the generals' plot against Hitler. Both were films of distinction.

Pabst died in Vienna in 1967, having been a chronic invalid for the last ten years of his life. Jean Renoir said of him in 1963: "He knows how to create a strange world, whose elements are borrowed from daily life. Beyond this precious gift, he knows how,

better than anyone else, how to direct actors. His characters emerge like his own children, created from fragments of his own heart and mind." A judgement that may be allowed to stand.

—Liam O'Leary

PAGNOL, MARCEL. French. Born in Aubagne, near Marseilles, 25 (or 28) February 1895. Educated at lycée Thiers, Marseilles; University of Montpellier, degree in letters. Married Jacqueline Bouvier, 1945; 2 sons. Career: 1911—with friends founds literary magazine *Fortunio*; 1912—begins teaching English at Tarascon (also taught at Pamiers sur Ariège and at lycée Saint-Charles, Marseilles); 1914-17—service with French infantry; 1922—appointed professor at lycée Condorcet, Paris; 1925—play *Les Marchands de Gloire* critical success; 1928—production of play *Topaze* establishes reputation as playwright; 1929—resigns teaching position after success of *Marius*, first play in "Marseilles trilogy" (*Marius*, *Fanny*, and *Cesar*); 1930—impressed with potential of talking pictures after seeing *Broadway Melody*; 1931—creates film company and founds magazine *Les Cahiers du film*; 1933—opens studio at Marseilles; 1940—military service; 1941—filming of *La Priere aux etoiles* begun in "free zone," interrupted in June 1942, film not completed; 1944-46—president of Society of French Dramatic Authors and Composers. Died 18 April 1974. Recipient: member, Academie française, 1947; Officer of the Légion d'honneur.

Films (as scriptwriter): 1931—*Marius* (Korda); 1932—*Fanny* (Allégret) (+co-pr); 1933—*Topaze* (Gasnier) (original play); *Un Direct au coeur* (Lion) (co-author of original play); *L'Agonie des aigles* (Richebé) (+co-pr); (as producer, director and scriptwriter): 1934—*Le Gendre de Monsieur Poirier*; *Jofroi*; *L'Article 330*; *Angele*; *Tartarin de Tarascon* (Bernand) (sc only); 1935—*Merlusse*; *Cigalon*; 1936—*Topaze* (2nd version); *Cesar*; 1937—*Regain*; 1938—*Le Schpountz*; *La Femme du boulanger*; 1939—*Monsieur Brotonneau* (Esway) (pr and sc only); 1940—*La Fille du puisatier*; 1945—*Naïs*; 1948—*La Belle Meunière*; 1950—*Le Rosier de Madame Husson* (Boyer) (sc only); 1951—*Topaze* (3rd version); 1952—*Manon des sources*; 1953—*Carnaval* (Vernauil) (pr and sc only); 1954—*Les Lettres de mon moulin*; 1962—*La Dame aux camélias* (Gir) (sc only); 1967—*Le Curé de Cucugnan* (for TV).

Publications related to cinema:

By PAGNOL:

Book—*Les Sermons de Pagnol* edited by Robert Morel, Paris 1968; articles—"Un Trésor qu'on gaspille", interview by Suzanne Chantal in *Cinémonde* (Paris), 4 December 1930; "Cinématurgie de Paris" in *Les Cahiers du film* (Paris), 16 December 1933, 15 January 1934, and 1 March 1934; collected in *Cahiers du cinéma* (Paris), no.173; "Je n'ai pas changé de métier", interview by Michel Gorel in *Cinémonde* (Paris), 17 August 1933; "Il n'y a rien de plus bête que la technique", interview by Maurice Bessy in *Cinémonde* (Paris), 6 October 1938; "Note" in *50 ans de cinéma* by Maurice Bessy and Lo Duca, Paris 1944; "Le Dramaturge" in *Livre d'or du cinéma française*, Paris 1945; "Mon ami René Clair" in *Cinémonde* (Paris), 23 April 1946; "Rx for Hollywood" in *The New York Times Magazine*, 21 November 1948;

"Adieu à Raimu" in *L'Ecran française* (Paris), 3 October 1951; "Souvenirs sur Raimu" in *Le Figaro Littéraire* (Paris), 7 September 1963; interview by J.-A. Fieschi and others in *Cahiers du cinéma* (Paris), December 1965; "Le Verbe et l'image", interview by Guy Braucourt in *Lettres françaises* (Paris), 13 March 1969; interview by Claude Beylie and Guy Braucourt in *Cinéma 69* (Paris), March 1969; "Le Cinéma selon Marcel Pagnol", interview by Claude Gauteur in *Image et son* (Paris), May 1969.

On PAGNOL:

Books—*Présences contemporains* by Pierre Leprohon, Paris 1957; *Cinéma d'hier, cinéma d'aujourd'hui* by René Clair, Paris 1970; *Marcel Pagnol* by P. Domeyne, Paris 1971; *Marcel Pagnol* by Claude Beylie, Paris 1972; *Marcel Pagnol m'a raconté...* by Raymond Castans, Paris 1975; *Marcel Pagnol* by Pierre Leprohon, Paris 1976; *Il etait une fois Marcel Pagnol* by R. Castans, Paris 1978; articles—"Mon ami Marcel Pagnol" by Fernandel in *Ciné-France* (Paris), 19 November 1937; "Pagnol, Pagnol, Pagnol et Cie" by Henri Jeanson in *Cinémonde* (Paris), 1 December 1937; "Suite au mythe du metteur en scène" by Claude Mauriac in *Le Figaro littéraire* (Paris), 23 June 1951; "Homage a Pagnol" by Hollis Alpert in *Saturday Review* (New York), 24 December 1955; entry in *Current Biography Yearbook 1956*, New York 1957; "Le Cas Pagnol" in *Qu'est-ce que le cinéma?* by André Bazin, Paris 1959; "Marcel Pagnol et la Cinématurgie" by Pierre Leprohon in *Radio-Cinéma* (Paris), 19 July 1959; special issue of *Livres de France* (Paris), March 1964; "Spécial Guitry-Pagnol" issue of *Cahiers du cinéma* (Paris), 1 December 1965; "The Marcel Pagnol Trilogy" by Harriet Polt in *Film Society Review* (New York), October 1967; "Marcel Pagnol revisité" by Arthur Cornand in *Image et son* (Paris), June 1969; "A la recherche de Pagnol" by Claude Gauteur in *Image et son* (Paris), June/July 1969; "La Saga Pagnol" by Michel Delahaye in *Cahiers du cinéma* (Paris), June 1969; "Marcel Pagnol" by Charles Ford in *Films in Review* (New York), April 1970; special issue of *Avant-Scène du cinéma* (Paris), July/September 1970; "Marcel Pagnol inconnu?" by C. Gauteur in *Image et son* (Paris), September 1973; "Marcel Pagnol" in *Les Grandes Rencontres* by P. Giannoli, Paris 1973; "Marcel Pagnol inconnu" by Claude Gauteur in *Image et son* (Paris), 1 September 1973; "Le Secret de Maître Pagnol" by Claude Beylie in *Ecran* (Paris), June 1974; "Marcel Pagnol: Un Cinéaste mineur?" by F. Gévaudan in *Cinéma* (Paris), June 1974; "Marcel Pagnol" by F. Debiesse in *Cinématographe* (Paris), June 1974; "Pagnol, prophète du chef-lieu" by Roland Duval in *Ecran* (Paris), October 1974; "Marcel, comme Pagnol" by G. Colpart in *Téléciné* (Paris), January 1976; "Le Rire qui vient du coeur" by Claude Beylie in *Télérama* (Paris), 28 January 1976; "Marcel Pagnol 1895-1974" by Pierre Leprohon in *Anthologie du cinéma* vol.9, Paris 1976; "Pagnol's Marseilles Trilogy" by E.B. Turk in *American Film* (Washington, D.C.), October 1980.

*   *   *

"The art of the theatre is reborn under another form and will realize unprecedented prosperity. A new field is open to the dramatist enabling him to produce works that neither Sophocles, Racine, nor Molière had the means to attempt." With these words, Marcel Pagnol greeted the advent of synchronous sound to the motion picture, and announced his conversion to the new medium. They also served to launch a debate, carried on for the most part with René Clair, in which Pagnol argued for the primacy of text over image in what he saw as the onset of a new age of filmed theater.

At the time Pagnol reigned supreme in the Parisien theater world. His plays, *Topaze* and *Marius*, both opened in the 1928-29 season to the unanimous acclaim of the critics and the public. Their success vindicated the theories of a group of playwrights which had gathered around Paul Nivoix, the drama critic for *Comoedia*. They were determined to develop an alternative to the predictable theater of the boulevards and the impenetrable experiments of the Surrealist avant-garde. The group pursued a dramatical ideal based on the well-made, naturalistic plays of Scribe and Dumas *fils*. The formula featured crisp dialogue, tight structures, and devastating irony. Its renewed popular appeal did not escape the notice of Bob Kane, the executive producer of the European branch of Paramount Pictures. Kane secured the rights for the screen versions of two plays, retaining Pagnol as writer for *Marius* to be directed by Alexander Korda, but then excluded him from any participation in the *Topaze* project. This neglect spurred the volatile young ex-schoolmaster from Provence to undertake his own productions.

With Pierre Braunberger and Roger Richebe, Pagnol produced and adapted his play, *Fanny*, a sequel to *Marius*, and hired Marc Allégret to direct. Then, in 1933, he formed his own production company, modelled on United Artists, which would control the production and distribution of all his future projects. At the same time he founded *Les Cahiers du film*, dedicated to the propagation of "cinematurgie," Pagnol's theories of filmed theater. *Jofroi* and *Angele*, the first two projects over which Pagnol exercised complete artistic control, established the tone for much of his ensuing career. Adapted from stories by Jean Giono and set in Provence in the countryside surrounding Marseilles where Pagnol was born and raised, the films treat the manners and lifestyle of the simple farmers and shopkeepers of the south and are executed with the precise principles of dramatic structure Pagnol had developed in his years with Nivoix. *Angele* is especially notable because it was shot on location on a farm near Aubagne. The film established a precedent followed by Jean Renoir in making *Toni*, a film produced and distributed by Pagnol's company, regarded by many as a forerunner of Italian neorealism. This is the formula to which Pagnol would return with increasing success in *Regain* and *Le Femme du boulanger*: a story or novel by Giono honed by Pagnol into a taut drama, elaborating the myths and folkways of "le coeur meridonale" and pivoting on the redemptive power of woman; set on location in Provence; and peopled with the excellent repertory company Pagnol had assembled from the Marseille music halls (including Raimu, Fernandel, Fernand Charpin, Orane Dumazis, and Josette Day).

Even after the formal break with Giono in an ugly squabble over money in 1937, Pagnol continued to exploit the formula in *La Fille du puisatier* and his masterpiece, *Manon des sources*. Running three hours and more, these films, even more than before, adopted the pace and flavor of the south which so colored Pagnol's approach to filmmaking. As Fernandel has put it: "With Marcel Pagnol, making a film is first of all going to Marseille, then eating some bouillabaise with a friend, talking about the rain or the beautiful weather, and finally if there is a spare moment, shooting...." Along with Clair and Cocteau, Pagnol has been inducted into the Academie Française. Every year his status grows among historians of cinema who once ridiculed his "canned theater."

—Dennis Nastav

PAKULA, ALAN J. American. Born Alan Jay Pakula in the Bronx, New York, 7 April 1928. Educated at Long Beach, Long Island, public schools, and Bronx High School of Science; Hill School, Pottstown, Pennsylvania; studied drama, Yale University, degree 1948. Married actress Hope Lange (divorced 1969); Hannah Cohn Boorstin, 1973; 5 stepchildren. Career: 1948—assistant, cartoon dept. of Warner Bros. directs Anouilh's *Antigone* at Circle Theatre, Los Angeles; 1950—becomes apprentice to producer-director Don Hartman at MGM, follows Hartman to Paramount the next year; 1957—produces *Fear Strikes Out*, begins association with director Robert Mulligan; 1962—*To Kill a Mockingbird* first production of Pakula-Mulligan Productions (active through 1969). Recipient: Best Direction, New York Film Critics, for *All the President's Men*, 1976. Agent: Stan Kamen, William Morris Agency, Beverly Hills, California. Address: Business: Gus Productions, 10889 Wilshire Blvd., Los Angeles, CA 90024.

Films (as producer): 1957—*Fear Strikes Out* (Mulligan); *To Kill a Mockingbird* (Mulligan); 1963—*Love with a Proper Stranger* (Mulligan); 1965—*Baby the Rain Must Fall* (Mulligan); 1966—*Inside Daisy Clover* (Mulligan); 1967—*Up the Down Staircase* (Mulligan); 1968—*The Stalking Moon* (Mulligan); (as producer and director): 1969—*The Sterile Cuckoo*; 1971—*Klute*; 1972—*Love and Pain and the Whole Damn Thing*; 1974—*The Parallax View*; 1976—*All the President's Men* (d only); 1978—*Comes a Horseman*; 1979—*Starting Over*; 1981—*Rollover*; 1982—*Sophie's Choice*.

Publications:

By PAKULA:

Articles—interview by Michel Ciment in *Positif* (Paris), March 1972; "Unlikely Elements", interview by Gordon Gow in *Films and Filming* (London), December 1972; "Not a Garbo or a Gilbert in the Bunch", interview by Tom Milne in *Sight and Sound* (London), spring 1972; "The Parallax View", interview by A.C. Bobrow in *Filmmakers Newsletter* (Ward Hill, Mass.), September 1974; interview by Michel Ciment in *Positif* (Paris), October 1976; "Mr. Pakula Goes to Washington", interview by R. Thompson in *Film Comment* (New York), September/October 1976; "Alan J. Pakula: l'enquête sur le Watergate", interview by A. Tournes in *Jeune Cinéma* (Paris), September/October 1976; "Making a Film About 2 Reporters" in *American Cinematographer* (Los Angeles), July 1976; interview by D. Cavett in *Cinemonkey* (Portland, Oregon), no.1, 1979.

On PAKULA:

Articles—"The Pakula Parallax" by R.T. Jameson in *Film Comment* (New York), September/October 1976; "Dossier: Hollywood 79: Alan J. Pakula" by P. Carcassonne in *Cinématographe* (Paris), March 1979; "Dialogue on Film" in *American Film* (Washington, D.C.), December/January 1978/79; entry in *Current Biography*, New York 1980.

*   *   *

Now considered by many a major cinematic stylist, Alan Pakula began his career as a producer. The quality of his films is rather uneven, ranging from the acclaimed *Fear Strikes Out* and *To Kill a Mockingbird* to the universally panned *Inside Daisy Clover*.

As a director, Pakula has been responsible for some very fine films; interestingly, his name is not as well-known as those of other directors, and yet the *films* often continue to receive critical and audience acclaim. Critic Guy Flatley noted that Pakula is affectionately acknowledged within the film industry as an "actor's director," eliciting "richly textured performances" from Liza Minnelli in *The Sterile Cuckoo*; Maggie Smith in *Love and Pain and the Whole Damn Thing*; Warren Beatty in *The Parallax View*; Robert Redford, Dustin Hoffman, and Jason Robards, Jr. in *All the President's Men*; Jane Fonda, James Caan, and Robards in *Comes a Horseman*; and Burt Reynolds, Candice Bergen, and Jill Clayburgh in *Starting Over*. Many filmgoers are surprised upon discovering that it was Pakula who directed all these films.

Pakula's self-effacement is deliberate. In the Oscar-winning *Sophie's Choice* (for Meryl Streep as Best Actress), the director's name is less known than the actors who worked so effectively under his direction, and far less known than the tragic personal, social, and historical themes of the film.

Pakula stresses the psychological dimension of his films. *Klute*, one of his most celebrated efforts, is highlighted by his use of taped conversation to both reveal character and heighten suspense. The film is noted for "visual claustrophobia" and unusual, effective mise-en-scène. For her performance, Jane Fonda received an Academy Award.

Klute was Pakula's first "commercial and critical gold." As one critic writes, "the attention to fine, authentic detail in *Klute* reflected the careful research done by both the director and the actress in the Manhattan demimonde, and many of the shadings of the complex character of the prostitute were developed improvisationally during the filming by...Fonda in collaboration with Pakula." Critical response to *Klute* is represented by such writers as Robin Wood, who said, "If it is too soon to be sure of Pakula's precise identity as an auteur, it remains true that *Klute* belongs, like any other great movie, to its director." Characteristically, Pakula believes that "the auteur theory is half-truth because filmmaking is very collaborative."

Pakula's other films have had equal success: *All the President's Men*, for example, was the top-grossing film of 1976, and won four academy awards. It was nominated for best picture and best director, as well. Even the critic called "Pakula's relentless nemesis," Stanley Kauffmann, "relented a little" concerning *All the President's Men*: he acknowledged that most scenes were shaved "as finely as possible."

Alan Pakula is a filmmaker whose work most notably features tautness in both narrative and performance; he is a director of "moods," and is often "congratulated for the moods he sustains." He has described his approach to filmmaking as follows: "I am oblique. I think it has to do with my own nature. I like trying to do things which work on many levels, because I think it is terribly important to give an audience a lot of things they may not get as well as those they will, so that finally the film does take on a texture and is not just simplistic communication."

—Deborah H. Holdstein

PAL, GEORGE. American. Born in Cegled, Hungary, 1 February 1908; became citizen of of the United States. Educated in architecture, Budapest Academy of Arts. Married Zsoka Grandjean, 1930. Career: before 1930—titler at Hunnia Films, Budapest; 1930-32—head of Ufa cartoon department; 1932—opens own studio; 1933—opens Prague studio; opens Paris studio, 1934, and one in Holland, 1935; 1939—comes to U.S., joins Paramount; 1949—begins producing feature films. Died 2 May 1980; buried at Holy Cross Cemetery, Culver City, California. Recipient: Special Academy Award for the development of novel methods and techniques in the production of short subjects known as Puppetoons, 1943; Special Effects Academy Award for *Destination Moon*, 1950; Special Effects Academy Award for *When Worlds Collide*, 1951; Special Effects Academy Award for *War of the Worlds*, 1953; Special Effects Academy Award for *Tom Thumb*, 1958; Special Effects Academy Award for *The Time Machine*, 1960.

Films (as director of Puppetoons at Paramount): 1941— *Western Daze*; *Dipsy Gypsy*; *Hoola Boola*; *The Gay Knighties*; *Rhythm in the Ranks*; 1942—*Jasper and the Watermelons*; *The Sky Princess*; *Mr. Strauss Takes a Walk*; *Tulips Shall Grow*; *The Little Broadcast*; *Jasper's Haunted House*; 1943—*Jasper and the Choo Choo*; *Bravo, Mr. Strauss*; *The 500 Hats of Bartholomew Cubbins*; *Jasper's Music Lesson*; *The Truck That Flew*; *Jasper Goes Fishing*; *Good Night, Rusty*; 1944—*A Package for Jasper*; *Say Ah, Jasper*; *And to Think That I Saw It on Mulberry Street*; *Jasper Goes Hunting*; *Jasper's Paradise*; *2 Gun Rusty*; 1945—*Hotlips Jasper*; *Jasper Tell*; *Hatful of Dreams*; *Jasper's Minstrels*; *Jasper's Booby Traps*; *Jasper's Close Shave*; *Jasper and the Beanstalk*; *My Man Jasper*; 1946—*Olio for Jasper*; *Together in the Weather*; *Jasper's Derby*; *John Henry and the Inky Poo*; *Jasper in a Jam*; *Shoe Shine Jasper*; 1947—*Wilbur the Lion*; *Tubby the Tuba*; *A Date with Duke*; *Rhapsody in Wood*; (as producer and special effects designer of feature films): 1949— *The Great Rupert* (Pichel); 1950—*Destination Moon* (Pichel); 1951—*When Worlds Collide* (Maté); 1953—*War of the Worlds* (Haskin); *Houdini* (Marshall); 1954—*The Naked Jungle* (Haskin); 1955—*The Conquest of Space* (Haskin); (as producer, director, and special effects designer): 1958—*Tom Thumb*; 1959—*The Time Machine*; 1960—*Atlantis, the Lost Continent*; 1962—*The Wonderful World of the Brothers Grimm* (co-d); 1964—*The 7 Faces of Dr. Lao*; (as producer): 1968—*The Power* (Haskin); 1975—*Doc Savage, the Man of Bronze* (Anderson).

Publications:

By PAL:

Articles—"George Pal and the Puppetoon", interview by Fred Von Bernewitz in *Castle of Frankenstein* (New York), June 1975; "*Logan's Run* Production", interview with George Pal and others by F.S. Clarke and others in *Cinefantastique* (Oak Park, Illinois), no.2, 1976; interview by Jay Duncan and Ted Bohus in *SPFX* (El Paso, Texas), January 1977; "Pal: Producing Special Effects Features—Without Special Budgets", interview by E. Zarmati in *Millimeter* (New York), February 1978.

On PAL:

Book—*The Films of George Pal* by G.M. Hickman, South Brunswick, New Jersey 1977; articles—"George Pal" by Marie Seton in *Sight and Sound* (London), summer 1936; "The Puppet and the Moppet" by Sondra Gorney in *Hollywood Quarterly*, July 1946; "The 5 Faces of George Pal" by D.S. Johnson in *Cinefantastique* (Oak Park, Illinois), fall 1971; "The Worlds of

George Pal" by Ed Naha in *Starlog* (New York), December 1977; "The Time Machine" by Ed Naha in *Starlog* (New York), May 1978; "The Disappearance" by P.S. Perakos and F.S. Clarke in *Cinefantastique* (Oak Park, Illinois), summer 1979; "Pal's Puppetoons" by James Burns in *Fantastic Films* (Chicago), October 1979; "George Pal's Puppetoons" by Jerry Back in *RBCC* (San Diego), September 1979; "George Pal" by Herbert Luft in *Films in Review* (New York), November 1980; "George Pal 1908-1980: from 'Puppetoons' to 'The Power'" by Samuel Maronie in *Starlog* (New York), September 1980.

*   *   *

George Pal's motion picture career can be divided into two different phases. He first achieved world-wide recognition as the creator of the Puppetoons. Pal was originally an illustrator and animator, but he felt that the two-dimensional cel cartoons were too flat. He preferred the three-dimensional look of puppets, which he brought to life in his studio through the process of stop-motion animation. The "actors" in the Puppetoons were quite complex characters, being sculpted in wood and constructed with wire limbs that made them easily posed. In addition, these puppets were designed to use replacement parts, particularly the heads. By replacing heads with different expressions, the puppets could talk and indicate emotions. Central characters in the Puppetoons could have as many as 100-200 different replacement heads.

The 42 Puppetoons which Pal made for Paramount (Pal estimated that he created over 200 such short films in Europe) are not your typical "cat-chase-mouse" cartoons. Even within these short eight minute films Pal tried to construct a meaningful story and, perhaps, a lesson. For example, he created at least two anti-Nazi propaganda films: *Tulips Shall Grow* and *Bravo, Mr. Strauss*. Both films emphasized man's struggle for individual freedom against the oppression of a mindless army. The theme of *John Henry and the Inky Poo* was the conflict between man and machine, proving man's will to dominate, rather than be dominated by machines. The Puppetoons remained extremely popular with the public through the 1940's, and in 1943 George Pal was awarded an Academy Award for the further "development of animation techniques." In 1948 the Puppetoons finally succumbed to skyrocketing production costs and Pal's studio at Paramount was closed. However, the end of the Puppetoons was also the beginning of George Pal's feature film career.

As a feature film producer Pal carried with him an immense enthusiasm for fantasy plus a wide knowledge of special effects techniques. (In fact, eight of his features won Academy Awards for special effects.) This combination paved the way for some of the classics of the science fiction genre, such as *Destination Moon*, *War of the Worlds*, and *The Time Machine*. Although these and other films can be catagorized as science fiction, Pal's films mainly emphasize the human quality of the story. Whereas most science fiction films are dark, pessimistic visions of the future, Pal's films hold forth hope for mankind. For example, the time traveler of *The Time Machine* is searching for a world without war; Dr. Lao of *The Seven Faces of Dr. Lao* shows us that there is good in everybody; the theme of *When Worlds Collide* is self-sacrifice amidst a struggle for survival.

Although Pal was never given the opportunity to work with a large budget (most of his films were produced for between

$500,000 and $1,000,000), his enthusiasm for his work produced the best possible product for the money, and the majority of his films were great financial successes. Today many of George Pal's feature films and Puppetoons continue to be revived in both theaters and on television. However, some of his Puppetoons, particularly those featuring a little black boy named Jasper, have met with criticism for being racist. Such criticism both surprised and saddened Pal who, in his innocence, was not aware of such possible interpretations when he made the films. In fact, it is this "innocent" quality in Pal's films that gives them much of the charm that other producer/directors find difficult to express in their work.

—Linda J. Obalil

PANFILOV, GLEB. Soviet. Born in Magnitogorsk, Urals, 1937. Educated at Urals Polytechnic Institute, degree in chemical engineering; in cinema at V.G.I.K. (State Cinema Institute). Married actress Inna Churikova. Career: works as factory foreman; sees Kalatozov's *The Cranes Are Flying*, becomes interested in filmmaking and begins shooting amateur films; 1960—becomes correspondence student at V.G.I.K., State Cinema Institute; 1968—directs first film; begins ongoing collaboration with actress wife Inna Churikova; 1970-76—attempts to make film on Joan of Arc; Recipient: Gold Medal, Moscow Festival, for *Vassa*, 1981.

Films (as director and scriptwriter): 1968—*V ogne broda net (There Is No Crossing Under Fire, No Ford in the Fire)*; 1970—*Nacala (Débuts, The Debut, A Girl from the Factory)*; 1976—*Ja prasu slova (I Ask for the Floor)*; 1980—*Tema (The Theme)*; 1981—*Valentina*; *Vassa*.

Publications:

By PANFILOV:

Article—interview in *Positif* (Paris), June 1977.

On PANFILOV:

Articles—"Hidden Star of All the Russias" by Frederick Brown in *The Guardian* (Manchester), 25 April 1981; article in *Sight and Sound* (London), summer 1983; article in *Soviet Film*, no.9, 1983.

*   *   *

Gleb Panfilov is one of the major young directors who blossomed during the Khrushchev thaw, but whose present difficulties illustrate the stiffening of the U.S.S.R.'s cultural policy. Trained as a chemical engineer, he abandoned his early profession to enter a two-year director's course at Mosfilm studios. He

directed his first three films for Lenfilm (Leningrad) which established his reputation. *No Ford in the Fire* (*V ogne broda net*) is on the surface a classic civil war story about a nurse working in an army train, taking care of the Red soldiers who have been wounded by the White army. The heroine (played by Inna Churikova, the director's wife who stars in all his films) is also an amateur painter whose work displeases a cultural commissar. Panfilov comments on the forthcoming socialist-realist aesthetics, and furthermore, depicts in subtle tones a White army officer. His style based on long shots is already conspicuous in this first film, but the characters are a bit too rationally conceived and the plot slightly mechanical, perhaps due the the influence of veteran screenwriter Evgeni Gabrilovitch. However, Panfilov's masterly direction and his complex reflections on art (two other important Soviet films, *Andrei Rubliov* and *Pirosmani* also deal with painters and their work) showed great promise confirmed by his next feature *Débuts* (*Nacala*), a further comment on artistic creation. A young worker in a factory town tries to escape from her boredom by playing in a small theatrical group. A film director hires her to star in Moscow in a new version of *Joan of Arc*. Panfilov shows the interplay between life and art; how the character she interprets influences her own personality and gives her strength to go on living, though at the end she is sent back to her dull provincial life. *I Want The Floor* (*Ja prasu slova*) is the third part of his trilogy of women characters. In his portrayal of the female mayor of a big town, Panfilov show the increasing conservatism that embalms the revolutionary values, the mechanics of loyal politics, and the attempts at censorship by his heroine who ultimately acknowledges her mistake. Panfilov's style is even more radical here with the use of long takes and static camera which creates a remarkable tension. His film, of course, stays within the limits of what he is allowed to say, but shows a keen perception of Soviet life.

In his next work, *Tema* (*The Theme*), about the problems of a writer, Panfilov seemed to have underestimated the bureaucratic watchdogs and his film was totally banned. The suggestion that emigration from the Soviet Union was not easy seems to have been one of the film elements that offended the authorities. Panfilov in his next two films had to play it safe, and resorted to the old solution of adapting classical plays. *Valentina* from Alexander Vampilov's *Last Summer in Tchoulimsk*, a Chekhovian chronicle of ten characters in a Taiga village inn, and *Vassa* from Maxim Gorki's *Vassa Gelznova*, about the decay of a petit bourgeois family, show an intelligence toward the material and a sensitivity for directing actors, but are far from fulfilling the hopes raised by the director's early career.

—Michel Ciment

PARADZHANOV, SERGEI. (Transliterations of name include "Paradjanov" and "Parajanov".) Soviet Georgian. Born in Tiflis (Tbilisi), Soviet Georgia, 1924. Educated at Kiev Conservatory of Music, 1942-45; studied under Igor Savchenko at Moscow Film Institute (V.G.I.K.), graduated 1951. Married Svetlana (Paradjanov), early 1950s (divorced after 2 years); son: Syrenchik. Career: 1953—begins directing at Kiev Dovzhenko Studio; 1965-66—*Shadows of Forgotten Ancestors* establishes international reputation; ten filmscripts prepared and rejected by authorities through 1974; 1974—indicted for a variety of crimes, convicted of trafficking in art objects; serves 4 of 5 year sentence at hard labor; 1977—international and Russian protests to Supreme Soviet of U.S.S.R. lead to release; lives in Tiflis, unable to work in films; 1981—reported selling family possessions to survive and begging on streets of Tiflis. Recipient: British Film Academy Award for *Shadows of Our Forgotten Ancestors*, 1966.

Films (as director and scriptwriter): 1951—*Moldavskaia skazka (Moldavian Fairy Tale)* (short); 1954—*Andriesh* (co-d); 1958—*Pervyi paren (The First Lad)*; 1961—*Ukrainskaia rapsodiia (Ukrainian Rhapsody)*; 1963—*Tsvetok na kamne (Flower on the Stone)*; 1964—*Dumka (The Ballad)*; 1965—*Teni zabytykh predkov (Shadows of Our Forgotten Ancestors)* (co-sc); 1972—*Sayat nova (The Color of Pomegranates)* (completed 1969); 1978—*Achraroumès (Retour à la vie)* [Return to Life] (short).

Publications:

By PARADZHANOV:

Articles—"*Shadows of Our Forgotten Ancestors*" in *Film Comment* (New York), fall 1968; "Perpetual Motion" in *Film Comment* (New York), fall 1968; interview by H. Anassian in *Le Monde* (Paris), 27 January 1980.

On PARADZHANOV:

Articles—"The Case of Sergo Paradjanov" by H. Marshall in *Sight and Sound* (London), winter 1974/75; "A Certain Cowardice" by Antonin Liehm in *Film Comment* (New York), July/August 1975; "Qui a peur de Paradjanov?" in *Cinéma* (Paris), September/October 1975; "Film Names Bid Soviets Be Kind to Paradzhanov" in *Variety* (New York), 17 November 1976; "Libérons Paradjanian" by J.-P. Fargier in *Cahiers du cinéma* (Paris), August/September 1977; "Un 'Ex-Cinéaste'" by A. Bosséno in *Image et son* (Paris), May 1980; "A Soviet Film-maker's Plight" by Richard Grenier in *The New York Times*, 26 July 1981.

*   *   *

After graduating in 1951 from the Directing Department of the Moscow Film Institute and working briefly as an assistant director, Sergei Paradzhanov began directing feature films at the Kiev Dovzhenko Studio. Paradzhanov himself considers his first five Ukrainian-language film failures—"albeit justified failures," but the validity of his appraisal is difficult to assess, since these films received little critical notice and have not been screened outside the Soviet Union.

In 1964, Paradzhanov made the remarkable *Teni zabytykh predkov (Shadows of Our Forgotten Ancestors)*, an unorthodox work by any standard, but especially so when seen in the context of other Russian films of the period. Although the film was supposedly "laughed off the screen by audiences" in Moscow, it achieved almost immediate international success, including the Grand Prize at the Mar del Plata and 15 other festival awards.

For this film, Paradzhanov was hailed as the inheritor of "the mantle of Sergei Eisenstein" by Western critics, including Herbert Marshall, one of Eisenstein's former students. Parad-

zhanov's filmic concerns, however, have little in common with the early Eisenstein of rational montage; instead the link between the two can be found in Eisenstein's concept of the monistic ensemble and in his dream of a fusion of the arts.

Shadows of Our Forgotten Ancestors, which is derived from a novel by 19th century Ukrainian writer M. Kotsiubinsky, is set in a small Carpathian village and concerns a blood-feud betweeen two families and the Romeo and Juliet-like love relationship between Ivan and Marichka. The plot itself, however, is the least important aspect of the film. Paradzhanov claims that "movie thinking" was alien to the material and that "we intentionally gave ourselves up to the material, its rhythm and style, so that literature, history, ethnography, and philosophy would fuse into a single cinematic image, a single act." Using a cyclical structure, multiple parallel incidents, fluid camera movements, and development of narrative through rituals, colors, folk songs, and dancing, Paradzhanov creates a world in this film that is sensous, erotic, exotic, and wondrous.

Clearly, the experience of making this film opened a new way of thinking for Paradzhanov. "We impoverish outselves by thinking only in film categories. Therefore I constantly take up my paintbrush... Another system of thinking, different methods of perception and reflection of life are opened to me. That's when you feel that the cinema is a synthetic art." The further realization of this synthetic art is found in *The Color of Pomegranates*, a "surreal icon come-to-life" depicting events in the life of the Armenian poet Aruthin Sayadin (1712-1795), known as Sayat Nova (King of Song). The film was finished in 1969, shelved, reedited by Sergei Yutkevitch, and finally given limited release in the Soviet Union in 1972. The film has only been screened in the West at various film festivals, including the New York festival in 1980.

In 1974, Paradzhanov was arrested on various charges, including trafficking in art objects, spreading venereal disease, homosexuality, and anti-Soviet agitation, and in a trial closed to the public he was sentenced to five years in prison. Near the end of his term, Paradzhanov was threatened with a ten-year extension of the sentence, but an international campaign was successful in securing his release in 1978. Since that time all of his proposed film projects have been rejected, and reports suggest that he is forced to survive by begging in the streets of Tiflis.

—Joseph A. Gomez

PASOLINI, PIER PAOLO. Italian. Born in Bologna, 5 March 1922. Educated at secondary school Reggio Emilia et Galvani, Bologna, graduated 1937; University of Bologna until 1943. Career: 1942—publishes *Poesie a Casarsa*, writes for *Corriere di Lugano*; 1943—conscripted; regiment taken prisoner by Germans following Italian surrender, escapes and takes refuge with family at Casarsa; 1944—with friends forms the "Academiuta di lenga furlana", publishes works in Friulan dialect; 1947—becomes secretary of Communist Party cell at Casarsa; 1949—accused of corrupting minors, is fired from Casarsa school where he has taught for several years, moves to Rome with mother; early 1950s—teaches in Ciampino, suburb of Rome; 1955—*Ragazzi di vita* published; he is indicted for obscenity; co-founds and edits review *Officina* (Bologna); 1963—prosecuted for "vilification of the Church" for directing "La ricotta" episode of *Rogopag*; 1978—exhibition of drawings, 1941-1975, presented at Milan. Died (bludgeoned to death) in Ostia, 2

November 1975; buried at at Casarsa. Recipient: Special Jury Prize, Venice Festival, for *Il vangelo secondo Matteo*, 1964.

Films (as co-scriptwriter): 1954—*La donna del fiume*; 1955—*Il prigioniero della montagna*; 1956—*Le notti di Cabiria*; 1957—*Marisa la civetta*; 1958—*Giovanni Mariti*; 1959—*La notte brava*; 1960—*La canta delle marane* (sc); *Morte di un amico*; *Il bell' Antonio*; *La giornata balorda*; *La lunga notte del '43*; *Il carro armato dell'8 settembre*; (as director and scriptwriter): 1961—*Accattone*; *La ragazza in vetrina* (co-sc only); 1962—*Mamma Roma*; *La commare secca* (sc only); 1963—"La ricotta" episode of *Rogopag*; *La rabbia* (part one); 1964—*Comizi d'amore*; *Sopralluoghi in Palestina*; *Il vangelo secondo Matteo (The Gospel According to Saint Matthew)*; 1966—*Uccellacci e uccellini (The Hawks and the Sparrows)*; "La terra vista dalla luna" episode of *Le Streghe (The Witches)*; 1967—"Che cosa sono le nuvole" episode of *Capriccio all'italiana*; *Edipo re (Oedipus Rex)*; 1968—*Teorema*; *La sequenza del fiore di carta* episode of *Amore e rabbia*; 1969—*Appunti per un film indiano*; *Appunti per una Orestiade africana (Notes for an African Orestia)*; *Porcile (Pigsty, Pigpen)*; *Medea*; *Ostia* (co-sc only); 1971—*Il decameron (The Decameron)* (+ro as Giotto); 1972—*12 dicembre* (co-d); *I racconti di Canterbury (The Canterbury Tales)* (+ro); 1973—*Storie scellerate* (co-sc only); 1974—*Il fiore delle mille e una notte (A Thousand and One Nights)*; 1975—*Salò o le 120 giornate di Sodome (Salo—The 120 Days of Sodom)* (co-sc).

Roles: 1960—*Il gobbo*; 1966—*Requiescat*.

Publications:

By PASOLINI:

Books—*Poesie a Casarsa*, Bologna 1942; *Dov'è la mia patria*, Casarsa 1949; *I parlanti*, Rome 1951; *Tal cour di un frut*, Tricesimo 1953; *Dal "diario" (1945-47)*, Caltanissetta 1954; *La meglio gioventù*, Florence 1954; *Il canto popolare*, Milan 1954; *Ragazzi di vita*, Milan 1955; *L'usignolo della Chiesa Cattolica*, Milan 1958; *Una vita violenta*, Milan 1959; *Passione e ideologia (1948-1958)*, Milan 1960; *Orestiade* by Aeschylus, translated by Pasolini, Urbino 1960; *Donne di Roma*, Milan 1960; *Roma 1950, diario*, Milan 1960; *Sonetto primaverile (1953)*, Milan 1960; *Accattone*, Rome 1961; *L'odore dell'India*, Milan 1962; *Mamma Roma*, Milan 1962; *Il sogno di una cosa*, Milan 1962; *La violenza*, with drawings by Attardi and others, Rome 1962; *Il vantone di Plauto*, Milan 1963; *Il vangelo secondo Matteo*, Milan 1964; *Poesie dimenticate*, Udine 1965; *Alì degli occhi azzurri*, Milan 1965; *Uccellacci e uccellini*, Milan 1965; *Edipo re*, Milan 1967; *The Ragazzi*, translated by Emile Capouya, New York 1968; *A Violent Life*, translated by William Weaver, New York 1968; *Teorema*, Milan 1968; *Pasolini on Pasolini*, interviews by Oswald Stack, London 1969; *Medea*, Milan 1970; *Ostia, un film di Sergio Citti*, with Sergio Citti, Milan 1970; *Poesie*, Milan 1970; *Entretiens avec Pier Paolo Pasolini* by Jean Duflor, Paris 1970; *Oedipus Rex*, London 1971; *Empirismo eretico*, Milan 1972; *Calderón*, Milan 1973; *Le poesie*, Milan 1975; *Il padre selvaggio*, Turin 1975; *Scritti corsari*, Milan 1975; *La nuova gioventù*, Turin 1975; *Trilogia della vita*, edited by Giorgio Gattei, Bologna 1975; *La divina Mimesis*, Turin 1975; *Giornate di Sodoma* by Uberto Quintavalle, Milan 1976; *'Volgar' eloquio* edited by A. Piromalli and D. Scarfoglio, Naples 1976; "L'arte del Romanino e il nostro tempo, with AA.VV., Brescia 1976; *I turcs tal Friùl*, Udine 1976; *Lettere agli amici*

(1941-1945), Milan 1976; *L'Experience heretique: langue et cinéma*, Paris 1976; *Le belle bandiere: dialoghi 1960-65*, Rome 1977; *Affabulazione, Pilade*, Milan 1977; *San Paolo*, Turin 1977; *I disegni, 1941-1975*, Milan 1978; *Friebeuterschriften*, Berlin 1978; *Theoreme*, Paris 1978; articles—"Intellectualism...and the Teds" in *Films and Filming* (London), January 1961; "Cinematic and Literary Stylistic Figures" in *Film Culture*, spring 1962; "Pier Paolo Pasolini: An Epical-Religious View of the World" in *Film Quarterly* (Berkeley), summer 1965; interview by James Blue in *Film Comment* (New York), fall 1965; "Pasolini—A Conversation in Rome" by John Bragin in *Film Culture* (New York), fall 1966; in *Interviews with Film Directors* edited by Andrew Sarris, New York 1967; interview by C.M. Cluny in *Cinéma* (Paris), March 1972; "Montage et sémiologie selon Pasolini" in *Cinéma* (Paris), March 1972; "Conversazione con Pier Paolo Pasolini" edited by A. Gennari in *Filmcritica* (Rome), August/September 1974; "Pasolini Today", interview by Gideon Bachmann in *Take One* (Montreal), September 1974; "Pasolini ne triche pas avec le public", interview by A. Tournès in *Jeune Cinéma* (Paris), November 1973; interview by Gideon Bachmann and D. Gallo in *Filmcritica* (Rome), August 1975; "Pier Paolo Pasolini: Cinema and Literature", interview by E. Wolfowicz in *Antaeus* (New York), winter 1976; "Divina Mimesis" in *London Magazine*, October/November 1976; "Pasolini's laatste interview" by Gideon Bachmann in *Skoop* (Amsterdam), January 1976; "The Scenario as a Structure Designed to Become Another Structure" in *Wide Angle* (Athens, Ohio), v.2, no.1, 1978; "Toto" in *Cahiers du cinéma* (Paris), March 1979.

On PASOLINI:

Books—*Pier Paolo Pasolini* by Marc Gervais, Paris 1973; *Directors and Directions* by John Taylor, New York 1975; *Vita di Pasolini* by Enzo Siciliano, Milan 1978; *Teoria e tecnica del film in Pasolini* by Antonio Bertini, Rome 1979; *L'ossessione e il fantasma: il teatro di Pasolini e Moravia* by Enrico Groppali, Venice 1979; *Pasolini*, seminar directed by Maria Macciocchi, Paris 1980; *Pier Paolo Pasolini* by Stephen Snyder, Boston 1980; articles—"Letter from Rome" by William Murray in the *New Yorker*, 21 April 1962; "Pasolini's Road to Calvary" by John Lane in *Films and Filming* (London), March 1963; "Pier Pailo Pasolini and the Art of Directing" by Gordon Hitchens in *Film Comment* (New York), fall 1965; "Pier Paolo Pasolini: Contestatore" by Marc Gervais in *Sight and Sound* (London), winter 1968/69; "Pier Paolo Pasolini: Poetry as a Compensation" by John Bragin in *Film Society Review* (New York), January, February and March 1969; "Pier Paolo Pasolini and the 'Rule of Analogy'" by Kevin Gough-Yates in *Studio International* (Lugano), March 1969; "Pasolini: Rebellion, Art and a New Society" by Susan Macdonald in *Screen* (London), May/June 1969; "Pasolini" by Roy Armes in *Films and Filming* (London), June 1971; "Dalla metodologia marxista alla visione classica" by E. De Paoli in *Cinema nuovo* (Turin), March/April 1972; "La Religione del suo tempo in Pier Paolo Pasolini" by F. Prono in *Cinema nuovo* (Turin), January/February 1972; "Quand le Christ, Marx et Freud se rencontrent..." by P. Sery in *Cinéma* (Paris), March 1972; "Pasolini in Persia: The Shooting of *1001 Nights*" by Gideon Bachmann in *Film Quarterly* (Berkeley), winter 1973/74; "Per una 'trilogia popolare, libera, erotica'" by G. Gambetti in *Cineforum* (Bergamo), March 1973; "L'Inspiration mythique chez Pasolini" by René Predal in *Cinéma* (Paris), September/October 1974; "L'Érotisme selon Pasolini" by H. Chapier in *Cinéma d'aujourd'hui* (Paris), winter 1975/76; "Sade-Pasolini" by Roland Barthes in *Le Monde* (Paris), 16 June 1976; "Lo Scandalo Pasolini", special issue edited by F. Di Giammatteo in *Bianco e nero* (Rome), v.37, no.1-4, 1976;

"Attraverso gli scritti l'impossibile scelta di Pasolini fra poesia e politica" edited by G. Pacchiano in *Cineforum* (Bergamo), April 1976; "Pier Paolo Pasolini", special issues of *Etudes cinématographiques* (Paris), no.109-111, 1976, and no.112-114, 1977; "Strutture dell'ipocrisia e tecniche del linciaggio" in *Cinema nuovo* (Turin), January/February 1976; special Pasolini issue of *Cinema* (Zurich), no.2, 1976; "Pornotisme et erographie" by V. Morin and others in *Ecran* (Paris), July 1976; "Pier Paolo Pasolini—temoignages" by E. Siciliano and others in *Cahiers du cinéma* (Paris), July/August 1976; "Pier Paolo Pasolini 1922-1975" by René Predal in *Avant-Scène du cinéma* (Paris), 1 and 15 November 1976; "Dossier: La Machine" by M. Amiel and others in *Cinéma* (Paris), August/September 1977; "Le 'dit' de Pasolini" by Noel Simsolo in *Cinéma* (Paris), May 1977; "Ankläger und Opfer", in 2 parts by W. Baskakov in *Film und Fernsehen* (Berlin), May and August 1978; "Pasolini par Laura Betti" by D. Rabourdin in *Cinéma* (Paris), January 1980; "Pier Paolo Pasolini", special section by J.L. Téllez and others in *Contracampo* (Madrid), September 1980; film—*Pasolini l'enragé* directed by Jean-André Fieschi, 1966.

* * *

Pier Paolo Pasolini, poet, novelist, philosopher, and filmmaker, came of age during the reign of Italian Fascism. His art is inextricably bound to his politics, which continued to grow and embody a criticism, even a contradiction of itself, throughout his life. Pasolini's films, like those of his early apprentice Bernardo Bertolucci, began under the influence of neorealism. He also did early scriptwriting with Bolognini and Fellini. Besides these roots in neorealism, Pasolini's works show a unique blend of linguistic theory and Italian Marxism. But Pasolini began transcending the neorealist tradition even in his first film *Accattone* (which means "beggar").

The relationship between Pasolini's literary work and his films has often been observed, and indeed Pasolini himself has said (in an introduction to a paperback selection of his poetry) "I made all these films as a poet." Pasolini was a great champion of modern linguistic theory and often pointed to Roland Barthes and Erich Auerbach in discussing the films many years before semiotics and structuralism became fashionable. His theories on the semiotics of cinema centered on the idea that film was a kind of "real poetry" because it expressed reality with reality itself and not with other semiotic codes, signs, or systems.

Pasolini's interest in linguistics can also be traced to his first book of poetry "Poems of Casarsa" which is written in his native Friuli dialect. This early interest in native nationalism and agrarian culture is also a central element in Pasolini's politics. His first major poem "The Ashes of Gramsci" (1954) pays tribute to the Italian Marxist and founder of the Italian Communist Party, Antonio Gramsci. It created an uproar unknown in Italy since the time of D'Annunzio's poetry and was read by artists, politicians and the general public.

The ideas of Gramsci coincided with Pasolini's own feelings, especially concerning that part of the working class known as the sub-proletariat, which Pasolini described as a prehistorical, pre-Christian, and pre-bourgeois phenomenon; a phenomenon which occurs for him in the South of Italy (the Sud) and in the Third World.

This concern with "the little homelands," the indigenous cultures of specific regions, is a theme linking all of Pasolini's films from *Accattone* to his final black vision, *Salò*. These marginal classes, known as *cafoni* (hicks or hillbillies), are among the main characters in Pasolini's novels *Ragazzi de vita* (1955) and *A*

Violent Life (1959), and appear as protagonists in many of his films, notably *Accattone*, *Mamma Roma*, *Hawks and Sparrows*, and *The Gospel According to Saint Matthew*. To quote Pasolini: "my view of the world is always at bottom of an epical-religious nature: therefore even, in fact above all, in misery-ridden characters, characters who live outside of a historical consciousness, these epical-religious elements play a very important part."

In *Accattone* and *The Gospel*, images of official culture are juxtaposed against those of a more humble origin. The pimp of *Accattone* and the Christ of *The Gospel* are similar figures. When Accattone is killed at the end of the film, a fellow thief is seen crossing himself in a strange backward way, it is Pasolini's indictment of how Christianity has "contaminated" the subproletarian world of Rome. Marxism is never far away in *The Gospel*, as in the scene where Satan, dressed as a priest, tempts Christ. In *The Gospel*, Pasolini has put his special brand of Marxism even into camera angles and has, not ironically, created one of the most moving and literal interpretations of the story of Christ. A recurrent motif in Pasolini's filmmaking, and especially prominent in *Accattone* and *The Gospel*, is the treatment of individual camera shots as autonomous units; the cinematic equivalent of the poetic image. It should also be noted that *The Gospel According to Saint Matthew* was filmed entirely in southern Italy.

In the 1960s Pasolini's films became more concerned with ideology and myth, while continuing to develop his epical-religious theories. *Oedipus Rex* (which has never been distributed in the Unites States) and *Medea* reaffirm Pasolini's attachment to the marginal and pre-industrial peasant cultures. These two films indict capitalism as well as communism for the destruction of these cultures, and the creation of a world which has lost its sense of myth.

In *Teorema* ("theorem" in Italian), perhaps Pasolini's most experimental film, a mysterious stranger visits a typical middle class family, sexually seduces mother, father, daughter and son and destroys them. The peasant maid is the only character who is transformed because she is still attuned to the numinous quality of life which the middle class has lost. Pasolini has said about this film: "a member of the bourgeoisie, whatever he does, is always wrong."

Pigpen, which shares with *Teorema* the sulphurous volcanic location of Mount Etna, is a double film. The first half is the story or parable of a 15th-century cult of cannibals and their eventual destruction by the Church. The second half concerns two former Nazis-turned-industrialists in a black comedy of rank perversion. It is the film closest in spirit to the dark vision of *Salò*.

In the 1970s Pasolini turned against his elite international audience of intellectuals and film buffs and embraced the mass market with his "Trilogy of Life": *Decameron*, *Canterbury Tales*, and *Arabian Nights*. The *Decameron* was the first major European box-office hit, due mainly to its explicit sexual content. All three films are a celebration of Pasolini's philosophy of "the ontology of reality, whose naked symbol is sex." Pasolini, an avowed homosexual, in *Decameron*, and especially *Arabian Nights*, celebrates the triumph of female heterosexuality as the epitome of the life principle. Pasolini himself appears in two of these films, most memorably in the *Decameron* as Giotto's best pupil, who on completion of a fresco for a small town cathedral says, "Why produce a work of art, when it's so much better just to dream about it."

As a result of his growing political pessimism Pasolini disowned the "Trilogy" and rejected most of its ideas. His final film *Salò* is an utterly clinical examination of the nature of fascism, which for Pasolini is synonomous with consumerism. Using a classical, unmoving camera, Pasolini explores the ultimate in human perversions in a static, repressive style. *Salò*, almost impossible to watch, is one of the most horrifying and beautiful visions ever created on film. Pasolini's tragic, if not ironic, death in 1975 ended a visionary career that almost certainly would have continued to evolve.

—Tony D'Arpino

PASSER, IVAN. Czech. Born in Prague, 10 July 1933. Educated in Film Faculty of the Academy of Musical Arts (FAMU), Prague. Career: 1961—assistant director to Milos Forman on *Audition* leads to scripting for Forman; and assistant directing; 1969—moves to U.S. in wake of Soviet invasion of Czechoslovakia; works in New York as longshoreman while studying English; 1971—U.S. directing debut with *Born to Win*. Recipient: Special Award, National Society of Film Critics, for *Intimate Lighting*, 1969; Rosenthal Foundation Award, National Society of Film Critics, for person working in cinema whose contribution to film art has not yet received due public recognition, 1972.

Films (as scriptwriter): 1963—*Konkurs (Talent Competition)* (Forman) (co-sc); *Cerný Petr (Black Peter, Peter and Pavla)* (Forman) (co-sc, +ass't d); 1965—*Lásky jedné plavovlásky (Loves of a Blonde, A Blonde in Love)* (Forman) (co-sc, +ass't d); (as director): 1965—*Fádní odpoledne (A Boring Afternoon)*; *Intimní osvětlení (Intimate Lighting)* (+co-sc); 1967—*Hoří, má panenko (The Firemen's Ball, Like a House on Fire)* (Forman) (co-sc only); 1971—*Born to Win*; 1974—*Law and Disorder* (+co-sc); 1976—*Crime and Passion (An Ace Up My Sleeve)*; 1978—*The Silver Bears*; 1981—*Cutter's Way (Cutter and Bone)*.

Publications:

By PASSER:

Article—interview in *Time Out* (London), 15-21 January 1982.

On PASSER:

Book—*Modern Czechoslovak Film 1945-1965* by Jaroslav Boček, Prague 1965; articles—"Ivan Passer" by A. Eyles in *Focus on Film* (London), autumn 1975; "Les Films américains d'Ivan Passer" by C. Benoit in *Jeune Cinéma* (Paris), April/May 1979; "Passer's Way" by R.T. Jameson in *Film Comment* (New York), July/August 1981; "Passer's Way" by J. Hoberman in *The Village Voice* (New York), 8 July 1981.

*   *   *

Hailed as one of the most promising directors of the Czech New Wave, Ivan Passer fled his homeland following the Russian invasion of August 1968, and after a brief stay in England, moved to the United States. After five films, his position as a director in this country is still being assessed, though many critics felt that *Cutter's Way* showed him to be one of the most promising talents of the eighties.

When Passer arrived in this country he had directed only one feature, but that film, *Intimate Lighting*, the story of a meeting of two former schoolmates as they prepared for a small town concert, brought him an international reputation through screenings at many important festivals including New York. Prior to the release of that film he had been known as a screenwriter whose reputation and career were closely aligned with that of fellow emigré and close friend Milos Forman, with whom he had written four of that director's five Czech films, In 1971 both directors made their American debuts, Forman with *Taking Off*, Passer with *Born to Win*; Forman's career bloomed, Passer's fell as his three subsequent features fared poorly at the box office.

Those three films, *Law and Disorder*, *Crime and Passion*, and *The Silver Bears*, are all flawed works, but not necessarily artistic failures. Each a curious satire on aspects of modern corruption, their commercial failure seems to have stemmed from the unresolved nature of their plots. Choosing to focus on the motivations and mysteries of the highly individualized misfits who are his central characters, Passer has generally neglected narrative clarity, matching unresolved plots to unfulfilled characters. In *Law and Disorder*, an examination of urban violence, a group of citizens take the law into their own hands by forming an auxiliary police force which turns out to be as corrupt as both the legal and criminal forces they wish to combat.

While these films work as character studies and display Passer's technical skill, the shifts between laughter and pain are often so unsettling subtle as to leave the spectator unsure of the director's moral position. All three films seem more interesting and their ideas clearer in light of *Cutter's Way*, his meditation on political and financial power, personal responsibility and the mysteries of friendship.

In this adaptation of Newton Thornburg's novel, Passer depicted his most successfully eccentric character—Alex Cutter—a multiple amputee and Vietnam vet whose anarchistic behavior is a result of his need to find a focus for his rage. In this devastatingly grim examination of the Vietnam nightmare which is masked by our insistent belief in the American dream, Passer unearths misconceptions of heroism and success, finding a corrupt mentality behind each while refusing to point the finger of blame in any particular direction. Alex Cutter's condition is a result of his having bought the dream; his revenge is the desire to bring down a powerful man, a synecdoche for the system which caused his martyrdom. The hauntingly unresolved nature of the films's ending is an achievement missing from Passer's earlier American films. The spectator here is forced to supply both the meaning and the outcome of the final action.

Cutter's Way was not only a personal achievement for Passer but became the film which demonstrated the viability of UA Classics, a subsidiary of the parent company which, in post-*Heaven's Gate* hysteria, had abandoned the film on its initial release. With special handling, *Cutter's Way* became a *cause celebré*, a minor financial success, and the hope of many for the recognition Passer deserves.

—Doug Tomlinson

PASTRONE, GIOVANNI. (Also known as Piero Fosco.); Italian. Born at Montechiaro d'Asti, 11 September 1883. Career: 1905—joins first Turin film company Rossi & C. as administrative assistant; 1907—company reorganized as Itala Film; named administrative director; 1910—begins directing; 1913-14—produces masterwork *Cabiria*; 1914—becomes production supervisor of Itala; early 1920s—abandons film industry, devotes efforts to medical research. Died in Turin, 27 June 1959.

Films (as producer and director): 1910—*Agnese Visconti*; *La caduta di Troia*; 1912—*Padre* (co-d); 1914—*Cabiria*; 1915—*Il fuoco*; *Maciste*; 1916—*Maciste alpino* (co-d); *Tigre reale*; 1919—*Hedda Gabler*; 1923—*Povere bimbe*.

Publications:

On PASTRONE:

Books—*Cinema ieri ed oggi* by Ettore Margadonna, Milan 1932; *Storia del cinema* by Francesco Pasinetti, Milan 1939; *Vecchio cinema italiano* by Eugenio Palmieri, Venice 1940; *Storia del cinema muto italiano* by Maria Prolo, Milan 1951; *Cinema italiano* by Mario Gromo, Milan 1954; *Il cinema italiano* by Carlo Lizzani, Florence 1954; *Storia del cinema muto* by Roberto Paolella, Naples 1956; articles—"Vita laboriosa e geniale di Giovanni Pastrone" by Mino Caudana in *Film* (Rome), 25 February and 4 March 1939; "D'Annunzio ed il cinema" by Luigi Bianconi in *Bianco e nero* (Rome), November 1939; "La tecnica rivoluzionaria nella 'Cabiria' di Pastrone" in *Cinema* (Milan), 15 March 1951; "Omaggio a Pastrone" issue of *Centrofilm* (Turin), no. 12 1961; "Pastrone, ultimo incontro" by Mario Verdone in *Bianco e nero* (Rome), June 1961; special Pastrone and Griffith issue of *Bianco e nero* (Rome), May/August 1975.

*   *   *

The firm Carlo Rossi and Company (of Turin) began in 1907 to manufacture films and apparatus, drawing their personnel from the Pathé Compnay of Paris. When Rossi left the Company, Sciamengo and Giovanni Pastrone took over what was by then Itala Films, and Pastrone soon proved himself an active and inspired manager. André Deed, the French comedian, was acquired in 1908 and proved a goldmine with his role of Cretinetti. Another valuable addition to the Company was Segundo de Chomon, the Spanish cameraman and a master of special effects. His first film for Itala was the sensational thriller *Tigris* in 1912. In the meantime Pastrone's ambitions led him into direction, and in 1910 he made *Agnese Visconti* and the sensational *Caduta del Troia*, which reached American cinemas in spite of an embargo on foreign films. His film *Padre* introduced the famous actor Ermete Zacconi to the screen. In 1913 Pastrone conceived a vast project set in the time of the Punic Wars when Scipio conquered Carthage. With a showman's instinct Pastrone approached d'Annunzio, and secured the approval and prestige of the great man's name for a tidy sum. Pastrone, under the name Piero Fosco, directed the film *Cabiria* with a script duly credited to the famous author, d'Annunzio. With dynamic thoroughness Pastrone did his homework. The period behavior, architecture and costumes were patiently researched. Vast structures were built. Shooting took six months, ranging from the Itala studios in Turin to Tunisia, Sicily and the Val de Lanzo where Hannibal is reputed to have crossed the Alps. Not only was the film spectacular but, artistically, it broke new ground. The striking camerawork by de Chomon made use of travelling shots with remarkable skill, and the effects of the eruption of Mount Etna and the naval battle of Syracuse were awe-inspiring. The charac-

ter of the strong man Maciste became a legend of the cinema. Later, Pastrone directed this ex-dock laborer in a further adventure, *Maciste*, and in the same year, he directed Pina Menichelli and Febo Mari in *Il Fuoco*, the love story of a young painter and a wealthy woman. The film's erotic atmosphere caused it to be banned and there were clerical demonstrations against the film.

In 1916 he again directed Menichelli in work by Verga, *Tigre reale*, and in 1919 he directed his former star of *Cabiria*, Itala Almirante Manzini, in *Hedda Gabler*. Before he retired at about that time he made several more films with his creation, Maciste. He abandoned the cinema to pursue researches in theraputic medicine.

—Liam O'Leary

———

PEARSON, GEORGE. British. Born in London, 1875. Career: January 1913—enters film industry with British Pathé as producer/director; April 1914—joins G.B. Samuelson company; May 1915—joins Gaumont; January 1918—with partner T.A. Welsh forms Welsh, Pearson company; 1929—goes to U.S. to supervise first Anglo-American co-production *Journey's End*; 1940—joins newly-formed Colonial Film Unit as producer, director, and writer; 1955—retires. Died 6 February 1973. Recipient: Officer, Order of the British Empire.

Films (as scenarist): 1912—*Peg Woffington*; (as documentary director): 1913—*Fair Sussex*; *In Dickens Land*; *Rambles Through Hopland*; *Lynmouth*; *Where History Has Been Written*; *Kentish Industries*; (as director): "Wonderful Nights of Peter Kinema" series (shorts); *A Lighter Burden* (short); *Mr. Henpeck's Dilemma* (short); *The Fool*; *Sentence of Death*; *Heroes of the Mine* (short); 1914—*A Fishergirl's Folly* (short); *The Live Wire*; *A Study in Scarlet*; *Christmas Day in the Workhouse* (short); *A Son of France* (short); *Incidents in the Great European War*; *The Cause of the Great European War*; *The Life of Lord Roberts VC*; 1915—*Buttons* (short); *For the Empire* (short); *A Cinema Girl's Romance*; *The True Story of the Lyons Mail*; *John Halifax Gentleman*; *Ultus the Man from the Dead*; 1916—*Ultus and the Grey Lady*; *Ultus and the Secret of the Night*; *Sally Bishop*; 1917—*Ultus and the 3 Button Mystery*; *The Man Who Made the Army* (documentary); *Canadian Officers in the Making* (documentary); 1918—*The Better 'ole*; *The Kiddies in the Ruins*; 1919—*Pallard the Punter* (sc only); *Angel Esquire* (sc only); *Hughie at the Victory Derby* (short); 1920—*Garryowen*; *Nothing Else Matters*; 1921—*Mary Find the Gold*; *Squibs*; 1922—*Mord Em'ly*; *The Wee MacGregor's Sweetheart*; *Squib Wins the Calcutta Sweep*; 1923—*Love Life and Laughter*; *Squibs M.P.*; *Squibs' Honeymoon*; 1924—*Reveille*; 1925—*Satan's Sister*; 1926—*The Little People*; *Blinkeyes*; 1927—*Huntingtower*; 1928—*Love's Option*; 1929—*Auld Lang Syne*; 1930—*Journey's End* (Whale) (supervising pr only); 1931—*East Lynne on the Western Front*; 1932—*The Good Companions* (Saville) (associate pr only); *The Third String*; 1933—*A Shot in the Dark*; *The Pointing Finger*; 1934—*River Wolves*; *4 Masked Men*; *Whispering Tongues*; *Open All Night*; 1935—*Ace of Spades*; *That's My Uncle*; *Gentleman's Agreement*; *Once a Thief*; *Jubilee Window*; *Checkmate*; 1936—*The Secret Voice*; *Wednesday Luck*; *Murder by Rope*; *Shipmates o' Mine* (sc only); 1937—*The Fatal Hour*; *Midnight at Madame Tussaud's*; *Command Performance* (sc only); 1938—*Follow Your Star* (sc only); *Souvenirs* (short); *Old Soldiers* (short); *Mother of Men* (short); (as documentary director): 1940—*Land of Water*; *Take*

Cover; Rural School; A British Family in Peace and War; 1941—*British Youth; An African in London.*

Publications:

By PEARSON:

Book—*Flashback: An Autobiography of a British Film Maker,* London 1957; article—"Lambeth Wall to Leicester Square" in *Sight and Sound* (London), winter 1938/39.

On PEARSON:

Articles—special issue of *Silent Picture* (London), spring 1969; "George Pearson: 1875-1973" by S. Peet in *Sight and Sound* (London), spring 1973; "Tribute to George Pearson" by Anthony Slide in *International Film Guide 1974,* London 1973; "Journey's End", letter by Anthony Slide in *Films in Review* (New York), March 1975.

*   *   *

George Pearson was a quiet, scholarly man, as far removed from the public image of a film director as it was possible to be. He had been a schoolmaster, and did not enter a film studio until he was 36 years old, but once Pearson decided he wanted to be a director he quickly became one of the best of the British silent cinema. Pearson never ceased expressing his admiration for D.W. Griffith, and he modeled his directorial style after the master, using the cinema to arouse an audience through emotion rather than technical virtuosity.

The director's first films offered little out of the ordinary for British silent shorts until 1914 when he was given the opportunity to direct *A Study in Scarlet,* the first major adaptation of a Sherlock Holmes story. *A Study in Scarlet* is also noteworthy for its ambitious use of locations, with the Cheddar Gorge standing in for the Rocky Mountains and the Southport Sands for the Salt Lake desert. With the "Ultus" series, produced between 1915 and 1917, George Pearson showed a grasp of the mystery film genre which led to a comparison with France's Louis Feuillade.

In 1918, George Pearson formed his own company in partnership with Tommy Welsh, and produced and directed *The Better 'Ole,* based on the cartoons of Bruce Bairnsfather. The film was perhaps the first to treat the First World War in the comic terms of the participating soldiers, and was widely reviewed and released in the United States, one of the first British features to receive international recognition. With *Nothing Else Matters,* George Pearson discovered Betty Balfour, who quickly became the British silent cinema's most popular star. She worked with Pearson on more than half-a-dozen films, notably the "Squibs" series which told of the comic adventures of a cockney flower seller and *Reveille,* a moving study of the after-effects of the First World War on a group of working-class Londoners.

With the coming of sound, George Pearson's career took a downward plunge, and he was kept busy in the Thirties directing a series of low-budget, quota-quickie films, which display little evidence of Pearson's earlier talent. With the Second World War, Pearson was back in demand in his old profession as a teacher with the Colonial Film Unit, educating young filmmakers from the emerging nations. Pearson's value to the British film industry as an instructor should not be overlooked, for many technicians learned their craft with him, notably Thorold Dick-

inson and Alberto Cavalcanti, who were associated with Pearson on *The Little People.* It is Thorold Dickinson who has noted, "Between Cecil Hepworth and Alfred Hitchcock, George Pearson was the outstanding personality in British silent cinema."

—Anthony Slide

PECKINPAH, SAM. American. Born David Samuel Peckinpah in Fresno, California, 21 February 1925. Educated at Fresno State College, B.A. in Drama 1949; University of Southern California, M.A. 1950. Married Marie Selland in 1947; children: Sharon, Kristen, Melissa and Matthew; married Begonia Palacios in 1964 (divorced); child: Lupita; married Joie Gould in 1972 (divorced). Career: 1943—enlists in Marine Corps; 1950-51—Director-Producer in Residence, Huntington Park (California) Civic Theatre; 1951-53—propman and stagehand, KLAC-TV, Los Angeles; assistant editor at CBS; 1954-57—assistant to Don Siegel on *Riot in Cell Block 11* and 4 more films; writes TV scripts for westerns including "Gunsmoke"; 1958-59—writes and directs "The Rifleman" pilot and other TV series episodes; 1963—works on scripts at Walt Disney Productions; 1964—fired as director of *The Cincinnati Kid;* 1966—writes and directs "Noon Wine" for ABC "Stage-67". Agent: Chasin-Park-Citron, Los Angeles, California.

Films (as director): 1961—*The Deadly Companions (Trigger Happy);* 1962—*Ride the High Country (Guns in the Afternoon)* (+co-sc, uncredited); 1965—*Major Dundee* (+co-sc); 1966—*Noon Wine* (+sc); 1969—*The Wild Bunch* (+co-sc); 1970—*The Ballad of Cable Hogue;* 1971—*Straw Dogs* (+co-sc); 1972—*Junior Bonner; The Getaway;* 1973—*Pat Garrett and Billy the Kid;* 1974—*Bring Me the Head of Alfredo Garcia* (+co-sc); 1975—*The Killer Elite;* 1977—*Cross of Iron;* 1978—*Convoy;* 1983—*The Osterman Weekend.*

Role: 1956—as Charlie the meter reader in *Invasion of the Body Snatchers* (Siegel).

Publications:

By PECKINPAH:

Articles—"A Conversation with Sam Peckinpah" by Ernest Callenbach in *Film Quarterly* (Berkeley), winter 1963/64; "Shoot!", interview by John Cutts in *Films and Filming* (London), October 1969; "Peckinpah's Return", interview by Stephen Farber, in *Film Quarterly* (Berkeley), fall 1969; "Talking with Peckinpah" by Richard Whitehall in *Sight and Sound* (London), autumn 1969; "Sam Peckinpah Lets It All Hang Out" in *Take One* (Montreal), January/February 1969; "Playboy Interview: Sam Peckinpah" by William Murray in *Playboy* (Chicago), August 1972; "Don Siegel and Me" in *Don Siegel: Director* by Stuart Kaminsky, New York 1974; "Mort Sahl Called Me a 1939 American" in *Film Heritage* (New York), summer 1976.

On PECKINPAH:

Books—*Horizons West* by Jim Kitses, Bloomington, Indiana 1970; *Sam Peckinpah: Master of Violence* by Max Evans, Vermilion, South Dakota 1972; *Pat Garrett and Billy the Kid* by

Rudolph Wurlitzer, New York 1973; *Peckinpah* by Valerio Caprara, Bologna 1976; *Sam Peckinpah* by Doug McKinney, Boston 1979; *Crucified Heroes: The Films of Sam Peckinpah* by T. Butler, London 1979; *Peckinpah: The Western Films* by Paul Seydor, Urbana, Illinois 1980; articles—"Sam Peckinpah's West" by Colin McArthur in *Sight and Sound* (London), autumn 1967; "The Ballad of Sam Peckinpah" by Rich Sassone in *Filmmakers Newsletter* (Ward Hill, Mass.), March 1969; "Sam Peckinpah" by Joel Reisner and Bruce Kane in *Action* (Los Angeles), June 1970; "Toward a Cinema of Cruelty" by William Blum in *Cinema Journal* (Evanston, Illinois), spring 1970; "Peckinpah's Progress: From Blood and Killing in the Old West to Siege and Rape in Rural Cornwall" by Dan Yergin in the *New York Times Magazine*, 31 October 1971; "Director Sam Peckinpah, What Price Violence?" by P.F. Kluge in *Life* (New York), 11 August 1972; "Sam Peckinpah in Mexico" by Grover Lewis in *Rolling Stone* (New York), 12 October 1972; "*The Wild Bunch* versus *Straw Dogs*" by Lawrence Shaffer in *Sight and Sound* (London), summer 1972; "Pat Garrett and Billy the Kid" by Jan Aghed in *Sight and Sound* (London), spring 1973; "Sam Peckinpah: The Survivor and the Individual" by Nigel Andrews in *Sight and Sound* (London), spring 1973; "*Cahiers du* Peckinpah" in *Esquire* (New York), February 1973; "Peckinpah's Obsession" in *Deeper into Movies* by Pauline Kael, Boston 1973; "Pat Garrett and Billy the Kid" by P. Biskind in *Film Heritage* (New York), winter 1973/74; "The Ballad of Sam Peckinpah" by R. Sassone in *Filmmakers Newsletter* (Ward Hill, Mass.), March 1973; Peckinpah issue edited by Anthony Macklin of *Film Heritage* (New York), winter 1974/75; "Sam Peckinpah's Television Work" by Garner Simmons in *Film Heritage* (New York), winter 1974/75; "*The Wild Bunch* and the Problem of Idealist Aesthetics..." by Cordell Strug in *Film Heritage* (New York), winter 1974/75; "Peckinpah in Mexico" by A. Madsen in *Sight and Sound* (London), spring 1974; "L'accettazione 'scientifica' di una realtà di sconfitta" by P. Mereghetti in *Cineforum* (Bergamo), July 1974; "In Defense of Sam Peckinpah" by Mark Miller in *Film Quarterly* (Berkeley), spring 1975; "Nightmare and Nostalgia: The Cinema West of Sam Peckinpah" by Arthur Pettit in *Western Humanities Review* (Salt Lake City), spring 1975; "Notes on the Nihilist Poetry oif Sam Peckinpah" by Pauline Kael in the *New Yorker*, 12 January 1976; "Peckinpah: il territorio sdoppiato" by E. Magrelli in *Filmcritica* (Rome), March 1976; "Truckin' with the Big Iguana" in *Time* (New York), 4 July 1977; "The Function of Mexico in Peckinpah's Films" by R. Humphries in *Jump Cut* (Berkeley), August 1978; "A Privilege to Work in Films: Sam Peckinpah Among Friends" by Sam Fuller in *Movietone News* (Seattle), February 1979; "La Critica e la sua adeguatezza: superficie e profondo" by R. Rosetti in *Filmcritica* (Rome), March 1979; "Sam Peckinpah: Cutter" by R. Gentner and D. Birdsall in *Film Comment* (New York), January/February 1981; "Midsection: Sam Peckinpah" by R.T. Jameson and others in *Film Comment* (New York), January/February 1981.

*   *   *

Though he has not made a western since 1973, it is as a director of westerns that Sam Peckinpah remains best known. This is not without justice. His non-western movies often lack the sense of complexity and resonance that he brings to western settings. He is adept at exploiting this richest of genres for his own purposes, explaining its ambiguities, pushing its values to uncomfortable limits. *Ride the High Country*, *Major Dundee*, and *The Wild Bunch* are the work of a filmmaker of high ambitions and rare

talents. They convey a sense of important questions posed, yet finally left open and unanswered. At their best they have a visionary edge unparalleled in American cinema, and it is hardly surprising that the declining popularity of the western has also seen a decline in Peckinpah's reputation.

His non-westerns lose the additional dimensions that the genre brings, as in, for example, *Straw Dogs*. A polished and didactic parable about a besieged liberal academic who is forced by the relentless logic of events into extremes of violence, it is somehow too complete, its answers too pat, to reach beyond its own claustrophobic world. Though its drama is entirely compelling, it lacks the referential framework that carries Peckinpah's westerns far beyond the realm of tautly-directed action. Compared to *The Wild Bunch*, it is a one-dimensional film.

Nevertheless, *Straw Dogs* is immediately recognizable as a Peckinpah movie. If a distinctive style and common theses are the marks of an *auteur*, then Peckinpah's right to that label is indisputable. His concern with the horrors and the virtues of the male group has been constant, as has his refusal to accept conventional movie morality. "My father says there's only Right and Wrong, Good and Evil, with nothing in between. But it's not that simple, is it?" asks Elsa in *Ride the High Country*. Judd's reply could almost be Peckinpah's: "No. It should be, but it isn't".

In traditional westerns, of course, right and wrong are clearly distinguishable. The westerner is, as Robert Warshow characterised him, the man with a code. In Peckinpah's westerns, as in some of his other movies such as *Cross of Iron*, it is the code itself that is rendered problematic. Peckinpah explores the ethic rather than taking it for granted, plays off its elements one against the other, uses his characters as emblems of those internal conflicts. He presents a world moral certainty is collapsing, leaving behind doomed variations of assertive individualism. In some modern westerns that theme has been treated as elegy; in Peckinpah it veers nearer to tragedy. His is a harsh world, softened only rarely in movies like *The Ballad of Cable Hogue* and *Junior Bonner*.

His richest achievements remain the two monumental epics of the sixties: *Major Dundee* and *The Wild Bunch*. In both, though *Major Dundee* was butchered by its producers both before and after shooting, there is ample evidence of Peckinpah's abililty to marshall original cinematic means in the service of a morally and aesthetically complex vision. He is a director who thinks in terms of film, not an adapter of pre-established literary or dramatic forms. It has become commonplace to associate Peckinpah with the rise of explicit violence in modern cinema, and it is true that few directors have rendered violence with such horrific immediacy. But his cinema is far more than that, his reflections upon familiar western themes technically sophisticated, elaborately constructed, and, at their best, genuinely profound.

—Andrew Tudor

PENN, ARTHUR. American. Born in in Philadelphia, 27 September 1922. Educated at at Olney High School, Philadelphia; Black Mountain College, North Carolina, 1947-48; studied at Universities of Perugia and Florence, 1949-50. Married actress Peggy Maurer, 1955; children: Matthew and Molley. Career: 1943—enlists in Army, befriends future collaborator Fred Coe; 1945—joins Soldiers Show Company, Paris; 1947—offers acting class at Black Mountain College; 1951-52—floor manager and assistant director on *The Colgate Comedy Hour*; 1953-55—directs *Gulf Playhouse: 1st Person* (NBC) and *Philco Television Playhouse* (NBC), New York; 1956-58—directs plays for *Play-*

house 90 (CBS) including *The Miracle Worker*; 1958—dismissed as director of *The Left-Handed Gun* after rough cut made; 1958-60—beginning with *2 For the Seesaw* directs series of Broadway hits; continues to alternate directing of stage plays and films. Agent: Sam Cohn, International Creative Management, New York.

Films (as director): 1958—*The Left-Handed Gun*; 1962—*The Miracle Worker*; 1965—*Mickey One* (+pr); 1966—*The Chase*; 1967—*Bonnie and Clyde*; 1969—*Alice's Restaurant* (+co-sc); 1970—*Little Big Man* (+pr); 1973—"The Highest" in *Visions of 8*; 1975—*Night Moves*; 1976—*The Missouri Breaks*; 1981—*4 Friends*.

Publications:

By PENN:

Articles—"Top Director Analyzes His Craft" in *Journal-American* (New York), 3 May 1960; "Rencontre avec Arthur Penn" by André Labarthe in *Cahiers du cinéma* (Paris), February 1963; "Rencontre avec Arthur Penn" by André Labarthe and others in *Cahiers du cinéma* (Paris), October 1965; interview by Jan Aghed and Stig Björkman in *Chaplin* (Stockholm), no. 64, 1966; "Arthur Penn Objects", letter in *The New York Times*, 20 February 1966; "Attention Harlan Ellison", letter in *Cinema* (Beverly Hills), March 1966; "An Interview with Arthur Penn" by Curtis Hanson in *Cinema* (Beverly Hills), summer 1967; "Bonnie and Clyde: Private Morality and Public Violence" in *Take One* (Montreal), vol.1, no.6, 1967; "Penn Replies" in *The New York Times*, 17 September 1967; "Sur *Bonnie and Clyde*" in *Positif* (Paris), November 1967; "Non faccio l'avvocato della violenza" in *Cineforum* (Bergamo), September 1968; "An Interview with Arthur Penn" by Michael Lindsay in *Cinema* (Beverly Hills), vol.5, no.3, 1969; interview in *The Director's Event* by Eric Sherman and Martin Rubin, New York 1970; "Entretien avec Arthur Penn" by Jan Aghed and Bernard Cohn in *Positif* (Paris), April 1971; "Arthur Penn", interview by Michael Billington in the *Times* (London), 10 April 1971; "Entretien avec Arthur Penn" by Guy Braucourt in *Cinema 71*,1971; "Incontri: Arthur Penn" by Mario Foglietti in *Rivista del Cinematografo*, December 1971; "Metaphor", interview by Gordon Gow in *Films and Filming* (London), July 1971; "On Directors and Technicians" in *Harper's Bazaar* (New York), July 1971; "Arthur Penn: Little Big Movie Miracle Worker?", interview by Deac Rossell in *Boston After Dark*, 23 March 1971; "Penn Pals with Film: Part 2" in *Boston After Dark*, 6 April 1971; "Arthur Penn at the Olympic Games", interview in *American Cinematographer* (Los Angeles), November 1972; "Night Moves", interview by T. Gallagher in *Sight and Sound* (London), spring 1975; "Arthur Penn ou l'anti-genre", interview by Claire Clouzot in *Ecran* (Paris), December 1976; "Now Is the Ideal Time for Theater", interview by G. Henry in *The New York Times*, 12 December 1976.

On PENN:

Books—*Arthur Penn* by Robin Wood, New York 1969; *Cinque Film di Arthur Penn* by Mauro Marchesini and Gaetano Stucchi, Turin 1972; *Focus on Bonnie and Clyde*, edited by John Cawelti, Englewood Cliffs, New Jersey 1973; *Arthur Penn* by Fabio Carlini, Milan 1977; articles—"Television: *State of the Union*" by Jack Gould in *The New York Times*, 17 November 1954; "Television Providing Directors for the Needy Movie

Industry" by Murray Schumach in *The New York Times*, 18 June 1958; "Can a Man Be Blamed for Wanting More than Memories?" by Bennett Schiff in the *Post* (New York), 7 September 1960; "An Untheatrical Director Takes the Stage" by Brock Brower in *The New York Times Magazine*, 20 May 1962; "*Mickey One*—2, 3, Go!" by Howard Thompson in *The New York Times*, 8 March 1964; "Arthur Penn et les symboles" by Marcel Martin in *Cinéma 65*, Paris 1965; "Penn: And Where Did All the *Chase*-ing Lead?" by Rex Reed in *The New York Times*, 13 February 1966; "Hollywood: The Shock of Freedom in Films" in *Time* (New York), 8 December 1967; "Filmographie de Arthur Penn" by Patrick Brion in *Cahiers du cinéma* (Paris), December 1967; "Arthur Penn à Paris" by Renaud Walter in *Cinéma* (Paris), April 1968; "Arthur Penn" by Jim Hillier in *Screen* (London), January/February 1969; "A Conversation with Arthur Penn" by Jacoba Atlas in *Rolling Stone* (New York), 19 March 1970; "Arthur Penn" in *The Film Director as Superstar* by Joseph Gelmis, New York 1970; "Director Penn: From *The Miracle Worker* to Penn and a Statement on Red Genocide" by Russell Deac in *Boston After Dark*, 7 January 1970; "Arthur Penn in Canada" by Robin Wood in *Movie* (London), winter 1970/71; "Filming the Olympics" by Lee Margulies in *Action* (Los Angeles), November/December 1972; "Le Gaucher", special issue of *Avant-Scène du cinéma* (Paris), November 1973; "Plot 'Attica' Sans Any Real Names" in *Variety* (New York), 2 April 1975; "Back in the Saddle" by Paul Zimmerman and Martin Kasindorf in *Newsweek* (New York), 11 August 1975; "What *Is* a Western?" by Stuart Byron and Terry Curtis Fox in *Film Comment* (New York), July/August 1976; "Mushville" by A. Lelchuk in *Atlantic Monthly* (Greenwich, Conn.), October 1976; "Rustling Up" by Robin Wood in the *Times Educational Supplement* (London), 23 July 1976; "Arthur Penn: The Flight from Identity" by T. Butler in *Movie* (London), winter 1978/79; films—*Arthur Penn Films "Little Big Man"* by Elliott Erwitt, Time-Life Films 1970; *Arthur Penn (1922-): Themes and Variants* by Robert Hughes, PBS 1970.

*   *   *

Arthur Penn has often been categorized—along with Robert Altman, Bob Rafelson and Francis Coppola—as one of the more "European" of American directors. Stylistically, this is true enough. Penn's films, especially after *Bonnie and Clyde*, tend to be technically experimental, and episodic in structure; their narrative line is elliptical, undermining audience expectations with abrupt shifts in mood and rhythm. Such features can be traced to the influence of the French New Wave, in particular the early films of François Truffaut and Jean-Lue Godard, which Penn greatly admired.

In terms of his thematic preoccupations, though, few directors are more utterly American. Consistently, throughout his work, Penn has been concerned to question and re-assess the myths of his country. His films reveal a passionate, ironic, intense involvement with the American experience, and can be seen as a uniquely illuminating chart of the country's moral condition over the past 25 Years. *Mickey One* is a dark film with the unfocused guilt and paranoia of the McCarthyite hangover, while the stunned horror of the Kennedy assassination reverberates through *The Chase*. The exhilaration, and the fatal flaws, of the 1960s anti-authoritarian revolt are reflected in *Bonnie and Clyde* and *Alice's Restaurant*. *Little Big Man* reworks the trauma of Vietnam, and *Night Moves* is steeped in the disillusioned malaise that pervaded the Watergate era. A wary, low-profile optimism, suited to the 1980s, emanates from *Four Friends*.

As a focus for his perspective on America, Penn often chooses an outsider group and its relationship with mainstream society. The Indians in *Little Big Man*, the Barrow Gang in *Bonnie and Clyde*, the rustlers in *The Missouri Breaks*, the hippies in *Alice's Restaurant*, the outlaws in *The Left-Handed Gun*, are all sympathetically presented as attractive and vital figures, preferable in many ways to the conventional society which rejects them. But ultimately they suffer defeat, being infected by the flawed values of that same society. "A society," Penn has commented, "has its mirror in its outcasts."

An exceptionally intense, immediate physicality distinguishes Penn's work. Pain, in his films, unmistakably *hurts*, and tactile sensations are vividly communicated. Often, characters are conveyed primarily through their bodily actions: how they move, walk, hold themselves or use their hands. Violence is a recurrent feature of his films—notably in *The Chase*, *Bonnie and Clyde*, and *The Missouri Breaks*—but it is seldom gratuitously introduced, and represents, in Penn's view, a deeply rooted element in the American character which has to be acknowledged.

Penn's reputation as a director was established by the enormous success of *Bonnie and Clyde*, widely agreed to be one of the most significant and influential films of its decade. Since 1970, though, he has made only three films, none of them commercially successful. Some critics have seen this as evidence of a declining talent. But almost invariably, those of Penn's films which have been poorly received on initial release—such as *The Left-Handed Gun*, *Night Moves*, or *The Missouri Breaks*—have subsequently gained steadily in critical esteem; and he has yet to make an uninteresting or negligible film. In the range, vitality, and sheer unpredictability of his output, Arthur Penn remains one of the most stimulating of American directors.

—Philip Kemp

PEREIRA DOS SANTOS, NÉLSON. Brazilian. Born in São Paulo, 1928. Educated in law; studied at I.D.H.E.C., Paris. Career: late 1940s—journalist; editor at *Jornal do Brasil*, Rio de Janeiro; 1951-53—assistant director on *O saci* (Nanni, 1951), *Agulha no palheiro* (Viany, 1952), *Balança mas não caid* (Vanderlei, 1953) and other films; 1954-55—directs first feature, *Rio, 40 Degrees*; 1956—begins teaching cinema at University of Brasilia; 1958—produces Roberto Santos's *O grande momento*; 1958-60—collaborates on short films with I. Rozemberg and J. Manzon; 1962—edits *Barravento* (Rocha) and *Pedreira de São Diogo* (Hirszman); beginning 1968—director of Dept. of Cinematographic Art, Federal University of Nitéroi; late 1970s—participates in founding of filmmakers' cooperative, which owns cinemas in major cities; editor and co-director of film revue *Luz e Açao*.

Films (as director and scriptwriter): 1950—*Juventude* (short); *Atividades políticas em São Paulo* (short); 1955—*Rio quarenta graus (Rio, 40 Degrees)*; 1957—*Rio, zona norte (Rio, zone nord)* (+co-pr); 1958—*Soldados do fogo* (short); 1960—part of a documentary on Karl Gass made in East Germany; 1961—*Mandacaru vermelho* (+co-pr, ro); 1962—*O Bôca de Ouro*; *Ballet do Brasil* (short); 1963—*Vidas sêcas (Sécheresse)* [Dry Lives]; *Um môco de 74 anos* (short); 1964—*Rio de Machado de Assis* (short); 1965—*Fala, Brasilia*; 1966—*Cruzada ABC*; 1967—*El justiciero (Le Justicier)* (+co-pr); 1968—*Fome de amor (Soif d'amour)*; *Abastecimento, nova política* (short); 1969—*Um*

asilo muito louco (Azyllo muito louco, L'Aliéniste) (+co-d); 1971—*Como é gostoso o meu francês (How Tasty Was My Little Frenchman, Comme il est bon mon français, Qu'il était bon mon petit français)* (+co-pr); 1972—*Quem e beta (Pas de violence entre nous)*; 1974—*Amuleta de ogum (The Amulet of Ogum)*; 1977—*Tenda dos milagres (Tent of Miracles, La Boutique des miracles)*; 1980—*Na estrada da vida (On the Highway of Life)*.

Publications:

By PEREIRA DOS SANTOS:

Articles—interview by Joaquim Pedro de Andrade and Claudio Mello e Sousa in *Supplemento Dominical do Jornal do Brasil* (Rio de Janeiro), 1 November 1959; interview by R. Grelier and G. Gauthier in *Image et son* (Paris), May 1966; interview by Marcel Martin in *Les Lettres françaises* (Paris), 6 January 1966; interview by Leo Murray in *Cahiers du cinéma* (Paris), March 1966; "Entretien avec Nélson Pereira dos Santos" by Federic de Cárdenas and Max Tessier in *Études cinématographiques* (Paris), no.93-96, 1972; r; "Bresil", interview by J. Frenais in *Cinéma* (Paris), October 1976; "Une Lutte de chaque jour", interview by A. Tournès in *Jeune Cinéma* (Paris), July/August 1978; interview by N. Carro in *Cine* (Mexico), April 1979; "Brazilian Cinema Reawakens", interview by S. Dominguez in *Film/Literature Quarterly* (Salisbury, Maryland), no.1, 1979; "Uma cooperativa de cirema", interview by A. Lima in *Filme cultura* (Rio de Janeiro), February 1979; "D'abord, le Brésil", interview by Charles Tessier in *Cahiers du cinéma* (Paris), November 1981.

On PEREIRA DOS SANTOS:

Book—*Revisão critica do cinema brasileiro* by Gláuber Rocha, Editôra Civilização Brasileira, 1963; articles—"*Vidas sêcas*" by Raymond Lefevre in *Cinéma 65* (Paris), November 1965; "L'Enfer, c'est un mauvais endroit" by Michel Petris in *Cahiers du cinéma* (Paris), November 1965; "L'Enfer sans diable" by Goffredo Fofi in *Positif* (Paris), February 1966; "Propos de N.P. dos Santos sur le cinéma brésilien" by Gérard Langlois in *Art et essai* (Paris), February 1966; "*Sécheresse*" by Guy Gauthier in *Image et son* (Paris), April 1967; "Nelson Pereira dos Santos" by José Monteiro, with filmography by Michel do Espirito Santo, in *Filme cultura* (Rio de Janeiro), September/October 1970; "O inventor do nôvo cinema" by Alex Viany in *Jornal do Brasil* (Rio de Janeiro), 21 May 1970; "Le 'cinema nôvo' brésilien (1)", edited by Michel Estève, in *Études cinématographiques* (Paris), no.93-96, 1972; "Dossies criticos: *Barre Pesada*" by O.L. Fassoni and others in *Filme Cultura* (Rio de Janeiro), February 1979.

PERIES, LESTER JAMES. Sri Lankan. Born in Colombo, Ceylon (now Sri Lanka), 5 April 1919. Educated at Catholic priests' college until 1938. Married editor and director Sumitra Gunawardana. Career: during WW II—works in theater and on radio as scriptwriter; 1946—sent to London by parents; invited to contribute to *The Times* of Ceylon; begins making short documentaries; 1950-52—makes 3 amateur shorts; 1952—returns to Ceylon, joins Government Film Unit; 1955—with cameraman William Blake and editor Titus De Silva (Titus Thotawatte), quits Film Unit, and begins work on first Sinhalese language feature shot on location; idle for several years after *The Line of*

Destiny, critically-acclaimed, is failure with audiences; 1960s—De Silva replaced as editor by wife Sumitra Peries.

Films (as director of short films): 1949—*Soliloquy*; 1950—*Farewell to Childhood*; *A Sinhalese Dance*; 1954—*Conquest in the Dry Zone*; 1955—*Be Safe or Be Sorry*; (as feature director): 1956—*Rekava (The Line of Destiny, The Line of Life)* (+pr, sc); 1960—*Sandesaya (The Message)* (+co-sc); 1961—*Too Many Too Soon* (short); 1962—*Home from the Sea* (short); 1964—*Forward into the Future* (short); *Gamperaliya (Changes in the Village)*; 1966—*Delovak Athara (Between 2 Worlds)* (+co-sc); 1967—*Ran Salu (The Yellow Robe)*; 1968—*Golu Hadawatha (Silence of the Heart)*; 1969—*Steel* (short); *Akkara Paha (5 Acres of Land)*; 1970—*40 Leagues from Paradise*; *Nidhanaya (The Treasure)*; 1971—*Kandy Perahera (The Procession of Kandy)* (short); 1972—*Desa Nisa (The Eyes)*; 1975—*The God King*; 1976—*Madol Duwa (Enchanted Island)*; 1978—*Ahasin Polawatha (White Flowers for the Dead)*; 1979—*Pinhamy* (short); *Veera Puran Appu (Rebellion)*; 1980—*Baddegama (Village in the Jungle)* (+co-sc); 1982—*Kaliyugaya (The Time of Kali)*; 1983—*Yuganthayo (End of an Era)*.

Publications:

By PERIES:

Articles—"A Filmmaker in Ceylon" in *Sight and Sound* (London), autumn 1957; interview by M. Sibra in *Cinéma* (Paris), December 1976; interview by A.J. Gunawardana in *Sight and Sound* (London), summer 1977; interview by J.-P. Hautin in *Positif* (Paris), November 1980; "A la découverte de Lester James Peries au Festival de La Rochelle", interview and article by I. Jordan and J.-P. Hautin in *Positif* (Paris), October 1980.

On PERIES:

Book—*The Lonely Artist* by Philip Coorey, Colombo, Ceylon (Sri Lanka) 1970; articles—"A Personal Cinema" by A.J. Gunawardana in *The Drama Review* (New York), spring 1971; "Lester James Peries: cinéaste de Sri Lanka" by G. Gauthier in *Image et son* (Paris), March 1981; "Lester James Peries" by Derek Elley in *International Film Guide 1983*, London 1982.

* * *

The film industry of Sri Lanka (formerly Ceylon), like those of many small countries, suffers from the proximity of a similar but much larger and more prolific industry which dominates both the home market, and potential export markets. For Sri Lankan filmmakers and their audience, film means Indian film, in particular the fantasy-formula movies so beloved of South Indian (Tamil) cinema. Home production has tended to rehash these movies in a Sinhalese version. When Lester James Peries broke away from the Government Film Unit, which largely made documentaries, with the aim of making "films that truly reflected the life of the people of this country...valid in terms of cinema as it is generally accepted in other countries," he initiated a revolution in the Sinhalese industry simply, as Philip Coorey remarks in his authoritative study of Peries, *The Lonely Artist*, by "making his films in the way he thought best."

"The way he thought best" took Peries out of the studio-bound industry, with its painted backcloths and equally painted actors,

into a world of real locations and real people. His first film, *Rekava (The Line of Destiny)*, was a commercial failure, though critically well-received abroad. As yet, Sri Lankan audiences were not prepared to accept a realistic view of themselves, instead preferring fantasies. But the barrier had been broken, and despite this setback, Peries and his associates persisted, encouraging others to break with the tradition.

In his subsequent films, Peries has endeavoured "to explore human relationships as truly as I can, even if that truth be unpalatable, to do so with sympathy and compassion"—thus producing films with both local relevance, and universal significance. Such works as *Gamperaliya (Changes in the Village)*, *Nidhanaya (The Treasure)*, and *Baddegama (Village in the Jungle)* are characterized by warmth, visual lyricism, and a powerful narrative instinct which occasionally (by western standards) verges on melodrama.

With some justification, critics have accused Peries of making films which are too slow, too uncommitted. His preoccupation is with the internal conflict of his characters, rather than with the external situations which have precipitated their angst. His is a contemplative cinema—in Coorey's words, "he eavesdrops on the inner and exterior life of his characters." Peries may not specifically condemn social conditions, or make political exposés of the corrupt influences in Sri Lankan society, but by concentrating on the lives of his characters he subtly shows how Sri Lanka, and to some extent every society, imposes on people through superstition, caste and/or class systems, and social mores, a way of life which can lead to much unhappiness, gross stupidity, and a general waste of human potential. A more serious charge against Peries might be that his films show a tendency towards the sentimental. The slow, lyrical style of his work can lead to a softness of approach, where a harder edge might give better dramatic results. However, such attempts at a more dynamic style of cinema as *The God King* (a co-production with Great Britain) have been less than convincing—although still fascinating.

In his compassionate portrayal of his people. Lester James Peries has earned a place beside Satyajit Ray, Flaherty, Renoir, Ozu, in the pantheon of humanist filmmakers. But his most distinctive achievement has been the creation, virtually single-handed, of a truly Sri Lankan cinema.

—Theresa FitzGerald

PERRAULT, PIERRE. Canadian. Born in Montreal, 29 June 1927. Educated in classical studies, Collège de Montréal and Collège Grasset, then at Collège Sainte-Marie; studied law, Université de Montréal, Université de Paris, and University of Toronto. Married Yolande Simard, 1951; children: Geneviève and Mathieu. Career: 1954-56—practices law in Montreal; 1956—becomes scriptwriter at Société Radio-Canada; 1959-60—directs *Au pays de Neufve-France* for TV; 1963—co-directs first cinema feature *Pour la suite du monde* with Michel Brault.

Films (as director): 1963—*Pour la suite du monde* (co-d); 1967—*Le Règne du jour*; 1969—*Les Voitures d'eau*; *Le Beau Plaisir*; 1970—*Un Pays sans bon sens*; *L'Acadie, l'Acadie!* (co-d); 1976—*Le Retour à la terre*; *Un Royaume vous attend*; *Le Goût de la farine*; 1977—*C'était un Québécois en Bretagne, madame!*; 1979—*Le Pays de la terre sans arbre*; *Gens d'Abitibi*; 1982—*La Bête lumineuse*; 1983—*Les Voiles bas et en travers*.

Publications:

By PERRAULT:

Books—*Portulan*, poems, Montreal 1961; *Ballades du temps précieux*, poems, Montreal 1963; *Toutes Isles*, stories, Montreal 1963; *Au coeur de la rose*, play, Montreal 1964; *La Règne du jour*, filmscript, Montreal 1968; *Les Voitures d'eau*, filmscript, Montreal 1969; *En désespoir de cause*, poems, Montreal 1971; *Un Pays sans bon sens*, filmscript, Montreal 1972; *Chouennes*, poems, Montreal 1975; *Gélivures*, poems, Montreal 1977; *Discours sur la condition sauvage et québécoise*, Montreal 1977; *La Bête lumineuse*, filmscript, Montreal 1982; *Caméramages*, Paris 1983; articles—"La mi-carême à l'Ile-aux-Coudres" in *MacLean* (Montreal), March 1964; "Discours sur la parole" in *Culture vivante* (Quebec), no.1, 1966 [also in *Cahiers du cinéma* (Paris), no.191, 1967, and in *Ar Vro* (Paris), no.4-5, 1967]; "La Parole est à Perrault", interview by M. Basset in *Cahiers de la Cinémathèque* (Paris), spring 1972; interview by G. Gauthier and L. Marcorelles in *Image et son* (Paris), January 1972; "La Femme dans la cinéma québécois" by G. Gauthier in *Image et son* (Paris), January 1973; "Prendre la parole pour briser le silence" in *L'Art et l'etat*, Montreal 1973; "A propos des voitures d'eau" in *Marins du Saint-Laurent* by Gérard Harvey, Montreal 1974; "L'Apprentissage de la haine" in *L'Homme dans son nouvel environnement* (IVe Colloque, Session Ross '74), University of Quebec at Rimouski, 1975; "Pierre Perrault et Bernard Gosselin: le gout de la parole québécois", interview by P. Demers in *Cinéma Québec* (Montreal), no.5, 1976; interview by J. Bouthillier Lévesque in *Positif* (Paris), October 1977; interview by N. Gauthier in *Image et son* (Paris), June/July 1977.

On PERRAULT:

Articles—"Paris Letter" by Geoffrey Minish in *Take One* (Montreal), January/February 1971; special issue by G. Gauthier and others of *Image et son* (Paris), January 1972; "The Political Situation of Quebec Cinema" by R. La Rochelle and G. Maggi in *Cineaste* (New York), summer 1972; "3 Aspects du cinéma québécois" by M. Martin and P. Staran in *Ecran* (Paris), April 1977; "The Film as Word (Perrault)" by P. Ohlin in *Ciné-Tracts* (Montreal), spring/summer 1978; "Faut-il bruler le cinéma quebecois?: le leçon du direct" by F. Dansereau and others in *Image et son* (Paris), February 1979; "Le Film ethnographique comme métaculture: la contribution de Pierre Perrault" by D. Clandfield in *Copie zéro* (Montreal), October 1981.

*   *   *

Canadian Peirre Perrault, along with Americans Richard Leacock and Frederick Wiseman and France's Jean Rouch has been the most exemplary practioner of cinema-verité, or candid-eye camera, which revolutionized cinema in the 1960s and introduced new ways of looking at reality. Living in Québec, he has suffered from a relative isolation so that his important work is not well known outside France or his own country. Colleague Jean Rouch defines his originality well when he states that "it is Bresson's camera coming out of Dziga Vertov's brain and falling on Flaherty's heart: it is *Man of Aran* with direct sound, *Farrebique* with a travelling camera."

The work of Pierre Perrault can be considered an ethnological investigation of the Canadian French community. It could only have been achieved by a man with wide cultural interests. Born in 1927 in Montreal, Perrault has been a lawyer, an athlete, a poet, a playwright. He also worked on the radio which explains his great interest in the spoken word (he did 300 broadcasts on the subject of popular traditions). His first documentary work, (13 thirty-minutes films for TV in 1959-1960), traditional in style, concerns the Northern side of the Saint Laurent River and prefigures his major work, the trilogy *Pour la suite du monde*, *Le Règne du jour*, and *Les Voitures d'eau*. These films center on the Ile aux Coudres (an island which is a microcosm of the French Canadian community), the conflicts of generations, and their search for an identity. With the major contribution of cameraman Michel Brault (who co-directed *Pour la suite du monde* and later *L'Acadie, l'Acadie*), Perrault has made his camera a participant in the life of his people while also attempting to catch their true selves in concrete action. For *Pour la suite du monde*, he asked the islanders to resume sea-hog fishing 38 years after it had been abandoned. Like Flaherty he lived with the community before starting to shoot and asked them to collaborate on the film thus making it possible for them to express their worries and their passions, going beyond surface realism toward their fantasies and even a collective unconscious.

The development of cinema techniques, particularly light-weight camera equipment and extremely faithful sound recording, have allowed a remarkable flexibility to the film shape, and made possible the recording of people as they see themselves and not as an outsider would see them. The importance of speech (the French Canadians' fight for their autonomy is based on a defense of their language) is paramount in Perrault's work, but we also witness *physically* the problems faced by the islanders. In *Pour la suite du monde*, we see the shaping of a human community through a collective project; in *Le Règne du jour*, the burial of French culture as a model to follow; in *Les Voitures d'eau* the necessity to adapt an ancient technique of building boats to a more modern usage. Later Perrault's films become much more politicized, even violent. *Un Pays sans bon sens* is a new affirmation of the Québec identity of the occasion of a trip to French Brittany, and *L'Acadie, l'Acadie* tells of the student fights at Moncton University.

In the 1970s Perrault has pursued his investigation of ethnic communities, particularly in a cycle of four films centered on the Abitibi region (*Un Royaume vous attend*, *Le Retour à la terre*, *C'était un Québecois en Bretagne, madame!*, *Gens d'Abitibi*). *Le Bête lumineuse*, a totally new experience, is about a hunting party which is given a mythological dimension, very much like Faulkner in his short story *The Bear*. The chase of an animal which we never see and will never be captured becomes a truculent saga where the members of the group reveal themselves through speech and behavior. Faithful to his methods, Perrault adds one more fascinating chapter to his human comedy.

—Michel Ciment

PETERSON, SIDNEY. American. Born in Oakland, California, 15 November 1905. Educated at University of California at Berkeley, 1928-30; California College of Arts and Crafts; California School of Fine Arts; Art Students League. Career: 1921—begins working as sculptor; 1932-34—lives in France (again in 1937-38), sees works of French avant-garde filmmakers; 1947-50—teaches filmmaking at California School of Fine Arts; makes 1st films as part of workshop class; 1952-54—director of a television project for the Museum of Modern Art, New York; investigates possible interaction of the museum and TV, also makes 3 commissioned films for TV; 1954-56—writes series of scripts for United Productions of America (UPA) animated films, some on artists; 1957-58—does script and storyboard for proposed Disney *Fantasia II*; 1961—publishes novel *A Fly in the Pigment*; 1980—teaches filmmaking workshop at the School of the Art Institute of Chicago, begins work on new film. Agent: Film-Makers' Cooperative, 175 Lexington Ave., New York NY 10016.

Films (as director): 1946—*The Potted Psalm* (with James Broughton); 1947—*The Cage*; *Horror Dream*; *Clinic of Stumble*; 1948—*Ah Nurture* (with Hy Hirsch); *The Petrified Dog*; *Mr. Frenhofer and the Minotaur*; 1949—*The White Rocker*; *The Lead Shoes*; *Adagio for Election Day*; (for Orbit Films): 1952—*Blunden Harbor*; *Chocolate Factory*; *Doll Hospital*; *Vein Stripping* (surgical procedure); (for the Museum of Modern Art): 1954—*Architectural Millinery*; *Manhole Covers*; 1955—*Japanese House*; (as scriptwriter for UPA animated films): 1954-55—*The Invisible Moustache of Raoul Dufy*; 1956—*The Merry-Go-Round in the Jungle* (on the Douanier Rousseau); *The Day of the Fox* (on Sharaku); *Columbus Discovers America*; *A Woman's Place* (on Belle Starr); *The 12 Days of Christmas*; *Rome Burns*; *The Greeks Take Troy*; *Lady Godiva*; *Grimaldi*; *The Night Watch* (on Rembrandt); *The Farm* (on Miro) (+storyboard); (for Disney): 1957—*Fantasia II* (+storyboard); 1980-82—*Man in a Bubble* (workshop production, School of the Art Institute of Chicago).

Publications:

By PETERSON:

Books—*A Fly in the Pigment*, Sausalito, California 1961; *The Dark of the Screen*, New York 1980; articles—"An Historical Note on the Far-out West" in *Contact*, August 1962; "A Note on Comedy in Experimental Film" in *Film Culture* (New York), summer 1963; "You Can't Pet a Chicken" in *The Atlantic* (New York), March 1963; "A Statement on Dance and Film" in *Dance Perspectives*, summer 1967; "A Visit with Sidney Peterson" by R. Del Tredici in *Cinemanews* (San Francisco), no.6, 1978/79.

On PETERSON:

Books—*Visionary Film* by P. Adams Sitney, New York 1974; *A History of the American Avant-Garde*, exhibition catalogue, by John Hanhardt and others, The American Federation of Arts, New York 1976; articles—"Sidney Peterson" by Parker Tyler in *Film Culture* (New York), no.19, 1959; "*The Potted Psalm* and Other Local Legends" by Jerome Tarshis in *San Francisco*, April 1974.

*   *   *

Sidney Peterson is one of the "first generation" of American avant-garde filmmakers. His group of films was made in the late 1940s in workshop classes at the California School of Fine Arts. Peterson drew on the varied interests and talents of his students, and combined their contributions in surprisingly disjunctive ways. There followed a decade of semi-commercial and commercial projects, over which he did not always have full control, and then a return to "personal" filmmaking with *Man in a Bubble* (1980-82), begun in another filmmaking workshop he was invited to teach.

Peterson's best early films (*Mr. Frenhofer and the Minotaur* and *The Lead Shoes* among them) are violently original works that open up possibilities for cinema that have still not been fully explored. Surrealism and allied European art movements were clearly an influence on these films, which enjamb several different and apparently unrelated narrative threads. The soundtracks are packed with spoken texts and other effects, combined in bizarre and often puzzling ways.

The uniqueness of Peterson's achievement lies in the fact that the viewer senses his films (especially on repeated viewings) as being much more than the playful amalgams that they may initially seem. Connections between sound and image grow more explicit; details of the stories told emerge; possible relations between the multiple stories are suggested. The humor that arises from Peterson's juxtapositions can have a Freudian suggestiveness to it; one senses several possible hidden meanings at work. While many of his successors have made films full of metaphoric connections, the notion of a cinema based primarily on concrete multiple meanings has not been as popular as has the notion that cinema should try to escape from such language-related specificities, via revelatory or visionary experience conveyed through film.

Peterson's films are as much, if not more, for the mind than for the eye. His imagery is often striking, but he never dwells on visual "beauty." Instead, black-and-white tones of his images are harsh and gritty, and the images are as visually congested as the overall effect of his editing and sound. "Congestion" is carried to an extreme in *The Lead Shoes*, in which an anamorphic lens is continually used to twist and distort imagery. The result is a cinematic space that, though it contains recognizable objects, denies the viewer any possibility of identification or entry.

With their direct appeal to the viewer's intellect, Peterson's films also deny entry on the level of their sound and image juxtapositions. At times, with the associations suggested by a film clustering ever more densely, the work can approach the condition of a mask, presenting the viewer with a fully detailed but knowingly deceptive surface, one which also allows him to proceed no further. At such moments, image, sound, and overall film all attain an awesome inscrutability.

Peterson's recent *Man in a Bubble* continues the tradition of his late 1940s films, and is a very fine work in itself. Its subject is urban life, and specifically the phenomenon of the radio/tape players that people carry with them in public places. The film is a strong depiction of "noise"—not merely of the noise that those machines make, but of a more generalized kind of noise, the multiple vibrations of social chaos and mechanized life that fill our streets and our brains.

—Fred Camper

PETRI, ELIO. Italian. Born Eraclio Petri in Rome, 29 January 1929. Educated in literature, University of Rome. Career: early 1950s—film critic for Communist daily *L'Unita*; through 1950s collaborates on scripts, notably on films of Giuseppe De Santis; also works as assistant director; 1961—directs first feature. Died summer 1982. Recipient: Best Foreign-Language Film Academy Award for *Investigation of a Citizen Above Suspicion*, 1970; Best Film (*ex aequo*), Cannes Festival, for *The Working Class Goes to Paradise*, 1972.

Films (as scriptwriter): 1952—*Roma ore undici (Rome 11 O'Clock)* (De Santis) (co-sc); 1953—*Un marito per Anna Zac-*

cheo (A Husband for Anna) (De Santis) (co-sc); (as director and co-scriptwriter): 1954—*Nasce un campione* (short); 1954—*Giorni d'amore (Days of Love)* (De Santis) (co-sc only); 1956—*Uomini e lupi (Men and Wolves)* (De Santis) (co-sc only); 1957—*I sette Contadini* (short); *L'Uomo senza domenica* (De Santis) (co-sc only); 1958—*Cesta duga godinu dana (La strada lunga un anno)* (De Santis) (co-sc only); 1960—*La Garçonnière* (De Santis) (co-sc only); 1961—*L'assassino (The Lady Killer of Rome)*; 1962—*I giorni contati*; 1963—*Il maestro di Vigevano* (d only); 1964—"Peccato nel pomeriggio (Sin in the Afternoon)" episode of *Alta infedeltà (High Infidelity)* (d only); 1965—*La decima vittima (The 10th Victim)*; 1967—*A ciascuno il suo (We Still Kill the Old Way)*; 1968—*Un tranquillo posto di campagna (A Quiet Place in the Country)*; 1970—*Indagine su un cittadino al di sopra di ogni sospietto (Investigation of a Citizen Above Suspicion)*; "Documenti su Giuseppe Pinelli" episode of *Ipotesi*; 1971—*La classe operaia va in paradiso (The Working Class Goes to Paradise, The Working Class Goes to Heaven, Lulu the Tool)*; 1973—*La proprietà non è piú un furto*; 1976—*Todo modo*; 1978—*Le mani sporche* (sc—for TV); 1979—*Le buone notizie.*

Publications:

By PETRI:

Books—*Roma ora undici*, filmscript, Rome and Milan 1956; *L'assassino*, filmscript, Milan n.d.; *Indagine su un cittadino al di sopra ogni sospetto*, filmscript with Ugo Pirro, Rome 1970; articles—interview by J.-A. Gili and C. Viviani in *Ecran* (Paris), June 1972; interview by C. Haustrate in *Cinéma* (Paris), July/August 1972; "Cinma Is Not for an Elite but for the Masses", interview by Joan Mellen in *Cinéaste* (New York), v.6, no.1, 1973; interview by J.-A. Gili in *Ecran* (Paris), December 1974; "La Propriété n'est plus le vol", interview by A. Garel and G. Colpart in *Image et son* (Paris), January 1975; "Actualité politique de Elio Petri", interview by A. Tournès in *Jeune Cinéma* (Paris), September/October 1976; "Todo modo", interview by J.A. Gili in *Ecran* (Paris), January 1977; "Elio Petri habla de su última pelicula", interview by A. Gómez Olea and A. Garciá del Vall in *Cinema 2002* (Madrid), January 1980; "L'Enfer selon Petri: bonnes nouvelles", interview by A. Tournès and A. Tassone in *Jeune Cinéma* (Paris), September/October 1980.

On PETRI:

Book—*Elio Petri* by Jean Gili, Nice 1974; articles—by Pascal Kane in *Cahiers du cinéma* (Paris), September/October 1972; article by James MacBean in *Film Quarterly* (Berkeley), spring 1972; article by James MacBean in *Film Quarterly* (Berkeley), spring 1973.

*   *   *

In his brief career, Elio Petri has become renowned as one of the major political filmmakers of the 1960s and 1970s. He was also among the directors who achieved an international stature for the Italian cinema for the third time in its history. From his first feature, an original variation on the police thriller, he maintained a consistently high quality of style and poignant subject matter. Even with the bitterness, grotesqueness and complexity of his films, many of them achieved a huge commercial success.

For example, *The Tenth Victim*, a stylized science fiction collage of Americanisms which concentrates on the voracious rapport between a man (Marcello Mastroianni) and a woman (Ursula Andress), plays repeatedly on American television. *Investigation of a Citizen Above Suspicion* (which won the Oscar for best foreign film) and *The Working Class Goes to Heaven* have enjoyed continued success with contemporary audiences through repertory screenings and 16mm distribution. With *Investigation*, Petri wanted to make a film against the police and the mechanisms that guaranteed immunity to the servants of power, yet intended no precise political references. His claim was that the state manifests itself through the police. Like his earlier film, *A ciascuno il suo*, it opens with a murder committed by a police official (Gian Marie Volonte) but, because of his position and manipulation of the system, it remains a crime without punishment. The film brilliantly studies the psychopathology of power whereas, with his other enormous success, *The Working Class...*, Petri wanted to return to what he considered was the real basis of Italian neorealism—a popular hero. Filmed in a factory whose director was serving a prison sentence, it investigates the reasons why a worker is driven to strike. Again the protagonist was played by Volonté (whose name in the film, Massa, means "the masses"). Although he is a highly individualized character, Petri continually stresses that his actions, thoughts, goals, and even his sexuality, are determined by society and its rules.

Two common themes running throughout Petri's work has been the alienation of modern man and investigations of the socio-political relationships between an individual and his/her society. Petri usually employs a highly stylistic form which he often describes as expressionist. This is most obvious, for example, in *Todo modo*, aptly described as a celebration of death, where some characters are referred to merely as "the president" and "him." Quite grotesque, the film was not well received in Italy where, despite its extreme stylization, it was read as a precise analogy of the ruling political party.

Petri began his film career as a scriptwriter, most notably for Giuseppe De Santis's *Rome Eleven O'Clock*: Petri often stated that De Santis was his only mentor and, like him, Petri directed relatively few films, carefully chosen for content and precisely planned in style and detail. Filmmaking was, in his opinion, the most popular tool with which a culture could understand itself. Thus, he is considered not an artisan, but an auteur, a filmmaker who closely identified the filmmaking process with personal, social, moral and political duties.

—Elaine Mancini

———

PICK, LUPU. (also known as "Lupu-Pick."); Romanian. Born in Iasi (Jassy), 2 January 1886. Married Edith Pasca. Career: 1914—acting debut in Romania; 1915—emigrates to Germany; acts in film, in Hamburg theaters and at Deutsches Theater, Berlin; 1917—founds production company Rex Filmgesellschaft; 1918—directs 1st film; 1922-23—makes *Scherben* and *Sylvester*, 1st 2 parts of triptych supposed to include *Der letzte Mann*; quits *Der letzte Mann* following disagreement with Carl Mayer over character of doorman which Pick was to have played; 1930—elected president of DACHO (German actors' union). Died in Berlin, 9 March 1931.

Films (as director): 1918—*Der Weltspiegel*; *Die Liebe des van Royk*; *Die Rothenburger*; *Die tolle Heirat von Laló*; *Mister Wu*; 1919—*Der Seelenverkäufer*; *Herr über Leben und Tod*; *Kitsch*;

Marionetten der Leidenschaft; *Mein Wille ist Gesetz*; *Tötet nicht mehr!*; *Misericordia* (+pr); 1920—*Der Dummkopf (The Idiot)* (+ro); *Niemand weiss es*; 1921—*Aus den Erinnerungen eines Frauenarztes* Part 2; *Grausige Nächte*; *Scherben (Shattered)*; 1922—*Zum Paradies der Damen*; 1923—*Sylvester (New Year's Eve)*; *Der verbotene Weg* (+ro); 1924—*La Péniche tragique*; 1925—*Das Haus der Lüge*; 1926—*Das Panzergewölbe (Armored Vault)* (+co-sc); 1928—*Eine Nacht in London (A Night in London)* (+pr); 1929—*Napoléon a Sainte-Hélène (Napoleon auf St. Helena)*; 1931—*Les Quatres Vagabonds*; *Gassenhauer*.

Roles: 1915—*Schlemihl*; *Hoffmanns Erzälungen*; *Die Pagode (Mr. Wu)*; 1916—*Nächte des Grauens* (Robison); *Homunculus* series; 1917—*Die Fremde*; 1917-18—*Es werde Licht* (3 episodes) (+sc); 1922—*Fliehende Schatten* (Lamprecht) (+co-sc); 1923—*Stadt in Sicht*; 1926—*Alte Herzen, neue Zeiten*; 1928—*Spione* (Lang).

Publications:

On PICK:

Books—*From Caligari to Hitler: A Psychological History of the German Film* by Siegfried Kracauer, Princeton, New Jersey 1947; *Le Cinéma réaliste allemand* by Raymond Borde, Freddy Bauche, François Courtade, and Marcel Tariol, Paris 1959; *The Haunted Screen: Expressionism in the German Cinema and the Influence of Max Reinhardt* by Lotte Eisner, translated by Robert Greaves, Berkeley and Los Angeles 1969; *Carl Mayer e l'espressionismo*, edition by *Bianco e Nero*, Rome 1969; *The German Cinema* by Roger Manvell and Heinrich Fraenkel, New York 1971.

* * *

Lupu Pick, a pioneer of the German *Kammerspielfilm* that led the way from expressionism to the new realism of the late twenties, came to the cinema from the Berlin stage where he worked as an actor under Piscator and Reinhardt. His first films as a director were segments of an adventure series for popular actor Bernd Aldor.

Two films that Pick created with scriptwriter Carl Mayer, *Scherben* and *Sylvester*, are the basis of his reputation. *Scherben* was the first German experiment in filmmaking without intertitles. Pick and Mayer adapted the name of Reinhardt's smallest stage—which had come to represent the intimacy and concentration of the plays staged there—in the subtitle of their first film together; *Scherben, ein deutsches Filmkammerspiel*. Critics often attribute the success of *Scherben* and *Sylvester* to Mayer. Indeed, Mayer wrote many of the films usually counted as *kammerspielfilme*, working with Murnau, Jessner and Gerlack. But, undeniably, Pick contributed his unique interpretation of Mayer's scripts.

Scherben uses a single intertitle and is distinguished by the extended use of a moving camera, especially in long tracking shots along railway ties. This movement contrasts sharply with the stationary plot, the slow movement of the actors and the long held, still shots. At times masks seem to be used in response to the expressionist punctuation Mayer used in his scripts. Diagonal slash masks isolate an image just as Mayer's one word sentences are set off by exclamation marks.

Pick was concerned to created a new, non-expressionist style, concentrating on naturalistic detail rather than on abstraction. Perhaps it was this enthusiasm for naturalism which lead Pick to linger over the process of mechanical tasks and everyday events. Yet his work remains tied to the Expressionist movement. The actors, especially his wife Edith Posca and Werner Krauss, operated within the range of theatrical Expressionist style. Shot at Pick's own Rex Studios in Berlin, *Scherben* is to a great extent manufactured in the studio, although its intent and its effect involve a realist illusion.

Unlike filmmakers truly caught up in Expressionism, Pick was concerned with portraying individual psychology. In his attempts to construct a drama without language he developed a system of irises and dissolves that is quite different from the psychological editing style then developing in Hollywood. Rather than cut to a reaction, Pick often masked the frame, isolating a single character. At other times he would compose a shot so that an object, framed in relation to a character, could represent a thought.

Perhaps it can be said that the style Pick developed had little influence on subsequent filmmaking, but nevertheless, it was a bold experiment in film narrative in its time.

Originally Pick and Mayer had planned a trilogy including *Scherben*, *Sylvester* and *Der letze Mann*, but a disagreement over the character of the doorman in the third film led to Pick's leaving the project.

The films Pick made after his collaboration with Mayer are not remembered by many. He continued to work as an actor both on stage and in films. His best known role is that of Dr. Matsumoto in Lang's *Spione*. Pick made a single sound film, *Gassenhauer*, reportedly an experiment in asynchronous sound.

—Ann Harris

POLANSKI, ROMAN. Polish. Born in Paris, 18 August 1933. Educated at Krakow Liceum Sztuk Plastycznych (art school), Cracow, Poland, 1950-53; State Film School, Lodz, 1954-59, diploma 1959. Married actress Barbara Kwiatkowska in 1959 (divorced 1961); married Sharon Tate in 1968 (died 1969). Career: 1947 through early 1950s—actor on radio and in theater; 1953—begins acting in films (often portraying a child); 1957—directs and appears in short *2 Men and a Wardrobe*; 1959—joins filmmaking group KAMERA as assistant to Andrzej Munk; 1963—*Knife in the Water* denounced by Polish Communist Party chief Gomulka, funding for subsequent films denied; moves to Paris; 1965—moves to London, completes *Repulsion*; 1968—takes home in Los Angeles; makes 1st U.S. film *Rosemary's Baby*; 1969—wife Sharon Tate and 3 friends murdered in Bel Air, California, home by members of Charles Manson cult; 1974—directs Berg opera *Lulu* at Spoleto Festival, Italy; 1976—makes *The Tenant* in France; 1977—arrested, charged with raping 13-year-old girl, serves portion of 90-day sentence; facing deportation, flees U.S. to France to avoid serving remainder of jail term. Recipient: Silver Bear, Berlin Film Festival, for *Repulsion*, 1965; Golden Bear, Berlin Film Festival, for *Cul-de-sac*, 1966; César award, French Academy, for *Tess*, 1980. Lives in Paris.

Films (as director): 1955—*Rower (The Bicycle)* (unfinished); 1957—*Rozbijemy zabawe (Break Up the Dance)* (+sc); *Morderstwo (The Crime)*; 1958—*Dwaj ludzie z szasa (2 Men and a Wardrobe)* (+sc, ro); 1959—*Lampa (The Lamp)* (+sc); *Gdy spadaja anioly (When Angels Fall)* (+sc, ro as old woman); 1961—*Le Gros et le maigre (The Fat and the Lean)* (+co-sc, ro as

Servant); 1962—*Nóż w wodzie (Knife in the Water)* (+co-sc); *Ssaki (Mammals)* (+co-sc); 1964—"La Rivière de diamants" episode of *Les Plus Belles Escroqueries du monde (The Beautiful Swindlers)* (+co-sc); 1965—*Repulsion* (+co-sc); 1966—*Cul-de-sac* (+co-sc); 1967—*The Fearless Vampire Killers or Pardon Me, But Your Teeth Are in My Neck (Dance of the Vampires)* (+co-sc, ro as *Alfred*); 1968—*Rosemary's Baby* (+sc); 1969—*A Day at the Beach* (Hesera) (pr only); 1971—*Macbeth* (+co-sc); 1972—*Weekend of a Champion* (Simon) (pr only); 1973—*What? (Che?, Diary of Forbidden Dreams)* (+co-sc, ro as *Mosquito*); 1974—*Chinatown* (+ro as *Man with Knife*); 1976—*Le Locataire (The Tenant)* (+co-sc, ro as *Trelkovsky*); 1979—*Tess* (+co-sc).

Roles: 1953—*Maly* in *Trzy opowiesci* (Nalecki, Poleska, Petelski); 1954—*Mundek* in *Pokolenie* (Wajda); 1955—*Adas* in *Zaczarowany rower* (Sternfeld); 1956—*Maly* in *Koniec wojny* (Dziedzina, Komorowski, Uszycka); 1957—in *Wraki* (Petelski); 1958—in *Zadzwoncie do mojej zony* (Mach); 1959—*Bandsman* in *Lotna* (Wajda); 1960—*Dudzio* in *Niewinni czarodzieje* (Wajda); *Romek* in *Do Widzenia Do Jutra* (Morgenstern); *Zezowate szczescie* (Munk); *Ostroznie yeti* (Csekalski); 1961—*Samson* (Wajda); 1970—*Man Listening to Lady Singer* in *The Magic Christian* (McGrath); 1972—*Interviewer* in *Weekend of a Champion* (Simon); 1974—*A Villager* in *Blood for Dracula* (Morrissey).

Publications:

By POLANSKI:

Books—*What?*, New York 1973; *3 Films*, London 1975; articles—"Entretien avec Roman Polanski" by Claude Costes in *Positif* (Paris), no.33, 1960; "A Pole Looks at Capitalistic TV", interview by Bill Greeley in *Variety* (New York), 2 October 1962; "View From a Local Vantage Point", interview by A.H. Weiler in *The New York Times*, 27 October 1962; "Interview with Roman Polanski" by Gretchen Weinberg in *Sight and Sound* (London), winter 1963/64; "Landscape of a Mind: Interview with Roman Polanski" by Michel Delahaye and Jean-André Fieschi in *Cahiers du Cinema in English* (New York), February 1966; "Entretien avec Roman Polanski" by Michel Delahaye and Jean Narboni in *Cahiers du cinéma* (Paris), January 1968; "Polanski in New York", interview by Harrison Engle in *Film Comment* (New York), fall 1968; "Entretien avec Roman Polanski" by Michel Ciment and others in *Positif* (Paris), February 1969; "Satisfaction: A Most Unpleasant Feeling", interview by Gordon Gow in *Films and Filming* (London), April 1969; "An Interview with Roman Polanski" by Joel Reisner and Bruce Kane in *Cinema* (Los Angeles), 5, no.2, 1969; "Roman Polanski" interview in *The Film Director as Superstar* by Joseph Gelmis, Garden City, New York 1970; "Playboy Interview: Roman Polanski" by Larry DuBois in *Playboy* (Chicago), December 1971; "Wajda & Polanski—Conversazione sul nuovo mondo" in *Filmcritica* (Rome), March 1972; "Andy Warhol Tapes Roman Polanski" in *Interview* (New York), November 1973; *Dialogue on Film: Roman Polanski*, American Film Institute, August 1974; "Penthouse Interview: Roman Polanski" by Richard Ballad in *Penthouse* (New York), August 1974; "The Restoration of Roman Polanski", interview by Tom Burke in *Rolling Stone* (New York), 18 July 1974; "Will Polanski Make a Star of Polanski?", interview by A. Alvarez in *The New York Times*, 22 February 1976; "Roman Polanski on Acting" by D. Brandes in *Cinema Papers* (Melbourne), January 1977; inter-

view by Serge Daney and others in *Cahiers du cinéma* (Paris), December 1979; "Perils of Polanski", interview by E. Behr in *Newsweek* (New York), 14 May 1979; "Face to Face: *Tess* Is the Film of My Mature Years", interview in *Vision* (London), no.1, 1979; "*Tess*", interview by Serge Daney and others in *Cahiers du cinéma* (Paris), December 1979; "Sur *Tess*", interview by Max Tessier in *Ecran* (Paris), 15 December 1979; interview by D. Maillet in *Cinématographe* (Paris), March/April 1981.

On POLANSKI:

Books—*The Cinema of Roman Polanski* by Ivan Butler, New York 1970; *Roman Polanski* by Pascal Kané, Paris 1970; *Roman Polanski* by Jacques Belmans, Paris 1971; *Roman Polanski: a Guide to References and Resources* by Gretchen Bisplinghoff and Virginia Wexman, Boston 1979; *The Roman Polanski Story* by Thomas Kiernan, New York 1980; *Polanski: A Biography* by Barbara Leaming, New York 1981; articles—"Nouveaux Cinéastes polonais: Roman Polanski" by Philippe Haudiquet in *Premier Plan* (Lyon), no.27, 1962; "Prélude à Polanski" by Jean-Paul Torok in *Positif* (Paris), March 1962; "Roman Polanski" by Philippe Haudiquet in *Image et son* (Paris), February/March 1964; "Polanski via Brach" by Gérard Brach in *Cinéma 65* (Paris), no.93, 1965; "Folie et autres rêves" by Jean-Louis Comolli in *Cahiers du cinéma* (Paris), January 1968; "Polanski" by Colin McArthur in *Sight and Sound* (London), winter 1968; "The Polanski Puzzle" by John McCarty in *Take One* (Montreal), May/June 1969; "Polish Imposition" by Kenneth Tynan in *Esquire* (New York), September 1971; "'If You Don't Show Violence the Way It Is,' says Roman Polanski, 'I Think That's Harmful. If You Don't Upset People Then That's Obscenity.'" by Bernard Weintraub in *The New York Times Magazine*, 12 December 1971; "Clubs" by P. Strick in *Films and Filming* (London), April 1972; "Hot Writer" by Martin Kasindorf in *Newsweek* (New York), 14 October 1974; "Le Bal des vampires", special issue of *Avant-Scène du cinéma* (Paris), January 1975; "Polanski In Guilty Plea to Sex Felony: Deportation Cloud" in *Variety* (New York), 10 August 1977; "Polanski Flees Sex Sentencing" in *Variety* (New York), 8 February 1978; "Notes on Polanski's Cinema of Cruelty" by J. Leach in *Wide Angle* (Athens, Ohio), v.2, no.1, 1978; "Sur Tess, Roman Polanski, Philippe Sarde" by Max Tessier in *Ecran* (Paris), December 1979; "*Tess*: Polanski in Hardy Country" by H. Kennedy in *American Film* (Washington, D.C.), October 1979; "Polanski to Return for Sentencing" by S.H. Anderson in *The New York Times*, 17 May 1979; "L'Univers de Roman Polanski", special section by M. Amiel and others in *Cinéma* (Paris), February 1980.

* * *

As a student at the Polish State Film School and later as a director working under government sponsorship, Roman Polanski learned to make films with few resources. Using only a few trained actors (there are but three characters in his first feature) and a hand-held camera (due to the unavailability of sophisticated equipment) Polanski managed to create several films which contributed to the international reputation of the burgeoning Polish cinema. These same limitations contributed to the development of a visual style which was well suited to the director's perspective on modern life: one which emphasized the sort of precarious, unstable world suggested by a hand-held camera, and the sense of isolation or removal from a larger society which follows the use of only small groupings of characters. In fact, Polanski's work might be seen as an attempt to map out the precise relationship between the contemporary world's instability and tendency to violence and the individual's increasing inability to overcome his isolation and locate some realm of meaning or value beyond himself.

What makes this concern with the individual and his psyche especially remarkable is Polanski's cultural background. As a product of a socialist state and its official film school at Lodz, he was expected to use his filmmaking skills to advance the appropriate social consciousness and ideology sanctioned by the government. However, Polanski's first feature, *Knife in the Water*, drew the ire of the Communist Pary and was denounced at the Party Congress in 1964 for showing the negative aspects of Polish life. Although less an ideological statement than an examination of the various ways in which individual desires and powers determine our lives, *Knife in the Water* and the response it received seem to have precipitated Polanski's subsequent development into a truly international filmmaker. In a career that has taken him to France, England, Italy, and finally the United State in search of opportunities to write, direct, and act, he has consistently shown more interest in holding up a mirror to the individual impulses, unconscious urges, and the personal psychoses of human life than in dissecting the different social and political forces he has observed.

The various landscapes and geographies of Polanski's films certainly seem designed to enhance this focus, for they pointedly remove his characters from most of the normal structures of social life as well as from other people. The boat at sea in *Knife in the Water*, the oppressive flat and adjoining convent in *Repulsion*, the isolated castle and flooded causeway of *Cul-de-sac*, the prison-like apartments of *Rosemary's Baby* and *The Tenant*, and the empty fields and deserted manor house in *Tess* form a geography of isolation that is often symbolically transformed into a geography of the mind, haunted by doubts, fears, desires, or even madness. The very titles of films like *Cul-de-sac* and *Chinatown* are especially telling in this regard, for they point to the essential strangeness and isolation of Polanski's locales, as well as to the sense of alienation and entrapment which consequently afflicts his characters. Brought to such strange and oppressive environments by the conditions of their culture (*Chinatown*), their own misunderstood urges (*Repulsion*), or some inexplicable fate (*Macbeth*), Polanski's protagonists struggle to make the unnatural seem natural, to turn entrapment into an abode, although the result is typically tragic, as in the case of *Macbeth*, or absurd, as in *Cul-de-sac*.

Such situations have prompted numerous comparisons, especially of Polanski's early films, to the absurdist dramas of Samuel Beckett. As in many of Beckett's plays, language and its inadequacy play a significant role in Polanski's works, usually forming a commentary on the absence or failure of communication in modern society. The dramatic use of silence in *Knife in the Water* actually "speaks" more eloquently than much of the film's dialogue of the tensions and desires which drive its characters and operate just beneath the personalities they try to project. In the conversational clichés and banality which mark much of the dialogue in *Cul-de-sac*, we can discern how language often serves to cloak rather than communicate meaning. The problem, as the director most clearly shows in *Chinatown*, is that language often simply proves inadequate for capturing and conveying the complex and enigmatic nature of the human situation. Detective Jake Gittes's consternation when Laura Mulraye tries to explain that the girl he has been seeking is both her daughter and her sister—the result of an incestuous affair with her father—points out this linguistic inadequacy for communicating the most discomfiting truths. It is a point driven home at the film's end when, after Mrs. Mulraye killed, Gittes is advised not to try to "say

anything." His inabililty to articulate the horrors he has witnessed ultimately translates into a symptomatic lapsing into silence by the protagonists of *The Tenant* and *Tess*, as they find themselves increasingly bewildered by the powerful driving forces of their own psyches and the worlds they inhabit.

Prompting this tendency to silence, and often cloaked by a proclivity for a banal language, is a disturbing force of violence which all of Polanski's films seek to analyze—and for which they have frequently been criticized. Certainly, his own life has brought him all too close to this most disturbing impulse, for when he was only eight years old Polanski and his parents were interned in a German concentration camp where his mother died. In 1969 his wife, Sharon Tate, and several friends were brutally murdered by Charles Manson's followers. The cataclysmic violence in the decidedly bloody adaptation of *Macbeth*, which closely followed his wife's death, can be traced through all of the director's features, as Polanski has repeatedly tried to depict the various ways in which violence erupts from the human personality, and to confront in this specter the problem of evil in the world. The basic event of *Rosemary's Baby*, Rosemary's bearing the offspring of the devil, a baby whom she fears yet, because of the natural love of a mother for her own child, nurtures, might be seen as a paradigm of Polanski's vision of evil and its operation in our world. Typically, it is the innocent or unsuspecting individual, even one with the best of intentions, who unwittingly gives birth to and spreads the very evil or violence he most fears. The protagonist of *The Fearless Vampire Killers*, for example, sets about destroying the local vampire and saving his beloved from its unnatural hold. In the process, however, he himself becomes a vampire's prey and, as a concluding voice-over solemnly intones, assists in spreading this curse throughout the world.

It is a somber conclusion for a comedy, but a telling indication of the complex tone and perspective which mark Polanski's films. He is able to assume an ironic, even highly comic attitude towards the ultimate and, as he sees it, inevitable human problem—an abiding violence and evil nurtured even as we individually struggle against these forces. The absurdist stance of Polanski's short films, especially *Two Men and a Wardrobe* and *The Fat and the Lean*, represents one logical response to this paradox. That his narratives have grown richer, more complicated, and also more discomfiting in their examination of this situation attests to Polanski's ultimate commitment to understanding the human predicament and to rendering articulate that which seems to defy articulation. From his own isolated position—as a man effectively without a country—Polanski tries to confront the problems of isolation, violence, and evil, and to speak of them for an audience prone to their sway.

—J.P. Telotte

POLLACK, SYDNEY. American. Born in South Bend, Indiana, 1 July 1934. Educated at South Bend Central High School; studied with Sanford Meisner, Neighborhood Playhouse, New York; Married Claire Griswold. children: Steven, Rebecca, and Rachel. Career: 1955-56—appears on Broadway in *A Stone for Danny Fisher* and *The Dark Is Light Enough*; appears in *Playhouse 90* TV productions; 1958-59—service in Army; 1960—moves to Los Angeles, begins TV directing with *Shotgun Slade* episode; directs 15 *Ben Casey* episodes; 1965—directs 1st film, *The Slender Thread*; 1975—begins producing his films. Recipient: Emmy Award for direction of "The Game" for Bob Hope-Chrysler Theatre. Business Manager: Michael Ovitz, Creative

Artists Agency, 1888 Century Park East, Los Angeles, CA 90067. Business: Mirage Enterprises, 4000 Warner Blvd., Burbank, CA 91522.

Films (as dialogue coach): 1961—*The Young Savages* (Frankenheimer); (as supervisor of dubbed American version): 1963—*Il gattopardo (The Leopard)* (Visconti); (as director): 1965—*The Slender Thread*; 1966—*This Property Is Condemned*; 1968—*The Swimmer* (Frank Perry) (d one sequence only); *The Scalphunters*; 1969—*Castle Keep*; *They Shoot Horses, Don't They?*; 1972—*Jeremiah Johnson*; 1973—*The Way We Were*; *Scarecrow* (Schatzberg) (pr only); 1975—*The Yakuza* (+pr); *Three Days of the Condor*; 1977—*Bobby Deerfield* (+pr); 1979—*The Electric Horseman*; 1980—*Honeysuckle Rose* (Schatzberg) (pr only); 1981—*Absence of Malice* (+pr); 1983—*Tootsie* (+pr).

Role: 1961—*War Hunt* (Sanders).

Publications:

By POLLACK:

Articles—"Entretiens avec Sydney Pollack et Robert Redford" by N. Arnoldi and Michel Ciment in *Positif* (Paris), October 1972; interview by G. Langlois in *Cinéma* (Paris), July/August 1972; interview by Max Tessier in *Ecran* (Paris), September/October 1972; interview on *Jeremiah Johnson* by C. Gili and others in *Cahiers de la Cinémathèque* (Paris), winter 1974; "Nos Plus Belles Années", interview by Max Tessier in *Ecran* (Paris), April 1974; "Sydney Pollack: The Way We Are", interview by Patricia Erens in *Film Comment* (New York), September/October 1975; interview by L. Salvato in *Millimeter* (New York), June 1975; "Les 3 Jours du condor", interview by Max Tessier in *Ecran* (Paris), December 1975; "De *Propriété interdite* à *Bobby Deerfield*" in *Positif* (Paris), December/January 1977/78; "Dialogue on Film: Sydney Pollack" in *American Film* (Washington, D.C.), April 1978; "Sydney Pollack, An Actor's Director", interview by P. Childs in *Millimeter* (New York), December 1979; interview by P. Carcassonne and J. Fieschi in *Cinématographe* (Paris), March/April 1981;

On POLLACK:

Book—*Sydney Pollack* by Jean A. Gili, Nice 1971; articles—"Pollack's Hollywood History" by Axel Madsen in *Sight and Sound* (London), summer 1973; "On achève bien les chevaux de Sydney Pollack", with interview, by J.-M. Lardinois in *Revue belge du cinéma* (Brussels), October 1977; "Dossier: Hollywood 79: Sidney Pollack" by M. Massuyeau in *Cinématographe* (Paris), March 1979; "Le Cavalier électrique", special issue of *Avant-Scène du cinéma* (Paris), 15 June 1980; "Je est un autre", special section by M. Henry in *Positif* (Paris), April 1980.

*   *   *

To date Sydney Pollack has directed 13 Hollywood features. He is especially noted for his ability to elicit fine performances from his actors and actresses and has worked with leading Hollywood stars, including Robert Redford who has appeared in five Pollack films, Jane Fonda, Barbra Streisand, Dustin Hoffman, Paul Newman and Burt Lancaster, among others.

Though Pollack has treated a cross-section of Hollywood

genres: the majority of his films divide into male-action dramas and female melodramas. Among the former are: *The Scalphunters*, *Castle Keep*, *Jeremiah Johnson*, *Three Days of the Condor*, and *The Yukuza*. Among the latter are: *The Slendor Thread*, *This Property is Condemned*, *The Way We Were*, and *Bobby Deerfield*. The remaining films are *They Shoot Horses, Don't They?*, *The Electric Horseman* and *Tootsie*.

The typical Pollack hero is a loner whose past interferes with his ability to function in the present. Throughout the course of the narrative, the hero comes to trust another individual and exchanges his isolation for a new relationship. For the most part, Pollack's heroines are intelligent women, often with careers, who possess moral strength, although in several cases they are victims of emotional weakness. Pollack is fond of portraying the attraction of opposites. The central issue in all of Pollack's work focuses on the conflict between cultural antagonists. This can be racial as in *The Slendor Thread*, *The Scalphunters* or *Jeremiah Johnson* (black vs. white; white vs. Indian), religious as in *The Way We Were* (Protestant vs. Jew), geographic as in *This Property is Condemned* and *The Electric Horseman* (city vs. town), nationalistic as in *Castle Keep* (Europe vs. America; East vs. West) or based on gender differences as in *Tootsie* (feminine vs. masculine).

Pollack's films do not possess a readily identifiable visual style. However, his works are generally noteworthy for their total visual effect, and he frequently utilizes the helicopter shot. Structurally the plots possess a circular form, often ending where they began. Visually this is echoed in the circular dance floor of *They Shot Horses, Don't They?*, but is also apparent in *Jeremiah Johnson* and *The Way We Were*.

Along with Sidney Lumet, Pollack is one of Hollywood's foremost liberals. His work highlights social and political issues, exposing organized exploitation rather than individual villainy. Most prominent among the issues treated are: racial discrimination (*The Scalphunters*), the destructiveness of war (*Castle Keep*), the Depression (*They Shoot Horses, Don't They*), Hollywood blacklisting (*The Way We Were*), CIA activities (*Three Days of the Condor*), commercial exploitation (*The Electric Horseman*), media exploitation (*Absence of Malice*) and feminism (*Tootsie*). Although Pollack has often been attacked for using these themes as background, rather than delving deeply into their subtlties, the French critics hold his work in high esteem.

—Patricia Erens

POLONSKY, ABRAHAM. American. Born in New York City, 5 December 1910. Educated at City College of New York; Columbia University, law degree. Career: 1930s—works as lawyer with Manhattan firm; giving technical advice to radio personality Gertrude Berg ("The Goldbergs") leads to writing for radio; gives up law practice; writes several novels, signs with Paramount as screenwriter before war; during WW II—serves in Europe with O.S.S. (Office of Strategic Services); 1946—writes script for Leisen's *Golden Earrings*; script completely rewritten by others, though retains credit; leaves Paramount; 1947—moves to Enterprise Productions, writes *Body and Soul* (Rossen); encouraged to direct *Force of Evil* by producer Bob Robertson and star John Garfield; following *Force of Evil* spends year in France working on novel, returns to Hollywood in 1950; 1950—signs for next picture with 20th Century-Fox; 1951—called to testify before House Un-American Activities Committee, invokes

5th Amendment; blacklisted through 1968 when writes police drama *Madigan*; 1970—directs 2nd film *Tell Them Willie Boy Is Here*; continues to write novels including *A Season of Fear* and *Zenia's Way* (1980). Agent: Phil Gersh Agency, Beverly Hills, California.

Films (as scriptwriter): 1947—*Golden Earrings* (Leisen); *Body and Soul* (Rossen); (as director and scriptwriter): 1948—*Force of Evil*; 1951—*I Can Get It for You Wholesale* (Gordon) (sc only); 1968—*Madigan* (Siegel) (sc only); 1970—*Tell Them Willie Boy Is Here*; 1971—*Romance of a Horsethief*.

Publications:

By POLONSKY:

Book—*Zenia's Way*, novel, 1980; articles—"Abraham Polonsky and *Force of Evil*", interview by William Pechter in *Film Quarterly* (Berkeley), spring 1962; interview in *Interviews with Film Directors* by Andrew Sarris, New York 1967; "Parts of Some Time Spent with Abraham Polonsky" by William Pechter in *Film Quarterly* (Berkeley), winter 1968/69; interview in *The Director's Event* by Eric Sherman and Martin Rubin, New York 1970; "How the Blacklist Worked in Hollywood" in *Film Culture* (New York), fall/winter 1970; interview by Jim Cook and Kingsley Canham in *Screen* (London), summer 1970; interview in *The Image Maker* edited by Ron Henderson, Richmond, Virginia 1971; "Making Movies" in *Sight and Sound* (London), spring 1971; "An Interview with Abraham Polonsky" in *Film Society Review* (New York), April 1971; "Nuits blanches pendant la liste noire: Extrait de journal" in *Positif* (Paris), December/January 1977/78.

On POLONSKY:

Article—"Polonsky" by Kingsley Canham in *Film* (London), spring 1970.

*   *   *

Abraham Lincoln Polonsky's filmography is quite thin: his second film as director, *Tell Them Willie Boy Is Here*, was released 21 years after his first, *Force of Evil*. "I was a left-winger," he told *Look* magazine in 1970. "I supported the Soviet Union. In the middle 1940s, we'd have meetings at my house to raise money for strikers and radical newspapers." For these crimes—and, equally, for the less than superficially patriotic qualities of his protagonists—a promising, perhaps even major, directorial career was squelched in its infancy by the insidious Hollywood blacklist.

A discussion of Polonsky would be incomplete without noting his collaborations with John Garfield, the American cinema's original anti-hero. Polonsky scripted *Body and Soul*, one of the best boxing films of all time, and both authored and directed *Force of Evil*, a "B film" ignored in its time, but now a cult classic highly regarded for its use of blank verse dialogue.

Garfield stars in *Force of Evil* as a lawyer immersed in the numbers racket. When his brother, a small-time gambler, is murdered by his gangster boss, he hunts the hood down and turns himself in to the police. In *Body and Soul*, the actor portrays a poor boy with a hard, knockout punch who rises in the fight game while alienating his family, friends, and the girl he

loves. In the end he reforms, defying the mob by refusing to throw a fight. "What are you gonna do, kill me?" he chides the chief thug. "Everybody dies." With that, he walks off into the night with his girl. The final cut of *Body and Soul* is as much Polansky's as it is director Robert Rossen's. Polonsky claimed to have prevented Rossen from altering the film's finale.

Both of Polonsky's protagonists become casualties of their desire for success. They seek out the all-American dream, but are corrupted in the process. They can only attain status by throwing fights, aligning themselves with lawbreakers. Fame and money, fancy hotels and snazzy suits, come not by hard work and honesty but by cheating, throwing the fight, fixing the books—the real American way.

Polonsky, and Garfield, were blacklisted as much for the tone of their films as their politics. Polonsky's heroes are cocky, cynical loner-losers, estranged from society's mainstream, who break the rules and cause others extreme sorrow—not the moral, honest, often comic book caricatures of American manhood that dominated Hollywood cinema. In addition, Polonsky created a character in *Body and Soul*, a washed-up boxer (lovingly played by Canada Lee) who was one of the earliest portraits of a black man as a human being with emotions and feelings, a man exploited. *Body and Soul* and *Force of Evil* played the nation's moviehouses in 1947 and 1948, when anything less than a positive vision of America was automatically suspect.

Polonsky's plight is particularly sad. His passport was revoked, and he could not escape to find work abroad. Years after others who had been blacklisted, had returned to the good graces of the cinema establishment, he toiled in obscurity writing television shows and perhaps dozens of film scripts—some Academy Award winners—under assumed names. His first post-blacklist directorial credit, *Willie Boy*, is a spiritual cousin of his earlier work. It is the tale of a nonconformist Paiute Indian (Robert Blake, who played Garfield as a child in *Humoresque*), victimized by an insensitive society after he kills in self-defense. The parallels between Polonsky and his character's fate are ever so clear.

Before the blacklist, Polonsky had hoped to film Thomas Mann's novella, *Mario and the Magician*; in 1971, he was again planning this project, among others. None were ever completed. But most significantly, the films that he might have made between 1948 and 1969—the prime years of his creative life—can now only be imagined.

—Rob Edelman

PONTECORVO, GILLO. Italian. Born Gilberto Pontecorvo in Pisa, 19 November 1919. Educated in chemistry, University of Pisa. Career: 1940s—journalist; fights during war as partisan in Milan, commands 3rd Brigade; 1946—after war joins Italian Communist Party, serves as Youth Secretary; plays role of partisan in Vergano's *Il sole sorge ancora*; late 1940s—Paris correspondent for Italian journals,; 1951—begins working on films as assistant to Yves Allegret on *Les Miracles n'ont lieu qu'une fois*; 1953-55—makes 10 shorts; 1956—leaves Communist Party following Soviet invasion of Hungary; 1970s—plans film *Time of the World's End* about life of Christ. Recipient: Golden Lion, Venice Festival, for *The Battle of Algiers*, 1966.

Films (as director): 1955—"Giovanna" episode of *Die Windrose*; 1957—*La grande strada azzurra* (*La lunga strada azzurra*, *The Long Blue Road*) (+co-sc); 1960—*Kapò* (+co-sc); 1966—*La bat-*

taglia di Algeri (The Battle of Algiers) (+co-sc, co-music); 1969—
Queimada (Burn!); 1979—*Ogro (Operation Ogre, Operacion
Ogro)*.

Roles: 1946—partisan in *Il sole sorge ancora* (Vergano).

Publications:

By PONTECORVO:

Articles—"Une si jeune paix", interview by Guy Hennebelle, in
Cinéma 65 (Paris), December 1965; "*The Battle of Algiers*: An
Adventure in Filmmaking" in *American Cinematographer* (Los
Angeles), April 1967; "An Interview with Gillo Pontecorvo" by
Joan Mellen in *Film Quarterly* (Berkeley), fall 1972; "Using the
Contradictions of the System", interview by H. Kalishman in
Cineaste (New York), v.6, no.2, 1974; "Political Terrorism in
Ogro", interview by C. Lucas in *Cineaste* (New York), fall 1980.

On PONTECORVO:

Book—*Filmguide to The Battle of Algiers* by Joan Mellen,
Bloomington, Indiana 1973; articles—"Le Cinéma algérien et *La
Bataille d'Alger*" by Pierre Porin in *Positif* (Paris), October 1966;
"Politics and Pontecorvo" by David Wilson in *Sight and Sound*
(London), fall 1970.

*　　*　　*

Gillo Pontecorvo is concerned with the oppressed, those kept
down by the unjust and cruel use of power—and who will eventually rebel against the oppressor. "I've always wanted to look at
man during the hardest moments of his life," the filmmaker has
stated. An examination of his filmography indicates that he has
been true to his goals and ideals.

Kapo, for example, is the story of a young Jewish girl and her
attempt to survive in a Nazi concentration camp. But Pontecorvo's masterpiece is *The Battle of Algiers*, a meticulous recreation
of the historical events surrounding the successful rebellion
against the French by Algeria between 1954 and 1962. Shot in
authentic locales with both actors and non-professionals in a
cinema-verité style, Pontecorvo's black-and-white images seem
like newsreels rather than staged sequences; the viewer can easily
forget that the film is not a documentary. Additionally, the
villains (chiefly, the French Colonel Mathieu, played by Jean
Martin) are not sadistic, one-dimensional imperialists, thugs and
goons who abuse the rights of those they have colonized. While
Mathieu is far from benevolent, he is believable and sympathetic,
as much the victim of an exploitive society as the Algerians; the
colonel even admits that the Algerians are destined to win—this
is a lesson of history—and his job is just to temporarily put off
the inevitable.

The same is true for the most visible tyrant in *Burn!*, Sir
William Walker (Marlon Brando), a confused, self-destructive
British adventurer who betrays the slaves that revolt on a
Portuguese-controlled, sugar-producing Caribbean island in the
mid-nineteenth century. Both Walker and Mathieu are depicted
as human beings—with misguided values, perhaps, but human
beings nonetheless. However, while *The Battle of Algiers* is a
near-flawless film, the scenario of *Burn!* is muddled in that
Walker's motives are never really clear. Both films are potent
politically in that the imperialists are not caricatured, yet at the

same time it is clear that Pontecorvo sides with the Algerians and
the slaves. At the beginning of *The Battle of Algiers*, for example,
a tortured Algerian is held up by French paratroopers. Despite
all that follows, this sequence is in an of itself a political statement, one that sets the tone for all that follows.

Pontecorvo is a Marxist: in 1941, at the age of 22, he became a
member of the Italian Communist Party. His initial film, the
"Giovanna" episode from *Die Windrose*, is a women's rights
movie shot in East Germany. And, in *The Battle of Algiers*,
which deals specifically with partisans of the Algerian National
Liberation Front who, via their actions, increase the political
awareness of their fellow citizens, Pontecorvo illustrates how a
group of individuals can unite into a political force and defeat a
common enemy. This is achieved by violent means: if freedom is
to be earned, suffering and physical force and even the deaths of
innocent people may be necessary.

Thematically, *The Battle of Algiers* is the successor to Eisenstein's *Battleship Potemkin* and the other Russian revolutionary
films, as well as a predecessor of Costa-Gavras's features, beginning with *Z*. Gillo Pontecorvo is a filmmaker whose art is
unscrupuliously true to his politics.

—Rob Edelman

———

PORTER, EDWIN S. American. Born Edwin Stratton Porter
in Connellsville, Pennsylvania, 21 April 1869. Career: quits
school at 14, takes various jobs including sign painter, theater
cashier, stagehand; 1893-96—serves in Navy, assists in development of gunnery range finder; 1896—working for Raff & Gam-
mon, marketers of Edison Vitascope, helps arrange first New
York screening of motion pictures (April 23, 1896); 1896-97—
works briefly for Edison, attempting to sell primitive projector;
1898-1900—invents and manufactures improved projector, business ruined by fire; 1899—begins making brief film clips of news
events; 1900—rejoins Edison Company; begins by designing and
building cameras; then becomes director and cameraman, and
soon supervises Edison production at New York City studio;
1903—makes *The Life of an American Fireman*, first known
example of intercutting in an American film and *The Great
Train Robbery*, most successful of early American films (until
The Birth of a Nation); 1909—quits Edison, founds Defender
Pictures; 1910—organizes Rex Film Company; 1912—sells
interest in Rex, with Adolph Zukor creates "Famous Players in
Famous Plays" company, becoming director general and treasurer, supervising production, and directing; 1915—sells share in
Famous Players; invests in Precision Machine Corp., manufacturer of Simplex projector, which he had helped develop, and
becomes president of firm. Died 30 April 1941.

Films (as director—also frequently scriptwriter, cinemato-
grapher, and editor—partial list): 1899—*The America's Cup
Race*; 1900—*Why Mrs. Jones Got a Divorce*; *Animated Lun-
cheon*; *An Artist's Dream*; *The Mystic Swing*; *Ching Lin Foo
Outdone*; *Faust and Marguerite*; *The Clown and the Alchemist*;
A Wringing Good Joke; *The Enchanted Drawing*; 1901—
Terrible Teddy the Grizzly King; *Love in a Hammock*; *A Day at
the Circus*; *What Demoralized the Barber Shop*; *The Finish of
Bridget McKeen*; *Happy Hooligan Surprised*; *Martyred Presi-
dents*; *Love by the Light of the Moon*; *Circular Panorama of the
Electric Tower*; *Panorama of the Esplanade by Night*; *The Mys-
terious Café*; 1902—*Uncle Josh at the Moving Picture Show*;
Charleston Chain Gang; *Burlesque Suicide*; *Rock of Ages*; *Jack*

and the Beanstalk; Happy Hooligan Turns Burglar; Capture of the Biddle Brothers; Fun in a Bakery Shop; 1903—The Life of an American Fireman; The Still Alarm; Arabian Jewish Dance; Razzle Dazzle; Seashore Frolics; Scenes in an Orphans' Asylum; The Gay Shoe Clerk; The Baby Review; The Animated Poster; The Office Boy's Revenge; Uncle Tom's Cabin; The Great Train Robbery; The Messenger Boy's Mistake; Casey and His Neighbor's Goat; 1904—The Ex-Convict; Cohen's Advertising Scheme; European Rest Cure; Parsifal; Casey's Frightful Dream; The Cop Fools the Sergeant; Elephant Shooting the Chutes at Luna Park; European Rest Cure; Capture of Yegg Bank Burglars; City Hall to Harlem in 15 Seconds via the Subway Route; 1905—The Kleptomaniac; Stolen by Gypsies; How Jones Lost His Roll; The Little Train Robbery; The White Caps; Seven Ages; The Life of an American Policeman; 1906—The Dream of a Rarebit Fiend; The Life of a Cowboy; 3 American Beauties; Kathleen Mavourneen; 1907—Daniel Boone; Lost in the Alps; The Midnight Ride of Paul Revere; Laughing Gas; Rescued from an Eagle's Nest; The Teddy Bears; 1908—Nero and the Burning of Rome; The Painter's Revenge; The Merry Widow Waltz Craze; The Gentleman Burglar; Honesty Is the Best Policy; Love Will Find a Way; Skinny's Finish; The Face on the Barroom Floor; The Boston Tea Party; Romance of a War Nurse; A Voice from the Dead; Saved by Love; She; Lord Feathertop; The Angel Child; Miss Sherlock Holmes; An Unexpected Santa Claus; 1909—The Adventures of an Old Flirt; A Midnight Supper; Love Is Blind; A Cry from the Wilderness; Hard to Beat; On the Western Frontier; Fuss and Feathers; Pony Express; Toys of Fate; The Iconoclast; Hansel and Gretel; The Strike; Capital versus Labor; 1910—All on Account of a Laundry Mark; Russia—the Land of Oppression; Too Many Girls; Almost a Hero; The Toymaker on the Brink and the Devil; 1911—By the Light of the Moon; On the Brink; The White Red Man; Sherlock Holmes Jr.; Lost Illusions; 1912—A Sane Asylum; Eyes That See Not; The Final Pardon; Taming Mrs. Shrew; 1913—The Prisoner of Zenda (co-d); His Neighbor's Wife; The Count of Monte Cristo (co-d); In the Bishop's Carriage (co-d); A Good Little Devil (co-d); 1914—Hearts Adrift; Tess of the Storm Country; Such a Little Queen (co-d); 1915—The Eternal City (co-d); Zaza (co-d); Sold (co-d); The Prince and the Pauper (co-d); Bella Donna (co-d); 1916—Lydia Gilmore (co-d).

Publications:

By PORTER:

Article—statement in Filmmakers on Filmmaking edited by Harry Geduld, Bloomington, Indiana 1967.

On PORTER:

Books—One Reel a Week by Fred Balshofer and Arthur Miller, Berkeley 1967; Spellbound in Darkness by George Pratt, Greenwich, Conn. 1973; articles—"English Influences on the Work of Edwin S. Porter" by Georges Sadoul in Hollywood Quarterly, fall 1947; "Edwin S. Porter" by Jack Spears in Films in Review (New York), June/July 1970; "Porter, or Ambivalence" by Noel Burch in Screen (London), winter 1978/79; "Detours in Film Narrative: The Development of Cross-Cutting" by A. Gaudreault and "Early Cinema of Edwin Porter" by C. Musser in Cinema Journal (Evanston), fall 1979; letter from Budd Schulberg in Variety (New York), 9 May 1979.

*   *   *

In the annals of film history, Edwin S. Porter is often credited as the first American film director. Although this may not be true in the literal sense, it is not unjustified to give Porter this title. Porter was first and foremost an engineer, an inventor, and a cameraman. In the early days of filmmaking, "cameraman" was synonymous with "director," and Porter found himself handling both jobs. He was also his own editor and discovered new ways of creating a narrative. While most early motion pictures were composed of a single shot showing only one continuous action from beginning to end, Porter began to combine and juxtapose his filmed images, creating new meanings as one scene "psychologically" led into another. Porter became one of the first American directors to tell a story in his films.

Porter acknowledged an influence in his filmmaking from Georges Méliès, the French filmmaker whose "trick films" were extremely popular in the United States. Being a designer of motion picture cameras, Porter was able to study and discover the secrets to many of Méliès's "tricks." Most importantly, Porter was struck by the fact that these films told a story. However, while Méliès's films told a straightforward, linear narrative, Porter expanded this idea with the use of cross-narrative (parrallel action) to depict two simultaneous events or points of view.

Porter's first film of major importance was The Life of an American Fireman, made in 1902 or early 1903. This film was largely composed of stock shots from earlier Edison Company films. Racing fire engines were a popular subject for early filmmakers and Porter had much footage at his disposal. To compliment these stock shots, Porter filmed additional footage, showing a mother and child trapped in a burning building. By editing these scenes together Porter created the story of the mother and child's rescue by the firefighters. Porter intercut the scenes of mother and child between stock footage of the racing fire engines, thereby creating a dramatic tension—will the firefighters rescue the two victims from the burning building in time? While this technique of storytelling may seem blasé by today's standards, it was innovative and exciting to 1903 audiences. The film was trendsetting in its style.

Porter continued to develop his film editing techniques in his best known and most popular film, The Great Train Robbery. On its most simplistic level, the film is a story of crime, pursuit, and capture. But it is perhaps the first great American chase film, a form still popular today. Again Porter edited his film using cross-cutting to show events that were supposedly occurring at the same time: the bandits begin their escape while the posse organizes a pursuit. The Great Train Robbery was an enormously popular film at a time when nickelodeons were just opening across the country and the film did a great deal of repeat business.

Surprisingly, after The Great Train Robbery, Porter did little else to advance the art of filmmaking. In 1912, he formed the Famous Players Film Co. with Adolf Zukor and David Frohman, acting as director-general of the company. However, his films of this period (such as The Count of Monte Cristo and The Prisoner of Zenda) contained none of the energy of his earlier films. In fact, they took several steps backward technically, being photographed in a very stagey, single point-of-view manner. Apparently, Porter was never really interested in directing films. He soon sold his shares in Famous Players and became more involved in designing motion picture cameras and projectors, including the Simplex. However, Porter's one important contribution to filmmaking—a freer style of editing—was a turning point in the development of film as a narrative art form.

—Linda J. Obalil

POWELL, MICHAEL AND PRESSBURGER, EMERIC.
British. Powell: born at Bekesbourne, near Canterbury, 30 September 1905; Pressburger: born in Miskolc, Hungary, 5 December 1902. Pressburger studied at the universities of Prague and Stuttgart. Career: 1922-31—Powell: works in various capacities (writing scenarios, as cinematographer, etc.) on films of Rex Ingram, Léonce Perret, Alfred Hitchcock, Lupu Pick; Pressburger works as journalist, then screenwriter on German and Austrian films; 1939—Powell, as director, begins collaboration with Pressburger as writer on *The Spy in Black* (final film together is *Intelligence Service*, 1956); 1943—Powell and Pressburger form producing, directing and writing team "The Archers", credited for most of their subsequent films together.

Films ("quota quickies" directed by Powell): 1931—*2 Crowded Hours*; *My Friend the King*; *Rynox*; *The Rasp*; 1932—*The Star Reporter*; *Hotel Splendide*; *C.O.D.*; *His Lordship*; *Born Lucky*; 1933—*The Fire Raisers* (+co-sc); 1934—*Red Ensign* (+co-sc); *The Night of the Party*; *Something Always Happens*; *The Girl in the Crowd*; 1935—*Lazybones*; *The Love Test*; *The Phantom Light*; *The Price of a Song*; *Someday*; 1936—*The Man Behind the Mask*; *Crown Versus Stevens*; *Her Last Affair*; *The Brown Wallet*; (as director of major feature films): 1937—*The Edge of the World* (+sc); 1939—*The Spy in Black (U-Boat)* (sc by Pressburger); *The Lion Has Wings* (co-d); 1940—*Contraband (Blackout)* (sc by Pressburger); *The Thief of Bagdad* (co-d); 1941—*49th Parallel (The Invaders)* (sc by Pressburger); 1942—*One of Our Aircraft Is Missing* (sc by Pressburger); (produced, directed and scripted by "The Archers"): 1943—*The Life and Death of Colonel Blimp*; *The Volunteer*; 1944—*A Canterbury Tale*; 1945—*I Know Where I'm Going*; 1946—*A Matter of Life and Death (Stairway to Heaven)*; 1947—*Black Narcissus*; 1948—*The Red Shoes*; 1949—*The Small Back Room (Hour of Glory)*; 1950—*Gone to Earth (The Wild Heart)*; *The Elusive Pimpernel (The Fighting Pimpernel)*; 1951—*The Tales of Hoffman*; 1955—*Oh! Rosalinda (Fledermaus '55)*; 1956—*The Battle of the River Plate (Pursuit of the Graf Spee)*; *Ill Met By Moonlight (Intelligence Service, Night Ambush)*; (films by Powell as producer and director): *Luna de miel (Honeymoon)*; 1960—*Peeping Tom*; 1961—*Queen's Guards*; 1964—*Bluebeard's Castle* (d only); 1966—*They're a Weird Mob*; 1968—*Sebastian* (co-pr only); 1969—*Age of Consent*; 1972—*The Boy Who Turned Yellow* (sc by Pressburger); 1974—*Trikimia (The Tempest)* (+sc); 1978—*Return of the Edge of the World*.

Publications:

By POWELL:

Articles—"Michael Powell: The Expense of Naturalism", interview by R. Collins and I. Christie in *Monogram* (London), no.3, 1972; interview by R. Lefevre and R. Lacourbe in *Cinéma* (Paris), December 1976; "Powell and Pressburger: The War Years", interview by D.J. Badder in *Sight and Sound* (London), no.1, 1979; "Redecouvrir Michael Powell", interview by R. Lacourbe in *Ecran* (Paris), 15 February 1979; Powell interview by P. Carcassonne and J. Fieschi in *Cinématographe* (Paris), May 1981; "Michael Powell's Guilty Pleasures" in *Film Comment* (New York), July/August 1981; "Retrospective" in *Positif* (Paris), April 1981; Powell interview by T. Williams in *Films and Filming* (London), November 1981.

On POWELL AND PRESSBURGER:

Book—*Powell, Pressburger, and Others*, edited by I. Christie, London 1978; articles—"Michael Powell" by O.O. Green in *Movie* (London), autumn 1965; "Private Madness and Public Lunacy" by Kevin Gough-Yates in *Films and Filming* (London), February 1972; "A Meeting of 2 Great Visual Stylists" by William K. Everson in *Films in Review* (New York), November 1977; "Michael Powell—Myths and Supermen" by J.R. Taylor in *Sight and Sound* (London), autumn 1978; "Peerless Powell" by N. Andrews and H. Kennedy in *Film Comment* (New York), May/June 1979; "Question de vie ou de mort", special issue of *Avant-Scène du cinéma* (Paris), 15 December 1980; "The Films of Michael Powell: A Romantic Sensibility" by D. Thompson in *American Film* (Washington, D.C.), November 1980; "Michael Powell" by William K. Everson in *Films in Review* (New York), August/September 1980; "Mark of the Red Death" by D. Thompson in *Sight and Sound* (London), autumn 1980; "Michael Powell: un orfèvre de l'objectif" by Raphaël Bassan in *Image et son* (Paris), May 1981; "Journals: Gilbert Adair from London" in *Film Comment* (New York), January/February 1981; "Aiming at the Archers" by Raymond Durgnat in *Positif* (Paris), February 1981; "Bio-biblio-filmographie de Michael Powell" in 2 parts by P. Gonzalez and C. Guiguet in *Positif* (Paris), March and April 1981; "Cinema of Enchantment: The Films of Michael Powell" by D. McVay in *Films and Filming* (London), December 1981; "Post-scriptum: le point du jour et les horizons perdus" by Y. Tobin in *Positif* (Paris), April 1981.

*   *   *

Between the years 1942 and 1957, English director Michael Powell and his Hungarian partner, Emeric Pressburger, formed one of the most remarkable, if relatively unheralded, partnerships in contemporary cinema. Under the collaborative pseudonym of the "The Archers," the two created a series of highly visual and imaginative treatments of romantic and supernatural themes that have defied easy categorization by contemporary film historians. Although both were listed jointly as director, screenwriter and frequently as producer, the extent of each one's participation on any given film is difficult to measure, it is probably most accurate to credit Powell with the actual visualization of the films, while Pressburger functioned primarily as a writer. The latter, in fact, had no background as a director before joining Powell and had drifted through the Austrian German and French film industries as a screenwritier before coming to England in 1936.

Many of the gothic, highly expressionistic characteristics of the films produced by the partnerhip seem to trace their origins to Powell's apprenticeship at Rex Ingram's studio in Nice in the 1920s. There he performed various roles on at least three of the visionary director's silent productions, *Mare Nostrum* (1926), *The Magician* (1926) and *The Garden of Allah* (1927). Working on these films and subsequently on his own features in the 1930s, Powell developed a penchant for expressionism that manifested itself in several rather unique ways. The most fundamental of these was in his use of the fantasy genre, as illustrated by *A Matter of Life and Death* with its problematic juxtaposition of psychiatry and mysticism. Another was in an almost philosophical sadism which permeated his later films, such as *Peeping Tom*, with a camera that impales its photographic subjects on bayonet-like legs. The mechanical camera, itself, in fact represents still another Powell motif, the use of machines and technology to create or heighten certain aspects of fantasy. For example, the camera obscura in *A Matter of Life and Death* and the German warship in the *Pursuit of the Graf Spee* (which is revealed through a slow camera scan along its eerie structure causing it to turn into a metalic killer fish) effectively tie machines into each film's set of symbolic motifs. In doing so, a technological mythology is created in which these objects take on near demonic proportions.

Finally, the use of color, which most critics cite as a trademark of the Powell-Pressburger partnership, is shaped into an expressionistic mode. Powell chooses his hues from a broad visual palette, and brushes them onto the screen with a calculated extravagance that becomes integrated into the themes of the film as a whole. In the better films, the visual and technological aspects complement each other in a pattern of symbolism. The mechanical staircase wich descends from the celestial vortex in *A Matter of Life and Death*, for example, blends technology and fantasy as no other image can. Similarly, when the camera replaces the young pilot's eye in the same film and the pink and violet lining of an eyelid descends over it, the effect is extravagant, even a bit bizarre, but it effectively serves notice that the viewer is closing his eyes to external reality and entering another world which, whether supernatural or psychological, is up to the audience to decide.

This world has been most palatable in popular Powell-Pressburger fantasies like *The Red Shoes*, a ballet film used as an allegory for the artist's unremitting dedication to his art; or *The Tales of Hoffman* in which the moody eccentricities of style have been kept in bounds by the built-in circumscriptions of the fantasy genre. However, at least one critic has noted a strange morbidity in *The Red Shoes* derived from the directors' use of certain pecularities of color, a criticism that has been magnified when some of Powell's and Pressburger's fantastic techniques occur in more realistic films. Their appearance usually upsets normal audience expectations when occurring in otherwise veracious contexts. *Black Narcissus* and Powell's *Peeping Tom* both had some problems with the critics for going to extremes in the exaggeration of otherwise plausible storylines.

Thematically, Powell and Pressburger operate in a limbo somewhere between romance and realism. The former, characterized by technical effects, camera angles and movements, and the innovative use of color, often intrudes in the merest of details in fundamentally naturalistic films. In the eyes of some, this weakens the artistic committment to realism. On the other hand, the psychological insights embodied in serious fantasies like *A Matter of Life and Death* are too often dismissed as simply entertainment. Most of the Powell-Pressburger efforts are, in fact, attempts at fundamental reconciliations between modern ideas and the irrational; between science and savagery; and religion and eroticism. This dichotomy usually occurs in one character's mind, as in Peter Carter's in *A Matter of Life and Death*, or in that of the sex-obsessed nun in *Black Narcissus*, and hinges upon a second character, as in *A Matter*'s Dr. Frank Reeves, who effects a degree of movement between the two sides of the dichotomy, particularly through his own death.

Although such mergings of reality and fantasy have met with approval by the moviegoing public, Powell and Pressburger have been less successful with the English film establishment. In a sense they are alienated from it through their exercise of a decidedly non-British flamboyance that does not conform to the manner in which the critics would like to perceive their artists. To some degree, the Clive Candy character in *The Life and Death of Colonel Blimp* embodies the English film community during the period after the war. Powell and Pressburger's visual and thematic extravagances of style conflicted with the self-consciousness of the English film industry's strivings for a rigid postwar realism not to be embellished by colorful and expressionistic ventures.

The team broke up in 1957 after *Ill Met by Moonlight*, and although Pressburger made some films by himself they were not well received. Powell, though, continued in the vein established by his collaboration with the Hungarian director. *Luna de Miel* and *The Queen's Guards* pursue all of the philosophical concerns of his earlier efforts while *Peeping Tom*, which is now regarded as his masterpiece, indicates a certain morbid refinement of his thematic interests. Unfortunately, it is perhaps still ahead of its time—a problem that has plagued the director and his collaborator for most of their careers.

—Stephen L. Hanson

PREMINGER, OTTO. American. Born in Vienna, 5 December 1905; became citizen of of the United States in 1943. Educated at University of Vienna, LL.D. 1926; studied acting in Max Reinhardt theater school. Married Marion Deutsch (stage name Marion Mill) in 1932 (divorced); married Mary Gardner in 1951 (divorced 1959); married Hope (Preminger) in 1960; children: Erik (by Gypsy Rose Lee), Victoria and Mark. Career: 1924—becomes actor with Max Reinhardt company; 1928—joins Theater in der Josefstadt; 1933—succeeds Max Reinhardt as director of Theater in der Josefstadt, Vienna; 1935—invited to Hollywood by Joseph Schenck; directs *Libel!* on Broadway; 1937—contract with Fox broken, moves to New York; 1938-41—directs plays in New York, beginning with *Outward Bound*; 1942—returns to Hollywood as actor; 1945—given 7 year contract with Fox following success of *Laura*; early 1950s—becomes independent producer; 1951—directs several Broadway productions; 1953—*The Moon is Blue* released without Production Code Seal of Approval; 1953—stages opera *The Trial* (Von Einem) in New York; 1973—directs *Full Circle* on Broadway. Address: office—Sigma Productions Inc., 129 East 64th Street, New York, NY 10021.

Films (as director): 1931—*Die grosse Liebe*; 1936—*Under Your Spell*; 1937—*Danger, Love at Work*; 1943—*Margin for Error* (+ro as Nazi consul Rudolf Forster); (as producer and director): 1944—*In the Meantime, Darling*; 1944 *Laura*; 1945—*Royal Scandal* (d only); *Fallen Angel*; 1946—*Centennial Summer*; 1947—*Forever Amber* (d only); *Daisy Kenyon*; 1948—*That Lady in Ermine* (d only); 1949—*The Fan (Lady Windermere's Fan)*; *Whirlpool*; 1950—*Where the Sidewalk Ends*; *The Thirteenth Letter*; 1952—*Angel Face* (d only); 1953—*The Moon is Blue* (co-pr); 1954—*River of No Return* (d only); *Carmen Jones*; 1955—*The Man with the Golden Arm*; *The Court Martial of Billy Mitchell (One Man Mutiny)* (d only); 1957—*Saint Joan*; *Bonjour Tristesse*; 1959—*Porgy and Bess* (d only); *Anatomy of a Murder*; 1960—*Exodus*; 1962—*Advise and Consent*; 1963—*The Cardinal*; 1964—*In Harm's Way*; 1965—*Bunny Lake is Missing*; 1966—*Hurry Sundown*; 1968—*Skidoo*; 1970—*Tell Me That You Love Me, Junie Moon*; 1971—*Such Good Friends*; 1975—*Rosebud*; 1980—*The Human Factor*.

Roles: 1942—*The Pied Piper*; *They Got Me Covered*; 1945—*Where Do We Go from Here*; 1953—camp commandant in *Stalag 17*.

Publications:

By PREMINGER:

Book—*Preminger: An Autobiography*, Garden City, New York 1977; articles—"Rencontre avec Otto Preminger" by Jacques Rivette in *Cahiers du cinéma* (Paris), December 1953; "Movie Critic Versus Movie Director", with Bosley Crowther, in *Esquire* (New York), October 1958; "Your Taste, My Taste ...and the Censors" in *Films and Filming* (London), November 1959; "Entretien avec Otto Preminger" by Gilbert Guez in *Ciné-monde* (Paris), 30 May 1961; "Sex and Censorship in Literature and the Arts", with Norman Mailer and others, in *Playboy* (Chicago), July 1961; "Entretien avec Otto Preminger" by Jacques Doniol-Valcroze and Eric Rohmer in *Cahiers du cinéma* (Paris), July 1961; "Interview express avec O.P." by Pierre Bretigny in *Image et son* (Paris), November 1962; "*The Cardinal* and I" in *Films and Filming* (London), November 1963; "A No-Holds Barred Interview with O.P." by Morris Renek in *Cavalier* (New York), February 1964; "Keeping Out of Harm's Way: Interview with O.P." in *Films and Filming* (London), June 1965; "Conversation Between Noel Coward and O.P." in *King* (London), July 1965; "An Interview with Otto Preminger" by Ian Cameron and others in *Movie* (London), summer 1965; in *Interviews with Film Directors* edited by Andrew Sarris, New York 1967; "Otto Preminger auteur de force", interview by D. Lyons in *Interview* (New York), July 1972; interview by L. Amos in *Lumiere* (Melbourne), March 1974; interview by D. Rabourdin in *Cinéma* (Paris), May 1975; "Cult and Controversy", interview by Gordon Gow in *Films and Filming* (London), November 1979; interview by Gene Phillips in *Focus on Film* (London), August 1979.

On PREMINGER:

Books—*All I Want is Everything* by Marion Mill Preminger, New York 1957; *Otto Preminger* by Jacques Lourcelles, Paris 1965; *The Cinema of Otto Preminger* by Gerald Pratley, New York 1971; *Behind the Scenes of Otto Preminger* by Willi Frischauer, London 1973; articles—"Otto Preminger" by Richard Gehman in *Theater Arts* (New York), January 1961; "Co-existence with the Ottocrat of the Silver Screen" by Burt Glinn in *Esquire* (New York), March 1961; "Both Sides of the Camera" and "Fabulous Saints and Sinners" by John Reid in *Films and Filming* (London), February and March 1961; special issue of *Présence du cinéma* (Paris), February 1962; special issue of *Movie* (London), September 1962; "Preminger and the Critics" in *Films and Filming* (London), May 1962; "Conférence Preminger à Cannes" by Bertrand Tavernier in *Cahiers du cinéma* (Paris), July 1962; special issue of *Movie* (London), no.1, 1963; special issue of *Visages du cinéma* (Paris), March 1963; special issues of *Interciné* (Toulouse), no.1 and no.2, 1963; special issue of *Film Ideal* (Madrid), November 1963; "Preminger's 2 Periods—Studio and Solo" by Andrew Sarris in *Film Comment* (New York), summer 1965; "Profiles: Anatomy of a Commercial Interruption" by Lillian Ross in the *New Yorker*, 19 February 1966; "Otto the Terrible" by Thomas Mehan in the *Saturday Evening Post* (Philadelphia), 8 April 1967; "Otto Preminger" by Richard McGuinness and "Otto Preminger" by Peter Bogdanovich in *On Film* 1970; articles in *Movie Reader* edited by Ian Cameron, New York 1972; "*Laura*: The Story Behind the Picture" by B. Borok in *Thousand Eyes* (New York), November 1976; "Laura", special issue by J. Lacourcelles of *Avant-Scène du cinéma* (Paris), July/September 1978.

*   *   *

The public persona of Austrian-born Otto Preminger has epitomized for many the typical Hollywood movie director: an accented, autocratic, European-born disciplinarian, terrorizing his actors, bullying his subordinates, and spending millions of dollars to insure that his films be produced properly, although economically. Before the *Cahiers du cinéma* critics began to praise Preminger, it may have been this public persona, more than anything else, which impeded an appreciation of Preminger's extraordinarily subtle style or thematic consistencies.

Preminger's career can be divided into two periods. Throughout the first period, Preminger worked as a studio director for Twentieth-Century Fox, where he had several well-publicized conflicts with Darryl F. Zanuck and found it difficult to conform to the studio demands or to collaborate without retaining overall artistic control. His evocative and romantic mystery *Laura* was his breakthrough film. Among the eclectic assignments he directed at Fox, the most interesting include a series of films noir in the late forties: *Whirlpool*, *Where the Sidewalk Ends*, *The Thirteenth Letter*, and *Angel Face*.

Throughout the second and far more interesting period of Preminger's career, Preminger worked as one of the first notable independent producer-directors, in the process successfully undermining the studio system in various way. He fought against institutional censorship by releasing several films without the Motion Pictures Association Seal (*The Moon is Blue*); he explored controversial subjects the studios might have been hesitant to touch (such as criticism of the war department in *The Court-Martial of Billy Mitchell* or homosexuality in *Advise and Consent*); he championed the independent producers movement by exploiting the Paramount Divorcement Decree and agressively marketing and arranging exhibition for his films; he incorporated fresh and authentic backgrounds by promoting location shooting away from Hollywood; he worked diligently to discover new performers (such as Jean Seberg) and to develop properties (such as *Carmen Jones* and *Hurry, Sundown*) which would allow the casting of Hollywood's under-used black performers; he even helped to break the studio blacklist by hiring and publicly crediting Dalton Trumbo as screenwriter on *Exodus*.

Preminger's tastes have always been as eclectic as the disparate sources from which his films have been adapted. Throughout the fifties and sixties, however, Preminger's films grew in pretention, displaying considerable interest in monolithic institutions (the military in *The Court Martial of Billy Mitchell* and *In Harm's Way*, the Senate in *Advise and Consent*, the Catholic Church in *The Cardinal*, the medical profession in *Such Good Friends*) as well as examining social and political problems (drug addiction in *The Man with the Golden Arm*; Jewish repatriation in *Exodus*; racial prejudice in *Hurry, Sundown*; political terrorism in *Rosebud*). A consistent archetype in Preminger's films is the quest for truth; indeed, a recurring image in Preminger's work is the courtroom. What has especially fascinated Preminger's admirers is the subtlety of his mise-en-scène; his most typical effort is a widescreen film with long takes, no pyrotechnical montage, few reaction shots, fluid and simple camera movements, and careful yet unselfconscious compositions. Preminger's style, though apparently invisible, is one which forces the audience to examine, to discern, to arrive at some ultimate position. Several critics have written persuasively on the ambiguity associated with Preminger's apparent objectivity, including Andrew Sarris, who has characterized Preminger as a "director who sees all problems and issues as a single-take two-shot, the stylistic expression of the eternal conflict, not between right and wrong, but between the right-wrong on one side and the right-wrong on the other, a representation of the right-wrong in all of us as our share of the human condition." If Preminger's formula seems somewhat to have floundered in the seventies and eighties—in this era in which the American cinema seems dominated by mainstream genre works and overt escapism, one cannot help but feel nostalgia for Preminger's serious subjects and profound respect for the artistry of his series of films beginning with *Bonjour, Tristesse* in 1957 and continuing through *Porgy and Bess*, *Anatomy of a Murder*, *Exodus*, *Advise and Consent*, *The Cardinal*, *In Harm's Way*, *Bunny Lake Is Missing*, and *Hurry, Sundown* in 1966, one of the longest strings of ambitious, provocative films in American cinema.

—Charles Derry

PROTAZANOV, YAKOV. Russian. Born Yakov Alexandrovitch Protazanov in Moscow, 4 February 1881. Educated in commercial school, Moscow. Career: 1905—begins working in films as actor; 1909—enters Gloria studios as translator, soon writing scenarios; 1910—directing debut; 1915—moves to Ermoliev company, begins collaborating with actor Ivan Mozhukhin; 1918—Ermoliev studios moved to Yalta following Revolution; 1919 or 1920—entire company moves to Istanbul, then Marseilles; 1920—moves to Paris, works in France and Germany until 1922; studio established at Montreuil-sous-bois; 1923—returns to Russia, joins Mezhrabpom-Rus Studio, Moscow; after 1928—object of increasing ideological criticism. Died in Moscow, 8 August 1945. Recipient: Merited Artist of the RSFSR, 1935.

Films (as director): 1909—*The Fountains of Bakhisarai*; 1911—*Pesnya katorzhanina (The Prisoner's Song)* (+sc); 1912—*Anfisa*; *Ukhod velikovo startza (Departure of a Grand Old Man)* (co-d); 1913—*Razbitaya vaza (The Shattered Vase)* (+sc); *Klyuchi shchastya (Keys to Happiness)* (co-d); *Kak khoroshi, kak svezhi byli rozi (How Fine, How Fresh the Roses Were)* (+sc); 1915—*Petersburgskiye trushchobi (Petersburg Slums)* (co-d, +co-sc); *Voina i mir (War and Peace)* (co-d, +co-sc); *Plebei (Plebeian)* (+sc); *Nikolai Stavrogin* (+sc); 1916—*Pikovaya dama (The Queen of Spades)*; *Zhenshchina s kinzhalom (Woman with a Dagger)*; *Grekh (Sin)* (co-d); 1917—*Prokuror (Public Prosecutor)*; *Andrei Kozhukhov* (+sc); *Ne nado krovi (Blood Need Not Be Spilled)* (+sc); *Prokliatiye millioni (Cursed Millions)*; *Satana likuyushchii (Satan Triumphant)*; 1918—*Otets Sergii (Father Sergius)*; 1919—*Taina korolevy (The Queen's Secret)* (+sc); 1924—*Aelita*; 1925—*Yevo prizyv (Broken Chains, His Call)*; *Zakroichik iz Torzhka (Tailor from Torzhok)*; 1926—*Protsess o tryokh millyonakh (The 3 Million Case)* (+co-sc); 1927—*Sorok pervyi (The 41st)* (+co-sc); 1928—*Byelyi orel (The White Eagle)* (+co-sc); *Dondiego i Pelaguya (Don Diego and Pelagea)*; 1929—*Chiny i liudi (Ranks and People)* (+co-sc); *The Man From the Restaurant*; 1930—*Prazdnik svyatovo Iorgena (Holiday of St Jorgen)* (+sc); 1931—*Tommy* (+sc); 1934—*Marionetki (Marionettes)*; 1937—*Bespridannitsa (Without Dowry)* (+co-sc); 1938—*Pupils of the 7th Grade*; 1941—*Salavat Yulayev*; 1943—*Nasreddin v Bukhare (Nasreddin in Bukhara)*.

Publications:

On PROTAZANOV:

Books—*Yakov Protazanov*, Moscow 1957; *Kino, A History of the Russian and Soviet Film* by Jay Leyda, London 1960; *Il cinema muto sovietico* by Nikolai Lebedev, Turin 1962; articles—"Priobžčenie k poesii" by N. Alisova in *Iskusstvo Kino*

(Moscow), April 1973; "Effect Protazanova" by I. Vajsfel'd and others in *Iskusstvo Kino* (Moscow), August 1981.

PTUSHKO, ALEXANDER. Russian. Born Alexander Lukich Ptushko in Lugansk, 6 April 1900. Educated at Plekhanov Institute of Economics. Career: 1920s—works as actor, newspaper correspondent, and painter in Don region; 1927—enters film industry, writing, directing, and animating shorts combining cartoon and trick work; 1935—makes *New Gulliver*, claimed to be first feature-length puppet (wax figure) animated film ever made; during WW II—becomes "combat director" of many films, continues to make animated and trick films; 1944—becomes Head of Animation Studios; 1946—instrumental in developing use of color, beginning with live-action *Stone Flower* (mostly shot at Barrandov Studios, Prague); 1956—makes first Soviet wide-screen feature, *Ilya Myromets*; 1958—pioneers in combining animation and special effects in Soviet-Finnish co-production *Sampo*. Recipient: Red Banner of Labor, 1944; First Prize for Color Film, Cannes Festival, for *Stone Flower*, 1946; State Prize for *Stone Flower*, 1947; Silver Lion, Venice Festival, for *Sadko*, 1953; People's Artist of the RSFSR, 1957.

Films (as director): 1928—*Chto delat'* [What to Do]; *Shifrovanny dokument* [Document in Cipher]; 1929—*Kniga v derevne* [Book in the Country]; *Sluchai na stadione* [Event in the Stadium]; *Stet priklyuchenni* [100 Adventures]; 1930—*Kino v derevne* [Cinema in the Country]; *Krepi oboronu*; 1932—*Vlasteli byta* [How Rulers Live]; *Begstvo Puankare* [The Flight (or Desertion) of Poincaré]; 1935—*Novy Gulliver (A New Gulliver)*; 1937—*Skazka o rybake i rybke* [Tale of the Fisherman and the Little Fish]; *Vesyoly musikanty* [The Jolly Musicians]; 1939—*Zolotoi klyuchik* [The Golden Key]; 1946—*Kamenny tsvetok (The Stone Flower)*; 1948—*Tri vstrechi (Three Encounters)* (co-d); 1952—*Sadko*; 1956—*Ilya Muromets*; 1958—*Sampo*; 1961—*Alye parusa* [Red Sails]; 1964—*Tale of Lost Time*; 1966—*The Tale of Czar Saltan*.

Publications:

By PTUSHKO:

Article—"Stepping Out of the Soviet" in *Films and Filming* (London), January 1960.

On PTUSHKO:

Article—"Ušel dobryj skazočnik" by G. Rošal in *Iskusstvo Kino* (Moscow), July 1973.

*   *   *

The "actors" in Alexander Ptushko's most important movies are neither flesh-and-blood professionals nor amateurs, but puppets—three-dimensional modelled figures. Ptushko expanded the artform initiated by Wladyslaw Starewicz, who first produced stop-motion films in Russia prior to the Revolution. Starewicz's works were ingeniously animated, and it is to his credit that three-dimensional figure animation is thought of as a native

Russian art. However, Ptushko added sound to the images, as well as more complex plotlines and feature-length running times.

Ptushko began his career as a cartoonist, one of the most sardonic of the 1920s. His first short sound films, also employing puppets, were only adequate, but he perfected his technique from year to year and project to project. His most famous film is his first full-length movie, *Novy Gulliver (The New Gulliver)*, based on Jonathan Swift's *Gulliver's Travels*—easily the best of all Soviet animated films, and the world's first feature starring puppets.

Unlike Dave Fleischer's 1939 animated cartoon, the scenario does not remain faithful to Swift. Instead, *The New Gulliver* is *Gulliver's Travels* with a twist. It is framed by a reading in a camp of Young Pioneers: Gulliver arrives in a Lilliput under the control of a dimwitted king and his secret police, and assists the oppressed during a workers' revolt. One human performer does appear: a boy (V. Konstantinov), who falls asleep and dreams himself into the story as Gulliver.

The New Gulliver took three years to produce, and was made before Walt Disney released his first animated feature, *Snow White and the Seven Dwarfs*. It is the first Soviet sound film to utilize extended multiplication and reproduction from models: the puppets—which are actually dolls—are not moved like marionettes but photographed motionless, in innumerable positions, a process similar to that in animation. They are modelled in clay, and there are no hidden mechanisms. Each has between two and 300 separate heads (or, if you will, masks), all interchangeable and featuring a wide array of gestures and expressions. These puppets feel and think, love and hate—in short, they become human: one contemporary reviewer predicted that they could successfully compete with Clark Gable and Joan Crawford in the Academy Awards competition. In its own modest way, *The New Gulliver* ranks with *Battleship Potemkin* in innovation. The film was Ptushko's first to be widely distributed outside the Soviet union. Portions were screened at the second film festival of Venice, in 1934.

"I have striven (in my films)," Ptushko wrote, "to portray the theme I love best—mankind's dream of a better life, of happiness for people in general." This is fulfilled in *The New Gulliver*—though within a "party line" framework—as the populace liberates itself from its crazed ruler. This spirit was also carried into Ptushko's later career, when he directed live-action features adapted from Russian folk stories.

Myths and legends are Alexander Ptushko's most prevalent subject matter, whether his films, feature puppets or actors. But those starring small figures cast in the likeness of the human form are regarded with special preference and affection.

—Rob Edelman

PUDOVKIN, VSEVOLOD. Russian. Born Vsevolod Illarionovitch Pudovkin in Penza, 16 February 1893. Educated in physics and chemistry at Moscow University; entered State Cinema School in 1920. Married actress and journalist Anna Zemtsova in 1923. Career: 1914—enlists in artillery; 1915—wounded and taken prisoner; 1918—escapes and returns to Moscow; 1919-20—works as writer and chemist; 1920—works with Vladimir Gardin on *Sickle and Hammer* and *Hunger ...Hunger...Hunger*; 1920-21—works on agit-films; 1922—becomes student in Lev Kuleshov's studio; 1923—quits State Cinema Institute (G.I.K.) to join Kuleshov's Experimental Laboratory; 1924—collaborates with Kuleshov on *Extraordi-*

nary Adventures of Mr. West in the Land of the Bolsheviks; 1925—meets Anatoly Golovnia, cinematographer on all but 4 of Pudovkin's films; 1925—begins association with scriptwriter Nathan Zarkhi on *Mother*; 1928—with Alexandrov signs Eisenstein's "Manifesto on Audio-Visual Counterpoint"; 1929—directs *The Living Corpse* in Berlin, attends conferences in Great Britain and Holland; 1932—joins Communist Party; 1935-38—injured in automobile accident, during recovery teaches at V.G.I.K., works on theoretic studies; 1937—with Mikhail Doller prepares film of *Anna Karenina* (unrealized); 1938—joins Mosfilm studios. Died in Riga, 30 June 1953. Recipient: Order of Lenin, 1935.

Films (as director): 1921—*Golod...golod...golod (Hunger... Hunger...Hunger)* (co-d, +co-sc, actor); (as scriptwriter): 1923—*Slesar i kantzler (Locksmith and Chancellor)* (co-sc); 1924—*Neobychainye priklucheniya Mistera Vesta v stranye bolshevikov (Extraordinary Adventures of Mr. West in the Land of the Bolsheviks)* (co-sc, +ass't, ro as the 'Count'); 1925—*Luch smerti (The Death Ray)* (+design, actor); (as director): 1925—*Shakhmatnaya goryachka (Chess Fever)* (co-d); 1926—*Mekhanikha golovnovo mozga (Mechanics of the Brain)* (+sc); *Mat (Mother)*; 1927—*Konyets Sankt-Peterburga (The End of St. Petersburg)*; 1928—*Potomok Chingis-khan (The Heir to Genghis-Khan)*; 1932—*Prostoi sluchai (A Simple Case)* (revised version of *Otchen kharacho dziviosta (Life's Very Good)* 1st screened in 1930); 1933—*Dezertir (Deserter)*; 1938—*Pobeda (Victory)* (co-d); 1939—*Minin i Pozharsky* (co-d); 1940—*Kino za XX liet (20 Years of Cinema)* (co-d, +co-ed); 1941—*Suvorov* (co-d); *Pir v Girmunka (Feast at Zhirmunka)* (co-d—for "Fighting Film Album"); 1942—*Ubitzi vykhodyat na dorogu (Murderers Are on Their Way)* (co-d, +co-sc); 1943—*Vo imya rodini (In the Name of the Fatherland)* (co-d); 1946—*Amiral Nakhimov (Admiral Nakhimov)*; 1948—*Tri vstrechi (3 Encounters)* (co-d); 1950—*Yukovsky* (co-d); 1953—*Vozvrachenia Vassilya Bortnikov (The Return of Vasili Bortnikov)*.

Roles: 1920—*V dni borbi (In the Days of Struggle)*; 1921—*Serp i molot (Sickle and Hammer)* (+ass't d); 1925—*Kirpitchiki (Little Bricks)*; 1928—Feodor Protassov in *Zhivoi trup (A Living Corpse)*; 1929—the illusionist in *Vessiolaia kanareika (The Cheerful Canary)*; 1944—as Nikolai the fanatic in *Ivan Grozny (Ivan the Terrible)*.

Publications:

By PUDOVKIN:

Books—*Film Technique*, translated by Ivor Montagu, London 1933; *Film-Acting*, translated by Ivor Montagu, London 1935; *Film Technique and Film Acting*, New York 1949; *Textes choisis*, Moscow 1955; *La settima arte*, Rome 1961; *Sobranie sochinenii v trekh tomakh*, Moscow 1974; articles—"Le Montage" in *Cinéa-Ciné pour tous*, Paris 1929; "Scénario et mise en scène" in *Revue du cinéma* (Paris), 1 September 1930; "Poudovkine parle du montage" by René Lévy in *Revue du cinéma* (Paris), 1 December 1931; "A Conversation with V.I. Pudovkin" by Marie Seton in *Sight and Sound* (London), spring 1933; "Le Montage" in *Cinéma d'aujourd'hui et de demain*, Cannes 1946; "Le Montage et le son" in *Le Magasin du spectacle* (Paris), April 1946; "Les Films historiques soviétiques" in *Cinémonde* (Cannes), special number, 1946; "The Global Film" in *Hollywood Quarterly*, July 1947; "Il faut développer les cinémas nationaux", interview by Anne Vincent in *L'Ecran Français* (Paris), 21 September 1948; "2 Conversations with Pudovkin" by C.H. Waddington in *Sight and Sound* (London), winter 1948/49; "Il faut développer les cinémas nationaux", interview by Anne Vincent in *L'Ecran français* (Paris), 21 September 1948; "Le Cinéma soviétique" in *Europe* (Paris), June 1950; "Michel Ange, ce méconnu" in *Les Lettres françaises* (Paris), 9 July 1953; "L'Homme nouveau et le drame ancien" in *Les Lettres françaises* (Paris), 21 September 1948; "Stanislavsky's System in the Cinema" in *Sight and Sound* (London), January/March 1953; "Le Travail de l'acteur de cinéma et le système de Stanislavski" in special "Recherches soviétiques" issue of *Cinéma* (Paris), April 1956; "La Force de la poésie" in *Le Cinéma soviétique par ceux qui l'on fait*, Paris 1966.

On PUDOVKIN:

Books—*Film Problems of Soviet Russia* by Winifred Bryher, London 1929; *Poudovkine, "Pouti Tvortchestva," "Les Voies de la création"* by N. Yezuitov, Moscow 1937; *Vsevolod Pudovkin* by A. Mariamov, Moscow 1952; *Kino: A History of the Russian and Soviet Film* by Jay Leyda, London 1960; *Vsevolod Poudovkine* by Luda and Jean Schnitzer, Paris 1966; *V.I. Poudovkine* by Barthélemy Amengual, Premier Plan, Lyon 1968; *Pudovkin's Films and Film Theory* by Peter Dart, New York 1974; articles—"Poudovkine parle du montage" by René Levy in *Revue du cinéma* (Paris), 1 December 1931; "Pudovkin and the Revolutionary Film" by Harry Potamkin in *Hound and Horn* (New York), April/June 1933; "Pabst, Pudovkin and the Producers" by Paul Rotha in *Sight and Sound* (London), summer 1933; "Index to the Creative Work of Vsevolod Pudovkin" by Jay Leyda in *Sight and Sound* (London), November 1948; "Vsevolod Poudovkine" by Jean-Pierre Darré in *L'Ecran français* (Paris), 11 September 1950; "Un Homme fait pour le jour" by Léon Moussinac and "Un Humaniste et un lyrique" by Georges Sadoul in *Les Lettres françaises* (Paris), 9 July 1953; special issue of *Cahiers du cinéma* (Paris), August/September 1953; "Poudovkine est mort" by Jacques Chevallier in *Image et son* (Paris), October 1953; "Vsevolod Pudovkin" by Herman Weinberg in *Films in Review* (New York), August/September 1953; "V.I. Pudovkin: 1893-1953" by Basil Wright in *Sight and Sound* (London), October/December 1953; "Film Image—Pudovkin" by Robert Herring in *Cinemage* (New York), May 1955; "Prose et poésie au cinéma" by Efim Dobine in *Esthétique* (Paris), July/August 1963; "Les Théories du langage et de l'expression filmiques selon Poudovkine" by Jacques-André Bizet in *Le Cinéma pratique* (Paris), September/October and November/-December 1966 and March 1967; "Souvenirs d'Inkijinoff" by J.-A. Bizet in *Cinéma* (Paris), June 1972; special Pudovkin issue of *Iskusstvo Kino* (Moscow), February 1973; "Wsewolod Pudowkin—Tradition und Neuerertum", in 2 parts by A. Karaganov in *Film und Fernsehen* (Berlin), May and June 1974; "Die wichtigste der Künste" by A. Karaganov in *Film und Fernsehen* (Berlin), April 1977; "Film Language: Pudovkin and Eisenstein and Russian Formalism" by E. Hudlin in *Journal of Aesthetic Education* (Urbana, Illinois), no.2, 1979; "V.I. Pudovkinh" by C. Losada in *Cinema 2002* (Madrid), February 1980; "Linkage: Pudovkin's Classics Revisited" by P.E. Burns in *Journal of Popular Film and Television* (Washington, D.C.), summer 1981.

*   *   *

Vsevolod Illarionovitch Pudovkin's background is quite unusual for a filmmaker. He studied chemistry and physics at Moscow University, enlisted in the artillery at the outbreak of World War I, and spent three years in a German prison camp. Pudovkin wanted to be an actor, and after the war went to Russia's State Film School where he learned all aspects of the cinema. He did appear in a number of films before commencing his career as director; and he chose to always play small roles in his own films, like Alfred Hitchcock, and even acted in Eisenstein's *Ivan the Terrible*.

Pudovkin's major contribution to the cinema is as a theorist. He was fascinated by the efforts of his teacher, the filmmaker Lev Kuleshov, in exploring the effects of montage. A famous example: a shot of an expressionless Mosjukhin, edited with shots of different images—first, a bowl of soup, then a child, finally a coffin. Each piece of film will strike contrasting response in the viewer. Pudovkin applied this to his own films, often creating highly emotional moments by rapidly intercutting shots of diverse content. Of course, the results could be manipulated: in *The End of St. Petersburg*, for instance, he mixed together shots of stock market speculation with those depicting war casualties. Occasionally, Pudovkin's images are uninspired: the above sequence looks static, even simplistic, today. Nevertheless, while other filmmakers may have advanced this technique, Pudovkin was one of the first to utilize it in a narrative.

Pudovkin's essays on film theory, "The Film Scenario" and "Film Director and Film Material," remain just as valuable as any of his works; these texts have become primers in film technique. Pudovkin wrote that it is unnecessary for a film actor to overperform, overgesture as he might in theater. There is no cause for him to constantly reach the audience member in the last row of the balcony. He can underplay: the director or editor, via montage, will communicate to the viewer the pervading feeling in the shots surrounding the actor. Meanwhile, he might concentrate on his internal emotions, transmitting the truths of his character in a more subtle manner.

Beyond this, an actor on screen is at the mercy of his director. The performer could be directed to cry, without knowing his character's motivations; the shots placed around him will pass along the cause of his grief. A non-actor could even be made to give a realistic performance as a result of perceptive editing. Pudovkin often integrated his casts with both actors and non-actors; the latter were utilized when he felt the need for realism over ability to perform. In *Chess Fever*, a two-reel comedy, Pudovkin even edited in shots of Jose Raoul Capablanca, a famous chess master, to make him seem an active participant in the scenario. As the filmmaker explained, "The foundation of film art is editing," and "The film is not shot, but built up from separate strips of celluloid that are its raw material."

Pudovkin's first significant credit, *The Death Ray*, was directed by Kuleshov. But he designed the production, wrote the scenario, assisted his teacher and acted a role. Before the end of the 1920s, he completed his three great silent features and best-remembered films, *Mother, The End of St. Petersburg* and *The Heir to Genghis-Khan*. While they were each concerned with various aspects of the Revolution, they are not totally propagandistic: each film does deal with human involvements, conflicts, and the effect that ideas and actions have on the lives of those involved. This is illustrated perfectly in *Mother*, based on a Maxim Gorky novel. Set during the 1905 Revolution, the film chronicles the plight of the title character (Vera Baranovskaya), who accidently causes her politically active, worker son (Nikolai Batalov) to be sentenced to prison. Eventually, Batalov is shot during an escape attempt and Baranovskaya, whose political consciousness has been raised, is trampled to death by the cavalry attacking a workers' protest.

Baranovskaya also appears in *The End of St. Petersburg*, filmed to mark the tenth anniversary of the 1917 Revolution and centering on the political education of an inexperienced young peasant (Ivan Chuvelyov). This film is significant in that it is one of the first to satisfactorily blend a fictional scenario into a factual setting; the graphic, carefully realized battlefield scenes here are reminiscent of those in *The Birth of a Nation*. And, typically, Pudovkin cast real pre-Revolution stockbrokers and exectives as stockbrokers and executives.

The Heir to Genghis-Khan (more commonly known as *Storm Over Asia*) is not as successful as the others, but is still worthy of note. The film, set in Central Asia, details the activities of the English army of occupation in Mongolia (called the White Russian army in foreign prints) and partisan revolutionaries. It focuses on a young Mongol trapper (Valeri Inkizhinov), whose fate is not dissimilar to that of Pudovkin's other heroes and heroines: he is radicalized by the unfolding events after he is cheated out of a prized fox fur by a European merchant.

Pudovkin continued making films after the advent of sound. *A Simple Case*, revised from his silent, *Life's Very Good*, was scheduled to be the Soviet cinema's first sound feature; instead, the honor went to Nikolai Ekk's *The Road to Life*. Pudovkin was not content to just add sound to his scenarios. His initial talkie was *Deserter*, in which he experimented with speech patterns: by editing in sound, he contrasted the dialogue of different characters in conversation to each other, and to crowd noises, traffic sounds, sirens, music and even silence. But Pudovkin did not abandon his concern for visuals: *Deserter* contains approximately 3,000 separate shots, and unusually high number for a feature film.

Pudovkin did make other sound films. His *Minin and Pozharsky*, released at the beginning of World War II, is set at a time during the 17th Century when Moscow was controlled by King Sigismund; it is the first major Soviet film to depict Poland as an invader. Nevertheless, his cinematic language is essentially one that is devoid of words. It is purely visual, and it is pure cinema.

—Rob Edelman

RADEMAKERS, FONS. Dutch. Born in Roosendaal, Brabant, 5 September 1920. Educated at Academy of Dramatic Art, Amsterdam. Career: mid-1950s—assistant to filmmakers in Italy (De Sica on *Il tetto*, 1956, and Fellini), to Jacques Becker in Paris, and David Lean in England; 1958—directing debut; begins collaboration with scriptwriter Hugo Claus.

Films (as director): 1958—*Dorp aan de rivier (Village on the River)*; 1960—*Makkers staakt uw wild geraas (That Joyous Eve...)* (+co-sc); 1961—*Het mes (The Knife)*; 1963—*Als 2 druppels water (The Spitting Image)* (+sc); 1966—*De dans van de reiger (The Dance of the Heron)*; 1971—*Mira*; 1973—*Because of the Cats (Niet voor de poesen, The Rape)*; 1976—*Max Havelaar*; 1978—*Mysteries*; 1979—*My Friend (The Judge's Friend)*.

Publications:

By RADEMAKERS:

Articles—"Ik ben een vijand van improvisatie", interview by G. Luijters and A. Haakman in *Skoop* (Amsterdam), v.8, no.9, 1973; "Een acteur moet iemand boven zich die weet wat hij wil", interview by A. de Jong in *Skoop* (Amsterdam), October 1976; interview, with others, by A. de Jong and W. Reisel in *Skoop* (Amsterdam), July 1979.

On RADEMAKERS:

Articles—"Talking About People" in *Film* (London), spring 1963; "Fons Rademakers" by Peter Cowie in *International Film Guide 1979*, London 1978; "History and Heroism Shape Rademakers's Epic *Havelaar*" in *Independent Film Journal* (New York), March 1979; "De raakpunten van film en toneel..." by A. de Jang and W. Reisel in *Skoop* (Amsterdam), April 1979.

RAFELSON, BOB. American. Born in New York City, 1935. Career: military service with Occupation forces in Japan; works as disc jockey for military radio station; acts as advisor to Shochiku Films on American market; late 1950s—works in television: reader and story editor for David Susskind (*Play of the Week*), Desilu, and Columbia Screen Gems; 1966—with Bert Schneider creates TV rock group the Monkees, produces series, and directs episodes of show; 1968—with Schneider and Steve Blauner forms BBS Productions; directs 1st feature *Head*, featuring Monkees. Recipient: Best Direction, New York Film Critics, for *Five Easy Pieces*, 1970. Business address: 1400 N. Fuller Ave., Hollywood, CA 90046.

Films (as director and co-producer): 1968—*Head* (+co-sc); 1969—*Easy Rider* (Hopper) (co-pr only); 1970—*Five Easy Pieces* (+co-story); 1971—*The Last Picture Show* (Bogdanovich) (co-pr only); 1972—*Drive, He Said* (Nicholson) (co-pr only); 1973—*The King of Marvin Gardens* (pr, +co-story); 1977—*Stay Hungry* (+co-sc); 1980—*Brubaker* (d 10 days only, then replaced by Stuart Rosenberg); 1981—*The Postman Always Rings Twice*.

Publications:

By RAFELSON:

Articles—"Le Monopoly est une métaphore très évidente du rêve américain...", interview by M. Grisolia in *Cinéma* (Paris), June 1973; "Staying Vulnerable", interview by John Taylor in *Sight and Sound* (London), no.4, 1976; interview by A.M. Tatò and Olivier Eyquem in *Positif* (Paris), May 1978; "Prodigal's Progress", interview by R. Combs and J. Pym in *Sight and Sound* (London), autumn 1981; "Raising Cain", interview by D. Thompson in *Film Comment* (New York), March/April 1981.

On RAFELSON:

Articles—"Bob Rafelson" in the *New Yorker*, 24 October 1970; "Petits meurtres américains ou nous et nos ciné-fantasmes" by Claire Clouzot in *Ecran* (Paris), June 1973; "Notes sur 3 films de Bob Rafelson..." by M. Lefanu in *Positif* (Paris), May 1978; "Dossier: Hollywood 79: Bob Rafelson" by P. Carcassonne in *Cinématographe* (Paris), November 1979; "Directors Series: Bob Rafelson—The Postman Always Rings Twice", interview by R. Edelman in *Films in Review* (New York), May 1981; "Bob Rafelson" by Tom Milne in *International Film Guide 1983*, London 1982.

*   *   *

Bob Rafelson is a neglected director mainly because he lays bare the myths essential to America. He does not sugarcoat the bitter dose of his satire, as do Coppola and Altman. A distaste on the part of mainstream critics has caused attacks upon, but mostly the neglect of, Rafelson's *The King of Marvin Gardens*, which is his most representative film and which will form a focus of this discussion of the director's output. *Head* is bound by the conventions of the teenage-comedy genre and shows few marks of Rafelson's authorship; *Stay Hungry* is a minor work which sustains his standard theme of the drop-out—this time it is a Southern aristocrat who falls into the underworld, which is ambiguously mixed with the business world above. Something of a popular success, *Five Easy Pieces* certainly demands attention.

Five Easy Pieces was the first expression of the burned-out liberalism that was to become the hallmark of American films of the seventies. Rafelson's film expresses the intelligentsia's dissatisfaction with its impotency in light of an overweening socio-economic structure. Either capitulating or dropping out seemed the only alternative. The films protagonist seeks escape, from a successful but unsatisfying career as a concert pianist, in the world of the working class—first as an oil-field worker and then, at the end of the film, as a logger. The film centers on his foray into the bourgeois bohemia of his family's home—a sort of *ad hoc* artist colony under the aegis of his sister. The world we see is both figuratively and literally one of cripples. His sister's lover is in traction. His father is a paralytic. All are emblems of a pseudo-class, without a vital motive force, that the protagonist rejects, but cannot replace. The protagonist's sole contribution to an intellectual discussion among his sister's friends is an obscene comment on the senselessness of their phrase-weaving. In the largest sense, *Five Easy Pieces* is about the American intellectual's self-hatred, his disorientation in an essentially anti-intellectual society, and his resulting inability to feel comfortable with his capacity to think and to create.

The King of Marvin Gardens cuts through the American dream—the belief that every man can achieve riches by ingenuity. The protagonist becomes drawn into his brother's success dream. Rafelson sets the film in pre-boom Atlantic City—an emblem of economic desolation. The locale's aptness is affirmed by the scene of the protagonist's sister-in-law throwing her make-up into a fire. Her aging face, without make-up, is seen against the dilapidated façade of boardwalk hotels, Her gesture (and in Rafelson's uncommitted world we daren't ask for more) of defiance is directed against what has been the female share of the American Dream: the male has traditionally taken for himself the power that comes of wealth and left woman the illusion called "glamor." Another symbol is the blowing up of an old hotel; it collapses in a heap like the dream of entrepreneurship the protagonist momentarily shares with his brother.

Rafelson has failed to gain critical approval because he does not soften brutal political deconstruction with dazzling techniques. He devotes his attention not only to the straightforward expression of his themes but to getting brilliant acting out of his casts. He forces them to explore the darker sides of their characters—each a microcosm of society.

—Rodney Farnsworth

RAINER, YVONNE. American. Born in San Francisco, 1934. Career: beginning 1957—trains as modern dancer in New York; 1960—begins choreographing own work; 1962—co-founder of Judson Dance Theater; 1962-75—presents choreographic work in U.S. and Europe; 1968—begins to integrate slides and short films into dance performances; 1972—completes 1st feature-length film, *Lives of Performers*; has taught extensively, at New School for Social Research, New York, California Institute of the Arts, Valencia, and numerous other colleges and universities. Recipient: First Prize in Independent Film, Los Angeles Film Critics, for *Journeys from Berlin/1971* (1980). Address: 72 Franklin St., New York, NY 10012.

Films (as maker of short films): 1967—*Volleyball (Foot Film)*; 1968—*Hand Movie*; *Rhode Island Red*; *Trio Film*; 1969—*Line*; (as director of feature-length films): 1972—*Lives of Performers*; 1974—*Film About a Woman Who...*; 1976—*Kristina Talking Pictures*; 1980—*Journeys from Berlin/1971* (+pr, sc, ed).

Publications:

By RAINER:

Book—*Work 1961-73*, New York 1974; articles—"A Quasi Survey of Some 'Minimalist' Tendencies in the Quantitatively Minimal Dance Activity Midst the Plethora, or An Analysis of Trio A" in *Minimal Art*, edited by Gregory Battcock, New York 1968; "The Performer as a Persona", interview in *Avalanche*, summer 1972; interview in *Monthly Film Bulletin* (London), May 1977; "Working Title: 'Journeys from Berlin/1971'", scenario in *October* (Cambridge, Mass.), summer 1979.

On RAINER:

Articles—"Performance: A Conversation" by Stephen Koch in *Artforum* (New York), December 1972; "Trisha Brown and Yvonne Rainer" by Lizzie Borden in *Artforum* (New York), June 1973; "Yvonne Rainer, Part One: the Dancer and the Dance" and "Part Two: Lives of Performers" by Annette Michelson in *Artforum* (New York), January and February 1974; "Yvonne Rainer: An Introduction" in *Camera Obscura* (Berkeley), fall 1976; "The Ambiguities of Yvonne Rainer" by Jonathan Rosenbaum in *American Film* (Washington, D.C.), March 1980.

*   *   *

Although Yvonne Rainer made her first feature-length film in 1972, she had already been prominent in the New York avant-garde art scene for nearly a decade. She moved to New York from San Francisco in 1957 to study acting, but started taking dance lessons and soon committed herself to dance. By the mid-1960's, she emerged as an influential dancer and choreographer, initially drawing the attention of critics and audiences through her work with the Judson Dance Theater.

Rainer saw a problem inherent in dance as an art form, namely its involvement with "narcissism, virtuosity and display." Her alternative conception was of the performance as a kind of work or task, as opposed to an exhibition, carried out by "neutral 'doers' " rather than performers. Thus the minimalist dance that she pioneered, which depended on ordinary movements, departed radically from the dramatic, emotive forms of both its classical and modern dance precursors.

Rainer was not long content with merely stripping dance of its artifice and conventions. She became interested in psychology and sexuality, in the everyday emotions that people share, and grew dissatisfied with abstract dance, which she found too limited to express her new concerns. To communicate more personal and emotional content, Rainer began experimenting with combining movements with other media, such as recorded and spoken texts, slides, film stills, and music, creating a performance collage. Language and narrative became increasingly important components of her performance.

Rainer's first films, shorts made to be part of these performances in the late sixties, were "...filmed choreographic exercises," as she wrote in 1971, "that were meant to be viewed with one's peripheral vision...not to be taken seriously." Her interest in the narrative potential of film and the director's dominance of the medium drew Rainer further into filmmaking.

Her first two feature films, *Lives of Performers*, and *Film About a Woman Who...*, both with cinematographer Babette Mangolte, originated as performance pieces. In these and in her two other films, *Kristina Talking Pictures* and *Journeys from Berlin/1971*, Rainer interweaves the real and the fictional, the personal and the political, the concrete and the abstract. She preserves the collagist methods of her performances, juxtaposing personal recollections, previous works, historical documents, and original dialogue and narration, her soundtracks often having the same richness, and the same disjunction, as the visual portions of her films.

Like Brecht, Rainer believes that an audience should contemplate what they see; they should participate in the creative process of the film rather than simply receive it passively. Thus, instead of systematically telling a story, she apposes and layers narrative elements to create meaning. The discontinuity, ambiguity, and even contradiction that often result keep Rainer's audience at a distance, so they can examine the feminist, psychological, political, or purely emotional issues she addresses. Consistent with her dance and performance, Rainer's films are theoretical, even intellectual, not dramatic, sentimental, or emotional, despite her subject matter, which is often controversial and emotion-laden.

—Jessica Wolff

RAY, NICHOLAS. American. Born Raymond Nicholas Kienzle in Galesville, Wisconsin, 7 August 1911. Educated in architecture and theater at the University of Chicago. Married Jean Evans in 1930 (divorced); Gloria Grahame in 1948 (divorced 1952); dancer Betty Schwab (divorced); married Susan (Ray); children: Anthony, Timothy and daughters Nicca and Julie. Career: early 1930s—director, Frank Lloyd Wright's Taliesin Playhouse; 1935-37—in Theater of Action; meets Group Theater figures; 1938—joins John Houseman's Phoenix Theater; accident results in loss of sight in right eye; 1942—named War Information Radio Program Director by John Houseman; 1943—directs *Back Where I Came From* and *Lute Song* on Broadway; 1944—Elia Kazan takes him to Hollywood as assistant director on *A Tree Grows in Brooklyn*; 1946—adapts *Sorry, Wrong Number* for CBS TV; 1962—walks off set of *55 Days at Peking*, takes residence in Paris; 1968—works on film in Chicago on 1968 Convention violence (some footage in Marcel Ophuls's *America Revisited*); 1971-73—teaches filmmaking at State University of New York, Binghamton, with students works on *You Can't Go Home Again* (unfinished); 1979—collaborates with Wim Wenders on *Lightning over Water*, a "documentary" based on the last months of his life. Died in New York, 16 June 1979.

Films (as director): 1948—*They Live By Night* (1st release in Britain as *The Twisted Road*, U.S. release 1949); *A Woman's Secret*; 1949—*Knock on Any Door*; 1950—*In a Lonely Place*; *Born to Be Bad*; 1951—*The Flying Leathernecks*; 1952—*On Dangerous Ground*; *The Lusty Men*; 1954—*Johnny Guitar*; 1955—*Run for Cover*; *Rebel Without a Cause* (+story); 1956—*Hot Blood*; *Bigger than Life*; 1957—*The True Story of Jesse James*; *Bitter Victory* (+co-sc); 1958—*Wind Across the Everglades*; *Party Girl*; 1959—*The Savage Innocents* (+sc); 1961—*King of Kings*; 1963—*55 Days at Peking* (co-d); 1975—*You Can't Go Home Again* (+sc, unfinished); 1981—*Lightning over Water* (co-d, +ro as himself).

Roles: 1977—*The American Friend* (Wenders); 1979—*Hair* (Forman).

Publications:

By RAY:

Articles—"Portrait de l'acteur en jeune homme" in *Cahiers du cinéma* (Paris), no.66, 1956; "Story into Script" in *Sight and Sound* (London), autumn 1956; "Entretien avec Nick Ray" by Charles Bitsch in *Cahiers du cinéma* (Paris), November 1958; "Conversations with Nicholas Ray and Joseph Losey" by Penelope Houston in *Sight and Sound* (London), autumn 1961; "Entretien avec Nick Ray" by Jean Douchet and Jacques Joly in *Cahiers du cinéma* (Paris), January 1962; "Interview with Nicholas Ray" by Adriano Aprà and others in *Movie* (London), May 1963; "La Fureur de vivre" in *Arts et spectacles* (Paris), 15 May 1967; in *Interviews with Film Directors* edited by Andrew Sarris, New York 1967; "Nicholas Ray Today", interview by J. Greenberg in *Filmmakers Newsletter* (Ward Hill, Mass.), January 1973; "Nicholas Ray: Rebel!", interview by M. Goodwin and N. Wise in *Take One* (Montreal), January 1977; interview by B. Krohn in *Cahiers du cinéma* (Paris), May 1978.

On RAY:

Books—*Underworld U.S.A.* by Colin McArthur, London 1972; *Nicholas Ray* by John Kreidl, Boston 1977; articles—"Generation Without a Cause" by Eugene Archer in *Film Culture* (New York), v.2, no.1, 1956; "Nicholas Ray" by Henri Agel in *New York Film Bulletin*, no.11, 1961; "The Cinema of Nicholas Ray" by Victor Perkins in *Movie Reader* edited by Ian Cameron, New York 1972; "Film Favorites" by Robin Wood in *Film Comment* (New York), September/October 1972; "Circle of Pain: The Cinema of Nicholas Ray" by Jonathan Rosenbaum in *Sight and Sound* (London), autumn 1973; "Cinemascope Before and After" by Charles Barr in *Film Theory and Criticism* edited by Gerald Mast and Mark Cohen, New York 1974; "Rebel Without a Cause: Nicholas Ray in the Fifties" by Peter Biskind in *Film Quarterly* (Berkeley), fall 1974; "Johnny Guitar", special issue of *Avant-Scène du cinéma* (Paris), March 1974; "Film as Experience: Nicholas Ray—The Director Turns Teacher" by Joseph Lederer in *American Film* (Washington, D.C.), November 1975; "Director in Aspic" by J. Cocks in *Take One* (Montreal), January 1977; obituary in *The New York Times*, 18 June 1979; obituary by Claude Beylie in *Ecran* (Paris), 15 September 1979; "Nicholas Ray, Without a Cause" by Terry Fox in *The Village Voice* (New York), 9 July 1979; "Nicholas Ray..." by T. Renaud in *Cinéma* (Paris), July/August 1979; "In a Lonely Place" by D. Thomson in *Sight and Sound* (London), no.4, 1979; "Nicholas Ray: The Last Movies" by T. Farrell and others in *Sight and Sound* (London), spring 1981; "Nicholas Ray (1911-1979)" by G. Langlois in *Avant-Scène du cinéma* (Paris), 1 May 1981; film—

I'm a Stranger Here Myself directed by David Helpern, Jr., 1974.

RAY, SATYAJIT. Indian. Born in Calcutta, India, 2 May 1921. Educated Ballygunj Government School; Presidency College, Calcutta; University of Santiniketan, 1940-42. Married Bijoya Das, 1949. Career: 1943—is hired by D.J. Keymer and Co., British ad agency, as commercial artist; 1944—begins writing film scenarios; 1947—co-founder, Calcutta Film Society, with Chidananda Das Gupta; 1949—meets Jean Renoir working on *The River* in India; 1950—sent to England by Keymer and Co.; 1951—begins putting together 1st film, *Pather Panchali*, but unable to obtain financial backing from production companies; 1951-55—completes *Pather Panchali* after receiving government support during filming; 1956-59—continues story begun in *Pather Panchali* in sequels *Aparajito* and *Apur Sansar*; 1961—directs 1st documentary film, *Rabindranath Tagore*; begins composing own music films beginning with *Teen Kanya (2 Daughters)*; 1977—makes 1st film in Hindi (as opposed to Bengali), *Shatranj Ke Khilari (The Chess Players)*. Recipient: Best Direction (Silver Bear), Berlin Festival, for *Mahanagar (The Big City)*, 1964; Best Direction (Silver Bear), Berlin Festival, for *Charulata (The Lonely Wife)*, 1965; Special Award of Honour, Berlin Festival, 1966. Address: Flat 8, 1/1 Bishop Lefroy Road, Calcutta 20, India.

Films (as director and scriptwriter): 1955—*Pather Panchali*; 1956—*Aparajito*; 1957—*Parash Pathar*; 1958—*Jalsaghar (The Music Room)*; 1959—*Apur Sansar (The World of Apu)*; 1960—*Devi (The Goddess)*; (as director, scriptwriter, and music composer): 1961—*Teen Kanya (2 Daughters)*; *Rabindranath Tagore*; 1962—*Abhijan (Expedition)*; *Kanchanjanga* 1963—*Mahanagar (The Big City)*; 1964—*Charulata (The Lonely Wife)*; 1965—*Kapurush-o-Mahapurush (The Coward and the Saint)* 1966—*Nayak (The Hero)*; 1967—*Chiriakhana (The Zoo)*; 1969—*Goopy Gyne Bagha Byne (The Adventures of Goopi and Bagha)*; 1970—*Pratidwandi (The Adversary)*; *Aranyer Din Ratri (Days and Nights in the Forest)*; 1971—*Seemabaddha* (+mu); *Sikkim*; 1972—*The Inner Eye*; 1973—*Asani Sanket (Distant Thunder)*; 1974—*Sonar Kella*; 1975—*Jana Aranya (The Middleman)*; 1976—*Bala*; 1977—*Shatranj Ke Khilari (The Chess Players)*; 1978—*Joi Baba Felunath*; 1979—*Heerak Rajar Deshe*; 1981—*Sadgati (Deliverance)* (for TV); *Pikoo* (short); 1982—*Ghare Bahire*.

Publications:

By RAY:

Book—*Our Films, Their Films*, New Delhi 1977; articles—"A Long Time on the Little Road" in *Sight and Sound* (London), spring 1957; "Satyajit Ray on Himself" in *Cinema* (Beverly Hills), July/August 1965; "From Film to Film" in *Cahiers du Cinema in English* (New York), no.3, 1966; interview in *Interviews with Film Directors* edited by Andrew Sarris, New York 1967; interview in *Film Makers on Filmmaking* by Harry M. Geduld, Bloomington, Indiana 1967; interview by J. Blue in *Film Comment* (New York), summer 1968; "Conversation with Satyajit Ray" by F. Isaksson in *Sight and Sound* (London), summer 1970; "Ray's New Trilogy", interview by C.B. Thomsen in *Sight and Sound* (London), winter 1972/73; "Dialogue on

Film: Satyajit Ray" in *American Film* (Washington, D.C.), July/August 1978; interview by Michel Ciment in *Positif* (Paris), May 1979; "Tourner" in *Positif* (Paris), May 1979; interview and article in *Positif* (Paris), June 1979.

On RAY:

Books—*Portrait of a Director* by Marie Seton, Bloomington, Indiana 1970; *The Apu Trilogy* by Robin Wood, New York 1971; *Directors and Directions: Cinema for the '70's* by John Russell Taylor, New York 1975; *Satyajit Ray*, Directorate of Advertising and Visual Publicity, New Delhi 1976; *Satyajit Ray's Art* by Firoze Rangoonwalla, Shahdara, Delhi, India 1980; articles—"Personality of the Month" in *Films and Filming* (London), December 1957; "3 Tendencies" by Guido Aristarco in *Film Culture* (New York), December 1957; "The Growing Edge: Satyajit Ray" by H. Gray in *Film Quarterly* (Berkeley, California), winter 1958; "Indian Movie Maker Who Flees Escape" by P. Grimes in *The New York Times Magazine*, 26 June 1960; "Talk with the Director" in *Newsweek* (New York), 26 September 1960; "Satyajit Ray: A Study" by Eric Rhode in *Sight and Sound* (London), summer 1961; "Satyajit Ray at Work on His Film *Kanchenjanga*" by Marie Seton in *Sight and Sound* (London), spring 1962; "Toughs and Taxi Drivers" by A. Malik in *Sight and Sound* (London), autumn 1962; "The World of Ray" by Alan Stanbrook in *Films and Filming* (London), November 1965; "A Reluctant God" by A. Malik in *Sight and Sound* (London), winter 1965-66; "Satyajit Soap Operas" by B. Hayeen in *Cinema, Television Digest*, spring 1966; "Satyajit Ray: Genius Behind the Man" by B. Hrusa in *Film* (London), winter 1966; "Maestro" in the *New Yorker*, 22 July 1967; "Ray and Tagore" by Chidananda Das Gupta in *Sight and Sound* (London), winter 1966-67; "On Ray" by Paul Glushanok in *Cineaste* (New York), summer 1967; "Satyajit Ray and the Alien" by A. Malik in *Sight and Sound* (London), winter 1967/-68; "At Home in Calcutta" by B. Taper in *Harper* (New York), December 1969; "Profiles" by V. Mehta in the *New Yorker*, 21 March 1970; "India's Chekhov" by W.S. Pechter in *Commonweal* (New York), 16 October 1970; "The Oriental Master" in *Film* (London), winter 1970; "Ray's New Trilogy" by Christian Braad Thomsen in *Sight and Sound* (London), winter 1972-73; "Cinema in India: An Interview with Satyajit Ray's Cinematographers" by K. Dutta in *Filmmakers Newsletter* (Ward Hill, Mass.), January 1975; "A Voyage in India: Satyajit Ray" by J. Hughes in *Film Comment* (New York), September/October 1976; "Tous les feux du Bengale" by Michel Ciment in *Positif* (Paris), June 1979; "Pather Panchali", special issue of *Avant-Scène du cinéma* (Paris), 1 February 1980; "Cinéma Bengali de Ray, cinéma Hindi de Bombay" by C. Haham in *Image et son* (Paris), July/August 1981; "La Longue Patience du regard dans l'oeuvre de Satyajit Ray" by H. Micciollo and others in *Cinéma* (Paris), March 1981.

*   *   *

From the beginning of his career as a filmmaker, Ray has been interested in finding ways to reveal the mind and thoughts of his characters. Because the range of his sympathy is wide, he has been accused of softening the presence of evil in his cinematic world; it has been observed that bad characters are seen in his films to be confused rather than malign. But a director who aims to represent the currents and cross-currents of feeling within people is likely to disclose to viewers the humanness even in reprehensible figures. In any case, from the first films of his early period, Ray devises strategies for rendering inner lives; he simplifies the surface action of the film so that the viewer's attention travels to (1) the reaction of people to one another, or to their environments, (2) the mood expressed by natural scenery or objects, and (3) music as a clue to the state of mind of a character. In the *Apu Trilogy* the camera often stays with one of two characters after the other character exits the frame. The viewer watches the character who remains in the frame to see what silent response to the departed personage wells up from within this character. Or else, after some significant event in the narrative, Ray presents correlatives of that event in the natural world. When the impoverished wife in *Pather Panchali* receives a postcard bearing happy news from her husband, the scene dissolves to water skates dancing on a pond. As for music, in his films Ray commissioned compositions from India's best classical musicians—Ravi Shankar, Vilayat Khan, Ali Akbar Khan—and constructed his sound track to allow full weight to these evocative compositions, but since *Teen Kanya* Ray has been composing his own music and has progressed towards quieter indication through music of the emotional experience of his characters.

Ray's work can be divided into three periods on the basis of his cinematic practice: the early period, 1955-66, from *Pather Panchali* through *Nayak*; the middle period, 1969-1977, from *Googy Gyne Bagha Byne* through *Shatranj Ke Khilari*; and the recent period, 1978-83, from *Joy Baba Felunath* and through *Sadgati* and *Ghare Bahire*. The early period is characterized by thoroughgoing realism: the mise-en-scène is rendered in deep focus; long takes and slow camera movements prevail. The editing is subtle, following shifts of narrative interest and cutting on action in the Hollywood style. Ray's emphasis in the early period on capturing realilty is obvious in *Kanchanjangha*, in which a hundred minutes in the lives of characters is rendered in a hundred minutes of film time. *The Apu Trilogy, Parash Pather, Jalsaghar*, and *Devi* all exemplify what Ray had learned from Hollywood's studio era, from Renoir's mise-en-scène and from the use of classical music in Indian cinema. *Charulata* affords the archetypical example of Ray's early style, the decor, the music, the long takes, the activation of various planes of depth within a composition, the reaction shots, all contributing significantly to a representation of the lonely wife's inner conflicts. The power of Ray's early films comes from his abililty to suggest deep feeling by arranging the surface elements of his films unemphatically.

Ray's middle period is characterized by increasing complexity of style; to his skills at understatement Ray adds a sharp use of montage. The difference in effect between an early film and a middle film becomes apparent if one compares the early *Mahanagar* with the middle *Jana Aranya*, both films pertaining to life in Calcutta. In *Mahanagar*, the protagonist chooses to resign her job in order to protest the unjust dismissal of a colleague. The film affirms the rightness of her decision. In the closing sequence, the protagonist looks up at the tall towers of Calcutta and says to her husband so that we believe her, "What a big city!" Full of jobs! There must be something somewhere for one of us!" Ten years later, in *Jana Aranya*, it is clear that there are no jobs and that there is precious little room to worry about niceties of justice and injustice. The darkness running under the pleasant facade of many of the middle films seems to derive from the turn in Indian politics after the death of Nehru. Within Bengal, many ardent young people joined a Maoist movement to destroy existing institutions, and more were themselves destroyed by a ruthless police. Across India, politicians abandoned Nehru's commitment to a socialist democracy in favor of a scramble for personal

power. In *Seemabaddha* or *Aranyer Din Ratri* Ray's editing is sharp but not startling. In *Shatranj Ke Khilari*, on the other hand, Ray's irony is barely restrained: he cuts from the blue haze of a Nawab's music room to a gambling scene in the city. In harsh daylight, commoners lay bets on fighting rams, as intent on their gambling as the Nawab was on his music.

Audiences in India who have responded warmly to Ray's early films have sometimes been troubled by the complexity of his middle films. A film like *Shatranj Ke Khilari* was expected by many viewers to reconstruct the splendors of Moghul India as the early *Jalsaghar* had reconstructed the sensitivity of Bengali feudal landlords and *Charulata* the decency of upper class Victorian Bengal. What the audience found instead was a stern examination of the sources of Indian decadence. According to Ray, the British seemed less to blame for their role than the Indians who demeaned themselves by colluding with the British or by ignoring the public good and plunging into private pleasures. Ray's point of view in *Shatranj* was not popular with distributors and so his first Hindi film was denied fair exhibition in many cities in India.

Ray's recent style, most evident in the short features *Pikoo* and *Sadgati*, pays less attention than earlier to building a stable geography and a firm time scheme. The exposition of characters and situations is swift: the effect is of great concision. In *Pikoo*, a young boy is sent outside to sketch flowers so that his mother and her lover can pursue their affair indoors. The lover has brought along a drawing pad and colored pens to divert the boy. The boy has twelve colored pens in his packet with which he must represent on paper the wealth of colors in nature. In a key scene (lasting ten seconds) the boy looks at a flower, then down at his packet for a matching color. Through that action of the boy's looking to match the world with his means, Ray suggests the striving in his own work to render the depth and range of human experience.

In focussing on inner lives and on human relations as the ground of social and political systems, Ray continues the humanist tradition of Rabindranath Tagore. Ray studied at Santiniketan, the university founded by Tagore, and was close to the poet during the poet's last years. Ray has acknowledged his debt in a lyrical documentary about Tagore, and through the Tagore stories on which he has based his films, *Teen Kanya, Charulata*, and the recent *Ghare Bahire*. As the poet Tagore was his example, Ray has become an example to important younger filmmakers (such as Shyam Benegal, M.S. Sathyu, G. Aravindan), who have learned from him how to reveal in small domestic situations the working of larger political and cultural forces.

—Satti Khanna

REED, SIR CAROL. British. Born in Putney, London, 30 December 1906. Educated at King's School, Canterbury. Married Diana Wynyard (divorced); actress Penelope Ward; sons: Max and Peter. Career: beginning 1924—appears on London stage; 1927—begins working with author Edgar Wallace as advisor on stage adaptation of Wallace's novels; acts in and directs resulting productions; 1929—stage directing debut in London; 1932—dialogue director for Associated Talking Pictures; 1933—release of first feature as director; during war serves in British Army Film Unit; 1946—begins collaboration with writer Graham Greene on *Odd Man Out*; 1961—replaced as director on

Mutiny on the Bounty by Lewis Milestone. Died in London, 1976. Recipient: British Film Academy Award, Best British Film for *Odd Man Out*, 1947; British Film Academy Award, Best British Film for *The Fallen Idol*, 1948; British Film Academy Award, Best British Film for *The Third Man*, 1949; Best Direction, New York Film Critics, for *The Fallen Idol*, 1949; Quarterly Award, Directors Guild of America, for *The Third Man*, 1949/50; Knighted, 1952; Golden Thistle Award, Scotland, 1967; Best Director Academy Award for *Oliver!*, 1968.

Films (as director): 1933—*Midshipman Easy (Men of the Sea)*; 1936—*Laburnum Grove*; *Talk of the Devil* (+story); 1937—*Who's Your Lady Friend?*; *No Parking* (Raymond) (story only); 1938—*Bank Holiday (3 on a Week-End)*; *Penny Paradise*; 1939—*Climbing High*; *A Girl Must Live*; *The Stars Look Down*; 1940—*Night Train to Munich (Night Train)*; *The Girl in the News*; 1941—*Kipps (The Remarkable Mr. Kipps)*; *A Letter from Home* (short documentary); 1942—*The Young Mr. Pitt*; *The New Lot*; 1944—*The Way Ahead*; 1945—*The True Glory* (collaboration with Garson Kanin); 1947—*Odd Man Out*; 1948—*The Fallen Idol*; 1949—*The Third Man*; 1951—*Outcast of the Islands*; 1953—*The Man Between*; 1955—*A Kid for 2 Farthings*; 1956—*Trapeze*; 1958—*The Key*; 1960—*Our Man in Havana*; 1963—*The Running Man* (+pr); 1965—*The Agony and the Ecstasy* (+pr); 1968—*Oliver!*; 1970—*Flap*; 1972—*Follow Me*.

Publications:

By REED:

Interview in *Encountering Directors* by Charles Samuels, New York 1972.

On REED:

Book—*The Movie Makers: Artists in an Industry* by Gene D. Phillips, Chicago 1973; articles—"Carol Reed" by E. Goodman in *Theatre Arts* (New York), May 1947; "I Give the Public What I Like" by Harvey Breit in *The New York Times Magazine*, 15 January 1950; "The Director: Carol Reed" by Basil Wright in *Sight and Sound* (London), summer 1951; "A Man with No Message" by Catherine De La Roche in *Films and Filming* (London), December 1954; "Carol Reed in the Context of His Time" in 2 parts by Andrew Sarris in *Film Culture* (New York), no.10, 1956 and no.11, 1957; "First of the Realists" and "The Stylist Goes to Hollywood" by Andrew Sarris in *Films and Filming* (London), September and October 1957; "Sir Carol Reed" by Marion Fawcett in *Films in Review* (New York), March 1959; "Pictures of Innocence: Sir Carol Reed" by M. Voigt in *Focus on Film* (London), spring 1974; obituary in *Cinéma* (Paris), June 1976; "Carol Reed" by Gene D. Phillips in *Films in Review* (New York), August/September 1982.

*   *   *

Carol Reed came to films from the theater. "As a young man," he recalled, "I became an assistant to Edgar Wallace, who wrote and produced so many melodramas on both stage and screen. I suppose that helped me to see the effectiveness and appealing value of melodrama, and thus gave me a penchant for filming

several thrillers later on." Reed served his apprenticeship in the film industry first as a dialogue director, and then graduated to becoming a director in his own right by making a series of low budget second features.

Reed's early films, such as *Midshipman Easy*, are not remarkable; but then few British films before World War II were. In the twenties and thirties British distributors were more interested in importing films from abroad, especially from America, than in encouraging film production at home. As a result British films were, with rare exceptions, bargain-basement imitations of Hollywood movies. In 1938, however, the British government stipulated that producers must allocate sufficient funds for the making of domestic films in order to allow an adequate amount of time for preproduction preparation, shooting, and the final shaping of each picture. Directors like Carol Reed took advantage of this increased support of British production to produce films which, though still modestly made by Hollywood standards, demonstrated the artistry of which British film makers were capable. By the late thirties, then, Reed had graduated to making films of considerable substance, like *Night Train to Munich*.

"For the first time," Arthur Knight has written, "there were English pictures which spoke of the British character, British institutions—even social problems such as unemployment and nationalization—with unexpected frankness and awareness." An outstanding example of this new trend in British film making was Reed's *The Stars Look Down*, an uncompromising picture of life in a Welsh mining community, which brought the director serious critical attention on both sides of the Atlantic.

Reed went on to work on some of the best documentaries to come out of the war, such as the Academy Award-winning *The True Glory*, as well as to direct the documentary-like theatrical feature, *The Way Ahead*, an unvarnished depiction of army life. The experience which Reed gained in making wartime documentaries not only influenced his direction of *The Way Ahead*, but also was reflected in his post-war cinematic style, enabling him to develop further in films like *Odd Man Out* the strong sense of realism which had first appeared in *The Stars Look Down*. The documentary approach that Reed used to tell the story of *Odd Man Out*, which concerns a group of anti-British insurgents in Northern Ireland, was one to which audiences were ready to respond. Wartime films, both documentary and fictional, had conditioned moviegoers in Britain and elsewhere to expect a greater degree of realism in postwar cinema, and Reed provided it.

The more enterprising English producers believed that British films should be made to appeal primarily to the home market rather than to the elusive American market which some of their colleagues were trying to conquer. It was the former, as things turned out, who won the day; for it was precisely British films such as Carol Reed was creating in the post-war years, films which were wholly English in character and situation, which were the first English movies to win wide popularity in the United States. Among these, of course, was *Odd Man Out*. This was the first film which Reed both produced and directed, a factor which guaranteed him a greater degree of creative freedom than he had enjoyed before the war.

For the first time, too, the theme that was to appear so often in his work was perceptible in *Odd Man Out*. In depicting for us in this and other films a hunted, lonely hero caught in the middle of a crisis usually not of his own making, Reed implies that man can achieve maturity and self-mastery only by accepting the challenges that life puts in his way and by struggling with them as best he can.

Reed won the best director award from the British Film Academy for *Odd Man Out*, and won the same prize for his next two consecutive films as well, *The Fallen Idol* and *The Third*

Man, a fact that clearly established him as one of the most distinguished British directors of his generation. *The Fallen Idol* was the first of a trio of masterful films which he made in collaboration with novelist-screenwriter Graham Greene, one of the most significant creative associations between a writer and a director in the history of film. The team followed *The Fallen Idol* with *The Third Man* and, a decade later, *Our Man in Havana*. *The Third Man*, which dealt with the black market in post-war Vienna, won the Grand Prize at the Cannes Film Festival. Commenting on his collaboration with the director, Greene has written that the success of these films was due to Reed, "the only director I know with that particular warmth of human sympathy, the extraordinary feeling for the right face for the right part, the exactitude of cutting, and not the least important, the power of sympathizing with an author's worries and an ability to guide him."

Because most of the films which Reed directed in the next decade or so were not comparable to the post-war films mentioned above, it was thought that he had passed his peak for good. *Oliver!* in fact proved that Reed was back in top form, for it won him the Academy Award as best director and was itself named best picture of its year. In her *New Yorker* review of the film, Pauline Kael paid Reed a tribute that sums up his entire career in the cinema: "I applaud the commerical heroism of a director who can steer a huge production and keep his sanity and perspective and decent human feelings as beautifully intact as they are in *Oliver!*."

A genuinely self-effacing man, Reed was never impressed by the awards and honors that he garnered throughout his career (he was knighted in 1952). Summarizing his own approach to filmmaking some time before his death at sixty-nine in 1976, he said simply, "I give the public what *I* like, and hope they will like it too." More often than not, he was right.

—Gene D. Phillips

REICHENBACH, FRANÇOIS. French. Born in Paris, 3 July 1922. Educated at lycée Janson-de-Sailly, Bachot. Career: after WW II—becomes art advisor to American collectors and museums; 1953—acquires 16mm camera, begins making amateur films; 1956—jury prize at Tours Festival; urged by cousin, producer Pierre Braunberger, to become professional filmmaker; 1960—first feature-length documentary, *L'Amérique insolite*. Recipient: Cannes Festival Award for *L'Amérique insolite*, 1960; Best Feature Documentary Academy Award for *Arthur Rubinstein—The Love of Life*, 1969.

Films (as director, scriptwriter, cinematographer, and sometimes sound recorder of short films): 1955—*Impressions de New York*; *New York ballade*; *Visages de Paris*; 1956—*Houston Texas*; *Novembre à Paris*; *Le Grand Sud*; 1957—*Au pays de Porgy and Bess*; *L'Américain se détend*; *Les Marines*; *Carnaval à la Nouvelle-Orléans*; *L'Eté indien*; 1958-60—*L'Amérique insolite (L'Amérique vue par un Français)* (feature); 1961—*Un Coeur gros comme ça (The Winner)* (feature); 1962—*Week-end en mer*; *Les Amoureux du "France"* (co-d—feature); *Retour à New York*; *A la mémoire du rock*; *Le Petit Café (Scènes de la vie de café)*; *L'Amérique lunaire*; *Le Paris des photographes*; *Le Paris des mannequins*; *Jeu 1 (Jeux)*; 1963—*Histoire d'un petit garçon devenu grand*; *La Douceur du village (Un Bol d'air à Loué)* (medium-length); *Illumination* (co-d); *Artifices*; *Enterrement de Kennedy* (for TV); 1964—*Les Cheveaux d'Hollywood*; *Mexico nuevo*; *Anges gardiens* (co-d); 1965—*Le Cinqième soleil* (co-d); *Lomelin (Portrait d'un novillero)*; *East African Safari*; *Boulez* (Fano) (ph only); *Lapicque*; *Dunoyer de Segonzac*; 1966—*Voyage de Brigitte Bardot aux U.S.A.*; *Reportage sur "Paris brûle-t-il?"* (medium-length); *Mireille Mathieu* (for TV); *Orson Welles* (for TV); *Jeanne Moreau* (for TV); *Herbert von Karajan* (for TV); *El Cordobès*; *Manitas de Plata*; *Aurora*; *Le Professeur de piano*; *Impressions de Paris*; 1967—*Concerto Brandenbourgeois*; *Gromaire*; *La Sixième Face du Pentagone* (Marker) (ph only); *Mexico, Mexico* (co-d—feature); 1968—*Treize Jours en France (Grenoble)* (co-d—feature); *Special Bardot (Show Bardot)* (co-d—for TV); *Musique en Méditerranée*; *Arthur Rubinstein, l'amour de la vie (Arthur Rubinstein—The Love of Life)* (co-d—feature); 1969—*L'Indiscret* (fiction feature); *Christian Dior*; *Festival dans le désert*; *A fleur d'eau (Vichy 1969)*; *France sur mer*; *Violence sur Houston (Prisons à l'américaine)*; *Kill Patrice, un shérif pas comme les autres*; *Parfums Revillon*; *Le Massacre* (feature); *Les Moisson de l'espoir (Israël)*; 1970—*Yehudi Menuhin—Chemin de lumière (Yehudi Menuhin—Road of Light, Yehudi Menuhin Story)* (co-d); *Soy Mexico*; *La Fête des morts*; *L'Opéra de quatre pesos*; *La Caravane d'amour (Medicine Ball Caravan)* (feature); 1971—*J'ai tout donné (Johnny's Days)* (feature); *Le Chasseur*; *Rêver ou Envol*; *Partir*; *Eliette ou instants de la vie d'une femme*; *Le Hold-up au crayon* (feature); (as director of feature-length documentaries): 1972—*La Raison du plus fou est toujours le meilleure* (co-d); *Mon amie Sylvie* (for TV); *Monte-Carlo*; 1973—*Vérités et mensonges (Nothing But the Truth)* (co-d); *La Passion selon les Coras* (short); 1974—*Entends-tu les chiens aboyer? (No oyes ladrar los perros?, Don't You Hear the Dogs Bark?)*; *Carlos Monzon*; *Portrait de Hildegard Knef* (for TV); 1975—*Lettre de Paris et d'ailleurs* (series of 6 films for TV); *Le Petit Cirque mexicain* (for TV); *Rolland Garros* (for TV); *F for Fake* (Welles) (d add'l footage, ro only); 1976—*Sex O'Clock U.S.A.*; *Portrait de Jacques Chirac* (for TV); *France inconnue* (series of 10 films for TV); *Le Roi Pelé*; *Club Méditerranée*; 1977—*Entre ciel et terre* (for TV); *L'Homme et le sport* (for TV); 1978—*Arts et arbres* (for TV); *Portrait de Diane Dufresne* (for TV); *Portrait de Barbara* (for TV); *Les Leçons de Slava* (series of 3 films for TV); 1979—*Vingt-cinq ans de l'Olympia* (series of 2 films for TV); *Grâce à la musique* (series for TV); *Valérie Giscard d'Estaing au Mexique (V.G.E.)*; *Arthur Rubinstein* (series of 5 films for TV); 1980—*Houston Texas*; *La Maison de Molière* (for TV); *La Belgique profonde* (for TV); *Jacques-Henri Lartigue*; 1981—*Le Japon insolite*.

Publications:

By REICHENBACH:

Books and scripts—"Les Marines", filmscript, in *Avant-Scène du cinéma* (Paris), December 1966; "Houston Texas (1956)", filmscript, in *Avant-Scène du cinéma* (Paris), February 1968; *François Reichenbach—Le Monde à encore un visage*, Paris 1981; *Houston Texas USA, un vrai crime*, filmscript, with Michel Rachline, La Table Ronde, Paris 1981. article—"Meeting La Nouvelle Vague" in *Films and Filming* (London), October 1959.

On REICHENBACH:

Articles—"The Men and Their Work" by G. Billard in *Films and Filming* (London), October 1959; "Visual De Tocqueville" in *Time* (New York), 19 December 1960.

*   *   *

After the war, Reichenbach left France for America. Interested in painting and art criticism, he became an advisor to art buyers. In 1953 he acquired a 16mm camera and became active as an amateur filmmaker. His first film, *Impressions de New York*, earned him the special jury prize at the Festival of Tours in 1956. This success allowed him to make other films which have, for the most part, been in color. Taking on the writing, photography, directing, and sometimes even sound recording, he created his own style, marked by poetry and authenticity.

A set of documentaries on America, in addition to two films on Paris, revealed his obvious talent as an observer. His report *Les Marines*, in particular, in which he represents the violent and dehumanizing aspects of the training of elite troops in America, attracted public and international critical attention. In 1960 he made his first feature-length film, *L'Amérique insolite*. He showed in a mosaic of well-chosen and cleverly-edited images, little-known aspects of the average American's daily life. Despite his somewhat thin analysis, the film was considered a success.

Returning to France, Reichenbach familiarized himself with the world of boxing in which he met black boxer Abdulah Faye to whom he devoted his second feature, *Un Coeur gros comme ça*. Despite winning the Prix Delluc in 1962, the film was poorly received. It was aboard the liner "France," on which he had made his first ocean crossing, that he returned once again to America. During the voyage he shot a documentary which would be incorporated into Pierre Grimblat's film *Les Amoureux du "France"*. After making various shorts in America, Reichenbach became interested in the daily life of Paris, and it was at Loué, in a little village of the Sarthe, that he directed his excellent portrayal of peasant life, *La Douceur de village*, which received the Grand Prix at Cannes in 1964.

Next he undertook a series of artists' portraits which still retain their value as historical documents. In 1966 Reichenbach and his camera followed Brigitte Bardot during her first trip to the U.S. Soon after he and Lelouch made a documentary on the winter Olympic games, *Treize jours à Grenoble*, then a feature with Patris on the celebrated pianist Arthur Rubinstein, which received the Oscar for Best Documentary. After attempting a fiction film, *L'Indiscret*, he went to Houston for a summer, following and filming the work of the police.

In France he next made *Le Massacre*, with Nathalie Delon, and *La Caravan d'amour* in the U.S. for Warner Brothers. He was in Mexico for several years and recorded, with deep sympathy, the life of its people. He made a feature, *Entends-tu les chiens aboyer?*, a mixture of fiction and documentary, which told of a long journey of a father and his sick son. The film represented Mexico at Cannes in 1974. After having portrayed the boxer Carlos Monzon in Argentina, he returned to the U.S. for an examination of the sexual revolution, *Sex O'Clock U.S.A.* In associating himself with the scandalous and sensational, he tended toward a complacency and commercialism for which a number of critics reproached him.

As a sought-after cineaste, Reichenbach came to meet numerous celebrities, especially in the world of music. He followed President Giscard d'Estaing on his trip to Mexico and again interviewed Rubinstein, for a televised series. In 1979 he returned for the third time to Houston, a city which holds a record for

criminality, intent on filming crime "en direct." A policeman having been killed, Reichenbach attempted to follow and record, point by point, the investigations and arrest of a young murderer. This documentary, which provoked an outpouring of opinion in favor of the accused, reveals in fact the limits of a cinematic approach based on spontaneity and intuition.

In 1981 Reichenbach made *Le Japon insolite* which attempted to show the connection between the traditions and future of this land: through alluring images, he manifested once again his penchant for the extraordinary and the unusual.

—Karel Tabery

REINIGER, LOTTE. British. Born in Berlin, 2 June 1899; became citizen of of Great Britain. Married Carl Koch, 1921 (died 1963). Career: 1915—meets Paul Wegener; 1916—creates silhouettes for intertitles of Wegener's *Rübezahls Hochzeit*; 1916-17—attends Max Reinhardt theater school, Berlin; 1918—introduced by Wegener to film group associated with Dr. Hans Cürlis; 1919—Cürlis's newly-founded Institut für Kulturforschung, Berlin, sponsor's Reiniger's first film; mid-1930s—with Koch moves to Britain, works with G.P.O. Film Unit with Len Lye and Norman McLaren; 1936—makes *The King's Breakfast*, first film in England; 1946—works with Märchentheater of city of Berlin at Theater am Schiffbauerdamm; beginning 1950—lives and works, mainly for TV, in England; 1950s and '60s—creates sets and figures for English puppet and shadow theater Hoghart's Puppets; 1953—Primrose Productions set up, sponsors productions for American TV; 1975—begins collaboration with National Film Board of Canada; 1979—*The Rose and the Ring* premiered at American Film Festival. Died 19 June 1981; buried at at Dettenheusen, near Tübingen, West Germany. Recipient: Silver Dolphin, Venice Biennale, for *Gallant Little Tailor*, 1955; Filmband in Gold, West Germany, for service to German cinema, 1972; Verdienst Kreuz, West Germany, 1978.

Films (contributions as indicated): 1916—*Rübezahls Hochzeit* (Wegener) (silhouettes for intertitles); *Die Schöne Prinzessin von China* (Gliese) (set decoration, props, and costumes); 1918—*Apokalypse* (Gliese) (silhouettes for intertitles); *Der Rattenfänger von Hameln (The Pied Piper of Hamelin)* (Wegener) (silhouettes for intertitles); (as director—principal collaborator Carl Koch, others include Berthold Bartosch and Arthur Neher): 1919—*Das Ornament des verliebten Herzens (The Ornament of the Loving Heart)*; 1920—*Der verlorene Schatten* (Gliese) (silhouette sequence only); *Amor und das standhafte Liebespaar*; 1921—*Der fliegende Koffer*; *Der Stern von Bethlehem*; 1922—*Aschenputtel*; *Dornröschen*; 1923—*Die Nibelungen* (Lang) (silhouette sequence only—not used); 1923-26—*Die Geschichte des Prinzen Achmed (Die Abenteuer des Prinzen Achmed, Wak-Wak, ein Märchenzauber, The Adventures of Prince Achmed)*; 1928—*Der scheintote Chinese* (originally part of *Die Geschichte des Prinzen Achmed*); *Doktor Dolittle und seine Tiere (The Adventures of Dr. Dolittle)* (in 3 parts: *Abenteuer: Die Reise nach Afrika, Abenteuer: Die Affenbrücke, Abenteuer: Die Affenkrankheit*); 1929-30—*Die Jagd nach dem Glück (Running After Luck)* (Gliese) (co-story, co-sc, co-sound only); 1930—*Zehn Minuten Mozart*; 1931—*Harlekin*; 1932—*Sissi* (intended as interlude for premiere of operetta *Sissi* by Fritz

Kreisler, Vienna 1932); 1933—*Don Quichotte* (Pabst) (opening silhouette sequence only); *Carmen*; 1934—*Das rollende Rad*; *Der Graf von Carabas*; *Das gestohlene Herz (The Stolen Heart)*; 1935—*Der kleine Schornsteinfeger (The Little Chimney Sweep)*; *Galathea*; *Papageno*; 1936—*The King's Breakfast*; 1937—*Tocher*; *La Marseillaise* (Renoir) (created shadow theater seen in film); 1939—*Dream Circus* (not completed); *L'elisir d'amore* (not released); 1944—*Die goldene Gans* (not completed); 1951—*Mary's Birthday*; (for U.S. TV): 1953—*Aladdin*; *The Magic Horse*; *Snow White and Rose Red*; 1954—*The 3 Wishes*; *The Grasshopper and the Ant*; *The Frog Prince*; *The Gallant Little Tailor*; *The Sleeping Beauty*; *Caliph Storch*; 1955—*Hansel and Gretel*; *Thumbelina*; *Jack and the Beanstalk*; (theatrical films): 1956—*The Star of Bethlehem*; 1957—*Helen la Belle*; 1958—*The Seraglio*; (interludes for theatrical performances): 1960—*The Pied Piper of Hamelin*; 1961—*The Frog Prince*; 1962—*Wee Sandy*; 1963—*Cinderella*; 1974—*The Lost Son*; 1976—*Aucassin et Nicolette*; 1979—*The Rose and the Ring*.

Publications:

By REINIGER:

Books—*Das Loch im Vorhang*, illustrations, Berlin 1919; *Venus in Seide*, Berlin 1919; *Die Abenteuer des Prinzen Achmed*, 32 pictures from film, with narration, Tübingen 1926 (reprinted 1972—text translated into English by Carman Educational Associates, Pine Grove, Ontario, Canada 1975); *Der böse Gutsherr und die guten Tiere*, Bristol 1934; *Der ewige Esel*, Zurich/Fribourg 1949; *King Arthur and His Knights of the Round Table*, London 1952; *Mondscheingarten—Gedichte*, Gütersloch 1968; *Shadow Theatres and Shadow Films*, London and New York 1970; *Das gestohlene Herz*, Tübingen 1972; articles—"Scissors Make Films" in *Sight and Sound* (London), spring 1936; "The Adventures of Prince Achmed" in *Silent Picture* (London), autumn 1970; "Lotte Reiniger et les ombres chinoises", interview by L. Bonneville in *Séquences* (Montreal), July 1975.

On REINIGER:

Books—*Walking Shadows* by Eric White, London 1931; *Experimental Animation* by Robert Russett and Cecile Starr, New York 1976; articles—"*Prince Achmed* and Other Animated Silhouettes" by Randolph Weaver in *Theatre Arts* (New York), June 1931; "Flatland Fairy Tales" by Guy Coté in *Film* (London), October 1954; "She Made 1st Cartoon Feature" in *Films and Filming* (London), December 1955; "The Films of Lotte Reiniger" in *Film Culture* (New York), no.9, 1956; "Animated Women" by H. Beckerman in *Filmmakers Newsletter* (Ward Hill, Mass.), summer 1974; "Lotte Reiniger at 80" by P. Gelder in *Sight and Sound* (London), no.3, 1979; "Lotte Reiniger's Fabulous Film Career" by Cecile Starr in *Sightlines* (New York), summer 1980; "Zum Tode Lotte Reiniger" by H. Hurst in *Frauen und Film* (Berlin), September 1981; "Lotte Reiniger au pays des ombres" in *Image et son* (Paris), December 1981; film—*You've Asked for It*, documentary, London 1953.

*   *   *

Lotte Reiniger's career as an independent filmmaker is among the longest and most singular in film history, spanning some sixty years (1919-1979) of actively creating silhouette animation films. Her *Adventures of Prince Achmed* is the world's first feature-length animation film, made when she was in her mid-twenties and winning considerable acclaim.

Silhouette animation existed before 1919, but Reiniger is its preeminent practitioner, transforming a technically and esthetically bland genre to a recognized art form, albeit a minor one. Since childhood she had excelled at free-hand cut-outs and shadow theaters. As a teenager at Max Reinhardt's acting studio, she was invited by actor-director Paul Wegener to make silhouette decorations for the credits and inter-titles of *The Pied Piper of Hamelin* (1918); she also helped animate the film's wooden rats, when live guinea pigs proved unmanageable. The rest of Reiniger's professional life was wholeheartedly devoted to silhoutte animation, with an occasional retreat to shadow plays or book illustrations when money was not available for films.

Prominent among Lotte Reiniger's talents was her transcendence of the inherent flatness and awkwardness of silhouette animation through her dramatic mise-en scène and her balletic movements. Her female characters are especially lively and original, displaying wit, sensuousness and self-awareness rarely found in animated cartoons (from whose creative ranks women animators were virtually excluded until the 1970s). Few real-life actresses could match the expressiveness with which Reiniger inspirited the gestures of her lead-jointed figures as she moved and filmed them fraction by fraction, frame by frame.

For over four decades, Lotte Reiniger shared her professional life with her husband, Carl Koch, who designed her animation studio and, until his death in 1963, served as her producer and camera operator. "There was nothing about what is called film-technique that he did not know," Jean Renoir wrote in his autobiography. (In the late 1930s, Koch collaborated on the scripts and production of Renoir's celebrated *Grand Illusion* and *Rules of the Game*, and on *La Marseillaise* for which Reiniger created a shadow-play sequence.)

Aside from *The Adventures of Prince Achmed*, Reiniger ventured into feature filmmaking only once, in *Running After Luck*, the story of a wandering showman, part animation and part live-action, which she co-directed with Rochus Gliese. It was a critical and financial failure, perhaps because of its imperfect sound system. The rest of her films were shorts, mainly one or two reels in length.

Lotte Reiniger worked outside commercial channels, with minimal support. She said she never felt discrimination because she was a woman, but she did admit resenting that great sums were spent on films of little or no imagination while so little was available for the films she wanted to make. In the 1970s she was coaxed from her retirement to make two films in Canada; she also toured much of Europe, Canada, and the United States under the auspices of the Goethe House cultural centers of the West German government, showing her films and demonstrating her cut-out animation technique.

Hans Richter, who knew Reiniger in the early Berlin years, later wrote that she "belonged to the avant-garde as far as independent production and courage were concerned," but that the spirit of her work seemed Victorian. Jean Renoir placed her even further back in time, as "a visual expression of Mozart's music." It is more likely that, like the fables and myths and fairy tales on which many of her films are based, her work transcends time and fashion.

—Cecile Starr

REISZ, KAREL. Czech. Born in Ostrava, Czechoslovakia, 21 July 1926. Educated Leighton Park School, Reading, England, 1938-44; Emmanuel College, Cambridge University, England, 1945-47. Married Julia Coppard (divorced); Betsy Blair, 1963; 3 sons. Career: 1938—arrives in England as a refugee from Nazi threat to Czechoslovakia; 1944-45—joins Czechoslovakian wing of RAF; 1947-49—teaches at London grammar school; 1950—begins writing film criticism on regular basis for *Sequence* and *Sight and Sound*; 1952—begins 3-year term as program director for the National Film Theatre; co-edits with Lindsay Anderson the last issue of *Sequence*; 1953—publishes *The Technique of Film Editing*; 1956—co-directs 1st film, *Momma Don't Allow*, with Tony Richardson; is associated with England's "Free Cinema" movement, a loosely knit group of documentary filmmakers; 1956-57—serves as "officer of commercials" in film division of Ford Motor Company in England; 1960—directs 1st feature, *Saturday Night and Sunday Morning*. Address: c/o Film Contrasts, 2 Lower James Street, London W 1, England.

Films (as director): 1956—*Momma Don't Allow* (co-d); 1957—*Every Day Except Christmas* (co-pr only); 1959—*We Are the Lambeth Boys*; 1960—*Saturday Night and Sunday Morning*; 1963—*This Sporting Life* (Anderson) (pr only); 1964—*Night Must Fall* (+co-pr); 1966—*Morgan, a Suitable Case for Treatment (Morgan!)*; 1968—*Isadora (The Loves of Isadora)*; 1974—*The Gambler*; 1978—*Who'll Stop the Rain (Dog Soldiers)*; 1981—*The French Lieutenant's Woman*.

Publications:

By REISZ:

Book—*The Technique of Film Editing*, revised by Gavin Miller, London 1968; articles—"Unfair to Eisenstein" with Marie Seton and L. McLeod in *Sight and Sound* (London), June 1951; "Interview with John Huston" in *Sight and Sound* (London), January/March 1952; "Hollywood's Anti-Red Boomerang" in *Sight and Sound* (London), January/March 1953; "Stroheim in London" in *Sight and Sound* (London), April/June 1954; "Experiment at Brussels" in *Sight and Sound* (London), summer 1958; "From 'Free Cinema' to Feature Film: Interview" in the *Times* (London), 19 May 1960; "Karel Reisz and Experimenters: An Exchange of Correspondence" in *Films and Filming* (London), December 1961; "Desert Island Films" in *Films and Filming* (London), August 1963; "How to Get into Films—By the People Who Got in Themselves" in *Films and Filming* (London), July 1963; "An Interview with Karel Reisz" by Gene D. Phillips in *Cinema* (Los Angeles), summer 1968; "Outsiders", interview by Gordon Gow in *Films and Filming* (London), January 1979; "Karel Reisz: permanence d'un personnage: le mal adapté", interview by J. Grissolange in *Jeune Cinéma* (Paris), October 1979.

On REISZ:

Books—*Non-Fiction Film* by Richard Barsam, New York 1973; *Hollywood U.K.: The British Film Industry in the 60's* by Alexander Walker, New York 1974; *Voices of Film Experience* edited by Jay Leyda, New York 1977; *A Critical History of the British Cinema* by Roy Armes, New York 1978; *Karel Reisz* by Georg Gaston, Boston 1980; articles—"Free Cinema" by Gavin Lambert in *Sight and Sound* (London), spring 1956; "*We Are the Lambeth Boys*" by Richard Hoggart in *Sight and Sound* (London), summer/autumn 1959; "Karel Reisz: Free Czech" in *Films*

and Filming (London), February 1961; "The Face of '63—Great Britain" by Peter Cowie in *Films and Filming* (London), February 1963; "Mad About the Boy" in *Time* (New York), 24 June 1966; "British Cinema Filmography" in *Film* (London), spring 1972; "*Saturday Night and Sunday Morning*" in *Masterworks of the British Cinema* by Boleshaw Sulik, New York 1974; "Cannes 78" by Betty Demby in *Filmmakers Newsletter* (Ward Hill, Mass.), September 1978; "*Dog Soldiers*: Novel into Film" by Stephen Zito in *American Film* (Washington, D.C.), September 1977; "Who'll Stop the Director" by Leigh Charlton in *The Village Voice* (New York), 4 September 1978; "Later On" by Stanley Kauffmann in the *New Republic* (New York), 30 September 1978; issue on Reisz in *Positif* (Paris), November 1978; "Outsiders: Karel Reisz in an Interview with Gordon Gow" in *Films and Filming* (London), January 1979; "Minute Reisz: 6 Earlier Films" by H. Kennedy in *Film Comment* (New York), September/October 1981; "Karel Reisz" by Roy Armes in *International Film Guide* edited by Peter Cowie, London 1982.

*   *   *

Karel Reisz came to filmmaking from the world of academia and scholarship. He had taught in an English grammar school, written film criticism, co-edited with Lindsay Anderson the last issue of the slightly snooty magazine *Sequence*, and written a theoretical textbook still in use today on *The Technique of Film Editing* (without having spent one working day in the industry). With such a background, it was obvious he would have preconceived notions about filmmaking, but they were notions without regard to established filmmaking practices. Reisz wanted to improve the British film industry which had also been the critical aim of *Sequence* and he had his first chance with two documentary shorts, *Momma Don't Allow* (co-directed with Tony Richardson) and *We Are the Lambeth Boys*. In these films, Reisz depicted contemporary Britain from a working-class viewpoint, and when they were first screened at London's National Film Theatre, they were presented along with films from Lindsay Anderson and others—as "British Free Cinema." In fact, these films were to herald a new wave in British filmmaking, which reached its zenith with Reisz's first feature, *Saturday Night and Sunday Morning*.

Jack Clayton's *Room at the Top* paved the way for *Saturday Night and Sunday Morning*, a study of a tough, young machinist, played by Albert Finney, who takes out his frustrations with his work and his life through sex and alcohol. He is the quintessential British rebel, the English answer to James Dean, who takes his revenge on society by impregnating his boss's wife. It is an uninhibited, fresh and frank look at British working class existence, and it brought critical fame to Karel Reisz.

The only problem was that Reisz seemed temporarily unable to follow up on that first success. (Reisz's output is pathetically small: seven films in 20 years, a sign perhaps not so much of a careful director as a director with whom producers feel uneasy.) Next, Reisz directed Albert Finney again in *Night Must Fall*, which had worked as a classic melodrama in the thirties but had little relevance to the sixties. The unconventionality of *Morgan* also seemed strained, and even a little pretentious (a claim that can easily be made against Reisz's outdated study of a Vietnam vet, *Who'll Stop the Rain?*) It was not until *Isadora* that Reisz began to demonstrate a new side to his work, a romantic side, obviously born of his Czech background (he did not come to Britain until he was twelve).

Both *Isadora* and the director's most recent success, *The French Lieutenant's Woman*, show that Reisz has now discovered how to successfully blend romanticism and the realism of his first films. In *Isadora* it is perhaps a little more subtly accomplished than in *The French Lieutenant's Woman*, where the two elements fight against each other for existence.

As to his directorial techniques, Reisz appears to be very willing to listen to others. He is quoted as saying, "For me the great thing about a film is to allow everyone to make their contribution and to keep the process fluid. The process of adaptation is a free process and the process of rehearsal is a free process and the process of shooting is a free process." Free process, free cinema, and a healthy freedom in his choice of subjects have marked Reisz's career to date.

—Anthony Slide

RENOIR, JEAN. French and American. Born in Paris, 15 September 1894; became citizen of United States (naturalized) in 1946, retained French citizenship. Educated at Collège de Sainte-Croix, Neuilly-sur-Seine, 1902; Ecole Sainte-Marie de Monceau, 1903; Ecole Massina, Nice, until 1912; University d'Aix-en-Provence, degree in mathematics and philosophy, 1913. Married Andrée Madeleine Heuschling ("Dédée", took name Catherine Hessling following 1924 appearance in *Catherine*) in 1920 (separated 1930); Dido Freire in 1944; child: Alain. Career: 1914-15—serves as 2nd lieutenant of cavalry, wounded 1915; 1916—transferred to French Flying Corps, demobilized 1918; 1920-23—works as potter and ceramicist; 1924—seeing *Foolish Wives* (von Stroheim) reportedly leads to decision to make films; 1930s—association with left-wing artists and intellectuals; 1936—*La Vie est à nous* refused censorship certificate permitting public showing; 1939—enters Service Cinématographique de l'Armée as lieutenant; *La Régle du jeu* banned by French government as demoralizing; 1940—Robert Flaherty arranges for Renoir's passage to U.S.; 1941—signs with 20th Century Fox; 1942—signs with Universal, terminates agreement later in year; 1951—reestablishes residence in Paris, retaining home in Beverly Hills; 1954—directs *Julius Caesar* in Roman arena at Arles for city's 2000th anniversary, continues to be active in theatre through 1950s; 1958—Compagnie Jean Renoir formed with Anne de Saint Phalle; 1960—teaches theatre at University of California, Berkeley; late 1960s—works on several novels and begins autobiography. Died in Beverly Hills, 12 February 1979. Recipient: Prix Louis-Delluc, La Jeune Critique Indépendante, for *Les Bas-Fonds*, 1936; Chevalier de la Légion d'Honneur, 1936; International Jury Cup, Venice Biennale, for *La Grande Illusion*, 1937; New York Critics Award for *Swamp Water*, 1941; Best Film, Venice Biennale, for *The Southerner*, 1946; Grand Prix de l'Académie du Cinéma for *French Cancan*, 1956; Prix Charles Blanc, Académie Française, for *Renoir*, biography of father; Honorary Doctorate in Fine Arts, University of California, Berkeley, 1963; Fellow of the American Academy of Arts and Sciences, 1964; Osella d'Oro, Venice Film Festival, 1968; Honorary Doctorate of Fine Arts, Royal College of Art, London, 1971; special Academy Award for career accomplishment, 1975.

Films (as producer and director): *La Fille de l'eau*; 1926—*Nana* (+adaptation); 1927—*Catherine (Une vie sans joie, Backbiters)* (co-pr, co-d, +sc, ro as sub-prefect—this is 1st film worked on by Renoir); *Sur un air de Charleston (Charleston, Charleston-Parade)* (+ed); *Marquitta* (+adaptation); *Le Petit Chaperon rouge* (Cavalcanti) (co-sc only +ro as the Wolf); 1928—*La Petite Marchande d'allumettes (The Little Match Girl)* (co-pr, co-d, +sc); (as director): 1928—*Tire au flanc* (+co-sc); *Le Tournoi dans la cité (Le Tournoi)* (+adaptation); 1929—*Le Bled*; 1931—*On purge bébé* (+co-sc); *La Chienne* (+co-sc); 1932—*La Nuit du carrefour (Night at the Crossroads)* (+sc); *Boudu sauvée des eaux* (+co-sc); 1933—*Chotard et cie.* (+co-sc); 1934—*Madame Bovary* (+sc); 1935—*Toni (Les Amours de Toni)* (+co-sc); 1936—*Le Crime de Monsieur Lange (The Crime of Monsieur Lange)* (+co-sc); *La Vie est à nous (The People of France)* (co-d, +co-sc); *Les Bas-Fonds (Underworld, The Lower Depths)* (+adaptation); 1937—*La Grande Illusion (Grand Illusion)* (+co-sc); *The Spanish Earth* (Ivens) (wrote commentary and narration for French version); 1938—*La Marseillaise* (+co-sc); *La Bête humaine (The Human Beast, Judas Was a Woman)* (+co-sc); 1939—*La Règle du jeu (Rules of the Game)* (+co-sc, ro as Octave); 1941—*La Tosca (The Story of Tosca)* (co-d, +co-sc); *Swamp Water*; 1943—*This Land is Mine* (+co-p, co-sc); 1944—*Salute to France (Salut à France)* (co-d, +co-sc); 1945—*The Southerner* (+sc); 1946—*(Une) Partie de campagne (A Day in the Country, Country Excursion)* (+sc: filmed 1936); *The Diary of a Chambermaid* (+co-sc); 1947—*The Woman on the Beach* (+co-sc); 1951—*The River* (+co-sc); 1953—*The Golden Coach* (+co-sc); 1955—*French Cancan (Only the French Can)* (+sc); 1956—*Elena et les hommes (Paris Does Strange Things)* (+sc); 1959—*Le Testament du Docteur Cordelier (The Testament of Dr. Cordelier, Experiment in Evil)* (+sc); *Le Déjeuner sur l'herbe (Picnic on the Grass, Lunch on the Grass)* (+sc); 1962—*Le Caporal épinglé (The Elusive Corporal, The Vanishing Corporal)* (co-d, +co-sc); 1970—*Le Petit Théâtre de Jean Renoir (The Little Theatre of Jean Renoir)* (+sc).

Roles: *Robert* in *Die Jagd nach dem Gluck* (Gliese); 1971—as himself in *The Christian Licorice Store* (Frawley).

Publications:

By RENOIR:

Books and scripts—*This Land is Mine* in *20 Best Film Plays* edited by Gassner and Nichols, New York 1943; *The Southerner* in *Best Film Plays—1945*, edited by Gassner and Nichols, New York 1946; *Orvet*, Paris 1955; *Renoir, My Father*, translated by Randolph and Dorothy Weaver, London 1962; *The Notebooks of Captain Georges*, translated by Norman Denny, Boston 1966; *La Grande Illusion*, screenplay, translated by Marianne Alexandre and Andrew Sinclair, London 1968; *Rules of the Game*, translated by John McGrath and Maureen Teitelbaum, New York 1970; *La Grande Illusion*, Paris 1971; *My Life and My Films*, translated by Norman Denny, New York 1974; *La Grande Illusion*, with Charles Spaak, Paris 1974; *Ecrits 1926-1971*, edited by Claude Gauteur, Paris 1974; *Jean Renoir: Essays, Conversations, Reviews* by Penelope Gilliatt, New York 1975; articles—"Il cinema e lo stato: intervista con Françoise Rosay e Jean Renoir" by Giuseppe Lo Duca in *Cinema* (Rome), 25 March 1939; "Jean Renoir à Hollywood", interview by Paul Gilson in *L'Ecran française* (Paris), 15 August 1945; "Pierre Sicard" in *"Paris and Versailles": Paintings by Pierre Sicard*, New York 1951; "Après la chasse (extrait de *La Règle du jeu*)" in *Cahiers du cinéma* (Paris), August/September 1954; "Enquête sur la censure et l'éroticisme: le public a horreur de ça" in *Cahiers du cinéma* (Paris), December 1954; "Paris-Provence": Inspiration pour un film" in *Cahiers du cinéma* (Paris), May 1954; "French Cancan" in *Cinéma 55* (Paris), December 1954; "Entretien avec Jean Renoir" by Jacques Rivette and François Truffaut in *Cahiers du cinéma* (Paris), April 1954; reprinted in part as "Renoir in America" in *Sight and Sound* (London), autumn 1954; "French Cancan" in *Cahiers du cinéma* (Paris), May 1955; "Carola ou les cabotins" in *Cahiers du cinéma* (Paris), Christmas 1957; "Nouvel entretien avec Jean Renoir" by Jacques Rivette and François Truffaut in *Cahiers du cinéma* (Paris), Christmas 1957; also in *La Politique des auteurs* by André Bazin and others, Paris 1972; "J'aime Simenon parce qu'il est riche..." in *Georges Simenon* by Bernard de Fallois, Paris 1961; "Elena y los hombres" in *Esquemas de películas* (Madrid), no.129, 1961; "Le Testament du Docteur Cordelier" in *L'Avant-Scène du cinéma* (Paris), July 1961; "Une amitié" in *Jacques Becker* by Jean Queval, Paris 1962; "Partie de campagne" in *Image et son* (Paris), April/May 1962; "Jean Renoir: propos rompus", interview by Jean-Louis Noames in *Cahiers du cinéma* (Paris), May 1964; *"La Regle du jeu"* in *L'Avant-Scène du cinéma* (Paris), Ocotber 1965; "La Grande Illusion" in *L'Avant-Scène du cinéma* (Paris), January 1965; "Hommages à l'artiste" in *Etudes cinématographiques* (Paris), no.48-50, 1966; "Renoir at 72", interview by Axel Madsen, in *Cinema* (Los Angeles), spring 1966; "The Situation of the Serious Filmmaker" in *Film Makers on Film Making* edited by Harry Geduld, Bloomington, Indiana 1967; "My Next Films", interview by Michel Delahaye and Jean-André Fieschi in *Cahiers du Cinema in English* (New York), March 1967; "C'est la révolution! (Crème de beauté)" in *Cahiers du cinéma* (Paris), May 1968; "Interview with Renoir" by Rui Nogueira and François Truchaud in *Sight and Sound* (London), spring 1968; "A Modern Parable" in *Journal of the Producers Guild of America* (Los Angeles), March 1969; "Conversation with Jean Renoir" by Louis Marcorelles in *Interviews with Film Directors* edited by Andrew Sarris, New York 1969; "Jean Renoir: Interview" by James Pasternak in *The Image Maker* edited by Ron Henderson, Richmond, Virginia 1971; "Q & A: Jean Renoir" by Digby Diehl in *Los Angeles Times West Magazine*, 16 April 1972; "The Grand Illusionist Turns 80" in *The New York Times*, 15 September 1974; "Pierre Sicard" in *Positif* (Paris), September 1975; articles in Renoir issue of *Positif* (Paris), September 1975; "La Chienne" in *L'Avant-Scène du cinéma* (Paris), October 1975; "An Interview with Jean Renoir" by James Silke in *The Essential Cinema* edited by P. Adams Sitney, New York 1975; "Entretien avec Jean Renoir" by Michel Ciment in *Positif* (Paris), September 1975; articles reprinted in *Image et Son* (Paris), March 1977.

Ꮎn RENOIR:

Books—*Jean Renoir* by Paul Davay, Brussels 1957; *Jean Renoir* by Armand-Jean Cauliez, Paris 1962; *Jean Renoir* edited by Bernard Chardère in *Premier Plan* (Lyon), no.22-24, May 1962; *Analyses des films de Jean Renoir*, Institut des Hautes Etudes Cinématographiques, Paris 1966; *Study Unit 8: Jean Renoir* by Susan Bennett, London 1967; *Renoir 1938 ou Jean Renoir pour rein. Enquête sur un cinéaste* by François Poulle, Paris 1969; *Jean Renoir und seine Film: eine Dokumentation* compiled and edited by Ulrich Gregor, Bad Ems 1970; *Jean Renoir* by Pierre Leprohon, New York 1971; *Humanidad de Jean Renoir* by Carlos Cuenca, Valladolid, Mexico 1971; *Jean Renoir: The World of his Films* by Leo Braudy, New York 1972; *Guerre et cinéma: grandes illusions et petits soldats, 1895-1971* by Joseph Daniel, Paris 1972; *Jean Renoir* by André Bazin, edited by François Truffaut, Paris, translated ed. 1973. *The Classic Cinema* by Stanley Solomon, New York 1973; *Filmguide to The Rules of the Game* by Gerald Mast, Bloomington, Indiana 1973; *Jean Renoir* by Raymond Durgnat, Berkeley, California 1974; *Jean Renoir: le spectacle, la vie* by Claude Beylie, Paris 1975; *Jean Renoir: A Guide to References and Resources* by Chris-

topher Faulkner, Boston 1979; *Jean Renoir: The French Films 1924-1939* by Alexander Sesonske, Cambridge, Mass. 1980; articles—"Grey Castles Stormed and Grave Grey Kings Bereft" by Carl Koch in *Sight and Sound* (London), winter 1937/38; "Omaggio a Renoir" by Michelangelo Antonioni in *Film Rivista* (Rome), 19 September 1946; "French Cinema: The New Pessimism" by Gavin Lambert in *Sequence* (London), summer 1948; special Renoir issue, *Cahiers du cinéma* (Paris), January 1952; "A Last Look Round" by Gavin Lambert in *Sequence* (London), no.14 1952; "Petit journal intime du cinéma" by André Bazin in *Cahiers du cinéma* (Paris), August/September 1954; "Jean Renoir" in *En marge du cinéma français* by Jacques Brunius, Paris 1954; "Renoir vu par André Bazin" in *Cinéma 56* (Paris), November 1956; special Renoir issue, *Cahiers du cinéma* (Paris), Christmas 1957; "Jean Renoir: 'Flaherty fut notre Villon, notre La Fontaine: une révolutionnaire d'une extrême douceur'" by Charles Bitsch in *Arts* (Paris), 26 November 1958; "Hommages à Renoir" in *Cahiers du Cinéma* (Paris), April 1958; "The Renaissance of the French Cinema—Feydor, Renoir, Duvivier, Carné" by Georges Sadoul in *Film: An Anthology* edited by Daniel Talbot, New York 1959; "Jeunesse de Jean Renoir" by Eric Rohmer in *Cahiers du cinéma* (Paris), December 1959; "Renoir and Realism" by Peter John Dyer in *Sight and Sound* (London), summer 1960; "Histoire d'une malédiction" by André G. Brunelin in *Cinéma 60* (Paris), February 1960; "Why Renoir Favors Multiple Camera, Long Sustained Take Technique" by Jean Belanger in *American Cinematographer* (Los Angeles), March 1960; "The Presence of Jean Renoir" by Ernest Callenbach and Roberta Schuldenfrei in *Film Quarterly* (Berkeley), winter 1960; "Renoir and Realism" by Peter Dyer in *Sight and Sound* (London), summer 1960; "Jean Renoir" by Lee Russell (Peter Wollen) in *New Left Review*, May/June 1964; "Le jeu de la vérité" by Philippe Esnault in *L'Avant-Scène du Cinéma* (Paris), October 1965; "Renoir, cinéaste de notre temps, à coeur ouvert" in *Cinéma 67* (Paris), May and June 1967; "Renoir, cinéaste de notre temps, à coeur ouvert" by Janine Bazin and others in *Cinéma 67* (Paris), May and June 1967; "Dialogue avec une salle" by Robert Grélier in *Cinéma 68* (Paris), March 1968; "The Autumn of Jean Renoir" by Daniel Millar in *Sight and Sound* (London), summer 1968; "To Love a Renoir Movie Properly" by Roger Greenspun in *The New York Times*, 6 September 1970; "Renoir in Calcutta" by Satyajit Ray in *Portrait of a Director: Satyajit Ray* by Marie Seton, Bloomington, Indiana 1971; "Directors Go to their Movies: Jean Renoir" by Digby Diehl in *Action* (Los Angeles), May/June 1972; "Jean Renoir and Television" by Jean-Luc Godard in *Godard on Godard*, London 1972; "The Cinema of the Popular Front in France (1934-38)" by Goffredo Fofi in *Screen* (London), winter 1972/73; "La Marseillaise" by Claude Gauteur in *Image et son* (Paris), February 1973; "Renoir par Renoir" by Claude Gauteur in *Positif* (Paris), July/August 1973; "La Règle du jeu et la critique en 1939" edited by Claude Gauteur in *Image et son* (Paris), March 1974; "Renoir 'auteur de films'" by Claude Gauteur in *Ecran* (Paris), December 1974; "House and Garden: 3 Films by Jean Renoir" by Roger Greenspun in *Film Comment* (New York), July/August 1974; "A Flight from Passion: Images of Uncertainty in the Work of Jean Renoir" in *6 European Directors* by Peter Harcourt, Harmondsworth, England 1974; "Pour saluer Renoir", special issue by Claude Beylie of *Cinéma d'aujourd'hui* (Paris), May/June 1975; Special Renoir issue of *Cinema* (Zurich), vol.21, no.4, 1975; "The Sorcerer's Apprentice: Bazin and Truffaut on Renoir" by P. Thomas in *Sight and Sound* (London), winter 1974/75; "A Masterpiece on 8th Street" by Marshall Lewis in *The Essential Cinema* edited by P. Adams Sitney, New York 1975; "Renoir at 80" by Scott Eyman in *Focus on Film* (London), autumn 1975; "Portraits de Jean Renoir" by

Roland Stragliati in *Positif* (Paris), September 1975; "Un Festival Jean Renoir" in *Les Films de ma vie* by François Truffaut, Paris 1975; "Renoir and the Illusion of Detachment" by D. Willis in *Sight and Sound* (London), autumn 1977; "Renoir, Roméo, l'Algérie et Juliette" by Claude Gauteur in *Ecran* (Paris), November 1978; "Un Séminaire Jean Renoir à Florence" in *Avant-Scène du cinéma* (Paris), 1 December 1979; "Renoir and the Popular Front" by E.G. Strebel in *Sight and Sound* (London), winter 1979/80; "Jean Renoir (1894-1979)" and "Jean Renoir face au cinéma parlant" by Claude Beylie in special Renoir issue of *Avant-Scène du cinéma* (Paris), 1 July 1980; "Discovering America: Jean Renoir 1941" by A. Sesonske in *Sight and Sound* (London), autumn 1981; films—*L'Album de famille de Jean Renoir* by Roland Gritti, Paris 1956; *La Direction d'acteurs par Jean Renoir* by Gisèle Braunberger, Paris 1970.

*   *   *

The Hollywood studio film has found its most alert viewers and cogent interpreters in France. It may be that North America provided the finest background for the breathtaking artistry of Jean Renoir. Renoir brings a sensibility to film absolutely unknown to our continent yet one, perhaps, that captures better than any other our endless fascination with space and history. The second son of the celebrated impressionist painter Auguste, Jean Renoir always held America in the forefront of his cinema. His maternal grandfather was one of the first settlers of the North Dakota plains, and as an aviator and cavalry officer in the First World War, Renoir acted out the stuff of the American western and airplane films of the first 30 years of our century. In fact, Renoir's obsessive admiration for an untrammelled, indifferent nature knowing no relation with man—a nature beyond and above our petty violence, our stupid sexual dramas, or farcical tragedies of history—may be located in his cinematic geography. Renoir's nature is something akin to the unconscious; it knows neither time nor contradiction; it embodies force that can never yield to the limiting frame of language, social change, writing or pictorial representation.

This is why Renoir is really the most ecologically committed—hence politically significant—film maker. He shows how murderous is the presence of image-making mechanisms that try to save or to record a fugacious glimpse of nature. They preserve, therefore they kill and ossify nature. Like Rousseau or Lévi-Strauss, Renoir uses the concept of nature as a working concept, as a protean shape, an analogue of love, a design of desire and as a pervasive foreground for all of his work. It is the unnameable vision shaping "Arizona Jim's" stories which brings effective political reform to a sick urban environment infected by capital and Christian religion in *The Crime of M. Lange* (the pun on *Lange* as both a social film derived from Lang's *M* and the notion of nature as a white, angelic *lange* or diaper sums up many of its tensions). And it may be that the great plains of the Northwest, where sky and ground (or any cardinal distincion, even the slightest linguistic or visual mark) are the same, are evoked in the masses of the white space enveloping the impoverished and desperate human beast at the end of many of his greatest films (*Boudu, Toni, Lange, The Grand Illusion*). The presence of a "western" is suggested in *The Rules of the Game* in which the social and symbolic intricacies of a post-medieval, post-revolutionary aristocracy are in part played out according to the conventions of the American western. A dazzling shoot-'em-up in an endless span of drawing rooms is registered through the contradictory optics of expansive and constricting space. Doors open onto vast salons and tiny cubicles in which characters spin through the steps of polite minuet and fox-trot; somewhat like barroom entries in the western that lead us from the abstract space of the plains and sagebrush into smoky, whiskey-ridden squalor, Renoir's camera tracks into space of the *petits appartements* of eighteenth century Versailles, acted out at Solognes, where characters obey the laws of the mimetic and biological mechanisms that direct them. It could be argued that a French viewer would see Musset's *Caprices de Marianne* inspiring *Rules*, Euripides or Racine and Pagnol at the bottom of *Toni*, and Maupassant, Flaubert and the nineteenth century realists at the beginnings of *Nana, Madame Bovary, Partie de campagne*, and the *Human Beast*. But visually, the formal tensions and wrenching drama of irreconcilable social contradiction of man as a corrupt agent in nature owe much to Renoir grafting an imaginary, unconscious American décor (perhaps inspired by the deserts Stroheim depicted in *Greed*) of endlessness onto peculiarly European obsessions with allegory of social upheaval and apocalypse.

Renoir's traits have absolutely no equivalent in American cinema, yet they are a primer for renewing our sense of volume and topography. Using extremely long shots in great depth of field, occasioned by outdoor and on-location photography, Renoir loses the subject or the narrative thread in spatial immensity. Then, by prolonging the same effect with shots of duration that only avant-garde cinema later dared to use in copying him, the director at once bores us and draws attention to our narrow span of attention and general passivity. He shoots in a fashion derivative, but also critical, of Impressionist painting. By capturing fugacious scenes of nature indifferent to the narrative that captures our imagination, he begins to loosen us from the grip of language, of plot or of cultural codes that are the stuff of every tale he tells. As in the painting of Manet and Monet, a scene of nature is always arrested or repressed by the optical conditions producing it. We need only recall the slow pan at the end of *Boudu* which follows the course of the bowler hat in the water; floating in closeup, then drifting into a long shot of the Marne river and its edge in deep focus, a shot which ends with a wrought-iron bridge framing derricks in the background behind a tuft of reeds in medium closeup. What degrades nature is always in the margins of his most inspired depictions of the outdoors.

Renoir laterally reframes the space of his narrative by shooting interiors and exteriors from varied angles and apposed points of view. On cursory viewing the spectator is lured into seeing a grandiose space of natural beauty, or an intimate infinity of visuals, but through his film work the familiar openness closes into a constrictive décor by virtue of the subtle, ever-varied repetition of space reframed. By the end of *The Rules of the Game* there is no space volume in which characters can hide. The viewer is *serré*, or tightened at the locus of murder by the *serre*, or greenhouse, adjacent to the Colinière chateau.

These formal approaches he brings to cinema are matched only by those of Welles and Lang. Renoir allows his compositions to exhaust their content through duration and recurrence. In this way his films quickly become instruments at once of cinematic and social theory that go beyond the historical frame of their narrative. To see Renoir is to engage in all of cinema and its most urgent problems concerning sequence, social contradiction (in its presentation of brutely closed ideological space) and pleasure. We derive the latter from judging the difference between the virtual invisibility of reality and the optical instruments that produce its tactility. The conjunction of France (its painting, its cuisine, its complex social orderings, its lurid history since early modern times) and America (our absence of any major tradition that would have known of a Dark or Middle

Age, our sense of Western expansion leading only to manifest destiny of celluloid infinity in Hollywood) might be an axis by which Renoir's work could be measured anew.

The phases of Renoir's career are a principal subject in the industry of criticism. Decidedly, as he admitted, Renoir spent his entire life "making one film," inflecting many subjects and genres with the same obsession with nature, pictorial depth and visual contradiction. But his silent period, including *La Fille de l'eau*, *Nana*, *Tir au flanc*, and *La Petite Marchande d'allumettes*, essays the optical properties of the medium and it allegiance (and resistance) to narrative. Seminal in this respect is the composition of *La Fille de l'eau*, where trees and lush riverbanks acquire more majestic beauty than humans sitting by them; day-for-night photography sets them in visual counterpoint and suggests presence of a cosmic order of seasonal change that will resonate in the pans of treetops, clouds and air, or in the closeups of percussive raindrops in *Partie de campagne* thirteen years later. In *La Fille de l'eau* Renoir already displays a cautiously intense use of the closeup. We see his first wife, Katharine Hessling (a former model for his father) in several portraits that dwell both on her luscious physiognomy, and doll-like, mechanical aspect (that will be developed at greater length in her impish and plastic look in *Nana*). Generally a shot that confers psychology or a lure of human plenitude to a film, the facial closeup acquires in this film traits opposite to what codes its function. Through it Renoir displays effects of a murderous voyeurism that selects the subject and holds it in a gaze of desire. The closeup is set in fugal counterpoint to the long shots in great depth of field; its effect is theorized and deprived of psychology. In his silent period, "human desire" is cast as our will to hold an object of love in close view instead of letting it roam or abandon itself to an indifferent world. The views of Hessling have the same violence that Renoir will invest in the closeups of Nora Grégor in *The Rules of the Game*. In the same period Renoir develops his fascination with collective physiology. No film maker has ever shot mealtime scenes with the such myriad and delicious contradiction. In *Tir au flanc*, Renoir sets long tables in extreme depth of field and catches both the joy of the archaic realm of people eating together and its quasi-Flaubertian opposite, where individuals of different orders are excluded from sharing the same space of nourishment or when they cannot bear to live in closure. He also essays focal inversion as an analogue to social reversal, both in the relation of servants to the frame of a composition structured by other classes in it, and in his development of the topos of the "world upside down," inverting the rapport of figure to ground in *Tir au flanc*.

Already the experience of image without sound conditioned Renoir's differential use of the two tracks in his second period that runs from *La Chienne*, the first sound film in France to be recorded on location, to *The Rules of the Game* in 1939. In this period Renoir made an uninterrupted series of masterpieces that include, *Boudu Saved from Drowning*, *Madame Bovary*, *Toni*, *Le Crime de M. Lange*, *Les Bas-Fonds*, *Partie de campagne*, *The Grand Illusion*, *La Marseillaise*, and *The Human Beast*. The films deal unremittingly with social and visual paradox, they explore the sardonic ironies in the order among humans and their relationship with nature through masterful silent compositions with punctuations of sound, and they continue to provide lush visuals with sources in the entire Western tradition of painting and representation. No director will ever equal the febrility of Renoir in the decade from 1930 to 1940.

With the onslaught of the Second World War Renoir fled to Italy and then emigrated to America. He made a number of films in Hollywood, including *Swamp Water* with 20th Century-Fox, shot on location in Georgia. At Universal he completed *This Land is Mine* in 1943 and the *Southerner* in 1945. *Diary of a Chambermaid* and *Woman on the Beach* round out the American venture. He shot *The River* in India and returned to Europe to make *The Golden Coach*, *French Cancan*, *Elena et les hommes*, *Le Dejeuner sur l'herbe*, *le Testament du Dr Cordelier*, *Le Caporal egingle* and, finally, *Le Petit Theatre* in 1970, nine years before his death.

In *Rules of the Game* the old general, representing the solid French nobless d'épée, applauds the masquerade and games of the Walpurgis night episode at La Colinière, the chateau belonging to the impure aristocrat, La Chesnaye. The general guffaws, "Why, we're not here to write our memoirs!" Nor was Renoir in 1939. But the films from that moment on do have a sense of being a testament and are imbued with nostalgia for the first two periods. They are memoirs of his former life, to the pre-war violence and to the antipathy of Renoir to signs of human progress that were like writing opposed to nature. They are a calm reminder and remake of the former years, all tender variants of the same film Renoir had been making all his life.

Writings on Renoir are legion. The best work includes Renoir's own memoir, *My Life and My Films*. Bazin's essays in the first volume of *What is Cinema?* and the posthumous *Jean Renoir* of the same author, assembled and edited by Francois Truffaut.

—Tom Conley

RESNAIS, ALAIN. French. Born in Vannes, Brittany, 3 June 1922. Educated at St.-François-Xavier, Vannes; attended Institut des Hautes Etudes Cinématographiques, Paris, 1943-45. Married Florence Malraux, 7 October 1969. Career: 1935—begins making movies with 8mm camera; 1940—moves to Paris; 1940-42—studies acting under René Simon; 1945—serves in the military with the occupation army in Germany and Austria, where he is a member of a travelling theatrical company, Les Arlequins; serves as lighting cameraman on *Le Sommeil d'Albertine* by Jean Ledoc; 1946—directs 1st feature film, *Ouvert pour cause d'inventaire*, in 16mm; 1946-48—directs a number of shorts in 16mm, mostly about artists; 1947—begins work as film editor, which he continues until 1958; 1948—directs 1st film in 35mm, a documentary short entitled *Van Gogh*; 1959—directs 1st 35mm feature, *Hiroshima mon amour*; 1960—teams with writer Alain Robbe-Grillet to direct *L'Année dernière à Marienbad (Last Year at Marienbad)*, released 1961; 1967—co-directs with Godard and others political film *Loin du Viêt-Nam*; 1970-72—lives and works in New York City; 1977—directs his 1st film in English, *Providence*. Address: 70 rue des Plantes, 75014 Paris, France.

Films (as editor): 1945—*Le Sommeil d'Albertine*; (as director of short films): 1946—*Ouvert pour cause d'inventaire*; *Schéma d'une identification*; 1947—*Visite à Lucien Coutaud*; *Visite à Félix Labisse*; *Visite à Hans Hartung*; *Visite à César Domela*; *Visite à Oscar Dominguez*; *Portrait d'Henri Goetz*; *La Bague*; *Journée naturelle*; *L'Alcool tue* (+ph, ed); *Paris 1900* (ed only); 1948—*Les Jardins de Paris* (+ph, ed); *Châteaux de France* (+sc, ph, ed); *Van Gogh*; *Malfray* (co-d); *Van Gogh* (35mm) (+ed); *Jean Effel* (ed only); 1950—*Gauguin* (+ed); *Guernica* (co-d, +ed); 1952—*Saint-Tropez, devoir de vacances* (ed only); 1953—*Les Statues meurent aussi* (co-d, +co-sc, ed); 1955—*Nuit et brouillard*; *La Pointe courte* (ed only); 1956—*Toute la mémoire du monde* (+ed); 1957—*Le Mystere de l'Atelier Quinze* (co-d); *L'Oeil du maître* (ed only); *Broadway by Light* (ed only); 1958—

Le Chant de Styrène (+ed); *Paris à l'automne* (ed only); (as feature director): 1959—*Hiroshima mon amour*; 1961—*L'Année dernière à Marienbad (Last Year at Marienbad)*; 1963—*Muriel, ou le temps d'un retour*; 1966—*La Guerre est finie (The War is Over)*; 1967—*Loin du Viêt-Nam (Far from Vietnam)* (co-d); 1968—*Je t'aime, je t'aime* (+co-sc); 1974—*Stavisky*; 1977—*Providence*; 1978—*Mon Oncle d'Amerique*; 1983—*La Vie est un roman*.

Publications:

By RESNAIS:

books and scripts—"*Nuit et brouillard*" in *Avant-Scène du cinéma* (Paris), February 1961; "*Le Chant du styrène*", script, in *Avant-Scène du cinéma* (Paris), February 1961; "*Guernica*", script, in *Avant-Scène du cinéma* (Paris), June 1964; "*Toute la mémoire du monde*", script, in *Avant-Scène du cinéma* (Paris), October 1965; "*Van Gogh*", script, in *Avant-Scène du cinéma* (Paris), July/September 1966; "*La Mystère de l'atelier*", script, in *Avant-Scène du cinéma* (Paris), July/September 1966; "*Hiroshima mon amour*", script, in *Avant-Scène du cinéma* (Paris), July/September 1966; *Repérages* with an introduction by Jorge Semprun, Paris 1974; articles—interview by François Truffaut in *Arts* (Paris), 20 February 1956; interview by Anne Phillipe in *Les Lettres françaises* (Paris), 12 March 1959; interview by Michel Delahaye in *Cinéma 59* (Paris), July 1959; "*Hiroshima, mon amour*, film scandaleux?, Interview" in *Les Lettres françaises* (Paris), 14 May 1959; "A Conversation with Alain Resnais" by Noël Burch in *Film Quarterly* (Berkeley, California), spring 1960; interview by Jean Carta and Michel Mesnil in *Esprit* (Paris), June 1960; interview by Max Egly in *Image et son* (Paris), February 1960; interview by Penelope Houston in *Sight and Sound* (London), winter 1961-62; interview by Peter Barker in *Films and Filming* (London), November 1961; "Introduction à la methode d'Alain Resnais et d'Alain Robbe-Grillet" by Hubert Juin in *Les Lettres françaises* (Paris), 10 August 1961; interview by André Labarthe and Jacques Rivette in *Cahiers du cinéma* (Paris), September 1961, reprinted in English in *Films and Filming* (London), February 1962; interview by Pierre Billard in *Cinéma 61* (Paris), no.61, 1961; interview by Pierre Uyterhoeven in *Image et son* (Paris), February 1962; interview by Eugene Archer in *The New York Times*, 18 March 1962; "Trying to Understand My Own Film" in *Films and Filming* (London), February 1962; "Last Words on Last Year: Discussion with Alain Resnais and Alain Robbe-Grillet" in *Films and Filming* (London), March 1969; "Alain Resnais Speaks at Random" in *New York Film Bulletin*, no.2 1962; "En attendant Harry Dickson", interview, by Robert Benayoun in *Positif* (Paris), no.50-52; interview by Marcel Martin in *Les Lettres françaises* (Paris), 21 February 1963; interview in *Filmkritik* (Munich), no.10 1964; interview by Marcel Martin in *Cinéma 65* (Paris), December 1964 and January 1965; interview by Robert Benayoun and others in *Positif* (Paris), no.79; interview in *Positif* (Paris), October 1966; interview by Adrian Maben in *Films and Filming* (London), October 1966; interviews in *Cinéma 66* (Paris), May 1966 and September/October 1966; interview by Guy Gauthier in *Image et son* (Paris), July 1966; interview by Yvonne Baby in *Le Monde* (Paris), 11 May 1966; "Comment" in *L'Avant-Scène du cinéma* (Paris), summer 1966; interview by Win Sharples, Jr. in *Filmmaker's Newsletter* (Ward Hill, Mass.), December 1974; "Alain Resnais, Jorge Semprun et *Stavisky*" by Claude Beylie in *Ecran* (Paris), July 1974; "Conversations with Alan Resnais" by James Monaco and "Facts Into

Fiction: Interview" by Richard Seaver in *Film Comment* (New York), July/August 1975; interview in *Positif* (Paris), February 1977; interview in *Positif* (Paris), June 1980; "Sacha Vierny et Alain Resnais: parallèles", interview by D. Goldschmidt in *Cinématographe* (Paris), July 1981.

On RESNAIS:

Books—*Alain Resnais, ou la création au cinéma* edited by Stéphane Cordier, Paris 1961; *Alain Resnais* by Bernard Pingaud, Lyon 1961; *Alain Resnais, Premier Plan* no.18, October 1961; *Alain Resnais* by Gaston Bournoure, Paris 1962; *Antonioni, Bergman, Resnais* by Peter Cowie, London 1963; "Alain Resnais" in *Cinema Eye, Cinema Ear* by John Russell Taylor, New York 1964; *French Cinema Since 1946: Vol. 2—The Personal Style* by Roy Armes, New York 1966; *The Cinema of Alain Resnais* by Roy Armes, London 1968; *Alain Resnais, or the Theme of Time* by John Ward, New York 1968; *Resnais: Alain Resnais* by Paolo Bertetto, Italy 1976; *Alain Resnais* by John Francis Kreidl, Boston 1977; *Alain Resnais: The Role of Imagination* by James Monaco, New York 1978; *Alain Resnais, arpenteur de l'imaginaire* by Robert Benayoun, Paris 1980; *The Film Narratives of Alain Resnais* by Freddy Sweet, Ann Arbor, Michigan 1981; articles—"Hiroshima, notre amours" in *Cahiers du cinéma* (Paris), July 1959; "Qu'est'ce que la Nouvelle Vague?" by Noël Burch in *Film Quarterly* (Berkeley), winter 1959; "Alain Resnais" in *Qu'est-ce que le cinéma* by André Bazin, Paris 1959; "Rebel with a Camera" by Louis Marcorelles in *Sight and Sound* (London), winter 1960; "Explorations in the Unconscious" by Cynthia Grenier in the *Saturday Review* (New York), 23 December 1961; "Fantasies of the Art House Audience" by Pauline Kael in *Sight and Sound* (London), winter 1961/62; "The Faces of Time: A New Aesthetic for Cinema" by Robert Gossner in *Theatre Arts* (New York), July 1962; "Les Malheurs du Muriel" in *Cahiers du cinéma* (Paris), October 1963; "The Left Bank" by Richard Roud in *Sight and Sound* (London), winter 1962/63; "The Time and Space of Alain Resnais" by Alan Stanbrook in *Films and Filming* (London), January 1964; special issue on Resnais of *L'Avant-Scène du cinéma* (Paris), summer 1966; "Dick Tracy Meets *Muriel*" by Francis Lacassin in *Sight and Sound* (London), spring 1967; "Alain Resnais: The Quest for Harry Dickson" by Francis Lacassin in *Sight and Sound* (London), summer 1967; "Un Cinéma politique: l'oeuvre de Resnais" by René Prédal in *Image et son* (Paris), November 1967; "Strain of Genius" by Hollis Alpert in *Saturday Review* (New York), 4 February 1967; "Interview with Delphine Seyrig in *Sight and Sound* (London), fall 1969; "Memories of Resnais" by Richard Roud in *Sight and Sound* (London), summer 1969; "Films of Alain Resnais" by F. Tuten in *Vogue* (New York), July 1969; "French Writers Turned Film Makers" by Judith Gollub in *Film Heritage* (Dayton, Ohio), winter 1968/69; "Resnais and Reality" by Roy Armes in *Films and Filming* (London), May 1970; "Ingrid Thulin Comments on Resnais" in *Dialogue on Film* (Washington, D.C.), no.3, 1972; "Memory is Kept Alive with Dream" by Peter Harcourt in *Film Comment* (New York), November/December 1973; "Journals: Paris" by Jonathan Rosenbaum in *Film Comment* (New York), March/April 1974; "Toward a Certainty of Doubt" by Peter Harcourt in *Film Comment* (New York), January/February 1974; "L'Année dernière à Chamonix" by Claude Beylie in *L'Avant-Scène du cinéma* (Paris), March 1975; "If It's Tuesday, It Must Be Belgium" by Richard Roud in *Sight and Sound* (London), summer 1976; article on Left Bank group in *Sight and Sound* (London), summer 1977; special issue on Resnais of *Cinéma* (Paris), July/August 1980; article on films by Resnais made in 1947 in *Positif* (Paris), July/August 1981; "Skin Games" by Raymond

Durgnat in *Film Comment* (New York), November/December 1981.

* * *

Alain Resnais is a prominent figure in the modernist narrative film tradition. His emergence as a feature director of international repute is affiliated with the eruption of the French New Wave in the late 1950s. This association was signaled by the fact that his first feature *Hiroshima mon amour* premiered at the Cannes Film Festival at the same time as François Truffaut's *Les 400 coups*. However, Resnais had less to do with the group of directors emerging from the context of the *Cahiers du cinéma* than he did with the so-called Left Bank group, including Jean Cayrol, Marguerite Duras, Chris Marker, and Alain Robbe-Grillet. This group provided an intellectual and creative context of shared interest. In the course of his film career Resnais frequently collaborated with members of this group. Marker worked with him on several short films in the fifties; Gayrol wrote the narration for *Nuit et brouillard* and the script for *Muriel*; Duras scripted *Hiroshima mon amour*; and Robbe-Grillet wrote *L'Année dernière à Marienbad*. All of these people are known as writers and/or filmmakers in their own right; their association with Resnais is indicative of his talent for fruitful creative collaboration.

Resnais began making films as a youth in 8 and 16mm. In the early 1940s he studied acting and filmmaking, and after the war, 1946-48, made a number of 16mm films including a series about artists. His first film in 35mm was the 1948 short, *Van Gogh*, which won a number of international awards. It was produced by Pierre Braunberger, an active supporter of new talent, who continued to finance his work in the short film format through the 1950s. From 1948-58 Resnais made eight short films, of which *Nuit et brouillard* is probably the best known. The film deals with German concentration camps, juxtaposing past and present, exploring the nature of memory and history. To some extent the film's reputation and sustained interest is due to its subject matter. However, many of the film's formal strategies and thematic concerns are characteristic of Resnais's work more generally. In particular, the relationship between past and present, and the function of memory as the mechanism of traversing temporal distance, are persistent preoccupations of Resnais's films. Other films from this period similarly reveal familiar themes and traits of Resnais's subsequent work. *Toute la memoire du monde* is a documentary about the Bibliothèque Nationale in Paris. It presents the building, with its processes of cataloguing and preserving all sorts of printed material, as both a monument of cultural memory and as a monstrous, alien being. The film almost succeeds in transforming the documentary film into a branch of science fiction. Indeed Resnais has always been interested in science fiction, the fantastic, and pulp adventure stories. If this interest is most overtly expressed in the narrative of *Je t'aime,je t'aime* (in which a human serves as a guinea pig for scientists experimenting with time travel), it also emerges in the play of fantasy/imagination/reality pervading his work, and in many of his unachieved projects (including a remake of *Fantômas* and *The Adventure of Harry Dickson*).

Through editing and an emphasis on formal repetition, Resnais uses the medium to construct the conjunctions of past and present, fantasy and reality, insisting on the convergence of what are usually considered distinct domains of experience. In *Hiroshima mon amour* the quivering hand of the woman's sleeping Japanese lover in the film's present is directly followed by an almost identical image of her nearly-dead German lover during World War II. Tracking shots through the streets of Hiroshima merge with similar shots of Nevers, where the woman lived during the war. In *Stavisky*, the cutting between events in 1933 and a 1934 investigation of those events presents numerous, often conflicting versions of the same thing; one is finally convinced, above all else, of the indeterminacy and contingency of major historical events. The central character in *Providence* is an aged writer who spends a troubled night weaving stories about his family, conjoining memory and fantasy, past, present, and future, in an unstable mix.

The past's insistent invasion of the present is expressed in many different ways in Resnais's films. In *Nuit et brouillard*, where the death camps are both present structures and repressed institutions, it is a question of social memory and history; it is an individual and cultural phenomenon in *Hiroshima mon amour*, as a French woman simultaneously confronts her experiences in occupied France and the Japanese experience of the atomic bomb; it is construed in terms of science fiction in *Je t'aime, je t'aime* when the hero is trapped in a broken time-machine and continuously relives moments from his past; and is a profoundly ambiguous mixture of an individual's real and imagined past in *L'Année dernière à Marienbad* (often considered Resnais's most avant-garde film) as X pursues A with insistence, recalling their love affair and promises of the previous year, in spite of A's denials. In all of these films, as well as Resnais's other work, the past is fraught with uncertainty, anxiety, even terror. If it is more comfortable to ignore, it inevitably erupts in the present through the workings of the psyche, memory traces, or in the form of documentation and artifacts.

Resnais's output has been relatively small; in the 24 years since *Hiroshima mon amour* he has made only nine films. He nonetheless stands as a significant figure in modernist cinema. His strategies of fragmented point of view and multiple temporality, as well as his use of the medium to convey past/present and fantasy/imagination/reality as equivocal and equivalent modes of experience have amplified our understanding of film's capacity for expression.

—M.B. White

RICHARDSON, TONY. English. Born Cecil Antonio Richardson in Shipley, England, 5 June 1928. Educated Wadham College, Oxford University, degree in English 1952. Married Vanessa Redgrave, 1962 (divorced 1967); 3 daughters. Career: 1949-51—president of Oxford University Drama Society; 1953—works as producer and director for BBC-TV; 1955—forms English Stage Company with George Devine; 1956—directs 1st play, *Look Back in Anger*, at London's Royal Court Theatre for the English Stage Company; this play marks beginning of collaboration with playwright John Osborne; co-directs film *Momma Don't Allow* with Karel Reisz, one of 1st "Free Cinema" documentary films; 1958—forms production company, Woodfall Films, with Osborne; 1959—directs 1st feature *Look Back in Anger*; 1969—resumes theatrical directing with London production of *Hamlet*; directs several London stage productions in early '70s; 1975—after completing over half of filming on *Mahogany*, Diana Ross vehicle, fired by producer Berry Gordy, Jr., for failure to "capture...black point of view." Recipient: Academy Award, Best Direction for *Tom Jones*, 1963; New York Film Critics' Award, Best Direction for *Tom Jones*, 1963. Address: 1478 North Kings Road, Los Angeles, California 90069.

Films (as director): 1955—*Momma Don't Allow* (co-d); 1959—*Look Back in Anger*; 1960—*The Entertainer*; *Saturday Night and Sunday Morning* (Reisz) (pr only); 1961—*Sanctuary*; *A Taste of Honey* (+pr, co-sc); 1962—*The Loneliness of the Long Distance Runner* (+pr); 1963—*Tom Jones* (+pr); 1964—*Girl with Green Eyes* (Davis) (exec pr only); 1965—*The Loved One*; *Madmoiselle*; 1967—*The Sailor from Gibraltar* (+co-sc); 1968—*Red and Blue*; *The Charge of the Light Brigade*; 1969—*Laughter in the Dark (La Chambre obscure)*; *Hamlet*; 1970—*Ned Kelly* (+co-sc); 1973—*A Delicate Balance*; *Dead Cert*; 1977—*Joseph Andrews* (+co-sc); 1978—*Death in Canaan*; 1982—*The Border*; 1984—*Hotel New Hampshire* (+sc).

Publications:

By RICHARDSON:

Articles—"The Films of Luis Bunuel" in *Sight and Sound* (London), January/March 1954; "The Metteur en Scene" in *Sight and Sound* (London), October/December 1954; "London Letter" in *Film Culture* (New York), no.8, 1956; "The Method and Why: An Account of the Actor's Studio" in *Sight and Sound* (London), winter 1956/57; "The Man Behind an Angry-Young-Man" in *Films and Filming* (London), February 1959; "Tony Richardson: An Interview in Los Angeles" by Colin Young in *Film Quarterly* (Berkeley), summer 1960; "Britain's Angry Young Directors: Interview" by Hollis Alpert in *Saturday Review* (New York), 24 December 1960; "The 2 Worlds of Cinema: Interview" in *Films and Filming* (London), June 1961; "Sous le signe de Jean Genet" in *Cinéma 65* (Paris), no.99, 1965; article in *Film Makers on Film-making* edited by Harry M. Geduld, Bloomington, Indiana 1967; interview in *Behind the Scene: Theatre and Film Interviews from Transatlantic Review* by Joseph F. McCrindle, New York 1971; "Within the Cocoon", interview by Gordon Gow in *Films and Filming* (London), June 1977.

On RICARDSON:

Books—*Tony Richardson* by Anne Villelaur, *Dossiers du cinéma*, Cinéastes I, Paris 1971; *Studies in Documentary* by Alan Lovell and Jim Hillier, New York 1972; articles—"2 New Directors" and "Look Back in Anger" by Penelope Houston in *Sight and Sound* (London), winter 1958/59; "A Free Hand" in *Sight and Sound* (London), spring 1959; "The Modern Hero: The Non-genue" by A.J. Alexander in *Film Culture* (New York), summer 1961; "The Cost of Independents" in *Sight and Sound* (London), summer 1961; "The Screen Answers Back" in *Films and Filming* (London), May 1962; "White Elephant Art vs. Termite Art" by Manny Farber in *Film Culture* (New York), winter 1962/63; "Entertainer" in *Time* (New York), 18 January 1963; "People Are Talking About" in *Vogue* (New York), 15 February 1963; "The Face of '63—Great Britain" by Peter Cowie in *Films and Filming* (London), February 1963; "Director" in the *New Yorker*, 12 October 1963; "Britain's Busiest Angry Young Man" by David Moller in *Film Comment* (New York), winter 1964; "*The Loved One*: An Interview with Jonathan Winters" by Curtis Lee Hanson in *Cinema* (Los Angeles), July/August 1965; article by Raymond Durgnat in *Films and Filming* (London), February 1966; "Recent Richardson: Cashing the Blank Check" by George Lellis in *Take One* (Montreal), September/October 1968; "Recent Richardson" by George Lellis in *Sight and Sound* (London), summer 1969; "Production of Hamlet" by B. Gill in the *New Yorker*, 10 May 1969; "Current Cinema" by Pauline

Kael in the *New Yorker*, 17 January 1970; "British Cinema Filmography" in *Film* (London), spring 1972; "*The Entertainer*: From Play to Film" by Joseph Gomez in *Film Heritage* (Dayton, Ohio), spring 1973.

*   *   *

Tony Richardson belongs to that generation of British film directors which includes Lindsay Anderson and Karel Reisz, all of them university-trained middle-class artists who were sympathetic to the conditions of the working classes and determined to use cinema as a means of personal expression, in line with the goals of the "Free Cinema" movement, founded by Lindsay Anderson. Like Anderson, Richardson, whose father was a pharmacist, was educated at Oxford (Wadham College), where he served as president of the Oxford Union Dramatic Society from 1949 to 1951. Thereafter, he enrolled in a directors' training program at the British Broadcasting Corporation before turning to theatre and founding, with George Devine, the English Stage Company in 1955 at London's Royal Court Theatre, a company that was to include writers Harold Pinter and John Osborne. Among Richardson's Royal Court productions were *Look Back in Anger* (which opened on May 8, 1956, influencing the course of British theatrical history for the decade), *A Taste of Honey*, and *The Entertainer*, dramatic vehicles that he would later transform into cinema.

Also in 1955, working with Karel Reisz, Richardson co-directed his first short film, *Momma Don't Allow*, funded by a grant from the British Film Institute and one of original productions of the "Free Cinema" movement. Richardson's realistic treatment of the works of John Osborne (*Look Back in Anger*), Shelagh Delaney (*A Taste of Honey*), and Alan Sillitoe (*Loneliness of the Long-Distance Runner*) would infuse British cinema with the "kitchen sink" realism Richardson had helped to encourage in the British theatre. Richardson's link with the "Angry Young Men" of the theatre was firmly established before he and John Osborne founded their film production unit, Woodfall, in 1958 for the making of *Look Back In Anger*. He effectively extended his flair for cinematic realism into the past for his 1968 rendering of *The Charge of the Light Brigade*, a film in which he added animation effects to punctuate his social criticism, though these points are better made by the realistic contrasts between the haves and the have-nots, and by the film's hideous demonstration of military "justice".

Richardson's strongest talent has been to adapt literary and dramatic works to the screen. In 1961 he turned to Hollywood, where he directed an adaptation of Faulkner's *Sanctuary*, which he later described as arguably his worst film. His most popular success, however, was his brilliant adaptation and abridgement of Henry Fielding's often rambling eighteenth-century novel, which in other hands would not have been a very promising film project but which, under Richardson's direction, won four Academy Awards in 1963—three for Richardson (Best Director, Best Producer, and Best Film) and one additionally for John Osborne's screenplay. (Albert Finney was also nominated for Best Actor, as were Hugh Griffith and Joyce Redman for Best Supporting Actor and Actress.) In 1977 Richardson tried to repeat his earlier success by adapting Fielding's other great comic novel, *Joseph Andrews*, to the screen, but, though the story was effectively shaped by Richardson (collaborating on the screenplay with Allan Scott and Chris Bryant) and the casting was splendid (Peter Firth as Joseph, Michael Hordern as Parson Adams, Beryl Reid as Mrs. Slipslop, Ann-Margret as Lady Booby, with additional support from Dame Peggy Ashcroft, Sir

John Gielgud, and Hugh Griffith, among others). the film was not the overwhelming commercial success that *Tom Jones* had been. Nonetheless, Vincent Canby singled out *Joseph Andrews* as "the year's most cheerful movie...and probably the most neglected movie of the decade."

Other adaptations and literary collaborations included *The Loved One* (Evelyn Waugh), *Mademoiselle* (Jean Genet), *The Sailor from Fibralter* (Marguerite Duras), *Laughter in the Dark* (Nabokov), and *A Delicate Balance* (Albee). Perhaps Richardson's most enduring dramatic adaptation, however, is his rendering of *Hamlet*, filmed in 1969, remarkable for the eccentric but effective performance by Nicol Williamson as Hamlet, which it captures for posterity, and also for Anthony Hopkins's sinister Claudius. Richardson's *Hamlet*, filmed at the Roundhouse Theatre in London where it was originally produced, is a brilliant exercise in filmed theater in the way it keeps the actors at the forefront of the action, allowing them to dominate the play as they would do on stage. Richardson has defined cinema as a director's medium, but his *Hamlet* effectively treats it as an actor's medium, as perhaps no other filmed production has done. In *Hamlet* Richardson was able to put his theatrical training and experience to intelligent, innovative use.

Other Richardson films seem to place a premium upon individualism, as witnessed by his treatment of the legendary Australian outlaw, *Ned Kelly* (starring Mick Jagger, a project Karel Reisz had first undertaken with Albert Finney.) This concern for the individual, running through several of Richardson's films, can also be discerned ten years later in *The Border*, a film Richardson completed for Universal Pictures in 1982, starring Jack Nicholson as a guard on the Mexican-American border, a loner who fights for human values against a corrupt constabulary establishment. Unfortunately *The Border*, which turned out to be a caricatured and flawed melodrama, according to *Variety* (27 January 1982), did not reflect the director's intentions in its released form, since Universal Studios apparently wanted—and got—"a much more up-beat ending where Nicholson emerges as a hero." That a talented director of considerable vision, intelligence, and accomplishment should experience such an impasse is a sorry commentary and a measure of an apparently declining career. Nonetheless, Richardson migrated to the Hollywood Hills by choice and claims to prefer California to his native England. By 1983 he had returned once again to theater directing Gardner McKay's psychological thriller *Toyer* (starring Brad Davis and Kathleen Turner) and was anticipating yet another film adaptation of a novel, John Irving's *Hotel New Hampshire*. He continues to work; whether he can regain success by Hollywood standards remains to be seen.

—James M. Welsh

RICHTER, HANS. German. Born in Berlin, 1888. Educated at Berlin Academy for Fine Arts, 1908; Weimar Academy of Art, 1909. Career: 1912-13—first encounter with modern art and literature through *Sturm* magazine; beginning 1915—collaborator on *Aktion* journal; 1915-16—military service and recovery from wounds; 1916—joins Dada group in Zurich; brief expressionist period followed by first experiments in abstract painting; 1918-19—with Viking Eggeling returns to Germany, does first scroll paintings; 1920—experimental focus shifts completely to film; 1923-26—publisher of art magazine *G*; 1940—emigrates to U.S.; 1942—Director of Film Institute, City College of New York; after 1942—very active as painter and writer,

continues to make films; 1948—resumes teaching. Died in Locarno, 1976.

Films (as director and graphic artist): 1921-24—*Rhythmus 21* (+ph) (original title: *Film ist Rhythmus*); 1923-24—*Rhythmus 23*; 1925—*Rhythmus 25*; 1926—*Filmstudie* (+co-ph); 1927-28—*Inflation* (+sc); *Vormittagsspuk (Ghosts Before Breakfast)* (co-d and graphic work, +co-story, ro); (as director and scriptwriter): 1928-29—*Rennsymphonie (Race Symphony)*; *Zweigroschenzauber (2-Penny Magic)*; *Alles dreht sich, alles bewegt sich (Everything Turns, Everything Revolves)* (co-sc); note: *Forty Years of Experiment*, Part 1 is comprised of experimental films and film fragments by Richter from 1921-30; 1944-47—*Dreams That Money Can Buy*; 1954-57—*8 x 8*; 1956-61—*Dadascope*; 1963—*Alexander Calder*.

Publications:

By RICHTER:

Books—*Filmgegner von heute—Filmfreunde von morgen*, Berlin 1929 (reprinted Zurich 1968); *Hans Richter by Hans Richter*, edited by Cleve.Gray, London 1971; *Der Kampf um den Film*, Munich and Vienna 1976; articles—"Prinzipielles zur Bewegungskunst" in *De Stijl* (Leiden), Jg.4, no.7, 1921; "Film" in *De Stijl* (Leiden), Jg.5, no.6, 1922; "Film" in *De Stijl* (Leiden), Jg.6, no.5, 1923; "Dimension", "Teil einer Partitur zu dem Film Rhythmus 25", "Die eigentliche Sphäre des Films", "Bisher", and "Die reine Form ist die Natürliche",in *G* (Berlin), no.5, 1926; "Neue Mittel der Filmgestaltung" and "Aufgaben eines Filmstudios" in *Die Form* (Berlin), Jg.4, H.3, 1929; "Der absolute Film braucht die Industrie. Ein Gespräch mit Hans Richter" in *Film-Kurier* (Berlin), 5 January 1929; "Avantgarde im Bereich des Möglichen" in *Film-Kurier* (Berlin), 1 June 1929; "L'Objet et mouvement" in *Cercle et Carré* (Paris), 15 March 1930; (reprinted in *Cercle et Carré*, 1971); "The Avant-Garde Film Seen From Within" in *Hollywood Quarterly*, fall 1949; "30 Years of Experimental Films", interview by Herman Weinberg in *Films in Review* (New York), December 1951; "8 Free Improvisations on the Game of Chess" in *Film Culture* (New York), January 1955; "*8 x 8*: A Sequence from Hans Richter's Latest Experimental Film" in *Film Culture* (New York), winter 1955; "Hans Richter on the Nature of Film Poetry", interview by Jonas Mekas in *Film Culture* (New York), no.11, 1957; "From Interviews with Hans Richter During the Last 10 Years" in *Film Culture* (New York), no.31, 1963/64; "Learning from Film History" in *Filmmakers Newsletter* (Ward Hill, Mass.), November 1973.

On RICHTER:

Books—*Hans Richter*, edited by Marcel Joray, Neuchâtel, 1965; *Viking Eggeling, 1880-1925, Artist and Filmmaker: Life and Work* by Louise O'Konor, Stockholm 1971; *Experimental Animation* by Robert Russett and Cecile Starr, New York 1976; articles—"Evidence of Conscience" by K. Boyle in *The Nation* (New York), 14 April 1956; "Clowning Out of the Void" in *Saturday Review* (New York), 1 February 1958; "Painter and Cinematographer Hans Richter: A Retrospective of 4 Decades" by Vernon Young in *Arts Magazine* (New York), September 1959; "Portrait: Hans Richter" by C. Gray in *Art in America* (New York), January 1968; "Fascination with Rhythm" in *Time* (New York), 16 February 1968; "In Memory of a Friend" in *Art in America* (New York), July 1969; "Richter e l'uomo visibile" by R. Codroico and L. Pezzolato in *Cinema nuovo* (Turin),

July/August 1972; "Se souvenir de Hans Richter" by H. Bassan and M. Roudevitch in *Ecran* (Paris), May 1977; "Appunti sul cinema e sulla teoria di Hans Richter" by G. Rondolino in *Bianco e nero* (Rome), January/February 1978.

*   *   *

Like many other filmmakers of the European avant-garde, Richter was initially a painter, influenced by such movements as futurism and cubism, and like his colleague Viking Eggeling, Richter came to extend his theoretical concerns beyond the limitations of paint and canvas to, first, abstract scrolls and then to film. Today he is highly regarded as a very early influence upon that major genre of production generally termed "experimental film," through his published theoretical writings (e.g. *Universelle Sprache*, with Viking Eggeling) and about a dozen films realized over four decades. Perhaps his most famous and most influential film was his first, *Rhythmus 21*.

Typical of experimental production, *Rhythmus 21* is a brief, a collaborative work, realized outside the financial and organizational constraints of the film industry. It is a silent, black and white film, running less than two minutes, an animated exploration of simple cut-out paper squares of various sizes and shades. The film's aesthetic force draws upon structures and strategies common to non-representational painting or graphic design. Part of the film's value comes from its explicit remove from theatrical or fictive prototypes, which dominated cinema in the 1920s as fully as today. Certainly *Rhythmus 21*'s value is as much predicated upon the later influence of its non-narrative structure (especially in international experimental film) as upon the lively dynamics of its simple yet stunning metamorphoses of shapes and tonalities. Richter went on to construct a number of companion pieces (e.g. *Rhythmus 23*). Later his film work took on more representational elements, as in his 1926 *Film Study* which employed animated suns, clouds, eyes, etc., with a somewhat surrealistic exchange of imagery. This embrace of film's representational resources grew more pronounced for Richter and, by 1930, he had largely ceased his concern with animated records of graphic materials. *Vormittagsspuk* (*Ghosts before Breakfast*) is a zany Dada story dependent upon shots of real objects and people. *Alles dreht sich, alles bewegt sich (All Revolves, All Moves)* embodies a somewhat documentary examination of a fairground. Still, such works clearly fall under the classification of the experimental genre, in part due to their fascination with a phenomenology of mental imagery—dream, fantasy, and reverie. This same concern also marks Richter's post-war production, such as the still surreal yet somewhat Jungian *Dreams that Money Can Buy*.

Richter's experimental film production has occurred during an extraordinarily long career. As recently as the 1960s he was still realizing new pieces, such as *Dadascope*. Yet his influence and importance to film historians and experimental filmmakers probably centers upon his early abstract, animated work. *Rhythmus 21* remains one of the best-known and most influential products of the European avant-garde.

—Edward S. Small

RIEFENSTAHL, LENI. German. Born Helene Berta Amalie Riefenstahl in Berlin, 22 August 1902. Attended Russian Ballet School, Berlin. Married Peter Jacob, 1944 (divorced 1946). Career: 1920—appears regularly on the stage as a dancer; 1926—signs contract with director Arnold Fanck to appear as dancer in film *Der heilige Berg*; 1926-31—stars in several of Fanck's "mountain films", also learns filmmaking from Fanck; 1931—establishes own production company, Riefenstahl Films; 1932—1st film, *Das blaue Licht*, released; meets Adolf Hitler for 1st time; 1933—is appointed "film expert to the Nationalist Socialist Party" by Hitler, and films Nazi rally for *Sieg des Glaubens* at Hitler's request; publishes *Kampf in Schnee und Eis*, an autobiographical account of her films; 1934—films Nuremberg Nazi rally (*Triumph des Willens (Triumph of the Will)* and in 1936 the Olympic games in Berlin (*Olympia*); 1945-48—detained in various prison camps by Allied Forces on charges of pro-Nazi activity; 1952—charges dismissed by Berlin court, allowed to work in film industry again; 1956—while working on documentary in Africa, suffers serious auto accident which may have been act of sabotage; 1956-72—attempts to revive filmmaking career, but no projects completed; 1972—commissioned by *Times* (London) to photograph Olympic Games in Munich; 1974—honored at Telluride Film Festival, Colorado; festival picketed by anti-Nazi groups. Recipient: Exposition Internationale des Arts et des Techniques, Paris, Diplôme de Grand Prix for *Triumph des Willens*, 1937; Polar Prize, Sweden, for *Olympia*, 1938. Address: lives in Munich, West Germany.

Films (as director): 1932—*Das blaue Licht (The Blue Light)* (+co-sc, ro as *Junta*); 1933—*Sieg des Glaubens (Victory of the Faith)*; 1935—*Triumph des Willens (Triumph of the Will)* (+pr); *Tag der Freiheit: unsere Wehrmacht* (+ed); 1938—*Olympia* (+ed); 1954—*Tiefland (Lowland)* (+sc, ed, ro as *Marta*) (produced 1944).

Roles: 1926—*Diotima* in *Der heilige Berg* (Fanck); 1927—*Der grosse Sprung* (Fanck); 1929—*Das Schicksal derer von Hapsburg* (Raffé); *Die weisse Hölle vom Piz Palü* (Fanck); 1930—*Stürme über dem Montblanc* (Fanck); 1931—*Der weiss Rausch* (Fanck); 1933—in *S.O.S. Eisberg* (Fanck).

Publications:

By RIEFENSTAHL:

Books—*Kampf in Schnee und Eis*, Leipzig 1933; *Hinter den Kulissen des Reichsparteitagsfilms*, Munich 1935 (uncredited ghost writer Ernst Jaeger); *Schönheit im Olypischen Kampf*, Berlin 1937; *The Last of the Nuba*, New York 1974; *Jardins du corail*, Paris 1978; articles—"An Interview with a Legend" by Gordon Hitchens in *Film Comment* (New York), winter 1965; "This Future is Entirely Ours" in *Film Comment* (New York), winter 1965; "Leni Riefenstahl" by Michel Delahaye in *Interviews with Film Directors* edited by Andrew Sarris, New York 1967; "Statement on Sarris-Gessner Quarrel about *Olympia*" in *Film Comment* (New York), fall 1967; "A Reply to Paul Rotha", with Kevin Brownlow, in *Film* (London), spring 1967; "Interview mit Leni Riefenstahl" by Herman Weigel in *Filmkritik* (Munich), August 1972; "Brève rencontre avec Leni Riefenstahl" by Y. Flot in *Ecran* (Paris), 9 November 1972; "Leni Riefenstahl Interviewed" by Gordon Hitchens in *Film Culture* (New York), spring 1973; "Why I Am Filming 'Penthesilea'" in *Film Culture* (New York), spring 1973; "Nie Antisemitin gewesen" in *Der Spiegel* (Germany), no.47, 1976.

On RIEFENSTAHL:

Books—*Screen Series: Germany* by Felix Bucher, New York 1970; *The German Cinema* by Roger Manville, New York 1971; *Histoire du cinéma Nazi* by Pierre Cadars and Francis Courtade, Paris 1972; *Er fürte Regie mit Gletschern, Stürmen, Lawinen* by Arnold Fanck, Munich 1973; *Film in the 3rd Reich* by David Stewart Hull, New York 1973; *Nazi Cinema* by Erwin Leiser, London 1974; *Film as a Subversive Art* by Amos Vogel, New York 1974; *Filmguide to 'Triumph of the Will'* by Richard Barsam, Bloomington, Indiana 1975; *Geschichte des Films* by Ulrich Gregor and Enno Patalas, Hamburg 1976; *Leni Riefenstahl, the Fallen Film Goddess* by Glenn Infield, New York 1976; *Leni Riefenstahl* by Charles Ford, Paris 1978; *The Films of Leni Riefenstahl* by David Hinton, Metuchen, New Jersey 1978; *Leni Riefenstahl et le 3e Reich* by G.B. Infield, Paris 1978; *Leni Riefenstahl* by Renata Berg-Pan, Boston 1980; articles—"Hitler's Dictator" in *Newsweek* (New York), 15 September 1934; "Nazi Pin-Up Girl: Hitler's no.1 Movie Actress" by Budd Schulberg in the *Saturday Evening Post* (New York), 30 March 1946; "Women Directors" by J. and H. Feldman in *Films in Review* (New York), November 1950; "Admired by Adolf" in *Time* (New York), 5 May 1952; "The Nazi Cinema" by Louis Marcorelles in *Sight and Sound* (London), autumn 1955; "Leni Riefenstahl" by David Gunston in *Film Quarterly* (Berkeley), fall 1960; "The Case of Leni Riefenstahl" in *Sight and Sound* (London), spring 1960; "Romantic Miss Riefenstahl" by R. Muller in *Spectator* (London), 10 February 1961; "Shame and Glory in the Movies" by J. Keller and A. Berson in the *National Review* (New York), 14 January 1964; "Can the Will Triumph?" by Robert Gardner in *Film Comment* (New York), winter 1965; "A Comeback for Leni Riefenstahl" by Ulrich Gregor in *Film Comment* (New York), winter 1965; "The Truth about Leni" by Arnold Berson in *Films and Filming* (London), April 1965; "Leni Riefenstahl" by Kevin Brownlow in *Film* (London), winter 1966; "I Deplore..." by Paul Rotha in *Film* (London), spring 1967; "Where Are They Now?" in *Newsweek* (New York), 28 October 1968; "Leni Riefenstahl—A Bibliography" by Richard Corliss in *Film Heritage* (Dayton, Ohio), fall 1969; "La Vérité sur Leni Riefenstahl et Le Triomphe de la volonté" by Erwin Leiser in *Cinéma 69* (Paris), February 1969; "Notes on Women Directors" by J. Pyros in *Take One* (Montreal), November/December 1970; "Leni Riefenstahl: Style and Structure" by J. Richards in *Silent Pictures* (London), autumn 1970; "Filmography of Leni Riefenstahl" by H. Linder in *Filmkritik* (Munich), August 1972; "The Lively Ghost of Leni" by Hollis Alpert in the *Saturday Review* (New York), 25 March 1972; "Leni Riefenstahl: Artifice and Truth in a World Apart" by R.M. Barsam in *Film Comment* (New York), November/December 1973; "4 Letters by Jean Cocteau to Leni Riefenstahl" in *Film Culture* (New York), spring 1973; "Propaganda as Vision: Triumph of the Will" by Ken Kelman in *Film Culture* (New York), spring 1973; "Letter to Gorden Hitchens" in *Film Comment* (New York), spring 1973; "The Rise and Fall of Leni Riefenstahl" in *Oui* (Chicago), May 1973; "Can We Now Forget the Evil That She Did?" by Amos Vogel in *The New York Times*, 13 May 1973; "Henry Jaworsky, Cameraman for Leni Riefenstahl Interviewed" by Gordon Hitchens and others in *Film Culture* (New York), spring 1973; "Dans les coulisses d'Olympia" by E. Leisen in *Ecran* (Paris), November 1973; "Leni" by L. Andrew Mannheim in *Modern Photography* (Cincinnati), February 1974; "Misguided Genius" in *Newsweek* (New York), 16 September 1974; "Footnote to the History of Riefenstahl's *Olympia*" by H. Barkhausen in *Film Quarterly* (Berkeley), fall 1974; "Fascinating Fascism" by Susan Sontag in the *New York Review of Books*, 6 February 1975; "Leni's Back and Bianca's Got Her" by Bianca Jagger in *Inter-*

view (New York), January 1975; "Über Nacht Antisemitin geworden?" by Harry R. Sokal in *Der Spiegel* (Germany), no.46 1976; "Blut und Hoden" in *Der Spiegel* (Germany), no.44 1976; "La Grande Dame blond aux petits gants blancs" by W. Aitken in *Take One* (Montreal), no.4, 1976; "Leni's Triumph of the Will" by P.D. Zimmerman in *Newsweek* (New York), 29 November 1976; "Lenis blühende Träume" by Peter Schille in *Der Stern* (Germany), 18 August 1977; "Zur Riefenstahl-Renaissance", special issue of *Frauen und Film* (Berlin), December 1977.

*   *   *

The years 1932 to 1945 define the major filmmaking efforts of Leni Riefenstahl. Because she remained a German citizen making films in Hitler's Third Riech, two at his request, she and her films were viewed as pro-Nazi. Riefenstahl claims she took no political position, committed no crimes. In 1948, a German court ruled that she was a follower of, not active in, the Nazi Party. Another court in 1952 reconfirmed her innocence of war crimes. But she is destined to remain a politically controversial filmmaker who made two films rated as masterpieces.

Film critics are pro-Leni or anti-Leni when explicating the political content and purpose of her films. All concur that she was a multiply-talented artist, aggressive and ambitious, a dancer, an athlete, who became an expert filmmaker. No matter what history may prove regarding Leni's politics in the years 1932 to 1945, her stature as a filmmaker of genius will not be diminished.

She began to learn filmmaking while acting in the mountain films of Arnold Fanck, her mentor. She made a mountain film of her own, *The Blue Light*, using smoke bombs to create "fog." She used a red and green filter on the camera lens over her cameraman's objections, to obtain a novel magical effect. This film is Leni's own favorite. She says it is the story of her own life. Hitler admired *The Blue Light*. He asked her to photograph the Nazi Party Congress in Nuremberg. She agreed to make *Victory of the Faith*, which was not publicly viewed. Hitler then asked her to film the 1934 Nazi Party rally.

Triumph of the Will, an extraordinary work, shows Hitler arriving by plane to attend the rally. He proceeds through the crowded streets of Nuremberg, addresses speeches to civilians and uniformed troops, reviews a five-hour parade. The question is: Did Riefenstahl make *Triumph* as pro-Nazi propaganda or not? "Cinematically dazzling and ideologically vicious," is R.M. Barsam's judgment. According to Barsam, three basic critical views of *Triumph* exist: (1) those who cannot appreciate the film at all, (2) those who can appreciate and understand the film, and (3) those who appreciate it in spite of the politics in the film.

Triumph premiered March 29, 1935, was declared a masterpiece, and subsequently earned three awards. *Triumph* poses questions of staging. Was the rally staged so that it could be filmed? Did the filming process shape the rally, give it meaning? Riefenstahl's next film, *Olympia*, posed the question of financing. Did Nazi officialdom pay for the film to be made? Riefenstahl claims the film was made independently of any government support. Others differ.

The improvisatory techniques Riefenstahl used to make *Triumph* were improved and elaborated to make *Olympia*. She and her crew worked 16-hour days, seven days a week. *Olympia* opens as *Triumph* does, with aerial scenes. Filmed in two parts, the peak of Olympia I is Jesse Owens's running feat. The peak of Olympia II is the diving scenes. In an interview with Gordon Hitchens in 1964, Riefenstahl revealed her guidelines for making *Olympia*. She decided to make two films instead of one because "the form must excite the content and give it shape.... The law of film is architecture, balance. If the image is weak, strengthen the sound, and vice-versa; the total impact on the viewer should be 100%." The secret of *Olympia*'s success, she affirmed, was its sound, all laboratory-made. Riefenstahl edited the film for a year and a half. It premiered April 20, 1938, and was declared a masterpiece, being awarded four prizes.

Riefenstahl's career after the beginning of World War II is comprised of a dozen unfinished film projects. She began *Penthesilea* in 1939, *Van Gogh* in 1943, and *Tiefland* in 1944, releasing it in 1954. Riefenstahl acted the role of a Spanish girl in it while co-directing with G.W. Pabst this drama of peasant-landowner conflicts. Visiting Africa in 1956, she filmed *Black Cargo*, documenting the slave trade, but her film was ruined by incorrect laboratory procedures. In the sixties, she lived with and photographed the Mesakin Nuba tribe in Africa.

—Louise Heck-Rabi

RISI, DINO. Italian. Born in Milan, 23 December 1917. Educated in medicine, specializing in psychiatry. Career: 1940-41—assistant to Mario Soldati on *Piccolo mondo antico* and to Alberto Lattuada on *Giacomo l'idealista*; toward end of war emigrates to Switzerland, studies filmmaking with Jacques Feyder in Geneva; after liberation returns to Milan; writes on cinema for various journals: *Milano sera*, *La nazione*, and *Tempo illustrato*; 1946-49—works in documentary, producing 13 films; 1950—producer Carlo Ponti sees short *Buio in sala*, leading to support for Risi's first feature.

Films (as assistant director): 1941—*Piccolo mondo antico* (Soldati); 1942—*Giacomo l'idealista* (Lattuada); (as director of documentary shorts): 1946—*I bersaglieri della signora*; *Barboni*; *Verso la vita*; 1947—*Pescatorella*; *Strade di Napoli*; *Tigullio minore*; *Cortili*; 1948—*Costumi e bellezze d'Italia*; *Cuore rivelatore*; *1848*; *La fabbrica del Duomo*; *Segantini, il pittore della montagna*; 1949—*La città dei traffici*; *Caccia in brughiera*; *La montagna di luce*; *Vince il sistema*; *Terra ladina*; *Il siero della verità* (feature-length); *Seduta spiritica* (feature-length); 1950—*L'isola bianca*; *Il grido della città*; *Buio in sala*; *Fuga in città*; (as co-scriptwriter): 1951—*Anna* (Lattuada); *Totò e i re di Roma* (Steno and Monicelli); 1952—*Gli eroi della domenica* (Camerini); (as feature director and collaborator on filmscript): 1952—*Vacanze col gangster (Vacation with a Gangster)* (+story); 1953—*Il viale della speranza (Hope Avenue)*; "Paradiso per 4 ore (Paradise for 4 Hours)" episode of *Amore in città (Love in the City)*; 1955—*Il segno di Venere (The Sign of Venus)*; *Pane, amore e... (Scandal in Sorrento)*; 1956—*Poveri ma belli (Poor but Beautiful)*; *Montecarlo* (Taylor) (co-sc only); 1957—*La nonna Sabella (Grandmother Sabella)*; *Belle ma povere (Beautiful but Poor, Irresistible)*; 1958—*Venezia, la luna e tu (I due gondolieri, Venice, the Moon, and You)*; *Poveri milionari (Poor Millionaires)*; 1959—*Il vedovo (The Widower)*; *Il mattatore (Love and Larceny)* (d only); 1960—*Un amore a Roma (Love in Rome)* (d only); *A porte chiuse (Behind Closed Doors)*; 1961—*Una vita difficile (A Difficult Life)* (d only); 1962—*La marcia su Roma (The March to Rome)* (d only); *Il sorpasso (The Easy Life, The Overtaking)*; 1963—*Il successo (The Success)* (Morassi) (co-d, uncredited, only); *I mostri (The Monsters, Opiate '67, 15 from Rome)*; *Il giovedì (Thursday)*; 1964—*Il gaucho (The Gaucho)* (d only); "La telefonata (The Telephone Call)" episode of

Le bambole (The Dolls) (d only); 1965—"Una giornata decisiva (A Decisive Day)" episode of *I complessi (The Complexes)*; *L'ombrellone (The Parasol, Weekend Italian Style, Weekend Wives)*; 1966—"Il marito di Attilia (or) Nei secoli fedele (Attilia's Husband or Forever Faithful)" episode of *I nostri mariti (Our Husbands)* (d only); *Operazione San Gennaro (Operation San Gennaro, Treasure of San Gennaro)*; 1967—*Il tigre (The Tiger and the Pussycat)*; *Il profeta (The Prophet, Mr. Kinky)*; 1968—*Straziami ma di baci saziami (Tear Me But Satiate Me with Your Kisses)*; 1969—*Vedo nudo (I See Everybody Naked)*; *Il giovane normale (The Normal Young Man)*; 1970—*La moglie del prete (The Priest's Wife)*; 1971—*Noi donne siamo fatte così (Women: So We Are Made)*; 1972—*In nome del popolo italiano (In the Name of the Italian People)* (d only); 1973—*Mordi e fuggi (Bite and Run)*; *Sesso matto (Mad Sex, How Funny Can Sex Be?)*; 1974—*Profumo di donna (Scent of a Woman, That Female Scent)*; 1975—*Telefoni bianchi (White Telephones, The Career of a Chambermaid)*; 1976—*Anima persa (Lost Soul)*; 1977—*La stanza del vescovo (The Bishop's Room)*; *I nuovi mostri (The New Monsters, Viva Italia)* (co-d only); 1978—*Primo amore (First Love)*; 1979—*Caro Papà (Dear Father)*; 1980—*Sono fotogenico (I Am Photogenic)*; 1981—*Fantasma d'amore (Ghost of Love)*; 1982—*Sesso e volentieri (Sex and Violence)*.

Publications:

By RISI:

Articles—interview by L. Codelli in *Positif* (Paris), September 1972; "A propos de Rapt à l'italienne", interview by L. Codelli in *Positif* (Paris), November 1974; "Sous le rire, des choses graves...", interview by J.-A. Gili in *Ecran* (Paris), November 1974; interview by G. Braucourt in *Ecran* (Paris), October 1975; interview by L. Codelli in *Positif* (Paris), October 1975; interview by A. Tassone in *Image et son* (Paris), June/July 1975; interview by A. Tassone in *Cinéma* (Paris), January 1976; "Le Cinéma: Dessins" in *Positif* (Paris), December/January 1977/78.

On RISI:

Book—*Dino Risi* by A. Vigano, Milan 1977; articles—"Au nom des monstres italiens (sur Dino Risi)" by L. Codelli in *Positif* (Paris), September 1972; *Sur 4 films de Dino Risi"* by A. Garel in *Image et son* (Paris), November 1974; "Parfum de femme" in *Avant-Scène du cinéma* (Paris), December 1975; "Dino Risi aujourd'hui et hier" by A. Tournès in *Jeune Cinéma* (Paris), September/October 1976; "Une Vie difficile", special issue of *Avant-Scène du cinéma* (Paris), 15 February 1977; "Minimaximes", special section by L. Codelli and A. Vigano in *Positif* (Paris), June 1978; "Film e figurazione: la riflessione metalinguistica" by G. Turroni in *Filmcritica* (Rome), January 1979; "Dino Risi" by Lorenzo Codelli in *International Film Guide 1983*, London 1982.

*   *   *

No other genre of Italian filmmaking has proliferated as successfully as the Italian comedy, a mixture of sexual farce, romantic comedy, and biting social satire. Dino Risi is one of the prime movers in this field. Brother of the poet and documentary filmmaker, Nelo Risi, he began work as a journalist before studying filmmaking with Jacques Feyder and becoming a screenwriter. Between 1946 and 1949 he directed 13 shorts and documentaries. Although Risi worked on important neorealist films (as assistant to Alberto Lattuada), his real interests were always determined by an unswerving belief that cinema meant entertainment and enjoyment for the ticket buyer. Undoubtedly, he was one of the youthful forces who helped steer the industry away from the provocative criticism of the neorealist film and toward the superficial but expertly-devised comedies in which it would become mired by the late fifties. Moving out of the catastrophic postwar period and into the surefooted capitalism of the "economic miracle," Italian audiences sought out more of the lighter fare, putting Risi in the mainstream of surefire profit-makers.

Generally adhering to simplicity of story line and concentrating on a representation of the "little man", the unexceptional character finding himself in a frustrating, misapprehending world, Risi's work often suggests the influence of neorealist dramaturgy. In "Paradiso per quattro ore," an episode in *Amore in città*, Risi's camera has all the scrutinizing inquisitiveness of direct cinema, and his capacity to draw characters deftly and economically rivals that of Fellini. By means of such characterizations, he sets up a group of satirical situations at a teenage dance which abjure any need for larger narrative structures. Couples are physically mismatched or too well-matched; "Gregory Peck," the local teenage sheik, enters and takes command of the field with feigned suavity; a mother checks out each boy who asks her daughter to dance, approving only the best-dressed. This brief episode is the first of a series of particularly Risian character studies, films composed of a quick succession of effective vignettes illustrating the defects and eccentricities of the Italian male, often starring the well-balanced, polished acting duet of Vittorio Gassman and Ugo Tognazzi, who alternately played friends and who brought a sense of personal tragedy to their work as well: and adversaries *I mostri*, *Vedo nudo*, *Sesso matto*, and *I nuovi mostri*.

In 1955 he made *Pane, amore, e...*, taking over from Comencini the popular series about the adventures of a *bersaglieri* marshall played by Vittorio De Sica and helping with it to launch the career of Sophia Loren. This was followed by *Poveri ma belli* and *Belle ma povere*, the story of two young "spivs" who court each other's sisters.

Seven films later, in 1961, Risi's satire assumed a serious edge and jettisoned much farcical frivolity. In *Una vita difficile* he takes stock of Italy's politico-economic transition in the story of a former partisan working as a left wing journalist (Alberto Sordi) who finds himself set upon by government, family, and colleagues alike. *La marcia su Roma* is a wry look at Mussolini's famous march to power, depicting the cowardice and selfishness of the King who made it easy for Mussolini. Tognazzi plays an incorruptible magistrate who destroys evidence that would acquit the dishonest industrialist (Gassman) in *In nome del popolo italiano*. Several films, including *Il gaucho* and *Telefoni bianchi* reflect Risi's desire to turn the satirical weapon of film on the film industry itself.

The high calibre of the director's projects can often be attributed to excellence in the script stage due to the work of writers like Ennio Flaiano, Age and Scarpelli, Bernadino Zapponi, and Ettore Scola.

—Joel Kanoff

RITCHIE, MICHAEL. American. Born 28 November 1938 in Waukesha, Wisconsin. Educated in history and literature at Harvard, graduated 1960. Married Georgina Tebrock, 1963; 3 children. Career: while student at Harvard stages 1st production of Arthur Kopit's *Oh Dad, Poor Dad, Mama's Hung You in the Closet and I'm Feelin' So Sad*; play attracts national attention, Ritchie hired by *Omnibus* TV series producer Robert Saudek; directs several film documentaries, works with Maysles brothers; becomes associate producer and director on Saudek's *Profiles in Courage* series; 1963-68—directs numerous segments of TV shows, including *Run for Your Life*, *The Man from U.N.C.L.E.*, *Dr. Kildare*, and pilot for *The Outsider*; 1969—begins directing feature films. Business: Miracle Pictures, 22 Miller Avenue, Mill Valley, CA 94941.

Films (as director of feature films): 1970—*Downhill Racer*; 1972—*Prime Cut*; *The Candidate*; 1975—*Smile*; 1976—*The Bad News Bears*; 1977—*Semi-Tough*; 1979—*An Almost Perfect Affair*; 1980—*The Island*; *Divine Madness*; 1983—*Survivors*.

Publications:

By RITCHIE:

Articles— "Snow Job" in *Action* (Los Angeles), September/October 1970; "Mon Film est avant tout une satire...", interview by M. Grisolia in *Cinéma* (Paris), September/October 1972; interview by L.O. Löthwall and A. Tournès in *Jeune Cinéma* (Paris), September/October 1972; "The Production of *Smile*" in *American Cinematographer* (Los Angeles), October 1975; interview by L. Salvato and D. Schaefer in *Millimeter* (New York), October 1975; "The Making of *Smile*", interviw by L. Sturhahn in *Filmmakers Newsletter* (Ward Hill, Mass.), October 1975; "Dialogue on Film: Michael Ritchie" in *American Film* (Washington, D.C.), November 1977; interview by B. Zito in *Millimeter* (New York), June 1979.

On RITCHIE:

Articles—"Realist Irony: The Films of Michael Ritchie" by James Monaco in *Sight and Sound* (London), summer 1975; "Michael Ritchie: Semi-Tough Satirist" by D. Jacobs in *Film Comment* (New York), November/December 1977; "Dossier: Hollywood 79: Michael Ritchie" by P. Carcassonne in *Cinématographe* (Paris), March 1979.

*   *   *

Michael Ritchie is himself a "semi-tough" filmmaker, a designation which might take in both the immediate pleasure in his ironies and the ultimate disapointments of his films. Yet despite his unvaryingly conventional narrative patterns and film style, Ritchie's films are immediately recognizable for their incisive (and ludicrous) confrontations of American institutions with his quirky characters. It would doubtless be to ask for other films altogether to quibble that they generally limit themselves to benign institutions—especially sports—and come around to an affable respect. That his earliest films (*Downhill Racer*, *Prime Cut*, *The Candidate*) are his toughest hints that Ritchie is moving away from his most interesting qualities.

Ritchie's recent failures are instructive. The personal project of *An Almost Perfect Affair* highlighted what his previous films nearly disguised—that he is at his most conventionally sentimental with sexual relations. At the other extreme, a commercial project like *The Island* fairly well swamped his delicate satire—one could imagine it being a personalized genre piece like Richard Lester's *Juggernaut*, but except for a little comic documentary on a Florida gunshop, it wasn't.

It seems to be the documentary infusions that so propel *Smile*, *Semi-Tough*, *Prime Cut*, and *The Bad News Bears* (in order of their success). Ritchie's most essential milieu is sunny suburban California, of the shopping malls and off-key high-school bands. His characters look slightly shell-shocked, as if they fail to notice how the self-created institutions have steamrolled over them. Ritchie is the Thomas Berger of filmmakers, with deft and ironic characterizations. The world is full of never-quite-successful business entrepreneurs: Bruce Dern in *Smile* trying to sell mobile homes with such pitches as "Thinking! That's the name of the game!" or the financier of the Bad News Bears trying to put a stop to the monster he's created, even the savage yet oddly pathetic Gene Hackman in *Prime Cut* trying to explain the literally cut-throat business world in "the heartland."

For all the sharp dissection of "middle" America in those films, comparisons are inevitable. Walter Matthau's curmudgeon in *The Bad News Bears* is a shadow of the same character under Billy Wilder. Ritchie covers something of the same territory as Alan Pakula, but without the paranoia—thus America is for Ritchie full of cute foibles, with never a hint of anything more vicious underneath.

—Scott Simmon

RITT, MARTIN. American. Born in New York City, 2 March 1920. Educated at Dewitt Clinton High School, New York City; attended Elon College, North Carolina; St. John's University, Brooklyn. Career: 1937—meets Elia Kazan while attending St. John's University; joins Group Theater; 1937-42—appears in several Group Theater productions; 1942-46—serves in U.S. Army Air Force; 1943-44—appears in play *Winged Victory* and George Cukor's film version, made for the armed forces; 1946—begins directing plays in New York City; 1948-51—directs and acts in live productions for CBS television, including series *Danger*; 1951—blacklisted by television industry when a Syracuse grocer charges him with donating money to Communist China; 1951-56—unable to find work, teaches acting at Actor's Studio; direct several plays, wins critical acclaim for staging *A Very Special Baby* and Arthur Miller's *A View from the Bridge*; 1956—directs 1st film, *Edge of the City*. Agency: Chasin-Park-Citron, Sunset Blvd., Los Angeles, California 90069.

Films (as director): 1957—*Edge of the City (A Man Is 10 Feet Tall)*; *No Down Payment*; 1958—*The Long Hot Summer*; 1959—*The Sound and the Fury*; *The Black Orchid*; 1960—*Jovanka e l altri (5 Branded Women)*; 1961—*Paris Blues*; 1962—*Adventures of a Young Man (Hemingway's Adventures of a Young Man)*; 1963—*Hud* (+co-pr); 1964—*The Outrage*; 1966—*The Spy Who Came in from the Cold* (+pr); 1967—*Hombre* (+co-pr); 1968—*The Brotherhood*; 1970—*The Molly Maguires* (+co-pr); *The Great White Hope*; 1971—*Sounder*; 1972—*Pete 'n' Tillie*; 1974—*Conrack* (+co-pr); 1976—*The Front* (+pr); 1978—*Casey's Shadow*; 1979—*Norma Rae*; 1980—*Back Roads*.

Roles: 1944—*Gleason* in *Winged Victory* (Cukor); 1975—in *Der Richter und sein Henker (End of the Game)* (Schell).

Publications:

By RITT:

Articles—interview in *The New York Times*, 1 June 1958; "It's the Freedom That Counts" in *Films and Filming* (London), May 1961; "Martin Ritt—Conversation" in *Action* (Los Angeles), March/April 1971; "The Making of Conrack", interview by B.J. Demby in *Filmmakers Newsletter* (Ward Hill, Mass.), April 1974; "Je suis un professionel, pas un génie...", interview by J.-C. Rubin in *Cinéma* (Paris), January 1974; interview by H. Béhar in *Image et son* (Paris), March 1977; "Paranoia Paradise", interview by A. Stuart in *Films and Filming* (London), March 1977; interview in *The New York Times*, 25 February 1979; interview by D. Chase in *Millimeter* (New York), June 1979; "Portrait of a Director: The Completely Candid Martin Ritt", interview by D.S. Reiss in *Filmmakers Monthly* (Ward Hill, Mass.), April 1981.

On RITT:

Book—*The Films of Martin Ritt* by Sheila Whitaker, London 1972; articles—"The Hollywood War of Independence" by Colin Young in *Film Quarterly* (Berkeley), spring 1959; "Personality of the Month" in *Films and Filming* (London), April 1960; "Talk with the Director" in *Newsweek* (New York), 2 October 1961; "The Photography of *Hud*" by Herb Lightman in *Action* (Los Angeles), July 1963; "The Best and Worst of Martin Ritt" by Douglas McVay in *Films and Filming* (London), December 1964; "*Outrage*: A Print Documentary on Hollywood Film-Making" by Sydney Field in *Film Quarterly* (Berkeley), spring 1965; "*Hombre* and *Welcome to Hard Times*" by Stephen Farber in *Film Quarterly* (Berkeley), fall 1967; "Tall When They're Small" by Lionel Godfrey in *Films and Filming* (London), August 1968; "Bio-filmography" in *Focus on Film, no.3* (Washington, D.C.), Summer 1970; "Norma Rae's Big Daddy" by B. Cook in *American Film* (Washington, D.C.), April 1980.

*   *   *

As his roots in the Group Theater would indicate, Martin Ritt is a man with a social conscience. He has himself known misfortune: he was blacklisted during the McCarthy hypocrisy of the 1950s and, in *The Front*, he poignantly attacks that odious practice. Often, the characters in his films are underdogs, victims of racism or sexism or capitalism who live lives of quiet dignity while struggling and occasionally triumphing over adversity.

Most refreshingly, Ritt's films are inhabited by odd couplings, characters from diverse backgrounds who unite for a common good while in the process expanding their own awareness. In *Norma Rae*, for example, Southern cotton mill, worker Sally Field and New York Jewish labor organizer Ron Leibman form a curious coalition as they unionize a factory. In a hilarious sequence, which symbolizes the cinema of Martin Ritt, Field joins the Lower East Side and Dixie when she petulantly utters the Yiddish word *kvetch* while complaining to Leibman. (The director also deals with the hardships of overworked, underpaid employees in *The Molly Maguires*, set in the Pennsylvania coal mines of the 1870s.)

Blacks and whites have regularly aligned themselves in Ritt films, from easy-going, hard-working railroad yard worker Sidney Poitier befriending confused army deserter John Cassavetes in *Edge of the City* to schoolteacher Jon Voight educating underprivileged black children in *Conrack*. In all of these, the black characters exist within a white society, their identities irrevocably related to whites. The exception is *Sounder*, released after Hollywood had discovered that black audiences do indeed attend movies; it was produced at a point in time when blacks on movie screens were able to exist solely within a black culture. *Sounder* pointedly details the struggles of a black family to overcome adversity and prejudice. Despite spending his youth in New York City, Ritt has set many of his films in the South: *Sounder, Conrack, Norma Rae, The Long Hot Summer, The Sound and the Fury*—the latter two based on William Faulkner stories.

While Ritt's films are all solidly crafted, they are in no way visually distinctive: Ritt cannot be called a great visual stylist, and is thus not ranked in the pantheon of his era's filmmakers. If anything, the best of his earliest films, *Edge of the City*, is intriguingly realistic.

—Rob Edelman

RIVETTE, JACQUES. French. Born Jacques Pierre Louis Rivette in Rouen, 1 March 1928. Educated at Lycée Corneille, Rouen. Career: 1949—shoots 1st film, *Aux Quatre Coins*, a 16mm short; moves to Paris; 1950—meets Godard, Truffaut, Rohmer, and Chabrol at cine-club in Paris; begins writing for *Gazette du cinéma*; directs short film, *La Quadrille*, produced by and starring Jean-Luc Godard; 1952—begins writing for *Cahiers du cinéma*; 1952-56—works on a number of films in various capacities, including as an apprentice on Jean Renoir's *French Cancan* and as cameraman on François Truffaut's *Une Visite*; 1956—directs *Le Coup du berger*, his 1st film in 35mm, which is co-produced and co-scripted by Chabrol and features Godard and Truffaut in small roles; 1958-60—directs 1st feature *Paris nous appartient*, released 1961; 1962-63—writes and directs play *La Religieuse*; 1963-65—editor-in-chief of *Cahiers du cinéma*; 1966—directs "Jean Renoir, le patron" for *Cinéastes de notre temps* series on French TV; 1970—directs lengthy *Out 1: noli me tangere* intending it as a TV series in 8 episodes, but the work is rejected by official French television organization; 1972—footage is edited into feature film *Out 1: spectre*, released in 1974. Address: 20 boulevard de la Bastille, 75012 Paris, France.

Films (as director): 1950—*Aux Quatre Coins*; *Le Quadrille*; 1952—*Le Divertissement*; 1956—*Le Coup du berger* (+co-sc); 1961—*Paris nous appartient (Paris Belongs to Us)* (+ro as part guest); 1966—*Suzanne Simonin, la religieuse de Denis Diderot (La Religieuse, The Nun)* (+co-sc); *Jean Renoir, le patron*; 1968—*L'Amour fou* (+co-sc); 1971—*Out 1: noli me tangere* (+co-sc) (never released); 1974—*Out 1: spectre* (+co-sc); *Céline et Julie vont en bateau (Céline and Julie Go Boating)* (+co-sc); 1976—*Duelle (Twilight)* (+co-sc); *Noroît (Northwest)* (+co-sc); 1979—*Merry-Go-Round* (+co-sc); 1981—*Le Pont du nord (North Bridge, The Northern Bridge)* (+co-sc); *Paris s'en va*; 1984—*L'Amour par terre*.

Roles: 1960—*Marilù's Boyfriend" in Chronique d'un été* (Morin and Rouch).

Publications:

By RIVETTE:

Articles—"*The Southerner*" in *Gazette du cinéma* (Paris), June 1950; articles on the Biarritz Festival and *Under Capricorn* in *Gazette du cinéma* (Paris), October 1950; articles on Soviet film and *Orphée* in *Gazette du cinéma* (Paris), November 1950; "*Chtche Droe Leto*" in *Cahiers du cinéma* (Paris), February 1953; "*I Confess*" in *Cahiers du cinéma* (Paris), August/September 1953; "*The Lusty Men*" in *Cahiers du cinéma* (Paris), October 1953; "*Madame De...*" in *Cahiers du cinéma* (Paris), November 1953; interview with Otto Preminger and article on *The Naked Spur* in *Cahiers du cinéma* (Paris), December 1953; article on Cinemascope in *Cahiers du cinéma* (Paris), January 1954; interview with Jacques Becker and article on *Angel Face* in *Cahiers du cinéma* (Paris), February 1954; interview with Jean Renoir in *Sight and Sound* (London), July/September 1954; "Renoir in America", with François Truffaut in *Sight and Sound* (London), summer 1954; interview with Abel Gance in *Cahiers du cinéma* (Paris), January 1955; interview with Roberto Rossellini, with François Truffaut in *Cahiers du cinéma* (Paris), April 1955; article on recent American cinema in *Arts* (Paris), October 1955; "*Les Mauvaises Rencontres*" in *Cahiers du cinéma* (Paris), November 1955; "*Land of the Pharaohs*" in *Cahiers du cinéma* (Paris), December 1955; "*Frau im Mond*" in *Cahiers du cinéma* (Paris), March 1956; article on Eisenstein in *Arts* (Paris), March 1956; "*The Trouble with Harry*" in *Cahiers du cinéma* (Paris), April 1956; interview with Joshua Logan in *Cahiers du cinéma* (Paris), December 1956; discussion of French cinema in *Cahiers du cinéma* (Paris), May 1957; interview with Max Ophuls in *Cahiers du cinéma* (Paris), June 1957; "*St. Joan*" in *Cahiers du cinéma* (Paris), July 1957; "*Beyond a Reasonable Doubt*" in *Cahiers du cinéma* (Paris), November 1957; article on Tours Festival in *Arts* (Paris), November 1957; interview with Jean Renoir in *Cahiers du cinéma* (Paris), Christmas 1957; "*Que Viva Mexico*" and "*Foolish Wives*" in *Cahiers du cinéma* (Paris), January 1958; article on Kenji Mizoguchi in *Cahiers du cinéma* (Paris), March 1958; "*Bonjour Tristesse*" in *Cahiers du cinéma* (Paris), April 1958; "*Sayonara*" in *Cahiers du cinéma* (Paris), May 1958; "*Sommarlek*" in *Cahiers du cinéma* (Paris), June 1958; interview with Gene Kelly in *Cahiers du cinéma* (Paris), July 1958; "*Paris nous appartient*" (dialogue) in *Cahiers du cinéma* (Paris), December 1958; interview with Roberto Rossellini in *Cahiers du cinéma* (Paris), April 1959; "*Les 400 Coups*" in *Cahiers du cinéma* (Paris), May 1959; "*Hiroshima, mon amour*" in *Cahiers du cinéma* (Paris), July 1959; interview with Fritz Lang in *Cahiers du cinéma* (Paris), September 1959; "*Trial*" in *Cahiers du cinéma* (Paris), November 1959; interview with Buster Keaton in *Cahiers du cinéma* (Paris), September 1960; article on art cinemas in *Cahiers du cinéma* (Paris), November 1960; interview with Alexandre Astruc in *Cahiers du cinéma* (Paris), February 1961; "*Kapo*" in *Cahiers du cinéma* (Paris), June 1961; "*The Hoodlum Priest*" in *Cahiers du cinéma* (Paris), September 1961; discussion on film criticism in *Cahiers du cinéma* (Paris), December 1961; interview with Rivette in *Les Lettres françaises* (Paris), December 1961; "*Splendor in the Grass*" in *Cahiers du cinéma* (Paris), June 1962; interview with Rivette in *Télérama* (Paris), April 1962; "*Proces de Jeanne d'Arc*" in *Cahiers du cinéma* (Paris), May 1963; "*Machorka-Muff*" in *Cahiers du cinéma* (Paris), July 1963; "*Monsieur Verdoux*" in *Cahiers du cinéma* (Paris), August 1963; interview with Roland Barthes in *Cahiers du cinéma* (Paris), September 1963; articles on *Muriel* and *Judex* in *Cahiers du cinéma* (Paris), November 1963; interview with Rivette in *Sight and Sound* (London), autumn 1963; articles on American cinema and American directors in *Cahiers du cinéma* (Paris), December-January 1964; articles on *Les Enfants Terribles* and *En Compagnie de Max Linder* and interview with Pierre Boulez in *Cahiers du cinéma* (Paris), February 1964; "*Le Journal d'une femme de chambre*" in *Cahiers du cinéma* (Paris), April 1964; article on Swedish cinema in *Cahiers du cinéma* (Paris), Máy 1964; interview with Claude Levy-Strauss in *Cahiers du cinéma* (Paris), June 1964; "*La Donna Scimmia*" in *Cahiers du cinéma* (Paris), October 1964; reply to letter from René Clair in *Cahiers du cinéma* (Paris), January 1965; article on Paris reception of *Gertrud* in *Cahiers du cinéma* (Paris), February 1965; articles on *Le Faux Pas, Island of the Blue Dolphins*, and on Soviet film in *Cahiers du cinéma* (Paris), March 1965; articles on *Les Pieds Dans Le Platre, Father Goose, The Troublemaker*, and *The Unsinkable Molly Brown* in *Cahiers du cinéma* (Paris), April 1965; "*Ring of Spies*" in *Cahiers du cinéma* (Paris), May/June 1965; interviews with Marcel Pagnol and members of Pagnol's crew in *Cahiers du cinéma* (Paris), December 1965; interview with Rivette in *Les Lettres françaises* (Paris), April 1966; interview with Vera Chytilova in *Cahiers du cinéma* (Paris), February 1968; press conference on "l'affaire Henri Langlois" in *Cahiers du cinéma* (Paris), March 1968; interview with Philippe Garrel in *Cahiers du cinéma* (Paris), September 1968; interview with Shirley Clark in *Cahiers du cinéma* (Paris), October 1968; interview with Rivette in *Le Monde* (Paris), 2 October 1968; article on Czech films in *Cahiers du cinéma* (Paris), January 1969; interview with Walerian Borowczyk and article on *Grazie Zia* in *Cahiers du cinéma* (Paris), February 1969; discussion on montage in *Cahiers du cinéma* (Paris), March 1969; articles on *The Touchables*, and Soviet film in *Cahiers du cinéma* (Paris), April 1969; "*Bice Skoro Propest Sveta*" in *Cahiers du cinéma* (Paris), June 1969; "*Dieu a Choisi Paris*" in *Cahiers du cinéma* (Paris), Ocotober 1969; interview with Marguerite Duras in *Cahiers du cinéma* (Paris), November 1969; interview with Rivette in *Cahiers du cinéma* (Paris), September 1968; interview with Rivette in *Positif* (Paris), April 1969; interviews with Rivette in *Le Monde* (Paris), 18 September and 14 October 1971; interview with Rivette in *Film Comment* (New York), September/October 1974; interview with Rivette in *Sight and Sound* (London), autumn 1974; interview with Rivette in *Film Quarterly* (Berkeley, California), winter 1974/75; article on Henri Langlois and the Cinémathèque Française in *Le Monde* (Paris), 21 January 1977.

On RIVETTE:

Books—*French Cinema Since 1946: Vol 2—The Personal Style* by Roy Armes, New York 1966; *The New Wave* by James Monaco, New York 1976; *Rivette: Texts and Interviews* edited by Jonathan Rosenbaum, translated by Amy Gateff and Tom Milne, London 1977; articles—"2 New Directors" by Penelope Houston in *Sight and Sound* (London), winter 1958/59; "*Paris Nous Appartient*" by Louis Marcorelles in *Sight and Sound* (London), winter 1958/59; "Qu'est-ce que la Nouvelle Vague?" by Noël Burch in *Film Quarterly* (Berkeley), winter 1959; "The Lady Called A: or, If Jules and Jim Had Only Lived at Marienbad" by Parker Tyler in *Film Culture* (New York), summer 1962; "Suzanne Simonin, Diderot's Nun" by E. Stein in *Sight and Sound* (London), summer 1966; "Jacques Rivette and *L'Amour Fou*" by P. Lloyd in *Monogram* (London), summer 1971; article in *Sight and Sound* (London), autumn 1974; article in *Film Comment* (New York), September/October 1974; "Biofilmographie" in *L'Avant-Scène du cinéma* (Paris), April 1975; special Rivette issue of *Cinéma* (Paris), March 1975; article in *Film Quarterly* (Berkeley), winter 1974/75; "Biofilmographie de Jacques Rivette" in *Image et son* (Paris), October 1981; "Sur l'oeuvre de Jacques Rivette" by Raphaël Bassan in *Image et son* (Paris), October 1981.

ROBISON, ARTHUR. American/German. Born in Chicago, 25 June 1888. Educated in medicine at University of Munich, M.D. Career: before 1914—actor in German and Swiss theaters; 1914—enters German film industry as dramaturg; 1916—feature directing debut; early 1930s—in Hollywood directs German and French versions of MGM films; then returns to Germany. Died 1935.

Films (as director): 1916—*Nächte des Grauens*; 1922—*Schatten (Warning Shadows)* (+co-story, co-sc); 1923—*Zwischen Abends und Morgens*; 1925—*Pietro, der Korsar (Peter the Pirate)* (+story, sc); 1926—*Manon Lescaut* (+co-sc); 1927—*Der letzte Walzer (The Last Waltz)*; 1928—*Looping the Loop*; 1929—*Frauenschicksal*; *The Informer*; 1930—*Jenny Lind* (French version of Sidney Franklin's *A Lady's Morals*); 1931—*Mordprozess Mary Dugan* (German version of Bayard Veiller's *The Trial of Mary Dugan*, 1929); *Quand on est belle* (French version of Jack Conway's *The Easiest Way*); 1933—*Des jungen Dessauers grosse Liebe*; *Tambour battant* (French version of preceding film); *Epoux célibataires*; *Monsieur le marquis*; 1934—*Fürst Woronzeff* (+sc); *Le Secret de Woronzeff* (French version); 1935—*Mach' mich glücklich* (+co-story, co-sc); *Der Student von Prag* (+co-sc).

*   *   *

While Dr. Arthur Robison was not a prolific director, the range of his work was interesting and varied. Born in Chicago in 1888 of German-Jewish parents, he studied medicine in Munich but the theatre became his first love and he gained experience as an actor in Germany and Switzerland. He entered the cinema in a literary capacity in 1914 and in 1916 he directed a horror film *Nachte des Grauens* with the distinguished actors Werner Krauss, Emil Jannings, and Lupu Pick. His second film *Schatten* made some seven years later was undoubtedly his masterpiece and is a classic of German cinema. Its visual beauty, its intense atmosphere, and the stylishness of its acting gave it a unique quality. The superb photography of Fritz Arno Wagner was again used to good effect in *Zwischen Abend und Morgen*, another horror film made in the same year, with Werner Krauss, Agnes Straub, and Fritz Rasp.

His *Pietro der Korsair* was a romantic costume drama with the popular Paul Richter (Lang's Siegfried) and Rudolph Klein-Rogge. For this spectacular film Robison used three ace cameramen—Fritz Arno Wagner, Georg Schneevoight, and Rudolph Maté. The next year he filmed Abbe Prevost's romance *Manon Lescaut* with a vivacious Lya de Putti in the title role. The film was embellished by the beautiful sets and costumes of Paul Leni and won universal appreciation. Marlene Dietrich appeared in a minor role as Lescaut's girlfriend. In a lighter vein, the Ruritanian *Der letzte Walzer*, based on the Oscar Strauss operetta, starred Willy Fritsch, Liane Haid, von Schlettow and Susy Vernon. Being a UFA-Paramount production it proved popular on two continents. His last silent German film was *Looping the Loop*, a story of jealousy in the entertainment world in the *Varieté* tradition, with Werner Krauss and Jenny Jugo.

In 1929 he directed the first version of *The Informer* by Liam O'Flaherty, which has been unjustly overshadowed by John Ford's later effort. Lars Hanson as Gypo Nolan and Lya de Putti as Katie Fox gave good performances, and the brooding sleazy atmosphere of the Dublin slums was far more acceptable in Robison's film. It was shot in Britain and, although silent, had a sound track added later which did nothing to improve it.

His sound films shot in France and Germany included *Mord-*

prozess Mary Dugan with Nora Gregor, Der junge Dessauers grosse Liebe, Fürst Woronzeff with Brigitte Helm, and his last film, Der Student von Prag, for which he returned to the classic German subject with Adolphe Wohlbruch in the title role, and Dorothea Wieck as his love. It was filmed in Austria, and he died the same year. Robison was very much the total director of his films, being also responsible for the scripts. His Schatten alone secures his place in film history.

—Liam O'Leary

ROBSON, MARK. American. Born in Montreal, 4 December 1913. Educated in political sciences and economics, University of California at Los Angeles; studied law at Pacific Coast University. Career: 1932—begins working in films as prop boy at Fox; becomes assistant in studio art dept.; 1935—joins RKO; works as sound cutter then editor; 1941—collaborates on editing of Citizen Kane with Robert Wise; also co-edits The Magnificent Ambersons; 1942—editing Cat People for Val Lewton leads to directing Lewton-produced horror films; 1949—directs 1st major production Champion for Stanley Kramer; 1971—with Robert Wise and Bernard Donnenfeld forms production company The Filmmakers Group; (corporation becomes Tripar partnership in 1974). Died in June, 1978.

Films (as director): 1943—The 7th Victim; The Ghost Ship; 1944—Youth Runs Wild; 1945—Isle of the Dead; 1946—Bedlam (+co-sc); 1949—Roughshod; Champion; Home of the Brave; My Foolish Heart; 1950—Edge of Doom; 1951—Bright Victory; I Want You; 1953—Return to Paradise; 1954—Hell Below Zero (+co-story); Phffft; The Bridges at Toko-Ri; 1955—A Prize of Gold; Trial; 1956—The Harder They Fall; 1957—The Little Hut (+co-pr); Peyton Place; 1958—The Inn of the 6th Happiness; 1960—From the Terrace (+pr); 1962—The Inspector (Lisa) (pr only); 1963—The Prize; 9 Hours to Rama (+pr); 1965—Von Ryan's Express (+exec pr); 1966—The Lost Command; 1967—Valley of the Dolls (+co-exec. pr); 1969—Daddy's Gone A-Hunting (+pr); 1971—Happy Birthday Wanda June; 1972—Limbo; 1974—Earthquake (+pr); 1979—Avalanche Express.

Publications:

By ROBSON:

Articles—"Why You Hear What You Hear at the Movies" in Good Housekeeping (New York), July 1955; "The Code Doesn't Stultify", with J. Wald in Films in Review (New York), December 1957; "9 Hours of My Life" in Films and Filming (London), November 1962; interview in The Celluloid Muse by Charles Higham and Joel Greenberg, London 1969; "Mark Robson Talks with Noel Black about Earthquake" in Action (Los Angeles), January/February 1975.

On ROBSON:

Articles—"Hollywood Director Speaks Out" by Robert Ellis in Negro Digest, January 1951; "Personality of the Month" in Films and Filming (London), March 1958; "Director's Way" in Saturday Review (New York), 20 December 1958; "Mark Rob-

son" by Herbert Luft in Films in Review (New York), May 1968; obituary in Ecran (Paris), September 1978.

*   *   *

Mark Robson's career has been schizophrenic. He directed his share of both classy and trashy melodramas, comedies and romances, yet also made films concerned with society's inequities. A couple in the latter category remain among the most honest and humane motion pictures of their era.

During the late 1940s, Robson both carried on the tradition of gritty, realistic social dramas initiated at Warner Bros. during the 1930s, and helped instigate the genre of racially-oriented films which attempted to destroy the negative stereotype of blacks in America. The first two of his four releases in 1949, shot for Stanley Kramer, are among the notable moralistic, issue-oriented films of the day. The tough, gripping Champion first brought Robson and his star, Kirk Douglas, to prominence. Douglas portrays a war veteran, constantly thwarted in his honest ambitions, who became a boxing champ and destroys the lives of everyone around him. He gains fame and wealth, but loses his humanity. The second, Home of the Brave, chronicles the effects of racial prejudice on a black GI while on a mission to a Japanese-held island; the role was solidly acted by the long-forgotten James Edwards. With Pinky, Lost Boundries, and Intruder in the Dust, it is the first attempt by Hollywood to focus a scenario on a black character, presenting him as a human being exploited by the racism inherent in American society.

Bright Victory effortlessly details the plight of disabled veterans, with Arthur Kennedy in one of his best roles as a blinded ex-GI. Trial, though overly melodramatic, is a thought-provoking drama about a Mexican boy accused of murdering an American girl solely because he was on the beach where she died. Another fight story, The Harder They Fall (Humphrey Bogart's final screen appearance), is a pungent exposé of corruption in the ring.

Limbo and Happy Birthday, Wanda June were filmed a generation later, near the end of Robson's career. Limbo is noteworthy for its honest attempt to depict the plight of women whose pilot-husbands are missing or imprisoned in North Vietnem. Even more tellingly, it was produced at a time, six years before Apocalypse Now, The Deer Hunter and Coming Home, when the war in Southeast Asia was taboo in Hollywood.

—Rob Edelman

ROCHA, GLÁUBER. Brazilian. Born in Vitoria da Conquista, Bahia, Brazil, 14 March 1938. Studied law, 1959-61. Career: 1957—founds production company "Lemanja-Filmes"; 1970—goes into exile; early 1970s—directs in Italy, France and Spain; 1976—returns to Brazil; 1981—preparing film in Portugal, succombs to pulmonary disease, returns to Brazil. Died in Rio de Janeiro, 22 August 1981.

Films (as director of short films): 1957—Um dia na rampa (co-d); 1958—O patio; A cruz na praça; (as director and scriptwriter): 1962—Barravento (co-sc); 1964—Deus e o diabo na terra do sol (The Black God and the Blond Devil) (+co-pr); 1965—Amazonas; Maranhão; A grande feira (d of pr only); Menino de engenho (pr only); 1966—A grande cidade (co-pr only); 1967—Terra em transe (Earth Entranced); 1968—Cancer (not completed);

1969—*Antônio das Mortes* (+co-pr, art d); 1970—*Der leone have sept cabecas (The Lion Has 7 Heads)* (co-sc, +co-ed); *Cabezas cortadas (Severed Heads)*; 1975—*Claro*; 1980—*A idade da terra (The Age of the Earth, L'Âge de la terre)*.

Publications:

By ROCHA:

Books—*Revisão critica do cinema brasileiro*, Brazil 1962; *Il cinema nôvo e l'avventura della creazione*, Italy 1968; *Riverao Sussuarana*, Brazil 1981; *Revoluçao do cinéma novo*, Brazil 1981; articles—interview by G. Gauthier in *Image et son* (Paris), July 1964; "L'Esthétique de la violence" in *Positif* (Paris), February 1966; "Culture de la faim, cinéma de la violence" in *Cinéma 67* (Paris), February 1967; "Cela s'appelle l'aurore" in *Cahiers du cinéma* (Paris), November 1967; "Un cinéma en transe" in *Image et son* (Paris), January 1968; on *Terre en transes* in *L'Avant-Scène du cinéma* (Paris), January 1968; interview by P. Arlorio and Michel Ciment in *Positif* (Paris), January 1968; "Luis Buñuel et Gláuber Rocha: échos d'une conversation", interview by A.M. Torres in *Cinéma 68* (Paris), February 1968; interview by M. Delahaye and others in *Cahiers du cinéma* (Paris), July 1969; "De la sécheresse aux palmiers" in *Positif* (Paris), March 1970; interview by N. Simsolo in *Image et son* (Paris), February 1970; "Cinema Novo vs. Cultural Colonialism: An Interview with Glauber Rocha" in *Cineaste* (New York), summer 1970; "Un Rêve libérateur" in *Le Monde* (Paris), 11 March 1971; interview by M. Martin in *Cinéma 71* (Paris), November 1971; interview by Guy Hennebelle in *Ecran* (Paris), June 1972; "Carta de Glauber Rocha" in *Cine Cubano* (Havana), no.71-72, 1972; "Somos los heraldos de la revoluciuón", interview in *Cine Cubano* (Havana), no.73-75, 1972; "La historia del Brasil según Glauber Rocha", interview in *Cine Cubano* (Havana), no.86-88, 1973; "Brève rencontre avec Glauber Rocha" in *Ecran* (Paris), March 1974; interview in *Jeune Cinéma* (Paris), June 1974; "Combats et mort du Cinema Novo", letter in *Jeune Cinéma* (Paris), June 1974; "Lumière, magie, action" in *Positif* (Paris), December 1974; "Conversazione con Glauber Rocha" edited by J. Aribar in *Filmcritica* (Rome), August 1975; "Glauber Rocha au Bresil" in *Ecran* (Paris), December 1976; "Amérique latine: 1—Bresil" in *Image et son* (Paris), June 1979; "Ma Tête a couper" in *Cahiers de la Cinémathèque* (Paris), special issue 1979; "Humberto Mauro and the Historical Position of Brazilian Cinema" and "Hunger vs. Profit Aesthetic" in *Framework* (Norwich, England), autumn 1979; "Bruit et fureur à Venise", with A. Tournès, in *Jeune Cinéma* (Paris), September/October 1980.

On ROCHA:

Articles—"Le Dieu, le diable et les fusils" by Michel Ciment in *Positif* (Paris), May 1967; "Cinema nôvo: nationalisme, révolution?" by Michel Houle and Gilbert Maggi in *Champ libre* (Montreal), spring 1971; "Pour une lecture de Gláuber Rocha" in *Les Cahiers de la Cinémathèque* (Paris), spring 1971; "Fantasia e polarità del simbolo in Glauber Rocha" by G. Cremonini in *Cinema nuovo* (Turin), January/February 1972; special Rocha issue of *Études cinématographiques* (Paris), no.97-99, 1973; "Analyse structurale d'un système textuel" by R. Gardies in *Image et son* (Paris), April 1973; "Structural Analysis of a Textual System: Presentation of a Method" by R. Gardies in *Screen* (London), spring 1974; "Ideology in the 3rd World Cinema: A Study of Ousmane Sembene and Glauber Rocha" by W.F. Van

Wert in *Quarterly Review of Film Studies* (Pleasantville, New York), no.2, 1979; "Music in Glauber Rocha's Films" by G. Bruce in *Jump Cut* (Berkeley), May 1980; "La Mort de Glauber Rocha", special section of *Cinéma 81* (Paris), October 1981; "The Incoherence of Underdevelopment" by Roy Armes in *Films and Filming* (London), November 1981; "Glauber Rocha: una mirada sobre su tumba" by A. García Ferrer in *Contracampo* (Madrid), October 1981; "Epitaphe pour Glauber Rocha" by M. Martin in *Image et son* (Paris), November 1981; "Gláuber: esa estética precaria, fea y violenta..." by M. Martínez Carril in *Cinemateca Revista* (Andes), September 1981.

ROEG, NICOLAS. English. Born Nicolas Jack Roeg in London, 15 August 1928. Educated Mercers School, England. Married Susan Rennie Stephen, 1957. Career: 1947—begins work at Marylebone Studio, dubbing French films and making tea; 1950—is hired at MGM's Boreham Wood Studios as part of camera crew on *The Miniver Story*; 1960—does 2nd unit work on *Lawrence of Arabia*; 1961-68—serves as director of photography on several well-known films, including Truffaut's *Farenheit 451*, Schlesinger's *Far From the Madding Crowd*, and Lester's *Petulia*; 1968—directs 1st feature, *Performance*, with David Cammell; 1971—1st solo direction on *Walkabout*. Address: Flat E, 2 Oxford and Cambridge Mansions, Old Marylebone Road, London N.W. 1, England.

Films (as camera operator): 1958—*The Great Van Robbery*; *A Woman Possessed*; *Passport to Shame*; *Moment of Indiscretion*; *The Child and the Killer*; *The Man Inside*; 1960—*The Trials of Oscar Wilde*; *The Sundowners*; *Jazz Boat*; 1962—*Lawrence of Arabia* (2nd unit ph only); *The Caretaker (The Guest)*; (as lighting cameraman): 1963—*Dr. Crippen*; *Information Received*; *Just for Fun*; *Nothing But the Best*; 1964—*The Masque of the Red Death*; *The System (The Girl Getters)*; *Every Day's a Holiday*; *Victim 5 (Code 7, Victim 5)*; 1965—*A Funny Thing Happened on the Way to the Forum*; *Judith* (2nd unit & add'l ph only); 1966—*Fahrenheit 451*; 1967—*Far from the Madding Crowd*; *Casino Royale* (some sections only); 1968 *Petulia*; (as director): 1970—*Performance* (co-d, +ph); 1971—*Walkabout* (+ph); 1973—*Don't Look Now*; 1976—*The Man Who Fell to Earth*; 1980—*Bad Timing*; 1982—*Eureka* (unreleased).

Publications:

By ROEG:

Articles—"An Interview with Nicolas Roeg" by Gordon Gow in *Films and Filming* (London), January 1972; "Don't Look Now", interview by Tom Milne and Penelope Houston in *Sight and Sound* (London), winter 1973/74; interview by D. Hay and E. Davis in *Cinema Papers* (Melbourne), April 1974; "Interview with Nicolas Roeg" by Tom Milne and Penelope Huston in *Sight and Sound* (London), winter 1974/75; "Nick Roeg...and the Man Who Fell to Earth" by John Lifflander and Stephan Shroyer in *Interview* (New York), March 1976; interview by G. Cohen in *Cinéma* (Paris), June 1976; "Roegian Thought Patterns", interview by J. Padroff in *Films* (London), September 1981.

On ROEG:

Book—*Nicolas Roeg* by Neil Feineman, Boston 1978; articles—
"The Nightmare Journey" by Stephan Farber in *Cinema* (Beverly Hills), fall 1970; "*Walkabout*" by Bill Nichols in *Cinema* (Beverly Hills), fall 1971; "Survival in Itself is Brutal" in *Films Illustrated* (London), October 1971; "The Ultimate Performance" in *Close-up: A Critical Perspective on Film* by Marsha Kinder and Beverle Houston, New York 1972; "British Cinema Filmography" in *Film* (London), spring 1972; "Nicholas Roeg: Permutations without Profundity" by Chuck Kleinhans in *Jump Cut* (Chicago), September/October 1974; "Story so far...*The Man Who Fell to Earth*" by Paul Mayersberg in *Sight and Sound* (London), autumn 1975; "No Sympathy for the Devil" in *Hollywood UK: The British Film Industry in the '60s* by Alexander Walker, New York 1976; "A Roeg's Gallery of Imagistic Motion Pictures" by Charles Champlin in the *Los Angeles Times Sunday Calendar*, 12 September 1976; "Film Apres Noir" by Larry Gross in *Film Comment* (New York), July/August 1976; "*The Man Who Fell to Earth*" by Tom Milne in *Sight and Sound* (London), summer 1976; "The Open Texts of Nicolas Roeg" by Robert Kolker in *Sight and Sound* (London), spring 1977; "Film as Science Fiction" by W.F. Van Wert in *Western Humanities Review* (Salt Lake City), no.2, 1979; "The Illusions of Nicholas Roeg" by H. Kennedy in *American Film* (Washington, D.C.), January/February 1980; "Pour rehabiliter Nicholas Roeg" by Jean-Louis Cros and Raymond Lefevre in *Image et son* (Paris), June 1981; "Another Look at Nicholas Roeg" by J. Gomez in *Film Criticism* (Edinboro, Penn.), fall 1981.

*   *   *

English-born Nicolas Roeg is one if the few filmmakers to successfully make the crossover from technician to director. He began as a clapperboy, at age 22, on *The Miniver Story* (1950) and for the next decade worked at various jobs in the industry, including second unit work on *Lawrence of Arabia*. With his far-ranging interests, Roeg found a successful place for himself in cinematography, first as a camera operator and then as a director of photography particularly noted for his brilliant lighting contributions in such films as *The Caretaker*, *The Masque of the Red Death*, *Far from the Madding Crowd*, and *Petulia* among others. The transition to directing was made gradually, with Roeg serving both as cinematographer and co-director (with Donald Cammell) on *Performance*. In his next venture, *Walkabout*, Roeg also did the cinematography but soloed as the director. *Don't Look Now* was his first effort strictly as a director and his first solid commercial success. This was followed by the controversial film *The Man Who Fell to Earth* and the equally controversial *Bad Timing*. For his latest film, *Eureka*, he has had trouble finding a distributor.

As a working director for 15 years, with only six completed films and only one solid commercial success to his credit, it is amazing that Nicolas Roeg continues to elicit interest. Within the framework of his films, there is a world explored with intensity and understanding but a world unsettling in its unresolved and uncontrolled implications. His films consistently explore realms of the psyche that other (safer) filmmakers have consistently avoided. It is certainly not that Roeg doesn't know how to win the adulation of audiences but that he refuses to compromise his vision. This is what makes Nicolas Roeg an intriguing, inconclusive, and ultimately an anachronistic explorer into the borderline territory of the contemporary cinema.

The central characters in Roeg's work are all aliens, in either a literal or figurative sense. His protagonists are outsiders who don't fit into the mainstream of conventional society. Whether thay are separated from society by heritage, or experience, or by preference, thay are all affected by their perceptions of the society which surrounds and absorbs them. The rock singer in *Performance*, the adolescent girl in *Walkabout*, the restoration designer in *Don't Look Now*, the intergalatic traveler in *The Man Who Fell To Earth*, and the psychiatrist in *Bad Timing* are all haunted by their differences from the normal.

From the beginning, but increasingly dominant in his films is the concept of fragmented time. Much like Alain Resnais, Roeg seems obsessed with the affect that the past and future have on the present. In *Don't Look Now*, for example, the child's death permeates events in the future, culminating when the child's father sees his own funeral pass in front of him. Or again in the same film, the scene of the couple making love is intercut with scenes of them dressing afterward, fluidity of time is especially evident in *Bad Timing*, where time is totally diffused and moves back and forth, through past, present, and future at leisure.

Whether one accepts Roeg's narrative, his visual style is always striking. Working as a cinematographer, Roeg was always brilliant in creative achievements with color and lighting. In *Masque of the Red Death*, for example, the masked ball sequence with its red motif stands as the harbinger of the terror to come. Again, in *Far from the Madding Crowd* Roeg imbues the film with bluish tones that emphasize in an understated way the sense of separation and distancing between the characters. As a director it seems consistent that Roeg bring to his films a highly disciplined sensitivity to the image. The red motif appears as an important visual warning in *Don't Look Now*: the girls' raincoat was red and the color red serves as a reminder and an omen. The images in *Bad Timing* are consistently framed with a painting nearby, the painting acting in a manner analogous to that of a Greek chorus—commenting on what is happening and what will happen.

If there is a reasonable explanation for Roeg's lack of commercial success, it is perhaps found in the problems of uniting his particular stylistic interests with his plots. For example, *The Man Who Fell to Earth* could have been a straight science-fiction story, but in Roeg's care it becomes less science fiction than a study of how society destroys what it does not understand. The popular failure of *Bad Timing*, although it contains some of cinema's most erotic lovemaking scenes, can be located in the concentration on form at the expense of plot; the fragmentation of events this film impairs the theme of uncontrollable sexual obsession.

—Stephen E. Bowles and Nat Chediak

ROHMER, ERIC. French. Born Jean-Marie Maurice Scherer in Tulle, 4 April 1920. Career: 1942-50—teaches literature at lycée, Nancy; 1950—with Godard and Rivette founds *La Gazette du cinéma*; 1951—makes short *Charlotte and Her Steak* with Godard as sole performer; 1951-present—cinema journalist and critic; 1957-63—editor-in-chief of *Cahiers du cinéma*; 1962-73—makes the "Six contes moraux" (6 Moral Tales) beginning with *Le Boulangère de Monceau*; 1980—with *La Femme de l'aviator* begins new series: "Comédies et proverbes." Recipient: Prix Max-Ophüls for *My Night at Maud's*, 1970; Prix Louis-Delluc, 1971; Prix Méliès for *Claire's Knee*, 1971; Prix Special du Jury, Cannes Festival, for *The Marquise of O...*, 1976; Officier des Arts et des Lettres. Address: office—26 av. Pierre-1er-de-Serbie, 75116 Paris, France.

Films (as director and scriptwriter): 1950—*Journal d'un scélérat*; 1951—*Présentation ou Charlotte et son steak (Charlotte* and Her Steak); 1952—Les Petites Filles modèles (co-d, unfinished); 1954—Bérénice; 1956—La Sonate à Kreutzer (The Kreutzer Sonata); 1958—Véronique et son cancre; 1959—Le Signe du lion (Sign of the Lion, The Sign of Leo); 1963—La Boulangerie de Monceau (1st of the "Contes moraux": following 5 identified here by "CM" and number Rohmer has assigned); La Carrière de Suzanne (Suzanne's Profession) (CM no.2); 1964—Nadja à Paris; 1964-69—films for educational television: Les Cabinets de physique au XVIIIème siècle, Les Métamorphoses du paysage industriel, Perceval, Don Quichotte, Edgar Poë, Pascal, La Bruyère, Mallarmé, La Béton dans la ville, Les Contemplations, Hugo architecte, Louis Lumière; 1965—films for television series "Cinéastes de notre temps": Carl Dreyer, Le Celluloid et la marbre; "Place de l'étoile" episode of Paris vu par... (6 in Paris); 1966—Une Étudiante d'aujourd'hui; 1967—La Collectionneuse (CM no.4); Fermière à Montfaucon; 1969—Ma Nuit chez Maud (My Night at Maud's) (CM no.3); 1970—Le Genou de Claire (Claire's Knee) (CM no.5); 1972—L'Amour l'après-midi (Chloe in the Afternoon) (CM no.6); 1976—Die Marquise von O. (The Marquise of O...); 1978—Perceval le Gaullois; 1980—La Femme de l'aviateur (The Aviator's Wife); 1982—Le Beau Mariage (The Perfect Marriage); 1983—Loup y es-tu? (Wolf, Are You There?).

Publications:

By ROHMER:

Books—Hitchcock, with Claude Chabrol, Paris 1957; 6 contes moraux, Paris 1974; articles—"Eric Rohmer", interview by Nicoletta Zalaffi and Rui Nogueira in Film (London), spring 1968; "Rohmer", interview by Rui Nogueira in Sight and Sound (London), summer 1971; "Eric Rohmer: An Interview" by Graham Petrie in Film Quarterly (Berkeley), summer 1971; interview by Rossell Deac in Cinema (Beverly Hills), fall 1971; "Eric Rohmer Talks About Chloe" in Interview (New York), November 1972; "Eric Rohmer parle de ses contes moraux", interview in Séquences (Paris), January 1973; "Riscoprire l'America" in Filmcritica (Rome), May/June 1973; interview by F. Barron in Take One (Montreal), January 1974; "Programme Eric Rohmer", article and interview by Claude Beylie in Ecran (Paris), April 1974; "La Marquise d'O..." in Avant-scène du cinéma (Paris), October 1976; interview by J. Fieschi in Cinématographe (Paris), June 1976; "Notes sur la mise en scène" in Avant-Scène du cinéma (Paris), 1 October 1976; "Rohmer Talks about Beauty and Box Office", interview by D. Yakir in The Village Voice (New York), 25 October 1976; interview by I. Pruks in Cinema Papers (Melbourne), October 1977; "Ein schweigsamer Regisseur", interview in Film und Fernsehen (Berlin), October 1977; "Rohmer's Perceval", interview by G. Adair in Sight and Sound (London), autumn 1978; "Rehearsing the Middle Ages", interview by N. Tesich-Savage in Film Comment (New York), September/October 1978; "Note sur la traduction et sur la mise en scène de Perceval" in Avant-scène du cinéma (Paris), February 1979; "Notes sur Le Petit Théâtre de Jean Renoir" in Cinéma (Paris), April 1979; "Un Allegorie policière", with Claude Chabrol, in Avant-scène du cinéma (Paris), June 1980; interview by P. Carcassonne and J. Fieschi in Cinématographe (Paris), May 1981.

On ROHMER:

Books—Women and Sexuality in the New Film by Joan Mellen, New York 1973; Eric Rohmer by G. Angeli, Milan 1979;

articles—"Views of the New Wave" by Louis Marcorelles in Sight and Sound (London), spring 1960; "Eric Rohmer" in Film (London), spring 1968; "L'Amour Sage" by Carlos Clarens in Sight and Sound (London), winter 1969/70; "The Moral Psychology of Rohmer's Tales" by Joan Mellen in Cinema (Beverly Hills), fall 1971; "The Reputation of Eric Rohmer" by William Pechter in Commentary (New York), August 1971; "Eric Rohmer: Choice and Chance" by Rui Nogueira in Sight and Sound (London), summer 1971; "From Maud to Claire to Chloe" by Vincent Canby in The New York Times, 8 October 1972; "Director of the Year" in International Film Guide 1972, London 1971; "Wenn man eine Erklärung findet..." by R. Koller in Filmkritik (Miunich), January 1972; "The Eyehole of Knowledge" by A. Appel, Jr., in Film Comment (New York), May/-June 1973; bibliography in Monthly Film Bulletin (London), December 1976; "My Night with Rohmer" by P. Gardner in New York, 8 November 1976; "Biofilmographie: Eric Rohmer" in Avant-Scène du cinéma (Paris), 1 October 1976; "The Ideology of Realism" by C. Crisp in Australian Journal of Screen Theory (Kensington, N.S.W.), March 1977; "Dossier: De Murnau à Rohmer" in 2 parts by M. Latil Le Dantec in Cinématographe (Paris), January and February 1977; "Dossier-auteur: Eric Rohmer a la recherche de la absolu" by M. Amiel and others in Cinéma (Paris), February 1979; "Dossier: le cinéma d'Eric Rohmer" by J. Fieschi and others in Cinématographe (Paris), February 1979; "Nei film di Rohmer le immagini transmettono pensiero scritto" by M. Milesi in Cineforum (Bergamo), April 1979; "Et Perceval rencontra la Marquise d'O..." by C. Oddos in Cinématographe (Paris), January 1980; "Rohmer Adds to His Intimate Comedies" by Joan Dupont in The New York Times, 26 September 1982.

*   *   *

By virtue of a tenure shared at Cahiers du cinéma during the fifties and early sixties, Eric Rohmer is usually classified with Truffaut, Godard, Chabrol, and Rivette as a member of the French New Wave. Yet, except for three shorts made with Godard in the early fifties, Rohmer's films seem to share more with the traditional values of such early directors as Renoir and Bresson than with the youthful flamboyance of his contemporaries. Much of this divergence owes to an accident of birth. Born Maurice Scherer at Tulle in 1920, Rohmer was at least ten years older than any of the other critic/filmmakers in the Cahiers group. By the time he arrived in Paris in 1948, he was an established teacher of literature at the Lycée in Nancy and had published a novel, Elizabeth (1946), under the pseudonym, Gilbert Cordier. When he joined Cahiers staff in 1951 Rohmer had already spent three years as a film critic with such prestigious journals as La Revue du cinéma and Sartre's Les Temps modernes. Thus Rohmer's aesthetic preferences were more or less determined before he began writing for Cahiers.

Still the move proved decisive. At Cahiers he encountered an environment in which film critics and filmmaking were thought of as merely two aspects of the same activity. Consequently, the critics who wrote for Cahiers never doubted that they would become film directors. As it turned out, Rohmer was one of the first to realize this ambition. In 1951 he wrote and directed a short 16mm film called Charlotte and Her Steak in which Godard as the sole performer plays a young man who tries to seduce a pair of offscreen women. Two of his next three films were experiments in literary adaption. These inaugurated his long association with Barbet Schroeder who produced or co-produced all of Rohmer's subsequent film projects.

In 1958 filmmaking within the *Cahiers* group was bustling. Rivette, Truffaut, and Chabrol were all shooting features. Rohmer, too, began shooting his first feature, *Sign of the Lion*. The result, however, would not be greeted with the same enthusiasm that was bestowed on Godard and Truffaut. Rohmer has always maintained that his films are not meant for a mass audience but rather for that small group of viewers who appreciate the less spectacular qualities of the film medium. Unfortunately, *Sign of the Lion* failed to find even this elite audience. And while Truffaut's *The 400 Blows* and Godard's *Breathless* were establishing the *Cahiers* group as a legitimate film force, it was not until 1963 that Rohmer was able to secure funding for a film of any length. That same year he ended his association with *Cahiers du cinéma*. The journal had for some time been moving away from the aesthetic policies of Bazin and towards a more leftist variety of criticism. Rohmer had always been viewed as something of a reactionary and was voted down as co-director. He chose to leave the magazine and devote his entire career to making films. At just this moment Barbet Schroeder was able to find money for a short 16mm film. While writing the scenrio for *Suzanne's Profession* Rohmer conceived the master plan for a series of fictional films (his moral tales) each a variation on a single theme: a young man on the verge of committing himself to one woman, by chance meets a second woman whose charms cause him to question his initial choice. His entire way of thinking, willing, desiring, that is to say, the very fabric of his moral life starts to unwind. The young man eventually cleaves to his original choice, his ideal woman against whom he measures all his other moral decisions but the meeting with the second woman, or as is the case in *Claire's Knee*, a trinity of women, creates a breathing space in the young man, a parenthesis in his life for taking stock. The vacillations of the young man, who often functions as the film's narrator, comprise the major action of the six films known as the moral tales. Rohmer recognizes the irony in his use of cinema, a medium which relies on objective, exterior images, to stage his inferior moral dramas. But by effecting minute changes in the exterior landscape he expresses subtle alterations in his protagonist's interior drama. This explains why Rohmer pays such scrupulous attention to rendering surface detail. Each film in the Six Moral Tales was shot on the very location and at the exact time of year in which the story is set. Rohmer was forced to postphone the shooting of *My Night at Maud's* for an entire year so that Jean-Louis Trintignant would be available during the Christmas season, the moment when the fiction was scripted to begin. The painter, Daniel, in *La Collectioneuse* is played by Daniel Pommereulle, a painter in real life. The Marxist historian and the priest who preaches the sermon at the end of *My Night at Maud's* are, in real life, historian and priest. The female novelist of *Claire's Knee* is a novelist and the married couple of *Chloe in the Afternoon* are man and wife. Such attention to detail allowed Rohmer to realize an advance in the art of cinematic adaption with his next two films, *The Marquise of O* and *Perceval*.

As he entered the eighties, Rohmer completed two films of a new series of moral tales which he calls "Parables." In contrast to the Six Moral Tales, the Parables are not played out on the interior landscape of a single character but rather engage an entire social milieu. In *The Aviator's Wife* a young postal clerk trails his mistress around Paris to spy on her affair with another man. During his peregrinations, he meets a young female student, loses track of his mistress, then decides he prefers the company of the young student only to discover her in the arms of another man. *The Perfect Marriage* chronicles the attempts of a young Parisian woman to persuade the man whom she had decided will make her a perfect husband that she will, in turn, make him the perfect wife. She discovers, too late, that he has

been engaged to another woman all along.

Emerging from the crucible of the French New Wave, Rohmer has forged a style that combines the best qualities of Bresson and Renoir with distinctive traits of the Hollywood masters. And though he was never as flamboyant as Godard or Truffaut, Rohmer's appeal has proved much hardier. The international success that met *My Night at Maud's* and *The Marquise of O* has built a following that awaits the new set of moral dilemmas limned by each further installment of the Parables with eagerness and reverence.

—Dennis Nastav

ROMERO, GEORGE A. American. Born in New York, 1940(?). Educated in drawing and painting, then acting. Career: 1954—begins making 8 mm films, receives prize for *Earthbottom*; mid-1960s—acts and directs in Pittsburgh; late 1960s—forms film publicity firm Filmmakers; after 1973—works in television as producer of sports and political programs and publicity spots; 1974—with Richard Rubinstein forms Laurel Group as production and distribution organization.

Films (as maker of short films): 1954-56—*The Man from the Meteor*; *Gorilla*; *Earthbottom*; 1958—*Curly*; *Slant*; 1960-62—*Expostulations*; (as feature film director): 1968—*Night of the Living Dead*; 1972—*There's Always Vanilla*; 1973—*Hungry Wives (Jack's Wife)*; *The Crazies*; 1977—*Martin*; 1978—*Zombie (Dawn of the Dead)*; 1979—*Knight Riders*; 1982—*Creep Show*.

Publications:

By ROMERO:

Articles—"Filming *Night of the Living Dead*", interview by A.B. Block in *Filmmakers Newsletter* (Ward Hill, Mass.), January 1972; "George Romero from Night of the Living Dead to The Crazies" in *Interview* (New York), April 1973; "Update on George (Night of the Living Dead) Romero or, What Happens After Your 1st Successful Film?", interview by R. Rubinstein in *Filmmakers Newsletter* (Ward Hill, Mass.), June 1973; "The Cult Movie Comes of Age", interview by D. Chase in *Millimeter* (New York), October 1979; "Die Zombies sind in uns", interview in *Film und Ton* (Munich), September 1979.

On ROMERO:

Articles—"A Pittsburg Horror Story" by P. McCollough in *Take One* (Montreal), November 1974; "Checklist 119—George A. Romero" by R.M. Stewart and others in *Monthly Film Bulletin* (London), February 1980.

*   *   *

Between 1968 and 1979, Romero produced a body of work comparable in distinction to that of Larry Cohen in the same period: both are centered in the horror genre, both extremely uneven, but achieving in certain instances an impressive intensity and concentration. Above all, both are rooted in (and appear significantly dependent upon) the disturbances in American society during that period.

Romero's first film, *Night of the Living Dead*, is a landmark in the evolution of the American horror film. It proved decisively that significant and commercially successful work in that genre could be produced outside Hollywood, on a low budget, independent of major studios. Thematically, it drew together the twin attitudes that underlie and motivate what must now be regarded as the golden age of horror film: general disillusionment with authority/government (this is the period of Vietnam), and specific disillusionment with the institution whereby authority/domination structures are transmitted, the patriarchal nuclear family. The film opens with a brother and sister driving to a remote country graveyard over which flies the American flag; they are reluctantly honoring a dead father neither of them cares about, on behalf of an invalid mother. They bicker, brother taunts sister in a repetition of childhood behavior patterns, sister responds with bitterness and helpless frustration; the first zombie lurches foward to attack sister and kill brother, the emanation of family tensions and the embodiment of the "living dead" that is the legacy of the American past. The film follows through from this premise with exemplary rigor, paralleling the zombies and the authorities as equally mindless and destructive, flouting all generic expectations (the young couple, traditionally the guarantee of the perpetuation of the family, are killed and devoured, the hero is mistaken for a zombie and casually shot down by the sheriff's posse, tracing the progress of the nuclear family's self-destruction, as zombie-daughter kills and eats her parents and "dead" brother leads the final assault on his sister.

The sequel, *Dawn of the Dead*, is even more remarkable, and among the few outstanding American films of the last decade. Here the Zombies are associated with entrapment in consumer-capitalism, from whose structures and characteristic relationship patterns the surviving humans must learn to extricate themselves or succumb to the "living dead." The heroine, Fran, ultimately rejects marriage (clearly depicted as an institution for the oppression of women); her lover—a traditional male needing the support of a subordinated woman for the confirmation of his identity—becomes a zombie. The ending of the film centers on two emblems of male authority: the surviving male surrenders his rifle to the zombies, Fran (cast earlier as helpless and dependent) flies the helicopter for their escape. The two have become mutually supportive but no future love-relationship is suggested. Fran is pregnant. They fly off to an uncertain destination and a precarious future, in which new male/female relationships must be constructed.

Romero's achievement so far is centered on those two films, though around them are grouped several related early works which are more distinguished than their neglect suggests. *The Crazies* takes up concerns from *Night of the Living Dead* and tentatively anticipates the more foward-looking potential of *Dawn of the Dead*; *Jack's Wife* and *Martin* are a closely linked pair of minor works concerned with their eponymous protagonists' striving for identity and dignity in a debased, materialistic world that offers them no recognition or autonomy, and their flight into roles (witch, vampire respectively) that offer false prestige and worse entrapment.

Since *Dawn of the Dead* Romero's career seems to have lost its sense of direction. Its powerful radical impulse, rooted in the Vietnam/Watergate syndrome of disillusionment, protest and subversion, has not sustained itself into the Reagan era. One may feel some sympathy (though little admiration) for the attempt in *Knight Riders* to convey liberal attitudes (and, regrettably,liberal platitudes) to the youth audience, but the film remains essentially a remake of *Alice's Restaurant*, ten years too late and with all the complexities ironed out. Nothing, however, had

prepared one for *Creep Show*, a five-part anthology film made in collaboration with Stephen King, virtually indistinguishable from the British Amicus horror films of the seventies: the same pointlessness, the same moral squalor: nasty people doing nasty things to other nasty people. It testifies to Romero's current uncertainty that, at time of writing, he is simultaneously planning *Day of the Dead* (the film that will complete the 'Living Dead' trilogy) and *Creep Show II*. Certainly, one's hopes are all focused on the former.

—Robin Wood

ROMM, MIKHAIL. Russian. Born in eastern Siberia, birth registered at Irkutsk, 24 January 1901. Educated in gymnasium, Moscow; master classes in sculpture with Golubkina, 1917; studied in atelier "Vkhoutemas", Fine Arts School, Moscow, 1921-25. Career: 1918-21—serves in Red Army; 1920s—pursues various arts-related professions including sculpture and translating (Zola, Flaubert); 1932—Alexander Macheret requests him as assistant director on *Jobs and Men*; 1956—begins teaching master class in film, State Cinema Institute; after 1962—works on documentary film project *The World Today* (unfinished). Died in Moscow, 1 November 1971.

Films (as scriptwriter): 1930—*Revanch (Revanche)* (co-sc); 1931—*Riadom s nami (On Our Side, A côté de nous)* (co-sc); 1932—*Dela i lyudi (Men and Jobs)* (ass't d only); 1933—*Konveyer smerti* [Conveyor of Death] (co-sc); (as director): 1934—*Pyshka (Boule de Suif)* (+sc); 1937—*Trinadtsat (The 13)* (+co-sc); 1939—*Lenin v 1918 godu (Lenin in 1918)*; 1943—*Metshta (The Dream)* (+co-sc); 1944—*Chelovek No.217 (Girl No.217)* (+co-sc); 1948—*Russkii vopros (The Russian Question)* (+sc); *Vladimir Ilyich Lenin* (co-d, compilation film); 1950—*Sekretnaia missiia (Secret Mission)*; 1953—*Admiral Ushakov (Amiral Tempête, Segel im Sturm)*; *Korabli shturmuiut bastioni (Attack from the Sea, The Ships Storm the Bastions)* (part 2 of *Admiral Ushakov*); 1956—*Ubiistvo na ulize Dante (Murder on Dante Street)* (+co-sc); 1962—*Deviat dnei odnovo goda (9 Days of One Year)* (+co-sc); 1965—*Obykhnovennyi fachizm (Ordinary Fascism)* (+co-sc, compilation film); 1966—*(Lost Letters)*; *(A Night of Thought)*.

Publications:

By ROMM:

Books—*Sovietskoe kinoiskusstvo*, edited with Leonid Trauberg, Moscow 1939; *Besedy o kino* [Talking About the Cinema], Moscow 1965; articles—"Clashes of Youth and Age", interview, in *Films and Filming* (London), September 1961; "Le Feu sur la terrasse" in *Positif* (Paris), February/March 1965; "Le Second Sommet" in *L'Avant-scène du cinéma* (Paris), July/September 1965; "Souvenirs" in *Le Cinéma soviétique par ceux qui l'ont fait* edited by Luda and Jean Schnitzer and Marcel Martin, Paris 1966; interview by Bernard Eisenschitz in *Cahiers du cinéma* (Paris), April 1970; "Propos liminaires sur le maître" in *Cahiers du cinéma* (Paris), April 1970; "Gespräche über Filmregie", special issue of *Filmwissenschaftliche Beitrage* (Berlin), v.18, no.1, 1977; "Stoff unserer Filme ist der Dialektik des Lebens", interview by H. Herlinghaus in *Film und Fernsehen* (Berlin), January 1981.

On ROMM:

Book—*La Vie de Lénine à l'écran* by Luda and Jean Schnitzer, Paris 1967; articles—"Soviet Kaleidoscope" by Nina Hibbin in *Films and Filming* (London), August 1966; "Sur Romm" by Bernard Eisenschitz in *Cahiers du cinéma* (Paris), April 1970; "Mikhaïl Romm" by Marcel Martin in *Cinéma 71* (Paris), December 1971; "Michail Romm" by Hans Lohmann in *Regiestühle*, Berlin 1972; "Souvenirs sur Mikhail Ilyitch Romm" by Andrei Mikhalkov-Konchalovski in *Positif* (Paris), March 1972; "'El Mundo de hoy', el último film de Mijail Romm" by I. Grigoriev in *Cine Cubano* (Havana), no.78-80, 1973; "Mikhail Romm (1901-1971)" by René Prédal in *Anthologie du cinéma* (Paris), January 1975; "Mikhail Romm" by René Prédal in *Anthologie du cinéma* vol.9, Paris 1976; "Primer M.I. Romma" by Gyorgy Chukhrai in *Iskusstvo Kino* (Moscow), January 1981.

ROOS, JØRGEN. Danish. Born in Gilleleje, 14 August 1922. Married Noemi Silberstein, 1957. Career: 1939-47—works as cameraman; 1945—with painter Albert Mertz founds Copenhagen film club; since 1947—scriptwriter, director, and cameraman on numerous documentaries and one feature film; 1956—co-founder of The Association of Danish Film Directors. Recipient: Silver Bear, Berlin Festival, for *Knud*, 1966. Address: Ved Amagerport 5, DK-2300 Copenhagen S, Denmark.

Films (as co-director with Albert Mertz): 1942—*Flugten (The Flight)*; 1943—*Kaerlighed paa Rulleskøjter*; *Hjertetyven (Thief of Hearts)*; 1944—*Richard Mortensens bevaegelige Maleri* (d alone); *Historien om en Mand (Story of a Man)* (unfinished); 1947—*Paa Besøg hos Kong Tingeling*; *Goddag Dyr!*; (as director): *Isen brydes* (co-d); *Johannes V. Jensen*; *Opus 1*; *Reflexfilm*; 1948—*Mikkel*; 1949—*Paris på to måder*; *Jean Cocteau*; *Tristan Tzara, dadaismens fader*; *Det definitive afslag på anmodningen om et kys* (co-d); 1950—*Spiste horisonter* (co-d); *Johannes Jørgensen i Assissi*; *Shakespeare og Kronborg (Hamlet's Castle)*; 1951—*Historien om et slot, J.F. Willumsen*; 1952—*Den strømlinjede gris*; *Slum*; *Feriebørn*; 1953—*Lyset i natten*; *Spaedbarnet*; *Goddag børn! (The Newborn)*; *Skyldig—ikke skyldig*; 1954—*Kalkmalerier*; *Inge bliver voksen*; *Avisen*; *Martin Andersen Nexos sidste rejse*; *Johannes Jørgensen i Svendborg*; 1955—*Mit livs eventyr (My Life Story)*; 1956—*Sølv*; 1957—*Ellehammer*; *Johannes Larsen*; 1958—*Magie du diamant (Magic of the Diamond)*; *6-dagesløbet (The 6 Days)* (feature); 1959—*Friluft (Pure Air)*; 1960—*En by ved navn København (A City Called Copenhagen)*; *Danish Design*; *Staphylokok-faren*; 1961—*Føroyar Faerøerne*; *Hamburg*; 1962—*Vi haenger i en tråd*; 1963—*Oslo*; 1965—*Støj*; 1966—*Carl Th. Dreyer*; *Knud*; *Sisimiut*; 1967—*En fangerfamilie i Thuledistriktet*; *17 minutter Grønland*; *Grønlandske dialektoptagelser og trommedanse fra Thuledistriktet*; *Et år med Henry*; 1968—*Ultima Thule*; 1969—*Det er tilladt at vaere åndssvag*; 1970—*Kaláliuvit (Er du grønlaender)*; 1971—*Andersens hemmelighed*; *Er i bange (Are You Afraid)* (ph only); 1972—*Huse til mennesker*; *Udflytterne*; *To maend i ødemarken*; *Ulrik fortaeller en historie*; 1974—*I den store pyramide*; *J. Th. Arnfred*; 1975—*Andersen hos fotografen*; 1977—*14 dage i jernalderen*; *Monarki og demokrati*; 1978—*Carl Nielsen 1865-1931*; 1979—*Nuuk 250 år*; 1980—*Slaedepatruljen Sirius*; *Grønland*; 1982—*Knud Rasmussens mindeekspedition til Kap Seddon*.

* * *

Jørgen Roos is the unrivalled master of the Danish documentary film, having worked for more than 40 years in this field. He has won international recognition and has received prizes at international short film festivals. Only once has he tried to direct a feature film.

He started out as a cameraman, taught by his brother, Karl Roos, and Theodor Christensen, the pioneer of the documentary film in Denmark. Karl Roos and Theodor Christensen were both active filmmakers, and also eminent film theoreticians. Christensen was influenced by the British documentary movement and considered himself a committed documentary filmmaker. Jørgen Roos was inspired by those two and he acquired a wide knowledge of the theory and the history of cinema. After having worked as a cameraman, he made his first experimental film in 1942 with the painter Albert Mertz, and this couple created the most interesting and original Danish avant-garde films of the forties. Since 1952 Jørgen Roos has made numerous documentaries for governmental institutions and private companies. Besides these commissioned films he has worked on projects of his own, and in recent years he has had his own production company.

To the commissioned film Jørgen Roos has brought a fresh and unconventional approach, and his way of solving the official tasks is often witty, surprising, and keen. His films are always one-man projects. He writes his own scripts, directs, and is often cameraman. And he is always the editor, because it is in the cutting room that he gives his films their definitive and personal form. Jørgen Roos is superior in the short form, his editing is rhythmical, and his films have a fascinating, fast-moving drive. He likes to tease, to find unusual points of view, and he has an eye for the curious. His brilliant technique however, can lead him into the superficial.

In 1955 he made one of his best films, *Mit livs eventry*, about Hans Andersen. In this film he brought the iconographic technique to perfection, and he used it in later films. One of his most popular and widely known films is *A City Called Copenhagen* from 1960, an untraditional and ironic tourist film. Jørgen Roos was asked to make similar city portraits of Hamburg and Oslo. Roos has portrayed Danish personalities such as Nobel laureate Johannes V. Jensen, Carl Th. Dreyer, Greenland explorer Knud Rasmussen, and composer Carl Nielson. In the last 15 to 20 years Jørgen Roos has shown a special interest in Greenland. He has lost his heart to this exceptional country and he has explored both the old and the new Greenland in many films. The cool and detached view, which was characteristic of Jøgen Roos's films, has been replaced by a deep-felt commitment to the land and the people, which he, more than anyone else, has brought to the screen.

—Ib Monty

ROSI, FRANCESCO. Italian. Born in Naples, 15 November 1922. Educated in law. Career: early 1940s—radio journalist in Naples, writes for U.S. Army radio, 1944-45; 1946—moves to Rome, begins to work in theater as actor, stage designer and assistant director; 1948—hired by Visconti as assistant on *La terra trema*; through 1956 works as assistant director on films of Luciano Emmer, Raffaello Matarazzo, Visconti, and Antonioni; also collaborates on scripts. Recipient: Special Jury Prize, Venice Festival, for *La sfida*, 1958; Silver Bear for Best Direction, Berlin Festival, for *Salvatore Giuliano*, 1963; Gold Lion, Venice Festival, for *Le mani sulla città*, 1963.

Films (as assistant director): 1947—*La terra trema*; 1949—*La domenica d'agosto*; 1951—*Bellissima* (Visconti) (+co-sc); 1952—*I vinti*; *Processo alla città* (sc only); *Camicie Rosse (Anita Garibaldi)* (co-d); 1954—*Carosello Napoletano*; *Proibiti*; *Senso*; (as director and co-scriptwriter): 1956—*Kean* (co-d); 1958—*La sfida (The Challenge)*; 1959—*I magliari*; 1961—*Salvatore Giuliano*; 1963—*Le mani sulla città (Hands Over the City)*; 1965—*Il momento della verità (The Moment of Truth)* (co-d, sc); 1967—*C'era una volta (More than a Miracle)*; 1970—*Uomini contro*; 1972—*Il caso Mattei (The Mattei Affair)* (co-sc); 1973—*A proposito Lucky Luciano (Re: Lucky Luciano)* (co-sc); 1976—*Cadaveri eccelenti (Illustrious Corpses, Cadavres exquis)* (co-sc); 1979—*Cristo si è fermato a Eboli (Christ Stopped at Eboli)* (co-sc); 1981—*Tre fratelli (3 Brothers)* (+co-sc).

Publications:

By ROSI:

Articles—"Francesco Rosi", interview, in *Film* (London), spring 1964; "Francesco Rosi: An interview" by Gideon Bachmann in *Film Quarterly* (Berkeley), spring 1965; interview by Michel Ciment and others in *Positif* (Paris), May 1965; "Moments of Truth", interview by John Lane, in *Films and Filming* (London), September 1970; interview by Michel Ciment in *Positif* (Paris), November 1970; "Un Homme contre: Francesco Rosi", interview by J.A. Gili in *Ecran* (Paris), December 1973; interview by Michel Ciment in *Positif* (Paris), January 1974; "Au cinéma la dénonciation devient vite un prêche...", interview by A. Tassone in *Cinéma* (Paris), January 1974; "The audience should not be just passive spectators", interview by Gary Crowdus in *Cineaste* (New York), v.7, no.1, 1975; "Entretien avec Francesco Rosi" by Aldo Tassone in *Image et son* (Paris), June/July 1976; interview by G. Robinson in *Thousand Eyes* (New York), November 1976; "Un Débat d'idées, de mentalités, de moralités" in *Avant-Scène du cinéma* (Paris), May 1976; interviews by Michel Ciment on *Christ Stopped at Eboli* in *Positif* (Paris), February 1979; "En travaillant avec Visconti: sur le tournage de *La Terra trema*" in *Positif* (Paris), February 1979; "Sono lo psicologico del film e non del personaggio: colloquio con Francesco Rosi" by F.D. Baker in *Cinema nuovo* (Turin), October 1979.

On ROSI:

Articles—"A Neapolitan Eisenstein" by John Lane in *Films and Filming* (London), August 1963; "*The Moment of Truth*" by John Lane in *Sight and Sound* (London), autumn 1964; "Francesco Rosi" by Maria Kornatowska in *Regiestühle*, Berlin 1972; special section on Rosi in *Image et son* (Paris), June/July 1976; "Found in Translation: Rosi in Context" by B. Amengual in *Thousand Eyes* (New York), November 1976; "Biofilmographie de Francesco Rosi" in *Avant-Scène du cinéma* (Paris), May 1976; "Entretien avec Tonio Guerra" by A. Tassone in *Positif* (Paris), February 1979; "Eisenstein, Rosi, Kieslowski und andere" by G. Netzeband in *Film und Fernsehen* (Berlin), no.12, 1979; special section on Rosi in *Positif* (Paris), May 1980.

ROSSELLINI, ROBERTO. Italian. Born in Rome, 8 May 1906. Married Marcella de Marquis (marriage annulled); children: Renzino and Romano (deceased); Ingrid Bergman, 1950 (divorced); children: Roberto Ingmar, and twins Isotta and Isabella; Somali Das Gupta (divorced); one son. Career: 1934—begins working on films in dubbing and sound effects, then editing; 1934-38—makes 2 short films on his own; 1940—directs 1st feature, *La nave bianca*; 1940-45—continues to direct and serve as technical director in official film industry; at same time, he and others are shooting documentary footage of Italian resistance fighters which is later incorporated into *Roma, città aperta* and *Paisà*; 1945—completes *Roma, città aperta*, inaugurating neorealist movement; 1946-49—refuses offer by David Selznick to make 7 films in Hollywood, but accepts offer by Howard Hughes to make film for RKO with Ingrid Bergman; 1949-57—scandals involving his affairs with Ingrid Bergman and later Indian screenwriter Somali Das Gupta result in unofficial public "boycott" of his films and subsequent decline in work and status; 1961—directs mainly documentary features for Italian and French television. Died 4 June 1977.

Films (as director and scriptwriter): 1936—*Daphne*; 1938—*Prelude à l'apres-midi d'une faune*; *Luciano Serra, pilota* (sc only); 1939—*Fantasia sottomarina*; *Il tacchino prepotente*; *La vispa Teresa*; 1941—*Il Ruscello di Ripasottile*; *La nave bianca* (co-sc); 1942—*Un pilota ritorna* (co-sc); *I tre aquilotta* (uncredited collaboration); 1943—*L'uomo della croce* (co-sc); *L'invasore* (supervised production); 1943—*Desiderio* (co-sc) (confiscated by police and finished by Marcello Pagliero in 1946); 1945—*Roma, città aperta (Open City)* (co-sc); 1946—*Paisà (Paisan)* (co-sc, +pr); 1947—*Germania, anno zero (Germany, Year Zero)* (co-sc); 1948—*L'amore (Woman, Ways of Love)*; *Il miracolo (The Miracle)* (co-sc); *La macchina ammazzacattivi* (co-sc, +pr); 1949—*Stromboli, terra di dio (Stromboli)* (co-sc, +pr); 1950—*Francesco—giullare di Dio (Flowers of St. Francis)* (co-sc); 1952—"L'Invidia" episode of *I sette peccati capitali (The 7 Deadly Sins, Les sept péchés capitaux)* (co-sc); *Europa '51 (The Greatest Love)* (co-sc); 1953—*Dov'è la libertà* (co-sc); *Viaggio in Italia (Voyage to Italy, Strangers, The Lonely Woman)* (co-sc); "Ingrid Bergman" episode of *Siamo donne* (d only); 1954—"Napoli '43" episode of *Amori di mezzo secolo*; *Giovanna d'Arco al rogo (Joan of Arc at the Stake)*; *Die Angst (Le Paura, Fear)* (d only); *Orient Express* (production supervision); 1958—*L'India vista da Rossellini* (10 episodes) (+pr); *India* (co-sc); 1959—*Il Generale della Rovere* (co-sc); 1960—*Era notte a Roma* (co-sc); *Viva l'Italia* (co-sc); 1961—*Vanina Vanini (The Betrayer)* (co-sc); *Torino nei centi'anni* (d only); *Benito Mussolini (Blood on the Balcony)* (production supervision); 1962—*Anima nera*; "Illibatezza" episode of *Rogopag*; 1963—*Le carabiniere* (co-sc only); 1964—*L'eta del ferro* (sc, pr only); 1966—*La Prise de pouvoir par Louis XIV (The Rise of Louis XIV)* (d only); 1967—*Idea di un'isola* (+pr); *La lotta dell'uomo per la sua sopravvivenza* (sc, +pr only); 1968—*Atti degli apostoli* (co-d, co-sc, +ed); 1970—*Socrate (Socrates)* (co-sc, +ed); 1972—*Agostino di Ippona* (d only); 1975—*Blaise Pascal* (d only); *Anno uno* (d only); 1978—*Il Messia (The Messiah)* (co-sc).

Publications:

By ROSSELLINI:

Books—*Era notte a Roma*, with others, Bologna 1961; "*India*" by Rossellini and others in *Roberto Rossellini* by Mario Verdone, Paris, Italy 1963; articles—"*Paisà*: 6th Sketch", with others in *Bianco e nero* (Rome), October 1947; "*Il miracolo*" by Rossellini and T. Pinelli in *Revue du cinéma* (Paris), June 1948;

"Interview with Rossellini" by Francis Koval in *Sight and Sound* (London), February 1951; "Coloquio sul neo-realismo" by Mario Verdone in *Bianco e nero* (Rome), February 1952; "*Viaggio in Italia*" (fragment), with V. Brancati in *Bianco e nero* (Rome), November 1953; "Entretien avec Roberto Rossellini" by Maurice Schèrer and François Truffaut in *Cahiers du cinéma* (Paris), July 1954; "10 ans de cinéma" in *Cahiers du cinéma* (Paris), August/September and November 1955, and January 1956; "Cinema and Television: Interview" by André Bazin in *Sight and Sound* (London), winter 1958-59; "Censure et culture" in *Cinéma 61* (Paris), October 1961; "Entretien avec Roberto Rossellini" by Jean Domarchi and others in *Cahiers du cinéma* (Paris), July 1962; "Conversazione sulla cultura e sul cinema" in *Filmcritica* (Rome), March 1963; "Cinema: nuove prospettive de conoscenza" in *Filmcritica* (Rome), July/August 1963; "*L'età del ferro* as *Il ferro*" in *Filmcritica* (Rome), November/December 1963; "Nouvel entretien avec Roberto Rossellini" by Eric Rohmer and Fereydoun Hoveyda in *Cahiers du cinéma* (Paris), July 1963; "*Viaggio in Italia*", with V. Brancati and "Intervista con Roberto Rossellini" by Adriano Aprà and Maurizio Ponzi in *Filmcritica* (Rome), April/May 1965; "Entretien avec Roberto Rossellini" by Jean Collet and Claude-Jean Philippe in *Cahiers du cinéma* (Paris), September 1966; "Comprimere nel tempo le esperienze di una vita" in *Cinema d'oggi*, June 1968; "Conversazione con Roberto Rossellini" by Michele Mancin, Renato Tomasino, and Lello Maiello in *Filmcritica* (Rome), August 1968; "Interview with Roberto Rossellini" by Toby Mussman and José Soltero in *Medium* (Frankfurt), winter 1967-68; "*Atti degli Apostoli*", with others in *Cinema e film*, summer 1969; "*Roma, città aperta*" by Rossellini and others in *L'Avant-Scène du cinéma* (Paris), 1971; "Roberto Rossellini" in *Cinema* (Beverly Hills), fall 1971.

On ROSSELLINI:

Books—*Roberto Rossellini* by Patrice Hovald, Paris 1958; *Ingrid Bergman: An Intimate Portrait* by Joseph Henry Steele, New York 1959; *Roberto Rossellini* by Massimo Mida, Parma 1961; *Roberto Rossellini* by Mario Verdone, Paris 1963; *Roberto Rossellini* by José Luis Guarner, translatd by Elizabeth Cameron, New York 1970; *Dibattio su Rossellini* by Gianni Menon, Rome 1972; *Roberto Rossellini* by Pio Baldelli, Rome 1972; *Roberto Rossellini* by Gianni Rondolino, Florence 1974; articles—"Prophet with Honor: Roberto Rossellini" by Peter Ordway in *Theatre Arts* (New York), January 1949; "Roberto Rossellini" by Lauro Venturi in *Hollywood Quarterly*, fall 1949; "Life in a Sausage Factory" in *Time* (New York), 7 February 1949; "Rossellini" in the *New Yorker*, 19 February 1949; "Ingrid's Rossellini" by G.Weller in *Colliers* (New York), 12 November 1949; "Difficulties in his Romance" in *Time* (New York), 26 December 1949; "The Stature of Rossellini" by Simon Harcourt-Smith in *Sight and Sound* (London), April 1950; "Ingrid Bergman Has a Baby" in *Life* (New York), 13 February 1950; "Basket of Ricotta" in *Time* (New York), 13 February 1950; "Stromboli Bambino" in *Newsweek* (New York), 13 February 1950; "Tempest on the Tiber" in *Life* (New York), 13 February 1950; "Roberto and the Rota" in *Newsweek* (New York), 27 February 1950; "Senor y Senora" in *Time* (New York), 5 June 1950; "Génie du christianisme" by Maurice Schèrer in *Cahiers du cinéma* (Paris), July 1953; "Good Old Roberto" in *Newsweek* (New York), 28 June 1954; "Rossellini" by François Truffaut in *Arts* (Paris), January 1955; "Lettre sur Rossellini" by Jacques Rivette in *Cahiers du cinéma* (Paris), May 1955; "2 images de la solitude" by Eric Rohmer in *Cahiers du cinéma* (Paris), May 1956; "Rossellini Story" in *Newsweek* (New York), 3 June 1957; "Not Forever Affair" in *Newsweek* (New York), 18 November

1957; "The Quest for Realism" by Gordon Gow in *Films and Filming* (London), December 1957; "La scelta assoluta di Roberto Rossellini" by Beniamino Joppolo in *Filmcritica* (Rome), April/May 1960; "New Meaning of Montage" by André Bazin in *Film Culture* (New York), no.22-23, 1961; "Dov'e Rossellini?" by Jean-André Fieschi in *Cahiers du cinéma* (Paris), May 1962; "The Face of '63—Italy" by J.F. Lane in *Films and Filming* (London), April 1963; "Rossellini Rediscovered" by Andrew Sarris in *Film Culture* (New York), no.32, 1964; "The Achievement of Roberto Rossellini" by Alan Casty in *Film Comment* (New York), fall 1964; "Le nouvel âge de Rossellini" by Adriano Aprà in *Cahiers du cinéma* (Paris), August 1965; "The 6th Montreal International Film Festival" by G. Weinberg in *Film Heritage* (Dayton, Ohio), winter 1965/66; "Age of Iron" by M. Mardore in *Cahiers du Cinema in English* (New York), no.3, 1966; "Duo e tre cose su Roberto Rossellini" by Maurizio Ponzi in *Cinema e film*, spring 1967; "The Legion of Decency" by Richard Corliss in *Film Comment* (New York), summer 1968; "If Elsa Could See Roberto Now" by Vincent Canby in *The New York Times*, 12 December 1971; "Rossellini's Materialist Mise-en-Scene" by J.R. MacBean in *Film Quarterly* (Berkeley), winter 1971/72; "Could Rossellini Work Here?" by J.J. O'Connor in *The New York Times*, 30 April 1972; "L'intelligenza del presente per Roberto Rossellini" by G. Aristarco in *Cinema nuovo* (Turin), September/October 1972; "Roberto Rossellini 1974" by J.H. Dorr in *Take One* (Montreal), May 1974; "Recent Rossellini" by J. Hughes in *Film Comment* (New York), July/August 1974; "Rossellini's Case Histories for Moral Education" by L. Norman in *Film Quarterly* (Berkeley), summer 1974; special issue of *Screen* (London), winter 1973/74; "Ingrid Bergman on Rossellini", interview, and "Rossellini" by Robin Wood in *Film Comment* (New York), July/August 1974; "Ingrid from Lorraine to Stromboli: Analyzing the Public's Perception of a Film Star" by J. Damico in *Journal of Popular Film* (Bowling Green, Ohio), vol.4, no.1, 1975; "Sulla lettera di Bazin a proposito del neorealismo" by G. Aristarco in *Cinema nuovo* (Turin), September/December 1975; special issue of *Filmcritica* (Rome), May/June 1976; "Roberto Rossellini" by L. Audibert in *Cinématographe* (Paris), July/August 1977; "Roberto Rossellini", with interview, by C. Beylie and C. Clouzot in *Ecran* (Paris), July 1977; "Un Débutant méconnu: Roberto Rossellini" by J. Demeure in *Positif* (Paris), October 1977; "In Memoriam: Roberto Rossellini" by J. Hughes in *Film Comment* (New York), July/August 1977; "Hommage à Roberto Rossellini" by J.-M. Lardinois in *Revue belge du cinéma* (Brussels), October 1977; "Rome, Open City; The Rise to Power of Louis XIV. Re-evaluating Rossellini" by M. Walsh in *Jump Cut* (Chicago), no.15, 1977; special issue by R. Gansera and W. Dütsch of *Filmkritik* (Munich), October 1978; "Rossellini oeuvre ouverte" by F. Gevaudan and J. Magny in *Cinéma* (Paris), March 1978; "Rossellini's Didactic Cinema" by H. Lawton in *Sight and Sound* (London), autumn 1978; "Rossellini dans le texte" by S. Trosa in *Cinématographe* (Paris), December 1978; "Documentary and Dullness: Rossellini According to the British Critic" and "Neo-realism—the Second Coming" by D. Ranvaud in *Monthly Film Bulletin* (London), February and March 1981.

* * *

Roberto Rossellini has been so closely identified with the rise of the postwar Italian style of filmmaking known as neorealism that it would be a simple matter to neatly pigonhole him as merely a practitioner of that technique and nothing more. So influential has that movement been on the filmmakers of the last quarter-century that the achievement ambodied in just three of his films, *Roma, città aperta*, *Paisà*, and *Germania, anno zero*, would be enough to secure the director a major place in film history. However, to simply label Rossellini a neorealist is to drastically undervalue his contribution to the thematic aspects of his art.

At its most basic level, his dominant concern appears to be a preoccupation with the importance of the individual within various aspects of the social context that emerged from the ashes of World War II. In his own words, "What matters to me is man. I have tried to express the soul, the light that shines inside people, their reality which is an absolutely personal, unique reality, secured by an individual, with a sense of the things around them. These things have meaning since there is someone observing them."

In his early films, which a number of historians have simplistically termed fascist, his concern for the individual was not sufficiently worldly to place his characters in the appropriate social context. Thus, a film like his first, *La nave bianca*, while portraying its sailors and hospital personnel as sensitive and caring, ignores the ideological and political milieu within its carry-over of the director's penchant for melodrama, that is properly considered as constituting Rossellini's "rites of passage" into the midst of the complex social issues confronting the individual in postwar Europe. The crude conditions under which it was shot, its authentic appearance and certain other naturalistic touches lent it an air of newsreel-like veracity, but its sheer raw power derived almost entirely from the individuals that Rossellini placed inside this atmospheric context. With the exception of Anna Magnani and Aldo Fabrizi, the cast was made up entirely of nonprofessionals who were so highly convincing that the effect upon viewers was electric. Many were certain that what they were viewing must have been filmed as it was actually occuring.

Despite legends about Rossellini's neorealistic style having arisen out of the scarcities and adverse shooting conditions immediately after the war, the director had undoubtedly begun to conceive the style as early as his aborted *Desiderio* of 1943, a small-scale forerunner to neorealism which Rossellini dropped in mid-shooting. Certainly, he continued the style in *Paisà* and *Germania anno zero*, the remaining parts of his war trilogy. In both of these, he delineates the debilitating effects of war's aftermath on the psyche of modern man. The latter film was a particularly powerful statement of the effect of Nazi ideology on the mind of a young boy, while criticizing the failure of traditional social institutions like the church to counter its corrupting influence.

The Rossellini films of the 1950s shed many of the director's neorealistic trappings and in doing so changed their emphasis somewhat to the spiritual aspects of man by revealing the instability of life and of human relationships. *Stromboli, Europa '51, Voyage to Italy*, and *Le paura* reflect a quest for a transcendent truth akin to the secular saintliness achieved by the priest in *Open City*. In the films of the fifties, however, his style floated unobtrusively between involvement and contemplation. This is particularly obvious in his films with Ingrid Bergman but best exemplified in *Voyage to Italy* with its leisurely-paced questioning of the very meaning of life. Every character in the film is ultimately in search of his soul. What little action there is has relatively little importance since most of the character development is an outgrowth of spiritual aspirations rather than a reaction to events. In this sense, its structure resembled the kind of neorealism practiced by De Sica in *Umberto D*, without its excessively emotional overtones and yet reaffirming Rossellini's concern for his fellow men and for Italy. At the same time, through his restriction of incident, he shapes the viewer's empathy for his characters by allowing the viewer to participate in the film only

to the extent of being companion to the various characters. The audience is free to intellectually wander away from the story, which it undoubtedly does, only to find its involvement in the character's spiritual development unchanged since its sympathy is not based upon the physical actions of a plot.

Such an intertwining of empathetic involvement of sorts with a contemplative detachment carried over into Rossellini's historical films of the 1960s and 1970s. His deliberately obtrusive use of zoom lense created in the viewer of such films as *Viva l'Italia* and *Agostino di Ippona* a delicate distancing and a constant but subtle awareness that the director's point of view was inescapable. Such managing of the viewers' consciousness of the historical medium turns his personages into identifiable human beings which, though involving our senses and our emotions, can still be scrutinized from a relatively detached vantage point.

This, then, is the seeming contradiction central to Rossellini's entire body of work. As most precisely exemplified in his early, pure neorealistic films, his camera is relentlessly fixed on the physical aspects of the world around us. Yet, as defined by his later works which both retain and yet modify much of this temporal focus, the director is also trying to capture within the same lens an unseen and spiritual landscape. Thus, the one constant within all of his films must inevitably remain his concern for fundamental human values and aspirations, whether they are viewed with the anger and immediacy of a *Roma, città aperta* or the detachment of a *Viaggio in Italia*.

—Stephen L. Hanson

ROSSEN, ROBERT. American. Born Robert Rosen in New York City, 16 March 1908. Attended New York University. Married Sue Siegal, 4 July 1954; children: Carol, Steven, and Ellen. Career: 1920s—while attending NYU, begins staging plays for Washington Square Players, later the Theatre Guild; 1929—directs 1st play, *The Tree*, in New York; 1930-35—acts, works as stage manager, directs and does summer stock in New York; 1935—writes and directs play *The Body Beautiful* in New York, a financial and critical failure; 1936-45—writes stories and collaborates on many screenplays, including *The Roaring Twenties* and *The Strange Love of Martha Ivers*, while under contract to Mervyn LeRoy and Warner Bros.; 1937-45—member of Communist Party in Hollywood; 1946—directs 1st film, *Johnny O'Clock*; 1947—subpoenaed by House Un-American Activities Committee (HUAC), but hearing suspended after arrest of Hollywood 10; 1949—produces 1st film, *The Undercover Man*; 1951-53—blacklisted after refusing to cooperate when called once again to testify before HUAC; 1953—requests special hearing, agrees to name names of other alleged Communists in Hollywood; as a result allowed to work again; 1961—makes brief commercial comeback with *The Hustler*. Died 18 February 1966. Recipient: Best Direction, New York Film Critics, for *The Hustler*, 1961.

Films (as scriptwriter): 1937—*Marked Woman* (co-sc); *They Won't Forget* (co-sc); 1938—*Racket Busters* (co-sc); 1939—*Dust Be My Destiny*; *The Roaring Twenties* (co-sc); 1940—*A Child is Born*; 1941—*Blues in the Night*; *The Sea Wolf*; *Out of the Fog* (co-sc); 1943—*Edge of Darkness*; 1946—*A Walk in the Sun*; *The Strange Love of Martha Ivers*; 1947—*Desert Fury*; (as director and scriptwriter): 1947—*Johnny O'Clock*; *Body and Soul* (d only); 1949—*The Undercover Man* (pr only); *All the King's Men* (+pr); 1951—*The Brave Bulls* (d only, +pr); 1955—

Mambo (co-sc); 1956—*Alexander the Great* (+pr); 1957—*Island in the Sun* (d only); 1959—*They Came to Cordura* (co-sc); 1961—*The Hustler* (co-sc, +pr); 1964—*Lilith* (co-sc, +pr).

Publications:

By ROSSEN:

Articles—"The Face of Independence" in *Films and Filming* (London), August 1962; "An Interview with Robert Rossen" in *Arts in Society* (Madison, Wisconsin), vol.4, 1967; "Lessons Learned in Combat: Interview" by Jean-Louis Noames in *Cahiers du cinéma in English* (New York), January 1967.

On ROSSEN:

Books—*Hearings Before the Committee on Un-American Activites, House of Representatives*, 1953 Volume, Washington, D.C. 1953; *The Films of Robert Rossen* by Alan Casty, New York 1969; articles—"Violence, 1947: 3 Examples" by John Houseman in *Hollywood Quarterly*, fall 1947; "His New Fangled Techniques" in *Time* (New York), 5 December 1949; "Notes on Rossen Films" by Henry Burton in *Films in Review* (New York), June/July 1962; "Notes on Robert Rossen" by Henry Hart in *Films in Review* (New York), June/July 1962; "A Rossen Index" by John Springer in *Films in Review* (New York), June/July 1962; "Minor Disappointments" by Andrew Sarris in *Film Culture* (New York), spring 1963; "Robert Rossen and the Filming of *Lilith*" by Saul Cohen in *Film Comment* (New York), spring 1965; "New American Gothic" by Stephen Farber in *Film Quarterly* (Berkeley), fall 1966; "Reminiscences" by John Bontemps and "Biofilmography" by Patrick Brion in *Cahiers du Cinema in English* (New York), January 1967; "The Films of Robert Rossen" by Alan Casty in *Film Quarterly* (Berkely), winter 1966/67; "The Unique Film" by J.-A. Fieschi and "Lilith and I" by Jean Seberg in *Cahiers du Cinema in English* (New York), January 1967; "Robert Rossen" by Alan Casty in *Cinema* (Beverly Hills), fall 1968; "Reflections of Robert Rossen" by C. Dark in *Cinema* (London), August 1970; "Fascism in the Contemporary Film" by Joan Mellen in *Film Quarterly* (Berkeley), summer 1971; "Robert Rossen" by M. Wald in *Films in Review* (New York), August/September 1972; "Private Madness and Public Lunacy" by Kevin Gough-Yates in *Films and Filming* (London), February 1972.

*   *   *

Robert Rossen died as he was beginning to regain a prominent position in the cinema, his premature death leaving us with a final film which pointed to a new, deepening devotion to the pictorialization of deteriorating psychological states.

As a contract writer for Warner Bros. in the late thirties and early forties, Rossen had worked on many excellent scripts which showed a strong sympathy for individuals destroyed by or battling the system. His first produced screenplay, *Marked Woman*, a little-known and highly underrated Bette Davis vehicle, deserves serious attention for its study of prostitution racketeering and the use of women to overthrow that corruption. His fifth film, *The Roaring Twenties*, is a thoughtful study of the obsessive drive for power and money amidst the harshness of the

post-World War I period and the beginnings of the Great Depression. While his early scripts occasionally displayed an idealism which bordered on naiveté, this fortunately never seriously dissipated his intention to depict economic and social injustice.

According to Alan Casty in his book *The Films of Robert Rossen*, Rossen was invited to direct his screenplay for *Johnny O'Clock*, a tale of murder among gamblers, at the insistence of the film's star, Dick Powell. Rossen followed this poorly-received directorial debut with two of his most critically and financially successful films: *Body and Soul* and *All the King's Men*, two male-centered studies of corruption and the drive for success, the first in the boxing ring, the second, the political arena. The success of *Body and Soul* (from a screenplay by Abraham Polonsky) allowed Rossen the financial stability to set up his own company with a financing and releasing contract through Columbia Pictures. As a result, he wrote, directed, and produced *All the King's Men*.

The unfortunate result of these back-to-back successes seems to have been a problem of directorial ego: production accounts of the later films detail Rossen's inability to openly accept collaboration. This paranoia was exacerbated by his deepening involvement with the HUAC proceedings. Despite a 1953 reprieve after naming names, he was unable to revive his Hollywood career. He seemed a particularly unlikely candidate to direct his next three films, the Ponti-DeLaurentiis melodrama *Mambo*, the historical epic *Alexander the Great*, and the interracial problem drama, *Island in the Sun*. The last of his fifties films, *They Came to Cordura*, is an interesting film which should have succeeded. Its failure so obsessed Rossen he spent many years unsuccessfully trying to re-edit it for re-release.

His final films, *The Hustler* and *Lilith*, showed a return to form, due in great part to the atmospheric cinematography of Eugene Schufftan. Rossen, firmly entrenched in the theatrical values of content through script and performance, had previously worked with strong cinematographers (especially James Wong Howe and Burnett Guffey), but had worked from the conviction that content was the prime area of concern. As he told *Cahiers du cinéma*, "Technique is nothing compared to content." In *The Hustler*, a moody film about winners and losers set in the world of professional pool-playing, the studied script was strongly enhanced by Schufftan's predominantly claustrophobic framings. Schufftan, long a respected European cameraman (best known for his work on Lang's *Metropolis* and Carné's *Quai des brumes*), had been enthusiastically recommended to Rossen by Jack Garfein who had brought Schufftan back to America for his *Something Wild*.

Schufftan's working posture was one of giving the director what he asked for and production notes from the set of *The Hustler* indicate he gave Rossen what he wanted, meanwhile achieving affects one feels were beyond Rossen's vision. There was no denying Schufftan's influence in the film's success (it won him an Oscar), and Rossen wisely invited him to work on his next film.

Lilith, an oblique and elliptical film in which a psychiatric worker ends up seeking help, signalled an advance in Rossen's cinematic sensibility. While several of the purely visual passages bordered on being overly symbolic, one feels that Rossen was beginning to admit the communicative power of the visual.

Less idealistic and with less affirmative endings, these last two films showed a deeper sense of social realism, one which strove to portray the effect of the psychological rather than social environment on his characters. His last project would have allowed him to portray both the social and psychological problems of people living in the vicinity of Cape Canaveral (then Cape Kennedy) and allowed him a further opportunity to break away from his tradition of dialogue-bound character studies.

—Doug Tomlinson

ROUCH, JEAN. French. Born Jean Pierre Rouch in Paris, 31 May 1917. Educated at lycée Henri IV, Paris, degree in literature; Ecole nationale des ponts et chaussées, Paris, degree in civil engineering. Married Jane Margaret Gain, 22 February 1952. Career: 1941—explores Africa's Niger River area as student of ethnology; 1945—buys 16mm film camera; 1946-47—becomes 1st to make descent of Niger River by dugout canoe, also begins making ethnographic films during this exploration; 1947-1960s—continues to make ethnographic films during travels through Africa; 1955—releases feature-length compilation of his earlier films; 1961—teams with Edgar Morin in making of *Chronique d'un été*, one of earliest examples of cinema verité; 1966—becomes Director of Research at Centre Nationale de la Recherche Scientifique; 1972—becomes Secrétaire Général du Comite du Film Ethnographique. Recipient: Cannes Film Festival, Critic's Prize for *Chronique d'un été*, 1961. Address: 4 rue de Grenelle, 75006 Paris, France.

Films (as director): 1946—*Chasse à l'hippopotame*; 1947—*Au pays des mages noirs* (co-d, +sc, ph); 1949—*Initiation à la danse des Possédés*; *Hombori*; *Les Magiciens de Wanzerbé* (co-d, +pr, ph); *La Circoncision* (+pr, ph); 1951—*Bataille sur le grand fleuve* (+ph); *Cimetière dans la falaise*; *Les Hommes qui font la pluie* (+ph); *Les Gens du mil* (+ph); 1955—*Les Fils de l'eau* (compilation of earlier films); *Les Maîtres fous* (+ph, narration); 1957—*Moro Naba* (+ph); 1958—*Moi, un noir* (+sc, ph); 1960—*Hampi*; 1961—*La Pyramide humaine* (+sc, co-ph); *Chronique d'un été* (co-d, +co-sc); 1962—*Urbanisme africain* (+sc); *Le Mil*; *Les Pêcheurs du Niger* (+sc); *Abidjan, port de pêche* (+sc); 1963—*Le Palmier à l'huile*; *Les Cocotiers*; *Monsieur Albert Prophète*; *Rose et Landry*; 1964—"Véronique et Marie-France" episode in *La Fleur de l'âge ou les adolescents (Les Veuves de quinze ans, The Adolescents, That Tender Age)* (+sc); "Gare du nord" episode of *Paris vu par (6 in Paris)* (+sc); *La Punition*; 1965—*La Chasse au lion a l'arc (The Lion Hunters)* (+sc, ph, narration); *Mammy Water*; *La Goumbe des jeunes noceurs* (+sc, ph); 1967—*Jaguar* (+ph); 1970—*Petit à petit* (+co-sc, co-ph); 1976—*Chantons sous l'Occupation* (co-ph only); *Babatu* (+ph); 1977—*Cocorico Monsieur Poulet* (+co-sc).

Publications:

By ROUCH:

Script—"*Moi, un noir*", special issue by M. Scheinfeigel of *Avant-Scène du cinéma* (Paris), 1 April 1981; articles—interview in *Movie* (London), April 1963; "Jean Rouch in Conversation" by James Blue in *Film Comment* (New York), fall/winter 1967; "Cocorico! Monsieur Poulet", interview by Guy Hennebelle in *Ecran* (Paris), March 1977; "The Politics of Visual Anthropology", interview by D. Georgakas and others in *Cineaste* (New York), summer 1978; "Jean Rouch erzählt" in *Filmkritik* (Munich), January 1978; "Ciné-transe: The Vision of Jean Rouch", interview by D. Yakir in *Film Quarterly* (Berkeley), spring 1978; "Blanco y negro en colores", interview by A.M. Amado in *Imagenes* (Mexico), December 1979; "Note sur les

problemes techniques souleves par l'experience Super 8" in *Cahiers du cinéma* (Paris), January 1979; "Jean Rouch: A Pastoral Perspective", interview by H. Naficy in *Quarterly Review of Film Studies* (Pleasantville, N.Y.), no.3, 1979; interview by J.-P. Oudart and Y. Lardeau in *Framework* (Norwich, England), autumn 1979; "5 Faces of Vertov" and "On Rossellini" in *Framework* (Norwich, England), autumn 1979; interview by B. Hervo in *Filmfaust* (Frankfurt), June 1980; "Superserious-8: Chronicle of a Master", interview by T. Treadway in *Filmmakers Monthly* (Ward Hill, Mass.), June 1981.

On ROUCH:

Books—*French Cinema Since 1946: Vol. 2—The Personal Style* by Roy Armes, New York 1966; *Cinema Verite* by M. Ali Issari, East Lansing, Michigan 1971; articles—"Recording Africa" by Alain Tanner in *Sight and Sound* (London), summer 1956; "Notes on a New Generation" by Georges Sadoul in *Sight and Sound* (London), summer/autumn 1959; "Films by Jean Rouch" by Roger Sandell in *Film Quarterly* (Berkeley), winter 1961/62; "The Face of '63—France" by Peter Cowie in *Films and Filming* (London), May 1963; "Cinéma Vérité in France" by Peter Graham in *Film Quarterly* (Berkeley), summer 1964; "The Films of Jean Rouch" by James Blue in *Film Comment* (New York), fall/winter 1967; "On Jean Rouch" by José Soltero in *Medium* (Frankfurt), winter 1967/68; "Prospects of the Ethnographic Film" by David MacDougall in *Film Quarterly* (Berkeley), winter 1969/70; "Jean Rouch" in *Documentary Explorations* edited by G. Roy Levin, Garden City, New York 1971; "Je suis mon premier spectateur", interview by L. Marcorelles in *Avant-Scène du cinéma* (Paris), March 1972; "Biofilmographie: Jean Rouch" in *Avant-Scène du cinéma* (Paris), March 1972; "Moi, un noir", special issue of *Avant-Scène du cinéma* (Paris), 1 April 1981.

ROY, BIMAL. Indian. Born in Dacca, 12 July 1909. Married to Manobina Bimal Roy; 3 daughters, one son. Career: 1932—joins New Theatres studio as assistant cameraman under Nitin Bose; 1935-42—cameraman for director P.C. Barua; 1944—directs 1st feature *Udayer Pathey*; after WW II—moves to Bombay; 1952—forms Bimal Roy Productions; 1960-62—president of the Indian Motion Picture Producers' Association. Died in 1966.

Films (as cameraman): 1934—*Daku Mansoor*; 1935—*Devdas*; *Nalla Thangal*; 1936—*Manzil*; *Grihadaha*; *Maya*; 1937—*Mukti*; 1938—*Abhagin*; 1939—*Badi Didi*; *Haar Jeet*; 1942—*Meenakshi*; (as director): 1943—*Bengal Famine* (+ph—short); 1944—*Udayer Pathey* (+sc, ph); 1945—*Hamrahi* (+sc, ph); 1948—*Anjangarh* (+sc); 1949—*Mantra-Mughdha*; 1950—*Pahela Admi* (+sc); 1952—*Maa*; 1953—*Parineeta*; *Do Bigha Zamin (2 Acres of Land, Calcutta Cruel City)* (+pr); 1954—*Baap Beti*; *Biraj Bahu*; *Naukri* (+pr); (as producer and director): 1955—*Devdas*; *Amanat* (Arbind Sen) (pr only); 1956—*Parivar* (Asit Sen) (pr only); 1957—*Aparadhi Kaun* (pr only); 1958—*Yahudi* (d only); *Madhumati*; 1959—*Sujata*; 1960—*Parakh*; *Usne Kaha Tha* (pr only); 1961—*Kabuliwala* (Hemen Gupta) (pr only); *Immortal Stupa* (pr only—documentary); 1962—*Prem Patra*; 1963—*Bandini*; 1964—*Benazir* (pr only); *Life and Message of Swami Vivekananda* (pr only—documentary); 1967—*Gautama the Buddha* (pr only—documentary); 1968—*Do Dooni Char* (pr only).

Publications:

On ROY:

Books—*Indian Film* by Erik Barnouw and S. Krishnaswamy, New York 1980; *The New Generation: 1960-1980* edited by Uma da Cuncha, New Delhi 1981; articles—"The Indian Film" by Marie Seton in *Film* (London), March 1955; "New Indian Directors" by S.K. Ray in *Film Quarterly* (Berkeley), fall 1960; "Discovering India" by Kolita Sarha in *Films and Filming* (London), December 1960; "The Bimal Roy Only I Knew" by Manobina Roy in *The Illustrated Weekly of India*, 3 August 1980.

*   *   *

Among Indian filmgoers Bimal Roy is regarded as a filmmaker of extraordinary integrity, as someone whose life and work are of a piece—a landowner's son who relinquished claims to the family property, a producer who provided unheard-of medical and pension benefits to his employees, and a filmmaker who addressed steadily the difficult social issues of casteism and the landless poor.

Bimal Roy started out as cameraman for New Theaters in Calcutta and worked on the famous Bengali film *Devdas* (1935), but the Second World War and the consequent decline of the Bengali film industry led him, like many other Bengali filmmakers, to the chief production center of Bombay. Here, Roy earned a national reputation for the realism of his film *Do Bigha Zamin*. The film tells the story of a poor peasant who tries to hold on to his two acres of farming land against the machinations of his landlord. The peasant fails to keep the land in spite of a heart-rending effort to make extra money as a rickshaw puller in Calcutta. Towards the end, the film piles misfortune on misfortune, but the early part of the film is modest and sober: the actor Balraj Sahni is quietly dignified as the peasant and the small domestic gestures between him and his wife are rendered naturally. Against the convention of most Hindi melodramas, *Do Bigha Zamin* ends on a note of despair, a note appropriate to the condition of marginal farmers in a newly-independent India.

Do Bigha Zamin was followed by the popular *Madhumati* and *Yahudi*. *Madhumati* dealt with the odd intimations of familiarity with strange places which Hindus attribute to acquaintance in a prior incarnation. *Yahudi* dealt with prejudice against Jews within the Roman Empire, a transposition of India's caste-related problems to the context of Rome. Both films revealed Roy's special skills as cameraman-director. Although Roy preferred to keep his camera static, he calculated the orbit of view very precisely and blocked movements as several elevations to lighten the sense of a fixed perspective.

Roy's next film *Sujata* harnessed all his energies as a filmmaker of conscience to a single end—that of exposing the evils of the caste system. *Sujata* tells the story of an outcaste girl who is raised "almost like a daughter" in a highcaste family. While the orphaned girl is young, she can be included in her new family without too much discrimination between her and the real daughter, but when the the real daughter becomes marriageable, there is pressure on the family to get the untouchable girl out of the way. Bimal Roy's camera views the family tensions with salutary detachment. The camera maintains a middle distance as the outcaste girl runs to her "father" to ask why she cannot sleep in a pretty bed like her sister; the camera maintains the same distance as the now older young woman walks near the windows of her room reflecting on arbitrary social distinctions. Where other Indian directors would cut from one dramatic scene to the next, Roy edits to include the undramatic moments which add substance to the drama. In a key scene by the river, Roy holds on

Sujata leaning against a wall, thinking (presumably) about the man she dare not hope to marry. When the man she is thinking of appears, her few words to him derive force from the pondering Roy has included in the sequence. Things turn out well at the end of *Sujata*, but not in the way of romances. No high birth or secret treasure is discovered to make the outcaste woman grander than she is. The social resistance to according her full status is strong; only an equally strong habit of self-respect in the woman and a strong act of *choosing* her by the young man allow their love to flower.

There are no art theaters in India. The older movies for which there is demand play in small commercial theaters in the morning. It is a clue to the enduring quality of Roy's work that *Do Bigha Zamin* and *Sujata* feature in these morning shows for *afficianados* of the cinema.

—Satti Khanna

RUGGLES, WESLEY. American. Born in Los Angeles, 11 June 1889. Married Arline Judge, 1931 (divorced 1937). Career: before 1914—actor with stock companies; 1914—begins acting in Keystone comedies; 1915-16—appears in Chaplin comedies including *The Bank*, *Shanghaied*, *Police*, and *Carmen*; 1917—directing debut. Died 8 January 1972.

Films (as director): 1917—*For France*; 1918—*The Blind Adventure*; 1919—*The Winchester Woman*; 1920—*Picadilly Jim*; *Sooner or Later*; *The Desperate Hero*; *The Leopard Woman*; *Love*; 1921—*The Greater Claim*; *Uncharted Seas*; *Over the Wire*; 1922—*Wild Honey*; *If I Were Queen*; 1923—*Slippery Magee*; *Mr. Billings Spends His Dime*; *The Remittance Woman*; *The Heart Raider*; 1924—*The Age of Innocence*; 1925—*The Plastic Age*; *Broadway Lady*; 1926—*The Kick-Off*; *A Man of Quality*; 1927—*Beware of Widows*; *Silk Stockings*; 1928—*Fourflusher*; *Finders Keepers*; 1929—*Street Girl*; *Scandal*; *Girl Overboard*; *Condemned*; *The Haunted Lady*; 1930—*Honey*; *The Sea Bat*; 1931—*Cimarron*; *Are These Our Children?*; 1932—*Roar of the Dragon*; *No Man of Her Own*; 1933—*Monkey's Paw*; *College Humor*; *I'm No Angel*; 1934—*Bolero*; *Shoot the Works*; 1935—*The Gilded Lily*; *Accent on Youth*; *The Bride Comes Home* (+pr); 1936—*Valiant Is the Word for Carrie* (+pr); 1937—*True Confession*; *I Met Him in Paris* (+pr); 1938—*Sing, You Sinners* (+pr); 1939—*Invitation to Happiness* (+pr); 1940—*Too Many Husbands* (+pr); *I Take This Woman* (co-d); *Arizona* (+pr); 1941—*You Belong to Me* (+pr); 1942—*Somewhere I'll Find You*; 1943—*Slightly Dangerous*; 1944—*See Here, Private Hargrove*; 1946—*London Town* (released in U.S. as *My Heart Goes Crazy*, 1953).

Publications:

By RUGGLES:

Articles—interview by B. Brown in *Photoplay* (New York), April 1934; "Prop Laughs" in *Lion's Roar* (Los Angeles), April 1943.

On RUGGLES:

Articles—sketch in *Motion Picture Classic* (Brooklyn), July

1929; article in *Movies and People*, no.2, 1940; obituary in *The New York Times*, 29 December 1971; obituary in *Classic Film Collector* (Indiana, Penn.), spring 1972.

*   *   *

Wesley Ruggles, brother of actor Charles Ruggles, was originally one of Mack Sennett's Keystone Kops. From this he branched out into directing silent films, the majority of which were comedies. His directorial career in the sound era is best defined by a series of eleven films authored by comedy writer Claude Binyon. The Binyon/Ruggles collaborations fit into the category of "screwball comedy," a type of film humor popular during the Depression years. The Binyon/Ruggles films were similar to others in the screwball tradition, with their host of zany characters involved in madcap adventures which frequently presented hilarious slapstick assaults on material property. Where the Binyon/Ruggles films varied from the majority of other screwball comedies was in their tendency to emphasize the female leading role over the male, and in presenting true romance in equal portion to the comedy. They are among the most romantic of the screwball comedies, and have a tendency to become "woman's films." In these films, Ruggles developed the comedy talents of several women stars who were famous for their beauty, glamour, and sex appeal. Carole Lombard, Claudette Colbert (who starred in three of these collaborations), and Lana Turner were three actresses he directed more than once, all of whom benefited from his seeing beyond their physical beauty a sense of fun, liveliness, and humor.

The Binyon/Ruggles films are in no way remarkable for style, but they do contain comedy sequences that are well written and well directed. Two of the best-remembered of these films are *I Met Him in Paris* (with Colbert playing a fashion designer pursued by three ardent suitors) and *True Confession* (with Lombard as a lying wife). These films illustrate the strengths and weaknesses of the collaboration. *I Met Him in Paris*, in its best scenes, provides an unpretentious, frequently truly funny situation well-played by the stars. It illustrates the collaboration at its best, and was selected by *The New York Times* as one of the ten best films of the year. However, like all eleven of the films, it is uneven in pacing. In any sequence involving physical comedy, as when the leads are asked to participate in a series of winter sports at which they have no ability, Ruggle's apprenticeship with Mack Sennett is put to good use. *True Confession*, which enjoys a reputation among people who apparently have not seen it since its initial release, is a film totally without charm and almost equally without any real humor. The one exception is the outrageous performance by John Barrymore. Ruggles was skilled at directing character portraits, and he allowed Barrymore to steal the movie with an almost cartoon-like performance of a down-and-outer who smugly comments on the heroine's chances of beating her murder rap: "She'll fry."

The difference between the good Ruggles film and the bad frequently is the margin of action, or physical comedy, presented. *I Met Him in Paris* holds up because of its slapstick sequences, and *True Confession* feels the lack of action. Outside the realm of comedy, Ruggles made a success of films with breathtaking action moments, as in *Cimarron* (1931 version) with its excellent Oklahoma land-rush sequence. *Cimarron* won the Oscar for best picture of the year, and Ruggles attempted to recreate his success with a similar picture in 1941, the sepia-toned *Arizona*. Both films contain rousing chases, feisty performances, and plenty of frontier humor. Both films represent examples of Ruggle's basic skill as a storyteller in the silent film tradition, as

well as his feeling for energetic American character and situation.

In his day, Ruggles was considered a top director, and his comedies were great favorites with reviewers. Today, his reputation cannot be said to have been devalued, because it does not really exist. His is a forgotten name. When his films are remembered at all, it is for the stars who are in them. In retrospect, he may be seen as a director whose work grew increasingly ponderous as his career developed. The simple, breezy style of his early comedies slowed down, and he seemed to lose his touch. He gave scripts he directed no particular life, and it is the script or the stars that now determines the success the film may have for a viewer. Although he made contributions to the careers of Irene Dunne, Jean Arthur, Lombard, Colbert, and Turner, today his poor reputation stands as an example of how critical tastes change over the decades.

—Jeanine Basinger

RUIZ, RAÚL. Chilean. Born in Puerto Montt, Chile, 25 July 1941. Educated in law and theology; spent year at Documentary Film School of Santa Fé, Argentina. Married to filmmaker Valeria Sarmiento, who edits most of Ruiz's films. Career: 1956-60—prolific writer of stage plays; 1960—shoots 1st film *La maleta* (unfinished) at Grupo Cine Experimental, University of Chile; 1967—works on 1st feature-length film, *El tango del viudo* (unfinished); 1971-72—cinema advisor for Socialist Party of Chile during Popular Unity government of Salvador Allende; 1973—forced into exile following coup, moves to Germany and completes *La expropriación*; 1974—moves to Paris; 1977—becomes regular filmmaker with France's National Audiovisual Institute which produces *La Vocation suspendue*; 1980—begins shooting 20-episode serial *Le Borgne*; films *The Territory* in Portugal. Recipient: Grand Prix at Locarno for *Tres Tristes Tigres*, 1969; César Award (France) for *Colloque de chiens*, 1978. Lives in Paris.

Films (as director and scriptwriter): 1960—*La maleta* [The Suitcase]* (unfinished); 1967—*El tango del viudo* [Widower's Tango] (unfinished); 1968—*Tres Tristes Tigres (3 Sad Tigers*; 1971—*La colonia penal (The Penal Colony)*; *Ahora te vamos a llamar hermano (Now We Will Call You Brother)**; *Nadie dijo nada (Nobody Said Nothing)*; 1972-73—*La expropriación (The Expropriation)*; *Los minuteros (The Minute Hands, The Street Photographer)**; *Nueva canción Chilena (New Chilean Song)**; *Realismo socialista (Socialist Realism)*; *Palomilla brava (Bad Girl)**; *Palomita blanca* [Little White Dove] (unfinished due to coup); *Abastecimiento (Supply)**; 1974—*Diálogo de exilados (Dialogue of Exiles)*; 1975—*El cuerto repartido y el mundo al revés (The Scattered Body and the World Upside Down, Utopia)*; 1976—*Sotelo**; 1977—*Colloque de chiens (Dog's Dialogue)**; *La Vocation suspendue (The Suspended Vocation)*; 1978—*L'Hypothèse du tableau vole (The Hypothesis of a Stolen Painting)*; *Les Divisions de la nature (The Divisions of Nature)**; 1979—*De Grands Evènements et des gens ordinaires (Of Great Events and Ordinary People)*; *Petit Manuel d'histoire de France (Short History of France)*; *Images du débat (Images of Debate)*; *Jeux (Games)*; 1980—*Le Jeu de l'oie (Snakes and Ladders)**; *La Ville nouvelle (The New Town)**; *L'Or gris (Grey Gold)*; *Teletests**; *Pages d'un catalogue (Pages from a Catalogue)**; *Fahlstrom**; 1981—4 episodes of *Le Borgne (The 1-Eyed Man)*; *The Territory (Le Territoire)* (co-sc); *Le Toît de la baleine (The Whale's Roof)*; 1982—*Classification de plantes (Classification*

of Plants)*; Les Ombres chinoises (Chinese Shadows)*; Querelle de (The War of the Gardens)*; Les Trois Couronnes du matelot (Les Trois Couronnes danois de matelots, The Sailor's 3 Crowns); Techo de la ballena (The Roof of the Whale).
Note: * denotes short features.

Publications:

By RUIZ:

Articles—interview by Federico de Cárdenas in *Positif* (Paris), January 1971; "Re-encuentro con Raúl Ruiz" by Federico de Cárdenas in *Hablemos de cine* (Lima), January/March 1972; "Prefiero registrar antes que mistificar el proceso chileno", interview in *Primer Plano* (Valparaiso), spring 1972; "Chili: le cinéma de l'unité populaire", interview by H. Ehrmann in *Ecran* (Paris), February 1974; "Cinémas en exil (1): Chili cinema venceremos", interview by A. Pâquet in *Cinéma Québec* (Montreal), April/May 1974; interview by Z.M. Pick in *Positif* (Paris), December 1974; "Présence du exil: Dialogues d'exilés", interview by G. Gervais in *Jeune Cinéma* (Paris), May/June 1975; "Notes sur *La Vocation suspendue*" in *Positif* (Paris), December/January 1977/78; "D'une Institution à l'autre", interview by P. Bonitzer and Serge Daney in *Cahiers du cinéma* (Paris), April 1978; "Les Relations d'objets au cinéma" in *Cahiers du cinéma* (Paris), April 1978; interview by T. Abadi and P. Coisman in *Image et son* (Paris), December 1978; interview by F. Cuel and P. Carcassonne in *Cinématographe* (Paris), June 1979; interview by D. Ranvaud in *Framework* (Norwich, England), spring 1979; interview by P. Carcassonne in *Cinématographe* (Paris), June 1979; interview by Francesco Llinás in *Contracampo* (Madrid), December 1979; "Image, Memory, Death: Imaginary Dialogues" and "Between Institutions", interview by I. Christie and M. Coad, in *Afterimage* (Rochester, New York), no.10, 1981.

On RUIZ:

Articles—"Le Cinéma chilien sous le signe de l'Unité Populaire (1970-1973)" by Zuzana Pick in *Positif* (Paris), January 1974; "Un Débat nécessaire (sur Dialogue d'exilés)" by Zuzana Pick in *Positif* (Paris), October 1975; "Turning Points: Ruiz & Truffaut" by Richard Roud in *Sight and Sound* (London), summer 1978; "Festival de Paris: Cinémas français et allemand" by Jacques Grant in *Cinéma* (Paris), December 1978; "Les Ruelles du conditionnel" by Jean-Paul Fargier, and articles by Yann Lardeau and Paul Bonitzer on *The Hypothesis of a Stolen Painting* in *Cahiers du cinéma* (Paris), July/August 1978; "L'Hypothese du tableau vole" by P. Carcassonne in *Cinématographe* (Paris), June 1979; "L'Hypothèse du tableau volé: l'illusion de la répresentation" by Gérard Courant in *Cinéma* (Paris), May 1979; "Presentación de...Raúl Ruiz" by M. de Orellana and A.R. Sanchez in *Imagenes* (Mexico), April 1980; "The Rubicon and the Rubik Cube" by G. Adair in *Sight and Sound* (London), winter 1982; "Exile and Cunning: Raul Ruiz", special section in *Afterimage* (Rochester, New York), no.10, 1981; "Rotterdam 82" by Charles Tesson in *Cahiers du cinéma* (Paris), March 1982; "Los cuadros vivientes" by Agustin Mahieu in *Cine Libre* (Buenos Aires), October 1982; "Raul Ruiz", special issue of *Cahiers du cinéma* (Paris), March 1983.

A prodigious storyteller, Raul Ruiz is also a prolific manufacturer of moving images. This Chilean filmmaker, now living in exile in Paris, has molded his films by a deeply personal concern with representation and discourse. His innovative and experimental work thus defies any attempt of classification.

The cinema of Ruiz is a cinema of ideas. He has unmasked ideological stereotypes (*Three Sad Tigers*, *Nobody Said Nothing*, and *Dialogue of Exiles*), has exposed the contradictions of despotic institutions (*The Suspended Vocation*), and unveiled his own tortured world (*The One-Eyed Man*) torn between his cultural origins and the false cosmopolitanism of forced exile (*The Whale's Roof*). His mise-en-scène is preoccupied with representation (*The Hypothesis of a Stolen Painting* and *The Divisions of Nature*) and the fragmentation of reality (*The Sailor's Three Crowns*). His narrative is imbued with an intense research into performance and the ambiguity of the spoken language. His storylines never appear to enjoy a privileged position within the overall narrative of his films (*The Expropriation*). The voice-over narration (*The War of the Gardens*), the commentary (*The Divisions of Nature*) or even the dialogue (*The Penal Colony*), by detaching themselves from the image track, acquire an independent life or serve to lure the spectator into the wilfull contradictions that Ruiz wants to explore. The spoken language, saturated with Chilean slang, often makes his films incomprehensible for non-Chilean spectators. In France Ruiz has found an audience for whom simulations of Cartesian logic are the playful components of a fictional labyrinth.

Few filmmakers have taken better advantage of commissioned work. His video essays and documentary films for television and the Centre Beaubourg are original experiments with technology and narrative which inform the strategies of his feature work. A didactic comparison of French and English-style gardens is displaced in favour of a playful suspense story (*The War of the Gardens*). A commissioned film on Beaubourg's cartography exhibition becomes a diabolic snakes-and-ladders game (*Snakes and Ladders*). Ruiz has a passionate affair with technology. Working with innovative directors of photography—Diego Bonancina in Chile, Sacha Vierny and Henri Alekan in France—he has brought back the magic of French poetic realism to explore a world of manipulation, impotence, and violence. He favors lighting, filters, and mirrors to deform filmic reality into a kaleidoscopic maze that traps his performers (*Snakes and Ladders*) and turns familiarity into fantastic exoticism (*The Territory*). Ruiz's originality stems from personal paradox. He is an exiled filmmaker in search of a territory, mastering a new language while stubbornly upholding his roots and confined in a culture he recognizes as having colonized his own.

Ruiz's contribution to Chilean cinema has been openly acknowledged since *Three Sad Tigers* in 1969. His innovative approach to film, his independence and his critical stance on political reductionism have often set him apart from the mainstream. A name rarely mentioned in discussions on the new Latin American cinema, despite avowed admiration, recent retrospectives of his work in Madrid, Edinburgh, London, Rotterdam, and Paris have finally brought Ruiz public recognition. After years of relative obscurity, critical acclaim has earned him a leading position within the French avant-garde. Chilean cinema in exile has found in Ruiz a respected and vital representative. A total filmmaker, for whom theater, music, literature, and visual arts are familiar territory, Ruiz successfully combines intellectual inquiry with Latin American hedonism.

—Zuzana Mirjam Pick

*   *   *

RUSSELL, KEN. English. Born Henry Kenneth Alfred Russell in Southampton, England, 3 July 1927. Educated Pangbourne Nautical College, Pangbourne, England, 1941-44. Married Shirley Ann Kingdon, 1957; children: James, Xavier, and Alexander. Career: 1945—serves in merchant navy; 1946-49—serves in Royal Air Force; 1950—dances with Ny Norsk ballet; 1951—joins Garrick Players as actor; 1957-58—makes several short films, leading to freelance work for BBC; 1958—is employed by BBC to work in documentaries; 1959-62—makes 20 short documentaries for BBC series *Monitor*; 1963—directs 1st feature film *French Dressing*; 1966—directs *Isadora Duncan: The Biggest Dancer in the World*, his 1st film for BBC television series *Omnibus*; 1969—directs *Women in Love* which gains worldwide attention.

Films (as director of amateur shorts): 1957—*Amelia and the Angel*; 1958—*Peep Show*; *Lourdes*; (as feature director): 1963—*French Dressing*; 1967—*Billion Dollar Brain*; 1969—*Women in Love*; 1970—*The Music Lovers* (+pr); 1971—*The Devils* (+sc, co-pr); *The Boy Friend* (+pr, sc); 1972—*Savage Messiah* (+pr); 1974—*Mahler* (+sc); *Tommy* (+co-pr, sc); 1975—*Lisztomania* (+sc); 1977—*Valentino* (+co-sc); 1979—*Altered States*.

(television films): 1959—*Poet's London*; *Gordon Jacob*; *Guitar Craze*; *Variations on a Mechanical Theme*; untitled film on Robert McBryde and Robert Colquhoun; *Portrait of a Goon*; 1960—*Marie Rambert Remembers*; *Architecture of Entertainment*; *Cranks at Work*; *The Miners' Picnic*; *Shelagh Delaney's Salford*; *A House in Bayswater*; *The Light Fantastic*; 1961—*Old Battersea House*; *Portrait of a Soviet Composer*; *London Moods*; *Antonio Gaudi*; 1962—*Pop Goes the Easel*; *Preservation Man*; *Mr. Chesher's Traction Engines*; *Lotte Lenya Sings Kurt Weill* (co-d); *Elgar*; 1963—*Watch the Birdie*; 1964—*Lonely Shore*; *Bartok*; *The Dotty World of James Lloyd*; *Diary of a Nobody*; 1965—*The Debussy Film*; *Always on Sunday*; 1966—*Don't Shoot the Composer*; *Isadora Duncan, The Biggest Dancer in the World*; 1967—*Dante's Inferno*; 1968—*Song of Summer*; 1970—*The Dance of the 7 Veils*; 1978—*Clouds of Glory, Parts I and II*.

Publications:

By RUSSELL:

Book—*An Appalling Talent: Ken Russell*, with John Baxter, London 1973; articles—"The Films I Do Best Are About People I Believe In" in *Friends* (London), 29 May 1970; "Shock Treatment: Interview" by Gordon Gow in *Films and Filming* (London), July 1970; "An Interview with Ken Russell" by Gene D. Phillips in *Film Comment* (New York), fall 1970; "Savage Saviour: Interview" by Peter Buckley in *Films and Filming* (London), October 1972; "I'm Surprised My Films Shock People" interview by Guy Flatley in *The New York Times*, 15 October 1972; "Ken Russell in the Port of New York" by Glenn O'Brien in *Interview* (New York), November 1972; "Ken Russell Writes on Raising Kane" in *Films and Filming* (London), May 1972; "Relax, It's Only a Ken Russell Movie: Interview" by Peter Mezan in *Esquire* (New York), May 1973; "Ideas for Films" in *Film* (London), January-February 1973; "Andre Previn Meets Ken Russell" in *Listener* (London), 19 September 1974; "Personal Choice 1974" in *Listener* (London), 19 and 26 December 1974; "Shirley and Ken Russell on Fashion, Film and Mountains" by Ruth Batchelor in the *Los Angeles Free Press*, 19 September 1975; "Ken Russell Faces the Music" by Janet Maslin

and Patrick McGilligan in *Take One* (Montreal), 2 December 1975; "The Big Scene Grabber Hits Again in the Movie *Tommy*: Interview by Gene Siskel in *Chicago Tribune*, 25 March 1975; "Ken Russell" by B. Wiener and C. Hemphill in *Interview* (New York), March 1975; "Fact, Fantasy, and the Films of Ken Russell" by Gene Phillips in *Journal of Popular Film* (Bowling Green, Ohio), v.5, no.3-4, 1976; "With Ken Russell on the Set of *Valentino*" by Herb Lightman in *American Cinematographer* (Los Angeles), November 1977.

On RUSSELL:

Books—*Ken Russell: A Director in Search of a Hero* by Colin Wilson, London 1974; *Ken Russell* by Thomas Atkins, New York 1976; *Ken Russell: The Adaptor as Creator* by Joseph Gomez, London 1976; *Ken Russell: A Guide to Reference Sources* by Diane Rosenfeldt, Boston 1978; *Ken Russell* by Gene D. Phillips, Boston 1979; articles—"*Women in Love*" by Ian Leslie Christie in *Sight and Sound* (London), winter 1969/70; "The Lonely Heart" in *Films and Filming* (London), July 1970; "Director in a Caftan" in *Time* (New York), 13 September 1971; "Ken Russell, a Director Who Respects Artists" by Saul Kahan in *Los Angeles Times Calendar*, 28 March 1971; "Russell and Trumbo: Shock for Shock's Sake?" by Deanna Kaufman in *Chevron* (Waterloo, Canada), 10 December 1971; "Russell Chooses Blood to Be Redder than Brown" by Leo Lerman in *Mademoiselle* (New York), November 1971; "Russell: Spoofing the Spoof" by Christopher Porterfield in *Time* (New York), 20 December 1971; "*The Music Lovers*" by Susan Rice in *Take One* (Montreal), March 1971; "Trust Me—Go See *The Music Lovers*" by Susan Rice in *Media and Methods* (Philadelphia), March 1971; "Great Lives on TV" by Richard Schickel in *Harper's* (New York), January 1971; "The World of Ken Russell" by Michael Dempsey in *Film Quarterly* (Berkeley), spring 1972; "3 Paintings of Sex: The Films of Ken Russell" by Jack Fisher in *Films Journal* (New York), September 1972; "Riflessioni sul musical (a proposito di un film 'inglese' di Ken Russell)" by Franco La Pollo in *Filmcritica* (Rome), November/December 1972; "On the Set with Ken Russell" by Tony Rose in *Movie Maker* (England), September 1972; "Other People's Pictures" by Tony Rose in *Movie Maker* (England), April 1972; "*The Devils*" by Dale Winogura in *Cinefantastique* (Oak Park, Illinois), spring 1972; "Ken Russell" in *The Film Business: A History of British Cinema, 1896-1972* by Ernest Betts, New York 1973; "Conversations with Ken Russell" by Terry Curtis Fox in *Oui* (Chicago), June 1973; "Ken Russell's Biopics: Grander and Gaudier" by Robert Kolker in *Film Comment* (New York), May/June 1973; "Le Messie sauvage" by Max Tessier in *Ecran* (Paris), February 1973; "Ken Russell" in *The Great British Picture Show* by George Perry, New York 1974; "Fantasists: Boorman, Russell" in *Hollywood UK* by Alexander Walker, New York 1974; "What the Blazes is Ken Russell Up to Now?" by William Hall in *The New York Times*, 23 June 1974; "Is Ken Russell Into Black Magic?" by Taurus in *Other Scenes* (Cannes), 1974; "Une Production télévisée passionnante" by G. Cogen in *Cinéma* (Paris), January 1974; "*Tommy*" by Robin Bean in *Films and Filming* (London), May 1975; "Daltrey's Good Vibrations" by David Castell in *Films Illustrated* (London), April 1975; "Ken Russell's Film Studies of Composers—Brilliance Gone Berzerk" by Peter Davis in *The New York Times*, 19 October 1975; "Russellmania" by Stephen Farber in *Film Comment* (New York), November/December 1975; "*Mahler* and the Methods of Ken Russell's Films on Composers" by Joseph Gomez in *Velvet Light Trap* (Madison, Wisconsin), winter 1975; "Analyzing Ken Russell" by Gene Phillips, Jeff Laffel, and Bernard Goldstein in *The New York Times*, 2

November 1975; "L'Avant Love" by R. Lefèvre in *Image et son* (Paris), June/July 1975; "Genius, Genia, Genium, Ho Hum" by Penelope Gilliatt in the *New Yorker*, 26 April 1976; "Interview: Oliver Reed" by Linda Merinoff in *Penthouse* (New York), January 1976; "Shirley Russell: Filmmaking: A Family Affair" by M. McAndrew in *Cinema* (Beverly Hills), no.35, 1976; "One-Take Jackson" by Gordon Gow in *Films and Filming* (London), January 1977; "Ken Russell, Again" by M. Dempsey in *Film Quarterly* (Berkeley), winter 1977/78; "Them and Us" by Gordon Gow in *Films and Filming* (London), October 1977; "Ken Russell's 'Rabelais'" by M. Yacowar in *Literature/Film Quarterly* (Salisbury, Maryland), v.8, no.1, 1980; "Ken Russell, au coeur des problèmes de son temps" by G. Dagneau in *Cinéma* (Paris), October 1981; "The Personal View of Ken Russell" by Gene D. Phillips, in *America* (New York), 16 May 1981; films—*Film Night—Confrontation* produced by BBC-TV, telecast 28 February 1971; "Ken Russell Interviewed by Colin Wilson" on *Camera 3*, produced by CBS-TV, telecast 23 and 30 September 1973.

*   *   *

British director Ken Russell was 42 when his film of D.H. Lawrence's *Women in Love* placed him in the ranks of movie directors of international stature. For more than a decade before that, however, British television viewers had been treated to a succession of his skilled TV biographies of great artists like Frederick Delius (*Songs of Summer*) and Isadora Duncan. Russell has always gravitated toward the past in choosing subjects for filming because, as he says, "topics of the moment pass and change. Besides, we can be more dispassionate and therefore more truthful in dealing with the past. And to see the past from the vantage point of the present is to be able to judge the effect of the past on the present."

His first TV documentaries, like that on Edward Elgar, correspond to what he calls "the accepted textbook idea of what a documentaty should be; you were supposed to extol the great artists and their work. Later I turned to showing how great artists transcended their personal problems and weakness in creating great art." But this more realistic approach, exemplified in his telefilm about Richard Strauss (*Dance of the Seven Veils*) and his feature film, *The Music Lovers*, about Tchaikovsky, upset some of the members of the audience for both his TV and theatrical films.

As he advanced from the small screen to the large in continuing to turn out what has come to be called his biopics, he has almost singlehandedly revolutionized the whole concept of the conventional film biography—to point where the genre will never be quite the same again. One need only recall the heavily romanticized Hollywood screen biographies on subjects like Cole Porter to grasp how Russell's biopics have come to grips with the problems of an artist's life in relation to his work, in a way that makes for much more challenging and entertaining films than the sugar-coated Hollywood screen biographies.

In addition to experimenting with the nature of biographical films, Russell has at the same time been seeking by trial and error to discover in all of his films, biopics or not, to what extent a motion picture can be cut loose from the moorings of conventional storytelling; and his mind-bending science fiction thriller *Altered States* is an excellent example of this experimentation. If these experiments in narrative technique account for occasional lapses in narrative logic, as in *Lisztomania*, they also account for the intricate and arresting blend of past and present, fact and fantasy, that characterize his best work.

Although Russell has often been looked upon as a maverick who makes films that are perhaps more subjective and personal than many directors working today, it is important to realize, he is the only British director in history ever to have three films playing first-run engagements in London simultaneously: *The Music Lovers*, *The Devils*, and *The Boy Friend*. This provocative and fascinating director has already assured himself a place in the history of world cinema.

—Gene D. Phillips

———————

RUTTMANN, WALTER. German. Born in Frankfurt am Main, 28 December 1887. Educated at Goethe-Gymnasium, Abitur 1905; architectural studies in Zurich beginning 1907; studied painting in Munich, 1909. Career: 1909—while studying in Munich becomes friend of Paul Klee and Lionel Feininger; WW I—serves on Eastern Front as artillery lieutenant; suffers severe nervous breakdown, sent to sanatorium and mustered out in 1917; 1917—makes 1st abstract images; 1919—begins filmmaking; 1919-23—collaborates on feature film productions, makes advertising films; 1923—moves to Berlin; 1925-26—collaborates with Lotte Reiniger and Carl Koch on *The Adventures of Prince Achmed*; 1929-31—works on *Don Quichotte* project in Paris (directed by G.W. Pabst); collaborates on *Le Fin du monde* with Abel Gance. Died in Berlin, 15 July 1941.

Films: 1921—*Opus I*; 1920-23—*Opus II, III, IV*; 1923—"Der Falkentraum (Dream of Hawks)" sequence in *Die Nibelungen* part 1 (Lang); 1923-26—*Die Abenteuer des Prinzen Achmed (The Adventures of Prince Achmed)* (Reiniger) (collaborated on making abstract, moving backgrounds); 1924—abstract Alps dream sequence for *Lebende Buddhas* (Wegener); 1925-26—*Opus V*; 1926-27—*Berlin, die Sinfonie der Grossstadt (Berlin, Symphony of a Great City)*; 1928—"Tönende Welle" episode for *Das weisse Stadion* (Fanck); 1929—*Melodie der Welt (World Melody)*; *Des Haares und der Liebe Wellen* (short fiction film); 1930—*Weekend (Wochenende)*; 1931—*In der Nacht (In the Night)*; *Feind im Blut* (documentary); 1932-33—*Acciaio*; 1933—*Blut und Boden*; 1934—short film incorporated into *Altgermanische Bauernkultur*; *Metall des Himmels*; prologue to *Triumph des Willens (Triumph of the Will)* (Riefenstahl); 1935—*Kleiner Film einer grossen Stadt—Die Stadt Düsseldorf am Rhein*; *Stadt Stuttgart, 100. Cannstatter Volksfest*; *Stuttgart, die Grossstadt zwischen Wald und Reben*; 1936—*Schiff in Not*; 1937—*Mannesmann*; 1938—*Henkel, ein deutsches Werk in seiner Arbeit*; *Weltstrasse See—Welthafen Hamburg*; *Im Dienste der Menschheit*; 1940—*Deutsche Waffenschmiede (Waffenkammern Deutschland)*; *Deutsche Panzer*; *Aberglaube*; 1941—*Ein Film gegen die Volkskrankheit Krebs—jeder Achte*....

Publications:

On RUTTMANN:

Books—*Experimental Animation* by Robert Russett and Cecile Starr, New York 1976; *Film as Film: Formal Experiment in Film, 1910-1975*, exhibition catalog, London 1979; articles—"Sound Montage: A Propos de Ruttmann" by Paul Falkenberg in *Film Culture* (New York), no.22-23, 1961; "*Berlin*" by Peter

Cowie in *Films and Filming* (London), August 1961; "Walter Ruttmann" in *Travelling* (Lausanne), summer 1979.

*   *   *

Walter Ruttmann is often associated with the films of others: he created the "Dream of the Hawks" sequence in Fritz Lang's *Die Nibelungen*, and directed several sequences in Paul Wegener's *Lebende Buddas*; later on, he assisted in the editing of Leni Riefenstahl's *Olympia*. Easily his most influential work is *Berlin, Symphony of a Great City*, one of the outstanding abstract documentaries of the 1920s.

Berlin is a visual essay on an average working day in the city, from dawn to the dead of night. The quiet, seemingly abandoned metropolis comes alive with a train on its way through the suburbs, workers on their way to factories, the wheels of industry set in motion, everyday occurrences in cafes and on streets. Night approaches, and Berlin becomes lit up like a birthday cake. Boys flirt with girls, chorus girls dance, an orchestra performs Beethoven. Lovers seek out privacy in a hotel. And it will all begin again with the sunrise.

Berlin is indeed a symphony, with Ruttmann stressing the movement of people and machinery in what amounts to a visual tapestry. The key is in the editing: for example, shots of people walking on a street are followed by those of cows' legs. Ruttmann makes no social commentary, as rich and poor, man and animal, exist side by side. His sole interest is the imagery, the creation of visual poetry—even when he contrasts poor children and the food in a restaurant. His use of montage was influenced by the Russian, Dziga Vertov. Yet while Vertov's newsreels depicted the progress of a post-Revolutionary Soviet society, the life in Berlin could just as well be the life in Brussels or Amsterdam or Paris. Ruttmann is concerned with the details of daily reality edited together to form a unified whole, but he never comments or editorializes on the lives of his subjects.

The filmmaker, who appropriately began his career as an abstract painter, preceded *Berlin* with a series of experimental "Opus" films. Siegfried Kracauer describes his *Opus I* as "a dynamic display of spots vaguely recalling X-ray photographs." Additionally, Ruttmann realized that the advent of sound in motion pictures was inevitable, and attempted to attune his images to the soundtracks that he felt would ultimately outweigh the visuals in importance. In *World Melody*, made after *Berlin*, music and sound effects are orchestrated to relate to the images; *In der Nacht* is a union of imagery and Schumann's music.

Because Ruttmann did not exhibit a social conscience in his early work, it is perhaps not surprising that, by the end of his life, he had coopted as a propagandist. An artist whose work was initially apolitical, Ruttmann neither protested nor went into exile with the advent of National Socialism. Instead, he conformed. His last documentaries were odes to Nazism, to Germany's military might.

—Rob Edelman

SANDRICH, MARK. American. Born in in New York City, 26 August 1900. Educated at Columbia University. Career: before 1922—writes numerous short stories and plays; 1922—began working as propman; 1927—starts directing comedy shorts;

directs Lupino Lane 2-reelers; 1928—feature directing debut; returns to directing shorts with coming of sound; 1933—winning Academy Award for short *So This Is Harris* leads to feature assignments; 1934—directs *The Gay Divorcee*, inaugurating series of Fred Astaire/Ginger Rogers musicals; 1940—begins producing as well as directing his films; 1945—dies during production of *Blue Skies*, completed by Stuart Heisler. Recipient: Academy Award, Short Subjects (Comedy), for *So This Is Harris*, 1932/33.

Films (as feature director): 1928—*Runaway Girls*; 1929—*The Talk of Hollywood* (+co-story); 1932—*So This Is Harris* (short); 1933—*Aggie Appleby, Maker of Men*; 1933—*Melody Cruise* (+co-sc); 1934—*Hips Hips, Hooray*; *Cockeyed Cavaliers*; *The Gay Divorcee*; 1935—*Top Hat*; 1936—*A Woman Rebels*; *Follow the Fleet*; 1937—*Shall We Dance?*; 1938—*Carefree*; 1939—*Man About Town*; (as producer and director): 1940—*Buck Benny Rides Again*; *Love Thy Neighbor*; 1941—*Skylark*; 1942—*Holiday Inn*; 1943—*So Proudly We Hail*; 1944—*Here Come the Waves*; 1944—*I Love a Soldier*.

*   *   *

His films bear the mark of their stars rather than of their director. He made *The Gay Divorcee*, *Follow the Fleet*, *Top Hat*, *Shall We Dance*, and *Carefree*, but these are more identifiable as Fred Astaire-Ginger Rogers musicals than as Mark Sandrich films. *A Woman Rebels* looks more like other Katharine Hepburn pictures than it resembles other films by Sandrich. *Cockeyed Cavaliers* and *Hips Hips, Hooray*, if known at all today, are remembered for the teaming of comedians Wheeler and Woolsey (and, in the latter film, for the performance of singer Ruth Etting). And *So Proudly We Hail* brings to mind such other high-gloss wartime melodramas as *Mrs. Minniver* and *Since You Went Away*, and is far more memorable for its impressive cast (Claudette Colbert, Paulette Goddard, and Veronica Lake) than as an example of its director's style.

But while it might be difficult to locate the "Sandrich touch," the director was nonetheless responsible for some of the most entertaining films of the Depression and wartime periods, with successes coming in several of Hollywood's major genres. Sandrich made musicals celebrating the never-never land of the impossibly rich and impeccably chic (*Top Hat*, *The Gay Divorcee*), and also with working-class heroes (*Follow the Fleet*). He contributed to the woman's melodrama with *A Woman Rebels*, a film with a heroine of remarkable strength and determination. During the 1940s, he made films in support of the war effort. *So Proudly We Hail*, which showed the heroism of women in the armed forces, was Sandrich's most notable film from this period, but he also made *I Love a Soldier*, about the difficulties of wartime marriages, and *Here Come the Waves*. This latter film, a musical about the navy, propagandizes in the gentlest and most entertaining way imaginable. Clearly, the song "Accentuate the Positive" provided a very special message to audiences living through a war.

So Sandrich emerges as a highly competent craftsman capable of making virtually any kind of film. But it is with the Astaire-Rogers cycle that he is most closely associated. RKO produced nine of the films, and Sandrich directed five of them, with these movies being largely responsible for keeping the studio on solid financial ground during the thirties. As a result, even though RKO employed, at various times during the decade, Katharine Hepburn, Howard Hawks, David O. Selznick, and others far more famous than Sandrich, it was he who made the films that kept the studio going during its first few years of operation.

But today, Sandrich has been completely overshadowed by the talents of the people with whom he worked on his most celebrated films, with the list including not only the stars, but also such behind-the-camera contributors as songwriter/composers Irving Berlin, Cole Porter, and George and Ira Gershwin, screenwriter Dudley Nichols, costume designer Walter Plunkett, and producer Pandro Berman.

—Eric Smoodin

SAURA, CARLOS. Spanish. Born in Huesca, 4 January 1932. Educated as engineer; studied at Instituto de Investigaciones y Experiencias Cinematográficos, Madrid, 1952-57. Career: beginning 1949—professional photographer; 1957-64—teaches at IIEC, film school; dismissed for political reasons; 1965—beginning with *La caza*, films produced by Elias Querejeta. Recipient: Silver Bear, Berlin Festival, for *La caza*, 1966; Silver Bear, Berlin Festival, for *Peppermint frappé*, 1968; Special Jury Award, Cannes Festival, for *La prima Angelica*, 1974; Special Jury Award, Cannes Festival, for *Cria cuervos*, 1976; Golden Bear, Berlin Festival, for *Hurry, Hurry*, 1981.

Films (as director of short films): 1957—*La tarde del domingo (Sunday Afternoon)* (+sc); 1958—*Cuenca* (+sc); (as feature director): 1962—*Los golfos (The Urchins, The Hooligans, Riff-Raff)* (+co-sc, ro—shown at Cannes 1960); 1964—*Llanto por un bandido (Lament for a Bandit)* (+co-sc); 1966—*La caza (The Hunt, The Chase)* (+co-sc); 1967—*Peppermint frappé* (+co-sc); 1968—*Stress es tres, tres (Stress Is Three, Three)* (+story, co-sc); 1969—*La madriguera (The Honeycomb)* (+story, co-sc); 1970—*El jardín de las delicias (The Garden of Delights)* (+story, co-sc); 1973—*Ana y los lobos (Ana and the Wolves)* (+story, co-sc); 1974—*La prima Angélica (Cousin Angélica)* (+story, co-sc); 1976—*Cría cuervos (Rear Ravens)* (+sc); 1977—*Elisa, vida mía* (+sc); 1978—*Los ojos vendados*; 1979—*Mama cumple cien años*; 1980—*Deprisa, deprisa (Hurry, Hurry)* (+sc); 1981—*Dulces horas (Sweet Hours); Bodas de sangre (Blood Wedding)*; 1982—*Antonieta*; 1983—*Carmen*.

Publications:

By SAURA:

Articles—interview by Guy Braucourt in *Ecran* (Paris), September/October 1973; "Dans le cercle magique de la réalité espagnole", interview by E. Brasó in *Positif* (Paris), October 1974; "Post-scriptum sur Ana y los lobos", interview by E. Brasó in *Positif* (Paris), May 1974; interview by F. Chevassu in *Image et son* (Paris), September 1974; interview by Claire Clouzot in *Ecran* (Paris), December 1974; interview by B. Cohn in *Positif* (Paris), May 1974; interview by G. Braucourt in *Thousand Eyes* (New York), October 1976; "Cria cuervos", interview by G. Braucourt in *Ecran* (Paris), July 1976; interview by E. Braso in *Positif* (Paris), June 1977; interview by M. Capdenac and others in *Ecran* (Paris), July 1977; interview by D. Maillet in *Cinématographe* (Paris), July/August 1977; interview by P.A. Paranagua in *Positif* (Paris), November 1979; "El cumpleaños de Saura", interview by J.L. Guerin in *Cinema 2002* (Madrid),

January 1980; "Mama wird hundert", interview by R. Heckmann in *Film und Fernsehen* (Berlin), May 1981; "Carlos Saura: bodas de prisa", interview by M. Pereira in *Cine Cubano* (Havana), no.99, 1981.

On SAURA:

Books—*Carlos Saura* by Enrique Brasó, Madrid 1974; *Venturas y desventuras de la prima Angélica* by Diego Galan, Valencia 1974; *Homenaje a Carlos Saura* by Roman Gubern, Huelva 1979; articles—"Spanish Films: Paradoxes and Hopes" by Richard Schickel in *Harper's* (New York), September 1967; "Saura Describes Film Spain Banned" by Richard Eder in *The New York Times*, 27 October 1971; "Anne et des loups", special issue of *Avant-Scène du cinéma* (Paris), November 1974; "Présence de l'Espagne chez Carlos Saura" by C. Chaboud in *Jeune Cinéma* (Paris), November 1975; "Dossier-auteur: Carlos Saura" by C.M. Cluny and J. Grant in *Cinéma* (Paris), September/October 1975; "Im Leben ist alles vermischt, Erinnerungen und Imaginationen" by H.M. Eichenlaub in *Cinema* (Zurich), December 1978; "Cria cuervos", special issue of *Avant-Scène du cinéma* (Paris), 15 October 1978; "Les Yeux bandés" by Marcel Martin in *Ecran* (Paris), July 1978; "Carlos Saura: The Political Development of Individual Consciousness" by Marcia Kinder in *Film Quarterly* (Berkeley), no.3, 1979; "Carlos Saura et la peinture, la photographie, le surrealisme, la musique, la littérature, le theatre et la representation" by J. Morder in *Image et son* (Paris), April 1979; "Les Loups et les agneaux" by P.A. Paranagua in *Positif* (Paris), November 1979; "España: Saura en la democracia, y que?" by H. Segura in *Cinemateca Revista* (Andes), August 1981; "Loss and Recuperation in *The Garden of Delights*" by Katherine Kovacs in *Cine-Tracts* (Montreal), summer/fall 1981; "Carlos Saura, Spain and Mama Turns 100" by S. Tate in *Cinema Papers* (Melbourne), April 1982; "Carlos Saura: Constructive Imagination in the Post-Franco Cinema" by Marvin D'Lugo; and "Soñar con tus ojos: Carlos Saura's Melodic Cinema" by Annette Insdorf in *The Quarterly Review of Film Studies* (Pleasantville, New York), spring 1983.

*   *   *

Over the past two decades, Carlos Saura has won numerous prizes at Berlin, Cannes, and other film festivals. He has attained international stature while exploring quintessentially Spanish themes. Saura was one of the first Spanish filmmakers to deal with the Spanish Civil War and its aftermath. In several films, he explored the impact of the war years and of the postwar period on the men and women of his generation, those who were born in the 1930s and who suffered emotional and psychological damage that affected them well into their adult years. In a number of movies, we witness the efforts of Saura's adult protagonists to resurrect their past memories in order to come to terms with them once and for all. In the course of their recollections, we see the negative effects not only of the war, but also of the repressive system of education and of the confining family structures that were consolidated by the triumph of Franco in the postwar period.

Until Franco's death in 1975, it was not possible to express this viewpoint openly. Films were censored first at the script stage and again upon completion. Nothing controversial was allowed. Even in the 1960s, during a period of liberalization when some experimentation was allowed and the New Spanish Cinema movement was born, Saura and the other young directors associated with this movement walked a delicate and difficult line trying to convey their ideas while avoiding the hurdles imposed by the censor.

It was in this atmosphere that Saura developed his cinematic style and method of working. In order to deal with taboo subjects, he (and the other young directors of that time) resorted to tactics of allusion, association, and allegory. In one of Saura's first movies, *The Hunt*, a hunting party arranged by four former comrades-in-arms under Franco is used to represent the legacy of the Civil War and the moral bankruptcy it has engendered. In other movies, Saura destroys the chronological sequence of events in order to show the impact of the past and its continued importance in explaining the present. Actions and events taking place in the present often recall or evoke corresponding past moments and Saura's protagonists come to exist in several temporal dimensions simultaneously. We participate in their memories as well as in their dreams and visions as Saura creates a fluid movement from present to past and in and out of dreams. What is original about these shifts in time and in perspective is that Saura dispenses with the dissolves and soft-focus shots usually used to effectuate a time change in films. In his movies present and past, reality and fantasy are deliberately fused together. Dream figures seem to be as palpable and as concrete as any of the "real" actors on screen. The audience learns to distinguish them through a series of narrative clues and through changes in clothing and in the actors' voices and facial expressions.

This method places substantial demands upon the actors with whom Saura works closely. He has often used the same actors in several movies. Saura has also worked with the same producer and crew for most of his career. There is a great deal of continuity from one of his movies to the next. Sometimes images or sequences from one movie recur in later ones. As Saura himself has said, "Every film is a consequence of the film before."

Every film is also a consequence of the particular political and social climate prevailing in Spain. With the death of Franco and the subsequent abolition of film censorship and restoration of democratic rule, Saura moved away from the complex, nonlinear narrative forms he had cultivated under Franco and began to make simpler, almost documentary-like movies. One of them, which dealt with juvenile delinquents in Madrid, was shot with nonprofessional actors from the slums of the capital (*De prisa, de prisa*). Two others are filmed versions of flamenco ballets that are based upon well-known literary works (*Bodas de sangre* and *Carmen*). In these as in other movies which contain references to Spanish plays, poems, and paintings, Saura affirms his ties to Spanish cultural traditions and shows their relevance to the Spain of today.

—Katherine Singer Kovács

SAUTET, CLAUDE. French. Born in Montrouge, Paris suburb, 23 February 1924. Educated at Ecole des Arts Décoratifs; entered IDHEC, 1948. Career: after WW II—music critic for newspaper *Combat*; 1951—makes experimental short *Nous n'irons plus au bois*; 1950s—assistant director to Pierre Montazel and Guy Lefranc, then to Georges Franju (on *Les Yeux sans visage*) and Jacques Becker (*Touchez pas au Grisbi*); also works in television as producer; beginning 1959—in addition to directing, collaborates on numerous scripts beginning with *Le Fauve est lâché*.

Films (as director and co-scriptwriter): 1951—*Nous n'irons plus au bois* (sc—short); 1956—*Bonjour sourire* (d only); 1960—*Classe tous risques (The Big Risk)*; 1965—*L'Arme à gauche (Guns for the Dictator)*; 1970—*Les Choses de la vie (The Things of Life)*; 1971—*Max et les ferrailleurs*; 1972—*César et Rosalie (Cesar and Rosalie)*; 1974—*Vincent, François, Paul... et les autres*; 1976—*Mado*; 1978—*Une Histoire simple*; 1980—*Un Mauvais Fils (A Bad Son)*; 1983—*Garçon*.

Publications:

By SAUTET:

Articles—"César et Rosalie", interview by Claude Beylie in *Ecran* (Paris), December 1972; interview by Guy Allombert in *Image et son* (Paris), November 1974; "Vincent, François, Paul...et les autres", interview by Claude Beylie in *Ecran* (Paris), November 1974; interview by Michel Ciment in *Positif* (Paris), November 1974; "Claude Sautet, c'est la vitalité" by François Truffaut in *Avant-Scène du cinéma* (Paris), December 1974; interview by Michel Ciment and M. Henry in *Positif* (Paris), December 1976; interview by D. Maillet in *Cinématographe* (Paris), December 1976; "Tournage: Une histoire simple, de Claude Sautet", interview by S. Frydman in *Cinématographe* (Paris), November 1978; interview by F. Guérif and S. Levy-Klein in *Cahiers de la Cinématheque* (Paris), spring/summer 1978; interview by D. Maillet and M. Devillers in *Cinématographe* (Paris), December 1978; interview by Michel Ciment and others in *Positif* (Paris), January 1979; "Romy Schneider: une actrice qui depasse le quotidien" in *Avant-Scène du cinéma* (Paris), 15 March 1979; interview by C. Béchade in *Image et son* (Paris), November 1980.

On SAUTET:

Articles—"Vom poetischen Realismus zum 'nouveau naturel'" by J.-P. Brossard in *Film und Fernsehen* (Berlin), May 1977; "Entretien avec Philippe Sarde sur Claude Sautet et quelques autres" by M. Sineux in *Positif* (Paris), January 1979.

*   *   *

The career of Claude Sautet was slow in getting under way but by the 1970s he had virtually become the French cinema's official chronicler of bourgeois life. He had made his directing debut with a solidly constructed thriller, *Classe tous risques*, in 1960, but a second film, *L'Arme à gauche*, did not follow until 1965 and was markedly less successful. Despite numerous scriptwriting assignments, his directing career did not really get under way until he completed *Les Choses de la vie* in 1969. This set the pattern for a decade of filmmaking. The core of any Sautet film is a fairly banal emotional problem—a man caught between two women in *Les Choses de la vie* or a married woman confronted with a former lover in *César et Rosalie*. Around this situation Sautet weaves a rich pattern of bourgeois life: concerns with home and family, with money and possessions, give these films their particular tone. This is a cinema of warm, convincingly depicted characters for whom Sautet clearly has great affection and more than a touch of complicity. Problems and motivations are always explicitly set out, for this is a style of psychological realism in which the individual, not the social, forms the focus of attention. The director's style is a sober, classical one, built on the model of Hollywood narrative traditions: action, movement, vitality. Though his style can encompass such set pieces as the boxing match in *Vincent, Francois, Paul...et les autres*, Sautet is more concerned with the unfolding of a strong and involving narrative line. A key feature of all his work are the confrontation scenes which offer such excellent opportunities for the talented stars and solid character players who people his films.

Sautet's films since the mid-1970s—*Mado*, *Une Histoire simple*, and *Un Mauvais Fils*—are all characterized by a total assurance and a mastery of the medium. This mastery, however, is exercised within very precise limits, not in terms of the subject matter, which widens to take in the problems of affluence, women's independence, and juvenile delinquency, but in the manner in which such issues of the moment are approached. Sautet's classicism of form and ability to communicate directly with his audience is not accompanied by the resonances of social criticism which characterize the best North American cinema. Seeking to move his audience rather than enlighten it, Sautet uses powerful actors cast to type in carefully constructed roles, but any probing of the essential contradictions is avoided by a style of direction which keeps rigidly to the surface of life, the given patterns of bourgeois social behaviour. His approach is therefore condemned to a certain schematism, particularly in the handling of dialogue scenes, but his work gets its sense of vitality from the vigor with which the group scenes—the meals and excursions—and the typical locations of café or railway station are handled. Sautet offers a facsimile of life, a reflection of current problems or issues, but contained within a form calculated not to trouble the spectator after he has left the cinema. This conformism may seem limiting to the contemporary critic, but it will offer future generations a rare insight into the manner in which the French middle classes liked to see themselves in the 1970s.

—Roy Armes

SAVILLE, VICTOR. British/American. Born Victor Salberg in Birmingham, 25 September 1897; became citizen of the United States, 1950. Educated at King Edward VI Grammar School, Camp Hill, Birmingham. Married Phoebe Vera Teller, 1920; children: David and Anne. Career: 1915—severely wounded at Battle of Loos; 1916—invalided out of army; hired by father's friend Sol Levy, Birmingham film distributor and cinema owner; manages small cinema in Coventry; 1917-19—joins Pathé Frères, London, works in Features and Newsreels Dept.; with Charles Wilcox runs film distribution company in Leeds; 1919—with Michael Balcon forms Victory Motion Pictures; 1923—directs and co-produces with Balcon *Woman to Woman*; 1924—severs relationship with Balcon; 1926-27—produces for Gaumont string of successful films with Maurice Elvey directing; 1927—launches independent production company Burlington Film Co. Ltd.; acts as Managing Director; 1929—travels to U.S. to make 1st sound films; 1930-35—beginning with *A Warm Corner* films produced by Michael Balcon; 1936—forms Victor Saville Productions, Ltd.; 1937—signs contract with Louis B. Mayer to produce exclusively for MGM; 1939-43—works at MGM in Hollywood; 1943—resigns, joins Columbia; success of *Tonight and Every Night* leads to MGM directing offer, makes 6 more films for MGM; 1952—forms Parklane Productions; 1960—returns to live in London; 1961—emerges from semi-retirement to make *The Greengage Summer* and last film *Mix Me a Person*. Died in London, 8 May 1979.

Films (as co-producer with Michael Balcon): 1923—*Woman to Woman* (Cutts); *The White Shadow* (Cutts); 1924—*The Prudes Fall* (Cutts); (as producer): 1926—*Mademoiselle from Armentieres* (Elvey); 1927—*Roses of Picardy* (Elvey); *The Glad Eye* (Elvey); *The Flight Commander* (Elvey); (as director): 1927—*The Arcadians* (+pr); 1928—*Tesha (Woman in the Night)*; 1929—*Kitty*; *Woman to Woman*; 1930—*The W Plan*; *A Warm Corner*; 1931—*The Sport of Kings*; *Hindle Wakes* (Elvey) (pr only); *Michael & Mary*; *Sunshine Susie (The Office Girl)*; 1932—*The Faithful Heart*; *Love on Wheels*; 1933—*The Good Companions*; *I Was a Spy*; *Friday the 13th*; 1934—*Evergreen*; *Evensong*; *The Iron Duke*; 1935—*The Dictator (The Loves of a Dictator)*; *Me and Marlborough*; *First a Girl*; 1936—*It's Love Again*; (as producer and director): 1937—*Dark Journey*; *Storm in a Teacup* (co-d); *Action for Slander* (Whelan) (pr only); 1938—*South Riding*; (as producer): 1938—*The Citadel* (Vidor); 1939—*Goodbye, Mr. Chips* (Wood); *Earl of Chicago* (Thorpe); 1940—*The Mortal Storm* (Borzage); *Bitter Sweet* (Van Dyke); 1941—*A Woman's Face* (Cukor); *Dr. Jekyll and Mr. Hyde* (Fleming); *Smilin' Through* (Borzage); *The Chocolate Soldier* (Del Ruth); 1942—*White Cargo* (Thorpe); *Keeper of the Flame* (Cukor); 1943—*Above Suspicion* (Thorpe); (as director): 1943—*Forever and a Day* (co-d); 1945—*Tonight and Every Night* (+pr); 1946—*The Green Years*; 1947—*Green Dolphin Street*; *If Winter Comes*; 1949—*The Conspirator*; 1950—*Kim*; 1951—*Calling Bulldog Drummond*; 1952—*24 Hours of a Woman's Life (Affair in Mont Carlo)*; 1953—*I, the Jury* (Essex) (pr); 1954—*The Long Wait*; 1955—*Kiss Me Deadly* (Aldrich) (exec. pr); *The Silver Chalice*; 1961—*The Greengage Summer* (Gilbert) (pr); 1962—*Mix Me a Person* (Norman) (exec. pr).

Publications:

On SAVILLE:

Book—*Victor Saville* by Cyril Rollins, London 1972; articles—obituary in *The New York Times*, 10 May 1979; obituary in *Variety* (New York), 16 May 1979; obituary in *Cine Revue* (Brussels), 23 May 1979.

* * *

A former film salesman who became a producer in partnership with Michael Balcon—both men were born in Birmingham—Victor Saville began his directorial career in the late twenties in England, and during the next decade became firmly established as one of that country's more stylish filmmakers. Unlike his contemporaries in the British film industry, Saville never made films that were particularly English in content or style; his manner of directing was quite definitely borrowed from Hollywood and he understood the need for glamor and sophistication in order to appeal to the international film market.

One of Victor Saville's earliest films, *Tesha* (released in the U.S. as *Woman in the Night*) is notable for its mature subject matter, a married woman who has a child by her husband's best friend. *Kitty* is a curiosity as one of Britain's first talkies, with the sound sequences shot at the Paramount Astoria Studios on Long Island. However, it was in the thirties that Victor Saville hit his stride as a director, with a series of romantic comedies featuring Jessie Matthews—*The Good Companions*, *Friday the Thirteenth*, *Evergreen*, *First a Girl*, and *It's Love Again*—and a brilliant First World War spy melodrama, *I Was a Spy*, which made an international star of Madeleine Carroll.

MGM recognized Victor Saville's internationality by selecting him to produce its first two prestigious British productions, *The Citadel*, and *Goodbye, Mr. Chips*. These films led to Saville's coming to the United States, where he produced (but did not direct) a string of quality films, notably *Bitter Sweet*, *Dr. Jekyll and Mr. Hyde*, *Smilin' Through*, and *Keeper of the Flame*. As with all of Saville's American films, they were solid, slightly dull, but always well-made entertainment pictures. The same may be said of the U.S. features which Saville directed, particularly *Green Dolphin Street* and *Kim*, which are heavy on production values and light on any originality in direction.

Victor Saville once remarked that films must "bounce off the times we live in," a philosophy which his early work upholds. If his later films have any linking continuity it is that they were derived from major literary works: *The Citadel* by A.J. Cronin, *Goodbye, Mr. Chips* by James Hilton, *Green Dolphin Street* by Elizabeth Goudge, *Kim* by Rudyard Kipling, *I, the Jury* and *The Long Wait* by Mickey Spillane, and *The Greengage Summer* by Rumer Godden. One project which never saw the light of day was Victor Saville's planned production of Agatha Christie's long-running play, *The Mousetrap*, which he had hoped to produce with Tyrone Power starring under the direction of Billy Wilder.

—Anthony Slide

SCHAFFNER, FRANKLIN J. American. Born in Tokyo, 30 May 1920. Educated at Franklin and Marshall College; studied law at Columbia University. Married Jean Gilchrist, 1948; daughters: Jennie and Kate. Career: 1941-45—serves in Navy; after war—assistant director for *March of Time* series; 1949-62—television director for CBS; directs *Studio One*, *Ford Theater*, and *Playhouse 90* productions; 1955—with Worthington Miner, George Roy Hill and Fielder Cook forms "Unit Four" production company to do *Kaiser Aluminum Hour*; among TV productions: "12 Angry Men," "Caine Mutiny Court Martial," "The Cruel Day"; 1960—directs *Advise and Consent* on Broadway; 1961—signs 3-picture contract with 20th Century-Fox, directs 1st feature film, *A Summer World* (incomplete); 1961-63—television counselor to President Kennedy. Recipient: Peabody Award for *The United Nations Telecast*, 1950; Emmy Award for *12 Angry Men*, 1954; Sylvania Award for *12 Angry Men*, 1954; Emmy Award for *The Caine Mutiny Court Martial*, 1955; New York Drama Critics Award for *Advise and Consent*, 1961; Emmy Award for *The Defenders*, 1962; Best Director Academy Award for *Patton*, 1970. Agent: Creative Artists Agency, Los Angeles, CA 90067.

Films (as feature director): 1961—*A Summer World* (incomplete); 1963—*The Stripper (Woman of Summer)*; 1964—*The Best Man*; 1965—*The War Lord*; 1967—*The Double Man*; 1968—*Planet of the Apes*; 1970—*Patton*; 1971—*Nicholas and Alexandra*; 1973—*Papillon* (+co-pr); 1977—*Islands in the Stream*; 1978—*The Boys from Brazil*; 1980—*Sphinx*; 1982—*Yes, Giorgio*.

Publications:

By SCHAFFNER:

Articles—"The Best and Worst of It", interview in *Films and Filming* (London), October 1964; interview by Gerald Pratley in *Cineaste* (New York), summer 1969; interview in *Cinema 70* (Paris), June 1970; interview in *Positif* (Paris), June 1970; "Inter/View with Franklin Schaffner" by R. Feiden in *Inter/-View* (New York), March 1972; "Chronicler of Power", interview by K. Geist in *Film Comment*, September/October 1972; interview in *Cinefantastique* (Oak Park, Illinois), summer 1972; interview in *Take One* (Montreal), September/October 1972; "Master Plans", interview by R. Appelbaum in *Films and Filming* (London), February 1979; "How to Lose Weight without Worrying", interview by D. Castelli in *Films Illustrated* (London), May 1979; interview in *Film News* (Ontario), no.8, 1979.

On SCHAFFNER:

Articles—"Franklin Schaffner" by David Wilson in *Sight and Sound* (London), spring 1966; "The Early Franklin Schaffner" by Stanley Kauffman in *Films in Review* (New York), August/-September 1969; "Director Franklin Schaffner: From *Planet of the Apes* to *Patton*" by Dale Munroe in *Show* (Hollywood), 6 August 1970; "Director of the Month—Franklin Schaffner: The Panoply of Power" by Andrew Sarris in *Show* (Hollywood), April 1970; article by Frank McCarthy in *Action* (Los Angeles), May/June 1971; "Papillon" by J. Delson in *Take One* (Montreal), January 1974; "On Location with *Islands in the Stream*" by Herb Lightman in *American Cinematographer* (Los Angeles), November 1976; "Franklin J. Schaffner" in *Kosmorama* (Copenhagen), autumn 1977; "The War Between the Writers and the Directors: Part II: The Directors" by B. Cook in *American Film* (Washington, D.C.), June 1979; "TV to Film—A Guide to 5 American Directors" in *Monthly Film Bulletin* (London), February 1983.

* * *

Franklin J. Schaffner has often been referred to as an "actors' director." A former actor himself, he spent over a decade directing television drama before making his first film. This experience proved invaluable when he arrived in Hollywood. All his films starred well-established professionals such as Fonda, Heston, Brynner, Scott, Hoffman, Peck, and Olivier.

His first film, *The Stripper*, was based on William Inge's play *A Loss of Roses*. Producer Jerry Wald died while it was being made, and after completion the film was taken out of Franklin's hands and re-edited. As a result the character of the "stripper," played by Joanne Woodward, was sadly lacking in contrast. Schaffner's experience working on political television programs stood him in very good stead when he directed his second film, *The Best Man*, a story of two contenders for the Presidential nomination at a political convention in Los Angeles. Set mainly in hotel rooms and corridors, it could have become very static. But Schaffner accepted the challenge and turned out a compelling drama.

After the intimacy of *The Best Man* came the vastness of *The War Lord*. A medieval costume picture was a complete change for Schaffner, but he succeeded in capturing the visual splendor of the outdoor sequences—particularly the first few minutes—and the excitement and gusto of the battle scenes. Although an "action" film, it had a literate script—and once again it was cut by the studio. *The Double Man*, shot in England and Austria was an average spy drama, but not a great film. His first big financial success was *Planet of the Apes*, in which he had to produce realistic performances from actors in monkey suits. Handled by another director it could easily have been turned into a farce, but

Schaffner's craftsmanship made it a science fiction satire.

In 1970 he directed George C. Scott in the role of General Patton. 27 years earlier Schaffner himself had taken part in the landings in Sicily under Patton. The film was shot in 70mm, but he insisted on cutting it in 35mm so as to avoid being influenced by the scope of 70mm. Scott's performance was widely praised, but he refused an Academy Award. (Schaffner accepted his!)

It was his interest in history that first attracted Schaffner to *Nicholas and Alexandra*. Here he told what was basically an intimate story of two people, but two people surrounded by the overflowing retinue of the court and the boundless expanse of the countryside. Schaffner used the contrast to great effect, and the film was nominated for an Oscar.

Papillon is the only film which Schaffner directed in sequence, and this was not by choice. Dalton Trumbo was rewriting the script as the film was being shot, often just managing to keep up with the production. This was the second time that Schaffner had worked with cinematographer Fred Koenekamp, and they were teamed again for his next feature, *Islands in the Stream*. This time he faced the problem of space and isolation, having to fill the large screen for a long time with just one man. He also found it necessary to use two cameras for some of the action sequences, something which he never did if it could be avoided. Several studios turned down *The Boys from Brazil* because it was impossssible to cast, but Schaffner thought it would work if he cast against type. So Gregory Peck, always known as a "good guy," played Mengele—the German doctor intent on producing clones of Hitler. Olivier, who had earlier played the German in "Marathon Man," was the Jewish doctor trying to track down the Nazi. In the early eighties Schaffner made *Sphinx*, an adventure story set amongst the pyramids, and *Yes, Giorgio*, his first "musical," with Luciano Pavarotti.

Schaffner has a reputation for getting the best out of his actors and coping well with intimate dramas. Yet he has also achieved success with large-scale epics and has been compared with David Lean because of the beauty of his compositions and the breadth of his dramatic power. He revels in films about men struggling to achieve a certain goal. A craftsman, he does his homework and prepares each scene before arriving on the set. He knows what he wants.

—Colin Williams

SCHATZBERG, JERRY. American. Born Jerrold N. Schatzberg in the Bronx, New York, 26 June 1927. Educated at Forest Hills, New York, High School; University of Miami. Formerly married; sons: Steven and Don. Career: works in family fur business; 1953—begins working as photographer; becomes assistant to fashion photographer Bill Helburn; mid-1950s—sets up own studio; by late '50s—shooting fashion pictures for *Vogue* and other publications; early '60s—begins directing commercials. Recipient: Best Film, Cannes Festival (*ex aequo*), for *Scarecrow*, 1973. Agent: William Morris Agency, 1350 Avenue of the Americas, New York, NY 10019.

Films 1970—*Puzzle of a Downfall Child*; 1971—*Panic in Needle Park*; 1973—*Scarecrow*; 1976—*Dandy, the All-American Girl (Sweet Revenge)*; 1979—*The Seduction of Joe Tynan*; 1980—*Honeysuckle Rose*; 1983—*Misunderstood*.

Publications:

By SCHATZBERG:

Articles—"L'Epouvantail", interview by Guy Braucourt in *Ecran* (Paris), June 1973; interview by Michel Ciment in *Positif* (Paris), June 1973; interview by D. Gain in *Image et son* (Paris), June 1973; "Les gens doivent apprendre à négocier avec la solitude...", interview by M. Grisolia in *Cinéma* (Paris), July/August 1973; "Entretien avec Anne S." in *Positif* (Paris), December/January 1977/78; "Jerry Schatzberg et *The Seduction of Joe Tynan*", interview in *Amis du film et de la télévision* (Brussels), November 1979.

On SCHATZBERG:

Articles—"L'Epouvantail", special issue of *Avant-Scène du cinéma* (Paris), October 1973; "Dossier: Hollywood 79: Jerry Schatzberg" by J. Fieschi in *Cinématographe* (Paris), March 1979.

*   *   *

Jerry Schatzberg is one of the very few important photographers who became an accomplished film director. In the sixties and the seventies, for *McCall's* and particularly *Vogue*, he proved himself a major talent of fashion photography, placing his models in everyday situations which gave his stills a sense of reality while retaining a rare sophistication. This proved to be a characteristic of his later cinematographic style. At the same time Schatzberg was making portraits of entertainment people (Bob Dylan, Roman Polanski, The Rolling Stones, Milos Forman, Catherine Deneuve, Claudia Cardinale, etc.) which allowed him not only to come into contact with the film world, but also through sessions with models to learn how to observe human beings and capture the revealing expression. Again, his direction of actors was to gain from this experience. In the same way the numerous street scenes and landscapes that he did during this early period of his life prepared him to shoot the background of films like *Panic in Needle Park* or *Scarecrow*.

He was given a break with *Puzzle of a Downfall Child*, starring Faye Dunaway, a highly complex movie, the fragmented portrait of a model recovering from a breakdown and telling her life to a photographer intending to make a film out of her confession. Schatzberg used to his advantage his first-hand knowledge of the fashion world and recreated in a highly elaborate style both the society in which his character, Lou Andreas Sand, lived and her distorted vision of reality. The refined photography, the elaborate interplay between the sound track and the images, the sensitive performance of Faye Dunaway, and the director's compassion for his heroine combined to make one of the most daring and original films of the early seventies, a period rich in experiments. The criticisms levelled at Schatzberg for his supposedly artificial style (in fact dictated by the subject matter) were to subside with his second film, *Panic in Needle Park*, inspired by a documentary account written by James Mills on the junkies in New York. Totally devoid of music, the film impresses by its raw quality, its intensity of feeling, and again the sensitivity shown by the director towards the predicament of his two characters, as lost in their physical degradation as the fashion model was in her emotional crisis. Al Pacino in his first screen role and Kitty Winn (best performance at the 1972 Cannes Film Festival) conveyed all the pathos of these lost souls in the modern city.

The Golden Palm awarded to Schatzberg's third film, *Scare-*

crow, at the 1973 Cannes Film Festival attracted world attention to his work. *Scarecrow*, along with *Puzzle* Schatzberg's most remarkable film, is a road movie, a new version of the American dream, with two tramps, Max (Gene Hackman) and Leo (Al Pacino) crossing America eastward, Max, after six years in prison, to open a carwash, and Leo, after a period on the sea, to see his child for the first time. Discarding classical dramatic construction and unity of mood, *Scarecrow* adopts a picaresque tone and mixes tragedy and humor, brutality and an invigorating sense of life. More modest in scope, *Dandy, the All-American Girl*, is the portrait of another outsider, a car thief in Seattle, played with wit and energy by Stockard Channing. Schatzberg's next film, *The Seduction of Joe Tynan*, was also his biggest commercial and critical success. Written by its male star, Alan Alda, it has a much more classical construction, a less flexible style, which may explain its greater popularity. Meryl Streep in one of her best performances is the mistress of a married senator. Schatzberg rediscovers the charm and the deft psychology of thirties comedies, but with a definite contemporary look, more detached and ambivalent.

Honeysuckle Rose, starring Willie Nelson, is again a road movie, showing empathy for the life of the Texan country singers, and a real sense of landscape and music. *Misunderstood*, Schatzberg's latest film, explores once more the director's primary concern: the relationship between people. A melodrama set in Tunisia, it concerns the triangular relationship between a father (Gene Hackman) and his two sons, one of whom he prefers and the other who will die. It reveals once more the delicacy of touch, infallible visual flair, and the rare sensitivity to human suffering which distinguish Schatzberg's work. Open and modern in his attitude towards morals, and manners, classical and inventive in his style, he has given his work a quality of feeling and a purity of form which should prove more lasting than the trendier qualities of other directors' work.

—Michel Ciment.

SCHLESINGER, JOHN. English. Born John Richard Schlesinger in London, 16 February 1926. Educated St. Edmunds School, London; Uppingham School, Rutland; Oxford University, 1945-50. Career: 1945—joins Oxford University Dramatic Society; 1948—directs 1st noteworthy short, *Black Legend*; 1950-52—joins Colchester Repertory Company in England and later tours Australia and New Zealand with Ngaio Marsh's theater troupe; 1952—makes 1st film appearance in *Single-handed (Sailor of the King)*; 1956—makes 1st appearance as television actor in dramatic series; 1956-61—directs 24 short documentaries for BBC series *Tonight* and *Monitor*; also works as 2nd unit director on television series *The 4 Just Men* and as interviewer for series *The Valiant Years*; 1962—directs 1st feature, *A Kind of Loving*; 1969—directs 1st American-made film, *Midnight Cowboy*; 1970—named Commander of the British Empire by Queen Elizabeth II for his contribution to British cinema; 1980—directs opera *Les Contes de Hoffmann*, in London. Recipient: Best Direction, New York Film Critics, for *Darling*, 1965; Best Direction British Academy Award for *Midnight Cowboy*, 1969; Best Director Academy Award for *Midnight Cowboy*, 1969; Director Award, Directors Guild of America, for *Midnight Cowboy*, 1969; Best Direction British Academy Award for *Sunday, Bloody Sunday*, 1971. Address: c/o Michael Oliver, Berger, Oliver & Co., 40 Picadilly, London W 1, England.

Films (as director): 1948—*Black Legend* (co-d, +co-pr, co-sc); 1950—*The Starfish* (co-d, +co-pr, co-sc); 1956—*Sunday in the Park* (co-d, +co-pr, co-sc); 1961—*Terminus* (+sc—documentary); 1962—*A Kind of Loving*; 1963—*Billy Liar*; 1965—*Darling*; 1967—*Far from the Madding Crowd*; 1969—*Midnight Cowboy* (+co-pr); 1971—*Sunday, Bloody Sunday*; 1972—"The Longest" section of *Visions of 8*; 1975—*The Day of the Locust*; 1976—*Marathon Man*; 1979—*Yanks*; 1981—*Honky Tonk Freeway*.

Roles include: 1953—*Singlehanded* (John and Roy Boulting); 1955—*Oh, Rosalinda* (Powell); 1956—*Brothers-in-Law* (John and Roy Boulting); *The Battle of the River Plate (Pursuit of the Graf Spee)* (Powell and Pressburger); 1957—*Holz* in *7 Thunders (The Beasts of Marseilles)* (Fregonese).

Publications:

By SCHLESINGER:

Articles—"Blessed Isle or Fool's Paradise: Interview" in *Films and Filming* (London), May 1963; "How to Get Into Films by the People Who Got in Themselves" in *Films and Filming* (London), July 1963; "John Schlesinger at the 6th Montreal International Film Festival" by Gretchen Weinberg in *Film Heritage* (Dayton, Ohio), fall 1965; "John Schlesinger" in *Directors in Action* edited by Bob Thomas, Indianapolis 1968; "John Schlesinger, A British Director Talks About Making Films in the United States" by N. Weaver in *After Dark* (Boston), no.5, 1969; "John Schlesinger Interviewed" by David Spiers in *Screen* (London), summer 1970; "John Schlesinger" in *Behind the Scenes: Theatre and Film Interviews from the Transatlantic Review* edited by Joseph McCrindle, New York 1971; "What the Directors Are Saying" in *Action* (Los Angeles), September/October 1974; "John Schlesinger parle..." by G.D. Phillips in *Sequences* (Paris), July 1974; "John Schlesinger" by Valerie Wade in *Interview* (New York), July 1974; "John Schlesinger" by Ken Kelley in *Penthouse* (New York), June 1975; "John Schlesinger Talks About 'Locust'" by Charles Loring in *American Cinematographer* (Hollywood), June 1975; "John Schlesinger Interview" by Gene Phillips in *Film Comment* (New York), May/June 1975; "I Both Hate and Love What I Do: An Interview with John Schlesinger" in *Literature/Film Quarterly* (Salisbury, Maryland); "John Schlesinger: 'I Can't Keep from Diving into the Deep End'" by Patrick Pacheco in *After Dark* (Boston), November 1979; "Dialogue on Film: John Schlesinger" by James Powers in *American Film* (Washington, D.C.), December 1979.

On SCHLESINGER:

Books—*The Movie Makers: Artists in an Industry* by Gene L. Phillips, Chicago 1973; *The Great British Picture Show: From the 90's to the 70's* by George Perry, New York 1974; *Hollywood UK: The British Film Industry in the 60's* by Alexander Walker, New York 1974; *Directing the Film: Film Directors on Their Art* by Eric Sherman, Boston 1976; *John Schlesinger: A Guide to References and Resources* by Nancy J. Brooker, Boston 1978; *John Schlesinger* by Gene D. Phillips, Boston 1981; articles—"John Schlesinger" in *Films and Filming* (London), June 1962; "The Face of '63—Great Britain" by Peter Cowie in *Films and Filming* (London), no.5, 1963; "A Buck for Joe" by Gordon Gow in *Films and Filming* (London), November 1969; "Schlesinger Released" by Penelope Mortimer in *The Observer* (London), 28 September 1969; "John Schlesinger, Social Realist" by Gene Phillips in *Film Comment* (New York), winter 1969; "John Schlesinger, Award Winner" by William Hall in *Action* (Los

Angeles), July/August 1970; "Film Union" in *The Times* (London), 14 July 1970; "The Personal Vision of John Schlesinger" by Gene D. Phillips in *America* (New York), 16 October 1971; "John Schlesinger at the Olympic Games" in *American Cinematographer* (Hollywood), November 1972; "Belles, Sirens, Sisters" by Lillian Gerard in *Film Library Quarterly* (New York), winter 1972; "Schlesinger—Back to TV" in *The Times* (London), 12 August 1973; "John Schlesinger and *The Day of the Locust*" by Andrew Bobrow in *Filmmakers Newsletter* (Ward Hill, Mass.), July 1975; "Photographing *The Day of the Locust*" by Conrad Hall in *American Cinematographer* (Hollywood), June 1975; "John Schlesinger's 2 Fascinating Dreams" by John Higgins in *The Times* (London), 25 February 1975; "Behind the Scenes of *Day of the Locust*" by Kenn Rand in *American Cinematographer* (Hollywood), June 1975; "Exile in Hollywood: John Schlesinger" by Gene Phillips in *Literature/Film Quarterly* (Salisbury, Maryland), spring 1977; "On *Yanks* and Other Films" by Gene D. Phillips in *Focus on Film* (London), fall 1978.

*   *   *

John Schlesinger began his professional career by making short documentaries for the BBC. His first major venture in the cinema was a documentary for British Transport called *Terminus*, about 24 hours at Waterloo Station, which won him an award at the Venice Film Festival. Schlesinger's documentaries attracted the attention of producer Joseph Janni; together they formed a creative association which has included all of Schlesinger's British films, beginning with *A Kind of Loving*, which won the Grand Prize at the Berlin Film Festival.

Schlesinger began directing feature films in Britain at the point when the cycle of low-budget, high-quality movies on social themes (called "Kitchen Sink" dramas) was in full swing. Because these films were made outside the large studio system, Schlesinger got used to developing his own film projects. He has continued to do so while directing films in Hollywood, where he has worked with increasing regularity in recent years, starting with his first American film, *Midnight Cowboy*, which won him the best director Academy Award from both the American and British film industries, as well as the American Directors' Guild Award.

"I like the cross-fertilization that comes from making films in both England and America,"he explains. "Although I am English and I do like to work in England, I have gotten used to regarding myself more and more as mid-Atlantic." As a matter of fact, foreign directors like Lang and Hitchcock and Schlesinger, precisely because they are not native Americans, are sometimes able to view American life with a vigilant, perceptive eye for the kind of telling details which home-grown directors might easily overlook or simply take for granted. Indeed, reviews of *Midnight Cowboy* by and large noted how accurately the British-born Schlesinger had caught the authentic atmosphere of not only New York City, but also of Miami Beach and the Texas Panhandle, as surely as he had captured the atmosphere of a factory town in his native England in *A Kind of Loving*.

"Any film that is seriously made will reflect the attitudes and problems of society at large," he says, and consequently possess the potential to appeal to an international audience, as many of his films have. "But it is inevitable that a director's own attitudes will creep into his films. For my part I try in my movies to communicate to the filmgoer a better understanding of other human beings by exploring the hazards of entering into a mutual relationship with another human being, which is the most difficult thing on earth to do, because it involves a voyage of discovery for both parties." Hence his prime concern as a director with examining complex human relationships from a variety of angles—ranging from the social outcasts of *Midnight Cowboy* to members of the jet set in *Darling*.

In sum, John Schlesinger is a member of the growing international community of filmmakers who are trying to speak to an equally international audience. That is the way the world cinema is headed, and directors like Schlesinger are helping to lead it there.

—Gene D. Phillips

SCHLÖNDORFF, VOLKER. German. Born in Wiesbaden, 31 March 1939. Educated at Lycée Henri Quatre, Paris; studied political science and economics; studied film directing at Institut des Hautes Etudes Cinématographiques, Paris. Married Margarethe von Trotta, 1969. Career: 1956—family moves to Paris; 1960-64—works as assistant to French directors including Louis Malle, Jean-Pierre Melville, and Alain Resnais; 1967—signed to 6-picture contract by Universal; 1969—forms Hallelujah-Film with Peter Fleischmann, goes into partnership with West German TV stations; 1969—begins ongoing collaboration with Margarethe Von Trotta on TV production *Baal*; 1973—with Reinhard Hauff forms Bioskop-Film; 1974—directs opera *Katja Kabanova* in Frankfurt, and in 1976 opera *Wir erreichen den Fluss* in Berlin; 1978—helps organize omnibus film *Deutschland im Herbst*. Recipient: FIPRESCI Prize, Cannes, for *Young Törless*, 1966; Best Film, Cannes Festival (*ex aequo*), for *The Tin Drum*, 1979; Foreign-Language Film Academy Award for *The Tin Drum*, 1979.

Films (as director): 1960—*Wen kümmert's... (Who Cares...)* (short—unreleased); 1966—*Der junge Törless (Young Törless)* (+sc); 1967—*Mord und Totschlag (A Degree of Murder)* (+co-sc); 1969—*Michael Kohlhaas—Der Rebell (Michael Kohlhaas—The Rebel)* (+co-sc); 1970—*Baal* (+sc—for TV); *Ein unheimlicher Moment (An Uneasy Moment)* (short—originally episode of uncompleted feature *Paukenspieler*, filmed 1967); *Der plötzlicher Reichtum der armen Leute von Kombach (The Sudden Fortune of the Poor People of Kombach, The Sudden Wealth of the Poor People of Kombach)* (+co-sc); 1971—*Die Moral der Ruth Halbfass (The Moral of Ruth Halbfass)* (+co-sc); *Strohfeuer (A Free Woman, Strawfire, Summer Lightning)* (+co-sc); 1974—*Übernachtung in Tirol (Overnight Stay in the Tyrol, Overnight in Tirol)* (+co-sc—for TV); 1975—*Georginas Grunde (Georgina's Reasons)* (for TV); *Die verlorene Ehre der Katharina Blum (The Lost Honor of Katharina Blum)* (co-d, +co-sc); 1976—*Der Fangschuss (Coup de grâce)*; 1977—*Nur zum Spass—Nur zum Spiel. Kaleidoskop Valeska Gert (Just for Fun, Just for Play, Only for Fun—Only for Play. Kaleidoscope Valeska Gert)* (+sc—documentary); 1978—*Deutschland im Herbst (Germany in Autumn)* (co-d); 1979—*Der Blechtrommel (The Tin Drum)*(+co-sc); 1980—*Der Kandidat (The Candidate)* (+co-sc—documentary); 1981—*Die Fälschung (The Forgery)* (+sc); *Circle of Deceit*; 1983—*War and Peace*.

Publications:

By SCHLÖNDORFF:

Books—*Die Blechtrommel, Tagebuch einer Verfilmung*, Neuwied 1979; *Die Blechtrommel als Film*, Frankfurt 1979;

articles—"Volker Schloendorff: The Rebel", interview by Rui Nogueira and Nicoletta Zalaffi in *Film* (London), summer 1969; interview by J.-L. Passek in *Cinéma* (Paris), January 1972; "Les Femmes sont sanctionées dès avant leur naissance", interview by M. Grisolia in *Cinéma* (Paris), February 1973; interview by D. Maillet in *Image et son* (Paris), February 1973; "Feu de paille", interview by M. Martin in *Ecran* (Paris), February 1973; "A propos de *Feu de paille*", interview by G. Langlois in *Téléciné* (Paris), March 1973; "Problemy kino", interview in *Iskusstvo Kino* (Moscow), June 1973; "Melville und der Befreiungskampf im Baltikum", interview by H. Wiedemann in *Film und Ton* (Munich), December 1976; "*Die Blechtrommel*" in *Film und Ton* (Munich), June 1979; "Volker Schlöndorff sur *Le Tambour*" in *Jeune Cinéma* (Paris), September/October 1979; "*Le Tambour*: journal d'un tournage" in *Cinématographe* (Paris), October 1979; "The Tin Drum: Volker Schlöndorff's 'Dream of Childhood'", interview by J. Hughes in *Film Quarterly* (Berkeley), spring 1981.

On SCHLÖNDORFF:

Articles—"Feu de paille", interview with Margarethe von Trotta in *Jeune Cinéma* (Paris), December/January 1972/73; "Gespräch zwischen Margarethe von Trotta und Christel Buschmann" in *Frauen und Film* (Berlin), June 1976; "Die verlorene Ehre der Katharina Blum" by Margarethe von Trotta and others in *Film und Fernsehen* (Berlin), no.8, 1976; "Le Coup de grâce", special issue of *Avant-Scène du cinéma* (Paris), 1 February 1977; "Den deutschen Film international machen: Volker Schlöndorff und *Die Blechtrommel*" by H.M. Eichenlaub in *Cinema* (Zurich), no.2, 1979; "Volker Schlöndorff" by Ronald Holloway in *International Film Guide 1982*, London 1981.

*   *   *

In discussions of the New German Cinema, Volker Schlöndorff's name generally comes up only after the mention of Fassbinder, Herzog, Wenders, and perhaps Straub, Syberberg, or von Trotta. Though his work certainly merits consideration alongside that of any of his countrymen, there are several reasons why he has stood apart from them.

As a teenager, Schlöndorff moved to France to study, earning academic honors and a university degree in economics and political science. He enrolled at IDHEC with an interest in film directing but chose instead to pursue an active apprenticeship within the French film industry. Eventually he served as assistant director to Jean-Pierre Melville, Alain Resnais, and Louis Malle. Schlöndorff then returned to Germany and scored an immediate triumph with his first feature, *Young Törless*. Like his mentor Louis Malle, then, he ushered in his country's new wave of film artists, but also like that of Malle, Schlöndorff's eclectic range of projects has defied easy categorization, causing his work to seem less personal than that of almost any other German filmmaker's. His decade in France also set Schlöndorff apart in other ways, not the least of which was his thorough professional training there that instilled in him an appreciation for the highly-crafted, polished filmmaking that marks his style. (The quality of the photography in his work—both black and white and in color, and whether by Sven Nykvist, Franz Rath, or Igor Luther—has been consistently exceptional.) While most of his contemporaries declared their antipathy toward the look and production methods of the declining German film industry of the sixties, Schlöndorff endeavored successfully to make larger-scaled features. Toward this end he helped form and continues to operate two production companies—Hallelujah-Film and Bioskop-Film—and has regularly obtained financing from German television and a variety of international producers. Yet he has met

shooting schedules of just three weeks, and his wide career includes shorts, documentaries, and television films (one is a production of Brecht's *Baal* with Fassbinder in the title role). In the mid-1970s he even turned to directing opera: Janáček's *Katya Kabanova* and a work by Hans Werner Henze.

Intellectual, literate, and fluent in several languages, he has chiefly been attracted to the adaption of literary works—a practice which attracts mixed critical reactions and which has yielded mixed results: *Young Törless*, from Robert Musil, remains one of his best films, and there is much to praise in *The Tin Drum*, the New German Cinema's foremost commercial success, which Günter Grass helped to adapt from his novel. Despite strengths in each, Kleist's *Michael Kolhaas* and Marguerite Yourcenar's *Coup de grace* turned out uneven for quite different reasons. The admirable *Lost Honor of Katharina Blum* comes from a Heinrich Böll story; the problematic *Circle of Deceit* from the novel by Nicolas Born.

Among "original" projects, on the other hand, are *A Degree of Murder*, a failure by all accounts; the fine *A Free Woman*; and the excellent *Sudden Wealth of the Poor People of Kombach*.

Despite the variety of his subjects, Schlöndorff is almost invariably drawn to material that allows him expression as social critic. All the films cited above share this characteristic. Some of his projects have been courageously political: *Katharina Blum* is an undisguised attack on Germany's powerful right-wing, scandal-mongering press, which serves large-scale social repression. As notable are his leading contributions to three collaborative documentaries: *Germany in Autumn*, a response to the authoritarian climate in the country in the wake of the Baader-Meinhof affair; *The Candidate*, shot during the election campaign and examining the career of ultra-conservative Christian Social Unionist Franz Josef Strauss; and *War and Peace*, an agit-prop film essay on the deployment of new American nuclear missiles in the Federal Republic.

Schlöndorff's major theme is the temptation toward moral and political equivocation within an ambiguous or malignant social order, and his films are wryly or skeptically realistic about any hoped-for solutions, even courting controversy. *A Free Woman* chastens unbridled feminist idealism; *Circle of Deceit* (made prior to the Israeli invasion of Lebanon) refuses to take sides in the Lebanese conflict.

Margarethe von Trotta, to whom he is married, has performed in a number of Schlöndorff's films and is a frequent collaborator on his scripts; interestingly, her own work as director is characterized not only by a polish equal to Schlöndorff's and similar political inspiration but also by a compelling intelligence and power of evocation.

—Herbert Reynolds

SCHOEDSACK, ERNEST B. American. Born Ernest Beaumont Schoedsack in Council Bluffs, Iowa, 8 June 1893. Married actress Ruth Rose, about 1926; son: Peter. Career: runs away from home, works with engineering road gangs in San Francisco area; becomes surveyor; before WW I—job as cameraman for Mack Sennett secured through brother Felix (G.F.) Schoedsack; 1916—enlists in Photographic Dept. of Signal Corps, goes to France; then captain in Red Cross photographic unit; 1918—following Armistice remains in Europe as freelance newsreel cameraman; 1919—meets Merian C. Cooper while on way to Poland to cover Russian invasion; 1922—invited by Cooper, covering world cruise for *The New York Times*, to replace project's cameraman; on return to U.S., collaborates with Cooper and newspaper correspondent Marguerite Harrison on film project about migratory tribes of Iran (*Grass*); 1924—Paramount takes up distribution of *Grass*, funds *Chang*; 1925—accompanies William Beebe expedition to Galapagos islands; during WW II—while in Air Force, testing photographic equipment at high altitudes, suffers severe eye injury when he drops face mask; subsequent operations fail to correct injury. Died 23 December 1979.

Films (as co-producer and co-director): 1925—*Grass* (+co-sc, co-ph—documentary); 1927—*Chang* (documentary); 1929—*The Four Feathers*; (as director): 1931—*Rango* (+pr); 1932—*The Most Dangerous Game (The Hounds of Zaroff)* (co-d, +co-pr); 1933—*King Kong* (co-d, +co-pr); *Son of Kong*; *Blind Adventure*; 1934—*Long Lost Father*; 1935—*The Last Days of Pompeii*; 1937—*Trouble in Morocco*; *Outlaws of the Orient*; 1940—*Dr. Cyclops*; 1949—*Mighty Joe Young*; 1952—*This Is Cinerama* (d prologue only, uncredited).

Publications:

On SCHOEDSACK:

Books—*The Making of King Kong* by Orville Goldner and George Turner, Cranbury, N.J. 1975; *The Girl in the Hairy Paw* edited by Ronald Gottesman and Harry Geduld, New York 1976; articles—"Prehistoric Monsters Roar and Hiss for the Sound Film" by Andrew R. Boone in *Popular Science Monthly* (New York), 1933. "Merian C. Cooper Is the Kind of Creative Showman Today's Movies Badly Need" by Rudy Behlmer in *Films in Review* (New York), January 1966; "Creating Film Magic for the Original *King Kong*" by L.G. Dunn in *American Cinematographer* (Los Angeles), January 1977; "The Making of the Original *King Kong*" in *American Cinematographer* (Los Angeles), January 1977; "RKO: They Also Served" in *Monthly Film Bulletin* (London), December 1979.

*   *   *

Ernest B. Schoedsack's initial fame as a filmmaker came from his work in the documentary mode, directing "natural dramas" as he and his partner Merian C. Cooper called the films. Schoedsack's spirit for adventure in these pictures can be traced to the kind of life he himself led. He began his film career simply enough as a cameraman with the Mack Sennett Keystone Studios. When World War I broke out Schoedsack enlisted with the photographic section of the Signal Corps. He was stationed in France where he gained a great deal of film experience as a newsreel cameraman. With the signing of the Armistice, Schoedsack decided to remain in Europe and aid the Poles in their battle against the Russians. While in Poland Schoedsack continued to make newsreels. However, this occupation was mainly a cover to disguise the fact that he was smuggling supplies and Poles out of Russian-occupied territory.

It was in Poland that Schoedsack met his future partner Merian C. Cooper. Like Schoedsack, Cooper was an American who wanted to help the Polish people in their struggle for freedom. Cooper's exploits during the Russian-Polish conflict resulted in his being imprisoned by the Russians as a spy. Fortunately he managed to escape before he could be executed. The true-life adventures of both Cooper and Schoedsack make it easy to see why these two sought out the most distant, difficult, and dangerous locations they could find for their films.

Their first motion picture collaboration, titled *Grass*, concerned the yearly migration of the Bakhtiari tribes in Persia as they crossed over the Zardeh Kuh mountain range to find graz-

ing land for their sheep and cattle. Although the trip was long and treacherous, Cooper and Schoedsack made the journey with the tribesmen, filming every step of the way. Back home *Grass* was an extremely successful film, and along with *Nanook of the North*, helped to set the style for documentary travelogues.

Their next project together, *Chang*, was a documentary film set in China, but with a more centralized story line than *Grass*. This film dealt with one man's efforts to protect his family from the dangers of nature. In order to help dramatize the story, some events in the film were staged. For example, the climactic elephant stampede toward the end of the film was directed at a mock village so that no lives would be endangered. However, audiences in America were none the wiser, and *Chang* played to large crowds on Broadway.

With each successive film Cooper and Schoedsack moved more and more toward fiction, although their films still retained a documentary look. For example, their next film, *The Four Feathers*, had background scenes filmed in Africa, while the principal actors were filmed on a Hollywood stage. Eventually Cooper and Schoedsack moved their filmmaking partnership entirely to Hollywood and away from real locations. However, they continued to make films in the documentary style, as shown by their most famous film of all, *King Kong*.

As a work of fiction, *King Kong* is a fantasy version of Cooper and Schoedsack's ultimate documentary adventure—a journey to a faraway uncharted island in search of the "Eighth Wonder of World." The film was the box-office surprise of 1933 and it is still popular 50 years later.

After *King Kong* Schoedsack directed little of any real note. He directed two more giant ape pictures, *Son of Kong* and *Mighty Joe Young*. An accident during World War II left Schoedsack partially blinded. However, his documentary films by themselves have earned Schoedsack an important place in the tradition of non-fiction filmmaking.

—Linda J. Obalil

SCHORM, EVALD. Czech. Born in Prague, 15 December 1931. Educated at FAMU Film Faculty, Prague, 1957-62. Married secretary Blanka Schormová. Career: 1949-56—works in construction; 1961—assistant director to Zdeněk Podskalský; 1962-71—senior lecturer on FAMU Film Faculty; begins directing documentaries at Short Film, Prague; 1963—TV directing begins; 1967—theatrical directing begins; 1974—begins experimental work with Magic Lantern theater. Address: Krkonošská 10, 120 00 Praha 2, Ceskoslovensko.

Films (as director): 1959—*Kdo své nebe neunese (Too Much to Carry)* (short); *Blok 15 (Block 15)* (+co-sc); 1961—"Kostelník" [Sexton] shot in *Zurnál FAMU (The FAMU Newsreel)*; *Spadla s měsíce (She Fell from the Moon)* (ass't d only); *Jan Konstantin* (+sc, ed); *Turista (The Tourist)* (+co-sc); 1962—*Země zemi (Country to Country)* (+sc); *Helsinky 62 (Helsinki 62)* (+sc); *Stromy a lidé (Trees and People)* (+sc); 1963—*Komorní harmonie (Chamber Harmony)* (+sc, for TV); *Zeleznicáři (Railwaymen)* (+sc); *Zít svuj život (To Live One's Life, Living One's Life)* (+sc); 1964—*Proč? (Why?)* (+sc); *Každý den odvahu (Every Day Courage, Courage for Every Day)*; "Dum radosti" [House of Pleasure] episode of *Perlicky na dně (Pearls in the Deep)*; 1965—*Zrcadlení (Reflection)* (+co-sc); *Odkaz (Heritage)* (+sc); *Sukovo trio (Suk's Trio)* (+sc, for TV); 1966—*Zalm (The Psalm)* (+co-sc); *Návrat ztraceného syna (The Return of the Prodigal Son)*

(+co-sc); *Gramo von Balet* (+co-sc, for TV); *Pět holek na krku (Five Girls to Cope With)*; 1967—*Král a žena (The King and the Woman)* (for TV); 1968—*Carmen nejen podle Bizeta (Carmen, Not According to Bizet)* (+co-sc); "Chlebové střevíčky" [Shoes Made of Bread] episode of *Pražské noci (Prague Nights)* (+co-sc); *Farářuv konec (The Priest's End)* (+co-sc); 1969—*Rozhovory (Dialogues)* (+co-sc, for TV); *Den sedmý, osmá noc (7th Day, 8th Night)* (+co-sc); 1970—*Psi a lidé (Dogs and People)*; *Koncert pro studenty (Concert for Students)* (for TV); *Z mého života (From My Life)* (for TV); *Lítost (Regret)* (for TV); *Sestry (Sisters)* (+sc, for TV); 1971—*Lepší pán (A Well-To-Do Gentleman)* (for TV); 1972—*Úklady a láska (Intrigue and Love)* (for TV); 1974—*Láska v barvách karnevalu (Love in Mardi Gras Colors)* (co-d, Magic Lantern program); 1976—*Etuda o zkoušce (An Essay on Rehearsing)* (+sc); 1977—*Kouzelný cirkus (The Magic Circus)* (co-d, +co-sc, Magic Lantern program); 1978—*Sněhová královna (The Snow Queen)* (Magic Lantern program); *Město mé naděje (The Town of My Hope)* (collaboration only); 1980—*Noční zkouška (The Night Rehearsal)* (Magic Lantern program).

Roles: 1966—Husband in *O slavnosti a hostech (An Account of the Party and the Guests)* (Němec); chaplain in *Hotel pro cizince (Hotel for Strangers)* (Máša); 1968—Kostka in *Zert (The Joke)* (Jireš); 1969—form in *Bludiště moci (The Labyrinth of Power)* (Weigl, for TV); 1974—Master Rudolf in *Bástyasétány 74 (Bastion Promenade 74)* (Gazdag); 1980—Jílek in *Útěky domu (Escapes Home)* (Jireš).

Publications:

By SCHORM:

Articles—interview in *Film a doba* (Prague), no.2, 1966; interview by Claude Sembain in *Image et son* (Paris), no.221, 1968.

On SCHORM:

Books—*3 ½ po druhé* by Jiří Janoušek, Prague 1969; *Evald Schorm* by Jan Bernard, Prague 1979 (unpublished ms.); article—"Nová vlna v odstupu" by Jaroslav Boček in *Film a doba* (Prague), no.12, 1966.

*   *   *

It was a noteworthy class that studied directing together at the Prague FAMU under the leadership of Otakar Vávra—Věra Chytilová, Jiří Menzel, Jan Schmidt, Evald Schorm. Each of these individuals had a personal but emphatic influence on the development of Czech cinema. Evald Schorm finished his studies with the short film *Turista (The Tourist)*, in which he attempts to depict the inner world of a worker who has failed both in his work and in his personal life. Upon receiving his certification, Schorm went off to Krátký film Praha and made, in rapid succession, *Helsinky 62 (Heksinki 62)*, a report on the Eighth World Youth Festival; *Země zemí (Country to Country)*, which saw the beginning of years of collaboration with cameraman Jan Spáta and composer Ivan Klusák; *Žit svuj život (To Live One's Life)*, an attempt at a portrait of the modern Czech photographer Josef Sudek; and the film *Proč (Why?)*, in which he tries to portray the conflict between the stated wishes of society and the facts of life, to expose the tension between appearance and substance. In the documentary inquiry *Zrcadlení (Reflection)*,

produced later, Schorm is interested in man at the boundary between life and death, his view on questions of the meaning of life, values, the way one lives, and one's attitude toward death.

He made his full-length debut in 1964 with *Každý den odvahu (Courage for Every Day)*. In this film he captures the inner crisis of a man who had devoted a piece of his life to false ideals, a man at the turning point between youth and maturity, and his disillusionment. Then came *Návrat ztraceného syna (The Return of the Prodigal Son)*, the drama of a neurotic trying to find himself, his lost inner values and confidence. His next film *Pět holek na krku (Five Girls to Cope With)* portrays the hopes and anxieties of a young girl growing up without friendships, sympathy and love during the period when a person's character is being molded. The film is an analysis of the mechanism of envy, malice and hostility and its effect on the human soul. The farce *Farářuv konec (The End of a Priest)*, which deals with a bogus priest, and the parable *Psi a lidé (Dogs and People)* mark the end of Schorm's work in fictional feature films.

In the 1970's Schorm collaborated in film only rarely. His major creative domain became opera and theater directing. Most notable were his film versions of Janáček's opera *Její pastorkyňa (Her Stepdaughter)*, Weber's *Der Freischütz (The Marksman)*, Mozart's *Die Zauberflöte (The Magic Flute)*, and Martinu's *Arianda (Arianda)*, *Tři přání (Three Wishes)*, and *Julieta aneb snář (Julieta or the Dreambook)*. His directing of Shakespeare (*Hamlet*), Dostoevsky (*The Brothers Karamazov, Crime and Punishment*), Brecht (*Don Juan*), and Hrabal (*Bambini di Praga*) confirms his standing as one of the most important Czech theatrical directors of our time.

Schorm's film oeuvre has met with varying critical responses both in Czechoslovakia and abroad. His documents are a meditation on a theme provided by real life, documentaristic essays that strive for a more profound, philosophical expression of reality. His works inquire into the meaning of man's world and life and examine man's relationship to society and to history. Schorm is a sensitive diagnostician of social life; his approach is characterized by emotional subtlety, integrity, and humility. He persistently and repeatedly pursues the meaning of things, the essence, and the truth about man and his world. Perhaps it is this creative type that best embodies the words of the writer Karel Capek: "...passionately and patiently you demand better vision and better hearing, clearer understanding and greater love. You create so you can recognize in your work the form and the perfection of things. Your service to things is a devine service."

—Vladimír Opěla

SCHRADER, PAUL. American. Born in Grand Rapids, Michigan, 22 July 1946. Educated in ministry of Christian Reformed religion at Calvin College, Grand Rapids, Michigan, graduated 1968; took summer classes in film at Columbia University, New York; University of California at Los Angeles film school, M.A. in Cinema. Career: while student at Calvin College, begins writing film reviews for school paper; church denounces movies for "worldliness," dismissed from paper; 1968—moves to Los Angeles to study at UCLA film school, begins writing film criticism for the Los Angeles *Free Press*; becomes editor of *Cinema* (Beverly Hills); 1972—begins writing *Taxi Driver* while hospitalized for ulcer; 1975—release of *The Yakuza*, first script filmed, a collaboration with Robert Towne. Agent: Jeff Berg, ICM.

Films (as scriptwriter): 1975—*The Yakuza* (Pollack) (co-sc); 1976—*Taxi Driver* (Scorsese); *Obsession* (DePalma); 1977—*Close Encounters of the Third Kind* (Spielberg) (co-sc, uncredited); 1977—*Rolling Thunder* (Flynn) (co-sc); (as director and scriptwriter): 1978—*Blue Collar*; 1979—*Raging Bull* (Scorsese) (co-sc—received screen credit); 1979—*Hardcore*; *American Gigolo*; *Old Boyfriends* (Tewkesbury) (co-sc, +exec. pr); 1982—*Cat People* (d only).

Publications:

By SCHRADER:

Articles—interview by F. Golchan in *Cinématographe* (Paris), June 1976; "*Taxi Driver*: Gespräch mit Drehbuchautor Paul Schrader" by M. Ratschewa and K. Eder in *Medium* (Frankfurt), July 1976; "Screenwriter: *Taxi Driver's* Paul Schrader" by R. Thompson in *Filmkritik* (Munich), October 1976; "Blue Collar" interview by Gary Crowdus and D. Georgakas in *Cineaste* (New York), winter 1977/78; "Robert Bresson, Possibly" in *Film Comment* (New York), September/October 1977; interview by J.-P. Le Pavec and D. Rabourdin in *Cinéma* (Paris), November 1978; interview by J.-M. Benard in *Cinématographe* (Paris), December 1979; interview by M.P. Carducci in *Millimeter* (New York), February 1979; "A Walk on the Dark Side...of Paul Schrader", interview by T. Crawley in *Films Illustrated* (London), February 1979; "Paul Schrader's Guilty Pleasures" in *Film Comment* (New York), January/February 1979; "Gigolos", interview by M. Tuchman in *Film Comment* (New York), March/April 1980; "The Conversation: John Gregory Dunne and Paul Schrader" in *Esquire* (New York), July 1982.

On SCHRADER:

Articles—"Trajectoire de Paul Schrader" by S. Toubiana and L. Bloch-Morhange in *Cahiers du cinéma* (Paris), November 1978; "Helden-Kino" by C. Lenssen in *Medium* (Frankfurt), May 1979; "Bilder amerikanischer Wirklichkeit" by W. Baer in *Film und Ton* (Munich), July 1979; "Hiring a New Gigolo" in *Films Illustrated* (London), September 1979; "Dossier: Hollywood 79: Paul Schrader" by F. Cuel in *Cinématographe* (Paris), March 1979; "Schrader's Inferno" by S. Kahan in *Focus on Film* (London), August 1979; "American Gigolo and Other Matters" by J. Wells in *Film Comment* (New York), March/April 1980; "That Schrader Boy! What's He Up To Now?" by Michael Blowen in the *Boston Globe*, 11 April 1982.

*   *   *

The conflict between artistic and intellectual integrity on the one hand and commercialism on the other has rarely been more evident than in the screenplays and films of Paul Schrader. If a filmmaker wants to make feature films which "say something" and which have "artistic merit," they must also make money at the box office. Profit is the primary factor in achieving directorial longevity in Hollywood and is especially important for talent just starting out.

What Schrader has in common with others of his generation of writers and directors (e.g. George Lucas, Francis F. Coppola, Martin Scorsese, Brian De Palma) is an independence of mind and spirit and an unwillingness, at least early on in their careers, to knuckle under to the Hollywood establishment. Schrader

wanted to bring to the screen a new kind of American cinema akin to the European tradition of poetic and personal films such as those of Bresson, Fellini, and Bergman. "We are trying to make the money so that we can direct and write pictures of artistic merit," he has said, "given our record of commerical success, perhaps the major studios will give us a chance to create our own personal, poetic films".

There is little doubt that Schrader is one of the most personal filmmakers working today in Hollywood. While his films are often badly flawed in plot and character development, one can sense a very strong, fresh and honest approach to themes which are important contemporary moral and ethical issues and are very deeply felt by the writer. The dilemmas, conflicts, and agonies of his characters seem, in many ways, to be his own. Film seems to be a working out of his own personal problems and confusions and it is this trait which connects him to the tradition of the European cinema.

He grew up in a very strict Calvinist home in the heart of middle America and did not see his first motion picture until he was 18 years old. He became a film addict, seeing many pictures a week and developing a strong affinity for the medium. He eventually left Grand Rapids for Los Angeles which brought out in him anxieties and frustrations that would find their way into his scripts and films in characters such as Travis Bickel (*Taxi Driver*), Jake Van Dorn (*Hardcore*), and Julian Kay (*American Gigolo*).

Schrader entered the film world as a critic, writing reviews for the Los Angeles *Free Press*. He also wrote serious academic criticism but none of this really satisfied his strong creative urge and the need to work out some of his inner conflicts through the film medium.

His first script sale was *The Yakuza*. It was a bittersweet success. Robert Towne, an already successful screenwriter and script doctor, was called in to rework parts of Schrader's script and he was forced to share writing credit with Towne. There was a bitter and unsuccessful legal fight to have Towne's name removed from the credits. *The Yakuza* is the story of Japanese gangsters and has little of what would later characterize Schrader's mature work except perhaps for the fascination with violence and a central character caught up in a life and death struggle while facing hard moral choices. *Obsession* was also a collaboration. It concerns a violent kidnapping, a theme appearing in several of Schrader's scripts and films, most importantly in *Taxi Driver* and *Hardcore*. In these two films the victim is rescued from bondage by an enraged and driven hero.

Of the films which Schrader wrote but did not direct (including *Rolling Thunder* and *Old Boyfriends*), *Taxi Driver* is the most significant. This film was the result of an uneasy collaboration between Schrader and Martin Scorsese. There were many personal and intellectual conflicts between the two, yet at that point in their careers they did share a similarly raw, violent view of urban American society. Scorsese's *Mean Streets* undoubtedly appealed to Schrader, and much of the crude, violent energy and anger in *Mean Streets* found its way into *Taxi Driver* as well as other Schrader scripts and films. With *Taxi Driver* we see all of the dilemmas and conflicts which will torture the flesh and the spirit of his protagonists in his later works. These themes include vengeance, sexual bondage and degradation, corruption, both political and personal, and explosive outrage. His films are characterized by much blood and gore, with characters living underground or on the very fringe of straight society. There is an overall sense in his work that the individual has no control even though he thinks he does for a time. Hostile forces are always ready to destroy the individual and the only weapon is that firestorm of rage, that superhuman burst of violent energy needed to fight off a superior enemy. Travis Bickel, Jake Van

Dorn, and *Rolling Thunder's* Charlie Rane are good examples of this aspect of his work.

Schrader's first directorial effort was *Blue Collar*. This film explores the relationship between the "American Dream" and the growing impossibility of its realization due to corruption and greed. The work is cynical and passive, lacking conviction in the writing and directing. *Hardcore* presents an even more improbable view of America. The contrasts which Schrader sets up in the film, between the straight-laced morality of middle America and the plastic sleaze of Los Angeles are artificial and unconvincing on the screen, yet the idea of separate societies within one culture is a fascinating one. The complexity of the theme is undercut by weak, predictable melodrama and preposterous plot situations which can not support the heavy ideas nor the characters. The romp through the sado-masochist sex den is more comic than shocking. It is so exaggerated and preposterous that Schrader undoes any sort of credibility he has gained with his audience.

American Gigolo is another case in point. Schrader has not managed to incorporate a serious subject within a commericial formula. Julian Kaye, the handsome gigolo, is totally bland. The director gives us nothing to love or hate. Julian just sits there on the screen modeling the latest designer clothes, ordering food in fancy restaurants, adjusting a print hanging on his wall, etc. *American Gigolo* could have been a brilliant film if Julian had been an active character instead of a passive one. He fits in well, however, with all the other visual trivia on the screen and the end result can only be a trivial film, unworthy of a man of Schrader's talent.

Cat People is perhaps the most atypical of Schrader's films. It fits into the early 1980s trend towards fantastic and exotic films, and while it reveals least of the filmmaker as a person it is the finest example of his writing and directing abilities. The socially realistic films seem to clutter Schrader's writing and directing, resulting in a lack of direction and focus. Not so with *Cat People*. His vision is fully realized in a smooth plot and with consistent characters who are fully believable. There is a lyricism and haunting beauty which colors even the most violent scenes. The underlying theme is the notion that we can not avoid being what we are. The tremendous urge to act in other Schrader characters is translated here, through the metaphor of the cat, into the need to be. The film is about the subconscious, repression and social conformity. *Cat People* is Schrader's most polished work in which he has managed to fuse his intellectual and commercial tendencies.

—Anthony T. Allegro

SCOLA, ETTORE. Italian. Born in Trevico, Avellino, 10 May 1931. Educated in law, University of Rome. Career: early 1950s—while student contributes to humor magazine *Marc' Aurelio*; 1953—begins working in films as scriptwriter; forms ongoing writing partnership with Ruggero Maccari; 1964—directing debut. Recipient: Cesar Award, France, for *C'eravamo tanto amati*, 1975; Best Director, Cannes Festival, for *Brutti, sporchi e cattivi*, 1976; Special Jury Prize, Cannes Festival, for *Una giornata particolari*, 1977.

Films (as co-scriptwriter with Ruggero Maccari): 1954—*Un americano a Roma* (Steno); *Due notti con Cleopatra (2 Nights with Cleopatra)*; *Una Parigina a Roma*; 1956—*Lo scapolo* (Pietrangeli); 1958—*Nata di marzo*; 1960—*Il mattatore (Love and*

Larceny); *Adua e le compagne (Love à la Carte)*; *Fantasmi a Roma (Ghosts of Rome)*; "La storia di un soldato (The Soldier)" episode of *L'amore difficile (Erotica, Of Wayward Love)* (Manfredi); 1962—*Anni ruggenti (Roaring Years)* (Zampa); *Il sorpasso (The Easy Life)* (Risi); 1963—*I mostri (The Monsters, Opiate '67, 15 from Rome)* (Risi); *La visita*; (as director and co-scriptwriter): 1964—*Se permette parliamo di donne (Let's Talk About Women)*; *La congiuntura*; *Il gaucho (The Gaucho)* (Risi) (co-sc only); *Alta infedeltà (High Infidelity)* (co-sc only); *Il magnifico cornuto (The Magnificent Cuckold)* (co-sc only); 1965—"Il vittimista" episode of *Thrilling*; *Io la conoscevo bene* (Pietrangeli) (co-sc only); *Made in Italy* (Loy) (co-sc only); 1966—*L'arcidiavolo (Il diavolo innamorato, The Devil in Love)*; *Follie d'estate* (co-sc only); 1967—*Le dolci signore (Anyone Can Play)* (co-sc only); 1968—*Il commissario Pepe*; *Riusciranno i nostri eroi a trovare il loro amico misteriosamente scomparso in Africa?*; 1970—*Dramma della gelosia—Tutti i particolari in cronaca (The Pizza Triangle, A Drama of Jealousy (and Other Things)*; 1971—*Permette? Rocco Papaleo (Rocco Papaleo)*; 1971—*Noi donne siamo fatte cosí (Women: So We Are Made)* (Risi) (co-sc only); 1972—*La piú bella serata della mia vita*; 1973—*Trevico-Torino...Viaggio nel Fiat Nam*; 1974—*C'eravamo tanto amati (We All Loved Each Other So Much)*; 1976—*Brutti, sporchi e cattivi (Down and Dirty)*; one episode of *Signori e signore, buonanotte*; 1977—*Una giornata particolari (A Special Day)*; one episode of *I nuovi mostri (The New Monsters, Viva Italia!)*; 1979—*Che si dice a Roma*; 1980—*La terrazza*; 1981—*Passione d'amore*; 1982—*Il mondo nuovo*; *La Nuit de Varennes*; 1984—*Le Bal*.

Publications:

By SCOLA:

Articles—"Se permettete parliamo di Scola" by J.A. Gili in *Ecran* (Paris), November 1976; interview by P. Carcassonne in *Cinématographe* (Paris), October 1977; interview by A. Tassone in *Image et son* (Paris), November 1977; "Ein besonderer Tag", interview by S. Michelli in *Film und Fernsehen* (Berlin), April 1978.

On SCOLA:

Articles—"Ettore Scola" in *Cinématographe* (Paris), August/-September 1976; "Nous nous sommes tant aimés", dossier in *Image et son* (Paris), no.331bis, 1978; "Biofilmographie d'Ettore Scola" in *Avant-Scène du cinéma* (Paris), 15 June 1979.

* * *

Before directing his own first feature in 1964 Ettore Scola was a writer and illustrator for satirical magazines, a writer for radio, and for movies, mainly comedy, directed by Nanni Loy, Antonio Pietrangeli, and Dino Risi, among others. His scripts have contributed to the fame of such Italian mainstays as Vittorio Gassman, Ugo Tognazzi, and Alberto Sordi.

Gassman speaks of Scola as "meticulous," delving "deeper into the psychology of characters"; Sophia Loren sees him as "continuing the tradition of De Sica and Rossellini . . . sensitive, intelligent," having "a lot of patience with actors" and "a great eye for detail." Stefania Sandrelli says he "understands women better than anybody."

Scola's scripts and 19 feature films confirm these actors' opinions as well as the variety of his subject matter and the intellectuality and humor of his approach. His work has progressed from a particularly Italian kind of comedy—bungling incompetents muddling through desperate situations, war's grotesqueries, life's ironies—to studies of Italians dealing with their history and social environment.

C'eravamo tanti amati, a tribute to Vittorio De Sica, is not only about the difficult and frustrating post-World War II years of three men with class and personal differences who had been close when they fought in the Resistance. It is also a complex survey of 30 years of Italian cinema and its relationship to Italian history, photographed in various appropriate cinema styles. *La terrazza* also examines the Italy-cinema relationship as well as the mores of Italian intellectuals, now middle-aged, no longer creative, and disappointed in their lives and professions.

In *Una giornata particolare* Scola accomplished a skillful integration of plot, theme, setting, acting and photography, demonstrating oppression in a super-organized society without depicting the usual overt violence of the genre. The fluid camera examines facade and interiors of a workers' dwelling. It is May 6, 1938; the Italian dictator is welcoming the German one to Rome. Family talk conveys the excitement and devotion to the Duce's program; the radio blares fascist self-confidence. Two marginal members of this society, a woman and an anti-fascist homosexual, meet by chance and share their humanity for a few hours.

Camera work, details of costume and milieu are integrated into Scola's cinema of ideas unobtrusively. (But see *Brutti, sporchi e cattivi*, literally "dirty, nasty, and bad, for the unavoidably disgusting appearance of everyone and everything in a community far below subsistence level, while *Riusciranno*, set in modern Angola and filmed on location, features an Italian bourgeois's leftover nineteenth century concept of a safari costume.)

In *La Nuit de Varennes* the French Revolution is happening, but there are no starving peasants center stage, and the King who is trying to flee the country does not appear. The film is an essay of thoughts and opinions, fears and worries of mostly upper class people, about monarchy and a changing world. Examining the past to interpret the present continues to be a Scola theme.

—Lillian Schiff

SCORSESE, MARTIN. American. Born in Queens, New York City, 17 November 1942. Educated at Cardinal Hayes High School, Bronx, 1956-60; New York University, 1960-66, B.S., M.A. Married Laraine Brennan, 1965 (divorced); children: Catherine and Terese; Julia Cameron (divorced); children: Domenica and Elizabeth; Isabella Rossellini, 1979. Career: 1960-64—makes a number of award-winning shorts while attending NYU; 1965-69—works on 1st feature, which begins as *Bring on the Dancing Girls* and is released as *Who's That Knocking at My Door*; 1967—makes short, *The Big Shave*, sponsored by Belgian Cinémathèque; 1968—makes several commercials in Britain; 1968-70—teaches filmmaking at NYU; 1969-71—serves as editor on *Woodstock* and in other capacities on other films; 1972—commissioned by Roger Corman to direct *Boxcar Bertha*; 1973—attains 1st critical notice at New York Film Festival with *Mean Streets*; 1976-78—directs 1st rock documentary in 35mm, *The Last Waltz*; 1978-79—stages and partially directs (with aid of Gower Champion) the Broadway musical, *The Act*, with Liza Minnelli. Recipient: Best Director, National Society of Film Critics, for *Taxi Driver*, 1976; Best Director, National Society of Film Critics, for *Raging Bull*, 1980. Agent: Ufland Agency, Beverly Hills, California.

Films (as director of short films): 1963—*What's a Nice Girl Like You Doing in a Place Like This?* (+sc); 1964—*It's Not Just You, Murray* (+co-sc); 1967—*The Big Shave* (+sc); (as feature director): 1969—*Who's That Knocking at My Door?* (+sc, ro as gangster); 1972—*Boxcar Bertha* (+ro as client of bordello); 1973—*Mean Streets* (+co-sc, ro as *Shorty the Hit Man*); 1974—*Italianamerican* (+co-sc—documentary short); *Alice Doesn't Live Here Anymore* (+ro as customer at Mel and Ruby's); 1976—*Taxi Driver* (+ro as *Passenger*); 1977—*New York, New York*; 1978—*The Last Waltz* (documentary); *American Boy*; 1979—*The Raging Bull*; 1982—*The King of Comedy*.

Roles (in films not directed): 1976—*Cannonball* (Bartel); 1979—interviewee in *Hollywood's Wild Angel* (Blackwood).

Publications:

By SCORSESE:

Articles—"The Filming of Mean Streets", interview by A.C. Bobrow in *Filmmakers Newsletter* (Ward Hill, Mass.), January 1974; interview by William Wolf in *Cue* (New York), 3 March 1975; Martin Scorsese seminar in *Dialogue on Film* (Washington, D.C.), April 1975; interview by Claude Beylie in *Ecran* (Paris), July/August 1975; "Martin Scorsese, Now They're Knocking at His Door!", interview by M. Carducci in *Millimeter* (New York), v.3, no.5, 1975; interview by Michel Ciment and M. Henry in *Positif* (Paris), June 1975; "The Making of *Alice Doesn't Live Here Anymore*", interview by S. Howard in *Filmmakers Newsletter* (Ward Hill, Mass.), March 1975; "It's a Personal Thing for Me", interview by F. Macklin in *Film Heritage* (New York), spring 1975; interview by M. Rosen in *Film Comment*, New York, March/April 1975; "Scorsese on *Taxi Driver* and Herrmann" by C. Amata in *Focus on Film* (London), summer/autumn 1976; interview in *Newsweek* (New York), 16 May 1977; interview by H. Béhar in *Image et son* (Paris), December 1977; "Taxi Dancer", interview by J. Kaplan in *Film Comment* (New York), July/August 1977; interview by David Sterritt in the *Christian Science Monitor* (Boston), 1 May 1978; "Martin Scorsese's Guilty Pleasures" in *Film Comment* (New York), September/October 1978; "American Boy", interview by L. Sweet and R. Combs in *Sight and Sound* (London), winter 1977/78; "Mes plaisirs coupables" in *Positif* (Paris), April 1981.

On SCORSESE:

Articles—"Martin Scorsese" by P. Gardner in *Action* (Los Angeles), May/June 1975; "La Passion de Saint Martin Scorsese" by M. Henry in *Positif* (Paris), June 1975; "Martin Scorsese" in *Hollywood Renaissance* by Diane Jacobs, New York 1977; "Une Nouvelle Vague américain: Martin Scorsese" by M. Elia in *Séquences* (Montreal), October 1979; "The Italian Connection in the American Film: Coppola, Cimino, Scorsese" by P. Rule in *America* (New York), 17 November 1979; "Color Fading: Raging Bull" by R. Edelman in *Films in Review* (New York), December 1980; "Un Patrimonie spirituel", special section by M. Henry in *Positif* (Paris), April 1980; "Scorsese gegen Eastman" in *Film und Fernsehen* (Berlin), June 1981; "Martin Scorsese vu par Michael Powell" in *Positif* (Paris), April 1981; film—*Movies Are My Life* by Peter Hayden, Great Britain 1978.

* * *

Evaluation of contemporary work must always be tentative: we lack the perspective that only the passage of time can give, and posterity may reverse out judgements. It is nonetheless necessary for the critic to single out what s/he feels to be of particular importance and stature. At present, with regard to the Hollywood cinema of the last ten years, two directors appear to stand out head-and-shoulders above the rest, and it is possible to argue high claims for their work on both formal and thematic grounds: Scorsese and Cimino. The work of each is strongly rooted in the American and Hollywood past, yet is at the same time audacious and innovative. Cimino's work can be read as at once the culmination of the Ford/Hawks tradition and a radical re-thinking of its premises; Scorsese's involves an equally drastic re-thinking of the Hollywood genres, either combining them in such a way as to foreground their contradictions (western and horror film in *Taxi Driver*) or disconcertingly reversing the expectations they traditionally arouse (the musical in *New York, New York*, the boxing movie and "biopic" in *Raging Bull*). Both directors have further disconcerted audiences and critics alike in their radical deviations from the principles of classical narrative: hence *Heaven's Gate* is received by the American critical establishment with blank incomprehension and self-defensive ridicule, while Scorsese is accused (by Andrew Sarris, among others) of lacking a sense of structure. Hollywood films are not expected to be innovative, difficult, and challenging, and must suffer the consequences of authentic originality (as opposed to the latest in fashionable *chic* that often passes for it).

The Cimino/Scorsese parallel ends at this shared tension between tradition and innovation. While *Heaven's Gate* can be read as the answer to (and equal of) *Birth of a Nation*, Scorsese has never ventured into the vast fresco of American epic, preferring to explore relatively small, limited subjects (though his current project is *The Last Temptation of Christ*), the wider significance of the films arising from the implications those subjects are made to reveal. He starts always from the concrete and specific—a character, a relationship: the vicissitudes in the careers and love-life of two musicians (*New York, New York*), the violent public and private life of a famous boxer (*Raging Bull*), the crazy aspirations of an obsessed nonentity (*King of Comedy*). In each case, the subject is remorselessly followed through to a point where it reveals and dramatizes the fundamental ideological tensions of our culture.

His early works are divided between self-confessedly personal works related to his own Italian-American background *Who's That Knocking at my Door?*, *Mean Streets*) and genre movies (*Boxcar Bertha*, *Alice Doesn't Live Here Anymore*). The distinction was never absolute, and the later films effectively collapse it. Each of the last four films takes as its starting point not only a specific character but a specific star: Robert De Niro. The Scorsese/De Niro relationship has proved one of the most fruitful director/star collaborations in the history of the cinema; its ramifications are extremely complex. De Niro's star image is central to this, poised as it is on the borderline between "star" and "actor"—the charismatic personality, the self-effacing impersonator of diverse characters. It is this ambiguity in the De Niro star persona that makes possible the ambiguity in the actor/director relationship: the degree to which Scorsese identifies with the characters De Niro plays, versus the degree to which he distances himself from them. It is this tension (communicated very directly to the spectator) between identification and repudiation that gives the films their uniquely disturbing quality.

This quality combined with their radicalism. Cimino (at least in *Heaven's Gate*) and Scorsese are the only two Hollywood directors of consequence who have succeeded in sustaining the radical critique of American culture that developed in the seventies into the Reagan era of retrenchment and recuperation.

Again, the approaches are completely different: where Cimino undertakes to rewrite American history/mythology, Scorsese probes the tensions within and between individuals until they reveal their fundamental, cultural nature. Few films have chronicled so painfully and abrasively as *New York, New York* the impossibility of successful heterosexual relations within a culture built upon sexual inequality. The conflicts arising out of the man's constant need for self-assertion and domination, the woman's bewildered alterations between rebellion and complexity are—owing to the peculiarities of the director/star/character/spectator relationship—simultaneously experienced and analysed.

Raging Bull goes much further in penetrating to the root causes of masculine aggression and violence, linking socially approved violence in the ring to socially disapproved violence outside it, violence against men to violence against women. It carries to its extreme that reversal of generic expectations so characteristic of Scorsese's work: a boxing melodrama/success story, it is the ultimate anti-*Rocky*; a filmed biography of a person still living, it flouts every unwritten rule of veneration for the protagonist, celebration of his achievements, triumph after tribulation, etc. Ostensibly an account of the life of Jake LaMotta, it amounts to a veritable case history of a paranoic, and can perhaps only be fully understood through Freud. Fundamental here is Freud's discovery of universal, constitutional bisexuality and its repression in our culture in the interests of constructing the social norms of "masculinity" and "femininity." More directly relevant to the film are Freud's assertion that every case of paranoia, without exception, has its roots in repressed homosexual impulse; that the primary homosexual love-objects are likely to be father and brothers; that there are four "principle forms" of paranoia, each of which amounts to a *denial* of homosexual attraction (see the analysis of the Schreber case and its postscript, *Case Histories*, Volume 2, Penguin edition). *Raging Bull* exemplifies all of this with startling (if perhaps largely inadvertent) thoroughness: all four of the "principle forms" are enacted in Scorsese's presentation of LaMotta, especially significant being the paranoid's projection of his repressed desires for men on to the woman he ostensibly loves. The film becomes nothing less than a statement about the disastrous consequences, for men and women alike, of the repression of bisexuality in our culture.

King of Comedy may seem at first sight a slighter work than its two predecessors, but its implications are no less radical and subversive: one of the most complete statements about the emotional and spiritual bankruptcy of patriarchal capitalism today that the cinema has given us. The symbolic Father (once incarnated in figures of mythic force, like Abraham Lincoln) is here revealed in his essential emptiness, loneliness, and inadequacy. The "children" (De Niro and Sandra Bernhard) behave in exemplary Oedipal fashion: he wants to *be* the father, she wants to screw the father. The film moves to twin climaxes. First, the father must be reduced to total impotence (to the point of actual immobility) in order to be loved; then Bernhard can croon to him "You're gonna love me/like nobody's loved me," and remove her clothes. Meanwhile, DeNiro tapes his TV act which (exclusively concerned with childhood, his parents, self-depreciation) culminates in a joke about throwing up over his father's new shoes: the shoes he is (metaphorically) now standing in. Ambivalence towards the father (the simultaneous desire to be him and vomit on him, make love to him and castrate him); the hatred-in-rivalry of "brother" and "sister'; the son's need for paternal recognition (albeit in fantasy) before he can announce himself to the woman he (very dubiously) loves; the irrelevance of the mother (a mere, intermittently intrusive, off-screen voice) to any "serious"—i.e. Oedipal patriarchal—concerns: *King of Comedy* constitutes one of the most rigorous assaults we have on the structures of the patriarchal nuclear family and the impossible desires, fantasies, frustrations, and violence those structures generate: an assault, that is, on the fundamental premises of our culture.

—Robin Wood

SEATON, GEORGE. American. Born George Stenius in South Bend, Indiana, 17 April 1911. Educated at Detroit Public Schools; one year at Phillips Exeter; graduated from Central High School, Detroit; Jesse Bonstelle Theatre School, Detroit. Married Phyllis Loughton, 1936; children: Mary and Marc. Career: 1930—moves to New York, tries acting on Broadway; begins writing stories for *True Confessions* and other publications; assumes nom de plume "George Seaton" from character in Philip Barry play *Holiday*; 1933—returns to Detroit, takes lead in new radio show being produced at WXYZ, "The Lone Ranger"; hired in New York by Sam Marx to write for MGM, moves to Los Angeles; 1934—with Robert Pirosh selected by Irving Thalberg to write *A Day at the Races* for Marx Brothers; 1940—begins association with producer William Perlberg on *The Doctor Takes a Wife* (through 1965); 1941—with Perlberg moves from Columbia to 20th Century-Fox; 1951—Seaton and Perlberg move to Paramount, given own producing unit; 1955-58—president of the Academy of Motion Picture Arts and Sciences; also served as president of the Screen Writers Guild, and vice president of the Screen Directors Guild and vice president of the Motion Picture Relief Fund. Died in Beverly Hills, 28 July 1979. Recipient: Best Screenplay Academy Award for *Miracle on 34th Street*, 1947; Best Screenplay Academy Award for *The Country Girl*, 1954; Jean Hersholt Humanitarian Award, Academy of Motion Picture Arts and Sciences, 1961; Laurel Award, Writers Guild of America, 1961.

Films (as scriptwriter): 1935—*Student Tour* (Riesner) (story only); *The Winning Ticket* (Riesner) (co-story only); 1937—*A Day at the Races* (Wood) (co-sc); 1940—*The Doctor Takes a Wife* (Hall) (co-sc); *This Thing Called Love* (Hall) (co-sc); 1941—*That Night in Rio* (Cummings) (co-sc); *Moon Over Miami* (Lang) (co-adapt); *Charley's Aunt* (Mayo); *Bedtime Story* (Hall) (contributed to treatment only); 1942—*10 Gentlemen from West Point* (Hathaway) (co-sc); *The Magnificent Dope* (Lang); 1943—*The Meanest Man in the World* (Lanfield) (co-sc); *Coney Island* (Lang); *The Song of Bernadette* (King); (as director and scriptwriter): 1945—*Billy Rose's Diamond Horseshoe*; *Junior Miss*; 1946—*The Cockeyed Miracle* (Simon) (play basis only); 1947—*The Shocking Miss Pilgrim*; *Miracle on 34th Street (The Big Heart)*; 1948—*Apartment for Peggy*; 1949—*Chicken Every Sunday* (co-sc); 1950—*The Big Lift*; *For Heaven's Sake*; (as co-producer with William Perlberg, director, and scriptwriter): 1951—*Rhubarb* (Lubin) (co-pr only); 1952—*Aaron Slick from Punkin Crick* (Binyon) (co-pr only); *Anything Can Happen* (co-sc); *Somebody Loves Me* (Brecher) (co-pr only); 1953—*Little Boy Lost*; 1954—*The Country Girl*; 1955—*The Bridges at Toko-Ri* (Robson) (co-pr only); 1956—*The Proud and the Profane*; 1957—*Williamsburg: The Story of a Patriot* (d only—short); *The Tin Star* (Mann) (co-pr only); 1958—*Teacher's Pet* (co-pr, d only); 1959—*But Not for Me* (Lang) (co-pr only); 1960—*The Rat Race* (Mulligan) (co-pr only); 1961—*The Pleasure of His Company* (co-pr, d only); 1962—*The Counterfeit Traitor*; 1963—*The Hook* (co-pr, d only); *Twilight of Honor* (Sagal) (co-pr only); 1965—*36 Hours*; (as director and scriptwriter): 1968—*What's So Bad About Feeling Good* (co-sc, +pr); 1970—*Airport*; 1973—*Showdown*.

Publications:

By SEATON:

Articles—"*Showboat*—Example of Well Planned Photography" in *American Cinematographer* (Los Angeles), August 1951; "Getting Out on a Limb" in *Films and Filming* (London), April 1961.

On SEATON:

Articles—"George Seaton" by Vanessa Brown in *Action* (Los Angeles), July/August 1970; "George Seaton Understands the Fundamental Needs of the Human Heart" by Jerome Simon in *Films in Review* (New York), November 1971; obituary in *Ecran* (Paris), 20 October 1979; obituary in *Variety* (New York), 1 August 1979; obituary in *Cinématographe* (Paris), no.50, 1979; obituary in *The New York Times*, 29 July 1979.

*   *   *

George Seaton's career as a director has been generally undistinguished, except for two films for which he also wrote the screenplays, *Miracle on 34th Street* and *The Country Girl*, and for which he received his two Oscars for best screenplay. The rest of his films have been entertaining, commercially successful, but "lightweight." Most of his movies have big name stars in roles which were ostensibly tailor-made for their particular talents, and thus the audience is more impressed by the actors than the director or story.

Yet there is some merit in the ability to allow (or make) popular box office stars, about whom audiences have a preconceived notion of how they should look and act, appear fresh. *The Country Girl* did this for William Holden and Bing Crosby, as well as providing Grace Kelly with her Oscar-winning role. The source material for the film was Clifford Odets's well-known play, *Winter Journey*, which could have been a dismal failure as a set-bound filmed play. Yet Seaton's screenplay, and light direction enabled the characters to come to life. The play was not "opened yet" with artificially imposed scenes but instead received movement by the backstage scenes. Most of the action took place in the theater, a small apartment, or hotel rooms, yet the theme of a "play within a play" worked to the story's advantage, rather than detriment. In addition, the acting is first rate, and, as critics have pointed out, the characters were not too lofty for the average moviegoer.

Another star film which was very successful was *Teacher's Pet*, which teamed Clark Gable and Doris Day. Gable was in his late fifties at the time of the film and had long since relinquished his title of "the king" yet the character which he plays, reminiscent of the reporter in *It Happened One Night*, retains the Gable charm. This was due in large measure to Seaton's fast-moving script and light direction of an amusing, if insignificant comedy.

Unquestionably Seaton's best-remembered film is *Miracle on 34th Street*, which is probably also his best work. The film is revived annually on television—either at Thankgiving or Christmas, and has been enjoyed by successive generations for over 35 years. The script is clever, if rather sentimental; it is witty, fast-paced, and created some very memorable characters. Even a cynical movie fan can appreciate the imbroglios created when a trial must rectify the errors of an incompetent store psychologist. The character roles in *Miracle on 34th Street*, Kris Kringle, the judge, the district attorney, and the campaign manager, are better developed than any others which Seaton would write. To make a film which tempts to prove that a kindly old man is indeed Santa Claus without making it overly maudlin is indeed an accomplishment.

—Patricia King Hanson

SEMBENE, OUSMANE. Senegalese. Born at Ziguinchor, Senegal, 8 January 1923. Career: 1937-38—works as mechanic; 1942—joins Free French forces fighting in Africa; 1945—demobilized at Marseilles; 1946—briefly returns to Senegal; 1948—leaves for France, works 3 months in Paris for Citroën, then goes to Marseilles; works on docks, becomes involved with union activities, elected Secretary General of black workers organization in France; begins career as writer; 1955—first novel published, *Le Docker noir*, followed in 1957 by *O Pays, mon beau peuple*; novels and other fiction include *L'Harmattan*, *Voltaïque* (collection of short stories), and *Vehi Ciosane*; 1960—returns to Senegal; 1962—leaves for Moscow to study cinema, takes courses of Gerasimov and Marc Donskoi; 1963—returns from Moscow, makes 16 mm film on Mali, *L'Empire Sonrai*.

Films (as director and scriptwriter): 1963—*Songhays (L'Empire Sonrai)* (documentary—unreleased); *Borom Sarret* (d only); 1964—*Niaye*; 1966—*La Noire de... (The Black Girl from...)*; 1968—*Mandabi (The Money Order)*; 1970—*Tauw (Taw)*; 1971—*Emitai*; 1974—*Xala (Impotence)*; 1977—*Ceddo (The People)*.

Publications:

By SEMBENE:

Books—*Le Docker noir*, Paris 1956; *O pays, mon beau peuple*, Paris 1957; *Les Bouts de bois de Dieu*, Paris 1960; *Voltaïque*, Paris 1962; *L'Harmattan*, Paris 1964; *Vehi Ciosane ou blanche genèse* suivi de *Mandat*, Paris 1965; *Xala*, Paris 1973; *Xala*, translated by C. Wake, Westport, Connecticut 1976; *Le Dernier de l'Empire*, novel, Paris 1981; articles—interview by Guy Hennebelle in *Jeune Cinéma* (Paris), November 1968; interview by Emile James in *Jeune Afrique* (Paris), 28 July 1970; "Ousmane Sembene at the Olympic Games", interview in *American Cinematographer* (Los Angeles), November 1972; "Ousmane Sembene. Les 'francs-tireurs' sénégalais", interview by A. Pâquet and G. Borremans in *Cinéma Québec* (Montreal), March/April 1973; interview by G.M. Perry in *Film Quarterly* (Berkeley), spring 1973; "Film-makers have a great responsibility to our people", interview by H.D. Weaver, Jr., in *Cineaste* (New York), v.6, no.1, 1973; "Ousmane Sembene, Carthage et le cinéma africain" and "Problématique du cinéaste africain: l'artiste et la révolution", interviews by T. Cheriaa in *Cinéma Québec* (Montreal), August 1974; interview by J.-C. Bonnet in *Cinématographe* (Paris), June 1977; interview by R. Grelier in *Image et son* (Paris), November 1977; "Ich will mit meinem Volk reden", interview by R. Richter in *Film und Fernsehen* (Berlin), February 1978; interview by C. Bosseno in *Image et son* (Paris), September 1979; "Ousmane Sembene: An Interview" by G.M. Perry and Patrick McGilligan in *Jump Cut* (Chicago), no.27.

On SEMBENE:

Books—*Ousmane Sembène, cinéaste. Première période 1962-1971* by Paulin Soumanou Vieyra, Paris 1972; *Evolution of an African Artist: Social Realism in the Works of Ousmane Sembene* by Carrie Moore, unpublished doctoral dissertation, Indiana University 1973; *Le Cinéma africain: dès origines à 1973* by Paulin Soumanou Vieyra, Paris 1975; articles—"Tonton Kafka" by Gilles Jacob in *Nouvelles littéraires* (Paris), 5 December 1968; "Le Cinéma et l'Afrique" by Paulin Vieyra in *Présence africaine*, Dakar 1969; "Le Cinéma africain" by Paulin Vieyra in *Présence africaine*, Dakar 1970; "Ousmane Sembene" by N. Ghali in *Cinématographe* (Paris), April 1976; "Ideology in the Third World Cinema: A Study of Ousmane Sembene and Glauber Rocha" by William Van Wert in *Quarterly Review of Film Studies* (Pleasantville, N.Y.), spring 1979; "Politics and Style in *Black Girl*" by Marsha Landy, "Female Domestic Labor and Third World Politics in *La Noire de...*" by Lieve Spass,; and "3 Faces of Africa: Women in *Xala*" by Francoise Pfaff in *Jump Cut* (Chicago), no.27.

*   *   *

Ousmane Sembene is one of the most important literary figures of sub-Saharan Africa and, at the same time, its premier filmmaker. Born in 1923 in Senegal, he received little formal education. His first literary work, autobiographical in nature, dates from 1956 and he has as its backdrop the port city of Marseilles where he worked as a docker. Sembene came to the film by necessity: painfully aware that he could not reach his largely pre-literate compatriots by means of a written art form, he studied film in Moscow in 1961 and began to work in this medium shortly thereafter. It is interesting and important to note that four of his films are based on texts, written by Sembene, which first appeared as novels or short stories. Between 1963 and 1977 he produced eight films while publishing three works of fiction. Following *Borom Sarret* and *Niaye*, Sembene made *La Noire de...*, the first feature-length film to come out of sub-Saharan Africa: it received several awards. While technically flawed, it is still a powerful piece which deals with the issue of neocolonialism in post-independence Africa, a common theme in Sembene's work. His next film, *Mandabi (The Money Order)*, marked an important breakthrough for Sembene: it is his first film in color, but, more importantly, it is the first work to use an African language—in this case Wolof, rather than French—and this allowed him to reach his primary audience in an even more direct manner than previously possible. His use of African languages continues with the creation of *Emitai*, which is made in Diola. It is noteworthy that this is the first full-length film by Sembene which is not an adaption from a written text.

The conditions of filmmaking in Africa are difficult and the lack of trained personnel and financial support have discouraged many African artists from working in this medium. Sembene has managed to overcome these problems and has even made a virtue of certain necessities: his almost exclusive reliance on non-professional actors and actresses, including those playing leading roles, is an example of this. He is able to increase both the general force of the film—the audience can more easily identify with them than with "stars"—and testify to his belief in the common man and the collective heroism of the masses.

Sembene's films are not innovative in a technical sense and their power and critical success come rather from the compelling portraits of Third World men and women struggling against forces, both internal and external, which would threaten dignity and, in fact, very existence. Sembene clearly sees himself as a Marxist-Leninist and sees art as necessarily both functional and politically committed. But this does not mean that he is a mere propagandist and, in fact, his art transcends narrow definition. His art is clearly African at base, despite his extensive contacts with the West: the filmmaker is the descendant of the traditional *griot*, recording the history of his society, criticizing its faults, finding strength in its people in the face of the denigration of African society and culture inherent in all forms of colonialism.

—Curtis Schade

SEN, MRINAL. Indian. Born in East Bengal (now Bangladesh), 4 May 1923. Educated in physics in Calcutta. Career: after leaving university, works as freelance journalist and medical representative in Uttar Pradesh; 1943-47—involved with Indian People's Theatres Association, sponsored by Communist Party of India, reads books on film theory and begins writing on film; 1956—directing debut. Recipient: Silver Bear (Special Jury Prize), Berlin Festival, for *Akaler Sandhane*, 1981.

Films (as director and scriptwriter of films in Bengali): 1956—*Raat Bhore (The Dawn, Night's End)*; 1959—*Neel Akasher Neechey (Under the Blue Sky)*; 1960—*Baishey Shravana (The Wedding Day)*; 1961—*Punnascha (Over Again)*; 1962—*Abasheshey (And at Last)*; 1964—*Pratinidhi (The Representative, Two Plus One)*; 1965—*Akash Kusum (Up in the Clouds)*; 1967—*Matira Manisha (2 Brothers)* (co-sc); *Moving Perspectives* (doc); 1969—*Bhuvan Shome (Mr. Shome)* (+pr, sc, in Hindi); 1970—*Ichhapuran (The Wish-Fulfillment)* (also Hindi version); 1971—*Interview* (co-sc); 1972—*Calcutta 71*; *Ek Adhuri Kahani (An Unfinished Story)*; 1973—*Padatik (The Guerrilla Fighter)* (co-sc); 1974—*Chorus* (co-sc); 1976—*Mrigaya (The Royal Hunt)* (co-sc—in Hindi); 1977—*Oka Oorie Katha (The Outsiders)* (co-sc—in Telugu); 1978—*Parashuram (The Man with the Axe)* (co-sc); 1979—*Ek Din Pratidin (And Quiet Rolls the Dawn)*; 1980—*Akaler Sandhane (In Search of Famine)*; 1981—*Chalachitra (The Kaleidoscope)*; 1982—*Kharij (The Case Is Closed)*.

Publications:

By SEN: Articles—"Ich möchte ein Kundschafter werden...", interview by A. Lipkov in *Film und Fernsehen* (Berlin), December 1975; "Introducing Mrinal Sen", interview by U. Gupta in *Jump Cut* (Berkeley), no.12/13, 1976; "'La Chasse royal' de Mrinal Sen", interview by M. Euvrard in *Cinéma Québec* (Montreal), v.6, no.1, 1978; "Der Sturm auf die Zitadelle", interview by M. Spoden in *Film und Fernsehen* (Berlin), no.4, 1979; interview by M. Wassef and A. Tournès in *Jeune cinéma* (Paris), June 1979; "Mrinal Sen et le cinéma indien", interview by H. Micin in *Cinématographe* (Paris), May 1980; "Mrinal Sen: cineasta de los humildes", interview by M. Pereira in *Cine Cubano* (Havana), no.99, 1981.

On SEN:

Book—*Film India: The New Generation 1960-1980*, edited by Uma da Cunha, New Delhi 1981; articles—"The Art Film in India: Report on Mrinal Sen" by Forrest Williams in *Film Culture* (New York), winter/spring 1970; bio-filmography in *Cinématographe* (Paris), September/October 1975; "Briser la

resignation" by A. Tournès in *Jeune cinéma* (Paris), June 1979; "Guerrilla Fighter" by D. Malcolm in *Sight and Sound* (London), autumn 1981; "Sen dossier", special section by L. Vreeswijk and others in *Skrien* (Amsterdam), October 1981.

*   *   *

Mrinal Sen's work is distinguished by the attention he pays to the lives of the underprivileged in India. The style of his films varies considerably, and even within individual films his achievements is uneven, but the body of his work adds up to an important attempt in India at making political films, films which point to prevailing injustices and urge people to change society. Sen is India's preeminent activist filmmaker.

Sen's early films testify to the influences of the Italian neorealists and of Satyajit Ray's first films. He filmed people at the ragged edge of society, using natural locations and employing non-professional actors. Nothing in his films touched up the drabness of poor villages. Unlike Ray, however, Sen's attitude had less humanism in it than political urgency. In a strong film like *Baishey Shravana*, Sen suggests that a bourgois mentality makes bad conditions worse by interposing the claims of respectability on matters of survival.

Although Sen established a reputation in Bengal with *Baishey Shravana*, he came to be known throughout India for the comic *Bhuvan Shome*, made in Hindi in 1969. The film describes a railway official's encounter with the wife of a ticket collecter under fire for accepting bribes. The prunish railway official (played in restrained slapstick by Utpal Dutt) is charmed by a country girl while on holiday in Gujarat and only later discovers that the girl is married to the offending ticket collector. The film is shot among sand dunes and sugarcane fields and reveals Sen's skill at sustaining a simple narrative. To some critics, *Bhuvan Shome* remains Sen's best film, an example of his little-used talents as a confectioner of cinema.

Conditions of near civil war in Calcutta in the late sixties led to three films known as the Calcutta trilogy—*Interview*, *Calcutta 71* and *Padatik*. In these films, Sen moved away from the surface realism of his previous work to allegorical characters and symbolic utterance. Sen turned to conventional narrative with the Hindi film *Mrigaya* in 1976 and has continued since then to present stories about marginal people, framing the story so that the viewer is led to discover his or her own complexity with oppression. His recent *Akaler Sandhane* describes the adventure of a film crew out to film a story about the Bengal famine of 1943. The villages in which the crew works are no more prosperous in 1980 than they were 40 years ago; an afternoon's shopping for the film team cleans out the village vegetable market. *Akaler Sandhane* is intensively effective in the film-within-film, when actors recreate the dire poverty of a disabled peasant's household. The wife has sold herself to the landlord in order to bring home a potful of rice. Sen cuts from a chilling night scene of the lame husband beating his wife to the crowd of onlookers; it is an open question whether the dissipation of intensity which follows this distancing serves a necessary political purpose.

Communist critics generally favor Sen's work; liberal critics point to characteristic weakness of structure. But Sen's caring and energy are never contested. In film after film he probes the fate of those people [tribals (*Mrigaya*), outcastes (*Oka Oorie Katha*), pavement dwellers (*Parashuram*), working women (*Ek Din Pratidin*), servants (*Kharij*)] who are treated as if they were sub-human. Sen's latest films (*Ek Din Pratidin, Chalachitra, Kharij*) affect a subdued tone and, unlike the Calcutta trilogy, trust the audience to draw its own moral from the films. Outside of India, too, critics discern a new phase of maturity in Sen's work.

—Satti Khanna

SENNETT, MACK. Canadian. Born Mikall (Michael) Sinnott in Danville, Quebec, Canada, 17 January 1880. Career: 1902-08—minor career in burlesque and as chorus boy on Broadway; 1908-10—appears in both minor and lead roles in Biograph films, some directed by Griffith; 1910-12—directs Biograph shorts, eventually moving to Hollywood with Biograph and Griffith; 1912—forms Keystone production company with Charles Bauman and Adam Kessell, where he develops the conventions of American slapstick comedy; 1914—Charlie Chaplin joins Keystone for a brief period; Sennett employs others, such as Clarence Brown, to direct; 1915—Keystone absorbed into Triangle Film Corporation with Thomas Ince's and Griffith's production companies; 1917—Triangle collapses and Sennett forms his own company, Mack Sennett Comedies, though his films are released by Paramount; 1923-28—his company is associated with Pathé; 1929-32—begins association with Educational Films, a small production company that releases only shorts; also returns to directing at this point; 1932—returns to Paramount where he produces and directs shorts for W.C. Fields and Bing Crosby; experiments with early color process called "Natural Color"; 1935—returns to Educational Films; subsequently retires from films and moves to Canada; 1939—returns to Hollywood for nominal postition at 20th Century Fox; makes cameo appearance in *Hollywood Cavalcade*; 1949—makes cameo appearance in *Down Memory Lane*. Died 1960. Recipient: Special Academy Award for his contributions to screen comedy, 1937.

Films (as director): 1910—*The Lucky Toothache* (+sc); *The Masher* (+sc); 1911—*Comrades*; *Priscilla's April Fool Joke*; *Cured*; *Priscilla and the Umbrella*; *Cupid's Joke*; *Misplaced Jealousy*; *The Country Lovers*; *The Manicure Lady*; *Curiosity*; *A Dutch Gold Mine*; *Dave's Love Affair*; *Their Fates Sealed*; *Bearded Youth*; *The Delayed Proposal*; *Stubbs' New Servants*; *The Wonderful Eye*; *The Jealous Husband*; *The Ghost*; *Jinks Joins the Temperance Club*; *Mr. Peck Goes Calling*; *The Beautiful Voice*; *That Dare Devil*; *An Interrupted Game*; *The Diving Girl*; *$500,000 Reward*; *The Baron*; *The Villain Foiled*; *The Village Hero*; *The Lucky Horseshoe*; *A Convenient Burglar*; *When Wifey Holds the Purse Strings*; *Too Many Burglars*; *Mr. Bragg, A Fugitive*; *Trailing the Counterfeit*; *Josh's Suicide*; *Through His Wife's Picture*; *The Inventor's Secret*; *A Victim of Circumstances*; *Their 1st Divorce*; *Dooley Scheme*; *Won Through a Medium*; *Resourceful Lovers*; *Her Mother Interferes*; *Why He Gave Up*; *Abe Gets Even With Father*; *Taking His Medicine*; *Her Pet*; *Caught with the Goods*; *A Mix-up in Raincoats*; *The Joke on the Joker*; *Who Got the Reward*; *Brave and Bold*; *Did Mother Get Her Wash*; *With a Kodak*; *Pants and Pansies*; *A Near-Tragedy*; *Lily's Lovers*; *The Fatal Chocolate*; *Got a Match*; *A Message from the Moon*; *Priscilla's Capture*; *A Spanish Dilemma*; *The Engagement Ring*; *A Voice from the Deep*; *Hot Stuff*; *Oh, Those Eyes*; *Those Hicksville Boys*; *Their 1st Kidnapping Case*; *Help, Help*; *The Brave Hunter*; *Won by a Fish*; *The Leading Man*; *The Fickle Spaniard*; *When the Fire Bells Rang*; *The Furs*; *A Close Call*; *Helen's Marriage*; *Tomboy Bessie*; *Algy, the Watchman*; *Katchem Kate*; *Neighbors*; *A Dash through the Clouds*; *The New Baby*; *Trying to Fool*; *1 Round*

O'Brien; *The Speed Demon*; *His Own Fault*; *The Would Be Shriner*; *Willie Becomes an Artist*; *The Tourists*; *What the Doctor Ordered*; *An Interrupted Elopement*; *The Tragedy of a Dress Suit*; *Mr. Grouch at the Seashore*; *Through Dumb Luck*; (as producer and director): 1912 *Cohen Collects a Debt (Cohen at Coney Island)*; *The Water Nymph*; *Riley and Schultz*; *The New Neighbor*; *The Beating He Needed*; *Pedro's Dilemma*; *Stolen Glory*; *The Ambitious Butler*; *The Flirting Husband*; *The Grocery Clerk's Romance*; *At Coney Island*; *Mabel's Lovers*; *At It Again*; *The Deacon's Troubles*; *A Temperamental Husband*; *The Rivals*; *Mr. Fix It*; *A Desperate Lover*; *A Bear Escape*; *Pat's Day Off*; *Brown's Seance*; *A Family Mixup*; *A Midnight Elopement*; *Mabel's Adventures*; *Useful Sheep*; *Hoffmeyer's Legacy*; *The Drummer's Vacation*; *The Duel*; *Mabel's Strategem*; 1913—*Saving Mabel's Dad*; *A Double Wedding*; *The Cure That Failed*; *How Hiram Won Out*; *For Lizzie's Sake*; *Sir Thomas Lipton Out West*; *The Mistaken Masher*; *The Deacon Outwitted*; *The Elite Ball*; *Just Brown's Luck*; *The Battle of Who Run*; *The Jealous Waiter*; *The Stolen Purse*; *Mabel's Heroes*; *Her Birthday Present*; *Heinze's Resurrection*; *A Landlord's Troubled*; *Forced Bravery*; *The Professor's Daughter*; *A Tangled Affair*; *A Red Hot Romance*; *A Doctored Affair*; *The Sleuth's Last Stand*; *A Deaf Burglar*; *The Sleuths at the Floral Parade*; *A Rural 3rd Degree*; *A Strong Revenge*; *The 2 Widows*; *Foiling Fickle Father*; *Love and Pain*; *The Man Next Door*; *A Wife Wanted*; *The Rube and the Baron*; *Jenny's Pearls*; *The Chief's Predicament*; *At 12:00*; *Her New Beau*; *On His Wedding Day*; *The Land Salesman*; *Hide and Seek*; *Those Good Old Days*; *A Game of Poker*; *Father's Choice*; *A Life in the Balance*; *Murphy's I.O.U.*; *A Dollar Did It*; *Cupid in the Dental Parlor*; *A Fishy Affair*; *The Bangville Police*; *The New Conductor*; *His Chum, the Baron*; *That Ragtime Band*; *Algie on the Force*; *His Ups and Downs*; *The Darktown Belle*; *A Little Hero*; *Mabel's Awful Mistake*; *Their 1st Execution* (pr only); *Hubby's Job* (pr only); *Betwixt Love and Fire* (pr only); *The Foreman and the Jury*; *Toplitsky and Company* (pr only); *The Gangster*; *Barney Oldfield's Race for a Life*; *Passions—He Had 3*; *Help! Help! Hydrophobia!*; *The Hansom Driver*; *Feeding Time* (pr only); *The Speed Queen*; *The Waiter's Picnic*; *The Tale of the Black Eye*; *Out and In*; *A Bandit*; *Peeping Pete*; *His Crooked Career*; *Largest Boat Ever Launched Sidewalks* (pr only); *For Love of Mabel*; *Rastus and the Game-Cock* (pr only); *Safe in Jail*; *The Telltale Light*; *Love and Rubbish*; *A Noise from the Deep*; *The Peddler*; *Love and Courage*; *Get Rich Quick* (pr only); *Just Kids* (pr only); *Professor Bean's Removal*; *Cohen's Outing*; *A Game of Pool* (pr only); *The Latest in Life Saving* (pr only); *A Chip Off the Old Block* (pr only); *The Firebugs*; *Baby Day*; *The Kelp Industry* (pr only); *Mabel's New Hero*; *Fatty's Day Off* (pr only); *Los Angeles Harbour* (pr only); *The New Baby* (pr only); *Mabel's Dramatic Career*; *The Gypsy Queen*; *What Father Saw* (pr only); *Willie Minds the Dog*; *The Faithful Taxicab* (pr only); *When Dreams Come True*; *Mother's Boy*; *The Bowling Match*; *Billy Dodges Bills* (pr only); *Across the Alley* (pr only); *The Abalone Industry* (pr only); *Schnitz the Tailor* (pr only); *Their Husbands* (pr only); *A Healthy Neighborhood* (pr only); *2 Old Tars* (pr only); *A Quiet Little Wedding* (pr only); *The Janitor* (pr only); *The Making of an Automobile Tire* (pr only); *The Speed Kings*; *Fatty at San Diego* (pr only); *Love Sickness at Sea*; *A Small Town Act* (pr only); *The Milk We Drink* (pr only); *Wine* (pr only); *Our Children* (pr only); *A Muddy Romance*; *Fatty Joins the Force* (pr only); *Cohen Saves the Flag*; *Zuzu the Band Leader*; (as producer): *The Woman Haters*; *The Rogues' Gallery*; *The San Francisco Celebration*; *A Ride for a Bride*; *The Horse Thief*; *The Gusher*; *Fatty's Flirtation*; *Protecting San Francisco from Fire*; *His Sister's Kids*; *A Bad Game*; *Some Nerve*; *The Champion*; *He Would A Hunting Go*; 1914—*A*

Misplaced Foot; A Glimpse of Los Angeles; Love and Dynamite; Mabel's Stormy Love Affair; The Under Sheriff; A Flirt's Mistake; How Motion Pictures Are Made; In the Clutches of the Gang (+d); *Too Many Brides; Won in a Closet; Rebecca's Wedding Day; Little Billy Triumphs; Mabel's Bare Escape; Making A Living; Little Billy's Strategy; Kid Auto Races at Venice; Olives and their Oil; Mabel's Strange Predicament* (+co-d); *A Robust Romeo; Raffles, Gentleman Burglar; A Thief Catcher; Love and Gasoline* (+d); *Twixt Love and Fire; Little Billy's City Cousin; Between Showers; A Film Johnnie; Tango Tangles; His Favorite Pastime; A Rural Demon; The Race (How Villains Are Made); Across the Hall; Cruel, Cruel Love; Barnyard Flirtations; A Back Yard Theater; Chicken Chaser; The Star Boarder; Mack at it Again* (+d); *Fatal High; The Passing of Izzy; A Bathing Beauty (A Bathhouse Beauty); Mabel at the Wheel* (+d); *20 Minutes of Love; Where Hazel Met the Villain; Bowery Boys; Caught in a Cabaret; When Villains Wait; Caught in the Rain; A Busy Day; The Morning Papers; A Suspended Ordeal; Finnegan's Bomb; Mabel's Nerve; The Water Dog; When Reuben Fooled the Bandits (When Ruben Fooled the Bandits); Acres of Alfalfa; Our Large Birds; The Fatal Flirtation; The Alarm; The Fatal Mallet; Her Friend the Bandit; Our Country Cousin; The Knockout* (+d); *Mabel's Busy Day; A Gambling Rube; A Missing Bride; Mabel's Married Life; The Eavesdropper; Fatty and the Heiress; Caught in Tights; Fatty's Finish; Love and Bullets; Row-Boat Romance; Laughing Gas; Love and Salt Water; World's Oldest Living Thing; Mabel's New Job; The Sky Pirate; The Fatal Sweet Tooth; Those Happy Days; The Great Toe Mystery; Soldiers of Misfortune; The Property Man; A New York Girl* (+d); *A Coat's Tale; The Face on the Barroom Floor; Recreation; The Yosemite; Such a Cook; That Minstrel Man; Those Country Kids; Caught in a Flue; Fatty's Gift; The Masquerader; Her Last Chance; His New Profession; The Baggage Smasher; A Brand New Hero; The Rounders; Mabel's Latest Prank; Mabel's Blunder; All at Sea; Bombs and Bangs; Lover's Luck; He Loved the Ladies; The New Janitor; Fatty's Debut; Hard Cider; Killing Hearts; Fatty Again; Their Ups and Downs; Hello Mabel; Those Love Pangs; The Anglers; The High Spots on Broadway; Zipp, the Dodger; Dash, Love and Splash; Santa Catalina Islands; The Love Thief; Stout Heart But Weak Knees; Shot in the Excitement; Doug and Dynamite; Gentlemen of Nerve; Lovers' Post Office; Curses! They Remarked; His Musical Career; His Talented Wife* (+d); *His Trysting Place; An Incompetent Hero; How Heroes Are Made; Tillie's Punctured Romance* (+d—feature); *Fatty's Jonah Day; The Noise of Bombs; Fatty's Wine Party; His Taking Ways; The Sea Nymphs; His Halted Career; Among the Mourners; Leading Lizzie Astray; Shotguns That Kick; Getting Acquainted; Other People's Business; His Prehistoric Past; The Plumber; Ambrose's First Falsehood; Fatty's Magic Pants; Hogan's Annual Spree; A Colored Girl's Love; Wild West Love; Fatty and Minnie-He-Haw; His Second Childhood; Gussle the Golfer; Hogan's Wild Oats; A Steel Rolling Mill; The Fatal Mallet* (+co-d); *1915—A Dark Lover's Play; Hushing the Scandal; His Winning Punch; U.S. Army in San Francisco; Giddy, Gay and Ticklish; Only A Farmer's Daughter; Rum and Wall Paper; Mabel's and Fatty's Wash Day; Hash House Mashers; Love, Speed, and Thrills; Mabel and Fatty's Simple Life; Hogan's Messy Job; Fatty and Mabel at the San Diego Exposition; Colored Villainy; Mabel, Fatty and the Law; Peanuts and Bullets; The Home Breakers; Fatty's New Role; Hogan the Porter; Caught in the Park; A Bird's a Bird; Hogan's Romance Upset; Hogan's Aristocratic Dream; Ye Olden Grafter; A Glimpse of the San Diego Exposition; Hearts and Planets* (+d); *A Lucky Leap; That Springtime Fellow; Hogan Out West; Ambrose's Sour Grapes; Wilful Ambrose; Fatty's Reckless Fling; From Patches To Plenty; Fat-*

ty's Chance Acquaintance; Love in Armor; Beating Hearts and Carpets; That Little Band of Gold; Ambrose's Little Hatchet; Fatty's Faithful Fido; A One Night Stand; Ambrose's Fury; Gussie's Day of Rest; When Love Took Wings; Ambrose's Lofty Perch; Droppington's Devilish Dream; The Rent Jumpers; Droppington's Family Tree; The Beauty Bunglers; Do-Re-Mi-Fa; Ambrose's Nasty Temper; Fatty and Mabel Viewing the World's Fair at San Francisco; Love, Loot and Crash; Gussie Rivals Jonah; Their Social Splash; A Bear Affair; Mabel's Wilful Way; Gussie's Backward Way; A Human Hound's Triumph; Our Dare Devil Chief; Crossed Love and Swords; Miss Fatty's Seaside Lover; He Wouldn't Stay Down; For Better—But Worse; A Versatile Villain; Those College Girls; Mabel Lost and Won; Those Bitter Sweets; The Cannon Ball; A Home Breaking Hound; The Little Teacher (+d); *Foiled By Fido; Court House Crooks; When Ambrose Dared Walrus; Dirty Work in a Laundry; Fido's Tin-Type Tangle; A Lover's Lost Control; A Rascal of Wolfish Ways; The Battle of Ambrose and Walrus; Only a Messenger Boy; Caught in the Act; His Luckless Love; Viewing Sherman Institute for Indians at Riverside; Wished on Mabel; Gussie's Wayward Path; Settled at the Seaside; Gussie Tied to Trouble; A Hash House Fraud; Merely a Married Man; My Valet* (+d); *A Game Old Knight; A Favorite Fool* (+d); *Stolen Magic* (+d); *Her Painted Hero; Saved by Wireless; Fickle Fatty's Fall; His Father's Footsteps; The Best of Enemies; A Janitor's Wife's Temptation; A Village Scandal; The Great Vacuum Robbery; Crooked to the End; Fatty and the Broadway Stars; The Hunt; A Submarine Pirate; 1916—The Worst of Friends; Dizzy Heights and Daring Hearts; The Great Pearl Tangle; Fatty and Mabel Adrift; Because He Loved Her; A Modern Enoch Arden; Perils of the Park; A Movie Star; His Hereafter; He Did and He Didn't (Love and Lobsters); Love Will Conquer; His Pride and Shame; Fido's Fate; Better Late Than Never; Bright Lights; Cinders of Love; Wife and Auto Troubles; The Judge; A Village Vampire; The Village Blacksmith; A Love Riot; Gipsy Joe; By Stork Delivery; An Oily Scoundrel; A Bathhouse Blunder; His Wife's Mistake; His Bread and Butter; His Last Laugh; Bucking Society; The Other Man; The Snow Cure; A Dash Of Courage; The Lion and the Girl; His Bitter Pill; Her Marble Heart; Bathtub Perils; The Moonshiners; Hearts and Sparks; His Wild Oats; Ambrose's Cup of Woe; The Waiter's Ball; The Surf Girl; A Social Club; Vampire Ambrose; The Winning Punch; His Lying Heart; She Loved a Sailor; His Auto Ruination; Ambrose's Rapid Rise; His Busted Trust; Tugboat Romeos; Sunshine; Her Feathered Nest; No One to Guide Him; Her 1st Beau; His 1st False Step; The Houseboat; The Fire Chief; Love on Skates; His Alibi; Love Comet; A la Cabaret; Haystacks and Steeples; A Scoundrel's Toll; The 3 Slims; The Girl Guardian; Wings and Wheels; Safety 1st Ambrose; Maid Mad; The Twins; Piles of Perils; A Cream Puff Romance; The Danger Girl; Bombs; His Last Scent; The Manicurist; 1917—The Nick of Time Baby; Stars and Bars; Maggie's 1st False Step; Villa of the Movies; Dodging His Doom; Her Circus Knight; Her Fame and Shames; Pinched in the Finish; Her Nature Dance; Teddy at the Throttle; Secrets of a Beauty Parlor; A Maiden's Trust; His Naughty Thought; Her Torpedoed Love; A Royal Rogue; Oriental Love; Cactus Nell; The Betrayal of Maggie; Skidding Hearts; The Dog Catcher's Love; Whose Baby; Dangers of a Bride; A Clever Dummy; She Needed a Doctor; Thirst; His Uncle Dudley; Lost a Cook; The Pawnbroker's Heart; 2 Crooks; A Shanghaied Jonah; His Precious Life; Hula Hula Land; The Late Lamented; The Sultan's Wife; A Bedroom Blunder; Roping Her Romeo; The Pullman Bride; Are Waitresses Safe; An International Sneak; That Night; Taming Target Center; 1918—The Kitchen Lady; His Hidden Purpose; Watch Your Neighbors; It Pays to Exercise; Sheriff*

Nell's Tussle; Those Athletic Girls; Friend Husband; Saucy Madeline; His Smothered Love; The Battle Royal; Love Loops the Loop; 2 Tough Tenderfeet; Her Screen Idol; Ladies First; Her Blighted Love; She Loved Him Plenty; The Summer Girls; Mickey; His Wife's Friend; Sleuths; Beware the Boarders; Whose Little Wife Are You; Her 1st Mistake; Hide and Seek Detectives; The Village Chestnut; 1919—Cupid's Day Off; Never Too Old; Rip & Stitch, Tailors; East Lynne with Variations; The Village Smithy; Reilly's Wash Day; The Foolish Age; The Little Widow; When Love is Blind; Love's False Faces; Hearts and Flowers; No Mother to Guide Him; Trying to Get Along; Among Those Present; Yankee Doodle in Berlin; Why Beaches Are Popular; Treating 'em Rough; A Lady's Tailor; Uncle Tom Without the Cabin; The Dentist; Back to the Kitchen; Up in Alf's Place; Salome vs. Shenandoah; His Last False Step; The Speak Easy; 1920—The Star Boarder; 10 Dollars or 10 Days; Gee Whiz; The Gingham Girl; Down on the Farm; Fresh from the City; Let 'er Go; By Golly; You Wouldn't Believe It; Married Life; The Quack Doctor; Great Scott; Don't Weaken; It's a Boy; Young Man's Fancy; His Youthful Fancy; My Goodness; Movie Fans; Fickle Fancy; Love, Honor, and Behave; A Fireside Brewer (Home Brew); Bungalow Troubles; 1921—Dabbling in Art; An Unhappy Finish; On a Summer's Day; A Small Town Idol (+sc); Wedding Bells Out of Tune; Officer Cupid; Away from the Steerage (Astray from the Steerage); Sweetheart Days; Home Talent (+sc); She Sighed by the Seaside; Hard Knocks and Love Taps; Made in the Kitchen; Call a Cop; Love's Outcast; Molly O (+sc); Oh, Mabel Behave (+co-d); 1922—By Heck; Be Reasonable; Bright Eyes; The Duck Hunter; On Patrol; Step Forward; Gymnasium Jim; The Crossroads of New York (+sc); Oh Daddy!; Home-Made Movies; Ma and Pa; Bow Wow; Love and Doughnuts; When Summer Comes; 1923—Suzanna; The Shriek of Araby (+sc); Where is My Wandering Boy This Evening; Nip and Tuck; Pitfalls of a Big City; Skylarking; Down to the Sea in Shoes; The Extra Girl (+co-sc); Asleep at the Switch; One Cylinder Love; The Dare-Devil; Flip Flops; Inbad the Sailor; 1924—10 Dollars or 10 Days (remake); One Spooky Night; Picking Peaches; The Half-Back of Notre Dame; Smile Please; Scarem Much; Shanghaied Ladies; The Hollywood Kid; Flickering Youth; Black Oxfords; The Cat's Meow; Yukon Jake; The Lion and the Souse; His New Mama; Romeo and Juliet; Wall Street Blues; The 1st 100 Years; East of the Water Plug (+sc); Lizzies of the Field; The Luck of the Foolish; 3 Foolish Wives; Little Robinson Corkscrew; The Hansom Cabman (Be Careful); Riders of the Purple Cows; The Reel Virginian (The West Virginian); Galloping Bungalows; All Night Long; Love's Sweet Piffle; The Cannon Ball Express; Feet of Mud; Off His Trolley; Bull and Sand; Watch Out; Over Here; The Lady Barber; North of 57; Love's Intrigue; The Stunt Man; 1925—The Sea Squaw; The Plumber; The Wild Goose Chaser; Honeymoon Hardships; Boobs in the Woods; The Beloved Bozo; Water Wagons; His Marriage Wow; The Raspberry Romance; Bashful Jim; Giddap; Plain Clothes; Breaking the Ice; The Marriage Circus; The Lion's Whiskers; Remember When; He Who Gets Smacked; Skinners in Silk; Good Morning, Nurse!; Super-Hooper-Dyne Lizzies; Don't Tell Dad; Isn't Love Cuckoo; Sneezing Breezes; Cupid's Boots; Tee for 2; The Iron Nag; Lucky Stars; Cold Turkey; Butter Fingers; There He Goes; Hurry, Doctor; A Rainy Knight; Love and Kisses; Over There-Abouts; Good Morning, Madam; A Sweet Pickle; Dangerous Curves Behind; The Soapsuds Lady; Take Your Time; The Window Dummy; From Rags to Britches; Hotsy Toty; 1926—The Gosh-Darn Mortgage; Wide Open Faces; Hot Cakes for 2; Whispering Whiskers; Saturday Afternoon; Funnymooners; Trimmed in Gold; Gooseland; Circus Today; Meet My Girl; Spanking Breezes; Wandering Willies; Hooked at the Altar; A Love Sundae; Soldier Man; The Ghost of Folly; Fight Night; Hayfoot, Strawfoot; A Yankee Doodle Dude; Muscle-Bound Music; Oh, Uncle!; Puppy Lovetime; Ice Cold Cocos; A Dinner Jest; A Sea Dog's Tale; Baby's Pets; A Bachelor Butt-in; Smith's Baby; Alice Be Good; When a Man's a Prince; Smith's Vacation; Hubby's Quiet Little Game; Her Actor Friend; Hoboken to Hollywood; The Prodigal Bridegroom; The Perils of Petersboro; Smith's Landlord; Love's Last Laugh; Smith's Visitor; Should Husbands Marry; Masked Mamas; A Harem Knight; Smith's Uncle; Hesitating Houses; The Divorce Dodger; A Blonde's Revenge; Flirty 4-Flushers; Smith's Picnic; 1927—Kitty from Killarney; Smith's Pets; Should Sleepwalkers Marry; Pass the Dumpling; A Hollywood Hero; Smith's Customer; Peaches and Plumbers; Plumber's Daughter; A Small Town Princess; A Dozen Socks; The Jolly Jilter; Smith's Surprise; Smith's New Home; Broke in China; Smith's Kindergarten; Crazy to Act; Smith Fishing Trip; His 1st Flame; Pride of Pickeville; Cured in the Excitement; Catalina, Here I Come; The Pest of Friends; Love's Languid Lure; College Kiddo; Smith's Candy Shop; The Golf Nut; Smith's Pony; A Gold Digger of Weepah; Smith's Cook; Daddy Boy; For Sale a Bungalow; Smith's Cousin; The Bull Fighter; Fiddlesticks; Smith's Modiste Shop; The Girl from Everywhere; Love in a Police Station; Hold that Pose; A Finished Actor (+d); 1928—Smith's Holiday; Run, Girl, Run; The Beach Club; Love at 1st Sight; Smith's Army Life; The Best Man; The Swan Princess; Smith's Farm Days; The Bicycle Flirt; The Girl From Nowhere; His Unlucky Night; Smith's Restaurant; The Good-bye Kiss; The Chicken; Taxi for 2; Caught in the Kitchen; A Dumb Waiter; The Campus Carmen; Motor Boat Mamas; The Bargain Hunt; Smith's Catalina Rowboat Race (Catalina Rowboat Race); A Taxi Scandal; Hubby's Latest Alibi; A Jim Jam Janitor; The Campus Vamp; Hubby's Week-end Trip; The Burglar; Taxi Beauties; His New Stenographer; The Lion's Roar (+d, sc); 1929—Clunked on the Corner; Baby's Birthday; Uncle Tom; Calling Hubby's Bluff; Taxi Spooks; Button My Back; Ladies Must Eat; Foolish Husbands; Matchmaking Mamas; The Rodeo; Pink Pajamas; The Night Watchman's Mistake; The New Aunt; Taxi Dolls; Don't Get Jealous; Caught in a Taxi; A Close Shave; The Bride's Relation (+d); The Old Barn (+d); Whirls and Girls (+d); Broadway Blues (+d); The Bee's Buzz (+d); The Big Palooka; Girl Crazy (+d); Motoring Mamas (+d); The Barber's Daughter (+d); Jazz Mamas (+d); The New Bankroll (+d); The Constable (The Constabule) (+d); Midnight Daddies (+d); The Lunkhead (+d); The Golfers (+d); A Hollywood Star (+d); Clancy at the Bat; The New Half-Back; Uppercut O'Brien; 1930—Scotch (+d); Sugar Plum Papa (+d); Bulls and Bears (+d); Match Play (+d); He Trumped Her Ace; Honeymoon Zeppelin (+d); Radio Kisses; Fat Wives for Thin (+d); Campus Crushes (+d); The Chumps (+d); Goodbye Legs (+d); Hello Television; Average Husband (+d); Vacation Loves (+d); The Bluffer (+d); Grandma's Girl (+d); Divorced Sweethearts (+d); Take Your Medicine; Don't Bite Your Dentist; Strange Birds; Racket Cheers (+d); A Hollywood Theme Song; Rough Idea of Love (+d); 1931—No, No, Lady; A Poor Fish (+d); Dance Hall Marge (+d); One Yard to Go; The College Vamp (remake); The Bride's Mistake; The Dog Doctor; Just a Bear (It's a Bear); Ex-Sweeties; In Conference; The Chiseler (+d); The Cowcatcher's Daughter; Ghost Parade (+d); Hollywood Happenings (+d); Hold 'er Sheriff (+d); Monkey Business in America (+d); Movie-Town (+d); Slide, Speedy, Slide; The Albany Bunch (+d); Fainting Lover; Too Many Husbands; The Cannonball; The Trail of the Swordfish; I Surrender Dear (+d); Poker Windows; The World Flier; Speed (+d); Who's Who in the Zoo; Taxi Troubles; The Great Pie Mystery; Wrestling Swordfish; One More Chance (+d); All American Kickback; Half Holiday; The Pottsville Palooka; 1932—Playgrounds of the

Mammals; Dream House; The Girl in the Tonneau; Shopping with Wife; Lady! Please!; Heavens! My Husband!; The Billboard Girl; The Flirty Sleepwalker; Speed in the Gay '90's; Man-Eating Sharks; Listening In; The Spot in the Rug; Divorce a la Mode; The Boudoir Brothers; Freaks of the Deep; The Candid Camera; Sea Going Birds; Hatta Marri; Alaska Love; For the Love of Ludwig; Neighbor Trouble; His Royal Shyness; Young Onions; The Giddy Age; Hypnotized (+d, sc); Lighthouse Love; Hawkins and Watkins; The Singing Plumber; Courting Trouble; False Impressions; Bring Back 'em Sober; A Hollywood Double; The Dentist; Doubling in the Quickies; The Lion and the House; Human Fish; 1933—Blue of the Night; The Wrestlers (A Wrestler's Bride); Don't Play Bridge with Your Wife; The Singing Boxer; Too Many Highballs; Easy on the Eyes; A Fatal Glass of Beer; Caliente Love; Sing, Bing, Sing; The Plumber and the Lady; Sweet Cookie; The Pharmacist; Uncle Jake; Dream Stuff; Roadhouse Queen; See You Tonight; Daddy Knows Best; Knockout Kisses; Husband's Reunion; The Big Fibber; The Barber Shop; 1935—Ye Olde Saw Mill (+d, sc); Flicker Fever (+d); Just Another Murder (+d, sc); The Timid Young Man (+d); Way Up Thar (+d).

Roles include: 1908—*Baked at the Altar* (Griffith); *Father Gets in the Game* (Griffith); *The Song of the Shirt* (Griffith); *Mr. Jones at the Ball* (Griffith); 1909—*Mr. Jones Has a Card Party* (Griffith); *The Curtain Pole* (Griffith); *The Politician's Love Story* (Griffith); *The Lonely Villa* (Griffith); *The Way of a Man* (Griffith); *The Slave* (Griffith); *Pippa Passes* (Griffith); *The Gibson Goddess* (Griffith); *Nursing a Viper* (Griffith); 1910—*The Dancing Girl of Butte* (Griffith); *All on Account of the Milk* (Griffith); *The Englishman and the Girl* (Griffith); *The Newlyweds* (Griffith); *An Affair of Hearts* (Griffith); *Never Again!* (Griffith); *The Call to Arms* (Griffith); *An Arcadian Maid* (Griffith); *A Lucky Toothache* (Griffith and Sennett); *The Masher* (Sennett and Griffith); 1911—*The Italian Barber* (Griffith); *Comrades* (Sennett); *Paradise Lost* (Griffith); *The Manicure Lady* (Sennett); *The White Rose of the Wilds* (Griffith); *A Dutch Gold Mine* (Sennett); *The Last Drop of Water* (Griffith); *That Dare Devil* (Sennett); *$500,000 Reward* (Sennett); *The Village Hero* (Sennett); *Trailing the Counterfeit* (Sennett); *Their 1st Divorce Case* (Sennett); *Caught with the Goods* (Sennett); 1912—*The Fatal Chocolate* (Sennett); *A Spanish Dilemma* (Sennett); *Their 1st Kidnapping Case* (Sennett); *The Brave Hunter; The Would-Be Shriner* (Sennett); *Pedro's Dilemma* (Sennett); *Stolen Glory* (Sennett); *The Ambitious Butler* (Sennett); *At Coney Island* (Sennett); *At It Again* (Sennett); *The Rivals* (Sennett); *Mr. Fix It* (Sennett); *A Bear Escape* (Sennett); *Pat's Day Off* (Sennett); *A Family Mix-up* (Sennett); *The Duel* (Sennett); 1913—*The Mistaken Masher* (Sennett); *The Battle of Who Run* (Sennett); *The Stolen Purse* (Sennett); *Mabel's Heroes* (Sennett); *The Sleuth's Last Stand* (Sennett); *The Sleuths at the Floral Parade* (Sennett); *A Strong Revenge* (Sennett); *The Rube and the Baron* (Sennett); *Her New Beau* (Sennett); *Mabel's Awful Mistake* (Sennett); *Barney Oldfield's Race for Life* (Sennett); *The Hansom Driver* (Sennett); *His Crooked Career* (Sennett); *Mabel's Dramatic Career* (Sennett); *Love Sickness at Sea* (Sennett); 1914—*Mack at It Again* (Sennett); *Mabel at the Wheel* (Sennett); *The Fatal Mallet* (Chaplin and Sennett); *The Knockout; The Property Man* (Chaplin); *A New York Girl* (Sennett); *His Talented Wife* (Sennett); 1915—*Hearts and Planets* (Sennett); *The Little Teacher* (Sennett); *My Valet* (Sennett); *Stolen Magic* (Sennett); *Fatty and the Broadway Stars* (Arbuckle); 1921—*Oh, Mabel Behave* (Sennett and Sterling); 1931—*Movie-Town* (Sennett); 1939—*Hollywood Cavalcade*; 1949—*Down Memory Lane.*

Publications:

By SENNETT:

Book—*Mack Sennett: King of Comedy, as Told to Cameron Shipp*, New York 1954; article—interview by T. Dreiser in *Photoplay* (New York), August 1928.

On SENNETT:

Books—*Mack Sennett* by C.A. Lejeune, London 1931; *Father Goose: the Story of Mack Sennett* by Gene Fowler, New York 1934; *Le Cinéma burlesque américain, 1912-30* by Jacques Chevallier, Paris 1964; *Mack Sennett* by David Turconi, Paris 1966; *Film Makers on Filmmaking* edited by Harry M. Geduld, Bloomington, Indiana 1967; *Mack Sennett's Keystone: The Man, the Myth, and the Comedies* by Kalton C. Lahue, South Brunswick, New Jersey 1971; *Dreams for Sale: The Rise and Fall of the Triangle Film Corporation* by Kalton C. Lahue, New York 1971; *Spellbound in Darkness* by George C. Pratt, Greenwich, Connecticut 1973; *Yesterday's Clowns* by Frank Manchel, New York 1973; articles—"Mack Sennett—Laugh Tester" by H.C. Carr in *Photoplay* (New York), May 1915; "Sketch" by E.W. Hewston in *Motion Picture Classic* (Brooklyn), January 1916; "The Psychology of Film Comedy" in *Motion Picture Classic* (Brooklyn), November 1918; "The Secret of Making Film Comedies" by H. Carr in *Motion Picture Classic* (Brooklyn), October 1925; "Maker of Comedies" by Jim Tully in *Vanity Fair* (New York), May 1926; "Dean of Custard College" by R. Wagner in *Colliers* (New York), 5 November 1927, or October 1929; "To Produce Talking Pictures" in *Photoplay* (New York), August 1930; "Defense of Low-Brow Comedy" by D. Manners in *Motion Picture Classic* (Brooklyn), October 1930; "A Star-Maker Whose Recipe is Anything for A Laugh" by Jerome Beatty in the *American* (New York), January 1931; "Inside Story Told by Mack Sennett's Rise to Fame" in *Newsweek* (New York), 27 October 1934; "Pie in Art" in *Nation* (New York), 7 November 1934; "Custard Pie Classics" in *The New York Times Magazine*, 8 June 1947; "Comedy's Greatest Era" by James Agee in *Life* (New York), 5 September 1949; "Then and Now" by Thomas Pryor in *The New York Times Magazine*, 22 February 1953; "Custard Pies" in *Newsweek* (New York), 6 December 1954; "Era of Great Comedians" by Arthur Knight in the *Saturday Review* (New York), 18 December 1954; "Mack Sennett's At It" in *Newsweek* (New York), 6 October 1958; "Galaxy of Present Day Stars in a Classic Mack Sennett Chase" in *Life* (New York), 22 December 1958; "Cops, Custard, and Keaton" by Peter John Dyer in *Films and Filming* (London), August 1958; entire issue on Sennett of *Cinéma 60* (Paris), August/September 1960; entire issue on Sennett of *Image et son* (Paris), April 1964; "The World of Comedy: Breaking the Laugh Barrier" by Raymond Durgnat in *Films and Filming* (London), October 1965; "Mack Sennett" by Robert Giroux in *Films in Review* (New York), December 1968; "King of Keystone" by J.R. Hoffner in *Classic Film Collector* (Indiana, Pennsylvania), summer 1971; "Festival Harry Langdon" by J.-J. Dupuich in *Image et son* (Paris), no.274, 1973; "All the Sad Young Bathing Beauties" by DeWitt Bodeen in *Focus on Film* (London), autumn 1974.

*   *   *

Mack Sennett was the outstanding pioneer and primitive of American silent comedy. Although Sennett's name is most commonly associated with the Keystone Company, which he founded in 1912, Sennett's film career begins four years earlier with the Biograph Company, the pioneering film company where D.W.Griffith established the principles of film narrative and rhetoric. Sennett and Griffith were colleagues and contemporaries, and Sennett served as actor, writer, and assistant under Griffith in 1908 and 1909, then, beginning in 1910, as director of his own films under Griffith's supervision. Sennett became associated with comic roles and comic films from the beginning under Griffith. In his first major role for Griffith, *The Curtain Pole* in 1908, Sennett played a comically drunk Frenchman who visits chaos upon all he meets and touches in a desperate race through town to replace a broken curtain rod. Already that film contains those traits that would become associated with the mature Sennett style: the breathless chase, the reduction of human beings to venal stereotypes, and the reduction of human society and its physical surroundings to chaotic rubble, and playing games with the cinema mechanism itself, through accelerated motion (by undercranking) and reverse motion. In other roles for Griffith, Sennett consistently played the comic rube or dumb servant—roles that took advantage of Sennett's shambling bulk and oafish facial expressions.

According to legend, Sennett founded the Keystone Company when he conned his bookies, Adam Kessel and Charles Bauman, to go double or nothing on his gambling debts and stake him to a film company. Kessel and Bauman, however, had been out of the bookmaking business and in the moviemaking business for a least five years as owners of Thomas Ince's flourishing Bison Motion Picture Company. Between late 1912 and early 1914, Sennett assembled the finest of raucous physical comedians and burlesque clowns in the film business. From Biograph he brought the pretty Mabel Normand, who was also an extremely agile and athletic physical comedienne, and the loomy Ford Sterling, with his big-gesturing burlesque of villainy and lechery. Among the other physical comedians he found in those years were the burly Mack Swain, the tiny Chester Conklin, the round Fatty Arbuckle, and the cross-eyed Ben Turpin. He also found such feature comic stars as Charles Chaplin, Harold Lloyd, and Harry Langdon, as well as the future director of sound comedies, Frank Capra. Perhaps more important than any artistic contribution was Sennett's managerial ability to spot comic talent and give it the opportunity to display itself.

At the root of Sennett's comic style was the brash, the vulgar, and the burlesque. His films parodied the serious film and stage hits of the day, always turning the serious romance or melodrama into outrageous nonsense. There was no serious moral, psychological, or social issues in Sennett films, simply raucous burlesque of social or emotional material. His short comedies were exuberantly impolite, often making public jokes out of ethnic, sexual, or racial stereotypes. Among the characters around whom he built film series were the German Meyer and Heinie, the Jewish Cohen, and the black Rastus. Many of these films were so brashly vulgar in their stereotypic humor that they cannot be shown in public today. As indicators of social attitudes of the 1910s, these films seem to suggest that the still largely immigrant American society of that time was more willing to make and respond to jokes openly based on ethnic and sexist stereotypes than they are today in an era of greater sensitivity to the potential harm of displaying, and hence preserving, these stereotypes. In defense of Sennett's making sport of ethnic types, it must be said that the method and spirit was consistent with his films' refusal to take any social or psychological matters seriously.

Sennett's Keystone films were extremely improvisational; a typical formula was to take a camera, a bucket of whitewash, and four clowns (two male, two female) out to a park and make a movie. Sennett's aesthetic was not so much an art that conceals art but an art that derides art. His many Keystone films reveal the same contempt for orderly, careful, well-crafted art that one can see in the Marx Brothers' Paramount films or W.C. Fields's Universal films two decades later. The one conscious artistic tool which Sennett exploited was speed, speed, speed—keeping the actors, and the action, and the gags, and the machines, and the camera in perpetual speeding motion. The typical Keystone title might be something like *Love, Speed, and Thrills* or *Love, Loot, and Crash*. Among other Sennett inventions were the Keystone Kops, a burlesque of attempts at social order, and the Bathing Beauties, a burlesque of attempts at pornographic sexuality. Sennett served his apprenticeship in the American burlesque theater, and he brought to the Keystone films that same kind of entertainment which took place at the intersection of vulgar lunacy and comic pornography. His most memorable films include a series of domestic films starring Mabel Normand, married either to Fatty Arbuckle or Charlie Chaplin, a series of films pairing the beefy Mack Swain and the diminutive Chester Conklin, a series featuring Ben Turpin as a cross-eyed burlesque of romantic movie stars, a series built around remarkably athletic automobiles and rampaging jungle beasts starring Billy Bevan, and a series of short films featuring the pixieish child-clown, Harry Langdon. Sennett also produced and personally directed the first comic feature film produced in America (or anywhere else), *Tillie's Punctured Romance*, starring Chaplin, Normand, and stage comedienne Marie Dressler in her first film role.

Sennett ceased to direct films after 1914, becoming the producer and overseer of every comic film made by his company for the next two decades. Although the Keystone company had folded by the late 1910s, Sennett's immensely long filmography is a testament to the sheer number of comic films he produced, well into the sound era. Sennett's real importance to film history, however, derives from that crucial historical moment between 1912 and 1915, a period when a comic assumption, the evolution of film technique, and a collection of talented physical clowns all came together under Sennett's stewardship to create a unique, memorable, and unduplicatable, type of comedy that has assumed its place, not only in the history of cinema, but in the much longer history of comedy itself.

—Gerald Mast

SHINDO, KANETO. Japanese. Born in Hiroshima Prefecture, 22 April 1922. Educated at Higher Elementary School (Middle School), graduated 1927. Married (first time), 1939 (wife died 1943); 2nd marriage ended in divorce after war; married actress Nobuko Otowa, 1978. Career: 1927—enters Shinko-Kinema Kyoto Studio, film developing section; 1928—moves to Shinko-Kinema Tokyo Studio art section; begins to write screenplays; 1936—wins 1st prize in scenario competition sponsored by magazine *Eiga Hyoron* with *Farmers Who Lost Earth*; *Hero's Face* wins studio's scenario competition; neither script filmed; joins Mizoguchi production *The Straits of Love and Hate* as assistant art director, is extremely impressed by director; 1939—moves to studio's scenario section, writes screenplay for Ochiai's 1st film, *South Advancing Girls*; 1941—decides to study scenario writing with Mizoguchi after working on *The 47 Ronin*; 1942—employed by Koa Film (absorbed by Shochiku-Ofuna Studio, 1943);

drafted, repatriated 1946; 1947—writes script for Yoshimura's very successful *Ball of the Anjo Family*, collaborates on series of films with Yoshimura; 1950—the two leave Shochiku, found independent production company Kindai Eiga Kyokai (Society of Modern Film), with producer Hisao Itoya, director Tengo Yamada, and actor Taiji Tonoyama; 1951—first film as director; besides films directed has written 193 filmscripts during career; 1972—becomes president of Japanese Association of Scenario Writers. Recipient: Grand Prix, Moscow Festival, for *Naked Island*, 1960; Asahi Prize, Japan, for activities in independent film production, 1975. Address: 4-8-6 Zushi, Zushi-City, Kanagawa, Japan.

Films (as scriptwriter—representative selection): 1939—*Nanshin josei (South Advancing Women)* (Ochiai); 1946—*Machiboke no onna (Woman Who Is Waiting)* (Makino); *Josei no shori (The Victory of Women)* (Mizoguchi); 1947—*Anjo-ke no butokai (The Ball of the Anjo Family)* (Yoshimura); 1948—*Yuwaku (Seduction)* (Yoshimura); *Waga shogai no kagayakeru hi (My Life's Bright Day)* (Yoshimura); 1949—*Waga koi wa moenu (My Love Burns)* (Mizoguchi) (co-sc); *Shitto (Jealousy)* (Yoshimura); *Mori no Ishimatsu (Ishimatsu of Mori)* (Yoshimura); *Ojosan kanpai (Toast to a Young Miss)* (Kinoshita); (as director and scriptwriter): 1951—*Aisai monogatari (Story of My Loving Wife)*; *Itsuwareru seiso (Deceiving Costume)* (Yoshimura) (sc only); *Genji monogatari (Tale of Genji)* (Yoshimura) (sc only); 1952—*Nadare (Avalanche)*; *Genbaku-no-ko (Children of the Atomic Bomb)*; 1953—*Shukuzu (Epitome)*; *A Life of a Woman*; 1954—*Dobu (Gutter)* (co-sc); 1955—*Ookami (Wolves)*; *Bijo to kairyu (The Beauty and the Dragon)* (Yoshimura) (sc only); 1956—*Gin-Shinju (Silver Double Suicide)*; *Ruri no kishi (Bank of Departure)*; *Joyu (An Actress)*; 1957—*Umi no yarodomo (Guys of the Sea)*; 1958—*Kanashimi wa onna dakeni (Sorrow Is Only for Women)*; *Hadaka no taiyo (Naked Sun)* (Ieki) (sc only); *Yoru no tsuzumi (Night Drum)* (Imai) (co-sc only); 1959—*Dai go fukuryu-maru* (co-sc); *Hanayome san wa sekai-ichi (The World's Best Bride)*; *Rakugaki kokuban (Graffiti Blackboard)*; 1960—*Hadaka no shima (Naked Island, The Island)*; 1962—*Ningen (Human Being)*; 1963—*Haha (Mother)*; *Shitoyakana kemono (Soft Beast)* (Kawashima) (sc only); 1964—*Onibaba*; *Kizudarake no sanga (Mountains and Rivers with Scars)* (Yamamoto) (sc only); 1965—*Akuto (A Scoundrel)*; 1966—*Honno (Instinct)*; *Totsuseki iseki (Monument of Totsuseki)*; *Tateshina no shiki (4 Seasons of Tateshina)*; 1967—*Sei no kigen (Origin of Sex)*; *Hanaoko Seishu no tsuma (Seishu Hanaoka's Wife)* (Masumura); 1968—*Yabu no naka no kuroneko (A Black Cat in the Bush)*; *Tsuyomushi onna (&) yawamushi otoko (Strong Woman and Weak Man)*; 1969—*Kagero (Heat Haze)* (co-sc); 1970—*Shokkaku (Tentacles)*; *Hadaka no jukyu-sai (Naked 19-year-old)* (co-sc); 1972—*Kanawa (Iron Ring)*; *Sanka (A Paean)*; *Gunki hatameku shitani (Under the Military Flag)* (Fukasaku) (sc only); 1973—*Kokoro (Heart)*; 1974—*Waga michi (My Way)*; 1975—*Aru eiga-kantoku no shogai: Mizoguchi Kenji no kiroku (Life of a Film Director: Record of Kenji Mizoguchi)* (documentary); 1977—*Chikuzan hitori-tabi (Life of Chikuzan)*; 1982—*Hokusai manga (Hokusai, Ukiyoe Master)*.

Publications:

On SHINDO:

Books—*Voices from the Japanese Cinema* by Joan Mellen, New York 1975; *The Waves at Genji's Door* by Joan Mellen, New

York 1976; *The Japanese Film* by Joseph Anderson and Donald Richie, expanded edition, Princeton 1982.

*   *   *

Shindo began his career in film as a scenario writer. An episode portraying his study of scenario writing, under the perfectionist director Kenji Mizoguchi, is included in his own first film as a director, *Story of My Loving Wife*. The rigorous influence of his mentor on Shindo's style is seen both in his scenarios and his direction. Such persistent influence, by one director on another, on mise-en-scène, and writing, is rarely found in the work of other filmmakers.

Shindo became a very successful scenario writer mainly for Kosaburo Yoshimura's films at Shochiku. However, after this team was subjected to commercial pressure from the studio, they left to produce their own films, establishing Kindai Eiga Kyokai, or the Society of Modern Film. Thus, they have been able to pursue their own interests and concerns in choosing subjects and styles.

Shindo, a Hiroshima native, frequently deals with the effects of the atomic bomb. He traced Hiroshima's aftermath in *Children of the Atomic Bomb* based on the compositions of Hiroshima children. This subject could be treated only after the American Occupation ended. *Mother* focuses on a surviving woman's decision to become a mother after much mental and physical trauma. *Instinct* deals with a middle-aged survivor whose sexual potence was revived by the love of a woman. *Dai go fukuryu-maru* is about the tragedy of the fishermen heavily exposed to nuclear fallout after American testing in the South Pacific. Shindo condemns nuclear weapons for causing such misery to innocent people, but also strongly affirms the survivor's will to live.

Shindo's best-known film internationally, *Naked Island*, is experimental in not using any dialogue but only music. It also uses local people except for a professional actor and actress who played roles of a couple living on a small island. We are impressed with the hardship of their farming life as well as with the beauty of their natural surroundings throughout the cycle of the seasons. The joy, sorrow, anger, and desperation of the hardworking couple is silently but powerfully expressed in a semi-documentary manner.

The peaceful atmosphere of this film is in contrast to many of Shindo's more obsessive works, such as *Epitome*, *Gutter*, *Sorrow Is Only for Women*, *Onibaba*, and *A Scoundrel*. These convey a claustrophobic intensity by using only a few small settings for the action, with much close-up camera work.

In 1975, Shindo expressed his life-long homage to his mentor, Mizoguchi, in a unique documentary: *The Life of A Film Director: Record of Kenji Mizoguchi*. In this film, he brought together many interesting and honest accounts of Mizoguchi by interviewing people who had worked for this master. These personal recollections along with sequences from Mizoguchi's films, are a testimony to the greatness of Mizoguchi's art, and to his intriguing personality.

Like Mizoguchi, Shindo creates many strong female figures who, by virtue of their love and the power of their will, try to "save" their male counterparts. While Mizoguchi's women seem to rely on their generous compassion to sustain their men, Shindo's women tend to inspire and motivate their men by their own energy and power. In much the same way, Shindo's own energy and perseverance have supported his artistic vision through a quarter-century of independent filmmaking.

—Kyoko Hirano

SHINODA, MASAHIRO. Japanese. Born in Gifu Prefecture, 9 March 1931. Educated in drama and literature at Waseda University, Tokyo. Married actress Shima Iwashita. Career: 1953—becomes assistant director at Shochiku's Ofuna studios; 1958—assists Ozu on *Twilight in Tokyo*, begins extensive study of Ozu and Mizoguchi camera technique and editing; 1960—given first directing assignments on "youth" films; begins working with composer Toru Takemitsu; 1965—quits Shochiku; 1967—*Clouds at Sunset* first release of independent production company, Hyogen-sha [Expression Company]. Address: 1-11-16 Kita-Senzoku, Ota-ku, Tokyo.

Films: (as director): 1960—*Koi no katamichi kippu (One Way Ticket to Love)* (+sc); *Kawaita mizuumi (Dry Lake, Youth in Fury)*; 1961—*Yuhi ni akai ore no kao (My Face Red in the Sunset, Killers on Parade)*; *Waga koi no tabiji (Epitaph to My Love)* (+co-sc); *Shamisen to otobai (Shamisen and Motorcycle, Love Old and New)*; 1962—*Watakushi-tachi no kekkon (Our Marriage)* (+co-sc); *Yama no sanka: moyuru wakamono-tachi (Glory on the Summit: Burning Youth)*; *Namida o shishi no tategami ni (Tears on the Lion's Mane)* (+co-sc); 1963—*Kawaita hana (Pale Flower)* (+co-sc); 1964—*Ansatsu (Assassination)*; 1965—*Utsukushisa to kanashimi to (With Beauty and Sorrow)*; *Ibun sarutobi sasuke (Samurai Spy, Sarutobi)*; 1966—*Shokei no shima (Punishment Island, Captive's Island)*; 1967—*Akanegumo (Clouds at Sunset)*; 1969—*Shinju ten no Amijima (Double Suicide)*; 1970—*Buraikan (The Scandalous Adventures of Buraikan)*; 1971—*Chinmoku (Silence)*; 1972—*Sapporo Orimpikku (Sapporo Winter Olympic Games)*; 1973—*Kaseki no mori (The Petrified Forest)*; 1974—*Himiko*; 1975—*Sakura no mori no mankai no shita (Under the Cherry Blossoms)* (+co-sc); 1976—*Nihon-maru (Nihon-maru Ship)* (documentary); *Sadono kuni ondeko-za (Sado's Ondeko-za)* (documentary); 1977—*Hanare goze Orin (The Ballad of Orin, Banished Orin)* (+co-sc); 1979—*Yashagaike (Demon Pond)*; 1980—*Akuma-to (Devil's Island)*.

Publications:

On SHINODA:

Books—*Sekai no eiga sakka 10: Shinoda Masahiro, Yoshida Yoshishige* [Film Directors of the World 10: Masahiro Shinoda and Yoshishige Yoshida], Tokyo 1971; *Voices from the Japanese Cinema* by Joan Mellen, New York 1975; *The Waves at Genji's Door* by Joan Mellen, New York 1976; *Japanese Film Directors* by Audie Bock, Tokyo 1978.

*   *   *

After his debut with *One Way Ticket to Love* in 1960, Shinoda (along with Oshima and Yoshida) was termed a "Japanese Nouvelle Vague" director. However, Shinoda's devotion to sensual

modernism contrasted with Oshima's direct expression of his political concerns. Shinoda's early films center on the fickle and frivolous entertainment world, petty gangsters, or confused student terrorists, ornamented by pop-art settings and a sensibility which may be largely attributed to his scenario writer, poet Shuji Terayama.

Being an intellectual and ideologue, Shinoda analyzes the fates of his marginal but likable characters with a critical eye on the social and political mileu. Even his work on Shochiku Studio home drama and melodrama projects show his critical views of the social structure.

His indulgent aestheticism, which appears in his films as incomparable sensuality, has been connected with images of death and destruction (*Assasination, With Beauty and Sorrow, Clouds at Sunset, Double Suicide, The Ballad of Orin*) and of degradation (*Silence, The Petrified Forest, Under the Cherry Blossoms*). This stance again contrasts with that of Oshima, whose sexual and political outlook ultimately affirms the value of life and survival. Shinoda's fundamental pessimism, represented by the image of falling cherry blossoms in his films, is rooted in the ephemerality of life.

The stylistic aspect of Shinoda's work originated in his long interest in the Japanese traditional theater. *Double Suicide* received the highest acclaim for his bold art direction (elaborate calligraphy on the set was done by his cousin, Toko Shinoda), ambitious experimentation as in his use of men dressed in black (recalling traditional Japanese puppeteers) appearing to lead the characters to their destinies, and the double roles of the contrasting and competing heroines, the prostitute and the wife. This black-and-white film presents a most imaginative adaptation of Bunraku, the Japanese puppet play. *The Scandalous Adventures of Buraikan* is an elaborate and colorful adaptation of Kabuki drama, playful in spirit. *Himiko* recalls the origin of Japanese theater in the primordial Japanese tribe's rituals, making use of avant-garde dancers. The two leading female roles in *Demon Pond* are played by the popular young Kabuki actor, Tamasaburo Bando.

Another unique aspect of Shinoda's work is his interest in sports. As an ex-athlete, he was well qualified for the assignment of making the official documentary, *Sapporo Winter Olympic Games*, and a documentary on runners, *Sado's Ondeko-za*. In these films, he succeeds in conveying in a beautiful visual manner the emotions of athletes in lonely competition.

Shinoda has also played an important role as the head of an independent film production firm, Hyogen-sha or Expressive Company, since he left Shochiku in 1965. Thus he has pursued his own concerns in choices of subjects and methods of expression, mostly through the adaption of traditional and modern Japanese literary works. He has developed many talented collaborators—actress Shima Iwashita (to whom he is married), music composer Toru Takemitsu, art directors Jusho Toda and Kiyoshi Awazu, and poet Taeko Tomioka, working as his scenario writer.

—Kyoko Hirano

SHUB, ESTHER. (Sub, Esfir). Soviet Ukrainian. Born Esfir Ilyianichna Shub in Chernigovsky district, Ukrainia, 3 March 1894. Educated in literature, Moscow; The Institute for Women's Higher Education, Moscow. Career: while studying at Institute for Women's Higher Education, takes administrative position with Theater Dept. of Narkompros (People's Commissariat of

Education); collaborates on stage works with Meyerhold and Mayakovsky; 1922—joins film company Goskino, begins reediting imported films for Soviet distribution; begins producing compilation and documentary films; 1925—works with Eisenstein on shooting scripts of *Strike* and *Battleship Potemkin*; 1927-28—release of trilogy on revolutionary transformation of Russia, *The Russia of Nicholas II and Lev Tolstoy*, *The Fall of the Romanov Dynasty*, and *The Great Road*; 1933-35—supervises workshop in montage for Eisenstein class at VGIK (film school); 1940—co-directs with Pudovkin *20 Years of Soviet Cinema*; 1942—leaves Goskino to become chief editor of *Novosti Dnya (The News of the Day)*, for Central Studio for Documentary Film, Moscow. Died in Moscow, 21 September 1959. Recipient: Honored Artist of the Republic, 1935.

Films (as editor): 1922-25—edited 200 foreign fiction films and 10 Soviet films, final one being *(The Skotinins)* (Roshal); 1926—*Krylya kholopa (Wings of a Serf)*; (as director, scriptwriter and editor): 1927—*Padenye dinastii romanovykh (The Fall of the Romanov Dynasty)*; *Veliky put' (The Great Road)*; 1928—*Rossiya Nikolaya II i Lev Tolstoi (The Russia of Nicholas II and Lev Tolstoy)*; 1930—*Segodnya (Today)*; 1932—*K-SH-E (Komsomol—Leader of Electrification, Komsomol—The Guide to Electrification)*; 1934—*Moskva stroit metro (Moscow Builds the Subway, The Metro By Night)*; 1937—*Strana Sovietov (The Country of the Soviets, Land of the Soviets)*; 1939—*Ispaniya (Spain)*; 1940—*Kino za XX liet (20 let sovetskogo kino, 20 Years of Cinema, 20 Years of Soviet Cinema)* (co-d, co-ed); 1941—*Fashizm budet razbit (Fascism Will Be Destroyed, The Face of the Enemy)*; 1942—*Strana rodnaya (The Native Country)*; 1946—*Po tu storonu Araksa (On the Other Side of the Araks, Across the Araks)*; *Sud v Smolenske (The Trial in Smolensk)*.

Publications:

By SHUB:

Books—*Krupnyn planom* [In the Close-Up], Moscow 1959; *Zhizn moya—kinematogra* [My Life—Cinema], Moscow 1972; articles—"Road from the Past" in *Sovietskoye Kino* (Moscow), November/December 1934; "Kuleshov, Eisenstein, and the Others: Part 1: On Kuleshov", interview by S.P. Hill in *Film Journal* (New York), fall/winter 1972.

On SHUB:

Book—*Kino: A History of the Russian and Soviet Film* by Jay Leyda, New York 1973; articles—"Esther Schub—ihre Bedeutung für die Entwicklung des Dokumentarfilms" by R. Halter in *Frauen und Film* (Berlin), October 1976; "Esther Shub: Cinema Is My Life" by Vlada Petric in *Quarterly Review of Film Studies* (Pleasantville, N.Y.), fall 1978.

*   *   *

In Russia, as directors traditionally do their own editing, famous film editors are rare. A great exception to this rule was Esther Shub. After gaining her reputation and experience in the early twenties, re-editing foreign productions and then working on a dozen Soviet features, she became, largely on her own initiative, a pioneer of the "compilation film," producing work that has seldom since been equalled. She brought to this genre far more than her speed, industry and flair: a positive genius for using all sorts of ill-considered oddments of old footage as a painter uses his palette and as if it had all been especially shot for her. For her first two brilliant compilations, *The Fall of the Romanov Dynasty*, and *The Great Road*, about the first decade of the revolution (both released in 1927), she scavenged everywhere with indefatigable determination: old newsreels, amateur footage shot by the imperial family and their friends, official footage from a pair of official imperial cinematographers, cellars, vaults and closets of wartime cameramen...even managing to purchase valuable material from the United States. All of this was against the original reluctance of her studios to go ahead with these projects, and they refused to recognize her rights as author when she had finished the films.

Originally planning, as her third work, a film biography of Tolstoy, even Shub failed to dig out more than a few hundred feet of material: undaunted she wove this with great effect into other early fragments and came out with *The Russia of Nicholas II and Lev Tolstoy*.

With the advent of sound Shub made an abrupt change in her methods. For *K-SH-E (Komsomol—Leader of Electrification)* she created her own version of the Communist Hero: young, passionate and dedicated—complete with high-necked Russian blouse and leather jerkin. She forsook her cutting table to become a sort of investigative journalist, deliberately turning her back on archive material, sweeping generalizations and bravura montage; forging instead a new, original style of ultra-realism, pre-dating by 30 years many of the practices and theories of cinema verité. 40 years later a Soviet film historian was to chide her for "indulging herself with a contemporary enthusiasm for the future of sound film and with the peculiar cult for film-apparatus." This was because she opened the film in a sound studio full of every kind of cinematic machinery with what she termed a "parade of film techniques," and occasionally cut back to this theme throughout the production. She purposely included shots in which people looked into the lens, screwed up their eyes at the arc-lamps, stumbled and stuttered in front of cameras and microphones visible in the scenes, and, in general, tried to augment reality by reminding the audience that the crew and camera were actually *there* instead of pretending that they were part of some all-seeing, omnipotent but unobtrusive eye.

Another important Shub film was *Spain*, a history of the Spanish Civil War, once more an "editor's film," which she put together from newsreels and the frontline camerawork of Roman Karmen and Boris Makaseyev, with a commentary by Vsevolod Vishnevski, who also collaborated on the script. In the following year Pudovkin collaborated on her compilation *Twenty Years of Cinema*, a history of the Soviet industry. She continued her documentary work through the war years and into the late forties.

Although as a woman and an editor she perhaps suffered some bureaucratic indifference and obstruction—"they only join pieces of film together"—Shub was an influential filmmaker who deserves at least a niche in the Soviet Film pantheon alongside such other originals (in both senses) as Pudovkin and Eisenstein, who certainly appreciated her work.

—Robert Dunbar

SIDNEY, GEORGE. American. Born in Long Island City, New York, 4 October 1916. Married dramatic coach Lillian Burns; married Jane Robinson (widow of Edward G. Robinson), 1978.

Career: late 1920s—works in circus, vaudeville; 1931—begins working at MGM as messenger boy; works in sound dept., as cutter, and assistant director; directs travelogues and Pete Smith shorts; 1940-41—directs 2 Academy Award-winning shorts: *Quicker 'n a Wink* (Pete Smith), and *Of Pups and Puzzles* (Passing Parade Series); directs numerous screen tests; awards lead to first feature assignment; 1951-58—President of Screen Directors Guild; 1957—begins producing independently, releasing through Columbia initially; president for several years of Hanna-Barbera Productions; 1965—directs for TV *Who Has Seen the Wind?*. Recipient: Academy Award, Short Subjects, for *Quicker 'n a Wink*, 1940; Academy Award, Short Subjects, for *Of Pups and Puzzles*, 1941. Address: Business address: 9301 Wilshire Blvd., Suite 412, Beverly Hills, CA 90210.

Films (as director of short films): 1936—*Polo*; 1937—*Pacific Paradise*; *Sunday Night at the Trocadero*; 1938—*Billy Rose's Casa Manana Review*; *Party Fever*; *Men in Fright*; *Football Romeo*; *Practical Jokers*; 1939—*Tiny Troubles*; *Duel Personalities*; *Love on Tap*; *Clown Princes*; *Cousin Wilbur*; *Hollywood Hobbies*; *Dog Daze*; *A Door Will Open*; *Alfalfa's Aunt*; 1940—*What's Your I.Q.? No.2*; *Quicker 'n a Wink*; *Third Dimensional Murder*; 1941—*Willie and the Mouse*; *Of Pups and Puzzles*; (as feature director): 1941—*Free and Easy*; 1942—*Pacific Rendezvous*; 1943—*Pilot No.5*; *Thousands Cheer*; 1944—*Bathing Beauty*; 1945—*Anchors Aweigh*; 1946—*The Harvey Girls*; *Holiday in Mexico*; 1947—*Cass Timberlane*; 1948—*The 3 Musketeers*; 1949—*The Red Danube*; 1950—*Annie Get Your Gun*; *Key to the City*; 1951—*Show Boat*; 1952—*Scaramouche*; 1953—*Kiss Me Kate*; *Young Bess*; 1955—*Jupiter's Darling*; 1956—*The Eddy Duchin Story*; 1957—*Pal Joey*; *Jeanne Eagels* (+pr); 1960—*Pepe* (+pr); *Who Was That Lady?*; 1963—*Bye-Bye Birdie*; *A Ticklish Affair*; 1964—*Viva Las Vegas* (+co-pr); 1966—*The Swinger* (+pr); 1968—*Half a Sixpence* (+co-pr).

Publications:

On SIDNEY:

Articles—"Directed Subtly by G. Sidney" by Barbara Berch in *The New York Times*, 28 October 1945; "George Sidney" by Charles Higham in *Action* (Los Angeles), May/June 1974; "George Sidney: A Matter of Taste" by G. Morris in *Film Comment* (New York), November/December 1977.

*   *   *

George Sidney is not a name that immediately comes to the mind of the average movie buff, yet in the course of his long career, principally at MGM, he directed a number of highly-regarded films. *Anchors Aweigh* and *The Harvey Girls* were two of the most popular, if not critically acclaimed musicals of the 1940's. In the 1950's, his versions of *Show Boat* and *Kiss Me Kate* were two of the most successful of the "big musicals" made in the last years of the genre.

Sidney began directing on his own in 1941 with the amusing if undistinguished *Free and Easy*, starring Robert Cummings. He made a few B movies at MGM during the war years, then became more successful with films such as *Bathing Beauty*, starring the studio's new box office star, Esther Williams. Most of his films during the 1940s and 1950s are regarded by film historians as superficial, attractive to look at, if unmeritorious programmers,

yet even the worst of his films are entertaining and they are frequently shown in MGM revivals and on television.

His 1948 version of *The Three Musketeers*, starring Gene Kelly and Lana Turner, has been dismissed by many critics, but like the 1974 version directed by Richard Lester, it successfully jumps back and forth between comedy and drama. In one of his few non-dancing roles of the period, Kelly comports himself well and Lana Turner even has some believable scenes as Milady de Winter. The major problems with the film lay more in the odd combination of actors, from June Allyson to Frank Morgan, all members of the so-called MGM stock company, who seemingly were thrown together without regard for their suitability. Yet with a number of major things wrong with it, the film still manages to be entertaining.

Perhaps his most highly praised film was *Show Boat*, a beautifully filmed version of the Edna Ferber novel. The story had been successful as a play and a 1936 film directed by James Whale. Sidney's version, though somewhat trite, has several gorgeous production numbers which were vividly filmed in Technicolor. Though less socially significant than the previous version, the Sidney film is still admired by devotees of the lavish MGM musicals.

One of his last films before retirement was the highly popular *Bye Bye Birdie* starring Dick Van Dyke and Ann-Margret. The acting in this film is almost invisible, but this take-off on the publicity surrounding Elvis Presley's induction into the Army a few years before has both comedy and some good musical numbers. *Bye Bye Birdie* combined satire with music to create some very entertaining specialty numbers, notably "Kids," and "Hymn for a Sunday Evening."

Interestingly, in 1964 Sidney directed Presley himself in the popular formula vehicle *Viva Las Vegas*, again starring Ann-Margret. Sidney's last film before retirement was *Half a Sixpence*, a less than memorable English-made musical starring Tommy Steele.

—Patricia King Hanson

———————

SIEGEL, DON. American. Born Donald Siegel in Chicago, 26 October 1912. Educated Jesus College, Cambridge University, England. Married Viveca Lindfors, 1948 (divorced 1953); 1 son; Doe Avedon, 1957; children: Nowell, Anne, Katherine, and Jack. Career: 1934—hired by Hal Wallis as film librarian at Warner Bros.; later becomes assistant editor at Warners, then moves to insert department; becomes involved with the Contemporary Theater in Los Angeles, headed by Hungarian actor J. Edward Bromberg; 1939—sets up montage department at Warners; 1940-45—works as 2nd unit director for Michael Curtiz and Raoul Walsh and others; 1945—directs 1st film, *Star in the Night*, wins Academy Award; 1946—directs 1st feature *The Verdict*; 1948-51—works as director for Howard Hughes at RKO; 1961-63—begins directing for television, mainly pilots but also series episodes; 1964—directs 1st made-for-TV film, *The Killers*; in wake of Kennedy assassination it is considered too violent for television and is released in theaters; 1965-67—produces series *The Legend of Jesse James* for TV. Address: c/o Capell, Flekman, Coyle & Co., 315 South Beverly Drive, Beverly Hills, California 90212.

Films (as director): 1945—*Star in the Night*; *Hitler Lives*; 1946—*The Verdict*; 1949—*Night Unto Night*; *The Big Steal*; 1952—*No Time For Flowers*; *Duel at Silver Creek*; 1953—*Count the*

Hours (Every Minute Counts); China Venture; 1954—Riot in Cell Block 11; Private Hell 36; 1955—An Annapolis Story (The Blue and the Gold); 1956—Invasion of the Body Snatchers; Crime in the Streets; 1957—Spanish Affair; Baby Face Nelson; 1958—The Gun Runners; The Line-Up; 1959—Edge of Eternity (+co-pr, ro as Man at the Pool); Hound Dog Man; 1960—Flaming Star; 1962—Hell is for Heroes; 1964—The Killers (+pr, ro as short-order cook in diner); The Hanged Man; 1967—Stranger on the Run; 1968—Madigan; 1969—Coogan's Bluff (+pr, ro as Man in Elevator); Death of a Gunfighter (uncredited co-d); 1970—2 Mules for Sister Sara; 1971—The Beguiled (+pr); Dirty Harry (+pr); 1973—Charley Varrick (+pr, ro as Murph); 1974—The Black Windmill (Drabble) (+co-pr); 1976—The Shootist; 1977—Telefon; 1979—Escape from Alcatraz (+pr); 1982—Jinxed.

Roles (in films not directed): 1971—Murphy the Bartender in Play Misty for Me (Eastwood); 1978—Cab Driver in Invasion of the Body Snatchers (Kaufman).

Publications:

By SIEGEL:

Articles—interview by Curtis Lee Hanson in Cinema (Los Angeles), spring 1968; interview by Peter Bogdanovich in Movie (London), spring 1968; "The Anti-Heroes" in Films and Filming (London), January 1969; "What Directors are Saying" in Action (Los Angeles), January/February 1970; "Conversation with Donald Siegel" by Leonard Maltin in Action (Los Angeles), July/August 1971; interview by Stuart Kaminsky in Take One (Montreal), June 1972; interview by Sam Fuller in Interview (New York), May 1972; "Stimulation", interview by Gordon Gow in Films and Filming (London), November 1973; "Charley Varrick", interview by W.E. Bühler in Filmkritik (Munich), March 1974; "Conversazione con Don Siegel" by A. Cappabianca and others in Filmcritica (Rome), October/December 1973; "Making The Shootist", interview by R. Appelbaum in Filmmakers Newsletter (Ward Hill, Mass.), October 1976; "The Man Who Paid His Dues", interview by B. Drew in American Film (Washington, D.C.), December/January 1977/78; "Escape from Alcatraz", interview by S. Mitchell in Filmmakers Monthly (Ward Hill, Mass.), June 1979.

On SIEGEL:

Books—Underworld, U.S.A. by Colin McArthur, London 1972; Don Siegel: Director by Stuart M. Kaminsky, New York 1974; articles—"Esoterica: Filmography" by Andrew Sarris in Film Culture (New York), spring 1963; article in Time (New York), 15 November 1968; "Out for the Kill" by David Austen in Films and Filming (London), May 1968; filmography in Movie (London), spring 1968; "Quotemanship" in Action (Los Angeles), July/August 1968; "Don Siegel: Time and Motion, Attitudes and Genre" by Robert Mundy in Cinema (London), February 1970; "The Films of Don Siegel and Sam Fuller" by Manny Farber in December (Los Angeles), no.1/2 1970; "Suddenly, Don Siegel's High Camp-us" by Charles Higham in The New York Times Biography Edition, 25 July 1971; "Saint Cop" by Pauline Kael in the New Yorker, 15 January 1972; "The Pod Society Vs. the Rugged Individualist" by Charles T. Gregory in Journal of Popular Film (Bowling Green, Ohio), winter 1972; "Siegel at 59: Director, Rebel, Star" by P. Gardner in The New York Times Biography Edition, 31 May 1972; "Don Siegel" by

Stuart Kaminsky and "The B-Movie as Art" by Peter Bogdanovich in Take One (Montreal), June 1972; "Suddenly, It's Siegel" by Norman Taylor in Film Review (London), December 1973; "Letter from Prison" by A.F. Nussbaum in Take One (Montreal), November 1973; "Siegel's Bluff" by D. Pirie in Sight and Sound (London), autumn 1973; "Don Siegel" by Judith M. Kass in The Hollywood Professionals, Vol. 4, London 1975; "Donald Siegel: cinéaste de la violence et du anti-héros" by Guy Allombert in Image et son (Paris), May 1976; "The Strange Romance of 'Dirty Harry' Callahan and Ann Mary Deacon" by A. Chase in Velvet Light Trap (Madison), winter 1977; "Biofilmographie de Donald (Don) Siegel" in Avant-Scène du cinéma (Paris), July 1979; "Less Is More: Don Siegel from the Block to the Rock" by R. Combs in Sight and Sound (London), spring 1980.

*   *   *

Siegel's virtues—tightly constructed narratives and explosive action sequences—have been apparent from the very beginning. Even his B pictures have an enviable ability to pin audiences to their seats through the sheer force and pace of the events they portray. Unlike some action movie specialists, however, Siegel rarely allows the action to overcome the characterization. The continuing fascination of Riot in Cell Block 11, for instance, stems as much from its central character's tensions as from the violent and eventful story. Dunn is a paradigmatic Siegel protagonist, caught between a violent inclination and the strategic need for restraint. Such incipient personal instability animates many Siegel films, finding material expression in the hunts and confrontations which structure their narratives. His people react to an unpleasant world with actions rather than words, often destroying themselves in the process. They rarely survive with dignity.

Siegel's singular distinction, however, lies in his refusal to strike conventional moral postures in relation to this depressing and often sordid material. Though one cannot fail to be involved in and excited by his action-packed stories, there is always a clear sense that he remains outside of them as something of a detached observer. In the fifties that seeming "objectivity" gave him a minor critical reputation as a socially conscious and "liberal" director, though this was a liberalism by implication rather than a direct and paraded commitment. In retrospect the fifties movies seem best described as individualistic, antagonistic to unthinking social conformity, rather than liberally sentimental after the fashion of "socially concerned" Hollywood movies of the period. These films are generalized warnings, not exercises in breast-beating. Their spirit is that of Kevin McCarthy's cry to his unheeding fellows in Siegel's original ending to Invasion of the Body Snatchers (United Artists added an epilogue): "You're next!"

In the sixties and seventies Siegel's reputation and his budgets grew. He struck out in new directions with such films as Two Mules for Sister Sara and The Beguiled, though his major concerns remained with action and with his emotionally crippled "heroes." The three cop movies (Madigan, Coogan's Bluff, and Dirty Harry) are representative, the latter especially encouraging the critical charge that Siegel had become a law-and-order ideologue. Its "wall-to-wall carpet of violence" (Siegel's description) easily lent itself to a "tough cop against the world" reading. Yet, just as his fifties films cannot be reduced to simple liberal formulae, so the later movies are far more complex than much criticism has suggested. A colleague remarks of Madigan: "For him everything's either right or wrong—there's nothing in between." In exploring his characters' doomed attempts to live by such absolutes Siegel refuses to make their mistake. And though he does not presume to judge them, that does not mean that he approves of their actions. As the less frenetic later films like *The Shootist* and *Escape from Alcatraz* make clear, his appreciation of character and morality is far more subtle than that.

More than any other action director of his generation Siegel has avoided the genre's potential for reductive simplification. He has combined entertainment with perception, skilled filmmaking economy with nicely delineated characters, and overall moral detachment with sympathy for his hard-pressed protagonists. His movie world may often seem uncongenial, but its creator has never appeared callous or unconcerned. His films have achieved much deserved commercial success; his skill and subtlety have deserved rather more in the way of critical attention.

—Andrew Tudor

SIODMAK, ROBERT. American/German. Born in Memphis, Tennessee, 8 August 1900. Educated at University of Marburg, Germany. Career: 1920—following graduation from university, acts in German repertory companies; 1921—quits acting to work in banking; 1923—bank closes due to economic collapse; 1925—begins working in films as titler for imported U.S. films; 1926-27—works for Herbert Nossen and Seymour Nebenzal re-editing 2-reel films into one-reelers; 1928—proposes comedy to Nossen and Nebenzal on how Berliners spend Sunday (*Menschen am Sonntag*); hired by Erich Pommer to scout for writers for UFA; 1930—talks Pommer into allowing him to direct; 1933—produces and directs *Brennende Geheimnis* for UFA; film attacked by Josef Goebbels in *Volkischer Beobachter*, removed from theaters; with brother Curt flees to Paris; 1933-40—based in Paris; 1940—leaves Paris for Hollywood just before German occupation; given 2-year contract at Paramount; moves to Universal under 7-year contract; 1951—hired to direct *The Crimson Pirate* in England and Spain, remains in Europe when filming completed; 1954—begins working for Arthur Brauner's CCC company. Died in 1973.

Films (as director): 1929—*Menschen am Sonntag (People on Sunday)* (co-d—documentary); 1930—*Abschied (So sind die Menschen)*; 1931—*Der Mann der seinen Mörder sucht (Looking for His Murderer)*; *Voruntersuchung (Inquest)*; 1932—*Stürme der Leidenschaft (The Tempest, Storm of Passion)*; *Quick (Quick—König der Clowns)*; 1933—*Brennendes Geheimnis (The Burning Secret)* (+pr); *Le Sexe faible*; 1934—*La Crise est finie (Finie la crise, The Slump Is Over)*; 1936—*La Vie parisienne*; *Le Grand Refrain (Symphonie d'amour)* (Mirande) (supervisor only); *Mister Flow (Compliments of Mr. Flow)*; 1937—*Cargaison blanche (Le Chemin de Rio, French White Cargo, Traffic in Souls, Woman Racket)*; 1938—*Mollenard (Hatred)*; *Ultimatum* (co-d—completed for Robert Wiene); 1939—*Pièges (Personal Column)*; 1941—*West Point Widow*; 1942—*Fly by Night*; *The Night Before the Divorce*; *My Heart Belongs to Daddy*; 1943—*Someone to Remember*; *Son of Dracula*; 1944—*Phantom Lady*; *Cobra Woman*; *Christmas Holiday*; 1945—*The Suspect*; *Conflict* (Bernhardt) (co-story only); *Uncle Harry (The Strange Affair of Uncle Harry, The Zero Murder Case)*; *The Spiral Staircase*; 1946—*The Killers*; *The Dark Mirror*; 1947—*Time Out of Mind* (+pr); 1948—*Cry of the City*; 1949—*Criss Cross*; *The Great Sinner*; 1950—*Thelma Jordan*; *Deported*; 1951—*The Whistle at Eaton Falls*; 1952—*The Crimson Pirate*; 1954—*Le Grand Jeu (Flesh and Woman)*; 1955—*Die Ratten*; 1956—*Mein Vater der Schauspieler*; 1957—*Nachts wann der Teufel kam (The Devil Strikes at Night)*; 1959—*Dorothea Angermann*; *The Rough and the Smooth (Portrait of a Sinner)*; 1960—*Katya (Un Jeune Fille un seul amour, Magnificent Sinner)*; *Mein Schulefreund*; 1962—*L'Affaire Nina B (The Nina B Affair)*; *Tunnel 28 (Escape from East Berlin)*; 1964—*Der Schut*; 1965—*Der Schatz der Azteken*; *Die Pyramide des Sonnengottes*; 1968—*Custer of the West (A Good Day for Fighting)*; 1968-69—*Der Kampf um Rom* (in 2 parts).

Publications:

By SIODMAK:

Article—"Hoodlums: The Myth and the Reality", with Richard Wilson in *Films and Filming* (London), June 1959.

On SIODMAK:

Book—*Underworld U.S.A.* by Colin McArthur, London 1972; articles—"Mister Siodmak" by D. Marshman in *Life* (New York), August 1947; "Encounter with Siodmak" by John Taylor in *Sight and Sound* (London), summer/autumn 1959; "Robert Siodmak" by Jack Nolan in *Films in Review* (New York), April 1969; "3 Faces of Film Noir" by Tom Flinn in *Velvet Light Trap* (Madison), summer 1972; "Robert Siodmak l'éclectique" by Claude Beylie in *Ecran* (Paris), May 1973; obituary in *Cinéma* (Paris), May 1973; "Checklist 112—Robert Siodmak" in *Monthly Film Bulletin* (London), June 1978.

* * *

Robert Siodmak is an example of the UFA-influenced German directors who immigrated to Hollywood when war threatened Europe. Less well known than his compatriots Billy Wilder and Fritz Lang, Siodmak demonstrated his cinematic skills early in his career with his innovative German movie, *Menschen am Sonntag*, which featured a non-professional cast, hand-held camera shots, stop motion photography, and the sort of flashbacks that later became associated with his work in America.

Siodmak carried with him to Hollywood the traditions and skills of his German film heritage, and became a major influence in American film noir of the forties. Deep shadows, claustrophobic compositions, elegant camera movements, and meticulously created settings on a grand scale mark the UFA origins of his work. Such themes as the treachery of love and the prevalence of the murderous impulse in ordinary people recur in his American films. The use of the flashback is a dominant narrative device, reflecting his fatalistic approach to story and character. *The Killers* (1946 version) presents a narrative that includes multiple flashbacks, each one of which is a part of the total story and all of which must be accumulated to understand the opening sequence of the film. This opening, based directly on Ernest Hemingway's famous short story, is a masterful example of film story-telling.

A typical Siodmak film of his noir period is *Phantom Lady*, a mini-masterpiece of mood and character, creating intense paranoia through lighting and setting. Two key sequences demonstrate Siodmak's method. In the first, the heroine follows a man into the subway, a simple action that sets off feelings of danger and tension in viewers, feelings that grow entirely out of sound, light, cutting, and camera movement. In the second, one of the most famous sequences in film noir, Siodmak uses jazz music and cutting to build up a narrative meaning that is implicitly sexual as the leading lady urges a drummer to a faster and faster beat.

Siodmak's work is frequently discussed in comparison with that of Alfred Hitchcock, partly because they shared a producer, Joan Harrison, for a period of time. Harrison produced two Siodmak films for Universal, *The Suspect* and *Uncle Harry*. In both films a seemingly ordinary and/or innocent man is drawn into a tangled web of murder, while retaining the audience's sympathy. *Criss Cross*, arguably Siodmak's best noir, ably demonstrates his ability to create depth of characterization through music, mood, and action, particularly in a scene in which Burt Lancaster watches his ex-wife, Yvonne DeCarlo, dance with another man. His fatal obsession with his wife and the victim/victimizer nature of their relationship is capably demonstrated through purely visual means.

In later years, Siodmak turned to such action films as *The Crimson Pirate* and *Custer of the West*, the former a celebrated romp, and one of the first truly tongue-in-cheek anti-genre films of its period. Although Siodmak's films were successful both critically and commercially in their day, he has never achieved the recognition which the visual quality of his work should have earned. An innovative and cinematic director, he explored the criminal or psychotic impulses in his characters through the ambience of his elegant mise-en-scène. The control of all cinematic tools at his command—camera angle, lighting, composition, movement, and design—was used to establish effectively a world of fate, passion, obsession, and compulsion. Although his reputation has been elevated in the past decade, his name deserves to be better known.

—Jeanine Basinger

SIRK, DOUGLAS. German/American. Born Claus Detlef Sierck in Hamburg, 26 April 1900; changed name to Hans Detlef Sierck at beginning of German acting career; changed name to Douglas Sirk after emigrating to U.S. Educated in law, philosophy, and art history in Copenhagen and Hamburg, until 1922. Career: spends childhood in Denmark and Hamburg; 1920—begins writing for *Neue Hamburger Zeitung*; begins involvement with theater as assistant dramaturg for Deutsches Schauspiele, Hamburg; 1921—made dramaturg; 1922—publishes translation of Shakespeare's sonnets; directs *Bahnmeister Tod* (Bossdorf), then directs Chemnitz "Kleinez Theater" (little theater), staging Molière, Strindberg, and others; 1923-29—artistic director, Bremen Schauspielhaus; 1929—named director of Altes Theater, Leipzig (through 1936); 1934—success of Berlin stage production leads to film directing in Berlin for UFA; 1936—made head of Leipzig drama school; 1937—leaves Germany, works on scripts in Austria and France (notably Renoir's *Partie de campagne*); 1939—directs *Boefje* in Holland; contacted by Warners; leaves Holland for U.S.; under contract to Warners prepares new version, unrealized, of *To New Shores*; 1940-41—inactive; 1942—writing contract with Columbia; working with group of German emigrés directs *Hitler's Madman* and *Summer Storm* as independent productions; 1950—begins directing for Universal; 1959—retires from filmmaking for health reasons, returns to Europe; 1960-69—active in theater (Residenz-Theater, Munich, and Thalia Theater, Hamburg).

Films (directed as Detlef Sierck): 1935—*'t Was een April* (Dutch version); *April, April* (German version); *Das Mädchen vom Moorhof*; *Stützen der Gesellschaft*; 1936—*Schlussakkord (Final Accord)* (+co-sc); *Das Hofkonzert* (+co-sc); *La Chanson du souvenir (Song of Remembrance)* (co-d—French version of *Das Hofkonzert*); 1937—*Zu neuen Ufern (To New Shores, Paramatta, Bagne de femmes)* (+co-sc); *La Habanera*; *Liebling der Matrosen* (Hinrich) (co-sc only); 1938—*Dreiklang* (Hinrich) (story only); 1939—*Accord final* (Bay) (supervision, uncredited); *Boefje* (+co-sc); (directed as Douglas Sirk): 1943—*Hitler's Madman*; 1944—*Summer Storm* (+co-sc); 1946—*A Scandal in Paris*; 1947—*Lured*; 1948—*Sleep My Love*; 1949—*Slightly French*; *Shockproof*; 1950—*Mystery Submarine*; 1951—*The First Legion* (+co-pr); *Thunder on the Hill*; *The Lady Pays Off*; *Weekend with Father*; 1952—*No Room for the Groom*; *Has Anybody Seen My Gal?*; *Meet Me at the Fair*; *Take Me to Town*; 1953—*All I Desire*; *Taza, Son of Cochise*; 1954—*Magnificent Obsession*; *Sign of the Pagan*; *Captain Lightfoot*; 1955—*All That Heaven Allows*; *There's Always Tomorrow*; 1956—*Never Say Goodbye* (Hopper) (d uncredited—completed film); *Written on the Wind*; 1957—*Battle Hymn*; *Interlude*; *The Tarnished Angels*; 1958—*A Time to Love and a Time to Die*; 1959—*Imitation of Life*.

Role: 1939—*Sehnsucht nach Afrika* (Zoch).

Publications:

By SIRK:

Articles—interview by Serge Daney and Jean-Louis Noames in *Cahiers du cinéma* (Paris), April 1967; "L'Homme au violoncelle" (story) in *Positif* (Paris), December/January 1977/78; "Douglas Sirk", with interview by D. Rabourdin and others in *Cinéma* (Paris), October 1978; "Het theater is fascistisch, film is goddank nog populair", interview by W. Verstappen in *Skoop* (Amsterdam), December/January 1978/79.

On SIRK:

Books—*Sirk on Sirk*, with Jon Halliday, New York 1972; *Edinburgh Film Festival 1972: Douglas Sirk*, Edinburgh 1972; articles—"L'Aveugle et le miroir, ou l'impossible cinéma de Douglas Sirk" by Jean-Louis Comolli in *Cahiers du cinéma* (Paris), April 1967; "2 Films by Douglas Sirk" by Paul Joannides in *Cinema* (Cambridge, Mass.), August 1970; "Sirk on Sirk" by Jon Halliday in *Cinema One* (London), no.18, 1971; special issue of *Screen* (London), summer 1971; "Towards an Analysis of the Sirkian System" by P. Willemen in *Screen* (London), winter 1972/73; "Sur Douglas Sirk", in 3 parts, by E. Bourget and J.-L. Bourget in *Positif* (Paris), April and September 1972; "Film Favorites" by M. McKegney in *Film Comment* (New York), summer 1972; "The Not So Tender Trap" by E. Keneshea in *Women and Film* (Santa Monica), no.2, 1972; "Begegnung mit D.S." by H.-G. Rasner and R. Wulf in *Filmkritik* (Munich), November 1973; "Douglas Sirk: Melo Maestro" by J. McCourt and "Fassbinder on Sirk" in *Film Comment* (New York), November/December 1975; "Patterns of Power and Potency, Repression and Violence" by M. Stern in *Velvet Light Trap* (Madison), fall 1976; "Douglas Sirk and Melodrama" by L. Mulvey in *Australian Journal of Screen Theory* (Kensington N.S.W.), no.3, 1977; "Notes on Sirk and Melodrama" by L. Mulvey in *Movie* (London), winter 1977/78; "Sirk's *The Tarnished Angels*: 'Pylon' Recreated" by P. Degenfelder in *Literature/Film Quarterly* (Salisbury, Maryland). summer 1977; "Douglas Sirk et le cinéma suisse" by P. Pithon in *Travelling* (Lausanne), spring 1977; "Les Noms de l'auteur" by J.C. Biette in

Cahiers du cinéma (Paris), October 1978; "Les Constantes d'un style" by R. Pithon and "Filmographie, Ausgewählte Bibliographie" in *Cinema* (Zurich), August 1978; "Idol der Münchner Filmstudenten: Douglas Sirk wieder in der HFF" by T. Honickel in *Film und Ton* (Munich), February 1979; "L'Imitazione 'specchio' della vita" by R. Vaccino in *Filmcritica* (Rome), March 1979; "Une Surface de verre" by E. Bourget in *Positif* (Paris), April 1980; "Courts métrages de Douglas Sirk" in *Positif* (Paris), February 1980; "Journals: James McCourt in New York" in *Film Comment* (New York), March/April 1980; "Stahl into Sirk" by T. Pulleine in *Monthly Film Bulletin* (London), November 1981.

*   *   *

Douglas Sirk's critical reputation has almost completely reversed from the time when he was a popular studio director at Universal in the 1950s. He was regarded by contemporary critics as a lightweight director of soap operas who showcased the talents of Universal name stars such as Rock Hudson and Lana Turner. His films often were labelled "women's pictures," with all of the pejorative connotations that term suggests. After his last film, *Imitation of Life*, Sirk retired to Germany, leaving behind a body of work which was seldom discussed or critiqued, but which was frequently revived on television late shows.

Standard works of film criticism either totally ignored or briefly mentioned him with words such as "not a creative film maker" (quoted from his brief entry in Georges Sadoul's *Dictionary of Film Makers*). In the early 1970s, however, a few American critics began to reevaluate his works. The most important innovators in Sirk criticism in this period were Jon Halliday whose lengthy interview in book form, *Sirk on Sirk* has become a standard work, and Andrew Sarris whose program notes on the director's films were compiled into the booklet *Douglas Sirk—The Complete American Period*. From the time of these two works, it became more and more appropriate to speak of Sirk in terms of "genius" and "greatness." By 1979, Sirk was even honored by BBC Television with a "Sirk Season" during which the now loyal following was treated to a weekly installment from the Sirk *oeuvre* as it now fashionably could be called.

Critics today see in Sirk's films more than melodrama with glossy photography and upper-middle-class houses. The word "expressionist" is frequently used to describe his technique, indicating not only the style of Sirk's work in the United States, but also his background in films within the framework of German expressionism in the 1920s and early 1930s. Sirk, who was born in Denmark, but emigrated to Germany in the teens, began work in the theater, then switched to films in the mid-1930s. Known for his "leftist" leanings, Sirk left Germany with the rise of Nazism, and eventually came to the United States in the early 1940s. The first part of his American career was characterized by low budget films which have gone into oblivion. His first well-known film was *Sleep My Love*, a variation on the *Gaslight* theme starring Don Ameche and Claudette Colbert. Soon he began directing films which starred several of the "hot" new Universal stars, among them Hudson and John Gavin, as well as many of the now middle-aged *grandes dames* of the 1930s and 1940s, such as Barbara Stanwyck, Lana Turner, and Jane Wyman. Although today he is known primarily for his dramas, Sirk did make a few lighter pieces, among them *Has Anybody Seen My Gal?*, a musical comedy set in the 1920s. This film is remembered by movie buffs as one of the first James Dean movies.

Many critics consider *Written on the Wind* to be his best film. It was also the one which was best received upon its initial release. All of Sirk's movies deal with relationships which are complicated, and often at a dead-end. In *Written on the Wind*, despite their wealth and attractiveness, the main characters are unhappy. They have little to interest them and seek outlets for their repressed sexuality. One of the four main characters, Kyle Hadley (Robert Stack), has always lived in the shadow of his more virile friend Mitch Wayne (Rock Hudson). He hopes to forget his own feelings of inadequacy by drinking and carousing, but his activities only reinforce his problems. Sexuality, either in its manifestation or repression, is a strongly recurrent theme in all of Sirk's works, but perhaps no where is it more blatantly dramatized than in *Written on the Wind*, where sex is the core of everyone's problems. Mitch is the only truly potent figure in the film, and thus he is the pivotal figure. Hudson's role as Mitch is very similar to that of Ron Kirby in *All That Heaven Allows*. Ron and Mitch both exhibit a strong sense of sexuality that either attracts or repels the other characters and initiates their action.

Kyle's feelings of sexual inadequacy and jealousy of Mitch are interrelated; Mitch is the manly son who Kyle's father always wanted and the virile lover who his wife Lucy (Lauren Bacall) loves. Kyle admires Mitch, yet hates him at the same time. Similarly, Carey Scott in *All That Heaven Allows* desires the earthy gardener Ron, yet she is shocked at her own sexuality, an apparent rejection of the conventions of her staid upper-middle-class milieu. In *There's Always Tomorrow*, Clifford Groves (Fred MacMurray) is faced with a similar situation. He seeks sexual and psychological freedom from his stifling family with Norma Vail (Barbara Stanwyck), yet his responsibilities and sense of morality prevent him from finding the freedom he seeks.

It is an ironic key to Sirk's popular acclaim now that exactly the same stars whose presence seemed to confirm his films as being "programmers" and "women's pictures" have ultimately added a deeper dimension to his works. By using popular stars of the 1930s through 1950s—stars who often peopled lightweight comedies and unregenerate melodramas, Sirk has revealed another dimension of American society. His films often present situations in which the so-called "happy endings" of earlier films are played out to their ultimate (and often more realistic) outcomes by familiar faces. For example, in *There's Always Tomorrow*, Clifford and his wife Marion (Joan Bennett) might very well have been the prototypes for the main characters of a typical 1930s comedy in which "boy gets girl" in the last reel. Yet, in looking at them after almost 20 years of marriage, their lives are shallow. The happy ending of a youthful love has not sustained itself. Similarly, in *All That Heaven Allows*, the attractive middle-aged widow of a "wonderful man" has few things in life to make her happy. Whereas she was once a supposedly happy housewife, the loving spouse of a pillar of the community, her own identity has been suppressed to the point that his death means social ostracism. These two examples epitomize the cynicism of Sirk's view of what was traditionally perceived as the American dream. Most of Sirk's films depict families in which a house, cars, and affluence are present, but in which sexual and emotional fulfillment are not. Many of Sirk's films end on a decidedly unhappy note; the ones that do end optimistically for the main characters are those in which traditions are shattered and the strict societal standards of the time are rejected.

—Patricia King Hanson

SJÖBERG, ALF. Swedish. Born in Stockholm, 21 June 1903. Educated at Royal Dramatic Theatre. Career: 1925—professional acting debut; 1927—begins stage directing; 1929—seeing Eisenstein film leads to first film directed, *The Strongest*; 1930s—continues working in theater; 1940—returns to filmmaking; 1944—*Torment*, scripted by Ingmar Bergman, receives international recognition. Died in 1980. Recipient: Best Film (*ex aequo*), Cannes Festival, for *Miss Julie*, 1951.

Films (as director): 1929—*Den starkaste (The Strongest)* (+story); 1940—*Med livet som insats (They Staked Their Lives)* (+co-sc); *Den blomstertid (Blossom Time)* (+sc); 1941—*Hem från Babylon (Home from Babylon)* (+co-sc); 1942—*Himlaspelet (The Road to Heaven)* (+co-sc); 1944—*Hets (Torment)*; *Kungajakt (The Royal Hunt)*; 1945—*Resan bort (Journey Out)* (+sc); 1946—*Iris och löjtnantshjärta (Iris and the Lieutenant)* (+sc); 1949—*Bara en mor (Only a Mother)* (+co-sc); 1951—*Fröken Julie (Miss Julie)* (+sc); 1953—*Barabbas* (+co-sc); 1954—*Karin Månsdotter* (+sc); 1955—*Vildfåglar (Wild Birds)* (+co-sc); 1956—*Sista paret ut (Last Pair Out)*; 1960—*Domaren (The Judge)* (+co-sc); 1966—*On (The Island)*; 1969—*Fadern (The Father)*.

Publications:

On SJÖBERG:

Book—*Filmregi Alf Sjöberg* by G. Lundin, Lund, Sweden 1979.

SJÖMAN, VILGOT. Swedish. Born David Harald Vilgot Sjöman in Stockholm, 2 December 1924. Educated in literary history, Stockholm University, late 1940s; attended UCLA, 1956. Career: at age 15 begins working as clerk in Swedish Cereals Company; later works as orderly in Långholm Prison; 1942—plays bit role in Ingmar Bergman stage production of *A Midsummer Night's Dream*, begins friendship with Bergman; late 1940s—begins to have novels published; early 1950s—begins scriptwriting; 1956—visits Hollywood, attends UCLA film course and is "intern" on George Seaton's *The Proud and the Profane*; 1961—begins film directing; has continued to do TV and stage work; 1967—*I Am Curious—Yellow* seized by U.S. Customs as pornography, released after lengthy legal battle, grosses more than any previous foreign film in U.S.

Films (as scriptwriter): 1952—*Trots (Defiance)* (Molander); 1958—*Lek på regnbågen (Playing on the Rainbow)*; 1962—*Siska* (co-sc); (as director and scriptwriter): 1962—*Älskarinnan (The Mistress, The Swedish Mistress)*; 1964—*491* (d only); *Klänningen (The Dress)* (d only); 1965—"Negressen i skåpet (Negress in the Wardrobe)" episode of *Stimulantia*; 1966—*Syskonbädd 1782 (My Sister My Love)*; 1967—*Jag är nyfiken—gul (I Am Curious—Yellow)*; 1968—*Jag är nyfiken—blå (I Am Curious—Blue)*; *Resa med far (Journey with Father)* (short); 1969—*Ni ljuger (You're Lying)*; 1970—*Lyckliga skitar (Blushing Charlie)* (co-sc); 1971—*Troll (Till Sex Do Us Part)* (+pr, co-sc); 1972—*Bröderna Karlsson (The Karlsson Brothers)* (+pr); 1974—*En handfull kärlek (A Handful of Love)*; *Kulisser i Hollywood* (short); 1975—*Garaget (The Garage)*; 1977—*Tabu (Taboo)*; 1979—*Linus*; 1982—*I Am Blushing*.

Role: 1968—TV interviewer in *Skammen (The Shame)* (Bergman).

Publications:

By SJÖMAN:

Books—*I Am Curious (Yellow)*, script, New York 1968; *I Am Curious (Blue)*, script, with Martin Minow and Jenny Bohman, New York 1970; articles—"Catching the Rare Moment", interview by Paul Grey in *Tulane Drama Review* (Louisiana), fall 1966; "From L 136: A Diary of Ingmar Bergman's Winter Light" in *Cinema Journal* (Evanston), spring 1974; "Vilgot Sjöman: Le Burlesque dans le sérieux", interview in *Jeune Cinéma* (Paris), May 1974; "Art is born at the frontiers of taboo", interview by D. Georgakas and Gary Crowdus in *Cineaste* (New York), fall 1977; "Att bygga upp ett filmarskap" in *Chaplin* (Stockholm), v.23, no.6, 1981.

On SJÖMAN:

Articles—"Convention Be Damned" by Sven Krohn in *Atlas*, August 1966; article by Clyde Smith in *Film Quarterly* (Berkeley), summer 1969; "Curiouser and Curiouser" by J. Morgenstern in *Newsweek* (New York), 24 March 1969; "Vilgot Sjöman" by T. Jungstedt and L. Löthwall in *Chaplin* (Stockholm), no.4, 1974; "Vilgot Sjöman" by Peter Cowie in *International Film Guide 1975*, London 1974.

SJÖSTRÖM, VICTOR. Swedish. Born Victor David Sjöström in Silbodal, Sweden, 20 September 1879. Attended high school in Uppsala, Sweden. Married Sascha Stjagoff, 1900 (died 1916); Lili Bech, 1916; Edith Erastoff, 1922 (died 1945); children: Karin and Gunn. Career: 1880—family moves to New York; 1887—returns to Sweden alone to live with an aunt; 1893—appears on stage for 1st time as amateur actor; 1896—becomes professional actor; 1896-1912—works as stage actor and director in Sweden and Finland; 1911—forms own theater company; 1912—hired as film director by Charles Magnusson, head of newly formed Svenska Biograf film studio, Stockholm; 1912-16—directs an average of 8 films per year for Svenska Biograf; 1916—gains international recognition with *Terje Vigen*; 1922—contracted by Goldwyn Pictures (soon to be MGM) to direct films in Hollywood and leaves following year; 1922-29—directs several silent films for MGM, including his most successful *The Wind*; name is "Americanized" as "Seastrom"; 1929—directs 1st sound film *The Lady to Love*; 1930—returns to Sweden, intending to make films, but returns to acting; 1943-49—artistic director, Svensk Filmindustri; 1957—appears in Ingmar Bergman's *Wild Strawberries*. Died in Stockholm, 3 January 1960.

Films (as director): 1912—*Trädgårdsmästaren (The Gardener)* (+ro); *Ett Hemligt giftermaål (A Secret Marriage)*; *En sommarsaga (A Summer Tale)*; 1913—*Löjen och tårar (Ridicule and Tears)*; *Blodets röst (Voice of the Blood)* (+sc, ro) (released 1923); *Lady Marions sommarflirt (Lady Marion's summer Flirt)*; *Äktenskapsbrydån (The Marriage Agency)* (+sc); *Livets konflikter (Conflicts of Life)* (co-d, +ro); *Ingeborg Holm* (+sc); *Halvblod (Half Breed)*; *Miraklet*; *På livets ödesvägar (On the Roads of Fate)*; 1914—*Prästen (The Priest)*; *Det var i Maj (It Was in May)* (+sc); *Kärlek starkare än hat (Love Stronger Than Hatred)*; *Dömen icke (Do Not Judge)*; *Bra flicka reder sig själv (A Clever Girl Takes Care of Herself)* (+sc); *Gatans barn (Children of the Street)*; *Högfjällets dotter (Daughter of the Mountains)* (+sc); *Hjärtan som mötas (Meeting Hearts)*; 1915—

Strejken (Strike) (+sc, ro); *En av de många (One of the Many)* (+sc); *Sonad oskuld (Expiated Innocence)* (+co-sc); *Skomakare bliv vid din läst (Cobbler Stay at Your Bench)* (+sc); 1916— *Lankshövdingens dottrar (The Governor's Daughters)* (+sc); *Rösen på Tistelön (Havsgammar, The Rose of Thistle Island, Sea Eagle)*; I. *Prövningens stund (Hour of the Trial)* (+sc, ro); *Skepp som motas (Meeting Ships)*; *Hon segrade (She Conquered)* (+sc, ro); *Therese* (+co-sc); 1917—*Dödskyssen (Kiss of Death)* (+co-sc, ro); *Terje Vigen (A Man There Was)* (+co-sc, ro); 1918—*Berg-Ejvind och hans hustru (The Outlaw and His Wife)* (+co-sc, ro); *Tösen från stormyrtorpet (The Lass from the Stormy Croft)* (+co-sc); 1919—*Ingmarsönerna, Parts I and II (Sons of Ingmar)* (+sc, ro); *Hans nåds testamente (The Will of His Grace)*; 1920—*Klostret I Sendomir (The Monastery of Sendomir)* (+sc); *Karin Ingmarsdotter (Karin, Daughter of Ingmar)* (+co-sc, ro); *Mästerman (Master Samuel)* (+ro); 1921—*Körkarlen (The Phantom Chariot, Clay, Thy Soul Shall Bear Witness)* (+sc, ro); 1922—*Vem dömer (Love's Crucible)* (+co-sc); *Det omringade huset (The Surrounded House)* (+co-sc, ro); 1923—*Eld ombord (The Tragic Ship)* (+ro); 1924—*Name the Man*; *He Who Gets Slapped*; 1925—*Confessions of a Queen*; *The Tower of Lies*; 1927—*The Scarlet Letter*; 1928—*The Divine Woman*; *The Wind*; *Masks of the Devil*; 1930—*A Lady to Love*; 1931— *Markurells I Wadköping* (+ro); 1937—*Under the Red Robe.*

Roles (in films not directed): 1912—*Lt. Roberts* in *Vampyren* (Stiller); *The Lieutenant* in *De svarta maskerna* (Stiller); I *livets vår* (Garbagni); 1913—*The Painter* in *När kärlekan dödar* (Stiller); *Medical Student* in *Barnet* (Stiller); 1914—*Borgen* in *För sin kädleks skull* (Stiller); *Högfjällets dotter* (Stiller); *Guldspindeln* (Magnusen); *Thomas Graal* in *Thomas Graals bästa film* (Stiller); *Thomas Graal* in *Thomas Graals bästa barn* (Stiller); 1934—*Synnove Solbakken* (T. Ibsen); 1935— *Valborgsmaässoafton* (Edgren); 1937—*John Ericsson*; 1939— *Gubben Kommer* (Lindberg); *Mot nya tider* (Wallen); 1941— *Striden går vidare* (Molander); 1943—*Det brinner en eld* (Molander); *Ordet* (Molander); 1944—*Kejsaren av Portugalien* (Molander); 1947—*Rallare* (Mattson); 1940's—*Farlig vår* (Mattson); 1950—*Till Glädje* (Bergman); *Kvartetten som sprängdes* (Molander); 1952—*Hård klang* (Mattson); 1955—*Nattens väv* (Mattson); 1957—*Professor* in *Smultronstället (Wild Strawberries)* (Bergman).

Publications:

On SJÖSTRÖM:

Books—*Film och Filmfolk* by Teddy Nyblom, Stockholm 1925; *40 Ans de cinéma nordique* by Georges Charensol, Paris 1935; *Den Svenska Filmens Drama: Sjöström och Stiller* by Bengt Idestam-Almquist, Stockholm 1938; *Greta Garbo* by E.E. Laing, London 1946; *Scandanavian Film* by Forsyth Hardy, London 1951; *Classics of the Swedish Cinema* by Bengt Idestam-Almquist, Stockholm 1952; *Garbo* by John Bainbridge, New York 1955; *The Lion's Share: the Story of an Entertainment Empire* by Bosley Crowther, New York 1957; *Swedish Cinema* by Rune Waldekranz, Stockholm 1959; *La Grande Aventure du cinéma suédois* by Jean Béranger, Paris 1960; *Garbo, A Biography* by Fritiof Billquist, New York 1960; *Swedish Film* by Einar Lauritzen, New York 1962; *The Films of Greta Garbo* by Michael Conway, New York 1963; *Sjöström et l'ecole suédois* by René Jeanne and Charles Ford, Paris 1963; *Swedish Cinema* by Peter Cowie, London 1966; *Anthologie du cinéma* Vol. I, Paris 1966; *Seastrom and Stiller in Hollywood* by

Hans Pensel, New York 1969; articles—"The Golden Age of Scandanavian Film" by M.C. Potamkin in *Cinema* (London), September 1930; "Le Cinéma nordique" in *L'Art cinématographique* edited by Felix Alian, Paris 1931; "Victor Sjöström" by Bengt Idestam-Almquist in *Biografbladet* (Stockholm), summer 1950; "Victor Sjöström and His Conversion" by Bengt Idestam-Almquist in *Biografbladet* (Stockholm), winter 1950; "Sweden in Film History" by Bengt Idestam-Almquist in *Biografbladet* (Stockholm), spring 1951; "Schedine per Sjöström" by Mario Verdone in *Cinema* (Milan), no.131, 1954; "Victor Sjöström and D.W. Griffith" by D. Vaughn in *Film* (London), January/February 1958; "Letter" by C. Shibuk in *Films in Review* (New York), May 1959; "Origin of the Swedish Cinema" by Bengt Idestam-Almquist in *Biografbladet* (Stockholm), spring 1960; "Victor Sjöström" by Charles L. Turner in *Films in Review* (New York), May and June 1960; "Victor Sjöström: Pioneer of the Swedish Film" by Frederic Fleisher in *American Scandinavian Review*, September 1960; "The Magic of 2 Heroes" by C. Duncan in *Film Journal* (Australia), March 1960; "Bergman on Victor Sjöström" in *Sight and Sound* (London), spring 1960; "Becker-Sjöström" in *Sight and Sound* (London), spring 1970; "As I Remember Him" in *Film Comment* (New York), summer 1970; "16mm Discovery: Under the Red Robe" by J. Richards in *Focus on Film* (London), spring 1972; "Swedish Retrospect" by J. Gillett in *Sight and Sound* (London), summer 1974; "Essays on the Swedish Cinema (Part 2)" by Robin Wood in *Lumiere* (Melbourne), April/May 1974; "Lost and Found" by Tom Milne in *Sight and Sound* (London), autumn 1975; "Sjöström, Stiller et L'Amérique" by Claude Beylie and M. Martin in *Ecran* (Paris), September 1978; "Victor Sjöström" in *Films and Filming* (London), no.9, 1979; "Seastrom: The Hollywood Years" by Herman Weinberg in *American Classic Screen* (Shawnee Mission, Kansas), fall 1979; "Allt går igen, även det onda" by B. Forslund and "Vem såg Victor Sjöströms mästerverk?" by J. Torbacke in *Chaplin* (Stockholm), v.22, no.6, 1980; "Svenska giganter 1" by B. Forslund in *Filmrutan* (Liding, Sweden), v.24, no.2, 1981; film—*Victor Sjöström—A Film Portrait* by Gösta Werner, Sweden 1980.

*   *   *

With a career in film that in many ways paralleled that of his close friend, Mauritz Stiller, Victor Sjöström entered the Swedish film industry at virtually the same time (1912), primarily as an actor, only to become almost immediately, like Stiller, a film director. However, whereas Stiller had spent his youth in Finland, Sjöström had spent six formative years as a child in America's Brooklyn; later, back in Sweden and after an unhappy childhood, his training for the theater had born fruit and he had become a well-established actor before entering the film industry at the age of 32: "The thing that brought me into filmmaking was a youthful desire for adventure and a curiosity to try this new medium," he once said in interview. The first films in which he appeared in 1912 were Stiller's *The Black Masks* and *Vampyren.*

Although Sjöström proved excellent as an actor in comedy, his innate seriousness of outlook was reflected in the films he directed. He developed a deep response to nature, to the spectacular northern landscape, the expanses of ice, snow, trees, and mountains in all their (to him as to other Scandinavians) mystical force. One of his earliest films was *Ingeborn Holm*, which exposed the cruelties of the forced labor system to which the children of paupers were still subjected. This film was produced partially outdoors; Sjöström's pantheistic response to nature was developed in *Terje Vigen*, his adaptation of Ibsen's ballad poem with its narrative set in the period of the Napoleonic confrontation with Britain. Sjöström himself played Terje, the bitter Norwegian sailor who had been imprisoned for a while by the British for attempting to break through their blockade at sea in order to bring food through to the starving people, including his wife and son, in his village. He fails, and they die in consequence. Terje's obsessive desire for vengeance is later purged as a result of his response to his British captor's child, whom he rescues in a storm.

Sjöström became a prolific director. He completed approaching 30 films between 1912 and 1918, the year he directed *The Outlaw and His Wife*, of which the French critic and filmmaker, Louis Delluc, wrote in 1921, "Here without doubt is the most beautiful film in the world. Victor Sjöström has directed it with a dignity that is beyond words...it is the first love duet heard in the cinema. A duet that is entire life. Is it a drama?.... I don't know.... People love each other and live. That is all." In this film a rich widow abandons her estate to live in the mountains with her outlaw lover until, hounded by his pursuers, they die together in the snow. It is typical of the Swedish film that winter, after the symbolic summer of love, should become the synonym for Death. Sjöström's intense feeling for nature expanded still further in his first adaptation of a novel by Selma Lagerlöf who, as a writer in the grand tradition, became one of the primary inspirers of the Swedish cinema of this period. This adaptation was from *The Lass from the Stormy Croft*, with its magnificent rustic setting which seems at once to transcend and embody the exigencies of human passion—the frustration of the poor peasant girl with her illegitimate child and the troubles that afflict the son of a landowner (played by Lars Hanson in his first important film role), who tries to befriend her. As Carl Dreyer, who in the same year made *The Parson's Widow* in Sweden, commented, "Selma Lagerlöf's predilection for dreams and supernatural events appealed to Sjöström's own somewhat sombre artistic mind."

Sjöström's most famous film before his departure for Hollywood in 1923 was *The Phantom Carriage* (also known as *Thy Soul Shall Bear Witness*), also based on a novel by Selma Lagerlöf. The legend had it that the phantom carriage came once each year, on New Year's Eve, St. Sylvester's Night, to carry away the souls of sinners. In the film the central character is David Holm, a violent and brutalized man who is brought to relive his evil past on St. Sylvester's Night, especially the ill-treatment he had given his wife, until his conscience is awakened. As Holm recalls his wicked deeds in flashback he is haunted by the approach of the phantom carriage, and is saved just in time through reunion with his wife, whose imminent suicide he prevents. Holm is played brilliantly by Sjöström himself, while Julius Jaenzen's multi-exposure camerawork emphasizes the distinction between body and soul in visuals that surpass virtually all that had been achieved in cinematography by 1920.

When, in the postwar era, Swedish films, with their comparatively heavy themes, began to prove less popular as exports, Sjöström, like Stiller, left for America on the invitation of Louis B. Mayer at MGM. He was to remain in Hollywood six years, and direct nine films under the name of Victor Seastrom. Of these *The Scarlet Letter*, with Lillian Gish as Hester Prynne and Lars Hanson as the priest, and *The Wind*, also with Lillian Gish and Lars Hanson, are the more significant, the latter ranking now as a masterpiece of the silent cinema. Lillian Gish has said of Sjöström that "his direction was a great education for me...the Swedish school of acting is one of repression." In *The Wind* she plays a sensitive girl from Kentucky forced into marriage with a coarse cattleman from Texas, a repellant marriage which, along with the harsh Texan environment, finally drives her nearly insane and impels her to kill a male intruder in self-defense. The

film, shot in the Mojave region, suffered some re-editing by the studio, and the imposition of a sound track. Sjöström's single attempt to recreate Sweden in America was *The Tower of Lies* (with Lon Chaney and Norma Shearer), an adaptation of Selma Lagerlöf's novel, *The Emperor of Portugal*, which at least one American reviewer praised for, "its preservation of the simplicity of treatment in *Thy Soul Shall Bear Witness*."

Sjöström returned to Sweden in 1928 and directed one good sound film, *Markurells i Wadköping*, in which he starred as a grim man, much like Terje Vigen, who is finally purged of his desire for revenge. Apart from directing a lame period romance in England, *Under the Red Robe*, with Raymond Massey and Conrad Veidt, Sjöström concentrated on his career as an actor, giving at the age of 78 a great performance as the aged professor in Bergman's *Wild Strawberries*.

—Roger Manvell

SKOLIMOWSKI, JERZY. Polish. Born in Warsaw, 5 May 1938. Educated in literature and history at Warsaw University, diploma 1959. Career: 1958—publication of 1st poetry collection, *Quelque part près de soi*; 1959—co-scriptwriter on Wajda's *Niewinni czardodzieje*; 1960—on recommendation of Andrzej Wajda enters State Cinema School at Lodz; 1960-64—makes *Rysopis* in course of fulfilling requirements as film student; 1961—collaborates with Polanski on script of *Knife in the Water*; 1967—*Hands Up!* banned by Polish authorities; leaves Poland; 1970—is invited by producer Gene Gutowski to direct *The Adventures of Gérard*. Recipient: Best Screenplay, Cannes Festival, for *Moonlighting*, 1982.

Films (as co-scriptwriter): 1959—*Niewinni czardodzieje (Innocent Sorcerers)* (Wajda); 1960—*Noz w wodzie (Knife in the Water)* (Polanski); *Przy Jaciel (A Friend)*; (as director and scriptwriter of short films): 1960—*Oko wykol (L'Oeil Torve)*; *Hamles (Le Petit Hamlet)*; *Erotyk (L'Érotique)*; 1961—*Boks (Boxing)*; *Piednadze albo zycie (La Bourse ou la vie)*; *Akt*; (as director and scriptwriter of feature films): 1964—*Rysopis (Identification Marks: None)* (+pr, art d, ed, ro as *Andrzej Leszczyc*); 1965—*Walkower (Walkover)* (+co-ed, ro as *Andrzej Leszczyc*); 1966—*Bariera (Barrier)*; 1967—*Le Départ (co-sc)*; *Rece do gory (Hands Up!)* (+co-art d, ro as *Andrzej Leszczyc*); 1968—*Dialog (Dialogue)* (+art d); 1970—*The Adventures of Gerard* (co-sc); *Deep End* (co-sc); 1971—*King, Queen, Knave* (co-sc); 1978—*The Shout* (co-sc); 1982—*Moonlighting* (+co-pr).

Publications:

By SKOLIMOWSKI:

Books—*Quelque part près de soi*, 1958; *La Hache et le ciel*, 1959; articles—"The 21st", interview, in *Cahiers du Cinema in English* (New York), January 1967; "Passages and Levels: Interview with Jerzy Skolimowski" by Michel Delahaye in *Cahiers du Cinema in English* (New York), December 1967; "'An Accusation That I Throw in the Face of My Generation'—A Conversation with the Young Polish Director, Jerzy Skolimowski" in *Film Comment* (New York), fall 1968; "Jerzy Skolimowski: A Conversation" by Peter Blum in *Film Culture* (New York), fall 1968; "Entretien avec Jerzy Skolimowski" by Michel Ciment and Bernard Cohn in *Positif* (Paris), February 1972; "Propos Rompus de Skolimowski", interview by J. Delmas in *Jeune Cinéma* (Paris), February 1972; interview by A. Cornand and R. Grelier in *Image et son* (Paris), February 1972; interview by Max Tessier in *Ecran* (Paris), February 1972; interview by E. Verdi in *Cinéma* (Paris), January 1972; interview in *Cahiers du cinéma* (Paris), July/August 1978; "Jerzy Skolimowski", with interview by P. Carcassonne and others in *Cinématographe* (Paris), June 1978; "El Grito", with interview by L. García Tsao in *Cine* (Mexico), December 1978; "Skolimowski's Cricket Match", interview by P. Strick in *Sight and Sound* (London), summer 1978; interview by Michel Ciment and H. Niogret in *Positif* (Paris), January 1979.

On SKOLIMOWSKI:

Articles—"Jerzy Skolimowski: Portrait of a Debutant Director" by Krzysztof-Teodor Toeplitz in *Film Quarterly* (Berkeley), fall 1967; "Skolimowski" by Christian Thomsen in *Sight and Sound* (London), summer 1968; "Adventures of Yurek" by Robin Bean in *Films and Filming* (London), December 1968; "Jerzy Skolimowski" by Michael Walker in *Second Wave*, New York 1970; "Director of the Year" in *International Film Guide 1970*, London 1969; "Bio-filmographie de Jerzy Skolimowski" by Michel Ciment in *Positif* (Paris), February 1972; "Profil de Skolimowski. Deep End" by J. Delmas in *Jeune Cinéma* (Paris), February 1972; "Le Pourpre et le jaune (*Deep End*)" by M. Sineux in *Positif* (Paris), February 1972; "Jerzy Skolimowski ou la poésie du dérisoire" by R. Lefèvre in *Cinéma* (Paris), September/October 1973.

* * *

Together with Roman Polanski, Jerzy Skolimowski is the most remarkable representative of the second generation of the Polish new wave. Younger than Wajda, Munk, or Kawalerowicz, those two did not share the hope for a new society after World War II and are more skeptical, to the point sometimes of cynicism. With Polanski, Skolimowski wrote *Knife in the Water*, which deals precisely with the relationship between two generations, after having also collaborated on the script of Wajda's *Innocent Sorcerers*, one of the director's rare attempts at portraying Poland's youth. A student in ethnography, a poet, an actor, and a boxer, Skolimowski went to the Lodz film school (1960-1964) and graduated with a diploma work that brought world attention to his talent. That film, *Rysopis (Identification Marks: None)*, and its totally controlled sequel *Walkover*, reveal an astonishing flexible style which follows a central character, Andrzej Leszczyc, played by Skolimowski himself. Without resorting to a subjective camera, the director nevertheless makes us see reality through his hero, refusing dramatic plot twists, and filming very much like a jazz musician—all rhythm and improvisation. *Rysopis* tells of the few hours before being called up for military service, and *Walkover* of the time preceding a boxing match. A limited number of shots (39 and 29 respectively!) gives an extraordinary sense of fluidity, of life caught in its most subtle shifts. *Bariera* is a much more literary and symbolic work. It offers the same themes and milieu (young people, often students), although with a dreamlike atmosphere, a somnambulistic quality which will reappear later in Skolimowski's work, but more successfully integrated into its realistic surface. "Our cynical and indifferent generation still possesses romantic aspirations," says one of the characters. And this sums up well the filmmaker's ambivalent attitude towards life.

If *Bariera* was, according to Skolimowski, influenced by Godard's *Pierrot le fou*, his next film, *Le Départ*, shot in Belgium, borrowed two actors, Jean-Pierre Léaud and Catherine Duport from the French director's *Masculin féminin*. It deals with a young hairdresser who dreams of becoming a rally driver and his relationship with a girl. The same sensitive portrait of youth will be found again in a more accomplished work, *Deep End*, a brilliant portrayal of a London swimming bath attendant and his tragic love affair. Skolimowski's very titles (*Walkover*, *Barrier*, *Departure*, *Hands Up*, *Deep End*) suggest the relationship to sports, movement and physical effort that characterizes his nervous and dynamic style. *Hands Up*, banned for fifteen years by the Polish authorites because of its bleak symbolic portrayal of a group of people shut up inside a railway carriage, determined Skolimowski to work in the West though he has always returned regularly to his home country. But the difficulties linked to an international career appeared quickly with the failure of *The Adventures of Gerard*, a spoof on Conan Doyle's Napoleonic novel, and the more evident one of *King, Queen, Knave*, shot in Munich from Nabokov's novel.

However, Skolimowski came back to the forefront of European filmmaking with *The Shout* and *Moonlighting*. The former, adapted from a Robert Graves short story, has a sense of the absurd which verges on creating a surrealistic atmosphere—a classic component of Polish culture. This film about a triangular relationship between a kind of sorcerer, the woman he is in love with, and her husband, is an intense, haunting piece of work. *Moonlighting*, arguably Skolimowski's best film to date, along with *Walkover*, was written and shot within a few months and looks deceptively simple. The tale of four Polish workers, sent from Warsaw to refurbish the house a rich Pole has bought in London, reveals, little by little, layers of meaning, contacts between East and West, and repression in Poland. The nightmare emerges slowly from a close scruntiny of reality and confirms that Skolimowski's materialism and lucidity do not contradict but rather refine his unique poetic sensibility.

—Michel Ciment

SMITH, HARRY. American. Born in in Portland, Oregon, 1923. Smith statement on the development of his filmmaking: "My cinematic excreta is of four varieties: batiked abstractions made directly on film between 1939 and 1946; optically printed non-objective studies composed around 1950; semi-realistic animated collages made as part of my alchemical labors of 1957 to 1962; and chronologically superimposed photographs of actualities formed since the latter year. All these works have been organized in specific patterns derived from the interlocking beats of the respiration, the heart and the EEG Alpha component and should be observed together in order, or not at all, for they are valuable works, works that will live forever—they made me gray.

Films: 1939?-47—*No.1* (5 min.); 1940-42?—*No.2* (10 min.); 1942-47—*No.3* (10 min.); 1950—*No.4* (6 min.); *No.5 (Circular Tensions)* (6 min.); 1951—*No.6* (20 min.); *No.7* (15 min.); 1954—*No.8* (5 min.—longer version became *No.12*); *No.9* (10 min.); 1956—*No.10* (10 min.—study for *No.11*); *No.11 (Mirror Animations)* (4 min.); 1943-58?—*No.12 (Heaven and Earth Magic, The Magic Feature)* (70 min.); 1962—*No.13* (180 min.); 1964-65—*No.14 (Late Superimpositions)* (30 min.); 1965-66—*No.15*; 1967—*No.16 (The Tin Woodman's Dream)* (15 min.).

Publications:

By SMITH:

Articles—"A Rare Interview with Harry Smith" by John Cohen in *Sing Out: The Folk Song Magazine* (New York), April/May and July/August 1969; "Harry Smith Interview" in *Cantrill's Filmnotes* (Melbourne), October 1974.

On SMITH:

Articles—"Death and Trancefiguration" by Ken Kelman in *Film Culture* (New York), no.34, 1964; "Dialogue without Words: The Work of Harry Smith" by Carol Berge in *Film Culture* (New York), no.37, 1965; "Mind, Medium, and Metaphor in Harry Smith's *Heaven and Earth Magic*" by Noel Carroll in *Film Quarterly* (Berkeley), winter 1977/78; "The Spatial Strategies of Harry Smith's *Heaven and Earth Magic*" by Judith Switzer in *Film Reader* (Evanston), no.3, 1978.

SNOW, MICHAEL. Canadian. Born in Toronto, 1929. Educated at Ontario College of Art, Toronto. Married to filmmaker Joyce Wieland. Career: early 1950s—pursues career first as painter, then as sculptor; sometimes supports self as jazz musician on trumpet and piano; 1955-56—works at Graphic Films, Toronto; at Graphic makes 1st film, animated short *A to Z*; 1957—first one-person show, Isaacs Gallery, Toronto; 1962—moves to New York City; 1964—makes *New York Eye and Ear Control* as part of series of works, in several media, based on "The Walking Woman" silhouette figure; about 1966—begins to concentrate on filmmaking; (culmination of series a set of sculptures executed for Expo '67, Montreal); 1969—collaborates with wife Joyce Wieland on *Dripping Water*; 1970—represents Canada at Venice Biennale with films and other art works; 1970—professor of Advanced Film Studies, Yale University; 1971—returns to Toronto; 1977—takes part in Documenta 6, Kassel. Recipient: Grand Prize, 4th International Experimental Film Festival, Knokke-le-Zoute, Belgium, for *Wavelength*, 1967. Address: lives in Toronto.

Films: 1956—*A to Z*; 1964—*New York Eye and Ear Control (A Walking Woman Work)*; 1965—*Short Shave*; 1966-67—*Wavelength*; 1967—*Standard Time*; 1968-69—◄──► *(Back and Forth)*; *One Second in Montreal*; *Dripping Water* (with Joyce Wieland); 1970—*Side Seat Paintings Slides Sound Film*; 1970-71—*La Region centrale (The Central Region)*; 1972 and 1976—*Breakfast (Table Top Dolly)*; 1974—*2 Sides to Every Story* (2-screen); 1972-74—*Rameau's Nephew by Diderot (Thanx to Dennis Young) by Wilma Schoen*; 1982—*Presents*; *This Is It*.

Publications:

By SNOW:

Books—*Michael Snow: A Survey*, exhibition catalogue, Art Gallery of Toronto, 1970; *Cover to Cover*, Nova Scotia 1976; articles—"Conversation with Michael Snow" by Jonas Mekas and P. Adams Sitney in *Film Culture* (New York), autumn 1967; "Letter from Michael Snow" in *Film Culture* (New York), no.46, 1967; "Michael Snow on 'La Region Centrale'" in *Film Culture*

(New York), spring 1971; "Passage" in *Artforum* (New York), September 1971; interview by M. Grande and others in *Filmcritica* (Rome), October 1972; "The Life and Times of Michael Snow", interview by J. Medjuck in *Take One* (Montreal), April 1972; "Snow's Sinema Soufflé", with interview, by A. Ibranyi-Kiss in *Cinema Canada* (Montreal), May/June 1975; interview by Jonas Mekas and P. Adams Sitney in in *Cahiers du cinéma* (Paris), January 1979; "Michael Snow in San Francisco", interview by P. Adams Sitney and others in *Cinemanews* (San Francisco), no.2/4, 1979; "The 'Presents' of Michael Snow", interview by Jonathan Rosenbaum in *Film Comment* (New York), May/-June 1981.

On SNOW:

Book—*A History of the American Avant-Garde*, exhibition catalogue, by John Hanhardt and others, The American Federation of Arts, New York 1976; articles—"The Act of Seeing" by John Perreault in *The Village Voice* (New York), 8 February 1968; "Critique: Glass and Snow" by Richard Foreman in *Arts Magazine* (New York), February 1970; article in *Negative Space* by Manny Farber, New York 1971; "Toward Snow" by Annette Michelson in *Artforum* (New York), June 1971; "Lo Schermo come soglia dell'infinito" by F. Pecori and "Teoria del cinema e cinema della teoria" by M. Grande in *Filmcritica* (Rome), October 1972; "A Note on Michael Snow, Written in a Minnesota Snowstorm" by Jonas Mekas in *Take One* (Montreal), April 1972; "Aspects of Cinematic Consciousness..." by Donald Skoller in *Film Comment* (New York), September/October 1972; "New Forms in Film" by Bill Simon in *Artforum* (New York), October 1972; "A Casing Shelved" by A. Hayum in *Film Culture* (New York), spring 1973; "Snow Storms Italy" by L. Marcorelles and T. Raneri in *Cinema Canada* (Montreal), February/March 1973; "Narrative Space" by S. Heath in *Screen* (London), no.3, 1976; "Hitting on 'A Lot of Near Mrs.'" by R. Cornwell in *Film Reader* (Evanston, Illinois), no.3, 1978; "Digne (À propos de Michael Snow)" by L. Bloch in *Cahiers du cinéma* (Paris), July/August 1978; "Digne" by G. Courant in *Cinéma* (Paris), August/September 1978; "Michael Snow: par le film une nouvelle vision de l'univers" by J. Delmas in *Jeune Cinéma* (Paris), March 1979; "Snow et la durée" by M. Martin in *Ecran* (Paris), 15 March 1979; "About Snow" by A. Michelson in *October* (Cambridge, Mass.), spring 1979; "Michael Snow et 'La Region centrale'" by M.-C. Questerbert in *Cahiers du cinéma* (Paris), January 1979.

*   *   *

After studies at the Ontario College of Art, Snow simultaneously pursued careers as a jazz musician and an artist, making sculpture, paintings, and photography. He began to make films while working for a commercial film company in Canada, but his first important film, *New York Eye and Ear Control* was made in New York, as an extension of his attempt to represent a graphic image (his "Walking Woman" outline) in a wide range of media. The film is notable for its use of a powerful jazz soundtract.

Snow's reputation as a filmmaker, however, crystallized with the release of his next film, *Wavelength*. There he built the entire film around the exploration of the illusionary properties of the zoom lens. That set the program for his most ambitious cinematic works, several of which examine the range of possibilities inherent in a given techinque. In ◄──►, the entire film consists of panning movements, first horizontally, then vertically, and finally a superimposed recapitulation for both. *One Second in*

Montreal brought the film composed wholly of stills to a new intensity of stasis, testing the possibilites of perceptual distinctions when shots are held unusually long, but for varying lengths of time.

The Central Region employs a specially built, remote-controlled equitorial mount to perform intricate movements, sweeping the entire, desolate landscape of the zone of northern Canada where it was set up, to present the visible worlds as if it were the inside of a great sphere. This three-hour-long film without human presence develops the tensions between cinematic time, as emphasized by the unequivocally mechanical camera gyrations, and the natural cycle of the solar day.

Rameau's Nephew by Diderot (*Thanx to Dennis Young*) by *Wilma Schoen* takes on an encyclopedic range of topics related to picture and sound, with a Duchampian "study" of language most prominent. For 285 minutes, in apparently 24 distinct sections, the film explores the human body as a source of sound. The inherent independence of picture and sound in all films becomes the justification for the invention of a series of totally improbable environments born of the disembodiment of sound: someone plays a sink, a voice roves around a room filled with people, a male/female urinating context is grotesquely simplified, a chair guffaws wildly; a piano moans out an orgasm, and so on. Like all of Snow's major films, his longest takes a technical fact as the generating force for a wholly cinematic presentation of space.

In *Presents* he directs his attention to editing. The results are somewhat less impressive than his earlier films, perhaps because of the enormity of this theme and the weight of original editing strategies by other filmmakers. After a hilarious parody of his own ◄—►, in which the stage rocks back and forth rather than the camera, he enters an extended series of very short takes, each glimpsing a different place. Then, with *This is it* he made a film of nothing but words. The film speaks to us one word at a time, about its own structure and aspirations, often lying outrageously.

Snow has also published a narrative, self-reflexive book of photographs, *Cover to Cover*, and has issued records of his own compositions, in jazz and concrete music.

—P. Adams Sitney

SOLANAS, FERNANDO AND GETINO, OCTAVIO. Argentine. Solanas born in Buenos Aires, 1936; Getino born in Spain (moved to Argentina in 1952). Solanas studied law, theater, and musical composition. Career: 1960s—Getino active as writer, book of short stories wins prize of Casa de las Americas (Cuba); Getino makes short documentary *Trasmallos*; 1962—Solanas makes first short film; works in advertising until 1966; 1966—both enter Cine Liberación group, making underground films; 1973—Perón returns to power; Getino accepts post on national film board; 1976—military coup against Perón; Solanas leaves Argentina for Paris where he continues to develop film projects; Getino goes to Peru, works on television projects dealing with education and rural development; 1982—Getino moves to Mexico, works with Film Dept. of the Universidad Autónoma de México.

Films (Solanas as director): 1968—*La hora de los hornos (Hour of the Furnaces)*; (co-directed by Solanas and Getino): 1971—*Perón: actualización política y doctrinaria para la toma del poder*; *Perón: La revolución justicialista* (both films made as part of Grupo de Cine Liberación); (Getino as director): 1973—*El familiar*; (Solanas as director): 1976—*Los hijos de Fierro* (not released per Solanas's request); (Getino as director): 1978—*La familia Pichilin* (not yet released).

Publications:

By SOLANAS:

Book—*Cine, cultura y descolonización*, Mexico City 1973; articles—"Cinema as a Gun", interview by Gianni Volpi and others in *Cinéaste* (New York), fall 1969; "Fernando Solanas: An Interview" in *Film Quarterly* (Berkeley), fall 1970; "Rundtischgespräch: Situation und Perspektiven des Films in Lateinamerika", with others, in *Information* (Wiesbaden), no.5-6, 1972; "Situation et perspectives du cinéma d'Amérique Latine", with others, in *Positif* (Paris), June 1972; "Dar espacio a la expresión popular", interview in *Cine Cubano* (Havana), no.86-88, 1973; "La Memoire critique de Fernando Solanas" in *Ecran* (Paris), 15 March 1979; "Les Fils de Fierro", with interview by F. Guerif and P. Merigeau in *Image et son* (Paris), January 1979; interview by A. Gumucio-Dagron and others in *Ecran* (Paris), 15 March 1979; "Argentina: Fernando Solanas—an Interview" by D. Ranvaud in *Framework* (Norwich, England), spring 1979; "Amerique latine: IV—Argentine" in *Image et son* (Paris), June 1979; "Round Table: The Cinema: Art Form or Political Weapon", with others, in *Framework* (Norwich, England), autumn 1979.

By GETINO:

Article—"Algunas observaciones sobre el concepto del 'Tercer Cine'" in *Comunicación y cultura*, January 1982.

On SOLANAS AND GETINO:

Articles—"Aspects of Latin American Political Cinema" by David Wilson in *Sight and Sound* (London), summer 1972; "The Camera as 'Gun': 2 Decades of Culture and Resistance in Latin America" by Julianne Burton in *Latin American Perspectives*, winter 1978.

*   *   *

Originators of the pivotal "third cinema" concept, Solanas and Getino demonstrated its practice in the only really important film they were to make—the influential *La hora de los hornos*. "Third cinema" was the product of a very specific context: the world-wide insurrections during the late 1960s. While U.S. students were burning banks in protest against the Vietnam war, Argentina moved close to genuine social revolution for the first time in its history. Solanas and Getino participated in that movement as cineastes, but they made it clear that their concern was with social change, not film art, in their first declaration as the Cine Liberacion Group: "Our commitment as cineastes in a dependent country is not with universal culture or art or abstract man; before anything else it is with the liberation of our country and the Latin American peoples."

As intellectuals and artists in a neo-colonial situation, Solanas and Getino were greatly influenced by the "Third Worldism" of the period, frequently citing ideologists from the African (Frantz Fanon) and Asian (Mao Tse-Tung) struggles. They contrasted "third cinema" to the "first cinema" of the Hollywood industry and to the auteurist "second cinema" in various ways, distinguishing it first of all for its ideological commitment to anti-imperialism and the struggle for socialism. Against the consumerism provoked by the hermetic narrative structures of Hollywood, they proposed a cinema which would require active audience participation. Thus, a film was important as a "detonator" or a "pretext" for assembling a group, not as an experience that was born and died on the screen. Likening themselves to guerillas who open paths with machete blows and to anonymous Vietnamese bicycle riders, submerged in a cruel and prolonged war, they perceived cinema as a provisional tool: "Our time is one of hypothesis rather than thesis, a time of works in process—unfinished, unordered, violent works made with the camera in one hand and a rock in the other."

The most realized description of "third cinema" can be found near the end of their often-reprinted essay, "Towards a Third Cinema." There they summarize it in the following manner: "The third cinema above all counters the film industry of a cinema of characters with one of themes, that of individuals with that of masses, that of the author with that of the operative group, one of neocolonial misinformation with one of information, one of escape with one that recaptures the truth, that of passivity with that of aggressions. To an institutionalized cinema, it counterposes a guerilla cinema; to movies as shows, it opposes a film act...to a cinema made for the old kind of human being, it proposes a *cinema fit for a new kind of human being, for what each one of us has the possibility of becoming.*"

Given their concern to produce a cinema of information rather than one of fantasies to be consumed, the obvious path led to the documentary. However, they conceived of the documentary as "not fundamentally one which illustrates, documents, or passively establishes a situation; rather it attempts to intervene in the situation as an element providing thrust or rectification...it provides discovery through transformation." *La hora de los hornos* may be a bit too didactic at times, but it was certainly more "revolutionary" than the documentaries they were to make as the official cineastes they became on the return of Juan Perón, the urban populist who was President of Argentina (1946-55 and 1973-74).

Because of the timeliness of *La hora de los hornos* and due to the extensive publication of Solanas and Getino's theoretical writings and interviews, they have received attention which may be disproportionate to that gotten by other Latin American cineastes of greater achievement, most notably the Cubans. Nonetheless, the French film critic, Guy Hennebelle, argued that "third cinema" is the concept that seems to be "most viable" as a counterpoint to traditional film study, stating, "According to this perspective, a vertitable 'counter-history' of the seventh art is yet to be written." In both their writings and their cinematic practice, Solanas and Getino have provided an alternative and a clearly articulated challenge to bourgeois cinema.

—John Mraz

SOLÁS, HUMBERTO. Cuban. Born in Havana, December 1942. Begins studying architecture, 1957. Career: 1957-59—active in insurrectionary movement against Batista government; 1959—experiments with 1st film; becomes member of Instituto Cubano del Arte e Industria Cinematografico (ICAIC); 1959-61—works on ICAIC's film magazine *Cine Cubano*; early 1960s—makes notes for Latin American ICAIC Newsreel and the Popular Encyclopedia; also serves as assistant director on *At the Club* and *Cuban Chronicle*; 1961—directs 1st film in collaboration with Hector Veitia and under the supervision of visiting Dutch documentarist Joris Ivens; 1964—travels to Europe; 1968—directs *Lucia* which brings international recognition; 1978—Licenciatur in History, University of Havana.

Films (as director): 1961—*Casablanca*; 1962—*Minerva traduce el mar* (co-d); 1963—*Variaciones*; *El retrato*; 1964—*El acoso*; 1965—*La acusation*; *Manuela*; 1968—*Lucia*; 1972—*Un dia de Noviembre*; 1974—*Simparele*; 1975—*Cantata de Chile*; 1977—*Nacer en Leningrado* (short); 1978—*Wilfredo Lam* (medium length); 1982—*Cecilia Valdés*.

Publications:

By SOLÁS:

Articles—"Que es *Lucía*? Apuntes acerca del cine por Humberto Solás" in *Cine Cubano* (Havana), no.52/3; interview by Pablo Mariñez in *Hablemos de cine* (Lima), July/August 1970; "L'Histoire du Chili comme allégorie", interview by G. Chijona in *Ecran* (Paris), January 1977; "Every Point of Arrival is a Point of Departure: An Interview with Humberto Solás" by Julianne Burton and Marta Alvear in *Jump Cut* (Chicago), December 1978; interview by G. Chijona in *Cine Cubano* (Havana), March 1978; "Cuba. 3. Humberto Solas", interview by J. King in *Framework* (Norwich, England), spring 1979; "Kantate über Chile" (photos) in *Film und Fernsehen* (Berlin), no.5, 1979; "Reflexiones" and "*Cecilia* o la busqueda de lo nacional", interview by Gerardo Chijona in *Cine Cubano* (Havana), no.102.

On SOLÁS:

Books—*Cuba: The Measure of a Revolution* by L. Nelson, Minneapolis 1972; *Memories of Underdevelopment: The Revolutionary Films of Cuba* by Michael Myerson, New York 1973; articles—"Cinema of Revolution—90 Miles From Home" by Elizabeth Sutherland in *Film Quarterly* (Berkeley), winter 1961-62; "The Cuban Cinema" by M.E. Douglas in *Take One* (Montreal), July/August 1968; "Propaganda Fills Cuban Newsreels" by R. Adler in *The New York Times*, 12 February 1969; "Cubans are Molding Movie Industry into a Pervasive Force" by R. Adler in *The New York Times*, 11 February 1969; "Cultural Life in Cuba Thriving Despite Rein" by R. Adler in *The New York Times*, 10 February 1969; "Solidarity and Violence" by A. Engel in *Sight and Sound* (London), autumn 1969; article on *Lucia* by G. Minish in *Take One* (Montreal), July/August 1969; "The Spring 1972 Cuban Film Festival Bust" by G. Crowdus in *Film Society Review* (New York), March/May 1972; "Cine Cubano" by P. Sauvage in *Film Comment* (New York), spring 1972; "*Lucia*: Style and Meaning in Revolutionary Film" by Steven Kovacs in *Monthly Review* (New York), June 1975; "*Lucía*: History and Film in Revolutionary Cuba" by John Mraz in *Film & History*, February 1975; "Introduction to Revolutionary Cuban Cinema" by Julianne Burton in *Jump Cut* (Chicago), December 1978; "*Lucia*: Visual Style and Historical Portrayal" by John Mraz in *Jump Cut* (Chicago), December 1978; "*Simparele*: The Heartbeat of a People" by Louise Diamond and Lyn Parker in *Jump Cut* (Chicago), December 1978.

*   *   *

Perhaps the foremost practitioner of the historical genre for which Cuban cinema has achieved international acclaim, Humberto Solás is a member of the first generation of directors to mature under the revolution. Of humble origins, Solás became an urban guerrilla at 14 and later left school altogether because, "It was a very unstable time to try to study. Either Batista (dictator of Cuba) closed down the university, or we did." Prior to the triumph of the revolution being a filmmaker "seemed like an unrealizable dream," but Solás financed a short film out of his savings and was invited to join the Cuban Film Institute (ICAIC) soon after its founding in 1959. Although it is customary for Cuban directors to serve an extensive apprenticeship in documentaries, Solás directed several early fiction shorts as well. He considers his imitating of European film styles in these works to be typical of feelings of cultural inferiority and alienation in the underdeveloped world, and affirms: "Neither me, nor my generation, nor my country can be seen in any of these films."

Historical subjects proved to be Solás's avenue to Cuban and Latin American realtiy. He believes that the importance attached to historical films in Cuba derives from the fact that, "Our history had been filtered through a bourgeois lens. We lack a coherent, lucid, and dignified appreciation of our national past." *Manuela*, a medium-length film on the guerrilla war in the mountains, was the first of Solás's works to embody "more genuinely Cuban forms of expression." His continuing search for national (and Latin American) cinematic idioms and themes led him to direct his masterpiece to date, *Lucia*, at age 26. Focusing on 3 periods of Cuban history through the characters of representative women, Solás used 3 different film styles to portray forms of experience and cognition during these epochs. In his later films, Solás interpretively analyzed the history of Haiti (*Simparele*), Chile (*Cantata de Chile*), and slavery in Cuba (*Cecilia Valdés*). These works are marked by an existing blend of music, dance, documentary footage, primative painting, and the re-enactment of historical events in an operatic style.

Solás considers his films "historical melodramas," in which a Marxist perspective provides a materialistic explanation for events and personal psychology. He contrasts this to common melodrama and its "particular world of valorative abstractions" which determine events, but lack the power to explain them. For example, although the travails suffered by the heroines of *Lucia* are experienced personally, they are depicted as deriving specifically from the colonial and neo-colonial situation of Cuba (and vestigial machismo), rather than from any "eternal passions" which have no relationship to concrete historical circumstances.

For Solás, historical cinema is always a dialogue about the present, and he has often chosen women as a central metaphor in his films because, as a dominated group, they feel more deeply and reflect more immediately the contradictons of society—for example, the maintenance of archaic forms as *machismo* in a revolutionary situation. As Solás states: "The sad masquerade of limited, archetyped, and suffocating human relations in defense of private property is most transparent in the case of the women—half of humanity. The pathetic carnival of economic exploitation begins there." To Solás, the past is only present insofar as it continues to condition (for both good and bad) the lives of people today. It is about this past/present that Humberto Solás has made and will go on making beautiful and moving cinema.

—John Mraz

SPIELBERG, STEVEN. American. Born in Cincinnati, Ohio, 18 December 1947. Educated California State College at Long Beach, BA in English, 1970. Career: 1960—wins amateur film contest with 40 min. film *Escape to Nowhere*; 1963—makes amateur film *Firelight*; late 1960s—on strength of film *Amblin'*, becomes TV director at Universal, working on series episodes as well as made-for-TV movies; 1971—directs TV film *Duel* which wins several awards upon its theatrical release in Europe; 1974—directs 1st theatrically released film *The Sugarland Express*; 1975—directs *Jaws* which breaks several box office records; 1979-81—directs *Raiders of the Lost Ark* in collaboration with producer George Lucas.

Films (as director): 1971—*Duel* (for TV); 1973—*Ace Eli and Rodger of the Skies* (Erman) (story only); 1974—*The Sugarland Express* (+co-sc); 1975—*Jaws*; 1977—*Close Encounters of the 3rd Kind* (+sc) (2nd version released 1980); 1978—*I Want to Hold Your Hand* (Zemeckis) (pr only); 1979—*1941*; 1981—*Raiders of the Lost Ark*; 1982—*E.T.—The Extraterrestrial*; Poltergeist* (Hooper) (pr only); 1983—episode of *The Twilight Zone* (+pr); 1984—*Indiana Jones and the Temple of Doom*.

Publications:

By SPIELBERG:

Book—*The Sugarland Express—Spielberg, Barwood and Robbins, Zsigmond* edited by Rochelle Reed, Washington, D.C. 1974; articles—"The Sugarland Express: Interview" by A.C. Bobrow in *Filmmakers Newsletter* (Ward Hill, Mass.), summer 1974; *Steven Spielberg Seminar* in *Dialogue on Film* (Washington, D.C.), July 1974; "On Location with *Jaws*—'Tell the shark we'll do it one more time'", interview by R. Riger in *Action* (Los Angeles), July/August 1974; interview by J. Moran in *Cinema Papers* (Melbourne), July/August 1975; "From Television to Features", interview by M. Stettin in *Millimeter* (New York), March 1975; "Close Encounter of the 3rd Kind: Director Steve Spielberg" by C. Austin in *Filmmakers Newsletter* (Ward Hill, Mass.), December 1977; interview in *Penthouse* (New York), February 1978; interview by H. Béhar in *Image et son* (Paris), April 1978; interview by G. Heathwood in *Cinema Papers* (Melbourne), April/June 1978; "The Unsung Heroes or Credit Where Credit is Due" and "Spielberg Speaks about 'Close Encounters'" in *American Cinematographer* (Los Angeles), January 1978; "The Mind Behind *Close Encounters of the 3rd Kind*", interview in *American Cinematographer* (Los Angeles), February 1978; interview by M. Tuchman in *Film Comment* (New York), January/February 1978; "Directing *1941*" in *American Cinematographer* (Los Angeles), December 1979.

On SPIELBERG:

Articles—"Steven Spielberg: Bio-filmography" by A. Eyles in *Focus on Film* (London), winter 1972; "Steven Spielberg" by A. Eyles in *Focus on Film* (London), winter 1972; "The New Panaflex Camera Makes Its Production Debut" by Herb Lightman in *American Cinematographer* (Los Angeles), May 1973; article in *Newsweek* (New York), 8 April 1974; "What Directors Are Saying" in *Action* (Hollywood), September/October 1974; "Films on TV" by A.H. Marill in *Films in Review* (New York), March 1975; "The Great American Eating Machine" by R.C. Cumbow in *Movietone News* (Seattle), 11 October 1976; article in *Newsweek* (New York), 21 November 1977; article in *The New York Times*, 15 May 1977; "Close Encounters with Steven Spielberg" by B. Cook in *American Film* (Washington, D.C.), November 1977; "Une Nouvelle Vague américaine. 3—Steven Spielberg" by M. Elia in *Séquences* (Montreal), April 1978; "Style vs. 'Style'" by R.T. Jameson in *Film Comment* (New

York), March/April 1980; "Spielberg's Express" by Veronica Geng in *Film Comment* (New York), July/August 1981.

*   *   *

Perhaps any discussion of Steven Spielberg must inevitably begin with the consideration that as of 1983, Spielberg is the most commercially successful director the world has yet seen—an incredible, if mind-boggling proposition which, in another time, might have immediately made the director's films ineligible for serious critical consideration. Yet the fact that Spielberg's combined films have grossed over one billion dollars attests to their power in connecting to the mass audience and offers the analyst an immediate conundrum which may take a more distanced generation of critics and filmgoers to answer fully: What does Spielberg know? And why does his work invite such audience approval?

In a cinematic career of little more than a decade, Spielberg has worked in a variety of genres: the television film *Duel* is a thriller; *Jaws* is a horror film; *1941* is a crazy comedy; *Close Encounters of the Third Kind* is a science-fiction film; *Raiders of the Lost Ark* is an adventure film patterned after film serials of the early fifties; and *E.T.—The Extraterrestrial* is a fantasy/family film combining elements from *The Wizard of Oz*, *Lassie*, and *Peter Pan*. And yet, virtually all of Spielberg's films are united by the same distinctive vision: a vision which is imbued with a sense of wonder and which celebrates the magic and mystery that imagination can reveal as an alternative to the humdrum and the everyday. The artistic consistency within Spielberg's work is demonstrated further by his narratives, which are structurally similar. In the typical Spielberg film, an Everyman protagonist has his conception of the world enlarged (often traumatically) as he comes face to face with some extraordinary and generally non-human antagonist who is often hidden from the rest of the world and/or the audience until the narrative's end. In *Duel*, a California businessman named Mann finds himself pitted against the monstrous truck whose driver's face is never shown; in *Jaws*, the water-shy sheriff must face an almost mythological shark whose jaws are not clearly shown until the final reel; in *Close Encounters*, a suburban father responds to the extra-sensory messages sent by outer-space creatures who are not revealed until the last sequence of the film; in *Raiders of the Lost Ark*, Indiana Jones quests for the Lost Ark which does not let forth its Pandora's Box of horrors until summoned up by those who would attempt to profit from it; and, of course, in *E.T.*, a small boy whose life is already in imagination keeps secret his adoption of a playful extra-terrestrial (although one could easily argue that the non-human antagonist here is not really the sensitive E.T., but the masked and terrifying government agents who, quietly working behind the scenes throughout the narrative, finally invade the suburban house and crystallize the protagonist's most horrific fears). Structural analysis even reveals that *Poltergeist*, the Spielberg-produced Tobe Hooper-directed film which relates to Spielberg's career in the same way the Howard Hawks-produced Christian Nyby-directed *The Thing* related to Hawks's career, is indeed a continuation of the Spielberg canon. In *Poltergeist*, a typical American family ultimately discovers that the antagonists responsible for the mysterious goings-on in their suburban home are the other-worldly ghosts and skeletons not shown until the end of the film when the narrative also reveals the villainy of the real estate developer who had so cavalierly disposed of the remains from an inconveniently located cemetery.

Technically proficient and dazzling, Spielberg's films are voracious in their synthesis of the popular culture icons which have formed the director's sensibilities: Hitchcock movies, John Wayne, comic books, *Bambi*, suburban homes, fast food, the space program, television, etc. His vision is that of the child-artist: the innocent and profound imagination that can summon up primeval dread from the deep as well as transcendent wonder from the sky. If Spielberg's films may sometimes be attacked for a certain lack of interest in, say, social issues or "adult concerns," they may be defended on the grounds that his films—unlike perhaps, so many of the "special effects" action films of the seventies and eighties—never seem to pander to their audience, but derive, rather, from a sensibility which is sincerely felt. If Spielberg is to be attacked at all, it might not be because his aspirations may ultimately lead to a reputation as a great artist of and for the bourgeois middle classes, but because his interest in objects and mechanical effects (as in *1941* and *Raiders of the Lost Ark*), though provocative, may not always be in perfect balance with his interest in sentiment and human achievement. Spielberg himself acknowledges his debt to Walt Disney, whose theme "When You Wish Upon a Star," a paean to faith and imagination, dictates the spirit of several Spielberg films. And yet certainly if intellectual and persuasive critical constructions are sought to justify our enjoyment of Spielberg's cinema, they can easily be found in the kind of mythic, Jungian criticism which analyzes his very popular work as a kind of direct line to the collective unconscious. *Jaws*, for instance, related to the primal fear of being eaten as well as to the archetypal initiation rite; *Close Encounters* is constructed according to the archetypal of the quest and the attendent religious structures of revelation and salvation; and of course *E.T.* has already been widely analyzed as a re-telling of the Christ story—complete with a sacred heart, a ritual death, a resurrection brought about by faith, and an eventual ascension into heaven as E.T. returns home.

If Spielberg is especially notable in any other way, it is perhaps that he represents the most successful example of what has been called the film school generation which is increasingly populating the new Hollywood: a generation which has been primarily brought up on television and film, rather than literature, and for whom film seems apparently to have replaced life as a repository for significant meaning. And yet if the old Hollywood's studio system is dead, it has been partially replaced by a solid, if informal matrix of friendships and alliances: between Spielberg and a greater fraternity of filmmakers including George Lucas, Francis Ford Coppola, Lawrence Kasden, John Millius, Bob Zemeckis, Robert Gale, Hal Barwood, Matthew Robbins, Melissa Mathison, and Harrison Ford. Worthy of note as well in regard to the community in which Spielberg finds himself is the fact that, although historically accused of an inordinate prejudice for box-office appeal over critical acclaim, Hollywood has nevertheless consistently refused—despite Spielberg's acquisition of both—to valorize publicly Spielberg's work: that the National Academy of Motion Picture Arts and Sciences has chosen four times to pass over Spielberg's films and direction—in 1975, bypassing *Jaws* in favor of *One Flew Over the Cuckoo's Nest* and Milos Forman; in 1977, bypassing *Close Encounters* for *Annie Hall* and Woody Allen; in 1981 bypassing *Raiders of the Lost Ark* for *Chariots of Fire* and Warren Beatty (as director of *Reds*); and in 1982 bypassing *E.T.* for *Ghandi* and Richard Attenborough—will someday require an explanatory footnote in film history texts.

—Charles Derry

———————

STAHL, JOHN M. American. Born in New York City, 21 January 1886. Educated in New York City public schools. Married Roxana Wray, 1932. Career: 1901—first stage appearance, in *DuBarry* with Mrs. Leslie Carter; 1901-14—plays juvenile roles and 2nd leads, works in Robert Edeson, Henrietta Crosman, and Belasco productions; 1914—hired by Vitagraph studios, Brooklyn; 1917—moves to Hollywood, joins Louis B. Mayer in independent productions; then works under Mayer at MGM; 1928-30—vice-president and directorial producer, Tiffany-Stahl Studios; supervises about 40 productions through 1930, then sells interest in studio; 1930—joins Universal. Died 12 January 1950.

Films (as director—incomplete listing prior to 1918): 1914—*The Boy and the Law*; 1917—*The Lincoln Cycle* (14-reeler distributed in 6 chapters including *My Mother, My Father, My Self, The Call to Arms*); 1918—*Scandal Mongers*; *Wives of Men* (+sc); *Suspicion*; 1919—*Her Code of Honor*; *A Woman Under Oath*; 1920—*Greater Than Love*; *Women Men Forget*; *The Woman in His House*; *Sowing the Wind*; *The Child Thou Gavest Me* (+pr); 1922—*The Song of Life*; *One Clear Call* (+pr); *Suspicious Wives*; 1923—*The Wanters* (+pr); *The Dangerous Age* (+pr); 1924—*Why Men Leave Home*; *Husbands and Lovers* (+pr); 1925—*Fine Clothes*; 1926—*Memory Lane* (+pr, co-sc); *The Gay Deceiver*; 1927—*Lovers?* (+pr); *In Old Kentucky* (+pr); 1930—*A Lady Surrenders*; 1931—*Seed*; *Strictly Dishonorable*; 1932—*Back Street*; 1933—*Only Yesterday*; 1934—*Imitation of Life*; 1935—*Magnificent Obsession*; 1937—*Parnell*; 1938—*Letter of Introduction* (+pr); 1939—*When Tomorrow Comes* (+pr); 1941—*Our Wife*; 1942—*The Immortal Sergeant*; 1943—*Holy Matrimony*; 1944—*The Eve of St. Mark*; *The Keys of the Kingdom*; 1946—*Leave Her to Heaven*; 1947—*Forever Amber* (replaced by Otto Preminger); *The Foxes of Harrow*; 1948—*The Walls of Jericho*; 1949—*Father Was a Fullback*; *Oh, You Beautiful Doll*.

Publications:

By STAHL:

Article—"Oh, the Good Old Days" in *The Hollywood Reporter*, 16 May 1932.

On STAHL:

Articles—obituary in *The New York Times*, 14 January 1950; "Esoterica" by Andrew Sarris in *Film Culture* (New York), spring 1963; "John M. Stahl: The Man Who Understood Women" by G. Morris in *Film Comment* (New York), May/-June 1977; "*Imitation of Life*" by Marjorie Baumgarten in *CinemaTexas Program Notes*, fall 1979; "Stahl into Sirk" by T. Pulleine in *Monthly Film Bulletin* (London), November 1981; "*Leave Her to Heaven*: The Double Bind of Post-War Women" by Michael Renov in *Journal of the University Film and Video Association*, winter 1983.

*   *   *

John Stahl was a key figure in the development of the Hollywood "women's melodrama" during the thirties and forties, and quite possibly in the teens and twenties as well. Although he began directing in 1914, and apparently made as many films before sound as after, only two of his silents (*Her Code of Honor* and *Suspicious Wives*) seem to have survived. Yet this is hardly the only reason that the ultimate critical and historical signifi-

cance of his work remains to be established. More pertinent is the critical disrepute of the "tearjerker" genre in which he worked almost exclusively—a genre which had to await the discovery of Douglas Sirk's melodramas and the reworking of the form by R.W. Fassbinder to attract serious critical attention.

Comparisons between Sirk's baroquely aestheticized and Stahl's straightforwardly unadorned treatments of equally improbable plots is somewhat useful, and virtually inevitable, given that Sirk remade three of Stahl's classic thirties' "weepies": *Imitation of Life* (1934/1959), *Magnificent Obsession* (1935/1954), and *When Tomorrow Comes* (1939), which became *Interlude* (1957). In a genre focusing on the problems presented by the social/sexual order for the individual (most frequently, the bourgeois female), Sirk tended to abstract dramatic conflicts in the direction of Brecht, while Stahl chose to emphasize the effects of social rigidities through the emotions of his characters.

Stahl's career seemed to flourish most at Universal in the thirties with the highly accomplished *Back Street*, *Only Yesterday*, and the three films Sirk remade, all of which present emotionally mimetic heroines buffeted by twists of fate which wreak havoc on their socially-determined modes of behavior. In his version of Fannie Hurst's *Back Street* (remade in 1941 and 1961), Stahl encourages sympathy with Irene Dunne, an independent working woman who gives up eveything to be "kept" in isolation by the respectible married man she loves. Audacious contradictions emerge from the very simplicity with which Stahl presents outrageous plot twists, Dunne meets the "kept woman" next door to her back street apartment, for example, only when the woman literally catches on fire and must be rescued. Recognizing a sister in shame, Dunne counsels the injured woman against allowing herself to be exploited by the man she loves; yet what seems to be a dawning moment of self-awareness on the part of our heroine is instantly obscured by a romantic haze when her own lover walks through the door in the middle of her diatribe. Similarly powerful contradictions abound in *Imitation of Life* (based on another Hurst novel), where best friends Claudette Colbert and Louise Beavers find themselves incapable, despite their best intentions, of breaking the social and radical molds which keep the black woman subservient to the white, even when the former is responsible for the latter's wealth and success.

Given material such as Fannie Hurst, the "inspirational" message of Lloyd C. Douglas's *Magnificent Obesession*, and the hopelessly romantic *Only Yesterday* (virtually remade as Max Ophuls's *Letter from an Unknown Woman*), and considering the period during which Stahl worked, the point of reference seems not to be Sirk so much as Stahl's better-appreciated contemporary Frank Borzage. It is Borzage's unrelenting romanticism which is usually assumed to characterize the "weepies" of the twenties and thirties; yet Stahl's work offers another perspective. While he clearly encourages emotional identification with his heroines, Stahl seems more interested in exposing their romantic illusions than in relishing them. In fact, his meditative restraint in such situations has prompted George Morris to suggest that "it is Carl Th. Dreyer whom Stahl resembles more than directors like Sirk or Borzage." Yet ultimately, Stahl's visual style seems largely dependent upon studio and cinematographer, a fact most clearly demonstrated by *Leave Her to Heaven*, a preposterously plotted drama of a psychotically duplicitous woman shot in Technicolor by Leon Shamroy on the modernesque sets of 20th Century-Fox, where the director's mise-en-scène emerges as florid and baroque as Sirk in his heyday—and a full decade earlier.

It seems that Stahl's films represent something of a missing link between Borzage's romanticism and Sirk's distanciation. Certainly, an examination of his work expands an understanding of the variety of Hollywood's strategies in personalizing overtly ideological questions of sex, status, and money. In fact, if film scholars are serious about studying the melodrama in any depth, then the films of John Stahl remian a top and current priority.

—Ed Lowry

STAUDTE, WOLFGANG. German. Born Wolfgang Georg Staudte in Saarbrücken, 9 October 1906. Educated as engineer; stage training with Max Reinhardt. Career: stage debut with Max Reinhardt; also works with Erwin Piscator; stage actor until 1933; 1931—film acting debut in Lupu Pick's *Gassenhauer*; mid-1930s—writes and directs advertising films and shorts; 1943—directs first feature, for Tobis Film; co-founds "Freie Film-Produktions-GmbH." with Harald Braun and Helmut Käutner; beginning 1945—works for DEFA studios (East Germany); directs 1st German postwar film *Die Mörder sind unter uns*; 1953—begins working in West Germany; 1970s—directs documentaries and series episodes (for *Der Kommissar* and *Tatort*) for West German TV. Recipient: Silver Lion, Venice Festival, for *Ciske de Rat*, 1955.

Films (as director): 1943—*Akrobat schö-ö-ön* (+sc); 1944—*Ich hab' von Dir geträumt*; 1945—*Der Mann, dem man den Namen stahl* (co-sc only); *Frau über Bord*; 1946—*Die Mörder sind unter uns (The Murderers Are Among Us)* (+sc); 1948—*Die seltsamen Abenteuer des Herrn Fridolin B.* (+sc); 1949—*Rotation* (+co-sc); *Schicksal aus zweiter Hand* (+sc); *Das Beil von Wandsbek* (co-sc only); *Der Untertan (The Submissive)* (+co-sc); 1953—*Die Geschichte des kleinen Muck (The Story of Little Mook)* (+co-sc); 1954—*Leuchtfeuer* (+co-sc); 1955—*Ciske—Ein Kind braucht Liebe (Ciske de Rat, Ciske—A Child Wants Love)* (+sc); 1957—*Rose Bernd*; 1958—*Kanonen-Serenade (The Muzzle)* (+co-sc); *Madeleine und der Legionär*; *Der Maulkorb*; 1959—*Rosen für den Staatsanwalt (Roses for the Prosecutor)* (+story); 1960—*Kirmes (Kermes)* (+sc); *Der letzte Zeuge (The Last Witness)*; 1962—*Die glücklichen Jahre der Thorwalds* (co-d); 1963—*Die Dreigroschenoper (The Threepenny Opera)*; 1964—*Herrenpartie (Men's Outing)*; *Das Lamm (The Lamb)*; 1966—*Ganovenehre (Hoodlum's Honor)*; 1968—*Heimlichkeiten* (+co-sc); 1970—*Die Herren mit der weissen Weste (Those Gentlemen Who Have a Clean Sheet)*; 1971—*Fluchtweg St. Pauli—Grossalarm für die Davidswache*; 1972—*Verrat ist kein Gesellschaftsspiel* (for TV); *Marya Sklodowska-Curie. Ein Mädchen, das die Welt verändert* (for TV); 1973—*Nerze Nachts am Strassenrand* (for TV); *The Seawolf*; 1974—*Ein herrliches Dasein*; 1978—*Zwischengleis (Yesterday's Tomorrow, Memories)*.

Roles: 1931—*Gassenhauer* (Pick); (other films): *Geheimnis des blauen Zimmers*; *Tannenberg*; *Der Choral von Leuthen*; *Heimkehr ins Glück*; *Pechmarie*; *Die Bande von Hoheneck*; *Schwarzer Jäger Johanna*; *Stärker als Paragraphen*; *Gleisdreieck*; *Susanne im Bade*; *Am seidenen Faden*; *Lauter Lügen*; *Pour le mérite*; *Mordsache Holm*; *Spiel im Sommerwind*; *Das Gewehr über*; *Die fremde Frau*; *Drei Unteroffiziere*; *Brand im Ozean*; *Legion Condor*; *Blutsbrüderschaft*; *Aus erster Ehe*; *Jud Süss*; *Jungens*; *Friedemann Bach*; *...reitet für Deutschland*; *Das grosse Spiel*.

Publications:

By STAUDTE:

Article—"Aber wenn geschlagen wird im diesem Land...", interview in *Film und Fernsehen* (Berlin), no.5, 1979.

On STAUDTE:

Articles—"Wolfgang Staudte" by J. Bachmann in *Film* (London), summer 1963; "Kurt Maetzig, Wolfgang Staudte" in *Information* (Wiesbaden), no.3-6, 1976; "Wolfgang Staudte" by K. Karkosch in *Film und Ton* (Munich), March 1976.

*   *   *

Wolfgang Staudte is one of the few important German directors of the postwar years. His debut during the war—two entertainment films—showed a command of his craft. Staudte already had experience working with Max Reinhardt and as a successful stage actor.

Die Mörder sind unter uns, the first German postwar film, remains today among the director's best works. A surgeon, Hans Mertens, returns home from the war, becomes an alcoholic, and lives hopelessly among the ruins. His girlfriend Susanne has survived a concentration camp and attempts to help him overcome his apathy. The apathy is quickly dispelled by the appearance of an industrialist, formerly a Nazi, whose outlook remains unchanged and who, just as before, uses deceptive phrases to justify the new situation.

This contemporary material was realized by Staudte in a thoroughly realistic style with expressionistic strokes, in a manner that suggests analogies with Rossellini's *Paisà*. An English critic identified the director as a successor to Lang and Pabst. The phrase "The murderers are among us" became a symbolic expression for the spirit of the time, in which progressive German intellectuals sought every means to reckon with the fascist past. It was not by chance that the film was made in the Soviet sector of Berlin and produced by the newly-founded DEFA studios. Staudte's efforts to interest cultural officials in the western zones in his project met with no success. This was also the case with *Rotation* and *Der Untertan*, a satiric version of Heinrich Mann's novel of the same title, set in an actual embassy.

Staudte is a political artist because, as he says, he is a political person. He has perfect command of a variety of means of expression and narrative forms, and uses a rich palette of symbolic images in realistically-structured filmic space. His films often led to comparisons with René Clément and Rossellini. Only his own country—the media and public as well as the authorities—could not accept him and systematically and conclusively thwarted him. In the beginning he was repeatedly labelled a communist because of his association with DEFA and urged to make West German films. In 1951 he decided to do this, and so began an unhappy period for him which consisted in attempting "to improve the world with the money of people who already find the world to be just fine." He was regularly reproached with fouling his own nest, and was reluctantly reduced to making entertainment films. In its headlong rush toward economic development, West German society wanted to see neither fundamental analysis of the Nazi past, nor pessimistic mistrust directed against the new, American-oriented NRD-model.

Years of harassment by the press and cultural authorities went by, Staudte working away, often in vain, writing unengaging comedies. He nevertheless made a few masterpieces: *Rosen für den Staatsanwalt*, *Kirmes*, and *Herrenpartie*. These films are united by Staudte's conviction that the present and the past are bound together and that man today remains inseparable from yesterday. The most imposing of these films is *Herrenpartie*: it confronts two worlds—that of today's German bourgeoisie, which would gladly bury Nazi memories, and that of a village of Yugoslavian widows who, despite everything, are better able to behave humanely than the Germans.

Wolfgang Staudte gets by today making TV detective stories. His case demonstrates that the new German cinema has worthy predecessors who remain unappreciated even by their colleagues. In the Federal Republic it's every man for himself and the system against all....

—Maria Racheva

STEVENS, GEORGE. American. Born George Cooper Stevens in Oakland, California, 18 December 1904. Attended high school in Lonoma, California, 1918-19. Married Joan (Stevens) (divorced); son: George Stevens, Jr.; married second time. Career: 1909—appears on stage for 1st time at Alcazar Theater, San Francisco; 1920-21—becomes actor and stage manager for father's theatrical company; 1921—travels to Hollywood and works as assistant and 2nd cameraman in films, eventually working his way up to full cameraman; 1927—joins Hal Roach as cameraman on Laurel and Hardy comedy shorts; 1929-30—begins to direct 2 reel comedies for Roach; 1932—directs shorts for Universal and RKO; 1933—directs 1st feature *The Cohens and Kellys in Trouble* for Universal; 1935—directs *Alice Adams* at Katharine Hepburn's insistence, which becomes his 1st critical and financial success; 1938—becomes producer for 1st time with *Vivacious Lady*; 1943—joins U.S. Army Signal Corps and becomes head of Special Motion Pictures Unit assigned to photograph the activities of 6th Army for national archives; 1945—Special Motion Pictures Unit is awarded citation from General Eisenhower for filming such important war events as D-Day and the freeing of inmates at the Dachau concentration camp; 1946-70—continues to be prominent director in Hollywood, winning several awards for his films; 1970—directs last film *The Only Game in Town*. Died in Paris, 9 March 1975. Recipient: Academy Award, Best Director for *A Place in the Sun*, 1951; Academy of Motion Picture Arts & Sciences, Irving G. Thalberg Award, 1953; Academy Award, Best Director for *Giant*, 1956.

Films (as cameraman include): 1924—*The White Sheep*; *The Battling Oriole*; 1925—*Black Cyclone*; 1926—*The Devil Horse*; *The Desert's Toll*; *Putting Pants on Philip*; 1927—*No Man's Law*; *The Valley of Hell*; *Lightning*; *The Battle of the Century*; 1928—*Leave 'em Laughing*; *2 Tars*; *Unaccustomed as We Are*; 1929—*Big Business*; (as director include): 1930—*Ladies Past*; 1931—*Call a Cop!*; *High Gear*; *The Kick-Off*; *Mama Loves Papa*; 1932—*The Finishing Touch*; *Boys Will Be Boys*; *Family Troubles*; 1933—*Should Crooners Marry*; *Hunting Trouble*; *Rock-a-bye Cowboy*; *Room Mates*; *A Divorce Courtship*; *Flirting in the Park*; *Quiet Please*; *Grin and Bear It*; *The Cohens and the Kellys in Trouble*; 1934—*Bridal Bail*; *Ocean Swells*; *Bachelor Bait*; *Kentucky Kernels*; 1935—*Laddie*; *The Nitwits*; *Alice Adams*; *Annie Oakley*; 1936—*Swing Time*; 1937—*Quality Street*; *A Damsel in Distress*; (as producer and director): 1938 *Vivacious Lady*; 1939—*Gunga Din*; 1940—*Vigil in the Night*; 1941—*Penny Serenade*; 1942—*Woman of the Year* (d only); *The Talk of the Town*; 1943—*The More the Merrier*; 1948—*I Remember Mama* (co-pr); 1951—*A Place in the Sun*; 1952—*Something to Live For*; 1953—*Shane*; 1956—*Giant* (co-pr); 1959—*The Diary of Anne Frank*; 1965—*The Greatest Story Ever Told*; 1970—*The Only Game in Town* (d only).

Publications:

By STEVENS:

Articles—interview in *Cinema* (Beverly Hills), December/January 1965; "George Stevens: Shorts to Features: Interview" by Leonard Maltin in *Action* (Los Angeles), November/December 1970.

On STEVENS:

Books—*George Stevens: An American Romantic* by Donald Richie, New York 1970; *The Movie Makers: Artists in the Industry* by Gene D. Phillips, Chicago 1973; articles—"Best Director in Hollywood" in *Time* (New York), 16 February 1942; "The Man Who Made the Hit Called *Shane*" by B. Martin in *Saturday Evening Post* (New York), 8 August 1953; "*Shane* and George Stevens" by Penelope Houston in *Sight and Sound* (London), fall 1953; "George Stevens: Letter" by N. Cecil in *Films in Review* (New York), February 1954; "New Pictures" in *Time* (New York), 22 October 1956; "George Stevens and the American Dream" by E. Archer in *Film Culture* (New York), no.1, 1957; "George Stevens: Filmography" by H.G. Luft in *Films in Review* (New York), November 1958; "Personality of the Month" in *Films and Filming* (London), July 1959; "The Lost Art of Editing" by Arthur Knight in *Saturday Review* (New York), 20 December 1958; "George Stevens" by Herbert Luft in *Films in Review* (New York), November 1958; "Letters" in *Films in Review* (New York), January 1959; "Hollywood Romantic" by J. Stang in *Films and Filming* (London), July 1959; "Sounds from the Westertoren" by Albert Johnson in *Sight and Sound* (London), spring 1959; "Hollywood Romantic" by Joanne Stasey in *Films and Filming* (London), July 1959; "George Who?" in *Atlantic* (New York), March 1960; "Faster, Faster" in *Saturday Review* (New York), 26 August 1961; "Cut!" in *Newsweek* (New York), 18 September 1961; "Modest Professional" in *Saturday Review* (New York), 8 September 1962; "Face of '63—United States" by G. Fenin in *Films and Filming* (London), March 1963; "3rd Line: Filmography" by Andrew Sarris in *Film Culture* (New York), spring 1963; "The Costumes of George Stevens" by J.R. Silke in *Cinema* (Beverly Hills), November/December 1963; "Sentiment and Humanism" by N. Bartlett in *Film* (London), spring 1964; "Sentiment and Humanism" by Nicholas Bartlett in *Film* (London), spring 1964; "*Greatest Story* Diaries" by Charlton Heston in *Cinema* (Beverly Hills), December/January 1964/65; "Monography of George Stevens' Films" and "The Picture" by J.R. Silke and "Greatest Stories Diaries" by Charlton Heston in *Cinema* (Beverly Hills), December/January 1965; "Greatest Stevens" by D. McVay in *Films and Filming* (London), April 1965; "Giant Stevens" by D. McVay in *Films and Filming* (London), May 1965; "A Place in the Sun" by Penelope Houston in *Sight and Sound* (London), winter 1955-56; "The Return of Shane" by Alan Stanbrook in *Films and Filming* (London), May 1966; "Very Model of a Modern Intellectual in *Saturday Review* (New York), 22 February 1969; "George Stevens" by B. Beresford in *Film* (London), summer 1970; "Letter Regarding Film Festival in South" by J. Spies in *Films in Review* (New York), May 1971; Stevens issue of *Dialogue on Film* (Washington, D.C.), no.1, 1972; "*Alice Adams*" by Elliott Sirkin in *Film Comment* (New York), winter 1971/72; obituary in *Action* (Los Angeles), March/April 1975; obituary by Claude Beylie in *Ecran* (Paris), May 1975; "George Stevens", special issue of *Dialogue on Film* (Washington, D.C.), May/June 1975; "A George Stevens Album" in *Action* (Los Angeles), May/June 1975; "George Stevens: The Wartime Comedies" by B. Petri in *Film Comment* (New York), July/August 1975; "George Stevens: A Piece of the Rock" by P. McGilligan and J. McBride in *Bright Lights* (Los Angeles), no.4, 1979.

*   *   *

When George Stevens returned from World War II, he was ready to plunge back into film production. He had left Hollywood in 1943, and returning home five years later, he wanted to take his time and re-accustom himself to the vagaries and pace of Hollywood. He had been regarded as one of the most promising young men behind the camera when he took off for special duties with the U.S. Army Signal Corps.

Katharine Hepburn had originally been responsible for bringing his talents to the attention of those in the front office. He had directed a great many two-reelers for Hal Roach, and was just entering films as a director of features when Hepburn met him, liked him, and asked that he be assigned as director to her next film, *Alice Adams*. It was a giant step forward, for Hepburn was the classiest new star in the business. *Alice Adams*, from the Booth Tarkington novel, was a project right up Stevens's alley.

Two years later Stevens directed Hepburn again in a charming version of Barrie's play, *Quality Street*, and then in 1941 Hepburn again got him over to MGM to direct her and Spencer Tracy in *Woman of the Year*, the first film they did together.

In the first half of his film career Stevens directed a Barbara Stanwyck feature, *Annie Oakley*, one of the best Astaire-Rogers dancing romances, *Swing Time*, and a delightful Ginger Rogers feature, *Vivacious Lady*. Astaire was never more debonair than in the adaption of Wodehouse's novel, *A Damsel in Distress*, with George Burns and Gracie Allen. Stevens then really hit his stride as director of *Gunga Din*, a Kiplingesque glorification of romantic derring-do, with Cary Grant, Victor McLaglen, and Douglas Fairbanks Jr. Two romances, *Vigil in the Night*, starring Carole Lombard, and *Penny Serenade*, co-starring Irene Dunne with Cary Grant, added to his repuation as an ideal director for romance, especially the weepy sort. His final feature before departing for wartime Europe was one of his best, with Joel McCrea, Jean Arthur, and Ronald Colman, a very funny comedy of the wartime housing situation in the national capital, *The More, The Merrier*.

After the war, Stevens decided that he would like to produce and direct something that glorified America's past, preferably a comedy. Fortunately, Stevens had been named by Irene Dunne as one of those she would like to work for as the projected star of *I Remember Mama*. It was an important decision for Miss Dunne, because she had made a name for herself as a romantic, glamorous star, and as Mama she would be playing a simple Norwegian wife and mother.

The film was in production for six months, and went far over schedule and budget. Stevens was a perfectionist, and determined not to be caught short of any piece of film he needed when making his first cut. He shot a master scene fully, with moving camera, and then he shot and kept shooting the same scene from every conceivable angle. Stevens was on scehdule for the first ten days of shooting, and then he came to a montage sequence involving Sir Cedric Hardwicke as Mr. Hyde, Mama's roomer. He became entranced with the sound of Sir Cedric's voice reading the classics, and for nearly ten days shot footage of Sir Cedric reading aloud while the family listened. It was admittedly no more than a montage sequence and was alloted half a day on the shooting schedule, but it is the first real evidence of how carefully and thoroughly Stevens filmed every sequence, regardless of schedule. He overshot, and it was expensive, but the end result was as near perfect as any movie could be. Because of an exces-

sive negative cost ($3,068,000), *I Remember Mama* did not realize the profit it might have earned, although it played five continuous weeks at Radio Music City Hall. where it premiered, gathering rave notices and honors for all concerned.

Stevens had proved that he was back in form and at the top. He moved over to Paramount, where he made two of his best pictures—*A Place in the Sun*, from Theodore Dreiser's American classic, *An American Tragedy*, with three perfectly-cast players, Montgomery Clift, Elizabeth Taylor, and Shelly Winters. He was the producer-director of one of the most unique westerns ever filmed, *Shane*, with Alan Ladd, Jean Arthur, Van Heflin, and a remarkable boy actor, Brandon De Wilde. It is all the more remarkable because it is a western told through the eyes of a young boy and has a disarming innocence in spite of its violence.

He was chided for his constant overshooting, and said that he could make a picture on time and not exceed the budget. He made a woman's story, *Something to Live For*, and the only thing that distinguishes it is that it looks as if it exceeded neither its budget nor its shooting schedule.

Stevens moved over to Warner Bros. to film Edna Ferber's novel about Texas, *Giant*, with Elizabeth Taylor, Rock Hudson, and James Dean. It was Dean's final credit, for he was killed in an auto crash directly after the shooting of his scenes was finished. Stevens's last three features, *The Diary of Anne Frank*, *The Greatest Story Ever Told*, and *The Only Game in Town*, were released by 20th Century-Fox. The last one, the best of the three, was virtually sloughed off in its release. When asked what the story was about, Stevens replied, "It's about an aging hooker and a losing gambler, if you think the world is ready for that." He had become embittered. The climate had changed in Hollywood, and it was difficult to get a first-class release for a picture made with the kind of extravagance Stevens was accustomed to.

—DeWitt Bodeen

STILLER, MAURITZ. Swedish, Russian. Born Mosche Stiller in Helsinki, Finland, 17 July 1883; became citizen of Sweden, 1921. Career: 1899—makes 1st stage appearance in a Swedish theater in Helsinki; 1900-03—plays small roles in Swedish theater in Turku, Finland; 1904-07—after escaping to Sweden to avoid Russian military draft, becomes actor in Swedish theater; 1911—manages small avant-garde theater in Stockholm, Lilla Teatern, enjoys moderate success; 1912—hired as film director by Charles Magnusson, head of newly formed Svenska Biograf film studio, Stockholm; 1912-17—writes, directs, or acts in over 30 thrillers and comedies for Svenska; 1918—gains international recognition with *Sången om den eldröda blomman (Song of the Scarlet Flower)*; 1923—discovers Greta Gustafsson (Garbo) and casts her in *Gösta Berlings saga (The Story of Gösta Berling)*; 1925—moves to Hollywood under contract to MGM; 1925-26—after several disputes with MGM is fired before he completes a film; 1926—hired by Erich Pommer at Paramount to direct *Hotel Imperial*; 1927—returns to Sweden after development of severe illness; presents musical *Broadway* for Oscar Theater in Stockholm. Died 8 November 1928.

Films (as director and scriptwriter): 1912—*Mor och dotter (Mother and Daughter)*; *När svärmor regerar (When the Mother-in-Law Reigns)*; *Vampyren (Vampire)*; *Barnet (The Child)* (d only); *De svarta maskerna (The Black Masks)* (co-sc); *Den tryanniske fästmannen (The Tyrannical Fiancée)*; 1913—

När kärleken dödar (When Love Kills) (co-sc); *När larmhlockan ljuder (When the Alarm Bell Rings)* (d only); *Den okända (The Unknown Woman)*; *Bröderna (Brothers)* (co-sc); *Den moderna suffragetten (The Suffragette)*; *På livets ödesväger (The Smugglers)* (d only); *Mannekägen (The Model)*; *För sin kärleks skull (The Stockbroker)*; *Gränsfolken (The Border Feud)* (d only); *Livets konflikter (Conflicts of Life)*; *Kammarjunkaren (Gentleman of the Room)*; 1914—*Lekkamraterna (The Play-mates)*; *Stormfågeln (The Stormy Petrel)* (d only); *Det röda tornet (The Master)* (co-sc); *Skottet (The Shot)* (d only); *När konstnärer älska (When Artists Love)* (d only); 1915—*Hans hustrus förflutna (His Wife's Past)* (d only); *Hämnaren (The Avenger)* (d only); *Madame de Thèbes (The Son of Destiny)* (d only); *Mästertjuven (The Son of Fate)* (d only); *Hans bröllops-natt (His Wedding Night)* (d only); *Minlotsen (The Mine Pilot)* (d only); *Dolken (The Dagger)* (co-sc); *Lyckonälen (The Motor-car Apaches)* (co-sc); 1916—*Balettprimadonnan (Anjuta, the Dancer)* (d only); *Kärlek och journalistik (Love and the Journalist)* (d only); *Kampen om hans hjärta (The Struggle for His Heart)* (d only); *Vingarne (The Wings)* (co-sc); 1917—*Thomas Graals bästa film (Thomas Graal's Best Picture)* (d only); *Alexander den Store (Alexander the Great)*; 1918—*Thomas Graals bästa barn (Thomas Graal's Best Child)* (co-sc); *Sången om den eldröda blomman (Song of the Scarlet Flower, The Flame of Life* (d only); 1919—*Fiskebyn (The Fishing Village)* (d only); *Herr Arnes pengar (Sir Arne's Treasure)* (co-sc); 1920—*Erotikon* (co-sc); *Johan*; 1921—*De Landsflyktige (The Exiles)* (co-sc); 1922—*Gunnar Hedes saga (Gunnar Hede's Saga, The Old Man-sion)*; 1923—*Gösta Berlings saga (Gosta Berling's Saga, The Story of Gösta Berling, The Atonement of Gösta Berling)* (co-sc); 1926—*The Temptress* (finished by Fred Niblo); 1927—*Hotel Imperial* (co-sc); *The Woman on Trial* (d only); *Barbed Wire* (finished by Rowland Lee); 1928—*The Street of Sin* (finished by Ludvig Berger).

Roles: 1912—*Count Raoul de Saligny* in *Mor och dotter* (Stiller); *Elias Petterson* in *Den tyranniskefästmannen* (Stiller); *The Pastor* in *När svärmor regerar* (Stiller).

Publications:

On STILLER:

Books—*Film och Filmfolk* edited by Teddy Nyblom, Stockholm 1925; *Den Svenska Filmens Drama: Sjöström och Stiller* by Bengt Idestam-Almquist, Stockholm 1938; *40 Ans de cinéma, 1895-1935* by Ove Brusendorff, Copenhagen 1940; *Greta Garbo* by E.E. Laring, London 1946; *Scandinavian Film* by Forsyth Hardy, London 1951; *Classics of the Swedish Cinema* by Bengt Idestam-Almquist, Stockholm 1952; *Garbo* by John Bain-bridge, New York 1955; *Swedish Cinema* by Rune Waldekranz, Stockholm 1959; *La Grande Aventure du cinéma suédois* by Jean Béranger, Paris 1960; *Garbo: A Biography* by Fritiof Bill-quist, New York 1960; *Hollywood Rajah: The Life and Times of Louis B. Mayer* by Bosley Crowther, New York 1960; *Swedish Film* by Einar Lauritzen, New York 1962; *The Films of Greta Garbo* by Michael Conway, New York 1963; *Sjöström et L'ecole suédois* by René Jeanne and Charles Ford, Paris 1963; *Swedish Cinema* by Peter Cowie, London 1966; *Anthologie du cinéma* Vol. III, Paris 1968; *Mauritz Stiller och hans filmer* by Gösta Werner, Stockholm 1969; *Seastrom and Stiller in Hollywood* by Hans Pensel, New York 1969; articles—"Le Cinéma nordique" in *L'Art cinématographique* edited by Felix Alian, Paris 1931; "Stiller, a Pioneer of the Cinema" by Bengt Idestam-Almquist in *Biografbladet* (Stockholm), fall 1950; "Sweden in Film History" by Bengt Idestam-Almquist in *Biografbladet* (Stockholm), spring 1951; "Stiller" by Mario Verdone in *Cinema* (Milan), no.126, 1954; "The Man Who Found Garbo" by Bengt Idestam-Almquist in *Films and Filming* (London), August 1956; "Origins of the Swedish Cinema" by Bengt Idestam-Almquist in *Bio-grafbladet* (Stockholm), spring 1960; "Greta Garbo and My Book" by A. Gronowicz in *Contemporary Review* (London), December 1960; "Herr Arne's Treasure" by Liam O'Laoghaire in *Films and Filming* (London), August 1960; "As I Remember Him" by Victor Sjöström in *Film Comment* (New York), summer 1970; "A Method of Reconstructing Lost Films" by G. Werner in *Cinema Journal* (Evanston), winter 1974/75; "Swed-ish Retrospect" by J. Gillett in *Sight and Sound* (London), summer 1974; "Essays on the Swedish Cinema (Part 2)" by Robin Wood in *Lumiere* (Melbourne), April/May 1974; "Checklist 110—Mauritz Stiller" and "Mauritz Stiller" by J. Robertson in *Monthly Film Bulletin* (London), December 1977; "Sjöström, Stiller et l'Amérique" by Claude Beylie and M. Mar-tin in *Ecran* (Paris), September 1978; "Svenska giganter 2" by G. Werner in *Filmrutan* (Lin, Sweden), v.24, no.3, 1981.

*   *   *

Like the other two distingushished pioneers of the early Swed-ish cinema, Sjöström and Sjöberg, Stiller had an essentially theatrical background. But it must be remembered he was reared in Finland of Russian-Jewish stock, did not emigrate to Sweden until he was 27, and remained there only 15 years before going to Hollywood. He responded, relatively late, to the Swedish cultu-ral tradition, so heavily influenced by the country's extreme northern climate and landscape, and by the fatalistic, puritanical literary and dramatic aura exerted most notably by the Swedish dramatist Strindberg and the Nobel prize-winning novelist Selma Lagerlöf, whose works, inspired by tradition and legend, *Herr Arne's Treasure*, *Gunnar Hede's Saga*, and *Gösta Berlings Saga*, were all to be adapted by Stiller for the silent screen.

After establishing himself as a talented stage actor, Stiller's work on film began in 1912. He proved at once a meticulous craftsman, with a strong visual instinct and a polished sense of timing and rhythm; his early work showed how much he had learned technically from the considerable number of D.W. Grif-fith's short narrative films shown in Sweden. For example, *The Black Masks*, made in 1912, is claimed by Forsyth Hardy, histo-rian of the Swedish cinema, as having, "over a hundred scenes, a constantly changing combination of interiors and exteriors, close-ups and panoramic shots." He even made in 1913 a film based on the activities of Mrs. Pankhurst, *Den moderna suffra-getten*, reflecting his reputation in the theater for avant-garde subjects.

He was to prove adept at comedy, as his films *Love and Journalism*, *Thomas Graal's Best Film*-one of the earliest films about filmmaking—and *Thomas Graal's First Child* reveal, with their skirmishing and coquetry that characterize the relationship of the sexes. Stiller insisted however on restraint in acting style; he was an autocratic perfectionist, and Emil Jannings, Ger-many's leading actor, termed him "the Stanislavski of the cinema." The second of these films had a complex structure, full of flashbacks and daydreams; the director Victor Sjöström starred in all three, as well as in other of Stiller's films and in certain of the earliest Stiller appeared himself. The climax to his career in the production of elegant and graceful comedies of sex manners was *Erotikon*; though better known, because of its alluring title, than its predecessors, it is somewhat less accomplished. Elaborately staged and full of sexual by-play—the wife of a preoccupied professor has two lovers in hot pursuit, a young sculptor and an elderly baron—it includes a specially commissioned ballet performed by the opera in Stockholm. These sophisticated silent films rank alongside the early comedies of Lubitsch, whose work in this genre in Germany in fact succeeded them. Lubitsch readily acknowledged his debt to Stiller. Again like Lubitsch (with whose career Stiller's can best be compared at this stage), Stiller was also to work on epic-style, historical subjects. He took over the adaptation of Selma Lagerlöf's novel, *Herr Arne's Treasure* from Sjöström, its original director. This was essentially an 18th-century story of escape and pursuit—three Scottish mercenaries in the service of King John III are imprisoned for conspiracy. They abscond in the depths of winter, undertaking a desperate journey overland to flee the country. In the process they become increasingly violent and menacing until they come on Arne's mansion. They steal his treasure, burn his house, slaughter its inhabitants except for an orphan girl, Elsalill, who survives the massacre, a haunted figure half-attracted to the leader of the Scottish renegades, but eventually betraying him and dying in the final confrontation in which the Scots are recaptured. The long, snake-like column of black-robed women moving over the icy waste in the girl's funeral procession is Stiller's concluding panoramic scene; one of the best-known spectacular shots in early cinema, it still appears in most history books. The film illustrates grandly the response of the early Swedish filmmakers to the menacing magnificence of the northern winter landscape.

After completing *Erotikon* and a Finnish subject, *Johan*—a dark and satiric study of the triangular relationship of husband, wife, and the visitant, stranger-lover, set in the desolate expanse of the countryside, with a climax worthy of Griffith as the guilty couple, chased by the husband, ride the rapids in a small boat—Stiller crowned his career in Sweden with his two further adaptations from Lagerlöf: *Gunnar Hedes Saga* and *Gösta Berlings Saga*. In the former—in every way an outstanding film of its period, in its immixture of dream and actuality—the hero, Nils (Einar Hansson), a violinist, is inspired to emulate his father, who made a fortune by driving a vast herd of reindeer south from the Arctic circle. Nils's adventure in realizing this dream only leads to severe injury resulting in amnesia; back home in the forests of the south he experiences hallucinations from which the girl who loves him finally liberates him. The film's duality is striking: the realism of the trek with the reindeer involving panoramic shots of the great herds and brilliant tracking shots of the catastrophic stampede which leads to Nils's accident, is in marked contrast to the twilit world of his hallucinations.

Gösta Berling's Saga, on the other hand, though famous for its revelation of the star quality of the young drama student, Greta Garbo, and its melodramatic story of the defrocked priest (Lars Hanson) fatally in love with Garbo's Italian girl, is clumsy in structure compared with *Gunnar Hede's Saga*, and was later destructively cut for export to half its original length of four hours.

Stiller travelled in 1925 to America at the invitation of Louis B. Mayer of MGM on the strength of his reputation as a sophisticated European director, but mostly (it would seem) because he was Garbo's Svengali-like and obsessive mentor. He very soon fell out with Mayer who endured him because he wanted Garbo as a contract player. All but mesmerized by Stiller, Garbo insisted he direct her in *The Temptress*; the inevitable difficulties arose and he was withdrawn from the film. His best film in America was made at Paramount, *Hotel Imperial* starring Pola Negri; it concerned a wartime love affair between a hotel servant and an Austrian officer and was notable for its spectacular, composite hotel set over which the camera played suspended from an overhead rail. After finishing a second film with Negri, *The Woman on Trial*, Stiller never managed to complete another film; the respiratory illness that was undermining his health forced him to part from Garbo and return to Sweden, where he died in 1928 at the age of 45.

—Roger Manvell

STORCK, HENRI. Belgian. Born in Ostend, 5 September 1907. Married photographer Virginia Lierens. Career: 1918—buys Pathé-Baby camera; mid-1920s—reads André Breton's *Manifeste du surréalisme*; acquainted with numerous artists and writers, including James Ensor, Leon Spilliaert, Constant Permeke; 1927—begins making films in 8mm; 1928—sees films of Robert Flaherty; organizes cine-club in Ostend; makes first "reportages"; 1931—works as assistant in France to Pierre Billon, Jean Croillon, and Jean Vigo; 1933—secretary of Brussels cine-club André Thirifays proposes film on striking coal miners; with Joris Ivens makes *Borinage*; 1936—begins making films about art; *La Belgique ancienne* pioneer folkloric film; 1951—directs feature *Le Banquet des fraudeurs*, first Belgian-international co-production; president for 15 years of the Association Belge des Auteurs de Films et Auteurs de Television; co-founder, Royal Film Archive of Belgium; 1972—series of 10 ethnographic films *Fêtes de Belgique*.

Films: 1927-28—amateur films on Ostend; 1929-30—*Pour vos beaux yeux; Images d'Ostende*; 1930—*Une Pêche au hareng; Le Service de sauvetage sur la côte belge; Les Fêtes du centenaire; Trains de plaisir; Tentative de films abstraits; La Mort de Vénus; Suzanne au bain; Ostende, reine des plages*; 1931—*Une Idylle à la plage*; 1932—*Travaux du tunnel sous l'Escaut; Histoire du soldat inconnu; Sur les bords de la caméra*; 1933—*Trois Vies une corde; Misère au Borinage* (co-d, +co-ph); 1934—*Création d'ulcères artificiels chez le chien; La Production sélective du réseau à 70*; 1935—*Electrification de la ligne Bruxelles-Anvers; L'Île de Pâques; Le Trois-Mâts; Cap du sud; L'Industrie de la tapisserie et du meuble sculpté; Le Coton*; 1936—*Les Carillons; Les Jeux de l'été et de la mer; Sur les routes de l'été; Regards sur la Belgique ancienne*; 1937—*La Belgique nouvelle; Un ennemi public; Les Maisons de la misère*; 1938—*Comme une lettre à la poste; La Roue de la fortune; Terre de Flandre; Vacances; Le Patron est mort*; 1939—*Voor Recht en Vrijheid te Kortrijk*; 1940—*La Foire internationale de Bruxelles*; 1942-44—*Symphonie paysanne* (co-d, +ph); 1944—*Le Monde de Paul Delvaux* (+ph); 1947—*La Joie de revivre*; 1947-48—*Rubens*; 1949—*Au carrefour de la vie*; 1950—*Carnavals*; 1951—*Le Banquet des fraudeurs* (feature); 1952—*La Fenêtre ouverte*; 1953—*Herman Teirlinck*; 1954—*Les Belges et la mer; Les Portes de la maison; Le Tour du monde en bateau-stop*; 1955—*Le Trésor d'Ostende*; 1956—*Décembre, mois des enfants*; 1957—*Couleur de feu*; 1957-60—*Les Seigneurs de la forêt*; 1960—*Les Gestes du silence*; 1961—*Les Dieux du feu; L'Énergie et vous*; 1962—*Variation sur le geste; Le Bonheur d'être aimée* (+co-pr, co-sc); *Les Malheurs de la guerre*; 1963—*Plastiques*; 1964—*Matières nouvelles*; 1965—*Le Musée vivant*; 1966—*Jeudi on chantera comme dimanche*; 1968—*Forêt secrète d'Afrique*; 1969-70—*Paul Delvaux ou les femmes défendues* (+ed); 1969-72—*Fêtes de Belgiques*; 1974-75—*Fifres et tambours d'Entre-Sambre-et-*

Meuse; *Les Marcheurs de Sainte Rolende*; *Les Joyeux Tromb-lons*; 1975—*Les Marcheurs de Sainte Rolende*.

Publications:

By STORCK:

Articles—interview in *Documentary Explorations* by G. Roy Levin, New York 1972; interview by Bert Hogenkamp in *Skrien* (Amsterdam), July/August 1977; interview by Bert Hogenkamp in *Ecran* (Paris), July 1978.

On STORCK:

Articles—"The Romantic Cinema of Henri Storck" by Oswell Blakeston in *Architectural Review* (New York), May 1931; "Storck le touche-à-tout" by R. Bassan in *Ecran* (Paris), September 1977; "Henri Storck" by R. Grelier in *Image et son* (Paris), September 1977; "Henri Storck—Nicht weit von Geel" by Bert Hogenkamp in *Filmfaust* (Frankfurt), December 1979; "Henri Storck à l'honneur" by P. Davay in *Amis du film et de la télévision* (Brussels), January 1979; monograph issue devoted to Storck of *Revue Belge du cinéma* (Brussels), August 1979; "Storck vu par un jeune Hudon" by J. De Bongnie in *Amis du film et de la télévision* (Brussels), November 1979.

*   *   *

After growing up in the seaside town of Ostend, Henri Storck naturally chose the beach and the sea, with the surrounding sand dunes, as background and subject for many of his early films. He became friendly with Ostend's resident and visiting artists, and they all apparently absorbed creative strength from the solid tradition of Flemish paintings as well as physical stamina from the invigorating North Sea air. Primarily a documentarist, Storck's profilic output of over 70 films does include a couple of fiction films: *Une Idylle à la plage*, a short film about adolescent love, and a feature film with a thriller framework, *Le Banquet des fraudeurs*. Storck has described the work of his mentor, Charles DeKeukeleire, another Belgian film pioneer, as having "..lyrical expression, faithfulness to authentic reality, and a sense of rhythm in editing." These words are just as applicable to Storck's own oeuvre. *Borinage*, a film about a coal miners' strike in the Borinage—a district southwest of Brussels—is a powerful revelation of the miners' living conditions. The film cinematically echoes the feelings that Van Gogh expressed in his drawings of an earlier period. *Borinage* is full of strong, intense images. A daring project made in collaboration with Joris Ivens, the film had to be shot covertly in order to evade the police. Banned from public showing in Belgium and Holland at the time it was released, *Borinage* became a time-tested classic and an inspiration to the "Grierson boys" in England. *Symphonie paysanne*, made in a completely different style, depicted the passage of the seasons on a Belgian farm. This pastoral eulogy again demonstrated Storck's ability to express his humane sensibility in a cinematic manner. After the war, Storck immensely enhanced a developing genre—films analyzing the visual arts. *Rubens*, (made in collaboration with Paul Haesaerts) and the *World of Paul Delvaux* are outstanding examples which were immediately recognized as *tours de force*. *The Open Window* and *The Sorrows of the War* were also worthy contributions to this category. A later film about Delvaux, *Paul Delvaux or the Forbidden Women* was, to

Storck's great amusement, promoted on Times Square as a pornographic film. In his films about art, Storck was particualrly innovative in his use of camera movement to display the details of the art works, and in some films used animated lines to demonstrate their structures of composition. Henri Storck's humanistic vision is revealed by his films and crosses all national and cultural boundaries.

—Robert Edmonds

———

STRAUB, JEAN-MARIE, AND HUILLET, DANIÈLE.
French, German. Jean-Marie Straub born in Metz, 8 January 1933. Straub educated in literature, Universities of Strasbourg and Nancy, 1950-54. Married in 1959. Career: 1954—Straub arrives in Paris, meets Danièle Huillet who becomes collaborator; 1954-58—Straub student and assistant to Abel Gance (*La Tour de Nesle*); assistant to Jean Renoir (*French Cancan, Eléna et les hommes*),Jacques Rivette (*Le Coup de berger*), Robert Bresson (*Un Condamné à mort s'est échappé*), and Alexandre Astruc (*Une Vie*); 1958—Straub leaves France to avoid military service in Algerian conflict; 1959—Straub and Huillet settle in Munich; 1966—meet Heinrich Böll while researching Bach film; since 1969 live in Italy; 1971—Straub amnestied in 1971 by French.

Films (Straub as director, Huillet as scriptwriter): 1963—*Machorka-Muff* (+co-ed, co-sound); 1965—*Nicht versöhnt oder Es hilft nur Gewalt, wo Gewalt herrscht (Es hilft nicht, wo Gewalt herrscht, Not Reconciled)* (+co-ph, co-ed); 1968—*Chronik der Anna Magdalena Bach (Chronicle of Anna Magdalena Bach)*; *Der Bräutigam, die Komödiantin und der Zuhälter (The Bridegroom, the Comedienne and the Pimp)* (+co-ed); (as co-directors, Huillet as scriptwriter): 1969—*Othon (Les Yeux ne veulent pas en tout temps se fermer ou Peut-être qu'un jour Rome se permettra de choisir à son tour, Die Augen wollen sich nicht zu jeder Zeit schliessen oder Vielleicht eines Tages wird Rom sich erlauben, seinerseits zu wählen, Eyes Do Not Want to Close at All Times or Perhaps One Day Rome Will Permit Herself to Choose in Her Turn, Othon)* (+co-ed, Straub in ro under pseudonym Jubarithe Semaran); *Einleitung zu Arnold Schoenberg Begleit Musik zu einer Lichtspielscene (Introduction to Arnold Schoenberg's Accompaniment for a Cinematographic Scene)* (+co-pr, co-ed—for TV); 1972—*Geschichtsunterricht (History Lessons)* (+co-pr, co-ed); 1975—*Moses und Aron (Moses and Aaron)* (+co-ed); 1976—*Fortini/Cani (I cani del Sinai)* (+co-ed); 1977—*Toute révolution est un coup de dés (Every Revolution Is a Throw of the Dice)*; 1979—*Della nube alla resistenza (From the Cloud to the Resistance)*.

Publications:

By STRAUB AND HUILLET:

Articles—"Frustration of Violence" in *Cahiers du Cinema in English* (New York), January 1967; interview with Straub and Huillet by A. Apon in *Skrien* (Amsterdam), May/June 1973; "Gespräch mit Danièle Huillet und Jean-Marie Straub" by W. Roth and G. Pflaum in *Filmkritik* (Munich), February 1973; "Filmografia di Jean-Marie Straub" by Danièle Huillet in

Filmkritik (Munich), January/February 1973; interview by J. Hribar in *Filmcritica* (Rome), February/March 1974; interview on *Moses and Aaron* by J. Bontemps and others in *Cahiers du cinéma* (Paris), July/August 1975; "'Moses und Aron' as an Object of Marxist Reflection", interview by J. Rogers in *Jump Cut* (Chicago), no.12-13, 1976; "Decoupage di Fortini/Cani" and "Pesaro: incontro con Straub e Huillet" in *Filmcritica* (Rome), November/December 1976; "Jean-Marie Straub et Danièle Huillet", interview by J.-C. Bonnet and others in *Cinématographe* (Paris), December 1977; "Straub/Huillet", interview by R. Gansera in *Filmkritik* (Munich), September 1978; interview by Serge Daney and J. Narboni in *Cahiers du cinéma* (Paris), November 1979.

On STRAUB:

Book—*Jean-Marie Straub* by Richard Roud, London 1971; articles—"Jean-Marie Straub" by B. Baxter in *Film* (London), spring 1969; "Jean-Marie Straub" by Andi Engel in *Second Wave*, New York 1970; "Jean-Marie Straub" by Roy Armes in *London Magazine*, September 1970; "Oltre l'iscrizione, la scrittura" by F. Casetti in *Bianco e nero* (Rome), July/August 1972; "Film Styles" by F. Zaagsma in *Lumiere* (Melbourne), May 1973; "Die Filmographie—Jean-Marie Straub" in *Information* (Wiesbaden), January 1974; "Political formations in the Cinema of Jean-Marie Straub" by M. Walsh in *Jump Cut* (Chicago), November/December 1974; special issue on *Moses und Aron* in *Cahiers du cinéma* (Paris), October/November 1975; issue devoted to Straub and Huillet of *Enthusiasm* (London), December 1975; "J.-M. S. et J.-L. G." by P. Bonitzer in *Cahiers du cinéma* (Paris), February 1976; "Report from Venice: Cinema and Ideology" by N. Greene in *Praxis* (Berkeley), no.2, 1976; "3 Cinéastes du texte" by J.-C. Bonnet in *Cinématographe* (Paris), October 1977; "Danièle Huillet Jean-Marie Straub's Fortini/Cani", special issue of *Filmkritik* (Munich), January 1977; "Straub/Huillet: The Politics of Film Practice" by S. Dermody in *Cinema Papers* (Melbourne), September/October 1976; "Jean-Marie Straub et Danièle Huillet" by Noel Simsolo in *Cinéma* (Paris), March 1977; "Gilbert Adair from Paris" in *Film Comment* (New York), March/April 1978; "The Films of Straub Are Not 'Theoretical'" by E. Bennett in *Afterimage* (Rochester), summer 1978; "Combat contre l'impression" by J. Grant in *Cinéma* (Paris), January 1978; "Le Plan Straubien" by Serge Daney in *Cahiers du cinéma* (Paris), November 1979; "Tribune: Cinéma, fragments d'expérience" by J.-P. Oudart in *Cahiers du cinéma* (Paris), February 1979; "Jean-Luc, Chantal, Danielle, Jean-Marie and the Others" by Jonathan Rosenbaum in *American Film* (Washington, D.C.), February 1979; "The Cinema of Jean-Marie Straub and Danièle Huillet", program notes with articles by Jonathan Rosenbaum and others, Film at the Public, Public Forum Theater, New York, 2-14 November 1982.

*   *   *

The films of Jean-Marie Straub and Danièle Huillet are best understood in the context of contemporary developments in radical, materialist cinema. They offer what many people see as a genuine alternative to both dominant narrative cinema and conventional art movies. Their work is formally austere and demands attentive, intellectual participation from audiences. However, it must be acknowledged that many people find their films nearly impenetrable and absolutely boring. This is explained in part by the fact that the films do not rely on standard narrative

construction or conventional characters. While the films of Straub and Huillet are by no means "abstract" it is nearly impossible to (re)construct a unified, imaginary, referential "world" through them.

In a sense their work might be explained in terms of strategies of displeasure, a wilful refusal to captivate audiences with a coherent fictional world, in favor of promoting a distanciated, intellectual interaction between viewer and film. Because of this insistence on critical distance, audiences must work with the film in a dialectical process of meaning construction. (In fact, Straub is notoriously critical of "lazy" viewers who are unwilling to engage in this activity.)

Straub and Huillet's films directly address the nature of cinematic signification and its political implications. This includes breaking away from conventional assumptions and practices of dominant narrative cinema. Their films exploit all channels of the medium—music, sounds, words, and images—as equivalent carriers of meaning, rather than privileging the "visual" or relegating music and sound effects to the task of support material. Thus, there are times when extremely long, static shots accompany lengthy, complex verbal passages (a singularly "uncinematic" practice according to conventional canons of film aesthetics). Sequences may be developed along the lines of montage construction, juxtaposing graphic material, verbal material, and moving images. Both of these strategies are used in *Introduction to Schoenberg's "Accompaniment for a Cinematographic Scene"*; and the starting point for this short film was a piece of music written by the composer. The major texts, read on-screen (though interrupted at intervals by black frames), are a letter from Schoenberg to Kandinsky explaining his reasons for not participating in the Bauhaus, and a text by Brecht elaborating the relationship between fascism and capitalism. The readings of these texts take up most of the film, which includes Straub and Huillet as on-camera narrators "placing" the texts, and concludes with a montage sequence. The political aspect of the film derives not only for the logical argument advanced, the Brecht analysis standing as a critique of Schoenberg's "liberal" position, but also from the film's rejection of documentary norms. At the same time it has been pointed out that Schoenberg's music stands in relation to classical rules of harmonic composition as Straub and Huillet films stand in relation to the conventions of dominant cinema.

The incorporation of musical works and verbal texts, as both a source for and signifying material within their films, is an important aspect of their work. The figure of Bertolt Brecht is perhaps the most pervasive presence in Straub and Huillet's films. His writing is included in *Introduction to Schoenberg* and provided the source for *History Lessons*. More crucially, the strategies of deconstruction and distanciation in their films derive from principles advanced in Brechtian theory. These include concepts of alienation and anti-illusionism elaborated in Brecht's theory of epic theater. Straub and Huillet have developed these ideas in the context of their films and their persistent concern with the politics of cinematic expression.

—M.B. White

STRICK, JOSEPH. American. Born in Pittsburgh, 6 July 1923. Educated at University of California at Los Angeles. Career: 1942-45—serves as Air Force pilot in submarine reconnaissance; after war works as copyboy on *Los Angeles Times*, becoming assistant telegraph editor; shooting film on weekends, assembles

Muscle Beach, film on bodybuilders; 1950s—works as promoter for companies specializing in development of high-precision instruments; in spare time assembles material for *The Savage Eye*; 1960—success of *The Savage Eye* makes possible full-time film career; 1965—moves to Dublin to prepare *Ulysses*. Recipient: Robert Flaherty Award (Best Feature Length Documentary), British Academy, for *The Savage Eye*, 1959; Academy Award, Documentary Short Subject, for *Interviews with My Lai Veterans*, 1970. Business: Trans-Lux Corp., 625 Madison Ave., New York, NY 10022. Address: 266 River Road, Grandview, New York 10960.

Films (as director): 1948—*Muscle Beach* (co-d—documentary); 1949—*Jour de fête* (documentary); 1953—*The Big Break* (+pr—documentary); 1959—*The Savage Eye* (co-d, +co-pr, co-sc, co-ed); 1963—*An Affair of the Skin* (associate pr only); *The Balcony* (+co-pr); 1966—*The Hecklers* (for British TV); 1967—*Ulysses* (+pr, co-sc); *The Legend of the Boy and the Eagle* (co-associate pr only); 1969—*Justine* (replaced as d by George Cukor); *Ring of Bright Water* (pr only); 1970—*Tropic of Cancer* (+pr, co-sc); *Interviews with My Lai Veterans* (+pr, sc—documentary); 1974—*Road Movie* (+pr); 1979—*A Portrait of the Artist as a Young Man*; 1981—*The Space Works*.

Publications:

By STRICK:

Articles—"The Blacklisting of Men and Ideas" in *Film Culture* (New York), fall/winter 1970; "I Can Be Pretty Insulting!", interview by G. Loney in *After Dark* (New York), July 1970.

On STRICK:

Articles—"Joy Censors Beware" in *Newsweek* (New York), 19 September 1966; "Things I Am Here to Read" in *Life* (New York), 31 March 1967; "Strick's Ulysses" by E. Rhode in *Encounter* (London), August 1967; "On the Scene: Joseph Strick" in *Playboy* (Chicago), September 1968; "Transliteration: Joseph Strick's *Tropic of Cancer*" by Louis Delpino in *Film Heritage* (New York), fall 1970; "Joseph Strick" by R. Nicholls in *Lumiere* (Melbourne), March 1974.

*   *   *

After making an amateur short about Pacific body-builders, *Muscle Beach*, Joseph Strick returned to filmmaking in 1959, with co-authors Ben Maddow and Sidney Mayers, to make *The Savage Eye*, a portrait of a lonely woman in the urban jungle. He demonstrated his documenatry skill and realistic, concise style in opposition to Maddow's poetic, mystical commentary. The fragmented, seemingly incoherent narrative method remarkably depicts the heroine's disorderly life.

In the early sixties, Strick was one of the unconventional, "angry" directors of the so-called "new American cinema." In his later films, he appeared on the margin of the official cinema, and could be regarded as a filmmaker in exile. He has always been noted for his audacity and originality in the choice of material. He was dismissed from two Hollywood productions (*The Heart Is a Lonely Hunter* and *Justine*) for his uncompromising attitudes.

His "literary films" of the sixties are praised by some critics and hated by others. The *Monthly Bulletin* reviewers are particularly hostile: Genet's *Balcony* is critized as too literal and stagy, Joyce's *Ulysses* and *A Portrait of the Artist as a Young Man* have a banal visual accompaniment to the monologues and dialogues, while Miller's *Tropic of Cancer* is flat, disjointed, and lacks the passion and poetry of the book. The visual aspect can, conversely, be regarded positively: Strick faithfully captures authentic Dublin locations and preserves a sense of timelessness by presenting both the Dublin of 1904 and of 1966.

Sex and its manifestations are a predominant feature in all Strick's films. Sexual power also plays a major role in *Janice*, a film about a prostitute soliciting truckdrivers. Strick maintains it is also a film about the destruction of the U.S. landscape by industry and bloated motorism.

His last film, *Interviews with My Lai Veterans*, an Oscar-winning short, attempts to show the feelings of five soldiers during the massacre and two years later back home, without trying to cut them off from other Americans. It asks fundamental questions about the human capacity to commit atrocities.

Strick is against violence but believes that "representation of it is purgative and infinitely better than the repression of it." A frequent foe of censors (e.g. for his retention of four-letter words in *Tropic of Cancer*), Strick rejects censorship and thinks that the obscenity laws encourage people to explore the borderline of permissiveness to see how much they can get away with. He says "one must always trust both the people and the critics to reject the cheap and shoddy."

—Veroslav Habá

STURGES, JOHN. American. Born in Oak Park, Illinois, 3 January 1911. Educated at Marin Junior College, California. Career: 1930 or 1932—enters RKO-Radio Pictures, where older brother employed in art dept.; works in blueprint dept.; becomes personal assistant to designer Robert Edmond Jones on first Technicolor films; works as production assistant to David O. Selznick; 1934-35—color consultant on Boleslavsky's *Garden of Allah*; 1935—begins working in RKO cutting rooms; 1942-45—serves in Army Air Corps, directs about 45 documentaries including *Thunderbolt*, co-directed and co-edited with William Wyler; 1946—signed as director by Columbia; 1949—joins MGM; 1960—begins working on independent productions; is co-founder of The Mirisch Company. Recipient: Outstanding Directorial Achievement, Directors Guild of America, for *Bad Day at Black Rock*, 1955. Agent: The William Morris Agency, Beverly Hills, California. Business: The Alpha Corp., 13063 Ventura Blvd., Suite 202, North Hollywood, CA 91604.

Films (as feature director): 1946—*The Man Who Dared*; *Shadowed*; 1947—*Alias Mr. Twilight*; *For the Love of Rusty*; *Keeper of the Bees*; 1948—*Best Man Wins*; *The Sign of the Ram*; 1949—*The Walking Hills*; 1950—*Mystery Street*; *The Capture*; *The Magnificent Yankee*; *Right Cross*; 1951—*Kind Lady*; 1951—*The People Against O'Hara*; *It's a Big Country* (co-d); 1952—*The Girl in White*; 1953—*Jeopardy*; *Fast Company*; *Escape from Fort Bravo*; 1954—*Bad Day at Black Rock*; 1955—*Underwater*; *The Scarlet Coat*; 1956—*Backlash*; 1957—*Gunfight at the O.K. Corral*; 1958—*The Old Man and the Sea* (took over direction from Fred Zinnemann); *The Law and Jake Wade*; 1959—*Last Train from Gun Hill*; *Never So Few*; 1960—*The Magnificent Seven*; 1961—*By Love Possessed*; 1962—*Sergeants Three*; *A Girl Named Tamiko*; 1963—*The Great Escape*; 1965—

The Satan Bug; The Hallelujah Trail; 1967—*The Hour of the Gun;* 1968—*Ice Station Zebra;* 1969—*Marooned;* 1972—*Joe Kidd;* 1973—*Valdez il mezzosangue (Chino, The Valdez Horses);* 1974—*McQ;* 1976—*The Eagle Has Landed.*

Publications:

By STURGES:

Article—"How the West Was Lost!" in *Films and Filming* (London), December 1962.

On STURGES:

Articles—"When the Twain Meet: *Seven Samurai* vs. *The Magnificent 7*" by Joseph Anderson in *Film Quarterly* (Berkeley), spring 1962; "Capsule of John Sturges" by Richard Cherry in *Action* (Los Angeles), November/December 1969; "The Merit of Flying Lead" and "The Power of the Gun" by D. Jones in *Films and Filming* (London), February 1974.

*   *   *

John Sturges has had a long and varied career in film. In the thirties he was an editor and then a producer. After working on documentaries during the war, he began directing in 1946. Popular film critics either pass over his work or they demean it. Andrew Sarris regards him as a mislabeled "expert technician," whose career is anything but "meaningful." Sturges has had success at the box office with some of the many action films he has done. *Gunfight at the OK Corral, The Magnificent Seven,* and *The Great Escape* were all major winners with audiences.

Sturges's films frequently deal with a group of men working towards a specific goal. In *The Great Escape* this theme is emphasized as each of the characters tries to escape from a German P.O.W. camp unsuccessfully. Only when they work together as a unit can success be achieved. While the goals are usually attained, the attempt is often costly. In several of the films, the group is decimated by the end of the mission. In *Marooned* only two of the astronauts survive and *The Magnificent Seven* is reduced to three by the end of the battle.

Sturges's work does not exclude women but the women are usually shown only as fringe characters. They are identified by the men they are associated with and react to what the men do or say. This is particularly clear in *Marooned.* In one sequence, each astronaut's wife is allowed a moment to talk to her husband via a television hook-up and say good-bye as the astronauts are trapped in their capsule in outer space.

Sturges holds a respected position in the film industry. His successes at the box office have helped him to gain that respect, but he also has an excellent eye for casting. His films have begun and furthered the careers of many actors. Steve McQueen's progress toward stardom can be traced in his films with Sturges—*Never So Few, The Magnificent Seven,* and *The Great Escape.* James Coburn, Charles Bronson, Ernest Borgnine, and Lee Marvin received career boosts from their roles in Sturges's films. Unlike Andrew Sarris, Hollywood appreciated Sturges's handling of wide-screen formats in his films of the fifties. It is thought that he was one of the first directors to develop the wide screen as a technique rather than use it as a gimmick. It is also very clear from Sturges's films that Hollywood feels confident in giving Sturges a project with a large cast and big budget. He capably handles large-scale projects, is able to deal with star egos (he has directed "rat pack" films with Frank Sinatra) and produces successes. Hollywood could not ask for more.

—Ray Narducy

———————

STURGES, PRESTON. American. Born Edmund P. Biden in Chicago, 29 August 1898; adopted by mother's second husband, Solomon Sturges. Educated in Chicago (Coulter School); Lycée Janson, Paris; Ecole des Roches, France; Villa Lausanne, Switzerland; and in Berlin and Dresden. Married Estelle Mudge (divorced 1928); married Eleanor Post Hutton, 1932 (annulled 1932); Louise Sergeant Tervis (divorced); actress Anne Nagle (known professionally as Sandy Mellen); sons: Thomas, Preston, Jr., and Solomon. Career: early teens—manages mother's cosmetic shop in Deauville, then in New York; 1914—works as runner for Wall Street brokerage firm; 1917—enlists in Air Corps, attends School of Military Aeronautics, Austin, Texas; 1919—returns to New York, goes into cosmetics business, invents kissproof lipstick; turns business over to mother; until 1927 works at various jobs and as inventor; 1927—undergoes appendectomy; during illness makes decision to become playwright; 1929—*The Guinea Pig* plays 16 weeks on Broadway; 1929-31—also writes plays *Strictly Dishonorable, Child of Manhattan, The Well of Romance;* writes 2 screenplays for Paramount; 1932—moves to Hollywood to work on script from Wells's *The Invisible Man* (unrealized) for Universal; 1940—begins directing own screenplays; also at this time manages Sturges Engineering Company which manufactures diesel engines; 1940-44—directs series of very successful comedies for Paramount; 1944—enters into association with Howard Hughes; dismissed by Hughes as director of *Vendetta;* 1949—moves to Paris. Died at the Algonquin Hotel, New York, 6 August 1959. Recipient: Best Original Screenplay Academy Award for *The Great McGinty,* 1940; Laurel Award for Achievement (posthumously), Writers Guild of America, 1974.

Films (as scriptwriter): 1930—*The Big Pond* (Henley) (co-dialogue); *Fast and Loose* (Newmeyer) (dialogue); 1931—*Strictly Dishonorable* (Stahl) (play basis); 1933—*The Power and the Glory* (Howard); *Child of Manhattan* (Buzzell) (play basis); 1934—*30 Day Princess* (Gering) (co-sc); *We Live Again* (Mamoulian) (co-sc); *Imitation of Life* (Stahl) (co-sc, uncredited); 1935—*The Good Fairy* (Wyler); *Diamond Jim* (Sutherland) (co-sc); 1936—*Next Time We Love* (Edward Griffith) (co-sc, uncredited); *One Rainy Afternoon* (Lee) (lyrics for "Secret Rendezvous" only); 1937—*Hotel Haywire* (Archainbaud); *Easy Living* (Leisen); 1938—*Port of 7 Seas* (Whale); *If I Were King* (Lloyd); 1940—*Remember the Night* (Leisen); (as director and scriptwriter) 1940—*The Great McGinty; Christmas in July;* 1941—*The Lady Eve; Sullivan's Travels;* 1942—*The Palm Beach Story;* 1944—*Hail the Conquering Hero; The Miracle of Morgan's Creek; The Great Moment;* 1947—*I'll Be Yours* (Seiter) (screenplay basis only); (as producer, director, and scriptwriter) 1947—*Mad Wednesday;* 1948—*Unfaithfully Yours;* 1949—*The Beautiful Blonde from Bashful Bend;* (in capacities as indicated): 1951—*Vendetta* (Ferrer) (co-d, uncredited); *Strictly Dishonorable* (Frank and Panama) (play basis); 1956—*The Birds and the Bees* (Taurog) (screenplay basis); 1957—*Les Carnets du Major Thompson (The French, They Are a Funny Race)* (d, sc); 1958—*Rock-a-bye Baby* (Tashlin) (screenplay basis).

Role: 1958—*Serge Vitry* in *Paris Holiday* (Oswald).

Publications:

By STURGES:

Articles—"Conversation with Preston Sturges" by Gordon Gow in *Sight and Sound* (London), spring 1956; interview in *Interviews with Film Directors* edited by Andrew Sarris, New York 1967.

On STURGES:

Articles—"When Satire and Slapstick Meet" by Bosley Crowther in *The New York Times Magazine*, 27 August 1944; "Preston Sturges" by A. King in *Life* (New York), 7 January 1946; "Preston Sturges" by Peter Ericsson in *Sequence* (London), summer 1948; "Preston Sturges or Laughter Betrayed" by Siegfried Kracauer in *Films in Review* (New York), February 1950; "Innovation by Sturges" in *Newsweek* (New York), 7 May 1951; "Then and Now" by A. Carey in *The New York Times Magazine*, 2 December 1956; "Preston Sturges" by Nel King and G.W. Stonier in *Sight and Sound* (London), summer/autumn 1959; article in *Current Biography Yearbook 1959*, New York 1960; "Preston Sturges and the Theory of Decline" by Eric Jonsson and "Preston Sturges: Success in the Movies" by Manny Farber and W.S. Poster in *Film Culture* (New York), no.26, 1962; "Preston Sturges" by Penelope Houston in *Sight and Sound* (London), summer 1965; "Notes on Preston Sturges and America" by Michael Budd in *Film Society Review* (New York), January 1968; "Preston Sturges in the 30s" by Andrew Sarris in *Film Comment* (New York), winter 1970/71; "Past Master" by R. Downey in *New York*, 17 August 1970; list of screenplays by P. Zucker in *Films in Review* (New York), March 1971; "Preston Sturges" by Richard Corliss in *Cinema* (Beverly Hills), spring 1972; "Johnny One Note, Souvenirs sur Preston Sturges" by R. Parrish in *Positif* (Paris), December/January 1977/78; "Hail the Conquering Sturges" by Andrew Sarris in the *Village Voice* (New York), 10 September 1979.

*   *   *

As a screenwriter, Sturges stands out for his narrative inventiveness. All of the amazing coincidences and obvious repetitions in such comedies as *Easy Living* and *The Good Fairy* show Sturges's mastery of the standard narrative form, and also his ability to exaggerate it, and to shape it to his own needs. And in *The Power and the Glory* (an early model for *Citizen Kane*), Sturges pioneered the use of voice-over narration to advance a story.

Along with John Huston, Sturges was one of the first of the sound-era screenwriters to become a director, and those films that he made from his own screenplays take even further the narrative experiments he began as a writer in the 1930s. He continued making comedies, but often he combined them with elements that more properly belonged to social dramas in the Warner Brothers tradition, even though Sturges himself worked primarily for Paramount. *The Great McGinty*, for instance, deals with big-city political corruption. *Christmas in July*, despite its happy end, analyzes an American dream perverted by dishonesty and commercial hype. And *Sullivan's Travels*, even as it mixes aspects of *It Happened One Night* and *I Am a Fugitive*

From a Chain Gang, examines the uses of comedy in a society burdened by poverty and social injustice.

With *The Palm Beach Story* and *The Lady Eve*, Sturges goes from combining genres to parodying the standard narrative form. Traditionally, in the classical narrative, elements repeat from scene to scene, but with slight differences each time. The story, then, becomes a series of episodes that are similar, but not obviously so. *The Palm Beach Story*, however (although we cannot be sure of this until the end), deals with two sets of twins, one pair male and the other female, and Sturges takes full advantage of a practically infinite number of possibilities for doubling and repetition.

In *The Lady Eve*, there are no twins to call out attention to how Sturges exaggerates the typical narrative. But the central female character, Jean, changes her identity and becomes Eve Harrington, an English aristocrat, so she can double-cross the man who jilted her when he found out she made her living as a con artist. So in this film, too, Sturges provides us with some obvious doubling. In fact, *The Lady Eve* divides neatly into two very similar parts: the shipboard romance of Charles and Jean, and then the romance, on land, of Charles and Jean-as-Eve. In this second half, the film virtually turns into a screwball comedy version of *Vertigo*. Charles falls in love with a woman who looks exactly like another woman he had loved and lost, and who, indeed, really is that woman.

The Lady Eve is most interesting in the way that it stands narrative convention on its head. Charles Pike, a wealthy ale heir, looks for snakes on the Amazon, but as soon as he leaves the jungle and heads back to civilization, the hunter becomes the hunted. This inversion itself is hardly remarkable, either in literature or the cinema. What does stand out as unusual is that the predators are all women. Pike boards a luxury liner steaming back to the United States, and every unmarried woman on board decides to end the voyage engaged to him, to have "caught" him just as Charles had been trying to capture reptiles. Certainly, there are few films from this period with such active, aggressive female characters.

Sturges works out the notion of feminine entrapment not only in his script but also through his visual style. On board, Jean plots to get Charles, and Sturges shows us her predatory skill by letting her capture Pike's image. In the dining room, Jean watches as various women attempt to attract Pike's attention. She does not want him to see her staring, so she turns away from Pike's table and holds a mirror to her face, as if she were giving a quick re-arrangement to her makeup. But instead she uses the mirror to watch Charles. Sturges cuts to a closeup of the mirror, and so we share Jean's point of view. As spectators, we are used to an appreciative male gaze, and to a woman as the subject of that gaze. But here, once again, Sturges reverses our expectations. It is Jean who plays the voyeur and, as an added show of her strength, it is Jean who apparently controls the images, since she holds the mirror, and it is she who captures an unknowing Charles within the frame of a looking-glass.

Sturges's most interesting achievement may be his 1948 film, *Unfaithfully Yours*. Here, he shows the same event three times. While fairly common in literature, this sort of narrative construction is extremely rare in the cinema. But even in literature, the repeated event almost always comes to us from the points of view of different characters. In Sturges's films, we see the event the first and second time through the eyes of the same man; an orchestra conductor plots revenge on his wife, whom he suspects of infidelity, and he imagines two different ways of getting it. Then, the next repetition, rather than being imaginary, is actual. We watch as the conductor attempts to murder his wife. So, since the conductor acts once again as the main character, even this last repetition comes to us from his point of view. The film stands out, then, as a remarkable case study of the thoughts and actions of a single character, and as one more of Sturges's experiments in narrative repetition.

During the early and mid-1940s, critics hailed Sturges as a comic genius. But after *Unfaithfully Yours*, over the last eleven years of his life, Sturges made only two more films. Upon leaving Paramount, he set out to make films for Howard Hughes, but the attempt was an ill-fated one, and Sturge's standing in the critical community declined rapidly. For several years, though, a reevaluation has been underway. Sturge's sophisticated handling of sexual relations (which the heiress in *The Palm Beach Story* refers to as "Topic A") make his films seem remarkably contemporary. There can be no doubting Sturges's screenwriting abilities, but only recently have critics come to appreciate Sturge's consummate skills as a filmmaker.

—Eric Smoodin

SUCKSDORFF, ARNE. Swedish. Born in Stockholm, 3 February 1917. Studied painting with Otto Skold and photography with Rudolf Klein-Rogge, Reimannschule, Berlin. Married Astrid Bergman. Career: late 1930s—after completing schooling, goes to Italy on tour, buys camera; photographs win first prize in film magazine contest; 1940—first 2 films attract attention of Svensk Filmindustri which produces next 11 shorts; 1953—feature directing debut; eventually settles in Brazil, directs Brazilian film school; becomes deeply involved in problem of extinction of Brazilian aboriginal peoples. Recipient: Short Subject (One Reel) Academy Award for *Symphony of a City*, 1948; Prize for Superior Technique, Cannes Festival, for *The Great Adventure*, 1954.

Films (as director of short films): 1939—*En Augustirapsodi (An August Rhapsody)*; 1940—*Din tillvaros land (This Land Is Full of Life, Your Own Land)*; 1941—*En Sommersaga (A Summer's Tale)*; 1943—*Vinden från våster (Wind from the West)*; *Sarvtid (Reindeer People)*; 1944—*Trut! (Gull!)*; 1945—*Gryning (Dawn)*; *Skugger över snön (Shadows on the Snow)*; 1947—*Människor i stad (Symphony of a City, Rhythm of a City)*; *Den drömda dalen (Soria-Moria, Tale of the Fjords, The Dream Valley)* (+ph); 1948—*Uppbrott (The Open Road)* (+ph, ed); *En kluven värld (A Divided World)* (+sc); 1950—*Strandhugg (Going Ashore)*; *Ett horn i norr (The Living Stream)*; 1951—*Indisk by (Indian Village)* (+pr); *Vinden och floden (The Wind and the River)* (+ph); (as director of feature-length films): 1953—*Det stora äventyret (The Great Adventure)*; 1957—*En djungelsaga (The Flute and the Arrow)*; 1961—*Pojken i trädet (The Boy in the Tree)*; 1965—*Mitt hem är Copacabana (My Home Is Copacabana)*; 1971—Antarctic animal sequences in *Forbush and the Penguins*.

Publications:

By SUCKSDORFF:

Article—interview and article in *Cinema* (Beverly Hills), July/August 1965.

On SUCKSDORFF:

Book—*The New Swedish Cinema* by Nils Sundgren, Stockholm 1970; articles—"The Films of Arne Sucksdorff" by Forsyth Hardy in *Sight and Sound* (London), summer 1948; "Producer-Director-Writer-Photographer Emerges as a New Talent Through a Series of Short Subjects" by Arthur Knight in *The New York Times*, 21 November 1948; "Arne Sucksdorff" by Peter Ericsson in *Sequence* (London), spring 1949; "Arne Sucksdorff's Adventure" by Catherine De La Roche in *Sight and Sound* (London), October/December 1953; "Arne Sucksdorff" by E. Ulrichsen in *Films in Review* (New York), October 1953; "Film-Maker on His Own" by Catherine De La Roche in *Sight and Sound* (London), November 1954; "Arne Sucksdorff" in *Image* (Rochester, New York), May 1955; entry in *Current Biography Yearbook 1956*, New York 1957; "Paradise Regained in Home Movies" by Cecile Starr in *House Beautiful*, February 1957.

* * *

Swedish filmmaker Arne Sucksdorff is what the French film critics call an *auteur*, or author of his work. He wrote, shot, edited, and/or supervised his films, and they bear the stamp of his personality. His films, taken as a whole, have similar themes and style, and they reflect his personal vision.

Sucksdorff, as a young man, studied both biology and art. After working with still photography, he combined his knowledge and love of nature with filmmaking. Working primarily in the documentary and semi-documentary traditions in the forties and fifties, he used the images and sounds of reality and shaped them as would a poet. His films are often set in the country (where he spent summers as a youth), and his characters are often wild animals and children (non-actors). He prefers black and white to color. Unlike Walt Disney's "true life adventures," where nature is often seen as comforting and even fun, and unlike Robert Flaherty's romantic films where outdoor life is presented as it should be, Sucksdorff shows how things are. "This is life," says Sucksdorff, "and whether we like it or not, this is the way life goes on." The spider web is almost a signature in a Sucksdorff film. It is at once beautiful and dangerous. A shadowy forest may hide a beautiful deer or a hungry bear. Animals chase and kill each other for survival. They prey upon each other. But life has its beautiful moments, too, and it is, as in the title of his most famous film, the great adventure.

Sucksdorff had considerable technical skill. Each frame of film is beautifully composed, from an extreme close-up of a gull's eye to an extreme long shot of an island cliff. Sucksdorff often used great depth-of-field and high-contrast lighting (the moon on a snowy lake) in order to create a poetic, yet realistic, mood. He also took great care in capturing foreground and background action for a sense of excitement. He spent months in the wilderness waiting for birds on the wing, rabbits washing their faces, and lynxes stalking their prey. He made much use of natural sounds, music, and narration with little, if any, dialogue. He then spent months in the cutting room on even his short films in order to present his vision. His technical skill, however, was never used to show off, but to help us see the natural world in new ways.

Svensk Filmindustri sponsored many of his early films, which often cost as much as a feature. His most famous short film is *Symphony of a City*, where people in Stockholm (rather than animals in the wilderness) are seen, sometimes through the eyes of a child. The fishing nets look like spider webs. There is beauty in the docks and a cathedral, but also disquiet in crowds, traffic, and the precarious angles of faces.

His most personal statement is the feature length *The Great*

Adventure, produced by his own company and filmed in central Sweden. The adventure of the title is life, and Sucksdorff presents it (as he does in many other films) through the eyes of young animals and children (his son and his son's friend). In the film, a fox must care for her young; two boys save an otter from a hunter and care for it. In spring, the young foxes are grown and the otter needs to be free. Although there is sorrow as the otter leaves for the wilderness, there is joy in seeing the cranes fly free overhead. Soon the boys will also be grown in the great adventure of life.

Sucksdorff went on to make *The Flute and the Arrow*, about the ancient Muria tribe in Central India. Surprisingly, he then made a dramatic fiction feature, *The Boy in the Tree*, and was shaken when it was unsuccessful.

He left Sweden and spent some years as a teacher of film in Rio de Janeiro. Several of his students became the leading directors of the Brazilian Cinema Novo. Sucksdorff's film *My Home is Copacabana* is about children in Rio and their gift for survival. Sucksdorff is presently retired from filmmaking.

Sucksdorff's films of the forties and fifties are the most critically acclaimed. Since many were made on his own (he has been described as one of the few lone wolf artists of the cinema world), and distributed in 16mm through the non-theatrical film industry to schools and libraries, his films live primarily in the classroom rather than on television or in theatres. But what more appropriate place for films that show "...the way life goes on."

—H. Wayne Schuth

SUTHERLAND, A. EDWARD (Eddie). American. Born Albert Edward Sutherland in London, 5 January 1895. Educated in numerous public and private schools; attended Rockhill College, Maryland. Married actress Louise Brooks (divorced); Edwina (Sutherland). Career: early teens—acting debut with Lindsay Morrison Stock Company, Lynn, Massachusetts; also toured with mother in vaudeville for year; 1914—begins acting in films with Signal Company, Pasadena; 1914-16—acts for Keystone Company, and for Triangle; 1917—enlists in Canadian Royal Flying Corps; 1923—becomes assistant director for Chaplin on *A Woman of Paris* and *The Gold Rush*; 1925—obtains contract with Paramount; late 1940s—begins producing and directing for television. Died in Palm Springs, California, 31 December 1973.

Films (as director): 1925—*Coming Through; Wild, Wild Susan; A Regular Fellow*; 1926—*Behind the Front; It's the Old Army Game; We're in the Navy Now*; 1927—*Love's Greatest Mistake; Fireman Save My Child*; 1928—*Figures Don't Lie; Tillie's Punctured Romance; The Baby Cyclone; What a Night!*; 1929—*Close Harmony* (co-d); *The Dance of Life* (co-d); *Fast Company; The Saturday Night Kid; Pointed Heels*; 1930—*Burning Up; Paramount on Parade* (d with 10 others); *The Social Lion; The Sap from Syracuse*; 1931—*Gang Buster; June Moon; Up Pops the Devil; Palmy Days* (with Busby Berkeley); 1932—*Sky Devils; Mr. Robinson Crusoe; Secrets of the French Police*; 1933—*Murders in the Zoo; International House; Too Much Harmony*; 1935—*Mississippi; Diamond Jim*; 1936—*Poppy*; 1937—*Champagne Waltz; Every Day's a Holiday*; 1939—*The Flying Deuces*; 1940—*The Boys from Syracuse; Beyond Tomorrow; One Night in the Tropics*; 1941—*The Invisible Woman; 9 Lives Are Not Enough; Steel Against the Sky*; 1942—*Sing Your Worries Away; Army Surgeon; The Navy Comes Through*; 1943—*Dixie*; 1944—*Follow the Boys; Secret Command*; 1945—*Having Wonderful Crime*; 1946—*Abie's Irish Rose*; 1956—*Bermuda Affair* (+co-sc).

Roles: 1916—*Love Under Cover; The Telephone Belle; Won by a Foot; Heart Strategy*; 1917—*Innocent Sinners; The Girl and the Ring; His Foothill Folly; Caught in the End; A Fallen Star; A Toy of Fate; His Cool Nerve; His Saving Grace; Dad's Downfall*; 1919—*The Viled Adventure*; 1920—*The Sea Wolf; The Round Up; All of a Sudden Peggy; Conrad in Quest of His Youth*; 1921—*The Dollar-a-Year Man; The Light in the Clearing; The Witching Hour; Everything for Sale; Just Outside the Door*; 1922—*The Loaded Door; Elope If You Must; Nancy from Nowhere; Second Hand Rose*; 1923—*The Woman He Loved; Girl from the West*; 1924—*Abraham Lincoln.*

Publications:

On SUTHERLAND:

Articles—sketch by D. Harden in *Photoplay* (New York), May 1926; "Man with a Megaphone" by C.M. Black in *Colliers* (New York), 16 July 1938.

SYBERBERG, HANS-JÜRGEN. German. Born in Nossendorf, Pomerania, 8 December 1935. Educated in literature and art history, Munich. Career: lives in East Germany until early 1950s; meets Bertolt Brecht, gains permission to film Berliner Ensemble at work; resulting 8mm sound film is only record of that group during Brecht period (blown up to 35mm and released 1970 as *My Last Move*); 1963-66—makes current affairs and documentary shorts for Bavarian television (185 films); 1965-69—makes 5 feature-length "character portraits" on actors Fritz Kortner, Romy Schneider, and on others; 1965—forms own production company; 1968—first feature *Scarabea*; 1972-77—makes "German Trilogy": *Ludwig—Requiem for a Virgin King, Karl May*, and *Our Hitler.*

Films (as director of feature-length documentaries): 1965—*Fünfter Akt, siebte Szene. Fritz Kortner probt Kabale und Liebe (Act Five, Scene Seven. Fritz Kortner Rehearses Kabale und Liebe); Romy. Anatomie eines Gesichts (Romy. Anatomy of a Face)*; 1966—*Fritz Kortner spricht Monologe für eine Schallplatte (Fritz Kortner Recites Monologues for a Record); Fritz Kortner spricht Shylock (Fritz Kortner Recites Shylock)* (short—extract from *Fritz Kortner spricht Monologe...*); *Fritz Kortner spricht Faust (Fritz Kortner Recites Faust)* (short—extract from *Fritz Kortner spricht Monologe...*); *Wilhelm von Kobell* (short); 1967—*Die Grafen Pocci—Einige Kapitel zur Geschichte einer Familie (The Counts of Pocci—Some Chapters Towards the History of a Family); Konrad Albert Pocci, der Fussballgraf vom Ammerland—Das vorläufig letzte Kapitel einer Chronik der Familie Pocci (Konrad Albert Pocci, the Football Count from the Ammerland—Provisionally the Last Chapter of a Chronicle of the Pocci Family)* (extract from the preceding title); (as feature director): 1968—*Scarabea—Wieviel Erde braucht der Mensch? (Scarabea—How Much Land Does a Man Need?)*; 1969—*Sex-Business—Made in Passing* (documentary); 1970—*San Domingo; Nach Meinem letzten Umzug (After My Last Move); Puntila* and *Faust* (shorts—extracts from the preceding title); 1972—*Ludwig—Requiem für einen jungfräuli-*

chen König (Ludwig—Requiem for a Virgin King); Theodor Hierneis oder: Wie man ehem. Hofkoch wird (Ludwig's Cook); 1974—Karl May; 1975—Winifred Wagner und die Geschichte des Hauses Wahnfried von 1914-1975 (The Confessions of Winifred Wagner); 1977—Hitler. Ein Film aus Deutschland (Hitler, a Film from Germany, Our Hitler) (in 4 parts: 1. Hitler ein Film aus Deutschland (Der Graal), 2. Ein deutscher Traum, 3. Das Ende eines Wintermärchens, 4. Wir Kinder der Hölle); 1981—Parsifal.

Publications:

By SYBERBERG:

Books—Le Film, musique de l'avenir, Paris 1975; Syberberg Filmbuch, Munich 1976; Hitler, ein Film aus Deutschland, Reinbek bei Hamburg 1978; Hitler, un film d'Allemagne, Paris 1978; articles—interview by A. Tournès in Jeune Cinéma (Paris), December/January 1972/73; "Hans-Jürgen Syberberg: Ludwig—Requiem für einen jungfräulichen König...", interview by F. Zaagsma in Skoop (Amsterdam), December 1973; "3 Cinéastes du texte", interview by J.-C. Bonnet in Cinématographe (Paris), October 1977; interview by J.-C. Bonnet and others in Cinématographe (Paris), June 1978; interview by M. Martin in Ecran (Paris), July 1978; "Form ist Moral: 'Holocaust' Indiz der grössten Krise unserer intellektuellen Existenz" in Medium (Frankfurt), April 1979; "Escuchar, pensar, dirigir" and interview by J.L. Téllez and J.V.G. Santamaría in Contracampo (Madrid), May 1980; "Aus keinem meiner Filme wird man jemandem hinaus-gehen sehen, der Taumelt", interview by R. Frey and K.L. Baader in Filmfaust (Frankfurt), April/May 1981.

On SYBERBERG:

Articles—"Ludwig's Cook" by D.L. Overbey in Sight and Sound (London), autumn 1974; "Le Renouveau du cinéma allemand (suite)", interview by J. Farren in Cinéma (Paris), no.195, 1975; "Forms of Address", article and interview by Tony Rayns in Sight and Sound (London), winter 1974/75; "Syberberg and the Tempter of Democracy" by J. Pym in Sight and Sound (London), autumn 1977; "Syberberg: dramaturgie, anti-naturaliste et germanitude" by D. Sauvaget in Image et son (Paris), January 1979.

*   *   *

The films of Hans-Jürgen Syberberg are at times annoying, confusing, overlong—but also ambitious and compelling. In no way is he ever conventional or commercial: critics and audiences have alternately labelled his work brilliant and boring, absorbing and pretentious, and his films today are still rarely screened. Stylistically, it is difficult to link him with any other filmmaker or cinema tradition. In this regard he is an original, easily the most controversial of all the New German filmmakers and at the vanguard of the resurgence of experimental filmmaking in his homeland.

Not unlike his contemporary, Rainer Werner Fassbinder, Syberberg's most characteristic films examine recent German history: a documentary about Richard Wagner's daughter-in-law, a close friend of Hitler (The Confessions of Winifred Wagner); his trilogy covering 100 years of Germany past (Ludwig II: Requiem for a Virgin King, Karl May, and, most fam-

ously, Our Hitler, A Film From Germany). These last are linked in their depictions of Germans as hypocrites, liars, egocentrics, and in the latter he presents the rise of the Third Reich as an outgrowth of German romanticism. Even more significantly, Syberberg is concerned with the cinema's relationship to that history. Our Hitler, seven hours and nine minutes long, in four parts and 22 specific chapters, is at once a fictional movie, documentary, three-ring circus (the "greatest show on earth"), and a filmed theatrical marathon. The Führer is presented with some semblance of reality, via Hans Schubert's performance. But he is also caricatured, in the form of various identities and disguises: in one sequence alone, several actors play him as a house painter, Chaplin's Great Dictator, the Frankenstein monster, Parsifal (Syberberg subsequently filmed the Wagner opera), and a joker. Hitler too becomes an object, a ventriloquist's doll, and a stuffed dog. In all, twelve different actors play the role, and there are 120 dummy Führers. The result: Syberberg's Hitler is both a fascist dictator who could have risen to power at any point in time, in any number of political climates (though the filmmaker in no way excuses his homeland for allowing Hitler to exist, let alone thrive), and a depiction of the Führer as a monstrous movie mogul, whose Intolerance would be the Holocaust.

Syberberg unites fictional narrative and documentary footage in a style that is at once cinematic and theatrical, mystical and magical. His films might easily be performed live (Our Hitler is set on a stage), but the material is so varied that the presence of the camera is necessary to thoroughly translate the action. The fact that his staging has been captured on celluloid allows him total control of what the viewer sees at each performance. Additionally, the filmmaker is perceptibly aware of how the everyday events that make up history are ultimately comprehended by the public via the manner in which they are presented in the media. History is understood more by catch-words and generalities than facts. As a result, in this age of mass media, real events can easily become distorted, trivialized. Syberberg demonstrates this in Our Hitler by presenting the Führer in so many disguises, so that the viewer is often desensitized to the reality that was this mass murderer.

"Aesthetics are connected with morals," Syberberg says. "Something like Holocaust is immoral because it's a bad film. Bad art can't do good things." And, also, "My three sins are that I believe Hitler came out of us, that he is one of us; that I am not interested in money, except to work with; and that I love Germany." Our Hitler, and his other films, clearly reflect these preferences.

—Rob Edelman

SZABÓ, ISTVÁN. Hungarian. Born in Budapest, 18 February 1938. Educated at Academy of Theatre and Film Art, Budapest, graduated 1961. Career: 1961—diploma film Koncert receives wide attention; subsequently directs 2 shorts for Béla Balázs Studio; 1964—directs 1st feature film; 1979-81—directs The Green Bird and Mephisto as Hungarian-West German co-productions. Recipient: Hungarian Film Critics Award for Concert, 1961; Hungarian Film Critics Award for Variations On a Theme, 1962; Silver Bear, Berlin Festival, for Confidence, 1980; Best Screenplay, Cannes Festival, for Mephisto, 1981; FIPRESCI Prize, Cannes Festival, for Mephisto, 1981; Best Screenplay, Cannes, Prize FIPRESCI, for Mephisto, 1982; Hungarian Film Critics Award for Mephisto, 1982; Academy Award, Best Foreign Film, for Mephisto, 1982.

Films (as director and scriptwriter): 1961—*Koncert (Concert)* (short); *Variációk egy témára (Variations on a Theme)* (short); 1963—*Te (You...)* (short); 1964—*Álmodozások kora (The Age of Daydreaming)*; 1966—*Apa (Father)*; 1967—*Ķegyelet (Piety)* (short); 1970—*Szerelmesfilm (Love Film)*; 1971—*Budapest, amiért szeretem (Budapest, Why I Love It)* (series of shorts: *Alom a házröl (Dream About a House)*, *Duna—halak— madarak (The Danube—Fishes—Birds)*, *Egy tukor (A Mirror)*, *Leányportre (A Portrait of a Girl)*, *Tér (A Square)*, *Hajnal (Dawn)*, *Alkony (Twilight)*); 1973—*Tüzoltó utca 25 (25 Fireman's Street)*; 1974—*Ösbemutató (Premiere)*; 1976—*Budapesti mesék (Budapest Tales)*; 1977—*Várostérkép (City Map)* (short); 1979—*Bizalom (Confidence)*; *Der grüne Vogel (The Green Bird)*; 1981—*Mephisto.*

Publications:

By SZABÓ:

Articles—interview by Yvette Biro in *Cahiers du cinéma* (Paris), July 1966; "Hungarian Director Szabo Discusses His Film *Father*" by Robert Siton in *Film Comment* (New York), fall 1968; "Conversation with István Szabó" in *Hungarofilm Bulletin* (Budapest), no.5, 1976; "Contes de Budapest", interview by René Predal in *Jeune Cinéma* (Paris), July/August 1977; "Mit adhat a magyar film a világnak?", interview in *Filmkultura* (Budapest), January/February 1978; "The Past Still Plays a Major Role", interview in *Hungarofilm Bulletin* (Budapest), no.2, 1979; "Regisseur István Szabó: 'Ik heb mijn neus vol van briljant gemaakte films'", interview by J. Rood in *Skoop* (Amsterdam), July 1981; "Mephisto—Erfolg—warum?", interview by Helmut Ullrich in *Filmspiegel* (Berlin), 1982.

On SZABÓ:

Book—*History Must Answer to Man: The Contemporary Hungarian Cinema* by Graham Petrie, London 1978; articles— "Movers" by Andrew Sarris in *Saturday Review* (New York), 23 December 1967; "Istvan Szabo: Dreams of Memories" by K. Jaehne in *Film Quarterly* (Berkeley), fall 1978; "Filmek családfája" by T. Hirsch in *Filmkultura* (Budapest), March/April 1981; "Méphisto de István Szabó" by Louis Marcorelles in *Le Monde* (Paris), July 1981; "Analízis jelképek nélkül" by György Szabó in *Filmkultura* (Budapest), no.3, 1982.

*   *   *

"What are Szabó's films noted for? For the fact that he works with a rich spectrum of possibilities and decisions, which only in their totality attain the poetic quality that becomes the viewer's primary experience after they have been looked at together. István Szabó reacts like a sensitive membrane to everything that has happened around him in the past or is just happening. At the same time he builds solely from motives that brand a film reel with the mark of an individual personality, even when he strives for seemingly objective symbols, for example, a streetcar—that constantly recurring, tangibly real and yet poetically long logogram for his individual and very special world." Such were the words of the noted Hungarian historian and film theoretician Josef Marx as he considered the work of director István Szabó. They underscore the most essential characteristic of Szabó's work, its inventiveness, which in his films takes on general forms in the broadest sense.

From his first feature film *Álmodozások kora*, which, together with Gaal's *Sordásban*, was the most expressive confession of an artistic generation and became a model for other artists, his entire work has built up an unprecedented picture of contemporary life and its activities. In his earliest period Szabó's starting point was his own experiences, which he transformed into artistic images. At the same time he carefully absorbed everything that was happening around him, made observations, and attempted to discern the essence of modern people, and to come to an understanding of their concerns, endeavors, and aspirations. He is interested in young engineers at the start of their careers; in the personal ideals of a young man on the threshold of maturity; in the changing relationship of two people, framed within a quarter-century of Hungarian history; in the dreams and locked-up memories of people living together in an old apartment building; in the "story" of an ordinary city streetcar with an allegorical resemblance to our contemporaries; in the love and distrust between a pair of completely different people in a charged wartime atmosphere; and in a deep probe into the character of a young actor whose talents are displayed and subordinated by the totalitarian power of nascent German fascism.

All of these films are linked by intimate confession sharply set off against historical reality. In the images of Szabó's films—full of poetry and the symbolism of dreamlike conceptions, the small dramas of plain folk, their disappointments, successes, loves, enthusiasms, moments of anxiety and ardor, joy and pain—the history of post-war Hungary passes by in contrapuntal details. István Szabó creates auteur films (except for his last) in which the shaping of the theme and the screenplay are just as important as the direction, so that the resulting works bears a unique stamp. The heroes of his films are not only people, but also cities, streets, houses, parks—his native Budapest, which is the point of intersection of human fates. Under Szabó's creative eye the city awakens, stirs, arises, wounded after the tumult of the war, and lives with its heroes.

Only recently has István Szabó deviated from the rule of auteur films (the model for his film *Mephisto* was a novel by Klaus Mann). This detracted nothing from the importance of the work, which won an Oscar, among other awards. Even in this film the director left his imprint and managed to develop it into a picture of personal tragedy painted into a fresco of historical events. At the same time, Szabó's last film is evidence that the creative process is a tireless search for pathways. Only a responsible approach to history and the way it is shaped can help the artist to complete understanding of today's world.

"To awaken an interest in the people I want to tell about; to capture their essence so that a viewer can identify with them; to broaden people's understanding and sympathy—and my own as well: That's what I'd like to do...," István Szabó once said in an interview. His films are an affirmation of this credo.

—G. Merhaut

TANNER, ALAIN. Swiss. Born in Geneva, 6 December 1929. Educated in economic sciences, Calvin College, Geneva. Career: 1951—begins university cine club, Geneva; after graduation works for shipping company in Geneva for year, then as clerk on cargo ships; 1955—moves to London, meets Lindsay Anderson, and through him obtains job at British Film Institute; 1956— meets Claude Goretta and together they make short *Nice Time*; 1958—becomes assistant producer at BBC, makes 6 films in series *Living with Dangers*; 1960—returns to Switzerland; early 1960s—co-founds Association Suisse des Réalisateurs; 1964-69—makes about 40 filmed reports for Swiss French TV, many co-produced by ORTF for its "Cinq Collones à la Une" program; 1966—first collaboration with writer John Berger on *Une Ville a Chandigarh*. Recipient: Experimental Film Prize, Venice Festival, for *Nice Time*, 1957; Best Screenplay (with John Berger), National Society of Film Critics, for *Jonah Who Will Be 25 in the Year 2000*, 1976; Special Jury Prize, Cannes Festival, for *Les Années lumière*, 1981.

Films (as director): 1957—*Nice Time* (co-d—short); 1959—*Ramuz, passage d'un poete* (short); 1962—*L'Ecole* (sponsored film); 1964—*Les Apprentis* (feature documentary); 1966—*Une Ville a Chandigarh*; 1969—*Charles mort ou vif (Charles, Dead or Alive)*; 1971—*La Salamandre (The Salamander)* (+pr, co-sc); 1973—*Le Retour d'Afrique*; 1974—*Le Milieu du monde*; 1976—*Jonas qui aura vingt cinq ans en l'an 2000 (Jonah Who Will Be 25 in the Year 2000)*; 1978—*Messidor*; 1980—*Light Years Away (Les Années Lumière)*; 1983—*Dans la ville blanche*.

Publications:

By TANNER:

Book—*Jonas qui aura 25 ans en l'an 2000*, Lausanne 1978; articles—interview by Michel Delahaye and others in *Cahiers du cinéma* (Paris), June 1969; interview by L. Bonnard in *Positif* (Paris), February 1972; "L'Objectivité empêche le pari sur l'avenir", interview by M. Boujut in *Jeune Cinéma* (Paris), January 1972; interview by Guy Braucourt in *Ecran* (Paris), September/October 1973; "Dossier cinéma suisse", interview and article in *Téléciné* (Paris), February 1973; "Le Succès me fait peur. J'essaie de prendre du recul", interview by Noel Simsolo in *Cinéma* (Paris), September/October 1973; interview by J.-P. Brossard in *Image et son* (Paris), January 1974; "Le Milieu du monde", interview by Noel Simsolo and Guy Braucourt in *Ecran* (Paris), October 1974; "Irony is a Double-Edged Weapon", interview by L. Rubinstein in *Cineaste* (New York), v.6, no.4, 1975; "Alain Tanner: 'Art is to Break with the Past'", interview by J. Klemesrud in *The New York Times*, 24 October 1976; "Au Milieu du monde", interview by James Monaco in *Movietone News* (Seattle), 29 August 1976; "Keeping Hope for Radical Change Alive", interview by L. Rubinstein in *Cineaste* (New York), winter 1976/77; "Dialektischen Spiel mit den Ausdrucksformen", interview by J.-P. Brossard in *Film und Fernsehen* (Berlin), December 1977; interview by N. Heinic in *Cahiers du cinéma* (Paris), January/February 1977; "Le Cinéma est un art et strictement rien d'autre", interview by D. Rabourdin in *Cinéma* (Paris), January 1977; "*Jonah Who Will Be 25 in the Year 2000*" (script extract) in *Ciné-tracts* (Montreal), fall/winter 1977-78; "Alain Tanner: After Jonah", interview by M. Tarantino in *Sight and Sound* (London), no.1, 1978/79; "Messidor", interview in *Film* (London), May 1979; "Der einzige Mythos die Gesellschaft", interview by K. Saurer in *Medium* (Frankfurt), November 1979.

On TANNER:

Articles—"Tanner, Goretta, la Suisse et nous" by J. Delmas in *Jeune Cinéma* (Paris), September/October 1973; "Das Zitat als Stilmittel" by G. Waeger, "Vier Temperamente" by M. Schaub and "Alain Tanner" in *Cinema* (Zurich), v.20, no.1, 1974; "The New Swiss Cinema" by F. Bucher in *Jeune/Young Cinema &*

Theatre (Prague), winter 1974; "The Screenwriter as Collaborator", interview of John Berger, in *Cineaste* (New York), summer 1980; "Tanner-Jonah-Ideology" by A.E. Harrild in *Film Directions* (Belfast), v.3, no.11, 1980; "Les Années lumière", special issue of *Avant-Scène du cinéma* (Paris), 15 June 1981.

*   *   *

Alain Tanner's involvement with film began while attending Geneva's Calvin College where he and Claude Goretta formed Geneva's first film society. Here Tanner developed an admiration for the ethnographic documentaries of Jean Rouch and fellow Swiss Henry Brandt, an influence that continued throughout his career. After a brief stint with the Swiss merchant marine, Tanner spent a year in London as an apprentice at the BFI, where, with Goretta, he completed an experimental documentary, *Nice Time*, chronicling the night life of Picadilly Circus. While in London he participated in the Free Cinema Movement, along with Karel Reisz, Tony Richardson, and Lindsay Anderson. Through Anderson, Tanner made the acquaintance of novelist and art critic, John Berger, who would later write the scenarios for *Le Salamandre*, *Middle of the World*, *Jonah Who Will Be 25 in the Year 2000*, and *Le Retour d'Afrique*.

Upon returning to Switzerland in 1960, he completed some 40 documentaries for television. Among these were: *Les Apprentis*, concerning the lives of teenagers (using the methods of Rouch's direct cinema); *Une Ville de Chandigarh*, on the architecture designed by Le Corbusier for the Punjab capital (the narration for this film was assembled by John Berger); and newsreel coverage of the events of May 1968 in Paris. This last provided the ammunition for Tanner (once again with Goretta) to form Groupe 5, a collective of Swiss filmmakers. They proposed an idea to Swiss TV for the funding of full-length narrative features to be shot in 16mm and then blown-up to 35mm for release. The plan enabled Tanner to make his first feature, *Charles, Dead or Alive*, which won first prize at Locarno in 1969. The film tells of a middle-aged industrialist who, on the eve of receiving an award as the foremost business personality of the year, discovers his disaffection for the institution-laden society in which he finds himself. Following an innate sense of anarchism that Tanner posits as universal, he attempts to reject this lifestyle. His retreat into madness is blocked by his family and friends who compel him, out of duty, to resume his responsibilities. All Tanner's films follow a similar scenario: individuals or a group become alienated from society; rejecting it, they try to forge a new society answerable to themselves alone, only to be defeated by the relentless pressures of traditional society's institutions, whose commerce they never cease to require. This theme receives its fullest and most moving expression in *Jonah*.... The failure of the collective and the survivors of 1968, who come together at Marguerite's farm outside Geneva, is not viewed as a defeat so much as one generation's attempt to keep the hope of radical social change alive by passing on the fruits of its mistakes, that is, its education or its lore, to the succeeding generation.

Tanner's style is a blend of documentary and fable. He uses techniques such as one scene/one shot, a staple of cinéma-vérité documentary, to portray a fable or folk-story. This tension between fact and fiction, documentary and fable, receives its most exacting treatment in *Le Salamandre*. Rosemonde's indomitable rebellious vitality repeatedly defeats the efforts of the two journalists to harness it in a pliable narrative form. After *Jonah*..., Tanner introduces a darker vision in *Messidor*, *Light Years Away*, and *Dans la ville blanche*. The possibility of escaping society by returning to nature is explored and shown to be equally provisional. The tyranny of physical need is portrayed as being just as oppressive and compromising as that of the social world.

—Dennis Nastav

———————

TARKOVSKY, ANDREI. Soviet Russian. Born in Moscow, 4 April 1932. Educated at Institute of Oriental Languages, enrolled 1952; All-Union State Cinematography Institute (VGIK), graduated 1960. Career: 1954-56—after studying Arabic at Institute of Oriental Languages, works as geological prospector in Siberia; 1960—makes diploma work *The Steamroller and the Violin*, begins ongoing collaboration with cameraman Vadim Yusov and composer Vyacheslav Ovchinnikov; 1967-71—release of *Andrei Rublev* delayed by authorities. Recipient: Lion of St. Mark (Best Film), Venice Festival, for *Childhood of Ivan*, 1962; International Critics Award, Cannes Festival, for *Andrei Rublev*, 1969; Special Jury Prize, Cannes Festival, for *Solaris*, 1972; Merited Artistic Worker of the RSFSR, 1974.

Films (as director): 1960—*Katok i skripka (The Steamroller and the Violin)* (+co-sc); 1962—*Ivanovo detstvo (Ivan's Childhood, Childhood of Ivan)*; 1965—*Andrei Rubliov (Andrei Rublev)* (+co-sc); 1971—*Solyaris (Solaris)* (+co-sc); 1975—*Zerkalo (A Mirror)* (+co-sc); 1979—*Stalker*; 1983—*Nostalghia (Nostalgia)*.

Publications:

By TARKOVSKY:

Articles—"Ich liebe sehr Dowshenko", interview by G. Netzeband in *Filmwissenschaftliche Beitrage* (Berlin), v.14, 1973; "Pered novymi zadačami", interview by O. Surkova in *Iskusstvo Kino* (Moscow), July 1977; interview by J. Fieschi and D. Maillet in *Cinématographe* (Paris), February 1978; "Against Interpretation", interview by I. Christie in *Framework* (Norwich, England), spring 1981; interview by I. Christie and M. Lefanu in *Positif* (Paris), December 1981.

On TARKOVSKY:

Book—*The Most Important Art: Eastern European Film After 1945* by Mira and Antonín Liehm, Berkeley, California 1977; articles—"Man and Experience: Tarkovski's World" by Ivor Montagu in *Sight and Sound* (London), spring 1973; "Tarkovski: retour à la science-fiction" by C. Benedetti in *Ecran* (Paris), May 1976; "De ethiek van Andrei Tarkovski en dde onderdrukking van de kunstfilm in Rusland" by G. Poppelaars in *Skoop* (Amsterdam), April/May 1980; "Itinéraire d'un démiurge: Andrei Tarkovsky" by Marcel Martin in *Image et son* (Paris), November 1981; special section on Tarkovsky in *Positif* (Paris), October 1981; "Tarkovski le rebelle: non-conformisme ou restauration" by Bernard Amengual in *Positif* (Paris), October 1981; "Troisième plongée dans l'océan, troisième retour à la maison" by E. Carrère in *Positif* (Paris), October 1981; "Sorting Out the Messages" by T. Hickey in *Film Directions* (Belfast), v.4, no.15, 1981; "Tarkovsky's Translations" by P. Strick in *Sight and Sound* (London), summer 1981.

———————

TASHLIN, FRANK. American. Born in Weehawken, New Jersey, 19 February 1913. Educated in public school, Astoria, Long Island. Married Mary Costa. Career: 1926-27—newspaper boy, errand boy for butcher, works in brassiere factory; 1928—errand boy for Max Fleischer, then working on *Out of the Inkwell* series; 1930—works on *Aesop's Fables* cartoons at RKO, rising to position of animator; until 1936 sells cartoons to magazines under pseudonym "Tish-Tash"; 1933—moves to Hollywood, works at Vitaphone Corp. on *Merrie Melodies* and *Looney Tunes*; 1934—comic strip *Van Boring* syndicated (until 1936); 1935—animates MGM's *Flip the Frog*, works in Hal Roach studio as gagman for Charlie Chase, Thelma Todd, and *Our Gang* series; returns to *Looney Tunes* series as scriptwriter and director, making one *Porky Pig* cartoon per month; 1939-40—story director at Disney studios for *Mickey Mouse* and *Donald Duck* series, writes 1st Mickey Mouse feature, *Mickey and the Beanstalk*; 1941—joins Columbia's Screen Gems Cartoon Studios as executive producer; 1942—returns to *Merrie Melodies* and *Looney Tunes*, works on Porky Pig and Bugs Bunny series; directs 1st *Private Snafu* cartoon for Army Signal Corps unit led by Frank Capra; 1944—first non-animated film credit as co-scriptwriter for *Delightfully Dangerous*; 1945—gag writer at Paramount; 1946—writes for Eddie Bracken's CBS radio shows; first cartoon book, *The Bear That Wasn't*; 1947—begins working principally as scriptwriter; 1950—takes over direction of *The Lemon Drop Kid* at request of Bob Hope; 1952—writes, produces and directs for NBC TV; 1954—also works for CBS TV. Died in Hollywood, 5 May 1972.

Films (as feature scriptwriter): 1944—*Delightfully Dangerous* (Lubin); 1947—*Variety Girl* (Marshall) (co-sc); *The Paleface* (McLeod) (co-sc); *The Fuller Brush Man (That Mad Mr Jones)* (Simon) (co-sc); 1948—*One Touch of Venus* (Seiter) (co-sc); *Love Happy* (Miller) (co-sc); 1949—*Miss Grant Takes Richmond (Innocence Is Bliss)* (Bacon) (co-sc); *Kill the Umpire* (Bacon); *The Good Humor Man* (Bacon); 1950—*The Fuller Brush Girl (The Affairs of Sally)* (Bacon); (as feature director and co-scriptwriter): 1950—*The Lemon Drop Kid* (co-d, uncredited); 1951—*The First Time*; *Son of Paleface*; 1953—*Marry Me Again* (sc); *Susan Slept Here* (co-sc uncredited); 1955—*Artists and Models*; *The Lieutenant Wore Skirts*; 1956—*The Scarlet Hour* (Curtiz) (co-sc only); *Hollywood or Bust* (co-sc uncredited); *The Girl Can't Help It* (+pr); 1957—*Will Success Spoil Rock Hunter?* (sc, +pr); 1958—*Rock-a-Bye Baby* (sc); *The Geisha Boy* (sc); 1959—*Say One for Me* (co-sc uncredited, +pr); 1960—*Cinderfella* (sc); 1962—*Bachelor Flat*; 1963—*It's Only Money*; *The Man from The Diner's Club* (d only); *Who's Minding the Store?*; 1964—*The Disorderly Orderly* (sc); 1965—*The Alphabet Murders* (d only); 1966—*The Glass Bottom Boat* (d only); *Caprice*; 1968—*The Private Navy of Sergeant O'Farrell* (sc).

Publications:

By TASHLIN:

Articles—"Frank Tashlin—An Interview and an Appreciation" by Peter Bogdanovich in *Film Culture* (New York), no.26, 1962; "Tashlin!", interview by Peter Bogdanovich in *Movie* (London), February 1963.

On TASHLIN:

Articles—"Frank Tashlin" by Roger Boussinot in *Cinéma 60*

(Paris), no.49, 1960; articles by Robert Benayoun and others in *Positif* (Paris), no.29; "Frank Tashlin and the New World" by Ian Cameron in *Movie* (London), February 1963; "Tashlin's Cartoons" by Peter Bogdanovich in *Movie* (London), winter 1968/69; "Le Chandler du slapstick" by Robert Benayoun in *Positif* (Paris), no.69; article in *Cahiers du cinéma* (Paris), no.150-151; "La Fin d'un amuseur" by Claude Beylie in *Ecran* (Paris), July/August 1972; "Frank Tashlin ou la poétique de l'objet" by M. Grisolia in *Cinéma* (Paris), July/August 1972; obituary in *The New York Times*, 9 May 1972; "Frank Tashlin" by Peter Bogdanovich in *The New York Times*, 28 May 1972; "Jerry Lewis. Films for Fun" by R. Gansera in *Filmkritik* (Munich), April 1974; "Looney Tunes and Merrie Melodies" by M.S. Cohen in *Velvet Light Trap* (Madison), autumn 1975; "Cartooned In" by J. Hoberman in *The Village Voice* (New York), 16-22 July 1980.

*   *   *

Frank Tashlin had achieved recognition as a children's writer when he entered the film industry to work in the animation units at Disney and Warner. Both of these early careers would have decisive import for the major films that Tashlin would direct in the 1950s. This early experience allowed Tashlin to see everyday life as a visually surreal experience, as a kind of cartoon itself, and gave him a faith in the potential for natural experience to act as a resistance to the increased mechanization of everyday life. Tashlin's films of the fifties are great displays of cinematic technique, particularly as it developed in a TV-fearing Hollywood: wide-screen, radiant color, frenetic editing, and a deliberate recognition of film as film. Tashlin's films often resemble live versions of the Warners cartoons. Jerry Lewis, who acted in many of Tashlin's films seemed perfect for such a visual universe with his reversions to a primal animality, his deformations of physicality, and his sheer irrationality.

Tashlin's films are also concerned with the ways the modern world is becoming more and more artificial; the films are often filled with icons of the new mass culture (rock and roll, comic books, television, muscle men, Jayne Mansfield, Hollywood) and are quite explicit about the ways such icons are mechanically produced within a consumer society. For example, in *Will Success Spoil Rock Hunter?*, the successful romance of Rita Marlow (Jayne Mansfield) will cause other women to engage in dangerous bust-expanding exercises to the point of nervous exhaustion. Yet the very critique of mass culture by an artist working in a commercial industry creates the central contradiction of Tashlin's cinema: if the danger of modern life is its increasing threat of mechanization, then what is the critical potential of an art based on mechanization? Significantly, Tashlin's films can be viewed as a critique of the ostentatious vulgarity of the new plastic age while they simultaneously seem to revel in creating ever better and more spectacular displays of sheer technique to call attention to that age. For example, *The Girl Can't Help It* chronicles the making of a non-talent (Jayne Mansfield) into a star, viewing the process with a certain cynicism, but at the same time participating in that process. These films are vehicles for Mansfield as Mansfield, and are thus somewhat biographical.

As with Lewis, serious treatment of Tashlin began in France (especially in the pages of *Positif*, which has always had an attraction to the comic film as an investigator of the Absurd). Anglo-American criticism tended to dismiss Tashlin (for example, Sarris in *American Cinema* called him "vulgar"). In such a context, Claire Johnston and Paul Willemen's *Frank Tashlin* has

the force of a breakthrough, providing translations from French journals, and analyses of the cinematic and ideological implications of Tashlin's work.

—Dana B. Polan

TATI, JACQUES. French. Born Jacques Tatischeff in Le Pecq, France, 9 October 1908. Educated at Lycée de St.-Germain-en-Laye; also attended a college of arts and engineering, 1924. Married Micheline Winter, 25 May 1944; children: Sophie and Pierre. Career: 1925-30—travels to England, plays professional rugby with the Racing Club team; 1930-35—begins working small cafés as a pantomimist/impressionist; 1931—experiments for 1st time with film, records one of his stage routines, "Oscar, champion de tennis"; 1934—appears in short *On demande une brute*, directed by Charles Barrois; 1935-39—enjoys some recognition when he plays the Ritz on the same bill as Maurice Chevalier, and later successfully tours European music halls and circuses; 1938—produces (for 1st time) and stars in *Retour à la terre*; 1939-45—serves in French Army; 1945—appears in minor roles in 2 of Claude Autant-Lara's films; 1946—begins directing himself in short films with *L'Ecole des facteurs*; 1949—directs and stars in first feature *Jour de fête*; 1953—his famous character "Mr. Hulot" appears for 1st time in *Les Vacances de Monsieur Hulot*; 1955-60—offered American TV series of 15 minute programs, refuses; 1961—creates play based on *Jour de fête* called "Jour de fête à Olympia"; 1973—directs and stars in production for Swedish TV, *Parade*. Died 5 November 1982. Recipient: Venice Film Festival, Best Scenario for *Jour de fête*, 1949; Max Linder Prize (France) for *L'Ecole des facteurs*, 1949; Louis Delluc Prix (France) for *Les Vacances de M. Hulot*, 1953; Cannes Film Festival, Special Prize for *Mon Oncle*, 1958; Grand prix national des Arts et des Lettres, Cinéma, 1979; Commandeur des Arts et des Lettres.

Films (as director and scriptwriter): 1947—*L'Ecole des facteurs* (+ro); 1949—*Jour de fête* (co-sc, +ro as *François* the postman)); 1953—*Les Vacances de Monsieur Hulot (Mr. Hulot's Holiday)* (co-sc, +ro as *M. Hulot*); 1958—*Mon Oncle* (co-sc, +ro as *M. Hulot*); 1967—*Playtime* (+ro as *M. Hulot*); 1971—*Trafic (Traffic)* (co-sc, +ro as *M. Hulot*); 1973—*Parade* (+ro as *M. Loyal*).

Roles: 1932—*Oscar, champion de tennis* (+sc); 1934—*On demande une brute* (Barrois) (+co-sc); 1935—*Gai Dimanche* (Berry) (+co-sc); 1936—*Soigne ton gauche* (Clément); 1938—*Retour à la terre* (+pr, sc); 1945—*Ghost* in *Sylvie et le fantôme* (Autant-Lara); 1946—*Soldier* in *Le Diable au corps* (Autant-Lara).

Publications:

By TATI:

Articles—"Talk with Tati" in *Newsweek* (New York), 10 November 1958; "Tati Speaks" by Harold Woodside in *Take One* (Montreal), no.6, 1969; interview by E. Burcksen in *Cinématographe* (Paris), May 1977; "Le Cinéma doit revenir au grand ecran!", interview in *Cine revue* (Brussels), 28 June 1979.

On TATI:

Books—*The French Film* by Georges Sadoul, London 1953; *Qu'est ce-que le cinéma* by André Bazin, London 1958; *Monsieur Hulot's Holiday* by Jeane-Claude Carriere, New York 1959; *New Cinema in Europe* by Roger Manville, New York 1966; *Jacques Tati* by Armand Cauliez, Paris 1968; *French Cinema Since 1946* Vol. I by Roy Armes, Cranbury, New Jersey 1970; *The Comic Mind* by Gerald Mast, New York 1973; *The Silent Clowns* by Walter Kerr, New York 1975; *Jacques Tati* by Penelope Gilliatt, London 1976; *The Films of Jacques Tati* by Brent Maddock, Metuchen, New Jersey 1977; articles— "Imports" in *Time* (New York), 31 March 1952; article by A.H. Weiler in *The New York Times*, 20 February 1952; "Letter from Paris" by Gênet in the *New Yorker*, 12 September 1953; "One Man's Movie" by Arthur Knight in the *Saturday Review* (New York), 19 June 1954; "Mr. Hulot" in the *New Yorker*, 17 July 1954; "Even Comics Ask 'Who's Tati?'" by Edwin Schallert in the *Los Angeles Times*, 13 March 1955; "The Art of Jacques Tati" by A.C. Mayer in *Quarterly of Film, Radio, and Television* (Berkeley), fall 1955; "Make Them Laugh" in *Films and Filming* (London), August 1957; "Jacques Tati" in *Film* (London), September/October 1958; "Torment of Mr. Tati" in *Life* (New York), 17 November 1958; article by Harold Hildebrand in the *Los Angeles Examiner*, 18 January 1959; "Conscience and Comedy" by Penelope Houston in *Sight and Sound* (London), summer/autumn 1959; "Tati (Hulot) Wants to Make Films Here, But with Control" in *Variety* (New York), 6 April 1959; "Hulot: or The Common Man as Observer and Critic" by John Simon in the *Yale French Review* (New Haven, Conn.), no.23, 1959; "Jacques Tati contre l'ironie française" by Pierre Marcabru in *Arts* (Paris), 8 March 1961; "French Comedy Writer..." in *Variety* (New York), 6 November 1963; "It's Tati Time in Paris" by A.H. Weiler in *The New York Times*, 10 January 1965; "Tati Back in Comic Mood for Latest Film" by Mary Blume in the *Los Angeles Times*, 6 September 1970; "The Comic Art of Jacques Tati" by Roy Armes in *Screen* (London), February 1970; "What Directors Are Saying" in *Action* (Los Angeles), November/December 1970; article by James Monaco in *Take One* (Montreal), September 1972; "Jacques Tati: Silent Comedy's Heir" by Kevin Thomas in the *Los Angeles Times*, 24 November 1972; "Playtime and Traffic, 2 New Tati's" by R.C. Dale in *Film Quarterly* (Berkeley), no.2, 1972-73; "Profiles" by Penelope Gilliatt in the *New Yorker*, 27 January 1973; "Tati's Democracy" by Jonathan Rosenbaum in *Film Comment* (New York), May/June 1973; "Parameters of the Open Film: Les Vacances de Monsieur Hulot" by K. Thompson in *Wide Angle* (Athens, Ohio), v.1, no.4, 1977; "Jacques Tati: l'autre monde de Hulot" by B. Boland in *Cahiers du cinéma* (Paris), September 1979; special issue of *Cahiers du cinéma* (Paris) September 1979.

*   *   *

Jacques Tati's father was disappointed that his son didn't enter the family business, the restoration and framing of old paintings. He shouldn't have been, for in Jacques Tati's films, the art of framing—of selecting borders and playing on the limits of the image—achieved new expressive heights. Instead of old paintings, Tati restored the art of visual comedy, bringing out a new density and brilliance of detail, a new clarity of composition. He is one of the handful of film artists—the others would include Griffith, Eisenstein, Murnau, Bresson—who can be said to have transformed the medium at its most basic level, to have found a new way of seeing.

After a short career as a professional rugby player, Tati entered the French music hall circuit of the early 1930s; his act consisted of pantomine parodies of the sports stars of the era. Several of his routines were filmed as shorts in the 1930s (and he appeared as a supporting actor in two films by Claude Autant-Lara), but he did not return to direction until after the war, with the 1947 short *L'Ecole des facteurs*. Two years later, the short was expanded into a feature, *Jour de fête*. Here Tati plays a village postman who, struck by the "modern, efficient" methods he sees in a short film on the American postal system, decides to streamline his own operations. The satiric theme that runs through all of Tati's work—the coldness of modern technology—is already well developed, but more importantly, so is his visual style. Many of the gags in *Jour de fête* depend on the use of framelines and foreground objects to obscure the comic event—not to punch home the gag, but to hide it and purify it, to force the spectator to intuit, and sometimes invent, the joke for himself. Tati took four years to make his next film, *Les Vacances de Monsieur Hulot (Mr. Hulot's Holiday)*, which introduced the character he was to play for the rest of his career—a gently eccentric Frenchman, whose tall, reedy figure was perpetually bent foward as if by the weight of the pipe he always kept clamped in his mouth. The warmth of the characterization, plus the radiant inventiveness of the sight gags, made *Mr. Hulot* an international success, yet the film already suggests Tati's dissatisfaction with the traditional idea of the comic star. Hulot is not a comedian, in the sense of being the source and focus of the humor; he is, rather, an attitude, a signpost, a perspective that reveals the humor in the world around him.

Mon Oncle is a transitional film: though Hulot had abdicated his star status, he is still singled out among the characters—prominent, but strangely marginal. With *Playtime*, released after nine years of expensive, painstaking production, Tati's intentions become clear. Hulot was now merely one figure among many, weaving in and out of the action much like the Mackintosh Man in Joyce's *Ulysses*. And just as Tati the actor refuses to use his character to guide the audience through the film, so does Tati the director refuse to use close-ups, emphatic camera angles, or montage to guide the audience to the humor in the images. *Playtime* is composed almost entirely of long-shot tableaux that leave the viewer free to wander through the frame, picking up the gags that may be occurring in the foreground, the background, or off to one side. The film returns an innocence of vision to the spectator; no value judgements or heirarchies of interest have been made for us. We are given a clear field, left to respond freely to an environment that has not been polluted with prejudices.

But audiences, used to being told what to see, found the freedom of *Playtime* oppressive. The film (released in several versions, from a 70mm stereo cut that ran over three hours to an absurdly truncated American version of 93 minutes) was a commercial failure, and plunged Tati deep into personal debt. His last theatrical film, the 1971 *Traffic*, would have seemed a masterpiece from anyone else, but for Tati it was clearly a protective return to a more traditional style. Tati's final project, a 60-minute television film titled *Parade*, has never been shown in America. Five films in 25 years is not an impressive record in a medium where stature is often measured by prolificity, but *Playtime* alone is a lifetime's achievement—a film that liberates and revitalizes the act of looking at the world.

—Dave Kehr

TAUROG, NORMAN. American. Born in Chicago, 23 February 1899. Married Susan (Taurog); 3 children. Career: 1912—

stage acting debut with Mary Pickford in David Belasco's *The Good Little Devil*; acts in regional theaters, returns to Broadway in *Potash and Perlmutter*; 1917—film acting debut at IMP Studios, New York; moves to Hollywood; with decline of acting career, begins working in production as property boy; begins directing 2-reel comedies with performers including Lupino Lane and Lloyd Hamilton; 1929—with coming of sound begins feature directing; directs first three at Tiffany before joining Paramount; 1936—moves to Fox for *Reunion*, then to MGM for *Boys Town* in 1938; following retirement teaches film at University of California. Died in Palm Desert, California, 7 April 1981. Recipient: Best Director Academy Award for *Skippy*, 1930/31.

Films (as feature director): 1929—*Lucky Boy* (co-d); 1930—*Troopers 3*; *Hot Curves*; *Sunny Skies*; *Follow the Leader*; 1931—*Finn & Hattie*; *Skippy*; *Newly Rich*; *Huckleberry Finn*; *Sooky*; 1932—*Hold 'em Jail*; *Phantom President*; *If I Had a Million* (co-d); 1933—*Way to Love*; *A Bedtime Story*; 1934—*We're Not Dressing*; *Mrs. Wiggs of the Cabbage Patch*; *College Rhythm*; 1935—*Big Broadcast of 1936*; 1936—*Reunion*; *Rhythm on the Range*; *Strike Me Pink*; 1937—*50 Roads to Town*; *You Can't Have Everything*; 1938—*The Adventures of Tom Sawyer*; *Mad About Music*; *Boys Town*; 1939—*The Girl Downstairs*; *Lucky Night*; 1940—*Young Tom Edison*; *Broadway Melody of 1940*; *Little Nellie Kelly*; 1941—*Men of Boys Town*; *Design for Scandal*; 1942—*Are Husbands Necessary?*; *A Yank at Eton*; 1943—*Presenting Lily Mars*; *Girl Crazy*; 1946—*The Hoodlum Saint*; 1947—*The Beginning of the End*; 1948—*The Big City*; *The Bride Goes Wild*; *Words and Music*; 1949—*That Midnight Kiss*; 1950—*Please Believe Me*; *Toast of New Orleans*; *Mrs. O'Malley and Mr. Malone*; 1951—*Rich, Young and Pretty*; 1952—*Room for One More*; *Jumping Jacks*; *The Stooge*; 1953—*The Stars Are Singing*; *The Caddy*; 1954—*Living It Up*; 1955—*You're Never Too Young*; 1956—*The Birds and the Bees*; *Pardners*; *Bundle of Joy*; 1957—*The Fuzzy Pink Nightgown*; 1958—*Onionhead*; 1959—*Don't Give Up the Ship*; 1960—*Visit to a Small Planet*; *G.I. Blues*; 1961—*All Hands on Deck*; *Blue Hawaii*; 1962—*Girls! Girls! Girls!*; 1963—*It Happened at the World's Fair*; *Palm Springs Weekend*; 1965—*Sergeant Deadhead*; *Tickle Me*; *Dr. Goldfoot and the Bikini Machine*; 1966—*Spinout*; 1967—*Double Trouble*.

Publications:

On TAUROG:

Articles—"His Success with Child Actors" by W.B. Courtney in *Colliers* (New York), 12 October 1935; "Pioneers '73: 4 Evenings with Directors Fritz Lang, Henry King, Norman Taurog, Rowland V. Lee" by C. Kirk in *Action* (Los Angeles), November/-December 1973; "Ils nous ont quittes: Norman Taurog" in *Cinéma* (Paris), June 1981; obituary in *Image et son* (Paris), June 1981; obituary in *The New York Times*, 10 April 1981.

*   *   *

Norman Taurog was perhaps the definitive "studio" or "contract" director. He made scores of motion pictures in his 40-year career, the vast majority of which were financially, if not critically successful. Taurog was not an *auteur* by any stretch of the imagination, but instead relied on his keen sense of entertainment for the thrust of his movies. If Taurog had one style which could be called his own, it was most probably his ability to work well with child actors. Many of his most notable and successful films were about children, or adolescents, among them *Boys Town*, *The Adventures of Tom Sawyer*, and *Room for One More*. His only major critical award, in fact, was his Oscar for Best Direction of the film *Skippy*, a tear-jerking story starring his young nephew, Jackie Cooper.

It is an irony of film criticism that directors such as Taurog who could successfully make musicals, dramas, comedies, and biographies are treated with disdain simply because they had no unilateral vision. His type of filmmaking, usually on assignment from the studio bosses at Paramount or MGM, was popular in the 1930s and 1940s, but has almost gone into oblivion in recent years. Being assigned a film rather than "finding a property" should not, however, detract from the intrinsic merits of the film. Rather than labelling Taurog and others of his type "studio hacks," the antitheses of auteurs, it would be more accurate in his case to simply call him versatile.

One of his better films was the musical *Girl Crazy*, an adaption of George Gershwin's Broadway hit. Working with Mickey Rooney and Judy Garland in young adult roles rather than in their previous teenage roles, Taurog proved that he could make a film on a par with other successful contemporary musicals. Some of the numbers are beautiful, especially Garland's solo, "But Not for Me," and "Bidin' My Time." These particular numbers actually seem more contemporary today than the traditionally staged grand finale, "I Got Rhythm," which had been shot by Busby Berkeley before that famous director of musicals was replaced on the film by Taurog. "But Not for Me" and "Embraceable You" are excellent examples of the bittersweet type of Garland solo that would be seen over and over in her later films directed by Vincente Minnelli. Seeing *Girl Crazy*, and knowing the role that Taurog played in its development, convinces one that he was certainly no hack.

Taurog continued to make financially successful movies well into the 1960s, but by the middle 1950s his assignments began to be dominated by stylistically unnoteworthy vehicles for big box office stars such as Dean Martin and Jerry Lewis and Elvis Presley. The Martin and Lewis, and later Presley films, were mostly formula movies made to cash in on the largely adolescent following of those stars. Of all of the films of this period, perhaps the most well known, if not the best movie was *G.I. Blues* with Presley. By the time of Taurog's retirement in the late 1960s, his output had deteriorated to such films as *Dr. Goldfoot and the Bikini Machine* and *Speedway*.

—Patricia King Hanson

———————

TAVERNIER, BERTRAND. French. Born in Lyons, 25 April 1941. Studied law one year. Career: early 1960s—writes extensively for film magazines, especially *Positif* and *Cahiers du cinéma*; co-founds film society Nickel-Odéon; interviewing Jean-Pierre Melville for *L'Etrave* leads to work on Melville's *Léon Morin, Priest*; hired as press agent by producer Georges de Beauregard; 1963—contributes sketch "Baisers de Judas" to de Beauregard production *Les Baisers*, and following year "Une Chance Explosive" to *La Chance et l'amour*; 1965—becomes freelance press agent associated with Pierre Rissient; 1972—quits publicity work to make *The Clockmaker*. Recipient: Prix Louis Delluc for *The Clockmaker*, 1974; Best Director and Best Original Screenplay (with Jean Aurenche) César Awards for *Let Joy Reign Supreme*, 1975; Best Original Screenplay (with Jean Aurenche) for *The Judge and the Assassin*, 1976.

Films (as director): 1963—"Baiser de Judas" episode of *Les Baisers*; 1964—"Une Chance Explosive" episode of *La Chance et l'amour*; (as scriptwriter): 1967—*Coplan ouvrte le feu a Mexico* (Freda); 1968—*Capitaine Singrid* (Leduc); (as director and co-scriptwriter): 1974—*L'Horloger de Saint-Paul (The Clockmaker)*; 1975—*Que la fête commence (Let Joy Reign Supreme)* (co-sc); 1976—*Le Juge et l'assassin (The Judge and the Assassin)*; 1977—*Des enfants gâtés (Spoiled Children)*; *La Question* (Heynemann) (pr only); 1979—*Death Watch (La Mort en direct)*; *Rue du Pied de Grue* (Grandjouan) (pr only); *Le Mors aux dents* (Heynemann) (pr only); 1980—*Une Semaine de vacances (A Week's Vacation, A Week's Holiday)*; 1981—*Coup de torchon (Clean Slate)*.

Publications:

By TAVERNIER:

Book—*Trente Ans de cinéma américain*, with Jean-Pierre Coursodon, Paris; articles—"Bertrand Tavernier: par delà Simenon, un univers personnel", interview by C. Benoit in *Jeune Cinéma* (Paris), March 1974; "L'Horloger de Saint-Paul", interview by G. Braucourt in *Ecran* (Paris), January 1974; interview by J. Demeure and P.-L. Thirard in *Positif* (Paris), February 1974; "Que la fête commence", interview by G. Braucourt in *Ecran* (Paris), May 1975; "Il n'y a pas de genre à proscrire ou à conseiller...", interview by D. Rabourdin in *Cinéma* (Paris), May 1975; "Les Rapports de la justice avec la folie et l'histoire" in *Avant-Scène du cinéma* (Paris), June 1976; interview by J. Demeure and others in *Positif* (Paris), September 1977; "Notes éparses" in *Positif* (Paris), December/January 1977/78; "Bertrand Tavernier: Des Enfants gâtés", interview by C. Benoit in *Jeune Cinéma* (Paris), September/October 1977; "Bertrand Tavernier: attaché de presse, critique et cinéaste", interview by M. Euvrard in *Cinéma Québec* (Montreal), v.6, no.2, 1978; interview by F. Guérif and S. Levy-Klein in *Cahiers de la Cinématheque* (Paris), spring/summer 1978; "Blending the Personal with the Political", interview by L. Quart and L. Rubinstein in *Cineaste* (New York), summer 1978; interview by F. Audé and others in *Positif* (Paris), February 1980; "3 Cinéastes en quête de l'histoire", interview by J.-P. Bertin-Maight in *Image et son* (Paris), July/August 1980; "Pouvoir de l'image et images du pouvoir (sur *La Mort en direct*)", interview by G. Cebe in *Image et son* (Paris), January 1980; "Une Semaine de vacances", interview by H. Desrues and G. Cèbe in *Image et son* (Paris), June 1980; "De personlijke films van Bertrand Tavernier", interview and article by A. van de Pas and others in *Skoop* (Amsterdam), March 1981.

On TAVERNIER:

Articles—"L'Horloger de Saint-Paul", special issue of *Avant-Scène du cinéma* (Paris), May 1974; "Le Cinéma de Bertrand Tavernier" by G. Hennebelle and others and by G. Alion and others in *Ecran* (Paris), September and October 1977; "Tavernier in Scotland" by M. Auty in *Sight and Sound* (London), winter 1976/77; "Bertrand Tavrenier: The Constraints of Convention" by W.R. and J. Magretta in *Film Quarterly* (Berkeley), summer 1978; "9 Questions aux nouveaux cinéastes" by J. Fieschi in *Cinématographe* (Paris), July 1979; "Round Table: The Cinema: Art Form or Political Weapon?" by F. Solanas and others in *Framework* (Norwich, England), autumn 1979.

* * *

It is significant that Bertrand Tavernier's films have been paid little attention by the more important contemporary film critics/theorists: his work is resolutely "realist" and realism is under attack. Realism has frequently been a cover for the reproduction and reinforcement of dominant ideological assumptions, and to this extent that attack is salutary. Yet Tavernier's cinema demonstrates effectively that the blanket rejection of realism rests on very unstable foundations. Realism has been seen as the borgeoisie's way of talking to itself. It does not necessarily follow that its only motive for talking to itself is the desire for reassurance (Tavernier's films are not reassuring); nor need we assume that the only position Realist fiction constructs for the reader/viewer is one of helpless passivity (Tavernier's films clearly postulate an alert audience ready to reflect and analyze critically).

Tavernier's three recent films (*Death Watch*, *Coup de torchon*, *A Week's Vacation*), if they do not unambiguously answer the attacks on realism, strongly attest to the inadequacy of their formulation. For a start, the films' range of form, tone and address provides a useful reminder of the potential for variety that the term "classical realist text" tends to obliterate. To place beside the strictly realist *A Week's Vacation*, on the one hand the futurist fantasy of *Death Watch*, and on the other the scathing, all-encompassing caricatural satire and irony of *Coup de torchon*, is to illustrate not merely a range of subject-matter but a range of strategy. Each film constructs for the viewer a quite distinct relationship to the action and to the protagonist, analyzable in terms of varying degrees of identification and detachment which may also shift *within* each film. Nor should my description of *A Week's Vacation* as "strictly realist" be taken to suggest some kind of simulated cinema-vérité: the film's stylistic poise and lucid articulation, its continual play between looking *with* the protagonist and looking *at* her, consistently encourage an analytical distance.

Through all his films, certainly, the bourgeoisie "talks to itself," but the voice that articulates is never reassuring, and bourgeois institutions and assumptions are everywhere rendered visible and opened to question. Revolutionary positions are allowed a voice and are listened to respectfully. This was clear from Tavernier's first film, *The Clockmaker*, among the screen's most intelligent uses of Simenon, in which the original project is effectively transformed by introducing the political issues that Simenon totally represses, and by changing the crime from a meaningless, quasi-existentialist *acte gratuit* to a gesture of radical protest. But Tavernier's protagonists are always bourgeois: troubled, questioning, caught up in social institutions but not necessarily rendered impotent by them, capable of growth and awareness. The films, while basically committed to a well-left-of-center liberalism, are sufficiently open, intelligent and disturbed to be readily accessible to more radical positions than they are willing actually to adopt.

Despite the difference in mode of address, the three films share common thematic concerns (most obviously, the fear of conformism and dehumanization, the impulse towards protest and revolt, the difficulties of effectively realizing such a protest in action). They also have in common a desire to engage, more or less explicitly, with interrelated social, political and aesthetic issues. The caustic analysis of the imperialist mentality and the kind of personal rebellion it provokes (itself corrupt, brutalized and ultimately futile) in *Coup de torchon* is the most obvious instance of direct political enagagement. *Death Watch*, within its science fiction format, is fascinatingly involved with contemporary inquiries into the construction of narrative and the objectification of women. Its protagonist (Harvey Keitel) attempts to create a narrative around an unsuspecting woman (Romy Schneider) by means of the miniature television camera surgically implanted behind his eyes. The implicit feminist concern here becomes the structuring principle of *A Week's Vacation.* Without explicitly raising feminist issues, the film's theme is the focusing of a contemporary bourgeois female consciousness, the consciousness of an intelligent and sensitive woman whose identity is not defined by her relationship with men, who is actively engaged with social problems (she is a schoolteacher), and whose fears (of loneliness, old age, death) are consistently presented in relation to contemporary social realities rather than simplistically defined in terms of "the human condition."

I do not wish to suggest that we should celebrate the resurgence of "bourgeois realism" in Tavernier's films (and they do not stand alone) without qualification or misgivings. Certainly, one regrets the failure of contemporary cinema substantially to follow up the radical experimentation with narrative that characterized the most interesting European films of the 1960s and 1970s and produced the best work of not just Godard, but Pasolini, Herzog, Bertolucci, Bergman, Buñuel, Rivette.... Nonetheless, Tavernier's work testifies to the continuing vitality and validity of a tradition many theorists have rejected as moribund. Taken together, his three latest films seem to me to constitute one of the most remarkable achievements in world cinema in the past five years.

—Robin Wood

TAVIANI, PAOLO AND VITTORIO. Italian. Paolo born in San Miniato, Pisa, 8 November 1931; Vittorio born in San Miniato, Pisa 20 September 1929. Educated at University of Pisa, Paolo in liberal arts, Vittorio in law. Career: 1950—with Valentino Orsini direct cine-club at Pisa; 1954—in collaboration with Cesare Zavattini direct short on Nazi massacre at San Miniato; 1954-59—together and in collaboration with Orsini make series of short documenatries; 1960—work on *L'Italia non è un paesa povero* with Joris Ivens; also work as assistants to Rossellini, Emmer, and Pellegrini; 1962—with Orsini direct first feature. Recipient: Best Film and International Critics Prize, Cannes Festival, for *Padre padrone*, 1977; Special Jury Prize, Cannes Festival, for *La notte di San Lorenzo*, 1982; Best Director Award (shared), National Society of Film Critics, for *The Night of the Shooting Stars*, 1983.

Films (as directors of documentary shorts, sometimes in collaboration with Valentino Orsini): 1954—*San Miniato, luglio '44*; 1955—*Voltera, comune medievale*; 1955-59—*Curtatone e Montanara*; *Carlo Pisacane*; *Ville della Brianza*; *Lavatori della pietra*; *Pittori in città*; *I Pazzi della domenica*; *Moravia*; *Carbunara*; 1960—episode of *L'Italia non è un paesa povero*; (as feature directors and scriptwriters): 1962—*Un uomo da bruciare (A Man for Burning)* (co-d, co-sc); 1963—*I fuorilegge del matrimonio* (co-d, co-sc); 1967—*Sovversivi* (+Vittorio in ro); 1969—*Sotto il segno dello scorpione (Under the Sign of Scorpio)*; 1971—*San Michele aveva un gallo*; 1974—*Allonsanfan*; 1977—*Padre padrone (Father Master)*; 1979—*Il prato (The Meadow)*; 1982—*La notte di San Lorenzo*; 1983—*The Night of the Shooting Stars.*

Publications:

By the TAVIANIS:

Book—*San Michele aveva un gallo/Allonsafan*, Cappelli, 1974; articles—"Le Pessimisme de la raison et l'optimisme de la

volonté", interview by J.-A. Gili in *Ecran* (Paris), December 1972; interview by G. Mingrone and others in *Filmcritica* (Rome), January 1972; interview by M. Amiel in *Cinéma* (Paris), June 1973; interview by J. Delmas in *Jeune Cinéma* (Paris), February 1973; interview by A. Tassone in *Image et son* (Paris), September 1974; "Les Frères Taviani sur leur film", interview in *Jeune Cinéma* (Paris), May/June 1975; "Très longue rencontre avec Paolo et Vittorio Taviani" by J.-A. Gili in *Ecran* (Paris), July/August 1975; interview by P. De Lara and others in *Cinématographe* (Paris), October 1977; "The Brothers Taviani", interview by V. Glaessner in *Cinema Papers* (Melbourne), January 1978; "Il Prato" in *Cinema nuovo* (Turin), October 1979; "Le Pré", interview by A. Tournès in *Jeune Cinéma* (Paris), February 1980.

On the TAVIANIS:

Articles—"Recherche et continuité: L'Oeuvre des Taviani" by J. Delmas in *Jeune Cinéma* (Paris), June 1973; "Dall'utile attraverso il vero verso il bello" by G. Aristarco in *Cinema nuovo* (Turin), September/October 1974; "Speciale Taviani", edited by S. Zambetti, in *Cineforum* (Bergamo), October 1974; "À propos de Padre Padrone: Du silence à la parole..." by C. Biegalski and C. Depuyper in *Cinéma* (Paris), August/September 1977; "Padre Padrone dans l'oeuvre des Taviani" by J. Delmas in *Jeune Cinéma* (Paris), September/October 1977; "Towards Utopia, By Way of Research, Detachment, and Involvement" by T. Mitchell in *Sight and Sound* (London), no.3, 1979; "Biofilmografia de Paolo e Vittorio Taviani" by F. Duarte in *Celulóide* (Portugal), April 1980.

*   *   *

Since the early sixties, after they realized that fiction feature films were going to be their main interest, Paolo and Vittorio Taviani have written scenarios and scripts, designed settings, developed a filmmaking style and philosophy, directed 10 features, and patiently explained their methods and concepts to many interviewers and audiences in Italy and abroad.

Although influenced to some extent by neorealism—*e.g.*, the films of Rossellini and De Santis characterized by on-location settings, natural lighting, authentic environmental sounds, nonprofessional actors, and an emphasis on "the people" as protagonists—the Tavianis want reviewers to see their films as invented and staged, as interpretations of history rather than as documentaries. They draw upon their early interests and background—as youngsters they saw musicals and concerts but not movies—using artistic and technical means and methods similar to those of theater and opera. Their films in which music is part of plot and theme reveal an inventory of flutes, accordions, record players, radios, human singing voices, folktunes, opera and oratorio (mostly Italian but also German), and even "The Battle Hymn of the Republic" in their latest film.

The photography in their films takes the eye back to the horizon, or across a huge field, far along a road or deep into the front of a church or schoolroom. Even casual viewers must realize the frequent alteration of intense close-ups and long shots that never cease to remind one of locale.

Thoughts and dreams are often given visual expression. A picture of a girl and her brother studying on a couch follows her interior monologue about missing the long yellow couch in her living room (*La notte di San Lorenzo*). A prisoner in solitary for

10 years creates a world of sound and sight expressed on the screen (*San Michele aveva un gallo*).

With theatrical form and technique as framework for their political cinema, and complex, individualistic characters as protagonists, the Tavianis are as concerned with corruption, abuse of power, poverty and suffering as were the neorealists and their successors. Struck by the autobiography of Gavino Ledda which became their well-received *Padre Padrone*, they investigate the abuse of power by a father, compelled by tradition and his own need to survive, to keep his son a slave. Amazingly, the illiterate, virtually mute shepherd boy whom a quirk of fate (army service) rescues from lifetime isolation, becomes a professor of linguistics through curiosity, will and energy. In *Un uomo da Bruciare* Salvatore, who wants to help Sicilian peasants break the Mafia's hold, is complex, intellectual and egotistical.

Other themes and topics in Taviani films are divorce, revolution as an ongoing effort interrupted by interludes of other activity, the changing ways of dealing with power and corruption, resistance in war, fascism, and the necessity of communal action for accomplishment. The Tavianis uses the past to illuminate the present, show the suffering of opposing sides, and stress the major role of heritage and environment. Their characters ask questions about their lives that lead to positive solutions, and sometimes to failure. The two directors believe that utopia is possible, eventually.

—Lillian Schiff

TESHIGAHARA, HIROSHI. Japanese. Born in Tokyo, 28 January 1927. Educated at Tokyo Geijutsu University in painting, graduated 1950. Career: 1953—given direction of film on painter Hokusai; later 1950s—meets writer Abe Kobo, who later becomes scriptwriter for Teshigahara's best-known films; becomes assistant to leftist documentarian Kamei Fumio; 1959—on trip to U.S. makes short on boxer José Torres; 1962—makes first feature; participates in activities of surrealist group Seiki no kai; forms own production company; 1970—suffers auto accident, makes no films for a number of years. Recipient: Special Jury Prize, Cannes Festival, for *Woman of the Dunes*, 1964.

Films (as director of documentary shorts): 1953—*Hokusai*; 1953-57—*Juninin no shashin-ka (12 Photographers)*; *Ikebana*; (as director of medium-length documentaries): 1958—*Tokyo 1958*; 1960—*José Torres*; (as feature director): 1962—*Otoshi ana (Pitfall)*; 1963—*Suna no onna (Woman of the Dunes, Woman in the Dunes)*; 1964—*Shiroi asa (White Morning)* (short); "Ako" episode of *La Fleur de l'age ou Les Adolescentes (The Adolescents, That Tender Age)* (episode deleted from American release print); 1965—*José Torres, Part II* (documentary); 1966—*Tanin no kao (The Face of Another)*; 1967—*Bakuso* (documentary); 1968—*Moetikuta chizu (The Man without a Map)*; 1970—*Ichinichi 240 jikan (One Day, 240 Hours)* (short—multi-screen for Expo 70); 1972—*Summer Soldiers*.

Publications:

By TESHIGAHARA:

Article—"Conversation avec quatre jeunes cinéastes japonais" by Georges Sadoul in *Cahiers du cinéma* (Paris) May/June 1965.

On TESHIGAHARA:

Articles—"*Woman in the Dunes*" by Adrienne Mancia in *Film Comment* (New York), winter 1965; "Documentary Fantasist" in *New Yorker*, 10 April 1965; "Introducing Teshigahara" by Fabienne Cousin in *Cinéma 65* (Paris), February 1965; "Un Beckett nippon" by Gilles Jacob in *Cinéma 65* (Paris), January 1965; "Akira Kurosawa—Hiroshi Teshigahara" by Felix Bucher in *Camera*, September 1966; "The Tao in *Woman in the Dunes*" by Dennis Giles in *Film Heritage* (New York), spring 1966.

*   *   *

Teshigahara belongs to a generation not simply reaping the consequences of Japan's defeat but suffering total disillusionment with modern modes of thought with which Western man has been coping for decades. Japan, until recently feudal, integrated, and insulated, suffered forced exposure to the contradictions of 20th century liberalism and change that have provoked an explosive reaction and a contemporary rejection of all values, occidental or oriental. Teshigahara represents one phase of this rejection. *Woman of the Dunes*, from a somewhat sophomoric novel by Abe Kobo, was more interesting as a movie. Teshigahara's visuals are concise where the corresponding images of the writer are didactic. A man stumbles into captivity in an unspecified barren landscape, works with Sisyphean effort to free himself, only to wander in a circle and return to the same pit: an unconsoling parable for man's condition. Teshigahara's style, bone-dry, maintains a photographic neutrality when framing a dune of sand, a woman's breast, a face, a object of furniture, thus robbing all things of their contextual associations, a fitting analogy to his mirthless existentialism. His subsequent films were more surreal and obscure; implicitly they are travesties of his society but they probe beyond to suggest the metaphysical solitude of man (Japanese man, at least). They are very Japanese, despite influence of Westerers such as Resnais, in their exactitude and their coldly aesthetic selection of images.

—Vernon Young

TORRE-NILSSON, LEOPOLDO. Argentine. Born in Buenos Aires, 5 May 1924. Married writer Beatriz Guido. Career: at age 15 begins to work with filmmaker father Leopoldo Torres Ríos; before 1949—makes short film and writes script for father before feature directing debut; 1949-53—collaborates with father on first 2 features; 1957—adapts Beatriz Guido's novel *La cas del ángel*, initiating collaboration with Guido as scriptwriter; 1959—with *Fin de fiesta* begins producing own films through company Producciones Angel; 1964—signs contract with Columbia to make *El ojo de la cerradura*. Died 8 September 1978. Recipient: International Critics Prize, Cannes Festival, for *Hands in the Trap*, 1961.

Films (as director of short film): 1947—*El muro (The Wall)*; (as feature director): 1949—*El crimen de Oribe (Oribe's Crime)* (co-d); 1953—*El hijo del crack (Son of the "Star")* (co-d); *La*

Tigra (The Tigress); 1954—*Días de odio (Days of Hate)*; 1955—*Para vestir (The Spinsters)*; 1956—*El protegido (The Protégé)*; *Graciela*; (as director, Beatriz Guido as scriptwriter): 1957—*La casa del ángel (End of Innocence, The House of the Angel)* (co-sc with Torre Nilsson, based on Guido novel); *Precursores de la pintura argentina* (short); *Los arboles de Buenos-Aires* (short); 1958—*El secuestrador (The Kidnapper)*; 1959—*La caída (The Fall)* (co-sc with Torre Nilsson); *Fin de fiesta (The Party Is Over, The Blood Feast)*; 1960—*Un guapo del 900* (Torre Nilsson d only, +co-pr); 1961—*La mano en la trampa (The Hand in the Trap)*; *Piel de verano (Summer Skin)* (+pr); 1962—*Setenta veces siete (The Female: 70 Times 7)*; *Homenaje a la hora de la siesta (Homage at Siesta Time)*; *La terraza (The Terrace)*; 1964—*El ojo de la cerradura (The Eavesdropper)*; 1965—*Once Upon a Tractor* (for United Nations); 1966—*La chica del lunes (Monday's Child)*; *Los traidores de San Angel (The Traitors of San Angel)*; *Cavar un foso (To Dig a Pit)*; 1968—*Martin Fierro*; 1969—*El santo de la espada (The Knight of the Sword)*; 1970—*Güemes—La terra en armas*; 1972—*La maffia (The Mafia)*; 1973—*Los siete locos (The 7 Madmen)*; 1974—*Boquitas pintadas (Painted Lips)*; 1975—*Diario de la guerra del cerdo (La guerra del cerdo, Diary of the Pig War)*; 1975—*El pibe cabeza*; *Los gauchos judíos (Jewish Gauchos)* (co-pr only); 1976—*Piedra libre*.

Publications:

By TORRE-NILSSON:

Book—*Entre sajones y el arrabal*, edited by Jorge Alvarez, Buenos Aires 1967; articles—in *Tiempo de cine* (Buenos Aires), October 1951; interview in *Cuadernos de cine* (Buenos Aires), October 1954; interview by Hector Grossi in *Mundo Argentino* (Buenos Aires), February 1957; interview in *Tiempo de cine* (Buenos Aires), October 1960; "How to Make a New Wave" in *Films and Filming* (London), November 1962; article in *Tiempo de cine* (Buenos Aires), August 1962; interview by José Soltero in *Medium* (Frankfurt), summer 1967; article in *Confirmado* (Buenos Aires), October 1971.

On TORRE-NILSSON:

Articles—"Torre-Nilsson and His Double" by Mario Trajtenberg in *Film Quarterly* (Berkeley), fall 1961; "An Argentine Partnership" by Domingo Di Nubila in *Films and Filming* (London), September 1961; article by Juan Cobos in *Temas de cine* (Madrid), April and May 1961; "Leopoldo Torre-Nilsson: The Underside of the Coin" by Keith Botsford in *Show* (Hollywood), November 1962; "Director of the Year" in *International Film Guide 1967*, London 1966; article by Juan Kreimer in *Cine & medios* (Buenos Aires), no.1, 1969; article in *Primera plana* (Buenos Aires), November 1970; article by Agustin Mahieu in *Cine & medios* (Buenos Aires), no.4, 1970; "Torre-Nilsson Remembered" by E. Cozarinsky in *Sight and Sound* (London), no.1, 1978/79; obituary by G. Alamo in *Celulóide* (Portugal), February 1979; "La Experiencia argentina durante el peronismo", interview by I.L. Frias and R. Bedoya in *Hablemos de Cine* (Lima), no.70, 1979.

TOURNEUR, JACQUES. American. Born in Paris, 12 November 1904; became citizen of of the United States, 1919.

Educated at Hollywood High School. Married actress Christianne (died). Career: 1914—family brought to U.S. by father, director Maurice Tourneur; 1924—begins working at MGM as office boy; 1926—signs with MGM as actor; works for father as script clerk on last 6 American films; 1928—moves to Paris with father, begins editing father's films; 1931—directing debut in France; 1935—begins working at MGM again as 2nd unit director; 1936—begins directing shorts, then B features in 1939; 1942—at RKO begins directing for producer Val Lewton; late 1950s—begins directing for TV; 1966—retired. Died in Bergerac, France, 19 December 1977.

Films (as director): 1931—*Un vieux garçon*; *Tout ça ne vaut pas l'amour*; 1933—*La Fusée*; *Toto*; *Pour être aimée*; 1934—*Les Filles de la concierge*; 1939—*They All Came Out*; *Nick Carter, Master Detective*; 1940—*Phantom Raiders*; 1941—*Doctors Don't Tell*; 1942—*Cat People*; 1943—*I Walked with a Zombie*; *The Leopard Man*; 1944—*Days of Glory*; *Experiment Perilous*; 1946—*Canyon Passage*; 1947—*Out of the Past (Build My Gallows High)*; 1948—*Berlin Express*; 1949—*Easy Living*; 1950—*The Flame and the Arrow*; *Stars in My Crown*; 1951—*Circle of Danger*; *Anne of the Indies*; 1952—*Way of a Gaucho*; 1953—*Appointment in Honduras*; 1955—*Stranger on Horseback*; *Wichita*; 1956—*Great Day in the Morning*; 1957—*Nightfall*; *Night of the Demon (Curse of the Demon)*; 1958—*The Fearmakers*; 1959—*Timbuktu*; *La battaglia di Maratona (The Battle of Marathon)*; *Frontier Rangers* (originally for TV); 1963—*The Comedy of Terrors*; 1965—*War Gods of the Deep (City Under the Sea)*.

Roles: 1923—*Scaramouche* (Ingram); 1927—*The Fair Co-ed* (Wood); *Love* (Goulding); 1929—*The Trail of '98* (Brown).

Publications:

By TOURNEUR:

Articles—"Taste without Clichés" in *Films and Filming* (London), November 1956; interview by Chris Wicking in *Midi-minuit fantastique* (Paris), May 1965; interview by Patrick Brion and Jean-Louis Comolli in *Cahiers du cinéma* (Paris), August 1966; interview in *The Celluloid Muse* edited by Charles Higham and Joel Greenberg, London 1969.

On TOURNEUR:

Books—*Val Lewton: The Reality of Terror* by Joel Siegel, London 1972; *Jacques Tourneur* by Michael Henry, *Dossiers du cinéma*, Paris 1974; articles—"Esoterica" by Andrew Sarris in *Film Culture* (New York), spring 1963; "Trois Tourneur" by Jean-Louis Noames in *Cahiers du cinéma* (Paris), May 1964; "Murmures dans un corridor lointain" and "Propos de Tourneur" by Bertrand Tavernier in *Positif* (Paris), November 1971; "The Shadow Worlds of Jacques Tourneur" by Robin Wood in *Film Comment* (New York), summer 1972; "Le Jardin aux sentiers qui bifurquent (Sur Jacques Tourneur)" by M. Henry in *Positif* (Paris), April 1973; "The Parallel Worlds of Jacques Tourneur" by John McCarty in *Cinefantastique* (Oak Park, Ill.), summer 1973; "Jacques Tourneur: les mondes parallele" by L. Dahan in *Cinématographe* (Paris), April/May 1976; "In einem Geisterhaus mit Direktion" by W.-E. Bühler in *Filmkritik* (Munich), March 1977; "3 Morts" by J.-C. Biette in *Cahiers du cinéma* (Paris), February 1978; obituary in *Cinématographe* (Paris), January 1978; "Chaplin/Hawks/Tourneur" by H.

Desrues and P. Mérigeau in *Image et son* (Paris), February 1978; "Jacques Tourneur, français d'Hollywood" by M. Massuyeau in *Cinématographe* (Paris), February 1978; "Jacques Tourneur" by J.L. Passek in *Cinéma* (Paris), February 1978.

*   *   *

The first director Val Lewton hired for his RKO unit was Jacques Tourneur, and the first picture made by that unit was *Cat People*, an original screenplay by DeWitt Bodeen.

When Tourneur's father, Maurice, returned to Paris to continue his directing career abroad, Jacques had gone with him, working as assistant director and editor for his father. In 1933, he made a few directorial solos in the French language and then returned to Hollywood, where he became an assistant director at MGM. It was at this time that he first met Val Lewton, and the two young men worked as special unit directors for Jack Conway on *A Tale of Two Cities*; it was Lewton and Tourneur who staged the storming of the Bastille sequence for that film.

Tourneur remained at MGM, directing over 20 short subjects, and Lewton eventually went on to become David O. Selznick's story editor. When Lewton left Selznick to head his own production unit at RKO, he had already made up his mind that Tourneur would direct his first production, *Cat People*. Tourneur came to RKO, where he served as director for Lewton's first three films—*Cat People*, *I Walked With a Zombie*, and *The Leopard Man*. The front office held his work in such esteem that he was given the "A" treatment—solo direction of a high budget film, *Days of Glory*, Gregory Peck's first starring film. It was not held against him that *Days of Glory* bombed. Tourneur had gone immediately into another high budget picture at RKO—*Experiment Perilous*, starring Hedy Lamarr with Paul Lukas and George Brent. Under Tourneur's skillful direction, it became a suspenseful mood period film, certainly one of his and Hedy Lamarr's best.

Tourneur stayed on at RKO to direct Robert Mitchum in one of his finest, *Out of the Past* (aka, *Build My Gallows High*), as well as an excellent melodrama, *Berlin Express*, starring Merle Oberon and Robert Ryan with Paul Lukas. It was filmed partially in Berlin, the first Hollywood picture to be made in Germany since the end of the war.

Tourneur then directed three excellent westerns for his friend, Joel McCrea—*Stars in My Crown*, *Stranger on Horseback*, and *Wichita* with McCrea as Wyatt Earp. He had directed *The Flame and the Arrow* starring Burt Lancaster; and then another western at RKO, *Great Day in the Morning* with Robert Stack and Virginia Mayo. He went back to make another horror picture in England, *Night of the Demon*, with Dana Andrews, which is rated as highly as those he made for Lewton.

Television direction occupied the greater part of his time for the next decade, but he retired in 1966, and returned to his native country, where he died in Bergerac on December 19, 1977. The best pictures which he directed were those of suspense and genuine terror, though he also did well with those that had a great deal of action. He resisted, wisely, scenes with long patches of dialogue, always frowning and saying "It sounds so corny."

—DeWitt Bodeen

TOURNEUR, MAURICE. French. Born Maurice Thomas in Paris, 2 February 1876; became citizen of United States in 1921. Educated at lycée Condorcet. Married Fernande Petit (stage name Van Doren) in 1904 (separated 1927); child: Jacques. Career: 1894—begins career as illustrator and graphic and interior designer; becomes assistant to Auguste Rodin and then Puvis de Chavannes; late 1890s—military service in artillery; 1900-12—actor and then stage director; associated with Antoine 1903-1909; 1912—Emile Chautard, directing for Eclair, casts Tourneur in several films; 1914—Chautard suggests Tourneur to head Eclair's studio at Fort Lee, N.J.; emigrates to U.S.; begins association with designer Ben Carré; 1915—becomes production head of Paragon studio; 1917—contract with Jesse Lasky for 3 Olga Petrova vehicles; 1918—forms own production company; 1919—moves to California; contract with Paramount; forms Associated Producers Inc. with Thomas Ince and others (failed 1921); 1920—moves to Universal after disagreements with Paramount; 1926—abruptly quits directing *The Mysterious Island* after MGM insists on putting him under supervision of producer; returns to France; 1929—makes last silent film in Germany, *Das Schiff der verlorene Menschen*; 1930—son Jacques Tourneur, formerly assistant, edits films beginning with *Accusée, levez-vous*. Died 1961.

Films (as director): 1912—*Le Friquet* (+sc); *Jean la poudre* (+sc); *Le Système du Docteur Goudron et du Professeur Plume*; *Figures de cire*; 1913—*Le Dernier Pardon* (+sc); *Le Puits mitoyen*; *Le Camee*; *Sœurette* (+sc); *Le Corso rouge*; *Mademoiselle 100 millions*; *Les Gaites de l'escadron* (+sc); *La Dame de Montsoreau* (+sc); 1914—*Monsieur Lecocq* (+sc); *Rouletabille I: Le Mystère de la chambre jaune* (+sc); *Rouletabille II: La Dernière Incarnation de Larsan* (+sc); *Mother* (+sc); *The Man of the Hour* (+ sc); *The Wishing Ring* (+sc); *The Pit*; 1915—*Alias Jimmy Valentine* (+sc); *The Cub*; *Trilby* (+sc); *The Ivory Snuff Box* (+sc); *A Butterfly on the Wheel*; *Human Driftwood*; 1916—*The Pawn of Fate*; *The Hand of Peril* (+sc); *The Closed Road* (+sc); *The Rail Rider*; *The Velvet Paw*; 1917—*A Girl's Folly*; *The Whip*; *The Undying Flame*; *Exile*; *The Law of the Land* (+sc); *The Pride of the Clan*; *The Poor Little Rich Girl*; *Barbary Sheep*; *The Rise of Jennie Cushing*; 1918—*Rose of the World*; *A Doll's House*; *The Blue Bird*; *Prunella*; *Woman*; *Sporting Life*; 1919—*The White Heather*; *The Life Line*; *Victory*; *The Broken Butterfly* (+co-sc); 1920—*My Lady's Garter*; *The County Fair*; *The Great Redeemer* (Brown) (supervised only); *Treasure Island*; *The White Circle*; *Deep Waters*; *The Last of the Mohicans*; 1921—*The Bait*; *The Foolish Matrons*; 1922—*Lorna Doone*; 1923—*While Paris Sleeps* (made in 1920); *The Christian*; *The Isle of Lost Ships*; *The Brass Bottle*; *Jealous Husbands*; 1924—*Torment* (+co-sc); *The White Moth*; 1925—*Never the Twain Shall Meet*; *Sporting Life* (+sc: remake); *Clothes Make the Pirate*; 1926—*Aloma of the South Seas*; *Old Loves and New*; *The Mysterious Island* (co-d, +sc); 1927—*L'Equipage* (+co-sc); 1929—*Das Schiff der verlorene Menschen (Le Navire des hommes perdus)*; 1930—*Accusée, levez-vous*; 1931—*Maison de danses*; *Partir...* or *Partir!*; 1932—*Au nom de la loi*; *Les Gaites de la escadron* (+co-sc); *L'Idoire* (+co-sc); 1933—*Les Deux Orphelines* (+co-sc); *L'Homme mysterieux (Obsession)*; 1934—*Le Voleur*; 1935—*Justin de Marseille*; 1936—*Königsmark*; *Samson*; *Avec le sourire*; 1938—*Le Patriote*; *Katia*; 1940—*Volpone*; 1941—*Peches de jeunesse*; *Mam'zelle Bonaparte*; 1942—*La Main du diable*; 1943—*Le Val d'enfer*; *Cecile est morte*; 1947—*Apres l'amour*; 1948—*L'Impasse des deux anges*.

Publications:

By TOURNEUR:

Articles—"Stylization in Motion Picture Direction" in *Motion Picture* (New York), September 1918; interview by M.S. Cheatham in *Motion Picture Classic* (Brooklyn), February 1920; interview by T.B. Handy in *Motion Picture* (New York), November 1920; interview by W. Goldbeck in *Motion Picture* (New York), January 1923; article reprinted from *Shadowland*, May 1920, in *Film Comment* (New York), July/August 1976.

On TOURNEUR:

Articles—"Monsieur Tourneur" by D. Nutting in *Photoplay* (New York), July 1918; "Work of Maurice Tourneur" by H. Haskins in *Motion Picture Classic* (Brooklyn), September 1918; "Maurice Tourneur" by George Geltzer in *Films in Review* (New York), April 1961; "Le Mort de Maurice Tourneur est passée presque inaperçue" by Jacques Siclier in *Télérama* (Paris), no.621, 1961; article in *Sight in Sound* (London), autumn 1961 (also notes and corrections, winter 1961); "Tombeau de Tourneur" by Claude Beylie in *Cahiers du cinéma* (Paris), January 1962; "Maurice Tourneur: The First of the Visual Stylists" by R. Koszarski in *Film Comment* (New York), March/April 1973; "De Curtiz à Tourneur" by Claude Beylie in *Ecran* (Paris), June 1977; "Maurice Tourneur—films parlants 1930/1948" by J. Deslandes in *Avant-Scène du cinéma* (Paris), 15 June 1977; article in *Lumière du cinéma* (Paris), July/August 1977; letter from Kevin Brownlow in *American Classic Screen* (Shawnee Mission, Kansas), fall 1979; article in *Classic Film/Video Images* (Muscatine, Iowa), May 1982.

*   *   *

Maurice Tourneur is one of the greatest pictorialists of the cinema, deriving his aesthetic from his early associations with Rodin and Puvis de Chavannes. Having worked for André Antoine as an actor and producer, he joined the Eclair Film Company in 1912 and travelled to their American Studios at Fort Lee, New Jersey, in 1941. Here he directed films based on successful stage plays. In *The Wishing Ring* it is possible to see the charm and visual beauty he brought to his work. His team consisted of John van der Broek, the cameraman who later tragically drowned during one of Tourneur's productions, Ben Carré, the art director, and Clarence Brown, his editor who would later achieve fame as Garbo's favorite director.

Tourneur was most literate in his pronouncements on the cinema, individualistic and iconoclastic at times. He saw the cinema in perspective and would not concede it a status equal to the other arts. He stated, "to speak of the future development of the art of the cinema is futile. It cannot be. It costs a great deal of money to produce a motion picture. The only way the financial backer can get his money back, to say nothing of a profit, is to appeal to the great masses. And the thing that satisfies millions cannot be good. As Ibsen once wrote, it is the minority which is always right." In practice, however, his own work belied this statement. To everything he did he brought a sense of beauty and great responsibility to his audiences.

He directed Clara Kimball Young in *Trilby*, Mary Pickford in *Pride of the Clan* and *Poor Little Rich Girl*, the latter a very successful film. He made three films with Olga Petrova. In 1918 five memorable films came from his hand: Elsie Ferguson appeared in his *The Doll's House*; two other stage plays, *The Bluebird* by Maeterlinck and *Prunella* by Granville Barker, gave Tourneur full scope for his visual style; *Woman* a film of episodes, dealt with Adam and Eve, Claudius and Messalina, Heloise and Abelard, a Breton fisherman and a mermaid and a

Civil War story; and, *Sporting Life* was significant for its absence of stars and its depiction of a fog-ridden London, anticipating Griffith's *Broken Blossoms* of the following year.

For Paramount, in 1919, he made Joseph Conrad's *Victory*, and in 1920, a delightful *Treasure Island* with Shirley Mason (as Jim Hawkins) and Lon Chaney, who also starred in *While Paris Sleeps*. For Associated Producers he made *The Last of the Mohicans*, which many consider to be his masterpiece although Clarence Brown took over direction when Tourneur fell ill during production.

Tourneur believed in location shooting and many of his films took him to far-off places. He shot in Puerto Rico, Big Bear Lake and the Marquesas.

His remaining Hollywood films included *Lorna Doone*, *The Christian*, *The Isle of Lost Ships*, *The Brass Bottle*, *The White Moth*, *Never the Twain Shall Meet* and *Aloma of The South Seas*. During the production of *The Mysterious Island* for M.G.M., Tourneur resented the interference of his work by a producer, walked off the set, and returned to France. He continued to work in films in Europe, his first being *L'Equipage*. In 1929 he made *Das Schiff der Verlorene* in Germany with Marlene Dietrich. This was his last silent film, but he accepted the coming of sound and, before his death in 1961, he had made over 20 sound films. The most important of these were *Les Deux Orphelines*, the delightful *Katia* with Danielle Darieux, *Volpone* with Harry Baur and Louis Jouvet, *La Main du diable* from a story by Gerard de Nerval and featuring Pierre Fresnay, and his last film *L'Impasse des deux anges*.

Tourneur was a man who had no illusions about working in films. He realized the limitations of Hollywood and the films he was given to direct. However, he brought his considerable talent as a designer to bear on his work, and did not hesitate to experiment. He stylized his sets, and was influenced by new movements in the theater, but he also used the effects of Nature to heighten his dramas. His awareness of the potentialities of the camera was profound, giving strength to his images.

—Liam O'Leary

TRNKA, JIRÍ. Czech. Born in Pilsen, 24 February 1912. Educated at Arts and Crafts School (UMPRUM), Prague, 1928-35. Married Ružena Trnková. Career: 1923—begins making puppets; 1926—becomes shop assistant, designer in modern puppet theater of Josef Skupa; 1928-35—while student at UMPRUM, works as newspaper cartoonist; 1936—founds puppet theater "Dřevěné divadlo" (Wooden Theatre); late 1930s—active as graphic artist, painter and book illustrator; 1937—Wooden Theatre fails; 1941-44—scenic artist at National Theatre; 1945—begins working in animation at invitation of members of studio that becomes "Bratři v triku" Studio; 1946—begins making puppet films. Died in Prague, 30 December 1969. Recipient: National Artist; Order of Labor.

Films (as director of cartoons): 1945—*Zasadil dědek řepu (Grandpa Planted a Beet)* (+art d); 1946—*Zvířátka a Petrovští (The Animals and the Brigands)* (+co-sc, art d); *Dárek (The Gift)* (+co-sc, art d); *Pérák a SS (The Springer and SS-Men)* (+co-sc, art d); (as director of puppet films): 1947—"Masopust" [Carnival], "Jaro" [Spring], "Legenda o svatém Prokopu" [Legend of St. Prokop], "Pouť" [Fair], "Posvícení" [Feast], "Betlém" [Bethlehem] episodes of *Spaliček (The Czech Year)* (+co-sc, art d); 1948—*Císařuv slavík (The Emperor's Nightingale)* (+sc, art d); 1949—*Román s basou (Novel with a Contrabass)* (+sc, art d); *Arie prérie (The Song of the Prairie)* (+co-sc, art d); 1950—*Certuv mlýn (The Devil's Mill)* (+sc, art d); *Bajaja (Bayaya)* (+sc, art d); *Veselý cirkus (The Merry Circus)* (+sc, co-art d, paper-cut animation); 1951—*O zlaté rybce (The Golden Fish)* (+sc, art d, cartoon); 1953—*Staré pověsti české (Old Czech Legends)* (+co-sc, art d); *Jak stařeček měnil až vyměnil (How Grandpa Changed Till Nothing Was Left)* (+sc, art d, cartoon); 1954—*Dva mrazíci (2 Frosts)* (+sc, art d); *Kuťásek a Kutilka, jak ráno vstávali (Kuťásek and Kutilka)* (+art d); 1955—"Z Hatvanu do Haliče" [From Putim to Putim], "Svejkovy nehody ve vlaku" [Schweik's Difficulties on the Train], and "Svejkova buďejovická anabase" [Schweik and Cognac] episodes of *Osudy dobrého vojáka Svejkova (The Good Soldier Schweik)* (+sc, co-art d); *Cirkus Hurvínek (Hurvínek's Circus)* (+art d); 1958—*Proč UNESCO? (Why UNESCO?)* (+co-sc, art d, cartoon); 1959—*Sen noci svatojánské (A Midsummer Night's Dream)* (+co-sc, art d); 1961—*Vášeň (Passion)* (+sc, art d); 1962—*Kybernetická babička (Cybernetic Granny)* (+sc, art d); 1964—*Archanděl Gabriel a paní Husa (Archangel Gabriel and Mistress Goose)* (+sc, art d); 1965—*Maxplatte, Maxplatten* (+sc, art d); *Ruka (The Hand)* (+sc, art d).

Art Direction: 1947—*Capkovy povídky (Tales by Capek)* (Frič); *Liška a džbán (The Fox and the Jug)* (Látal) (+co-sc); 1951—*Perníková chaloupka (Gingerbread Hut)* (Pojar, puppet film); *Císařuv pekař—Pekařuv císař (The Emperor's Baker, The Baker's Emperor)* (Frič); 1953—*O skleničku víc (One Glass Too Much)* (Pojar, puppet film); 1954—*Byl jednou jeden král (Once Upon a Time There Was a King)* (Bořivoj Zeman); *Jan Hus* (Vávra); 1955—*Spejbl na stopě (Spejbl on the Trail)* (Pojar, puppet film); *Jan Žižka (A Hussite Warrior)* (Vávra) (co-costume des only); 1957—*Proti všem (Against All)* (Vávra) (co-costume des only); *Paraplíčko (The Brolly)* (Pojar, puppet film) (des'd only puppet of magic grandpa); 1959—*Bombomanie (Bombomania)* (Pojar, puppet film); 1960—*Pulnoční příhoda (The Midnight Event)* (Pojar, puppet film); 1966—*Blaho lásky (The Bliss of Love)* (Brdečka, cartoon).

Publications:

By TRNKA:

Articles—"The Puppet Film as an Art", interview by J. Brož in *Film Culture* (New York), no.5-6, 1955; "20 let Cs.filmu-vypovídá Jiří Trnka", interview by Jaroslav Brož in *Film a doba* (Prague), no.6, 1965.

On TRNKA:

Books—*Od Spalíčku ke Snu noci svatojánské* by Marie Benešová, Prague 1961; *Jiří Trnka, Artist and Puppet Master* by Jaroslav Boček, Prague 1963; *Cas se nevrací!* by Adolf Hoffmeister, Prague 1965; *Jiří Trnka*, brochure, by Marie Benešová, Prague 1970; *Muj syn* by Ružena Trnková and Helena Chvojková, Prague 1972; articles—"4 European Illustrators" by E. Metzl in *American Artist*, December 1955; "An Interview with the Puppet-Film Director, Jirí Trnka" by Jaroslav Brož in *Film* (London), January/February 1956; "Trnka's Little Men" by Bernard Orna in *Films and Filming* (London), November 1956; "The Czechoslovak Animated Film" by Harriet Polt in *Film Quarterly* (Berkeley), spring 1964; "Trnkaland" in *Newsweek* (New York), March 1966; "Trnkovské postskriptum" by Jaroslav Boček in *Film a doba* (Prague), no.3, 1966; obituary in *The New York Times*, 31 December 1969; obituary in *Newsweek* (New York), 12 January 1970; "O Jiřím Trnkovi se Stanislavem Látalem a Břetislavem Pojarem" by Miloš Fiala in *Film a doba* (Prague), no.4, 1970; "O Jiřím Trnkovi s Václavem Trojanem a Jiřím Brdečkou" by Miloš Fiala in *Film a doba* (Prague), no.5, 1970; films—*Loutky Jiřího Trnky (Jiří Trnka's Puppets)* directed by Bruno Sefranka, 1955; *Skutečnost noci svatojánské (Reality of a Midsummer Night's Dream)* directed by Václav Táboprský, 1959; *Jiří Trnka* directed by Jiří Lehovec, 1967.

*   *   *

A puppeteer at heart, a skilled painter and renowned illustrator, Jiří Trnka was 33 years old in June of 1945 when associates at the animated film studio (later the "Bratři v triku" Studio) asked him to collaborate with them. He began work on the 15th of June, little knowing at the time that fate would allot him a mere 20 years for his career in film.

In one year's time he created four animated films in rapid succession, making a strong impact on the development of the genre. With their naive charm and an artistic conception based on unfettered drawing and a new method of film narration that was well received by the international moviegoing public, these works demonstrated that animated films could be done differently from before and broke the monopoly in this area of art previously enjoyed by Walt Disney. However, Trnka did not find animated films artistically satisfying, and after leaving the studio he went off to a small atelier to attempt a film with puppets. He immediately produced a magnificent work, *Spalíček (The Czech Year)*, in which he dipicted the Czech year from spring through winter in the customs, rituals, work, holidays, and legends of country life. *Spalíček* is a key work which portrays the Czech's attitudes towards life, work, love, faith, and death. It anticipates a number of motifs from his later work, motifs which Trnka will develop at various places in various genres and which will resonate throughout his oeuvre.

Along the pathway of the puppet film Trnka would create his own world, but he would also show that the expressive possibilities of the puppet film are boundless. He depicts ancient times in legends and myths, visions of the future, and the worlds of fairy tales and of modern times. He switches genres from comedy through parody, satire, and pantomime to drama and parable. He translates into cinematic form the works of Andersen [*Císařuv slavík (The Emperor's Nightingale)*], Chekhov [*Román s basou (Novel with a Contrabass)*], Němcová [*Bajaja (Bayaya)*], Hašek [*Osudy dobrého vojáka Svejkova (The Good Soldier Schweik)*], Shakespeare [*Sen noci svatojánské (A Midsummer Night's Dream)*], and Boccaccio [*Archanděl Gabriel a paní Husa (Archangel Gabriel and Mistress Goose)*]. He recognizes the encroachment of technology into human life as one of the greatest threats to mankind [*Císařuv slavík (The Emperor's Nightingale)*] and returns to this theme again in the film *Vášeň (Passion)* and in the science fiction film *Kybernetická babička (Cybernetic Grandma)*. In his last work, the philosophical study *Ruka (The Hand)*, Trnka creates a timeless parable about man and power, a theme that has been so tragically felt so many times in our twentieth century. *Ruka* marks the end of his work in film.

Until the end of his life, however, he continued to devote himself to illustrating, woodcarving, sculpture, and painting, in order, as he put it, "to capture a story, but in a single phase." He was awarded the Andersen Prize *in memoriam* for his work in illustrating.

Trnka was an extraordinarily talented and hard-working individual. He painted and wrote and was a woodcutter, a sculptor, and an illustrator. In all his films he was not only a writer and graphic artist but also an editor, a designer and builder of puppets, and a designer of puppet costumes. Often misunderstood and attacked by the critics, he never bent to any pressures.

The work he produced was well-rounded, full of human warmth, tenderness, wisdom, humor, and grace. He succeeded in bringing the puppet film out of the periphery and into mature prominence. He brought the masterworks of literature into the purview of the puppet film and expressed philosophical ideas and emotions with such urgency that his films have become not only a landmark but also a yardstick for puppet films yet to be made.

Truly a unique genius of Czech culture in the second half of the twentieth century, Trnka has demonstrated by his work that the animated film can convey all the conditions of the human spirit.

—Vladimír Opěla

TROELL, JAN. Swedish. Born at Limhamn, in Skåne, 23 July 1931. Career: early 1950s—teacher in elementary school in Malmö; about 1960—begins making documentaries for Swedish TV; begins collaborating, as cinematographer, with director Bo Widerberg; mid-1960s—begins association with producer Bengt Forslund on *Here Is Your Life*.

Films (as director and photographer of documentaries): 1960—*Stad* (short); 1961—*Baten (The Ship)*; *Sommartag (Summer Train)*; *Nyarsafton pa skanska slatten (New Year's Eve on the Skåne Plains)*; 1962—*Pojken och draken (The Boy and the Kite)* (co-d); *Var i Dalby hage (Spring in Dalby Pastures)* (short); *De kom tillbaka (The Return)*; 1963—*Barnvagnen (The Pram, The Baby Carriage)* (Widerberg) (ph only); 1964—*De gamla kvarnen (The Old Mill)* (shot in 1962); *Johan Ekberg*; *Trakom (Trachoma)*; 1965—"Uppehall i myrlandet (Stopover in the Marshland, Interlude in the Marshland)" episode of *4 X 4* (+co-sc, ed); (as feature director, co-scriptwriter, photographer, and editor): 1966—*Här har du ditt liv (Here Is Your Life)*; 1968—*Ole dole doff (Eeny Meeny Miny Moe, Who Saw Him Die?)*; 1971—*Utvandrarna (The Emigrants)*; 1972—*Nybyggarna (The New Land)*; 1974—*Zandy's Bride*; 1977—*Bang!*; 1979—*Hurricane* (not ph); 1981—*Ingenjör Andrées luftfärd (The Flight of the Eagle)* (sc).

Publications:

By TROELL:

Articles—"John Simon on Jan Troell", interview in *Film Heritage* (New York), summer 1974; "Filmmaking in Sweden" in *Interview* (New York), no.1, n.d.

On TROELL:

Articles—"Director of the Year" in *International Film Guide 1972*, London 1971; "Les Émigrants. Le Nouveau Monde" by A. Cornand in *Image et son* (Paris), April 1974; article by Michael Sragow in *Rolling Stone* (New York), June 1983.

TRUFFAUT, FRANÇOIS. French. Born in Paris, 6 February 1932. Educated at Lycée Rollin, Paris. Married Madeleine Morgenstern, 29 October 1957 (divorced); children: Laura, 1959 and Eva, 1961. Career: 1947—founds own cine-club in Paris; lack of funds causes closing, is jailed for inability to pay debts and André Bazin has him released; 1949—meets Jean-Luc Godard, Jacques Rivette, and Claude Chabrol while attending the Ciné-club du Quartier Latin; 1951—enlists in army but deserts on eve of departure for Indochina, later is released for "instability of character"; 1953—employed by the Service Cinématographique of the Ministry of Agriculture but is fired after a few months; through Bazin begins writing film criticism for *Cahiers du cinéma* and later *Arts*; 1954—writes 1st theoretical article for *Cahiers*, "Une Certain Tendance du cinéma français", which becomes focus for discussion of "politique des auteurs"; 1955—makes *Une Visite*, short 16mm film, with Jacques Rivette and Alain Resnais; 1956-58—assistant to Roberto Rossellini, works on 3 of his unreleased films; 1959—directs 1st feature *Les Quatre Cents Coups (The 400 Blows)*; writes script for Godard's 1st film *À bout de souffle*; 1966—publishes *Le Cinéma selon Hitchcock*; 1968—helps to organize protests over the dismissal of Henri Langlois, head of Cinémathèque Française; with Godard and Claude Lelouche, instigates shutting down of 1968 Cannes Film Festival in wake of May uprisings; 1975—publishes *Les Films de ma vie*. Recipient: Best Director, Cannes Festival, for *The 400 Blows*, 1959; Prix Louis Delluc for *Stolen Kisses*, 1969; Best Director, National Society of Film Critics, for *Stolen Kisses*, 1969; Best Foreign-Language Film Academy Award for *Day for Night*, 1973; Best Director, National Society of Film Critics, for *Day for Night*, 1973; Best Direction, New York Film Critics, for *Day for Night*, 1973; Best Direction British Academy Award for *Day for Night*, 1973. Address: 5 rue Robert-Estienne, 75008 Paris, France.

Films (as director and scriptwriter): 1955—*Une Visite* (+co-ed); 1957—*Les Mistons* (co-sc); 1958—*Une Histoire d'eau* (d only); 1959—*Les Quatre Cents Coups (The 400 Blows)*; 1960—*Tirez sur le pianist (Shoot the Piano Player)* (co-sc); 1961—*Jules et Jim (Jules and Jim)* (co-sc); 1962—"Antoine et Colette" episode of *L'Amour a vingt ans (Love at 20)* (+ro); 1964—*La Peau douce (The Soft Skin)* (co-sc); 1966—*Fahrenheit 451* (co-sc); 1967—*La Mariée était en noir (The Bride Wore Black)* (co-sc); 1968—*Baisers volés (Stolen Kisses)* (co-sc); 1969—*La Sirène du Mississippi (Mississippi Mermaid)*; *L'Enfant sauvage (The Wild Child)* (co-sc, +ro as *Dr. Jean Itard*); 1970—*Domicile conjugal (Bed and Board)* (co-sc); 1971—*Les Deux Anglaises et le continent (Two English Girls)* (co-sc); 1972—*Une Belle Fille comme moi (Such a Gorgeous Kid Like Me)* (co-sc); 1973—*La Nuit américaine (Day for Night)* (co-sc, +ro as *Ferrand*); 1975—*L'Histoire d'Adèle H. (The Story of Adele H.)* (co-sc); 1976—*L'Argent de poche (Small Change)* (co-sc); 1977—*L'Homme qui aimait les femmes (The Man Who Loved Women)* (co-sc); 1978—*La Chambre verte (The Green Room)* (co-sc, +ro as *Julien Davenne*); 1979—*L'Amour en fuite (Love on the Run)* (co-sc); 1980—*Le Dernier Métro (The Last Metro)*.

Role (in film not directed): 1977—*French Scientist* in *Close Encounters of the 3rd Kind* (Spielberg).

Publications:

By TRUFFAUT:

Books—*Les Quatre Cents Coups* by François Truffaut and

Marcel Moussy, Paris 1959; *Le Cinéma selon Alfred Hitchcock*, Paris 1967; *Hitchcock*, New York 1967; *Ce n'est qu'un début*, Paris 1968; *Jules and Jim*, translated by Nicholas Fry, New York 1968; *The 400 Blows: A Film By François Truffaut*, translated screenplay by David Denby (plus articles and interview), New York 1969; *The Adventures of Antoine Doinel: 4 Autobiographical Screenplays*, New York 1971; *La Nuit américaine et le journal de tournage de Fahrenheit 451*, Paris 1974; *Les Films de ma vie*, Paris 1975; *Day for Night* (script plus footnotes by translator), New York 1975; *The Wild Child*, translated by Linda Lewin and Christine Lémery, New York 1975; *Small Change*, translated by Anselm Hollo, New York 1976; *The Story of Adele H.*, translated by Helen G. Scott, New York 1976; *L'Homme qui aimait les femmes*, Paris 1977; *The Films in My Life*, New York 1978; *Hitchcock*, with H.G. Scott, London 1979; articles—"Une Certain Tendance du cinéma français" in *Cahiers du cinéma* (Paris), January 1954; "Renoir in America", with J. Rivette in *Sight and Sound* (London), July/September 1954; "La Crise d'ambition du cinéma français" in *Arts* (Paris), 30 March 1955; article on Cayatte and the scriptwriters in *Arts* (Paris), 25 May 1955; article on critics in *Arts* (Paris), 6 July 1955; article on the "scriptwriters cinema" in *Arts* (Paris), 28 September 1955; interview, with M. Scherer, of Rossellini in *Film Culture* (New York), March/April 1955; article in *Arts* (Paris), 19 December 1956; article on Cannes 1957 in *Arts* (Paris), 15 May 1957; article on new directors in *Arts* (Paris), 8 January 1958; article on *Les Amants* and *En cas de malheur* in *Arts* (Paris), 19 November 1958; "André Bazin" in *Arts* (Paris), 19 November 1958; "On the Death of André Bazin" in *Cahiers du cinéma* (Paris), January 1959; "Charles Aznavour" in *Cinémonde* (Paris), 5 May 1960; "On Film: Truffaut Interview" in the *New Yorker*, 20 February 1960; "Tomorrow—the Artists", interview, in *Films and Filming* (London), October 1960; "*Les Mistons*" in *L'Avant-Scène du cinéma* (Paris), no.4, 1961; "*Histoire d'eau*" in *L'Avant-Scène du cinéma* (Paris), no.7, 1961; "L'Agonie de la Nouvelle Vague n'est pas pour demain" in *Arts* (Paris), 20 December 1961; "*Jules et Jim*" in *L'Avant-Scène du cinéma* (Paris), June 1962; interview in *Cahiers du cinéma* (Paris), December 1962; interview in *Les Lettres françaises* (Paris), 25 January 1962; "*Vivre sa vie*" in *L'Avant-Scène du cinéma* (Paris), October 1962; "Sex and Life" in *Films and Filming* (London), July 1962; interview in *Les Lettres françaises* (Paris), 24 October 1963; interview in *Cinéma 64* (Paris), May/October 1964; "*Le Testament d'Orphée*" in *Cahiers du cinéma* (Paris), February 1964; "Sur le cinéma américaine" in *Cahiers du cinéma* (Paris), December 1963 and January 1964; "Skeleton Keys" in *Film Culture* (New York), spring 1964; "*La Peau douce*" in *L'Avant-Scène du cinéma* (Paris), May 1965; "*Farenheit 451*" (working notes by Truffaut) in *Cahiers du cinéma* (Paris), February/July 1966; interview in *Cinéma 67* (Paris), January 1967; interview in *Cahiers du cinéma* (Paris), May 1967; interview in *Les Lettres françaises* (Paris), 20 April 1967; "Jean-Luc Godard" in *Les Lettres françaises* (Paris), 16 March 1967; "Georges Sadoul" in *Les Lettres françaises* (Paris), 18 October 1967; interview in *Les Lettres françaises* (Paris), 11 April 1968; "Ernst Lubitsch" in *Cahiers du cinéma* (Paris), February 1968; "Jean Renoir" in *Le Monde* (Paris), 18 January 1968; "Françoise Dorlèac" in *Cahiers du cinéma* (Paris), April/-May 1968; "L'Antimémoire courte" in *Combat* (Paris), 12 February 1968; "La Résistible Ascension de Pierre Barbin" in *Combat* (Paris), 16 February 1968; "Toujours la Cinémathèque" in *Combat* (Paris), 15 March 1968; interview in *Arts* (Paris), 29 April 1969; "Vive 'Glenariff!'" in *Le Monde* (Paris), 17 October 1969; "Life Style Homo Cinematicus—François Truffaut" by Sanche de Gramont in *The New York Times Magazine*, 15 June 1969; "*Farenheit 451*" (synopsis of action only) in *L'Avant-*

Scène du cinéma (Paris), October 1970; "*L'Enfant Sauvage*" in *L'Avant-Scène du cinéma* (Paris), October 1970; interview in *Télé-Ciné* (Paris), March 1970; "Is Truffaut the Happiest Man on Earth? Yes" in *Esquire* (New York), August 1970; "Intensification", interview by Gordon Gow in *Films and Filming* (London), July 1972; interview by P. Thomas in *Cinéma* (Paris), January 1972; "Mes Deux Anglaises, mon onzième film", interview by P. Thomas in *Avant-Scène du cinéma* (Paris), January 1972; "2 Filme von Truffaut: Une Belle Fille comme moi" in *Filmkritik* (Munich), July 1972; interview by Dominique Maillet in *Cinématographe* (Paris), summer 1973; "Perchè" and interview by M. Mancini and C. Tiso in *Filmcritica* (Rome), September 1973; interview by C. Beylie in *Ecran* (Paris), July/August 1973; "A Portrait of Francois Truffaut", interview by S. Mallow in *Filmmakers Newsletter* (Ward Hill, Mass.), December 1973; interview by S. Rosenthal in *Focus on Film* (London), autumn 1973; "La Conférence de presse: Un Art qui se cherche" by J.-P. Tadros in *Cinéma Québec* (Montreal), July/August 1973; "The Lesson of Ingmar Bergman" in *Take One* (Montreal), July 1973; "I Wish", interview by Donna Dudinsky in *Take One* (Montreal), March 1974; "François Truffaut: le métier et le jeu", interview by E. Ballerini and others in *Jeune Cinéma* (Paris), March 1974; interview by Charles Higham in *Action* (Los Angeles), January/February 1974; "Le Cinéma est un jeu", interview by A. Leroux and L. Gagliardi in *Cinéma Québec* (Montreal), December/January 1973/74; interview by Dominique Maillet in *Cinématographe* (Paris), October/November 1975; "Adèle H.", interview by G. Adair in *Sight and Sound* (London), summer 1975; "François Truffaut: The Romantic Bachelor" by Melanie Adler in *Andy Warhol's Interview* (New York), March 1976; "Dialogue on Film: Interview with Truffaut" in *American Film* (Washington, D.C.), May 1976; "Kid Stuff: François Truffaut on *Small Change*" by J. McBride and T. McCarthy in *Film Comment* (New York), September/October 1976; "De l'abstrait au concret" in *Avant-Scène du cinéma* (Paris), April 1976; "Mr. Hitchcock, wie haben Sie das gemacht?", interview in *Film und Ton* (Munich), January 1976; "Non conosco Isabelle Adjani" in *Filmcritica* (Rome), January/February 1976; "Truffaut, Part V", interview in the *New Yorker*, 18 October 1976; interview by J. Fieschi in *Cinématographe* (Paris), May 1977; "François Truffaut: Feminist Filmmaker?" by Annette Insdorf in *Take One* (Montreal), January 1978; "Hitchcock—His True Power is Emotion" in *The New York Times*, 4 March 1979; "My Friend Hitchcock" in *American Film* (Washington, D.C.), March 1979; "Truffaut: 20 Years After", interview by D. Allen in *Sight and Sound* (London), no.4, 1979; interview by P. Carcassonne in *Cinématographe* (Paris), February 1979.

On TRUFFAUT:

Books—*The New Wave* edited by Peter Graham, New York 1968; *The Cinema of François Truffaut* by Graham Petrie, New York 1970; *François Truffaut* by C.G. Crisp and Michael Walker, New York 1971; *François Truffaut* by C.G. Crisp, London 1972; *Le Cinéma en question* by Jean Collet, Paris 1972; *L'Univers de François Truffaut* by Dominique Fanne, Paris 1972; *3 European Directors* edited by James M. Wall, Grand Rapids, Michigan 1973; *Truffaut* by Don Allen, New York 1974; *The New Wave: Truffaut, Godard, Chabrol, Rohmer, Rivette*, by James Monaco, New York 1976; *Le Cinéma de François Truffaut* by Jean Collet, Paris 1977; "François Truffaut" by Annette Insdorf, Boston 1978; *François Truffaut* by Annette Insdorf, London 1981; articles—"Qu'est-ce que la Nouvelle Vague?" by Noël Burch in *Film Quarterly* (Berkeley), winter 1959; "Notes on a New Generation" by Georges Sadoul in *Sight and Sound* (London), October 1959; "François Truffaut—The Anarchist Imagination" by Judith Shatnoff in *Film Quarterly* (Berkeley), spring 1963; "White Elephant Art vs. Termite Art" by Manny Farber in *Film Culture* (New York), winter 1962-63; "The Literary Sophistication of François Truffaut" by Michael Klein in *Film Comment* (New York), summer 1965; "After the Nouvelle Vague" by Stephen Taylor in *Film Quarterly* (Berkeley), spring 1965; "Hitchcock, Truffaut, and the Irresponsible Audience" by Leo Braudy in *Film Quarterly* (Berkeley), summer 1968; article in *Life* (New York), 7 March 1969; "10 Years of Truffaut" in *Newsweek* (New York), 10 March 1969; "Chabrol and Truffaut" by Robin Wood in *Movie* (London), winter 1969-70; article by Molly Haskell in *The Village Voice* (New York), 16 April 1970; "Will the Real François Truffaut Please Stand Up" by J.J. O'Connor in *Making Films* (New York), October 1970; "A Man Can Serve 2 Masters by David Bordwell in *Film Comment* (New York), spring 1971; "Truffaut: The Educated Heart" by Julian Jebb in *Sight and Sound* (London), summer 1972; "Le Continent, Truffaut et le deux anglaises" by C. Beylie and others in *Ecran* (Paris), January 1972; "Chabrol, Truffaut, après 15 ans" by J.P. Jeancolas in *Jeune Cinéma* (Paris), January 1972; "Truffaut and Itard: The Wild Child" by J. Gerlach in *Film Heritage* (New York), spring 1972; "Truffaut & Marx" by R. Tomasino in *Filmcritica* (Rome), September 1973; "Truffaut's Gorgeous Killers" by Beverle Houston and Marsha Kinder in *Film Quarterly* (Berkeley), winter 1973/74; "Art and Film in François Truffaut's *Jules and Jim* and *2 English Girls*" by B. Coffey in *Film Heritage* (New York), spring 1974; "La Politique des auteurs: Part 2: Truffaut's Manifesto" by J. Hess in *Jump Cut* (Chicago), July/August 1974; "The Cinema of Irony: Chabrol, Truffaut in the 1970s" by M. Lefanu in *Monogram* (London), no.5, 1974; "20 ans après: une certaine constante du cinéma français" by M. Martin in *Ecran* (Paris), January 1974; "Les Films de ma vie" by R. Duval in *Ecran* (Paris), June/July 1975; "The Sorcerer's Apprentice: Bazin and Truffaut on Renoir" by P. Thomas in *Sight and Sound* (London), winter 1974/75; "Les Enfants de Truffaut" by J. Beaulieu in *Séquences* (Montreal), October 1976; "From *The 400 Blows* to *Small Change*" by Gerald Mast in the *New Republic* (New York), 2 April 1977; "Valérie Bonnier", interview by C. Bechtold in *Cinématographe* (Paris), May 1977; "Truffaut le narrateur" by P. Carcassonne in *Cinématographe* (Paris), November 1977; "La Chambre vert", special issue of *Avant-Scène du cinéma* (Paris), 1 November 1978; "François Truffaut en compagnie de Maurice Jaubert" by F. Porcile in *Image et son* (Paris), April 1978; "Das Gesicht hinter der Glasscheibe: das enttäuschende Ende der Geschichte Antoine Doinels" by B. Giger in *Cinema* (Zurich), no.2, 1979; "Ein Mann, der Film liebt: über François Truffaut" by V. von Wroblewsky in *Film und Fernsehen* (Berlin), no.4, 1979; "Bazin Defended Against His Devotees" by B. Henderson in *Film Quarterly* (Berkeley), no.4, 1979; "Interview met Suzanne Schiffman over Truffaut" by H. Hosman in *Skoop* (Amsterdam), October 1979; "François Truffaut: The Man Who Loved Movies" by W. Kowinski in *Rolling Stone* (New York), 14 June 1979; "Truffaut's La Chambre vert" by A.R. Tintner in *Literature/Film Quarterly* (Salisbury, Maryland), v.8, no.2, 1980.

*   *   *

François Truffaut was one of five young French film critics, writing for Andre Bazin's *Cahiers du cinéma* in the early 1950s, who became one of the leading French filmmakers of his generation. It was Truffaut who first formulated the *politique des auteurs*, a view of film history and film art that defended those directors who were "true men of the cinema"—Renoir, Vigo, Tati in France; Hawks, Ford, Welles in America—rather than those more literary, script-oriented film directors and writers associated with the French "tradition of quality." Truffaut's original term and distinctions were subsequently borrowed and translated by later generations of Anglo-American film critics, including Andrew Sarris, Robin Wood, V.F. Perkins, and Dave Kehr. When Truffaut made his first feature in 1959, *Les Quatre Cent Coups*, he put his ideas of cinema spontaneity into practice with the study of an adolescent, Antoine Doinel, who breaks free from the constrictions of French society to face an uncertain but open future. Since that debut, Truffaut's career has been dominated by an exploration of the Doinel character's future (five films) and by the actor (Jean-Pierre Léaud) whom Truffaut discovered to play Antoine. In Truffaut's 25 years of making films, the director, the Doinel character, and Léaud have all grown up together.

The rebellious teenager of *Quatre Cent Coups* becomes a tenative, shy, sexually clumsy suitor in the "Antoine et Collette" episode of *Love at Twenty*. In *Baisers Volés*, Antoine is older but not much wiser at either love or money making. In *Domicile conjugal* Antoine has married but still on the run toward something else—the exotic lure of other sexual adventures. And in *L'Amour en fuite*, Antoine is still running (running became the essential metaphor for the Doinel character's existence, beginning with the lengthy running sequence that concludes *Les Quatre Cent Coups*. Although Antoine is now divorced, the novel which he has finally completed has made his literary reputation. That novel, it turns out, is his life itself, the entire Doinel saga as filmed by Truffaut, and Truffaut fills his films with film clips that are both visual and mental recollections of the entire Doinel cycle. Truffaut deliberately collapses the distinction between written fiction and filmed fiction, between the real life of humans and the fictional life of characters. The collapse seems warranted by the personal and professional connections between Truffaut the director, Doinel the character, and Léaud the actor.

Many of Truffaut's non-Doinel films are style pieces that similarly explore the boundaries between art and life, film and fiction. The main character of *Tirez sur le pianist* tries to turn himself into a fictional character, as does Catherine in *Jules et Jim*. Both find it difficult to maintain the consistency of fictional characters when faced with the demanding exigencies of real life. *La Mariée etait en noir* was Truffaut's elegy to Hitchcock, a deliberate style piece in the Hitchcock manner, while *Fahrenheit 451*, his adaption of the Ray Bradbury's novel, explores the lack of freedom in a society in which books—especially works of fiction—are burned. Adele H in *L'Histoire d'Adele H*, attempts to convert her passion into a book, her diary, but life can neither requite nor equal her passion, driving her to madness and a total withdrawal from life into the fantasy of her romantic fiction. In *L'Homme qui aimait les femmes*, an incurable womanizer translates his desire into a successful novel, but the existence of that work in no way diffuses, alleviates, or sublimates the desire that vivified it. *The Green Room* is Truffaut's homage to fiction and the novelist's craft—a careful, stylish adaption of a Henry James story. Given his conscious commitment to film and fiction, it was not surprising that Truffaut devoted one of his films to the subject of filmmaking itself. *La Nuit americaine* is one of the most loving and revealing films about the business of making films, an exuberant illustration of the ways in which films use artifice to capture and convey the illusion of life. This film, in which Truffaut himself plays a film director, is a comically energetic defense of the joys and pains of filmmaking, in deliberate responses to the more tortured visions of Fellini's *8 ½* or Bergman's *Persona*.

Those Truffaut films not concerned with the subject of art are frequently about education. *L'Enfant sauvage* explores the beneficial power and effects of civilization on the savage passions of a child who grew up in the forest, apparently raised by beasts. Truffaut again plays a major role in the film (dedicated to Jean-Pierre Léaud), the patient scientist who effects the boy's conversion from savagery to humanity. Like the director he played in *La Nuit americaine*, Truffaut is the wise and dedicated patriarch, responsible for the well-being of a much larger enterprise. *L'Argent de poche* examines the child's life at school and the child's relationships both to adults and other children. As opposed to the imprisoning restrictions which confined children in the world of *Quatre Cent Coups*, the now adult Truffaut realizes that adults—parents and teachers—treat children with far more care, love, and devotion than the children (like the younger, rebellious Truffaut himself) are able to see,

Unlike his friend and contemporary, Jean-Luc Godard, Truffaut has remained consistently committed to his highly formal themes of art and life, film and fiction, youth and education, art and education, rather than venturing into radical political critiques of film forms and film imagery. Truffaut seems to state his position in *Le Dernier Metro*, his most political film, examining a theater troupe in Nazified Paris. The film director seems to confess that, like those actors in that period, he can only continue to make art the way he knows how, that his commitment to formal artistic excellence will eventually serve the political purposes that powerful art always serves, and that for him to betray his own artistic powers for political, programmatic purposes would perhaps lead to his making bad art and bad political statements. In this rededication to artistic form, Truffaut is probably restating his affinity with the Jean Renoir he wrote about for *Caheirs du cinéma*. Renoir, like Truffaut, progressed from making more rebellious black-and-white films in his youth to more accepting color films in his maturity; Renoir, like Truffaut, played major roles in several of his own films; Renoir, like Truffaut, believed that conflicting human choices could not be condemned according to facile moral or political formulae; and Renoir, like Truffaut, saw the creation of art (and film art) as a genuinely humane and meaningful response to the potentially chaotic disorder of formless reality.

—Gerald Mast

ULMER, EDGAR G. Austrian. Born Edgar Georg Ulmer in Vienna, 17 September 1904. Educated in architecture at Academy of Arts and Sciences, Vienna; studied stage design at Burgteater, Vienna. Married Shirley Castle; child: Arianne. Career: 1918—designer for Decla-Biosope film company; 1919-22—works as designer for Max Reinhardt, Vienna; 1923—comes to New York with Reinhardt, signs with Universal as designer; 1924—returns to Germany, is designer and set-builder for *Der letzte Mann* and *Faust* for Murnau; 1925—returns to U.S. as assistant to Murnau, through 1929; works as art director and production assistant at Universal, then assistant director to William Wyler; 1929—returns to Berlin to make *Menschen am Sonntag* with Robert Siodmak; 1930-33—art director at MGM and stage designer for Philadelphia Grand Opera Co.; mid-1930s—makes public health doumentaries for minority groups, produces and directs foreign-language feature films in New York; 1942—returns to Hollywood, writes and directs for Producers' Releasing Corp. (PRC) through 1946; late 1940s, 1950s—works in Mexico, Italy, Germany and Spain as well as U.S. Died in Woodland Hills, California, 30 September 1972.

Films (as director—of 128 films Ulmer claimed to have directed, the following titles are reported in current filmographies): 1929—*Menschen am Sonntag (People on Sunday)* (co-d, +co-sc); 1933—*Damaged Lives* (+co-sc); *Mr. Broadway*; 1934—*The Black Cat* (+co-sc); *Thunder over Texas* (d as 'John Warner'); *Little Man, What Now?* (set design only); 1937—*Green Fields* (co-d); 1938—*Natalka Poltavka* (+sc, assoc. p); *The Singing Blacksmith* (+p); *Zaporosch Sa Dunayem (Cossacks in Exile, The Cossacks Across the Danube)*; 1939—*Die Tlatsche (The Light Ahead)* [original title: *Fishe da Krin*] (+p); *Moon Over Harlem*; *Americaner Schadchen (The Marriage Broker, American Matchmaker)*; *Let My People Live*; 1940—*Cloud in the Sky*; 1941—*Another to Conquer*; 1942—*Prisoner of Japan* (story only); *Tomorrow We Live*; 1943—*My Son, the Hero* (+co-sc); *Corregidor* (co-sc only); *Girls in Chains* (+story); *Isle of Forgotten Sins* (+story); *Danger! Women at Work* (co-story only); *Jive Junction*; 1944—*Bluebeard*; 1945—*Strange Illusion (Out of the Night)*; *Club Havana*; *Detour*; 1946—*The Wife of Monte Cristo* (+co-sc); *Her Sister's Secret*; *The Strange Woman*; 1947—*Carnegie Hall*; 1948—*Ruthless*; 1949—*I pirati de Capri (Pirates of Capri)*; 1951—*St. Benny the Dip*; *The Man from Planet X*; 1952—*Babes in Bagdad*; 1955—*Naked Dawn*; *Murder Is My Beat (Dynamite Anchorage)*; 1957—*The Daughter of Dr. Jekyll*; *The Perjurer*; 1960—*Hannibal*; *The Amazing Transparent Man*; *Beyond the Time Barrier*; *L'Atlantide (Antinea, L'amante della città Sepolta, Journey Beneath the Desert)* (co-d); 1964—*Sette contro la morte (Neunzig Nächte und ein Tag)*; 1965—*The Cavern*.

Publications:

By ULMER:

Articles—interview in *Cahiers du cinéma* (Paris), August 1961; interview in *Midi-Minuit fantastique* (Paris), November 1965; "Edgar G. Ulmer, an Interview" by Peter Bogdanovich in *Film Culture* (New York), no.58-60, 1974.

On ULMER:

Book—*The Hollywood Professionals* vol.3 by John Belton, New York 1974; articles—"Edgar G. Ulmer" by Luc Moullet in *Cahiers du cinéma* (Paris), April 1956; "Esoterica" by Andrew Sarris in *Film Culture* (New York), spring 1963; "Prisoners of Paranoia" by John Belton in *Velvet Light Trap* (Madison, Wisconsin), summer 1972; "Edgar G. Ulmer, dandy de grand chemin" by Claude Beylie in *Ecran* (Paris), December 1972; "Prisoners of Paranoia" by J. Belton in *Velvet Light Trap* (Madison), winter 1977.

*   *   *

The films of Edgar G. Ulmer have generally been classified as "B" pictures. However, it might be more appropriate to reclassify some of these films as "Z" pictures. On an average, Ulmer's pictures were filmed on a six-day shooting schedule with budgets as small as $20,000. He often worked without a decent script, adequate sets, or convincing actors. But these hardships did not prevent Ulmer from creating an individual style within his films.

Part of the look of Ulmer's films was, naturally, a result of their small budgets. The cast was kept to a minimum., the sets were few and simple, and stock footage helped to keep costs down (even when they didn't quite match the rest of the film). The length of the scripts was also kept to a minimum. Most of Ulmer's films ran only 60 to 70 minutes and it was not uncommon for his pictures to open upon characters who were not formally introduced. Ulmer often plunged his audience into the middle of the action, which would add to their suspense as the story finally did unfold.

It is a common element of Ulmer's films for the characters to find themselvs in strange and distant surroundings. This plight is especially true for the title character of *The Man from Planet X*. This curious being is stranded on earth (which from his point of view is an alien world) and is at the mercy of the strangers around him. In another example, the Allisons, a young couple on their honeymoon in *The Black Cat*, find themselves trapped in the futuristic home of the bizarre Mr. Poelzig. They are held against their will with all avenues of escape blocked off. Many of Ulmer's characters find that they are prisoners. Some of them are innocent, but many times they live in prisons of their own making.

Another theme that is prevalent in Ulmer's films is fate. His characters rarely have control over their own destiny, an idea verbalized by Al Roberts in *Detour* who says, "whichever way you turn, Fate sticks out its foot to trip you." In *The Amazing Transparent Man*, a scientist who has been forced to work against his will on experiments with nuclear material, explains that he "didn't do anything by choice." The Allisons in *The Black Cat* have no control over their destiny, either—their fate will be determined by the outcome of a game of chess. In most cases the characters in Ulmer's films find themselves swept away in a series of circumstances that they are unable to stop.

The critical recognition of Ulmer's work has been a fairly recent "discovery." Initial reviews of Ulmer's films (and not all of his films received reviews) were far from complimentary. Part of the reason for their dismissal may have been their exploitative nature. Titles like *Girls in Chains* and *Babes in Bagdad* could conceivably have some difficulty in finding a respectable niche in the film world. However, taken as a whole, the work of Edgar Ulmer reveals personal vision that is, at the very least, different and distinctive from the mainstream of film directors.

—Linda Obalil

VADIM, ROGER. French. Born Roger Vadim Plemiannikov in Paris, 26 January 1928. Educated in political science; studied acting with Charles Dullin. Married Brigitte Bardot (divorced); Annette Stroyberg (divorced); one child; child by Catherine Deneuve; married Jane Fonda (divorced); child by Catherine Schneider. Career: 1944-47—stage actor; early 1950s—becomes assistant to Marc Allégret, works on *Juliette* (1953), writes dialogue for *Futures vedettes* (1954); co-adapts *En effeuillant la Marguerite* (1956); 1953-55—journalist, writing especially for *Paris-Match*; also directs for TV, notable *Entrée des artistes*; 1956—Raoul Lévy produces first film; first three films written for and starring Brigitte Bardot.

Films (as director and co-scriptwriter): 1956—*Et... Dieu créa la femme (And... God Created Woman)*; 1957—*Sait-on jamais? (No Sun in Venice)* (sc); 1958—*Les Bijoutiers du clair de lune (The Night Heaven Fell)*; 1959—*Les Liaisons dangereuses*; 1960—*Et mourir de plaisir (Blood and Roses)*; 1961—*La Bride sur le cou (Please Not Now!)*; 1962—"L'Orgueil (Pride)" episode of *Les Sept Pechées capitaux (7 Deadly Sins)*; *Le Repos du guerrier (Love on a Pillow)*; 1963—*Le Vice et la vertu (Vice and Virtue)* (+pr); *Château en Suede (Nutty Naughty Chateau)*; 1964—*La Ronde (Circle of Love)* (co-adapt); 1966—*La Curée (The Game Is Over)* (+pr); 1968—"Metzengerstein" episode of *Histoires extraordinaires (Spirits of the Dead)*; *Barbarella*; (as director): 1971—*Pretty Maids All in a Row*; 1972—*Hellé* (+story); 1973—*Don Juan 1973 ou si Don Juan était une femme (Ms. Don Juan)* (+co-sc); 1974—*La Jeune Fille assassinée (Charlotte)* (+pr, sc, ro); 1976—*Une Femme fidèle* (+co-sc); 1979—*Night Games*; 1980—*The Hot Touch*.

Publications:

By VADIM:

Book—*Les Liaisons dangereuses*, script, with Roger Vailland and Claude Brulé, New York 1962; articles—"Pretty Maids" in *Playboy* (Chicago), April 1971; "4 de la forfanterie" by Claude Beylie in *Ecran* (Paris), October 1975; "Conversation with Roger Vadim" in *Oui* (New York), October 1975; "Vadim's Theory on Pic Mayhem, Erotica" in *Variety* (New York), 27 October 1976.

On VADIM:

Books—*Brigitte Bardot and the Lolita Syndrome* by Simone de Beauvoir, London 1961; *The Brigitte Bardot Story* by George Carpozi, Jr., New York 1961; *Roger Vadim* by Maurice Frydland, Paris 1963; *French Cinema Since 1946: Vol.2—The Personal Style"* by Roy Armes, New York 1966; *Jane: An Intimate Biography* by Thomas Kiernan, New York 1973; articles— "Qu'est-ce que la Nouvelle Vague?" by Noël Burch in *Film Quarterly* (Berkeley), winter 1959; "Ban on Vadim" by G. Billard in *Films and Filming* (London), November 1959; "Roger Vadim" by Michel Mardore in *Premier Plan* (Lyon), October 1959; "Pygmalion of Sex" in *New Statesman* (London), 3 September 1960; "The French Fonda" in *Playboy* (Chicago), August 1966; "Blonde Black Panther" in *Time* (New York), 9 September 1966; "Vadim and Zola" by A. Maben in *Films and Filming* (London), October 1966; "Meeting the Gallic Svengali", interview by M. Rosen in *Millimeter* (New York), October 1975.

*   *   *

With *Et...Dieu créa la femme* Roger Vadim created the commercial climate which made the *nouvelle vague* possible. Despite this, his reputation as director has always lagged behind that as a connoisseur of the beautiful women who inhabit his films. His relationships with Brigitte Bardot, Annette Stroybert, Catherine Deneuve, Jane Fonda and others established him, in English-speaking countries at least, as the archetypal "French" director. The American retitling of *Le Repos du guerrier* as *Love on a Pillow*, and *Chateau en Suede* as *Nutty, Naughty Chateau* glumly emphasizes his raffish image.

Vadim claims in his fanciful autobiography that a prostitute provided by producer Raoul Levy to relieve the tedium of screenwriting furnished him with rationale for Bardot's character in *Et...Dieu créa la femme*—unselfishness. "If she's not interested in money, people won't think she's a whore." This motive recurs in Vadim's work, where generous, warm-hearted and sensual women lavish their favors on indifferent, often evil love objects. Fulfilment comes only with death. In *La Jeune Fille assassiné*, Vadim even makes death in the throes of orgasm the sole ambition of his heroine, and his only American film, *Pretty Maids All in a Row*, casts Rock Hudson as an improbable mass-murdering psychiatrist in a girls' college.

For an artist with a single subject, Vadim has proved remarkably imaginative. *Sait-on jamais* exploits Venice with style, the Modern Jazz Quartet's chiming score harmonizing precisely with Vadim's romantic thriller. His lesbian vampire melodrama, *Et mourir de plaisir*, is among the lushest of horror films, enlivened by a clever use of color and a surrealist dream sequence which reminds one that he knew Cocteau and acted in *La Testament d'Orphée*. Jane Fonda never looked more beautiful than in the incest drama *La Curée*, and in *Barbarella* he turned Jean-Claude Forest's comic strip into something between Grand Guignol and an erotic *tableau vivant*.

He is at his best in the high style, as in the melodrama *L'Amour fou*, where the material encourages grand gestures. Bardot in *Le Repos du guerrier* standing like the Winged Victory in a ruined church, face turned into a torrent of wind; Stroyberg in an 18th-century white gown gliding through the cypresses of Hadrian's Villa to Jean Prodromides's score of harp and pizzicati strings in *Et mourir de plaisir*— these are images that briefly transcend the novelettish material from which they spring.

—John Baxter

VANDERBEEK, STAN. American. Born in New York City, 1927. Married; 2 children. Career: early 1960s—begins making collage-films; mid-1960s—builds dome-studio ("the Movie-Drome") in Stony Point, New York; active as university guest lecturer; teaches film courses at State University of New York, Stoneybrook, and The Media Center, Houston (now Institute of the Arts of Rice University); late 1960s—works at Bell Telephone Laboratory, Murray Hill, New Jersey, on experiments in computer graphics; 1970—creates *Violence Sonata*, combining television, live drama, and telephone feedback for Boston WGBH-TV; holds positions as Artist in Television at WGBH-TV and Artist in Residence, Massachusetts Institute of Technology; currently Chairman of the Dept. of Visual Arts, University of Maryland. Recipient: Bronze Medal, Brussels International Experimental Film Competition, for *Mankinda* and *What Who How*, 1958; First Prize in Animation, Bergamo Festival, for *Mankinda*, 1960.

Films: 1957—*What Who How*; *Mankinda*; *Astral Man*; 1957-58—*One and Yet*; 1958—*Ala Mode*; *Wheeeeels No.1*; *Visioniii*; 1959—*Wheeeeels No.2*; *Dance of the Looney Spoons*; *Science Friction*; *Achoo Mr. Keroochev*; *Street Meat* (documentary—not completed); 1960—*Skullduggery*; *Blacks and Whites in Days and Nights*; 1961—*Snapshots of the City*; 1961-62—*Misc. Happenings* (documentaries of Claus Oldenberg happenings); *Summit*; 1964—*Breathdeath*; *Phenomenon No.1*; 1965—*The Human Face Is a Monument*; *Variations No.5*; *Feedback*; 1966—*Poem Field No.2*; 1967—*See, Saw, Seems*; *Poem Field No.1*; *Man and His World*; *Panels for the Walls of the World*; *Poem Field No.5: Free Fall*; *Spherical Space No.1*; *The History of Motion in Motion*; *T.V. Interview*; *Poem Field No.7*; 1968—*Newsreel of Dreams No.1*; *Vanderbeekiana*; *Oh*; *Super-Imposition*; *Will*; 1968-70—*Found Film No.1*; 1969—*Newsreel of Dreams No.2*; 1970—*Film Form No.1*; *Film Form No.2*; *Transforms*; 1972—*Symmetricks*; *Videospace*; *Who Ho Ray No.1*; *You Do, I Do, We Do*; 1973—*Computer Generation*;

1977—*Color Fields*; 1978—*Euclidean Illusions*; 1980—*Mirrored Reason*; *Plato's Cave Inn*; *Dreaming*; 1981—*After Laughter*.

Publications:

By VANDERBEEK:

Articles—"The Cinema Delimina: Films from the Underground" in *Film Quarterly* (Berkeley), summer 1961; "On 'Science Friction'" in *Film Culture* (New York), summer 1961; "If the Actor is the Audience" in *Film Culture* (New York), spring 1962; "Antidotes for Poisoned Movies" in *Film Culture* (New York), summer 1962; "Simple Syllogism" in *Film Culture* (New York), no.29, 1963; "Interview: Chapter One" in *Film Culture* (New York), no.35, 1964/65; "'Culture: Intercom' and Expanded Cinema" in *Film Culture* (New York), spring 1966; "Re: Vision" in *American Scholar* (Washington, D.C.), spring 1966; "Compound Entendre" in *Film: A Montage of Theories* edited by Richard MacCann, New York 1966; "A Statement on Dance and Film" in *Dance Perspectives*, summer 1967; "Movies: Disposable Art" in *Take One* (Montreal), January/February 1969; "Disposable Art—Synthetic Media—and Artificial Intelligence" in *Take One* (Montreal), January/February 1969; "Poem, Notes, and a Letter to Lenny Lipton" in *Film Culture* (New York), winter/spring 1970; "Re Computerized Graphics" in *Film Culture* (New York), no.48-49, 1970; "The Future Is Not What It Used to Be" in *Film Culture* (New York), no.48-49, 1970; "Media (W)rap-around: Or a Man with No Close" in *Filmmakers Newsletter* (Ward Hill, Mass.), March 1971; "Re-Vision" in *Perspectives on the Study of Film* edited by John Katz, Boston 1971; "Social-Imagistics: What the Future May Hold" in *American Film Institute Report*, Washington, D.C. May 1973; "Animation Retrospective" in *Film Comment* (New York), September/October 1977.

On VANDERBEEK:

Book—*A History of the American Avant-Garde*, exhibition catalogue, by John Hanhardt and others, The American Federation of Arts, New York 1976; articles—"Vanderbeek: Master of Animation" by Robert Christgau in *Popular Photography* (Boulder, Colo.), September 1965; "Culture: Intercom" in *Tulane Drama Review* (Louisiana), fall 1966; "Vanderbeek" by Robert Christgau in *Cavalier* (New York), July 1967; "4 Artists as Filmmakers" by A. Manica and W. Van Dyke in *Art in America* (New York), January 1967; "New Talent: the Computer" in *Art in America* (New York), January 1970.

*   *   *

Stan Vanderbeek was born in 1927 in New York City. Typical to a great number of experimental filmmakers, he studied painting before actually beginning his film production. Indeed his earliest films are animated collage pieces which embody his background in graphics (e.g. *Breathdeath*).

Vanderbeek's career now spans about a third of a century, a period of almost constant creativity with extraordinary amalgamations of media. As such, it is a difficult career to summarize, especially in light of the fact that no definitive list of his truly countless productions seems to exist. Vanderbeek appears to exude creations at a rate that escapes even his own cataloguing.

Soon after his early animation work, he was to focus upon a

unique multi-projection apparatus of his own design. This "Movie-Drome" (at Stony Point, New York) provided the presentation of a number of "Vortex-Concerts," prototypes for a satellite-interconnected "Culture Intercom" that might allow better (and quicker) international communication. At the same time, he continued experiments with dance films, paintings, polaroid photography, architecture, 195-degree cinematography, and intermedia events.

However, Vanderbeek's more recent explorations of computer generated images and video graphics not only provide a clear contemporary perspective for his career, but moreover signal a technostructural metamorphosis which marks the ongoing evolution of that major genre generally known as the "experimental film." Experimental filmmakers of Vanderbeek's prestige and prominence have, at times, found the fortune of industry support. In the late 1960s, Vanderbeek came to collaborate with computer specialists like Ken Knowlton of New Jersey's Bell Telephone Laboratories. The result was a number of cathode-ray-tube mosaics called *Poem Fields*. Today these early exercises with computer graphic possibilities still retain aesthetic power as transparent tapestries in electronic metamorphosis. Typically brief, non-narrative and abstract, the various *Poem Fields* often reveal subtle, stunning *mandala* patterns, strikingly similar to classic Asian meditative devices with their symmetrical concentricity.

Vanderbeek's most recent work retains his address of electronically constructed imagery. Some of this work (e.g. *Color Fields*) employs the same painterly interest in abstraction which characterized *Poem Fields*. Others (e.g. *Mirrored Reason*, made in video and released in film) are more representational and narrative. Still others (e.g. *After Laughter*) recall the rapidly paced irony that marked Vanderbeek's earliest animation like *Breathdeath*.

This noteworthy quanity, quality, and extraordinary technological diversity of output has resulted in exceptional institutional support for Vanderbeek throughout the years. He has been artist-in-residence at USC, Colgate, WGBH-TV, and NASA. His work has been presented on CBS, ABC, and such CATV showcases as "Night Flight." His performances outside the United States have taken him to such cities as Berlin, Vienna, Tokyo, Paris, and Toronto; he has been a U.S.I.A. speaker in nations like Israel, Iran, Turkey, Greece, and England. His grants and awards are equally numerous and prestigious.

Finally, his academic recognition has provided Vanderbeek not only with guest lectures and screenings throughout the United States, but faculty appointments at such schools as Columbia, Washington, and M.I.T. He is currently Chairman of the Department of Visual Arts, University of Maryland in Baltimore County, where he continues his dynamic and distinctive creative work.

—Edward S. Small

VAN DYKE, WILLARD. American. Born Willard Ames Van Dyke in Denver, 5 December 1906. Educated University of California. Married Mary Gray Barnett, 2 January 1938 (divorced 1950); children: Alison and Peter; Margaret Barbara Murray Milikin, 17 June 1950; children: Murray and Cornelius. Career: 1934—serves as photographer on WPA Art Project in San Francisco; 1935—works as photographer for *Harper's Bazaar*; 1936-37—works as cameraman on Pare Lorentz's documentary *The River*; 1939—directs *The City*, with Ralph Steiner;

1941-45—serves as producer for Office of War Information's Motion Picture Bureau, and acts as liason officer between OWI and group of Hollywood writers providing scripts for OWI; 1945—*San Francisco* used as the official film on establishment of the United Nations; 1946-65—makes many films for sponsors including the Rockefeller Foundation, Ford Foundation, and for TV—*Omnibus* series and *The 20th Century* series; 1965-73—serves as director of film department of Museum of Modern Art; currently serving as vice-president of International Federation of Film Archives. Address: 505 West End Avenue, New York City 10024.

Films (as director): 1937—*The River* (ph only); 1939—*The City* (co-d, +co-pr, co-ph); 1940—*Valley Town* (+co-sc); *The Children Must Learn* (+sc); *Sarah Lawrence*; *To Hear Your Banjo Play*; *Tall Tales*; 1942—*The Bridge*; 1943—*Oswego*; *Steeltown*; 1944—*Pacific Northwest* (+co-ph); 1945—*San Francisco*; 1946—*Journey into Medicine*; 1947—*The Photographer*; 1948—*Terribly Talented*; 1949—*This Charming Couple*; *Mount Vernon*; 1950—*Years of Change*; 1952—*New York University*; 1953—*Working and Playing to Health*; *There is a Season*; 1954—*Recollections of Boyhood: An Interview with Joseph Welch*; *Cabos Blancos*; *Excursion House*; *Toby and the Tall Corn*; 1957—*Life of the Molds*; 1958—*Skyscraper* (co-d); *Tiger Hunt in Assam*; *Mountains of the Moon*; 1959—*Land of White Alice*; *The Procession*; 1960—*Ireland, the Tear and the Smile*; *Sweden*; 1962—*So That Men Are Free*; *Search into Darkness*; *Harvest*; 1963—*Depressed Area*; 1964—*Rice*; *Frontiers of News*; 1965—*Pop Buell, Hoosier Farmer in Laos*; *Taming the Mekong*; *The Farmer: Feast or Famine* (co-d); *Frontline Cameras 1935-1965*; 1968—*Shape of Things to Come*.

Publications:

By VAN DYKE:

articles— "The Interpretive Camera in Documentary" in *Hollywood Quarterly*, July 1946; "The American Documentary—Limitations and Possibilities: An Interview with Willard Van Dyke" by Edouard De Laurot and Jonas Mekas in *Film Culture* (New York), no.3, 1956; "30 Years of Social Inquiry: An Interview with Willard Van Dyke" by Harrison Engle in *Film Comment* (New York), spring 1965; "Letters from *The River*" in Film Comment (New York), spring 1965; "Interview" by B.L. Kevles in *Film Culture* (New York), fall 1965; "The Role of the Museum of Modern Art in Motion Pictures" in *Film Library Quarterly* (New York), winter 1967/68; "Glancing Backward...Without Nostalgia" by Lora Hays in *Film Library Quarterly* (New York), summer 1971; "Willard Van Dyke" in *Documentary Explorations* edited by G. Roy Levin, Garden City, New York 1971.

On VAN DYKE:

Articles—"Director on Location" in the *Saturday Review* (New York), 10 September 1949; "Focus on Willard Van Dyke" by Art Zuckerman in *Popular Photography* (Boulder, Colorado), April 1965; film—*Conversations with Willard Van Dyke* by Amalie Rothschild, U.S. 1981.

*　　*　　*

During the 1930s and 1940s, an American documentary tradition was established by a group of filmmakers concerned with then-current issues and crises: the Depression-era Dust Bowl (in Pare Lorentz's *The Plow That Broke the Plains*); the destruction of the Mississippi River basin (Lorentz's *The River*); the advantages of electricity in the rural Midwest (Joris Iven's *Power and the Land*); and the construction of oil rigs in the Louisiana swamp (Flaherty's *Louisiana Story*). One of the seminal filmmakers of this period was Willard Van Dyke, who photographed *The River*, and, with Ralph Steiner, made *The City*, a plea for the necessity of city planning.

The City, produced by the American Institute of Planners for screening at the New York World's Fair, is as revelant to 1983 as 1939. The focus is on the need for, and development of, model cities with a stress on human and social considerations. Communities must be livable; they must be by, of, and for people. Van Dyke and Steiner trace the development of modern urban America, with an emphasis on the manner in which city planners had erred in judgement; at the finale, they present an ideal planned community. There is a minimum of narration: scenes of New York City tenements and subways—and, specifically, a sequence in which a man attempts to cross a street in traffic—are ample proof of the filmmakers' argument. While the film's strength remains its visuals, at the same time the soundtrack music (by Aaron Copland) poignantly expresses emotion. As with Virgil Thompson's score for *The River* and Marc Blitzstein's for Van Dyke's next documentary, *Valley Town*, the music is as meaningful as the images or words in communicating ideas and feelings. The New York *Herald-Tribune* reported, weeks after the film's premiere, "Already several thousand persons have seen *The City*, many of whom had never before seen a documentary film, and it may be predicted that its cordial reception by critics and public alike will benefit greatly the already widening beginnings of the documentary form in this country."

In *Valley Town*, a stylized examination of the results of automation on the people in a Pennsylvania steel town, Van Dyke had his narrator serve as the town's mayor, who discusses the problems of his municipality. Rarely were any of his later films as trenchant as his first two. He shot documentaries for a variety of sources, including the Office of War Information (during World War II), the U.S. State Department, the Ford Motor Company, the United Church of Christ, and the television shows *Omnibus*, *High Adventure* and *Twentieth Century*. Van Dyke's subjects ranged from the folk music of Pete Seeger, Josh White and Burl Ives (*To Hear Your Banjo Play*, *Tall Tales*) to the establishment of the United Nations (*San Francisco*); recreational therapy in a mental hospital (*Working and Playing to Health*) to life in Africa (*Tiger Hunt in Assam*, *Mountains of the Moon*) and Appalachia (*Depressed Area, U.S.A.*).

However, Willard Van Dyke's most typical subject matter does relate to the social implications of change, whether again examining the lives of steelworkers (in *Steeltown*), or auto workers (*There Is a Season*), or farmers in Puerto Rican cooperatives (*Cabos Blancos*), or Protestant clergymen (*The Procession*). All have their roots in *The City* and *Valley Town*.

—Rob Edelman

VAN DYKE, W.S. American. Born Woodbridge Strong Van Dyke II in San Diego, California, 21 March 1889 (known by childhood name "Woody"). Career: 1892—makes debut as child actor in San Francisco; 1903-15—besides theatrical activities is miner, electrician, music hall performer and mercenary in Mexico; 1907—following trip to Alaska, joins mother's theatrical

company, "The Laura Winston Players"; also performs with companies of Vin Moore, Del Lawrence and Alexander Pantages; 1915—quits theater to become ass't director for Essanay Studios, Chicago; 1916—introduced to D.W. Griffith, becomes his ass't and close friend; 1917—becomes ass't to James Young at Paramount and begins directing low-budget westerns; 1926—signed by Thalberg for MGM; 1927-28—co-directs *White Shadows in the South Seas* with Robert Flaherty; 1929—leads expedition of over 200 to Africa for filming of *Trader Horn* (Van Dyke is the original of *Carl Denham* in Schoedsack's *King Kong*); 1941—mobilized as Marine Corps officer. Died 4 February 1943.

Films (as assistant director or scenarist): 1915—*The Raven* (ass't d); *A Daughter of the City* (Windom) (sc); 1916—*The Little Girl Next Door* (Windom) (sc); *The Little Shepherd of Bargain Row* (Barthelet) (sc); *Orphan Joyce* (Berthelet) (sc); *The Chaperon* (Berthelet) (co-sc); *The Discard* (Windom) (sc); *The Return of Eve* (Berthelet) (co-sc); *The Primitive Strain* (Berthelet) (sc); *Intolerance* (Griffith) (ass't d); *Oliver Twist* (Young) (ass't d); *Sins of the Parents* (Nichols) (sc); (as director): 1917—*Her Good Name* (+sc); *Clouds*; *Mother's Ordeal* (+sc); *The Land of Long Shadows* (+sc); *The Range Boss* (+sc); *The Open Places* (+sc); *The Men of the Desert* (+sc); *Our Little Nell*; *The Gift o' Gab* (+sc); *Sadie Goes to Heaven* (+sc); 1919—*Lady of the Dugouts* (+co-sc); 1920—*Daredevil Jack* (+co-sc); *The Hawk's Trail* (+co-sc); 1921—*Double Adventure* (+co-sc); *The 40th Door* (unfinished); *The Avenging Arrow* (co-d, +co-sc); 1922—*White Eagle* (co-d, +co-sc); *Ruth of the Range* (d: Warde; Van Dyke directed action scenes); *The Milky Way*; *According to Hoyle*; *Forget Me Not*; *The Boss of Camp 4*; 1923—*The Girl Next Door (You Are in Danger)*; *The Destroying Angel*; *The Miracle Makers*; *Half-a-Dollar Bill*; 1924—*Loving Lies*; *The Battling Fool*; *The Beautiful Sinner*; *Winner Takes All*; *Gold Heels*; 1925—*The Chicago Fire (Barriers Burned Away)*; *Ranger of the Big Pines*; *The Trail Rider*; *Hearts and Spurs*; *The Timber Wolf*; *The Desert's Price*; 1926—*The Gentle Cyclone*; *Eyes of the Totem*; *The Heart of the Yukon* (+co-sc); (as director at Metro-Goldwyn-Mayer): 1926—*War Paint (Rider of the Plains)*; *Winners of the Wilderness*; 1927—*Under the Black Eagle*; *California*; *Foreign Devils*; *The Adventurer (The Gallant Gringo)* (d: Tourjanski; Van Dyke finished film); *Spoilers of the West*; *Wyoming* (+co-sc); *Riders of the Dark* (Grindé) (sc only); 1928—*White Shadows in the South Seas* (co-d); 1929—*The Pagan*; 1931—*Trader Horn* (+co-dialogue); *Guilty Hands*; *Never the Twain Shall Meet*; *The Cuban Love Song (Rumba)*; 1932—*Tarzan the Ape Man*; *Night Court (Justice for Sale)*; 1933—*Penthouse*; *The Prizefighter and the Lady (Every Woman's Man)* (+co-pr); *Eskimo (Mala the Magnificent)* (+co-sc); 1934—*Laughing Boy*; *Manhattan Melodrama*; *The Thin Man*; *Hide Out*; *The Painted Veil* (d: Boleslawski; Van Dyke finished film); *Forsaking All Others*; 1935—*Naughty Marietta*; *I Live My Life*; *A Tale of 2 Cities* (co-d; Van Dyke replaced Jack Conway); *Rose Marie*; 1936—*His Brother's Wife (Lady of the Tropics)* (+pr); *San Francisco* (+co-pr); *The Devil Is a Sissy (The Devil Takes the Count)*; *Love on the Run*; *After the Thin Man (Nick, Gentleman Detective)*; 1937—*Personal Property (Man in Possession)*; *They Gave Him a Gun*; *The Prisoner of Zenda* (Cromwell and Cukor; Van Dyke directed action scenes); *Rosalie*; 1938—*Marie Antoinette* (Julien Duvivier directed Revolution scenes); *Sweethearts*; *Stand Up and Fight*; 1939—*It's a Wonderful World*; *Andy Hardy Gets Spring Fever*; *Another Thin Man*; *I Take This Woman* (film begun in 1938 by von Sternberg, then Borzage as *New York Cinderella*); 1940—*I Love You Again*; *Bitter Sweet*; 1941—*Rage in Heaven*; *The Feminine Touch*; *Shadow of the Thin Man*; *Dr. Kildare's Victory (The Doctor and the Debu-*

tante); *I Married an Angel*; *Cairo*; *Journey for Margaret*; 1943— *Dragon Seed* (completed by Jack Conway and Harold Bucquet).

Publications:

By VAN DYKE:

Book—*Horning into Africa*, Los Angeles 1931; articles—"Dans les Mers du Sud avec le char de soleil" in *Ciné Magazine* (Paris), March 1930; "From Horse Opera to Epic" in *Cue* (New York), 16 March 1935; "The Motion Picture and the Next War" in *Hollywood Reporter*, 8 June 1936; "Rx for a Thin Man" in *Stage* (New York), January 1937; "Addio alle avventure" in *Cinema* (Rome), no.24, 1937.

On VAN DYKE:

Books—*Van Dyke and the Mythical City of Hollywood* by Robert Cannom, Culver City, California 1948; *The Lion's Share: The M-G-M Story* by Bosley Crowther, New York 1957; *Thalberg, Life and Legend* by Bob Thomas, New York 1969; articles—"He Brings 'Em Back in Cans" by Jerome Beatty in *American*, August 1934; "Van Dyke—Lord Fauntleroy in Hollywood" by Alva Johnston in *New Yorker*, 28 September 1935; "Van Dyke's Choice Locations" by F. Condon in *Collier's* (New York), 18 May 1935; "Hollywood Helmsmen: W.S. Van Dyke and Frank Capra" by Cornelia Penfield in *Stage* (New York), 13 April 1936; "Van Dyke, the Unorthodox" by B. Rodgers in *Cinema Progress* (New York), August 1937; "Storia di Van Dyke II" by Domenico Meccoli in *Cinema* (Rome), 24 April 1938; obituary in *Time* (New York), 15 February 1943; "Damn the Crocodiles, Keep the Camera Rolling!" by Byron Riggan in *American Heritage* (New York), June 1968; "Up From Assistant Director" by Lesley Selander in *Action* (Los Angeles), January/-February 1971; "Woody S. Van Dyke et l'âge d'or d'Hollywood" by Hervé Dumont in *Travelling* (Lausanne), no.37, 1973; "W.S. Van Dyke (1889-1943)" by H. Dumont in *Anthologie du cinéma* (Paris), July/September 1975.

*   *   *

The one thing that best characterizes the style of W.S. Van Dyke is exemplified by his famous nickname, "One Take" Van Dyke. Known for the speed and economy such an epithet indicates, Van Dyke was the unofficial "house director" at Metro-Goldwyn-Mayer for most of his career. Because he died before the collapse of the studio system, he did not face the economic constraints many former MGM directors, accustomed to lavish budgets, were forced to deal with during the 1950s. Based on his record for swift and skillful set-ups, and his experience directing series films which involved a recurring set of characters, he presumably would not only have survived the collapse of the studios, but might also have become one of the biggest names in television. As it is, his career stands as a tribute to the studio system and what it could turn out in as little as three weeks. His films not only pleased those who saw them upon initial release, but they continue to delight new audiences today with their careless charm.

Van Dyke is not an artist. His work is sometimes downright sloppy, with poorly matched cuts and an improvisational quality that is more desperate than deliberate. However, he was a confident craftsman, and his best films are pure fun. Whether he

worked with a typical Metro big budget (as in *Marie Antoinette*) or found himself with less money and time (the *Thin Man* films), he stressed story and character, and getting the job done without sacrificing too much of the Metro gloss. He became a favorite with studio bosses, and directed some of MGM's most successful series film, among them the first Johnny Weismuller/Maureen O'Sullivan Tarzan film, *Tarzan the Ape Man*, and the first Nelson Eddy/Jeanette MacDonald pairing, *Naughty Marietta*. He also directed an Andy Hardy, a Dr. Kildare, and several others in the Eddy/MacDonald series. He is generally given credit for the idea of casting William Powell and Myrna Loy as Nick and Nora Charles in the first *Thin Man* movie, which he directed along with several others in the series.

Van Dyke's first movie (circa 1917) taught him the out-in-the-field improvisational filmmaking of the silent era. When he became a contract director at MGM, he was able to use these skills, as in his 1926 costume film, *Winners of the Wilderness*, one of Joan Crawford's first starring vehicles. It is an effective combination of location shooting, action sequences, and lavish costume drama built around a beautiful female star. Such movies as *White Shadows of the South Seas*, *Trader Horn*, and *Eskimo* continued his penchant for out-of-door filming, and for the fresh, open quality such movie-making required.

The interesting thing about Van Dyke's career is that, given the restrictions of working at MGM during the 1930s, he never lost his breezy, off-hand approach to films. Although he seemed willing to assume any assignment, and his overall work does not add up to a personal cinema, he was adept at directing the great female stars that MGM had under contract during those years. He was able to make significant contributions to their personae by seeing in them qualities that were the opposite of those that had originally brought them stardom. For instance, instead of restricting Myrna Loy to roles as an exotic, Oriental beauty, he suggested her for the lead in a modern comedy, helping her to reveal her "good pal" side in order to play the perfect wife of *The Thin Man*. The serious side of Jean Harlow, whose intelligence he respected, and the comic side of Joan Crawford were explored in *Personal Property* and *Love on the Run*, respectively. Norma Shearer's experience as a silent film actress was allowed to flower in the final scenes of *Marie Antoinette*, as he saw her as being more than just a glamorous clothes horse. He also helped turn the unlikely combination of Nelson Eddy and Jeanette MacDonald into one of the most successful screen teams in the history of musical films.

Van Dyke is more or less a forgotten director today. Yet his films are revived regularly, and as Andrew Sarris correctly perceived in *American Cinema*, "he made more good movies than his reputation for carelessness and haste would indicate." Van Dyke made entertainment films, not art, but he is a perfect example of a man who could survive in the studio system. His films are unique, in that they have stood the test of time without having stood the test of the art form.

—Jeanine Basinger

VAN PEEBLES, MELVIN. American. Born Melvin Peebles in Chicago, 1932. Educated at Ohio Wesleyan. Career: military service in Air Force as navigator on B-47; mid-1950s—earns living as cable car grip in San Francisco; paints, writes book with photos about experience working on cable cars; also works in post office; 1958—having made short films in San Francisco, approaches several Hollywood producers; 1959—moves to New York, then begins graduate studies in astronomy, Holland; early

1960s—moves to Paris at invitation of Mary Meerson and Lotte Eisner who had chanced to see his early shorts; makes short film *500 balles*; begins writing novels in French after learning that French authors have right to adapt own works as screenplays; signed by Edouard Luntz as technical advisor; 1967—visits U.S. as French delegate to San Francisco Film Festival; contracted by Columbia to make *Watermelon Man*; 1968—first feature released in France, *The Story of a 3-Day Pass*; 1970—invests salary from *Watermelon Man* in privately-financed *Sweet Sweetback's Baadasssss Song*; 1970s—directs and writes stage productions including *Ain't Supposed to Die a Natural Death*; 1981—adapts John Williams's novel *Sophisticated Gents* for NBC-TV mini-series; 1982—writes book and songs for, directs, produces and stars in *Waltz of the Stork* on Broadway. Business: Yeah, Inc., 850 7th Avenue, suite 1206, New York, NY 10019.

Films (as director, scriptwriter and composer): 1968—*La Permission (The Story of a 3-Day Pass)* (co-composer); 1970—*Watermelon Man* (d and co-composer only); 1971—*Sweet Sweetback's Baadasssss Song* (+pr, ed, ro); 1977—*Greased Lightning* (co-sc only).

Publications:

By VAN PEEBLES:

Articles—interview by J. Euvrard in *Image et son* (Paris), February 1980; interview by S. Le Peron in *Cahiers du cinéma* (Paris), February 1980.

On VAN PEEBLES:

Articles—"Van Peebles Story" by Hollis Alpert in *Saturday Review* (New York), 3 August 1968; "Story of a 3-Day Pass" in *Ebony* (Chicago), September 1968; "An Afro-American in Paris: The Films of Melvin Van Peebles" by Charles Peavy in *Cineaste* (New York), summer 1969; "On the Scene: Melvin Van Peebles" in *Playboy* (Chicago), September 1970; "Sweet Song of Success" in *Newsweek* (New York), 21 June 1971; "The Decolonizer of the Black Mind" by M. Rubine in *Show* (Hollywood), July 1971.

*   *   *

Melvin Van Peebles is an extremely talented filmmaker. He can direct, write, act; he can compose music and produce and, last but most assuredly not least, promote. Unfortunately, his filmography is pitifully thin: he has directed only three features in 15 years. His last, *Sweet Sweetback's Baadasssss Song*, is a milestone in the histories of both black and independent cinemas. The film is one of the all time top-grossing, independently produced features, proof that a filmmaker can reap profits while working completing outside the studio system. Even more impressively—although some might prefer distressingly—*Sweetback* almost singlehandedly created the black exploitation genre of the early 1970s.

Van Peebles is a hustler, a nonconformist who has, out of choice, worked outside the mainstream. It is not surprising that early in his career Van Peebles abandoned the United States for Europe, where he wrote novels and directed his first film, *The Story of a Three-Day Pass*, about a black American GI and his affair with a French shopgirl. Earlier, Van Peebles had attempted

to find employment in Hollywood, but had only been offered jobs sweeping floors. In France, he was allowed a director's card because the film was based on his novel and writers are allowed the privilege of directing adaptations of their own work.

Van Peebles's second film, *Watermelon Man*, the outrageous story of a white bigot who turns black, was made for Columbia Pictures. *Watermelon Man*, however, is almost reactionary when compared to *Sweetback*, on which Van Peebles is credited as writer, composer, editor, producer, promoter, distributor and star.

In the early 1970s, Hollywood was belatedly discovering a previously untapped audience: blacks. Major studios came out with entertaining cops-and-robbers adventures (*Cotton Comes to Harlem*), exciting private eye dramas (*Shaft*) and touching Depression-era weepers (*Sounder*). All were fashioned for black viewers, while remaining inoffensive to whites. Van Peebles made *Sweetback* totally outside the confines of the white studio system, utilizing his *Watermelon Man* salary, a bank loan, and $50,000 from Bill Cosby. In *Sweetback*, the title tells all: the film unfolds completely in a black milieu, and from a totally black point of view, with Van Peebles evoking a militant, violent sensibility unallowable in a Columbia or Paramount production. He stars as Sweetback, a pimp and stud, an outsider populating a gritty landscape of violence and graphic, raw sex. The character beats up a pair of white policemen, mashing their heads with their own handcuffs. He wins a sex stamina contest against a Hell's Angels hoodlum. (Van Peebles, in fact, claimed to have come down with gonorrhea after filming a "love scene.") Ultimately, he survives by outwitting the honky world and making it across the Mexican border at the finale. A message then appears on screen: "Watch out, a baadasssss nigger is coming back to collect some dues."

Van Peebles himself admitted that his two earlier films, although focusing on blacks, were essentially "white" films lacking any real black sensibility. So *Sweetback* is a first. It does glorify the unsavory aspects of ghetto streetlife, and its hero is a shoddy role-model; the film is a reverse-racist diatribe in that it depicts blacks as "bad," whites as fools, with nothing in between. Unsurprisingly, the film was either ignored or critically roasted in the white media, and condemned by many in the black community.

Audiences, however, loved *Sweetback*. Shot for $500,000, it grossed $14-million—despite the absence of the major studio publicity machine. At one point it was the nation's number one box office attraction, even outgrossing *Love Story*. And it spawned an entire cinematic genre, from *Black Belt Jones* and *Foxy Brown* to *Willie Dynamite*.

Since *Sweetback*, Van Peebles has fashioned several Broadway productions. His *Ain't Supposed to Die a Natural Death* and *Don't Play Us Cheap*, though earning mixed reviews, garnered a total of 11 Tony Award nominations. While black exploitation movies have, thankfully, lost their appeal, it is not gratuitous to say that the theater's gain is still the cinema's loss.

—Rob Edelman

VARDA, AGNÈS. Belgian. Born in Brussels, 30 May 1928. Educated in literature and psychology at the Sorbonne, Paris; studied art history at the Ecole du Louvre; took classes in photography at night school. Married director Jacques Demy; children: Rosalie and Mathieu. Career: 1947—while student becomes stage photographer for Theater Festival of Avignon; when festival's director Jean Vilar made head of Theatre National Popu-laire, Paris, hires Varda as photographer; commissioned to do a number of magazine photo stories; 1954—directing debut with *La Pointe courte*; 1955—accompanies Chris Marker to China as advisor for *Dimanche à Pekin*; 1968—directs 2 shorts in U.S., subsequently works both in California and France; 1977—founds production company Ciné-Tamaris to produce *One Sings, the Other Doesn't*. Recipient: Prix Méliès for *Cléo de 5 à 7*, 1961; Prix Louis Delluc for *Le Bonheur*, 1966; Special Award, Berlin Festival, for *Le Bonheur*, 1966.

Films (as director): 1954—*La Pointe courte* (+pr, sc); 1957—*O saisons, o châteaux* (documentary short); 1958—*L'Opera-Mouffe* (short); *Du côté de la Côte (short)*; 1961—*Cléo de cinq à sept* (+sc); 1963—*Salut les Cubains (Salute to Cuba)* (+text—short documentary); 1965—*Le Bonheur* (+sc); 1966—*Les Créatures*; 1967—*Uncle Yanco*; episode of *Loin du Vietnam (Far From Vietnam)*; 1968—*Black Panthers (Huey)* (documentary); 1969—*Lion's Love* (+pr); 1970—*Nausicaa* (for TV); 1971—*Last Tango in Paris* (Bertolucci) (co-dialogue only); 1975—*Daguerrotypes* (+pr); *Réponses de femmes* (8mm); 1977—*L'Une chante l'autre pas (One Sings, the Other Doesn't)*; 1978—*Lady Oscar* (Demy) (pr only); 1980—*Mur Murs (Wall Walls, Mural Murals)* (+pr); 1981—*Documenteur: An Emotion Picture* (+pr);

Publications:

By VARDA:

Articles—"*Cleo de 5 a 7*: Script Extract" in *Films and Filming* (London), December 1962; "Pasolini—Varda—Allio—Sarris—Michelson" in *Film Culture* (New York), fall 1966; "Le Bonheur" in *Cinema* (Beverly Hills), December 1966; "The Underground River", interview by Gordon Gow in *Films and Filming* (London), March 1970; "Mother of the New Wave", interview by J. Levitin in *Women and Film* (Santa Monica), v.1, no.5-6, 1974; "One Sings, the Other Doesn't", interview by R. McCormick in *Cineaste* (New York), winter 1977/78; "Agnès Varda Sings", interview by Yang Yu Ying in *Take One* (Montreal), November 1977; interview by M. Martin in *Ecran* (Paris), May 1977; "L'Une chante, l'autre pas", interview by J. Narboni and others in *Cahiers du cinéma* (Paris), May 1977; interview by N. Dugal and V. Godard in *Cine* (Mexico), December 1978; interview by P. Carcassonne and J. Fieschi in *Cinématographe* (Paris), March/April 1981.

On VARDA:

Book—*French Cinema Since 1946: Vol.2—The Personal Style* by Roy Armes, New York 1966; articles—"Agnès Varda" by P. Strick in *Film* (London), spring 1963; "Notes on Women Directors" by J. Pyros in *Take One* (Montreal), November/December 1970; article in *Current Biography Yearbook 1970*, New York 1971; "The Left Bank Revisited" by Richard Roud in *Sight and Sound* (London), summer 1977; "Les Chardons ardents d'Agnès Varda" by Claude Beylie in *Ecran* (Paris), 15 April 1979.

* * *

Agnès's Varda's startlingly individualistic films have earned her the title "grandmother of the New Wave" of French filmmak-ing. Her statement that a filmmaker must exercise as much

freedom as a novelist became a mandate for New Wave directors, especially Chris Marker and Alain Resnais. Varda's first film, *La Pointe courte*, edited by Resnais, is regarded, as Georges Sadoul affirms, as "the first film of the French *nouvelle vauge*. Its interplay between conscience, emotions, and the real world make a direct antecedent of *Hiroshima, mon amour*."

The use of doubling, and twin story lines; the personification of objects; the artistic determination of cinematic composition, color, texture, form, and time; and the correlation of individual subjectivity to societal objectivity to depict socio-political issues are denominators of Varda's films, which she writes, produces, and directs.

While pursuing art studies and work, Varda made her first film, *La Pointe Courte*, inspired by Faulkner's novel *The Wild Palms*. The film tells two stories: a couple visit a seaport trying to save their failing marriage, while local fishermen struggle against the domination of large fisheries. Charles Ford (*Femmes cinéastes*, p. 110) comments: "The slow action, the imperfect rhythm, the refinement of the psychological discussions excited the critics. Varda has a penetrating feel for point-of-view, announcing a talented filmmaker."

Varda made three documentaries in 1957-8. The best of these was *L'Opera-Mouffe*, portraying the Mouffetard district of Paris, as seen by Varda, who was then pregnant. Segments of the film are prefaced by handwritten intertitles, a literary element Varda is fond of using.

In 1961-2, Varda began but did not complete two film projects: *La Cocotte d'azur* and *Melangite*. Her next film, *Cléo de cinq à sept*, records the time a pop singer waits for results of her exam for cancer. Varda used physical time in *Cleo*: events happening at the same tempo as they would in actual life. The film is divided into chapters, using Tarot cards which symbolize fate. Varda next photographed 4,000 still photos of Castro's revolution-in-progress, resulting in *Salute to Cuba*.

Le Bonheur is considered Varda's most stunning and contro-versial achievement. Critics were puzzled and pleased. Of her first color film, Varda says it was "essentially a pursuit of the palette...Psychology takes first place." A young carpenter lives with his wife and children. Then he takes a mistress; when his wife drowns, his mistress takes her place. The film was com-mended for its superb visual beauties, the use of narrative in *le nouveau roman* literary pattern, and its tonal contrasts and spatial configurations. Critics continue to debate the film's theme.

Elsa is an essay portraying authors Elsa Triolet and her hus-band Louis Aragon. *Les Creatures* uses a black and white with red color scheme in a fantasy-thriller utilizing an inside-outside plot that mingles real and unreal events. As in *La Pointe courte*, a young couple retreat to a rural locale. The pregnant wife is mute, due to an accident. Her husband is writing a book. He meets a recluse who operates a machine forcing people to behave as his or her subconscious would dictate. The wife gives birth, regaining her speech.

Visiting the United States, Varda and her husband Jacques Demy each made a film. Varda honored her *Uncle Janco* in the film so named. *The Black Panthers* (or *Huey*) followed. Both documentaries were shown at the London Film Festival in 1968. She next directed a segment of the anti-war short, *Far From Vietnam*.

Using an American setting and an English-speaking cast, including the co-authors of the musical *Hair*, Varda made *Lions Love* in Hollywood. This jigsaw-puzzle work includes a fake suicide, and images of a TV set reporting Robert Kennedy's assassination. G. Roy Levin declared that it was hard to distin-guish between the actual and the invented film realities. *Nausicaa* dealt with Greeks living in France. Made for television, it was not shown, Varda says, because it was against military-ruled Greece.

In 1971, Varda helped write the script for *Last Tango in Paris*. Varda's involvement in the women's movement began about 1972; a film dealing with feminist issues, *Réponses de femmes*, has yet to be shown. Made for German television, *Daguerreotypes* has no cast. Varda filmed the residents and shops of the Rue Daguerre, a tribute to L.J.M. Daguerre.

In 1977, Varda made *One Sings, the Other Doesn't* and established her own company, Ciné-Tamaris, to finance it. This "family" of workers created the film. Chronicling the friendship of two women over 15 years, it earned mixed reviews, some referring to it as feminist propaganda or as sentimental syrup. But Varda, narrating the film and writing the song lyrics, does not impose her views. In *One Sings*, she wanted to portray the happiness of being a woman, she says. With three decades of filmmaking experience, Varda's reputation as a filmmaker dazzles and endures.

—Louise Heck-Rabi

VASILIEV, SERGEI AND GEORGI. Soviet. Georgi Nikolaievitch Vasiliev born in Vologda, 25 November 1899; Sergei Dmitrievitch Vasiliev born in Moscow, 4 December 1900. Though not related, they came to be known as the Vasiliev brothers because of a shared surname and because they worked together. Georgi educated at technical institute, Warsaw, and theatre course in Moscow 1922-23; Sergei educated in filmmaking, Moscow. Career: 1917—Sergei takes part in storming of the Winter Palace, serves in Red Army after 1917; 1918-22—Georgi serves with Red Army; 1922-23—Georgi active as journalist and film critic while attending school; Sergei joins Sevzapkino as film editor; 1924-29—Georgi works as film editor for Goskino studios; 1928—Goskino and Sevzapkino merged, the brothers find themselves working together; first film assembled from documentary footage brought back by Soviet parties sent to Arctic to attempt rescue of party lost with dirigible *Italia*; 1930—direct first film; 1944—Sergei becomes administrator at Lenfilm Studios; 1955—Sergei directs *The Heroes of Shipka*; 1965—Council of Ministers of the RSFSR creates a prize for artistic achievement named for the Vasiliev brothers. Georgi Vasiliev died 8 June 1946; Sergei Vasiliev died 16 December 1959. Recipient: Order of Lenin, 1935; Georgi named Artist of Merit of the RSFSR, 1940; State Prize for *Chapayev*, 1941; State Prize for *The Defense of Tsaritsyn*, 1942; Order of the Red Star for *The Front*, 1944; bronze medal, Venice Festival, for *Chapayev*, 1946; Sergei named People's Artist of the U.S.S.R., 1948; best direction for *Heroes of Chipka*, Cannes Festival, 1955.

Films (as directors and scriptwriters): 1928—*Podvig vo idach (An Exploit on the Ice, The Ice-Breaker Krassnin)* (d only); 1930—*The Sleeping Beauty (The Woman of the Sleeping Forest, La Belle au bois dormant)* (co-sc); 1932—*A Personal Affair (A Personal Matter, Une Affaire personnelle)* (d only); 1934—*Chapayev*; 1937—*Volochayevskiye dni (The Days of Volochayev, Far East, Intervention in the Far East, Les Jours de Volotchaïev)*; 1942—*Oborona Tsaritsina (The Defense of Tsaritsyn, La Défense de Tsaritsyne)*; 1943—*Front (The Front)*; (Sergei directing alone): 1954—*Geroite na Shipka (The Heroes of Shipka, Les Héros de Chipka)* (d only); 1958—*Oktiabr' dni (October Days, The Days of October, Les Jours d'Octobre)* (co-sc).

Publications:

By the VASILIEVS:

Books—*Chapayev*, Moscow 1936; *Tchapaïev, La Défense de Tsaritsyne, Les Jours de Volotchaïev* in *Scénarios choisis du cinéma soviétique* vol.2, Paris 1951.

On the VASILIEVS:

Articles—"Les Frères Vassiliev" by E. Schmulevitch in *Avant-Scène du cinéma* (Paris), 1 and 15 January 1977; "Les Frères Vassiliev" by Eric Schmulévitch in *Anthologie du cinéma* vol.10, 1979; "Brat'ja Vasil'evy: put' i metod" by D. Pisarevsky in *Iskusstvo Kino* (Moscow), November 1980.

VERNEUIL, HENRI. French. Born Achod Malakian in Rodosto, Turkey, 15 October 1920. Educated in civil engineering, Ecole Nationale des Arts et des Métiers, Marseilles, degree 1943. Married Françoise Bonnot, 1961; children: Patrick and Sophie. Career: after war works as journalist and in radio; film critic for Marseilles radio station; 1947—directs first short, *Escale au soleil*; 1951—feature directing debut, *La Table au crèves*, initiates period of collaboration with actor Fernandel; 1963—*Weekend à Zuydcoote* leads to Hollywood offer; makes *The Battle of San Sebastian* with Anthony Quinn; 1979—beginning with *I...comme Icare* produces as well as directs.

Films (as director of shorts): 1947-51—*Escale au soleil; Entre deux trains; Fantaisies pour clarinette; Compositeurs et chansons de Paris; L'Art d'être courtier; Maldonne; Kermesse aux chansons; Musique tropicale; On demande un bandit; Les Nouveaux Misérables; Un Curieux Cas d'amnèsie; La Légende de Terre Blanche; A qui le bébé?; Pipe, chien; A la culotte de zouave; Les Chansons s'envolent; Cuba à Montmartre; Rhythmes de Paris; Un Jurébavard; 33e chambre; Avedis Aharonian, le dernier président arménien; Une Journée avec Jacques Hélian et son orchestre; Variétés; Paris mélodies*; (as assistant director): 1949—*Véronique* (Vernay); (as director): 1951—*La Table aux crèves*; 1952—*Brelan d'as; Le Fruit défendu; Le Boulanger de Valorgue*; 1953—*Carnaval; L'Ennemi public no.1*; 1954—*Le Mouton à cinq pattes; Les Amants du Tage*; 1955—*Des gens sans importance*; 1956—*Paris Palace Hôtel* (+co-sc); 1957—*Une Manche et la belle*; 1958—*Maxime* (+co-sc); *Le Grand Chef*; 1959—*La Vache et le prisonnier*; 1960—*L'Affaire d'une nuit*; "L'Adultère" episode of *La Française et l'amour; Le Président*; 1961—*Les Lions sont lâchés*; 1962—*Un Singe en hiver; Mélodie en sous-sol*; 1963—*Cent Mille Dollars au soleil* (+co-sc); 1964—*Week-end à Zuydcoote*; 1966—*La Vingt-cinquième heure (The 25th Hour)* (+co-sc); 1967—*La Bataille de San Sebastian*; 1969—*Le Clan des Siciliens* (+co-sc); 1971—*Le Casse*; 1972—*Le Serpent* (+co-sc); 1974—*Peur sur la ville* (+co-sc); 1976—*Le Corps de mon ennemi* (+co-sc); 1979—*I...comme Icare* (+sc, ro); 1981—*Mille Milliards de dollars* (+sc).

Publications:

By VERNEUIL:

Interview in *Amis du film*, April 1982.

On VERNEUIL:

Book—*V... comme Verneuil* by Christian Rousso, with interviews, Paris 1981; film—*Portrait d'Henri Verneuil* directed by André Halimi, for TV, France 1981.

* * *

After his studies at the School of Industrial Arts in Aix-en-Provence, Verneuil began to work as a journalist. Interested by the cinema, he soon went to Paris where, from 1947 to 1951, he made several short films which honed his professional technique.

More than anything else, it was meeting Fernandel, who appeared in Verneuil's first film, *Escale au soleil*, which proved decisive for his film career. In 1951 he made his first feature, *La Table aux crèves*, with Fernandel, based on the novel by Marcel Aymé; then *Brelan d'as*, with Michel Simon in the role of Maigret. The collaboration with Fernandel continued with *Le Fruit défendu*, and in Verneuil's next three films. In 1954 he offered the great comedian six different roles in *Le Mouton à cinq pattes*. To this series of films he added *Le Grand Chef* in 1958 and *La Vache et le prisonnier* in 1959. Fernandel's playfulness lends this film a humor and *drôllerie*, and it's among Verneuil's best efforts.

In the course of his films, Verneuil developed and set his own style, based on the choice and direction of the great actors, applying in France the recipes of the American cinema. His scenarios, taken for the most part from literary works, elaborately embroidered, are rendered infallible by his collaboration with the best scriptwriters. Having mastered a narrative technique founded in the classical tradition, he addresses himself to a mass audience in productions that are frequently international.

With *Le Président*, based on a Simenon novel, the Jean Gabin era began. The director entrusted him with other great roles in the psychological drama *Un Singe en hiver* at the side of Belmondo, and in the crime comedy *Mélodie en sous-sol*, with Alain Delon, where Gabin gave proof of his remarkable talent. This last film became a classic of the genre.

Cent Mille Dollars au soleil charmed part of the public with its aspect of adventure, but the intellectual critics continued to reproach the director for his commercial side as well as his reliance on stars. The success of *Mélodie en sous-sol*, as well as that of *Weekend à Zuydcoote*, with Belmondo, earned him an invitation to Hollywood. He directed the Occupation drama *La Vingt-cinquième Heure* in 1966 and *La Bataille de San Sebastian*, done in Mexico, the following year, both starring Anthony Quinn.

Returning to France, he made *Le Clan des Siciliens*, a crime and adventure film played by the trio Gabin, Delon, and Lino Ventura, which became one of his greatest successes. True to his conception of a cinema of spectacle and entertainment, he added to his oeuvre *Le Serpent*, which had international distribution. Next came *Peur sur la ville* in 1974, further enriching the Belmondo series. In the two following films, for which he also served as producer, *I...comme Icare* with Montand in 1979, and *Mille Milliards de dollars* with Patrick Dewaere in 1981, he treated the difficult themes of submission to authority and the power of international capitalism.

Television, which he had always avoided, then devoted to his work a program, and critics began to discover more than ambitions in this director, which his success before the public had made, in fact, a reality.

—Karel Tabery

VERTOV, DZIGA. Russian. Born Denis Arkadievitch Kaufman in Byalistok, Poland (then annexed to Russia), 2 January 1896. Educated at the music academy in Byalistok, Poland, 1912-1915; also attended medical school in St. Petersburg/Petrograd, 1916-17. Married Elizoveta Svilova. Career: 1915—Kaufman family moves to Moscow; 1915-17—while attending medical school in St. Petersburg/Petrograd, he sets up a lab for the study of sound; 1916—becomes involved with Futurists and other avant-garde artistic groups; 1917—adopts pseudonym "Dziga Vertov," which translates roughly as "spinning top"; becomes editor and writer for newsreel section of Moscow Cinema Committee; 1919—makes his 1st personal film, compilation documentary *Godovshchina revoliutsiya (Anniversary of the Revolution)*; publishes Kinoks-Revolution Manifesto, a position paper against fiction films and for reportage-type films; 1921—organizes film activities on agit-steamboats and agit-trains, which spread the government's message by bringing newsreels and films to outlying areas; 1922—begins developing theory of "Kino-Glaz" (Kino-Eye); 1922-25—works on *Kino-pravda* and *Goskinokalender* newsreel series; 1924—wife begins to collaborate with him on various compilation films; 1931—makes his 1st sound film, *Entuziazm: Simfoniia Donbassa (Enthusiasm: Symphony of the Don Basin)*; 1937—makes his last feature length film, *Kolibel'naya (Lullaby)*; 1947-54—directs the newsreel series *Novosti dnia*. Died 1954.

Films (as co-director): 1918-19—*Kino-Nedelia (Weekly Reels)* series, no. 1-43 (according to Sadoul, he did not take part in the production of no.38-42); (as director): 1919—*Godovshchina revoliutsiya (Anniversary of the Revolution)* (+ed); *Protsess Mironova (The Trial of Mironov)*; *Vskrytie moschei Sergeia Radonezhskogo (Exhumation of the Remains of Sergius of Radonezh)*; 1920—*Boi pod Tsaritsinom (Battle for Tsaritsin)* (+ed); *Vserusski starets Kalinin (All Russian Elder Kalinin)*; *Instruktorii Parokhod 'Krasnaia Zvezda' (Instructional Steamer 'Red Star')*; 1921—*Agitpoezd VTsIK (The VTIK Train, Agit-Train of the Central Committee)*; 1922—*Istoriia grazhdenskoi voini (History of the Civil War)* (+ed); *Protsess Eserov (Trial of the Social Revolutionaries)*; *Univermag (Department Store)*; 1922-23—*Kino-pravda (Cinema-Truth, Film-Truth)* series, no.1-23; 1923-25—*Goskinokalender* series, no.1-53; *Sevodiya (Today)*; 1924—*Sovetskie igrushki (Soviet Toys)*; *Iumoreski (Humoresques)*; *Daesh vozkukh (Give Us Air)*; *Khronika-molniya (Newsreel-Lightning)*; *Kino-glaz (Kino-Eye)*; 1925—*Zagranichnii pokhod sudov Baltiiskogo flota kreisere 'Aurora' i uchebnogo sudna 'Komsomolts,' August 8, 1925*; *The 7th Anniversary of the Red Army*; 1926—*Shagai, Soviet! (Stride, Soviet!)*; *Shestaya chast' mira (A Sixth of the World)*; 1928—*Odinnadtsatii (The 11th Year)*; 1929—*Chelovek s kinoapparatom (The Man With a Movie Camera)*; 1931—*Entuziazm: Simfoniia Donbassa (Enthusiasm: Symphony of the Don Basin)*; 1934—*Tri pensi o Lenine (3 Songs of Lenin)*; 1937—*Kolibel'naya (Lullaby)* (+narration); *Pamyati Sergo Ordzhonikidze* (In Memory of Sergo Ordzhonikidze); *Sergo Ordzhonikidze* (co-d); 1938—*Slava Sovetskim Geroiniam (Famous Soviet Heroes)*; *Tri geroini (3 Heroines)* (+co-sc); 1941—*Krov' za krov', smert' za smert': slodeianiya Nemetsko-Fashistkih zakhvatchikov na territorii C.C.C.P. mi ne zabudem (Blood for Blood, Death for Death)*; *Soiuzkinozhurnal No. 77*; *Soiuzkinozhurnal No. 87*; 1943—*Tebe, Front: Kazakhstan Front (For You at the Front: The Kazakhstan Front)*; 1944—*V gorakh Ala-Tau (In the Mountains of Ala-Tau)*; *Kliatva molodikh (Youth's Oath, The Oath of Youth)*; 1944-54—*Novosti dnia* series (contributed various issues through 1954).

Publications:

By VERTOV:

Books—*Statii, dnevniki, zamysly* edited by S. Drobashenko, Moscow 1966; *Dsiga Wertow: aus den Tagebüchern*, edited by Peter Konlechner and Peter Kubelka, Vienna 1967; *Articles, Journaux, Projects*, edited and translated by Sylviane and Andree Robel, Paris 1972; articles—"Iz rabochikh tetradei Dziga Vertov" in *Iskusstvo Kino* (Moscow), no.4, 1957; "Tvorcheskaya deyatel'nost'" G.M. Boltyanskogo" in *Iz Istorii Kino* (Moscow), no.2, 1959; "Vespominaiia o s'emkakh V.I. Lenin" in *Iz Istorii Kino* (Moscow), no.2, 1959; "Shagai, Soviet" in *Iz Istorii Kino* (Moscow), no.6 1965; "Manuscrit sans titre", translated by J. Aumont in *Cahiers du cinéma* (Paris), May/June 1970; "Doklad na pervoi vsesoyuznoi..." in *Iz Istorii Kino* (Moscow), no.8 1971; various articles in *Film Comment* (New York), spring 1972; "From the Notebooks of Dziga Vertov", translated by Marco Carynnyk in *Artforum* (New York), March 1972; "Was ist 'Kino-Auge?'" in *Film und Fernsehen* (Berlin), February 1974.

On VERTOV:

Books—*Film Problems of Soviet Russia* by Winnifred Bryher, Terrutent, Switzerland 1929; *Voices of October: Art and Literature in Soviet Russia* by Louis Lozowick, Joseph Freeman, and Joshua Kunitz, New York 1930; *Soviet Cinema* by Herbert Marshall, London 1945; *Soviet Cinema* by Thorold Dickinson and Catherine De La Roche, London 1948; *Film Form* by Sergei Eisenstein, edited and translated by Jay Leyda, New York 1949; *Soviet Films: Principle Stages of Development* by V.I. Pudovkin, G. Alexandrov and I.Piryev, Bombay, India 1951; *The Soviet Film Industry* by Paul Babitsky and John Rimberg, New York 1955; *Dziga Vertov* by N.P. Abramov, Moscow 1962; *Dziga Vertov* by Nikolai Abramov, edited and translated by B. Amengual, French ed., Lyon 1965; *Dziga Vertov* by V. Borokov, Moscow 1967; *The October Revolution and the Arts* by Yuri Davydov, translated by Byron Bean and Bernard Meares, Moscow 1967; *Film Makers on Filmmaking* edited by Harry Geduld, Bloomington, Indiana 1967; *Sowjetischer Dokumentarfilm*, edited by Wolfgang Klaue and Manfred Lichtenstein, Leipzig 1967; *Istorii Sovetskogo Kino* by Kh. Abdul-Kacimeva and others, Moscow 1969; *Politics and Film* by Folke Isaksson and Leif Furhammar, translated by Kersti French, New York 1971; *Dziga Verov* by Georges Sadoul, Paris 1971; *Cinema Verité* by M. Ali Issari, East Lansing, Michigan 1971; *Marx, le cinema et la critique de film* by Guido Aristarco, translated by B. Amengual, Paris 1972; *Documentary: A History of the Non-Fiction Film* by Erik Barnouw, New York 1974; *Kuleshov on Film* by Lev Kuleshov, translated and edited by Ronald Levaco, Berkeley, California 1974; *Evolution of Style in the Early Work of Dziga Vertov* by Seth Feldman, New York 1977; articles— "Notes on Movies" by Jere Abbott in *Hound and Horn* (London), December 1929; "Vertov, His Work and His Future" by Jean Lenauer in *Close-Up* (London), December 1929; "2 Vertov Films" by Oswell Blakeston in *Close-Up* (London), August 1929; "First Russian Sound Film" by A. Kraszna-Krausz in *Close-Up* (London), December 1931; "The New Kino" by Harry Alan Potamkin in *Close-Up* (London), March 1931; "Vertov ad Absurdum" by Pennethorne Hughes in *Close-Up* (London), September 1932; "Dziga Vertov" by Simon Koster in *Experimental Cinema* (New York), no.5, 1934; "Le fonti di due 'Novatori,' Dziga Vertov e Lev Kuleshov" by Guido Aristarco in *Cinema nuovo* (Turin), January/February 1959; "The Man with the Movie Camera" by Dai Vaughan in *Films and Filming* (London), November 1960; "Dziga Vertov es a dokumentufilm muveszete" by Nikolai Abramov in *Filmkultura* (Budapest),

January 1961; "Dziga Wertow: Publizist und Poet des Dokumentarfilms" by Erika Richter in *Filmwissenschaftliche Mitteilungen*, March 1961; "The Writings of Dziga Vertov", translated by Val Telberg and S. Brody in *Film Culture* (New York), summer 1962; "Actualite de Dziga Vertov" by Georges Sadoul in *Cahiers du cinéma* (Paris), June 1963; "Bio-Filmographie de Vertov" by Georges Sadoul in *Cahiers du cinéma* (Paris), August 1963; "Wertow, die Thorndikes und das "Russische Wunder" by Antonin Navratil in *Film* (Germany), no.2, 1964; "Dziga Vertov, i futuristi italiani, Apollinaire e il montaggio delle reistrazini" by Georges Sadoul in *Bianco e nero* (Rome), July 1964; "Dziga Vertov et les Pravdisty" by A. Fevralski, translated by Eric Schmulevitch in *Cahiers du cinéma* (Paris), December 1965; "The Man With the Movie Camera" by Herman G. Weinberg in *Film Comment* (New York), fall 1966; "O Vertove" by R. Yurenev in *Iskusstvo Kino* (Moscow), no.6, 1967; "La 'produttività' dei materiali di Ejsenstejn e Dziga Vertov" by Gianni Toti in *Cinema & Film* (Rome), vol.1, no.3, 1967; "Dziga Vertov, Poet and Writer of the Cinema" by Nikolai Abramov in *Soviet Film* (Moscow), no.11, 1968; *Documentary Film* by Paul Rotha and Richard Griffith, New York 1968; "Dziga Vertov" by Christopher Giercke in *Afterimage* (Rochester), April 1970; "Maiakovski et Vertov" by Bernard Eisenschitz in *Cahiers du cinéma* (Paris), May/June 1970; "The Idea of Montage in Soviet Art and Cinema" by David Bordwell in *Cinema Journal* (Evanston, Illinois), spring 1972; "The So-Called 'Formal Method'" by Osop Brik, translated by Richard Sherwood, in *Screen* (London), winter 1971/72; "Dziga Vertov: notas sobre su actualidad" by Victor Casaus in *Cine Cubano* (Havana), no.76-77, 1972; "A Quantitative View of Soviet Cinema" by Stephen P. Hill in *Cinema Journal* (Evanston, Illinois), spring 1972; "Dziga Vertov: An Introduction" by David Bordwell in *Film Comment* (New York), spring 1972; "The Vertov Papers" by M. Carynnyk in *Film Comment* (New York), spring 1972; "The Man with the Movie Camera: From Magician to Entomologist" by Annette Michelson in *Artforum* (New York), March 1972; article in *Cinema in Revolution* edited by M. Martin and L. and J. Schnitzer, translated with additional material by David Robinson, New York 1973; "Dziga Vertov" by Marsha Enzensberger in *Screen* (London), winter 1972/73; "The Man without a Movie Camera" by Jean Vronskaya in *Film* (London), May 1973; "Cinema Weekly and Cinema Truth: Dziga Vertov and the Leninist Proportion" by S. Feldman in *Sight and Sound* (London), winter 1973/74; "Wertow— Majakowski—Futurismus" by H. Herlinghaus in *Filmwissenschaftliche Beitrage* (Berlin), v.14, 1973; "Mayakovsky and the Literary Movements of 1917-30" by Osip Brik, translated by Diana Matias, in *Screen* (London), autumn 1974; "Problems of Film Stylistics" by Boris Eichenbaum, translated by T.L. Aman, in *Screen* (London), autumn 1974; "Dziga Vertov: Yesterday and Today" by J. Skwara in *Young/Jeune Cinema & Theatre* (Prague), winter 1974; "Chaplin: Die Professoren sollten ihm lernen" by A. Krautz and "...und eines Tages flog er durch die Luft", interview with Elisaveta Vertova-Svilova in *Film und Fernsehen* (Berlin), February 1974; "Sur 2 films de Dziga Vertov: *Kino Glaz* et *L'Homme àla caméra*" by J. Cornand in *Image et son* (Paris), June/July 1975; "O pis'me iz Petrograda 'Avtokino' i Vertove" by V. Listov in *Iskusstvo Kino* (Moscow), January 1975; "Linguistic Models in Early Soviet Cinema" by H. Denkin in *Cinema Journal* (Evanston), fall 1977; "Enthusiasm: from Kino-eye to Radio-eye" by L. Fischer in *Film Quarterly* (Berkeley), winter 1977/78; "Kino-truth and Kino-praxis: Vertov's *Man with a Movie Camera*" by J. Mayne in *Ciné-Tracts* (Montreal), summer 1977; "Film's Institutional Mode of Representation and the Soviet Response" by Noel Burch, "Dr. Crase and Mr. Clair" by A. Michelson, and "An Interview with

Mikhail Kaufman" in *October* (Cambridge, Mass.), winter 1979; "Dziga Vertov" in *Travelling* (Lausanne), summer 1979; "5 Faces of Vertov" by Jean Rouch in *Framework* (Norwich, England), autumn 1979.

* * *

Dziga Vertov, pioneer Soviet documentarist, was born Denis Arkadievitch Kaufman. He and two younger brothers, Mikhail and Boris, were sons of a librarian in the Polish city of Byalistok, which at the time was within the Tsarist empire. When World War I broke out, the parents took the family to what seemed the comparative safety of Petrograd—St. Petersburg renamed to expunge the Germanic link. When the Bolshevik revolution began, Denis, who was twenty-one, and Mikhail, who was nineteen, became involved. Denis volunteered to the cinema committee and became a newsreel worker. Soon he was editing footage of revolutionary upheaval and the struggles against American, British, French, and Japanese intervention forces. His hastily assembled reels went out as war reports and morale boosters. He was now Dziga Vertov; both names suggesting a spinning top, and perhaps meant to convey perpetual motion. The newsreel, titled *Kino-Nedelia* (Film Weekly), continued until the end of the hostilities in 1920. Vertov used selected footage for the multi-reel *Godovshchina revoliutsiva* (Anniversary of the Civil War) and other compilations.

He now hoped to launch a more ambitious series of film reports on the building of a new society, but a period of frustration followed. A New Economic Policy, introduced as a temporary measure, permitted limited private enterprise to stimulate the prostrate economy. Cinemas could import foreign features, and were soon filled with old American, German, French and English films. Vertov, outraged, turned polemicist, a writer of fiery manifestos. Addressing the film world, he wrote: " 'Art' works of pre-revolutionary days surround you like icons and still command your prayerful emotions. Foreign lands abet you in your confusion, sending into the new Russia the living corpses of movie dramas garbed in splendid technological dressing." He tended to look on these films, and even on fiction films in general, as dangerous corrupting influences, another "opium of the people." He urged producers to "come to life."

His vitriol won Vertov enemies in the film world, but he also had support in high places. Early in 1922 Lenin is said to have told his Commissar of Education, Anatoli Lunacharsky, "Of all the arts, for us film is the most important." Lenin emphasized newsreels and proclaimed a "leninist film-proportion": along with fiction, film programs should include material reflecting "Soviet reality." All this enabled Vertov to launch, in May 1922, the famous *Kino-Pravda* (Film Truth), which continued as an official monthly release until 1925. His wife Elizoveta Svilova became film editor. Mikhail Kaufman, giving up a planned law career, became chief cameraman.

The *Kino-Pravda* group scorned prepared scenarios. Vertov outlined ideas but left wide latitude to Mikhail and other cameramen. Sallying forth with cameras, they caught moments when a Moscow trolley line, long defunct in torn-up streets, was finally put back into action. Army tanks, used as tractors, were seen leveling an area for an airport. A children's hospital was trying to save war-starved waifs. A travelling film team was seen arriving in a town, unpacking gear, and preparing an outdoor showing—of *Kino-Pravda*. The reels were always composed of "fragments of actuality" but Vertov also put emphasis on their provocative juxtaposition. Superimpositions, spilt screens, slowed or speeded motion could play a part in this. If the fragments were "truths,"

the manipulations were to bring out other "truths"—relationships and meanings.

For a time the *Kino-Pravda* releases were virtually the only item in cinema programs that touched the historic movement, and they therefore gained wide impact. Footage was from time to time reused, with new footage, in feature documentaries. Among the most successful was *Shestaya chast' mira* (One Sixth of the World), in which Vertov made impressive use of subtitles. Short, intermittent subtitles formed a continuing apostrophe addressing the people of the Soviet Union. "You in the small villages ...You in the tundra...You on the ocean." Having established, via footage and words, a vast geographic dispersion, the catalog turned to nationalities: "You Uzbeks...You Kalmiks." Then it addressed occupations, age groups, sexes. The continuing sentence went on for minutes, then ended with: "You are the owners of one sixth of the world." The incantation style, reminiscent of Walt Whitman—much admired by Vertov—continued throughout the film, projecting the destiny forseen for the "owners." To men and women with only a dim awareness of the scope and resources of their land, the film must indeed have been a prideful pageant.

Vertov's career gradually became clouded, especially in the Stalin years. His aversion to detailed scenarios, which he said were inapplicable to reportage documenataries, marked him as "antiplanning." He agreed to write "analyses" of what he had in mind, but his proposals were often rejected. Articulated social doctrine was increasingly mandatory; experiments in form were decried. Ironically, Vertov remains best known for one of his most experimental films, *Chevolek s kinoapparatom* (Man with a Movie Camera). Featuring Mikhail in action, and intended to demonstrate the role of the cameraman in showing "Soviet reality," it also became an antholgy of film devices and tricks. Eisenstein, usually a Vertov supporter, criticized it for "unmotivated camera mischief" and even "formalism."

During the following years Vertov and Kaufman worked in the Ukraine studios, apparently a reflection of disfavor in Moscow. But in the Ukraine Vertov created one of the most inventive of early sound films, *Entuziazm: Simfoniia Donbassa* (Enthusiasm: Symphony of the Don Basin), a virtuoso exploration of the possibilites of nonsynchronus sound. Another such exploration was the moving *Tri pesni o Lenine* (Three Songs About Lenin), utilizing the precious fragments of Lenin footage. But Vertov had lost standing. In his final years he was again a newsreel worker, arriving and leaving the job on schedule, no longer writing manifestos.

His ideas were, however, echoed in later years in cinema verité, the movement of the 1960s named after Vertov's *Kino-Pravda*. The 1960s and 1970s saw an international revival of interest in Vertov. It included rehabilitation in the Soviet Union, with retrospectives of his films, biographical works, and publication of selections from Vertov's journals, manifestos, and other writings.

—Erik Barnouw

VIDOR, CHARLES. Hungarian/American. Born in Budapest, 27 July 1900. Educated at Universities of Budapest and Berlin. Married actress Karen Morley, 1932 (divorced 1943); son: Michael; Mrs. Doris Warner Leroy, 1945; sons: Quentin and Brian. Career: WW I—serves as infantry lieutenant; early 1920s—works as assistant cutter and assistant director at UFA studios, Berlin; 1924—moves to U.S.; sings with English Grand Opera company; also works in Broadway chorus and as longshoreman; late 1920s—moves to Hollywood, works as assistant to Alexander Korda; works as assistant director, editor, and scriptwriter; 1931—makes short film *The Bridge* independently; 1932—begins directing for MGM; 1949—leaves Columbia in dispute with Harry Cohn after directing there for many years; resulting breach-of-contract suit settled out of court; moves to MGM; 1956—forms Aurora Productions; 1959—suffers heart attack in Vienna while filming *Magic Flame* (completed as *Song without End* by George Cukor). Died in Vienna, 4 June 1959.

Films (as director): 1931—*The Bridge* (short); 1932—*The Mask of Fu Manchu* (co-d, uncredited); 1933—*Sensation Hunters*; 1934—*Double Door*; 1935—*Strangers All*; *The Arizonian*; *His Family Tree*; 1936—*Muss 'em Up*; 1937—*A Doctor's Diary*; *The Great Gambini*; *She's No Lady*; 1939—*Romance of the Redwoods*; *Blind Alley*; *Those High Grey Walls*; 1940—*My Son, My Son!*; *The Lady in Question*; 1941—*Ladies in Retirement*; *New York Town*; 1942—*The Tuttles of Tahiti*; 1943—*The Desperadoes*; 1944—*Cover Girl*; *Together Again*; 1945—*A Song to Remember*; *Over 21*; 1946—*Gilda*; 1948—*The Loves of Carmen* (+pr); 1952—*It's a Big Country* (co-d); *Hans Christian Andersen*; 1953—*Thunder in the East*; 1954—*Rhapsody*; 1955—*Love Me or Leave Me*; 1956—*The Swan*; 1957—*The Joker Is Wild*; 1958—*A Farewell to Arms*; 1960—*Song without End* (completed by George Cukor).

Publications:

On VIDOR:

Articles—"Vidor Graph" by Thomas Pryor in *The New York Times*, 5 November 1944; "No Swansong for Director Charles Vidor" by Martin Gray in *Films and Filming* (London), June 1956; obituary in *The New York Times*, 5 June 1959.

*   *   *

Charles Vidor's filmography is as unremarkable as it is varied: an average musical (*Cover Girl*) enhanced by the charm of Gene Kelly, the presence of Rita Hayworth, and the comedy of Phil Silvers and Eve Arden; Grace Kelly's final screen credit (*The Swan*); a cute comedy of a middle-aged man in the military (*Over 21*); a turgid Alan Ladd adventure (*Thunder in the East*); a fine gothic melodrama (*Ladies in Retirement*); a solid Randolph Scott western (*The Desperadoes*); a campy Boris Karloff vehicle (*The Mask of Fu Manchu*, co-directed with Charles Brabin); a clumsy Hemingway remake (*A Farewell to Arms*); and programmers for various studios during the 1930s.

A majority of his credits are romances and musicals, and he also specialized in cinematizing the lives of the famous. Vidor's two show-business biographies mix entertainers and mobsters: *The Joker Is Wild*, the life of the nightclub performer Joe E. Lewis, featuring one of Frank Sinatra's better performances; *Love Me or Leave Me*, with Doris Day good as Ruth Etting and James Cagney great as "The Gimp." He also chronicled the lives of *Hans Christian Andersen*, Fredric Chopin (*A Song to Remember*) and Franz Liszt (*Song without End*, completed by George Cukor on his death). Other films also have classical settings or origins: *Rhapsody* (wealthy Elizabeth Taylor torn between pianist John Ericson and violinist Vittorio Gassman); *The Loves of Carmen* (again with Hayworth, but without Bizet's music).

Vidor's one fascinating—and very atypical—credit is *Gilda*, starring Hayworth, his favorite actress. It is exceptionally erotic for 1946, highlighted by Rita's energetic nightclub dance in which she peels off her long white gloves. *Blind Alley* is another noteworthy film, one of Hollywood's initial features which seriously deals with psychology: mobster Chester Morris is analyzed by his hostage, psychiatrist Ralph Bellamy.

Vidor occasionally elicits above-average performances from his stars, and many of his films are enjoyable. But they cannot compare with similar films by other filmmakers, and his actors—with the exception of Hayworth in *Gilda*—give their most characteristic performances elsewhere. *Cover Girl*, by no means a classic musical, is far from Gene Kelly's cinematic zenith. *The Swan* is more of a footnote to Grace Kelly's career. *Ladies in Retirement* is no *Wuthering Heights* or *Rebecca*. *Rhapsody*, next to *Intermezzo*, is hokum. His classical biographies are not as grotesque as those of Ken Russell, but this is certainly no recommendation. None of his biographies rank with *Yankee Doodle Dandy*, or *The Great Ziegfeld*, or *The Glenn Miller Story*, or *Funny Girl*, or *Isadora*, or *Lust for Life*, or *I'll Cry Tomorrow*, or *Moulin Rouge*, or *The Jolson Story*, or *Pride of the Yankees*, or *Sergeant York*, or *The Life of Emile Zola*, or *The Story of Louis Pasteur*, or any one of a dozen others. *Love Me or Leave Me* comes closest, but just misses. Of course, Cagney's quintessential gangster roles are all earlier in his career.

Charles Vidor is, at best, an entertainer whose films are enhanced by the talents of those in his casts. He cannot be truthfully considered an artist.

—Rob Edelman

———————

VIDOR, KING. American. Born King Wallis Vidor in Galveston, Texas, 8 February 1894. Attended Peacock Military Academy, San Antonio, Texas. Married Florence Arto, 1915 (divorced 1924); Eleanor Boardman, 1926 (divorced 1932); Elizabeth Hall, 1932. Career: 1909-10—works in Galveston's 1st movie house as ticket-taker and part-time projectionist; 1910-15—becomes amateur newsreel photographer, shooting local events and selling them to newsreel companies; also makes 1st film, a 2-reeler called *In Tow*; 1915—drives to Hollywood in Model T, financing trip by shooting footage for Ford Company's advertising newsreel; wife Florence is hired by Thomas Ince to work in Vitagraph comedies; 1915-18—works at various jobs in the film industry, selling scenarios to Universal and directing shorts for Judge Willis Brown; 1918—directs 1st feature, *The Turn in the Road*, financed by Brentwood Film Corp. which consisted of a group of doctors and dentists; 1920—is hired by 1st National; builds own studio called Vidor Village; 1922—after Vidor Village shuts down, is hired by MGM to direct *Peg-O-My-Heart*; 1923—joins Goldwyn studios and is later absorbed by newly formed MGM as another director on the staff; 1925—success of *The Big Parade* secures reputation; allowed to choose his own subjects and stories; 1929—directs his 1st sound film, *Hallelujah*; 1959—retires from directing; 1960s—teaches graduate course in cinema at UCLA. Died 1 November 1982. Recipient: Venice Film Festival, Best Direction for *Wedding Night*, 1935; Edinburgh Film Festival, Special prize for his cumulative work, 1964; Honorary Academy Award, 1978.

Films (feature films as director): 1919—*The Turn in the Road* (+sc); *Better Times* (+sc); *The Other Half* (+sc); *Poor Relations* (+sc); 1920—*The Jack Knife Man* (+pr, co-sc); *The Family*

Honor (+co-pr); 1921—*The Sky Pilot; Love Never Dies* (+co-pr); 1922—*Conquering the Woman* (+pr); *Woman, Wake Up* (+pr); *The Real Adventure* (+pr); *Dusk to Dawn* (+pr); 1923—*Peg-O-My-Heart; The Woman of Bronze; 3 Wise Fools* (+co-sc); 1924—*Wild Oranges* (+co-sc); *Happiness; Wine of Youth; His Hour;* 1925—*Wife of the Centaur; Proud Flesh; The Big Parade;* 1926—*La Bohème* (+pr); *Bardelys, The Magnificent* (+pr); 1928—*The Crowd* (+co-sc); *The Patsy; Show People;* 1929—*Hallelujah;* 1930—*Not So Dumb; Billy the Kid;* 1931—*Street Scene; The Champ;* 1932—*Bird of Paradise; Cynara;* 1933—*Stranger's Return;* 1934—*Our Daily Bread* (+pr, co-sc); 1935—*Wedding Night; So Red the Rose;* 1936—*The Texas Rangers* (+pr, co-sc); 1937—*Stella Dallas;* 1938—*The Citadel* (+pr); 1940—*Northwest Passage* (+pr); *Comrade X* (+pr); 1941—*H.M. Pulham, Esq.* (+pr, co-sc); 1944—*American Romance* (+pr, co-sc); 1946—*Duel in the Sun;* 1949—*The Fountainhead; Beyond the Forest;* 1951—*Lightning Strikes Twice;* 1952—*Ruby Gentry* (+co-pr); 1955—*Man Without a Star;* 1956—*War and Peace* (+co-sc); 1959—*Solomon and Sheba.*

Publications:

By VIDOR:

Books—*King Vidor on Filmmaking*, New York 1972; *A Tree is a Tree*, New York, reprinted 1977; articles—"Easy Steps to Success" in *Motion Picture Classic* (New York), August 1919; "Credo" in *Variety* (New York), January 1920; interview by J. Tully in *Vanity Fair* (New York), June 1926; interview by S.M. Keller in *Motion Picture Classic* (New York), spring 1927; interview by B. Beach in *Motion Picture Classic* (New York), June 1928; interview by M. Cheatham in *Motion Picture Classic* (New York), June 1928; "2 Story Conferences", with R. Brooks, in *Sight and Sound* (London), October/November 1952; "The Story Conference" in *Films in Review* (New York), June/July 1952; "The End of an Era" in *Films and Filming* (London), March 1955; "Lillian Gish in Opera" in *Films and Filming* (London), January 1955; "Me...and My Spectacle" in *Films and Filming* (London), October 1959; "Interview" by V.F. Perkins and M. Shivas in *Movie* (London), July/August 1963; "War, Wheat and Steel" by J. Greenburg in *Sight and Sound* (London), autumn 1968; "King Vidor at N.Y.U.", interview in *Cineaste* (New York), spring 1968; "King Vidor" by D. Lyons and G. O'Brien in *Inter/View* (New York), October 1972; special issues of *Positif* (Paris), September and November 1974; "King Vidor on D.W. Griffith's Influence", interview by A. Nash in *Films in Review* (New York), November 1975.

On VIDOR:

Books—*The Parade's Gone By...* by Kevin Brownlow, New York 1968; *The Celluloid Muse: Hollywood Directors Speak* edited by Charles Higham and Joel Greenberg, London 1969; *King Vidor* by John Baxter, New York 1976; articles—"A Young Crusader" in *Photoplay* (New York), December 1919; "A Young Crusader" by Adela Rogers St. John in *Photoplay* (New York), December 1919; "Story of" by A.R. St. John in *Photoplay* (New York), August 1923; "Collectivism More or Less" by W. Troy in *Nation* (New York), 24 October 1934; "Steel Comes to the Films: Vidor's Film America" by F. Daugherty in *Christian Science Monitor Magazine* (Boston), 8 May 1943; "1929: Year of Great Transition" by Arthur Knight in *Theatre Arts* (New York), September 1949; "From Flickers to Fischinger" by Rudolph Arnheim in *Saturday Review* (New York), 18 Febru-

ary 1950; "Sovereign Audience" by R. Griffith in *Saturday Review* (New York), 24 October 1953; "King Vidor's Hollywood Progress" by C. Harrington in *Sight and Sound* (London), April/June 1953; "The Big Screens" in *Sight and Sound*, spring 1955; "Man Who Did It" in *Newsweek* (New York), 30 July 1956; King Vidor" by Kevin Brownlow in *Film* (London), winter 1962; "2nd Line" by Andrew Sarris in *Film Culture* (New York), spring 1963; "The Directors Choose the Best Films" in *Cinema* (Beverly Hills), August/September 1963; "King Vidor" by G.J. Mitchell in *Films in Review* (New York), March 1964; "King Vidor" by C. Higham in *Film Heritage* (Dayton, Ohio), summer 1966; "King Vidor at NYU: Discussion" in *Cineaste* (New York), spring 1968; "Godard in Hollywood" in *Take One* (Montreal), June 1968; "King Vidor" by C. Barr in *Brighton* (London), March 1970; "A Career that Spans Half a Century" by H.G. Luft in *Film Journal* (New York), summer 1971; "Long Live Vidor, A Hollywood King" by C. Higham in *The New York Times*, 3 September 1972; "Il mito di fronte alla storia" by M. Buffa in *Filmcritica* (Rome), May/June 1973; "King Vidor", in 2 parts, by Raymond Durgnat in *Film Comment* (New York), July/August and September/October 1973; special issues of *Positif* (Paris), September and November 1974; "Notre pain quotidien", special issue of *Avant-Scène du cinéma* (Paris), 1 May 1977; "Tribute to King Vidor" by B. Dover in *Films in Review* (New York), June/July 1978; reprinted articles from *Ciné-Magazine* in *Avant-Scène du cinéma* (Paris), 15 October 1980; "Hommage à King Vidor" by J. Lang in *Cinéma* (Paris), November 1981.

*   *   *

King Vidor's first job in the movies was as a ticket-taker and part-time projectionist at the Globe Theater in Galveston, Texas, where he claims he learned a great deal from French pantomime comedy and the feature *Ben Hur*. Vidor made his first motion picture with a friend's home-made camera, built from cigar boxes and an old projector. This first film pictured the destruction of a Galveston beachhouse in gale winds, for which Mutual Weekly awarded him a newsreel contract. Vidor's next project was his first fiction film, called *In Tow*, which took advantage of an actual road race in Galveston for its setting. Following *In Tow*, Vidor produced two one reelers with Edward Sedgwick, an experienced vaudevillian, who later became a director of comedies in Hollywood. Sedgwick wrote, directed, and starred in the short comedies, while Vidor handled the business aspects. Vidor, now married to Florence Arto, travelled to New York to sell the films to a distributor. He returned to Galveston having procured a distribution contract with a company that shortly thereafter went bankrupt.

Finally, Vidor decided to venture to Hollywood. He and Florence and a friend spent six weeks on the road in a Model T, shooting footage for the Ford Motor Company, and arriving in San Francisco with little over a dollar. Unsuccessful in finding employment in San Francisco, King and Florence went to Santa Monica, where she became a star with Vitagraph, and King wrote scenarios and worked as an extra. After writing 52 scripts, he sold one, *When it Rains it Pours*, designed to keep the studio working during an unusually long month of rainy weather. While Florence's career was mushrooming, King's was barely underway.

Vidor subsequently began work as a company clerk for Universal, submitting original scripts under the pseudonym Charles K. Wallis. (Universal employees weren't allowed to submit original work to the studio.) Vidor eventually confessed his wrongdoing and was fired as a clerk, only to be rehired as a comedy writer. Within days, he lost this job as well when Universal discontinued comedy production.

Vidor next worked as the director of a series of short dramatic films detailing the reform work of Salt Lake City Judge Willis Brown, a Father Flanagan-type. Vidor tried to parlay this experience into a job as a feature director with a major studio but was unsuccessful. He did manage, however, to find financial backing from nine doctors for his first feature, a picture with a Christian Science theme titled *The Turn in the Road*. Vidor spent the next year working on three more features for the newly-christened Brentwood Company, including the comedy *Better Times*, starring his own discovery Zasu Pitts.

In 1920, Vidor accepted an offer from First National and a check for $75,000. He persuaded his father to sell his business in order that he might build and manage "Vidor Village," a small studio which mirrored similar projects by Chaplin, Sennett, Griffith, Ince, and others. Vidor directed eight pictures at Vidor Village, but was forced to close down in 1922. The following year, he was hired by Louis B. Mayer at Metro to direct aging stage star Laurette Taylor in *Peg-O-My-Heart*. Soon after, he went to work for Samuel Goldywn, attracted by Goldywn's artistic and literary aspirations. In 1924, Vidor returned to Metro with the merger that resulted in MGM. He would continue to work there for the next 20 years, initially entrusted with molding the careers of rising stars, John Gilbert, and Eleanor Boardman, soon to be Vidor's second wife.

The Big Parade changed Vidor's status from contract director to courted screen artist. Produced by Irving Thalberg, the film grew from a minor studio production into one of MGM's two biggest hits of 1926, grossing $18 million. *The Big Parade* satisfied Vidor's desire to make a picture with lasting value and extended exhibition. It was the first of three films he wanted to make on the topics of "wheat, steel, and war." Vidor went on to direct Gilbert, and the studio's new acquisition Lillian Gish, in *La Boheme*.

Encouraged by the popularity of German films of the period and their concern with urban life, Vidor made *The Crowd*, "The Big Parade* of peace." It starred unknown actor James Murray, whose life would end in an alcoholic suicide, and who inspired one of Vidor's projects, an unproduced picture titled *The Actor*. Like *The Big Parade*, *The Crowd* presented the reactions of an everyman, this time to the anonymity of the city and the rigors of urban survival. Vidor's silent career continued with two of Marion Davies's comedies *The Patsy* and *Show People*, and extended into "talkies" with a third comedy, *Not So Dumb*. Though only moderately succesful, Vidor became a favorite in William Randolph Hearst's entourage.

Vidor was in Europe when the industry announced its conversion to sound. He quickly returned to propose *Hallelujah*, with an all-black cast. Although considered a politically-astute director for Hollywood, the film exposes Vidor's political shortcomings in its paternalistic attitude toward blacks. With similar political naiveté, Vidor's next great film, the pseudo-socialist agricultural drama *Our Daily Bread*, was derived from a *Reader's Digest* article.

By this point in his career, Vidor's thematics were fairly intact. Informing most of his lasting work is the struggle of Man against Destiny and Nature. In his great silent pictures, *The Big Parade* and *The Crowd*, the hero wanders through an anonymous and malevolent environment, war-torn Europe and the Amercan city, respectively. In his later sound films, *The Citadel*, *Northwest Passage*, *Duel in the Sun*, and *The Fountainhead* various forms of industry operate as a vehicle of Man's battle to subdue Nature. Unlike the optimism in Ford's and Capra's films, Vidor's follow a Job-like pattern, in which victory comes, if at all, with a great deal of personal sacrifice. Underlying all of Vidor's great work are the biblical resonances of a Christian Scientist, where Nature is ultimately independent from and disinterested in Man, who always remains subordinate in the struggle against its forces.

Following *Our Daily Bread*, Vidor continued to alternate between films that explored this personal thematic and projects seemingly less suited to his interests. In more than 50 features, Vidor worked for several producers, directing *Wedding Night* and *Stella Dallas* for Samuel Goldwyn, *The Citadel*, *Northwest Passage*, and *Comrade X* for MGM, *Bird of Paradise*, where he met his third wife Elizabeth Hill, and *Duel in the Sun* for David O. Selznick, *The Foutainhead*, *Beyond the Forest*, and *Lightning Strikes Twice* for Warner Brothers, and late in his career, *War and Peace* for Dino De Laurentiis. Vidor exercised more control on his films after *Our Daily Bread*, often serving as producer, but his projects continued to fluctuate between intense metaphysical drama and light-weight comedy and romance.

In the fifties, Vidor's only notable film was *Ruby Gentry*, and his filmmaking career ended on a less-than-praiseworthy note with *Solomon and Sheba*. Vidor is credited with the direction of one television show, "Light's Golden Jubilee," produced by Selznick for General Electric, and in the sixties he made two short documentaries, *Truth and Illusion*, and *Metaphor*, about his friend Andrew Wyeth.

He wrote a highly praised autobiography in 1953, *A Tree Is a Tree*, and in 1979, he received an honorary Oscar, following his nomination as a director five times. In the last years of his life, he was honored in his hometown of Galveston with an annual King Vidor film festival.

—Michael Selig

VIGO, JEAN. French. Born in Paris, 26 April 1905, the son of anarchist Miguel Alemreyda (Eugéne Bonaventure de Vigo). Attended a number of boarding schools including the Boys School of St. Cloud until 1917; also attended a boarding school in Nîmes, after the death of his father, under the name Jean Sales. Married Elisabeth Lozinska, 24 January 1929; child: Luce, 1931. Career: 1917—father found dead under mysterious circmstances in his jail cell; 1923—mother confined to a hospital; 1923-29—experiences a variety of health problems and eventually enters clinic in Montpellier; 1929—moves to Nice because of his tuberculosis; directs his 1st film, *À propos de Nice*; 1932—with family returns to Paris to live; 3rd film, *Zéro de conduite* removed from circulation by censors because it is considered "anti-France"; 1933—becomes seriously ill with leukemia. Died 5 October 1934.

Films (as director) 1930—*À propos de Nice*; 1931—*Taris (Taris roi de l'eau, Jean Taris champion de natation)*; 1933—*Zéro de conduite*; 1934—*L'Atalante*.

Publications:

By VIGO:

Article—"Towards a Social Cinema" in *Millenium* (New York), winter 1977/78.

On VIGO:

Books—*An Index to the Creative Work of Jean Vigo* by Harry

and Joseph Feldman, supplement to *Sight and Sound*, index series, London 1951; *Le Surréalisme au cinéma* by Ado Kyrou, Paris 1953; *Amour, erotisme et cinéma* by Ado Kyrou, Paris 1957; *Jean Vigo* by P.E. Salès-Gomès, Paris 1957; *Miroirs de l'insolite dans le cinéma français* by Henri Agel, Paris 1958; "Le Rêve et le fantastique dans le cinéma français by Charles Pornon, Paris 1959; *Les Grands Cinéastes* by Henri Agel, Paris 1960; *Hommage à Jean Vigo* edited by Freddy Buache and others, Lausanne 1962; *Anarchist Cinema* by Alan Lovell, London 1967; *Jean Vigo* by Pierre Lherminier, Paris 1967; *Jean Vigo* by Marcel Martin, *Anthologie du cinéma* vol.2, Paris 1967; *Jean Vigo* by John Smith, New York 1971; *Jean Vigo* by P.E. Salès-Gomès, revised English ed., Los Angeles 1971; *Jean Vigo* by P.E.S. Gomes, Milan 1979; *Jean Vigo* by Luis Filipe Rocha, Porto Portugal 1982; articles—"Jean Vigo" by Alberto Cavalcanti in *Cinema Quarterly* (Edinburgh), winter 1935; "Jean Vigo" by Mario Verdone in *Bianco e nero* (Rome), March 1939; "Scoperta di un registra: Jean Vigo" by Luigi Comencini in *Cine-tempo* (Rome), 6 December 1945; "Jean Vigo" by Siegfried Kracauer in *Hollywood Quarterly*, April 1947; "Life and Work of Jean Vigo" by J. Agee in *Nation* (New York), 12 July 1947; "The Films of Jean Vigo" by H.G. Weinberg in *Cinema* (Beverly Hills), July 1947; "Films in Review" by H.R. Isaacs in *Theatre Arts* (New York), August 1947; "Remembrances of Jean Vigo" by G. Zilzer in *Hollywood Quarterly*, winter 1947/48; special issue of *Ciné-club* (Paris), February 1949; "A proposito di Jean Vigo" in *Bianco e nero* (Rome), March 1949; "Rettrospettive" by Carlo Doglio in *Cinema* (Milan), 15 June 1951; "D'un Duvivier à Jean Vigo" by Jean-Paul Marquet in *Positif* (Lyon), June 1952; special issue of *Positif* (Lyon), no.7, 1953; "The 5th Columnists" by Roy Edwards in *Sight and Sound* (London), July/September 1953; article by Barthélemy Amengual in *Positif* (Paris), May 1953; "Souvenir de Jean Vigo" by Pierre de Saint-Prix in *Cinéma 55* (Paris), March 1955; "Le Mort de Jean Vigo" by P.E. Salès-Gomès in *Cahiers du cinéma* (Paris), August/September 1955; "Portrait of Vigo" by D.S. Ashton in *Film* (London), December 1955; "An Interview with Boris Kaufman" by Edouard De Laurot and Jonas Mekas in *Film Culture* (New York), summer 1955; "Jean Vigo et ses films" by Bernard Chardère in *Cinéma 55* (Paris), March 1955; "Dossier Jean Vigo" by François Tranchant in *Image et son* (Paris), October 1958; "The French Film: Discussion" in *Film* (London), November/December 1955; special issue of *Premier Plan* (Lyon), no.19, 1961; "Jean Vigo" by François Chevassu in *Image et son* (Paris), February 1961; "The Anarchism of Jean Vigo" by John Ellerby in *Anarchy 6* (London), August 1961; "Sensibilité au génie de Vigo" by Freddy Buache in *Michel Simon*, Switzerland 1962; article by Bernard Chardère in *Jeune Cinéma* (Paris), February 1965; special issue of *Études cinématographiques* (Paris), no.51-52, 1966; "Anarchy, Surrealism, and Optimism in *Zéro de conduite*" by B. Mills in *Cinema* (London), no.8, 1971; "The Playground of Jean Vigo" by B. Teush in *Film Heritage* (New York), fall 1973.

*   *   *

It is difficult to think of another director who made so few films and yet had such a profound influence on other filmmakers. Jean Vigo's *À propos de Nice*, his first film, is his contribution to the French Surrealist movement. The film itself is a direct descendant of Vertov's *Man with a Movie Camera*. Certainly, his films make political statements similar to Vertov's. Vertov's documentary celebrates a people's revolution, while Vigo's chastizes the bourgeois vacactioners in a French resort town. Even

more importantly, both films revel in the pyrotechnics of the camera and the editing room. They are filled with dizzying movement, fast cutting, and the juxtaposition, from frame to frame, of objects that normally have little relation to each other. In yet another link between the two directors, Vertov's brother, Boris Kaufman, photographed *À propos de Nice*, as well as Vigo's other three films.

À propos de Nice provides a look at a reality beyond the prosaic, common variety that so many films give us. The movie attempts nothing less than the restructuring of our perception of the world by presenting it to us not so much through a seamless, logical narrative, but rather through a fast-paced collection of only tangentially related shots.

After *À propos de Nice*, Vigo began combining his brand of surrealism with the poetic realism that would later be so important to a generation of French directors, such as Jean Renoir and Marcel Carné. For his second film, he made another documentary, *Taris*, about France's champion swimmer. Here Vigo takes his camera underwater as Taris clowns at the bottom of a pool and blows at the lens. *Taris* certainly has some striking images, but it is only eleven minutes long. Indeed, if Vigo had died in 1931, after finishing *Taris*, instead of in 1934 (and given the constantly precarious state of his health, this would not have been at all unlikely), he would have been remembered, if at all, as a director who had shown great potential, yet who could hardly be considered a major talent.

However, Vigo's third film, *Zéro de conduite*, stands out as one of the cinema's most influential works. Along with films such as Sagan's *Mädchen in Uniform* and Wyler's *These Three*, it forms one of the more interesting and least studied genres of the 1930s—the children's boarding school film. Although it is Vigo's first fiction film, it continues the work he began with *À propos de Nice*. That first movie good-naturedly condemns the bourgeoisie, showing the rich as absolutely useless, their primary sin being banality rather than greed or cruelty. In *Zéro de conduite*, teachers, and not tourists are the representatives of the bourgeoisie. But like the Nice vacationers, they are not so much malicious as they are simply inadequate, instructing their schoolboys in nothing important, and prizing the school's suffocating regulations above all else. Vigo lets the schoolboys rebel against this sort of mindless monotony, having them engage in an apocalyptic pillow fight, and then allowing them to bombard their teachers with fruit during a stately school ceremony. The film's anarchic spirit led to its being banned in France until 1945. But during the 1950s, it became one of the inspirations for the French New Wave directors. In subject matter, it somewhat resembles Truffaut's *400 Blows*. But it is the film's style—the mixture of classical Hollywood visuals with the dreamlike illogic of slow motion, fast action, and quick cutting—that particularly influenced a new generation of filmmakers.

Vigo's last film, *L'Atalante*, is his masterpiece. It is a love story that takes place on a barge, with Vigo once again combining surrealism with poetic realism. The settings are naturalistic and the characters lower-class, and bringing to mind Renoir's poetic realist films, for instance *Toni* and *Les Bas-Fonds*. There is also an emphasis on the imagination and on the near-sacredness of banal objects that places the film strongly in the tradition of such surrealist classics as *Un Chien andalou*. After Juliette leaves Jean, the barge captain, Jean jumps into the river, and sees his wife's image everywhere around him. The underwater sequence not only makes the viewer think of *Taris*, but also makes us aware that we are sharing Jean's obsession with him. This dreamy visualization of a character's thoughts brings to mind the priority that the surrealists gave to all mental proceses. The surrealists prized, too, some of the more mundane aspects of everyday life, and Vigo's film is full of ordinary objects that take on (for Juliette) a magical status. They are only puppets, or fans, or gramophones piled in a heap in the room of Père Jules, Jean's old assistant, but Juliette has spent her entire life in a small town, and for her, these trinkets represent the mysteries of faraway places. They take on a special status, the banal being raised to the level of the exotic.

Despite the movie's links to two film movements, *L'Atalante* defies categorization. It is a masterpiece of mood and characterization, and along with *Zéro de conduite*, it guarantees Vigo's status as a great director. But he was not granted that status by the critical community until years after his death. Because of the vagaries of film exhibition and censorship, Vigo was little known while he was making films, receiving nowhere near the acclaim given to his contemporaries Jean Renoir and René Clair.

—Eric Smoodin

VISCONTI, LUCHINO. Italian. Born Count Don Luchino Visconti di Modrone in Milan, 2 November 1906. Educated at private schools in Milan and Como; also attended boarding school of the Calasanzian Order, 1924-26. Career: 1926-28—serves in Reggimento Savoia Cavalleria, cavalry regiment; 1928-29—designs sets for play directed by G.A. Traversi, begins to do some acting; 1936—moves to Paris, meets Jean Renoir through an introduction by Coco Chanel; 1936-37—becomes a member of Renoir's semi-permanent production crew, at first in charge of costumes and later as assistant director; 1939—returns to Italy to assist Renoir on *La Tosca*; 1942—directs 1st film *Ossessione*; 1945—directs 1st play, Cocteau's *Parenti terrible (Les Parents terribles)*, in Rome; 1954—directs 1st opera *La vestale* in Milan; 1956-57—involved in the production of 2 ballets, *Mario e il mago* and *Maratona di danza*. Died 17 March 1976. Recipient: Venice Film Festival, International Prize for *La terra trema*, 1948; Cannes Film Festival, 25th Anniversary Award, 1971.

Films (as assistant director): 1936—*Les Bas-fonds*; 1937—*Une Partie de campagne*; 1940—*La Tosca*; (as director): 1942—*Ossessione* (+co-sc); 1945—*Giorni di gloria* (asst d only); 1947—*La terra trema* (+sc); 1951—*Bellissima* (+co-sc); *Appunti su un fatto di cronaca* (2nd in series *Documento mensile*); 1953—"We, the Women" episode of *Siamo donne* (+co-sc); 1954—*Senso* (+co-sc); 1957—*Le notti bianche (White Nights)* (+co-sc); 1960—*Rocco e i suoi fratelli (Rocco and His Brothers)* (+co-sc); 1962—"Il lavoro (The Job)" episode of *Boccaccio '70* (+co-sc); 1963—*Il gattopardo (The Leopard)* (+co-sc); 1965—*Vaghe stelle dell'orsa (Of A Thousand Delights, Sandra)* (+co-sc); 1967—"Le strega bruciata viva" episode of *Le streghe*; *Lo straniero (L'Etranger)* (+co-sc); 1969—*La caduta degli dei (The Damned, Götterdämmerung)* (+co-sc); 1970—*Alla ricerca di Tadzio*; 1971—*Morte a Venezia (Death in Venice)* (+pr, co-sc); 1973—*Ludwig* (+co-sc); 1974—*Gruppo di famiglia in un interno* (+co-sc); 1976—*L'innocente (The Innocent)* (+co-sc).

Publications:

By VISCONTI:

Books—*Senso*, Bologna 1955; *Le notti bianche*, Bologna 1957; *Rocco et ses frères* edited by Michèle Causse, Paris 1961; *Rocco ei suoi fratelli*, Bologna 1961; *Il gattopardo*, Bologna 1963;

Vaghe stelle dell'orsa (Sandra), Bologna 1965; *3 Screenplays*, New York 1970; *Morte a Venezia*, Bologna 1971; *Il mio teatro*, in 2 volumes, Bologna 1979; articles—"Cadaveri" in *Cinema* (Rome), 10 June 1941; "Il cinéma antropomorfico" in *Cinema* (Rome), 25 September 1943; "*La terra trema*" in *Bianco e nero* (Rome), March 1951; "*La Terra tremble*" in *L'Ecran français* (Paris), January 1952; "*Marcia nuziale*" in *Cinema nuovo* (Turin), 1 May 1953; "*Senso*" in *Les Lettres français* (Paris), 9 February 1956; "*Bellissima*" in *Radio, cinéma, télévision* (Paris), 7 November and 16 December 1956; interview by Claude Sarraute in *Le Monde* (Paris), 15 June 1956; interview by Jacques Doniol-Valcroze and Jean Domarchi in *Cahiers du cinéma* (Paris), March 1959; interview by Jean Slavik in *Cahiers du cinéma* (Paris), April 1960; interview by Yvonne Baby in *Le Monde* (Paris), 9 March 1961; "The Miracle That Gave Men Crumbs" in *Films and Filming* (London), January 1961; "*Le Guèpard*" in *Cinéma 63* (Paris), September/October 1963; "Drama of Non-Existence" in *Cahiers du Cinema in English* (New York), no.2, 1966; "Au royaume de Visconti", interview by L. Spagnoli in *Ecran* (Paris), April 1975; "Violence et passion", special issue of *Avant-Scène du cinéma* (Paris), June 1975.

On VISCONTI:

Books—*Cinema Italiano* by Mario Gromo, Milan 1954; *Le Cinéma italien* by Carlo Lizzani, Paris 1955; *Il nuovo cinema italiano* by Giuseppe Ferrara, Florence 1957; *Luchino Visconti* by Lorenzo Pellizzari, Milan 1960; *I film di Luchino Visconti* by Pio Baldelli, Manduria, Italy 1965; *Visconti* by Yves Guillaume, Paris 1966; *Les Grands Cinéastes que je propose* by Henri Agel, Paris 1967; *Man and the Movies* by W.R. Robinson, Baton Rouge, Louisiana 1967; *Luchino Visconti* by Geoffrey Nowell-Smith, New York 1968; *Le Cinéma italien, d'Antonioni à Rosi* by Freddy Bauche, Yverdon, Switzerland 1969; *Visconti* by Giuseppe Ferrara, translated by Jean-Pierre Pinaud, Paris, 2nd ed. 1970; *A Discovery of Cinema* by Thorold Dickinson, Toronto 1971; *Luchino Visconti* by Pio Baldelli, Milan 1973; *Callas* by John Ardoin and Gerald Fitzgerald, New York 1974; *Burt Lancaster* by Tony Thomas, New York 1975; *Visconti: il cinema*, edited by Adelio Ferrero, Modena 1977; *Lettere e taccuini di Regina Coeli* by Mario Alicata, Turin 1977; *Maestri del cinema* by Pietro Bianchi, Milan 1977; *Album Visconti* edited by Lietta Tornabuoni, foreward by Michelangelo Antonioni, Milan 1978; *A Screen of Time: A Study of Luchino Visconti* by Monica Stirling, New York 1979; *Luchino Visconti* by Gaia Servadio, New York 1983; articles—"Mitologia e contemplasione in Visconti, Ford ed Eisenstein" by Renzo Renzi in *Bianco e nero* (Rome), February 1949; "Notes sur Visconti" by Philippe Demonsablon in *Cahiers du cinéma* (Paris), March 1954; "Verismo litterario e neorealismo" by Pietro Speri in *Cinema* (Rome), 15 March 1954; "The Hurricane Visconti" by John Francis Lane in *Films and Filming* (London), December 1954; "Pour saluer Visconti" by Willy Archer in *Cahiers du cinéma* (Paris), March 1956; "Visconti et le réalisme au théâtre" by Roland Barthes in *Théâtre populaire* (Paris), September 1956; "La questione del dialetto" by Luigi Chiarini in *Cinema nuovo* (Turin), 10 April 1956; "Luchino Visconti" by Giulio Castello in *Sight and Sound* (London), spring 1956; "Visconti—The Last Decadent" by John Francis Lane in *Films and Filming* (London), July 1956; "3 Tendencies: A Postscript to the Venice Film Festival" by Guido Aristarco in *Film Culture* (New York), December 1957; "The Vision of Visconti" by Peter John Dyer in *Film* (London), March/April 1957; "Luchino Visconti e il melodramma" by Luigi Pestalozza in *Cinema nuovo* (Turin), January/February 1959; "Composers' Director" by C.G. Pepper in *Theatre Arts* (New York), March 1959; "Il naturalismo di Visconti" by Rino Dal Sasso in *Filmcritica* (Rome), October 1960; "Luchino Visconti and the Italian Cinema" by Gianfranco Poggi in *Film Quarterly* (Berkeley), spring 1960; special issue of *Premier Plan* (Paris), May 1961; "Why Neo-Realism Failed" by Eric Rhode in *Sight and Sound* (London), winter 1960/61; "Italy: The Moral Cinema: Notes on Some Recent Films" by Vernon Young in *Film Quarterly* (Berkeley), fall 1961; "Rebirth in Italy" by C.G. Pepper in *Newsweek* (New York), 10 July 1961; "Visconti and Rocco" by P. Armitage in *Film*, winter 1961; "...on safari with Visconti" by Colquhoun in *Films and Filming* (London), October 1962; "New Old Master" by L. Minoff in *Saturday Review* (New York), 29 December 1962; special issue of *Etudes cinématographiques* (Paris), no.26-27, 1963; "Visconti et l'histoire" by Marcel Martin and "Visconti et le temps retrouvé by Jean-Paul Torok" in *Cinéma 63* (Paris), September/October 1963; "A Case of Artistic Inflation" by John Francis Lane in *Sight and Sound* (London), summer 1963; "The Auteur Theory and the Perils of Pauline" by Andrew Sarris in *Film Quarterly* (Berkeley), summer 1963; "People Are Talking About" and "Visconti, the Leopard Man" in *Vogue* (New York), July 1963; "Luchino Visconti: morte o resurrezione?" by Renzo Renzi in *Cinema nuovo* (Turin), January/February 1964; "Le sud dans le cinéma italien" by Goffredo Fofi in *Image et son* (Paris), no.195, 1966; "Memories of Resnais" by R. Roud in *Sight and Sound* (London), summer 1969; special issue of *Cinema* (Rome), April 1970; "Visconti" by K. Radkai in *Vogue* (New York), 1 November 1970; "Visconti in Venice" by H. Alpert in *Saturday Review* (New York), 8 August 1970; "Luchino Visconti" by T. Elsaesser in *Brighton* (London), February 1970; "The Earth Still Trembles" by Guiso Aristarco in *Films and Filming* (London), January 1971; "Marxism and Formalism in the Films of Luchino Visconti" by Walter Korte in *Cinema Journal* (Evanston, Illinois), fall 1971; "Fascism in the Contemporary Film" by Joan Mellen in *Film Quarterly* (Berkeley), summer 1971; "Ingrid Thulin Comments on Visconti" in *Dialogue on Film* (Washington, D.C.), no.3, 1972; "Le Nom-de-l'auteur" by Serge Daney and J.-P. Oudart in *Cahiers du cinéma* (Paris), January/February 1972; "A propos de Mort à Venise" by J.-C. Guiguet in *Image et son* (Paris), February 1972; "Luchino Visconti" by Drahomira Novotnà in *Filmkultura* (Budapest), no.1, 1973; "Notes sur Luchino Visconti" by J.-C. Bonnet in *Cinématographe* (Paris), summer 1976; "Visconti le magnifique" by F. Gevaudan in *Cinéma* (Paris), July 1976; "Luchino Visconti, 1906-1976" by J. Cabourg in *Avant-Scène du cinéma* (Paris), 1 and 15 March 1977; "Visconti années quarante" by J. Fieschi in *Cinématographe* (Paris), December 1978; "Le Tyran à la rose" by P. Soli in *Lumière du cinéma* (Paris), February 1977; article in *The New York Times*, 7 January 1979; articles in *Cine* (Mexico), March 1979; "Nachkomme eines alten Herrschergeschlechts", 5-part series by G. Bogemski in *Film und Fernsehen* (Berlin), October and December, 1979, and January, April and June 1980; "L'Air de la folie" by J. Fieschi in *Cinématographe* (Paris), November 1979; "Visconti's Magnificent Obsessions" by D. Lyons in *Film Comment* (New York), March/April 1979; "En travaillent avec Visconti: sur le tournage de *La Terra trema*" by Francesco Rosi in *Positif* (Paris), February 1979; "Luchino Visconti's Legacy" by Andrew Sarris in *The Village Voice* (New York), 15 January 1979; "Luchino Visconti et la symbolique de l'aliment" by J.-C. Bonnet in *Cinématographe* (Paris), March 1979; "Dossier: cinéma et opéra: l'air et la folie" by J. Fieschi in *Cinématographe* (Paris), November 1979; "Le Diable au corps" by E. Decaux in *Cinématographe* (Paris), June 1980.

*   *   *

The films of Luchino Visconti are among the most stylistically and intellectually influential of postwar Italian cinema. Born a scion of ancient nobility, Visconti integrated the most heterogeneous elements of aristocratic sensibilty and taste with a committed Marxist political consciouness, backed by a firm knowledge of Italian class structure. Stylistically, his career follows a trajectory from a uniquely cinematic realism to an operatic theatricalism, from the simple quotidian eloquence of modeled actuality to the heightened affect of lavishly appointed historical melodramas. His career fuses these interests into a mode of expression uniquely Viscontian, prescibing a potent, double-headed realism. Visconti turned out films steadily but rather slowly from 1942 to 1976. His obsessive care with narrative and filmic materials is apparent in the majority of his films.

A debate still rages over when to date the inception of neorealism. Whether or not we choose to view the wartime *Ossessione* as a precursor or a determinant of neorealism or merely as a continuation of elements already present in Fascist period cinema, it is clear that the film remarkably applies a realist mise-en-scène to the formulaic constraints of the genre film. With major amendations, the film is, following a then-contemporary interest in American fiction of the 1930s, a treatment (the second and best) of James M. Cain's *The Postman Always Rings Twice*. In it the director begins to explore the potential of a long-take style, undoubtedly influenced by Jean Renoir for whom Visconti had worked as assistant. Having met with the disapproval of Vittorio Mussolini and the Fascist censors for its depiction of the shabbiness and desperation of Italian provincial life, *Ossessione* was banned from exhibition.

For *La terra trema*, Visconti further developed those documentary-like attributes of story and style generally associated with neorealism. Taken from Verga's late nineteenth century verist masterpiece *I malavoglia*, the film was shot entirely on location in Sicily and employs the people of the locale, speaking in their native dialect, as actors. Through them, Visconti explores the problems of class exploitation and the tragedy of family dissolution under economic pressure. Again, a mature long-shot/long-take style is coupled with diverse, extensive camera movements and well-planned actor movements to enhance the sense of a world faithfully captured in the multiplicity of its activites. The extant film was to have become the first episode of a trilogy on peasant life, but the other two parts were never filmed. However, *Rocco e i suoi fratelli*, made over a dozen years later, continues the story of this Sicilian family or at least one very much like it. Newly arrived in Milan from the South, the Parandis must deal with the economic realities of their poverty as well as survive the sexual rivalries threatening the solidarity of their family unit. The film is episodic in nature, affording time to each brother's story (in the original version), but special attention is given to Rocco, the forebearing and protective brother who strives at all costs to keep the group together, and Simone, the physically powerful and crudely brutal one, who is unable to control his personal fears, insecurities, and moral weakness. Unable to find other work, they both drift into prize fighting, viewed here as class exploitation. Jealousy over a prostitute, Nadia, causes Simone to turn his fists against his brother, then to murder the woman, but Rocco impelled by strong traditional ties would still act to save Simone from the police. Finally, the latter is betrayed to the law by Ciro, the fourth youngest and a factory worker who has managed to transfer some of his familial loyalty to a social plane and the labor union. Coming full circle from *La terra trema*, Luca, the youngest dreams of a day when he will be able to return to the Southern place of his birth. *Rocco* is perhaps Visconti's greatest contribution to modern tragedy, crafted along the lines of Arthur Miller and Tennessee Williams (whose plays he directed in Italy). The Viscontian tragedy is saturated with melodramatic intensity, a stylization incurring more than a suggestion of decadent sexuality and misogyny. There is, as in other Visconti works, a rather ambiguous intimation of homosexuality (here between Simone and his manager.)

By *Senso* Visconti had achieved the maturity of style that would characterize his subsequent work. With encompassing camera movements—like the opening shot moving from the stage of an opera house across the audience, taking in each tier of seats where the protest against the Austrians will soon erupt—and with a melodramatic rendering of historical fact, Visconti begins to mix cinematic realism with compositional elegance and lavish romanticism. Against the colorful background of the Risorgimento, he paints the betrayal by an Austrian lieutenant of his aristocratic Italian mistress who, in order to save him, has compromised the partisans. The love story parallels the approaching betrayal of the revolution by the bourgeois political powers. Like Gramsci who often returned to the contradictions of the Risorgimento as a key to the social problems of the modern Italian state, Visconti explores that period once more in *Il gattopardo* from the Lampedusa novel. An aristocratic Sicilian family undergoes transformation as a result of intermarriage with the middle-class at the same time that the Mezzogiorno is undergoing unification with the North. The bourgeoisie, now ready and able to take over from the dying aristocracy, usurps Garibaldi's revolution; in this period of *transformismo*, the revolutionary process will be assimilated into the dominant political structure and defused.

Still another film that focuses on the family unit as a barometer of history and changing society is *La caduta degli dei*. This treatment of a German munitions industry family (much like Krupp) and its decline into betrayal and murder in the interests of personal gain and the Nazi state intensifies and brings up-to-date an examination of the social questions of the last mentioned films. Here again a meticulous, mobile camera technique sets forth and stylistically typifies a decadent, death-surfeited culture.

Vaghe stelle dell'orsa removes the critique of the family from the social to the psychoanalytic plane. While death or absense of the father and the presence of an uprising surrogate is a thematic consideration in several Visconti films, he here explores it in conjunction with Freudian theory in this deliberate yet entirely transmuted re-telling of the Elektra myth. We are never completely aware of the extent of the relationship between Sandra and her brother, and the possibility of past incest remains distinct. Both despise Gilardini, their stepfather, whom they accuse of having seduced their mother and having denounced their father, a Jew, to the Fascists. Sandra's love for and sense of solidarity with her brother follows upon a racial solidarity with her father and race, but Gianni's love, on the other hand, is underpinned by a desire for his mother, transferred to Sandra. Nevertheless, dramatic confrontation propels the dialectical investigations of the individual's position with respect to the social even in this, Visconti's most densely psychoanalytic film.

Three films marking a further removal from social themes and observation of the individual, all literary adaptions, are generally felt to be his weakest: *Le notte bianche* from Dostoevski's "White Nights" sets a rather fanciful tale of a lonely man's hopes to win over a despairing woman's love against a decor that refutes, in its obvious, studio-bound stageness, Visconti's concern with realism and material verisimilitude. The clear inadequacy of this Livornian setting, dominated by a footbridge upon which the two meet and the unusually claustrophobic spatiality that results, locate the world of individual romance severed from large social and historical concerns in an inert, artificial perspective that borders on the hallucinatory. He achieves similar results with location shooting in *Lo straniero*, where—despite alterations of the original Camus—he perfectly captures the difficult

tensions and tone of individual alienation by utilizing the telephoto lens pervasively. Rather than provide a suitable Viscontian dramatic space rendered in depth, it reduces Mersault to the status of a Kafkaesque insect-man observed under a microscope. Finally, *Morte a Venezia* based on Thomas Mann, among Visconti's most formally beautiful productions is one of his least critically successful. The baroque elaboration of mise-en-scène and camera work does not rise above self-pity and self-indulgence, and is cut off from social context irretrievably.

—Joel Kanoff

VON STERNBERG, JOSEF. Austrian. Born Jonas Sternberg in Vienna, 29 May 1894. Educated briefly at Jamaica High School, Queens, New York; returned to Vienna to finish education. Married Riza Royce, 1926 (divorced 1930); married Jeanne Annette McBride, 1943; children: 1 son, 1 daughter. Career: 1911—works as film patcher for World Film Co. in Ft. Lee, New Jersey; 1917—joins U.S. Army Signal Corps to make training and indoctrination films; cited by War College for his efforts; 1918-24—works as scenarist and assistant for directors including Hugo Ballin, Harold Shaw, Emile Chautard, and Lawrence Windom; 1924—directs his scene in William Neill's *Vanity's Price* starring Anna Nilsson at FBO Studios; attaches "von" to his name at suggestion of actor Elliot Dexter while working as scenarist and assistant on *By Divine Right*; directs 1st film *The Salvation Hunters* as an independent; film purchased by Douglas Fairbanks for United Artists Co.; signs 8 picture contract with MGM, but after 2 abortive projects the contract is mutually terminated; 1926—directs *The Sea Gull (Woman of the Sea)* for Charlie Chaplin, but Chaplin does not release it; 1926-35—directs films for Paramount, beginning with *Underworld*; 1928—edits *The Wedding March* for Erich von Stroheim; 1929—directs 1st sound film *Thunderbolt*; 1930—directs UFA studio's 1st sound film *Der blaue Engel* in Berlin at request of Emil Jannings; discovers Marlene Dietrich who moves to U.S. to work with von Sternberg on future projects; 1935—last film with Dietrich, *The Devil is a Woman*; 1937—attempts to direct *I, Claudius* for Alexander Korda but production problems and accident of star Merle Oberon halt project; 1938—honored by Austrian government for furthering Austrian culture; 1941—offers services to U.S. Office of War Information, makes documentary *The Town*; 1947—teaches class in film direction at USC; 1950-52—makes 2 films for Howard Hughes, neither released as von Sternberg intends; 1953—directs *The Saga of Anatahan* at request of Japanese film industries; mid-1950s—retires from directing, begins lecturing and teaching at universities; appears at retrospectives of his work in major film centers around the world. Died 22 December 1969. Recipient: George Eastman House Medal of Honor, 1957; Honorary Member, Akademie der Künste, Berlin, 1960.

Films (as assistant director—partial list): 1919—*The Mystery of the Yellow Room*; *By Divine Right* (+sc, ph); *Vanity's Price*; (as director): 1925—*The Salvation Hunters* (+pr, sc); *The Exquisite Sinner* (+co-sc) (remade by Phil Rosen); *The Masked Bride* (remade by Christy Cabanne); 1926—*The Sea Gull (Woman of the Sea)* (+sc); 1927—*Children of Divorce* (d add'l scenes only); *Underworld*; 1928—*The Last Command* (+sc); *The Drag Net*; *The Docks of New York*; 1929—*The Case of Lena Smith*; *Thunderbolt*; 1930—*Der blaue Engel (The Blue Angel)*; *Morocco*; 1931—*Dishonored*; *An American Tragedy*; 1932—*Shanghai*

Express; *Blonde Venus* (+co-sc); *I Take This Woman*; 1934— *The Scarlet Empress*; 1935—*The Devil is a Woman* (+co-ph); *Crime and Punishment*; 1936—*The King Steps Out*; 1939— *Sergeant Madden*; *New York Cinderella* (remade by Frank Borzage and W.S. Van Dyke); 1941—*The Shanghai Gesture* (+co-sc); 1943-44—*The Town*; 1946—*Duel in the Sun* (d several scenes only); 1951—*Macao* (re-shot almost entirely by Nicholas Ray); 1953—*Anatahan (The Saga of Anatahan)* (+sc, ph); 1957—*Jet Pilot* (completed 1950).

Publications:

By VON STERNBERG:

Books—*Daughters of Vienna*, free adaptation of stories by Karl Adolph, Vienna 1922; *Fun in a Chinese Laundry*, New York 1965, published in France as *Souvenirs d'un montreur d'ombres*, Paris 1966; *The Blue Angel* (screenplay), New York 1968; articles—interview by Erich Krünes in *Film-Magazin* (Berlin), 25 August 1925; interview in *Motion Picture Classic* (New York), May 1931; "Come studio i mei film" in *Cinema* (Rome), no.3, 1936; "On Life and Film" in *Films in Review* (New York), October 1952, reprinted in *Cinémonde* (Paris), Christmas 1959; "Acting in Film and Theater" in *Film Culture* (New York), winter 1955; "More Light" in *Sight and Sound* (London), autumn 1955; "Pluie de lumière" in *Cahiers du cinéma* (Paris), October and November 1956; "Le jeu au théâtre et au cinéma" in *Cahiers du cinéma* (Paris), Christmas 1956; "Crèer avec l'oeil" in *L'Art du cinéma* by Pierre Lherminier, Paris 1960; interview by Philippe Esnault and Michèle Firk in *Positif* (Paris), January/- March 1961; interview by D. Freppel and B. Tavernier in *Cinéma 61* (Paris), March 1961; "A Taste for Celluloid" in *Films and Filming* (London), July 1963; "The von Sternberg Principle" in *Esquire* (New York), October 1963; "Sternberg at 70" by John Pankake in *Films in Review* (New York), May 1964; interview by Peter Bogdanovich in *Movie* (London), summer 1965; interview in *Cahiers du cinéma* (Paris), July 1965; "Total Recall" by John Nugent in *Newsweek* (New York), 29 March 1965; "L'Ange bleu" in *L'Avant-Scène du cinéma* (Paris), March 1966; interview by Kevin Brownlow in *Film* (London), spring 1966; interview by F.A. Macklin in *Film Heritage* (Dayton, Ohio), winter 1965-66; interview in *Positif* (Paris), March 1967.

On VON STERNBERG:

Books—*Marlène Dietrich, femme-énigme* by Jean Talky, Paris 1932; *Hollywood d'hier et d'ajourd-hui* by Robert Florey, Paris 1948; *An Index to the Films of Josef von Sternberg* by Curtis Harrington, London 1949; *Marlene Dietrich—Image and Legend* by Richard Griffith, New York 1959; *The Films of Josef von Sternberg* by Andrew Sarris, New York 1966; *Josef von Sternberg, Dokumentation, eine Darstellung*, Mannheim, Germany 1966; *Josef von Sternberg* by Herman G. Weinberg, Paris 1966; *The Celluloid Sacrifice* by Alexander Walker, New York 1967; *Josef von Sternberg: A Critical Study* by Herman G. Weinberg, New York 1967; *Film Makers on Filmmaking* edited by Harry M. Geduld, Bloomington, Indiana 1967; *Interviews with Film Directors* by Andrew Sarris, New York 1967; *Anthologie du cinéma* Vol.6, Paris 1971; *The Cinema of Josef von Sternberg* by John Baxter, New York 1971; articles—"The Luck of von Sternberg" by E.E.B. in *Picture Goer* (London), January 1925; special issue on von Sternberg in *Filmcritic* (Tokyo), 1928; "Josef von Sternberg" by Jim Tully in *Vanity Fair* (New York), July 1928; "Le cas de Josef von Sternberg" by Louis Chavance in

Revue du cinéma (Paris), July 1930; "10 Jours à Berlin" by Jean Lenauer in *Revue du cinéma* (Paris), June 1930; "Hollywood Has Nothing to Learn" by William Ortoni in *Atlantic Monthly* (New York), June 1931; "Profile of Josef von Sternberg" by Henry Pringle in the *New Yorker*, 28 March 1931; "Un Ethique du film" by Denis Marion in *La Revue du cinéma* (Paris), January 1931; "Les grands rôles de Marlène Dietrich" in *Ciné-monde* (Paris), 4 February 1932; "Field Generals of the Film" by H.A. Potamkin in *Vanity Fair* (New York), March 1932; special issue on von Sternberg in *Filmcritic* (Tokyo), 1933; "J.v.S.— Stylist" by Andre Sennwald in *The New York Times*, 23 September 1934; "Comment Marlène Dietrich est devenue star" by Maurice Dekobra in *Cinémonde* (Paris), 16 April 1939; "The Dangerous Compromise" by Curtis Harrington in *Hollywood Quarterly*, no.4, 1949; "Director's Return" by Herman G. Weinberg in *The New York Times*, 6 November 1949; "Escape" by Robert Florey in *Cinémonde* (Paris), 7 February 1949; "A Native Returns" in *The New York Times*, 10 September 1950; "Arrogant Gesture" by Curtis Harrington in *Theatre Arts* (New York), November 1950; "Josef von Sternberg" by Curtis Harrington in *Cahiers du cinéma* (Paris), October/November 1951; "Has von Sternberg discovered a Japanese Dietrich?" by Herman G. Weinberg in *Theatre Arts* (New York), August 1953; "Sternberg, le donne e i gangsters" by Giovanni Scognamillo in *Bianco e nero* (Rome), November/December 1954; "Filmografia di von Sternberg" in *Bianco e nero* (Rome), no.11-12, 1954; "Un Coeur mis à nu" by Philippe Demonsablon and "Un metteur en scène baudelairien" by André Labarthe in *Cahiers du cinéma* (Paris), April 1956; article in *Bianco e nero* (Rome), August/September 1959; "The Lost Films, Part 1" by Herman G. Weinberg in *Sight and Sound* (London), August 1962; "Pantheon Directors" by Andrew Sarris in *Film Culture* (New York), spring 1965; "A Belated Appreciation of von Sternberg" by Jack Smith in *Film Culture* (New York), winter 1963/64; filmography in *Cahiers du cinéma* (Paris), July 1965; "6 Films of Josef von Sternberg" by O.O. Green in *Movie* (London), no.13, 1965; "Josef von Sternberg ou le cinéma de l'enthousiasme" in *Cahiers du cinéma* (Paris), July 1965; filmography in *Movie* (London), summer 1965; "Josef von Sternberg" by Herman G. Weinberg in *Film Heritage* (Dayton, Ohio), winter 1965; article on von Sternberg and Dietrich in *Positif* (Paris), May 1966; "Sternberg and Strohiem—Letter" by Herman G. Weinberg in *Sight and Sound* (London), winter 1965/66; "L'Oeuvre de Josef von Sternberg" by Bernard Eisenschitz in *L'Avant-Scène du cinéma* (Paris), March 1966; "Sternberg, avant, pendant, après Marlene" by Ado Kyrou in *Positif* (Paris), May 1966; "On Sternberg" by Herman G. Weinberg in *Sight and Sound* (London), summer 1967; "Reflections on the Current Scene" by Herman G. Weinberg in *Take One* (Montreal), July/August 1969; article in *Image et son* (Paris), April 1970; "In Memoriam" by J. Jubak in *Focus* (Los Angeles), spring 1970; "Thoughts on the Objectification of Women" by Barbara Martineau in *Take One* (Montreal), November/December 1970; article by Jules Furthman and Richard Koszarski in *Film Comment* (New York), winter 1970-71; "Essays on Film Style" by F. Camper in *Cinema* (London), no.8, 1971; "Joe, Where Are You?" by T. Flinn in *Velvet Light Trap* (Madison, Wisconsin), fall 1972; "Josef von Sternberg: The Scientist and the Vamp" by Joyce Rheuban in *Sight and Sound* (London), autumn 1973; "Petite Suite russe" by Bernard Amengual in *Cahiers de la Cinématheque* (Paris), winter 1974; "Alchemy: Dietrich + Sternberg" by Gordon Gow in *Films and Filming* (London), June 1974; "Shanghai-Express" by M. Humbert in *Image et son* (Paris), June/July 1975; "Sternberg's Empress: The Play of Light and Shade" by Robin Wood in *Film Comment* (New York), March/April 1975; "L'Éclat du regard" by L. Audibert in *Cinématographe* (Paris), March 1977; "Joe

Where Are You?" by T. Flinn in *Velvet Light Trap* (Madison), winter 1977; "Sternberg: The Context of Passion" by D. Willis in *Sight and Sound* (London), spring 1978; articles from *Ciné-Magazine* reprinted in *Avant-Scène du cinéma* (Paris), 15 March 1980; "Some Observations on Sternberg and Dietrich" by C. Zucker in *Cinema Journal* (Evanston), spring 1980; special section of *Contracampo* (Madrid), June/July 1981; "Josef von Sternberg" by Herbert Luft in *Films in Review* (New York), January 1981; film—*The Epic That Never Was—"I, Claudius"* directed by Bill Duncalf for BBC-TV, London 1966.

*   *   *

There is a sense in which Jonas Sternberg never grew up. In his personality, the twin urges of the disturbed adolescent towards self-advertisement and self-effacement fuse with a brilliant visual imagination to create an artistic vision unparalleled in the cinema. But Sternberg lacked the cultivation of Murnau, the sophistication of his mentor von Stroheim, the humanity of Griffith or the ruthlessness of Chaplin. His imagination remained immature, and his personality malicious, obsessive. His films reflect a schoolboy's fascination with sensuality and heroics. That they are sublime visual adventures from an artist who contributed substantially to the sum of cinema technique is one paradox to add to the stock that make up his career.

Much of Sternberg's public utterance, and in particular his autobiography, was calculated to confuse; the disguise of his real Christian name under the diminutive "Jo" is typical. Despite his claims to have done so, he did not "write" all his films, though he did *re*-write the work of some skilled collaborators, notably Jules Furthman and Ben Hecht. While his eye for art and design was highly developed he never designed sets, merely "improved" them with props, veils, nets, posters, scribbles, but above all with light. Of this last he was a natural master, the only director of his day to earn membership of the American Society of Cinematographers. Given a set, a face, a camera and some lights, he could create a mobile portrait breath-taking in its beauty.

Marlene Dietrich was his greatest model. He dressed her like a doll, in feathers and sequins, in a gorilla suit, in a tuxedo, in a succession of gowns by Paramount's master of couture, Travis Banton. She submitted to his every demand with the skill and complaisance of a great courtesan. No other actress provided him with such malleable material. With Betty Compson, Gene Tierney and Akemi Negishi he fitfully achieved the same "spiritual power," as he called the mood of yearning melancholy which was his ideal, but the effect never equalled that of the seven Dietrich melodramas.

Sternberg was born too early for the movies. The studio system constrained his fractious temperament; the formula picture stifled his urge to primp and polish. He battled with MGM, who offered him a lucrative contract after the success of his von Stroheim-esque expressionist drama *The Salvation Hunters*, fell out with Chaplin, producer of the still-suppressed *Woman of the Sea*, and fought constantly with Paramount until Ernst Lubitsch, acting studio head, "liquidated" him for his intransigence; the later suppression of his last Paramount film, *The Devil Is a Woman*, in a political dispute with Spain merely served to increase Sternberg's alienation.

For the rest of his career, Sternberg wandered from studio to studio, country to country, lacking always the facilities he needed to achieve his best work. Even Korda's lavish *I Claudius*, dogged by disaster and finally terminated in a cost-cutting exercise, shows in its surviving footage only occasional flashes of Sternbergian brilliance. By World War II, he had already achieved his best work, though he was able to live for another 30 years.

Sternberg alarmed a studio establishment whose executives thought in terms of social and sexual stereotypes, formula plotting, stock happy endings; whose narrative idea was a *Saturday Evening Post* novelette. No storyteller, he derided plot; "the best source for a film is an anecdote," he said. From a single coincidence and a handful of characters, edifices of visual poetry could be constructed. His films leap years in the telling to follow a moral decline or growth of an obsession.

The most important film of his life was one he never made. After the humiliation of the war years, when he produced only the propaganda short *The Town*, and the nadir of his career, as close-up advisor to King Vidor on *Duel in the Sun*, he wrote *The Seven Bad Years*, a script that would, he said, "demonstrate the adult insistence to follow the pattern inflicted on a child in its first seven helpless years, from which a man could extricate himself were he to realize that an irresponsible child was leading him into trouble." He was never to make this work of self-analysis, nor any film which reflected a mature understanding of his contradictory personality.

Sternberg's theories of cinema were not especially profound, deriving largely from the work of Reinhardt, but they represented a quantum jump in an industry where questions of lighting and design were dealt with by experts who jealously guarded this prerogative. In planning his films not around dialogue but around the performances' "dramatic encounter with light," in insisting that the "dead space" between the camera and subject be filled and enlivened, and above all in seeing every story in terms, not of star quality, but "spiritual power," he established a concept of personal cinema which presaged the *politique des auteurs* and the Movie Brat generation.

In retrospect, his contentious personality, the self-conscious affecting of uniforms and costumes on the set, the epigrammatic style of communicating with performers which drove many of them to frenzy all reveal themselves as reactions against the banality of his chosen profession. Sternberg was asked late in life if he had a hobby. "Yes. Chinese philately." Why that? "I wanted," he replied in the familiar weary, uninflected voice, "a subject I could not exhaust."

—John Baxter

VON STROHEIM, ERICH. Austrian. Born Erich Oswald Stroheim in Vienna, 22 September 1885; became citizen of United States, 1926. According to von Stroheim he attended Maria-hilfe Military Academy, but many biographers doubt this; he did serve briefly in the Austro-Hungarian Army. Married Margaret Knox, 1914 (died 1915); May Jones, 1916 (divorced 1918); son: Erich von Stroheim, Jr.; married Valerie Germonprez, 1918 (separated about 1945); son: Josef Erich von Stroheim. Career: between 1906 and 1909—arrives in America; 1909-14—works at various odd jobs including salesman, clerk, short story writer, railroad worker, and travel agent; 1914—appears in 1st film, *Captain McLean*, in a bit part; 1914-15—works for D.W. Griffith as actor, assistant, and military advisor on *Birth of a Nation* and *Intolerance* among others; 1915—first major role in *Old Heidelberg*; 1915-17—works as assistant director, military advisor, and occasionally set designer for director John Emerson; 1917—appears for first time as a Prussian officer in *For France* and becomes known as "the man you love to hate"; 1918—directs *Blind Husbands* for Carl Laemmle at Universal; 1922—association with Universal terminated due to problems with producer Irving Thalberg on set of *Merry-Go-Round*; 1923—

directs *Greed* for Goldwyn Co.; his version cut to 10 reels by studio; 1933—publishes 2 novels adapted from film projects never realized; stars in *La Grande Illusion* by Renoir, and helps script role; 1940—returns to U.S. after plans for a directorial comeback fall through due to outbreak of war; 1941-43—only stage play appearance in *Arsenic and Old Lace*; 1945-57—lives and works in France, returning to the U.S. to appear in Wilder's *Sunset Boulevard* in a part especially written for him. Died 12 May 1957; buried at Maurepas, near Paris.

Films (as assistant director): 1915—*Old Heidelberg* (Emerson) (+military advisor, ro as *Lutz*); 1916—*Intolerance* (Griffith) (+ro as *Second Pharisee*); *The Social Secretary* (Emerson) (+ro as *A Reporter*); *Macbeth* (Emerson) (+ro); *Less Than the Dust* (Emerson) (+ro); *His Picture in the Papers* (Emerson) (+ro as *The Traitor*); 1917—*Panthea* (Dwan) (+ro as *Russian policeman*); *Sylvia of the Secret Service* (Fitzmaurice) (+ro); *In Again—Out Again* (Emerson) (+art d, ro as *Russian officer*); 1918—*Hearts of the World* (Griffith) (+ military advisor, ro as *German officer*); (as director and scriptwriter): 1918—*Blind Husbands* (+art d, ro as *Lieutenant von Steuben*); 1919—*The Devil's Passkey* (+art d); 1921—*Foolish Wives* (+co-art d, co-costume, ro as *Count Wladislas Serge Karamazin*); 1922—*Merry-Go-Round* (+co-art d, co-costume) (completed by Rupert Julian); 1923—*Greed* (+co-art d); 1925—*The Merry Widow* (+co-art d, co-costume); 1927—*The Wedding March* (+co art d, co-costume, ro as *Prince Nicki*); *The Tempest* (sc only); 1928—*The Honeymoon* (+ro as *Prince Nicki*—part 2 of *The Wedding March* and not released in U.S.); *Queen Kelly* (+co-art d) (completed by others); 1933—*Walking Down Broadway* (mostly reshot by Alfred Werker and Edwin Burke and released as *Hello Sister!*); (as scriptwriter or co-scriptwriter) 1934—*Fugitive Road* (+military advisor); 1935—*Anna Karenina* (military advisor only); 1936—*Devil Doll*; *San Francisco*; 1937—*Between 2 Women*; 1947—*La Danse de mort* (Cravenne) (co-adapt, co-dialogue only, +ro as *Edgar*).

Roles: 1914—*Captain McLean* (Conway); 1915—*Ghosts* (Emerson); *The Birth of a Nation* (Griffith); 1917—*Prussian officer* in *For France* (Ruggles); 1918—*German officer* in *The Unbeliever* (Crosland); *German officer* in *The Hun Within* (Cabanne); 1929—*Gabbo* in *The Great Gabbo* (Cruze); 1930—*3 Faces East* (del Ruth); 1931—*Friends and Lovers* (Schertzinger); 1932—*The Lost Squadron* (Archimbaud and Sloane); *As You Desire Me* (Fitzmaurice); 1934—*German pilot* in *Crimson Romance* (Howard) (+military advisor); 1935—*Dr. Crespi* in *The Crime of Dr. Crespi* (Auer); 1936—*German officer* in *Marthe Richard* (Bernard); 1937—*von Rauffenstein* in *La Grande Illusion* (Renoir); *Col. Mathesius* in *Mademoiselle Docteur* (Gréville); *Winkler* in *L'Alibi* (Chenal); 1938—*Tschou-Kin* in *Les Pirates du rail* (Christian-Jaque); *Denis* in *L'Affaire Lafarge* (Chenal); *German professor* in *Les Disparus de Saint-Agil* (Christian-Jaque); *Général Simovic* in *Ultimatum* (Wiene and Siodmak); *Marson* in *Gibraltar (It Happened in Gibraltar)* (Ozep); *Eric* in *Derrière la façade* (Lacombe); 1939—*Hoffman* in *Menaces* (Gréville); *Stanley Wells* in *Rappel immédiat* (Mathot); *Pears* in *Pièges* (Siodmak); *Emile Lasser* in *La Révolte des vivants* (Pottier); *Kohrlick* in *Tempête sur Paris* (Bernard-Deschamps); *Knall* in *Macao l'enfer* (Delannoy); *Paris—New York* (Heymann and Mirande); 1940—*I Was an Adventuress* (Ratoff); *So Ends Our Night* (Cromwell); 1943—*Field Marshall Rommel* in *5 Graves to Cairo* (Wilder); *German medic* in *The North Star* (Milestone); 1944—*The Lady and the Monster* (Sherman); *Storm over Lisbon* (Sherman); 1945—*Flamarion* in *The Great Flamarion* (Mann); *Scotland Yard Investigation* (Blair); *Dijon* in *The Mask of Dijon* (Landers); 1946—*Eric von Berg* in *On ne meurt pas comme ça* (Boyer); 1948—*Le Signal rouge* (Neubach); 1949—*Portrait d'un assassin* (Bernard-Roland); 1950—*Max* in *Sunset Boulevard* (Wilder); 1952—*Minuit, quai de Bercy* (Stengel); *Alraune (La Mandragore)* (Rabenalt); 1953—*O'Hara* in *L'Envers du paradis* (Gréville); *Alerte au sud* (Devaivre); 1954—*Beethoven* in *Napoléon* (Guitry); 1955—*Série noire* (Foucaud); *La Madone des sleepings* (Diamant-Berger).

Publications:

By VON STROHEIM:

Books—*Paprika*, New York 1935; *Les Feux de la Saint-Jean: Veronica* (Part 1), Givors, France 1951; *Les Feux de la Saint-Jean: Constanzia* (Part 2), Givors, France 1954, reissued 1967; *Poto-Poto*, Paris 1956; *Greed* (full screenplay), Cinémathèque Royale de Belgique, Brussels 1958; articles—interview in *Motion Picture Classic* (Brooklyn), January 1920; interview in *Motion Picture* (New York), August 1920; interview in *Motion Picture* (New York), October 1921; interview in *Motion Picture* (New York), May 1922; interview in *Motion Picture* (New York), September 1923; interview in *Motion Picture* (New York), April 1927; interview in *Motion Picture Classic* (Brooklyn), April 1930; "Charges Against Him and His Reply" by C. Belfrage in *Motion Picture Classic* (Brooklyn), June 1930; "My Own Story" in *Film Weekly* (London), April/May 1935; "Ma première rencontre avec Jean Renoir" in *Cinémonde* (Paris), Christmas 1936; "Sexe et cinéma" in *Cinémonde* (Paris), 9 April, 16 April, and 23 April; "Da Vienna a Hollywood" in *Sequenze* (Rome), October 1948; "Suis-je vraiment le metteur en scène le plus cher et le plus salaud du monde?" in *Ciné-club* (Paris), April 1949; "Homage to D.W. Griffith" in *Hollywood Scapegoat* by Peter Noble, London 1951; "Stroheim in London" by Karel Reisz in *Sight and Sound* (London), April/June 1954; "Synopsis of *Queen Kelly* and *Walking Down Broadway*" in *Film Culture* (New York), January 1955; article in *Film Culture* (New York), April 1958; "*La Dame Blanche*" (2 scenes) in *Bianco e nero* (Rome), February/March 1959; "Erich von Stroheim" in *Interviews with Film Directors* edited by Andrew Sarris, New York 1967; "*Les Rapaces (Greed)*" (scenario) in *L'Avant-Scène du cinéma* (Paris), September 1968; "Citizen Kane" in *Positif* (Paris), March 1968 (reprinted from 1941); "Erich von Stroheim zum Tod von D.W. Griffith" in *Filmkritik* (Munich), April 1975.

On VON STROHEIM:

Books—*Erich von Stroheim* by P. Atasceva and V. Korolevitch, Moscow 1927; *The Life and Adventures of Carl Laemmle* by John Drinkwater, New York 1931; *Film* by Rudolph Arnheim, London 1933; *Erich von Stroheim, sa vie, ses films* by Georges Fronval, Paris 1939; *An Index to the Creative Work of Erich von Stroheim* by Herman G. Weinberg, supplement to *Sight and Sound*, index series, London 1943; *Hollywood Scapegoat: The Biography of Erich von Stroheim* by Peter Noble, London 1951; *Erich von Stroheim* by Bob Bergut, Paris 1960; *Erich von Stroheim* by Jan Barna, Vienna 1966; *Hommage à Erich von Stroheim* edited by Charlotte Gobeil, Ottawa 1966; *Erich von Stroheim* by Michel Ciment, Paris 1967; *Stroheim* by Joel Finler, Berkeley 1968; *The Parade's Gone By...* by Kevin Brownlow, New York 1968; *Erich von Stroheim* by Thomas Quinn Curtiss, Paris 1969; *Erich von Stroheim* by Freddy Buache, Paris 1972; *Spellbound in Darkness* by George C. Pratt, Greenwich, Conn. 1973; *Stroheim: A Pictorial Record of His 9 Films* by Herman

G. Weinberg, New York 1975; articles—"Gosh, How They Hate Him!" by Robert Yost in *Photoplay* (New York), December 1919; *Erich von Stroheim" by Jim Tully in Vanity Fair* (New York), March 1926; "The Don Quixote of Pictures" in *Motion Picture Classic* (Brooklyn), May 1926; "The Seamy Side of Directing" in *Theatre* (New Haven), November 1927; "Erich von Stroheim" by Denis Marion in *Revue du cinéma* (Paris), 15 November 1929; "Another Film Carnage" by Herman G. Weinberg in *Cinema Quarterly* (London), summer 1933; "Erich von Stroheim" by Herman G. Weinberg in *Film Art* (London), spring 1937; "*5 Graves to Cairo*" in *Life* (New York), 14 June 1943; "Work of Erich von Stroheim" in *Newsweek* (New York), 31 May 1943; "L'Homme que vous aimeriez haïr" by E.T. Gréville in *Ecran français* (Paris), Christmas 1945; "Tribute to Stroheim" in *Film Quarterly* (London), spring 1947; "Stroheim at the Crossroads" by John Florquin in *Film Quarterly* (London), spring 1947; "Lament of the Bad Men" by Harry Wilson in *Screen* (London), autumn 1947; "The Man You Love to Hate" by Peter Noble in *Film Quarterly* (London), spring 1947; "Erich von Stroheim, His Work and Influence" in *Sight and Sound* (London), winter 1947-48; "The Fabulous Von" by Peter Noble in *Motion Picture Spy* (London), winter 1947-48; special issue of *Ciné-club* (Paris), April 1949; "The Man You Love to Hate: A Study of Stroheim" by Peter Noble in *Theatre Arts* (New York), January 1950; "The Resurgence of von Stroheim" by Jules Schwerin in *Films in Review* (New York), April 1950; "Le Bouc émissaire" by Denis Marion in *Cahiers du cinéma* (Paris), December 1952; "Cloudland Revisited" by S.J. Pearlman in the *New Yorker*, 20 September 1952; "Lunch with Erich von Stroheim" by O. Jensen in *Vogue* (New York), 15 October 1953; "En travaillant avec Erich von Stroheim" by Renée Lichtig in *Cahiers du cinéma* (Paris), no.37, 1954; "Stroheim Revisited: The Missing Third in American Cinema" by Gavin Lambert in *Sight and Sound* (London), April/June 1955; "Le Mythe" by Etienne Chaumeton in *Cinéma 57* (Paris), February 1957; "Hommage à Stroheim" by Henri Langlois in *Cinéma 57* (Paris), June 1957; "Notes sur le style de Stroheim" by Lotte Eisner in *Cahiers du cinéma* (Paris) January 1957; "The Career of Erich von Stroheim" by W.K. Everson in *Films in Review* (New York), August/September 1957; "Stroheim poète de l'amour" by Marcel Martin and "Stroheim le créateur" by Jean Mitry in *Cinéma 57* (Paris), February 1957; "Tendre Stroheim" by Claude de Givray in *Cahiers du cinéma* (Paris), January 1957; obituary in *Time* (New York), 27 May 1957; "Stroheim" by G. Mitchell in *Films in Review* (New York), October 1957; special issue of *Film Culture* (New York), April 1958; "Lovers in the Shadows" by Peter John Dyer in *Films and Filming* (London), April 1958; special issue of *Bianco e nero* (Rome), February/March 1959; "Cinémathèque" by Jacques Rivette in *Cahiers du cinéma* (Paris), January 1959; "The Legion of Lost Films" by H.G. Weinberg in *Sight and Sound* (London), autumn 1962; "Stroheim, the Legend and the Fact" by Denis Marion in *Sight and Sound* (London), winter 1961/62; special issue of *Premier Plan* (Lyon), August 1963; interview with H.G. Weinberg in *Objectif* (Montreal), October/November 1964; special issue of *Etudes cinématographiques* (Paris), no.48/50, 1966; "*Queen Kelly*" by Arthur Lennig in *Film Heritage* (Dayton, Ohio), fall 1966; "Sternberg and Stroheim" by Herman Weinberg in *Sight and Sound* (London), winter 1965-66; "Erich von Stroheim" by Marianne Sabatier in *Image et son* (Paris), January 1967; "Erich von Stroheim: Zwischen zwei Legenden" by François Bondy in *Der Monat* (Berlin), February 1967; "Count von Realism" by R. Lee in *Classic Film Collector* (Indiana, Pennsylvania), spring 1969; "*Hello Sister*" by Richard Koszarski in *Sight and Sound* (London), autumn 1970; "Stroheim et l'enigme de *Walking Down Broadway*" by Michel Ciment in *Positif* (Paris), October

1971; "The Scabrous Poet from the Estate Belonging to No One" by Penelope Gilliatt in the *New Yorker*, 3 June 1972; "Hommage à Erich von Stroheim, martyr et comédien" by Freddy Buache in *Cinéma* (Paris), June 1972; "Erich von Stroheim", special issue of *Cinema* (Zurich), December 1973; "Second Thoughts on Stroheim" by Jonathan Rosenbaum in *Film Comment* (New York), May/June 1974; "Stroheim's Last 'Lost' Film: The Making and Remaking of *Walking Down Broadway*" by Richard Koszarski and William K. Everson in *Film Comment* (New York), May/June 1975; "Les Rapaces d'Erich von Stroheim" by L. Dahan in *Cinématographe* (Paris), April 1977; "William Daniels on von Stroheim, Garbo and Others" by G.C. Pratt in *Image* (Rochester), no.1, 1979; articles from *Ciné-Magazine* reprinted in *Avant-Scène du cinéma* (Paris), 15 March 1980.

* * *

Erich von Stroheim had two complementary careers in cinema, that of actor-director primarily during the silent period, and that of distinguished character actor when his career as a director was frustrated through inability to bring his genius to terms with the American film industry.

After edging his way into the industry in the humblest capacities, his lengthy experience as bit player and assistant to Griffith paid off. His acceptance during the pioneer period of American cinema as Prussian "military adviser," and his bullet-headed physical resemblance to the traditional monocled image of the tight-uniformed Hun-officer, enabled him to create a more established acting career and star in his own films, and with his first personal film, *Blind Husbands*, he became the prime creator in Hollywood of witty, risqué, European-like sex-triangle comedy-dramas. His initial successes in the early 1920s were characterized by subtle acting touches, and a marked sophistication of subject that impressed American audiences of the period as essentially European and facsinatingly decadent. *Blind Husbands* was followed by other films in the same genre, the 12-reel *The Devil's Pass Key* and the critically successful *Foolish Wives*. In all three, women spectators could easily identify with the common character of the lonely wife, whose seduction by attractively wicked Germanic officers and gentlemen (usually played by Stroheim, now publicized as "the man you love to hate") provided the essential thrill. Stroheim also cunningly included certain beautiful but excitingly unprincipled women characters in both *The Devil's Pass Key* and *Foolish Wives*, played by Maude George and Mae Busch. Details of bathing, dressing, and the ministration of servants in the preparation of masters or mistresses in boudoir or dressing room were recurrent, and the Stroheim scene always included elaborate banquets, receptions and social ceremonies.

Stroheim's losing battle with the film industry began in his clashes with Irvin Thalberg at Universal. His obsessive perfectionism over points of detail in setting and costume had pushed the budget for *Foolish Wives* to the million dollar mark. Though the publicists boasted of Stroheim's extravagance, the front office preferred hard profits to such self-indulgent expenditure. Thalberg also refused Stroheim's demands that his films should be of any length he determined, and *Foolish Wives* (intended to be in two parts) was finally taken out of his hands and cut from 18/20 to some 12/14 reels. Although a critical success, the film lost money.

Foolish Wives was Stroheim's most discussed film before *Greed*. In it he played a bogus aristocratic officer, in reality a swindler and multi-seducer. His brilliant, sardonic acting "touches" brought a similar psychological verisimilitude to this grimly satiric comedy of manners as Lubitsch was to establish in his *Kammerspielfilme* (intimate films). He also specialized in decor, photographic composition and lighting. Unforgettable is the latticed light and shadow in the sequence when the seducer in full uniform visits the counterfeiter's underworld den with hope of ravishing the old man's mentally defective daughter.

Greed, Stroheim's most important films, was based meticulously on Norris's Zolaesque novel, *McTeague*. Stroheim's masterpiece, it was eventually mutilated by the studio because of its unwieldy length; under protest by Stroheim it was reduced from 42 reels to 24 (between 5 and 6 hours), and then finally cut to 10 reels by the studio. Stroheim's stress on the ugly and bizarre in human nature emerged in his psychologically naturalistic study of avarice and degradation in the mis-matched couple—McTeague, the impulsive, primitive (but bird-loving) lower-class dentist, and Trina, the pathologically avaricious spinster member of a German-Swiss immigrant family and winner of a $5,000 lottery. After their marriage, Trina hoards her money as their circumstances decline to the point where the husband becomes drunk and brutal, and the wife mad. After he murders her, and becomes a fugitive, McTeague ends in the isolated wastes of Death Valley, handcuffed to Marcus, his former friend whom he has killed. Using the streets of San Francisco and the house where the actual murder that had inspired Norris had taken place, Stroheim anticipated Rossellini in his use of such locations. But his insistence on achieving an incongrous and stylized realism, starting with McTeague's courtship of Trina sitting on a sewerpipe and culminating in the macabre sequence in Death Valley goes beyond that straight neorealism of the future. Joel W. Finler in his book, *Stroheim*, analyzes the wholesale cutting in the 10-reel version, exposing the grave losses that render the action and motivation of the film unclear. But the superb performance of Zasu Pitts and Gibson Gowland compensate, and the grotesque Sieppe family provide a macabre background, enhanced by Stroheim's constant reminder of San Francisco's "mean streets." The film was held to be his masterpiece by many, but also condemned as a "vile epic of the sewer."

Stroheim was to work as director on only five more films: the Ruritanian *Merry Widow* (adapted from the operetta), *The Wedding March* (in two parts, and again severely cut), the erotic *Queen Kelly* (directed for Gloria Swanson, but never completed by Stroheim, though released by Swanson with her own additions), and the sound films *Walking Down Broadway* (*Hello, Sister* reworked and never released in Stroheim's original version), and *The Emperor's Candlesticks* on which it appears he collaborated only in direction. The silent films portray the same degenerate Imperial Viennese society Stroheim favored, half romantic, half grotesque fantasy, and once again presented with Stroheim's meticulous attention to detail in decor and characterization. *The Wedding March* (in spite of studio intervention) is the high point in Stroheim's career as a director after *Greed*. Subsequently he remained content to star or appear in films made by others, some 50 appearances between 1929 and 1955, most notably Renoir's *La Grande Illusion* and Wilder's *Five Graves to Cairo* and *Sunset Boulevard*, in which his past as a director is almost ghoulishly recalled.

—Roger Manvell

VON TROTTA, MARGARETHE. German. Born in Berlin, 21 February 1942. Educated in Romance languages and literature and German studies, Munich and Paris; studied acting in Munich. Married Volker Schlöndorff. Career: 1960s—performs in theaters at Dinkelsbül, Stuttgart, and Frankfurt; 1969—since 1969 works entirely in TV and film; 1970—begins appearing in and collaborating on films of Volker Schlöndorff. Recipient: Golden Lion, Venice Festival, for *Die bleierne Zeit*, 1981.

Films (as director and co-scriptwriter—also see "Roles" below): 1975—*Die verlorene Ehre der Katherina Blum (The Lost Honor of Katharina Blum)* (co-d); (as director and scriptwriter): 1977—*Das zweite Erwachen der Christa Klages (The Second Awakening of Christa Klages)*; 1979—*Schwestern oder Die Balance des Glücks (Sisters, or The Balance of Happiness)*; 1981—*Die bleierne Zeit (Leaden Times, Marianne and Julianne, The German Sisters)*; 1983—*Heller Wahn (Sheer Madness)*.

Roles: 1968—*Schräge Vögel* (Ehmck); 1969—*Brandstifter* (Lemke); *Margarethe* in *Götter der Pest* (Fassbinder); 1970—*Sophie* in *Baal* (Schlöndorff); *Maid* in *Der amerikanische Soldat* (Fassbinder); 1971—*Heinrich's Woman* in *Der plötzliche Reichtum der armen Leute von Kombach* (Schlöndorff) (+co-sc); *Doris Vogelsang* in *Die Moral der Ruth Halbfass* (Schlöndorff); 1972—*Elisabeth* in *Strohfeuer* (Schlöndorff) (+co-sc); 1973—*Desaster* (Hauff); *Katja* in *Übernachtung in Tirol* (Schlöndorff); 1974—*Paulette* in *Invitation à la chasse* (Chabrol—for TV); *Kate Theory* in *Georgina's Gründe* (Schlöndorff—for TV); 1975—*Filmschauspielerin* (film actress) in *Das andechser Gefühl* (Achternbusch); 1976—*Sophie von Reval* in *Der Fangschuss* (Schlöndorff) (+co-sc).

Publications:

By VON TROTTA:

Articles—"Feu de paille", interview with Margarethe von Trotta in *Jeune Cinéma* (Paris), December/January 1972; "A propos de *Feu de paille*", interview by G. Langlois in *Téléciné* (Paris), March 1973; "Les Femmes sont sanctionées dès avant leur naissance", interview by M. Grisolia in *Cinéma* (Paris), February 1973; "Problemy kino", interview in *Iskusstvo Kino* (Moscow), June 1973; "Gespräch zwischen Margarethe von Trotta and Christel Buschmann" in *Frauen und Film* (Berlin), June 1976; "Die verlorene Ehre der Katharina Blum" in *Film und Fernsehen* (Berlin), no.8, 1976; "Melville und der Befreiungskampf im Baltikum", interview by H. Wiedemann in *Film und Ton* (Munich), December 1976; "Frauen haben anderes zu sagen...", interview by U. Schirmeyer-Klein in *Film und Fernsehen* (Berlin), no.4, 1979; "Die politische Dimension der privaten Themen", interview by B. Geisel in *Medium* (Frankfurt), November 1979; "Retrouver la force du rêve", interview in *Jeune Cinéma* (Paris), March 1980.

On VON TROTTA:

Book—*Schwestern oder die Balance des Glücks: ein Film*, edited by W. Baer and H.J. Weber, Frankfurt 1979; articles—"Le Coup de grâce", special issue of *Avant-Scène du cinéma* (Paris), 1 February 1977; "Von Trotta Feeling Vindicated on Film" in *Variety* (New York), 20 January 1982.

*　　*　　*

An important aspect of Margarethe von Trotta's filmmaking which effects not only the content but also the representation of that content, is her emphasis on women and the relationships that can develop between them. For example, von Trotta chose as the central theme in two of her films, *Sisters or the Balance of Happiness* and *Marianne and Juliane*, one of the most intense and complex relationships that can exist between two women, that of sisters. Whether von Trotta is dealing with overtly political themes as in *The Second Awakening of Christa Klages* (which is based on the true story of a woman who robs a bank in order to subsidize a daycare center) and *Marianne and Juliane* (which is based on the experiences of Christine Ensslin and her "terrorist" sister) or with the lives of ordinary women as in *Sisters or the Balance of Happiness* or *Sheer Madness*, von Trotta shows that the relationships between women are political. By paying close attention to these relationships von Trotta brings into question the social and political systems which either sustain them or do not allow them to exist. She examines these systems through close psychological analysis of her female characters.

Although the essence of von Trotta's films is political and critical to the status quo, their structures are quite conventional. Her films are expensively made and highly subsidized by the film production company Bioskop, which was started by her husband, Volker Schlöndorff, and Reinhart Hauff, both filmmakers. Von Trotta joined the company when she started making her own films. She did not go through the complicated system of incentives and grants available to independent filmmakers in Germany. Rather, she began working for Schlöndorff as an actress and then as a scriptwriter, and finally on her own as a director and co-owner in the production company which subsidizes their films.

Von Trotta has been criticized by some feminists for working too closely within the system and for creating characters and structures which are too conventional to be of any political value. Other critics find that a feminist aesthetic can be found in her choice of themes. For although von Trotta uses conventional women characters she does not represent them in traditional fashion. Nor does she describe them with stereotyped, sexist clichés, rather she allows her characters to develop on screen through gestures, glances and nuances. Great importance is given to the psychological and subconscious delineation of her characters by von Trotta's constant attention to dreams, visions, flashbacks and personal obsessions. In this way, her work can be seen as inspired by the films of Bresson and Bergman, filmmakers who also use the film medium to portray psychological depth.

"The unconscious and subconscious behavior of the characters is more important to me than what they do", says von Trotta. For this reason, von Trotta spends a great deal of time with her actors and actresses to be sure that they really understand the emotions and motivations of the characters which they portray. This aspect of her filmmaking caused her to separate her work from that of her husband, Volker Schlöndorff. During their joint direction of *The Lost Honor of Katharina Blum*, it became apparent that Schlöndorff's manner of directing which focused on action shots, did not mix with her own predilections for exploring the internal motivation of the characters. Her films are often criticized for paying too much attention to the psychological, and thus becoming too personal and inaccessible.

Von Trotta has caused much controversy within the feminist movement and outside of it. Nevertheless, her films have won several awards not only in her native Germany but also internationally, drawing large diverse audiences. Her importance cannot be minimalized. Although she travels within the well used and accepted structures of popular filmmakers, her message is quite different. Her main characters are women and her films treat them seriously and innovatively. Such treatment of women inside a traditional form has in the past been undervalued or ignored. Her presentation of women has opened up possibilties

for the development of the image of women on screen and in turn the development of film itself.

Von Trotta's choice of conventional structures and characters indicates that change can happen anywhere there is uneasiness brewing under the surface of people's lives.

—Gretchen Elsner-Sommer

WAJDA, ANDRZEJ. Polish. Born in Suwalki, Poland, 6 March 1927. Educated Fine Arts Academy, Kraków, Poland, 1945-48; High School of Cinematography, Lódź, Poland, 1950-52. Career: 1940-43—during occupation of Poland by Germany, works at odd jobs including assistant in restoration of paintings in a church in Radom; 1942—joins the A.K. (Home Army) directed by the Polish government in exile, against the Germans; 1950-52—directs several shorts as part of schooling; 1954—becomes assistant to director Aleksander Ford on *Piatka z ulicy Barskiej* (5 Boys from Barska Street); begins work on his 1st feature, *Pokolenie (A Generation)*, in which Roman Polanski appears; 1959—directs 1st play, *A Hatful of Rain*, in Gdańsk; 1961-62—first film outside Poland, *Sibirska Ledi Magbet (Lady Macbeth of Mtsensk)* for Avala Films, Belgrade; 1962—contributes "Warszawa" episode to French-Italian-Japanese-Polish production *L'Amour à 20*, which includes episodes by Truffaut and Marcel Ophuls; 1967—death of Polish actor and close friend to Wajda, Zbigniew Cybulski, leads to making of *Everything for Sale*; 1972—directs *Pilatus und andere (Pilate and Others)* for West German television; 1981—following imposition of martial law, concentrates on theatrical projects in Poland and on film productions in cooperation with non-Polish studios; 1983—government dissolves Wajda's Studio X film production group; 1984—government demands Wajda's resignation as head of filmmakers' association in return for allowing continued existence of organization. Recipient: Palme d'or, Cannes Festival, for *Man of Iron*, 1981.

Films (as director and scriptwriter): 1950—*Kiedy ty śpisz* [While You Sleep]; *Zły chłopiec* [The Bad Boy]; 1951—*Ceramika Ilzecka* [The Pottery of Ilzecka]; 1955—*Pokolenie (A Generation)*; *Ide ku słońcu (Ide do słonca)* [I Walk to the Sun]; 1957—*Kanał (They Loved Life)* [Sewer]; 1958—*Popiół i diament (Ashes and Diamonds)* (co-sc); 1959—*Lotna* (co-sc); 1960—*Niewinni czarodzieje (Innocent Sorcerers)*; 1961—*Samson*; 1962—*Sibirska Ledi Magbet (Lady Macbeth of Mtsensk, Fury is a Woman)* [Siberian Lady Macbeth]; "Warszawa" episode of *L'Amour à 20*; 1965—*Popioły (Ashes)*; 1967—*Bramy raju (Gates to Paradise, The Gates of Heaven, The Holy Apes)* (co-sc); 1968—*Wszystko na sprzedaz (Everything for Sale)*; *Przekładaniec* [Roly-Poly]; 1969—*Polowanie na muchy (Hunting Flies)*; *Makbet (Macbeth)* (for Polish TV); 1970—*Krajobraz po bitwie (Landscape After the Battle)* (co-sc); *Brzezina* [The Birch-wood] (d only); 1972—*Pilatus und andere—ein Film für Karfreitag (Pilate and Others)*; *Wesele (The Wedding)* (d only); 1974—*Ziemia obiecana (Promised Land)* (also as series on Polish TV); 1976—*Smuga cienia (The Shadow Line)* (co-sc); 1978—*Człowiek z marmuru (Man of Marble)*; *Bez znieczulenia (Without Anesthetic)* (co-sc); *Zaproszenie do wnetrza (Invitation to the Inside)* (documentary); 1979—*Dyrygent (The Conductor, The Orchestra Conductor)*; *Panny z Wilka (Maidens from Wilko, The Girls from Wilko)*; 1981—*Człowiek z zelaza (Man of Iron)*; 1982—*Danton*.

Publications:

By WAJDA:

Articles—"Destroying the Commonplace" in *Films and Filming* (London), November 1961; interview by Stanislas Janicki and Jean Sirodeau, translated by Gail Naughton, in *Positif* (Paris), March 1966; interview by Boleslaw Michalek in *Kino* (Warsaw), no.1, 1968; "Andrzej Wajda Speaking" in *Kino* (Warsaw), no.1, 1968; "Wajda & Polanski: conversazione sul nuovo mondo" in *Filmcritica* (Rome), March 1972; "Realyser filmowy i świat współczesny: Andrzej Wajda w rozmowie z Romanem Polańskim" in *Kino* (Warsaw), February 1972; "Living in Hope", interview by Gordon Gow in *Films and Filming* (London), February 1973; "O 'Lotnej' domu rodzinnym okresie wojny i studiach", edited by S. Janicki in *Kino* (Warsaw), March 1973; "Les Noces", interview by M. Martin in *Ecran* (Paris), February 1974; interview by J.-L. Passek in *Cinéma* (Paris), February 1974; "Filmer les noces" in *Positif* (Paris), February 1974; interview by W. Wertenstein in *Kino* (Warsaw), May 1974; interview by P. Haudiquet in *Image et son* (Paris), April 1976; interview by J.-L. Passek in *Cinéma* (Paris), April 1976; interview by W. Wertenstein in *Kino* (Warsaw), June 1976; interview by K.K. Przybylska in *Literature/Film Quarterly* (Salisbury, Md.), winter 1977; "3 Schritte in die Zukunft", interview in *Film und Fernsehen* (Berlin), January 1977; interview by M. Devillers in *Cinématographe* (Paris), November 1978; interview by M. Martin in *Ecran* (Paris), November 1979; "Robie filmy, ktore sam chcialbym zobaczyc", interview by M. Dipont in *Kino* (Warsaw), February 1979; "5 cinéastes pour Cannes: propos d'Andrzej Wajda", interview by J. Plazewski in *Ecran* (Paris), 15 May 1979; "Co przed nami" in *Kino* (Warsaw), January 1979; "Dlaczego *Panny z Wilka*?", interview by W. Wertenstein in *Kino* (Warsaw), June 1979; "L'uomo di celluloide", interview by D. Ferrario in *Cineforum* (Bergamo), April 1979; "Pologne: l'état de la question", interview by M. Martin in *Ecran* (Paris), 20 November 1979; "Andrzej Wajda parle de *Sans anesthesie*" by B. Michalek in *Positif* (Paris), June 1979; "Testimonianze: la rabbia ai *Senza anestesia*" in *Filmcritica* (Rome), May 1979; "Between the Permissible and the Impermissible", interview by D. Bickley and L. Rubinstein in *Cineaste* (New York), winter 1980/81; "Je complète mon curriculum vitae", interview by K. Klopotowski in *Positif* (Paris), June 1981; "Wajda August '81", interview and article by G. Moszcz in *Sight and Sound* (London), winter 1982.

On WAJDA:

Books—*Film Makers on Filmmaking* edited by Harry M. Geduld, Bloomington, Indiana 1967; *Andrzej Wajda: Polish Cinema* edited by Colin McArthur, London 1970; *The Cinema of Andrzej Wajda* by Bolesław Michatek, translated by Edward Rothert, London 1973; articles—article in *Positif* (Paris), February 1957; "Against and For" by Kazimierz Dbnicki in *Film* (Poland), no.19, 1957; "The Tragedy of a Generation" by Roman Szydlowski in *Film* (Poland), no.46, 1958; "Romantic Reportage" by Jerzy Peltz in *Film* (Poland), no.45, 1958; "For *Lotna*, Against *Lotna*" in *Film* (Poland), no.44, 1959; article in *Cahiers du cinéma* (Paris), no.102, 1959; "Polish Notes" by Bolesław Michalek in *Sight and Sound* (London), winter 1958-59; "Personality of the Month" in *Films and Filming* (London), March 1960; "Samson Among the Philistines" by Konrad Eberhardt in *Film* (Poland), no.42, 1961; "The Hounds that Won't Take to the Woods" by Andrzej Zuławski in *Film* (Poland), no.11, 1964; "Off the Ground" by Andrzej Zuławski in *Film* (Poland), no.28-29, 1964; "Zeromski Alive" by Wiktor Woros-zylski in *Film* (Poland), no.41, 1965; "Climates" by Andrzej Zułlawski in *Film* (Poland), no.26, 1965; "Poetry and Social Fashion" by Stefan Zolkiewski in *Film* (Poland). no.42, 1965; "*Ashes* Falsified" by Jan Jakubowski and "*Ashes* Simplified" by Zbigniew Zaluski in *Ekran* (Ljubljana, Yugoslavia), no.42, 1965; "Grasping the Nettle: The Films of Andrzej Wajda" by C. Higham in *Hudson Review* (Nutley, New Jersey), autumn 1965; special issue of *Etudes cinématographiques* (Paris), no.69-72, 1968; "A Wajda Generation" by David Austen in *Films and Filming* (London), July 1968; "Some Recent Polish Films" by Steven Hill in *Film Society Review* (New York), February 1968; "Everything for Sale" by Colin McArthur in *Sight and Sound* (London), summer 1969; "Wajda Redivivus" by K. Toeplitz in *Film Quarterly* (Berkeley), winter 1969/70; "Wajda Play for London" in *Films and Filming* (London), June 1972; "Andrzej Wajda—polnischer Film par excellence" by K. Aeschbach in *Cinema* (Zurich), v.19, no.1, 1973; "Andrzej Wajda...ou la fidélité" by J. Delmas in *Jeune Cinéma* (Paris), February 1974; "Pologne: Wajda et Zanussi" by J. Plazewski in *Ecran* (Paris), April 1975; "I istorija i sovremennost" in *Iskusstvo Kino* (Moscow), December 1975; "Wajda Redux" by Peter Cowie in *Sight and Sound* (London), winter 1979/80; "Gielgud and Wajda Find Joint Production Enhances Productivity" in *The New York Times*, 5 June 1979; "Interpretacja filmowych znaczen w krakowskiej inscenizacji *Emigrantow* w rezyserii Andrzeja Wajdy" by A. Pilch in *Kino* (Warsaw), January 1979; "Andrzej Wajda" by M. Dipont in *Polish Film Polonaise* (Warsaw), no.4, 1979; "Between the Conception and the Re-creation Falls *The Shadow Line*" by John Simon in *Hudson Review* (New York), no.2, 1979; "La libertad del artista: Wajda" by M. Martínez Carril in *Cinemateca revista* (Andes), July 1980; dossier by R. Grelier and others in *Image et son* (Paris), December 1980; special issue of *Avant-Scène du cinéma* (Paris), 1 January 1980; "Polish Film Makers Fearful Over Curb on Wajda" in *The New York Times*, 4 January 1984.

*   *   *

The history of Polish film is as old as the history of filmmaking in most European countries. For entire decades, however, its range was limited to Polish territory and a Polish audience. Only after the Second World War, at the end of the 1950s, did the phenomenon known as the "Polish school of filmmaking" make itself felt as a part of world cinema. The phenomenon went hand in hand with the appearance of a new generation of film artists who, despite differences in their artistic proclivities, have a number of traits in common. They are approximately the same age, having been born in the 1920s. They spent their early youth in the shadow of the fascist occupation, and shared more or less similar postwar experiences. This is also the first generation of cinematically accomplished artists with a complete grasp of both the theoretical and practical sides of filmmaking.

Their debut was conditioned by the social climate, which was characterized by a desire to eliminate the negative aspects of postwar development labelled as the cult of personality. The basic theme of their work was the effort to come to grips with the painful experience of the war, the resistance to the occupation, and the struggle to put a new face on Polish society and the recent past. Temporal distance allowed them to take a sober look at all these experiences without schematic depictions, without illusions, and without pathetic ceremony. They wanted to know the truth about those years, in which the foundations of their contemporary life were formed, and express it in the specific destinies of the individuals who lived, fought, and died in those crucial moments of history. And one of the most important traits uniting all the members of the "school" was the attempt to debunk the myths and legends about those times and the people who shaped them.

The most prominent representative of the Polish school is Andrzej Wajda. In the span of a few short years he made three films, *Pokolenie*, *Kanał*, and *Popiół i diament*, which form a kind of loose trilogy and can be considered among the points of departure for the emergence of popular Poland. *Pokolenie* tells of a group of young men and women fighting in occupied Warsaw; *Kanał* is a tragic story of the 1944 Warsaw Uprising; *Popiół i diament* takes place at the watershed between war and peace. Crystallized in these three films are the fundamental themes of Wajda's work, themes characteristic of some other adherents of the "school" as well. In these films we also see the formation of Wajda's own artistic stamp, his creative method, which consists of an emotional approach to history, a romantic conception of human fate, a rich visual sense, and dense expression that is elaborate to the point of being baroque. In his debut *Pokolenie* he renounces the dramatic aspect of the battle against the occupation and concentrates on the inner world of people for whom discovering the truth about their stuggle was the same as discovering the truth about love. In *Kanał* he expresses disagreement with a myth long ago rooted in the consciousness of the Polish people and propounded in portrayals of the Warsaw Uprising—that the greatest meaning of life is death on the barricades. In the film *Popiół i diament* we hear for the first time in clear tones the theme of the Pole at the crossroads of history and the tragedy of his choice. Wajda expresses this theme not in abstract constructions but in a concrete reality with concrete heroes.

Wajda returns to the war experience several times. *Lotna*, in which the historical action precedes the above-mentioned trilogy, takes place in the tragic September of 1939, when Poland was overrun. Here Wajda continues to take a critical view of national tradition. Bitterness and derision toward the romanticization of the Polish struggle are blended here with sober judgment, and also with understanding for the world and for the people playing out the last tragicomic act on the historical stage. In the film *Samson*, the hero, a Jewish youth, throws off his lifelong passivity and by this action steps into the struggle. Finally, there is the 1970 film *Krajobraz po bitwie*, which, however, differs sharply from Wajda's early films. The director himself characterized this difference in the following way: "It's not I who am drawing back [from the war]. It's the war. It and I are growing old together, and therefore it is more and more difficult for me to discover anything in it that was close to me."

Krajobraz po bitwie has apparently become Wajda's definitive farewell to the war. This does not mean, however, that the fundamental principles of the artistic method found in his early films have disappeared from his work, in spite of the fact that his work has developed in the most diverse directions over the course of almost thirty years. The basic principles remain and, with time, develop, differentiate, and join with other motifs brought by personal and artistic experience. Some of the early motifs can be found in other contexts. Man's dramatic attitude towards history, the Pole at the crossroads of history and his tragic choice—these we can find in the film *Popioły*, in the image of the fate of Poland in the period of the Napoleonic Wars, when a new society was taking shape in the oppressive atmosphere of a defeated country divided up among three victorious powers. People living in a time of great changes are the main heroes of *Ziemia obiecana*, which portrays the precipitous, drastic, and ineluctable course of the transition from feudalism to the capitalist order. A man's situation at dramatic historical moments is also the subject of several of his latest films (*Człowiek z marmuru*, *Człowiek z zelaza*, *Danton*), which have met with more controversy than the preceding works.

Wajda's work reveals many forms and many layers. Over time, historical films alternate with films on contemporary subjects; films with a broad social sweep alternate with films that concentrate on intimate human experiences. Wajda is conscious of these alternations. From history he returns to contemporaneity, so as not to lose contact with the times and with his audience. After a series of war films, he made the picture *Niewinni czarodzieje*, whose young heroes search for meaning in their lives. In the film *Wszystko na sprzedaz*, following the tragic death of his friend, the actor Zbigniew Cybulski, he became absorbed in the traces a person leaves behind in the memories and hearts of friends; at the same time he told of the problems of artistic searching and creation. Wajda's attitudes on these questions are revealed again in the next film *Polowanie na muchy*, and even more emphatically in *Dyrygent*, where they are linked to the motif of faithfulness to one's work and to oneself, to one's ideals and convictions. The motif links *Dyrygent* with *Popiół i diament*. Another theme of *Dyrygent*—the inseparability of one's personal, private life from one's work life and the mutual influence of the two—is the basic problem treated in *Bez znieczulenia*. In Wajda there are many such examples of the migration of themes and motifs from one film to another. They affirm the unity of his work despite the fact that alongside great and powerful works there are lesser and weaker films. Such, for example, is Wajda's sole attempt in the genre of comedy, *Polowanie na muchy*, or the adaptation of Joseph Conrad's novel *Heart of Darkness*, which underwent a cinematic transformation. Another unifying element in Wajda's oeuvre is his faithfulness to literary and artistic sources. A significant portion of his films came from literature, while the pictorial aspect finds its inspiration in the romantic artistic tradition. In addition to such broad historical frescoes as *Popioły* or *Ziemia obiecana*, these include, for example, Stanisław Wyspianski's drama of 1901, *Wesele*, important for its grasp of Poland at a bleak point in the country's history. Wajda translated it to the screen in all the breadth of its meaning, with an accent on the impossibility of mutual understanding between disparate cultural milieus. The director also selected from the literary heritage works that would allow him to address man's existential questions, attitudes towards life and death. This theme resonates most fully in adaptations of two works by the writer Jarosław Iwaszkiewicz, *Brzezina* and *Panny z Wilka*, in which the heroes are found not in history but in life, where they are threatened not by war but by old age, illness, and death, and where they must struggle only with themselves. To address such existential tension he also developed a transcription of Mikhail Bulgakov's prose work *The Master and Margarita*, filmed for television in the German Democratic Republic under the title *Pilatus und andere-ein Film für Karfreitag*.

Wajda's oeuvre, encompassing artistic triumphs and failures, forms a unified but incomplete whole. The affinity among his films is determined by a choice of themes which enables him to depict great historical syntheses, metaphors, and symbols. He is constantly drawn to those moments in the destinies of individuals and groups that are crossroads of events with tragic consequences. In his films the main motifs of human existence are interwoven—death and life, love, defeat and the tragic dilemma of having to choose, the impossibility of realizing great aspirations. All these motifs are subordinated to history, even a feeling as subjective as love.

Wajda's films have not been, and are not, uniformly received by audiences or critics. They have always provoked discussions in which enthusiasm has confronted condemnation and agreement has confronted disagreement and even hostility; despite some failures, however, Wajda's films have never been met with indifference.

—Mrs. B. Urgošíková

WALSH, RAOUL. American. Born in New York City, 11 March 1887. Educated Public School 93, New York; attended Seton Hall College. Married Miriam Cooper, 1916 (divorced 1927); Mary Edna Simpson, 1941. Career: 1903—sails to Cuba with uncle, captain of a trading ship; 1903-04—learns riding and roping in Mexico and begins work as a wrangler; 1904-10—drifts across the West working at a number of jobs from surgeon's assistant to undertaker; 1910—acquires small part in play *The Clansman* in San Antonio; 1910-12—becomes cowboy actor in silent films, 1st for Pathé Studio in New Jersey, and then Biograph; 1912—actor and assistant director for D.W. Griffith at Biograph; moves to Hollywood with Griffith company; 1913-14—Griffith sends him to Mexico to shoot documentary footage of Pancho Villa and his march on Mexico City; Villa footage later becomes part of *The Life of Villa* starring Walsh as the young Villa; 1914-15—works as assistant director and appears as John Wilkes Booth in *Birth of a Nation*; 1916—hired by William Fox as director, works with Theda Bara among others; 1916-28—while under contract to Fox, loaned out to other studios as a director, working with prominent actors such as Fairbanks, Sr. and Valentino; 1928—while on location on his 1st sound film, loses an eye in an auto accident when jackrabbit smashes through windshield; 1930—introduces John Wayne as feature actor in *The Big Trail*; 1930-64—continues to work for various studios, most notably making action films with actors such as Errol Flynn, James Cagney, Clark Gable, and Humphrey Bogart. 1964—retires to his ranch. Died 31 December 1980; buried at Simi Valley, California.

Films (as director): 1912—*The Life of General Villa* (co-d, +ro as *Young Villa*); *Outlaw's Revenge*; 1913—*The Double Knot* (+pr, sc, ro); *The Mystery of the Hindu Image* (+pr, sc); *The Gunman* (+pr, sc—credit contested); 1914—*The Final Verdict* (+pr, sc, ro); *The Bowery*; 1915—*The Regeneration* (+co-sc); *Carmen* (+pr, sc); *The Death Dice* (+pr, sc—credit contested); *His Return* (+pr); *The Greaser* (+pr, sc, ro); *The Fencing Master* (+pr, sc); *A Man for All That* (+pr, sc, ro); *11:30 P.M.* (+pr, sc); *The Buried Hand* (+pr, sc); *The Celestial Code*; *A Bad Man and Others* (+pr, sc); *Home from the Sea*; *The Lone Cowboy* (+co-sc); 1916—*Blue Blood and Red* (+pr, sc); *The Serpent* (+pr, sc); *Pillars of Society*; 1917—*The Honor System*; *The Silent Lie*; *The Innocent Sinner* (+sc); *Betrayed* (+sc); *The Conqueror* (+sc); *This is the Life*; 1918—*Pride of New York* (+sc); *The Woman and the Law* (+sc); *The Prussian Cur* (+sc); *On the Jump* (+sc); *I'll Say So*; 1919—*Should a Husband Forgive* (+sc); *Evangeline* (+sc); *Every Mother's Son* (+sc); 1920—*The Strongest* (+sc); *The Deep Purple*; *From Now On*; 1921—*The Oath* (+pr, sc); *Serenade* (+pr); 1923—*Lost and Found on a South Sea Island* (*Passions of the Sea*); *Kindred of the Dust* (+pr, sc); 1924—*The Thief of Bagdad*; 1925—*East of Suez* (+pr); *The Spaniard* (+co-pr); *The Wanderer* (+co-pr); 1926—*The Lucky Lady* (+co-pr); *The Lady of the Harem*; *What Price Glory*; 1927—*The Monkey Talks* (+pr); *The Loves of Carmen* (+sc); 1928—*Sadie Thompson* (*Rain*) (+co-sc, ro); *The Red Dance*; *Me Gangster* (+co-sc); 1929—*In Old Arizona* (co-d); *The Cock-eyed World* (+co-sc); *Hot for Paris* (+co-sc); 1930—*The Big Trail*; 1931—*The Man Who Came Back*; *Women of all Nations*; *The Yellow Ticket*; 1932—*Wild Girl*; *Me and My Gal*; 1933—*Sailor's Luck*; *The Bowery*; *Going Hollywood*; 1935—*Under Pressure*; *Baby Face Harrington*; *Every Night at Night*; 1936—*Klondike Annie*; *Big Brown Eyes* (+co-sc); *Spendthrift*; 1937—*O.H.M.S. (You're in the Army Now)*; *When Thief Meets Thief*; *Artists and Models*; *Hitting a New High*; 1938—*College Swing*; 1939—*St. Louis Blues*; *The Roaring 20's*; 1940—*The Dark Command* (+pr); *They Drive by Night*; 1941—*High Sierra*; *The Strawberry Blonde*; *Manpower*; *They Died With Their Boots On*; 1942—*Desperate Journey*; *Gentleman Jim*; 1943—*Background to Danger*; *Northern Pursuit*; 1944—*Uncertain Glory*; *San Antonio* (uncredited co-d); *Salty O'Rourke*; *The Horn Blows at Midnight*; 1946—*The Man I Love*; 1947—*Pursued*; *Cheyenne*; *Stallion Road* (uncredited co-d); 1948—*Silver River*; *Fighter Squadron*; *One Sunday Afternoon*; 1949—*Colorado Territory*; *White Heat*; 1950—*The Enforcer* (uncredited co-d); *Montana* (uncredited co-d); 1951—*Along the Great Divide*; *Captain Horation Hornblower*; *Distant Drums*; 1952—*The World in his Arms*; *The Lawless Breed*; *Blackbeard the Pirate*; 1953—*Sea Devils*; *A Lion in the Streets*; *Gun Fury*; 1954—*Saskatchewan*; 1955—*Battle Cry*; *The Tall Men*; 1956—*The Revolt of Mamie Stover*; *The King and 4 Queens*; 1957—*Band of Angels*; 1958—*The Naked and the Dead*; *The Sheriff of Fractured Jaw*; 1959—*A Private's Affair*; 1960—*Esther and the King* (+pr +sc); 1961—*Marines, Let's Go* (+pr +sc); 1964—*A Distant Trumpet*.

Roles: 1910—*Bank Clerk* in *The Banker's Daughter*; *Young man* in *A Mother's Love*; *Paul Revere* in *Paul Revere's Ride* (Emile Cocteau); 1915—*John Wilkes Booth* in *Birth of a Nation* (Griffith).

Publications:

By WALSH:

Books—*Each Man in His Time*, New York 1974; *Un Demi-siècle à Hollywood*, Paris 1976; articles—interview by Paul Mas and others in *Contrechamp* (Paris), May 1962; interview by Jean-Louis Noames in *Cahiers du cinéma* (Paris), April 1964; "Can You Ride the Horse?", interview by J. Childs in *Sight and Sound* (London), winter 1972/73; interview by Guy Braucourt in *Ecran* (Paris), September/October 1972; interview by Olivier Eyquem and others in *Positif* (Paris), February 1973; "Raoul Walsh Remembers Warners", interview by P. McGilligan and others in *Velvet Light Trap* (Madison), autumn 1975; "Raoul Walsh Talks About D.W. Griffith" by P. Montgomery in *Film Heritage* (New York), spring 1975.

On WALSH:

Books—*The Parade's Gone By...* by Kevin Brownlow, New York 1968; *Raoul Walsh* by Michael Marmin, Paris 1970; *The Hollywood Professionals* by Kingsley Canham, New York 1973; *Raoul Walsh* edited by Phil Hardy, Colchester, England 1974; articles—article by I. St. Johns in *Photoplay* (New York), September 1925; article by W. Mizner in *Photoplay* (New York), November 1928; article by L.O. Parsons in *Cosmopolitan* (New York), June 1947; "Le Monde de Walsh est celui de l'aventure" by Raymond Ravanbaz in *Radio-Cinéma-Télévision* (Paris), 22 February 1959; special issue of *Présence du Cinéma* (Paris), 1962; "Méconnaissance de Raoul Walsh" by Claude Beylie in *Cinématexte* (Paris), May/June 1963; filmography by Andrew Sarris in *Film Culture* (New York), spring 1963; "Raoul Walsh: l'Aventure et la grandeur humaine" by Michel Marmin in *Télé-*

rama (Paris), 25 October 1964; special issue of *Cahiers du cinéma* (Paris), April 1964; "Hitch Your Genre to a Star" by Harris Dienstfrey in *Film Culture* (New York), fall 1964; "Where are they now?" in *Newsweek* (New York), 14 December 1964; "L'Esprit d'aventure" by Jean-Louis Comolli in *Cahiers du cinéma* (Paris), April 1964; "Raoul Walsh" by Bertrand Jeraques in *Téléciné* (Paris), December 1965; "3 Films de Raoul Walsh" by Gérard Legrand in *Positif* (Paris), January 1965; "Raoul Walsh" by Kevin Brownlow in *Film* (London), autumn 1967; "Raoul Walsh" by R. Lloyd in *Brighton* (London), November, December, and January 1970; "Good days, good years" by R. Schickel in *Harper* (New York), October 1970; "Raoul Walsh— His Silent Films" by W. Conley in *Silent Picture* (London), winter 1970/71; "What Directors are Saying" in *Action* (Los Angeles), May/June 1972; "Action All the Way", "Going Hollywood" and "Hollow Victories" by J. Fox in *Films and Filming* (London), June, July and August 1973; "Au soleil (quelquefois noir) de Raoul Walsh" by G. Legrand in *Positif* (Paris), February 1973; "Raoul Walsh: 'He Used to Be a Big Shot'" by Manny Farber in *Sight and Sound* (London), winter 1974/75; "The Western Landscape of Raoul Walsh" by R. McNiven in *Velvet Light Trap* (Madison), autumn 1975; "Aspects of British Feminist Film Theory" by E. Ann Kaplan in *Jump Cut* (Chicago), no.12/13, 1976; "Raoul Walsh: filmographie" by P. Guinle and others in *Avant-Scène du cinéma* (Paris), 15 October 1976; "Raoul Walsh filmographie: l'oeuvre 'parlante' 1929/1961" by J. Cocchi and others in *Avant-Scène du cinéma* (Paris), April 1976; "William Keighley, Raoul Walsh et le style Warner" by J.-P. Bleys in *Cahiers de la Cinémathèque* (Paris), spring/summer 1978; "Raoul Walsh, rien que l'action" by G. Cèbe in *Image et son* (Paris), March 1981; "Trying to Remember an Afternoon with Raoul Walsh" by J. Halliday in *Framework* (Norwich, England), spring 1981; "Ils nous ont quittés" in *Cinéma* (Paris), April 1981; "Raoul Walsh: 1887-1981" by R. McNiven in *Film Comment* (New York), July/August 1981; "Raoul Walsh" by M. Marinero and others in *Casablanca* (Madrid), February 1981; "Merci, Monsieur Walsh!" by D. Rabourdin in *Cinéma* (Paris), February 1981; "Print the Legend (Custer, vakulinchuk, Tejero)" by P. Viota in *Contracampo* (Madrid), March 1981; films—"Raoul Walsh ou le bon vieux temps" produced for television by André-S. Labarthe and Janine Bazin in *Cinéastes de notre temps* series, 4 October 1966; "Un sujet—trois films" produced by Armand Panigel in *Cinéma-Variations* series, 20 January 1969.

*   *   *

Raoul Walsh's extraordinary career spanned the history of the American motion picture industry from its emergence, through its glory years in the thirties and forties, and into the television era. Like his colleagues Alan Dwan, King Vidor, John Ford, and Henry King, whose careers also covered 50 years, Walsh continuously turned out popular fare, even several extraordinary hits. Movie fans have long appreciated the work of this director's director. But only when auteurists began to closely examine his films was Walsh "discovered," first by the French (in the 1960s), and then by American and British critics (in the 1970s). To these critics Walsh's action films come to represent a unified view, put forth by means of a simple, straightfoward technique. Raoul Walsh is now accepted as an example of a master Hollywood craftsman who worked with a naive skill, and an animal energy, both frustrated and buoyed by the studio system.

Unfortunately, this view neglects Walsh's important place in the silent cinema. Raoul Walsh began his career with an industry still centered in and around New York City, the director's birth place. He started as an actor in Pathé westerns filmed in New Jersey, and then journeyed to California to be with D.W. Griffith's Fine Arts production company. Walsh apprenticed with Griffith as an actor, appearing in his most famous role as John Wilkes Booth in *Birth of a Nation*.

Walsh then turned to directing, first for the fledgling Fox Film Company. For the next five years (interrupted by World War I service experience) Walsh would master the craft of filmmaking, absorbing lessons which would last him more than forty years. His apprenticeship led to major assignments, and his greatest financial successes came in the 1920s. Douglas Fairbanks's *The Thief of Bagdad* was directed by Walsh at the height of that famous star's career.

Walsh took advatage to this acclaim by moving for a time to the top studio of that era, Paramount, and then signed a lucrative long-term contract with Fox. At that point Fox began expanding into a major studio. Walsh contributed to that success with hits like *What Price Glory?* and *The Cockeyed World*. The introduction of new sound-on-film technology, through its Movietone Newsreels, helped Fox's ascent. Consequently, when Fox was about to convert to all-sound features, corporate chieftains turned to Walsh to direct *In Old Arizona*, in 1929. (It was on location for that film that Walsh lost his eye.) Through its experience with newsreel shooting, only Fox at the time could film and record quality sound on location. Walsh's next film used the 70mm "Grandeur" process on a western, *The Big Trail*. The film did well but could not save the company from succombing to the Great Depression.

Walsh's career stagnated during the 1930s. He and Fox never achieved the heights of the late 1920s. When Darryl F. Zanuck came aboard with the Twentieth Century merger in 1935, Walsh moved on, freelancing until he signed with Warners in 1939. For slightly more than a decade, Walsh functioned as a contract director at Warners, turning out two or three films a year. Walsh never established the degree of control he had over the silent film projects, but he seemed to thrive in the restrictive Warners environment. Walsh's first three films at Warners fit into that studio's mode of crime melodramas: *The Roaring Twenties*, *They Drive By Night*, and *High Sierra*. *The Roaring Twenties* was not a classic gangster film, like Warners' *Little Caesar* and *Public Enemy*, but a realistic portrait of the socio-economic environment in the United States after World War I. *High Sierra* looked ahead to the film noir of the 1940s. In that film the gangster became a sympathetic character trapped by forces he did not understand. During the World War II era Walsh turned to war films with a textbook example of what a war action film ought to be. Walsh continued making crime melodrama and war films in the late 1940s and early 1950s. *Battle Cry*, *The Naked and the Dead*, and *Marines, Let's Go* proved that he could adapt to changing taste within familiar genres.

Arguably Walsh's best film of the post-war era was *White Heat* made for Warners in 1949. The James Cagney character is portrayed against type: we see the gangster hiding and running, trying to escape his past and his social, economic, and psychological background. *White Heat* was the apex of Walsh's work at Warners, at once fitting into an accepted mode, and transcending the formula. *White Heat* has come to symbolize the tough Raoul Walsh action film. Certainly that same sort of style can also be seen in his westerns at Warners, *They Died With Their Boots On*, *Pursued*, and the remake of *High Sierra*, *Colorado Territory*. But there are other sides of the Walsh oeuvre, usually overlooked by critics, or at most awkwardly positioned among the action films. *The Strawberry Blonde* is a warm, affectionate, turn-of-the-century tale of small town America. *Gentleman Jim* of 1942 also swims in sentimentality. This action director certainly had a soft touch when required. Indeed, when closely examined, Walsh had the ability to adapt to many different themes and points of view.

The 1950s seemed to have passed Walsh by. Freed from the confines of the rigid studio system Walsh's output became less interesting. But a survivor he was, completing his final feature, a cavalry film for Warners in 1964, *A Distant Trumpet*, at age 72 or 77 depending on which biographical reports one believes. By then Raoul Walsh had truly become a Hollywood legend, having reached two career peaks in a more than fifty-year career. To carefully examine the career of Raoul Walsh is to study the history of the American film in toto, for the two are nearly the same length and inexorably intertwined.

—Douglas Gomery

WALTERS, CHARLES. American. Born in Pasadena, California, 17 November 1911. Educated at the University of Southern California. Career: 1934—Broadway debut as actor and dancer in *New Faces*; also appears in *Fools Rush In*, *Parade*, and *Jubilee*; 1938—begins choreographing on Broadway with *Sing Out the News*; shows choreographed include *Let's Face It*, and *Banjo Eyes*, both 1941; 1942—first film appearance in *7 Days Leave*; begins choreographing for films at suggestion of Robert Altman on *DuBarry Was a Lady*, working with Gene Kelly; 1944—shoots as well as stages "Brazilian Boogie" number, with Lena Horne, in *Broadway Rhythm*; 1945—directs short *Spreadin' the Jam*; 1947—Arthur Freed offers direction of first feature *Good News*. Died in Malibu, California, 13 August 1982.

Films (as choreographer—appearances indicated by "ro" are as actor/dancer): 1942—*Seven Days Leave* (Whelan) (+ro); 1943—*DuBarry Was a Lady* (Del Ruth); *Presenting Lily Mars* (Taurog) (co-choreo, +ro); *Best Foot Forward* (Buzzell); *Girl Crazy* (Taurog) (+ro); 1944—*Broadway Rhythm* (Del Ruth) (co-choreo); *Three Men in White* (Goldbeck); *Meet Me in St. Louis* (Minnelli); 1945—*Thrill of a Romance* (Thorpe); *Her Highness and the Bellboy* (Thorpe); *Weekend at the Waldorf* (Leonard); *The Harvey Girls* (Sidney); *Abbott & Costello in Hollywood* (Simon); (as director): 1945—*Spreadin' the Jam* (short); 1946—*Ziegfeld Follies* (Minnelli and others) (choreo Judy Garland's "An Interview" sequence only); 1947—*Good News*; 1948—*Summer Holiday* (Yates) (choreo only); *Easter Parade*; 1949—*The Barkleys of Broadway*; 1950—*Summer Stock (If You Feel Like Singing)* (+choreo); 1951—*Three Guys Named Mike*; *Texas Carnival*; 1952—*The Belle of New York*; 1953—*Lili* (+choreo, ro); *Dangerous When Wet*; *Torch Song* (+choreo, ro); *Easy to Love*; 1955—*The Glass Slipper*; *The Tender Trap*; 1956—*Don't Go Near the Water*; 1957—*High Society* (+choreo); 1959—*Ask Any Girl*; 1960—*Please Don't Eat the Daisies*; 1961—*Two Loves (Spinster)*; 1962—*Billy Rose's Jumbo*; 1964—*The Unsinkable Molly Brown*; 1966—*Walk, Don't Run*.

Publications:

By WALTERS:

Articles—"On the Bright Side", interview by John Cutts in *Films and Filming* (London), August 1970; interview by P. Sauvage in *Positif* (Paris), November/December 1972.

On WALTERS:

Articles—"Likable but Elusive" by Andrew Sarris in *Film Culture* (New York), spring 1963; special issue of *Positif* (Paris), November/December 1972; "Charles Walters" in *Positif* (Paris), February 1973; article in *Variety* (New York), 5 November 1975; "Charles Walters" by D. McVay in *Focus on Film* (London), no.27, 1977; obituary in *Variety* (New York), 25 August 1982; obituary in *Films and Filming* (London), October 1982.

*   *   *

Before going to Hollywood Charles Walters spent about eight years on Broadway. For the most part he was a dancer, then in 1938 he choreographed his first show. A few years later Robert Altman introduced him to MGM and he began to stage routines for the screen. He worked with Gene Kelly on a number for *Du Barry Was A Lady*, then began staging musical numbers for some of Metro's leading ladies such as June Allyson, Gloria De Haven, Lucille Ball, and Judy Garland. Judy became a great friend and he worked on a number of her films, sometimes dancing with her. His first effort at directing was Lena Horne's "Brazilian Boogie" number in *Broadway Rhythm*. The following year he directed a short film called *Spreadin' the Jam*, but it was not until 1947 that he made his first feature, *Good News*.

As a dancer, movement was very much on his mind. As a director he moved not only the performers but also the camera, making full use of tracking shots, pans, and crane shots. The studio was impressed with the result and gave him *Easter Parade* with Astaire and Garland. The budget was twice that of his first film, and notable for the "Couple of Swells" number—which Walters danced with her when she did her memorable show at the Palace a few years later. *The Barkleys of Broadway* should have starred Astaire and Garland again, but Judy was ill and Ginger Rogers returned to the screen in her stead. These first three films were made under his original contract as a choreographer, and at the same fee. But by now he had proved himself, and was recognized as a director of musicals ready to follow into the footsteps of those other MGM stalwarts Stanley Donen and Vincente Minnelli. *Summer Stock* began with the pleasantly relaxed number "If You Feel Like Singing," as the camera moved through the window into the shower, and followed Judy into the dressing-room. But the rest of the filming was far from relaxed as Walters had to cope with Judy's nerves and weight problems. The final song, "Get Happy," was staged by Walters after the film was finished because they needed a good number for the climax, and Judy's loss of weight was quite noticable.

In 1951 he directed his first straight picture, *Three Guys Named Mike*, a passable romantic comedy. His least favorite film, *The Belle of New York*, was followed by his favorite, *Lili*. In this light, whimsical piece he drew a charming performance from Leslie Caron and received an Oscar nomination. *Dangerous When Wet* was one of three films he made with Esther Williams. Walters staged the lively opening number with each character taking up the song, and "Ain't Nature Grand," with Charlotte Greenwood showing great vitality in her high kicks. In the dramatic musical *Torch Song* Walters was the first to direct Joan Crawford in a color film. He got to know her well, and put a lot of the real Joan Crawford into the character of Jenny. His careful handling of Frank Sinatra in *The Tender Trap* was most opportune. After a string of dramatic roles, this film confirmed Sinatra's talent as a comedy actor. In 1957 he was reunited with Sinatra for what is arguably his best film, *High Society*. Every number in this film is significant, yet they are all completely different. One of the high spots was Crosby and Sinatra's "Well, Did You Evah," which Walters himself had introduced years before with Betty Grable. It took place in two rooms and was shot without a single cut. In the early sixties he made *The Unsinkable Molly Brown* and *Billy Rose's Jumbo*, the latter being by far the better of the two.

Walters was a sincere director whose musicals had a style of their own. He was equally at home with a field full of dancers as he was with soloist or a group on a bandstand. He not only moved his cameras and his performers, but staged many numbers on moving vehicles—a car, a carriage, a coach, a trolly, a boat, and even a tractor. His use of color and his sudden cuts produced striking effects, and the energy and spirit of his work contributed a great deal to the Hollywood musical.

—Colin Williams

WARHOL, ANDY (WITH PAUL MORRISSEY). American. Warhol born in McKeesport, Pennsylvania, 6 August 1928; Morrissey born in New York City, 1939. Warhol studied at Carnegie Institute of Technology, Pittsburgh, 1945-49, B.F.A. 1949; Morrissey studied at Fordham University. Career: 1949-50—Warhol works as illustrator for *Glamour Magazine* (New York); 1950-57—commercial artist, New York; beginning 1957—concentrates on making paintings derived from strip comics and advertisements; 1960-61—first silk-screen paintings; Morrissey makes short underground films; 1963—Warhol begins making films; Morrissey joins Warhol's "Factory" as assistant and sometimes cameraman; 1968—Warhol seriously wounded by former "Factory" regular Valerie Solanas; while recovering, Morrissey takes over principal directing responsibility while Warhol acts mainly as producer; 1977—Morrissey embarks on separate directing career, making version of *The Hound of the Baskervilles*. Agent: (Warhol) c/o Leo Castelli Gallery, 4 East 77th Street, New York, NY 10021.

Films (Warhol as producer and director, Morrissey as sometime assistant): 1963—*Tarzan and Jane Regained...Sort Of*; *Sleep*; *Kiss*; *Andy Warhol Films Jack Smith Filming Normal Love*; *Dance Movie (Roller Skate)*; *Salome and Delilah*; *Haircut*; *Blow Job*; 1964—*Empire*; *Batman Dracula*; *The End of Dawn*; *Naomi and Rufus Kiss*; *Henry Geldzahler*; *The Lester Persky Story (Soap Opera)*; *Couch*; *Shoulder*; *Mario Banana*; *Harlot*; *Taylor Mead's Ass*; 1965—*13 Most Beautiful Women*; *13 Most Beautiful Boys*; *50 Fantastics*; *50 Personalities*; *Ivy and John*; *Screen Test I*; *Screen Test II*; *The Life of Juanita Castro*; *Drunk*; *Suicide*; *Horse*; *Vinyl*; *Bitch*; *Poor Little Rich Girl*; *Face*; *Restaurant*; *Afternoon*; *Prison*; *Space*; *Outer and Inner Space*; *Camp*; *Paul Swan*; *Hedy (Hedy the Shoplifter or The 14 Year Old Girl)*; *The Closet*; *Lupe*; *More Milk, Evette*; 1966—*Kitchen*; *My Hustler*; *Bufferin (Gerard Malanga Reads Poetry)*; *Eating Too Fast*; *The Velvet Underground*; *Chelsea Girls*; 1967—***** (Four Stars)*; [parts of ******** : *International Velvet*; *Alan and Dickin*; *Imitation of Christ*; *Courtroom*; *Gerard Has His Hair Removed with Nair*; *Katrina Dead*; *Sausalito*; *Alan and Apple*; *Group One*; *Sunset Beach on Long Island*; *High Ashbury*; *Tiger Morse*]; *I, a Man*; *Bike Boy*; *Nude Restaurant*; *The Loves of Ondine*; 1968—*Lonesome Cowboys*; *Blue Movie (Fuck)*; (Warhol as producer, Morrissey as director): 1968—*Flesh*; 1970—*Trash*; 1972—*Women in Revolt* (co-d with Morrissey); *Heat*; 1973—*L'Amour* (co-d, co-sc with Morrissey); 1974—*Andy Warhol's Frankenstein*; *Andy Warhol's Dracula*; 1977—*Andy*

Warhol's Bad; (Morrissey as director): 1977—*The Hound of the Baskervilles*.

Publications:

By WARHOL OR MORRISSEY:

Books—*Blue Movie*, script, New York 1970; *The Philosophy of Andy Warhol (From A to B and Back Again)*, New York 1975; articles—interview by Gerard Malanga in *Kulchur* (New York), winter 1964/65; interview by David Ehrenstein in *Film Culture* (New York), spring 1966; "Nothing to Lose", interview by Gretchen Berg in *Cahiers du Cinema in English* (New York), May 1967; numerous interviews conducted by Warhol in *Interview* (New York); interview by Tony Rayns in *Cinema* (London), August 1970; interview with Warhol in *The Film Director as Superstar* by Joseph Gelmis, Garden City, New York 1970; "It's Hard to Be Your Own Script" in *Vogue* (New York), 1 March 1970; interview by Ralph Pomeroy in *Afterimage* (Rochester), autumn 1970; "Filming Andy Warhol's *Trash*", interview by F.W. Howton in *Filmmakers Newsletter* (Ward Hill, Mass.), June 1972; "Les Américains ne pensent qu'à ça...", interview by G. Langlois in *Cinéma* (Paris), December 1972; "Gesprek met Andy Warhol en Paul Morrissey over Heat" by A. de Jong in *Skoop* (Amsterdam), June 1973; "Paul Morrissey Seminar" in *Dialogue on Film* (Washington, D.C.), November 1974; "Realisme van het toeval: Paul Morrissey: Alles draait om het personage", interview by Gideon Bachmann in *Skoop* (Amsterdam), November 1974; interview by P. Maraval in *Cinématographe* (Paris), January 1979.

On WARHOL AND MORRISSEY:

Books—*Andy Warhol* by John Coplans, New York 1970; *Andy Warhol* by Rainer Crone, New York 1970; *Andy Warhol* by Peter Gidal, New York 1970; *The Autobiography and Sex Life of Andy Warhol* by John Wilcox, New York 1971; *Stargazer: Andy Warhol and His Films* by Stephen Koch, New York 1973; articles—article by Jonas Mekas in *The Village Voice* (New York), 13 August 1964; "Andy Warhol, Movie Maker" by Howard Junker in *The Nation* (New York), 22 February 1965; "The Detached Cool of Andy Warhol" by John Wilcock in *The Village Voice* (New York), 6 May 1965; "Beyond Cinema: Notes on Some Films by Andy Warhol" by James Stoller in *Film Quarterly* (Berkeley), fall 1966; "Dragtime and Drugtime: or Film à la Warhol" by Parker Tyler in *Evergreen Review* (New York), April 1967; "Whitehall with Warhol" in *Cinema* (Beverly Hills), winter 1967; "Warhol" in *Film Culture* (New York), summer 1967; "Superstar—Superset" by Gregory Battcock in *Film Culture* (New York), summer 1967; "On Andy Warhol" by Andrew Lugg in *Cineaste* (New York), winter 1967/68 and spring 1968; "Andy" by Gretchen Berg in *Take One* (Montreal), no.10, 1968; "The Shot that Shattered the Velvet Underground" by Howard Smith in *The Village Voice* (New York), 6 June 1968; "Andy Warhol's Films Inc.: Communication in Action" by Tony Rayns in *Cinema* (London), August 1970; "Notes on Seeing the Films of Andy Warhol" by Lee Heflin in *Afterimage* (Rochester), autumn 1970; "Warhol as Filmmaker" by David Bourdon in *Art in America* (New York), May/June 1971; "Il Materiale gestuale" by E. Rasy in *Filmcritica* (Rome), June/July 1972; "Andy Warhol: Iconographer" by D.J. Cipnic in *Sight and Sound* (London), summer 1972; "A Retrospective Look at the Films of D.W. Griffith and Andy Warhol" by R. Larson in *Film Journal* (New York), fall/winter 1972; "La Persistenza dell'oggetto (note su alcini film di Warhol e di Morrissey)" by E. Bruno in *Filmcritica* (Rome), October/December 1973; "You Name It, I'll Eat It" by G. Ford in *Cinema* (Beverly Hills), spring 1973; essay on Morrissey in *Directors and Directions: Cinema for the 70s* by John Taylor, New York 1975.

*   *   *

By the time he screened his first films in 1963, Andy Warhol was well on his way to becoming the most famous "pop" artist in the world, and his variations on the theme of Campbell's soup cans had already assumed archetypal significance for art in the age of mechanical reproduction. Given Warhol's penchant for the automatic and mass-produced, his movement from sculpture, canvas, and silk-screen into cinema seemed logical; and his films were as passive, as intentionally "empty," as significant of the artist's absence as his previous work or as the image he projected of himself. One of his earlist films, *Kiss*, was no more nor less than a series of people kissing in closeup, each scene running the 3-minute length of a 16mm daylight reel, complete with flash frames at both ends. But it was his 1963 film *Sleep*, a 6-hour movie comprised of variously framed shots of a naked sleeping man, which made Warhol a star on the burgeoning New York underground film scene. As though to display any doubts that his message was the medium, Warhol followed *Sleep* with *Empire*, an 8-hour stationary view of the Empire State Building, creating a kind of cinematic limit case for the Bazinian integrity of the shot; a film of such conceptual significance that if it did not exist it would have to be invented; yet a film which was equally unwatchable (even Warhol refused to sit through it).

During the period 1963 to 1967, Warhol made some 55 films, ranging in length from 4 minutes (*Mario Banana*, 1964) to 25 hours (****, 1967). All were informed by the passive, mechanical aesthetic of simply turning on the camera to record what was in front of it. Generally, what was recorded were the antics of Warhol's E. 47th Street "factory" coterie—a host of friends, artists, junkies, transvestites, rock singers, hustlers, fugitives, and hangers-on. Ad-libbing, "camping," being themselves (and often more than themselves) before the unblinking eye of Warhol's camera, they became "superstars"—underground celebrities epitomizing Warhol's consumer-democratic ideal of five minutes' fame for everyone.

Despite Warhol's cultivated image as the "tycoon of passivity," his films display a cool, but very dry wit. *Blow Job*, for example, consisted of thirty minutes of a closeup of the expressionless face of a man being fellated outside the frame—a coyly humorous presentation of a forbidden act in an image perversely composed as a denial of pleasure (for the actor and the audience). *Mario Banana* simply presented the spectacle of transvestite Mario Montez eating bananas while in drag. *Harlot*, Warhol's first sound film, featured Mario (again eating bananas) sitting next to a woman in an evening dress, with the entirety of the virtually inaudible dialogue coming from three men positioned off-screen.

In the course of his films, Warhol seemed to be retracing the history of the cinema, from silence to sound to color (*Chelsea Girls*); from a fascination with the camera's "documentary" capabilities (*Empire*) to attempts at narrative by 1965. *Vinyl*, an adaption of Anthony Burgess's *A Clockwork Orange*, invoived a single high-angle camera position tightly framing a group of mostly uninvolved factory types, with protagonist Gerard Malanga sitting in a chair, reading his lines off a script on the floor, and being tortured with dripping candle wax and a "popper" overdose. When the camera accidently fell over in the middle of the proceedings, it was quickly returned to its original position without a break in the action. *My Hustler* offered a modicum of story, audible dialogue, and two shots—one of them a repetitive pan from a gay man talking to friends on the deck of a Fire Island beach house to his hired male prostitute sunning himself on the beach. The second shot, which fails to reveal the outcome of a wager made in the first section, shows the hustler and another man taking showers and grooming themselves in a crowded bathroom (a scene which made the pages of *Life* magazine for its brief male nudity).

It was *Chelsea Girls*, however, which provided Warhol's break-through to national and international exposure. A 3-hour film in black-and-white and color, shown on two screens at once, it featured almost all the resident "superstars" in scenes supposedly taking place in various rooms of New York's Chelsea Hotel. After *Chelsea Girls'* financial success, subsequent Warhol films like *I, A Man*, *Bike Boy*, *Nude Restaurant*, and *Lonesome Cowboys* became a bit more technically astute and conventionally feature-length; and the scenes taking place in front of the camera, while maintaining their bizarre, directionless, ad-libbed quality, became more sensational in their presentation of nudity and sex. Warhol's last hurrah, *Lonesome Cowboys* was actually shot in Arizona, featuring a number of "superstars" dressing in western garb, posing and walking through a nearly non-existent story amongst western movie sets. It was the last film Warhol completed before he was seriously wounded in an assassination attempt by marginal factory character Valerie Solanis.

Warhol's shooting marked the beginning of a period of reclusiveness for the artist. Subsequent "Warhol" films were the product of cohort and collaborator Paul Morrissey, who has been credited with the increasing commercialism of the 1967 films (not to mention the decline of the factory "scene"). While Warhol lay in the hospital recovering from gunshot wounds, Morrissey completed a film on his own entitled *Flesh*—a series of episodes basically recounting a day in the life of Joe Dallesandro (who appears nude more often than not), featuring Warhol-like performances and camera work, but adding a discernible story line and even character motivations. From 1970 to 1974, Morrissey's films under Warhol's name quickly became not only more commercial, but more technically accomplished and traditionally plotted as well. After *Trash*, a kind of watershed film featuring Joe and Holly Woodlawn in a narrative comedy about some marginal New York junkies and low-lifes, Morrissey even began to tone down the nudity. *Women in Revolt* was virtually a full-fledged melodrama, but with three transvestites playing the women of the title. *Heat*, shot in Los Angeles, had Dallesandro and New York cult actress/screenmaker Sylvia Miles playing out a sleazy remake of *Sunset Boulevard*. *L'Amour* took the whole Morrissey coterie to Paris.

Morrissey's big step into mainstream filmmaking came with the 1974 production of *Andy Warhol's Frankenstein*, a preposterously gory, tongue-in-cheek horror rendered in perfectly seamless, classical Hollywood style, and in a highly accomplished 3-D process. As outrageous as it was in its surrealistically bloody excess, and for all its "high-camp" attitude, the film bore almost no resemblance to the films of Andy Warhol; nor did Morrissey's *Blood for Dracula*, made at the same time, with virtually the same cast, but without 3-D. Since that time, Morrissey has pursued a career apart from Warhol's name, as an independent commercial filmmaker; his most significant subsequent film being a version of *The Hound of the Baskervilles*, starring Peter Cook and Dudley Moore.

—Ed Lowry

WATKINS, PETER. English. Born in Norbiton, Surrey, 29 October 1935. Educated at Christ College, Brecknockshire; studied acting at Royal Academy of Dramatic Art, London, beginning 1953. Career: military service with East Surrey Regiment, involved with local repertory company; late 1950s—works as assistant producer of TV shorts and commercials for London ad agency; with group of friends, begins making 16mm amateur films, wins several awards; this activity leads to job with BBC; 1961-67—works as assistant editor, producer, and director of documentaries; 1965—BBC bans British showing or international distribution of *The War Game*, documentary about possible effects of nuclear war; BBC subsequently gives rights to British Film Institute and film is shown theatrically but not on TV; 1967—makes first fiction feature *Privilege*; 1968—moves to Sweden after British support for *The Gladiators* falls through; 1969-71—works in U.S., makes *Punishment Park*; 1970s—series of film projects begun then cancelled by production organizations because of controversial subject matter; 1972—returns to Scandinavia; 1978—undertakes film biography of playwright August Strindberg at invitation of Swedish Film Institute; 1981—project reported abandoned due to financial disagreements. Address: c/o Swedish Film Institute, Film House, Box 271 26, 102 52 Stockholm, Sweden.

Films (as amateur filmmaker): 1956—*The Web*; 1958—*The Field of Red*; 1959—*Diary of an Unknown Soldier*; 1961—*The Forgotten Faces*; 1962—*Dust Fever* (unfinished); (as professional filmmaker): 1964—*Culloden*; 1966—*The War Game*; 1967—*Privilege*; 1969—*Gladiatorerna (The Gladiators, The Peace Game)*; 1971—*Punishment Park*; 1974—*Edvard Munch* (released in U.S. 1976); 1975—*70-Talets Människor (The Seventies People)*; *Fällen (The Trap)*; 1977—*Aftenlandet (Evening Land)*.

Publications:

By WATKINS:

Book—*The War Game*, script, New York 1967; articles—"Left, Right, Wrong" in *Films and Filming* (London), March 1970; "Peter Watkins Talks About the Suppression of His Work within Britain" in *Films and Filming* (London), February 1971; interview in *Film Society Review* (New York), March/May 1972; "Ne pas noyer le poisson", interview by J. Grant in *Cinéma* (Paris), December 1973; interview by H. Desrues in *Images et son* (Paris), September 1973; "Le règne de la télévision est celui du silence collectif", interview by G. Langlois in *Téléciné* (Paris), December/January 1973/74; interview by M. Martin in *Ecran* (Paris), November 1973; "Edvard Munch, la danse de la vie", interview by H. Béhar in *Images et son* (Paris), December 1976; "'Punishment Park' and Dissent in the West" in *Literature/Film Quarterly* (Salisbury, Md.), no.4, 1976; "Force de frappe—Watkins: 'l'avenir, le passé et le présent en même temps'", interview by B. Nave in *Jeune Cinéma* (Paris), April/May 1978; "Force de frappe" in *Images et son* (Paris), April 1978; interview by Scott MacDonald in *The Journal of the University Film and Video Association*, summer 1982.

On WATKINS:

Articles—"Peter Watkins Discusses His Suppressed Nuclear Film *The War Game*" by James Blue and Michael Gill in *Film Comment* (New York), fall 1965; "On the Scene: Peter Watkins" in *Playboy* (Chicago), June 1968; "Peter Watkins: Cameraman at World's End" by B.F. Kawin in *Journal of Popular Film* (Washington), summer 1973; "Peter Watkins' Edvard Munch" by J.A. Gomez in *Film Quarterly* (Berkeley), winter 1976/77; "Edvard Munch: A Director's Statement" in *Literature/Film Quarterly* (Salisbury, Md.), winter 1977; "Peter Watkins and Those 'Vital' Amateur Days", interview by J.A. Gomez in *Movie Maker* (England), February 1979; "Tense, Address, Tendenz: Questions of the Work of Peter Watkins" by Stuart Cunningham in *Quarterly Review of Film Studies* (Pleasantville, N.Y.), fall 1980; "The Modern Apocalypse: *The War Game*" by James Welsh in *Journal of Popular Film and Television* (Bowling Green, Ohio), spring 1983.

*   *   *

From his early amateur days to his most recent unfinished projects, Peter Watkins has attempted to make uniquely personal films which delineate disturbing social and political dimensions. Like George Orwell, he is preoccupied with the growth of a repressive world order, the suppression of individual freedoms, and the dangerous spread of a soothing conformity. Beyond these obvious thematic concerns in his work, Watkins has also made significant contributions to the area of film as art. Almost all of his films push beyond the traditions of conventional cinema. Over the years he has developed a particular style of "documentary reconstruction" which often blends realistic and expressionistic structure to the point that his editing techniques have become a stylistic hallmark, and, since *Punishment Park*, he has managed to create sound montages equal in complexity to his visual arrangements. Finally, Watkins, in his films, in various essays, and on numerous world-wide lecture tours, has offered perceptive analysis and stinging criticism of the dangers of media in today's world.

As early as *The Forgotten Faces*, Watkins subverted the deep-seated cinematic conventions that actors do not see the camera and that the camera always knows what will happen next and therefore is accurately focused and properly framed. On the basis of this amateur film reconstruction of the 1956 Hungarian uprising (which was actually filmed in the back streets of Canterbury), Watkins was hired by the BBC, where he further developed his techniques of reconstruction (the use of amateur actors, extensive cross-cutting, a distinctive interview method, etc.) in *Culloden* and *The War Game*. Part of the impact of the latter film, which chillingly depicts the possible effects of a nuclear attack on Great Britain, derives from what Watkins calls the film's "block structure." This structure juxtaposes the strategies of the present with the supposed "fantasy" of the future, but Watkins cleverly reverses the usual presentation of fantasy and reality. The future in Watkins's films becomes the "reality" and is graphically depicted via newsreel-like techniques. The "fantasy" element of present-day opinions about the aftermath of a nuclear attack is reinforced by the artificiality of the presentation of authority figures and by the use of printed captions and quotations.

Although *The War Game* won an Academy Award for the Best Documentay of 1966, the BBC has never lifted the world-wide ban it placed on the screening of the film on television. After the suppression of *The War Game*, Watkins resigned from the BBC, and, after making *Privilege*, he left England because he felt that he could no longer make films there. During this period of exile, which has lasted to the present, he made films in Sweden, Norway, Denmark, and the United States.

The most controversial of these works is *Punishment Park*, a metaphorical depiction in documentary style of the polarization of political attitudes in the U.S. during the war in Vietnam.

Through experiments with improvisation and a further development of his interview style in order to elicit direct emotional response from his audience, Watkins hoped to create a film that would serve as a catalyst for the viewer to seek "a new and more meaningful solution to the present human dilemma posed within Western Society."

The intense hostility to this film in the United States has almost been matched by the hostility of Scandinavian critics to *The 70s People* and *Evening Land*, but a majority of film critics on both sides of the Atlantic seem to agree that Watkins's crowning achievement is *Edvard Munch*. This epic, yet paradoxically personal, work manages to provide a unique balance between the actuality of Munch's statements and the improvisations of nonprofessional actors expressing their own feelings and concerns. As such, the film functions on multiple levels—it delineates Munch's own fears and anxieties, provides penetrating insight into the nature of his artistic creation, captures accurately the historical nuances of that era in which he lived, and finally allows the viewers to perceive, in this intricate amalgam, problems of contemporary society which touch them directly.

Unfortunately, Peter Watkins still remains very much the outsider whose work is usually either viciously attacked ("offensive," "hysterical," and "paranoid") or simply ignored. His role in film history, however, is significant, and as Raymond Durgnat rightly notes "Watkins is as crucial as John Grierson in the development of documentary."

—Joseph A. Gomez

WATT, HARRY. Scottish. Born in Edinburgh, 18 October 1906. Educated Edinburgh University. Career: 1931 or 1932—joins Empire Marketing Board (EMB) film unit under John Grierson; 1934—joins General Post Office (GPO) film unit after EMB film unit is dissolved and transferred to GPO; assists Robert Flaherty on *Man of Aran*; 1939—with outbreak of war, Ministry of Information is formed and incorporates GPO film unit into its organization; 1939-42—works on various war documentaries for Ministry of Information and for Army Film Unit; 1942—joins Ealing Studios; 1945-48—directs films in Australia; 1951-53—directs films in West Africa; 1955—joins Granada TV as producer (in England); 1956—again joins Ealing Studios; 1958—directs documentary, *People Like Maria*, for UNESCO; 1974—writes autobiography, *Don't Look at the Camera*.

Films (as director): 1934—*BBC: Droitwich* (co-d); *6:30 Collection* (co-d); 1936—*Night Mail* (co-d); *The Saving of Bill Blewitt* (+sc); 1937—*4 Barriers* (co-pr only); *Big Money* (co-d); 1938—*North Sea*; *Health in Industry*; 1939—*The 1st Days* (co-d); 1940—*Squadron 992*; *London Can Take It* (co-d); *The Front Line*; *Britain at Bay*; 1941—*Target for Tonight* (+sc); *Christmas Under Fire*; 1942—*Dover Revisited*; *21 Miles*; 1943—*9 Men* (+sc); 1944—*Fiddlers 3* (+sc); 1946—*The Overlanders* (+sc); 1949—*Eureka Stockade (Massacre Hill)* (+sc); 1951—*Where No Vultures Fly (Ivory Hunter)*; 1954—*West of Zanzibar* (+co-sc); 1958—*People Like Maria*; 1959—*The Siege of Pinchgut* (+co-sc).

Publications:

By WATT:

Book—*Don't Look at the Camera*, New York 1974.

On WATT:

Books—*Studies in Documentary* by Alan Lovell and Jim Hillier, New York 1972; *The Rise and Fall of British Documentary: The Story of the Film Movement Founded by John Grierson* by Elizabeth Sussex, Berkeley, California 1975; articles—on *North Sea* by Robert Flaherty in *Sight and Sound* (London), Summer 1938; article on *Where No Vultures Fly* by Bradner Lacey in *Films in Review* (New York), June/July 1952; "Filmography" in *Film* (London), November/December 1957; "British Feature Directors: An Index to Their Work" in *Sight and Sound* (London), autumn 1958; "Personality of the Month" in *Films and Filming* (London), June 1959; article on *The Siege of Pinchgut* by Dai Vaughn in *Films and Filming* (London), October 1959.

*   *   *

Watt was a member of the Grierson documentary group who, during World War II, moved over into feature film directing, carrying his documentary heritage with him. He was one of the two most talented directors to come out of British documentary of the 1930s; Humphrey Jennings being the other. Whereas Jennings was the poet, Watt was the story teller.

He early demonstrated his flair for narrative, for characterization, and for humor—an ability rare among documentary filmmakers. It first became evident in *Night Mail*. Though the creative origins of that film seem to be genuinely collective, it was unquestionably Watt who drew the engaging performances—the naturalness, the bits of banter and occasional tension—from the cast of mailmen. Next, *The Saving of Bill Blewitt* offered a comic anecdote concocted by Watt about a Cornwall fishermen and the Post Office Savings Bank. In *North Sea*, which followed, Watt's attraction to the dramatic is given full reign. Though a short like the others, the situation—of a disabled fishing trawler awash in high seas, loved ones waiting at home, efforts to aid the stricken ship—has all of the ingredients for a feature. *Squadron 992* continued Watt's feeling for narrative, humor, and excitement into the beginning of the war.

But it was *Target for Tonight* that emerged as Watt's major contribution: it became the prototype for the British wartime semi-documentary feature. This form involved a real situation, though it might be composite and representative rather than actual; in this case it was a typical British bombing raid into Germany. The nonactors, here RAF airmen, were given some characterization and dialogue. The exposition, conflict, climax, and denouement follow narrative/dramatic convention. (The bomber on which the film concentrates is hit with flack and the main question becomes whether its crew will return safely.) The semi-documentary was, in other words, half fact and half fiction.

As one can infer from his charming autobiography, *Don't Look at the Camera*, Watt had always thought that filmmaking was really the making of fiction feature films for the theaters. Since the semi-documentary form was picked up and developed by the commercial studios as well as by the government Crown Film Unit, when Watt moved over to Ealing Studios in 1942 he continued along the semi-documentary lines he had begun. Of his features made for Ealing, *The Overlanders* is the most successful, certainly in critical and probably in commercial terms as well. It was shot in Australia and chronicles a cattle drive across the awesome Outback occasioned by the fear of Japanese invasion after Japan's entry into World War II. Though actors play the roles, it is a recreation of an actual occurrence. Watt once said of himself as a filmmaker: "I am a dramatic reporter."

—Jack C. Ellis

***

WEBER, LOIS. American. Born in Allegheny City, Pennsylvania, 1882. Married Phillips Smalley, about 1906 (divorced about 1922). Career: 1890s—tours as concert pianist; becomes Church Home Missionary in Pittsburgh, singing hymns on streetcorners and working in industrial slums; goes on stage in touring company of *Zig Zag*; 1905—joins road company of melodrama *Why Girls Leave Home*; meets and subsequently marries company's manager Phillips Smalley; 1908—begins writing and directing for Gaumont Talking Pictures; soon joined by Smalley, and form together acting-writing-directing partnership; move to Reliance, then Rex, being studio's dramatic leads and serving as directors under Edwin S. Porter; 1912—Porter leaves, the Smalleys (as they are known), take over Rex, a member of the Universal conglomerate; about 1914—Weber emerges as dominant figure of the two; in all directs between 200 and 400 pictures (about 50 positively identified); 1914—joins Hobart Bosworth's company; 1915—Universal finances private studio for Weber at 4634 Sunset Boulevard; 1917—founds own studio; 1920—signs contract with Famous Players-Lasky for $50,000 per picture and a percentage of profits; 1921—dropped by company after 3 unprofitable films; subsequently loses company, divorced from Smalley, suffers nervous collapse; late 1920s—briefly resumes directing; early 1930s—works as script-doctor for Universal, does screen tests; 1934—directs last film. Died in Hollywood, 13 November 1939.

Films (as director—partial list): 1912—*The Troubadour's Triumph*; 1913—*The Eyes of God*; *The Jew's Christmas* (co-d, +sc, ro); *The Female of the Species* (+ro); 1914—*The Merchant of Venice* (co-d, +ro as *Portia*); *Traitor*; *Like Most Wives*; *Hypocrites!* (+sc); *False Colors* (co-d, +co-sc, ro); *It's No Laughing Matter* (+sc); *A Fool and His Money* (+ro); *Behind the Veil* (co-d, +sc, ro); 1915—*Sunshine Molly* (co-d, +sc, ro); *A Cigarette, That's All* (sc only); *Scandal* (co-d, +sc, ro); 1916—*Discontent* (short); *Hop, the Devil's Brew* (co-d, +sc, ro); *Where Are My Children?* (co-d, +sc); *The French Downstairs*; *Alone in the World* (short); *The People Vs. John Doe* (+ro); *The Rock of Riches* (short); *John Needham's Double*; *Saving the Family Name* (co-d, +ro)); *Shoes*; *The Dumb Girl of Portici* (co-d); *The Flirt* (co-d); 1917—*The Hand That Rocks the Cradle* (co-d, +pr, ro); *Even As You and I*; *The Mysterious Mrs. M*; *The Price of a Good Time*; *The Man Who Dared God*; *There's No Place Like Home*; *For Husbands Only* (+pr); 1918—*The Doctor and the Woman*; *Borrowed Clothes*; 1919—*When a Girl Loves*; *Mary Regan*; *Midnight Romance* (+sc); *Scandal Mongers*; *Home*; *Forbidden*; 1921—*Too Wise Wives* (+pr, sc); *What's Worth While?* (+pr); *To Please One Woman* (+sc); *The Blot* (+pr, sc); *What Do Men Want?* (+pr, sc); 1923—*A Chapter in Her Life* (+co-sc); 1926—*The Marriage Clause* (+sc); 1927—*Sensation Seekers* (+sc); *The Angel of Broadway*; 1934—*White Heat*.

Publications:

By WEBER:

Interview by Aline Carter in *Motion Picture Magazine* (New York), March 1921.

On WEBER:

Articles—"Notes on Women Directors" by J. Pyros in *Take One* (Montreal), November/December 1970; "The Years Have Not Been Kind to Lois Weber" by Richard Koszarski in *The Village Voice* (New York), 10 November 1975; (reprinted in *Women and the Cinema* edited by Karyn Kay and Gerald Peary, New York 1977).

*   *   *

Lois Weber was a rather unique silent film director. Not only was she a woman and certainly the most important female director the American film industry has known, but, unlike many of her colleagues up to the present, her work was regarded in its day as equal to, if not a little better than that of most male directors. She was a committed filmmaker in an era when commitment was virtually unknown, a filmmaker who was not afraid to make features with subject matter in which she devoutly believed, subjects as varied as Christian Science (*Jewel* and *A Chapter in Her Life*) or birth control (*Where Are My Children*). *Hypocrites* was an indictment of hypocrisy and corruption in big business, politics, and religion, while *The People vs. John Doe* opposed capital punishment. At the same time, Lois Weber was quite capable of handling with ease a major spectacular feature, such as the historical drama, *The Dumb Girl of Portici*, which introduced Anna Pavlova to the screen.

During the teens, Lois Weber was under contract to Universal where she appears to have been given total freedom as to the subject matter of her films, all of which were among the studio's biggest moneymakers and highly regarded by the critics of the day. (The Weber films, however, did run into censorship problems and the director was the subject of a vicious attack in a 1918 issue of *Theatre Magazine* over the "indecent and suggestive" nature of her titles.) Eventually the director felt the urge to move on to independent production, and during 1920 and 1921 she released a series of highly personal intimate dramas dealing with married life and the types of problems which beset ordinary people. None of these films was particularly well received by the critics, who unanimously declared them dull, while the public displayed an equal lack of enthusiasm. Nonetheless, features such as *Too Wise Wives* and *The Blot* demonstrate Weber at her directorial best. In the former she presents a study of two married couples. Not very much happens, but in her characterizations and attention to detail (something for which Weber was always noted), the director is as contemporary as a Robert Altman or an Ingmar Bergman. *The Blot* is concerned with "genteel poverty" and is marked by the underplaying of its principals—Claire Windsor and Louis Calhern—and an enigmatic ending which leaves the viewer uninformed as to the characters' future, an ending unlike any in the entire history of the American silent film. These films, as with virtually all of the director's work, were also written by Lois Weber.

Through the end of her independent productions in 1921, Lois Weber worked in association with her husband Phillips Smalley, who usually received credit as associate or advisory director. After the two were divorced, Lois Weber's career went to pieces. She directed one or two minor program features together with one talkie, but none equalled her work from the teens and early twenties. She was a liberated filmmaker who seemed lost without companionship both at home and in the studio of a husband. Her career and life is in many ways as enigmatic as the ending of *The Blot*.

—Anthony Slide

WEIR, PETER. Australian. Born in Sydney, 21 August 1944. Educated in Arts/Law course at Sydney University. Career: leaves school to enter family realty business; 1966—first visit to Europe; 1967—joins TV station ATN 7, Sydney; 1969—joins Commonwealth Film Unit (now Film Australia) as assistant cameraman and production assistant; 1980—signs multi-film contract with Warner Brothers. Recipient: Grand Prix, Australian Film Institute for *Three to Go* (shared with Brian Hannant and Oliver Howes); Grand Prix, Australian Film Institute for *Homesdale*, 1971.

Films (as director of short films): 1967—*Count Vim's Last Exercise*; 1968—*The Life and Times of the Rev. Buck Shotte*; 1970—"Michael" episode of *Three to Go*; 1971—*Homesdale*; 1972—*Incredible Floridas*; 1973—*Whatever Happened to Green Valley?*; (as feature director): 1974—*The Cars That Ate Paris*; 1975—*Picnic At Hanging Rock*; 1977—*The Last Wave*; 1978—*The Plumber*; 1981—*Gallipoli*; 1982—*The Year of Living Dangerously*.

Publications:

By WEIR:

Articles—"Weir, Weird and Weirder Still", interview by D. Castell in *Films Illustrated* (London), November 1976; interviews by H. Béhar in *Images et son* (Paris), January and February 1978; "Naissance d'un cinéma australien", interview by A. Tournès in *Jeune Cinéma* (Paris), March 1978; "It Doesn't Take Any Imagination at All to Feel Awed", interview by J.M. Kass in *Movietone News* (Seattle), December 1979; "New Wave Director Peter Weir Rides *The Last Wave* into U.S. Market", interview by P. Childs in *Millimeter* (New York), March 1979; "His Subject—Mysteries of Different Cultures", interview by D. Jacobs in *The New York Times*, 14 January 1979; "Peter Weir: Towards the Centre", interview by B. McFarlane and T. Ryan in *Cinema Papers* (Melbourne), September/October 1981.

On WEIR:

Articles—"Peter Weir" by R. Nicholls in *Lumiere* (Melbourne), March 1973; "The Cars That Ate Paris—Production Report" by G. Glenn and S. Murray and "Peter Weir" by R. Brennan in *Cinema Papers* (Melbourne), January 1974; "The Films of Peter Weir" by B. McFarlane in *Cinema Papers* (Melbourne), April/-May 1980; "Peter Weir" by M. Magill in *Films in Review* (New York), October 1981.

* * *

The Australian new wave's most sophisticated director, Peter Weir brings to his films a European elegance and fantasy. Many derive from discoveries made while on foreign journeys. The

Cars That Ate Paris was suggested by an unexpected diversion from a main French auto route, *The Last Wave* by the discovery of an ancient sculptured head on a Tunisian beach. Even his apprentice short films, one for a university revue, the other a private joke for the Australian Broadcasting Commission's staff party, show a flair for the grotesque. *Michael*, with its vision of Australia gripped by revolution, and the macabre *Homesdale*, set in an isolated retirement home, display an imagination uncharacteristic of the largely documentary-oriented Australian cinema. His documentary *Incredible Floridas*, on the other hand, dipped into dream imagery for its picture of composer Richard Meale's chamber work, a tribute to Rimbaud.

The Cars That Ate Paris established Weir as a major talent. This absurdist black comedy about a country town preying on motorists whose vehicles are cannibalized and made into spiked battle taxis by the local youth alarmed Australian audiences while attracting the unwelcome attention of foreign producers anxious to steal the idea. But universal acclaim greeted *Picnic At Hanging Rock*, a Victorian fantasy that has become a cornerstone of Australian cinema. Drowsy, sensual, and cryptic, it emphasized Weir's increasing eminence among his less thoughtful contemporaries.

Belligerent Australian reaction to *The Last Wave* may have been fuelled by a resentment of Weir's internationalism. He imported American Richard Chamberlain for this story of ancient aboriginal cults foretelling the world's end in a new flood. Almost in reaction, *The Plumber*, made for TV, is prosaic, recognizable as Weir only in the surrealist premise of an unsummoned plumber overturning the cosy home environment of a baffled surburban housewife. Weir was even then preoccupied with a project about Australia's first international military adventure, the disastrous Dardenelles campaign of 1916, which he was finally to make after four years as *Gallipoli*.

Given mass release, *Gallipoli* established Weir's name. He again worked with Hollywood to make *The Year of Living Dangerously* about a journalist in Indonesia struggling to report and survive during the collapse of the Sukarno regime. The result confirmed him as a director of substantial skill, but little of his original grotesque vision and humor was apparent; without this, he risks sinking into the crowd of talented but undirected newcomers who inhabit the international film scene.

—John Baxter

WEISS, JIRI. Czech. Born in Prague, 29 March 1913. Educated in law, Charles University, Prague. Career: 1935—leaves school, becomes advertising writer and makes 1st documentary; 1936—success of film leads to offer from Barrandov Studios, Prague; 1939—escapes to London following Nazi occupation; 1940s—works with British documentarists, volunteers for army, assigned to Crown Film Unit; shoots battlefield documentaries in Europe after 2nd front opened; 1945—returns to Prague; 1963—teaches at film school in West Berlin; 1968—at Venice Film Festival at time of Soviet invasion of Czechoslovakia, requests political asylum in Italy. Recipient: Artist of Merit, Czechoslovakia.

Films (as director): 1935—*People in the Sun*; 1936—*Give Us Wings*; 1937—*Song of a Sad Country*; 1938—*Journey from the Shadows*; 1939—*The Rape of Czechoslovakia*; 1941—*Eternal Prague*; 1943—*Before the Raid*; 1945—*Věrni zustaneme (Interim balance)* (+sc); 1947—*Uloupená hranice (The Stolen Frontier)* (+co-sc); 1948—*Dravci (Wild Beasts, Beasts of Prey)* (+co-sc); *Ves v pohraničí (The Village on the Frontier)*; 1949—*Píseň o sletu I, II (Song of the Meet, I and II, High Flies the Hawk, I and II)*; 1950—*Vstanou noví bojovníci (New Warriors Will Arise)*; *Poslední výstřel (The Last Shot)*; 1953—*Muj přítel Fabián (My Friend Fabian, My Friend the Gypsy)* (+co-sc); 1954—*Punt'a a čtyřlístek (Punta and the Four-Leaf Clover, Doggy and the 4)* (+co-sc); 1956—*Hra o život (Life at Stake, Life Was at Stake)* (+co-sc); 1957—*Vlčí jáma (Wolf Trap)* (+co-sc); 1959—*Taková láska (Appassionata, That Kind of Love)* (+co-sc); 1960—*Romeo, Julie a tma (Romeo, Juliet and the Darkness, Sweet Light in the Dark Window)* (+co-sc); 1962—*Zbabělec (Coward)* (+co-sc); 1963—*Zlaté kapradí (The Golden Fern)* (+co-sc); 1965—*Třicet jedna ve stínu (90 in the Shade)* (+co-sc); 1966—*Vražda po našem (Murder Our Style, Murder Czech Style)* (+co-sc); 1968—*Prípad pro Selwyn (Justice for Selwyn)* (for Czech tv).

Publications:

By WEISS:

articles— "Czech Cinema Has Arrived" in *Films and Filming* (London), March 1959; "Mixing It" in *Films and Filming* (London), June 1965; interview in *Closely Watched Films* by Antonín Liehm, White Plains, New York 1974.

On WEISS:

Books—*Modern Czechoslovak Film* by Jaroslav Boček, Prague 1965; *Leksykon rezyserow filmowych* by Zbigniew Pitera, Warsaw 1978.

*   *   *

Jiři Weiss is one of the most significant and certainly most interesting Czech directors of the last 50 years. He studied at Jura and had worked as a journalist before making his first film in 1934, a documentary which received a prize at Venice that year. Until the outbreak of war he continued to work on documentaries.

In 1939 Weiss fled the Nazis to England, befriended an English documentarist and made several films including *Before the Raid*. Later, as a film specialist, he took part in the battles of the Czech exile army. He returned to his homeland in 1945. His first theatrical film, *Uloupená hranice*, dealt with the Munich accord of 1938, shortly before the fascist occupation of his country. A subsequent film, *Vstanou noví bojovníci*, depicted the establishment of the worker's movement in Czechoslovakia, and brought the director not only official recognition at home but also attention abroad. Afterward Weiss made films dealing with contemporary problems and people's everyday life. In the 1953 *My Friend Fabian* he described how the gypsies have adjusted, with many difficulties, to a new life in socialist Czechoslovakia. *Hra o život* appeared in 1956, a critical film about the destruction of a bourgeois family in the period of the German occupation. *Taková láska*, a dramatic psychological work, displayed the director's ability to develop richly human characterization.

Vlčí jama impressed further through the deep psychological treatment of the characters and the careful attention to cultural surroundings by which he delineated the *Zeitgeist*, the atmosphere and the milieu of the petit bourgeoisie prior to World War I. An honorable mayor of a small city, who feels a devotion for his aging wife, nevertheless falls in love with a young girl that lives in the same house.

This film revealed the full range of Jiři Weiss's style. It is based in a solid critical realism, rooted in the epic novels of the 19th century. This approach sets out fully-realized and many-sided human figures within an accurately-described milieu. The cinema of Weiss draws on Czech cultural tradition, and at the same time strives toward broader European dimensions. In this way his works attain to a certain cosmopolitanism.

On the one hand, Weiss was strongly influenced by neorealism as were all the other filmmakers of his generation. Although not so pathetically inclined as, for example, Andrzej Wajda, Weiss showed in his masterpiece *Romeo, Julie a tma* the influences of the neorealist aesthetic, especially in the case of the theme, again broadly European, of the tragic fate of two young lovers in Prague in 1942. The Jewish schoolgirl Hanna is hidden by young Pavel, a tender love develops, and is cut short by Hanna's death. Weiss had created a tragic and poetic work, without filmic innovation, but nevertheless a serious, noble film.

In the sixties Weiss made *Zlaté kapradí*, *Trícet jedna ve stínu*, and *Vražda po našem*, which attained a high standard in terms of craft, but broke no new ground formally or thematically. Living since 1968 in the West, he has made an occasional film for television and at the moment finds himself in California.

—Maria Racheva

WELLES, ORSON. American. Born in Kenosha, Wisconsin, 6 May 1916. Educated at Todd School in Woodstock, Illinois, 1926-1931. Married Virginia Nicholson in 1934 (divorced 1939); child: Christopher; Rita Hayworth in 1943 (divorced 1947); child: Rebecca; Paoli Mori in 1955; child: Beatrice. Career: 1931—auditions for the Gate Theatre, Dublin, Ireland, winning a leading role in *Jew Suss*; 1931-34—later appears in and directs several plays there; 1934—joins Katherine Cornell's road company in the U.S., debuting on Broadway as Tybalt in *Romeo and Juliet*; co-directs his first film, 4 minute short *The Hearts of Age*; also performs on radio for 1st time; 1935—collaborates with John Houseman on productions of the Phoenix Theatre Group; both subsequently produce and direct for the Federal Theater Project; 1937—Houseman and Welles form Mercury Theatre Group, in which they perform, direct; 1938—Mercury Theatre moves into radio with "Mercury Theatre on the Air"; on Halloween, 1938, Welles's famous dramatization of H.G. Wells's *War of the Worlds* is broadcast; 1939—given contract by RKO, works on several unrealized projects; 1941—*Citizen Kane* is released; 1942—begins documentary *It's All True* in Latin America for RKO, but the film is never completed; Welles and his staff are removed from RKO; 1947—employed by Columbia Studios and directs *The Lady from Shanghai*; 1948—hired by Republic Pictures and directs *Macbeth*; 1949—disenchanted with Hollywood, leaves for Europe to act in several films, including *The 3rd Man* by Carol Reed; begins working on the first of several of his own films in Europe; except for *Touch of Evil*, Welles completes no more films in U.S.; 1970—fire at home in Spain destroys only print of *Too Much Johnson*; 1970s to present—appears in commercials and continues to act, attempts to complete film *The Other Side of the Wind*. Recipient: Cannes Film Festival, 20th Anniversary Tribute, 1966; Honorary Academy Award for "Superlative artistry and versatility in the creation of motion pictures," 1970; American Film Institute, Life Achievement Award, 1975.

Films (as director): 1934—*The Hearts of Age* (16mm short) (co-d); 1938—*Too Much Johnson* (+co-pr, sc) (unedited, not shown publicly, destroyed in 1970 fire); 1941—*Citizen Kane*

(+pr, co-sc, ro as *Charles Foster Kane*); 1942—*The Magnificent Ambersons* (+pr, sc); 1942—*It's All True* (+pr, co-sc) (not completed and never shown); 1943—*Journey into Fear* (co-d, uncredited, +pr, co-sc, ro as *Colonel Haki*); 1946—*The Stranger* (+co-sc, uncredited, ro as *Franz Kindler* alias *Professor Charles Rankin*); 1948—*The Lady from Shanghai* (+sc, ro as *Michael O'Hara*) (produced in 1946); *Macbeth* (+pr, sc, co-costumes, ro as *Macbeth*); 1952—*Othello* (+pr, sc, ro as *Othello* and narration); 1955—*Mr. Arkadin (Confidential Report)* (+sc, art d, costumes, ro as *Gregory Arkadin* and narration); *Don Quixote* (+co-pr, sc, ass't ph, ro as himself and narration) (not completed); 1958—*Touch of Evil* (+sc, ro as *Hank Quinlan*); 1962—*The Trial* (+sc, ro as *Hastler* and narration); 1966—*Chimes at Midnight (Falstaff)* (+sc, costumes, ro as *Sir John Falstaff*); 1968—*The Immortal Story* (+sc, ro as *Mr. Clay*); 1970—*The Deep* (+sc, ro as *Russ Brewer*); 1972—*The Other Side of the Wind* (+sc) (filming begun in 1972, uncompleted); 1975—*F for Fake* (sc).

Roles: (in films not directed): 1940—off-screen narrator of *Swiss Family Robinson* (Ludwig); 1943—*Edward Rochester* in *Jane Eyre* (R. Stevenson); 1944—revue appearance with Marlene Dietrich in *Follow the Boys* (Sutherland); 1945—*John McDonald* in *Tomorrow is Forever* (Pichel); 1946—off-screen narrator of *Duel in the Sun* (Vidor); 1947—*Cagliostro* in *Black Magic* (Ratoff); 1948—*Cesare Borgia* in *Prince of Foxes*; 1949—*Harry Lime* in *The 3rd Man* (Reed); 1950—*General Bayan* in *The Black Rose* (Hathaway); 1951—himself in *Return to Glennascaul* (Edwards); 1953—*Sigsbee Manderson* in *Trent's Last Case* (Wilcox); *Benjamin Franklin* in *Si Versailles m'était conté* (Guitry); *The Beast* in *L'uomo, la bestia e la virtu* (Steno); 1954—*Hudson Lowe* in *Napoléon* (Guitry); *Lord Mountdrago* in "Lord Mountdrago" segment of *3 Cases of Murder* (O'Ferrall); 1955—*Samin Cejador y Mengues* in *Trouble in the Glen* (Wilcox); narrator in *Out of Darkness* (documentary); 1956—*Father Mapple* in *Moby Dick* (Huston); 1957—*Virgil Renckler* in *Pay the Devil* (Arnold); *Will Varner* in *The Long Hot Summer* (Ritt); 1958—*Cy Sedgwick* in *The Roots of Heaven* (Huston); off-screen narrator of *Les Seigneurs de la forêt* (Sielman and Brandt); narrator of *The Vikings* (Fleischer); 1959—*Saul* in *David e Golia* (Pottier and Baldi); *Jonathan Wilk* in *Compulsion* (Fleischer); *Captain Hart* in *Ferry to Hong Kong* (Gilbert); off-screen narrator of *High Journey* (Baylis); off-screen narrator of *South Sea Adventure* (Dudley); 1960—*Fulton* in *Austerlitz* (Gance); *Hagolin/Lamorcière* in *Crack in the Mirror* (Fleischer); *Barundai* in *I tartari* (Thorpe); 1961—*Benjamin Franklin* in *Lafayette* (Dréville); off-screen narrator of *King of Kings* (Ray); *Désordre* (short); 1962—narrator of *Der grosse Atlantik* (documentary); 1963—*Max Buda* in *The V.I.P.s* (Asquith); *The Film Director* in *Rogopag* (Pasolini); 1964—*Ackermann* in *L'Echiquier de Dieu (La Fabuleuse Aventure de Marco Polo)* (de la Patellière); narrator of *The Finest Hours* (Baylis); 1965—*The Island of Treasure* (J. Franco); narrator of *A King's Story* (Booth); 1966—*Is Paris Burning?* (Clément); *Cardinal Wolsey* in *A Man for All Seasons* (Zinnemann); 1967—*Casino Royale* (Huston and others); *The Sailor from Gibralter* (Richardson); *I'll Never Forget Whatshisname* (Winner); 1968—*Tiresias* in *Oedipus the King* (Saville); *Emperor Justinian* in *Kampf um Rom*; *The Southern Star* (Hayers); 1969—*Tepepa*; narrator of *Barbed Water* (documentary); *Una su 13*; *Michael the Brave*; *House of Cards* (Guillermin); 1970—*General Dweedle* in *Catch-22* (Nichols); *Battle of Neretva* (Bulajia); narrator in *Start the Revolution without Me* (Yorkin); *The Kremlin Letter* (Huston); *King Louis XVIII* in *Waterloo* (Bondarchuk); 1971—narrator of *Directed by John Ford* (Bogdanovich); narrator of *Sentinels of Silence*; *A Safe Place* (Jaglom); 1972—*La Decade prodi-*

gieuse; *Malpertius*; *I racconti di Canterbury* (Pasolini); *Long John Silver* in *Treasure Island* (Hough); *Get to Know Your Rabbit* (De Palma); 1973—*Necromancy* (Gordon); 1975—narrator of *Bugs Bunny Superstar* (Jones); 1976—narrator of *Challenge of Greatness* (documentary); *Voyage of the Damned* (Rosenberg); 1977—*It Happened One Christmas* (Thomas—for TV); 1979—on-camera narrator in *The Late Great Planet Earth*; *J.P. Morgan* in *The Muppet Movie* (Frawley); *Yug* in *Tesla*; 1981—*The Judge* in *Butterfly* (Cimber).

Publications:

By WELLES:

Books—*Everybody's Shakespeare*, New York 1933, revised as *The Mercury Shakespeare*, 1939; *Une Grosse Légume*, translated by Maurice Bessy, Paris 1953; *A bon entendeur*, translated by Serge Greffet, Paris 1953; *Mr. Arkadin*, Paris 1954; *Sed de mal e Il processo* (scripts for *Touch of Evil* and *The Trial*), Madrid 1962; *The Trial*, script, New York 1970; *Citizen Kane*, script, in *The Citizen Kane Book* by Pauline Kael, New York 1971; *The Films of Orson Welles* by Charles Higham, Berkeley 1970; *This is Orson Welles* by Peter Bogdanovich and Orson Welles, New York 1972; articles—"La Splendeur des Amberson" in *Revue du cinéma* (Paris), December 1946; interview by André Bazin and Jean-Charles Tacchella in *L'Ecran français* (Paris), 21 September 1948; "Interview with Welles" by Francis Koval in *Sight and Sound* (London), December 1950; preface to *He That Plays the King* by Kenneth Tynan, New York 1950; preface to *Les Truquages au cinéma* by Maurice Bessy, Paris 1951; "Je combats comme un géant dans un monde de nains pour le cinéma universal" in *Arts* (Paris), 25 August 1954; "The 3rd Audience" in *Sight and Sound* (London), January/March 1954; "For a Universal Cinema" in *Film Culture* (New York), January 1955; "The Scenario Crisis" in *International Film Annual*, London 1957; "Un Ruban de rêves" in *L'Express* (Paris), 5 June 1958, reprinted in *International Film Annual* London 1958; interview by André Bazin and Charles Bitsch in *Cahiers du cinéma* (Paris), June 1958; interview by André Bazin in *France-Observateur* (Paris), 12 June 1958; "Nouvel entretien avec Orson Welles" by André Bazin, Charles Bitsch, and Jean Domarchi in *Cahiers du cinéma* (Paris), September 1958; "Orson Welles s'explique" by Henry Magnan in *Les Lettres françaises* (Paris), 19 June 1958; "Conversation at Oxford" by Derrick Griggs in *Sight and Sound* (London), spring 1960; "Citizen Kane" in *L'Avant-Scène du cinéma* (Paris), January 1962; "Le Procès" in *L'Avant-Scène du cinéma* (Paris), February 1963; "The Life and Opinions of Orson Welles" by Dilys Powell in *The Sunday Times* (London), 3 February 1963; "A Trip to Don Quixoteland: Conversations with Orson Welles" by Juan Cobos and others in *Cahiers du Cinema in English* (New York), June 1966; "Interview: Orson Welles" by Kenneth Tynan in *Playboy* (Chicago), March 1967; interview in *The Americans* by David Frost, New York 1970; "1st Person Singular" by Joseph McBride in *Sight and Sound* (London), winter 1971-72; "Heart of Darkness" in *Film Comment* (New York), November/-December 1972; "Ansichten" in *Film und Fernsehen* (Berlin), no.2, 1979.

On WELLES:

Books—*Orson Welles, A First Biography* by Roy A. Fowler, London 1946; *Orson Welles* by André Bazin, Paris 1950; *Put Money in Thy Purse* by Micheál MacLiammóir, London 1952;

The Fabulous Orson Welles by Peter Noble, London 1956; *The Cinema of Orson Welles* by Peter Bogdanovich, New York 1961; *Orson Welles* by Maurice Bessy, *Cinéma d'aujourd'hui* series, Paris 1963; *Orson Welles, l'éthique et l'esthétique* by various authors in *Etudes cinématographiques* (Paris), 1963; *The Cinema of Orson Welles* by Peter Cowie, London 1965; *The Films of Orson Welles* by Charles Higham, Berkeley 1971; *The Citizen Kane Book* by Pauline Kael, New York 1971; *Orson Welles* by Maurice Bessy, New York 1971; *This Is Orson Welles* by Peter Bogdanovich and Orson Welles, New York 1972; *Orson Welles* by Joseph McBride, London 1972; *Run Through: A Memoir* by John Houseman, New York 1972; *A Ribbon of Dreams* by Peter Cowie, New York 1973; *Orson Welles: Actor and Director* by Joseph McBride, New York 1977; *Orson Welles: A Critical View* by André Bazin, translated by Jonathan Rosenbaum, New York 1978; *The Magic World of Orson Welles* by J. Naremore, New York 1978; articles—"Le Cinéma à la recherche du temps perdu" by Jacques Bourgeois in *Revue du cinéma* (Paris), December 1946; "Essai dur le style d'Orson Welles" by Jacques Manuel in *Revue du cinéma* (Paris), December 1946; "Les Films à la première personne et l'illusion de la réalité au cinéma" by Jean-Pierre Chartier in *La Revue du cinéma* (Paris), January 1947; "L'Opérateur de prises de vues" by Gregg Toland in *Revue du cinéma* (Paris), January 1947; "L'Apport d'Orson Welles" by André Bazin in *Ciné-Club* (Paris), May 1948; profile of Welles by Jean Cocteau in *Cinémonde* (Paris), 6 March 1950; "Wonder Boy Welles" by Walter Kerr in *Theatre Arts* (New York), September 1951; "Les Vertes Statues d'Orson Welles" by Maurice Bessy in *Cahiers du cinéma* (Paris), May 1952; "Orson Welles" by Micheál MacLiammóir in *Sight and Sound* (London), July/September 1954; "Orson Welles from *Citizen Kane* to *Othello*" by Roberto Pariante in *Bianco e nero* (Rome), March 1956; "Winged Gorilla" in *New Statesman and Nation* (London), 21 January 1956; "Orson Welles chez les Jivaros" by André Bazin in *Cahiers du cinéma* (Paris), October 1958; "Welles a n'en plus finir" by Jean Domarchi in *Cahiers du cinéma* (Paris), July 1958; "L'Oeuvre d'Orson Welles" in *Cahiers du cinéma* (Paris), September 1958; "All is Not Welles" by Sergei Gerasimov in *Films and Filming* (London), September 1959; "Welles contra Hitchcock" in *Film Forum* (Voorhout, Holland), no.3, 1959; "Orson Welles" by Jean-Claude Allais in *Premier Plan* (Lyon), 16 November 1961; "Orson Welles" by Peter Cowie in *Films and Filming* (London), April 1961; "Retour de Welles" by Max Egly in *Image et son* (Paris), March 1961; "My Name is Orson Welles" by André-S. Labarthe in *Cahiers du cinéma* (Paris), March 1961; "The Heroes of Welles" by Alan Stanbrook in *Film* (London), no.28, 1961; entire issue of *Image et son* (Paris), no.139, 1961; articles by Kenneth Tynan in *Show* (Hollywood), October and November 1961; "Citizen Welles" by Jean Béranger in *Kosmorama* (Copenhagen), October and December 1962; "My Name is Orson Welles" by Stig Björkman in *Chaplin* (Stockholm), no.33, 1962; "The Legion of Lost Films" by Herman Weinberg in *Sight and Sound* (London), autumn 1962; entire issue of *Cine forum* (Venice), no.19, 1962; "Le Procès d'Orson Welles" in *Cinéma 62* (Paris), no.71 1962; "Case for the Defense" by Richard Fleischer in *Films and Filming* (London), October 1962; "Interview with John Houseman" by Penelope Houston in *Sight and Sound* (London), autumn 1962; "Orson Welles and the Big Experimental Film Cult" by Parker Tyler in *Film Culture* (New York), summer 1963; "Trials" by William Pechter in *Sight and Sound* (London), winter 1963/64; interview with Everett Sloane in *Film* (London), no.37, 1965; "Orson Welles: Of Time and Loss" by William Johnson in *Film Quarterly* (Berkeley), fall 1967; "Welles in Power" by Serge Daney in *Cahiers du Cinema in English* (New York), September 1967; "Special Report: Orson Welles" in *Action* (Los Angeles), May/-

June 1969; "Welles Before Kane" by Joseph McBride in *Film Quarterley* (Berkeley), spring 1970; "It's Not Quite All True" by Richard Wilson in *Sight and Sound* (London), autumn 1970; "Orson Welles' Use of Sound" by Phyllis Goldfarb in *Take One* (Montreal), July/August 1971; "The Long Take" by Brian Henderson in *Film Comment* (New York), summer 1971; article by Joseph McBride in *Film Heritage* (Dayton, Ohio), fall 1971; "Orson Welles" by Mike Prokosch *Film Comment* (New York), summer 1971; "The Heart of Darkness in Citizen Kane" by H. Cohen in *Cinema Journal* (Evanston), fall 1972; "Heston on Welles" and "Orson Welles's Use of Sound" by P. Goldfarb in *Take One* (Montreal), October 1972; "The Voice and the Eye" by Jonathan Rosenbaum in *Film Comment* (New York), November/December 1972; "'The Citizen Kane Book'" by George Coulouris and Bernard Herrmann in *Sight and Sound* (London), spring 1972; "A Touch of Orson" by Gordon Gow in *Films and Filming* (London), December 1974; "Welles and the Logic of Death" by N. Hale in *Film Heritage* (New York), fall 1974; "On the AFI Tribute to Orson Welles" in *Millimeter* (New York), May 1975; "Howard, Hugh, Walt et sardoniquement Orson" by Robert Benayoun in *Positif* (Paris), March 1975; "Orson Welles (sur *Nothing But the Truth* and *The Other Side of the Wind*)" by M. Bessy and others in *Ecran* (Paris), February 1975; "Neighborhood Grocer?" by D. Bowie in *Take One* (Montreal), May 1975; "Orson Welles, le théâtre et 'La Tragique Histoire du docteur Faust'" by John Houseman in *Positif* (Paris), March 1975; "Hollywood Salutes its 'Maverick' Genius Orson Welles", special issue of *American Cinematographer* (Los Angeles), April 1975; "Orson Welles, interprète et continuateur de Shakespeare" by R. Marienstras in *Positif* (Paris), March 1975; "Orson Welles, itinéraire d'un poète maudit" by J.-C. Allais in *Cahiers de la Cinématheque* (Paris), summer 1976; "3 Regards critiques" by L. Audibert in *Cinématographe* (Paris), April 1977; "Director in Aspic" by Jay Cocks in *Take One* (Montreal), January 1977; "The Lost Film of Orson Welles" by F. Brady in *American Film* (Washington, D.C.), November 1978; "All's Welles" by J. McBride in *Film Comment* (New York), November/December 1978; "The Great God Orson: Chabrol's '10 Days' Wonder'" by Lee Poague in *Film Criticism* (Edinboro, Pa.), no.3, 1979; "Von einem, der Karriere macht: Orson Welles im Hollywood der dreissiger Jahre" by J. Toeplitz in *Film und Fernsehen* (Berlin), no.2, 1979; "Orson Welles existe-t-il?" by J. Magny in *Cinéma* (Paris), October 1981.

*   *   *

References to Orson Welles as one of American's most influential directors and *Citizen Kane* as one of the great American films have become a simplistic way to capsulize Welles's unique contribution to cinema. It is a contribution which seems obvious but is difficult to adequately summerize without examining his complex career.

Welles began as an actor in Ireland at Dublin's famous Gate Theater, bluffing his way into the theater's acting troupe by claiming to be well-known on the Broadway stage. He began directing plays in New York, and worked with John Houseman in various theatrical groups. For the Federal Theater Project, they attempted to stage Marc Blitzstein's leftist, pro-labor *The Cradle Will Rock*, but government agents blocked the opening night's production. Performers and audience moved to another theater in one of Broadway's most famous episodes. The incident led to Houseman being fired and Welles's resignation from the Project. Houseman and Welles formed the Mercury Theater Group with a manifesto written by Houseman declaring their intentions to foster new talent, experiment with new types of plays, and to appeal to the same audiences that frequented the Federal Theater plays. Welles's work on the New York stage has been described as generally leftist in its political orientation, and inspired by the expressionist theater in the 1920s, prefiguring the look of his films. He became known for adapting the classics, particularly Shakespeare. For his all-black production of *Macbeth*, performed in Harlem, he set the play in Haiti, with voodoo priestesses replacing the witches.

Welles and his Mercury Theater Group expanded into radio as the Mercury Theater on the Air. In contrast to most theater-oriented shows on radio, which consisted merely of plays read aloud, the Mercury group adapted their works in a more natural, personal manner. Welles was interested in telling stories to the audience as though he were talking to each individual one-to-one; most of the plays were narrated in the first person. His desire to eliminate the impersonal elements of radio theater and pursue a more realistic approach gained him a reputation as an experimenter. Shrewd imitations of news announcements and technical breakdowns heightened the realism of his 1938 Halloween *War of the Worlds* broadcast to such a degree that the show has become famous for the panic it caused as Americans thought New Jersey was actually being invaded by Martians. This event itself has become a pop culture legend, shrouded in exaggeration and half-truths, and was the subject of a 1975 made-for-television film, *The Night That Panicked America*.

RKO studios hired Welles in 1939 hoping he could repeat the success on film for them that he had enjoyed on stage and in radio. Welles, according to most sources, accepted the job because his Mercury Theater needed money to produce an elaborate production called *5 Kings*, an anthology of several of Shakespeare's plays. Whatever the reason, his contract with RKO began an erratic and rocky relationship with the Hollywood industry that would, time and again, end in bitter disappointment for Welles, leading finally to his self-imposed exile in Europe.

The film on which Welles enjoyed the most creative freedom was his first and most famous, *Citizen Kane*. At the time the film created a controversy over both its subject matter and style. Loosely based on the life of newspaper magnate William Randolph Hearst, the film supposedly upset Hearst to such a degree that he attempted to stop the production, and then the distribution and exhibition. In the end, his anger was manifested in the scathing reviews critics gave the film in all his newspaper. Some Welles scholars maintain that actress Marion Davies, Hearst's mistress, on whom the Susan Alexander character was supposedly modeled, was the most upset by *Kane*, and that Hearst's efforts to dull the impact of the film were on her behalf. The film's innovative structure consisting of flashbacks from the differing points-of-view of the various characters, in addition to other formal devices so different from the classic Hollywood cinema, contributed to *Kane*'s financial failure and commercial downfall, though critics other than those on Hearst's papers generally gave the film positive reviews. Other controversies surrounding the film include that over the correct scriptwriting credit. Originally Welles claimed solo credit for writing the film, but the Writer's Guild forced him to acknowledge Herman Mankiewicz as co-author. Each writer's *exact* contributions remain unknown, but the controversy was revived during the early 1970s by critic Pauline Kael, who attempted to prove that Mankiewicz was most responsible for the script. Whatever the case, the argument becomes unimportant and even ludicrous given the unique direction which shapes the material, and which is undeniably Welles's.

Due to the failure of *Kane*, Welles was supervised quite closely on his next film, *The Magnificent Ambersons*. After shooting was completed, Welles went to South America to begin work on a documentary, *It's All True*, designed to help dispel Nazi propaganda in Latin America. He took a rough cut of *Ambersons* with him, hoping to coordinate cutting with editor Robert Wise. However, a sneak preview of Welles's *Ambersons* proved disastrous and the studio cut his 140-minute-plus version to 88 minutes, adding a "happy ending." The film was a critical and commercial failure, and was sometimes placed on a double bill with *The Mexican Spitfire Sees a Ghost*, starring Lupe Velez. As a result, the entire Mercury staff was removed fom the RKO lot.

Welles spent the remainder of his career in Hollywood, for the most part, sparring with various producers or studios over the completed versions of his films and his uncredited direction on films in which he starred. For example, *Journey Into Fear* was begun by Welles but finished by Norman Foster, though Welles claims he made contributions and suggestions throughout. *Jane Eyre*, which made Welles a popular star, was directed by Robert Stevenson, but the gothic overtones, the mise-en-scène, and other stylistic devices, suggest a Wellesian contribution. With *The Stranger*, directed for Sam Spiegel, he adhered closely to the script and a preplanned editing schedule, evidently to prove that he could turn out a Hollywood product on time and on budget. However, Welles refers to *The Stranger* as "the worst of my films," and several Welles scholars agree that it is too conventional and fairly mediocre. Welles directed one of his best films, *The Lady from Shanghai*, for Harry Cohn of Columbia. The film, a loose, confusing, noirish tale of double-crosses and corrupted innocence, starred Welles's wife at the time, Rita Hayworth. Cohn was supposedly already dissatisfied with their marriage, because he felt it would reduce Hayworth's box-office value, but was furious with what Welles did to her image in *Shanghai*. The film, shot mostly on location, was made under stressful circumstances with Welles often re-writing during the shooting. It was edited several times, and finally released two years after its completion, but failed commercially and critically. His final Hollywood project, a version of *Macbeth* for Republic Studios, was also considered a commercial flop.

Disenchanted with Hollywood, Welles left for Europe where he began the practice of acting in other director's films in order to finance his own projects. His portrayal of Harry Lime in Carol Reed's *The Third Man* is considered his finest work from this period, and Welles continued to create villainous antagonists who are often more interesting, complex, or exciting than the protagonsits of the films. In the roles of Col. Haki in *Journey Into Fear*, Will Varner in Martin Ritt's *The Long Hot Summer*, Quinlan in *Touch of Evil* and *Mr. Arkadin*, Welles has created a sinister persona for which he has become as famous as for his direction of *Citizen Kane*. His recent roles are often caricatures of that persona, as in Marlo Thomas's *It Happened One Christmas*, or parodies as in *The Muppet Movie*.

Welles's European ventures include his *Othello*, shot over a period of years between acting assignments, often under chaotic circumstances. The difficulties of the film's production are often described as though they were the madcap adventures of a roguish artist, but in reality it must have been an extreme hardship to assemble and reassemble the cast over the course of the film's shooting. At one point, he "borrowed" equipment under cover of night from the set of Henry King's *The Black Rose* (in which Welles was starring) to quickly shoot a few scenes. Welles later obtained enough financial backing to make *Mr. Arkadin*, a *Kane*-like story of a powerful man who made his fortune as a white slaver, and also *Chimes at Midnight*, a combination of four Shakespeare plays. He returned to America in the late 1950s to direct *Touch of Evil*, starring Charlton Heston. Originally approached only to star in the film, Welles mistakenly thought he was also to direct. Heston intervened and insisted he be allowed to do so. Welles immediately threw out the original script, rewriting it without reading the book upon which the script was based, *Badge of Evil*. Welles's last works include *The Immortal Story*, a one-hour film made for French television, and *F for Fake*, a strange combination of documentary footage shot by another director, some Welles footage from earlier ventures, and Welles's own narration.

Welles's outsider status in connection with the American film industry is an interesting part of cinema history in itself, but his importance as a director is due to the innovations he has introduced through his films and the influence they have had on filmmaking and film theory. Considering the turbulent relationship Welles experienced with Hollywood and the near-chaotic circumstances under which his films were made in Europe, it is surprising there is any thematic and stylistic consistency in his work at all.

The central character in many of his films is often a powerful, egotistical man who lives outside or above the law and society. Kane, Arkadin, and Mr. Clay (*The Immortal Story*) are enabled to do so by their wealth and position; Quinlan (*Touch of Evil*) by his job as a law enforcer, which allows him to commit injustices to suit his own purposes. Even George Minafer (*Ambersons*) becomes an outsider as a modern, industrialized society supercedes his aristocratic, 19th-century way of life. These characters are never innocent, but seem to be haunted by an innocence they have lost. *Kane*'s "Rosebud," the emblem of childhood that he clings to, is the classic example, but this theme can also be found in *Mr. Arkadin* where Arkadin is desperate to keep his daughter from discovering his sordid past. Many parallels between the two films have been drawn including the fact that the title characters are both wealthy and powerful men whose past lives are being investigated by a stranger. Interestingly, just as Kane whispers "rosebud" on his deathbed, Arkadin speaks his daughter's name at the moment of his death. Quinlan, in *Touch of Evil*, is confronted with his memories and his past when he runs into Tanya, now a prostitute in a whorehouse. Though he knew her when he was young, she does not recognize him. The ornaments and mementoes in her room (some of them from Welles's personal collection), seem to jog his memory of a time when he was not a corrupt law official. In *Shanghai*, it is interesting to note that Welles does not portray the egotist, Bannister, but instead the "innocent" Michael O'Hara, who is soiled by his deaings with Bannister's wife. That the corrupt antagonist is doomed is often indicated by a prologue or introductory sequence which foreshadows his destruction—the newsreel sequence in *Kane*; the opening montage of *Ambersons* which condenses 18 years of George Minafer's life into 10 minutes to hint that George will get his "comeuppance" in the end; the opening funeral scene of *Othello*; and the detailing of Mr. Clay's sordid past in *The Immortal Story*. The themes of lost innocence and inescapable fate often shroud Welles's films with a sense of melancholy, which serves to make these characters worthy of sympathy.

Much has been made of Welles's use of deep-focus photography, particularly in *Kane* and *Ambersons*. Though a directorial presence is often suggested in the cinema through the use of editing, with Welles it is through mise-en-scène, particularly in these two films. Many Welles scholars discuss the ambiguous nature of long-shot/deep-focus photography, where the viewer is allowed to sift through the details of a scene and make some of his own choices about what is important to the narrative, plot devlopment, etc. However, Welles's arrangement of actors in specific patterns, his practice of shooting from unusual angles, and use of wide-angle lenses which distort the figures closest to them, are all intended to convey meaning. For example, the exaggerated perspective of the scene where Thatcher gives young Charles Kane a sled makes Thatcher appear to tower over the boy, visually suggesting his unnatural and menacing hold on him (at least from young Kane's point of view).

Welles also employed rather complex sound tracks in *Kane* and *Ambersons*, perhaps a result of his radio experience. The party sequence of *Ambersons*, for example, makes use of overlapping dialogue, as the camera tracks along the ballroom, as though one were passing by, catching bits of conversation.

His visual style becomes less outragous and he is less concerned with effects as his career continues. There seems to be an increasing concentration on the acting, particularly in the Shakespeare films. Welles had a lifelong interest in Shakespeare and his plays, and is well known for his unique handling and interpretations of the material. *Macbeth*, for example, was greatly simplified, with much dialogue omitted and scenes shifted around. A primitive feel is reflected by badly synchronized sound, and much of the impact of the spoken word is lost. *Othello*, shot in Italy and Morocco, makes use of outdoor locations in contrast to the staginess of *Macbeth*. Again, Welles was quite free with interpretation: Iago's motives, for example, are suggested to be the result of sexual impotency. His most successful adaptation of Shakespeare is *Chimes at Midnight*, an interpretation of the Falstaff story with parts taken from *Henry IV*, parts one and two, *Henry V*, *Merry Wives of Windsor*, and *Richard II*. In *Chimes*, Falstaff, as with many of Welles's central characters, is imprisoned by the past. Like George Minafer, he straddles two ages, one medieval and the other modern. Falstaff is destroyed not only by the aging process but also by the problems of being forced into a new world, as are Minafer, and perhaps Kane. Again Welles is quite individualistic in his presentation of the material, making Falstaff a true friend to the king and an innocent, almost childlike, victim of a new order.

In recent years, Welles has become known for his appearances on commercials and talk shows, playing the role of the celebrity to its maximum. It is unfortunate that this latter-day persona often overshadows his contributions to the cinema.

—Susan Doll

WILLIAM WELLMAN; American. Born William Augustus Wellman in Brookline, Massachusetts, 29 February 1896. Attended Newton High School, Newton Highlands, Massachusetts, 1910-14. Married Helene Chadwick, 1918 or 1919 (divorced 1920); 3 other marriages 1920—1933; Dorothy Coonan, 1933; children: Pat, William Jr., Tim, Kitty, Cissy, Michael, and Margaret (Maggie). Career: 1914—becomes professional ice hockey player for minor league team; 1917—during WW I, joins volunteer ambulance corps destined for France; upon arrival, joins French Foreign Legion where he learns to fly planes; when U.S. enters war, becomes member of Lafayette Flying Corps, an arm of the Lafayette Escadrille; 1918-19—breaks into film as an actor through friendship with Douglas Fairbanks, Sr.; 1919—appears in 1st film, *Knickerbocker Buckaroo*; decides he doesn't like acting and seeks to direct; 1920—Fairbanks gets him job as a messenger for Goldwyn Pictures; works his way up to assistant director for Bernie Durning, a director of westerns; directs 1st film *The Twins of Suffering Creek*; 1923—hired by 20th Century Fox as director; 1927—signed by Paramount; *Wings* noted for its use of aerial photography becomes 1st film to win Academy Award. Died 9 December 1975. Recipient: Academy Award, Best Writing (Original Story) for *A Star is Born* (shared with Robert Carson), 1937.

Films (as director): 1920—*The Twins from Suffering Creek*; 1923—*The Man Who Won*; *2nd Hand Love*; *Big Dan*; *Cupid's Fireman*; 1924—*The Vagabond Trail*; *Not a Drum Was Heard*; *The Circus Cowboy*; 1925—*When Husbands Flirt*; 1926—*The Boob*; *The Cat's Pajamas*; *You Never Know Women*; 1927—*Wings*; 1928—*The Legion of the Condemned*; *Ladies of the Mob*; *Beggars of Life*; 1929—*Chinatown Nights*; *The Man I Love*; *Woman Trap*; 1930—*Dangerous Paradise*; *Young Eagles*; *Maybe It's Love*; 1931—*Other Men's Women*; *The Public Enemy*; *Night Nurse*; *Star Witness*; *Safe in Hell*; 1932—*The Hatchet Man*; *So Big*; *Love is a Racket*; *The Purchase Price*; *The Conquerors*; 1933—*Frisco Jenny*; *Central Airport*; *Lilly Turner*; *Midnight Mary*; *Heroes for Sale*; *Wild Boys of the Road*; *College Coach*; 1934—*Looking for Trouble*; *Stingaree*; *The President Vanishes*; 1935—*The Call of the Wild*; 1936—*The Robin Hood of El Dorado* (+co-sc); *Small Town Girl*; 1937—*A Star is Born* (+co-sc); *Nothing Sacred*; 1938—*Men With Wings* (+pr); 1939—*Beau Geste* (+pr); *The Light That Failed* (+pr); 1941—*Reaching for the Sun* (+pr); 1942—*Roxie Hart*; *The Great Man's Lady* (+pr); *Thunder Birds*; 1943—*The Ox-Bow Incident*; *The Lady of Burlesque*; 1944—*Buffalo Bill*; 1945—*This Man's Navy*; *The Story of G.I. Joe*; 1946—*Gallant Journey* (+pr, co-sc); 1947—*Magic Town*; 1948—*The Iron Curtain*; 1949—*Yellow Sky*; *Battleground*; 1950—*The Next Voice You Hear*; 1951—*Across the Wide Missouri*; 1952—*Westward the Women*; *It's a Big Country* (co-d); *My Man and I*; 1953—*Island in the Sky*; 1954—*The High and the Mighty*; *Track of the Cat*; 1955—*Blood Alley*; 1958—*Darby's Rangers*; *Lafayette Escadrille* (+pr +co-sc).

Role: 1919—*Juvenile lead* in *Knickerbocker Buckaroo* (Parker).

Publications:

By WELLMAN:

Book—*A Short Time for Insanity: An Autobiography*, New York 1974; articles—"Director's Notebook—Why Teach Cinema?" in *Cinema Progress* (Los Angeles), June/July 1939; "A Memorable Visit to an Elder Statesman: Interview" in *Cinema* (Beverly Hills), July 1966.

On WELLMAN:

Book—*The Parade's Gone By* by Kevin Brownlow, New York 1968; articles—"Screwball Bill" by H.F. Pringle in *Collier's* (New York), 26 February 1938; "Wyler, Wellman, and Huston" by Richard Griffith in *Films in Review* (New York), February 1950; "War in Hollywood" in *Newsweek* (New York), 16 September 1957; "Yank in the Black Cat Squadron" by E.M. Miller in *Flying*, August 1961; "Fallen Idols" by Andrew Sarris in *Film Culture* (New York), spring 1963; "William Wellman" by Kevin Brownlow in *Film* (London), winter 1965/66; "The Essential Wellman" by J.M. Smith in *Brighton* (London), January 1970; "William Wellman: Director Rebel" by William Wellman, Jr. in *Action* (Los Angeles), March/April 1970; "The Current Cinema" by Penelope Gilliatt in *New Yorker*, 25 September 1971; "On Location with Billy Wellman" by Louise Brooks in *Film Culture* (New York), spring 1972; "Bulletin Board" by Frank Capra in *Action* (Los Angeles), March/April 1973; "A Man's World", in 2 parts, by J. Fox in *Films and Filming* (London), March 1973; "'Wild Bill' William A. Wellman" by S. Eyman and A. Eyles in *Focus on Film* (London), no.29, 1978; "William Wellman 1896-1975" by G. Langlois in *Avant-Scène du cinéma* (Paris), 1 March 1978.

*   *   *

William Wellman's critical reputation is, in many respects still in a state of flux long after reevaluations and recent screenings of his major films should have established some consensus of opinion regarding his place in the pantheon of film directors. While there is some tentative agreement that he is, if nothing else, a competent journeyman director capable of producing entertaining male-dominated action films, other opinions reflect a wide range of artistic evaluations ranging from comparisons to D.W. Griffith to outright condemnations of his films as clumsy and uninspired. His own preferred niche, as is indicated by his flamboyant personality and his predilection for browbeating and intimidating his performers, would probably be in the same general class with highly masculine filmmakers like Howard Hawks, John Ford, and Raoul Walsh. While those three enjoy a distinct auteur status, a similiar designation for Wellman is not so easily arrived at since much of his early work for Warner Bros. in the late 1930s is, at first glance, not easily distinguishable from the rest of the studio's output of sociological problem films and exposés of organized crime. In addition, his later films do not stand comparison, in many scholars' opinions, to treatments of similiar themes (often employing the same actors and locales) by both Ford and Hawks.

It might be argued, however, that Wellman actually developed what has come to be regarded as the Warner Bros. style to a degree greater than that of the studio's other directors. His 1931 *Public Enemy*, for example, stands above most of the other gangster films of the era in its creative blend of highly vivid images and in the subtle manner in which it created a heightened impression of violence and brutality by giving only hints of it on the screen. Exhibiting similar subtlety, Wellman's depiction of a gangster beginning with his childhood, graphically alluded to the sociological roots of organized crime. While many of his more typical treatments of men in adversity, like 1927's Academy Award-winning *Wings*, were somtimes artificial, everything worked in *Public Enemy*.

In his later films like *The Ox-Bow Incident*, *The Story of G.I. Joe*, and *Battleground*, the interactions of men in various groupings are shaped in such a way as to determine the direction and thematic force of each story. In others, like *Track of the Cat*, the emphasis focuses instead on one individual and his battle with forces of nature beyond his control. Yet in all cases, the issue is one of survival, a concept that manifests itself in some manner in all of Wellman's films. It is overt and recognizable in war dramas like *Battleground* or in a disaster film like *The High and the Mighty*, but it is reflected at least as much in the pyychological tensions of *Public Enemy* as it is in the violence. It becomes even more abstract in a complex picture like *Track of the Cat* when the issue concerns the family unit and the insecurity of its internal relationships. In the more heavy-handed propaganda films, *The Iron Curtain* and *Blood Alley*, the theme centers on the threat to democratic forms of government, and finally, in the *Ox-Bow Incident*, the issue is the very fragility of society itself in the hands of a mob.

Wellman's supporters feel that these concerns arise from the latent cynicism of a disappointed romantic but are expressed by an instinctive artist with a keen awareness of the intellectual force of images conveyed with the raw power of many of those in *Public Enemy*. Yet it is the inconsistency of these images and a corresponding lack of inspiration in his work overall that clouds his stature as an auteur of the first rank. While, ultimately, it is true Wellman's films cannot be easily separated from the man behind them, his best works are those that sprang from his emotional and psychological experiences. His lesser ones have been overshadowed by the cult of his personality and are best remembered for the behind-the-scenes fistfights, parties, and wild stunts, all detracting from the production. Perhaps he never got the chance to make the one film that would thematically support all of the seemingly irreconcilable aspects of his personality and allow him to create an indisputable masterpiece to firmly establish him as a director of the first magnitude.

—Stephen L. Hanson

WENDERS, WIM. German. Born Wilhelm Wenders in Düsseldorf, 14 August 1945. Educated in medicine and philosophy; studied at Hochschule für Fernsehen und Film, Munich, 1967-70. Career: late 1960s—film critic in Munich for *Süddeutsche Zeitung* and *Filmkritik*; 1971—commences professional filmmaking.

Films (as director of short films): 1967—*Schauplätze (Locations)*; *Same Player Shoots Again*; 1968—*Silver City*; *Victor I*; 1969—*Alabama—2000 Light Years*; *3 amerikanische LPs (3 American LP's)*; 1970—*Polizeifilm (Police Film)*; (as feature director): 1970—*Summer in the City (Dedicated to the Kinks)* (diploma film); 1971—*Die Angst des Tormanns beim Elfmeter (The Goalie's Anxiety at the Penalty Kick)*; 1972—*Der scharlachrote Buchstabe (The Scarlet Letter)*; 1973—*Alice in den Städten (Alice in the Cities)*; 1974—*Aus der Familie der Panzerechsen* [From the Family of the Crocodilia] (short—for TV); *Die Insel* [The Island] (short—for TV); *Falsche Bewegung (Wrong Movement)*; 1976—*Im Lauf der Zeit (Kings of the Road, In the Course of Time)*; 1977—*Der amerikanische Freund (The American Friend)*; 1981—*Lightning Over Water (Nick's Film)*; 1982—*Hammett*; *Der Stand der Dinge*.

Publications:

By WENDERS:

Book—*The Film by Wim Wenders: KINGS OF THE ROAD (In the Course of Time)*, with Fritz Müller-Scherz, translated by Christopher Doherty, Munich 1976; articles—"Die Angst des Tormanns beim Elfmeter", interview by H.R. Blum in *Filmkritik* (Munich), February 1972; "Alice in den Städten", interview by W.-E. Bühler and P.B. Kleiser in *Filmkritik* (Munich), March 1974; interview by H. Niogret in *Positif* (Paris), November 1976; "A Young German Filmmaker and His Road Movie", interview by B. Thompson in *Thousand Eyes* (New York), November 1976; "Wim Wenders über *Im Lauf der Zeit*", interview by H. Wiedemann and F. Müller-Scherz in *Film und Ton* (Munich), May 1976; "Filming Highsmith", interview by J. Dawson in *Sight and Sound* (London), winter 1977/78; "King of the Road", interview by Carlos Clarens in *Film Comment* (New York), September/October 1977; interview by L. Dahan in *Cinématographe* (Paris), June 1977; interview by A. Masson and H. Niogret in *Positif* (Paris), October 1977; "Wenders on Kings of the Road" in *Monthly Film Bulletin* (London), July 1977; "Das grosse Geld, die Angst und der Traum vom Geschichten erzählen", interview by W. Adler in *Filmkritik* (Munich), December 1978; "'At Home on the Road' Wim Wenders", interview by J.M. Kass in *Movietone News* (Seattle), 22 February 1978; interview by P. Lehman and others in *Wide Angle* (Athens, Ohio), v.2, no.4, 1978; "Cinéma d'Allemagne de l'ouest: Wenders/Lang: sa mort n'est pas un solution" in *Cinéma* (Paris), December 1979; "Big money, la peur et la rêve de racon-

ter des histoires", interview by W. Adler in *Cahiers du cinéma* (Paris), June 1979; "Ecrits" in *Positif* (Paris), April 1979; interview by J.-C. Bonnet and others in *Cinématographe* (Paris), December 1980; "Pour jeter l'ancre", interview by Michel Ciment in *Positif* (Paris), November 1980; "Lightning Over Water", interview by J.-L. Cros and V. Tolédano in *Image et son* (Paris), December 1980; "Wim Wenders en de laatste dagen van Nicholas Ray", with J. Rood and G. Poppelaars, in *Skoop* (Amsterdam), March 1981; interview by J. Vega and M. Vidal Estévez in *Contracampo* (Madrid), April/May 1981; "Cinéma et vidéo dans Nick's Movie", interview by H. Welsh in *Jeune Cinéma* (Paris), April/May 1981.

On WENDERS:

Articles—"German Underground" by A. Thoms in *Afterimage* (Rochester), autumn 1970; "Forms of Address" by Tony Rayns in *Sight and Sound* (London), winter 1974/75; "Die Filmographie—Wim Wenders" by U. Storch in *Information* (Wiesbaden), February 1974; "Dossier-auteur: Wim Wenders" by N. Ghali in *Cinéma* (Paris), December 1976; "Entretien avec Rudiger Vogler" by J. Grant in *Cinéma* (Paris), December 1976; "Bilderarbeit" by M. Schaub in *Cinema* (Zurich), no.3, 1976; "Voyage au pays de Wenders" by G. Dagneau in *Image et son* (Paris), December 1977; "Le Cinémasse de Wim Wenders" by E. Mairesse in *Cahiers du cinéma* (Paris), October 1977; "Wim Wenders: A Worldwide Homesickness" by M. Covino in *Film Quarterly* (Berkeley), winter 1977/78; "Wenders at Warners" by P. Stamelman in *Sight and Sound* (London), autumn 1978; "Wim Wenders Bibliography" by J.M. Welsh in *Wide Angle* (Athens, Ohio), v.2, no.4, 1978; "De emotionele reizen van Wim Wenders" by L.d. Winter in *Skrien* (Amsterdam), April 1978; "Detour par l'Amerique: sur les traces de Wim Wenders" by P. Kral in *Positif* (Paris), April 1979; "Wenders en Californie" by S. Toubiana in *Cahiers du cinéma* (Paris), June 1979; "The Realist Gesture in the Films of Wim Wenders: Hollywood and the New German Cinema" by T.J. Corrigan in *Quarterly Review of Film Studies* (Pleasantville, N.Y.), spring 1980; "Avatares del desplazamiento" by J.M. Company in *Contracampo* (Madrid), April/May 1981; "Todo sobre *Hammett* de Wim Wenders" by G. Hocquenguem in *Casablanca* (Madrid), January 1981; "Alice dans les villes", special issue of *Avant-Scène du cinéma* (Paris), 1 May 1981; special issue of *Caméra/Stylo* (Paris), January 1981.

*   *   *

The first thing that everyone says about him is that he belongs to the "new German cinema"; the second is that he has mastered very well a film language oriented toward the American cinema. The lightning-quick career he's made, the rapidity of his recognition, is due to his ability to couple his films to various highly contemporary trends. He has supplied the audience with what it already knows and likes—American pictures. To young filmgoers he offers pretentious attitudes and restless, empty human figures, full of doubt; to post-industrial society sad and pretty films without social or political significance, a kind of film that reaches the eyes and the heart without disturbing the mind.

The German critic Peter Buchke writes about Wenders's aesthetic, "Wenders had from the beginning a boundless faith in film, more than any other medium or art form. The most transient impressions could be preserved for all time. He has scarcely concerned himself about meaning and purpose; significance would be derived solely from such images."

This characteristic accounts for the essential fascination of these films. The films of Wenders live by static, perfectly composed, arresting, and strong imagery. The story of a film plays no important role for him. On account of this his films have very disparate sources: from his first effort, *The Goalie's Anxiety at the Penalty Kick* from Peter Handke, through *Wrong Movement*, inspired by Goethe's *Wilhelm Meisters Lehrjahre* and again written by Handke, through *The American Friend*, a filming of Patricia Highsmith's thriller *Ripley's Game*, to *Hammett*, a biographical essay on the famous author.

All these works are stamped, through rich, impressive imagery, with the unmistakable Wenders style. Although content is unimportant to him, his more personal films like *Alice in the Cities, Im Lauf der Zeit, Lightning Over Water (Nick's Film)*, or *Der Stand der Dinge*, are better and more fully realized than the rest. The amazement of a girl confronted by the skyscrapers of America (*Alice*), the hopeless journey of two cinema mechanics in a dying region, the border area between the two Germanies, and especially his look at the last days before Nicholas Ray's death (*Nick's Film*), communicate real feeling and the perplexity of the director who in these cases is humanly engaged.

Thus Wim Wenders, both to his advantage and his detriment, belongs to the modern film, to cinema at the end of the seventies. He is the typical representative of filmmakers who find their creative inspiration not in reality, but ultimately in the cinema itself. His world had been the old Hollywood films, where he learned to compose his images: he doesn't shoot everything that comes in front of his camera, but only those snippets of reality that correspond with something in his filmic memory.

After the foundations of his filmmaking were laid, and having received remarkably rapid recognition, Wenders sought to advance his career in the U.S. and was invited by Francis Ford Coppola to make a film at Zoetrope studio. Thus began a painful time for Wenders, a series of disillusioning experiences, which he immediately knew to note down, and later, with his own resources, used to make *Der Stand der Dinge*: a film about the realizations of a filmmaker who is forced to give up his belief in the magic film land of America. The sincerity we feel in the truthful experiences worked out in the film brought Wenders the Golden Lion at Venice in 1982, a confirmation of his European identity as an artist. Hopefully he has finally grasped this.

—Maria Racheva

WERTMÜLLER, LINA. Italian. Born Arcangela Felice Assunta Wertmüller von Elgg Spanol von Braueich in Rome, 14 August 1928. Attended several private Catholic primary schools; Academy of Theatre, Rome, 1947-51, graduated with degree in theater. Married artist Enrico Job, 1968. Career: 1951—produces and directs avant-garde plays; 1951-52—joins Maria Signorelli's puppet troupe; 1952-62—works as actress, stage manager, set designer, publicist and writer in theater and later radio and television; 1962—works as assistant to Fellini on *8 1/2*, but quits to do documentary film about making of *8 1/2*; 1963—directs 1st feature film *I basilischi (The Lizards)*; 1964—returns to theater and television because of lack of funding for her 3rd film; 1968—attains 1st commercial success and critical notice when she sells script for *2 + 2 Are No Longer 4* as theatrical production to Franco Zeffirelli; 1973—directs her 1st film to be released in U.S., *Film d'amore e d'anarchia*; 1977—is hired by Warner Bros. to direct 4 films, but contract is mutually terminated after financial failure of first of those films.

Films (as assistant director): 1963—*Otto e mezzo (8 1/2)* (Fellini); (as director and scriptwriter) 1963—*I basilischi (The Lizards)*; 1965—*Questa volta parliamo di uomini (Now Let's Talk About Men, This Time Let's Talk About Men)*; 1966—*Rita la zanzara (Rita the Mosquito)* (d musical numbers only, +sc); 1967—*Non stuzzicate la zanzara (Don't Tease the Mosquito)*; 1972—*Mimì metallurgio ferito nell'onore (The Seduction of Mimi, Mimi the Metalworker, Wounded in Honour)*; 1973—*Film d'amore e d'anarchia, ovvero stamattina alle 10 in Via dei fiori nella nota casa di toleranza (Love and Anarchy, Film of Love and Anarchy, or This Morning at 10 in the Via dei fiori at the Well-Known House of Tolerance)*; 1974—*Tutto a posto e niente in ordine (Everything's in Order but Nothing Works, All Screwed Up)*; *Travolti da un insolito destino nell'azzurro mare d'agosto (Swept Away by a Strange Destiny on an Azure August Sea, Swept Away)*; 1976—*Pasqualino settebellezze (Pasqualino Seven Beauties, Seven Beauties)*; 1978—*The End of the World in Our Usual Bed in a Night Full of Rain*; *Shimmy lagano tarantelle e vino*; 1979—*Revenge.*

Publications:

By WERTMÜLLER:

Book—*The Screenplays of Lina Wertmüller* with introduction by John Simon, translated by Steven Wagner, New York 1977; articles—interview in *Woman and Film* (Santa Monica), no.5-6, 1974; interview in *Interview* (New York), March 1975; interview in *The New York Times*, 5 March 1976; "Look, Gideon—Gideon Bachmann Talks with Lina Wertmüller" in *Film Quarterly* (Berkeley), spring 1977; "Lina Sweeps in", interview by G. Ott in *Cinema Canada* (Montreal), March 1978.

On WERTMÜLLER:

Articles—on 1st film by Raymond Durgnat in *Films and Filming* (London), October 1964; article on 1st film by Elizabeth Sussex in *Sight and Sound* (London), spring 1964; "Lina Wertmüller: The Politics of Private Life" by Peter Biskind in *Film Quarterly* (Berkeley), winter 1974/75; article in *New York*, 2 February 1976; article in *Time* (New York), 16 February 1976; "Lina Wertmüller" in *Current Biography Yearbook*, New York 1976; "How Left is Lina?" by L. Quacinella in *Cineaste* (New York), fall 1976; "Is Lina Wertmuller Just One of the Boys?" by Ellen Willis in *Rolling Stone* (New York), 25 March 1976.

*   *   *

Pitifully few women have throughout cinema history been allowed to make movies, let alone make great movies. One, Lina Wertmüller, had by the mid-1970s directed a series of features which brought her fame in America. In recent years, though, her critical reputation has been tarnished: her detractors have dubbed her a reactionary, labelling her films as grotesque and self-absorbed, with little love for people; meanwhile, her champions call her a feminist and socialist, a defender of the downtrodden, an idealistic anarchist who realizes anarchy is impractical but still cherishes the notion of total individual freedom. Actually, upon examining her films, one realizes that most of her characters are indeed caricatures, but at the same time also sympathetic human beings. It all depends upon the interpretation.

Wertmüller's films most characteristically focus on the eternal battle of the sexes, fought in the setting of a class war via noisy screaming matches and comical seductions. Her most typical features may be found in the midsection of her filmography, from *The Seduction of Mimi* through *Swept Away*.... These are all uneven: for every inspired sequence—most notably, in *The Seduction of Mimi*, Giancarlo Giannini's antics between the sheets with a ridiculously obese woman—there are long stretches of repetitious ax-grinding on sex, love, anarchy, fascism, and the class struggle. All but *All Screwed Up* star Giannini, Wertmüller's favorite actor. His characters think they are suave, lusty studs, but are really just stubborn and stupid, in constant trouble both politically and sexually. An example: in *Love and Anarchy*, set in 1932, he plays an anarchist, riding in a brothel, who falls for a prostitute while planning to assassinate Mussolini. Wertmüller's women on the other hand, are not politically aware and are uninterested in struggling for self-sufficiency.

Seven Beauties, crammed with stunning images, is a searing drama about survival in a surreal, insane world. Its reputation has suffered primarily because Wertmüller's most recent features have been misfires: *The End of the World in Our Usual Bed in a Night Full of Rain*, her first English language effort, an overly verbose marital boxing match pitting journalist/communist Giannini and photographer/feminist Candice Bergen; and *Revenge*, also known as *Blood Fued*, the overdone tale of a radical lawyer (Marcello Mastroianni) and a gangster (Giannini) who both love widow Sophia Loren during the early years of fascist rule in Italy.

—Rob Edelman

WHALE, JAMES. English. Born in Dudley, England, 22 July 1889 (some sources state 1896). Career: 1910—begins job as cartoonist for *The Bystander* (England); 1914-17—begins acting in the army during WW I while in a prisoner-of-war camp; 1917-25—after the war, joins the Birmingham Repertory Theatre, as an actor; also designs sets; 1925—acts on London stage for 1st time in *A Comedy of Good and Evil* at the Ambassador Theatre; 1928—directs 1st play *Journey's End* on London stage; 1930—moves to Hollywood to direct film version of his stage success *Journey's End*; 1931—directs his 1st American horror film *Frankenstein* for Universal; 1931-41—continues to direct mostly horror films for Universal; 1941—retires from films to pursue painting; 1949—attempts comeback with *Hello Out There* but the project is abandoned before completion; 1949-57—directs a few plays; 1957—begins to design sets for a science-fiction operetta based on the works of Ray Bradbury and Max Beerbohm, but dies before completion. Died 30 May 1957.

Films (as director): 1930—*Journey's End*; 1931—*Waterloo Bridge*; *Frankenstein*; 1932—*The Impatient Maiden*; *The Old Dark House*; 1933—*The Kiss Before the Mirror*; *The Invisible Man*; 1934—*By Candlelight*; *One More River*; 1935—*The Bride of Frankenstein*; *Remember Last Night*; 1936—*Showboat*; 1937—*The Road Back*; *The Great Garrick*; 1938—*The Port of 7 Seas*; *Sinners in Paradise*; *Wives Under Suspicion*; 1939—*The Man in the Iron Mask*; 1940—*Green Hell*; 1941—*They Dare Not Love*.

Publications:

On WHALE:

Books—*Le Fantastique au Cinéma* by Michel Laclos, Paris 1958; *Horror* by Drake Douglas, New York 1966; *An Illustrated History of the Horror Film* by Carlos Clarens, New York 1968; *Hollywood in the 30's* by John Baxter, New York 1970; *Science Fiction in the 30's* by John Baxter, New York 1970; *Horror in the Cinema* by Ivan Butler, 2nd revised ed., New York 1970; *Cinema of the Fantastic* by Burt Goldblatt and Chris Steinbrunner, New York 1972; *James Whale's 'Frankenstein'* by Richard Anobile, New York 1974; *The Films of Boris Karloff* by Richard Bojarski and Kenneth Beale, Secaucus, New Jersey 1974; *Classics of the Horror Film* by William Everson, Secaucus, New Jersey 1974; *Horror Movies* by Alan Frank, London 1974; *Horror and Fantasy in the Movies* by Tom Hutchinson, New York 1974; *The Horror People* by John Brosnan, New York 1976; *Horror Films* by R.H.W. Dillard, New York 1976; *Mary Shelley's Monster: The Story of Frankenstein* by Martin Tropp, Boston 1976; *Dark Dreams: A Psychological History of the Modern Horror Film* by Charles Derry, New York 1977; *Journey into Darkness: The Art of James Whale's Horror Films* by Reed Ellis, New York 1980; articles—"James Whale and Frankenstein" in *The New York Times*, 20 December 1931; "*The Bride of Frankenstein*" in *Time* (New York), 29 April 1935; "Movie Gothick: A Tribute to James Whale" by Roy Edwards in *Sight and Sound* (London), autumn 1957; obituary in *The New York Times*, 30 May 1957; "James Whale" by Robert Fink and William Thomaier in *Films in Review* (New York), May 1962; "The Subconscious: From Pleasure Castle to Libido Motel" by Raymond Durgnat in *Films and Filming* (London), January 1962; "Memories of a Monster" by Boris Karloff in *Saturday Evening Post* (Philadelphia), 3 November 1962; "Frankenstein, Or the Modern Prometheus: A Review" by Harold Bloom in *Partisan Review* (New Brunswick, New Jersey), fall 1965; "Film Clips" by Arkadin in *Sight and Sound* (London), winter 1967/68; "James Whale" by Paul Jensen in *Film Comment* (New York), spring 1971; "Monster Movies: A Sexual Theory" by Walter Evans in *Journal of Popular Film* (Bowling Green, Ohio), fall 1973; "One Man Crazy: James Whale" by Tom Milne in *Sight and Sound* (London), summer 1973; "Monster Movies and Rites of Initiation" by Walter Evans in *Journal of Popular Film* (Bowling Green, Ohio), spring 1975; "Rediscovery" by William K. Everson in *Films in Review* (New York), December 1977; "The Poetics of Horror: More than Meets the Eye" by D.L. White in *Film Genre: Theory and Criticism* edited by Barry Grant, Metuchen, New Jersey 1977; "Designed for Film: The Hollywood Art Director" by Carlos Clarens and Mary Corliss in *Film Comment* (New York), May/June 1978.

*   *   *

Although he is primarily remembered as the director of the cult horror films *Frankenstein*, *The Old Dark House*, *The Invisible Man*, and *The Bride of Frankenstein*, James Whale contributed much more to the cinema with his handling of such stylish and elegant productions as *Waterloo Bridge* and *One More River*, which had little critical impact when they were first released and are, unfortunately, largely unknown today.

A quiet, introspective man, James Whale's background was the stage, notably the original London and New York productions of R.C. Sheriff's pacifist play *Journey's End*. Aside from some work assisting Howard Hughes with the direction of *Hell's Angels* (work which is both negligible and best forgotten), James Whale made his directorial debut with *Journey's End*, a film which illustrates many of the qualities which were to mark Whale's later work: close attention to acting and dialogue, a striving for authenticity in settings and a thoughtful use of camera (here somewhat hampered by the limits imposed on early talkies).

From 1930 through 1937, while Whale was under contract to Universal and under the patronage of studio production head Carl Laemmle, Jr., the director was able to turn out a group of literate and accomplished features. Among his varied productions was the First World War melodrama *Waterloo Bridge*, later remade in a gaudy Hollywood fashion by Mervyn LeRoy, but in this version noteworthy for its honest approach to its leading character's prostitution and a stunning performance by Mae Clarke (a favorite Whale actress). Both *The Invisible Man* and *The Bride of Frankenstein* are influenced by the director's earlier *Frankenstein*, but both contain an element of black humor which lifts them above the common horror film genre . *The Kiss Before the Mirror* and *By Candlelight* possess an intangible charm, while *One More River* is simply one of Hollywood's best depictions of upper class British life, memorable for the ensemble playing of its cast, headed by Diana Wynyard, and the one-liners from Mrs. Patrick Campbell. *Show Boat* demonstrates that Whale could handle a musical as easily as a romantic drama and is, without question, the finest screen version of the Jerome Kern-Oscar Hammerstein hit. All of Whale's Universal features were well received, with the exception of his last, *The Road Back*, based on an Erich Maria Remarque novel, intended as a sequel to *All Quiet on the Western Front*. *The Road Back* today appears badly constructed, a problem created in part by the studio's interference with the production out of concern that the German government might find the film unacceptable.

Whale's final films after leaving Universal are uniformly without interest, and contemporary response to them was lukewarm at best. The director simply grew tired of the hassels of filmmaking and retired. It has been suggested that Whale's homosexuality may have been unacceptable in Hollywood and helped to end his career, but he was a very private man who kept his personal life to himself, and it seems unlikely that his sexual preference created any problem for him or his employees; certainly Whale's homosexuality is not evident from his films, unless it be in the casting of the delightfully "camp" Ernest Thesiger in *The Old Dark House* and *The Bride of Frankenstein*.

—Anthony Slide

WICKI, BERNHARD. Austrian. Born in St. Pölten, 28 October 1919. Studied acting with Gustaf Gründgens, Staatliche Schauspielhaus, Berlin, and at Max-Reinhardt-Seminar, State Academy, Vienna. Married actress Agnes Fink. Career: debuts as Faust, Schönbrunner-Schlosstheater, Vienna; acts in Zurich, Basel, Vienna, and Munich; also stage director in Vienna, Bremen, and elsewhere; 1945-50—with Stadttheater, Basel; 1950s—active as still photographer; 1958—makes documentary *Warum sind sie gegen uns?*; 1959—feature directing debut. Recipient: Best Direction, Berlin Festival, for *The Wonder of Father Malachias*, 1961.

Films (as director): 1958—*Warum sind sie gegen uns?* (+co-sc—documentary); 1959—*Die Brücke (The Bridge)* (+co-sc); 1961—*Das Wunder des Malachias (The Miracle of Father Malachias)* (+co-sc); 1962—*The Longest Day* (co-d); 1964—*Der Besuch (The Visit, La rancune, La vendetta della signora)*; 1965—

Morituri (The Saboteur—Code Name Morituri); 1966—*Transit*; 1967—"Militarischer Spuk" episode of *Quadriga* (+sc); 1971—*Das falsche Gewicht* (+co-sc); 1977—*Die Eroberung der Zitadelle* (+co-sc).

Roles: 1950—*Der fallende Stern* (Braun); 1953—*Junges Herz voll Liebe* (May); 1954—*Rummelplatz der Liebe (Circus of Love)* (Neumann); *Die letzte Brücke (The Last Bridge)* (Käutner); *Gefangene der Liebe* (Jugert); *Die Mücke* (Reisch); *Das zweite Leben (Double destin)* (Vicas); *Johann Strauss* in *Ewiger Walzer (The Eternal Waltz)* (Verhoeven); 1955—*Es geschah am 20 Juli* (Pabst); *Kinder, Mutter und ein General* (Benedek); *Du mein stilles Tal* (Steckel); *Rosen im Herbst (Effi Briest)* (Jugert); 1956—*Frucht ohne Liebe* (Erfurth); *Weil du arm bist, musst du früher sterben* (May); *Skandal un Dr. Vlimmen* (Rabenalt); 1957—*Königin Luise* (Liebeneiner); *Flucht in die Tropennacht* (May); *Die Zürcher Verlobung (The Affairs of Julie)* (Käutner); *Es wird alles wieder gut* (von Bolvary); 1958—*Madeleine und der Legionär* (Staudte); *La Chatte (The Cat)* (Decoin); *Unruhige Nacht (Restless Night)* (Harnack); 1959—*Eine Frau im besten Mannesalter* (von Ambesser); 1960—*Lampenfieber* (Hoffmann); 1961—*La notte* (Antonioni); 1962—"Il serpente" episode of *L'Amore difficile (Erotica)* (Bonucci); 1963—*Les Vacances portugaises (Les Sourires de la destinée)* (Kast); *Elf Jahre und ein Tag* (Reinhardt); 1966—*Crime and Passion*; 1967—*Die linkshändige Frau (The Left-Handed Woman)*; 1969—*Deine Zärtlichkeiten* (Schamoni).

Publications:

By WICKI:

Book—*Zwei Gramm Licht*, preface by Friedrich Dürrenmatt, 1960 (photographs); article—"Lesson of the Hate Makers" in *Films and Filming* (London), April 1962.

On WICKI:

Article—"Personalien—Oktober 1974" in *Information* (Wiesbaden), September 1974.

*   *   *

Bernhard Wicki's best film is his first, *The Bridge* a savage, clear-headed account of seven German teen-agers drafted into service in, literally, the last seconds of World War II. They are trained for a day, and their schoolmaster pleads that they be given nonhazardous assignments. The boys are ordered to guard an old stone bridge: finally, they are routed in a grim, bloody, sobering sequence—quite graphically gory for 1959. Wicki does not gently kill off his child-soldiers; their deaths are not meant to titillate (as in so many gratuitously violent melodramas and horror films of the past decade) but to confront the viewer with the reality of war. *The Bridge* is not really about Germans or Americans or a specific time in history, but is universal in its anti-war sentiment. The film is in no way nationalistic: the older German soldiers are cynical about their leadership; an American GI dies while shouting that he does not want to fight with children.

Beyond *The Bridge*, Wicki's career is undistinguished. He competently handled the German sequences in Darryl F. Zanuck's *The Longest Day*. *The Visit*, from Friedrich Dürrenmatt's play is an uneven melodrama of vengeance and evil. *The Saboteur, Code Name Morituri* is a ridiculous tale of a German who aids the British during World War II. These last films feature top stars—Ingrid Bergman, Anthony Quinn, Marlon Brando, Yul Brynner, Trevor Howard—to no great advantage. After *Morituri*, Wicki did not direct for another six years.

Wicki's roots are in the theater. He started out as an actor on the German, Austrian and Swiss stage. Later, he played a partisan leader in Helmut Kautner's *The Last Bridge*, a suitor in Kautner's *The Affairs of Julie*, and a dying man in Antonioni's *The Night*. With the exception of *The Bridge*, his acting is more exceptional than his directing.

In 1962, Wicki was quoted in *The New York Times*, "We need more 'small' pictures—small in budget and narrow in scope. People are looking for answers. Perhaps we can't give them. But, at least, we can present the questions. We can stimulate thought and generate emotions. It is a function that is not at all at odds with a film's designed function to entertain as well."

Very well put. But, unfortunately, Wicki's films barely reflect this sentiment.

—Rob Edelman

WIDERBERG, BO. Swedish. Born in Malmö, 8 June 1930. Career: briefly works in mental hospital, then as night editor for small-town newspaper; 1950—begins writing short stories, publishes in 1951 collection of stories and novel; 1960—becomes film critic for newspaper; in 1962 *The Vision of Swedish Cinema* published, severely criticizing Swedish film industry and its domination by Ingmar Bergman; 1962—feature directing debut; 1970—directs *Joe Hill* in U.S. Recipient: Special Jury Prize, Cannes Festival, for *Ådalen 31*; Special Jury Prize, Cannes Festival, for *Joe Hill*, 1971.

Films (as director and scriptwriter): 1962—*Pojken och draken* (for TV); 1963—*Barnvagnen (The Baby Carriage, The Pram)*; *Kvarteret Korpen (Raven's End)*; 1965—*Karlek 65 (Love 65)*; 1966—*Heja Roland (30 Times Your Money)*; 1967—*Elvira Madigan*; 1968—*Ådalen 31 (The Adalen Riots)* (+ed); 1969—*Den vita sporten (The White Game)* (documentary made as member of collective "Group 13"); 1971—*Joe Hill* (+co-pr); 1974—*Fimpen (Stubby)*; 1977—*Man on the Roof* (+sc, co-ed); 1979—*Victoria*.

Publications:

By WIDERBERG:

Articles—interview by Gérard Langlois in *Les Lettres françaises* (Paris), 9 July 1969; interview by G.M. Loney in *Interview* (New York), vol.1, no.7, n.d.; interview by B. Cohn in *Positif* (Paris), January 1972; "Ni naetter for otte sekunder-Widerberg om *Manden på taget*", interview by C. Hesselberg in *Kosmorama* (Copenhagen), spring 1977.

On WIDERBERG:

Articles—"Director of the Year" in *International Film Guide 1968*, London 1967; "Counting the Gains" in *Films Illustrated* (London), October 1971; "Filmmaking in Sweden" in *Interview*

(New York), vol.1, no.7, n.d.; "Bio-filmographie de Bo Widerberg" by J. Béranger in *Positif* (Paris), January 1972; "Bo Widerberg: Filmographie" in *Avant-Scène du cinéma* (Paris), April 1972; "Red Membranes, Red Banners" by J.P. Gay in *Sight and Sound* (London), spring 1972; "Lettre ouverte à Bo Widerberg à propos de Joe Hill" by G. Haustrate in *Cinéma* (Paris), January 1972; "Lyriken Widerberg? Nej, hverdagsrealisten Widerberg" by S. Kjørup in *Kosmorama* (Copenhagen), spring 1977.

WIELAND, JOYCE. Canadian. Born in Toronto, 1931. Educated at Central Technical Vocational High School, Toronto. Married Michael Snow, 1957. Career: 1950s—pursues careers as independent artist and commercial artist working for Toronto firms; 1955-56—works as animator for Jim McKay and George Dunning's Graphic Films; meets artist Michael Snow; 1963—with Snow moves to New York City; about 1964—forms company Corrective Film; 1967—camerawoman on Shirley Clarke's *Vosnesensky*; begins making films that lead to association with Structural Cinema movement; 1971—moves back to Toronto; 1976—following release of *The Far Shore* ceases active filmmaking. Agent: Isaacs Gallery, Toronto, Ontario. Film Distributor (U.S.): Film-Makers Cooperative, 175 Lexington Avenue, New York, NY 10016.

Films (as director): 1958—*Tea in the Garden* (co-d); 1959—*Assault in the Park* (co-d); 1963—*Larry's Recent Behaviour*; 1964—*Peggy's Blue Skylight*; *Patriotism* (Parts 1 and 2); 1964-65—*Watersark*; 1965—*Barbara's Blindness* (co-d); 1967-68—*Sailboat*; *1933*; *Hand-tinting*; 1968—*Catfood*; *Rat Life and Diet in North America*; 1968-69—*La Raison avant la passion (Reason over Passion)*; 1969—*Dripping Water* (co-d with Michael Snow); 1972—*Pierre Vallières*; *Birds at Sunrise*; 1973—*Solidarity*; 1976—*The Far Shore*.

Roles: 1967—*Sky Socialist* (Jacobs); *Wavelength* (Snow); *Standard Time* (Snow); 1972—*Knocturne* (George and Mike Kuchar); *"Rameau's Nephew" by Diderot (Thanx to Dennis Young) by Wilma Schoen* (Snow).

Publications:

By WIELAND:

Book—*True Patriot Love/Veritable Amour patriotique*, with interview by Pierre Théberge, Ottawa 1971; articles—"North America's Second All-Woman Film Crew" in *Take One* (Montreal), December 1967; film outline of *True Patriot Love* in *Film Culture* (New York), spring 1971; "Kay Armatage Interviews Joyce Wieland" in *Take One* (Montreal), February 1972; "Jigs and Reels" in *Form and Structure in Recent Film*, edited by Dennis Wheeler, Vancouver Art Gallery 1972; interview by Anne Wordsworth in *Descant*, spring/summer 1974; interview by Lauren Rabinovitz in *Afterimage* (Rochester, N.Y.), May 1981.

On WIELAND:

Articles—"Joyce Wieland" by Manny Farber in *Artforum* (New York), February 1970; "There Is Only One Joyce" by P. Adams

Sitney in *Artscanada* (Toronto), April 1970; "Canadian Women Directors" by Alison Reid in *Take One* (Montreal), November/-December 1970; *"True Patriot Love:* The Films of Joyce Wieland" by Regina Cornwell in *Artforum* (New York), September 1971; "Wieland: An Epiphany of North" by Hugo McPherson in *ArtsCanada* (Toronto), August/September 1971; "La Raison avant la passion" by George Lellis in *Form and Structure in Recent Film*, edited by Dennis Wheeler, Vancouver Art Gallery, 1972; "The Far Shore: A Film About Violence, A Peaceful Film About Violence" by B.H. Martineau in *Cinema Canada* (Montreal), April 1976; "An Essay on Canadian (Film)" by D. Ord in *Cinema Canada* (Montreal), June/July 1977; "Wielandism: A Personal Style in Full Bloom" by Marshall Delaney in *Canadian Film Reader*, edited by Feldman and Nelson, Ontario 1977; "Ragged History and Contemporary Scatterings" by B.H. Martineau in *Cinema Canada* (Montreal), January/February 1981; "The Development of Feminist Strategies in the Experimental Films of Joyce Wieland" by Lauren Rabinovitz in *Film Reader* (Evanston), no.5, 1982; film—*A Film About Joyce Wieland* directed by Judy Steed, Canada 1972.

*   *   *

Joyce Wieland achieved her reputation as one of a group experimental filmmakers who contributed to the creation of an avant-garde film style in the middle and late 1960s. Wieland's films formally investigate the limitations and shared properties of several media while they develop increasingly pointed themes regarding Canadian nationalism and feminism.

When Toronto developed into a leading Canadian art center in the late 1950s and 1960s, Wieland became the only woman who achieved artistic prominence among the new group of Canadian painters influenced by Abstract Expressionism and Pop Art. Concerned about being even closer to the most recent developments among vanguard artists, Wieland and Snow moved to New York City in 1963. Although they remained expatriates until 1971, Wieland continued to exhibit her work throughout Canada and established a reputation during the next decade as the country's leading woman artist.

In New York City, Wieland became friendly with many members of the "underground" film community, a group whose bohemian behavior and outrageously styled home movies were gaining increased notoriety. Influenced by underground filmmakers Harry Smith, Ken Jacobs, and George Kuchar, Wieland began making short, personal films, and her movies were soon included in the group's regular Greenwich Village screenings.

The cinematic style that evolved out of several underground filmmakers' works became known by the late 1960s as "structural film." These films addressed the nature of the film viewing experience itself and created self-reflexive statements about such basic materials of filmmaking as projected light, celluloid, and the camera apparatus. Structural filmmaking paralleled painterly developments in minimal art and received internationl recognition as the new radical forefront of avant-garde film. Wieland's films, often grouped and discussed with those by such other structural filmmakers as Snow, Jacobs, Hollis Frampton, and Ernie Gehr, played at museums, film festivals, and colleges in Europe and North America.

In 1969, Wieland directed a feature-length movie that wedded the highly conceptual and experimental concerns of structural film with her own political feelings regarding Canada. The result, *Reason Over Passion* is an experimental documentary film about the country of Canada, Canadian culture and identity. Following the film's release, Wieland expressed and developed the same themes in an art show entitled "True Patriot Love" at the National Gallery of Canada in 1971. The show's Pop Art styled quilts, embroideries, and knittings served as patriotic banners for nationalism and feminism.

Because of the direction her work was taking, and because of her increased involvement in Canadian artists' political groups and causes, Wieland returned in 1971 to Toronto. There she completed two additional short structural documentaries. *Pierre Vallières* is about a French-Canadian revolutionary and the problems between French and English Canada. *Solidarity* is about a labor stike at an Ontario factory whose workers were mostly women. At the same time, Wieland co-wrote, co-produced, and directed a theatrical feature-length film. *The Far Shore* is a romantic melodrama that tells the story of a French Canadian women whose failing marriage to a stuffy Toronto bourgeois results in her liberating affair with a Canadian painter. The film was not commercially successful but has subsequently been featured at film festivals, colleges, and museums in North America and Europe. After the completion of *The Far Shore*, Wieland returned to drawing, painting, and printmaking and has since produced several series of new works.

—Lauren Rabinovitz

WIENE, ROBERT. German. Born in Dresden, 1881. Career: before 1913—active as actor, writer, and director, Lessing-Theater, Berlin; 1913—discovered by producer Kolowrat, makes film directing debut; 1915—collaborates with Walter Turszinsky on several comic films; 1916—directs a number of Henny Porten films; 1924-26—works in Austria; 1934—leaves Nazi Germany. Died in Paris, 17 July 1938.

Films (as director): 1912—*Die Waffen der Jugend* (d: Wiene or Friedrich Müller, +sc); 1915—*Frau Eva (Arme Eva)* (+co-sc); *Die Konservanbraut*; *Der springende Hirsch (Die Diebe von Günsterburg)* (co-d?); (as scenarist): *Fräulein Barbier* (Albes) (co-sc); *Arme Marie* (Zeyn and Mack); *Flucht der Schönheit (Seine schöne Mama)* (Rector, i.e. Zeiske) (co-sc); *Die büssende Magdalena* (Albes) (co-sc); *Lottekens Feldzug* (Ziener) (co-sc); *Der Schirm mit dem Schwan* (Froelich); (as director): 1916—*Der Sekretär der Königin* (+sc); *Der Liebesbrief der Königin* (+sc); *Das wandernde Licht*; *Die Räuberbraut*; *Der Mann Spiegel* (+sc); *Gelöste Ketten* (Biebrach) (sc only); 1917—*Der standhafte Benjamin* (+sc); *Das Leben—ein Traum* (+co-sc); *Frank Hansens Glück* (Larsen) (sc only); *Die Prinzessin von Neutralien* (Biebrach) (sc only); 1918—*Der Umweg zur Ehe* (d: Wiene or Fritz Freisler, +co-sc); *Die Millionärin* (alternate title of preceding?); (as scenarist): *Die Heimkehr des Odysseus* (Biebrach); *Das Geschlecht derer von Rinwall* (Biebrach); *Opfer der Gesellschaft* (Grunwald); *Die Dame, der Teufel und die Probiermamsell* (Biebrach); *Am Tor des Lebens (Am Tor des Todes)* (Conrad Wiene); (as director): 1919—*Die verführte Heilige* (+sc); *Ein gefährliche Spiel* (+sc); *Um das Lächeln einer Frau* (alternate title for preceding?); *Satanas* (Murnau) (artistic supervision only); *Ihr Sport* (Biebrach) (sc only); *Die lebende Tote* (Biebrach) (sc only); 1920—*Die drie Tänze der Mary Wilford* (+co-sc); *Das Kabinett des Dr. Caligari (Das Cabinet des Dr. Caligari, The Cabinet of Dr. Caligari)*; *Genuine*; *Die Nacht der Königin Isabeau* (+sc); (as scenarist): *Das Blut der Ahnen* (Gerhardt) (co-sc); *Die Jagd nach dem Tode* and *Die verbotene Stadt* (Gerhardt—in 2 parts) (co-sc); *Die Abenteuer des Dr. Kircheisen* (Biebrach); (as director): 1921—*Die Rache einer Frau*; *Das Spiel mit dem Feuer* (+co-sc); 1922—*Die höllische Macht*;

1923—*Raskolnikow (Schuld und Sühne)* (+sc); *Der Puppenmacher von Kiang-Ning*; *I.N.R.I. (Ein Film der Menschlichkeit)* (+sc); *Die Macht der Finsternis* (Conrad Wiene) (sc only); 1924—*Orlacs Hände*; *Pension Groonen*; *Das Wachsfigurenkabinett (Waxworks)* (Leni) (artistic supervision only); 1925—*Der Leibgardist (Der Gardeoffizier)*; *Der Rosenkavalier* (+cosc); *Die Königin vom Moulin-Rouge*; 1927—*Die Geliebte*; *Die berühmte Frau*; *Le Tombeau sous l'Arc de Triomphe*; 1928—*Die Frau auf der Folter*; *Die grosse Abenteuerin*; *Leontines Ehemänner*; *Unfug der Liebe*; *Heut Spielt der Strauss (Der Walzerkönig)* (Conrad Wiene) (sc only); (sound films): 1930—*Der Andere* (French version: *Le Procureur Hallers*); 1931—*Der Liebesexpress (Acht Tage Glück)* (French version: *Huit Jours de bonheur*); *Panik in Chicago*; 1933—*Polizeiakte 909 (Der Fall Tokeramo)* (+sc); 1934—*Eine Nacht in Venedig* (+sc); 1936—*The Robber Symphony* (Feher) (artistic supervision only); 1938—*Ultimatum* (completed by Robert Siodmak).

Publications:

By WIENE:

Book—*The Cabinet of Dr. Caligari* translated and description of action by R.V. Adkinson, New York 1972.

On WIENE:

Books—*From Caligari to Hitler: A Psychological History of the German Film* by Siegfried Kracauer, Princeton, New Jersey 1947; *50 Years of German Cinema* by Hans H. Wollenberg, London 1948; *The Haunted Screen* by Lotte Eisner, Berkeley 1969; *The German Cinema* by Roger Manvell and Heinrich Fraenkel, New York 1971; *Weimar: A Cultural History 1918-1933* by Walter Laqueur, New York 1974; article—"*Le Cabinet du Docteur Caligari*" (plus photos) by Carl Mayer in *L'Avant-Scène du cinéma* (Paris), July/September 1975.

*   *   *

Robert Wiene's name will ever be associated with his most famous film although there are critics who would minimize his responsibilty for this masterpiece of the cinema. His work is uneven and often blatantly commercial but in spite of this many of his film show some originality of theme and distinguished performances by actors who worked under him.

Das Cabinet des Dr. Caligari, originally intended for Fritz Lang, put Wiene's name on the map. It is the most important of the expressionist films and today its power seems undiminished and its daring timeless. It ran continuously in Paris for seven years, thereby creating a record, and at the Brussels Worlds Fair of 1958 it was chosen by 117 film historians from 26 countries as one of the top twelve most important films of all time.

In *Genuine* Wiene failed to repeat his success in the same genre although the film was also scripted by the talented Carl Mayer. In 1923 three films show an interesting range of subject matter. *I.N.R.I.* dealt with the death of Christ and was mounted on a grand scale, with the cream of German acting in the leading roles, and with settings by the promising young Hungarian designer,

Ernö Metzner. *Der Puppenmacher von Kiang-Ning*, a tragicomedy with a script by Carl Mayer, and *Raskolnikow* with fantastic sets by the Russian designer Andreiev completed an interesting trilogy. The latter used emigreé actors in an adaptation of Dostoievsky's *Crime and Punishment*.

From 1924 to 1926 Wiene worked in Austria where he made other distinguished films—*Orlacs Hände*, a horror film with Conrad Veidt as a sensitive musician who has the hands of a murderer grafted on to him, and *Der Rosenkavalier* a film adaptation of the Strauss opera, co-scripted by Hugo von Hoffmanstahl and with a special score arranged by the composer, who personally conducted the orchestra when it had its premiere at the Dresden State Opera House and at the Tivoli Cinema in London. The leading roles were taken by the French stars Huguette Duflos and Jaque Catelain.

Wiene returned to Germany but his later work showed no special qualities and consisted of lightweight comedies with artists like Lily Damita, Dina Gralla, and Maria Jacobini. He directed Mady Christians and Andre Roanne in a French production *La Duchesee de Les Folies*. Of his sound films the Johann Strauss operetta *Eine Nacht in Venedig* merits attention. He died in Paris in 1938 while directing Erich von Stroheim and Dita Parlo in *Ultimatum* which was completed by Robert Siodmak. In 1935 he had supervised in England *The Robber Symphony* directed by his former actor from *Caligari*, Friedrich Feher.

While he covered a wide range of material in his films he never developed a personal style. His merit lay in encouraging many diverse talents and often securing outstanding contributions from them. He controlled his productions, in most cases writing the scripts himself. He lived in a great period of cinema which he served in his fashion.

—Liam O'Leary

———————

WILCOX, HERBERT. British. Born in Cork, 19 April 1891. Educated in Brighton, England, schools. Married actress Anna Neagle, 1943. Career: before 1914—works on newspaper; serves as pilot in RAF during World War I; 1919—begins selling stories to film companies; becomes secretary and director of Astra Films; 1920—with Graham Cutts forms Graham Wilcox Productions; 1922—begins producing with *The Wonderful Story*; about 1929—organizes British and Dominion Productions; 1932—begins making films with Anna Neagle; 1937—organization of Imperator Film Productions, Ltd., becomes chairman and managing director; 1938—signs agreement with RKO-Radio for distribution of his films; 1940—begins directing in Hollywood for RKO; 1942—returns to England; 1945—signs contract with 20th Century-Fox for series of pictures; 1964—forced into bankruptcy. Died in London, 15 May 1977.

Films (as producer): 1922—*The Wonderful Story* (Cutts); *Flames of Passion* (Cutts); (as director): *Whispering*; 1923—*Chu-Chin-Chow*; *Paddy-the-Next-Best-Thing* (Cutts) (pr only); 1924—*Southern Love*; *Decameron Nights*; 1926—*The Only Way*; 1927—*Tip Toes*; *London*; *Mumsie*; *Nell Gwynne*; 1928—*The Scarlet Pimpernel*; *Madame Pompadour*; 1929—*The Woman in White*; *The Rosary*; *The Bondman*; 1930—*The Loves of Robert Burns*; *Mountains of Mourne*; 1931—*The Blue Danube*; *The Chance of a Night Time*; 1932—*The Little Damozel*; *Carnival*; *Goodnight Vienna*; *The Flag Lieutenant*; *The Love Contract*; *The King's Cup*; *Thark* (pr only); *The Flag*

Lieutenant (Edwards) (pr only); *The Love Contract* (Selpin) (pr only); 1933—*Bitter Sweet*; *Say It with Music* (Raymond) (pr only); 1934—*The Queen's Affair*; *Sorrell and Son* (Raymond) (pr only); 1935—*Nell Gwynne*; *Brewster's Millions* (Freeland) (pr only); 1936—*Peg of Old Drury*; *Fame*; *Limelight*; 1937—*The Three Maxims*; *Millions*; *This'll Make You Whistle*; *London Melody*; *Victoria the Great*; *The Gang Show* (Goulding) (pr only); *The Rat* (Goulding) (pr only); *Our Fighting Navy* (Walker) (pr only); *The Frog* (Raymond) (pr only); 1938—*60 Glorious Years*; *Sunset in Vienna* (Walker) (pr only); *Blondes for Danger* (Raymond) (pr only); 1939—*Nurse Edith Cavell*; 1940—*No No Nanette*; *Irene*; 1941—*Sunny*; 1942—*They Flew Alone*; 1943—*The Yellow Canary*; *Forever and a Day* (co-d); 1945—*I Live in Grosvenor Square*; 1946—*Picadilly Incident*; 1947—*The Courtneys of Curzon Street*; 1948—*Spring in Park Lane*; 1949—*Elizabeth of Ladymead*; *Maytime in Mayfair*; 1950—*Odette*; 1951—*The Lady with a Lamp*; *Into the Blue*; *Derby Day*; 1952—*Trent's Last Case*; 1953—*Laughing Anne*; 1954—*Lilacs in the Spring*; *Trouble in the Glen*; 1955—*King's Rhapsody*; 1956—*My Teenage Daughter*; 1957—*These Dangerous Years*; *Yang-tse Incident* (Anderson) (pr only); 1958—*The Man Who Wouldn't Talk*; *Wonderful Things*; 1959—*The Lady Is a Square*; *The Heart of a Man*.

Publications:

By WILCOX:

Book—*25,000 Sunsets: The Autobiography of Herbert Wilcox*, London 1967.

On WILCOX:

Books—*It's Been Fun* by Anna Neagle, London 1949; *There's Always Tomorrow* by Anna Neagle, London 1974; articles—in *Current Biography* (New York), November 1945; "Herbert Wilcox" by J.-L. Passek in *Cinéma* (Paris), August/September 1977.

*   *   *

In the opening chapter of his autobiography, Herbert Wilcox wrote, "I was born starry-eyed on 19 April, with Aries at its zenith, and I've lived with stars in my eyes ever since." In fact, Wilcox had only one star in his eyes through most of his career, and that star was his wife Anna Neagle, who was featured in virtually every film that Wilcox made from 1932 onwards. They were a team, whose charms helped override some of their basic deficiencies as director and actress. What is apparent from the films, as Nöel Coward noted in his diary, was "the unimpaired 'niceness' of both of them." Herbert Wilcox was an affable, easy-going director, with an eye to the box office, who thought he could transform Anna Neagle into any character from history: Nell Gwynne, Queen Victoria (in *Victoria the Great* and *Sixty Glorious Years*), Nurse Edith Cavell, Amy Johnson (in *They Flew Alone*), French spy Odette, or Florence Nightingale (in *The Lady with the Lamp*). Sometimes he succeeded.

A film salesman turned producer in the early twenties, Herbert Wilcox's silent career was notable for his realization that it was stars who brought commercial fame, and as Britain had so few film stars it was necessary to import them from the States. To this end he brought over Mae Marsh, Dorothy Gish, Blanche Sweet,

and even Will Rogers. Those early films were light and frothy affairs, but Wilcox began to take himself seriously with *The Only Way* (featuring Sir John Martin Harvey in his famous stage version of Dickens's *A Tale of Two Cities*), and *Dawn*, with Sybil Thorndike as Edith Cavell. Both were surprisingly well-made, but Wilcox professed a strong dislike for realism and insisted that entertainment must always be the chief component in his productions. In the thirties, therefore, he made musicals with Jack Buchanan and Anna Neagle, until struck by a sense of patriotism (and perhaps a desire to prove that Miss Neagle could act) which led to two features dealing with the life of Queen Victoria and a remake of *Dawn* (*Nurse Edith Cavell*), obviously intended as anti-German propaganda.

The success of the Wilcox-Neagle films in the United Stated led to a RKO contract in Hollywood, and more "entertainment" through remakes of *Irene*, *No, No Nanette*, and *Sunny*. Returning to a Britain governed by Socialists, Herbert Wilcox embarked on another series of films, billed as filled with "Music, Gaiety, Laughter and Romance," this time concerned with upper middle-class Londoners who existed in Park Lane and Curzon Street, in a world far removed from the reality of rationing and postwar depression.

It was not until the fifties that Herbert Wilcox began to lose his grip on the audience. He tried unsuccessfully to turn Errol Flynn into an Ivor Novello matinee idol with *Lilacs in the Spring* and *King's Rhapsody*. Anna Neagle was forced to come to grips with teenage rebellion and rock-and-roll in *My Teenage Daughter*, *These Dangerous Years*, and *The Lady Is a Square*. Audiences were not interested. In 1964 Wilcox was declared bankrupt, and his last years were spent in futile attempts to obtain funding for film projects which would once again glorify England, as he had done in the thirties.

For almost half a century, Herbert Wilcox was Britain's most successful producer/director, and while it is perhaps easy to sneer at many of his films, one should not overlook his understanding of the audience, and the professionalism and care which are obvious in all of his features (qualities lacking from the works of many of his English contemporaries).

—Anthony Slide

WILDER, BILLY. American. Born Samuel Wilder in Sucha, Austria (now part of Poland), 22 June 1906; became citizen of United States, 1933 or 1934. Educated in law one year, University of Vienna. Career: works as journalist in Vienna after leaving university; 1926—travels to Berlin, writes for various newspapers and magazines, gaining prominence as crime reporter; 1929—collaborates with Robert and Kurt Siodmak, Edgar Ulmer, Fred Zinnemann, and Eugen Schüfftan on *Menschen am Sonntag*; 1929-33—scriptwriter mainly for UFA studios; 1933—flees to Paris, co-directs *Mauvaise graine*, 1st directorial effort; moves to Hollywood, hired by script department at Columbia, and then 20th Century-Fox; 1937—Paramount hires him as a scriptwriter; begins 13 year collaboration with Charles Brackett on *Bluebeard's 8th Wife*; 1939—Brackett and Wilder gain notice as scriptwriters for *Ninotchka*; 1942—directs 1st American film, *The Major and the Minor*; 1945—serves in U.S. Army as Colonel in Psychological Warfare Division of the Occupational Government, Berlin; 1955—begins making films as independent producer/director with *The Seven Year Itch*; 1957—teams for 1st time with writer I.A.L. Diamond on *Love in the Afternoon*; 1974—contracted by Universal, directs *The Front Page*; 1977—

Universal drops contract, directs *Fedora* as independent. Recipient: Academy Award, Best Direction for *Lost Weekend*, 1945; Academy Award, Best Screenplay (with Charles Brackett) for *Lost Weekend*, 1945; New York Film Critics' Award, Best Direction for *The Lost Weekend*, 1945; Academy Award, Best Story and Screenplay (with Charles Brackett) for *Sunset Boulevard*, 1950; Academy Award, Best Story and Screenplay for the Screen (with I.A.L. Diamond) for *The Apartment*, 1960; Academy Award, Best Direction for *The Apartment*, 1960; New York Film Critics' Award, Best Direction for *The Apartment* (co-winner), 1960; New York Film Critics' Award, Best Writing (with I.A.L. Diamond) for *The Apartment*, 1960.

Films (as co-scriptwriter—in Germany): 1929—*Menschen am Sonntag (People on Sunday)*; *Der Teufelsreporter*; 1930—*Seitensprünge* (story); 1931—*Ihre Hoheit befiehlt*; *Der falsche Ehemann*; *Emil und die Detektive (Emil and the Detectives)* (sc); *Der Mann der seinen Mörder sucht*; 1932—*Es war einmal ein Walzer*; *Ein blonder Traum*; *Scampolo, ein Kind der Strasse*; *Das Blaue von Himmel*; 1933—*Madame wünscht keine Kinder*; *Was Frauen träumen*; *Mauvaise Graine* (co-d only); (in the U.S.): *Adorable* (co-story, based on *Ihre Hoheit befiehlt*); 1934—*Music in the Air*; *One Exciting Adventure* (co-story); 1935—*Lottery Lover*; 1937—*Champagne Waltz* (co-story); 1938—*Bluebeard's 8th Wife*; 1939—*Midnight*; *What a Life*; *Ninotchka*; 1940—*Arise My Love*; 1941—*Hold Back the Dawn*; 1941—*Ball of Fire*; (as director and co-scriptwriter): 1942—*The Major and the Minor*; 1943 *5 Graves to Cairo*; 1944—*Double Indemnity*; 1945—*The Lost Weekend*; 1948—*The Emperor Waltz*; *Foreign Affair*; 1950—*Sunset Boulevard*; 1951—*Ace in the Hole (The Big Carnival)* (+co-pr); (as producer, director, and co-scriptwriter): 1953—*Stalag 17*; 1954—*Sabrina*; 1955—*The Seven Year Itch* (co-pr); 1957—*The Spirit of St. Louis* (d, co-sc only); *Love in the Afternoon*; 1958—*Witness for the Prosecution* (d, co-sc only); 1959—*Some Like It Hot*; 1960—*The Apartment*; 1961—*One, Two, Three*; 1963—*Irma La Douce*; 1964—*Kiss Me, Stupid*; 1966—*The Fortune Cookie*; 1970—*The Private Life of Sherlock Holmes*; 1972—*Avanti!*; 1974—*The Front Page* (d, co-sc only); 1978—*Fedora* (co-pr).

Publications:

By WILDER:

Articles—"Wilder Sees Films 'With Bite' to Satisfy 'Nation of Hecklers'" by Philip Scheuer in *Los Angeles Times*, 20 August 1950; "Why Not Be In Paris" in *Newsweek* (New York), 26 November 1956; "Wilder in Paris" by John Gillett in *Sight and Sound* (London), winter 1956; "I Head is Better than 2" in *Films and Filming* (London), February 1957; "The Old Dependables" by Colin Young in *Film Quarterly* (Berkeley), fall 1959; "Billy Wilder Eats Some Crow" by Art Buchwald in *Los Angeles Times*, 7 August 1960; "Charming Billy" by Richard Gehman in *Playboy* (Chicago), December 1960; "Fast Talker" in *The New York Times*, 4 March 1961; "Entretien avec Billy Wilder" by Jean Domarchi and Jean Douchet in *Cahiers du cinéma* (Paris), August 1962; "Interview: Billy Wilder" in *Playboy* (Chicago), June 1963; "The Jury Already Has Ruled I Have No Talent" in the *Herald-Examiner* (Los Angeles), 6 November 1966; "Meet Whiplash Wilder" by Charles Higham in *Sight and Sound* (London), winter 1967; "Movie Maker Billy Wilder is Ready for Sherlock Holmes" by Roderick Man in the *Herald-Examiner* (Los Angeles), 10 March 1968; "Interview with Billy Wilder" by Robert Mundy and Michael Wallington in *Cinema* (London),

October 1969; "Wilder—'Yes, We Have No Naked Girls'" by Mark Shivas in *The New York Times*, 12 October 1969; "Billy Wilder: Broadcast to Kuala Lampur" by Vanessa Brown in *Action* (Los Angeles), November/December 1970; "Entretien avec Billy Wilder" by Michel Ciment in *Positif* (Paris), October 1970; "Petit Dictionaire Wildérien" in *Positif* (Paris), May 1971; "Wilder in Italy: Order Among the Extroverts" by William Touhy in *Los Angeles Times*, 30 April 1972; "Wilder Still Working Without Net" by Charles Champlin in *Los Angeles Times*, 14 July 1974; "In the Picture: *The Front Page*" by Joseph McBride in *Sight and Sound* (London), autumn 1974; interview by Michel Ciment in *Positif* (Paris), January 1974; "Interview with Billy Wilder" by Gene Phillips in *Film/Literature Quarterly* (Salisbury, Md.), winter 1975; "Wilder Bewildered", interview by G. Adair in *Sight and Sound* (London), winter 1976/77; "2 ou 3 comtesses", interview by G. Legrand and others in *Positif* (Paris), September 1978; "Going for Extra Innings", interview by J. McBride and T. McCarthy in *Film Comment* (New York), January/February 1979; interview by H.-G. Rasner in *Filmkritik* (Munich), February 1980.

On WILDER:

Books—*From Caligari to Hitler: A Psychological History of the German Film* by Siegfried Kracauer, Princeton, New Jersey 1947; *Billy Wilder* by Oreste del Buono, Parma, Italy 1958; *Billy Wilder* by Axel Madsen, Bloomington, Indiana 1969; *The Bright Side of Billy Wilder, Primarily* by Tom Wood, New York 1970; *Hollywood* by Garson Kanin, New York 1974; *Talking Pictures: Screenwriters in the American Cinema* by Richard Corliss, New York 1975; *Billy Wilder in Hollywood* by Maurice Zolotow, New York 1977; *The Film Career of Billy Wilder* by Steve Seidman, Boston 1977; articles—"The Happiest Couple in Hollywood: Brackett and Wilder" by Lincoln Barnett in *Life* (New York), 11 December 1944; "End of a Journey" by Thomas Pryor in *The New York Times*, 23 September 1945; "I registi: Billy Wilder" by Giulio Cesare Castello in *Cinema* (Rome), May 1949; "Old Master, New Tricks" by Herb Lightman in *American Cinematographer* (Los Angeles), September 1950; "Putting *Life* into a Movie: *Ace in a Hole*" in *Life* (New York), 19 February 1951; "L'audacia de Billy Wilder" by Fernaldo Di Giammatteo in *Bianco e nero* (Rome), November 1951; "Un Bovaryste à Hollywood" by Jean Myrsine in *Cahiers du cinéma* (Paris), April 1952; "High Key vs. Low Key" by Frederick Foster in *American Cinematographer* (Los Angeles), August 1957; "In the Picture: Bergman and Wilder" in *Sight and Sound* (London), summer/autumn 1959; "Policeman, Midwife, Bastard" in *Time* (New York), 27 June 1960; "The Wilder Shores of Hollywood" in *Variety* (New York), 8 June 1960; "Wilder Touch" in *Life* (New York), 30 May 1960; "The Eye of the Cynic" by Douglas McVay in *Films and Filming* (London), January 1960; "The Wilder—and Funnier—Touch" by Murray Schumach in *The New York Times Magazine*, 24 January 1960; "Wilder Hits at Stars, Exhibs, Sees Pay-TV as 'Great Day'" in *Daily Variety* (New York), 13 December 1961; "The 2 Faces of Shirley" by Robin Bean in *Films and Filming* (London), February 1962; "Belts and Suspenders" by John Simon in *Theater Arts* (New York), July 1962; "Cast a Cold Eye: The Films of Billy Wilder" by Charles Higham in *Sight and Sound* (London), spring 1963; "Billy Wilder: Hating People for Fun and Profit" by Jim Murray in *Los Angeles Magazine*, October 1963; "Fallen Idols" by Andrew Sarris in *Film Culture* (New York), spring 1963; "Bright Diamond" by Murray Schumach in *The New York Times Magazine*, 26 May 1963; "The Films of Billy Wilder" in *Film Comment* (New York), summer 1965; "For Billy Wilder, the Words Are Foremost" in *Motion Picture Herald* (New York), 20 July

1966; "Billy Wilder: Why He Chose Hollywood" by Marika Aba in *Los Angeles Times*, 3 March 1968; "Wilder, Billy (tournage)" by Bernard Cohn in *Positif* (Paris), no.109, 1969; "In Search of Sherlock" by John Gillett in *Sight and Sound* (London), winter 1969; "Wilder Reappraised" by Robert Mundy in *Cinema* (London), October 1969; "Interview with I.A.L. Diamond" by Robert Mundy and Michael Wallington in *Cinema* (London), October 1969; "Review of Axel Madsen's *Billy Wilder*" by Michael Walker in *Screen* (London), March/April 1969; "Billy Wilder: A Filmography" in *Film Comment* (New York), winter 1970; "The Private Life of Billy Wilder" by Joseph McBride and Michael Wilmington in *Film Quarterly* (Berkeley), summer 1970; "Sept Réflexions sur Billy Wilder" by Michel Ciment in *Positif* (Paris), May 1971; "The Films of Billy Wilder" by Stephen Farber in *Film Comment* (New York), winter 1971; "*Private Life of Sherlock Holmes*" by Joseph McBride and Michael Wilmington in *Film Quarterly* (Berkeley), spring 1971; "Billy Wilder" by Tom Onosko in *Velvet Light Trap* (Madison, Wisconsin), winter 1971; "Interview with I.A.L. Diamond" in *The Screenwriter Looks at the Screenwriter* by William Froug, New York 1972; "Arsenic and Old Directors" by Noel Berggren in *Esquire* (New York), April 1972; "La Dernier Carfe" by Jean-Loup Bourgét in *Positif* (Paris), April 1973; "2 Old Men's Movies" by Stephen Farber in *Film Quarterly* (Berkeley), summer 1973; "Landmarks of Film History: *Some Like It Hot*" by Stanley Kauffmann in *Horizon* (Los Angeles), winter 1973; "La maschera come opposizione e come integrazione in Billy Wilder" by F. La Polla in *Filmcritica* (Rome), May/June 1973; "The Importance of Being Ernst" by J. McBride in *Film Heritage* (New York), summer 1973; "Raymond Chandler and the World You Live In" by Paul Jensen in *Film Coment* (New York), November/December 1974; "Notes sur Billy Wilder" by Nöel Simsolo in *Image et son* (Paris), March 1974; "Le Rose et le noir" by Olivier Eyquem in *Positif* (Paris), January 1974; "Notes sur Billy Wilder" by Noel Simsolo in *Image et son* (Paris), March 1974; "Wilder à la 'une'" by Claude Beylie in *Ecran* (Paris), April 1975; "Un Pas de deux (*Spécial Première*) by Gerard Legrand in *Positif* (Paris), April 1975; addenda to filmography in April issue, in *Ecran* (Paris), May 1975; "Dialogue on Film: Billy Wilder and I.A.L. Diamond" in *American Film* (Washington, D.C.), July/August 1976; "Billy Wilder: Closet Romanticist" by Andrew Sarris in *Film Comment* (New York), July/August 1976; "Fedora", special issue of *Avant-Scène du cinéma* (Paris), 15 November 1978; "The Life and Hard Times of *Fedora*" by R. McGee in *American Film* (Washington, D.C.), February 1979; "At 73, Billy Wilder's Bark Still Has Plenty of Bite" by A. Harmetz in *The New York Times*, 29 June 1979; "The Private Films of Billy Wilder" by G. Morris in *Film Comment* (New York), January/February 1979; "Some Versions of Billy Wilder" by Lee Poague in *Cinemonkey* (Portland), no.1, 1979; "Berlanga—B. Wilder: Buscando un punto común" by J.L. Acosta in *Cinema 2002* (Madrid), March/April 1980; "Retrospectives in Berlin" by R. Traubner in *Films in Review* (New York), August/September 1980.

WISE, ROBERT. American. Born in Winchester, Indiana, 10 September 1914. Educated in journalism at Franklin College. Career: 1933—forced to quit college for lack of money; hired as assistant editor at RKO where brother employed; 1939—

becomes full-fledged film editor; early 1940s—edits *Citizen Kane* and *The Magnificent Ambersons* among other prominent films; 1944—takes over direction of *The Curse of the Cat People* when Gunther von Fritsch fails to meet production schedule; 1959—becomes independent producer for Mirisch Corporation and in 1963 for Fox. Recipient: Best Direction Academy Award (with Jerome Robbins) for *West Side Story*, 1961; Best Direction Academy Award for *The Sound of Music*, 1965; Director Award, Directors Guild of America, for *The Sound of Music*, 1965; Irving G. Thalberg Memorial Academy Award, 1966. Agent: Phil Gersh Agency, Beverly Hills, California. Business: Robert Wise Productions, Sunset Gower Studios, 1438 North Gower St., Suite 562, Hollywood, CA 90028.

Films (as director): 1944—*The Curse of the Cat People* (co-d); *Mademoiselle Fifi*; 1945—*The Body Snatchers*; 1946—*A Game of Death*; *Criminal Court*; 1947—*Born to Kill*; 1948—*Mystery in Mexico*; *Blood on the Moon*; 1949—*The Set-Up*; 1950—*3 Secrets*; *2 Flags West*; 1951—*The House on Telegraph Hill*; *The Day the Earth Stood Still*; 1952—*Destination Gobi*; *Something for the Birds*; 1953—*The Desert Rats*; *So Big*; 1954—*Executive Suite*; 1955—*Helen of Troy*; *Tribute to a Bad Man*; 1956—*Somebody Up There Likes Me*; 1957—*This Could Be the Night*; *Until They Sail*; 1958—*Run Silent, Run Deep*; *I Want to Live*; 1959—*Odds Against Tomorrow* (+pr); 1961—*West Side Story* (co-d); 1962—*2 For the Seesaw*; 1963—*The Haunting* (+pr); 1965—*The Sound of Music* (+pr); 1966—*The Sand Pebbles* (+pr); 1968—*Star!*; 1970—*The Andromeda Strain* (+pr); 1971—*2 People* (+pr); 1975—*The Hindenburg*; 1977—*Audrey Rose*; 1979—*Star Trek: The Motion Picture*.

Publications:

By WISE:

Articles—interview in *Directors at Work* edited by Bernard Kantor and others, New York 1970; "Impressions of Russia" in *Action* (Los Angeles), July/August 1971; "Robert Wise at RKO", interview by Ruy Nogueira in *Focus on Film* (London), winter 1972; "Wise Side Story", interview by Ruy Nogueira in *Ecran* (Paris), February 1972; "Robert Wise at Fox", interview by Ruy Nogueira in *Focus on Film* (London), spring 1973; "Robert Wise Continued" by Ruy Nogueira and A. Eyles in *Focus on Film* (London), autumn 1973; "Newsmaker: Robert Wise" in *Action* (Los Angeles), March/April 1974; "Robert Wise to Date", interview by Ruy Nogueira in *Focus on Film* (London), autumn 1974; "Director Robert Wise at the 10th Chicago International Film Festival", interview in *American Cinematographer* (Los Angeles), January 1975; "Robert Wise Talks About 'The New Hollywood'" in *American Cinematographer* (Los Angeles), July 1976; "The Production of *The Hindenburg*" in *American Cinematographer* (Los Angeles), January 1976; "Audrey Rose: In Search of a Soul", interview by R. Appelbaum in *Films and Filming* (London), November 1977; interview by D. Rabourdin in *Cinéma* (Paris), January 1978; "*Star Trek: The Motion Picture*", interview by P.N. Jones in *Cinefantastique* (Oak Park, Illinois), no.2, 1979; "Time and Again", interview in *Monthly Film Bulletin* (London), November 1979; "Techniques of the Horror Film: Or a Decline of Technique?", interview by R. Appelbaum in *Filmmakers Monthly* (Ward Hill, Mass.), September 1980; "An AFI Seminar with Robert Wise and Milton Krasner ASC" in *American Cinematographer* (Los Angeles), March 1980; "Rumbo a lo desconocido", interview by L.G. Tsao in *Cine* (Mexico), June/July 1980.

On WISE:

Articles—"Robert Wise" by Samuel Stark in *Films in Review* (New York), January 1963; "Wise in Hollywood" by Arthur Knight in *Saturday Review* (New York), 8 August 1970; "The Future...A Slight Return" by Roy Pickard in *Films and Filming* (London), July 1971; special issue of *Dialogue on Film* (Washington, D.C.), v.2, no.1, 1972; "Robert Wise: The Hindenburg" by J. Biegel in *Action* (Los Angeles), November/December 1975; "Robert Wise and *The Hindenburg*" by P. Stamelman in *Millimeterr* (New York), November 1975; "Nous avons gagné ce soir" by F. Guérif in *Avant-Scène du cinéma* (Paris), 1 March 1980; "Lexique des réalisateurs de films fantastiques américains (5)" by J.-P. Piton in *Image et son* (Paris), September 1981.

*   *   *

In the early forties there were two young men in the editorial department at RKO who worked as editors on Val Lewton pictures: Robert Wise and Mark Robson. The latter was promoted to a full directorship of Lewton's *Seventh Victim*, a moody script by DeWitt Bodeen and Charles O'Neal, about a cult of devil worshippers in modern Manhattan.

Meanwhile, Robson's immediate superior in the editorial department, Robert Wise, got his first directorial opportunity when the front office was displeased with Gunther von Fritsch, who was halfway through *Curse of the Cat People*, and was dismissed because he was behind schedule, a cardinal sin in the days of the studios. It was natural that Robert Wise, being the editor of *Curse of the Cat People*, should take over and complete the film, for only he knew the continuity of what had already been shot. Wise did so admirable a job that Lewton immediately got him assigned to his unit as full director for *Mademoiselle Fifi* with Simone Simon and *The Body Snatcher* with Boris Karloff.

Wise had edited two Orson Welles films for RKO—two that became classics, *Citizen Kane* and *The Magnificent Ambersons*. After now being made a full director, he diligently went into an acting class because he felt that actors had a special knowledge and language of their own; it was the ideal way of seeing film from the actor's point of view. It paid off almost immediately; he got an assignment as director for *The Set-Up*, a realistic picture of the prize ring that made a top star of Robert Ryan and a top director as well of Wise. *The Set-Up* won him the Critics Prize at the Cannes Film Festival.

In 1950 he was at Warner Bros., where he directed a distinguished mood film, *Three Secrets*, and went on to direct a remake of Edna Ferber's *So Big* with Jane Wyman, and *The Desert Rats* at 20th Century-Fox with Richard Burton. *Executive Suite* at MGM raised his status a notch higher, as did *Tribute to a Bad Man* with James Cagney. *Somebody Up There Likes Me* was an excellent prize ring picture starring Paul Newman, while *Run Silent, Run Deep* was a splendid submarine thriller for Gable and Lancaster. *I Want to Live* at long last won Susan Hayward an Acadeny Award as Best Actress for 1958. A couple of years later Wise shared an Academy Award as Best Director with Jerome Robbins for *West Side Story*.

He returned to the mood horror film to make one of the most memorable of all time, *The Haunting*, which he also produced. He was director/producer again for *The Sound of Music*, which won him once more the Academy's Oscar as Best Director, and still stands as a top box-office winner. *The Sand Pebbles*, with the late Steve McQueen, also earned him admiration.

—DeWitt Bodeen

WISEMAN, FREDERICK. American. Born in Boston, 1 January 1930. Educated Williams College; Yale Law School, law degree; Harvard University. Career: 1954-56—military service in Army; 1956-58—practices law in Paris, begins experimenting with 8mm filmmaking; 1958-61—teaches at Boston University Law School; 1963—buys rights to *The Cool World* by Warren Miller, and produces documentary film version directed by Shirley Clarke; 1966—directs 1st film, *Titicut Follies*, documentary on Bridgewater, Massachusetts, prison-hospital; 1967—receives foundation grant to do *High School*; 1968-71—directs 3 films funded in part by PBS and WNET Channel 13 in New York; 1971—contracted by WNET to do one documentary each year for 5 years; 1976—contract renewed by WNET for another 5 years. Recipient: Emmy Award for Best Documentary Direction of *Hospital*, 1970; Catholic Broadcasters' Association, Personal Achievement Gabriel Award, 1975.

Films (as producer, director, and editor): 1964—*The Cool World* (Clarke) (pr only); 1967—*Titicut Follies*; 1968—*High School*; 1969—*Law and Order*; 1970—*Hospital*; 1971—*Basic Training*; 1972—*Essene*; 1973—*Juvenile Court*; 1974—*Primate*; 1975—*Welfare*; 1975—*Meat*; 1977—*Canal Zone*; 1981—*Model*; 1982—*Seraphita's Diary*.

Publications:

By WISEMAN:

Articles—"The Talk of the Town: New Producer" in the *New Yorker*, 14 September 1963; "An Interview with Frederick Wiseman" by Janet Handelman in *Film Library Quarterly* (New York), summer 1970; "An Interview with Frederick Wiseman" by Ira Halberstadt in *Filmmaker's Newsletter* (Ward Hill, Mass.), February 1974; interview by L. Lindeborg in *Chaplin* (Stockholm), no.6, 1975; "An Interview with Frederick Wiseman" by Ira Halberstadt in *Nonfiction Film Theory and Criticism* edited by Richard Barsam, New York 1976; "Vérités et mensonges du cinéma américain", interview by M. Martin and others in *Ecran* (Paris), September 1976; "Wiseman's Latest Film is Another 'Reality Fiction'", interview by J.J. O'Connor in *The New York Times*, 7 November 1976; "Frederick Wiseman ou le cinéma du constat", interview by J. Roy in *Cinéma* (Paris), June 1976; "Propos" in *Positif* (Paris), February 1977; "Wiseman on Polemic", interview by A.T. Sutherland in *Sight and Sound* (London), spring 1978; interview by D. Bergoughan and others in *Cahiers du cinéma* (Paris), September 1979.

On WISEMAN:

Books—*Cinema Verite* by M. Ali Issari, Ann Arbor, Michigan 1971; *The Celluloid Curriculum: How to Use Movies in the Classroom* by Richard A. Maynard, New York 1971; *Nonfiction Film: A Critical History* by Richard Barsam, New York 1973; *Frederick Wiseman* edited by Thomas Atkins, New York 1976; *Frederick Wiseman: A Guide to References and Resources* by Liz Ellsworth, Boston 1979; articles—"*The Cool World*" by Harriet Polt in *Film Quarterly* (Berkeley), winter 1963; "Shirley Clarke at Venice: An Interview with Harriet Polt" in *Film Comment* (New York), no.2, 1964; "Bay State in Move to Bar Prison Film" in *The New York Times*, 27 September 1967; "Court Here Refuses to Bar Film at New York Film Festival" in *The New York Times*, 29 September 1967; "Tempest in a Snake Pit" in *Newsweek* (New York), 4 December 1967; "US Court Refuses to Ban *Titicut Follies* to Public" in *The New York*

Times, 1 December 1967; "Cinema Verite and Film Truth" by Arthur Knight in the *Saturday Review* (New York), 9 September 1967; "Whose Truth?" by Jose Yglesias in *Nation* (New York), 23 October 1967; "Film Stirs Furor in Mass., Legislators See *Follies* Made at Memorial Hospital" by John H. Fenton in *The New York Times*, 18 October 1967; "Stripped Bare at the *Follies*" by Robert Coles in the *New Republic* (New York), 20 January 1968; "*Titicut Follies* is Barred to Bay State Public" in *The New York Times*, 25 June 1969; "2...But Not of a Kind" by Paul Bradlow in *Film Comment* (New York), no.3, 1969; "Popular Conventions" by Nancy Dowd in *Film Quarterly* (Berkeley), spring 1969; "The Kids of *High School*" by Charles Faucher in *Media and Methods* (Philadelphia), September 1969; "Movie on Police Censored by NET, *Law and Order* Program Cut to Remove Obscenities" by George Gent in *The New York Times*, 27 February 1969; "A Verite View of High School" by Richard Schickel in *Life* (New York), 12 September 1969; "Movies: Shooting It Like It Is" by Paul Zimmerman in *Newsweek* (New York), 17 March 1969; "I Was Fed Up with Hollywood Fantasies" by Beatrice Berg in *The New York Times*, 1 February 1970; "Frederick Wiseman" by Donald Williams in *Film Quarterly* (Berkeley), fall 1970; "The New Documentaries of Frederick Wiseman" by Stephen Mamber in *Cinema* (Beverly Hills), summer 1970; "Documentary America" by David Denby in *Atlantic Monthly* (Greenwich, Conn.), March 1970; "Frederick Wiseman Documents the Dilemmas of Our Institutions" by Thomas Atkins in *Film News* (New York), October 1971; "The Media: Public Documents" by Robert Mamis in *Newsweek* (New York), 4 October 1971; "Frederick Wiseman" in *Documentary Explorations* edited by G. Roy Levin, New York 1971; "The Film is About Killing" by John O'Connor in *The New York Times*, 3 October 1971; "Documentary" by K. Gay in *Films and Filming* (London), July 1972; "The Documentary Maker" by Thomas Meehan in the *Saturday Review* (New York), 2 December 1972; "TV Verite" by Jane Crain in *Commentary* (New York), December 1973; "Cinema Verité and Social Concerns" by Stephen Mamber in *Film Comment* (New York), November/December 1973; "American Institutions: The Films of Frederick Wiseman" by Thomas Atkins in *Sight and Sound* (London), autumn 1974; "Frederick Wiseman" in *Cinema Verite in America: Studies in Uncontrolled Documentary* by Stephen Mamber, Cambridge, Mass. 1974; "The Woes of Welfare" by Gregg Kilday in the *Los Angeles Times*, 22 September 1975; "The Advent of Magnetic Sounds" by James Scott in *Film: The Medium and the Maker*, New York 1975; "Watching Wiseman Watch" by David Eames in *The New York Times Magazine*, 2 October 1977; "Wiseman-retrospectief" in *Skrien* (Amsterdam), April 1977; "Fred Wiseman's Documentaries: Theory and Structure" by Bill Nichols in *Film Quarterly* (Berkeley), spring 1978; "Wiseman" by P. Jong and others in *Skrien* (Amsterdam), November 1978; "Fred Wiseman's Documentaries: Theory and Structure" by B. Nichols in *Film Quarterly* (Berkeley), spring 1978; "Frederick Wiseman's Cinema of Alienation" by R. Tuch in *Film Library Quarterly* (New York), v.11, no.3, 1978; "Fred Wiseman" by S. Le Peron in *Cahiers du cinéma* (Paris), September 1979; "Frederick Wiseman, c'est aussi l'Amérique" by P. Pilard in *Image et son* (Paris), November 1981; "Rétrospective Frederick Wiseman" by C. Varène in *Cinématographe* (Paris), November 1981.

*   *   *

Wiseman's documentaries are comprehensively anti-traditional. They feature no commentary and no music; their sound-tracks carry no more than the sounds Wiseman's recorder encounters; they are long, in some cases over three hours; and they are monochrome. Like the Drew/Leacock "direct cinema" filmmakers, Wiseman uses lightweight equipment and high-speed film to explore worlds previously inaccessible. In direct cinema the aim was to achieve more honest reportage. Wiseman's insight, however, has been to recognize that there is no pure documentary, and that all filmmaking is a process of imposing order on the filmed materials.

For this reason he prefers to call his films "reality fictions." Though he shoots in direct cinema fashion (operating the sound system, usually in tandem with cameraman William Brayne), the crucial stage is the imposition of structure during editing. As much as 40 hours of film may be reduced to one hour of finished product, an activity he has linked to that of a writer structuring a book. This does not mean that Wiseman's films "tell a story" in any conventional sense. The pattern and meaning of Wiseman's movies seem to slowly emerge from events as if somehow contained within them. Only after seeing the film do the pieces fall into place, their significance becoming clear as part of the whole system of relations that forms the movie. Thus, to take a simple example, the opening shots of the school building in *High School* make it look like a factory, yet it is only at the end when the school's principal reads out a letter from a former pupil in Vietnam that the significance of the image becomes clear. The soldier is, he says, "only a body doing a job," and the school a factory for producing just such expendable bodies.

Wiseman is not an open polemicist; his films do not appear didactic. But as we are taken from one social encounter to the next, as we are caught up in the leisurely rhythms of public ritual, we steadily become aware of the theme uniting all the films. In exploring American institutions, at home and abroad, Wiseman shows us social order rendered precarious. As he puts it, he demonstrates that "there is a gap between formal and actual practice, between the rules and the way they are applied." What emerges is a powerful vision of people trapped by the ramifications of their own social institutions.

Some critics, while recognising Wiseman's undoubted skill and intelligence, attack him for not propagandizing more overtly. They argue that when he shows us police violence (*Law and Order*), army indoctrintion (*Basic Training*), collapsing welfare services (*Welfare*), or animal experiments (*Primate*) he should be more willing to apportion blame and make his commitments clear. Wiseman avoids the easy taking of sides for he is committed to the view that our institutions overrun us in more complex ways than we might imagine. By forcing us to piece together the jigsaw that he offers, he ensures that we understand more profoundly how it is that our institutions can go so terribly wrong. To do that at all is a remarkable achievement. To do it so uncompromisingly over so many years is quite unique.

In 1982 Wiseman turned to "fiction," though *Seraphita's Diary* is hardly orthodox and it is an intelligible extension of his interests. His abiding influence, however, remains in being the most sophisticated documentarist of modern cinema, with *Welfare* his most compelling achievement.

—Andrew Tudor

WOLF, KONRAD. German. Born in Hechingen/Württemberg, 20 October 1925. Educated at Institute of Cinematography (VGIK), Moscow, 1949-54; studied with Grigori Alexandrov. Career: 1934—Father, Friedrich Wolf, emigrates with family to

Moscow; 1945—returns to Germany with Soviet Army; helps found *Berliner Zeitung*; correspondent for Saxony; early 1950s—assistant director to Kurt Maetzig and Joris Ivens among others; 1965—becomes President of Deutschen Akademie der Künste (GDR); 1975—Wolf film retrospective held in Moscow. Died 7 March 1982. Recipient: First Jury Prize, Cannes Festival, for *Stars*, 1959.

Films (as director): 1955—*Einmal ist keinmal*; 1956—*Genesung*; 1957—*Lissy* (+co-sc); 1958—*Sonnensucher*; 1959—*Sterne (Stars, Etoiles)*; 1960—*Leute mit Flügeln*; 1961—*Professor Mamlock* (+co-sc); 1964—*Der geteilte Himmel (Le Ciel partagé)*; 1966—*Der kleine Prinz (The Little Prince)* (for TV); 1967—*Ich war neunzehn (I Was 19)* (+co-sc); 1971—*Goya*; 1977—*Der nackte Mann auf dem Sportplatz (The Naked Man on the Athletic Field)* (+co-sc); *Mama ich lebe*.

Publications:

By WOLF:

Articles— "In Amerika", interview by G. Netzeband in *Film und Fernsehen* (Berlin), September 1975; "Auf der Suche nach dem Lebenszentrum" and "Für die Offensive des sozialistischen Films", interviews by K. Wischnewski in *Film und Fernsehen* (Berlin), April and May 1975; "Die letzte Mahnung: Auszug aus dem Drehbuch zu *Lissy*" in *Film und Fernsehen* (Berlin), no.7, 1976; "In diesen Tagen: Nachhilfeunterricht" in *Film und Fernsehen* (Berlin), no.6, 1979.

On WOLF:

Articles—"The Face of '63—Germany" by R. Bean in *Films and Filming* (London), June 1963; "Konrad Wolf" by Hans-Dieter Tok in *Regiestühle*, Berlin 1972; "Goya de Konrad Wolf", with interview, by André Cornand in *Image et son* (Paris), February 1972; "Das Fotoporträt: Konrad Wolf" by A. Fischer and "Eine ungewöhnliche Rückschau" by R. Herlinghaus in *Film und Fernsehen* (Berlin), April 1975; "Ein Frauenschicksal" by I. Rubanowa in *Film und Fernsehen* (Berlin), no.7, 1976; "Über bequeme Sessel und unbequeme Filme", interview by G. Netzeband in *Film und Fernsehen* (Berlin), June and July 1977; "Ein gewisser Konrad Wolf" by W. Bergmann in *Film und Fernsehen* (Berlin), July 1978; "Erinnerungen und Fragen eines Kameramannes" by W. Bergmann in *Film und TV Kameramann* (Munich), December 1979; "Cinéma de R.D.A.: dictionnaire des réalisateurs" in *Cinéma* (Paris), September 1979.

WOOD, SAM. American. Born Samuel Grosvenor Wood in Philadelphia, 10 July 1884. Educated at Stanton School, Philadelphia. Married Clara Roush; daughters: Jeane and Gloria. Career: heads west in gold rush of 1900, settles in Reno; 1904—moves to Los Angeles, becomes real estate broker; about 1908—makes film acting debut as "Chad Applegate" in *A Gentleman of Leisure* for Famous Players Company; 1914—begins working as assistant to Cecil B. De Mille; 1916—promotion to director; 1919—becomes director at Paramount; 1926—signs with newly-formed MGM; directs for MGM until 1939; 1939—directs final scenes of *Gone With the Wind*; 1944—named president of Motion Picture Alliance for the Preservation of American

Ideals; 1947—testimony before House Un-American Activities Committee helps to spread notion of Communist infiltration of Hollywood. Died 22 September 1949.

Films (as director): 1920—*Double Speed*; *Excuse My Dust*; *What's Your Hurry?*; *Sick Abed*; *The Dancing Fool*; *City Sparrow*; *Peck's Bad Boy* (+sc); 1921—*Her First Elopement*; *The Snob*; *Her Beloved Villain*; *The Great Moment*; *Under the Lash*; *Don't Tell Everything*; 1922—*Impossible Mrs. Bellew*; *Her Husband's Trademark*; *Beyond the Rocks*; 1923—*My American Wife*; *Prodigal Daughters*; *Her Gilded Cage*; *Bluebeard's 8th Wife*; *His Children's Children*; 1924—*Bluff*; *The Female*; *The Next Corner*; *The Mine with the Iron Door*; 1925—*The Re-Creation of Brian Kent*; 1926—*Fascinating Youth*; *One Minute to Play*; 1927—*The Fair Co-ed*; *Rookies*; *A Racing Romeo*; 1928—*Telling the World*; *The Latest from Paris*; 1929—*It's a Great Life*; *So This Is College*; 1930—*Way for a Sailor*; *The Richest Man in the World*; *Sins of the Children*; *The Girl Said No*; *They Learned About Women* (co-d); *Paid*; 1931—*A Tailor Made Man*; *New Adventures of Get-Rich-Quick Wallingford*; 1932—*Prosperity*; *Huddle*; 1933—*Hold Your Man* (+pr); *The Barbarian*; *Christopher Bean*; 1934—*Stamboul Quest*; 1935—*A Night at the Opera*; *Let 'em Have It*; 1936—*Whip Saw*; *The Unguarded Hour*; 1937—*Navy Blue and Gold*; *Madame X*; *A Day at the Races* (+co-pr); 1938—*Stablemates*; *Lord Jeff* (+co-pr); 1939—*Goodbye, Mr. Chips*; 1940—*Raffles*; *Our Town*; *Kitty Foyle*; *Rangers of Fortune*; 1941—*King's Row*; *The Devil and Miss Jones*; 1942—*The Pride of the Yankees*; 1943—*For Whom the Bell Tolls* (+pr); 1944—*Casanova Brown*; *Address Unknown* (pr only); 1945—*Guest Wife*; *Saratoga Trunk*; 1946—*Heartbeat*; 1947—*Ivy* (+co-pr); 1948—*Command Decision*; 1949—*The Stratton Story*; *Ambush*.

Publications:

On WOOD:

Books—*A Day at the Races*, script, by Robert Pirosh and others, New York 1972; *A Night at the Opera*, script, by George S. Kaufman and others, New York 1972; *The Hollywood Professionals—Vol.2* by Clive Denton and others, New York 1974; articles—in *Time* (New York), 2 February 1942; article in *Current Biography Yearbook 1943*, New York 1944; obituary in *The New York Times*, 23 September 1949; "Sam Wood" in *Contracampo* (Madrid), October/November 1980.

*   *   *

Samual Grosvenor Wood was one of the more prolific directors in Hollywood history. Working continously at his craft from 1916 to 1949, he created an average of nearly three films per year. His most noted motion pictures came during tha last fifteen years of his career: *A Night at the Opera*, *A Day at the Races*, *Goodbye Mr. Chips*, *Kitty Foyle*, *King's Row*, and *For Whom the Bell Tolls*. Wood also worked on, uncredited, *Gone With the Wind*. Yet in all these films Sam Wood seemed unable to develop an identifiable personal style. He knew the Hollywood system, created clean crisp narratives, but never transcended the system to create complex films as did his contemporaries, John Ford and Howard Hawks.

In 1908, at age 23, Sam Wood established his career as a Los Angeles real estate agent. But through a chance meeting, he did try acting in motion pictures, and gradually worked his way up to substantial roles for the Famous Players Company. In 1914 he became an assistant to Cecil B. De Mille; in 1916 he was promoted to director. Sam Wood directed films for Famous Players (later Paramount) until 1926. Then he signed on with the newly formed Metro-Goldwyn-Mayer Company. He remained with MGM through the studio's salad days of the 1930s. But after his experience with *Gone With the Wind*, Wood struck out on his own. During the 1940s he worked for RKO, Paramount, Warner Bros., MGM, and independent producers Sol Lesser and Sam Goldwyn.

Sam Wood's directorial career seems to be divided into two parts. Until 1935 he was a traditional contract director at two of Hollywood's more important studios: Paramount and MGM. He directed many noted stars (Wallace Reid, Gloria Swanson, Jackie Coogan, Norma Shearer, Robert Montgomery, John Gilbert, Ramon Novarro, Clark Gable, Jean Harlow, and Maria Dressler), and earned a reputation as a solid, dependable director, one who brought films in on time. Sam Wood rose to the top echelon of Hollywood's contract directors through his association with Irving Thalberg and the Marx Brothers. *A Night at the Opera* became one the of the major revenue generators of the 1935-36 movie season. From then on Sam Wood was able to pick and choose his projects. By 1939 he was considered a "money director," only taking on projects with million dollar budgets. From 1939 on his films consistently finished among the top box office draws of the year. He was nominated for the Academy Award for best director in 1939 (*Goodbye Mr. Chips*), 1940 (*Kitty Foyle*), and 1942 (*King's Row*), but never won.

However Sam Wood is more often in film history books for his part in organizing the anti-Communist group, the Motion Picture Alliance for the Preservation of American Ideals. Named president in 1944, Wood carried a campaign to purge the film industry of left-wing sympathizers. Along with Walt Disney, Gary Cooper, King Vidor, and others, Wood pushed the Alliance against all proponents of progressive politics. Indeed, on the morning of his fatal heart attack he was quarreling with Columbia Pictures about the necessity of expelling a screenwriter. In his will Wood specified no heir could inherit anything unless he (or she) swore that they "are not now, nor ever have been, a Communist." Sam Wood, a former supporter of Franklin Roosevelt, died amidst front page debate concerning Hollywood's witchhunt against progressives, and thus is now remembered more for his right-wing politics than his nearly one hundred films.

—Douglas Gomery

WRIGHT, BASIL. English. Born in London, 12 June 1907. Educated in Classics and Economics, Corpus Christi College, Cambridge. Career: 1930—joins Empire Marketing Board (EMB) film unit as assistant under John Grierson; 1931—begins directing for EMB; 1933—transfers with Grierson to General Post Office (GPO) Film Unit after EMB film unit is dissolved; 1937—forms Realist Film Unit with John Taylor; joins Film Centre; 1940—begins making films for Ministry of Information after GPO film unit is absorbed by them; during WW II spends some time in Canada as adviser on information technique and policy; 1945—works as producer in charge of Crown Film Unit; later works at UNESCO under Sir Julian Huxley and John Grierson; 1946-49—forms own production company, International Realist, and produces several documentaries; 1951-60—

directs documentaries for various organizations and companies; 1960s—lectures on filmmaking at University of California; 1974—writes critical history of film, *The Long View*. Address: lives in Freith, Henley-on-Thames, Oxfordshire.

Films (as director): 1931—*The Country Comes to Town* (+co-ph, sc); 1932—*O'er Hill and Dale* (+ph, sc); *Gibraltar* (+ph, sc); 1933—*Windmill in Barbados* (+ph, sc); *Liner Cruising South* (+ph, sc); *Cargo from Jamaica* (+ph); 1934—*Song of Ceylon* (+ph, co-sc, ed); *Pett and Pott* (ass't d only); 1936—*Night Mail* (co-d, +co-sc, co-ed); 1937—*Children at School* (+co-pr); *The Smoke Menace* (ass't pr only); 1938—*The Face of Scotland* (+sc); 1939—*The Londoners* (co-pr only); 1940—*Harvest Help*; 1945—*This Was Japan*; 1948—*Bernard Miles on Gun Dogs* (+pr, sc); 1950—*Waters of Time* (co-d); 1953—*World Without End* (co-d); 1955—*Stained Glass at Fairford* (+pr); 1958—*The Immortal Land* (+co-pr); 1959—*Greek Sculpture* (co-d); 1960—*A Place for Gold* (+pr).

Publications:

By WRIGHT:

Books—*The Use of Film*, London 1948; *The Long View*, London 1974; articles—"The Documentary Dilemma" in *Hollywood Quarterly*, summer 1951; article on *World Without End* in *Sight and Sound* (London), summer 1953; "Basil Wright on the Big Screen" in *Film* (London), December 1955; "Which Way is Ahead?" in *Film* (London), November/December 1957; "Basil Wright and *Song of Ceylon*", interview by Cecile Starr in *Filmmakers Newsletter* (Ward Hill, Mass.), November 1975; "Basil Wright on Art, Anthropology and the Documentary" by S. Thomas in *Quarterly Review of Film Studies* (Pleasantville, N.Y.), fall 1979.

On WRIGHT:

Books—*Grierson on Documentary* by Forsyth Hardy, revised edition London 1966; *Studies in Documentary* by Alan Lovell and Jim Hillier, New York 1972; *Documentary Explorations* by G. Roy Levin, Garden City, New York 1972; *The Rise and Fall of British Documentary: The Story of the Film Movement Founded by John Grierson* by Elizabeth Sussex, Berkeley, California 1975; *John Grierson: A Documentary Biography* by Forsyth Hardy, London 1979; articles—on *Waters of Time* in *Sight and Sound* (London), May 1951; article on *World Without End* by Paul Rotha in *Sight and Sound* (London), summer 1953; article on *World Without End* in *Films in Review* (New York), April 1954; article on *World Without End* by Forsyth Hardy in *Sight and Sound* (London), January/March 1954; article on *Stained Glass at Fairford* by John Gillett in *Sight and Sound* (London), winter 1956/57; article on *The Immortal Land* by Ken Gay in *Films and Filming* (London), December 1958; article on *The Immortal Land* by Kenneth Cavender in *Sight and Sound* (London), winter 1958/59; "Basil Wright" by O. Barrot in *Cinéma d'aujourd'hui* (Paris), February/March 1977.

*   *   *

Of the young men hired by Grierson at the Empire Marketing Board, at the beginning of British documentary, Wright was the first. He came from a wealthy liberal family and, like many of the others, had recently completed his education at Cambridge University. Wright became one of Grierson's most loyal colleagues, remaining in touch and being involved with him on various projects over many years.

His apprenticeship consisted of editing together bits of stock footage for what were called "poster films." In the first films that he directed Wright's special talent for poetic observation became evident; e.g., *O'er Hill and Dale*, and *Cargo from Jamaica*. It achieved its fullest expression in *Song of Ceylon*, which is not only Wright's masterpiece but one of the few British documentaries of the 1930s with the kind of aesthetic value to have kept it in active circulation ever since. *Song of Ceylon* is untypical of early British documentary not only in its extraordinary formal experimentation, but in its subject (an exotic foreign culture) and theme (admiration for the religious spirit of that culture and sadness and perhaps anger at the impact of Western commerce on it). Though a number of people played important roles in its creation (Grierson as producer, Walter Leign as composer, Cavalcanti as sound editor), *Song of Ceylon* is very much Wright's film, including most of its marvelous cinematography.

Wright shares directorial credit for *Night Mail* with Harry Watt. The original script seems largely to have been Wright's and the completed film contains some of the poetic touches one associates with him working at his best. But the strong narrative line and deft bits of characterization and humor seem much more in the directorial style Watt was developing.

In his work which followed, Wright moved into an obvious imitation of the American *March of Times* series, which was greatly admired by Grierson and other British documentarians. *Children at School*, one of a program of shorts sponsored by the British Commercial Gas Association, was an example. Though competent in technique and hard-hitting as exposé, in its impersonality it might have been directed by any number of other documentarians. It represents Wright's deep and genuine social concern arrived at intellectually rather than the emotional core of his being out of which his most personal and best work has come.

In the 1951 *Waters of Time* he returned to the poetic; but by then what earlier would have been gentle reflectiveness seems to have become slack. It was made after the Grierson tradition had become diffused. *World Without End*, which had both some poetry and some force, was the last of the films with which Wright was involved that are concerned clearly with the Griersonian main line. A big and ambitious film, it was made on behalf of UNESCO in collaboration with Paul Rotha, another veteran of the early Grierson group. Rotha shot in Mexico and Wright in Thailand, with their material being intercut. Ultimately the film says that the world has grown together and that a low water level in a Mexican lake and a terrible tropical disease are of concern to us all, a very Griersonian idea.

—Jack C. Ellis

WYLER, WILLIAM. American. Born Willy Wyler in Mulhouse (Mülhausen), Alsace-Lorraine, 1 July 1902; became citizen of United States, 1928. Attended briefly Ecole supèrieure de commerce, Lausanne, Switzerland, 1919. Married Margaret Sullavan, 1934 (divorced 1936); married Margaret Tallichet in 1938; children: Judith, Melanie, David, and Catherine. Career: 1920—invited by cousin Carl Laemmle to come to America; 1921—works for Laemmle in publicity department at Universal in New York, then is transferred as office boy to Universal City in Hollywood; 1923—assists the assistant directors on Universal's *The Hunchback of Notre Dame*; 1924—begins as assistant director on 2-reel Westerns for Universal, also serves as assistant director on *Ben-Hur*; 1925—directs 1st film *Crook Buster*, 2-reel Western in Universal's "Mustang" series; 1926—directs 1st feature, *Lazy Lightning*, in Universal's "Blue Streak" series; 1930—directs his 1st all-talking film, *Hell's Heroes*; 1936—signs contract with Samuel Goldwyn, directs *Dodsworth*, receiving his first Academy Award nomination; 1942-45—serves as major in U.S. Army Air Corps and directs two documentaries; becomes partially deaf when injured in a flight over Italy; 1947—helps found Committee for the First Amendment with John Huston and Phillip Dunne to counteract Hollywood investigations by House Un-American Activities Committee; 1963—visits Soviet Union at invitation of Union of Cinema Workers; 1966—"Hommage à William Wyler" organized by Henri Langlois at the Cinémathèque française; 1972—retires from directing during preparations for *40 Carats*. Died 29 July 1981. Recipient: Academy Award, Best Direction for *Mrs. Miniver*, 1942; Academy Award, Best Direction for *The Best Years of Our Lives*, 1946; New York Film Critics' Award, Best Direction for *Best Years of Our Lives*, 1946; Academy Award, Best Direction for *Ben Hur*, 1959; Motion Picture Academy, Irving G. Thalberg Award, 1965; American Film Institute, Life Achievement Award, 1976.

Films (as director): 1925—*Crook Buster*; 1926—*The Gunless Bad Man*; *Ridin' for Love*; *Fire Barrier*; *Don't Shoot*; *The Pinnacle Rider*; *Martin of the Mounted*; *Lazy Lightning*; *Stolen Ranch*; 1927—*2 Fister*; *Kelly Gets His Man*; *Tenderfoot Courage*; *The Silent Partner*; *Galloping Justice*; *The Haunted Homestead*; *The Lone Star*; *The Ore Riders*; *The Home Trail*; *Gun Justice*; *Phantom Outlaw*; *Square Shooter*; *The Horse Trader*; *Daze in the West*; *Blazing Days*; *Hard Fists*; *The Border Cavalier*; *Straight Shootin'*; *Desert Dust*; 1928—*Thunder Riders*; *Anybody Here Seen Kelly*; 1929—*The Shakedown*; *The Love Trap*; 1930—*Hell's Heroes*; *The Storm*; 1931—*A House Divided*; 1932—*Tom Brown of Culver*; 1933—*Her First Mate*; *Counselor at Law*; 1934—*Glamour*; *The Gay Deception*; 1936—*These Three*; *Dodsworth*; *Come and Get It*; 1937—*Dead End*; 1938—*Jezebel*; 1939—*Wuthering Heights*; 1940—*The Westerner*; *The Letter*; 1941—*The Little Foxes*; 1942—*Mrs. Miniver*; 1944—*Memphis Belle*; 1946—*The Best Years of Our Lives*; 1947—*Thunder-Bolt*; 1949—*The Heiress*; 1951—*Detective Story*; 1952—*Carrie*; 1953—*Roman Holiday*; 1955—*The Desperate Hours*; 1956—*Friendly Persuasion*; 1958—*The Big Country*; 1959—*Ben-Hur*; 1962—*The Children's Hour*; 1965—*The Collector*; 1966—*How to Steal a Million*; 1968—*Funny Girl*; 1970—*The Liberation of L.B. Jones*.

Publications:

By WYLER:

Articles—interview in *The New York Times*, 17 November 1946; "William Wyler: Director with a Passion and a Craft" by Hermine Isaacs in *Theater Arts* (New York), February 1947; "Talk with the Director" in *Newsweek* (New York), 12 March 1962; "Interview at Cannes" in *Cinema* (Beverly Hills), July/August 1965; interview by Charles Higham in *Action* (Los Angeles), September/October 1973; "Wyler on Wyler" by Alan Cartnel in *Interview* (New York), March 1974; "William Wyler at the Tehran Film Festival", interview in *American Cinematographer* (Los Angeles), February 1975; "No Magic Wand" in *Hollywood*

Directors: 1941-76 edited by Richard Koszarski, New York 1977; "Dialogue on Film" in American Film (Washington, D.C.), April 1976; interview by P. Carcassonne and J. Fieschi in Cinématographe (Paris), March/April 1981; lecture excerpts in Films and Filming (London), October 1981; "Jeg var kjent som en tyrann", interview by R. Rynning in Film & Kino (Oslo), v.49, no.7, 1981.

On WYLER:

Books—The Life and Adventures of Carl Laemmle by John Drinkwater, New York 1930; Samuel Goldwyn: The Producer and His Films by Richard Griffith, New York 1956; William Wyler, an Index edited by Karel Reisz, London 1958; Directors at Work edited by Bernard Kantor and Irwin Blacker, New York 1970; Hollywood in the 30's by John Baxter, New York 1970; William Wyler by Axel Madsen, New York 1973; Filmmaking: The Collaborative Art edited by Donald Chase, Boston 1975; Uil'iam Uailer by V. Kolodiazhnaia, Moscow 1975; Samuel Goldwyn Presents by Alvin R. Marill, South Brunswick, New Jersey 1976; Close-up: The Hollywood Director edited by John Tuska, Metuchen, New Jersey 1978; William Wyler by Michael A. Anderegg, Boston 1979; articles—on his marriage by D. Hogart in Motion Picture (New York), February 1935; article in Time (New York), 29 June 1942; "Gregg Toland Film-Maker" by Lester Koenig in Screen Writer (London), December 1947; "The Work of Gregg Toland" by Douglas Slocombe in Sequence (London), summer 1949; "Wyler, Wellman, and Huston" by Richard Griffith in Films in Review (New York), February 1950; "Willy Makes the Stars Tremble" by D. Chandler in Collier's (New York), 4 February 1950; "The Later Films of William Wyler" by Karel Reisz in Sequence (London), no.13, 1951; "Personality of the Month" in Films and Filming (London), July 1957; "The Questions No One Asks About Willy" by Charlton Heston in Films and Filming (London), August 1958; "A Little Larger Than Life" by John Howard Reid in Films and Filming (London), February 1960; "A Comparison of Size" by John Howard Reid in Films and Filming (London), March 1960; "Fallen Idols" by Andrew Sarris in Film Culture (New York), spring 1963; "The Early Days of William Wyler" by Kevin Brownlow in Film (London), autumn 1963; "William Wyler" by Curtis Hanson in Cinema (Beverly Hills), summer 1967; "Working with William Wyler" by Charlton Heston in Action (Los Angeles), January/February 1967; "The Lady and the Director: Bette Davis and William Wyler" by Gary Carey in Film Comment (New York), fall 1970; "William Wyler" by Ken Doeckel in Films in Review (New York), October 1971; "William Wyler" by Charles Higham in Action (Los Angeles), September/October 1973; "Oltre la maschera" by A. Rinaldo in Filmcritica (Rome), January/February 1975; "A Life in Film" by Larry Swindell in American Film (Washington, D.C.), April 1976; "William Wyler" by Gene Phillips in Focus on Film (London), spring 1976; "The Ben-Hur Journal" by Charlton Heston in American Film (Washington, D.C.), April 1976; "Les Hauts de Hurlevent" in Avant-Scène du cinéma (Paris), April 1976; "Les Immortels du cinéma: William Wyler" by J. von Cottom in Ciné revue (Brussels), 30 August 1979; "William Wyler: 'L'Homme qui ne fit pas jamais un mauvais film'" by T. Renaud in Cinéma (Paris), September 1981; "Wyler, o el talento de un artesano creativo" by G. Zapiola in Cinemateca Revista (Andes), August 1981.

*   *   *

Willaim Wyler's career is an excellent argument for nepotism. Wyler went to work for "Uncle" Carl Laemmle, the head of

Universal, and learned the movie business as assistant director and then director of programmers, mainly westerns. One of his first important features, A House Divided, demonstrates many of the qualities that mark his films through the next decades. A transparent imitation of Eugene O'Neill's Desire under the Elms, it contains evidence of the staging strategies that identify Wyler's distinctive mise-en-scène. The film's premise holds particular appeal for a director who sees drama in claustrophobic interiors, the actors held in expressive tension by their shifting spatial relationships to each other, the decor, and the camera. In A House Divided Wyler extracts that tension from the dynamics implicit in the film's principal set, the downstairs room that confines the crippled father (Walter Huston), the stairs leading to the landing between the rooms of the son (Kent Douglass) and the young step-mother (Helen Chandler). The stairway configuration is favored by Wyler for the opportunity it gives him to stack the agents of the drama and to fill the frame both vertically and in depth. When he later collaborates with cinematographer Gregg Toland, the potential of that depth and height is enhanced through the varying degrees of hard and soft focus. (Many critics, who are certainly unfamiliar with Wyler's early work, have unjustly credited Toland for the staging in depth that characterizes the partnership.)

The implications of focus in Wyler's stylistics goes far beyond lighting procedures, lenses, even staging itself. Focus directs the viewer's attention to varieties of information within the field, whatever its shape or extent. Focus gives simultaneous access to discordant planes, characters, objects that challenge us to achieve a full, fluctuating reading of phenomena. André Bazin, in his important essay on Wyler in the French edition of What Is Cinema?, speaks of the director's "democratic" vision, his way of taking in the wholeness of a field in the unbroken time and space of the "plan-sèquence," a shot whose duration and complexity of staging goes far beyond the measure of the conventional shot. Bazin opposes this to the analytic montage of Soviet editing. In doing so he perhaps underestimates the kind of control that Wyler's deep field staging exerts upon the viewer, but he does suggest the richness of the visual text in Wyler's major films.

Counselor At Law is a significant test of Wyler's staging. The Broadway origins of the property are not disguised; they are made into a virtue. The movement through the law firm's outer office, reception room and private spaces reflects a fluidity that is a function of the camera's mobility and a challenge to the fixed frame of the proscenium. Wyler's tour de force rivals that of the film's star, John Barrymore. Director and actor animate the attorney's personal and professional activites in a hectic, ongoing present, sweeping freely through the sharply delineated (and therefore sharply perceived) vectors of the cinematic/theatrical space.

Wyler's meticulousness and Samuel Goldwyn's insistence on quality productions resulted in the series of films, often adaptations of prestigious plays, that most fully represent the director's method. In Dodsworth, the erosion of a marriage is captured in the opening of the bedroom door that separates husband and wife; the staircase of These Three delimit the public and private spaces of a film about rumor and intimacy; the elaborate street set of Dead End is examined from a dizzying variety of camera angles that create a geometry of urban life; the intensity of The Little Foxes is sustained through the focal distances that chart the shape of family ties and hatreds. After the war, the partnership of Wyler and Toland is crowned by The Best Years of Our Lives, a film whose subject (the situation of returning servicemen) is particularly pertinent, and whose structure and staging are the most personal in the director's canon.

In his tireless search for the perfect shot, Wyler was known as the scourge of performers, pushing them through countless retakes and repetitions of the same gesture. Since performance in his films is *not* pieced together in the editing room but is developed in complex blockings and shots of long duration, Wyler required a high degree of concentration on the part of the actors. Laurence Olivier, who was disdainful of the medium prior to his work in *Wuthering Heights*, credits Wyler for having revealed to him the possibilities of the movies. But it is Bette Davis who defines the place of the star actor in a Wyler film. The three she did with Wyler demonstrate how her particular energies both organize the highly controlled mise-en-scène and are contained within it. For *Jezebel* she won her second Academy Award. In *The Letter*, an exercise in directorial tyranny over the placement of seemingly every element in its highly charged frames, the viewer senses a total correspondence between the focus exercised by director and performer.

During the last decades of Wyler's career many of the director's gifts that flourished in contexts of extreme dramatic tension and the exigencies of studio shooting were dissipated in excessively grandiose properties and "locations." There were, however, exceptions. Wyler's presence is strongly felt in the narrow staircase of *The Heiress* and the dingy station house of *Detective Story*. He even manages to make the final shootout of *The Big Country* adhere to the narrowest of gulches, thereby reducing the dimensions of the title to his familiar focal points. But the epic scope of *Ben Hur* and the ego of Barbra Streisand (in *Funny Girl*) escape the compact economies of the director's boxed-in stackings and plane juxtapositions. Only in *The Collector*, a film that seems to define enclosure (a woman is kept prisoner in a cellar for most of its duration) does Wyler find a congenial property. In it he proves again that the real expanse of cinema is measured by its frames.

—Charles Affron

YATES, PETER. British. Born in Aldershot, Surrey, 24 July 1929. Educated at Charterhouse school; studied acting at Royal Academy of Dramatic Art. Career: after graduation from RADA works as actor, stage manager, and director with repertory companies; manages racing car drivers for two years, works with Stirling Moss and Peter Collins; also does stunt driving for film companies; 1957-60—begins doing film production work editing documentaries and dubbing foreign films; 1959-62—works as assistant director to Tony Richardson on *The Entertainer*, J. Lee Thompson on *The Guns of Navarone* and others; also works as stage director in London and directs for British TV; 1962—feature film directing debut; 1967—brought to Hollywood by Steve McQueen to direct *Bullitt*, on strength of car chase sequence in *Robbery*; remains in U.S. after success of *Bullitt*. Recipient: Best Assistant Director, Directors Guild of America, for work on *Sons and Lovers* (Cardiff). Agent: Tom Chasin, Chasin-Park-Citron Agency, Hollywood. Business: Tempest Productions, Inc., 1775 Broadway, Suite 621, New York, NY 10019.

Films (as assistant director): 1960—*The Entertainer* (Richardson); *Sons and Lovers* (Cardiff); 1961—*A Taste of Honey* (Richardson); *The Roman Spring of Mrs. Stone* (Quintero); *The Guns of Navarone* (Thompson); (as director): 1962—*Summer Holiday*; 1964—*One Way Pendulum*; 1967—*Robbery* (+co-sc); 1968—*Bullitt*; 1969—*John and Mary*; 1971—*Murphy's War*; 1972—*The Hot Rock (How to Steal a Diamond in 4 Uneasy Lessons)*; 1973—*The Friends of Eddie Coyle*; 1974—*For Pete's Sake*; 1976—*Mother, Jugs & Speed* (+co-pr); 1977—*The Deep*; 1979—*Breaking Away* (+pr); 1980—*Eyewitness* (+pr); 1982—*Krull*; 1984—*The Dresser*.

Publications:

By YATES:

Articles—"The Suggestive Experience", interview in *Films and Filming* (London), August 1969; "Pressure", interview by Gordon Gow in *Films and Filming* (London), April 1971; "The Hot Rock", interview by R. du Mée and G. Luijters in *Skoop* (Amsterdam), v.8, no.2, 1972; "The Making of *Friends of Eddie Coyle*", interview by A.C. Bobrow in *Filmmakers Newsletter* (Ward Hill, Mass.), October 1973; "Making *The Deep*" in *Filmmakers Newsletter* (Ward Hill, Mass.), May 1977; interview by J. von Cottom in *Ciné revue* (Brussels), 6 December 1979; "Breakaway", interview by Gordon Gow in *Films and Filming* (London), February 1980.

On YATES:

Articles—"A Hot Director Breaks Away from the Mainstream" by S. Considine in *The New York Times*, 15 July 1979; "Peter Yates" by Peter Cowie in *International Film Guide 1981*, London 1980.

*　　*　　*

Not since Alfred Hitchcock has a British director so successfully assimilated to American movie-making as Peter Yates. It seems an unexpected destiny for someone whose first film was a vehicle for so anodynely British a figure as Cliff Richard. But Yates has always been a thoroughgoing professional, ready to take on unpromising material and make an accomplished, impersonal job of it—especially if by doing so he can gain the money and reputation needed to make the kind of films he really wants.

A chance combination of circumstances gave him his breakthrough. His third British film, *Robbery*, otherwise a drably downbeat account of the Great Train Robbery, included a car chase filmed with exceptional pace and flair. This sequence attracted the attention of Steve McQueen, who invited Yates to direct his next film. Yates, sharing the actor's enthusiasm for fast cars (he was once racing manager for Stirling Moss), readily agreed. So did the studio, who wanted to sink McQueen, and reckoned an unknown British director a sure guarantee of disaster. Instead, *Bullitt* proved a massive box-office success, thanks largely to the brilliantly handled San Francisco car chase sequence, and became highly influential. For some years no crime movie was thought complete without careening hub-caps, and Yates reputation was made.

On the strength of *Bullitt*, he directed *John and Mary*, a quietly humorous conversation piece with Dustin Hoffman and Mia Farrow. One of Yates's own favorite films, it was a total flop at the box-office. "I'd much prefer to develop simplicities and nuances than decide which lamppost a car is going to hit," Yates remarked, but bowed to financial necessity. Since then, his recurrent aim has been to reconcile his bankable skills as virtuoso action director with his predilection for low-key social realism—either by using one to finance the other, or by attempting, from time to time, to combine the two in the same film.

Hot Rock came close to it, mixing pleasingly offbeat comedy with some spectacular helicopter sequences; although other attempts to blend humor with action—*Murphy's War*, *For Pete's Sake*, *Mother, Jugs and Speed*—fell flat. But in the dourly atmospheric *The Friends of Eddie Coyle* Yates displayed a rare feel for locale (in this case a bleak and wintry Boston), as well as eliciting one of Robert Mitchum's finest performances. Despite critical acclaim, it attracted meagre audiences.

Yates redeemed himself in the eyes of the studio accountants with the sub-aqueous hokum of *The Deep*, a thumping commercial success which ensured him the backing for *Breaking Away*. Engagingly scripted by Steve Tesich, and filmed around the scriptwriter's home town of Bloomington, Indiana, this is probably Yates's best movie to date, offering a fresh and unaccustomed view of class-ridden middle America, and climaxing in an exhilarating bicycle race. *Eyewitness*, a thriller also scripted by Tesich, again proved quirky and consistently diverting, though sometimes to the detriment of the suspense.

Peter Yates's career looks set to continue in the same pattern, with his big-budget science fiction film, *Krull*, being followed by *The Dresser*, a small-scale intimate adaption of Ronald Harwood's play, and the director's first British subject in 15 years. Despite his box-office triumphs, Yates's critical reputation seems likely to rest on his "small" films such as *Breaking Away* and *Eddie Coyle*. Which is, no doubt, how he would prefer it.

—Philip Kemp

YOSHIMURA, KOZABURO. (Also known as Kimisaburo Yoshimura). Japanese. Born in Shiga Prefecture, 9 September 1911. Educated at Nihon High School, Tokyo, graduated 1929. Married Tomoko Oouchi, 1940. Career: 1929—entered Shochiku-Kamata Studio, becomes assistant director to Yasujiro Shimazu; 1932—drafted into military; 1934—after return from service, offered direction of silent comedy *Sneaking*, film fails and is demoted to assistant director until 1939; during this period works for Shimazu, Heinosuke Gosho, Shiro Toyota, and Mikio Naruse; 1936—moves to newly-established Shochiku-Ofuna studios; 1939—resumes directing; 1940—career established with *The Story of Tank Commander Nishizumi*; 1944—drafted, sent to Thailand, serves in machine gun unit, then as information officer on general staff; 1945—repatriated, spends year in prison and repatriation camp; 1947—begins collaboration with scriptwriter Kaneto Shindo on *The Ball of the Anjo Family*; 1950—the two leave Shochiku, found independent production company Kindai Eiga Kyokai (Society of Modern Film), with producer Hisao Itoya, director Tengo Yamada, and actor Taiji Tonoyama; 1956—contracted by Daiei Studio; 1963—suffers serious illness; 1960s—begins directing for TV; 1972—has stomach operation; 1974—reemerges with independent production *Ragged Flag*. Recipient: Eiga Seikai-sha New Director's Prize, for *Danryo*, 1939; *Kinema Jumpo* Number One film, *Anjo-ke no bukokai*, 1947; Mainichi Director's Prize for *Itsureru seiso*, 1951; Shiju-Hosho Decoration, Japanese Government, 1976. Address: 4-3-37 Zushi, Zushi-City, Kanagawa, Japan.

Films (as director): 1934—*Nukiashi sashiashi (Sneaking)*; 1939—*Onna koso ie o momore (Women Defend the Home!, Women Should Stay at Home)*; *Yokina uramachi (Cheerful Alley, Gay Back Alley)*; *Asu no odoriko (Tomorrow's Dancers, Dancers of Tomorrow)*; *Gonin no kyodai (Five Brothers and Sisters)*; *Danryu (Warm Current)*; 1940—*Nishizumi sanshacho den (The Story of Tank Commander Nishizumi)*; 1941—*Hana (Flower)*; 1942—*Kancho mada shinazu (The Spy Has Not Yet Died, Yet Spies Haven't Died)* (+story); *Minami ni kaze (South Wind)*; *Zoko minami no kaze (South Wind: Sequel)*; 1943—*Laisen no zenya (The Night Before the War)*; *Tekki kushu (Enemy Air Attack, An Attack of the Enemy Planes)*; 1944—*Kessen (A Decisive Battle)*; 1947—*Zo o kutta renchu (The Fellows Who Ate the Elephant)*; *Anjo-ke no butokai (A Ball at the Anjo House, The Ball of the Anjo Family)*; 1948—*Yuwaku (Temptation, Seduction)*; *Waga shogai no kagayakeru hi (The Day Our Lives Shine, The Bright Day of My Life)*; 1949—*Shitto (Jealousy)*; *Mori no Ishimatsu (Ishimatsu of the Forest, Ishimatsu of Mori)*; *Mahiru no enbukyoku (Waltz at Noon)*; 1950—*Shunsetsu (Spring Snow)*; *Senka no hate (The Height of Battle, The End of Battle Fire)*; 1951—*Itsuwareru seiso (Clothes of Deception, Deceiving Costume)*; *Jiyu gakko (The School of Freedom, Free School)*; *Genji monogatari (A Tale of Genji)*; 1952—*Nishijin no shimai (Sisters of Nishijin)*; *Boryoku (Violence)*; 1953—*Senba-zuru (A Thousand Cranes)*; *Yokubo (Desire)*; *Yoake mae (Before the Dawn)*; 1954—*Ashizuri misaki (Cape Ashizuri)*; *Wakai hitotachi (Young People)*; 1955—"*Hanauri musume (The Flower Girl, The Girl Who Sells Flowers)*" episode of *Aisureba koso (If You Love Me, Because I Love)*; *Ginza no onna (Women of the Ginza)*; *Bijo to kairyu (The Beauty and the Dragon)*; 1956—*Totsugu hi (Day of Marriage, The Day to Wed)*; *Yoru no kawa (Night River, Undercurrent)*; *Yonjuhassai no teiko (48-Year-Old Rebel, Protest at 48 Years Old)*; 1957—*Osaka monogatari (An Osaka Story)*; *Yoru no cho (Night Butterflies, Butterfly of Night)*; *Chijo (On the Earth)*; 1958—*Hitotsubu no mugi (One Grain of Barley)*; *Yoru no sugao (The Naked Face of Night)*; 1959—*Denwa wa yugata ni naru (Telephone Rings in the Evening)*; *Kizoku no kaidan (Aristocrat's Stairs)*; 1960—"*Koi o wasureta onna (A Woman's Testament, The Woman Who Forgot Love)*" episode of *Jokei (Women's Scroll)*; *Onna no saka (Woman's Descent)*; 1961—*Konki (Marriage Time)*; *Onna no kunsho (Woman's Decoration)*; 1962—*Kazoku no jijo (A Night to Remember, Family's Situation)*; *Sono yo wa wasurenai (I Won't Forget That Night)*; 1963—"*Shayo nigo (Company's Business)*" episode of *Echizen take ningyo (Bamboo Doll of Echizen)*; 1966—*Kokoro no sanmyaku (The Heart of the Mountains)*; 1967—*Daraku suru onna (A Fallen Woman)*; 1968—*Nemureru bijo (Sleeping Beauty, The House of the Sleeping Virgins)*; *Atsui yoru (A Hot Night)*; 1971—*Amai himitsu (Sweet Secret)*; 1973—*Konketsuji Rika (Rika, the Mixed-Blood Girl)*; *Hamagure no komoriuta (Lullaby of Hamagure)*; 1974—*Ranru no hata (Ragged Flag)*.

Publications:

By YOSHIMURA:

Book—*Eiga no gijutsu to mikata* [Film Technique and How to Look at Films], 1952.

On YOSHIMURA:

Books—*Voices from the Japanese Cinema* by Joan Mellen, New York 1975; *The Waves at Genji's Door* by Joan Mellen, New York 1976; *The Japanese Film* by Joseph Anderson and Donald Richie, expanded edition, Princeton 1982.

*   *   *

Although Kozaburo Yoshimura's early work followed the drama and comedy conventions of the Shochiku Studio productions of the 1930s, he gradually proved himself an ambitious artist who broke away from these conventions through his varied selections of themes and subjects, and his bold exploration of styles. His technical maturity has been consistent over the years and through all genres, from the melodramatic *Warm Current* which first brought Yoshimura recognition, through the wartime production *The Story of Tank Commander Nishizumi* which successfully portrayed the decent, human side of the war hero with exciting action scenes, to the patriotic spy film *The Night Before the War Begins* which stylistically resembles an American suspense film.

The postwar liberation allowed him to employ more freely his favorite American film styles and techniques. Typical of this period is *The Ball of the Anjo Family*, which surprised the Japanese postwar audience not only with its fresh techniques, but also with its striking theme of the contrasts between the falling and emerging social classes of the time.

The challenges of the varied subjects of his subsequent films confirmed his energy and versatility, as in *The Bright Day of My Life*, which illustrated a flamingly passionate love, unusual in Japanese films, between a couple who had belonged to opposing political groups before the war. *Ishimatsu of Mori* is regarded as one of the first successful postwar films. From the familiar legend, Yoshimura made a satirical comedy which alludes critically to the contemporary gangster's mentality. *Deceiving Costume*, a postwar adaption of Mizoguchi's prewar masterpiece, *Sister of Gion*, demonstrated a similar emotional intensity and powerful social criticism through the life of geisha sisters. *The Beauty and the Dragon* is a new adaptation of a popular Kabuki play, made with the assistance of the innovative theater troupe, Zenshin-za.

Scenario writer Kaneto Shindo's collaboration with Yoshimura was indispensable to Yoshimura's success, from *The Ball of the Anjo Family* to *The Day to Wed*, during which time they produced 22 films together. When in 1950 Shochiku Studio subjected the pair to commercial pressures, they decided to establish an independent production company, Kindai Eiga Kyokai or Society of Modern Film. It enabled the two to pursue their artistic experimentation and thus produce many masterpieces which attracted critical attention.

Yoshimura became well known for literary adaptations—*A Tale of Genji*, *A Thousand Cranes*, *Before the Dawn*, *Sleeping Beauty*, and *Cape Ashizuri*—as well as for light comedy—*Free School*, about contemporary social life, *Desire*, *Young People*, and *One Grain of Barley*, among others. Particularly noteworthy is a series of films on the life of contemporary women using many of Daiei Studio's prime actresses, *Night River*, *Night Butterfly*, *Naked Face of Night*, etc.

He has continued his independent efforts, notably with funds raised by a local PTA, in making *Heart of the Mountains* and his most recent film, *Ragged Flag*, which powerfully depicts the life of a pioneering opponent of pollution in Japan in the early years of this century.

Yoshimura has consistently shown excellent story-developing skill which has won popular support for his films. His best films often contain social criticism, but at the same time do not preach, relying instead on the depiction of heightened emotions among the characters to successfully appeal to the audience.

—Kyoko Hirano

YUTKEVICH, SERGEI. Soviet Russian. Born Sergei Iosipovich Yutkevich in Kiev, 28 December 1904. Studied painting in Kiev and Moscow; took experimental direction course under K.A. Mardzhanov; joined Eisenstein Master Class at what became VGIK (Moscow Film School), 1923. Career: works as set designer, Foregger Theater; 1922—with Kozintsev and Trauberg founds Factory of the Eccentric Actor (FEKS), Leningrad; 1923—returns to Moscow, joins Meyerhold's workshop, works as set designer; 1925—joins Abram Room as set designer and assistant director on *The Traitor* and *Bed and Sofa*; also works as assistant director on the latter; 1926—assists Abram Room on *Traitor*; 1933—put in charge of training program for young directors; 1938—joins faculty of State Film Institute, Moscow; early 1940s—heads Soyuzdetfilm Studio, helps to improve children's films; 1945-46—works on *Light Over Russia*, suppressed for unknown reasons and not appearing in official filmographies; career suffers from being named an "internationalist" during period of artistic purges; 1967—supervises reconstruction of Eisenstein's *Bezhin Meadow*. Recipient: Red Banner of Labor, 1939; State Prize for *Yakov Sverdlov*, 1941; State Prize for *Molodost nashei strany*, 1947; International Prize and Diploma of Honor for Best Direction, Cannes Festival, 1954; Best Director, Cannes Festival, for *Othello*, 1956; People's Artist of the Soviet Union, 1962; Hero of Socialist Labor, 1974; Corresponding Member of the Academy of Fine Arts, German Democratic Republic.

Films (as director): *Daesh radio! (Give Us Radio!)*; 1928—*Kruzheva (Lace)* (+co-sc); 1929—*Chyorni parus (The Black Sail)*; 1931—*Zlatye gori (Golden Mountains)* (+co-sc); 1932—*Vstrechnyi (Counterplan)* (co-d with Ermler, +co-sc); 1934—*Ankara—serdche Turkiye (Ankara, Heart of Turkey)* (co-d); 1936—*Semero smelykh (The Bold 7)* (co-sc only); 1937—*Kak budet golosovat' izbiratel' (How the Elector Will Vote)*; *Shachtery (Miners)*; 1938—*Chelovek s ruzhyom (The Man with a Gun)*; 1940—*Yakov Sverdlov* (+co-sc); 1941—*Noviye rasskazy bravogo soldata Shveika (Schweik in the Concentration-Camp)*, *Eleksir bodrosti (Elixir of Courage)* and *Belaya vorona (The White Raven)* segments of *Boyevoye kinosbornik n.7 (Fighting Film Album No.7)*; 1943—*Noviye pokhozdeniya Shveika (New Adventures of Schweik)*; 1944—*Osvobozhdennaya Frantsei (Liberated France)*; 1945—*Zdravstvuy Moskva! (Greetings Moscow!)*, *Molodost nashei strany (Our Country's Youth)*; 1947—*Svet nad Rossiei (Light over Russia)*; 1948—*Tri vstrechi (3 Encounters)* (co-d); 1951—*Przhevalsky*; 1953—*Velikiy voin Albanii Skanderberg (The Great Warrior)*; 1955—*Otello (Othello)*; 1957—*Rasskazi o Lenine (Stories about Lenin)*; *Poet Iv Montan (Yves Montand Sings)* (co-d with Slutski); 1960—*Vstrecha s Frantsei (Meeting with France)*; 1962—*Banya (Bath)* (with Karanovich); 1963—*(Peace to Your House)*; 1964—*Lenin v Polshe (Lenin in Poland)*; 1967—*O samon chelovekhnom* (compilation film); 1969—*Siuzhet dliya nebolshogo rasskaza (Subject for a Short Story)*; 1973—*Poet na ekrane (Baryshnya i chuligan)* (for TV); *Ilyinskiye o Mayakovskom* (for TV); 1975—*Mayakovski smeyetsia (Mayakovski Laughs)*; 1981—*Lenin v Paridzhe (Lenin in Paris)*.

Publications:

By YUTKEVICH:

Books—*Le Cinéma soviétique*, with Dziga Vertov, edited by Marcel Lapierre, Anthologie du cinéma, Paris 1946; *Chelovek na ekrane* [Man on the Screen], Moscow 1947; *Chelovek na ekrane. Chetyre besedy o kinoiskusstve. Dnevnik rezhissera* [Man on Screen. Four Conversations About Film Art. Director's Diary], Moscow 1947; *La figura e l'arte di Charlie Chaplin*, with Eisenstein and others, 1949; *Kontrapunkt rezhizora* [Counterpoint of the Director], Moscow 1960; *Izbrannye, proizvedenea, vshestitomah* by Sergei Eisenstein, edited by Yutkevich, in 6 volumes, Moscow 1964—; *Eisenstein: risunki raznykh let*, edited by Yutkevich, Moscow 1968; *Shekspir i kino* [Shakespeare and Cinema], Moscow 1973; *Sergei Yutkevich*, Moscow 1974; *Kino—eto pravda 24 kadra v sekundu* [Film—Truth at 24 Frames Per Second], Moscow 1974; articles—"Lettre ouverte a Marcel Carné" in *Cinéma d'aujourd'hui et de demain*, Sovexportfilm, 1946; "My Way with Shakespeare" in *Films and Filming* (London), October 1957; "Cutting It to Style" in *Films and Filming* (London), March 1962; "Majakowski spottet", interview by S. Certok in *Film und Fernsehen* (Berlin), June 1974; "Iz opita na tvorčeskoto tridesetiletie" in *Kinoizkustvo* (Sofia), April 1974.

ZAMPA, LUIGI. Italian. Born in Rome, 2 January 1905. Educated in engineering; studied at Centro Sperimentale di Cinematografia, Rome. Career: 1928—quits studies to pursue career as actor and playwright; 1930-32—plays produced; 1933—directing debut with documentary *Risveglio di una città*; attends film school; 1939—collaborates on scripts for Max Neufeld, Mario Soldati, and Carlo Bragaglia; 1941—first feature film; 1946— *Vivere in pace* establishes reputation as leading neorealist. Recipient: Best Foreign Film, New York Film Critics, for *To Live in Peace*, 1947.

Films (as director): 1933—*Risveglio di una città*; (as scriptwriter): 1939—*Il capiano degli ussari*; *La danza dei milioni*; *Un mare di guai*; *Tutta per la donna*; *Manovre d'amore*; *Dora Nelson*; (as assistant director): *Mille lire al mese*; (as director and co-scriptwriter): 1941—*L'attore Scomparso*; *Fra' Diavolo*; 1942—*Signorinette*; *C'e sempre un ma...*; 1943—*L'abito Nero da sposa*; 1945—*Un Americano in vacanza (A Yank in Rome)*; 1946—*Vivere in pace (To Live in Peace)*; 1947—*L'onorevole Angelina (Angelina)*; 1948—*Anni difficili (Difficult Years)*; 1949—*Campane a Martello (Children of Change)*; 1950—*Cuori senza frontiere (The White Line)*; *E più facile che un cammello (His Last 12 Hours)*; 1951—*Signori in carrozza*; 1952—*Processo alla città (City on Trial)*; "Isa Miranda" episode of *Siamo donne (We the Women)*; 1953—*Anni facili (Easy Years)*; 1954—"La patente" episode of *Questa e la vita*; *La Romana (Woman of Rome)*; *L'arte di arrangiarsi*; 1955—*Ragazze d'oggi*; 1957—*La ragazza del Palio (The Love Specialist)*; ; 1958—*Ladro lui, ladro lei*; 1959—*Il magistrato (The Magistrate)*; 1960—*Il vigile*; 1962—*Gli anni ruggenti (Roaring Years)*; 1963—*Frenesia dell'estate*; 1965—*Una questione d'onore (A Question of Honor)*; 1966—"Il marito di Olga" episode of *I nostri mariti*; 1967—*Le dolci signori (Anyone Can Play)*; 1968—*Il medico della Mutua*; 1971—*Bello onesto emigrato Australia sposerebbe compaesana illibata (A Girl in Australia)*; 1973—*Bisturi: la mafia bianca*; 1975—*Gente di rispetto*; 1977—*Il mostro*; 1979—*Letti selvaggi*.

Publications:

By ZAMPA:

Book—*Il succeso*, novel, 1948; article—interview by George Bluestone in *Film Quarterly* (Berkeley), winter 1958.

On ZAMPA:

Book—*Luigi Zampa* by Domenico Meccoli, Rome n.d.; articles—by Gian Luigi Rondi in *Italian Cinema Today*, Rome 1950; colloquium in *Cinema* (Rome), 15 March 1954.

*   *   *

A journeyman director of the Italian cinema, Luigi Zampa specializes in comedy and satire. His ironic observations are always directed at specifically Italian situations and customs, but his complete control and understanding of these subjects renders them more universal and understandable than other directors' films that attempt to deal with more general themes. Unfortunately, film distributors have not often appreciated this fact; thus most of his work is scarcely known outside his native country. Zampa's mastery of comedy is based on two fundamental aspects: lively well-drawn characterizations and the ability to rapidly describe a situation. This craftsmanship can be seen, for example, in his 1971 film about an Italian who has emigrated to Australia a dozen years before but doesn't marry until he can save up the money to pay for the travel of an Italian mail-order bride. Alberto Sordi, as the protagonist, gives one of his finest performances as does Claudia Cardinale who plays the prostitute trying to be a virginal fiancée. Zampa here uses his typical framework of short introductory scenes, lasting but a few minutes, that quickly establish the characters and the social milieu in which they live.

Zampa is most famous for the films he directed during the period of neorealism when a much larger percentage of Italian films were receiving world-wide distribution. This also coincided with Zampa's close and fruitful collaboration with the satirical novelist Vitaliano Brancati, covering the years 1948 until the latter's death in 1954.

The 1941 *L'attore Scomparso*, set in a theater, and the 1942 *Signorinette*, a light comedy about female adolescents, had established Zampa as good box-office in Italy and his *Un Americano in vacanza*, a love story of an ex-GI and an Italian woman, was well-received in the States and in London when it was shown in March 1949. *Vivere in pace*, honored by the New York Critics Award for best film of 1947, as well as receiving awards in Italy and Brussels, remains one of Zampa's finest achievements. Set mainly in an Italian household during the war, it relies on the strength of the characterizations of the cautious uncle (Aldo Fabrizi), his hysterical wife (Ave Ninchi), the two prisoners-of-war given refuge by them (Gar Moore and John Kitzmiller) and the German officials who come to "visit." Stressing moral purpose, the film depicts the effects of war on the individual sensibility, the clash between whom one is told to think of as enemies and human understanding for those enemies, and the tension between conformism and fear on the one hand and progressivism and bravery on the other. Immediately after came *L'onorevole Angelina*, starring Anna Magnani (who won the Golden Lion at Venice for best actress), set in a poor neighborhood of Rome and dealing with personal and political responsibility. The next film began a trilogy of works beginning with the word "years" which cover long periods in the lives of a group of characters. *Anni difficili*, adapted by Brancati from one of his stories, relates 20 years of a Sicilian family's life during Fascism. It too received an award at the Venice festival but, due to its penetrating psychological study and audacious realism, it caused an outrage among political parties and came close to being banned in Italy. *Anni facili*, a satire of bureaucracy, is also set in Sicily, although filmed almost entirely in the studio. It too caused divided opinions between the political left who liked it and the right who didn't.

Gli anni ruggenti was liberally adapted from Gogol's *The Inspector General* in order to deal directly with Italian Fascism.

—Elaine Mancini

ZANUSSI, KRZYSZTOF. Polish. Born in Warsaw, 17 June 1939. Educated in physics, Warsaw University, 1955-59; Faculty of Philosophy, University of Cracow, 1959-62; directing course, State Film School, Lodz, graduated 1966. Career: 1955-59—attends lectures on film at the Institute of Arts of Polish Academy of Science while student at Warsaw University; makes films as member of student amateur film club; 1973—appointed to faculty of Lodz film school; named vice-president of Association of Polish Filmmakers; 1980—chosen by Pope John Paul II to make his film biography *From a Far Country*; following suppression of Solidarity labor movement in Poland, directs mainly in western Europe. Recipient: Best Film, Polish Film Critics, for *The Structure of Crystals*, 1970; State Award, Polish Minister of Culture and Arts, 1973.

Films (as director): 1958—*Droga do nieba (The Way to the Skies)* (amateur film in collaboration with Wincenty Ronisz); 1966—*Smierc prowincjala (The Death of a Provincial)* (short-diploma film); *Przemysl; Maria Dabrowska*; 1967—*Komputery (Computers)*; 1968—*Twarza w twarz (Face to Face)* (+co-sc—for TV); *Krzysztof Penderecki* (for TV); 1969—*Zaliczenie (An Examination, Pass Mark)* (+co-sc—for TV); (as feature director): *Struktura krsztalu (The Structure of Crystals)* (+co-sc); 1970—*Gory o zmierzchu (Mountains at Dusk)* (for TV); *Zycie rodzinne (Family Life)* (+sc); 1971—*Rola (Die Rolle)* (+sc—for West German TV); *Za sciana (Behind the Wall)* (+co-sc—for TV); 1972—*Hipoteza (Hypothesis)* (+sc—for TV); 1973—*Illuminacja (Illumination)* (+sc); 1974—*The Catamount Killing*; 1975—*Milosierdzie platne z gory (Nachtdienst, Night Duty)* (for TV); *Bilans kwartalny (A Woman's Decision)* (+sc); 1976—*Barwy ochronne (Camouflage)* (+sc); 1977—*Anatomie stunde (Lekcja anatomii, Anatomy Lesson)* (for TV); *Haus der Frauen (House of Women)*; *Penderecki, Lutoslawa*; *Brigitte Horney*; 1978—*Spirala (Spiral)* (+sc); 1979—*Wagen in der Nacht (Ways in the Night, Paths into the Night)* (+sc); 1980—*Constans (The Constant Factor)*; 1981—*Kontrakt (The Contract)* (+sc); *From a Far Country*; 1982—*Imperative*.

Role: 1978—as himself in *Amator (Camera Buff)* (Kieslowski).

Publications:

By ZANUSSI:

Articles—interview by J. Demeure and H. Niogret in *Positif* (Paris), May 1973; "Réfléchir, en moraliste, à une deuxième phase révolutionnaire", interview by F. Dufour in *Cinéma* (Paris), April 1973; "Illumination", interview by M. Martin in *Ecran* (Paris), December 1974; "The Ethics of Being Krzysztof Zanussi", interview by S. Murray in *Cinema Papers* (Melbourne), September/October 1976; "*La Part du feu*: Ebauche de script pour un projet de long métrage" in *Positif* (Paris), December/January 1977/78; "Opcja przekorna: za świadomościa", interview by T. Krzemień in *Kino* (Warsaw), February 1977; interview by J. Delmas and G. Gervais in *Jeune Cinéma* (Paris),

February 1978; interview by F. Audé and others in *Positif* (Paris), December 1980; interview by J.-C. Bonnet and P. Carcassonne in *Cinématographe* (Paris), November 1980; "Zanussi ou le refus du camouflage", interview by G. Haustrate in *Cinéma* (Paris), October 1980; "L'Oeuvre de Zanussi: le refus de la compromission", interview by René Predal in *Jeune Cinéma* (Paris), November 1980; "Z dalekiego kraju—czyli stad", interview by M. Malatyńska in *Kino* (Warsaw), March 1981; "The Workings of a Pure Heart", interview by J. Weiss in *Cineaste* (New York), v.11, no.2, 1981.

On ZANUSSI:

Articles—"Krzysztof Zanussi und sein Film *Illumination*" by J. John in *Film und Fernsehen* (Berlin), December 1973; "The Cinema of Krzysztof Zanussi" by M. Boleslaw in *Film Quarterly* (Berkeley), spring 1973; "Krzysztof Zanussi: l'ancien, le nouveau et le temps présent" by J. Demeure in *Positif* (Paris), May 1973; "Zanussiego ćwiczenia z życia" by M. Hopfinger in *Kino* (Warsaw), January 1973; "Pologne: Wajda et Zanussi" by J. Plazewski in *Ecran* (Paris), April 1975; "Krzysztof Zanussi" in *International Film Guide 1976*, London 1975; special section by A. Tassone and others in *Positif* (Paris), December 1979; "Zanussi, un reflexivo en busca de lo vital" by L. Elbert in *Cinemateca revista* (Andes), June 1980; "Made in Poland: The Metaphysical Cinema of Krzysztof Zanussi" by Peter Cowie in *Film Comment* (New York), September/October 1980; "Les Constantes de Krzysztof Zanussi", special section by M. Martin and others in *Image et son* (Paris), September 1980.

*   *   *

The cinema of Krzysztof Zanussi explores a continuum of conflict ranging from the individual and interpersonal to the larger social order. He explores the relationship of the individual's conscience to society's norms of morality. Appearing as himself in Krzysztof Kieslowski's *Camera Buff*, Zanussi says that he feels an obligation to question why the corrupt manipulators are the survivors. His is a provocative, cerebral cinema, objectifying its characters through both attention to detail and cool observation of the stages of conflict. During this process Zanussi demands the intellectual participation of his audience, and ultimately its response. The spectator should attain the level of self-awareness that his protagonists reach.

Zanussi has worked chiefly under a system of government subsidy in his native Poland. He has headed one of the three Polish film units. Active in Solidarity, he has been directing mostly abroad since its demise. West German television has produced many of these non-Polish films, but they are still subject to Polish government approval. His films have therefore occupied a space between individual self-expression and government tolerance. Prior self-censorship has been a factor in both his message and the discourse which conveys it. No clear separation exists between the private world of Zanussi the artist-intellectual and the public realm in which he operates.

Three major types of conflicts permeate the films. The first is between determinism and free will (often clouded by chance). He elaborates this as the bridgeable gap between empiricism (rational analysis) and Catholicism (grace) in, for example, *Illumination*, *The Constant Factor*, and *Imperative*. Zanussi's background in physics and philosophy strongly influences these films. Conflict between the individual and the corruption of (contemporary Polish) society occurs in *Camouflage*, *The Constant Factor*, and *Contract*. Zanussi masks the conflict in *Ways in the Night*, which presents the dilemma of an intelligent, sensitive young German officer who must uphold the policies of the National Socialists. The third major opposition is between the individual's self-awareness and the invisible (yet pervasive) pressures of the immediate social milieu; this is strongest in *Spiral* and *The Contract*.

From a Far Country, his biography of the Polish Pope John Paul II, is an important key to understanding Zanussi's world view. In this film no separation exists between the actions of the individual and the larger network of social forces in which he moves. The dichotomy of free will and determinism underlies the entire project.

Although Zanussi sets his films in a precise historical context, he does explore some of the issues that have been universally debated by artists and intellectuals for many centuries. What distinguishes him as a filmmaker is his particular deployment of the technology of the cinema as a vehicle for his thematic concerns. His orchestration is meticulous. *Spiral* exemplifies the plight of the solitary individual living disharmoniously with himself and those around him. Zanussi follows the tortured protagonist with a jerky handheld camera through the maze of rooms and characters in a ski resort. In *Family Life* an individual in conflict with his family must resolve his dilemma, which will otherwise haunt him in his interaction with the larger social order. He introduces the protagonist through a carefully plotted series of zooms, pans, and tilts, contextualizing the different spheres of conflict. In *Contract* Zanussi adds both an aural and a visual dimension to the conflict between the son and his family. The handheld camera follows his attempt to burn down the family home. Zanussi intercuts this obsessive behavior with the repetitive sound of bells from a sleigh which carries his family. At the end of *The Constant Factor*, a stone falls in slow motion from where the protagonist, who has fallen from occupational grace because of his incorruptibility, is cleaning windows. It strikes a child playing below; chance plays a hand in a universe beyond the individual's control. Zanussi then cuts to the majestic, desolate mountains, as if to say there is no rational method for solving the existential dilemma.

In all of his films these moments of cinematic self-consciousness alternate with long takes of intellectual debate and questioning. During these probing conversations Zanussi is least obtrusive in the application of cinematic techniques. The irony is that during these verbal conflicts, the ideological imprint of the director is most overt.

—Elliott Feinstein

ZECCA, FERDINAND. French. Born in Paris, 1864. Career: 1896—hired by Maison Pathé to record phonograph cylinders; specializes in imitations of religious sermons, official speeches, and monologues of all sorts; begins making films for Pathé; 1899—begins appearing in films, interpreting scenes recorded on cylinders, to make "talking" films; makes first film *Le Muet mélomane*; 1900—engaged by Charles Pathé, begins working at Studio de Vincennes; performs functions of director, scenic artist, scenarist, and actor; imitates films of Méliès, and Englishman Paul Smith; 1907—collaborates in creation of the *Pathé Journal*, documentary series; 1910—becomes Director General of Production; 1913—sent to U.S. to supervise Pathé Exchange in New Jersey; 1914—supervises construction of Pathé studios at Fort Lee; 1920—returns to France, becomes artistic director of Pathé Baby and Pathé Rural, companies surviving Pathé corporate reorganization; 1939—retires. Died in Paris, 1947.

Films (as director and in other capacities—partial list of several hundred films): 1899—*Le Muet mélomane*; 1900—*Le Mégère récalcitrante*; *La Loupe de gran'maman*; *Comment Fabien devient architecte*; *Drame au fond de la mer*; 1901—*Les Sept Chateaux du diable*; *La Baignade impossible*; *Tempête dans une chambre à coucher*; *A la conquête de l'air*; *Idylle aous un tunnel*; *L'Assassinat de McKinley*; *Quo Vadis*; *Histoire d'une crime*; *L'agent plongeur*; *Rêve et réalité*; *Discussion politique*; *L'illusioniste mondain*; *Chagrin d'amour* (co-d); *Le Supplice de Tantale*; *Une Demande en mariage mal engagée* (co-d); *Le Salut de Dranem* (co-d); 1902—*Les Victimes de l'alcoolisme* (co-d); *L'Affaire Dreyfus*; *L'Amour à tous les étages*; *Ce que je vois dans mon telescope*; *Catastrophe de la Martinique*; *Ali Baba et les 40 voleurs*; 1903—*La Vie d'un joueur*; *Don Quichotte*; *Le Chat botte*; 1904-05—*La Grève*; *Au pays noir*; *Pour l'honneur d'un pére*; *Roman d'amour*; *Le Rêve dans la lune*; 1905—*La Passion*; 1907—*Metempsychose*; *Un Drame à Venise* (co-d); *La Legende de Polichinelle*; 1910—co-directs with Leprince series *Scenes de la vie cruelle*.

ZEFFIRELLI, FRANCO. Italian. Born Gianfranco Corsi in Florence, 12 February 1923. Educated in architecture, University of Florence; at Accademia di Belle Arti, Florence. Career: 1945—begins designing for theater; 1946—designs first opera, *Livietta e Tracolle*; 1947—directs Anouilh's *Eurydice*; makes only film acting appearance in Zampa's *Angelina*; 1948—assistant director on Visconti's *La terra trema*; (also on *Bellissima* and *Senso* in 1951 and 1954); 1949-52—works as stage designer with Visconti on *A Streetcar Named Desire*, *Troilus and Cressida*, and *The Three Sisters*; 1953—opera directing debut with *La Cenerentola*, La Scala, Milan; subsequently stages series of famous opera productions; also becomes well-known for Shakespearian productions.

Films (as director): 1957—*Camping* (+co-sc); 1966—*The Taming of the Shrew* (+co-sc); 1968—*Romeo and Juliet* (+co-sc); 1972—*Fratello sole sorella luna (Brother Sun, Sister Moon)* (+co-sc); 1977—*Gesú di Nazareth (Jesus of Nazareth)* (+co-sc); 1979—*The Champ*; 1981—*Endless Love*; 1982—*La Traviata*.

Publications:

By ZEFFIRELLI:

Book—*Jesus*, Paris and Montreal 1978; articles—interview by B.J. Demby in *Filmmakers Newsletter* (Ward Hill, Mass.), September 1973; "Versatility", interview by Gordon Gow in *Films and Filming* (London), April 1973; "Knowing, Feeling, Understanding, then Expression", interview by A. Stuart in *Films and Filming* (London), August 1979.

On ZEFFIRELLI:

Articles—"*The Taming of the Shrew*" by John Lane in *Films and Filming* (London), October 1966; "I Know My Romeo and Juliet" by P. Devlin in *Vogue* (New York), 1 April 1968; "The Champ: Round 2" by D. Chase in *American Film* (Washington, D.C.), July/August 1978; "The Film that Lived in Franco Zeffirelli's Memory for 45 Years" by T. Buckley in *The New York Times*, 30 March 1979.

*   *   *

Franco Zeffirelli imbues his theater, opera and film productions with a dazzling array of baroque imagery, visual pyrotechnics, sumptous sets and costumes, and overt eroticism. Of his seven major motion pictures, nearly all are adaptions of classical derivation set in another era. To many of films are hollow, banal, and superfluous romantic exercises, but Zeffirelli defends his love of the past and tradition by saying: "We have no guarantee for the present or the future. Therefore the only choice is to go back to the past and respect traditions. I have been a pioneer in this line of thinking, and the results have proven me right.... The reason I am box-office everywhere is that I am an enlightened conservative continuing the discourse of our grandfathers and fathers, renovating texts but never betraying them."

After studying architecture at the University of Florence, Zeffirelli took up acting. Luchino Visconti saw him in a production of Jean Cocteau's *Les Parents terribles* and hired him to act in two stage productions—*Eurydice* by Jean Anouilh and *Crime and Punishment* by Dostoevsky. Zeffirelli also involved himself in designing sets and costumes for Visconti's stage presentations and appeared in the film *L'onorevole Angelina*, directed by Luigi Zampa and starring Anna Magnani. As a result of that film he was offered a seven-year acting contract at RKO-Radio by screenwriter Helen Deutsch but turned it down to become Visconti's assistant on three films—*La terra trema*, *Bellissima*, and *Senso*.

His natural talent at set and costumes design and his love of opera provided an obvious segue into staging opera productions. These productions gained a reputation for opulence and for the focusing of attention on the lead female singers. Zeffirelli says he "adores fun, fantasy and women," and he emphasized these elements in his operas. His most famous and successful association in opera was with the volatile Maria Callas for whom he staged productions of *La Traviata*, *Lucia de Lammermoor*, *Norma*, and *Tosca*.

He also made opera history by staging the opening production for the new Metropolitan Opera in 1966. The opera was Samuel Barber's *Antony and Cleopatra* starring Leontyne Price; it was ambivalently received by critics and Zeffirelli says he hates it because it did not evolve the way he had envisioned.

His lengthy apprenticeship in the various theatrical arts earned Zeffirelli a reputation as a Renaissance man of sorts. He turned to feature film directing in 1967 bringing his romanticized traditionalism to *The Taming of the Shrew* starring Elizabeth Taylor and Richard Burton. While unarguably a bowdlerization of Shakespeare, its slapstick and boisterous merriment was engaging.

Romeo and Juliet was another matter entirely. Here the very heart of Shakespeare was replaced with Romeo and Juliet as flower children. It was an unabashed combination of theatricality, nude love scenes, and a Mercutio which Zeffirelli describes as "a self-portrait of Shakespeare himself as a homosexual." The film was tremendously popular with the young movie-going audience and received Academy Awards for cinematography and costume design.

Fratello sole sorella lune (Brother Sun Sister Moon) was also aimed at the young, this time the Jesus freaks, but this outrageous portrait of St. Francis of Assisi was a complete flop.

Zeffirelli's 1978 Easter television presentation, *Jesus of Nazareth*, employed a star-studded cast and surprised many serious critics with its sensitivity and restraint. This was not the case, however, with his syrupy diminishing of *The Champ*, a sentimental classic which should never have been updated.

Zeffirelli disavows the explicitly erotic *Endless Love*, a vehicle for Brooke Shields, which, he says, was a beautiful story of the tragedy of two families in its original three-hour-version. He labels the truncated version "trash" and vows he is finished with

trying to capture the young audience. Appropriately, his latest motion picture was the opulent and admirably cinematic presentation of *La Traviata* and he plans to film more operas in the future.

Zeffirelli defends his extravagant approach to filmmaking by saying, "I am a flag-bearer of the crusade against boredom, bad taste and stupidity in the theater," but he is still the target of critical barbs such as those from the *Time* magazine reviewer who stated he was "a director in need of a director."

—Ronald Bowers

ZEMAN, KAREL. Czech. Born in Ostroměř, 3 November 1910. Career: 1930-36—works in France as poster designer, window dresser, artist with various advertising agencies; 1943—becomes animator in Baťa Film Studio at Zlín (now Gottwaldov); assistant director to Hermína Týrlová; 1945—becomes director, organizer of 2nd production group for puppet films at Gottwaldov Film Studio; 1955—*A Journey into Primeval Times* establishes international reputation. Recipient: National Artist, Order of the Republic, Order of Labor, Order of February Victory; twice received Klement Gottwald State Prize. Address: 761 79 Gottwaldov—Kudlov, Ceskoslovensko.

Films (as director of puppet films unless otherwise noted): 1946—*Vánoční (The Christmas Dream)* (co-d, +co-sc, comb. puppet and feature); *Podkova pro štěstí (A Horseshoe for Luck)* (+sc, art d); *Křeček (The Hamster)* (+sc, art d); 1947—*Pan Prokouk úřaduje (Mr. Prokouk in the Office)* (+sc, art d); *Pan Prokouk v pokušení (Mr. Prokouk in Temptation)* (+sc, art d); *Brigády (Mr. Prokouk Leaves for Volunteer Work)* (+sc, art d); 1948—*Pan Prokouk filmuje (Mr. Prokouk is Filming)* (+sc, art d); *Pan Prokouk vynálezcem (Mr. Prokouk, the Inventor)* (+sc, art d); 1949—*Inspirace (Inspiration)* (+sc); 1950—*Král Lávra (King Lavra)* (+sc, art d); 1952—*Poklad Ptačího ostrova (The Treasure of Bird Island)* (+sc, art d); 1955—*Cesta do pravěku (A Journey into Prehistory, A Journey into Primeval Times)* (+co-sc, art d, "trick-film"); *Strakonický dudák (The Piper of Strakonice)* (co-special effects only); *Cerný démant (The Black Diamond)* (sc, art d only); *Pan Prokouk, přítel zvířátek (Mr. Prokouk, the Animal Lover)* (+sc, art d); 1957—*Pan Prokouk detektivem (Mr. Prokouk, the Detective)* (sc only); 1958—*Vynález zkázy (An Invention for Destruction)* (+co-sc, art d, "trick-film"); *Pan Prokouk akrobat (Mr. Prokouk, the Acrobat)* (sc, art d only); 1961—*Baron Prášil (Baron Munchhausen)* (+sc, co-art d, "trick-film"); 1964—*Bláznova kronika (A Jester's Tale)* (+sc, co-art d); 1966—*Ukradená vzducholod (The Stolen Airship)* (+co-sc, art d, "trick-film"); 1970—*Na kometě (On the Comet)* (+co-sc, art d, "trick-film"); 1972—*Pan Prokouk hodinářem (Mr. Prokouk, the Watchmaker)* (sc, art d only); (as director of paper-cut animations): 1974—*Pohádky tisíce a jedné noci (A Thousand and One Nights)* (+sc, co-art d); 1977—*Carodějuv učen (Krabat)* (+sc, co-art d); 1980—*Pohádka o Honzíkovi a Mařence (The Tale of John and Mary)* (+sc, co-art d).

Publications:

By ZEMAN:

Articles—"Comment j'ai tourné *Une Invention diabolique*" in *Image et son* (Paris), November 1959; interview by R. Lethem in *Midi-Minuit fantastique* (Paris), December/January 1966/67.

On ZEMAN:

Books—*Karel Zeman* by Marie Benešová, Prague 1968; *Karel Zeman* (in French), Ceskoslovensky Filmexport, Prague 1968; *Karel Zeman* by J. Hořejši, Prague 1970; *Fantastičeskij kinomir Karela Zemana* by Sergei Asenin, Moscow 1979; articles— "Aventures fantastiques" by Michel Delahaye in *Cinéma 59* (Paris), no.38, 1959; "Karel Zeman ou L'Impossible n'est pas tchèque" by Marcel Martin in *Cinéma 59* (Paris), no.34, 1959; "Le Diabolique Karel Zeman" by P.-L. Thirard in *Les Lettres françaises* (Paris), 15 January 1959; "Putting on a Style" by Konradova Libuse in *Films and Filming* (London), June 1961; "Le Baron de Crac rencontre le mage Zeman" by P. Philippe in *Les Lettres françaises* (Paris), 26 April 1962; "The Czechoslovak Animated Film" by Harriet Polt in *Film Quarterly* (Berkeley), spring 1964; "Karel Zeman ce nouveau Méliès" by Marie Benešová in *Jeune Cinéma* (Paris), December/January 1964/65; "Karel Zeman—Puvab chlapecké romantiky", in 3 parts, by J. Hrbas in *Film a doba* (Prague), January, February and March 1974; "Odpovědnost umělcova—odpovědnost k umělci" by J. Kliment in *Film a doba* (Prague), October 1974; "Zlínští po osvobození" by Jaroslav Boček in *Panoráma* (Prague), no.3, 1978; "Zápas o tvar" by M. Benešová in *Film a Doba* (Prague), December 1980; film—*Kouzelný svět Karla Zemana (Magic World of Karel Zeman)* directed by Zdeněk Rozkopal, 1962.

stories, "that enchantment from naiveté, poetry, and geniality of Verne's novels that anticipated technical discoveries at the end of the century" (M. Benešová). In a perfect form he joined the techniques of the cartoon, animated, and live-action film and created a film in which actor, cartoon figure, structure, and scenery are a part of the graphic style. With this work Zeman revived and refined the forgotten Mèliés mode of filmmaking and created his own style—that of the graphic special-effects film. Encouraged by the film's world-wide success, Zeman made another in the same style. This time he chose Bürger's novel *Baron Prášil (Baron Munchhausen)*. Here, too, the graphic design is based on the original illustrations for the novel. Unlike its predecessor, however, this film was devoted more to the acting, while the graphic aspect was enriched through the emotive use of color. In subsequent films of this tendency the live-action component began to predominate.

In the 1970s he returned to the animated film and experimented with three-dimensional technique. He filmed folk tales for children. Along with Jiří Trnka and Hermína Týlová, Karel Zeman is co-creator of the Czech animated film. The outstanding features of his talent are technical ingenuity and an experimental searching, which have led him to the graphic special-effects film. His supreme work *Vynález zkázy (An Invention for Destruction)* is a unique landmark of world cinematography. It has revived and refined the forgotten Méliès tradition.

—Vladimír Opěla

* * *

After 1945 Karel Zeman, Hermína Týlová's assistant, began independent work with a piece promoting the salvaging of old material, *Podkova pro štěstí (A Horseshoe for Luck)*. Everyone in the studio was surprised at the positive response. The main animated character in the film, Mr. Prokouk, a sort of indifferent citizen with petty bourgeois traits, enjoyed tremendous popularity. Thus there emerged over the course of two years a series of five cartoons that respond to the needs of the time, nimble, tendentious grotesques with rapid-fire gags and Mr. Prokouk in the leading role. Zeman conceived the theme and wrote the script, and worked as graphic artist, animator, and director. In complete contrast to the preceding work, he then hastily produced a remarkable piece, a cinamatic poem devoted to the work of Czech glassmakers in which he brought to life the fragile beauty of figures of blown glass. *Inspirace (Inspiration)* possesses the beauty of a perfect work of art and is one of the pinnacles of his creation. Here, Zeman demonstrated great technical resourcefulness and an ability to experiment. The folk tale *Poklad Ptačího ostrova (The Treasure of Bird Island)*, an evening-long animated film with a combination of flat and three-dimensional figures and an artistic form inspired by Persian miniatures was intended for children. Also made for children was his next film, *Cesta do pravěku (A Journey into Prehistory)*. This is the story of four boys sailing against the current of time and encountering on their journey the natural world of past geological eras. The film's creative form gives it a special place: it is a popular science film, a scientific fantasy film, and combines animation, special effects, and live action. Here again, Zeman showed his abilities as an experimenter.

While in *Cesta do pravěku* Zeman attempted to reconstruct a world that once existed, in his new work *Vynález zkázy (An Invention for Destruction)*, based on Jules Verne's novel *Face au drapeau*, he creates a new world inspired by the illustrations that accompanied the first editions of Verne's novels. With considerable grace, Zeman attained in this film the magic of the old Verne

ZETTERLING, MAI. Swedish. Born in Västeras, 24 May 1925. Educated at Royal Dramatic Theater School, Stockholm, 1942-45. Married actor Tutte Lemkow (divorced); son and daughter; married writer David Hughes. Career: stage debut at age 16 in Per Lagerkvist play at Blanche Theater; 1944—appears in Alf Sjöberg's *Torment*, attracting international attention; 1945-47—in company of Royal Dramatic Theater, Stockholm; 1946—invited to star in Relph and Dearden's *Frieda* in Britain; 1960—begins collaborating on TV documentaries with husband David Hughes. Recipient: Golden Lion, Venice Festival, for *The War Game*, 1963.

Films (as director of documentary shorts): 1960—*The Polite Invasion* (for BBC TV); 1961—*Lords of Little Egypt* (for BBC TV); *The War Game* (+pr); 1962—*The Prosperity Race* (for BBC TV); 1963—*The Do-It-Yourself Democracy* (for BBC TV); (as co-director, with David Hughes, of feature-length films): 1964—*Alskande par (Loving Couples)*; 1966—*Nattlek (Night Games)*; 1967—*Doktor Glas*; 1968—*Flickorna (The Girls)*; 1971—*Vincent the Dutchman* (+pr—documentary); 1973—"The Strongest" episode of *Visions of 8*; (as director): 1976—*We har manje namn (We Have Many Names)* (+ed, ro); 1977—*Stockholm* (+ro—for Canadian TV); 1978—*The Rain's Hat* (+ed—for TV); 1982—*Scrubbers* (+co-sc).

Roles: 1941—*Lasse-Maja* (Olsson); 1943—*Jag drapte* (Molander); 1944—*Hets (Torment, Frenzy)* (Sjöberg); *Prins Gustaf* (Bauman); 1946—*Iris och Lojtnantshjarta (Iris and the Lieutenant)* (Sjöberg); *Frieda* (Relph); *Driver dagg faller Regn (Sunshine Follows Rain)*; 1948—*Musik i morker* (Bergman); *Nu borjar livet* (Molander); *Quartet* (Smart and others); *The Bad*

Lord Byron (MacDonald); *Hildegard*; 1949—*Portrait from Life (The Girl in the Painting)* (Fisher); *The Romantic Age* (Gréville); *The Lost People* (Knowless); 1950—*Blackmailed* (Marc Allégret); *The Ringer* (Hamilton); 1952—*The Tall Headlines (The Frightened Bride)* (Young); 1953—*The Desperate Moment* (Bennett); *Knock on Wood* (Frank and Panama); 1954—*Prize of Gold* (Robson); *Dance Little Lady* (Guest); 1956—"Ett dockhem (A Doll's House)" episode of *Giftas* (Henriksson); *Abandon Ship (7 Waves Away)* (Sale); 1957—*The Truth About Women* (Box); 1958—*Lek pa regnbagen* (Kjellgren); 1959—*Jet Storm* (Endfield); *Faces in the Dark* (Eady); 1960—*Picadilly Third Stop* (Rilla); *Offbeat* (Owen); 1961—*Only 2 Can Play* (Gilliat); 1962—*The Main Attraction* (Petrie); *The Man Who Finally Died* (Lawrence); 1963—*The Bay of St. Michel* (Ainsworth); 1965—*The Vine Bridge* (Nykvist).

Publications:

By ZETTERLING:

Book—*Bird of Passage*, New York 1976; articles—"Some Notes on Acting" in *Sight and Sound* (London), October/December 1951; "Mai Zetterling at the Olympic Games", interview in *American Cinematographer* (Los Angeles), November 1972.

On ZETTERLING:

Book—*Film in Sweden, the New Directors* by Stig Bjorkman, London 1979; articles—"Meeting with Mai Zetterling" in *Cahiers du Cinema in English* (New York), December 1966; "Notes on Women Directors" by J. Pyros in *Take One* (Montreal), November/December 1970; "Mai is Behind the Camera Now" by C. McGregor in *The New York Times*, 30 April 1972; "Hiding it Under a Bushel: Free Fall" by D. Elley in *Films and Filming* (London), April 1974.

*   *   *

Mai Zetterling's career as a filmmaker stemmed from her disillusionment with acting. Trained at Stockholm's Royal Dramatic Theater, Zetterling debuted on stage and screen in 1941. She considered the film *Torment* her best acting achievement. She worked in British theater, enacting roles from Chekhov, Anouilh, and Ibsen plays, and in British films. After one part in a Hollywood film, *Knock on Wood* with Danny Kaye, she spurned contract offers and returned home.

With her husband, David Hughes, she made several documentaries in the 1960s dealing with political issues. Zetterling's feature films depict the social status and psyche of women, reflecting her feminist concerns. The uncompromising honesty of perception and technical virtuosity in her films correspond to the pervasive and dominant themes of loneliness and obsession. Zetterling says: "I want very strongly to do things I believe in. I can't do jobs for the money. I just can't do it."

In 1960, Roger Moorfoot of the BBC financed her idea for a film on the immigration of Swedes to Lapland, *The Polite Invasion*. Three more followed: *The Lords of Little Egypt* depicted the gypsies at Saintes-Maries-de-la-Mer; her view of Swedish affluence in *The Prosperity Race* was not appreciated in Stockholm; and *Do-It-Yourself Democracy* commented on Icelandic society and government. Her first independent effort was the 15-minute anti-war film *The War Game*, in which two boys

tussle for possession of a toy gun.

Her first feature film, *Loving Couples* was based on the fifth volume of Swedish author Agnes von Krusenstjerna's seven-volume novel, *The Misses von Pahlen*. Zetterling wrote the script in one year, with sketches of each shot to indicate camera positions. In it, three expectant mothers in a Stockholm hospital recall their lives in the moment of, and then beyond, the births of their babies. Critic Derek Elley suggests that Zetterling developed her theories and themes of film in *Loving Couples*, and rarely deviated from them in later works. She employs elaborate time lines as well as flashbacks, which she uses often and well, intertwining them one within another. Her films peak emotionally in scenes of parties and social gatherings. Her films are cohesive compositions, with a literary base, filmed in the stark contrasts of black to white, with a range of grays intervening. Zetterling's scenes of sexual behavior are integral to her themes of loneliness and obsession. *Loving Couples* exemplifies these characteristics.

Night Games, derived from Zetterling's novel with the same title, was banned from the Venice Film Festival. The critics who saw it were angered by the Marxist and Freudian elements in it; shocked by scenes of vomiting, masturbation, and childbirth. Based on Hjalmar Soderberg's 1905 novel, her next film, *Doktor Glas*, records the haunted love of a young physican for a pastor's wife. Even though the wife does not respond to the physician's erotic overtures, he administers a lethal drug to the pastor. It is Zetterling's grimmest study of loneliness, as Derek Elley observes, and her most pessimistic film, told in one extended flashback, "a far cry from *Night Games*." Stanley Kauffmann notes that the film takes place in Doctor Glas's mind. But the film's "irony is familiar and its final impact small." In Vincent Canby's view *Doktor Glas* was "technically good, handsomely photographed...totally devoid of passion."

She returned to a strongly feminist story in *Flickorno* and, as in *Loving Couples*, it contains three female roles of equal weight. In *Flickorna* three actresses perform *Lysistrata* on tour, acting out the views of the play in their private lives. Some critics reacted negatively finding it self-indulgent, a mix of Greek comedy and soap opera, with heavy symbolism and confusing time structures. Other critics liked the various forms of humor effectively employed, and the arresting imagery. Marjorie Rosen called it "a rich, exciting, political work."

In 1971, Zetterling filmed a documentary in color about Vincent Van Gogh. Titled *Vincent the Dutchman*, it was shown on American and British television. David Wolper then asked her to film any phase of the 1972 Olympics she chose; she filmed the weightlifting sequence, "The Strongest" for *Visions of Eight*.

In the 1970s, Zetterling published three novels, pursuing creative tracks other than filmmaking. She also continued making documentaries: one on Stan Smith, tennis champion, one dealing with Stockholm, another on marriage customs. A seven-hour adaptation for French television of Simone de Beauvior's *The Second Sex* is her most recent effort, and she plans a second film on Iceland in the future. Zetterling re-asserts that whatever she films, "It will be something I believe in."

—Louise Heck-Rabi

ZINNEMANN, FRED. Austrian/American. Born in Vienna, 29 April 1907. Educated in law, University of Vienna, degree 1927; studied one year at the Ecole Technique de Photographie et Cinématographie, Paris. Career: works as assistant cameraman in Paris and Berlin; 1928—joins Robert Siodmak, with Bily Wilder and Eugen Schüfftan, in making *Menschen am Sonntag*; 1929—moves to Hollywood; works as assistant cameraman and cutter for Berthold Viertel; 1931—accompanies Robert Flaherty to Berlin to work on unrealized documentary project; 1934-35—works in Mexico with Paul Strand on *Los Redes (The Wave)*; 1937—hired by MGM to direct short subjects. Recipient: Short Subject Academy Award for *That Mothers Might Live*, 1938; Short Documentary Academy Award for *Benjy*, 1951; Best Direction, New York Film Critics, for *High Noon*, 1952; Best Directing Academy Award for *From Here to Eternity*, 1953; Best Direction, New York Film Critics, for *From Here to Eternity*, 1953; Director Award, Directors Guild of America, for *From Here to Eternity*, 1953; Best Direction, New York Film Critics, for *The Nun's Story*, 1959; Best Directing Academy Award for *A Man for All Seasons*, 1966; Best Direction, New York Film Critics, for *A Man for All Seasons*, 1966; Director Award, Directors Guild of America, for *A Man for All Seasons*, 1966. Agent: Stan Kamen, William Morris Agency, Beverly Hills, California.

Films (as assistant cameraman): 1927—*La Marche des machines* (Deslaw); 1929—*Ich küsse Ihre Hand, Madame* (Land); *Sprengbagger 1010* (Achaz-Duisberg); *Menschen am Sonntag (People on Sunday)* (Siodmak); (as assistant director to Berthold Viertel): 1930—*Man Trouble*; 1931—*The Spy*; 1932—*The Wiser Sex*; *The Man from Yesterday*; (as assistant to Busby Berkeley): *The Kid from Spain*; (as director): 1934-35—*Los Redes (The Wave)*; (as director of short subjects at MGM): 1938—*A Friend Indeed*; *The Story of Dr. Carver*; *That Mothers Might Live*; *Tracking the Sleeping Death*; *They Live Again*; 1939—*Weather Wizards*; *While America Sleeps*; *Help Wanted!*; *One Against the World*; *The Ash Can Fleet*; *Forgotten Victory*; 1940—*The Old South*; *Stuffie*; *The Way in the Wilderness*; *The Great Meddler*; 1941—*Forbidden Passage*; *Your Last Act*; 1942—*The Lady or the Tiger?*; (as feature director): *The Kid Glove Killer*; *Eyes in the Night*; 1944—*The Seventh Cross*; 1945—*Little Mr. Jim*; 1946—*My Brother Talks to Horses*; 1947—*The Search*; 1948—*Act of Violence*; 1950—*The Men*; 1951—*Teresa*; *Benjy* (short); 1952—*High Noon*; *The Member of the Wedding*; 1953—*From Here to Eternity*; 1955—*Oklahoma*; 1957—*A Hatful of Rain*; 1958—*The Nun's Story*; (as producer and director): 1960—*The Sundowners*; 1963—*Behold a Pale Horse*; 1966—*A Man for All Seasons*; 1973—*The Day of the Jackal*; 1977—*Julia*; 1982—*Five Days One Summer*.

Role: 1930—bit role in *All Quiet on the Western Front* (Milestone).

Publications:

By ZINNEMAN:

Articles—"Different Perspective" in *Sight and Sound* (London), autumn 1948; "Choreography of a Gunfight" in *Sight and Sound* (London), July/September 1952; "The Impact of Television on Motion Pictures", interview by Gideon Bachmann in *Film Culture* (New York), no.2, 1957; "A Conflict of Conscience" in *Films and Filming* (London), December 1959; interview by J.R. Taylor in *Sight and Sound* (London), winter 1960/61; "From Here to Eternity", letter in *Films in Review* (New York), November 1961; "A Discussion: Personal Creation in Hollywood: Can It Be Done?" in *Film Quarterly* (Berkeley), spring 1962; "Zinnemann Talks Back", interview in *Cinema*

(Beverly Hills), October/November 1964; "Revelations" in *Films and Filming* (London), September 1964; "Zinnemann—True or False?" in *Cinema* (Beverly Hills), February/March 1964; "Montgomery Clift" in *Sight and Sound* (London), autumn 1966; "Some Questions Answered" in *Action* (Los Angeles), May/June 1967; interview by G. Phillips in *Focus on Film* (London), spring 1973; "Fred Zinnemann and *Julia*", interview by Cecile Starr in *Filmmakers Newsletter* (Ward Hill, Mass.), November 1977; "Individualism Against Machinery", interview by Gordon Gow in *Films and Filming* (London), February 1978;

On ZINNEMAN:

Books—*Fred Zinnemann* by Richard Griffith, New York 1958; *High Noon*, script by Carl Foreman, New York 1971; "*High Noon*" in *3 Major Screenplays* by Malvin Wald and Michael Werner, New York 1973; *The Movie Makers: Artists in an Industry* by Gene Phillips, Chicago 1973; "*High Noon*" in *Values in Conflict* edited by Richard Maynard, New York 1974; articles—"Fred Zinnemann" by Arthur Knight in *Films in Review* (New York), January 1951; "Zinnemann on the Verge" by Henry Hart in *Films in Review* (New York), February 1953; article in *Current Biography Yearbook 1953*, New York 1953; "The Old Dependables" by C. Young in *Film Quarterly* (Berkeley), fall 1959; "Fred Zinnemann: Quiet Man on the Set" by Richard Schickel in *Show* (Hollywood), August 1964; "A Man for All Movies" by John Reid in *Films and Filming* (London), May and June 1967; "A Man for All Movies: The Films of Fred Zinnemann" by Alan Stanbrook in *Films and Filming* (London), June 1967; "Zinnemann's Fate" by D. Adler in *Show* (Hollywood), May 1970; "The Sound Track" by P. Cook in *Films in Review* (New York), December 1977.

*   *   *

In 1928 Fred Zinnemann worked as assistant to cinematographer Eugene Schüfftan on Robert Siodmak's *Menschen am Sonntag* (*People on Sunday*), along with Edgar Ulmer and Billy Wilder, who wrote the scenario for this semi-documentary silent feature made in the tradition of Flaherty and Vertov. Having been strongly influenced by realistic filmmaking, particularly the work of Erich von Stroheim, King Vidor, and Robert Flaherty, Zinnemann immigrated to the United States in 1930 and worked with Berthold Viertel, Robert Flaherty ("probably the greatest single influence on my work as a filmmaker," he later stated), and the New York photographer-documentarist Paul Strand on *Los Redes*, the first of a proposed series intended to document everyday Mexican life. *Los Redes* told the story of the struggle of impoverished fishermen to organize themselves against economic exploitation. The film was shot in Vera Cruz, and Zinnemann was responsible for directing the actors.

Zinnemann's documentary training and background developed his style as a "social realist" in a number of early pictures (several shorts he directed, for example, in MGM's *Crime Does Not Pay* and *The Passing Parade* series) during the years 1937-1942. His medical short *That Mother Might Live*, won an Academy Award and enabled Zinnemann to direct feature films. His first feature at MGM was a thriller, *The Kid Glove Killer*, with Van Heflin and Marsha Hunt. *The Seventh Cross*, was adapted from Anna Segher's anti-fascist World War II novel. The central character, played by Spencer Tracy, escapes from a Nazi concentration camp and attempts to flee Germany in the plot of this film, which was notable for its atmosphere and documentary style. *The Search*, shot on location in Europe in 1948, with Montgomery Clift, gave a realistic portrayal of children who had been displaced by the turmoil of World War II and was a critical as well as a commercial success. *The Men* was the first of a three-picture contract Zinnemann signed with Stanley Kramer and dealt with the problem of paraplegic war veterans, marking Marlon Brando's debut as a film actor. Zinnemann filmed *The Men* on location at the Birmingham Veteran's Hospital and used a number of patients there as actors.

Zinnemann's next film for Kramer, *High Noon* was destined to become a classic, significant because of the way Zinnemann's realistic style turned the genre of the western upside down. It featured Gary Cooper in an Oscar-winning performance as Will Kane, a retired marshal who has taken a Quaker bride (Grace Kelly), but whose marriage is complicated by the anticipated return of paroled desperado Frank Miller, expected on the noon train. Zinnemann treated his "hero" as an ordinary man beset with doubts and fears in an existential struggle to protect himself and the community of Haddleyville, a town that proves to be undeserving of his heroism and bravery. Zinnemann created a tense drama by coordinating screen time to approximate real time, which is extended only when the fateful train arrives, bearing its dangerous passenger. Working against the stylized and mythic traditions that had come to dominate the genre, *High Noon* established the trend of the "psychological" western and represents one of Zinnemann's finest accomplishments.

Zinnemann's last Kramer picture was *The Member of the Wedding*, a Carson McCullers novel that had been adapted to a popular Broadway production by Carson McCullers herself. Zinnemann's film for the most part follows the structure of the play version, opening the play slightly towards the end by filming action that is described in the novel and heightening the psychological realism of the piece. The film utilized the same cast that had made the stage production successful (Julie Harris, Brandon de Wilde, and Ethel Waters) and created cinematically an effective atmosphere of entrapment. *Member of the Wedding* is a model of effective theatrical adaption. Zinnemann went on to adapt the 1955 movie version of the Rodgers and Hammerstein classic *Oklahoma!*, removing the exclamation point, as one wit noted, in a spacious and lyrical, but also rather perfunctory effort.

In 1953 Zinnemann moved to Columbia Pictures to direct the adaption of the popular James Jones novel *From Here to Eternity*, a huge popular success starring Montgomery Clift, Frank Sinatra, and Ernest Borgnine, that won Zinnemann an Academy Award for Best Director. Zinnemann's approach effectively utilized newsreel footage of the Japanese attack on Pearl Harbor and his realistic style both tightened and dramatized the narrative. *A Hatful of Rain* applied Zinnemann's documentary approach to the problem of drug addiction in New York. *The Nun's Story* (with Audrey Hepburn and Peter Finch) has been linked to *A Man For All Seasons* in that both reflect conflicts of conscience, a recurring motif in Zinnemann's films. *A Man for All Seasons*, adapted from Robert Bolt's play, won Paul Scofield an Academy Award for his portrayal of St. Thomas More and was regarded as one of the year's most outstanding films.

Among Zinnemann's political films are *Behold a Pale Horse*, starring Gregory Peck and set during the Spanish Civil War, a picture that also incorporated newsreel authenticity, and *The Day of the Jackal*, a story about an assassin's attempt on the life of Charles de Gaulle, shot on location "like a newsreel," Zinnemann told Gene D. Phillips, "in France, Italy, and Austria with a cast made up largely of unknowns." A later and in many ways impressive political film involving a conflict of conscience was Zinnemann's *Julia*, adapted by Alvin Sargent from Lillian Hellman's *Pentimento*, concerning Hellman's love affair with the writer Dashiell Hammett (Jason Robards) and her long-standing friendship with the mysterious Julia (Vanessa Redgrave), the daughter of a wealthy family who becomes a socialist-intellectual politicized by events in Germany under the Nazi regime. Jane Fonda delivered one of her most effective performances as Lillian Hellman, dramatizing her building political and moral awareness and her coming of age as a writer and mature human being. *Julia* is a perfect Zinnemann vehicle, impressive in its authenticity and historical reconstruction, and also psychologically tense, particularly in the way Zinnemann films Hellman's suspense-laden journey from Paris to Moscow via Berlin. It demonstrates the director's sense of psychological realism and his apparent determination to make worthwhile pictures that are highly entertaining.

—James M. Welsh

ZURLINI, VALERIO. Italian. Born in Bologna, 19 March 1926. Educated in law, Rome. Career: 1948-54—makes about 15 short documentaries; 1954—feature directing debut; 1968—completed *Come, quando è perché* following death of Antonio Pietrangeli. Recipient: Golden Lion, Venice Festival, for *Cronaca familiare*, 1962.

Films (principal documentary shorts): 1950—*Storia di un quartiere*; 1951—*Pugilatori*; 1952—*Il blues della domenica*; *Il Mercato delle facce*; 1953—*Soldati in città*; (as director): 1954—*La ragazze di San Frediano*; (as director and co-scriptwriter): 1959—*Estate violenta (Violent Summer)*; 1960—*La ragazza con la valigia (Girl with a Suitcase)*; 1962—*Cronaca familiare (Family Diary)*; 1965—*Le soldatesse (The Camp Followers)*; 1968—*Seduto alla sua destra (Black Jesus)*; 1972—*La prima notte di quiete*; 1976—*Il deserto dei tartari* (d only).

Publications:

By ZURLINI:

Articles—interview by Massimo D'Avack in *Cinema e letteratura* (Rome), Rome 1964; interview by Blaise Duport in *Contre-Champ* (Paris), no.6-7, 1964; interview in *Cinema international*, May/July 1964; "Zurlini, Delon et *Le Professeur*" in *Positif* (Paris), March 1973; interview by J.-A. Gili in *Ecran* (Paris), December 1976; interview by F. Cuel and B. Villien in *Cinématographe* (Paris), November 1981.

On ZURLINI:

Article—"Encuentro con dos cineastas italianos" by A. Garcia del Vall and A. Gomez Olea in *Cinema 2002* (Madrid), February 1980.

NOTES ON ADVISERS
AND CONTRIBUTORS

AFFRON, Charles. Essayist. Professor of French, New York University, since 1965. Author of *Star Acting: Gish, Garbo, Davis*, 1977, and *Cinema and Sentiment*, 1982. **Essays:** Capra; Goulding; Lean; Le Roy; Wyler.

AFFRON, Mirella Jona. Essayist. Associate Professor, Program in Cinema Studies since 1973, and Chairperson, Department of Performing and Creative Arts since 1977, College of Staten Island, City University of New York. Member of the Executive Council, Society for Cinema Studies, since 1981. **Essay:** Castellani.

ALLEGRO, Anthony T. Essayist. Assistant Professor of Film, University of Miami, since 1980. Also, experimental filmmaker; titles include: *Touch*, 1978; *Minimal Moves*, 1979; *Toxic Shock*, 1983; *Cellular Role Analysis*, 1983; and *Circular Deficiency Anemia*, 1983. **Essays:** Milius; Schrader.

ANDERSON, Joseph. Adviser. Manager for Operations, WGBH, Boston; President, Mass Comm/Masu Komi media consultants. Author, with Donald Richie, of *The Japanese Film: Art and Industry*, 1959, 1982.

ANDREW, Dudley. Adviser and Essayist. Professor since 1981 and Head of the Film Division, University of Iowa, Iowa City (joined faculty, 1969). Author of *Major Film Theories*, 1976; *André Bazin*, 1978; *Kenji Mizoguchi: A Guide to References and Resources* (co-author), 1981; *Concepts in Film Theory*, 1984; and *Film in the Aura of Art*, 1984. **Essays:** Marc Allégret; Yves Allégret; Astruc; Becker; Benoit-Lévy; Cayatte; Christian-Jaque; Clément; Clouzot; Delannoy; Duvivier; Grémillon; Leenhardt; Mizoguchi.

ARMES, Roy. Essayist. Reader in Film and Television at the Middlesex Polytechnic, London. Author of *French Cinema since 1946*, 1966, 1970; *The Cinema of Alain Resnais*, 1968; *French Film*, 1970; *Patterns of Realism*, 1972, 1983; *Film and Reality*, 1974; *The Ambiguous Image*, 1976; *A Critical History of British Cinema*, 1978; *The Films of Alain Robbe-Grillet*, 1981; and *A History of French Cinema*, 1984. **Essays:** Allio; Benegal; Carné; Chahine; Cocteau; Delluc; Dickinson; Epstein; Feuillade; Gance; Güney; L'Herbier; Melville; Sautet.

BARDARSKY, Dimitar. Adviser. With the Short Films Department, Bulgarian Cinematography, Sofia, since 1982. With The Programming and Publications Department, Bulgarian National Film Archive, Sofia, 1978-81. Contributor to and editor of the biographical section, *In the World of Cinema*, 3 volumes, 1982-83.

BARNOUW, Erik. Adviser and Essayist. Professor Emeritus of Dramatic Arts, Columbia University, New York City, since 1973 (joined faculty, 1946; organized and chaired the film division of the School of the Arts). Head, Writers Guild of America, 1957-59. Film and Television Specialist, 1977, and Chief of the Motion Picture, Broadcasting and Recorded Sound Division, 1978-81, Library of Congress, Washington, D.C. Author of *Indian Film*, with S. Krishnaswamy, 1963, 1980; *Documentary: A History of the Nonfiction Film*, 1974, 1983; *Tube of Plenty: The Evolution of American Television*, 1975; *The Sponsor: Notes on a Modern Potentate*, 1978; and *The Magician and the Cinema*, 1981. **Essay:** Vertov.

BASINGER, Jeanine. Essayist. Professor of Film Wesleyan University, Middletown, Connecticut, since 1969. Trustee, American Film Institute; Member of the Advisory Board, Foundation for Independent Video and Film and Association of Independent Video and Filmmakers Inc. Author of *Working with Kazan*, 1973; *Shirley Temple*, 1975; *Gene Kelly*, 1976; *Lana Turner*, 1977; *Anthony Mann: A Critical Analysis*, 1979. **Essays:** De Toth; Fleming; Ruggles; Siodmak; W.S. Van Dyke.

BAXTER, John. Essayist. Novelist, screenwriter, and film historian. Visiting Lecturer, Hollins College, Virginia, 1974-75; programmed seasons at the National Film Theatre, London, and worked as broadcaster with B.B.C. Radio and Television, 1976-81. Author of six novels, two anthologies of science fiction (editor), various screenplays for documentary films and features, and works of film criticism: *Hollywood in the Thirties*, 1968; *The Australian Cinema*, 1970; *Science Fiction in the Cinema*, 1970; *The Gangster Film*, 1970; *The Cinema of Josef von Sternberg*, 1971; *The Cinema of John Ford*, 1971; *Hollywood in the Sixties*, 1972; *Sixty Years of Hollywood*, 1973; *An Appalling Talent: Ken Russell*, 1973; *Stunt*, 1974; *The Hollywood Exiles*, 1976; *King Vidor*, 1976; and, with Brian Norris, *The Video Handbook*, 1982. **Essays:** Bogdanovich; Richard Brooks; John Ford; Frankenheimer; Jewison; Leisen; Malle; Vadim; von Sternberg; Weir.

BOCK, Audie. Essayist. Freelance author and lecturer; visiting lecturer posts held at Harvard, Yale, University of California, etc., 1975-83; Assistant Producer of the international version of Kurosawa'a *Kagemusha*, 1980. Author of *Japanese Film Directors*, 1978, and *Mikio Naruse: un maître du cinema japonais*, 1983; translator of *Something Like an Autobiography* by Kurosawa, 1982. **Essay:** Kurosawa.

BODEEN, DeWitt. Adviser and Essayist. Screenwriter and film critic. Author of: screenplays—*Cat People*, 1942; *Seventh Victim*, 1943; *Curse of the Cat People*, 1944; *The Yellow Canary*, 1944; *The Enchanted Cottage*, 1945; *Night Song*, 1947; *I Remember Mama*, 1948; *Mrs. Mike*, 1959; *Billy Budd*, 1962; also numerous teleplays, 1950-68; film criticism/history—*Ladies of the Footlights*; *The Films of Cecil B. De Mille*; *Chevalier*; *From Hollywood*; *More from Hollywood*; *13 Castle Walk* (novel); editor—*Who Wrote the Movie and What Else Did He Write?* **Essays:** Borzage; Brown, Cromwell; Guitry; Korda; Murnau; Stevens; Jacques Tourneur; Wise.

BORDWELL, David. Essayist. Professor of Film, University of Wisconsin, Madison, since 1973. Author of *Filmguide to "La Passion de Jeanne d'Arc,"* 1973; *Film Art: An Introduction*, with Kristin Thompson, 1979; *French Impressionist Cinema*, 1980; *The Films of Carl-Theodor Dreyer*, 1981; *The Classical Hollywood Cinema: Film Style and Mode of Production to 1960*, with Janet Staiger and Kristin Thompson, 1984; and *Narration in the Fiction Film*, 1985. **Essay:** Ozu.

BOWERS, Ronald. Essayist. Financial Editor, E.F. Hutton and Company, since 1982. Editor, Films in Review, 1979-81. Author of *The MGM Stock Company*, with *James Robert Parish*, 1973; and *The Selznick Players*, 1976. **Essays:** Dwan; King; Litvak; Molander; Negulesco; Zeffirelli.

BOWLES, Stephen E. Essayist. Associate Professor of Film, University of Miami, since 1976. Author of *An Approach to Film Study*, 1974; *Index to Critical Film Reviews from British and American Film Periodicals 1930-1971*, 3 volumes, 1974-75; *Sidney Lumet: References and Resources*, 1979; and *Index to Critical Film Reviews: Supplement I, 1971-1976*, 1983; associate editor of *The Film Book Bibliography 1940-1975*, 1979. **Essays:** Lumet; Roeg.

BRITO, Rui Santana. Adviser. Film Historian, Cinemateca Portuguesa, Lisbon.

BROESKE, Pat H. Essayist. Freelance journalist and film critic, Los Angeles. **Essay:** Beresford.

BURGOYNE, Robert. Adviser and Essayist. Lecturer in Film Theory, New York University. Editor, *Enclitic*. Author of *Film Semiotics: A Lexicon of Terms*, 1983. **Essay:** Bertolucci.

BURTON, Julianne. Essayist. Associate Professor, Merrill College and the Board of Studies in Literature, University of California at Santa Cruz, since 1982 (Assistant Professor, 1974-82). Author of more than 40 publications on the Latin American cinema. **Essay:** Birri.

CAMPER, Fred. Essayist. Independent filmmaker and writer on film, since 1965. Assistant Professor, 1976-83, and Chairperson of the Filmmaking Department, 1977-81, School of the Art Institute of Chicago. **Essays:** Baillie; Breer; Frampton; Gehr; Peterson.

CHEDIAK, Nat. Essayist. Specialist in the exhibition of foreign films in the United States. **Essay:** Roeg.

CIMENT, Michel. Adviser and Essayist. Associate Professor in American Studies, University of Paris (7). Member of the Editorial Board, *Positif*, Paris. Author of *Erich von Stroheim*, 1967; *Kazan by Kazan*, 1973; *Le Dossier Rosi*, 1976; *Le Livre de Losey*, 1979; *Kubrick*, 1980; *Les Conquerants d'un nouveau monde* (collected essays), 1981; *Schatzberg, de la photo au cinéma*, 1982; co-author, with Annie Tresgot, *Portrait of a 60% Perfect Man: Billy Wilder*, 1980; *Elia Kazan, An Outsider*, 1982; *All about Mankiewicz*, 1983. **Essays:** Angelopoulos; Brocka; Comencini; Guerra; Iosseliani; Mikhalkov-Konchalovsky; Panfilov; Perrault; Schatzberg; Skolimowski.

CONLEY, Tom. Essayist. Professor and Chairman, Department of French and Italian, University of Minnesota, Minneapolis. Editor, *Enclitic*, since 1977. Author of *Cesures, estudios cinematographicos*, 1984. **Essay:** Renoir.

D'ARPINO, Tony. Essayist. Freelance writer. Author of *The Tree Worshipper*, 1983, and *Untitled Zodial*, 1984. **Essay:** Pasolini.

DERRY, Charles. Essayist. Head of Motion Pictures Studies, Wright State University, Dayton, Ohio, since 1978. Author of *Dark Dreams: A Psychological History of the Modern Horror Film*, 1978, and *The Film Book Bibliography 1940-1975*, with Jack Ellis and Sharon Kern, 1980. **Essays:** Altman; Chabrol; Lewis; Mulligan; Preminger; Spielberg.

DOLL, Susan. Essayist. Assistant Editor, *International Dictionary of Films and Filmmakers*. **Essay:** Welles.

DUNAGAN, Clyde Kelly. Essayist. Instructor in Mathematics, University of Wisconsin Center, Sheboygan. **Essay:** Eisenstein.

DUNBAR, Robert. Adviser and Essayist. Freelance film critic and historian; has held various visiting professorships and lectureships since 1975. Worked for Gainsborough and Gaumont-British Studios, 1933-38, 1948-49; Director of Public and Cultural Relations, British Embassy, Moscow, 1944-47; General Manager, Imperadio Pictures, 1949-51; independent producer of feature films and documentaries, 1952-63; Chairman, London School of Film Technique, 1963-74. **Essays:** Gerasimov; Kozintsev; Shub.

EDELMAN, Rob. Essayist. Editor, reporter and freelance writer, specializing in the arts, New York City. Associate Editor of *Leonard Maltin's TV Movies*. **Essays:** Blier; Broca; Coppola; Costa-Gavras; Crosland; Cruze; Czinner; Dassin; Disney; Donskoi; Dovzhenko; Ferreri; Garnett; Hiller; Lelouch; Leni; Logan; Mazursky; Micheaux; Niblo; Polonsky; Pontecorvo; Ptushko; Pudovkin; Ritt; Robson; Ruttmann; Syberberg; Willard Van Dyke; Van Peebles; Charles Vidor; Wertmuller; Wicki.

EDMONDS, Robert. Essayist. Professor-at-Large, Columbia College, Chicago, since 1975 (joined faculty, 1971). Author of *About Documentary: Anthropology on Film*, 1974; *Scriptwriting for the Audio-Visual Media*, 1978; and *The Sights of Sounds of Cinema and Television*, 1982; editor of the English translation of *The Aesthetics and Psychology of the Cinema* by Jean Mitry, 1976. **Essay:** Storck.

ELLIS, Jack C. Adviser and Essayist. Professor of Film since 1956, and Chairman of the Department of Radio, Television and Film since 1980, Northwestern University, Evanston, Illinois. President, Chairman of the Board of Directors, and Newsletter Editor, American Federation of Film Societies, 1955-75; President, Treasurer, and Council Member, Society for Cinema Studies, 1959-82; Editor, *Cinema Journal*, 1976-82. Author of *A History of Film*, 1979; compiler, with Charles Derry and Sharon Kern, *The Film Book Bibliography 1940-1975*, 1979; editor, with Richard Dyer MacCann, *Cinema Examined*, 1982. **Essays:** Grierson; Jennings; Lorentz; Watt; Wright.

ELSNER-SOMMER, Gretchen. Essayist. Freelance film critic. Associate Editor of *Jump Cut* magazine. **Essay:** von Trotta.

ERENS, Patricia. Associate Professor, Rosary College, River Forest, Illinois, since 1977. Author of *Akira Kurosawa: A Guide to References and Resources*, 1979, and *The Jew in America Cinema*, 1984; editor of *Sexual Stratagems: The World of Women in Film*, 1979. **Essays:** Hani; Ichikawa; Nemec; Pollack.

ESTRIN, Mark W. Essayist. Professor of English and Director of Film Studies, Rhode Island College, Providence (joined faculty, 1966). Author of *Lillian Hellman: Plays, Films, Memoirs*, 1980. **Essay:** Nichols.

EVERSON, William K. Adviser. Film critic/historian: teaches at New York University, the New School for Social Research, and the School of Visual Arts, New York City. Author of *The Art of W.C. Fields*; *Classics of the Horror Film*; *The Western*; etc.

FALLER, G.S. Essayist. Instructor at Northwestern University, Evanston, Illinois. Editor/Production Manager, Filmmakers of Philadelphia, 1977-78. Assistant Editor, *Film Reader 5*, 1982. **Essays:** Donen; Fosse; Lubitsch.

FARNSWORTH, Rodney. Member of the Associate Faculty, English and Linguistics, Indiana University-Purdue University, Fort Wayne, Indiana (member, visiting faculty, comparative literature and film studies, 1981-82). **Essays:** Herzog; Rafelson.

FEINSTEIN, Howard. Essayist. Researcher and Archivist,

Department of Film, Museum of Modern Art, New York, since 1979; Instructor, New York University Department of Cinema Studies, and University of Bridgeport, Connecticut, since 1983. **Essay:** Zanussi.

FITZGERALD, Theresa. Adviser and Essayist. Managing Director and Writer-Producer-Director, Camden Productions Ltd., London, since 1982. Secretary, London Screenwriters Workshop, since 1983. Researcher, Academic Information Retrieval, London, 1974-82; Part-Time Administrator, Association of Independent Producers, London, 1982. Lecturer in Film and Television, Barking College of Technology, Romford, Essex, 1978-80. Co-author of the forthcoming (1986) *International Film Index*. **Essays:** Clayton; Dearden; Ivory; Peries.

FONSECA, M.S. Essayist. Researcher, Programming Department, Cinematica Portuguesa, Lisbon, since 1981. Film Critic, *Expresso* newspaper, Lisbon, 1981-83. Contributor to numerous Portuguese film journals. **Essay:** Oliveira.

FOREMAN, Alexa L. Essayist. College Programmer, Films Incorporated, Atlanta, since 1980. Manager, American Film Institute Theatre, Washington, D.C. 1979-80. Author of *Women in Motion*, 1983. **Essay:** Malick.

GIANNETTI, Louis D. Adviser. Member of the faculty, Case-Western Reserve University, Cleveland. Author of books and articles on the cinema.

GOMERY, Douglas. Adviser and Essayist. Associate Professor of Radio-TV-Film, University of Maryland, College Park. Author of *High Sierra*, 1979, and the forthcoming books, *Film History*, with Robert Allen, and *The Hollywood Studio System* **Essays:** Bacon; Curtiz; Walsh; Wood.

GOMEZ, Joseph. Essayist. Member of the faculty, Wayne State University, Detroit. **Essays:** Paradzhanov; Watkins.

HABÁ, Věroslav. Essayist. Film historian, Prague. **Essays:** Robert Kramer; Strick.

HANSON, Patricia King. Essayist. Associate Editor, Salem Press, Fort Lee, New Jersey, since 1978. Bibliographer for History and Romance Languages, University of Southern California, 1971-78. Associate Editor, with Stephen L. Hanson, *Magill's Bibliography of Literary Criticism*, 4 volumes, 1979; *Magill's Survey of Cinema*, series I, 4 volumes, 1980, series II, 6 volumes, 1981; *Silent Films*, 3 volumes, 1982; *Foreign Language Films*, 6 volumes, 1984; also, *Magill's Annual Survey of Cinema*, 1982, and 1983; editor of the *American Film Institute Catalogue of Films 1911-1920*. **Essays:** Daves; Franklin; Mamoulian; Seaton; Sidney; Sirk; Taurog.

HANSON, Steve. Essayist. Humanities Bibliographer, University of Southern California, Los Angeles, since 1969. Associate Editor, with Patricia King Hanson, *Magill's Bibliography of Literary Criticism*, 4 volumes, 1979; *Magill's Survey of Cinema*, series I, 4 volumes, 1980, series II, 6 volumes 1981; *Silent Films*, 3 volumes, 1981; *Magill's Annual Survey of Cinema*, 1982; *Foreign Language Films*, 6 volumes, 1984. **Essays:** Fellini; Germi; La Cava; Milestone; Powell and Pressburger; Rossellini; Wellman.

HARRIS, Ann. Essayist. Doctoral student in cinema studies, New York University. **Essay:** Pick.

HECK-RABI, Louise. Essayist. Freelance writer. Public and special librarian, 1955-70. Author of *Women Filmmakers: A Critical Reception*, 1983. **Essays** Deren; Guy; Meszaros; Riefenstahl; Varda; Zetterling.

HIRANO, Kyoko. Essayist. Doctoral student in cinema studies, New York University, since 1982. Editor of *Cinema Gras*, Tokyo, 1977-79. **Essays:** Gosho; Imai; Kinoshita; Shindo; Shinoda; Yoshimura.

HOLDSTEIN, Deborah H. Essayist. Assistant Professor of English, Illinois Institute of Technology, Chicago, since 1980. **Essays:** Asquith; Pakula.

KAMINSKY, Stuart M. Essayist. Professor and Head of the Division of Film, Northwestern University, Evanston, Illnois. Author of *Don Siegel, Director*, 1973; *Clint Eastwood*, 1974; *American Film Genres*, 1977; *John Huston: Maker of Magic*, 1978; *Coop: The Life and Legend of Gary Cooper*, 1980; and, with Dana Hodgdon, *Basic Filmmaking*, 1981; editor of *Ingmar Bergman: Essays in Criticism*, 1975. Also, a novelist; works include: *Bullet for a Star*, 1977; *Murder on the Yellow Brick Road*, 1978; *You Bet Your Life*, 1980; *The Howard Hughes Affair*, 1980; *Never Cross a Vampire*, 1980; *Death of a Dissident*, 1981; *High Midnight*, 1981; *Catch a Falling Crown*, 1982; and *He Done Her Wrong*, 1983. **Essays:** *Mel Brooks; Richard Fleischer; Hathaway; Huston; Leone.*

KANOFF, Joel. Essayist. Lecturer in the Visual Arts, Princeton University, New Jersey, since 1983. **Essays:** De Sica; Visconti.

KAPLAN, E. Ann. Adviser. Teacher of Film and Literature, Rutgers University, New Brunswick, New Jersey. Author of *Women in Film Noir; Fritz Lang: A Guide to References and Resources; Women in Film: Both Sides of the Camera; Regarding Television;* etc.

KATZ, Ephraim. Adviser. Filmmaker, writer and critic. Has written, directed and produced documentary, educational and industrial films. Author of *The Film Encyclopaedia*, 1979.

KEHR, Dave. Adviser and Essayist. Film Critic, *The Reader*, Chicago, since 1974, and *Chicago* magazine, since 1979. **Essays:** Edwards; Tati.

KEMP, Philip. Adviser and Essayist. Freelance writer and screenwriter, London. **Essays:** Clair; Hamer; Kobayashi; Mackendrick; Penn; Yates.

KHANNA, Satti. Adviser and Essayist. Research Associate, Center for South and Southeast Asia Studies, University of California, Berkeley, since 1976. Author of *Indian Cinema and Indian Life*, 1980. **Essays:** Kapoor; Satyajit Ray; Roy; Sen.

KOVÁCS, Katherine Singer. Essayist. Assistant Professor, Department of Comparative Literature, University of Southern California, Los Angeles. Editor, Humanities in Society; Member of the Executive Committee, *The Quarterly Review of Film Studies*. Author of *Le Reve et la Vie: A Theatrical Experiment* by Gustave Flaubert, 1981. **Essays:** Bardem; Borau; Garcia Berlanga; Saura.

LIMBACHER, James L. Essayist. Audio-Visual Librarian, Dearborn, Michigan Department of Libraries, 1955-83. National President, American Federation of Film Societies,

1962-65, and Educational Film Library Association, 1966-70; host of the television series *Shadows on the Wall* and *The Screening Room*. Author of *Using Films*, 1967; *Four Aspects of the Film*, 1968; *Film Music: From Violins to Video*, 1974; *Haven't I Seen You Somewhere Before?*, 1979; *Keeping Score*, 1981; *Sexuality in World Cinema*, 1983; and *Feature Films on 8mm, 16mm and Video*, 7 editions. **Essays:** Fischinger; Markopoulos.

LOCKHART, Kimball. Essayist. Member of the faculty, Department of Romance Studies, Cornell University, Ithaca, New York. Founding Editor, *Enclitic*, 1977-80. Member, Editorial Board, *Diacritics*, Cornell University, since 1978. **Essay:** Antonioni.

LORENZ, Janet E. Essayist. Contributing Writer, *Magill's Survey of the Cinema*, since 1980, and *SelecTV Programming Guide*, since 1981. Assistant Supervisor, Cinema Library, University of Southern California, Los Angeles, 1979-82. **Essay:** Losey.

LOWRY, Ed. Essayist. Assistant Professor of Film Studies, Southern Illinois University, Carbondale, since 1983. Contributor to various film periodicals. **Essays:** Aldrich; Anger; Demme; Minnelli; Stahl; Warhol and Morrissey.

MacCANN, Richard Dyer. Adviser. Professor of Film, University of Iowa, Iowa City, since 1970. Editor, *Cinema Journal*, 1967-76. Author of *Hollywood in Transition*, 1962, and *The People's Films: A Political History of U.S. Government Motion Pictures*, 1973; editor of *Film and Society*, 1964; *Film: A Montage of Theories*, 1966; *The New Film Index*, 1975; and *Cinema Examined*, 1982.

MANCINI, Elaine. Essayist. Teacher of film at the College of Staten Island, New York, and film history and art history at St. John's University, New York. Author of the forthcoming books, *The Films of Luchino Visconti: A Reference Guide; D.W. Griffith at Biograph*; and *The Struggles of the Italian Film Industry During Fascism*. **Essays:** De Santis; Gallone; Lattuada; Monicelli; Petri; Risi; Zampa.

MANVELL, Roger. Essayist. University Professor and Professor of Film, Boston University. Director, British Film Academy, London, 1947-59, and a Governor and Head of the Department of Film History, London Film School, until 1974; Bingham Professor of the Humanities, University of Louisville, 1973. Editor, *Penguin Film Review*, 1946-49, and the Pelican annual *The Cinema*, 1950-52; Associate Editor, *New Humanist*, 1968-75, and Member of the Board of Directors, Rationalist Press, London, since 1966; Editor-in-Chief, *International Encyclopedia of Film*, 1972. Vice-Chairman, National Panel of Film Festivals, British Council, London, 1976-78. Author of *Film*, 1944; *The Animated Film*, 1954; *The Film and the Public*, 1955; *On the Air*, 1955; *The Technique of Film Music*, 1957, 1976; *The Technique of Film Animation*, with John Halas, 1959; *The Living Screen*, 1961; *Design in Motion*, with John Halas, 1962; *What Is a Film?*, 1965; *New Cinema in Europe*, 1966; *This Age of Communication*, 1967; *New Cinema in the U.S.A.*, 1968; *New Cinema in Britain*, 1969; *Art in Movement*, 1970; *The German Cinema*, with Heinrich Fraenkel, 1971; *Shakespeare and the Film*, 1971; *Films and the Second World War*, 1975; *Love Goddesses of the Movies*, 1975; *Theatre and Film*, 1979; *Art and Animation: Halas and Batchelor 1940-1980*, 1980; *Ingmar Bergman*, 1980; also novels, biographies of theatrical personalities and of personalities of the Third Reich. **Essays:** Bergman; Halas and Batchelor; Méliès; Sjöström; Stiller; von Stroheim.

MARCHETTI, Gina. Essayist. Researcher in film theory in Paris, on government grant, 1982-83; Instructor, University of North Carolina, Chapel Hill, 1983-84. Editor of *Film Reader 5*, 1982. **Essay:** Makavejev.

MAST, Gerald. Adviser and Essayist. Professor of English and General Studies in the Humanities, University of Chicago, since 1978. Member of the faculty, Richmond College, New York, 1967-78. Author of *A Short History of the Movies*, 1971, 3rd edition 1981; *The Comic Mind: Comedy and the Movies*, 1974, 1979; *Film/Cinema/Movie: A Theory of Experience*, 1977, 1982; and *Howard Hawks, Storyteller*, 1982; editor, with Marshall Cohen, *Film Theory and Criticism: Introductory Readings*, 1974, 1979; editor of *The Movies in Our Midst: Documents in the Cultural History of Film in America*, 1982. **Essays:** Allen; Chaplin; Hawks; Keaton; Sennett; Truffaut.

MERHAUT, G. Essayist. Film historian. Member of staff, Film Archives of Czechoslovakia, Prague. Author of *Actors and Actresses of the Italian Cinema*. **Essays:** Gaál; Kachyňa; Kawalerowicz; Szabó.

MERRITT, Russell. Essayist. Professor, University of Wisconsin, Madison. **Essay:** Griffith.

MICHAELS, Lloyd. Essayist. Associate Professor of English, Allegheny College, Meadville, Pennsylvania. Editor, *Film Criticism*, since 1977. Author of the forthcoming book *Elia Kazan*. **Essay:** Kazan.

MONTY, Ib. Adviser and Essayist. Director of Det Danske Filmmuseum, Copenhagen, since 1960. Literary and Film Critic for the newspaper *Morgenavisen Jyllands-Posten*, since 1958. Editor-in-Chief of the film periodical *Kosmorama*, 1960-67; Member, Danish Film Council, 1965-69. Author of *Leonardo da Vinci*, 1953; editor, with Morten Piil, *Se- det er film I-iii* (anthology of articles on film), 1964-66, and *TV-Broadcasts on Films and Filmmakers*, 1972. **Essays:** Blom; Carlsen; Christensen; Dreyer; Gad; Henning-Jensen; Holger-Madsen; Roos.

MRAZ, John. Essayist. Coordinator of Graphic History, Center for the Historical Study of the Mexican Labor Movement (CEHSMO), since 1982. Lecturer in Film Studies, University of California at Santa Cruz, 1978-79; Video Coordinator, Multi-Ethnic School Environments, National Institute of Education (U.S.), 1980-81; Lecturer in Communications and History, Universidad Nacional Autonoma de Mexico, 1981-82. **Essays:** Alvarez; De Fuentes; Fernández; Manuel Octavio Gómez; Sara Gomez; Leduc; Solanas and Getino; Solás.

MURPHY, William T. Essayist. Chief, Motion Picture, Sound and Video Branch, National Archives, Washington, D.C., since 1976. Author of *Robert Flaherty: A Guide to References and Resources*, 1978. **Essay:** Flaherty.

NARDUCY, Ray. Essayist. Film critic and historian, Chicago. **Essays:** Ashby; Friedkin; George Roy Hill; Lester; Miller; John Sturges.

NASTAV, Dennis. Essayist. Documentary filmmaker, 1976-79. **Essays:** Pagnol; Rohmer; Tanner.

NICHOLS, Bill. Essayist. Professor and Head, Department of Film Studies, Queen's University, Kingston, Ontario, since 1976 (joined faculty, 1974). Author of *Ideology and the Image*, 1981, and *Newsreel: Documentary Filmmaking on the American*

Left, 1981; editor of *Movies and Methods*, 1976. **Essays:** Dmytryk; Stanley Kramer.

OBALIL, Linda J. Essayist. Assistant (Special Visual Effects Unit), Dreamscape, Bruce Cohn Curtis Productions/Bella Productions, since 1983. Associate Editor, *Film Reader 4*, 1979. **Essays:** Avery; Bakshi; Boorman; Cohl; Fisher; Jones; McLeod; Pal; Porter; Schoedsack; Ulmer.

O'KANE, John. Essayist. Film critic and historian, Minneapolis. **Essay:** Fassbinder.

O'LEARY, Liam. Adviser and Essayist. Film Viewer, Radio Telefis Eireann, Dublin, since 1966; Director, Liam O'Leary Film Archives, Dublin, since 1976. Producer, Abbey Theatre, Dublin, 1944; Director of the Film History Cycle at the National Film Theatre, London, and Acquisitions Officer, National Film Archive, London, 1953-66. Co-Founder, 1936, and Honorary Secretary, 1936-44, Irish Film Society. Director of the films *Our Country*, 1948; *Mr. Careless*, 1950; and *Portrait of Dublin*, 1951. Author of *Invitation to the Film*, 1945; *The Silent Cinema*, 1965; *Rex Ingram, A Master of the Silent Cinema*, 1980. **Essays:** Dieterle; Dupont; Feyder; Ingram; Olcott; Pabst; Pastrone; Robison; Maurice Tourneur; Wiene.

OPELA, Vladimír. Essayist. Film Historian, Czechoslovakian Film Archives, Prague. **Essays:** Fric; Jireš; Schorm; Trnka; Zeman.

PEÑA, Richard. Adviser and Essayist. Director, Film Center of the School of the Art Institute of Chicago. **Essays:** Bellocchio; Imamura; Mauro.

PHILLIPS, Gene D., S.J. Essayist. Professor of English, Loyola University, Chicago (joined faculty, 1970). Contributing Editor, *Literature/Film Quarterly*, since 1977, and *American Classic Screen*, since 1979. Author of *The Movie Makers: Artists in an Industry*, 1973; *Graham Greene: The Films of His Fiction*, 1974; *Stanley Kubrick: A Film Odyssey*, 1975; *Evelyn Waugh's Officers, Gentlemen, and Rogues*, 1977; *Ken Russell*, 1979; *The Films of Tennessee Williams*, 1980; *Hemingway and Film*, 1980; *John Schlesinger*, 1981; *George Cukor*, 1982. **Essays:** Cukor; Kubrick; Reed; Russell; Schlesinger.

PICK, Zuzana Mirjam. Essayist. Assistant Professor, Film Studies Department, Carleton University, Ottawa, since 1976. Editor of *Latin American Film Makers and the Third Cinema*, 1978. **Essay:** Ruiz.

POLAN, Dana B. Essayist. Film critic and historian, Pittsburgh. **Essays:** Fuller; Tashlin.

PORTON, Richard. Essayist. Graduate student in film studies, New York University. **Essays:** Goretta; Loach.

RABINOVITZ, Lauren. Adviser and Essayist. Assistant Professor, Department of History of Architecture and Art, University of Illinois at Chicago, since 1980. **Essays:** Clarke; Max and Dave Fleischer; McCay; Wieland.

RACHEVA, Maria. Adviser and Essayist. Selector of films for the International Film Festival, Munich, since 1983. Teacher of Film History, High School for Cinema, Sofia, Bulgaria, 1974-81; Editor of the cultural review *Westermanns Monatshefte*, Munich, 1981-82. Author of *Presentday Bulgarian Cinema*, 1970; *Nowa fala i nowa powiesc*, 1974; *Der bulgarische Film*,

with Klaus Eder, 1977; *Andrzej Wajda*, with Klaus Eder, 1980; *Neostariavashti filmi*, 1981. **Essays:** Hauff; Kluge; Kovács; Staudte; Weiss; Wenders.

REYNOLDS, Herbert. Essayist. Historian and Project Coordinator, Museum of Modern Art Department of Film, New York City, since 1981; Consultant, American Federation of Arts Film Program, since 1982. Member, Curatorial Staff of the Film Archives, George Eastman House, Rochester, New York, 1976-81. **Essay:** Schlöndorff.

ROBSON, Arthur G. Essayist. Professor and Chairman, Department of Classics, and Professor of Comparative Literature, Beloit College, Wisconsin, since 1966. Editor of *Latin: Our Living Heritage, Book III*, 1964; author of *Euripides' "Electra": An Interpretive Commentary*, 1983; and author, with Rodney Farnsworth, of *Alexandre Alexeieff and Claire Parker: The Artistry of Animation* (forthcoming). **Essay:** Alexeieff and Parker.

RUBINSTEIN, E. Essayist. Coordinator of the Program in Cinema Studies, College of Staten Island, City University of New York (joined faculty, 1978). Author of *Filmguide to "The General,"* 1973. **Essay:** Buñuel.

SAELI, Marie. Essayist. Tutor in Developmental Education, Triton College, River Grove, Illinois, since 1982. **Essay:** Anderson.

SCHADE, W. Curtis. Essayist. Associate Director of Admissions, Beloit College, Wisconsin, since 1980. **Essay:** Sembene.

SCHIFF, Lillian. Essayist. Freelance film critic; consultant to high school and college film departments. English Teacher, Schreiber High School, Port Washington, New York, 1947-78; Author of *Getting Started in Filmmaking*, 1978. **Essays:** Akerman; Leacock; Maysles; Scola; Taviani.

SCHUTH, H. Wayne. Essayist. Professor, Department of Drama and Communications, University of New Orleans, since 1979 (joined faculty, 1973). Member, Board of Directors, University Film and Video Association, 1983-85. Author of *Mike Nichols*, 1978. **Essay:** Sucksdorff.

SELIG, Michael. Essayist. Assistant Professor, University of Vermont, since 1983. Contributor to *Film Reader*, *Jump-Cut*, and *Journal of Popular Film and Television*. **Essay:** King Vidor.

SILET, Charles L.P. Essayist. Associate Professor of English, Iowa State University, Ames, since 1979. Co-author of *The Literary Manuscripts of Upton Sinclair*, 1972; author of *Hamlin Garland and Henry Blake Fuller: A Reference Guide*, 1977; *Lindsay Anderson: A Guide to References and Resources*, 1979; and *Paul Rosenfeld: An Annotated Bibliography*, 1981; co-editor of *The Worlds Between Two Rivers: Perspectives on American Indians in Iowa*, 1978; and *The Pretend Indians: Images of the Native Americans in the Movies*, 1980. **Essay:** Lang.

SIMMON, Scott. Essayist. Film Programmer, Mary Pickford Theatre, Library of Congress, Washington, D.C., since 1983. Contributor to *Film Comment*, *Journal of Popular Film and Television*, and *Literature/Film Quarterly*. **Essays:** Boetticher; Cimino; Ritchie.

SITNEY, P. Adams. Adviser and Essayist. Director of Library and Publications at Anthology Film Archives; teacher at Princeton University, New Jersey. Author of *Film Culture Reader*; *Essential Cinema*; *The Avant-Garde Film*; *Visionary Film*; etc. **Essays:** Brakhage; Bresson; Broughton; Kubelka; Landow; Mekas; Olmi; Snow.

SKVORECKÝ, Josef. Essayist. Professor of English and Film, University of Toronto. Formerly, Member, Central Committee, Czechoslovakian Film and Television Arts and of the Czechoslovakian Writers Union. Author of *The Bass Saxophone*; *The Cowards*; *Miss Silberstein's Past*; etc. **Essays:** Chytilová; Forman; Menzel.

SLIDE, Anthony. Adviser and Essayist. Freelance writer. Associate Film Archivist, American Film Institute, 1972-75; Resident Film Historian, Academy of Motion Picture Arts and Sciences, 1975-80. Author of *Early American Cinema*, 1970; *The Griffith Actresses*, 1973; *The Films of D.W. Griffith*, with Edward Wagenknecht, 1975; *The Idols of Silence*, 1976; *The Big V: A History of the Vitagraph Company*, 1976; *Early Women Directors*, 1977; *Aspects of American Film History Prior to 1920*, 1978; *Films on Film History*, 1979; *The Kindergarten of the Movies: A History of the Fine Arts Company*, 1980; *Fifty Great American Silent Films 1912-1920*, with Edward Wagenknecht, 1980; *The Vaudevillians*, 1981; and *Great Radio Personalities*, 1982; editor of the five-volume series, *Selected Film Criticism 1896-1950*. **Essays:** Blackton; Brenon; Browning; Fejös; Florey; Hepworth; Howard; Lye; Neilan; Pearson; Reisz; Saville; Weber; Whale; Wilcox.

SMALL, Edward S. Essayist. Associate Professor of Radio-TV-Film since 1979, and Chairman of the Interdisciplinary Program in Film Studies since 1983, University of Missouri, Columbia (joined faculty, 1972). Associate Editor, *Journal of the University Film and Video Association*. **Essays:** Connor; Eggeling; Emshwiller; Le Grice; Richter; Vanderbeek.

SMOODIN, Eric. Essayist. Doctoral candidate, film studies, University of California at Los Angeles. Contributor to *Film Studies Annual* and *Journal of the University Film and Video Association*. **Essays:** De Mille; Mankiewicz; Sandrich; Preston Sturges; Vigo.

SNYDER, Thomas. Freelance writer, Chicago. Reviewer for *Video Movie Magazine*, Chicago. **Essays:** De Palma; Lucas.

STARR, Cecile. Adviser and Essayist. Freelance writer, lecturer, and filmmaker. Film Reviewer, *The Saturday Review*, New York, 1949-59. Author of *Discovering the Movies*, 1972, and, with Robert Russett, *Experimental Animation*, 1976. **Essays:** Arzner; Dulac; Reiniger.

TABERY, Karel. Essayist. Currently, researcher on the French cinema, collaborating on a film encyclopaedia. Historian/Archivist, Czechoslovakian Film Archives, Prague, 1974-82. **Essays:** Fábri; Reichenbach; Verneuil.

TELOTTE, J.P. Essayist. Assistant Professor of English, Georgia Institute of Technology, Atlanta, since 1979. Contributor to *Film Quarterly*, *Journal of Popular Film*, *Film Criticism*, etc. Member of the Editorial Board, *Film Criticism* and *Literature/Film Quarterly*. **Essay:** Polanski.

THORPE, Frances. Adviser. Librarian, British Film Institute, London. Formerly, Editor, *International Index to Film Periodicals*.

TOMLINSON, Doug. Essayist. Assistant Professor of Film Studies, Montclair State College, and Lecturer, Princeton University, New Jersey, since 1983. Lecturer, New York University, 1979-82. Principal Researcher for *Voices of Film Experience*, edited by Jay Leyda, 1977. **Essays:** Berkeley; Bolognini; Passer; Rossen.

TUDOR, Andrew. Essayist. Sociologist: has lectured on sociology at the University of York. Contributor to various film journals. Author of *Theories of Film*. **Essays:** Walter Hill; Peckinpah; Siegel; Wiseman.

URGOSIKOVÁ, Mrs. B. Essayist. Film Historian, Czechoslovakian Film Archives, Prague. Author of *History of Science Fiction Films*. **Essays:** Munk; Wajda.

VERDAASDONK, Dorothee. Essayist. Film Reviewer for the Dutch feminist monthly *OPZIJ*, since 1979; Lecturer in Film and Television, Utrecht University, since 1982. Secretary, Department of Film, Dutch National Arts Council, 1975-82. Author of *The First Wave*, 1983; editor of *Bert Haanstra: The Moved Eye*, 1983. **Essays:** Haanstra; Ivens.

WEINBERG, Herman. Essayist. Teacher of Film History, City College, New York. Columnist, *Films in Review*. Author of *Josef von Sternberg: A Critical Study*; *The Lubitsch Touch*; *Saint Cinema*; *The Complete "Greed"*; *The Complete "Wedding March"*; *Stroheim: A Pictorial Record of His Nine Films*; etc. Died in December 1983. **Essay:** D'Arrast.

WELSH, James M. Essayist. Teacher at Salisbury State College, Maryland; Arts Editor and Reviewer, television station WBOC: Co-Editor, *Literature/Film Quarterly*. Co-author of *His Majesty the American: The Cinema of Douglas Fairbanks Sr.*, 1977, and *Abel Gance*, 1978. **Essays:** Richardson; Zinnemann.

WEST, Dennis. Essayist. Associate Professor, University of Idaho, Moscow, since 1981. Director, Indiana University Film Studies Program, 1976-77. Contributor on Latin American and Spanish cinema to such journals as *Latin American Research Review*, *Cineaste*, *New Scholar*, etc. **Essays:** Gutiérrez Alea; Guzmán.

WHITE, M.B. Essayist. Assistant Professor, Department of Radio-TV-Film, Northwestern University, Evanston, Illinois, since 1982. Contributor to *Enclitic*, *Purdue Film Studies Annual*, etc. **Essays:** Autant-Lara; Duras; Resnais; Straub and Huillet.

WILLIAMS, Colin. Essayist. Researcher and writer, London, since 1961. **Essays:** Schaffner; Walters.

WINE, Bill. Essayist. Assistant Professor of Communications, LaSalle College, Philadelphia, since 1981. Film, Theatre and Television Critic, *Camden Courier-Post*, 1974-81. **Essays:** Cassavetes; Kershner.

WOLFF, Jessica R. Essayist. Freelance researcher, writer and editor, New York City. **Essay:** Rainer.

WOOD, Robin. Adviser and Essayist. Professor of Film Study, Department of Fine Arts, Atkinson College, York University, Toronto, since 1977. Member of the film studies department, Queen's University, Kingston, Ontario, 1969-72, and University of Warwick, Coventry, England, 1973-77. Author of *Hitchcock's Films*, 1965; *Howard Hawks*, 1967; *Arthur Penn*, 1968; *Ingmar Bergman*, 1969; *Antonioni*, with Ian Cameron, 1970; *Claude Chabrol*, with Michael Walker, 1971; *The Apu Trilogy of Satyajit Ray*, 1971; *Personal Views: Explorations in Film*, 1976; *The American Nightmare: Essays on the Horror Film*, with Richard Lippe, Andrew Britton and Tony Williams, 1979. **Essays:** Carpenter; Demy; Franju; Godard; Hitchcock; Mann; McCarey; Max Ophüls; Romero; Scorsese; Tavernier.